Author-Title Index
to
Joseph Sabin's

Dictionary of Books
Relating to America

compiled by

JOHN EDGAR MOLNAR

Vol. III: Q-Z

The Scarecrow Press, Inc.
Metuchen, N.J.   1974

Copyright 1974 by John Edgar Molnar

Key to original volumes of Sabin

v. 1.	A - Bedford, Pennsylvania.
v. 2.	Bedinger - Brownell, H. H.
v. 3.	Brownell, H. H. - Chesbrough
v. 4.	Cheshire, New Hampshire - Costa Pereira
v. 5.	Costa Rica - Dumorter
v. 6.	Du Moulin - Franklin, A. W.
v. 7.	Franklin, Benjamin - Hall, Joseph
v. 8.	Hall, Joseph - Huntington, Jedediah V.
v. 9.	Huntington, Joseph - Lacroix, Francois J. P. de.
v. 10.	Lacroix, Frederic - M'Clary
v. 11.	McClean - Memoire justificatif
v. 12.	Memoire justificatif des hommes - Nederland (Articulen)
v. 13.	Nederland (Besoignes) - Omai
v. 14.	Omana y Sotomayor - Philadelphia City Tract Society
v. 15.	Philadelphia Club - Providence, Rhode Island (Measures)
v. 16.	Providence Mechanics' and Apprentices' Library - Remarks relative
v. 17.	Remarks respecting - Ross, C. K.
v. 18.	Ross, D. B. - Schedae
v. 19.	Schedel - Simms, W. G.
v. 20.	Simms, W. G. - Smith, Seba.
v. 21.	Smith, Sebastian Bach - Solis y Valenzuela, Bruno de.
v. 22.	Solis y Valenzuela, Pedro de - Spiritual manifestations
v. 23.	Spiritual maxims - Storrs, R. S.
v. 24.	Storrs, R. S. - Ternaux-Compans, H.
v. 25.	Ternaux-Compans, H. - Tucker, J.
v. 26.	Tucker, J. - Vindex, pseud.
v. 27.	Vindex, pseud. - Weeks, Levi.
v. 28.	Weeks, William Raymond - Witherspoon, J.
v. 29.	Witherspoon, J. - Z.

Key to numbered entries in Sabin

A	1 - 2546	N	51671 - 56364
B	2547 - 9740	O	56365 - (58050)
C	9741 - (18220)	P	58051 - 66883
D	18221 - 21607	Q	(66884) - 67372
E	21608 - 23576	R	67373 - (74601)
F	(23577) - 26265	S	74602 - 94141
G	26266 - 29387	T	94142 - 97659
H	(29388) - 34140	U	97660 - 98253
I	34141 - 35325	V	98254 - 100860
J	(36326) - 36967	W	100861 - 105711
K	36968 - 38373	X	105712 - 105742
L	(38374) - 42894	Y	105743 - 106228A
M	42895 - 51670	Z	106229 - 106413

Q. pseud. You have heard of them. see Rosenberg, G. C.

Q., H. V. pseud. tr. see Quellenburgh, H. V. tr.

Q., P. pseud. Observations on the West India Dock salaries. 102779

Q., Q. P. pseud. Sketches of the character of the New-York press. see Worth, Gorham A.

Q., T. pseud. Wall-street bear in Europe. see Young, Samuel, fl. 1855.

Q. C. S., D. M. pseud. Triunfo de la justicia. see Quiros y Campo Sagrado, Manuel de.

Q. Garcia, Jose de J. see Garcia, Jose de J. Q.

Q. B. V. 103033

Q. D. V. B. Dissertatio geographica de terra australi. (78049)

Q. D. B. V. Disputatio geographica-historia. 67386

Q. F. F. Q. S. Comparatio inter potiores terrae. 98390

Q. F. F. Q. S. Dissertatio historica politica. 93770

Q. K. Doesticks, Philander. pseud. see Thomson, Mortimer, 1832-1875. and Underhill, Edward Fitch, 1830-1898.

Q. M. D. 36022

Q. P. Q. pseud. see Worth, Gorham A.

Qa palos wowapi kage ciqon. 18291, 71336

Q'jeamooltoowhwee uhkaghkeendwaukunul. 79221

Qu' est-ce que la constitution de 93? 40911

Qu' est-ce que les gens comme il faut? 83512

Quack doctor. A Negro farce. 83022

Quackenbergius, Dr. pseud. see Dr. Quackenbergius. pseud.

Quackenbos, George P. 66885-66888

Quackenbosh, Henry. 33523

Quackenboss, Quincy. 88417

Quackery of the age. 45424

Quaden, Matthias. 66889-66894

Quadrado y De-Roo, Francisco de Paula. 66895

Quadraginta et octo conclusionum manus in Peruvini Regni Collegio. 66896

Quadrat, Nonpareil. pseud. "Happy new year!" see Holden, J. G. P.

Quadrat. (66897)

Quadrennial confederacy. 58147

Quadrennial register of the Methodist Episcopal Church. 25382

Quadro chronologico das pecas. 88712

Quadro de receita e despeza da provincia. 85631

Quadro das iltimas revolucoes do Brasil. (75223)

Quadro elementar das relacoes politicas e diplomaticas. (76847)

Quadro historico politico de la capital del Peru. (66899)

Quadro sinoptico de las ciencias. 97731

Quadroon. pseud. Colored man round the world. see Door, David F.

Quadroon of Louisiana. 93636

Quadroon; or, a lover's adventures in Louisiana. (69063)

Quadroon; or, adventures in the far west. 69064

Quadroona; or, the slave mother. 75256

Quadroone. 66900

Quadros, Luiz Miguel. 66901-66902

Quadrupeds. 71026

Quadrupeds of North America. 2368

Quae convenientia saguarum Americae Septentrionalis cum Islandica. 69242

Quae sao so limites naturaes. 17012

Quaestie van vrijen arbeid en immigratie in de West-Indie toegelicht. 52348

Quaestio de imperatoria vel regia potestate. 11235, (11240)

Quaestiones aliquae desumptae et disputatae. (25687)

Quaestiones novae in libellum de sphera. 32681

Quaestiones pro modulo discutiendae. 105828

Quaesitor. pseud. Warning voice. 66903

Quaife, M. M. ed. 89367

Quaissain, --------. 3978, 101895

Quaker, pseud. Beames of eternal brightness. 4116

Quaker a Christian. 59726

Quaker-almanack for this year 1705. 39817

Quaker and methodist compared. 28794

Quaker, being a series of sermons. 66931

Quaker city. 41396

Quaker de Philadelphie. 25052

Quaker in Pennsylvania. pseud. Copy of a letter. see Bringhurst, Joseph.

Quaker in Road-Island [sic]. pseud. New and further narrative. 52445

Quaker laws of Plymouth and Massachusetts. 6010

Quaker no Christian. 59726

Quaker partisans. A story of the revolution. 81249

Quaker quiddities. 15470

Quaker scout of Wyoming. 22297

Quaker soldier. 41398

Quaker spy. 36582

Quaker unmask'd. 2464A, 41946, 66932-(66933), (66935), 69495, 1st note after 97104

Quaker vindicated. (66933)

Quakerism. 66934

Quakerism a judicial infatuation represented. 103069

Quakerism a new nick-name for old Christianity. 59727

Quakerism anatamiz'd, and confuted. 103659

Quakerism no Christianity. 59708, 59727

Quakerism not Christianity. 17270, 68660

Quakerism, or the story of my life. 66934, 70284

Quakerism verson Calvanism [sic]. 68660

Quakers. see Friends, Society of.

Quaker's address, versify'd. 3961

Quakers' almanach for the year 1705. 28453

Quakers antient testimony revived. 39818, 66741

Quakers assisting to preserve the lives of the Indians. (66935)-(66936)

Quakers assisting, to preserve the lives of the Indians, in the barracks, vindicated. (66936), 1st note after 97104

Quakers at Philadelphia. see Friends, Society of. Philadelphia Monthly Meeting. Friends, Society of. Philadelphia Yearly Meeting.

Quakers farewel to England. (66937)

Quakers from their origin till the present time. 17964

Quakers grossly insulted. 66938

Quakers in Bermuda tryed, &c. (21671)

Quakers in Pennsylvania. see Friends, Society of. Philadelphia Monthly Meeting. Friends Society of. Philadelphia Yearly Meeting.

Quakers no apostates. 106101

Quaker's opinions. 59683

Quakers plainness. 95527

Quakers quibbles, in three parts. 95527

Quaker's sea-journal. 25318

Quakerstadt und ihre Geheimnisse. 41397

Qual Tratta della piu marauegliosi cose. 44229

Qualification for voting in the provincial charter of Massachusetts. 66939

Qualifications of missionaries. 85934

Quality and characteristics of the cereals exhibited. 73959

Quand et comment l'Amerique a-t-elle ete pueplee d'hommes et d'animaux? 22568

Quandary, Christopher. pseud. Some serious considerations. 66940

Quando el nueuo camino no fuero tan rico
prouechoso. 68363
Quandt, C. 66941
Quantite d'anecdotes amusantes. 5270
Quantite de remarques historiques. (7739)
Quantities of cereals produced in different
countries compared. 73959
Quantrell, the terror of the west. 66942
Quantum Sufficit. pseud. Reply. 66943
Quapaw Indians. Treaties, etc. 48086, 96634,
96689, 96697
Quarantine Convention, Philadelphia, 1857.
49381
Quarantine laws for the harbor of Quebec, etc.
67039
Quarantine laws for the use of pilots attending
at the Narrows. 53433
Quarantine laws in force in South-Carolina.
87707
Quarantine regulations. (66944)
Quaritch (Bernard) firm publisher 70891,
99371-99372
Quaritch's reprints of rare boosk, I. 99371
Quaritch's translations of rare books. I.
99372
Quarles, Francis. 39820, (66428)-66430, 1st
note after 94666
Quarles, James Minor, 1823-1901. 66945-66946
Quarles van Ufford, Jakob Karel Willem, 1818-
1902. 66947
Quarles van Ufford, W. 66948
Quarll, Philip. 66949-66952
Quarrel between Governor and the Council of
the provisional government. 84858
Quarta [Junta Publica de la Real Sociedad
Economica de Guatemala.] 29085
Quarta parte del teatro Mexicano. 99386,
99388
Quarta relacion que Fernando Cortes Gouernador
y Capitan General por Su Majestad. 16936
Quarta relacio que Fernando Cortes Gouernador
y Capitan General por Sumahestad. 16937
Qvarta y qvinta parte de la Aravcana. (57801)-
57802
Quartenta libros d' el compendio historial.
26666
Quarter-centennial Celebration of the Establish-
ment of Normal Schools in America,
Framingham, Mass., 1864. (47686)
Quarter-centennial celebration of the Newton
Sabbath School Union. 55094
Quarter centennial discourses: the parish-the
pulpit. 9058
Quarter-centennial sermon, by the Rt. Rev.
William Rollinston Whittingham. 66152
Quarter century. 83344
Quarter-century anniversary discourse, March
18, 1870. 52688
Quarter century celebration at Illinois College.
93281
Quarter century discourse. [By B. C. Cutler.]
18161
Quarter century discourse. Delivered in the
Tenth Presbyterian Church. 6079
Quarter century discourse, delivered June 26th,
1867. 35533
Quarter century memorial of the Eliot Sabbath
School. 73641, note after 95465
Quarter-century sermon, . . . in the First
Baptist Church in New Haven. 61398
Quarter-century sermon; or, pastorate of 25
years. 89099
Quarter-century sermon, preached in behalf of
the American Tract Society. 89770
Quarter-day. 105178
Quarter-day, or the horrors of the first of
May. A poem. 105194

Quarter of a century of Jamaica legislation.
42655
Quarter race in Kentucky, and other sketches.
66953
Quarterly and annual communications of the
Grand Lodge. (43992)
Quarterly anti-slavery magazine. 66954
Quarterly catalogue of the Young Ladies'
Department . . . [of the Newark Academy.]
54876
Quarterly catalogues of the . . . Young Ladies,
at Newark Academy. 54876
Quarterly Christian spectator. 2671, (12925),
66955, (70214), 93138
Quarterly church journal. 54848
Quarterly circular of the Central Division of
the New England Protective Union.
66956
Quarterly educational news. 35316
Quarterly homoeopathic journal. 66957-66958
Quarterly journal, conducted by the Knights of
Richmond Castle. 27580
Quarterly journal of agriculture. 66960
Quarterly journal of education. 77887
Quarterly journal of science. 5359
Quarterly journal of the [American Unitarian]
Association. 1255
Quarterly journal, . . . of the Chester and
Delaware County Medical Societies.
47325
Quarterly journal of the Grand Division of the
Sons of Temperance, of the State of
Maine. 87029
Quarterly journal of the Grand Division of the
Sons of Temperance, State of Massa-
chusetts. 87032
Quarterly journal of the New York State His-
torical Association. 94200
Quarterly law journal. 66961
Quarterly magazine and review. 93134, 93144
Quarterly magazine of medicine and the
auxiliary sciences. 55547
Quarterly miscellany. 55345
Quarterly museum of questions and answers.
66962
Quarterly of the Historical and Philosophical
Society of Ohio. 105499
Quarterly of the Methodist Episcopal Church,
South. 84740
Quarterly of the Society of California Pioneers.
105053
Quarterly of the Texas Historical Association.
84858
Quarterly of the Young Men's Christian Associa-
tions of America. 66963
Quarterly of the Young Men's Christian Associa-
tions of the United States and British
Provinces. 66964
Quarterly publication of the State Historical
Society. 34973
Quarterly publications [of the American Statis-
tical Association.] 83566
Quarterly publications of the Historical and
Philosophical Society of Ohio. 94103
Quarterly record. 40954
Quarterly register and journal of the American
Education Society. 1198
Quarterly register of the [American Education]
Society. 1198
Quarterly report . . . see Report . . .
Quarterly reporter for the Young Men's Christian
Associations in North America. (66965)
Quarterly reports . . . see Reports . . .
Quarterly repository of literature. (66966)
Quarterly returns of the banks. (52922)

Quarterly review. 4603, 10645, (21555), 23933, (25198), 31142, note after 39323, (50944), 52245, 59215, 64219, 65414, 70251, 84174, 85700, 98678, 98722, 98925, 99774, 102795
Quarterly review. plaintiffs 66969
Quarterly review. see also Brownson's quarterly review. Methodist Magazine and quarterly review.
Quarterly review of the American Protestant Association. 66967
Quarterly review of the Methodist Episcopal Church, South. 66968
Quarterly review versus the state of New York. 66969
Quarterly reviewer. pseud. Letter to John Barrows, Esq., F. R. S. 3671
Quarterly special relief report of the U. S. Sanitary Commission. 76615
Quarterly theological magazine. (66970)
Quarterly theological review. 66971
Quarterman, James. 66972-(66973)
Quartermaster General's Office, General orders, no. 70 [i. e. 69½.] 1430, (45016), 72820
Quartermaster's Department. Sketch of its organization. 73835
Quartermaster's guide; being a compilation from the army regulations. (5989)
Quartermaster's guide . . . . By Col. Theo. S. Case. 11302
Quartermaster's report of the Department of the Cumberland. 20588
Quarti, Pablo Maria. 58840
Quartier, Jacques. see Cartier, Jacques.
Quarto notion. 71890
Quarto, or second book in geography. 83951-83955
Quartz Hill Gold Mining Company. 66975
Quartz mining. (66976)
Quashy; or the coal-black maid. 50805
Quatemoczin, Juan Rosillo de Mier. see Mier, Quatemoczin, Juan Rosillo de.
Quateroone. 69065
Quatre ans a Cayenne. 2328
Quatre ans de campagnes a l'armee du Potomac. 68813
4000 J. G. du Cap de la secte d'Emmanuel. 10750
Quatre lettres d'un Bourgeois de New-Heaven [sic]. 47206
Quatre lettres, ecrites par un Francais a un Hollandais. 16023
Quatre lettres sur le Mexique Exposition. 7423, (7437)
Quatre relations veritables du Sieur Serres de Montpellier. 79318
Quatre Stuarts. 12248
92 resolutions, et debats sur icelles. 10503
Quatremere, -------. 67931
Quatrieme lettre. 5652
Quatrieme voyage au Bresil. 75234
Quatriesme voyage fait par le Capitaine Gourges. 39234-39235
Quatro cartas de Hernan Cortes. 3350
Quatro derradeiras noites dos inconfidentes de Minas Geraes. 58988
Quatro libros. De la naturaleza y virtudes de las plantas y animales. 31514, 105727
Quatro libros primeros de la Cronica general de Espana. 56619-56620
Quatro partes enteras de la Cronica de Espana. 56618
Quatro sentenciados a morte. pseud. defendants 97697
Qvatvor Americi Vespvtii Navigationes. note before 99327, 99354-99355, 101017

Quaw, James E. supposed author 14266, 89906
Quay, John. plaintiff (72621), note after 96921
Quay, Joseph F. (62299)
Que aquella provincia manifesto los reverentes obsequios. 86442
Que aura mas de dos anos y medio. 87184
Que auiendo acabado su oficio de Virrey de la Nueua Espana. 98161
Que con la obediencia de Su Superior. 87188
Que con el motivo de las questiones. 86515
Que desde su ninez ha estado en la Nueua-Espana. 87156
Que Don Francisco de Solis Ossorio, su padre. 86438
Que el ano de 1641. 86516
Que el dicho Reyno le embia a dar quenta a V. Magestad. 87186
Que el Virrey del Piru ha escrito a V. M. 98332
Que en el ano de 1633. 81479
Que en virtud de los poderes. 87187
Que estado la dicha su prouincia preseguida y oprimida. 96757
Que estando prohibido por cedulas. 74030
Que ha hecho quanto ha sido de su parte. 87185
Que ha 38. anos q[ue] sirue a V. M. 98722
Que haviendo servido. 86379
Que la dicha su prouincia ha has de setenta anos. 3557
Que, la mayor de mi vida. 98333
Que la riqueza que se ha sacado dello cerro de Potosi. 68357
Que la Villa de Moquegua. 86514
Que las tierras referidas en su relacion. 87237
Que l'Europe soit attentive aux evenements possibles en Amerique. 25909
Que los religiosos de la Co[m]pania de Iesus se emplea. 98805
Que muera el papel moneda ya que cómenzo a enfermar. 66977
Que preciosa va la danza. 99714
Que siendo V. M. informado. 98331
Que son tan fuertes y concluyentes las razones y causes. 87238
Que tratandose en la Corte Romana la beatificacion. 98368
Queal, Robert F. 4242
Quebec, Bishop of. see Mountain, George Jehosaphat, successively Bishop of Montreal, and Quebec, 1789-1863. Mountain, Jacob, Bishop of Quebec. Stewart, Charles James, Bishop of Quebec, 1775-1837.
Quebec (Archdiocese) 10510, 67004, (67036), 105708
Quebec (Archdiocese) Archives. 7431
Quebec (Archdiocese) Bishop (Capse) 10766 see also Capse, Charles Froncois de, Bp.
Quebec (Archdiocese) Bishop (Pontbriand) 38164 see also Pontbrinand, Henri Marie Dubreuil de, Bp., 1709-1760.
Quebec (Archdiocese) Bishop (Saint Vallier) 23037, 38506, 66978-66980 see also Saint Vallier, Jean Baptiste de la Croix de Chevrieres de, Bp., 1653-1727.
Quebec (Archdiocese) Church Society. see Church Society of the Diocese of Quebce.
Quebec (Archdiocese) Clergy. 10512
Quebec (Archdiocese) Diocesan Committee. (67043)
Quebec (Archdiocese) Incorporated Church Society. see Church Society of the Diocese of Quebec.

Quebec (Archdiocese) Religieuses Hospitalieres.
see Hospitalieres. Quebec.
Quebec (Archdiocese) Secretariat. 10510
Quebec (City) (66998)
Quebec (City) Comite General du Chemin de
Fer du Nord. see Comite General du
Chemin der Fer du Nord, Quebec.
Quebec (City) Conference, 1862-1863. 40232
Quebec (City) Congregation de Notre-Dame.
see Congregation de Notre-Dame de
Quebec.
Quebec (City) Congregation des Hommes. see
Congregation de Notre-Dame de Quebec.
Quebec (City) Council. (57399)
Quebec (City) Gough Division, No. 2. see
Sons of Temperance of North American.
Quebec (Province) Gough Division, No. 2,
Quebec.
Quebec (City) Hospital de la Misericorde.
Mere Superieure. see Hospitalieres.
Quebec. Mere Superieure.
Quebec (City) Hospitalieres. see Hospitalieres.
Quebec.
Quebec (City) Ordinances, etc. 67039, 67044,
82912
Quebec (City) Petit Seminaire. see Seminaire
de Quebec.
Quebec (City) Presbyterian Chapel. 88958
Quebec (City) St. Patrick's Society. see St.
Patrick's Society of Quebec.
Quebec (City) Seminaire. see Seminaire
de Quebec.
Quebec (City) Seminary. see Seminaire de
Quebec.
Quebec (City) Societe dor the Encouragement
of Arts and Sciences in Canada. see
Society for the Encouragement of Arts
and Sciences in Canada, Quebec.
Quebec (City) Stadacona Club. see Stadacona
Club, Quebec.
Quebec (City) Treasurer. (66998)
Quebec (City) Trinity House. 96988
Quebec (City) Ursuline Convent. plaintiffs
98140
Quebec (Diocese) see Quebec (Archdiocese)
Quebec (French Province) see New France.
Quebec (Province) 2519, 10526, (12937), 4th
note after 42522, 42524, 66993, 67030,
(67038), (70234), 75443
Quebec (Province) petitioners 10386, (56545),
61286, 67032
Quebec (Province) Agent. 67032, 42807 see
also Lymburner, --------.
Quebec (Province) Army. Courts Martial.
93241
Quebec (Province) Assemblee Legislative. see
Quebec (Province) Legislature. Legisla-
tive Assembly.
Quebec (Province) Assembly. see Quebec
(Province) Legislature. Legislative
Assembly.
Quebec (Province) Attorney General. 4778,
15495, 27567, note after 90679, 93174
see also Stuart, Sir James, Bart.,
1780-1853.
Quebec (Province) Board of Agriculture. (10342),
10346
Quebec (Province) Board of Trade. 66992
Quebec (Province) British Inhabitants. petitioners
see Quebec (Province) Citizens.
petitioners
Quebec (Province) Bureau de Comtes. see
Quebec (Province) Bureau of Accounts.
Quebec (Province) Bureau d'Hypotheques. see
Quebec (Province) Bureau of Mortgages.
Quebec (Province) Bureau of Accounts. 38609

Quebec (Province) Bureau of Mortgages. 38609
Quebec (Province) Census, 1831. 10400
Quebec (Province) Chambre d'Assemblee. see
Quebec (Province) Legislature. Legisla-
tive Assembly.
Quebec (Province) Citizens. petitioners 61286,
67000
Quebec (Province) Commissaire des Terres de
la Couronne. see Quebec (Province)
Commissioner of Crown Lands.
Quebec (Province) Commissaires des Travaux
Publics. see Quebec (Province) Com-
missioners of Public Works.
Quebec (Province) Commissaires Pour Explorer
le Saguenay. see Quebec (Province)
Commissioners to Explore the Saguenay
River.
Quebec (Province) Commissaires s'enquirer de
l'Origine et des Causes de l'Incendie que
a Consume l'Hospice des Soeurs de la
Charite, 1854. see Quebec (Province)
Commissioners to Enquire Into the Origin
and Cause of the Fire at the Grey Nun-
nery, or "Hospice des Soeurs de la
Charite,", 1854.
Quebec (Province) Commissaires s'Enquirer
de la Cause de l'Incendie que a Detruit
l'Hotel du Parlement, 1854. see Quebec
(Province) Commissioners to Enquire Into
the Cause of the Fire at the Parliament
Buildings, 1854.
Quebec (Province) Commissary General of
Provisions and Stores. 66994
Quebec (Province) Commission of Inquiry Con-
cerning French Laws Still in Force in
Canada. 67720
Quebec (Province) Commissioner of Crown
Lands. (10412)
Quebec (Province) Commissioners of Public
Works. 67923
Quebec (Province) Commissioners for Revising
the Acts and Ordinances. (10498)
Quebec (Province) Commissioners to Enquire
Into the Cause of the Fire at the Parlia-
ment Buildings, 1854. 67051
Quebec (Province) Commissioners to Enquire
Into the Origin and Cause of the Fire at
the Grey Nunnery, or "Hospice des Soeurs
de la Charite," 1854. 67052
Quebec (Province) Commissioners to Explore
the Saguenay River. 74939
Quebec (Province) Commissioners to Visit the
United States' Penitentiaries. 69780
see also Mondelt, D. Neilson, J.
Quebec (Province) Commons House of Assembly.
see Quebec (Province) Legislature.
Legislative Assembly.
Quebec (Province) Convention, 1835. petitioners
95372
Quebec (Province) Council. see Quebec
(Province) Legislature. Council.
Quebec (Province) Counsel Superieur. see
Quebec (Province) Legislature. Council.
Quebec (Province) Cour d'Appel. see Quebec
(Province) Court of Appeals.
Quebec (Province) Cour Seigneuriale. see
Quebec (Province) Seigneurial Court.
Quebec (Province) Cour Speciale d'Oyer et
Terminer. see Quebec (Province)
Court of Oyer and Terminer.
Quebec (Province) Court of Appeals. 99598
Quebec (Province) Court of Common Pleas.
Judges. 66990, 67007
Quebec (Province) Court of King's Bench.
9902, 21292, 67028, 79623, 96814, 96930,
101168

Quebec (Province) Court of Oyer and Terminer.
43485, 69111, 81378, note after 96856,
96902
Quebec (Province) Court of Queen's Bench.
see Quebec (Province) Court of King's
Bench.
Quebec (Province) Courts. 10495, 67720,
70360, 98394, 96924
Quebec (Province) Divers Tribunaux. see
Quebec (Province) Courts.
Quebec (Province) General Court Martial,
1838-1839. 10588, 93241
Quebec (Province) House of Assembly. see
Quebec (Province) Legislature. Legislative Assembly.
Quebec (Province) Institut Canadien. see
Institut Canadien de Quebec.
Quebec (Province) Investigation Into the Past
Administration of Justice, 1787. 90622
Quebec (Province) Laws, statutes, etc. 10409,
10433, 10475, 10477-(10478), 10480,
10482, 10485, 10488, 10490, 10495-10499,
10502, 10601-(10603), 11737, 38609,
41690, (42507)-42508, (42510)-42514,
(42517), 42522, 42525, (43095), 50286,
67029-67030, (67031), 67062, 67720,
69469, 85811, 85785, 88697, 93126,
98394
Quebec (Province) Legislature. 31137, 42525,
98067
Quebec (Province) Legislature. Legislative
Assembly. (10491), 10538, 10540, 10601-
10602, 10611, 19456, 25176, 42518,
(67009), 67055, 69718, (74590), (75311),
75312, 96927, 99597, 99598, 99600
Quebec (Province) Legislature. Legislative
Assembly. petitioners 93175
Quebec (Province) Legislature. Legislative
Assembly. Agent. 99597-99598 see also
Morin, Augustin Norbert. Viger, Denis
Benjamin.
Quebec (Province) Legislature. Legislative
Assembly. Certain Members. 58489
Quebec (Province) Legislature. Legislative
Assembly. Committee on Elections.
(42138)
Quebec (Province) Legislature. Legislative
Assembly. Committee on Finances.
10454
Quebec (Province) Legislature. Legislative
Assembly. Committee on the Saguenay,
Argenteuil, Kamouraska, and Laval Con-
tested Elections, 1854. 49369
Quebec (Province) Legislature. Legislative
Assembly. Committee on the Settlement
of Crown Lands. 10410-10411
Quebec (Province) Legislature. Legislative
Assembly. Committee to Which Was
Referred That Part of the Speech of the
Governor In Chief Which Relates to the
Act of 2d. Will. IVth, Cap. 16. 67113
Quebec (Province) Legislature. Legislative
Assembly. Court of Impeachment. 42518,
96864, 96926-96927
Quebec (Province) Legislature. Legislative
Assembly. Library. 66996
Quebec (Province) Legislature. Legislative
Assembly. Select Committee on the
Emigration Which Takes Place Annually
From Lower Canada to the United States.
10439
Quebec (Province) Legislature. Legislative
Assembly. Select Committee on the Politi-
cal State of the Provinces of Upper and
Lower Canada. 80438

Quebec (Province) Legislature. Legislative
Assembly. Select Committee to Enquire
Into the Present System and Management
of the Public Lands. 10413
Quebec (Province) Legislature. Legislative
Assembly. Special Committee Appointed
to Enquire Into the Causes Which Retard
the Settlement of the Eastern Townships.
10564, (10595), 42519
Quebec (Province) Legislature. Legislative
Assembly. Special Committee on the
Petitions of Complainants. 10568
Quebec (Province) Legislature. Legislative
Assembly. Special Committee on the
Roads and Other Interior Communications.
10566
Quebec (Province) Legislature. Legislative
Assembly. Special Committee on the
State of Agriculture. 10347, 42523
Quebec (Province) Legislature. Legislative
Assembly. Special Committee to Enquire
Into the Expediency of Establishing the
System of Credit Foncier. 19114
Quebec (Province) Legislature. Legislative
Assembly. Special Committee to Enquire
Into the Function of the Act Concerning
Municipalities and Roads. 10567
Quebec (Province) Legislature. Legislative
Assembly. Special Committee to Enquire
Into the State of Education. 10428,
10430, 10431
Quebec (Province) Legislature. Legislative
Council. 10476, 23503, 38609, 42522,
66990, 67002, 67007, 67010, (67031),
88697, 98065C, 99598
Quebec (Province) Legislature. Legislative
Council. defendants 96930
Quebec (Province) Legislature. Legislative
Council. Committee on Education.
10428, 10430
Quebec (Province) Legislature. Legislative
Council. Committee on Promoting the
Means of Education. 67056
Quebec (Province) Legislature. Legislative
Council. Committee on the Financial
Concerns. 10454
Quebec (Province) Legislature. Legislative
Council. Library. 66996
Quebec (Province) Legislature. Library.
(66995)
Quebec (Province) Literary and Historical
Society. see Literary and Historical
Society of Quebec.
Quebec (Province) Minister of Agriculture.
10347
Quebec (Province) Minister of Finance. 69884
Quebec (Province) Minister of Public Instruc-
tion. 67057
Quebec (Province) Old and New Subjects.
petitioners see Quebec (Province)
Citizens. petitioners
Quebec (Province) Post Office. 41690
Quebec (Province) Secretary's Office. 100763
Quebec (Province) Seigneurial Court. 42004-
(42005)
Quebec (Province) Societe Amicale. see
Societe Amicale de Quebec.
Quebec (Province) Societe Bienveillante. see
Societe Bienveillante de Quebec.
Quebec (Province) Societe Bienveillante des
Ouvriers. see Societe Bienveillante des
Ouvriers de Quebec.
Quebec (Province) Societe de Construction.
see Societe de Construction, Quebec.
Quebec (Province) Societe de Construction du
Peuple. see Societe de Construction du
Peuple, Quebec.

Quebec (Province) Societe de Construction
Mutuelle. see Societe de Construction
Mutuelle, Quebec.
Quebec (Province) Societe de Discussion. see
Societe de Discussion de Quebec.
Quebec (Province) Societe Litteraire. see
Societe Litteraire de Quebec.
Quebec (Province) Societe Litteraire et His-
torique. see Literary and Historical
Society of Quebec.
Quebec (Province) Societe Permanente de
Construction des Artisans. see Societe
Permanente de Construction des Artisans,
Quebec.
Quebec (Province) Society for Propagating the
Gospel Among the Destitute Settlers and
Indians. see Society for Propagating
the Gospel Among the Destitute Settlers
and Indians in Lower Canada.
Quebec (Province) Superintendent of Education.
10428, 10432, 10433, 42515-(42517)
Quebec (Province) Superior Court. 21292
Quebec (Province) Tribunaux. see Quebec
(Province) Courts.
Quebec: a poetical essay. 59075
Quebec Agricultural Society. 10344-10345,
10347
Quebec Agricultural Society. Special Committee.
42508
Quebec almanac. 67040
Quebec and its environs. 67041
Quebec and its environs, historically, panorami-
cally, and locally exhibited. 90035
Quebec: as it was, and as it is. 72606, 74408
Quebec and New York. 67042
Quebec and Saguenay Railway Company. (69769)
Quebec and Saguenay Railway Company. Chief
Engineer. (69769) see also Fosdick,
H. M.
Quebec Benevolent Society. see Societe
Bienveillante de Quebec.
Quebec business directory. 67045
Quebec directory, and city and commercial
register. 67045
Quebec Committee of the SPCK. see Society
for Promoting Christian Knowledge.
Quebec Diocesan Committee.
Quebec directory and stranger's guide to the
city & environs. 67045
Quebec directory, or strangers' guide in the
city, for 1826. 67044, 82912
Quebec directory, for 1848-9. 67045
Quebec directory for 1866-7. 67045
Quebec guide. 67046
Quebec guide, being a concise account of all the
places. 67047
Quebec Hill. 43363
Quebec Jail Association. 67048
Quebec journal of education. see Journal of
education, Province of Quebec.
Quebec Literary and Historical Society. see
Literary and Historical Society of Quebec.
Quebec School of Medicine. 67050
Quebec Societe de Construction Permanente de
Levis. see Societe de Construction
Permanente de Levis, Quebec.
Quebec. The harp, and other poems. (30986)
Quebec to Halifax, via Gaspe and Pictou. 42527
Quebecois. pseud. Rapport. 67053
Quebrada, Innez di. (38757), 67064
Queen Anne's County, Md. Court. 67065
Queen Charlotte Islands. (64029)
Queen City. (13107)
Queen Elizabeth's heroic speech. 68259
Queen of islands. 50134
Queen of the ocean unqueen'd. 14011

Queen vs. Eyre. 23561
Queen's College, Kingston, Ontario. see
Kingston, Ontario. Queen's University.
Queen's College, New Brunswick, N. J. see
Rutgers University, New Brunswick,
N. J.
Queens County, N. Y. 67070
Queens County, N. Y. petitioners 95462
Queens County, N. Y. Agricultural Society.
see Queens County Agricultural Society.
Queens County, N. Y. Board of Supervisors.
67067
Queens County, N. Y. Citizens. petitioners
84556
Queens County, N. Y. Court of Common Pleas.
67071
Queens County, N. Y. Inhabitants. petitioners
see Queens County, N. Y. Citizens.
petitioners
Queens County, N. Y. Society for the Promo-
tion of Agricultural and Domestic Manu-
factures. see Queen's County Society,
for the Promotion of Agricultural and
Domestic Manufactures.
Queens County Agricultural Society. 67068
Queens County Agricultural Society. Annual
Exhibition, 16th, Jamaica, N. Y., 1839.
67068
Queens County enrollment list. 67070
Queen's County in olden times. 57314
Queen's County Society, for the Promotion of
Agriculture and Domestic Manufactures.
67069
Queen's heart. 67072
Queens of American society. 22212
Queens of England. 92810
Queen's rangers. 67073
Queen's University and College, Kingston,
Ontario. see Kingston, Ontario. Queen's
University.
Queenston. A tale of the Niagara Frontier.
67075
Queer almanac, 1836. 67076
Queilhe, L. le Meynard de. see Meynard de
Queilhe, L. le.
Queimado Companhia. see Companhia de
Queimado.
Queipo, Manuel Abad, Bp. (67078)-(78080),
99500 see also Michoacan (Archdiocese)
Bishop (Queipo)
Queipo, Manuel de Abad y. see Queipo,
Manuel Abad, Bp.
Queipo, Vaszuez. 67081
Queiros, Pedro Fernandes de, d. 1615. 5905,
11607, 31503-31504, 33489-33491, 43760,
52359, 66686, 67355, 67357-67359, 67736-
67739, 68346, (72372)
Queiros, Pedro Fernandes de, d. 1615.
petitioner 67353-67356
Queiroz Coitinho Mattoso Camare, Eusebio de.
see Mattoso Camare, Eusebio de
Queiroz Coitinho.
Quejas de la Nueva Espana. 67082
Quejas de los Mexicanos a su ilustre Presidente.
67083
Quejas justas de los chupadores. 67084
Quelch, John. defendant 67085-67086
Quelen, Augustus van. see Guelen, Auguste
de.
Quellen des Susquehannah. 16504
Quellen und Untersuchingen zur Fahrt der ersten
Duetschen nach dem Portugiesischen
Indien. 99363
Quellenburgh, H. V. tr. 26310-26311
Quellensammlung zur Darstellung des Amerikanis-
chen Lebens. (22042)

Quincy, Ill. Illinois Association. see Congregational Churches in Illinois. Illinois Association, Quincy.
Quincy, Ill. Needle Pickets. see Illinois. Militia. Needle Pickets, Quincy.
Quincy, Ill. New England Society. see New England Society of Quincy, Ill.
Quincy, Ill. Washington Military Union of the American Army. see Washington Military Union of the American Army, Quincy, Ill.
Quincy, Mass. 67290
Quincy, Mass. Adams Academy. see Adams Academy, Quincy, Mass.
Quincy, Mass. Auditor. 67285
Quincy, Mass. Christ Church. Committee. 67286
Quincy, Mass. Committee to Consider the Subject of an Academy. (67296)
Quincy, Mass. Evangelical Church. (67284)
Quincy, Mass. Evangelical Congregational Church. 67287, (67291)
Quincy, Mass. Library. see Thomas Crane Public Library, Quincy, Mass.
Quincy, Mass. National Soldiers' Home. see National Soldiers' Home, Quincy, Mass.
Quincy, Mass. Public Library. see Thomas Crane Public Library, Quincy, Mass.
Quincy, Mass. School Committee. 67295
Quincy, Mass. Thomas Crane Public Library. see Thomas Crane Public Library, Quincy, Mass.
Quincy, Mass. Town Meeting, 1835. 67292
Quincy city directory. 67281
Quincy directory. 67281
Quincy Homestead Association. 67265
Quincy in 1857. 32615
Quincy Mining Company. (67298)
Quincy, Weymouth, and Braintree directory for 1876-7. 67294
Quindaro. 67299
Quiner, E. B. 67300-67301
Quinet, Edgar. 47292, 67302-67303
Quinland. (67304)
Quinn, Arthur Hobson, 1875- 83788, 97617
Quinn, David. 67305
Quinn, David. petitioner 67306
Quinn, Henry. 67307
Quinografia Portugueza. 98834
Quinohequin Lodge, Jamaica Plain, Mass. see Odd Fellows, Independent Order of. Massachusetts. Quinohequin Lodge, Jamaica Plain.
Quinologia. 74003, 74005
Quinones, Jose Garcia. 67308
Quinones, Juan Jose. 67309
Quinones, Nicolas. 67310
Quinones, Pedro de Loaisa y. see Loaisa y Quinones, Pedro de.
Quinones, Pedro de Solis y. see Solis y Quinones, Pedro de.
Quiñonez, --------, fl. 1852. 50527
Quinquennial catalogue of the . . . North Granville Ladies' Seminary. (55715)
Quinquennial register and circular [of the New York State Normal School.] 53967
Quint, Alonzo H. 15479, (67311)-(67316)
Quint Fernandez Davila, Diego. 67317
Quinta carta pastoral. 26719
Quinta esencia de la virtud. (78165)
Quinta junta publica de la Real Sociedad Economica de Amantes de la Patria de Guatemale [sic]. 29085, 85750
Quinta normal de la republica de Chile. 67318
Qvinta parte delle historie memorabili [di] Alessandro Zilioli. 106333

Quintal, Joao Dias do. 67319
Quintana, Andres Narino de. 67321
Quintana, Augustin de. (67320)
Quintana, Manuel Josef. 67322-67325
Quintana Roo, Andres. see Roo, Andres Quintana.
Quintana Warnes, Jose Maria. 67327-67329 see also Havana. Regidor.
Quintana y Guido, Antonio de. (67330)
Quintanilla, Angel Miguel de. 67331
Quintanilla y Malo de Molina, Camillo. 67332
Quintard, Charles Todd. 67333-67335
Quintela, Augustin de. 67336-67337
Quinten, Richard St. see St. Quinten, Richard.
Quintero, Angel. 67338
Quintero, Cayetano de Cabrera y. see Cabrera y Quintero, Cayetano de.
Quintero, Francisco Diaz. tr. 33726
Quintero, J. A. (67339)
Quintero, Marian Yuste de. 67340
Quintessence of long speeches. 67341
Quintessence of Lorenzo's works. 20757
Quintessence of universal history. (77437)
Quintianus Stoa, --------. 50058, 1st note after 106378
Quintilla, Ignacio de Costa. (67342)
Quintillas en elogio de S. Juan de Dios. (76262)
Qvinto, y sexto pvnto de la relacion. 12799, 27785
Quinton McKell, of Irongray, Soothsayer. pseud. see McKell, Quinton. pseud.
Quintus, J. 67343
Quinze ans de voyages autour du monde. (38605)
Quinze jours de traverse. 44133
Quir, Pedro Fernandes de. see Queiros, Pedro Fernandes de, d. 1615.
Quir, Petrus Fernandez de. see Queiros, Pedro Fernandes de, d. 1615.
Quir, Pierre Fernand de. see Queiros, Pedro Fernandes de, d. 1615.
Quirino, Pietro. see Queiros, Pedro Fernandes de, d. 1615.
Quirinus, Petrus. see Queiros, Pedro Fernandes de, d. 1615.
Quirk Ogee. pseud. see Ogee, Quirk. pseud.
Quirno, Gregorio J. 67344
Quiroga, Diego Gonzales de. 27809, (67345)
Quiroga, Domingo. 67346
Quiroga, Juan Facundo. defendant (67438)
Quiroga, Jacinto de Salas y. see Salas y Quiroga, Jacinto de.
Quiroga, Jose. 67347
Quiroga, Vasco de, Bp., ca. 1470-1565. 50611 see also Michoacan (Archdiocese) Bishop (Quiroga)
Quiroga y Lossada, Diego de. 84384
Quiros, --------, fl. 1859. 58566
Quiros, Anselmo. 67349
Quiros, Blas de. plaintiff 98150
Quiros Campo Sagrado, Manuel. see Sagrado, Manuel Quiros Campo.
Quiros, Diego Herranz y. see Herranz y Quiros, Diego.
Quiros, Jose Maria. 67350-67351
Quiros, Pedro Fernandes de. see Queiros, Pedro Fernandes de, d. 1615.
Quiros y Campo-Sagrado, Manuel de. 67360-67361, 74607, 97019
Quiros y Millan, Jose Maria. 67362
Quita, Domingos dos Reis. see Reis Quita, Domingos dos.
Quite correct; a comedy—in two acts. 83779, 83780, 83787
Quitman, Frederick H. 67363-67364

Quitman, John Anthony, 1799-1858. 13191,
(67367)-67368, 90643
Quito. Conferencia Tenida Entre Los Ministros
Plenipotentiarios del Peru y Del Ecuador
Nombrados Para Transijir las Diferencias
que Existen Entre Una y Otra Republica.
61095
Quito. Real Audiencia. Presidente y Oydores.
98809
Quito. Real Audiencia. Visitador. (44359),
98809 see also Manozca, Juan de. and
Catholic Church in Peru. Inquisidor
Apostolico.
Quito (Diocese) Bishop (Pena Montenegro)
59623-(59624) see also Pena Montenegro,
Alonso de la, Bp.
Quito (Diocese) Dean y Cabildo. 77141
Quito (Ecclesiastical Province) 76110
Quivera Society. 99641
Quixano, ---------, fl. 1813. 20251, 67370
Quixano, Emmanuel Ignatius Beye Zisnoros y.
see Beye Zisnoros y Quixano, Emmanuel
Ignatius.
Quixano, Ignacio Beye Cisneros y. see Beye
Cisneros y Quixano, Ignacio, 1718-1787.
Quixote, Don. pseud. Ichneumon. see
Tupper, --------.
Quixotic guardian. 23019
Quod, John. pseud. Attorney. see Irving,
John Treat.
Quod, John. pseud. Harry Harson. see
Irving, John Treat.
Quod correspondence. 67371
Quoddy hermit. 67372
Quodlibet. 37417
Qvodlibeticae qvaestiones ex diuersis sacri
eloquii. 87183
Quodlibets, lately come over from New
Britaniola. 31037
Quoit Club carols. 101971
Quola atsinosidv etlusi anehi widuwowelanelvhi.
12454
Quotation from George Wallis's system of the
laws. (4686)
Quoy, ----------. 21210, 25916
Quozziana: or letters from Great Goslington,
Mass. (18916), 20005, 37654, 70574

R****

R***. pseud. tr. see Suard, Jean Baptiste
Antoine. tr.
R****. pseud. L'Ameriquiade. 38760
R. pseud. Bigarures d'un citoyen de Geneve.
see Rousseau, Jean Jacques, 1712-1778.
supposed author and Wilkes, John, 1727-
1797. supposed author
R. pseud. Naval. see Ruschenberger,
W. S. W.
R***. pseud. Six months ago. 67373
R., A. pseud. Marrow of history. see Ross,
A. ed.
R., A. pseud. Suggestions on the military
resources of Canada. see Roche,
Alfred R.
R., B. pseud. William B. Reed. see Rush,
Benjamin.
R., C. H. pseud. Incidents of travel. 67374
R., D. pseud. Baptistes. (46229)
R., D. pseud. Rasgos biograficos. 71608
R., D. pseud. 1671. An almanack of
coelestial motions. see Russell, Daniel.
R., E. pseud. Narrative. see Ritchie,
Elizabeth.
R., E. pseud. Revolution in New England
justified. see Rawson, Edmand.
supposed author
R., E. B. pseud. Poem. 63579
R., F. A. pseud. tr. (77795)
R., F. G. M. pseud. Pequeno catecismo.
80883
R., G. pseud. Gruendlicher Unterricht.
(67375)
R., G. pseud. Sol de Chile. 86217
R., G. A. pseud. Mother Goose's melodies.
see Wheeler, W. A.
R., H. pseud. Ovr Ladys retorne to England.
see Roberts, Henry.
R., H. pseud. Report of the Trustees of
Hanover College. 88137
R., H. pseud. Trvmpet of fame. see
Roberts, Henry.
R., H. O. pseud. Governing race. 28156,
67376
R., H. R. pseud. Sketches in verse. see
Rose, H. R.
R., I., sieur. pseud. tr. (10358)
R., J. pseud. Epistle to the reader. see
Rogers, John, 1649?-1721.
R——, J. pseud. Humble representation.
see Rivington, James. spurious author
R., J. pseud. Necessity of a well experienced
souldiery. see Richardson, John.
R***, J. pseud. Reise nach der Insel
Martinique. see Romanet, J.
R., J. pseud. 1670. An almanack of coeles-
tiall motions. 62743
R., I. pseud. Spy. see Rhodes, John.
R********, J. pseud. Supplecation. see
Rivington, James. spurious author
R., I. pseud. Trades increase. see Roberts,
J. supposed author
R***, J. pseud. Voyage a la Martinique.
see Romanet, J.
R., J. A. pseud. Series of poems. see
Richey, J. A.
R., J. D. pseud. Earth twice shaken. see
Roussignac, Jacques de.
R., J. E. pseud. Short, faithful, and concise
development. (67379)

R., J. G. pseud. Cuestion Talambo ante la
America. (61108), 67380
R., J. G. pseud. Triunfo de la libertad.
see Roscio, J. G.
R., J. J. pseud. Bigarures d'un citoyen de
Geneve. see Rousseau, Jean Jacques,
1712-1778. supposed author and Wilkes,
John, 1727-1797. supposed author
R., J. J. pseud. Uniform national currency.
97749
R., L. A. pseud. Histoire generale. see
Roubaud, Pierre Joseph Andre.
R******, M. pseud. Voyages to the Madeira,
and Leeward Carribean isles. see
Riddell, Maria. supposed author
R., N. pseud. Poem. see Mather, Cotton,
1663-1728.
R., P. D. pseud. Mercvre Indien. see
Rosnel, Pierre de.
R., R. pseud. ed. 10158
R., R. pseud. True state of the case. see
Richardson, Rebecca. plaintiff
"R., S." pseud. Extract from a sermon.
see Reed, Sylvanus.
R., T. pseud. Contraband Christmas. 16174,
67381
R., T. pseud. Preface. see Rand, Thomas.
R., T. C. pseud. Mexitli. 67382
R., T. H. pseud. Fragments of family and
contemporary history. see Robinson,
Thomas H.
R., W. pseud. Authentic memoir of the life
of the late Rev. G. Whitefield. 103615
R., W. pseud. Briefe narration. see
Rathband, William.
R., W. pseud. Narration. see Rathband
William.
R., W. pseud. Preface. see Richmond,
William.
R., W. pseud. Remarks on the report of
the Commissioners. see Roscoe,
William.
R., W. pseud. Several epistles. see
Robinson, William.
R., W. S. W. pseud. Brief history of the
existing controversy. see Ruschenberger,
W. S. W.
R., W. S. W. pseud. Principles of naval
staff rank. see Ruschenberger, W. S. W.
R. y C L., A. pseud. see L., A. R. y C.
pseud.
R. A. pseud. see A., R. pseud.
R. A. pseud. see Allen, Richard.
R. A. F. pseud. see F., R. A. pseud.
R. A. P. pseud. see Paige, Rhode Ann.
R. B. pseud. see Bache, Richard. supposed
author
R. B. pseud. see Baird, Robert. supposed
author
R. B. pseud. see Beverley, Robert.
R. B. pseud. see Burton, Robert.
R. B. pseud. tr. see Crouch, Nathaniel,
1632?-1725?
R. B., Author of the English empire in America.
pseud. see Crouch, Nathaniel, 1632?-
1725?
R. B. A. pseud. see Anderson, R. B.
supposed author
R. C. pseud. see C., R. pseud.
R. C. pseud. see Chamberlaine, Richard.

2230

R. C. B. pseud. see Rutledge, Jean Jacques.
R. C. C. A. M. pseud. see Reed, John.
supposed author
R. C. C. A. M. pseud. see Smith, William.
supposed author
R. C. Hellrigle & Co's Springfield, Urbana,
Piqua, Sidney and Bellefontaine city
directories. 89892
R. C. Smith's reply to the charges of Daniel
Adams. 83958
R. Coope's letter to the South Sea Proprietors.
16399
R. D. S***. pseud. see Rousselot de Surgy,
Jacques Philibert.
R. E. C. pseud. see Colston, R. E.
R. F. pseud. see F., R. pseud.
R. F. Loper to Hon. E. M. Stanton. 41967
R. G. pseud. see Gray, Robert, 17th cent.
supposed author
R. G. pseud. see Green, Roger, 17th cent.
supposed author
R. G. pseud. see Greene, Robert. supposed
author
R. G. H. pseud. see H., R. G. pseud.
R. G. Z. pseud. see Z., R. G. pseud.
R. H. pseud. see H., R. pseud.
R. H. pseud. tr. see Hakluyt, Richard,
1552?-1616. tr.
R. H. pseud. see Harlakenden, Richard.
R. H. pseud. see Hayman, Robert.
R. H. pseud. see Hutchinson, Richard.
supposed author
R. H. S. pseud. see Stoddard, Richard
Henry.
R. H. W. pseud. see Wilde, R. H.
R. J. pseud. tr. see Johnson, Robert. tr.
R. L. pseud. see Lingard, R.
R. M. pseud. see M., R. pseud.
R. M. Johnson, to the colored citizens of the
American republic. 36276
R. N. pseud. see N., R. pseud.
R. N. pseud. see Noble, Robert.
R. P. pseud. see Price, Richard.
R—h Ph——ps. pseud. see Ph——ps,
R——h. pseud.
R. P. Andriani Knudde, dicti Crespi, elogium.
4644, 5101, (69246)
R. P. Cornelij Beudinij, dicti Godinez,
martyrium. (69246)
R. P. Petri Jarrici Tholosani Societ. Jesu
Thesaurus rerum Indicarum. 35791
R. R. M. pseud. see Madden, R. R.
RR. PP. Antonii Sepp, und Antonii Bohm der
Societat Jesu Priestern Teuscher Nation,
deren der erste aus Tryol. 79162,
(79164)
RR. PP. Antonii Sepp, und Antonii Bohm, . . .
Reiss-Beschreibung. (79163)
RR. PP. Antonij Sepp, und Antonij Bohm, der
Societat Jesu Priestern. 79165
R—— S——. pseud. see S——, R——.
pseud.
R***** S*****. pseud. see S*****, R*****.
pseud.
R. S. pseud. see Paltock, Robert.
R. S. pseud. tr. see Samber, R. supposed
tr.
R. S. pseud. see Sears, Robert, 1810-
R. S. pseud. see Steere, Richard.
R. S., a passenger in the Hector. pseud. see
Paltock, Samuel. supposed author
R. S. T. pseud. see T., R. S. pseud.
R. Volaterrani Commentariorvm urbanorum.
43763
R. W. pseud. see Ames, William.
R. W. pseud. see Whitbourne, Sir Richard.
R. W. pseud. see Williams, Roger, 1604?-
1683.

Raadgevingen aan de ingezetenen van Suriname.
67383
Raalte, A. C. van. see Van Raalte, A. C.
Rasloff, ---------. 35807
Raban, Louis Francois, 1795-1870. 67384
Rabe, die Glocken, und Lenore. 63547
Rabe. Mit einer biographischen Skizze. 63548
Rabe. Von Edgar Allen Poe. 63549
Rabelais, Francois, 1494?-1553. 31037
Rabello, Agostinho. defendant 67385
Raben-Geschrey. 77732
Rabener, Justus Gottfried, 1634-1699. 67386
Rabenerus, Justus Gotofredus. see Rabener,
Justus Gottfried, 1634-1699.
Rabinal-achi vepu xahoh-tun. 7423, 7427
Rablais, Francis, see Rabelais, Francois,
1494?-1553.
Rabnerus, Justus Gotofredus. see Rabener,
Justus Gottfried, 1634-1699.
Rabshakek's proposals considered. 5977,
102427
Rabun, William. 49073
Raccolta Colombiana. 99281, note after 99383C
Raccolta completa degli scritti di Christoforo
Colombo. 14645
Raccolta de' viaggi piu interessanti. 102543
Raccolta di viaggi. 46994, 95146, 98793,
100694, 105725
Raccolta di viaggi dalla scoperta del nuovo
contiennte. 44647, note after 99383C
Raccolta di vocaboli del Brasile. (62804)
Racconti incredibili. 63568
Racconto del mare relativo ai tempi della
guerra Americana. 16498
Racconto della grande a tetra palude. 92405
Race fairly run. 43638
Race for life. 57294
Race for the mitre. 89632
Races Aryennes du Perou. 42001
Races of man. (62623)-62624
Races of mankind. (67387)
Races of men: a fragment. (38172)
Rachel . . . a tale of truth. 41725
Rachel and the New World. 4210
Rachel Dyer: a North American story. 52156
Rachel et le Nouveau Monde. 4209
Rachel Kell. (49699)
Rachel's sepulchre. 104502
Raciad and other occasional poems. (17344)
Raciad, and other poems. 17346, note after
93564
Racine, A. (67388)-67389
Racine, Louis Joseph. 67390
Racine, Wisc. Board of Education. 67394
Racine, Wisc. Racine College. see Racine
College, Racine, Wisc.
Racine, Wisc. Racine Division No. 4. see
Sons of Temperance of North America.
Wisconsin. Racine Division No. 4, Racine.
Racine advocate. 67391
Racine and Mississippi Railroad Company.
67395-(67396)
Racine and Rock River Plank Road. 67392
Racine Baptist Association. see Baptists.
Wisconsin. Racine Baptist Association.
Racine College, Racine, Wisc. 67397-67398
Racine directory, for . . . 1858. (67400)
Racine Division No. 4., Racine, Wisc. see
Sons of Temperance of North America.
Wisconsin. Racine Division No. 4, Racine.
Racine, Janesville, and Mississippi Railroad
Company. (67399)
Racional d'l officio y vso de la razon. 98502
Rack, Edmund. 21048-21049
Rada, Francisco de Elorza y. see Elorza y
Rada, Francisco de.
Rada, Joseph Lorenz de. plaintiff (67401)

Rada y Delgado, Juan de Dios de la. 63306
Radcliff, --------. 67403
Radcliff, Ebenezer. see Radcliffe, Ebenezer.
Radcliff, G. 67404
Radcliff, Jacob. ed. 53745
Radcliff, T. ed. 43846
Radcliffe, ----------. 37475
Radcliffe, Ebenezer. 67405, 97565
Raddi, Giuseppe. 67406-67407
Radel, D. Petit. see Petit-Radel, D.
Radermacher, Jacques Corneille Matthieu.
　67408
Raders, J. E. W. F. van. 67409
Raders, R. F. van. 67410-(67415), 1st note
　after 93855
Raders, R. F. van. supposed author 93863
Raders, W. van. 67416
Radet, J. B. 67417
Radical. pseud. Letter. 82007
Radical (Newbern, N. C.) 67420
Radical (Virginia City, Nevada) (69658)
Radical. A continuation of the working man's
　advocate. 67418
Radical: a monthly magazine, devoted to
　religion. 67419
Radical: and advocate of equality. 67421
Radical cause of the present distresses.
　89293
Radical common sense—the President and
　Congress. 22092
Radical deficiency of the existing circulating
　medium. 28619
Radical democracy of New York. 12200
Radical falsehood exposed! Grant's Attorney
　General exposes the falshoods of Senator
　Morton. 84808
Radical falsehood exposed. U. S. troops sent
　to North Carolina. 84807
Radical Governor of Alabama confirms the
　statements. 84808
Radical reconstruction on the basis of one
　sovereign republic. 67422
Radical reformer, and working man's advocate.
　8397
Radical Union Party. Missouri. 20817,
　(49576)
Radical, weekly stamped newspaper. 97534
Radical words of the Mohawk language. 8779
Radicalism and conservatism—the truth of
　history vindicated. 36885
Radicalism and conservatism: their influence
　on the development. 50454
Radicalism and the national crisis. 89100
Radicalism in religion, philosophy, and social
　life. (42705), 58758, 67423
Radicalism the nation's hope. 36885
Radicalism vindicated. 20817
Radices verborum Iroquaeorum. 8779
Radiguet, Max. (67424)
Radlof, J. G. (67425)
Radtler, B. 74829
Rae, John, 1796-1872. 67426
Rae, John, 1813-1893. 67427-(67429)
Rae, Julio H. 61606
Rae, W. F. 67430
Raegos memoraveis do Senhor Dom Pedro I.
　58988
Raei de Jonge, Joh. de. 67431
Raemdonck, J. van. 67432
Rae's Philadelphia pictorial directory. 61606
Raetzel. pseud. Catalogue des livres et
　manuscrits. see Ternaux-Compans,
　Henri.
Rafael de Jesus. see Jesus, Rafael de.
Rafael, Tomas de San. see San Rafael,
　Tomas de.
Rafaeli, Jose Maria. defendant (71615)

Raff, George W. 67433-67435
Raffles, Thomas. 67436
Rafinesque, Constantine Samuel, 1783-1840.
　12430, 13079, 44780, 50004, 67437-
　67465, 72031, note after 105488
Rafinesque-Schmaltz, Constantine Samuel. see
　Rafinesque, Constantine Samuel, 1783-
　1840.
Rafn, Carl Christian, 1795-1864. (4117), 55464,
　67466-(67486), 81698, 83424
Rafter, Hermann. 67487
Rafter, M. 67488
Rageneau, Paul. 39957
Raggvaglio d'alcvne missioni dell' Indie
　Orientali, & Occidentali. 44964, 89536,
　89538
Raggvaglio d'alcuni avisi notabili dell' Indie
　Orientali y Occidentali. 18658, 89537
Ragguaglio della navigazione alle Indie Orientale.
　(62804)
Ragguaglio scritto per mano di Mormon.
　83134
Ragine, A. 67489
Ragionamenti di Francesco Carletti Fiorentino.
　10908
Ragionamento nel quale si conferma l'opione
　generale. 14662, 79309
Ragland, Thomas. defendant at court martial
　67490
Ragnet, Conoly. ed. 3212, 31497, 69433,
　94090, 96433
"Rags! Rags! Rags!" 32182
Ragueneau, Paul. 39992, (67491)-67500, note
　after 69259, 96969 see also Jesuits.
　Canada. Superior des Missions.
Raguenet, Francois, 1660?-1772. ed. 74820
Raguet, Condy, 1784-1842. 23373, 24349,
　67501-67507
Rahnen, Johann Rudolff. ed. 99534
Raid of the dog-days. 81209, 81211
Raids and romances of Morgan and his men.
　25069
Rail road and route book for the western and
　southern states. (28885), 35715
Rail roads, canals, bridges, &c. 60166
Rail Road Commissioners report. 70630
Rail Road Conspirators. defendants see Fitch,
　Abel F. defendant
Rail road excursion. 32230, 74900
Rail road freight tariff between Boston and
　Albany. 67509
Rail road to New Orleans for transporting the
　mail. 95746
Rail roading at Erie. 22738, 82146
Rail-roads and canals. 67511
Rail roads, canals, bridges, &c. 60166, 92813
Rail roads in the United States. (67512)
Railroad and insurance almanac for 1865.
　67508
Railroad and route book, for the western and
　southern states. (28885), 35715
Railroad and steam-boat companion. 104392
Railroad and steamboat directory. (9374)
Railroad and steamboat directory; . . . by
　Burton Kendrick. 37374
Railroad and steamboat sketches. 72139
Railroad Celebration, Boston, 1851. 6766,
　6768, 12513, 1st note after 94186
Railroad communication. A west proposed line.
　85240
Railroad Companies Owning the Lines Between
　Washington and New York. 90675
Railroad Conspirators. defendants see Fitch,
　Abel F. defendant
Railroad Convention, Decatur, Ala., 1853.
　petitioners 87328
Railroad Convention, Harrisburg, Pa., 1838.
　60428

Railroad economy. 39023
Railroad edition, no. 46. 83896
Railroad from Lake Superior to the Pacific.
  (43171)
Railroad from the banks of the Ohio River to
  the tide-waters. 67510
Railroad from the Mississippi to the Pacific.
  29383
Railroad gazetteer for gratuitous distribution.
  17559
Railroad grants and land monopoly. 33349
Railroad iron. 79545
Railroad Jubilee, Boston, 1851. see Railroad
  Celebration, Boston, 1851.
Railroad jubilee. An account of the celebration.
  6766
Railroad jubilee: two discourses. 37847
Railroad laws and charters of the United
  States. 28722
Railroad monopoly. 10828
Railroad policy of Pennsylvania. 92909
Railroad question. [By Henry C. Carey.]
  10842
Railroad question. State ownership no remedy
  for existing evils. 89572
Railroad reading. (9692)
Railroad register and general advertiser.
  91736
Railroad, steamboat, and stage guide and hand-
  book. 29759
Railroad, steamboat, and telegraph book.
  20325
Railroad to the Pacific. 7088
Railroad to the Pacific . . . July 7. 29862
Railroad to the Pacific. Northern route.
  36207
Railroad to the Pacific Ocean. 83832
Railroads are private property, and subject
  to legislative control. 64107
Railroads considered in regard to their effects
  on the value of land. 36459
Railroads, history and commerce of Chicago.
  12664
Railroads in Canada. 10560
Railroads in New Jersey. (36269)
Railroads in the states. (20611)
Railroads of the United States: by Henry V.
  Poor. (64057)
Railroads of the United States; their history
  and statistics. 24769
Railton, ---------, fl. 1858. (41863)
Railton, J. 67513
Railton's directory, for the city of London,
  C. W. (41863)
Railway anecdote book. 67514
Railway business directory and shippers' guide.
  34209
Railway Committee evidence. (67515)
Railway communication between New York and
  Washington. (67516)
Railway correspondence. (67517)
Railway directory for 1858. 42399
Railway extension. Mr. Laurie's report.
  56164
Railway manual containing railroad maps.
  73501
Railway. Remarks at Belfast, Maine, July 4,
  1867. 64065
Railway ride to it. 83331
Railway shilling edition. 92491
Railway system of Massachusetts. 67270
Railway to the Pacific. 57934
Railways: an introductory sketch. 91323
Railways. Extension correspondence. 56165
Railways in Canada. 10560
Railways in New Brunswick. 7112

Railways: their capital and dividends. 91323
Raimond, Julien. (67518)-67522, 78720
  see also France. Commission aux
  Isles Sous le Vent.
Raimondi, Antonio. 67523-67525
Raimondo da Roma, F. 67526
Rain imbibed, or emblem of grace. 83450
Rainbow (H. M. Ship) 19775, note after 96363
Rainbow. 91673
Rainbow bird of Carolina. 38008
Rainbow; first series. 67527, note after
  104881
Rainbow, or lights and shadows of fashionable
  life. 67528
Rainbow side. 21917
Rainey, Thomas. (57012), 67529, 71468 see
  also Companhia Ferry do Rio de
  Janeiro e de Nictheroy. Emprezario.
Rains, George W. 67530
Rains, John. 34461
Rainsford, Marcus. 67531-67535
Rainsford Island Hospital, Boston. see Mas-
  sachusetts. Rainsford Island Hospital,
  Boston.
Rainville, Cesar de. 67537
Rainy day in camp. 67538
Raio, Joanne. see Ray, John, 1627-1705.
Raiol, Domingos Antonio. 67539-67540
Raising by Lt.-Col. Johnstone Livingston de
  Peyster, of the first real American flag
  over Richmond. 67541
Raising of money to be used in impeachment.
  9615
Raisonie ou douce demeure. 94385
Raisons de la Grande Bretagne d'avoir forme
  une colonie. 4936
Raisons que font voir combien il est important
  au Roi et a son etat. 10362
Raisons qui font voir combien il est important
  au Roy & son estat. (56080)
Ralegh, Gvalthervm, see Raleigh, Sir Walter,
  1552?-1618.
Ralegh, Sir W. see Raleigh, Sir Walter,
  1552?-1618.
Ralegh, Walther. see Raleigh, Sir Walter,
  1552?-1618.
Raleigh, Carew. 67599
Raleigh, Phillip. (67543)-67544, 67589
Raleigh, W. 17351
Raleigh, Walter. pseud. Observations on the
  public affairs of Great-Britain. see
  Bolingbroke, Henry St. John, Viscount,
  1678-1751.
Raleigh, Sir Walter, of Lincoln's Inn. (22976),
  67599
Raleigh, Sir Walter, 1552?-1618. (8784),
  14349, 14957, (14958), 16781, 20518,
  21919, 33658-33659, 33672, 37686-37691,
  67542-67544, 67546, (67551)-67558,
  67560-67566, 67572-67573, 67574-(67585),
  67587-67591, 67595-67599, 73312, (73325),
  78994, 82979, 97558, 97595-97597,
  98513
Raleigh, Sir Walter, 1552?-1618. supposed
  author (22976), 67599
Raleigh, Sir Walter, 1552?-1618. defendant
  35784, 67545, (67547), 67560, (67567),
  67569, (67570), 67590
Raleigh, N. C. Administration Convention,
  1827. see Administration Convention,
  Raleigh, N. C., 1827.
Raleigh, N. C. Constitutional Convention, 1835.
  see North Carolina. Constitutional
  Convention, Raleigh, 1835.
Raleigh, N. C. Constitutional Convention, 1868.
  see North Carolina. Constitutional
  Convention, Raleigh, 1868.

Raleigh, N. C. Convention, 1861-1862. see North Carolina. Convention, Raleigh, 1861-1862.
Raleigh, N. C. Convention, 1865-1866. see North Carolina. Convention, Raleigh, 1865-1866.
Raleigh, N. C. Convention of Freedmen of North Carolina, 1865. see Convention of Freedmen of North Carolina, Raleigh, 1865.
Raleigh, N. C. Episcopal School of North-Carolina. see Episcopal School of North Carolina, Raleigh.
Raleigh, N. C. Freedmen's Convention, 1866. see Freedmen's Convention, Raleigh, N. C., 1866.
Raleigh, N. C. Institution for the Deaf and Dumb and the Blind. see North Carolina. School for the Blind, Raleigh. and North Carolina. School for the Deaf and Dumb, Raleigh.
Raleigh, N. C. School for the Blind. see North Carolina. School for the Blind, Raleigh.
Raleigh, N. C. School for the Deaf and Dumb. see North Carolina. School for the Deaf and Dumb, Raleigh.
Ralfe, J. 91842
Ralfe, James. 67601-(67602)
Rallier, ---------. 67603-(67605)
Ralling, John. 67606-67607
Rally, ----------. tr. (26050)
Rallying-point, for all true friends of their country. 81322
Ralph, James, 1705?-1762. 67608-(67609), 99257
Ralph Doughby's Esq. Brautfahrt. 64544
Ralph Earle and his descendants. 21628
Ralph Norwood. 93106
Ralph Raven. pseud. see Raven, Ralph. pseud.
Ralph Sprague, in Charlestown in 1628. 89678
Ralpho Risible. pseud. see Risible, Ralpho. pseud.
Ralphs, E. S. 67610
Ralphton; or, the young Carolinian of 1776. 8003
Ralston, G. 67611
Ralston, W. C. 67612
Ramalhete poetico do Parnaso Italiano. 81303
Ramanzo, the conscience stricken brigand. 83006
Rambach, Friedrich Eberhard. 90027
Rambau, Alfred Xavier. 67614
Ramble, James. 67615
Ramble, Robert. pseud. City scenes. 67616
Ramble in the footsteps of Alexander Selkirk. 8657
Ramble of six thousand miles. 24161
Ramble through the United States. 79926
Rambler. 36295A
Rambler! His guide to, and around the Cauderskill and Haines's Falls. 11552
Rambler in Mexico. (39221)
Rambler in North America. 39222
Rambler in the west. pseud. Letters. (34260)
Rambler, or a tour through Virginia, Tennessee, &c. 67617
Rambler's recollections. (5558), 61177
Rambler's magazine and New-York theatrical register. 67618
Rambles about Portsmouth. 7774
Rambles about the country. 22214

Rambles among the blue-noses. 89156
Rambles and scrambles in North and South America. 93482
Rambles and scrambles in Texas and New Estremadura. 88599, 93969, note before 95109
Rambles by land and water. 55493
Rambles in Brazil. 59279
Rambles in Chili. 12800
Rambles in Cuba. (17798), 67619
Rambles in the Mammoth Cave in 1844. 17590
Rambles in mission-fields. 84059
Rambles in the path of the steam horse. 7054
Rambles in the Rocky Mountains. 50853
Rambles in the United States and Canada. 73859
Rambles in Westchester County. 18396
Rambles in Yucatan. 4608, (55494)
Rambles of a journalist. (30110)
Rambles of a naturalist. 27663, 27664
Rambles of Fudge Fumble. (67620)
Rambles through the city. 21742
Rambleton. 64551
Rambling poem. 68644, 101234
Rambling recollections of a trip to America. 84326
Rambling reflections in Greenwood. 28696
Ramblings in California. (79954)
Rambosson, K. 67621
Rame, Alfred. 11141-11142
Rame, Louis. 32200
Rameau, E. 67622-67623
Rameau, S. 67624
Ramel, Jean Pierre, 1768-1815. (1534), 26839, (27337), 29157, 67625-67633
Ramez, Louis. 26883
Ramezay, Jean Baptiste Nicolas Roch, sieur de, 1708-1777. 67021
Ramires de Arellano, R. 67634
Ramires de Castillo, Pedro. 67635, 74044
Ramirez, Alejandro. 26436, 67636 see also Cuba. Indendente de Ejercito. Cuba. Superintendente.
Ramirez, Antonio. 60904
Ramirez, Antonio de Guadalupe. 67637-67638
Ramirez, Geronimo. 39140
Ramirez, I. ed. 69596
Ramirez, José Antonio Alzate. see Alzate Ramirez, Jose Antonio, 1738-1799.
Ramirez, Jose Fernando. 21405, (34156), 56008, 62878, 65267, 67639-67645, 80978, 80987, 85760 see also Mexico. Museo Nacional de Antiguedades. Conservador. Sociedad Mexicana de Geografia y Estadistica. Comision Nombrada Para Examiner la Obra de D. Francisco Pimentel.
Ramirez, Joseph Gil. 67647
Ramirez, Jose H. 67649
Ramirez, Jose Maria. 67650
Ramirez, Jose Miguel. (67651)
Ramirez, Josephus. supposed author 59523, 67647
Ramirez, Juan. ed. 40959, (64915)
Ramirez, Lucas. 67652
Ramirez, Manuel. 67653
Ramirez, Manuel Maria Doming y. 67654
Ramirez, Miguel. 23436, 67655
Ramirez, Pedro. 63652, 73861
Ramirez, Ramon. 67656
Ramirez, Sebastian. 70459
Ramirez, Aparicio, Manuel. 67657
Ramirez de Feunleal, S., BP. 94854 see also Santo Domingo (Archdiocese) Bishop (Ramirez de Feunleal)

Randel, J. F. 33887
Randel, John. 67807
Randing, Ambrosius. (67808)
Randolph, Anson D. F. 67809-67810
Randolph, Bernard. 67811
Randolph, Beverley. 100217-100219 see also
Virginia. Governor, 1788-1791 (Beverley
Randolph)
Randolph, Edmund, 1820-1861. 67820-67822
Randolph, Edmund Jennings, 1753-1813.
(13896), (34385), 34900, note after
53697, 63818, 67812-67818, note after
83791, 96446, 1st note after 99797,
100213-100216, 100405, 2d note after
101709 see also U. S. Department of
Justice. U. S. Department of State.
Virginia. Governor, 1786-1788 (Edmund
Randolph)
Randolph, Francis. 67823-(67824), 82006
Randolph, Henry. 100380 see also Virginia
(Colony) General Assembly. House.
Clerk.
Randolph, J. Thornton. pseud. Cabin and
parlor. see Peterson, Charles J.
Randolph, Jacob. 67825
Randolph, Jessie. 67826
Randolph, Sir John, 1693?-1737. 99909-
99911, 99913 see also Virginia (Colony)
General Assembly. House of Burgesses.
Speaker.
Randolph, Sir John, 1693?-1737. reporter
99975
Randolph, Sir John, 1693?-1737. supposed
author 99911
Randolph, John, 1727?-1784. 55170, 91860,
96739, 100448-100449, 101737-101743
Randolph, John, 1773-1833. (67827)-67847,
68198, (69814), 69817, 77320, (78388),
91241, 104027, 105157
Randolph, Joseph Fitz, 1803-1873. 67850
Randolph, Mary. 100557
Randolph, Paschal Beverly. 67851-67852
Randolph, Peter. 100006 see also Virginia
(Colony) Commissioners to the Catawba
and Cherokee Indians.
Randolph, Peter. a slave 67853
Randolph, Peyton, 1721?-1775. 40292, (40388),
85243, 100007, 100008, 3d, and 7th notes
after 100483 see also Virginia (Colony)
Convention, Aug. 1-6, 1774. Moderator.
Randolph, R. K. 70663
Randolph, Sarah N. (67854)
Randolph, Thomas Jefferson, 1792-1875. 232,
35891-35892, (67856)-67857, 96015
Randolph, Thomas Jefferson, 1792-1875.
petitioner 67855
Randolph, W. B. (67859)
Randolph, Warren. (67858)
Randolph. firm see Frazier & Randolph.
Firm
Randolph, Mass. School Committee. 67861
Randolph, Mass. Selectmen. 67861
Randolph, Vt. Washington Benevolent Society.
see Washington Benevolent Society.
Vermont. Randolph.
Randolph County, Indiana. Citizens. petitioners
(47651), 69829
Randolph epistles. 67860
Randolph Macon College, Ashland, Va. 67862,
84743
Randolph's abridgment. 100405
Random recollections. 90430
Random recollections of a long medical life.
84266
Random recollections of Albany, from 1800 to
1808. 36513, 105498-105499

Random recollections of Albany, Hudson &
Cincinnati. 105499
Random shot. 67863
Random sketches in relation to the ancient
town of Hull, Mass. 33648
Random sketches of Buenos Ayres. 67864
Random sketches, . . . of Hull, . . . Boston.
32722
Random sketches upon witches, dreams, love
and romance. 17557
Rangel, J. A. 67866
Rangel, Joaquin. defendant at court martial
67865
Rangel, Joseph Francisco Dimas. 67867
Ranger, pseud. Hunter's experiences. see
Flack, Captain. pseud.
Rangers. 95485
Rangers and regulators of the Yanaha. 2108A,
note after 93619
Rangers of the Mohawk. 22297
Rango, F. L. von. 67868
Ranken, George, 1828-1856. 67869-67870
Ranken, W. Bayne. ed. 67869
Rankin, A. 67872
Rankin, Adam, 1755-1827. 67871, 95382
Rankin, Adam, 1755-1827. defendant before
presbytery 96459
Rankin, Andrew. 67873
Rankin, Christopher. 67874-67875
Rankin, Jeremiah Eames. 67876-67881
Rankin, John. (39554), (67882)
Rankin, John C. 67883-67884
Rankin, Melinda. 67885
Rankin, R. G. 67886
Rankin, Thomas. 51829, (67887), 100437
Rankin, William. (67888)
Rankin, William, Jr. 67889
Rankin, William C. 67890
Ranking, John. (28181), 67891-(67892), 2d
note after 93802
Ranklin, Benjamin. supposed author 60742,
note after 97095
Ranlet, Henry. 83398-83399
Ranlett, William H. 67893
Ranney, J. A. 67894
Ranney, Waitstill R. 67895
Ranney Family Reunion. see Family Reunion
of the Descendants of Waitstill Ranney
and Jeremiah Atwood. 8th, Chester, Vt.,
1866.
Ransford, Rogers. 106070
Ransom, C. R. 83857
Ransom, William Merwin. 86981
Ransonnet, ------ de. 50131, 67898-67899,
4th note after 99504
Ranst, C. W. van. see Van Ranst, C. W.
Ranter. 54944
Rantoul, Robert, 1805-1852. (11925), 20539,
46072, (46084), 67900-67908, 92068
Ranuzzi, Annibale. 67909
Raorihwadogennhti ne Shongwayaner Yesus
Keristus. 49848
Raousset-Boulbon, G. de. 38459, (38700),
67910
Raowenna teyoninhokarowan Shakonadonire ne
rondaddegenshon. 49849, 95145
Rap for the rappers. 16338
Rapatea Friderici Augusti und Saxo-Fridericia
Regalis. note after 77796
Rape of Bethesda. 36234
Rapelje, George. 67911
Raphael: a member of the Astronomical Society
of London. pseud. Royal book of dreams.
see Smith, R. C., 1795-1832.
Raphael, de Jesus. 36088-36089, (67912)
Raphael, Morris Jacob, 1798-1868. (8488)

Raphall, Morris Jacob, 1798-1868. (22088), 57492, 67913
Rapida ojeada. 67914
Rapida ojeada al estado de Sonora. 106402
Rapida ojeada sobre la Compana & segunda parte. 76747
Rapida ojeada sobre nuestros disturbios, sus causas y remedios. 44899
Rapido esboco da futura rede geral de suas vias navegareis. 50485
Rapine, ---------. illus. 6982
Rapine, Charles. 67915
Raport de la premiere ascention areostatique. 95307
Raport van sijn administratie. 98248
Rapp, George. 67916-67917, 95698
Rapp, Wilhelm. 67918
Rappers. 67919
Rapport a la Chambre des Pairs. 47968
Rapport a mes amis. 15926
Rapport a M. le Ministre de l'Intereur des Etats-Unis, par M. le Chef du Bureau des Affaires Indiennes. (32746), (44438)
Rapport a M. le Ministre de l'Interieur des Etats-Unis sur les hommes rouges. 49974
Rapport adresse a l'Empereur Charles V. 94853
Rapport adresse a M. le Garde des Sceaux Hebert. 40956
Rapport adresse a M. le Ministre de la Marine et des Colonies. 61023
Rapport adresse au Directoire Executif. (42350), 96343
Rapport adresse au gouvernement de S. M. Britannique. 70047
Rapport annuel du Maitre-General des Postes. (10548)
Rapport annuel de la Societe de Construction du District de Montreal. 85796
Rapport annuel des Directeurs de la Societe de Construction Mutuelle. 85800
Rapport annuel des Inspecteurs du Penitencier Provincial. (10553)
Rapport . . . au Departement Militaire Suisse. 39659
Rapport au Departement Militaire Suisse. (39660)
Rapport au nom de la Commission Chargee de Presenter les Lois Organiques. 21762
Rapport . . . dans l'Assemblee General. 39675
Rapport de . . . [A. de Mendoza] Vice-Roi de la Nouvelle-Espagne. 94854
Rapport de E. G. Squier. 89958
Rapport de Julien Raimond. 67520
Rapport de la Commission des Onze. 28132
Rapport [de la Commission . . . Pour l'Examen des Questions Realtive a l'Esclavage et a la Constitution Politique des Colonies.] 14717
Rapport de la Division des Sauvages du Departement du Secretaire d'Etat. 67920
Rapport de la Societe d'Agriculture du Bas-Canada. 10347
Rapport [de la Societe Francaise de Bienfais-sance de Philadelphie.] 62248
Rapport de l'ingenieur de la Societe de l'Amerique Meridionale sur l'exploitation des plages auriferes du Rio-Tipuani. 67921
Rapport de l'Inspecteur des Chemins. 50274
Rapport de Lord Durham. 58489
Rapport de Lord Durham, Haut-Commissaire de Sa Majeste. 38749
Rapport de M. Barnave sur l'affaire de Saint-Domingue. 49083

Rapport de M. Drouyn de Lhuis. 20964
Rapport de M. Guillemin au Ministre de l'Agriculture. 67922
Rapport de M. Theophile Barnoin. 3549
Rapport de MM. le Marquis de Cadusch, Brulley, et De Pons. 9833
Rapport de Philippe-Rose Roume. 73471
Rapport de progres depuis son commencement jusqu'a 1863. 41810
Rapport definitif des Commissaires Charges de l'Enquete. 10428
Rapport des Commissaires de la Societe Royale de Medecine. 11624
Rapport des Commissaires des Travaux Publics pour 1851. 67923
Rapport des Commissaires des Travaux Publiques pour l'anne 1855. 10561
Rapport des Commissaires Nommes Pour s'Enquerir de la Cause de l'Incendie. 67051
Rapport des Commissaires Nommes Pour s'Enquerir de l'Origine et des Causes de l'Incendie. 67052
Rapport des Commissaires pour Explorer le Saguenay. 74939
Rapport des Commissaires Speciaux, Nommes le 8 de Septembre, 1856. 67924
Rapport des seances annuelles de 1848-1851. 85827
Rapport des seances annuelles de 1838 et de 1839. 85826
Rapport du Bureau d'Ingenieurs et de W. E. Logan. 41816
Rapport du Capitaine de la Marine Royale Sir James Clark Ross. 73385
Rapport du Capitaine MacClintock. 43044, 44171
Rapport du Commissaire des Terres de la Couronne du Canada. (10412)
Rapport du Commissaire du Bureau General des Terres Publiques. 67925
Rapport du Comite Charge de Prendre et Recueillir des Informations. 33547
Rapport du Comite Charge, en Vertue de la Resolution Prise par les Deux Chambres de la Legislature. 42286
Rapport du Comite Choise sur le Gouvernement Civil de Canada. 10563
Rapport du Comite de la Chambre des Com-munes Sur le Gouvernement Civil du Canada. 10562
Rapport du Comite des Six. 14056-14057
Rapport du Comite du Conseil, sur l'objet d'augmenter les moiens d'education. 10428
Rapport du Comite Sepcial de la Chambre d'Assemblee du Bas-Canada. 10428
Rapport du Comite Special Nomme Pour s'Enquerir des Causes de l'Emigration du Canada. 10440
Rapport du Comite Special sur la Rapport de la Societe d'Agriculture. 10347
Rapport du Comite Sepcial sur l'Etat de l'Agriculture du Bas-Canada. 42523
Rapport du Superintendant de l'Education pour le Bas-Canada. Pour 1853. 10428
Rapport du Surintendant [sic] de l'Education pour le Bas-Canada . . . 1855. 42516
Rapport d'un Quebeccois. 67053
Rapport d'un temoin oculaire. 67926
Rapport et projet de decret presentes par le citoyen Dornier. 75173
Rapport et projet de decret, sur les approvisionnemens des colonies. 67927
Rapport et projet de decret, sur les lettres-du-charge. 44826

Raymond, James. (68058)
Raymond, John H. 68059-68060 see also
Vassar College. President.
Raymond, Julien. see Raimond, Julien.
Raymond, Miner. 68062
Raymond, Robert R. 68063
Raymond, Rossiter W. 68064-68067 see also
U. S. Bureau of Mines.
Raymond, Samuel G. 68068
Raymond, William. 68069
Raymond Institute, Carmel, N. Y. 68071
Raymondi, Antonio. see Raimondi, Antonio.
Raymundo Pasqual, Antonio. see Pasqual,
Antonio Raymundo.
Raymonds, Edmund A. 72353 see also Roch-
ester, N. Y. City Attorney.
Raynal, Guillaume Thomas Francois, 1713-
1796. 1361, 4479, 4688, 4928, 7929,
10883, 11824, 24017, 47206, 56308-
56310, 58222-58223, 58239, (61313),
(68072)-(68075), 68077-68085, 68087-
68098, 68101-68116, 80675, 91304,
92197, 97507, 99302
Raynal de la juenesse. 69098
Raynal demasque. 68099
Raynal parmi les quadrupedes. 56061, (68086)
Rayner, B. L. (68117)-68118
Rayner, Kenneth, 1808-1884. 68119-68121,
90338
Rayner, Menzies. 68122
Rayner, Menzies. plaintiff 96922
Rayneval, J. M. Gerard de. supposed author
4182, 56580, 68123-68124
Raynham, Mass. School Committee. 68125-
68126
Raynham, Mass. Selectmen. 68126
Raynham, Mass. Treasurer. 68126
Raynolds, Freegrace. 68127
Raynolds, Peter. 68128
Raynolds, W. F. (68129)
Raynouard, Francois Juste Marie, 1761-1836.
11237
Rayo a lo que quiere la Habana. (29452)
Rayo azul en la naturaliza y en la historia.
72778
Rayon, Ignacio Lopez. 48287, 67646, 93580
Rayon, J. Sancho. 26385
Rayon, Sancho. ed. 69211
Rayon-de-soleil. 4903D
Rays of sunlight from South America. (26636),
68131
Razgo biografico que consagra a la memoria.
86252
Raziones y derechos que tienen los pontifices
Romanos. 14547
Razoes de appellacao por parte de A. de S. R.
88800
Razoes de recurso interposito para o Superior
Tribunal do Relacio. 68330
Razon annual de los progresos y trabajos del
mineral de Tauricocha. 68134
Razon de la fabrica allegorica. 99400
Razon de la residencia, y sentencia. 73850
Razon de la sentencia. 22841, (70795)
Razon de las guerras dilatadas de Chile.
12754
Razon de lo acaecido en la ciudad de San
Francisco de Quito. 68135
Razon de Mexico. Periodico politico y
literario. 68133
Razon particular de los templos. 27811
Razon periodico independiente de politica.
(68132)
Razon puntual de los successos mas mem-
orables. 27811
Razonamiento de los embaradores de Espana.
94623

Razones que apoyan la translacion. 68136
Razvael, M. pseud. Dedication. see
Alvarez, M.
Re d'Ormus. 64014
Rea, Alexander W. 78076
Rea, John. USN 68137
Rea, John, fl. 1816. 68138
Read, Alexander. 68139
Read, Benjamin. 68140
Read, C. H. 68141
Read, Charles. 22192, 40280, 68142, 68143
Read, Collinson. 59769, 68144
Read, D. F. 68157
Read, Daniel, 1757-1841. 68145
Read, Daniel, 1805-1878. 68146-68147
Read, David. 68148
Read, George, 1733-1798. 52569, 68194 see
also Delaware. Convention, Newcastle,
1776. President.
Read, George, 1765-1836. 68149
Read, H. Y. 68155
Read, Harriette Fanning. 68150
Read, Hollis. 68151-68154
Read, Hugh G. ed. 43128
Read, J. 68156
Read, J. A. 68157
Read, Jesse. (9322)-(9323)
Read, Joel. (68158)
Read, John. 68159, 73398-73340, (73402)
Read, John, 1769-1854. 56542, 84842 see
also U. S. Agent Under the Sixth Article
of the Treaty of Amity, Commerce, and
Navigation, Between His Britannic
Majesty and the United States of America.
Read, John Dickinson. 68160
Read, John K. 68161, 100473, note after
100474
Read, John Meredith, 1797-1874. 18838, 61891,
68162-68169
Read, John Meredith, 1837-1896. 68170
Read, M. S. 68171
Read, Marie. 16930
Read, N. C. (68172)
Read, O. A. 55020, (68173)
Read, Thomas Buchanan, 1822-1872. 51437,
68174-(68186), 95753
Read, W. G. 22587
Read, W. J. see Read, William Thompson.
Read, William. 68187-68188 see also
Boston. Health Department. City
Physician.
Read, William C. 68189
Read, William George. 45079, 68190-68193
Read, William J. see Read, William
Thompson.
Read, William Thompson. 68194-68195
Read, Y. 68196
Read and circulate. 91015
Read and circulate! 91012
Read and circulate. City missions. 62112
Read and circulate. Published under authority
of the National and Jackson Democratic
Association Committee. 91633
Read and circulate. Speech of Hon. A. H.
Stephens. 27111, 91254
Read and decide for yourself. 65208
Read and judge for yourself. 18832
Read and judge. Shall the society or the
committee rule? (47241), 93816
Read, and lend to your neighbor. 85895,
91008-91009
Read and let neighbors read. 88295
Read and ponder. 57276, 63768
Read and reflect. 68197
Read—and then choose. 62301
Read carefully; reflect, decide, and then act.
93460

Read for yourselves. (34691)
Read, Jerseymen! Pause, and reflect!!!
68198
Read, ponder, and pass it to your neighbor.
82041
Read, read. 90765
Read, reflect and vote. (68199)
Read this before you vote! (68200)
Read, try, decide, on the charge of Washington. 73829, 1st note after 101879
Reade, J. K. defendant 100229
Reader for beginners in the English and German languages. (6131)
Reader for the use of primary schools. (12286)
Reader is desired to take notice. 65689
Readfield, Me. Bowdoinham Baptist Association Meeting, 1793. see Baptists. Maine. Bowdoinham Baptist Association.
Reading, M. B. illus. 21446
Reading, Philip. 68201, 106354
Reading, Mass. 58710, 68203, 68205, 68208, (68211)-68212
Reading, Mass. Bi-centennial Celebration, 1844. (24776)
Reading, Mass. Ecclesiastical Council, 1847. see Congregational Churches in Massachusetts. Ecclesiastical Council, Reading, 1847.
Reading, Mass. Public Library. 68206
Reading, Mass. Public Library. Trustees. 68206
Reading, Mass. School Committee. 68205, 68209
Reading, Mass. Second Congregational Church. 71003, note before 90710
Reading, Mass. Superintending School Committee. (68204)
Reading, Pa. Christ Church. 65838
Reading, Pa. Convention of Democratic Young Men, 1838. see Democratic Party. Pennsylvania. Convention of Democratic Young Men, Reading, 1838.
Reading, Pa. Convocational Congress, 1867. see Protestant Episcopal Church in the U. S. A. Pennsylvania (Diocese) Convocational Congress, Reading, 1867.
Reading & Lehigh Rail Road. 68214
Reading & Lehigh Rail Road. Charter. 68214
Reading city and business directory for 1867-8. 68213
Reading directory for 1866. 68213
Reading farce, in two acts. 81925
Reading Hall and Circulating Library, Rhinebeck, N. Y. see Rhinebeck, N. Y. Reading Hall and Circulating Library.
Reading no preaching. 68202
Reading rail-road: its advantages for the cheap transportation of coal. 68214
Reading Railroad Company. 78080
Reading Railroad Company. 68214
Reading Railroad Company: their policy and prospects. 68214
Reading upon the personal liberty laws of Massachusetts. 42078
Readinger Magazin fur Freunde der Deutschen Literatur in Amerika. (68216)
Readings in American history. 82850
Ready reckoner; or, the American measurer's guide. 71912
Ready reckoner; or the trader's useful assistant. 68217
Ready reckoner; or, trader's useful assistant. 68217
Ready way to true content. (70899)
Ready way to unpopularity. 95734

Reagan, John Henninger, 1818-1905. (15234), 15245, 15282, 15314, 15387-(15388), 68218 see also Confederate States of America. Post Office Department.
Reagles (C.) & Sons. firm 68219
Real, Christoval de Villa. see Villa Real, Christoval de.
Real, Diogo de Mendoca Corte. see Mendoca Corte-Real, Diogo de, 1658-1736.
Real, Gaspar Corte. see Corte-Real, Gaspar, 1450-1501.
Real, Joao Pereira Corte. see Corte-Real, Joao Pereira.
Real, Joseph Remi Vallieres de St. see Vallieres de St. Real, Joseph Remi.
Real Transporte, ---------, Marques del. defendant 29425
Real Audiencia de Cuentas, Havana. see Havana. Real Audiencia de Cuentas.
Real advantages which ministers and people may enjoy. 4093, 102573
Real American. 68221
Real and genuine school for scandal, a comedy. 80343
Real and ideal: a collection of metrical compositions. 50092
Real and ideal: a poem by W. Gordon McCabe. 68161
Real and personal estate, 1852. (18518)
Real and vital religion served. 46569, note after 98241
Real Casa de Moneda de las Indias. see Spain. Real Casa de Moneda de las Indias.
Real Casa de Moneda de Mexico. see Mexico (Viceroyalty) Real Casa de Moneda.
Real cedula concerniente a las carceles y reos de la ciudad de Mexico. 48634
Real cedula concerniente la celebracion de Concilios Provinciales. 68222
Real cedula dada en Madrid. (61088)
Real cedula de 10 de Mayo de 1776. 68873
Real cedula de 17 de Junio de 1794. 67108, 76861
Real cedula, de 19 de enero de 1769. 17808
Real cedula de ereccion del Colegio de Escribanos. 17800
Real cedula de ereccion del consulado de Buenos-Ayres. 9031
Real cedula de ereccion del consulado de Chile. 68223
Real cedula de ereccion del consulado de Guadalaxara. 29028
Real cedula de ereccion del consulado de la Habana. 29450
Real cedula de incorporacion de el Banco de Potosi. 68224
Real cedula de 9 de Febrero de 1811. 68225
Real cedula de Poligamia. (68226)
Real cedula de S. M. que contiene el reglamento. 68227
Real cedula de S. M. y Senores del Consejo. 68228
Real cedula de S. M. y Senores del Real y Supremo Consejo. 29029
Real cedula de Su Magestad, expedida para que en la ciudad de San Christoval de la Habana. 16668, 29422
Real cedula de Su Magestad sobre la educacion. 68229
Real cedula de 21 de Octubre de 1817. 17799, 68230
Real cedula despachada en 11 Sept. 1767. 68231
Real cedula expedida por S. M. de Noviembre de 1773. 68232

Real cedula para la fundacion de la Confradia de Santiago. 48635
Real cedula sobre privilegios de inventos artisticos. 68233
Real character of a certain great orator. 41945
Real Chicago platform. 12662, 68234
Real Christian. 24400
Real Christianity. 93207
Real Christians hope in death. 106391
Real Compania de Comercio para las Islas de Santo Domingo. 68236, 1st note after 75184
Real Compania Guipuzcoana de Caracas: noticias historiales. 68237
Real crisis. 70342
Real declaracion de 17 de Junio de [1]773. 68860
Real declaracion de Su Magestad, de 17 de Junio de 1733. 68238
Real decreto de 15 de Febrero de 1810. 17747
Real e Ilustre Colegio de Abogados de San Ignacio de Loyola, Puerto Principe. 66587
Real estate and building company. 68239
Real estate and the beterment law. (13172)
Real Estate and Stock Exchange, Denver. see Denver Real Estate and Stock Exchange.
Real estate publisher. 68240
Real estate record. 68241
Real friend to legal liberty and the constitution. pseud. Reflections on the present combination. 68707
Real glory of a church. 73568
Real historia a la milagrosa imagen de Maria Santisima Senora. 59029
Real liberty song. 5818
Real life in the backwoods. 24640
Real life in the west. 57986, 37988
Real motives of the rebellion. 57594
Real motives of the rebellion. The slave-holders' conspiracy. 19505, 68242
Real object of charity. 72732
Real orden comunicada por el Excmo. S. Virey del Reyno. (68243)
Real orden de 9 de Junio de 1798. 56747
Real orden de 20 de Febrero 1765. 68873
Real orden de 27 de Abril. 98650
Real orden de 22 de Setiembre de 1820. 17774
Real orden expedida en S. Lorenzo. (56292)
Real orden que expidieron las Cortes Ordinarias. 68244
Real ordenanza para el establicimiento e instruccion de Intendentes. de Exercito y Provincia en el reino de la Nueva-Espana. 56259
Real ordenanza para el establicimiento e instruccion de Intendentes de Exercito y Provincia en el Virreinato de Buenos-Aires. (68245)
Real picture of slavery. 5218
Real proclamacion de su augusto hijo el Senor D. Carlos IV. 28254
Real question stated. 56660
Real questions before the country. (68246)
Real religion. 83896
Real resolucion sobre terrenos realengos y valdios. 17801
Real Robinson Crusoe. 75543
Real state of parties. 6816
Real state of the case. 95957
Real story for real boys and girls. 84749

Real Tribunal de Protomedicato de Esta Nueva Espana. see Mexico (Viceroyalty) Real Tribunal del Protomedicato.
Real y Conciliar Colegio Seminario, Havana. see Havana. Real y Conciliar Colegio Seminario.
Real y Distinguida Orden Espanola de Carlos III. see Orden de Carlos III. Mexico.
Real y Pontifica Universidad, Mexico. see Mexico (City) Universidad.
Real zedula. Para las audiencias y gobernadores de Indias &c. &c. 68247
Reales, -----------, Baron de Juras. see Juras Reales, --------, Baron de.
Reales, Pedro. 27802, 68248
Reales aranzeles de los Ministros de la Real Avdiencia. (9891), note after 96350
Reales cedulas y bula apostolica. 68249
Reales disposiciones que Nuestro Amado Soberano Fernando VII. 68250
Reales exequias. (64336)
Reales exequias celebradas en la Santa Iglesia Catedral de Mexico. 68251
Real exequias de Maria Magdalena Barbara de Portugal. 72540, 1st note after 96790
Reales exequias del Da. Maria Amalia de Saxonia. (44542)
Reales exequias, por el Senor Don Carlos III. 28254
Reales exequias, que por el fallecimiento del Senor Don Carlos III. (68252), 71247
Reales ordenanzas para la direccion, regimen y gobierno. 56260
Reales ordenes de 8 de igual mes de 1851. 66593
Reales ordenes, y cartas del Gobernador Don Juan de Prado. 16670
Reality versus fiction. A review of a pamphlet. 19662.
Reality versus fiction. By Hinton Rowan Helper. 31272
Reams, John W. 45512
Re-annexation of Texas. 95110
Reaper. 79546
Rear Admiral Goldsborough and the retiring laws of the Navy. 36019
Reason, Charles L. (68253)
Reason against railing, and truth against fiction. 59728
Reason against the emancipation proclamation. 56030
Reason and revelation. (64671)
Reason satisfied: and faith established. 46476
Reason the only oracle of man. (802), 57424, 79287
Reason why. 83459
Reason why Coleman Yellott, state senator of Baltimore. 55571
Reasonable religion. 46477
Reasonable vindication of the propriety. 2d note after 96428
Reasonableness of Christianity. (20062)
Reasonableness of nonconformity to the Church of England. (20062)
Reasonableness of personal reformation. 24682
Reasonableness of, regular singing. 94117
Reasonableness of setting forth the most worthy praise. 46478
Reasonableness of the abolition of slavery. 59765
Reasoner tracts, no. 38 and 40. 69375
Reasons against a national bank. (3182)
Reasons against a separation from the Church of England. 102685
Reasons against giving a territorial grant. 68254

Reasons humbly offer'd to the Honourable
House of Commons, by the merchants
and traders in Tobacco. 100517
Reasons humbly offered to the Hon. House of
Commons for passing the clause. 68286
Reasons humbly submitted to the consideration.
87935
Reasons in support of an opinion offered to
the public respecting the votes of Otsego
County. 30566, (68287), note after
83791
Reasons of Andrew Miller. 62237
Reasons of dissent. 12857, 29853
Reasons of dissent from the judgment of a
council, respecting the doctrines of Rev.
Mr. Bacheller. 2602, 12857, 29853
Reasons of my withdrawing my vote. (79447)
Reasons of the . . . Directors of the Pennsyl-
vania Railroad Company. 60358
Reasons of the government of the United
States. 96020
Reasons offered by Samuel Eddy. 21814-21815
Reasons offered to the House of Commons.
68288
Reasons offered to the Legislature of Massa-
chusetts. (82042)
Reasons on which were founded, the protest.
84586
Reasons, principally of a public nature.
(6603), (12116), 93541, 1st note after
101499
Reasons proposed to the House of Commons.
(68289)
Reasons shewing it is the interest of the
nation. 68290
Reasons submitted in favor of allowing a
transit of merchandize. 8859
Reasons to encourage a trade from Great-
Britain. 40404, 88186
Reasons to shew, that there is a great possi-
bility of a navigable passage. 68291
Reasons why distilled spirits should be
banished. 27850
Reasons why John Smith should not change
his name. 36147
Reasons why Lord **** should be made a
public example. 68292
Reasons why Mr. Byles left New London.
74633
Reasons why New London has not a navy yard
to-day. (69283)
Reasons why no deductions ought to be made.
68294
Reasons, why, not anabaptist plunging but
infants-believer's baptism. (42038)
Reasons why state aid should be granted.
(68295)
Reasons why the approaching treat of peace
should be debated. 68296
Reasons why the British colonies, in America,
should not be charged with internal
taxes. 15801, 24588, note after 68296
Reasons why the directors of the Stony Brook
Railroad should not be authorized. 92167
Reasons why the government of the United
States should aid. 68297
Reasons why the Hon. Elisha R. Potter should
not be a senator. 9233
Reasons why the illegal transactions in relation to dividing the Grand Division.
87958
Reasons why the independence of Texas should
be immediately recognized. 103113
Reasons why the Legislature should grant "the
petition of Wm. Aspinwall and others."
69298

Reasons why the measure of value established
by law. (52339)
Reasons why the Mexican treaty should be
accepted. 68299
Reasons why the New Haven and Northampton
Railroad should terminate. 68300
Reasons why the north should opposed Judge
Douglas. 41148
Reasons why the people called Quakers, cannot
so fully unite. 62475
Reasons why the people called Quakers do not
pay tythes. 68301, 97584
Reasons why the present system of auctions
ought to be abolished. 68302
Reasons why the supplement to the act incor-
porating the Susquehanna Canal Company,
should pass. 93926
Reasons why the transfer of the entire copy-
right. 68303
Reasons why the United States government
should be upheald. 68304
Reasonus. pseud. Theatre. 95280
Reavis, L. U. (68305)-(68314)
Rebau, Heinrich. pseud. Bibliothek der
Lander- und Volkerkunde. see Berghaus,
Heinrich Karl Wilhelm.
Rebecca. pseud. Tramps in New York. 68315
Rebel barbarities. 68316
Rebel brag and British bluster. 58028, 68317
Rebel conditions of peace and the mechanics
of the south. 68318
Rebel conscript. 64092
Rebel cotton loan. 68319
Rebel friend. 70550
Rebel invasion of Missouri and Kansas. 31969
Rebel of Dorchester. 81223-81224
Rebel pirate's fatal prize. 68320
Rebel Quakeress. 90522
Rebel rhymes and rhapsodies. 50367
Rebel saint. pseud. specimen of southern
devotion. 89124
Rebel states are organized conspiracies. 5447
Rebel states. The President and Congress.
68321
Rebel terms of peace. (27453), 68322
Rebel war clerk's diary at the Confederate
capital. 36531
Rebelion en Aznapuquio. 67323
Rebelle. (68814)
Rebelliad. 30755, 59539
Rebellion against democracy. 21475, 28451,
(35097)
Rebellion against free government. 80447
Rebellion against the United States. 30019
Rebellion; an historical poem. 37803
Rebellion and its purposes. 6931
Rebellion and opposition. 68324
Rebellion and our foreign relations. 68053
Rebellion and recognition. (23042)
Rebellion and witchcraft. 52418
Rebellion cannot abate the state governments.
71262
Rebellion cannot succeed. 55463
Rebellion de 1837 a Saint-Eustache. 58495,
94638
Rebellion in America. 55400
Rebellion in Tennessee. 43534
Rebellion in the north!! 68324
Rebellion in the United States. (26021)
Rebellion—its causes and consequences. (2189)
Rebellion: its character, motive, and aim.
20817
Rebellion: its consequences, and the Congres-
sional Committee. (34964), 68326
Rebellion: its origin and life in slavery. 20817
Rebellion: its origin, and the means of sup-
pressing it. 55361

Rebellion of '61. A domestic and political
tragedy. (2818), 19455, 86512
Rebellion of the cavaliers. 68327
Rebellion: our relations and duties. 43631
Rebellion record; a diary of American events.
7965, 40590, 41029, (43011), 43370,
50356, 50368, note after 69327, 74401,
89506, 89687-89688
Rebellion record. Part I. Supplementary
volume. 89506
Rebellion. Speech of Gerrit Smith in Montreal.
82654
Rebellion—the mistakes of the past—the duty
of the present. 36885
Rebellion. Two speeches. 43631
Rebellious nation reproved. 74829
Rebellious states. 61046
Rebello, Amador. 68328-68329, 72499
Rebello, Francisco Justiniano de Castro.
68330
Rebello, Jose Silvestre. 7530, 56371, 68331-
68332 see also Brazil. Legation.
United States.
Rebels. 6487, 12725
Rebels, and not the Republican Party, destroyed
slavery. (20611)
Rebels and tories. (38449)
Rebels, or Boston before the revolution. 12725
Rebolledo, Juan de. 68333-68334
Reboltijo del Padre Soto. 87220
Reboucas, Antonio Pereira. 68335-(68336)
Rebuke of secession doctrines by southern
statesmen. 68337
Rebuke of the Lord. (51254)
Rebuke to Daniel Leeds. (39819)
Rebuke to the worldly ambition of the present
age. (45438)
Rebuker rebuked in a brief answer to Caleb
Pusey. (39819)
Rebullosa, Jayme. 6810, (68338)
Rebuznos del Tio Bartolo que no seran los
ultimos. 68340
Recabarren, Martin de. 86439
Recalled; in voices of the past. 41725
Recantation; being an anticipated valedictory
address. 68341
Recantation; or four letters written by him.
105629
Recantation; or four letters, written by the
prophet. 105630
Recapitulati ou des propositions et transactions.
7543
Recapitulation of wonderfull passages which
have occurr'd. (46509)
Recapitulation, reflexions arising from a
retrospect of a late case. 39925-39926,
1st note after 87356, note after 87824
Recapitulations and conclusion. 99597
Reccho, Nardo Antonio. 31514-31516, 105727
Receipt from Middleborough. 7790
Receipt to make a speech. (68342)
Receipts and disbursements for the year
ending 105857
Receipts and disbursements of Siloam Lodge,
No. 2. (81071)
Receipts and expenditure of the subscription
of 1831. 68343
Receipts and expenditures for eleven months.
105857
Receipts and expenditures in the treasury of
Pennsylvania. 60443
Receipts and expenditures of . . . North
Reading. 55729
Receipts and expenditures of . . . Portsmouth.
64429
Receipts and expenditures of the county of
Norfolk. (55481)

Receipts and expenditures of the town of
Franklin. 25661
Receipts and expenditures of the town of Groton.
28971
Receipts and expenditures of the town of
Reading. 68208
Receipts and payments at the treasury of
Pennsylvania. 60443
Receipts for the cure of most diseases. 43413
Receivers and Exporters of American Leaf
Tobacco. petitioners (61276), 65002
Receivers and Exporters of American Leaf
Tobacco. Meeting, New York, 1865.
65002
Recensement des Canadas. 10401
Recent attempt to defeat the constitutional
provisions. 6649, 42457
Recent case of infamous and horrible abduction.
85225
Recent contest in Rhode Island. 68344, 70632
Recent discovery of the wreck. 41560, (42112),
note after 89026
Recent exploring expeditions to the Pacific.
36013
Recent history of the [American Peace] Society.
5830
Recent letter of Dr. Taylor in the Christian
spectator. 97594
Recent letters from the United States. 34401
Recent occurrences in Canada. 10570
Recent progress of astronomy. 41955
Recent recollections of the Anglo-American
church. 68345
Recent speech of the Hon. Daniel Webster.
35863, 60952, 82074, 93197
Recent speeches and addresses, by Charles
Sumner. 93648, 93664, 93670
Recent speeches and writings of William H.
Seward. 79547
Recent speeches, rehearsing his [i.e. William
G. Brownlow's] experience with secession.
8704
Recent tour of four thousand miles in the
United States. 18752
Recent tourist. pseud. Right of recognition.
71352
Recent travelers. pseud. Domestic manners
of the Americans. 97914
Recentes Novi Orbis historiae. 68346
Recept, von aine, Holtz zubrauchen fur die
Kranckhait. 68348
Recept von ainem Holtz su Brauche fur die
Kranckhait. 68347
Recept-Calender und Familien Wegweiser fur
das Jahr 1854. 68349
Reception and Dinner in Honor of George
Peabody, Danvers, Mass., 1856. see
Danvers, Mass. Reception and Dinner
in Honor of George Peabody, 1856.
Reception . . . by . . . Citizens of New-York
to the Survivors of the Officers and
Crews of the United States Frigates
Cumberland and Congress, 1862. see
New York (City) Reception . . . by . . .
Citizens of New-York to the Survivors
of the Officers and Crews of the United
States Frigates Cumberland and Congress,
1862.
Reception by the clergy and laity of Baltimore.
88912
Reception of an electoral vote from that state.
42263
Reception of General T. M. Logan. 88109
Reception of George Thompson in Great Britain.
9324, 95509
Reception of Goldwin Smith, by the Union
League Club of New York. 82686

Reception of Gov. Andrew Johnson, of Tennessee. (60444)
Reception of Senator Wilson. 89627
Reception of the American Medical Association. (61461)
Reception of the delegates from the Society for the Propagation of the Gospel in Foreign Parts. 66204
Reception of the Oneida Volunteers at the city of New-York. 68350
Reception of the President of the United States. (9174)
Reception of the Sons of Portsmouth. 64427
Reception speeches on his return from the Bastile. (57165)
Rechabite recorder. (17743)
Rechabites, Independent Order of. see Independent Order of Rechabites.
Rechberg und Rothelowen, Bernhard, graf von, 1806-1899. (36199)
Recherches curieuses sur la diversite des langues. 7733
Recherches et doutes sur le magnetisme animal. 25579, 92135
Recherches et experiences sur les poisons d'Amerique. 43701, 71251
Recherches experimentales sur la polarisation atmospherique. 63667
Recherches faites par ordre de S. M. Brit. 7326
Recherches historiques, critiques, et bibliographiques. (76850)
Recherches historiques et geographiques sur le Nouveau-Monde. (77608)
Recherches historiques et medicales sur la fievre jaune. 18333
Recherches historiques et politiques sur les Etats-Unis de l'Amerique Septentrionale. 47206, 97457
Recherches historiques sur la systeme de John Law. 40739
Recherches in Guayana in 1837-9. 77794
Recherches into the physical history of man. 65476
Recherches into the physical history of mankind. 65480
Recherches, memoires et observations. 68351
Recherches naturelles, chimiques et physiologiques sur le curare. 70458
Recherches philosophiques sur la decouverte de l'Amerique. 44238-44239
Recherches philosophiques sur la decouverte du Mouveau-Monde. 44238, note after 89135
Recherches philosophiques sur les Americains. (10914), 59239-(59247), (59251), 60994, 60995, 3d note after 100862, 2d note after 102210
Recherches practiques sur la fievre jaune. 18579
Recherches qui ont ete faites depuis Fernand Cortez jusqu'a present. 25910
Recherches . . . . Second supplement aux memoires. 68352
Recherches statistiques sur l'esclavage colonial. 50558
Recherches sur Americ Vespuce. 76849
Recherches sur la constitution des naturels de Saint Domingue. (2127)
Recherches sur la fievre jaune. 72373
Recherches sur la nature et les causes de la richesse des nations. 82306-(82311)
Recherches sur la priorite de la decouverte des pays. 76838, 76834, 76851
Recherches sur la situation des emigrants aux Etats-Unis. 92727

Recherches sur l'ancienne population de l'Amerique. 68443
Recherches sur le pays de Fou Sang. 38033
Recherches sur les antiquites de l'Amerique du Nord. 40038, 101364
Recherches sur les antiquites de l'Amerique Septentrionale. 101365
Recherches sur les antiquites des Etats-Unis. 68443
Recherches . . . sur les causes de l'acrete de l'huile de ricin. 6970
Recherches sur les empoisonnemens pratiques par les negres a la Martinique. 73930
Recherches sur les enfants trouves. 28146
Recherches . . . sur les Etats-Unis. 15194
Recherches sur les lois. 91851
Recherches sur les mines de Haiti. 84487
Recherches sur les moyens de perfectionner les canaux de navigation. 26202
Recherches sur les principaux phenomenes de meteorologie. 75526
Recherches sur les ressources de cet empire. 92624
Recherches sur les ruins de Palenque et sur les origine. 7435
Recherches sur les ruins de Palenque et sur les origines. (7439)
Recherches sur les terres australes de Drake. 24751, note just before 44492
Recherches sur les voyages et decouvertes des navigateurs Normands. 23035
Recherches sur l'ile Antillia. 8831, (47542)
Recherches sur l'organization de la peau de l'homme. 26771
Recherches sur l'origine du despotisme oriental. 6884
Recherches sur sa flora et sa geographie physique. (56735)
Recherches zoologiques pour servir a l' histoire. (24424)
Rechte Weg ausz zu Faren von Liszbona gen Kallakuth. 68354
Rechten Weg ausz su Faren vo Liszbona gen Kallakuth. 68353
Rechteren, -------- van. 14957-14960, 68455
Rechtmassige Deutsche Ausgabe des Univers pittoresque. 26848A
Rechtsgeleerde memorie. see Reghtsgeleerde memorie.
Rechtsgeleerd advis in de zaak van den gewezen stadhouder. 100768
Recibimiento del General Paez en Washington. 58139
Recife (Brazilian Province) Presidente (Peretti) 69315 see also Peretti, Anselmo Francisco.
Recio de Leon, Juan. 40075, 68355-68365
Recipe for the cure of schism. 69340
Reciprocal duties and obligations. 24764
Reciprocal obligations of professors and pupils. 49725
Reciprocal obligations of religion and civil government. 16342
Reciprocity. 31022
Reciprocity discussed. 8348
Reciprocity treaty between the United States and Great Britain. (6582)
Reciprocity treaty; its advantages to the United States. 30769
Reciprocity treaty, its history. 33313
Reciprocity treaty. Report of the Special Committee of the Detroit Board of Trade. (19791)
Reciprocity treaty. Speech . . . June 15, 1860. (22378)

Reciprocity treaty. Speech of Hon. F. W.
Kellogg. 37292
Reciprocity with British North America
vindicated. 57834
Recit de evenements arrivees a la Martinique.
(5649)
Recit de l'estat present des celebres colonies.
72318
Recit de l'origine, des progres et de l'etat
actuel. 58266
Recit de l'origine, de progres et de l'etat
actuel de la guerre entre l'Espagne et
l'Amerique Meridionale. 70352
Recit de ma captivite par A. Guinnard. (29241)
Recit de mesures prises dans differentes
parties. 10886
Recit de voyages. 74748
Recit des evenemens arrives a la Martinique.
68366
Recit des evenemens qui ont eu lieu sur le
territoire des Sauvages. 68367
Recit des journees de 9 et 10 Noviembre
dernier. 94901
Recit des voyages et des decouvertes du R.
Pere Jacques Marquette. (44665)
Recit ecrit de la main de Mormon. 83122-
83123
Recit du martyre d'onze religieux du mesme
ordre. 17187
Recit d'un chercheur d'or. 9988
Recit fidele. (11743)
Recit fidele et abrege de toutes les par-
ticularitez. 68368
Recital, and concise view, of uncontroverted
facts. 101126
Recital of the events connected with their lives
and actions. 4429
Recitative ode on events of revolutionary times.
47274
Recits Americains. 7803
Recits du bivouac. (69041)
Recits et faits remarquables tires des plus
celebres voyageurs. 88695
Recits et types Americains. 18242
Recits instructifs et moreaux. 11819
Reck, P. G. F. von 38365, 68369-(68370)
Reclamacion de la intervencion del Colonel Sr.
Alejandro Macdonald. (43143)
Reclamacion de la Junta de Inspeccion y
Gobierno. 76323
Reclamacion y protesta del supremo gobierno
del estado de Guatemala. (29093)
Reclamation a la Cour de France. 11643
Reclamation de M. l'Intendant de Saint-
Domingue. (68372)
Reclamation des citoyens de couleur. 68373
Reclamation des Heritiers Renaut. 69604
Reclamation des Negres libres, colons
Ameriquains. 28736
Reclamation of fugitives from service. 12197
Reclamation of the Florida Everglades. 84092
Reclamations de M. Bury Fedon. 24001
Reclamations et observations des colons. 68374
Reclamo de descuidos. 76222
Reclamos de la nacion a su Congreso y
monarca. 94146
Reclus, E. (68375)
Recluse. pseud. Art of domestic happiness.
2119
Recluse: a semi-monthly literary journal.
68376
Recluse of Jamestown. (11172), 100443
Reco de Leon, Juan. see Leon, Juan Reco de.
Recognitio, svm mularum Reuerendi Patris
Illdephonsi a Vera Crvce. 98918
Recognition. A chapter from the history. 27298

Recognition and the Monroe doctrine. 88854
Recognition: its international legality. 57826
Recognition of Crete. 79751
Recognition of Cuba. 51317
Recognition of friends in heaven. (79795)
Recognition of friends in heaven: a discourse.
79794
Recognition of God in the facts of our history.
85462
Recognition of Hayti and Liberia. Speech . . .
June 3, 1862. (37270)
Recognition of Hayti and Liberia. Speech . . .
June 2, 1862. 27828
Recognition of Liberia and Hayti. 43476
Recognition of the republic of Liberia. (13254)
Recognition of the southern confederacy. 68377
Recollections and experiences of an abolitionist.
(73337)
Recollections and private memoirs of Gen.
Washington. (18156)
Recollections and private memoirs of Washing-
ton. (18157)
Recollections and reflections. 55186
Recollections and sketches of notable lawyers.
83725
Recollections from Madeira. 91161
Recollections, historical, biographical, and
antiquarian. 77235
Recollections of a backwoodsman. 67962
Recollections of a Boston police officer. 77227
Recollections of a burnt journal in California.
44695
Recollections of a busy life. 7072, 28491
Recollections of a congressional life. 83691
Recollections of a forest life. 16720
Recollections of a house-keeper. 58102
Recollections of a journey to Wyoming in 1742.
68992
Recollections of a life of adventure. 90116
Recollections of a lifetime. 27919, 85431
Recollections of a literary life. 49752
Recollections of a mute. (38102)
Recollections of a New England bride. (27430)
Recollections of a ramble from Sydney to
Southampton. (68378)
Recollections of a service of three years.
14618, 2d note after 98882
Recollections of a six years residence. 52297
Recollections of a southern matron. (27430)-
27431
Recollections of a ten-months' ramble. 25047,
2d note after 96992
Recollections of a tour in the United States of
America. 2208
Recollections of a visit to the falls of Niagara.
93615
Recollections of a visit to the United States and
British provinces. 63373
Recollections of Albany. 37481
Recollections of Albany and of Hudson. 36513,
105498
Recollections of Alexander H. Stephens. 91279
Recollections of an artillery officer. 31810
Recollections of an early Philadelphian. 84855
Recollections of an old man. 36382
Recollections of an old soldier. 61028
Recollections of Bishop England. 88110
Recollections of by-past times. 64685, 99631
Recollections of Central America and the west
coast of Africa. 25025
Recollections of Cincinnati. 105499
Recollections of departed friends. 4975
Recollections of early ministers. 91813
Recollections of field service with the 20th
Iowa Infantry Volunteers. 3536
Recollections of fifty years since. 2647

Recollections of Henry Watkins Allen. 20660
Recollections of Italy, England, and America. (12270)
Recollections of itinerant life. 8477
Recollections of John Jay Smith. 82986
Recollections of Jotham Anderson. 101393-101394
Recollections of Jotham Anderson; and May morning. 101392
Recollections of Jotham Anderson, minister of the Gospel. 101391
Recollections of Labrador life. 6151, 18110
Recollections of Mary Lyon. 24521
Recollections of maternal influence. (49699)
Recollections of men and things at Washington. 27624
Recollections of Mexico. 95537
Recollections of Mr. James Lenox. 91520
Recollections of my childhood. 41403
Recollections of my life. 47028
Recollections of Nettleton. 83758
Recollections of Newark. 85144
Recollections of North America. 93912
Recollections of old Texas days. 85099
Recollections of our neighborhood in the west. 10824
Recollections of persons and events. 46845
Recollections of persons and places in the west. 7171
Recollections of Rev. David Hayden. 104670
Recollections of Rev. F. W. P. Greenwood. 26068
Recollections of scenes and small adventures. 31416, note after 96968
Recollections of seventy years. 23883, 106147
Recollections of the campaign of the 14th Regiment Indiana Volunteers. (64025)
Recollections of the court of Louis Philippe. 74274
Recollections of the days of '76. 101841
Recollections of the early days of the National Guard. 45456
Recollections of the early settlement of the Wabash Valley. 17272
Recollections of the gold mines. 9978, 9981
Recollections of the Jersey prison ship. 20948-(20949), 28582, note just before 68379
Recollections of the last ten years. (24794)
Recollections of the life of John Binns. (5507)
Recollections of the morals, habits, &c. of that country. 10616
Recollections of the outlines of a sermon on the death of Mrs. Waterman. 42718
Recollections of the private life of General Lafayette. 13773
Recollections of the siege of Rivas. 91711
Recollections of the stage. 4929
Recollections of the United States Army. 68379
Recollections of the west. (26698)
Recollections of two distinguished persons. 83565
Recollections of William Theophilus. 37707
Recollections of Windsor Prison. (70417)
Re-commencement. 5347
Recommendation by the Society in Scotland for Propagating Christian Knowledge. 85993
Recommendation for a subscription for relieving Friends of Great Britain. 86071
Recommendation of inoculation according to Baron Dimsdale's method. 50651
Recommendation of the subject to the serious attention of people in general. (17335), 80691-80692
Recommendation of William Smith. 84646
Recommendations. 88643
Recommendatory advertisement. 21939

Recommendatory epistle (in verse) 103920
Recommendatory preface, by Dr. Ryland, Mr. Fuller, and Mr. Sutcliff. 32951
Recommendatory preface by five . . . clergymen. 12331, 13350
Recommendatory preface by Gilbert Burnet. (78444)
Recommendatory preface by Ralph Wardlaw. 102189
Recommendatory preface, by the Rev. Gilbert Tennent. 21664, 94709
Recommendatory preface by the Rev. I. Watts. 91150
Recommendatory preface, by the Rev. John Eustace Giles. 21427
Recommendatory preface, by the Rev. Thomas Snow. 97628
Recompensa del merito. 86872
Recompense. A sermon for country and kindred. 3794
Reconcilable, Sam. pseud. Friendly address. see Young, Samuel, fl. 1690-1700.
Reconciliation; or, the triumph of nature. 44623
Reconciliation respectfully recommended. 29311
Reconnaissance du sud. 28271
Reconnaissance geologique au Nebraska. 44505
Reconnaissance hydrographique des cotes occidentales du Centre-Amerique. (56720), 68380
Reconnoissance from Bottom's Bridge to Seven Pines. 68381
Reconnoissance of a new route through the Rocky Mountains. 90370
Reconocimiento de la Bahia de Panzacola en Florida. 80971
Reconocimiento del istmo de Tehuantepec. 26550, 50771, 7th note after 94592
Reconocimiento del Rio Pepiri-Guazu. 9811
Reconstructed city. 83368
Reconstruction, a letter to President Johnson. 26730
Reconstruction: a poem. (55197)
Reconstruction. A speech of Hon. James A. Cravens. 17431
Reconstruction!! An appeal to the patriotic National Republican members of Congress. 20153
Reconstruction an Andrew Johnson. 34737
Reconstruction and its relation to the business of the country. (6977)
Reconstruction and Negro suffrage. 51020
Reconstruction and suffrage. 36279, 36885
Reconstruction and the executive power of pardon. 68321
Reconstruction—branch mint in Oregon. (31322)
Reconstruction. . . . [By Charles G. Loring.] 42078, 105613
Reconstruction. By Oliver B. Bunce. 9157
Reconstruction. [By William Oland Bourne.] 6933
Reconstruction Convention, Austin, Texas, 1866. see Texas. Constitutional Convention, Austin, 1866.
Reconstruction in America. 37894, (68382)
Reconstruction: industrial, financial, and political. 10842
Reconstruction: its true basis. (6977)
Reconstruction letter. 91066
Reconstruction. Letter from Peter Cooper to President Johnson. 16595
Reconstruction; liberty the corner-stone. 2072
Reconstruction measures constitutional. 8453
Reconstruction of Mississippi. Speech of Hon. Alexander H. Jones. 36452
Reconstruction of Mississippi. Speech of Hon. Thomas Fitch. 24590

2249

Record of facts, and reply to a pamphlet entitled "Belize." 55912

Record of facts concerning the persecutions of Madeira. 55878

Record of facts, without comment being memoranda. (68396)

Record of Fort Sumter. 30538

Record of George Wm. Gordon. (27978)

Record of Heister Clymer. (13808)

Record of heroism, patriotism and patience. 8162

Record of Hon. Stephen A. Douglas on the tariff. (20606)

Record of inscriptions in the cemetery and building of the . . . Unitarian . . . Church. 68397

Record of interesting events, traditions, and anecdotes. 59434

Record of John G. Sinclair. 81405

Record of musical science, literature and intelligence. 51581

Record of munificence. (27887), 1st note after 96962

Record of New Sweden. 65692

Record of news, history and literature. 68398

Record of past and present members of the Second Congregational Church. 55090

Record of pioneer life in California. 91787

Record of private practice. 7997

Record of proceedings at the fifth annual reunion. 86099

Record of proceedings of a Board of Clergy. 35054

Record of proceedings of a naval court martial. 47084

Record of proceedings of the first annual reunion. 86097

Record of proceedings of the investigation. 45313

Record of such as adjoyned themselves. 95639

Record of the adventures, habits of animals. 3932A

Record of the adventures of that renowned partisan ranger. 17440

Record of the births marriages and deaths in Worcester Vermont. 44

Record of the Boston stage. (13231)

Record of the campaigns, sieges, etc. 57394

Record of the causes and events which produced, and terminated in the establishment and independence of the American republic. 1592, 50927

Record of the centennial celebration of the incorporation. 21248

Record of the civil and military history. 21818

Record of the civil and military patriotism of the state. 67301

Record of the class of 1821. 105883

Record of the Coe family. (14148)

Record of the Commissary General for 1861. 56892

Record of the commissioned officers, noncommissioned officers and privates. 53888, note just before 68399

Record of the Cope family. 16656

Record of the court at Upland. 19596, 68399

Record of the Democratic Party. 68400

Record of the descendants of Samuel Spalding. 88863

Record of the descendants of Silence Holbrook. 32444

Record of the distribution and sale of lots. 42108

Record of the evangelical labours in the United States. (21623)

Record of the events of fifty-six years. 80533

Record of the experience of a nine month's regiment. (29560)

Record of the families in New England. 32346

Record of the families of Robert Patterson. 21017

Record of the family of Louis Du Bois. (21016)

Record of the family of Thos. Ewing. 21018, 23332

Record of the federal dead. 68401

Record of the First Church of Christ. 21819

Record of the first exhibition of the Metropolitan Mechanics' Institute. (48219)

Record of the funeral and memorial services of the Rev. Cornelius Springer. 89832

Record of the greal rebellion. (10849)

Record of the Hon. James R. Doolittle. (20611)

Record of the inscriptions on the tablets and grave-stones. 13275

Record of the life, assassination and obsequies of the martyred president. 41206, 80017

Record of the M'Clellan Copperheads. 11886

Record of the Massachusetts Volunteers. 45964

Record of the Metropolitan Fair in aid of the United States Sanitary Commission. (68402), 76665

Record of the munificence, self-sacrifice, and patriotism of the American people. (27887), 1st note after 96962

Record of the New-England Anti-slavery Society. 52655, 81731

Record of the proceedings before the Senate of Ohio. 48702

Record of the proceedings of a general court martial, holden at the Court-House in Salem, in the county of Essex. 96874

Record of the proceedings of a general court martial, holden at the Court House in Salem, Sept. 28, 1812. 27838

Record of the proceedings of the Court of Bishops. 20394

Record of the proceedings of the Trustees. 59385

Record of the Progressive Gardner's [sic] Society. 62096

Record of the Second Massachusetts Infantry. (67315)

Record of the service of the Fifty-Fifth Regiment of Massachusetts Volunteer Infantry. (25334)

Record of the Sharpe family in England and America. 79854

Record of the "Society for Promoting the Gospel among the Seamen in the Port of New York." 85860

Record of the soldiers. 33503

Record of the soldiers of Southborough. 104562

Record of the testimony taken in the trial of Commodore T. T. Craven. 17430

Record of the trial [of Brigadier General George Talcott.] 89356, note before 94236A, note after 96929

Record of the trial of Joshua Hett Smith. 83423

Record of the trial of Selden Braynard. 96835

Record of the votes of Franklin Pierce. 29428

Record of the voyages, travels, labours, and successes. 12891

Record of travel across the plains. (42649)

Record of travel in English-speaking countries. 20155

Record of twelve month's travel in the United States. 73931, 4th note after 96452

Record of typography. (65690)

Record of unfulfilled prophecies. 58028, 68317

Record of visits to the primary schools. 31202

Record of William Governeur [sic] Morris. 50885

Recordacoes de vida parlamentar do advogado Antonio Pereira Recoucas. (68336)

Recorder. 30997

Recorder of the City of New York. see New York (City) Recorder.

Recorder of the progress of Christianity. 81858

Recording of Michael Taintor. 14285

Records and results of a magnetic survey. (2588), 85072

Records of a tourist. 38919

Records of a village pastor. 68403

Records of an old mission station. (36490)

Records of British enterprise beyond sea. 3219

Records of Colchester. 14265, 1st note after 94219

Records compared. 43785, 45197

Records of conventions in the New Hampshire Grants. 1st note after 98997

Records of families of the name of Rawlins or Rollins. 72866

Records of five years. (41404)

Records of freemasonry in the state of Connecticut, compiled from the journals. 92193

Records of freemasonry in the state of Connecticut, with a brief account of its origin in New England. 92192

Records of His Majesty's 87th Regiment. 68404

Records of living officers. 29943

Records of longevity. 2753

Records of Massachusetts Bay and the colony of New Plymouth. 45966, 63488, 80788

Records of New-England Yearly Meeting Boarding School. 52637

Records of patriotism and love of country. 2755

Records of Rev. Roger Viets. 99541

Records of Salem witchcraft. (68405)

Records of some of the descendants of John Fuller. (13457)

Records of some of the descendants of Richard Hull. 13458

Records of some of the descendants of Thomas Clarke. 13456

Records of the Bubbleton Parish. 68406

Records of the church, in Foxborough. 104387

Records of the church in the case of Deacon James G. Carter. 95259

Records of the Church of England in Rawdon. 31821

Records of the City Inspector's Department. 54689, note after 94172

Records of the colony and plantation of New Haven. 53004

Records of the colony of New Plymouth in New England. 53388, 63488

Records of the colony of Rhode Islands and Providence Plantations. 3748, (79633)

Records of the colony or jurisdiction of New Haven. 53005

Records of the Columbia Historical Society. 39533, 64584, 82954, 101944

Records of the Company of the Massachusetts Bay. 45965

Records of the Council for New England. 19051, (52625), 68407

Records of the Council of Safety and Governor and Council of Vermont. 803, 1st note after 98997, 98999, 99005, 2d note after 99005, 99008, note after 99008, 99053 see also Records of the Governor and Council of Vermont.

Records of the descendants of Hugh Clark. 13311

Records of the descendants of Thomas Nash. (51854)

Records of the descendants of William Curtis. 13459

Records of the eleventh annual meeting of the Maine Medical Association. 43982

Records of the First Congregational Church in East Windsor, Ct. 68408

Records of the Grand Chapter of the State of Vermont. 99180

Records of the Grand Lodge of Virginia. 100472

Records of the Governor and Company of the Massachusetts Bay in New England. 45966

Records of the Governor and Council of Vermont. 801, 806, 7286, 12851, 52791, 56564, 66514, 98998-note after 98998, 2d note after 99000, 99001-99002, 1st note after 99003, 2d note after 99003, 3d-4th notes after 99005, 6th note after 99005, 99009, 99018-99019, 99054, 99056, 99058, 99059, 99068, 99073, 99090, 101077 see also Records of the Council of Safety and Governor and Council of Vermont.

Records of the late provincial congress, held at Cambridge. 23533, 45731

Records of the life, character and achievements of Adoniram Judson. 48867

Records of the life of the Rev. John Marig. (44573)

Records of the life of the Rev. John Murray. 51524

Records of the New-York . . . Mission and Tract Society. 54190

Records of the New York stage. 35058

Records of the Northern O. S. Assembly. 65223

Records of the Ohio Company. 31799

Records of the Presbyterian Church in the United States of America. By W. M. Engles. 22602

Records of the Presbyterian Church in the United States of America: embracing the minutes of the Presbytery of Philadelphia. (65209)

Records of the proceedings and debates at the sixty-first annual convention. 53881

Records of the Proprietors of Narraganset Township, No. 1. 68509

Records of the Provincial Congress, held at Cambridge. 45731

Records of the revolutionary war. 74870

Records of the Synod of Mississippi. 49500

Records of the town of Lynn. 42838

Records of the town of Newark, New Jersey. 54883

Records of the 24th Independent Battery. 48000

Records of the Virginia Company of London. 1st note after 99856, note after 99857, 4th note after 99888

Records of William Spooner. 89625

Recos Jepphi. pseud. Ministerial almanack. 68410

Recovery of America demonstrated to be practicable. 68411

Recovery of some materials for the early history of Rochester. 20881

Recreacao Brasileira. 93833

Recreacion poetica. 63306

Recreador mineiro. 88713

Recreations in agriculture. 101735-101736

Recreations of a long vacation. 4213

Recreations of a southern barrister. 36612, (68412), note after 88311
Recreations of George Taletell, F. Y. C. 94254
Recreo de las familias. (68413)
Recruiting Committee, Boston. see Boston. Recruiting Committee.
Recruiting in the United States. 68414
Recruiting system of the city of Boston. 6549
Recruits for Caledonia. 78230
Recruito, a comic opera. (35411)
Rectification of a new mollusk. 39492
Rectification of Mr. T. A. Conrad's "Synopsis of the family of Naiades." 39491
Rectitude in national policy essential to national prosperity. 106084
Rectitude of the divine administration. 84546
Rector. pseud. [Two letters.] 80391
Rector, Philo Cor-. pseud. see Philo Corrector, Esq. pseud.
Rector, William. 68415
Rector and Assistant Minister of Trinity Church, Boston. see Boston. Trinity Church. Rector and Assistant Minister.
Rector and Inhabitants of the City of New York. see New York (City) Trinity Church.
Rector detected. 1st note after 100484
Rector detected or the colonel reconnoitred. 70255
Rector [of Christ Church, Boston.] pseud. Historical Account of Christ Church. see Eaton, Asa.
Rector [of Grace Church, Galena.] pseud. Christian patriot. see Egar, John H.
Rector of St. Bardolph's. (80152)
Rector rectified. 4973, 2d note after 96984
Rector vindicated. 10173, 100444
Rectories of Upper Canada. 10571
Rector's Christmas offering for 1835. 20391
Rector's cure of souls. 80088, 1st note after 96985
Rector's offering, February 11, 1857. (2577)
Rector's offering for MDCCCL. (77421)
Rector's offering for MDCCCXLII. 77420
Rector's reply to sundry requestions and demands. 23317
Rectus, --------. 68416
Recueil A [-Z, etc.] Collection de pieces curieuses d'histoire. (68417)
Recueil abrege des privileges de cette ville. 47541
Recueil amusant de voyages en vers et en prose. 68418
Recueil complet des traites. 10089
Recueil consacre a la discussion des interets de tous les etats orientaux. 70359
Recueil d'anciennes cartes Europeenes et Orientales. 36432, 77804
Recueil d'anecdotes, bon mots, reflexions, maximes et observations. (25668)
Recueil d'arrests. 68419, 69299
Recueil d'arrests du Roi. 68419
Recueil d'arrests et autres pieces pour l' etablissement de la Compagnie d'Occident. 25999, 68419
Recueil de arrests. 25999
Recueil de cantiques. 68425
Recueil de cartes geographiques. 71864
Recueil de ce qui s'est passe en Canada. 67023
Recueil de chansons Canadiens et Francaises. (10569)
Recueil de chansons nouvelles. 68426
Recueil de differentes pieces pour & countre l'admission des etrangers. 68427
Recueil de divers traitez de paix. 68429
Recueil de divers voyages. 41058

Recueil de divers voyages faits en Afrique et en l'Amerique. 36944, 68430
Recueil de diverses pieces, concernant la Pensylvanie. 60445
Recueil de diverses pieces et des discussions qui eurent lieu. 68428
Recueil de documents et de memoires relatifs a l'etude des monuments. 70355
Recueil de documents et memoires originaux. 94853
Recueil de documents pouvant servir a l' histoire de la guerre des Etats-Unis. 64717
Recueil de jurisprudence coloniale. 68431
Recueil de la diuersite des habits qui sont de present en usaige tout es pays d'Europe. 19689, 68432
Recueil de la politique. (70363)
Recueil de litterature Canadienne. 34041, 69661
Recueil de litterature nationale. 86215
Recueil de lois et ordonnances royales. 1585
Recueil de memoires contenus dans les anciens manuscrits. (67469)
Recueil de memoires et de notices scientifiques et industriels. 47476, 49982, 80864
Recueil de memoires hydrographiques pour servir d'analyse. 38329
Recueil de pieces diverses. 68433
Recueil de pieces en proces-verbaux. 68434
Recueil de pieces officielles, memoires et morceaux historiques. 77752
Recueil de pieces, pour servir d'addition & de preuve a la relation. 63904
Recueil de pieces pour servir d' addition & de preuve a la relation abregee, donnes par l'auteur. 63907, 1st note after 98174
Recueil de pieces relatives a la conquete du Mexique. 94852, 94854, 98647
Recueil de pieces relatives a la fievre jaune d' Amerique. 68435
Recueil de pieces sur la Floride. 24894, note after 94854, 94856, note after 99605
Recueil de pieces sur la negociation. 20929, 68436
Recueil de pieces touchant l'histoire de la Compagnie de Jesus. (36767)
Recueil de plans des cotes et des portes de celle ile. (62965)
Recueil de planches coloriees d'animaux du Bresil. 47025
Recueil de prieres. 6296
Recueil de prieres catechisme et cantiques. 68437
Recueil de quelques missions des Indes-Orientales et Occidentales. 44965, note after 89538
Recueil [de regionibus septentrionalibus.] 6119, 106330
Recueil de reglemens, concernant le commerce des isles & colonies. 68438
Recueil de reglemens, edits, declarations et arrets. (68420), (68439), 68459
Recueil de romans, poesie Canadienne, &c., inedits. 73876
Recueil de tares et usages des principales villes. 9269
Recueil de toutes les pieces et nouvelles. 68440
Recueil de traites d'alliance. (44843)
Recueil de traites de paix, de treve, de neutralite, de confederation. 40104
Recueil de traites de paix, &c. 75477
Recueil de traites, status imperiaux et autres actes publics. 68441
Recueil de traittez de paix, treves et neutralite entre les couronnes. 12689

Recueil de voiages au nord. 4935-4937, 25999, 31355, 38970-38971, 38975, 68419, note after 68441-68442, 69172, note after 69262, 69299, 96172

Recueil de voyages dans l'Amerque Meridionale. 4937A, 16782, note after 68442

Recueil de voyages de M^r. Thevenot. 31370-31372, 44666, 95332

Recueil de voyages et de documents. 100828

Recueil de voyages et de memoires. 68443

"Recueil de voyages," etc. (28181)

Recueil de vues de l'Amerique Septentrionale. 77467

Recueil de vues des lieux principaux. 50578

Recueil d'edits, declarations et arrests de Sa Majeste. (68420), (68439), 68459

Recueil des cartes generales et particulieres. 4554

Recueil des declarations, arrests, status, ordonnances et reglemens. 68444

Recueil des decrets apostoliques. (58529), note after 68444, 99324

Recueil des descriptions pittoresques, des recits curieux, des scenes variees, des decouvertes scientifiques. 30849

Recueil des divers memoires Anglois. 34862

Recueil des edits, declarations, lettres-patent. 68445

Recueil des isles nouvelles trouveee en la grande mer oceane. 34542

Recueil des lettres au Roi. 21044

Recueil des lettres de eveques et des missionnaires. (68446)

Recueil des lois publiees dans tous les etats de l'Europe. 41962

Recueil des lois relatives a la marine et aux colonies. (68447)

Recueil des loix constitutives des colonies Angloises. 68448

Recueil des memoires qui ont ete publies avec les cartes hydrographiques. 4556

Recueil des ordres donnees pour le bannissement des religieux. 68449

Recueil des ordres permanens du Conseil Legislatif. 88697

Recueil des pensees extraites de l'Histoire philosophique des deux Indes. 68077

Recueil des pieces pour servir d'addition & de preuve a la relation abregee. 63907

Recueil des pieces relatives a la conquete du Mexique. 994

Recueil des plans de l'Amerique Septentrionale. 40143, 68450

Recueil des plusieurs cartes geographiques. 68451

Recueil des principaux traites d'alliance. 44841

Recueil des principaux traites de meme nature. 30866

Recueil des reglemens rendus jusqu'a present. 14125

Recueil des relations les plus interessants des naufrages. 19619, 19621, note after 32022

Recueil des relations originales inedites. 56093

Recueil des traites de commerce et de navigation de la France. 30866

Recueil des traites de paix Europeens. 27262

Recueil des traitez de paix, de treve, de neutralite, de confederation. 68452

Recueil des traitez de paix, de treve, de neutralite, de suspension d'armes. 68453

Recueil des voyages de la Compagnie des Indes. 55448

Recueil des voyages interessants. 10305

Recueil des voyages qui ont servi a l'etablissement. 89451

Recueil des voyages qui ont servi a l'etablissement et aux progres de la Compagnie des Indes Orientales. 68454

Recueil des voyages qui ont servi a l'etablissement et aux progrez de la Compagnie des Indes Orientales. 68455

Recueil d'estampes representant les differents evenemens. 27650, (63966), 68421

Recueil d'evenemens curieux et interessans. 68423

Recueil d'experiences faites dans les Academies Royales. (63350)

Recueil diplomatique du commerce. 68456

Recueil d'observations astronomiques. (33757)

Recueil d'observations curieuses. 68424

Recueil d'observations de zoologie et d'anatomie. 33755

Recueil d'observations faites en plusieurs voyages. 71110

Recueil du discours fait par Monsieur de Brun. 19125

Recueil general des lois et actes du gouvernement d'Haiti. 29585, 41382

Recueil general des traites de commerce. (21123)

Recueil historique-chronologique de tous les actes. 26806

Recueil historique complet des traites. 10090-10091

Recueil historique d'actes, negotiations, memoires et traitez. 73495

Recueil historique et chronologique de faits memorables. 20543, note after 68456

Recueil les plus interessantes naufrages. 23567

Recueil litteraire et historique. 10455, (12573), (41510)

Recueil manuel et pratique des traites. 44833

Recueil mensuel. 60367

Recueil mensuel de la politique. 70362

Recueil trimstriel de documents. 70361

Recueil van authenticque stukken. 93862

Recueil van de tractaten gemaeckt ende geslooten. 68457

Recueil van egte stukken. 68458, 1st note after 93862

Recueils de reglemens, edits, declarations et arrets. (68420), (68439), 68459

Recuerdo de las obligaciones del ministerio apostolico de curas. 57101, 68461

Recuerdo del priorato de Monserrate de Mexico. 68462

Recuerdo, o colleccion de verdades. 17802

Recuerdo politico por el religioso. 68463

Recuerdo que el Ayuntamiento Constitucional de Mexico dirige. (68464)

Recuerdo seminario de literatura y variedades. 68460

Recuerdos de la invasion Norte-Americana. 71705

Recuerdos de la monarquia Peruana. 74955

Recuerdos de provincia. (77084)

Recuerdos de provincia por el autor de Civilizacion y barbaria. (68465)

Recuerdos de un viaje hecho en las provincias meridionales de Chile. 20558

Recuerdos de viaje a los Estados-Unidos. 44670

Recuerdos del Chamberlin. 34433

Recuerdos del 9. de Julio de 1820. 105744

Recverdos historicos y politicos. (75813)

Recuerdos sobre la rebelion de Caracas. 10183, 19967, 68466, 3d note after 98882

Recvil des isles. (16952)

Recurso al tribunal de la razon. 68467
Recurso de atentado que algunos de los duenos
    de la Mina de la Luz. 73864
Recurso del Dr. R. Ramires de Arellano.
    67634
Recurso humilde y religioso. 76024
Recurso, y reverente suplica. (74854)
Red, Charles. 68142-68143
Red book. (68468)
Red book. State of New-York. 68469
Red brothers. 68470
Red coats. 91329
Red eagle. 47366
Red fawn of the flower land. 69059
Red flag in John Bull's eyes. 13863
Red Hook Building Company. 68471
Red Jacket. Seneca Indian Chief (41630),
    68472-68473, 89175, 89187, 89206
Red-letter days in Applethorpe. 20506
Red man: a lecture. (74411)
Red mark. 19826
Red men of the Ohio valley. 20499
Red queen. 75257
Red race of America. 77852, 77867, 77872
Red River country, Husdon's Bay & North-
    West Territories. 74298-74299
Red River expedition. 69870
Red River insurrection. 68474
Red River settlement. (33546)
Red River settlement—correspondence relating
    to recent disturbances. (68475)
Red River settlement; its rise, progress, and
    present state. 73328
Red River settlement. . . . Message of the
    President. (68475)
Red Rover. 16520
Red Rover. A tale. 16518
Red Rupert, the American buccaneer. 51532
Red-sea freedmen. 13245
Red-skins, or Indians and Injin. 16525
Red-tape and pigeon-hole generals. 50630
Red Top Ranch. 83632
Red, white and blue; a short treatise. 82955
Red, white and blue. Sketches of military life.
    68477
Red white and blue songster. (68479)
Red white and blue songster. No. I. 68478
"Red, white, and blue" warbler. 67944
Red wing. 34776
Redaccion politica. 77135
Redacterus du voyage pittoresque autour du
    monde. pseud. eds. 57458
Redactor da Malagueta. pseud. see Malagueta.
    Redactor. pseud.
Redactor de Nueva-York. 51244
Redactor Mexicano. 68480
Redactor municipal. 68481
Redactor, no. 2. 68685
Redactor poblano. 68482
Redactores del Clamor publico. pseud. trs.
    92607
Redburn; his first voyage. 47482
Redburn; or the schoolmaster of a morning.
    68483
Redden, Laura C. 68484-68485
Redding, Cyrus. 32152, 68486
Reddington, D. (68487)
Reddition de l'armee du Lord Cornwallis.
    27650, (63966), 68421
Reddy, William. 85348
Rede, Carteret. (68488), 2d note after 96107
Rede, William Leman. 68489
Rede bei dem Trauer-Gottesdienste zum
    Andenken. 91987
Rede bei der Begrabnissfeier der Prasidenten
    Abraham Lincoln. 88843

Rede beim Trauergottesdienst in der Zions
    Kirche zu Philadelphia. 88842
Rede der Miss Polly Baker. (17987)
Rede des Ehrbaren Charles Sumner. 93686
Rede des ehrwurdigen Vatters Antonius Viejra.
    99526
Rede . . . 3. Februar 1862. 32877
Rede gehalten am Abend der Vorfeier des
    Humbolt-Gestes. 22777
Rede gehlaten bie der Einweihung des Uni-
    versitats-Gebaudes. 91988
Rede, ueber den Todt unseres unsterblichen
    Waschington's. 101542
Rede vom Ursprunge d. Bevolkerung in Amerika.
    97676
Rede, womit or seinen Vorschlag einer
    Ausssohnung. 69549
Rede zum Anderken an Abraham Lincoln. 38311
Rede sur Feyer des Maximilians-Tages. 89547
Re-dedication. A discourse. 43496
Redeemed captive: a narrative of the captivity.
    104273
Redeemed captive, being a narrative. 55891
Redeemed captive returning to Zion. 93077,
    94499, 104262-104271, 104274
Redemptio. pseud. Flying roll. see Smith,
    Richard Ransom.
Redemption of labor. 80541
Redemption of oppressed humanity! 85126
Redemption of the great national Whig and
    Democratic parties. 68490
Redemption of the seed of God at hand. 50431
Reden, Friedrich Wilhelm von. 68491-68492
Reden: On American taxation und On conciliation
    with America. 9297
Reden van dat die VVest-Indische Compagnie.
    68493, 1st note after 102910
Reden waeromme de West-Indische Compagnie.
    49828, (68495)
Redeneering, aanwysende, hoe tollen op eenige
    koopmanschappen. 100770
Redenen, ende verscheyde notable omstandigheden.
    68494
Redenen waerom het oorbaerder is dat de Ver-
    eenichde Nederlanden. (68496)
Redevoering, gehouden in de openbarren ver-
    gadering. 4362
Redevoering over de oorzaken van het verval.
    73100
Redevoering, ter gedanchtenis der roemrijke
    gebeurtenis. 98476
Redfield, Amasa A. 68497
Redfield, David A. 34534, (56995), 68498
Redfield, Isaac F. 68499-68502, 104180
Redfield, J. S. 68509
Redfield, James W. 68503-68504
Redfield, John Howard. 68505
Redfield, Lewis H. (68506)
Redfield, Richard W. 68509
Redfield, Timothy P. 68507
Redfield, William C. 2293, 2295A, 48174,
    (57238), 68505, 68508-(68512), 72476
Redfield; a Long Island tale. 68513
Redfield's Ohio railway gazetteer. (56995)
Redford, A. H. 68514
Redford, George. 89737
Redgate. firm see Almong & Redgate. firm
Redgrave, Samuel. 51527
Redhead, Henry. 68515
Redi, Franc. 68516-(68517)
Redigees calculees. (33757)
Reding, Charles W. 68518
Redington, James. (68519)
Redivivus, Junius. pseud. Tale of Tucuman.
    see Adams, William Bridges. supposed
    author

REDIVIVUS

Redivivus, Quevedo, Jr. pseud. Vision of
    judgment. see Wright, Robert William.
Redman, John. 66737, 68520-68521
Redman, Patrick H. 32615, (68522)
Redningsanstalterne. 18724
Rednitz, L. 68523
Redouer, Marthurin de. tr. 50059-50064,
    99379, note after 99383C, 3d and 5th
    notes after 106378
Redpath, James. (28520), (42356), (68524)-
    (68530)
Redres van de Abuysen ende Faulten in de
    Colonie van Rensselaers-wijck. 98545
Redskins. 16515
Redstick. 50122
Reduccion universal. 50037
Reducciones de estancias. 80987
Reducciones de plata. 4818
Reduced rates on ships discharged. 68531
Reduction of all the genera contained in the
    catalogue of North American plants.
    82788
Reduction of all the genera of plants contained
    in the Catalogus plantarum Americae
    Septentrionalis. 51249
Reduction of Cape Breton. 7300
Reduction of Louisbourgh, a poem. (52417)
Reduction of tariff and taxes. 89321
Reduction of the currency. 9615
Redwood, William. 51752
Redwood. 78772, 78775, 78792, 78800-78801,
    78806-78807, 96483
Redwood Library and Athenaeum, Newport, R.
    I. see Newport, R. I. Redwood Library
    Company.
Redwood Library Company, Newport, R. I. see
    Newport, R. I. Redwood Library Company.
Reed, ---------, fl. 1836. (60516), 62136
Reed, ---------, fl. 1844. 95124
Reed, ---------, fl. 1851. plaintiff (38087)
Reed, ---------, fl. 1882. 83961
Reed, Andrew, 1787-1862. 3534, (39840),
    (68537)-(68538)
Reed, Andrew, fl. 1835. (68535)-(68536)
Reed, Anna C. 27502, (35191), 1st note after
    99504, 101840, 101845, 101888, 101904
Reed, B. T. 86807-86808
Reed, Benjamin F. H. 68539
Reed, Caleb. 68540
Reed, Charles. 22192, 40280, 68143
Reed, Emily Hazen. 68541
Reed, Fitch. 68542
Reed, George E. (68543)
Reed Harrison, 1813- (24890), 68544, 95814
    see also Florida. Governor, 1868-1872
    (Reed)
Reed, Henry. of Cincinnati 68549-68551,
    78709
Reed, Henry, 1808-1854. (68545)-68548, 90289
Reed, J. M. 33491
Reed, James. 7827, 68553
Reed, James Whittemore. (68552)
Reed, John, 1751-1831. 55533, 68555-68556,
    68559, 76514
Reed, John, fl. 1768. plaintiff 68567
Reed, John, fl. 1774-1785. 68554
Reed, John, 1777-1845. (68558)
Reed, John, 1777-1845. supposed author 96804
Reed, John, 1781-1860. (68560)-68563, 90330
Reed, John, 1786-1850. 68564
Reed, John, fl. 1823. 68557
Reed, John J. 33176, (68565)
Reed, Jonas. 68566

Reed, Joseph. 9836-9837, 25279, (68568)-
    (68570), 68579, 68610, 68826, 82725,
    84611, 84612, 89000, 105365 see also
    Pennsylvania. Supreme Executive Council.
    President.
Reed, Joseph. defendant 68567
Reed, Mary T. 43228
Reed, N. A. 68572
Reed, P. Fishe. 68573-68574
Reed, Philip. 68575
Reed, Ralph J. 68576
Reed, Rebecca Theresa. 12097, 45038, 68578-
    68580, 75208, note after 93800, 2d note
    after 98167, 98168, 3d note after 98168
Reed, Sampson. 68581
Reed, Samuel R. 68582
Reed, Seth. 68583
Reed, Silas. 40632, 68584
Reed, Sylvanus. 68585-68586
Reed, Thomas B. 68587
Reed, Thomas C. (68588)-68590
Reed, Villeroy D. 68591-68592
Reed, William. proprietor of the "Grocer"
    68594
Reed, William, fl. 1805. 68593
Reed, William, fl. 186-. 68595
Reed, William, fl. 1864. 68596
Reed, William Bradford, 1806-1876. (20212),
    (24242), 34725, 36242, 37771, 40359,
    56319, 68569, (68597)-68625, 84611,
    89000, 2nd note after 94129
Reed, William Howell. (68626)
Reed controversy. 68571
Reeder, Andrew Horatio, 1807-1864. 58852,
    68627-(68629), 91268 see also Kansas
    (Territory) Governor, 1854-1855 (Reeder)
Reeder, Robert S. 68630
Reeder en Handelaar op de West-Indien. pseud.
    Reeder en handelaar op de West-Indien,
    aan zijne medereeders. (22010), 68631
Reeder en Handelaar op de West-Indien, aan
    zijne medereeders. (22010), 68631
Reedifacion de la iglesia martriz parroquial.
    68630
Reefer of '76. 11600
Reeks van brieven aan den Heer Necker. 97333
Reelfs, C. Schemering. 68633
Reemelin, Charles. (44759)
Rees, -------. 68650
Rees, Abraham. 59775, (68634), 102369
Rees, James. 68635-68644, 101234, note after
    102311
Rees, O. van. 68645-(68647), note before 98186
Rees, Thomas. 856, 40829-40830
Rees, William. 68648-68649, 92620
Rees' description of Keokuk. 68649
Reese, David Meredith. 54808, 68651-68660,
    (73941), (81887)
Reese, H. D. 12464
Reese, John. 68661
Reese, Levi R. 68662
Reese, Thomas. (68663)
Reese, W. B. 68664
Reeside case. 52136
Rees's cyclopaedia. 102369
Re-establishment of the apostolic church. 89369
Re-establishment of the flag. 6062
Reeve, Henry. tr. 29269, 96062-96065
Reeve, J. 68665
Reeve, John. 59720
Reeve, Lovell. 4389, 28400
Reeve, Tapping. 68666
Reeve, William, 1757-1815. 86928, 105527

Reeves, Henry. 68667
Reeves, Henry A. 68668
Reeves, James E. 68669-68670
Reeves, John. (68671)-(68675), (69711), 3d
note after 97583
Reeves, John. petitioner 68676
Reeves, M. S. 84343-84344
Reeves, W. 14346
Reeves on Americans. (68675), 3d note after
97583
Reexamination of American minerals. 82997,
82999-83000
Referee Sale of Real Estate, Hillsboro, Oregon,
1869. see Hillsboro, Ore. Referee Sale
of Real Estate, 1869.
Reference and distance map of the United
States. (49715)
Reference book and directory of the architects.
51467
Reference-book of the state of Maine. (42036)
Reference for officials of the nation. 83848
Reference handbook of medical sciences. 84276
Reference to the history and prophecy of the
past. 68677
References to the Book of Mormon. 83038
References to the civil and other systems of
foreign law. 6981
References to the decisions of the Supreme
Court. (42209)
References to the plan of the island of Domin-
ica. 9705
References to the plan of the island of St.
Vincent. 9706
Refined poetry of the south. 5523
Reflecciones sobre el dictamen. 68678
Reflecciones sobre la aparicion. 87243
Reflecciones sobre la invasion. 86237
Reflecciones sobre la nacionalidad. 68679
Reflecsiones al Congreso de Zacatecas. 68680
Reflecsiones militares sobre la organizacio.
57522
Reflecsiones que hace al supremo gobierno.
68681
Reflecsiones sobre algunas reformas. (68682)
Reflecsiones sobre el articulo primero. 26584
Reflecsiones sobre el manifesto de D. Anastasio
Bustamente. 9565
Reflesciones sobre un informe del Cabildo
Eclesiastico de Lima. 41123
Reflecteur organe de l'Eglise de Jesus-Christ
de Saints-des-Derniers-Jours. 68683
Reflectio supra quintam libri tertij magist.
58391
Reflection of ten years travells. 24684
Reflection on death and eternity. 7485
Reflectiones que se hicieron por su autor.
68684
Reflections against the Baptists refuted. 79796
Reflections and critical remarks. 68686
Reflections and maxims relating to the conduct
of human life. (68687)
Reflections and suggestions in regard to what
is called the catholic press. 33593
Reflections and suggestions on the present
state of parties. 68688
Reflections applicable to the present dangerous
crisis. 18348
Reflections concerning the future settlement of
these colonies. 3644A
Reflections critical and moral. note before
90223
Reflections excited by the present state of
banking operations. 3183
Reflections, for the consideration of the Congress. 68689
Reflections for the new year. 62626

Reflections moral and political on Great Britain
and her colonies. 103221
Reflections, occasioned by the late disturbances
in Charleston. 62909
Reflections of a few friends of the country upon
several circumstantial points; in a conference between Sandy, Pady, Simon and
Jonathan, and the parson; or, a looking
glass for overturning the ballance of power
and liberties of Europe. 68690
Reflections of a few friends of the country,
upon several circumstantial points; in a
conference between Sandy, Pady, Simon
and Jonathan, with the Parson: or a
looking-glass for the Americans. 68691
Reflections of a minister in a day of declension.
105945
Reflections of Col. Lillingston. 9207
Reflections of the state of society in the south-
west. 22364
Reflections offertes aux capitalistes de l'Europe.
98538
Reflections on a country church yard. 100663
Reflections on courtship and marriage. 68692-
68693
Reflections on David Humphrey's essay. 24022,
94058
Reflections on Dr. Samuel Johnson's defence of
Aristocles. (20062)
Reflections on domestic slavery. 103316
Reflections on extortion. 37650
Reflections on fever. 88906
Reflections on foreign trade in general, and the
future prospects of America. 413, 8456
Reflections on French atheism and English
Christianity. (79894)
Reflections on French atheism and on English
Christianity. 70791
Reflections on gold, silver and paper passing
as mony. [sic] 65678, 103121
Reflections on government. 68694
Reflections on His Majesty's . . . speech from
the throne. 40467
Reflections on hypocrisy. 78699
Reflections on intemperance. 102598
Reflections in itinerary parliaments. 37638
Reflections on its actual state in Europe.
(37136)
Reflections on Lieutenant Ogilvie's case. 106040
Reflections on Lord Clive. 60346
Reflections on Mr. Burchett's memoirs. 41072
Reflections on Mr. Walls history of infant
baptism. 69522
Reflections on Monroe's view. 29982, 69421-
69422
Reflections on Monroe's view of the conduct of
the executive on the foreign affairs.
29983, 96422
Reflections on nullification. 87949
Reflections on our present critical situation.
68695
Reflections on passing events. 29898, 68696
Reflections on peace and war. (35435)
Reflections on political society. 36244
Reflections on slavery, addressed to Lord Darce.
68697
Reflections on slavery, etc. (5339)
Reflections on slavery in general. 22933
Reflections on slavery; with recent evidence.
33683
Reflections on some of the results of the late
American war. 3634
Reflections on the American contest. 42900
Reflections on the Boston and Quebec acts.
11152

Reflections on the cause of the Louisianians. (42288)

Reflections on the causes which led to the formation of the colonization society. 10889

Reflections on the cession of Louisana to the United States. 81132, 94100

Reflections on the changes which may seem necessary. (40983)

Reflections on the character and public services of Andrew Jackson. 35387

Reflections on the commercial system. 8439

Reflections on the consequence of the banks. 10889

Reflections on the conservatory elements of the American republic. 68698

Reflections, on the constitution and management of the trade to Africa. 86735

Reflections on the death of a sister. 91541

Reflections on the different states and conditions of society. 33923, 98698

Reflections on the domestic and foreign policy of Great Britain. 68699

Reflections on the domestic policy. 68700

Reflections on the embargo. 9851

Reflections on the goodness of God. (44233)

Reflections on the importation of bar-iron. 68701

Reflections on the inconsistency of man. 68702

Reflections on the late war with America. 34814

Reflections on the law of 1813. 43385

Reflections on the loss of the steam-boat Home. 85338

Reflections on the manner in which property in Great Britain. 68703

Reflections on the mistakes the French have committed. 12140

Reflections on the moral and civil condition. 85549

Reflections on the most proper means of reducing the rebels. 68704

Reflections on the mysterious fate of Sir John Franklin. 58887

Reflections on the . . . objects of all science and literature. 28862

Reflections on the observations on the importance of the American revolution. 49402

Reflections on the operation of the present system of education. 1486

Reflections on the patent laws. 22182, 59045

Reflections on the perils and difficulties of the winter navigation. 19400

Reflections on the policy and necessity of encouraging the commerce. 68705, 97381

Reflections on the preliminary and provisional articles. 68706

Reflections on the present combination of the American colonies. 68707

Reflections on the present contest between France and Great Britain. 11586

Reflections on the present state and prosperity of the British West Indies. 28019

Reflections on the present state government of Virginia. 100518

Reflections on the present state of affairs at home and abroad. 106064

Reflections on the present state of the American war. (30149), 68708

Reflections on the present state of the province of the Massachusetts-Bay. 45967

Reflections on the present state of the slaves. 68709

Reflections on the present system of banking. 10889

Reflections on the present treaty of peace. 104140

Reflections on the printed case of William Penn. 68710

Reflections on the proclamation of the second of July, 1783. (68711)

Reflections on the proposition to communicate. 68712

Reflections on the protestation. 7663

Reflections on the renewal of the charter. 10889

Reflections on the rise and principles of the Society of Friends. (68713)

Reflections on the rise and progress of the American rebellion. (68714), note after 102685

Reflections on the rise, progress, and probable consequences, of the present contentions with the colonies. 22791

Reflections on the slave-trade. 58056

Reflections on the state of affairs in the south. (68715)

Reflections on the state of parties. 11829-11830

Reflections on the state of the late Spanish Americas. 68716

Reflections on the state of the union. (68717)

Reflections on the statements and opinions published in the Free enquirer. 62439

Reflections on the subject of a division of the Mississippi Territory. 68718

Reflections on the subject of emigration. 10871

Reflections on the subject of emigration from Europe. 10889

Reflections on the sudden death of seven persons. 91541

Reflections on the system of the Union Benevolent Association. 62349

Reflections on the terms of peace. 68719

Reflections on the tomb of Columbus. 14669

Reflections on the value of the British West India colonies. 68720

Reflections on West India affairs. 18148

Reflections on yellow fever periods. 88907

Reflections physical and moral. 68721

Reflections previous to the establishment of a militia. (68722)

Reflections sobre las notas insertas en el Redactor No. 2. 68685

Reflections sommaires sur le commerce. 67020

Reflections suggested by a second visit. 84009-84010

Reflections suggested by reading history and biography. 31618

Reflections suggested by the obsequies of John Adams. 68723

Reflections theologicae XII. 100618

Reflections . . . touching the several interests of the United States. 1341

Reflections upon a farewell. 63852, 100804

Reflections upon a pamphlet entitled Salvation for all men. (13424)

Reflections upon Mr. Whtmore's letter. (20062)

Reflections upon reflections. (68724)

Reflections upon the administration of justice in Pennsylvania. 60446

Reflections upon the appearance of a foreign war. 50045, 72155

Reflections upon the constitution and management of the trade to Africa. 68725

Reflections upon the law of libel. (37753), 57856

Reflections upon the late correspondence between Mr. Secretary Smith and Francis James Jackson. 30257

Reflections upon the military preparations. 68726

Reflections upon the peace. 18983, 18985

Reflections upon the perils and difficulties of the winter navigation. 36622, note after 68726

Reflections upon the present state of affairs, at home and abroad. 68737

Reflections upon the present state of England, and the independence of America. 18983, 18986

Reflections upon the present state of the currency. 185, 68728

Reflections upon the value of the British West Indian colonies. 85238

Reflections while descending the Ohio. 95393

Reflector, Philo. pseud. see Philo Reflector. pseud.

Reflexien over 't Noord-Amerikaansch bestier 68729

Reflexion generale sur l'etat present de la colonie de Surinam. 75838

Reflexion sobre su causa y estado. 99702

Reflexiones al ultimo impreso del Dr. D. Tomas Gutierrez de Pineres. 93304

Reflexiones de J. M. Alvirez. 10097

Reflexiones de M. de Cocherel. 14057

Reflexiones de un Habanero sobre la independencia. 17804

Reflexiones de un incognito a los magistrados y jurisconsultos. (68731)

Reflexiones de un patriota Americano. 76226

Reflexiones del Capitan Chinchilla. 105749

Reflexiones del Contador D. Joseph de Villa-Senor y Sanchez. 23606

Reflexiones del Gefe de Escuadra Don Juan Ruiz de Apodaca. 74022

Reflexiones du un Espanol Europeo. 68730

Reflexiones en contestacion al articulo comunicado. 68732

Reflexiones historico criticas sobre la insurrecion de Caracas. 10771, 10784

Reflexiones imparciales acerca del folleto titulado Da seroiebte de moises. 68733

Reflexiones imparciales sobre la humanidad de los Espanoles en las Indies. (56309)-57310

Reflexiones que con el interesante objeto de la reconsiliacion. 63185

Reflexiones que el Arzobispo de Caracas y Venezuela. 47804

Reflexiones que se hazen de vn papel. 96277

Reflexiones sobre el bando de 25. de Junio ultimo. (66581)

Reflexiones sobre el comercio de Espana. 68734

Reflexiones sobre la carta secrita por F. de Arrangoiz y Berzabal. 47036

Reflexiones sobre la consulta de la Excma. Diputacion Provincial. 79185

Reflexiones sobre la critica del P. Fr. Honorato de Sta. Maria. 76018

Reflexiones sobre la cuestion de la paz. 49409

Reflexiones sobre la importante cuestion. (17480)

Reflexiones sobre la inobservancia de la constitucion. 68735, 4th note after 98882

Reflexiones sobre la ley de 17 de Mayo. 68736

Reflexiones sobre la memoria del Ministerio de Relaciones. 95111

Reflexiones sobre la urgencia de que la representacion nacional decida. (68737), 5th note after 98882

Reflexiones sobre los decretos episcopales. 73159

Reflexiones sobre varios articulos del proyecto de constitucion. 68738

Reflexions addresses aux Canadiens Francais. 4165

Reflexions adressees aux Haytiens. 98673

Reflexions au sujet du tremblement de terre. 75527

Reflexions de M. de Cocherel. 14056

Reflexions detachees. 25052

Reflexions du bon citoyen. 68741

Reflexions d'un cultivateur Americain. 35511, 68739

Reflexions d'un Portugaus. (68740)

Reflexions d'un vieillard du pays de Medoc. 40001

Reflexions d'un vieillard sur l'admission des etrangers. 21035

Reflexions extraites d'un memoire. 47205

Reflexions historiques et politiques. 103081

Reflexions impartiales d'un citoyen. 94308

Reflexions impartiales sur l'Amerique. 68742

Reflexiones impartiales sur les consequences. 26426

Reflexions on a pamphlet. 68743

Reflexions on representation in Parliament. 68744

Reflexions on the blacks and whites. 98674

Reflexions on the proposed plan. 10889

Reflexions on the state of the union. 17302

Reflexions philosophiques et historiques. 80818

Reflexions politiques sur la guerre actuelle. 68745

Reflexions politiques sur quelques ouvrages et journaux Francais. 98669, 98675

Reflexions preliminaires des vrais principes politiques. 21195

Reflexions redigees en 1776. 97457

Reflexions sommaires adresses a la France. 38432

Reflexions sur la cession de la Guadeloupe. 23916

Reflexions sur la colonie de Saint-Domingue. 3312

Reflexiones sur la colonie Francoise de la Guyane. 29193

Reflexions sur la deportation des citoyens Verneuil, Ballio, Fournier et Gervais. (58613)

Reflexions sur la guerre en reponse a reflexions sur la paix. 35302

Reflexions sur la loi du Congres des Etats-Unis. 68747

Reflexions sur la paix. 35302

Reflexions sur la traite et l'esclavage des negres. 17858.

Reflexions sur la traite et l'esclavage des noirs. 68748

Reflexions sur l'abolition de la traite et de l' esclavage des Negres. 68746

Reflexions sur le code noir. (68751)

Reflexions sur le commerce, la navigation, et les colonies. 21035, 68752

Reflexions sur le despotisme qu'exercent a Saint-Domingue. (75185)

Reflexions sur le livre de M. Cochin. 27501

Reflexions sur le nouveau decrit. 8037

Reflexions sur le projet d'une colonie de cultivateurs Europeens. 29194

Reflexions sur le sort des noirs dans nos colonies. 68753

Reflexions sur la traite des noirs. (59579)

Reflexions sur les colonies. (58163)

Reflexions sur les debats, entre les accusateurs & les accuses. 58983, 75182

Reflexions sur les despotisme qu'exercent a Saint-Domingue. (58163)

Reformed Church of France. 25027, 91384

Reformed Church of Geneva. 91384

Reformed Church of Switzerland. 91384

Reformed common-wealth of bees. (30701), 1st note after 100518

Reformed drunkard. pseud. Sketch of the life of John Bishop. see Bishop, John.

Reformed Dutch Church. see Reformed Church in America.

Reformed Dutch Church, Hyde Park, N. Y. see Hyde Park, N.Y . Reformed Dutch Church.

Reformed Dutch Church, New York. see New York (City) Collegiate Church.

Reformed Dutch Church, Sleepy Hollow, N. Y. see Sleepy Hollow, N. Y. Reformed Dutch Church.

Reformed Dutch Church in North America. see Reformed Church in America.

Reformed Dutch Church in the Netherlands. see Nederlandsche Hervormde Kirke.

Reformed Dutch Church in the United States of America. see True Reformed Dutch Church in the United States of America.

Reformed Dutch Church in Williamsburgh. An historical discourse. 64238

Reformed Dutch Church of North America. see Reformed Church in America.

Reformed Dutch Protestant Church, New York. see New York (City) Collegiate Church.

Reformed Episcopal Church. Book of Common Prayer. 83518

Reformed Episcopal Church. General Council, 6th, 1878. 83250

Reformed Episcopal Church. Secretary. 83518

Reformed German Church lottery. . . . New-York, April 13. 1772. 68774

Reformed Low Dutch Church. see Reformed Church in America.

Reformed man. pseud. Sketch of the life. 81526

Reformed Presbyterian Church in North America. (68760), 68761, 72118, 81558

Reformed Presbyterian Church in North America. Eastern Subordinate Synod. Minority. 27320

Reformed Presbyterian Church in North America. General Synod. 93, (59400), 65121, 65180, (65188)

Reformed Presbyterian Church in North America. Presbytery of the Middle District. 96879

Reformed Presbyterian Church in North America. Southern Reformed Presbytery. 65227

Reformed Presbyterian Church in North America. Southern Reformed Presbytery. Several Ministers. pseud. see Several Ministers of the Southern Presbytery. pseud.

Reformed Presbytery in North America. see Reformed Presbyterian Church in North America. General Synod.

Reformed Protestant Dutch Church. see Reformed Church in America.

Reformed Protestant Dutch Church, New York. see New York (City) Collegiate Church.

Reformed Protestant Dutch Church, Schenectady, N. Y. see Schenectady, N. Y. Reformed Protestant Dutch Church.

Reformed Protestant Dutch Church in North America. see Reformed Church in America.

Reformed Quakers old friend, Trepidantium Malleus. pseud. Second friendly epistle. see Young, Samuel, fl. 1690-1700.

Reformed Society of Israelites, Charleston, S. C. 12092, 68782

Reformed stock gambler. pseud. Stocks and stock-jobbing in Wall Street. see Armstrong, William.

Reformed Virginian silk-worm. 30700-(30701), 1st note after 100518

Reformer. 68783

Reformer and the conservative. 62772

Reformers and intercessors sought by God. 58798

Reforms and reformers. 28491

Refreshment for the memory of Wm. Cobbet. [sic]. (7258), 14026, note after 95800, 12th note after 95843

Refuge in the City of Boston. Directors. (59670)

Refugee Commission, Louisville, Ky. see Louisville Refugee Commission.

Refugee. pseud. Letter to the President of the United States. see Barnard, Frederick Augustus Porter.

Refugee. pseud. Letters to the President of the United States. see Barnard, Frederick Augustus Porter.

Refugee: being the life of political exiles. 68784

Refugee in America: a novel. 97034

Refugee; or the narratives of fugitive slaves in Canada. (20931)

Refugee Relief Commission of Ohio. (57033)

Refugees from slavery in Canada West. (33333)

Refugees Home Society. 68785

Refugee's niece. 31580

Refugees of Martinique. 93417

Refugee's testimony. 6180

Refugies de St. Domingue, Baltimore. see Francais Refugies de St. Domingue, Baltimore.

Refutacao da carta de Talleyrand. 76325

Refutacao das doutrinas hereticas e falsas. 76320

Refutacao das mentiras e calumnias. 76322

Refutacao do segundo relatorio. (76318)

Refutacion a la America en peligro. (23065)

Refutacion al cuaderno titulado. 76747

Refutacion al cuaderno titulado: Ojeada sobre la campana. 57522

Refutacion al informe de la Comision del Senado. 68786

Refutacion al papel titulado Bosquejo de la marcha. (43796)

Refutacion, comentario, replica, folleto, etc. 77061

Refutacion, con notas interesantse. 56730

Refutacion contra la memoria presentada por Don Miguel Cabrera Nevares. 42673

Refutacion de la acta acordada por los diputados. 68787

Refutacion de la guarnicion de Veracruz. 57661

Refutacion de la inculpaciones hechas al C. Matias Romero. (70328)

Refutacion de la obra titulada Curso de derecho natural. 73164

Refutacion de las ideas del siglo diez y neuve. 38825

Refutacion de las memorias de Lord Cochrane. 61117

Refutacion de una leccion del Dr. Gustavo Minelli. (23068)

Refutacion del discurso que en favour de la toleracion religiosa. (9209)

Refutacion del folleto escrito en Arequipa. 35079

Refutacion del folleta titulado "Manifestacion del Vice-Presidente." 68788

Refutacion del papel publicado en Chile. 68789, 94833

Refutacion del papel publicado en la Habana. 68790

Refutacion del tercer manifiesto de D. Gabriel Claudio Sequeira. 1885

Refutacion dirigida al gobierno Frances. 99834

Refutacion documentada del folleto titulado "Cuestion de limites." 42916

Refutacion en la parte historica del articulo. 52332, 68791

Refutacion que hace el ciudadano Andres Torres. 96239

Refutatio argumentorum quae a DD. Directoribus Societatis tum Orientalis tum Occidentalis in Foederato Belgio. 40712, 68792, 102442

Refvtatio objectorvm in librvm de homine. 66471

Refutation a una atroz calumnia. 23237

Refutation and exposure of clerical misrepresentation. (35340)

Refutation, by his friends, of the calumnies against David Henshaw. (31423)

Refutation complete des accusations portees par MM. Ruste et Corio. 5850

Refutation d'assertions erronees publiees par le Moniteur universel. 50228

Refutation de cette adresse. 94901

Refutation de la lettre du General Francois Dauxion Lavaysse. 65419

Refutation de la Note collective. (57944)

Refutation de l'escrit intitule: Coup d'oeil sur l'etat politique. 4158

Refutation de l'opinion emise par Jomard. 58554

Refutation de quelques assertions d'un discours. 96348

Refutation des argumens avances de la parte de M^{rs} les Directeurs des Compagnies d'Orient. 40712, 68792, 102442

Refutation des argumens et raisons alleguees par M. Diogo de Mendoca Corte-Real. 47824, 102441

Refutation des calomnies relatives aux affaires du Bresil. 1444

Refutation des inculpations calomnieuses faites aux colons par l'auteur. 17507, 97507

Refutation des prospectus publies par MM. Laisne de Villeveque, Giordan et Baradiere. 44062, 44391

Refutation des reproches faits au Capitaine-General Rochambeau. (39231)

Refutation du livre de M. V. Schoelcher sur Haiti. 5652

Refutation du livre de M. Victor Schoelcher. 5652

Refutation du manifeste du General Oribe. 3245

Refutation du projet des amis des noirs. (75033)

Refutation du rapport de Lord Durham. 58489

Refutation d'un ecrit de Charrault. 12027

Refutation [d'un ecrit des ex-colons.] 65420

Refutation. Notes et observations financieres et politiques. 67624

Refutation of a certain pamphlet. 13867

Refutation of a dangerous & hurtful opinion. (37179), 37211, 104070

Refutation of a false aspersion. 98690

Refutation of a false, cruel and gross libel. (68793)

Refutation of a pamphlet, called Thoughts on the late transactions. (36312)

Refutation of Andrew Stewart's fabrication against General Lewis Cass. 91633

Refutation of aspersions on "Stuart's three years in North America." 93179

Refutation of calumnies, misrepresentations and fallacies. (8651)

Refutation of certain calumnies. (59154)

Refutation of certain misrepresentations. (30393)

Refutation of Dr. Price's statement of the national debt. 18347, 27145, note after 71369

Refutation of fallacious arguments anent [sic] the American question. 68794

Refutation of John C. Rives' statements. (71576)

Refutation of Mr. Charles O'Connor's defence of slavery. 13291

Refutation of Mr. Colden's "Answer" to Mr. Sullivan's report. 93532, 93535

Refutation of Mormonism. 80134

Refutation of R. S. Coxe's assertions. 102123

Refutation of several misstatements that have been published in the "Nautical magazine" of 1837. 21639, 93948

Refutation of sundry aspersions in the "Vindication" of the present trustees. (25775)

Refutation of sundry charges of Rev. R. Kearney against Peter Gough. 68795

Refutation of that illegitimate letter. 12348

Refutation of the calumnies . . . against the West India planters. 41037

Refutation of the calumnies circulated against the southern & western states. (32500), 5th note after 88114

Refutation of the charge brought against Admiral Knowles. 17611, (38152)

Refutation of the charge of abolitionism. (51011)

Refutation of the charges against John Frazee. 25691

Refutation of the charges brought by the Roman Catholics. (19992), 76454, 96419

Refutation of the charges in Mr. Marryat's "Thoughts on the abolition of the slave trade, &c." 102148

Refutation of the charges in the proclamation of President Jefferson. 104647

Refutation of the charges made by a writer. 98977

Refutation of the charges made by Dr. Caldwell. 17654

Refutation of the charges preferred against His Excellency Daniel D. Tompkins. 96150

Refutation of the claim of John Livingston. 41621

Refutation of the claims of the West India colonists. (42951), 86736, 1st note after 102832

Refutation of the false statements of Mary Dyer. 57844, note after 97893, note after 105575

Refutation of the letter to an Honble Brigadier-General. 36094-36905, 95766

Refutation of the misstatements contained in a pamphlet. 60311

Refutation of the pamphlet which Colonel Picton lately addressed. 26154

Refutation of the principles of abolition. 68796

Refutation of the reasons assigned by the arbitrators. 78820

Refutation of the several calumnies and falsehoods. 9829

Refutation of the several misstatements that have been published in the "Nautical magazine" of 1837. 21639, 93948

Refutation of the sophisms. 105610

Refutation of the three oppressers of the truth. 37212

Refutation of the various calumnies against the West India colonies. 68797

Refutation of two passages in the writings of Thomas Jefferson. 4037, 20458

Refutation of various calumnies against the West India colonies. 102796

Refutation que el Dr. Antonio Jose Sucre hace. 56450

Refutation sommaire pour les Sieurs Walpole & Consorts. 101149

Refutation victorieuse du rapport soumis a la Convention Anti-seigneuriale. 67614

Refutations de nouvelles allegations du Ministere. 4515

Regal boke of dreemes. 83735

Regalia, Antonio Joseph Alvarez de Abreu, Marques de la. see Abreu, Antonio Joseph Alvarez de, Marques de la Regalia.

Regalis justitia Iacobi. 78189

Regan, John. 68798-68799

Regards due to such as have been eminent & useful. 103791

Regards due to the memory of faithful ministers. 78278

Regein fur die Duetsche Gesellschaft im dem Staate von Neu-York. 101242

Regeling van den geneeskundigen dienst. 68800

Regeln der Incorporirten Deutschen Gesellschaft zur Unterstutzung. 60055

Regeln der Teutschen Gesellschaft in Philadelphia. (62305), 68801

Regeln und Articuls zu besserer Regierung und Anfuhrung. (68802)

Regencia del reyno se ha servido dirigirme el decreto que sigue. 68519

Regenerador. Periodico politico, literario y comercial. (68803)

Regeneration and the testimony of the spirit. (26595)

Regeneration before reconstruction. 36885

Regeneration des colonies. 6318

Regenspurger Exemplar. 96792

Regent van een voornaame Stad. pseud. Politiek vertoog over het waar sistema. see Van Goens, Rijklof Michael.

Regent's office and duties in Harvard University. 88999

Regi pacifico, Ludovico XVI. 44693

Regia parentatio exorans pios manes. 11449

Regicides. 94250

Regicides sheltered in New England. 71787

Regidor D. Jose Ramon Martelo y Otero. 44827

Regier, Geh. ed. 4643

Regierungsbericht uber die Zustande Canada's. 21753

Regierungsrath, ---------. 24013, 51076

Regierungsverfassung der Republik Pennsylvanien, wie solche von der General Convention. 60447

Regierungsverfassung der Republik Pennsylvanien wie solche von der zu dem Zweck erwahlten und vom 15ten July. 68804

Regil, J. M. (68805)

Regil, Pedro Manuel. 68806

Regil Velasco, Pedro. 68807

Regime municipal des capitales. 14063

Regimental history. 80135

Regimental orders. 68808

Regimental record. (74873)

Regimento da navegacao e conquestas do Brasil, Angola, etc. 7619

Regimento das caramas municipaes. 16977

Regimento de pilotos. 44607

Regimento interno da Assemblea Legislativa da Provincia da Bahia. 68810

Regimento nautico. 39232

Regimento, & leyes sobre as missionens do estado do Maranhao. 44461

Regimentos e ordenacoes da fazenda. 68809

Regiments-Verfassung von Pennsylvania. 68811

Regimento or denacoes da fazenda. 68809

Regimiento de navigacion. (11718)

Regina Maria. (51033)

Reginald Reverie. pseud. see Mellen, Grenville.

Regiomontanus, Johannes. see Mueller, Johannes, Regiomontanus, 1436-1476.

Region of the Ohio. 59132

Regions nouvelles. 73466

Regionvm Indicarum per Hispanos olim devastatarum. 11285

Regis, Augustin. 68812

Regis Salazar, Juan Francisco. 68815, 75579

Register and almanack for the state of Connecticut. (15829)

Register and circular of the State Normal School, Albany. 53966

Register and circular of the State Normal School at Salem, Mass. 75749

Register, and Connecticut almanack. for . . . 1775. 92980

Register, and Connecticut almanack, for . . . 1776. 15669, 92981

Register and manual for the use of the members. 88233

Register and pocket almanack. (24688)

Register and western calendar, for 1818. 42723

Register der resolutien van de Hoog Mog: Heeren Staten Generaal. 93834

Register der resolutien van de Hoog Mogende Heeren Staten Generaal. 102889A

Register der resolutien van de Hoogh Mog. Heeren Staten Generael. 102892

Register der resolutien van Haer Hoogh Moog. 486, 102877

Register der resolutien van Ridderschap en Steden. de Staaten van Overyssel. 93834

Register der resolutien vande Hoogh Mogh. Heeren Staten Generaal. 23513

Register des Buchs der Croniken vnd Geschichtens. 77525

Register for 1846-7. 20083

Register for New England and Nova Scotia; and an almanack for 1768. 47408

Register for New-England and Nova-Scotia. With all the British lists. 24685, 67243

Register for the state of Connecticut. (15829)

Register for the state of Connecticut: with an almanack, for the year of Our Lord, 1785. 15828

Register for the state of Connecticut: with an almanack for the year of Our Lord 1794. 28560

Register of arts. 24215

Register of baptisms in the Presbyterian Church. 83423

Register of canal boats, in the Comptroller's Office. (53563)

Register of canal boats, kept in the Canal Department during the year 1847-8. (53564)

Register of canal boats, kept in the Canal Department, showing the names of the boats registered. (53563)

Register of civil, judicial, military and other officers in Connecticut. 15666, 68816

Register of coelestial configurations &c. 62743
Register of debates; being a report of the
    speeches. 28517, 68817
Register of debates in Congress. 1229, 4783,
    15587, (15607), 90365
Register [of De Veaux College.] 19806
Register of federal officers and salaries.
    20194
Register of Hobart College. 32313
Register of Indian affairs. 43110
Register of Indian affairs within the Indian (or
    Western) Territory. (43111)
Register of inventions and improvements.
    47283
Register of lodges in South Carolina and
    Georgia. 25812
Register of lost, stolen and missing securities.
    68818
Register of Mattapoisett Academy. 46879
Register of members of the Moravian Church.
    68993
Register of naval actions. 21251
Register of New-Hampshire. 15143, (18062)
Register of New Netherland. 56615
Register of North Carolina troops. 55675
Register of officers and agents, civil, military
    and naval, in the service of the United
    States; corrected to November, 1862.
    20317
Register of officers and agents, civil, military,
    and naval, in the service of the United
    States, in 1802. 68819
Register of officers and agents, civil, military,
    and naval, in the service of the United
    States on the third day of September,
    1815. 68820
Register of officers and agents, civil, military,
    and naval, in the service of the United
    States, on the thirtieth day of September,
    1816. 68821
Register of officers and students, 1901. 83004
Register of official papers. 25057
Register of Pennsylvania. (6107), (31103),
    31106, 83983, 101219
Register of Racine College. 67398
Register of rural affairs. 88273
Register of St. John's College. 75288
Register [of St. Mary's Hall.] 75439
Register of state papers, history and politics.
    (1260)
Register of the army and navy of the United
    States. 25058
Register of the city of Boston. 6550
Register of the college. 9337
Register of the college of St. James. 75237
Register of the Collegiate Department, Western
    Military Institute. 51880
Register of the commissioned and warrant
    officers of the navy. 15347
Register of the commissioned and warrant
    officers of the navy of the United States.
    32688
Register of the commissioned officers and
    privates of the New Jersey Volunteers.
    53209
Register of the Confederate dead, interred in
    Hollywood Cemetery. 68822
Register of the deaths in Northampton. (55768)
Register of the decrees of the Committee of
    Public Safety. 96568
Register of the Department of State. 68823
Register of the descendants of Adam Todd.
    (28609)
Register of the executive and legislative depart-
    ments. (44007)

Register of the executive and legislative depart-
    ments of the government of Massachusetts.
    54628, 64028
Register of the faculty, officers and students
    of the Academic Department. (45389)
Register of the House of Representatives of
    . . . Maine. 44008
Register of the inhabitants of Framingham
    before 1800. (3691)
Register of the Kentucky State Historical
    Society. 84940, 105053
Register of the lodges of Masons in South
    Carolina and Georgia. 25812, 87840
Register of the members of the Union Philo-
    sophical Society. 20082
Register of the . . . Metropolitan Academy and
    Gymnasium. 54396
Register of the Military Order of the Loyal
    Legion of the Massachusetts Commandery.
    (45833)
Register of the militia of the District of
    Columbia. 20312
Register of the officers and graduates of the
    Military Academy. 17866
Register of the officers and students for 1854-5.
    61061
Register of the officers and students of Lehigh
    University. 39884
Register of the officers and students, with
    programme of the course of study. 69641
Register of the Pelletreau family. 59585
Register of the premiums and bounties given
    by the Society Instituted at London. 68824
Register of the proceedings of the Western
    Literary Institute. 102989
Register of the Rensselaer Polytechnic Institute.
    96941
Register of the Rensselaer Polytechnic Institute,
    Troy, N. Y. 69641
Register of the Senate of Maine. (44009)
Register of the Southern British American
    colonies. 87755
Register of the Southern British American
    provinces. 87753
Register of the . . . State Normal School [of
    New Jersey.] 53195
Register of the Superior Council of Quebec.
    17852, (66984)
Register of the times. 68825
Register of the times, and literary review.
    68825
Register of the weather . . . for the last
    twenty-five years. 925
Register of the weather, in Hingham, Massa-
    chusetts. 89676
Register of the weather kept according to
    Farenheit's scale. 89677
Register of trade of the colored people.
    (62113)
Register office. A comedy. 68826
Register; or Odd Fellows' guide. 68827
Register resolutien van de Ho. Mog. Heeren
    Staten Generaal. 93836
Register: together with an almanack. 87760
Registrar's book of Governor Keith's Court
    of Chancery. 68004
Registration of births, marriages and deaths.
    90124
Registration report. . . . 1st February, 1867
    56167
Registratur von der Sechsten Versammlung
    der Evangelischen Arbeiter in Pennsyl-
    vania. 51293, 4th note after 97845
Registre de deliberations du Comite Colonial
    de Saint Domingue. 75119

Registre des deliberations de la Deputation de Saint-Domingue. 75120

Registre des Etats Generaux des Pais Bas Unis. (68750)

Registres de deliberations et de correspondence. 85787

Registres de l'Assemblee Provinciale . . . de l'Quest. 75116

Registres des Baptesmes et sepultures. 68828

Registres des deliberations de l'Assemblee Provinciale du Sud. 75117

Registres des deliberations de l'Assemblee Provinciale du Sud de Saint-Domingue. 75115

Registres du Conseil d'Estat. (56085), (56089), 56091, 75057, 75059

Registres du Conseil Priue du Roy. 56088, 72043

Registres du Conseil Superieur et des registres d' Intendance. 17851

Registres du Parlement. 68074

Registro diplomatico del gobierno de Buenos-Aires. 9033, (68829)

Registro estadistico de Buenos Aires. 9035, 106365

Registro estadistico de la provincia de Buenos Aires. 68831

Registro estadistico de la republica Arjentina. Bajo la direccion de Damian Hudson. 68830

Registro estadistico de la republica Arjentina, 1864. 68830

Registro estadistico del estado de Buenos Aires. 9034

Registro nacional. Provincias Unidas del Rio de la Plata. 68832

Registro oficial de la republica Peruana. 68833

Registro oficial del gobierno de Buenos Aires. (9036)

Registro oficial del gobierno de los Estados-Unidos Mexicanos. 48638, 68834

Registro trimestre. 68835

Registro Yucateco. 68836

Registrum ecclesiae parochialis. 9357

Registrum huius operis libri cronicarum. 77523

Registrvm alphabeticvm. (66472)

Registry law. 34572

Registry laws affecting lands in Upper Canada. 81674

Registry of American and foreign shipping. 68837

Regla consuenta. 68838

Regla de la gloriosa Santa Clara. 68839

Regla de la Purissima Concepcion de Nuestra-Senora. 68840

Regla de los Frayles Menores. 68841

Regla de S. Agustin, que han de guardar las religiosas. 24150

Regla de S. Augustin. Constituciones de la orden. (68842)

Regla de San Francisco. 68843

Regla, y constituciones de la Sagrada Religion Bethlemitica. 68845

Regla y constituciones de las Religiosas de Santa Brigida. 68844

Regla y constituciones del Orden Tercero del Real y Militar de Nuestra Senora de la Merced. 62601

Regla y constituciones que han de guardar las religiosas. 68847-68848

Regla y constituciones que han de guardar las religiosas del Convento del Glorioso Padre San Geronimo. 68846

Regla, y constituciones, que observa la Sagrada Religion de la Charidad. 68849

Regla y ordenaciones de las religiosas de la Limpia. 44393

Regla, y ordenanzas de las religiosas y canonigas regulares. 41124

Reglamento concerniente al teatro de Mexico. (26476)

Reglamento consular do imperio do Brasil. 88770

Reglamento de administracion y contrabilidad militar. 68850

Reglamento de aduanas maritimas frontarizas y de cabotage. 48639

Reglamento de aduanas para los almacenes de deposito. (68851)

Reglamento de aduanas y resguardos del estado de Chile. 12801

Reglamento de auxiliares para la seguaridad de las personas. 48640

Reglamento de comercio de la republica del Peru. 61159

Reglamento de correos del Peru. (68852)

Reglamento de la Academia de Jurisprudencia. 68853

Reglamento de la Casa de Misericordia. 10785

Reglamento de la Caja de Ahorros de la Gran Sociedad. 68854

Reglamento de la Compania General Mexicana. 48641

Reglamento de la Junta Superior. 68855

Reglamento de la milicia activa. 48644

Reglamento de la milicia nacional Mexicana. 48642

Reglamento de la Sociedad (aprobado en junta general.) 85724

Reglamento de la Sociedad Artistica. 85717

Reglamento de la Sociedad de Beneficencia. 85723

Reglamento de la Sociedad de los Fundadores de la Independencia del Peru. 85728

[Reglamento de la Sociedad de San Felipe de Jesus.] 85731

Reglamento de la Sociedad Economica empleados de aduana. 85754

Reglamento de la Sociedad Filarmonica de Santa Cecilia. 85755

Reglamento de la Sociedad Patriotica de Carabobo. 68856

Reglamento de libertad de imprenta de la republica Mejicana. 48643

Reglamento de libertad de imprenta mandado observar en la republica Mexicana. 48643

Reglamento de los mayorales y mayordomos de ingenios. 29453

Reglamento de los tributos de esta capital. 70285

Reglamento de milicias de la isla de Cuba. 17805

Reglamento de policia. 98857

Reglamento de policia de la Habana. 29454

Reglamento del Colegio de Ingenieros de la republica. 68857

Reglamento del Colegio Militar. 48644

Reglamento del Cuerpo de Serenos. 68858

Reglamento del Gremio de Panaderos de Mexico. 48644

Reglamento del metodo con que deben usarse las mulas asignadas a los Cuerpos del Ejercito. 68859

Reglamento del Monte Pio de Viudas. 68860

Reglamento del Monte Pio Militar. 68238

Reglamento del Tribunal de Revision de Cuentas. 48644

Reglamento e instruccion de la infanteria de linea i tiradores. (14619)

Reglamento, e instruccion para los presidios. 56262

Reglamentos particulares de la R. L. de San Juan de Esococia. 68893

Reglas ciertas para jueces de las Indias. 50477

Reglas ciertas, y precisamente necessarias. (50605)

Reglas de gobierno de la Sociedad de Subscritores del Teatro. 48645, 85735

Reglas de la Compania de Jesus. 68894

Reglas de orthographia, diccionario, y arte del idioma Othomi. 52413

Reglas de ortografia. (52414)

Reglas de ortografia para instruccion de los que comienzan a escribir. 105740

Reglas de ortographia dicionario y arte del ydioma Othomi. 49896

Reglas para el domicilio de nuevos colonos y sus auxilios. 17809

Reglas para la extraccion licita del numerario de los puertos. 73455

Reglas para la inteligencia de la lengua de los Indios de Piritu. 74017

Reglas para que los naturales de estos reynos sean felices. 42066

Reglas y constituciones de la Sancta Congradia d[e] los Iuramentos. 68895

Reglas, y constitvciones, qve han de gvardar los Senores Inqvisidores. 68896

Reglas y ordenanzas del choro de esta Santa Iglesia Cathedral. (66575)

Reglas y ordenanzas para el gobierno de los Hospitales de Santa Fe de Mexico. 50611

Reglas y patentes de la entrada y profesion de los Hermanos de Tercer Orden de los Siervos de Maria Santisima de los Dolores. (68897), note after 94835

Regle proportionelle. 33563

Reglement au sujet des engagez et fusiles. 68898

Reglement by de West-Indische Compagnie het open-stellen vanden handel. 102928

Reglement by de VVest-Indische Compagnie, ter vergaderinge vande negentiene. 68889, note after 102926, 102927

Reglement concernant les prises que des corsaires Francois conduiront. 68901

Reglement concernant les sieges d'amiraute. 68902

Reglement concernant l'exploitation de la peche de la Morue. (68900), 73817

Reglement, contineerende restrictien en bepaalingen. 22996

Reglement de la Societe. 85806

Reglement [de la Societe Bienveillante de Notre Dame de Bonsecours.] 85783

Reglement de la Societe des Amis des Noirs. 85805

Reglement [de la Societe du Magnetisme de la Nouvelle-Orleans.] 85812

Reglement de police sur les Negres de la Guyane. 29195

Reglement des droits & salaires des officiers des sieges d'amiraute des Isles du Vent de l'Amerique. 68906

Reglement des droits & salaires des officiers du siege d'amiraute a l'Isle-Royale. (68904)

Reglement des droits & salaires des officiers du siege de l'amiraute de l'Isle Royale. (68903)

Reglement des droits & salaires des officiers du siege de l'amiraute de Quebec. (68905)

Reglement des droits, salaires & cavations des officiers des sieges d'Amiraute des Isles du vent de l''amerique. 68907

Reglement du Roy. Du vingtieme Aoust 1698. 68908

Reglement dv Roy pour la conduite, police et discipline. 68909

Reglement, et lettres-patentes sur icelui. 68910

Reglement general des douanes maritimes et frontieres. 48646

Reglement militaire, concernant la police et la discipline. 68911

Reglement og foreening indgaaet og sluttet d. 26 Sept., 1733. 102939

Reglement op de administratie der justitie en de manier van procedeeren. 68912

Reglement op het beleid van de regering. (68914)

Reglement op het belied van de regering, het hustitie-wezen, enz. te Suriname. 68913

Reglement pour etablir un bon ordre de police au Canada. 73741

Reglement pour le siege de l'amiraute a l'Isle Royale. 68916

Reglement pour les farines de Canada. 68917

Reglement pour les paquebots etablis par arret du Conseil. 68919

Reglement pour les paquebots etablis pour communiquer avec les Etats-Unis d' Amerique. 68918

Reglement pour l'etablissement & l'entretien des chemins royaux. 68915

Reglement que le Roy veut & entende estre observe. 68920

Reglement sur la police a observer a l'egard des matelots. 68921

Reglementen op het beleid van de regering. 68922

Reglements consulaires des principaux etats maritimes. (18144)

Reglements [de la Societe Amicale de Quebec.] 85782

Reglements de la Societe de Construction Metropolitaine. 85799

Reglements [de la Societe Permanente de Construction des Artisans, Quebec.] 85820

Reglements de la Societe Permanente de Construction Jacques-Cartier. 85821

Regles de la Congregation de Notre-Dame de Quebec. 67054

Regles de la Societe Bienveillante de Quebec. 85785

Regles et reglemens de la Societe du Feu a Montreal. 85810

Regles et reglements de la Societe Bienveillantes des Ouvriers de Quebec. 85786

Regln fur die Ordhung und Disciplin der Vereingten Staaten. 91419

Reglo de ano neuvo para el Senor. 72281

Regnault, Elias. (68923)-68925

Regnault, Eugene. see Regnault, Elias.

Regnault-Warin, Jean. 68926-68928

Regne animal. 18210

Regne de Toussaint-Louverture. 60969, 96344

Regni Collegio, Peru. see Peru (Viceroyalty) Regni Collegio.

Regni Hispaniae post omnivm editiones locvpletissima descriptio. 32005, 77901

Regnicola recien llegado a esta capital. pseud. Carta. 11097

Regnier, --------, fl. 1778. tr. 68448

Regnier, --------, fl. 1798. 97026

Regno Gesuitico del Paraguay dimonstrato. (58530)

Regnorum aquilonarium, Daniae, Sueciae, Norvagiae chronica. 38299, 106294, 106330

Regnum animale. 100783

Regnum Gutschi. 99365

Rego, Antonio Jose de Souza. see Souza Rego, Antonio Jose de.
Rego, Jose Pereira. 68929
Rego Abranches, Antonio Manuel do. ed. 68930
Rego Barreto, Luis do. 68930
Regocijo Mexicano por la deseada y feliz entrada. 68931
Regon, M. C. 56444, 68932
Regt ingezetenen van deezen staat. (68933)
Regtsgeleerde bedenkingen over het tractaat. 68934
Regtsgeleerde memorie. 22011-22012, 42747, 102499
Regtuit, Jan. (77977)
Regvla Beatissimi Patris Nostri Augustini Episcopi. (68936)
Regula, et constitutiones pro clericis. 68937, 98642
Regula, et distinctio primo constitutionum Sacri Ordinis Praedicatorum. 68938
Regulamento da Secretaria do Conselho Director do Imperio Instituto de Agricultura. 85630
Regulamento do imposto do sello e da sua arrecadacao. 67668
Regulamento geral das escolas primarias. 88746
Regulamento para a instruccao primaria da provincia do Rio Grande do Norte. 71478
Regular and skilful music in the worship of God. (55386)
Regular hymns. 104115
Regular series of chronology. 78348
Regulated slave trade. 92005
Regulation of fees. 99094
Regulation versus prohibition. (13256)
Regulations adopted by the corporation. (30749)
Regulations adopted by the Massachusetts Medical Society. 45874
Regulations. . . . Adopted May, 1846. 73670
Regulations and course of study. 44218
Regulations and general laws of the Independent Order of Rechabites. 68939
Regulations and instructions for the field service. 43016
Regulations as approved by the National Quarantine and Sanitary Association of the United States. (52017)
Regulations by the Standing Committee of Companies A. B. and C. 61989
Regulations for common school districts. 60449
[Regulations for Field Relief Agency Corps.] (76607), 76647
Regulations for light infantry and riflemen. 26639
Regulations for maintaining the cleanliness, &c., of the streets. 73669
Regulations for navigating the Chesapeake and Ohio Canal. 12510
Regulations for the administration of justice. 22997
Regulations for the interior police and discipline. 53889
Regulations for the army of the Confederate States. 68941
Regulations for the army of the Confederate States. By W. T. Mecklin. 68963
Regulations for the army of the Confederate States, 1864. 15350
Regulations for the army of the Confederate States, 1862. 15348
Regulations for the army of the Confederate States, with a full index. (15349)
Regulations for the army of the United States, 1857. 68942

Regulations for the assessment of the income tax. 68943
Regulations for the better government of His Majesty's subjects. (9362)
Regulations for the Board of School Committee. 68944
Regulations for the Commissariat of . . . Georgia. 27090
Regulations for the Commissary's Department of the state of Virginia. 15351
Regulations for the Consular Corps of the United States of America, in Japan. 68945
Regulations for the dining hall. 105833
Regulations for the field exercise. (68946), 85187-85188
Regulations for the general and internal division of the Soldiers' Home. 86338
Regulations for the government of students. 88099
Regulations for the government of the Naval Academy. 68947
Regulations for the government of the New Bedford Alms-House. 52499
Regulations for the government of the Ordnance Department. 68948
Regulations for the government of the Ordnance Department of the Confederate States of America. 15352
Regulations for the government of the Social School. (52498)
Regulations for the government of the Territory North-West of the River Ohio. 16101
Regulations for the government of the Transportation Department of the Western Rail Road Corporation. 103005
Regulations for the government of the United States Navy. 68949
Regulations for the Grammar School of St. Augustine's College. 68950
Regulations for the Library [of the Massachusetts Historical Society.] (45858)
Regulations for the Medical Department of the Confederate States Army. 15353
Regulations for the Medical Department of the C. S. Army. 15354
Regulations for the navy, 1862. 15355
Regulations for the order and discipline of the troops of New-Hampshire. 93510
Regulations for the order and discipline of the troops of the state of Vermont. 99060
Regulations for the order and discipline of the troops of the United States. 91395, 91397-91418, 91420-91431, 91433-91434, 91437, 91439, 91443-91458, 91458-91463
Regulations for the order and discipline of the volunteer army of the United States of America. 91438, 91440
Regulations for the Pay Department of the Army of the United States. 68951
Regulations for the public schools, of . . . Lowell. 42479
Regulations for the public schools . . . [of the City of Salem.] Adopted . . . [by the School Committee,] April, 1840. (75741)
Regulations for the public schools of the city of Salem. Adopted by the School Committee, May 1836. (75741)
Regulations for the public schools of the town of Salem. (75741)
Regulations for the Quartermaster's Department of the state of Georgia. 27090
Regulations for the Quartermaster's Department of the United States Army. 68952
Regulations for the recruiting service. 68953
Regulations for the Subsistence Department. 15356

Regulations for the Subsistence Department of the Army of the United States. (68954)

Regulations for the superintendence, government, and instruction of the public schools. . . . adopted, 1847. (75741)

Regulations for the superintendence, government and instruction of the public schools. . . . adopted, 1842. (75741)

Regulations for the sword exercise of the cavalry. 17368

Regulations for the uniform and dress of the Army of the United States. (68956)

Regulations for the unifrom & dress of the Army of the United States. June, 1851. 68957

Regulations for the uniform & dress of the Marine Corps of the United States. 68958

Regulations for the uniform and dress of the Massachusetts Volunteer Militia. 46148. 92038

Regulations for the uniform and dress of the military forces. 68959

Regulations for the uniform and dress of the Navy and Marine Corps. 68960

Regulations for the uniform and dress of the United States Navy. 68961

Regulations for the uniform of the militia. 53890

Regulations for the uniform of the United States Navy. (68962)

Regulation for voluntary studies. 105835

Regulations lately made concerning the colonies, and the taxes imposed upon them, considered. (5859), 10243, 28770-28771, 3d note after 103122

Regulations of police, &c. &c. in force in this district. 67044, 82912

Regulations of St. Aloysius Sunday School. 106132

Regulations of the Beverly Second Social Library. 5122

Regulations of the Canal Board in relation to engineers. (53564)

Regulations of the Children's Asylum. 54178

Regulations of the College of New Jersey. 53088

Regulations of the Common Council for the citizens watching in rotation. 77596

Regulations of the Confederate States School-Ship Patrick Henry. 15357

Regulations of the Economical School in . . . New York. 54257

Regulations of the Evangelical Lutheran Church of St. Peter. 70489

Regulations of the Field Relief Corps. 68940

Regulations of the free schools of . . . Northborough. 55777

Regulations of the Friendly Fire Society. 10153

Regulations of the Governor and Council [of the Massachusetts State Prison.] 45902

Regulations of the Grand Lodge of New Hampshire. 52835

Regulations of the Grand Royal Arch Chapter of . . . New York. (53692)

Regulations of the Grand Royal Arch Chapter of the state of Vermont. 99181

Regulations of the Grand Royal Arch Chapter of the state of Vermont. With the additions and amendments since adopted. 99181

Regulations of the Laurel Hill Cemetery. 39255

Regulations [of the Library of Brown University.] 8624

Regulations of the military academies of South Carolina. 87390

Regulations [of the New Bedford City Library.] 52467

Regulations of the New York Agency. 76570, 76647

Regulations of the Ordnance Department of the Confederate States. 15358

Regulations of the Quartermaster's and Pay Departments of the Confederate States. 68964

Regulations of the School Committee of Dorchester. (20628)

Regulations of the School Committee of New Bedford. (52483)

Regulations of the School Committee of Roxbury. 73670

Regulations of the School Committee of the town of Concord. 15134

Regulations of the School Committee of the town of Dorchester. (20628)

Regulations of the Selectmen. (15465)

Regulations of the Smithsonian Institution. 85051

Regulations of the South Dining Hall, Yale College. 105830

Regulations of the Supply Department. 68965

Regulations of the United States Naval Academy. 68966

Regulations of the U. S. Naval Academy, at Annapolis, Maryland. 68947

Regulations of the Virginia Military Institute at Lexington. 100559

Regulations, ordered by Congress for the government . . . of the troops. 91459

Regulations prescribed by the President for consular officers. (68967)

Regulations relating to public health. 56168

Regulations, relative to the procession for rendering funeral honors. 101814

Regulations relative to the waste lands of the crown. 10409

Regulations respecting board. I. All who 105832

Regulations respecting board. I. The steward engages. 105831

Regulations respecting the issue and transfer of certificates of stock. (53564)

Regulations, studies, and system of the common schools. (10929)

Regulations to be observed by vessels navigating the Chesapeake and Delaware Canal, and Bank Creek. 12498

Regulations to be observed by the Syndics and Alcalds. 102764

Regulations under which the inhabitants may purchase the enumerated articles. 68968

Regulator for Crazy Will's death-watch. 68969

Regulatoren in Arkansas. 27194

Regulus. pseud. Fan for fanning. (55611), 68970

Regulus. pseud. On the dismemberment of Canada. see Smyth, John Ferdinand Dalziel, 1745-1814.

Regulus. pseud. To the freemen of Pennsylvania. (60696)

Regulus. 15523, (19253)

Rehfeus, P. I. tr. 104707

Rehfues, Ph. J. von. tr. 19986

Rehoboth, Mass. 68971

Rehoboth, Mass. Petitioners 46051

Rehoboth, Mass. Congregational Church. (68973), 95524

Rehoboth, Mass. Ex-parte Council, 1st-3d, 1825. see Congregational Churches in Massachusetts. Ex-parte Council, 1st-3d, Rehoboth, 1825.

Rehoboth, Mass. School Committee. 68975
Rehoboth, Mass. Superintending School Committee. 68976
Rehoboth in the past. 55020
Rei de los volcanes. 72770
Reibaud, Francisco. (11176)
Reich, J. H. Zur-. see Muller, W. J.
Reichard, H. A. O. 68977
Reichardt, C. F. 68978-68979
Reichardt, Theodore. 68980
Reichart, Johann Peter. 68981
Reiche, Charles Christopher. 68982
Reiche Schweden General Compagnie. see Soder Compagniet.
Reiche Schweden General Compagnies handlungs Contract. (68983), 98199, note after 98207, 98210
Reichel, Edward H. 32082, (68984)
Reichel, Leven T. 68985-68986
Reichel, William C. 47671, 50523, 68987-68993
Reichenbach, ----------, Graf. 68994
Reichert, Edward T. 85072
Reickles, John H. defendant 68995
Reid, ----------. supposed author (5198)
Reid, A. Illus. 16584
Reid, Adam. 68996-69000
Reid, David Boswell. (69001)
Reid, David S. 69002
Reid, Dennis. 69003
Reid, H. 69004-69006
Reid, H. L. 42828
Reid, Hiram A. 69007-69009
Reid, Horace H. 69010
Reid, Hugo. 69011-69012
Reid, Mrs. Hugo. see Reid, Marion (Kirkland)
Reid, J. 69015
Reid, James D. 36745, 69014
Reid, John. 1061, 21731, (69016)-note after (69016)
Reid, Marion (Kirkland) 69013
Reid, Mayne. 2108A, 2694, (57374), 69017-69086, note after 93619
Reid, Patrick. appellant 69087
Reid, Samuel C. 14391, 69088-(69090)
Reid, Whitelaw, 1837-1912. 69091-(69092), 84789, 84791
Reid, William. 69093
Reid, Sir William, 1791-1858. (69094)
Reid, William, 1814-1896. 69095
Reid, William Hamilton. (69096)
Reid. firm see Russ & Reid. firm
Reide, Thomas Dickson. 69097
Reiersen, Chr. S. 55486
Reiersen, Johan Reinert. (69098)
Reiff, --------, fl. 1731. 102509
Reigart, J. Franklin. 60111, 60513, 69099-(69101)
Reigert, J. Franklin. see Reigart, J. Franklin.
Reign of Doctor Joseph Gaspard Roderick de Francia. 69615
Reign of felicity. 69102, 89288
Reign of George III. to 1783. 43099
Reign of Jesus Christ. 104321
Reign of reform. 69103
Reign of terror in Kansas. 37080
Reign of terror in Missouri. 37327
Reign of woman. 87131
Reigning abominations. 104732
Reihe von Abhandlungen uber Brasiliens Gold-Diamanten- und andere mineralogischen Reichtum. 22830
Reihe von Briefen an Freunde in England. 30534
Reiley, James. 69104
Reilly, C. Leslie. (69105)

Reilly, H. plaintiff (20260), 69106
Reilly (W. W.) & Co. firm publishers 57002
Reilly's hymns. 66444
Reimann, Eduard. 69107-69109
Reimarus, A. tr. 73322
Reimbursment of loyal states. 5733
Reimers, I. C. 69110
Reimpresion del articulo en la Miscelanea. 50476
Reimpression fidele d'une lettre de Jean Schoner. 77800, 77807
Reinado e ultimos momentos de Sua Magestado o Senhor D. Pedro V. 1448
Reincke, Abraham. 68993
Reincorporation de Santo Domingo a Espana. 75186
Reine des Antilles. 31613
Reinel Hernandez, Marcos. see Santa Maria, Miguel de.
Reinhard, Charles de. see De Reinhard, Charles.
Reinhardt, Johannes Christopher Hagemann, 1776-1845. (69112)-69116, 71433, 71435
Reinhardt, Karl. Illus. 27182
Reinhold, C. L. 69117
Reining, Jan Erasmus. (69119), note after 91357
Reinisch, Leon. (72812)
Reinosa, D. J. 50482
Reinoso, D. see Reynoso, D.
Reintrie, Henry Ray de la. see La Reintrie, Henry Ray de.
Reintzel, A. 69120
Reintzell, D. 102020
Reipublicae, Amicus. pseud. Address to the public. see Thurston, Benjamin.
Reis, Francisco Sotero dos. see Sotero dos Reis, Francisco.
Reis, Manuel Basilio da Cunha. see Cunha Reis, Manuel Basilio da.
Reis Quita, Domingos dos. 69121
Reis annr de eilanden der Zuidzee, 1827-28. 20177
Reis-beschrijvinge door Frankrijk, Spagnie, Italien. 69133
Reis-beschryving door de Zuid-Zee. 25927
Reis-beschryving door een groot gedeelte van de Spannse West-Indien. 14099
Reis door de republik van Columbia. 49920
Reis door de Vereenigde Staten van Noord-Amerika. (40737)
Reis door de Vereenigten Staten van Nord Amerika en Canada. 27251
Reis door Noord Amerika, gedaan door den Heer Pieter Kalm. (36988)
Reis i Columbia. 28065
Reis in de Vereenigde Staten en Canada. 103079
Reis na Guinea en de Caribische eilanden in Columbien. 35245
Reis naar Columbia. 28067
Reis naar da Ijszee. 38222
Reis naar de landen hij den equator. 33772
Reis naar de nord-west kust van Amerika. 64395
Reis naar de zuidpool en romdom de weereld. 16275
Reis naar de zuidzee, met aanteekeningen wegens Brazilien. 91669
Reis naar den zuidpool en romdom de weereld. 30945
Reis naar Peru. 4044
Reis om de wereld. 11822
Reis rondom de weereld. 1641, 4th note after 101185
Reis rondom de weereldt. 6872

Reis rondom den aardkloot gedaan in den jaren 1765 en 1766. 9739
Reis ter ontdekking van een noordwestelijke doorvaart. (58863)
Reis van het schip de Wager. 1642A
Reis van Humboldt en Bonpland. 33737
Reis van Humboldt en Bonpland naar de keerkringen. 33736
Reis von Fort Prinz Wallis in der Hudsonbai nach den nordlichen weltmeer. 31186
Reisbeschrijving van de zelve schrijver naar Brasil. (50580)
Reisbeschrijvingen voor de jeugd. (10306)
Reisbeskrivelse til oester Groenland opdagelse, 1786-87. 22039
Reisch, Gregorius. 69122-69132
Reise-Beschreibung der Saltzburg Nurnberger Emigranten nach Holland. 24422
Reise blandt de Norske Emigranter. 20131
Reise d. Herrn Olof Toree nach Surate und China. 96191
Reise der Oesterreichischen Fregatte Novara um die Erde, in den Jahren 1857, 1858, 1859, unter den Befehlen des Commodore B. von Wullerstorf-Urbair. [Beschreibender Theil.] 77619
Reise der Osterreichischen Fregatte Novara um die Erde in den Jahren 1857, 1858, 1859, unter den Befehlen des Commodore B. von Wutterstorf-Urbair.—Linguistischer Theil von Dr. Friedrich Muller. 51284
Reise der Osterreichischen Fregatte Novara um die Erde in den Jahren 1857, 1858, 1859, unter den Befehlen des Commodore B. von Wullerstorf-Urbair. Zoologischer Theil. Erster Band Vogel. Von August von Pelzeln. 59596
Reise der Russ.-Kaiserl. Flotten Officiere Chwostow und Dawydow. 13036
Reise der Kaiserlich-Russischen Flotten-Lieutenants Ferdinand v. Wrangel. 105519
Reise des Kupfer-Schmiede-Meisters Friedrich Hohne in Weimer. 32375
Reise des Onkels Franz durch alle Welttheile. 72229
Reise des Vasco de Gama. (69369)
Reise desz Edlen vnd Vesten Thomas Candish. (8784)
Reise door de provincie San Salvador. 29500
Reise door Indien. 19446
Reise durch Amerika. 12232
Reise durch die Felsengebirge und die Humboltgebirge nach dem Stillen Ocean. 77632
Reise durch die Florida's. 8217
Reise durch die innern provinzen von Columbien. 30024
Reise durch die La Plata-Statten geschildert. 9350
Reise durch die La Plata-Staaten mit besonderer rucksicht. 9347
Reise durch die Mexikanischen Provinzen Tumalipas. 42639
Reise durch die Nordamerikanischen Freistaaten und durch Ober- und Unter-Canada. 102537
Reise durch die Prairien. 35144
Reise durch die Provinzen von Rio de Janeiro. 9349
Reise durch die Vereinigten Staaten von Nord-America. 11414
Reich durch die Verienigten Staaten von Nord-Amerika. (8038)
Reise durch die Vereinigten Staaten von Nord-Amerika in den Jahren 1818 und 1819. 31202

Reise durch die Vereinigten Staaten von Nord-amerika. (43805)
Reise durch die Vereins-Staaten von America. Aus dem Englischen. 43352
Reise durch die Vereinsstaaten von Amerika. 37122
Reise durch die Westlichen Gebiete von Nord-America. 62839
Reise durch die Wueste Atacama. 62452
Reise durch einem Theil der Vereinigten Staaten von Nordamerika. 38198
Reise durch einige der mittlern und sudlichen Vereinigten Nordamerikanischen Staaten. 77757
Reise durch Nord-Amerika. (2615)
Reise durch Nord-Brasilien. (2473)
Reise durch Sud-Brasilien. 2471
Reise durch Surinam. 24120
Reise eines Rheinlanders durch die Nord-Amerikanischen Staaten. 97922
Reise einiger Missionarien der Gesellschaft Jesu in Amerika. 51480, (51482), 98777
Reise-Erinnerungen aus den Vereinigten Staaten von Amerika. 77650
Reise-Erinnerungen und Abenteuer aus der Neuen Welt. 58263
Reise i Peru og Chili. 63630
Reise im Innern von Brasilien. 63680
Reise in Amerika. 12263
Reise in Amerika und Asien. 41777
Reise in Brasilien. 40156
Reise in Brasilien auf Befehl Sr. Majestat Maximilian Joseph I. 44996, 44999, 89549
Reise in Brasilien . . . fur die Jugend. 89548
Reise in Brasilien, Peru und Caracas. 4858A
Reise in Brasilien von Dr. Joh. Bapt. von Spix. 89550
Reise in Brazilien. 38241
Reise in Canada und einem Theile der Vereinigten Staaten von Nord-Amerika. 94230
Reise in Chile, Peru und auf dem Amazonenstrome. 63629
Reise in Columbia in den Jahren 1823 und 1824. 14073
Reise in Columbien, in den Jahren 1825 und 1826. 28066
Reise in das innere der Nordamerikanischen Freistaaten. 48707
Reise in das Innere Nord-Amerika in den Jahren 1832 bis 1834. 47014
Reise in das Innre von Amerika. 63060
Reise in das sudliche Stille Meer. 49481, note after 104633
Reise in das Sudmeer, ein Beitrag zu Ansons Reisen. 69135
Reise in das Sudmeer. Nebst J. F. de Surville's Reise. 5912
Reise in dem ostlichen Theil von Terrafirme in Sud-Amerika. 19645
Reise in den beyden Louisianen. 61014
Reise in den Vereinigten Staaten und Canada. 103080
Reise in die Aequinoctial-Gegenden des neuen Continents. 33738
Reise in die Aequinoctial-Gegenden des neuen Continents und Reisen im Europaischen und Asiatischen Russland. 33739
Reise in die Missionen nach Paraguay. (59173)
Reisen in Guiana und am Orinoko. (77791)
Reise in New-Andalusien. 38241
Reise in Nord-Amerika. 42762
Reise in Ober-Pensylvanien und in Staate Neu York. (17502), 69136
Reise in Sudamerika. 5216
Reise in Westindien. 101113

Reise in Westindien mit verschiedenen Anek-
doten und Carakterschilderungen. 69137
Reise-Journal von Mehr als Tausend Meilen.
10957, 39453
Reise naar Groenland. 44197
Reise naar Guatemala. 29500
Reise naar Guatemala in 1829. 29501
Reise naar het Rotsgebergte. 82269
Reise naar Surinamen. 91077
Reise nach Amerika. (69138)
Reise nach Brasilien, durch die Provinzen von
Rio de Janeiro. 9348
Reise nach Brasilien in den Jahren 1816 bis
1817. (47018)-47019
Reise nach Brasilien und Aufenthalt daselbst in
den Jahren 1802 und 1803. 41297
Reise nach Californien. 38241
Reise nach Cayenne aus dem Franzosischen.
41830
Reise nach Cayenne in Nord und Sud Amerika.
63061
Reise nach Central-America. (44674)
Reise nach Chili. 1864
Reise nach Columbia. (49919)
Reise nach dem Brittischen Westindien. 43457
Reise nach dem Demarary. 6183
Reise nach dem Eissmeer. 91218
Reise nach dem Nordpol. 62575
Reise nach dem Staat Ohio in Nordamerika.
36671
Reise nach dem Stillen Ocean. 4348
Reise nach dem Stillen Ocean. 16264
Reise nach dem Sudpol und nach Ozeanien.
21218
Reise nach dem Sudpol und Oceanien. 21219
Reise nach dem Antillen und nach Sudamerika.
39607
Reise nach den Inseln Teneriffa. 39688
Reise nach den Inseln Trinidad. 18672
Reise nach den Spanischen Landern in Europa
und America. 41773
Reise nach den unbekandten Sud-Landern. 4377
Reise nach den Vereinigten Staaten von Nord-
Amerika. 52062
Reise nach der Insel Martinique. 72988
Reise nach der Magellansstrasse, nebst einem
Berichte uber die Sitten und Gebrauche
der Einwohner und die Naturerzeugnisse
von Patagonien. 98613
Reise nach der Magellanstrasse, nebst einem
Bericht uber die Sitten und Gebrauche
der Einwohner von Patagonien. 16771
Reise nach der Schwedisch West-Indischen
Insel St. Bartholemi. (23107)
Reise nach der Sud-See. 25929
Reise nach Gronland. 44196
Reise nach Guaxaca in Neu-Spanien. 95348
Reise nach Guiana und Cayenne. 29196
Reise nach Guinea und dem Caribaischen
Inseln. 35243
Reise nach Hudsons Meerbusen. (22314)
Reise nach Island im Sommer 1860. 65418
Reise nach Kentucke und Nachrichten von
dieser neu angebaueten Landschaft.
(24339)
Reise nach Lima, San Francisco . . . 7393
Reise nach Mexico im Jahre 1864. 38230
Reise nach Mexico im Jahre 1823. 9143
Reise nach Mexico und Californien im Jahre
1769. 38398
Reise nach Neufoundland und der sudlichen
Kuste von Labrador. (12007)
Reise nach Nord America. 78105
Reise nach Nord-Amerika und dessen erste
Ansiedelung dasellbst. 94639
Reise nach Nordamerika. 22581

Reise nach Ost- und West-Indien. 106347
Reise nach Paraguay. 69616
Reise nach Pennsylvanien im Jahr 1759. 49761
Reise nach Peru. 4043
Reise nach Siberien. (77154)
Reise nach Sud-America. 36810, 1st note after
97689
Reise nach Sud-Amerika in d. J. 1781-1801.
(2544)
Reise nach Sudamerika. 67974
Reise nach Sudamerika, in den Jahren 1817-18.
7181
Reise nach Texas. 21342
Reise om de Wereld. 5835
Reise omkring Jordkloden i Aarene 1768-1771.
26273
Reise-Scenen aus Amerika. 467
Reise seiner Durchlaucht. 90510
Reise Sr. Hoheit des Herzogs Bernhard zu
Sachsen-Weimar-Eisenach. 4953
Reise Seiner Koniglichen Hoheit des Prinzen
Adalbert von Preussen nach Brasilien.
38050
Reise-Skizzen in Poesie und Prosa. 49923
Reise-Tagebuch des Missionars Johann August
Miertsching. 48892
Reise til Sydamerika. 64019
Reise uber England und Portugal. 102444
Reise um die Erde ausgefuhrt auf dem Koniglich
Preussischen Seehandlungs-Schiffe Prinzess
Louise. 48667
Reise um die Erde durch Nord-Asien. 22770
Reise um die Erde nach Japan. 31241
Reise um die Welt, 1806-1812. 10211
Reise um die Welt, auf dem Wege durch die
Grosse Sudsee. 80160
Reise um die Welt. Ein Lesebuch fur Kinder
und junge Leute. 18390
Reise um die Welt in den Jahren 1803, 1804,
1805 und 1806. 38328
Reise um die Welt in den Jahren 1772 bis 1775.
25129
Reise um die Welt, mit Capitain Cook. 106346
Reise um die Welt mit der Romanzoffischen
Entdeckungs-Expedition. 11817, 38284
Reise um die Welt und drei Fahrten der
Koniglich Britischen Fregatte Herald.
78868
Reise, um die Welt, von Westen nach Osten
durch Sibirien. 69139
Reise um die Welt wahrend den Jahren 1772
bis 1775. 25131
Reise um die Welt, welche er als Obserbefehl-
shaber uber ein Geschwader. 1640, 2d
note after 101187
Reise um die Welt, welche mit der Fregatte
la Boudeuse. 6871
Reise- und Lebensbilder aus Neuholland.
78016
Reise unter die Wilden in Nord-America.
39584
Reise von Berlin nach Rui de Janeiro. 39943
Reise von Bethlehem in Pensilvanien. 31207
Reise von den Prinz von Wallis Fort an der
Hudsons Bay. 31185
Reise von Hamburg nach Philadelphia. 69140
Reise von Kamtschatka nach Amerika. 91218
Reise von New-York nach Paris. 42661
Reise von Wien nach Brasilien. 61336
Reise zur Entdeckung einer nordwestlichen
Burchfahrt. 58862
Reise zwischen Sud- und Nord-Amerika. 27696
Reisebemarkungen uber die Vereinigten Staaten.
58361
Reisebericht der Familie Kopfli & Suppiger.
75372, 93793

Relacam verdadeira de todo o svccedido na
restauracao da Bahia de Todos os
Sanctos. 16835, 69166
Relacam verdadeira dos trabalhos que ho
Gouernador do Fernado d'Souto e certos
fidalgos Portugueses passarom. 24895,
87206
Relacam verdadeira, e breve da tomada da
ville de Olinda. (69167)
Relacam verdadeira, em que se dam a ler as
victorias. (69168)
Relac, ao abbreviada da republica. 63895
Relac, ao abbreviada da republica. 63895
Relacao breve e verdadeira da memoravel
victoria. 677
Relacao da acclamacao que se fez na capitania
do Rio de Janeiro. 7620
Relacao da conquista do genito Xavante. 25824,
72555
Relacao da conversao do R. Senhor Joao
Thayer. 95252
Relacao da embaixada que o poceroso Rei de
Angome. 45408
Relacao de huma batalha, succedida no campo
de Lake Giorge. 38661, 3d note after
(69168)
Relacao da republicia que os Jesuitas das
Provincias de Portugal e Gespanha esta-
belecerao. (63896)
Relacao de um prodigio succedido. 45408
Relacao da viagem que fez ao Brasil. 8132
Relacao da victoria que os Portuguezes alcan-
caram no Rio de Janeiro. 47854
Relacao de sitio de nova colonia do Sacra-
mento. 74791
Relacao diaria do sitio e tomada da forte
praca do Recife. 2584
Relacao do naufragio que fez Jorge Coelho.
94595
Relacao do naufragio que passon Jorge de
Albuquerque Coelho. 27754
Relacao do succedido na ilha de S. Miguel.
69169
Relacao do successo e hatalhas que teve com
a nau S. Juliao. 47858
Relacao dos festejos. 24167
Relacao dos festivos applausos. 62984
Relacao dos procedimentos que teve sendo
Commissario Geral da Bulla. 45403
Relacao dos publicos festejos que tiveram
logar. 7621
Relacao dos successos da Armada. 44425, 3d
note after 69170
Relacao historico-geografia do Reino do
Brazil. 11640
Relacao summaria das cousas do Maranhao.
81120
Relacao summara dos funebres obsequios.
(3650)
Relacao verdadeira de todo o succedido.
16835
Relacao verdadeira dos svcessos do Conde de
Castelmelhor. 69171
Relacio dela muerte de Francisco Draque.
77289
Relacio do sitio. 24173
Relacion apologetica en defensoria satisfacion.
69172
Relacion breve de la vida exemplar de F. A.
Margil de Jesus. 29120
Relacion breve y verdadera de algunas cosas.
63965
Relacion cierta, y avtencica de vn milagro.
(39014)
Relacion cierta, y verdadera de los que
sucedio. 16185, (44392)

Relacion circunstandiada de todas las obras
publicas. (66600)
Relacion cierta y verdadera, del famoso suc-
esso y vitoria. (50084), 69173
Relacion circumstanciada de todas las oper-
aciones. 2959, 69174
Relacion comica. (69175)
Relacion completa, y exacta del Avto Publico
de Fe. 33397
Relacion cronologica de lo que han padecido y
padecen. 76109
Relacion de algunos mercaderes. 3350
Realcion de ce qvi s'est passe de plvs remar-
qvables. 6413, 39995, note after 69259
Relacion de como martirizaron los hereges
Olandeses. 69570
Relacion de el martyrio que seis padres.
76787
Relacion de el santuario de Tecique. 47840
Relacion de juramenso que hizieron los reinos
de Castilla, y Leon. 27765
Relacion de la agaecido con el Sr. D. Mariano
Otero. 57840
Relacion de la carta que embio a Su Magestad.
96110
Relacion de la conquista de esta Nueva Espana.
74945
Relacion de la conquista de la provincia de
Los Nayaritas. 52134
Relacion de la conquista de Mexico. 34153
Relacion de la consagracion del sumtuoso
templo de la Catedral. 75815
Relacion de la conversion del Sr. Juan Thayer.
95253
Relacion . . . [de] la detencion de la flota
deste reyno. (11694)
Relacion de la entrada del Presidente D.
Alonso de Ribera. 42671
Relacion de la exemplar, y religiosa vida del
Padre Nicolas de Guadalaxara. 24818,
29033, 39891
Relacion de la felix entrada en Mexico del
Marques de Villena. 47351, 99400
Relacion de la Florida para el Ilmo. Senor
Visorrei de la Na. Espana. 84379
Relacion de la funebre ceremonia y exequias.
30411
Relacion de la gloriosa y singular victoria.
69176
Relacion de la gran fiesta civicia celebrada
en Chile. 69177
Relacion de la inundacion de la laguna de
Mexico. 50123
Relacion de la iornada de las vaccas de
Erbela. 69210
Relacion de la iornada, expugnacion, y con-
questa de la isla Tercera. 76759
Relacion de la jornada que hizo a descubrir
en la Mar del Sur. 84379
Relacion de la iornada qve la armada de Su
Magestad a hecho. 69178
Relacion de la literatura, grandos, meritos,
y servicios. 94624
Relacion de la marcha de la Brigada Gonzalez.
69179
Relacion de la milagros aparicion de la Santa
Imagen. 17737
Relacion de la mision apostolica de los Moxos.
22068, 22715
Relacion de la muerte, y entiero del Rey N. S.
69180
Relacion de la Nueva Mexico. 60875
Relacion de la obediencia, que los Indios de
Nayarit dieron. 9883
Relacion de la persecvcion qve [t]vvo en la
yglesia de Iapon. 69181

Relacion de la prodigiosa imagen de el Santo
Christo. 69182

Relacion de la prodigiosa imagen de el Santo
Christo de los Milagros, sacada del
archivo de el Observantissimo Monasterio de Religiosas Carmelitas Nazarenas
de esta ciudad de Lima. 69183

Relacion de la real tragi-comedia con que los
padres de la Compania de Jesus de
Lisboa recibieron a Felipe II de Portugal. 69184

Relacion de la sacra festiva pompa que en el
reverente accion de gracias. 60855

Relacion de la salvd milagrosa. 38271

Relacion de la segunda y tercera ascension
aereostatica. 95308

Relacion de la solemnidad con que se estreno
la Iglesia de Santo Cristo. 24143

Relacion de la sorprecha hecha por los
Franceses. (51204), 69185

Relacion de la toma de Parayba. 58555

Relacion de la victoria que han tenido las
armas. 4951

Relacion de la vida de la V. Madre Sor. Maria
de Jesus. 105733

Relacion de la vida y gloriosa muerte del P.
Leorenzo Carranco. 2984, 11028

Relacion de la vida y virtudes del P. Antonio
Herdonana. 47198, 69186

Relacion de la vida y virtudes del V. Hermano
Pedro de San Joseph Bentacur. 41712

Relacion de la vitoria de las armas. 47850

Relacion de la vitoria qve alcanzaron las
armas catolicas. (69187)

Relacion de la vitoria qve dios Nevestro Senor
fve servido. 69188

Relacion [de Las Casas.] 11267

Relacion de las causas que influyeron en los
desgraciados sucesos. 48633, 69189

Relacion de las cosas de Iucatan y informe
contra los idolatros. 527

Relacion de las cosas notables succedidas en
la ciudad de Lima. 41126

Relacion de las demonstraciones con que la
ciudad de Durango explico. (52250)

Relacion de las demonstraciones con que la
ciudad de San Luis Potosi. 76152

Relacion de las demonstraciones funebres que
la hecho. 69190

Relacion de las exequias del Ill$^{mo.}$ S$^{or.}$ D. D.
Diego Antonio de Parada. 62995

Relacion de las exequias funerales por el alma
de Rey D. Carlos IV. 69191

Relacion de las exequias que a la memoria de
N. SS. P. Clemente XIV. 96192

Relacion de las exequias que D. Juan de
Mendoza. 40085

Relacion de las exequias q[ue] el Exmo S^{r}. D.
Iuan de Mendoza y Luna. 69193

Relacion de las exequias que se hicieron en
la S. Iglesia Catedr. de Guatemala.
(39086)

Relacion de las exequias y funebre pompa.
71639

Relacion de las fiestas de la Congregacion de
Lima. 40055

Relacion de las fiestas de Lima. 41127

Relacion de las fiestas de Lima en el octavario
de los 23 martyres. 39473

Relacion de las fiestas qve a la Immacvlada
Concepcion. (72538)

Relacion de las fiestas que el Comercio, Consulado de los Mercaderes de Lima.
41128

Relacion de las fiestas que hizo la ciudad de
Lima. (2515)

Relacion de las fiestas triumphales que la
insigne Universidad de Lima. 29334

Relacion de las fiestas, y magnificos aparatos
conque la Muy Illustre, y Leal Ciudad de
Durango. 69194, 98383

Relacion de las funciones qve hicieron. 69195

Relacion de las grandezas del Peru. 39292

Relacion de las honras funerales. 76138

Relacion de las islas Filipinas. 12836

Relacion de las milagrosas apariciones de
Christo N. S. 69196

Relacion de las minas de coubre. (26805)

Relacion de las missiones de los Indios.
24135, 1st note after 98488

Relacion de las obras y fiestas publicas.
29455

Relacion de las prouincias descubiertas el ano
1598. 69210

Relacion de las provincias de Tipuane. 40075

Relacion de las solemnes exequias con que la
cuidad de Ica honro. 72798

Relacion de las violencias qve han padecido.
87208

Relacion de las vitorias qve Don Diego de
Arroyo y Daca. 2115, 69197

Relacion de les [sic] reales exequias a la
memoria. (6404)

Relacion de lo acaecido en la celebridad.
(72535)

Relacion de lo acaecido en la ciudad de Granada.
(69198)

Relacion de lo ejecutado en la ciudad de
Mexico. (69199)

Relacion de lo que hicieron los religiosos
Augustinos. 69200

Relacion de lo qve svcedio en el Reyno de
Chile. 98330

Relacion de lo que sucedio en la jornada que
hizimos el Senor Presidente. 98330

Relacion de lo svcedido a la armada de Barlo-
vento. 69201

Relacion de lo svcedido a la armada real de
la Guarda de la Carrera. 69202

Relacion de lo sucedido en la isla de Terceyra.
69203, 76759

Relacion de lo svcedido en las provincias de
Nexapa, Yztepex, y la Villa Alta. 11424,
50109, note after 96260

Relacion de lo svcedido en los galeones y
flota de Terrafirme. 69204

Relacion de los autos de reconocimiento.
27881

Relacion de los debates de la Convencion de
California. 8660

Relacion de los estrahos y ruynas. 34192

Relacion de los loables trabajos. 69205

Relacion de los meritos y servicios de D.
Diego Miguel Bravo de Rivero y Zavala.
7464, (71649)

Relacion de los martyres que ha havido en la
Florida. 57541

Relacion de los meritos de P. Bustamente.
9595

Relacion de los meritos del Dr. D. Joseph
Xavier de Tembra, y Simanes. 94637

Relacion de los meritos, grados, y ecercisios
literarios. 94820

Relacion de los meritos, grados, y literatura
del Doctor Don Francisco Xavier Tello
de Mayorga. 94630

Relacion de los meritos, servicios, grados, y
literatura del Doctor D. Joseph Tellez
Calderon. 94625

Relacion de los meritos, y circumstancias de
D. Mateo de Toro Zambrano y Ureta.
96211

Relacion de los meritos y exercicios liter-
arios. 71647
Relacion de los meritos, y grados del Doctor
de Medicina Don Francisco Thenessa.
95302
Relacion de los meritos, y grados del Doctor
Don Pedro Thamaron y Romeral. 95211
Relacion de los meritos, y servicios del Doctor
Don Juan Diego Teruel. 94896
Relacion de los meritos y servicios de D.
Diego Miguel Bravo de Rivero y Zavala.
(71648)
Relacion de los meritos, y servicios de Don
Luis Telaya y Santiso. 94600
Relacion de los milagros qve Dios Nuestro
Senor ha obrador. 98602
Relacion de los muertos, y heridos que huuo
en la real Armada de la Guardia de las
Indias. 69206
Relacion de los naufragios. 3350
Relacion de los particvlares seruicios que ha
hecho. (41974), 1st note after 96979
Relacion de los pasajes mas celebres. 99496
Relacion de los servicios del Capitan Don
Pedro Porter y Casanate. 64325
Relacion de los servicios del Maesse de Campo
Don Antonio de Vrrutia de Vergara.
98158
Relacion de los servicios qve hizo a Sv Magie-
stad del Rey D. Felipe Segundo y Ter-
cero. 10952
Relacion de los servicios y meritos del Dr.
Jose Rafael Quarez Pereda. 93336
Relacion de los socorros, que ha remitido a
Tierra-Firme. 40012
Relacion de los svcedido en las provincas de
Nexapa. 11424
Relacion de los sucessos de la Flota contra
los Olandeses. 76421
Relacion de los succesos que tuvo D. Luis
Faxardo. 69207
Relacion de los trabajos fisicos y meteorolo-
gicos. 74935
Relacion de los viajes por la America Meri-
dional y Septentrional. 97674
Relacion de lost [sic] meritos, virtvd, y liter-
atvra. 94936
Relacion de meritos pertenecientes al Doctor
Don Athanasio Joseph de uruena. 98174
Relacion de meritos y servicios. 71633
Relacion [de Palacio.] 31559
Relacion de servicios de al Capitan, y Castel-
lano Don Iuan Fra[n]cisco Teran. 94832
Relacion de servicios de D. Pedro Tellez
Carvajal. 94626
Relacion de servicios del Doctor D. Antonio
Terreros Oxhoa. 94875
Relacion de servicios, y exercicios literarios
del Licenciado Don Pedro Alexandro de
Texeda. 95137
Relacion de todo lo precedido. 95309
Relacion de todo lo succedido en Nueva Espana.
10325
Relacion de todo los sucedido en la provincia
del Piru. 69209
Relacion de todo los svcedido en estas pro-
vincias de la Nveva Espana. (69208)
Relacion de ultimo viage. 16765, 98613,
note after 98613
Relacion de un pais que neuvamente se ha
descubierto. 31374
Relacion del atentado sacrilegio. 94276
Relacion del Avto de Fe. 60856
Relacion del desengano de la guerre de Chile.
12799, 27785

Relacion del descrvbimiento [sic] del Nvovo
Mexico. 69210
Relacion del espantable terremoto. 69211
Relacion del estado en que el Marques de
Gelues hallo. 69212
Relacion del exemplar castigo qve embio Dios
a la ciudad de Lima. 41130
Relacion del feliz viaje. 94283
Relacion del funebre entierro. 50610
Relacion del gobierno superior y capitania
general de la Isla de Cuba. 17810, 94194
Relacion del gran terremoto . . . 1868. 63667
Relacion del martirio de los Padres Roque
Goncalez de Santa Cruz. 24195
Relacion del milagro que obro Dios por inter-
cession. (69213)
Relacion del Nuevo Modo. 60876
Relacion del origen y fundacion del Monasterio
del Senor San Joaquin. 69214
Relacion del pleyto seguido por el Ilust. S.
Obispo de Arequipa. 29258
Relacion del reconocimiento de la costa de
Guatemala. 64188
Relacion del restablecimiento de la Compania
de Jesus. 11393
Relacion del restablecimiento de la Sagrada
Compania de Jesus. 27814
Relacion del sanctuario de Tecaxique. 69215
Relacion del sitio, toma y desalojo de la
colonia. 69216
Relacion del suceso de la jornada que Fran-
cisco Vazquez hizo. 84379, 98723
Relacion del suceso de la jornada que hizo
Hernando de Soto. 84379
Relacion del svcesso del armada, y exercito
qve fve al socorro del Brasil. 96111
Relacion del svcesso del armada, y exercito
que fue al socorro del Brazil. 69217,
96112
Relacion del svcesso qve tvvo Francisco Diaz
Pimienta. 62885-(62886)
Relacion del temblor y terremoto. 18214
Relacion del tercero avto particvlar de fee.
(69218)
Relacion del tierromoto que succedio en Lima.
41131
Relacion del transito qve hizieron a las Indias.
69219
Relacion del ultimo viage al estrecho de
Magallanes. 16765, note after 98613
Relacion del ultimo viaje del autor. (74920)
Relacion del viage al Magallanes de la Fragata
de Guerra Santa Maria de la Cabeza.
1729, note after 98611
Relacion del viage de M^r. Courtois Saint Clair.
(69220)
Relacion del viage hecho por las goletas Sutil
y Mexicana. 681, (69221)
Relacion del viage, que por orden de Su Mage-
stad. (55395)
Relacion del viage, svcessos qve tvvo desde
qve salio de la civdad de Lima. 54330
Relacion del viaie, y svcesso de la armada.
(69222)
Relacion del viaje al Nuevo Megico. 69210
Relacion del viaje que hizo el Senor Capitan
Hernnado Picarro. 105724
Relacion del viaje qve por orden de Sv Mag^d.
55394
Relacion des glorieus evenemens qui ont prote
Leurs Majestes Royales. (41139)
Relacion descriptiva de la cuidad y provincia
de Truxillo del Peru. 24256
Relacion descriptiva de la fundacion, dedicacion
. . . de las iglesias. 48647

Relacione del viaggio, che fece il Capitan Fernando Pizarro. 105724

Relaciones, cartas, y otros documentos. 52104

Relaciones de los Vireyes del Nuevo Reino de Granada. 26574

Relaciones de los Vireyes y Audiencias que han gobernado el Peru. 69239

Relaciones exteriores de la Nueva Granada. 56287

Relaciones toscanas de Juan Botero Benes. (68338)

Relaciones vniversales del mundo de Iuan Botero Benes. 6809, 69240

Relaes en contradictie op den motiven. 102911

Relaes ende 't cargo van 't silver ende coopmanschappen. 69241

Reland, Hadrian. 1371, (38646), 69242

Reland, John. see Riland, John, 1778-1863.

Relandi, H. see Reland, Hadrian.

Relandus, H. see Reland, Hadrian.

Relapse. 69244

Relatio de Academia Bostonicensi sive Neo-Cantabrigiensi in America. 104961

Relatio de Caaiguarum gente. 5101

Relatio . . . de maximo sua marina peregrinatione. 99363

Relatio historica Habspurgico-Austraica. 105640

Relatio historica . . . navigationis Sebalti de Weert. (8784)

Relatio historico-botanico medica de avellana Mexicana. 8731

Relatio de Caaiguarum gente. 4644, 5101, (69246)

relatio itineris in Marylandiam. 103353

Relatio memorialis. 67355

Relatio quam Philippo IV. 4638, 76813

Relatio rervm gestarum in Novo-Francia missione annis 1613 & 1614. 69245

Relatio super detectione. 67355, 68346

Relatio super freto per M. Hudsonum Anglum quaesito. 67355

Relatio triplex de rebvs Indicis. 4644, 5101, (69246)

Relatio. Welche Philippo IV. Kinig in Hispanien. 76814

Relation. 21354

Relation abregee. (63900)

Relation abregee concernant la republique etablie par les Jesuites dans les domaines d'outre-mer. 63904

Relation abregee concernant la republique etablie par les Jesuites dans l'Uruguai, & de Paraguai. 63907, 1st note after 98174

Relation abregee, concernant la republique que les religieux, nommes Jesuites, des provinces de Portugal & d'Espagne, ont etablie. 63897-(63899)

Relation abregee de ce que la Societe etablie en Angleterre. 69247

Relation abregee de quelques missions des S. Peres de la Compagnie de Jesus. (7735)

Relation abregee du voyage de La Perouse. 38959, note after 99740

Relation abregee d'un voyage fait dans l'intereur de l'Amerique Meridionale. 27660, (38482), 38484-38485

Relation abregee, &c. qu'on vient de donner au publique. 63908

Relation abregee sur la Nouvelle-Espagne. 94854

Relation adressee a Sa Majeste. 94853

Relation and duty of the lawyer to the state. 78824

Relation authentique de la guerre. (51427), (58535), (63900)

Relation authentique de tout ce qui s'est passe a Saint Domingue. 75187

Relation authentique du voyage du Capitaine de Gonneville. 27788

Relation between the races at the south. 48933

Relation bien circonstanciee de l'origine. 97653

Relation concernant l'empire et le gouvernement du Japon. 4935-4936

Relation curieuse des Caraibes sauvages. 31354

Relation curieuse des voyages du Sieur de Montauban. (11274), note after 39117

Relation de ce que les Jesuites ont fait. 7652

Relation de ce qui, d'apres la volonte de Dieu, est arrive. 94854

Relation de ce qui est arrive a deux religieux de la Trappe. 99770

Relation de ce qui s'est fait a la prise de Cartagene. 63701

Relation de ce qui s'est passe a la defaite de l'Armee Navale de France. 69253

Relation de ce qvi s'est passe a la defaite de l'escadre de vaisseaux Hollandois, a Tabago. 69254

Relation de ce qui s'est passe au Fort S. Pierre. 69255

Relation de ce qui s'est passe au siege de Quebec et de la prise du Canada. 69256-69257

Relation de ce qui s'est passe au voyage de Ferdinand de Soto. 98749

Relation de ce qui s'est passe aux Hurons, en . . . 1635. 39950-39951, note after 69249

Relation de ce qui s'est passe dans la decouverte de ce pays. 98748

Relation de ce qui s'est passe dans la mission de l'Immaculee Conception. (28360)

Relation de ce qvi s'est passe dans le pays des Hvrons. 99748

Relation de ce qui s'est passe, dans les isles & terre-ferme de l'Amerique. 13768, note after 98248

Relation de ce qvi s'est passe de plvs remarqvable avx missions des Peres de la Compagnie des Iesvs, en la Novvelle France, aux annees mil six cent soixante cinq, & mil six cent soixante six. (6413), 39995, 67013, note after 69259

Relation de ce qvi s'est passe de plvs remarqvable aux Missions des Peres de la Compagnie de Iesvs, en la Novvelle France, aux annees mil six cens soixante sept. & mil six cens soixante huit. 39997, 67014, note after 69259

Relation de ce qvi s'est passe de plvs remarqvables avc missions des Peres de la Compagnie de Iesvs, en la Novvelle France, es annees mil six cent cinquante neuf & mil six cent soixante. note after 69259

Relation de ce qvi s'est passe de plvs remarqvable avx missions des PP de la Compagnie de Iesvs en la Novvelle France, es annees 1657. & 1658. note after 69259

Relation de ce qvi s'est passe de plvs remarqvable avx missions des Peres de la Compagnie de Iesvs, in a Novvelle France, es annees mil six cens cinquante six & mil six cens cinquante-sept. 39957

Relation de ce qvi s'est passe de plvs remarqvable avx missions des Peres del a Compagnie de Iesvs, en la Novvelle France, es annees 1660. & 1661. 39958

Relation de ce qvi s'est passee en la mission des Peres de la Compagnie de Iesvs, en la Novvelle France, es annees 1653. & 1654. 39993

Relation de choses de Yucatan. 38826

Relation de cinq annees des courses et d' observations. 91083

Relation de deux caravelles envoyees en 1618. 50539

Realtion de deux voyages dans les Mers Australes & des Indes. 37618

Relation de divers voyages dans l'Afrique, l' Amerique, et aux Indes Occidentales. 69260

Relation de divers voyages faits dans l'Afrique, dans l'Amerique, et aux Indes Occidentales, &c. (20885)

Relation de divers voyages faits dans . . . l' Amerique. 28273

Relation de evenemens qui suivirent a la Guiane. (1534), (27337)

Relation de Frere Jerome d'Escobar. 94853

Relation de . . . [G. de Godoi] a Fernand Cortes. 94854

Relation de Ghanat et des coutumes de ses habitans. 68443

Relation de Guillaume de Rubruck. 68443

Relation de Henri de Tonty. 96172

Relation de la Baie de Hudson. 68419

Relation de la bataille de Tabago. 69263

Relation de la conversion de M. Jean Thayer. 95247

Relation de la conversion de Mr. Thayer. 95248

Relation de la decouverte de la terre de Jesso. 4935-4936

Relation de la decouverte du sort de La Perouse. 20176

Relation de la deffaite des Anglois a S. Domingo. 69264

Relation de la deportation a Cayenne. 67632

Relation de la deportation et de l'exile a Cayenne. 24124

Relation de la descente fait par M^r. Cassard. 69265

Relation de la fete de S. M. la Reine d'Hayti. 98677

Relation de la funebre ceremonia y exequias. 9790

Relation de la grande Riviere des Amazones. (72759), note after 93778

Relation de la Guiane. 36944, 68430

Relation de la Guiane de Walter Raleigh. 16781

Relation de la Guiane, du Lac de Parime. 4937A

Relation de la Guaine, et du commerce qu'on y peut faire. 72757, (72759), note after 93778

Relation de la levee du siege de Quebec. 69266-69267

Relation de la Louisiane, et du Mississipi. 4935, 69299, 96172

Relation de la Louisiane ou Mississipi. 4936, 69299

Relation de ma mission du Mississippi. 9079, note before 95222

Relation de la mort de quelques religieux. 106368

Relation de la Novvelle-France. 6844

Relation de la Novvelle France, de ses terres, naturel dv pais, & de ses habitans. 5136, 69268, (69300)

Relation de la prise de la Grenade. 69269

Relation de la prise des forts de Choueguen, ou Oswego. 69270

Relation de la prise des isles de Goree au Cap-Vert et de Tabago. (69271)

Relation de la prise du Fort Georges, ou Guillaume-Henry. 69272

Relation de la prize des forts de Choueguen, ou Oswego. 69270, (80023)

Relation de la riviere de Amazones. 151, 72757, (72759), note after 93778

Relation de la riviere du Nil. 36944, 68430

Relation de la Societe Etablie pour la Propagation de l'Evangile. (69273)

Relation de la surprise qui voulut faire la garrison de Fribourg. 26770, note after 94151

Relation de la Tartarie, de Jean du Plain de Carpin. 68443

Relation de la Tartarie Orientale. 4935-4936

Relation de l'Amiral de Fonte. 8834

Relation de l'emeute populaire de cuenca au Peru. 38485

Relation de l'enlevement du navire le Bonty. 5909

Relation de l'etablissement de la Compagnie Francoise Pour le Commerce des Indes Orientales, dediee au Roi. (69261)

Relation de l'etablissement des Francois depvis l'an 1635. 6948

Relation de l'etablissement d'vne colonie Francoise. 21396

Relation de l'etat actuel de la Nouvelle Ecosse. 32545

Relation de l'expedition aux Indes Occidentales. (26629)

Relation de l'expedition de Carthagene. 63700, 2d note after (69261)

Relation de l'expedition de la corvette la Creole. 31256

Relation de l'expedition Francaise au Mexique. 5832, 76139

Relation de l'expedition partie d'Angleterre en 1817. 29477

Relation de l'horrible tremblement. 69262

Relation de l'islande. 4935-4936, 38975, note after 69262

Relation de l'isle de Barbades. 36944, 68430

Relation de l'isle de Tabago. 72323

Relation de l'origine, moeurs, coustumes, religion, guerres et voyages des Caraibes. 36944, 68430

Relation de los meritos, y servicios de D. Joseph de Teron y Prieto. 94857

Relation de mission Abnaquise de St. Francois de Sales. 5356

Relation de Nuno de Guzman. 16951

Relation de quelques particularitez. 39950-39951, (61004), note after 69259

Relation de sa captivite parmi les Onneiouts en 1690-1. 48944

Relation de ses voyages et aventures dans le Mexique. 5390

Relation de Terre-Neuve, par White. 4935-4936

Relation de Yucatan. (14676)

Relation. Del espantoso terro-moto. 41129

Relation derniere de ce qvi s'est passe av voyage du Sievr de Povtrincovrt. 40178

Relation des affaires du Canada, en 1696. 10572, 69274

Relation des avantages remportes par les armes du Roi. 69275

Relation des aventures arrivees a quatre matlots Russes. 40145

Relation des avantures et voyages de Mathieu Sagean. 74898

Relation des combats et des evenemens de la guerre maritime. 37615

Relation d'un voyage fait aux Indies Orientales. 19444

Relation d'un voyage fait en Europe et dans l'Ocean Atlantique. 75417

Relation d'un voyage fait en 1695. 1696. & 1697. 26001-26002

Realtion d'un voyage fait par ordre de S. M. Danoise. 42504

Relation d'un voyage fait recemment dans les provinces de la Plata. 9038, 9747

Relation d'un voyage recent des Espagnols. 6902

Relation d'une conspiration tramee par les Negres. 68251

Relation d'une descente des Espagnoles. 4935-4936

Relation d'une isle nouvellement habitee. 69260

Relation d'une traversee fait en 1812. 69252

Relation ecrite par l'epouse d'un Mormon. 23215

Relation en forme de journal. 4937A

Relation Espagnole, de la mission des Moxes. 4937A

Relation et lettres inedites publies par le P. Auguste Carayon. (10790)

Relation et naufrages d'Alvar Nunez Cabeca de Vaca. 9770

Relation, &c., made use of by two parties claiming land in Nantucket. 32964

Relation exacte de circumstances qui ont accompagne le debarquement. 35288

Relation exacte dv voyage de Gvill. Schovten, dans les Indes. 77952-77954

Relation fatta per Diego Godoy a Fernando Cortese. 67740

Relation fidel d'un nombre de cruautes inouis. 99596

Relation fidele de l'expedition de Cartagene. 69286

Relation Hern. Petri Fernandez de Quir. 67354

Relation historique de la decouverte de l'isle de Madere. 679, 69287

Relation historique de la Guinee. (4690)

Relation historique de la Virginie. 74606, 2d note after 100518

Relation historique de l'expedition. 84647

Relation historique du Colonel Boon. 24338

Relation historique et descriptive d'un sejour de vingt ans. 79334, 91613-91614

Relation historiqve et geographiqve, de la grande riviere des Amazones. 58141

Relation oder Beschreibung der Rheisz vnd Schiffahrt ausz Engellandt. 20837, 93588

Relation of a discovery lately made on the coast of Florida. (31919)

Relation of a remarkable providence which fell out at Port-Royale. 11748

Relation of a remarkable providence, which fell out at the time of the great earthquake at Jamaica. 69288

Relation of a storm and great deliverance at sea. 67811

Relation of a voyage from Boston to New-foundland. 104856

Relation of a voyage made by the Sieur de Montauban. 96171

Relation of a voyage made in the years 1695, 1696, 1697. (26004)

Relation of a voyage of the Sieur de Montauban. (23489)

Relation of a voyage of the Sieur de Montauban, Captain of the Freebooters in Guinea. 23486-23487

Relation of a voyage of the Sieur de Montaubon. 23483-23485

Relation of a voyage to Acadia. 3605, 69148

Realtion of a voyage to Gviana. 30296-30297, 67599

[Relation of a] voyage to Guiana. 30394

Relation of a wonderful voiage made by William Cornelison Schovten. 77962

Relation of Alex. Ursino in 1581. 66686

Relation of Alvaro Nunez Capo di Vacca. 66686

Relation of an assault made by divers papists. 38886, 92940

Relation of Captain Parry's voyages. 55829, 3d note after 97726

Relation of Christianity. 16210

Relation of Christianity to civil government in the United States. 221

Relation of Christianity to politics. 29530

Relation of Colonel Beeston. 79781

Relation of commerce to literature. 50041, 92272

Relation of fovre seuerall discoueries. (51198), note after 104797

Relation of Maryland. 45315

Relation of Maryland; together, with a map of the countrey. 45314

Relation of master and servant. 94538

Relation of Mr. R. M.'s voyage to Buenos Ayres. 42918

Relation of more particular wicked plots. 78364

Relation of pastor and people. 24095

Relation of poverty to human discipline. 92021

Relation of property and labor. 93471

Relation of religion to the war. (10994)

Relation of seismic disturbances. 84533

Relation of slavery to a republican form of government. note after (58767)

Relation of some former and later proceedings of the Hollanders. 20779

Relation of some of the many tragical disasters. 6428

Relation of some yeares travaile. 31471

Relation of the Academy to the educational system. 43844

Relation of the action at Cadiz. (67543)-67544

Relation of the beginning, continuance, and end of the late disturbances. 76501

Relation of the Bible to science. 71077

Relation of the cause which produced the effects. (35046)

Relation of the Christian experience and triumphant death of Jane Cameron. (73348)

Relation of the church to children. 88871

Relation of the colony of the Lord Baron of Baltimore. 103352-103353

Relation of the conquest of Mexico, etc. 66686

Relation of the cruel and bloody sufferings of the people called Quakers. 5630

Relation of the detention of Mr. Lovis Rame. 53402

Relation of the Earl of Essex and Sir Arthur Gorges. 66686

Relation of the expougnable attempt and conquest of the ylande of Tercera. 76760

Relation of the fearful state of Francis Spira. 2678, 89463-89465

Relation of the first discovery of the New World called America. 9499

Relation of the first voyages and discoveries made by the Spanish. 39119

Relation of the gouernement of Sir Walter Raleigh's fleete. 67576

Relation of the government to slavery. 69289

Relationi universale. 94185

Relationi universali. 98222

Relationi vniversali di Giovanni Botero. 6804, 6806

Relationi vniversali divise in quattro parti. 6805

Relationi vniversali, nella quale si contiene la descrittione. (6800)

Relationis historicae continuatio. (69296)

Relations. (18247)

Relations and duties of free colored men in America. 17727

Relations between America_and England. A reply to the late speech. (82688)

Relations between America and England, an address delivered. 82687

Relations between the Boston and Maine and Cocheco Railroads. 29671

Relations between the Cherokees, and the government. 69297

Relations curieuses de differens pays nouvellement decouverts. 21148, 69298

Relations de divers voyages curieux. 26308, 42918. 95333-95334

Relations de la Louisiane, et du fleuve Mississipi. 25999, 69299, 96172

Relations [de la Venerable Marie de l'Incarnation.] 44861, 5th note after 99504

Relations de S. de Eslaba. 36689

Relations des Jesuites contenant ce qui s'est passe de plus remarquables dans les missions. 39958, 69268, (69300), 99753

Relations des Jesuites sur les decouvertes et les autres evenements. 56612

Relations des missions et des voyages des evesques. (69301)

Relations des missions et des voyages des evesques, vicaires apostoliques et de leurs ecclesiastiques es annees 1676 et 1677. (69302)

Relations des quatres voyages entrepris par Christophe Colomb. 52105

Relations d'infortunes sur mer. 19620

Relations diverses sur la bataille du Malangueule. 69303

Relations d'un voyage au Texas et en Haiti. (44601)

Relations et memoires inedits. 96172

Relations et memoires inedits pour servir a l'histoire de la France. (44534)

Relations, etc., of Virginia, by George Percy. 66686

Relations inedites de la Cyrenaique. 68443

Relations inedites de la Nouvelle-France. 10522, 10573, 44869, note after 69259

Relations of Algiers by Nich. Nicholay. 66686

Relations of Brasil by Thomas Turner. 66686

Relations of Brasill and the Amazones by William Davies. 66686

Relations of China by Gaspar da Cruz and Galeotta Perera. 66686

Relations of Christianity and science. 70853

Relations of Christianity to labor and capital. 72643

Relations of Christianity to law and the legal profession. 72636

Relations of Christianity to war. 85316

Relations of Ethiopia by Nunnez, Baretus, and Andrea Oviead. 66686

Relations of expeditions and pilgrimages to Jerusalem. 66686

Relations of faith and philosophy. (82711)

Relations of God's people to Him. 104365

Relations of Guiana and the West Indies. 66686

Relations of liberal Christianity to . . . the west. 47181

Relations of Ormuz. 66686

Relations of slavery to the war. 70409

Relations of states. Speech of Judah P. Benjamin. (4704)

Relations of states. Speech of the Hon. James Chesnut Jr. 12522

Relations of states. Speech of the Hon. Jefferson Davis. 18836

Relations of the American lawyer to the state. 35442

Relations of the American scholar to his country and his times. 68054

Relations of the Bible to the civilization of the future. 61364

Relations of the British and Brazilian governments. 69304

Relations of the business men of the United States. (31825)

Relations of the conquest of Peru. 66686

Relations of the constitution and the public law to rebellion. 80141

Relations of the discoveries, regions, and religions, of the New World. 66678

Relations of the discoveries, regions, and religions, of the New World. Of New France, Virginia, Florida. 66678

Relations of the educated man with American nationality. 9133

Relations of the federal government to slavery. 21849, 22047

Relations of the federal government to the states. 90799

Relations of the industry of Canada, with the mother country. 8852

Relations, of the most famovs kingdoms and common-weales throvgh the world. .36283

Relations of the most famous kingdoms and common-wealths throwout the world. 6812

Relations of the past to the present. (13383)

Relations of the Phillippinas. 66686

Relations of the Presbyterian Church to the work of home missions. 65210

Relations of the pulpit to slavery. 69306

Relations of the Summer Islands. 66686

Relations of the temperance reformation. 16284

Relations of the world and the religions observed. 66678-66682

Relations of the voyages to the South Sea. 66686

Relations of war to medical science. 35999

Relations par de Biedma et de Beteta. 24894, note after 94854, 94856

Relations veritables et curieuses de l'isle de Madagascar. (50579), 50724

Relations with Great Britain. Speech . . . in the . . . Senate, April 19, 1869. 11887

Relations with Great Britain. Speech . . . in the Senate . . . March 12-13, 1856. 8437

Realtions with Mexico, and the continental railroad. (79549)

Relations with Mexico. Speech . . . February 15, 1853. 29640

Relative. pseud. Short biography of D. M. Hoyt. 51643

Relative duties of ministers and people. 92934

Relative position in our industry of foreign commerce. (14914)

Relative position of the finances of various European countries. 74611

Relative powers of the Senate and House of Representatives. 79550

Relative rank in the navy. (69307)

Relative state of the civilized world at a future period. 62581, 77689

Relatorio acerca da exposicao Maranhense de 1871 e 1872. 88701

Relatorio acerca da saude publica. (10669)

Relatorio annual da directoria, acompanhado dos seguientes annexos. 85775

Relatorio apresentado a Assemblea Geral dos Accionistas do Banco do Brasil. 69309

Relatorio apresentado a Assemblea Geral dos Instituidores do Monte-Pio Geral. (57900)

Relatorio apresentado a Assemblea Geral Legislativa na quarta sessao da nona Legislatura. 24165

Relatorio apresentado a Assemblea Geral Legislativa na terceira sessao da decima Legislatura. 7623

Relatorio apresentado a Assemblea Geral Legislativa, . . . pelo Ministro e Secretario d'Estado dos Negocios da Justica. 46906

Relatorio apresentado a Assemblea Legislativa da Provincia de Sao Paulo. (76903)

Relatorio apresentado a Assemblea Legislativa da Provincia do Para. 58499

Relatorio apresentado a Assemblea Legislativa Provincial de Sao Paulo. 85620

Relatorio apresentado a Assemblea Legislativa Provincial de Sergipe. 79218

Relatorio apresentado a Assemblea Legislativa Provincail em o 1.° de Marco de 1866. 60991

Relatorio apresentado a Assemblea Legislativa Provincial na 1ª sessao ordinaria da 15ª Legislatura. 69309

Relatorio apresentado a Assemblea Provincial de S. Paulo. (69310)

Relatorio apresentado aos accionistas da Companhia do Mucury . . . em 1860. (57900)

Relatorio apresentado aos accionistas da Companhia do Mucury . . . em 8 de Julho de 1855. (57900)

Relatorio apresentado aos accionistas da Companhia do Mucury . . . em 1 de Outubro de 1858. (57900)

Relatorio apresentado aos accionistas da Companhia do Mucury . . . em 15 de Junho de 1853. (57900)

Relatorio apresentado aos accionistas da Companhia do Mucury . . . em 15 de Octubro de 1857. (57900)

Relatorio apresentado aos accionistas da Companhia do Mucury . . . em 7 de Agosto de 1854. (57900)

Relatorio apresentado aos accionistas da Companhia do Mucury . . . [em 23 de Outubro de 1856.] (57900)

Relatorio apresentado aos accionistas da Companhia do Mucury no dia 10 de Maio de 1860. 51229

Relatorio apresentado aos accionistas da Companhia Ferro do Rio de Janeiro e de Nictheroy. 71468

Relatorio apresentado pela Direccao da Sociedade Portugueza de Beneficencia. (69311)

Relatorio com que ao Exm. Snr. Dr. Jose Antonio Saraiva. 69312

Relatorio com que no dia 1° de Fevereiro de 1866. 69313

Relatorio com que o Exm. Conselheiro Dr. Jose Bento da Cunhae Figueiredo. 69314

Relatorio com que o Exm. Sr. Desembargador Anselmo Francisco Peretti. 69315

Relatorio com que o Exm. Snr. Dr. Esperidiao Eloy de Barros Pimentel. 62876

Relatorio com que o Exm. Sr. Dr. Galdino Augusto da Nactividade e Silva. 69316

Relatorio com que o Exm. Snr. Dr. Galdino Augusto da Natividade Silva. 60888

Relatorio com que o Exm. Snr. Vice-Presidente Barao de Propria. 79217

Relatorio com que o 2.° Vice-Presidente o Exm. Snr. Dr. Dionizio Rodriguez Dantas. (79219)

Relatorio com que S. Exc. o Sr. Senador Barao de Ituana. 69317

Relatorio da Commissao da Praca do Commercio do Para. (58500)

Relatorio da Commissao de Exame Contas da Sociedade de Vehiculos Economicos. 85771

Relatorio da Commissao de Exame de Cortas da Companhia Ferry. 71469

Relatorio da Commissao de Inquerito. 7624

Relatorio da Commissao en Carregada do Revisao da Tarifa. 7568

Relatorio da Commissao Liquidadora da Companhia do Mucury. 69318

Relatorio da Companhia de Minas de Ouro e Cobre ao Sul do Brazil. 88785

Relatorio da Companhia de Navegacao e Commercio do Amazonas. 69319

Relatorio da fundacao da Bibliotheca Popular Itaborahyense. 85670

Relatorio da Junta Directora da Associacao Commercial da Praca da Bahia. 69320

Relatorio da reparticao dos negocios da fazenda. 69321

Relatorio da reparticao dos negocios da justica. 85643

Relatorio da reparticao dos negocios estrangeiros. 85644

Relatorio da reparticao dos negocios estrangeiros, apresentado a Assemblea. 69322

Relatorio da 2a. Exposicao Nacional de 1866. 88799

Relatorio da Sociedade de Vehiculos Economicos. 85772

Relatorio. [17 de Maio de 1852.] (57900)

Relatorio do estado da instruccao primaria e secundaria. 69324

Relatorio do estado da instruccao publica e particular. 88747

Relatorio do Gabinete Estadistico Medico-Cirurgico. 81102

Relatorio do Gremio Litterario Portuguez. 50214

Relatorio do Ministerio dos Negocios Estrangeiros. 85648

Relatorio do Museo Nacional. 88786

Relatorio do Presidente da Provincia do Para. 58501

Relatorio do Presidente da Provincia do Rio de Janeiro. 85645

Relatorio do Secretario da Provincia. 58503

Relatorio do Thesouro Provincial. 85620

Relatorio dos fiscaes do Banco do Brasil. 69325

Relatorio feito ao Excellentissimo 1.° Vice-Presidente da Provincia da Bahia. (69326)

Relatorio feito pelo Exm.° Snr. Conselheiro Jeronimo Francisco Coelho. 58502

Relatorio lido perante a Assemblea Legislativa da Provincia das Alagoas. 69237

Relatorio motisado sobre a estatistica da provincia de S. Pedro do Rio Grande do Sul. (72298)

Relatorio que a Assemblea Legislativa de Pernambuco apresentou. (60992)

Relatorio que a Assemblea Legislativa Provincial de Pernambuco. 60993

Relatorio que o Exm. Presidente da Provincia do Espirito Santo. 51844

Relatorio que o Presidente da Provincia de Santa Catharina. (69328)

Relatorio sobre a Exposicao Internacional de 1862. 50585

Relatorio sobre a instruccao publica da Provincia de S. Paulo. 85620

Relatorio. Sobre alguns logares da Provincia do Amazonas. 81104

Relatorio sobre as medidas mais importantes. 17008

Relatorio sobre medidas de salubridade reclamadas. 59183

Relatorio sobre o melhoramento do systema de pesos. 96264

Relatorios com que os Excellentissimos Senhores. 85621

Relatorios do estado da instruccio publica e particular. 63953

Relazione breve della republica. (63902)-63903

Relazione de terribili terremoti. 69329

Relazione de viaggio. (12555)

Relazione del conquisto del Peru. 105725

Relazione della battagla del di Ottobre, 1759. 58532

Relazione della gloriosa morte di ducento e cinque beati martiri. 6122

Relazione delle principali scoperte esequite per mare. 69330

Relazione delle scoperte fatte da C. Colombo. 69331

Relazione di cinque anni di corse e di osservazioni. 91081

Relazione istorica della Nuova Christianita degl' Indiani detti Chichiti. 24136, 1st note after 98488

Relazioni del viaggio e missione di Congo. 106394

Relazioni universali. (36282), 36287, 1st note after 96483

Relecciones teologicas. 100622

Relectiones morales duobus Tomis comprehensae. 100621

Relectiones theologicae. 100622

Relectiones theologicae tredecim partibvs. 100620

Relhan, N. H. see Enfield, N. H.

Reliable and descriptive guide to the Adirondacks. 82695

Reliable and thrilling narrative. 58376

Reliable guide. 27623

Reliable Troy directory. 97072

Reliance on God, our hope of victory. 28014

Relic library devoted to the reproduction. 83289

Relic of the past. 87439

Relic of the revolution. 31456

Relief and Hospital Association of Georgia. see Georgia Relief and Hospital Association.

Relief Association, Portsmouth, Va. see Portsmouth Relief Association, Portsmouth, Va.

Relief Association for East Tennessee. see Pennsylvania Relief Association for East Tennessee.

Relief Association of the Maryland Penitentiary. Committee. 45233

Relief Association of the Maryland Penitentiary. Committee on Prison Manufactures. 45233

Relief Association of the Maryland Penitentiary. Committee to Prepare Plans for the . . . Penitentiary. 45233

Relief Committee For the Relief of Sufferers by the Fire in Portland, Ore. 64388

Relief Committee for the Relief of the Families and Dependants of Volunteers and Drafted Soldiers, Providence, R. I. 66344

Relief Fire Society, Newburyport, Mass. 54926

Relief Committee to Collect Funds for the Sufferers by Yellow Fever, at Norfolk and Portsmouth, Va., Philadelphia, 1855. see Philadelphia. Relief Committee to Collect Funds for the Sufferers by Yellow Fever at Norfolk and Portsmouth, Va., 1855.

Relief for hard times. 93817

Relief for West-Indian distress. 17620

Relief from the pressure. 25941

Relief laws. 94965, 94970

Relief of sufferers by the fire in Portland. 64388

Relief of the Army of the Cumberland. 84771

Relief of the Franklin Expedition. 93186

Relief of the persecuted protestants of Saltzburgh. 5055

Relief Society of New York. 54617

Relief to the afflicted. 93954

Relieve the oppressed. 96376

Religieuse de l'Hospital General de Quebec. pseud. Relation de ce qvi s'est passe au siege de Quebec. 69256-69257

Religieuse de l'Hospital General de Quebec. pseud. Relation du siege de Quebec en 1759. 67020

Religieuses Hospitalieres de Quebec. see Hospitalieres. Quebec.

Religieux Augustin. pseud. Lettre sur les superstitions [sic] du Perou. 94853

Religieux de L'Ordre de S. Francois. pseud. tr. see Paludanus, Francois.

Religio medici. 8677

Religion, a principle, not a form. (26240)

Religion and business. 29350

Religion and education. An oration delivered at . . . Iowa City. 64471

Religion and education in America. 38866

Religion and liberty. (81644)

Religion and loyalty. 95759

Religion and morality united in the duty of man. 65105

Religion and patriotism in '76. 82951

Religion and patriotism the constituents of a good soldier. 18760, 18763

Religion and politics. A discourse delivered in thanksgiving day. 16804

Religion and politics. A discourse . . . March 20th, 1859. (26240)

Religion and public spirit. 18770

Religion and rank. 89744

Religion and righteousness the basis of national honor. 8930

Religion and state; not church and state. 105666

Religion and superstition of the North American Indians. 84162

Religion and the church. 24953

Religion, and the present revival. (74540)

Religion and the state. A discourse delivered in . . . Savannah. 64226

Religion and the state; or, Christianity the safeguard of civil liberty. 77988

Religion and the state, or, the Bible and the public schools. 89101

Religion at home. 104170, 104174

Religion aux Etats-Unis d'Amerique. 2793

Religion de los Indios. 38381, 56007, (75765)

Religion del dinera. 65976

Religion der That. 90130
Religion et patrie! 20892
Religion, histoire, litterature, sciences, arts. 70370
Religion in common schools. 74416
Religion in our public schools. 3794
Religion in politics. 22052
Religion in public instruction. 31864
Religion in public life. (72637)
Religion in public schools. 4655
Religion in the common schools. 47178
Religion in the making. 84069
Religion in the United States of America. (2792)
Religion is the life of God's people. (22006)
Religion, la independencia, y la razon. 69332
Religion, les loix, & les coutumes des Indiens naturels. 5115-5117, 2d note after 100478
Religion of an oath. (46478)
Religion of Jesus Christ the only true religion. 40191
Religion of politics. (26532)
Religion of reason. 82673
Religion of science. 5819
Religion of the ancient Brachmans. 69333
Religion of the Bible the basis and the bulwark of our nationality. 88858
Religion of the Bible, the only preservative of our civil government. 104740
Religion of the closet. 46479
Religion of the cross. (46480)
Religion of the heart. 85479
Religion of the northmen. 37697
Religion of the revolution. (8343)
Religion perseguida por los anarquistas. (29377)
Religion productive of music. 47446
Religion pura. 46481
Religion raisonnable. 22906
Religion rebuking sedition. 12931
Religion recommended to the soldier. 58899
Religion recommended to youth. 95226
Religion supported by reason and divine revelation. 22140
Reason, the only preservative of national freedom. (21571)
Religion the only safeguard of national prosperity. 32933
Religion the only source of national prosperity. 89427
Religion to be minded under the greatest perils of life. 13348
Religion true wisdom. (74371)
Religion und sonderbare Aberglaube der Gronlander. (17987)
Religions and religious ceremonies of all nations. (55302)
Religions de l'Oceanie et de l'Amerique. 8876
Religions du monde. 73318
Religions of the world. (55215)
Religions of the world and their relations to Christianity. 46953
Religionszustand der verschiedenen Lander der Welt. 7707
Religiosa. pseud. Monicion caritativa. (69334)
Religiosa Sociedade de Amigos. see Friends, Society of.
Religiosas de esta Noble Capital. petitioners see Lima (Archdiocese) petitioners
Religiosas de la Limpia, e Immaculada Concepcion de la Virgen Sant. Nra. Senora. see Orden de las Religiosas de la Limpia, e Immaculada Concepcion de la Virgen Sant. Nra. Senora.
Religiosas de Santa Brigida. see Bridgettines.

Religioso de la Co[m]pania de Iesus. pseud. Zodiaco regio, templo politico. 99400, 106366
Religioso de la misma Compania. pseud. ed. 96271
Religioso de la Orden de S. Francisco, de la Provincia de Guathemala. pseud. Pvntero apvntado con apvntes breves. 66669
Religioso de la Orden de Predicadores. pseud. ed. Relacion de la prodigiosa imagen. 69183
Religioso del Sacro Orden de Nuestra Senora de la Merced Redemption de Captiuos. pseud. Breve tratado que ensena el camino de la vida perfecta. 74799, 98897
Religioso Portugues. de la Orde[n] d'el Serafico Padre Sa[n]t Fra[n]cisco. pseud. Con priulegio imperial . . . libro llamado Tesoro de virtudes. note after 27585, 40960, note after 47850
Religious address to the Supreme Being. 84678C
Religious and literary gem. 69335
Religious and literary intelligencer. 82783
Religious and literary journal. 25943, 83829
Religious and moral wants of the west. (22178)
Religious and political persecution of the late Rev. John Smith. 82910
Religious Anti-slavery Convention, Boston, 1846. 81950
Religious aspects of the age. 69336
Religious cabinet. (69337)
Religious celebration of independence. 89744
Religious ceremonies and customs. 27875
Religious ceremonies and customs of the several nations. 4934
Religious ceremony; and other customs of the Mandans. 11543
Religious character of a people the true element. (21137)
Religious character of Washington. 30286
Religious Charitable Society, in the County of Worcester. 105408
Religious Charitable Society of Worcester County, Mass. 105408-105409
Religious Charitable Society of Worcester County, Mass. Charter. 105410
Religious Charitable Society of Worcester County, Mass. Committee. 105410
Religious Charitable Society of Worcester County, Mass. Directors. 105410
Religious constitution of colleges. 13219, note after 105924
Religious colloquy. 48192
Religious condition of colleges. (69338)
Religious creeds and statistics of every denomination. 31077
Religious denominations in the United States. 104771
Religious denominations in the United States, their history, doctrine, government, and statistics. 4402
Religious denominations of the world. (49129)
Religious discourse delivered in the Synagogue in this city. 78950
Religious dogmas and customs of the ancient Egyptians. 24021
Religious duty of obediency to law. 89327
Religious education of children recommended. 8641
Religious educator. 69339
Religious element in education. 92391
Religious endowments in Canada. 31932
Religious experience and counsels of Mrs. Ruth Stanley. 90316

Religious experience of Eunice Winchester
Smith. 79330
Religious experience of Norris Stearns. 90921
Religious fear of God's tokens. 103933
Religious freedom. (43719)
Religious harmonist. 69340
Religious herald. 40799, 92868-92869
Religious husbandman. 46220
Religious ignorance. 69341
Religious improvement of the death of great
men. (30635)
Religious improvement of the harvest. 32825
Religious informer. 69342
Religious inquirer. 69343
Religious inquirer, published by an association
of gentlemen. (69344)
Religious instruction enforced. (73883)
Religious instruction in common schools.
69345
Religious instruction of the Negroes. (36470)
Religious instruction of the slaves in the West-
India colonies. 102151-102152
Religious instructor. 94439
Religious intelligence and seasonable advice
from abroad. 69346
Religious intelligencer. see Connecticut evan-
gelical magazine and religious intelli-
gencer.
Religious intelligencer for the year ending May,
1817. (69347)
Religious keepsake. 69348
Religious liberties of the Christian laity
asserted. 4214
Religious liberty. A discourse delivered in
the Congregational Church at Hanson.
25759
Religious liberty. . . . A sermon preached
. . . at Washington. 4575
Religious liberty. A sermon, preached on the
day of the annual fast. (14221)
Religious liberty an invaluable blessing. 172
Religious liberty, and protection of American
citizens abroad. (69349)
Religious liberty: being a letter to the editor
of the "Palladium." 71718
Religious liberty. Equality of civil rights amid
native and naturalized citizens. 69350
Religious liberty in danger. 69351
Religious life of Francis Markoe. 81645
Religious, literary and agricultural journal.
88361
Religious magazine. see Unitarian review and
religious magazine.
Religious magazine and family miscellany.
69353
Religious magazine, for 1833-4. 69352
Religious magazine, or spirit of the foreign
theological journals and reviews. 69354
Religious marriner. 69355
Religious miscellany. see Christian examiner
and religious miscellany. Unitarian
advocate, and religious miscellany.
United Brethren's missionary intelli-
gencer, and religious miscellany.
Religious monitor. Publisher. pseud. Exhibition of some of the dishonorable means
used. see Webster, Chauncy.
Religious monitor and evangelical repository.
69356
Religious movement in the United States.
69357
Religious offering, for MDCCCXXXV. 98051
Religious opinions and character of Washington. (43296)
Religious principle—a source of public prosperity. 35461

Religious principle, the foundation of personal
safety. 97596
Religious principles, and forms of government.
56838
Religious prisoner in Newgate. pseud. Scrip-
tures and reasons. see Murton, John.
supposed author
Religious regards we owe to our country.
14512
Religious repository. see Quarterly theological
magazine, and religious repository.
Religious repository. Published by the New
Hampshire Missionary Society. 69358
Religious retreat sounded to a religious army.
70082, 101322
Religious sentiments proper to our national
crisis. 82701
Religious services by the Right Reverend
William White, D. D. 60778
Religious singing into schools of common edu-
cation. 94439
Religious, social, and political history of the
Mormons. 77713, 85168
Religious societies. 46482
Religious Society of Friends. see Friends,
Society of.
Religious Society of Spring Valley, N. J. see
Spring Valley, N. J. Religious Society.
Religious soldier. 37650
Religious souvenir, a Christmas, new year's and
birth day present. 69348, (69359)
Religious souvenir, for MDCCCL. 73250
Religious souvenir, for 1841. 73249
Religious souvenir for 1839. (69360)
Religious tale. 98468
Religious tract. 92832
Religious Tract and Book Society of Upper
Canada. see Upper Canada Religious
Tract and Book Society.
Religious Tract Society, Albany, N. Y. see
Albany Religious Tract Society.
Religious Tract Society, London. 49477
Religious Tract Society, New York. see New
York Religious Tract Society.
Religious Tract Society, Philadelphia. (62114)
Religious Tract Society of Baltimore. 86568
Religious Tract Society of Vermont. see
Vermont Religious Tract Society.
Religious tracts in the Choctaw language.
(69361), (104308)
[Religious tracts] no. 47 [of the New Hampshire
Tract Society.] 99138
[Religious tracts] no. IV [of the New Hampshire
Tract Society.] 99138
Religious tracts. no. I[-VIII.] Published by the
Society for Promoting Christian Knowl-
edge, Piety and Charity. 85854
Religious tracts. No. XIII [of the Vermont
Religious Society.] 99138
Religious trader. 69362, 91149
Religious tradesman. 91149-91150
Religious ultraism. 89744
Reliquae. 69363
Reliquae liturgicae. 6349, 69364
Reliquiae Baldwinianae. 18559
Reliquiae Baxterianae. 4013-4014
Reliquiae Haenkeanae, sive descriptiones et
icones graminum in America. 29503,
65360
Reliquiae Houstounianae. 33196
Reliquiae Turellae. (14513), 97451
Reliquien. 49916
Relly, James. 66444, 69365
Relly, John. 66444, 69365
Relph, John. 69366
Relyea, B. J. 69367-(69368)

Rem, Lucas. (69369)

Remack, Edmund. tr. 58947

Remainder of the observations promised. 60450, (69370)

Remainder of the tryals at the late Court of Oyer and Terminer. 96849

Remains and sermons of Rev. Asahel Nettleton. (52353)

Remains of giants, &c. 15076

Remains of Japhet. 58886

Remains of Joseph A. H. Sampson. 75939

Remains of Maynard Davis Richardson. 71075

Remains of Melville B. Cox. (17264)

Remains of my early friend. 69371

Remains [of Nathaniel Appleton Haven.] 30890, 95803

Remains of Rev. Edmund D. Griffin. (28816)

Remains of Rev. Joshua Wells Downing. 20778

Remains of Samuel B. Paris. 58594

Remains of Samuel Bartlett Parris. 58842

Remains of Sir Walter Raleigh. 67577-67584, 67588, 67599

Remains of the Rev. Carlos Wilcox. 103967, 103968

Remains of the Rev. Charles Henry Wharton. 103094

Remains of the Rev. James Marsh. 44739

Remains of the Rev. William Jackson. 35483

Remains of William Sloan Graham. 28242

Remak, Stephen S. 69372

Remark on the disputes and contentions in this province. 14833, 44577

Remarkable account, of a young lady of fortune. 69373

Remarkable account of Mrs. Rachel Lucas. 42616

Remarkable adventures of Alexander Selkirk. (35704), 79018

Remarkable adventures of Jackson Johonnet. (69374)

Remarkable adventures of Jackson Johonnot. 36403, 44258, 105687-note after 105690

Remarkable adventures of the Mormon prophet. 69375

Remarkable and extraordinary narrative of the revivication of young Joseph Taylor. 94520

Remarkable captivity and surprising deliverance of Elizabeth Hanson. 69376

Remarkable cases of criminal jurisprudence. 11649-11650

Remarkable delusions. 69377

Remarkable dream, or vision, which was experienced on the night of the 20th of May, 1799. 101432

Remarkable events in the history of America. (26049), 26052

Remarkable extracts and observations on the slave trade. 69378

Remarkable extracts, &c. &c. 99831

Remarkable historical facts. 7488

Remarkable incidents in the life of Rev. J. H. Fairchild. (23682)

Remarkable journal of Christian Frederic Post. 95562

Remarkable judgments of God. 46540

Remarkable life, adventures and discoveries of Sebastian Cabot. 55185

Remarkable manufactories at the present time. 5606

Remarkable mercies should be faithfully published. 104262, 104264-104267

Remarkable narrative of an expedition against the Indians. 38110

Remarkable narrative of Mary Spaulding. 89050-89051

Remarkable narrative of the captivity and escape of Mrs. Frances Scott. 78263, note before 97104

Remarkable narrative of Whiting Sweeting. 94051

Remarkable occurrences in regard to the first exhibition. 86230

Remarkable occurrences, lately discovered among the people called Shakers. 82768-82769, 82770A

Remarkable prophecy of a certain hermit who lived fifteen years. 85607

Remarkable prophecy, of a certain hermit, who lived twelve years. 85606

Remarkable prophecy. Presented to our readers as we received it. 69379

Remarkable prophecy, relating to twelve great men. 66667, 92711

Remarkable providences illustrative of the earlier days of American colonization. 46528, 46678, 46680, (46728)

Remarkable relation of certain pirates. 46577, 1st note after 99407

Remarkable shipwrecks. (69380)

Remarkable speech of Sir Benjamin Rudyerd. 89176

Remarkable speeches of good old Roger Pindar, Esq. 102394

Remarkable trial of Richard Lawrence. 39366

Remarkable trials of all countries. 21336

Remarkable tryal and sufferings of a protestant. (53403)

Remarkable vision shewing the sudden and surprising appearance. 100595, 2d note after 105939

Remarkable visions. 64959

Remarkable voyages and travels, consisting of Anson's voyage. 69381

Remarkable voyages and travels into Brazil. 13015, (55278)

Remarks, accompanying the reading of the declaration of American independence. 44316

Remarks addressed to the citizens of Charleston. 62904

Remarks addressed to the citizens of Illinois. (69382)

"Remarks," addressed to the governor of Maine. 32779

Remarks against the bill. 31595

Remarks, and a discourse on slavery. 5725

Remarks and conjectures on the voyage of the ships Resolution and Discovery. 16252, (69383)

Remarks and criticisms on the Hon. John Quincy Adams' letter to Hon. Harrison Gray Otis. 14313

Remarks and directions for navigation and pilotage. 3608

Remarks and documents concerning the location of the Boston and Providence Railroad. 18265, 21643

Remarks and documents relating to the Massachusetts State Prison. 7247

Remarks and documents relating to the preservation and keeping of public archives. 3775

Remarks and historical notices, relating to emancipation. 13098

Remarks and illustrations relative to lawful government. 89314

Remarks and observations made in the inland parts. 97702

Remarks and observations on several passages. 5631

Remarks and observations on the constitution
of the Canadas. 69385
Remarks and ode by John H. Sheppard. 80322
Remarks and reflections upon the trial of
Colonel Talbot Chambers. (11802)
Remarks and resolutions commemorative of
the Hon. Josiah Quincy. 67234
Remarks and statistics on . . . cheap postage
and postal reform. 39563
Remarks and strictures on the misstatements.
8075
Remarks and suggestions on the agriculture
of Nova Scotia. (73363)
Remarks . . . April 14, 1866. 26664
Remarks . . . April 25th, 1860. 24803
Remarks as to the true canal policy. 3846
Remarks at a dinner in Charleston, S. C.
32653
Remarks at a hearing before the Joint Com-
mittee on Education, February 4, 1848.
23271
Remarks at a hearing before the Joint Com-
mittee on Education, 1 February, 1848.
30765, 69386
Remarks . . . at a public meeting . . . in . . .
Boston. 30859
Remarks at a Union Meeting in Albany. 68057
Remarks at Belfast, Maine, July 4, 1867.
64065
Remarks at Central Falls, R. I. (59277)
Remarks . . . at Cooper Institute, . . . New
York. 50635
Remarks . . . at . . . Cooper Institute, New
York. 50636
Remarks . . . at . . . Geneva, N. Y. (31388)
Remarks . . . at . . . Macon County, Ga.
49073
Remarks at Rutland, Vermont, June 24, 1869.
(64068)
Remarks . . . at Tammany Hall. 64622
Remarks at the celebration dinner. 35849
Remarks . . . at the celebration of the fourth
of July. 9235
Remarks . . . at the funeral of Jonas H. Lane.
37976
Remarks at the funeral of Mary and Martha
Calvin. 93616
Remarks . . . at the funeral of the Hon.
Benjamin Thompson. 22309
Remarks at the inaugural meeting of the
American Freedmen's Aid Union. 35849
Remarks at the Indianapolis Exposition. 31026
Remarks . . . at the Mass Meeting of Working-
men in Faneuil Hall. 62528
Remarks, at the meeting of the friends of the
administration. 92237
Remarks at the New Hampshire State Agricul-
tural Convention. 76240
Remarks . . . at the opening of the Convention
of Tobacco Planters. 35983
Remarks at the Plymouth Festival, on the first
of August, 1853. In commemoration of
the embarkation of the pilgrims. By
Charles Sumner. 93656
Remarks at the Plymouth Festival, on the first
of August, 1853, in commemoration of the
embarkation of the pilgrims. [By Edward
Everett.] 23271
Remarks . . . at the Workingmen's Institute,
Boston. (11790)
Remarks . . . at Wilmington, Del., Nov. 6,
1863. 68057
Remarks before the Association for Aged
Indigent Females. (72652)
Remarks before the Committee of Public
Health. 84276

Remarks . . . before the committee of the
Legislature. 62712
Remarks before the Committee of Ways and
Means. 37626
Remarks before the Joint Committee on the
Petition of Samuel Hinkley. 31884
Remarks before the Judiciary Committee of
the Senate of Massachusetts. 7004
Remarks . . . before the Sanitary Association.
23317
Remarks . . . by a member of the Massa-
chusetts bench. 64851
Remarks by an inhabitant of St. Nevis. (10895),
12026, 80599
Remarks by Charles Blanchard, of Ottawa,
Illinois. 5821
Remarks by Committee of the Boston Board
of Trade. 34920
"Remarks" [by Cotton Mather.] 28052, 28506,
65689
Remarks by Edward Brooks. 8344
Remarks by Elizabeth T. Stone. 92056
Remarks . . . by F. G. Skinner. 37885
Remarks by George Prince. 73289
Remarks [by James Morse.] 50920
Remarks . . . by John D. Defrees. 19295
Remarks by Mr. Woodbury. 105101
Remarks by Mrs. Inchbald. 17876
Remarks . . . [by N. B. Shurtleff.] (45545)
Remarks by the Boston Board of Trade. 20807
Remarks [by the committee of the New York
Coal Company.] 54581, note after 97065
Remarks by the compiler. 102346
Remarks by the "Examiner" on this . . . sub-
ject. 57860
Remarks by the Hon. R. C. Kirk. 41236, 6th
note after 96964
Remarks . . . by the Hon. T. H. Perkins.
60976
Remarks, calculated to assist in ascertaining
the causes. 72869
Remarks comprising in substance Judge Hert-
tell's argument. 31595
Remarks concerning stones said to have fallen
from the clouds. 37798
Remarks concerning the government and laws.
42925
Remarks concerning the late Dr. Bowditch.
58325
Remarks concerning the means to re-establish
the declining state of commerce. 69387
Remarks concerning the savages of North
America. 25578, (25594)
Remarks, critical and historical, on an article.
36343
Remarks . . . December 1, 1856. 28996
Remarks . . . December 19, 21, and 22, 1870.
36615
Remarks . . . delivered in the House of Repre-
sentatives, April 3 & 4, 1834. 43205
Remarks . . . delivered in the Ohio House of
Representatives. 24658
Remarks . . . delivered in the Tennessee House
of Representatives. (23333)
Remarks . . . delivered . . . January 13, 1834.
9936
Remarks, delivered My 31, 1838. 30016
Remarks during a journey through North Amer-
ica. (32358)
Remarks . . . embracing a statement of the
necessity. 26697
Remarks . . . February 4, 1869. 37272
Remarks . . . February 19, 1870. 51317
Remarks, . . . February 17, 1859. (28280)
Remarks . . . February 17, 1849. 54968
Remarks for my own race. 50818

Remarks of Hermon S. Conger. 15473
Remarks of Hiland Hall. 29781
Remarks of Hon. A. A. Sargent. 76947
Remarks of Hon. A. C. Dodge. 20493
Remarks of Hon. A. H. Tanner. 90828
Remarks of Hon. Aaron A. Sargent and Hon.
John M. Coghlan. 76947
Remarks of Hon. C. L. L. Leary. 39541
Remarks of Hon. Charles Sumner. 93646
Remarks of Hon. D. E. Sickles. 80846
Remarks of Hon. David K. Hitchcock. 32240
Remarks of Hon. E. Stanly. 90327
Remarks of Hon. Edward Everett. (45858)
Remarks of Hon. Ellis H. Roberts. 71885
Remarks of Hon. F. S. Richards. 70914
Remarks of Hon. Franklin Pierce. 37859
Remarks of Hon. Frederick A. Sawyer. (77306)
Remarks of Hon. G. S. Boutwell. (6977)
Remarks of Hon. Galusha A. Grow. 28997
Remarks of Hon. George William Curtis.
(18053)
Remarks of Hon. H. B. Anthony. 65536
Remarks of Hon. H. D. Henderson. (31322)
Remarks of Hon. Henry W. Corbett. 16748
Remarks of Hon. Isaac I. Stevens. 91532
Remarks of Hon. Isaac I. Stevens . . . made
before the Committee of Military Affairs.
91532
Remarks of Hon. J. Ellis Bonham. 6300
Remarks of Hon. James F. Dowdell. 20762
Remarks of Hon. James Redington. (68519)
Remarks of Hon. John Sherman. 80383
Remarks of Hon. John Young Brown of Ken-
tucky. 8529
Remarks of Hon. Lansing Stout, of Oregon.
92357
Remarks of Hon. M. Strong. 92949
Remarks of Hon. Owen Lovejoy. 42369
Remarks of Hon. R. F. Stockton, of New
Jersey. 91898
Remarks of Hon. R. F. Stockton . . . upon non-
intervention. 91899
Remarks of Hon. R. L. Burrows. 9477
Remarks of Hon. Richard C. McCormick.
(43102)
Remarks of Hon. S. W. Barnes. 3526
Remarks of Hon. Samuel Ames. 1310
Remarks of . . . Hon. Samuel M. Moore.
50435
Remarks of Hon. Stephen Fairbanks. 64990
Remarks of Hon. W. A. Hall. 29859
Remarks of Hon. W. H. Kelsey. 37326
Remarks of Hon. W. McKee Dunn. 21327
Remarks of Hon. W. R. Steele. 91163
Remarks of Hon. W. S. Miller. 49079
Remarks of Hon. William D. Kelley. 37269
Remarks of Hon. William F. Smith. 84767
Remarks of Hon. Wm. H. Seward. 79530
Remarks of Hon. William Sprague, of Rhode
Island. 89726
Remarks of Hon. William Sprague, upon the
presentation of the statue. 89727
Remarks of I. D. Jones, June 16, 1842. 36515
Remarks of J. G. Palfrey. 20256, 45711
Remarks of James P. Hardin in the House of
Representatives. 30327
Remarks of James W. Stone. 92067
Remarks of John E. Devlin. 101418
Remarks of John Hunter. 33919
Remarks of John L. Mason and Joseph S.
Bosworth. 45459
Remarks of John M. Read. 68167
Remarks of John R. Cox. 17262
Remarks of Joseph Blunt. 6041
Remarks of Logan H. Roots. 73139
Remarks of M. W. Gray. (28402)

Remarks of Messrs. Clemens, Butler, and
Jefferson Davis. 13621
Remarks of Messrs. Everett, Mason [and
others.] 71351
Remarks of Messrs. Millson, . . . and [others.]
49125
Remarks of Messrs. Rhett, Belser, and A. V.
Brown. 70481
Remarks of Messrs. Seward, Hale, and Chase.
79554
Remarks of Mr. A. H. H. Stuart, of Virginia.
93121
Remarks of Mr. Allen. 65098, 69392
Remarks of Mr. Babcock. 2572
Remarks of Mr. Banks. 3206
Remarks of Mr. Beadsley. 4138
Remarks of Mr. Berrien. 4980
Remarks of Mr. Biddle. 5249
Remarks of Mr. Brewer. 7762
Remarks of Mr. Cass. 11349
Remarks of Mr. Crosby. 17643
Remarks of Mr. Dellet. 19441
Remarks of Mr. Dent. 19610
Remarks of Mr. Dickson. 20089
Remarks of Mr. Dixon. (47257)
Remarks of Mr. Duer. 21110
Remarks of Mr. Duncan. 21250
Remarks of Mr. Everett [and others] in the
Senate. (23267)
Remarks of Mr. Everett on the bill. 23271
Remarks of Mr. F. A. Conkling. 15625
Remarks of Mr. Fillmore. 53049
Remarks of Mr. Goggin. 27697
Remarks of Mr. [Heman] Allen's counsel.
65098, 69392
Remarks of Mr. John Welsh. 62115
Remarks of Mr. Johnson. 65863
Remarks of Mr. Johnston, of Louisiana. 36380
Remarks of Mr. L. Beardsley. 4137
Remarks of Mr. Leete. 39836
Remarks of Mr. McClernand. 43040
Remarks of Mr. Stockton. 91901
Remarks of Mr. N. P. Tallmadge. 94268
Remarks of Mr. Ogle. 56841
Remarks of Mr. Owen. 58010
Remarks of Mr. Phelps. 61394
Remarks of Mr. Ritchie as referred to. 94091
Remarks of Mr. Ritchie . . . with an introduc-
tion. 39912
Remarks of Mr. Rives. 71656
Remarks of Mr. Rusk, of Texas. 74182
Remarks of Mr. Russell. 74322
Remarks of Mr. S. G. Haven. 30897
Remarks of Mr. Schenck. (77579)
Remarks of Mr. Seger. 78883
Remarks of Mr. Sims. 81380
Remarks of Mr. Slidell. (82139)
Remarks of Mr. Smith, of Maryland. 83990
Remarks of Mr. Smith, of Virginia, delivered
in the House. 84718
Remarks of Mr. Smith, of Virginia, on the
organization of the House. 84719
Remarks of Mr. Stanly, (of North Carolina.)
90328
Remarks of Mr. Stanly, on the bill. 90329A
Remarks of Mr. Stanly, on the branch mint.
90330
Remarks of Mr. Stilwell. 91820
Remarks of Mr. Stockton . . . on Pirsson's
condenser. 91900
Remarks of Mr. Stockton . . . on the Indian
appropriation bill. 91902
Remarks of Mr. Storer. 92186
Remarks of Mr. Tallmadge. 94269
Remarks of Mr. Truman Smith. 84452

Remarks of Mr. Wager, in relation to the legislative power. 100951

Remarks of Mr. Wager, in Senate, May 21st, 1836. 100951

Remarks of Mr. Webster and Mr. Wright. 102319

Remarks of Mr. Webster in the Senate of the United States, May 9, 1828. 102270

Remarks of Mr. Webster, on different occasions. 102286

Remarks of Mr. Webster on the following resolution. 102306

Remarks of Mr. Webster, on the removal of the deposites. 102285

Remarks of Mr. Wetmore. 103072

Remarks of . . . Moses W. Field. 24286

[Remarks] of Professor Silliman. 14535, (69758), 102319

Remarks of R. W. Russell. 74365

Remarks of Rev. Dr. Brainerd. 7351

Remarks of Rev. Dr. Gurley. (41226)

Remarks of Rev. James C. Fletcher. 7591, 53586

Remarks of Rev. Thos. A. Starkey. 90527

Remarks of Richard H. Dana, Jr., Esq., at a dinner. 18450, 89718

Remarks of Richard H. Dana, Jr., Esq., before the Committee on Federal Relations. 18445

Remarks of Richard Smith. 83767

Remarks of Rob't. E. C. Stearns, and resolutions. 90932

Remarks of Robert E. C. Stearns on the death of Dr. William Stimpson. 90933

Remarks of Senator Doolittle. 78028

Remarks of Senators Brown and Toombs. 8438

Remarks of Senators Pugh of Ohio, and Stuart of Michigan. 93154

[Remarks] of T. H. Seymour and S. Eliot. 23271

Remarks of the Chinese Merchants of San Francisco. 76077

Remarks of the Committee of St. Paul's Congregation. 75463

Remarks of [the Hon. Daniel S. Dickinson] upon Mr. Clemen's resolutions. 20031

Remarks . . . of the Hon. Daniel Webster. 14535, (69768), 102319

Remarks of the Hon. F. J. Moses. 51056

Remarks of the Hon. John B. Haskin. 30804

Remarks of the Hon. Peleg Sprague. 89706

Remarks of the Hon. Robert T. Conrad. 15897

Remarks of the Hon. William M. Gwin. 29383

Remarks of the Plymouth Company. 63498

Remarks of the press concerning the outrage. 37808, 97098

Remarks of the Rev. Joshua Wells Downing. 20789

Remarks . . . of the route and its importance. 38656

Remarks of the United States catholic magazine. 37411

"Remarks of thirty-one Boston schoolmasters." 44324

Remarks of Ward Nicholas Boylston. 7140

Remarks of Washington Hunt. 33897

Remarks of William D. Northend. 55784

Remarks of William Dewey in Assembly. 19864

Remarks of William H. Seward, in memory of Thomas J. Rusk. 79552

Remarks of William H. Seward, in the Senate, June, 1856. 79551

Remarks of William H. Seward, in the Senate of the United States, February 22, 1855. 79545

Remarks of Wm. M. Bradford. (7266)

Remarks offered in illustration of a report on the doctrine. 43569

Remarks . . . on a bill to reorganize the staff. 43631

Remarks on a British railway. 69393

Remarks on a certain publication. (26766)

Remarks on a dangerous mistake. 42289, 2d note after 98684

Remarks on a discourse of Dr. Waterland's. (20062)

Remarks on a discourse of the Rev. Jona. Parsons. 79747

Remarks on a discourse of the Rev. Jonathan Parsons. 97319

Remarks on a late appeal from the Trustees of the East Windsor Institute. 105891-105892

Remarks on a late pamphlet, entitled, "A vindication of Governor Parr, and his Council." (34763), 58833-(58834), 99410-99411

Remarks on a late pamphlet entitled Common sense. 10671, 84642

Remarks on a late pamphlet entitled Plain truth. (74423)

Remarks on a late pamphlet entitled "Some considerations." 69394

Remarks on a late pamphlet entitled, "The opinion of one that has perused the Summer-morning's conversation." 13350

Remarks on a late pamphlet intitul'd the Two great questions consider'd. 69516, 97560

Remarks on a late pamphlet, wrote by Mr. Hobart. (30648)

Remarks on a late piece. 55, 58896

Remarks on a late proposition from the Boston and Roxbury Mill Corporation. 2398

Remarks on a late protest against the appointment of Mr. Franklin. 25576-25577, 84586

Remarks, on a late publication in the Independent gazetteer. 9836-9837, 68568, 82725

Remarks on a late tract entitled, "Discourses on the publick revenues." 69395

Remarks on a Latin inscription found at Castine. 24961

Remarks on a letter from Joseph John Gurney. 51789, 55959

Remarks on a letter from the Hollis-Street Society. 6655

Remarks on a letter of Elder Galusha. 92869

Remarks on . . . a letter relating to the divisions of the First Church in Salem. 8505

Remarks on a letter to the Rt. Hon. Lord Kenyon. 37588, 69396

Remarks on a method lately published for procuring a fermentation. 22249, 5th note after 102832

Remarks on a pamphlet, by 'Pacificus,' addressed to the Society of Friends. 58094

Remarks on a pamphlet by the Associate Presbytery of Albany. 90514

Remarks on a pamphlet, called, Considerations on the present German war. 95722

Remarks on a pamphlet entitled A review. 92832

Remarks on a pamphlet entitled 'A true narrative. 103661, 103665

Remarks on a pamphlet, entitled "An enquiry respecting the capture of Washington by the British." (22650), 104746

Remarks on a pamphlet, entitled, "Considerations on the Bank of North-America." 69398

Remarks on a pamphlet, entitled, Considerations on the present state of our affairs at home and abroad. 64143, 69687,
86737

Remarks on a pamphlet entitled "Proceedings
of the Board of Overseers of Harvard
University, 1834." 69399

Remarks on a pamphlet entitled "Prof. Hale
and Dartmouth College." 29615, 57202

Remarks on a pamphlet entitled, The case
between Mr. Whitefield and Dr. Stebbing
stated. 26596

Remarks on a pamphlet, entitled "The state
of religion in New England." 69400,
90595-90597, 103594

Remarks on a pamphlet, entituled "A dissertation on the political union and constitution." 69397, 80405, 102402

Remarks on a pamphlet, intitled, An examination of the commercial principles.
15031

Remarks on a pamphlet, intitled, "Objections
to the taxation of the American colonies,
&c. considered." 6218

Remarks on a pamphlet, intitled Observations
on the conduct of Great Britain. 17351

Remarks on a pamphlet intitled, Thoughts on
the present state of affairs with America.
1777

Remarks on a pamphlet lately published by Dr.
Price. 24089, 1st note after 69400

Remarks on a pamphlet, printed by the Professors and Tutors of Harvard University.
23271, 30756, (42458)

Remarks on a pamphlet published by a Committee of the Citizens of Berkshire.
69401, 2d note after 104432

Remarks on a pamphlet said to be offered to
the churches by a convention of ministers.
360, 11968, 3d note after 96741

Remarks on a passage from the River Balise.
16285

Remarks on a passage in the Bishop of London's sermon. 65456

Remarks on a passage in the opinion of Judge
Daniel. 69402, 105215

Remarks on a passage in the preface to his
direction to his people. 97454

Remarks on a petition from certain inhabitants. 102957

Remarks on a piece wrote by Mr. Isaac
Backus. 24439

Remarks on a plan entitled Plan for a general
legislative union. 69403, 79623, 93181

Remarks on a plan for a general legislative
union. 69403, 79623, 93181

Remarks on a poem, called "The scourge of
fashion. 69404

Remarks on a popular letter. 69405

Remarks on a printed discourse of Rev. Mr.
Fish. 25199

Remarks . . . on a proposition to devise means
for the preservation of life and property.
54968

Remarks on a protective tariff. (23943)

Remarks on a publication entitled, "The result
of an ecclesiastical council in Simsbury."
73138

Remarks on "A roaster for Peter Porcupine."
14003

Remarks on a recent letter of Dr. Taylor.
97594

Remarks on a report of a Committee of the
Overseers of Harvard College. (37057),
2d note after 69405

Remarks on a report . . . on the subject of the
House of Reformation. 6727

Remarks on a "Reprint of the original letters
from Washington to Joseph Reed." 68621,
89000

Remarks on a review of Symmes' theory.
70433

Remarks on a second publication of B. Henry
Latrobe. 60451, 62116, 84648

Remarks on a sermon . . . before the Plymouth
Association. 55333

Remarks on a sermon of the Rev. Aaron
Hutchinson. (34058), 97320

Remarks on a sermon preached by G. K. 37213

Remarks on a sermon, published by the Rev.
Isaac Robinson. 72085

Remarks on a speech made to the National
Assembly of France. 44134

Remarks on a volunteer navy. 69406

Remarks on a war with America. 69407

Remarks on African colonization. 69408

Remarks on Allston's paintings. 69409

Remarks on American debts. (28071)

Remarks on American history. 89001

Remarks on American lands in general. 30437-
30439

Remarks on "American Unitarianism." 77231

Remarks on an absurd and abusive letter.
17671

Remarks on an account in the Boston evening-
post. 11967

Remarks . . . on . . . "An act for the trial of
certain offenders." 36185

Remarks on an act of Parliament. 48941

Remarks on "An act to establish the Superior
Court of the City of Boston." (6777),
67235, 67254

Remarks on an address . . . before the New
England Society. (44734)

Remarks on an address delivered at Washington.
24052, 2d note after (69432), 93573

Remarks on an address to the members of the
new Parliament. (69410), (69491), 93796,
102863

Remarks on an anonymous tract. 47144-(47145)

Remarks on an article from the Christian examiner. 2290, 58757

Remarks on an article in the Austin state
gazette. 10842

Remarks on an article in the Bible repertory
and Princeton review. 58624

Remarks on an article in the North American
review. (4759)

Remarks on article IX., in the . . . North
American review. (69411)

Remarks on banks and banking. 3184, 104231

Remarks on Bishop Hopkins' letter on the
Bible view of slavery. 47062

Remarks on Bishop Ravenscroft's answer.
49684

Remarks [on Blackstone's commentaries.] 5697

Remarks on bridging the upper Mississippi.
(28826)

Remarks on British relations. 69412, 4th note
after 98684

Remarks . . . on canals and state finances.
(42646)

Remarks on capital punishment. (33640)

Remarks on capital punishments and the penitentiary system. 93702

Remarks on cellular separation. 25277

Remarks on certain statements purporting to be
Bishop Chase's defence. 102726

Remarks on changes lately proposed or adopted.
95805

Remarks on Com. Johnstone's account. 5792, 36395

Remarks on common schools. 92389

"Remarks" on considerations suggested by the establishment of a second college in Connecticut. 15721, 36444, note after 101999

Remarks on contagion and quarantine. 84416

Remarks on coolie and African emigration. 33223

Remarks on currency and banking. 1817-1818

Remarks on Des Barres' chart of Boston Harbor. 3607

Remarks on Dr. Bray's memorial, &c. 105652

Remarks on Dr. Channing's slavery. 2414-2415, (11920), 64948, 81162, 94057

Remarks on Dr. Edwards' notion of the freedom of the will and system of universality. 21930

Remarks on Dr. Edwards' notion on the freedom of the will. 21930

Remarks on Dr. Gale's letter to J. W. Esq. 26351-26352, 21587

Remarks on Dr. Griffin's requisition. 28818

Remarks on Dr. Mayhew's incidential reflections relative to the Church of England. 8641, 47140, 5th note after 69412

Remarks on Dr. Moore's address. 41348

Remarks on Dr. Price's additional observations. 104706

Remarks on Dr. Price's observations. 24090

Remarks on Dr. Roger's vindication of the civil establishment. 11870

Remarks on Dr. Ware's answer. 105135

Remarks on Dr. Ware's answer to the preceding reply. 105132

Remarks . . . on Dunn's and Haven's bills on Kansas. 30897

Remarks on education, by Hon. Daniel Brenan. 7717

Remarks on education. . . . First published in the North American review. 67908

Remarks on education: illustrating the close connection. 84079

Remarks on . . . emancipation and colonization. 2886

Remarks on emigration from the United Kingdom. 92656

Remarks on emigration to Jamaica. 3353, (69413)

Remarks on emigration, with a draft of a bill. 79134

Remarks on entomology. 7986

Remarks . . . on . . . "Equality of all men before the law." 33380

Remarks on Europe. 8340

Remarks on female infidelity. 97580

Remarks . . . on flogging in the navy. 64273

Remarks on Frothingham's history of the battle. 26080

Remarks on G. Keith's sermon. 104256

Remarks on G. W's. sheet. 95527

Remarks on General Burgoyne's state of the expedition from Canada. 9265

Remarks on Gen. Washington, trade, &c. 98635

Remarks on "General Wm. Hull's memories of the campaign." 85417

Remarks on Governor Johnstone's speech in Parliament. (68570)

Remarks on Hayti as a place of settlement. (33840), (81989)

Remarks on his observations on the nature of civil liberty. 41286, 1st note after 95742

Remarks on his sermon preached at Newbury-Port. 97323

Remarks on his services in America. 21864

Remarks on important theological controversies. 21967

Remarks on insanity. 58804

Remarks on its system of instruction and management. 89828

Remarks on Jay's treaty. 69414

Remarks . . . on . . . John Bass's . . . narrative. 55332

Remarks on Judge Thacher's sentence. 19583, (69415)

Remarks on laying the corner-stone of the Mechanic Institution. 47897

Remarks on legislation and jurisprudence. 3854, (56570)

Remarks on liberty of conscience. 69416, 98496

Remarks on library construction. 84980

Remarks on literary property. 55327

Remarks on Lord Howe's extraordinary gazette. 52069

Remarks on Lord Sheffield's observations. 32637, 1st note after 69417, (74428)

Remarks on Lord Viscount Goderich's dispatch. 69417

Remarks on lotteries. (44185)

Remarks on marine life-saving inventions. 49023

Remarks on Mentor's reply. (29964)-29965

Remarks on Mr. Adams's sermon. 11967

Remarks on Mr. Baldwin's sermon. 82492

Remarks on Mr. Baring's examination. 2262

Remarks on Mr. Biddle's discourse. 71856

Remarks on Mr. Binney's treatise. 5485

Remarks on Mr. Birkbeck's "Notes" and "Letters." 23956

Remarks on Mr. Birkbeck's opinions upon this subject. 87307

Remarks on Mr. Bouldin's resolution of inquiry. (1819)

Remarks on Mr. Chatfield's report. 69418

Remarks on Mr. Chilton's resolution. 79205

Remarks on Mr. Espy's theory of centripetal storms. (68512)

Remarks on Mr. Forster's account. 25128, 25130, 101031

Remarks, on Mr. Gaston's address to the freemen. 105118

Remarks on Mr. Horace Mann's report on education. 28612

Remarks on Mr. Huskinsson's letter. (25622)

Remarks on Mr. Isherwood's defence. (35249)

Remarks on Mr. Jeremie's conduct. 36057, 69419

Remarks on Mr. John Fitch's reply. 3521

Remarks on Mr. Marks' "Memorial." (48569)

Remarks on Mr. Mason's speech. 2908

Remarks on Mr. Motley's letter. 51103, 69420

Remarks on Mr. Nathan Bassett's appendix. (24469)

Remarks on Mr. Norton's 'Statement of reasons.' 90713

Remarks on Mr. Schlegel's works. 17594

Remarks on Mr. Stuart's book. 60952, 93197

Remarks on Mr. Whitefield. 103646

Remarks on Mr. Whitefield's second letter. 26596

Remarks on Mr. Whitefield's two letters. 26596

Remarks on money. 60452

Remarks on Mormonism. 64960

Remarks on musical conventions in Boston. (42612)

Remarks on native silver from Michigan. 77873

Remarks on New-York banking. 9749

Remarks on the Lord Bishop of Clogher's account. 11496

Remarks on the Lyme dispute. 101216

Remarks on the majority and minority reports. 45317

Remarks on the manufacture of bank notes. 69471

Remarks on the manufacturing of maple sugar. (69472)

Remarks on the memorial of the New England clergymen; United States Senate, March 14, 1854. [By Sam Houston.] 33195

Remarks . . . on the memorial of the New England clergymen; United States Senate, March 14, 1854. [By Stephen Douglas.] 20693

Remarks on the "Merchants' Bank." 12384

Remarks on the militia bill now before Congress. 69473

Remarks on the militia of Canada. 11164

Remarks on the militia system. 69474

Remarks on the mineralogical character of the Seigneury of Rigaud Vandreuil. 17959

Remarks on the mineralogy and geology of Nova Scotia. 35402

Remarks on the minutes of the Warren Association. 82483

Remarks on the moral and religious character of the United States. (56601)

Remarks on the Narragansett patent. 2217

Remarks on the nature and bad effects of spirituous liquors. (4673), 4679-4680, note just before 69475, 79260

Remarks on the nature and extent of liberty. 69475

Remarks on the nature and probable effects of introducing the voluntary system in the studies of Latin and Greek. 67239

Remarks . . . on the navy appropriation bill. 18095

Remarks . . . on the necessity of organizing governments. 50581

Remarks . . . on the neutrality bill. 18095

Remarks on the new essay of the Pennsylvanian farmer. 20047

Remarks on the new separate school agitation. 74570

Remarks on the new system of medical education. 59753

Remarks on the new sugar-bill. (69476), 1st note after 102863

Remarks on the north eastern boundary question. 31144

Remarks on the northern whale fishery. 43142

Remarks on the number of Unionidae. 39493

Remarks on the observation of the Lord's day. 69477, 1st note after 97653, note after 105674

Remarks on the observations made in the late voyage to the north pole. 33056, 69478

Remarks on the observations made in the late voyage towards the North pole. 33056, 69478

Remarks on the opinions of Messrs. Hunter and Greene. 66239

Remarks on the ordinance of nullification. 69479, 6th note after 88114

Remarks on the ordonnance issued at Paris. 69480

Remarks on the organization and constitutional powers. 36961

Remarks on the pamphlet of Sir Howard Douglass. 70156

Remarks on the past and its legacies to American society. 56058

Remarks on the past and present policy of Great Britain. 13252, 4th note after 96480

Remarks on the Patriot. 36301, note after 69480, 78302

Remarks . . . on the pay of navy officers. 8454

Remarks on the penal system of Pennsylvania. 25277

Remarks on the persecution for libel instituted against the author. 8514

Remarks on the petition for an act. 69481

Remarks on the petition of the convention. 95372

Remarks on the plan and extracts of deeds. (69482)

Remarks on the plan of a college to exclude the Latin and Greek studies. 76404

Remakrs on the police of Boston. 6750

Remarks on the policy and practice of the United States and Great Britain. 11349, 69483

Remarks on the policy of prohibiting the exportation of cotton. 69484

Remarks on the policy of recognizing the independence of the southern states of North America. 52327, 69485

Remarks on the political state of things. 103119

Remarks on the Popham Celebration of the Maine Historical Society. 30896

Remarks on the post establishment in the United States. 69486

Remarks on the practicability and expediency of establishing a rail road. (29653)

Remarks on the practicability and expediency of rail roads. 69487

Remarks on the practicability of Indian reform. 43113

Remarks on the pre-emption bill. 102307

Remarks on the preface, by the late John Fothergill. 58788

Remarks on the preface of a pamphlet published by John Presbyter. 69488

Remarks on the "Preliminary history" of two discourses. (3700)

Remarks on the present position of the Hoosac Tunnel enterprise. 30859, 32890

Remarks on the present project of the city government. 72653

Remarks on the present situation of Yale College. 105795

Remarks on the present state of currency. 104984

Remarks on the present state of Jamaica. 47051

Remarks on the present state of our West India colonies. 69489

Remarks on the present state of the American navy. 19677

Remarks on the preservation of the public archives. 52872

Remarks on the pretended country-man's answer to the book. 14537

Remarks on the prevailing storms of the Atlantic coast. (68512)

Remarks on the principal acts of the thirteenth Parliament. 41284

Remarks on the principles and practice of road-making. 73754

Remarks on the probability of reaching the north pole. 78182

Remarks on the probable conduct of Russia and France. 69490

Remarks on the proceedings as to Canada. 10574, 28787

Remarks on the slave registry bill. 14726, (21855)

Remarks on the slave trade and African squadron. 46874

Remarks on the slave-trade, and the slavery of the Negroes. 69505

Remarks on the slavery of the black people. 58844

Remarks on the slavery question. 11917

Remarks on the so-called pigmy race. (51024)

Remarks on the social and economical aspects. 54744

Remarks on the Society for the Extinction of the Slave-Trade. 93257

Remarks on the speech attributed, by Mr. Jefferson, to Logan. 3823

Remarks on the state of commerce in the French and British West India islands. 31973

Remarks on the state of education in the province of Canada. 10429, 38463

Remarks on the state of society, religion, morals, and education, at Newfoundland. 50858

Remarks on the . . . state of the laws in Massachusetts. 45968

Remarks on the state of the sugar trade, &c. 69506

Remarks on the statistics and political institutions of the United States. 57946

Remarks on the steam-power, rig, &c. 25051

Remarks on the strictures of Reverend Joseph Lyman. 42791, 104117

Remarks on the subject of a ship canal. (69507)

Remarks on the subject of slavery in America. 2791

Remarks on the supplement to the African Company's case. (73777)

Remarks on the supply of water, to the city of Mobile. 91195

Remarks, on the supposed tides. 103692

Remarks on the tariff bill. 41839

Remarks . . . on the tariff. Delivered . . . May 7, 1844. 67951

Remarks . . . on the ten million bank question. 67908

Remarks on the theatre, and on the late fire at Richmond. 727, (71189)

Remarks on the theories of Divine right of Hobbes and others. 302

Remarks on the theories of Malthus and Godwin. 23233

Remarks on the times. 58972

Remarks on the tornado which visited New-Brunswick in New-Jersey. (68512)

Remarks on the "Tour around Hawaii." (76380)

Remarks on the tragedy of Jacob Leisler. 39936

Remarks on the travels of the Marquis de Chastellux. 12233, 69508, 81137

Remarks on the treaty with Spain. (70269)

Remarks on the trial of John-Peter Zenger. 106314

Remarks on the trial of the Earl of Stirling. 38829, 91841A

Remarks on the two last reports of the Land Agent. 43947-(43948)

Remarks on the United States factories. 69509

Remarks on the United States of America, drawn up from his own observations. 33638

Remarks on the United States of America, with regard to the actual state of Europe. (21166)

Remarks on the utility and necessity of asylums or retreats for the victims of intemperance. 69510

Remarks on the voyage of John Meares. 20361

Remarks . . . on the warehouse bill. 20341

Remarks on the Washington Tontine. 91980

Remarks on the West-India station. 5871

Remarks on the western states of America. 69511

Remarks on the work of grace. 7343

Remarks on tides and the prevailing currents of the ocean and atmosphere. (68512)

Remarks on Trinity Church bill before the Council of Revision. 96982, 97066

Remarks on two late, noted sermons. 39530, 102571

Remarks on two pamphlets, lately published. 86764A

Remarks on two sermons . . . by Dr. Mayhew of Boston. 32955

Remarks on typhus fever. 26497

Remarks on university education in Nova Scotia. 69012

Remarks on Washington College, and on the "Considerations" suggested by its establishment. 15720, 15721, (69512), 1st and 2d notes after 101998, 103167, 103169

Remarks on West India affairs. 28935

Remarks on Whitefield's journals. 26596

Remarks on William C. Rives of Virginia. 71668

Remarks [on Worcester's first letter.] 96412

Remarks [on Worcester's second letter.] 96412

Remarks. I. On the position of barracks in the West Indies. 80564

Remarks, propositions and calculations. 103117

Remarks relative to the construction of a rail road. 29652

Remarks . . . relative to the remarkable phenomenon. 26754

Remarks respecting the Sodus Canal. 69513

Remarks sent to the people who celebrated the fourth of July, 1835. 9235

Remarks, . . . September, 1864. 30022

Remarks . . . showing the unconstitutionality . . . of the bill. 31595

Remarks suggested by the case of the Creole. 11924

Remarks suggested by the speech of the Hon. F. P. Blair. 5741, (25845)

Remarks sur la partie de la relation du voyage du Capitaine Cook. 22576

Remarks to accompany a comparative vocabulary. 77792

Remarks to his neighbors on leaving Springfield. 89850

Remarks to the bar of Philadelphia. 5490

Remarks to the young. (70435)

Remarks touching the Wheeling Bridge suit. 22209

Remarks . . . 24th of February, 1849. 51466

Remarks upon a book, entituled, The present state of the sugar colonies consider'd. (65328), (69514)

Remarks upon a book, intitled, A short history of Barbados. 3281

Remarks upon "A discourse delivered at the installation." 66780

Remarks upon a discourse intitled An overture. 20060, 69515, 95581

Remarks upon a discourse preached December 15th 1774. (28005)

Remarks upon a late pamphlet intitul'd The two great questions consider'd. 69516, 97560

Remarks upon a letter addressed by M. Mazeres. 98674

Remarks upon a letter published in the London Chronicle. 10732

Remarks upon a letter to the Bishop of Massachusetts. (17683)

Remarks upon a letter written by Mr. Luis C. Vanuxem. 97000

Remarks upon a memorial circulated by the agents of the Forest Improvement Company. 60455

Remarks upon a message sent by the Upper to the Lower House of Assembly. 45069, 45318

Remarks upon a pamphlet, entitled A letter to a friend. 25527, 31295-31296

Remarks upon a pamphlet, entitled, A letter to a friend in the country. 31296, 69518

Remarks upon a pamphlet entituled, A discourse shewing. 69517

Remarks upon a pamphlet intitled "An address from the Baptist Church in Philadelphia." 69519, note after 104732

Remarks upon a pamphlet, intitled, The considerations in relation to trade considered. 69520

Remarks upon a pamphlet published at Bath, Me. (20226), (37853), 37856, 104779

Remarks upon a plan for the total abolition of slavery. (69521)

Remarks upon a protestation presented to the Synod of Philadelphia. 17662, 62106, 94686, 94700

Remarks upon a scandalous libel. 80329, 88168

Remarks upon a scandalous piece. (60861), 91305

Remarks upon a sermon preached in Brooklyn. 104558

Remarks upon an essay, intituled, The history of the colonization. 94124

Remarks upon an oration delivered at Cambridge. 66784

Remarks upon an oration delivered by Charles Sumner. (66786)

Remarks upon Capt. Middleton's defence. 20406

Remarks upon coral formation in the Pacific. 17196

Remarks upon Gen. Howe's account of his proceedings. 46919

Remarks upon inland navigation. 5700, 105386

Remarks upon men, manners, religion, and policy. 22664

Remarks upon Mr. Appleton's remarks. 1818

Remarks upon Mr. Binney's letter. 5491

Remarks upon Mr. Carter's outline. 11117

Remarks upon Mr. Gale's reflections. 69522

Remarks upon Mr. Mills's proposals. (50807)

Remarks upon Mr. Pickering's letter. 282

Remarks upon Mr. S. Swett's sketch. (12696), 94058

Remarks, upon Mr. Smith's preface and sermon. 24470

Remarks upon recent publications against Rt. Rev. Philander Chase. 12208

Remarks upon several pamphlets writ in opposition. 69523

Remarks upon slavery. 69524

Remarks upon slavery and the slave trade. 13563, note after 69523

Remarks upon some things advanced by Mr. Sandeman. 4495

Remarks upon that part of the President's message which relates to the revenues and finances. 102318

Remarks upon that portion of Durham's report relating to Prince Edward's Island. 38750

Remarks upon that portion of the message of Gov. Seymour, relating to military arrests. 51466

Remarks upon the application of the Bank of Mutual Redemption. (69526)

Remarks upon the advice to the freeholders &c. 60456, (69525)

Remarks upon the auction system. 69527

Remarks upon the Bank of the United States. (31424)

Remarks upon the Bishop of London's late pastoral letter. (78594)

Remarks upon the changes of a dying world. 46533

Remarks upon the controversy between the commonwealth of Massachusetts and the state of South Carolina. 101331

Remarks upon the cultivation of the sugar-cane. 4248

Remarks upon the cutting of the great ship canal. 9699

Remarks upon the danger and inconveniences of the principal defects of the constitution of Pennsylvania. 10062, 59956

Remarks upon the defence of the Reverend Mr. Hemphill's observations. (36017)

Remarks upon the delineated Presbyterian play'd hob with. 2464A, 69528

Remarks upon the disputed points of boundary. (12830), note after 69528

Remarks upon the doctrine of perseverance. (78292)

Remarks upon the emigration of hill coolies. 69529

Remarks upon the epistle of St. Ignatius to the Trallians. 69517

Remarks upon the establishment of the American prime meridian. 18807

Remarks upon the evidence given by Thomas Irving, Esq. (35122)

Remarks upon the first [familiar conference upon some Antinomian tenets.] 4095, 78730

Remarks upon the growth and culture of the cotton plant. 19909

Remarks upon the historical memorial published by the court of France. 47516-47517, 69530

Remarks . . . upon the Indian appropriation bill. 52341

Remarks upon the legality of the income tax. (69531)

Remarks upon the life and writings of Charles Sprague. 102092

Remarks upon the life, character and behavior of the Rev. George Whitefield. 30399

Remarks upon the list of British ships in a pamphlet. 65959

Remarks upon the manner and form of swearing and kissing the Gospels. (13374)

Remarks . . . upon the Nebraska resolutions. 66817

Remarks upon the necessity and effect of general bankrupt law. (69532)

Remarks upon the new doctrine of England. 50827, 101270

Remarks upon the North American insects. 30522

Remarks upon the objects and advantages of the Anglo-Brazilian Canal, Road, Bridge and Land Improvement Company. 7625

Remarks upon the oration delivered by Charles Sumner. 93683

Remarks . . . upon the Pacific Railroad. 12200

Remarks upon the pamphlet published by the Tabernacle Church. 105323

Remarks upon the postscript to the defence. (12363), (20061)

Remarks upon the practical working of the U. S. drug law. 89946

Remarks upon the principles of instruction. 11117

Remarks upon the "proceedings of the Trustees of the Greene Foundation." 69533

Remarks upon the progress of Canada. 11789

Remarks upon the proposed federation of the provinces. (56197), 69534

Remarks upon the remedy for slavery. 90865

Remarks upon the report of a peace. 69535

Remarks upon the report of His Honor the Mayor of Boston. 67907, (11925)

Remarks upon the report of the Committee appointed by the Carlisle Presbytery. 69536

Remarks upon the report of the Committee of the Legislature. 510

Remarks upon the rights and powers of corporations. (31425)

Remarks upon the situation of Negroes in Jamaica. 4251

Remarks upon the social and economical aspects of the southern political crisis. (14909)

Remarks upon the use of anthracite. 98697

Remarks upon the usury laws. 69537

Remarks upon United States intervention in Hayti. (13254)

Remarks upon usury and its effects. 37287

Remarks, which the author of the Compendious extract, &c. 106352, 106361

Remarque sur la destruction des plantes indigenes au Bresil. 52358

Remarques critiques sur le tableau historique et politique. 69538

Remarques d'un Republicain. 42923

Remarques d'un voyageur sur la Hollande. 69539

Remarques et observations pour la navigation de France a Quebec. 96456

Remarques generales sur l'Amerique Septentrionale. 44238, 44240, note after 89135

Remarques historiques pour l'esclaircissement de la langue. (7739)

Remarques par l'auteur Francois. 49393

Remarques plus particulieres. (20785)

Remarques succinctes et deduction faites par les deputes. 20783

Remarques succinctes, etc. 57532, 69540

Remarques sur la carte de duite de l'Ocean Septentrional. 4338

Remarques sur la carte de l'Amerique Septentrionale. 4559

Remarques sur la declaration du Marquis de Barvacena. 3294

Remarques sur la partie de la relation du voyage du Capitaine Cook. 22575

Remarques sur la revolution Americaine. 44236

Remarques sur le detroit de Belle-Isle. 4557

Remarques sur le tableau historique et politique de Surinam. 24120

Remarques sur les avantages et les desavantages de la France et de la Gr. Bretagne. 63439

Remarques sur les erreurs de l'histoire philosophique et politique. 58239

Remarques, sur les malades veneriennes. (48901)

Remarques sur les notes de M. Lafontaine. 39106

Remarques sur les rapports naturels des genres viscum. 67458

Remarques sur les theories de Godwin, Malthus, Say, Sismundi, &c. (23234)

Remarques sur plusieurs branches de commerce et de navigation. 69451

Remarques uber den Mississippischen Actien-Handel. (32104), note after 42194

Remarques uber die jetziger Zeit Welt. 69542

Remarques van Bewinthebberen der Geoctroyeerde West-Indische Compagnie. 69543, 1st note after 102911

Remarques vande Gedeputeerden vande H: Mog: Heeren Staten Generael. 20786, note after 98953

Rembert, S. S. 69544

Rembert, W. R. (69545)

Remedio natural para precaverse de los reyos. 26374

Remedios . . . [de Las Casas.] 11239

Remedy against dispair. 104102

Remedy: being a sequel to the African slave trade. 9691

Remedy by state interposition. 30446

Remedy for duelling. 4330, 4337

Remedy for the blues. 63933

Remedy for war. 69546

Remedy, in a national bank of the people. 69547

Remember; a word for soldiers. 31307

Remember that the islands of the West-Indies are incapable of emulating your noble example. 102870

Remembrance of former times of this generation. 35330, 69548

Remembrance of his works. 93407

Remembrancer. pseud. To the public. 95997

Remembrancer. (491), 806, 955, 34087, (47395), 50830, (52446), 63784, note after 92858

Remembrancer for 1775. 243

Remembrancer of beloved companions. 57132

Remembrancer of filial obligations. 13696

Remembrancer of former times of this generation. 35330, 69548

Remembrancer of the departed heroes & statesmen of America. (72735)

Remembrancer of the departed heroes, sages, and statesmen, of America. 72736

Remer, Julius August. 1286, 9259, 39709, 41285, 65454, 69549, 91056, 97350

Remesal, Antonio de. (69550)-(69551)

Remey, R. Lepelletier de Saint. see Lepelletier de Saint-Remy, R.

Remi, R. Lepelletier de Saint. see Lepelletier de Saint-Remy, R.

Remick, Martha. 69552

Remington, A. G. 54841, (69553)

Remington, Dewitt C. 70629 see also Rhode Island. Quartermaster General.

Remington, E. F. 69554

Remington, J. R. 69556

Remington, James. (69555)

Remington, R. P. 20470, 55805, (69557)-(69558)

Remington, S. (69559)

Reminiscence of Sleepy Hollow. (29218)

Reminiscence of the blood an successful adventures. 69560, note after 102493

Reminiscences. 71279

Reminiscences, anecdotes and statistics of . . . Sherburne. 30836

Reminiscences and conclusions. (14118)

Reminiscences at home and abroad. 1908

Reminiscences by Hon. O. H. Smith. 83689

Reminiscences et confessions d'un ancien chirurgien de corsaires. 10108

Reminiscences, historical and biographical.
(6115)
Reminiscences of a campaign in Mexico.
69561, 71957
Reminiscences of a campaign in Mexico: an
account of the operations. 82742
Reminiscences of a country congregation.
65536, 65539
Reminiscences of a country pastorate. 12678
Reminiscences of a fifty-years' pastorate.
25874
Reminiscences of a 46 years' residence. 55356
Reminiscences of a half-century pastorate.
92092
Reminiscences of a long life, historical, politi-
cal, personal and literary. 84891, 84895
Reminiscences of a New England church and
people. 84131
Reminiscences of a quarter of a century.
31244
Reminiscences of a ruined generation. 13268
Reminiscences of a tour through New Bruns-
wick and Nova Scotia. 89156
Reminiscences of a trans-Atlantic traveller.
42920
Reminiscences of a Virginia physician. (74431)
Reminiscences of a voyage to British Columbia.
10168
Reminiscences of a voyage to India. 27664
Reminiscences of Albert Gallatin. 3749
Reminiscences of America in 1869. 69562
Reminiscences of Amherst College. (32248)
Reminiscences of an annual conference. 5627
Reminiscences of an old Yorker. 21116
Reminiscences of Bishop Chase. 12193
Reminiscences of Boston. 19081
Reminiscences of Carpenters' Hall. 62118
Reminiscences of Catskill. (62905)
Reminiscences of Charleston. By J. N.
Cardozo. (10818)
Reminiscences of Charleston, lately published
in the Charleston courier. 25675
Reminiscences of Col. John Ketchman. 32971
Reminiscences of Col. Joseph Durfee. 21428
Reminiscences of Congress. 44485
Reminiscences of early and later times.
13329, 84484
Reminiscences of early Methodism in Indiana.
82925
Reminiscences of Elizabeth Cady Stanton.
90405
Reminiscences of forty years. 62730
Reminiscences [of Gen. John Hancock.] 93714,
93717
Reminiscences of Gen. Warren and Bunker
Hill. 93716
Reminiscences of George La Bar. 38395
Reminiscences of Georgia. 9307
Reminiscences of Gustavus Fellowes Davis.
84548
Reminiscences of him, by a fellow student.
35427
Reminiscences of James A. Hamilton. 30018
Reminiscences of Joseph Smith. 83316
Reminiscences of La Fayette's visit to Boston.
83718
Reminiscences of Lucius Manlius Sargent.
(80317)
Reminiscences of medical teachings and
teachers in New York. (51120)
Reminiscences of men and things in Northfield.
51374
Reminiscences of Meshach Browning. (8693)
Reminiscences of Methodism in New Jersey.
68037

Reminiscences of Mrs. Margaret Prior.
65698
Reminiscences of Old Gloucester. (48818)
Reminiscences of our work for fifteen years.
58371
Reminiscences of past and present times.
69563
Reminiscences of pioneer life in the Missis-
sippi valley. 89361
Reminiscences of Quebec. (69564), 69565
Reminiscences of Rev. Edward Payson. 103046
Reminiscences of Rufus Choate. 58660
Reminiscences of Samuel Dexter. 77021
Reminiscences of Samuel Latham Mitchell.
25448
Reminiscences of Saratoga or twelve seasons
at the "States." 83317
Reminiscences of scenes and characters in
college. (49699)
Reminiscences of seven years of early life.
83792
Reminiscences of seventy years. 89566
Reminiscences of seventy years of a busy life
in Pittsburgh. 83702
Reminiscences of Sharp and Wilberforce.
13499
Reminiscences of some of the events of the
war of 1812. 69566
Reminiscences of South America. 30974
Reminiscences of South Carolina. 95387
Reminiscences of Syracuse. (12429)
Reminiscences of the American revolution.
5985
Reminiscences of the city of Albany. 22084
Reminiscences of the city of New-York.
(69567)
Reminiscences of the civil war and other
sketches. 83744
Reminiscences of the French war. 72730, note
after 90518
Reminiscences of the late Rev. Samuel Hopkins.
59126
Reminiscences of the late Waitstill R. Ranney.
67895
Reminiscences of the last days, death and
burial of General Henry Lee. 36480
Reminiscences of the last sixty-five years.
95387
Reminiscences of the life and character of
Benjamin Woolsey Dwight. 21514
Reminiscences of the life and character of
Col. Phineas Staunton. 58924
Reminiscences of the life of a former merchant.
55412
Reminiscences of the life of Joseph Gatchell.
26755
Reminiscences of the military life and suffer-
ings of Col. Timothy Bigelow. 31588
Reminiscences of the navy. (52129)
Reminiscences of the original associates. 41258
Reminiscences of the park and its vicinity.
18941
Reminiscences of the past sixty years. (25446)-
25447
Reminiscences of the Rev. Samuel Hopkins.
59125
Reminiscences of the Texas republic. 82346
Reminiscences of the Vaughan family. 80318
Reminiscences of thirteen years spent there.
50622
Reminiscences of two epochs. 84267
Reminiscences of Wilmington. 50138
Reminiscences; or extracts from the catalogue
of General Jackson's juvenile indiscre-
tions. 35386

Remonstrances faictes a la Royne Mere du Roy. 99726

Remonstrancie aen Sijn Konicklijcke Majesteyt van Portugael. 60987

Remonstrant. pseud. Arguments and statements addressed to the . . . Legislature. 6782, note after 6785

Remonstranten t'onrecht bewerpt in sijn derde deel. 98247

Remonstrantie, aen de Ho: Mo: Heeren de Staten Generael. 69585, 2d note after 102911

Remonstrantie ende consideratien aengaende de vereeninghde vande Oost ende West-Indische Compagnien. 69586, 3d note after 102911

Remonstrantie, om, van wegen den Conig van Bohemen. 102888

Remonstrantie, van de Hooft-Partijcipanten. 69588, 4th note after 102911

Remonstrantie van Syn Koninklyke Majest. van Bohemen. 15931-15932, 102888

Remonstrantie, van vveghen den Coninck van Bohemen. 69589

Remonstrantie, vande Bewinthebberen der Nederlantsche West-Indische Compagnie. 69587, 5th note after 102911

Remonville, ------ de. (25854)

Removal of ancient landmarks. 9099

Removal of Brunside. 15212, 69849

Removal of disibilities. (77307)

Removal of Indians. 34663

Removal of Judge Loring. 92067

Removal of political disabilities. 72612

Removal of public disabilities. 77164

Removal of the Cherokees west of the Mississippi. 30496

Removal of the City Council of New Orleans. 53362

Removal of the Indians. (69590)

Removal of the remains of James Smithson. 84990

Removal of the seat of government. 20314, 94403

Removal of the Sioux Indians. 9327

Removal of the Surgeon-General. 30116

Removal public deposites. 5492

Removals and appointments to office. 7205

Remove not the ancient landmark! 70926

Remove the Indians westward. 43518

Remsen, Henry. 96021, 100787

Remson, --------, fl. 1856. (82107)

Remur, Simon Guillaume Gabriel Brute de. see Brute de Remur, Simon Guillaume Gabriel, Bp., 1779-1839.

Remusat, Charles Francois Marie, Comte de, 1797-1875. 11907, 11924, 11927, (32513), 52105, (69592)

Remy, Dick St. see St. Remy, Dick.

Remy, Joseph Saint. see Saint-Remy, Joseph.

Remy, Jules. 69593-(69595)

Remy, R. Lepelletier de Saint. see Lepelletier de Saint-Remy, R.

Renacimiento. 69596

Renan, Ernest. (69597)

Renard, Louis. 69598-69600

Renat, --------, fl. 1815. 3978, 101895

Renato de Grosourdy, --------. see Grosourdy, Rene de.

Renato, episodo do genio do Christianismo. (12268)

Renatus. (46483)

Renaud, Alexandre. (69603)

Renaudiere, Philippe Francois de la. see La Renaudiere, Philippe Francois de, 1781-1845.

Rencher, Abraham, 1798-1883. 69605 see also New Mexico (Territory) Governor, 1857-1861 (Rencher)

Render to all their dues. 75651, 2d note after 94170

Rendicion de Panzacola. 72805

Rending of the vail of the temple. (14525)

Rendition of Anthony Burns. 13416

Rendition of Anthony Burns. [By William Ingersoll Bowditch.] 7009

Rendition of Anthony Burns. Murderers, thieves, and blacklegs employed by Marshal Freeman! 9401

Rendition of fugitive slaves. (69606)

Rendon, Jose D. Espinosa. see Espinosa Rendon, Jose D.

Rendon, Sebastian Gomez. see Gomez Randon, Sebastian.

Rendorp, J. 69607

Rendu, Alp. 69608

Rene. 12248-12251, (12261)-12263

Rene a tale. 12266

Rene Lefebvre. pseud. see Laboulaye, Edouard.

Rene, ou les effets des passions. 12265

Renewal of covenant the great duty incumbent. (46729)

Renewed remarks. 38463

Reney, William. 69609

Renfermant las matieres suivants. 26328

Renfrew Gold Mining and Crushing Co. (69610)

Renger, --------. publisher 90016

Rengger, A. ed. 69616

Rengger, J. R. 4815, 69611-69616

Renne, George Wymberley Jones de. see De Renne, George Wymberley Jones, 1827-1880

Rennefort, Urbain Souchu de, ca. 1630-ca. 1689. (19447)

Rennell, James, 1742-1830. 38022, 69617

Renner, Daniel. petitioner 69618

Renner, John. 69619

Renneville, Rene Auguste Constantin de. 68454-68455, 89451

Renny, Robert. (69620)

Reno, Lydia M. (69621)

Reno Oil and Land Company. 69622

Renouard, Felix. (69623), 75537

Renouard de Sainte-Croix, Carloman Louis Francois Felix. see Sainte-Croix, Carloman Louis Francois Felix Renouard de, Marquis.

Renouf, Sidney. 69624

Renovacion por si misma de la soberana imagen. 98788

Renovales, Mariano de. 69625-69627

Renovation of politics. 2378

Renseignemens sur la navigation des cotes occidentales d'Amerique. (39103)

Renseignemens sur l'Amerique. 16616

Renseignemens tendant a prouver la continuation de ce trafic illegal. 96444

Renseignements fideles sur les Etats-Unis. 29204

Renseignements generaux. (76883)

Renseignements nautiques sur les cotes de Patagonie. 74990

Renseignements sur la Nouvelle Zelande. 72241

Renseignements sur la partie comprise. 6030

Renseignements sur la partie de la cote comprise. (6029)

Renseignements sur la partie des Etats-Unis de l'Amerique du Nord. 69630

Renseignements sur l'artillerie navale de l'Angleterre. 959

Rensiegnements sur le Centre-Amerique. (69631)

Renseignment [sic] sur les affaires de la Plata. 39983

Renselaar, A. van. 69632

Renselaer, James van. see Van Renselaer, James.

Renshaw, James. defendant 75957, note after 96922

Renshaw, James. defendant before naval court of enquiry 75957, note after 96922

Renson, G. tr. 35175, 65286, 65293, 65295

Rensselaer, ------- van. see Van Rensselaer, ---------.

Rensselaer, Anne van. see Van Rensselaer, Anne.

Rensselaer, C. van. see Van Rensselaer, C.

Rensselaer, Cortlandt van. see Van Rensselaer, Cortlandt.

Rensselaer, Jeremiah van. see Van Rensselaer, Jeremiah.

Rensselaer, John S. van. see Van Rensselaer, John S.

Rensselaer, Kiliaen van, 1580?-1646. 98544-98546

Rensselaer, Philip S. van. see Van Rensselaer, Philip S.

Rensselaer, S. van. see Van Rensselaer, S.

Rensselaer, Solomon van. see Van Rensselaer, Solomon.

Rensselaer, Stephen van. see Van Rensselaer, Stephen.

Rensselaer County, N. Y. Agricultural Society. see Rensselaer County Agricultural Society.

Rensselaer County, N. Y. Board of Supervisors. 69633, 69635-69636

Rensselaer County, N. Y. Medical Society. see Renssealer County Medical Society.

Rensselaer County, N. Y. School Association. see School Association of Rensselaer County, N. Y.

Rensselaer County, N. Y. Washington Benevolent Society. see Washington Benevolent Society. New York. Rensselaer County.

Rensselaer Agricultural Society. see Rensselaer County Agricultural Society.

Rensselaer County Agricultural Society. 69637-69638

Rensselaer County Board of Supervisors' defence. 69636

Rensselaer County Medical Society. 69639

Rensselaer Institute. Announcement of the fifty-second semi-annual session. 69641

Rensselaer Institute: established especially to instruct students. 69641

Rensselaer Polytechnic Institute, Troy, N. Y. 69641

Rensselaer Polytechnic Institute, Troy, N. Y. petitioners 69641

Rensselaer Polytechnic Institute, Troy, N. Y. Board of Trustees. 69641

Rensselaer Polytechnic Institute, Troy, N. Y. Charter. 69641

Rensselaer Polytechnic Institute, Troy, N. Y. Class of 1856. 69641

Rensselaer Polytechnic Institute, Troy, N. Y. Division B. 69641

Rensselaer Polytechnic Institute, Troy, N. Y. Preparatory School. see Rensselaer Polytechnic Institute, Troy, N. Y. Troy Academy.

Rensselaer Polytechnic Institute, Troy, N. Y. Semi-centennial Celebration, 1874. 69641

Rensselaer Polytechnic Institute, Troy, N. Y. Training School. see Rensselaer Polytechnic Institute, Troy, N. Y. Troy Academy.

Rensselaer Polytechnic Institute, Troy, N. Y. Troy Academy. 69641

Rensselaer Polytechnic Institute. Graduating exercises of the class of 1856. 69641

Rensselaer Polytechnic Institute, Troy, N. Y. [Course of study, etc.] 69641

Rensselaer School. see Rensselaer Polytechnic Institute, Troy, N. Y.

Rensselaer School exercises in the fall. 69641

Rensselaerville Baptist Association. see Baptists. New York. Rensselaerville Baptist Association.

Rente, Jose Guell y. see Guell y Rente, Jose.

Renuncia justificada del Gobernador Interino del Estado de Michoacan. 48816

Renvncia qve huzo la religion de S. Francisco. (69643)

Renunciation of free-masonry. By the Rev. Edward B. Rollins. 72851

Renunciation of free masonry, with his [i. e. Nathaniel Very's] answers. 99319

Renunciation of freemasonry, and appeal to the public. 103825

Renunciation of freemasonry. By Hiram B. Hopkins. (32918)

Renunciation of popery. 84029

Renunciation of universalism. 96096

Renville, John B. 19285, (69644)-69645

Renville, Joseph. 18288-18289, 18292, 69646-69649

Renville (J.) and Sons. firm eds. 69645

Renwick, Henry B. 69650

Renwick, J. 86908, 96505

Renwick, James. 69650-69654, 90792

Renzi, A. 69655-69656

Re-opening of the Tennessee River near Chattanooga. 84772

Reorganization of civil government. 62755

Re-organization of Florida. 78630

Reorganization of the Central High-School. (61529)

Reorganization of the judiciary. 24274

Re-organization of the rebel states. 69657

Reorganized Church of Jesus Christ of Latter Day Saints. (50732), 50737-50738, 69156, 75544, 83048, 83053-83054, 83074-83075, 83081-83082, 83089-83090, 83095-83096, 83099, 83104, 83108-83109, 83113, 83119, 83129, 83132, 83160, 83166-83167, 83176, 83179-83180, 83184, 83187, 83190, 83191, 83195, 83199, 83202, 83205, 83206, 83210, 83212, 83226, 83230-83234, 83247-83251, 83282, 83284, 83287, 83292-83293, 83297, 83299-83300, 83497, 83498, 83499, 84426-84429, 84431

Reorganized Church of Jesus Christ of Latter Day Saints. Annual Conference, 1870. (50746), 83294

Reorganized Church of Jesus Christ of Latter Day Saints. Board of Publication. 83166

Reorganized Church of Jesus Christ of Latter Day Saints. Committee on the Claims and Faith of the Church. (50746), 83294

Reorganized Church of Jesus Christ of Latter Day Saints. President. (50746), 83294 see also Smith, Joseph, 1832-1914.

Reorganized republic. (69658)

Repairing the breach. 13327

Reparations de certains edifices publics. (10453)

Reply of H. M.'s subjects, the principal inhabitants of the Mosquito Shore. (32364)-32365, note after 96027, 96028, note after 103448

Reply of His Majesty's subjects, the principal inhabitants of the Mosquito-Shore. (32364-32365, note after 96027, 96028, note after 103448

"Reply" of Hon. H. Mann. (80269)

Reply of Hon. Onslow Stearns. 90930

Reply of Hon. Reverdy Johnson. 36262

Reply of Hon. Thos. L. Jones. 36615

"Reply" of . . . Horace Mann. 44324

Reply [of J. F. Johnson.] 84739

Reply of J. P. Kennedy. (37410)

Reply [of James Buchanan, ex-President of the United States.] (78429)

Reply [of James Buchanan to Andrew Jackson's reply to Mr. Clay.] 35348

Reply of James P. Heath. 31188

Reply [of James Ramsay.] 96056

Reply of Joab Houghton. 33162

Reply of John Crookshanks. 17611

Reply [of John G. Plafrey.] 37683

Reply of John T. McLaughlin. 43500

Reply [of John Wesley.] (23139)

Reply of Judge Sprague of Massachusetts. 89707

Reply of Lt. Col. Maynadier. 47159

Reply of Lieut.-Col. Pilsen. (6287)

Reply [of Lord Glenelg.] 33138

Reply of Maj. Gen. Sherman to the Mayor of Atlanta. 80417-80418

Reply of Maj.-Gen. William B. Franklin. 25639

Reply of Messrs. Sterns & Taylor. 91357

Reply of Mr. Joseph Harvey. 58654

Reply of Mr. McDuffie. 43205

[Reply of Mr. Moore.] 11958

Reply of Mr. Trimble. 96973

Reply [of Mrs. Ann S. Stephens.] 33620, note before 91289

Reply of N. P. Trist, Consul at Havana, to the Preamble. 97001

Reply of Nicholas P. Trist, Consul at Havana, to the resolutions. 97002

Reply, October 7, 1864. 55840

Reply of Pres. Joseph Smith. 83298

Reply of Prof. Morse. (17630)-17631

Reply of Rev. Wm. G. Starr. 90566

Reply of Sir George Downing. (20787)

Reply of the Board of Directors of the Union Bank of Florida. 97757

Reply of the Canada Wesleyan Conference. 69673

Reply of the Central Committee of the Republican Party of So. Carolina. 88078, 1st note after 94434

Reply of the Chief Engineer of the B. and O. R. R. Co. 2992

Reply of the Church of the Puritans to the protest. 12403, 54184

Reply of the Cincinnati Chamber of Commerce. 13072

Reply of the Columbia Typographical Society. 28516, 1st-2d notes after 101931, note after 101967

Reply of the Congregational Church in Whitesboro. 103683

Reply of the Court [of Oyer and Terminer of Baltimore County, Md.] 3011

Reply of the Delegates of the Cherokee Nation. (12472)

Reply of the Delegates of the Cherokee Nation to the pamphlet. 12471

Reply of the Directors to the charges against the penitentiary [of Maryland.] 45233

Reply of the Directors to the "Report of the Directors of the Boston and Maine Railroad." 14047

Reply of the English Commissaries. note after 96403

Reply of the Executive Committee of the Camden and Amboy Railroad Company. 69674

Reply of the Free Church of St. Mary, for Sailors, Boston. 72137

Reply of the friends of Rev. John Pierpont. (62777)

Reply of the Genesee Consociation. (22449), 26921

Reply of the Grand Master. 69675

Reply of the Hawes-Place Congregational Society. 10743

"Reply" of the Hon. Horace Mann. 44324

Reply of the International Ocean Telegraph Company. 69676, 84773

Reply of the Judge Advocate, H. L. Burnett. 9381

Reply of the Judge Advocate, John A. Bingham. 5452

Reply of the majority of the representatives from the state of Massachusetts. 69677, 98641

Reply of the Managers to the communications of Mr. James R. Hale. 85954

Reply of the memorialists. 52997

Reply of the New York evening post. 34456

Reply of the President of the . . . [Philadelphia, Wilmington and Baltimore] Railroad. 62051

Reply of the Proprietor. 11924

Reply of the Rev. Mr. Harold. 10889, 30414

Reply of the Rev. W. V. Harold. 10889

Reply of the Southern Cherokees. 12473

Reply of the Trustees of the . . . [Public School] Society. 54615

Reply of the Union Bank of Tennessee. 94811

Reply of the Vestry of St. Paul's Church, Castleton. 11439, 52516

Reply of the Vestry of St. Paul's Church, Cincinnati. 69678

Reply of the Vestry of St. Paul's Church, to the statement. 75464

Reply of the Trustees of Kenyon College. 20708, 37590

Reply of two of the brethren to A. S. (69679), 91383

Reply of Washington A. Bartlett. 3781

Reply of William Cunningham, & Co. (17976), 84842

Reply on the Kent's Hill tragedy. 28605

Reply, on the presentation of a testimonial to S. P. Chase. 12200

Reply "Point by point" to the special report. 95657, 95660

Reply relating to witchcraft. 9926

Reply, relative to this question. (17101)

Reply. Sept. 29, 1864. 55840

Reply. Speech of Hon. Samuel Shellabarger of Ohio. 80139

Reply to a book called, "A plain discovery of many gross falshoods, &c." 24278

Reply to a book entitl'd Anguis flagellatus. 40197

Reply to a book lately published, entitled, A display of God's special grace. 17675

Reply to a brief statement on his naval history. 35721

Reply to a British pamphlet. 48580

Reply to a certain publication circulated through the district. 105068

Reply to a circular issued by the Glasgow Association for the Abolition of Slavery. 23056

Reply . . . to a circular of . . . members of the Faculty of Yale College. 33458

Reply to a communication signed by three hundred and twenty-eight laymen. 57309

Reply to a confutation of some grounds for infants baptisme. 62483

Reply to a critique on "Uncle John's cabin." 69680

Reply to a defence of the divine right of infant baptism. 13350

Reply to a discourse concerning episcopacy. 101194

Reply to a feeble and unfounded attack. 19357

Reply to a few observations. 90351

Reply to a friendly letter. 105248

Reply to A. Hamilton's letter. 13135

Reply to a late work by the Bishop of Vermont on slavery. 27936

Reply to a lecture on the north and the south. 24458

Reply to a letter addressed to Mr. Van Buren. 37451, 74141

Reply to a letter from a gentleman in New York. 40289, (69681), 86592, note after 96961

Reply to a letter in the Christian examiner. 16338

Reply to a letter, lately addressed to the . . . Earl of Selkirk. 43146

Reply to a letter of the Rt. Rev. the Lord Bishop of Montreal. 31255

Reply to a letter published by Henry Orne. 28608

Reply to a letter remonstrating against the consecration of Rev. H. U. Onderdonk. 69682

Reply to a letter to the Right Rev. Bishop Hobart. 32304

Reply to a modest paper, &c. 86632

Reply to "A narrative of the proceedings of the Board of Trustees of Dickinson College." 20081, 99393

Reply to a pamphlet by Thomas Allen. 102208

Reply to a pamphlet entitled, "A brief exposition of matters." (36271)

Reply to a pamphlet entitled "A statement of facts." (54732), 69683

Reply to a pamphlet entitled "A statement of the facts." 60312-60313

Reply to a pamphlet entitled "Advantages of League Island for a naval station." 39517, 69684

Reply to a pamphlet, entitled "An answer of a friend in the west, &c." (26354), 3d note after 105937

Reply to a pamphlet entitled "Belize." 55912

Reply to a pamphlet, entitled "Bondage, a moral institution." (24909)

Reply to a pamphlet, entitled, Considerations on the Society. 69685

Reply to a pamphlet, entitled, "Objections to Unitarian Christianity considered." 63928

Reply to a pamphlet, entitled, "Observations arising from the declaration." (69686)

Reply to a pamphlet, entitled, "The answer of a friend in the west, &c." 13213, (26354), (38374), note after 105924

Reply to a pamphlet intitled, Popular prejudices against the convention. 69687, 94143

Reply to a pamphlet issued by the Assistant Secretary of the Navy. (69688)

Reply to a pamphlet on the subject of "assimilated rank." 71589

Reply to a pamphlet printed at Glasgow. 64960

Reply to a pamphlet, purporting to be an answer to a letter. 40265, (45634), 45970

Reply to a pamphlet recently circulated by Mr. Edward Brooks. 42465

Reply to a pamphlet recently published by Sidney George Fisher. 24504

Reply to a pamphlet, written by George Wotherspoon. 22225

Reply to a piece called the Speech of Joseph Galloway, Esq. 20051

Reply to a piece wrote by Israel Holly. 2632

Reply to a pretended answer. (59729)

Reply to a quibbling answer of G. Whiteheads. 95527

Reply to a remonstrance and answer of the Bethel Free School. 54115, 69689

Reply to a resolution of the Georgia Historical Society. (22280)

Reply to a review of Webster's system. 76952

Reply to a review of Whitman's letters to Professor Stuart. 63990, 103728

Reply to a scandalous pamphlet lately published. 10065

Reply to a scurrilous publication in the Kentucky Whig. 3198

Reply to a second letter to the author. 35867

Reply to a sermon preached by the Rev. Mr. Bradford of Rowley. 7240, 94361

Reply to "A spectator." (60457)

Reply to a speech in Congress. 26403

Reply to Alexander Campbell. 91764

Reply to 'American's examination' of the 'right of search.' 11346, 23369, (69691), 71353

Reply to an address of Capt. R. F. Stockton. 106236

Reply to an address of the London Anti-slavery Society. 69690

Reply to an address to the author of a pamphlet. (26423), 26442

Reply to "An address to the people of Barnwell District." 96177

Reply to an address to the Roman Catholics. 103090, 103095

Reply to "an advocate for water." 8327

Reply to an "American's examination" of the "right of search." 11346, 23369, (69691), 71353

Reply to 'An answer' . . . by another Episcopalian. 32296

Reply to an answer to "Taxation of learning, charity, and religion." 62119, 65434

Reply to an apology for protesting. 85439

Reply to an article in the Edinburgh review. 35662, note after 90597

Reply to an article in the June number of the Millenial harbinger. 91764

Reply to an attack by John Jay. 18943

Reply to an attack on Delaplaine's repository. 9899

Reply to "An Episcopalian's review of a sermon." 64692

Reply to an epistle. 86052

Reply to "An examination of the banking system of Massachusetts." (69692)

Reply to an inquiring friend. 28492

Reply to an inquiry into the origin of American Methodism. 11436

Reply to . . . an opinion, of the Hon'ble William Wirt. 71384, 104880

Reply to argument of special counsel. 89232

Reply to "Ariel," Drs. Young and Blackie, on the Negro. 74626

Reply to Aristides. 12385

Reply to article X., no. LVIII, in the North American review. 50960

Reply to articles in the Springfield republican. (69693)

Reply to Asa Rand. 13840

Reply to B. R. Curtis. 79874

Reply to Bishop Hopkins' view of slavery. 6231

Reply [to Breckenridge's second defence.] 103873

Reply to "Brief historical sketches." 69694

Reply to Brownson's "Review of the sermon of Dr. Potts." 64692

Reply to Capt. Middleton's answer. 20407

Reply to Censor. 87936

Reply to certain calumnious strictures. 104681

Reply to certain insinuations. note after 39323

Reply to certain misrepresentations and mistakes. 81262, note after 88005

Reply to certain oral and written criticisms. 27323, 59151

Reply to certain portions of the minority report. (33797)

Reply to certain queries of the . . . Canal Committee. 8385

Reply to charges against the French reformers of 1789. 105588

Reply to charges of disloyalty by the Potter Investigating Committee. 65398

Reply to charges of Prof. R. S. M'Culloh. (6384)

Reply to Chas. Stearns. 66866, 90873

Reply to Col. Benton. 9936

Reply to Col. Clap's vindication. (13210)-13211

Reply to Col. Drayton's late address. (31042)

Reply to Col. Pickering's attack upon a Pennsylvania farmer. 64747

Reply to Colonel Picton's address. 26155

Reply to Col. Troup's defence of the agency. 29542

Reply to "Considerations and arguments proving the inexpediency." 371

Reply to Dr. Chandler's "Appeal defended." (12326)

Reply to Dr. Dewey's address. 28427

Reply to Dr. Eberle. 102326

Reply to Dr. Hare's further objections. (68512)

Reply to Dr. Hare's objections. (68512)

Reply to Dr. John Gill's book. 13350

Reply to Dr. Mayhew's letter of reproof. (13597)

Reply to Dr. Miller's letter to a gentleman in Baltimore. 49051

Reply to Dr. Noah Webster's calumniators. 64049

Reply to Dr. Price's Observations on the nature of civil liberty. 32790

Reply to Dr. Seybert's strictures. 105107

Reply to Dr. Ware. 105132

Reply to Dr. Ware's letters to Trinitarians and Calvinists. 105136

Reply to Francis Herr's pamphlet. 45425

Reply to "Fremont and McClellan, their political and military careers reviewed." 43025

Reply to G. & C. Merriam's attack. (69695)

Reply to General Andrew Jackson's letter. (14929)

Reply to General Cass. 33593

Reply to General Joseph Reed's remarks. 9836-9837, 82725

Reply . . . to George Northrop, Esq. 37271

Reply to Greene's pamphlet. 28605

Reply to Henry A. Wise. 38148

Reply . . . to Henry M. Fuller's attack. 36542

Reply to 'Hints on the re-organization of the navy.' 31978, 69696, 74187

Reply to his first latter to Hon. Reverdy Johnson. (33569)

Reply to his [i. e. Robert Wickliffe's] printed speech. 7687

Reply to Hon. Charles G. Loring. 105613

Reply . . . to Hon. Montgomery. 32653

Reply to Hon. Z. Chandler's speech in the U. S. Senate. 64249

Reply to Horace Binney on the privilege of the writ. 8463

Reply to Horace Binney's pamphlet on the habeas corpus. 5486, (28936)

Reply to Horace Greeley's lecture. 24182

Reply to . . . James Spence. 22339

Reply to John Earle's letter. 21622, 81461

Reply to John P. Campbell's strictures on atonement. 92030

Reply to Jonathan Dickinson's remarks. 4095

Reply to . . . Josiah Smith's answer to a postscript. (24469)

Reply to Kosciusko Armstrong's assault. 43405

Reply to Lawyer G. F. Borch. 5397

Reply . . . to . . . Legislature of Massachusetts of 1868. 30859

Reply to "Letters to Joseph Sturge." 93261

Reply to Lieutenant General Burgoyne's letter. 9266, 18348, 27144

Reply to Longfellow's Theologian. 68667

Reply to Lucius Junius Brutus' examination of the President's answer. (40117)

Reply to Messrs. Daniel W. Coxe and Henry Turner's remarks. 27509

Reply to Mr. Abbot's statement of proceedings. 18, 3d note after 96123

Reply to Mr. Adams's answer to my [i. e. Ebenezer Chaplin's] former treatise. 360, 6254, 11968, 3d note after 96741

Reply to Mr. Biddle. 92701

Reply to Mr. Borthwick's lectures on colonial slavery. 96400

Reply . . . to Mr. Buchanan, of Pennsylvania. 18846

Reply to Mr. Chancy's first part. 104183

Reply to Mr. Chandler's statement. 55827

Reply to Mr. Clay. 35348

Reply to Mr. Colden's vindication. (21117)

Reply to Mr. Colman's notes. 16795, 70266

Reply to Mr. Dobb's answer. 48856-(48857)

Reply to Mr. Duponceau. 95346

Reply to Mr. Espy. (68512)

Reply to Mr. George Bancroft and others. 68619

Reply to Mr. George Whitefield's letter. 32670

Reply to Mr. Greenhow's answer. 23725

Reply to Mr. Heathcote's letter. 31193

Reply to Mr. . . . Humphrey's remarks. 31595

Reply to Mr. Increase Mather's printed remarks. 37213

Reply to Mr. Isaac Backus. 104716

Reply to Mr. James Rumsey's pamphlet. 3521, 24582, 74126

Reply to Mr. James Spence. 68009

Reply to Mr. Jeremie's pamphlet. 36057

Reply to Mr. Jonathan Ward's vindication. 94523

Reply to Mr. Lindsay's speech. 27640

Reply to Mr. Polk. 8348

Reply to Mr. Roebuck's speech. (27639)

Reply to Mr. Rutherfurd. 46782

Reply to Mr. Samuel Harker's appeal. 94127

Reply to Mr. Thurlow Weed. 23658, 3d note after 97148

Reply to Mr. Urquhart's letters on impressment. 98145

Reply to Mr. Wales's remarks. 25128, 101031

Reply to Mr. Whitefield's remarks on the first edition. 90596, 103594, 3d note after 103650

Reply to Mr. Williams answer. 17045

Reply to Mr. Williams, his examination. 17077

Reply to Nicholas P. Twise. (13277)

Reply to objections of the Secretary of War. 69697

Reply to O'Connell. 12200

Reply to Orson Pratt, by Joseph Smith. 83299

Reply to "Palmetto." 87937

Reply to part of the report of the Diocesan Convention of New Jersey. 5493

Reply to parts of the Bishop's statement. (35842)

Reply to Phocion's letter. (5459), 29963-29965, 47872

Reply to Pickering's letter on the embargo. 69698

Reply to President Lincoln's letter. 69699

Reply to Professor Bledsoe's essay on liberty and slavery. 5894, 79900

Reply to Professor Hodge, on the "State of the country." 28427, (32330)

Reply to Prof. O. A. Brownson's lecture on non-intervention. 90111

Reply to Professor Parker's letters. 2670

Reply to Professor Stuart and President Nott. 93209

Reply to Professor Stuart's letter. 89744

Reply to Prof. Tayler Lewis' review. 515

Reply to Prof. Tyndall's latest attack. 76966

Reply to remarks of Rev. Moses Stuart. 35863

Reply to remarks on a late pamphlet. (34763), 58833-(58834), 99410-99411

Reply to remarks on the fourth volume of the Commentaries. (65513)

Reply to Rev. Francis Brown. 74430

Reply to Rev. Moses Mather's "The visible church." (4486)

Reply to Sedgewick's impartial narrative. 78767

Reply to Senator Phelps' appeal. 61394, 81679

Reply to Senor Saco on annexation. (37766)

Reply to Sir Henry Clinton's narrative. 16814, note before 95301-95301

Reply to six letters of Archdeacon Strachan. 50881, 82650

Reply to Six months in a convent. 68580, 3d note after 98168

Reply to some essays lately published. 71756

Reply to some exceptions against war. 94695

Reply to some of the objections of Mr. Winchester. 30247

Reply to some remarks . . . by Prof. Swallow. (47371)

Reply to some remarks on a letter to a gentleman. 69700, 86603

Reply to strictures on Fessenden's essay. (24216)

Reply to strictures on that system. 8118

[Reply] to "Substance of remarks." 14419

Reply to sundry defamatory letters. 105577

Reply to "T. W. H." in Boston advertiser. 84037

Reply to T. W. P. Taylder's pamphlet. 64949

Reply to that letter [by Clark Brown.] 92785

Reply to that letter [by John Lowell.] 98558

Reply to the above, May 19, 1766. 43638

Reply to the abstract of Unitarian belief. 89002

Reply to the address, by the Hon. George Muter and Benjamin Sebastian. (44778)

Reply to the address of Gen. Peter B. Porter. 4061

Reply to the address of the women of England. 13864

Reply to "The alarming developments." 13255, 33944

Reply to the allegations and complaints. 14800

Reply to "The American war, the whole question explained." (23752)

Reply to the . . . answer of Mr. Cotton. 104331

Reply to the arguments contained in various publications. 44708

Reply to the arguments submitted to the Judiciary Committee. 53189

Reply to the articles of error alleg'd. 7268, 27584, 103399

Reply to the attack of C. J. Ingersoll. 2205

Reply to the attacks in the Boston morning post. (69701), 1st note after 97258

Reply to the author of the letter on South America and Mexico. 69702

Reply to the Bible view of slavery. 20955

Reply to the Board of Managers. 14848

Reply to the Centinel review. 2415

Reply to the charge lately delivered by the Archdeacon of Colchester. (56601)

Reply . . . to the charge of misrepresenting Mr. Buchanan's argument. 18846

Reply to the charges and accusations of the Rt. Rev. Philander Chase. 89024

Reply to the charges brought against it [i. e. the American Colonization Society.] 32351, 93132

Reply to the charges of Daniel Adams. 83958

Reply to the Christian examiner on catholicity and naturalism. (69703)

Reply to the circular of the Committee of the Baptist Missionary Society. 3624

Reply to the Committee of Ohio Democrats. 41153

Reply to the communication signed D. H. Mulvany. 8239, 62120

Reply to the congregational methodistical question. 82494

Reply to the Connecticut gentleman's plea, &c. 102755

Reply to the Correspondent. 94074-94075, 102523

Reply to "The crisis." 60458, 69704

Reply to the criticism of Inchiquin's letter. 59215

Reply to the criticisms of J. N. Barker. 47270

Reply to the criticisms of James D. Dana. 44505

Reply to the declaration of a number of ministers. 17675

Reply to the declaration of the 1200 masons. 69705

Reply to the defence of Major Ripley. 71527

Reply to the defense of the Earl of Shelburne. (80109)

Reply to the defence of the majority. 41679

Reply to the discourse of episcopacy. 69517

Reply to the Earl of Suffolk. 63069

Reply to the Edinburgh review on Clarkson's treatise. 13499

Reply to the Episcopal recorder. 71285

Reply to the essay on silver and paper currencies. 20723, 34810, 4th note after 98549

Reply to . . . the Southern Presbyterian review. 28135

Reply to the speech, &c. 60006

Reply to the speech of Dr. Lushington. (69713)

Reply to the speech of Governor Cosby. 94092

Reply to the speech [of Isaac Norris.] 60645, 93252

Reply to the speech of Mr. Charles Francis Adams, Jr. 89572

Reply . . . to the speech of Senator Douglas. 18837

Reply to the speech of Sir Roundell Palmer. 4626

Reply to the speech of the Hon. J. C. Breckenridge. 11065

Reply to the speech of the Rev. F. L. Hawks. (66973)

Reply to the statement of Hon. Samuel Hooper. 27892

Reply to the "Statement" of the late Bishop of New York. 71138

Reply to the statement of the Rev. Mr. Wiggins. 28394

Reply to the "Statement of the Trustees" of the Dudley Observatory. (28096)

Reply . . . to the strictures of "Another who also knows." 12216

Reply to the "Strictures" of Ebenezer Newcomb. 93080

Reply to the strictures of Lord Mahon and others. 89003-89004, 90291

Reply to the strictures of Mr. J. S. a layman. 93506, 95173

Reply to the strictures on his military character. 65414

Reply to the third address of the Rev. Robert Heys. 94506A

Reply to the "Vindication" of "the land agent." 32779, 43947-(43948)

Reply to the vindication of the representation of the case of the planters of tobacco. 69714, note after 100519

Reply to the vindication of the result of the late Council at Ipswich. 44510

Reply to the Virginian girl's address to her Maryland lover. 88492

Reply to the work of Mr. Chalmers. (81893), note after 102820

Reply to those answers of the gentlemen of the Council. (53693), 98435

Reply to Trumbull on the improvement of Connecticut River. 105712

Reply to two discourses of the Rev. Thomas Smyth. 85330

Reply to two letters of William Roscoe. 98707

Reply to U.S. Senator M. S. Wilkinson's challenge. 66943

Reply to W. Wilberforce. (7823)

Reply to Webster, in a letter from Hon. William Jay. 35867

Reply to Webster, March 3 [1840.] 9936

Reply to Wm. B. Read. (20212), 56319, (68603)

Replys to the letters of George F. Farley. (13256)

Reponse a cette question. 5027

Reponse a des calomnies. 20633

Reponse a deux adresses. 10502

Reponse a deux adresses a l'Honorable Assemblee Legislative. 10502

Reponse a divers ouvrages publies contre le Mormonisme par MM. Guers. 91222

Reponse a Jean Skei Eustace. 49413

Reponse a la brochure de M. Dubouchet. 3245B

Reponse a la brochure de M. Fleuriau. 5652

Reponse a la brochure, intitulee "Le pour et contre." 21034

Reponse a la censure de la Faculte de Theologie. (68075), 68100

Reponse a la declaration du Congres Americain. 15589, 41282

Reponse a la justification de M. La Fayette. 69716

Reponse a la lettre de G.-T. Raynal. (68072)

Reponse a la lettre de M. l'Abbe Raynal. (68072)

Reponse a la lettre d'un colon. 93353

Reponse a la lettre d'un homme de la race Latine. 6130

Reponse a M. de Lally-Tolendal. 40728

Reponse a Mr. Du Ponceau. 95347

Reponse a M. Edmound Blanc. 6905

Reponse a M. Philippart. 19729

Reponse a preface critique du livre intitule: Journal des observations physiques. 25930

Reponse a quelques imputations contre les Etats-Unis. 98294

Reponse a son dernier message. (56054)

Reponse a un des articles des Annales politique de M. Linguet. 9267, note after 41332, 69717

Reponse a un ecrit. 98667

Reponse a un memoire de M. Maury. 1541

Reponse a une adresse pour les noms des personnes nommees. 10575

Reponse a une adresse au subjet d'un entendue de terre. 69718

Reponse a une adresse de l'Assemblee Legislative. 67055

Reponse au champion Americain. 19300

Reponse au contradicteur de la brochure. 69719

Reponse au discours d'un soi-disant bon Hollandois. (56478), 2d note after 93480

Reponse au factum de M. Schoelcher. 4542

Reponse au memoir de l'Abbe Morellet. (52216)

Reponse au memoire concernant la prise & detention des vaisseaux Hollandois. (47510), 69720

Reponse au memoire du Sieur Rossignol Desdunes. 21220

Reponse au memoire publie contre lui. (19762)

Reponse au pamphlet de MM. Lacharriere et Foignet. 5652

Reponse au Patriote Hollandois. 40660

Reponse aux allegations de MM. les Docteurs Hosack et Townsend. 12482

Reponse aux calomnies coloniales de Saint-Domingue. 39286

Reponse aux considerations de M. Moreau, dit Saint-Mery. 67522

Reponse aux inhures de la Minerve. 62609

Reponse avx libelles d'Inivres. 99727

Reponse aux libelles seditieux. 75181

Reponse aux observations d'un habitant. (17167), (28733)

Reponse aux opinions de cet auteur. 38762

Reponse aux principales questions. 6324

Reponse de J.-P. Brissot. 8015

Reponse de l'Amerique Septentrionale. 69721

Reponse de l'Assemble Generale de la Partie Francoise de Saint-Domingue. 7737, 40668

Reponse de l'Assemblee Provinciale du Nord de Saint-Domingue. 7737

Reponse de l'Empereur aux explications demandees par le Roi. (69722)

Reponse de Mathieu, Lord Aylmer. (10535)

Reponse de MM. Bissette et Favien. 5653

Reponse de MM. de Gasparin, Laboulayne, Martin et Cochin. 26734

Reponse de M. Duchilleau. 21063

Reponse de M. Franklin. 5691, 65025, 96091

Reponse de Mr. J. de Pinto. 62988, (62991)

Reponse de Mr. le Ministre [de Relations Exterieures.] 9027

Reponse de M. Libri au rapport de M. Boucly. 40956

Reponse de M. N[ecker] au memoire de M. l'Abbee Morellet. 50595

Reponse de Mylord Suffolk. 93427

Reponse de Pinchinat. 62892

Reponse des citoyens Commissaires de Saint-Domingue. (40676)

Reponse des colons de Saint-Domingue. 99242

Reponse des condamnes de la Martinique. 5656

Reponse des Deputes des Manufactures & du Commerce du France aux motions de MM. de Cocherel et de Reynaud. Appercu sur la constitution. 14052

Reponse des Deputes des Manufactures et du Commerce de France, aux motions de MM. de Cocherel et de Reynaud, Deputes de l'isle de St. Domingue. 14059

Reponse d'Etienne Laveaux. 39289

Reponse du General Rochambeau. 99746

Reponse du Sieur Breard. 7650

Reponse en parallele a l'Abbe Raynal. (68072)

Reponse par des pieces justificatives. 38698, 42753, note after 93793

Reponse, point de grace a Monsieur de la Fayette. 69715

Reponse provisoire aux brillans extraits du Memoire justificatif. 42752

Reponse succinte des Deputes de St. Domingue. 75190

Reponses a ces doutes. 15915

Reponses academiques. 8747, 1st note after 96990

Report . . . accompanied with a statement of certain banks. 59905

Report, address and proceedings of the Pittsburgh Sanitary Committee. 63141

Report addressed by the Royal Society of Northern Antiquaires. 85828

Report, addressed to the American Unitarian Association. 97393

Report, adopted at the spring meeting of the South Middlesex Conference of Churches. 63765, note after 88147

Report adopted by the San Francisco Chamber of Commerce. 76040

Report adopted in the Convention of the trade. 9306

Report against the prohibitive liquor law of Massachusetts. 64269, 89627

Report also of the Trustees, and several interesting things. 89802

Report . . . amendments to act of 1852. 45979

Report, analysis, and medical properties. 82992

Report, and accompanying documents. 42970

Report and accompanying documents of the Minnesota State Railroad Bond Commission. 49291

Report and accompanying documents on the petition. 6604

Report and address, delivered by the President, to the Medical Society. 54376

[Report and address of] a Committee of the Bunker Hill Monument Association. (9174)

Report and bill concerning licenced houses. 40964

Report and bill on the petition of the Seekonk Branch Railroad Company. 78854

Report and bills relating to the abolition of capital punishment. 67908

Report and catalogue of the Reading Hall and Circulating Library. (70490)

Report and charts of the cruise of the U. S. Brig Dolphin. 39800

Report and circular of the New Orleans School of Medicine. (53358)

Report and collections of the Wisconsin Historical Society. 83026, 83029, 85428, 85433, 92227, 3d note after 94249

Report and constitution of the Providence Infant School Society. (66329)

Report and constitution or plan of organization of the Democratic Party. 69723

Report and correspondence of the Commissioners for Promoting the Internal Improvement of the State. 60459

Report and despatches (British North America) 31141

Report and despatches of the Earl of Durham. (38748)

Report and documents of the Committee Appointed to Inquire into the Conduct of the Cashier and Directors of the Bank [of Pennsylvania.] 59910

Report and documents of the Union Defence Committee. (54658)

Report and documents relating to the loan. 74271

Report and documents relating to the public schools of Rhode Island. 70636, 70723

Report and documents, relative to the fine imposed. 35388

Report and documents submitted by the committee appointed to confer. 2992

Report and estimate for avoiding the inclined plane. note just before 60250

Report and explanation of a survey. 59060

Report and extracts relating to colored schools. 14751

Report and journal of proceedings of the Joint Commissioners. 45090

Report and . . . memorial. 36623

Report and memorial . . . . Made . . . to the Legislature. 60750

Report & memorial of county superintendents of the poor. (53935)

Report and memorial . . . [of the Union Canal Company of Pennsylvania.] 60750, note after 97766

Report and minutes of the . . . Teachers' Association of Ontario. 57366

Report and observations, on the banks. 69724

Report and ordinance submitted by the Committee on Ways and Means. 45396

Report and plan for a wire suspension bridge. 22209

Report and plan of sewerage for the city. 12512, 12653

Report . . . and plans of supplying the city with water. 62370

Report and proceedings at a town meeting. 6552

Report and proceedings in relation to the Baltimore and Susquehannah Railroad. 2994

Report and proceedings of the Auxiliary Foreign Missionary Society. 105336

Report and proceedings of the first annual meeting of the Providence Anti-slavery Society. 66302

Report and proceedings of the second annual meeting of the [Young Men's Education Society.] 106173

Report from the United States of America. 34935

Report G. of the annual report of the [Canadian Geological] Survey. 84802

Report given by G. A. Mix. 21042

Report giving the name of all stock corporations. 53618

Report; a half year, ending January 31, 1865. 28478

Report, historical and statistical, of Fidelity Division, No. 2, S. of T. 87056

Report, House of Representatives, relating to the . . . use of spirituous liquors. 45979

Report in Chancery. George Codwise Jr. and others vs. Comfort Sands. 96853

Report, in Congress, on the memorial of the General Assembly of Illinois. (34203)

Report in favor of engraving the map and printing the memoir. 83534

Report in favor of lithographing the map. 83534

Report in favor of the abolition of capital punishment. 69734

Report, in part, of the committee to whom was referred . . . the memorial. 69735

Report, in part, of Samuel L. Mitchill. 49748

Report (in part) of the Committee appointed on so much of the message of the President as relates to the military establishment. 69737

Report in relation to a geological survey of the state of New York. 20341

Report . . . in relation to an Asylum for the Insane Poor. 60332

Report in relation to difficulties between the Eastern and Western Cherokees. 4459

Report in relation to district officers and district police. 87392

Report . . . in relation to light houses. 13826

Report . . . in relation to passage of certain railroad bills. 53928

Report . . . in relation to protections to American seamen. 43441

Report in relation to the Antietam National Cemetery. (60461)

Report . . . in relation to the circulation of paper currency. 59905

Report . . . in relation to the Delaware Rail Road. 61970

Report in relation to the International Agricultural Exhibition. 73973

Report . . . in relation to the northeastern boundary. 43941

Report . . . in relation to the purchase and publication of the Madison papers. 43717

Report . . . in relation to the railroad bridge over the Mississippi River. 36072

Report . . . in relation to the revenue, debt, & financial policy. 99278

Report . . . in relation to the road through Ohio. 71713

Report in relation to the working of copper ores. (33581)

Report . . . in reply to certain charges. 34207

Report in the case of Henry O'Neal. 57329

Report in the Common Council, on the "Act for suppressing immorality." 54621

Report in the Legislature on imprisonment for debt. 45980

Report in the Senate, of the Committee appointed to . . . report. 53891

Report, in the Senate of the United States, by Mr. Sanford. 76500

Report, in the Senate of the United States, by Mr. Sanford, on commerce and manufactures. 76499

Report . . . including the catalogue for the academic year. 34517

Report intended to illustrate a map of the hydrographical basin. (55257)

Report . . . January, 1862 [of the Maryland State Agricultural Chemist.] 45158

Report . . . January 10, 1860 [of the Iowa Institution for the Education of the Blind.] 34996

Report laid before Congress, by Judge Bland. 5865

Report, . . . Lieutenant Michler's report. (48806)

Report made at an adjourned meeting. 105418

Report made by a committee of the citizens of Port Deposite. 93925

Report, made by a committee of the General Assembly in South Carolina. 56845-56846, 87853, 2d note after 87848

Report, made by a committee of the House of Representatives of Pennsylvania. 60095

Report made by a committee specially appointed. (81979)

Report made by Leverett Salstonstall [sic]. 98556

Report, made by Mr. Wheeler. 103196

Report made by order of the Common Council of the city of Brooklyn. 8291, 94072

Report made by the Board of Trade against the Grenada laws. 28760

Report made by William Rawle. 101686

Report made by William Strickland. 92811, 94407

Report made in 1828, by the Canada Committee of the House of Commons. 10600, 95373

Report made in 1823, to the War Department of the United States. 96319

Report . . . made . . . the 17th of February, 1870. 42815

Report made to a meeting of the citizens of Hamilton and Rossville. 69738

Report made to the Academy of Sciences. 1865

Report made to the American Geographical and Statistical Society. 24346

Report made to the American Medical Association. 64157

Report made to the Beet Sugar Society of Philadelphia. 59509

Report made to the Board of Council. 64428

Report made to the Boston Prison Discipline Society. 33330

Report made to the Chamber of Deputies on the abolition of slavery. 96072

Report made to . . . the city of Brooklyn, April 14th, 1852. 42933

Report made to the Conference of the Evangelical Alliance. (2796)

Report made to the Crown Lands Department. 75844

Report made to the Directing Senate. 90063

Report made to the Executive Committee of the Salem Providence Association. 75732

Report made to the General Assembly of New Jersey, Aug. 20, 1855. 53053

Report made to the General Assembly of . . . Rhode Island, at their January session, 1861. 15434, 59404

Report made to the General Assembly of the state of Louisiana. 41614

Report made to the High Street Congregational Sabbath School. 66268

Report made to the Historical & Literary Committee of the American Philosophical Society. 21383

Report made to the Hon. John Forsyth. 13439

Report made to the House of Representatives. (8973)

Report made to the House of Representatives of . . . Massachusetts. 45981

Report made to the Legislature of New Hampshire. 52899

Report made to . . . the Lieutenant-Governor of . . . New Brunswick. (52533)

Report made to the Maryland and New York Coal and Iron Company. 81034

Report made to the Maryland Mining Company. 81033

Report made to the Platte County Self-Defence Association. 92866

Report, made to the Senate of New York. 21107, 99821

Report made to the Senate relative to the enlistment of boys. 70637

Report . . . made to the Watering Committee. 22209

Report made to the Yearly Meeting of Friends. 53662

Report made under authority of the Legislature of Vermont. 44737

Report . . . March 5th, 1866. 45217

Report . . . March 19, 1831. 54793

Report, March 29, 1858. 86974

Report . . . March 21, 1862. 38061

Report . . . May, 1866. 76690

Report . . . May 1820. (37820)

Report . . . May 10, 1853. 58084

Report (Mr. John Cotton Smith) from the Committee of Claims. 82939

Report. Mr. Lacock . . . reported. 38471, note before 92843

Report. New-York Branch Freedman's Union Commission. 53803

Report . . . November 1855. 54392

Report . . . November 7, 1867, to consider the subject of obstructions. (53592)

Report no. 1, of the Civil and Military Engineer. 87393

Report, no. 31. (27705)

Report, October, 1852. 64357

Report . . . Oct. 1, 1863. 38061

Report of a bill to prevent officers of the Army and Navy. 69739

Report of a Board of Army Officers upon the claim of Maj. Gen. William Farrar Smith, U. S. V. 84771-84772

Report of a Board of Army Officers upon the claim of Maj. Gen. William Farrar Smith, U. S. V., Major, U. S. Army (Retired.) 84774

Report of a boarding school. 28628

Report of A. C. Buchanan. 8840

Report of a case argued and determined. 102624

Report of a case before William N. Green. 96936

Report of a case, decided on Saturday, the 16th of November, 1793. 36994, 94411, note after 96882, 3d note after 96891

Report of a case tried in the Court of King's Bench. 84409

Report of a cause, John Jessup vs. John Ifirth. (36077)

Report of a commission appointed for the revision of the revenue system of the United States. 70173-(70174)

Report of a commission of inquiry appointed by the U. S. Sanitary Commission. 34341, 76651

[Report of a committee and opinion of Hon. Richard Fletcher.] 75648

Report of a committee, and resolutions of the Legislature of Georgia. 64808

Report of a committee, and resolutions of the Legislature of the state of Georgia. 34655

Report of a committee appointed April 29, [1829.] 85929

Report of a committee appointed at a meeting held . . . December 3d, 1852. (62122)

Report of a committee, appointed August 4, 1834. 10135

Report of a committee, appointed by a Convention of Republican Citizens of the County of Addison. 99174

Report of a committee appointed by the Common Council of . . . New York. 54622

Report of a committee appointed by the Guardians for the Relief . . . of the Poor. 61503

Report of a committee appointed by the House of Assembly of Quebec. 10411

Report of a committee appointed by the . . . [Massachusetts Historical] Society. (45858)

Report of a committee appointed by the Pennsylvania Society for Discouraging the Use of Ardent Spirits. (60363)

Report of a Committee appointed by the Society for the Prevention of Pauperism. 85957

Report of a committee appointed by the Society . . . on . . . erecting an institution for the reformation of juvenile delinquents. 54670

Report of a committee appointed by the Synod of the Presbyterian Church of Nova-Scotia. (65212)

Report of a committee appointed by the Trustees of the town of Milwaukee. 69740

Report of a committee appointed Dec. 23, 1844. 90818

Report of a committee appointed for the purpose of ascertaining the most eligible route. 22762

Report of a committee appointed Jan. 4, 1855. (54755)

Report of a committee, appointed to explore the western waters of the state of New-York. (22754), 69741, 102983

Report of a committee appointed to inquire into the state of Columbia College. 14842

Report of a committee appointed to investigate the evils of lotteries. 60462, 62123

Report of a committee appointed . . . to investigate the ministerial fund of Lexington. 40890

Report . . . of a committee . . . appointed to prepare the draught of a plan. 65213

Report of a committee . . . appointed to visit the Farmers' High School. 60376

Report of a committee at a meeting of the citizens of Providence. 66345

Report of a committee concerning the requirements for admission to the University. (30759A)

Report of a committee from "St. George's Church in the city of New York." (75211)

Report of a committee in favor of incorporating Amherst College. (1231), note after 93362

Report of a committee in the House of Representatives. (82047)

Report of a committee of citizens of Dedham. 19220

Report [of a committee of citizens of Schenectady] on the present alarming state of our national affairs. 77598

REPORT

Report of a committee of Congress containing the evidence. 6001
Report of a committee of Directors of the Bank of the United States. 3189
Report of a committee of investigation [of the Philadelphia and Reading Railroad Company.] 61948
Report of a committee of stockholders of the Boston and Portland Railroad. 6768
Report of a committee of stockholders of the Columbia Bridge Company. 14848
Report of a committee of the Abolition Society of Delaware. 58482
Report of a committee of the African Institution. (68265)
Report of a committee of the American Convention. 82048
Report of a committee of the Associate Medical Members of the Sanitary Commission. 84268
Report of a committee of the Baltimore Young Men's Society. 3064
Report of a committee of the Bank [of Pennsylvania.] 59910
Report of a committee of the Board of Directors of the African Institution. 70222
Report of a committee of the Board of Directors of the Planters' and Mechanics' Bank of South Carolina. 87913
Report of a committee of the Board of Overseers respecting the state of the university. 30758
Report of a committee of the Board of Supervisors of the County of Kings. 8316
Report of a committee of the Board of Trustees, presented Sept. 27, 1860. 37589
Report of a committee of the Board of Washington College. 102007
Report of a committee of the Boston Board of Trade upon the cotton tax. 6584, 17129
Report of a committee of the citizens of Boston and vicinity, opposed to a further increase of duties on importations. 23363, 27637, (39756), 1st note after 69741, 70258
Report of a committee of the Centre School District in Worcester. 105341
Report of a committee of . . . the Church connected with the Owego Congregational Society. 58005
Report of a committee of the Church in the North Parish in Wrentham. 105523
Report of a committee of the City Council. 66346
Report of a committee of the Connecticut Medical Society. 15783
Report of a committee of the Council of Barbadoes. 3283
Report of a committee of the Council on promoting the means of education. 10430
Report of a committee of the Council on the subject of promoting the means of education. 67056
Report of a committee [of the Danville and Pottsville Rail Road Company.] 59967
Report of a committee of the Delaware County Institute of Science. 19420
Report of a committee of the Directors [of the Middlesex Canal.] (48841)
Report of a committee of the Directors [of the Middlesex Canal] . . . 1811. (48841)
Report of a committee of the Directors, September, 1842. 24599
Report of a committee of the East Cambridge Union Temperance Society. 10153

Report of a committee of the First Church in Braintree. (67191)
Report of a committee of the First Ecclesiastical Society of New Haven. 53007
Report of a committee of the General Assembly, appointed for revising the form of government. 65215
Report of a committee of the General Assembly of the Presbyterian Church. 65214
Report of a committee of the Governors of the New York Hospital. 86157
Report of a committee of the High School Society. 54312
Report of a committee of the Home League. 32710
Report of a committee of the . . . House of Assembly of Jamaica. (35656)
Report of a committee of the House of Commons on the extinction of slavery. 81848
Report of a committee of the House of Representatives, appointed to "examine and report, whether monies drawn from the treasury." 104982
Report of a committee of the House of Representatives, appointed upon the application of James Clarke. (60307)
Report of a committee of the House of Representatives of the United States. 17458
Report of a committee of the House of Representatives, transmitting a report. 48780
Report of a committee of the Humane Society, appointed to inquire into the number of tavern licences. 35854, (69742)
Report of a committee of the Humane Society of New York, appointed to inquire into the number of tavern licences. 53696
Report of a committee of the inhabitants of Boston. 69743
Report of a committee of the Linnaean Society of New England. 41351
Report of a committee of the Massachusetts Legislature. 45983
Report of a committee of the . . . Massachusetts Medical Society. 45861
Report of a committee of the . . . [Massachusetts] Society [for the Suppression of Intemperance.] (45898)
Report of a committee of the Medical Society of South-Carolina. 87888
Report of a committee of the Medical Society . . . on . . . medical education. 53765
Report of a committee of the New England Annual Conference. 2484
Report of a committee of the . . . [New England Historic-Genealogical] Society. 52688
Report of a committee . . . [of the New York Chamber of Commerce.] (53591)
Report of a committee of the Overseers, and a memorial. (30759A)
Report of a committee of the Overseers of Harvard College. (30759A)
Report of a committee of the Overseers of Harvard College, . . . May 4th, 1824. (37057), 2d note after 69405
Report of a committee of the Overseers . . . on the memorial. (30759A)
Report of a committee of the Peace Convention. 45984, 69933
Report of a committee of the Pennsylvania Society for Promoting the Abolition of Slavery. 60397
Report of a committee of the Pennsylvania Society for Promoting the Abolition of Slavery, &c. 62072
Report of a committee of the pewholders of the Independent Presbyterian Church. 77260

[Report of a meeting of the Associate Members.] 76668

Report of a meeting of the Massachusetts Soldiers' Relief Association. 45899

Report of . . . a meeting [of the Pennsylvania Freedmen's Relief Association.] (60324)

Report of a military reconnaissance. 69946

Report of a missionary tour. 49122

Report of a plan for extending & more perfectly establishing. (54375)

Report of a preliminary scheme of improvements. 90789

Report of a preliminary survey of the camps. 76539, 76549, 76647

Report of a public meeting held at Finsbury Chapel. 20716

Report of a public meeting held at the Kingston Conference. 74580

Report of a public meeting of the colored citizens of Oberlin, Lorain Co., O. (56418)

Report of a railway suspension bridge. 22209

Report of a reconnaissance and survey in California. 69900, 69946

Report of a reconnaissance made in April, 1865. 59964

Report of a reconnaissance made in April, 1865, of the coal property. 40186

Report of a reconnaissance of a route for a road. 84774

Report of a reconnaissance of the Missouri River. 71925

Report of a reconnaissance of the Sacramento Mountains. 36377, 84774

Report . . . of a route for a railroad. 29801

Report of a search made in England. 82407

Report of a select committee of the House of Assembly. 10580

Report of a select committee of the House of Commons, on the state of the West India colonies. 17617, 70259, 102841, 3d note after 102863

Report of a select committee of the House of Representatives. 51032

Report of a select committee . . . [of the New York Chamber of Commerce.] (53592)

Report of a select committee of the Senate . . . [of Pennsylvania.] 60464

Report of a select committee of the Trustees of Union College. 97785

Report of a select committee on a geological and agricultural survey. 85144

Report of a select committee on a ship canal. 55131

Report of a special committee. 61650

Report of a special committee of the Boston Board of Trade. (6582)

Report of a special committee of the Common Council. (54729), 105560

Report of a special committee of the Grammar School Board. 6760

Report of a special committee of the House of Assembly. 10431

Report of a special committee . . . [of the New York Chamber of Commerce.] (53592)

Report of a special committee of the Senate, of South-Carolina. 87529

Report of a special committee of the U. S. Naval Lyceum. 52079, 97982

Report of a special committee . . . on national finances and taxation. 61970

Report of a special committee on schools. (20628)

Report of a special committee . . . on the decline of American commerce. (53592)

Report of a special committee . . . on the present quarantine laws. (53885)

Report of a special committee to the Commissioners of the Girard Estate. (27494)

Report of a speech on the increase of bank capital. (9614)

Report of a sub-committee to the general committees on Indian Concerns. 69746

Report of a survey for a rail road from the city of Boston. (31064)

Report of a survey for canals between St. Peter's Bay. 23665, note after 69942

Report of a survey of a route for the Genesee Valley Canal. 36623

Report of a survey . . . of coal and ore lands. 36334

Report of a survey of the public schools of Leavenworth. 84522

Report of a survey of the Tonewanda Canal route. 103310A

Report of a trial in the Superior Court of the State of New-York. 96908

Report of a trial in the Supreme . . . [Judicial] Court, . . . at Boston. (42801), 102321, 1st note after 103741

Report of a trial: Miles Farmer, versus Dr. David Humphreys Storer. 23841, 92191

Report of a visit to Canada and Nova Scotia. 9408

Report of a visit to some of the tribes of Indians. 38868, 3d note after 94534

Report of a visit to Spotted Tail's tribe of Brule-Sioux Indians. 69747

Report . . . of a visit to the locations. 55733

Report of a visit to the Luray Cavern. 85053

Report of A. W. Craven. 17428

Report of a western tour. 16291

Report of Adj. Gen. Fuller. 34306

Report of Admiral R. Fitzroy. 89971

Report of affair at Port Royal Ferry. 59617

Report of Albert Gallatin on roads and canals. 106114

Report of Albert Pike. 15292

Report of Alexander H. Arthur. 2128

Report of Alexander Hamilton. 97751

Report of Alexander Vattemare. 53616

Report of Alfred Kelly. 37303

Report of all such English statutes as existed. 45320

Report of Allen Campbell. 22763

Report of Amos B. Corwin. (16986), 58408

Report of an action of assault, battery and wounding. 25124, 96305

Report of an address delivered . . . Feb. 7th, 1870. (56925)

Report of an anti-slavery meeting . . . in . . . Leeds. 29236, (39828)

Report of an educational tour in Germany. 44324

Report of . . . an examination in . . . 1846. 33368

Report of an examination of the Bristol Copper Mine. 81055

Report of an examination of the Ohio Diamond Coal Co. (81056)

Report of an expedition down the Zuni and Colorado Rivers. 35765, 81472-81473, 105714

Report of an expedition into the interior of British Guayana. 77793

Report of an expedition to the territory of Minnesota. (64117)

Report of an experimental survey of the Mississippi and Atlantic Railroad. 49521

Report of an exploration and survey of the territory. (32598)

Report of commissioners appointed under a resolve of the Legislature of Massachusetts. 45988

Report of commissioners appointed under resolve of 1856. 24448

Report of commissioners concerning an agricultural school. 45989

Report of commissioners, &c. Executive Department, February 7, 1835. 53211

Report of commissioners for a settling cartel for the exchange of prisoners. 18775

Report of Commissioners for 1864-5 [of the Kentucky Institution for Feeble-Minded Children.] 37506

Report of Commissioners for 1869-70 [of the Illinois Southern Insane Asylum.] 34258

Report of commissioners for settling a cartel for the exchange of prisoners. 69750

Report of . . . Commissioners of the Pine Grove Cemetery. 42845

Report of Commissioners on the Culture of the Grape-Vine. 30282

Report of commissioners on the revision and consolidation of the statute laws. 87400

Report of commissioners relative to encroachments and preservation of the harbor of New-York. 54624

Report of commissioners relative to the eastern boundary of . . . New York. (53774)

Report of committee and proposed law. 54903

Report of committee appointed by the Legislative Council. 10454

Report of committee appointed by the New-York Board of Underwriters. 54750

Report of committee appointed to examine the new Saint Louis jail. 75373

Report of committee appointed to inquire how much of the legislation of Congress is abrogated by the secession of the state. 87486

Report of . . . committee appointed to visit the charitable institutions. 53927

Report of committee in relation to the official conduct of the harbor masters. 54307

Report of committee, January, 1848. 30597

Report of committee of Senate of South-Carolina. 28861

Report of committee of South Carolina Legislature. 87487

Report of committee of the Assembly on the slave trade. 35658

Report of committee of the House of Correction and Employment. 61727

Report of . . . committee of the Senate. (53929)

Report of . . . committee of the Senate on the electoral law. 53933

Report of committee [of the Southern Railroad Company.] 88456

Report of committee of the Vestry of Christ Protestant Episcopal Church. 54180

Report of Committee of Ways and Means. 48781

Report of Committee on Canals. 53566

Report of Committee on Claims. 15376

Report of Committee on Commerce and Navigation. 54625

Report of committee . . . on correspondence of Madison and Monroe. (43721)

Report of committee on courses of study and faculty. (34236)

Report of Committee on Deceased Soldiers' Claims. 15377

Report of Committee on Fairmount Park Contribution. 61650

Report of Committee on Foreign Relations. 45449

Report of Committee on Housatanic Railroad Company. 15800

Report of Committee on Indian Affairs, May 20, 1834. 34671

Report of Committee on Indian Affairs, on petitions. 53893

Report of committee on joint resolutions to Congress. 10009

Report of Committee on Military Surgery. 54423

Report of committee on petition of Tufts College. 45990

Report of Committee on Police. (62126)

Report of Committee on Public Court. 73673

Report of Committee on Public Highways. 62127

Report of Committee on the First Church of the Pilgrims. 23016

Report of committee on the petition of the President and Fellows. (30759A), (45991)

Report of Committee on the Supply of Water. 66347

Report of Committee on Transportation and Intercommunication. 90790

Report of Committee . . . to Inspect the Books of the Bank. 3189

Report of Committee to Recruit the Ninth Army Corps. (69751)

Report of committee to the stockholders of the Saco Water Power Company. 74779

Report of . . . committee to which was referred . . . the Governor's message. 53932

Report of committee to which was referred the subject of a fresh water basin in the harbor of Portland. 64371

Report of Commutation Commission. 70639

Report of contested elections, in the House of Representatives. 45992

Report of Convention, 1852 [of the Unitarian Church Association of Maine.] 44050

Report of crown law cases. 103185

Report of D. Ridgely, State Librarian. 45370

Report of D. Ridgely to the Executive of Maryland. 71283

Report of Davis S. Bates. 96352

Report of deaths in the city and county of New-York. 54086

Report of decisions of the Commission of Claims. 69752

Report of Delegates from the General Aid Society for the Army. (33100)

Report of Directors of Housatonic Rail Road Company. 33174

Report of Directors of the Boston and Worcester Rail Road Corporation. 6768

Report of Directors of the Experimental School. 34238

Report of Directors [of the Harewood Iron and Mining Company.] 30370

Report of Directors [of the Insane Asylum of North-Carolina.] 55625

Report of Dr. Benjamin Franklin, and other commissioners. 25579

Report of Dr. J. S. Newberry. 76623

Report of Dr. John A. Veatch. 98731

Report of Dr. Peters . . . on the longitude and latitude of Ogdensburgh. 56832, 61189

Report of Dr. Peters, . . . on the longitude of Elmira. 61189

Report of Dr. Rae on the Arctic Searching Expedition. 67427, (67429)

Report of Dr. T. Sterry Hunt. 33893

Report of Drs. W. H. Coggeswell and W. M. White. 15787

Report of E. Everett. 23271

Report of E. F. Johnson. 54723

Report of E. L. Pierce. 62711

Report of E. L. Viele. 54655

Report of E. S. Philbrick. 62435

Report of Ed. B. Dalton. 18349

Report of education in Europe. (2588)

Report of Edward C. Anderson. 77261

Report of Edward Hoogland. (37081)

Report of Edward Miller, civil engineer. 78086

Report of Edward Miller, Engineer in Chief. 93731

Report of Elder Orson Spencer. 89373

Report of engagements at Knoxville. 15330

Report of evacuation of Little Rock. 15330

Report of evidence taken before a Joint Special Committee. 15370

Report of examinations and surveys of a route for a rail-road. (62617)

Report of examinations made in 1856-7. 12653

Report of expedition to Beverly. 15330

Report of . . . expenditures of the town of Hyde Park. 34128

Report . . . of expense of maintaining the West Boston and Canal Bridges. 51615

Report of experiments and observations on the Concord and Sudbury Rivers. 15150

Report of experiments to navigate the Chesapeake and Delaware Canal. (2588)

Report of experiments with American Guano. 69753

Report of exploration . . . from San Francisco Bay to Los Angelos [sic]. 69946

Report of exploration . . . near the 38th and 39th parallels. 69900, 69946

Report of exploration . . . near the thirty-second parallel. 69900, 69946

Report of exploration of a route for the Pacific Railroad. 4258

Report of exploration of a route for the Pacific Railroad, near the thirty-second parallel. 64115

Report of explorations across the great basin. 81355

Report of explorations and surveys. 80759

Report of explorations . . . by Capt. J. W. Gunnison. 69900, 69946

Report of explorations for a route for the Pacific Railroad. 69900, 69946

Report of explorations for that portion of a railway route. 58641

Report of explorations in California for rail-road routes. 69900, 69946

Report of explorations in 1873. 64754

Report of explorations . . . near the forty-seventh and forty-ninth parallels. 69900, 69946

Report of explorations . . . near the thirty-fifth parallel. 69900, 69946

Report of explorations . . . near the thirty-fifth parallel. 69946

Report of explorations. . . . near the thirty-second degree of north latitude. 69900, 69946

Report of explorations . . . near the thirty-second parallel. 69900, 69946

Report of explorations of a route for the Pacific Railroad. 4258

Report of explorations . . . on the line of the forty-first parallel. 69900, 69946

Report of explorations . . . on the line of the fifty-first parallel. 69900, 69946

Report of F. W. Landry of a survey. 69900

Report of Finance Committee of the House of Representatives. 70640

Report of . . . firewood, anthracite, Virginia and charcoal. (54278)

Report of Forest Shepherd, Esq. (80277)

Report of Forest Shepherd, Esq., on the mineral lands. 80278

Report . . . [of Franklin B. Hough.] 33154

Report of free white schools at Richmond. (71209)

Report of Freedman schools in the Department of Tennessee and Arkansas. 21728

Report of Fund Commissioner. (34524)

Report of G. M. Dodge, Chief Engineer. (20496)

Report [of General Carrington.] 16129

Report of General G. T. Beauregard of the defence of Charleston. 4199, 15363

Report of General Joseph E. Johnston. 15366, (36376)

Report of Gen. Raynolds. 70427

Report of General Robert E. Lee, and subordinate reports. 15364

Report of General Robert E. Lee, of operations at Rappahannock Bridge. 15365

Report of George C. Williams, W. A. Sanborn, and John M. Whipple. 52901, 52950

Report of Geo. H. Cook, State Geologist. 53120

Report of George H. Cook upon the geological survey of New Jersey. 53119

Report of George H. Cook upon the geology and agricultural resources. 53118

Report of George L. Schuyler. 78054

Report of George Turner, Amherst Everett and J. Russell Bullock. 70641

Report of George W. Miller. 53993

Report of Gershom Powers. (53976)

Report of gold and silver coins. 14236

Report of H. Allen. 87962

Report of H. Franklin. (53894)

Report of H. H. Eames. 49247

Report of H. Haupt. 60358

Report of H. W. Halleck, General in Chief. 29883

Report of H. W. Halleck, . . . on the treatment of Kansas troops. 29882

Report of Hanchett and Clark. 49247

Report of Hartman Bache. note after 60249, note after 104493

Repotr of Henry M. Naglee. (51719)

Report of Henry O. Kent. 37471, (52943)

Report of . . . [his, i. e. Henry Naglee's] command. 51720

Report of His Excellency Ambrose E. Burnside. 70642

Report of His Honor the Mayor of Boston. (11925), 67907

Report of His Majesty's Commissioners for Inquiring into the Administration and Operation of the Poor Laws. 23527

Report of His Majesty's Most Honorable Privy Council. 73459

Report of his [i. e. Captain Cook's] march from Santa Fe to San Domingo. 58

Report of his operations on the Peninsula. 43850

Report of his survey for an interoceanic ship canal. (48806)

Report of his survey of a road. 41375

Report of his tour in the western states. 35497

Report of Hon. C. J. Faulkner. (23926)

Report of Hon. David L. Swain. 55676

Report of Hon. G. R. Mitchell. 58082

Report of . . . Hon. Horace Mann. 44324

Report of Hon. Horace Maynard. (47190)

Report of Hon. Ichabod Goodwin. 52902

Report of Hon. Israel T. Harch. 30834

Report of Hon. James Meacham. 85054

Report of the Adjutant-General of . . . Oregon. 57569

Report of the Adjutant-General of Pennsylvania. 59865

Report of the Adjutant-General of . . . Rhode Island. 70541

Report of the Adjutant General of the Massachusetts Militia. 45620

Report of the Adjutant-General [of the Republic of Texas.] 94960

Report of the Adjutant-General of the state of California. 10033-10034

Report of the Adjutant General of the state of Connecticut. 15784

Report of the Adjutant General of the state of Illinois. 34299-34300

Report of the Adjutant General of the state of Iowa. (35025)

Report of the Adjutant General of the state of Kentucky. 37552-37553

Report of the Adjutant General of the state of Maine. 43998

Report of the Adjutant-General of the state of New Hampshire. 52903, 64621

Report of the Administration Committee of the U. S. Naval Lyceum. 97981

Report of the Administrators of the University of Louisiana. 42310

Report of the affairs and condition of the Branch of the Bank of the State of Alabama at Mobile. (26335)

Report of the affairs of the New-Hampshire Iron Factory Co. (52873)

Report of the African Institution. 95657

Report of the Agent of the city. (64362)

Report of the Agent of the Clinton State Prison. 53603

Report of the Agent of the Colonization Society. 34501

Report of the Agent of the Martha's Vineyard Camp Meeting. (14188)

Report of the Agent of the Middlesex Canal. (48831)

Report of the Agent of the New State Prison. 53897

Report of the Agent of the State of New York. 8176, 53669

Report of the Agent to the Trustees of the Cambridge Humane Society. 10152

Report of the Agricultural Meeting, held in Boston. 14535, 69758, 102319

Report of the Agricultural Society of . . . New Jersey. 53062

Report [of the Alleghany Railroad and Coal Company.] 779

Report of the . . . Allegheny Cemetery. (63107)

Report of the Allotment Commissioners. 34564

Report of the Alms House Commissioner. 54073

Report of the American Abolition Society. 82103

Report of the American Academy of Music. 61458

Report of the American and Foreign Anti-slavery Society. 81820

Report of the American Anti-slavery Society. 81856

Report of the American Anti-slavery Society, with the speeches delivered. (68652), 81823

Report of the American Board of Commissioners for Foreign Missions. 90107

Report of the American Colonization Society. 81831

Report [of the American Education Society.] 21880

Report of the American Emigrants' Friend Society. 61459

Report of the . . . American Female Education Society. (61460)

Report of the American Female Guardian Society. 54076

Report of the American Freedmen's Inquiry Commission. (58023)

Report of the American Historical Association. 85455, 87328, note before 95044, 95075, 98409, 98425, 103113

Report of the American Historical Society. 84791, note before 87347

Report [of the American Scenic and Historic Preservation Society.] 99281

Report of the American Society for Colonizing the Free People of Colour in the United States. 81842

Report [of the American Society for Educating Pious Youth for the Ministry.] 12680

Report of the American Society for Meliorating the Condition of the News. 89744

Report of the American Society for Promoting the Civilization and General Improvement of the Indian Tribes of the United States. 34606

Report of the annual dinner of the New England Society. (52746)

Report of the annual exhibition, 1850 [of the Illinois State Agricultural Society.] 34198

Report [of the Antioch Baptist Church, New York.] 54087

Report of the Apalachicola Land Company. 1727

Report, . . . of the Apprentices Library Company. 61475

Report of the appropriations and expenditures of the government. 95052

Report of the architect [of the Athenaeum, Philadelphia.] 61496

Report of the Argilite and Greenup Coal and Iron Company. (1960)

Report of the arguments and judgment in Herrick v. the Grand Trunk Railway Company of Canada. 85421

Report of the arguments in the case of the United States vs. Heth. 31619

Report of the arguments of counsel, and of the opinion of the court. 2490

Report of the arguments of counsel, and opinions of the Court of Appeals. 87449

Report of the arguments of counsel, in the case of Prudence Crandall. (17391), 2d note after 96854

Report of the arguments of the Attorney of the Commonwealth. 38091

Report of the arguments on the application of the Attorney-General. 34419

Report of the Army Committee of the Boston Young Men's Christian Association. 6787

Report of the Army Committee of the United States Christian Commission. 63144

Report of the assays and experiments made on the gold. (69759)

Report of the Assistant Postmaster General on unproductive post roads. 64482

Report of the Assistant Secretary of State [of Minnesota.] 49310

Report of the Associated Banks of Massachusetts. 45642

Report of the Associated Executive Committee of Friends on Indian Affairs. 34608

Report of the Association for the Benefit of Colored Orphans. 54100

Report of the Board of Foreign Missions of the Reformed Church in America. 68778

Report of the Board of Health, . . . of Louisiana. 42196

Report of the Board of Health of Lynn. 42831

Report of the Board of Health [of Massachusetts.] 45650

Report of the Board of Health of . . . New Orleans. 53308

Report of the Board of Health of Philadelphia. 61504

Report of the Board of Health, of the births, marriages and deaths, in the city of Richmond. (71165)

Report of the Board of Health of the city of Saint Louis. 75336

Report of the Board of Health of the Health Department [of New York.] 54124

Report of the Board of Health of the town of Gloucester. (27596)

Report of the Board of Health, on cholera, as it appeared in Rochester. (72351)

Report of the Board of Immigration of . . . Missouri. 49582

Report of the Board of Indian Commissioners, appointed by the President. 69763

Report of the Board of Indian Commissioners . . . for 1809. 34680

Report of the Board of Indian Commissioners to the President. (34609)

Report of the Board of Indian Commissioners to the Secretary of the Interior. 69763

Report of the Board of Inspectors of the Mount-Pleasant State Prison. 53545

Report of the Board of Inspectors of the Provincial Penitentiary. 10551

Report of the Board of Inspectors of the Rhode Island State Prison. (70557)

Report of the Board of Internal Improvement, in answer to resolutions. 37572

Report of the Board of Internal Improvement [of Michigan.] 48720

Report of the Board of Internal Improvement of the state of Kentucky. 37572

Report of the Board of Internal Improvement on the same, February 28, 1829. 4946

Report of the Board of Management of the Veterans of the National Guard. (54125)

Report of the Board of Managers and Treasurer of the Maryland Institute. 45222

Report of the Board of Managers [of St. Luke's Hospital.] 75413

Report of the Board of Managers of the Association of Banks. (3178)

Report of the Board of Managers of the Association of Friends. 86032

Report of the Board of Managers [of the Boston Mechanics' Institution.] 6743

Report of the Board of Managers of the Colonization Society of Virginia. 100447

Report of the Board of Managers of the Education and Missionary Society of the Protestant Episcopal Church in the State of New-York. (54126), 66144

Report of the Board of Managers of the Episcopal Missionary Association for the West. 22688, 66147

Report of the Board of Managers of the Evangelical Educational Society. 66149

Report of the Board of Managers of the Five Points Mission. 54280

Report of the Board of Managers, of the Industrial School Department. 76049

Report of the Board of Managers of the Industrial School for Girls. (20628)

Report of the Board of Managers of the Lehigh Coal . . . Company. (39881)

Report of the Board of Managers of the Maryland State Bible Society. 45242

Report of the Board of Managers of the Maryland State Colonization Society. 45246

Report of the Board of Managers of the [Massachusetts Colonization] Society. 45832

Report of the Board of Managers, of the New-Bedford Port Society for the Moral Improvement of Seamen. 52485, 85545

Report of the Board of Managers of the New-England Anti-slavery Society. 52655

Report of the Board of Managers of the N. H. Colonization Society. 52867

Report of the Board of Managers . . . [of the New York Protestant Episcopal Sunday-School Society.] 54530

Report of the Board of Managers [of the Pennsylvania Hospital.] 60330

Report of the Board of Managers of the Prison Discipline Society, Boston. 45936

Report of the Board of Managers of the Protestant Episcopal Church Missionary Society for Seamen. 66191

Report of the Board of Managers [of the Protestant Episcopal Orphan Asylum of the City of Louisville.] 43241

Report of the Board of Managers of the Society for Improving the Condition and Elevating the Character of Industrious Females. 85845

Report of the Board of Managers of the Society for the Encouragement of Faithful Domestics. 85899

Report of the Board of Managers of the Society for the Establishment and Support of Charity Schools. 62253

Report of the Board of Managers of the Society for the Relief of Destitute Children of Seamen. 85963

Report of the Board of Managers of the Spring Garden Institute. 89821

Report of the Board of Managers of the Temperance Society of Fishkill-Landing. 94655

Report of the Board of Managers [of the Temperance Union of Washington, D. C.] 20311, note after 94656

Report of the Board of Managers of the Trenton Delaware Falls Company. 96776

Report of the Board of Managers [of the Washington City Bible Society.] 101959

Report of the Board of Managers of the Washington City Orphan Asylum." 101962

Report of the Board of Managers of the [Young Men's City Bible Society of New-York] Auxiliary to the American and Foreign Bible Society. 106167

Report of the Board of Managers of the Young Men's Colonization Society of Pennsylvania. 106170

Report of the Board of Managers of . . . Trinity Church. (55067)

Report of the Board of Metropolitan Police of the District of Columbia. 20314

Report of the Board of Military Claims. 59920

Report of the Board of Missions of the Diocese of Pennsylvania. (59921)

Report of the Board of Missions of the . . . Presbyterian Church. 65143

Report of the Board of Missions of the Reformed Church in America. 68778

Report of the Board of Officers, appointed to decide between League Island and New London, for a naval station. 69764

Report of the [Boston] City Physician on the Cholera Hospital. 6634

Report of the Boston Committee of Policy-Holders. 56056

Report of the Boston Committee [on the removal of the U. S. Bank deposites.] 69766

Report of the Boston Committee, upon the aid to complete the same [i. e. the Bytown and Prescott Railway.] 17398

Report of the Boston Female Anti-slavery Society. (6704), 81910-81912

Report of the Boston Female Anti-slavery Society; being a concise history of the cases. 6703, 81910

Report of the Boston Female Anti-slavery Society; with a concise statement of events. 11994, 81909

Report of the [Boston Mercantile Library Association.] 6744

Report of the [Boston] School Committee. 2237

Report of the Boston Society of Natural History. 6774

Report [of the Boston Warren Street Chapel.] 6682

Report of the Boundary Commissioners. 45999

Report of the Bowery Savings Bank. 54109

Report of the British and Foreign Anti-slavery Society. 8082, 81917

Report of the British Association for the Advancement of Science. 39167

Report of the Brooklyn Association in Aid of the Grand-Ligne Mission. 8334

Report [of the Brooklyn Athenaeum and Reading Room.] (8264)

Report [of the Brooklyn Young Men's Christian Association.] 8268

Report [of the Buffalo Horticultural Society.] 9063

Report [of the Buffalo Orphan Asylum.] 9063

Report of the Building Committee and Architect [of Girard College.] (27494)

Report of the Building Committee [of Girard College] to the Select and Common Councils of Philadelphia. 27493, 101199

Report of the Building Committee of the House of Refuge. 85953

Report of the Building Committee [of the Howard Sunday School, Philadelphia.] 89744

Report of the Bureau of Animal Industry. 84332

Report of the Bureau of Free Labor. 16223

Report of the Bureau of Immigration . . . of Louisiana. 42200

Report of the Bureau of Statistics of Labor. 46000

Report of the Canada Education and Home Missionary Society. 50240

Report of the Canada Mission. 10524

Report of the Canal Appraisers of the state [of New York.] 53558

Report of the Canal Board [of New York.] 73977

Report of the Canal Commissioners as to supply of water. (53564)

Report of the Canal Commissioners . . . in relation to the Ohio Canal. 56888

Report of the Canal Commissioners in reply to the strictures of Mr. Robinson. 41888

Report of the Canal Commissioners of Illinois. 34202

Report of the Canal Commissioners of New York. (53559), (53564)-53565, 53921, 70189

Report of the Canal Commissioners [of Ohio.] 56888

Report of the Canal Commissioners of Pennsylvania. 59955, (59996), note just before 60250

Report of the Canal Commissioners on a navigable communication. 22761

Report of the Canal Commissioners on a resolution of the Assembly. (53564)

Report of the Canal Commissioners on the Delaware and Raritan Canal. 19414

Report of the Canal Commissioners on the Erie and Champlain Canals. 22760

Report of the Canal Commissioners relative to the amount paid for repairs. 59955

Report of the Canal Commissioners relative to the extension of the Pennsylvania Canal. 59955

Report of the Canal Commissioners, relative to the number of officers and agents. 59955

Report of the Canal Commissioners . . . relative to the Pennsylvania canals and rail-roads. 59955

Report of the Canal Commissioners relative to the superintendents, engineers, &c. 59955

Report of the Canal Commissioners to the Governor. 34208

Report of the Canal Engineer on the subject of a canal. 56929

Report of the case between the Rev. Cave Jones, and the Rector and Inhabitants of the City of New-York. 18867, 1st note after 96891

Report of the case Call vs. Clark. 13249

Report of the case ex parte Dorr. (20647), note after 96509

Report of the case in the Court of Errors. 28147

Report of the case, Nicholds, . . . against Wells. 55182

Report of the case of alleged contempt. (12698)

Report of the case of Belchertown election. (23243)

Report of the case of Charles Stearns against J. W. Ripley. 90872

Report of the case of Edward Prigg. 61207

Report of the case of Ezra A. Bourne. 72744

Report of the case of George B. Sloat. (82175)

Report of the case of Gloucester election. 27597

Report of the case of Heman Allen v. Hathaway and Pierson. 69392

Report of the case of Ives vs. Hazard. 35314

Report of the case of John Dodge. 96859

Report of the case of John Dorrance. 20652

Report of the case of John M. Trumbull. 97250

Report of the case of John W. Webster. 4627

Report of the case of Joshua Stow. 92380

Report of the case of Pennsylvania against Tench Coxe. 17303, 17313, 60471, 1st note after 96854

Report of the case of Rev. Moses Thatcher [sic]. 95157

Report of the case of Shelden Hawley. 96883

Report of the case of the Bank of Maryland. 45079

Report of the case of the Belchertown election. 4405

Report of the case of the Canadian prisoners. 25915

Report of the case of the Commonwealth of Pennsylvania, versus John Smith. 60470, 82884

Report of the Commissary General of . . .
Pennsylvania. 59992

Report of the Commissary-General of South
Carolina. 87395

Report of the commission appointed by the
Governor . . . to investigate the alleged
army frauds. 60472

Report of the Commission Appointed by the
Sanitary Board of the City Councils.
62131

Report of the Commission appointed . . . 1863.
40356

Report of the Commission appointed . . . to
Determine and Ascertain the Quota of
This State. 53616

Report of the Commission Appointed to Visit
Canada. (35460)

Report of the Commission Appointed Under
Act of Congress Approved April 23, 1873.
69774

Report of the Commission Appointed Under
Act of Congress Approved June 1, 1872.
69772

Report of the Commission Appointed Under
Act of Congress Approved March 3, 1873.
69773

Report of the Commission Appointed Under
Resolution of the Legislature. (43114),
87716

Report of the Commission, by Henry G. Clark.
76581

Report of the Commission of Inquiry to Santo
Domingo. 75191

Report of the Commission of Fisheries. 25257

Report of the Commission of Ordnance and
Ordnance Stores. 70260

Report of the Commission . . . [on] the Affairs
of the Grand Trunk Railway. (28269)

Report of the Commission on the Code. 87399

Report of the Commissioned Officers, Non-
Commissioned Officers and Privates.
53888

Report of the Commissioner Appointed to
Ascertain the Number, Ages, Hours of
Labor, and Opportunities for Education
of Children. 70645

Report of the Commissioner Appointed to
Complete the Examination and Deter-
mination of All Questions of Titles to
Land. 59469

Report of the Commissioner book II. 87705

Report of the Commissioner General Land
Office. 94982

Report of the Commissioner of Agriculture.
(69775)

Report of the Commissioner of Common
Schools . . . of New Hampshire. (52906)

Report of the Commissioner of Common
Schools of the Territory of Nebraska.
52187

Report of the Commissioner of Crown Lands.
(10412)

Report of the Commissioner of Education.
21884

Report of the Commissioner of Fish and Fisheries. 84125, 84231-84232

Report of the Commissioner of Indian Affairs
of Nova Scotia. 56178

Report of the Commissioner of Indian Affairs
[of the Confederate States.] 15397

Report of the Commissioner of Indian Affairs
[of the United States.] 12443, 34648,
(79113), note after 94525

Report of the Commissioner of Indian Affairs
to the President. 34630

Report of the Commissioner of Indian Affairs,
transmitted with the message of the
President. 34607

Report of the Commissioner of Internal Revenue.
34913

Report of the Commissioner of Patents. (69775)

Report of the Commissioner of Patents, Richmond, January, 1863. 15374

Report of the Commissioner of Public Schools,
in Rhode Island. 70565

Report of the Commissioner of Public Schools,
of Rhode Island. 70555, 70565, (70695)

Report of the Commissioner of Public Schools,
of the State of Rhode Island. 70565

Report of the Commissioner of Public Works
and Internal Improvements. (69761)

Report of the Commissioner of Public Works
for the Province of Ontario. 57364

Report of the Commissioner of Railroads and
Telegraphs. 56893

Report of the Commissioner of Rhode Island
on the Soldiers' National Cemetery.
(70636)

Report of the Commissioner of Shell Fisheries.
70566

Report of the Commissioner of Statistics [of
Minnesota.] (49279)-49280

Report of the Commissioner of Statistics [of
Missouri.] 49579

Report of the Commissioner of Statistics [of
Ohio.] 56894

Report of the Commissioner of Taxes. 69899

Report of the Commissioner of the General
Land Office. 38818-38819A, 42290

Report of the Commissioner of the Land Office
[of Michigan.] 48721

Report of the Commissioner on the Narragansett
Tribe of Indians. 70646

Report of the Commissioner, on the subject of
the lien of the commonwealth. 59827

Report of the commissioner . . . relating to
the public encouragement of Agriculture.
52553

Report of the Commissioner to Visit Almshouses and Asylums. (70647)

Report of the Commissioners and Chief Engineer of the Charlestown Water Works.
(12116)

Report of the . . . Commissioners and Officers
of the Houses of Refuge. 53310

Report of the Commissioners and views of the
minority. 62132

Report of the Commissioners, appointed . . .
April, 1824. (53977)

Report of the Commissioners appointed . . .
April 21, 1825. (53899)

Report of the Commissioners appointed at the
last session of the General Assembly.
87396

Report of the Commissioners appointed . . .
August 26, 1844. 6785

Report of the Commissioners appointed by an
act of the General Assembly of New York,
April, 1807. 69776

Report of the Commissioners, appointed by an
act of the Legislature of . . . New-York.
50833

Report of the Commissioners appointed by an
act of the Legislature [of Pennsylvania.]
60473

Report of the Commissioners appointed by the
British Government. 69777

Report of the Commissioners appointed by the
City Councils of the cities of Roxbury
and Boston. (73676)

Report of the Committee in relation to the licence laws. 15834

Report of the Committee . . . in 1740. 88005

Report of the Committee . . . made Feb. 8, 1858. 43690

Report of the Committee of Accounts. 75687

Report of the Committee of Advice. 58538

Report of the Committee of Agriculture. 53062

Report of the Committee of Aldermen. 29706

Report of the Committee of Arrangement of the Second Annual Exhibition. 101932

Report of the Committee of Arrangements of the Common Council of . . . New York, upon the funeral ceremonies in commemoration of the death of Gen. Andrew Jackson. 54632

Report of the Committee of Arrangements of the Common Council of the City of New York, of the obsequies in memory of the Hon. Henry Clay. 13565

Report of the Committee of Assembly relative to the creation of a sinking fund. 53220

Report of the Committee of both branches of City Council. 6702

Report of the Committee, of both Houses of Assembly of the Province of South-Carolina. 87349-87350, 88005

Report of the Committee of both Houses to whom was referred the message. 70654

Report of the Committee of British Merchants. 9037

Report of the Committee of By-laws. 45846

Report of the Committee of Citizens. 15152

Report of the Committee of Claims, on a motion. 69803

Report of the Committee of Claims, on the alterations and repairs. 46035

Report of the Committee of Claims, on the memorial of Alexander Burray. (51484)

Report of the Committee of Claims, on the petition of Charles Bean. (4118)

Report of the Committee of Claims . . . on the . . . petition of Jared Shattuck. 79875

Report of the Committee of Claims, on the petition of Stephen Sayre. 77417

Report of the Committee of Claims on the petition of the Corporation of Rhode Island College. 70716

Report of the Committee of Claims, on the petition of the heirs. 69804

Report of the Committee of Claims to the Legislature of Maryland. 45324

Report of the Committee of Claims to whom was referred. 77418

Report of the Committee of Claims, to whom were referred the petitions. 73625

Report of the Committee of Claims, who were instructed. 69805

Report of the Committee of Commerce and Manufactures, . . . on . . . the memorial of Henry Messonier. 48161

Report of the Committee of Commerce and Manufactures, on the petition of Anthony Buck. 8880

Report of the Committee of Commerce and Manufactures, on the petition of Armroyd, &c. 2014

Report of the Committee of Commerce and Navigation. 10037

Report of the Committee of Commerce on manufactures. (22964)

Report of the Committee of Common Councils. 61553

Report of the Committee of Conference. Delivered in the Senate. 93157

Report of the Committee of Conference in the House of Representatives. 46027

Report of the Committee of Conference, to whom was referred an act. 60498

Report of the Committee of Correspondence and Publication. (66153)

Report of the Committee of Correspondence with southern ecclesiastical bodies. 82051

Report of the Committee of Council and Assembly. 96043

Report of the Committee of . . . Councils of Philadelphia. 62138

Report of the Committee of Defence. 15830

Report of the Committee of Delegates. 6580

Report of the Committee of Directors and Stockholders of the South-Carolina Canal and Rail Road Company. 87963

Report of the Committee of Directors of the Bank of the United States. 3189

Report of the Committee of Directors of the St. Louis Gas Light Company. 75388

Report of the Committee, of Drs. W. H. Van Buren and C. R. Agnew. 76546, 76647

Report of the Committee of Education. 37507

Report of the Committee of Elections, and statement. 44020

Report of the Committee of Elections [of the Rockingham Convention, 1812.] 72390, 93487, 102319

Report of the Committee of Elections on the Boston elections. 46027

Report of the Committee of Elections, to whom was referred, on the 8th inst. 69806

Report of the Committee of Elections, to whom was referred . . . the petition. 60499

Report of the Committee of Fifteen Citizens. (61239)

Report of the Committee of Finance [of New Bedford, Mass.] 52502

Report of the Committee of Finance of the city of Richmond. 71191

Report of the Committee of Finance [of the Winchester and Potomac Railroad Company.] 104743

Report [of] the Committee of Finance . . . [on] the Bank of the United States. 2189

Report of the Committee of Foreign Relations. 46031, 67832-67833

Report of the Committee of Grievances and Courts of Justice of the House of Delegates of Maryland. 3072

Report of the Committee of Grievances and Courts of Justice, relative to the official conduct of the Honorable Abraham Shriver. 80752

Report of the Committee . . . of Harvard College. 36035

Report of the Committee of his Majesty's Council, appointed to make inquiry. 730

Report of the Committee of His Majesty's Council for the province of New-York. (53909)

Report of the Committee of His Majesty's Council, to whom it was referred, to examine and make enquiry, toching a letter. 30378, 30380

Report of the Committee of His Majesty's Council, to whom it was referred to examine and make inquiry touching a letter. 731, 30380, 84558

Report of the Committee of Holders of Union Canal Bonds. 60750

Report of the Committee of Inquiry. 60500

Report of the Committee of the Contraband's Relief Commission of Cincinnati. 13113

Report of the Committee of the Convention of the Union and State Rights Party. 14852, 88087-88088, 1st-2d notes after 97754

Report of the Committee . . . of the Convention of Wool Manufacturers. 51935

Report of the Committee of the Corporation of Brown University. 8630

Report of the Committee of the corporation, on the subject of fortifying the harbor of New York. (54636)

Report of the Committee of the Council of Censors. 69810-69811

Report of the Committee of the Democratic Society. 60051

Report of the Committee of the Essex Institute. 75688

Report of the Committee of the First Parish in Cambridge. 10125

Report of the Committee of the First Parish [in Portland, Me.] 64375

Report of the Committee . . . of the Friends of Education. 53219

Report of the Committee of the General Assembly appointed to draught a plan. 65218

Report of the Committee of the General Assembly at their special session. 15832

Report of the Committee of the General Assembly in relation to the Geological Survey. 53117

Report of the Committee of the General Assembly of the state of Delaware. 69812

Report of the Committee of the Historical Society of Pennsylvania. 36510

Report of the Committee of the House of Assembly. 10410

Report of the Committee of the House of Representatives. (18453)

Report of the Committee of the House of Representatives of Congress on the petition of Oliver Evans. (23182)

Report of the Committee of the House of Representatives of Congress upon so much of the President's message as relates to Louisiana. 42291

Report of the Committee of the House of Representatives of Massachusetts. 46029

Report of the Committee of the House of Represenatative of the 8th of February, 1830. 10110

Report of the Committee of the House of Representatives of the United States, appointed 30th Nov. 1818. 3189

Report of the Committee of the House of Representatives of the United States appointed to prepare and report articles of impeachment. (6003)

Report of the Committee of the House of Representatives of the United States on the memorial. 14732

Report of the Committee of the . . . House . . . to whom was referred the message of the Governor. 60503

Report [of] the Committee of the Judiciary. 41175

Report of the Committee . . . of the Lawrence Machine Shop. 39397

Report of the Committee fo the Legislature, in relation to the northeastern boundary. 84039

Report of the Committee of the Legislature of Dominica. (20578)

Report of the Committee of the Legislature . . . [on] the Kennebec and Portland Railroad. 44021

Report of the Committee of the Legislature on the petitions. 1328

Report of the Committee of the Legislature on the subject of the war. 46030

Report of the Committee of the Massachusetts Emigrant Aid Company. 52198

Report of the Committee of the Massachusetts Homoeopathic Medical Society. 45861

Report of the Committee of the Massachusetts Legislature. 32653

Report of the Committee of the Medical Society . . . appointed to investigate the subject of a secret medical association. 54376

Report of the Committee of the Medical Society . . . explanatory of the causes and character of the epidemic fever. 54376, note after 96392

Report of the Committee of the Medical Society of Philadelphia, on epidemic Cholera. 61810

Report of the Committee of the Medical Society . . . on the epidemic fever of Bancker Street. 54376, note after 96392

Report of the Committee of the Medical Society . . . to enquire into the pestilential disease. 54376

Report of the Committee . . . [of the New York Chamber of Commerce.] (52592)

Report of the Committee of the New York Meeting of Friends. 14752

Report of the Committee of the Overseers appointed to confer with a like committee of the President and Fellows. (30749)

Report of the Committee of the Overseers appointed to consider what measures, if any, may be adopted. (30759A)

Report of the Committee of the Overseers to procure a perfect copy. (30759A)

Report of the Committee of the Overseers . . . appointed to visit the Lawrence Scientific School. (30759A)

Report of the Committee of the Overseers . . . appointed to visit the library. 30730

Report of the Committee of the Overseers.. . . appointed to visit the University in 1849. (30759A)

Report of the Committee of the Overseers of Harvard College, appointed to visit the Law School. 93671

Report of the Committee of the Overseers of Harvard College appointed to visit the library for the year 1861. 30730

Report of the Committee of the Overseers, on the state of the University. (30759A)

Report of the Committee of the Overseers . . . to revise the by-laws and rules. (30749)

Report of the Committee of the Privy Council. (41657), note after 102630

Report of the Committee of the Proprietors. 62778

Report of the Committee of the Proprietors upon the "Result." 6656

Report of the Committee of the Providence Association for the Promotion of Temperance. (66304)

Report of the Committee of the Relief Association. 45233

Report [of the Committee of the Rhode Island Legislature.] (70655)

Report of the Committee of the said [Brookfield] Association. (8247)

Report of the Committee of the Senate appointed on the judiciary system. 60504

Report of the Committee on Salt Supply.
(15384A)

Report of the Committee on Salvages. (69824)

Report of the Committee on Schools of the
Council. 49304

Report of the Committee on Sewerage and
Drainage. 77263

Report of the Committee on Slavery, presented
May 30, 1849. 45696

Report of the Committee on Slavery, to the
Convention of Congregational Ministers
of Massachusetts. Presented May 30,
1849. 45817, (82052)

Report of the Committee on State Lands.
43951

Report of the Committee on Statistics. 12637,
52211

Report of the Committee on Substitutes and
Relief. 54128, 54638

Report of the Committee on Supplying Water.
53010

Report of the Committee on Territories. In
the Senate. 52180

Report [of] the Committee on Territories [on]
a constitution for Kansas. 37041

Report [of] the Committee on Territories, to
whom was referred a bill. 37040

Report of the Committee on the accounts.
75275

Report of the Committee on the action of the
General Assembly. 70663

Report of the Committee . . . on the annual
apportionment. 54121

Report of the . . . Committee . . . on . . .
the Annual Fair. 45829

Report of the Committee . . . [on the] Bill . . .
to divide the city. 53011

Report of the Committee . . . on the charges
at Quarantine. (53592)

Report of the Committee on the Coal Lands.
13851

Report of the Committee on the coal-trade nad
iron interests. 37575

Report of the Committee on the collection of
the revenue. 49538

Report of the Committee on the Coloured
Population. 45331

Report of the Committee on the Commerce of
the State. 53913

Report of the Committee on the complaint of
George Logan. 24499, 62134

Report of the Committee on the Conduct of the
War on the attack on Petersburg. (69826)

Report of the Committee on the Conduct of the
War, on the condition of the Union
prisoners. 69825

Report of the Committee on the Conduct of the
War relative to the Peninsula Campagin.
37646

Report of the Committee on the contested election case. (71284)

Report of the Committee on the correspondence
between Governor Clinton and Governor
Williamson. 13747

Report of the Committee on the destruction of
churches. 87929

Report of the Committee on the distribution of
lunatic hospital reports. (2242)

Report of the Committee . . . on the existing
revenue laws. 61970

Report of the Committee on the financial affairs
of the state. (49634)

Report of the Committee on the financial affairs
of the town of Hingham. 31957

Report of the Committee on the Fire Department. (73687)

Report of the Committee on the fortification
of the ports. 69827

Report of the Committee on the fugitive slave
case. (45332)

Report of the Committee on the judicial department. 52818

Report of the Committee on the judicial reform.
(46039)

Report of the Committee on the Judiciary
(General) of the Senate. 60522

Report of the Committee on the Judiciary, in
relation to the repeal. 64272

Report of the Committee on the Judiciary, on
refunding the fine. 35389

Report of the Committee on the Judiciary, on
Senate bill, no. 150. 15383

Report of the Committee on the Judiciary
relative to the abolition of slavery. 60522

Report of the Committee on the Judiciary
relative to the sale of intoxicating liquors.
43898

Report of the Committee on the Judiciary
System. 60523

Report of the Committee on the Judiciary
System, relative to the penal code. 60523

[Report of] the Committee on the Judiciary to
whom was referred the message of the
Governor. (44028)

Report of the Committee on the Judiciary, upon
the suspension of the habeas corpus.
69828

Report of the Committee on the Kilby Bank.
37738

Report of the Committee on the Library. 6759

Report of the Committee on the Logan Evening
School. (61796)

Report of the Committee . . . [on the] memorial
and petition of Aaron Ogden. (56798)

Report of the Committee on the memorial of
Cornelius Coolidge. (16370)

Report of the Committee [on] the memorial of
the Illinois and Wabash Land Company.
34294

Report of the Committee . . . on the memorial
of the St. Augustine Catholic Church.
(75001)

Report of the Committee on the message of the
Governor. (45263), 45266

Report of the Committee on the meteorology and
hygiene. 81294

Report of the Committee on the Military Fund.
(73688)

Report of the Committee on the Militia System.
(60524)

Report of the Committee on the Negro and
Aborigines Fund. 86065

Report of the Committee on the North-Eastern
Boundary. 44019

Report of the Committee on the official conduct
of the Judges. (37576)

Report of the Committee [on the Oregon Territory.] 57564

Report of the Committee on organization. 49312

Report of the Committee . . . [on] the origin
and spread of the yellow fever. 4909

Report of the Committee on the petition of
Cornelius Coolidge. 16371

Report of the Committee on the petition of
Elijah Gould. 28103

Report of the Committee on the petition of Henry
J. Duff. 21129, 80410

Report of the Committee on the petition of Peter
Soumans. 53221

Report of the Committee on the petition of
sundry inhabitants. 69829
Report of the Committee on the petition of
the town of East Hartford. (21648),
30672
Report of the Committee . . . on the petitions
for and the remonstrances against a
bridge. 33528
Report of the Committee . . . on the present
alarming state. (46025)
Report of the Committee on the present position
of Swan Point Cemetery. (66374)
Report of the Committee on the President's
message relating to Hamet Carramalli.
11027
Report of the Committee on the President's
message, relating to the United States
Bank. 13581
Report of the Committee on the proposed
division of the Diocese of Maryland.
45308
Report of the Committee,. . . [on] the propriety of admitting the Mississippi
Territory. 49537
Report of the Committee on the Public Lands,
on the petition of Joab Garret. (26691)
Report of the Committee on the Public Lands
to whom was referred on the eighth
instant. 69830
Report of the Committee on the punishment
and reformation of juvenile offenders.
(15793)
Report of the Committee on the question of
the episcopate of Maryland. 45309
Report of the Committee . . . on . . . the
relation of apprentices. 45829
Report of the Committee . . . [on] the religious
instruction. 65220
Report of the Committee on the remonstrance
of Wm. R. Huston. 73689
Report of the Committee, on the representation
of the House of Representatives. 69831
Report of the Committee on the revision &
amendments. 73690
Report of the Committee on the Sinking Fund,
. . . 1838. 37510
Report of the Committee on the Sinking Fund,
made 1830. 62243
[Report of the Committee on the state of the
business in the High Court of Chancery.]
100107
Report of the Committee on the state of the
. . . [New York Free School] Society.
54285
Report of the Committee . . . [on] the state
of the water works. 62369
Report of the Committee on the subject of a
new canal, to the Proprietors of the
Locks and Canals of Merrimac River.
69832
Report of the Committee on the Subject of a
new canal, to the Proprietors of the
Locks and Canals on the Merrimac River.
48016
Report of the Committee on the subject of an
extension of suffrage. 31092, 42730
Report of the Committee on the subject of
appropriations for the Indian Department.
34673
Report of the Committee on the subject of
Judge Symme's purchase. 62149
Report of the Committee on the subject of
pauperism. 69833
Report of the Committee on the subject of the
embargo. 46040

Report of the Committee on the temporary
organization. 45168
Report of the Committee on Tolls. 78089
Report of the Committee on United States
District Courts. 76037
Report of the Committee on Vice and Immoral-
ity, relative to intemperance. 60525
Report of the Committee on Vice and Immo-
rality, relative to the appointment of a
moral instructor. 60525
Report of the Committee on Ways and Means.
(45335)
Report of the Committee on Wharves. 54639
Report of the Committee recommending that
a pension be granted. 9406
Report of the Committee, relating to the des-
truction of the Ursuline Convent. 12115,
2d note after 98168
Report of the Committee . . . relating to the
southern boundary. 46042
Report of the Committee . . . relative to a
bridge. 33528
Report of the Committee relative to a new
organization. (30759A)
Report of the Committee relative to the Gettysburg Rail Road. 60122
Report of the Committee relative to the purchase
of the Hancock Estate. (30181)
Report of the Committee relative to the subject.
(60526)
Report of the Committee sent to Georgia.
(27839)
Report of the Committee . . . "To enquire into
the expediency." 42292
Report of the Committee . . . to inspect the
condition of New-Gate Prison. (15793)
Report of the . . . Committee . . . to investigate certain charges. 53610
Report of the Committee to investigate the loan
made by this state. 62051
Report of the Committee . . . to investigate the
local causes of cholera. 61478
Report of the Committee . . . to investigate . . .
the Plainfield Bank. 63251
Report of the Committee . . . to meet the
exigency. 46026
Report of the Committee to prevent the admis-
sion of Texas. 46041
Report of the Committee to the House of As-
sembly. 10411
Report of the Committee to whom the petition
of the Deputies of the United Moravian
Churches was referred. 69731, 1st note
after 97845
Report of the Committee to whom was committed the proceedings of sundry of the other
states. 15005, 100077, 100081
Report of the Committee to whom was referred
a bill. (69842)
Report of the Committee to whom was refererd
His Excellency's speech. 15831
Report of the Committee, to whom was referred
on the 7th ultimo. 69839
Report of the Committee to whom was referred
on the sixteenth instant. 69841
Report of the Committee to whom was referred,
on the twentieth of Dec. last. (69835)
Report of the Committee to whom was referred,
on the 26th ultimo. (15688)
Report of the Committee . . . to whom was
referred so much of the Governor's
message. 60513
Report of the Committee to whom was referred,
so much of the President's speech as
relates to "A revision and amendment of
the judiciary system." 69838

Report of the Committee to whom was referred so much of the President's speech as relates to the naval establishment. 69837

Report of the Committee to whom was referred sundry memorials. 62150

Report of the Committee to whom was referred sundry petitions. 62151

Report of the Committee to whom was referred the communication of Patrick Magruder. (15563)

Report of the Committee to whom was referred the correspondence. 12489

Report of the Committee to whom was referred the memorial of the Boston Sanitary Association. 46043

Report of the Committee to whom was referred the memorial of the representatives of the people south of the Ohio. note after 94720

Report of the Committee to whom was referred the message from the President of the United States. 69734, note after 94720

Report of the Committee to whom was referred the message of the Governor. 60528

Report of the Committee to whom was referred the motion of the 17th of January last. 69836

Report of the Committee to whom was referred the remonstrance and petition. 94745

Report of the Committee to whom was referred . . . the report of a Select Committee. (69840)

Report of the Committee to whom was referred the report of the Commissioners of Common Schools. 56895

Report of the Committee to whom was referred the several petitions. 36278, 70196

Report of the Committee to whom was referred the subject of steam communication. 53312

Report of the Committee to whom was referred the subject of the Delaware and Raritan Canal. 19415

Report of the Committee to whom were referred certain memorials. (69843)

Report of the Committee . . . to whom were referred . . . the memorial of Return Jonathan Meigs. 47399

Report of the Committee to whom were referred . . . the memorials and petitions. 69844

Report of the Committee under the act. 804

Report of the Committee under the resolutions of 1862. 25804

Report of the Committee upon the petition of William Paterson. 18565

Report of the Committee . . . upon the subject of an Agricultural College. (52915)

Report of the Committee who presented the report. 54640

Report of the Committee who were instructed. 69845

Report of the Common Council. 78064

Report of the Common, Superior, Academic, and Normal and Model Schools. (56113)

Report of the Comptroller, and the report of the Commissioners of the Sinking Fund. (54212)

Report of the Comptroller, exhibiting the revenues. (54212)

Report of the Comptroller-General of the state of Georgia. 27098

Report of the Comptroller General, on the claims of the State. 87411

Report of the Comptroller General to the Legislature of South Carolina. 87412

Report of the Comptroller [of Milwaukee.] 49160

Report of the Comptroller of . . . New York. (54212)

Report of the Comptroller of Public Accounts to the General Assembly [of Connecticut.] 15842

Report of the Comptroller of Public Accounts [of North Carolina.] 55677

Report of the Comptroller of the city of Brooklyn. 8281

Report of the Comptroller, on the condition of the several insurance companies. 53618

Report of the Comptroller of the Currency to the first session of the 39th Congress. 69847

Report of the Comptroller of the Currency to the second session of the 29th Congress. 17994

Report of the Comptroller . . . of the receipts. (54212)

Report of the Comptroller of the state [of New York.] 53618

Report of the Comptroller of the Treasury Department [of Maryland.] 45380

Report of the Comptroller of the Treasury [of Ohio.] 56900

Report of the Comptroller, to the Commissioners of the Sinking Fund. (54212)

Report of the Comptroller, with the accounts of the corporation. (54212)

Report [of the Concord Female Anti-slavery Society.] 72714

Report of the condition and improvement of the common schools. 20901

Report of the condition and operations of the Free Academy. 54121

Report of the condition of the Academy of Natural Sciences. 74194

Report of the condition of the Bank of the United States. 3189

Report of the condition of the Common Schools. (13087)

Report of the condition of the New Jersey State Prison. 53063

Report of the condition of the advance of the column. 51720

Report of the Confederate Commissioners. 65358

Report of the Conference Committee on the Kansas question. 44781

Report of the Conference Committee on the exemption bill. 15385

Report of the Congregational Board of Publication. (15478)

Report of the Congressional Committee [on St. Clair's defeat.] (75020)

Report of the Congressional Committee on the Conduct of the War. 69848

Report of the Congressional Committee on the operations of the Army of the Potomac. 15212, 69849

Report of the Congressional Committee, presented in the House of Representatives, July 1, 1856. 37083

Report of the Congressional Committee, presented in the House of Representatives, on . . . July 1, 1856. 37092, 93347

Report of the Congressional Committee upon the question of reconstruction. 24222

Report of the Congressional Temperance Society. 101934

Report of the Conneaut & Beaver, and Beaver & Conneaut Rail Roads. 60007

Report of the Connecticut delegation to the Convention. 80405

Report of the Directors of the . . . [Young Men's Auxiliary Education Society of the City of New-York.] 106160

Report of the . . . Directors of the Young Men's Christian Union. 66341

Report of the Directors to the stockholders [of the Boston & Maine Rail Road.] 6768

Report of the . . . Directors to the stockholders of the Naugatuck Railroad Company. (52060)

Report of the Directors to the stockholders of the Quincy Mining Company. (67298)

Report of the Directors to the stockholders of the South-Eastern Mining Company of Canada. 88263

Report of the Directors to the stockholders of the South-Western Mining Co. of Canada. 88263

Report . . . of the discussion at Brunswick. 37369

Report of the discussion at Danvers, Mass. between the Rev. Milton P. Braman. 103802

Report of the discussion at Danvers, Mass. on November 6, 1853. (18515), 103797

Report of the discussion at Pottsville. 60529

Report of the District Grand Committee. (53692)

Report of the doings of the ecclesiastical council. 32627

Report of the doings of the First State Convention of Sabbath School Teachers. 15733

Report of the Domestic Committee of the Board of Missions. 66142

Report of the Dorchester Temperance Society. (20628)

Report of the Dublin schools. 21006

Report of the Dutchess County & Poughkeepsie Sanitary Fair. 21455

Report of the Earl of Durham. 29693

Report of the East River Industrial School for Girls. 54254

Report of the Eastern Auxiliary Foreign Missionary Society. 72387

Report of the Eastern Dispensary of . . . New York. 54255

Report of the ecclesiastical council convened at Portsmouth. 64431

Report of the Edgeworth Chapel Sunday School. 12098

Report of the Education Society of Connecticut. (15723)

Report of the Education Society of the Presbyterian Church. 65159

Report of the Educational Commission for Freedmen. 25739, 52685

Report of the effect of freemasonry on the Christian religion. 50682, 97958

Report of the 8th of January, 1838. 38118

Report of the Employment Society, Providence, R. I. 66258

Report of the engagement at Drainesville. (20809)

Report of the engagement at Staunton River. 15386, (23808)

Report of the engineer and artillery operations. 3484

Report of the Engineer and General Superintendent [of the Philadelphia and Reading Rail Road Company.] 61948

Report of the engineer and geologist in relation to the new map. (45156)

Report of the engineer appointed by the Commissioners. (3074), 45098

Report of the Engineer in Chief of the Georgia Rail Road and Banking Co. 95573

Report of the Engineer-in-Chief of the Illinois and St. Louis Bridge Company. 34324

Report of the Engineer [of the Boston and Providence Railroad Company and Lowell Railroad Corporation.] 6768

Report [of the Engineer of the Springfield and Mansfield Railroad Company.] 89900

Report [of the Engineer of the Springfield, and Mount Vernon & Pittsburg Railroad Company.] 89901

Report of the Engineer [of the Worcester County Committee on the Blackstone Canal.] 5700, 105386

Report of the Engineer on the proposed line of a canal. 72159

Report of the Engineer on the route surveyed. 55826

Report of the Engineer on the survey of the Valley Railroad, in Vermont. 97541, 1st note after 99216

Report of the Engineer, to the Association for the Promotion of Internal Improvements in the State of Kentucky. 104291

Report of the Engineer to the Cincinnati, Columbus and Wooster Turnpike Company. 104292

Report of the Engineer to the President of the Hanging Rock and Lawrence Furnace Railroad Company. 104293

Report of the Engineer upon the . . . location for the Hartford and Springfield Railroad. 58357

Report of the Engineer, upon the preliminary surveys. 97542

Report of the Engineer upon the several definitive locations. 30670

Report of the Engineers, employed to re-survey the location. (43326)

Report of the Engineers of the Naumkeat Steam Cotton Company. 75675

Report of the Engineers [of the Philadelphia and Reading Railroad Company.] 61948

Report of the Engineers on the reconnoissance and surveys. 2992

Report of the Engineers to the Naumkeag Steam Cotton Company. 75675

Report of the . . . Episcopal Missionary Society of Philadelphia. 61620

Report of the Episcopal Sunday School Society. (54261)

Report of the Erie Canal Company. 60089

Report [of the Erie County Penitentiary.] 22734

Report of the establishment of Grace Free Church. 29245

Report of the Evansville Board of Trade. 23198

Report of the evidence & arguments of counsel. 37455

Report of the eivdence and points of law. 38066

Report of the evidence and reasons for the award. (57622)

Report of the evidence, arguments of counsel, charge and sentence. (13370), 96848

Report of the evidence at the trial of Levi & Laban Kenniston. 37454

Report of the evidence delivered on the trial of the case. 23168, note before 105987

Report of the evidence in the case, John Atkins, appellant. 2276, 56235

Report of the evidence in the case of John Stephen Bartlett. 3756

Report of the evidence [in the case of the commonwealth vs. Dennie.] 19583, (69415)

Report of the Examining Committee on the management. 55828

Report of the examination and survey of the coal fields. (26056)

Report of the Geological Survey in Kentucky. 37513

Report of the Geological Survey of Canada for 1863-66. 33894

Report of the Geological Survey of Canada, on the north shore of Lake Huron. 38663

Report of the Geological Survey of Indiana. 17254, 37527

Report of the Geological Survey of Kansas. 37033

Report [of the Geological Survey of Missouri.] 49593

Report of the Geological Survey of . . . New Jersey. 53115, 53121

Report of the Geological Survey of Ohio. 56928, 84797

Report of the Geological Survey of . . . Pennsylvania. 60118

Report of the Geological Survey of the province of New Brunswick. 27226

Report of the Geological Survey of the state of Iowa. (35000), 35003

Report of the Geological Survey of the state of Michigan. 48734

Report of the Geological Survey of the state [of New Hampshire.] (52832)

Report of the Geological Survey of Wisconsin. 18498

Report of the Geologist of Maryland. 45153

Report . . . of the Georgia Penitentiary. 27099

Report of . . . the Georgia Relief & Hospital Association. 27100

Report of the Glasgow Emancipation Society. 27550

Report of the Glasgow New Association for the Abolition of Slavery. 27550

Report of the government, presented to the Board. 74734

Report of the Governor and Directors. 93927

Report of the Governors of the Alms House. 54073

Report of the Grace Church Education Society. 54295

Report of the Grand Committee appointed to investigate. 60530

Report of the Grantees of the Boston and Providence Railroad Company. 6768

Repotr of the Grantees [of the Nashua and Lowell Rail Road Corporation.] 51859

Report of the great conspiracy case. 24559, 48784

Report of the "Guardian for Friendless Girls." 29061

Report of the Guardians of the Washington Asylum. 101963

Report of the Halifax Diocesan Committee. 85849

Report of the Hamilton County Sabbath School Association. 30067

Report of the . . . Harbor Commissioners [of Massachusetts.] 45762

Report of the Harbor Committee in relation to an increase. 9060

Report of the Harbor Master of the city of Roxbury. 73692

Report [of the Harrisburg and Hamburg Railroad.] 30542

Report [of the Hartford County Peace Society.] 103166

Report of the Hartford Evangelical Tract Society. 30654

Report of the Hartford Soldiers' Aid Association. 30673

Report of the heads of departments, to the Governor. (60577)

Report [of the Health Department of New York City.] 84263

Report of the Health Officer. 8334

Report of the hearing before the Massachusetts Legislature. 32890

Report of the herbaceous flowering plants of Massachusetts. (19845)

Report of the Historical Society of the University of North Carolina. 55701

Report of the Holden slave case. 96937

Report of the Home Committee. 37084

Report of the Home for Aged Women. 66271

Report of the Home for Destitute Colored Children. (61725)

Report of the . . . Home for Friendless Children. 55036

Report of the Home for the Friendless, New Haven. 52979

Report of the Hon. D. A. Wells. 10842

Report of the Hon. Elisha Whittlesey. 40763

Report of the Hon. Horace Mann. 22429, 44324

Report of the Hon. James M. Edmands. 58089

Report of the Hon. Mosely Baker, Chairman of the Committee. 94966

Report of the Hon. Mosely Baker, [on] the disposal of Gen. Santa Anna. 76747

Report of the Hon. Paul Dillingham. 20164

Report of the Hon. Thomas E. Powers. 64806

Report of the Hornell Library Association. 33034

Report of the Horticultural Exhibition held in Salem. 75689

Report of the . . . Hospital for the Insane. 34536

Report of the . . . Hospital [of the Protestant Episcopal Church.] 61726

Report of the House Committee on Agriculture. 53062

Report . . . of the House of Lords. 56560

Report of the House of Reformation [in Providence, R. I.] 66272

Report of the House of Refuge [of Cincinnati, Ohio.] 13076

Report [of the House of Refuge, Philadelphia.] 61729

Report of the House of Representatives [of Alabama.] 568

Report of the Howard Association of New Orleans. 53330

Report of the Howard Association [of Philadelphia.] 55483

Report [of the Howard Benevolent Society, Boston.] 6728, 92021

Report of the Hudson River Industrial School Association. 33533

Report of the Huron Fishing Company. 34010

Report of the Illinois Central Railroad Company. (34320)

Report [of the Illinois Commissioners of Public Charities.] 34217

Report of the Illinois State Hospital for the Insane. 34254-34256

Report of the important hearing on the memorial. 69865

Report of the important trial of Shermer v. Rusling. 96925

Report of the Incorporated Church Society of the Diocese of Quebec. 67006

Report of the Incorporated Society for the Conversion and Religious Instruction and Education of the Negro Slaves. 85879

Report of the Indian Peace Commissioners. (69754)

Report of the Indiana Canal Company. 34494

Report of the Joint Committee of the General Assembly on finance. 57037
Report of the Joint Committee of the General Assembly upon public institutions and buildings. (57038)
Report of the Joint Committee of the House of Bishops. 26910
Report of the Joint Committee of the Legislature, appointed to examine. 59773
Report of the Joint Committee of the Legislature of Connecticut. (30658)
Report of the Joint Committee of the Legislature on the petition. 53919
Report of the Joint Committee of the Legislature . . . on the State Prison. 46044
Report of the Joint Committee of the Legislature, on the subject of the canals. 22758
Report of the Joint Committee of the Legislature . . . relative to the Eastern State Penitentiary. 60532
Report of the Joint Committee of the Legislature, respecting the University. (45389)
Report of the Joint Committee . . . of the province of New-Brunswick. 52554
Report of the Joint Committee of the Select and Common Councils. (62155)
Report of the Joint Committee of the Senate and Assembly, relative to Governor Clinton's charge. 53920
Report of the Joint Committee of the Senate and Assembly, relative to the internal improvements of the state. 53921
Report of the Joint Committee of the Senate and House . . . on the publication of the Geological Survey. 60533
Report of the Joint Committee of the Senate and House . . . to which was referred so much of the Governor's message. 60534
Report of the Joint Committee of the two houses, appointed at the last session. 87491
Report of the Joint Committee of the two houses of the . . . Legislature. 60535
Report of the Joint Committee of Valuation. 3189, note after 57037
Report of the Joint Committee on Accounts. 54641
Report of the Joint Committee on Banks [of Kentucky.] 37493, 37495
Report of the Joint Committee on Federal Relations of the State of South Carolina. 87478
Report of the Joint Committee on Federal Relations, . . . proposing an amendment. (45336)
Report of the Joint Committee on Highways. 73693
Report of the Joint Committee on Internal Improvements. 15836
Report of the Joint Committee on Public Instruction. 73694
Report of the Joint Committee on Public Lands. 6754
Report of the Joint Committee on Reconstruction. 24222
Report of the Joint Committee on Reconstruction, at the first session thirty-nineth Congress. 15593
Report of the Joint Committee . . . [on] Superintending and Directing the Water Works. 62369
Report of the Joint Committee on the Affairs of the James River & Kanawha Co. 35726

Report of the Joint Committee on the Conduct of the Present War. 69867
Report of the Joint Committee on the Conduct of the War. 69869
Report of the Joint Committee on the Conduct of the War, and the origin, progress, and results of the late expedition to Florida. 69868
Report of the Joint Committee on the Conduct of the War, at the second session thirty-eighth Congress. 69870
Report of the Joint Committee on the Conduct of the War. . . . Massacre at Fort Pillow. 25164
Report of the Joint Committee on the Erection of a House of Correction. 61727
Report of the Joint Committee . . . on the extension of Fairmount Park. 61650
Report of the Joint Committee on the memorial of the Regents. (45389)
Report of the Joint Committee on the State Library. 45370
Report of the Joint Committee on the State Prison accounts. 53222
Report of the Joint Committee on the subject of the fire in New Street. 54642
Report of the Joint Committee on Treasurer's Accounts. (53223)
Report of the Joint Committee, relative to calling a convention. (46046)
Report of the Joint Committee relative to frauds upon volunteers. 60536
Report of the Joint Committee relative to the Geological Survey. 48738
Report of the Joint Committee, to whom was referred so much of the Governor's message. 15833
Report of the Joint Committee, to whom was referred that part of the Governor's message. 10739
Report of the Joint Committee upon the boundary line. (70667)
Report of the Joint Delegation appointed by the Committee on the Indian Concern of the Yearly Meetings of Baltimore, Philadelphia and New York. (69871)
Report of the Joint Delegation appointed by the Committee on the Indian Concern of the Yearly Meetings of Ohio and Genesee. (34611)
Report of the Joint Library Committee of the Legislature. 53924
Report of the Joint Select Committee appointed . . . to inquire. (55678)
Report of the Joint Select Committee [of the Confederate States.] 69873
Report of the Joint Select Committee of the Legislature. 44024
[Report of the Joint Select Committee of the Salem City Council.] 75649
Report of the Joint Select Committee of the Senate and House of Representatives. 44023
Report of the Joint Select Committee on Common Schools. 15718
Report of the Joint Select Committee on Federal Relations. (69872)
Report of the Joint Select Committee on so much of His Excellency's message. 15841
Report of the Joint Select Committee on so much of the Governor's message. 15843
Report of the Joint Select Committee, on the defalcation. 44026
Report of the Joint Select Committee on the infraction of the Treaty of Washington. (44025)

REPORT

Report of the Lincoln Freedmen's Aid Society. 73646
Report of the Little Schuylkill Navigation Railroad and Coal Company. 41545, (60219)
Report of the Loan Committee of the Associated Banks of New York. (54363)
Report of the locating survey. 59120, 75032
Report of the . . . Locust Mountain Coal and Iron Company. (60222)
Report . . . of the London Anti-slavery Society. 66666
Report of the Long-Island Bible Society. 41893
Report of the . . . Long Island Historical Society. 41897
Report [of the Lords Commissioners for Trade and Plantations.] 41656, note after 102630
Report of the Lords Commissioners for Trade and Plantations on the petition of the Honourable Thomas Walpole. 101150
Report of the Lords Committees, appointed by the House of Lords. 69877
Report of the Lords Committees on the condition and treatment of the colonial slaves. (81747)
Report of the Lords of the Committee of Council, appointed for the consideration of all matters relating to trade and foreign plantations. (69878)
Report of the Lords of the Committee of Council appointed for the consideration of all matters relating to trade and foreign plantations; submitting . . . the evidence. 69879
Report of the Lords of the Committee of Council, relative to the slave trade. 23301, (81744)
Report of the Lords of the Committee of the Privy Council. 69880
Report of the Lords of the Committee, upon Governour Shute's memorial. (80807)
Report [of the Louisiana Rock-Salt Company.] 42280
Report [of the Louisville, Cincinnati, and Charleston Railroad.] 42325
Report of the Louisville Refugee Commission. 42334
Report of the Louisville Temperance Society. 42335
Report of the Lowell Hospital Association. 42489
Report . . . of the Lowell Sabbath School Union. (42492)
Report of the Loyal and Patriotic Society of Upper Canada. 92649
Report of the Lykens Valley Rail Road and Coal Co. 60225
Report of the Lyster Copper Company. (42887)
Report of the McLean Asylum for the Insane. (43520)
Report of the . . . Macon & Brunswick Railroad Co. 43620
Report of the Macon and Western Railroad Company. 43621
Report of the Madison and Indianapolis Railroad Company. (43747)
Report of the . . . Madras School. 43752
Report of the Magdalen Society of New York. (54367)
Report of the Maine Board of Agriculture. (43939)
Report of the Me. Missionary Society. 82892
Report of the majority and minority of the Committee of the Legislative Council. 53226
Report of the majority and minority of the Committee of the Senate. 64510

Report of the majority and minority of the Committee on Indian Affairs. 69881
Report of the majority and minority of the Committee on Western Connections. 2992
Report of the majority and minority of the Select Committees. 60539
Report of the majority of the Committee on Banks. 1529, 53925
Report of the majority of the Committee on Cities and Villages. (54645)
Report of the majority of the Committee on Secret Societies. 45337
Report of the majority of the Committee . . . [on] . . . the bill. (45389)
Report of the majority of the Committee . . . relative to . . an act. 60523
Report of the majority of the Committee . . . to examine the route. 60122
Report . . . [of the Malone Sandstone Company.] (44144)
Report of the Managers and Trustees of the San Francisco Ladies' Protection and Relief Society. 76093
Report of the Managers [of Erie Cemetery.] 22737
Report of the Managers of St. Joseph's Hospital. 62212
Report of the Managers of the . . . [Apprentices Library] Company. 61475
Report of the Managers of the Association for Aged Indigent Women. 13089
Report of the Managers of the Children's Home and Home for Aged Females. (73635)
Report of the Managers of the Cincinnati Orphan Asylum. (13115)
Report of the Managers of the Colonization Society of the State of Connecticut. 15697
Report of the Managers of the Cooper Shop Soldiers' Home. (61562)
Report of the Managers of the Eastern Lunatic Asylum. 37489
Report of the Managers [of the Elmira and Williamsport Railroad Company.] 60085
Report of the . . . Managers of the Episcopal Education Society of Pennsylvania. 22687, 60088
Report of the Managers, of the Free Produce Association of Friends. 69882
Report of the Managers of the Girard Trust. (27494)
Report of the . . . Managers of the Gurney Evening School. 61713
Report of the Managers [of the Haverford School.] 30905
Report of the Managers of the Horticultural Fair. 52994
Report of the Managers of the Kensington and Penn Township Rail-Road Company. (61752)
Report of the Managers of the Ladies' Benevolent Society. 53332
Report of the Managers of the Ladies' Depository. 61757
Report of the Managers of the Lancaster and Schuylkill Bridge Company. 38800
Report of the . . . Managers of the Lehigh Valley Rail-Road Company. 60201
Report of the Managers of the "Lincoln Institution." 61790
Report of the Managers of the Lunatic Asylum [of Kentucky.] (37491)
Report of the Managers of the Magdalen Asylum. 61800
Report of the . . . Managers of the Marine and City Hospitals. (60609)

2366

Report of the New Hampshire Bible Society. (52860)
Report of the New Hampshire Branch of the American Education Society. 52862
Report of the New-Hampshire Society for the Promotion of Temperance. 52887
Report of the New-Hampshire Unitarian Association. 52890
Report of the New-Haven County Bible Society. 52989
Report of the New Haven County Medical Society. 52996
Report of the . . . New Haven Hopkins Grammar School. 52993
Report of the New Haven Ladies' Greek Association. 52995
Report of the . . . New Haven Young Men's Institute. 53000
Report of the New Jersey Commissioners upon . . . a canal. (53227)
Report of the New Jersey Howard Society. 53178
Report of the New Jersey Prison Reform Association. 53186
Report of the N. J. Railroad and Trans. Co. (53185)
Report of the New Jersey State Board of Education. (53192)
Report of the New Jersey State Prison. 53196
Report of the New Orleans and Nashville Railroad Company. 53339
Report . . . of the New Orleans Canal and Banking Company. 53342
Report of the New York and Brooklyn Auxiliary Society. 54727
Report of the New York and Lake Superior Mining Company. 54735
Report of the New York and Texas Land and Emigration Association. 54743
Report of the New-York Anti-tobacco Society. 54426
Report of the New-York Association for the Improvement of the Condition of the Poor. 54429
Report of the New-York Association for the Suppression of Gambling. 54430
Report [of the New York Asylum for Insane Convicts.] 53535
Report of the New York Bible Society. 54433
Report of the New-York Book Society. (54434)
Report [of the] New-York Branch Freedman's Union Commission. 53803
Report of the [New York] Canal Commissioners. 22745
Report of the New York Central College Association. 54754
Report of the New York Central Homoeopathic Dispensary. 54435
Report of the New-York Central Railroad Company. (54755)
Report of the . . . New York Chamber of Commerce. (53594)
[Report of the New York City Board of Commissioners of the Central Park.] 54158
Report [of the New York City Health Department.] 84262-84263
Report of the [New York City] Metropolitan Board of Health. 53598
Report of the New York City Mission and Tract Society. (54444)
Report [of the New York City Street Commissioner.] 54684
Report of the . . . [New York City] Temperance Society. 54448
Report of the New-York Colonization Society. 54437

Report of the New York Committee of Vigilance. 54452
Report of the New-York Eye Infirmary. 54462
Report of the New York Female Auxiliary Bible Society. 54463
Report of the New York Female Union Society (54465)
Report of the New York House and School of Industry. 54487
Report of the New York House of Mercy. 54485
Report of the New York Infirmary for Women and Children. 54497
Report of the . . . [New York] Juvenile Asylum. 54503
Report of the New-York Ladies' Home Missionary Society. 54504
Report of the New-York Life Insurance Company. 54792
Report of the . . . New York Lyceum. (54507)
Report of the New-York Magdalen Female Benevolent Society. (54509)
Report of the New York Maternal Association. 54511
Report of the New York Medical Association for the Supply of Lint. 54805
Report of the New York National Freedman's Relief Association. 54827
Report of the New York Opthalmic and Aural Institute. 54519
Report . . . of the New-York Opthalmic Hospital. 54520
Report of the New York Philharmonic Society. 54523
Report of the New York Protestant Church Missionary Society. 54525
Report of the New-York Protestant Episcopal Missionary Society. 54527
Report of the New-York Protestant Episcopal Tract Society. 54531
Report of the New York Religious Tract Society. 54532
Report of the N. Y. Sacred Harmony Society. 54534
Report of the New York Society for the Encouragement of Faithful Domestic Servants. 54537
Report of the New York Society for the Promotion of Knowledge and Industry. (54539)
Report of the New York Society for the Relief of the Ruptured and Crippled. 54540
Report of the New York Southern Sunday School Union. 54856
Report of the New York State Commissioner to the Paris Exposition. 53817
Report of the New York State Inebriate Asylum. 53821
Report of the . . . New York State Institution for the Blind. 53822
Report of the New-York State Society for the Promotion of Temperance. (53840)
Report of the . . . [New York State Woman's] Hospital. 53978
Report of the New-York Sunday School Union Society. 54548
Report of the New-York Temperance Alliance. 54447
Report of the New-York Tract Society. 54449
Report of the New-York Unitarian Book Society. 54553
Report of the New-York Young Men's Christian Association. 54561
Report of the New York Young Men's Society. 54562
Report of the New York Washing and Bathing Association. 54554
Report [of the Newark Bible Society.] (49080)

Report of the . . . Newburyport Railroad
Company. 54923
Report of the Newcastle District Committee.
85852
Report of the Newfoundland School Society.
54974
Report of the Newsboys' Aid Society. 61865
Report of the . . . Norfolk County Bible Society.
55479
Report of the Normal and Training School.
(57836)
Report of the Normal, Model, and Common
Schools in Upper Canada. 10419, 74545
Report of the Normal School Committee. 60541
Report [of the North American Provinces
Commissioners.] 85234
Report of the North-Carolina Geological Survey.
55617
Report of the North-Middlesex Sunday-School
Society. 55721
Report of the North Street Union Mission.
55731
Report of the . . . North-Western Dispensary.
55740
Report of the . . . North Western Mining
Company. 55749
Report of the . . . North Western Railroad
Company. (60279)
Report [of the Northern Academy of Arts and
Sciences.] 55785
Report of the Northern Baptist Education
Society. 55788
Report . . . of the Northern Central Railway
Company. (60280)
Report of the Northern Dispensary. (55793)
Report of the Northern Educational Union.
23874
Report of the Northern Home for Friendless
Children. 55798, (61870)
Report of the . . . Northern Ohio Lunatic
Asylum. 56963
Report of the Northern Pennsylvania Railroad
Company. 55824
Report of the Northwestern Freedmen's Aid
Commission. 55743
Report of the Northwestern Sanitary Commis-
sion. 55954
Report of the . . . Norwich Mining Company.
(55929)
Report [of the Nova Scotia Board of Works.]
(56115)
Report of the Nova Scotia Commissioner for
the International Exhibition. 56173
Report of the number of men furnished by the
town of Rockport. 72410
Report of the Nurse Charity. 61870
Report of the Nursery for the Children of
Poor Women. 56341
Report of the occupation of Cumberland Gap.
50643
Report of the Oceanic Oil and Guano Company.
56641
Report of the Odd Fellows' Library Associ-
ation. (76063)
Report of the Officers and Trustees [of the
Manchester Public Library.] 44216
Report of the Officers Constituting the Light-
House Board. (41048)
Report of the Officers of Committees of the
city of Burlington. (9339)
Report of the Officers of the House of Refuge,
for Western Pennsylvania. 60149
Report of the Officers of the House of Refuge,
St. Louis. (75351)
Report of the Officers of the Iowa Soldiers'
Orphans Home. 35030

Report of the Officers of the Mississippi
Penitentiary. 49529
Report of the Officers of the New Jersey State
Lunatic Asylum at Trenton. (53194)
Report of the . . . Ogdensburth and Lake
Champlain Railroad. 56829
Report . . . of the Ohio and Indiana Railroad
Company. 56956
Report of the . . . Ohio Asylum for . . .
Idiotic and Imbecile Youth. 56970
Report of the . . . "Ohio Bible Society." 56972
Report of the . . . Ohio Institution for the
Education of the Blind. 11961
Report of the . . . Ohio Penitentiary. 56991
Report of the Ohio State Horticultural Society.
57006
Report of the . . . Old Colony and Fall River
Rail Road Company. 57119
Report of the Old Colony Railroad Company.
57121
Report of the Oneida Association. (47337)
Report of the [Oneida Bible] Society. 98230
Report of the Onondaga Commissioners. 23362
Report of the operations of the Cincinnati
Branch. 13113, 76568, 76647
Report of the operations of the Sanitary Com-
mission. 27245
Report of the Ophir Mining Co. 57396
Report of the opinion of the Supreme Court.
(30089), note after 96853
Report of the opinions and decision of the Court.
101436
Report of the opinions of the judges. (59653)
Report of the opinions of the three judges.
60589
Report of the Organization Committee of the
Smithsonian Institution. 85025
Report of the Organization Committee of the
Smithsonian Institution: with the resolutions
accompanying the same. 85058
Report of the organization of the Ladies' National
League. 75352
Report of the . . . Orphan Asylum Society.
54570
Report of the Orphan's Home of the Protestant
Episcopal Church. 54572
Report of the Orphan's Home, Pittsburgh, Pa.
57648
Report of the Overseer of the Poor [of Provi-
dence, R. I.] 66288
Report of the Overseers of the Poor of . . .
New Bedford. 52503
Report of the Overseers of the Poor [of Salem,
Mass.] 75679
Report of the Overseers of the Poor of the
city of Portland. 64351, (64353)
Report of the Overseers of the Poor, of the
city of Roxbury. 73713, 73716
Report of the Pacific Railroad [of Missouri.]
(58090)
Report of the pamphlet of "Oswego." (22766)
Report of the Parliamentary Select Committee
on Aboriginal Tribes. 34675
Report of the parochial meeting of St. Andrew's
Church. 62206
Report of the Pastoral Aid Society. 53855,
66181
Report of the . . . Patriot Orphan Home.
59087
Report of the Paymaster General of Missouri.
49636
Report of the Paymaster General [of New York.]
53856
Report of the Paymaster General . . . of
Pennsylvania. 60291

Report [of the President of the Richmond and
Danville Rail Road Company.] 71196
Report of the President [of the Schuylkill
Navigation Company.] 78079
Report of the President of the Southern Rail-
road Company. 88457
Report of the President of the Third Avenue
Railroad Company. 54692
Report of the President . . . [of the Union
Canal Company.] 60750
Report of the President [of the University of
Michigan.] 48804
Report of the President of the Young Men's
Association for Mutual Improvement in
the City of Schenectada.[sic] 77602, 2d
note after 106156
Report of the President [of the Young Men's
Association for Mutual Improvement, of
the City of Albany.] 106154
Report of the President Richard G. Sneath.
(76041)
Report of the President to the Board of Direc-
tors. 88022
Report of the President to the Directors.
44296
Report of the President to the . . . Directors.
51607
Report of the President to the Stockholders
[of the Lynchburg and Tennessee Railroad.] 42822
Report of the President to the Stockholders
[of the Pacific Mail Steamship Co.]
58084
Report of the President to the Stockholders
of the Pickell Mining Company. 62618
Report of the President, Vice-Presidents, and
several directors. (9174)
Report of the Principal of the Free Academy.
72366
Report of the Principal of the Normal School.
61867
Report of the Principal of the State Normal
School. 45135
Report of the Prison Association of New York.
53861
Report of the Prison-Discipline Society. 45902
Report of the Prison Inspectors and Prison
Agent. 62073
Report of the Prison Society [of Philadelphia.]
62073
Report of the probable revenue. 12509
Report of the proceedings and speeches at the
dedication. (79740)
Report of the proceedings and testimony at the
Coroner's Inquest. 69890
Report of the proceedings and the examination
of Charles G. Davis. 18801
Report of the proceedings and views of the
Taunton Union. 94421
Report of the proceedings at a banquet. 24265
Report of the proceedings at the annual meeting
of the Massachusetts Historical Society.
(45858)
Report of the proceedings at the centennial
celebration. 82322
Report of the proceedings at the formation of
the African Education Society. 69891,
note before 101926
Report of the proceedings at the meetings
held . . . May 17, 1865. (8101)
Report of the proceedings before the Court of
King's Bench. 96930
Report of the proceedings connected with the
disputes between the Earl of Selkirk.
(20701), 79016, note after 96860, 2d
note after 106023

Report of the proceedings in relation to the
case. 105843
Report of the proceedings in relation to the
contested election. 104777
Report of the proceedings in the cases of the
Bank of South Carolina. 87448
Report of the proceedings in the District Court
of the United States. 90364
Report of the proceedings in the Supreme
Judicial Court. 75691
Report of the proceedings of a convention and
conference. 69892
Report of the proceedings of a convention com-
posed of delegates. 62164
Report of the proceedings of a convention of
delegates. 37049
Report of the proceedings of a meeting held
. . . Philadelphia. 62165
Report of the proceedings of a meeting of the
Friends and Admirers of Lord Metcalfe.
48168
Report of the proceedings of an Ecclesiastical
Council held in Boscawen. 6446, 7779
Report of the proceedings of an Indian Council,
at Cattaraugus. 34676
Report of the proceedings of professed spiritual
agents and mediums. 42706, 89533
Report of the proceedings of the Anti-slavery
Conference. 82055
Report of the proceedings of the Board of
Trade. 12636
Report of the proceedings of the Canada Edu-
cation and Home Missionary Society.
10433
Report of the proceedings of the Convention
of Delegates from the National Association
of Wool Manufacturers. 51935
Report of the proceedings of the Convention
[to Improve the Condition of the Indians
in the United States.] 37660
Report of the proceedings of the fourth session
[of the International Statistical Congress.]
34835
Report of the proceedings of the Franklin Insti-
tute. 25656
Report of the proceedings of the Fruit Growers'
Society. 60110
Report of the proceedings of the Glasgow Ladies'
Auxiliary Emancipation Society. 95756
Report of the proceedings of the Great Anti-
slavery Meeting. 69893
Report of the proceedings of the Joint Committee
Appionted to Prepare and Present Medals.
69894
Report of the proceedings of the late jubilee
at Jamestown. 35739, 1st note after
100520
Report of the proceedings of the Medical and
Surgical Society. (54000)
Report of the proceedings of the Mixed Com-
mission on Private Claims. 33030
Report of the proceedings . . . of the Muster-
In. 34303
Report of the proceedings [of the National
Academy of Sciences.] 51915
Report of the proceedings of the National Con-
vention of Fire Underwriters. (69895)
Report of the proceedings of the National Con-
vention of Silk Growers. 81014
Report of the proceedings of the New Haven
Ladies' Greek Association. 52995
Report of the proceedings of the . . . [New
York State Anti-slavery] Society. 53801
Report of the proceedings of the Queens County
Agricultural Society. 67068

Report of the proceedings of the Rensselaer
  Agricultural Society. 69637
Report of the proceedings of the Sanatory
  [sic] Committee. 54124
Report of the proceedings of the second Ameri-
  can Health Convention. 69896
Report of the proceedings of the second annual
  exhibition of the Colorado Agricultural
  Society. 17449
Report of the proceedings of the second annual
  meeting of the Iowa Soldiers' Orphans
  Home. 35030
Report of the proceedings of the seventh year
  of the Mariner's Church. 61805
Report of the proceedings of the Society for
  the Relief of Strangers in Distress.
  85976
Report of the proceedings of the Society of
  the Army of the James. 86095
Report of the proceedings of the Society of
  the Army of the Tennessee. 86098
Report of the proceedings of the town meeting.
  (62166)
Report of the proceedings of the Tract Associ-
  ation of Friends. 96409
Report of the proceedings of the triennial
  meeting of the Stockholders. 3189
Report of the proceedings of the Trustees of
  the Evangelical Missionary Society.
  (45724)
Report of the proceedings of the Williamsport
  Convention. 59924
Report of the proceedings, on the occasion of
  the reception. (7320)
Report of the proceedings, on the petition of
  Mrs. Sarah M. Jarvis. 35817
Report of the proceedings on the writ of habeas
  corpus. 10696
Report of the proceedings upon the late project.
  60542
Report of the production and manufacture of
  cotton. 17131
Report of the Professors of the Newton Theo-
  logical Institution. (55095)
Report of the progress and present state.
  55615
Report of the progress of the geological survey
  of Michigan. 48735
Report of the progress of the geological survey
  of Missouri. 49593
Report of the progress of the geological survey
  of North Carolina. 55621
Report of the progress of the Pennsylvania
  Lyceum. 60344
Report of the property. 12359
Report of the Proprietors of the Bowditch
  Library. 7012
Report of the Proprietors of the Merrimack
  Manufacturing Company. (48013)
Report of the the [sic] Protective War Claim
  Association. (66098)
Report of the Protestant Episcopal Association.
  (66186)
Report of the Protestant Episcopal Missionary
  Association for the West. 66196
Report of the Protestant Episcopal Sunday and
  Adult School Society. 62104
Report of the Protestant Half Orphan Asylum
  Society. 85966
Report of the Protestant Orphan Asylum Society.
  (76071)
Report of the Providence Aid Society. 66297
Report of the Providence Association for the
  Benefit of Colored Orphans. (66303)
Report of the [Providence] Athenaeum. (66308)

Report of the Providence Auxiliary Bible
  Society. 66310
Report of the Providence Auxiliary Unitarian
  Association. 66311
Report of the Providence Bible Mission. 66314
Report of the Providence Domestic Missionary
  Society. 66321
Report of the Providence Evangelical Seamen's
  Friend Society. (66322)
Report of the Providence Female Tract Society.
  66325
Report of the Providence, Hartford and Fishkill
  Railroad Co. (66328)
Report [of the Providence Reform School.]
  66334
Report of the Providence Society for the En-
  couragement of Faithful Domestic Servants.
  66335
Report of the Providence Washington Total
  Abstinence Society. 66337
Report of the Providence Young Men's Bible
  Society. 66339
Report of the Provident Association for Friend-
  less Females. 66343
Report of the Provident Association of Portland.
  (64370)
Report of the Provident Society for the Employ-
  ment of the Poor. (62107)
Report of the Provost to the Trustees of the
  Peabody Institute. (59393)
Report of the . . . Public Library, of . . .
  Newburyport. 54922
Report of the Public Library of Quincy. 67293
Report of the Public Library of the city of
  Boston. 6759
Report of the public school system of the city
  of Saint Paul. 75460
Report of the public schools in the town of
  Dover. 20745
Report of the public schools of Galveston.
  26473
Report of the public schools [of Lawrence,
  Mass.] 39396
Report [of the public schools of Rochester.]
  72366
Report of the public schools of the city of
  Nashville. 51867
Report of the Public Treasurer, to the Legis-
  lature of North Carolina. 55681
Report of the Quartermaster General, Dewitt
  C. Remington. 70629
Report of the Quartermaster General, George
  Lewis Cooke. 70629
Report of the Quartermaster General [of
  Indiana.] 34565
Report of the Quartermaster General [of
  Kentucky.] 37554
Report of the Quartermaster General [of Mary-
  land.] 45267
Report of the Quartermaster General [of
  Michigan.] 48785
Report of the Quartermaster General [of
  Missouri.] (49637)
Report of the Quartermaster General [of New
  Hampshire.] (52919)
Report of the Quartermaster General of . . .
  New York. 53886
Report of the Quartermaster General [of Ohio.]
  57031
Report of the Quartermaster General of the
  Commonwealth [of Pennsylvania.] (60441)
Report of the Quartermaster General [of the
  United States.] 66974
Report of the Quartermaster General to the
  General Assembly [of Connecticut.] 15788

Report of the Quartz Hill Gold Mining Company. 66975

Report of the Quebec Diocesan Committee. (67043), 85850

Report of the Quebec Jail Association. 67048

Report of the Racine and Mississippi Railroad Company. 67395

Report of the Racine, Janesville and Mississippi Railroad Company. (67399)

Report of the Railroad Commissioners, made to the General Assembly, of the state of Rhode Island. 70631

Report of the Railroad Commissioners [of New York.] 53887

Report [of the Railroad Commissioners of Rhode Island.] 70630

Report of the Railway Commissioners of . . . New Brunswick. 52558

Report of the receipts and expenditures [of Lynn, Mass.] 42832

Report of the receipts and expenditures [of Marblehead, Mass.] 44470

Report of the receipts and expenditures [of Medfield, Mass.] 47298

Report of the receipts and expenditures [of Medway, Mass.] 47361

Report of the receipts and expenditures [of Methuen, Mass.] 48208

Report of the receipts and expenditures [of Milford, Mass.] 48945

Report of the receipts and expenditures of . . . Nashua. 51858

Report of the receipts and expenditures of . . . Natick. (51907)

Report of the receipts and expenditures of . . . Newbury. (54907)

Report of the receipts and expenditures [of Portland, Me.] 64351

Report of the receipts & expenditures of the city of Concord. (15146), 15155

Report of the receipts and expenditures of the city of Portland. 64342

Report of the receipts and expenditures of the city of Roxbury. 73716

Report of the receipts and expenditures of the city of Salem. 75633, 75636

Report of the receipts and expenditures of the Green-Wood Cemetery. 28697

Report of the receipts and expenditures of the town of Billerica. 5405

Report of the receipts and expenditures of the town of Braintree. 7354

Report of the receipts and expenditures of the town of Brighton. 7974, 7976

Report of the receipts and expenditures of the town of Dover. 20745

Report of the receipts and expenditures of the town of Lincoln. 41274

Report of . . . the receipts and expenditures of the town of Nahant. 51721

Report of the receipts and expenditures of the town of Quincy. 67285

Report of the receipts and expenditures of the town of Reading. 68205

Report of the receipts and expenditures of the town of Royalston. 73826

Report of the receipts and expenditures of the town of Salem. 75633, (75692)

Report of the receipts, expenditures, and financial condition of the town of Rowley. 73600

Report of the receipts, expenditures, &c. [of Beverley, Mass.] 5123

Report of the receipts, expenditures, &c. [of Ipswich, Mass.] 35043

Report of the Receiver [of the La Crosse and Milwaukee Rail Road Company.] 38508

Report of the Receivers to the Trustees of the St. Louis, Alton and Chicago Rail Road. 75382

Report of the reconnaissance of a railroad. 69946

Report of the Record Commissioners. 6696, note after 102733

Report of the Recording Secretary [of the National Institute.] 51988

[Report of the Rector and Visitors of the University of Virginia.] 100537

Report of the Reform School Commissioners of Ohio. 56996

Report of the Reform School for Girls. 57032

Report of the Refugee Relief Commission of Ohio. (57033)

Report of the Refugees Home Society. 68785

Report of the Regent [of the Illinois Industrial University.] (34234)

Report of the Regents [of the Smithsonian Institution] to Congress. 85060

Report of the Regents of the University [of the State of New York.] (53996)-53998, (54000)

Report of the Register-General on the state of the finances of Pennsylvania. 60448

Report of the Register of the Maryland Agricultural College. (45199)

Report of the Register of the State Land Office. 35032

Report of the Registrar of the Lietchfield South Association. (41473)

Report of the registry and return of births. 53228

Report of the Resident Physician of the Colored Home. 54200

Report of the Resident Physician of . . . [The Lunatic Asylum, Blackwell's Island, New York.] (54662)

Report of the Restigouche Agricultural Society. 70102

Report of . . . of the result of the survey. 28290

Report of the results of examinations made. 12511

Report of the Revenue Commission on distilled spirits. 70175

Report of the Revenue Commissioners. 60588

Report of the revenues and expenditures of the city [of New York.] (54212)

Report of the Rev. Asa Eaton. (45842)

Report of the Rev. Dr. Ethan Allen. 45339

Report of the Rev. John P. Robinson. 72138

Report of the Rev. Thomas Cooper. 81972

Report . . . [of the Rhode Island Commissioner of Public Schools.] 70565

Report of the Rhode Island Peace Society. 70730

Report of the Rhode-Island State Temperance Society. 70737

Report of the Rhode-Island Sunday School Union. 70740

Report of the Richmond and Petersburg Rail Road Company. 71199

Report of the Richmond and York River Rail Road. 71200

Report of the Ridgway Farm and Land Company. (71295)

Report of the Right Honourable the Earl of Durham. 38751

Report of the Rt. Rev. George M. Randall. 67784

Report of the Roanoke Island Investigation Committee. 15389

Report of the Rochester and Chatham Anti-slavery Society. 72370

Report of the Secretary of the Treasury, read
in the House. (29980)
Report of the Secretary of the Treasury . . .
relative to the claim. (38264)
Report of the Secretary of the Treasury . . .
respecting the direct tax. 26399
Report of the Secretary of the Treasury to
the House of Representatives. (69498)
Report of the Secretary of the Treasury, to
whom was referred the memorial. 26399
Report of the Secretary of the Treasury . . .
transmitting. 3189
Report [of the Secretary of War] 70731
Report of the Secretary of War and Marine
[of Texas.] 95062
Report of the Secretary of War, communicating
a copy of Major-General Rosecrans'
report. (73259)
Report of the Secretary of War, communicating
a report and map of the examination of
New Mexico, made by Lieut. J. W. Abert.
57
Report of the Secretary of War, communicating
a report and map of the examination of
New Mexico; with Col. Cook's report.
58
Report of the Secretary of War, communicating, in compliance with a resolution.
83434
Report of the Secretary of War, communicating
information. 83706
Report of the Secretary of War, communicating
the report of an expedition. (64117)
Report of the Secretary of War, communicating
the report of Capt. George B. McClellan.
(43017)
Report of the Secretary of War communicating
the several Pacific Railroad Explorations
69900
Report of the Secretary of War, in answer to
a resolution. (76081)
Report of the Secretary of War, in further
compliance with the resolution of the
Senate. 83533
Report of the Secretary of War, in further
compliance with the resolitions of the
Senate. 83706
Report of the Secretary of War on the several
railroad explorations. 69946
Report of the Secretary of War [of Texas.]
95056, 95060-95061
Report of the Secretary of War [of the Con-
federate States.] 15396-15400, 15419
Report of the Secretary of War [of the United
States.] 29883, 34703, 69900, 70731
Report of the Secretary . . . under the act
of March, 1842. 46076
Report of the Secretary with regard to the
probable origin. (76674)
Report of the Select Committee appointed by
the Legislature. (53926)
Report of the Select Committee appointed by
the Planters' Convention. (69901)
Report of the Select Committee appointed . . .
March 27, 1832. (53607)
Report of the Select Committee appointed to
confer with the authorities. 60543
Report of the Select Committee appointed to
consider. 45340
Report of the Select Committee appointed to
enquire into the condition. 60133
Report of the Select Committee appointed to
enquire into the present system. 10413
Report of the Select Committee appointed . . .
to investigate into the management of
the canals. (53568)

Report . . . of the Select Committee appointed
to investigate matters connected with the
New Orleans massacre. 53367
Report of the Select Committee appointed to
investigate matters connected with the
publication. 22518
Report of the Select Committee, chosen by
ballot. 87938
Report of the Select Committee in relation to
Sunbury and Erie Railroad. 60551
Report of the Select Committee in relation to
the fraudulent abstraction. 24913
Report of the Select Committee . . . in relation
to the resources. 45341
Report of the Select Committee, made in the
Senate. 60552
Report of the Select Committee (Majority) of
the Board of Governors. 54073
Report of the Select Committee . . . of Colum-
bia College. 73977
Report of the Select Committee of the Assembly
of 1851. (53977)
Report of the Select Committee of the Assembly
on the Library. (2723)
Report of the Select Com. of the B. & O. R. R.
Co. 2992
Report of the Select Committee of the Board
of Ten Governors. 54073
Report of the Select Committee of the Board
. . . to which was referred a communi-
cation. 54121
Report of the Select Committee of the College.
85923
Report of the Select Committee of the Common
Council. 9061, note after 91136
Report of the Select Committee of the Constitutional Convention. 49538
[Report of the Select Committee of the House
in relation to the colonial records of
Pennsylvania.] 60550
Report of the Select Committee of the House
of Assembly of Upper Canada. 43439
Report of the Select Committee of the House
of Assembly, on the embarrassments of
the country. 69902
Report of the Select Committee, of the House
of Assembly, on the political state of
the provinces of Upper and Lower Canada.
80438
Report of the Select Committee of the House
of Commons. 52260
Report of the Select Committee of the House
[of Representatives of Pennsylvania.]
note just before 60250
Report of the Select Committee of the House of
Representatives [on the Memphis riots.]
47782
Report of the Select Committee of the House
of Representatives on the subject of building an insane hospital. 52920
Report of the Select Committee of the House
of Representatives, to which were referred
the messages. 69903
Report of the Select Committee of the House
. . . on the . . . alleged frauds. 60553
Report of the Select Committee of the House
. . . on the constitution of Maryland.
45113
Report of the Select Committee of the House
. . . relative to the exemption. 60554
Report of the Select Committee of the Legislative Assembly. 10439
Report of the Select Committee of the Legislative Council of Upper Canada. 10578
Report of the Select Committee of the Legislative Council on the subject of the state of
the Lunatic Asylum. 53229

REPORT

Report of the Solicitor of the Protective War Claim and Pension Agency. 62168, 66097, 76652

Report of the Somerville Horse Railroad. 86831

Report of the South & North Alabama Railroad. 87326

Report of the South-Carolina Canal and Rail Road Company. 87954

Report of the South Carolina Commissioners. 87408

Report of the South-Carolina Domestic Missionary Society. 88003

Report of the South Massachusetts Education Society. 88147

Report of the South Reading Branch Railroad. 88161

Report of the South Shore Railroad Company. 88207

Report of the Southern Aid Society. 88274

Report of the Southern Baptist Publication Society. 88310

Report [of the Southern Board of Foreign Missions.] 88313

Report of the Southern Female College. 88349

Report of the Southern Protestant Educational Association. 88450

Report of the Southwestern Bible Society of New-Orleans. (53376)

[Report of the Southwestern Railroad Company (Georgia)] 88624

Report of the Special Agent [of the Little Rock and Fort Smith Railroad Company.] 41543

Report of the Special and Joint Committee appointed at the last session. 87492

Report of the Special Commission on the Hours of Labor. 46057

Report of the Special Commissioner and Auditor of State [of Ohio.] 57062

Report of the Special Commissioners, appointed on the 8th of September, 1856. 10467

Report of the Special Committee, appointed at the session of 1838. 87520

Report of the Special Committee appointed by the Board of Education. 63158

Report of the Special Committee appointed by the Chairman. 86080

Report of the Special Committee, appointed by the Common Council of the city of New York. 38267

Report of the Special Committee appointed by the Common Council on a communication from the Board of Trustees. (27494)

Report of the Special Committee appointed by the Common Council . . . relative to the catastrophe in Hague Street. 54648

Report of the Special Committee appointed by the Legislative Assembly. 19114

Report of the Special Committee, appointed by the Mayor and Aldermen. 15153

Report of the Special Committee, appointed by the Select Council. 62169

Report of the Special Committee appointed for the purpose of examining all books. 62170

Report of the Special Committee appointed for the purpose of examining the condition of the public records of this state. 45345

Report of the Special Committee, appointed October 6, 1868. 86159

Report of the Special Committee appointed to enquire and report as to the condition, management, and prospects. (28269)

[Report] of the Special Committee appointed to inquire into the causes which retard the settlement. 42519

Report of the Special Committee appointed to inquire into the military expenditures. 48786

Report of the Special Committee appointed . . . to investigate the proceedings, &c. 48787

Report of the Special Committee appointed to investigate the troubles in Kansas. 37087

Report of the Special Committee concerning the City Bank. 53013

Report of the Special Committee in relation to weights and measures. (70675)

Report of the Special Committee in the matter of the application. 55828

Report of the Special Committee of Common Council. 62171

Report of the Special Committee of Nine. (69906)

Report of the Special Committee of the Assembly. 53230

Report of the Special Committee of the Board of Councilmen. 54649

Report of the Special Committee of the Board of Education. 54121

Report of the Special Committee of the Board of Regents of the Smithsonian Institution. 85059-85060

Report of the Special Committee of the Board of Regents on the communication of Prof. Henry. 85024

Report of the Special Committee of the Board of Regents on the proposal. 85061

Report of the Special Committee of the Chamber of Commerce of the State of New York on the confiscation of cotton. 17130, 53940

Report of the Special Committee of the Chamber of Commerce on testimonials. 37132

Report of the Special Committee of the Common Council in relation to the reorganization. 54584

Report of the Special Committee of the Common Council, on supplying the city with water. 8330

Report of the Special Committee [of the Controllers of the Public Schools.] 62173

Report of the Special Committee of the County Board on Public Schools. 62172

Report of the Special Committee of the Detroit Board of Trade. (19791)

Report of the Special Committee of the General Assembly of South Carolina. 87493

Report of the Special Committee of the General Assembly relative to the deleterious substances. 70676

Report of the Special Committee of the Grand Lodge. (53692)

Report of the Special Committee of the House appointed to inquire. 28157, 69907

Report of the Special Committee of the House of Assembly. 53196

Report of the Special Committee of the House of Representatives, of South Carolina, on so much of the message. 87521

Report of the Special Committee of the House of Representatives of South Carolina, relative to the organization of that body. 87522

Report of the Special Committee of the House of Representatives [of the Confederate States.] (69908)

Report of the Special Committee of the House on so much of the message. 87523

Report of the State Geologist of the state of Colorado. 82752-82753

Report of the State Historian. 60630

Report of the State Insurance Commissioner [of Rhode Island.] 70680, (70747)

Report of the State Librarian of Michigan. 48788

Report of the State Librarian of Nevada. 52398

Report of the State Librarian [of Pennsylvania.] 60632

Report of the State Librarian, relating to the registration. 15851

Report of the State Librarian to the New Hampshire Legislature. 52921

Report of the State Library . . . of . . . Louisiana. 42257

Report of the State Lunatic Hospital, at Northampton, Mass. 46138

Report . . . of the State Lunatic Hospital [of Pennsylvania.] 60633

Report of the State Mineralogist of . . . Nevada. 52396

Report of the State Normal and Training School at Cortland. 53967

Report of the State Normal and Training School at Oswego. 53967

Report of the State Normal and Training School at Potsdam. 53967

Report of the state of education in Pennsylvania. 60373

Report of the state of Grace-Church Charity School. 54295

Report of the . . . state of the missions. 102707

Report of the State Paymaster of the Indiana Volunteer Militia. 34564

Report of the . . . State Reform School [of Michigan.] (48772)

Report of the State Registrar [of California.] (10043)

Report of the State Superintendent of Common Schools of . . . Maine. (43934)

Report of the State Superintendent of Public Instruction [of Maryland.] 45137

Report of the State Temperance Committee 46143

Report of the State Treasurer [of Arkansas.] (69761)

Report of the State Treasurer [of Iowa.] 35034

Report of the State Treasurer [of Louisiana.] 42297

Report of the State Treasurer [of Maine.] 44049

Report of the State Treasurer [of Michigan.] (48796)

Report of the State Treasurer [of Missouri.] (49646)

Report of the State Treasurer [of Nevada.] 52410

Report of the State Treasurer [of New Hampshire.] (52922)

Report of the State Treasurer [of Pennsylvania.] 60443

Report of the State Treasurer on the finances. (60639)

Report of the State Treasurer, shewing the receipts and expenditures. (60639)

Report of the State Treasurer to the General Assembly [of Connecticut.] 15673

Report of the state trials before the General Court Martial. 10588

Report of the State Trustee of the Illinois & Michigan Canal. 56394

Report of the State's Agent of the Western Shore of Maryland. 45381

Report of the Stockholders' Committee of the South Shore Railroad Company. 88205

Report of the Stockholders of the Dauphin and Susquehanna Coal Company. 18670

Report of the Stockholders of the . . . [Mohawk and Hudson Rail Road] Company. 49853

Report of the Stockholders of the Richmond Female Institute. 71206

Report of the Street Railway Commissioners. 46147

Report of the Sub-committee deputed to visit Erie. 62177

Report of the Sub-committee on Agriculture. (70736)

Report of the Sub-committee on cleansing the city. 62178

Report of the sub-committee on consolidation of bonds and stocks. 55828

Report of the Sugar River Valley Railroad Company. 93458

Report of the suit against the Rock Island Bridge. 72395

Report of the suit of Henry B. Bascom and others. 48191, note after 93976

Report [of the Sunday School Association of Somerset County.] 86810

Report of the Sunday-School Union of the Methodist Episcopal Church. 48205

Report of the Superintendent and Inspector of Salt. 53989

Report of the Superintendent and Secretary of the Board of St. Joseph Public Schools. 75295

Report of the Superintendent and Secretary to the Board of the St. Louis Public Schools. 75365

Report of the Superintendent of Alien Passengers. (45630)

Report of the Superintendent of Buildings. 54687

Report of the Superintendent of Common Schools of Connecticut. 15724

Report of the Superintendent of Common Schools [of Illinois.] 34225

Report of the Superintendent of Common Schools . . . of Indiana. 34507

Report of the Superintendent of Common Schools [of Missouri.] 49638

Report of the Superintendent of Common Schools [of New York.] 53990

Report of the Superintendent of Common Schools of North Carolina. 55694

Report of the Superintendent of Common Schools [of Ohio.] 57058

Report of the Superintendent of Common Schools [of Pennsylvania.] 60565, 60648

Report of the Superintendent of Common Schools of the City of Cincinnati. (13088)

Report of the Superintendent of Education for Lower Canada. 10432, 42515

Report of the Superintendent of Education on the schools of Nova Scotia. 56183

Report of the Superintendent of Health of . . . Providence. 66370

Report of the Superintendent of Health upon the subject of fat and lard melting. (66350)

Report of the Superintendent of Lights. (66371)

Report of the Superintendent of Negro Affairs. 35701

Report of the Superintendent of Public Buildings. 66372

Report of the Superintendent of Public Education [of Louisiana.] 42223-42224

Report of the Superintendent of Public Instruction of Indiana. 34508

Report . . . of the Superintendent of Public Instruction [of Iowa.] 34990

Report of the survey of a section of the River Delaware. (43069), 62179

Report of the survey of extension of the European and North American Railway. 9418

Report of the survey of the Colorado of the West and its tributaries. 85062

Report of the survey of the Colorado of the West. Letter from the Secretary of the Smithsonian Institution. 85062

Report of the survey [of the geology of Canada.] 84802

Report of the survey of the isthmus of Tehuantepec. 26549, note after 93913, 8th note after 94592

Report of the survey of the Little South Division. 88232

Report of the survey [of the Mohawk Valley Railroad.] 49855

Report of the survey of the Neenah or Fox River, Wisconsin. 61287

Report of the survey of the north and northwest lakes. 47233

Report of the survey of the Rivers Atrato, Pato, and Baudo. (38855)

Report of the survey of the roads in Cambridge. (10144)

Report of the survey of the route of the Galena and Chicago Union Rail Road. 50673

Report of the survey of the route of the Ithaca and Owego Rail-Road. 94073

Report of the survey of the route of the New York and Erie Railroad. (54729), 105560

Report of the Surveyor General of California. 10019

Report of the Surveyor-General of . . . Nevada. 52397

Report of the Surveyor-General [of Pennsylvania.] (60655)

Report of the Surveyor-General on the Oneida Purchases. 57342

Report of the Surveyor of Highways of . . . Providence. (66373)

Report of the Surveyor of Highways [of Roxbury, Mass.] 73720

Report of the surveys and estimates of the Potsdam & Watertown Railroad. 64598

Report of the surveys and location for the extension. 45396

Report of the surveys of the Kennebeck River. 37388

Report of the Susquehanna Commissioners. (60609)

Report of the Susquehannah Commissioners. 93938

Report of the Synod of Ohio. 32429

Report of the Tax Committees of the New York, Boston, and Philadelphia Clearing House Associations. 3188

Report of the Teachers' Institute, . . . of Philadelphia. 62302

Report of the Temporary Home Association. (62303)

Report of the tenth exhibition [of the Pennsylvania Horticultural Society.] 60326

Report of the Territorial Secretary, Auditor, etc. [of Nevada Territory.] 52410

Report of the Territorial Superintendent of Common Schools. Kansas, 1859. 37031

Report of the testimony in the case of Harry Ingersoll. 60278

Report of the . . . Theological Seminary of St. Charles Borromeo. 62308

Report of the third annual fair of the American Institute. (54080)

Report of the third meeting of the National Conference of Unitarian and Other Christian Churches. (51952)

Report of the Topographical Commissioners. 62180

Report of the town convention [of Boston, 1804.] 6715

Report of the Town Council on the expenses. 30549

Report of the Town Temperance Committee [of New Bedford, Mass.] 52505

Report of the Town Treasurer of the town of Smithfield. 84976

Report of the Town's Committee on the petition of Isaac P. Davis. 6748, 69912

Report of the Town's Committee, on the subject of city government. (75693)

Report of the trade and commerce of the British North American colonies. 16985

Report of the trade and commerce of the city of Albany. 612

Report of the Training, or Preparatory School (Troy Academy.) 69641

Report of the transactions of the . . . [Massachusetts Horticultural] Society. 45862

Report of the transactions of the Pennsylvania State Agricultural Society. 60376

Report of the Treasurer [of Marlboro', Mass.] 44633

Report of the Treasurer of . . . Maryland. 45158, 45380

Report of the Treasurer [of Mississippi.] 49539

Report [of the Treasurer of Savannah, Ga.] 77261-77262

Report of the Treasurer of State [of Indiana.] 34526

Report of the Treasurer of State [of Iowa.] 35034

Report of the Treasurer of State [of Ohio.] 57061

Report of the Treasurer of the city of Montreal. 50242

Report of the Treasurer [of the Lawrence Machine Shop.] 39397

Report of the Treasurer of the Meadville Theological School. 47247

Report of the Treasurer of the Metropolitan Fair. 54401

Report of the Treasurer of the Naumkeag Steam Cotton Company. (75676)

Report of the Treasurer [of the Norwich Mining Company.] (55929)

Report of the Treasurer of the Republic of Texas. 95053

Report of the Treasurer of the [School] Board [of Charlestown, Mass.] 12095

Report of the Treasurer of the state of Georgia. (27101)

Report of the Treasurer of the state of Illinois. (34251)

Report of the Treasurer of the state [of New York.] 53995

Report of the Treasurer of the W[estern] Shore [of Maryland.] 45381

Report of the Treasurer. To the Honorable House of Representatives of Massachusetts. (46059)

Report of the Treasury Board on a mint. 49334

Report of the Treasury Department. 95055

Report of the trial an action on the case brought by Silvanus Miller. 55375

Report of the trial and acquittal of Edward Shippen. (30039), 1st note after 96927

Report of the trial and acquittal of the Hon. Robert Porter. 64311

Report of the trial and conviction of John Earls. 21630

Report of the trial and conviction of John Haggerty. 29519

Report of the trial, before Judges Thompson and Betts. 88951

Report of the trial by impeachment of James Prescott. 62643

Report of the trial for riot. 62181, 96940

Report of the trial of Abner Rogers, Jr. 5292

Report of the trial of Abraham Prescott, for the murder of Mrs. Sally Cochran. 65235

Report of the trial of Abraham Prescott, on an indictment for the murder of Mrs. Sally Cochran. 65234

Report of the trial of Albert S. Field. 24263

Report of the trial of Alexander Humphreys or Alexander. 33827, 91841A, 94084

Report of the trial of an action brought by persons. 48190, 74566

Report of the trial of an action by Mr. W. Dawe. 30001

Report of the trial of an action for libel. 96898

Report of the trial of an action on the case. 49074

Report of the trial of an indictment for libel. 69824, 100796

Report of the trial of an indictment, prosecuted at the instance of the West India Dock Company. 102781

Report of the trial of an officer. 64788

Report of the trial of Andrew Wright. 105543

Report of the trial of Arthur Hodge. 4425, 32327

Report of the trial of Bradbury Ferguson. 64621

Report of the trial of Brig. General William Hull. 25045, 33645

Report of the trial of Castner Hanway for treason. (71820)

Report of the trial of Catharine N. Forrest vs. Edwin Forrest. 25109

Report of the trial of Charles N. Baldwin for a libel, in publishing charges of fraud and swindling. 2879, 72619, 101441

Report of the trial of Charles N. Baldwin, for a libel, in publishing, in the Republican chronicle, certain charges. 2879, 101441

Report of the trial of Col. Jos. D. Learned. 39537

Report of the trial of Commodore David Porter. 64222

Report of the trial of Daniel H. Corey. 16784, 96854

Report of the trial of Dr. Samuel Thomson. 95602

Report of the trial of Dominic Daley. 18303

Report of the trial of Edward Williams. 104196

Report of the trial of Ephraim Wheeler. 103183

Report of the trial of Eunice Hall. 72620, note after 96880

Report of the trial of Evan Poultney, on the charge of felony. 64724

Report of the trial of Evan Poultney, William M. Ellicott, and Samuel Poultney. 45079

Report of the trial of fourteen Negroes. 69913

Report of the trial of Friends, at Steubenville. 28119, note after 96937

Report of the trial of Friends, in the city of Philadelphia. 28120, 96938

Report of the trial of George Bowen. 7059

Report of the trial of George Ryan. 74530

Report of the trial of George W. Williams. 104224

Report of the trial of Henry Bedlow. (69914)

Report of the trial of Henry Eckford. 3392

Report of the trial of Henry Phillips. 96919

Report of the trial of J. O. Beauchamp. 18431, 79848

Report of the trial of Jacob Cochrane. 82578, note after 96852

Report of the trial of James H. Peck. 59476, 1st note after 90364

Report of the trial of James Jameson. 69889

Report of the trial of James Johnson. (36227), (75954), note after 96890

Report of the trial, of James Sylvanus M'Clean. 43007

Report of the trial of Jason Fairbanks. 23672, 96862

Report of the trial of Jereboam O. Beauchamp. 18431, 79848

Report of the trial of John Boies. 6148

Report of the trial of John Hodges. 32341

Report of the trial of John Quay. (72621), note after 96921

[Report] of [the trial of] John Sinclair. (36227)

Report of the trial of John Wade. 100902

Report of the trial of Joshua Nettles. 11005

Report of the trial of Levi Weeks. 102461

Report of the trial of McLaurin F. Cooke. (16326)

Report of the trial of Michael & Martin Toohey. 92878

Report of the trial of Miss Prudence Crandall. 17392, 2d note after 96854

Report of the trial of Mr. John N. Maffitt. 43790

Report of the trial of Nathan Foster. (25259), 73045

Report of the trial of . . . [Oliver Dana Thompson.] 95518

Report of the trial of Pedro Gibert. 69915, 96948

Report of the trial of Pedro Gilbert [sic]. 27309

Report of the trial of Prof. John W. Webster. 102329

Report of the trial of Richard D. Croucher. 96856

Report of the trial of Richard Dennes the younger. 19591

Report of the trial of Robt. J. Breckenridge. 7690

Report of the trial of Robert S. Field. 29890, note after 96863

Report of the trial of S. M. Andrews. (18802), 1st note after 96812

Report of the trial of Samuel Tulley. 97443

Report of the trial of Sherman Converse. (16211)

Report of the trial of the cause of John Taylor. 19369, note after 94503

Report of the trial of the engine America. 103008

Report of the trial of the Hon. Samuel Chase. 12204

Report of the trial of the King v. John Hatchard. 30841

Report of the trial of the late Rev. D. Graham. 96879

Report of the trial of the Rev. David Brigham. 96836

Report of the trial of the Rev. Ephraim K. Avery. (31792), 96818

Report of the trial of the Rev. Theodore Clapp. 13230

Report of the trial of the Spanish pirates. 93808

Report of the trial of Thomas Wilson Dorr, for treason against the state of Rhode Island. 20650

Report of the trial of Thomas Wilson Dorr, for treason; including the testimony at length. 20649, 1st note after 97484

Report of the trial of William Coleman. 14314

Report of the trial on an indictment for libel. 100796

Report of the trial, Timothy Upham vs. Hill & Barton. 98052

Report of the trial trip of the United States Steamer Wampanoag. 55224

Report of the trial, Washburn vs. Knight. 101522

Report of the trials of Capt. Thomas Wells. 102604

Report of the trials of Charles de Reinhard. 69111

Report of the trials of Charles Denney and Patrick Bryne. 96939

Report of the trials of Dr. John Stratton. 92736

Report of the trials of Oliver Cummins. 17941, 30345

Report of the trials of the causes of Elisha Jenkins. (35991), 98547

Report of the trials of the murderers of Richard Kennings. 36046

Report of the Trinity Hall Sunday School. 57874

Report of the . . . true boundary line. (46001)

Report of the Trustees and other officers of the village of Rutland. 74468

Report of the Trustees and Principal of the Illinois Institution for the Education of the Deaf and Dumb. 34231

Report of the Trustees, and speech of J. M. Lovejoy. 55683

Report of the Trustees and Superintendent of the . . . [Pennsylvania State Lunatic] Hospital. 60379

Report of the Trustees, appointed to receive contributions for the ransom of the captives taken by the Indians at Hatfield. 91929

Report of the Trustees of Beliot College. (4589)

Report of the Trustees [of Boston City Hospital.] (6692)

Report of the Trustees of Columbia College. (14839)

Report of the Trustees of Donations for Education in Liberia. 40923

Report of the Trustees of Hanover College. 88137

Report of the Trustees [of Iowa State University.] 34993

Report of the Trustees of McDonogh Estate. 43177

Report of the Trustees [of Marietta College.] (44569)

Report of the Trustees of Oak Dale Cemetery. 56377

Report of the Trustees of Pine Grove Cemetery. 62926

Report of the Trustees of Rutgers College. 74440

Report of the Trustees of St. Johnland. 86084

Report of the Trustees of the Antietam National Monument. (70681)

Report of the Trustees [of the Astor Library.] 2255

Report of the Trustees [of the Bank for Savings, New York.] 54108

Report of the Trustees of the Bible Society of Salem and Vicinity. 100925

Report of the Trustees [of the Boston Public Library.] 6759

Report of the . . . Trustees [of the Broad Street Baptist Church.] 61508

Report of the Trustees of the Cooper Union. (16596)

Report of the Trustees of the Douglas Houghton Mining Company. 20730

Report of the Trustees [of the Evangelical Missionary Society of Massachusetts.] 45648

Report of the Trustees [of the Female Missionary Society of the Western District of New York.] 24050

Report of the Trustees of the Five Points House of Industry. 54280

Report of the Trustees of the Hampshire Missionary Society. (30137), 63926, 94206

Report of the Trustees of the High-School Society. 54312

Report of the . . . Trustees of the House of Reformation. 52923

Report of the Trustees of the Indiana Asylum for the Education of the Deaf and Dumb. 34511

Report of the Trustees [of the Indiana Institute for the Education of the Blind.] 34510

Report of the Trustees of the Kentucky Institution for the Deaf and Dumb. (37491)

Report of the Trustees of the Lake Superior Copper Mining Company. 38674

Report of the Trustees [of the Lane Theological Seminary.] 38861

Report of the Trustees of the M'Donogh Educational Fund and Institute. (69916)

Report of the Trustees [of the Maine Insane Hospital.] (43973)

Report of the Trustees [of the Maine Missionary Society.] (5978), 43983, 101313

Report of the . . . Trustees of the Manual Labour Academy. 60230

Report of the Trustees of the Marietta Collegiate Institute. 44570

Report of the Trustees of the Massachusetts School. 45893

Report of the Trustees of the . . . [Massachusetts] Society . . . [for Promoting Agriculture.] (45896)

Report of the Trustees [of the Massachusetts State Reform School.] 46141

Report of the Trustees of the Michigan Asylum for the Insane. 48759

Report of the Trustees of the Missionary Fund. 73654

Report of the Trustees of the Montreal Mining Company. 50266

Report of the Trustees of the Museum of Comparative Zoology. (51572)

Report of the Trustees of the Nautical Branch of the State Reform School. 46141

Report of the Trustees of the New-Bedford City Library. 52467

Report of the Trustees of the New England Institution for the Education of the Blind. 52691

Report of the Trustees of the New Hampshire Asylum for the Insane. 52857

Report of the . . . Trustees of the New Hampshire College of Agriculture. (52866)

Report of the Trustees of the New Hampshire Missionary Society. (52879)

Report . . . of the . . . Trustees of the New Jersey State Normal School. 53195

Report of the Trustees of the New-York and Lake Superior Mining Company. 54735

Report of the Trustees of the New-York and Michigan Mining Company. 54737

Report of the . . . Trustees of the New-York Baptist Union. (54749)

Report of the Trustees of the [New York City Free School] Society. 54285

Report of the Trustees of the . . . [New York] Society Library. 54544

Report of the Trustees of the New-York State Asylum for Idiots. 53802

Report of the Trustees of the [New York] State Library. (53824)

Report of the Trustees of the . . . [New York State Lunatic] Asylum. 53831

Report of the . . . Trustees . . . of the Northern Ohio Lunatic Asylum. 55817

Report of the Trustees of the Oneida Institute of Science and Industry. 57341

Report of the Trustees of the Parochial Fund. (66207)

Report of the Trustees of the Peabody Academy of Science. 59385

Report of the Trustees of the Peabody Institute, Danvers. 59395

Report of the . . . Trustees of the Philadelphia Association for the Relief of Disabled Firemen. 61956

Report of the Trustees of the Philadelphia Gas Works. 62000

Report of the Trustees of the Public Library of the city of Charlestown. 12103

Report of the Trustees of the Public Library of the city of Fall River. 23744

Report of the Trustees of the Public Library of the town of Reading. 68206

Report of the Trustees of the . . . [Public School] Society of [New York.] 54615

Report of the Trustees of the Roxbury Athenaeum. 73725

Report of the Trustees of the Roxbury Missionary Fund. (61569)

Report of the Trustees of the School Fund of . . . New Jersey. 53064

Report of the . . . Trustees of the . . . Schools of Louisville. 42321

Report of the Trustees of the Second Mortgage Bond Holders. 55828

Report of the Trustees of "The Sheltering Arms." 80149

Report of the . . . Trustees of the Society of the Protestant Episcopal Church, for the Advancement of Christianity. 60618

Report of the Trustees of the State Industrial School for Girls. 46135

Report of the Trustees of the State Library [of New Hampshire.] 52921

Report of the Trustees of the State Library [of New York.] 101353

Report of the Trustees of the State Lunatic Hospital, at Northampton. 46138

Report of the Trustees of the State Lunatic Hospital, at Taunton. 46138

Report of the . . . Trustees of the State Lunatic Hospital [of Pennsylvania.] 60633

Report of the Trustees of the State Normal School [of Connecticut.] 15734

Report of the Trustees of the State Reform School [of California.] 10001

Report of the Trustees of the State Reform School [of Connecticut.] 15732

Report of the Trustees of the Subscription Fund for the Benefit of the Cambridge Volunteers. 10153, 69917

Report of the Trustees [of the University of Alabama.] (570)

Report of the Trustees [of the University of Maryland.] (45389)

Report of the . . . Trustees of the Young Man's Institute [of Philadelphia.] 62399

Report of the Trustees, . . . to the Female Oneida Missionary Society. 57342

Report of the Trustees, Treasurer and Library of the Manchester City Library. 44213

Report of the trvth of the fight about the Isles of Acores. 58038, 67575, (67585)

Report of the twentieth annual exhibition of the . . . [Massachusetts Horticultural] Society. 45862

Report of the [28th] anniversary banquet. 30856

Report of the twenty-first National Anti-slavery Bazaar. 51922

Report of the twenty-fourth National Anti-slavery Festival. 45817

Report of the Ulverston will cause. 97700

Report [of the Union Benevolent Association, Philadelphia.] note after 97764

Report of the Union College Anti-slavery Society. 97799

Report of the "Union Committee" appointed by the meeting of the signers of the memorial to Congress. 54653, 69918, note after 97799

Report of the Union Committee in relation to national banks. 51938

Report of the Union Committee of the Sunday Schools. 79797

Report of the "Union Committee" on the National Bank. 26399

Report . . . of the Union League [of Philadelphia.] 62352

Report of the Union Temporary Home for Children. 62356

Report of the United Domestic Missionary Society. 54078, 97869

Report of the United Foreign Missionary Society. 97874

Report of the United States and Mexican Boundary Survey. 22538

Report [of the United States Christian Commission.] 45385

Report of the U.S. civil engineer employed. 38658

Report of the United States Commissioners [to the Paris Universal Exposition, 1867.] (58595)

Report of the United States Guano Company. 29056

Report [of the U.S. Historical Manuscripts Commission.] note before 95044, 98425

Report of the United States Provost Marshall, of Rhode Island. 70682

Report of the United States Revenue Commission. 70170, 70173

Report of the United States Revenue Commission in respect to copper mining. 16703

Report of the United States Revenue Commission on distilled spirits. (20295), 70173

Report of the U. S. Senate on the Nebraska bill. 52201

Report of the Universal Lyceum. 98002

Report of the Universalist Sabbath School Association. 81625, 98016

Report of the Upper Canada Clergy Society. 98093

Report of the Upper Canada Religious Tract & Book Society. 98095

Report [of the Utica and Oswego Railroad Company.] 98236

Report [of the Utica and Schenectady Railroad Company.] 98237

Report of the Valuation Committee. (46022)

Report of the Van Wyck Committee. (17913)

Report of the Vermont Anti-slavery Society. 99220

Report of the Vermont Bible Society. 89744, 99222

Report of the [Young Men's Missionary Society of the Reformed Dutch Church.] 106179

Report of the [Young Men's New-York Bible Society.] 106181

Report [of the Young Men's Temperance Association in Salisbury and Amesbury, Mass.] 106185

Report of the [Young Men's Temperance Society of New Haven.] 106189

Report of the [Young Men's Temperance Society of Philadelphia.] 106190

Report of the [Young Men's Temperance Society, Washington, D. C.] 106191

Report of the Youth's Missionary Society. 62404, 106209

Report of the Youths' Tract Society. 62405, 106211

Report of their [i. e. the African Institution's] Committee. 95689

Report of Theodore B. Samo. (75907)

Report of Theodric Bland. 5864

Report of Thomas B. Akins, Commissioner of Public Records. (56184)

Report of Thomas B. Akins . . . February 24th, 1864. 56166

[Report of Thomas Bennett.] 87387

Report of Thomas Butler King. 37837

Report . . . [of Thomas Butler King.] (37840)

Report of Thomas Purse. 77262

Report of Thomas S. Fernon. 60358

[Report of Thomas S. Grimke.] 87531

Report of Thos. W. Conway. 16223

Report of three nights' public discussion in Bolton. 64962

Report of tolls, trade and tonnage. 53560

Report of town officers [of Marblehead, Mass.] (44473)

Report of transactions [of the Illinois State Sanitary Bureau.] 34266

Report of Treasurer of Committee of Relief for Sufferers of the Pemberton Mill. (39392)

Report of trials in the courts of Canada. (1346)

Report of Trinity Church. 20341, 69710, 4th note after 96984

Report of Trustees of McDonogh Estate. 43177

Report of . . . Trustees of the Illinois and Michigan Canal. 34207

Report of vessels sunk or burnt. 69919

Report of Vice-President and Managing Directors. (28268)

Report of Vincent Colyer, on the reception. 14921

Report of Vincent Colyer, Superintendent N. Y. State Soldiers' Depot. 14919

Report of W. B. Robbins. 71853

Report of W. G. Veazey. 27249

Report of W. H. Gist. 87471

Report of W. H. H. Terrell. 34526

Report of W. Milnor Roberts, Chief Engineer. 60132

Report of W. Milnor Roberts on the survey and imporvement. 71940

Report of Walter Shanly. 57887, 79757

Report of Ways and Means. The Committee of Ways and Means further report. 87498

Report of Ways and Means. The Committee of Ways and Means report. 87497

Report of West-India planters and merchants. 102794

Report of Wm. B. Foster. 55578, 60275

Report of William B. Frue. 88156

Report of Wm. C. Drake. (35028)

Report of William Crawford. 17443

Report of William E. Morris. (60561)

Report of William H. Crawford. 16117, 17446, note after 92827

Report of William H. Marshall. 10716

Report of Wm. H. Smith. 84866

Report of Wm. Howard. 87958

Report of Wm. J. Aydelott. 45090

Report of Wm. J. McAlpine. 52493

Report of William Lambert. 38739

Report of William Milnor Roberts. 60031

Report of William P. Blake . . . and Charles T. Jackson. 5804, 18278

Report of William P. Blake, . . . upon the gold placers. 5805, 12526

Report of William Weston. 54654, 103057

Report of Woman's Rights Convention. 90397

Report . . . Ohio Teachers' Association. (23677)

Report . . . on a continuous water line of transportation. 51941

Report on a direct route for the eastern termination. 10209

Report on . . . a high school for girls. (2588)

Report on a light house off Nantucket. 51754

Report on a memorial of the Alumni of Dartmouth. 18626

Report . . . on a national name. 54476

Report on a proposition to modify the plan. 3459

Report on a railroad from Boston to the Hudson River. 6768

Report on a railway suspension bridge. 79316

Report on a re-examination of the economic geology. 45753

Report on a ship canal between Lake Michigan and the Mississippi River. 38665

Report . . . on a survey and examination of the various plans. 57068

Report on a survey for the railway bridge. 37146

Report on a survey of the Genesee Valley Canal. 44730

Report on a suspension bridge across the Potomac. 22209

Report . . . On a system for the . . . relief. 57539

Report on a system of public elementary instruction. 74571

Report on a topographical and geographical exploration. 31938

Report on a uniform system of weights, measures, &c. 27285

Report on almshouses and pauperism. 81292

Report on ambulance and camp-hospital corps. 54640

Report on American manufactures. 10889

Report on American meteorites. 80168

Report on American slavery. 814, 70068

Report on amputations through the foot. 30113, 76657

Report on an exploration of the country. 85161

Report on barracks and hospitals. 69920

Report on by-laws, rules of order, and principles of discipline. 87077

Report . . . on canals and internal improvements. 53921

Report on . . . Cape Cod Harbor. 10734

Report on capital punishment. (46059)

Report . . . on capital punishment. Made . . . March 14, 1851. (53934)

Report on capital punishment made to the Maine Legislature. 66722

Report . . . on capital punishments. 45980

Report on cereals. 73959

Report on certain documents. 45346

Report on certain mineral lands. 19151

Report on certain points in the geology of
Massachusetts. 45756
Report on Chiriqui. 70990
Report on cholera and emigration. 8570
Report on church building. 73749
Report, on city affairs. 64350
Report on civil engineering and public works.
(58595)
Report on collegiate education. 44303
Report on colonization and emigration. 49689,
49701
Report on commerce and navigation. (10111)
Report on condition of troops, hospitals, etc.
34304
Report on conditions and prospects [of the]
Ascot Mining Company. 2164
Report on congregationalism. 15486, 69921
Report . . . on . . . continued fevers. 30113,
76657
Report . . . on convictions for criminal
offences. 53956
Report on cooperative educational and research
work. 85063
Report on criminal statistics in the state of
New York. 31161
Report . . . on criminal statistics of . . . New
York. 53956
Report on Crustacea of the United States
Exploring Expedition. 18422
Report on currency and corporations. 34735
Report on currency. [By George McDuffie.]
(27641)
Report on diminishing the cost of instruction.
(30759A)
Report on drainage and sewerage. 62183
Report . . . on dysentery. 30113, 76657
Report on education by John W. Hoyt. 33408
Report on . . . education in . . . Louisville.
42321
Report on education in Lower Canada. 42515
Report on . . . education, read in the Senate.
60568
Report on elementary public instruction in
Europe. 92387, 92392
Report on emigration by a Select Committee of
the Chamber of Commerce. 22506
Report on epidemic cholera. 17214
Report on epidemic cholera and yellow fever.
22684
Report on epidemic cholera, in the Army of
the United States. 22683
Report . . . on evening schools. 54121
Report . . . on . . . excision of joints for
traumatic causes. 30113, 76657
Report . . . [on] executive patronage. 9936
Report on executive patronage; . . . May 4,
1826. 49426
Report . . . on external hygiene. (66944)
Report on fellowship with slavery. 82057
Report on food and diet. (28114)
Report on foreign correspondence. 58975
Report on foreign missions. 85318
Report on free labour. 93258
Report on free white schools in Richmond.
(71209), 86344
Report . . . [on] French spoliations. 50583
Report [on French spoliations, January 14,
1831.] (41617)
Report on gambling in New York. 28535
Report on gaols and houses of correction.
(56061)
Report on granting public lands. 7703
Report on harbors and rivers. 33898
Report on health in the schools. 66267
Report . . . on home evangelization. 45740

Report . . . on idleness and sources of employ-
ment. 54670
Report on Illinois coal. 34252
Report on Indian affairs. [By Horace Everett.]
(23282)
Report on Indian affairs. [By Lewis Cass.]
48099
Report on Indian missions. (34468), 82261
Report on insanity and idiocy in Massachusetts.
(46062)
Report on internal revenue frauds. 18589
Report on interoceanic canals and railroads.
18805
Report on its commerce, and the navigation of
Lake Michigan, 49163
Report on Kentucky River. 2845
Report on land titles in California. (36629)
Report on laying a railroad. 18141
Report on legislation regulating the practice
of pharmacy. 44061
Report on leins of the commonwealth. 59827,
60562
Report on limited partnerships. 60563
Report . . . [on martial law.] 101918
Report . . . on . . . memorial of David Hatch
on San Domingo affairs. 33253
Report on meteorology, to the Secretary of the
Navy. 22917
Report on meteorology, to the Surgeon-General.
22917
Report on meteorology, with directions for
mariners. 22917
Report on Mexico and her financial questions.
48649
Report . . . on . . . miasmatic fevers. 30113,
76657
Report on military hygiene and therapeutics.
30113, 76657, 76676
Report on . . . [Missouri] prisons. 49640
Report on Mystic Pond. 33051
Report on Neversink River. 13739
Report on normal schools. 69922
Report on Nova Scotia gold fields. 64033
Report on observations of the total eclipse of
the sun. (76435)
Report on operations during and after the
battles at Gettysburg. 20718
Report . . . on petitions to prevent slave
hunting. 53937
Report . . . on . . . pneumonia. 30113, 76657
Report on portions of the Williams Lake and
Cariboo Districts. 58355
Report on postal telegraph. 33422
Report on providing for the appointment of a
Board of Agriculture. (45648)
Report . . . on public expenditures of the
House of Representatives. 23901
Report on public instruction. 42223
Report on public instruction in Pennsylvania.
50644
Report on public schools in Rhode Island.
70565
Report . . . [on] quinine as a prophylactic.
30113, 76657
Report on registration. 85501
Report . . . on relief of the family. (53592)
Report . . . on report & memorial of county
superintendents. (53935)
Report on roads, bridges and canals. 60564
Report on Sabbath mails. 36278, 41843
Report on school-houses. 25820
Report on schools for freedmen, 1866. 25743
Report on schools for freedmen, July, 1867.
(9217)
Report . . . on . . . scurvy. 30113, 76657

Report . . . on side walks. 52502

Report . . . on so much of the Governor's message as relates to the investment and distribution of the surplus revenue. 53922

Report . . . on so much of the Governor's message as relates to the school fund. 46036

Report on standard weights. 21409

Report on state certificates. (70549)

Report on stopping the United States mail. 36277

Report on sundry petitions. 41267

Report on . . . supply of water from Lake Erie. 22765

Report on supplying Chicago with water. 42934

Report on supplying the city of Charlestown with pure water. 2891, note after 91588

Report on supplying the city of Hamilton, C. W., with water. 30059

Report on supplying the city of Quebec with pure water. 67058

Report on surveys for the extension of the Hartford, Providence and Fishkill Railroad. 56051

Report on surveys for the extension of the Providence, Hartford and Fishkill Railroad. (66328)

Report on surveys for the Picton Branch Railway. (62685)

Report . . . [on] "That part of the speech of . . . the Governor." 53939

Report on the abolition of capital punishment. (46084)

Report on the accounts of the Treasurer of Trinity Church. 6675

Report on the address of a portion of the members of the General Assembly of Georgia. 27093, 27102, 87436, 87443

Report on the administrative changes in France. (76485)

Report on the affairs of British North America, from the Earl of Durham. 38746-38747

Report on the affairs of the Bank of Bangor. 3159

Report on the affairs of the Indians in Canada. 10468

Report on the affairs of the Mohawk and Hudson Railroad Company. 49853

Report on the African apprentice system. 33583

Report on the agency of intemperance. 62184, 97765

Report on the agricultural capabilities. 36370

Report on the agriculture and geology of Mississippi. 49540

Report on the agriculture and industry of the county of Onondaga. 26824

Report on the agriculture of Massachusetts. 14535

Report on the agriculture of the province of Canada. 10347

Report on the Albert Coal Mine. 35401

Report on the Alcinda Gold Mine. (24495)

Report on the alleged outrages in the southern states. (78313)

Report on the annexation of Texas. 46063

Report on the apportionment bill. 299

Report, on the appropriation of public lands for schools. 89005

Report on the Ashburton murder. 47233

Report . . . [on] the attempt to circulate, through the mail. 9936

Report on the Bahamas. (68017)

Report on the battle of Murfreesboro', Tenn. 73260

Report on the battle of Ridgeway, Canada West. 57348

Report . . . on the bill to settle and adjust the western boundary line. 45090

Report on the births, marriages and deaths, in . . . Providence. 66255

Report on the Board of Police of Baltimore. 45346

Report on the botany. 69946

Report on the boundary line between Massachusetts and Rhode Island. 45921

Report on the breadstuffs of the United States. 4234

[Report on the Browne, Choate, and Forrester Funds.] (75647)

Report on the Brunswick Canal and Railroad. 2903

Report on the burial of Massachusetts dead. 46064

Report on the case of A. C. Rhind. (70488)

Report on the case of indigent pious students in Yale College. 105844

Report on the case of Laura Bridgman. 33332

Report . . . on the case of T. C. A. Dexter. 32653

Report on the case of the Canadian prisoners. 10589

Report on the case of the Queen vs. Edward John Eyre. 24371

Report on the causes which retard the progress. 28939

Report on the change of route west of Omaha. 81357

Report on the chemical examination of several waters. 81057

Report on the Chesapeake & Ohio Canal. 91634

Report on the "Circumstances attending the surrend of the Navy Yard at Pensacola." (69923)

Report . . . on the city charter. 52502

Report on the claim of John Browne Cutting. 18204

Report on the claim of the Iroquois Indians. 68507

Report on the claims of William Milton, and others. 49145

Report on the clarification of cane-juice. 80474

Report on the classification of the schools. 46065

Report on the coal lands. 36334

Report on the coal lands of the Mount Carmel and Shamokin Rail Road Company. 72660

Report on the coal lands of the Zerbe's Run and Shamoken Improvement Company. 72661

Report on the coal mines. 69924

Report . . . on the coasting and lake trade. (53592)

Report . . . on the colonial agency. 53936

Report on the commerce and improvement of western lake harbors. (28218)

Report on the commerce of the United States. 69925

Report on the commercial regulations of the United States with all foreign nations. 24650

Report on the commercial regulations of the United States with foreign countries. 14984

Report on the commercial regulations of the United States with foreign nations. (69926)

Report . . . on the Commissioners appointed by the Legislature of Maryland. 65473

Report . . . on the . . . common continued fever of New-England. (35429)

Report . . . on the common school system. 25682

Report on the common schools. 60565

Report on the concerns of the New Hampshire Cent Institution. 52865

Report on the condition and improvement of the common schools. 20901

Report on the condition and improvement of the public schools of Rhode Island. 3468, 70683-70684

Report on the condition, capacity and resources. (19661)

Report on the condition of camps and hospitals at Cairo and vicinity, Paducah and St. Louis. 76562, 76647

Report on the condition of camps and hospitals at Cairo and vicinity, St. Louis, etc. 59168

Report on the condition of common schools. 57058

Report on the condition of government cotton. 69927

Report on the condition of military hospitals at Grafton, Va. 76565, 76647

Report on the condition of our wounded fellow-citizens. (39070)

Report . . . on the condition of returned prisoners. 25164

Report on the condition of the camps and hospitals at Cairo and Vicinity. 76562, 76647

Report on the condition of the Charity Fund. 45760

Report on the condition of the Fire Department of . . . Providence. (66260)

Report on the condition of the Freedmen, of the Department of the Gulf. 16223

Report on the condition of the people of color in . . . Ohio. 57043

Report on the condition of the public records. (45347)

Report on the condition of the south. 61214

Report on the condition of the State Prison. 53196

Report on the condition of the troops. 54892, 76560, 76647

Report on the connection at various times. 10125

Report on the construction of a military road. 51275

Report on the construction of a railway bridge. 50257

Report on the continuation of the Little Schuyl-kill Rail Road. 60566

Report on the Contoocook Valley Plumbago Mine. 35401

Report on the copper mine of the North Carolina Copper Company. 35401

Report on the country between Frampton. 69928

Report on the country between the Saguenay. 74940

Report on the cretaceous and tertiary plants. 31004

Report on the criminal law at Demerara. 31398

Report [on the Crooked Lake and Chemung Canals.] 106109

Report . . . on . . . the cultivation of tropical plants. (41340)

Report on the cultivation of spring wheat. 14535

Report on the Cumberland Gap and Price's Turnpike Road. 17717

Report on the Cumberland Road. 17887

Report on the currency. 17993, 57390

Report on the cypress Timber. 20022

Report on the debate in the House of Commons. 39629

Report . . . on the debts and revenues of the city of Memphis. 47787

Report on the Decapod Crustacea of the Albatross dredgings. 84231-84232

Report . . . on the decificency in the Treasurer's accounts. 46029

Report, on the derivation and definition of the names. 98387

Report on the development. 82754

Report on the disastrous effects of the destruction. 38979

Report on the discussion on American slavery. 95500

Report on the Dismal Swamp Canal, . . . a history. 37762

Report on the Dismal Swamp Canal, its cost, condition, and resources. 58664

Report, on the diversion of the water. 44729

Report on the eastern terminus of the Pennsylvania Rail Road. 60358

Report on the economic geology of southern Ohio. (56924)

Report on the educational policy of the state of New York. 33305

Report . . . on the encroachments upon the bay and harbor of New York. 54655

Report on the enlargement of the water works. 22209

Report on the epidemic small pox and chicken pox. 53765, 69929

Report on the epidemics of Tennessee and Kentucky. 93978-93979

Report on the establishment . . . in Philadelphia. 62185

Report on the establishment of a farm school. 35394

Report on the establishment of a state agricultural school. 8908

Report on the establishment of one or more union schools. 62355

Report on the evidence. 96848

Report on the examination of the canal routes. 24515

Report . . . [on] the expediency of adopting measures. 23268

Report on the expediency of celebrating in future. 69930, 77236

Report . . . on the expediency of filling up the basin. (39220)

Report on the expediency of laying a direct tax. 20314

Report on the expediency of providing better tenements for the poor. 60975

Report on the expediency of publishing the journal of the Provincial Congress. 41267

Report on the expedition to procure seeds and plants. 89922

Report on the expenses of general education. (60609)

Report on the experiments with turbine wheels. 62370

Report on the exploration of Lakes Superior & Huron. 73447

Report on the exploration of the country between Lake Superior and the Red River Settlement, and between the latter place and the Assiniboine. 18958

Report on the exploration of the country between Lake Superior and the Red River settlement. Printed by order of the Legislative Assembly. 10590

Report on the exploration of the Yellowstone River. (68129)

Report on the insects of Massachusetts. 30523

Report on the Intercolonial Railway Exploratory Survey. (24707)

Report on the introduction of manual labor. 85856

Report on the introduction of soft water. (21813)

Report on the Invertebrata of Massachusetts. 28086-28087

Report on the iron of Dodge and Washington Counties. 60869

Report on the Joint Standing Committee on the Public Domain. 15837

Report on the keeping of swine in the city of Providence. (66351)

Report on the lands of the East Tennessee Mining Company. 21655

Report on the libels contained in the Boston newspapers. (45645)

Report . . . on the Library Department of the Maryland Institute. 45225

Report on the location and expenses of the Niagara Falls Ship Canal. 55131

Report on the location and survey of the Potomac and Annapolis Canal. (33581)

Report, on the location of the Choctaw Claims. 38815

Report on the location of the line between Fishkill and Albany. 36072

Report on the Londonderry Iron and Coal Deposits. 27226

Report on the McCauley Mountain coal lands. 71933

Report . . . on the M'Donogh bequest. 43177

Report on the McDonogh Estate. 53370

Report on the malignant disease. 49015

Report on the management of the Indians in British North America. 34677

Report on the manufacture of iron. (45348)

Report on the manufactures, unimproved mill seats, &c. 12544

Report on the Massachusetts resolutions: House of Representatives, April 4, 1844. 300

Report on the Massachusetts resolutions, 28th Congress. 34750

Report on the massacres committed by Seminoles. 79070

Report on the Medical Department [of the University of Pennsylvania.] 60758

Report on the medical topography and epidemic diseases of Rhode Island. 58877

Report on the medical topography and epidemics of California. (41807)

Report on the medical topography and epidemics of the state of New York. 83363

Report on the medical topography and the epidemic diseases of Kentucky. 93980

Report on the memorial of Fulwar Skipwith. 81655

Report on the memorial of sundry merchants and traders. (62186)

Report on the memorial of T. J. Randolph. 67855

Report on the memorial of Tobias Lear. 39533

Report on the memorials of the Seneca Indians. (46067)

Report on the merits of the claim of . . . Massachusetts. 46068

Report on the Mexican war. 8907

Report . . . on the Micmac Mission. (48820)

Report on the minerals and mineral waters of Chile. 83001

Report . . . on the mines, iron works . . . Clearfield Coke and Iron Company. 36334

Report on the mines known in the eastern division of Hayti. 101226

Report on the mines of New Mexico. 58014

Report on the mines of the Connecticut Cupper Company. 25430

Report on the mollusca of Long Island. 84127

Report on the Mt. Pleasant Coal Mine. 78469

Report on the National Bank Currency Act. 69934

Report on the national defences. 21388

Report on the Navy Yard at League Island. 39519

Report on the new map of Maryland, 1835. (45156)

Report on the new map of Maryland, 1834. (45156)

Report on the new town at the foot of Lake Huron. (32973)

Report on the new treasury buildings. 101200

Report on the Nicaragua route. 86964

Report on the Northern Pacific Railroad. 6586

Report on the Nova-Scotia Railway. 56185

Report on the noxious, beneficial and other insects, of the state of Missouri. 49645, 71391

Report on the noxious, beneficial and other insects, of the state of New York. 24562

Report on the operations of the Inspectors and Relief Agents. 25696

Report on the operations of the Sanitary Commission. 76597, 76647

Report on the operations of the U. S. Sanitary Commission in North Carolina. 76613, 76647

Report on the operations of the U. S. Sanitary Commission in the valley of the Mississippi, for the quarter ending Oct. 1st, 1864. 54893, 76610, 76647

Report on the operations of the U. S. Sanitary Commission in the valley of the Mississippi, made September 1st 1863. 76601, 76647

Report on the organization and campaigns of the Army of the Potomac. 43010, 43018

Report on the organization of an evening school. 62187

Report on the organization of the Army of the Potomac. (43014)

Report on the origin and increase of the Paterson Manufactories. 59061, 93532, 93535

Report on the origin of the yellow fever in Norfolk. 55484

Report on the Ottawa and French River Navigation Project. 79758

Report on the Painter Tract. 42776

Report on the Palaeontological Department. 15906

Report on the palaeontology [of Southern California.] (1712)

Report on the parish schools of New Brunswick. 52559

Report on the part of the Committee of Privileges. 20994

Report on the passage of a general law concerning Indians. 34678

Report. [On the pauper laws of Massachusetts.] 45971

Report . . . [on] the penal code of Massachusetts.] 46150

Report on the penitentiary system. (60566A)

Report on the penitentiary system in the United States. (29552)

Report on the pension systems. 76593, 76647

Report on the petition of S. W. Hall. 29849

Report on the petition of the Trustees of Amherst College. (45895)

Report on the petition of William Forsyth. 10577

Report on the petitions of Franklin and Wrentham. 16140

Report on the physical condition of the Rhode Island Regiments. 51008, 70686

Report on the plan of instruction. 54312

Report on the poor and insane in Rhode-Island. 31112, 70687

Report . . . [on] the practicability and expediency of establishing a university of active instruction. 53938

Report on the practicability of forming a communication. 50767

Report on the practicability of navigating with steamboats. (26198)

Report on the practical operation of the law. 2745

Report on the preliminary surveys and estimates. 88626

Report on the preliminary surveys, by F. Harbach. 30283

Report on the present state and recent progress of ethnographical philology. 39167

Report on the present state of our knowledge. 11002

Report on the present state of the Chesapeake and Ohio Canal. 29656, 94073

Report on the present state of the Society in Scotland for Propagating Christian Knowledge. 94427

Report . . . on the present system of keeping and dispursing the public money. (3187)

Report on the principal fisheries of the American seas. 74736

Report on the proceedings against the late Rev. J. Smith. 82905

Report on the production and manufacture of cotton. 17127, 35449

Report on the progress and present condition of the Chester County Cabinet of Natural Science. 12545

Report on the progress of library architecture. 84980

Report on the progress of settlement in the townships. 6945, 10591

Report on the progress of the Geological Survey of Ohio. 54894

Report on the project of uniting the great bays. (41900)

Report on the projected canal. 41748

Report on the projected survey. 45155

Report on the projects for supplying the city. 42935

Report on the property of the Arlington Gold Mining Co. (81058)

Report on the property of the Atlantic Gold Mining Company. 81059

Report on the property of the California Borax Company. 62459

Report on the property of the Champlain Copper Mining Company. 11843

Report on the property of the Chebucto Gold Mining Company. 81060

Report on the property of the Colonial Gold Mining Company. (14686), 81061

Report on the property of the Halifax Gold Mining Company. 81062

Report on the property of the Waverley Gold Mining Co. 81063

Report on the proposed alterations in the constitution. (66153)

Report of the proposed canal. 105561

Report on the proposed city park. 57246

Report on the proposed connection of the West Branch Improvements. 2507

Report on the proposed rail-road. (31064)

Report on the proposed railroads. 60567

Report on the proposed railway in the province of Pernambuco. 50764

Report on the proposed trunk line of railway. 69935

Report on the proposed works. 14089

Report on the public departments of Upper Canada. 10581

Report on the public schools. 42146

Report on the Quadrupeds of Massachusetts. 46069

Report on the question of bridging the Missouri River. 20400

Report [on the recently discovered petroleum region in California.] 10000

Report on the Red Slate Quarry. 45473

Report on the region of Mineral de Veraguas. (48020)

Report on the relation of Mystic Pond and River. 6726

Report on the relation of the auxiliaries to the Central Board. 76667

Report on the relative powers, duties, and responsibilities. (30759A)

Report on the removal of the deposites. [By John Middleton Clayton.] (13576)

Report on the removal of the deposites, made by Mr. Webster. 102288

Report on the removal of the . . . [General Theological] Seminary. (66153)

Report on the reptiles and amphibians of Ohio. 84797

Report on the resolutions of 8th ultimo. (40339)

Report on the resources of Iceland and Greenland. (59542)

Report on the resources of the United States. 73963

Report . . . on the returns of the seventh census. 37430

Report on the rights and dutes of the President and Fellows. 101056

Report . . . on the Rochester and Corning Railroad. 93150

Report on the rock oil, or petroleum. 81064

Report on the Sailors' Snug Harbor. 74976

Report on the same. 49341

Report on the sandstone of the Connecticut Valley. 32244

Report on the sanitary condition of the city of New York. 22389

Report on the sanitary condition of the United States Troops in the Mississippi Valley. 54896, 76551, 76647

Report on the Sanitary Survey of the State. 79886

Report on the Saratoga Seltzer Spring. 11854

Report on the season of 1846. 3586

Report . . . on the Seminole War. 38471, note before 92843

Report on the Sherbrooke Gold District. 31936

Report on the silver mines of the Macate Valley, Peru. (43226)

Report on the small pox, in . . . Providence. (66352)

Report on the soil, climate, etc., of Oregon. 33369

Report on the soils, from the St. John's Colleton Agricultural Society. 87534

Report on the soils of Powhatan County. 27380

Report on the South Pennsylvania Railroad. 88155

Report on the standards of weight and measure. 45359

Report on "The Star-spangled banner." 105959, 105966

Report on the state beneficiaries. 3752, 70688

Report . . . on the state finances. 45980

Report on the state house artesian well. (46814)

Report on the state of education in Pennsylvania. 60373, 98707

Report on the state of public instruction in Prussia. 94510

Report on the state of religion, &c. 15820

Report on the state of the Grand Lodge. 45760

Report on the state of the Grand Lodge of Massachusetts. 20379

Report on the state of the Land Office. 43952

Report on the state of the militia. 10520

Report on the state of the Mint. 69936

Report on the state of the Patent Office. 59047

Report on the state of the representation. 10592

Report . . . on the state pauper laws. 46048

Report . . . on the State Reform School. 46141

Report on the Stockbridge Indians. 46070

Report, on the subject of a communication. (69937)

Report . . . [on] the subject of a home. 60339

Report on the subject of a House of Reformation. 66353

Report on the subject of cotton and woolen manufactories. 55684

Report on the subject of introducing pure water. 2902

Report . . . on the subject of jurors. (46039)

Report on the subject of land titles in California. (36629)

Report on the subject of manufactures. 29979

Report . . . on the subject of manufactures . . . on the 15th day of January, 1790. 29976

Report on the subject of paying interest on current deposits. 54656

Report on the subject of the boundary line. 3750

Report on the subject of the chancery records. (45350)

Report on the . . . subject of the free bridge. 6605

Report on the subject of the national road. 71715

Report on the subject of the ship canal across Cape Cod. 10734

Report on the subject of the state census. 79886

Report on the Sudbury fight. 37717

Report on the survey by J. C. Trautwine. (38466)

Report on the survey, estimates and revenues. 60186

Report on the survey of a canal from the Potomac to Baltimore. 33283, 64593

Report on the survey of a route for the proposed Susquehanna and Delaware Rail-Road. 93919

Report on the Survey of South Carolina. 87719-87722

Report on the survey of the Bangor, Orono and Oldtown Rail-Road. 50993

Report on the survey of the boundary between Maryland and Virginia. 45090

Report on the Survey of the Colorado of the West. 85048

Report on the survey of the European and North American Railway. 50993

Report on the survey of the Lackawanna and Lanesboro' Railroad. 60187, note after 96479

Report on the survey of the Portsmouth & Newburyport Rail Road. 3542

Report on the surveys and definite location of the Eastern Railroad. (21666), (24207)

Report on the surveys for a railroad from Stonington, Connecticut. 92163

Report on the surveys of the Providence and Plainfield Railroad. 66300

Report on the surveys, undertaken with a view to the establishment of a rail road. 60569, 94527, 94529

Report on the suspension bridge at Middletown. 48870

Report on the suspension of specie payments. 46071

Report on the Susquehanna Coal Company's lands. 93931

Report on the system of popular education in the city of New York. 54657

Report on the tariff of toll. 22209

Report . . . on the Tioga Coal & Iron Mines. (33581)

Report on the topographical features and character of the country. 69946

Report on the topography and epidemic diseases of New Jersey. 83503

Report on the Toronto and Guelph Railway. 79758

Report on the trade and commerce of Montreal. 50282

Report on the trade in foreign corn and on the agriculture of the north of Europe. 35492

Report on the transportation of the mail. 36278

Report on the trees and shrubs. 22429

Report . . . on the Universal Exposition at Paris. (53592)

Report . . . on the use of Quinine as a prophylactic. 30113, 76555, 76647

Report on the vessels. (9062)

Report on the viaduct. 62231

Report on the wealth and resources of the state of Oregon. 11687

Report on the Wheeling and Belmont Suspension Bridge. 22209

Report . . . on the Wills legacy. 62391

Report on the yellow fever of 1867. 32469

Report on the zoology. 69946

Report on thorough-drainage. 80473

Report on Toronto harbour. 79758

Report on trade and commerce. 10593

Report . . . on . . . treatment of fractures. 30113, 76657

Report . . . on . . . vaccination. 30113, 76657

Report on venereal diseases. 30113, 76657

Report on Victoria Bridge. 91322

Report, on water [by Dewitt Clinton.] 93511

Report on water for locomotives. 11854

Report . . . on weights, measures, and coins. (58595)

Report . . . on . . . yellow fever. 30113, 76657

Report on Zoophytes of the U. S. Exploring Expedition. (18423)

Report, ordinance, and addresses of the Convention. 87428

Report . . . Our taxes, markets, streets and sanitary condition. (54188)

Report preliminary for continuing the survey. 85086

Report, prepared by authority of the Delegates. 75343

Report prepared by Mr. Botts. 6832

Report, . . . prepared for the Executive Council. 61970

Report . . . presented at the annual meeting. 45860

Report, presented Oct. 29, 1834. (13115)

Report presented to the Anti-slavery Society of Canada. 81865

Report to the Board of Directors of the
Southern Pacific Railroad Company.
88434

Report to the Board of Missions. 66132

Report to the Board of Overseers . . . on
the condition, needs, and prospects of
the university. (30759A)

Report to the Board of Regents of the University of Michigan. 48804

Report to the Board of Trade. (34586)

Report to the Booth Association. 83491

Report to the Boston Board of Trade. 2282

Report to the Brown Association, U. S. A.,
made by C. M. Fisher. 24454

Report to the Brown Association, U. S. A.
made by Columbus Smith. 82408

Report to the Building Committee of the
Girard College for Orphans. 101199

Report to the California State Board of Agriculture. 5801

Report to the Canada Temperance Society.
51270

Report to the Canal Commissioners, in reply
to strictures. (60572)

Report to the Canal Commissioners of Ohio.
26825

Report to the Chamber of Commerce. 45034

Report to the City Council of Providence.
66354

Report to the City Council of Providence,
presented June 1, 1846. 66355

Report to the City Council of Savannah. 101427

Report to the Commission. 76581, 76647

Report . . . to the . . . Commissioners of
Emigration. 37101

Report to the Commissioners of the Central
Park. 54158

Report to the Committee, by Henry G. Clark.
34822, 76591, 76647

Report to the "Committee for Promoting the
Better Observance of the Sabbath."
74657

Report to the Committee, May, 1863. 76605

Report to the Committee of the City Council.
(79883)

Report to the Common Council [of Washington,
D. C.] 61314

Report to the Congress of the United States
of America. 29949

Report to the Congress on the comparative
population and cereal product. 73954

Report to the contributors to the Pennsylvania
Relief Association. 60360, 61474

Report to the Controllers of the Public Schools,
on the reorganization. (2588), 61561

Report to the Corporation of Brown University.
(8631)

Report to the Councils of Philadelphia on
insects. 39908

Report to the . . . Councils, on the progress
and state of the water works. 62369

Report to the creditors. 22220

Report to the Delegates of the Benevolent
Societies of Boston. 3444

Report to the Department of State by Samuel
B. Ruggles. 73954

Report to the Directors . . . by a Committee.
34317

Report—to the Directors of the Honduras
Inter-oceanic Railway Company. 89992

Report to the Directors of the Pequa Railroad and Improvement Company. (60844)

Report to the Directors of the Utica and
Schenectady Rail Road Company. 98239

Report to the Earl of Clarendon. (24625)

Report to the East Tennessee Relief Association
at Knoxville. 21656, 33782

Report to the Emperor of the French. 21357

Report to the Executive Committee of New
England Yearly Meeting. 86064

Report to the Executive Committee of the
American Unitarian Association. 91044

Report to the Faculty of South Carolina College.
87990

Report to the Female Missionary Society for
the Poor. 54274, 90079

Report to the Follansbee Association. 82410

Report to the Foreign Office. 41692

Report to the Freedmen's Inquiry Commission.
(33333)

Report to the French government. 84504

Report to the General Assembly, June session,
1799. 70689

Report to the General Assembly . . . of its
Trustees. 65222

Report to the General Assembly of Rhode
Island, of the Committee on Education.
70690

Report to the General Assembly of Rhode
Island relative to the registry and returns of births. (70634)

Report to the General Assembly of the state of
Rhode Island, on the Soldier's National
Cemetery at Gettysburg. 3751

Report to the General Assembly on the condition of the railroads. 59291

Report to the General Association of Massachusetts. (34816)

Report to the General-in-Chief of the Army.
80844

Report to the Gibson Association of Vermont.
(82411)

Report to the government of the United States
on the munitions of war. 55872

Report to the Governor. . . . concerning the
Indians of the commonwealth. 21626

Report to the Governor [of Illinois by the State
House Commissioners.] 34264

Report to the Governor [of New Jersey by the
Treasurer.] (53223)

Report [to the Governor of New York] on
Antietam Cemetery. 35849

Report to the Governor of the state of Michigan.
27249, 48791

Report [to the Governor] relative to establishing
a state university. 10001

Report. To the Honorable Senate and House
of Representatives. 87401

Report to the Houghton Association. 82412

Report to the House . . . from the Committee
on the Judiciary. 64622

Report to the House of Representatives of the
commonwealth of Massachusetts. 12699,
note after 98561

Report to the House of Representatives of the
United States. 90329

Report to the House . . . on the Seventh Day
Baptists. 60573

Report to the Hudson River Railroad Committee.
50673

Report to the Indiana State Medical Society.
93975

Report to the International Statistical Congress
at Berlin. 73966

Report to the International Statistical Congress
at The Hague. 73958

Report to the inventors of the United States.
(51113)

Report to the Jennings Association. 82413

Report to the Legislature by the Pennsylvania
Institution for the Deaf and Dumb. 102545

Report to the Legislature of Kentucky. 9899

Report . . . to the Legislature of Massachusetts, upon idiocy. (33333)

Report to the Legislature of . . . New-Hampshire on the culture of silk. 30420

Report to the Legislature of Pennsylvania, containing a description. 4120

Report to the Legislature of Pennsylvania, containing a description of the Swatara Mining District. 92910

Report to the Legislature of South Carolina on the expediency of a code. 28862

Report to the Legislature of South Carolina, relating to the registration. 87723

Report to the Legislature of Virginia on scientific education. 82558

Report, to the Legislature, on the Juniata and Conemaugh Canal. 36898

Report to the Legislature on the state of affairs in Baltimore. 3077

Report to the Legislature, on the subject of a canal. 15845

Report to the Legislature relating to the registry and returns. 79886

Report to the lot holders of the Cemetery of Spring Grove. (13115), 98922

Report to the Louisiana State Medical Society. (3838)

Report to the Massachusetts Legislature. (46077)

Report to the Mayor and Aldermen of Boston. 96509

Report to the Mayor of New Orleans. (30484)

Report to the . . . [Mine Hill & Schuylkill Haven Rail Road] Company. 60252

Report to the National Convention of the Home League. 6042

Report to the Navy Department, by Captain Dalghren. 18277

Report to the Navy Department of the United States. 36334

Report to the patrons and friends of the City Mission of Salem. 75646

Report to the patrons of the Salem City Mission. 75646

Report to the Pennsylvania Legislature. 7669

Report to the people of Rochester. 72366

Report to the President and Directors of the Mohawk and Hudson Railway Company. 24705, 49853

Report to the President and Directors of the South-Carolina Canal and Railroad Company. 87960

Report to the Proprietors of the Boston Athenaeum. (6595)

Report to the Proprietors of the Lowell Cemetery. 42485

Report to the Proprietors of the Middlesex Canal. 93536

Report to the provincial government. (33218)

Report to the Prudential Committee. (1418)

Report to the purchasers of coal and salt lands. 56923

Report to the Right Hon. the Lords Commissions of Trade and Plantations. 37239

(Report to the Secretary of the Smithsonian Institution.) By Lorin Blodget. 5949

Report to the Secretary of the Smithsonian Institution on the fishes of New Jersey. 2805

Report to the Secretary of the Treasury. By Rossiter W. Raymond. (68066)

Report to the Secretary of the Treasury from the Chief of the First Division National Currency Bureau. 69940

Report to the Secretary of the Treasury in relation to the foreign commerce. 55340

Report to the Secretary of War, of July, 1861. 3482

Report to the Secretary of War of the operations of the Sanitary Commission. (76574), 76647

Report to the Secretary of War of the United States. 50945

Report to the Secretary of War on the operations of the Sanitary Commission. (76564), 76647

Report to the Secretary of War . . . upon the sanitary condition of the volunteer army. 57245

Report. To the Select Council. (62188)

Report . . . to the Senate of Massachusetts. 58660

Report to the Senate [of New York.] 53536

Report to the Senate of the 14th January, 1850. 69418

Report to the Society for Propagating the Gospel Among the Indians and Others in America. 77610

Report to the Society in Scotland for Propagating Christian Knowledge. 94428

Report to the Standing Committee, of the United States Sanitary Commission. 76622, 76647

Report to the Standing Committee, United States Sanitary Commission. 4575

Report to the stock and bond holders. 76445

Report to the stock and bondholders . . . made April 7, 1858. 76445

Report to the Stockholders in the New York County Bank. 53013

Report to the Stockholders [of the Cumberland Coal and Iron Company.] 17883

Report to the Stockholders of the East Boston Company. 21644

Report to the Stockholders of the N. H. Iron Factory Company. (52873)

Report to the Stockholders of the New Jersey Mining Company. 53184

Report . . . to the stockholders of the Pittsburgh and Connellsville Railroad Company. 63126

Report to the Stockholders [of the Portland, Saco & Portsmouth Rail Road Company.] 64367

Report to the Stockholders of the Wilmington & Susquehanna Rail Road Company. 104587

Report to the Superintendent of the U. S. Coast Survey. 28097

Report to the Supreme Court of the State of New-York. 73956, 73977

Report to the Swiss Military Department. 39661

Report to the Trustees and friends of the Baltimore Ministry at Large. 18307

Report to the Trustees in possession of the Rancine and Mississippi Railroad. (67396)

Report to the Trustees of the Apalachicola Land Company. 5878

Report to the Trustees of the Ascension Association. 82943

Report to the Trustees of the College of New Jersey. (28505)

Report to the Trustees of the Emlen Institution. (61616)

Report to the Trustees of the Lake Superior Copper Company. 35401

Report . . . to the . . . Trustees of the University of Pennsylvania. 55237

Report to the U. S. Sanitary Com., July 1, 1862. 86316

Report to the U. S. Sanitary Commission on a system. 76668
Report to the Vestry of St. George's Church, N. Y. 75212
Report to the Vestry of St. Peter's Church, Albany, of the lay delegates appointed by them. 35847
Report to the Vestry of St. Peter's Church, Albany, of the lay delegates to the Diocesan Convention. 637, 35847, 89353
Report to the Vestry of St. Peter's Church, Albany, of their delegate to the Diocesan Convention. 89354
Report to the Vestry of Trinity Church. 4976
Report. To the Watering Committee. 62371
Report to the Willoughby Association. 82414
Report to the Wilson Association. 82694
Report to the Yearly Meeting of Friends. 53662
Report . . . transmitting [the names of the foreign stockholders.] 3189
Report. Ulster Mine at Glenville. 32332
Report, United States Senate [on the] memorial [of the Hartford Argillo Manufacturing Company.] 30664
Report . . . a code for the support of common schools. 45137
Report upon a plan for the organization of colleges. 66609
Report upon a projected improvement of the state. 57246
Report upon a route from San Diego to Port Yuma. 69946
Report upon a supply of water for the city of Baltimore. 80839
Report upon coinage and segnorage. 8348
Report upon collections. (47371), 85072
Report upon cotton. 51236
Report upon education in Upper Canada. 21268
Report upon international exchanges. 85065
Report upon loan and fund associations. 45776
Report . . . upon memorials from the city of New York. 53956
Report upon . . . nullification. (60574)
Report upon opening the Reading Room. 6759
Report upon public schools and education in Rhode Island. 70692
Report upon public schools and education [in Rhode Island.] (70695)
Report upon public schools and education, in the state of Rhode Island. 70691
Report upon sundry documents relating to Asiatic cholera. 66356
Report upon the autographical manuscript. 45370
Report . . . upon the bills relating to the manufacture and duty on salt. 53912
Report upon the . . . Black River Mines. 35401
Report upon the census of Rhode Island. 70693
Report upon the Colorado River of the West. 35308
Report upon the condition . . . of the Lehigh and Delaware Water Gap Rail Road. 60199
Report upon the constitutional rights and privileges of Harvard College. (30759A), note after 102262
Report upon the contemplated metropolitan railroad. (72050)
Report upon the Convention of Cattle Commissioners. 85502
Report upon the cost of transporting troops and supplies. 69900, 69946
Report upon the disabled Rhode Island Soldiers. 18279, 70694

Report . . . upon the epidemic of 1853. 71255
Report upon the extension of the water works [of Philadelphia.] 62369
Report upon the finances and internal improvements of the state of New-York. (73964), 73977, 103010
Report . . . upon the financial condition of the . . . [Massachusetts General] Hospital. 45846
Report upon the Geological Survey of New Jersey. 16238
Report upon the Geological Survey of Newfoundland. 54988
Report upon the geology and mineralogy of . . . New Hampshire. (52832)
Report upon the gold placers. 5807
Report upon the Huntington and Board Top Rail Road and Coal Company's coal lands. (60152), 92911
Report upon the Indian tribes. 69946
Report upon the international exchanges. (29267)
Report upon the invertebrate animals of Vineyard Sound. 84233
Report . . . upon the investigation of frauds. (53930)
Report upon the memorial of the Chamber of Commerce of Sheffield. (52832)
Report upon the merits of the Great Western Railroad. 28478
Report upon the merits of the Michigan Central Railroad. 48761
Report upon the military and hydographical chart. 28216
Report upon the mineral resources of the Illinois Central Railroad. 25246
Report upon the natural history and geology of the state of Maine. (43939)
Report upon the oil property. 81054
Report upon the . . . Oxford Plumbago Mining Company. 35401
Report upon the physics and hydraulics of the Mississippi River. (33797)
Report upon the plan of construction of several of the principal rail roads. 38118
Report upon the population of Barbados. 68018
Report upon the prevention of disease in . . . Providence. 66357
Report upon the property of the Mount Lebanon Cemetery Company. (61847)
Report . . . upon the provision made by law. 10594
Report upon the registration of births, marriages, and deaths. (70634)
Report upon the removal of swill and house offal. 66358
Report upon the Reptilia of the North Pacific Exploring Expedition. 29914
Report upon the resolutions for the amendment of the law. 87382
Report upon . . . the . . . road from Cumberland to the District of Columbia. 71711
Report upon the sailing directions for the port of New-York. (2588)
Report upon the sanitary effects of filling the Cove Basin. 66359
Report upon the survey and cost of constructing a railroad. 91497
Report upon the surveys . . . of the Baltimore and Ohio Rail Road. 2992, (39220)
Report upon the Tomhicken Mining Property. (71934)
Report upon the Tonawanda Railroad Company. 96158
Report upon the value of the company's land. 75422

Report upon the wealth, internal resources, and commercial prosperity. (53371)

Report . . . whether the Seneca Indians have sustained losses. 79114

Report . . . with accompanying documents. 45090

Report . . . with constitution . . . officers and members [of the New Mexico, Arizona and Colorado Missionary Association.] 53282

Report with sundry resolutions. 47010

Report . . . with the constitution and by-laws of the Young Men's Christian Association, of Natick. (51907)

Report, with the report of the Chief Engineer [of the Clinton Line Railroad Company.] (13760)

Reporter, a partial imitation of the sixth satire. 69941

Reporter. A periodical devoted to religion, law, legislation, and public events. 66137, 66942, 88394

Reporter: a satire. 65086

Reporter for Common Council. pseud. Daguerreotype sketches. see Coleman, Thomas M.

Reporter of the New York Court of Appeals. pseud. Political status of the rebellious states. 63809

Reporter of the New York press. pseud. Matrimonial brokerage. 46872

Reporters. pseud. Life of Eliza Sowers. 88828

Reportorio de los tiempos. 12351

Reports and bills of the Select Committee of the Senate. 60575

Reports and bills relating to spirituous liquors. 46078

Reports and dissertations, in two parts. 99132

Reports and documents of the Union Defence Committee of the Citizens of New York. 54702

Reports and documents relative to the Morris Canal. 50889

Reports and documents relative to the Stuyvesant Meadows. 93290

Reports and documents respecting the University of Virginia. 100540

Reports and documents upon public schools and education. (70695)

Reports and epistles from America. 34596

Reports and estimates for a ship canal and basin. 42936

Reports and estimates, for uniting Lake Ontario with the Erie Canal. 94072

Reports and estimates made . . . August 24th, 1837. 49709

Reports and estimates [of the Philadelphia, Germantown, and Norristown Railroad Company.] 62001

Reports and letters from the engineers employed on the reserved location. 12510

Reports and letters to the . . . [Philadelphia] Society [for Promoting Agriculture.] 62036

Reports and maps by Professors J. W. Foster and J. D. Whitney. 25248

Reports and negotiations on the north-eastern boundary of the state. 44030

Reports and ordinances, of the Convention of the People of South Carolina. 87429

Reports and other documents relating to the State Lunatic Hospital. 46138

Reports and other documents respecting public lands in Providence. (66360)

Reports and papers relating to a canal. 23665, note after 69942

Reports and proceedings of Col. McKenney. (43406)

Reports and public letters [of J. C. Calhoun.] 9936

Reports and realities from the sketch-book. 62198

Reports and resolutions [of the General Assembly of South Carolina.] 87411, 87445, 87500, 87515, note before 87535, 87655, 87659-87660, 87662, 87668, 87673, 87713, 87727

Reports and resolutions [of the House of Representatives of South Carolina.] 87515

Reports and resolutions of the Joint Committee of the Senate and House of Delegates of Maryland. 3078

Reports and resolutions [of the Senate of South Carolina.] 87526

Reports and resolutions, together with the journals of both houses of the General Assembly of South Carolina. 87500

Reports and resolves of the Bahama Assembly. 11768, (81893), note after 102820

Reports and resolves of the Massachusetts Peace Society. 45882

Reports, and statistical documents pertaining to the Ohio and Mississippi Railroads. (69443)

Reports and statistics of Northborough. 55779

Reports and surveys of the mountain mining lands. 86809, 96505

Reports as Minister at Large in Boston. 97399

Reports as to the coal production in the British colonies. 69958

Reports by Directors, Trustees . . . etc. [of the Mammoth Vein Consolidated Coal Company.] 44181

Reports by George W. Brega. 7705

Reports [by Lieut. Abbot.] 69946

Reports by P. W. Sheafer. (55750)

Reports by P. W. Sheafer, engineer. 44181

Reports by Professor George I. Chace. (49210)

Reports by Prof. George I. Chace . . . and Wm. Petherick. 8768

Reports by Sir John Randolph. 99975

Reports by the Presidents of the So. Ca. Rail Road Company. 88029

Reports communicated to both branches of the Legislature. (37579)

Reports concerning property in trusts. 46079

Reports concerning the State Normal School. 53195

Reports delivered by the Court of Directors of the Sierra Leone Company. 80885-80886, 93373, 93375, 93377

Reports delivered by the Directors of the Sierra Leone Company. 93377

Reports, estimates, maps, &c. 75312

Reports, &c. of the City Council [of Salem, Mass.] 75695

Reports, etc., of the Smithsonian Institution. 85066

Reports from Brevet Major General Smith. 83706

Reports from Committees of the House of Commons. 33548, 85232, 2d note after 85232

Reports from the Committee appointed to enquire. 54989

Reports from the Western Department. 76580, 76647

Reports in reference to the Codrington College. 14146

Reports in relation to the annexation of
Roxbury to Boston. 6770
Reports in the Legislature of Massachusetts.
98561
Reports in the Legislature on the reduction
of salaries. 46080
Reports in the Supreme Court of Alabama.
80280
Reports, including messages, and other com-
munications. 57044
Reports . . . Land Office. 75489
Reports made by P. M. Butler. 9658
Reports made to the City Council of Rockland.
(72398)
Reports made to the General Assembly. 70543
Reports made to the General Superintendent
of the Baltimore & Ohio Rail Road.
84848
Reports made to the House of Representatives.
(34573)
Reports made to the Senate and House of
Representatives. (34322)
Reports of A. D. Hager. 41820
Reports of a journey of survey. 58355
Reports of A. P. Robinson. 57977
Reports of addresses at a meeting. 25715
Reports of admiralty cases tried in Halifax.
91682
Reports of Alexander Hamilton. (29981)
Reports of all the commanders. 8181
Reports of cases adjudged in the District
Court of South Carolina. 87456
Reports of cases adjudged in the Superior
Court and Supreme Court of Errors.
(73132)
Reports of cases adjudged in the Supreme
Court of Pennsylvania. (5497), 60471
Reports of cases argued and adjudged in the
Court of Errors and Appeals. 94737
Reports of cases argued and adjudged in the
Superior Court of Judicature. 67193
Reports of cases argued and adjudged in the
Supreme Court of Errors and Appeals.
94736
Reports of cases argued and adjudged in the
Supreme Court of the United States.
(17390), (33241), 103162
Reports of cases argued and determined in the
Court of Appeals of South Carolina.
87461
Reports of cases argued and determined in the
Court of Appeals of Virginia. 100038,
note after 101528
Reports of cases argued and determined in the
Court of Chancery of the state of South-
Carolina. 87457
Reports of cases argued and determined in the
High Court of Errors and Appeals for
the state of Mississippi. 82248
Reports of cases argued and determined in the
Superior Court of Chancery of the state
of Mississippi. 82247
Reports of cases argued and determined in the
Superior Courts of Law in the state of
South-Carolina. 87458-87459
Reports of cases argued and determined in the
Supreme Court of Rhode Island. 70696-
70697
Reports of cases argued and determined in the
Supreme Court of the state of Illinois.
77443
Reports of cases argued and determined in
the Supreme Judicial Court of Massa-
chusetts. 97622
Reports of cases determined in the Circuit
Court of the United States. note after
101528

Reports of cases determined in the Constitu-
tional Court of South-Carolina. 87460-
87462
Reports of cases determined in the Supreme
Court of Nevada. 52409
Reports of cases determined in the Supreme
Court of the state of Vermont. 99132
Reports of cases in prize. 5879
Reports of cases . . . in the Court of
Chancery of the state of New York.
33442
Reports of cases . . . in the Supreme Court
of Judicature and Court for the Trial of
Impeachments and Correction of Errors.
103382
Reports of cases in the Supreme Court of
Massachusetts. 83881
Reports of cases . . . in the Supreme Court
of Pennsylvania. 103111
Reports of cases in the Supreme Court of the
state of Indiana. 84403
Reports of cases . . . in the Supreme Judicial
Courts of New-Hampshire. 11886
Reports of cases ruled and adjudged in the
courts of Pennsylvania. 17303, 18313,
60471, 1st note after 96854
Reports of cases, ruled and decided by the
Supreme Court of Errors and Appeals.
94738-94739
Reports of Charles T. Whippo and Charles De
Hass. (59996)
Reports of Commander, now Captain, James
Clark Ross. 73381, 73384
Reports of Committees appointed to visit the
county societies. (24765)
Reports of Committees in relation to the Long
Island Canal Company. 41895
Reports of Committees [of the Connecticut River
Valley Agricultural Society.] 77314
Reports of Committees [of the Friends of
Domestic Industry.] (54675)
Reports [of Comstock.] 15617
Reports of contested elections. 18119
Reports of controverted elections. 46081
Reports of criminal law cases decided at the
City-Hall. 103185, 103188
Reports of criminal law cases, with notes and
references. 103188
Reports of criminal trials in the Circuit, State
and United States Courts. 33371
Reports of decisions in the Circuit Courts
Martial. 44031
Reports of decisions in the Supreme Court of
the state of Alabama. 84896
Reports of determinations in the several courts
of law. 79823
Reports of divine kindness. 104262, 104264-
104267
Reports of Dr. Charles T. Jackson. 42006
Reports of E. F. Beale. 88607
Reports of Edward Keating. 87028
Reports of Edward Miller, Chief Engineer.
60278
Reports of Edward Miller, Esq., Chief Engineer.
62078
Reports of equity cases. 87463
Reports of experiments on the strength and
other properties of metals. (72488)
Reports of experiments with the Williams'
patent bullet. (69945)
Reports of explorations and surveys, to ascertain the most practicable and economical route for a railroad. 2804, 5809,
69946, 83724
Reports of explorations and surveys to ascertain the practicability of a ship-canal.
79013

Reports of General De Peyster. 19634

Reports of General Steedman. 91088

Reports of Gold Commissioner of Nova Scotia. (14686), 81061

Reports of his service as a Minister at Large. 97395

Reports of hospital physicians. (69947)

Reports of J. Dutton Steele. 91120

Reports of J. W. Foster. 25247

Reports of judges and premiums awarded. 60376

Reports of judicial decisions in the Constitutional Court. 87454-87465

Reports of Major General J. E. B. Stuart. 15364

Reports [of Major General Sherman.] 80415

Reports [of Messrs. Poole and Campbell.] 56109

Reports of missions to the Cherokees. 34650

Reports of Moncure Robinson. 59955

Reports of preliminary surveys for the Union Pacific Railway. 80559

Reports of Professor Charles U. Shepard. 80169

Reports of Prof. George I. Chace. 4583

Reports of Prof. Henry to the Regents. 70474, 85090

Reports of progress. (31937)

Reports of public officers and state institutions [of Illinois.] 34326

Reports of Sundry Commissioners appointed to view and explore the rivers Susquehanna and Juniata. 60576

Reports of the African Institution. 46857, 95656

Reports of the Agents and Commissioners of the McDonogh Estate. 43177

Reports of the American Anti-slavery Society. 81823

Reports of the American Baptist Home Mission Society. 3241

Reports of the American Steamship Company. (31825)

Reports of the Annual Visiting Committee of the Public Schools of the city of Boston for 1845. 6763, 77770

Reports of the Annual Visiting Committees of the Public Schools of the city of Boston. 6762-6763

Reports of the Auditor of Public Accounts of the state of Illinois. 34250

Reports of the Auditor of State [of Ohio.] (13140)

Reports of the Bank and Judiciary Committee. 97757

Reports of the Bank Commissioners [of New Hampshire.] 52916

Reports of the Benevolent Association of the County of Hampden. 30129

Reports of the Benevolent Societies and Conference of Churches in Cheshire County. (12515)

Reports of the Board of Direction of the Mercantile Library Association. 54390

Reports of the Board of Directors of the Theological and Religious Library Association of Cincinnati. 13092

Reports of the Board of Selectmen . . . of Lewiston. (40873)

Reports of the Board of Treasury relative to finance of the United States. 69948

Reports of the Board of Trustees and Officers of the Longview Asylum. (41938)

Reports of the Board of Visitors, . . . Trustees, and . . . Superintendent [of the New Hampshire Asylum for the Insane.] 52857

Reports of the Boston Sunday School Society. 93743

Reports of the Branch Associations of Antigua and St. Christopher's. 85880

Reports [of the California State Geologist.] 10009

Reports of the Canal Commissioners [of New York.] (53563)

Reports of the cases, the state vs. Samuel Small. (52925)

Reports [of the Chicago, Burlington and Quincy Railroad Company.] 12665

Reports of the Chief of Engineers, U. S. A. 84774

Reports [of the Cincinnati Public Library.] 13093

Reports of the city departments of Richmond, Va. (71167)

Reports of the city departments of the city of Cincinnati. 13064

Reports of the City Engineer and Special Committee. 75377

Reports of the City Treasurer to the Military Commandant. 54230

Reports of the Commissioner and Architect of the new state capitol. 87403

Reports of the Commissioner of Indian Affairs. 34668

Reports of the Commissioner of the School Fund. 15735

Reports of the Commissioners and Secretary of the Hydrographic Survey. (44052)

Reports of the Commissioners, appointed by . . . the Legislature of New Jersey. (53233)

Reports of the Commissioners appointed to inquire into the grievances. 10582

Reports of the Commissioners appointed to prepare the revised statutes. (53942)

Reports of the . . . Commissioners . . . in the Fire District. 63159

Reports of the Commissioners of Agriculture and Arts. 10347

Reports of the Commissioners of Emigration. 53610

Reports of the Commissioners of Fisheries. 44032

Reports of the Commissioners of the Sinking Fund. 56897

Reports of the Commissioners of the Zoological Survey. 46082

Reports of the Commissioners on Portland Harbor. 64376

Reports of the Commissioners on the controversy with the state of New York. 53234

Reports of the Commissioners on the Geological Survey. 45754

Report of the Committee of Bondholders [of the Union Canal Company.] 60750

Reports of the Committee of Finance and the School Committee. 10142

Reports of the Committee of Inquiry. 3189

Reports of the Committee of Investigation. (61988)

Reports of the Committee of Secrecy. 88168, 88204

Reports of the Committee on Central High School. (61529)

Reports of the Committee on Indian Affairs at Philadelphia. 26255, 34652

Reports of the Committee on the Judiciary. 69949

Reports of the Committee on the Sing Sing and Auburn Prisons. 53943

Reports of the Committee to whom was referred the message of Gov. James H. Adams. 87524

Reports of the Committees for 1858. 70721

Reports of the Committees for 1852. 45862

Reports of the Committees of both houses. 87481

Reports of the Committees of Council [of Philadelphia.] 62200

Reports of the Comptroller and Treasurer of Kansas Territory. 37089

Reports of the County School Commissioners. 45135

Reports of the Directors and Treasurer of the Sullivan Railroad Company. 93564

Reports of the Directors of the African Institution. 81966

Reports of the Directors of the Imperial Brazilian Mining Association. 7627

Reports of the Directors of the Little Miami Riailroad Company. 41537

Reports of the Directors [of the New York Institution for the Instruction of the Deaf and Dumb.] 54500

Reports of the Directors of the State Library [of Nevada.] 52398

Reports of the discovery of Peru. 105720

Reports of the Engineers of the Danville and Pottsville Rail Road Company. 59967

Reports of the Engineers of the Western Rail Road Corporation. 103009

Reports of the Engineers [on a rail-road from Boston to the Hudson River.] 45998

Reports of the . . . Engineers on the . . . location of the summit level. 60750

Reports on the Engineers on the new waterworks [of Montreal.] 50280

Reports of the Evening Free School. 75646

Reports of the Executive Board . . . of the [Union Benevolent] Association. 62349

Reports of the Fellenberg Academy. (24015)

Reports of the Female Orphan Asylum. 3958

Reports of the first Exhibition of the Middlesex Mechanic Association. 42496

Reports of the first Exhibition of the Salem Charitable Mechanic Association. 75720

Reports of the foreign insurance companies. (70498)

Reports [of the French Canadian Missionary Society.] 10523

Reports of the General and Deputy Superintendents of the Metropolitan Police. 54400

Reports of the Geological Survey of Missouri. 49593

Reports of the Geological Survey taken from the "Colonist" newspaper. 77294

Reports of the Gold Commissioner of Nova Scotia. (14686)

Reports of the heads of departments [of Pennsylvania.] 85465

Reports of the Honourable the Committee of Secrecy. 88197

Reports of the Illinois State Penitentiary. 34309

Reports [of the Indiana State Board of Colonization.] 34501

Reports of the Inspectors made to the Judges. 10390

Reports of the Inspectors [of the Eastern Penitentiary.] 60080

Reports of the Inspectors of the Free Ports. 26740

Reports of the Joint Commissioners, and of Col. Graham. 60246

Reports of the Joint Commissioners and of Lieut. Col. Graham. (45089)

Reports of the Joint Commissioners, and of Lt. Col. Graham. 45088

Reports of the Joint Special Committee on the whole matter. 70698

Reports of the Kentucky Commissioners. 37547

Reports . . . of the Leeds Copper Mining . . . Company. 39829

Reports of the majority and minority of Special Committee. (54659)

Reports of the majority and minority of the Committee appointed . . . 1861. 60358

Reports of the majority and minority of the Committee on Foreign Affairs. 23271

Reports of the majority and minority of the Joint Committee on Canal Lettings. 53569

Reports of the majority and minority of the Select Committee on . . . Intemperance and the Sale of Intoxicating Drinks. 53944

Reports of the majority and minority of the Select Committee on the Pacific Railroad. 69950

Reports of the majority and minority of the Select Committee relative to the estates of J. Nicholson. 60578

Reports of the majority and minority of the Select Committee . . . to View the Line of the Gettysburg Extention. 60122

Reports of the [Manganese Mining] Company, New Brunswick. 44248

Reports of the . . . Massachusetts Baptist Missionary Society. 45823

Reports of the . . . meetings. 2235

Reports of the Mexican Pacific Coal and Iron Mining and Land Company's exploring expedition. (48572)

Reports of the Ministry at Large in Providence. 66283, 92046

Reports of the minority and majority of the Financial Commission. 53372

Reports of the minority of the Committee, and of Mr. Adams. 51897

Reports of the . . . Natchez Institute. 51897

Reports of the National War Committee. 54418

Reports of the naval engagements on the Mississippi River. 53373

Reports of the New England Mutual Life Insurance Company. 52709

Reports of the New Jersey Zinc Company. (53197)

Reports of the New York Harbor Commission. 53806

Reports of the Newcastle District Committee. 85852

Reports [of the Northern Baptist Society.] 3236

Reports of the officers of the city of Burlington, Vt. (9338)

Reports of the officers of the institution [of the Massachusetts State Prison.] 45902

Reports . . . of the Ohio & Mississippi Railroad Co. 56968

Reports of the . . . Ohio Institution for the Education of the Deaf and Dumb. 56984

Reports of the operations of the Army of Northern Virginia. 15403, (39790)

Reports of the Paris Industrial Exhibition of 1855. 10445

Reports of the . . . parish work of Grace Parish. 54295

Reports of the Parliamentary Select Committee. 34675

Reports [of the Pennsylvania Supreme Court.] (5497)

Reports of the Presbyterian Hospital. 54587

Reports of the President and Board of Trustees [of the Medical College of South Carolina.] 87872

Reports of the President and Directors and the General Superintendent of the South Carolina Railroad Company. 88023

Reports of the Prison-Discipline Society. 65706

Reports of the proceedings and debates of the Convention of 1821. 53945, note after 92151

Reports of the Railroad Commissioners, of . . . New-Hampshire. 52926

Reports of the Rail-Road Corporations of Massachusetts. 45963

Reports of the receipts and expenditures of the city of Salem. 75636

Reports of the School Committee [of the General Society of Mechanics and Tradesmen, New York.] 54290

Report of the School Committees of Bedford, Mass. 4278

Reports of the schools in the city of Concord. 15139

Reports of the second Exhibition of the Middlesex Mechanic Association. 42496

Reports of the Secretaries of State of the republic of Colombia. 14622, 1st note after 90588

Reports of the Secretary of the Navy. 39519

Reports [of the Secretary of the Treasury.] 3191

Reports of the Secretary of War. 36377, 84774

Reports of the Select Committee of the Legislative Assembly. (10451)

Reports of the Select Committee of the Senate. 96985

Reports [of the Select Committee of the Society for Propagating the Gospel among the Indians and Others in North America.] 34610

Reports of the Select Committee of Thirty-Three. 69952

Reports of the Select Committee on Secret Societies. 45317

Reports of the Selectmen and other officers of the town of Concord. 15125

Reports of the Selectmen and . . . School Committee [of Nashua, N. Y.] 51858

Reports of the Selectmen and the Overseers of the Poor of Concord. 15135

Reports of the Selectmen, and the Superintending School Committee. 35530

Reports of the Selectmen of Achushnet. 154

Reports of the Selectmen [of Manchester, N.H.] 44219

Reports of the Selectmen . . . of . . . New Ipswich. 53026

Reports of the Selectmen, Overseers of Poor, Treasurer, and Cemetery Committee of the town of Clinton. 13763

Report of the Selectmen, Overseers of the Poor, Superintendent of Public Grounds, and Chief Engineer of the Fire-Department [of Concord, Mass.] 15136

Reports of the Selectmen, Treasurer, and School Committee, of the town of Raynham. 68126

Reports of the Selectmen, Treasurer, and School Visitors of the town of Putnam. 66845

Reports of the several banks. 59905

Reports of the several departments, committees, &c., of the city of Salem. 75696

Reports of the several departments, for the preceding municipal year. 75696

Reports of the several departments [of Meriden, Conn.] 47966

Reports of the several departments, of the city government [of Portland, Me.] 64339, 64351

Reports of the several departments of the city of Salem. 75672

Reports of the several departments of the town government [of Saco, Me.] (74782)

Reports of the several railroad companies. 59905

Reports of the several Superintending School Committees of . . . Portsmouth. (64415)

Reports of the Sierra Leone Company. 95656

Reports of the Smithsonian Institution. 85007, 85088

Reports of the Society for the Propagation of the Gospel in Foreign Parts. 14145, 85947

Reports of the Society of the Burnside Expedition. 86100

Reports of the Soldiers' Memorial Society. 86342

Reports of the Special Committee appointed to inquire into the causes. 42519

Reports of the Special Committee appointed to make suitable arrangements. 54660

Reports of the Special Committee . . . [on] the causes which retard. (10595)

Reports of the Special Committees on the Governor's messages. 87501

Report of the state directors of the joint companies. 53065

Reports of the state officers, boards and committees [of South Carolina.] 87500

Reports of the Superintendent and Engineer [of the North Branch Canal.] 60276

Reports of the Superintendent of Public Instruction of . . . Michigan. 48725

Reports of the Superintendent of the Illinois State Penitentiary. 34308

Reports of the Superintending School Committee of Rehoboth. 68976

Reports of the Superintending School Committees of the city of Concord. 15154

"Reports" of the Supreme Court and of the Court for Trial of Impeachments. 102624

Reports of the surveys for the Pacific Railroad. 20554

Reports of . . . the timber trade. 56561

Reports of the Town Clerk and School Committee [of Scituate.] 78131

Reports of the . . . Town of Chicopee. 12683

Reports of the town of Plymouth. 63472

Reports of the Town Officers . . . of Leicester. 39900

Reports of the . . . Town Officers of . . . Millbury. 48997

Reports of the Town Officers of the town of Rehoboth. 68971

Reports of the Treasurer and Principal [of the Pennsylvania Training School for Idiotic and Feeble-Minded Children.] 60385

Reports of the Treasurer and Secretary of the Soldiers' Relief Fund Committee. 76082, 76669

Reports of the Treasurer for the years 1854-55 [of Framingham, Mass.] 25423

Report of the Treasurer, Secretary and Superintendent [of the Milwaukee and Mississippi Rail Road Company.] 49167

Reports of the trial of Col. Aaron Burr. 9434

Reports of the trials of David T. Chase. 12172

Reports of the trials of Michael Mellon. 47464

Reports of the trials of the causes of Elisha Jenkins vs. Solomon Van Rensselaer. (35991)

Reports of the Trustees and Superintendent of the Butler Hospital. 66243

Reports of the Trustees, and the Executive Committee, of the Rhode Island Hospital. (70722)

Reports of the Trustees, Steward, and Treasurer, and Superintendent of the Insane Hospital [of Maine.] (43973)

Reports [of the Union Benevolent Association, Philadelphia.] note after 97764

Reports of the United States Commissioner. 21868

Reports of the United States Commissioners. Extracts from the report. (58595)

Reports of the United States Commissioners. Introduction, with selections. (58595)

Reports of the United States Commissioners. Report upon cotton. 51236

Reports of the United States Commissioners to the Paris Universal Exposition, 1867. 23534, 40200, (51235)-51236, (58595), 73959

Reports of the United States Commissioners . . . upon wool. (51235)

Reports of the United States Engineers. (35727)

Reports of the various Standing Committees of the South Carolina Convention. 87445

Reports of the Warden and Inspectors of the Maine State Prison. (44028)

Reports of the Watering Committee [Philadelphia.] 81539

Reports of the Watering Committee to Councils. 62371, (78083)

Reports of the Western Committees. 50683

Reports of the work of the State Temperance Alliance. 46142

Reports of Thomas Petherick. 49458

Reports of two cases determined in the prize Court. 98533

Reports of Wm. A. Burt and Bela Hubbart. 9486, 38676

Reports on a geological survey. 10460

Reports on canals, railways, roads, and other subjects. 92815

Reports on city lands. 73723

Reports on contested elections. 46083

Reports on education. (44317), 44321

Reports on experiments on the properties of metals for cannon. (72488)

Reports on free white schools at Richmond. (71209), 86344

Reports on Indian affairs. 30193

Reports on revolutionary claims. 29781

Reports on schools of Nova Scotia. 18955

Reports on the accounts of the corporation [of Montreal.] 50281

Reports on the accounts of the corporation of the city of Saint John. 75276

Reports on the analysis of the soils. 34529

Reports on the Bear Mountain Rail Road. (36257)

[Report] on the coal and iron ores of the Bear Valley coal basin. (36257)

Reports . . . on the coal properties. (60844)

Reports on the combustible qualities of the semi-anthracites. 72668

Reports on the course of instruction in Yale College. 105794

Reports on the diseases of cattle in the United States. 69953

Reports on the exploration of British North America. (58333)

Reports on the extent and nature of the materials available. 30116, 57853, 69954

Reports on the fishes, reptiles and birds of Massachusetts. (46085), 59383

Reports on the free school system. 87502

Reports on the Geognostic Survey of South Carolina. 87722

Reports on the geology and topography. 25249

Reports on the geology of Jamaica. (35584)

Reports on the geology of the coast, mountains, and part of the Sierra Nevada. 10006

Reports on the Halifax and Quebec Railway. (29707)

Reports on the herbaceous plants. 46086

Reports . . . on the late Treasury's accounts. (45589)

Reports on the laws of New England. 18878

Reports on the memorial of David Jones. 36485

Reports on the New York Central Park. (28499)

Reports [on the noxious, beneficial and other insects, of the state of New York.] 24562

Reports on the operations and relief agents of the Sanitary Commission. 20718

Reports on the operations of the inspectors and relief agents of the Sanitary Commission. 76582, 76647

Reports on the petition of Tristram Burges and others. (78855)

Reports on the present state of the United Provinces of South America. 72494

Reports on the progress nad local advantages of the city. 50282

Reports on the property of the Chatham Mining Company. 12282

Reports on the property of the copper mines. 21288

Reports on the property of the Nelson Copper Mining Company. 69956

Reports on the property of the North Sutton Mining & Smelting Co. (55732)

Reports on the property of the Nyko Silver-Mining Company. (69955)

Reports on the property of the South Bedford Copper Mining Co. 87332

Reports on the prosperity of the Brome Mining Company. 8191

Reports on the reservation system of California. 2728

Reports on the sea and river fisheries of New Brunswick. 60984

Reports on the stepping or discipline mill. 69957

Reports on the subject of a licence law. 46087

Reports presented and read at the third annual meeting. (66308)

Reports received from Her Majesty's Secretaries of Embassy and Legation. 69958

Reports relating to . . . a railroad and line of electro-magnetic telegraph. 69959

Reports relating to colored schools. 14750

Reports, relating to the failure of the Rio de la Plata Mining Association. 9191

Reports relating to the failure of the Rio Plata Mining Association. 31136

Reports relative to the surveys of routes. 63127

Reports relative to the Woodlands Cemetery 62394

Reports relative to the Yellow Creek, Carrollton and Zoar Rail-Road. 106009

Reports, resolutions, and proceedings of the Commissioners of Health. 54203

Reports . . . September 23, 1861. 38061

Reports, specifications, and estimates of public works. 92816

Reports to Congress of the progress of the Coast Survey. (2588)

Reports to the Board [of Public Improvements of North Carolina.] 55593

Reports to the Boston Board of Trade. (31825)
Reports to the Chamber of Commerce of San Francisco. 76037
Reports to the General Assembly of Rhode Island. 70544
Reports to the Legislature, and an annual register. 19806
Reports to the Legislature of S. C. 87524
Reports . . . to the Metropolitan Board of Health. 11854
Reports to the President and Board of Trustees [of the Medical College of the state of South Carolina.] 87872
Reports to the President and Directors of the Welland Canal Company. 22935, 102555
Reports to the Saint Paul Chamber of Commerce. (75457)
Reports to the Yearly Meeting of Friends. 34679
Reports upon bridging the Delaware. 69960
Reports upon . . . St. Margaret's Copper Mine. 35401
Reports upon the mineral resources of the United States. 8664
Reports upon the plan of re-constructing the Fairmount Dam. 61650
Reports upon the property of the Naumkeag Mining Company of Lake Superior. (69961)
Reports upon the property of the Ramsay Lead Mining and Smelting Co. 67722
Reports upon the surveys, location, and progress of construction. 1595
Repositorium fur die Neueste Geographie, etc. 8759
Repository. Containing a . . . view of the most considerable transactions. 69962
Repository; containing various political, philosophical, literary, and miscellaneous articles. 69964
Repository. Devoted to the cause of truth. 69965
Repository of amusement. (66077)
Repository of ancient and modern fugitive pieces. 1162
Repository of entertaining knowledge. see Lady's magazine and repository of entertaining knowledge.
Repository of entertainment and knowledge. (35598)
Repository of history, politics and literature. 97972
Repository of knowledge, historical, literary, miscellaneous and theological. (69966)
Repository of national and foreign literature. 75303
Repository of original articles, written exclusively by females actively employed in the mills. 42491, 2d note after 95375
Repository of original and selected American poetry. 90002
Repository of political truths. 42858
Repository of religion and literature. 69967
Repository of religious intelligence. (54820)
Repository of religious, literary, and entertaining knowledge. 23290
Repository of religious, literary and entertaining knowledge for families. 23288
Repository of science & literature. 64329
Repository of the lives and portraits of distinguished American characters. 9899, 19357-19358
Repository of the songs of the day. 52009
Repository of useful and polite literature. 84363-84364
Repository of useful information. 80754
Repository of useful knowledge. see Alleghany magazine; or repository of useful knowledge. Canadian almanac, and repository

of useful knowledge. Confederate States almanac, and repository of useful knowledge. Scobie's Canadian almanac, and repository of useful knowledge.
Repository: or treasury of politics and literature. 69963
Reposta que o filho do compadre do dio de Janeiro da. 76326
Repplier, Agens. 84510
Reprasentaten der Vereinigten Staaten von Amerika. (69968), 70002
Represailles, episode de la guerre d'Amerique 23093, note after 98620
Represailles, fait historique. 98956
Represailles militaires. 39594
Representacao dirigida a Assemblea Geral Legislativa. 78956
Representacao dirigida pelo Arcebispo da Bahia. 78955
Representacio a Assemblea Geral Constituente. 1445
Representacion a la Camara de Disputados. 26479
Representacion a las Camaras Representavas del Peru. 71605
Representacion a los Americanos del Sud y Mexicanos. 31316
Representacion al Congreso de varios comerciantes. 101294
Representacion al Exmo. Sr. Presidente de la Republica. 69969
Representacion al Rey N. S. Don Fernando VII. 24158
Representacion al Rey N. Senor D. Phelipe V. 106282
Representacion al Rey sobre la continuacion de 12,000 pesos. (75985)
Representacion al Rey sobre la divison del Obispado de la Puebla de los Angeles. 72560
Representacion al Rey sobre la libre extraccion del cacao. 76228
Representacion al Soberano Congreso de la Union. 96232
Representacion al Supremo Magistrado de la Nacion. 9588
Representacion al Virey de Nueva Granada. 67650
Representacion calumniosa que unos emigrados de la villa. 48527
Representacion de D. Jean Orpen. 69970
Representacion de la Diputacion Americana. 69971
Representacion de la Junto de Fomento de Comercio. 29030
Representacion de los Capoteros al Senor Gobernador. 69972
Representacion de los fundamentos de hecho, y derecho. 69973
Representacion de los Haciendos de Buenos Ayres. 69974
Representacion de varios ciudadanos al Esc. Sr. Presidente. 69975
Representacion del Exmo Ayuntamiento de la capital de Puebla. 66576
Representacion del Ilmo. Sr. Arzobispo de Mejico concernente a algunos sucesos anteriores. 24995
Representacion del Ilmo. Sr. Arzobispo de Mejico concerniente a algunos sucesos anteriores. 48651
Representacion del Illmo. Sr. Obispo de Michoacan al Supremo Gobierno, pidiendo la revocacion de la ley. 51325
Representacion del Illmo. Sr. Obispo de Michoacan al Supremo Gobierno, protestando contra varios articulos. 51325

Representacion del M. N. Y. L. Ayuntamiento de Guatemala. 29096
Representacion del M. R. Arzobispo de Bogota. 51067
Representacion del Rafael D. Merda. 47941
Representacion del Senor Rafael D. Merida. 47962
Representacion del Sindico Lic. Ramon Gamboa. 63697
Representacion del Y. Ayuntamiento de Tepec. 94828
Representacion dirigida a la Camara de Diputados. (69976)
Representacion dirigida al Congreso General. 69978
Representacion dirigida al Congreso Nacional. 76747
Representacion dirigida al Congreso Nacional por . . . Ignacio Sierra y Rosso. 80895
Representacion dirigida al . . . Presidente Provisional. 69977
Representacion dirigida al Rey de Espana. 69979
Representacion dirigida al Sr. Superintendente de la Hacienda Publica. (69980)
Representacion dirigida al Suprema Gobierno. 24326
Representacion dirigida al Supremo Gobierno por la Direccion. 69982
Representacion dirigida al Virey de Nueva Espana. 48652
Representacion dirijida al Soberano Congreso General. 57621, 69981
Representacion elevada al Soberano Congreso. 26592
Representacion hecha por el Conde de Miravalle. 96758
Representacion juridica, allegato reverente. (69983)
Representacion juridica, con el Senor Fiscal. 17738
Representacion legal al Rei Nitro. Sr. 72542
Representacion political legal. 69984
Representacion por el Clero de Mexico. 69985
Representacion por la Provincia de San Hipolito de Oaxaca. 96240
Representacion que a favor de libre comercio. 60902
Representacion que a nombre de la Mineria de esta Nueva Espana. 39135, 42724, note after 98814
Representacion que dirige a S. M. la Cortes Generales. 6305
Representacion que dirigen al Gobierno Ramon Olarte. 17840, 57104, 1st note after 94592
Representacion que el ciudadano Pedro de la Portilla hace. 64335
Representacion que el Clero de Caracas hace. 47804
Representacion que el Clero de Caracas preparo. 47804
Representacion que el Clero dirigio al Illmo. y Venerable Cabildo Sede-Vacante. 26577
Representacion que el Vecindario de Morelia dirige. 69986
Representacion que eleva al Soberano Congreso. (71311)
Representacion, que en nombre de los actuales Curas Beneficiados. 95138
Representacion que hace al Congreso en 27. de Febrero de 1826. (64168)
Representacion que hace Don Rafael Davila a S. M. I. 69987
Representacion que hace el Ayuntamiento de esta capital. 69988

Representacion que hace su autor al Excmo. Sr. Gefe Politico. 93789
Representacion que han elevado a las Camaras de la Nacion. (69989)
Representacion qve haze el R. P. Lector Fray Francisco de Tapia. 94347
Representacion que la Junta de Industria de Puebla eleva. 66577
Representacion que los eclesiasticos de Guadalajara dirigen. 29032
Representacion que los eclesiasticos de Guadalajara diriges. 29031
Representacion que los Espagnoles Americanos residentes en esta ciudad han entregado. 98373
Representacion que los subditos Inglese hacen. 69990
Representacion, que ofrece a los Reales Pies de la Magestad. 86378
Representacion, que pone reverente a los Reales Pies. (49908)
Representacion tocante a su salario. 75897
Representacion urgentisima de un ciudadano. 97169
Representacion y manifesto de los Espanoles Americanos. 69991
Representaciones de D. Manuel de Vidaurre. 99497
Representaciones del Real Tribunal de Mineria. 69992
Representaciones del Sr. D. Juan Jurado. 36937
Representaciones documentadas del Ayuntamiento de Santiago. 31447
Representaciones que la viuda de Don Agustin de Itrubide ha dirigido. 35295
Representans de S. Domingue. see Santo Domingo (French Colony) Deputes a l' Assemblee Nationale de France.
Representation. 49824
Representation addressed to the Supreme Government. 24323
Representation addressee a M. le Ministre de France. 41136
Representation and address of several members. 10978
Representation and memorial of the Council. 35660, 105080
Representation and memorials of sundry citizens of Massachusetts. 27092, 69728
Representation and petition of Ebenezer Wadsworth. 100928
Representation and petition of the Council-General of the Indian and African Company to the Parliament. 18566, 69993, 78231
Representation and petition of the representatives elected. 42298
Representation and petition of the subscribers. 97952
Representation by the creditors of the island of Tobago. 96047
Representation du monde universel. 47884
Representation from the Commissioners for Trade and Plantations. 69994
Repretention from the Diocese of New Jersey. (20385), 88253
Representation in Congress. 8886
Representation of all, and representation of the majority only. 48988
Representation of Arkansas. 43119
Representation of Dr. Samuel Page. (58160)
Representation of facts. 50342
Representation of matters of fact. 19946, 53253
Representation of minorities to act with the majority. 69995

Representation of New Netherland. 69996, note after 98474

Representation of some of our sea damages. 86681

Representation of Stephen Fuller. (26179)

Representation of sundry citizens of Providence. 66361

Representation of the Assembly of the said province. 60701

Representation of the Board of Trade. 16727, (69997)

Representation of the case of Oliver Pollock. 105154-105155

Representation of the case of the planters. 69714, note after 100519

Representation of the Commissioners of the Alms-House. 54073

Representation of the Council and Company of Scotland. 18567

Representation of the English merchants at Bruges. 86742, 94070

Representation of the injustice and dangerous tendency of tolerating slavery. 79809, 79818-79819, 79830

Representation of the injustice of slavery. 4689

Representation of the Lords Commissioners for Trade and Plantations. 54981

Representation of the Lords Commissioners for Trade and Plantations to the King. 69998

Representation of the miserable state of Barbadoes. 3285

Representation of the Philadelphia Chamber of Commerce. (61975)

Representation on behalf of the people called Quakers. 60579, 69999

Representation to the King and Parliament. (70000)

Representation to the President and Executive Council and General Assembly. 60580

Representations against the title of the Seminary. 50289

Representations du Comte de Welderen. 93427

Representations du system des zones habitables. 76838

Representations faites par les Creanciers Anglois des colons de Tabago. 73469, 96048

Representations of Governor Hutchinson and others. (34085)

Representations of Messrs. Halstead, Perkins, Coppuck and Gill. 20395

Representations of the anomaly existing. 1477

Representative actors. 74380

Representative American orations. 93665

Representative American plays. 83788, 97617

Representative and leading men of the Pacific. (80755)

Representative democracy in the United States. 9611

Representative from Chester County. pseud. Desultory remarks. see Darlington, William.

Representative government and electorial reform. 70001

Representative life of Horace Greeley. 68311

Representative men. Seven lectures. 22460

Representative plays by American dramatists. 92513

Representative Reform Association, Columbia, S. C. General Committee. 87733

Representative reform—the cumulative vote. 8886

Representative women. 2889

Representatives Elected by the Freemen of the Territory of Louisiana. petitioners see Louisiana (Territory) Representatives. petitioners

Rep. no. 420. Tariff. (33482)

Representatives of F. Pelletreau. claimants 59584

Representatives of the Freeholders of Nova Scotia. petitioners see Nova Scotia. General Assembly. petitioners

Representatives of the people—please read this statement. 98555

Representatives of the United States of America, in Congress assembled. (69968), 70002

Representatives of the Yearly Meeting of Friends for New England. see Friends, Society of. New England Yearly Meeting. Representatives.

Representatives of Wade Hampton. petitioners 30152

Reprimand delivered by the President of the Senate. 94971

Reprimand for the author of a libel. 106104

Reprint from the New-York journal of commerce. 54231

Reprint of a London gazette. 41858

Reprint of a short biography of Col. Ebenezer Allen. 789, 3525

Reprint of an article on "Uncle Tom's cabin." 79130-79131, (81837), note after 92624

Reprint of Rev. Thomas Symmes's sermon. (37711)

Reprint of the Journal of George Washington. 101710

Reprint of the original letters from Washington to Joseph Reed. 68621, 89000

Reprint of the Reed and Cadwalader pamphlets. 68569, (68602)

Reprint of the . . . result of ex parte council. 56049

Reprint, with additions of two articles. (29885)

Reprinted copy of a pamphlet published in New-York. 70003

Reprints of rare books. I. 99371

Reprints of southern tracts, II. 16234

Reprise du paiement en especies. (81304)

Reproach of Christ. 22222

Reproduction of his globe of 1523 long lost. 77803

Reproduction series [of the Bulletin of the Lloyd Library.] 83710, 95605

Reproof to Dr. McFarland. 58105

Reproof to heedless youth. 21735

"Reptiles." 69946

Reptiles and amphibia. 43785

Reptiles by John Edward Gray and Albert Gunther. 28401, 71032

Reptiles, by S. F. Baird. 22538

Reptiles. [By Sir John Richardson.] 71033

Reptiles, by Spencer F. Baird. 69946

Reptiles, by Thomas Bell. 18649

Reptiles coll. on an explor. exped. from the Missouri to Utah Lake. 2805

Reptiles coll. on an explor. exped. from the Sacramento Valley. 2805

Reptiles coll. on an explor. exped. in Upper-California. 2805

Reptiles de l'ile de Cuba. 14113

Reptiles et poissons. 21353

Reptiles, fishes, and crustacea. 27419

Reptiles of Australia. 28401, 71032

Reptiles of the western part of North America. 2805

Reptiles. Par MM. Cocteau et Bibron. 74922

Reptiles, poissons, mossusques, zoophytes, et foraminiferes. 57457

Republican court, or American society in the days of Washington. 28897

Republican crisis. 70028

Republican dissected. 29955, 6th note after 104016

Republican documents. Massachusetts Republican resolutions, 1855. 46089

Republican documents. Official proceedings of the Republican Convention. 70029

Republican economy. 14905, 102396

Republican education. 70030

Republican farmer. pseud. Address to the freemen of Rhode Island. 70531

Republican farmer. pseud. Address to the freemen of Rhode Island on the subject of the spring elections. 70533

Republican farmer. pseud. Past, present, and future of greenbacks. see Alvord, C. supposed author

Republican farmer. pseud. To the citizens of the United States. 97937

Republican farmer (Staunton, Va.) 89160

Republican Festival, proclamation, and new Jerusalem. 2402

Republican form. 35993

Republican form of government: definition. 19511, 80444

Republican form of government; its definition, manhood suffrage. 70031

Republican General Committee of Young Men of the City . . . of New York. see Democratic Party. New York. New York City. General Committee of Young Men.

Republican herald (Providence, R. I.) 2485, 35314, note after 92848

Republican homes. 32994

Republican imperialism is not American liberty. 70032

Republican judge. (13880), 14013

Republican landmarks. (76406)

Republican legislative address and resolutions. 53973

Republican Legislative Meeting, Albany, 1834. see Democratic Party. New York. Albany. Legislative Meeting, 1834.

Republican magazine. 70033

Republican magazine for Oct. 1785. 1152

Republican magazine; or, repository of political tracts. 42858

Republican manual. 43192

Republican manual. History, principles, early leaders, achievements. 82212

Republican meeting in Hartford. 70034

Republican meeting of the Citizens of Albany and Colonie. 626

Republican meeting of the citizens of Washington City. 101952

Republican member of the Legislature. pseud. Considerations in favor. see Van Buren, Martin, Pres. U. S., 1782-1862.

Republican Methodism contrasted with Episcopal Methodism. 14346

Republican military system. 91087

Republican nominations. 78038

Republican notes on religion. 35914, 100344

Republican of Connecticut. pseud. Compromise by a compensation. 15063

Republican of 1800. pseud. Appeal for a union of parties. 1769

Republican of Massachusetts. pseud. Review of political affairs. (70215)

Republican of Norfolk. pseud. Address to the citizens of Norfolk County. see Ruggles, Nathaniel.

Republican of the Jefferson school. pseud. Voice from the interior. see Henshaw, D. supposed author

Republican opinions about Lincoln. 41229, 70036

Republican; or, a series of essays. 35819

Republican Party. 19497, 28493, (70019)-70021, 70040, 79530, 89495, 89496 see also National Andrew Johnson Club.

Republican Party. National Committee, 1856. 51955, 63113

Republican Party. National Committee, 1896. 83366

Republican Party. National Convention, Pittsburgh, 1856. 51955, 59842, 63113, 70029

Republican Party. National Convention, Chicago, 1860. 12661, 56351, 64407, 65894, 70035, 93679, 93681

Republican Party. National Convention, Baltimore, 1864. 63348

Republican Party. California. Convention, 1863. 76067

Republican Party. California. San Francisco. 76067, 93690 see also Young Men's Democratic Republican Club of the City and County of San Francisco.

Republican Party. Colorado. 90708

Republican Party. Connecticut. Convention, Hartford, 1856. (65353), 70034

Republican Party. Illinois. State Central Committee. (20696)

Republican Party. Louisiana. Convention, New Orleans, 1865. 42284

Republican Party. Louisiana. State Campaign Committee. 42186

Republican Party. Louisiana. State Central Committee. 90641

Republican Party. Louisiana. New Orleans. 53318 see also John Brown Pioneer Radical Republican Club, New Orleans.

Republican Party. Maryland. State Central Committee. 34362, 45054, 45382, (47091)

Republican Party. Massachusetts. 46089

Republican Party. Minnesota. Second Congressional District Committee. (49236)

Republican Party. New Hampshire. 52927

Republican Party. New York. New York City. 1424, 25816, 36181, 40940, 40941, 54661, 55416, 70043 see also Central Fremont and Dayton Glee Club of the City of New York. Eighteenth Ward Republican Festival, New York, 1860. Fremont & Dayton Central Club of the City of New York. Republican Union Festival, New York, 1862. Young Men's Republican Union, New York.

Republican Party. New York. New York City. Union Festival, 1862. see Republican Union Festival, New York, 1862.

Republican Party. Ohio. Executive Committee. 90582

Republican Party. Pennsylvania. Convention, Williamsport, 1867. (60585)

Republican Party. Pennsylvania. State Central Committee. 59845, 60751

Republican Party. Rhode Island. State Central Committee. 70524

Republican Party. Rhode Island. State Committee. 70525

Republican Party. South Carolina. 87941

Republican Party. South Carolina. petitioners 87939

Republican Party. South Carolina. Convention, 1868. 87940

Republican Party. South Carolina. State Central Committee. 87942, 88078, 1st note after 94434

Republican Party. Tennessee. Convention, Nashville, 1870. 70037

Republican Party. Washington, D. C. Republican Association, 70020

Republican Party. Wisconsin. Convention, Milwaukee, 1894. 83675

Republican Party. Wisconsin. State Central Committee. Press Secretary. 83675 see also Smith, Nicholas.

Republican Party and its presidential candidates. 29733

Republican Party and the Republican candidate. (21328)

Republican Party in Tennessee reorganized. 70037

Republican party—its history and policy. 80380

Republican Party; its origin, necessity & performance. 93672

Republican Party—the message. 64675

Republican Party the result of southern aggression. 78811

Republican Party vindicated. 41160

Republican Party; what the north has to do with slavery. 22175

Republican platform. 93681

Republican platform. Revised speech of Hon. E. G. Spaulding. 89039

Republican pocket pistol. 9329

Republican principles. 41161

Republican prize songster. (70038)

Republican quarterly review. (70039)

Republican rally. 15471

Republican review. 52000

Republican scrap book. 70040

Republican songs for the people. 20935

Republican songster. Being a collection. 70041

Republican songster, for 1860. Edited by George W. Bungay. 9161

Republican songster, for . . . 1860. Edited by John W. Hutchinson. (34065)

Republican songster, for the campaign of 1864. 70042

Republican spy. 104114, 105543

Republican success secures reform. 90535

Republican ticket. 46090

Republican Union Festival, New York, 1862. 40941, 54661, 70043

Republican Union Festival, New York, February 22, 1862. 40941, 54661, 70043

Republican watch-tower. 70044

Republicanas. 39013

Republicanism and aristocracy contrasted. 44437

Republicanism backwards and Christianity reversed. 28350

Republicanism in America. 43031

Republicanism, liberality, and catholicity of Presbytery. 85287

Republicanism of Methodism. (70045)

Republicanisme oligarchique desapointe. 42637

Republicano. pseud. Notas. 65928

Republicano. pseud. ed. Poesias de D. Unis G. Ortis. 57721

Republican's manual for the use of a free people. (82238)

Republicas de Centro America. 86246

Repvblicas del mvndo. 72895

Republicas del mundo divididas en XXVII libros. 72894

Republication of Baptist works. 93622

Republication of standard Baptist works. 86855

Republication of the celebrated letters of Phocion. 29948, 84818

Republication of the sentiments of several authors. 4689

Republication of voyages, travels, history, biography, science, tales, and poems. (28572)

Republick der Jesuiten des umgesturzten Paraguay. 51426

Republics established and thrones overturned by the Bible. 11799, 17695

Republiek Colombia. 70900

Republiek van Venezuela. 77129

Republik Chili. (22778)

Republik der Jesuiten. 58534, 63901

Republik Mexico. 92807

Republikanische Calender. 70046

Republken Chile aren 1821-28. 5712

Republique Americaine. (23554)

Republique Argentine. 101350

Republique Argentine. De la salubrite du climat des Andes. 78501

Republique Argentine. Documents officiels. (70048)

Republique Argentine. Finances, commerce, industrie lainiere, immigration. 70047

Republique Argentine. [Par Charles Beck-Bernard.] 4241

Republique de Bolivar. 101350

Republique de Buenos-Ayres. 74610

Republique de Colombie. 101350

Republique de Costa-Rica. 17018

Republique de Equateur (Exposition Universelle de 1867.) 70049

Republique de Nicaragua. 9148A

Republique des Etats-Unis d'Amerique. 47201

Republique des Jesuites. (51427), (58535), (63900)

Republique du Honduras. 4594

Republique du Paraguay. 21161

Republique du Salvador. 4592

Republique d'Haiti renaissant. (3545)

Republique Haitienne. 21010

Republique sans impot. (39297)

Republiques de l'Amerique Espagnole. 29059

Republiques de l'Amerique Latine. 70050

Repuesta a la contestacion. 47804

Repuesta a un papel anonyma contra el libro. (36797)

Repuesta al impreso que dio a luz el P. Provincial de San Diego. 19261

Repuesta del Marques de Grimaldi. 28846

Reputable farmer. pseud. Letter. 12483

Reputed wife of Michael Robinson. 72054

Requa, W. C. 57737, note after 101510

Requena, Cayetano. 97660

Requena, Martin de. 70051

Requena, Tomas. 70052

Request. 106198

Request der Gecommitteerdens van de Groen-landsche en Straat Davidsche Vischeryen. 70053

Request, for a dismission. 8461, note just before 69458

Request from the Committee on Internal Improvements. 45110

Request of the Society for the Propagation of the Gospel in Foreign Parts. 85945

Requeste aan de Staten Generael der Neder-landen. 4813, 58396

Requeste, als de zoo genaamde grieven. 93836

Requeste, met memorie en bijlagen van P. Pama. 4813

Requeste oft, verhael d'welck den . . . Pater . . . J. de Santander. (76812)

Requeste presentee a la Chambre d'Assemblee. 10512

Requeste presentee au Roy Charles Neufiesme. 39630

Reqveste presentee av Roy d'Espagne. 67356

Requeste presentee au Roy en son Conseil. 72043

Reqveste presentee au Roy par Jeanne Francois. 39609

Reqveste remonstrative av Roi d'Espagne. 4637, 76811

Reqveste remonstrative que la Reuerendissime Pere, Frere Jean de Santander. 7637, 76811

Requeste van de Burgerije ende Negotianten. (16680), (57320), 1st note after 102889A

Requeste van de dolerende Burgeren aen de E. E. Heeren. (16680), (57320), 1st note after 102889A

Requeste van de Predicanten. (16680), (57320), 1st note after 102889A

Requeste vande West Indische Compagnie. (16680), (57320), 1st note after 102889A

Requesten van de goede gehoorsame Burgeren. (16680), (57320), 1st note after 102889A

Requeste argumentative en faveur des prisonniers. 93241

Reqvete av Roy, faite en forme de complainte. (39632)

Reqeute de plusieurs chefs Indiens d'Atitlan. 94854

Requiem. 77469

Requiem to the memory of A. Lincoln. 37251

Requier, Augustus Julian. (70054)-70055

Requier, J. Baptiste. (81446), 81448

Requiescat. pseud. see Eliot, John Fleet.

Requirement in a lexicographer of the English language. (20541)

Requirements of American village homes. 13591

Requisites for admission to the freshman class. 105786

Requisites of female education. 18139

Requisites to our country's glory. 62731

Requisition for seven hundred thousand ministers. 28818

Requisition now announced shortly to be made on us. 87536

Requited Labor Convention, Philadelphia, 1838. (49355)

Re-re-commencement: a kind of poem. 5348

Rerum a Soc. Jesu in India gestarum. 31382

Rerum ab Hispanis in India Occidentali. 68346

Rerum ab illustrissimo heroe Ioanne Navritio. 63319

Rerum et urbis Amstelodamensium historia. 64002

Rerum Hispanicarum ordine sequuntur. 77904

Rerum medicarum novae Hispaniae thesaurus. (31515)-31516

Rerum memorabilium libri II. 58411

Rerum memorabilium sive deperditarum. 58412

Rerum morumque in regio Chinensi. 27782

Rervm vrbivmque Hispaniae. 32005, 77901-77902

Rerum Venetiarum. 74667

Res et personas memoralibes. 20939

Resa til Norra America. 36986

Resa til Norra Americas Ishaf. 97702

Resa til Spanska landerna uti Europa och America. (41772)

Resa till Montevideo och Buenos Ayres. 5713

Resa uti Guiana. 21004

Rescript of the Court of Madrid. 69499

Rescue. 53020

Rescued chief. 51656

Rescued fragments of cabin memorandums. 29912

Researches, chemical and physiological. 36577

Researches, concerning the institutions & monuments. (33751)

Researches into the origin and history of the red race. 7233

Researches into the physical history of mankind. 65477

Researches on America. (43132)-43133

Researches on electrical rheometry. 85072

Researches on the ammonia-cobalt bases. 85072

Researches on the tides. 103259

Researches, philosophical and antiquarian. 43134

Researches relative to the planet Neptune. 85072, 101075

Researches respecting Americus Vespucius. 76852

Researches upon Nemertians and Planarians. 27484

Researches upon the anatomy and physiology of respiration. 85072

Researches upon the venom of the rattlesnake. 85072

Researches upon the venoms of poisonous serpents. 85072

Researches upon the vital dynamics of civil government. 20764

Reseignemens authentiques sur l'abolition de l' esclavage. 42952

Reseignements complementaires. 14720

Reseignements nautiques sur la Nouvelle-Caledonie. 28862

Reseignements sur la cote meridionale du Bresil. 3583

Resemblance between Moses and Christ. 72643

Resena de las festividades nacionales. 48653

Resena de los partidos. (70056)

Resena de los principales puertos y puntos. (77795)

Resena de los trabajos cientificos. 73036

Resena de su vida publica. 27770

Resena historica de la formacion y operaciones. 36791

Resena historica de las negociaciones diplomaticas. 70057

Resena historica de los principales concordatos celebrados. 44559

Resena historica del derecho de ultramar. 41972

Resena historica del establicimiento de ciencias medicas. 70058

Resena historica y esplicativa. 70059

Resende, Angelo Andrea de. 70060

Resende, Antonio Telles da Silva Caminha e Menezes, Marquez de. see Telles da Silva Caminha e Menezes, Antonio, Marquez de Resende, 1790-1875.

Resende, Garcia de. 70061-(70063)

Resendio, A. A. de. see Resende, Angelo Andrea de.

Reserved power. A sermon. (66787)

Resguardo contra el Olvido. 72248

Residence at the court of London. 74272-74274

Residence at the court of London, comprising incidents. 74273

Residence at the Great Salt Lake City. 24186

Residence in Lima. 82330

Residence in the Sandwich Islands. 91664, 91670

Residence in the south. 81520

Residence in the West Indies and America.
(75024)

Residence of twenty-one years in the Sandwich
Islands. 5432

Residence on a Louisiana plantation. (38177)

Resident. pseud. New Orleans as it is.
(53341)

Resident. pseud. Salmon-fishing in Canada.
734, 75833

Resident. pseud. Sketches and recollections of
the West Indies. (81546), 4th note after
102866

Resident and business directory of Saint
Joseph. 75297

Resident at the Cape of Good Hope. pseud.
Remarks on the demoralizing influence
of slavery. 69456

Resident at the falls. pseud. Guide to travellers. 55119

Resident beyond the frontier. pseud. Tales of
the northwest. see Snelling, William
Joseph, 1804-1848.

Resident Canadian. pseud. Narrative of the
rebellion in the Canadas. 10528

Resident emigrant, late from the United States.
pseud. History of Texas. see Stille,
----------.

Resident in Jamaica. pseud. Obi. 56420, 4th
note after 95756

Resident in the south; and a tour in the west.
2958, 81520

Resident in the West Indies for thirteen years.
pseud. British West India colonies. see
Campbell, ------ (Bourne)

Resident in the West Indies for thirteen years.
pseud. Suggestions realtive to the
improvement of the British West India
Colonies. see Campbell, ------ (Bourne)

Resident of Boston. pseud. Yankee chronology.
21309, 105957

Resident of twelve years at Marietta. pseud.
Brief sketch of the state of Ohio. see
Ward, Nahum.

Resident of Washington. pseud. Disunion and
its results. see Hodge, William L.

Residing member of the Society for Promoting
Christian Knowledge in London. pseud.
Letter. 40311

Resignation, a funeral sermon. (36601)

Resignation. An American novel. 70064

Resignation and address, in a circular letter.
101532

Resignation and address to the citizens of the
United States. 101571, 101601

Resignation, of General Washington. 101567

Resignation of His Excellency General Washington. 101569

Resignation of the Presidency of the United
States. 101588

Resignation; or the fox out of the pit. 70065

Resignation to the afflictive dispensations of
divine providence. 104964

Resistance no rebellion: in answer to Dr.
Johnson's Taxation no tyranny. 36307

Resistance no rebellion. In which the right
of the British Parliament. 70066

Resistance to evil. 38086

Resistance to laws of the United States.
40048, 70067

Resistance to slavery every man's duty. 814,
70068

Resolucion de la Diputacion Provincial. 33119

Resolucion de la H. Diputacion Provincial.
10780

Resolucion de las cuestiones sobre America.
68732

Resolucion de V. Magestad. 51044

Resolucion que tomo el Consejo en Sala de
Justicia. 98150

Resolutie op de memorie van d. Groot-Brittan.
Ambasss. (36569)

Resolutie van de Ed: Groot Mo: Heeren Staten
van Hollant. 102912

Resolutie van de Heeren Burgemeesteren ende
Raden tot Amsterdam. 16732-(16734),
23344, 3d note after 102889A, 7th note
after 102890

Resolutie van de Staten-Generall in d. 4. Oct.
1764. 4814

Resolutie van Haar Hoog Mogende de Heeren
Staten Generaal. 22998

Resolutie vande Ed. Mo. Heeren Staten van
Vriesland. 70069

Resolutie . . . 17 Nov. 1779. 36570

Resolutien ende proceduren by de Ed. Mog.
Heeren Staten van Stadt Groningen en
Ommelanden. (78001)

Resolutien van Haar Hoog Mogende en van de
Societeit daar toe betrekkelyk. 68458,
1st note after 93862

Resolution and speech of Hon. Thomas C.
McCreery. 43119

Resolution, calling on the government for
evidence. 55323

Resolution de L. H. P. les Etats de Zeland
justifiee. 70070

Resolution from the Committee of Elections.
91259

Resolution from the Senate. 91820

Resolution in relation to the proceedings.
76083

Resolution of an aged minister. 104527

Resolution of Congress expressive of their
high sense. 16098

Resolution of Congress, of the 26th of May,
1781. 50866

Resolution [of Mr. Foote.] (23732)

Resolution of the American Congress. 52783-
52784, 1st note after 52940

Resolution, of the Assembly of Grenanda,
104904

Resolution of the Assembly of the 23d February.
(53564)

Resolution of the Board of Trustees [of St.
Stephen's College.] (75494)

Resolution of the Convention of August fourth.
94981

Resolution of the directors of the [American
Education] Society. 104503

Resolution of the General Assembly of Indiana.
34574

Resolution of the General Assembly of May,
1868. 89261

Resolution of the General Assembly of the
state of Indiana. 34575

Resolution of the Georgia Historical Socety.
(22280)

Resolution of the High Court of Errors and
Appeals. 60582, 94236

Resolution of the House of Commons. 57400

Resolution of the House of 9th instant. 53362

Resolution of the House of Representatives
and of the Senate. 88100

Resolution of the House of Representatives
[of Alabama.] (49785)

Resolution of the inhabitants of Petersburg.
61221

Resolution of the Judiciary Committee. (59430)

Resolution of the Legislative Assembly of the
Territory of Washington. 101922

Resolution of the Legislature of North Carolina.
55685

Resolution of the "National Labor Congress." 24287

Resolution of the Pennsylvania Assembly. 60629

Resolution of the Roxbury Yeoman Association. 73734

Resolution of the Senate for information. (76081)

Resolution of the Senate [of Ohio.] 56881

Resolution of the Senate [of the state of Indiana.] 34501

Resolution offered by Mr. Foot. 4787

[Resolution prohibiting the sale within the United States of property.] 83987

Resolution providing for state scholarships. 8599

Resolution relative to an amendment to the constitution. 60583

Resolution relative to the abduction or enslavement of citizens. 53616

Resolution relative to the market property of the city. (54212)

Resolution relative to the public lands. 3832

Resolution reported by the Committee of Elections. (66732)

Resolution to expel Mr. Long, of Ohio. 59646

Resolutions, acts and orders of Congress for the year 1780. 15545

Resolutions, acts, and orders of Congress, 1760 [sic]. 15591

Resolutions, address, and journal of proceedings. 88331

Resolutions, addresses and remonstrances of the free people of color. (26709)

Resolutions adopted at a meeting held in Washington, D. C. 88471

Resolutions adopted at a meeting of citizens held in Providence, R. I. 3695, 8524, note after 89213

Resolutions adopted at a meeting of citizens of Boston. 82060

Resolutions adopted at a meeting of the Episcopalians. (70071)

Resolutions adopted at a meeting of the Grand Council U. L. A. 10011

Resolutions . . . adopted, at the first annual meeting. 51941

Resolutions adopted at the Mass Meeting of the Loyal National League. 54663

Resolutions adopted by Bratton's Brigade. 87803

Resolutions adopted by . . . his constituents. (50376)

Resolutions adopted by the Anti-masonic members of the Legislature. 46091

Resolutions adopted by the Common Council of the city of Alton. 968

Resolutions adopted by the Native American Association. (61860)

Resolutions adopted by the Senior Class. 58197

Resolutions adopted by various public bodies. 35313

Resolutions adopted in the Convention of Texas. 95114

Resolutions adopted in the House of Representatives. 37548

Resolutions adopted on that occasion. 13550

Resolutions and address adopted by the Southern Convention. 88332-88333

Resolutions and address of a meeting at Martlings. 43615, 49335

Resolutions and address of a meeting convened at Martlings. 43615, 49335, note after 103267

Resolutions and address of the American Congress. 106-107, 1657, 2760, 15523, (19253), 36302-36303, 36306-36307, 36309, 50452, 56060, 58399, 63216, 63771, 78302, (80441), 90317, note before 94431, note before 94434, 96184, 97635, 102647

Resolutions and addresses of the Anti-duelling Association of New York. 4337

Resolutions and circular address of the Convention of Perfectionists. 60921

Resolutions and discourse. 18136

Resolutions and extracts from the journals of the Hon. the Congress. 70072

Resolutions and instructions of the Legislature. 69677, 98641

Resolutions and memorial adopted at the session. 87939

Resolutions and memorial adopted by the Southern Republican Association. 88471

Resolutions and memorial of citizens of New York. 70073

Resolutions and memorial of the miners of California. 10038

Resolutions and private acts passed by the General Assembly. 15777

Resolutions and protests. 88912

Resolutions and remonstrances of the people of colour. 14732

Resolutions and report of a Committee of the General Assembly. 57045

[Resolutions appointing finance committee.] 76528, 76647

Resolutions at a meeting in Boston. 97002

Resolutions. At a meeting of Delegates from the several towns. (23007)

Resolutions by the Diocesan Convention. 30972

Resolutions . . . by the General Assembly of Georgia. 27103

Resolutions containing the amendments to be made. 42525

Resolutions, . . debated from January 17 to February 18. 87651

Resolutions [denouncing the tariff acts of 1824 and 1828.] 87503

Resolutions directing the mode of levying taxes. 70074

Resolutions entered into by the Delegates from the several towns. 83439

Resolutions expressive of sympathy. (80470)

Resolutions expressive of the determination of Georgia. 70075

Resolutions expressing their sentiment. 322

Resolutions, from the Committee on Federal Relations. 45351

[Resolutions from the counties of Caroline, Orange, Louisa.] 100071

Resolutions from the state of South Carolina. 87479

Resolutions giving notice to Great Britain. 11771

Resolutions in the Senate on . . . calling a convention. 60584

Resolutions introduced by Mr. Bayles. 9659

Resolutions, . . . January, 1841. 37572

Resolutions, laws, and ordinances. 15592, 70076

Resolutions of a meeting in St. Thomas' Parish. 33572

[Resolutions of] Boston Chamber of Commerce. 96754

Resolutions of certain Episcopalians. (70071)

Resolutions of Congress. January, 1862. (15404)

Resolutions of Congress, of the 18th of April 1783. 15590

Resolutions of Congress of the 5th of December last. 99073

Resolutions of Congress under the confederation. 33820

Resolutions [of Daniel Webster.] (29016)

[Resolutions of House of Delegates respecting the settlement.] 100096

Resolutions [of Mr. Crowninshield.] 17711

Resolutions of Mr. Welch. 29279

Resolutions of South Carolina. 46058

Resolutions of thanks to Major General Rosecrans. 57046

Resolutions of the American Congress. 52784

Resolutions of the [American Library] Association. 84980

Resolutions of the Baltimore Democratic Convention. 20428

Resolutions of the Baltimore Whig Convention. 20428

Resolutions of the Board [of Trustees of Dudley Observatory.] 21100

Resolutions of the California Academy of Natural Sciences. 90932

Resolutions of the Committee of Philadelphia. 62190

Resolutions of the Committee on Federal Relations. (45352)

Resolutions of the [Connecticut Medical] Society. 16783

Resolutions of the Democratic Hickory Club of Philadelphia. 61572

Resolutions of the Democratic League. 80445

Resolutions of the Democratic Meeting of Delegates of Washington County. 102011

Resolutions of the Diocesan Convention [of New York.] 30972, 5th note after 96966

Resolutions of the Fraternity and Twenty Eighth Congregational Society. 58768, 12th note after 96966

Resolutions of the General Assembly [of Alabama. (50375)

Resolutions of the General Assembly of . . . Georgia. 46056

Resolutions of the General Assembly of Kentucky. (37579)

Resolutions of the General Assembly of South Carolina, in relation to the controversy. 87504

Resolutions of the General Assembly of South Carolina, on the subject of the distribution. 87505

Resolutions of the General Assembly of the Mississippi Territory. (49541)

Resolutions of the General Assembly, of 21st Dec., 1788. 23453

Resolutions of the General Conference. 48207

Resolutions of the General Council of War. 2455, 11131, 1st note after 99245

Resolutions of the House of Commons [of North Carolina.] 55686

Resolutions of the House of Commons, on the great and constitutional questions. 70077

Resolutions of the Legislative Council for the construction. 49176

Resolutions of the Legislature of California. 10039

Resolutions of the Legislature of Georgia. 27104

Resolutions of the Legislature of Maine. 43922

Resolutions of the Legislature of Maryland. 45353

Resolutions of the Legislature of Massachusetts. (16095)

Resolutions of the Legislature of New Jersey. 91898

Resolutions of the Legislature of New York. 53946

Resolutions of the Legislature of the state of Georgia. 34655

Resolutions of the Legislature of the state of Maine. 44033

Resolutions of the Legislature of the state of South Carolina. 87506

Resolutions of the manufacturers. 42827

Resolutions of the meetings of planters. (35621)

Resolutions of the missionaries. 106096

Resolutions of the Noble and Great Mighty Lords. 102912A

Resolutions of the Press Conference. 70263

Resolutions of the Provincial Congress, of the colony of New-York. 53948, 70078

Resolutions of the Provincial Congress, September 1, 1776. 53947

Resolutions of the Republican citizens of Boston. 6553

Resolutoins [sic] of the Roman Catholics of New York. (70079)

Resolutions of thee several [sic] parishes. 70080

Resolutions of the several states. (22237), note after 100545A

Resolutions of the Society of Paper Makers. 60617

Resolutions of the state of Georgia. 17458

Resolutions of the States General. 36636

Resolutions of the Stockholders of the Delaware and Schuylkill Canal. 60046

Resolutions of the Trustees for Establishing the Colony of Georgia. 27104

Resolutions of the Union and State Rights Party. 97752

Resolutions of the Union Republican State Convention. (60585)

Resolutions of Virginia and Kentucky. (43720)

Resolutions on national affairs [by the New Hampshire Legislature.] 52928-52929

Resolutions . . . on national affairs [by the New York Legislature.] 53593

Resolutions on the death of President Lincoln. 6822

Resolutions on the late decease of Hon. Joseph Story. 92320

Resolutions . . . November and December session, 1791. 87652

Resolutions passed at a meeting of Republicans. 97413

[Resolutions passed] at a meeting of "The Maryland Society." 45241

Resolutions passed . . . at the second annual meeting. 71193

Resolutions passed by the citizens of Baltimore. 3080

Resolutions passed by the . . . Councils. 62191

Resolutions passed by the General Assembly of the state of Rhode Island. (8599)

Resolutions passed by the late Philadelphia Annual Conference. 72124

Resolutions passed by the Sanitary Committee. 76543, 76549, 76647

Resolutions [relating to the public lands.] 45354

Resolutions relative to national affairs. 60586

Resolutions relative to slavery. 89355

Resolutions relative to slavery passed by the Legislatures. 60247

Resolutions relative to the Bank of the United States. (60037)

Resolutions relative to the death of Abraham Lincoln. 59863

Resolutions relating to the subject of the militia. 99205

Resolutions submitted by him [i. e. Thomas Jefferson.] 18836

Resolutions submitted by Mr. Alexander Smyth. 85189

Resolutions submitted by Mr. Ramsal. 87529

Resolutions submitted by the Hon. Jefferson Davis, March 1, 1860. (4704)

Resolutions submitted by the Hon. Jefferson Davis, of Miss. 12522

Resolutions suggested by Mr. Olmsted. 76670

[Resolutions that the General Assembly of Virginia will cooperate.] 100076

Resolutions to retrench the expenditures. 8862

Resolutions concerning the boundary line between the states. 46092

Resolve for districting the commonwealth. (46093)

Resolve of His Majesty's Council relating to the disorders. (46094)

Resolve of the House of Representatives, Dec. 4, 1794. 19618

Resolve of the Provincial Congress for taking up government in form. 52783-52784, 1st note after 52940

Resolved by the Senate. 85064

Resolved Christian. 46486

Resolved, that a committee be appointed to prepare an address. 100495

Resolved, that an application be made. 100055

Resolved, that Col. Joseph Marsh. 99014

Resolved, that it be recomme[nded that all those citizens.] 105395

Resolved, that the Captain-General's orders. 99074

Resolved, that the following vindication be forthwith published. 803, 2d note after 99005

Resolved . . . that the President of the United States. note after 94720

Resolved, that the Senators and Representatives of this state. 99048

Resolved, that the thanks of this committee. 85996

Resolved. That this meeting do unanimously nominate Daniel Webster. 103275

Resolved, that three thousand extra copies be printed. 80500

Resolved, that two hundred copies of the reports. 90045

Resolved, that—Whereas, during no age in our past history. 86162

Resolved . . . to maintain and defend the constitution. 100105

Resolved unanimously, that a copy of the memorial. 100090

Resolved unanimously, that the proceedings. 100091

Resolves and orders of the Congress and General Court. 46095

Resolves and orders of the Congress, Council, and General Court. 46096, 70081

Resolves and orders of the Council of War. 70516, 70699

Resolves and private acts of the state of Connecticut. 15848

Resolves and private laws of the state of Connecticut. 15776

Resolves concerning the boundary line. 45686, 46097

Resolves in relation to petitions. (20313)

Resolves of a convention held on the New-Hampshire Grants. 66514, 1st-2d notes after 99003

Resolves of Congress concerning trade. 46098

Resolves of the citizens in Town Meeting [of Baltimore.] 13158

Resolves of the citizens in Town Meeting. Particulars. 3025

Resolves of the Committee for the province of Pennsylvania. 20040, (20046), 84678C

Resolves of the eighth Legislature of . . . Maine. (44035)

Resolves of the General Assembly of the colony of Massachusetts-Bay. 46099

Resolves [of the General Assembly of the state of Vermont.] 66514, 1st-2d notes after 99003

Resolves of the General Court of . . . Massachusetts, respecting the sale of eastern lands. 46101

Resolves of the General Court of . . . Massachusetts, . . . 1781. 46100

Resolves of the House of Burgesses. 99925

Resolves of the Legislature of the state of Maine. (44034)

Resolves of the Massachusetts House of Representatives. 46102

Resolves of the state of Maine. (44036)

Resolves, respecting the militia of the colony. 87353, 87612

Resona Recessus. 70082

Resort and remedy of those that are bereaved. 21967

Resort of piety. 46487

Resource of war. 89033, 89040

Resources, advantages, and productions of the counties. 70083

Resources and prospects of America. 61289

Resources and statistics of nations. 43289

Resources, character, and condition. 77062

Resources of California. 32272

Resources of Colorado. 19614

Resources of Mexico. 78592

Resources of Santo Domingo. (23589)

Resources of South-Carolina. 87943

Resources of the Canadas. 10596

Resources of the Ottawa Valley. 82201

Resources of the Pacific Slope. 8662

Resources of the Philadelphia and Erie Railroad region. 61947

Resources of the southern fields and forests. 64157

Resources of the union. 10842

Resources of the United States of America. 8050

Resources of the United States. Report to the International Statistical Congress at Berlin. 73966

Resources of Vallejo. 32273

Respect for the remains of the dead. 90912

Respectable Federalists of the County of Hampshire. see Federal Party. Massachusetts. Hampshire County.

Respectable Federalists of the county of Hampshire, indignant at the base and infamous practices. 92884

Respectable minister of the Gospel. pseud. Increase of piety. see March, Angier.

Respectable residents in the various townships of Upper Canada. pseud. Statement of the satisfactory results. 10609, note after 90758

Respected friend. . . . 61935

Respected friend, the time has arrived. 105439

Respectful address of C. P. M'Ilvaine. 43324

Respectful address to the Protestant Episcopalians. 43321

Respectful address to the Trinitarian clergy. 105271

Respectful memorial of the subscribers. 95928

Respectful observations on . . . the bill.
(70084)
Respectful remonstrance, on behalf of the white
people. 87817
Respective pleas and arguments. 97358
Responce par le Chevalier de Villegaignon.
99726
Respondent the Governor's case. 103894
Respondent's case. 91849, 101262
Respondents' case. 47918, 69087, note before
98976
Respondents' case. 1810. 104160
Respondents case. The merchants, factors,
and agents. 35603
Respondent's case. To be heard before the
Right Honourable the Lords of the Com-
mittee of Council, at the Council Chamber.
103894
Respondent's case. To be heard before the
Right Honourable the Lords of the Com-
mittee of Council at the Council Chamber
at the Cockpit. 92362
Respondents case. To be heard before the
Right Honourable the Lords of the Com-
mittee of His Majesty's Most Honourable
Privy-Council. 101002
Respondiendo a los memoriales. 76026
Response a la preface critique. (25925)
Response aux calomnies de Jaques Beaufe.
35792
Response aux lettres de Nicolas Durant. 99725
Response aux libelles d'iniures. 99728
Response by Benjamin B. Minor. 49651
Response from the Diocese of New York.
70085, 85946
Response of the Public Treasurer. 55686
Response of the Adjutant General of Kentucky.
37556
Response of the Bank of Kentucky. 37493
Response of the Judges of the Court of Ap-
peals. 37581
Response of the ministers of the Massachu-
setts Association. 66883
Response of the people of the northwest Ohio.
15877
Response of the Treasurer [of Kentucky.]
37511
Response to Bishop Potter. 47700, 70086
Response to Charleston. 70087
Response to Mr. Binney. 55173
Responses aux objections contre le systeme
colonial. 57793
Responsibilities of a republical government.
(11946)
Responsibilities of American merchants. 35733
Responsibilities of Congress. 51634
Responsibilities of rulers. 6966
Responsibilities of the American citizen.
(46939)
Responsibilities of the founders of the re-
public. 59139
Responsibilities of the mother country. 92628
Responsibility for organizing the House. 28997
Responsibility of the church. A discourse.
92022
Responsibility of the church in Richmond.
94537
Responsibility of the north in regard to slavery.
(70088)
Responsible government for Canada. 10597
Responsible government for colonies. 9125
Responsible or parliamentary government.
28166
Responsio ad dissertationem secundam Hvgonis
Grotii. 38562

Responsio ad totam quaestionum syllogen a
Clarissimo Viro Domino Guilianmo
Apollonio. 55888
Responsione. 22188
Respost ao Marquez de Olinda. 85646
Resposta do Arcebispo da Bahia. 78957
Resposta do Sr. Conselheiro Nabuco. 85773
Resposta que o Reverendo Deputado P. Diogo
Antonio Feijo. 76329
Respostas dadas por D. Jose Joaquim da Cunha
de Azeredo Coutinho. 17955
Respublica. 65392
Respublicas del Peru, Chile, etc. 63676
Respuesta a dicho papel por el Dr. Echeverria.
21775
Respuesta a la manifestacion. 63438
Respuesta a la memoria de las quinas de Santa
Fe. 74005
Respuesta a la memoria que presento en 16 de
Enero de 1776. 70089
Respuesta a las cartas del Doctor Alberdi.
26273
Respuesta a las dudas sobre gobierno de la
Iglesia. 70090
Respuesta a las imposturas de un folletista
Espanol. (70091)
Respuesta a los fundamentos con que el Senor
Fiscal. 70092
Respuesta a los fundamentos de el Senor Doct.
Jose de Torres, y Vergara. 97707
Respuesta al duelo vindicado. 70093
Respuesta al libelo titulado "Caso de conciencia."
(73165)
Respuesta al papel de Da Carmen Maiz publi-
cado hoy. 44065
Respvesta al papel de el Padre Lector de
Theologia. 86416
Respuesta de algunos proprietarios de fincas
rusticas. 70094
Respvesta de D. Geronimo de Ayanz. 70095
Respuesta de Jose Mariano de Anzorena.
34187-34189
Respuesta de los Senores Fiscales. 70090
Respuesta del Autor del Duelo de la Inquisicion.
94824
Respuesta del General Jose Maria Tornel y
Mendivil. 96205
Respuesta del Jeneral Paez. 14621
Respuesta del Oidor Decano de la Real Au-
diencia. 70097
Respuesta del P. Soto al Pensador Mejicano.
87221
Respuesta del Payo Rosario al del Tejocote.
99706
Respuesta del Senor Doctor Antonio Go[n]calez.
70098
Respuesta juridica al Senor Dean D.ʳ D. Rodrigo
Garcia Flores de Valdes. 96277-96278
Respuesta para desengano del publico. 74004
Respuesta que da D. D. Antonio Duarte y Zenea.
21003
Respuesta que dio como Fisca en Primer
Ayudante. 106348
Respuesta, que D. Joseph Antonio de Villa-Senor,
y Sanchez. 99685
Respuesta que la Suprema Junta Provisional.
97044
Respuesta satisfactoria a la carte apologetica.
(40063)-40064
Respuesta satisfactoria que a las anotaciones
hechas a su ephemeris. 106404
Respuesta unica que debe darse. 98389
Respvesta, y satisfaccion, a la pretencion del
P. Fr. Iuan Guerrero. 86142
Respuesta, y satisfacion dada por . . . D. Juan
Antonio de Vizarron, y Eguiarreta. 100638

RESPUESTAS

Respuestas de los Fiscales del Consejo Real de las Indias. 36952
Respuestas del Payo de Rosario. 99715
Ressende, Garcia de. see Resende, Garcia de.
Rest in reserve for the righteous. 95760
Rest of the faithful departed. 88575, 91719
Rest of the nations: a poem. (47442)
Restablecimiento de las fabricas. 97690
Restablecimiento de las fabricas, y comercial Espanol. 97690
Restablecimiento de las fabricas y commercio Espagnol. 98249
Re-statement of Mr. Chalmer's opinion. 11764, 68674-(68675), 3d note after 97583
Restauracao de Portugal prodigiosa. 22835
Restavracion de la civdad del Salvador. 94280
Restavracion del estado de Aravco. 94899
Restauracion y reparos del Peru. (71454)
Restaurador Mexico. (70099)
Restauration de l'evangile ancien. 85531
Reste, Bernard de. tr. 70100, 101231-note after 101231, 1st note after 106377
Restell, Anna. alias see Lohman, Anna (Trow) 1812-1878.
Restigouche Agricultural Society. 70102
Restituta. 8829, 25999, 79342
Restitution of all things. 8498
Restitution sought in Spayne. 100439, 4th note after 102831
Restitutus. 46488
Restivo, Paulo. 74032-74033
Restoration and the President's policy. 86055
Restoration and the Union Party. 68057
Restoration of Georgia. 20795
Restoration of legitimate authority. 81497
Restoration of the currency. 62820
Restoration of the rebellious states. 54968
Restoration of union. 79553
Restorationist. 70103
Restorer of the union of the United States. 36652
Restrepo, Jose Manuel. 14592, 43757, 70104-70105 see also Colombia. Secretaria de Relaciones Esteriores. Colombia. Secretaria del Interior.
Restrepo, Vicente. tr. 1st note after 100947
Result. 16297
Result, and proceedings of the mutual ecclesiastical councils. 5992
"Result," &c. 37695
Result of a careful visitation. 97549
Result of a . . . council, . . . May, 1820. 57602, 1st note after 105357, 105358
Result of a Council of Churches at Concord, Mass. 15137
Result of a Council of Churches at Grafton. (28200), 103935
Result of a Council of Nine Churches met at Northampton. 21967, 55771
Result of a Council of Ten Churches. 23391, 70106
Result of a Council of the Consociated Churches of the county of Windham. 104763
Result of a late Ecclesiastical Council. 7357
Result of a Mutual Ecclesiastical Council. 57602, 105358
Result of a Synod at Cambridge. 17059, (70107)
Result of an Ecclesiastical Council at Bolton. 6254
Result of an Ecclesiastical Council at Dorchester. 7095, (20624)-20625, 69500
Result of an Ecclesiastical Council at Exeter. 23392-(23393)

Result of an Ecclesiastical Council, at North Yarmouth. 70108
Result of an Ecclesiastical Council at Princeton. 27695, 70109
Result of an Ecclesiastical Council convened at Bolton. 6253
Result of an Ecclesiastical Council, convened at Exeter, N. H. 70110
Result of an Ecclesiastical Council convened at Groton, Mass. (4338), 9623, 28965, 28976, 42760
Result of an Ecclesiastical Council convened at North Wrentham. 24096
Result of an Ecclesiastical Council convened at Plymouth, Mass. 70111
Result of an Ecclesiastical Council convened at Reading. (68210)
Result of an Ecclesiastical Council, convened at Salem. 75698
Result of an Ecclesiastical Council, convened in the Vestry. (75697)
Result of an Ecclesiastical Council convened on call of the First Society. 81389
Result of an Ecclesiastical Council, held at Sandwich. (76449)
Result of an Ecclesiastical Council in Simsbury 73138
Result of an Ecclesiastical Council [Ipswich, Mass.] 35047
Result of an Ecclesiastical Council publickly declared. 32989
Result of an Ex-Parte Council. 70112
Result of an Ex-Parte Ecclesiastical Council. 70113
Result of astronomical observations. 70114
Result of Council, and addresses to the Society. (80370)-80371, note after 100602, 102522
Result of Council at Princeton. 70115
Result of Council held in the Lecture Room. 70116
Result of manufactures at Lowell. 11219
Result of some researches. 20882
Result of the Consociation of the county of Windham. 94075, 102523
Result of the Convention of Delegates holden at Ipswich. 58906, 99826
Result of the Council at Billingsgate. 21669
Result of the deliberations of the Federal Convention. (70117)
Result of the Ecclesiastical Council convened at Brimfield. 7984
Result of the Ecclesiastical Council convened at North Wrentham. 24096, 95158
Result of the Ecclesiastical Council, holden at Pomfret. 94075, 102523
Result of the N. Y. state election. (70118)
Result tested. 4305
Resultado de las exploraciones practicadas. 50708
Resultants de l'abolition de l'esclavage. (14064)
Resultat au point de vue hydrographique. 40915
Resultat d'observations faites dans les ports de mer. (48689)
Resultat du Conseil du 24 May. 57904, 70119
Resultats de la liberte des noirs a Cayenne. (1999)
Resultats de la revolution quant au commerce. (60721)
Resultats de l'emancipation Anglaise. 77743
Results of a series of meterological observations. 33151
Results of the survey made by Order of the Lords Commissioners. 4045
Results of a voyage of exploration. 5933
Results of an examination of the shells. (28088)

Resurrection. 79254
Resurrection illustrated. 30637
Resurrection of a glorious Jesus demonstrated. 46476
Resurrection of good men a blessed immortality. 79967
Resurrection of James the Apostle. 28043
Resurrection of Laurent Ricci. 64576
Resurrection of Lazarus. 103515, 103593
Resurrection of liberty. 70128
Resurrection of the blue-laws. 70129
Resurrection of the body. 84116
Ressurrection of the just. 90913
Resurreicao, Lourenco da. 70130
Retablissement des manufactures et du commerce d'Espagne. 97691
Retana, J. D. de. defendant 57674
Retchforde, W. 17059
Retchir, Whilhelm. (72235)
Retired barrister. pseud. Review of Du Ponceau on the jurisdiction of the courts. 21377
Retired barrister of Lincolnshire, England. pseud. White acre vs. black acre. see G. J. pseud.
Retired Christian. 46489
Retired common councilman. pseud. Chronicles of the city of Gotham. see Paulding, James Kirke, 1770-1860.
Retired editor. pseud. Brother Jonathan's wife. 8391
Retired governor of Juan Fernandez. pseud. Sixteen years in Chile and Peru. see Sutcliffe, Thomas.
Retired governor of that colony. pseud. Crusoniana. see Sutcliffe, Thomas.
Retired governor of that island. pseud. Earthquake of Juan Fernandez. see Sutcliffe, Thomas.
Retired governor of the islands of Juan Fernandez. pseud. Foreign loans. see Sutcliffe, Thomas.
Retired military officer. pseud. Jamaica as it is, and as it may be. 35594
Retired pastor's annual. 80268
Retirement, and the retired list of the army. 83367
Retort, Dick. pseud. Tit for tat. see Clifton, William. supposed author Cobbett, William, 1763-1835. supposed author Davies, Benjamin. supposed author
Retort, Jack. pseud. Humble attempt at scurrility. see Franklin, William.
Retour du Bresil. 3337A
Retraction of his former opinion. 17079
Retraction of Mr. Cha. Chauncy. (12308)
Retraction of reflections contained in a congressional report. 70131, 82453
Retrato de Bolivar. 99482
Retrato de los Jesuitas. 39016
Retratos de los Espanoles. 70134
Retrato de los R. R. P. P. Jesuitas. 70133
Retrato de Manuel de Faria y Sousa. (64154)
Retratos de varoes Portuguezes. 43299
Retraites de la Venerable Mere Marie de l' Incarnation. 70132
Retreat beaten backward. 70082
Retreat for the Insane, Hartford, Conn. Directors. 30674
Retreat for the Insane at Hartford, Conn.: third report. 30674
Retreat from town. 70135
Retrenchment, economy, reform. 89840
Retribution. 84067
Retribution and other addresses. 84064, 84067
Retro-prospectus. 51255, 75279-75280

Retrorsum. 70975
Retrospect. 85222
Retrospect after thirty years ministry. 64463
Retrospect and other poems. 70136
Retrospect into the King's revenue. 10823
Retrospect of early quakerism. 48711
Retrospect of forty years of military and naval service. 70179
Retrospect of the Boston tea-party. 6778, 70137
Retrospect of the operations of the Society for the Propagation of the Gospel in North America. 104968
Retrospect of the summer and autumn of 1832. 51187
Retrospect of thirty-six years' residence. 11081
Retrospect of western travel. (44940)
Retrospect on the ministry and church of Saybrook. 33128
Retrospect, or, sentimental review. 38791
Retrospect: or the ages of Michigan. 77876, 103695
Retrospect. Two sermons preached . . . Oct. 24, 1841. 58885
Retrospection. 32250
Retrospections of the stage. 4929
Retrospective glance at the progressive state. 38463
Retrospective of four score years. 80268
Retrospective view of the causes of the difference. 70138
Retrospecto de anno de 1866. 59228
Retrospecto dos erros do Brasil. 88773
Retslag, Carl. 70139
Return. 63582, 100804
Return . . . 5 February, 1850. 25633
Return. For Copies of documents. 67055
Return for statements relative to applications. (28269)
Return from the Quarter Master General's Department. 46104
Return in compliance with Mr. Sergeant's request. 14479, 79194
Return of all documents relating to the postal service. (28269)
Return of an old man to his native place. 94062
Return of deaths in . . . New York. (54664)
Return of departed spirits. (70140)
Return of paupers. 45549
Return of peace. 85460
Return of post routes. (56186)
Return of Quarter-Master-General's stores in _____. 70141
Return of Quarter-Master-General's stores in the _____. 70142
Return of the claim of British subjects. 70143
Return of the commissions under the acts. 632
Return, of the militia [of Massachusetts.] 93720
Return of the number of inhabitants in . . . Connecticut. 93034
Return of the whole number of persons within the several districts of the United States, according to "An act providing for the enumeration of the inhabitants of the United States." 11662, 70144-(70145)
Return of the whole number of persons within the several districts of the United States, according to "An act providing for the second census or enumeration of the inhabitants." 20994, 70146-(70147)

Revelations of a slave smuggler; being the
autobiography of Capt. Richard Drake.
20865
Revelations of a slave trader. 47102
Revelations of an opera manager in America.
44524
Revelations of inside life and experience.
(25332)
Revelations of James J. Strang. 92687
Revelations of July 12th, 1843. 83284
Revelations of politics. 97540
Revelations of Potter Christ. 64618
Revelations on the death of Sir John Franklin.
13200
Revelations on the Paraguyan War. 70162
Revelations sur l'intervention Francaise. 38405
Revelations sur l'occupation Francaise au
Mexique. 70163
Revelator. A new church monthly periodical.
70164
Revelator: being an account of the twenty-one
days' entrancement. 70165
Revelli, Salvatore, 1816-1859, illus. 73421
Revello, J. F. Bovo de. 70166
Revels, Hiram Rhodes, 1827-1901. 70167
Revely, William. tr. 17020
Revenga, Jose R. 14594, 70168 see also
Colombia. Secretaria de Estado.
Revenga, Lino J. 70169
Revenu du Canada et paiements faits a meme
ce revenue. (10453)
Revenu et depenses du Departement de la Poste.
(10453)
Revenue and American labor. 71886
Revenue and expenditures. (80381)
[Revenue bill passed by the General Assembly
of 1787-88.] 100053
Revenue book. (36443)
[Revenue laws.] 100395
Revenue laws and custom-house regulations.
19304
Revenue laws of Maryland. 45355
Revenue system. (12039)
Revenue taxes. 100414
Revenues and expenditures for the year 1860.
54665
Reverberator. 84576
Revere, John. 70176-70177
Revere, Joseph Warren. 43179, 70179, 70182
Revere, Joseph Warren. defendant at court
martial 70180-70181
Revere, Paul. engr. 73782, 84617, 90939-
90942
Revere (Ship) in Admiralty 89704
Revere Copper Company. Agent. petitioner
47731, 85541 see also Snow, Samuel T.,
d. 1901. petitioner
Revere House, Boston. see Boston. Revere
House.
Revere Lodge, Boston. see Freemasons.
Massachusetts. Revere Lodge, Boston.
Reverence for law. (74875)
Reverend, A. P. 70185
Reverend ____ ____. pseud. see _____,
Reverend _____. pseud.
Rev. A. B. Cross' account of the Battle of
Gettysburg. 45385
Rev. A. Ganilh's Check checked. 70857
Rev. Aaron Hutchinson's reply to the remarks
on her sermon. 97323
Reverend and learned divine. pseud. Brief
discourse. see Mather, Increase, 1639-
1723
Rev. Anthony Verren, Pastor of the French
Episcopal Church. 99283
Rev. Antoine Verren, Pasteur de l'Eglise
Episcopale Francaise. 99283

Reverend Association in the County of New
Haven. see Congregational Churches in
Connecticut. New Haven County Associ-
ation.
Reverend author of the three former sermons.
pseud. Copy of the letter. see Norton,
John.
Rev. Bela Jacobs' report of his tour. 35497
Rev. Bishop James Osgood Andrew. 84992
Rev. Brother Ripley's prayer. 71515
Rev. divine of the Church of England. pseud.
America dissected. see Macsparran,
James.
Reverend divine there. pseud. Account of the
late earthquake in Jamaica. (35559),
35665, 97172
Rev. Dr. Baker. pseud. see Hines, David
Theodore.
Rev. Dr. Hall's lectures. 29836
Rev. Dr. Honeyman's geological survey. 56187
Rev. Dr. M. J. Raphall's Bible view of
slavery reviewed. (22088)
Reverend Dr. N. Whitaker's neighbour is come.
13594, 103322
Rev. Dr. Richard Furman's exposition of the
views. (26227)
Rev. Dr. Ryerson's defence against the at-
tacks. 74573
Rev. Dr. Ryerson's defence of the Wesleyan
petitions. (74581)
Rev. E. Spencer's defence and testimony.
89314
Rev. George Junkin. 36930
Rev. J. Goldsmith. pseud. see Phillips, Sir
Richard.
Rev. J. Gordon Lorimer's 'Church and state'
in America exposed. (42071)
Rev. J. W. Loguen as a slave and as a free-
man. (41824)
Rev. Jamess [sic] M. Cook. 90780
Rev. John C. Smith. 82954
Rev. John Fletcher's arguments. 24727
Rev. John N. Campbell. 10256, 89744
Rev. L. H. Cobb's discourse. 89897
Rev. M. Keith and the Society of Friends.
20392
Rev. M. Stone's semi-centennial discourse.
92092
Reverend Matson Meier-Smith. 83571
Rev. Menzies Rayner vs. Col. Agur Hudson.
96922
Rev. Mr. Beman. pseud. see Hines, David
Theodore.
Rev. Mr. Brown's request. 8461, note just
before 69458
Rev. Mr. Carey's fast day sermon. 10844
Rev. Mr. Cooper and his calumnies against
Jamaica. (16626), 1st note after 102803
Rev. Mr. Haynes' sermon. 31054
Reverend Mr. Jacob Duche's (late chaplain to
the Congress) letter. 101739-101740
Rev. Mr. Jacob Henderson's fifth letter. 31313
Reverend Mr. James Davenport's confession &
retractions. 18701
Rev. Mr. M'Ilvaine in answer to the Rev.
Henry U. Onderdonck. 43324
Rev. Mr. Pickering's letters. 62646
Reverend Mr. Smith vindicated. (32780)
Rev. Mr. Smith's installation sermon. 84293
Rev. Mr. Snodgrass' funeral discourse. 85483
Rev. Mr. Whitefield's answer. 103577
Rev. Mr. Worcester's sermon. 105302, 105306
Rev. Nathaniel Colver. 83464
Reverend pastor of Roxbury. pseud. Thanks-
giving discourse. see Gordon, William,
1728-1807.

Reverend Pere de Smet et la ville de Tremonde. 82277

Reverend Pere P. J. de Smet. 82277

Reverend President's answer to the things charg'd upon him. 103901

Rev. S. F. Smith. 84047

Rev. S. K. Lothrop. 91604

Rev. Samuel Arnold cast and tried for his cruelty. 62426

Rev. Samuel Peters' LL. D. General history of Connecticut. 61210

Rev. Samuel Willard's confession of faith. 28628, 104118

Reverend Sir and dear brother in Jesus Christ! 95164

Rev. Sir, I take the liberty to inclose you a proposal. 95412

Rev. Sir, our destitute state bespeaks your compassion. 103323

Reverend T. Wilson. pseud. see Clark, Samuel.

Rev. Thomas Bray, his life and selected works. 105651

Rev. Thomas Smith, D. D. 84353

Rev. Tobias Spicer's election sermon. 89427

Rev. W. W. Patton's decennial and farewell sermons. 59167

Reverendi Do. Francisco Mavrolyci, Abbatis Messanensia. 96108

Reverendi Patris F. Francisci de Victoria. 100618

Reverendi Patris F. Fra[n]cisci Victoriae. 100619

Reuerendissimo in Christo Patri ac Domino. 77804

Reverendos Padres Bethlemitas del Convento de Nuestra Senora de Bethlem, y San Francisco Xavier, Mexico. see Mexico (City) Convento de Nuestra Senora de Bethlem y S. Francisco Xavier (Bethlemite)

Reveridi, A. supposed author 94175

Reverie, Reginald. pseud. Sad tales and glad tales. see Mellen, Grenville.

Reveries d'un celibataire. 49678

Reveries d'un Suisse. 70186

Reveries in rhyme. 52328

Reveries of a bachelor. 49672, 49677

Reveron, Luis Felipe Garcia y. see Garcia y Reveron, Luis Felipe.

Reverses needed. A discourse. 9546

Review. A weekly periodical. 70187

Review and a study. (77430)

Review and exposition. (70188), 106112

Review and herald. 84472

Review and refutation of the statements made. 70189, 99779

Review, by a Pittsburgher, of a pamphlet. 70190

Review by a plebeian of the western hemisphere. 82128

Review by a stockholder of the Morris Canal. 91881, 105641

Review by C. Glen Peebles of New York. 70191

Review [by Daniel Defoe.] 19277, 22969

Review, by E. H. Derby. 11219

Review by Ellwood Morris. 71937

Review . . . by Gerrit Smith. 13536

Review. By J. A. Mowatt. 51207

Review by Judge Pierrepont. 62784

Review by Samuel B. Ruggles. 73947

Review by the company. 62459

Review by the Judge Advocate General, of the case. 30116

Review by the Judge Advocate General of the proceedings. 32653

Review, by "The people's friend." 60822

Review by Thomas Henning. 31377

Review, devoted to the restoration of the southern states. 19116

Review. Examination of the Russian claims. 93270

Review (extracted from the Panoplist.) 3105

Review, financial, statistical, & commercial. 93287

Review from the London times. note after 92624

Review in "The Christian disciple" of Professor Stuart's letters. 93205

Review of a correspondence between the Archbishop and Mayor of Baltimore. 3079

Review of a declaration of sentiments. 64692

Review of a Democratic pamphlet. (23236), 42448, 92886

Review of "A discourse occasioned by the death of Daniel Webster." 36924, note before 90886

Review of a history of Connecticut. 61213

Review of a late pamphlet. 30055, 70192

Review of a law recently enacted. (76977)

Review of a "Letter from a gentleman in Boston." (70193)

Review of a letter from Bishop Hopkins. (44755)

Review of a letter from Gen'l Ripley. 71529

Review of a letter, from the Presbytery of Chillicothe. 85179-85180

Review of a "Letter from the Right Rev. John H. Hopkins." (32928)

Review of a letter written by the Rev. Charles T. Torrey. (28349)

Review [of a memoir by Rev. James M. Cook.] 2653

Review of a memoir of the U. S. Artillery. 55979

Review of a narrative by Rev. John Keep. 57167

Review of "A narrative of the anti-masonic excitement." 101166

Review of a "Narrative of the siege of New Orleans." 11349

Review of a pamphlet by the Hon. John C. Spencer. 35847

Review of a pamphlet, called "A testimony, and epistle of advice." 34498, 70194

Review of a pamphlet entitled "A report of the evidence in the case." 56235

Review of a pamphlet, entitled An appeal to the public. 52236, (61730)

Review of a pamphlet, entitled, "An epistle and testimony." 58904, (70195)

Review of a pamphlet entitled "Rights of Congregationalists in Knox College." 2738

Review of a pamphlet entitled "The rights of the Congregational Churches of Massachusetts." 42460

Review of a pamphlet, entitled "Trial of the action." 74372

Review of a pamphlet on a trust deed. 6650

Review of a pamphlet proporting to be documents. 22270

Review of a pamphlet published at Charleston, S. C. 19662

Review of a pamphlet published by Dr. T. T. Moorman. 9318

Review of a pamphlet purporting to be "A statement of facts." 90688

Review of a pastoral address by the Right Rev. T. N. Stanley. 90107

Review of a "Poem in three cantos." 57154, 96317

Review of a portion of the geological map. 5808

Review of a report of the Committee. 36278, 70196

Review of a report, presented to the Warren Baptist Association. 70197

Review of a report to the House of Representatives. 12699, note after 98561

Review of a sermon, by Novanglus. 4345

Review of a sermon, by the Rev. Wm. S. Potts. 64692

Review of a sermon delivered at New York. 55862

Review of a sermon, entitled, "The Christian Bishop approving himself unto God." 104918

Review of a sermon on the "Danger of being overwise." 77007, 89744

Review of a slave case. 82061

Review of a statement of facts. 70280

Review of a tract entitled "Secret societies in colleges." (35481)

Review of a treatise on expatriation by George Hay. 30998

Review of a vindication of the disciplinary proceedings. 70198

Review of a work entitled, "A popular life of George Fox." (44754)

Review of abolitionism. 40849

Review of address in respect to a late ordination. (56602)

Review of all that hath pass'd. 70199

Review of American birds in the museum. 2805

Review of American Unitarianism. 11924, 50946, 96412

Review of an action for a libel. 14030

Review of an address of the Joint Board of Directors. 10828

Review of an address of the minority in Congress. 70200

Review of an "Address," professing to be a vindication. 20657

Review of "An address" respecting slavery. (70201)

Review of "An address to the citizens of Philadelphia." 62192

Review of "An address to the working-men of New-England." 5318

Review, of an anonymous publication styled Strictures. 92832

Review of an anti-abolition sermon. 103896

Review of an article in the North American [review.] 70202

Review of an article in the North American review. 102208

Review of "An oration . . . before the young men of Boston." 57873

Review of Attorney-General Black's report on land titles in California. (36629)

Review of Attorney General Clifford's report. 64269, 89627

Review of Bishop Brownell's fourth charge. 8691, 52763

Review of Bishop Hobart's sermon. (32301)

Review of Bishop Hopkins' Bible view of slavery. 42695

Review of Bishop Hughes's sermon. 48934

Review of Bishop Meade's counter statement. 47238

Review of books, register of events. 41495

Review of Capt. Basil Hall's travels in North America. 5247

Review of certain remarks. 70203

Review of Clifford's report. 64269, 89627

Review of "Considerations." 67210

Review of Cox on Quakerism. 40801

Review of Dr. Adison's sermon on Sabbath keeping. 91585

Review of Dr. Bancroft's appendix. 3105

Review of Dr. Bancroft's vindication. 3105, 27695, 70115

Review of Dr. Beecher's sermon at Worcester. 4344, 101057

Review of Dr. Boardman's address against Kossuth. 42979

Review of . . . Dr. Channing's discourse. 11909

Review of Dr. Channing's letter to Hon. Henry Clay. 11913

Review . . . of Dr. Charles A. Lee. (39716)

Review of Dr. Cleaveland's anniversary sermon. 64304

Review of Dr. Cleaveland's reply to the New-Englander. 64304

Review of Dr. Dana's remonstrance. (18407)

Review of Dr. J. Prescott's "Brief extracts." 90462

Review of Dr. John M. Mason's oration. 45460

Review of Dr. Mayhew's remarks. 1856

Review of Dr. Morse's "Appeal to the publick." 42461, 70204

Review of Dr. Price's writings. (50675)

Review of Dr. Wayland's elements of moral science. 94538

Review of Dr. Wyatt's sermon. 102563

Review of documents and records. 87944

Review of Du Ponceau on the jurisdiction of the courts. 21377

Review of ecclesiastical proceedings in the Congregational Church and Society in Brooklyn. 104559

Review of Edward A. Raymond's address. 11299

Review of Ellet's "Mississippi and Ohio Rivers." 19018

Review of Ellwood [sic] Fisher's lecture. 24458, 51593

Review of Evangeline. 41911

Review of facts and circumstances. 95134

Review of facts and observations. 36491

Review of facts relative to the late ecclesiastical proceedings. 95623

Review of the financial affairs in the United States. 70205

Review of Forster's observations. 25146

Review of . . . fugitive poems of Miss Amanda A. P. Capers. (52237)

Review of General Wilkinson's memoirs. 2025

Review of Gliddon and Nott's 'Types of mankind. 56040

Review of Governor Andrew's veto. (49198)

Review of Gov. Banks' veto. 5539

Review of Gov. Seymour's message. (2723)

Review of Governor Seymour's message, in the Assembly. 30901

Review of Governor Snyder's objections. 60452

Review of Hamilton's edition of the Federalist. 5494

Review of Hammond's and Fuller's letters. 30099, 82096

Review of His Grace's life and character. 78718

Review of his wars and debts. 25672

Review of Hon. Caleb Butler's History of the ecclesiastical affairs of Pepperell. 1492, 60842

Review of Hon. Henry Winter Davis on freesoilism. 18833

Review of Hon. Joseph Howe's essay. 30028

Review of Horace Binney's essay on the writ. 5484, 48675

Review of Inchiquin's letters. (21555), (50944)

Review of Jacksonian fanaticism and its influence. (70206)

Review of Jacksonism. 35383

Review of Jubilee College. 12208

Review of Judge Advocate General Holt. (36267)

Review of Judge Story's Commentaries on the constitution. 7866

Review of Kirwan. 33593

Review of . . . L. Potter's appeal. 65683

Review of la France, le Mexique, et les Etats-Confederes. 37893

Review of lectures. 64773, 84742A

Review of "Letters to the Rev. Wm. E. Channing." 11919, 93205

Review of Lord Bute's administration. (70207), (70212)

Review of Lord Mahon's History of the American revolution. 58325, 89004

Review of Lord Vis. Clare's conduct. 97359

Review of Lovejoy's lecture. 39334

Review of [Lyman Beecher's sermon at Worcester.] 4344

Review of Lynn. 42843, 70208

Review of Lysander Spooner's essay. 62524

Review of M. Hookers survey of church-discipline. 11615

Review of McClellan's campaigns. 70209

Review of Mary M. Dyer's publication. 21595, 97895, note after 104781

Review of "Men and manners in America." 55863

Review of Miss Martineau's work on "Society in America." 103993

Review of Mr. Ames's works. 42459, 43375

Review of Mr. Binney's pamphlet. 9131

Review of Mr. Burke's conduct. 9304

Review of Mr. Calhoun's Report on the Memphis memorial. 28566

Review of Mr. Cambreling's report. 37418, 47878

Review of Mr. Hooper's pamphlet. 42465

Review of Mr. Howe's pamphlet. 31932, (33315)

Review of Mr. Knapp's defence of masonry. 76255

Review of Mr. Marcy's letter. 74368

Review of Mr. Mitchell's sermon. 70210

Review of Mr. Pearson's sermon. 59443

Review of Mr. Pitt's administration. 70211, 70213

Review of Mr. Pitt's administration. By the author of Lord Bute's. (70207), (70212)

Review of Mr. Ryan's address. (10998)

Review of Mr. Seward's diplomacy. 37771, (68603), 68622, 2d note after 94129

Review of Mr. Seward's foreign correspondence of 1862. 34725, 68604

Review of Mr. Whitman's letters. 63990, 103728, 103730

Review of M. de Tocqueville's work. 96061

Review of New England politics. 95572

Review of New York. 21742

Review of northern assertions and southern facts. 96799

Review of pamphlets on slavery and colonization. 2671, (70214), 93138

Review of Pierce County, Wisc. 62748

Review of Pierce's administration. 11064

Review of political affairs during the last half year. (70215)

Review of political opinions. 3197

Review of President Pierce's annual message. 4785

Review of Prof. Frisbie's inaugural address. (55864)

Review of Professor Palfrey's sermon. 58316

Review of Professor Stuart. 36848

Review of recent publications on that subject. 70001

Review of remarks. 72085

Review of reports to the Legislature of S. C. 87524

Review of Rev. Dr. Lord's thanksgiving sermon. 42030

Review of Rev. Dr. Raphael's discourse. (8488)

Review of Rev. Henry J. Van Dyke's discourse. 82173

Review of Rev. Henry J. Van Dyke's sermon. 515

Review of Rev. Mr. Cushman's "Calm review." 12948

Review of Rev. Mr. Lovejoy's 'Lecture on the subject.' 42367

Review of Rev. R. C. Waterston's letter. 76992, note after 97137

Review of Rev. W. W. Ell's thanksgiving sermon. 14464

Review of Ripley's "Defence." 71527

Review of Robert Smith's address to the people of the United States. 83828

Review of Rosanna. 94652

Review of Secretary Marcy's letter. 74366

Review of Secretary Walker's report. 1823

Review of Senate Committee report, no. 289. 5526

Review of Senator Doolittle's speech. 83029

Review of Senator Morton's . . . bill and his speech. 66624

Review of some of the arguments. 70216

Review of some of the doings of the Legislature of Maine. 70217

Review of some of the writings of "Peter Porcupine." (7258), 14026, note after 95800, 12th note after 95843

Review of some portions of Gen. Garfield's speech. 77994

Review of Symmes' theory. 70433

Review of T. L. McKenney's narrative of the causes. 2030, 43405

Review of the action of the Wisconsin Annual Conference. 83755

Review of the address delivered at the Merchants' Exchange. (73948)

Review of the address delivered by Hon. John Q. Adams. 268, 89629

Review of the address of the Free-Trade Convention. 10889, 30052, 70218

Review of the "Address of the Lay Association." 72574

Review of the administration and civil police. 59576

Review of the administration of General Pierce. 16361

Review of the administration of the government. (70219)

Review of the administrations of Lords Durham and Sydenham. (71037)

Review of "The African slave trade." 9689

Review of the American contest. 58212-58213

Review of the annual message of the President. 48574

Review of the apologies of Dr. Seabury and Mr. Haight. 65970

Review of the argument of President Lincoln. (55179)

Review of the argument of the Judge Advocate. 82576

Review of the argument which His Excellency Alexander G. McNutt. 2407, 43609

Review of the arguments of counsel. 59502

Review of the arguments of Lord Kames in favor of war. 105254-105255, 105260

Review of the arguments which His Exc. Alexander G. McNutt. 2407, 43609

Review of the article in the Southern review, for 1830. 31044

Review of the article on continental money. 16163, 62490

Review of the authorities as to the repression of riot. 24372

Review of the battle of the Horse Shoe. 70220

Review of the Berkley case. 21820, 70221

Review of the "Biographical sketch" of John Vanderlyn. 98481

Review of the biographical sketch of the Hon. Samuel Dexter. 19903

Review of the Bishop of London's reply. 14767

Review of the Bishop of Oxford's counsel to the American clergy. 4992

Review of the Book of Mormon. 31922

Review of the case of Alexander McLeod. 62634

Review of the case of Brigadier-Gen. Joseph W. Revere. 70180

Review of the case of Moses Thacher versus Preston Pond. 95158

Review of the case of the Antelope. 274

Review of the case of the free bridge. 12119

Review of the cause and the tendency of the issues. 66830

Review of the cause of the New Orleans batture. 21383

Review of the causes and consequences of the Mexican war. 35864

Review of the centennial memorial of St. Andrew's Lodge. 80319

Review of the city of Burlington, Iowa. 9335

Review of the colonial slave registration acts. 497, 70222

Review of the commerce, manufactures, and the public and private improvements of Galesburg, Ill. 79033

Review of the commerce, manufactures, public and private improvements of Chicago. 12628

Review of the commerce of Chicago. 70223

Review of the commerce of Cincinnati. 13066

Review of the commerce of St. Louis. 75330

Review of the commerce of St. Louis, together with a list of steamboat disasters. 75332

Review of the commerce of St. Louis, together with a very full list of steamboat disasters. 75333

Review of the communication of S. Lawrence and W. W. Stone. 63686

Review of the conduct of the administration. 423

Review of the conduct of the late ministers. 17521

Review of the "Constitution and associate statutes of the Theological Seminary in Andover." 1441, 70224, 95190

Review of the constitution of Maine. 44038

Review of the consitution proposed by the late convention. 70225

Review of the 'Constitutional history of the Presbyterian Church." 31866

Review of the constitutions of the principal states of Europe. 19328, 38501

Review of the controversy between Great Britain and her colonies. (1969), (3111), 38180, 56562, 2d note after 103122

Review of the controversy between the Federalists and Republicans. 70226

Review of the controversy between the Methodists and Presbyterians. 70227

Review of the controversy on a question of rank. 40543, 78414

Review of the correspondence between Richard Fuller. 29526

Review of the correspondence between the Archbishop and Mayor of Baltimore. 70228

Review of the correspondence between the Hon. John Adams and the late Wm. Cunningham. 62658, 84906

Review of the correspondence between the Hon. John Adams, late President of the United States, and the late Wm. Cunningham. 62658, 84906

Review of the "correspondence" of Messrs. Fuller & Wayland. 28944

Review of the course of Judge James B. McKean. 24590

Review of the course of the leading periodicals. 82706

Review of the court's decision. 64222

Review of the criminal law [of Kentucky.] 96328

Review of the criticisms of the Congregationalist. (55072)

Review of the Crittenden and other revolution. 70229

Review of the Court of Equity. 104663

Review of the debate in the Virginia Legislature. 19836

Review of the decate, 1857-67. 10842

Review of the decision of . . . the case of Dred Scott. 56050

Review of the decision of the Court of Appeals. 70230

Review of the decision of the Supreme Court of the United States. (78262)

Review of the decision of the United States Supreme Court. 49087

Review of the D'Hauteville case. 19916, 70231

Review of the diplomatic policy adopted. 70232

Review of the diseases of Dutchess County. (80427)

Review of the efforts and progress of nations. 81459

Review of the encouragement now held out. 34408

Review of the eve of eternity. (13435)

Review of the events. 104904

Review of the evidence against Richard Busteed. 83872

Review of the evidence taken on charges against Richard Busteed. 83873

Review of the excise-scheme. 70233

Review of the fancies, fallacies, mistakes. 96396

Review of the fifth annual report of the Northern Educational Union. 23874

Review of the financial affairs in the United States. 24344, 70205

Review of the first session [of the twenty-ninth Congress.] 8346

Review of the foreign missions [of the Moravian Church, from] 1872 to . . . 1873. 86173

Review of the foreign missions of the Moravian Church, from July 1st, 1871, to July 1st, 1872. 86173

Review of the general and particular causes. 14093

Review of the government and grievances of the province of Quebec. (70234)

Review of the Governor's message. (14452)

Review of the governor's veto. 70235
Review of the history and contents of the Book of Mormon. 79628
Review of the history and law of servitude. 70236
Review of the history of maritime discovery. 5248
Review of the Hon. John P. Kennedy's discourse. 37409-(37410)
Review of the improvements, progress and state of medicine. 67706
Review of the Lady Superior's reply. 68580, 3d note after 98168
Review of the late canvass. (13533)
Review of the late case of the Rt. Rev. W. R. Whittingham. 90878
Review of the late correspondence and documents. 14310
Review of the late decision of the Supreme Court of Ohio. 89832
Review of the late message of the President. 70237
Review of the late negociations and arrangement. 70238, 2d note after 102863
Review of the late opinion and decision of the United States Supreme Court. 70239
Review of the late report of Commissioner Wells. 50780
Review of the late report of the Secretary of the Treasury. 70240
Review of the late temperance movements in Massachusetts. 104952
Review of the late war. 32203
Review of the laws of England. 1968
Review of the laws of the United States of North America. 70241
Review of the leading measures of the General Assembly. 65231
Review of the lectures of W. A. Smith. (64773)
Review of the letter addressed by W. A. Duer. 14281
Review of the letter of General Cox. 20098
Review of the "Letter of Leonard Jarvis." 82566
Review of the letter of the Hon. Henry A. Wise. (32207), 87110
Review of the letters of the late Rev. John Bowden. 104638
Review of the life and character of Archbishop Secker. 64328, (78715)
Review of the life and fragments of Miss Elizabeth Smith. 82505
Review of the life and writings of M. Hale Smith. 83585, 83598
Review of the life of Horace Mann. 44327
Review of the "Life of Michael Martin." 44903
Review of the manifesto of the majority. 3878
Review of the Maryland report. 89005
Review of the measures of the administration. 28003, 1st note after 101265
Review of the memoir of Josiah Quincy, Jr. (67219)
Review of the memoir on the U. S. Artillery. 69712
Review of the memorial of Dr. John Bell. 35459
Review of the message of Jefferson Davis. 58700
Review of the Mexican war, embracing the causes of the war. 64211
Review of the Mexican war on Christian principles. (4993)
Review of the military operations in North-America. 14649, (41650), note after 91855, 101710

Review of the militia policy of the present administration. (19570)
Review of the mining, agricultural, and commercial interests. 10936
Review of the minority report. 70242
Review of the most important events relating to the rise and progress. 97882, 105576
Review of the national banking law. 42024
Review of the negociations between the United States. 94551
Review of the New Haven theology. 95205
Review of the new water documents. 8327
Review of the New York and Massachusetts systems. (9077)
Review of the New-York Central Road's official expose. (54755)
Review of the noted revival in Kentucky. 67871, 95381
Review of the official apologies of the American Tract Society. 70243
Review of the operation and results. 13825
Review of the opinion of Charles O'Conor. 33610, 56660, 70244
Review of the opinion of Chief Justice Taney. 58696
Review of the opinion of Hon. Edward King. 35336
Review of the opinion of Judge Cowen. 17241, 43529
Review of the opinion of the Attorney General of the U. S. (37681)
Review of the opinion of the Supreme Court of the United States. (30089)
Review of the opinion of the Supreme Judicial Court of Massachusetts. (21627)
Review of the opinions of the justices of the Supreme Court. 43255
Review of the opinions of the three judges. 60589
Review of the origin, progress, present state and future prospects. 48024
Review of the pamphlet entitled "An antidote." 71913
Review of the pamphlet of Henry Winter Davis. 18832
Review of the pamphlet of "Oswego." (22741), (22766), 92863
Review of the pamphlet of W. N. P. Fitzgerald. 90022
Review of the parliamentary and forensic eloquence. 23520
Review of the past. 14134
Review of the plan of education in South Carolina. 87945
Review of the policy of the United States government. 21537
Review of the political life and opinions of Martin Van Buren. 105456
Review of the "Portraiture of Shakerism." 21595, 97895, note after 104781
Review of the position of parties in the union. 29933
Review of the Post Office establishment. 7055
Review of the power assumed by rulers. 105253, 105257, 105260, 105263
Review of the present administration. 70245
Review of the present condition of the State Penitentiary. (20336A)
Review of the present state of the nation. 70246
Review of the principal events of the last ten years. 37932
Review of the principal facts objected to [in] the first volume. 52147
Review of the proceedings in the Massachusetts Legislature. 46106

Review of the proceedings of a Council at
Georgetown, Mass. 4305
Review of the proceedings of Joel Parker.
(72214)
Review of the proceedings of the alumni of
Columbia College. 70247
Review of the proceedings of the Arctic
Searching Expedition. 70248
Review of the proceedings of the Catholics.
70249
Review of the proceedings of the Court of
Enquiry. (36270)
Review of the proceedings of the Detroit Con-
vention. (31825)
Review of the proceedings of the General
Assembly. 65224
Review of the proceedings of the General
Assembly of the Presbyterian Church.
65208
Review of the proceedings of the Legislature
of Lower Canada. 93128
Review of the proceedings of the Navy Depart-
ment. 70250
Review of the proceedings of the Nunnery Com-
mittee. 29620
Review of the proceedings of the Reform Con-
vention. 32422
Review of the progress of England. 43286
Review of the prosecution against Abner Knee-
land. 38091
Review of the protest and appeal of Bishop
Doane. 20395
Review of the Quarterly review. 70251
Review of the question, in whom has the con-
stitution vested the treaty power? 70252
Review of the question of an outlet lock. 5684,
60590, 70253
Review of the question whether the common
law of England. 94357
Review of the Racine and Mississippi Rail
Road project. 92945
Review of the reasons given. (68265), 70254,
91242
Review of the reasons offered by S. Eddy.
21815
Review of the Rector detected. 70255
Review of the reign of George the Second.
70256
Review of the relations between the United
States and Mexico. 17292
Review of the relative commercial progress.
70257
Review of the remarks on Dr. Channing's
slavery. 2415, (11920), 81162
Review of the reply. 73535
Review of the report by Maj.-Gen. William
Farrar Smith. 84774
Review of the report made in 1828. 10600,
95373
Review of the report of a Committee of the
Citizens of Boston and vicinity. 70258
Review of a report of a Select Committee of
the House of Commons. 17617, 70259,
102841, 3d note after 102863
Review of the report of Hon. Horace Maynard.
(47190)
Review of the report of I. W. P. Lewis. 40865
Review of the report of Mr. Edward Miller.
60278
Review of the report of the Board. 84774
Review of the report of the Board of Engi-
neers. 57068
Review of the report of the Commission on
Ordnance and Ordnance Stores. 70260
Review of the report of the Committee of Ways
and Means. 3138

Review of the report of the Committee on
Foreign Affairs. 39393
Review of the report of the Committee on the
Conduct of the War. 37646
Review of the report of the Committee on the
President's message. 13581
Review of the report of the Court convened
for the trial. 37728
Review of the report of the Hon. D. A. Wells.
10842
Review of the report of the Judiciary Com-
mittee. 70261
Review of the report of the late Commissioners
for Investigating the Affairs of the Joint
Companies. 10828
Review of the report of the President. 58083
Review of the report of the Secretary of the
Treasury. 70262
Review of the report of the Select Committee
of the House of Commons. 52260
Review of the report . . . on the returns of
the seventh census. 37430
Review of the reports of the Annual Visiting
Committee of the Public Schools of the
City of Boston. 6762-6763, 77770
Review of the reports to the Legislature of
South Carolina. 459
Review of the resolutions of the Press Con-
ference. 70263
Review of the result of an Ecclesiastical
Council . . . by one who listened to . . .
the public hearing. 70110
Review of the result of an Ecclesiastical
Council, convened at Exeter. (23393)
Review of "The result of an Ecclesiastical
Council convened at Salem, Mass."
75698-75699
Review of the result of the "Council at Dan-
vers." 70264
Review of the revenue system. (24363), 70265
Review of the Reverend Aaron Pickett's "Reply."
(62666)
Review of the Rev. Dr. Channing's letter to
Jonathan Phillips. 2415, 11917
Review of the Rev. Dr. Junkin's synodical
speech. 36933
Review of the Rev. Dr. Putnam's discourse.
(7008)
Review of the Rev. Horace Bushnell's discourse.
27409
Review of the Rev. J. W. Cooke's pamphlet.
51262
Review of the Rev. Jared Sparks' letters on
the Protestant Episcopal Church. 88979,
105646
Review of the Rev. Mr. Colman's sermon.
16795, 70266
Review of the Rev. Mr. Matthews's pamphlet.
46848, (46900), 102024
Review of the Rev. Moses Stuart's pamphlet
on slavery. 13362, 93197
Review of the Rev. Thomas Smyth's two sermons. 85330
Review of the Rev. U. C. Burnap's sermon.
(78480)
Review of the Rev. William Croswell's letter.
(17683)
Review of the reviewers and repudiators. 203,
92624
Review of the revolutionary elements of the
rebellion. (66831)
Review of the rise and progress of the Church
of England in Nova Scotia. 31821
Review of the rise, progress and tendency of
the present system. 70267
Review of the same. (76388)

Review of the scandalous and impertinent Beale pamphlet. (42660)

Review of the Sectional Dock Company's pamphlet. 70268

Review of the sermon, by Wm. B. Fowle. 83572

Review of the sermon of Dr. Potts. 64692

Review of the short view. (70269)

Review of the slave question. 70270, 2d note after 100580

Review of "The slavery of the British West India colonies delineated." 102798

Review, of the southern and western states. 19116

Review of the southern review on Mr. Foot's resolution. (23732)

Review of the speech in . . . Philadelphia. 16298

Review of the speech of Harrison Gray Otis. (70271)

Review of the speech of Hon. J. R. Chandler. 63063

Review of the speech of Hon. Joseph R. Chandler. 4837

Review of the speeches delivered in Dr. Beattie's Chapel. (78726)

Review of the "Spiritual manifestations." 4300

Review of the state of Great Britain. 70272

Review of the state of the British nation. 55065

Review of the systems of superintendency. 51924, 90871

Review of the tariff of 1846. 2831

Review of the tariff of 1832. 10889, 96073

Review of the testimony . . . against Elias Hichs. 40802

Review of the testimony given before the General Court Martial. 89356, note before 94236A, 1st note after 96929

Review of the testimony taken before the Second Inquest. 64373, 71823

Review of the times. 6231

Review of the tract controversy. (70273)

Review of the trade and commerce and of the condition and traffic. 12629

Review of the trade and commerce of Albany. 631

Review of the trade and commerce of Cincinnati. 84725

Review of the trade and commerce of Detroit. 19784

Review of the trade and commerce of New York. 70274

Review of the trade, commerce & manufactures of Cincinnati. 83766

Review of the trial and acquital of the Rev. S. Phillips. 84739

Review of the trial, conviction and final imprisonment. 38091

Review of the trial, conviction and sentence of George F. Alberti. 70275

Review of the trial of John Alley. 70276

Review of the trial . . . with remarks. 79895

Review of the tribute to the pilgrims, &c. 30925

Review of the Unitarian controversy. 50947

Review of the veto. 35359

Review of the veto message of President Pierce. 11585, 70277

Review of the views of the minority. 70278

Review of the war which was terminated. 43249

Review of the warnings of Jefferson. 64127

Review of the Water Commissioners' report. (43227)

Review of the whole political conduct of the late eminent patriot. 70279

Review of the year. 47181

Review of three pamphlets. 10889

Review of twenty years. 83458

Review of two masonic addresses. 90900

Review of two pamphlets. (20626), note after 70279

Review of Town's speculative masonry. 45501, 96366

Review of W. C. Brownlee on Quakerism. 8698

Review of Webster. 58765

Review of Webster's American dictionary. By Isaiah Dole. (20541)

Review of Webster's American dictionary. [By James Luce Kingsley.] 37892

Review of Webster's speech on slavery. 62525

Review of Webster's system in the Democratic review. 76952

Review of Winthrop's journal. 20884

Review of Wyse on the necessity of a national system of education. (25200)

Review, opinions, &c., of Dr. Charles A. Lee. 31331

Review reviewed in a letter to David Andrews. (9625)

Review. The tomb of the martyrs. 72887

Review upon review. 13886

Reviewer of Mrs. E. Willard reviewed. 104049

Reviewer (in the Christian observer) reviewed. 98836

Reviewer of the remarks on Dr. Channing's slavery. (11920)

Reviewer reviewed. 3670

Reviewer reviewed. A defence of an oration. 57874

Reviewer reviewed. A few remarks. 58758

Reviewer reviewed; being a reply to a feeble and unfounded attack. 19357

Reviewer reviewed: being an examination of a pamphlet. 70280

Reviewer reviewed, or a reply to . . . the Southern Presbyterian review. 28135

Reviewer reviewed: or an answer to an attack made by Rev. J. L. Hodge. 70281

Reviewer reviewed: or Doctor Brownlee, versus the Bible. 80453

Reviewer reviewed: or strictures and testimony on M. Thacher's review. 63993

Reviewer reviewed; reply to an attack on Delaplaine's repository. 9899

Reviewer reviewed. Republished from the Knickerbocker. 101879

Reviewer reviewed. [By Alexander H. Stephens.] 91279

Reviewers reviewed. [By Anna Cora Mowatt.] 70282

Reviewers reviewed, or British falsehoods detected. 70283

Reviews and brief remarks. 70283

Reviews, communications, &c., American and home correspondence. 58448, (72576)

Reviews, narratives, essays, and poems. 57816

Reviews of a part of Prescott's 'History of Ferdinand and Isabella.' 76381

Reviews of Lord Durham's report. 10625

Reviews upon the cultivation, commerce, and manufacture of cotton. 19115

Revilers of H. A. Muhlenberg. 51251

Revilla, Joa. 57421

Revilla, Jose de la. 86471, 86473

Revillagigedo, Juan Vicente de Guemes Pacheo de Podilla, Conde de. see Guemes Pacheo de Podilla, Juan Vicente de, Conde de Revillagigedo.

Reville, Albert. (58752), 58763, (70289)-70291

Revilliod, Gustave. tr. 27188, 78599

Revisal of all the public acts. 94781

Revisal of all the public acts of the state of North-Carolina and the state of Tennessee. 94774-94775, 94782

Revisal of the intreagues of the triumvirate. 60591, 70292

Revisal of the laws of . . . North Carolina. (55687)

Revisal of the public acts to 1807. 94774

Revisals of the laws of . . . North Carolina. 94509

Revised abstract, exhibiting the condition of the banks. 46108

Revised acts and ordinances of Lower Canada. (10498)

Revised almanac. 84948

Revised catalogue of . . . the Sunday School Library. 55102

Revised charter and ordinances of the city of Kenosha. 37460

Revised charter of the city of Rochester. 72353

Revised charter . . . passed April 10, 1850. 72353

Revised charter . . . with other acts. 72353

Revised city charter, to be submitted to the citizens. 6633, 6719

Revised civil code. (42299)

Revised code of college laws. (30749)

Revised code of laws of Illinois. 34287

Revised code of laws of Illinois, enacted by the fifth General Assembly. 34286

Revised code of North Carolina. (55688)

Revised code of the laws of Mississippi. 49542, 63686

Revised code of the statute laws of . . . Mississippi. (49543)

Revised compendium of Methodism. 64269

Revised constitution . . . as finally adopted. 100514

Revised constitution of Michigan. (48793)

Revised discipline approved by the Yearly Meeting of Friends. (45364)

Revised edition of the citizens' hand book. 84911

Revised edition, with census of 1850. 83935

Revised general instructions for camp inspections. 76576, 76647

Revised index to the statute law of . . . Ohio. (57047)

Revised laws concerning passengers in vessels. 53949

Revised laws of Illinois. 34285, 34288

Revised laws of Indiana, . . . adopted and enacted by the General Assembly. 34546

Revised laws of Indiana, adopted . . . by the General Assembly. 34545

Revised laws of the state of Vermont. 99090

Revised laws [of Vermont.] note after 99131

Revised militia law. (52929)

Revised orations of R. Choate and J. S. Holmes. 6519

Revised orders of the city and county of San Francisco. 76084

Revised ordinances of the city of Detroit. (19792)

Revised ordinances of the city [of Manchester, N. H.] (44220)

Revised ordinances of the city of Saint Louis. 75378

Revised ordinances of the city of St. Louis, together with . . . the charter. (75379)

Revised ordinances of the Mayor, Alderman, and Commonalty. (54666)

Revised regulations for the Army of the United States. 70293

Revised regulations for the collection. (70294)

Revised report made to the Legislature. 60592

Revised report of the Select Committee relative to the Soldiers' National Cemetery. 27247

Revised rules of the National Division of North America. 87017

Revised school law, approved March 24, 1866. 10001

Revised school law of the state of Indiana. 34520

Revised speech of Hon. H. G. Spaulding. 89039

Revised statute laws of . . . Louisiana. 42301

Revised statutes . . . as altered by subsequent legislation. 53952

Revised statutes . . . from 1828 to 1835. (53951)

Revised statutes of Connecticut of 1849. 15778

Revised statutes of . . . Indiana, adopted and enacted. 34547

Revised statutes of . . . Indiana passed at the twenty-seventh session. (34548)

Revised statutes of Jamaica. 35628

Revised statutes of Kentucky. 90436

Revised statutes of Kentucky, approved and adopted. 37539

Revised statutes of Kentucky, by C. A. Wickliffe. 37538

Revised statutes of . . . Louisiana. 42300

Revised statutes of Maine. (80290)

Revised statutes of Massachusetts. 45107

Revised statutes of . . . Michigan. 48794

Revised statutes of . . . Missouri. (49643)

Revised statutes of New Brunswick. 52561

Revised statutes of . . . New Hampshire. 52930

Revised statutes of . . . New York. 53432

Revised statutes of . . . North Carolina. 55689

Revised statutes of Nova-Scotia. (56188)

Revised statutes of Nova-Scotia. Second series. 56189

Revised statutes of the state of Illinois. 34289

Revised statutes of the state of Indiana. 34549

Revised statutes of the state of Maine. 44039

Revised statutes of the state of Missouri. 49642

Revised statutes of the state of Missouri, revised. 49641

Revised statutes of the state of Rhode Island. 70700

Revised statutes of the state of South Carolina. 87708

Revised statutes of the state . . . passed during the years. 53950

Revised statutes of the Territory of Minnesota. (49305)

Revised statutes of the Territory of Nebraska. 52202

Revised statutes of the Territory of New Mexico. 53284

Reviser of the work. pseud. Some remarks. (21065)

Revisio myrtacearum Americae hucusque cognitae. 4840

Revision and confirmation of the social compact. 97896

Revision des constitutions coloniales. 40129

Revision des Graminees. 33766

Revision documents of the Constitutional Convention. 53953

Revision of 1860. 35019

Revision of Swift's Digest of the laws of Connecticut. 15779

Revision of the canons of the Protestant Episcopal Church. 66208

Revision of the delegate system. 62193
Revision of the hitherto known species. 78532
Revision of the laws. 31030
Revision of the North American Tailed-
Batrachia. 2805
Revision of the statutes and laws. (30749)
Revisor de la politica y literatura Americana.
70295
Revista (Caracas) 70296
Revista Americana. 70297
Revista Argentina. 70298
Revista bimestre Cubana. 17814, 70321
Revista Brazileira. (7628)
Revista cientifica del Colegio de Ingenieros
de Venezuela. (70299)
Revista cientifica y literaria de Mejico. 70300
Revista contemporanea. 6822
Revista contemporanea de Portugal e Brasil.
7629
Revista de administracion de comercio y de
jurisprudencia. (29457)
Revista de agricultura. (9018)
Revista de Buenos-Aires. 9040, (67124)
Revista de Buenos-Aires. Fundadores. 1957,
9021
Revista de ciencias i letras. 70301
Revista de Colombia y Venezuela. (70302)
Revista de Colombia y Venezuela unida y
separada. 95812
Revista de Espana, de Indias y del extrangero.
70303
Revista de Espana y del Estrangero. 70303
Revista de Espana y sus provincias de
ultramar. 70304
Revista de la Casa de Pereira Gamba i Com-
pania. 60892
Revista de la cronica. 70305
Revista de la Habana. 47813, 70307
Revista de la Habana, periodico quincenal, de
ciencias, literatura, artes, modas, teatros,
etc. 70306
Revista de legislacion y jurisprudencia. 25104
Revista de lejislacion y jurisprudencia. 70308
Revista de Lima. (41132)
Revista de los documentos relativos al llama-
miento hecho. 59515
Revista de los escritos publicados en Chile.
35079
Revista de los estados del Plata. 63329
Revista de los dos mundos. (70341), 4th note
after 99402
Revista de minas. 48273
Revista del Archivo General de Buenos Aires.
70309
Revista del Parana. 58544
Revista del Plata. 70310
Revista del Rio de la Plata. (70311)
Revista do Instituto Polytechnico Brasileiro.
70312
Revista Espanola de Ambos Mundos. 70313
Revista general de fantasia. 70314
Revista general de la economica policia.
96237
Revista Hispano-Americana. 70316
Revista Hispano-Americana, periodico quin-
cenal. (70315)
Revista Hispano-Americana, politica, cientifica,
y literaria. 70316
Revista juridica. (70317)
Revista literaria. (27817)
Revista Mexicana. Periodico cientifico y
literario. (70318)
Revista politica. (50484)
Revista politica sobre la historia de la revo-
lucion. 39043, 72296

Revista segunda de las declamaciones contra
el poder judicial. 70319
Revista semanaria dos trabalhos legislativos.
7631
Revista trimensal de historia e geografia.
7630, 2d note after 70319
Revista trimensal do Instituto Historico e
Geografico Brasileiro. see Revista trimensal do Instituto Historico Geographico
e Ethnographico do Brasil.
Revista trimensal do Instituto Historico Geo-
graphico e Ethnographico do Brasil.
7630, 13263, 60879, note after 70319,
76904, 85635, 88806, note after 90061,
93595, 98828-98829, 99512, note after
99383C
Revista trimestre de Filadelfia. 48582, 96434
Revista universal Brasileira. 7632
Revista universal Lisbonense. 70320
Revista y repertorio bimestre de la isla de
Cuba. 17814, 70321
Revista Yucateca. Periodico politico y noti-
cioso. 70322
Revius, J. 70323-70324
Revival sermons delivered during his twentieth
visit. 83896
Revival . . . in the days of Wesley. 38115
Revival melodies. (18259)
Revival of Bishop Berkeley's Bermuda College.
28407
Revival of education. 47078
Revival of religion in the United States of
America. 34434, 44483, 105172
Revival of religion which we need. note after
(58767)
Revival or directions for a sculpture. 70325
Revival sermons. 42705, 58758, 67423
Revival sketches and manual. 33794
Revivalism and the church. (70326)
Revivalist (London) 70327
Revivalist (Nashville) 82783
Revivals. (26240)
Revived almanack. 34049
Revived puritan. 103678
Revivication of young Joseph Taylor. 94521
Reviw [sic] of his life and character. 78719
Revoil, Benedict Henry. 27194, 69027, 69077,
(70328)-70336, note after 101315
Revolte de Boston. (3710)
Revolte des Negres. 19086, (75094)
Revoltes du Para. 11045
Revolucao e o imperialismo. 70337
Revolucion (Mexico) (70338)
Revolucion. 99482
Revolucion comenzada el dia 14 de Abril de
1837. 76153
Revolucion de Mayo 1810. 55499
Revolucion de Santa-Anna. 96765
Revolucion: diario politico, literario y comercial.
70340
Revolucion en la republica Argentina. (70341),
4th note after 99402
Revolucion Espanola en Cuba. 88946
Revolucion. 1865. 70339
Revolucion. Por Monsenor Segur. (78914)
Revolution, William. 70342
Revolution. (70344), 90405
Revolution Americaine devoilee. 59505
Revolution and reconstruction. 58699
Revolution de Brumaire. 6269
Revolution de l'Amerique. 24017, 58222-58223,
68101-68103
Revolution in MDCCLXXXII. 70346
Revolution in France. 70345, 102395
Revolution in Hell. (62592)

Rey tres vecos coronado. 93346
Reybauld, Charles. 70385-70387
Reybauld, Louis, i. e. Marie Roch Louis,
　1799-1879. 21211-21215, 70388-70391
Reybauld, Marie Roch Louis. see Reybauld,
　Louis, i. e. Marie Roch Louis, 1799-
　1879.
Reyero, Juan N. (70392)
Reyes, Antonio de los. 70393-70394
Reyes, Antonio Garcia. (70395)
Reyes, Jose Maria. 70396
Reyes, Jose Maria de los. see De los Reyes,
　Jose Maria.
Reyes Angel, Gaspar de los. 70397
Reyes, Ciudad de los. see Lima, Peru.
Reygadas, Fermin. 70398
Reyna de la America. 76109
Reynal, Rafael. (70399), 99402
Reynaud, -------, Comte de. 14052, 14059,
　70400-70401
Reynard, Nicolas. see Baynard, Nicholas.
Reynell, Carew. (70402)
Reyner, E. supposed author 32834-32835
Reynie de la Bruyere, J.-B.-M.-L. La. see
　La Reynie de la Bruyere, J.-B.-M.-L.
Reyno, Juan N. 70403
Reynolds, -------, fl. 1795. 102346
Reynolds, -------, fl. 1839. 87735
Reynolds, Alexander G. 70404
Reynolds, Andrew J. 70405
Reynolds, Caesar, 1803-1833. defendant
　94617
Reynolds, E. Winchester. 70408-70411
Reynolds, Edward. 70406-(70407)
Reynolds, George. 83037-83038
Reynolds, Grindall. 70412-(70413)
Reynolds, H. G. ed. 45533
Reynolds, Henry D. 70414
Reynolds, Ignatius Aloysius. 22588
Reynolds, J. 70416
Reynolds, J. A. 70415
Reynolds, J. J. 70427
Reynolds, J. L. 87979
Reynolds, Miss J. P. (70435)
Reynolds, J. V. (70436)
Reynolds, Jack. Alias. see Reynolds, John.
　defendant
Reynolds, Jeremiah N., 1799-1858. 70428-
　70434
Reynolds, John. defendant (70423)
Reynolds, John, of Vermont. (70417)-70418
Reynolds, John, fl. 1624. supposed author
　78372-78375, 2d note after 100788,
　100799
Reynolds, John, 1788-1865. 70419-70422,
　96673-96674 see also Illinois. Gov-
　ernor, 1830-1834 (Reynolds) U. S. Com-
　missioners to the Confederated Tribes
　of Sauk and Fox Indians. U. S. Com-
　missioners to the Winnebago Indians.
Reynolds, John George. defendant at court
　martial 70425-70426
Reynolds, John George. reporter 70424
Reynolds, John N. ed. 27551, 101879
Reynolds, Joseph. 70437-70438
Reynolds, L. E. 70440
Reynolds, Laurence. 70439
Reynolds, Marcus T. 97773
Reynolds, Peter. see Raynolds, Peter.
Reynolds, Richard, successively Bishop of
　Bangor, and Lincoln, 1674-1744. (70441)
Reynolds, Samuel. (70442)
Reynolds, T. 70443
Reynolds, Theophilus. (70444)
Reynolds, Thomas. 70445

Reynolds, Thomas C. 70446 see also
　Missouri. Lieutenant Governor (Reynolds)
Reynolds, W. M. ed. 23132
Reynolds, W. T. 31004
Reynolds. William. 84411
Reynolds, William B. (54212)
Reynolds, William D. 70448
Reynolds, William M. (70451)-70452
Reynolds (Samuel and T. F.) firm publishers
　104437
Reynolds (T. F.) publishers see Reynolds
　(Samuel and T. F.) firm publishers
Reynolds (William C.) firm publishers (70447)
Reynold's history of Illinois. 70420
Reynold's pamphlet. (29969)-29970
Reynolds' political map of the United States.
　(70447)
Reynoso, Alvaro. 70453-70458
Reynoso, Diego de. 70459
Reynst, -------. 70460
Reys-beschryving op het schip de Vrouw Maria.
　62800
Reys-beschryvinghe door de Koninckrycken van
　Spanien. 106296
Reys-boek van het rijcke Brasilien. 7633
Reys-gheschrift van de navigatien der Portugal-
　oysers in Orienten. 41356, (41359),
　41361-41363
Reys-journael van een Amsterdamse kapitein.
　70461
Reyse. 33664
Reyse desz Edlen vnd Besten Thomas Candisch.
　(8784)
Reyse door Nieuwe Ondekte Landen. 31358
Reyse durch den Commandeur Turck Alberts
　Raven. 6340
Reyse na Groenlandt. 54550
Reyse van Indien. 99363-99364
Reyse van Lissebone. 99366
Reyse van Lissebone. note before 99327,
　99363-99364
Reyse van Lissobone. 99365
Reysen in Afrique. 49701
Reysen na de vier gedeeltens den werelds.
　28176
Reysen na West-Indien. (17873A)
Reysgheschrift. 41356
Reystogt rondom de Werreld. 18385
Reystogten rondom de Waereldt. 18388
Reyze na Groenland. 6337
Reyze naar het Zuydland. 72770
Rezabal y Ugarte, Joseph de. 70462
Rezard de Vouves, P. L. C. F. 70463
Rezzonico, Carlo de la Torre. see Clement
　XIII, Pope, 1693-1769.
Rham, Henry C. de. see De Rham, Henry C.
Rhand, Tally. pseud. Guttle and gulpit. 70464
Rhapsodical execration on the slave trade.
　102701
Rhapsodies, hyperboles, and incongruities of the
　sacred and profane. (30398)
Rhapsodies of restless hours. 30598
Rhapsody. (70465)
Rhea, John, 1753-1832. 70467
Rhea, John, fl. 1772. 70466, 62327
Rhea, Samuel A. (70468)
Rhees, B. Rush. 70469
Rhees, Morgan H. 70470-(70473)
Rhees, William H. 84985, 84987
Rhees, William Jones. 70474-70476, 84989,
　85007, 85037, 85076-85077, 85080, 85089-
　85090, 85097 see also Smithsonian Insti-
　tution. Chief Clerk.
Rhein, Franco von. (69138)
Rheinisch Archiv. (14638)

Rheinlander, pseud. Nachrichten und Erfah-
rungen. see G., G. A. pseud.
Rhetorica Christiana. 25934
Rhetorica Christiana ad concionandi. 98300
Rhetorical dialogues. 42379
Rhetorical grammar of the English language.
80347
Rhetorical manual. 73345
Rhett, Robert Barnwell, 1800-1876. 9950,
15064, 70477-70486, 83853-83854,
87480
Rhett, Robert Barnwell, fl. 186-. 70487
Rhetvm epistola. 63957
Rhexies. (33763)
Rhind, A. C. defendant (70488)
Rhinebeck, N. Y. Reading Hall and Circulating
Library. (70490)
Rhinebeck, N. Y. St. Peter Evangelical
Lutheran Church. 70489
Rhinebeck, N. Y. Starr Institute. see Starr
Institute, Rhinebeck, N. Y.
Rhinelander, John R. (70491)-70492
Rhoades, Sumner. 70493
Rhoads, Asa. 70494
Rhoads, Samuel N. ed. 106129
Rhoads, Thomas Y. 70495
Rhode Island (Colony) 3748, 32968, (70633)
Rhode Island (Colony) respondent 45665
Rhode Island (Colony) Census, 1744. 3737
Rhode Island (Colony) Charter. 1069, 12162-
12163, (41430), 70510-70512, 70514,
70582, 70626-70628, 1st note after
99889
Rhode Island (Colony) Council. 99808
Rhode Island (Colony) Deputy Governor, 1767
(Brown) 103308 see also Brown,
Elisha.
Rhode Island (Colony) General Assembly.
3740, 65849, 70617, 90478
Rhode Island (Colony) Governor, 1698-1727
(Cranston) 99808 see also Cranston,
Samuel, 1659-1727.
Rhode Island (Colony) Governor, 1765-1767
(Ward) 101335 see also Ward, Samuel,
1725-1776.
Rhode Island (Colony) Laws, statutes, etc.
3741, 39410, 39414, 55053, 65849,
68534, 70510-70517, 70589, 90478
Rhode Island (Colony) Militia. Courts Martial.
68392
Rhode Island (Colony) Secretary. 70516,
99808 see also Ward, R. Ward, Thomas.
Rhode Island. 3752, 20468, 45717, 56779,
58453, 70541, 70578, 70611, 70621,
83353-83355, 84975
Rhode Island. defendants 45682, 46149,
(46151)-46154, 66240, 70546, 70752-
70753
Rhode Island. plaintiffs (31093), 45686, 46154,
70497, 70550, 70751
Rhode Island. Adjutant General. 70541 see
also Mauran, Edwin C.
Rhode Island. Attorney General. 66348
Rhode Island. Auditor. (70545), 70679,
70746 see also Collins, James C.
Watson, William R.
Rhode Island. Bank Commissioners. 70553
Rhode Island. Bar. 92287
Rhode Island. Board of Cattle Commissioners.
70556
Rhode Island. Board of Education. 70555
see also Rhode Island. Office of Com-
missioner of Education.
Rhode Island. Board of Inspectors of the
State Prison. see Rhode Island. State
Prison. Board of Inspectors.

Rhode Island. Board of State Charities and
Corrections. 70558
Rhode Island. Cenus, 1865. 70693
Rhode Island. Census, 1875. 70693
Rhode Island. Citizens. petitioners (20647),
note after 96509
Rhode Island. College. see Brown University.
Rhode Island. Commissioner, Appointed to
Ascertain the Number, Ages, Hours of
Labor, and Opportunities for Education of
Children, Employed in the Manufacturing
Establishments of Rhode Island. 70645,
77410 see also Sayles, W. B.
Rhode Island. Commissioner for Adjusting the
Accounts of the State Against the United
States. 9135, 70643 see also Bullock,
Jonathan Russell, 1815-1899.
Rhode Island. Commissioner of Public Schools.
see Rhode Island. Office of Commissioner
of Public Schools.
Rhode Island. Commissioner of Shell Fisheries.
70566
Rhode Island. Commissioner on the Narragan-
sett Tribe of Indians. 70646
Rhode Island. Commissioner on the Physical
Condition of the Rhode Island Regiments,
Now in the Field, 1863. 51008, 70686
see also Morton, Lloyd.
Rhode Island. Commissioner on the Soldiers'
National Cemetery, at Gettysburg. 27243,
(70636) see also Bartlett, John Russell.
Rhode Island. Commissioner to the Universal
Exposition at Paris, 1867. 70644 see also
Perry, John G.
Rhode Island. Commissioner to Visit Almshouses
and Asylums, for the Insane Poor, Indi-
gent Persons, or Paupers. (70647)
Rhode Island. Commissioner to Visit the
Hospitals, 1863. 18279, 70694 see also
Dailey, Charlotte F.
Rhode Island. Commissioners on the Boundary
with Massachusetts. (46001), (70648)
Rhode Island. Commissioners on the Boundary
with Massachusetts. Minority. (46001)
Rhode Island. Commissioners to Establish the
Boundary Line of East Providence.
70649
Rhode Island. Commissioners to Investigate
the Practicability of Re-stocking the
Waters of the State with Salmon and
Other Migratory Fish. 70650
Rhode Island. Commissioners to the Convention
of Commissioners From the Several
States, Washington, D. C., 1861. see
Rhode Island. Commissioners to the
Peace Convention, Washington, D. C.,
1861.
Rhode Island. Commissioners to the Peace
Convention, Washington, D. C., 1861.
15434, 59404
Rhode Island. Committee on the Registered
State Debt. 70641 see also Bullock,
Jonathan Russell, 1815-1899. Everett,
Amherst. Turner, George.
Rhode Island. Constitution. 1269, 1271, 2071,
5316, 6360, 16086-16092, 16097, 16099-
16103, 16107, 16113, 16118-16120, 16133,
(19476), 25790, 33137, (47188), 59771,
(66397), 70562, 70569-70573, 70579,
70620, 70626-70628, 70700, 100342,
104198
Rhode Island. Constitutional Convention, 1834.
70537
Rhode Island. Constitutional Convention,
Providence, 1841. 60551, 70579

Rhode Island. Constitutional Convention, Newport, 1842. 70590
Rhode Island. Convention, 1790. 22233, 70628, 90478, note after 106002
Rhode Island. Counsel. 70497
Rhode Island. Court of Common Pleas. 20652
Rhode Island. Courts. 20649, 20650
Rhode Island. General Assembly. 3735, 3737, 3741, 3748, (8599), 18673, 70509, 70517, 70519, 70541, (70549)-70550, 70561-70562, 70575, 70580, (70595), 70597, 70604, 70614, 70622, 70651, 70654, 71292, 90477, 90478, 98638
Rhode Island. General Assembly. Committee Appointed to Inquire Into the Situation of the Farmers' Exchange Bank in Gloucester. 27585, 70651
Rhode Island. General Assembly. Committee of Claims. 70716
Rhode Island. General Assembly. Committee on a Monument to the Rhode Island Soldiers and Sailors. (70656)
Rhode Island. General Assembly. Committee on an Extension of Suffrage. 31092
Rhode Island. General Assembly. Committee on Education. 70607, 70658-70659, 70690
Rhode Island. General Assembly. Committee on Education. Minority. 70606
Rhode Island. General Assembly. Committee on Elections. Minority. 55055
Rhode Island. General Assembly. Committee on Indian Tribes. (70661)
Rhode Island. General Assembly. Committee on Public Schools. 70662
Rhode Island. General Assembly. Committee on Schools. 70638
Rhode Island. General Assembly. Committee on Suffrage. 31092, 42730
Rhode Island. General Assembly. Committee on the Constitution. 70663
Rhode Island. General Assembly. Committee to Investigate Freemasonry. 29888, 45506, 70652, (70655)
Rhode Island. General Assembly. Committee to Visit and Examine the Banks. (70653)
Rhode Island. General Assembly. Commutation Commission. 70639
Rhode Island. General Assembly. Democratic Members. see Democratic Party. Rhode Island.
Rhode Island. General Assembly. Finance Committee. (70664)-70665, 70583
Rhode Island. General Assembly. Joint Committee on the Disputed Boundary Between Rhode Island and Massachusetts. Majority. 70594
Rhode Island. General Assembly. Joint Committee upon the Boundary Line Between the State of Rhode-Island and Massachusetts. (70667)
Rhode Island. General Assembly. Joint Select Committee Upon a Division of the Town of Smithfield. 84975
Rhode Island. General Assembly. Joint Special Committee on the Affairs in the Quartermaster-General's Department. 70671
Rhode Island. General Assembly. Joint Special Committee on the Affairs in the Quartermaster-General's Department. Minority. 70608

Rhode Island. General Assembly. Joint Special Committee on the State Asylum for the Insane. 70672
Rhode Island. General Assembly. Joint Special Committee on the Whole Matter of the Central Bridge Location, &c. 70698
Rhode Island. General Assembly. Joint Special Committee to Examine Into the Fisheries of Narragansett Bay. 70669
Rhode Island. General Assembly. Joint Special Committee to Proceed to Washington, for the Purpose of Procuring an Extension of the Draft. 70668
Rhode Island. General Assembly. Joint Special Committee Upon the Special Message of the Governor, 1866. 70670
Rhode Island. General Assembly. Minority. 70623
Rhode Island. General Assembly. Select Committee on the Bill "To Abolishment Imprisonment for Debt." 70674
Rhode Island. General Assembly. Special Committee on Equity Powers of Supreme Court. 35314
Rhode Island. General Assembly. Special Committee on the Memorial of Certain Citizens of Providence. 33003
Rhode Island. General Assembly. Special Committee on the Petition of Charles T. Hazard. 31094
Rhode Island. General Assembly. Special Committee in Relation to Weights and Measures. (70675)
Rhode Island. General Assembly. Special Committee Relative to the Deleterious Substances Deposited in the Public Waters of the State. 70676
Rhode Island. General Assembly. House of Representatives. 70562, (70576), 70590, 85502
Rhode Island. General Assembly. House of Representatives. Committee on Corporations. 70657
Rhode Island. General Assembly. House of Representatives. Committee on Corporations. Minority. 70605
Rhode Island. General Assembly. House of Representatives. Committee on Masonry. Minority. 89720, 2d note after 97484
Rhode Island. General Assembly. House of Representatives. Committee on the Petition of H. J. Duff and Others. 21129, 80410
Rhode Island. General Assembly. House of Representatives. Committee to Inquire Into the Expediency of Increasing the Banking Capital. (31093)
Rhode Island. General Assembly. House of Representatives. Finance Committee. 70640
Rhode Island. General Assembly. House of Representatives. Judiciary Committee. (70673)
Rhode Island. General Assembly. House of Representatives. Special Finance Committee. 70677
Rhode Island. General Assembly. Senate. 70562, 70593, 70637, 70642
Rhode Island. General Assembly. Senate. Committee on Finance. 70660
Rhode Island. General Treasurer's Office. see Rhode Island. Treasury Department.
Rhode Island. Governor, 1790-1805 (Fenner) 70559 see also Fenner, Arthur, 1745-1805.

Rhode Island. Governor, 1811-1817 (Jones) 33150 see also Jones, William, 1753-1822.

Rhode Island. Governor, 1839-1843 (King) 70577 see also King, Samuel Ward, 1786-1851.

Rhode Island. Governor, 1857-1859 (Dyer) 33150 see also Dyer, Elisha, 1811-1890.

Rhode Island. Governor, 1860-1863 (Sprague) 70601 see also Sprague, William, 1830-1915.

Rhode Island. Governor, 1863-1866 (Smith) 66356, 70567, (70602), 70609, 82798-82799 see also Smith, James Youngs, 1809-1876.

Rhode Island. Governor, 1866-1869 (Burnside) 70602, 70642, 70658 see also Burnside, Ambrose Everett, 1824-1881.

Rhode Island. Governor, 1869-1873 (Padelford) (70603) see also Padelford, Seth, 1807-1878.

Rhode Island. Insurance Commissioner. (70747)

Rhode Island. Laws, statutes, etc. 3741, 8054, 16078, 18117, 23765, 31030, 31101, 38722, 39414, 52051, 54839, 55033-55034, 55038, 55053, (55056), 59261, 66241-66243, 66247, 66249-66250, 66263, (66271), 66305, (66307), (66309), (66312), 66326, 66331, 66369, (66374), 70501-70509, 70516-70520, 70554, 70560-70561, (70564), (70576), 70580, 70582, 70587, (70589), 70591, 70604, 70626-70628, 70684, 70689, (70695), 70699, 70700, 70715, 70718-70719, 70727, 70743, 70748, 70820-70821, (81943), 82438, 84975, 85831, 87134, 89066, 1st note after 91736, note after 94020, 101493-101495, 102022, 103255

Rhode Island. Militia. 56779, 70611

Rhode Island. Militia. Courts Martial (Brown) 8584-8585

Rhode Island. Militia. Courts Martial (Maxwell) 62977, 96942

Rhode Island. Militia. Courts Martial (Pinniger) 62977, 96942

Rhode Island. Militia. Courts Martial (Tillinghast) 62977, 96942

Rhode Island. Militia. Courts Martial (Whiting) 62977, 96942

Rhode Island. Militia. Drafted Regiment in the War of 1812. petitioners 70597

Rhode Island. Militia. First Light Infantry Company, Providence. (55256)

Rhode Island. Militia. Rhode Island Brigade. 9235, 90726-90727

Rhode Island. Militia. Rhode Island Brigade. Claims Agent. 90727 see also Barton, William.

Rhode Island. Militia. Rhode Island Brigade. Officers and Soldiers. petitioners 9235, 70599

Rhode Island. Office of Commissioner of Education. 3468, 8623, 70555, 70565, 70635, 70683-70684, 70691-70692, (70695) (70735), 83908 see also Allyn, Robert. Barnard, Henry, 1811-1900. Potter, Elisha Reynolds, 1811-1882.

Rhode Island. People's Convention, Providence, 1841. see Rhode Island. Constitutional Convention, Providence, 1841.

Rhode Island. Public Schools. 70500, 70635-70636, (70695), 70723

Rhode Island. Quartermaster General. 70629 see also Cooke, George Lewis. Remington, Dewitt C.

Rhode Island. Railroad Commissioners. 70630-70631

Rhode Island. School Commissioners. see Rhode Island. Office of Commissioner of Education.

Rhode Island. Secretary of State. 3741, 3748, 3752, 70496, (70498)-(70499), 70537, 70546, (70589), (70595), (70633)-(70634), 70688, 70744-70745 see also Addeman, Joshua M. Bartlett, John Russell. Potter, Asa. Robbins, Christopher E. Smith, William Henry, d. 1860.

Rhode Island. Soldiers' Monument, Providence. see Providence, R. I. Soldiers' Monument.

Rhode Island. State Allotment Commissioner. (70678)

Rhode Island. State Auditor. see Rhode Island. Auditor.

Rhode Island. State Insurance Commissioner. 70680 see also Watson, William R.

Rhode Island. State Prison. 70544, 70749

Rhode Island. State Prison. Board of Inspectors. (70557)

Rhode Island. State Prison. Inspectors. 70543

Rhode Island. State Prison. Physician. 70543

Rhode Island. State Prison. Warden. 70543

Rhode Island. Sundry Citizens. petitioners see Rhode Island. Citizens. petitioners

Rhode Island. Superintendent of the Census. 70693 see also Snow, Edwin Miller, 1820-1888.

Rhode Island. Supreme Court. 1310, (2482), 2483, 2485-2486, 5785, 20649-20650, (31792), 35314, 70508, (70576), 70696-70697, 89104, note after 92848, 96818, 1st note after 97484, 1st note after 99826, 101131

Rhode Island. Treasury Department. (70666)

Rhode Island. Trustees of the Antietam National Monument. (70681)

Rhode Island. United States Provost Marshall. see United States. Provost Marshall for Rhode Island.

Rhode Island. Various Merchants. petitioners see Various Merchants of Rhode Island. petitioners

Rhode Island. 22369

Rhode-Island almanac. 88633

Rhode-Island almanac, for . . . 1804. (70707)

Rhode-Island almanac, for . . . 1802. 70706

Rhode-Island almanack for 1791. 70704

Rhode-Island almanack for the year, 1738. 90073

Rhode-Island almanack for the year, 1735. (70702)

Rhode-Island almanack for the year, 1737. 90072

Rhode-Island almanac, for the year 1728. 70701

Rhode-Island almanack, or astronomical diary, for . . . 1772. 70703

Rhode Island almanac, with an ephemeris for the year 1794. 70705

Rhode Island Anti-masonic State Convention, Providence, 1830. see Anti-masonic State Convention of Rhode Island, Providence, 1830.

Rhode Island Anti-masonic State Convention, Providence, 1835. see Anti-masonic State Convention of Rhode Island, Providence, 1835.

Rhode Island Anti-masonic State Convention, Providence, 1836. see Anti-masonic State Convention of Rhode Island, Providence, 1836.

Rhode-Island Anti-slavery Convention, Providence, 1836. 70619

Rhode Island Art Association. 70708

Rhode Island Art Association. Exhibition, 1st, Providence, 1854. 70708

Rhode Island Association for Freedmen. 70709

Rhode Island Baptist. 70710

Rhode Island Baptist State Convention. see Baptists. Rhode Island. State Convention.

Rhode Island Baptist Sunday School Convention, 14th, Providence, 1854. 70712

Rhode Island Bible Society. Board of Trustees. 70750

Rhode Island bill of rights. 70582

Rhode-Island book. 70713

Rhode Island Brigade. see Rhode Island. Militia. Rhode Island Brigade.

Rhode-Island clerk's magazine. 70714

Rhode-Island Cloth Hall Company. Charter. 70715

Rhode Island College. see Brown University.

Rhode Island colonial records. 1521, 3740

Rhode Island Congregational Conference. see Congregational Churches in Rhode Island.

Rhode Island conservative. pseud. Letter to the Hon. James F. Simmons. 40481, 81171

Rhode Island controversy. 35314

Rhode Island cottage. 71140-(71141)

Rhode Island educational magazine. (70695), 70718, 70743

Rhode Island Evangelical Consociation. see Evangelical Consociation of Rhode Island.

Rhode Island freeman. pseud. To the freemen of Rhode Island. 70756

Rhode Island historical collections. see Collections of the Rhode Island Historical Society.

Rhode Island Historical Society. (10076), 21981, (28046), 64633, 70719, 90475, 104330, 104340,

Rhode Island Historical Society. Board of Trustees. 70719

Rhode Island Historical Society. Charter. 70719

Rhode Island historical tracts. 32968, 1st note after 97146, 104334

Rhode Island Home Missionary Society. see Congregational Churches in Rhode Island. Home Missionary Society.

Rhode-Island Homoeopathic Society. 70720

Rhode Island Horticultural Society. Committees. 70721

Rhode Island Hospital, Providence, R. I. see Providence, R. I. Rhode Island Hospital.

Rhode Island in the Continental Congress. 90478

Rhode Island in the war of the revolution of 1776. 9235, 63427

Rhode Island Infantry. see Rhode Island. Militia.

Rhode Island Institute of Instruction. 70635, 70723

Rhode Island Institute of Instruction. Annual Meeting, 23d, Providence, 1848. 70723

Rhode Island Institute of Instruction. Executive Committee. 70723

Rhode Island Institute of Reward. 34824, 70724

Rhode Island Institute of Reward, auxiliary to the "Institute of Reward for Orphans of Patriots. 70724

Rhode Island—Interference of the executive in the affairs of. June 7, 1844, 70725

Rhode Island Library. Burrillville. (37126)

Rhode-Island literary repository, a monthly magazine. (70726)

Rhode Island Medical Society. 70727, 85493, 85502

Rhode Island Medical Society. Charter. 70727

Rhode Island memorial. June 17, 1844. 70725, 70728

Rhode Island Numismatic Association. 70729

Rhode Island Peace Society. 70730

Rhode Island pension roll. 70731

Rhode Island politics, and journalism. 18889

Rhode-Island Protestant Association. 104389

Rhode-Island protestantism. 104389

Rhode-Island question. 70732

Rhode-Island register, and United States calendar. 70733

Rhode Island register, for the year 1853. 70734

Rhode Island reports. 70697

Rhode Island repudiation. 71148

Rhode Island repudiation of her registered state debt. 71147

Rhode Island schoolmaster. 8623, (70735)

Rhode Island Society for the Encouragement of Domestic Industry. (70736), 85493

Rhode Island Society for the Encouragement of Domestic Industry. Charter. (70736)

Rhode Island Society for the Encouragement of Domestic Industry. Sub-committee on Agriculture. (70736)

Rhode Island Society of Colonial Wars. see Society of Colonial Wars in the State of Rhode Island and Providence Plantations.

Rhode Island Society of the Cincinnati. see Society of the Cincinnati   Rhode Island.

Rhode Island State Temperance Society. 70737

Rhode Island State Total Abstinence Society. 70738

Rhode Island State Total Abstinence Society. Corresponding Secretary. 70738

Rhode-Island Suffrage Association. 70739

Rhode-Island Sunday School Union. 70740

Rhode Island tales. 70741

Rhode Island Temperance Society. see Rhode Island State Temperance Society.

Rhode Island Total Abstinence Society. see Rhode Island State Total Abstinence Society.

Rhode Island Union Conference magazine. (70742)

Rhode Island vs. John and William Gordon. (27985)

Rhode Island vs. Massachusetts. Papers put into the case by Massachusetts. 46154

Rhode Island vs. Massachusetts. Papers put into the case of Rhode Island vs. Massachusetts. 70751

Rhode Island vs. Massachusetts, pending in the Supreme Court. 70497

Rhode-Islander. pseud. Jeremy Bentham and the usury law. see Whipple, John.

Rhode Islander. pseud. Might and right. 48898

Rhode Islander. pseud. Mr. Harris reviewed. 70757

Rhode Islander. pseud. Some considerations touching the proposed change. 70758

Rhodes, C. C. 86971

Rhodes, J. R. 70759

Rhodes, Jacob. 70760

Rhodes, James A. 70761
Rhodes, John, fl. 1606. (70762)
Rhodes, John, fl. 1726. 59698
Rhodes, John, b. 1755. 70763-70765, 71709,
    93907-93908 see also Roach, John, b.
    1748.
Rhodes, N. C. 70766
Rhodes, Rufus R. 15374, 15405-15407, 74072
    see also Confederate States of America.
    Patent Office.
Rhodes, William. 63476
Rhodes, William H. (70767)
Rhodes (Charles C.) firm publishers 37374
Rhodes railroad and steamboat directory.
    37374
Rhododendron and "American plants." 67751
Rhodomanthus. (70768)
Rhodospermeae. 30782
Rhody, Sister. pseud. Whatcheer, a story of
    olden times. see Child, Anna P.
Rhone (Department) Prefet. 84478
Rhyme and reason of country life. 16606
Rhyme of dark and daybreak. 90564
Rhyme of the war. 65375
Rhymed eulogy. 41725
Rhymed lesson. 32621
Rhymed tactics. (70769)
Rhymer, Robert. (70770)
Rhymers' club. 70771
Rhymes. 96394
Rhymes addressed to the friends of liberty.
    82111
Rhymes of contrast on wisdom and folly.
    74251
Rhymes of travel. 94440
Rhymes of twenty years. 50630
Rhymes relating to the present times, &c.
    70772
Rhymes with reason and without. 80480
Rhys, Ernest. ed. 84316
Rhys, Horton. 70773
Rhythme descasyllabicall. 79341
Rhythmical history of the Fifteenth N. Y.
    Volunteer Engineers. 41019
Rhythmical romance of Minnesota. 14682,
    44358
Rhythmics of many moods and quantities.
    80477
Rianzuela, --------, Marques de. 70774
Riba, J. P. (70775)
Ribadeneira, Petrus. 712, 70776-70784
Ribadeneyra, Antonio de Solis y. see Solis
    Ribadeneyra, Antonio de, 1610-1686.
Ribadeneyra, Diego Portichuelo de. see Por-
    tichuelo de Ribadeneyra, Diego.
Ribadeneyra, Marcello de. 76787
Ribadeneyra, Pedro. see Ribadeneira, Petrus.
Ribadeneyra y Barrientos, Antonio Joaquin.
    (70785)-(70786)
Ribald, H. (8784)
Ribald, Jean. see Ribaut, Jean.
Ribaldus, Petrus. 70787
Ribas, Alonso Rubio de. see Rubio de Ribas,
    Alonso.
Ribas, Andres-Perez de, 1576-1655. 70895,
    70788-70789
Ribas, Antonio Joaquin. 70790
Ribas, Diego Rodriguez de. see Rodriguez de
    Ribas, Diego, Abp., d. 1771.
Ribas Baldwin, Angel E. (76782)
Ribas y Palacios, Jose Felix. petitioner
    70791
Ribault, ------. 39234-39236
Ribaut, Jean, ca. 1520-1565. 24894, 24902,
    39236, 39634-(39635), 70792, note after
    94854, 94856, note before 99284

Ribeira da Sabrosa, ---------, Baron de.
    95144, note before 96272
Ribeiro, -------. 7610
Ribeiro, Antonio de Souza. see Souza Ribeiro,
    Antonio de.
Ribeiro, Cacharel Annibal Andre. 70793
Ribeiro, Joao Pinto. supposed author 98253
Ribeiro, Sanctiago Nunes. 56427
Ribeiro de Andrada, Antonio Carlos. 1444,
    62954, 106062
Ribeiro de Andrada, Martin Francisco. 1444
Ribeiro de Andrada Machado e Silva, Antonio
    Carlos. 88767
Ribeiro de Sa, S. J. ed. 70320
Ribeiro de Sampajo, Francisco Xavier. 70794
Ribera, ------. 29276
Ribera, Antonio de. 22841, (70795)
Ribera, Antonio Flores de. see Flores de
    Ribera, Jose Antonio.
Ribera, Diego de. (70797)-70798
Ribera, F. Payo de. see Payo de Ribera, F.
Ribera, Fr. Fernando de Carvajal y. see
    Carvajal y Ribera, Fr. Fernando de.
Ribera, J. B. de. 70800
Ribera, Jose Antonio Flores de. see Flores de
    Ribera, Jose Antonio.
Ribera, Juan Antonio. 70799
Ribera, Miguel P. de. (70801)
Ribera, Payo Henriquez de, Abp. 50110,
    59305, (70802)-70804, 93586 see also
    Guatemala (Archdiocese) Bishop (Ribera)
    Mexico (Archdiocese) Archbishop (Ribera)
    Mexico (Viceroyalty) Virrey, 1673-1680
    (Ribera) Vera Paz (Diocese) Bishop
    (Ribera)
Ribera Florez, Dionysio de. 69224
Ribera Valdes, Leonor. defendant (76336)
Ribera y Colindres, Luys de. (70805)
Riberio de Andrada, Martim Francisco. 88767
Ribero, Diego. cartographer 76838, 89762
Ribero, J. see Ribero, Diego.
Ribero, L. Miguel. 70806
Ribero, Pedro Bravo del. respondent 61136
Ribero, Sebastian, Bp. (70807)
Ribero Sanchez, Antonio. see Sanchez, Antonio
    Ribero.
Ribeyre, Felix. 70808
Ribeyro, Joao Pinto. see Ribeiro, Joao Pinto.
Ribeyrolles, Charles. (70809)-70810
Ricara Indians. Treaties, etc. 96643
Ricard, Fortune. 65450
Ricardo, Antonio. 20565, 32492, (67160),
    100643
Ricardo, David. (82311)
Ricaut, Sir Paul. 18563
Ricci, Juan Jos. Matraya y. see Matraya y
    Ricci, Juan Jos.
Riccioli, Giovanni Battista, 1598-1671. 51478,
    (70811)-70812
Riccius, ------. 66686
Riccoboni, --------. 100727
Rice, A. H. 70816
Rice, A. T. ed. 55562
Rice, Abner. 70814
Rice, Alexander Hamilton, 1818-1895. 70815-
    70818 see also Boston. Mayor, 1856-
    1857 (Rice)
Rice, Benjamin Holt. 70844
Rice, Charles B. 16224, 70818-(70819)
Rice, Clinton. 70820-70821
Rice, D. 70822
Rice, Daniel. 70823-70825
Rice, David. 5618, 70826-70827
Rice, Miss E. D. ed. 89882
Rice, E. L. 70828-70829
Rice, George Edward. 70830-(70831)

Rice, Harvey, 1800-1891. 16224, 70832-70833
Rice, Henry L. 70834
Rice, Isaac. petitioner 70607
Rice, Isaac J. 70835
Rice, James. 70836
Rice, James C. 70837-70838
Rice, John A. (70839)
Rice, John H. 70846
Rice, John Holt, 1777-1831. 70840-70845,
   82852
Rice, John Hovey, 1816-1911. 52127
Rice, Luther. (70847)
Rice, Nathan L. 5825, 62438, 70848-70857,
   (77444), 82243, 92818, 98169
Rice, Nathan L. defendant 70848
Rice, Nathan P. 70858
Rice, Roswell. 70859
Rice, Spooner M. 70860
Rice, Spring. 93176
Rice, Thomas M. 70861
Rice, Thomas O. 70862
Rice, Victor M. 36167, (53741)
Rice, William, fl. 1838. 70864, 87693
Rice, William, fl. 1861. 70863
Rice Creek Springs, S. C. Richland School
   see Richland School, Rice Creek Springs,
   S. C.
Ricerche istorico-critiche circa alle scoperte
   d'Amerigo Vespucci. 3799-3800, 99383C
Rice's orations and poems. 70859
Rich, A. B. 85913
Rich, A. Judson. 70865
Rich, Charles, 1771-1824. 70866
Rich, Elihu. 30971, 44508, 70867-(70868), 1st
   note after 96498
Rich, Elisha. 70869-70870
Rich, Ezekiel. 70872-(70874)
Rich, Ezekiel. petitioner 70871
Rich, John. supposed author 89470
Rich, John B. supposed author 26807
Rich, Obadiah, 1783-1850. 28306, 70875-
   70887, 95332
Rich, Oliver O. (70888), 1st note after 94129
Rich, Richard, fl. 1610. 70889-70891, note
   after 99857, 100483
Richard, Robert, 1587-1658. see Warwick,
   Robert Rich, 2d Earl of, 1587-1658
Rich, Robert, d. 1679. 70892-70896
Rich, Robert, fl. 1725. (70897)
Rich, W. A. 70898
Rich and Sons. firm 70887
Rich and poor. (76989)
Rich and poor meet together. 21507
Rich and Sons' catalogue for 1848. 70887
Rich men of Massachusetts. (25034), 46109
"Rich men of Philadelphia." (61736), 62194
Rich newes from Jamaica. 9461
Rich treasure at an easy rate. (70899)
Rich Trinity. A layman's answer. 32934
Richard, Achille. 21210, 74921-74922
Richard, Carl. 70900
Richard, Christian. 25997, (38973)-38974
Richard, Gaspard. (70901)
Richard, Henry. 70902
Richard, James. 66724
Richard, Jerome. 2580, 70904
Richard, L. 70903
Richard, M. F. see Richard, Jerome.
Richard, Mondesir. 5654
Richard, Pierre. 70905, 1st note after 94551
Richard, Poor. pseud. see Franklin, Benjamin,
   1706-1790.
Richard, Uncle. pseud. see Uncle Richard.
   pseud.
Richard Burton. pseud. see Crouch, Nathaniel.

Richard Cobden . . . a biography. (43269)
Richard Cortambert. 16930
Richard Edney and the governor's family.
   36842
Richard Hurdis. 81191, 81197, 81199, 81272,
   (81279)
Richard Hurdis, a tale of Alabama. 81251
Richard Hurdis; or, the avengers of blood.
   70907, 81250
Richard Ireton. 69552
Richard Mather's journal. 106052
Richard Ploughjoffer. pseud. see Ploughjoffer,
   Richard.
Richard Rum. pseud. see Rum, Sir Richard.
   pseud.
Richard Saunders. pseud. see Franklin,
   Benjamin, 1706-1790.
Richard Snowden Andrews. 84468
Richarderie, Gilles Boucher de la. see Boucher
   de la Richarderie, Gilles, 1733-1810.
Richards, Mr. --------. supposed author
   15792, 15826, note just before 63828
Richards, Mrs. A. M. 47562, 70909
Richards, Alfred Bate. 70908
Richards, Antonio D. (70910), note just before
   (73261)
Richards, "Boss." pseud. Richardsiana. (70978)
Richards, C. A. L. 35679
Richards, Christian. (38973)-38974, note after
   100853, note after 100854
Richards, Ezra F. tr. 83136-83137
Richards, F. S. 70914
Richards, Franklin D. 70912-70913, 83044,
   83258, 85563
Richards, G. W. 70942-70943
Richards, George. reporter 32232
Richards, George, fl. 1770. respondent 15748-
   15752
Richards, George, d. 1814. 64433, 65383,
   66444, 70915-70929, 1st -2d notes after
   101825
Richards, George, 1816-1870. 70930-(70939)
Richards, George H. 70940-70941
Richards, Giles. (63390), 70944 see also
   College Hill, Ohio. Farmers' College.
   Committee on the College. Chairman.
Richards, Guy. plaintiff 102578
Richards, Henry. defendant 72374
Richards, J. H. 70955
Richards, J. W. 70952
Richards, James. (70945)-70950
Richards, James. defendant 70951
Richards, John. 70953-(70954)
Richards, Karsten. see Richards, Christian.
Richards, Lucy. (70956)
Richards, Paul R. 84037
Richards, Peter. 62275 see also Philadelphia
   County, Pa. Sub-Lieutenant.
Richards, S. (70957)
Richards, T. Addison. 1798, 22085, 70958-
   (70969)
Richards, T. T. 70970
Richards, Willard. 83283
Richards, William, 1749-1818. 70971
Richards, William, d. 1819. 23170
Richards, William, fl. 1863. 55078
Richards, William C. 70976
Richards, William Carey, 1818-1892. 57618,
   (70963), 70972-70975, 88391
Richards, Zalmon, 1811-1899. 70977 see also
   U. S. Office of Education.
Richards (John) firm publishers 89508
Richard's botanical dictionary. 21706, 44408
Richards' weekly gazette. 88391
Richardsiana. (70978), note before 94463

Richardson, ---------. engr. 3784, 3787,
8899, note after 104504, 104505
Richardson, ----------, fl. 1776. 94569
Richardson, ----------, fl. 1863. ed. 89845
Richardson, A. A. ed. (45748)
Richardson, Abby (Sage) 1837-1900. 70979,
(70982)
Richardson, Albert D. 70980, (70982)-70985
Richardson, Albert D. reporter (70981)
Richardson, Mrs. Albert D. see Richardson,
Abby (Sage) 1837-1900.
Richardson, Charles, 1775-1865. (70989),
102370
Richardson, Charles S. 70990
Richardson, Chauncey. 70991
Richardson, D. M. 70992-70994
Richardson, Daniel S. 70995-70996
Richardson, David. 70997-(71001)
Richardson, E. J. 71002
Richardson, Emily. defendant before church
court 71003, note before 90710
Richardson, Freeman. 71004
Richardson, George, fl. 1844. 71005
Richardson, George, Jr., fl. 1862. (71006)
Richardson, George F. 71007 see also Lowell,
Mass. Mayor 1867-1868 (Richardson)
Richardson, H. H. 90788
Richardson, J. S. 71069
Richardson, J. S. defendant at impeachment
(71070)
Richardson, J. W. 71071
Richardson, Jabez. 71008
Richardson, James, 1771-1858. (71009)-71013
Richardson, James, fl. 1848. 71014-71015
Richardson, James, fl. 1849. 71016
Richardson, James, fl. 1865. 39044
Richardson, James, fl. 1873. 71017-(71018)
Richardson, James Burchill. 87539 see also
South Carolina. Governor, 1802-1804
(Richardson)
Richardson, James Daniel, 1843-1914. 104205
Richardson, Jasper. pseud. True and faithful
account. 97090
Richardson, Jeffrey. (71019)-71020
Richardson, John, 1647-1696. 71021-(71022)
Richardson, John, 1667-1753. 71023-71024
Richardson, Sir John, 1787-1865. 4389, (25624),
25628-25629, 28400, 28401, 31945,
37963, 39843, 71025-71033
Richardson, John, 1796-1852. 71036-71046,
94578, 100881
Richardson, John, 1796-1852. supposed author
98978
Richardson, John, fl. 1829. 71034
Richardson, John fl. 1831. 71035
Richardson, John B. 71047
Richardson, John G. 71048
Richardson, Joseph, 1778-1871. 15580, (31958),
71049-(71068), note just before 71069,
89503, 1st note after 99820
Richardson, Joseph Wilberforce. 71072
Richardson, Luther. 71073-(71074)
Richardson, Maynard Davis. 71075
Richardson, Merrill. 71076-71077
Richardson, N. (71078)-(71079)
Richardson, N. L. 30972, 5th note after
96966
Richardson, N. S. (71081)
Richardson, Nathaniel. ed. 71080, note after
92321
Richardson, R. H. 71084-71085
Richardson, Rebecca. plaintiff 71082
Richardson, Robert. 71083
Richardson, T. G. ed. 55552
Richardson, W. ed. 88324
Richardson, W. engr. 82829-82830, 82857

Richardson, W. A. ed. (45748)
Richardson, W. G. 571
Richardson, William, fl. 1739. 99249
Richardson, William, fl. 1744. 71086, 78981,
79330
Richardson, William, 1743-1814. 9821, 71087-
(71089)
Richardson, William Alexander, 1811-1875.
71090-71092
Richardson, William H. 71093-71095
Richardson, William H. of Boston 71096
Richardson, William Merchant, 1774-1838.
12601, 71097-71099
Richardson. firm publishers see Campbell &
Richardson. firm publishers
Richardson (W.) firm publishers 82823
Richardson-McFarland tragedy. 70987
Richardson's American reader. note just before
71069
Richardson's monitor of freemasonry. 71008
Richardson's Virginia and North Carolina
almanac. 70998
Richardson's Virginia & North Carolina almanac.
(71001)
Richardson's Virginia, North Carolina, Mary-
land and District of Columbia almanac.
70997
Richel, Dionisio. 71100-71101
Richelet, P. tr. 36812, 2d and 4th notes after
97689, 98748-98749
Richelot, Henri. 77607
Richelieu, Armand Jean du Plessis, Cardinal,
Duc de, 1585-1642. 71102-71103, 75014,
75016
Richer, Adrien, 1720-1798. (44825), (71104)-
71108
Richer, Edmundo. 71109
Richer, Jean. 71110
Richer-Serisy, -------. (1534), (27337)
Riches and honour. 71111
Riches without wings. 82516
Richesse de la Hollande. 32521, 48905, 79236
Richey, J. A. 67378
Richey, Matthew. 71112-71114
Richey, Matthew H. 71115
Richey, Thomas. 71116
Richie, ----------. defendant 89212
Richison, Melvins. ed. 83151
Richland District, S. C. Citizens. 71117
Richland District, S. C. Citizens. petitioners
71118
Richland School, Rice Creek Springs, S. C.
71119
Richmond, Allen. 71120
Richmond, Charles Lennox, 3d Duke of, 1735-
1806. (15052)
Richmond, Edward. 71121-71129
Richmond, George B. 71130 see also New
Bedford, Mass. Mayor, 1870 (Richmond)
Richmond, J. F. 71142
Richmond, James. 71131
Richmond, James. petitioner 71131
Richmond, James Cook. 40516, 64678, 71132-
(71134), 71136-(71141), 88113
Richmond, John M. 71143
Richmond, John W. 71144-71148
Richmond, Thomas. 71149
Richmond, Thomas T. 71150
Richmond, Wellington Harrison. 71151-71152
Richmond, William, 1797-1858. (71153), 94202
Richmond, William, fl. 1833. 71154
Richmond, William E. 35385, 65667, 71155-
71157
Richmond, Indiana. Board of Education. 71158
Richmond, Indiana. Public Schools. 71158

Richmond, Indiana. Public Schools. Board of Instructors. 71158

Richmond, Indiana. Public Schools. High School Department. 71158

Richmond, Indiana. School Examiners. 71158

Richmond, Indiana. Superintendent of Public Schools. 71158

Richmond, Mass. Congregational Church. (71160)

Richmond, Mass. School Committee. (71161)

Richmond, Mass. Selectmen. 71162

Richmond, Va. (71167)

Richmond, Va. Academie des Sciences et Beaux-Artes des Etats-Unis de l'Amerique. see Academy of Sciences and Fine Arts, Richmond, Va.

Richmond, Va. Academy of Sciences and Fine Arts. see Academy of Sciences and Fine Arts, Richmond, Va.

Richmond, Va. Anti-Jackson Convention, 1827-1828. see National Republican Party. Virginia.

Richmond, Va. Athenaeum. Library. 71207

Richmond, Va. Bank Convention of the Confederate States, 1861. see Bank Convention of the Confederate States, Richmond, 1861.

Richmond, Va. Banks. plaintiffs 89232

Richmond, Va. Board of Health. (71165)

Richmond, Va. Charter. (71170)

Richmond, Va. Circuit Court. 33371

Richmond, Va. Citizens. petitioners 69575

Richmond, Va. Coal-Owners and Iron-Masters. petitioners 71184

Richmond, Va. Colporteur Convention, 1852. see Colporteur Convention, Richmond, 1852.

Richmond, Va. Committee of Finance. 71191

Richmond, Va. Committee of Twenty-Four. see Meeting for Devising Means to Suppress . . . Gambling, Richmond, 1833. Committee of Twenty-Four.

Richmond, Va. Common Council. (71170)

Richmond, Va. Convention, March 20-27, 1775, see Virginia (Colony) Convention, Richmond, March 20-27, 1775.

Richmond, Va. Convention, July 17-Aug. 26, 1775. see Virginia. Convention, Richmond, July 17-Aug. 26, 1775.

Richmond, Va. Convention, Dec. 1, 1775-Jan. 20, 1776. see Virginia. Convention, Williamsburg, Dec. 1, 1775-Jan. 20, 1776.

Richmond, Va. Convention, 1788. see Virginia. Convention, Richmond, 1788.

Richmond, Va. Convention of Ministers, 1863. see Convention of Ministers, Richmond Va., 1863.

Richmond, Va. Council. 71190

Richmond, Va. Democratic Party Convention, 1839. see Democratic Party. Virginia. Convention, Richmond, 1839.

Richmond, Va. Domestic Missionary Society. see Domestic Missionary Society of Richmond, Va.

Richmond, Va. Female Humane Association. see Female Humane Association, Richmond, Va.

Richmond, Va. Female Institute. see Richmond Female Institute, Richmond, Va.

Richmond, Va. Free White Schools. see Soldiers' Memorial Society, Boston. Free White Schools, Richmond.

Richmond, Va. Grand Convocation and Supreme Grand Lodge of the Independent Order of the Sons of Malta, 1860. see Independent Order of the Sons of Malta. Virginia. Grand Convocation and Supreme Grand Lodge, Richmond, 1860.

Richmond, Va. Juvenile Library Company. see Juvenile Library Company, Richmond, Va.

Richmond, Va. Meeting for Devising Means to Suppress . . . Gambling, 1833. see Meeting for Devising Means to Suppress . . . Gambling, Richmond, 1833.

Richmond, Va. Meeting of the National Board of Trade, 2d, 1869. see National Board of Trade. Annual Meeting, 2d, Richmond, Va., 1869.

Richmond, Va. Mrs. Mead's School. see Mrs. Mead's School, Richmond.

Richmond, Va. Mutual Assurance Society. see Mutual Assurance Society, Richmond.

Richmond, Va. Ordinances, etc. (71170), 71186, 71202

Richmond, Va. Presbyterian Committee of Publication. see Presbyterian Church in the U. S. Committee of Publication.

Richmond, Va. Richmond College. see Richmond, Va. University. Richmond College.

Richmond, Va. School Board. 71166

Richmond, Va. Southern Baptist Convention, 1846. see Southern Baptist Convention, Richmond, 1846.

Richmond, Va. Southern Commercial Convention, 1856. see Southern Commercial Convention, Richmond, 1856.

Richmond, Va. Southern Female Institute. see Southern Female Institute, Richmond.

Richmond, Va. State Library. see Virginia. State Library, Richmond.

Richmond, Va. Superintendent of Public Schools. 71166

Richmond, Va. Theatre. 71180

Richmond, Va. Union Theological Seminary. 63298, 97820-97821

Richmond, Va. Union Theological Seminary. Library. 65644

Richmond, Va. University. Richmond College. 71203, 100550-100552

Richmond, Va. Washington Statue. (71183)

Richmond, Va. William Park Club. see William Park Club, Richmond, Va.

Richmond, Va. Young Mens Christian Association. see Young Mens Christian Association, Richmond, Va.

Richmond (District), Philadelphia. 61852

Richmond (Diocese) Synod, 1856. 72965

Richmond County, Ga. Public Meeting, 1860. 71214

Richmond County, N. Y. Board of Supervisors. 71215

Richmond County, N. Y. Medical Society. see Richmond County Medical Society.

Richmond County, N. Y. Society for Charitable and Religious Purposes. see Richmond County Society for Charitable and Religious Purposes.

Richmond age. 68398, (71194)

Richmond age, a southern electic magazine. (71194)

Richmond alarm. 71195

Richmond and Danville Rail Road Company. Chief Engineer. 71196

Richmond and Danville Rail Road Company. President. 71196

Richmond and Danville Rail Road Company. Stockholders. 71196

Richmond and Louisville medical journal. (71208)

Richmond and Manchester Colonization Society. Managers. 71196

Richmond and Ohio Railroad Company. Charter. 71198

Richmond and Petersburg Railroad Company. 71199

Richmond and Petersburg Railroad Company. Stockholders. 71199

Richmond and Washington in December, 1863. 63862

Richmond and York River Rail Road. 71200

Richmond Baptist Foreign and Domestic Missionary Society. 71201

Richmond city directory for 1866. (71174)

Richmond city ordinances. 71202

Richmond College, Richmond, Va. see Richmond, Va. University. Richmond College.

Richmond County Medical Society. 84093

Richmond County Society for Charitable and Religious Purposes. Board of Directors. 71216

Richmond directory and business advertiser, for 1850-1851. (71174)

Richmond directory and business advertiser, for 1856. (71174)

Richmond directory and business reference-book for 1845-46. (71174)

Richmond directory for 1855. (71174)

Richmond Domestic Missionary Society. 71177

Richmond during the war. 71204

Richmond eclectic. 88395

Richmond enquirer. 4366, 59645, 67039, 67527, 71577, 78888, 85198, 94494, 94091, 100555, 104878, note after 104881

Richmond enquirer and sentinel. 83775

Richmond examiner. 59645, 71205

Richmond examiner during the war. (18493), 71205

Richmond Female Institute, Richmond, Va. 71206

Richmond Female Institute, Richmond, Va. Stockholders. 71206

Richmond Garden, a poem. 99743

Richmond: her glory and her graves. 36642

Richmond in by-gone days. 50533

Richmond in ruins. 71135

Richmond, January 25, 1794. 100223

Richmond journals. 55834

Richmond lady. pseud. Richmond during the war. see Brock, Sallie A.

Richmond Library, Richmond, Va. see Richmond, Va. Athenaeum. Library.

Richmond medical journal. see Richmond and Louisville medical journal.

Richmond, state of Virginia. In convention . . . the 25th of June, 1788. 100034

Richmond, state of Virginia. In convention . . . the 25th of June, 1788. The convention . . . resolved itself into a committee. 100033

Richmond Street Church, Providence, R. I. see Providence, R. I. Richmond Street Congregational Church.

Richmond Street Congregational Church, Providence, R. I. see Providence, R. I. Richmond Street Congregational Church.

Richmond, Supervisor's-Office, Dec. 31st, 1795. 100413

Richmond, the capital of Virginia: its history. (41520)

Richmond times. 86294

Richmond whig. 78877

Richmond's book of legal forms and law manual. 77152

Richmond's pamphlets reviewed. 40516, 88113

Richmondville, N. Y. Lodge no. 446, Independent Order of Odd Fellows. see Odd Fellows, Independent Order of. New York. Richmondville Lodge no. 446.

Richmondville, N. Y. Union Seminary. see Richmondville Union Seminary, Richmondville, N. Y.

Richmondville Lodge no. 446, Independent Order of Odd Fellows. see Odd Fellows, Independent Order of. New York. Richmondville Lodge no. 446.

Richmondville Union Seminary, Richmondville, N. Y. 71218

Richszhoffer, Abrosius. 71219

Richter, Eugene. 16647, (71220)

Richter, Gustav. 71221

Richter, Karl Ernst. 71222

Richter, Moritz August. 51330, (57278), 71222-71224

Richthofen, Emil Karl Heinrich, Freiherr von. 71225-71226

Richthofen, Ferdinand, Freiherr. 9959, 71227-71228

Richtige Gegenmittle. 93686

Richtschnur und Regel eines Streiters Jesu Christi. 71229

Rickard, F. Ignacio. 71230-71231

Rickard, Truman. 71232-(71234)

Rickel, Dionisio. see Richel, Dionisio.

Ricker, Peter. 53473, 54042, 83604

Ricketson, Daniel. (71235)-71236

Ricketson, Shadrach. 71237

Rickey, Anna S. 71238

Rickey, Mallory and Company. firm 71239

Rickey, Mallory and Company's catalogue raisonne. 71239

Rickman, Thomas Clio. 22496, 71241-71244

Ricks, J. W. (71245)

Ricks, Joel. 83105

Ricla, Ambrosio Funes Villapando Abarca de Bolea, Conde de. see Abarca de Bolea, Ambrosio Funes Villapando, Conde de Ricla.

Rico, Francisco Cerda y. see Cerda y Rico, Francisco.

Rico, Juan. (68252), 71246-71247

Rico, Juan Joseph. 71248

Rico Frontaura, Placido. 71249

Rico, Villademoros, Domingo. see Villademoros, Domingo Rico.

Ricolo, --------. 40708

Ricon, Antonio del, d. 1601. (71412)-71413

Ricord, Elizabeth (Stryker) 1788-1865. 68391, 71250

Ricord-Madiana, J. B. 43701, 71251

Ricordi di un viaggio scientifico. 10738

Ricous, --------. 71252

Ricque, Camille. 71253

Riddel, Maria. see Riddell, Maria.

Riddel, Samuel Hopkins, 1800-1876. 1198, 97393

Riddell, John L. 56919, 67461, 71254-71255

Riddell, Maria. supposed author 67795, note after 71155

Riddell, V. P. (71156)

Riddle, Albert Gallatin, 1816-1902. 71258-71265

Riddle, Adam N. 84743

Riddle, D. H. 71266-(71269)

Riddle, George Read, 1817-1867. 71270

Riddle, John A. 71271

Riddle, M. S. 71272

Riddle, Samuel. 60273

Riddle. 60593, 71257, 103490

Riddle of riddles unriddled. 90150

Rimas de Bartolome Mitre. 49759
Rime di Gabriello Chiabrera. 12614
Rimes varias. (4949)
Rimius, Henry. 31583, 71404-(71410)
Rimouski vs. Bic et Chemin de Fer. 82786
Rinaldi, Piervincentio Dante de. tr. 32683
Rinaldini, Benito. 71411
Rincon, Jose. 71414
Rincon, Jose Antonio. (71415)
Rincon, Juan de Medina. see Medina Rincon, Juan de.
Rincon, Lucas del. (71416)
Rincon, Manuel. 71417-71418
Rincon, Manuel. defendant 71419
Rincon Gallardo, Francisco. defendant 81080
Rincon Gallardo, Teresa. plaintiff 81080
Rincon de las Salinas, part of the Bernal Rancho. 71420
Rind, William. ed. 23500, 90521, 99967, 100465
Rindge, N. H. Congregational Church. 71421
Ring, F. D. 71422
Ring, J. 71423
Ringgold, Cadwalader. 71424-(71425)
Ringgold, Cadwalader. defendant at court of inquiry (71426)
Ringgold, G. H. 71427
Ringier, John Henry. 80901
Ringmann, Matthias, 1482?-1511. (66478), 69125, 69126, 99333, 101017, 101022, 101025-101026
Ringrose, Basil. (23469), (23479), 23481-23484, 23486-23487, (23489)
Ringwalt, J. Luther. 71428
Ringwood, Thomas. 71429
Ringwood the rover. 31466
Rink, Heinrik Johannes. 23099, 71430-71440
Rink, Heinrik Johannes. tr. 71440
Rio, A. M. de el. see De el Rio, A. M.
Rio, Alphonso Mariano del. 71441
Rio, Andres del. 71442
Rio, Andres Manuel del, 1765-1849. 37108, 71443-71444
Rio, Antonio del. 71445-71447
Rio, Antonio Ferrer del. 71448-(71449)
Rio, Guillermo del. 71450
Rio, Ignacio Jordan de Asso y del. see Asso y del Rio, Ignacio Jordan de, 1742-1804.
Rio, J. Garcia del. see Garcia del Rio, J.
Rio, Jose Rivera y. see Rivera y Rio, Jose.
Rio, Joseph de Araujo y. 71451-71452
Rio, Juan de Aguilar del. petitioner 71453-(71454)
Rio, Manuel del. 71455 see also Peru. Ministerio de Relaciones Esteriores.
Rio, Manuel Rojo del. see Rojo del Rio, Manuel, 1708-1764.
Rio, Pedro Jimenez de Gongara y Lujan, Duque de Almodovar del. see Almodovar del Rio, Pedro Jimenez de Gongara y Lujan, Duque de, d. 1794.
Rio de la Loza, L. see Loza, L. Rio de la.
Rio de Loza, Augustin Joseph Mariano. 48391, 71474
Rio-Frio, Miguel Maria de. 99487
Rio Laubyan y Vieyra, E. R. del. see Laubyan y Vieyra, E. R. del Rio.
Rio de Janeiro (Archdiocese) Archbishop [ca. 1867] 79145
Rio de Janeiro (Archdiocese) Bishop (Monte Rodrigues de Araujo) 47590, 72500-72503 see also Monte Rodrigues de Araujo, Manuel do, Bp., 1798-1863.
Rio de Janeiro (Capitania) 7620
Rio de Janeiro (City) 71462
Rio de Janeiro (City) Academia. 79186

Rio de Janeiro (City) Academia Imperial das Bellas Artes. see Academia Imperial das Bellas Artes, Rio de Janeiro.
Rio de Janeiro (City) Bibliotheca Nacional. 74029
Rio de Janeiro (City) British Commissioner. see Great Britain. Consulate. Rio de Janeiro.
Rio de Janeiro (City) British Subscription Library. see British Subscription Library, Rio de Janeiro.
Rio de Janeiro (City) Capella Imperial. 81117
Rio de Janeiro (City) Cathedral. 81117
Rio de Janeiro (City) Convento de Sato Antonio 11736, 66386
Rio de Janeiro (City) Escolas. 69324
Rio de Janeiro (City) Gabinete Portuguez de Leitura. see Gabinete Portuguez de Leitura, Rio de Janeiro.
Rio de Janeiro (City) Huma Associacao de Litteratos. see Huma Associacao de Litteratos, Rio de Janeiro.
Rio de Janeiro (City) Imperial Instituto de Agricultura. see Imperial Instituto de Agricultura, Rio de Janeiro.
Rio de Janeiro (City) Imperial Instituto dos Meninos Cegos. see Imperial Instituto dos Meninos Cegos, Rio de Janeiro.
Rio de Janeiro (City) Instituto Historico e Geographico Brasileiro. see Brazil. Instituto Brasileiro de Historico e Geographico.
Rio de Janeiro (City) Instituto Polytechnico Brasileiro. see Instituto Polytechnico Brasileiro, Rio de Janeiro.
Rio de Janeiro (City) Museu Imperial e Nacional. see Rio de Janeiro (City) Museu Nacional.
Rio de Janeiro (City) Museu Nacional. 52358, (71459), 88783, 98833
Rio de Janeiro (City) Obsterreischischen Gesandtschaft. see Austria. Gesantschaft, Rio de Janeiro.
Rio de Janeiro (City) Palestra Scientifica. see Palesta Scientifica, Rio de Janeiro.
Rio de Janeiro (City) Sancta Egreja Cathedral. see Rio de Janeiro (City) Cathedral.
Rio de Janeiro (City) Santa Casa da Misericordia e Enfermarias Publicas. Hospital Geral. Gabinete Estadistico Medico-Cirurgico. 81102
Rio de Janeiro (City) Santa Casa da Misericordia e Enfermarias Publicas. Hospital Geral. Gabinete Estadistico Medico-Cirurgico. Director. 81102 see also Silva Brandao, Luiz da.
Rio de Janeiro (City) Sociedad Internacional de Immigracao. see Sociedad Internacional de Immigracao, Rio de Janeiro.
Rio de Janeiro (City) Sociedade Auxiliadora da Industria Nacional. see Sociedade Auxiliadora da Industria Nacional, Rio de Janeiro
Rio de Janeiro (City) Sociedade da Bibliotheca Popular Itaborahyense. see Sociedade da Bibliotheca Popular Itaborahyense, Rio de Janeiro.
Rio de Janeiro (City) Sociedade Internacional de Immigracao. see Sociedade Internacional de Immigracao, Rio de Janeiro.
Rio de Janeiro (Province) 71457, 71462
Rio de Janeiro (Province) Camara dos Deputados. 85649
Rio de Janeiro (Province) Constitution. 16977

Rio de Janeiro (Province) Laws, statutes, etc. 16977
Rio de Janeiro (Province) Presidente, 1839-1840 (Soares de Souza) 85645 (see also Soares de Souza, Paulino Jose, Visconde do Uruguay, 1807-1866.
Rio Amazonas y las comarcas que forman su hoya, vertientes hacia el Atlantico. 71456
Rio de Janeiro Anglo-Brazilian times. see Anglo-Brazilian times.
Rio de Janeiro, Buenos Ayres, ride through the pampas. 27179
Rio de Janeiro und seine Umgebungen, (71740)
Rio de Janeiro wie es ist. 71471, 77653
Rio de la Plata (Viceroyalty) Laws, statutes, etc. 8991, 26483, (68245)
Rio de la Plata (Viceroyalty) Real Audiencia. Senores Fiscales. 70090
Rio de la Plata Agricultural Association. 39001
Rio de la Plata, Buenos-Ayres, Montevideo. 19326
Rio de la Plata. Die revolutionare Politik. 71473
Rio de la Plata e Tenerife, viaggi e studi. 44398
Rio Grande, Brazil (Dutch Province) Regidoor. 58548 see also Paraupaba, Antonio.
Rio Grande do Norte (Mexican Province) Laws, statutes, etc. 71478
Rio Grande do Sul (Brazilian State) Presidente (Souza e Oliveira) 88765, 88768 see also Souza e Oliveira, Saturnino de, 1803-1848.
Rio Grande, Mexican, and Pacific Railroad Company. President. 71476
Rio Grande, Mexican, and Pacific Railroad Company. President. petitioner 71477 see also Lea, Luke. petitioner
Rio-Janeiro. 39300
Riofrio, Bernardo de. 71481
Riolano, Conradino. 45015
Riom de Prolhiac de Fourt de Pradt, Dominique Georges Frederic de. see Pradt, Dominique Georges Frederic de Riom de Prolhiac de Fourt de, Abp., 1759-1837.
Rionda, D. M. defendant 71482
Rios, A. F. de los. see De los Rios, A. F.
Rios, Epitacio J. de los. 71483
Rios, J. P. de los. 71484
Rios, Jose Amador de los. see De los Rios, Jose Amador.
Rios, Thomas Theran de los. see Theran de los Rios, Thomas.
Rios, Tomas. 71485
Rios Sanchez y Zarzoas, Manuel de Godoy Alvarez de Faria. see Godoy Alvare de Faria Rios Sanchez y Zarzosa, Manuel de, Principe de la Paz, 1767-1851.
Rios y Rosas, Antonio de los, 1808-1873. 67141
Riot act of 1855. 7336
Riot and outrage of the 9th June, in Montreal. 50285
Riot, murder, & arson. 5987
Riots in Congress. 85505
Riou, E. illus. 5134, (44507)
Rip van Bigham. 32994
Rip van Winkle. 35186, (35193)-35194, 71486
Rip van Winkle and his wonderful nap. 91067
Rip van Winkle Club of Westchester County, N. Y. 63817

Rip van Winkle's nap. 91067
Ripalda, Geronimo de, d. 1618. 27794, (71487)-(71491)
Riparian Association of New Jersey. see New Jersey Riparian Association.
Riparian rights on the Potomac. (36269)
Ripia, Juan de la. 71493
Ripley, Charles. 71494
Ripley, David B. (71495)
Ripley, Dorothy. 71496-(71497)
Ripley, Eleazar Wheelock. 70501
Ripley, Eleazar Wheelock. supposed author 23634, 55425, 71500
Ripley, Ezra, 1751-1841. 33109, 71502-71515
Ripley, Ezra, d. 1863. 71516
Ripley, George, 1802-1880. 19920, 52439, (71517)-71523, 83857
Ripley, H. W. (71526)
Ripley, Henry J. 71524-71525
Ripley, James Wolfe. 71528-71529, 91522 see also U. S. Army. Ordnance Department.
Ripley, James Wolfe. defendant 90872
Ripley, James Wolfe. defendant at court of inquiry 71527
Ripley, Roswell Sabine, 1823-1887. 15360, 71530
Ripley, Samuel. 71531-(71532)
Ripley, Thomas B. 71533
Ripley, William B. 71534
Ripley Female College, Poultney, Vt. 66959
Ripoli, Jaime Torrubiano. tr. 100622
Ripon, Frederick James Robinson, Earl of, 1782-1859. (22504), 69417, 72072 see also Great Britain. Colonial Office.
Ripon, Wisc. Ripon College. see Ripon College, Ripon, Wisc.
Ripon College, Ripon, Wisc. 71535
Ripperda, Joan Willem van, Duque, d. 1737. 71536-71537
Rippon, John. 71538-71539
Ripsnorter comic almanac. (71540)
Riquet, Georges Joseph Victor, Comte de Caraman. see Caraman, Georges Joseph Victor Riquet, Comte de.
Riquetti, Honore Gabriel. see Mirabeau, Honore Gabriel Riquetti, Comte de, 1749-1791.
Riquetti, Jean Antoine Joseph Charles Elzaer. see Mirabeau, Jean Antoine Joseph Charles Elzaer Riquetti, 1717-1784.
Riquetti, Victor. see Mirabeau, Victor Riquetti, Marquis de, 1715-1789.
Riqueza entre-riana. 79315
Rische, A. 6110
Rise, Julius. 71307-(71308)
Rise and continance of the substitutes. 71541
Rise and decline of oligarchy in the West. 58968
Rise and fall of pot-ash in America. 71542, 91309
Rise and fall of the Democratic Party. 5453
Rise and fall of the Emperor Maximilian. (37609)
Rise and fall of the grand South Sea bubble. 33198-33199
Rise and fall of the late projected excise. 70233
Rise and fall of the pro-slavery Democracy. 35849
Rise and operations of the Religious Charitable Society. 105410
Rise and progress of a remarkable work of grace. 7339-(7340), 85994
Rise and progress of error in the Church of Rome. 71956

Rise and progress of Methodism in Canada. (47211)

Rise and progress of Methodism in Cobleskill Centre. (79748)

Rise and progress of Minnesota Territory. 49306

Rise and progress of perfectionism in western New York. 2693

Rise and progress of revolution. 380, 105045

Rise and progress of Royal African and Assiento Companies. 33198-33199

Rise and progress of the doctrines of abolitionism. 71543

Rise and progress of the General Trades' Union. 71544

Rise and progress of the Methodist Society. 71545

Rise and progress of the people called Quakers. 59682, 59730

Rise and progress of the recent popular movements. 10407, (71546)

Rise and progress of the Young Ladies' Academy of Philadelphia. 62398, 2d note after 106135

Rise and progress of Trinity College, Toronto. 47479

Rise and progress of St. George's Church. 10940

Rise and progress of the bloody outbreak at Harper's Ferry. (30451)

Rise and progress of the Hoosac Tunnel. 30859

Rise and progress of the serpent. 21597

Rise and progress-the usurped dominion. 18717

Rise and travels of death. 105228

Rise of Canada. 72607

Rise of federal judicial supremacy. 84398

Rise of goods at vendue. 95964

Rise of the American constitution. 71312

Rise of the Dutch republic. 51109

Rise . . . of the New York Medical Institution. 4099

Rise of the republic of the United States. 26086

Rise of the west. 77876, 103695

Rise, progress and downfall of aristocracy. (46818)

Rise, progress, and effect of the claim. 15691

Rise, progress, and present state of medicine. 102065

Rise, progress, and present state of the dispute. (35471), 71547

Rise, progress, and present state of the Mormons. 11478

Rise, progress and present status of dentistry. 5605

Rise, progress, and prospects of the republic of Texas. 37440

Rise, progress and travels of the Church of Jesus Christ. 82585, 83283

Rise, spring and foundation of the Anabaptists. 7785, 78439

Risible, Ralph. pseud. Pickeroniad. 71548

Rising glory of America. 7190

Rising of the sun in the west. 97655

Rising-Star Lodge, no. 393, Yonkers, N. Y. see Freemasons. New York. Rising-Star Lodge, no. 393, Yonkers.

Rising Village, with other poems. 27720

Risk, T. F. 71549

Risler, Jeremias. 71550-71551

Risley, ------. illus. 83010-83011

Risley, Hanson A. 71552

Rispin, Thomas. 72113

Risposta ad alcune lettere. 71553

Risposta alla lettera scritta da un Gesuita. 71553

Risposta dello Eccellentissimo Messer Hieronimo Fracastoro. 67730

Risposta di Felice Isnardi. 35262

Risposta prima d'un Italiano. 71553

Ristretto delle historie Genovese. 34905

Rita Bastos, Rancisco Xavier de Sancta. see Sancta Rita Bastos, Francisco Xavier de.

Ritch, J. W. 71554

Ritchey, George W. 85072

Ritchie, A. H. illus. 71555, 101686

Ritchie, Andrew, 1782-1862. 71556-71557

Ritchie, Andrew, fl. 1857-1861. 71558-71559

Ritchie, Andrew, fl. 1857-1861. supposed author 86273

Ritchie, Anna Cora (Ogden) Mowatt, 1819-1870. 51206, 70282, 71560-71562, 81245

Ritchie, Archibald Tucker. 71563

Ritchie, David, fl. 1792. (71564)

Ritchie, David, 1812-1867. (71565)-71567

Ritchie, Elizabeth. 71568, 94539-94540, 103662

Ritchie, J. S. 71571, note before 93775

Ritchie, James. (71569)-71570, 73632

Ritchie, James S. 71571-71572

Ritchie, John, 1831-1887. 71573

Ritchie, John W. 56161, (56188)

Ritchie, Samuel S. defendant 8466, 89212

Ritchie, Thomas, 1778-1854. 39912, 71575-71577, 94091, 94494

Ritchie, Thomas, 1820?-1854. defendant 71578

Ritchie, William. 71579-71581

Ritchie's historical picture. 71555

Rites of funeral. (51443)

Rithaymer, George. 71582

Ritner, Joseph, 1780-1869. (45141), (59996), note just before 60250, (60509), 60528, 71585, note after 104493 see also Pennsylvania. Governor, 1835-1839 (Ritner)

Ritner, Joseph, fl. 1829. 71586

Rito Durao, Jose de Santa. see Durao, Jose de Santa Rito.

Ritratti et elogii di Capitani illustri. 71587

Ritson, Mrs. --------. 63648

Rittenhouse, David. 38792, (69759), (71588), 79775-79780, 82978, 84602, 84678C

Rittenhouse, J. B. 71589

Rittenhouse Academy, Washington, D. C. 71590

Rittenhouse's Executrices. defendants 57236

Ritter, Abraham. 71591-(71592)

Ritter, Carl. see Ritter, Karl, 1779-1859.

Ritter, Charles. 71593

Ritter, Henry. illus. 35196

Ritter, Karl, 1779-1859. 7457, (6988), 19987, 39977, 71594-71595, 89957, 105518-105519

Ritter, Stephan. 71596

Ritter, W. L. tr. 92519

Ritters von Chastellux Reisbeobachtungen uber America. 12231

Rittner, Heinrich. 71597

Ritual and illustrations of freemasonry. 71598

Ritual and songs of the col-water legions. 71599

Ritval formvlario. 6096

Ritual of degrees. (71600)

Ritual of the Methodist Episcopal Church. 48207

Ritual over Kirke-Forretningerne ved den Danske Mission. 22846

Ritual para la recta administracion. 76274
Ritvale, sev manvale Pervanvm. 57542
Ritualism of law. 9630
Ritualistic melody in four parts. 75306
Ritz, Philip. 71601
Ritzema, Johannes. 66448, (71602)
Riva-Aguero, Jose de la. 523, (66413),
    71603, 98755
Riva-Aguero, Jose de la. petitioner 71604-
    71606
Riva-Agues, ---------. 61127
Riva Palacio, Mariano. see Palacio, Mariano
    Riva.
Riva Palacio, Vicente. see Palacio, Vicente
    Riva.
Riva Villalon, Pedro de. 71633
Rivadavia, Bernardino. 71607-71608
Rivadeneira, Pedro de. see Ribadeneira,
    Petrus.
Rival administrations. 63862
Rival belles. A tale. 36537
Rival belles; or, life in Washington. 36532
Rival platforms. (71609)
Rival scouts. 22297
Rival volunteers. 33321
Rival war-chief. 72079
Rivals: a Chickahominy story. 29397, 71610
Rivals: a tale of the times of Aaron Burr.
    13620
Rivals of Acadia. 71611
Rivardi's Seminary, Philadelphia. see Mrs.
    Rivardi's Seminary, Philadelphia.
Rivarol, P. de. (71612)
Rivas, Diego Rodriguez, Bp. 71613 see also
    Guadalajara (Diocese) Bishop (Rivas)
Rivas, Federico. 71614
Rivas, Fidel. (71615)
Rivas, Manuel Joseph de la. see La Rivas,
    Manuel Joseph de.
Rivas-Cacho, Jos. M. (Franco Soto) de. 71616
Rivas-Cacho, Manuel de. plaintiff 71616
Rivas-Cacho, Manuel de. defendant 71616
River Amazons. 3933
River and harbor improvements. Letter of
    Senator Douglas. (29693A), (71617)
River and the sound. 71618
River communications of the British North
    American provinces. 61032
River guide. (35716)
River Improvement Convention, St. Louis,
    1867. 65907
River Improvement. Mississippi Valley
    memorial. 71619
River of God. 64625
River Plate as a field for emigration. 39003
River Plate. Further correspondence. 39002
River Plate hand-book. 71621
River Plate (South America) a field for
    emigration. 71620
River railroads. 84036
River St. Lawrence. 75321
Rivera, Alejandro Tapia y. see Tapia y
    Rivera, Alejandro.
Rivera, Antonio de. 98018
Rivera, Gregorio. 71622
Rivera, Jos. de. 71623
Rivera, Juan S. tr. 77364
Rivera, Manuel. (71624)-71626
Rivera, Mariano Galvan. see Galvan Rivera,
    Mariano.
Rivera, Pedro de. 19955 see also Spain.
    Visitador General de Precidios.
Rivera Bermudes, Joseph de. see Rivera
    Bermudez, Joseph de, Conde de Santiago
    de la Laguna.

Rivera Bermudez, Joseph de, Conde de Santiago
    de la Laguna. 4950, (71629), 76862
Rivera Cambas, Manuel. 71630
Rivera Indarte, Jose. see Indarte, Jose
    Rivera.
Rivera Maestro, M. 71631
Rivera Marquez, Pedro de. 71632
Rivera y Rio, Jose. 71634-(71637)
Rivero, Eladio Ramon del. 71638
Rivero, Joseph Bravo de. 71639
Rivero, Luis Manuel del. 71640
Rivero, Mariano Eduardo de. 71641-71645
Rivero, Nicanar. 25177
Rivero Cordero, Manuel. ed. 93346
Rivero y Ustariz, Mariano Eduardo de. 71646
Rivero y Zavala, Andres Bravo de. 71647
Rivero y Zavala, Diego Miguel Bravo de.
    7464, (71648)
Rivers, --------. tr. 1639, 100803
Rivers, David. 71649
Rivers, William James. (71650)-71652,
    87805A, 1st note after 87949, 88005,
    88086
Rivers and harbors. Speech . . . in the
    House. 11517
Rivers and harbors. Speech of Hon. E. G.
    Spaulding, of New York. 89041
Riverside Cemetery, Gouverneur, N. Y. see
    Gouverneur, N. Y. Riverside Cemetery.
Riverside in 1871. 71653
Riverside magazine for young people. (71655)
Rives, Alexander. 71656
Rives, Eugene de. pseud. Notice biographique.
    see Casgrain, H. R.
Rives, F. 71657
Rives, Francis E. 71658
Rives, J. 71657
Rives, John C. 4783, (15607), (71576)
Rives, William Cabell, 1793-1868. 71659-71682
Rives, William Cabell, 1825-1889. 71684
Rives, Mrs. William Cabell. 71683, 3d note
    after 94244
Rives. firm defendants see Blair & Rives,
    Washington, D. C. firm defendants
Rives et Compagnie. see Brown Rives et
    Compagnie.
Rivet, L. Banet. see Banet-Rivet, L.
Riviere, -------- Brutel de la. see Brutel de
    la Riviere, --------.
Riviere, E. 71685
Riviere, Leon. 71686
Riviere Paraguay. 51197
Rivieres Beaubien, Henry des. see Des
    Rivieres Beaubien, Henry.
Rivingstone. 34776
Rivington, Alexander. 71687
Rivington, James. ed. and publisher 1499,
    39708, 41456, (54420), 71688-71692,
    84565, 84653, 84842, 85104-85106, 89627,
    86929, 95916, 101739, 102835
Rivington, James. spurious author 93814
Rivington's army list. 41456
Rivington's gentleman and lady's pocket
    almanack. 71688
Rivington's new almanac for 1774. 71689
Rivington's New-York gazette. 71690, 101739
Rivington's New York gazette and universal
    advertiser. 71690
Rivington's New-York gazetteer. 39708, (54420),
    71690-71692, 84653, 84842
Rivington's New York loyal gazette. see
    Rivington's New York gazette.
Rivington's royal gazette. 1449, 71690, 84565,
    85104, 89627, 86929, 95916, 102835
Rivinus, Eduard Florens. 2305, 61455

Rivolta dei negri di San Domingo. (33613)
Rivors, C. 71693
Rivot, L. E. (71694)-71695
Rivulet. 71696
Rix, S. Wilton. 6144
Ro., Ric. 13033
Roa, Alonso de. 71697
Roa, Victoriano. 71698-71699
Roa Barcena, Jose Maria. 71700-71705
Roa Barcena, R. 71706
Roach, A. C. 71707
Roach, Isaac. plaintiff (7770)
Roach, John, b. 1748. 70763-70764, 71709,
    93907-93908 see also Rhodes, John, b.
    1755.
Roach, John, 1813-1887. 71710
Road—Cumberland to District of Columbia.
    71711
Road laws of South Carolina. 87709
Road—Little Rock to Cantonment Gibson.
    71712
Road through Ohio, Indiana, and Illinois.
    71713
Road to happiness. 74672
Road to peace, commerce, wealth and
    happiness. (42462)
Road to peace through Pennsylvania via
    Washington. 71714
Road to ruin. 5540
Road to safety. 80805
Road. Zanesville to Columbus. 71715
Roads and railroads. 71716
Roads and walks. 71717
Roads and walks of the Central Park. 71717
Roaf, John. 71718
Roane, --------. 100581
Roane, Spencer. 23453, 2d note after 100462
Roanoke College, Salem, Va. (75760)
Roaster for Peter Porcupine. 14003
Roaster; or, a check to the progress of
    political blasphemy. 14031, 94025
Roath, David L. (71719)
Rob of the bowl. (37419), (37423)
Roback, C. W. (71720)
Robaglia, J. tr. 44699
Robarts, Henry. see Roberts, Henry, fl.
    1585-1616.
Robaud, J. L. Audibert. 71721
Robb, Charles. 31939, 41820
Robb, James, of Fredericton, N. B. 52557,
    71722-71724
Robb, James, 1814-1881. (71725)-71728
Robb, James B. 71728
Robb, John S. 71729-71730, 94822
Robb, T. P. 71732 see also Illinois. Sani-
    tary Commissioner.
Robber. 65490
Robberds, J. G. 71733
Robbers of Calabria. 97465
Robberte, ye Sonne ov Robberte, Duc ov
    Normandie. pseud. Ane poemme. see
    Robertson, Robert
Robbery justly rewarded. 100952
Robbery of the Bank of Pennsylvania. 42867
Robbins, Ammi Ruhamah, 1740-1813. (29905),
    51841, 71734-71737, 92962
Robbins, Archibald. 71738, 101008
Robbins, Asher, 1757-1845. 63685, (71739)-
    71751, 89222
Robbins, Chandler, of New York. 71803-
    71804
Robbins, Chandler, 1738-1799. (16101), 71752-
    71764
Robbins, Chandler, 1738-1799. reporter
    103350
Robbins, Chandler, 1801?-1836. (71765)

Robbins, Chandler, 1810-1882. 57935, (71766)-
    (71802), 101400
Robbins, Charles. 71805
Robbins, Christopher E. see also Rhode Island.
    Secretary of State.
Robbins, E. W. 71811
Robbins, E. Y. 71812-71814
Robbins, Eliza. 71807-71809, 5th note after
    94244
Robbins, Ephraim. 71810
Robbins, Frank L. 71815
Robbins, Gilbert. 71816
Robbins, George Robbins, 1808-1875. 71817
Robbins, Gurdon. 71818
Robbins, Harvey. 71819
Robbins, J. W. 71822
Robbins, James. defendant 6326, 1st note after
    96956, 1st note after 97284
Robbins, James J. (71820)
Robbins, James Murray, 1796-1885. (20619),
    (71821)
Robbins, John. 71824
Robbins, Jonathan. plaintiff 62898-62899
Robbins, Louis S. incorrectly supposed author
    71825, note after 91969, 2d note after
    94296
Robbins, Nathaniel. (71826)-71828
Robbins, Philemon. 71829-71831, 96091
Robbins, Robert. 71832, 104373
Robbins, Royal, 1787-1861. 11801, 71833-
    71834
Robbins, S. J. ed. (60342)
Robbins, Samuel D. 71835
Robbins, Samuel P. 71836
Robbins, Thomas. 71837
Robbins, Thomas, 1777-1856. 71838-71852,
    73140
Robbins, William B. 71853
Robbins' journal. 101008
Robe, James. (80666)-80667
Robeck, ------. 77124
Robello da Costa, Agost. see Costa, Agost.
    Robello da.
Roberdeau, Daniel. 61492
Roberdeau, Isaac. 71854-71855
Roberjot, -------. 71856
Roberjot's remarks on Mr. Biddle's discourse.
    71856
Robert, a slave. 71857, 97198
Robert, of Normandy. 66686
Robert, the Hermit of Massachusetts see
    Roberts, a slave.
Robert, --------, Chevalier de Saint. see
    Saint-Robert, -------, Chevalier de.
Robert, B. H. 83246
Robert, C. W. tr. 26734
Robert, Carlos. defendant 70124
Robert, Charles E. (71858)-(71859)
Robert, E. 26330
Robert, Joseph Lavallee, Marquis de Bois-.
    see Lavallee, Joseph, Marquis de Bois-
    Robert, 1747-1816.
Robert, Pedro. 15196, (34151)
Robert, T. 71860
Robert de Vaugondy, Gilles, 1688-1766. 38022,
    71861-71869
Robert de Vaugondy, Didier, 1723-1786. 8831,
    25913-25914, 38022, (47542), 71864-
    71866, 71870-71876, note after 98694
Robert and Harold. 28130
Robert Blake admiral and general at sea.
    20375
Robert Burton. pseud. see Crouch, Nathaniel.
Robert C. Schenck, U. S. A. 77584
Rob. Cobb Kennedy, the incendiary spy. 29482

Robert Dexter Romaine. pseud. see Payson, George.

Robert Dinwiddie, Esq; His Majesty's Lieutenant-Governor. 99990

Robert E. Lee. In memoriam. 39792

Robert Earle of Essex his ghost. 78369, 78379

Robert F. Stockton, Esq. 96929

Robert Fulton. 97936

Robert Fulton, an historical novel. 30853

Robert Fulton; roman historique. 30852

Robert Graham. 31436

Robert H. Ives vs. Charles T. Hazard and others. 35314

Robert Harris and his descendants. 30488

Robert Hermann Schomburgk's Reise in Guiana. (77791)

Robert Macaire of journalism. 49766

Robert Morris' property. 50869

Robert Morton. 74247

Robert Ramble. pseud. see Ramble, Robert. pseud.

Robert Ramble's scenes in the country. 67616

Robert Rusty-Turncoat. pseud. see Croswell, Harry.

Robert S. Paschall to John Moss. 50869

Robert Severne. 30114

Robert Slender's journey from Philadelphia to New York. (25894)

Robert Smith and the navy. 83828

Robert Smith's address to the people of the United States. 83818-83823

Robert Stanser. pseud. see Croke, Sir Alexander.

Robert White Smith vs. the Mutual Life Insurance Company of New York. 83881

Robert Comtaei Nortmanni De origine gentium Americanarum dissertatio. 15079

Roberts, ----------. engr./illus. 50185, 82375, 82379

Roberts, ---------, fl. 1692-1696. 29473

Roberts, A. pseud. Never caught. see Hobart-Hampden, Augustus Charles, 1822-1886.

Roberts, A. tr. 98299

Roberts, B. S. 71878

Roberts, B. T. defendant before church conference 71879

Roberts, Browne H. E. 71880

Roberts, Daniel. (71881)

Roberts, David, 1804-1879. (71882)-71883

Roberts, Deborah S. 78861

Roberts, E. J. 48794

Roberts, Edmund. 71884

Roberts, Ellis Henry, 1827-1918. 71885-71887

Roberts, F. J. 61864, 94335

Roberts, George, fl. 1726. 28539, (71888)

Roberts, George, fl. 1794. 71889, 104315

Roberts, George C. M. (71891)-71892

Roberts, H. tr. 35144

Roberts, Henry, fl. 1585-1616. 57926, (71893)-71896, 1st note after 97255

Roberts, J. supposed author 30394, 71899

Roberts, James Austin. 71897

Roberts, Job. 71898

Roberts, Jonathan. 60297

Roberts, Joseph. 71900-(71902)

Roberts, Joseph Jenkins, Pres. Liberia, 1809-1876. 71903-(71904)

Roberts, Lemuel. 71905

Roberts, Lewes. 71906-(71910)

Roberts, Louis A. illus. 91006

Roberts, Mary. (71911)

Roberts, Mary E. 52330

Roberts, Nathan, fl. 1824. 22935, 102555

Roberts, Nathan, fl. 1838. 71912

Roberts, O. 71913

Roberts, Oran Milo, 1815-1898. 71914

Roberts, Orlando W. 71915

Roberts, P. engr. 84357, 101820

Roberts, R. Biddle. 60375 see also Pennsylvania. State Agent, Washington, D. C.

Roberts, Robert. 71906

Roberts, Robert Ellis, 1809-1888. (1142), (19792)

Roberts, Samuel, b. 1800. (71918)

Roberts, Samuel, fl. 1818. (60060), 71916-71917

Roberts, Samuel W. (60218), 71920-71923 see also Little Schuylkill and Susquehanna Rail Road Company. Chief Engineer.

Roberts, Sarah C. plaintiff 93642

Roberts, Sidney. 71919

Roberts, Thomas. 71924

Roberts, Thomas P. 71925

Roberts, W. B. ed. 54763

Roberts, William, fl. 1763. 24841, 71926

Roberts, William, 1798- 71927-71929

Roberts, William C. 71930

Roberts, William F. (4121), 42006, (55750), (60152), (60219), (71931)-71935, 80027, note after 92907, 92911

Roberts, William L. 71936

Roberts, William Milnor. 60031, 60132, 73127, 71937-71940 see also Cumberland Valley Rail Road Company. Chief Engineer. Harrisburg and Lancaster Rail Road Company. Chief Engineer.

Roberts, William Randall, 1830-1897. (71941)

Roberts, Zophar. 71942

Roberts. firm engrs. see Butler & Roberts. firm engrs.

Roberts (George) firm publishers 71890

Roberts (Sylvester) firm publishers (62196), 62236

Roberts' excursions in Central America. 16045

Roberts' Fund and China Mission Society. 37558

Roberts his welcome of good will. 71896

Roberts' ready reckoner. 71912

Roberts' second edition of the secret "customs." (62196)

Roberts' semi-monthly magazine. 71890

Robertson, --------. 71943

Robertson, ----------. intervenor 82145

Robertson, Rev. Mr., of Nevis. see Robertson, Robert.

Robertson, Alexander. ed. 73780

Robertson, Charles Franklin, 1835-1886. (71944)

Robertson, D. F. 71945

Robertson, David. reporter 9434-(9435), 10072, 100029

Robertson, F. M. 87907

Robertson, Felix. 94790

Robertson, George, 1790-1874. 13550, 71947-71951, 85376

Robertson, George, fl. 1815. 71946

Robertson, H. M. 71952

Robertson, Ignatius Loyola. pseud. Sketches of public characters. see Knapp, Samuel Lorenzo.

Robertson, J. supposed author 100564

Robertson, J. B. 69561, 71957

Robertson, James, minister of Pottsburgh Church, Edinburgh 71955

Robertson, James, of Halifax. 71956

Robertson, James, of Manchester, Eng. 71954

Robertson, James, wool merchant defendant 71953

Robertson, James, fl. 1770-1780. 60594, 73780, (73803)

Robertson, James, fl. 1840. 64962
Robertson, John. (71959)
Robertson, John, 1787-1873. 71958
Robertson, John L. 71980
Robertson, John Parish. 71961-71965
Robertson, Joseph Clinton. 60870, 71966
Robertson, Margaret. 71967
Robertson, Peter. alias see Hanly, Peter.
Robertson, Robert. 3291, 10894, (27313),
 71968-71969, note before 93803, 105937
Robertson, Samuel. (71970)
Robertson, Thomas Bolling, 1784-1828.
 (71971)-(71972) see also Louisiana.
 Governor, 1820-1824 (Robertson)
Robertson, W. S. (51587), 51589, 72017-72020
Robertson, William, 1721-1793. 1558, 26881,
 40952, 50222, 56308-56310, 65295,
 69144, 71973-72015, 85593, 91674,
 96144, 96333
Robertson, William, 1753-1835. ed. 71974
Robertson, William Parish. 71961-71965,
 72016
Robertson, William Spence. 83640
Robertson, Wyndham. 72021-(72022), 82823
Robertson, firm see Robertson, Mills and
 Hicks. firm publishers
Robertson, Mills and Hicks. firm publishers
 73780 see also Mills and Hicks. firm
 publishers
Robertson's tracts. 3291, note before 93803
Robertus Monachus. 72023
Roberval, ------ de. 11143
Robeson, George Maxwell, 1829-1897. 72024
 see also U. S. Navy Department.
Robie, Joseph. 72713
Robie, Thomas, 1689-1729. 40378, 62743,
 72025-72029
Robin, Ch. 72030
Robin, Claude C. 67461, 72031-72041, 3d
 note after 100807
Robin, Jean. 32024, 72042
Robin, Poor. pseud. see Poor Robin. pseud.
Robin Hood and Captain Kidd. 37704
Robin Hood, or, Sherwood Forest. 86926
Robin-Hood Society, New York. (54233)
Robina, Juan Joseph. defendant 86377 see
 also Lima, Peru. Tribunal de Quentas.
 Contador. defendant
Robineau, Rene, Sieur de Bethencourt.
 petitioner 72043
Robinet, --------. supposed ed. (491)
Robins, --------. 8582
Robins, Benjamin. 419, 1629, 72044, 101175
Robins, E. 17216
Robins, Gurdon. 72045
Robins, James, d. 1836. 78349
Robins, John. defendant 96887
Robins, Seelin. 72046
Robins, Thomas E. 72047
Robinson, -------. illus. 36666
Robinson, -------. plaintiff 96923
Robinson, -------, fl. 1735. 69403, 79623,
 93181
Robinson, -------, fl. 1778. 4746, 4th note
 after 99800
Robinson, -------, fl. 1802. 59316
Robinson, -------, fl. 1816. supposed author
 59634
Robinson, -------, fl. 1831. 41888, (60572)
Robinson, A. P. 57977, (72050)
Robinson, Alfred. (10031), 72048
Robinson, Alvan. (72049)
Robinson, Anne Steele. 72051
Robinson, Anthony. 72052
Robinson, Benjamin. 72053

Robinson, Charles. 72055-72056 see also
 Charlestown, Mass. Mayor, 1865-1866
 (Robinson)
Robinson, Charles, 1818-1894. 37034-37035
 see also Kansas. Governor, 1861-1863
 (Robinson)
Robinson, Charles, 1818-1894. defendant at
 impeachment 72057 see also Kansas.
 Governor, 1861-1863 (Robinson) defendant
 at impeachment
Robinson, Charles, fl. 1836. 105883
Robinson, Charles D. 72058
Robinson, Charles S. 72059-(72060)
Robinson, Christopher, 1806-1889. (72061)
Robinson, Conway. ed. 22975, 72062-72064,
 72117, 4th note after 99888
Robinson, D. G. 72066
Robinson, Daniel. 43969, 72065
Robinson, E. T. 72068
Robinson, Edward. defendant 6326, 1st note
 after 96956, 1st note after 97284
Robinson, Edward, 1794-1863. 72067, 82708,
 72819
Robinson, Mrs. Edward. see Robinson,
 Therese Albertine Louise (von Jacob)
 1797-1869.
Robinson, Fay. tr. (12591)
Robinson, Fayette. 72069-(72071)
Robinson, Frederick, fl. 1831-1832. 72073-
 72077
Robinson, Frederick James. see Ripon,
 Frederick James Robinson, Earl of,
 1782-1859.
Robinson, G. 72078
Robinson, G. W. 72079
Robinson, George D. 85212 see also Massa-
 chusetts. Special Commissioner on the
 Appeal of Egbert C. Smyth from the
 Visitors of the Theological Institution
 in Phillips Academy in Andover.
Robinson, H. H. 57068
Robinson, Heaton Bowstead. 72081
Robinson, Henry, 1605?-1664? 72082-72083
Robinson, Henry, fl. 1865. 84900
Robinson, Howard S. 86510
Robinson, Isaac. 72084-72086
Robinson, J. tr. 12242
Robinson, James. 72087
Robinson, James, fl. 1802-1804. 2998, 61606
Robinson, John, of Richmond, Va. ed. 72117
Robinson, John. portrait painter 72116
Robinson, John, 1575-1625. 29818, 56357,
 72088-72102, 72104-72110, (74456)
Robinson, John, fl. 1655-1657. (72111)-72112
Robinson, John, 1727-1802. 34846, 72113
Robinson, John, 1768-1843. 72114
Robinson, John, 1782-ca. 1833. 72115, (77255)
Robinson, John, 1814-1848. 72118
Robinson, John Bell. 431, 72122-72124 see
 also Maj. Gen. Geo. B. McClellan Club,
 Philadelphia. Corresponding Secretary.
Robinson, Sir John Beverley, Bart., 1791-1863.
 33075, 72119-72121, 79623, note after
 104595 see also Ontario. Attorney
 General.
Robinson, John H. (72125)
Robinson, John Hovey, 1825- (72126)-72133
Robinson, John Larne, 1813-1860. 72135
Robinson, John P. 72136-72138, 75420
Robinson, John W. 72139
Robinson, John W. defendant at impeachment
 72057 see also Kansas. Secretary of
 State (Robinson) defendant at impeachment
Robinson, Joshua D. 72140
Robinson, Lucius. (72141) see also New York
 (State) Comptroller's Office.

Robinson, Lucius Franklin. 72142

Robinson, M. M. 72143

Robinson, Mark. 72144

Robinson, Mary S. (72145)-72148

Robinson, Matthew. see Montagu, Matthew
Robinson,

Robinson, Merritt M. 72156

Robinson, Michael. 62054

Robinson, Moncure. (42172), 59955, 60566,
61948, 72157-72159

Robinson, Montague. 62051

Robinson, Morgan Poitiaux, 1876- 91860

Robinson, Moses. 99062 see also Vermont.
Governor, 1789-1790 (Robinson)

Robinson, Peter, d. 1841. defendant 72160-
72164, 1st note after 97085

Robinson, Phinehas. 72165

Robinson, R. H. P. 15272, 26896, 72174

Robinson, R. T. (72175)

Robinson, Richard P. defendant (72166)-72168

Robinson, Robert, 1735-1790. 72169-72172

Robinson, Robert C. 72173

Robinson, Samuel. 61280, 2d note after
98997 see also Proprietors of the
New Hampshire Grants. Attorney.

Robinson, Dr. Samuel. 72176

Robinson, Samuel, fl. 1754. petitioner
100928

Robinson, Sara T. L. 72178

Robinson, Sarah. 72177

Robinson, Simon W. 72179

Robinson, Solon. 48230, (54083), 55796,
72180-72183, 88276 see also American
Widows Relief Association, New York.
Secretary.

Robinson, Stuart. 72184

Robinson, T. B. (71972)

Robinson, Tancred. (72185)-72187

Robinson, Therese Albertine Louise (von
Jacob) 1797-1869. 62636, 72188-72191,
2d note after 94271

Robinson, Thomas. 71926

Robinson, Thomas H. 72192-(72196)

Robinson, Thomas Romney. 72197

Robinson, Tracy. 72198

Robinson, William, fl. 1669. 5629, 28099,
72199, 91318-91320

Robinson, William Davis. 72200-72206

Robinson, William Erigena, 1814-1892.
72207-72212

Robinson, William L. 19958, 72213

Robinson, William S. (72214)-72217

Robinson and Jones. firm publishers 13085

Robinson Americain. 16527, 61428

Robinson and Jones' Cincinnati directory for
1846. 13085

Robinson Bresilien. 77896

Robinson Crusoe. pseud. Serious reflections.
79266

Robinson Crusoe. 16303, 19286-19287, 19554,
note after 72217

Robinson Crusoe: or, the bold buccaniers.
63516

Robinson Crusoe's almanac for 1813. 72239

Robinson Crusoe's island down to the present
time. 72224, note before 93805

Robinson Crusoeus. 72233

Robinson der Jungere. 72233

Robinson der Jungere. Ein Lesebuch fur
Kinder. 72232

Robinson der Oberosterreicher. 72234

Robinson Female Seminary, Exeter, N. H.
72240

Robinson, vs. Lorillard. 96923

Robinson's Erlebnisse, Abenteuer und Fahrten.
2694

Robinson's original annual directory for 1817.
61606

Robinson's Philadelphia register and city
directory. 61606

Robinson's Reise um die Welt. 10308

Robiquet, A. 72241

Robison, John. 72242, (72244)

Robledo, --------. supposed author 68790

Robeldo, Maria de las Nieves. 72245

Robeldo, Miguel. 72246

Robles, Antonio de. (48440), 72247-72248

Robles, Francisco. (72249)

Robles, Juan. of Antequera 72251

Robles, Juan de, d. 1698. 72250

Robles, Nicolas. 72252

Robles Dominguez de Mazariegos, Mariano.
72254

Robles Pezuela, Luis. see Pezuela, Luis
Robles.

Robles Pezuela, Manuel. 72253

Robley, John. supposed author 60985, 72255,
1st note after 102858

Roblot, Charles. 72256

Robolsky, H. ed. 24754

R'ob'ons'in Kruzo'z il'and. (72223), note
after 93791

Robredo, Antonio. 72257-(72258)

Robson, Elizabeth. 103059

Robson, Joseph. (72259)-72260

Robson, Mary. see Hugh, Mary (Robson)

Robson, W. 72261

Roby, John. (72262)-72263

Roby, Joseph. 72264-72265

Robynson, Raphe. tr. 50544, 50545

Roca, J. J. de la. plaintiff 71616

Roca, Ramon de la. 18671, 72266-72267

Rocafuerte, Vicente. 6456, 29132, 34178, 1st
note after 72267, 72268-72281, 98947

Rocaful, Melchor de Navarra y. see Navarra
y Rocaful, Melchor de, Duque de la
Palata.

Rocamora y Torrano, Gines. 72282

Rocca, F. A. 72283

Rocchietti, Joseph. 72284-(72285)

Roch, E. 72286

Roch, Patrick. appellant 72287

Rocha, Diego Andres. 72288-(72290)

Rocha, Francisco de Rojas y. see Rojas y
Rocha, Francisco de.

Rocha, Jesus de la. 72291-72292

Rocha, Jose. (72293)

Rocha, Jose Gomes da. 72294

Rocha, Juan Ignacio de la. (72295)

Rocha, Juan Sanchez de la. see Sanchez de la
Rocha, Juan.

Rocha, P. F. la. see La Rocha, P. F.

Rocha, Pedro Francisco de la. 72296

Rocha Cabral, Jose Marcellino da. 72297-
(72298)

Rocha Ferreira Lapa, Ludgero da. see Lapa,
Ludgero da Rocha Ferreira.

Rocha Leao, Jose da. see Leao, Jose da
Rocha.

Rocha Loureiro, Joao Bernardo da. see
Loureiro, Joao Bernardo da Rocha.

Rocha Pitta, Sebastiao da, 1660-1738. 72299-
72301

Rocha Vianna, Antonio da. 72302

Rocha y Benavides, Pedro de Peralta Barneuvo.
see Peralta Barneuvo Rocha y Benavides,
Pedro de.

Rochambeau, Donatien Marie Joseph de Vimeur,
Vicomte de. 99745-99746

Rochambeau, Jean Baptiste Donatien de Vimeur,
Comte de. 72303-72304, 1st-2d notes
after 99746, 99747

Rochdale. 89481
Roche, -------- de. 39046, 72305
Roche, A. la. see La Roche, A.
Roche, Alfred R̲. 72306-72307, 93469 see
    also London Morning Post. Canada
    Correspondent.
Roche, Benjamin la. see Laroche, Benjamin,
    1797-1852.
Roche, Edward. 72308
Roche, H. P. 31125
Roche, J. L. 72310
Roche, James. (72309)
Roche, John. 72311
Roche, Martin. 72312
Roche, Pierre Marie Sebastien Catineau de la.
    see Catineau-Laroche, Pierre Marie
    Sebastien.
Roche, R. la. see La Roche, R.
Roche, Richard W̲. 72313
Roche, Sophie von la. see La Roche, Sophie
    von.
Roche Gallichon, F. C. de la. see La Roche
    Gallichon, F. C. de.
Roche-Heron, C. de la. e̲d̲. 19202
Roche-Tillac, Jean Charles Poncelin de la.
    see Poncelin de la Roche-Tillac, Jean
    Charles, 1746-1828.
Rochefort, Cesar de. incorrectly supposed
    author 72314
Rochefort, Charles de. 5040, 72314-72326,
    (77989)
Rochefort, Henri. 72327
Rochefoucauld, Francois, D̲u̲c̲ de la, 1613-1680.
    72328-72329
Rochefoucauld-Liancourt, Francois Alexandre
    Frederic, D̲u̲c̲ de la, 1747-1827. see La
    Rochefoucauld-Liancourt, Francois
    Alexandre Frederic, D̲u̲c̲ de la, 1747-
    1827.
Rochelle, Jean Baptiste Gaspard Roux de.
    see Roux de Rochelle, Jean Baptiste
    Gaspard, 1762-1849.
Rochelle, Jean Francois Nee de la. see Nee
    de la Rochelle, Jean Francois, 1751-
    1838.
Rochemore, -------- de. 47509 see also
    France. Ministere de la Marine.
Rochemore, Sieur de. see Rochemore,
    Vincent-Gaspard Pierre de, Sieur.
Rochemore, Vincent Gaspard Pierre de,
    Sieur. 72330
Rochemore, Vincent Gaspard Pierre de, Sieur.
    plaintiff 47509, 72330
Roches, V. de. 72331
Roches de Parthenay, ------- des. see Des
    Roches de Parthenay, ---------.
Rochester, Archdeacon of. see Denne, John.
Rochester, Bishop of. see Bradford, Samuel,
    successively Bishop of Carlisle, and
    Rochester, 1652-1731. Dampier, Thomas,
    successively Bishop of Rochester, and
    Ely, 1748-1812. Horsley, Samuel, suc-
    cessively Bishop of St. Davids, Roch-
    ester, and St. Asaph, 1733-1806.
    Thomas, John, Bishop of Rochester,
    1712-1793. Turner, Francis, succes-
    sively Bishop of Rochester, and Ely,
    1638?-1700. Wilcocks, Joseph, succes-
    sively Bishop of Gloucester, and Roch-
    ester, 1673-1756.
Rochester, Mass. Herring Inspectors. 72337
Rochester, Mass. School Committee. 72334-
    72337
Rochester, Mass. Selectmen. 72334, 72337
Rochester, Mass. Superintendent of Schools.
    72336

Rochester, N. Y. Athenaeum and Mechanics'
    Association. 72355
Rochester, N. Y. Athenaeum and Mechanics'
    Association. Board of Directors. 72355
Rochester, N. Y. Athenaeum and Mechanics'
    Association. Library. 72355
Rochester, N. Y. Athenaeum and Mechanics'
    Association. President. 72355
Rochester, N. Y. Athenaeum and Mechanics'
    Association. Standing Committees.
    72355
Rochester, N. Y. Athenaeum—Young Men's
    Association. (72354)-72355
Rochester, N. Y. Athenaeum—Young Men's
    Association. Charter. 72355
Rochester, N. Y. Board of Common Council.
    see Rochester, N. Y. Common Council.
Rochester, N. Y. Board of Education. 72366
Rochester, N. Y. Board of Health. (72351)
Rochester, N. Y. Board of Water Commission-
    ers. 72369
Rochester, N. Y. Charter. 72338, 72345,
    72353
Rochester, N. Y. City Attorney. (72346),
    72353 see also Raymonds, Edmund A.
    Shepherd, Jesse.
Rochester, N. Y. City Library. 72355
Rochester, N. Y. Colored National Convention,
    1853. see Colored National Convention,
    Rochester, N. Y., 1853.
Rochester, N. Y. Committee of the Friends
    of the Present Administration, 1842.
    see Whig Party. New York. Rochester.
Rochester, N. Y. Common Council. 72349,
    72353, 72365
Rochester, N. Y. Convention Upon the Subject
    of an Immediate Enlargement of the
    Erie Canal, 1837. see Convention Upon
    the Subject of an Immediate Enlargement
    of the Erie Canal, Rochester, 1837.
Rochester, N. Y. Free Academy. see Free
    Academy, Rochester, N. Y.
Rochester, N. Y. Health Officer. (72343)
    see also Langworth, Henry H.
Rochester, N. Y. Industrial School. see
    Industrial School, Rochester, N. Y.
Rochester, N. Y. Ingham University. see
    Ingham University, Rochester, N. Y.
Rochester, N. Y. Inhabitants Interested in the
    Use of the Waters of the Genesee, for
    Hydraulic Purposes. petitioners 72344
Rochester, N. Y. Junior Pioneer Association.
    see Junior Pioneer Association of the
    City of Rochester and Monroe County,
    N. Y.
Rochester, N. Y. Juvenile Reform Society.
    see Rochester Juvenile Reform Society.
Rochester, N. Y. Ladies Anti-slavery Sewing
    Society. see Rochester Ladies Anti-
    slavery Sewing Society.
Rochester, N. Y. Ladies Anti-slavery Society.
    see Rochester Ladies Anti-slavery
    Society.
Rochester, N. Y. Ladies' Hospital Relief
    Association. see Ladies' Hospital Relief
    Association, Rochester, N. Y.
Rochester, N. Y. Libraries. 72339
Rochester, N. Y. Meeting of the Citizens
    With Reference to the Improvement of
    the Erie Canal, 1839. see Western
    Canal Convention, Rochester, N. Y.,
    1839.
Rochester, N. Y. Ordinances, etc. 72345-
    72346, 72353, 72366
Rochester, N. Y. Pioneers. see Pioneers of
    Rochester.

Rochester, N. Y. Plymouth Church. (72347).
Rochester, N. Y. Printers' Festival, 1847.
see Printers' Festival, Rochester,
N. Y., 1847.
Rochester, N. Y. Public Meeting to Consider
the Condition of the Public Schools,
1838. Committee. 72366
Rochester, N. Y. Public Schools. 72366
Rochester, N. Y. Sabbath Convention, 1842.
see Sabbath Convention, Rochester,
N. Y., 1842.
Rochester, N. Y. State Convention for
Rescuing the Canals from the Ruin With
Which They are Threatened, 1859. see
New-York State Convention for Rescuing
the Canals from the Ruin With Which
They are Threatened, Rochester, 1859.
Rochester, N. Y. State Convention to Con-
sider Measures for Reforming the
Management and Improving the Trade
of the . . . Canals, 1870. see State
Convention to Consider Measures for
Reforming the Management and Im-
proving the Trade of the . . . Canals,
Rochester, N. Y., 1870.
Rochester, N. Y. State Industrial School.
see New York (State) State Industrial
School, Rochester.
Rochester, N. Y. Superintendent of Public
Schools. 72366
Rochester, N. Y. Theological Seminary.
see Rochester Theological Seminary,
Rochester, N. Y.
Rochester, N. Y. Trinity Church. 72367
Rochester, N. Y. University. 72363, 72368
Rochester, N. Y. University. Board of
Trustees. 72368
Rochester, N. Y. University. Collegiate
Department. 72368
Rochester, N. Y. University. Theological
Seminary. see Rochester Theological
Seminary.
Rochester, N. Y. Western Canal Convention,
1839. see Western Canal Convention,
Rochester, N. Y., 1839.
Rochester, N. Y. Western House of Refuge
for Juvenile Delinquents. see New York
(State) State Industrial School, Rochester.
Rochester, N. Y. Woman's Rights Convention,
1848. see Woman's Rights Convention,
Rochester, N. Y., 1848.
Rochester, N. Y. Young Men's Association.
see Young Men's Association, Rochester,
N. Y.
Rochester, N. Y. Young Men's Christian
Association. see Young Men's Christian
Association, Rochester, N. Y.
Rochester, Vt. 104393
Rochester (Diocese) Synod, 1875. 72966
Rochester, a satire. 46849
Rochester and Brockport directory. 72340
Rochester and Chatham Anti-slavery Society.
72370
Rochester and Monroe County business
directory. 72340
Rochester Athenaeum and Mechanics' Associa-
tion. see Rochester, N. Y. Athenaeum
and Mechanics' Association.
Rochester Athenaeum—Young Men's Association.
see Rochester, N. Y. Athenaeum—Young
Men's Association.
Rochester Athenaeum—Young Men's Association.
Catalogue of the Rochester City Library.
72355

Rochester Athenaeum—Young Men's Association.
Proceedings of the Young Men's Associa-
tion. (72354)
Rochester directory. 72340
Rochester city directory and register. 72340
Rochester city directory, 1857-58. 72340
Rochester directory, containing a general
directory. 72340
Rochester directory for 1863-4. 72340
Rochester directory, for the year ending July
1, 1868. 72340
Rochester directory, no. 21, 1870. 72340
Rochester Free Academy. see Free Academy,
Rochester, N. Y.
Rochester in 1835. (57593)
Rochester in 1827. 72356
Rochester Juvenile Reform Society. 72357
Rochester knockings! (72358)
Rochester Ladies' Anti-slavery Sewing Society.
72359
Rochester Ladies' Anti-slavery Society. 72359
Rochester Lake View Water-Cure Institution.
72360
Rochester magazine, and theological review.
72361
Rochester, Monroe County, N. Y., January —
1859. 50667
Rochester, Monroe, Co., N. Y., October 1,
1869. 50668
Rochester mystery. 72362
Rochester new monthly. 54797
Rochester Presbytery. see Presbyterian Church
in the U. S. A. Presbytery of Rochester.
Rochester public schools. Thirtieth annual
report. 72366
Rochester reprints. 103202, 103205-103208,
103211-103212
Rochester Theological Seminary, Rochester,
N. Y. 72363
Rochester Theological Seminary, Rochester,
N. Y. Trustees. (54749)
Rochester Theological Seminary. University
of Rochester. 72363
Rochester token. 50640
Rochester Water Works Company. 72369
Rochester Water Works Company. Charter.
72369
Rochester Young Men's Christian Association.
see Young Men's Christian Association,
Rochester, N. Y.
Rochomerus, Ludochus. 77804
Rochon, Alexis Marie de, 1741-1817. (11716),
44594, 52580, (59572), 62957, 64396,
72371-(72372)
Rochoux, J.-A. 72373
Rock County Agricultural Society and Mechanics'
Institute. 29117
Rock County almanac and business directory.
72380
Rock formations. 21702, (53688), 3d note
after 98549
Rock Hill College, Ellicott City, Md. 72384
Rock Island, Ill. Board of Trade. (72397)
Rock Island, Ill. Citizens. petitioners 51925
Rock Island, Ill. Medical School. 72394
Rock Island and its surroundings. 72396
Rock Island Bridge Company. defendants 72395
Rock Island directory and advertiser. 89395
Rock Island: her present and future. (72397)
Rock me to sleep. 50955
Rock of ages. 84060
Rock oils of Ohio. 54895
Rock River Baptist Association. see Baptists.
Illinois. Rock River Baptist Association.

Rock-River Conference of the Methodist Episcopal Church. see Methodist Episcopal Church. Illinois. Rock-River Conference.

Rock River Seminary, Mount Morris, Ill. 72411

Rock River Valley Union Rail Road Company. 72413

Rockafield, H. A. 72374

Rockaway, N. J. Church. 72375

Rockbridge Alum Springs, Virginia. 72377

Rockford, Ill. Burnham's Commercial and Mathematical Institute. see Burnham's Commercial and Mathematical Institute, Rockford, Ill.

Rockford, Ill. Female Seminary. see Rockford Female Seminary, Rockford, Ill.

Rockford, Ill. Seminary. see Rockford Female Seminary, Rockford, Ill.

Rockford Female Seminary, Rockford, Ill. 72382-72383

Rockford parish. 55904

Rockford Seminary, Rockford, Ill. see Rockford Female Seminary, Rockford, Ill.

Rockford Seminary . . . a collegiate institute for young women. 72383

Rockingham County, N. H. Agricultural Society. see Rockingham Agricultural Society.

Rockingham County, N. H. Convention, Brentwood, 1812. see Brentwood, N. H. Convention, 1812.

Rockingham County, N. H. Convention, Kingston Plains, 1812. see Brentwood, N. H. Convention, 1812.

Rockingham County, N. H. Convention Relative to the Observance of the Lord's Day, and to the Suppression of Vice, Exeter, 1815. (72389)

Rockingham County, N. H. Court of Common Pleas. 98052-98053

Rockingham County, N. H. Democratic Convention, 1812. see Democratic Party. New Hampshire. Rockingham County.

Rockingham County, N. H. Fair. 72392

Rockingham County, N. H. Teacher's Institute, Exeter. (72385)

Rockingham County, Va. Circuit Court. 48146

Rockingham Agricultural Society. 72386

Rockingham Charitable Society, in New-Hampshire. 72391

Rockingham Conference of Churches. Annual Meeting, Chester, N. H., 1851. 72388

Rockingham Conference of Churches. Annual Meeting, Portsmouth, N. H., 1866. 72388

Rockingham Convention, Relative to the Observance of the Lord's Day, and to the Suppression of Vice, Exeter, N. H., 1815. see Rockingham County, N. H. Convention Relative to the Observance of the Lord's Day, and to the Suppression of Vice, Exeter, 1815.

Rockingham County Eastern Auxiliary Foreign Missionary Society. see Eastern Auxiliary Foreign Missionary Society of Rockingham County, New-Hampshire.

Rockingham County Convention. 72390

Rockingham County handbook for . . . 1856. 64424

Rockland, Me. Charter. 72399

Rockland, Me. City Council. 72399

Rockland, Me. Mayor, 1860. (72398)

Rockland, Me. Ordinances, etc. 72399

Rockland County, N. Y. Female Institute. see Rockland County Female Institute, Nyack, N. Y.

Rockland, Belfast, Camden & Thomaston directory. 72400

Rockland County Female Institute, Nyack, N. Y. 72402-(72403)

Rockland Female Institute, Nyack, N. Y. see Rockland County Female Institute, Nyack, N. Y.

Rockland Mining Company. Board of Directors. 72401

Rockman, Constant. 72404-72405

Rockport, Mass. 72410

Rockport, Mass. Auditing Committee. 72409

Rockport, Mass. First Congregational Church. 72408

Rockport, Mass. School Committee. 72406

Rockwell, Charles, 1806-1882. 72417-72420

Rockwell, Charles, fl. 1842. (72416)

Rockwell, E. F. 72421

Rockwell, Henry Ensign. (72422)

Rockwell, Joel Edson. 72423-72429

Rockwell, John A. 72430, 90793

Rockwell, John Arnold, 1803-1861. 72431-(72440)

Rockwell, Julius, 1805-1888. (72441)-72445

Rockwell, Lathrop. 72446

Rockwell, T. A. supposed author 101235

Rockwell, William S. 72447-72448

Rockwell family in America. (72422)

Rockwood, E. L. 72454

Rockwood, Elisha. (72449)-(72453)

Rockwood, L. B. 72455, 90777 see also New England Tract Society. District Secretary.

Rocky-Bar Mining Company. 72456

Rocky Hill, Conn. Congregational Church. 72457

Rocky Hill and rolling prairie. 72458

Rocky Mountain directory and Colorado gazetteer. 72459

Rocky Mountain Gold Mining Company of Colorado. 72460

Rocky Mountain Gold Mining Company of Colorado and New York. 72460

Rocky Mountain life. 74890-74891

Rocky Mountain saints. 91222

Rocky Mountain song book. 72461

Rocky Mountains. By Albert Bierstadt. (5266)

Rocky Mountains; or, scenes, incidents, and adventures in the far west. 35195

Rococo. 62965

Rocoles, Jean Baptiste de. 18911, 26858, note after 69259

Rocque, -------- de la. see La Rocque, --------- de.

Rocque, C. la. see La Rocque, C.

Rocque (Mary Ann) firm publishers 79332

Rocum, C. 72462

Rod for a fool's back. 102396

Rod for Dagonites. 82924

Rod, for the backs of the critics. 13877, 64161

Rod for the fool's back. 5598, 83831, 102396

Rodas, Andres. 72463

Rodd, D. tr. 26378

Rodd, Thomas. 49026

Roddan, John T. 72465

Rode. Indian chief 628, 66062 see also Three Maquas Castles (Indians) Sachems.

Rode, Charles R. 54459, 72466

Rode Fribytaren. 16524

Rodenbough, Theodore F. 72467

Roderic Rover, Esq. pseud. see Prentiss, Charles.

Roderick Roundelay. pseud. see Roundelay, Roderick. pseud.

Rodero, Antonio. 72468

Rodero, Gaspar. 72469

Rode's New York City directory. 54459
Rode's United States Post Office directory. 72466
Rodet, D. L. 72470-(72471)
Rodgers, Charles T. 72472
Rodgers, Esther. defendant 72691
Rodgers, J. Kearney. 84093
Rodgers, James E. Thorold. (13040)
Rodgers, John, 1727-1811. 40455, 41630, 47276, 65149, 72473-(72474), (78736), 97107, 104942, 104946 see also Eighteen Presbyterian Ministers in America. pseud.
Rodgers, John, 1771-1838. 72476
Rodgers, John, 1771-1838. defendant at court of inquiry 72475
Rodgers, John R. B. 72477
Rodgers, Nathaniel. 42037
Rodgers, Ravaud K., 1796-1879. 72478-72479
Rodiger, G. F. W. tr. 21185
Roding, Carl Nicolaus. 6184, 21068, 14891, 72480-72482
Rodman, Benjamin. 72484
Rodman, Benjamin. petitioner 72483
Rodman, J. 25415, 35146, 72485
Rodman, John. 72486
Rodman, Ruth. (52634)
Rodman, Samuel. 52505
Rodman, Samuel. petitioner 72487
Rodman, T. J. (72488)
Rodman, Thomas P. 72489-(72490)
Rodman, W. M. 72492
Rodman, Washington. 72491 see also Standard bearer. Editor.
Rodman, William M. 37757
Rodney, Caesar Augustus, 1772-1824. 31500, 72493-72494 see also U. S. Legation. Buenos Aires (Province)
Rodney, Daniel, 1764-1846. 33150 see also Delaware. Governor, 1814-1817 (Rodney)
Rodney, George Brydges Rodney, Baron, 1719-1792. 8828, 44972, 51314
Rodney, W. G. (26936)
Rodo, Juan Lope del. (72495)
Rodolph. A fragment. 62966, 72496
Rodrigo de S. Jose. 56427
Rodrigues, Francisco. cartographer 76838
Rodrigues, Jose Carlos. ed. (70317), 72497
Rodrigues, Miguel de Manuel y. see Manuel y Rodrigues, Miguel de, fl. 1780.
Rodrigues, Pedro, 1542-1628. 4826-(4827), 4829, 4833, 68329, 72499
Rodrigues de Araujo, Manuel do Monte. see Monte Rodrigues de Araujo, Manuel do, Bp., 1798-1863.
Rodrigues de Campos, Jose Paulo. see Campos, Jose Paulo Rodrigues de.
Rodrigues de Mello, Jose, 1704-1783. 47461-47462
Rodrigues de Mello, Jose, 1704-1783. supposed author (16831), 1st note after 100616
Rodrigues Seixas, Domingos. see Seixas, Domingos Rodrigues.
Rodrigues Velloso de Oliveira, Antonio. see Velloso de Oliveira, Antonio Rodrigues.
Rodriguez, Antonio Marquez. (72504)
Rodriguez, Carlos. 72505
Rodrigues, Casimira. defendant 98150
Rodriguez, E. illus. (48590)
Rodriguez, Eugenio. 72507-72508

Rodriguez, Francisco. 72509
Rodriguez, Gabriel, 1830-1901. 85710
Rodriguez, Galvan Ignacio. 72510-72511
Rodriguez, Ignacio. 72512
Rodriguez, Jose Carlos. 16052
Rodriguez, Jose Ignacio. (72513)-72515
Rodriguez, Jose M. de Cardenas y. see Cardenas y Rodriguez, Jose M. de.
Rodriguez, Jose Manuel. 69229, 72516-(72520)
Rodriguez, Jose Maria. (72521)
Rodriguez, Juan. 69211
Rodriguez, Juan Antonio. 72522
Rodriguez, Juan Francisco. 72523
Rodriguez, Manuel. 72524-72526
Rodriguez, Manuel. petitioner 72525
Rodriguez, Manuel del Socorro. 72527
Rodriguez, Marcos Jose. defendant 93402 see also Caracas. Administracion General de Tabaco. Fiel de Almacenes.
Rodriguez, Maria Moreno. see Zeballos, Maria Moreno (Rodriguez)
Rodriguez, Mathias. 72528
Rodriguez, Pedro. 72529
Rodriguez, Y. 72530
Rodriguez, Zorobabel. 86250
Rodriguez, Zorobabel. supposed author 86560
Rodriguez Cabrillo, Juan. see Cabrillo, Juan Rodriguez.
Rodriguez Carrazedo, Juan. 72531
Rodriguez Dantas, Dionizio. see Dantas, Dionizio Rodriguez.
Rodriguez de Arizpe, Pedro Joseph. 24154, 72532-72536
Rodriguez de Fonseca, Bartolóme Augustin. 72537
Rodriguez de Leon, A. J. 99689
Rodriguez de Leon, Antonio. (72538)
Rodriguez, de Leon Pinelo, Antonio. see Leon Pinelo, Antonio Rodriguez de, d. 1660.
Rodriguez de Mello, Jose. see Rodrigues de Mello, Jose, 1704-1783.
Rodriguez de Ribas, Diego, Bp., d. 1771. 29074, 72541-72542 see also Guatemala (Archdiocese) Bishop (Rodriguez de Ribas)
Rodriguez de San Miguel, Juan. 48906, 58417, 72543-72550
Rodriguez de Santo Tomas, Miguel. 72551
Rodriguez de Toro, Francisco. see Toro, Francisco Rodriguez de.
Rodriguez del Toro, J. 72540, 1st note after 96790
Rodriguez Delgado, Augustin, Bp. 16070, 72539 see also La Paz (Diocese) Bishop (Rodriguez Delgado)
Rodriguez-Ferrer, Miguel. 24179, 70304, (72553)-72554
Rodriguez Fernandez, Francisco. 72552
Rodriguez Freire, Jose. see Freire, Jose Rodrigues.
Rodriguez Guillien, Pedro. see Guillen, Pedro Rodriguez.
Rodriguez Lamego, Manuel. 72556
Rodriguez Leon, Juan. 72557-72559
Rodriguez Leon, Juan. petitioner 72560
Rodriguez Medrano, Balthasar. (72561)
Rodriguez Mello, Jose. see Rodriguez de Mello, Jose.
Rodriguez Monino, Antonio R. ed. 105724
Rodriguez Navarijo, Ignacio. see Navarijo, Ignacio Rodriguez.
Rodriguez Rivas, Diego. see Rivas, Diego Rodriguez, Bp.
Rodriguez Saenz de Pedroso, Pedro Josef. 48519
Rodriguez Sampedro, Joaquin. 72562

Rodriguez Santivanez, Alonso Antonio. tr.
99525
Rodriguez Santos, Francisco. see Santos,
Francisco Rodriguez.
Rodriguez Ucares, Jose. 72563-72564
Rodriguez Velasco, Francisco de Paula.
72565
Rodriguez y Arguelles, Anacleto. (72566)
Rodriguez y Calero, Jose Antonio. (72569)-
72570
Rodriguez y Cos, Jose Maria, 1823-1899.
72567-72568, 98852
Rodschied, Ernst Karl. 47353, 82571
Roe, E. A. 72572
Roe, F. A. 72573
Roe, Henry. 72574
Roe, Sir Thomas. 66686
Roebling, John A., 1806-1869. 55125, 58448,
72575-72577
Roebling, W. A. (72578)
Roebuck, Arthur. 10638
Roebuck, John. (72580)-72582
Roebuck, John Arthur, 1801-1879. (27639),
72583-72584
Roebuck: a novel. 72579, 74317
Roeder, Ole Munch. 72585
Roehig, F. L. O. 2251, 72586
Roel, Juan. 72587, 99654
Roelandszoon, J. van Wijk. see Wijk, Jacobus
van.
Roekler, Bernard. 72589
Roem-Waardige Zee- end Land-togten na
Nieuw-Spajne en Mexico. 16962
Roemeling, C. A. 72590
Roemer, Ferdinand. 82591-72594
Roemer, J. 72595
Roemer, J. J. (72597)
Roemer, Jean, 1815?-1894. 72596
Roep, van de doot, tot het leven. 91319-91320
Roer, Coopmans. engr. 97664
Roesby, Mary. see Roesly, Mary.
Roeser, Charles. (72598)
Roesgen von Floss, Ph. von. 72599
Roesly, Mary. 72600
Rofe, George. 72601-72602
Roff, Amos B. defendant 27438
Rog, John P., d. 1819. defendant (41584),
96944, 104281-note after 104281
Roger. pseud. Observator's trip to America.
56596, 67997
Roger, Mr. see Rogers, John, 1684-1755.
Roger, Abraham. 72603
Roger, Aime. 9045-9046, 72604 see also
France. Consulat. Buenos Aires.
Roger, Charles. 72605-72607
Roger Brooke Taney. 84515
Roger Clap's memoirs. 106052
Roger Pindar. pseud. see Pindar, Roger.
pseud.
Roger Plowman. pseud. see Plowman, Roger.
pseud.
Roger Williams. 92124
Roger Williams and the Baptists. 21807
Roger Williams in banishment. (21426)
Roger, Williams in Banishment. 21427
Roger Wren. pseud. see Wren, Roger. pseud.
Rogers, --------, fl. 1736. 11870
Rogers, Abner, Jr. defendant 5292
Rogers, Abraham. see Roger, Abraham.
Rogers, Ammi. 72608
Rogers, Andrew Jackson, 1828-1900. 72609-
(72610)
Rogers, Anthony Astley Cooper, 1821-1899.
72611-72612
Rogers, Artemas. reporter 23817
Rogers, Augustus Dodge. 72613

Rogers, Charles, 1800-1874. 72614
Rogers, Charles, 1800-1874. supposed author
90035
Rogers, Clark. 72615
Rogers, D. 62646
Rogers, Daniel. 72618
Rogers, Daniel. reporter 2879, 72617, 72619-
(72621), 82620, 96876, note after 96880,
note after 96921, 97250, 101441
Rogers, David. (72622)
Rogers, David W. (72623)
Rogers, E. 32860
Rogers, Edward Coit. 25773, (72642)
Rogers, Edward H. 72643
Rogers, Ebenezer Platt. 72624-72641
Rogers, George. 72644-72648
Rogers, Henry. 21974
Rogers, Henry B. 6574, 38788, 72649-72653,
97387 see also Association of Delegates
from the Benevolent Societies of Boston.
Secretary.
Rogers, Henry B. supposed author 12859,
(67211), 72651
Rogers, Henry D. 53113-53114, 60118-60119,
(72654)-72672, 86814 see also New
Jersey. State Geologist. Pennsylvania.
State Geologist.
Rogers, Henry J. 72673-72676
Rogers, Henry W. (72677)
Rogers, Horatio. 72678
Rogers, Isaac. 72679
Rogers, Isaac. illus. 22178A
Rogers, Israel L. 83160
Rogers, J. A. 42822
Rogers, J. G. 45994 see also Massachusetts.
Commissioners to Reduce the . . . Law
of Crimes and Punishments into a Syste-
matic Code.
Rogers, J. K. petitioner/claimant 90113
Rogers, James. 103661, 103665
Rogers, James E. Thorold. ed. 82303-82304
Rogers, John, d. 1555. 12541, note after
52712
Rogers, John, 1649?-1721. 72680-72687
Rogers, John, fl. 1654. 40120, 66211
Rogers, John, 1666-1745. 72691-72693
Rogers, John, 1674-1753. (46484), 64973,
72688-72689, 72692, 2d note after 97559
Rogers, John, 1684-1755. 72694
Rogers, John, 1712-1789. (72695)-(72696)
Rogers, John, 1800-1867. 18741, 72701, 92027
Rogers, John, fl. 1803-1812. 72697-(72698)
Rogers, John, fl. 1825. 72699
Rogers, John, fl. 1827. 72700
Rogers, John B. 72702
Rogers, John Henry. 72703
Rogers, John M. 72704
Rogers, John Smyth. 72705
Rogers, John W. 38599, 72706
Rogers, Josias. 27467
Rogers, Julia. 72707
Rogers, M. L. 72709
Rogers, Medad. 72710
Rogers, Molton Cropper, 1786-1863. 39172
Rogers, Nathaniel, 1598-1655. 72711
Rogers, Nathaniel, 1704-1775. 42037, 62646,
72692, (72712)-72713, 92099, 2d note
after 97559, 105074-105077
Rogers, Nathaniel Peabody. 72714-72716
Rogers, Nicholas. 45377, 72718, note after
95746
Rogers, Nicholas. incorrectly supposed author
50336, 72717
Rogers, Patrick Kerr. 72719
Rogers, Ransford. 72720-72722, 106070

Rogers, Robert, 1731-1795. 19788, 33138, 72723-72730, 84616-84618, 85254, note after 90518

Rogers, Robert Possac. (72731)

Rogers, Sally. illus. 72732

Rogers, Samuel. 72733, 2d note after 100814

Rogers, Sion Hart, 1825-1874. 72734

Rogers, Thomas J. (72735)-72737

Rogers, Timothy. (72738)

Rogers, Timothy Foster. 72739

Rogers, William. reporter 72744

Rogers, William, fl. 1687. 71906

Rogers, William, 1751-1824. 10221, 72740-72743

Rogers, William B., 1804-1882. 72670-72671, (72745)-72746

Rogers, William H. (72747)-(72749)

Rogers, William Matticks. 72750-(72752)

Rogers, Woods, d. 1732. (18386), 20518, 31389, 38163, (54897), 72753-(72761), note after 93778

Rogers' American code of marine signals. 72674

Rogers and Black's American semaphoric signal book. 72676

Rogers' marine telegraphic list. 72675

Rogerson, A. E. 61456

Rogerson, William. 14092

Rogge, H. C. tr. 63887

Roggeveen, Arent. (72762)-72766

Roggeveen, Jacob. 72767, 72768, 2d note after 100873

Rogniat, Calvet. 72771

Rogues and rogueries of New York. 72772

Rohan, Henrique de Beaurepaire. see Beaurepaire-Rohan, Henrique, Visconde, 1812-1894.

Roi des tropiques. 23555

Roisel, -------. 72775

Rojas, ------. 72776

Rojas, Alonso. see Roxas, Alonso de.

Rojas, Aristides. 72778-72789, 83947

Rojas, F. Michelena y. see Michelena y Rojas, F.

Rojas, Jose M. 72790-72794

Rojas, Pedro Jose. 72795-72797

Rojas y Andrade, Francisco. 72799-72803, 73622

Rojas y Canas, Ramon. (72804)

Rojas y Rocha, Francisco de. 26478, 72805

Rojo, Juan Jose. 72806

Rojo Costa, Juan. 72807

Rojo del Rio, Manuel, 1708-1764. 72808

Rojo y Calderon, Andres. see Roxo y Cale Calderon, Andres Joseph.

Roland, Bartholome. 72811-(72812)

Roland, William F. 72810

Roldan, Francisco Bermejo y. 72813

Roldan, Francisco Pasqual. (52250)

Roldan, Juan. 72814

Roldan de la Cueva, Jose. 72815

Roles, John. 72816

Rolet, A. tr. 92535

Rolf, Charles A. 77031

Rolfe, John. 52287

Rolker, Bernard. ed. and tr. 18116

Roll call. 72817

Roll call; or, how will you answer it? 48973

Roll of Company "C." 52506

Roll of former members of Chauncy-Hall School. 18122, 12341

Roll of honor. 1430, (45016), 51875, 72818-(72845)

"Roll of honor," being a catalogue of the names, &c. 26610

Roll of honor; comprising the names of all soldiers. 37822, 80997

Roll of honor; list of members of Bowdoin College. 7037

Roll of missing men. (3829)

Roll of state officers. 15850

Roll of students of Harvard University. 8471, 30760

Roll of the officers of the Virginia Line. 100521

Roll of the original, hereditary, and honorary members. 13127

Roll of the persons having office or employ- ment. 72847

Roll of the Senate and House of Representa- tives. 15849

Rolla and Cora. 8137, 80342

Rolla: or, the Peruvian hero. 38283

Rolla's Tod. 97573

Rolland, Jean Roth. 98394

Rolle, Denys. 92223

Rolle, Denys. petitioner 72848

Rollin, -----. (44825)

Rollin, Frank A. 72849

Rolling thunder. 72079

Rollins, A. P. 72950

Rollins, Edward B. 72851-72853

Rollins, Edward W. 72854

Rollins, Edward Henry, 1824-1889. 72855-72856

Rollins, James Sidney, 1812-1888. 72857-72863

Rollins, John R. (55960), 72864-72866

Rollinson, --------. engr. 101742-101743

Rollner, A. T. 41170, 72867

Rollo, E. M. 72868

Rollo, John. 31336, 72869-72870

Rolph, John. 41309, 72871-72873

Rolph, Thomas. 72874-72879 see also Canada. Government Agent for Emi- gration.

Rolt, Richard. 72880-(72883)

Roma, F. Raimondo da. see Raimonda da Roma, F.

Romagne, ------. 72885

Romagnesi, ------. 100727

Romain-Desfosses, ------. 20964

Romaine, Benjamin. (72886)-72889

Romaine, Robert Dexter. pseud. New age of gold. see Payson, George.

Romaine, Samuel B. 72891

Romaine, W. (72892)

Roman, Andrew Bienvenu, 1795-1866. 72893 see also Louisiana. Governor, 1839- 1843 (Roman)

Roman, Antonio de San. see San Roman, Antonio de.

Roman, Hieronymo. 72984-72995

Roman, James Dixon, 1809-1867. 72896

Roman de Nogales, Miguel. defendant 74860

Roman i Polanco, Gabriel. see Polanco, Gabriel Roman i.

Roman Allemand traduit par Benedict H. Revoil. 27194

Roman Americain, traduit de l'Anglais. 78801

Roman American traduit de l'Anglais par Lamst. 83512

Roman aus Amerika's Urwaldern. 4536

Roman aus dem Leben der Sklaven in Amerika. 92552

Roman aus dem Nordamerikanische Revolutions- kriege. 16535

Roman aus Kentucky. 5555

Roman Catholic Church and free thought. 66675

Roman Catholic element in American history. 26195

Roman Catholic manual, or collection of prayers. 72976

Roman Catholic population of our world. 4618

Roman Catholic prayer book. 19378

Roman Catholic Orphan Asylum Ladies' Association, New York. see New York (City) Roman Catholic Orphan Asylum Ladies' Association.

Roman Catholic Society of St. Joseph, Philadelphia. see Society of St. Joseph, Philadelphia.

Roman Catholics in Hawaii. see Hawaii (Diocese)

Roman Catholics of America. petitioners see Carroll, John, Abp.

Roman Catholics of New York. (54059), 54615 see also New York (Archdiocese)

Roman de moeurs Canadiennes. [Par P. J. O. Chauveau.] 12344

Roman de moeurs Canadiennes. Par Philippe Aubert de Gaspe. 26739

Roman et la realite dans la guerre du Paraguay. 13232

Roman father. 101866

Roman historique de C. Hauch. 30852

Roman historique. Par Ferdinand Denis. 19549

Roman historique, par M. Hilliard-D'Auberteuil. 31904

Roman history. 86491

Roman Indien. 12257

Roman maritime et de moeurs Creoles. 11519

Roman politique sur l'etat present des affaires de l'Amerique. 42896, (75520)-75521

Roman serio-philosophico-politico-bouffon. 16482

Roman traduit de l'Allemand par Gustave Revilliod. 78599

Roman tribute, a tragedy. 82517

Roman uit het tijdperk der Amerikaansche omwenteling. (16572)

Roman- und Nouvellen-Zeitung. 17936

Roman-Zeitung. 92402

Romance. 5553, 30190, 30994, 37767, 54960, 57888, (71719), (72071), 74166, (80152), 81245, 84890, 100443, 101417, 104923

Romance and beauty of the hills. 83336

Romance and humor of the rail. 84245, 84248

Romance and humor of the road. 84247

Romance; and other poems. 51700

Romance and realities of soldier life. 68573

Romance Brasileiro. 79128

Romance. By the author of "Francis Berrian." (24795), 80735

Romance corriente. 74607, 97019

Romance Cubano. 98827

Romance de D. Francisco Joseph de Soria. 87155

Romance de Veracruz. 100695

Romance dust from the historic placer. 47197

Romance en elogio de S. Juan de Dios. 76889

Romance, en que se procura pintar. 98380

Romance heroico. 98309, 98317

Romance heroico en elogio del M. R. P. Mtro. Fr. Juan Villa Sanchez. (76292)

Romance historico do Alto-Amazonas. 81100

Romance historico en que se refieren los sucesos acaecidos. 10811

Romance historico, por el autor del titulado La Invasion de Cardenas. 10812

Romance, in four cantoes. 82127

Romance in verse. 98340

Romance joco-serio descriptivo. 74016

Romance lastimoso. 10318

Romance lirico. 72978

Romance moral escripto em Inglez. 92598

Romance of a piano. 72979

Romance of aboriginal New England. 21155

Romance of American history. (7653)

Romance of American history, as illustrated in the early events. 3232

Romance of American landscape. 70967

Romance of border life. (64922)

Romance of business. 37767

Romance of Cambridge. (12728)

Romance of Carolina. 81278-(82179), 1st note after 106011

Romance of days not far distant. 35697

Romance of fashionable life in New-York. 64551

Romance of Hayti. 44937

Romance of Indian history. 72980

Romance of Indian life. By J. Springer. 89833

Romance of Indian life; with other tales. (21686)

Romance of Kentucky. (30191)

Romance of metrimony. 72981

Romance of Mexico. 5549-(5550)

Romance of military life. 16339

Romance of natural history. 28064

Romance of New England life. 51652

Romance of New-York. 23947

Romance of Old Bermuda. 83631

Romance of our own country in its ancient days. 8838, 36829

Romance of real life. 91287

Romance of southern life. 61254

Romance of the age. 21232

Romance of the Ashley. (70054)

Romance of the Blue Ridge. 88662-88663

Romance of the Canadas. (71040)

Romance of the Charter Oak. 79340

Romance of the Cuyahoga Valley. 71261

Romance of the frontier. 72183, 48230

Romance of the great rebellion. 18131

Romance of the Hartz Prison. (80152)

Romance of the history of Louisiana. 26797

Romance of the Indian country. (21916)

Romance of the Massachusetts colony. 51108

Romance of the Mohawk. 32385

Romance of the New World. 81270-81271

Romance of the nineteenth century. 105179

Romance of the ocean. 24947

Romance of the plains. 69071

Romance of the prairie. 69079

Romance of the present day. 46840

Romance of the Red Indians. 37319

Romance of the republic. (12727)

Romance of the revolution, and other poems. 92905

Romance of the revolution:·being a history of the personal adventures. 9158, 72982-72984

Romance of the revolution: being true stories. 72985

Romance of the revolution. By George Lippard. 41391

Romance of the revolution. By James Rees. 68643

Romance of the revolution. By W. Gilmore Simms. 81244

Romance of the revolution. With an appendix. 9214

Romance of the ring. 51700

Romance of the rivers. 9093

Romance of the road. 72133

Romance of the sea-serpent. 3906

Romance of the war. A poem. 74628
Romance of the war. [By James D. McCabe.] 42962
Romance of the west. 72133
Romance of the West Indies. 93417
Romance of trade. 95735
Romance of travel, comprising tales of five lands. 104514
Romance of Washington's aide and young Abigail Adams. 84904
Romance of western history. 29792
Romance of yachting. 30630
Romance of the philosophy of politics. 8003
Romance par Eugene de St. Quinton. (75479)
Romance tiree du roman et de la piece de ce nom. 92542
Romances en verse. 25052
Romances of southern landscape. (70969)
Romances of the sea. (2976)
Romances por Joaquim Manoel de Macedo. 43214
Romancist and novelist's library. 81217, 93418
Romand, H. 42715
Romane, I. B. 72986
Romanet, J. 72987-72988, 4th note after 100802
Romanism against republicanism. 58658
Romanism and republicanism incompatable. 2875
Romanism exposed. 86557
Romanism in America. 13362
Romanism in Mexico. 47103
Romanism in the United States. 4428
Romanism incompatible with republican institutions. 72989
Romanism not Christianity. 70854-(70855)
Romanism, the enemy of education. (70855)
Romano, Manuel. 72990
Romans, ---------. 1147
Romans, Bernard. (72991)-72997
Romans, Charles. cartographer 1147, 7326
Romans populaires illustres. 92531
Romantic adventures in field and forest. 70333
Romantic adventures in northern Mexico. 69069
Romantic incidence. (72998)
Romantic incidents in the life of James Fisk, Jr. 72999
Romantic incidents of a New-England town. 3904
Romantic passages in southwestern history. 47367
Romantic tale of high American life. 92741
Romanus, Andrianus. 63000
Romanzo maritimo. 16544
Romay, Tomas. 11292, 73001-73012, 85742
Romayne, James T. B. 73013
Romayne, Nicholas. 54376, (73014)-73015 see also Medical Society of the County of New York. President.
Romayne, Nicholas. supposed author (32961), 73016
Rombauer, R. J. 70317
Rombert: a tale of Carolina. 73018, 81252
Rombusto Pogommega. pseud. see Borbazza, Andrea.
Rome, George. petitioner 93593, 3d note after 105598-9 [sic]
Rome. 17157
Rome. Archi-Confradia de la Minerva. see Archi-Confradia de la Minerva de la Santa Ciudad de Roma.
Rome. R. Societa Geografia Italiana. see R. Societa Geografia Italiana, Rome.

Rome, N. Y. Cemetery. 73020
Rome, N. Y. Democratic Party State Convention, 1849. see Democratic Party. New York (State) Convention, Rome, 1849.
Rome, N. Y. Free Democratic State Convention, 1849. see Free Soil Party. New York (State) Convention, Rome, 1849.
Rome, N. Y. Free Soil Party State Convention, 1849. see Free Soil Party. New York (State) Convention, Rome, 1849.
Rome and Oneida County business directory. 73019
Rome, Camden and Oneida directory. 73019
Rome capital. 89554
Rome directory, 1857. 73019
Rome directory, with a business directory of Oneida County. 73019
Rome in America. 35849
Rome to America. 64129
Rome, Watertown and Ogdensburgh Railroad Company. 73021
Romer, F. see Roemer, F.
Romer, Jonathan. 47197
Romeral, Pedro Thamaron y. see Thamaron y Romeral, Pedro.
Romero, Anselmo Suarez y. see Suarez y Romero, Anselmo.
Romero, C. A. 99633, 99635, 99637, 105724
Romero, Elias. 73031
Romero, Francisco. 61076, (73032)
Romero, Jose Guadalupe. 10097, 62878, 73033-73037, 85760 see also Sociedad Mexicana de Geografia y Estadistica. Comision Nombrada Para Examiner la Obra de D. Francisco Pimentel.
Romero, Jose Mariano. 73038
Romero, Jose Valentin. 73039
Romero, Matias, 1837-1898. 54594, 73022, 73025, (73027)-(73031)
Romero, Miguel. 73040-73041
Romero, Tomas Munoz y. see Munoz y Romero, Tomas.
Romero, Vicente. tr. (49188)
Romero de Mella, Nicolas. 73042
Romero de Mella, Nicolas. plaintiff 73042
Romero de Terreros y Trebuesto, Maria Micaela. see Terreros y Trebuesto, Maria Micaela Romero de, Marquesa de San Francisco.
Romero Lopez Arbizu, Miguel. 73043-(73044)
Romey, Charles. (1933), (11041), 16480, 92535
Romeyn, Herman M. reporter (25259), 73045
Romeyn, James. 73046-73047
Romeyn, John Brodhead, 1777-1825. 73048-73058, 81522, 103231
Romeyn, T. 105055
Romeyn, Theodore. 73059
Romeyn, Theodore Bayard, 1827-1885. (73060)
Romilly, Charles, 1808-1887. ed. (73063)
Romilly, Edward, 1804-1870. ed. (73063)
Romilly, Frederick, 1810-1887. ed. (73063)
Romilly, Henry, 1805-1884. ed. (73063)
Romilly, Lord John, 1802-1874. ed. (73063)
Romilly, Sir Charles, 1757-1818. 49394, 56487, 73061-(73073)
Romilly, William, 1799-1855. ed. (73063)
Romish and prelatical rite of confirmation examined. 85319
Romish church opposed to the liberties of the American people. 11065
Romish intrigue! (25845)
Romish priest in Canada. pseud. Letter. see Seguenot, ---------.
Romme, Ch. see Romans, Charles.

Romney, George. illus. (71242), (73064)
Romney, John. (73064)
Romo, Nicolas Mahy y. see Mahy y Romo, Nicolas.
Romualdo Amaro, J. see Amaro, Juan Romualdo.
Romulus and Remus Silver Mine. 73065
Romyen, Abraham. 73066
Romyen's Johnstown calendar. 73066
Romyn de Hooge, -------. 32805, 73067
Ron, Antonio Joseph Alvarez de. plaintiff/ petitoner (69983)
Ronald, ---------, fl. 1784-1785. 100083, note after 100084
Ronald, William. 100093
Ronaldson, James. 3177, 73069-73070
Ronaldson, Richard. ed. 3177, 73069
Ronaldson (James) firm (73068)
Ronchini, Amadio. 73071
Ronda, Jose. 73072
Rondborstige, doch onpartijdige aenmerkingen op de memorien. 69607
Rondborstige wildeman. 100746
Ronde, Lambertus de. 16124, 73073-73076
Rondeau, James. 73077
Rondelay celebrating American independency. 50003
Ronderos, Vicente. (73078)-73079
Rondin de la libertad. 73080
Rondthaler, Edward. 73081
Ronmy, -------. (73082)
Ronna, Eugenio de Ochoa y. see Ochoa y Ronna, Eugenio de, 1814-1872.
Ronne, -------- von. 73083
Ronwennenni nok ronwathitharani. 104213
Ronzeau, R. 73084
Roo, Andreas Quintana. 67326, 73085-73086
Roo, Francisco de Paula Quadrado y de. see Quadrado y de Roo, Francisco de Paula.
Rood, A. 58705
Rood, H. 73087
Rood, Ogden N. 73088
Rooder zeeroover. 16523
Roof, Katharine Metcalf. 84904
Rooker, ---------. illus. 77467
Rooker, A. 73089
Rooker, W. Y. (73090)
Rooms of the National Executive Committee. 16142
Rooney, Alderman. pseud. Alderman Rooney at the Cable Banquet. see Townley, Daniel O'Connell.
Rooney, Barney. speud. Barney Rooney's letters. see Garvie, William.
Roorbach, Orville A. 37310, 73091-73098
Roorbach's list of booksellers in the United States. 73098
Roos, Frederick Fitzgerald de. see De Roos, Frederick Fitzgerald.
Roos, P. F. 73099-73101
Roosbroeck, Gustave L. van. see Van Roosbroeck, Gustave L.
Roosen, Gerhard. (73102)
Roosevelt, Clinton. (73103)-73105
Roosevelt, James J. defendant 72589
Roosevelt, Robert Barnwell. (29920), 73106-(73115) see also New York (State) Commissioners of Fisheries.
Roosevelt, S. Weir. 73116
Roosevelt Hospital, New York. see New York (City) Roosevelt Hospital.
Roosevelt Hospital, New York. First annual report. 73117
Root, David. (73118)-73123, 105032 see also New Hampshire Anti-slavery Society. President.

Root, Elihu, 1845-1937. 84774 see also U. S. War Department.
Root, Erastus, 1773-1846. 30094, 73124-73126
Root, George F. (73127)
Root, James. 73128
Root, James Pierce. 73129-73130
Root, Jeriel. 73131
Root, Jesse. (73132)
Root, Joseph Mosley, 1807-1879. 73133-73137
Root, N. W. T. ed. 86945
Root, O. E. 67281
Root. firm publishers 18723, (60833), 67281
Root genealogical records. 73129
Root of the evil. 91054
Roots, Benajah. 73138
Roots, Logan Holt, 1841-1893. 73139
Roots, Peter Philanthropos, d. 1828. 73140
Root's Davenport city directory. 18723
Roots' Peoria city directory. (60833)
Root's Quincy city direction. 67281
Roper, ---------. plaintiff 104413
Roper, Moses. (65464), 73141
Roper, Robert William. 73142
Ropes, Hannah Anderson. 73143
Ropes, Joseph S. 73144-73147
Roque, ------ de la. see La Roque, ------ de.
Roquefort, -----------, Marquis de Bausset-. see Bausset-Roquefort, --------, Marquis de.
Roquefeuil, Camille de. 62509, 73149-73150
Roques de Montgaillard, Juan Gabriel Maurice. see Montgaillard, Juan Gabriel Maurice Roques de.
Roquete, J.-Ignacio. 10299
Roquette, J. J. ed. 99521
Roquette, Jean Baptiste Marie Alexandre Dezos de la. see La Roquete, Jean Baptiste Marie Alexander Dezos de, 1784-1868.
Rordans, J. 73152
Rordansz, C. W, 73153
Rosa. pseud. Clamor de la justicia. see Verdugo, Manuel Jose.
Rosa. pseud. Justicia en defensa de la verdad. see Verdugo, Manuel Jose.
Rosa. pseud. Patriotismo. see Verdugo, Manuel Jose.
Rosa, Agustin de la. 73155-(73165)
Rosa, Gabriele. 73166
Rosa, Hipolito Buena de la. see La Rosa, Hipolito Buena de.
Rosa, Joao Ferreira de. (73167)
Rosa, Jose de la. see Sierra, Jose de.
Rosa, Jose Nicolas de la. 73168
Rosa, Luis de la. 39064-39065, 73169-73174 see also Mexico. Ministro de Relaciones.
Rosa, Manuel Toribio Gonzalez de la. 73175 see also Peru. Inspector Especial de Todos los Establecimeintos Departamentales.
Rosa Figueroa, Francisco Antonio de la. see Figueroa, Francisco Antonio de la Rosa.
Rosa Maria, Pedro Beltran de Santa. see Beltran de Santa Rosa Maria, Pedro.
Rosa Toro, Agustin de la. see La Rosa Toro, Agustin de.
Rosa, a melo-drama, in three acts. 73154
Rosa de el Perv. 98606
Rosa de S. Maria virgo Limensis. 73187
Rosa del Palermo S. Rosalia. 86444
Rosa laureada entre los santos epitalamios sacros de la corte. 58838
Rosa Peruana. (30249)
Rosabower: a collection of essays and miscellanies. 39072
Rosaccio, Gioseppe. 66507, 73194-73198

Rosains, Juan Nepomuceno. see Nepomuceno
    Rosains, Juan.
Rosal, Antonio. 97826
Rosal, Juan de Dios. 73200
Rosal, Juana Albares de. see Pinto de Ulloa,
    Juana (Albares de Rosal) de Valverde.
Rosal, Maria Theresa de Valverde y. see
    Valverde y Rosal, Maria Theresa de.
Rosales, Diego de, b. 1600? 73201
Rosales, F. T. 73202
Rosales, Francisco Xavier. (73203)
Rosales, Jose Vicente Solis y. see Solis y
    Rosales, Jose Vicente.
Rosales, Joseph, ed. 61074
Rosales, Vicente Perez. 60917, 73204
Rosamel, ------ de. 14720, 94850, 95786
    see also France. Ministre de Marine.
Rosamond Culbertson. 84031
Rosamond: or, a narrative of the captivity and
    sufferings of an American female.
    73205, 84030, 84032
Rosanna, or scenes in Boston. 39738, 94652
Rosario, Antonio do, d. 1704. 63206
Rosario, Paulo do. see Paulo do Rosario.
Rosario, Payo del. pseud. see Villavicencio,
    Pablo de.
Rosario de la Virgen Maria Nuestra Senora.
    76275
Rosario de Peruanos. 73208
Rosary. 101883
Rosary. By E. W. Parsons. 58881
Rosary. Introduced to the preceding farce.
    89593
Rosas, Antonio de los Rios y. see Rios y
    Rosas, Antonio de los, 1808-1873.
Rosas, Juan Manuel de, 1793-1877. 9022,
    9043, 34437, 44278, 44281, 73210-73211,
    73215-73217, 93807 see also Argentine
    Republic. Gefe Supreme, 1835-1852
    (Rosas) Argentine Republic. Ministro
    del Interior. Buenos Aires (Province)
    Governor (Rosas)
Rosas, Juan Manuel de, 1793-1877. defendant
    73209
Rosas, Juan Manuel de, 1793-1877. plaintiff
    73214
Rosas, Landa. 73222
Rosas and his calumniators. 44126
Rosas and the River Plate. 73219
Rosas et Montevideo devant la Cour d'Assises.
    73220
Rosas y sus opositores. 34437
Rosas'sche Schreckensperiode in Sud-Amerika.
    28183
Rosati, Joseph, Bp. 72970 see also St.
    Louis (Archdiocese) Bishop (Rosati)
Roscio, J. G. (73223)-73224, note after 97019
Roscius, Julius. 33068, 73225
Roscoe, Henry. ed. 21659, 89130
Roscoe, William. (53977), 69497, 73226-
    73232, 98707, 2d note after 105630
Roscoe, William. supposed author 95694
Roscoe Mining Company, Canada East. (73233)
Roscommon. pseud. To the author of those
    intelligencers printed at Dublin. 95908
Rose, A. B. 87738
Rose, Aquila. 73234-73235
Rose, E. M. P. 73236
Rose, George, 1744-1818. 7869-7870, 73237-
    (73240)
Rose, George, 1817-1882. 73241-73243
Rose, Sir George Henry, 1771-1855. 12486,
    12489, 73244, 96020 see also Great
    Britain. Legation. United States.
Rose, John. 73245-73246
Rose, Joseph. ed. 73235

Rose, Julius D. 73247
Rose Mather. 32617
Rose, R. H. 67377, 73248
Rose Roume, Philip. see Roume, Philip Rose.
Rose Beneficent Association. plaintiffs 21543
Rose bud, or youth's gazette. 88483
Rose Carney. 84377
Rose Clark. 58961
Rose de Smyrne et l'ermite de Niagara, poemes.
    47925
Rose de Timosthenes. 76838
Rose-hill; a tale of the Old Dominion. 94169,
    note after 100581
Rose of Sharon. 93765
Rose of Sharon: a religious souvenir, for
    MDCCCL. 73250
Rose of Sharon: a religious souvenir, for 1841.
    73249
Rose of the Rio Grande. (18061)
Rose of the valley. 73251
Rose of Wisconsin. 75261
Rose: or affection's gift. 73252
Rose tree. 105961-2 [sic]
Rose von Puebla. 28183
Roseau, Dominica. Court. 61188
Rosecrans, William Starke, 1819-1898. (50308),
    57046, 73253-(73256), 73258-73260, note
    just before (73261), 95753
Rosecrans, William Starke, 1819-1898. petitioner
    73257
Rosecrans (W. S.) & Company. firm 73253
Rosecrans' campaign with the Fourteenth Army
    Corps. 5223
Rosecrans Gold Mining Company. (73261)
Rosehill Cemetery, Chicago. see Chicago.
    Rosehill Cemetery.
Roselius, Christopher. (69916), (73263)
Rosell, Cayetano. ed. and tr. 65292
Roselli, Francisco. cartographer 76838
Rosellini, Massimina Fantastici. 73264
Roselly de Lorgues, Antoine Francois Felix,
    Comte, 1805-1898. 73256-(73273), 76522
Rosemond de Beauvallon, Jean Baptiste.
    (73274)
Rosen, W. von. 5399-5400
Rosenbach, A. S. W. 102376
Rosenberg, ------. illus. 16778
Rosenberg, C. G. 73275-73277
Rosencrantz, Herman. defendant 73278
Rosende, Antonio Gonzalez de. see Gonzalez
    de Rosende, Antonio, 17th cent.
Rosenfeld, Jo. Hartmannus. 99538
Rosengarten, J. G. 73281
Rosenthal, Alfredo. 73282
Rosenthal, J. Th. H. Nedermeyer van. see
    Nedermeyer van Rosenthal, J. Th. H.
Rosenthal, L. lithographer 91293
Rosenwald, Victor. ed. 40234
Roses-des-vents en usage au Moyen-Age.
    76838
Rosette, John E. defendant 89841
Rosewain, Edward. defendant 96949
Rosewood, J. B. pseud.?? Life of Greeley.
    see Sellen, Theodore B.
Rosica de Caldas, Sebastian Alvarez Alfonso.
    73286
Rosicrucian. pseud. Dealings with the dead.
    see Randolph, Paschal Beverly.
Rosier, E. 73287
Rosier, James, 1575-1635. 66686, (73288)-
    (73290)
Rosiers, --------, Comte de. 73291
Rosignon, J. see Rossignon, Julio.
Rosier's account of Waymouth's voyage.
    66686
Rosier's narrative of Waymouth's voyage. 73289

Rosier's relation of Waymouth's voyage.
(73290)
Rosillo, Andres. 73292
Rosillo de Mier Quatemoczin, Juan. see
Mier Quatemoczin, Juan Rosillo de.
Rosina Meadows, the village maid. 77171
Rosine Association, Philadelphia. 62198
Rosine Association, Philadelphia. Manager.
pseud. see Manager of the . . . Rosine
Association. pseud.
Rosine Association, Philadelphia. Managers.
62198
Rosine Laval: a novel. 83788
Rosing, J. 73293
Rosique, Miguel Tacon y. see Tacon y
Rosique, Miguel, Marques de la Union
de Cuba, 1777-1854.
Roslern, W. E. Burkhard. see Berkhard
Roslern, W. E.
Roslin, Helisaeus. 73294-73295
Roslin Castle. A song. (73296)
Roslyn, N. Y. Bryant School. see Bryant
School, Roslyn, N. Y.
Rosnel, Pierre de. 40242, 73297-73298
Rosny, Leon de. 1612, 70373, 70376-(70378),
73299-(73309), 85781, 85791
Rosny, Lucien de. (14634), 73310, 85781
Rospigliosi, Giulio. see Clement IX, Pope,
1600-1669.
Ross, ----------. cartographer 35953,
35954, 35962, (40141)
Ross, A. ed. 67599
Ross, A. M. 42982
Ross, Alexander, 1590-1654. 73312-(73325)
Ross, Alexander, 1783-1856. (73326)-73328
Ross, Alexander Milton. 73329-73340
Ross, Arthur A. (73341)
Ross, Charles. (16812), (17904)
Ross, Charles J. 73342
Ross, Christian K. (73343)-73344
Ross, D. Barton. 73345
Ross, David. 47904, 92841
Ross, Dunbar. 17511, (73346)-73347
Ross, Duncan. (73348)
Ross, Edmund Gibson, 1826-1907. 73349-
73352
Ross, Ezra, d. 1778. defendant 105350-
105350A
Ross, F. A. 32360
Ross, Fitzgerald. 24612, 73353
Ross, Frederick A. 73354-73356
Ross, G. M. von. 73357-73358
Ross, George. defendant 6326, 1st note after
96956, 1st note after 97284
Ross, H. J. 73359
Ross, Hugh. 78197 see also Company of
Scotland Trading to African and the
Indies. Council. Secretary.
Ross, J. tr. 52146
Ross, James, of Madison, Wisc. 73364-73365
Ross, James, of Nova Scotia (73363)
Ross, James, 1744-1827. 73361-(73362),
73889, 99448
Ross, James, 1762-1847. 73360
Ross, Sir James Clark, 1800-1862. 28401,
71032, 73366-73367, 73381-73382, 73384-
73385
Ross, Joel H. 73368
Ross, John, Bp. of Exeter, 1719-1792. 73369
Ross, Sir John, 1777-1856. 19582, 36014,
73370-73388, 100825
Ross, John, fl. 1785. (38801) see also
Lancaster County, Pa. Lieutenant.
Ross, John, Cherokee Chief, 1790?-1866.
6859, 12449, 12473, 47657, 73389, 73391-
73393, see also Cherokee Nation.
Principal Chief.

Ross, John, Cherokee Chief, 1790?-1866.
petitioner 73390
Ross, John, fl. 1862. 73394
Ross, Lewis Winans, 1812-1895. 73395-73396
Ross, M. D. (73397)
Ross, R. 71731
Ross, Rhomasina. tr. (33771)
Ross, Robert, 1726-1799. 36859, 73398-73408
Ross, Thomas, 1806-1865. 73409
Ross, W. P. ed. 12439
Ross, William. defendant 96924
Ross, William P. petitioner (70351), 73410
Ross, Zeph. 73411
Ross, Johnson, H. C. see Johnson, H. C.
Ross.
Rossa, Vitale Terra. see Terra Rossa, Vitale.
Rossal, J. A. de. plaintiff 62944
Rosse, J. Willoughby. 5747, 73412
Rosse, John, Bp. of Exeter see Ross, John.
Bp. of Exeter, 1719-1792.
Rosseel, James A. 73413
Rossel, ------ de. (22671), 52105
Rossel, Elisabeth Paul Edouard de. 73414
Rosser, I. L. (19568)
Rosser, W. H. 73415-73417
Rossett, Lewis Henry de. see De Rossett,
Lewis Henry.
Rossi, G. Giacomo. 73418
Rossi, L. 73419-73420
Rossi, Stefano. 73421
Rossie Lead Mining & Smelting Company.
73422
Rossignol Desdunes, -------. 21220
Rossignon, Julio. 73423-(73424)
Rossiter, T. P. illus. 73425
Rossitter, E. W. defendant 73426
Rosslyn, Alexander Wedderburn, 1st Earl of,
1733-1805. 22706, 34072, note before
102432
Rosso, Ignacio Sierra y. see Sierra y Rosso,
Ignacio.
Rossville, Ohio. Meeting of the Citizens on
the Subject of a Western National Armory,
1841. see Meeting of the Citizens of
Hamilton and Rossville, Ohio, on the
Subject of a Western National Armory,
1841.
Rost, Pierre A. 73427-73428
Rost fran landet Zion. 85511
Rostaing, Jules. 92547
Roster, Hermann. tr. 58947
Roster of Company C. First Maine Heavy
Artillery. 84941
Roster of general officers. 88370
Rostoff, Alexandre Labanoff de. see Labanoff
de Rostoff, Alexandre.
Roswag, C. 73429
Rosz, John. see Ross, Sir John, 1777-1856.
Rota, Diego. pseud. Dialogo. see Valencia,
P. F.
Rotalde, Francisco de. 73430
Rotatory eldership. (73431)
Roteiro chorographico. (11452)
Roteiro da cidade de Sancta Maria de Belem do
Grao-Para. 57198
Roteiro da viagem de Vasco de Gama. (58261)
Roteiro da viagem que em descobrimento da
India. 98649
Roteiro do cidade de Santa Maria. 3900
Roteiro dos collectores. 73432
Roteiro e descripcao hydrographica da mesma
costa. 38620
Roteiro e mappa da viagem da ciudade de S.
Luis do Maranhao. 81101
Roteiro e navagacao das Indias Occidentalis.
(73433)

Roteiro geral des costas. 17010
Roterigvs, Petrvs. see Rodrigues, Pedro, 1542-1628.
Roth, J. tr. 80013
Rothe, C. E. 55613
Rothelin, -------. (8784), 73435
Rothelin, --------- d'Orleans de. see Rothelin, ---------.
Rothelowen, Bernhard, Graf von Rechberg und. see Rechberg und Rothelowen, Bernhard, Graf von, 1807-1899.
Rotheram, John. 73436
Rothermel, H. A. 73437-73438
Rothermel, P. F. illus. 73439-73440
Rotours, Noel Francois Arnot des. see Des Rotours, Noel Francois Arnot.
Rotteck, Karl von. 73443-73445
Rottenness of the paper money banking system exposed. 24536
Rotterdam. 36563
Rottermund, --------, Comte de. 73446-73447
Rou, Lewis, d. 1750. (73448)-73449, 2d note after 97148
Rouard y Paz-Soldan, Manuel. 59326, 59335, 73450-(73451)
Rouargue, ------. illus. (73271)
Roubard, --------. supposed author 40006
Roubard, J. L. Audibert. 73452, 2d note after 101785
Roubard, Pierre Joseph Andre. 73453
Roubaud, Rafael Gomez. 11099, 73454-73455, 86819 see also Cuba. Intendente de Exercito, Havana.
Rouby, Jules. (73456)
Roucher, J. A. tr. 82308
Rouelle, John. 73457
Rouen, France. 57538
Rouen, France. Aldermen. 73458
Rouen, France. Cour de Aydes. 56086
Rouen, France. Fete Bresilienne, 1550. 19556, 73458
Rouen, France. Parlement. see France. Parlement (Rouen)
Rouge et noir. 19768
Rough, William. complainant 73459
Rough and ready annual. 73460
Rough and ready melodist. (73461)
Rough and ready songs. 73462
Rough and ready songster. 73463
Rough hewer. pseud. Political papers. see Yates, Abraham, 1724-1796.
Rough-hewer, devoted to the support of the Democratic principles. 73464
Rough hewer extra. 95818
Rough hewer, Jr. pseud. Political papers. see Yates, Abraham, 1724-1796.
Rough notes of an exploration. 96480
Rough notes taken during some rapid journeys. 31134
Rough sketches of the life. 39507
Rough sketches on the borders of the picture picturesque. 41020
Rough trip to the border. 7765
Roughing it in the bush. 50306, 2d note after 98090
Roughley, Thomas. (73465)
Rougisme en Canada. 33986
Rouhaud, Hippolyte. 73466
Rouhaud, Pedro. 17153, 19463-19464, 21178-21179
Rouhette, -------. 94390-94391
Roujoux, M. de. 38632
Roulin, ------. 73467
Roulin, F. tr. 65478
Roulin, Francois Desire, 1796-1874. 6941

Roulstone, George. 94776
Roulstone, John. 94086
Roume, Sieur. see Roume, Philippe Rose.
Roume, Philippe Rose. 2931, 73468-73469, 73471 see also France. Commission aux Isles Sous le Vent. Tobago (French Colony) Commissaire et Ordonnateur.
Roume, Philippe Rose. petitioner 73470
Round Hill School, Northampton, Mass. see Northampton, Mass. Round Hill School.
Round pack. A tale of the forked deer. 72133
Round table, a weekly record. 73473
Round table. No. 2. 73472
Round the block. 6946, 73474
Round the world. 37887
Roundelay, Roderick. pseud. Little bit of a tid-re-i. 41530
Roundell, Charles Saville. 73475
Roundhill scholars. 14218
Roupell, George. plaintiff 23532, 39925, 1st note after 87356, note after 87824, note after 96924
Rouqeutte, Adrien E. 73476-73479
Rouqeutte, Francois Dominique. (73480)-73481
Roure, P. 73482
Rous, George, 1744?-1802. 56540
Rous, Jean Isidore. 73486
Rous, John. 32480, (73483)-73485, 78753
Rous, John. supposed author 42756, 62756
Rouse, E. S. S. 73487
Rouse, T. H. 35736
Rouso d'Eres, Charles Dennis, b. 1761. (22731)
Rousseau, Jean Jacques, 1713-1778. 17033
Rousseau, Jean Jacques, 1713-1778. supposed author 5270, note after 104001
Roussel, Napoleon. (73488)-73489
Rousselot de Surgy, Jacques Philibert. 1408A, 26978, 36991, 65402, 73490-73492, 100838
Rousset de Missy, Jean. 73493-73495
Roussignac, Jacques de. 73496
Roussillon, ------. (75174)
Roussillon, F.-P. Vigo. see Vigo Roussillon, F.-P.
Roussin, Albin Rene, Baron, 1781-1854. (73497)-(73500)
Rout from Philadelphia to Fort-Pitt. 84617
Route across the Rocky Mountains. 36260
Route and city guides. 89903
Route and distances to Oregon and California. 80555
Route de la Californie a travers l'isthme de Panama. 74986
Route from Liverpool to Great Salt Lake Valley. (41325)
Route from the Gulph of Mexico and the lower Mississippi Valley. 17492
Route near the thirty-second parallel of north latitude. 69900, 69946
Route north from Boston. 73501
Route to the Pacific Ocean. 88607
Routes a suivre pour evite les abordages en mer. 46972
Routes and tables of distances. (73502)
Routes to California. 5809
Routes to the White Mountains. 73503
Routh, Martha. 73504
Routier des iles Antilles. 1701, (73505)-73506
Routier des Indes Orientales et Occidentales. 18655
Routledge (George) & Co. firm publishers 73507, 92494
Routledge (George) & Sons. firm publishers 84305-84306
Routledge's American handbook. 73507
Routledge's excelsior series. 84305

Routledge's standard library. 84306
Routledge's standard novels. 92494
Rouvellat de Cussac, Jean-Baptiste. 73508-73509
Rouvellet, J. D. R. defendant 73510
Rouville, ------- Delafosse de. see Delafosse de Rouville, --------.
Roux, Sergeant Major. 35512, 73511
Roux, A. A. 73512
Roux, Charles Frederic. 73513
Roux, F. A. 73514
Roux, P. 29567, 73515
Roux de Rochelle, Jean Baptiste Gaspard, 1762-1849. 73516-73519, 102622
Rouxel, H. 73520-(73521)
Rouzeau, A. 73522
Rover. pseud. Rambles in Chili. see Will the Rover. pseud.
Rover, Riley. pseud. Early settlers in the west. (73523)
Rover, Roderic, Esq. pseud. Thistle. see Prentiss, Charles.
Rover: a dollar weekly magazine. 73524
Rover: a weekly magazine of tales, poetry, and engravings. 84154, 84162
Rover of Cuba. (67664)-67665
Rovers, M. A. N. 58739
Roville, -----. 75172 see also France. Ministere de la Marine.
Roving editor. 68529
Roving printer. pseud. Adventures in the South Pacific. see Jones, -------.
Roving printer. pseud. Life and adventures in the South Pacific. see Jones, --------.
Rovings in the Pacific. 73525
Row, Augustus. 73526
Rowan, --------, fl. 1839. 40240
Rowan, Archibald Hamilton. 73527
Roan, Frederica. tr. (81007)
Rowan, John, 1773-1843. 37561, (73528)-(73530)
Rowan, Stephen N. 73531-73537
Rowcroft, Charles. 73538
Rowe, D. Watson. (73539)
Rowe, Elizabeth. 73540-73543, 80720
Rowe, G. 73544
Rowe, John. (73545)
Rowe, Mass. School Committee. 73546
Rowe-Street Baptist Church, Boston. see Boston. Rowe-Street Baptist Church.
Rowed, Richard. 101207
Rowell, Edward T. (73547)
Rowell, George P. (47793), 73551
Rowell, Hopkins. 73552
Rowell, I. 73553
Rowell, Joseph. 73554
Rowell (George P.) & Company. firm publishers (47793), 73458-73551
Rowett, W. 73555
Rowland, David Sherman. 25232, 73556-73562, 102947
Rowland, Henry A. 73563-73566, 73568-(73570)
Rowland, James. 73571
Rowland, John. 73572, 94688
Rowland, John. supposed ed. 78362
Rowland, Thomas. 45207
Rowland, William F. 73573-73576
Rowlandson, Joseph. 73577, 73579
Rowlandson, Mary. (73578)-73592, 104266, 104272
Rowlandson, Thomas. 73593-73594
Rowles, R. 66686
Rowles, W. P. 73595
Rowlett, John. 73596-73598
Rowlett's tables of discount, or interest. 73597

Rowley, William. 73599
Rowley, Mass. 73600
Rowley, Mass. School Committee. 73601
Rowson, Susanna. 51885, (73602)-73619
Rowson, Susanna Haswell. 97284
Rowson, William. ed. 86925
Roxas, Alonso de. petitioner 72777, (73620)
Roxas, Francisco de. 84384
Roxas, Ignacio de. 73621
Roxas y Andrade, Francisco. see Rojas y Andrade, Francisco.
Roxborough, Mass. Church of Christ. 95639
Roxborough, Pa. Baptist Church. (73624)
Roxborough, Pa. High School. 73623
Roxburgh, Alexander. petitioner 73625
Roxbury, Mass. (73631), 73637, 73647, 73691, 73716
Roxbury, Mass. Aldermen. see Roxbury, Mass. City Council. Board of Aldermen.
Roxbury, Mass. Artillery. see Massachusetts. Militia. Roxbury City Guard.
Roxbury, Mass. Athenaeum. 73725
Roxbury, Mass. Athenaeum. Trustees. 73725
Roxbury, Mass. Auditors. 73633
Roxbury, Mass. Bicentennial Celebration, 1830. 73659
Roxbury, Mass. Charitable Society. see Roxbury Charitable Society, Roxbury, Mass.
Roxbury, Mass. Charter. 73627, 73629, 73657
Roxbury, Mass. Children's Home and Home for Aged Females. see Roxbury Home for Children and Aged Females, Roxbury, Mass.
Roxbury, Mass. City Council. 319, 73657, 73721-73723
Roxbury, Mass. City Council. Committee on a Public Common. 73679
Roxbury, Mass. City Council. Committee on a Sewer in Fellows Street. (73680)
Roxbury, Mass. City Council. Committee on Police. (73681)
Roxbury, Mass. City Council. Committee on Public Court. 73673
Roxbury, Mass. City Council. Committee on Public Property. 73686
Roxbury, Mass. City Council. Committee on the Military Fund. (73688)
Roxbury, Mass. City Council. Committee on the Remonstrance of William R. Huston. 73689
Roxbury, Mass. City Council. Committee on the Remonstrance of William R. Huston. Minority. (73655)
Roxbury, Mass. City Council. Committee on the Revision and Amendments of the City Ordinances. 73690
Roxbury, Mass. City Council. Joint Committee on Highways. 73693
Roxbury, Mass. City Council. Joint Committee on Public Instruction. 73694
Roxbury, Mass. City Council. Joint Special Committee in the Matter of the Roxbury Color and Chemical Company. 73696
Roxbury, Mass. City Council. Joint Special Committee on a Public Cemetery. 73697
Roxbury, Mass. City Council. Joint Special Committee on Annexation. 73701
Roxbury, Mass. City Council. Joint Special Committee on Gas. 73698
Roxbury, Mass. City Council. Joint Special Committee on Public Squares. 63799
Roxbury, Mass. City Council. Joint Special Committee on Rules and Orders. 73700
Roxbury, Mass. City Council. Joint Special Committee on Salaries of City Officers. 73674

Roxbury, Mass. City Council. Joint Special Committee on the Appointment of a City Physician. 73702

Roxbury, Mass. City Council. Joint Special Committee on the Buildings at Brook Farm. 73703

Roxbury, Mass. City Council. Joint Special Committee on the City Marshal. 73695

Roxbury, Mass. City Council. Joint Special Committee on the Expediency of a Survey of the City. 73707

Roxbury, Mass. City Council. Joint Special Committee on the Removal of the Alms-House and the Purchase of "Brook Farm." 73704

Roxbury, Mass. City Council. Joint Special Committee on the Subject of the Donation of Hon. Linus B. Comins. 73705

Roxbury, Mass. City Council. Joint Special Committee to Oppose the Petition of Isaac T. Allard and Others. 73706

Roxbury, Mass. City Council. Joint Standing Committee on Burial Grounds. 73668, 73708

Roxbury, Mass. City Council. Joint Standing Committee on Finance. 73709

Roxbury, Mass. City Council. Joint Standing Committee on Parks or Squares. 73710

Roxbury, Mass. City Council. Joint Standing Committee on Police Court Minority. 73712

Roxbury, Mass. City Council. Joint Standing Committee on Sewerage. (73672)

Roxbury, Mass. City Council. Joint Standing Committee on the Fire Department. 73711

Roxbury, Mass. City Council. Board of Aldermen. 73667

Roxbury, Mass. City Council. Board of Aldermen. Committee on the Fire Department. (73687)

Roxbury, Mass. City Guard. see Massachusetts. Militia. Roxbury City Guard.

Roxbury, Mass. City Marshal. 73636

Roxbury, Mass. City Registrar. 73671

Roxbury, Mass. City Treasurer. 73716

Roxbury, Mass. Commissioners Appointed on the Union of Boston and Roxbury. see Commissioners Appointed by the City Councils of the Cities of Roxbury and Boston, Respectively, On the Union of the Two Cities Under One Municipal Government.

Roxbury, Mass. Committee on Accounts and Expenditures. 73716

Roxbury, Mass. Committee on Public Instruction. (73682)-73685

Roxbury, Mass. Committee on Public Instruction. Majority. 73648

Roxbury, Mass. Committee on Public Instruction. Minority. 73648

Roxbury, Mass. Division No. 78, Sons of Temperance. see Sons of Temperance in North America. Massachusetts. Roxbury Division, no. 78.

Roxbury, Mass. Dudley Street Baptist Church. 73638

Roxbury, Mass. Eastern Grammar School. Perambulating Committee. 37314

Roxbury, Mass. Eliot Church. 73640

Roxbury, Mass. Eliot Sabbath School. 73641, note after 95465

Roxbury, Mass. Fire Department. Chief Engineer. 73716

Roxbury, Mass. First Unitarian Church of Christ. 73643

Roxbury, Mass. First Universalist Society. 73643

Roxbury, Mass. First Universalist Society. Charter. 73643

Roxbury, Mass. Forest Hills Cemetery. 25078-25079

Roxbury, Mass. Forest Hills Cemetery. Board of Commissioners. 73644, 73675

Roxbury, Mass. Grammar School in the Eastern Part of the Town. see Roxbury Mass. Eastern Grammar School.

Roxbury, Mass. Harbor Master. 73692

Roxbury, Mass. Home for Children and Aged Females. see Roxbury Home for Children and Aged Females, Roxbury, Mass.

Roxbury, Mass. Horse Guard. see Massachusetts. Militia. Roxbury Horse Guard.

Roxbury, Mass. Lincoln Freedmen's Aid Society. see Lincoln Freedmen's Aid Society, Roxbury, Mass.

Roxbury, Mass. Mayor, 1846-1847 (Clarke) 73649 see also Clarke, John J.

Roxbury, Mass. Mayor, 1847-1851 (Dearborn) 73630 see also Dearborn, Henry Alexander Scammell, 1783-1851.

Roxbury, Mass. Mayor, 1853-1854. 73667

Roxbury, Mass. Mayor, 1856-1858 (Sleeper) 73550, (73687), 73701, 82116, 82123 see also Sleeper, John Herburne, 1794-1878.

Roxbury, Mass. Mechanics' Co-operative Association. see Mechanics' Co-operative Association of Roxbury, Mass.

Roxbury, Mass. Ministry at Large. 73654

Roxbury, Mass. Ministry at Large. Trustees of the Missionary Fund. 73654

Roxbury, Mass. Missionary Fund. see Roxbury Missionary Fund, Roxbury, Mass.

Roxbury, Mass. Ordinances, etc. 73626, 73628, 73658, 73660-73666, 73669, 73670, 73695

Roxbury, Mass. Overseers of the Poor. 73713, 73716

Roxbury, Mass. Physician to the Alms-House. 73715-73716 see also Cotting, B. E.

Roxbury, Mass. St. James' Church. Benevolent Society. 73736

Roxbury, Mass. School Committee. 73670, 73685, (73717), 73738

Roxbury, Mass. School Committee. Special Committee. (73718)-73719

Roxbury, Mass. Surveyors of Highways. 73720

Roxbury, Mass. Trustees of the Missionary Fund. see Roxbury, Mass. Ministry at Large. Trustees of the Missionary Fund.

Roxbury, Mass. Universalist Church. 73737

Roxbury, Mass. Yeoman Association. see Roxbury Yeoman Association, Roxbury, Mass.

Roxbury, Mass. Young Men's Christian Association. see Young Men's Christian Association, Roxbury, Mass.

Roxbury almanac and business directory for the year 1847. 73724

Roxbury Artillery. see Massachusetts. Militia. Roxbury City Guard.

Roxbury Charitable Society, Roxbury, Mass. (73726)

Roxbury Charitable Society, Roxbury, Mass. Charter. (73726)

Roxbury Charitable Society, Roxbury, Mass. Executive Committee. (73726)

Roxbury City Guard. see Massachusetts. Militiia. Roxbury City Guard.

Roxbury Democrat—extra. 73728

Roxbury directory. 73724, 73727

Roxbury Division, no. 78, Sons of Temper- ance. see Sons of Temperance in North America. Massachusetts. Roxbury Division, no. 78.

Roxbury Gas Light Company. (73731)

Roxbury Gas Light Company. Charter. (73731)

Roxbury Home for Children and Aged Females, Roxbury, Mass. 71570

Roxbury Home for Children and Aged Females, Roxbury, Mass. Managers. (73635)

Roxbury Horse Guard. see Massachusetts. Militia. Roxbury Horse Guard.

Roxbury Missionary Fund, Roxbury, Mass. Trustees. (61569)

Roxbury Verd-Antique Marble Company. (73733)

Roxbury Yeoman Association, Roxbury, Mass. 73734

Roxbury Young Men's Christian Association. see Young Men's Christian Association. Roxbury, Mass.

Roxbury Young Men's Christian Association of Boston. see Young Men's Christian Association, Roxbury, Mass.

Roxo Mexia y Ocon, Juan. see Mexia y Ocon Juan Roxo.

Roxo y Calderon, Andres Joseph. 72809, 73740

Roy, -------, Clair. see Clair Roy, ---------.

Roy, ------- Fitz. see Fitz-Roy, ----------.

Roy, Albert de. see De Roy, Albert.

Roy, E. 73742

Roy, J. J. E. 27485, 73751

Roy, Herman le. see Le Roy, Herman. appellant

Roy, J. B. tr. 30040

Roy, Jennet. 73743-73745

Roy, Joseph. E. 73746-(73750)

Roy, Maria le. 73752

Roy, P. L. le. see Le Roy, P. L.

Roy, Rammohun. 73753, 81776

Roy, Thomas. 73754

"Roy ayant par son arrest du dernier Febrier 1682." 56090

Roy estant en son Conseil, la Reyne . . . Paris. 73741

Roy estant informe par les remonstrances. 56092

Royal & Clyde. firm publishers 60033

Royal Academy, London. (63350)

Royal Academy, Paris. see Academy des Sciences, Paris.

Royal Acadian School, Halifax, N. S. 56133

Royal African. 73755

Royal African Company and separate traders agreed. 73775

Royal African Company of England. 1650, 73756, 73758, (73777), 79370, note before 93802

Royal African Company of England. petitioners 73771

Royal African Company of England. Creditors. 73757, (73772)

Royal African Company of England. Directors. (19780), 73768

Royal African Company of England. General Court. 73776

Royal Agricultural Society of Prince Edward Island. (65640)

Royal American gazette. 73780

Royal American magazine. 34077, 73781- 73782, 84617, 2d note after 95414

Royal ape: a dramatic poem. 73783, 84892

Royal Arch Mason, K. T.—K. of M.—&c. &c. pseud. Freemason's monitor. see Webb, Thomas Smith.

Royal Arctic theatre. 73784

Royal Bahama gazette. 73785

Royal book of dreams. 83735

Royal burial. 17438

Royal Canadian Yacht Club, Toronto. 73786

Royal College of Physicians, London. 85250

Royal commentaries of Peru. (2308), 98760

Royal decrees of Scanderoon. 71825, note after 91969, 2d note after 94296

Royal fishing revived. 73788

Royal gazette (Charleston, S. C.) 73790

Royal gazette (Kingston, Jamaica.) 73789

Royal gazette (New York) see Rivington's royal gazette.

Royal gazette and universal chronicle. 73791

Royal gazette extraordinary. 102835

Royal gazette extraordinary. Respecting the defeat of the French. 102835

Royal genealogies. 1398

Royal Geographical Society, London. 4857A, 73792, 77793-77794, 78998

Royal Geogria gazette. 73793

Royal Granada gazette. 73794

Royal Horticultural Society, London. (32865)

Royal Institution, London. see Royal Institution of Great Britain, London.

Royal Institution of Great Britain, London. (72667), 84576

Royal Institution of Great Britain. Weekly evening meeting. (72667)

Royal institutions. 33164

Royal Insurance Company. firm publishers (73795)

Royal Insurance Company Fire and life Capital two million sterling. (73795)

Royal Irish Academy, Dublin. 21322

Royal Irish Society. see Royal Irish Academy, Dublin.

Royal kalendar. 73796

Royal kalendar, or correct annual register. 73796

Royal law, by which all mankind will be judged! 79824

Royal magazine or gentleman's monthly com- panion. 73798

Royal Mail Steam Packet Company. 73799- 73800

Royal Mail Steam Packet Company, under contract with Her Majesty's government. 73800

Royal Mail Steam Packet Company, under contract with Her Majesty's government, for the conveyance of the mails. 73799

Royal melody. 101196

Royal melody complete. 94333-94339

Royal military chronicle or British officers' monthly register. 73801

Royal military chronicle; or, the British military officers' monthly register. 73802

Royal navy biography. 44797

Royal penitent. 64316

Royal Pennsylvania gazette. 60594, (73803)

Royal perseverance. 73804, 97634

Royal police. A tale of 1773-75. (72126)

Royal primer. 73806

Royal primer improved. 73805

Royal road to fortune. 49016

Royal road to wealth. 62199

Royal scriptural magazine. 73807

Royal slave. 88530
Royal slave. A tragedy. 88538
Royal slave. A true history. (4371)
Royal Society, London. 3868, 3892, 9389, (13575), 28689, 74700-74704, 84985, 104851
Royal Society of Arts, London. 40857, 65052-65055, 68824
Royal Society of London. see Royal Society, London.
Royal Society of Medicine, Paris. see Academie de Medecine, Paris.
Royal Society of Northern Antiquarians, Copenhagen. see K. Nordske Oldskrift-Selskab, Copenhagen.
Royal supremacy. 86824
Royal treasury of England. (73808)
Royal truths. 4321
Royal water lily of South America. (39445)
Royale esclave. 4373
Royalisme de la Guadeloupe devoile. 2351
Royalist's daughter and the rebels. 51435
Royall, Anne. 73818-73825, 4th note after 96481
Royalston, Mass. 73828
Royalston, Mass. Auditor. 73826
Royalston, Mass. School Committee. 73827
Royalston, Mass. Wendell Baptist Association Meeting, 1825. see Baptists. Massachusetts. Wendell Baptist Association. Meeting, Royalston, 1825.
Royalty in the new world. 16821
Royalty of federalist! 73829, 1st note after 101879
Royaume de Guatemala. 101350
Royaume d'Hayti. Le Comte de Limonade . . . a ses concitoyens. 41140
Royaume d'Hayti. L'Olivier de la paix. 73831
Royaume d'Hayti. Manifeste du Roi. 73830
Royaume d'Hayti. Refutation d'un ecrit de Charrault. 12027
Royce, Andrew. 73832, 73234
Royce, H. A. 73835
royce, Moses S. 73836
Roye, Edward James. 73837
Royer, A. H. 73838
Royer, C. Barbault. 73839
Royer, John. 73840
Royle, J. Forces. 73841
Royou, J. C. 10754
Roys, Auren. 73842
Royse, N. K. 73843
Royse, P. E. 73844
Royse, Vere. 94109
Royston, Philip Yorke. Lord. see Hardwick, Philip Yorke, 2d Earl of, 1720-1790.
Royston, S. Watson. 73845
Rozas, Manuel Gaspar de. 86507
Rozas e goivos. Poezias. 10670
Rozoi, ----- de. see Farmian de Rois, known as Durosi.
Rua, Hernando de la. 69172, 73847-73850
Ruanova, Estanislao. 73851
Rub from Snub. 14032, 85597, 94025
Rubalcava, Joseph Gutierrez de. 29359-29360, 63862, 66408, 73852
Rubbi, Andrea. 73853
Rubeck, Sennoia. anagram see Burke, John.
Rubel, J. C. 65868
Robens, Christian. 90090
Rubens, Peter Paul. ed. 62688
Rubi, Diego. 73854
Rubi, J. F. Mas y. see Mas y Rubi, J. F.
Rubi, Ramon Puchpalat y. see Puchpalat y Rubi, Ramon.

Rubim, Braz da Costa. see Costa Rubim, Braz da, 1817-
Rubin, Jose Mario. 73856-73857
Rubin, Pedro de Teran. see Teran Rubin, Pedro de.
Rubin de la Torre, Matias. (73858)
Rubino Salinas, Manuel. ed. 94353
Rubio. pseud. Rambles in the United States and Canada. 73859
Rubio, Antonio. 63652, (73860)-73861
Rubio, C. 73862
Rubio, Carlos Maria Colina y. see Colina y Rubio, Carlos Maria.
Rubio, Cayetano. 15083, 75781
Rubio, Diego de Torres. see Torres Rubio, Diego de.
Rubio, Juan. 73863
Rubio, Manuel. 73864
Rubio, Nicolas Antonio Guerrero Martinez. 73865
Rubio, P. Torres. see Torres Rubio, P.
Rubio de Aunon, Alfonso Carrio y Morcillo. see Carrio y Morcillo Rubio de Aunon, Alfonso.
Rubio de Aunon, Pedro Morcillo. see Morcillo Rubio de Aunon, Pedro.
Rubio de Ribas, Alonso. 41134, 73866, 98931
Rubio y Salinas, Manuel Joseph, Abp. (48448), 48469, 73867-73872, 94171 see also Mexico (Archdiocese) Archbishop (Rubio y Salinas)
Rubion, Geronimo. 73873
Ruble, Johannes Casparus. (73874)
Rubridge, Charles. 73875
Rubriquis, William. see Ruysbroek, Willem van.
Rubruck, Guillaume de. see Ruysbroek, Willem van.
Ruchamer, Jobsten. tr. 50056-50057, note after 99383C, 2d note after 106378
Ruche litteraire illustre. 73876
Rvcioli, Antonio. tr. 32678, 72810
Ruckblick auf deren erstes Jahrhundert. 8722
Ruckblick auf die Zustande der Vereinigten Staaten. 29676
Ruckblick auf einige der alteren Reisen in Norden. 29940
Ruckert, Friedrich. (73877)
Rucksicht auf die Lage des dortigen Duetschen Militars. 71471, 77653
Rudd, E. B. 73878
Rudd, John C. 73879-73884
Rudd, Sayer. (73885)
Ruddell, Maria. 67795, note after 71255, note after 100844
Rudder, William. 73886-(73887)
Ruddiman, --------. ed. 73888
Ruddiman, Thomas, 1674-1757. 73398-73400, (73402), 73889
Ruddiman's weekly mercury. 73888
Ruddock, Samuel A. 73890-73891, 87782-87783
Rude stone monuments in all countries. 24104
Rude veins of a poetic conformation. 89438
Ruder, F. A. 21127, 73892, 96066, 101301
Rudge, E. (73893)
Rudimentc cosmographia. 32793-32794, 98281
Rvdimentorum cosmographiae. 69130
Rudimentorum cosmographiae libri duo. 32792
Rudimentorum cosmographicorum Ioan Honteri Coronensis. 32795-32797
Rvdimentorum cosmographicorum libri III. (32798)-32799
Rudiments of English grammar. 102367, 102375, note after 102396
Rudiments of English grammar, illustrated by parsing lessons. 88861

Rudiments of geography. 33435
Rudiments of Latin prosody. 57867
Rudiments of Latin syntax and prosody. 73405
Rudiments of law and government. 73894, note after 87945
Rudiments of mental philosophy. 91495
Rudiments of music. 89423
Rudiments of national knowledge. 73895
Rudiments of political science. 42943
Rudiments of taste. 73896
Rudiments of the Latin tongue. 73889
Rudimentum nuvitiorum. 76838
Ruding, Rogers. 73897-73898
Rudisill, Abraham. 85183
Rudo ensayo. (73899)
Rudolph, ---------. 73900-73901
Rudolph, Ludwig. 5135, 4540
Rudolph. 97465-97466
Rvdolphi Agricolae Ivnioris rheti. 98283
Rudoux, Henry. illus. 100745
Rudyard, Thomas. (53078), (59679) see also Board of Proprietors of the Eastern Division of New Jersey.
Rudyer, Sir Benjamin. see Rudyerd, Sir Benjamin, 1572-1658.
Rudyerd, Sir Benjamin, 1572-1658. 11398, 57765, 89176
Rue, Amelie Eugenie (Caron de Beaumarchais) Toussaint de la. see Toussaint de la Rue, Amelie Eugenie (Caron de Beaumarchais)
Rue, F. A. H. la. see La Rue, F. A. H.
Rue, Warren de la. see De la Rue, Warren.
Rueda, Bernardo. 73902
Rueda, Jose Ignacio. 73903
Rueda, Juan. 73904
Rueda Beranejos, Casandro. 73905
Ruel Daggs vs. Elihur Frazier et als. 26127
Ruelle-Pomponne, ------. 73906
Rufahl, Ludwig. see Kufahl, Ludwig. 73907
Rufende wachter Stimme. (73908)
Ruffian released. 26074
Ruffin, Edmund, 1794-1865. 1689, (9721), 23857, 73909-73919, 87374 see also South Carolina. Agricultural Surveyor.
Ruffin, Frank G. 73920
Ruffin, Thomas, 1787-1870. 73921
Ruffner, Henry. 73922-73923, 81797
Ruffner, William Henry. 73925
Rufiana. (73926)
Rufus, J. J. tr. 46910
Rufus, William. (73926)
Rufz, E. 73927-73930
Rufz de Lavison, Etienne, 1806-1884. 13645
Rugama, Laenciado da Jose Maria. 32771 see also Honduras. Ministro Jeneral.
Rugbaean. pseud. Transatlantic rambles. see Dixon, --------. supposed author
Rugeley, Rowland. supposed author 92337-92338, 2d note after 102599
Rugendas, Maurice. 73933-73935
Rugendas, Moritz. illus. 77121
Rugg, Charles P. 73936
Rugg, Henry W. 73937
Ruggle, George. supposed tr. 31998, 35676, 99886
Ruggles, A. G. 52026, 73938
Ruggles, Benjamin. 73939
Ruggles, C. Lorain. 73940
Ruggles, David. (73941)-73942
Ruggles, Edward. 73943
Ruggles, Henry. 8326
Ruggles, John, 1789-1874. 73944
Ruggles, Nathaniel. (73945)-(73946)
Ruggles, Samuel, fl. 1745. 86726, 2d note after 103650

Ruggles, Samuel Bulkley, 1800-1881. 640, 34923, 34935, 53660, 53768, 53895, (58410), (58595), 54109, 73947-73977, 88410, 103010 see also New York (State) Commissioner on the Englargement of the Canals for National Purposes. New York (State) Referee on Compensation to Owners of Vaults in Cemeteries, and to Relatives of Individuals Buried in Graves, Disturbed by Legal Proceedings. Southern Minnesota Railroad Company. Trustees. U. S. Delegate to the International Statistical Congress, Berlin, 1863. U. S. Delegate to the International Statistical Congress, The Hague, 1869.
Ruggles, Thomas. 73978-(73981)
Ruhl, Karl. 73982
Ruhrende Erzahlung. (70449)
Ruhrende Lektur. (22806)
Ruin and restoration. 73571
Ruin of Callao. 73983
"Ruin" of Jamaica. (31792)
Ruin of the Democatic Party. 73984
Ruin or separation from Anti-Christ. 58609
Ruin seize thee, ruthless king! 73985
Ruina de la Nueva Espana. 10652, 41986
Ruina de Tula. 71703
Ruina y destruccion de la profesa. 73986
Ruinas de mi convento. 73987
Ruinas del monasterio. 87244
Ruinous effects of civil war. 20099
Ruinous tendency of auctioneering. 73988
Ruins of Athens; Titania's banquet, a mask. (73989), 2d note after 100820
Ruins of Athens, with other poems. (73989)
Ruins of innocence. 101458
Ruins of Paestum. 62627, 62630
Ruins of Port Royal in 1801. 28724
Ruins of Tenampua, Honduras. 89993
Ruiz, Antonio. ed. 74001, 74029
Ruiz, Antonio. see Ruiz de Montoya, Antonio.
Ruiz, Domingo. 73990
Ruiz, Francisco. defendant 27309, (51797), 69915, 93808, 96948
Ruiz, Gaspar Soler. see Soler Ruiz, Gaspar.
Ruiz, Hipolito. see Ruiz Lopez, Hipolito, 1754-1815.
Ruiz, J. J. Larriva y. see Larriva y Ruiz, J. J.
Ruiz, Jose, fl. 1858. 74007
Ruiz, Jose, fl. 1861. (74008)
Ruiz, Juan, fl. 1759. 74009
Ruiz, Manuel. 74010
Ruiz, Nicolas. 74011
Ruiz, Santiago Jose Lopez. 41102, 41998, 74012-74013
Ruiz, Sebastian Josef Lopez. 74014
Ruiz, Telesforo. (74015)
Ruiz, Thomas Antonio. 74016
Ruiz Blanco, Matias, 1643-1705? 5852-5854, 74017-74019, 105954
Ruiz Blanco, Matias, 1643-1705? petitioner 74019
Ruiz Calado, J. I. 67108, 67861
Ruiz Guerra y Morales, Christoval. 67635, 74044
Ruiz Cano y Galiano, Antonio. 74020
Ruiz Davila, Manuel. (74021)
Ruiz de Apodaca, Juan. 74022
Ruiz de Conejares, Francisco Alonso y. 74023
Ruiz de Conejares, Francisco Alonso y. supposed author 98861
Ruiz de Conejares, Joseph. 74024
Ruiz de Esparza, Mariano. see Esparza, Mariano Ruiz de.
Ruiz de Leon, Francisco. 74025

Ruiz de Montoya, Antonio. 74026-(74041)
Ruiz de Padron, Antonio Joesph. 74043,
94286
Ruiz de Villafranca y Cardenas, Jose. see
Ruiz Villafranca y Cardenas, Joseph.
Ruiz Guerra y Morales, Christoval. 74044
Ruiz Lopez, Hipolito, 1754-1815. 38728,
73991-74006
Ruiz Lozano, Antonio. 74045
Ruiz Morales, Carlos. 74046
Ruiz Perea, Miguel. 74047
Ruiz Villafranca y Cardenas, Joseph. 74048,
99625
Ruiz y Cervantes, Jose Manuel. 74049-74050
Ruiz Montoya en Indias. 105717
Rule and measure of Christian charity. 85320
Rule and misrule of the English in America.
29694
Rule Britannia. 101771
Rule establish'd in Spain. 98781
Rule in Minot's case again. 76797
Rule of divine providence applicable. (21137)
Rule of life. 12150
Rule of the new-creature. 74051
Rule or ruin. 74052
Rulers are a terror. 92102
Ruler's duty and honor. 104216
Rulers feeding & guiding their people. 100914
Rulers highest dignity. 13349
Rulers must be just. (79428)
Rulers should be benefactors. 30168
Rulers the ministers of God. 104895
Rules adopted by the . . . Directors. 62352
Rules adopted by the President and Directors.
12510
Rules and articles for governing troops in
forts and garrisons. 91426-91427
Rules and articles for the better government
of His Majesty's Horse and Foot Guards.
74053
Rules and articles for the better government
of the troops . . . of the United States.
100375
Rules and articles for the better government
of the troops of the United States.
(74060)
Rules and articles, for the better government
of the troops raised, or to be raised,
and kept by and at the joint expence.
74054, 74055
Rules and articles for the better government
of the troops, raised, or to be raised,
and kept in pay, by and at the expense
of the United States of America. (74058)-
74059, 74161-74164, 91431
Rules and articles, for the better government
of the troops raised, or to be raised,
and kept in pay by and at the joint expense of the English colonies of North-
America. 74057
Rules and articles for the better government
of the troops raised, or to be raised,
and kept in pay by and at the joint
expence of the thirteen United English
colonies. 74056
Rules and articles for the government of the
armies of the republic of Texas. 95059
Rules and articles for the government of the
armies of the United States. 74065-
74066
Rules and articles for the government of the
army of Virginia. 74067
Rules and articles for the government of the
Pennsylvania forces. 74068
Rules and articles of the [Massachusetts Charitable Mechanic] Society. 45829

Rules and articles of the Worcester Mutual
Fire Insurance Company. 105434
Rules and articles of war. 26903, 91454,
91458
Rules and articles of war, and the military
laws. 94786
Rules and articles of war, for the government
of the troops of the United States. 74069
Rules and bye-laws of the Society of Cincinnati.
86138
Rules and by-laws [of Boston Pier.] (6731)
Rules and by-laws of the Charleston Library
Society. 12040
Rules and by-laws [of the Fall River Athenaeum
Library.] 23743
Rules and by-laws of the First Universalist
Society. 73643
Rules and by-laws of the Overseers of Harvard
College. (30749)
Rules and by-laws of the St. Louis Chamber
of Commerce. 75338
Rules and by-laws of the St. Louis Chamber
of Commerce, with the act of incorpora-
tion. 75339
Rules & by-laws of the Salem Evangelical
Library. 75724
Rules and catalogue of the Social Law Library.
(6773)
Rules and constitution of the Society of St.
George, in Maryland. 86081
Rules and constitution of the Society of the
Sons of St. George. 86167
Rules and constitutions of the Society of English-
men. (74070)
Rules and constitutions of the Society of the
Sons of St. George. 74071
Rules and constitutions of the Society of the
Sons of St. George, established at Phila-
delphia. 62260
Rules and decisions of the General Assembly.
60595
Rules and decisions of the General Assembly
of Pennsylvania. 85177
Rules and decisions of the General Assembly
of Pennsylvania. Legislative directory.
85176
Rules and directions for proceedings in the
Patent Office. 59048
Rules and direction for the Confederate States
Patent Office. 15405
Rules and directions for proceedings in the
Confederate States Patent Office. 74072
Rules & directions respecting damages to the
college buildings. 105836
Rules and discipline of the Yearly Meeting of
Friends, held in Virginia. 100526
Rules and forms in bankruptcy in . . .
Massachusetts. 46110
Rules and joint rules of the Senate and House
. . . of Illinois. 34277
Rules, and list of members, of Garden-Street
Church. 6646
Rules, and names of members [of the Maverick
Church, Boston.] 6657
Rules and orders for establishing a fund of
charity. 25814
Rules and orders for regulating the practice
of the Supreme Court of Pennsylvania.
(60596)
Rules and orders for regulating the practice
of the Supreme Court of Pennsylvania,
the Circuit Court of the United States.
60597
Rules and orders for the management of the
House of Correction. (10144)

Rules and regulations, for the government of the Protestant Episcopal Church. 87930

Rules and regulations for the government of the public schools. 64432

Rules and regulations for the government of the School Board. (13088)

Rules and regulations for the government of the Union Bank of the State of Tennessee. 94812, note after 97760

Rules and regulations for the government of the United Fire Society. 97873

Rules and regulations for the introduction of gas. 9063

Rules and regulations for the management of the Philadelphia, Wilmington and Baltimore, and the Newcastle and Frenchtown, Rail Roads. 62051

Rules and regulations for the Massachusetts army. (46117)

Rules and regulations for the Massachusetts army. Published by order. 74082

Rules and regulations for the . . . Philadelphia Club. (61981)

Rules and regulations for the Philadelphia Public Schools. 62201

Rules and regulations for the sword exercise of the cavalry. 74083

Rules and regulations for . . . the Wills Hospital. 62390

Rules and regulations in bankruptcy. 74084

Rules and regulations made by the Controllers [of the Public Schools, Philadelphia.] 61561

Rules and regulations of Bowdon Collegiate Institution. 7041

Rules and regulations of Harvard College. (30749)

Rules and regulations of Her Majesty's Colonial Service. 74085

Rules and regulations of said Board [of Health.] (10144)

Rules and regulations of the Ancient and Honourable Artillery Company. 74086

Rules and regulations of the Assembly of New York. 53954

Rules and regulations of the Bar in the county of Essex. (23009)

Rules and regulations of the Bar in the county of Norfolk. (55474)

Rules and regulations of the Bar, in the county of Suffolk. 93431

Rules and regulations of the Bar, in the county of Waldo. 101013

Rules and regulations of the Board of Education of the city of Chicago. (12644)

Rules and regulations of the Board of Education of the city of Detroit. (19792)

Rules and regulations of the Board of Health [in Dorchester, Mass.] (20628)

Rules and regulations of the Board of Health [of Boston.] (6610)

Rules and regulations [of the Boston Board of Health.] 45796

Rules and regulations of the Boston Chamber of Commerce. 6628

Rules and regulations of the Boston Hussars. 74087

Rules and regulations of the Brotherhood of St. Vincent of [sic] Paul. 86087

Rules and regulations of the Cemetery of the Evergreens. (23293)

Rules and regulations of the Charlestown Gas Company. (12117)

Rules and regulations of the Christian Society called the Church of Christ. 21923

Rules and regulations . . . of the City Library [of Manchester.] 44213

Rules and regulations of the College. 14251

Rules and regulations of the Confederate Army. 12846

Rules and regulations of the Convention for the Amendment and Revision of the Constitution. (42276)

Rules and regulations of the Corporation of Malden Bridge. (44100)

Rules and regulations of the District Medical Society. 93940

Rules and regulations of the Fire Department of . . . Lowell. 42487

Rules and regulations of the Franklin United Fire Society. 97872

Rules and regulations of the government of the Grand Army of the Republic. 74088

Rules and regulations of the Governors of the Alms House. 54073

Rules and regulations of the Green-Wood Cemetery. 28698

Rules and regulations of the Laurel Hill Cemetery. 61764

Rules and regulations of the Louisville Jockey Club. 42328

Rules and regulations of the . . . [Maple Grove Cemetery] Association. 44451

Rules and regulations of the . . . [Massachusetts Rifle] Club. 45889

Rules and regulations of the . . . [Massachusetts] Society [for Promoting Agriculture.] (45896)

Rules and regulations of the Medical College of South Carolina. 87878

Rules and regulations of the medical societies [in New Jersey.] 74089

Rules and regulations of the Mercantile Club. 61835

Rules and regulations of the Most Worshipful Grand Lodge. 87844

Rules and regulations of the Mutual Assistance Bag Company. 54409

Rules and regulations of the Navy. 15527

Rules and regulations of the Newton Theological Institution. (55095)

Rules and regulations of the Overseers. (30749)

Rules and regulations [of the Philadelphia Almshouse.] 61455

Rules and regulations of the Portland Rifle Company. 64366

Rules and regulations of the Providence Dispensary. 66320

Rules and regulations of the Public Library. 54922

Rules and regulations of the public schools. 42480

Rules and regulations of the Public Schools of . . . Nantucket. 51753

Rules and regulations [of the Public Schools of Richmond, Ind.] 71158

Rules and regulations of the quarantine. 42302

Rules and regulations of the Rhode Island Hospital. (70722)

Rules and regulations of the Rome Cemetery. 73020

Rules and regulations, of the School Committee, of . . . Lawrence. 39396

Rules and regulations of the School Committee [of Salem, Mass.] (75743)

Rules and regulations of the Society for Political Enquiries. (62249)

Rules and regulations of the Theological School at Cambridge. (30749)

Rules and regulations of the . . . Trustees. 59396

Rules and regulations of the Union Club of Philadelphia. 62350

Rules and regulations of the Washington Jockey Club. 101968

Rules and regulations of the Worcester Associate Library Company. 105379

Rules and regulations prescribed by the Mayor. 54584

Rules and regulations promulgated by the President. 95017

Rules and regulations relating to the several laws of Bowdoin College. 7038

Rules and regulations, to be observed in the Library. 45370

Rules and regulations . . . with Mr. Cleaveland's descriptive notices. 28700

Rules and regulations with regard to the qualifications. 86118

Rules and regulations . . . with suggestions respecting the purchases. 28699

Rules and statutes of the professorships in the University of Cambridge. (30749)

Rules and statutes of the University [of Pennsylvania.] 60758

Rules, articles of faith . . . and names of members. 6645

Rules, by-laws, etc., of Trustees. 34207

Rules for a holy life. (78447)

Rules for behaviour during meals. 90221

Rules for conducting business in the Senate. 94973

Rules for conducting business in the Senate of the third Congress. 94972

Rules for conducting business in the Senate of the Confederate States of America. 15407

Rules for conducting the business of the Senate of the United States. 74090

Rules for drill and the evolutions of the light cavalry. 17368

Rules for establishing rank of precedence. 60598

Rules for the exercises and manoeuvres of the cavalry. 87370

Rules for governing the Proprietors. (66330)

Rules for hearing the word of God. 9238

Rules for keeping the principal record books. 74091

Rules for preserving the health of the soldier. 30113, 76540, 76647, 76657, 76695

Rules for reducing a great empire to a small one. 25580, 74092

Rules for the art of eloquence. (5431)

Rules for the compilation of the catalogue. 91514

Rules for the Court of Common Pleas. 95852

Rules for the discerning of the present times. 104103

Rules for the Executive Service. 76608, 76647

Rules of the exercise and manoeuvres of the United States Infantry. 78411

Rules for the government of principals and seconds. 104661

Rules for the government of the Alms-House. 54073

Rules for the government of the Board of Guardians. 61503

Rules for the government of the Common Council. 61553

Rules for the government of the Democratic Party. 62203

Rules for the government of the National Union Party. 61859

Rules for the government of the Orphan-House, at Charleston. 12083

Rules for the government of the . . . [Pennsylvania] Hospital. 60330

Rules for the government of the School Committee. (75743)

Rules for the government of the Select and Common Councils. 62205

Rules for the government of the Select Council. 62204

Rules for the government of this Congress. 74093

Rules for the . . . Grammar, Secondary, and Primary Schools. (61502)

Rules for the House of Representatives of the Confederate States. 15408

Rules for the Incorporated South-Carolina Society. 12085

Rules . . . for the medical relief of the poor. 54460

Rules for the regulation of practice in Chancery. (74094)

Rules for the regulation of the [Pennsylvania] Society [for the Promotion of the Abolition of Slavery.] 60364

Rules for the regulation of the Society for the Relief of Free Negroes. 62255

Rules for the St. Andrew's Society, in New-York. (74995)

Rules for the St. Andrew's Society in Philadelphia. (62210)

Rules for the Society of Negroes. 74095

Rules [for the use of Clinton Cemetery.] 13758

Rules for waiters. 105834

Rules governing the National Academy of Sciences. 51915

Rules in civil causes of admiralty and maritime jurisdiction. 74096

Rules, maxims, and observations. 74098

Rules of a visit. 46492

Rules of College Wood-Yard. 105837

Rules of discipline and Christian advices. 60599

Rules of discipline of the Yearly-Meeting, held on Rhode-Island. (74099)-74100

Rules of discipline of the Yearly Meeting of Friends, for Pennsylvania, New-Jersey, Delaware, and the eastern part of Maryland. (60600)

Rules of discipline of the Yearly Meeting of Friends, for Pennsylvania, New-Jersey, Delaware, and the eastern parts of Maryland. 74101

Rules of discipline of the Yearly Meeting of Friends, held in Philadelphia. 62202, 74102

Rules of discipline of the Yearly Meeting of Philadelphia. 62202

Rules of equity practice. 60601

Rules of examination. 105839

Rules of order and discipline. 87311

Rules of order and regulations, adopted by the Board of Commissioners. 3082

Rules of order for the . . . Senate and House of Commons. (55690)

Rules of practice for the Vice-Admiralty Court of Jamaica. 31926

Rules of practice of the Court of Claims of the United States. 74103

Rules of practice of the Court of Equity. 74104

Rules of practice of the Court of Equity of the United States. 74105

Rules of practice, to be observed in the discipline of the church. (76446)

Rules of practice under the Sequestration Act. 15409

Rules of prosody. 74106

Rum and dynamite. 83716
Rumball, Thomas. 74122
Rumbo, Antonio. (74123)
Rumbo seguro y vnico para traer las Indias. 87204
Rumford, Sir Benjamin Thompson, Count, 1753-1814. 95466
Rumford Society, Harvard University. see Harvard University. Rumford Society.
Rvmori moderni di Francia. 106333
Rumpus, Roger. pseud. At a meeting of the true Sons of Liberty. 86983
Rumseller's money. 77023
Rumseller's victim. (16823)
Rumsey, James. 3521, 24581-24582, 74126-74129
Run and read library. 92500
Run-away last Sunday night. 93972
Run through the United States. 47047
Runaway boy. 30162
Runaway fight of the regulars. 40888
Runckler, Seb. 74130
Rundall, Thomas. (74131)
Rundle, T. (74132)
Runge, G. 61888
Runkel, William. 74133
Runkle, Benjamin P. (74134) see also U. S. Bureau of Refugees, Freedmen, and Abandoned Lands. Department of Kentucky. Chief Superintendent.
Runkle, Benjamin P. defendant at court martial (74135)-74137
Runkle, John D. 85072
Runnell, E. B. 74139
Runnells, E. B. 74140-74141
Runnells, M. T. 74142-74144
Running sketches of men and places. (16721)
Running the gauntlet. 85433
Runyon, Theodore. 74145
Rupert, -----. 16747
Rupert Redmond. 88606
Rupert, Vt. Congregational Church. 74146
Rupert, Vt. Ecclesiastical Council, 1815. see Congregational Churches in Vermont. Ecclesiastical Council, Rupert, 1815.
Ruperti, F. 58263
Ruperto, -----. 94839
Rupert's Land, Bishop of. see Anderson, David, Bishop of Rupert's Land.
Rupert's Land, Canada. Inhabitants. petitioners see People of Rupert's Land and North-West Territory, British Canada. petitioners
Rupp, I. Daniel. 74150-74164, 74200, 83289, 84617, 89175, 101710
Ruppaner, -------. defendant 90759
Ruppius, Otto. 74165-74167
Ruprecht, Theodor. 74168
Rural cemeteries of America. 13606, (28695), 51149, 74169
Rural Cemetery, New Bedford, Mass. see New Bedford Rural Cemetery.
Rural Cemetery, Pittsfield, Mass. see Pittsfield, Mass. Rural Cemetery.
Rural Cemetery, Poughkeepsie, N. Y. see Poughkeepsie, N. Y. Rural Cemetery.
Rural cemetery and public walk. 101076
Rural code of Haiti; in French and English. (29586)
Rural code of Haiti. Literally translated. 29587
Rural code of the province of Buenos Ayres, 51269
Rural economist. see Journal of the American Silk Society and rural economist.
Rural economy. 106065

Rural essays. 20775
Rural harmony. 37756
Rural hours; a poem. (26222)
Rural hours, by a lady. 16605
Rural lays and sketches. 65563
Rural life in America. 59639
Rural life in New England. 74170
Rural magazine and farmer's monthly museum. 74171, 101012
Rural magazine, and literary evening fireside. 74172
Rural magazine: or, Vermont repository. (74173), 1st note after 99205, 104347
Rural manuals, no. 1. 24683, 50344
Rural New-Yorker. 50344
Rural poem. With miscellaneous poems. (32561)
Rural poem, written for the centennial celebration. 90889
Rural poems. By John Hayes. 31023
Rural poems. By Thomas Buchanan Read. 68182
Rural register and almanac. (38846)
Rural repository, devoted exclusively to polite literature. (74174)
Rural repository, or bower of literature. (74175)
Rural scenes. 68037
Rural sketches of Minnesota. 30012
Rural Socrates. (74176), 3d note after 98684
Rural studies with hints for country places. 49679
Rural visitor. 74177
Rural walks in cities. 6689
Rurality. Original desultory tales. 94234
Rus de Cea, Genaro. 74178-(74180)
Ruscelli, Girolamo. tr. 66503-66505, 66507, 73198
Ruschenberger, W. S. E. (23360), 31978, 69696, 74181-74197, 1st note after 93829, 3d note after 96756
Ruschenberger's series. First books of natural history. 74197
Rusco. pseud. Teone. see Smith, Mary Ann.
Rusdorfer, Bernard. (22821)
Rush, Benjamin, 1745-1813. 9837, 10876, 17861, 18000, (20221), 31877, 56592, 60010, 60393, 61299, (74198)-74241, (78619), 79268, (82106), 84602, 90240, note after 99798
Rush, Benjamin, 1745-1813. supposed author 9836, 67712, 74215, 82725
Rush, Benjamin, 1745-1813. plaintiff 14030
Rush, Benjamin, 1811-1877. 74243-(74245), 74274
Rush, Caroline E. 55570, 74246-74247
Rush, Christopher. 74248
Rush, Jacob, 1746-1820. 14993, 74249-74250, 83764
Rush, James. 74251
Rush, Richard, 1780-1859. (25794), (26931), 36894, 64402, 67848, 74253-74278, 89359, 99301, 2d note after 101951, 104874 see also U. S. Legation. Great Britain. U. S. Treasury Department.
Rush, Richard, 1780-1859. supposed author 60682, (74252), 103155
Rush-light. 14030
Rush-light. 15th Feb., 1800. 14015
Rush Medical College, Chicago, Ill. (74279)
Rushton, Edward. 74280-(74281), 3d note after 101806
Rushton, Edward. supposed author 102805
Rushworth, John, 1612?-1690. 31095
Rusk, Thomas Jefferson, 1803-1857. 74282-74285, 89926

Russkos Geograficheskoe Obshchestvo, St.
Petersburg. 19577
Russwurm, H. 7725
Russwurm, Johannes. 75767
Rust, Albert, d. 1780. (74413)-74414
Rust, Richard S. 74415-74416
Ruste, ------. (5849)-5850, 56471
Rustic, Ruth. pseud. Forget-me-nots. 74418
Rustic bard. pseud. Incidental poems. see
Dinsmoor, Robert.
Rustic rhymes. 74417
Rusticatio Mexicana. 38839
Rusticus. pseud. Alazon. see Smith
William Wye, 1827-1917.
Rusticus. pseud. Friendly debate. (74419)
Rusticus. pseud. Good of the community.
27833, 74420, 3d note after 97116
Rusticus. pseud. Hints for the people.
(74424)
Rusticus. pseud. Letter from the country.
40342
Rusticus. pseud. Letter to a merchant in
Boston. 27833, 40415, 74420, 3d note
after 97116
Rusticus. pseud. Liberty. 74421-(74422)
Rusticus. pseud. Long Island miscellanies.
see Furman, Garrett.
Rusticus. pseud. Remarks on a late pamph-
let. see Dickinson, John, 1732-1808.
supposed author
Rusticus, Nicholas. pseud. Pride or a touch
at the times. (74426)
Ruston, Thomas. (74427)-(74428)
Ruston, Thomas. supposed author 32637, 1st
note after 69417, (74428)
Rusty-Turncoat, Robert. pseud. Wasp. see
Croswell, Harry, 1778-1858. defendant
Rus-urban tale. 36842
Ruszisch-Kaiserlichen Generalmajors von der
Flotte. 77125
Ruter, Martin. (74429)-74430
Ruter, Michael. 9153
Ruter, P. S. (74431)
Rutgers, Anthony. 53473, 54042, 83604
Rutgers, Elizabeth. plaintiff 53473, 74432-
74433, 83604
Rutgers Female College, New York. 74443,
74445
Rutgers Female College, New York. Board of
Trustees. 74445
Rutgers Female College, New York. Board of
Trustees. President. 74442
Rutgers Female College, New York. Charter.
74445
Rutgers Female College, New York. Inaugu-
ration Meeting, 1867. 74444
Rutgers Female College, New York. President.
74442
Rutgers Female Institute, New York. see
Rutgers Female College, New York.
Rutgers literary miscellany. 74446
Rutgers Medical College, New York. see
Geneva College, Geneva, N. Y. Rutgers
Medical College, New York.
Rutgers Medical College, Duane Street. 74447
Rutgers Scientific School, Trenton, N. J. 74449
Rutgers University, New Brunswick, N. J.
30791, 74436, 74438, (74441)
Rutgers University, New Brunswick, N. J. Cen-
tennial Celebration, 1870. 74437
Rutgers University, New Brunswick, N. J.
Charter. 52520
Rutgers University, New Brunswick, N. J.
Students. 74436
Rutgers University, New Brunswick, N. J.
Trustees. 74440

Rutgers vs. Waddington. 53473, 83604
Ruth Churchill. 74450
Ruth Hall. 58961
Ruth Rustic. pseud. see Rustic, Ruth. pseud.
Rutherfoord, John, 1792-1865. (28415) see
also Virginia. Governor, 1841-1842
(Rutherfoord)
Rutherfoord, John C. see Rutherford, John C.
Rutherford, -------, fl. 1830. (74453)
Rutherford, John. 74452
Rutherford, John C. (74453)-(74454)
Rutherford, Samuel. 17091, 32861, 46782,
74455-(74460)
Rutherford, Walter. (7884), 95936
Rutherford, Williams. 27022, 27114
Rutherfurd, John. 74461
Rutherfurd, Livingston. 84557
Rutherfurd, Samuel. see Rutherford, Samuel.
Ruth's sacrifice. 59445, 64092
Ruth's vision. 74451, 75920
Ruthven, A. S. 74462
Rutland, Charles Manners, 4th Duke of, 1754-
1787. 89210
Rutland, Mass. 74464
Rutland, Mass. School Committee. 74463
Rutland, Vt. 74468, 74471
Rutland, Vt. Association of Underwriters. see
Association of Underwriters of Rutland, Vt.
Rutland, Vt. Charter. 74465-74466
Rutland, Vt. Circuit Court. 106058
Rutland, Vt. Citizens. 25012
Rutland, Vt. Free Convention, 1858. see Free
Convention, Rutland, Vt., 1858.
Rutland, Vt. Ordinances, etc. 74465-74466
Rutland, Vt. Selectmen. 74469
Rutland, Vt. Trustees. 74468
Rutland and Burlington Railroad Company.
defendants (74472), 91108
Rutland and Burlington Railroad Company.
Charter. (74472)
Rutland and Burlington Railroad Company.
Directors. (74472)
Rutland and Stamford Auxiliary Bible Society.
74473
Rutland and Whitehall Railroad. 74474
Rutland County Agricultural Society. Annual
Fair, 11th, 1856. (74475)
Rutland county almanac 1862. 74476
Rutland herald. 93898, 99142
Rutland Marble Company. 74477
Rutland Railroad Company. Managers. (74479)
Rutledge. pseud. Mr. Douglas and the doctrine
of coercion. (74480)
Rutledge. pseud. Reply to "Palmetto." 87937
Rutledge. pseud. Resources of South-Carolina.
87943
Rutledge. pseud. Separate state secession
practically discussed. 74481, 87946
Rutledge, Capt. pseud. see Hines, David
Theodore.
Rutledge, Edward, 1749-1800. 48052, 87538
see also South Carolina. Governor,
1798-1800 (Edward Rutledge)
Rutledge, Edward, 1798-1832. 74482-74484
Rutledge, Henry M. 74485
Rutledge, Jean Jacques. 74486
Rutledge, John, 1739-1800. 20985, 22202,
74487-74489, 87535, 87854 see also
South Carolina. Governor, 1779-1782
(John Rutledge)
Rutt, John Towill. (9867), 74490
Ruttan, Henry. 74491
Ruttenber, E. M. 74492-74496
Rutter, -------. 74497
Rutter's political quarterly. 74497
Ruttimann, ------. 74498

S., G.

S., G. pseud. Temperance. 74611
S., G., Brussels. pseud. Present financial position of the United States. 74611
S., G., Brussels. pseud. Relative position of the finances. 74611
S., G. B. pseud. Alliance of British cotton spinners. see Stebbins, Giles Badger.
S——, G—— H——. pseud. Song. see Spierin, George Heartwell.
S., G. W. pseud. Descripiton of the Eastern Penitentiary. 74612
S., G. W. pseud. View and description of the Eastern Penitentiary. 60080, note after 99542
S., H. pseud. History of the Davenport family. 74613
S., H. pseud. Journal on board H. M. Ship Cambridge. 74614
S., H. M. pseud. Financial suggestions. 74615
S., H. M. pseud. Financial suggestions. No. 2. 74615
S., H. R. pseud. Rise of the west. see Schoolcraft, Henry Rowe, 1793-1864.
S., H. W. pseud. Record of a happy life. see Smith, Horace Wemyss.
S., I. pseud. Discovery of Fonseca. 20248, (74617)
S., I. pseud. Epistle from Yarico to Inkle. see Story, Isaac, 1774-1803. incorrectly supposed author
S., I. pseud. Mirror of merit and beauty. see Smith, James, d. 1812.
S., I., an eye-witness. pseud. Brief and perfect journal. 7854, 74616
S., I. A. pseud. Stradavits reyse. 74618
S., I. C. E. pseud. Physikalisch Untersuchung. see Springer, Johann Christoph Eric.
S., J. pseud. tr. 43832
S., J. pseud. tr. see Scottow, Joshua.
S., J. pseud. Mirror of merit and beauty. see Smith, James, d. 1812.
S., J. pseud. Narrative of the planting. see Scottow, Joshua.
S., J. pseud. Old mens tears. see Scottow, Joshua.
S., J. pseud. Seven hints for all who will take them. 62238, 79356
S., J. pseud. 1674. An almanack. see Sherman, John, 1613-1685.
S., J. pseud. 1676. An almanack. see Sherman, John, 1613-1685.
S., J. pseud. Some account of J. S. (74619)
S., J. pseud. Second Spira. (78740)
S., J. pseud. Strictures on the abolition of the slave trade. see Sabine, James.
S., J. pseud. To the Reverend Mr. William Hubbard. (33445)-33446, 106052
S., J. a layman. pseud. Strictures on the Rev. Mr. Thatcher's pamphlet. see Sullivan, James, 1744-1808.
S., J. A. B. D. M. F. P. E. pseud. Relacam do estrango. 69164
S., J. B. pseud. tr. 92604
S., J. C. E. pseud. Physikalisch Untersuchung. see Springer, Johann Christoph Eric.
S., J. E. pseud. Vollstandige Beschreibung der Spanischen Handlung. (74620)
S., J. F. pseud. Algemeine Geschichte. see Schroter, Johann Fredrich.
S., J. G. pseud. tr. 14320, 2d note after 102874, 2d note after 106324
S., J. G. pseud. Selection of trials. 74621
S., J. H. pseud. Essay on the Red Sulphur Springs. 74622

S., J. I. H. Y. pseud. Sermon panegirico. see Heredia y Sarmiento, Jose Ignacio.
S., J. J. pseud. Letter from a gentleman of Baltimore. see Speed, Joseph J.
S., J. J. pseud. Vindicacion del Senador D. Jose Domingo Martinez Zurita. 99792
S**, J. L. pseud. Neue Nachrichten. see Schulze, Johan Ludwig.
S., J. Norberto de S. pseud. Brasileiras celebres. see Souza Silva, Joaquim Norberto de, 1820-1891.
S., J. R. Y. pseud. Coleccion de decretos. (48352)
S., J. W. pseud. To the public. 103973
S., John. pseud. tr. see Sechla, John. tr.
S., L. pseud. Noticias de la Provincia de Californias. see Sales, Luis.
S., L. pseud. Porcupine alias the Hedge-Hog. 74623
S., L. pseud. "Times" and the American war. see Stephen, Leslie.
S., L. C. pseud. Seaweeds from the shores of Nantucket. see Starbuck, Lucy Coffin.
S., L. H. pseud. Farmer and soldier. see Sigourney, Lydia (Huntley) 1791-1865.
S., L. M. pseud. Extracts of letters. see Sargent, Lucius M.
S., M. pseud. Adamic race. 74626
S., M. pseud. Enchiridion geographicum. 74625
S., M. pseud. Fundament. see Menno Simons.
S., M. pseud. Greevovs grones for the poore. see Sparke, Michael.
S., M. pseud. M. S. to A. S. see Goodwin, John. supposed author
S. M. pseud. Safe home. see Stoddard, Mrs. M.
S., M. B . . . . de. pseud. Memoire de la Guadeloupe. (74627)
S., M. D. pseud. Histoire naturelle et politique de la Pensylvanie. see Rousselot de Surgy, Jacques Philibert.
S., M. D. L. pseud. Dictionnaire Galibi. see Sauvage, ------- de la.
S., M. J. pseud. Vocabulario da lingua indigena. geral. see Seixas, Manuel Justiniano Justiniano de.
S., M. M. pseud. incorrectly supposed tr. 11235, 11287, 1st note after 39118
S., M. P. pseud. Mara. 74628
S., M. Q. C. pseud. Triunfo de la justicia. see Quiros y Campo-Sagrado, Manuel de.
S***, M. R. D. pseud. Melanges interessans. see Rousselot de Surgy, Jacques Philibert.
S., M. R. D. pseud. Oriental pearls at random strung. see Smith, Mary Rebecca Darby, 1814-1886.
S——, Martha. 26245, 30710
S., N. pseud. see Strong, Nehemiah.
S., N. pseud. Continuation of the state of New England. (52623)
S., N. pseud. New and further narrative. 52445
S., N. pseud. Present state of New-England. 65324
S., N., Presbyter. pseud. Strike but hear! 92862
S., N. B. pseud. John Beal of Hingham. see Shurtleff, Nathaniel Bradstreet, 1810-1874.
S., N. L. pseud. Tales of St. Augustine. see Smith, Nina L.
S., P. pseud. Biographical sketch of Rev. Preserved Smith. see Smith, Preserved, 1789-1881.

S., P. pseud. Clava del Indio. 74629

S., P. pseud. Hungarian exile, and his adventures. see Stojadirouicx, P. and Stehenson, P. incorrectly supposed author

S., P. de. pseud. Memorias da viagem. see Souza, Bernardo Xavier Pinto de.

S., P. M. D. pseud. Histoire naturelle. see Rousselot de Surgy, Jacques Philibert.

S., P: P: v: pseud. Seldsamme en noit gehoorde wal-vis-vangst. 74630, 78978

S., P. S. T. pseud. Astounding disclosures and frauds. 2257

S., P. V. pseud. engr. 84647

S----, R-----. pseud. reporter 104518

S*****, R*****. pseud. reporter 104519

S., R. pseud. tr. see Samber, R. supposed tr.

S., R. pseud. Daniel catcher. see Steer, Richard.

S., R. pseud. Pictorial history of the American revolution. see Sears, Robert, 1810-

S., R., a passenger in the Hector. pseud. Life and adventures of Peter Wilkins. see Paltock, Samuel. supposed author

S***, R. D. pseud. Melanges interessans et curieux. see Rousselot de Surguy, Jacques Philibert.

S., R. H. pseud. Life travels and books of Alexander von Humboldt. see Stoddard, Richard Henry.

S., S. pseud. Answer to the seditious and scandalous pamphlet. see Starling, Samuel.

S., S. pseud. Immanuel. see Shaw, Samuel, 1635-1697. and Stoddard, Solomon. incorrectly supposed author

S., S. pseud. Revolution in New England justified. see Sewall, Samuel, 1652-1730. supposed author

S., S. pseud. Upon the drying up of that ancient river. see Sewall, Samuel, 1652-1730. supposed author

S., S., a friend to justice, and courts of justice. pseud. Answer to the seditious and scandalous pamphlet. see Starling, Samuel.

S., S. C. pseud. Dover directory. see Stevens, Samuel C.

S., S. C. pseud. Legend of the Manitou Rock. (39857), 74632

S., S. S. pseud. Aunt Sophie's stories. see Simpson, S. S.

S., S. S. pseud. Flaming sword. see Snow, Samuel Sheffield.

S., S. S. pseud. Two hundred years ago. see Simpson, S. S.

S., T. pseud. tr. (25283)

S., T. pseud. Canada. see Sockett, Thomas, 1778?-1859.

S., T. pseud. Cool reply. see Stanley, Thomas.

S., T. pseud. Reasons why Mr. Byles left New London. 74633

S., T. pseud. Second part of Vox populi. see Scott, Thomas, 1580?-1626.

S., T. pseud. MDCLVI an almanack for the year of Our Lord 1656. 62743

S., T. pseud. Spoils system. see Smith, Truman, 1791-1884.

S., T. pseud. Thoughts on the proposed annexation. see Sedgwick, Theodore, 1811-1859.

S., T., of U. pseud. Second part of the Vox populi. see Scott, Thomas, 1580?-1626.

S., T., of V. pseud. Vox popvli. see Scott, Thomas, 1580?-1626.

S., T. H. pseud. Floating flowers. see Stockton, Thomas Hewlings.

S., T. R. C. S. C. pseud. tr. 37675

S., W. pseud. engr. see Saltonstall, Wye. engr.

S., W. pseud. ed. Discourse on the English constitution. 20243

S., W. pseud. Instructions for the increasing of mulberie trees. see Stallenge, William.

S., W. pseud. Joyful tidings. see Smith, William, d. 1673.

S., W. pseud. Liberty regain'd. (74636)

S----, W----. pseud. Mr. Aislabie's two speeches considered. see Sheppard, W.

S., W. pseud. Mysterious nothing. (74635)

S., W. pseud. Observations occasion'd by reading a pamphlet. 56481

S., W. pseud. Proceedings of the English colonie in Virginia. see Strachey, William. incorrectly supposed author and Symonds, William.

S., W. A. B. pseud. Antigionian and Boston beauties. see Chauncy, Charles, 1705-1787.

S., W. A. B. pseud. Some thoughts from Seneca. see Chauncy, Charles, 1705-1787.

S., W. H. pseud. Similarity of Washington and Harrison. see Smith, William Henry, d. 1860.

S., W. T. P. pseud. Τα 'Αεθλαάγγλαμερίκανα ὅρα δη Προγομναζρατα της φραγκίης. see Shortt, William T. P.

S., Y. O. pseud. Anecdota importante. 74637

S. Benoit Dinouart, Chanoine de. see Dinouart, Chanoine de S. Benoit.

S. de A., J. pseud. see A., J. S. de. pseud. tr.

S. S., J. Norberto de. pseud. Brasileiras celebres. see Souza Silva, Joaquim Norberto de, 1820-1891.

S. y A. pseud. Triunfo de la religion. see Sul y Amira, ---------.

S. y L., M. C. pseud. Espresiones de sincero y tierno efecto. 74638

S. A. T. pseud. see Thomas, Sidney A.

S. and S. Salisbury, continued importing from London. 105359

S. B. pseud. see B., S. pseud.

S. B. P. pseud. see Page, Stephen Benson.

S. B. Union for the Sake of the Union. 16128

S. C. pseud. see C., S. pseud.

S. C. pseud. see Cheever, Samuel.

S. C. pseud. see Conant, Shubael. supposed author

S. C. pseud. see Crisp, Stephen.

S. C. B. pseud. tr. see B., S. C. pseud. tr.

S. C. S. pseud. see S., S. C. pseud.

S. C. S. pseud. see Stevens, Samuel C.

S. D. pseud. see Danforth, Samuel.

S. D. C. pseud. see C., S. D. pseud. tr.

S---- de C----. pseud. see C----, S---- de. pseud.

S. de. V. pseud. see Vries, Simon de.

S. E. pseud. see E., S. pseud.

S. F. Business directory. 76092

S. Fernando III. Pey [sic] de Castilla. 86433

S. G. pseud. tr. see Goulard, Simon.

S. G. pseud. see Groome, S.

S. G. B. pseud. see B., S. G. pseud.

S. H. pseud. see Hume, Sophia.

S. H. of Boston in New-England. pseud. see Hutchinson, Samuel.
S. H. L. pseud. see L., S. H. pseud.
S. J. H. pseud. see Honeywood, St. John.
S. I. L. pseud. see L., S. I. pseud.
Sl K. pseud. see Fenno, John.
S. L. J. pseud. see Jones, Sarah L.
S. M. la Emperatriz Carolta en Veracruz. 10930
S. N. pseud. engr. see N., S. pseud. engr.
S. N. pseud. see Nowel, Samuel.
S. O. pseud. see Scott, Thomas, 1580?-1626.
S. O. B. pseud. see Beeton, S. O.
S. of U., T. pseud. see Scott, Thomas, 1580?-1626.
S. R. pseud. see Reed, Sylvanus.
S. R. N. I. pseud. see Scott, Thomas, 1580?-1626.
S. S. pseud. see Sewall, Samuel, 1652-1730.
S. S. pseud. see Shaw, Samuel, 1635-1696.
S. S. pseud. see Starling, Samuel.
S. S. S. pseud. see Simpson, S. S.
S. S. S. pseud. see Snow, Samuel Sheffield.
S. S. Seward Institute, Florida, N. Y. 24905, 79600
S. Southwick's address. 88649
SS. de la Junta Censoria Interna de esta siudad. 1886
S. T. pseud. see Walpole, Horace, 4th Earl of Orford, 1717-1797.
S―― T――. pseud. petitioner see T――, S――. pseud. petitioner
S. T. C. pseud. see C., S. T. pseud.
S. T. O. G. pseud. see Satariengo-Teran-Obregon, G.
S. von N. pseud. see N., S. von. pseud.
S. von V. pseud. see Vries, Simon de.
S. W. pseud. see W., S. pseud.
S. W. M. pseud. see M., S. W. pseud.
Sa, Luis de Franca Almeida e. see Franca Almeida e Sa, Luis de.
Sa, Manoel Jose Maria de Costa e. see Costa e Sa, Manoel Jose Maria de.
Sa, Manoel Tavares de Sequeira e. see Sequeira e Sa, Manoel Tavares de.
Sa, S. J. Ribeiro de. see Ribeiro de Sa, S. J.
Sa de Menezes, Francisco de. see Menezes, Francisco de Sa de.
Sa e Albuquerque, A. C. de. 678
Sa e Menezes, Estacio de. 74640
Sa Pereira de Castro, Eduardo de. 74641
Saa, Jacobus a. (74642)
Saabye, Hans Egede. (22030), 74643-74646
Saacke, F. 74647
Saakaldte "Ottawahistorie" upartisk belyst af S. Sommer. 86852
Saam, Moses Ben. pseud. Speech. see Robertson, Robert.
Saavedra, Bernardo Carrasco y. see Carrasco y Saavedra, Bernardo.
Saavedra, Diego. 74648
Saavedra, Francisco Arias. 74649
Saavedra, Francisco Javier Venegas de. see Venegas de Saavedra, Francisco Javier.
Saavedra, Marcos de, d. 1631. 74650
Saavedra Guzman, Antoine de. see Guzman, Antoine de Saavedra.
Saba, Onuphrio Prat de. see Prat de Saba, Onuphrio.
Sabanas de Barinas. 10193, note after 94254, note after 98870
Sabatier, -------. illus. 48916, 73935
Sabatier, William. 74651

Sabatina universal. Periodico politico y literario. 74652
Sabau y Blanco, J. (44550)
Sabau y Larroya, Pedro. tr. 65284
Sabbath. A discourse on the duty of civil government. 104554
Sabbath . . . . A sermon, . . . at the annual election. (50459)
Sabbath among the Tuscarora Indians. (74653)
Sabbath and free institutions. 32943
Sabbath and the pulpit. (74654)
Sabbath and the sanctuary. 82935
Sabbath Association, Philadelphia. see Philadelphia Sabbath Association.
Sabbath at home. 22148, 74655
Sabbath Committee, New York. see New York Sabbath Committee.
Sabbath Convention, Harrisburg, Pa., 1844. see State Sabbath Convention, Harrisburg, Pa., 1844.
Sabbath Convention, Rochester, N. Y., 1842. 72350
Sabbath Convention, Saratoga Springs, N. Y., 1844. see New York State Sabbath Convention, Saratoga Springs, 1844.
Sabbath-day's rest asserted. 46209
Sabbath desecration. 74656
Sabbath in New York. 74657
Sabbath lyrics. (81253)
Sabbath of the Jews. 93742
Sabbath-profanity. 105230
Sabbath School Association, Hamilton County, Ohio. see Hamilton County Sabbath School Association.
Sabbath School Association of Minnesota. see Minnesota State Sabbath School Association.
Sabbath School Association of Philadelphia. see Philadelphia Sabbath School Association.
Sabbath School Convention, Salem, Mass. see Baptists. Massachusetts. Salem Baptist Association.
Sabbath-school index. (58559)
Sabbath school premium. 89799
Sabbath School Society of Massachusetts. see Massachusetts Sabbath School Society.
Sabbath School Teachers Convention, West Boylston, Mass. see Baptists. Massachusetts. Worcester Baptist Association. Sabbath School Teachers Convention, West Boylston, Mass.
Sabbath School Teachers of Massachusetts. Annual Convention, 4th, 1858. (46119)
Sabbath School Union, Lowell, Mass. see Lowell Sabbath School Union, Lowell, Mass.
Sabbath School Union, Newton, Mass. see Newton Sabbath School Union, Newton, Mass.
Sabbath School Union of Massachusetts. see Massachusetts Sabbath School Union.
Sabbath School Union of New England. see New England Sabbath School Union.
Sabbath School Union of the Reformed Protestant Dutch Church in North America. see Reformed Church in America. Sabbath School Union.
Sabbath School Union of Vermont. see Vermont Sabbath School Union.
Sabbath School Union of Worcester and Middlesex North. see Worcester and Middlesex North Sabbath School Union.
Sabbath School of Waterville, Me. see Waterville, Me. Sabbath School.
Sabbaths in the Arctic regions. 78176
Sabbatismos. A discussion and defence of the Lord's Day. (36934)

Sabellico, Marco Antonio Coccio, called, 1436?-
1506. 74658-74667
Sabellicus, M. A. C. see Sabellico, Marco
Antonio Coccio, called, 1436?-1506.
Sabin, C. B. 74668-74669
Sabin, Elijah R. (74670)-74672
Sabin, Joseph, 1821-1881. 9709, 11709, 16981,
22147, 22150, (36512), 45315, (70839),
72313, 74673-(74694), 73696, 80206-
80208, 84593, 91862, 92801, 101330,
101710, 103689, note after 104653
Sabin (Joseph) & Co. firm 74647
Sabin (Joseph) & Sons. firm publishers
61196, 74695
Sabine, Sir Edward, 1788-1883. 23923, (25624),
(33727), 37826, 39843, (55714), 73371,
73777, (74699)-(74716), 105518
Sabine, Mrs. Edward. see Sabine, Elizabeth
Juliana (Leeves) 1807-1879.
Sabine, Elizabeth Juliana (Leeves) 1807-1879.
tr. 33707, (33727), 105518
Sabine, James. 74718-(74729), 92848, 97772A
Sabine, Joseph. 74730
Sabine, Lorenzo. 74731-74736 see also Bos-
ton. Board of Trade. Secretary.
Sabine, Robert. 74737-74738
Sabine, William T. 74739-74740
Sabin's reprints. Octavo series. 4748, (36512),
36488, 74697, 84593, 91862, 101710
Sabin's reprints. Quarto series. 9709, 11709,
21611, 22147, 22150, 45315, 52759,
74696, 80206-80208, 92801, 101330,
103689, note after 104653
Sabin's reprints. Second series. 23779, 74698
Sabino. pseud. Popham colony. see Ballard,
Edward.
Sabio manifiesto de XIII. de Abril de 1811.
92096
Sable cloud. 340, 74741
Sable Venus. 94565
Sabliere, Trudaine de la. tr. 23993
Sabourin, A. D. 74742
Sabre, G. E. (74743)-74744
Sabrosa, --------, Baron da Ribeira de. see
Ribeira de Sabrosa, -------, Baron da.
Sac and Fox Indians. see Fox Indians. and
Sauk Indians.
Sacaza, Daniel. 74745
Saccheuse, --------. illus. 89541
Sacedon, Antonio de Jesus. 74746
Sacerdocio y la civilizacion. 47425
Sacerdos in aeternvm. 50108
Sacerdote. pseud. Carta familiar. 11098
Sacerdote. pseud. Clara y sucinta exposicion.
13233
Sacerdote. pseud. Devocionario hecho. see
Serruto y Nava, Jose.
Sacerdote de la Compania de Jesvs. pseud.
Manual para administrar a los Indios.
44418
Sacerdote de la misma Congregacion. pseud.
ed. Svma de vna platica. 93576
Sacerdote del Obispado de la Puebla de los
Angeles. pseud. Lecciones espirituales.
34191, 39628
Sacerdote del Obispado de Puebla. pseud.
Compendio del confessionario en idioma
Mexicano. (15035)
Sacerdote della Compagnia di Gesu. pseud.
Vita del Venerabile P. Fr. Francisco
Camacho. see Santagata, Saverio.
supposed author
Sacerdote della medesima Compagnia. pseud.
Della vita del Ven. servo di Dio P.
Guiseppe Ancheta. see Oddi, Longaro
degli.

Sacerdote della medesima Compagnia. pseud.
Vita del Venerabile Servio di Dio P.
Giuseppe Anchieta. see Oddi, Longaro
degli.
Sacerdote en el Peru. pseud. Carta. see
U., Y. A. pseud.
Sacerdote Mexicano. pseud. Segundas obser-
vaciones. 78908
Sacerdote Peruano en Chile. pseud. Contesta-
cion. see Requena, Cayetano.
Sacerdote religioso. pseud. Noticias de la
Provincia de Californias. see Sales,
Luis.
Sacerdote religioso hijo del Real Convento de
Predicadores del Valencia. pseud.
Noticias de la Provincia de Californias.
see Sales, Luis.
Sachems of the Three Maquas Castles. see
Three Maquas Castles (Indians) Sachems.
Sachem's-wood. 74747
Sachot, Octave. 74748
Sachsen. pseud. Freie Auswanderung. see
Bromme, Traugott.
Sachsen-Weimer-Eisenach, Karl Bernhard,
Herzog zu. see Karl Bernhard, Herzog
zu Sachsen-Weimer-Eisenach.
Sachtzung keine Tirauner. 69549
Sack, -------. 74752
Sack, Albert, Baron von. 74749-74751
Sack and destruction of the city of Columbia,
S. C. 81254
Sack of Unquowa. 91329
Sacken, R. Osten. see Osten-Sacken, R.
Sacket's Harbor and Ellisburgh Rail Road.
74753
Sacket's Harbor & Saratoga Rail-Road. (74754)
Sackett, John H. 74755
Sackett, Nathaniel. petitioner 74756
Sackett, William Augustus, 1821-1895. 74757-
(74758)
Sackett, William Post. defendant 74759
Sacks and Foxes of the Missouri. see Fox
Indians. and Sauk Indians.
Sackville, George Sackville Germain, 1st Vis-
count, 1716-1785. 8738, 13751, 16814,
27140, 27144, 64572, note before 95301-
95301
Sackville, George Sackville Germain, 1st Vis-
count, 1716-1785. supposed author 2761,
9266, 18347, 18348, 27145, 27188, note
after 41286, (62991), note after 71369
Sackville, John Frederick. see Dorset, John
Frederick Sackville, 3d Duke of, 1745-
1799.
Saco, Jose Antonio. 519, (37766), 74750-
74775
Saco, Maine. 74778, (74782)
Saco, Maine. Charter. 74777
Saco, Maine. City Council. 74777
Saco, Maine. Mayor, 1867. 74777
Saco, Maine. Mayor, 1870. 74778
Saco, Maine. Ordinances, etc. 74777
Saco, Maine. Superintending School Committee.
74776
Saco Indians. see Pequawket Indians.
Saco Water Power Company. 74781
Saco Water Power Company. Committee.
74779
Sacones de la lealtad clausulas. (11441)
Sacra Congregatio Rituum. see Catholic
Church. Congregation Sacrorum Rituum.
Sacra Rituum Congregatione Cardinali Nigrono
Oxomen. 74783
Sacra Rituum Congregatione Emo, & Rmo.
Domino Card. Nigronio. 74784

Sacra Ritum Congregatione Emo. et Rmo. Domino Cardinale Odescalchi. 64174

Sacra Rituum Congregatione Oxomen. Beatificationis. (74785)

Sacracenicall empire. 66682

Sacramena, Juan Jose. 74786

Sacramental controversy brought to a point. 78734

Sacramental discourse had at Boston. (14525)

Sacramental exercises. 21625

Sacramental sermon on the Lamb of God. 93207

Sacramento, Leondro do. see Leandro do Sacramento.

Sacramento, Lorenzo. 74787-74789

Sacramento, Lorenzo del Santo. see Lorenzo del Santo Sacramento.

Sacramento, Calif. California Medical Society Convention, 1856. see California Medical Society. Convention, Sacramento, 1856.

Sacramento, Calif. Citizens. 37808, 97098

Sacramento city and country directory. 74792

Sacramento Medical Society, Sacramento, Calif. 74793

Sacramento Valley Railroad Company. 74794

Sacred and miscellaneous verse. 84056

Sacred architecture. 90205

Sacred books of New Testament. note after 101417

Sacred circle. 74795

"Sacred concerts" unmasked. 93745

Sacred covenant of our heavenly parents. 91701

Sacred dignity of the Christian priesthood. 1758, 43664, (52608)

Sacred dirges, hymns, and anthems. 32475, 51578, note after 74795, note after 101879, 104278

Sacred exorcisms. 46230

Sacred Harmonic Society, New York. see New York Sacred Harmonic Society.

Sacred hymns and spiritual songs. 74797

Sacred hymns and spiritual songs for the Church of Jesus Christ of Latter Day Saints in Europe. (74796)

Sacred lines for thanksgiving day. 28251

Sacred memories. 84756-84756A

Sacred minister. (46801)

Sacred mirror. 84363-84365

Sacred Music Society, Madison, Wisc. 43739

Sacred music, to be performed in St. Paul's Church. 101880

Sacred Musical Society of Strafford County, N. H. see Strafford Sacred Musical Society.

Sacred ode. 105332

Sacred performances at the dedication of the Baptist Meeting-House in Charlestown. 12121, (50948), 91812

Sacred philosophy of earthquakes. 74798

Sacred poem on Dives and Lazarus. 89526, 89530

Sacred poems, and private ejaculations. (31457)

Sacred poetry. 73479

Sacred poetry and music reconciled. 104115

Sacred poets of England and America. (28898)

Sacred reminiscences. 43138

Sacred rhetoric. 71525

Sacred roll and book. 79707

Sacred sympathy of sorrow. 20391

Sacred to the memory of the illustrious champion of liberty. 101881

Sacred to the memory of the Reverend George Whitefield. 83452

Sacred writings of the apostles and evangelists. 10206

Sacredness of human life. 32881

Sacredness of learning. 85473

Sacredness of personality the shield of liberty. 11784

Sacri Ordinis Praedicatorum. see Dominicans. Sacripantes. 43301

Sacro Bosco, Joannes de, fl. 1230. 32677-32684, 74800-74810

Sacro Orden de Nuestra Senora de la Merced. see Mercedarians.

Sacrobosco, Joannes de. see Sacro Bosco, Joannes de, fl. 1230.

Sacrobusto, Giovanni de. see Sacro Bosco, Joannes de, fl. 1230.

Sacs and Foxes of Missouri Indians. see Fox Indians. and Sauk Indians.

Sacy, Claude Louis Michel de. 74811

Sad, and deplorable newes from New England. 74813

Sad and deplorable news from New England. 74812

Sad and dreadful news from New-England. 74814

Sad case; a great wrong! 67852

Sad effects of sin. 46493

Sad estate of the unconverted. 74815

Sad history of the unparallel'd cruelty. 4003

Sad tales and glad tales. (47442)

Sad tendency to divisions and contentions in churches. 104366

Sada, Luis. 74816-74817

Sadd, H. S. engr. 168, 84905

Saddi, Nathan Ben. pseud. Chronicle of the Kings of England. see Chesterfield, Philip Dormer Stanhope, 4th Earl of, 1694-1773. supposed author

Saddi, Nathan Ben. pseud. Chronicles of the Kings of England. see Dodsley, Robert 1703-1764. supposed author

Saddi, Nathan Ben. pseud. Fragment of the chronicles. see Dodsley, Robert, 1703-1764. supposed author

Saddle placed on the right horse. 60602

Saddle-trip on the south-western frontier. (57243)

Saddlebags, Jeremiah. pseud. Journey to the gold diggins. see Read, D. F. and Read, J. A.

Sadeur, Jacques. pseud. Aventures de Jacques Sadeur. see Foigny, Gabriel de.

Sadeur, Jacques. pseud. Terre australe connue. see Foigny, Gabriel de.

Sadia: a heroine of the rebellion. 36862

Sadleir, M. 97028

Sadler, Mrs. J. 43263, 74824-74826

Sadlier (D. & J.) & Co. firm publishers 74827-74828, (82267)

Sadlier (J.) & Co. firm publishers see Sadlier (D. & J.) & Co. firm publishers

Sadlier's catholic almanac and ordo. 74827

Sadlier's catholic directory. 74828

Sadlier's Household library. (82267)

Saeghman, Gillis Joosten. ed. and publisher 4804, 11263, 11264, 31507, 38257, 41364, 41365, 55431, 55444, 61334, 67981, (74830)-(74850), 78896, 89449, 97528-97529, 98740, 102500

Saenz, Agustin. 74851

Saenz, Diego. 74852

Saenz, Jose. 74853

Saenz, Manuel. petitioner (74854)

Saenz, Mateo. 74855

Saenz, Matias San Antonio. see San Antonio Saenz, Matias.

Sailing directions for the coast of North America, from New York to Cape Florida. 74959

Sailing directions for the coasts and harbours of North America. 5665

Sailing directions for the coasts of eastern and western Patagonia. (37827)

Sailing directions for the east coast of North America, from Boston to the Mississippi. 74960

Sailing directions for the east coast of North America, from Cape Canso to Cape Cod. 74961

Sailing directions for the Gulf and River St. Lawrence. 4045

Sailing directions for the Gulph and River of St. Lawrence. 5666

Sailing directions for the Gulf of St. Lawrence. 76322

Sailing directions for the island of Newfoundland. 74962

Sailing directions for the North American pilot. 34862

Sailing directions for the North American pilot: containing the Gulf and River St. Lawrence. 74965

Sailing directions for the River St. Lawrence. (38744)

Sailing directions for the west coast of North America. 74966

Sailing directions for the west coast of North America, from Bodega to Cape San Lucas. 6032

Sailing directions for the West Indies. 50413

Sailing directions from sea to Sandy Hook. 46974

Sailing directions, general and particular. 91090

Sailing directions of Henry Hudson. 19198

Sailing directories for the eastern coasts and islands of America. 66695-66696

Sailing directory for all the coasts of Brasil, &c. (66690)

Sailing directory for the American coasts. 66692-66694

Sailing directory for the Bermuda Islands. 66695

Sailing directory for the islands and banks of Newfoundland. 66691

Sailing directory for the northern part of the West Indies. 66696

Sailing directory for the windward and gulf passages. 66704

Sailing in the low-lands. 67599

Sailings over the globe. (74967)

Saillet, Alexandre de. 74968-74969

Sailor. pseud. Letter to the Right Honourable the Earl of Sandwich. 40529, 74970

Sailor boy a favorite [sic] song. 92175B

Sailor boy; or Jack Somers in the navy. 57216

Sailor boy's first voyage. 74971

Sailor boy's voyage to see the world. 55463

Sailor Crusoe. 75258

Sailor lov'd a lass. 92176

Sailor on board the Shrewsbury. pseud. Vernon's glory. 99259

Sailor's advocate. 74972

Sailor's advocate, numb. 11. 74972

Sailors & their hardships on shore. 74973

Sailor's companion. 74974

Sailor's letters. 95488

Sailor's magazine and naval journal. 74973, 74975

Sailor's medley. 94130

Sailor's revenge. 90522

Sailors' Snug Harbor, Boston. 6771, 74976

Sailors' Snug Harbor, Boston. Charter 74976

Sailors' Snug Harbor, New York. 67798, 74977

Sailors' Snug Harbor, New York. Charter. 67798, 74977

Sailors' Snug Harbor, New York. Trustees. 74977

Sailors' Snug Harbor of Boston. 74976

Sailours companion and counsellour. (46494)

Sain de Boislecomte, Andre Olivier Ernest. see Boislecomte, Andre Olivier Ernest Sain de.

Sains de la Pena, Francisco. 99785

Sainsbury, W. Noel. ed. 74979-74980, 88005

Saint, L. le. see Le Saint, L.

Saint Abe and his seven wives. 74982

Saint-Adolphe, J. C. R. Milliet de. see Millet de Saint-Adolphe, J. C. R.

St. Albans, Francis Bacon, Viscount. see Bacon, Francis, Viscount St. Albans.

St. Albans, Vt. First National Bank. plaintiffs 88829

St. Alban's Lodge, Wrentham, Mass. see Freemasons. Massachusetts. St. Alban's Lodge, Wrentham.

St. Albans raid. Investigation by the Police Committee. 74983

St. Albans raid; or, investigation into the charges. 4710, 74983

Saint-Albin, J. pseud. Voyage au centre de la terre. see Collin de Plancy, Jacques A. S.

St Albin, Jacques de. pseud. Voyage au centre de la terre. see Collin de Plancy, Jacques A. S.

Saint-Allias, Nicolas Viton de, 1773-1842. 101348-101350

Saint Aloysius Juvenile Society, Newport, R. I. 55055A

St. Aloysius Sunday School, Boston. see Boston. St. Aloysius Sunday School.

Saint-Amand, -------. 74984

Saint-Amant, Ch. de. 74985-74989, note after 100812

Saint and the sinner. 74981

Saint-Andre, Dupin de. 74990

St. Andrew's Church, Philadelphia. see Philadelphia. Church of St. Andrew.

St. Andrew's Church, Pittsburgh. see Pittsburgh. St. Andrew's Church.

St. Andrew's Church allotment, Woodlands Cemetery. 62206

St. Andrew's Club, Charleston, S. C. see St. Andrew's Society of the City of Charleston.

St. Andrew's journal and colonial miscellany. 74991

St. Andrew's journal and La-Baye miscellany. 74991

St. Andrew's Lodge, Boston. see Freemasons. Massachusetts. Boston. St. Andrew's Lodge.

St. Andrew's Parish, Staten Island, N. Y. see Staten Island, N. Y. St. Andrew's Parish.

St. Andrew's Society, Albany, N. Y. see St. Andrew's Society of Albany.

St. Andrew's Society, Charleston, S. C. see St. Andrew's Society of the City of Charleston.

St. Andrew's Society, Philadelphia 62207

St. Andrew's Society, Philadelphia Charter. 84745

St. Andrew's Society of Albany. 634

St. Andrew's Society of the City of Charleston. 12087

St. Andrew's Society of the State of new York. 74992-(74995), note after 95589

St. Johnbury, Vt. Academy. see St. Johnbury
    Academy, St. Johnbury, Vt.
St. Johnbury, Vt. Second Congregational
    Church. 75292
St. Johnbury, Vt. St. Johnbury Academy. see
    St. Johnbury Academy, St. Johnbury, Vt.
St. Johnbury Academy, St. Johnbury, Vt. 75293
St. Johnland, Smithtown, N. Y. see Society
    of St. Johnland, Smithtown, N. Y.
St. Johnland. 75280
St. Johnland as it is. 51255, 75280
St. Johnland: Part I. A retro-prospectus.
    51255, 75280
St. John's Antigua. Missionary Meeting, 1840.
    see United Brethren. Antigua. Mission-
    ary Meeting, St. John's, 1840.
St. John's Church, Providence, R. I. see
    Providence, R. I. St. John's Church.
St. John's College, Annapolis, Md. 75284,
    (75286), 75288-75290
St. John's College, Annapolis, Md. Library.
    75287
St. John's College, Annapolis, Md. Visitors
    and Governors. 75285
St. John's College, Fordham, New York. see
    Fordham University, Fordham, New York
    (City) St. John's College.
St. John's Colleton Agricultural Society,
    Edisto Island, S. C. see Agricultural
    Society of St. John's Colleton, S. C.
St. John's Episcopal Church, Portsmouth, N. H.
    see Portsmouth, N. H. St. John's Epis-
    copal Church.
St. John's Lodge, Bridgeport, Conn. see
    Freemasons. Connecticut. St. John's
    Lodge, Bridgeport.
St. John's Lodge, no. 31, Charleston, S. C.
    see Freemasons. South Carolina. York
    Rite. St. John's Lodge, no. 31, Charles-
    ton.
St. John's Lutheran Church, Philadelphia. see
    Philadelphia. St. John's Lutheran Church.
St. John's Indians. 15435
St. John's Orphan Asylum, Philadelphia.
    Managers. 62211
St. John's vision. 26781
St. Jonathan, the lay of a scald. 75294
St. Joseph, Florida. Constitutional Convention,
    1838. see Florida (Territory) Consti-
    tutional Convention, St. Joseph, 1838.
St. Joseph, Missouri. Board of Public Schools.
    Secretary. 75295
St. Joseph, Missouri. Soldiers' Orphans' and
    Widows' Home. see Soldiers' Orphans'
    and Widows' Home, St. Joseph, Mo.
St. Joseph, Missouri. Superintendent of Public
    Schools. 75295
St. Joseph and St. Helena (Snow) in Admiralty
    81390
St. Joseph city directory and business mirror
    for 1865-66. (75296)
St. Joseph medical & surgical journal. (75298)
St. Joseph's Academy, Frederick County, Md.
    75299
St. Joseph's Cathedral, Buffalo, N. Y. see
    Buffalo, N. Y. St. Joseph's Cathedral.
St. Joseph's Cathedral, Buffalo, N. Y. 75300
St. Joseph's College, Bardstown, Ky. 75301-
    75303
St. Joseph's College, Mobile, Ala. see Spring
    Hill College, Mobile, Ala.
Stl Joseph's College, Perry County, Ohio.
    (75304)
St. Joseph's College minerva. 75303
St. Joseph's Home for Sick and Destitute Ser-
    vant Girls, Boston. see Boston. St.

    Joseph's Home for Sick and Destitute
    Servant Girls.
St. Joseph's Hospital, Philadelphia. see Phila-
    delphia. St. Joseph's Hospital.
St. Jude's Protestant Episcopal Free Church,
    New York. see New York (City) St.
    Jude's Protestant Episcopal Free Church.
St. Katharine's spire. 75306
St. Landry Parish, La. Ordinances, etc. 75307
St. Laurent, Quebec. Assemblee des Electeurs
    du Comte de Montreal, 1837. see Mon-
    treal (Comte) Assemblee des Electeurs,
    St. Laurent, 1837.
St. Lawrence County, N. Y. Board of Super-
    visors. (75314)
St. Lawrence County, N. Y. Citizens. petition-
    ers (47666)
St. Lawrence Academy, Potsdam, N. Y. 75308
St. Lawrence and Atlantic Railroad. (75309)
Saint Lawrence and Atlantic Railroad. A letter
    to the Chairman. (26453)
St. Lawrence and the Saguenay. 76518-76519
St. Lawrence Baptist Association. see Baptists.
    New York. St. Lawrence Baptist Associa-
    tion.
St. Lawrence County directory. 75315
St. Lawrence County Mutual Insurance Company.
    75316
St. Lawrence County Mutual Insurance Company.
    Charter. 75316
Saint Lawrence Land Company. 75317
St. Lawrence pilot, for the Gulf and River.
    4045
St. Lawrence Street Church, Portland, Me. see
    Portland, Me. St. Lawrence Street Church.
St. Lawrence University, Canton, N. Y. 75323
St. Lawrence University, Canton, N. Y. Charter,
    75323
St. Lawrence University, Canton, N. Y. Theo-
    logical Department. (75324)
St. Lawrence University, Canton, N. Y. Theo-
    logical Department. Charter. 75323
Saint-Leger, B. Mercier. ed. (68417)
Saint Leger, or the treats of life. 37767
St. Lo, George. 75324-75325
St. Louis. petitioners 75356
St. Louis. Academy of Science. see St. Louis
    Academy of Sciences.
St. Louis. Anniversary Celebration of the
    Landing of the Pilgrims, 1845. 65763
St. Louis. Bellefontaine Cemetery. 4505A
St. Louis. Board of Civli Engineers to Consider
    the Subject of the Construction of a Rail
    or Highway Bridge Across the Mississippi
    River, 1867. 75363
St. Louis. Board of Directors of the St. Louis
    Public Schools. see St. Louis. Public
    Schools. Board of Directors.
St. Louis. Board of Health. 75336
St. Louis. Board of Public Schools. Committee
    on Books and Accounts. (75367)
St. Louis. Board of Public Schools. Secretary.
    75365
St. Louis. Certain Presbyters. pseud. see
    Certain Presbyters of St. Louis. pseud.
St. Louis. Chamber of Commerce. 11792,
    75338-75339, (75341)
St. Louis. Chamber of Commerce. petitioners
    75340
St. Louis. Chamber of Commerce. Charter.
    85338-75339
St. Louis. Chamber of Commerce. Committee
    on Trade, Commerce, and Manufactures.
    75342
St. Louis. Chamber of Commerce. Merchants'
    Exchange and Reading Room. 75339

St. Louis. Chamber of Commerce. Secretary. 75332 see also Baker, W. B.

St. Louis. Chamber of Commerce. Special Committee to Which was Referred the Memorial of the Officers of the United States Navy to Congress. 75342

St. Louis. Charter. 75329, 75345, 75378-(75379), 75404

St. Louis. Citizens. petitioners (75355)

St. Louis. City Engineer. 75375, 75377

St. Louis. Colored People's Educational Convention, 1870. see Colored People's Educational Convention, St. Louis, 1870.

St. Louis. Committee of Citizens, Appointed at a Public Meeting, Held Aug. 18th, 1860, on the Practicability of Manufacturing Railroad Iron at or Near St. Louis. (35091), 75328

St. Louis. Committee on Improvement of the Mississippi River and Tributaries. 75376

St. Louis. Committee to Examine the New St. Louis Jail. 75373

St. Louis. Common Council. 75345

St. Louis. Common Council. Special Committee in Relation to a Bridge Across the Mississippi River. 75377

St. Louis. Convention, 1861-1863. see Missouri. Convention, St. Louis, 1861-1863.

St. Louis. Convention, 1865. see Missouri. Convention, St. Louis, 1865.

St. Louis. Delegates to the Chicago Convention, 1847. see Chicago. Mississippi Valley Convention, 1847. St. Louis Delegation.

St. Louis. Direktoren-Rathes der Offentlichen Schulen. see St. Louis. Public Schools. Board of Directors.

St. Louis. First Independent Church. 75348

St. Louis. Franklin Society. see Franklin Society, St. Louis.

St. Louis. General Superintendent of the St. Louis Public Schools. see St. Louis. Public Schools. Superintendent.

St. Louis. High School. 75390

St. Louis. House of Refuge. see St. Louis House of Refuge.

St. Louis. Merchants' Bank. see Merchants' Bank of St. Louis.

St. Louis. Merchants' Exchange and Reading Room. see St. Louis. Chamber of Commerce. Merchants' Exchange and Reading Room.

St. Louis. Mississippi Valley Convention Delegation, 1847. see Chicago. Mississippi Valley Convention, 1847. St. Louis Delegation.

St. Louis. Mississippi Valley Railroad Convention, 1852. see Mississippi Valley Railroad Convention, St. Louis, 1852.

St. Louis. Missouri Medical College. see Missouri Medical College, St. Louis.

St. Louis. Missouri State Convention, 1865. see Missouri. Convention, St. Louis, 1865.

St. Louis. Missouri State Sunday School Convention, 1st 1866. see Missouri State Sunday School Convention. 1st, St. Louis, 1866.

St. Louis. Normal School. 75390-(75391)

St. Louis. O'Fallon Polytechnic Institute. see O'Fallon Polytechnic Institute, St. Louis.

St. Louis. Ordinances, etc. 75345, 75361, 75378-75380

St. Louis. Pine Street Presbyterian Church. Union Members. 85344

St. Louis. Police Commissioners. 75362

St. Louis. Public Meeting, Aug. 18, 1860. Committee. see St. Louis. Committee of Citizens, Appointed at a Public Meeting, Held Aug. 18, 1860, On the Practicability of Manufacturing Railroad Iron at or Near St. Louis.

St. Louis. Public School Library. 75368-75369

St. Louis. Public School Library. Librarian. 75369 see also Bailey, Jonathan Jay.

St. Louis. Public Schools. Board of Directors. 75365-75366

St. Louis. Public Schools. Superintendent. 75365

St. Louis. River Improvement Convention, 1867. see River Improvement Convention, St. Louis. 1867.

St. Louis. Societa di Mutuo Soccorso. see Societa di Mutuo Soccorso, St. Louis.

St. Louis. Sodality Lyceum. see Sodality Lyceum, St. Louis.

St. Louis. State Sunday School School Convention, 1866. see Missouri State Sunday School Convention. 1st, St. Louis, 1866.

St. Louis. Sunday School Convention, 1866. see Missouri State Sunday School Convention. 1st, St. Louis, 1866.

St. Louis. Union Merchants' Exchange. 65907

St. Louis. Union Merchants' Exchange. Secretary. 75335 see also Morgan, George H.

St. Louis. Washington University. see Washington University, St. Louis.

St. Louis. Young Men's Sodality. see Sodality Lyceum, St. Louis.

St. Louis (Archdiocese) Archbishop (Kenrick) 72971 see also Kenrick, Peter Ricardo, Abp.

St. Louis (Archdiocese) Bishop (Rosati) 72970 see also Rosati, Joseph, Bp.

St. Louis (Archdiocese) Synod, 1839. 72970

St. Louis (Archdiocese) Synod, 1850. 72971

St. Louis (Ecclesiastical Province) Council, 1858. 72921

St. Louis County, Mo. Circuit Court. 27614

St. Louis County, Mo. County Court. (75406)

St. Louis County, Mo. Criminal Court. (27613), 75407

St. Louis County, Mo. House of Refuge. see St. Louis House of Refuge.

St. Louis County, Mo. Ordinances, etc. (75406)

St. Louis Academy of Sciences. 75326-(75327), 74244

St. Louis Academy of Sciences. Library. 75369

St. Louis Agricultural and Mechanical Association. Annual Fair, 2d, 1857. 75381

St. Louis Agricultural and Mechanical Association. Annual Fair, 3d, 1858. 75381

St. Louis Agricultural and Mechanical Association. Annual Fair, 4th, 1859. 75381

St. Louis Agricultural and Mechanical Association. Annual Fair, 7th, 1867. 75381

St. Louis, Alton and Chicago Rail Road. Receivers. 75382

St. Louis American. Carriers. (75373)

St. Louis and New Orleans Telegraph Company. 75384

St. Louis and New Orleans Telegraph Company. Charter. 75384

St. Louis beacon. Carriers. 75385

St. Louis Bridge Company. 75364

St. Louis bulletin. 85374

St. Louis business directory, for 1859. 75346

Saint Louis business directory for 1859-60. 75346

St. Louis business directory, for 1847. 75346

St. Louis Capital Committee. 75337
St. Louis Chamber of Commerce. see St. Louis. Chamber of Commerce.
St. Louis Church, Buffalo. Documents. 9063
St. Louis Copper Company. 75386
St. Louis Copper Company of Lake Superior. . . . Office, 43 City Exchange, Boston. 75386
Saint Louis directory, for the year 1842. 75346
St. Louis directory for the years 1838-'39. 75346
St. Louis Gas-Light Company. 75389
St. Louis Gas-Light Company. Charter. 75387
St. Louis Gas-Light Company. Board of Directors. 75387-75388
St. Louis Gas-Light Company. Board of Directors. Committee. 75388
Saint Louis Historical Society. 75350
St. Louis House of Refuge. 75405
St. Louis House of Refuge. Charter. 75405
St. Louis House of Refuge. Officers. (75351)
Saint Louis in 1846. 81590
St. Louis' Isle, or Texiana. 32892
St. Louis Ladies' National League. see Ladies' National League of St. Louis.
St. Louis Ladies Union Aid Society. see Ladies Union Aid Society of St. Louis.
St. Louis Law Library Association. see Law Library Association of St. Louis.
St. Louis Law School. see Washington University, St. Louis. School of Law.
St. Louis Library Association. (75392)
St. Louis Library Association. Charter. (75392)
St. Louis liminary. 85513
Saint Louis magnet. (75393)
St. Louis Magnetic Spring. (75394)
St. Louis medical and surgical journal. 75395
Saint Louis medical and surgical journal. Edited, in conjunction with M. L. Linton, M. D. . . . by G. Baumgarten, M. D. (75396)
Saint Louis medical reporter. 75397
St. Louis Medical Society of Missouri. 75398
St. Louis Mercantile Library Association. 75358-75359
St. Louis Mercantile Library Association. Board of Directors. 75357
St. Louis Mercantile Library Hall Company. see St. Louis Mercantile Library Association.
St. Louis Missouri republican. see Missouri republican.
St. Louis Prison Discipline Association. (75399)
St. Louis Public School Library Society. see Public School Library Society, St. Louis.
St. Louis: the future great city of the world. 68312
St. Louis University. 75400
St. Louis University. Medical Department. 75401
St. Louis Young Men's Christian Association. see Young Men's Christian Association, St. Louis.
Saint-Luc de la Corne, ------. see La Corne, St. Luc de.
St. Lucia. Census, 1825. 75410
St. Lucia, historical, statistical, and descriptive. 7700
St. Luke's Home for Indigent Christian Females, New York. 75411
St. Luke's Hospital, Cincinnati. see Cincinnati. St. Luke's Hospital.

St. Luke's Hospital, New York. see New York (City) St. Luke's Hospital.
St. Luke's Hospital Association of the Church of the Ascension, New York. see New York (City) Church of the Ascension. St. Luke's Hospital Association.
Saint-Marc, Haiti. 75102
Saint Marc, Haiti. Citoyens de Couleur. Commissaires. 75161
Saint-Marie, ----- Poyen. see Poyen Saint-Marie, -------.
St. Mark. 105709
St. Mark's Church, Frankford, Pa. see Frankford, Pa. St. Mark's Church.
St. Mark's of the Bowery Church, New York. see New York (City) St. Mark's of the Bowery Church.
Saint Mars, Gabrielle Anne Cisterne de Courtiras, Vicomtesse de, 1804-1872. 21184, 27476-27477
Saint-Martin, ----- Baillot de. see Baillot de Saint-Martin, ---------.
Saint-Martin, Antoine Jean. 52105, 75417
Saint-Martin, Louis Vivien de. see Vivien de Saint-Martin, Louis.
St. Martin (Antilles) Laws, statutes, etc. 61019
St. Martin (Antilles) Societe des Etangs Salins. see Societe des Etangs Salins, St. Martin (Antilles)
St. Mary, Ky. St. Mary's College. see St. Mary's College, St. Mary, Ky.
St. Mary's Canal Mineral Land Company. 75421-75423
St. Mary's Canal Mineral Land Company. Charter. 75423
St. Mary's Canal Mineral Land Company. Reports upon the value of the company's land. 75422
St. Mary's Church, Philadelphia. see Philadelphia. St. Mary's Church (Roman Catholic)
St. Mary's College, Baltimore. 75424
St. Mary's College, St. Mary, Ky. 75425
St. Mary's Copper Mining Company. 75426-75427
St. Mary's Falls Ship Canal Company. (75428)-75430
St. Mary's Falls Ship Canal Company. Directors. 75432-75433
St. Mary's Falls Ship Canal Company. Superintendent. 75431, 75433
St. Mary's Hall, Burlington, N. J. 20391, (55993), (75434)-75439
St. Mary's Hall, Green Bank, Burlington, N. J. see St. Mary's Hall, Burlington, N. J.
St. Mary's Hall register. 75439
St. Mary's Mutual Benevolent Catholic T. A. Society, Boston. 75440
St. Mary's Seminary and catholics at large vindicated. 75441, 87004
St. Matthew's Church, Bedford, Mass. see Bedford, Mass. St. Matthew's Church.
St. Matthew's Church, New York. see New York (City) St. Matthew's Church (English) Lutheran)
Saint-Maurice, Charles. 10296
St. Meinard, Indiana. Benedictine Abbey. 37116, 80015
St. Memin, ---------. illus. 50185, (75444), 82375, 82379
St. Memin collection of portraits. (75444)
Saint-Mery, Mederic Louis Elie Moreau de. see Moreau de Saint-Mery, Mederic Louis Elie, 1750-1819.
St. Mesmin, E. Menu de. see Menu de Saint-Mesmin, E.

St. Michaels (Ship) in Admiralty 105162
St. Michael's Church, Philadelphia. see Philadelphia. St. Michael's Church (Evangelical Lutheran)
St. Michael's day. 66900
St. Michel, ------- Mavrile de. see Mavrile de Saint Michel, ---------.
St. Michel, Quebec. Societe Ecclesiastique. see Societe Ecclesiastique de St. Michel, Quebec.
St. Michel's Church, Trenton, N. J. see Trenton, N. J. St. Michel's Church.
St. N., J. pseud. History of baptism. see St. Nicholas, John.
St. Nicholas, John. 75445
St. Nicholas. (75446), 83959
St. Nicholas Hotel, N. Y. see New York (City) St. Nicholas Hotel.
Saint-Nicholas Hotel: its plan and arrangements. 75447
St. Nicholas Society of Nassau Island. 51891
St. Nicholas Society of the City of New York. 75448
St. Nicholas Society of the City of New York. Charter. 75448
St. Onge, L. N. 75449
St. Patrick, Order of the Friendly Brothers of. see Ancient and Most Benevolent Order of the Friendly Brothers of St. Patrick, Boston.
St. Patrick and the Irish. (72210)
St. Patrick Benevolent Society, Philadelphia. 62217
St. Patrick's Society of Quebec. 67059
St. Paul, Henry. (75451)
Saint-Paul, P. de. 75452
St. Paul, Minn. Baldwin School. see Baldwin School, St. Paul, Minn.
St. Paul, Minn. Board of Education. 75460-75461
St. Paul, Minn. Chamber of Commerce. petitioners 69884
St. Paul, Minn. Chamber of Commerce. Directors. (75457)
St. Paul, Minn. Chamber of Commerce. Secretary. (75457)
St. Paul, Minn. College. Academic Department. 75453
St. Paul, Minn. Constitutional Convention, 1857. see Minnesota. Constitutional Convention, St. Paul, 1857.
St. Paul, Minn. Dakota Mission. see Dakota Mission, St. Paul, Minn.
St. Paul, Minn. Deutscher Verein. see Saint Paul Deutscher Verein.
St. Paul, Minn. Editorial Convention, 1868. see Minnesota Editorial Convention, 2d, St. Paul, 1868.
St. Paul, Minn. Grand Celebration Commemorative of the Successful Laying and Working of the Atlantic Telegraph Cable, September 1, 1858. (28257)
St. Paul, Minn. House of Hope Presbyterian Church. (49263), (75455)
St. Paul, Minn. Library Association. see St. Paul Library Association.
St. Paul, Minn. Mercantile Library Association. see St. Paul Mercantile Library Association, St. Paul, Minn.
St. Paul, Minn. Public Meeting of Citizens of Minnesota, in Favor of a Semi-Weekly Overland Mail from Saint Paul to Puget Sound, 1850. see Public Meeting of Citizens of Minnesota, in Favor of a Semi-Weekly Overland Mail from Saint Paul to Puget Sound, St. Paul, 1850.

St. Paul, Minn. Public Schools. 75460
St. Paul, Minn. Societe de Bienfaisance Franco-Canadienne. see Societe de Bienfaisance Franco-Canadienne de Saint Paul.
St. Paul, Minn. Societe of St. Vincent de Paul. see Society of St. Vincent de Paul, St. Paul, Minn.
St. Paul, Minn. State Library. see Minnesota. State Library, St. Paul.
St. Paul, Minn. Young Men's Christian Association. see Young Men's Christian Association, St. Paul, Minn.
Saint Paul (Diocese) Synod, 1874. 72969
St. Paul & Chicago Railway Co. 75456
Saint Paul Deutscher Verein. 75458
Saint Paul Deutscher Verein. Minnesota, der Pioneer-Staat. 75458
St. Paul directory, and statistical record for 1866. 75454
St. Paul Library Association, St. Paul, Minn. 75459
St. Paul Mercantile Library Association, St. Paul, Minn. 75459
St. Paul's Agricultural Society, Charleston, S. C. 87518
St. Paul's Church, Boston. see Boston. St. Paul's Church.
St. Paul's Church, Brookline, Mass. see Brookline, Mass. St. Paul's Church.
St. Paul's Church, Castleton, N. Y. see Castleton, N. Y. St. Paul's Church.
St. Paul's Church, Cincinnati. see Cincinnati. St. Paul's Church.
St. Paul's Church, Detroit. see Detroit. St. Paul's Church.
St. Paul's Church, New York. see New York (City) St. Paul's Church (Lutheran) New York (City) St. Paul's Church (Methodist Episcopal) New York (City) St. Paul's Church (Protestant Episcopal)
St. Paul's Church, Philadelphia. see Philadelphia. St. Paul's Church.
St. Paul's Church, Springfield, Ill. see Springfield, Ill. St. Paul's Church.
St. Paul's College, College Point, N. Y. 14405, 75465-(75466), 75468-(75469)
St. Paul's College, College Point, N. Y. Fund for the Education of Teachers in the Protestant Episcopal Church. 75467
St. Paul's College, Flushing, N. Y. 24921-24922, 51256
St. Paul's College. 51256
St. Paul's Methodist Episcopal Church, New York. see New York (City) St. Paul's Church (Methodist Episcopal)
St. Paul's Missionary Society, New Haven, Conn. 53015
Saint Paul's School, Concord, N. H. see Concord, N. H. St. Paul's School.
St. Peter, Minn. Hospital for the Insane. see Minnesota. State Hospital, St. Peter.
St. Peter, Minn. State Hospital. see Minnesota. State Hospital, St. Peter.
St. Peter Evangelical Lutheran Church, Rhinebeck, N. Y. see Rhinebeck, N. Y. St. Peter Evangelical Lutheran Church.
St. Peter's Church, Albany. see Albany. St. Peter's Church.
St. Peter's Church, Auburn, N. Y. see Auburn, N. Y. St. Peter's Church.
St. Peter's Church, Baltimore. see Baltimore. St. Peter's Church.
St. Peter's Church, Beverly, Mass. see Beverly, Mass. St. Peter's Church.
St. Peter's Church, Great Valley, Pa. see Great Valley, Pa. St. Peter's Church.

St. Peter's Church, Philadelphia. see Philadelphia. St. Peter's Church.

St. Peter's Church, Salem, Mass. see Salem, Mass. St. Peter's Church.

St. Peter's College, Chambly County, Quebec. 11809

St. Peter's exhortation to fear God and honor the king. 78576

St. Peter's Parish, Philadelphia. see Philadelphia. St. Peter's Church.

St. Petersburg, Russia. Russischen Geohischen Gesellschaft. see Russkos Geografischeskoe Obshchestvo, St. Petersburg.

St. Petersburg, Russia. Russkos Geografischeskoe Obshchestvo. see Russkos Geografischeskoe Obshchestvo, St. Petersburg.

St. Petrus-Vereins, Albany. 75472

St. Philip's Church, Charleston, S. C. see Charleston, S. C. St. Philip's Church.

St. Philip's Church, New York. see New York (City) St. Philip's Church.

Saint-Pie, --------. tr. (38303)

S. Pierre, --------, Comte de. 40711

Saint Pierre, Jacques Henri Bernardin de, 1734-1814. 12249-(12250), 75474, 78774, 105527

Saint Pierre, Louis de. 62782, 75475

St. Pierre. Assemblee Coloniale. 66213

St. Pierre. Citoyens. petitioners 66213

St. Pierre. Peuple. petitioners see St. Pierre. Citoyens. petitioners

St. Pierre-Miquelon (French Colony) Commune. 75476

Saint-Prest, Jean Yves de. 75477

Saint Priest, Alexis de Guignard, Comte de, 1805-1851. 23795, 40038

Saint-Quentin, Edouard de. (75479)

Saint-Quentin, Eugene de. (75479)

Saint-Quentin, J. Bellon de. see Bellon de Saint-Quentin, J.

St. Quinten, Richard. defendant 89626

Saint-Quintin, Alfred de. 75478-(75479)

Saint-Quintin, Auguste de. (75479)

St. Real, Joseph Remi Vallieres de. see Vallieres de St. Real, Joseph Remi.

St. Remy, Dick. 75480

Saint-Remy, Joseph. 6160, 42355, 75481-75484

Saint Remy, R. Lepelletier de. see Lepelletier de Saint-Remy, R.

Saint Robert, -------, Chevalier de. 73213, 75486

St. Sauveur, Charles Poyen. see Poyen St. Sauveur, Charles.

Saint Sauvier, Grasset de. see Grasset Saint Sauvier, J.

St. Sauvier, J. Grasset. see Grasset St. Sauvier, J.

Saint Solitaire des Indes. 42583

St. Stephens, Ala. Land Office. 75489

St. Stephens Brotherhood, Boston. 75490

St. Stephen's Church, Philadelphia. see Philadelphia. St. Stephen's Church.

St. Stephen's College, Annandale, N. Y. see Columbia University. St. Stephen's College, Annadale, N. Y.

St. Stephen's College, Annandale. The following portion of the Warden's report is published. (75494)

St. Tammany, Society of. see Tammany Society. New York.

St. Tammany's magazine. (75495), 3d note after 94296

St. Thomas, Mary, Mother. see Mary St. Thomas, Mother.

St. Thomas' Church, New York. see New York (City) St. Thomas' Church.

St. Thomas Dansk Amerikansk O. 33026

St. Thomas in the East Branch Association of the Incorporated Society for the Conversion and Religious Instruction and Education of Negro Slaves, London. see Society for the Conversion and Religious Instruction and Education of Negro Slaves. St. Thomas in the East Branch Association, London.

St. Thomas' Parish, S. C. Meeting, 1832. 33572

St. Thomas treaty. 75500

St. Thomas's Church, Brooklyn. see Brooklyn. St. Thomas's Church.

St. Timothy's Hall, Baltimore, Md. 75501

St. Ursula's Convent. (75502)

Saint Valier, -------, Sieur Joly de. see Joly de St. Valier, --------.

Saint Vallier, Jean Baptiste de la Croix de Chevrieres de, Bp., 1653-1727. 23037, 38506, 66978-66980, (77502)-(77503), 105708 see also Quebec (Archdiocese) Bishop (Saint Vallier)

Saint-Vel, O. 75504-75505

Saint-Venant, Barre. see Barre Saint-Venant, Jean.

Saint-Venant, Jean Barre. see Barre Saint-Venant, Jean.

Saint-Veran, Louis Joseph, Marquis de Montcalm. see Montcalm Saint-Veran, Louis Joseph, Marquis de, 1712-1759.

Saint-Victor, J. B. de. 75507

Saint Vincent, Jacques Maximilien Benjamin Bins de. 7928, 40721, 75508-75509

Saint Vincent, J. B. G. M. Bory de. see Bory de St. Vincent, J. B. G. M.

St. Vincent, John Jervis, Earl, 1735-1823. 7728, 95299

St. Vincent. 75510

St. Vincent. Council. 8005

St. Vincent. Courts. 80270

St. Vincent. Governor (Brisbane) 8005, (20578), 75512 see also Brisbane, Sir Charles, 1769?-1829.

St. Vincent, Governor (Morris) 50879 see also Morris, Valentine.

St. Vincent. House of Assembly. 8005, 75512

St. Vincent. Laws, statutes, etc. 75513

St. Vincent. Treaties, etc. 106124

St. Vincent's College, Cape Girardeau, Mo. 75516

St. Vincenz in Pennsylvanien. 50473

Saint waiting his change. 80530

St. Xavier College, Cincinnati, Ohio. 75516-75517

Saintard, P. 42896, 75518-75521

Sainte Bonnaventure de Jesus, Marie de. see Marie de Saint Bonaventure. Mere Superieure

Saint-Beuve, Charles Auguste, 1804-1869. (12261)

St. Ignace, Mere Francoise Juchereau de. see Juchereau de St. Ignace, Mere Francoise.

Sainte-Claire Deville, Charles. see Sainte-Claire Deville, Charles Joseph, 1814-1876.

Sainte-Claire Deville, Charles Joseph, 1814-1876. 19820, 75522-75528

Sainte-Croix, Carloman Louis Francois Felix Renouard de, Marquis. (69623), 75535-75537

Sainte-Croix, Guillaume Emmanuel Joseph Gyilhem de Clermont-Lodeve, Baron de. 56582, 75529-75534

Sainte-Marie, --------- Poyen. see Poyen Sainte-Marie, ---------.

Sainte-Lucie. Assemblee. 95733

Sainte Lucie. Planteurs et Citoyens. petitioners 75408

Sainte Pierre, Martinique. Officiers Municipaux. 5848

Saintes, Amand. 75538

Saintes. 101350

Saintete de Christophe Colomb. 75539

Sainthill, -------. 75541

Sainthorent, --------. 75540 see also France Corps Legislatif. Conseil des Cinq-Cents. Commission des Colonies. Saintin, --------. illus. 14940

Saintine, X.-B. pseud. Seul! see Boniface, Jose Xavier.

Saintine, X.-B. pseud. Solitary of Juan Fernandez. see Boniface, Jose Xavier.

Saintonage, Alfonse de. see Fonteneau, Jean.

Saintrac, Louis Nadal de. see Nadal de Saintrac, Louis.

Saints' advocate 83296

Saints anchor-hold, in all storms and tempests. 18710

Saints and servants of God. (73193)

Saints compleat in glory. 104686

Saints' cordialls. 32847

Saints dignitie, and dutie. 32848

Saint's duty and exercise. 74292

Saints' harmony. 83300

Saints' harp. 75544, 83300

Saints' herald. 83038, 83040, 83048, 83160, 83166, 83175-83176, 83179-83180, 83190, 83195, 83202, 83206, 83232, 83233, 83247, 83250, 83251, 83282, 83284, 83287, 83289, 83291, 83295, 83297, 83301, 83302, 83497, 84425, 84426, 84427, 84428, 84429, 84430-84431, 84549-84550

Saints imperfect whilst on earth. 104686

Saint's jewel. 80216, 80227-80229, (80231), 80233-80235, 80238

Saints jewell. 80226

Saints' jubilee. 75545

Saints' portion. 65369

Saints support & comfort. 17078

Saints united confession. 25408

Saints' victory and triumph over sin and death. 95163

Sainz de Alfaro y Beaumont, Isidro. (48338) see also Mexico (Archdiocese) Gobernador de la Sagrada Mitra.

Sainz de Baranda, Pedro. (52099)

Saissy, J. A. 83664

Sal-o-quah. 28130

Sala, George Augustus. 8647, 30339, 75545-75547, 84181-84183, 84185-84187

Sala, Juan. 75548-75552

Sala adicionado. 75549

Sala Hispano-Chileno. (75550)

Sala Hispano-Mejicano. 75551

Sala Mexicano. 75552

Salad for the social. 77180

Salad for the solitary. 77176-77177, 77181

Salad for the solitary and the social. 77182

Salade nouuellemet imprimee a Paris. 39110

Salamanca, Ignatius de. 72809, 73740

Salamanca, Juan Velez de Guevara y. see Velez de Guevara y Salamanca, Juan.

Salamanca (Diocese) Bishop (Bertran) 5024 see also Bertran, Felipe, Bp.

Salamander. 82518

Salander and the dragon. (80152)

Salaries of the officers of the city of Lowell. (42500)

Salary grab. (72215)

Salary of certain officers. 60278

Salas, Diego Arellano y. (75553)

Salas, Joseph Prefecto de. 98150

Salas, Petro de. (75554)

Salas y Quiroga, Jacinto de. 75555, 99404

Salas y Valdes, Juan B. 75556

Salathe, -------. illus. 88693, note before 91212

Salazar, A. de. (75557)

Salazar, Antonio. 75558-75560

Salazar, Antonio Cardenas. 75561

Salazar, Antonio M. (75562)

Salazar, C. Carlos. (75563) see also Guatemala. Ministro del Estado.

Salazar, Domingo de. ed. 94221

Salazar, Francisco. (75564)

Salazar, Francisco Cervantes. (75565)-75569

Salazar, Francesco Cervantes de. see Salazar, Francisco Cervantes.

Salazar, Gonzalo. (75570)

Salazar, J. F. Regis. see Regis Salazar, J. F.

Salazar, Jose Antonio Lopez. plaintiff 75571

Salazar, Jose Cavero y. see Cavero y Salazar, Jose.

Salazar, Jose Maria. 75572-75576

Salazar, Joseph de. 75577

Salazar, Juan, fl. 1737-1738. 75578

Salazar, Juan, fl. 1759. see Regis Salazar, Juan Francisco.

Salazar, Juan de la Rynaga. see Rynaga Salazar, Juan de la.

Salazar, Juan de Onate y. see Onate y Salazar, Juan de.

Salazar, Juan Francisco Regis. see Regis Salazar, Juan Francisco.

Salazar, Juan Jose. 75580

Salazar, Juan Joseph de. 75581

Salazar, Juan Velzaquez de. see Velazquez de Salazar, Jaun.

Salazar, Manuel M. (75582)

Salazar, Nicolas. 75583-75585

Salazar, Remijio. (75586)

Salazar de Mazarredo, Josef. 75587

Salazar de Mendoza, Pedro. 75588

Salazar Maxiscatzin Citlalpopoca, Nicolas. 75589

Salazar Munatones, Lorenzo. 75590-(75591)

Salazar Varona, Jose. 75592

Salazar y Cordoba, B. see Salinas y Cordova, B

Salazar y Mazarredo, Eusebio de. 11710, (59323)

Salazar y Olarte, Ignacio de. 75594-75595

Salazar y Torres, Agustin, 1642-1675. 75596-(75597)

Salazar y Vicuna, Manuel de. 98935

Salazar y Zevallos, Alonso Eduardo de. (41093)

Salazar Ylarregui, Jose. 75598

Salbanke, Joseph. 66686

Salceda, Pablo. 75599

Salcedo, Bruno Diaz. (75600)

Salcedo, Ferdinand Camargo y. see Camargo y Salcedo, Ferdinand.

Salcedo, Francisco Ugarte de la Hermosa y. see Ugarte de la Hermosa y Salcado, Francisco.

Salcedo, Juan de Dios. 75601

Salcedo, Juan de Solorzano y. see Solorzano y Salcedo, Juan de.

Salcedo, M. 75602

Salcedo, Mateo. 75603-75604

Salcedo, Matias. 75605

Salcedo Fita, Juan. 75606

Salcedo y Mernandez, Manuel. 61128
Salcedo y Sierra Alta, Miguel de. 24173
　see also Buenos Aires (Province) Gob-
　ernador, 1734-1742 (Salcedo y Sierra
　Alta)
Saldana, Antonio Murcia. 75607
Saldana, Antonio Murcia. incorrectly supposed
　author note after 98317-98318
Saldana, Ignacio. 75608
Saldana y Ortega, Antonio de. 75609-75612
Saldana y Ortega, Antonio de. petitioner
　56396, 79138
Saldanha, ----------, Cardinal 63907, 1st
　note after 98174
Saldanha, Joao Carlos de Saldanha Oliveira
　e Daun, 1. Duque de, 1790-1876. 57196,
　82917
Saldanha, Jose de la Natividad. 75613
Saldanha da Gama, J. see Saldanha da Gama,
　Jose da.
Saldanha da Gama, Joao de. see Saldanha
　da Gama, Jose da.
Saldanha da Gama, Jose da. 26490, 75614-
　75620, 88782
Saldanha Oliveira e Daun, Joao Carlos de.
　see Saldanha, Joao Carlos de Saldanha
　Oliveira e Daun, 1. Duque de, 1790-1876.
Saldos contra o paiz. 44497
Salduendo, Francisco Xavier. 75621
Sale and separation of a family. 75622
Sale list of publications. 85037
Sale of mineral lands. 36885
Sale of public lands. 20602
Sale of South Cove lands. 88119
Sale of surplus gold. 91019
Sale of the estate Clairmount in the island of
　St. Croix. 5398
Sale of town lots at Pensacola. 60803
Salem, Ahab. pseud. New maid of the oaks.
　see Murray, James.
Salem, Mass. 75623, 75629, 75631, (75647),
　75672, 75686, 75696, 75757, 101882
Salem, Mass. Alms-House. 75709
Salem, Mass. Alms-House. Board of Over-
　seers. 75704
Salem, Mass. Anti-slavery Society. see
　Salem Anti-slavery Society.
Salem, Mass. Association for the Relief of
　Aged and Destitute Women. see Asso-
　ciation for the Relief of Aged and
　Destitute Women in Salem, Mass.
Salem, Mass. Association of Housewrights.
　see Association of Housewrights, Salem,
　Mass.
Salem, Mass. Athenaeum. see Salem
　Athenaeum, Salem, Mass.
Salem, Mass. Auditor. 75633, 75636, 75658,
　(75692), 75750-(75752)
Salem, Mass. Bank. see Salem Bank, Salem,
　Mass.
Salem, Mass. Baptist Church of Christ.
　75637, 93595
Salem, Mass. Bible Society. see Bible
　Society of Salem and Vicinity.
Salem, Mass. Bible Translation and Foreign
　Missionary Society. see Salem Bible
　Translation and Foreign Missionary
　Society, Salem, Mass.
Salem, Mass. Board of Trade. see Salem
　Board of Trade.
Salem, Mass. Charitable Mechanic Association.
　see Salem Charitable Mechanic Associa-
　tion.
Salem, Mass. Charter. 75629, 75644-75645,
　75674, 75701, 75703

Salem, Mass. Church. see Salem, Mass.
　First Church.
Salem, Mass. Citizens. petitioners 75673,
　92309
Salem, Mass. City Council. 7946, 75626,
　75644-75645, 75650, 75674, 75695, 75700-
　75703
Salem, Mass. City Council. Joint Select Com-
　mittee in Relation to Establishing a
　System of Water Rates. 75649
Salem, Mass. City Council. Joint Special
　Committee on the Subject of a Supply of
　Water. (75690)
Salem, Mass. City Mission. see Salem City
　Mission, Salem, Mass.
Salem, Mass. City Solicitor. 75684
Salem, Mass. Classical and High School. see
　Salem Classical and High School, Salem,
　Mass.
Salem, Mass. Committee Concerning the By-
　laws. 75686
Salem, Mass. Committee of Accounts. 75636,
　75687
Salem, Mass. Committee of Arrangements for
　the Visit of the President of the United
　States, 1789. 101784
Salem, Mass. Committee on a Supply of Water
　from Wenham Pond. (75683)
Salem, Mass. Committee on Accounts. see
　Salem, Mass. Committee of Accounts.
Salem, Mass. Committee on City Government.
　(75693)
Salem, Mass. Committee on the Rights of the
　City to the Flats on the North River.
　74648
Salem, Mass. Committee on the Salem Alms-
　House. (75708)
Salem, Mass. Committee to Enquire Into the
　Practicability and Expediency of Estab-
　lishing Manufactures in Salem. (75685)
Salem, Mass. Court. 46563, 2d note after
　97085
Salem, Mass. Dinner to Charles Peabody, 1856.
　(59370)
Salem, Mass. Dispensary. see Salem Dispen-
　sary, Salem, Mass.
Salem, Mass. East India Marine Society. see
　East India Marine Society, Salem, Mass.
Salem, Mass. Ecclesiastical Council, 1734.
　see Congregational Churches in Massa-
　chusetts. Ecclesiastical Council, Salem,
　1734.
Salem, Mass. Ecclesiastical Council, 1784.
　see Congregational Churches in Massa-
　chusetts. Ecclesiastical Council, Salem,
　1784.
Salem, Mass. Ecclesiastical Council, 1816.
　see Congregational Churches in Massa-
　chusetts. Ecclesiastical Council, Salem,
　1784.
Salem, Mass. Ecclesiastical Council, 1831.
　see Congregational Churches in Massa-
　chusetts. Ecclesiastical Council, Salem,
　1831.
Salem, Mass. Ecclesiastical Council, 1849.
　see Congregational Churches in Massa-
　chusetts. Ecclesiastical Council, Salem,
　1849.
Salem, Mass. English High School. 75657
Salem, Mass. Essex gazette. see Essex
　gazette, Salem, Mass.
Salem, Mass. Essex Historical Society. see
　Essex Historical Society, Salem, Mass.
Salem, Mass. Essex Institute. see Essex
　Institute, Salem, Mass.

Salem, Mass. Evangelical Library. see
Salem Evangelical Library, Salem, Mass.
Salem, Mass. Evening Free School. see
Salem Evening Free School.
Salem, Mass. Exhibition of Antique Relics,
&c., Held by the Ladies' Centennial
Committee, 1875. see Salem, Mass.
Ladies' Centennial Committee. Exhibi-
tion of Antique Relics, &c., 1875.
Salem, Mass. Female Charitable Society.
see Salem Female Charitble Society.
Salem, Mass. First Church. 24532, 31744,
75654, 75666, 79415, 103366
Salem, Mass. First Church. Library. (75661)
Salem, Mass. First Church of Christ. see
Salem, Mass. First Church.
Salem, Mass. Funeral Honours Bestowed on
the Remains of Capt. Lawrence and
Lieut. Ludlow, 1813. 39355
Salem, Mass. Harmony Grove Cemetery.
75663
Salem, Mass. Henfield Division, no. 2. see
Sons of Temperance of North America.
Massachusetts. Henfield Division, no. 2,
Salem.
Salem, Mass. Horticultural Exhibition, 1850.
see Horticultural Exhibition, Salem,
Mass., 1850.
Salem, Mass. Housewrights. see Association
of Housewrights, Salem, Mass.
Salem, Mass. Howard Street Church. 80617
Salem, Mass. Inhabitants. petitioners see
Salem, Mass. Citizens. petitioners
Salem, Mass. Ladies' Centennial Committee.
Exhibition of Antique Relics, &c., 1875.
105963
Salem, Mass. Ladies' Fair for the Benefit
of the New-England Asylum for the
Blind, 1833. 52658, 75463
Salem, Mass. Marine Society. see Marine
Society, Salem, Mass.
Salem, Mass. Mayor, 1836-1837 (Saltonstall)
(75630), 75856 see also Saltonstall,
Leverett, 1783-1845.
Salem, Mass. Mayor, 1840-1841. 75631
Salem, Mass. Mayor, 1850-1851 (Silsbee)
81072 see also Silsbee, N. jr.
Salem, Mass. Mayor, 1857-1858. 75652
Salem, Mass. Mayor, 1859-1860. 75672
Salem, Mass. Mayor, 1869-1870 (Goswell)
75626 see also Goswell, William.
Salem, Mass. Mechanic Library. see Salem
Mechanic Library, Salem, Mass.
Salem, Mass. Merchants. petitioners 47680,
1st note after 92309
Salem, Mass. Moral Reform Society. see
Moral Reform Society, Salem, Mass.
Salem, Mass. Normal School. see Massachu-
setts. State Normal School, Salem.
Salem, Mass. North Church. (75660)
Salem, Mass. Ordinances, etc. 75641-75642,
75644-75645, 75674, (75678), 75700-
75703, 75706, 75746
Salem, Mass. Overseers of the Poor. 75679
Salem, Mass. Peabody Academy of Science.
see Peabody Academy of Science, Salem,
Mass.
Salem, Mass. Plummer Farm School. see
Plummer Farm School, Salem, Mass.
Salem, Mass. Plummer Hall. see Plummer
Hall, Salem, Mass.
Salem, Mass. Police. 75746
Salem, Mass. Providence Association. see
Salem Providence Association.
Salem, Mass. Public Schools. (75741)

Salem, Mass. Sabbath School Convention. see
Baptists. Massachusetts. Salem Baptist
Association. Sabbath School Convention.
Salem, Mass. St. Peter's Church. 75667,
75707
Salem, Mass. Salem Division, no. 61. see
Sons of Temperance of North America.
Massachusetts. Salem Division, no. 61.
Salem, Mass. Salem Sanitary Society. see
Salem Sanitary Society, Salem, Mass.
Salem, Mass. School Committee. 75739-
(75743)
Salem, Mass. Seamen's Orphan and Children's
Friend Society. see Salem Seamen's
Orphan and Children's Friend Society,
Salem, Mass.
Salem, Mass. Seamen's Widow and Orphan
Association. see Seamen's Widow and
Orphan Association, of Salem, Mass.
Salem, Mass. Social Library. see Social
Library, Salem, Mass.
Salem, Mass. State Normal School. see
Massachusetts. State Normal School,
Salem.
Salem, Mass. Superintendent of Schools. 75740
Salem, Mass. Tabernacle Church. 75651,
75665, (75753)-75754, 2d note after 94170,
103366, 105323
Salem, Mass. Tabernacle Church. Pastor.
88890, 105323 see also Spalding, Joshua,
1760-1825. Worcester, Samuel Melanch-
thon.
Salem, Mass. Third Church. 103323
Salem, Mass. Third Church of Christ. 75755
Salem, Mass. Treasurer. 75636
Salem, Mass. Tribute to the Memory of Wash-
ington, 1800. 101887
Salem, Mass. Tribute to the Memory of Wash-
ington, 1800. Committee of Arrangement.
101887
Salem, Mass. Town Meeting, 1831. Committee.
75682
Salem, Mass. 200th Anniversary Celebration,
1828. (75624), 75725
Salem, Mass. Washington Fire Club. see
Washington Fire Club, Salem, Mass.
Salem, Mass. Water Commissioners. Chairman.
75626 see also Phillips, W. P.
Salem, Mass. Water Committee. 75694
Salem, Mass. Young Men's Union. see Salem
Young Men's Union, Salem, Mass.
Salem, N. H. Old Nutfield Celebration, 1869.
see Celebration of the One Hundred and
Fiftieth Anniversary of the Settled Part
of Old Nutfield, N. H., 1869.
Salem, N. Y. Theological Seminary. see
Washington Academy, Salem, N. Y. Theo-
logical Seminary.
Salem, N. Y. Washington Academy. see
Washington Academy, Salem, N. Y.
Salem, Ohio. Union School. see Salem Union
School, Salem, Ohio.
Salem, Ore. Meeting of the Congregational
Association of Oregon, 1864. see Con-
gregational Churches in Oregon. Oregon
Association.
Salem, Va. Roanoke College. see Roanoke
College, Salem, Va.
Salem, Va. Virginia Collegiate Institute. see
Roanoke College, Salem, Va.
Salem. 89557
Salem Alms-House. 75709
Salem & Danvers Aqueduct. 75710
Salem Anti-slavery Society. 75634
Salem Athenaeum, Salem, Mass. 75711

Salinas y Cordova, Buenaventura, d. 1653. petitioner 75785 see also Franciscans. Mexico. Comissario General. petitioner

Salinas y la Cerda, Juan Fernandez de. petitioner (75788)

Saline Coal and Manufacturing Company. 75789

Salisbury, Edward E. 75790

Salisbury, Guy H. 9056, 75791, note after 95451

Salisbury, J. H. 75792-75793

Salisbury, Robert Cecil, 1st Earl of, d. 1612. 67545

Salisbury, S. 75794

Salisbury, Samuel. 31331, (39716), 75795-(75796)

Salisbury, Stephen. 75797-75798

Salisbury (Samuel and Stephen) firm 105359

Salisbury, Bishop of. see Barrington, Shute, successively Bishop of Salisbury, and Durham, 1734-1826. Burgess, Thomas, successively Bishop of St. Davids, and Salisbury, 1756-1837. Burnet, Gilbert, Bishop of Salisbury, 1643-1715. Douglas, John, successively Bishop of Carlisle, and Salisbury, 1721-1807. Drummond, Robert Hay, Archbishop of York, 1711-1776. Gilbert, John, Archbishop of York, 1693-1761. Hume, John, successively Bishop of Bristol, Oxford, and Salisbury. Sherlock, Thomas, successively Bishop of Salisbury, and London, 1678-1761. Thomas, John, successively Bishop of Lincoln, and Salisbury, 1691-1766. Thomas, John, successively Bishop of Peterborough, Salisbury, and Winchester, 1696-1781. Ward, Seth, Bishop of Salisbury, 1617-1689.

Salisbury, Mass. Young Men's Temperance Association. see Young Men's Temperance Association in Salisbury and Amesbury, Mass.

Salisbury, N. H. 75800

Salisbury, N. H. Baptist Church. 75799

Salisbury, N. H. School Committee. 75800

Salisbury Mansion School, Worcester, Mass. 75801

Salisbury Mills. Charter. 75802

Salisbury Mills. Act of incorporation and by-laws. 75802

Salizar, C. Carlos. (75563) see also Guatemala. Ministro del Estado.

Salizar, Salvador Jose de Muros y. see Someruelos, Salvador Jose de Muros y Salazar, Marques de, 1754-1813.

Salkeld, J. ed. 23289

Salkeld family of Pennsylvania. (75803)

Salle, A. de la. see La Salle, A. de.

Salle, Abraham. defendant 105702

Salle, Adrien Nicolas la. see La Salle, Adrien Nicolas.

Salle, Antoine de la. see La Salle, Antonie de.

Salle, Robert Cavelier, Sieur de la. see La Salle, Robert Cavelier, Sieur de, 1643-1687.

Salle de l'Estang, Simon Philibert de la. see La Salle de l'Estang, Simon Philibert de, d. 1765.

Salle de l'Estange, Simon Philippe de la. see La Salle de l'Estang, Simon Philibert de, d. 1765.

Salles, Euesebe Fr. de. 74804

Salles, Jose Agostinho de. 59656

Salles la Terriere, Pierre de. see La Terriere, Pierre de Salles.

Salley, A. S. 2d note after 87347, note after 87355

Sallieth, M. illus. see Salieth, M. illus.

Salluste, Guillaume de. see Du Bartas, Guillaume de Salluste, Seigneur, 1544-1590.

Sallusti, Giuseppe. (75805)

Salm, Felix de Salm. see Salm-Salm, Felix de.

Salm, Ines de Salm. see Salm Salm, Ines de.

Salm-Salm, Felix de. ed. 55490, 75806-(75808)

Salm Salm, Ines de. 75809-75811

Salmagundi. 35224, (68468)

Salmagundi; or, the whim-whams and opinions of Launcelot Langstaff, Esq. 35222-35223, (59211)

Salmagundi. Second series. (35225)

Salmeron, Marcos, Bp. 75812-(75813)

Salmeron, Pedro. 75814-75817

Salmeron y Castro, Jose de Escobar. 75818, 80977

Salmon, D. E. 84331

Salmon, Edward, 1830- defendant 10997 see also Wisconsin. Governor, 1862-1864 (Salmon) defendant

Salmon, Edmond. see Salmon, Edward, 1830-

Salmon, Leon N. supposed author 16362, 89058

Salmon, N. 66686

Salmon, Thomas, 1679-1767. 10330, 17661, 20726, (56847), 75819-75829, 87900, 3d note after 93596

Salmon, Thomas, fl. 1853. 75830

Salmon and sea fisheries. 75832

Salmon Falls directory, business directories, etc. 20745

Salmon fisheries of the River St. Lawrence and its tributaries. 52351

Salmon-fishing in Canada. 734, 75833

Salmuth, Henry. 58411-58413, 58415

Salodiano, Givan Paolo Gallvcci. tr. 124, 69132

Salomon, --------. 75834

Salomon, Edward. 38979

Salomon, John C. Fr. 75835

Salomonib okalagataningit prefeteniglo. (75836)

Salomons, David. 75837

Salong-Bibl. 92407

Salontha, ------- de. 75838

Salt and fishery. 14440

Salt Company of Onondaga. 75839

Salt Lake City, Utah. Charter. (28464), 75840

Salt Lake City, Utah. Citizens. (32882)

Salt Lake City, Utah. City Council. (28464), 75840

Salt Lake City, Utah. Deseret Sunday School Union. see Deseret Sunday School Union, Salt Lake City.

Salt Lake City, Utah. Ordinances, etc. (28464), 75840, 98221

Salt Lake County, Utah. Coroner's Court. 72134

Salt Lake City directory. (75841)

Salt Lake City directory and business guide. 75842

Salt Lake City. Illustrated. 75843

Salt Sulphur Springs, Monroe Co., Va. (51604)

Salt water bubbles. 82121

Salter, A. P. 75844

Salter, J. W. 4389

Salter, Richard. 75845-75846

Salter, William. 75847-75849

Saltmarsh, John. 74459

Saltmarsh, S. (75850)

Saltmarsh returned from the dead. 28041, 82043

Salto de Agua (Parroquia) Mexico (City) Congregation del Esclavos Cocheros del Santiss. Sacramento. 48378

Saltonstall, Charles. 75851-75852
Saltonstall, Gurdon, 1666-1724. 15823, 68808, (72684), 75853-75854 see also Connecticut (Colony) Governor, 1708-1724 (Saltonstall)
Saltonstall, Gurdon, 1666-1724. plaintiff (72684)
Saltonstall, Leverett, 1783-1845. (72214), (75630), 75855-(75861), 98556 see also Salem, Mass. Mayor, 1836-1837 (Saltonstall)
Saltonstall, Richard. (21090), 33698, 78431, 104846
Saltonstall, Winthrop. 75862
Saltonstall, Wye. engr. 32750, 47885, 82816, 82823, 82829
Saltonstall Division, no. 37, East Haven, Conn. see Sons of Temperance of North America. Connecticut. Saltonstall Division, no. 37.
Saltworks case. 85190
Salud Dn. Jose Manuel Selva Mayo 10 de 1852. 79036
Salud, por el Dr. Genaro Guen. 29107
Salutaris lux evangelii toto orbi exoriens. 23599
Salutation of Gospel love. (14954)
Salutation of love, and tender invitation. 95528
Salutation of love to the seed of God everywhere. 20034
Salutation to the Britains. 66608
Salutatory address delivered at a public exhibition. 11070
Salutatory oration. 84595
Salutatory sermon. 6223
Salute of the Americans. 98276
Salutem in Domino sempiternam. 98913
Salutory address. 20350
Salva, Miguel. (52099)
Salva, Vincent. 75551, (75862)
Salva y Mallen, Pedro. 74864
Salva (Vincent) e Hijo. firm (75863)
Salvador, Agustin Pomposo Fernandez de San. see San Salvador, Agustin Pomposo Fernandez de.
Salvador, Jos. de. 74865
Salvador. 32762, 76191, 76194, 76196, 76199, 76206
Salvador. Camara de Diputados. 76209
Salvador. Camara de Senadores. (76190)
Salvador. Comisionados. (76204), (76208)
Salvador. Constitution. 76192-76193
Salvador. Laws, statutes, etc. 76211
Salvador. Legislatura. Senado. 76209
Salvador. Legislatura. Senado. Presidente. 76198
Salvador. President, 1851. 64345
Salvador. President, 1860-1862 (Barrios) 3636, 76189 see also Barrios, Gerardos, Pres. Salvador, d. 1865.
Salvador. President, 1863-1871 (Duenas) 65346 see also Duenas, Francisco, Pres. Salvador.
Salvador. Treaties, etc. (21123), 63172, (76204), (76208)
Salvages o la caridad. 73031
Salvago, Antonio. (75866)
Salvandy, Narcisse Achille de. 75867
Salvatierra, Andres Bernal y. see Salvatierra, Andres Vernal de.
Salvatierra, Andres Vernal de. 75868
Salvatierra, Cristobal. 75869
Salvatierra, Juan Maria. (75870)
Salvatierra Garnica, Bernanrdino. 75871-75873
Salvation by Christ. 78298

Salvation by grace through faith. 85440
Salvation by Jesus Christ. 75874
Salvation for all men, illustrated and vindicated, as a scripture doctrine. (13424), (21975), 75875, 8th note after 100870
Salvation for all men, put out of all dispute. 880
Salvation of all men . . . by Charles Chauncy. 12331
Salvation of all men strictly examined. (21975)
Salvation of Great Britain in embryo. (59095)
Salvation of the country secured by immediate emancipation. (12406)
Salvation of the sour considered. 46495
Salvations of God in 1746. (65610)
Salvatore, Michele del. (75876)
Salve for New-England's sore. 19563
Salve of divinity. 78720
Salve regina, en lengua Mexicana. 73202
Salverte, Eusebe. (50530), 75877-(75878)
Salvin, H. S. 75879
Salvin, Osbert. 78138, 78141-78142
Salyards, Richard S. 83095
Salzburgers and their descendants. 92879
Salzburgers in Georgia. 85848
Salzedo, Joseph de. defendant 75880
Salzmann, C. G. 75881
Sam. pseud. Life and times of Sam. 41011
Sam Houston and his republic. 40229
Sam. Reconcilable. pseud. see Young Samuel, fl. 1690-1700.
Sam Sansculotte. pseud. see "Scotch Runaway." pseud. supposed author and Swanwick, John. supposed author
Sam Sharpley's iron-clad songster. 79858
Sam Simple. pseud. see Wilburn, George T. supposed author
Sam Slick. pseud. see Haliburton, Thomas Chandler.
Sam Slick in England. 29696
Sam Slick in search of a wife. 29696
Sam Slick in Texas. 30082
Sam Splicem. pseud. see Splicem, Sam. pseud.
Samana Bay Company. 75882
Samana Bay, San Domingo and Hayti Steamship Company. 75883
Samaniego, Francisco de, Bp., 1598-1645. 75884-75890, 75894-75897
Samaniego, Francisco de, Bp., 1598-1645. petitioner 75891-75893
Samaniego, Jose Ximenez. see Ximenez Samaniego, Jose.
Samaritan Institute, no. 1, Boston. see United Order of Independent Odd Ladies. Samaritan Institute, No. 1, Boston.
Samber, R. supposed tr. 86917
Sambo and Toney. 75900
Sambo & Toney, a dialogue in three parts. (75899)
Sambo's call. 8447
Sambrano, Joseph de. see Zambrano Bonilla, Jose.
Same hand. pseud. Following written to the young people. see Teall, Benjamin.
Same hands with the former. pseud. Querists, part III. 67117
Same person who . . . September 21, 1771, delivered a small poem. pseud. Poem on divine revelation. see Brackenridge, Hugh Henry.
Samen-spraeck, tusschen teeuwes ende keesje maet. 99317
Samenspraak in het rijck der dooden tusschen Admiraal Piet Heyn. 31662

Samuel Purchas to his friend Captaine Iohn
   Smith. 82824
Samuel Purchas pelgrimagie. (66687)
Samuel R. Smith Infirmary, New York. see
   New York (City) Staten Island Hospital.
Samuel Sombre. see Gerard, James Watson.
Samuel Urlspergers in seinem 82 sten Jahre
   durch Gottes Gnade. 98131
Samuel Waldo—appellant. 101002
Samuel Waldow of Boston, merchant. 101003
Samuels, Edward A. 75967-(75969)
Samuelston witches of 1678. 11650
Samwell, David. 75970
San Agustin de las Cuevas, Mexico. Colegio
   y Escuelas Lancasterianas del Instituto
   Literario de Mexico. see Instituto
   Literario de Mexico. Colegio y Escuelas
   Lancasterianas, San Agustin de las
   Cuevas, Mexico.
San Alberto, Joseph Antonio de, Abp., 1727-
   1804. 669-670, 75971-75981 see also
   La Plata (Archdiocese) Archbishop (San
   Alberto)
San Alberto (Ecclesiastical Province) 36800
San Anastasio, Juan de. 75982-75983
San Anton Munon Chimalpain, Juan Buatista de.
   see Chimalpain, Juan Bautista de San
   Anton Munon.
San Antonio, Agustin. 75984-(75985)
San Antonio, Francisco de. 61165, (75986)
San Antonio, Juan Francisco de. 75987
San Antonio Moreno, Martin de. 75990
San Antonio Ortega, J. de. see Ortega, J.
   de San Antonio.
San Antonio Saenz, Matias. 75991-75993
San Antonio, Brazil (Ecclesiastical Province)
   75989
San Antonio Silver Mining Company. 76994
San Augustin, Andres de. (75995)
San Augustin, Gaspar de. (75996)
San Augustino Macedo, Francisco a. see
   Macedo, Francisco a San Augustino.
San Bartolome, Jose de. 75998, 94824
San Benito, Jose. 63599, 75999
S. Benedicto, Josephum a. see San Benito,
   Jose.
San Bernardino Botehlo, Jose de. see Botelho,
   Jose de San Bernardino.
San Bernardino County, California, its history,
   climate and resources. 76001
San Bernardo, Juan. 76002
San Bernardo, Juan de. see Juan de San
   Bernardo.
San Blas, Caesario. pseud. Voyage to the
   island of philosophers. see Woodruff,
   Sylvester. supposed author
San Buenaventura. see Bonaventura. Saint
San Buenaventura, F. de. 76006
San Buenaventura, Gabriel de. 76007-(76008)
San Cayetano, Herman Jose. 76010
San Cirilo, Francisco de. (76011)-76020
San Cirilo, Pedro de. see Pedro de San
   Cirilo.
S. Crisostomo, M. de. see Crisostomo, M.
   de S.
San Cristoval, ---------, Marques de. (76021)
San Damasco, Juan. 76022
San Diego y Villalon, Juan. 76025
San Diego y Villalon, Juan. petitioner 76026
San Diego, Calif. Chamber of Commerce.
   petitioners 88507
San Diego (Ecclesiastical Province) 76023
San Diego (Ecclesiastical Province) petitioners
   76024
San Domingo. see Santo Domingo.
San Domingo. 82641

San Domingo. Pen pictures and leaves of
   travel. 37171
San Felipe, Academia de. see Academia de
   S. Felipe Neri, Mexico City.
San Felipe de Austin, Texas. see Austin,
   Texas.
San Felipe de Jesus, Patron de Mexico. 71685
San Fermin, Antonio de. (76030)-(76031)
S. Fiora, Paolo Mariani da. see Fiora, Paolo
   Mariani da S.
San Francisco, Juan de. 76107
San Francisco, Maria Micaela Romero de
   Terreros y Trebuesto, Marquesa de.
   see Terreros y Trebuesto, Maria Micaela
   Romero de, Marquesa de San Francisco.
San Francisco, Melchor. 76108
San Francisco, Pedro. 76109
San Francisco. 76078, 76096, 76097, 76101,
   103174
San Francisco. plaintiffs 76046
San Francisco. Auditor. 76033 see also Hale,
   Henry M.
San Francisco. Ayuntamiento. 76062 see also
   San Francisco. City Council.
San Francisco. Board of Education. 76074
San Francisco. Board of Education. Commit-
   tee. 76076
San Francisco. Board of Engineers. 76079
San Francisco. Board of Supervisors. 76044,
   76062, 76084, 76096-76097
San Francisco. Chamber of Commerce. 76036-
   76039, 76040
San Francisco. Chamber of Commerce. peti-
   tioners 76037, 76039
San Francisco. Chamber of Commerce.
   Charter. 76038
San Francisco. Chamber of Commerce. Com-
   mittee on Dockage and Wharfage. 76037
San Francisco. Chamber of Commerce. Com-
   mittee on Earthquakes. Sub-committee.
   76037
San Francisco. Chamber of Commerce. Com-
   mittee on Laws Relating to Pilots and
   Pilotage. 76037
San Francisco. Chamber of Commerce. Com-
   mittee on United States District Courts.
   76037
San Francisco. Chamber of Commerce. Libra-
   rian. 76038
San Francisco. Chamber of Commerce. Presi-
   dent. 76036, 76038, (76041) see also
   Dibblee, Albert. Sneath, Richard G.
San Francisco. Chamber of Commerce. Re-
   presentative to the Interoceanic Canal
   Convention, Paris, 1879. see Inter-
   oceanic Canal Convention, Paris, 1879.
   Representative for San Francisco County
   and City and Chamber of Commerce.
San Francisco. Chamber of Commerce. Secre-
   tary. 76038
San Francisco. Chamber of Commerce.
   Treasurer. 76038
San Francisco. Charter. 76043-76044
San Francisco. Chinese Merchants. 76077
San Francisco. Citizens. petitioners 76056
San Francisco. City Council. 76070
   see also San Francisco. Ayuntamiento.
San Francisco. City Engineers. 76042
San Francisco. Committee of Vigilance. see
   San Francisco. Vigilance Committee.
San Francisco. Customs House. see U. S.
   Customs House, San Francisco.
San Francisco. First Congregational Church.
   Sunday School. 76034
San Francisco. First Congregational Church.
   Sunday School. Library. 76034

San Francisco. Grace Church. Sunday School Library. 76035
San Francisco. Grand Mass Meeting of the Citizens, 1863. see Republican Party. California. San Francisco.
San Francisco. Great Mass Meeting in Favor of the Union, 1861. 76068
San Francisco. Holders and Owners of the Floating Debt. petitioners see Holders and Owners of the Floating Debt of San Francisco. petitioners
San Francisco. Humboldt Savings and Loan Society. see Humboldt Savings and Loan Society, San Francisco.
San Francisco. Industrial School Department. 76049
San Francisco. Industrial School Department. Board of Managers. 76049
San Francisco. Ladies' Aid and Protection Society, for the Benefit of Seamen. see Ladies' Aid and Protection Society, for the Benefit of Seamen, of the Port of San Francisco.
San Francisco. Mercantile Library. see Mercantile Library Association of San Francisco. Library.
San Francisco. Odd Fellows' Library Association. see Odd Fellows, Independent Order of. California. Library Association of the City of San Francisco.
San Francisco. Ordinances, etc. 76032, (76064)-76065, 76084
San Francisco. Panama-Pacific International Exposition, 1915. see Panama-Pacific International Exposition, San Francisco, 1915.
San Francisco. Pilgrim Sunday School. Teachers' Association. (76100)
San Francisco. Produce Exchange. 76098
San Francisco. Public Schools. 76074
San Francisco. Representative to the Interoceanic Canal Convention, Paris, 1879. see Interoceanic Canal Convention, Paris, 1879. Representative for San Francisco County and City and Chamber of Commerce.
San Francisco. St. Ignatius' College. see St. Ignatius' College, San Francisco.
San Francisco. Sanitary Commission. 2697
San Francisco. Santa Clara College. see Santa Clara College, San Francisco.
San Francisco. Smith's Cash Store. see Smith's Cash Store, San Francisco.
San Francisco. Society of California Pioneers. see Society of California Pioneers, San Francisco.
San Francisco. Society of First Steamship Pioneers. see Society of First Steamship Pioneers, San Francisco.
San Francisco. Soldiers Relief Fund Committee. see United States Sanitary Commission. Soldiers Relief Committee, San Francisco.
San Francisco. Sons of Revolutionary Sires. see Sons of the American Revolution. California Society.
San Francisco. Superintendent of Public Schools. 76072-(76073), 76075 see also Pelton, John C.
San Francisco. Teachers' Association of the Pilgrim Sunday School. see San Francisco. Pilgrim Sunday School. Teachers' Association.
San Francisco. Town Council. see San Francisco. Ayuntamiento. and San Francisco. City Council.

San Francisco. Union Ratification Meeting, 1867. 76069
San Francisco. Vigilance Committee. 37808, 76047-76048, 94889, 97098
San Francisco. Young Men's Democratic Republican Club of the City and County. see Young Men's Democratic Republican Club of the City and County of San Francisco.
San Francisco (District) Legislative Assembly, 1849. 76062
San Francisco (Diocese) Synod, 1862. 72967
San Francisco (Ecclesiastical Province) Council, 1874. 72919
San Francisco (Ecclesiastical Province) Council, 1882. 72929
San Francisco County, Calif. see San Francisco.
San Francisco almanac for the year 1859. 76088
San Francisco and around the bay. (27254)
San Francisco & Washoe Railroad. Chief Engineer. 5602
San Francisco Baptist Association. see Baptists. California. San Francisco Baptist Association.
San Francisco bulletin. 1573, 51959
San Francisco business directory, for 1863. 76092
San Francisco Chamber of Commerce. see San Francisco. Chamber of Commerce.
San Francisco city directory. 76092
San Francisco city directory for the year commencing October, 1856. 76092
San Francisco College. 76090
San Francisco Commercial Association. (76091)
San Francisco daily herald. 52436
San Francisco de Quito (Ecclesiastical Province) see Quito (Ecclesiastical Province)
San Francisco directory for the year commencing July, 1860. 76092
San Francisco directory for the year commencing June 1859. 76092
San Francisco directory for the year commencing September, 1861. 76092
San Francisco directory for the year 1858. 76092
San Francisco directory, for the year 1852-53. 76092
San Francisco Ladies' Protection and Relief Society. 76093
San Francisco Ladies' Protection and Relief Society. Managers. 76093
San Francisco Ladies' Protection and Relief Society. Trustees. 76093
San Francisco Ladies' Seamen's Friend Society. see Ladies' Seamen's Friend Society of the Port of San Francisco.
San Francisco, May 12, 1854. 76079
San Francisco Mechanics' Institute. see Mechanics' Institute of San Francisco.
San Francisco Medical Society. 76094
San Francisco Medical Society. President. 76094
San Francisco Mercantile Library Association. see Mercantile Library Association of San Francisco.
San Francisco municipal reports: 1859-60. 76096
San Francisco municipal reports, for the fiscal year 1861-62. 76097
San Francisco, Order of. see Franciscans.
San Francisco Produce Exchange. see San Francisco. Produce Exchange.

San Francisco Protestant Orphan Asylum
Society. see Protestant Orphan Asylum
Society, San Francisco.
San Francisco Savings Union. 76099
San Francisco Union Ratification Meeting,
1867. see San Francisco. Union Rati-
fication Meeting, 1867.
San Francisco Young Men's Christian Associ-
ation. see Young Men's Christian
Association, San Francisco.
San Ignacio, Maria Anna Agueda de, 1695-1756.
76112-76114
S. Jago de la Vega, Jamaica. Supreme Court
of Judicature. see Jamaica. Supreme
Court of Judicature, St. Jago de la Vega.
San Jose, A. M. de. ed. 21776, (24140), note
after 99395
San Jose, Baltasar de. 76120
San Jose, Francisco de. see Francisco de
San Jose, d. 1701.
San Jose, Juan de. see Juan de San Jose.
Fray
San Jose, Juana Maria. 76122
San Jose, Manuel. 76123
San Jose, Prudencia de. (76124)
S. Jose, Rodrigo de. see De S. Jose, Rodrigo.
San Jose Muro, Antonio. 76125
S. Jose Muro, Antonio de. see Muro, Antonio
de S. Jose.
San Jose (Parroquia), Mexico (City) Congre-
gacion de Esclavos del Divinisimo Senor
Sacramentado. 47378
San Jose city directory. 76119
San Jose del Cabo, Mexico. 48298
San Joseph, Francisco de. see Francisco de
San Jose, d. 1701.
S. Joseph, Marcelo de. see De S. Joseph,
Marcelo.
San Jose Betancur, Pedro de. see Betancur,
Pedro de San Joseph.
San Juan, Alexandro Bonilla y. see Bonilla
y San Juan, Alexandro.
San Juan, Pedro Antonio Castillo y. see
Castillo y San Juan, Pedro Antonio.
San Juan Bautista, Elias de, d. 1605. 3242-
3243, 3993-3999, 36132-36134, 36784-
36786
San Juan Bautista, Matias de. 76134-76138
San Juan Hermoso, Fuastino de. see Hermoso,
Faustino de S. Juan.
San Juan, Puerto Rico. Gremio de Jente de
Mar. see Gremio de Jente de Mar,
San Juan, Puerto Rico.
San Juan, Puerto Rico. Sociedad de Socorros
Mutuos "Los Amigos del Bien Publico."
see Sociedad de Socorros Mutuos "Los
Amigos del Bien Publicao," San Juan,
Puerto Rico.
San Juan (Archdiocese) Archbishop (Haro) 30410
see also Haro, Damian Lopez de, Abp.
San-Juan. 76128
San Juan de Ulua ou relation de l'expedition
Francaise. 5832, 79139
San Juan del Norte, Nicaragua. Ordinances,
etc. 51328
San Juan island. Speech . . . April 16, 1869.
33253
San Juan Logia, no. 4, Caracas. see Free-
masons (Scotch Rite) Venezuela. San
Juan Logia, no. 4, Caracas.
S. Leone (Diocese) Bishop (Dati) see also
Dati, Giliano, Bp., 1445-1524.
San Luis Obispo, Calif. Ordinances, etc.
76140
San Luis Potosi, Mexico (City) Collegio.
defendants 106281A

San Luis Potosi, Mexico (City) Ordinances, etc.
(75600)
San Luis Potosi, Mexico (Diocese) 76150
San Luis Potosi, Mexico (State) Audiencia.
76145
San Luis Potosi, Mexico (State) Comision
Segunda de Puntos Constitucionales.
76144
San Luis Potosi, Mexico (State) Constitution.
(76143)
San Luis Potosi, Mexico (State) Junta Inspec-
tora de Instruccion Primaria. 47749,
76148
San Luis Potosi, Mexico (State) Laws, statutes,
etc. (40898), 76141
San Luis Potosi, Mexico (State) Legislatura.
76146
San Luis Potosi, Mexico (State) Legislatura
Constitucional. 76141
San-Martin, ---------. tr. 23225
San Martin, Jose de, 1778-1850. 26112, 44291,
76158
San Martin, Jose de, 1778-1850. plaintiff
14078
San Martin, Jose Maria. 76160
S. Michel, ------- Mavrile de. see Mavrile
de S. Michel, --------.
San Miguel, Andres de, 1665-1742. 76161-
76168
San Miguel, Jose Peregrino. see Sanmiguel,
Jose Peregrino.
San Miguel, Juan. 76169-76172
San Miguel, Juan de. see Juan de San Miguel.
San Miguel, Juan Rodriguez de. see Rodriguez
de San Miguel, Juan.
San Miguel, Matias Sanz de. 76181
San Miguel, N. A. Diez de. see Diez de San
Miguel, N. A.
San Miguel, Phelipe Sico de. see Sico de
San Miguel, Phelipe, Bp.
San Miguel, Vicente Tofino de. see Tofino de
San Miguel, Vicente.
San Miguel, Ysidro de. 76182
San Miguel (Parroquia), Mexico (City) Archico-
fradia de San Miguel. 48383, (48386),
65731
San Milian, Francisco Lorenzo de. see Lorenzo
de San Milian, Francisco.
San Miguel, Juan Rodriguez de. see Rodriguez
de San Miguel, Juan.
San Nicolas, Andres de. 76184-76186
San Nicolas, Gabriel de. see Gabriel de San
Nicolas.
San Nicolas de Michoacan (Ecclesiascial Prov-
ince) see Michoacan (Ecclesiastical
Province)
San Paulo (Brazilian Province) Presidente
(Bastos) (69310) see also Bastos, Jose
Tavares.
San Paulo (Brazilian Province) Presidente
(Itauna) 69317 see also Ituana, Barao
de.
San Paulo (Brazilian Province) Presidente
(Soares) 85620 see also Soares, Joao
Crispiniano.
San Paulo (Brazilian Province) Thesouro.
85620
San Pedro, Diego Antonio Menendez de. see
Menendez de San Pedro, Diego Antonio.
San Pedro, Francisco de. 76187
San Pedro, Nicolas de. 56646
San Rafael, Tomas de. 99451
San Roman, Antonio de. (76188)

San Salvador, Augustin Pomposo Fernandez de. 1025, (24145)-24148, 49796, (63962), 76216-76222, 93358

San Salvador, Augustin Pomposo Fernandez de. supposed author 24146, 60902, 76217

San Salvador (Republic) see Salvador.

San Salvador und Honduras im Jahre 1576. 58271

San Sebastian (Parroquia), Mexico (City) Congregacion del Alumbrado y Vela Continua al Santissimo Sacramento. 34685

San souci. (76703), 101487

San souci, alias Free and easy. (76703), 101487

San souci songs. 76704

San Teresa, Giovanni Guiseppe di. see Giovanni Giuseppe di S. Teresa.

San Thomas, Domingo. 26564-26565

San Vicente, Juan Manuel de. 76227

San Vicente, Nicolas Garcia de. see Garcia de San Vicente, Nicolas.

San Xavier, ----------, Conde de. 76228

Sana, Gaspar. 76229

Sanabria, Marcos Munoz. 76230

Sanadon, David Duval. see Duval-Sanadon, David.

Sanative influence of climate. 13302

Sanavria, Tomas Jose. (76231)-76232

Sanborn, A. 76233

Sanborn, Charles H. (76234)-76235

Sanborn, Charles W. 12179

Sanborn, Edwin D. 76237-76247

Sanborn, Franklin Benjamin. 46126, 76248-76251 see also Massachusetts. Board of State Charities. Secretary.

Sanborn, J. C. 76252

Sanborn, Nathan. 76253

Sanborn, Peter. (76254)-76256

Sanborn, R. S. 76258-(76259)

Sanborn, Reuben. 76257

Sanborn, Solomon H. 76260

Sanborn, W. A. 52901, 52950 see also New Hampshire. Commissioners to Make Examination of the Public Lands.

Sanborn, Walter Henry, 1845-1928. 84518-84519

Sanbornton, N. H. Congregational Church. 74742

Sancere, Adelaide de. 76261

Sancha, Francisco Gonzalez. (76262)

Sancha, Lorenzo Gonzalez. 76263-76266

Sanches Guerrero, B. see Guerrero, B. Sanches.

Sanchez, --------, fl. 1761. 65931

Sanchez, Alejo. 76267

Sanchez, Alejo Ramon. (40063)-40064, 50617

Sanchez, Antonio Ribero. 76268-76270

Sanchez, B. 76271

Sanchez, Francisco, fl. 1673-1691. 76272-76276

Sanchez, Francisco, fl. 1825. 76277

Sanchez, Gaspar. 76278-76279

Sanchez, Hipolito. 76280-76281

Sanchez, Ignacio. 76282

Sanchez, Jose. 76283

Sanchez, Jose Antonio de Villasenor y. see Villasenor y Sanchez, Jose Antonio de.

Sanchez, Jose Maria. 76284

Sanchez, Joseph de Villa-Senor y. see Villa-Senor y Sanchez, Joseph de.

Sanchez, Juan. 76285

Sanchez, Juan de Villa. see Villa Sanchez, Juan de.

Sanchez, Manuel. 76286

Sanchez, Miguel, 1594-1674. 17737, 76287-76291, 97024

Sanchez, Miguel, fl. 1738. (76292)

Sanchez, Santos. 76293

Sanchez, Sebastian. 76294

Sanchez de Aguirre, J. see Aguirre, J. Sanchez de.

Sanchez de Aguilar, Pedro. 527, (76295)

Sanchez de Barreda y Vera, Francisco. 86439

Sanchez de Bustamante, Antoine. 9562, 96068

Sanchez de Bustamante, D. A. see Sanchez de Bustamante, Antoine.

Sanchez de Castro, Jose Geronimo. 76296

Sanchez de Guevara, Cristoval. 76297-76298

Sanchez de la Rocha, Juan. petitioner 76299

Sanchez de Munon, Sancho. (76300)

Sanchez de Ocampo, Andres. 58292, note after 86444

Sanchez de Sotomayor, Diego. see Sotomayor, Diego Sanchez de.

Sanchez del Arco, Francisco. 63746

Sanchez Marmol, M. see Marmol, M. Sanchez.

Sanchez Mora, Andres. 76301

Sanchez Munoz de Velasco, Joaquin de la Pezula y. see Pezula y Sanchez Munoz de Velasco, Joaquin de la, l. Marques de Viluma, 1761-1830.

Sanchez Pareja, Bartolome. 76302

Sanchez Pereira, Diego. 76303-76305

Sanchez Pereyra, Diego Joseph. 76305 see also Spain. Contaduria General.

Sanchez Trujillo, Jose. (76307)

Sanchez Valverde, Antonio. 76308-76309

Sanchez Vergara, Vicente. see Vergara, Vicente Sanchez.

Sanchez y Zarzosa, Manuel de Godoy Alvarez de Faria Rios. see Godoy Alvarez de Faria Sanchez y Zarzosa, Manuel de, Principe de la Paz, 1767-1851.

Sancho, Ignatius. 76310

Sancho, Jose Maria Garcia. 76311

Sancho, Pedro. 66686, 105724

Sancho de Melgar, Esteban. see Melgar, Esteban Sancho de.

Sancho Rayon, J. see Rayon, J. Sancho.

Sancion pragmatica de Su Magestad. 76312

Sancta Anna, Joaquim de. 76313

Sancta Anna Esbarra, Joaquim Jose de. see Esbarra, Joaquim Jose de Sancta Anna.

Sancta Cruz, Manuel Fernandez de. see Fernandez de Sancta Cruz, Manuel.

Sancta Gerturdes Magna, Francisco de Paula de. see Gertrudes Magna, Francisco de Paula de Sancta.

Sancta Maria, Goncalo Garcia de. see Garcia de Sancta Maria, Goncalo.

Sta. Maria de Loreto, ----------, Conde de. 21775

Sancta-Maria Jaboatam, Antonio de. see Jaboatam, Antonio de Sancta-Maria.

Sancta Rita Bastos, Frnacisco Xavier de. 76314

Sancta Egreja Cathedral, Rio de Janeiro. see Rio de Janeiro. Cathedral.

Sancti Francisci Salesii De confessionibus scrupulosorum brevis tractatus. 75763

Sanctification of the Sabbath. 80255-(80257)

Sanctiss. in Christo Patris. 76315

Sanctissimi Domini Nostri Pii Divina providentia Papae IX. 63172

Sanctity of a Christian temple. 97604

Sanctity of national pledges. (11866)

Sanctius, Alfonsus. 76316

Sanctius, Josephus Eusebius. (76317)

Sancto, Antonio del Espiritu. see Antonio del Espiritu Sancto.

Sanctos, Joao dos. see Joao dos Sanctos.
Sanctos, Luis Goncalves dos. (76318)-76330
Sanctos e Silva, Thomas Antonio dos. 76331
Sanctos Marrocas, F. H. dos. 11383-11384
Sanctuario Marianno. 76784
Sanctuary. A sermon, preached at the dedi-
cation of the Congregational Meeting-
House, Claremont. 88675
Sanctuary. A sermon, preached at the dedi-
cation of the Congregational Meeting-
House in Franklin. 88676
Sanctuary: a story of the civil war. (55198)
Sanctuary of God, consulted in the present
crisis. 66229
Sanctuary, the design of its services. 63851
Sanctvm Provinciale Concilivm Mexici cele-
bratvm anno dni milless.mo qvingen-
tess.mo octvagessimo qvinto. 76332,
note after 90828
Sanctus Joannis Baptistae del Peru (Ecclesias-
tical Province) 61074
Sand, George, pseud. of Mme. Dudevant, 1804-
1876. 4523, 92534
Sand-Lake, N. Y. Collegiate Institute. see
Sand-Lake Collegiate Institute, N. Y.
Sand-Lake Collegiate Institute, N. Y. 76419
Sandars, Joseph. 76333
Sandby, Paul. 76334, 81486
Sande, Fernando Fernandez de Cordoba y.
see Fernandez de Cordoba y Sande,
Fernando.
Sande, J. Van de. 76335
Sande, Mateo. (76336)
Sandeman, Patrick. 76337
Sandeman, Robert, 1718-1771. 2632, 4495,
72404, 76338-(76340)
Sandemanian. 57140
Sander, Constantin. 76345-76347
Sandercock, Edward. 76348
Sanders, Alvin. 52181 see also Nebraska
(Territory) Governor, 1861-1867
(Sanders)
Sanders, Charlotte. 76349
Sanders, D. S. supposed author 94252
Sanders, Daniel Clarke. 32174, 76350-76377
Sanders, Elizabeth (Elkins) (16206), 76378-
76382
Sanders, Elizabeth (Elkins) incorrectly sup-
posed author 12714, (76379)
Sanders, George N. 46962, 76383-76386
Sanders, John. 76387-(76388)
Sanders, Prince. see Saunders, Prince, d.
1840.
Sanders, R. 76390
Sanders, Sandra. tr. 83136-83137
Sanderson, George. 76391
Sanderson, J. M. 76392-(76393)
Sanderson, James M. (76394)-76395
Sanderson, James M. defendant before military
commission 76395
Sanderson, John, 1560-1627? 66686, 78871
Sanderson, John, 1783-1844. 76397-76405,
84866, 101140
Sanderson, John, fl. 1812. (76396)
Sanderson, John P. (76406)
Sanderson's biography of the signers. 76400-
76403
Sanderus, Joshua. tr. 73319
Sandford, Edward. 76407
Sandford, John F. A. defendant 5751, (18036),
25009, 33240, (78261)
Sandford, Mrs. Nettie. see Sanford, Mrs.
Nettie.
Sandford, P. P. 76409
Sandford, Robert. see Sanford, Robert.
Sandfords, --------. 101435

Sandham, Alfred. (76410)-76412
Sandheds-røst. 75512
Sandi, Francisco de. 70098
Sandi, Juan Jose. 76413
Sandiford, Ralph. (76414)-76415
Sandifort, G. 76416
Sandige, John Milton, 1817-1890. 76417
Sandisfield, Conn. School Committee. (76418)
Sandmark, Car. Gust. 76420
Sandoval, Geronimo de. 76421
Sandoval, Juan Zapata y. see Zapata y
Sandoval, Juan.
Sandoval, Pedro. 76422
Sandoval, Prudencio de. 76423-(76429)
Sandoval, Rafael Tiburcio. 76430
Sandoval y Cavellero, Maria de. plaintiff
34710, 1st note after 99650
Sandoval y Guzman, Sebastian de. 76431
Sandoval y Zapaya, Luis. 76432
Sandry, --------. illus. 77467
Sands, A. B. 74330, 76433
Sands, Alexander Hamilton. 76434
Sands, Alexander Hamilton. supposed author
36612, (68412), note after 88311
Sands, Austin L. 90725
Sands, B. F. 21678, (76435)
Sands, Comfort. defendant 96853
Sands, D. 47330, 76433
Sands, David. 76436
Sands, Elisha. 76437
Sands, George W. 76438
Sands, Henry. defendant 96853
Sands, Joshua. 90725
Sands, Lewis. defendant 96853
Sands, Nathaniel. 76439
Sands, Robert Charles, 1799-1832. 16939,
21659, 76440-76442, 89130, 94247, 94258,
note after 99271, note after 99276
Sands, Samuel. 95810
Sandtner, Fr. Ed. ed (18362)
Sandusky, Ohio. Citizens. petitioners 16304
Sandusky City and Cedar Point Company. 76444
Sandusky City Manufacturing Company. 76444
Sandusky, Dayton and Cincinnati Railroad.
Committee. 76445
Sandusky directory, city guide and business
mirror. (76442)
Sandwich, Edward Montagu, 1st Earl of, 1625-
1672. 3254, (67375)
Sandwich, John Montagu, 4th Earl of, 1718-1792.
64572
Sandwich, Mass. Calvinistic Congregational
Church. (76446)
Sandwich, Mass. Collegiate Institute. see
Sandwich Collegiate Institute, Sandwich,
Mass.
Sandwich, Mass. Committee on Accounts.
(76447)
Sandwich, Mass. Ecclesiastical Council, 1817.
see Congregational Churches in Massa-
chusetts. Ecclesiastical Council, Sandwich,
1817.
Sandwich, Mass. School Committee. 76448
Sandwich, Mass. Spring Hill Boarding School.
see Spring Hill Boarding School, Sand-
wich, Mass.
Sandwich Collegiate Institute, Sandwich, Mass.
(76450)
Sandwich Collegiate Institute: a boarding school
for boys and misses. (76450)
Sandwich Islands. Extracts from a journal.
90108
Sandwich Islands: progress of events. 81340
Sandy. pseud. Reflections of a few friends of
the country. 68690-68691
Sandy foundation shaken. 92860

Santa Anna. Historischer Roman aus dem Burgerkriege in Mexico. 28183

Santa Casa de Misericordia e Enfermarias Publicas, Rio de Janeiro. see Rio de Janeiro. Santa Casa de Misericordia e Enfermarias Publicas.

Santa Catharina (Brazilian State) Presidente (Aranjo Lima) (69328) see also Aranjo Lima, Andre Cordeiro de.

Santa Catharina de Sena. (62939)

Santa Clara, Sulfras de. see Sulfras de Santa Clara.

Santa Clara College, San Francisco. 76750-(76751)

Santa Clara Mining Association of Baltimore. (76752)

Santa Clara Mining Association of Baltimore. Charter. (76752)

Santa-Claus and Jenny Lind. 76753

Santa Cruz, Alvaro de Bacan, Marquis de. 76755-76764

Santa Cruz, Andres, Pres. Bolivia, 1794-1865. 6195, 6203, 55450, 61146, 76766-76771 see also Bolivia. President, 1829-1839 (Santa Cruz) Peru. President, 1836-1839 (Santa Cruz)

Santa Cruz, Baltasar de. 76772

Santa Cruz, Fernando de. plaintiff 99619

Santa Cruz, Gabriel Beltran de. petitioner (76773)

Santa Cruz, Ioqauin de, Marquez. 99619

Santa Cruz, Manuel Fernandez de. see Fernandez de Santa Cruz, Manuel.

Santa Cruz, Miguel Perez de, Marques de Buenavista. plaintiff 75583

Santa Cruz, Nicolas Maria. 76774

Santa Cruz, Pedro Agustin Morel de. see Morel de Santa Cruz, Pedro Agustin, Bp.

Santa Cruz de Marcenado, Alvaro de Navia Osorio, Marques de, 1684-1732. 76765

Santa Cruz Merlin, Mercedes de. see Merlin, Mercedes de Santa Cruz.

Santa Cruz y Sahagun, Manuel Fernandez de. 76775-76777

Santa Fe (Viceroyalty) see Nueva Granada (Viceroyalty)

Santa Fe, Argentina. Convencion Nacional, 1860. see Argentine Republic. Convencion Nacional, Santa Fe, 1860.

Santa Fe, Argentina (Province) Gobierno. plaintiffs 41983

Santa Fe, Colombia. Ayuntamiento. petitioners 24158

Santa Fe, Colombia. Cabildo. petitioners 24158

Santa Fe, Colombia (Archdiocese) 72968

Santa Fe, Colombia (Archdiocese) Archbishop (Azura e Yturgoyen) 65553 see also Azura e Yturhoyen, Phelipe de, Abp.

Santa Fe, Mexico. Curas Beneficiados. see Curas Beneficiados de la Ciudad de Santa Fee Real, y Minas de Guanaxuato.

Santa Fe, New Mexico (Diocese) Bishop (Lamy) 72968 see also Lamy, John B., Bp.

Santa Fe and back. (47427)

Santa Fe de Bogota. see Bogota.

Santa Fe de Guanaxuato. see Guanajuato, Mexico (City)

Santa Fe gazette. plaintiffs 76778

Santa Fe gazette vs. the citizens of Dona Ana County. 76778

Santa Gertrudis, Francisco. 76779

Santa Gertrudis, Jose Agustin. 76780-76781

Santa Iglesia Cathedral, Guatemala (City) see Guatemala (City) Santa Iglesia Cathedral

Santa Ines, Melchior Oyanguren de. see Oyanguren de Santa Ines, Melchior.

Santa Isabel, Gonsalo de. 75989

Santa Maria, Agostinho de, 1642-1728. 76783-76785

Santa Maria, Bernardo de. see Bernardo de Santa Maria.

Santa Maria, Domingo, Pres. Chile, 1825-1889. 39151, (76786), 76857

Santa Maria, Juan de. 76787

Santa Maria, Miguel. 76789

Santa Maria, Miguel de. 76788

Santa Maria, Pedro de. see Pedro de Santa Maria.

Santa Maria de Lorento, ---------, Penalver, Conde. see Penalver, --------, Conde de Santa Maria de Lorento

Santa Maria de Puerto Principe. see Puerto Principe.

Santa Maria de Todos-Santos de Mexico, Colegio Mayor de. see Colegio Mayor de S. Maria de Todos-Santos de Mexico.

Santa Maria Iaboatam, Antonio de. see Jaboatam, Antonio de Sancta Maria.

Santa Maria Maraver, Juan de. 76790-76791

Santa Maria y Sevilla, Manuel. 76792

Santa Rito Durao, Jose de. see Durao, Jose de Santa Rito.

Santa Rosa, Curacao. see Curacao. Heilige Rosa Kirke.

Santa Rosa del Peru. 50618

Santa Rosa Maria, Pedro Beltran de. see Beltran de Santa Rosa Maria, Pedro.

Santa Rosa, religiosa de la Tercera Orden de S. Domingo. (42056)

Santa Teresa, Giovanni Gioseppe di. 27474, 55498, (76793)-76794

Santa Teresa, Luis de. 76795

Santa Teresa, Manuel de. 76796-76801

Santa Teresa de Jesus Silver Mining Company. 76802

Santa Verracruz (Parroquia), Mexico (City) Archicofradia de Ciudadanos. 86371, 96275

Santacilia, Jorge Juan y. see Juan y Santacilia, Jorge.

Santacilia, Pedro. (76805)

Santagata, Saverio. supposed author 100611

Santalla, Thirso Goncalez de. see Goncalez de Santalla, Thirso.

Santamaria, Miguel. 105749

Santamana, Miguel. 31568, (76806) see also Colombia. Legacion. Mexico.

Santander, Francisco de Paula, 1792-1840. 14609-14611, 14621, 19678, (25459), 58138, 76809, 93812, 1st note after 98873, 99498 see also Colombia. Vice President, 1824-1828 (Santander)

Santander, Juan de. 4637-4638, (76810)-76814 see also Franciscans. Mexico. Comissario General.

Santander, Juan de. petitioner 4636, (76810) see also Franciscans. Mexico. Comissario General. petitioner

Santander y Torres, Sebastian. (76815)-76822

Santangelo, Orazio Donatio Gideon de Attelis, b. 1774. 76823-76830, 76832-76833, 95429, 102321

Santangelo, Orazio Donatio Gideon de Attelis, b. 1774. defendant 76831

Santangelo's trial for libel. 76831

Santarem, Manuel Francisco de Barros e Sousa de Mesquita de Macedo Leitao e Carvalhosa, Visconde de. see Santarem, Manuel Francisco de Barros, 2. Visconde de, 1791-1856.

Santarem, Manuel Francisco de Barros, 2.
Visconde de, 1791-1856. 76833-76852,
77804
Santaren, Jose. 76853
Santayana y Spinosa, Rodrigo Saenz de. see
Saenz de Santayana y Spinosa, Rodrigo.
Sante, Gerret van. 76854
Santee Indians. Treaties, etc. 96662, 96714
Santiago. pseud. Letter. 76855
Santiago Cerro y Zamudio, Jose. see Cerro
y Zamudio, Jose Santiago.
Santiago de la Laguna, Joseph de Rivera
Bermudez, conde de. see Rivera
Bermudez, Joseph de, Conde de Santiago
de la Laguna.
Santiago de Chile. petitioners 98301
Santiago de Chile. Cabildo. 12754
Santiago de Chile. Cabildo Eclesiastico.
100608
Santiago de Chile. Comision de Negocios
Constitucionales. 76859
Santiago de Chile. Esposicion Nacional de
Agricultura, 1869. see Esposicion
Nacional de Agricultura, Santiago, Chile,
1869.
Santiago de Chile. Ordinances, etc. (76856)
Santiago de Chile. Sociedad de la Union
Americana. see Sociedad de la Union
Americana de Santiago de Chile.
Santiago de Chile. Sociedad Sericicola Ameri-
cana. see Sociedad Sericicola Americ-
ana, Santiago de Chile.
Santiago de Chile (Diocese) Bishop (Carrasco
y Saavedra) 11036 see also Carrasco
y Saavedra, Bernardo, Bp.
Santiago de Chile (Diocese) Synod, 1688.
11036
Santiago de Cuba. Ayuntamiento. 31447
Santiago de Cuba. Sociedad Economica. see
Sociedad Economica de Santiago de Cuba.
Santiago de Guatemala. see Guatemala (City)
Santiago de Queretaro, Mexico, see Quere-
taro, Mexico (City)
Santiago, Orden de. see Orden de Santiago.
Santiago, principe hereditario de este reino.
78905
Santibanez, Juan Antonio Ramirez. 67660,
76863-76866
Santidad prudente de San Gregorio Thaumaturgo.
74843
Santie Indians. see Santee Indians.
Santillan, Matias. 76867-76868
Santillana, Ignacio de Hoyos. 76869
Santin y Valcarce, Joseph Bruno Magdalena.
see Magdalena Santin y Valcarce,
Joseph Bruno.
Santiso, Luis Telaya y. see Telaya y Santiso,
Luis.
Santisteban, Jose Silva. 76870-76873
Santisteuan Osorio, Diego de. see Osorio,
Diego de Santisteuan.
Santivanez, Alonso Antonio Rodriguez. see
Rodriguez Santivanez, Alonso Antonio.
Santo, Antonio del Espiritu. see Antonio
Antonio del Espiritu Santo.
Santo, Francisco dos. defendant 86863
Santo-Domingo, -------- de. (76874)
Santo Domingo, Antonio. 76876
Santo Domingo, Garcia de. 76877
Santo Sacramento, Lorenzo del. see Lorenzo
del Santo Sacramento.
Santo Stephano, Hieronimo da. 67730
Santo Thomas, Diego de. 76885
Santo Thomas, Domingo de. see Domingo de
Santo Tomas.
Santo Tomas, Manuel de. petitioner 76886

Santo, Tomas, Miguel Rodriguez de. see
Rodriguez de Santo Tomas, Miguel.
Santo Angel Custodia (Parroquia), Havana.
29435
Santo Domingo (French Colony) 65980, (75125)
see also Colons de Saint-Domingue Qui
Resident en France. petitioners Colons
Francois de Saint-Domingue, Reunis a
Paris. petitioners Comite Colonial de
Saint Domingue, Paris, 1789. Compagnie
de Colons de Saint Domingue, Paris.
Assemblee de Colons Americains, Paris,
1789.
Santo Domingo (French Colony) Assemblee
Coloniale. see Santo Domingo (French
Colony) Assemblee Generale.
Santo Domingo (French Colony) Assemblee
Generale. 7737, 28152, 40668, 40669,
56096, 75048, 75054, 75068-75070, 75088,
75089, 75096, 75102, 75105, 75140,
75147, (75180)
Santo Domingo (French Colony) Assemblee
Generale. Archives. 75144
Santo Domingo (French Colony) Assemblee
Generale. Comites. 75090, 85090
Santo Domingo (French Colony) Assemblee
Generale. Commissaires. (40676), 75104
Santo Domingo (French Colony) Assemblee
Generale. President. 19366 see also
Delaval, ---------.
Santo Domingo (French Colony) Assemblee
Provinciale de l'Ouest. 28152, 65980,
75116
Santo Domingo (French Colony) Assemblee
Provinciale du Nord. 28152, 29564,
75036, 75040, 75043, 75063, 75064,
75087, 75088, 75096, 75141, 75148,
75150, 75189
Santo Domingo (French Colony) Assemblee
Provinciale du Nord. Deputes. 75106
Santo Domingo (French Colony) Assemblee
Provinciale du Sud. 27152, 75088, 75113,
75115, 75117
Santo Domingo (French Colony) Citoyens Blancs.
Treaties, etc. see Santo Domingo (French
Colony) Province de l'Ouest. Treaties,
etc.
Santo Domingo (French Colony) Citoyens de
Couleur. petitioners 61267, (67518),
75142
Santo Domingo (French Colony) Colons. peti-
tioners 75041
Santo Domingo (French Colony) Commissaires.
19807, 28153, 47519, (58163)-58165,
65022, 75143, 75149, 75178 see also
Brulley, C. A. Choiseul-Praslin, -------,
Duc de. Page, --------. Vaudreuil,
--------, Comte de.
Santo Domingo (French Colony) Commissaires.
Rapporteur. 47519 see also Gouy
d'Arsy, Louis Henri Marthe, Marquis de,
1753-1794.
Santo Domingo (French Colony) Commissaires
des Colons. 40930 see also Clausson,
---------. Millet, F. A.
Santo Domingo (French Colony) Commissaires
des Patriotes, Deputes Pres la Convention
Nationale. see Commissaires des
Patriotes de S. Domingue, Deputes Pres
la Convention Nationale.
Santo Domingo (French Colony) Commissaires
et Deputes des Citoyens de Couleur. see
Commissaires & Deputes des Citoyens de
Couleur, des Isles & Colonies Francoises.
petitioners

Santo Domingo (French Colony) Comites
75090, 85789
Santo Domingo (French Colony) Conseil
Superieur du Cap-Francois. 75061
Santo Domingo (French Colony) Constitution.
38430
Santo Domingo (French Colony) Deputes a
l'Assemblee Nationale. 28152, 28154,
38698, 42753, 44143, 58932, 65032,
75081, 75090, 75109, 75145, (75146),
75149, 75151-75152, note after 75175,
(75179), 75190, 85090, 85789, note after
93793 see also Gouy d'Arsy, Louis
Henri Marthe, Marquis de, 1753-1794.
Santo Domingo (French Colony) Governeur
General, 1788-1789 (Airvault) 3312A,
12062-12063, (68372), 75059-75060,
75141, 75149 see Airvault, Marie
Charles du Chilleau, Marquis d'.
Santo Domingo (French Colony) Habitans de
la Partie du Nord. see Santo Domingo
(French Colony) Province du Nord.
Habitans.
Santo Domingo (French Colony) Intendant.
see Santo Domingo (French Colony)
Governeur General.
Santo Domingo (French Colony) Laws, statutes,
etc. 3312A, 29569, 38430, 75059, 75060-
75061, 75063-75064, 75078, note after
98577
Santo Domingo (French Colonly) Ordonnateur
des Finances. 44826
Santo Domingo (French Colony) Proprietaires,
Residans a Paris. see Proprietaires
de Saint-Domingue, Residans a Paris.
petitioners
Santo Domingo (French Colony) Province de
l'Ouest. Citoyens de Couleur de Quatorze
Paroisses. Treaties, etc. see Santo
Domingo (French Colony) Province de
l'Ouest. Treaties, etc.
Santo Domingo (French Colony) Province de
l'Ouest. Treaties, etc. 75083, 96738
Santo Domingo (French Colony) Province du
Nord. Deputes. 75144
Santo Domingo (French Colony) Province du
Nord. Habitans. 75042
Santo Domingo (French Colony) Province du
Nord. Laws, statutes, etc. 75141
Santo Domingo (French Colony) Province du
Sud. Treaties, etc. 75084
Santo Domingo (French Colony) Representans
Venus en France sur le "Leopard."
(75082)
Santo Domingo (Republique Francaise) see
Haiti.
Santo Domingo (Spanish Colony) Audiencia.
(11946), 19145-19147
Santo Domingo (Spanish Colony) Audiencia.
Fiscal. 99437 see also Prada, Fran-
cisco de.
Santo Domingo (Spanish Colony) Chancilleria.
(11946), 50107
Santo Domingo (Spanish Colony) Gobernador,
1653-1655 (Montemayor y Cordova de
Cuenca) 93586 see also Montemayor
y Cordova de Cuenca, Juan Francisco
de, 1620-1685.
Santo Domingo (Spanish Colony) Laws, statues,
etc. 20575, 75079
Santo Domingo (Spanish Colony) Real Audiencia.
see Santo Domingo (Spanish Colony)
Audiencia.
Santo Domingo (Archdiocese) 34836
Santo Domingo (Archdiocese) Arbishop (Fernandez Navarrete) 52095 see also

Fernandez Navarrete, Domingo, Abp., d.
1689.
Santo Domingo (Archdiocese) Archbishop
(Portes e Infantes) 81433 see also
Portes e Infantes, Tomas de, Abp.
Santo Domingo (Archdiocese) Bishop (Ramirez
de Feunleal) 94854 see also Ramirez
de Feunleal, S., Bp.
Santo Domingo (Archdiocese) Provincial. 76878
Santo Domingo (Archdiocese) Synod, 1683. 52095
Santo Domingo (Archdiocese) Synod, 1851.
81433
Santo Domingo de Guzman. 78922
Santo Domingo en el Peru. 76879
Santo Domingo, Puerto Rico y Margarita. 76880
Santo Evangelio (Mexican Province) Laws,
statutes, etc. 76881
Santos, Francisco Rodriguez. 76887
Santos, Juan. 76888
Santos, Pedro. 76889
Santos Barretto, Joao P. dos. 85642
Santos de la Hera, Jose. see Hera, Jose
Santos de la.
Santos de la Paz, Francisco. 29373, 76890
Santos dela Paz, Francisco. see Santos de la
Paz, Francisco.
Santos Guardiola, --------. (35822)
Santos Magana, Juan. 76891
Santos Neves, A. J. see Neves, A. J. Santos.
Santos Ortiz, Jose. see Ortiz, Jose Santos.
Santos Saurez, Leonardo. see Suarez, Leonardo
Santos.
Santoyo, Felipe. 76892-76895
Santuario de N. Senora de Copacabana en el
Peru. 98404
Santval, P. 76896
Santvoord, Cornelius van. see Van Santvoord,
Cornelius.
Santvoort, -------. illus. 32886
Sanuto, Giulio. engr. 76897
Sanuto, Livio. 76897
Sanuto, Mariano. 76838
Sanuto, Marinus. 76838
Sanvitores, Diego Luis de. (76898)-76900
Sanvitores, Diego Luis de petitioner 76901
Sanz, Lorenco Matheu y. see Matheu y Sanz,
Lorenco.
Sanz de San Miguel, Matias. see San Miguel,
Matias Sanz de.
Sao Leopoldo, Jose Feliciano Fernandes Pinheiro,
Visconde de. see Fernandes Pinheiro,
Visconde de S. Leopoldo, 1774-1847.
Sao Paulo (Brazilian Province) Governo Pro-
vizorio. 76902
Sao Paulo (Brazilian Province) Presidente
(Mendonca) (76903) see also Mendonca,
Joao Jacyntho de.
Sapame unukut atugagssat ardlait. 76905
Sapido, Sulpicio. 76906
Sapp, William R. (75907)-(76908)
Sapphic, Pindaric and common odes. (36483)
Sapphire. 76962
Sappington, John. 76909
Sapsikuatpama timash mamachatumki. 75449
Saqueo de Oaxaca y motin de Mexico. (76910)
Sara J. Spencer vs. the Board of Registrators.
89380
Sarabia, Agustin de Ugarte y. see Ugarte y
Sarabia, Agustin de, Bp.
Saraceni, Giovan Carlo. 76897
Saracenial histoire. 66682
Sarah. a pious woman in Connecticut. (47491),
76911
Sarah, an African woman. 93215
Sarah E. Webster vs. the Judge of Election.
89380

Sarah, or the exemplary wife. (73614)
Saraiva, Jose Antonio. 69312 see also
Alagoas (Brazilian Province) Presidente
(Saraiva)
Saranacs and racket. 92775
Sarate, Augustine. see Zarate, Augustin de.
Saratoga, N. Y. National Sabbath Convention,
1863. see National Sabbath Convention,
Saratoga, N. Y., 1863.
Saratoga, N. Y. Nationalen Sonntags-Convention,
1863. see National Sabbath Convention,
Saratoga, N. Y., 1863.
Saratoga County, N. Y. Bible Society. see
Saratoga County Bible Society.
Saratoga County, N. Y. Board of Supervisors.
76928-76929
Saratoga County, N. Y. Convention of Republi-
can Antimasonic Delegates, Ballston Spa,
1831. see Anti-masonic Party. New
York. Saratoga County. Convention,
Ballston Spa, 1831.
Saratoga County, N. Y. Convention of Republi-
can Anti-masonic Delegates From the
Several Towns in the County, Ballston
Spa, 1831. see Anti-masonic Party.
New York. Saratoga County. Con-
vention, Ballston Spa, 1831.
Saratoga County, N. Y. Court. (16421)
Saratoga County, N. Y. Meeting of the Inhab-
itants, Cornish, 1846. see Meeting of
the Inhabitants of Saratoga and Warren
Counties, Cornish, N. Y., 1846.
Saratoga County, N. Y. Washington Benevolent
Society. see Washington Benevolent
Society. New York. Saratoga County.
Saratoga. 27650, (63966), 68421
"Saratoga." 86564
Saratoga. A story of 1787. 80274
Saratoga; a tale of the revolution. 76931
Saratoga; an Indian tale of frontier life. 80275
Saratoga and how to see it. A complete de-
scription. 76919
Saratoga and how to see it. Containing a
description of the watering place. 76920
Saratoga and how to see it. Containing a full
account of its mineral springs. 76918
Saratoga and what is to be seen there. 76921
Saratoga and Warren Railroad. (76922)
Saratoga Baptist Association. see Baptists.
New York (State) Saratoga Baptist Asso-
ciation.
Saratoga County Bible Society. 76930
Saratoga County Society for the Promotion of
Agricultural and Domestic Manufactures.
see Society for the Promotion of Agri-
cultural and Domestic Manufactures in
the County of Saratoga, N. Y.
Saratoga empire spring. 22518
Saratoga Female Seminary, Saratoga Springs,
N. Y. (76924)
Saratoga: its mineral waters. 18928
Saratoga New York republican. 106115
Saratoga sentinel. 106110
Saratoga Springs, N. Y. Convention Relative
to the St. Lawrence and Champlain Ship
Canal, 1849. see Convention Relative
to the St. Lawrence and Champlain Ship
Canal, Saratoga Springs, N. Y. 11849
Saratoga Springs, N. Y. Female Seminary.
see Saratoga Female Seminary, Saratoga
Springs, N. Y.
Saratoga Springs, N. Y. National Temperance
Convention, 1851. see National Tem-
perance Convention, Saratoga Springs,
N. Y., 1851.

Saratoga Springs, N. Y. State Sabbath Conven-
tion, 1844. see New York State Sabbath
Convention, Saratoga Springs, N. Y., 1844.
Saratoga Springs, N. Y. Young Men's Associa-
tion for Mutual Improvement. see Young
Men's Association for Mutual Improve-
ment, Saratoga Springs, N. Y.
Saratoga standard. see Schenectady and
Saratoga standard.
Saratoga waters. 55523
Saravia, Joseph Diego de Medina y. see
Medina y Saravia, Joseph Diego de.
Saraza y Arce, Francisco. ed. (76933)
Sarcasmos mvndo, or the frontispice [sic]
explained [sic]. 78189
Sard, Antonio de. 76934
Sardanete, Jose. 76935
Sardinia. 44605
Sardinia. Treaties, etc. 96543
Sardo, Joaquin. 76936
Sardon, Francisco Cipriano. 76937
Sargeant, E. ed. 21658, 47278
Sargeant, John. see Sergeant, John, 1777-
1852.
Sargeaunt, W. C. (14694)
Sargent, Aaron, 1822-1913. 76939
Sargent, Aaron Augustus, 1827-1887. (76940)-
76947
Sargent, Charles Lenox. 76948
Sargent, Charles Lenox. supposed author
(82323)
Sargent, Epes, 1813-1880. 1036, 13559, 25587,
30290, (53291), (76949)-76966, 84783-
84784
Sargent, Fitz William. 76967-76968
Sargent, George B. 76969-(76972)
Sargent, Henry Jackson. 76973
Sargent, Henry Winthrop. (20776)
Sargent, Horace Binney. 76974, 77026
Sargent, Ignatius. 93269
Sargent, John. petitioner 101150
Sargent, John. of London 84611-84612
Sargent, John, fl. 1826. 76975
Sargent, John, d. 1836. 76976
Sargent, John Osborne. (76977)-76980
Sargent, John T. 29061, 76981-76992, 91372,
note after 97137
Sargent, Joseph. supposed author 76993,
105638
Sargent, Lucius Manlius, 1786-1867. 1240,
6784, 7702, 30765, 54980, (63893), 76994-
77026, 89539, 89744, 90038, 91376,
93203, 93206, note after 94655, 2d note
after 98269, note after 98576
Sargent, Lucius Manlius, 1786-1867. supposed
author 77003, 89539, 89919, note after
96474, note after 96475
Sargent, Nathan, 1794-1875. 41335, (77027)-
77029
Sargent, Thomas. 77030
Sargent, William. 77031
Sargent, Winthrop, 1753-1820. (3821), (6480),
(18173), 58452, 63780, 77032-77041 see
also Mississippi (Territory) Governor,
1798-1801 (Sargent) Ohio Company.
Agent. Ohio Company. Secretary.
Sargent, Winthrop, 1825-1870. 1502, 1545,
7211, (42560), 77035, (77042)-77044,
90375
Sargent prize-medal essay. 84611-84612
Sargent's new monthly magazine of literature.
76963
Sargent's school monthly. (76964)
Sargent's standard school primer. 76966
Sargent's standard series. 76966

Sargent's standard series of speakers. 76966
Saricheff, Gavrila Andreevich. see Sarychef, Gavrila Andreevich.
Sarinana, Isidro, 1630-1696. 48596, 77045-77057
Sarinana, Severo M. 77058
Sarinara, Ysidro. see Sarinana, Isidro, 1630-1696.
Saris, John. 66686
Sarjeant, T. 77059
Sarles, John W. 77060
Sarmatha. 34100-34107
Sarmenticidio. 77061
Sarmiento, A. Belin. ed. 77087
Sarmiento, Domingo Faustino, Pres. Argentine Republic, 1811-1888. (38992), (41237), 49757, 53590, (68465), 77062-77087, 93404 see also Argentine Republic. Legacion. United States. Argentine Republic. President, 1868-1874 (Sarmiento)
Sarmiento, Ferdinand L. (77088)-77089
Sarmiento, Jose. 77089-77090
Sarmiento, Jose Ignacio Heredia y. see Heredia y Sarmiento, Jose Ignacio.
Sarmiento, Martin. 77092
Sarmiento, Pedro. 77093
Sarmiento de Gamboa, Pedro. 77094
Sarmiento Valladares, Jose. see Valladares, Jose, Sarmiento, Conde de Montezuma.
Sarmint agin bull fights. 77095
Sarnow, Emil. 99334, 99378
Sarrans, Bernard. (77096)-(77098)
Sarrazin, M. engr. 87349
Sarria, Francisco Xavier. 77100
Sarria, Juan de. see Sarria y Alderete, Juan.
Sarria y Alderete, Juan. 77101-(77103)
Sarrut, Germain. 77104
Sarsfield, Dalmacio Velez. 77105
Sartain, John, 1808-1897. 63637, (77106), 84678C, 85162, 85466, 101686
Sartain (John) & Co. firm (77107)
Sartain's union magazine of literature and art. (77107)
Sarti, Antonio. 77108
Sartiges, E. de. 77109
Sartines, ------- de. 34179
Sarto, Giuseppe Melchiorre. see Pius X, Pope, 1835-1914.
Sartolo, Bernardo. 77110
Sartori, Louis C. petitioner (77111)
Sartorio, Jose Manuel. 77112-77117
Sartorius, C. (77118)-77121
Sartorius, J. C. engr. 71219
Sarum, Bishop of. see Salisbury, Bishop of.
Sarychef, Gavrila Andreevich. 62506-62507, (77123)-77126
Sarytschew, G. A. see Sarychef, Gavrila Andreevich.
Sa-sa-na. Mohawk maiden see Loft, Sa-sa-sa.
Saskatchewan and the Rocky Mountains. 88529
Sasnett, William J. 77127
Sass, Job. pseud. Trackt for the soldiers. 77128
Sassen, H. 77129
Sastre, Marcos. 77130-77131
Satan contre Christophe Colomb. 73270
Satan des Urwaldes. 5556
Satan dis-rob'd. 103655
Satan strip'd of his angelic robe. 24391
Satan transform'd into an angel of light. 40195, 85464-85365, 105650
Satan unbound. 77132
Satan's harbinger encountered. 66741
Satan's kingdom aristocratical. 17261

Satanstoe, or the Little-page manuscripts. 16525, 16528
Satanstoe ou la famille Littlepage. 16529
Satariengo-Teran-Obregon, G. 14932
Satchel. 77134
Satchel. Issued at the Public Latin School. 77133
Satelite del Peruano. 77135
Satira. 16155
Satire. 56833, (59096), 62414, 62915, 63654, 65086, 66711, (77345), 80151, (81279), 84995, 90648, 93095, 95294, note after 97028, 2d note after 97036, 101134
Satire; and other miscellaneous poems. 46849
Satire . . . and other poems. 101140
Satire, by a youth of thirteen. 8815, 22409, 2d note after 106203
Satire, by an unknown. 51458, note after 92624
Satire, containing some characteristical strokes. 40287, 84627
Satire, delivered before the . . . alumni of Union College. 61371
Satire on somebody. 55392
Satire on the times. 74052
Satire on the times. By Augustus Mason. 45424
Satire. Respectfully dedicated to all the "Saints." 75545
Satire, written with a view to prove the wickedness. 51671
Satires, and other poems. 77136
Satires, imitations, and sonnets. (10370)
Satiric poem. 49977
Satiric poem; shewing, that slavery still exists. 12042
Satirical allegorical novel. 89916
Satirical ballads, &c. on the times. 77137
Satirical effusion. 42912, 44885
Satirical epistle. 33785, 77885
Satirical hits on the people's education. 94514
Satirical parody in rhime. 21782, 63005
Satirical poem. 47441, 85375
Satirical poem, addressed to all genuine reformers. (74426)
Satirical poem. By J. G. Saxe. 77344
Satirical poem. By Juvenal Junius, of New Jersey. 36922
Satirical poem, by Sir Anthony Avalanche. 5887, 1st note after 104829
Satirical poem on the virtuous ten. 21780
Satirical poem with notes. 49857
Satirical poem, written during the American revolution. 56713
Satirical poetic-hodge-podge. 57177
Satirical view of London. (16913)
Satisfaccion a la vindicacion y manifiesto. 62937
Satisfaccion a las dudas propuestas. 77138
Satisfaccion a una calumnia imaginaria. 99667
Satisfaccion al libro de Visitador, D. Juan de Palafox. 72777, (73620)
Satisfaccion dada por el Ministro de Hacienda. 77140
Satisfaccion del Conde de Superunda, Theniente General. 29459, 93778
Satisfaccion del Coronel D. Dion. Soler. 29459
Satisfaccion del Coronel Don Dionysio Soler. 29458
Satisfaccion del Marscal de Campo D. Juan de Prado. 29459
Satisfaccion del Payo del Rosario. 99716
Satisfaccion legal a los motivos representados. 23338, 96309
Satisfaccion legal del D. D. Nicolas Pastrana, y Monteserin. 77141
Satisfaccion pundonorosa. 978, note after 96117

Satisfaccion, qve el Bachiller Ivan Ortiz de Castro. 87229
Satisfaccion que el que suscribe da al publico. 96794
Satisfacion al memorial de los religiosos de la Compania del nombre de Iesus. 56265, 58280, (77142)
Satisfacion que se da sobre el derecho. 24943
Sator, H. H. 77143
Satry [sic] on politics. 67175
Satterlee, Alfred H. 77144
Saturday chronicle. 72056
Saturday courier. 34776, 92751, 93773
Saturday evening post. 105929
Saturday, February 28, 1778. Theatre. 62224
Saturday magazine. (52020), 52027, 77145-77146
Saturday museum extra. 96382
Saturday-night musings and thoughtful papers. 63932
Saturday review. 11317
Saturday review of politics, literature, science, and art. (77147)
Saturday visitor. 85466
Saturniad. (2849), (77147)
Satyr. (41003), 57606
Satyr: by nobody. 71139
Satyr. In which is describ'd the laws. 16234, note after 80002
Satyrar, liber I. 70787
Saucy carrier. pseud. Address. 77148
Saucy carrier's address for the year 1833. 77148
Saudade a memoria do Dr. Antonio Navarro de Abreu. 88771
Saudade pela sentidissima morte do Senhor D. Pedro I. 99735
Saudades de Lisboa no coracao Brasileiro. (22808)
Saudosa cantilena que repetiram. (22809)
Sauer, George. 77149-(77151)
Sauer, Martin. (77152)-(77154)
Sauerwein, Wilhelm. 77155
Sauger, Calvin, & al., executors. 2276
Saugrain, Claude Marin. 77156
Saugus, Mass. 77158
Saugus, Mass. School Committee. 77157
Sauk County, Wisc. Old Settlers' Association. see Old Settlers' Association, Sauk County, Wisc.
Sauk Indians. Chief. see Keokuk, Chief of the Sauk and fox Indians
Sauk Indians. Treaties, etc. 96591, 96616, 96633, 96647, 96662, 96674, 96708, 96712-96713, 96722 see also Michigan Indians. Treaties, etc.
Sauk Indians of Missouri. see Sauk Indians.
Saul. A mystery. (77160)
Saul—an apostle of liberty. 77161
Saules, Carlos Luiz de. 77162
Saulnier, Sebastien Louis, 1790-1835. 77163
Saul's conversion. 103573
Savls prohibition staide. 65421
Saulsbury, Eli. 77164
Saulsbury, Willard. 77165-77168
Sault St. Marie (Diocese) 72972
Saumarez, James Saumerez, 1st Baron de. see De Saumarez, James Saumerez, 1st Baron.
Saunders, Ann. 77169-77170
Saunders, C. 82910
Saunders, C. H. 77171
Saunders, Charles. 26620, (35961), 75318
Saunders, Daniel, fl. 1792. 77172
Saunders, Daniel, fl. 1863. 77173

Saunders, Elizabeth (Elkins) see Sanders, Elizabeth (Elkins)
Saunders, Frederic. 54490, 77174-77182
Saunders, Jack. 77183
Saunders, James M. (77184)
Saunders, Maria L. petitioner 77185
Saunders, Prince, d. 1840. 29578, 76389, 77186
Saunders, Richard. pseud. Father Abraham's speech. see Franklin, Benjamin, 1706-1790.
Saunders, Richard. pseud. Note, this almanack . . . . see Franklin, Benjamin, 1706-1790.
Saunders, Richard. pseud. Pocket almanack for the year 1742. see Franklin, Benjamin, 1706-1790.
Saunders, Richard. pseud. Poor Richard, 1733. see Franklin, Benjamin, 1706-1790.
Saunders, Richard. pseud. Way to wealth. see Franklin, Benjamin, 1706-1790.
Saunders, Rolfe S. 77190
Saunders, Romulus Mitchell, 1791-1867. 77187-(77189)
Saunders, W. (77191)
Saunders, William, 1743-1817. 77192
Saunders, William, fl. 1859. 77193
Saunderson, Henry H. 77195
Sauorguan de Foruile, Pierre. see Foruile, Pierre Sauorguan de.
Saur, A. 73000
Saur, Christoph, 1693-1758. see Sower, Christopher, 1693-1758.
Saur, Christoph, 1721-1784. see Sower, Christopher, Bp., 1721-1784.
Saurel, ------. 77200
Saurius, Abraham. 77201
Sausseret, -------. 77202
Saussure, Henri Louis Frederic de, 1829-1905. 77203-77217
Saussure, Henry William de. see Desaussure, Henry William.
Saussure, W. F. de. see De Saussure, W. F.
Sauvage. pseud. Dialogues. 29142, (38643)
Sauvage, ------- de la. supposed author (65038), 1st note after (74627), (77219)-77220
Sauvage, Jehan. (38494), 77218
Sauvage du Canada. 100745
Sauvages de la Croix, Pierre Augustin de Boissier de. see Boissier de Sauvages de la Croix, Pierre Augustin de.
Sauvages des Canada. 20735
Sauvages, parodie de la tragedia d'Alzire. 100727
Sauveur, Charles Poyen st. see Poyen St. Sauveur, Charles.
Sauveur, Grasset de Saint. see Saint Sauveur, Grasset de.
Sauveur, J. Grasset St. see Saint Sauveur, Grasset de.
Sauveur, Jacques Grasset de Saint. see Grasset de Saint Sauveur, Jacques.
Sauvier, Grasset de Saint. see Grasset St. Sauvier, J.
Sauvier, J. Grasset St. see Grasset St. Sauvier, J.
Sauvigny, Louis Edme Billardon de. see Billardon de Sauvigny, Louis Edme.
Savage, ------. illus. 101742-101743
Savage, Mrs. ------. 77223
Savage, Arthur. defendant 62457
Savage, Charles C. 77224-(77225)
Savage, Edward. (66313), 77226

Savage, Edward Hartwell, 1812-1893. 77227-
77228
Savage, Ezekiel. 77229, 101882
Savage, Faith. defendant 62457
Savage, Faith. respondent 92694
Savage, George. 6512, (77230)-77231
Savage, Habijah. defendant 62457
Savage, Hannah. defendant 62457
Savage, J. R. 61606
Savage, James, 1784-1873. 20884, 24037,
69930, 77232-77236, 104845, 104847
see also Pilgrim Society, Boston.
Committee.
Savage, John, 1779-1863. 614
Savage, John, 1828-1888. 68048, 77237-77239
Savage, John A. 77240
Savage, John Houston, 1815-1904. 77241-77243
Savage, M. J. (77244)
Savage, Sarah. 77245
Savage, Thomas, 1640-1706. 77246
Savage, Thomas, 1793-1866. (4279), 77247-
77248
Savage, Thomas S. 77249
Savage, Timothy. 77250
Savage, William. 77251
Savage, William T. 77252-77253
Savage, Mrs. William T. 77254
Savage. firm publishers see Hill & Savage.
firm publishers
Savage. (77255)
Savage beauty, a novel. 89915, note after
103973
Savage beauty, a satirical allegorical novel.
89916
Savage, by Piomingo. 72115
Savages of America. (72729)
Savanes, poesies Americaines. 73477
Savanna tune. 103526
Savannah, Ga. (77259)
Savannah, Ga. Bailiffs. 103575
Savannah, Ga. Bethesda Orphan House. 22221,
103575, 103640, 103648
Savannah, Ga. Bethesda Orphan House. Child-
ren. 103513
Savannah, Ga. Bethesda Orphan House. Super-
intendent of Temporal Affairs. 29468
see also Habersham, ----------.
Savannah, Ga. Bethesda Orphan House. Super-
intendents. 103513
Savannah, Ga. Census, 1848. 77256
Savannah, Ga. Chatham Academy. see Chat-
ham Academy, Savannah, Ga.
Savannah, Ga. City Council. 77256, 101427
Savannah, Ga. Committee on Sewerage and
Drainage. 77263
Savannah, Ga. Convention, 1861. see Georgia.
Convention, Milledgeville and Savannah,
1861.
Savannah, Ga. Court. 27113, 91313, 91315-
91316
Savannah, Ga. Customs Comptroller. see
Great Britain. Customs Comptroller,
Savannah, Ga.
Savannah, Ga. Freedmen. 15430
Savannah, Ga. Grand Jury. 27052
Savannah, Ga. Independent Presbyterian Church.
Committee of the Pewholders. 77260
Savannah, Ga. Liberty Society. see Liberty
Society, Savannah, Ga.
Savannah, Ga. Mayor, 1855 (Anderson) 77261
see also Anderson, Edward C.
Savannah, Ga. Mayor, 1862 (Purse) 77262
see also Purse, Thomas.
Savannah, Ga. Mayor, 1865. 77265
Savannah, Ga. Mayor, 1879. 101427

Savannah, Ga. Meeting of the Teachers' Society
of Georgia. see Teachers' Society of
Georgia.
Savannah, Ga. Ordinances, etc. 77257
Savannah, Ga. Orphan House. see Savannah,
Ga. Bethesda Orphan House.
Savannah, Ga. Orphan House Academy. see
Savannah, Ga. Bethesda Orphan House.
Savannah, Ga. Southern Commercial Convention,
1856. see Southern Commercial Con-
vention, Savannah, Ga., 1856.
Savannah, Ga. Southern Medical College. see
Southern Medical College, Savannah, Ga.
Savannah, Ga. Southern Railroad Convention,
1855. see Southern Railroad Convention,
Savannah, Ga., 1855.
Savannah, Ga. Treasurer. 77261-77262
Savannah, Ga. Union Society. see Union
Society, Savannah, Ga.
Savannah, a poem in two cantos. 14902
Savannah, Albany and Gulf Rail Road Company.
President and Directors. 77264
Savannah and Boston. 77265
Savannah and Charleston Railroad Company.
Charter. 87679
Savannah and Memphis Railroad. 77266
Savannah Baptist Association. see Baptists.
South Carolina. Savannah Baptist Asso-
ciation.
Savannah city directory for 1867. 77258
Savannah, Ga. directory, and general advertiser.
77258
Savannas of varinas. 10193, note before 94254,
note after 98870
Savardan, Augustin. 77268
Savaresy, A. M. Th. 77269
Savary, Jacques, 1622-1690. (77270)
Savary, Philemon Louis. (77270)-77271, 77273
Savary des Brulons, Jacques, 1677-1716. 77271-
77278
Savery, William. 23173, 77279-77288
Savile, Henrie. 77289
Saville, Sir George. 25335
Saville, M. H. ed. 103397
Saving Fund Society, Philadelphia. 62225
Saving remedy. 36885
Savings banks, life insurance, and other papers.
(24350)
Savings Institution, Cambridge, Mass. see
Cambridge, Mass. Savings Institution.
Savings Institution in the Town of Cambridge,
Mass. see Cambridge Savings Institution,
Cambridge, Mass.
Savings Union, San Francisco. see San Fran-
cisco Savings Union.
Saviour with his rainbow. 46496, 46551
Saviour's presence with his ministers. 89783
Savoie-Carrignan, Eugene, Prince of. see
Eugene, Prince of Savoie-Carrignan,
1663-1736.
Savonarola, Raffaello. 39133, 2d note after
98594
Savorgnanus, Peter. tr. 16947-16948, 16951,
16957, 16961
Savory, William. see Savery, William.
Savoury dish for loyal men. 77290
Savoy, Mass. Selectmen. (77292)
Savoy, Mass. Schools. 77291
Savoy. (16890), 44605
Savoy. Treaties, etc. 96540
Saw ye my hero George. 101883
Sawin, Thomas E. (77293)
Sawkins, James Gay, 1806-1878. (35584),
46101, 77294
Sawney, pseud. Friendly debate. see Walter,
Thomas, 1696-1725.

Sawney, Scots. pseud. see Scots Sawney. pseud.

Sawney, Redivivus et restaurantus. 5349

Sawny. pseud. Friendly debate. see Walter, Thomas, 1696-1725.

Sawtell, E. N. 13672, (77295)-77296

Sawtelle, I. B. 77297-77299

Sawyer, A. F. 77300

Sawyer, Asa. 77301

Sawyer, Augustus. (77302)

Sawyer, Mrs. C. M. see Sawyer, Caroline Mehetabel (Fisher) 1812-1894.

Sawyer, Caroline Mehetabel (Fisher) 1812-1894. 73250, 77303

Sawyer, E. A. 39517, 69684

Sawyer, Esther. (77302)

Sawyer, Eugene T. 77304

Sawyer, Frederic William. 77309-77311

Sawyer, Frederick Adolphus, 1822-1891. 65336, 77305-77308

Sawyer, George S. 77312

Sawyer, J. B. 77313

Sawyer, Joseph. 77314

Sawyer, Joseph W. (73315)

Sawyer, Leicester A. 77316-77318

Sawyer, Lemuel, 1777-1852. 77319-77321

Sawyer, Matthias E. 77322

Sawyer, Milton. (77323)-(73324)

Sawyer, R. P. 77325

Sawyer, Thomas J. 77326, 84281, 84284

Sawyer, William, 1803-1877. (77327)-77333

Saxby, Henry. 77334

Saxe, Burton. 77335

Saxe, John Godfrey. (77336)-77346

Saxe, Maurice, Comte de, 1696-1750. 68016

Saxe-Weimar-Eisenach, Bernhard, Duke of. see Karl Bernhard, Herzog zu Sachsen-Weiner-Eisenach.

Saxische Robinson. (72235)

Saxon, Isabelle. 77347

Saxonville, Mass. Edwards Church. 77348

Saxton, Charles. 77349

Saxton, Joseph. 21787

Saxton, Luther Calvin. 77351

Saxton (C. M.) firm publishers 77350

Saxton's handbook on tobacco culture. 77350

Say, Benjamin. ed. (77365)

Say, Charles. 77352

Say, Horace. 77353, (77357), 77361-77362

Say, Jean Baptiste. (23230), (23234), 77354-77364, (82311), 93602

Say, Thomas, 1709-1796. (77365)-77366

Say, Thomas, 1787-1834. 12430, 35682-(35683), (37137), 77367-77390

Say how can words a passion feign. 92175, 92176A

Saybrook, Conn. Collegiate School. 105855

Saybrook, Conn. Synod, 1708. see Congregational Churches in Connecticut. Saybrook Synod, 1708.

Saye, James H. (77396)

Sayere, Jamey. see Sayre, James.

Sayers, Edward. 77397-77400

Sayers, Joseph. 77401

Sayings and doings at the Tremont House. 82193

Sayings and doings in America. 77404

Sayings and doings of Samuel Slick, Esq. 29695

Sayings and doings of Samuel Slick, of Slickville. 29684

Sayings and doings of volunteers. 43051

Sayings and doings, with the history of one day. 61573

Sayings of Dr. Bushwhacker and other learned men. 17325

Sayings of the little ones. 80967

Sayings. With comic illustrations. 79912

Sayler, Milton. (77405)-77408

Sayles, John. 77409

Sayles, W. B. 70645, 77410 see also Rhode Island. Commissioner, Appointed to Ascertain the Number, Ages, Hours of Labor, and Opportunities for Education of Children, Employed in the Manufacturing Establishments of Rhode Island.

Sayre, --------. plaintiff 90759

Sayre, Daniel. 77411

Sayre, James. 6935, (77412)

Sayre, John. 77413-(77414)

Sayre, Stephen. petitioner 77415-77419

Sayre-Ruppaner case. 90759

Sayres, Gilbert H. 77420-(77421)

Sayres, Samuel W. 77422

Says I to myself—how is this? 13717

Sayve, --------, Comte de. 77423

Sayward, W. T. 77424

Sazie, L. ed. 70301

Scadding, Henry. 77425-77434, 85205

Scaeva. pseud. Hartford in the olden time. see Stuart, Isaac William.

Scaevola. pseud. Letters of a Nova Scotian. (40604)

Scaevola. pseud. To the Commissioners appointed by the East-India Company. 95912

Scald. pseud. St. Jonathan. see Coxe, Arthur Cleveland.

Scale of 250 toises. 50185, 82379

Scales, Jacob. 77435

Scales, W. B. 34290

Scales, William. 77436-(77437)

Scales dropt from the eyes of the people. 98021

Scaliger, Joseph. 6118, 94273

Scaliger, Julius. 77438

Scaligerius, Jos. see Scaliger, Joseph.

Scalona Aguero, Gaspar de. see Aguero, Gaspar de Escalona.

Scalp-hunters. 69029, 69069-69071

Scalpeur des Ottavas. 4903E

Scalpjager. 2694, (69072)

Scamler, Robert. 77440

Scammon, Charles M. (77441)

Scammon, J. Young. 12621, (77442)

Scammon, J. Young. reporter 77443

Scammon, McCagg & Fuller. firm 87299

Scandaloser prozess. 57309

Scanderoon. pseud. Royal decrees. see Stoddard, William Osborn. and Robbins, Louis S. incorrectly supposed author

Scank, Philemon. pseud. Few chapters to Brother Jonathan. 63438, (77444), 98169

Scanlan, Michael. (77445)

Scapel, M. D. pseud. Terrible mysteries of the Ku-Klux-Klan. see Dixon, Edward H.

Scapel: a journal of health. 20358, 77439

Scarabee d'or. 63530

Scarborough, John. (77446)

Scarborough, W. S. 77447

Scarburgh, Edmond. 77448

Scarcity of seamen. 93547

Scare-crow. 14016

Scarlet flag. 51532

Scarlet letter. A romance. 30994

Scarlett, P. Campbell. 77449

Scatacook Indians. see Scaticook Indians (Connecticut)

Scaticook Indians (Connecticut) (15440)

Scaticook Indians (Connecticut) Treaties, etc. 85217

Scautacook Indians. see Scaticook Indians
   (Connecticut)
Scattergood, David. illus. 63543
Scattergood, John. 77450
Scattergood, Joseph. petitioner 77451
Scattergood, Thomas, d. 1814. (77452)-77453
Scawen, John. 77454
Scelta di curiosita letterarie. 69331
Scelter, Helter von. pseud. Schemer. see
   Ridley, J.
Scene comica original. (62985)
Scene della schiavitu dei Negri in America.
   92587
Scene du Nouveau=Monde. 77455
Scene from a new play call'd the Bully. 89119
Scene in Jamaica. 78339, 96128
Scene in the first act of the new farce. 77456
Scene in the High Court of Admiralty. 8514
Scene of Christ in the Garden of Gethsemane.
   76473
Scene off Bermuda. 78339, 96128
Scenen aus dem Kampfen der Mexicaner und
   Nordamerikaner. 93107
Scenen aus dem Mexicanischen Befreiungskriege.
   4519
Scenen aus dem Mexicanischen Waldleben.
   4539
Scenen aus dem Volksleben in I Act. 77155
Scenen aus den Kampfen der Indianer Floridas.
   29676
Scenen aus der jungsten Rebellion. 40116
Scener och skildringar fran Nordamerikanska
   Fristaterna. 98243
Scenery American. 49423
Scenery of Ithaca. 35278, 89381
Scenery of the Catskill Mountains. 11553
Scenery of the mountains of western North
   Carolina. 14792
Scenery of the plains, mountains, and mines.
   (38904)
Scenery of the United States. 77457
Scenery of the White Mountains. 56387, 57099
Scenery of the Windward and Leeward Islands.
   9824
Scenery, science, and art. 1648
Scenery-shower. 9507
Scenery-showing, and other writings. 9505
Scenes Americaines. 57225
Scenes and adventures. 17267
Scenes and adventures in an overland journey
   to California. (10032), 41030
Scenes and adventures in Central America.
   30343
Scenes and adventures in Mexico. (64553)
Scenes and adventures in the army. 16339
Scenes and adventures in the semi-alpine
   region. 77877, 77881
Scenes and adventures in the southwest. 30344
Scenes and characters. 94255
Scenes and incidents illustrative of religious
   faith. (29475)
Scenes and incidents in the western prairies.
   (28713)
Scenes and incidents of American history.
   (11950)
Scenes and incidents of the war in Arkansas.
   4017
Scenes and narratives from German history.
   77458
Scenes and narratives from the early history
   of the United States. 77458
Scenes and scenery in the Sandwich Islands.
   (35800)
Scenes and sketches among the descendants of
   the pilgrim fathers. 92425

Scenes and sketches of the late American and
   Mexican war. 64538
Scenes and songs of social life. 80185
Scenes and studies of savage life. 89910
Scenes at the fair. 77459
Scenes at Washington. 77460
Scenes behind the curtain. 37308
Scenes beyond the Rocky Mountains. 35125
Scenes d'esclavage d'apres Mme. H. Beecher
   Stowe. 92545
Scenes de la guerre de l'independance du
   Mexique. 4518
Scenes de la nature dans les Etats-Unis. 2371
Scenes de la nature sous les tropiques. 19555
Scenes de la vie Canadienne. 12562
Scenes de la vie Californien. 27188
Scenes de la vie des esclaves. 23553
Scenes de la vie des Etats-Unis. 2244
Scenes de la vie des Indiens. (23552)
Scenes de la vie Mexicaine. Par Gabriel Ferry.
   4524
Scenes, de la vie Mexicaine. Par Lucien Biart.
   5142
Scenes de la vie militaire au Mexique. 4525
Scenes de la vie sauvage au Mexique. 4530
Scenes de la vie sauvage en Amerique. 4266
Scenes de la vie Sud-Americaine. 32598
Scenes de moeurs et de voyages dans le
   Nouveau-Monde. 23556
Scenes de moeurs Mexicaines. 5141
Scenes et aventures de voyage. 11542
Scenes et paysages dans les Andes. 44506
Scenes from American history. 77461
Scenes from American history. By William H.
   Barnes. 3531
Scenes from the life of an actor. 77462
Scenes from the past; a series of poems.
   63453
Scenes from the past; and other poems. 63453
Scenes in a mad-house. (19667)
Scenes in a metropolis. 52162
Scenes in a vestry. 103042
Scenes in Africa and America. 94468
Scenes in America, for the amusement and
   instruction. 94469
Scenes in Boston. A story. 39738, 94652
Scenes in Chusan. 77463
Scenes in Europe and Asia. 94468
Scenes in Georgia. (20981)
Scenes in Ireland, America, &c. 31810
Scenes in my native land. 80951
Scenes in New Orleans. 47120
Scenes in Nova Scotia. 28986
Scenes in "old Ironsides." 41012
Scenes in our parish. 32597
Scenes in pioneer life. (13328)
Scenes in the Caribbean Sea. 5890
Scenes in the country. 67616
Scenes in the Frigate United States. 44606
Scenes in the Hawaiian Islands and California.
   1413
Scenes in the Indian country. 77463
Scenes in the Isle of Mount Desert. 19199
Scenes in the life of a Halifax belle. 31468
Scenes in the life of Gen. Scott. 78425
Scenes in the Old Dominion. 59441
Scenes in the practice of a New York surgeon.
   20359
Scenes in the Rocky Mountains, and in Oregon.
   74892-74894
Scenes in the south, and other miscellaneous
   pieces. (17457)
Scenes in the south. By R. R. Montesano.
   50122
Scenes in the south west. 41018, 64545

Scenes in the west. 47289, 59440
Scenes in the West Indies. 77474
Scenes in the work of a western pastor. 32450
Scenes, incidents, and adventures in the far
  west. 35195
Scenes, incidents, and adventures in the Paci-
  fic Ocean. 35506
Scenes, incidents, and lessons of the great
  Chicago fire. 79617
Scenes of American wealth and industry.
  77465
Scenes of British wealth. 94468
Scenes of Indian life. 18583
Scenes of the primitive forest of America.
  30772
Scenes of wonder and curiosity in California.
  10041, 34045
Scenes of youth. A poem. 102167
Scenes on the Mississippi. 97031-97032
Scenes on the shores of the Atlantic. 20091,
  77466
Scenic dialogue in five parts. 74874
Scenographia Americana. 77467
Scenographical geology. 45755
Sceptick. 67573, 67577-67578, (67579)-67584,
  67588, 67598
Schaack, Peter van. 53733
Schaad, J. Christian. 77468-77469
Schabalie, Johann Philip. 77470
Schabelski, Achille. 77471
Schad, Georg Friedrich Casimir. tr. 38416
Schade, Louis. (77472)-(77473)
Schadtler, -------. tr. 92517
Schadtler, Gustavo. (77474)
Schaduwbeelden uit Suriname. 1577
Schaede die den staet der Vereenichde Neder-
  landen. (77475)
Schaeffer, -------. 77476
Schaeffer, -------, Ritter von. 77486-(77487)
Schaeffer, C. F. 77477
Schaeffer, C. W. 77478-77479
Schaeffer, D. F. 23128, 77480-(77481)
Schaeffer, Fred. Chris. 77482-77483
Schaeffer, G. C. ed. 47283
Schaeffer, J. C. 77484
Schaeffer, L. M. 77485
Schaefmyer, John Jacob. 96078
Schaff, Philip. 77488-77497
Schaffer, David. 96004
Schaffer, David F. 77717
Schaffer, David F. supposed tr. 102481
Schaffer, Joannem. tr. 55437
Schaffer und Maund's Calender. 77476
Schaffner, T. F. 77498
Schaffner, Tal. P. see Shaffner, Taliaferro
  Presto, 1818-1881.
Schaffter, C. A. 88282
Schaft, H. E. (77500)
Schagen, Jan van. (77501)-77502 see also
  Curacao. Raad Fiscaal.
Schaick, C. Van. 77503
Schaldemose, F. tr. (16509), 16554, (16566),
  63630
Schall, Emil. (62870), 77504-77505
Schall und Gegendschall der Wahrheit und des
  gesundten Verstandes. 77506
Schaller, Frank. tr. 44651
Scharf, John Thomas, 1843-1898. 77507-77511,
  83793, 84589
Sachsler, Max. 92580
Schasz, J. A. pseud. Engelsche en Amerika-
  ansche kaart-spel. see t'Hoen, Pieter.
Schasz, J. A. pseud. Geplaagde Hollander.
  see t'Hoen, Pieter.

Schasz, J. A. pseud. Misrekening. see
  t'Hoen, Pieter.
Schasz, J. A. pseud. Verdrag, zijnde het
  derde vervolg. see t'Hoen, Pieter.
Schasz, J. A. pseud. Verdrukte wildeman.
  see t'Hoen, Pieter.
Schat-en woordt-boeck des aerdtrycks. 67431
Schatz, G. tr. 25520
Schau-Buhne der Welt. 77517
Schaues, Adam. 2462, 4th note after 97845
Schaufuss, L. W. (77518)
Schaumburg, James W. 77519
Schaumburg, James W. petitioner 77521
Schauplatz der gantzen Welt. (55306)
Schauplatz der Welt. 77522
Schawbuch der Erdtkreys. 57707
Schawplatz des Erdbodems. 57706
Schedae ara prests froda vm Island. (34158)
Schedel, Hartmann. 77523-77527
Schediasma hocce etymologico-philologicum
  prodromum Americano Gronlandicum.
  22867
Schedule, R. I. 31092, 42730
Schedule exhibiting the condition of the banks
  in Massachusetts. 45629
Schedule exhibiting the condition of the banks
  of Massachusetts. 77528
Schedule of a revenue tariff. 90827
Schedule of duties payable by law. 98391
Schedule of furnace property. 75026
Schedule of his [i. e. George Washington's]
  property, directed to be sold. 101752-
  101753, 101755-101756, 101758-101759,
  101761
Schedule of lands. &c. 37386
Schedule of lots laid out in the cemetery.
  51152
Schedule of premiums for the third annual fair.
  75381
Schedule of prizes offered. 45862
Schedule of property, late of Adolphus Ulrich
  Wertmuller. 102641
Schedule of the acts of the Legislature of South
  Carolina. 12088
Schedule of the ancient colored inhabitants of
  Charlestown. 77529
Schedule of the charges for survey. 98058A
Schedule of the number of persons. 11665
Schedule of the ordinances of the City Council
  of Charleston. 12088
Schedule of the rates of storage. 8723
Schedule of the real estate owned by the corpo-
  ration. (62226)
Schedule of the several companies incorporated.
  10560
Schedule of vouchers. 94412
Schedule. Resolutions containing the amend-
  ments. 42525
Scheeberger, Barbara. 77733
Scheepe-Thiefe. 77530
Scheeps-togt na West-Indien. 4807
Scheeps-togt na Ysland en Groenland. 5905,
  47383, 52359
Scheeps-togt van Anthony Chester na Virginia.
  12528
Scheeps-togt van Johan de Verrazano. 99281
Scheeps-togt van Johan Smith na Virginia.
  82822
Scheeps-togt van Johan Smith, na Virginia, in
  het jaar 1606. 82838
Scheeps-togt van M. Pringe gedaan in't jaar
  1603. (10690)
Scheffer, Arnold. 77531
Scheffer, C. A. tr. 79632
Scheffer, Ed. tr. 17940

Scheffer, J. G. de Hoop. 77532
Scheibert, J. 77533-77536
Scheibler, Carl Friedrich. 77537-77538
Schele de Vere, Maximilian, 1820-1898. tr. 35908
Schelechof, Grigori. (77539), 91218
Scheliha, ------- von. 77540
Schelke, Dominikus. tr. (24746)
Schell, Mary L. 51717
Schelling, -------. 8548
Schellinger, W. 77541
Schem, Alexander J. (77542)-77544
Schema conjugationis Gronlandicae verborum in ok. 95617
Scheme (by striking twenty thousand pounds, paper money). 77545
Scheme for a national currency. 30366
Scheme for a new marriage act. 106040
Scheme for amending and systematizing the medical department. (3862)
Scheme for an additional stock to the Royal African Company. 73776
Scheme for employing masters or teachers in the mean time. 84672
Scheme for improving the mines. (77546)
Scheme for the abolition of slavery. 78727
Scheme, for the relief of the South Sea sufferers. 94404
Scheme for the revival of Christianity. 77547
Scheme is, that this lottery consist of four classes. 97970-97971
Scheme of a convention between His Most Christian Majesty and the United States. 77548
Scheme of a lottery, consisting of three classes. (77549)
Scheme of a lottery, &c. 52570
Scheme of a lottery, for deposing of the following houses. (77550)
Scheme of a lottery. For raising the sum of seven hundred and fifty pounds. 77552
Scheme of a lottery for raising the sum of three hundred and seventy-five pounds. 52571
Scheme of a lottery, for the benefit of East Tennessee College. 94741
Scheme of a lottery, granted by the Honorable General Assembly. 101492
Scheme of a lottery to raise $39,900. 77553
Scheme of Christ-Church lottery. 77554
Scheme of government. (56101)
Scheme of such theological and other heads. 7474
Scheme of such theological heads both general and particular. 7474
Scheme of the exercises at the exhibition of the Brothers' Society, Yale-College. 105861
Scheme of the exercises at the exhibition of the Linonian Society. 105900
Scheme of the exercises at the Junior Exhibition of Yale College. 105893
Scheme of the exercises, at the public commencement of Yale College. 105783
Scheme of the exercises for the public commencement, Yale-College. 105783
Scheme of the exercises of the candidates for the baccalaureate. 105783
Scheme of the exhibitions at the public commencement at Yale College. 105783
Scheme of the exhibitions at the public commencement in New-Haven. 105783
Scheme to drive the French out of all the continent. 77555-(77556)
Scheme to pay off the national debt. 77557
Schemer. 77558

Schemering, Daniel. 77559
Schemes for colonization. 82179.
Schemes of a lottery. 99049
Schemes of the South-wea Company and the Bank of England. 88198
Schem's statistics of the world. 77543
Schem's universal statistical table. 77544
Schenando, -------. 55812
Schenck, Abraham H. 77560
Schenck, B. S. ed. 59562
Schenck, Hubert G. 84529
Schenck, J. H. 77561-77562
Schenck, Noah Hunt. 77563-77567
Schenck, Peter A. appellant 96868-96869
Schenck, Peter A. plaintiff 96869
Schenck, Peter H. 77577
Schenck, Robert Cumming, 1809-1890. 77578-77584
Schenck, William, 1740-1823. (77585)
Schenck, William Edward, 1819-1903. (77586)-77588
Schenectady, N. Y. Board of Education. 77590
Schenectady, N. Y. Charter. 77591
Schenectady, N. Y. Citizens Watching in Rotation. 77596
Schenectady, N. Y. Committee of Citizens. 77598
Schenectady, N. Y. Common Council. 77594
Schenectady, N. Y. Court of General Sessions of the Peace. 97773
Schenectady, N. Y. First Protestant Dutch Church. 77593
Schenectady, N. Y. First Reformed Dutch Church. 77593
Schenectady, N. Y. Inhabitants' Meeting Against the Change of the Route of the Erie Canal, 1836. petitioners 22753, 77597
Schenectady, N. Y. Meeting Against the Change of the Route of the Erie Canal, 1836. see Schenectady, N. Y. Inhabitants' Meeting Against the Change of the Route of the Erie Canal, 1836. petitioners
Schenectady, N. Y. Ordinances, etc. 77591, 77595-77596
Schenectady, N. Y. Reformed Protestant Durch Church. 77592
Schenectady, N. Y. Schenectady Institute. see Schenectady Institute, Schenectady, N. Y.
Schenectady, N. Y. Social Society. see Social Society, Schenectady, N. Y.
Schenectady, N. Y. Union College. see Union College, Schenectady, N. Y.
Schenectady, N. Y. Young Men's Association for Mutual Improvement. see Young Men's Association for Mutual Improvement, Schenectady, N. Y.
Schenectady and Saratoga Standard. 65760, 94516
Schenectady and Troy Railroad Company. 77604
Schenectady cabinet. 101524
Schenectady city and county directory. 77599
Schenectady city directory for 1867-8. 77599
Schenectady city directory for 1866. 77599
Schenectady County Bible Society. 77605
Schenectady directory and city register. 77599
Schenectady directory . . . for 1857, by W. H. Boyd. 77599
Schenectady directory for 1868-9. 77599
Schenectady directory for 1865. 77599
Schenectady Institute, Schnectady, N. Y. (77600)
Scherdiger, Abel. tr. 4799, 12959
Scherer, Henri. ed. and tr. 77607
Scherer, Henricus. 77606
Scherer, Jean-Benoit. (77608)
Schermerhorn, J. 15008, 49121

Schermerhorn, J. W. 77612
Schermerhorn, John Freeman, 1786-1851.
  77609-77611, 96684-96686, 96688-96689
  see also U. S. Commissioner to the
  Seminole Indians. U. S. Commissioners
  to the Cherokee Nation of Indians, West
  of the Mississippi. U. S. Commissioners
  to the Muskogee or Creek Nation of
  Indians. U. S. Commissioners to the
  Seneca and Shawnee Indians. U. S.
  Office of Indian Affairs.
Scherpf, George A. (77613), 95122
Scherr, Johannes. 65294, 77614
Scherzer, C. ed. 32045, 105727
Scherzer, Karl. 77615-77625
Schetky, George P. 77626
Schets om te strekken ten betooge. 93863
Schets van de natuur- en staatkundige aardrijks-
  beschrijving. (51075)
Schets van een ontworp tot behoud van Suri-
  name. 22396, 38934, 2d note after
  93855
Schetsen en portretten. 35201
Schetsen en tafereelen uit de wouden en
  prairien. 4540
Schetsen en tooneelen uit den Mexicaanschen
  Vrijheidsoorlog. 4519B
Schetsen en verhalen uit het Noord-Amerika-
  ansche volksleven. 74165
Schetsen uit de 17de eeuw. 32787
Schetsen voor een ontwerp van kolonisatie in
  de Vereenigde Staten. 77772
Schettler, Paul A. 85504
Scheuer, C. A. 77627
Schevichaven, S. R. J. van. (77628)
Schiaffinati, Nicolai Antonii. 77629
Schiavitu nuovissimo romanzo. 92586
Schibel, K. tr. 4579
Schicksale und Abenteuer der aus Sachsen
  nach Amerika. 77630
Schieble, -------- Erhard. see Erhard-
  Schieble, --------. engr.
Schiedam, Netherlands. 36563
Schieffelin, Samuel B. 77631
Schiel, J. 4257, 77632
Schiff-fahrt: Beschreibungen einer hochst-
  muhseligen vnd gantz gefahrlichen Reyse.
  33679
Schiffahrt nach dem Konigreich Chili. 7465
Schiffart der Hollander vnder dem Admiral
  Jacob Eremiten. (8784)
Schiffbruch des Jagd-Schiffes der Schelling.
  8548
Schiffbruch und Grangsale von John Byron.
  29590
Schiffs-Lieutenants Bourne Gefangenschaft.
  72231
Schiffung mitt dem Laandt der Gulden Insel.
  1560, (45009)
Schilder, Karel vander Mander. tr. (4802)-
  4803
Schilderung der arktischen Gegeden. 38038
Schilderung der Auswanderung nach Nord-
  amerika. 6461
Schilderung der gegenwartigen Zustandes.
  9878
Schilderung der neuen Colonie Leopolidna.
  25922
Schilderung der Vereinigten Staaten von Nord-
  amerika. 100690
Schilderung des gegenwartigen Zustandes von
  Grossbritannien. 42407
Schilderung des hauslichen Lebens. (50621)
Schilderung des Mississippithales. 1938
Schilderung des Nordens von Amerika. 25129

Schilderung einer Reise nach Californien's
  Goldminen. 38241
Schilderung von Louisiana. 4964
Schilderungen aus dem Leben in den Sklaven-
  staaten Nordamerika's. 92556
Schilderungen des Treibens im Leben und
  Handel. (71308)
Schiller, -------. 78097
Schiller, Johann Christoph Friedrich von, 1759-
  1805. 30942-(30943), 71998, 77633
Schilperoort, T. Olivier. see Olivier-
  Schilperoort, T.
Schiltberger, Johannes. 77634
Schiodte, Jorgen Matthias Christian, 1815-1884.
  71433, 71435
Schipbreuk in lotgevallen. 99414
Schipvaert naer Oost ofte Portugaels Indien.
  41361-41363
Schirach, G. B. von. 32103, 77635
Schirmbeck, Adam. 48157, 77636
Schism among the Quakers. 77637
Schism the offspring of error. 77638
Schlager, E. 77639
Schalgintweit, Robert von. 77640-77642
Schlange als Mythe. (17987)
Schlatter, Charles L. 60608 see also Penn-
  sylvania. Board of Canal Commissioners.
  Principal Engineer.
Schlatter, Michael. (77643)
Schlechtendal, Diedrich Franz Leonhard von,
  1794-1866. 77644-77645
Schlegel, Johan Friedrich Vilhelm, 1765-1836.
  11594, 77646-77648
Schleicher, F. cartographer 2313, 38348
Schleidem, Em. 40901
Schleiden, R. 77649-77650
Schleirmacher and De Wette. 71519
Schlesier, G. 38047
Schlesischen Provinzialblattern. 106396
Schley, J. van der. cartographer 65404
Schley, John. 77651
Schley, William, 1756-1858. 18096, 27028,
  34867, 77652 see also Georgia. Gover-
  nor, 1835-1837 (Schley)
Schlichthorts, C. 71471, 77653
Schlieben, Wilhelm Ernst August von. (77654)
Schlosser, Friedrich Christoph. (77655)-(77657)
Schlozer, August Ludwig. 52365, 77658-(77659),
  99311
Schlussel zu Onkel Tomm's Hutte. 92415-
  92416
Schmackhaftes Gericht fur Loyale Manner.
  77660
Schmaus, Leonard. (77661)
Schmettow, W. F. von. 77662
Schmick, H. 10269
Schmid, Theophilus. 77662
Schmid, Vlrich. see Schmidel, Ulrich, 1510?-
  1579?
Schmidel, Huldericus. see Schmidel, Ulrich,
  1510?-1579?
Schmidel, Ulrich, 1510?-1579? 3350, (8784),
  25471-25472, 33656-33657, 66686, (67562),
  77677-77686, 90039
Schmiden, Johann. see Smith, John, 1581-1630.
Schmidt, -------. 89758
Schmidt, Carl. (77664)-77665
Schmidt, Carl Christian Gottlieb. 77666
Schmidt, E. ed and tr. 62917
Schmidt, Er. A. tr. 61153
Schmidt, Ernst Reinhold. 77667
Schmidt, Ferdinand. 77668-77670
Schmidt, Gustavus. (42253), (77671)
Schmidt, Henry J. 77672-77675
Schmidt, Henry Immanuel. 82716

Schmidt, Johann. see Smith, John, 1581-1630.
Schmidt, Marcus Fredericus. 77676
Schmidt, Nicolaus. tr. 3412
Schmidt, Ulrich, 1510?-1579? see Schmidel, Ulrich, 1510?-1579?
Schmidt-Phiseldek, Conrad Friedrich von. 62581, 77687-(77691)
Schmidt Geschichte der Deutschen 18. Band. 89758
Schmidtmeyer, Peter. 77692
Schmidts, C. L. 77693
Schmiedlein, Jacob. (77694)
Schmohl, Johann Christoph. 97667
Schmolder, B. 52379, 77695-77698
Schmouth, J. E. 77699
Schmucker, B. M. ed. 78014
Schmucker, S. S. 77715-(77727)
Schmucker, Samuel Mosheim, 1823-1863. 6010, (15761), 25839, 31066, 63325, (77700)-77714, 85145-85170
Schnabel, L. C. ed. (12250)
Schnake, Friedrich. 77728-(77729)
Schnap, Julius. pseud. Old times and new. 77730
Schneck, Benjamin Shrader, 1806-1874. 65721, 77731
Schneeberger, Andreas. 77732
Schneider, Carol Catherine (Smith) 95355
Schneider, J. G. 97689
Schneider, L. 77734
Schneller, J. A. 77735-77737
Schnellers, Conrad. 98137
Schnetzler, Kreisr. tr. 12263
Schnitzer, Johannes. cartographer (66472)
Schobert, -------, Baron. 77738
Schobri, G. 10623
Schodack, N. Y. Mutual Insurance Association. see Mutual Insurance Association of Nassau, Schodack and Chatham, N. Y.
Schoebel, --------. 85781
Schoeben, Johann Georg. tr. 49793
Schoeffer, C. H. (43761), 77739
Schoelcher, Victor. 5652, (77740)-77751
Schoeler, ------. 47292
Schoell, Fr. tr. (49919)
Schoell, Maximilian Samson Friedrich. 26601, 38201, 77752-77753
Schoener, Jean. cartographer 76838
Schoenfeld, Friedrich W. tr. 83223-83224
Schoepf, Johann David. 77754-77757
Schoeppe, Paul. defendant 77758-77759
Schoeppe murder trial. 77758
Schofield, G. 77760
Schofield, W. J. 77762
Schofield, William. 77761
Schofield's Commercial College, Providence, R. I. 77769
Schoharie, N. Y. Schoharie Academy. see Schoharie Academy, Schoharie, N. Y.
Schoharie County, N. Y. Court of Oyer and Terminer. 33424, 98405-98406
Schoharie Academy, Schoharie, N. Y. 77763
Schoharie County Bible Society. 77764
Schoharie County Teachers' Institute, Schoharie Court House, 1850. 77765
Schoharie County Teachers' Institute, Sharon Springs, N. Y., 1861. 77765
Schoharie County Teachers' Institute (2d District), Cobleskill, N. Y., 1862. 77765
Schoharie County Teachers' Institute, held at Schoharie Court House. 77765
Schoharie Court House, N. Y. Teacher's Institute, 1850. see Schoharie County Teachers' Institute, Schoharie Court House, 1850.
Schoharie scout. 85611

Scholar in the republic. 11784
Scholar of to-day. 44489
Scholar, the jurist, the artist, the philanthropist. 93673
Scholar's almanack, and farmer's daily register. (39555)
Scholar's assistant. (82286)
Scholar's companion. 102370
Scholar's manual. 77766
Scholar's vocation in the new republic. (47179)
Scholastic education and biblical interpretation. 92922
Scholcher, V. see Schoelcher, Victor.
Scholefield, James. 77767
Scholer, L. 77768
Scholia in sphaerum. 32680
Scholiast. pseud. Review of the reports. 6763, 77770
Scholiast schooled. 6763, 77770
Scholl, Aurelien. 5662, 26417
Scholte, Henry P. 77771-77774
Scholte, Henry P. petitioner 77775
Scholtens, Godefreed. 77776
Scholtz, K. A. (77777)
Schomberg, Isaac. 77778-77779
Schomburgk, O. A. tr. 77784, (77791)
Schomburgk, Moritz Richard, 1811-1891. 77780
Schomburgk, Sir Robert Hermann, 1804-1865. 162, 4770, 8103, (62550), 67555, 77780-note after 77796, 92808
Schon hubsch Lesen von etlichen Inszlen. (14638)
Schon lustig Reiszbuch. 40727
Schon Weltlich Lied. 77797
Schonborn, Anton. 72476
Schondia. 38299, 106330
Schone kurtzweilige Historia. 23997
Schone newe Zeytung. 16956
Schone Richtige vnd Volkomliche Cosmographie. 67978
Schone richtige und vollkommene Beschreibung. 67977
Schonenburgh, Wouter van. 7564 see also Brazil (Dutch Colony) President (Schonenburgh)
Schoner, -------. 76838
Schoner, Joannis, 1477-1547. (26856), 77798-77808
Schonfeld, Friedrich W. ed. 83127-83128
Schonhoven, Jacobus van. 33523
Schoning, Gerhard. (77809)-77810
School. 8959
School act of Prince Edward Island. 65642
School advocate. 70422
School & family catechist. 84713
School and family geography. 49722
School and family visitor. 77811
School and financial reports, for the year ending March, 1862. 21006
School and financial reports of . . . Jaffrey. 35531
School and the schoolmaster. 64617
School architecture. 3469
School Association of Rensselaer County, N. Y. 69634
School atlas. 49722
School boy. pseud. School boy's oration. 51000, 77812
School-boy's instructor. 92720
School boy's introduction to the geography and statistics. 88850
School boy's oration on the state of the country. 51000, 77812
School Committee, Blackstone, R. I. see Blackstone, R. I. School Committee.

School of the . . . [Massachusetts] Institute [of Technology.] (45867)
School of the prophets. 94442
School of wisdom. 77831
School Presentation Meeting, Boston, 1855. see Boston. Presentation Meeting, 1855.
School question. A correspondence. (37311)
School question in the United States. 49964
School report of Savoy, for the school year 1858-9. 77291
School report of the town of Hubbardston. 33456
School report of the town . . . [of Milton, Mass.] 49146
School returns, 1829. 45544
School system of Maryland. 98408
School Visitors of the First School Society of New Haven, Conn. see First School Society, New Haven, Conn. School Visitors.
"Schoolboy freak, unworthy praise or blame." 84874
Schoolcraft, Mrs. Henry R. see Schoolcraft, Mary (Howard)
Schoolcraft, Henry Rowe, 1793-1864. 7417, (11185), 34661, 32062, (48718), 49962, 54476, 62509, 65495, (77832)-77841, 77843-(77882), 84162, 3d note after 96452, 96704, 96716, 96728, 103695-103696 see also New York (State) Agent to Take the Census or Enumeration of the Indians, 1846. U. S. Commissioner to the Chippewa Indians. U. S. Commissioner to the Swan Creek and Black River Bands of the Chippewa Indians. U. S. Office of Indian Affairs.
Schoolcraft, Mary (Howard) 40621, 77883-(77884
Schoolmaster: a tale. 95481
Schoolmaster. Essays on practical education. 77887
Schoolmaster in the eastern country. pseud. Personal satire. see Humphrey, Asa.
Schoolmaster of a morning. 68483
Schoolmate. 77888
Schools demanded by the present age. 38515
Schools of Cincinnati, and its vicinity. 25024
Schools of journalism. (69092)
Schools of Ohio at the centennial exposition. 77889
Schools; or, a comparative statement. 5729
Schoonmaker, Marias, 1811-1894. 77890-77891
Schooten, Henry. (77892)-77893
Schopf, Johann David. see Schoepf, Johann David.
Schoppe, Amelie. 25937, (77894)-77896
Schoppe, Sigismondus van. 7564 see also Brazil (Dutch Colony) Militie. Luytenant Generael.
Schoppe, Sigismvnd van. 77897-77898
Schori, P. 77899
Schott, Andreas. 32005, 44545, 70778, 77900-77904, 79179
Schott, Arthur. 22538
Schott, Charles Anthony. 13612, 31021, (31800), 37003, 43042, (77905)-77912, 85072
Schott, Franc. ed. 44545, 77904
Schott, Friedrich. 9144
Schott, Guy Bryan. 77913
Schott, Heinrich Wilhelm, 1794-1865. 7607, (77973)
Schott, James. 77914
Schott, Theodor. 77915
Schottus, And. see Schott, Andreas.

Schouler, James. 77916
Schouler, William. 77917-77919 see also Massachusetts. Adjutant General.
Schout, Wilhelm. see Schouten, Willem Corneliszoon, d. 1625.
Schouten, Cornelius. 31543
Schouten, Guatier. 68454
Schouten, Gvillelmo Cornelio. see Schouten, Willem Corneliszoon, d. 1625.
Schouten, Joost. 105639
Schouten, Willem Corneliszoon, d. 1625. (8784), 33669, 44058, 66686, 77920-77964, 89448
Schoutenius, Guilielmo Cornelius. see Schouten, Willem Corneliszoon, d. 1625.
Schouwtooneel der aertsche Schepselen. 56361
Schouw-tooneel van wederwaardigheden of verzameling van rampspoedige en ongelukkige reistochten. 77965
Schoyen, David Monrad. (77966)
Schrader, A. ed. 92416, 92435, 92559
Schram, -------. 14957-14960
Schramke, T. 77967
Schramm, Hugo. 77968
Schrammius, Jonas Conradus. 77969
Schreber, ------. 2348
Schreiben an die Einwohner der Provinz Quebec. (77970)
Schreiben an einen guten Freund. 77971
Schreiben an seiner Bruder. 95250
Schreiben des Evangelisch-Lutherisch und Reformirten Kirchen-Rathes. 77972
Schreiben eines Russischen Officers. 41418
Schreiben von demselben aus den Uebersetzer. 49396
Schreibens an die Hoc-Mogende Heeren Staden General. 100934
Schreibens von einem Spanischen Minister. (58531)
Schreibers, Carl Franz Anton von, 1775-1852. ed. 7607, (77973) see also Austria. K. Hofnaturalienkabinets Director.
Schreibers, K. von. see Schreibers, Carl Franz Anton von, 1775-1852.
Schreiner, Hermann L. 4200, 77974-77975
Schreyack, Johannes. see Shryock, John.
Schreyack, Johannes. of Chambersburg, Pa. see Shyrock, John.
Schrifftmassig dargelegt von einem Teutschen Geringen Handwercks Mann. (38036)
Schrift von den Streitigkeiten mit des Colonien in Amerika. 107, 102647
Schrift zur Belehrung uber die wahren Verhaltnisse. (7931)
Schriftelicke contestatie. 78000
Schriftelicke doleantie. 102913
Schriftelycke notificatie en protest. 49410
Schriften. (21186)
Schfirten der bewahrtesten Vieh-Aerzte. 104977
Schriften gesammelt von der Gesellschaft zur Verbreitung Politischer Kenntnisse. 85888
Schriften [von C. F. van der Velde.] 98819-98820
Schrik niet! 77976
Schrik wel deegelyk! (77977)
Schroder, Henry W. 87833
Schroderus, Ericus. tr. 98211
Schroeder, Henry. supposed author (9670), 95755
Schroeder, John Friedrick. 11882, 32302, 77978-77988, note after 96981
Schroter, Johann Friedrich. ed. (38594A), (77989)
Schryock, J. K. 77731
Schryvers welke over de kolonie Suriname. 77990
Schubert, F. W. 77991

Schuckers, J. W. (77992)-77998
Schulden und Hulfequellen der Vereinigten
   Staaten. 22095
Schuldigstes Liebes-und Ehren-Denkmahl.
   91203
Schulenborch, Johan. see Schulenburgh, Johan.
Schulenburgh, Johan. 78002
Schulenburgh, Johan. defendant 77999-(78001)
Schulgebrauch mit einem Worterbuche. 24754
Schulgebrauch mit einer Einleitung und Anmer-
   kungen versehen. 9297
Schulgeographie. 10687
Schuller, Rudolph. 99362
Schultz, C. W. H. 78004
Schultz, Christian. (77803)
Schultz, F. tr. 43372
Schultz, F. A. ed. 11923
Schultz, J. H. S. 78005
Schultz, Jackson S. 78006
Schultz, Theodore, 1770-1850. tr. 2099,
   80762
Schultz, Thomas. tr. 2099
Schultze, Benjamin. 25986, 78007-78008
Schultze, J. H. 78010
Schultze, John Andrew. 78009
Schultze, Pet. 2431
Schulz, Friedrich. 78011
Schulz, J. L. see Schulze, Johann Ludewig.
Schulz, Johann Ephraim. 78012
Schulz, M. Chr. tr. 91073
Schulze, Franz. 99363
Schulze, G. E. (31208)
Schulze, Johann Ludewig. 25919, 51694,
   (52367), 78013-78015
Schulze, John A. 97949
Schulze, W. 78016
Schumacher, Hermann A. 78017
Schumacher, J. G. (78018)
Schumacher, P. H. 78019
Schumann, Victor. 85072
Schumard, B. F. 68476
Schurtzer, J. H. ed. and tr. 27262
Schurz, Carl. 10190, 78020-(78040), (78042)-
   78058, 93644
Schuster, -------. ed. 10283
Schuster, Michael. (78049)
Schutz, -------. 104704
Schutz, F. tr. 33232
Schutz, Fredreick. 78050
Schutz's allgemeine Erdkunde. 104704
Schuylenborgh, G. v. 21929
Schuyler, Anthony. (78051)
Schuyler, George L. (78052)-78054
Schuyler, Lydia. (78055)
Schuyler, Montgomery. 78056-78058
Schuyler, Philip. 78061
Schuyler, Philip John, 1733-1804. 33523,
   (78060), 94675, 101698, 102985-102986
Schuyler, Philip John, 1733-1804. defendant
   at court martial 78059
Schuyler, Pieter. 628, 66062 see also Al-
   bany. Mayor, 1690 (Schuyler)
Schuyler, Robert Livingston. 11310, note before
   97328, 1st note after 97332, 97341,
   97352, 97364, 97366
Schuyler. firm see Jones & Schuyler. firm
Schuyler County, N. Y. Board of Supervisors.
   78062
Schuyler ov Hobokuk. pseud. Aene songe.
   see Moore, Nathaniel Schuyler.
Schuylerville, N. Y. Convention of the Soldiers
   of the War of 1812, 1856. see Convention of the Soldiers of the War of
   1812. New York. Convention, Schuylerville, 1856.

Schuylkill County, Pa. Prison. Board of
   Commissioners. 78074
Schuylkill and Delaware Canal Company. peti-
   tioners 78069
Schuylkill and Susquehanna Canal Company.
   President and Directors. 50865, 84620
Schuylkill and Susquehanna Navigation Company.
   see also Delaware and Schuylkill Canal
   Navigation. Union Canal Company of
   Pennsylvania.
Schuylkill and Susquehanna Navigation Company.
   petitioners 60725, 78072
Schuylkill and Susquehanna Navigation Company.
   President and Managers. 50865, 84620-
   84621
Schuylkill Bridge Company. 62230-62231
Schuylkill Bridge Company. petitioners 62231
Schuylkill Bridge Company. Charter. (59794),
   62230
Schuylkill Bridge Company. Committee. (61468)
Schuylkill Bridge Company. Directors. Com-
   mittee. 62229
Schuylkill Canal Boatmen. see Boatmen of the
   Schuylkill Canal.
Schuylkill Canal navigator. (78071)
Schuylkill Coal Company organized under the
   laws. 78073
Schuylkill Fishing Company. 62232
Schuylkill Fishing Company. Charter. 62232
Schuylkill Haven and Lehigh River Railroad
   Company. Commissioners. 78076
Schuylkill Navigation Company. 61451, 61556,
   61889, 62371, (78083)
Schuylkill Navigation Company. Boat Loan
   Holders. see Holders of the Schuylkill
   Navigation Company's Boat Loan.
Schuylkill Navigation Company. Charter. 59801
Schuylkill Navigation Company. Chief Engineer.
   78086 see also Miller, Edward.
Schuylkill Navigation Company. Committee on
   Tolls. 78089
Schuylkill Navigation Company. Committee to
   View the Improvements, of the Navigation
   of the Connecticut River. 78082
Schuylkill Navigation Company. Loanholders.
   see Schuylkill Navigation Company.
   Stockholders and Loanholders.
Schuylkill Navigation Company. President.
   78079
Schuylkill Navigation Company. President and
   Managers. 78079, 78090
Schuylkill Navigation Company. Stockholders
   and Loanholders. Committee. 78088
Schuylkill Navigation Company. 78092
Schuylkill Permanent Bridge Company. 78067
Schuylkill permanent bridge. Dec. 12, 1833.
   62231
Schwabe, J. J. ed. 913, 65406, 84560
Schwaegrichen, D. F. ed. 78104
Schwalbe, J. F. G. 78093
Schwartz, Franz. see Nigrinuo or Schwartz,
   Franz.
Schwartz, Joachim. pseud. Reflexions sur
   l'esclavage des Negres. see Condorcet,
   Marie Jean Antoine Nicolas Caritat,
   Marquis de.
Schwartz, John, 1793-1860. 78096
Schwartz, L. J. C. (11655)
Schwartz, Sprotto y Compania. firm 66522
Schwartze, J. George. illus. 93192
Schwarz, J. L., fl. 1775. 78097
Schwarz, J. L., fl. 1849. 78098
Schwarze, C. A. (78099)
Schwarze, W. N. ed. note after 106203
Schwarzenberg, F. A. 78100

Schweden General Compagnie. see Suder Companey.
Schweichel, Robert. 7078
Schvveigker, Solomon. 17730
Schweinitz, Edmund Alexander de. see De Schweinitz, Edmund Alexander, 1825-1887.
Schweinitz, Lewis D. de. see Schweinitz, Lewis David von, 1780-1834.
Schweinitz, Lewis David von, 1780-1834. 67461, (78103)-78104
Schweitzer, Johann. 78105
Schweizer Schutzen-Compagnie im Nord-amerikanischen Kriege. (2167)
Schwenckfeld, Caspar. 60090
Schwere Arbeiten und reiffe Seelen-Fruchten. 47108
Schwert der Revolution. 42661
Schwur. 4527
Schyn, H. 78106-78107
Scian Dubh. pseud. Ridgeway. 78108
Science. 82810, 85095
Science. A poem. By Francis Hopkinson. 32982
Science: a poem dedicated to the American Association for the Advancement of Science. 92774
Science and religion. 32943
Science and scientific schools. 18427
Science des personnes de la cour de l'epee et de robe. 12604
Science du Bonhomme Richard. 25567, 25583-25585, 25596, 78109-78117
Science du cultivateur Americain. 12234
Science in America with remarks on the modern methods of science. 83003
Science news. 84797
Science of business. 83884-83886, 83890
Science of education. (24537)
Science of government. 106060
Science of government as exhibited in the institutions of the United States. 27877
Science of government, founded on natural law. 73105
Science of government in connection with American institutions. 700
Science of political economy. 48862
Science of the sciences. 80465
Science v. modern spiritualism. 26734
Sciences naturelles. 21210
Sciencia da Bon Homem Riccardo. 78118
Scientific American. 78119
Scientific American; an illustrated journal of art, science, and mechanics. 78120
Scientific and descriptive catalogue of Peale's Museum. 59419
Scientific and industrial education. 91013
Scientific Commission, Albany, 1852. petition-ers 47701
Scientific geology. 45751
Scientific journal. (60320)
Scientific library. 84363-84364
Scientific monthly. 85144
Scientific reports made by A. la Roche and James Richardson. 39044
Scientific repository. 54794
Scientific results of a journey in Brazil. 30714
Scientific schools in Europe. 27433
Scientific Students' Association, Manchester, Eng. 89284
Scientific writings of James Smithson. 84985, 84987, 84989
Scillacio, Niccolo. 73071, 74659, 94095-94096
Scimitar. 78121
Scintille d'un Brasiliana di Floresta Augusta Brasileira. 78122

Scioto Company. see Compagnie du Scioto, Paris.
Scipio. pseud. Reflections on Monroe's view. see Tracy, Uriah. and Hamilton, Alexander, 1755-1804. incorrectly sup-posed author
Scipio Africanus, P. 24340
Scipio Americanus. pseud. Address to Sir John Cust. 78127
Scipio's reflections on Monroe's view. 29983, 96422
Scituate, Mass. 78130
Scituate, Mass. First Trinitarian Congrega-tional Church of Christ. 78128
Scituate, Mass. School Committee. 78131
Scituate, Mass. Selectmen. 78131-78132
Scituate, Mass. Town Clerk. 78131
Scituate, R. I. 78133
Sclater, Philip Lutley. (78134)-78148
Sclaverei und Freiheit. (20715)
Scobel, Henry. (78149), 97129 see also Great Britain. Council. Secretary. Great Britain. Parliament. Clerk.
Scobell, Henry. see Scobel, Henry.
Scobie, Hugh. (10624), 78150
Scobie's Canadian almanac. (10624), 78150
Scoble, A. R. (29266)
Scoble, John. 728, 1426, 67184, 78151-78154, 92002
Scoffern, John. 78155
Scofield, Alanson. 48777
Scofield, B. B. 78156
Scofield, Glenni W. (78157)-78163
Scofield, Orrin. ed. 20755
Scofield, Samuel. 78164
Scofield, William C. 78165
Scoles, John. engr. (16915), 83422, 84363, 101842
Scondia illustrata. 48150
Scoperta dell' America. 94287
Scoptera dell' America fatta nel secolo X. (5515)
Scoperte artiche narrate. (49224)
Scoprimento dello Stretto Artico. 78166
Score wip'd off. 78452, note after 95867
Scoresby, William, 1789-1857. 3628, 12410, 78167-78183
Scoresby-Jackson, R. E. (35452), 78184
Scroyer, Richard. 78185
Scot, Dred. see Scott, Dred.
Scot, Edmund. 66686
Scot, George. 78186
Scot, John. 22149, 59561
Scot, Patricke. 78187
Scot, Phil. pseud. Defence of the Scots Abdi-cating Darien. see Ferguson, Robert, d. 1814. Harris, Walter. supposed author Hodges, James. supposed author
Scot, R. 25363-(25364)
Scot, Thomas, fl. 1605. (78188)-78191
Scot, W. Lithgow. see Lithgow, W.
Scot, William. defendant 6326
Scot abroad and the Scot at home. 74997, note after 95589
Scotch answer to a yankee question. 78192
Scotch Irish, and their first settlements. 33296
Scotch marine. 78193
Scotch poetic genius. pseud. Scotch answer. 78192
Scotch politics defended in America. (44187)
Scotch Presbyterians of New York. petitioners (54141)
"Scotch Runaway." pseud. supposed author Roaster. 14031, 94025
"Scotch Runaway." pseud. supposed author Rub for Snub. 14032, 85597, 94025

Scotian. pseud. Confederation considered on its merits. 15426
Scotland, ------. 44124
Scotland. Arbiters on the Submission. 104487
Scotland. Church. see Church of Scotland.
Scotland. Congregational Union. see Congregational Union in Soctland.
Scotland. Established or Parochial Schoolmasters. see Established or Parochial Schoolmasters in Scotland.
Scotland. Great Seal. 57392
Scotland. Laws, statutes, etc. 18544-(18545), 18555, 18560, 78220, 78224, 2d note after 98925
Scotland. Lord Advocate. 18570, 78196, 2d note after 91386 see also Steuart, Sir James, 1635-1715.
Scotland. Lord President of the Session. 18570, 78196, 2d note after 91386 see also Berwick, Sir Robert.
Scotland. United Associate Synod. see United Associate Synod of Scotland.
Scotland Trinitarian Congregational Church, Bridgewater, Mass. see Bridgewater, Mass. Scotland Trinitarian Congregational Church.
Scotland's grievances, relating to Darien, &c. 18568, (78194)-78195
Scotland's present duty. 18569
Scotland's right to Caledonia. 18570, 78196, 2d note after 91386
Scots colony in Darien. 18556
Scots Company in Darien in the West-Indies. 78218
Scots gentleman. pseud. Memoirs, life, and character of the great Mr. Law. 39311
Scots-Irishman. pseud. Poems, chiefly in the Scottish dialect. see Bruce, David, d. 1830.
Scots Lords and Gentlemen met at St. James's, 1688. 9372, 81492
Scots magazine. 84628
Scots peerage. 85261
Scots Proprietors of East New Jersey. see Board of Proprietors of the Eastern Division of New Jersey. Scots Proprietors.
Scots Sawney. pseud. Letter. 78240
Scots Thistle Society of Philadelphia. (62233)
Scots weaver. pseud. Speech. 89185
Scott, ------, fl. 1831. 101281
Scott, --------, fl. 1857. 14325
Scott, Alexander. petitioner (78241)
Scott, Allen M. 78242-78243
Scott, Andrew. plaintiff 68169
Scott, Benjamin. 78244-78246
Scott, Charles. 78247
Scott, Charles C. defendant 78246
Scott, Charles Lewis, 1827-1899. 78248
Scott, David. 78249-78252
Scott, David B. 78253-78255
Scott, Dorothy (Quincy) Hancock. 93717
Scott, Dred. plaintiff 5751, (18036), 25009, 33240, 56050, 69402, 78256-78259, (78261)-(78262), 105215
Scott, Edward. 94777
Scott, Frances. 38109, 78263, note before 97104
Scott, Frank J. 78264-78266
Scott, Genio C. (78267)
Scott, George. petitioner 44766
Scott, George G. (78268)
Scott, George W. 78269-78270
Scott, Helenus. (78271)
Scott, Hervey. 78272
Scott, J. M. (41650), note after 91855

Scott, J. T. engr. 82420, 3d note after 94805
Scott, J. W. 78273-78274
Scott, J. W. USA 78275
Scott, J. W., fl. 1868. (78276)
Scott, J. Walter. 78277
Scott, James, 1649-1685. see Monmouth and Buccleuch, James, Duke of, 1649-1685.
Scott, James, fl. 1816. 78278
Scott, James, d. 1858. 78279
Scott, James L. 78280
Scott, Job, b. 1751. 78281-78298, 102638
Scott, John, 1730-1783. (36296), 36301, note after 69480, 78299-78392
Scott, John, of Centreville, Ind. 34532-34533, 78304-78305, 94532
Scott, John, 1785-1861. 78303
Scott, John, 1820-1907. 78307-78309
Scott, John, 1824-1896. 78310-78314
Scott, John, fl. 1848. 78306
Scott, John B. 78315
Scott, John F. 78316
Scott, John Morin, 1789-1858. (78317)-78319, 84576, 90011, 95990
Scott, John Morris. (7884), 54368, 63210, 95935 see also New York (Colony) Agents on the Boundary Line Between New York and New Jersey, 1769.
Scott, John Welwood. 78320
Scott, John Witherspoon, 1800-1892. 78321
Scott, Jonathan, fl. 1784. 78322
Scott, Jonathan, fl. 1808. 78323-(78324)
Scott, Jonathan M. 78325-(78326)
Scott, Joseph. geographer 78327-78331
Scott, Joseph, fl. 1841. 78332
Scott, Joseph M. 78333
Scott, Julia H. 77303, (78334)
Scott, L. 78335
Scott, Levi. defendant 84738
Scott, M. Y. (54082)
Scott, Martin B. 78336-(78338)
Scott, Michael, 1789-1835. 78339, 96128
Scott, Moses Y. (69154), (78340)-78341, 83665
Scott, N. 78342
Scott, Nancy N. 78343
Scott, Obadiah. petitioner 36485
Scott, Orange, 1800-1847. (46866), 78344-78346
Scott, Otho. 45207
Scott, R. E. 23930, 78721, 103287, note after 103287 see also Whig Party. Virginia. Fauquier County. Central Committee.
Scott, Robert. pseud. History of England during the reign of George III. see Robins, James, d. 1836.
Scott, Robert, 1761?-1834. 78347-78348, 104523
Scott, Robert, d. 1854. defendant 78350
Scott, Robert E. 78351
Scott, Robert Kingston, 1826-1900. 78352-(78353), 79963, 87562 see also South Carolina. Governor, 1868-1874 (Scott)
Scott, Robert W. 78354
Scott, Samuel. (78355)
Scott, Sarah. 78356
Scott, T. Parkin. 78380-78381
Scott, Thomas. of Utrecht. see Scott, Thomas, 1580?-1626.
Scott, Thomas, 1580?-1626. 17105, 78357-78379, 88936, 2d note after 100788, 100799, 100801
Scott, Thomas, 1580?-1626. supposed author (67586)
Scott, U. 99908 see also Virginia (Colony) Council. Clerk.
Scott, W. K. 60007
Scott, Walter. pseud. Lay of the Scottish fiddle. see Paulding, James Kirke, 1778-1860.

Scriptural examination of the institution of slavery. 13841
Scriptural interpreter. 78488
Scriptural notices respecting bondmen. (78489)
Scriptural plea for the revolted colonies. (24724)
Scriptural policy. 88872
Scriptural refutation of a pamphlet lately published. (30492)
Scriptural researches of the licitness of the slave trade. 18504
Scriptural researches on the licitness of the slave-trade. (30492), (33606), 67714, (79498)
Scriptural rights of the members of Christ's visible church. 74574
Scriptural temperance. (25185)
Scriptural view of politics. 78490
Scriptural view of slavery and abolition. 24614
Scriptural view of the character, causes, and ends of the present war. 43529
Scriptural view of the moral relations of American slavery. 23310
Scriptural view of the wine-question. 93209
Scriptural account of the Sechinah. 79462
Scripture and reasons. 17056
Scripture biography. 26409
Scripture bishop. (78492), 78494
Scripture-bishop, examin'd in two letters. 22115, (78492)-78493
Scripture-bishop or the divine right of Presbyterian ordination. (78491)
Scripture-bishop vindicated. 22115, 78493
Scripture catechism; by a clergyman of Massachusetts. 78495
Scripture-catechism, or, the principles of the Christian religion. 78496
Scripture characters or marks of false prophets. 9907
Scripture disproof and syllogistical conviction. 26314
Scripture doctrine of atonement examined. 30150
Scripture doctrine of election, considered. (70928)
Scripture-doctrine of original sin. 12331, 13350
Scripture doctrine of regeneration. 2623
Scripture doctrine of santification stated. 85480-85481
Scripture doctrine with regard to slavery. 78497
Scripture evidence of the sinfulness of injustice and oppression. 21086, 51733, note after 78497
Scripture exalted, and priestcraft eradicated. (79494)
Scripture-grounds of the baptism of Christian infants. 13350
Scripture history relating to the overthrow of Sodom and Gomorrah. 79463
Scripture-precept of subjection to civil government. 65074
Scripture prophecies explained. 12390
Scripture readings. 86299
Scripture the friend of freedom. (30492), (78498)
Scripture tract for the times. 78499
Scripture truths and precepts. 78500, note after 96397
Scriptures and reasons written . . . by a . . . prisoner in Newgate. 104331
Scripturista. pseud. Answer to Paulinus. (18419)
Scrivener, ------. 78501

Scrivenor, Harry. 78502-78503
Scrog, ------. (19715)
Scroggs, G. A. 78504
Scroggs, Sir William, 1623?-1683. (30463)
Scrope, G. Poulett Thompson, 1797-1876. (10444), 78506-78509
Scrutator. pseud. Impracticability of a north-west passage. 34407
Scudder, David Coit. 78521
Scudder, Evarts. 78510
Scudder, Henry. 78511-78514
Scudder, Henry A. 78515-78517
Scudder, Henry J. 78518
Scudder, Henry Martyn. 78519-78520
Scudder, Horace E. 78521
Scudder, John. ed. 54498, 78522
Scudder, John, 1798-1855. 78523
Scudder, M. L. 78524
Scudder, Samuel H. (78525)-78532
Scudder, William. (78533)
Scudder, Zeno. 78534
Scull, ------. cartographer 35954, (40141)
Scull, Joseph H. tr. 98387
Scull, Nicholas. supposed author 37121, 78535
Scull, Nicholas. surveyor 62065
Scull, William. 35953-35954, 35962, 35969
Scully, William. 78536-(78537)
Sculptures of Santa Lucia Cosumalwhuapa. 85072
Scurilous piece of Philander dissected. 19239
Scurry, William R. (57155)
Scweinitz, Ludovici Davidis de. see Schweinitz, Lewis David von, 1780-1834.
Scylla and Charybdis. 25020
Se Cristoforo Colombo abbia studiato all' Universita di Pavia. 76522
Se nos ha entregado en Tejas como borregos de ofrenda. 95112
Sea. 78538
Sea and her famous sailors. (27886)
Sea and its living wonders. 30720
Sea as an emblem. 85546
Sea-atlas being a book of marine charts. 95631
Sea atlas describing the sea coasts. (79023)
Sea-atlas of the watter-world [sic]. 106290
Sea-atlas or the water-world. 78539
Sea coast of Nova Scotia. 3608
Sea grammar. 82813-82814, 82824, 82830, 82839-82841, 82851
Sea journal of William Moulton. (51136)
Sea kick, for a land cuff. 95866
Sea lark. 93636
Sea life. 93560
Sea lions. 16530
Sea-mans grammar. 82814, 82840-82841
Sea-mans grammar and dictionary. 82841-82843
Sea marke. 82815
Sea mirrour, containing the sea-coasts. 41051
Sea mirrour, or lightning columne. 78540
Sea of ice. (75259)
Sea officer. pseud. Concise account of voyages. see Pickersgill, ---------.
Sea officer. pseud. Voyages and travels. see Vernon, Francis V.
Sea-officer who went out with Commodore Hughes. pseud. Genuine account. see Walpole, Horace, 4th Earl of Orford, 1717-1797. supposed author
Sea piece. 38008
Sea serpent, or Gloucester hoax. 78541
Sea-service. 78542
Sea-spray: a Long-Island village. (33978)
Sea voyage. 83784
Seabord [sic] and Roanoke Railroad Company. 78543

Seaborn, Adam. (78544)

Seabra da Silva, Jose de. see Silva, Jose de Seabra da.

Seabrook, E. Bayard. (78545)-78546

Seabrook, I. D. supposed author 87822

Seabrook, Whitemarsh B. 78547-78522, 87402, 87547, 87922 see also South Carolina. Governor, 1848-1850 (Seabrook)

Seabrook, Whitemarsh B. supposed author 81884, 81885, note before 88112

Seabrook's memoir on the origin, cultivation and uses of cotton. 78551

Seabury, Charles. supposed author 96921

Seabury, Samuel, 1706-1764. 78553-78554

Seabury, Samuel, Bp., 1729-1796. (15009), (15654), 29955-29956, 39529, 65970, 78555-78581, 2d note after 99553, 4th note after 100862

Seabury, Samuel, 1801-1872. 78582-78589, 96965

Seabury, William J. 90659

Seabury College. 96123, 1st note after 105926

Seacliff, or the mystery of the Westeroefts. 19292

Seafarer's library. 98126, 101044

Seager, D. W. 78592

Seager, Mrs. E. S. 78593

Seagrave, Robert, 1693-1760? 15027, (78594)- (78596), note after 103616

Sealed servants of our God. 46511

Sealfield, Charles. pseud. see Postl, Karl, 1793-1864.

Sealsfield, Charles. pseud. see Postl, Karl, 1793-1864.

Seall, Robert. 78597

Seally, John. (78598)

Seals of the southern hemisphere. 28401, 71032

Sealy, Celer. pseud. Echoes from the garrett. [sic] (78600)

Seaman. pseud. Journals of the ocean. see Weaver, William Augustus.

Seaman. pseud. Observations and closer remarks. 36396

Seaman, Ezra C., 1805-1880. 78601-78607

Seaman, Henry John, 1805-1861. 78608-(78611)

Seaman, Jordan. 78612

Seaman, L. 78613

Seaman, Lazarus. 3213, note after 92800, note before 93797, 3d note after 103687

Seaman, Maria. alias see Shade, Maria.

Seaman, Valentine, 1770-1817. 78614-78617, 102346

Seaman's companion. (52068)

Seaman's complete guide. 44119

Seaman's friend. pseud. School of reform. 77828

Seaman's Lyceum of Philadelphia. 62234

Seaman's narrative. 89057

Seaman's new daily assistant. 50412

Seaman's practical guide for Barbadoes and the Leeward Islands. 3286

Seaman's preacher, being a sermon on the right improvement. 96107

Seaman's Retreat, New York. 78618

Seaman's safe pilot to the Cape of Good Hope. 77828

Seaman's secrets. 18842

Seaman's spiritual directory. 27629

Seamanship. 42623

Seamen. pseud. Journals of the ocean. see Weaver, William Augustus.

Seamen's Aid Society, Boston. 6772

Seamen's Friend Society, Philadelphia. see Philadelphia Seamen's Friend Society.

Seamen's Orphan and Children's Friend Society, Salem, Mass. see Salem Seamen's Orphan and Children's Friend Society, Salem, Mass.

Seamen's signal book. 72676

Seamen's Widow and Orphan Association, of Salem. 75744

Seance annuelle du 26 Janvier 1837. 85829

Seance de la Societe Litteraire de Quebec. 85817

Search, Simon. pseud. Spirit of the times. (78619)

Search after Sir John Franklin's expedition. 57759

Search for Franklin. 61183

Searcher. 78620

Searcher after truth. pseud. 95254

Searcher after truth. pseud. Rappers. 67919

Searchfield, Rowland, Bishop of Bristol, 1565?-1622. 103330-103331

Searching analysis. 41209

Seares, Alexander. 42778, 78621-(78622), 95166

Searing, Edward. 78623

Searl, John, 1723-1787. 58895, (78624)-78626

Searle, Ambrose. 79269

Searle, Mrs. L. C. 78627

Searle, Roger. (78628)

Searles, Mrs. R. A. 78629

Searls, W. 90990

Sears, ------. illus. 92479

Sears, Alfred F. 54877, 78630

Sears, B. 59389 see also Peabody Education Fund. General Agent.

Sears, Barnas, 1802-1880. 35496, 78632

Sears, C. defendant 19915, 49067

Sears, Clinton W. 78633

Sears, David. 16175, 78634-78635

Sears, David. defendant 19915, 49067, 70231

Sears, E. I. tr. (12572)

Sears, Edmund H., 1810-1876. 78636-78644

Sears, Edmund Hamilton. 71789

Sears, Edward I. ed. 52018

Sears, Freeman. 78645

Sears, Hiram. 78646

Sears, Isaac. 95990

Sears, M. 78647

Sears, Miriam C. defendant 19915, 49067, 70231

Sears, Reuben. 78648-(78649)

Sears, Robert, 1810-1892. 53383, 78650-(78656)

Sears, W. T. 17919

Sears, William G. tr. 83138

Sears Fund connected with St. Paul's Church. (6672)

Sears' pictorial magazine. (78654)

Searsburgh poetry. 21745

Searson, John. 78657-(78660), 2d note after 97555, note after 101799

Seaside and the fireside. (41926)

Seasonable account of the Christian and dying-words. 78661

Seasonable address of a militia-man. 78662

Seasonable address to the more serious part. 102686

Seasonable advice to a neighbour. 62517

Seasonable advice to Sir R—— W——. 18511

Seasonable advice to the inhabitants of the province of Pennsylvania. 60606, 78663

Seasonable advice, to the members of the British Parliament. 78664

Seasonable and affecting observations on the mutiny bill. 78665

Seasonable and candid thoughts. (78666)

Seasonable and ernest address. 35753

Seasonable and serious word of faithful advice. 56382

Seasonable cautions against mistakes and
  abuses. 78700
Seasonable caveat against believing every
  spirit. 103903
Seasonable caveat against meddling with them.
  91757
Seasonable caveat against popery. 78667
Seasonable considerations for the inhabitants.
  25558, 83984
Seasonable considerations on the expediency
  of a war with France. 9450
Seasonable defence of the old protestant doc-
  trine. 17675
Seasonable discourse wherein sincerity &
  delight in the service of God. 56383
Seasonable discourses upon some common but
  woful distempers. 46505
Seasonable discourses upon som common, but
  woful instances. 46230
Seasonable information and caveat. 37214
Seasonable information, &c. 22351
Seasonable meditations both for winter and
  summer. (46705)
Seasonable meditations for the last day of the
  year. 12822
Seasonable memento for New-Year's day.
  25403
Seasonable observations on the trade to Africa.
  (78668)
Seasonable plea for the liberty of conscience.
  22990, 104221
Seasonable proposition for propagating the
  Gospel. (58030)
Seasonable testimony to good order. 46733
Seasonable testimony to the glorious doctrines
  of grace. 46498
Seasonable thoughts on human creeds or
  articles of faith. 78669
Seasonable thoughts on the state of religion in
  New-England. 12322, (12327), 103563
Seasonable thoughts upon mortality. 46499
Seasonable truths. 46681
Seasonable warning to these churches. 17103,
  50996
Seasonable vvatch-vvord unto Christians.
  104654
Seasons. 95574
Seasons, an interlocutory exercise. 42378,
  78670
Seasons with the sea-horses. (38768)
Seat, W. H. (78671)
Seat of empire. 14170
Seat of government. 67573, 67588, 67598-
  67599
Seat of government of Canada. 73347
Seat of the muses. 78672
Seatfield, Charles. see Postl, Karl, 1793-
  1864.
Seaton, C. W. 53577
Seaton, John Colborne, 1st Baron, 1778-1863.
  10517, 10528 see also Canada. Gover-
  nor General, 1838-1839 (Seaton)
Seaton, firm publishers see Gales and
  Seaton. firm publishers.
Seatsfield, Charles. pseud. see Postl, Karl,
  1793-1864.
Seattle, Wash. Alaska-Yukon-Pacific Exposition,
  1909. see Alaska-Yukon-Pacific Expo-
  sition, Seattle, 1909.
Seaver, Anna Maria. 78673
Seaver, Benjamin. 78674-78675 see also
  Boston. Mayor, 1852-1853 (Seaver)
Seaver, E. 68827
Seaver, Ebenezer. 78676, note after 90763
Seaver, Henry. (78677)

Seaver, James E. 78678-(78682), 105548,
  105555
Seaver, Norman. (78683)-78684
Seaver, Richard. petitioner 100928
Seaver, William. 78685
Seaver. firm auctioneers see Whitwell &
  Seaver. firm auctioneers
Seavy, W. H. ed. 10262, 27871
Seaward, Sir Edward. pseud. Sir Edward
  Seward's narrative. see Porter, William
  Ogilvie.
Seaweeds from the shores of Nantucket. 90507
Seaworthy, Gregory. pseud. Bertie. 78686
Seaworthy, Gregory. pseud. Nag's head.
  (78687)
Seba, Albertus, 1665-1736. 78688-78689
Sebastian, Benjamin. (44778)
Sebastian, John. plaintiff (56999)
Sebastian, Pedro Cubero. see Cubero Sebas-
  tian, Pedro.
Sebering, Daniel. 25755, 25974, 98572
Sebring, Jacob L. defendant 96886
Secchi, A. 85072
Secchia. 94402
Secchia poema eroicomico d'Androvinci Melisone.
  94402
Seccion del Callao y Lima a la Oroya. 41108
Seccombe, Joseph, 1706-1760. 21608, (14525),
  78696-78702, 89125, note after 102194
Seccombe, Thomas. 82857
Seccome, John, 1708-1793. (78690)-78695,
  86781
Seceding Masons. Convention, Le Roy, N. Y.,
  1828. see Convention of Seceding Masons,
  Le Roy, N. Y., 1828.
Secession. 62916
Secession: a folly and a crime. 34748
Secession, a national crime and curse. 21808
Secession an absurdity. 96510
Secession and reconstruction. 19508
Secession and slavery. A lecture delivered at
  Timstall, Staffordshire. 64121
Secession and slavery: or the constitutional
  duty of Congress. 5608A
Secession and slavery: or, the effect of seces-
  sion. 5608
Secession aux Etats Unis et son origine.
  50989, (78703)
Secession, coercion, and the civil war. 78704
Secession, concession, or self-possession.
  13417
Secession considered as a right. (78705)
Secession ferocity. 19607
Secession from Parliament vindicated. 105706
Secession in Switzerland. 19637
Secession in the future. 78706
Secession is rebellion. 55463
Secession: its cause and cure. (21137)
Secession. Letters of Amos Kendell. 37354
Secession of a large body of Friends from the
  Yearly Meeting of Indiana. 34500, 78707
Secession of the cotton states. 12216
Secession of the rats. (78708)
Secession of the whole south an existing fact.
  68550, 78709
Secession or, prose in rhyme and east Tennes-
  see. 78710
Secession resisted. 34750
Secession; shall it be peace or war? 21820
Secession: the remedy and result. 20510
Secession unmasked. 13704
Secessionists. 78711
Seche, Leon. 78712
Sechla, John. tr. (80879)
Sechs Jahre in Surinam. 37102

Sechs Monate in Mexiko. 9144

Sechste Fortsetzung. 78013-78014

Sechste Theil Americae. (8784)

Sechste Theil der Neuwen Welt. (8784)

Sechste Theil, kurtze warhaffitge Relation. (11608), 33660

Sechster Theil Americae. (8784)

Sechzehende Schiffahrt. 33669, 77956

Secker, Thomas, Abp. of Canterbury, 1693-1768. 5689, 17550, (11877)-11879, 64328, 78713-78719, 84646, 97341

Secker, William. 78720

Secoli dei due sommi Italiani Dante e Colombo. 18464

Secomb, Daniel Franklin, 1820-1895. 83897

Second address . . . see Address . . .

Second addrese a l'Assemblee Nationale. (78744)

Second advent hymns. 78723

Second advent tracts. 101299

Second and third letter to the Whigs. 40548

Second and third letters to the Rev. Samuel Miller. 89006

Second and Third Street Passenger Railway Co. (62235)

Second and Third Street Passenger Railway Co. Charter. (62235)

Second anniversary of the Merchants Fund. 91580

Second annual announcement of the Polytechnic College. 60396

Second annual catalogue . . . see Catalogue . . .

Second annual exhibition of the Society of Artists of the United States. 60616

Second annual fair of the St. Louis Agricultural and Mechanical Association. 75381

Second annual message . . . see Message . . .

Second annual report . . . see Report . . .

Second annual reports . . . see Reports . . .

Second Annual State Convention of the Young Men's Christian Association of New Hampshire, Nashua, 1869. see Young Men's Christian Association of New Hampshire. State Convention, 2d Nashua, 1869.

Second annual statement of the . . . National Bank of Commerce. 54413

Second answer to Mr. John Wesley. 18239

Second appeal to the justice and interests of the people. 39704

Second appeal to the people of Pennsylvania. (60607)

Second appendix to facts and documents. 68972, 95524

Second article in the Princeton review. 58625

Second Baptist Church, Cambridge, Mass. see Cambridge, Mass. Second Baptist Church.

Second Baptist Church, Galway, N. Y. see Galway, N. Y. Second Baptist Church.

Second biennial report . . . see Report . . .

Second book in arithmetic. 83908

Second book in geography. 83951-83955

Second book of records of the town of South-hampton. 88230

Second book of the art of metals. 3254

Second book of the "Washington benevolents." 101993

Second Brigade. 78724

Second calm address. 41780

Second catechism for children. 12878, 105534

Second catechism for children in the Dakota language. 69649

Second century lecture of the First Church. 98044

Second Chahta book. 105536

Second chapter from the secret history of the war. 51720

Second charge, to the clergy of his diocess. [sic] 78560

Second charge to the clergy of Massachusetts. 21663

Second charge to the clergy of the diocese of New Jersey. 20391

Second Church, Boston. see Boston. Second Church.

Second Church, Bradford, Mass. see Bradford, Mass. Second Church.

Second Church, Hartford, Conn. see Hartford, Conn. Second Church.

Second Church, Ipswich, Mass. see Ipswich, Mass. Second Church.

Second Church, Stafford, Conn. see Stafford, Conn. Second Church.

Second Church, West Stafford, Conn. see West Stafford, Conn. Second Church.

Second Church and Parish, Dorchester, Mass. see Dorchester, Mass. Second Church.

Second Church of Christ, Woodstock, Conn. see Woodstock, Conn. Second Church of Christ.

Second collection of papers. 81492

Second commandment like to the first. 79429

Second communication in answer to the same. 54428

Second conference. 20057, (20271)

Second Congregational Church, Boscawen, N. H. see Boscawen, N. H. Second Congregational Church.

Second Congregational Church, Cohasset, Mass. see Cohasset, Mass. Second Congregational Church.

Second Congregational Church, New London, Conn. see New London, Conn. Second Congregational Church.

Second Congregational Church, Newton, Mass. see Newton, Mass. Second Congregational Church.

Second Congregational Church, Reading, Mass. see Reading, Mass. Second Congregational Church.

Second Congregational Church, St. Johnsbury, Vt. see St. Johnsbury, Vt. Second Congregational Church.

Second Congregational Church, South Windsor, Conn. see South Windsor, Conn. Second Congregational Church.

Second Congregational Church, Southborough, Mass. see Southborough, Mass. Second Congregational Church.

Second Congregational Church, Southville, Mass. see Southborough, Mass. Second Congregational Church.

Second Congregational Church in St. Johnsbury, Vermont. 75292

Second Congregational Society, Worcester, Mass. see Worcester, Mass. Second Congregational Society.

Second Congregational Unitarian Church, New York. see New York (City) Church of the Messiah.

Second Congress of the United States. At the first session. note after 94720

Second crisis of America. 78725

Second Dakota reading book. 63996

Second defence of a sermon preach'd at Newark. (20062)

Second defence of Church establishment. (78726)

Second defence of Robert J. Breckenridge. 7687

Second defence, of the episcopal government, of the church. 39531

Second defence of the old protestant doctrine of justifying faith. 17675
Second defence, or, the third and last part of the Snake in the grass. 40197
Second dialogue, between a minister and his parishoner. 4497, 94524
Second dialogue of the dead. 78727
Second discours d'un bon Hollandais. 78728
(Second edition.) A sketch of the life of Randolph Fairfax. 81709
Second edition. An account of the insurrection in St Domingo. 32990
Second edition. An oration . . . on the occasion. 35709
Second edition corrected. The revolutionary officers. (70349)
Second edition. Mr. Russell on Bull Run. 74401
Second edition of George W. Hawes' Indiana state gazetteer. 34535
Second edition of the speech of the D-ke of A---le. 10229
Second edition, with additions, of a remonstrance. 32781
Second edition (with necessary improvements.) 39342, 78729
Second epistle of Orson Pratt. (64963)
Second epoch of grandfather's chair. 30990
Second essay on free trade and finance. 102405
Second Evangelical Congregational Church, Cambridgeport, Mass. see Cambridge, Mass. Second Evangelical Congregational Church.
Second Exhibition of the Kentucky Mechanics' Institute, Louisville, 1854. see Kentucky Mechanics' Institute, Louisville. Exhibition, 2d, 1854.
Second Exhibition of the South-Carolina Academy of the Fine Arts. 87951
Second familiar conference. 4095, 78730
Second Festival of the Sons of New Hampshire, celebrated in Boston. 78731
Second friendly epistle to Mr. George Keith. 106105
Second genuine speech. 99247
Second Grinnell Expedition in search of Sir John Franklin. 37001
Second incendie du Cap par les Noirs. 19086, (75094)
Second inquiry, into the nature and design of Christian baptism. 92897
Second Jefferson Benevolent Institution, of Pennsylvania. 60169
Second Joe Miller. 41207
Second joint debate. 55840
Second journal of Christian Frederick Post. 64453
Second journal of the Stated Preacher. 22384
Second letter . . . [by John Henry Hopkins.] (32931)
Second letter, from a gentleman in Barbadoes. 8099
Second letter from an English gentleman residing at China, to the Earl of ***. 90255
Second letter from an English gentleman, residing in China, to the Earl of ******. 90257
Second letter from Barbadoes. 70896
Second letter . . . [from John Bowden.] 6987, 91749
Second letter from Oberea, Queen of Otaheite. 3205
Second letter from one in the country. 78733
Second letter from Philopatrios. 62558
Second letter from Phocion. (29964)-29965

Second letter from the Church of England minister. 86752
Second letter [from the Rev. Mr. Whitefield.] 103506
Second letter, occasion'd by what has past since. 100604
Second letter [of Samuel Worcester.] 96412
Second letter on Dawson's introduction to the Federalist. 35844
Second letter . . . on Negro slavery. (33074), note after 104595
Second letter on the condition and prospects of the Reading Railroad. (76393)
Second letter on the subject of lay ordination. 4259
Second letter . . . on the subjects of cheap money. 51978
Second letter to —— —— merchant in London. 78735
Second letter to a friend. 25407, 99800
Second letter to a friend, giving a more particular narrative. (12328), 97569
Second letter to a friend in London. 84594
Second letter to a radical member of Congress. 62858
Second letter to Deacon Moses Grant. (31792)
Second letter to George W. Jones. 50465
Second letter to his fellow-citizens of the United States. 3430
Second letter to J. Bellamy. 78734
Second letter to Lord John Russell. (35493)
Second letter to ministers of the Gospel. (42044)
Second letter to Mr. Andrews Norton. 71518
Second letter to Mr. Chandler. 97322
Second letter to Mr. Channing. 11924
Second letter to Mrs. E—— B——. 101218
Second letter to the author. 35867
Second letter to the citizens of . . . Pennsylvania. (61663)
Second letter to the congregations of the eighteen Presbyterian (or New-Light) ministers. 47276, (78736), 97107
Second letter . . . [to the Hon. Howell Cobb.] 20162
Second letter. To the ministers and elders of the Presbyterian Church in Kentucky. 5579
Second letter to the people of England. 80056
Second letter to the people of Pennsylvania. 10671, 15526, note after 63244, 84642
Second letter to the Reverend Mr. George Whitefield. 103648
Second letter to the Reverend Mr. George Whitefield, urging upon him the duty of repentance. 103649
Second letter [to the Rev. Samuel Miller.] (49063)
Second letter to the Rev. William E. Channing. 105312
Second letter to the Right Honourable Charles Jenkinson. (40520)
Second letter to the Right Hon. Earl of Liverpool. 77767
Second letter [to the Right Honourable the Earl of B***.] (40527)
Second letter . . . [to the Right Hon. the Earl of Derby.] 99256
Second letter to the Rt. Hon. W. E. Gladstone. 90306
Second letter to the Special Commissioner of the Revenue. 71804
Second lettre de M. de Pinto. (62989)
Second Louisiana. May 27th, 1863. 6172
Second manvdvction for Mr. Robinson. 72103
Second memoire pour le Sr. Cazotte & la Dlle. Fouque. 94391

Second memoire relatif aux anciens colons de Saint-Domingue. 105643

Second memorial in case of Ship Hunter. 33939, 103717

Second memorial of Joseph W. Brackett. 78737, 103717

Second . . . message [of Governor Cummings to the Legislature of the Territory of Colorado.] 14740

Second mortgage of the South Carolina Rail Road Company. 88030

Second narrative of the proceedings at Turners-Hall. (37191)

Second neighbour. pseud. Letter, to the reverend author. see Bellamy, Joseph.

Second number of the Times, a solemn elegy. 95841

Second pamphlet in the case of Bishop H. U. Onderdonk. 47239

Second Parish, Worcester, Mass. see Worcester, Mass. Second Parish.

Second part. Being meditations and observations. 66688

Second part of Cooke's centuries. 16330

Second part of memoirs and considerations. 2193-2194

Second part of Mr. Ogle's speech. 56841

Second part of Noua Britannia. (36286)

Second part of Philomythie, or Philomythologie. 78191

Second part of Robert Earle of Essex his ghost. 78369, 78379

Second part of Spanish practices. 78379

Second part of Spanish practices. Or, a relation of more particular wicked plots. 78364

Second part of the catalogue [of the Library Company of Philadelphia.] 61788

Second part of the Dvply to M. S. 91382

Second part of the interest of the country. 100770

Second part of the memorial. 38828

Second part of the mystery of Foxcraft. 66743

Second part of the Quaker qubbles. 95527

Second part of the South-Sea stock. 78738

Second part of the Synoptical flora Telluriana. 78451

Second part of the tract on missions. 76382

Second part of the tragedy of Amboyna. 1002

Second part of the unfortunate shipwright. (3404)

Second part of the Wilmingtoniad. 19421

Second part of Vox popvli. 78377, 78379, 100801

Second part. The privilege of the writ of habeas corpus. 5482

Second pastoral address to the parishioners. 20391

Second Presbyterian Church, Albany, N. Y. see Albany. Second Presbyterian Church.

Second Presbyterian Church, Charleston, S. C. see Charleston, S. C. Second Presbyterian Church.

Second Presbyterian Church, Columbus, Ohio. see Columbus, Ohio. Second Presbyterian Church.

Second Presbyterian Church, New York. see New York (City) Second Presbyterian Church.

Second Presbyterian Church, Philadelphia. see Philadelphia. Second Presbyterian Church.

Second Presbytery of Philadelphia. see Presbyterian Church in the U. S. A. Presbytery of Philadelphia.

Second printed speech of the 22d of March, 1775. 80042

Second protest, with a list of the voters. 66103, 78739

Second publication in favor of Calvin and Calvinism. 74430

Second publication of B. Henry Latrobe. 60451, 62116, 84648

Second rapport sur l'exploration des Lacs Superieur et Huron. 73447

Second reader for the use of primary schools. (12286)

Second reception of the sons and daughters of Portsmouth. 64427

Second recueil de pieces. 63905

Second recueil de pieces sur le Mexique. 94852

Second relation of the unjust proceedings. 1617

Second reply to Mr. Jonathan Parsons. 82723

Second report . . . see Report . . .

Second review of the speeches. (78726)

Second revolution. 47078

Second semi-annual report . . . see Report . . .

Second series of Afloat and ashore. 16471

Second series of letters addressed to Trinitarians and Calvinists. 101375, 101380

Second series of the black book. 73822-(73823)

Second series of the Breitmann ballads. (39963)

Second series of the present and future prospects of Jamaica considered. (52295)

Second series of voyages to various parts of the world. 14197

Second sermon, delivered Lord's Day, January 5, 1800. 8929

Second sermon, preached at Wallingford. 82216

Second session of the Parliament. 96042

Second Social Library, Beverley, Mass. see Beverley, Mass. Second Social Library.

Second solemn appeal to the church. 35055

Second solemn call to Mr. Zinzendorf. 71406-71407

Second speaker of the Children's Primary Association. 85507

Second speech in reply to Mr. Webster. (31042)

Second speech, in the House of Representatives of the United States. 67224

Second speech, July 24 [1721.] 548, 80328

Second speech of Hon. Daniel Webster. 102275

Second speech of Mr. Smith. 84453

Second speech of Solon Borland. (6430)

Second speech of the Hon. J. Randolph. 67840

Second speech on Mr. Foot's resolutions. 102273

Second speech . . . on the coalition in Massachusetts. 67908

Second speech on the report of the Committee of Foreign Relations. 67833

Second speech on the same subject, Dec. 2, 1808. 27376

Second speech on the sub-treasury bill. 102309

Second Spira; being a fearful example of an atheist. (78740)

Second Spira; or, the blasphemers justly reproved. 78741

Second statement of facts relative to the session. 65225

Second statement of facts [relative to the session . . . of the Reformed Presbyterian Church, New York.] 20683

Second statement on the part of Great Britain. 44046, note before 90764

Second supplement au code [de la Martinique.] 61263

Second supplement aux memoires. 68352

Second supplement [to the catalogue of the Free Public Library, New Bedford, Mass.] 52466

Second supplement [to the catalogue of the Library of the Young Men's Association of the City of Milwaukee.] 49182

Second supplement [to the catalogue of the Northampton Public Library.] 55763

Second supplement [to the probability of reaching the North Pole.] 3632

Second supplement [to the public laws of Rhode Island.] 70700

Second thoughts. 65-66, (11767)

Second treatise. 66754

Second treatise on church-government. 360, 6254, 11968, 3d note after 96741

Second trial . . . August 14, 1830. 38066

Second triennial catalogue [of Hanover College.] 30242

Second Turnpike Road in New-Hampshire. Proprietors. see Proprietors of the Second Turnpike Road in New Hampshire.

Second Unitarian Society, Newton, Mass. see Newton, Mass. Second Unitarian Society.

Second vindication of God's sovereign free grace. Against Mr. John Beach. (20062)

Second vindication of God's sovereign free grace indeed. 4095

Second visit to the United States of North America. 42763

Second voiage de Linschoten. 4935-4936

Second voiage d'Et. van der Hagen. 68455

Second voice from America. 11563

Second volvme of the Principal navigations. 29596-29597

Second voyage a la Louisiane. 3980

Second voyage de J. van Neck aux Indes Orientales. 68455

Second voyage round the world. 16246

Second war of independence in America. 33488

Second war of revolution. (78742), 100582

Second war of the revolution. (78742), 100582

Second war with England. (31160)

Second warning. 3431, 78743

Second warning to America. (64626)

Second year of the war. 63860-(63861)

Seconda lettra di Andrea Corsali Fiorentino. 67730

Seconda parte della Geografia di Cl. Tolomeo. 66506, 66508

Seconda parte delle Histoire dell Indie. 13049

Seconda parte delle Historie dell' Indie. 13052

Seconda parte delle Historie generali dell' India. 27737

Seconda relatione della Nvova Spagna. 67740

Secondary education. 30092

Seconde campagne de Saint-Domingue. 40011

Seconde et tierce narrationes. (16962)

Seconde et troisieme notices. 98352

Seconde lettre de M. Malouet. 44149

Seconde lettre de Mr. de Pinto. 56095

Seconde note sur une pierre gravee. 36435

Seconde partie dv voyage de Francois Pyrard. 66880-(66881)

Seconde sounde. 44820

(Secondo) Libro di Mattheo di Micheovo. 67738

Secondo viaggio. 99504

Secondo volvme delle Navigationi et viaggi nel qvlae si contengono. 67736

Secondo volume delle Navigationi et viaggi raccolto gia da M. Gio. Battista Ramvsio. (67737)-67738

Secondsight, Solomon. pseud. Spectre of the forest. see McHenry, James.

Secondsight, Solomon. pseud. Wilderness. see McHenry, James.

Secondthoughts, Solomon. pseud. Quodlibet. see Kennedy, John Pendleton, 1795-1870.

Secor, Gilbert. 81532

Secrecy: a poem. 64778-(64779)

Secret anecdotes of the revolution. 67633

Secret band of brothers. 28534

Secret book of the elders. 102602

Secret cabal. 72133

Secret chapter in the history of the war. 59669

Secret correspondence illustrating the condition of affairs in Maryland. 45358

Secret corresponding vocabulary. (82570)

Secret "customs," and revenue of the Sheriff's Office. (62196), 62236

Secret debates of the Federal Convention. (26931)

Secret du flux et reflux de la mer. 23560

Secret enemies of true republicanism. 85121, 85126-85127

Secret expedition thither in 1740. 33198-33199

Secret expedition to Peru. note after 97687

Secret history and misfortunes of Fatuma. 105985

Secret history of the emancipation in the English West Indies. 4862

Secret history of the late Directors of the South-Sea-Company. 94668

Secret history of the peninsular campaign. 78745

Secret history of the perfidies, intreagues, and corruptions. 17908, 78746

Secret history of the revolutions. (32644)

Secret history of the South Sea Directors. (34371)

Secret history; or, the horrors of St. Domingo. 30807, note after 78746

Secret instructions of the Jesuits: with an appendix. 78748

Secret instructions of the Jesuits. With an historical essay. 78747

Secret journals of the acts and proceedings of Congress. (15594)

Secret journals of the Senate of the republic [of Texas.] 94970

Secret of success. 78750

Secret prayer inculcated and incouraged. 103402

Secret proceedings and debates of the Convention. 78749, note after 106002

Secret proposal of the insurgents to revive it. 4703, 81812

Secret report. 100940

Secret service. 70985

Secret societies. 85322

Secret societies and oaths. 8346

Secret societies in colleges. (35481)

Secret societies, their use and abuse. 78751

Secret springs of the late charges in the ministry. 78752

Secret workes of a cruel people. 78753

Secretary Chase scheming for the Presidency. 5741

Secretary of State's duty. 99089

Secretary of the (late) mission to La Plata. pseud. Voyage to South America. see Brackenridge, Henry Marie.

Secretary to the Spanish Embassy at the Hague. pseud. Voice of peace. 100667

Secretary Van Tienhoven's answer. 20597, note after 98474

Secretary's guide. 78754-(78760), 106148

Secretary's Office, Brattleborough, March 20, 1787. 99104

Secretary's Office, November 20, 1784. 99098

Secretaryships of Aberdeen and Palmerston. (43477)

Secrete resolutien van de Edele Groot. Mog. Heeren Staten. 78761

Secretos de chirurgia. 4639

Secrets of curing diseases. 89408
Secrets of government. 67599
Secrets of masonry. (13395)
Secrets of the American Bastile. 104747
Secrets of the great city. 44865
Secrets of the great conspiracy. (21579)
Secrets of the Mt. Pleasant State Prison
    exposed. 7793
"Secrets worth knowing." 37860
Sectarian stratagem. 91592
Sectarian thing. 77024
Sectarianism is heresy. 105667
Sectarianism; its evils and its remedy. 66416
Section on legal education. 84516
Section II, Part First, of our political practice.
    105566
Sectional agitation. 20031
Sectional controversy. 25329
Sectional difficulties. 47072
Sectional Dock Company. 70268
Sectional equilibrium. 78308
Sectional maps showing the location of one
    million acres. 88154
Sectional plan of Prospect Park. 8290
Sectionalism in Pennsylvania during the revo-
    lution. 84857
Secular and ecclesiastical history of the town
    of Worthington. 70837
Secular history, 1853-1874 [of Worthington,
    Mass.] 70838
Secular history to 1854 [of Worthington, Mass.]
    70838
Secular state of the church. 92657
Secular view of religion in the state. 33998
Secularia. 42619
Secvnda pars Enneadvm Marci Antonii Sabel-
    lici. 74659
Secunda parte de las obras patrioticas. 51217
Secunda parte de los comentarios reales.
    98755, 98758
Secundus. pseud. Animadversions on a late
    publication. 102752
Secundus, Junius. pseud. Constantine and
    Eugene. see Kelsall, Charles.
Secundus, Plinius. pseud. Curiae Canadenses.
    see Plinius Secundus. pseud.
Securities of Robert McCallem. petitioners
    53919
Security for the living. 69453
Security of a nation. 32229
Security of Englishmen's lives. 86799-86800
Security of God's people in times of trouble.
    30975
Security of the rights of citizens. 15854
Seda en Guatemala. 39011
Seddon, James Alexander, 1815-1880. 15397,
    78762-78765 see also Confederate
    States of America. Secretary of War.
Seddon, T. ed. 14869, note after 97998
Sedeno, Gregorio. 78766
Sedgely Park Estate. 61650
Sedgely Park scheme. 62237
Sedgewick, J. 78767
Sedgewick, Robert. 78768
Sedgewick's impartial narrative. 78767
Sedgwick, Catharine Maria, 1789-1867. 18057,
    18734, 78769-78807, note before 92209,
    2d note after 94244, 94247, 96483,
    101086
Sedgwick, Mrs. Charles. 78808
Sedgwick, Charles Baldwin, 1795-1882. 78809-
    78813, 84956 see also U. S. Congress.
    House of Representatives. Committee on
    Naval Affairs. Chairman.
Sedgwick, Charles F. 78814-78816

Sedgwick, Henry Dwight, 1785-1831. 22620,
    (54091), 78818-78822
Sedgwick, Henry Dwight, 1824-1903. 78823-
    78824
Sedgwick, John. 78825
Sedgwick, Obadiah. (13865)
Sedgwick, Robert, 1787-1841. 21108, 78827
Sedgwick, Susan Ann (Livingston) Ridley, 1789-
    1867. 909, 78828-78829, 106134
Sedgwick, Theodore, 1746-1813. 40696, 78830,
    note after 101839
Sedgwick, Theodore, 1780-1839. 78831-(78837)
Sedgwick, Theodore, 1811-1859. 39863, 78843-
    78845, 84576, note before 95127, note
    after 95722, note after 99394, 3d note
    after 103115
Sedgwick, Mrs. Theodore. see Sedgwick,
    Susan Ann (Livingston) Ridley, 1789-1867.
Sedillot, L. P. E. A. tr. 83512
Sedition and defamation display'd. 66643
Sedley, Henry, 1835- 78846
Sedley, William Henry. see Smith, William
    Henry, 1806-1872.
Sedwick & Co. 10069
See-Capitans, merckwurdige Reisen und Begeben-
    heiten. (4001)
See-farth nach der Neuen Welt. 44076
See-Helden, Admiralen und Land Erfinder.
    25464
See-Reisen von Englandern, Hollandern, Franzo-
    sen, Spaniern, Danen and Russen. 62576
"See, the conquering hero comes." (20696)
See- und Land-Reisen. 41881
Seebohm, Benjamin. 28748, (78847)
Seebohm, Frederick. 78848
Seebohm, Ludwig. tr. 59740
Seeckere naedere missive. 7634
Seeckere remonstratie aen Hare Hoogh Moghende
    de Heeren Staeten Generael. 7635
Seeckere reypltque vander Heer George Downing.
    20786, note after 98953
Seeckeren brief gheschreven uyt Loando St.
    Paulo. 23514
Seed of the woman and the seed of the serpent.
    103573
Seeds and shells. 26079
Seeger, C. L., 1763-1848. 78849-78851
Seehanen Buch. 42392
Seeing it hath pleased God. 99861
Seekampf zwischen den Panzerschiffen Merrimac
    und Monitor. 78852
Seeking the golden fleece. 91787
Seekonk, Mass. petitioners 46051
Seekonk Branch Railroad Company. petitioners
    78853-78854, 78856, 89697
Seeley, L. W. 78857
Seeley, R. H. 78858-78859
Seelowen. 16532
Seely, Catharine. 78860-78861
Seelye, Edward E., 1819-1865. 78862, 89744
Seelye, Julius H., 1824- 78863
Seelye, L. Clarke. 84961
Seelye, S. T. 78864
Seemann, Berthold Carl, 1825-1871. 38025,
    58925, 62871, 78865-(78869)
Seemingly experimental religion or war. 5529
Seer. 64961, (64963), 83283
Seer. By Mrs. E. Oakes Smith. (82519)
Seer cort verhael. 11227-11228, 11233, (11249)-
    11251
Seer gedenckwaerdige vojagien. 78871
Seer naukeurige beschryving der genoemde
    landen. (488), 47474, 2d note after
    102813
Se'er, or, the American prophecy. 78870

Seitz, Don Carlos, 1862-1935. ed. 90002
Seixas, Daniel G. 78945
Seixas, Domingos Rodrigues. 78946
Seixas, Francisco Aguiar. 78947-78948
Seixas, Gershom. 78949-78950
Seixas, Manuel Justiniano de. (78951)
Seixas, Romualdo Antonio de, Abp. 47590, 72503, 78952-78954, 79857-78959 see also Bahia (Archdiocese) Archbishop (Seixas)
Seixas, Romualdo Antonio de, Abp. petitioner 78955-78956
Seixas y Lovera, Francisco de. (78960)-78963
Seize annees de clinque chirurgicale civlie au Presil. 17003
Seizure of slave vessels. (27978)
Seizure of the Bark Maury. (53594)
Seizure of the Black Warrior. 11314
Seizure of the "Peterhoff." 61180
Seizure of the ship Industry. 7099, 25368
Seizure of the Southern Commissioners considered. 78964, 83714
Sejour d'un artiste Francais. 19122
Seker articulen beraemt. 16731, 2d note after 102889A
Seker extract. 41356
Seker Heere. pseud. Propositie ende vertooninghe. 98248, 5th note after 102913
Seker vriendt ende liefhebber van de welstandt des vader-landts. pseud. Discours. 20233, 49557-49558, 5th note a after 102890, 102898
Selah. pseud. Major-General Israel Putnam. (18939)
Selbstbiographie. 9674
Selbstbiographie. Aus dem Englischen von W. Kapp. 35915
Selby, Benjamin. 78965 see also Kentucky. Auditor of Public Accounts.
Selby, Julian A. ed. 81254
Selby, William. 78966
Selden. pseud. Letters. 78967
Selden, -------. 100084
Selden, -------. plaintiff 97308
Selden, H. M. 84482
Selden, Henry R. 78970
Selden, R. E. 49929, 78976-78977
Seldon, Almira. 78968
Seldon, Dudley. 78969
Seldon, Johannis. (78971)-(78975)
Seldon, R. E. 49929, 78977
Seldsamme en noit gehoorde wal-vis-vangst. 74630, 78978
Seleccion de lecturas ejemplares. 77131
Select American speeches. 11005, 84837, 104632
Select and fugitive poetry. 20200
Select anthems, &c. 94014
Select anthems, &c. &c. 94015-94016
Select antiquities, curiosities, and beauties of nature and art. 33631
Select cases, adjudged in the courts of the state of New-York. (78979)
Select cases from the records of the Supreme Court of Newfoundland. (54990)
Select cases resolved. 80258
Select circulating library. (29722), 33202, 71041, 73381, 77097, 82983, 82987, 83491, 84984, 96381, 97401, 99419, 100998
Select circulating library for town and country. 21321, 33202, 82987, 83491, 84984
Select collection of letters of the late Reverend George Whitefield. 103579
Select collection of poems. 78980

Select collection of scarce and valuable economical tracts. 99560
Select collection of scarce and valuable tracts on commerce. 71086, 78981, 97330
Select collection of scarce and valuable tracts on money. 78982
Select collection of Scottish, English, Irish, and American songs. 28225
Select collection of the most interesting tracts. 106311
Select Committee, charged with the memorial of Dr. James Smith. 82780
Select Committee of Canadian Gentlemen. pseud. eds. Abstract of those parts of the custom. (66985)
Select Committee of Canadian Gentlemen. pseud. eds. Sequel of the abstract. 67061
Select Committee of Canadian Gentlemen, Well Skilled in the Laws of France. pseud. Abstract of the Loix de Police. (66983)
Select Committee, to which was referred the message of the President of the United states. 85070
Select contributions to the papal controversy. 7683
Select discourses. 21527
Select discourses from the American preacher. 78983, 83802, 84096
Select discourses on practical subjects. 95169
Select discourses on the functions of the nervous system. 82921
Select dissertations on colonies and plantations. 78984
Select English and Classical Boarding and Day School, Philadelphia. 83769
Select English and Classical School, Philadelphia. 83769
Select essays. 78985
Select essays on rural economy. 21456, 86016
Select essays, with some few miscellaneous copies of verses. 78986
Select Family School for Boys, South Williamston, Mass. 88216
Select historical memoirs of the Religious Society of Freinds. 32370-(32371)
Select letters of Christopher Columbus. 14670
Select letters of Columbus. 14628, (14635)
Select letters of . . . Columbis. 14671
Select letters of Major Jack Downing of the Downingville Militia. 84155
Select letters of Major Jack Downing, written by himself. 18800, note after 84162
Select letters on the English nation. 80057
Select letters on the trade and government of America. 4925, 78987
Select letters, written by the late Right Honourable Philip Dormer Stanhope. 90226
Select library. 82987
Select manual almanac. (47161)
Select miscellanies. 2006
Select number of choice hymns. 46322
Select observations of the incomparable Sir Walter Raleigh. 67599
Select pamphlets [Carey's]. 10066, 10876, 10883-10884, 13875, note after 63795, (78988), 97092, 104186
Select pamphlets . . . Duane's collection. 94304
Select passages from the Holy scriptures. 12475, 78989
Select passages from the Old Testament. 78993
Select passages in the Old and New Testaments. (17990)
Select pieces on religious subjects. 101434
Select poems. [By Harvey Rice.] 70833

Select poems. By Mrs. L. H. Sigourney.
80952-80953

Select poems. By Sir John Smyth. 85239

Select poems on various times and countries.
1063

Select poems on kindness to animals. 78990

Select portions of his [i. e. John Carroll's]
writings. 7719

Select remains. 8515

Select remains of James Meikle. 47402

Select remains of the Rev. William Nevins.
52424

Select reviews, and spirit of the foreign magazines. 78991

Select series [of John Barclay.] 9416

Select sermons of the Rev. Worthington Smith.
84929

Select sermons of William Smith, D. D. 84649,
84678C

Select sermons on doctrinal and practical
subjects. 91798

Select speeches [edited by Dr. Chapman.]
11005

Select speeches, forensic and parliamentary.
11997

Select speeches of John Sergeant. 76938,
79206

Select speeches of Kossuth. 38268

Select speeches [of William Windham and
William Huskisson.] 101166

Select speeches. With a biographical sketch.
34029

Select tracts relating to colonies. 78992

Select works of Benjamin Franklin. 25587,
76966

Select works of Edgar Allan Poe. (63551)

Select works of . . . George Whitefield. 103678

Select works [of James Fenimore Cooper.]
16559

Select works of John Witherspoon. 104942

Select works of Robert Goodloe Harper. 30442

Select works of Simon Clough. 13781

Select works of William Penn. (59731)

Selectae dissertationes Mexicanae. 22065

Selectae e veteri testamento historiae. 78993

Selectae e veteri testamento, historiae. 78993

Selectarum epistolarum ex India libri quatuor.
43770, 43775-43776

Selectarum stirpium Americanarum historia.
20942

Selectas dissertationes Mexicanas. 22065

Selected catalogue of publications in the English
language. 30521

Selected for the soldiers. No. 15. 86262

Selected poems. 63550

Selected poems of William Wye Smith. 84919

Selected political essays of James Wilson.
104627

Selected songs sung at Harvard College.
(30761)

Selected speeches and reports of finance and
taxation. 80382

Selection and use of acceptable words. 79798

Selection from fields old and new. 16606

Selection from his [i. e. John Caldwell Calhoun's] speeches. 9954

Selection from his [i. e. Jesse Appleton's]
sermons. 1808

Selection from juvenile poems. 59287

Selection from the Annals of virtue. 26952,
81027

Selection from the female poetic writers.
29670

Selection from the Harleian miscellany of
tracts. 78994

Selection [from] the "Lettres edifiantes."
34872

Selection from the Lowell offering. 49193

Selection from the manuscripts of Colonel
Theodorick Bland. 5867

Selection from the miscellaneous writings of
the late Isaac Harby. 30294

Selection from the poems of Cheever's manuscript. 46273

Selection from the revelations . . . and narratives of Joseph Smith. (59437)

Selections from the revelations, translations
and narratives of Joseph Smith. 83285

Selection from the sermons of the Rev. Jacob
Kirkpatrick. 38007

Selection from the works of William E.
Channing. 11918

Selection from the writings of Henry R. Cleveland. (13660)

Selection from the writings of the late Jonathan
Lawrence. 39360

Selection from various authors on the present
condition. 9139

Selection, in prose and poetry. 17345

Selection of all the laws of the United States.
7794

Selection of American poetry. 14874

Selection of curious, rare, and early voyages
and histories. 100460

Selection of devotional pieces in verse and
prose. 100678

Selection of eulogies pronounced in the several
states. 258, 83996, 84222, 89690, 89701,
97609, 102269, 104873

Selection of hand-bills. 78995

Selection of hymns. 82527

Selection of hymns and other sacred poems.
(66764)

Selection of hymns and poems for the use of
the believers. 79718, 97889, 98797

Selection of hymns, &c. &c. 95386

Selection of hymns from the best authors.
71539

Selection of items illustrative of American
slavery. 81860

Selection of laws, &c. passed at the first session. 78996

Selection of lessons for reading and speaking.
note just before 71069

Selection of letters, written on various occasions. 43506

Selection of masonick, sentimental, and humorous songs. 99835

Selection of orations and eulogies. 78997,
82800, 2d note after 101883

Selection of papers laid before Congress. 10067

Selection of papers on Arctic geography and
ethnology. 73792, 78998

Selection of papers on various branches of
husbandry. 29703, 2d note after 85847

Selection of passages from the speeches,
addresses, and letters of Abraham Lincoln.
29628

Selection of pieces, in prose and verse. (78388)

Selection of poems, from the diary of Cole.
(78999)

Selection of sepulchral curiosities. 37930

Selection of sermons from the note book of
the octogenarian traveller. 84901

Selection, of some of the most interesting
narratives. 42165, 101219

Selection of songs for children. 48553

Selection of such acts and resolutions of the
General Assembly of South-Carolina, as
relate to the city of Charleston. 87710

Selection of the curious, rare, and early voyages. 29600

Selection of the miscellaneous works of C. S. Rafinesque. 67565

Selection of the most approved songs, duets, &c. 94020

Selection of the most important and interesting events which have transpired since the discovery of this country. (3326)

Selection of the most interesting anecdotes. 35681

Selection of the most memorable passages in his writings. 84318-84319

Selection of the patriotic addresses. 259, 79000

Selection of the public and private correspondence of Vice-Admiral Lord Collingwood. 14428

Selection of the sketches of the work. (12893)

Selection of trials, causes, and important occurrences. 74621

Selection of war lyrics. 18583, 79001

Selections from a discourse. 89007

Selections from American and English orators. 44770

Selections from Arcturus. 46840

Selections from Canadian poets. 19838

Selections from Cobbett's political works. 14017

Selections from conversations and unpublished writings. 59310

Selections from his [i. e. Joseph John Gurney's] journals. 7361

Selections from his [i. e. Tristram Burges'] speeches. 7060

Selections from les recherches philosophiques. (59251), 3d note after 100862, 2d note after 102210

Selections from letters written during a tour. 33372

Selections from M. Pauw. 59252, 3d note after 102210

Selections from notices of the press. 79002

Selections from Sydney Smith. 84316

Selections from the American poets. 79003

Selections from the Annals of virtue. 26952, 81027

Selections from the autobiography of Elizabeth Oakes Smith. 84162

Selections from the Book of Common Prayer. (6355)

Selections from the chronicle of Boston. 6554, 79004, note after 102419

Selections from the correspondence of General Washington. 101735-101736

Selections from the correspondence of the Executive of New Jersey. 53235

Selections from the correspondence of the late William Baldwin. 18599

Selections from the court reporters. 79005

Selections from the diary and other writings of Mrs. Almira Torrey. 96280

Selections from the epistles of George Fox. (25353)

Selections from the journal of Thomas story. 92327

Selections from the letters of Thomas B. Gould. 28125, (32371)

Selections from the Madison papers, &c. (43721)

Selections from the New England fathers. 24037

Selections from the papers of Lord Metcalfe. 48168

Selections from the poetical literature of the west. 26382, 79006

Selections from the political works of William Cobbett. 14017

Selections from the private correspondence of James Madison. (43721)

Selections from the public documents of the province of Nova Scotia. 56190

Selections from the sermons, addresses, etc., of S. C. Fessenden. 24210

Selections from the sermons and writings of Joseph F. Smith. 83347

Selections from the speeches and writings of prominent men in the United States. 79007

Selections from the speeches of eminent Americans. 1173

Selections from the testimony taken before the United States Revenue Commission. 17132

Selections from the various authors. 51191

Selections from the works of Isaac Penington. 80035

Selections from the works of Joseph Story. 92317

Selections from the works of the Baron von Humboldt. (33740), note after 94501

Selections from the works of the late Sylvester Genin. 26943

Selections from the works of Washington Irving. 35196

Selections from the writings and speeches of William Lloyd Garrison. 26707

Selections from the writings of James Kennard. 37378

Selections from the writings of John Woolman. 105206

Selections from the writings of Mrs. M. M. Davidson. 18735

Selections from the writings of Mrs. Sarah C. Edgarton Mayo. (47195)

Selections from the writings of Mrs. Sarah Hall. 29845

Selections from the writings of the late Thomas Hedges Genin. (26944)

Selections from the writings of the Rev. John Wesley. 11435

Selections from the writings of the Rev. Sydney Smith. 84314-84315

Selections from various sources. 80954

Selections in prose and verse. 70713

Selections of his [i. e. Jeremy Belknap's] correspondence. 4441

Selections of scripture in Nez Perces. 88878

Selections of some of the most interesting narratives. 42165, 101219

Selectmen's report of the expenditures of the town of Lexington. 40892

Selectmen's report of the receipts and expenditures [of Epping, N. Y.] 22710

Selectmen's report of the receipts and expenditures of the town of East Bridgewater. 21645

Selectmen's report of the town of Dorchester. (20628)

Selectmen's report . . . of the town of Hanover. 30243

Selectmen's report to the town of Rutland. 74469

Selectorum stirpium Americanarum historia. 35519, 35521-(35523)

Selenopolitani Dissertatio ludicro. 38417

Self-condemnation. 35082

Self-Defence Association, Platte County, Mo. see Platte County Self-Defence Association.

Self-defence, with a refutation of calumnies. (8651)

Self-defensive war, lawful. (10939)

Self development. (81256)
Self disclaimed and Christ exalted. (6789)
Self-emancipation. 43177
Self-enquiry concerning the work of God.
 103510
Self-examination. 91541
Self-examination . . . urged and applied. 32317
Self-flatterer discovered. 79008
Self-imployment in secret. 16746
Self instructor. 79009
Self interpreting Bible. 8511
Self-justiciary convicted and condemned.
 (46789)
Self-justification. 35082
Self-made men. 79640
Self-moving forces of the universe. 64954
Self-preservation. Artillery election sermon,
 1802. 15
Self-preservation the right and duty of the
 general government. 5447
Self-sacrifice, or the pioneers of Fuegia.
 51639
Self-training. 78792-(78793)
Self vindication, of Col. William Martin. 44925
Selfish temper. 94435
Selfridge, Thomas Oliver, d. 1816. 79010
Selfridge, Thomas Oliver, d. 1816. defendant
 24728, 79011-(79012)
Selfridge, Thomas Oliver, 1837- 79013
Selim. pseud. New-Haven, a poem. see
 Woodworth, Samuel.
Selin's Grove, Pa. Evangelical Lutheran
 Missionary Institute. see Evangelical
 Lutheran Missionary Institute, Selin's
 Grove, Pa.
Selish or flat-head grammar. 47861
Selkirk, Alexander, 1676-1723. 35704, 72753-
 72755, (79017)-79018
Selkirk, Edward, 1809- 79019-79020
Selkirk, Thomas Douglas, 5th Earl of, 1771-
 1820. 20697-20704, (22080), 68367,
 69460, 79015, note before 90767
Selkirk, Thomas Douglas, 5th Earl of, 1771-
 1820. plaintiff (20701), 79016, note
 after 96860, 2d note after 106023
Sell, J. J. 79021
Sellar, Richard. 79031
Sellen, Theodore B. supposed author 73284-
 73285
Seller, John. 79022-79030
Seller, John. supposed author 22616-22619,
 88221, 95631
Seller, Richard. 82871
Sellers, David W. (61586)
Sellers, John. 84678C
Sellers, Richard. see Sellar, Richard.
Sellers, W. 60754
Selling of Joseph. 74871, 79446
Selling white men for debt! 103490A
Sellius. tr. 1408
Sello del pasaporte para Londres al ciudano
 Teran. 73199, 79032
Sellon, C. J. 79033
Sellon, J. 79034
Sells, William. 79035
Selma weekly reporter. 84896
Selskabet for Trykkefrihedens Rette Burg,
 Kjobenhavn. note after 96061
Selva, Jose Manuel. 79037
Selva, Juan de la. 79038
Selva de varia lettione. (48240)
Selwyn, Alfred R. C. ed. 84802
Selwyn, William. (24957) see also Jamaica.
 Governor, 1702-1711 (Selwyn)
Selye, Lewis, 1803-1883. (79039)-(79040)
Selys-Longchamps, Walthere de. 79041

Semalle, Rene de. 79042-79045
Semana Cristiana. 76774
Semana de ejercicios en la profesa. (38386)
Semana de la senoritas Mejicanas. 79046
Semana de Nuestro Senora del Refugio. 81087
Semana literaria de "el Porvenir." 79047
Semana Santa tratados de los comentarios.
 99674-99675
Semanario artistico para la educacion y fomento.
 79048
Semanario de agricultura. 79049
Semanario de historia. (29255)
Semanario de la industria Megicana. 79050
Semanario de la Nueva Granada. 9876, 79051
Semanario de las senoritas Mejicanas. 79052
Semanario de Santiago. 79053
Semanario del Nuevo Reyno de Granada. 79054
Semanario judicial de la federacion Mexicana.
 79055
Semanario politico y literario de Mejico. 79056
Semanario politico y mercantil de Mexico.
 48399
Semanario de religion, literatura y variedadas.
 20562
Semblanzas de los diputados a cortes de 1820
 y 1821. 93782
Semblanzas de los individuos de la Camara
 Disputados. 48658
Semblanzas de los miembros que componen el
 honorable Congreso. 48658
Semblanzas de los miembros que han compuesto
 la Camara de Diputados. 79057
Semblanzas de los representantes. 79058
Semenario de la Nueva Granada. 9876
Semeria, J. B. 79059
Semeur Canadien. 79060
Semi-annual address before the Medical and
 Chirurgical Faculty of Maryland. 83664
Semi-annual examination papers for . . . 1865-
 66. (45867)
Semi-annual merit roll of the under-graduate
 classes in Columbia College. 14841
Semi-annual report . . . see Report . . .
Semi-annual reports . . . see Reports . . .
Semi-annual statement . . . see Statement . . .
Semi-centenary and the retrospection of the
 African Meth. Episcopal Church. 59280
Semi-centenary discourse. 11558
Semicentenary review. 89260
Semi-centennial address. 64320
Semi-centennial address before the American
 Colonization Society. 13385
Semi-centennial address to the alumni of Yale
 College. 73960
Semi-centennial address . . . before the Medi-
 cal Society of . . . New-York. 44482
Semi-centennial Anniversary, Knoxville, Tenn.,
 1842. see Knoxville, Tenn. Semi-
 centennial Celebration, 1842.
Semi-centennial anniversary, celebrated at
 Lowville, N. Y. (42543)
Semi-centennial catalogue of officers and
 students [of the Rensselaer Polytechnic
 Institue.] 69641
Semi-centennial catalogue of the . . . [Theo-
 logical] Seminary [of the Presbyterian
 Church.] (65657)
Semi-centennial Celebration, Knoxville, 1842.
 see Knoxville, Tenn. Semi-centennial
 Celebration, 1842.
Semi-centennial celebration, Rensselaer Poly-
 technic Institute, 1874. see Rensselaer
 Polytechnic Institute, Troy, N. Y. Semi-
 centennial Celebration, 1874.
Semi-centennial celebration. Fiftieth anniver-
 sary of the founding of the . . . [New
 York] Historical Society. 54477

Semi-centennial celebration of the First Sab-
bath School Society in Massachusetts.
12098
Semi-centennial celebration of the New England
Society. (52746)
Semi-centennial celebration . . . of the New
York Historical Society. 3136
Semi-centennial celebration of the Park Street
Church and Society. (6669), 79061
Semi-centennial celebration of the Park Street
Church and Society; held on the Lord's
Day, February 27, 1859. (6669), 79061
Semi-centennial of the Providence journal.
66364
Semi-centennial celebration of the South-
Carolina College. 87991
Semi-centennial discourse. 52279
Semi-centennial discourse, delivered before
the Massachusetts Home Missionary
Society. 92255
Semi-centennial discourse, delivered by Rev.
David Spear. 89074
Semi-centennial discourse, delivered November
24, 1854. 92066
Semi-centennial discourse, delivered October 1,
1851. 64209
Semi-centennial discourse, Marlborough, Mass.
(8919)
Semi-centennial discourse preached in the
South Dutch Church. 46844
Semi-centennial discourse, with other exercises
on the occasion. 92092
Semi-centennial historical discourse. 83628
Semi-centennial jubilee. (59557)
Semi-centennial memorial discourse. (24191)
Semi-centennial memorial of the Universalist
Church, Roxbury. 73737
Semi-centennial of York County Conference.
85487
Semi-centennial oration, by the Hon. Jas. L.
Petigru. 87991
Semi-centennial report . . . see Report . . .
Semi-centennial retrospect. 94065
Semi-centennial sermon. 24546
Semi-centennial sermon, . . . before the Brook-
field Associational Conference. 60935
Semi-centennial sermon, by the Rev. William
Berrian. 4977
Semi-centennial sermon, containing a history
of Middlebury, Vt. 48006
Semi-centennial sermon, First Presbyterian
Church, Rome, N. Y. 38185
Semi-centennial sermon of the Seventh Presby-
terian Church. 18959, 84414
Semi-centennial sermon, preached before the
Oneida Annual Conference. 68542
Semi-centennial sermon, preached June twenty-
second and twenty-ninth. 24434
Semi-centennial services of the Sunday School.
90117
Semi-centennial supper . . . February 4, 1857.
53765
Semi-colon. 79062
Semi-globular publication. 77018, note after
98576
Semi-monthly journal. see New Orleans
Medical news and hospital gazetteer. A
semi-monthly journal.
Semi-monthly journal, devoted to agriculture.
52677
Semi-monthly journal, devoted to southern
agriculture. 88334
Semi-monthly literary and entertaining journal.
(74175)
Semi-monthly literary journal. 68376

Semi-monthly magazine, for town and country.
71890
Semi-monthly record. (47326)
[Semi-monthly] record of law reports and pro-
ceedings. 51937
Semi-monthly record of medicine and surgery.
75397
Seminarie de Quebec. 67060
Seminarie de Quebec. Superior and Directors.
petitioners 67060
Seminaire des Missions Etrangeres, Paris.
Directors. (69302)
Seminaire d'Enfans a la Savane des Juifs,
Paramaribo. see Maison d'Education
ou Seminaire d'Enfans a la Savane des
Juifs, Paramaribo.
Seminario, Jose. 99499
Seminario Conciliar, Oazaca, Mexico. see
Oazaca, Mexico. Seminario Conciliar.
Seminario de la Madre Santissima de la Luz,
Leon, Mexico. 40090
Seminario de Santo Toribio, Lima. see Lima,
Peru. Seminario de Santa Toribio.
Seminario judicial. (48637)
Seminary, Buffalo, N. Y. see Buffalo Seminary.
Seminary for Female Teachers, Ipswich, Mass.
see Ipswich Seminary for Female Teach-
ers.
Seminary of divinity. 24542
Seminary of Quebec. see Seminaire de Quebec.
Seminole Indians. Treaties, etc. 96672, 96688
Seminoles, Negroes, &c., captured from Indians.
79071
Semi-serious poem. 82290, 83799
Semi-Virgilian husbandry. 67791
Semi-weekly Eagle, Brattleboro, Vt. see
Brattleboro' (Semi-weekly) Eagle.
Semler, Johann Salomon. 79072
Semmedo, Joao Curvo. 79073-79074
Semmes, J. 15383
Semmes, R. T. defendant before military
commission 9381
Semmes, Raphael. 79075-79083
Semmes, T. J. 15231
Semmes, Thomas. (79085)
Semmes, the pirate. 79084
Semonetti, Antonio. defendant 74943
Sempe, Edouard. 79086
Semper eadem Iohn Hvighen Van Lindschoten.
(41374)
Sempertegui, Lorenzo. 79087
Semple, Henry C. 83873
Semple, Robert. 79088
Semple, Robert B. 79089-79090
Semple, William. 3866, 95976
Semple Lisle, J. G. see Lisle, J. G. Semple.
Sena, Manuel Garcia de. see Garcia de Sena,
Manuel.
Senado y Camara de Diputados a sus comitentes.
76209
Senador Megicano. 72245
Senador que suscribe. pseud. Voto. see
Torres, Geronimo.
Senancourt, Laignel. 10754
Senate bill for the administration of Kansas.
35271
Senate debates. (19093), 33195
Senate journal of the Legislative Assembly of
the state of Kansas. (37091)
Senate journal of the state Legislature of
Nebraska. 52203
Senate of the United States, July 18, 1798.
Gentlemen of the Senate. 101712, 101716
Senate report no. 177. 64337
Senator. 79092

Senor D. Porfiado. pseud. see Porfiado,
   Senor D. pseud.
Senor. El Ayuntamiento . . . de Tlaxcala.
   95878
Senor. El Bachiller D. Diego de Valladolid,
   Presbitero. 98368
Senor. El Capitan Don Francisco Solis y
   Casanova. 86442
Senor, el Capitan Francisco de Vitoria
   Baraona. 100624
Senor, el Capitan Francisco de Vitoria
   Baraona dize. 100625
Senor el Capitan Pedro Fernandez de Quiros.
   67353
Senor. El Capitan y Almirante Mateo de
   Vesga. 99326
Senor. El Dean, y Cabildo sedevacante de
   la Santa Yglesia Cathedral de Antequera
   Valle de Oaxaca. 56396, 79138
Senor. El Doctor Alonso Vazquez de Cisneros.
   98722
Senor. El Dr. D. Antonio de Texeda. 95136
Senor. El Dr. D. Antonio Joachin de Urizar,
   y Bernal, Colegial Huesped en el Mayor,
   y Viejo de Santa Maria de Todos Santos.
   98129
Senor, el Dr. D. Antonio Joachin de Urizar,
   y Bernal. Colegial Huesped mas antiguo
   en el Insigne Viejo, y Mayor de Santa
   Maria de Todos Santos. 98128
Senor. El Dr. D. Joseph Maria Solano y
   Marcha. 86248
Senor. El Dr. D. Pedro Alexandro de Texeda
   Clerigo Presbytero. 95139
Senor, el Doctor D. Pedro Vgariz. 97670
Senor. El General Gonzalo de Solis, Holguin,
   dize. 86437
Senor el Licdo. Don Antonio Domingo Thello,
   y Barbero. 95298
Senor. El Lic. D. Pedro Alexandro Texeda.
   95140
Senor, el Lic. D. Pedro de Teran Rubin.
   94835
Senor. El Maesse de Campo Don Antonio
   Vrrutia de Vergara, dize. 98159
Senor. El Maesse de Campo Don Antonjo
   Vrrutia de Vergara dize. 98160
Senor. El Maesse de Campo Don Antonio
   Vrrutia de Vergara, dize: que auiendo
   acabado su oficio. 98161
Senor. El Maesse de Campo Iuan Recio de
   Leon. Dize que el principal efecto.
   68360
Senor. El Maesse de Campo Iuan Recio de
   Leon . . . propose. 68359
Senor. El Maestro de Campo Iuan Recio de
   Leon, dize. 68361
Senor. El Maestro Fr. A. Bazquez Despinosa.
   98725
Senor. El Maestro Fray Bernardino de
   Solorcano. 86514
Senor. El Maestro Fray Fracisco de Herrera.
   96757
Senor. El Padre Luis de Valdiuia de la
   Compania de Iesus. 98331
Senor. El Padre Luis de Valdiuia, de la
   Compania de Iesus, dize. 98332
Senor. El Padre Luys de Valdiuia Vice-
   prouincial de la Compania de Iesus.
   98333
Senor, el Prior y Consules de la Universidad
   de los Mercaderes. 98020
Senor. El Prior, y Consules de la Vniuersidad
   de los Mercaderes de la Nueua-Espana:
   dizen. 79139

Senor, el Sargento Major D. Diego Gomez de
   Ocampo. 56617
Senor Excel.mo. Medios en servicio de Sv
   Magestad. 97673
Senor. Fr. Bernardino de Solorcano. 86515
Senor. Fray Matias Ruiz Blanco. 74019
Senor. Fray Pedro de Sosa de la Orden de
   San Francisco. 87184
Senor. Fray Pedro de Sosa, de la Orden de
   San Fra[n]cisco. Dize. 87185
Senor. Fray Pedro de Sosa Guardian del
   Conuento de S. Francisco de Santiago.
   87188
Senor. . . . . Fray Pedro de Sossa de la Orde[n]
   de S. Francisco. 87186
Senor. Fray Pedro de Sossa de la Orden de
   S. Francisco, Predicador y Guardian del
   Conuento de la misma Orden de Santiago.
   87187
Senor. Haviendo dado cuenta a V. Mag. 86439
Senor. Ivan Recio de Leon . . . haze relacion.
   68362
Senor. La muy noble, y leal ciudad de Santiago
   de Chile. 98301
Senor. La resolucion de V. Magestad. 51044
Senor. Los Arcobispos de Obispos de las
   Indias Occidentales. 102866
Senor. Los Procuradores Generales de las
   Ordenes de Santo Domingo, S. Francisco,
   S. Agustin, y las demas religiones.
   106408
Senor, los sueldos y salarios. 86509
Senor, los vassallos de V. M. 98815
Senor. Manuel Rodriguez de la Compania de
   Iesvs. 72525
Senor. Medios para V. Magestad ahorrar lo
   mucho. (7401)
Sr. Ministro, Senores hermanos. 49417
Senor. Pedro de Velasco de la Compania de
   Iesus. 98805
Senor Pensador Mejicano. 98264
Senor: por cumplir con la obligacion. · 84384
Senor por que se que aureis plazer. 14639
Senor. Quando el nueuo camino no fuera tan
   rico. 68363
Senor. Relacion que Iuan Recio de Leon.
   (68364)
Senor Rodrigo Barnueuo, de la Compania de
   Jesus. 3557
Senor. Siendo tan notorio. 98803
Senor Sivorio Siuori dize. 81479
Senor. Tres cosas son las que obligan a
   credito. 93321
Senora Americana. pseud. Cartas sobre la
   educacion del bello sexo. 11106
Senora de poucos annos. pseud. Carta. see
   Pitt, Miss --------.
Senora. El Maestre de Campo D. Juan
   Fernandez de Salinas y la Cerda. (75788)
Senora. Fray Mateo de Heredia de la orden de
   S. Francisco. 73850
Senores editores del Salvador rejenerado. 76210
Senores Presidente, y Oidores de la Real
   Audiencia. 79140
Senorita. pseud. Dialogo. 19922
Senorita Inglesa que abjuro sus errores. pseud.
   Carta. see Pitt, Miss -----------.
Senour, F. 79141-(79144)
Senovert, -------. 104584
Senovert, ------- de. ed. and tr. (39314)
Sens (Archdiocese) Archbishop. 81946
Sens-commun. (58217)
Sens commun, addresse [sic] aux habitants de
   l'Amerique. (58216)
Sense. 63932

Sense of the beautiful. 81257

Sense of the city relative to the landing. 95984

Sensible sinners invited to come to Christ. 104209

Sensuyt le nouueau monde et nauigacions. 50062, note after 99383C, 3d note after 106378, 5th note after 106378

Sensuyt le nouueau monde & nauigations. 50061, 50064, note after 99383C, 5th note after 106378

Sensuyt le nouveau monde & navigations faictes par Emeric Vespuce Florentin. 50059, 99379, note after 99383C, 5th note after 106378

Sensuyt le nouueau mo[n]de et nauigations. 50060, 50063, note after 99383C, 5th note after 106378

Sensuytle nouueau mo[n]de & nauigations: faictes par Emeric de Vespuce Florentin. 50059, note after 99383C, 5th note after 106378

Sentenca de excommunhao e desautoricao fulminada. 15102, 79145

Sentenca de morte. 67945

Sentence [by Chief Justice Spencer.] 33424, 98405

Sentence in the case of the Commonwealth vs. Dennie. (69415)

Sentence of excommunication passed on two that were members. 42037, 92099

Sentencia del 20 de Febrero dada por los Jueces Plenipotenciaros. 11698

Sentencia en la residencia del Virey Vizarron Arzobispo de Mexico. 100639

Sentencia pronunciada por los Senores del Consejo Real. 70804

Sentencias Catholicas del divi poeta Dant. 24174

Sentencias de vista, y revista. 79146

Sentencias pronunciadas por D. Manuel Siliceo. (44966)

Sententie ende executie over eenighe schippers. 2443

Sententie gepronunchieert tegens Johan Schulenburgh. 78002

Sententie ghegeven tot Paris den 30 Nov. 1663. 79147

Senter, Isaac. 79148

Senter, Nathaniel G. M. 79149-79150

Sentimens d'un republicain. 79151

Sentiment d'un patriote Hollandois. (23343), 40660, (79152)

Sentimental and descriptive poem. 99418

Sentimental and honourous essays. 102397

Sentimental journey through France and Italy. 91346-91351, 91355-91356

Sentimental lucubrations. 60795

Sentimental novel. 77814

Sentimental philosopher. pseud. Fragment of a journal. see Irving, Washington, 1783-1859. supposed author and Rodman, J. supposed author

Sentimental review. 83791

Sentimental satire. (13435)

Sentimentos publicos de Pernambuco. (7317)

Sentiments and conduct proper to the present crisis. 35440

Sentiments and information respecting the slave trade. 90446

Sentiments and plan of the said [Danbury Baptist] Association. (18458)

Sentiments and plan of the Stonington Association. 92165

Sentiments and plan of the Warren Association. 101498

Sentiments and resolutions of an association of ministers. 53311, 92107, 101174

Sentiments, concerning the coming and kingdom of Christ. 88893

Sentiments des colons de Saint-Domingue. 4961

Sentiments of a British American. 95160

Sentiments of a foreigner. 68105

Sentiments of a free and independent elector. 99828

Sentiments of a principal freeholder. 79153, 98434

Sentiments of a West India savage. 53404

Sentiments of an American woman. 79154

Sentiments of an impartial member of Parliament. 79155

Sentiments of Lord Chatham on the American measures. 63072

Sentiments of Prince Eugene and Count Sinzendorf. 86742, 94070

Sentiments of Samuel B. Wylie. 105669

Sentiments of the free. 81983

Sentiments of the humours & amusements of the times. 105521

Sentiments on liberty. 4479

Sentiments on resignation. 48155

Sentiments on the small pox inoculated. 46741, 104243

Sentiments on what is freedom. 4480

Sentiments on what is freedom, and what is slavery. 4479

Sentiments relating to the late negotiation. 79156

Sentiments respecting slavery in the West Indies. 102843

Sentiments upon the religion of reason and nature. 79157-79158, 86635

Sentiments, upon the subject of state rights. 9936

Sentiments veritables du Ministre Swartz. 15193

Sentimiento que ha causado la infausta quanto sensible muerto. 98268

Sentimientos de la Nueva Espana. 76222

Sentimientos sublimes de religion. 64192

Sentinel. pseud. Who goes there? see Bogart, William H.

Sentinel (1768) 84678C

Sentinel (186-) 15421

Sentinel & gazette, extra. 92237

Sentinel. [By Richard Penn Smith.] 83779-83780

Sentinelle du peuple. (75180)

Sentinelle, garde a vous! 58164

Sentinels. 83788

Sentir del R. P. Fr. Augustin de Vetancurt. 76007

Sentmanat, Antonio de, Cardinal. 79159

Sentmanat, Manuel de Herrera y. see Herrera y Sentmanat, Manuel de.

Separat-Abdruck aus der National-Zeitung. 71473

Separate no. 147 [of the Wisconsin Historical Society.] 84132

Separate report of Mr. Blake's speech. 5798

Separate state secession. 74481, 87946

Separate-traders queries. (73772)

Separation from slavery. 79160

Separation of Israel. 73355

Separation of the Jewish tribes. 28009

Separation of the tares and wheat reserved to the day of judgment. 17103

Separation: war without end. 38445

Separations from the Religious Society of Friends. 38023

Separatists. United States. 79161

Separatists scheme. 72100-72101

Separazione una follia, ed un diletto. 34749

Sepp, Alphonso. 79168

Sepp, Antonio. 13015, 79162-79168

Seep, Gabriel. 79162, (79164), 79166

Sepp, J. C. (79169)

Sepp, Steph. Ign. 79165

Sept-Fontaines, H. C. Emmery de. see Emmery de Sept-Fontaines, H. C.

Sept dialogves. (48243)

Septe giornate della geographia di Francesco Berlingeri Fiorentino. 66500-66501

September 18, 1758. To the Honorable Francis Fauquier, Esq; His Majesty's Lieutenant-Governor, and Commander in Chief, of the Colony and Dominion of Virginia: the humble address of the Council. 99906

September 18, 1758. To the Honorable Francis Fauquier, Esq; His Majesty's Lieutenant-Governor, and Commander in Chief, of the Colony and Dominion of Virginia: the humble address of the House of Burgesses. 99924

September the eleventh, 1777. 41391

September 22d, 1756. 99904

Septenario devoto. (74008)

Septenary catalogue of the class of 1843. 18627

Septentrio novantiquus. 5905, 47383

Septenville, Edouard de. 79170

Septien, Pedro Antonio. 79171

Septimo Juguetillio. 79172

Septuagenaire. pseud. Projet pour tenter la decouverte. 79173

Septuagenarian. pseud. Army abuses. 79174

Septuagenarian dinner. 63160

Sepulchral service. 104278

Sepulveda, Diego Ortiz. plaintiff 86405

Sepulveda, Gines de. 11234, 39115

Sepulveda, Joannis Genesius, 1490?-1573. (79175)-79180

Sequeira, Gabriel. 79181

Sequeira, Gabriel Claudio de. 1885, 79181-79185

Sequeira, Gabriel Claudio de. defendant 79182

Sequeira e Sa, Manoel Tavares de. 79186

Sequel. 59252

Sequel, including the voyage of the "Fox." 5817

Sequel of Hon. Horace Mann. 83586

Sequel of the abstract of those parts of the custom. 67061

Sequel of the Indian queen. 20979

Sequel or appendix to the sacred roll and book. 32664, 79707-79708, note after 91701

Sequel to Afloat and ashore. 16475

Sequel to "American mines and mining." 68067

Sequel to American popular lessons. 71809

Sequel to an Appeal to the Society of Friends. 3463, 25264

Sequel to an essay on the yellow fever. 3113

Sequel to apostolical succession examined. 64692

Sequel to Barnum's parnassus. (41279)

Sequel to Bulkley and Cummins' voyage to the South Sea. 10205

Sequel to Common sense. 79187

Sequel to Linda. 31436

Sequel to Mrs. Kemble's journal. 28430, 37331, note after 95596, 2d note after 103115

Sequel to "Morals of manners." 78770

Sequel to Old Hicks the guide. 102248

Sequel to Politicks on both sides. 22636

Sequel to Riley's narrative. (71400)

Sequel to the African slave trade. 9691

Sequel to the Butterfly's ball. 59413

Sequel to the end of the irrepressible conflict. 34180

Sequel to the Farmer of New-Jersey, a tale. 101236

Sequel to the Forayers. 81209

Sequel to the History of John Bull the Clothier. 4433

Sequel to the History of the Six Nations. 92137

Sequel to the Indian-slayer. 89834

Sequel to the late visit of the Russian fleet to the United States. 79188

Sequel to the Plea for the Indians. 4361

Sequel to the "Prairie flower." (4724)

Sequel to the report of the 8th of January, 1838. 38118

Sequel to the so called correspondence between Rev. M. H. Smith and Horace Mann. 44324, 83572

Sequestration act of the Confederate States. 15410

Sequestration cases before the Hon. A. G. Magrath. 79189, 87467

Sequitada de la cabana Indiana. 12249

Sequoiyah. see Guess, George, or Sequoya, Cherokee Indian, 1770?-1843.

Sequuntur versae vivaeque imagines. (8784)

Seraiah, the Scribe. pseud. Chronicles of the fire-eaters. 12964, 79190

Serapeum. (8784)

Seraphical young shepherd. 11631

Seraphine. 79191

Serchfield, Rouland. see Searchfield, Rowland, Bishop of Bristol, 1565?-1622.

Serdonati, Francesco. tr. 43777-43780

Serenata para cantar-se no felix dia natalicio de Serenissima Senhora D. Carlota Joaquina. 88832

Serenata para cantar-se no feliz dia natalicio do Serenissimo Senhor D. Joao. 88835

Serenissimum Magnae Britanniae regem maris circumflui. (78971)-78972

Serf. 71486

Sergeant, Henry J. 79192

Sergeant, John, d. 1749. 14478-14479, (40566), 79193-79196

Sergeant, John, 1779-1852. 76938, 79197-79211, 97768

Sergeant, Jonathan D. (34385), note after 53697, note after 83791

Sergeant, Mrs. R. A. 77464

Sergeant, Thomas, 1782-1860. 21380, (79212)-79216

Sergeant Major of Gen. Hopson's Grenadiers. pseud. Journal of the expedition. (36723), 67022, 67024

Sergeant of the 1st Maryland, a prisoner. pseud. Four months of prison life. 19956

Sergeant slasher. (36220)

Sergeant's stratagem a war drama. (19423)

Sergipe (Brazilian Province) Presidente (Ferreira da Veiga) 79218 see also Ferreira da Veiga, Evaristo.

Sergipe (Brazilian Province) 2° Vice-Presidente (Dantas) (79219) see also Dantas, Dionizio Rodriguez.

Sergipe (Brazilian Province) Vice-Presidente (Barao) 79217 see also Barao, --------.

Sergipe (Brazilian Province) Vice-Presidente (Coelho e Mello) 69313 see also Coelho e Mello, Antonio Dias.

Seria, Jose Ignacio Negreyros y. see Negreyros y Seria, Jose Ignacio.

Seria ac jocosa. (71959)

Seriah the Scribe. pseud. see Seraiah,
    the Scribe. pseud.
Serie de articula editoriales dados a luz.
    70017
Serie de articulos publicados en "El provenir."
    64015
Serie de articulos publicados en la "Nacion
    Argentina." 38946
Serie de lettre ecrites de Bombay. 84006
Serie de mappemondes. 76838
Series of addresses. 104043
Series of agricultural essays. 94483-94484
Series of American historians. 93804, 105938
Series of American school biographies, for
    youth. 101844
Series of American tales. 104828
Series of amusing adventures of a Masonic
    Quixot. 95474
Series of answers to certain popular objections.
    97360
Series of answers to questions. 82585
Series of appeals. 52330
Series of articles and discourses. 13781
Series of articles communicated to the Journal
    of commerce. 9638
Series of articles in defence of the national
    sentiments. 8852
Series of articles on man and woman. 60794
Series of articles on the Cuban question.
    79220
Series of articles on the financial and political
    condition of the United States. 31101,
    (57938)
Series of articles on the value of the union.
    89749
Series of articles originally published in the
    Anti-slavery reporter. 93459
Series of articles originally published in the
    Evening post. 9639
Series of articles published in the Daily news.
    93721
Series of articles published originally in the
    Edgefield advertiser. 74481
Series of articles re-printed from the Sheffield
    free press. 55008
Series of articles . . . upon constitutional
    guarantees. (37656)
Series of articles which appeared in the Jour-
    nal of commerce. 63826
Series of biographical sketches of American
    artists. 40218
Series of books for systematic instruction in
    the English language. 102398
Series of brief historical sketches of the
    Church of England. 73836
Series of candid letters. 105330
Series of catechisms. 79221
Series of chapters on present-day conditions.
    84065
Series of charts. (71425)
Series of communications published in the
    Kingston herald. 47873, note before
    93160
Series of communications to the Boston daily
    advertiser. 28092
Series of comprehensive biographies. (50361)
Series of conversations on the natural history
    of Lower Canada. (28061)
Series of dialogues between a minister and his
    friend. 104734
Series of dialogues between a Presbyterian
    minister and a young convert. 84762
Series of dialogues between a Presbyterian
    minister and a young convert, on some
    prominent and most commonly disputed
    doctrines. 84761

Series of discourses. 18212
Series of discourses delivered before the
    Historical Society of Michigan. 32062,
    103692
Series of discourses delivered before the
    Literary and Philosophical Society of
    Manchester. 84106
Series of discourses, delivered in view of a
    dissolution of the pastoral relation. (18899)
Series of discourses, . . . from representative
    men. 50453
Series of . . . discourses on the laws of Moses.
    72184
Series of designs for rural cottages. (20773)
Series of doctrinal lectures. 83759
Series of eight letters. 32445
Series of eight sketches in colour. 17490
Series of elementary principles. (57744)
Series of English grammars. 85354
Series of essays, addressed to Congress.
    51975
Series of essays, addressed to Thomas Ritchie.
    100463
Series of essays and reports originally published
    in the New-England galaxy. 85425
Series of essays containing strictures upon the
    late correspondence. 42451
Series of essays, critical, moral, and miscel-
    laneous. 104951
Series of essays, letters, and discourses, &c.
    13442
Series of essays on civil and social duties.
    65991
Series of essays on morals and the diffusion
    of knowledge. 96290
Series of essays on the principles and policy
    of free states. 35819
Series of essays, originally published in the
    Connecticut herald. 96123, 1st note after
    105926
Series of essays, published in the Western
    Reserve chronicle. 58092
Series of essays recently published in the
    Charleston courier. 106004
Series of essays showing the great similarity
    between George Keith and his followers.
    58846
Series of essays, under the signature of Phocion.
    23994, 84832
Series of evenings with the poets. 77176
Series of extemporaneous discourses. 31714
Series of extracts from "The principles and
    results." 97385
Series of extracts illustrative of the proceedings
    and principles of the "Liberty Party."
    81822
Series of facts connected with the life of the
    author. (58363)
Series of familiar letters. 81515
Series of familiar letters and remarks. 81581
Series of familiar letters, illustrating the
    scenery. 81488, 2d note after 100605
Series of familiar letters . . . on the right of
    a state. (51378)
Series of familiar letters to a friend. 27919
Series of fourteen sketches. 47083
Series of geographies. 49722
Series of highly finished line engravings. 51149,
    74169
Series of historical sketches relative to Onon-
    daga. 13329, 84484
Series of historical tableaux. 89445
Series of humorous illustrations. 49214
Series of humorous sketches. 71730, 94822
Series of Indian narratives. 101219

Series of intercepted letters. (79222), 83867, 83868

Series of intercepted Mexican letters. 83869

Series of lectures. 26797

Series of lectures delivered in Edinburgh. 104001

Series of lectures on orthodoxy and heterodoxy. 105577

Series of lectures . . . on the position . . . of Chili. 33912, 1st note after 99449

Series of lectures on the signs of the times. 83843

Series of letters. 69505

Series of letters addressed by Frederick List. 41427

Series of letters addressed to a friend. 10852

Series of letters, addressed to a young lady. 95226

Series of letters addressed to . . . Earl Grey. 50859

Series of letters addressed to George D. Prentice. 37498, (65065)

Series of letters addressed to J. Fenimore Cooper. 57312

Series of letters addressed to J. Soule. 82350

Series of letters addressed to John Solan. 101456

Series of letters, addressed to Mrs. Beecher Stowe. 91233

Series of letters addressed to Mons. Michel Chevalier. 10842

Series of letters, addressed to Monsieur Necker. 97334-97336

Series of letters addressed to Sir Fitzroy Kelley. 8199

Series of letters addressed to some gentlemen of this city. (74720), 97772A

Series of letters, addressed to the citizens of New-York. 82772

Series of letters addressed to the citizens of the United States. (33643)

Series of letters, addressed to the Earl of Liverpool. 43641

Series of letters, addressed to the editor of the Times. 102796

Series of letters addressed to the greatest politician in England. (79223)

Series of letters addressed to the people of the United States. By a native of Virginia. 27376, 66513

Series of letters addressed to the people of the United States. By Timothy Pickering. (26257)

Series of letters addressed to the public. 10063

Series of letters addressed to the Rev. A. W. McLeod. 80744

Series of letters addressed to the Rev. Allen Steele. 6222, 91104

Series of letters addressed to the Rev. Samuel Miller. (33226)

Series of letters, addressed to Thomas Herttell. 88643

Series of letters, addressed to Thomas Jefferson. 23186, 94189

Series of letters and journals. 100898

Series of letters and notes. 11537

Series of letters and other documents. 3083, (79224)

Series of letters, between a friend and his correspondent. 62891

Series of letters, between a young man and a minister. 90191

Series of letters between Enoch Emerson and Joseph Boyce. (22426)

Series of letters, between Junius and Sir William Draker. (36911)

Series of letters. By a citizen of Pennsylvania. (26388), 2d note after 102806

Series of letters. By a physician of Philadelphia. 56533, 1st note after 100506

Series of letters. By an officer. 1366, 2d note after 96502

Series of letters. By Calvin Kingsley. 37887

Series of letters. By Egerton Ryerson. 74550

Series of letters. By George F. Pierce. 62718

Series of letters. [By Henry Holcombe.] (32464)

Series of letters. [By James Biggs.] 5333-5334, 9117

Series of letters. By John Scoble. 78154

Series of letters by Levin Lawrence. 39361

Series of letters, by Rev. P. J. de Smet. 82277

Series of letters, by Socrates. (19067), 86193

Series of letters. By the late Hon. William Sullivan. 93559

Series of letters containing a faithful state of many important and striking facts. 40100

Series of letters descriptive of Prince Edward Island. 36400

Series of letters from a cosmopolite to a clergyman. 16893, 20275

Series of letters from a field hospital. 87262

Series of letters from a gentleman, resident there. 22496, 71241

Series of letters from a gentleman to his friend. 53643, 59284, 104441-104442

Series of letters from a partaker in the American revolution. (34383)

Series of letters from a resident in Jamaica. 56420, 4th note after 95756

Series of letters from a young gentleman who went to reside there. 99423

Series of letters from Canada and the United States. (6433)

Series of letters from Dr. Pleasant Jones to Major Joseph Jones of Georgia. 36595, 82069, note after 90541, note after 95543, note after 95665

Series of letters from Lebanon Springs. 59506, 79716, note after 97880, 3d note after 100605

Series of letters from Mexico. 104188

Series of letters from Mrs. Manvill. 44435

Series of letters from that country to a friend in England. 18640-18641, note after 99589-99590, 105557

Series of letters from the Brandywine and Constitution Frigates. 81564

Series of letters from Upper Canada. 4483

Series of letters from Washington. 16074

Series of letters, in answer to a question. 95669

Series of letters in reference to the building of a monster hotel. 33132

Series of letters, including an account of Harper's Ferry. 9917, 1st note after 96334, 4th note after 100532

Series of letters, inviting the Rev. Eli Smith to compare his own statements with fact. 105235

Series of letters of the Second Annual Hunting Expedition. 88608

Series of letters on education. 104943

Series of letters on financial, commercial, and colonial policy. 96233

Series of letters on free masonry. (17558)

Series of letters on North America. 12596

Series of letters on . . . the "legislative choice." 9740

Series of letters on the mode and subjects of baptism. 11958

Series of letters on the subject of the "legislative choice." 45096

Series of letters, published in different gazettes. 98924

Series of letters to a Baptist minister. 105274

Series of letters to a friend. . . . By A. Thomason. 4447, 95454

Series of letters to a friend. By G. W. Snyder. 95600

Series of letters to a friend, by Roderick Mackenzie. 43431, 94397

Series of letters to a freind. By William Carter. 11124

Series of letters to a friend in England. 30533

Series of letters to a lady. 1258, 1st note after 100566

Series of letters to a respectable citizen of Philadelphia. 32255

Series of letters to an instructor. 98895

Series of letters to Aristippus, from Aristander. 91857

Series of letters to Barton W. Stone. 92025

Series of letters to Earl Bathurst. 56520

Series of letters to F. W. Allston. 67789

Series of letters to Harriet Beecher Stowe. 7982, note after 92624

Series of letters to his friends. 31950

Series of letters to Hon. W. L. Yancey. 68046

Series of letters to Mr. Zephariah Slick. (82135), 91282

Series of letters to Peter S. Duponceau. 79731

Series of letters to T. Clarkson. 90174

Series of letters to the Boston daily advertiser. 75500

Series of letters to the Duchess of Lesdiguieres. 12139

Sereis of letters to the editor of the United States gazette. 104774

Series of letters to the ex-acting President. 17908, 78746

Series of letters to "The Hackettstown gazette." 84220

Series of letters to the London Times. 10339, 74544

Series of letters to the Rev. Dr. Miller. 88975

Series of letters to the Rev. James Flint. (24794)

Series of letters which appeared in the "New times." 70251

Series of letters which appeared in the Star newspaper. 99774

Series of letters with editorial remarks on the existing differences between England and America. (23709)

Series of letters, written by a lady of Cape Francois. 30807, note after 78746

Series of letters, written by Amaziah Bumpas. 9154

Series of letters written by an American youth. 97621, 3d note after 105973

Series of letters written by an officer, employed on the expedition. 4511, 34378

Series of letters, written by Colonel John Taylor. 94494

Series of letters, written during a journey through Pennsylvania, Ohio, Indiana, and into the states of Illinois and Kentucky. 103020

Series of letters, written during a visit to Austin's colony. (32528)

Series of letters, written from America, in the years 1777 and 1778. (32064)

Series of letters written from Bombay in the spring of 1863. 84005

Series of letters, written in the years 1831-2. 97401

Series of letters, written originally to the Right Honourable the Earl of **** ****. 13796

Series of letters wrote . . . in . . . 1774, & 1775. 43655

Series of lights and shadows. (72998)

Series of local American history. 47105, 51371, 51887, (71302)

Series of maps to Willard's history of the United States. 104046

Series of numbers on prison discipline. 79225

Series of numbers, originally published in the Schenectady cabinet. 101524

Series of numbers upon three theological points. 103231-103232

Series of observations . . . on the expediency of Great Britain entering into commercial regualtions with the South American states. 31315

Series of oil-colour views. 38659

Series of original designs for cottages. (82164)

Series of original designs. 67893

Series of original essays, moral and amusing. 105628

Series of original sermons. 82781

Series of original sermons by clergymen of the Protestant Episcopal Church. 66197

Series of outline maps. 49722

Series of pamphlets [by Orson Pratt.] 64952, 64956, 64957, 64959, 64962

Series of pamphlets, principally written by Rev. Joseph Lyman. 28628, 104118

Series of papers. 102786

Series of papers, addressed to the citizens of Maryland. 22337, 99771

Series of papers first published in the Boston commonwealth in 1851. (12012), 24636

Series of papers relating to the expeditions from Canada. 33144

Series of papers under the signature of "Hampden." 23453, 2d note after 100462

Series of papers written by federal prisoners. 3950, note after 90573

Series of photographic views, with letter-press sketches. 77561

Series of pieces partly heretofore published. 1691, 14021

Series of poems, by a citizen of South Carolina. 14888, 26949

Series of poems by a South Carolinean. 14888

Series of poems, by J. A. R. 67378

Series of poems. [By Robert G. Haliburton.] 29678

Series of poems. [By William Plumer.] 63453

Series of poems, on some of the most important and interesting subjects. (32239)

Series of political papers, proving the injurious and debasing consequences of republican government. (64166), 2d note after 96805

Series of popular lectures, in which popery and protestantism are contrasted. 70854

Series of popular letters. 32512

Series of portraits of eminent persons. 101816

Series of the present and future prospects of Jamaica considered. (52295)

Series of questions. 94684

Series of quiet talks about the singers and their songs. 77175

Series of reminiscential letters from Daniel
Drake. 20824
Series of reprints of early American poetry.
104986
Series of sermons, by members of the Society
of Friends. 66931
Series of sermons by Rev. E. D. Bryan.
46901
Series of sermons in defence of the doctrine
of universal salvation. 81631
Series of sermons on some of the internal
and distinctive peculiarities of the Pro-
testant Episcopal Church in America.
91999-91200
Series of sermons on the divinity of Christ.
71852
Series of sermons on the doctrine of ever-
lasting punishment. 79034
Series of seven letters. 90823
Series of seven pictures, in nine colors, in
oil. 89510
Series of short and familiar essays. 67504
Series of [672] stereoscopic views of most of
the points of interest. 9977, 33180
Series of sketches. 41042
Series of sketches demonstrative of the mental
powers and intellectual capacities of the
Negro race. 216, 27628
Series of sketches for young folks. 75967
Series of sketches, humorous and descriptive.
9509
Series of sketches in the shape of a connected
narrative. 87143
Series of sketches of prominent men of the
House of Representatives. 68485
Series of sketches . . . of whims and women.
41016
Series of sketches, picturesque and historical.
(81232)
Series of stereoscopic views. 9977, 33180
Series of tables of the several branches of
American manufactures. 79225
Series of tales and sketches. (46835), 46840
Series of tales and sketches of American life.
46836, 46840
Series of ten letters. 90823
Series of three letters. 90823
Series of three letters, addressed to His
Royal Highness the Prince Regent.
(17529), 101267
Series of thrilling tales and sketches. 68379
Series of tracts on the doctrines, order and
polity of the Presbyterian Church. 85311
Series of twelve essays. 9305
Series of useful lessons. 103012
Series of views taken on the spot. (9184)
Series of wisdom and policy: being a full
justification of all our measures. 79228
Series of wisdom and policy, manifested in a
review of our foreign negotiations and
transactions. 79227
Series of wonderful facts and startling revela-
tions. 73285
Seriman, Zaccaria. 79230-79232, note after
99404-99405, note after 101249-101251
Serionne, Joseph Accarias de. see Accarias
de Serionne, Joseph, 1706-1792.
Serious actual dangers of foreigners and
foreign commerce. (36649)
Serious address and farewell charge to the
members of the Church of England.
99540
Serious address of the Consociation of the
Western District of Vermont. 99171
Serious address to all serious Christians.
79237

Serious address to lay-Methodists. (28793),
(79238)
Serious address to part of the Congregational
Church in Newbury-port. (11861), 97315,
97321-97322
Serious address to professing Christians.
(32953), note after 102754
Serious address, to such of the inhabitants of
Pennsylvania, as have cannived [sic] at,
or do approve of, the late massacre.
79239
Serious address, to such of the inhabitants of
Pennsylvania, as have connived at, or do
approve of, the late massacre of the
Indians at Lancaster. 79240-79242
Serious address to such of the people called
Quakers. 28790, 79243
Serious address to the candid members of the
Methodist communion. (79244)
Serious address to the clergy; by a minister
of the Church of England. 62430, 79245
Serious address to the freeholders and other
inhabitants. 60610
Serious address to the inhabitants of the colony
of New-York. 79246
Serious address to the members of the Epis-
copal Separation in New England, being
an attempt. 79247
Serious address to the members of the Epis-
copal Separation in New-England, occa-
sioned by Mr. Wetmore's vindication.
32310-(32311)
Serious address to the Methodist community
of New England. 23454
Serious address to the people of England.
102687
Serious address to the Presbytery of Oneida.
60944
Serious address to the rulers of America.
4694
Serious address to the rulers of America and
Virginia. 55360
Serious address to the rulers of America, on
the inconsistency of their conduct respect-
ing slavery. (79248)-(79250)
Serious address to the youths of Boston.
102742
Serious address to those who unnecessarily
frequent the tavern. 46500
Serious address to young people. 62517
Serious advice to delivered ones from sickness.
829
Serious and affectionate address to the citizens
of the United States. 85986
Serious and candid letters to the Rev. Thomas
Baldwin. 105313
Serious and earnest address to the gentry,
clergy, and the other inhabitants. 79251
Serious and expostulatory letter to the Revd.
Mr. George Whitefield. 103565
Serious and impartial observations on the
blessings of liberty and peace. 79252
Serious and seasonable improvement of that
great example of magistratical piety.
(49660)
Serious and short address, to those Presby-
terians. 19938, 60057, 64448
Serious and suitable counsels for them that
go to sea. 13205, 106289
Serious answer to Mr. Wesley's Calm address.
105746
Serious apology for the principles of the people
call'd Quakers. 103659
Serious appeal on the necessity of mutual for-
giveness. 10851, (10877)

Serious appeal to all the more sober, impartial & judicious people. (37215)

Serious appeal to the wisdom and patriotism of the Legislature. 22767

Serious call and admonition to watchfulness and diligence. (14508)

Serious call* from the city to the country. (79253)

Serious call in Christian love. 79254

Serious call, or masonry revived. 79255

Serious call to the Quakers. 79256, 103660

Serious call to those who are without the pale of the Episcopal Church. (79257), 85660, 97597

Serious cautions against excess in drinking. 97551

Serious charge and accusation against Mr. Edw. Winslow. 7487

Serious charges against Captain Oliver H. Perry. 31189

Serious Christian. 46501

Serious comedy. (79258)

Serious consideration of two very important cases. 46440

Serious consideration, that God will visit. 104410

Serious considerations addressed to the electors of New-Jersey. 79259

Serious considerations on several important subjects. 4680, 79260

Serious considerations on the election of a President. 13724, 35932, 41347, 79263, note after 99831, 105513

Serious considerations on the political conduct of Lord North. 8914

Serious considerations on the present state of the affairs. 37394, 79261

Serious considerations on the present state of the city of Philadelphia. 25522, 25558, 25563, 88824, 2d note after 96428

Serious considerations on various subjects of importance. 105207-105208

Serious debate with himself what course he shall take. 63581

Serious examination of George Keith's pretended serious call to the Quakers. 103660

Serious exhortation. 46640-(46641), 46677

Serious exhortation to the present and succeeding generation. (46627)

Serious exhortations address'd to young men. 16640

Serious expostulation with the followers of Elias Hicks. 24455

Serious expostulation with the members of the House of Representatives. 48897, 79262

Serious expostulation with the Society of Friends, in Pennsylvania. 58094, 62564

Serious facts, opposed to "Serious considerations." 35932, 79263

Serious fall in the value of gold ascertained. 36098

Serious inquiry into the nature and effects of the stage. 104944

Serious letter to the public. (36913)

Serious letter to the young people of Boston. 46819

Serious opera. 30851

Serious question stated. 24401

Serious questions for the new year. 76990

Serious reflections. 79266

Serious reflections addressed to all parties. 105494

Serious reflections affectionately recommended. 79264-(79265)

Serious reflections during the life and surprising adventures of Robinson Crusoe. 19284, 79266

Serious reflections for the citizens of South-Carolina. 87818

Serious reflections on late publick concernments in these churches. 92103

Serious reflections on the slave trade and slavery. (79831)

Serious reflections on the times. A poem. (79267)

Serious reflections on the times. By Anthony Benezet. 4681

Serious refutation of the idolatrous divinity of Ann Lee. 13263

Serious remonstrances, addressed to the citizens of the northern states. 7384

Serious remonstrance to the people of Connecticut. 15859, note after 90848

Serious review, affectionately recommended to the careful examination of Friends. 46931

Serious thoughts on the late administration of episcopal orders. 36463

Serious thoughts on the subject of taking the lives of our fellow creatures. 21923

Serious thoughts on the traffick in and use of distilled spirituous liquors. 79268

Serious warning to Great Britain and her Colonies. 79826, 93140

Serious word to the posterity of holy men. 104275

Serious word to the present and su-ceeding generation of New England. 44006

Serisy, ------- Richer. see Richer-Serisy, ---------.

Sermam, que pregou o P. Antonio Vieira. 99527

Sermao das dores de N. Senhora. 43216

Sermao de accao de gracas. 78958

Sermao em memoria do faustissimo dia, em que Sua Alteza Real desembarcou n'esta cidade da Bahia. 27200

Sermao em memoria do faustissimo dia en que Sua Alteza Real entrou a barra da Bahia. 43211

Sermao na Cathedral da Bahia. 29322

Sermao no procissao da gracas que a muito nombre villa de Villo-Real. 16837

Sermao pregado em accao de gracas. 7621

Sermao pregado na Capella Catholica de Stonehouse. 65395

Sermao que pregou na Se da Bahia. 7318

Sermao sobre a piedade de Nossa Senhora. 49991

Serment, J. H. 79270-(79271)

Serment prononce par les naturels de la Nouvelle-Espagne. 94854

Sermoes e panegyricos recitados. 78959

Sermoes das tardes das Domingas da Quaresma. 81076

Sermon. 49296

Sermon a las exeqvias del Ilvstrissimo Senor Don Fr. Gabriel de Zatate. 112

Sermon, adapted to the occasion, by Samuel Stillman. 12121, (50948), 91812

Sermon, addressed to a military company. 103762

Sermon addressed to De Witt Clinton. 13736

Sermon addressed to the congregation in Franklin, Mass. 88671

Sermon addressed to the First Church in Brookfield. (61372)

Sermon, addressed to the Fourth Presbyterian Congregation in Albany. 89744

Sermon, addressed to the Legislature of . . . Connecticut. 8690

Sermon, addressed to the Legislature of the state of Connecticut, at the annual election in Hartford, May 7, 1823. 94525

Sermon addressed to the Legislature of the state of Connecticut, at the annual election in New Haven, May 5, 1830. 6056

Sermon addressed to the Mather Church and Society. (67311)

Sermon, addressed to the Second Congregational Church. 89744

Sermon addressed to the Second Presbyterian Congregation, Albany. 89744

Sermon addressed to the Second Presbyterian Congregation, Albany, Sabbath morning, March 14, 1858. 89744

Sermon addressed to the Second Presbyterian Congregation, Albany, Sunday afternoon, May 9, 1858. 89744

Sermon addressed to the Second Presbyterian Congregation, Albany, Sunday morning, April 2, 1865. 89744

Sermon addressed to the Second Presbyterian Congregation in Albany, April 23, 1837. 89744

Sermon addressed to the Second Presbyterian Congregation in Albany, February 3, 1839. 89744

Sermon addressed to the Second Presbyterian Congregation in Albany, March 4, 1838. 89744

Sermon addressed to the Second Presbyterian Congregation in Albany, November 26, 1843. 89744

Sermon, addressed to the Second Presbyterian Congregation in Albany, on the fourth of July, 1830. 89744

Sermon addressed to the Second Presbyterian Congregation in Albany, Sunday morning, August 27, 1854. 89744

Sermon, addressed to the temperate. (47216)

Sermon after his funeral . . . by . . . Mr. Colman. 59602

Sermon, . . . after the calamitous death of Mr. Charles Austin. 22465

Sermon [after the death of Daniel Webster.] 26074

Sermon . . . after the death of J. G. Stevenson. 26074

Sermon, . . . after the death of Joseph P. Bradlee. 26074

Sermon . . . after the death of Marshall Sears Perry. 26536

Sermon, . . . after the death of Mrs. Mehitabel Gerrish. (46387)

Sermon . . . after the death of Nathaniel Ward. 30892

Sermon after the death of . . . Thomas Steel. 14505

Sermon after the decease of the very Reverend and Learned Cotton Mather. 46793

Sermon after the earthquake. [By Eliphalet Williams.] 104214

Sermon . . . after the . . . earthquake which occur'd . . . between the 29th and 30th of October, 1727. 3472

Sermon after the funeral of Dame Bridget Usher. 25408

Sermon . . . after the funeral of Madam Lydia Hutchinson. 12370

Sermon after the funeral of Mrs. Abigail Stearns. 79451, 90905

Sermon . . . after the funeral of . . . Simeon Stoddard. (14480)

Sermon . . . after the funeral of the Honourable Penn Townsend. 25408

Sermon . . . after the funerals of the Rev. Dr. Harris, and the Hon. Daniel Sargent. 26074

Sermon, after the great fire of 1835. 21660

Sermon . . . after the interment of the Hon. John Winthrop. 38875

Sermon, . . . after the proclaiming of King George the Second. 14485

Sermon against absolute election. 103617

Sermon against profane cursing and swearing. 28202

Sermon against the dangerous and sinful practice of inoculation. 46176

Sermon, against Universalism. 103798

Sermon al glorioso San Francisco de Borja. 70397

Sermon . . . Albany, . . . a plea for home missions. 24503

Sermon . . . Albany . . . General Synod of the Reformed Dutch Church. 48998

Sermon and address . . . at the induction of the Rev. John Waddell. 28208

Sermon and address on the death of Dea. Oren Sage. 55844

Sermon and addresses, at the installation of . . . Rev. Jacob M. Manning. 44350

Sermon and its answer. 82087

Sermon . . . [and] memoirs of Mrs. Gale and . . . Mrs. Esther Peak. (59415)

Sermon and memorial, delivered at the funeral. (79390)

Sermon and narrative of the dangers and deliverances at sea. 36335

Sermon and other exercises, at the ordination and installation of Alexander McKenzie. 70937

Sermon and other exercises at the ordination of Alex. McKenzie. 43419

Sermon and speeches at the settlement of Rev. Wm. C. Whitcomb. 37976

Sermon . . . annual election. 31809

Sermon, . . . annual fast, April 7, 1859. 26647

Sermon . . . annual thanksgiving, by Alexander McLean. 43508

Sermon . . . annual thanksgiving, November 20, 1794. 57776

Sermon . . . April 11, 1841. 43271

Sermon . . . April 5, 1799. 19818

[Sermon] April, 1799, at a quarterly meeting. 2921

Sermon . . . April 16, 1857. (29830)

Sermon . . . April 3, 1859. 42045

Sermon, April 30, 1863. 43340

Sermon, April 30, 1863, at Detroit, Michigan. 22784

Sermon . . . April 30, 1863, national fast day. (64208)

Sermon, April 20, 1841. 57317

Sermon . . . April 28, 1861. By Albert Barnes. 3504

Sermon . . . April 28, 1861. [By L. Merrill Miller.] 49036

Sermon . . . April 21, 1850. (38784)

Sermon . . . April 24, 1864. 33964

Sermon, . . . April 24, 1822. (23951)

Sermon . . . April 27, 1858. (21878)

Sermon, . . . April 23, 1837. 26074

Sermon artillery . . . election . . . Boston, June 2, 1806. 37366

Sermon at a fast kept by the First Gathered Church in Boston. 104073

Sermon at a meeting of the Grand Lodge of Free-Masons. 50097

Sermon at a private meeting of the Society of Young Men for Religious Exercise. 40773

Sermon at a wedding in Edmonton. 78720

Sermon at Abington, Mass. 14256

Sermon . . . at Acworth, N. H. (3700)

Sermon . . . at Alexandria. (51260)

Sermon at Alstead, N. H. 31734

Sermon, . . . at Concord, before . . . the Governor, . . . at the annual election, June 6th, 1805. (58178)

Sermon . . . at Concord, before . . . the Legislature of . . . New-Hampshire. 58717

Sermon . . . at Concord, before the Senate and House of Representatives of . . . New Hampshire. 58717

Sermon at Concord Dec. 29, 1737. 42088

Sermon at Concord, in New-Hampshire, Sabbath Day, April 25, 1813. 43240

Sermon . . . at Concord, June 5, 1828. 6966

Sermon . . . at Concord, June 6th, 1799. (59317)

Sermon . . . at Concord . . . June 3, 1818. 8470

Sermon . . . at Concord . . . June 25th, 1798. 71515

Sermon . . . at Concord, . . . New-Hampshire, election, June 5, 1788. 38875

Sermon, . . . at Concord, New-Hampshire, June 22, 1806. 43240

Sermon, . . . at Crawfordsville. 49099

Sermon at Cummington, March, 1811. 28978

Sermon at Danbury, Nov. 8, 1789. 38876

Sermon at Danvers at the interment of the Rev. B. Wadsworth. (18453)

Sermon at Danville, June 25, 1798. (25156)

Sermon at Dedham, Mass. 18055

Sermon . . . at Deerfield, — Jan. 1, A. D. 1799. 42791

Sermon . . . at Dennis, January 2, 1805. 37366

Sermon . . . at Dorchester . . . after the interment of Mr. Nathaniel Topliff. 30521

Sermon . . . at Dorchester . . . following the decease of Mrs. Rebecca Stetson. (29830)

Sermon . . . at Dorchester, . . . Jan. 27, 1861. (29830)

Sermon . . . at Dorchester, June 25, 1817. 43379

Sermon at Dorchester, Mass., January 1, 1796. 30521

Sermon . . . at Dorchester, Nov. 26, 1807. 30521

Sermon . . . at . . . Dorchester, on Sunday, Feb. 2, 1862. 9091

Sermon at Dover, N. H., Aug. 9, 1797. 43050

Sermon . . . at Dover, N. H. on the 28th of June, 1846. 42159

Sermon . . . at Dunkeld. 59136

Sermon . . . at Dunstable, Mass. 31672

Sermon at East Haddam, Conn. 33961

Sermon at East Haddam, Oct. 23, 1816. 24763

Sermon at East Hampton. 8984

Sermon at East-Hartford, Nov. 3, 1806. 24763

Sermon . . . at East-Haven, January 13, 1808. 28127

Sermon at East Windsor. (43066)

Sermon . . . at Epping, N. H., December 27, 1850. 59354

Sermon . . . at Epping, N. H., September 21, 1854. 59354

Sermon . . . at Epson, New-Hampshire. 43240

Sermon at Exeter, N. H. 72810

Sermon . . . at Exeter, October 15. 1798. 8930

Sermon at Exon, Jan. 30, 1716-17. 62722

Sermon . . . at Falmouth, at the ordination of the Reverend Mr. Samuel Dean. (47954)

Sermon . . . at Farmington, Connecticut. (58189)

Sermon at first preached in Latine at Oxford. 103440

Sermon at Fitchburg. 21746

Sermon at Fort Midway. 923

Sermon at Franklin, Dec. 31, 1820. 21977

Sermon, . . . at Franklin, on the day of annual thanksgiving. 22525

Sermon . . . at Freetown, Dec. 2. 1747. (64275)

Sermon . . . at Freyeburg, Me. 12678

Sermon at gathering of a church at New Salem. (2198)

Sermon, . . . at Glassenbury. 41749

Sermon at Grafton. 34059

Sermon at Greenfield, Mass., Sept. 24, 1826. 2757

Sermon . . . at Greenland. 43050

Sermon at Hackensack. 16793

Sermon at Haddam, Dec. 14, 1813. 24273

Sermon . . . at Haddam, June 14, 1797. 33961

Sermon . . . at Halifax; on behalf of the Incorporated Society for the Propagation of the Gospel in Foreign Parts. 34771

Sermon . . . at Halifax, 25 April, 1794. (34766)

Sermon at Hallowell, October 21, 1795. 28791

Sermon . . . at Hamden, Sept. 9th, 1802. 42806

Sermon . . . at Hamilton, on the day of the national fast. (18177)

Sermon . . . at Hampton Falls, N. H. 79948

Sermon at Hanover, before the Franklin Lodge of Free and Accepted Masons. 43240

Sermon at Hanover, Mass. 11954

Sermon at Hartford, Conn. May 30, 1813. 18125

Sermon . . . at Hartford in Connecticut in N. E. 24579

Sermon, . . . at Hartford, in Connecticut, on the general election. 56041

Sermon, at Hartford, May 12th, 1726. 24529

Sermon . . . at Hartford; on the day of the anniversary election. 20641

Sermon . . . at Harvard, June 3, 1801. 39199

Sermon . . . at Harwich, January 21, 1791. 47449

Sermon . . . at Hatfield, Nov. 4, 1804. 42791

Sermon, . . . at Hatfield, October 20, 1807. (42790)

Sermon . . . at Haverhill, December 21, 1808. (18435)

Sermon . . . at Haverhill, Mass., 17 December, 1837. 79329

Sermon . . . at Hebron, . . . Connecticut. (43066)

Sermon, . . . at Hingham, March 19, 1837. 47078

Sermon . . . at Hingham, . . . October 12, 1768. 26785

Sermon at Hingham on his [i. e. John White Brown's] death. (8636)

Sermon . . . at his [i. e. Henry A. Rowland's] funeral. 73567

Sermon at his [i. e. Samuel Hopkins'] funeral. 32953, note after 102754

Sermon at his [i. e. Seth Coleman's] funeral. (14309)

Sermon at his [i. e. Elisha Rockwood's] interment. (72453)

Sermon at his [i. e. David Brainerd's] ordination. 21927

Sermon at his [i. e. John Graham's] ordination. (28223)

Sermon at his [i. e. Hugh Knox's] own ordination. 38162

Sermon . . . at Holden, Mass. 27694

Sermon . . . at Holliston, August 20, 1812. (65108)

SERMON

Sermon . . . at Holliston, . . . September 19.
1802. (65109)
Sermon at Hopkinton, April 9, 1735. 42088
Sermon . . . at Hopkinton . . . Feb. 28, 1808.
33324
Sermon at installation of Rev. James W.
Thompson. 28687
Sermon at installation of Stephen Chapin.
30528
Sermon at Inverness. 10931
Sermon . . . at Ipswich, Nov. 7, 1765. 58902
Sermon . . . at Keene, at the first opening
of the Inferior Court. (26776)
Sermon at Keene, N. H., 15 August, 1819.
3105
Sermon at Keene, N. H. June 24, 1789. 24211
Sermon . . . at King's Chapel . . . Boston.
59351
Sermon . . . at Kingston, Sept. 29. 1725.
56724
Sermon . . . at Lebanon . . . at the dedication.
42806
Sermon at Lebanon, Con. March 4, 1776.
14217
Sermon . . . at Lebanon Goshen, May 7, 1807.
42806
Sermon at lecture, Boston, Dec. 14, 1694.
(46358)
Sermon . . . at Lee . . . December 20th,
1807. 34117
Sermon . . . at Lee, December 22d, 1820.
34117
Sermon . . . at Leicester. 42315
Sermon at Leominster, Mass. 3882
Sermon, . . . at Lexington, April 19, 1780.
(60788)
Sermon at Lexington, to implore the blessing
of God. 42088
Sermon at Litchfield, at a public meeting of
singers. 49120
Sermon . . . at Litchfield, at the execution of
John Jacob. 63043
Sermon at Littleton. 25216
Sermon . . . at Long Meadows. 36150
[Sermon] at Longmeadow. 2623
Sermon . . . at Lyme. 42806
Sermon . . . at . . . Lynn . . . June 11, 1854.
36313
Sermon . . . at Manchester, Vermont. 31054-
31055
Sermon . . . at Mansfield. 58377
Sermon . . . at Marblehead, . . . 5th of April,
1838. 55324
Sermon, . . . at Marblehead, on the fifth of
April, 1838. 55324
Sermon . . . at Marborough, Feb. 7. 17$\frac{30}{31}$.
42086, 94067
Sermon at Marlborough, July 9. 1734. 37467
Sermon . . . at Marshfield, Feb. 21, 1753.
28550
Sermon . . . at Marshfield, Sept. 5. 1759.
18110
Sermon . . . at Mason, April 11, 1803. 31813
Sermon . . . at Medfield, . . . Feb. 6, 1820.
26517
Sermon . . . at Medfield, June 6, 1773. 65104
Sermon . . . at Medfield, November 6th, 1748.
(21241)
Sermon . . . at Medway, West Parish, Oct. 31,
1771. (55325)
Sermon at Middleborough East-Precinct. 65602
Sermon at Middleborough, Feb. 5, 1769. 2632
Sermon, . . . at Middleborough . . . June 9,
1822. 58185
Sermon at Middleborough, Mass. 2632
Sermon at Middlefield. (51848)

Sermon at Middletown, April 10, 1786. 33960
Sermon . . . at Middletown, July 20th, A. D.
1775. 33961
Sermon at Middletown, June 20, 1816. 24273
Sermon at Middletown, occasioned by the death
of Mr. Hezekiah Hulbert. 33961
Sermon . . . at Morris-Town. 56823
Sermon, . . . at Natick. 50423
Sermon, . . . at Needham, December 12, 1821.
37752
Sermon . . . at Needham, March 12, 1815.
56236
Sermon . . . at Needham, November 7, 1792.
30887
Sermon at New Braintree, June 13, 1769. 25042
Sermon at New Braintree, Mass. 24546
Sermon . . . at New-Braintree, October 26,
A. D. 1796. 24791
Sermon . . . at New-Cambridge, in Bristol.
63044
Sermon . . . at New Castle, (Del.) on the thir-
teenth day of April, 1815. 39227
Sermon . . . at New-Castle, in New-Hampshire.
58898
Sermon . . . at New Gloucester, February 10th,
1802. (36164)
Sermon at New Haven, Con. June 4, 1760.
4095.
Sermon at New Ipswich, Aug. 6, 1811. 31813
Sermon . . . at New-Ipswich, June 3, 1811.
31813
Sermon . . . at New-London, November 27,
1794. (11899)
Sermon . . . at New York, July 4th, 1794.
43474
Sermon . . . at . . . New York, November 20,
1851. 64608
Sermon . . . at New York, October 31, 1817.
77483
Sermon . . . at New York, Sunday, May 30,
1860. (12406)
Sermon at Newark, June 2, 1736. (20062)
Sermon . . . at Newbury, . . . April 18th, 1774.
36114
Sermon, . . . at Newbury, March 26, 1758.
42439
Sermon, . . . at Newbury, May 22. 1755. (42440)
Sermon . . . at Newbury-Port, April 23d, 1767.
(34057)-(34058)
Sermon . . . at . . . Newbury-Port, Jan. 26,
1788. (51518)
Sermon . . . at . . . Newbury-Port: occasioned
by the death of Mrs. Phebe Lane. (51518)
Sermon . . . at Newburyport, before the Merri-
mack Bible Society. 18415
Sermon . . . at Newburyport, December 19,
1794. (18435)
Sermon . . . at Newburyport . . . December 9,
1818. 6234
Sermon . . . at Newburyport, Dec. 30, 1856.
28568
Sermon . . . at . . . Newburyport, Dec. 25th,
1812. (50979)
Sermon, . . . at Newburyport, July 20, 1803.
(50897)
Sermon at Newent in Norwich. (46210)
Sermon . . . at Newport, in Rhode-Island.
63883
Sermon at Newport, R. I. June 12, 1745. 10684
Sermon at Newport, R. I. Oct. 24, 1773. 5641
Sermon . . . at . . . Newport, Rhode-Island,
on the day of Pentecost. 37103
Sermon at Newport, R. I., 22. Jan., 1854.
7756
Sermon at Newton, Aug. 9, 1741. 1845

Sermon . . . at Newton . . . December 7, 1792. 32729

Sermon at Newton January, 1804. 28199

Sermon . . . at Newtown, Pennsylvania. 50873

Sermon . . . at North-Woodstock. 39535

Sermon at North Yarmouth. 11955

Sermon . . . at Northampton. 42791

Sermon . . . at Northampton, before the Hampshire Missionary Society. 38063

Sermon, . . . at Northaption, . . . fast day, September 1, 1837. (49699)

Sermon at Northampton, in 1738. 21967

Sermon . . . at Northampton . . . March 31, 1812. 36151

Sermon, . . . at Northampton, Nov. 11, 1819. 42789

Sermon at Northampton, Nov. 29, 1759. 27354

Sermon at Northborough. 846

Sermon at Northfield, Massachusetts. 8461

Sermon, . . . at Northfield, on the day of . . . thanksgiving. 45483

Sermon, . . . at Norton, July 3, 1793. 65107

Sermon . . . at Norwich, April 2, 1784. 14217

Sermon at Norwich, Vermont, February 2, 1848. 9644

Sermon at Nottingham, December 13, 1776. 65074

Sermon at ordination of Benj. Tappan. 1808

Sermon at ordination of Rev. Ebenezer Sparhawk. 8923

Sermon at ordination of Rev. Elisha Kent. 20063

Sermon . . . at ordination of Rev. Hiram Withington. (29830)

Sermon at ordination of Rev. John Mass. 30170

Sermon at ordination of Rev. Joseph Fowler. (23021)

Sermon . . . at . . . ordination of the Reverend Mr. Ephraim Ward. 30888

Sermon . . . at . . . ordination of the Reverend Mr. Joseph Woodman. (29645)

Sermon at Oxford, April 23, 1791. 22525

Sermon at Oxford, Mass., Oct. 7, 1818. 3915

Sermon, at Oxford, Mass., September 13, 1798. 30521

Sermon at Oxford, May 31st, 1761. 62580

Sermon at Oxford, N. H., May 20, 1801. 26180

Sermon at Oxford, O., in 1849. 43567

Sermon at Paule's Crosse. 37811

Sermon at Pelham, Aug. 30. 1744. 21967

[Sermon] at Pelham, N. H., Oct. 31, 1798. 2623

Sermon, . . . at Pendleton, . . . on . . . the death of Rev. Jasper Adams. 62901

Sermon at . . . Philadelphia, April, 1841. 7349

Sermon . . . at Philadelphia, April 21, 1861. 35440

Sermon at Philadelphia, Jan. 14, 1834. 20391

Sermon, . . . at Pictou. 43131

Sermon . . . at Pittsburgh. 28741

Sermon . . . at Pittsfield, (Mass.) December 22, 1820. 33789

Sermon, . . . at Pittsfield, on the day of the annual fast. 33794

Sermon, . . . at Plainfield, June 14, 1743. 42009

Sermon . . . at Plymouth . . . after the interment of Deacon Ephraim Spooner. 37366

Sermon at Plymouth Church, Milwaukee. 46889

Sermon . . . at Plymouth December 22d, 1774. 32261

Sermon, at Plymouth, July, 29th. 1724. (22007)

Sermon . . . at Plymouth, on the twenty-second of December, 1846. 32943

Sermon at Plymouth, on the twenty-second of December, 1827. 4333

Sermon at Plymouth, Sept. 21, 1800. 37366

Sermon . . . at Portland, Maine. 59354

Sermon . . . at Portland . . . September 9, 1851. (71269)

Sermon . . . at Portsmouth. 8641

Sermon . . . at Portsmouth, N. H., by Andrew P. Peabody. 59352

Sermon at Portsmouth, N. H., June 14, 1772. 43050

Sermon . . . at . . . Portsmouth, N. H. on the anniversary of the City Missionary Society. (50385)

Sermon . . . at Portsmouth, on thanksgiving day. (32647)

Sermonn. . . at Putney, June 25, 1807. 39199

Sermon . . . at Quebec, Dec. 30, 1832. 51187

Sermon . . . at Quebec, . . . January 10th, 1799. (51188)

Sermon . . . at Racine, Wisconsin. 64234

Sermon . . . at Randolph, before the Norfolk Auxiliary Education Society. 2744

Sermon . . . at Reading . . . August 13, 1851. 27850

Sermon, at Reading, Mass., before Mount Moriah and Good Samaritan Lodges. 21679

Sermon at Ripton, Oct. 27, 1773. 22387

Sermon at Rochester, Oct. 10, 1793. 22525

Sermon . . . at Rockaway . . . December 31, 1848. 37782

Sermon . . . at Rowley, . . . June 7, 1797. 58378

Sermon . . . at Roxbury, in Morris County. 56825

Sermon, . . . at Rutland, . . . 1805. (31056)

Sermon at Rutland, Mass. on a haymow. 9468

Sermon . . . at Rye, August 20, 1812. 64260

Sermon . . . at Rye, 1812. 64259

Sermon, . . . at Saco, Maine, May 16, 1852. 55209

Sermon at St. Andrew's 2 Septr., 1763. 11396

Sermon at St. John's, N. B. (5640)

Sermon . . . at St. Mary's Church, Castleton. 58378

Sermon at St. Paul's Cathedral. 8507

Sermon . . . at St. Paul's, New-York. 56409

Sermon . . . at St. Peter's Church, Charleston. 65109

Sermon . . . at Salem, . . . after the death of the Reverend, Mr. George Curwin. 3471

[Sermon] at Salem, April 20, 1803. 2425

Sermon at Salem. By E. Wilson. (8636)

Sermon at Salter's Hall. 26230

Sermon at Salter's Hall, before the Correspondent Board in London. 38891

Sermon at Salter's Hall, for the spreading of the Gospel. 35510

Sermon . . . at Sandisfield, Mass. 76496

Sermon at Sandwich, October 20, 1813. 28818

Sermon . . . at Saybrook. 35816

Sermon at Scituate, Mass. 19062

Sermon . . . at Shrewsbury, June 18, 1850. (34753)

[Sermon] at Somers, Conn., Nov., 1793. 2623

Sermon . . . at Somers, Conn., Sept. 18, 1859. 57982

Sermon . . . at South Carver, Mass. 49196

Sermon . . . at South-Hampton, December 2, 1784. 56227

Sermon at Southampton, May 28, 1758. 36837

Sermon . . . at Southborough, July 17, 1827. 58686

Sermon at Southborough, October 21, 1730. 28692

Sermon . . . at the dedication of the Church of the Unity. 31446

Sermon . . . at the dedication of the Church presented to the town of Stetson. 31218

Sermon at the dedication of the Clifton Springs Water-Cure. 13701

Sermon at the dedication of the College Chapel. 33794

Sermon . . . at the dedication of the Congregational Church in Hatfield. 30500

Sermon . . . at the dedication of the Congregational Meeting-House. 39799

Sermon at the dedication of the English Lutheran Church called Zion. 38531

Sermon . . . at the dedication of the Evangelical Congregational Meeting-House in Northborough. 33166

Sermon at the dedication of the First Baptist Meeting-House, Salem. 6233

Sermon . . . at the dedication of the First Congregational Church in Natick. 51888

Sermon . . . at the dedication of the First Unitarian Church in Marietta, Ohio. 22309

Sermon at the dedication of the First Universalist Meeting-House. 2969

Sermon . . . at the dedication of the Free-Will Baptist Meeting-House. (32569)

Sermon at the dedication of the Independent Congregational Church. 14535

Sermon . . . at the dedication of the Indian Street Congregational Church, . . . December 12, 1847. (25376)

Sermon . . . at the dedication of the Lee-Street Church, Cambridge. 51614

Sermon, at the dedication of the Meeting-House, in Foxborough. 104387

Sermon . . . at the dedication of the Meeting-House, in Spencer. 58120

Sermon . . . at the dedication of the Meeting-House of the Oliver-Street Baptist Church. 79793

Sermon, . . . at the dedication of the Meeting House of the Second Parish in Saco. 28687

Sermon at the dedication of the new building. 102579

Sermon . . . at the dedication of the new house of worship erected by the Third Presbyterian Church. 33962

Sermon . . . at the dedication of the New House of Worship . . . Second Congregational Society in Newton, Ms. 27353

Sermon . . . at the dedication of the new meeting-House erected by the Congregational Society in Wenham. 44363

Sermon, at the dedication of the new meeting house, in Dover. 56236

Sermon at the dedication of the new meeting house in Tewksbury, Mass. 14205

Sermon at the dedication of the new meeting-house in Vassalboro. 27401

Sermon . . . at the dedication of the new meeting house of the First Congregational Society in Charlestown. 17637

Sermon . . . at the dedication of the new meeting house, . . . Oxford, Mass. 54992

Sermon . . . at the dedication of the New South Meeting-House. 39187

Sermon at the dedication of the North Congregational Church. 30925

Sermon . . . at the dedication of the Orthodox Congregational Meeting House. 28278

Sermon . . . at the dedication of the Presbyterian Meeting-House in Hunter. (64216)

Sermon . . . at the dedication of the Reformed Dutch Church of Raritan. (48158)

Sermon . . . at the dedication of the Second Congregational Church in Bilton. note after 42429

Sermon . . . at the dedication of the Second . . . Congregational Church, in Hartford. 41378

Sermon . . . at the dedication of the Second Congregational Church in Worcester. 3105

Sermon . . . at the dedication of the Second Congregational Church, in Durcham, Conn. 25330

Sermon . . . at the dedication of the South Congregational Church in Natick. note after 42429

Sermon . . . at the dedication of the South Congregational Church, Pittsfield, Mass. 32943

Sermon, . . . at the dedication of the Third Congregational Church in Cambirdge, Dec. 25, 1827. 42427

Sermon . . . at the dedication of the Trinitarian Church, in Concord. 28555

Sermon at the dedication of the Twelfth Congregational Church in Boston. 58325

Sermon . . . at the dedications of the "Union Street Brick Church." 33983

Sermon . . . at the dedication of the Unitarian Church in Augusta, Geo. (27436)

Sermon . . . at the dedication of the Unitarian Church in Jersey City. 26079

Sermon . . . at the dedication of the Universalist Meeting-House at Shirley. 2969

Sermon . . . at the dedication of the vestry of the Second Congregational Parish in Cohasset. (50424)

Sermon . . . at the Dudleian lecture. 13350

Sermon . . . at the East Church in Pembroke. (3512)

Sermon at the execution of Moses Paul. 56636

Sermon . . . at the forty-eighth anniversary of the Society. 50801

Sermon . . . at the Friend Street, Chapel. [sic] 29389

Sermon . . . at . . . the funeral of A. Lee. 56043

Sermon . . . at the funeral of Adoniram Foot. (58880)

Sermon at . . . the funeral of Bethiah, wife of Capt. William Huntington. 22393

Sermon at the funeral of Caleb Webster. 73087

Sermon at the funeral of Col. C. Codrington. 28004

Sermon at the funeral of Col. Christopher Avery. (36222)

Sermon . . . at the funeral of Col. Edwards Whipple. 52315

Sermon at the funeral of Daniel Morse. 105117

Sermon . . . at the funeral of Deacon Cyrus Stowell. 38120

Sermon . . . at the funeral of Deacon Daniel Wiley. 34175

Sermon . . . at the funeral of Doct. William Cogswell. 37312

Sermon, . . . at the funeral of Gen. Jedediah Huntington. (43231)

Sermon . . . at the funeral of George Elliot. 44361

Sermon . . . at the funeral of Harry S. Richards. 59454

Sermon . . . at the funeral of Helen Hanchett. 7074

Sermon at the funeral of Henry D. Ward. 28512

Sermon at the funeral of his [i. e. Samuel Buell's] son. (8985)

Sermon . . . at the funeral of Hon. Laban Wheaton. 32627

Sermon . . . at the funeral of Hon. Nathaniel O. Kellogg. 82319

Sermon at the funeral of Hon. W. W. Ellsworth. 28104

Sermon, at the funeral of Hon. William Pennington. 64053

Sermon . . . at the funeral of Jasper Bradley. 36321

Sermon . . . at the funeral of John Lowe. 25042

Sermon . . . at the funeral of Loyal Scranton. 62780

Sermon . . . at the funeral of Martin Rockwell. 22103

Sermon . . . at the funeral of Mr. Alpha Child. (28353)

Sermon . . . at the funeral of Mr. Cyrus Babcock. 39720

Sermon, at the funeral of Mr. Jedidiah Wilbur. 63917

Sermon at the funeral of Mr. Samuel Rhoades. 58901

Sermon, . . . at the funeral of Mr. Shadrack Standish. 32627

Sermon . . . at the funeral of Mr. Silas May. (28353)

Sermon . . . at the funeral of Mr. Simeon Burge. (43066)

Sermon at the funeral of Mr. Warren Fay Stone. 55299

Sermon at the funeral of Mrs. A. Kendall. (51484)

Sermon . . . at the funeral of Mrs. Angelina Charlotte Yeatman. 64692

Sermon at the funeral of Mrs. Anna Strong. (11899)

Sermon at the funeral of Mrs. Anne Mason. 24580

Sermon at the funeral of Mrs. Bennett. 62665

Sermon . . . at the funeral of Mrs. Esther Strong. 33973

Sermon . . . at the funeral of Mrs. Joanna Strong. (32235)

Sermon . . . at the funeral of Mrs. Jerusha Woodbridge. 41756

Sermon at the funeral of Mrs. Lathrop. 62665

Sermon . . . at the funeral of Mrs. Lucy Parmelee. 58822

Sermon at the funeral of Mrs. Martha Roads. 30530

Sermon . . . at the funeral of Mrs. Ruth Hart. 71834

[Sermon] at the funeral of Oliver Wolcott. 2622

Sermon . . . at the funeral of Rev. Daniel Thomas. 17134

Sermon . . . at the funeral of Rev. David Long. 34175

Sermon . . . at the funeral of Rev. Elias Cornelius. 30925

Sermon at the funeral of Rev. George Stewart. (24520)

Sermon . . . at the funeral of Rev. Hervey Talcott. 19559

Sermon . . . at the funeral of Rev. James Burt. 43510

Sermon . . . at the funeral of Rev. James Rowland. 32263

Sermon . . . at the funeral of Rev. John E. Farwell. 43080

Sermon at the funeral of Rev. Joseph Bellamy. (4663)

Sermon . . . at the funeral of Rev. Joshua Huntington. 21528

Sermon . . . at the funeral of Rev. Lewis P. Bayard. 57308

Sermon at the funeral of Rev. Lyman Beecher. 2675

Sermon . . . at the funeral of Rev. Nathan S. Haseltine. 35878

Sermon . . . at the funeral of Rev. Orange Scott. (46866)

Sermon at the funeral of Rev. T. Gray. 26074

Sermon . . . at the funeral of Rev. Timothy Tittle. 80530

Sermon at the funeral of Rev. W. I. Putnam. 19896

Sermon . . . at the funeral of Rev. William Andrews. (64794)

Sermon at the funeral of the Hon. Col. Francis Collingwood. 31612

Sermon at the funeral of the Honble John Winthrop. (46601)

Sermon, . . . at the funeral of the Honorable Oliver Ellsworth. (73569)

Sermon . . . at the funeral of the late Mrs. Abigail Newton. 38149

Sermon . . . at the funeral of the Rev. Ammi Ruhamah Robbins. 39720

Sermon . . . at the funeral of the Rev. Araetius B. Hull. 52315

Sermon . . . at the funeral of the Rev. Benjamin R. Wisner. (23951)

Sermon at the funeral of the Rev. Daniel Crosby. (28592)

Sermon at the funeral of the Rev. David Butler. 20391

Sermon . . . at the funeral of the Rev. David Osgood. 23588

Sermon . . . at the funeral of the Rev. David Peabody, A. M. 42045

Sermon . . . at the funeral of the Rev. Jarvis Gregg. 41869

Sermon, at the funeral of the Rev. John Rodgers Coe. 72478

Sermon, . . . at the funeral of the Rev. Levi Pilsbery. (59317)

Sermon . . . at the funeral of the Rev. Moses C. Welch. 56043

Sermon, . . . at the funeral of the Rev. Timothy Fuller. (50391)

Sermon . . . at the funeral of the Right Reverend John Henry Hobart. 57308

Sermon . . . at the funeral of Thomas Greene. 32880

Sermon . . . at the funeral of William Henry Harrington. 41576

Sermon at the gathering of a church at Biddesford. 58205

Sermon at the gathering of a new church. 46391

Sermon . . . at the gathering of the second Congregational Church. 62733

Sermon . . . at the . . . General Convention of the Protestant Episcopal Church in the United States. (29991)

Sermon, . . . at the inauguration of the Rev. Archibald Alexander. (49064)

Sermon . . . at the inauguration of the Rev. Ebenezer Porter. 32588

Sermon at the inauguration of the Rev. Edward D. Griffin. 89800

Sermon at the induction of the Rev. Frederick Van Horn. 9631

Sermon . . . at the installation of A. Judson Rich. 59354

Sermon at the installation of Andrew Govan. 11853

Sermon at the installation of Andrew Rankin. (32647)

Sermon . . . at the installation of Caleb D. Bradlee. 37848

Sermon at the installation of Daniel Breck. (9490)

Sermon at the installation of Ezra Carpenter. 26785

Sermon at the installation of Humphrey C. Perley. 21737

Sermon at the installation of James Thurston. 8930

Sermon at the installation of John Brown, D. D. 18405

Sermon . . . at the installation of John Stelle. (48159)

Sermon at the installation of Nathaniel Sherman. 18268

Sermon . . . at the installation of . . . Rev. Abiel Holmer [sic]. (18419)

Sermon at the installation of Rev. Abiel Holmes. (18419)

Sermon at the installation of Rev. Andrew Bigelow. 3105

Sermon at the installation of Rev. C. Cravens. 47181

Sermon at the installation of Rev. Calvin Park. 21977

Sermon . . . at the installation of Rev. Charles. E. Grinnell. 59354

Sermon . . . at the installation of Rev. Charles Lowe. 59354

Sermon, at the installation of Rev. Dan Huntington. 42791

Sermon . . . at the installation of Rev. E. B. Willson. 29632

Sermon at the installation of Rev. Ezekiel L. Bascom. (25239)

Sermon . . . at the installation of Rev. Flaviel Griswold. 32250

Sermon, . . . at the installation of Rev. George W. Briggs. 50715

Sermon . . . at the installation of Rev. H. Alger. 22309

Sermon at the installation of Rev. John T. Sargent. (26240)

Sermon at the installation of Rev. John Todd. 18770

Sermon . . . at the installation of Rev. N. M. Gaylord. (40096)

Sermon . . . at the installation of Rev. Nathaniel S. Folsom. 59354

Sermon . . . at the installation of Rev. Samuel Hunt. 34175

Sermon, . . . at the installation of Rev. Samuel Kirkland Lothrop. 58325

Sermon at the installation of Rev. Thomas Williams. 22525

Sermon . . . at the installation of Rev. Townsend P. Abell. 81626

Sermon, . . . at the installation of . . . Rev. William Bascom. 51436

Sermon at the installation of the Morning Star-Lodge of Freemasons. (43066)

Sermon at the installation of the Rev. B. Boardman. 27884

Sermon . . . at the installation of the Rev. Caleb Alexander. 22525

Sermon . . . at the installation of the Rev. David Avery. 22525

Sermon . . . at the installation of the Rev. E. E. Hale. 33964

Sermon . . . at the installation of the Rev. Ebenezer Peck Sperry. 25875

Sermon . . . at the installation of the Rev. Eldekin Boardman. 64792

Sermon . . . at the installation of the Rev. George R. Noyes. 3622

Sermon . . . at the installation of the Rev. Henry Blatchford. 18405

Sermon . . . at the installation of the Rev. Horatio N. Brinsmade. 33794

Sermon . . . at the installation of the Rev. Hosea Ballou. 19038

Sermon at the installation of the Rev. Isaac Bridggs. 25875

Sermon . . . at the installation of the Rev. Jacob Frieze. 62626

Sermon . . . at the installation of the Rev. Jacob M. Manning. 58625

Sermon at the installation of the Rev. James Miltimore. 8930

Sermon . . . at the installation of the Rev. Joel T. Benedict. (64216)

Sermon at the installation of the Rev. John A. Stevens. 7239

Sermon, . . . at the installation of the Rev. John B. Romeyn. 48998

Sermon . . . at the installation of the Rev. Luther Willson. 3105

Sermon at the installation of the Rev. Mr. Solomon Wolcott. 60968

Sermon at the installation of the Rev. William Frothingham. (71512)

Sermon . . . at the installation of the Rev. William L. Stearns. (33100)

Sermon . . . at the installation of the Rev. William M. Cornell. (44153)

Sermon at the installation of Thomas Williams. 22525

Sermon . . . at the installment of the Rev. Grindal Rawson. 26785

Sermon . . . at the instalment of Rev. Elias Hull. 65060

Sermon . . . at the instalment of Rev. Joseph Willard. 65060

Sermon at the instalment of Samuel Buel. 21931

Sermon . . . at the instalment of the Reverend Mr. Joseph Green. 21341

Sermon . . . at the instalment of the Reverend Nathanael Whitaker. 42013

Sermon at the institution of Philander Chase as rector of Christ Church. 103715

Sermon . . . at the institution of the Rev. George Upford. (32301)

Sermon at the institution of the Rev. John Wragg Shackelford. 20391

Sermon at the interment of Deacon J. Hunt. 56043

Sermon . . . at the interment of Miss Susan Winchester. 58822

Sermon . . . at the interment of Mr. Walter Moor. 2479

Sermon . . . at the interment of Mrs. Betsey Bartlett. 38120

Sermon, . . . at the interment of Mrs. Lydia Kilburn. (25221)

Sermon, at the interment of Mrs. Phebe Foster. 90858

Sermon . . . at the interment of Mrs. Priscilla Elvira Bascom. 37737

Sermon . . . at the interment of Rev. John Lathrop. 58800

Sermon . . . at the interment of Rev. Timothy Pitkin. 60968

Sermon . . . at the interment of the Rev. Eliphalet Williams. (43066)

Sermon . . . at the interment of the Rev. Joseph Eckley. 39187

Sermon at the ordination of J. H. Fairchild. 22377

Sermon at the ordination of J. T. Sargeant. 28687

Sermon . . . at the ordination of James Thurston. 41558

Sermon at the ordination of . . . James Welman. 12210

Sermon at the ordination of Joel Bordwell. 39769

Sermon at the ordination of Joel Foster. 24233

[Sermon] at the ordination of John B. Whittlesey. 2622

Sermon at the ordination of John Boardman. 7367

Sermon . . . at the ordination of John C. Kimball. 26536

Sermon at the ordination of John C. March. 18405

Sermon at the ordination of John Dane. 27401

Sermon at the ordination of John Hancock. (30169)

[Sermon at the ordination] of John Milton Whiton. 2425

[Sermon at the ordination] of John Nelson. 2425

Sermon at the ordination of John Owen. 200

Sermon at the ordination of John Smith. 22525

[Sermon at the] ordination of John Sparhawk. 1845

Sermon at the ordination of Jonathan Dickinson. 50660

Sermon . . . at the ordination of Jonathan L. Pomeroy. 58878

Sermon, . . . at the ordination of Joseph Angier. 19862

Sermon at the ordination of Joseph Avery. 30888

Sermon at the ordination of Joseph Emerson. 22525

[Sermon] at the ordination of Joseph Russell. 2623

Sermon at the ordination of Joshua Bradley. (26541)

Sermon at the ordination of Joshua Knapp. 71737

Sermon at the ordination of Josiah Bayley. 3489

Sermon at the ordination of Josiah Cotton. 1845

Sermon at the ordination of Kiah Bailey. 22427

Sermon at the ordination of Lemuel Capen. 30521

Sermon at the ordination of Lemuel P. Bates. (50459)

[Sermon at the ordination] of Leonard Worcester. 2425

Sermon, at the ordination of . . . Linus Hall Shaw. 14535

[Sermon at the] ordination of Matthew Bridge. 1845

Sermon at the ordination of Milton Palmer Braman. 7367

Sermon . . . at the ordination of Mr. Chas. B. Ferry. 29632

Sermon, . . . at the ordination of Mr. Charles T. Torrye. 34173

Sermon . . . at the ordination of Mr. Ebenezer Thresher. 79798

Sermon . . . at the ordination of Mr. Edgar Buckingham. 26074

Sermon . . . at the ordination of Mr. Franklin P. Appleton. (29830)

Sermon . . . at the ordination of Mr. Freeman P. Howland. 32627

Sermon at the ordination of Mr. George Beckwith. (46210)

Sermon . . . at the ordination of Mr. George Wadsworth Wells. note after 42429

Sermon . . . at the ordination of Mr. H. F. Jenks. 59354

Sermon . . . at the ordination of Mr. Horatio Stebbins. 59354

Sermon . . . at the ordination of . . . Mr. James Varney. 31302

Sermon . . . at the ordination of Mr. Jonathan Calef. 31288

Sermon . . . at the ordination of Mr. Lyman Cutler. 61365

Sermon . . . at the ordination of Mr. Samuel Webster. 58900

Sermon at the ordination of Mr. Stephen Williams. 104402

Sermon . . . at the ordination of Mr. Thomas B. Fox. note after 42429

Sermon, . . . at the ordination of Mr. Thomas Barnard. 42441

Sermon . . . at the ordination of Mr. William Barry. note after 42429

Sermon at the ordination of Nathan Parker. 3105

Sermon . . . at the ordination of Noah Porter. 64292

Sermon . . . at the ordination of . . . Noah Welles. (32311)

Sermon . . . at the ordination of Oliver Hayward. 37366

[Sermon at the] ordination of Oliver Peabody. 1845

Sermon . . . at the ordination of Oliver Wetmore. 60968

Sermon at the ordination of Prof. Timothy Dwight. 30925

Sermon at the ordination of Reuben Nason. 1808

Sermon at the ordination of Reuben Parmelee. (31056)

Sermon . . . at the ordination of Rev. Amos Smith. 58800

Sermon at the ordination of Rev. C. Frost. 22224

Sermon . . . at the ordination of Rev. C. Tingley. (29848)

Sermon [at the ordination of Rev. Charles C. Shackford.] 23684, 87341

[Sermon at the ordination] of Rev. Daniel Merrill. 2921

[Sermon at the ordination] of Rev. David Leonard. 2921

Sermon at the ordination of Rev. Ebenezer Allen. 841

Sermon . . . at the ordination of Rev. Frederick D. Huntington. (66794)

Sermon . . . at the ordination of Rev. Harrison G. O. Phipps. 42714

Sermon . . . at the ordination of Rev. Heman Ball. 39199

Sermon, . . . at the ordination of . . . Rev. Hezekiah May. (50953)

Sermon . . . at the ordination of Rev. Hezekiah N. Woodruff. 60968

[Sermon at the ordination] of Rev. Hosea Beckley. 11943

Sermon at the ordination of Rev. Isaac Weston. 22224

Sermon at the ordination of Rev. James Adams. 42978

Sermon . . . at the ordination of Rev. James Augustus Kendall. 37366

SERMON

Sermon at the ordination of the Rev. James
  Boyd. 48155
Sermon . . . at the ordination of Rev. James
  Thurston. (49136)
Sermon . . . at the ordination of Rev. Joel L.
  Dickinson. (38019)
Sermon . . . at the ordination of Reverend
  John Burt Wight. 43378
Sermon at the ordination of Rev. John Gano.
  21726
Sermon . . . at the ordination of . . . Rev.
  John Parkman. 58800
Sermon, . . . at the ordination of Rev. Josel
  Wright. (59317)
Sermon at the ordination of Rev. Joseph
  Hasard. (8985)
Sermon . . . at the ordination of Rev. Josiah
  Moore. (31806)
Sermon at the ordination of Rev. Nathan
  Strong. (28224)
Sermon, . . . at the ordination of Rev. O. B.
  Frothingham. 26074
Sermon . . . at the ordination of Rev. Oliver
  M. Sears. 30500
Sermon . . . at the ordination of Rev. Oliver
  W. B. Peabody. 59384
[Sermon at the] ordination of Rev. Samuel
  Kendall. (2198)
Sermon at the ordination of Rev. Samuel
  Tobey. 24203
Sermon, . . . at the ordination of . . . Rev.
  Samuel Whittelsey. 11943
Sermon, . . . at the ordination of . . . Rev.
  Simeon Colton. (50459)
Sermon . . . at the ordination of Rev. Thomas
  Brattle Gannett. 32588
Sermon at the ordination of Rev. Thomas
  Lancaster. (11861)
Sermon at the ordination of Rev. W. B.
  Sprague. 24763
Sermon at the ordination of Rev. William
  Bates. 3941
Sermon . . . at the ordination of Rev. William
  L. Gaylord. 37976
Sermon at the ordination of Rev. Wm. Muzzy.
  (13317)
Sermon . . . at the ordination of Rev. William
  W. Hall. (29848)
Sermon at the ordination of Samuel Goodrich.
  · 27884
Sermon at the ordination of Samuel Kendall.
  2200
Sermon at the ordination of Samuel May, Jr.
  28687
Sermon at the ordination of Shearjasbub Town-
  send. 21832
Sermon at the ordination of Stanley Griswold.
  (43066)
Sermon . . . at the ordination of Stephen
  Barker. 4575
Sermon . . . at the ordination of Sylvester
  Burt. 39199
Sermon . . . at the ordination of ten candidates.
  32933
Sermon . . . at the ordination of the Rev.
  Abiel Abbot. (25870)
Sermon . . . at the ordination of the Rev.
  Abijah Cook. 58663
Sermon . . . at the ordination of the Rev.
  Allen Pratt. 33238
Sermon, . . . at the ordination of the Rev.
  Ariel Parish. 58606
Sermon, . . . at the ordination of the Rev.
  Avery Williams. 37347
Sermon . . . at the ordination of the Rev.
  Benjamin Kent. 25440

Sermon . . . at the ordination of the Rev.
  Benj. R. Woodbridge. 33239
Sermon at the ordination of the Rev. Beriah
  Green. (33155)
Sermon . . . at the ordination of the Rev.
  Caleb Hamilton Shearman. 30512
Sermon, at the ordination of the Rev. Charles
  C. Sewall. 38776
Sermon . . . at the ordination of the Rev.
  Charles Lowell. 64245
Sermon at the ordination of the Rev. Charles
  Moulson Browne. 11949
Sermon at the ordination of the Reverend
  Converse Francis. 57778
Sermon at the ordination of the Rev. Cornelius
  Adams. 39535
Sermon . . . at the ordination of the Rev.
  Daniel Emerson. 32317
Sermon . . . at the ordination of the Reverend
  Daniel Stone. 28405
[Sermon] at the ordination of the Rev. David
  Crosby. 21979
Sermon . . . at the ordination of the Rev.
  David Holman. 32570
Sermon . . . at the ordination of the Rev.
  David Thurston. 58609
Sermon at the ordination of the Rev. Ebenezer
  Fitch. 36864
Sermon . . . at the ordination of the Rev.
  Ebenezer Hill. (59317)
Sermon . . . at the ordination of the Rev.
  Ephraim Abbot. 59444
Sermon, . . . at the ordination of the Rev.
  Henry Edes. 22169
Sermon, at the ordination of the Rev. Henry
  Lord. 42791
Sermon at the ordination of the Rev. Holland
  Weeks. 36864
Sermon . . . at the ordination of the Rev.
  Hosea Hildreth. 32588
Sermon, . . . at the ordination of the Rev.
  Hugh Wallis. 27401
Sermon . . . at the ordination of the Rev.
  James Beach. 32812
Sermon . . . at the ordination of the Rev.
  James D. Farnsworth. 64796
Sermon . . . at the ordination of the Rev.
  James Flint. 24771
Sermon . . . at the ordination of the Reverend
  James Kendall. (25870)
Sermon . . . at the ordination of the Rev.
  Jared Sparks. 11919, 93205
[Sermon] at the ordination of the Rev. Jeremiah
  Chaplin. 2921
Sermon at the ordination of the Rev. Jeremiah
  Noyes. (49136)
Sermon . . . at the ordination of the Rev.
  Jesse Appleton. 43050
Sermon . . . at the ordination of the Rev.
  Jesse Fisher. 39199
Sermon at the ordination of the Rev. Job Strong.
  21967
Sermon . . . at the ordination of the Rev.
  John Bartlett. 32588
Sermon, at the ordination of the Rev. John
  Codman. 11919
Sermon . . . at the ordination of the Rev.
  John Gorham Palfrey. 64245
Sermon at the ordination of the Rev. John
  Kelly. 31288
Sermon at the ordination of the Rev. John
  Willard. 37978
Sermon . . . at the ordination of the Reverend
  Jonathan Strong. 36864
Sermon . . . at the ordination of the Rev.
  Jonathan Whitaker. 32588

Sermon . . . at the ordination of the Rev.
Joseph Brown. (59317)
Sermon . . . at the ordination of the Reverend
Joseph Perry. (64314)
Sermon . . . at the ordination of the Rev.
Josiah B. Andrews. 24763
Sermon . . . at the ordination of the Reverend
Joshua Bates. 24771
Sermon . . . at the ordination of the Reverend
Josiah Bridge. (13431)
Sermon . . . at the ordination of the Rev.
Levi Hart. 42013
Sermon . . . at the ordination of the Rev.
Levi Hartshorn. 18405
Sermon . . . at the ordination of the Rev.
Lyman Colman. 30925
Sermon . . . at the ordination of the Rev.
Mathew Waldo. 58609
Sermon at the ordination of the Rev. Mr.
Aaron Brown. 9803
Sermon at the ordination of the Rev. Mr.
Benjamin Bradstreet. 97418
Sermon . . . at the ordination of the Rev.
Mr. Benj. Green. 18108
Sermon . . . at the ordination of the Rev'd.
Mr. Bunker Gay. 26785
Sermon . . . at the ordination of the Reverend
Mr. Cotton Brown. 16349
Sermon . . . at the ordination of the Rev.
Mr. Daniel Grosvenor. 28947
Sermon, . . . at the ordination of the Reverend
Mr. Daniel Oliver. (25870)
Sermon, at the ordination of the Reverend
Mr. Ebenezer Hubbard. 92051
Sermon, . . . at the ordination of the Reverend
Mr. Eleazer May. 41749
Sermon at the ordination of the Reverend
Mr. Elijah Brown. 18105
Sermon, . . . at the ordination of the Reverend
Mr. Enos Hitchcock. 32261
Sermon . . . at the ordination of the Reverend
Mr. Gideon Richardson. 42087
Sermon . . . at the ordination of the Rev.
Mr. Henry True. 3456
Sermon . . . at the ordination of the Reverend
Mr. Henry Wight. 65106
Sermon . . . at the ordination of the Rev.
Mr. Isaac Bailey. 28945
Sermon . . . at the ordination of the Reverend
Mr. Isaac Story. 59609
Sermon . . . at the ordination of the Rev'd
Mr. Jacob Burnap. 30898
Sermon at the ordination of the Rev. Mr.
John Page Hawke. 4049
Sermon . . . at the ordination of the Reverend
Mr. John Payson. 59315
Sermon . . . at the ordination of the Reverend
Mr. Jonathan Dorby. 26785
Sermon . . . at the ordination of the Reverend
Mr. Jonathan Eames. 58649
Sermon at the ordination of the Rev. Mr.
Jonathan Leavitt. 39557
Sermon at the ordination of the Reverend Mr.
Joseph Sumner. 66753
Sermon . . . at the ordination of the Rev.
Mr. Moses Everett. 30888
Sermon . . . at the ordination of the Reverend
Mr. Samuel McClintock. 38875
Sermon at the ordination of the Reverend
Mr. Samuel Williams. 18107
Sermon . . . at the ordination of the Rev.
Mr. Seth Payson. 59315
Sermon . . . at the ordination of the Reverend
Mr. Thaddeus Maccarty. (28383)
Sermon . . . at the ordination of the Reverend
Mr. Walter Wilmot. 59609

Sermon . . . at the ordination of the Rev.
Moses G. Thomas. 3622
Sermon, . . . at the ordination of the Rev.
Nathan Holman. 49100
Sermon . . . at the ordination of the Reverend
Nathanael Robbins. 16347
Sermon . . . at the ordination of the Reverend
Nathaniel Langdon Frothingham. 43379
Sermon, . . . at the ordination of the Rev.
Nathaniel Thayer. 57778
Sermon . . . at the ordination of the Rev.
Nathaniel Whitman. 24779
Sermon . . . at the ordination of the Rev.
Nicholas Bowes Whitney. 103777
Sermon . . . at the ordination of the Rev.
Nymphas Hatch. 41250
Sermon at the ordination of the Rev. Oliver
Ayer. 56043
Sermon, . . . at the ordination of the Rev.
Oliver C. Everett. 62772
Sermon . . . at the ordination of the Reverend
Oliver Everett. 23284
Sermon . . . at the ordination of the Rev.
Robinson Smiley. 22564
Sermon . . . at the ordination of the Rev.
Royal A. Avery. 30799
Sermon . . . at the ordination of the Rev.
Samuel Gilman. 97399
Sermon . . . at the ordination of the Rev.
Samuel Osgood. 30521
Sermon . . . at the ordination of the Rev.
Samuel Stearns. 25440
Sermon . . . at the ordination of the Rev.
Sewall Harding. 34175
Sermon . . . at the ordination of the Reverend
Stephen Farrar. (39373)
Sermon . . . at the ordination of the Reverend
Thomas Green. 26337
Sermon, . . . at the ordination of the Rev.
Thomas Mason. (65109)
Sermon, at the ordination of the Rev. Thomas
Robbins. 92962
Sermon . . . at the ordination of the Rev. W.
B. Peabody. 59384
Sermon . . . at the ordination of the Rev.
Warren Benton. 28687
Sermon . . . at the ordination of the Rev.
William Gregg. (49136)
Sermon . . . at the ordination of the Reverend
William L. Strong. 17667
Sermon . . . at the ordination of the Rev.
William Parsons Lunt. 28687
Sermon at the ordination of Thomas Allen.
32819
Sermon at the ordination of Thomas Beveridge.
27269
Sermon at the ordination of Thomas Clap.
200
[Sermon] at the ordination of Thomas Snell.
2623
[Sermon] at the ordination of Timothy Mather
Cooly. 2623
[Sermon] at the ordination of Vinsor Gould.
2623
[Sermon at the ordination] of Warren Fay.
2425
Sermon . . . at the ordination of William
Bentley. 39187
Sermon at the ordination of William Brown.
(21975)
Sermon . . . at the ordination of William F.
Miller. 60968
Sermon at the ordination of William Gafer.
200
Sermon . . . at the ordination of . . . William
Jenison. 13350

[Sermon] at the ordination of Zephaniah S.
Moore. 2623
Sermon at the ordination of Zolva Whitmore.
21977, 22525
Sermon . . . at the public fast, in West-
Springfield. 39199
Sermon at the public lecture in Boston, July
25, 1728. 65587
Sermon at the public lecture in Boston. July
xxvii, 1732. 65597
Sermon . . . at the public lecture in Boston
. . . Sept. 16, 1742. 58895
Sermon at the public lecture, March 1, 1738-
39. 16640
Sermon at the publick lecture in Boston Jan.
viii. 1729, 30. 65611
Sermon . . . at the re-opening and dedication
of the French Protestant Church. 33244
Sermon . . . at the re-opening of St. Andrew's
Church. 49123
Sermon . . . at the re-opening of the First
Baptist Church. 61398
Sermon at the re-opening of the House of
Worship of the Congregational Society
in Quincy. 13340
Sermon . . . at the request of the Ancient
and Honourable Artillery Company.
57778
Sermon . . . at the South Church in Boston.
32955
Sermon at the South Church in Boston, Nov.
27, 1846. (65610)
Sermon at the South Church in Boston, Thurs-
day, Aug. 24. 1749. 65606
Sermon, . . . at the South Precinct in Brain-
tree. 64274
Sermon . . . at the State Prison, in Massa-
chusetts. note after 42429
Sermon . . . at the Thursday-lecture, in
Boston, N. E. (21246)
Sermon at the Thursday lecture in Boston,
October 17th. 1734. 102221
Sermon at the Tuesday-evening lecture in . . .
Boston. 43293
Sermon at Thompson, Con. Oct. 17, 1742.
9803
Sermon . . . at Townsend, March 3, 1808.
31813
Sermon . . . at Trinity Church, in Boston.
26624
Sermon . . . at Trinity Church, March 25,
1810. 26624
Sermon at Troy, on the death of General
Zachary Taylor. 29893
Sermon at Tyringham, July 10, 1831. 20748
Sermon . . . at Unity. (43252)
Sermon, . . . at Utica, . . . December 10th,
1835. 44232
Sermon at Ware Factory Village. (22120)
Sermon . . . at . . . Watertown. 13350
Sermon at Weathersfield, July 6, at a public
thanksgiving. 41749
Sermon . . . at West Bloomfield, N. J. 65483
Sermon . . . at Westerly, R. I. 58632
Sermon . . . at Westfield, January 1, 1800.
39199
Sermon . . . at Westfield November 8th 1817.
38063
Sermon at Westhampton, in time of sickness.
(28126), 55388, 104528
Sermon . . . at Wethersfield, December 13th,
1782. 44743
Sermon . . . at Weymouth, August 19, 1719.
58205
Sermon . . . at . . . Weymouth, October 29,
1814. 39187

Sermon at Weymouth . . . on the twenty-fifth
anniversary. 22469
[Sermon] at Wilbraham, Mass., May 2, oc-
casioned by six young persons being
drowned. 2623
Sermon at Williamsburg, May v. 1777. 31345
Sermon at Williamsburgh, N. Y. 30806
Sermon . . . at Williamsburgh, Nov. 30, 1828.
(42026)
Sermon at Williamstown, Mass. Feb. 20, 1830.
10695
[Sermon] at Wilmington, Mass., Oct. 29, 1795.
2623
Sermon . . . at Windham, . . . at the ordination
of . . . Reverend Mr. Peter Thacher.
38875
Sermon at Windsor, Dec. 14, 1720. 44752
Sermon . . . at Windsor . . . July 4, 1819.
40106
Sermon at Woodstock, Vt. Feb. 8, 1818. 11960
Sermon at Wolcot Sept. 21, 1814. 4344
Sermon . . . at Worcester, August 10, 1731.
(65070)
Sermon at Worcester, Jan. 1817. 3105
Sermon [at Worcester] . . . July 9th, 1826.
3102
Sermon at Worcester, July 2, 1778. 42995
Sermon at Worcester, Mass. Oct. 15, 1823.
4331
Sermon . . . at Worcester, Mass., October 9,
1816. (27893)
Sermon [at Worcester], . . . November 22,
1818. 3105
Sermon . . . at Worcester, . . . November 23d,
1775. 42995
Sermon at Worcester, Oct. 15, 1823. 4344,
101057
Sermon . . . at Worcester, October the
twentieth, 1768. 42995
Sermon . . . at Worcester, October 25th, 1770.
42995
Sermon at Worcester on the annual fast. 2425
Sermon . . . at Worthington, October 20th,
1799. 63928
Sermon . . . [at] Yale-College. (49032)
Sermon . . . at Yarmouth, Jan. 1, 1795. 47449
Sermon, . . . at Yarmouth, November 13, 1796.
47449
Sermon . . . at York, Me. 48155
Sermon . . . at York, March 16, 1810. 31288
Sermon . . . Athens, on the Sunday following
the interment. (65072)
Sermon, . . . August 18, 1850. 32937
[Sermon] . . . August 15, 1855. 32937
[Sermon] . . . August 15, 1852. 32937
[Sermon] . . . August 1, 1858. 32937
[Sermon] . . . August 1, 1860. 32937
[Sermon] . . . August 4, 1857. 32937
Sermon . . . August 14, 1798. (24539)
[Sermon] . . . August 2, 1863. 32937
Sermon August 2. 1715. (14525)
[Sermon] . . . August 17, 1851. 32937
[Sermon] . . . August 3, 1856. 32937
Sermon August 20, 1765. 10684
Sermon . . . August 21, 1842. 43138
Sermon . . . August 21, 1825. 26289
Sermon . . . August 26th, 1815. (64216)
Sermon . . . Augusta, Geo. 9091
Sermon . . . Augusta, Me. 36842
Sermon, . . . Baltimore, October 31, 1826.
(49064)
Sermon . . . Baltimore, on thanksgiving day,
November 28, 1861. 43340
Sermon . . . Baptist Church, Thanksgiving . . .
November 24, 1864. 31059

Sermon . . . Bath, (Maine,) July 4, 1822.
31210
Sermon . . . before . . . Artillery Company.
26624
Sermon . . . before Brig. Gen. Hoke's Brigade.
58592
Sermon . . . before C. Strong, Esq., Governor.
2918
Sermon . . . before . . . Caleb Strong, Esq.,
Governor. 37345
Sermon . . . before . . . Edward Everett,
Governor. 32942
Sermon before . . . Free Masons in Lyme.
33129
Sermon, . . . before His Excellency . . . at
the annual election. 32245
Sermon . . . before His Excellency John
Brooks. 36035
Sermon before His Excellency John Hancock.
361
Sermon, before His Excellency, the Honourable
Council, and Representatives. 18470,
(19157), 104088
Sermon before Isaac Tichenor. 38736
Sermon . . . before . . . John Brooks, Esq.
(33948)
Sermon . . . before . . . May 28th. 1746.
3473
Sermon . . . before Mount Moriah Lodge.
65060
Sermon . . . before . . . Parliament. 61196
Sermon . . . before the African Society.
26624
Sermon, before the Albany Moral Society.
12534
Sermon before the American Board of
Commissioners for Foreign Missions,
at . . . Salem, Mass. October 3, 1871.
64471
Sermon before the American Board of Com-
missioners for Foreign Missions, at
their meeting in Brooklyn, N. Y. 90908
Sermon before the American Board of Com-
missioners for Foreign Missions, at
. . . Worcester, Mass. 15183
Sermon, before the American Board of Com-
missioners for Foreign Missions . . .
October 2, 1860. 24500
Sermon before the American Church Union.
90526
Sermon . . . before the American Education
Society of Norfolk County. 14224
Sermon . . . before the American Sunday
School Union, May 24, 1863. (72060)
Sermon before the American Sunday-School
Union, Philadelphia. 17404
Sermon . . . before the Ancient and Honorable
Artillery Company, in Boston, June 1,
1795. 38005
Sermon . . . before the Ancient and Honourable
Artillery Company, in Boston, June 7,
1819. 28412
Sermon, . . . before the Ancient & Honourable
Artillery Company, in Boston, June 6,
1803. (50953)
Sermon, . . . before the Ancient and Honourable
Artillery Company, . . . June 4, 1810.
42422
Sermon before the Ancient and Honourable
Artillery Company . . . June 4, 1820.
14137
Sermon before the Ancient and Honorable
Artillery Co., on its CCXXVII anniver-
sary, June 5, 1865. 67784

Sermon before the Ancient and Honorable
Artillery Company on the CCXXI anniversary, June 6, 1859. 31444
Sermon . . . before the annual convention of
ministers of the Massachusetts-Bay.
3456
Sermon . . . before the annual convention of
the Congregational ministers of Massa-
chusetts, in Boston. 28818
Sermon . . . before the annual convention of
the Congregational ministers of Massa-
chusetts . . . May 29, 1845. 32943
Sermon before the annual convention of the
Diocese of Massachusetts, in . . . Boston.
20391
Sermon before the annual convention of the
Protestant Episcopal Church, at Waterbury,
Connecticut. 14238
Sermon before the annual convnetion of the
Protestant Episcopal Church in Massa-
chusetts, May 28, 1799. 30530
Sermon, . . . before the . . . Artillery Com-
pany, on their CCXIX. anniversary.
47253
Sermon before the Association at Philadelphia.
30642
Sermon before the Association of Litchfield
County, Goshen. 3713
Sermon, . . . before the Auxiliary Education
Society of Norfolk County. 59379
Sermon . . . before the Auxiliary Education
Society of Norfolk County at their annual
meeting in Stoughton. 60960
Sermon, . . . before the Auxiliary Education
Society of Norfolk County, at their . . .
Meeting in Wrentham. 17327
Sermon before the Auxiliary Education Society
of Norfolk County, delivered in Medway.
14224
Sermon . . . before the Axuiliary Foreign
Missionary Society, of Farmington and
Vicinity. 56804
Sermon before the Berkshire and Columbian
Missionary Society, Canaan. 12534
Sermon, . . . before the Bible and Common
Prayer Book Society. (50329)
Sermon . . . before the Bible Society of Salem
and Vicinity. 3493
Sermon before the Bishop Seabury Association
of Brown University. 78590
Sermon before the Bishops, Clergy, and Laity.
43324
Sermon, before the Bishops, Clergy and Laity,
constituting the Board of Missions.
92073
Sermon . . . before the Boston Society for the
Prevention of Pauperism. 29632
Sermon . . . before the Church Union of . . .
Massachusetts. 33979
Sermon before the Churchmen's Missionary
Association for Seamen. 64617
Sermon . . . before the Classis of New
Brunswick. (48159)
Sermon before the Clergy and Laity of the
Eastern Shore of Maryland. 45448
Sermon . . . before the Columbian Lodge, at
Nottingham, N. H. (56819)
Sermon before the . . . Commissioners of
Common Schools, Salem, N. Y. 66228
Sermon . . . before the Congregational
Charitable Society of Maine. 63964
Sermon . . . before the . . . congregations of
Jamaica Plain. (41249)
Sermon . . . before the . . . Congress of the
colony of the Massachusetts-Bay. 38872

Sermon . . . before the Conn. Baptist Education Society. 51439

Sermon before the "Connecticut Society for Promoting Good Morals." 11943

Sermon, before the Convention at Middletown, August 3d. 1795. (15654), 39529, 78555

Sermon before the Convention, Oct. 2, 1844. 35311

Sermon, . . . before the Convention of Congregational Ministers in Boston, . . . May 28, 1812. (50953)

Sermon . . . before the Convention of Congregational Ministers of Massachusetts, in . . . Boston, May 26, 1831. 14137

Sermon . . . before the Convention of Congregational Ministers of Massachusetts, May 26, 1859. 61365

Sermon . . . before the Convention of Congregational Ministers of Massachusetts . . . XXVII May MDCCCXIX. 32588

Sermon . . . before the Convention of the Clergy of Massachusetts, in Boston, May 30, 1799. 25042

Sermon . . . before the Convention of the Clergy of Massachusetts, May 29, 1817. 34116

Sermon, . . . before the Convention of the Congregational Ministers of Massachusetts, . . . May 30, 1821. 58609

Sermon . . . before the Convention of the Congregational Ministers of Massachusetts, on . . . May 27, 1858. 22309

Sermon, before the Convention of the Diocese of New Jersey. 20391

Sermon, before the Convention of the Diocese of New Jersey, in . . . Newark. 55509

Sermon . . . before the Convention of the . . . Episcopal Church in the state of Connecticut, . . . Stratford. 8233

Sermon before the Convention of the Protestant Episcopal Church, in the state of New York. 50448

Sermon before the Convocation of the clergy, at Morristown. 20391

Sermon . . . before the Convocation of the Protestant Episcopal Church, in Virginia. 35789

Sermon before the Corporation for the Relief of Widows and Children of Clergymen. 2358

Sermon . . . before the . . . Council and . . . Legislature of . . . New Hampshire, June 8, . . . being the anniversary sermon. 33306

Sermon . . . before the . . . Council and . . . Senate. 43050

Sermon before the Cumberland Society for the Suppression of Public Vices. 1808

Sermon, . . . before the . . . Diocese of New Jersey. 56835

Sermon before the Directors of the Protestant Episcopal Society for the Promotion of Evangelical Knowledge. 89022

Sermon, before the Domestic and Foreign Missionary Society. 43324

Sermon . . . before the Eastern Association of Farifield County. 16344

Sermon before the Ecclesiatical Convention of New Hampshire. 8930

Sermon . . . before the . . . Education Society of Norfolk County. 46891

Sermon before the 18th, or Royal Regiment of Ireland. 84673

Sermon before the Episcopal clergy of New England. 8641

Sermon before the execution of a young Negro Servant. (9717)

Sermon before the Female Charitable Society, Newark. (43681)

Sermon . . . before the Female Charitable Society of Newburyport. 58609

Sermon before the Fifth Regiment of New York State Infantry. 49681

Sermon before the first annual Convention of the Church Union. 2567

Sermon . . . before the First Congregational Society, in New-Bedford. 50714

Sermon, . . . before the Foreign Missionary Society of New York and Brooklyn. (45438)

Sermon . . . before the General Assembly . . . 1855. (81648)

Sermon . . . before the General Assembly of . . . Connecticut . . . anniversary election, May 8. 1760. 24437

Sermon . . . before the . . . General Assembly of . . . Connecticut, at Hartford, . . . May 12th, 1725. 46207

Sermon before . . . the General Assembly of Connecticut, at Hartford, on the day of election, May 10th, 1787. 27883

Sermon . . . before the General Assembly of . . . Connecticut, at Hartford; on . . . their anniversary election, May 12th, 1774. (41753)

Sermon before the General Assembly of Connecticut, Hartford, May 9, 1754. 41749

Sermon . . . before the General Assembly of . . . Connecticut . . . on the . . . anniversary election, May 14th, 1747. 33836

Sermon . . . before the General Assembly of . . . Connecticut, on the day of their election, . . . May 13. 1736. 44751

Sermon . . . before the General Assembly of the colony of Connecticut, at Hartford, May 9. 1717. 18187

Sermon . . . before the General Assembly, of the colony of Connecticut, at Hartford, May 12th, 1720. 33112

Sermon . . . before the General Assembly of the colony of Connecticut at Hartford on the day of the anniversary election, May 8, 1766. 39770

Sermon . . . before the General Assembly of the Presbyterian Church in the United States of America. 38227

Sermon . . . before the General Assembly of the Presbyterian Church . . . May 19, 1806. 56036

Sermon . . . before the General Assembly of . . . Vermont: October 9, 1857. (43394)

Sermon before the General Association of Connecticut, at New Haven, June 18, 1827. 33794

Sermon . . . before the General Association of Connecticut, at Saybrook. 18969

Sermon . . . before the General Board of Missions. 67784

Sermon before the General Convention . . . in . . . New York. 43324

Sermon before the General Convention, May 23, 1814. 17581

Sermon . . . before the General Convention of the Baptist Denomination. 79790

Sermon before the General Convention of the Protestant Episcopal Church . . . in . . . New York. 32933

Sermon, . . . before the General Convention of the Protestant Episcopal Church in . . . New-York, . . . September 12, 1804. (50329)

Sermon before the Merrimac Humane Society, at Newburyport. (3887)

Sermon before the Merrimac Humane Society, 4th Sept. 1804. (18419)

Sermon before the Ministerial Conference of the Monroe Baptist Association. 12991

Sermon . . . before the ministers of the Central Association. 42791

Sermon . . . before the ministers of the province of the Massachusetts-Bay. 58798

Sermon before the Missionary Society of the Synod of South Carolina and Georgia. 31415

Sermon before the New England Society of New York. 30517

Sermon before the New-York Auxiliary to the Protestant Episcopal Society for the Promotion of Evangelical Knowledge. 92074

Sermon . . . before the New-York Bible Society. (36153)

Sermon, . . . before the New York Missionary Society, . . . April 6th, 1802. 49059

Sermon before the New York Missionary Society, April 24, 1799. 43474

Sermon, . . . before the New-York Missionary Society, . . . November 7, 1797. 45463

Sermon, . . . before the Northern Missionary Society. 25116

Sermon . . . before the officers and students of Waterville College. 55073

Sermon . . . before the officers of the Forty-Third Regiment. 44350

Sermon before the Oliver Street Baptist Church. 79801

Sermon, . . . before the Oneida and Wyoming Conferences. 59472

Sermon . . . before the Orange County Conference. (43394)

Sermon before the Parliament, Oct. 8, 1656. (73545)

Sermon . . . before the Pastoral Association of Massachusetts. 52315

Sermon, . . . before the Penitent Females Refuge Society. 21979

Sermon before the Phi Beta Kappa at Dartmouth College. (9490)

Sermon . . . before the Plymouth Association of Ministers. 55333

Sermon, before the Presbyterian Education Society, in New York. 24497

Sermon . . . before the Presbytery of Detroit, October 13, 1842. (21137)

Sermon . . . before the Presbytery of St. Louis, . . . 1842. 64692

Sermon, . . . before the Protestant Episcopal Brotherhood of Baltimore. 67784

Sermon . . . before the Protestant Episcopal Church in . . . Virginia. note after 43706

Sermon . . . before the Right Worshipful Lodge of Free and Accepted Masons. 8641

Sermon before the sacrament. (14525)

Sermon . . . before the Schoharie Bible Society. 77611

Sermon . . . before the 70th Convention of the Diocese of New Hampshire. 58735

Sermon, . . . before the Society for Propagating the Gospel among the Indians and Others in North America. 50951

Sermon before the Society for Propagation of the Gospel in Foreign Parts, Feb. 15, 1788. 16818

Sermon before the Society for Propagation of the Gospel in Foreign Parts, Feb. 20, 1756. 16817

Sermon before the Society for Propagation of the Gospel in Foreign Parts, Feb. 23, 1759. 22289

Sermon before the Society for Propagation of the Gospel in Foreign Parts, on the 21st of February, 1728. 22045

Sermon before the Society for Propagation of the Gospel in Foreign Parts, 1763. 17482

Sermon before the Society for the Prevention of Pauperism. 59364

Sermon before the Society for the Promotion of the Gospel in Foreign Parts. 16694

Sermon before the Society for the Propagation of the Gospel, by the Lord Bishop of Litchfield and Coventy [sic]. 33135

Sermon before the Society for the Propagation of the Gospel . . . by the Lord Bishop of Oxford. 42542

Sermon before the Society for the Propagation of the Gospel. [By William Cleaver, Bishop of Chester.] 13614

Sermon . . . before the . . . Society for the Propagation of the Gospel in Foreign Parts . . . by Right Reverend Mathew, Lord Bishop of Bangor. 34109

Sermon before the Society for the Propagation of the Gospel in Foreign Parts. By Thomas Hayley. 31034

Sermon . . . before the . . . Society for the Propagation of the Gospel in Foreign Parts; . . . February 18, 1742-43. 46997

Sermon before the Society for the Propagation of the Gospel . . . February 19, 1768. (28540)

Sermon before the Society for the Propagation of the Gospel in Foreign Parts, February, 1748. 26992

Sermon . . . before the . . . Society for the Propagation of the Gospel in Foreign Parts . . . February 17, 1734-4. (27352)

Sermon . . . before the . . . Society for the Propagation of the Gospel in Foreign Parts, . . . February 17, 1769. (55084)

Sermon . . . before the . . . Society for the Propagation of the Gospel in Foreign Parts . . . February 16 1781. 33991

Sermon . . . before the . . . Society for the Propagation of the Gospel in Foreign Parts; . . . February 16, 1770. (37596)

Sermon . . . before the . . . Society for the Propagation of the Gospel in Foreign Parts, . . . February 20, 1761. 54938

Sermon . . . before the Society for the Propagation of the Gospel in Foreign Parts, Feb. 20, 1735. 42814

Sermon . . . before the Society for the Propagation of the Gospel in Foreign Parts; . . . February 21, 1752. 57740

Sermon . . . before the . . . Society for the Propagation of the Gospel in Foreign Parts, . . . February 21, 1723. 28614

Sermon . . . before the . . . Society for the Propagation of the Gospel in Foreign Parts; . . . 15th of February, 1733. 43700

Sermon . . . before the Society for the Propagation of the Gospel in Foreign Parts, . . . on . . . the 15th of February, $17\frac{11}{12}$. 37448

Sermon before the Society for the Propagation of the Gospel in Foreign Parts. 1754. 20976

2570

Sermon before the Society for the Propagation
of the Gospel in Foreign Parts, 1757.
37154
Sermon before the Society for the Propagation
of the Gospel in Foreign Parts, 1747.
41422
Sermon before the Society for the Propagation
of the Gospel in Foreign Parts, 1763.
22046
Sermon [before the Society for the Propagation
of the Gospel in Foreign Parts, 1712.]
85939
Sermon . . . before . . . the Society for the
Propagation of the Gospel in Foreign
Parts, . . . 1727. (70441)
Sermon before the Society for the Relief of
the Widows and Orphans of Deceased
Clergymen of the Protestant Episcopal
Church. 33964
Sermon . . . before the Society in Scotland
for Propagating Christian Knowledge
. . . in . . . Edinburgh. (39814)
Sermon . . . before the Society in Scotland
for Propagating Christian Knowledge,
. . . January 1, 1759. (44458)
Sermon . . . before the Society in Scotland
for Propagating Christian Knowledge
. . . June 5, 1773. 31409
Sermon before the Society in Scotland for
Propagating Christian Knowledge, 1799.
4717
Sermon before the Society of Bath and
Vicinity for the Suppression of Public
Vices. 1808
Sermon, . . . before the Society of United
Christian Friends. 49681
Sermon . . . before the Synod of New Jersey,
for the benefit of the African School.
(49064)
Sermon before the Synod of New Jersey,
Oct. 21, 1862. 43271
Sermon . . . before the Synod of New York
and New Jersey. 82340
Sermon . . . before the Synod of New-York,
at . . . Newburgh. (45438)
Sermon before the Synod of New York, New-
Ark, N. J. 21967
Sermon before the Third Congregation in
Greenfield. 2757
Sermon . . . before the Vermont Colonization
Society, at Montpelier, October 18, 1866.
(33155)
Sermon before the Vermont Colonization
Society, at Montpelier, October 17, 1833.
96419
Sermon . . . before the Vermont Domestic
Missionary Society. 48008
Sermon . . . before the Washington Bible
Society, Granville. 66228
Sermon . . . before Thomas Gage, Esq.
32260
Sermon . . . Boonville, Missouri, January 4,
1861. 58259
Sermon . . . Boston, . . . April 11, 1858.
note after (58767)
Sermon . . . Boston . . . April 2, 1799.
(2917)
Sermon . . . Boston, . . . April 23, 1865.
19896
Sermon, . . . Boston, before the Society of
. . . Free and Accepted Masons. 22169
Sermon . . . Boston, December 1, 1831. 32933
Sermon, . . . Boston . . . February 18, 1843.
21663
Sermon, . . . Boston, . . . July 4, 1858.
note after (58767)

Sermon . . . Boston . . . June 1, 1856. 37976
Sermon . . . Boston, May 31, 1826. 14137
Sermon . . . Boston, November 21. 1734.
30167
Sermon . . . Bristol, Rhode Island, on . . .
Feb. 28, 1855. 21663
Sermon, . . . Brooklyn, L. I. May 14, 1843.
(23813)
Sermon, . . . Burlington. 20391
Sermon by A. P. Putnam. 66758
Sermon . . . by a presbyter of New Jersey.
80364
Sermon . . . . [By A. T. Hopkins.] (32907)
Sermon by Abraham Hellenbrock. 94697
Sermon [by Albert W. Duy.] (13367)
Sermon . . . [by Andrew Croswell.] 17675
Sermon by . . . Arthur Swazey. 8384
Sermon . . . [by B. W. Morris.] 50801
Sermon, by Benjamin T. Onderdonk. 57308
Sermon by Bishop Hobart. (54261)
Sermon by C. M. Cordley. 16760
Sermon. By Citoyen de Novion. 93493
Sermon, by Conrad Speece. 89093
Sermon [by Daniel Haskell.] 99227
Sermon [by Dr. Wyatt.] 105646
Sermon by E. D. Griffin. 28818, 92835
Sermon, . . . [by Ebenezer Porter.] (64233)
Sermon . . . . [By Edward Cleveland.] 13656
Sermon . . . . [By Edward D. Griffin.] 28818
Sermon by Elizabeth Robson. 103059
Sermon. [By F. C. Ewer.] 23317
Sermon . . . [by Festus Foster.] (25221)
Sermon . . . [by Frederick G. Clark.] 13280
Sermon, by G. W. Eaton. 21721
Sermon by George Duffield. 21138
Sermon . . . [by George Jehosaphat Mountain.]
51187
Sermon. By George Putnam. (66787)
Sermon. [By George Whitefield.] 103509,
103586, 103612
Sermon [by H. Carner.] (20062)
Sermon. [By Horace James.] 35702
Sermon. [By Horatio Potter.] (64646)
Sermon by Hugh Peters. 61196
Sermon. [By Hugh Stowell.] 92628
Sermon [by John Beach.] (20062)
Sermon by John Bidlake. 5252
Sermon . . . [by John Cotton.] 17103
Sermon, by John Cotton. 17065
Sermon . . . [by John Danforth.] 18470
Sermon. [By John Hancock.] 30168
Sermon . . . by John McVickar. 43679
Sermon. [By John Marsh.] (44749)
Sermon. By John Rogers. (72695)
Sermon. By John T. Sargent. (76989)
Sermon, by Joshua Lacy Wilson. 104674
Sermon. [By Josiah Smith.] 83447
Sermon . . . [by L. J. Livermore.] (41577)
Sermon, by Lebbeus Armstrong. 2035
Sermon. [By Lemuel Haynes.] 31054
Sermon by Rev. M. J. Savage. (77244)
Sermon: by Miss R. Watkins. 102113
Sermon. By Mr. Samuel Davies. 18770
Sermon. [By Nathaniel L. Frothingham.]
26074
[Sermon by Nicolas de San Pedro.] 56646
Sermon . . . [by O. B. Frothingham.] 26079
Sermon . . . [by O. E. Daggett.] 18269
Sermon . . . by Phil. P. Neely. 49357
Sermon, by Rev. C. B. Boynton. (7148)
Sermon by Rev. Caleb Bradlee. 29827
Sermon by Rev. Dr. Spring. 32435, note after
89770
Sermon . . . by Rev. G. W. Perkins. (60950)
Sermon, . . . by Rev. Geo. Wilhelmus Mancius.
44227

Sermon . . . by Rev. H. Darling. 18585

Sermon by Rev. H. J. Van Dyke. 28013

Sermon. By Rev. H. R. Bromwell. 8223

Sermon by Rev. Henry W. Lee. 39761

Sermon by Rev. J. P. Lundy. (42694)

Sermon by Rev. J. P. Thompson. 95517

Sermon . . . by Rev. James O. Murray. 51514

Sermon by Rev. John Jenkins. 35995, (35997)

Sermon, by Rev. John L. Girardeau. 85323

Sermon . . . by Rev. John Little. 41518

Sermon . . . by Rev. John M'Cron. 43120

Sermon. By Rev. John Reynolds. 70418

Sermon, . . . by Rev. Jonathan L. Pomeroy. 63926

Sermon . . . . By Rev. Joseph Morgan. 50659

Sermon, by Rev. M. Hale Smith. 83572

Sermon . . . by Rev. Robert W. Lewis. 40846

Sermon. By Rev. Samuel J. May. 47076

Sermon by Rev. T. H. Robinson. (72196)

Sermon. By Rev. W. H. Ryder. (74540)

Sermon, by Rev. W. Macaulay. 42950

Sermon . . . . By Rev. William A. Miller. 49078

Sermon by Rev. William A. Snively. 63118, 85462

Sermon. [By Richard Watson.] 102151

Sermon . . . by Right Rev. Stephen Elliott. 63846

Sermon . . . by Robert Robinson. 72172

Sermon . . . by Robert W. Hill. 31859

Sermon, by S. T. Spear. 89093

Sermon [by S. Ward.] 97551

Sermon [by Samson Occom.] 21971

Sermon. [By Samuel Cooper.] 16603

Sermon by Samuel Willard. 104077, 104100, 104105

Sermon [by Stephen Farley.] 92790

Sermon by T. H. Rouse. 35736

Sermon. By the late Reverend George Whitefield. 103551

Sermon by the late Reverend John Clarke. (13424)

Sermon . . . . By the late Right Rev. Theodore Dehon. 19314

Sermon, by the Rev. Dr. A. Thomson. 95560

Sermon by the Rev. Dr. Raphall. 57492

Sermon, by the Rev. E. Punderson. (66665)

Sermon . . . by the Rev. Geo. W. Bassett. 3894

Sermon by the Rev. Henry Budd. 8950, 54987

Sermon by the Rev. J. H. Fairchild. 103792

Sermon [by the Rev. Mr. Ashley.] (23584)

Sermon by the Reverend Mr. George Whitefield. 103580

Sermon by the Rev. Mr. Symmes of Bradford. 94107

Sermon . . . by the Rev. Noah Atwater. 2341

Sermon, . . . by the Rev. Paul Couch. 17135

Sermon by the Rev. President Edwards. 21960

Sermon by the Rev. Samuel Seabury. (78586)

Sermon, by the Rev. Thomas Richey. 71116

Sermon, by the Rev. Thomas Smyth. 84296

Sermon . . . by the Rev. William Scott. 78387

Sermon by the Venerable Edward Wix. 104967

Sermon, by the Venerated President Edwards. 21959

Sermon by Thomas De Witt. (38166)

Sermon, by Thomas L. Harris. (30527)

Sermon. [By Thomas Wentworth Higginson.] 31755

Sermon, by W. F. Brand. 7390

Sermon. By William H. Green. 28567

Sermon, by William W. Spear. 89107

Sermon . . . by William Warburton. (17674)

Sermon . . . celebrada en la Santa Iglesia Metropolitana de Mexico. (44539)

Sermon . . . celebration of the third semi-centennial jubilee. 39511

Sermon . . . characteristics of the Reformed Dutch Church. (24191)

Sermon, charge, and pastoral letter of the late Bishop. 92077

Sermon . . . Charleston . . . November 11, 1860. 26292

Sermon . . . Charlestown, December 9, 1860. 22309

Sermon . . . Charlestown, September 20, 1863. 22309

Sermon, Christian unity, Board of Missions. 35816

Sermon commaunded at Paul's Crosse. 65421

Sermon commemorative of Edward M. Pell. 83526

Sermon, commemorative of Mrs. Mary H. Chittenden. 92271

Sermon commemorative of national events. 42653

Sermon, commemorative of our national bereavement. 71960

Sermon commemorative of Rev. William Ward Merriam. 51514

Sermon, commemorative of the death of Mrs. Mary A. Brown. (71269)

Sermon commemorative of the late Rev. John Cotton Smith. 82947

Sermon commemorative of the life and labor of the Rev. Charles Ridgely Howard. 77572

Sermon commemorative of the life and labors of the Rev. William Kirby. 93280

Sermon commemorative of the life . . . of the Rev. Samuel H. Turner. 36321

Sermon commemorative of the Rev. E. G. Prescott. 20391

Sermon commemorative of the Rev. Edmund Quincy Sewall. 32345

Sermon commemorative of the Rt. Rev. . . . William Heathcote De Lancy. 31909

Sermon, commemorative of the . . . virtues and public services of . . . De Witt Clinton, late governor of . . . New-York. 66224

Sermon. Composed by the late Daniel Burgess. 9237

Sermon con motivo de la jura de independencia. 57712

Sermon con motivo del regresso de la republica. 55348

Sermon concerning assurance of the love of Christ. 46740

Sermon concerning obedience & resignation of the will of God in every thing. (46734)

Sermon concerning, the day of judgement [sic]. 46453

Sermon concerning the glory of the throne of the Lord Jesys Christ. 46694

Sermon concerning the laying of deaths of others to heart. 16640

Sermon concerning the obligations we are under to love and delight in the public worship of God. (36295)

Sermon concerning the sin and misery of the fallen angels. 46630

Sermon . . . Concord, November 9th, 1856. 26017

Sermon connected with the re-opening of the Church of the South Parish. 59353

Sermon containing a brief history of the
South Church of the parish in Dedham.
14223
Sermon . . . containing a brief sketch of the
life and death of Mrs. L. E. Stowell.
92625
Sermon, containing a general history of the
parish of Westfield. 33985
Sermon, containing a general history of the
town of East-Hampton. 4341
Sermon, containing a history of the origin of
the First Baptist Church in the city of
New York. 58790
Sermon containing reflections on the solar
eclipse. 39199
Sermon, containing, scriptural instructions to
civil rulers. 80456
Sermon containing the history of the First
Unitarian Church. 16220
Sermon . . . Convention of the Diocese of
Delaware. (39694)
Sermon . . . Convocation of the Protestant
Episcopal Church in Virginia. 47242
Sermon . . . day of national fast. (50953)
Sermon . . . day of public thanksgiving . . .
December 1st, 1814. 32627
Sermon . . . day of public thanksgiving,
November 29, 1838. 32960
Sermon de accion de gracias, con motivo de
la restauracion de Buenos-Ayres. 94870
Sermon de accion de gracias por el recibi-
miento del Excel. Senor D. J. de la
Pezuela y Sanchez. 39099
Sermon de accion de gracias, que con el
plausible motivo de la restauracion de
la ciudad. 94869
Sermon de accion de gracias, que con motivo
de haberse recibido con extraordinario
el dia de Agosto del presente ano de
1807. 94871
Sermon de capitulo provincial. 78932
Sermon de dedicacion de Iglesia. 78933
Sermon de el glorioso martyr San Felipe de
Jesus. 36790
Sermon de Fray Sulfra dedicado a los Es-
panoles. 93446
Sermon de gracias con que el Ill. Cabildo de
la ciudad de Santa Fe Real. 44959
Sermon de gracias en la solemne proclamacion
y jura de Fernando VII. 76413
Sermon de gracias por el feliz prenado de la
Reina Dona Maria Luisa de Saboya.
76176
Sermon de gracias por la restitucion a su
trono del Sr. Don Fernando VII. (72801)
Sermon de gracias por la restitucion del Sr.
Fernando VII. 76284
Sermon de gracias predicado en la dedicacion
del Templo Mayor de Mexico. 77052
Sermon de gracias que en la exaltacion al
trono de N. Catolico Monarca D. Carlos
IV. 63306
Sermon de honras de su difunto Arzobispo D.
Alonzo Nunez de Haro y Peralta. 27795
Sermon de la Concepcion Inmaculada de Maria.
74867
Sermon de la dedicacion del Hospital de los
Terceros Hijos de S. Francisco. 50077
Sermon de la Epifania. 11033
Sermon de la fe. 5424
Sermon de la milagrosa imagen de N. S. de
Guadalupe de Mexico. 99621
Sermon de la primera dominica de adviento.
75865
Sermon de la profesion solemne de Sor Maria
del Carmen. 76019

Sermon de la publicacion de la bula de la Sta
Cruzada. 6099, 6101
Sermon de la Pvrificacion de Maria SSma.
86435
Sermon de la Purissima Concepcion de Maria.
87232
Sermon de la Santa Casa de Loreto. (23069)
Sermon de la Sanitada el Sen. San Pedro.
50085
Sermon de la soledad de Maria Santissima N.
Sen. 39680
Sermon de la Transfiguracion del Senor.
(73858)
Sermon de las honoras, etc. 11459
Sermon de las lagrimas de el Principe de los
Apostoles. 36793, (76177)
Sermon de las necesidades que padecio Maria
Ssma. 75612
Sermon de las penas del purgatorio. 75612
Sermon de los dolores de la Virgen Maria.
76781
Sermon de N. P. San Pedro Nolasco. 28027
Sermon de Ntra Sra. de Guadalupe. (36092)
Sermon de Ntra. Sra. de la Soledad. 77091
Sermon de Nuestra Santissima Guadalupana
Senora. 58575
Sermon de Nuestra Senora del Rosario. 76178
Sermon de ramos que para el dia veinte de ano
de 1755. 80898
Sermon de rogativa por el feliz parto de la
Serenisima Reina de Espana. 75560
Sermon de rogativa por la falta de aguas.
72509
Sermon de S. Cosme y S. Damian. 67321
Sermon de San Felipe de Jesus. 44954
Sermon de San Hermenigildo Martir. 75865
Sermon de un Padre Santo. 93447
Sermon . . . death of Mr. George W. Barber.
34175
Sermon, . . . death of Mrs. Carile Mary
Whitmore. 58885
Sermon . . . death of Mrs. Delia Williams.
30925
Sermon . . . death of Mrs. Mary Codman.
47254
Sermon . . . death of Mrs. Susannah Hull.
33924
Sermon, . . . death of Rev. Gerardus A.
Kuypers. 38165
Sermon . . . death of William Gould. 33962
Sermon . . . death of William Seaver. (41524)
Sermon . . . December 5, 1832. (31707)
Sermon . . . December 5, 1792. 29306
Sermon . . . Dec. 15, 1861. 42149
Sermon . . . December 1, 1814. 55879
Sermon . . . December 1, 1833. 59325
Sermon, . . . December 4th, 1853. 51737
Sermon . . . December 2, 1821. 45462
Sermon, Dec. 17, 1865. 32613
Sermon . . . December 10, 1800. 32588
Sermon . . . December 10, 1829. 36349
Sermon . . . December 13. 1779. 33991
Sermon . . . December 13, 1776. 39616
Sermon . . . December 20, 1842. 37976
Sermon . . . December 28, 1845. 33964
Sermon . . . December 28, 1817. 43526
Sermon, . . . December 25, 1827. 59486
Sermon . . . December 29, 1844. 63388
Sermon . . . December 27, 1863. 43419
Sermon . . . December 27th, 1832. 30925
Sermon . . . December 26, 1858. (43394)
Sermon, Dec. 30, 1860. 38336
Sermon, . . . Dec. 31, 1854. 47181
Sermon, dedication of Reformed Dutch Church,
Farmerville, N. Y. 28743

Sermon . . . dedication of the Meeting-House. (16334)

Sermon defending slavery. 2669

Sermon del glorisos transito de la Virgen Maria. (76124)

Sermon del Gran Padre, y Dr. S. Augustin. 99622

Sermon del Padre Santo. 93449

Sermon del Patrocinio de la Virgen Maria. 17737

Sermon del Santisimo Sacramento de la Eucaristia. [Por Juan San Miguel.] 76172

Sermon del Santisimo Sacramento de la Eucaristia. [Por Juan Serna.] 79302

Sermon del Santo Martyr y Pontifice Marcelo. 58335

Sermon . . . Delaware and Chester Convocation. 48672

Sermon delivered April 19, 1772. 11968

Sermon, delivered April 7, 1819. (82423)

Sermon delivered . . . April 13, 1815. 5882

Sermon delivered, . . . April 25, 1847. 13648

Sermon delivered April 22, 1845. 89744

Sermon delivered April 27, 1785. (31895)

Sermon, delivered at a singing-lecture. 92931

Sermon, delivered at Abingdon in Pomfret. (71495)

Sermon delivered at Acton. 71502

Sermon delivered at Acworth. 93954

Sermon, delivered at Albany. 89744

Sermon, delivered at Andover. 94122

Sermon, delivered at Ansonia, Conn. 92779

Sermon, delivered at Augusta, Georgia. 7416

Sermon, delivered at Bedford, Mass. 90970

Sermon delivered . . . at Bethlehem. 18969

Sermon, delivered at Beverly. 105302, 105306-105307

Sermon delivered at Boston, before the Great and General Assembly. 103930

Sermon delivered at Boston, in the audience of the Great and General Court. (65071)

Sermon deliver'd at Boston, . . . June 3d. a. m. 1753. 63517

Sermon, delivered at Boston, March 12th, 1789. 102747

Sermon, delivered at Bridge-Hampton, (L. I.) (62480)

Sermon delivered at Bridgehampton. 105219

Sermon delivered at Brimfield. 3105

Sermon delivered at Brookfield, October 19, 1779. 24553

Sermon, delivered at Brooklyn, New York. 4304

Sermon, delivered at Brunswick, April 13, 1815. 1806

Sermon, delivered at Buxton, June 8th, 1821. 24733

Sermon delivered at Cainhoy, in the province of South-Carolina. 83451

Sermon delivered at Cairo. 64214

Sermon delivered at Cambridge. 65607, 92351

Sermon delivered at Canastota, N. Y. 91722

Sermon delivered at Candia, N. H. 65073

Sermon, delivered at Catskill. 98587

Sermon deliver'd at Charles-Town, in South Carolina. 83446

Sermon, delivered at Charlestown, in the afternoon. 7241, 94361

Sermon delivered at Charlestown, July 23, 1797. 11213

Sermon delivered at Chelmsford. 93706

Sermon delivered at Chelsea. 59314

Sermon delivered at Christ's Church, West Haven. 11941

Sermon, delivered at Concord, before His Excellency the Governor. 104321

Sermon, delivered at Concord, before the Bible Society in the County of Middlesex. 90859

Sermon delivered at Concord, before the . . . General Court of . . . New Hampshire. 23165

Sermon, delivered at Concord, before the . . . General Court of the state of New-Hampshire. (59377)

Sermon delivered at Concord, before . . . the Governor, . . . Council, and . . . Legislature of . . . New Hampshire. 22298

Sermon, delivered at Concord, Massachusetts, December 26, 1799. (71609)

Sermon delivered at Concord, New-Hampshire. 43240

Sermon, delivered at Dennis, December 17, 1795. 92108, 97741

Sermon, delivered at Dover, state of New Hampshire. (50718)

Sermon delivered at Dudley, Massachusetts. 89744

Sermon, delivered at East-Windsor. 43065

Sermon delivered at Easton, Mass. 92246

Sermon, delivered at Ellington. 93088

Sermon, delivered at Ellington in Connecticut. (43066)

Sermon, delivered at Exeter. 73576

Sermon, delivered at Fort Griswold. 97525

Sermon, delivered at Fredericksburg. 89163

Sermon delivered at Friends' Meeting, Green Street, Philadelphia. 90020A

Sermon, delivered at Fryeburg, Maine. 64942

Sermon, delivered at Goffstown, N. H. 92626

Sermon, delivered at Goshen, at the ordination. 33796

Sermon, delivered at Greensburgh, Ia. 85101

Sermon, delivered at Groton February 21, 1775. 5977, 102427

Sermon delivered at Groton Jan. 12, 1815. 11965

Sermon delivered at Guilford. 104219

Sermon delivered at Hallowell. (78324)

Sermon, delivered at Hampton, July 28th, 1791. 14217

Sermon delivered at Hartford, before the Legislature. 102546

Sermon, delivered at Hartford, January 6, 1807. 92957

Sermon, delivered at Hartford, Sept. 17, 1806. 24763

Sermon, delivered at Hartland, the 29th of June, 1768. 92934

Sermon, delivered at Haverhill, N. Hampshire. 93953

Sermon delivered at Haverhill, New Hampshire, July 28, 1796. 105272

Sermon, delivered at her funeral, by Rev. J. Butler. 96280

Sermon, delivered at Hingham. 101381

Sermon delivered at Hopkinton. 28404

Sermon, . . . delivered at Independence, Mo. 83302

Sermon delivered at Irasburgh, Vt. 4082

Sermon, delivered at Ireland Parish, West Springfield. 82721

Sermon delivered at Johnstown. 89744

Sermon delivered at King's Chapel, Boston. 11205

Sermon, delivered at Lamoni, Iowa. 83302

Sermon, delivered at Lancaster, Dec. 29, 1816. 95260

Sermon, delivered at Lenox. 80194

SERMON

Sermon delivered at Leominster, October 15, 1823. 15086
Sermon delivered at Leominster on leaving the Old Meeting-House. 15085
Sermon, delivered at Lexington. 71121
Sermon delivered at Linebrook Parish, Rowley, May 2, 1813. 104225
Sermon delivered at Lisbon, Maryland. 82952
Sermon, delivered at Loudon, August 17, 1806. 97310
Sermon, delivered at Lunenburg, December 2, 1827. 18364
Sermon, delivered at Lunenburg, March 4, 1801. 103777
Sermon, delivered at Lynn, on the general fast. 72265
Sermon, delivered at Lynn, on the general fast, May 3d, 1781. 72264
Sermon deliver'd at Medfield, October 25. 1759. 96388
Sermon, delivered at Medway, November 4, 1813. 105616
Sermon, delivered at Mendon, Lord's-Day March 25, 1781. 104057
Sermon delivered at Middlefield, Mass. 13399
Sermon delivered at Middlefield, on the Lord's Day, April 1799. 105093
Sermon, delivered at Middletown, Conn. 9483
Sermon, delivered at Milton, February 18, 1807. 90969
Sermon delivered at Monroe, (Conn.) 68122
Sermon, delivered at Montpelier, Lord's Day evening. 97078
Sermon, delivered at Montpelier, October 28th, 1812. 105569
Sermon delivered at Nassau Hall. 18765
Sermon delivered at New Haven, April 27, 1759. 5559
Sermon delivered at New-Haven . . . October 27, 1812. 4336
Sermon delivered at New York, December 7, 1826. 55862
Sermon, delivered at Newark, by John E. Latta. 98979
Sermon delivered at Newark, during the session of the Synod of New-York and New-Jersey. 4332
Sermon, delivered at Newburgh, on Thursday the twenty-fourth day of June. 89433
Sermon, delivered at Newbury, April 29, 1792. 21619
Sermon, delivered at Newbury, Vt. 93954
Sermon, delivered at Newbury-Port, August 14th 1788. 97324
Sermon, delivered at Newburyport, Nov. 26, 1812. 102330
Sermon, delivered at Newburyport, on the 22nd of February. 6111
Sermon, delivered at Newport, New-Hampshire. 73554
Sermon delivered at Newton, . . . October, 1812. 28199
Sermon, delivered at Norfolk, Conn., Nov. 30, 1843. 22104
Sermon, delivered at North Bridgewater, Oct. 31, 1821. 92259
Sermon delivered at North-Haven, December 11, 1783. 97187
Sermon delivered at North Mendon, April 30, 1843. 79947
Sermon, delivered at Northborough February 22d, 1800. 103771, 105017
Sermon delivered at Northborough, Mass. 25255
Sermon, delivered at Oakham, September 7, 1810. 85396

Sermon, delivered at Palmer. 101406
Sermon, delivered at Peacham. 105241
Sermon, delivered at Peterville Church. 89164
Sermon delivered at Philadelphia, on January 1, 1770. 21982
Sermon delivered at Pisgah. 6051
Sermon delivered at Pittsfield, New-Hampshire. 65073
Sermon delivered at Plymouth before the Robinson Congregation. 13838
Sermon delivered at Plymouth, December the Twenty-Second, 1826. 92263
Sermon delivered at Plymouth, December 21st, 1804. 7230
Sermon, delivered at Plymouth, December 22, 1803. 92925
Sermon delivered at Plymouth, December 22, 1801. 934
Sermon, delivered at Plymouth, N. H., July 4, 1825. 101312
Sermon, delivered at Plymouth, September 4, 1803. 37366
Sermon, delivered at Pomfret, July 18, 1819. 64265
Sermon, delivered at Portland, Nov. 19, 1818. 1807
Sermon delivered at Portsmouth, in the province of New-Hampshire. 36114
Sermon, delivered at Princeton, before the Board of Trustees. (72474)
Sermon delivered at Providence, R. I. (23811)
Sermon, delivered at Putney, Vermont, on the sixteenth day of November, 1797. 102606
Sermon, delivered at Quebec Village. 21082
Sermon, delivered at Royalston, Vermont. 97436
Sermon delivered at Rutland, Wednesday, January 1st, 1800. 2936
Sermon, delivered at S. Reading. 22461
Sermon delivered at St. John, New Brunswick. 74597
Sermon delivered at St. John's, New Brunswick. (9718)
Sermon, delivered at Salem, Dec. 21, 1786. 88892
Sermon delivered at Salem, January 14, 1796. (24480)
Sermon, delivered at Salem, on March 31, 1796. 3493
Sermon deliver'd at Salem-Village, the 24th of March, 1692. 39443
Sermon, delivered at Salisbury, Conn., Dec. 14th, 1859. 69000
Sermon delivered at Salisbury, July 14, 1774. 102421
Sermon delivered at Schoharie. 17910
Sermon, delivered at Shrewsbury. 93707
Sermon delivered at Somers, January 12, 1819. 93087
Sermon delivered at Southborough, December 17, 1806. 58686, 103771
Sermon delivered at Stamford. 82417
Sermon delivered at Stockland, Dorset. 59401
Sermon delivered at Stoughton. (21246)
Sermon, delivered at Suffield. (28906)
Sermon delivered at Taunton. 15092
Sermon, delivered at the annual election, in Trinity Church. 103168
Sermon delivered . . . at the annual election, . . . January 3, 1844. 11947
Sermon, delivered at the annual fast, April 5, 1838. 20531
Sermon delivered at the annual fast at Salem, N. H. 82888
Sermon, delivered at the Branch Church in Salem. 97437

Sermon delivered at the Bulfinch-Street
Church, Boston. (29399)

Sermon delivered at the Church in Brattle-
Street. (13424)

Sermon, delivered at the consecration of the
New Brick Church. 92963

Sermon, delivered at the dedication of the
American Chapel in Paris. 78858

Sermon delivered at the dedication of the
Baptist Meeting-House. 79796

Sermon delivered at the dedication of the
Baptist Meeting-House in New Haven.
31809

Sermon delivered at the dedication of the
Baptist Meeting House in this town.
79800

Sermon, delivered at the dedication of the
Brick Meeting House. 100932

Sermon delivered at the dedication of the
Christian Church. 21870

Sermon delivered at the dedication of the
Eastern Methodist Meeting House. 74672

Sermon delivered at the dedication of the First
Congregational Church. 13452

Sermon, delivered at the dedication of the
Meeting House of the Second Church and
Congregation in Beverly. 90246

Sermon delivered at the dedication of the New
Brick Meeting House. 6088

Sermon delivered at the dedication of the new
chapel of Bowdoin College. 32268

Sermon delivered at the dedication of the New
Jerusalem Temple. 20154

Sermon delivered at the dedication of the new
Meeting House in North Brookfield.
85387

Sermon, delivered at the dedication of the new
Meeting-House in Waterville Village.
11957

Sermon delivered at the dedication of the new
Meeting-House of the First Evangelical
Congregational Church. 90993

Sermon delivered at the dedication of the new
Universalist Meeting House in Norway
Village. 105037

Sermon, delivered at the dedication of the
North Congregational Meeting-House.
14136

Sermon, delivered at the dedication of the
South Meeting House in Dorchester.
(30518)

Sermon, delivered at the dedication of the
Universalist Meeting House in Halifax,
Mass. 62626

Sermon delivered at the dedication of the
Washington Street Church. 84930

Sermon delivered at the Diocesan Convention,
May 19, 1847. (47069)

Sermon, delivered at the East Meeting House
in Boscawen. 90294

Sermon delivered at the First Church in
Boston. (12329)

Sermon, delivered at the First Parish in
Brookfield. 101290

Sermon, delivered at the First Presbyterian
Church in Hartford. 91619

Sermon, delivered at the First Presbyterian
Church, October 18, 1880. 83391

Sermon, delivered at the funeral of a young
woman of Lyman. 93954

Sermon delivered at the funeral of Benjamin
Franklin Nichols. 18976

Sermon, delivered at the funeral of Col. John
Anderson. 104778

Sermon, delivered at the funeral of Deacon
Stephen Baldwin. 70948

Sermon delivered at the funeral of Gen. Stephen
Badlam. 14137

Sermon delivered at the funeral of Henry
Obookiah. 4342

Sermon, delivered at the funeral of His Excellency Samuel Huntington. 92935

Sermon delivered at the funeral of Hon.
Charles Paine. 26536

Sermon delivered at the funeral of Hon. Thomas
Fitch. 20063

Sermon delivered at the funeral of . . . M.
Griswold. 72446

Sermon, delivered at the funeral of Miss
Abigail Reed. 92789

Sermon delivered at the funeral of Miss Nabby
Frothingham. 17839

Sermon, delivered at the funeral of Mr. Nathan
Ball. 34117

Sermon, delivered at the funeral of Mr. Samuel
Phillips. 1495

Sermon, delivered at the funeral of Mrs.
Almira James. 90003

Sermon, delivered at the funeral of Mrs.
Elizabeth Mason. 71534

Sermon, delivered at the funeral of Mrs. Sarah
Williams. 92964

Sermon, delivered at the funeral of Rev. David
Tenny Kimball. 24606

Sermon, delivered at the funeral of Reverend
Eliab Stone. 90971

Sermon, delivered at the funeral of Rev. Royal
Robbins. 89814

Sermon, delivered at the funeral of the Hon.
John Treadwell. (64297)

Sermon delivered at the funeral of the Honorable Roger Sherman. 21973

Sermon, delivered at the funeral of the Reverend Alfred V. Bassett. 103803

Sermon delivered at the funeral of the Rev.
Cotton Mather Smith. 61029

Sermon delivered at the funeral of the Rev.
Ezra Ripley. 26016

Sermon, delivered at the funeral of the Rev.
Levi Hart. 4659

Sermon delivered at the funeral of the Rev.
Paul Litchfield. 12989

Sermon, delivered at the funeral of the Rev.
Samuel Goodrich. 71833

Sermon, delivered at the General Convention
of Universalists. 36610

Sermon delivered at the house of Major Jacob
Mann. 13598

Sermon, delivered at the installation of . . .
Ezekiel Rich. 17403

Sermon delivered at the installation of Rev. A.
Dumont Jones. 26296

Sermon delivered at the installation of Rev.
Edwin Jennison. 84293

Sermon delivered at the installation of Rev.
Frederick Freeman. 21979

Sermon, delivered at the installation of Rev.
Henry Bacon. 11947

Sermon, delivered at the installation of Rev.
Josiah W. Powers. 92253

Sermon delivered at the installation of the
Rev. Artemas B. Muzzey. 7938

Sermon delivered at the installation of the
Rev. Edward B. Hall. 19862

Sermon delivered at the installation of the
Rev. Elias Cornelius. 4329, 4344

Sermon delivered at the installation of the
Rev. Horace Holley. (21792)

Sermon delivered at the installation of the
Rev. Lorenzo D. Johnson. 12427

Sermon, delivered at the installation of the
Rev. Orin Fowler. 89744

Sermon delivered at the installation of the
Rev. Reuben Emerson. 74896
Sermon delivered at the installation of Thomas
Mather Smith. 84408
Sermon, delivered at the institution of the
Rev. Charles Mason. 92079
Sermon delivered at the interment of Mrs.
Susannah Porter. 8930
Sermon, delivered at the interment of Rev.
Dr. Moore. 85392
Sermon delivered at the interment of the Hon.
Jacob Abbot. 21737
Sermon, delivered at the interment of the Rev.
Jeremy Belknap. 38005
Sermon, delivered at the interment of the
Reverend Jesse Appleton. 94360
Sermon, delivered at the interment of the
Reverend William Emerson. 8934
Sermon delivered at the introduction of the
Rev. Peter Thatcher. 57778
Sermon delivered at the lecture in Boston,
Sept. 18, 1729. 3471
Sermon delivered at the lecture in Newbury-
Newton. 8506
Sermon, delivered at the Meeting-House in the
First Parish in Hingham. 80803
Sermon delivered at the North Congregational
Church in Newbury-port. 89801
Sermon, delivered at the North Parish in
Brookfield. 85390
Sermon delivered at the Old South Church,
Boston. 104810
Sermon, delivered at the opening of the
Branch Church in Salem. 88888
Sermon, delivered at the opening of the
General Assembly. 73054
Sermon delivered at the opening of the
General Synod, at York. 89753
Sermon, delivered at the opening of the
Independent Congregational Church, in
Barton Square, Salem. 16795, 70266
Sermon delivered at the opening of the Lecture
Room. 91596
Sermon, delivered at the opening of the New
Meeting-House in Piermont. 93954
Sermon delivered at the ordination and instal-
lation of Rev. J. Younglove. 11999
Sermon delivered at the ordination of Mr.
Timothy Dwight. (21975)
Sermon delivered at the ordination of Rev.
Chandler Robbins. 101395
Sermon, delivered at the ordination of Rev.
James I. T. Coolidge. 26536
Sermon delivered at the ordination of Rev.
John Emery Abbot. 11919
Sermon, delivered at the ordination of Rev.
Josiah Webster. 58378
Sermon delivered at the ordination of Rev.
Leonard Withington. 14137
Sermon delivered at the ordination of Richard
Varick Dey. 73536
Sermon, delivered at the ordination of the
Reverend Aaron Woolworth. (8985)
Sermon, delivered at the ordination of the
Reverend Abner Morse. (24443)
Sermon delivered at the ordination of the
Rev. Alexander Gillet. 92933
Sermon, delivered at the ordination of the
Rev. Alvin Tobey. 88898
Sermon, delivered at the ordination of the
Rev. Benjamin Bell. 89798
Sermon delivered at the ordination of the Rev.
Bezaleel Pinneo. 8169
Sermon delivered at the ordination of the
Reverend Caleb Hobart. 92260

Sermon delivered at the ordination of the Rev.
Daniel Hall. (37852)
Sermon, delivered at the ordination of the Rev.
Daniel L. Carroll. 90385
Sermon, delivered at the ordination of the Rev.
Edmund Quincy Sewall. 71515
Sermon delivered at the ordination of the Rev.
Ezra Stiles Gannett. 11919
Sermon, delivered at the ordination of the
Reverend Henry Channing. 6987, 91745
Sermon delivered at the ordination of the Rev.
Henry Wilber. 18405
Sermon, delivered at the ordination of the Rev.
Ichabod Lord Skinner. 92965
Sermon delivered at the ordination of the Rev.
Jacob Weed Eastman. 18405
Sermon, delivered at the ordination of the Rev.
James Porter. 21233
Sermon delivered at the ordination of the Rev.
John Robinson. 22525
Sermon, delivered at the ordination of the
Reverend John Taylor. 2340
Sermon, delivered at the ordination of the Rev.
John White. 71514
Sermon delivered at the ordination of the Rev.
Lathrop Rockwell. 92127
Sermon, delivered at the ordination of the Rev.
Levi White. 92926
Sermon, delivered at the ordination of the Rev.
Martin Moore. 24519
Sermon, delivered at the ordination of the
Reverend Matthew Noyes. 27884
Sermon, delivered at the ordination of the Rev.
Micah Stone. 92052
Sermon delivered at the ordination of the
Reverend Mr. Joel Benedict. 20632
Sermon delivered at the ordination of the
Reverend Mr. Nathanael Huntington.
19830
Sermon delivered at the ordination of the
Reverend Mr. Stephen Peabody. 78626
Sermon, delivered at the ordination of the Rev.
Mr. Zephaniah H. Smith. 92898
Sermon delivered at the ordination of the Rev.
Moses Bradford. 7242
Sermon delivered at the ordination of the Rev.
Nathan Tilton. 7231
Sermon delivered at the ordination of the Rev.
Otis Thompson. 3398
Sermon delivered at the ordination of the Rev.
Reed Paige. 32657
Sermon, delivered at the ordination of the Rev.
Richard Salter Storrs. 92239
Sermon, delivered at the ordination of the Rev.
Robert Page. 42045
Sermon delivered at the ordination of the Rev.
Samuel P. Robbins. 71837
Sermon, delivered at the ordination of the Rev.
Samuel Sumner. 93705
Sermon delivered at the ordination of the Rev.
Shubael Bartlett. 22394
Sermon, delivered at the ordination of the Rev.
Stephen Williams. 92241
Sermon, delivered at the ordination of the Rev.
Thomas Ruggles. 21465
Sermon, delivered at the ordination of the Rev.
Thomas Skelton. 90972
Sermon delivered at the ordination of the
Reverend Wales Tileston. 89744
Sermon delivered at the ordination of the
Reverend William Bascom. 32588
Sermon delivered at the request of Harmony
Lodge. 24583
Sermon delivered at the request of the African
Benevolent Society. 59126

Sermon delivered at the request of the American Sunday School Union. 102187

Sermon, delivered at the request of the Elders. 50720

Sermon, delivered at the request of the Young Men's Christian Association. 91583

Sermon delivered at the semi-annual meeting. 29775

Sermon delivered at the South Church in Boston, N. E. 65612

Sermon delivered at the South-Church in Boston, on the Lord's-Day. 65583

Sermon delivered at the South Church in Portsmouth. 708

Sermon delivered at the Tabernacle in Salem. 105137

Sermon, delivered at the Third Parish in Newbury. 94363

Sermon delivered at the University of Pennsylvania. 104729

Sermon, delivered at the West-Farms. 104366

Sermon delivered at Thomastown. (5978)

Sermon delivered at Topsfield, January 5, 1800. 33945

Sermon, delivered at Topsfield, Mass. 21737

Sermon, delivered at Townshend. 97417

Sermon delivered at Upton. 105023

Sermon, delivered at Wallingford. 82214

Sermon, delivered at Wallingford, Connecticut. 28907

Sermon, delivered at Waltham. 17700

Sermon, delivered at West-Springfield. 89744

Sermon, delivered at Weston. 37347

Sermon delivered at Williamstown. 32906

Sermon deliver'd at Worcester, November 24th, 1737. 10226

Sermon delivered at Worcester, on the day of public thanksgiving. 2425

Sermon, delivered at Wrentham, at the ordination. (32257)

Sermon delivered at Wrentham, October 26, 1773. 4119

Sermon delivered at York. 71513

Sermon, delivered August 20, 1812. 95261

Sermon, delivered August 20, 1793. 92053

Sermon delivered August 25, 1835. 89744

Sermon delivered August 25, 1822. 82889

Sermon delivered August 27, 1845. 89744

Sermon delivered before His Excellency . . . and the Legislature of Massachusetts. 62824

Sermon delivered before His Excellency . . . at the annual election. 61364

Sermon, delivered before His Excellency Caleb Strong. 66603

Sermon delivered before His Excellency Edward Everett. 92261

Sermon delivered before His Excellency Emory Washburn. 39203

Sermon delivered before His Excellency George N. Briggs. (66788)

Sermon delivered before His Excellency Henry J. Gardner. 78859

Sermon, delivered before His Excellency John Brooks. 101382

Sermon delivered before His Excellency John H. Clifford. 68062

Sermon delivered before His Excellency Levi Lincoln, Esq. Governor. 93210

Sermon delivered before His Excellency Levi Lincoln, Governor. 106012

Sermon delivered before His Excellency Levi Lincoln Governor, His Honor Thomas L. Winthrop Lieutenant Governor, the Hon. Council. 101058

Sermon delivered before His Excellency Levi Lincoln, Governor . . . of . . . Massachusetts. (24537)

Sermon delivered before the A. B. C. F. M. 18826

Sermon, delivered before the American Board of Commissioners for Foreign Missions, at . . . Springfield, Massachusetts. (50953)

Sermon, delivered before the Ancient and Honorable Artillery Company, in Boston. 95262

Sermon, delivered before the Ancient and Honourable Artillery Company, June 6th, 1825. 26069

Sermon delivered before the Ancient and Honorable Artillery Company, on their CCXX. anniversary. 82945

Sermon, delivered before the Annual Convention of the Congregational Ministers of Massachusetts. (18435)

Sermon, delivered before the Anti-slavery Society of Haverhill. (73118)

Sermon, delivered before the Associated Congregational Ministers of Salem and Vicinity. 74723

Sermon delivered before the Association, by Sebastian Streeter. 98016

Sermon, delivered before the Association of Massachusetts Proper. 85399

Sermon delivered before the Auxiliary Education Society of Norfolk County, at their annual meeting in South Braintree. 76475

Sermon delivered before the Auxiliary Education Society of Norfolk County . . . in Walpole. 13250

Sermon, delivered before the Bishop White Prayer Book Society. 91581

Sermon delivered before the Boston Baptist Association. 12181

Sermon delivered before the Boston Baptist Foreign Missionary Society. 102189

Sermon delivered before the Boston Episcopal Charitable Society. (78577)

Sermon delivered before the citizens of Brandon. 25072

Sermon delivered before the civil and military officers. 22780

Sermon, delivered before the Congregational Ministers of . . . Massachusetts. 3493

Sermon delivered before the Congregational Society at Thomastown. 7229

Sermon delivered before the Connecticut Society for the Promotion of Good Morals. 21465

Sermon, delivered before the Convention of Congregational Ministers in Massachusetts. 90860

Sermon, delivered before the Convention of the Clergy of Massachusetts. 4438

Sermon delivered before the Convention of the Protestant Episcopal Church in the state of New York. (4141)

Sermon delivered before the Convention of the Protestant Episcopal Church in Maryland. 37338

Sermon delivered before the executive and legislative departments of the government of Massachusetts, at the annual election . . . Jan. 4, 1860. 1422

Sermon delivered before the executive and legislative departments of the government of Massachusetts, at the annual election, . . . Jan. 3, 1866. (67316)

Sermon delivered before the executive and legislative departments of the government of Massachusetts, at the annual election, Wednesday, January 5, 1870. 78673

Sermon delivered before the executive and legislative departments of the government of Massachusetts, at the annual election, Wednesday, Jan. 6, 1864. 90994

Sermon delivered before the executive and legislative departments of the government of Massachusetts, at the annual election, Wednesday, Jan. 6, 1869. (13256)

Sermon delivered before the First Church and Society in Nashua. 83573

Sermon, delivered before the First Church and Society in Nashua, N. H. on Sabbath, April 20, 1845. 83570

Sermon delivered before the Foreign Missionary Society of New-York and Brooklyn. 89090

Sermon, delivered before the General Assembly of South Carolina. 84543

Sermon delivered before the General Assembly of the colony of Connecticut, at Hartford, on the day of the anniversary election, May 13th, 1762. (4496)

Sermon delivered before the General Assembly of the colony of Connecticut, at Hartford, on the day of their anniversary election, May 14, 1772. (39547)

Sermon delivered before the General Assembly of the colony of Connecticut at Hartford on the day of their anniversary election May 9th 1776. 11828

Sermon delivered before the General Assembly of the colony of Connecticut, on the anniversary election at Hartford, May 14th, 1752. 105084

Sermon, delivered before the General Convention of the Protestant Episcopal Church. 103466

Sermon delivered before . . . the General Court of Massachusetts. 29631

Sermon delivered before the Gloucester Female Society for Promoting Christian Knowledge. 18405

Sermon delivered before . . . the Governor, . . . Council, and House of Representatives of . . . Vermont. 74897

Sermon delivered before . . . the Governor . . . Council, and . . . Representatives of Vermont. 31057

Sermon delivered . . . before the Governor, . . . Council, etc., of New-Hampshire. 7253

Sermon, delivered before the Governor, the Lieutenant-Governor, the Council and the two houses composing the Legislature. 59199

Sermon, delivered before the Honorable General Court. 73575

Sermon, delivered before the Honorable Legislature of the state of Vermont, at Montpelier, October 9, 1823. (81652)

Sermon, delivered before the Honorable Legislature of the state of Vermont, met at Montpelier. 89427

Sermon, delivered before the Howard Benevolent Society of Boston. 92258

Sermon delivered before . . . the Legislature of Massachusetts, at the annual election, January 5, 1843. (26532)

Sermon delivered before . . . the Legislature of Massachusetts at the annual election, January 1, 1840. (14130)

Sermon delivered before. . . . the Legislature of Massachusetts, at the annual election . . . Jan. 6, 1847. (5587)

Sermon delivered before the Maine Missionary Society, at their annual meeting in Portland. 101313

Sermon delivered before the Maine Missionary Society, . . . in Bath. 27401

Sermon delivered before the Maine Missionary Society . . . in Gorham. 8470

Sermon delivered before the Maine Missionary Society, . . . June 23, 1815. 4054

Sermon, delivered before the Massachusetts Missionary Society, at their annual meeting May 25, 1802. 89802

Sermon, delivered before the Massachusetts Missionary Society, . . . Boston, May 25, 1818. (22449)

Sermon delivered before the Massachusetts Missionary Society, on their thirteenth anniversary, May 26, 1812. 105138

Sermon delivered before the Massachusetts Society for the Suppression of Intemperance. 36035

Sermon, delivered before the members of the graduating class of the Medical College of Georgia. 72634

Sermon, delivered before the members of the New North Religious Society. 22169

Sermon delivered before the Merrimac Humane Society. (18435)

Sermon delivered before the military officers. 14150

Sermon, delivered before the New-England Society. 30517, (78821), 2d note after 69442, 89782

Sermon, delivered before the New-York Missionary Society. (41630)

Sermon delivered . . . before the nintieth Convention of the Diocese of New York. 79645

Sermon, delivered before the Orange Bible and Tract Society. 90359

Sermon, delivered before the Pastoral Association of Massachusetts, in . . . Boston, May 24, 1838. 14137

Sermon, delivered before the Pastoral Association of Massachusetts, in Central Church, Boston. 90992

Sermon delivered before the Peace Society of Temple. 72679

Sermon, delivered before the people who were collected to the execution of Moses Dunbar. 92961

Sermon delivered before the Presbytery of Long-Island. 4337

Sermon delivered before the Proprietors of the Second Church. 71788

Sermon delivered before . . . the representatives of Vermont. 24584

Sermon, delivered before the Second Christian Church. 3103

Sermon delivered before the Second Rev. Presbytery of New-Castle. 83803

Sermon, delivered before the Second Society in Danvers. 101072

Sermon delivered before the Society for Promoting the Gospel Among the Indians and Others in North America, November 5, 1829. 104913

Sermon, delivered before the Society for Propagating the Gospel Among the Indians and Others in North America, at their anniversary, November 7, 1811. 37366

Sermon, delivered before the Society for Propagating the Gospel Among the Indians and Others in North America, in . . . Boston. 14131

Sermon delivered before the Society for Propagating the Gospel Among the Indians and Others in North America, Nov. 4, 1813. 3941

Sermon delivered before the . . . Society . . . June 3, 1723. 104764

Sermon, delivered before the State Convention of Universalists. 82758

Sermon delivered before the Synod of New York. 72426

Sermon. Delivered before the Synod of Virginia. 89168

Sermon delivered before the Third Presbytery of New-York. 91999-92000

Sermon, delivered before the Vermont Colonization Society. 105750

Sermon, delivered before the Worcester Baptist Association. 83306

Sermon delivered . . . Billerica, Mass. (18366)

Sermon delivered by Andrew Eliot. (22123)

Sermon, delivered, by appointment, at the opening of the Annual Convention. 20391

Sermon delivered by appointment of the Albany Bible Society. 79934

Sermon delivered by appointment of the Committee of Missions. 73055

Sermon, delivered by Jeremiah Day. 18969

Sermon delivered by request before the Third Religious Society. 7274

Sermon, delivered by request of the Female Charitable Society in Salem. 93211

Sermon, delivered by Rev. Dr. Snell, June 27th, 1848. 85400

Sermon, delivered by Rev. Dr. Snell, June 27th, 1858. 85401

Sermon, delivered by Rev. Dr. Snell, on the last Sabbath in June, 1838. 85402

Sermon delivered by Rev. Mr. Smith. 84013

Sermon delivered by the Rev. Aaron Bancroft, November 30, 1794. 3105, 97296, 105243

Sermon delivered by the Rev. Mr. N-O-Y-E-S. (56232)

Sermon delivered by the Rev. R. B. Claxton. 13529

Sermon delivered by the Rev. Samuel B. Bell. (4481)

Sermon delivered by Thomas Prince, M. A. (65613)

Sermon, delivered December 15, 1819. (74726)

Sermon delivered December 19, 1838. 89744

Sermon, delivered Dec. 9th, 1812. 103715

Sermon, delivered December 17, 1834. 103827

Sermon, delivered December 17th, 1795. 92108, 97741

Sermon, delivered December 10, 1806. (25239)

Sermon delivered December 10, 1788. (31895)

Sermon, delivered December 13, 1820. 34175

Sermon, delivered Dec. 30, 1834. 79453

Sermon, delivered Dec. 31, 1820. 22525

Sermon, delivered December 12, 1822. 70950

Sermon, delivered December 29, 1819. 34175

Sermon, delivered Dec. 29, 1799. At the Second Church. 24556

Sermon delivered December 29, 1799; occasioned by the death of General George Washington, late President. (49058)

Sermon, delivered December 29, 1799; occasioned by the death of General George Washington, who died December 14, 1799. 47227

Sermon delivered Dec. 23, 1835. 76491

Sermon, delivered . . . December 23, 1832. 20391

Sermon delivered during the Second Plenary Council. 79289

Sermon, delivered February 4, 1824. 66820

Sermon delivered Feb. 19, 1795, being a day of general thanksgiving. (18434)

Sermon, delivered Feb. 19, 1795, being a day of public thanksgiving. 1505

Sermon, delivered February 19, 1795; being a day set apart by the President. 101376

Sermon delivered February 19, 1795. Being the day of public thanksgiving. 2919

Sermon, delivered February 19, M,DCC,XCV, on occasion of a thanksgiving. 13354

Sermon delivered February 12, 1818. 92088

Sermon delivered February 28, 1796. 8931

Sermon delivered February 22d, 1800, commemorating the death of George Washington. 55355

Sermon, delivered February 22d, 1800, in . . . Albany. 36239

Sermon delivered February 22d, 1800, the day of national mourning. 14172

Sermon delivered February 23, 1829. 93086

Sermon delivered February 23, 1827. 22377

Sermon delivered, in accordance with the late proclamation. 5688

Sermon, delivered in Adams, N. Y. 79331

Sermon delivered in . . . Albany, . . . August 24, 1856. 32943

Sermon delivered in . . . Albany, . . . October 5, 1856. 78864

Sermon delivered in . . . Albany, on the occasion of the funeral. 24503

Sermon, delivered in America, September, 1816 [i. e. 1815.] 95191, note after 97996

Sermon delivered in Amory Hall. 13418

Sermon, delivered in an honourable audience, at Boston. 46411

Sermon, delivered in Andover. 12989

Sermon, delivered in . . . Augusta, (Geo.) 82728

Sermon, delivered in Baltimore-Town, on the 22d day of April, 1792. 104566

Sermon delivered in Bangor, June 23d, 1824. (28497)

Sermon delivered in behalf of the Warren Street Chapel. 33964

Sermon delivered [i]n . . . Beverly. 24779

Sermon delivered in . . . Boston, at the first meeting of the Convention of the Eastern Diocese. (28881)

Sermon, delivered in Boston, before the African Society. 28412

Sermon delivered in Boston before the Massachusetts Society for Promoting Christian Knowledge; . . . June 1, 1815. 11965

Sermon delivered in Boston, before the Massachusetts Society for Promoting Christian Knowledge, Oct. 21, 1812. (18435)

Sermon delivered in . . . Boston, February 18, 1855. 81620

Sermon, delivered in . . . Boston, . . . Jan. 1, 1818. 14137

Sermon delivered . . . in Boston, July 19, 1840. 26536

Sermon delivered in Boston, May 26, 1829. 12989

Sermon delivered in Boston, Nov. 29, 1804. 2868

Sermon delivered . . . in Boston, October 9, 1842. 26536

Sermon, delivered in Boston, September 18, 1814. 11919

Sermon delivered in Boxford, April 19, 1829. 21737

Sermon delivered in Brookfield, at the formation of a Missionary Society. 85408

Sermon delivered in Calais, Maine. 92122

Sermon, delivered in . . . Cambridge, in Maryland. 37338

Sermon delivered in . . . Charleston, S. C. (42410)

Sermon delivered in Charlestown, in the province of South-Carolina. 83441

Sermon delivered in Christ Church, Alexandria. 104577

Sermon, delivered in Christ-Church, on the 21st day of June, 1786. 103467

Sermon, delivered in Christ Church, Savannah. 82730

Sermon delivered in Colchester, April 21, 1861. 18058

Sermon delivered in connection with the anniversary of the American Society for Meliorating the Condition of the Jews. 89744

Sermon delivered in connection with the anniversary of the Foreign Evangelical Society, in the Reformed Dutch Church. 89744

Sermon delivered in Danvers. 89812

Sermon delivered in . . . Detroit. 95532

Sermon delivered in Dorchester, Dec. 7, 1845. 14134

Sermon delivered in Dorchester, May 14, 1841. 14132

Sermon delivered in . . . Dorchester, . . . Nov. 5, 1854. 84043

Sermon delivered in Durham, at the ordination. 36864

Sermon delivered in Durham, Connecticut. 82737

Sermon, delivered in East-Hampton. (28126), 55388, 104528

Sermon delivered in Essex. 24606

Sermon delivered in Francestown, N. H. 18164

Sermon delivered in Gorham. (17918)

Sermon delivered in Grace Church, Galena. 22016

Sermon delivered in Grace Church, Providence. 13385

Sermon delivered in Hallowell. (36492)

Sermon, delivered in Hartford. 83576

Sermon delivered in Haverhill, Dec. 22, 1820. 20502

Sermon, delivered in Haverhill, Mass. 26297

Sermon delivered in Henniker. 25195

Sermon delivered . . . in Hingham. 71062

Sermon, delivered in Holliston, February 19, 1839. 92240

Sermon delivered in Holliston, on the day of the annual thanksgiving. 24564

Sermon delivered in Hudson, Ohio. 32263

Sermon delivered in Huntsville, Alabama. 73355

Sermon delivered in Ipswich, Second Parish. 17699

Sermon, delivered in King's Chapel, Boston. 101383

Sermon delivered in Lexington, Kentucky. 18466

Sermon, delivered in . . . Lowell, on the day of annual thanksgiving. 9367

Sermon delivered in Madisonville. 84366

Sermon delivered in Manlius, N. Y. 43268

Sermon delivered . . . in Marblehead. 24779

Sermon, delivered in Needham. 58378

Sermon delivered in New-Haven. 40810

Sermon, delivered in . . . New-York, April 1, 1810. 73049

Sermon, delivered in . . . New-York, . . . January 28, 1810. (73052)

Sermon, delivered in New-York, on the 22d of December, 1821. 73050

Sermon delivered in Newburyport, February 18, 1827. 105128

Sermon delivered in Newburyport, March 20, 1827. 20193

Sermon, delivered in . . . Newburyport, Ms., April 19, 1852. (81628)

Sermon, delivered in Newton, Oct. 13, 1816. 32728

Sermon, delivered in . . . Newton, March 6th, 1815. 68122

Sermon delivered in North Brookfield, April 23d, 1818. 85388

Sermon, delivered in North Brookfield, November 26, 1846. 85403

Sermon, delivered in North-Yarmouth, June 28, 1837. 92119

Sermon, delivered in Northampton, August 24, 1815. 37162

Sermon, delivered in Northampton, March 6, 1828. 2031

Sermon deliver'd in Norwich Second Society. 95760

Sermon deliver'd (in part) at a family-meeting in pricate. 25408

Sermon, delivered . . . in Petersham. (25221)

Sermon delivered in Philadelphia at the opening of the Baptist Association. 30642

Sermon delivered in . . . Philadelphia, . . . 27th of December, 1793. 43804

Sermon, delivered in . . . Pittsburgh, July 1846. (71267)

Sermon, delivered in Plymouth, Dec. 23, 1821. 96306

Sermon delivered in Plymouth, New-Hampshire, on fast day. 23662

Sermon delivered in . . . Portland, on the annual thanksgiving. 5586

Sermon, delivered in presence of His Excellency John Taylor Gilman. (73574)

Sermon, delivered, in publick, to the Assembly of Ministers. 3474

Sermon delivered in Rochester, N. H. 92792

Sermon delivered in St. Andrews Church, Hanover. 18184

Sermon delivered in St. Andrew's Church, Quebec. 88956

Sermon, delivered in St. George's Church, Flushing. 82935

Sermon delivered in St. Paul's Church, Hoboken. 8729

Sermon: delivered in St. Paul's Church, on the fourth of July, 1813. 104578

Sermon, delivered in . . . Salem . . . March 13. (4774)

Sermon delivered in Salem, Sept. 25, 1823. 16795

Sermon delivered in . . . Springfield, Mass. 57786

Sermon delivered . . . in Springfield, May 10, 1846. 74324

Sermon, delivered in Stafford, on the anniversary of American independence, July 4th, A. D. 1793. 104313

Sermon delivered in . . . Stamford, . . . November 28, 1861. (49727)

Sermon delivered in the audience of His Exellency the Earl of Bellomont, Captain General and Governour in Chief, and of the Council, and Representatives of the General Assembly of the Province of Massachusetts-Bay, convened at Boston in New-England, May 31st. 1699. (46751)

Sermon delivered in the audience of His Excellency, the Earl of Bellomont, Captain General, and Governor in Chief, and of the Council & Representatives, of the General Assembly of the Province of the

Massachusetts-Bay, convened at Boston, in New-England. On May 29 1700. 46458

Sermon delivered in the audience of the General Assembly of the colony of Connecticut, at New Haven Oct. 18. 1719. 18185

Sermon delivered in the audience of the General Assembly of the colony of Connecticut, at New Haven Octob. 22, 1727. 104220

Sermon delivered in the audience of the ministers of . . . Massachusetts-Bay. 62513

Sermon delivered in the Baptist Meeting House in Sansom-Street. 90839

Sermon delivered in the Baptist Meeting House, in the village of Troy. 56839

Sermon delivered in the Brick Meeting House in Danvers. 100920

Sermon, delivered in the capitol of the United States. 90841

Sermon delivered in the Central Presbyterian Church, Charlestown. 18456

Sermon, delivered in the Chapel, Boston, before the Society of Antient and Honorable Free and Accepted Masons. 101469

Sermon delivered in the Chapel of Rhode-Island College. 47005

Sermon delivered in the Chapel of Yale College. (49032)

Sermon, delivered in the Chapel in Essex-Street. 74721

Sermon, delivered in the Church of the Covenant. 74739

Sermon delivered in the Church of the Holy Innocents, Albany. 68686

Sermon delivered in the College Chapel in New Haven. 82218

Sermon, delivered in the Collegiate Institution, Amherst. 32250

Sermon delivered in the East Church, in Salem. 24778

Sermon, delivered in the east, north, and south. 102080

Sermon, delivered in the First Church in Portsmouth. 8929

Sermon, delivered in the First Church in Portsmouth, on the Lord's Day after the melancholy tidings of the death. 8929

Sermon delivered in the First Congregational Church in New Orleans. 13229

Sermon, delivered in the First Parish in Springfield. 7662, 104270

Sermon delivered in the First Presbyterian Church, Newark. 103229

Sermon delivered in the First Presbyterian Church, Utica, N. Y. 64210

Sermon, delivered in the First Presbyterian Meeting House in Cincinnati. 104675

Sermon, delivered in the First Society in Lebanon. 104363

Sermon, delivered in the First Society in Lebanon, May 31, 1780. 92130

Sermon, delivered in the First Society of Chatham. 92893

Sermon delivered in the First Universalist Church, Lombard Street. 84287

Sermon delivered in the Fourth Baptist Church, Providence. (28279)

Sermon delivered in the Fourth Universalist Church in Boston. 103792

Sermon . . . delivered in the Greene St. Hebrew Synagogue. 67913

Sermon, delivered in the Hollis Street Meeting-House, Boston. (25185)

Sermon delivered in the M. E. Church, Mount Vernon, N. Y. 6369

Sermon delivered in the Masonic Temple on fast day. (13409)

Sermon, delivered in the North Presbyterian Church in Hartford. 92967

Sermon, delivered in the Old South Church, Boston. (74725)

Sermon delivered in the Old South Church, in Boston. 104906

Sermon, delivered in the Pearl-Street Presbyterian Church. 73566

Sermon, delivered in the Presbyterian Church at Caldwell, N. J. 89682

Sermon delivered in the Presbyterian Church, Natchez. 92739

Sermon, delivered in the presence of His Excellency Samuel Huntington. 71734

Sermon, delivered in the presence of His Excellency Samuel Huntington, Esq. L. L. D. Governor. 92966

Sermon, delivered in the Roman Catholic Church, New-York. (24080)

Sermon delivered in the South Congregational Church, Newport. 59124

Sermon delivered in the Second Congregational Church, Norwich. 20036

Sermon delivered in the Second Presbyterian Church, Albany. 89744

Sermon delivered in the Second Presbyterian Church, Albany, on Sabbath afternoon, July 20, 1854. 89744

Sermon delivered in the Second Presbyterian Church, Albany, on Sabbath morning, August 20, 1854. 89744

Sermon delivered in the Second Presbyterian Church, Albany, September 3, 1854. 89744

Sermon delivered in the Second Presbyterian Church, Albany, Sunday morning, November 6, 1859. 89744

Sermon: delivered in the Second Presbyterian Church, Charleston. 85338

Sermon delivered in the Second Presbyterian Church in Charleston, (S. C.) on Sabbath morning. 85279

Sermon delivered in the Second Presbyterian Church in the city of Albany. 89744

Sermon delivered in the South Parish in Andover, April 5, 1810. 12988

Sermon delivered in the Trinitarian Church on fast day. 17369

Sermon, delivered in the Warren Street Church, Sunday, November 14, 1852. (81622)

Sermon delivered in the West Church, Boston. 3792

Sermon, delivered in Tolland, on the public fast. 71889, 104315

Sermon delivered in Trinity Church, Boston. 21552

Sermon, delivered in Trinity Church, Easton. 72704

Sermon delivered in Trinity Church, Milton. 36514

Sermon, delivered in Trinity Church, New-Haven. 103464

Sermon delivered in Trinity Church, New York. 30530

Sermon, delivered in Union Village, Paris, (N. Y.) 84286

Sermon, delivered in Warwick, Mass. 83730

Sermon delivered . . . in West-Bridgewater. 32345

Sermon, delivered in West-Springfield. 39199

Sermon delivered in . . . Williamsburgh, L. I. 64237

Sermon, delivered, in Windham. 102521

Sermon, delivered in Winthrop. 82892
Sermon, delivered in Wiscasset. 104388
Sermon, delivered in Woburn. 4735
Sermon, delivered in Worcester Jail. 102090
Sermon delivered in Worcester, January 31, 1836. 3104
Sermon delivered in Yale College. 18267
Sermon, delivered January 11, 1810. 67746
Sermon, . . . delivered Jan. 10, 1830. 43225
Sermon delivered Jan. 3, 1759. 42013
Sermon delivered January 13, 1861. (29839)
Sermon delivered January 26, 1803. 24932
Sermon, delivered July 1, 1789. 21791
Sermon delivered . . . July 4, 1852. 82385
Sermon, delivered July 4, 1802. 24211
Sermon . . . delivered, July fourth 1830. 105666
Sermon, delivered July 4, 1826. 6055
Sermon delivered July 2, 1806. (4776)
Sermon delivered . . . July 31, 1842. 43790
Sermon, delivered July 31, 1816. 17403
Sermon delivered July 31st, 1768. 15094
Sermon delivered July 20, 1796. 11213
Sermon, delivered July 29, 1829. 76369
Sermon delivered July 23, 1812. 8470
Sermon . . . delivered June, 1825. 22461
Sermon delivered . . . June 1st, 1865. 36359
Sermon delivered June 13, 1827. 89744
Sermon, delivered Lord's Day, January 6, 1828. 93089
Sermon, delivered March 1st, 1840. 82953
Sermon, delivered March 2, 1803. 22465
Sermon delivered March 7, 1802. 18405
Sermon, delivered March 6th, 1760. (9718)
Sermon, delivered March 12, 1828. 5317
Sermon, delivered . . . March 21, 1819. 73056
Sermon, delivered March 21st, 1798. 32550
Sermon, delivered March 22, 1837. 89744
Sermon, delivered March 27th, 1776. (73560)
Sermon, delivered May 14, 1841. (26240)
Sermon delivered May 3, 1812. 105139
Sermon, delivered May 13, 1790. 104055
Sermon, delivered May 26, 1808. 11965
Sermon, delivered May 23, 1792. 71504
Sermon delivered next Lord's Day after the interment. 50787
Sermon, delivered . . . November 5, 1809. 26624
Sermon, delivered November 19, 1827. 17700
Sermon, delivered November 19, 1823. 11956
Sermon delivered November 6th, 1808. (72474)
Sermon delivered November 3, 1821. 103410
Sermon delivered November 13, 1855. 24605
Sermon, delivered November 13th, 1814. 92128
Sermon, delivered, November 30, 1804. 97477
Sermon, delivered November 20, 1816. 71122
Sermon, delivered November 20, 1794. 91808
Sermon delivered November 22, 1809. (71506)
Sermon delivered Nov. 22, 1832. 55384
Sermon delivered November 26, 1808. 1507
Sermon delivered October 1, 1801. 1506
Sermon, delivered, October 9, 1793. 103937
Sermon delivered October 7, 1801. (18435)
Sermon, delivered October 17th, 1824. 71062
Sermon delivered October 12, 1851. 89744
Sermon, delivered October 24, 1819. 73573
Sermon, delivered October 27th, 1813. 92927
Sermon delivered October 27, 1833. 59077
Sermon delivered on fast day, April 6, 1826. 74724
Sermon delivered on fast day at Church Green, Boston. 19860
Sermon delivered on Sabbath evening, April 23, 1865. 82701

Sermon, delivered on Sabbath morning, Jan. 4, 1846. 89744
Sermon delivered on Sabbath, P. Lachor, 5824. (22089)
[Sermon] delivered on Sunday evening, July 4, 1875. 85202
Sermon, delivered on Sunday morning, June 22, 1851. 21661
Sermon delivered on thanksgiving day, at Mattapoisett. (8827)
Sermon delivered on thanksgiving day, in Baltimore. 17928
Sermon delivered on thanksgiving day: in . . . Peoria. 36384
Sermon delivered on thanksgiving day, November 26th, 1863. (22089)
Sermon, delivered . . . on the anniversary election, May 26, 1819. 21737
Sermon delivered on the anniversary of the Female Benevolent Society. (67989)
Sermon delivered on the annual fast in Massachusetts. 27401
Sermon delivered on the annual thanksgiving, November 29, 1798. 25869
Sermon delivered on the day of annual thanksgiving, November 19, 1795. 92928
Sermon, delivered on the day of annual thanksgiving, November 20, 1794. 22169
Sermon, delivered on the day of general election, at Montpelier. (77315)
Sermon, delivered on the day of general election, at Montpelier, October 12, 1815. 18826
Sermon delivered on the day of general election, . . . Oct. 13. 3776
Sermon delivered on the day of general election . . . Oct. 13, 1814. 42779
Sermon delivered on the day of national humiliation. 17927
Sermon, delivered on the day of national thanksgiving. February 19, 1795. .By Ebenezer Bradford. 7240-7241
Sermon, delivered on the day of national thanksgiving, February 19, 1795. [By Thomas Barnard.] 3493
Sermon delivered on the day of prayer. (48709)
Sermon, delivered on the day of public humiliation and prayer. 7241
Sermon, delivered on the day of public thanksgiving, at Deerfield. 94499
Sermon, delivered on the day of the annual fast, April 6, 1820. 103164
Sermon delivered on the day of the annual fast in Massachusetts. 101307
Sermon, delivered on the day of the annual thanksgiving. 3493
Sermon: delivered on the day of the national fast, May 14th, 1841. 65381
Sermon delivered on the death of the Rev. Joseph Lane. 92032
Sermon, delivered on the late fast day. 90361
Sermon delivered on the Lord's Day succeeding the interment. 103776
Sermon delivered on the national fast day, January 4, 1861. 12612
Sermon, delivered on the national thanksgiving, April 13, 1815. 104372
Sermon, delivered on the 9th of May, 1798. (4440)
Sermon delivered on the occasion of the annual thanksgiving, Dec. 12, 1827. 2887
Sermon delivered on the occasion of the death of John Nitchie. 103388
Sermon, delivered on the public fast, April 9th, 1801. 102753

Sermon en las exequias de Joseph de la Puente. 78924

Sermon en las honorificas y sumptuoas exequias. 11322

Sermon en las honras de Dona Hypolita de Cordova. 7459

Sermon en las honras de el Chr. Munoz de la Concepcion. 77057

Sermon en las honras de el Doctor Don Andres Gonzalez Calderon Arcediano. 27825

Sermon en las honras funebres que hizo el Religiosissimo Convento de S. Phelippe de Jesus. 24828

Sermon en lengva de Chile. 98334

Sermon en solemne dedicacion del Oratorio de S. Felipe Neri. 76290

Sermon, entitled The principles of the revolution vindicated. 102145

Sermon, entitled "The remedy for duelling." 4330

Sermon entituled, The marks of the new birth. 103569, 103581

Sermon, entituled, The wise and foolish virgins. 103582

Sermon, entituled, What think ye of Christ? 103583

Sermon epidictico que en las honras. 22834

Sermon eucaristico por el nacimiento del Principe Luis I. (76179)

Sermon eucharistico por la felicidad que locro la ciudad de Durango. 22925

Sermon exhibiting some of the principal doctrines. 88979, 102563, 105646

Sermon, exhibiting the present dangers. 50950

Sermon . . . fast day. 39218

Sermon . . . Feb. 18, 1818. 64232

Sermon . . . February 15, 1826. 58718

Sermon . . . February 5, 1860. (43394)

Sermon, . . . February 5th, 1799. (49064)

Sermon . . . February 14, 1836. 37366

[Sermon] Feb. 19th, 1804. 2921

Sermon . . . February 19th. 1795. being a day. 19058

Sermon . . . February 19, 1795, the day of public thanksgiving. (25981)

Sermon . . . February 2d, 1845. (45438)

Sermon . . . February 17, 1811. 32570

[Sermon] Feb. 17, 1813. 13854

Sermon, February 7, 1822.3. (14525)

Sermon . . . February 3d, 1839. 5085

Sermon . . . February 28, 1821. (23951)

Sermon . . . February 28, 1790. (50953)

Sermon, Feb. 25. 1722. (25397)

Sermon . . . February 21, 1847. 33964

Sermon; . . . Feb. 24th, 1808. 24497

Sermon . . . Feb. 24, 1802. (59317)

Sermon . . . February 24, 1731, 32. 83978

Sermon . . . February 22, 1863. (36246)

Sermon . . . Feb. 26, 1817. 3941

Sermon . . . February 23, 1730, 31. 83978

Sermon . . . 5 March, 1854. 32397

Sermon . . . following the death of Rev. James F. Brown. (29830)

Sermon for all times. 13246

Sermon for country and kindred. 3794

Sermon for December 15, 1796. 25765

Sermon for midsummer day. note after (58767)

Sermon for thanksgiving day, 1861. 83570

Sermon . . . for the benefit of the New-York Bible and Common Prayer Book Society. 42765

Sermon . . . for the benefit of the Portsmouth Female Asylum. 28818

Sermon for the Boston Prison Discipline Society. 92016

Sermon for the Church of the Redeemer. 7275

Sermon, for the day of publick thanksgiving. 105109

Sermon, for the day of thanksgiving. 3574

Sermon for the fourth of July, 1862. 90471

Sermon for the General Theological Seminary. 43679

Sermon for the new year. note after (58767)

Sermon for the Presbyterian Sunday School Society of St. Louis. 64692

Sermon for the reformation of manners. 14517

Sermon for the relief of the widows and children. (5645)

Sermon for the rich to buy. 22384

Sermon for the time. 31218

Sermon for the times. By Joseph A. Seiss. 78939

Sermon for the times. By Rev. Alexander Clark. 13241

Sermon for the times. By Rev. W. Y. Rooker. (73090)

Sermon for the times, by Rev. William P. Breed. 7697

Sermon for the times. . . . By the Rev. Alexander Duncanson. 21266

Sermon for the times. Civil War, no remedy for secession. 64941

Sermon for the times . . . fast day, April 7, 1864. 42014

Sermon for the times . . . Jackson, July 28, 1854. 82234

Sermon for the times. June, 1862. 13279

Sermon for the times . . . on fast day, April 7, 1864. 3794

Sermon for the times. Preached at Jacksonville, Fla. 28708

Sermon for the times. . . . preached in aid of the "Jacobins in Maryland." 38167

Sermon for the times; . . . September 22, 1850. note after (58767)

Sermon founded on Jer. 28: 16. 76495

Sermon . . . 14th January, 1817. 11943

Sermon, . . . fourth anniversary of the Auxiliary Education Society. 21979

Sermon, fourth of March, 1813. 104382

Sermon from Eccles. iv. 9, 10, 11, 12. 103572

Sermon from Gal. ii. 19. 22322, 36951

Sermon from Joh. III, 3. 94705

Sermon from I. Joh. III. 94705

Sermon. From I Peter 2, 17. 95759

Sermon from I. Tim. ii. 4. (1838)

Sermon from Philipp. ii, 12, 13. (20529)

Sermon, from Psal 103, 15, 16. 100913

Sermon from Psalms CXXII. I. (14525)

Sermon from Psalm CXXII. 7. 92275

Sermon from Rev. II: 3. 2632

Sermon from the capitol. 91916

Sermon from the Independent whig. (17350)

Sermon from Zech. VII., 10. 1845

Sermon funebre a las piadosas memorias de J. Alonso de Cuevas Davalos. 81000

Sermon funebre, a los piadosas memorias del Illmo. y Rmo. Sr. Dr. D. Alonso de Cuevas. 62248

Sermon fuenbre, celebro en Mexico dia 28. Febrero. 18330

Sermon fuenbre, de Francisco Xavier Lazcano. 62874

Sermon funebre en las exequias de los militares difuntos Espanoles. (22816)

Sermon funebre en las exequias que el Colegio de Pachuca hizo. 74048

Sermon funebre en las exequias, que el Observantissimo Convento de San Juan de la Penitencia de Mexico. 75608

Sermon funebre en las honras al Capitan D. Gaspar de Villalpando Centeno. 19977

Sermon funebre en las honras de la piadosa Sra. Dona Teresa Bernaldo de Palacio. 73851

Sermon funebre en las honras, que el dia 26 de Oct. 1825. 36087

Sermon funebre en las solemn. exequias de Sen Cayet Ant. de Torres. 26387

Sermon funebre en memoria del F. Mathias de Escobar y Llamas. 23805

Sermon funebre, por A. C. de Montenegro. 80880

Sermon funebre predicado en la Santa Iglesia Catedral de Mejico. 72802

Sermon funebre que en el aniversario de difuntos. 59340

Sermon funebre que en las exequias a la tierna. 39291

Sermon funebre que en las exequias del P. San Phelipe Neri. 48994

Sermon funebre que en las exequias, que el Convento de San Francisco Xavier. 26387

Sermon funebre, que en las honras, que a la memoria. 98374

Sermon funebre, que en las honras, que hicieron en 29. de Mayo. 96274

Sermon funebre, que en las honras que hizo la Insigne Real Colegiata de Nuestra Senora de Guadalupe de Mexico. 27805

Sermon funebre y panegyrico en las honras. 31725

Sermon funebris, por J. M. Velez de Ulivarri y Olasasso. (44542)

Sermon funeral en las honras del D. Andreas de Carvajal y Tapia. 64169

Sermon funeral en las honras del Dr. D. Pedro Bernardino Primo y Jordan. 68815, 75579

Sermon . . . funeral of Capt. Simeon A. Mellick. (36507)

Sermon . . . funeral of John Hubbard, Nov. 28, 1794. 42791

Sermon funeral que predico el R. P. F. Gaspar Joseph de Solis. 86423

Sermon giving an historical account of St. John's Church. 9630

Sermon giving historical notices of St. Mark's Church. 1673

Sermon: giving thanks for union victories. 8474

Sermon, Granville, May 1, 1805. 16366

Sermon had in private, Octob. 15, 1722. (14525)

Sermon; . . . Hall of the House of Representatives. 33593

Sermon . . . Hallowell. 27401

Sermon . . . Hartford, Sept. 14, 1836. 14137

Sermon, . . . Hatfield, November 7th, A. D. 1793. 42788

Sermon having some reference to the character of the late Rev. Cortlandt Van Rensselaer. 89744

Sermon . . . Hingham, December 6, 1770. 26785

Sermon, historical sketch, addresses, &c. 35736

Sermon, historical papers, addresses. 63944

Sermon historico apologetico de Nuestra Senora de Guadeloupe. 27792

Sermon: . . . history of the Methodist Church in Hartford. 17435

Sermon, illustrating the human and official inferiority and supreme divinity of Christ. 72085

Sermon . . . in . . . Albany, August 26, 1829. (49064)

Sermon . . . in . . . Albany, N. Y. 47176

Sermon . . . in . . . Albany, on thanksgiving day, November 24, 1853. (44233)

Sermon . . . in . . . Albany, on thanksgiving day, Nov. 29, 1855. 43866

Sermon . . . in . . . Albany, 22d February, 1822. 38457

Sermon . . . in . . . Alexandria, . . . 18th of Sept. 1825. 47242

Sermon, in Argyle, County of Washington. 29893

Sermon . . . in Bainbridge, Pennsylvania. 33599

Sermon . . . in Baltimore, January 13, 1861. 31244

Sermon in . . . Baltimore . . . May 14, 1837. 9364

Sermon, . . . in . . . Baltimore, October 19, 1820. 49062

Sermon . . . in Baltimore . . . September 18, 1859. 26536

Sermon . . . in . . . Baltimore, September 15, 1836. (49064)

Sermon . . . in Barkhemstead. 44752

Sermon . . . in behalf of the American Colonization Society. July 4, 1830. 43790

Sermon, . . . in behalf of the American Colonization Society, . . . New-York, July 10, 1825. 43585

Sermon, in behalf of the American Education Society, . . . May 23, 1853. 22100

Sermon, in behalf of the American Education Society, . . . May 29, 1854. 35702

Sermon . . . in behalf of the American Home Missionary Society . . . January 2, 1848. (45438)

Sermon in behalf of the American Home Missionary Society . . . May, 1849. 3502

Sermon in behalf of the American Home Missionary Society, . . . May 10, 1870. 44350

Sermon in behalf of the American Home Missionary Society, preached in . . . New York and Brooklyn, May, 1851. 71268

Sermon in behalf of the American Home Missionary Society. Preached in . . . New-York and Brooklyn, May, 1848. 37970

Sermon, in behalf of the American Sunday-School Union, delivered at Philadelphia, May 15, 1853. 64678

Sermon, in behalf of the American Sunday-School Union. Delivered at Philadelphia, May 16, 1847. 5084

Sermon, in behalf of the Bethesda Society of Boston, delivered in Park Street Church. 92020

Sermon in behalf of the General Episcopal S. S. Union. 13385

Sermon in behalf of the mission work of St. Mark's Chapel. 21507

Sermon . . . in . . . Bleecker-St. . . . Church. 39837

Sermon . . . in Boston, after the funerals. (14493)

Sermon . . . in Boston, . . . after the interment. 22465

Sermon . . . in Boston, . . . anniversary of the American Education Society. (64233)

Sermon . . . in Boston, . . . April 3, 1729. (24926)

Sermon . . . in Boston at the Annual Convention of the Congregational Ministers of Massachusetts, May 30, 1811. 66604

Sermon . . . in Boston at the Annual Convention of the Congregational Ministers of Massachusetts, May 31st, 1810. 64245

Sermon, . . . in Boston, at the Annual Convention of the Warren Association. 47005

Sermon . . . in Boston, August 20, 1812. 11919

Sermon in Boston, August 26. 1742. 22442

Sermon . . . in Boston, before the American Society for Educating Pious Youth for the Gospel Ministry. 59443

Sermon . . . in Boston, before the Conference of Baptist Ministers. 79782

Sermon . . . in Boston, before the Massachusetts Society for Promoting Christian Knowledge, Nov. 27, 1811. 59444

Sermon . . . in Boston before the Massachusetts Society for Promoting Christian Knowledge, Sept. 15, 1813. (65109)

Sermon . . . in Boston, December 24. 1741. 32880

Sermon . . . in Boston, February 2, 1862. (25021)

Sermon . . . in Boston, . . . Febr. 28th. 1719, 20. 25408

Sermon . . . in Boston, in the audience of the General Court. 25408

Sermon . . . in Boston, June 1st, 1812. 64245

Sermon, . . . in Boston, . . . June 4, 1854. note after (58767)

Sermon . . . in Boston, March 17th. 1744, 5. 43036

Sermon, . . . in Boston, May 10, 1812. 39199

Sermon . . . in . . . Boston, May 22, 1768. (51518)

Sermon . . . in Boston, November 18, 1791. 33279

Sermon . . . in Boston . . . Nov. 29, 1866. (64639)

Sermon, . . . in . . . Boston, . . . Oct. 31, 1819. 58901

Sermon . . . in . . . Boston. On 8 d. XI m. 1716, 17. 46618

Sermon . . . in Boston, on fast day, April 7, 1808. 26624

Sermon, . . . in Boston, on October, 21st. 1773. 46802

Sermon . . . in . . . Boston, on the death of Mary E. Robbins . . . June 26, 1870. 50716

Sermon, . . . in . . . Boston, September 25, 1807. (50953)

Sermon . . . in Boston, Sept. 21. 12371

Sermon, in . . . Boston . . . thanksgiving day, November 29, 1850. (81623)

Sermon . . . in Bradford, Feb. 2, 1742.3. 2873

Sermon, in Braintree. 47068

Sermon . . . in Brookline. 31218

Sermon . . . [in] Brooklyn . . . April 23, 1853. 41933

Sermon in Brooklyn, Conn., April 14, 1824. 22377

Sermon in . . . Brooklyn . . . June 5th, 1870. 66765

Sermon . . . in . . . Brooklyn, N. Y., February 11, 1849. (36320)

Sermon . . . in . . . Brooklyn, N. Y., . . . June 26, 1853. (23813)

Sermon . . . in . . . Brooklyn, New York, on thanksgiving day. 36321

Sermon . . . in Buffalo. 42032

Sermon, . . . in Burlington. 59459

Sermon in Cambridge. 32588

Sermon . . . in Catskill. (36935)

Sermon . . . in Charles-Town in South-Carolina. 23164

Sermon . . . in . . . Charleston, December 15th, 1861. (33346)

Sermon in Charleston, S. C., Dec. 27, 1817. (18299)

Sermon in Charleston, S. C., March 22, 1778. 30642

Sermon, . . . in Charlestown, October 21st, 1866. (48931)

Sermon . . . in . . . Charlestown, on fast day. (48931)

Sermon, . . . in Chester, May 21, 1814. (51848)

Sermon . . . in Christ's Church, Hartford. 20391

Sermon . . . in Clermont. 40092

Sermon, . . . in Clinton. 55859

Sermon in commemoration of Daniel Webster. 90985

Sermon in commemoration of Rev. Edmund Hamilton Sears. 71789

Sermon, in commemoration of the benevolence of the citizens of Boston. 74727

Sermon in commemoration of the death of Abraham Lincoln. (23240)

Sermon in commemoration of the fiftieth anniversary of his [i. e. Charles Wellington's] ordination. 102579

Sermon, in commemoration of the landing. 12533

Sermon in commemoration of the Right Reverend William White. 20391

Sermon in commemoration of the sixth anniversary of the commencement. 18702

Sermon in commemoration of the virtues of Abraham Lincoln. (70436)

Sermon in commemoration of William Bartlet. 18405

Sermon . . . in . . . Concord, DNcember 10, 1858. 48928

Sermon . . . in Cummington, Mass. 18429

Sermon . . . in Dalton, March 4, 1808. 36039, 102755

Sermon . . . in . . . Davenport, Iowa, on thanksgiving day. (39760)

Sermon . . . in . . . Davenport, on . . . thanksgiving. 39761

Sermon . . . in Dedham, January 10, 1847. 38776

Sermon . . . in Dedham, September 13, 1801. 30521

Sermon . . . in . . . Dorchester, after the death of Lieutenant William R. Porter. 47254

Sermon . . . in . . . Dorchester, . . . June 19, 1870. (29830)

Sermon . . . in Easton, at the interment of Mr. Isaac Lothrop. 32570

Sermon, . . . in . . . Elizabeth, N. J. (43820)

Sermon, . . . in . . . Elmira on the . . . death of Milton Partridge. 51435

Sermon . . . in Farmington, at the Freeman's Meeting. 64296

Sermon, . . . in Fitchburg, Mass. 66839

Sermon . . . in . . . Fredericksburgh. (43295)

Sermon, . . . in . . . Frederickton. 51187

Sermon . . . in Geneva. 57308

Sermon, . . . in Goshen. 42806

Sermon, . . . in Granville. (16365)

Sermon . . . in . . . Greenfield, Massachusetts, . . . June 17, 1855. 39759

Sermon in Greenfield, Massachusetts, October 16, 1825. 2757

Sermon, . . . in Hackney, March 30, 1794. (65513)

Sermon, . . . in Hadley, March 12, . . . 1811. 42791

Sermon . . . in Halifax, (Vt.) Sept. 17, 1806. 42791

Sermon . . . in Hartford, Ct. 68122

Sermon . . . in . . . Hartford . . . May 30, 1847. 35814

Sermon . . . in . . . Hartford, on thanksgiving day. 59765

Sermon . . . in Harvard University, July 13, 1845. 59354

Sermon . . . in Haverhill, February 20, 1774. 58649

Sermon . . . in Hingham, August 12. 1730. 26785

Sermon . . . in Hingham, January 8, 1865. 41244

Sermon . . . in Holles, New-Hampshire, April 19, 1804. 82468

Sermon . . . in Hollis Street Church, . . . 8th Dec. 1833. 62772

Sermon . . . in Hollis Street Church, fast day . . . April 2, 1840. 62772

Sermon . . . in Hopewell, New Jersey. 30642

Sermon . . . in Hopkinton, New-Hampshire. 82532

Sermon . . . in . . . Iowa. 39761

Sermon . . . in . . . Jamaica, L. I. (56388)

Sermon . . . in . . . Kensington. 50699

Sermon . . . in Kingston, N. H. (47454)

Sermon . . . in Lancaster. 47447

Sermon . . . in Littleton. 54953

Sermon . . . in Lowell, Mass., July 12th, 1846. 55324

Sermon . . . in Lowell, on the Sabbath following the funeral. 2957

Sermon . . . in Lowell, on the Sabbath following the funeral of the Hon. Luther Lawrence. 48928

Sermon . . . in Lyme. 14420

Sermon . . . in Lynn. 62781

Sermon . . . in Malden, November 25th, 1821. (28498)

Sermon in Malden, October 20th 1738. 22443

Sermon . . . in Marblehead . . . June 12, 1796. 33420

Sermon . . . in Marlborough, at the ordination. 13355

Sermon in Marlborough, July 9, 1734. 37467

Sermon in memory of Abraham Lincoln. 38812

Sermon in memory of Captain F. A. Root. 34777

Sermon in memory of Henrietta Lamson. (17833)

Sermon . . . in memory of Mrs. Adaline Hasklins. 36321

Sermon in memory of the late Samuel Bradlee. 22327

Sermon in memory of the Rev. George Champlin Shepard. 58735

Sermon in memory of the Rev. Samuel Bacon. 51256

Sermon in memory of the Right Reverend George Washington Doane. 43868

Sermon in memory of Thomas T. Guion. 36076

Sermon . . . in Middleborough, at the annual fast. (17738)

Sermon . . . in . . . Milton, June 4, 1854. 50716

Sermon . . . in Natick, June 13, 1819. (50424)

Sermon . . . in Needham, . . . March 22, 1812. 58378

Sermon . . . in Needham, Nov. 16, 1811. 58378

Sermon . . . in . . . New Albany, Indiana. 36321

Sermon . . . in . . . New-Brunswick, N. J. 66229

Sermon . . . in New-Haven: April 19th, 1741. 59609

Sermon, . . . in New-Haven, at the ordination of the Rev. Eleazer Thompson Fitch. 22272

Sermon, . . . in . . . New Haven, Conn., Oct. 9th, 1860. 67784

Sermon . . . in New Haven, Sept. 12, 1822. 66228

Sermon . . . in New London, Dec. 2, 1784. 59126

Sermon, . . . in . . . New Milford, Conn. 51434

Sermon . . . in . . . New-York . . . April 11th, 1841. 38315

Sermon, . . . in . . . New-York, . . . August 8, 1810. 48998

Sermon, . . . in . . . New-York, August 20th, 1812. (58793)

Sermon . . . in . . . New-York, July fourth, 1795. (49064)

Sermon, . . . in New-York, July 4th, 1793. 49057

Sermon . . . in . . . New-York, May 28, 1809. (49064)

Sermon . . . in . . . New-York, . . . November, 1817. 49131

Sermon in New York, Nov. 17, 1861. 26079

Sermon . . . in . . . New York . . . October 31, 1858. 4088

Sermon . . . in New York, . . . October 20, 1840. 57308

Sermon in . . . New-York, on the . . . consecration of . . . John H. Hopkins. 57317

Sermon . . . in . . . New York, on the . . . consecration of the Rev. Charles Franklin Robertson. 39466

Sermon . . . in . . . New-York, on the . . . death of Mrs. Mary Delezenne. 43502

Sermon, . . . in . . . Newark, before the Annual Convocation of the Church. 45447

Sermon . . . in Newbury-port, April 7, 1793. (49136)

Sermon in . . . Newburyport, . . . April 1, 1824. 20193

Sermon . . . in . . . Newburyport, January 6th, 1811. 50977

Sermon, . . . in . . . Newburyport, January 23, 1791. 51517

Sermon . . . in Newburyport, Mass., Nov. 25, 1813. 64138

Sermon in . . . Newburyport, November 9th, 1806. 59126

Sermon . . . in North Wilbraham. 39199

Sermon, . . . in Northyarmouth. (42774)

Sermon, . . . in . . . Norway Village. 51488

Sermon . . . in . . . Norwich, on . . . the death of Edward B. Chappell. 50690

Sermon, . . . in . . . Norwich, . . . Sept. 24th, 1853. 48128

Sermon . . . in . . . Perth-Amboy, May 16, 1786. 56825

Sermon, . . . in . . . Philadelphia, . . . April 9th, 1854. 55083

Sermon . . . in . . . Philadelphia, as a memorial of . . . Reverend Benjamin Dorr. (39823)

Sermon . . . May 3, 1840. 34175
Sermon . . . May 13. 1742. 12331
Sermon . . . May 13. 1733. (14525)
[Sermon] May 30, 1804. 2921
Sermon . . . May 31. 1721. 50302
Sermon . . . May 12, 1816. 34175
Sermon . . . May 20, 1863. 33964
Sermon . . . May 28, 1843. (39694)
Sermon . . . May 28, 1800. 43390
[Sermon] May 28, 1809. 2921
Sermon . . . May 25, 1802. 26624
Sermon, . . . May 25th. 1757. 59609
Sermon . . . May 25th. 1737. 42084
Sermon . . . May 26, 1851. 34119
Sermon . . . May 26th. 1756. 16598
Sermon . . . May 26th. MDCCXXXI. 24531
Sermon, . . . May 26. 1736. 32669
Sermon . . . May 23, 1831. 33794
Sermon-memoir of Mrs. Harriet Cutler.
    (77571)
Sermon. Memorial of the Rev. Henry
    William Duchalet. 23317
Sermon moral. 20136
Sermon moral del fuego vengador de la
    caridad. 11039
Sermon moral en la primera misa. 77055
Sermon moral en la solemne dedicacion del
    retablio del sagririo. 64021
Sermon moral para el Capitulo Provincial de
    Zacatecas. 76180
Sermon moral predicado en oposicion a la
    Canongia Magistral. 77054
Sermon moral, que en la rogacion solemne
    hecha por los Cuerpos Militares. 86249
Sermon moral sobre el Evangelio. (77103)
Sermon . . . Nashville, Tenn. 62717
Sermon . . . national fast, January 4, 1861.
    (47898)
Sermon . . . national independence, 1852.
    30500
Sermon, . . . national thanksgiving, February
    19, 1795. 37346
Sermon . . . New Bedford, April 21, 1861.
    17371
Sermon . . . New Bedford, Jan. 2, 1870.
    64670
Sermon . . . New Bedford, . . . September
    15th, 1850. 33079
Sermon . . . New Britain, Conn., thanksgiving
    day, November 26, 1863. (27845)
Sermon, . . . New London, Conn., on the day
    of thanksgiving. 43232
Sermon, . . . New-York, July 4th, 1799.
    (49064)
Sermon . . . New York, June 10, 1860. 26079
Sermon, . . . New York . . . March 19, 1843.
    21663
Sermon . . . New-York . . . May 14, 1841.
    38315
Sermon, . . . Newark, July 24th, 1825. 30047
Sermon . . . Newton Ms. on the anniversary
    of the landing. 39570
Sermon, 19th May, 1727. 27312
Sermon . . . 9th of May, 1798. 57778
Sermon . . . North Fairfield, Connecticut.
    29764
Sermon, . . . Northampton, before the Hamp-
    shire Missionary Society. 22433
Sermon, . . . Norwalk, Conn. 29764
Sermon not preached on the late general fast.
    (13001)
Sermon . . . Nov. 11, 1802. 58118
Sermon . . . November 11, 1772. 58902
Sermon, . . . Nov. 5, 1857. (3700)
Sermon, . . . Nov. 1, 1809. 43568

Sermon, . . . November 4, 1812. (50391)
Sermon . . . Nov. 19, 1854. 3794
Sermon . . . November 2, 1856. 26323
Sermon . . . November 2, 1825. 18405
Sermon Nov. 17, 1773. 36114
Sermon . . . November 16th, 1859. (43394)
Sermon . . . November 3, 1861. 3794
Sermon . . . Nov. 3, 1812. 59444
Sermon . . . November 13, 1858. (3508)
Sermon . . . November 13, 1839. 37976
Sermon . . . Nov. 30, 1837. 51539
Sermon . . . Nov. 30, MDCCXCV. 3105
Sermon . . . Nov. 12th, 1837. (45438)
Sermon, . . . November 12, 1812. 26624
Sermon . . . November 21, 1858. (43394)
Sermon . . . November 21st. 1758. 10685
Sermon . . . November 22d, 1835. 28687
Sermon . . . November 27, 1814. 58800
Sermon . . . Nov. 27, 1864. 3794
Sermon . . . November 26, 1837. 42032
Sermon, November 26, 1812. (18403)
Sermon—No. V.—Jan. 1831. 84288
Sermon, occasioned by her [i. e. Eleanor Emer-
    son's] death. 105302, 105306
Sermon occasioned by her [i. e. Susan Hunting-
    ton's] death. 104909, 104912
Sermon occasioned by her [i. e. Louisa Adams
    Leavitt's] death, and a supplementary
    sketch. 82337
Sermon occasioned by his [i. e. John Wither-
    spoon's] death. 104946
Sermon occasioned by that awfull providence.
    46753
Sermon, occasioned by that branch of British
    commerce. 4144
Sermon occasioned by the Alton outrage.
    96416
Sermon occasioned by the burning of the
    Episcopal Church. 21323
Sermon, occasioned by the burning of the
    steamer Lexington. 92082
Sermon occasioned by the catastrophe. (32816)
Sermon occasioned by the completion of the
    new college edifice. 93212
Sermon occasion'd by the death of a religious
    matron. 46428
Sermon occasioned by the death of Abel
    Chittenden. 7486
Sermon occasioned by the death of Abraham
    Lincoln. 91160
Sermon occasioned by the death of Adeline
    Rider. 64236
Sermon occasioned by the death of Alexander
    Henry. 43196
Sermon occasioned by the death of Andrew
    Pepperell. 91483
Sermon occasioned by the death of Arthur H.
    Prichard. (43394)
Sermon occasioned by the death of Barnabas
    Bidwell. 82751
Sermon occasioned by the death of Benjamin
    Stevens. 30892
Sermon occasioned by the death of Calvin
    Smith. 85201
Sermon, occasioned by the death of Calvin
    Whiting. 58378
Sermon, occasioned by the . . . death of Capt.
    Jonathan Parsons. (51518)
Sermon occasioned by the death of Capt. Lewis
    Smith. 76509
Sermon occasioned by the . . . death of Charles
    Whittelsey. 18415
Sermon, occasioned by the . . . death of Col.
    Moses Titcomb. 42441
Sermon occasioned by the death of Daniel
    Hildreth. 55206

Sermon occasioned by the death of Daniel
Webster. 90914

Sermon, occasioned by the death of David
Bates Douglass. 29615

Sermon occasioned by the death of Deacon
Samuel Staples. 33271

Sermon . . . occasioned by the death of D^r
A. Stone. 2906

Sermon, occasioned by the death of Dr.
Phineas Bradley. 82949

Sermon occasioned by the death of Edward
Everett. 66759

Sermon occasioned by the death of Elisabeth
Price. 12331

Sermon, occasioned by the death of General
George Washington, and preached Feb.
22, 1800. 95174

Sermon, occasioned by the death of Gen.
George Washington, Commander in Chief
of the Armies of the United States.
105116

Sermon occasioned by the death of Gen.
Shepard Leach. 32622

Sermon occasioned by the death of General
Washington, delivered at Greenbush.
(49006)

Sermon, occasioned by the death of Gen.
Washington, late President of the United
States. 13021

Sermon occasioned by the death of George II.
30892

Sermon, occasioned by the death of George
Washington, late Commander in Chief of
the Armies. 102746

Sermon, occasioned by the death of George
Washington, late Commander in Chief
of the Armies of the United States.
91799

Sermon, occasioned by the death of George
Washington, Supreme Commander of the
American forces. 101384

Sermon occasioned by the death of His Excellency DeWitt Clinton. 49131

Sermon occasioned by the death of His Excellency General George Washington. 26225

Sermon occasioned by the death of His Excellency, George Washington. 723

Sermon occasioned by the death of Hon. Jabez
W. Huntington. 6278

Sermon occasioned by the death of Hon. John
Davis. 26536

Sermon occasioned by the death of Hon.
William Hale. 58805

Sermon occasioned by the death of . . . Hon.
William Reed. 17328

Sermon occasioned by the death of James
Greene. 91492

Sermon, occasioned by the death of John
Adams. (13451)

Sermon occasioned by the death of John
Gorham. 58325

Sermon . . . occasioned by the death of John
Ogilvie. (34766)

Sermon occasioned by the death of Jonathan
Nicols. 105665

Sermon, occasioned by the death of Josiah
Hartwell. 25216

Sermon, occasioned by the death of Lieutenant-
General George Washington. (32464)

Sermon occasioned by the death of Lieut. John
Hammond. (33212)

Sermon occasioned by the death of Major Gen.
Alexander Hamilton. 52

Sermon occasioned by the death of Major James
Owen Law. 51577

Sermon occasioned by the death of Major
Thomas Savage. 104073

Sermon, occasioned by the death of Miss Mary
S. Dwight. 24503

Sermon occasioned by the death of Miss Susan
Allibone. 91569

Sermon occasioned by the death of Mr. Abiel
Abbot. 3474

Sermon occasioned by the death of Mr. Amos
Fuller. 58378

Sermon, occasioned by the death of Mr. Amos
Pettingell. 20193

Sermon, occasioned by the death of Mr. Charles
Bealer. 32463

Sermon occasioned by the death of Mrs.
Jeremiah Fuller. 58378

Sermon occasioned by the death of Mr.
William Combs. 18405

Sermon, occasioned by the death of Mrs.
Abigail Davison. 12527

Sermon, occasioned by the death of Mrs. Abigail
Noyes. 103789

Sermon; occasioned by the death of Mrs.
Barrent Van Buren. (64239)

Sermon occasioned by the death of Mrs. Betsy,
wife of Deacon Matthews Thacher. 33271

Sermon occasioned by the death of Mrs. Beulah
Clarke. 21803

Sermon, occasioned by the death of Mrs.
Clarissa Webber. 49138

Sermon occasioned by the death of Mrs.
Elizabeth Watson. 71764

Sermon occasioned by the death of Mrs.
Eunice T. Smith. 62577

Sermon occasioned by the death of Mrs. Hariot
Putnam. 18405

Sermon occasioned by the death of Mrs.
Isabella Graham. 45463

Sermon occasioned by the death of Mrs. Lydia
Hovey. 71754

Sermon, occasioned by the death of Mrs.
Margaret Green. (78693)

Sermon occasioned by the death of Mrs.
Mariam Phillips. 104914

Sermon occasioned by the death of Mrs. S.
Agnes Smith. 8577

Sermon occasioned by the death of Mrs. Sarah
Gill. (33783)

Sermon occasioned by the death of Mrs. Sarah
Maria Potter. (68588)

Sermon, occasioned by the death of Mrs. Sarah
Whitman. (79952)

Sermon occasioned by the death of President
Taylor. 91917

Sermon occasioned by the death of Rev.
Alexander Phoenix. 6926

Sermon occasioned by the death of Rev. Dr.
Auchmuty. (50329)

Sermon occasioned by the death of Rev. Dr.
James Sproat. (28505)

Sermon occasioned by the death of . . . Rev.
Dr. John N. Abeel. 29281

Sermon occasioned by the death of Rev. Dr.
Samuel Auchmuty. (34766)

Sermon occasioned by the death of Rev. Edwin
H. Crane. (70468)

Sermon occasioned by the death of Rev. George
Bradford. 66763

Sermon occasioned by the death of Rev.
Nathaniel Gage. 8900

Sermon occasioned by the death of . . . Rev.
Samuel Foxcroft. 51052

Sermon occasioned by the death of Rev. Samuel
Gay. (21423)

Sermon occasioned by the death of Rev.
Theophilus Lindsay. 4599

Sermon occasioned by the death of Rev.
William Ramsay. 28521

Sermon occasioned by the death of Richard
Marvin, Esq. 89744

Sermon occasioned by the death of Robert
Ralston. 18211

Sermon, occasioned by the death of Royal W.
Smith. 104119

Sermon occasioned by the death of several
who were drowned. 46470

Sermon occasioned by the death of several
worthy members. 12331

Sermon occasioned by the death of the
Honorable Abigail Belcher. 78692

Sermon occasioned by the death of the Hon.
Alfred Dwight Foster. 82209

Sermon occasioned by the death of the Hon.
Ambrose Spencer. 64640

Sermon occasioned by the death of the Hon.
. . . John Burrill. 31302

Sermon occasioned by the death of the Honble.
Judge Wilds. (24759)

Sermon, occasioned by the death of the
Honorable Major General Alexander
Hamilton. 86130

Sermon, occasioned by the death of the
Honorable Major-General Israel Putnam.
103763

Sermon occasioned by the death of the
Honourable Mary Belcher. 65584

Sermon occasioned by the death of the
Honorable Mrs. Abigail Belcher. 105073

Sermon, occasioned by the death of the Hon.
Richard Penn. 21052

Sermon occasioned by the death of the
Honourable Sir William Pepperell.
91484

Sermon occasioned by the death of the
Honourable Wait Winthrop. (79408)

Sermon occasioned by the death of the Hon.
William Phillips. 104915

Sermon occasioned by the death of the Hon.
William Williams. 36039, 102755

Sermon occasioned by the death of the late
Mr. Edmund P. Sanford. 34175

Sermon occasioned by the death of the late
Reverend Mr. Gilbert Tennent. (24390)

Sermon, occasioned by the death of the mother
of the late Judge Story. 71782

Sermon occasioned by the death of the Rev.
Alexander H. Crosby. 30493

Sermon occasion'd by the death of the
Reverend & Learned, Mr. Ebenezer
Pemberton. (79426)

Sermon occasioned by the death of the Rev.
George Cowles. 58626

Sermon occasioned by the death of the Rev.
George Phillips Smith. 82208

Sermon occasioned by the death of the Rev.
George Whitefield. 22222

Sermon, occasioned by the death of the Rev.
James Patterson. (3508)

Sermon occasioned by the death of the Rev.
John H. Livingston. 18212

Sermon occasioned by the death of the Rev.
John Martin Connell. 6070

Sermon occasioned by the death of the Rev.
Joseph S. Christmas. 89773

Sermon, occasioned by the death of the Rev.
Joseph Snow. 25639

Sermon, occasioned by the death of the Rev.
L. L. Bonnell. 92881

Sermon occasioned by the death of the Rev.
Matthias Bruen. 81646

Sermon occasioned by the death of the Rev.
Mr. John Moorhead. 43293

Sermon occasioned by the . . . death of the
Reverend Nathanael Hooker. (61040)

Sermon, occasioned by the death of the Rev.
Noadiah Russel. 103764

Sermon, occasioned by the death of the Rev.
Oliver Hart. 72743

Sermon, occasioned by the death of the Rev.
Peter S. Wynkoop. 32595

Sermon, occasioned by the death of the Rev.
Samuel Worcester. 16795

Sermon occasioned by the death of the Rev. W.
Croscombe. 71114

Sermon, occasioned . . . by the death of the
Rev. William Horton. 11982

Sermon occasioned by the death of the Rev.
William Redfield Stocking. 60963

Sermon occasioned by the death of the Rev.
Zabdiel Bradford. 28284

Sermon, occasioned by the death of the Rt.
Rev. William White. 92081

Sermon occasioned by the death of the wife of
Rev. Jeremiah Day. 82417

Sermon occasioned by the death of William
Henry Harrison, by S. F. Smith. 84061

Sermon occasioned by the death of William
Henry Harrison, the late President.
6081

Sermon occasioned by the death of William
Hickling Prescott. (22326)

Sermon occasioned by the death of young
Mr. Daniel Oliver. 65617

Sermon occasioned by the death of Zachary
Taylor. (82388)

Sermon occasion'd by the decease of Mrs.
Anna Cary. 65075

Sermon occasioned by the decease of Mrs.
Deborah Prince. 65616

Sermon occasioned by the decease of Mrs.
Hannah Fayerweather. 65579

Sermon occasion'd by the decease of Mrs.
Martha Stoddard. 65598

Sermon occasioned by the decease of Mrs.
Mary Stillman. 91800

Sermon occasion'd by the decease of some
desirable Friends. (46523)

Sermon occasioned by the decease of the Rev.
Oliver Hart. (26227)

Sermon . . . occasioned by the dedication of a
Grammar School House. 25042

Sermon occasioned by the destruction of Pennsylvania Hall. 26238

Sermon, occasioned by the devastating fire of
16th December. 82729

Sermon occasioned by the earth-quakes in
Spain and Portugal. 12331

Sermon occasioned by the earthquake. 3471

Sermon occasioned by the execution of a man
found guilty of murder. 46735, 50296

Sermon occasioned by the execution of Samuel
Frost. 3105

Sermon occasioned by the explusion of six
young gentlemen. 65499, (79890)

Sermon occasion'd by the fall of the brave
Capt. John Lovewell. (37711), 94107-
94108, 94111-94112

Sermon occasioned by the great and publick
loss in the death. (65608)

Sermon occasioned by the great & publick loss
in the decease. (65588)

Sermon occasioned by the great fire, Boston,
N. England, 1760. (46761)

Sermon occasioned by the great fire in Boston,
New-England, . . . March 20. 1760.
47137

Sermon occasioned by the heavy sufferings of
our fellow subjects. 44618

Sermon occasioned by the horrid murder of Messieurs Samuel Gray, Samuel Maverick, James Caldwell, and Crispus Attucks. 39184

Sermon occasion'd by the inexpressible loss in the death of His Late Royal Highness Frederick. 65601

Sermon, occasioned by the lamentable fire which which was in Boston. 46644

Sermon occasioned by the late earthquake in New England. 9716

Sermon, occasioned by the late great earthquake. 18469

Sermon occasioned by the late riot in New York. 4575

Sermon, occasioned by the loss of the Harold and the Lexington. (72752)

Sermon, occasioned by the much lamented death of Col. Joseph Trumbull. 103457

Sermon, occasioned by the much lamented death of the Honorable William Pitkin. 10426

Sermon, occasioned by the much-lamented death of the Reverend Mr. Aaron Burr, A. M. 82364

Sermon occasion'd by the much lamented death of the Reverend Mr. William Waldron. 101016, 102218

Sermon, occasioned by the present excitement respecting the gold in California. 13589

Sermon occasion'd by the present rebellion. 12331

Sermon, occasioned by the present religious attention. (19847)

Sermon occasioned by the raging of a mortal sickness. 46499

Sermon occasioned by the recent election in Massachusetts. (75850)

Sermon. Occasioned by the sickness . . . at Alexandria. 51259

Sermon occasion'd by the success of the late expedition. 94698

Sermon occasioned by the sudden and much lamented death of the Reverend George Whitefield. 59606, 103131

Sermon, occasioned by the sudden death of Mr. Elisha Lyon. 91732

Sermon, occasioned by the sudden death of Mrs. A. Fisher. 24519

Sermon occasion'd, by the sudden drowning of six persons. 100908

Sermon occasion'd by the very sorrowful tidings. 100911

Sermon occasioned by the very sudden death of two young gentlemen. 65605

Sermon occasion'd by the very sudden deaths of Mr. Thomas Lewis. 79414

Sermon . . . October 18, 1845. (3508)

Sermon . . . October 15, 1828. 43392

Sermon . . . October 5th, 1777. 37649

Sermon . . . October 1, 1843. 17270

Sermon . . . Oct. 1, 1816. 35816

Sermon . . . October 4, 1732. 2873

Sermon . . . October 19, 1862, at the funeral. 41717

Sermon, . . . October 19th, 1862, in . . . Brooklyn. 32612

Sermon . . . Oct. 19th, 1834. (45438)

Sermon . . . October 9th, 1842. note after (58767)

Sermon . . . October 17, 1847. 26536

Sermon, Oct. 6, 1830. 19877

Sermon . . . October 30, 1805. 39773

Sermon . . . October 30th, 1827. 21132

Sermon . . . Oct. 30, 1771. 2632

Sermon . . . October 20, 1802. 32588

Sermon . . . Oct. 28, 1855. 40107

Sermon, October 28, 1853. 9243

Sermon, . . . October 28, 1795. 24538

Sermon, . . . October 25, 1849. (25213)

Sermon . . . October 25, 1838. 37162

Sermon . . . October 21, 1818. 37162

Sermon . . . October 24, 1787. (31895)

Sermon . . . October 22d, 1812. 58378

Sermon . . . October 27th, 1814. 64229

Sermon, October 26, 1817. 28818

Sermon, . . . October 23, 1793. 37347

Sermon . . . Odelltown, Nov. 9, 1829. 16398

Sermon, oder Predigt. 103613

Sermon of a Dutch divine. 94697

Sermon of a new kind. 79272

Sermon of merchants. note after (58767)

Sermon of Rev. O. B. Frothingham. 26077

Sermon [of Samuel Smith.] 86574

Sermon of slavery. note after (58767)

Sermon of thanksgiving. 16691, 2d note after 99888

Sermon of the consequences of an immortal principle. note after (58767)

Sermon of the dangerous classes in society. note after (58767)

Sermon of the memorable Mr. John Higginson. (49658)

Sermon of the moral condition of Boston. note after (58767)

Sermon of the moral dangers incident to prosperity. note after (58767)

Sermon . . . of the ordination of the Rev. Jonathan Cole. 7495

Sermon of the perishing classes of Boston. note after (58767)

Sermon of the possibility of God's forsaking a people. 73579

Sermon of the public function of woman. note after (58767)

Sermon of the Rev. John C. Young. (47241), 93816

Sermon of the Rev. Philip F. Mayer. 47114

Sermon of the Reverend William E. Channing. 105131

Sermon of the spiritual condition of Boston. note after (58767)

Sermon of war. note after (58767)

Sermon, offer'd unto the Anniversary Convention of Ministers. (46416)

[Sermon] on a day of fasting. 13854

Sermon on a day of prayer, kept by the North Church. 14501

Sermon, on a day of prayer, kept with a religious family. 46443

Sermon on a day of prayer, March 5, 1723. 16640

Sermon on a day of prayer, previous to the choice. 97324

Sermon . . . on a day of public thanksgiving. 12148

[Sermon on a fast day.] 4397

Sermon on a general thanksgiving. 75937

Sermon on American affairs. 106388

Sermon on American slavery. (21137)

Sermon on an afflictive occasion. 64138

Sermon on Ash-Wednesday. 65456

Sermon, . . . on assuming the duties of Pastor. 47181

Sermon on . . . attending public worship. 22169

[Sermon] on beneficence. 30239

Sermon on Bible servitude. (78480)

Sermon on Biblical slavery. 515

Sermon, on board of the fleet at Whitehall. 21295

Sermon on brotherly love. 33270
Sermon on censoriousness and evil speaking. 99541
Sermon on certain popular amusements. 64692
Sermon, on Christian union. 102533
Sermon on church government. 36859, 73408
Sermon on civil government. 90301
Sermon, on conversion. 71064
Sermon on covenanting. (24361), 105669
Sermon on Daniel Webster. 47180
Sermon on death of Mrs. A. Fowler. 94893
Sermon on Deuteronomy, V. 29. 27960, 30153, note after 95748
Sermon on duelling. 21563
Sermon on Ecclesiastes XII. 10. 89165
Sermon on education. 61201
Sermon, on Ezekiel I. 16. 102691, 102693
Sermon on Ezek. XXXIII. 2. 40843, 106353
Sermon on family prayer. 89803
Sermon . . . on fast day, April 18, 1839. (3259)
Sermon.. . . on fast-day, April 10 [1851. By C. A. Bartol.] 3794
Sermon . . . on fast-day, April 10, 1851. [By Theodore Parker.] note after (58767)
Sermon [on fast day.] August 20, 1812. (22419)
Sermon . . . on fast day. [By Stephen N. Rowan.] 73537
Sermon . . . on fast day . . . in Burlington, Vermont. 34742
Sermon . . . on fast day morning, April 3, 1828. 2968
Sermon . . . on fast-day, Sept. 26, 1861. (10994)
Sermon on foundation principles. 36467
Sermon, on general education; . . . Canandaigua, Sept. 8th, 1816. 57317
Sermon on . . . her death, an account of the American missions. 54956
Sermon on his life and death. 104386
Sermon on holding communion with extortioners. 66821
Sermon on human depravity. 79392
[Sermon] on Jan. 1, 1811. 2921
Sermon, on Job I. 21. 65594
Sermon . . . on July 4th, 1794. 39196
Sermon on July 23. 1640. 32810-32811
Sermon on justification. 17671
Sermon on life and character of Rev. Joseph Eastburn. 18652
Sermon on Luke 8th, 18. 103584
Sermon on man's primitive state. 18770
Sermon on Mark VI. 34. 94686
Sermon on Matth. XVI. 18. 24438
Sermon on Matth. XII. 28. 24386
Sermon on military duty. 4439
Sermon on military institutions. 90996
Sermon on national righteousness and sin. 5673
Sermon on natural election. 71810
Sermon, on Nebachadnezzar's dream. 82496
Sermon on occasion of constituting a church. 22377
Sermon, on occasion of the death of George W. Heard. 88582
Sermon on occasion of the death of Henry C. Parkhurst. 82334
Sermon, on occasion of the death of Mr. Martin Harmon. (76370)
Sermon, on occasion of the death of Mrs. George W. Heard. 88583
Sermon on occasion of the death of the Rev. Samuel C. Stratton. (17330)

Sermon on occasion of the decease of Mr. Samuel Aspinwal. 917
Sermon on occasion of the fast appointed . . . by the President. 20525
Sermon on occasion of the late calamity at Washington. 19862
Sermon, on occasion of the late fire. (19861)
Sermon . . . on occasion of the ordination of Mr. Zachariah Thayer. 25388
Sermon, on occasion of the present encroachments of the French. 68201
Sermon on one baptism. 82478
Sermon, on I Chronicles XXIX. 28. 94701
Sermon, on I. John VI. I. 103325
Sermon on I Thess: V, 12, 13. 83429
Sermon on opening of the Methodist Church in John St. 48036
Sermon on our liberties. 5085
Sermon on prayer, preached at Dorchester, Mass. 14137
Sermon on Psal. LXXXVIII. 15. 65580
Sermon on Psalm CXLVII. 2. 91758
Sermon on Ps. CXIX. 109. 13348
Sermon on Psalms LXXVIII, 2-8. 70952
Sermon on regeneration. 103585
Sermon on regular singing. 101197
Sermon . . . on requiring a collection to be made. 102176
Sermon on revivals of religion. 104531
Sermon on Sabbath keeping. 91585
Sermon, on St. John's Day, 5817. (18299)
Sermon on San Felipe de Jesus. 38455
Sermon on self-denial. 103586
Sermon on slander. 84117
Sermon on slavery. By Rev. John Liddon. 40971
Sermon on slavery, . . . Norwich, Ct. (29271)
Sermon on some of the internal and distinctive peculiarities of the Protestant Episcopal Church in America. 91999
Sermon on speculative free-masonry. (71970)
Sermon . . . on Sunday, April 9, 1865. 6077
Sermon . . . on Sunday, Jan. 30th. note after (58767)
Sermon on tea. 79273
Sermon on temperance. 85404
Sermon, on temporal and spiritual salvation. 84650
Sermon . . . on . . . thanksgiving . . . at Lexington. (41577)
Sermon . . . on thanksigving day. [By George G. Ingersoll.] 34742
Sermon . . . on thanksgiving day . . . New Bloomfield, Pa. 24935
Sermon on thanksgiving day, Nov. 27, 1851. 2675
Sermon . . . on thanksgiving day, November 27, 1862. 39569
Sermon . . . on . . . Thanksgiving, December 7, 1865. (50385)
Sermon . . . on . . . Thanksgiving for national victories. 58147
Sermon . . . on . . . Thanksgiving . . . in . . . Philadelphia. 55083
Sermon, . . . on . . . Thanksgiving; Leicester, December 5, 1822. 52315
Sermon . . . on thanksgiving day, November 25, 1847. 3794
Sermon . . . on . . . Thanksgiving . . . November 29th, 1860. 43324
Sermon on that great occasion, at Boston, New-England. 46507
Sermon on the accursed thing that hinders success. 99754
Sermon . . . on the . . . admission of Mr. Richard F. Putnam. 67784

Sermon, on the anniversary of ordination.
7495

Sermon, . . . on the annual election, May 31,
1797. 47449

Sermon . . . on . . . the annual fast, April
15, 1847. 59354

Sermon, . . . on the annual fast, . . . April
4, 1844. 42367

Sermon on . . . the annual fast, April 12, 1850.
65683

Sermon on the annual thanksgiving in this
state. 8461

Sermon . . . on the . . . "Anti-rent" disturbances. 30455

[Sermon] on the appearance of a comet. 221

Sermon on the assassination of Abraham
Lincoln. (29837)

Sermon on the burning of the First Church in
Somerville. (64106)

Sermon . . . on the burning of the Theatre at
Richmond. 49061, 104944

Sermon on the capture of Lord Cornwallis.
16816

Sermon on the causes and remedy of the
national troubles. 42050

Sermon on the causes and uses of the present
civil war. 31679

Sermon on the centenary of Methodism. 94190

Sermon on the character and death of Leonard
Donham. 33964

Sermon on the character and influence of
Washington. 42031

Sermon on the character of Dr. Andrew
Nichols. 1799

Sermon on the character of Joseph Stephens
Abbot. 21616

Sermon on the character of Rev. Ephraim
Peabody. 3794

Sermon, on the character, preaching, &c. of
the Rev. Mr. Whitefield. 83433, 103514,
103601

Sermon on the Christian necessity of war.
27925

Sermon on the civil war in America. 33593

Sermon, on the comparative happiness and
duty of the United States. 43096

Sermon, on the conclusion of the second century. 104389

Sermon on the crime against freedom. 25212

Sermon on the danger of political strife.
89744

Sermon on the dangers and duties of a seafaring life. 8445

Sermon on the dangers of the times. 39199

Sermon on the dangers which threaten the
rights of man. (58759)

Sermon on the day appointed for a general
fast. 1211, 79280

Sermon . . . on the day of annual thanksgiving.
26644

Sermon . . . on the day of election, 1817.
27884

Sermon on the day of election, May 10, 1759.
41749

Sermon . . . on the day of general election,
at Montpelier. (37375)

Sermon on the day of prayer with fasting.
79421

Sermon . . . on the day of the interment of the
Reverend Mr. William Waldron. 25408,
101016

Sermon . . . on the day of the national fast,
Sept. 26th, 1861. 30923

Sermon on the death, and Doctor's [sic]
Welsh's eulogy. 95175

Sermon on the death of Abraham Lincoln,
April 15th, 1865. 18269

Sermon on the death of Abraham Lincoln,
April 16, 1865. 33029

Sermon on the death of Abraham Lincoln,
late President. 70856

Sermon on the death of Bishop J. H. Hobart.
29247

Sermon on the death of C. S. Sterling. 13529

Sermon on the death of C. T. Torrey. 92385

Sermon . . . on the death of Capt. Daniel
Goodwin. 59121

Sermon on the death of Capt. J. Sewall Reed.
50716

Sermon on the death of Capt. Skerry. 85390

Sermon on the death of Charles I. S. Hazzard.
90200

Sermon on the death of Charles M. Jenkins.
22520

Sermon on the death of Daniel Webster. 9630

Sermon on the death of Dr. A. Brigham.
(27881)

Sermon on the death of Dr. Daggett. 91746

Sermon on the death of Dr. Kane. 66789

Sermon . . . on the death of Dr. Seth Coleman.
60969

Sermon on the death of E. P. Brown. 77318

Sermon on the death of Ebenezer Daggett.
(24097)

Sermon on the death of Elijah Hunter. 90185

Sermon on the death of Frederick A. Raybold.
7352

Sermon on the death of General George Washington. By Thomas Morrell. 50782

Sermon on the death of General George Washington, delivered at Cape May. 90151

Sermon on the death of General George Washington; delivered Lord's Day, January 5,
1800. 26539

Sermon, on the death of General George
Washington, . . . delivered on the twelfth
of January, one thousand eight hundred.
37231

Sermon on the death of Gen. George Washington,
preached February 22, 1800. 22524

Sermon on the death of Gen. George Washington;
the substance of which was delivered at
Thyatira. (43097)

Sermon on the death of General Harrison.
38401

Sermon on the death of General Lafayette.
26070

Sermon on the death of Gen. Taylor. 9130

Sermon on the death of Gen. Zachary Taylor.
(43820)

Sermon on the death of George Bryan. 23327

Sermon on the death of Geo. J. Strout. 85521

Sermon on the death of George M. Ramsaur.
6086

Sermon on the death of Geo. Whitefield. 21918

Sermon on the death of Gov. Noah Noblet.
4346

Sermon on the death of his mother. 91800

Sermon on the death of Hon. John Davis.
(31806)

Sermon on the death of Hon. Robert H. Gardiner.
9243

Sermon on the death of Hon. Samuel Hubbard.
536

Sermon on the death of Hugh Brodie. 46853

Sermon on the death of J. J. Fabyan. 200

Sermon on the death of Jeremiah Evatts.
105140

Sermon on the death of Johannes Theodorus
Wilhelmus Maas. 38162

Sermon on the death of John Atwood. 3471
Sermon, on . . . the death of John G.
Gollond. 59457
Sermon on the death of John Lowell. 28687
Sermon on the death of John M. Jackson.
43471
Sermon . . . on . . . the death of John
Nicoll. 59609
Sermon . . . on the death of . . . John Walley.
59602
Sermon on the death of Jos. Warren Fearing.
13222
Sermon on the death of Leonard E. Lathrop.
(31707)
Sermon on the death of Levi Eldridge. 7347
Sermon on the death of Levi Hartshorn.
18405
Sermon on the death of Lieutenant-General
George Washington. 5748
Sermon on the death of Miss Dorwin. (22200)
Sermon on the death of Miss Marietta Ingham.
58924
Sermon on the death of Miss Sibyl Richardson.
58118
Sermon on the death of Mr. Davies. 18766
Sermon on the death of Mr. Ebenezer Grant
Marsh. 21563
Sermon . . . on the death of Mr. John Coney.
16637
[Sermon on the death of Mr. John Hart.]
12237
Sermon on the death of Mr. Jonathan Leech.
22393
Sermon on . . . the death of Mr. Joseph
Brewster. 82336
Sermon on the death of Mr. Robert Watson.
46853
Sermon on the death of Mr. William Steile.
(30607)
Sermon . . . on the death of Mrs. Abigail
Sewall. (46567)
Sermon on the death of Mrs. Cornelia S.
Lansing. 92780
Sermon on the death of Mrs. Elizabeth
Hendren. 89166
Sermon . . . on the death of Mrs. Hannah
Sewall. 46571
Sermon on the death of Mrs. Jane Steel.
(14525)
Sermon on the death of Mrs. L. Adams. 200
Sermon on the death of Mrs. M. Buckley.
200
Sermon on the death of Mrs. Martha Nicholas.
89167
Sermon on the death of Mrs. Mary Kelley.
88859
Sermon on the death of Mrs. Ruth Sage.
92899
Sermon on the death of . . . Mrs. Sarah
Byfield. (12323)
Sermon on the death of Mrs. Thomas Worthing-
ton. (26723)
Sermon on the death of N. Wattles. (2654)
Sermon on the death of Oliver Cobb. 19889
Sermon on the death of Otis Pettee. 43650
Sermon on the death of our late President.
6125
Sermon on the death of President Abraham
Lincoln. 5508
Sermon on the death of President Lincoln,
April 23, 1865. 27406
Sermon on the death of President Lincoln,
preached at St. Catherines. 55909
Sermon on the death of President Lincoln,
preached in . . . Rootstown. 38721

Sermon . . . on the death of President Taylor.
(64646)
Sermon [on] the death of Prof. Ebenezer Kel-
logg. 32943
Sermon on the death of Rev. Chas. J. Smith.
(8985)
Sermon on the death of Rev. Charles T. Torrey.
(39158)
Sermon . . . on the death of Rev. Frederick
T. Gray. 59364
Sermon on the death of Rev. John Thomas of
Charleston. 83449
Sermon on the death of Rev. Samuel Moodey.
50303
Sermon on the death of Rev. William B. Davies.
5616
Sermon on the death of Samuel Couch. 11974
Sermon on . . . the death of Samuel Prentiss.
42050
Sermon on the death of Sarah Constance Green.
(75964)
Sermon on the death of the Hon. Caleb Ellis.
23815
Sermon on the death of the Hon. David Mitchell.
27437
Sermon on the death of the Hon. Henry Shel-
burne. 30892
Sermon on the death of the Honourable Richard
Cartwright. 92658
Sermon on the death of the Hon. William
Paterson. 13321
Sermon on the death of the Lord Bishop of
Quebec. 74549
Sermon on the death of the Rev. Abijah Wines.
23815
Sermon on the death of the Rev. Benjamin C.
C. Parker. 18162
Sermon . . . on the . . . death of the Rev.
David S. Bogart. 19875
Sermon on the death of the Rev. Francis
Asbury. 87271
Sermon on the death of the Rev. Henry Ware.
28390
Sermon on the death of the Rev. J. Green.
6009
Sermon on the death of the Rev. Mr. George
Whitefield. 102688
Sermon on the death of the Reverend Mr.
Joseph Emerson. (22444)
Sermon on the death of the Rev. Samuel Jones.
90842
Sermon on the death of the Reverend Thomas
Clap. 18268
Sermon on the death of the Rev. William
McDonald. 71114
Sermon on the death of the Rev. William
M'Kendree. 87272
Sermon on the death of the Rt. Rev. Samuel
Bowman. 49927
Sermon . . . on the death of the Right
Reverend Samuel Parker. 26624
Sermon on the death of . . . William Eustis.
28411
Sermon on the death of Wm. H. Harrison. By
S. G. Bulfinch. 9091
Sermon on the death of William Henry Harri-
son. . . . By Joseph Richardson. 71065
Sermon on the decease of the Rev. Peter
Thatcher. 22465
Sermon on the decline of protestantism. 48934
Sermon, on the dedication of the First Pres-
byterian Church. 74722
Sermon, on the departure of Mrs. Frances
Webb. 46334

Sermon on the departure of the Venerable and Memorable Dr. Increase Mather. 46326

Sermon on the divine origin of civil government. 16389

Sermon on the divine use of vocal music. (13424)

Sermon on the divinity of Christ. 71852

Sermon, on the doctrine of the New-Jerusalem Church. 104571

Sermon, on the due celebration of the festival. 103468

Sermon on the duties and advantages of affording instruction. 26409

Sermon on the duties of citizens with respect to the fugitive slave law. 37653

Sermon, on the duty and dignity of woman. (71066)

Sermon, on the duty of attending the public worship of God. 99541

Sermon on the duty of civil disobedience. 103469

Sermon on the duty of loving our enemies. 4095

Sermon on the duty of loyalty. 5074

Sermon on the duty of the Presbyterian Church in Missouri. 64692

[Sermon] on the eclipse of the sun. 221

Sermon on the eternity of hell-torments. 103587

Sermon on the evacuation of Charlestown. 79274

Sermon on the . . . exposition at Fales and Gray's Car Manufactory. 13385

Sermon, on the fanaticism of the present age. 24738

Sermon, on the federal fast. 103982

Sermon . . . on the Federal-Street Meeting House. 26536

Sermon on the fifth of November, 1719. 7208

Sermon on the first sabbath after his [i. e. Ezra Styles Ely's] ordination. 22384

Sermon on the following subjects. 20099

Sermon, . . . on the 14th July, 1850. 45437

Sermon on the frailty of man. 79394

Sermon on the freedom and happiness of America. 32584

Sermon on the freedom and happiness of the United States. 18738

Sermon on the fruits of our breavement. 17370

Sermon on the fugitive slave law. [By B. M. Hall.] 29737

Sermon on the fugitive slave law. By Charles Beecher. 4297

Sermon on the golden rule of justice. 24576

Sermon on the great American sin of speaking evil of rulers. 84447

Sermon on the great schism of 1844. 49690

Sermon on the horrible crime of self-murder. 46646

Sermon on the importance of sinners coming immediately to Christ. 89808

Sermon on the inscription over the entrance to Mount Auburn. 25440

Sermon on the "irrepressible conflict." 90472

Sermon on the late general fast. 91003

Sermon on the . . . late William Ellery Channing. 31218

Sermon, on the leading doctrines of the New Jerusalem Church. 30375

Sermon on the lecture in Boston. 104095

Sermon on the life and character of Abraham Lincoln. 30091

Sermon on the life and character of Hon. John Aiken. 82383

Sermon on the life and death of Abraham Lincoln. (16302)

Sermon, on the life and death of Henry Clay. 88254

Sermon on the liquor law of Massachusetts. 38905

Sermon, . . . on the loss of the Lexington. 46845

Sermon on the manifestation of God. 71067

Sermon on the Mexican war. 58760

Sermon on the moral aspect of the Kingston tragedy. 48017

Sermon, . . . on the moral importance of cities. 19862

Sermon on the moral uses of the pestilence. 19862

Sermon on the much-lamented death of Mr. Eben'r Grant Marsh. (18419)

Sermon . . . on the "national crisis." 78862

Sermon . . . on the national fast . . . April 30, 1863. 40788

Sermon . . . on the national fast day, April 30, by the . . . Rev. J. E. Caruthers. 11170

Sermon . . . on the . . . national fast day, August 3d, 1849. 18006

Sermon on the national fast day, January 4, 1861. 29248

Sermon on the national fast, 1861. 7959

Sermon on the national fast occasioned by the death of General Harrison. 90386

Sermon, on the nature and criminality of man's inability to serve the Lord. 88899

Sermon on the nature and importance of conversion. (9717)

Sermon, on the nature of Christian courage. 66822

Sermon on the Nebraska bill. 4301

Sermon . . . on the 19th of February, 1795. 45463

Sermon, . . . on the 9th of May, 1798. 38005

Sermon . . . on the 9th of September, 1813. 39227

Sermon on the occasion . . . by J. McVickar. 70085

Sermon on the occasion. By William Scoresby. 78179

Sermon on the occasion of fasting and prayer on account of the cholera morbus. 8770

Sermon, on the occasion of the annual fast, April 5, 1838. 97370

Sermon on the occasion of the assassination of President Lincoln. 2877

Sermon on the occasion of the centenary of Wesleyan Methodism. 84547

Sermon on the occasion of the death of Charles F. Allison. 51842

Sermon on the occasion of the death of John Adams. 26063

Sermon on the occasion of the death of Lt. Col. Alexander Ramsay Thompson. 38165

Sermon on the occasion of the death of President Lincoln. 17396

Sermon . . . on the occasion of the death of Rachel Hillhouse. 31881

Sermon on the occasion of the death of the late Chief Justice Reid. 5087

Sermon on the occasion of the death of the late Washington Irving. 17469, note after 89333

Sermon on the occasion of the execution of William Enoch. 96994

Sermon . . . on the occasion of the fiftieth anniversary of the ordination of Rev. Theophilus Packard. 58121

Sermon on the occasion of the funeral of Mrs. Mary Ann Phelps. 7490

Sermon on the occasion of the funeral of Rev. P. Thacher. 16640

Sermon on the occasion of the lamented death of the Rev. Joseph Galluchat. (10749)

Sermon on the occasion of the national fast. 78633

Sermon: on the occasion of the 25th anniversary of his rectorship. 78058

Sermon . . . on the ordination of J. Lockhart. 29254

Sermon on the ordination of the Rev. Henry Adams. 17629

Sermon on the ordination of William K. Talbot. 18405

Sermon on the origin of the war, delivered at Genesee, Illinois. (16280)

Sermon on the political tendencies of popery. 91472

Sermon on the premature and lamented death of General Alexander Hamilton. (43157)

Sermon on the pleasure and advantages of church music. 38876

Sermon on the present national troubles. (24548)

Sermon on the present situation of American affairs. (27219), 84651-84662

Sermon, on the present situation of the affairs of America. 79275

Sermon on the prevailing vice of intemperate drinking. 29281

Sermon on the priestly-office of Christ. 94697

Sermon on the principles, means and blessings, of union and peace. 77435

Sermon, . . . on the public fast, April 4, 1816. (64233)

Sermon . . . on the public fast in . . . Massachusetts, April 11, 1793. (43389)

Sermon on the . . . public thanksgiving. For the happy termination of the late civil dissensions in Rhode Island. (59534)

Sermon on the qualifications, the authorities, and the duties. 103470

Sermon, on the reciprocal influence of civil policy and religious duty. 103471

Sermon on, the refuge of the distressed. 46512

Sermon on the relations of the Christian ministry. 103096

Sermon on the religious education of children. 104945

Sermon, . . . on the religious tendencies of the age. (64646)

Sermon on the re-opening of Christ Church, Cambridge, Mass. (33001)

Sermon on the repeal of the stamp-act. 91796

Sermon on the responsibilities of Englishmen in the colonies. 51187

Sermon on the restoration of peace between the United States and Great Britain. (13022)

Sermon on the resurrection of Our Lord. (79276)

Sermon on the right improvement of such mercies. 96107

Sermon on the same subject. 35752

Sermon on the scriptural doctrine of a change of heart. 91999

Sermon on the scriptural, ecclesiastical, and political obligations, in regard to the use of certain prayers. 29246

Sermon on the "scriptures." 101197

Sermon, on the seasons, time and eternity. 64138

Sermon on the services and death of Abraham Lincoln. 5778

Sermon on the slave trade. By Abraham Booth. 6383

Sermon on the slave trade. By Rev. James Dore. 20629

Sermon on the sorrowful occasion of the death of His Late Majesty King George. 65614

Sermon . . . on the spread of the Gospel among the heathen. 37958

Sermon on the state of the country. (25308)

Sermon on the subject of the slave trade. (65513)

Sermon on the suppression of the late unnatural rebellion. (27981)

Sermon on the supreme divinity of Christ. 82488

Sermon . . . on the third day of January, A. D. 1759. 62517

Sermon . . . on the 13th of November, 1751. 62511

Sermon on the times. (3356)

Sermon on the traffic in intoxicating liquors. 37976

Sermon on the trial of the spirit. 43293

Sermon on the trial of the spirits, &c. 9907

Sermon . . . on the twelfth of January, 1815. 39227

Sermon on the twenty-fifth anniversary of his ministry. 21471

Sermon . . . on the twenty-fifth anniversary of his settlement. (44153)

Sermon . . . on the twenty-fifth anniversary of the Boston Female Asylum. 28687

Sermon, on the 29th November, 1759. 95711

Sermon on the victory of Fort Donelson. 29298

[Sermon] on the virtue of charity. 94697

Sermon on the war, delivered in Amesbury. 47228

Sermon on the war, preached at Patterson. 9636

Sermon on the war, . . . to the soldiers at Exeter, N. H. 51888

Sermon, on the way of peace. 105246

Sermon on theatrical exhibitions. 43419

Sermon, on Thursday, Novemb. 29th, 1759. 95710

Sermon, on Titus, 2d Chapter, 13th and 14th verses. 85438

Sermon on universal charity. (81410)

Sermon, on war. 69553

Sermon on withdrawing from the congregational ministry. 1518

Sermon on Zechariah 6:13. 92157

Serm. I. On Wednesday, July 29, 1789. 84675-84675A

Sermon . . . ordination of Rev. Eliakim Phelps. (50953)

Sermon, . . . ordination of the Rev. Ezra Stiles Ely. 22393

Sermon . . . ordination of the Reverend Mr. William Vinal. 24440

Sermon panegir del glor. Padre Bern. Abad. 11039

Sermon panegirico de accion de gracias. 31569

Sermon panegirico de la gloriosa aparicion de Nuestra Senora de Guadelupe. 31479

Sermon panegirico de la peregrina imagen de Jesus Nazareno. (35591)

Sermon panegirico de las glorias de los Religiosos Betlemitas. 73903

Sermon panegirico de S. Francisco de Asis. 76108

Sermon panegirico de Santa Ines virgen y martir. 27803

Sermon penegirico de Santjago el Mayor. 11039

Sermon panegirico del ang. Doct. S. Tomas de Aquino. 31479

Sermon panegirico del Apostol S. Pedro. (77056)

Sermon panegirico del glorioso Apostol y Evangelico S. Mateo. 51556

Sermon panegirico del grand Padre S. Francisco de Aves. 27804

Sermon panegirico del precursos de Cristo S. Juan Bautista. 76866

Sermon panegirico del SS. Patriarca S. San Joseph. 19990

Sermon panegirico en la dedicacion de la Nueva Iglesia del Convento. 44959

Sermon panegirico en la funcion anual de orden dal Supremo Consejo de Castilla. 57658

Sermon panegirico en la solemne dedicacion de la suntuosa Capilla. 74773

Sermon panegirico moral, predicado en esta Santa Metropolitana. (35052)

Sermon panegirico moral predicado en la Santa Iglesia Metropolitiana. 35051

Sermon panegirico predicado el dia 6 de Junio de 1819. 73803

Sermon panegirico predicado en la Catedral de Chiapa. 76877

Sermon panegirico que el dia 25 de Setiembre de 1814. 35050

Sermon panegyrico al celestial cingulo. (24821)

Sermon panegyrico con motivo de la celebracion. 57658

Sermon panegyrico de la Santa Casa de Loreto. 105735

Sermon panegyrico de las glorias de San Francisco. 76161

Sermon panegyrico del ange. joven San Luis Gonzaga. 50615

Sermon panegyrico del gloriosissimo martyr S. Juan Nepomuceno. 17001

Sermon panegyrico, en la accion de gracias. 50601

Sermon panegyrico en la primera solemne festividad. 41425

Sermon panegyrico en las magnificas honras celebro. 26562

Sermon panegyrico funebre. 50491

Sermon panegyrico-funeral. 35283

Sermon panegyrico, que dijo el Fr. Man. Maria Doming y Ramirez. 67654

Sermon panegyrico, que el dia tres de Octubre de el ano de 1728. 87174

Sermon panegyrico, qve el R. P. presentado Fr. Alvaro de Soria Briviesca. 87158

Sermon panegyrico, que en la Sancta Iglesia Cathedral de la Puebla. 94636

Sermon panegyrico, que en su dia y templo de la ciudad de Santiago. 71474

Sermon, par Citoyen de Novion. 93492

Sermon para publicar la Sancta Bulla. (36795)

Sermon . . . Pastoral Association of Mass. 16338

Sermon patriotico en la funcion publica. 35870

Sermon . . . Philadelphia . . . June 1st, 1865. (35952)

Sermon . . . Philadelphia, November, 1862. 44487

Sermon politico-moral para dar principio a la mision extraordinaria. 7988

Sermon por la exaltacion al trono de N. Catol. Monarca D. Carlos IV. (60813)

Sermon . . . Portland, Nov. 9, 1825. 21525

Sermon, . . . Portsmouth, Va. 30224

Sermon preach'd a month after it happened. (16631)

Sermon preached after his [i. e. F. W. P. Greenwood's] death. 26068

Sermon preached after the death of Benjamin R. Gilbert. (71798)

Sermon preached after the death of Cornelia F. Fiske. (71791)

Sermon preached after the death of Mrs. Eliza Frothingham. 71790

Sermon preach'd after the funeral of Mr. Cornelius Thayer. 12331

Sermon preached . . . after the funeral of Mrs. Ann Foxcroft. 12331

Sermon, preach'd . . . after the funeral of . . . Nathanael Byfield. 12325

Sermon preached after the funeral of Noah Lincoln. 71792

Sermon preached after the funeral of Rev. G. Cooper. 10761

Sermon preached . . . after the interment of William Lawrence. 42149

Sermon preached after the terrible fire. (46216)

Sermon, preached April 8, 1788. 19830

Sermon, preached April 15, 1807. (71123)

Sermon, preached April 5, 1757. 84596

Sermon preached April 4th, 1820. 25066

Sermon preached April 9, 1865. 39570

Sermon preach'd April 9. 1760. 16603

Sermon, preached April 17, 1811. 62973

Sermon, preached April 6, and 13, 1851. 92266

Sermon preached . . . April the 17th, 1735. (59436)

Sermon, preached . . . April 13, A. D. 1815. 32299

Sermon preached April 13, 1815. 82887

Sermon, preached April 13, 1862. 29632

Sermon preached, April 21, 1811. 89783

Sermon preached April 21, 1861. [By J. R. Hibbard.] 31679

Sermon preached . . . April 21, 1861. [By Morgan Dix.] 20349

Sermon, preached April 29, 1789. (18419)

Sermon preached April 27, 1810. 81333

Sermon preached . . . April 23, 1865. 37151

Sermon preached . . . as an improvement of the calamity. 4995

Sermon, preached at a fast, in Marlborough. 90978

Sermon preached at a lecture in Westfield. 2950

Sermon preached at a meeting of the people called Quakers. 69660

Sermon preached at a public association-lecture at West Haven. (74371)

Sermon preached at a public lecture in Attle-borough. 30878

Sermon preached at a service of commemoration held in All Saints' Memorial Church. 71402

Sermon preached at a singing lecture, in Braintree. 102534

Sermon preached at a singing lecture in Warwick. 13219

Sermon, preached at Aberdeen, December 12, 1776. 10217

Sermon preached at Alstead. 2085

Sermon preached at . . . Amesbury. (18435)

Sermon preach'd at an anniversary Convention of Ministers. 91482

Sermon: preached at an exhibition of sacred musick. 90861

Sermon preach'd at Annapolis in Maryland. 37206

Sermon, preached at Arundel, at ordination. 8506

Sermon preached at Arundel at the ordination of Mr. John Hovey. 104112

Sermon, preached at Arundel, January 12, 1800. 50320

Sermon, preached at Aurelius. 104533

Sermon preached at Baltimore in the state of Maryland. 102644

Sermon, preached at Barnstable, February 14, 1807. 9441

Sermon preach'd at Barnstable, May 12, 1755. 26785

Sermon preached at Barrington, R. I. 56236

Sermon preached at Biddeford, November 22d. 1741. 95539, 104112

Sermon, preached at Billerica, April 9th, 1801. 17900

Sermon preached at Billerica, November 29, 1798. (17899)

Sermon preached at Black-Heath and Philadelphia. 103570

Sermon preached at Bolton. 17901

Sermon, preached at Boston, April 25, 1799. 91801

Sermon preached at Boston, at the ordination of the Rev. Mr. Joseph Bowman. 12331

Sermon preached at Boston, before the American Board of Commissioners. 42791

Sermon preach'd at Boston, before the Great and General Assembly. 94068

Sermon preached at Boston, before the Great and General Court or Assembly. 91485

Sermon preached at . . . Boston, Dec. 18th, 1808. 8933

Sermon preached at Boston, Decemb. 29. 1689. 46528

Sermon, preached at Boston, Dec. 23, 1744. (9717)

Sermon, preached at Boston in New-England, by George Keith. (46746), 104256

Sermon preached at Boston in New-England. June 5th. 1710. (46658)

Sermon preached at Boston in N. E. May 15. 1667. (49661)

Sermon preached at Boston in New-England, May 26, 1751. 47146

Sermon preached at Boston in New England on the day of the artillery election there, June 1. 1674. 50299

Sermon preached at Boston in New England, on the day of the artillery election there, June 3d, 1672. 56385

Sermon preached at Boston, in the audience of His Excellency Jonathan Belcher, Esq. 102219

Sermon preach'd at Boston: in the audience of His Excellency William Shirley, Esq; Governour. 40789

Sermon preach'd at Boston, in the audience of His Honour Spencer Phips. 62512

Sermon preach'd at Boston, in the presence of His Excellency William Shirley. (22006)

Sermon preached at Boston, in the province of the Massachusetts-Bay. 15217

Sermon, preached at Boston, July 3rd, 1701. 91956

Sermon preached at Boston lecture, Decemb, 5, 1706. 104262

Sermon preached at Boston lecture, July 3d. 1712. 91964

Sermon preacht [sic] at Boston-lecture on August 16. 1722. 100916

Sermon preached at Boston, May 17 [i. e. 18] 1766. 91796

Sermon preached at Boston, May 30, 1703. 91963

Sermon preached at Boston, New England. 21198

Sermon preach'd at Boston, on the death of Mr. Benjamin Landon. 15216

Sermon, preached at Boston, on the lecture; January 30. 1700, 1. 94080

Sermon preach'd at Boston . . . the 23d of August. 1716. 14515

Sermon; preached at Boston upon a lecture day. 91967

Sermon preached at Braintree . . . after the burial of . . . Mrs. Ann Niles. 58205

Sermon, preached at Brandon, (Vt.) 101037

Sermon, preached at Brattleborough, Vermont. 102607

Sermon preached . . . at Bridgwater. (37235)

Sermon preached at Bristol, R. I. (28881)

Sermon preached at Bristol, the Lord's Day after a very terrible earthquake. 9482

Sermon preached at Brook Haven on Long Island. (65529)

Sermon preached at Brookfield, March 6, 1778. 24552

Sermon preached at Brookfield, Mass. Sept. 13, 1749. 8939

Sermon preached at Brookfield, October 16. 1717. 91946

Sermon, preached at Brookfield on the last day of the year 1776. (24551)

Sermon, preached at Brooklyn, (Conn.) June 9th, 1814. 24545

Sermon, preached . . . [at] Brooklyn, N. Y., . . . August 8, 1841. (23813)

Sermon preached at . . . Brooklyn, N. Y., January 1st, 1865. 66762

Sermon preached at . . . Brooklyn, N. Y. . . . July 16, 1848. (23813)

Sermon preach'd at Burlington in New-Jersey. 94702

Sermon preached at Burlington, on the day of the anniversary election. 2339

Sermon preach'd at Cainhoy, in the province of South-Carolina. 83445

Sermon preached at Cambridge, before His Excellency Thomas Hutchinson. 97325

Sermon preached at Cambridge, before . . . Thomas Hutchinson. 58902

Sermon, preached at Cambridge, . . . December 29, 1799. 32586

Sermon preached at Cambridge in New-England. Decemb. 6. 1696. (46662)

Sermon preached at Cambridge in New-England, upon a day of publick fasting and prayer. 80261

Sermon, preached at Cambridge, January 4, 1801. 32588

Sermon preach'd at Cambrige, [sic] March 24 1716, 17. 91548

Sermon, preached at Cambridge, May 5th, 1788. 82739

Sermon preached at Cambridge, on the ordination of His Honor Thomas Hutchinson, Esq. 16292

Sermon preach'd at Cambridge, September 15th. 1738. 104410

Sermon preach'd at Cambridge, September 12. 1739. 97452

Sermon preach'd at Cambridge, soon after the death of the Reverend & Honourable John Leverett. (1834), 95737, 100915

Sermon preached at Cambridge the day after the commencement. 12306

Sermon preached at Cambridge, the Lord's-Day after the death of the Reverend & Learned John Leverett. (1834), 95737, 100915

Sermon preach'd at Cambridge upon the death of the Reverend Mr. Benjamin Wadsworth. (79434), 103899

Sermon preached at Cambridge upon the sudden death of the Reverend & Learned John Leverett. 14499, 95737, 100915

Sermon, preached at Carlisle. 3849

Sermon preached at . . . Castle William, March 26. 1738. 16382

Sermon preached at Charles-Town, June 24, 1785. 91789

Sermon preached at Charleston, October 7, 1802. 91802

Sermon preached at Charlestown, February 15. 1681. 104081

Sermon preach'd at Charlestown, in the province of South-Carolina. 83454

Sermon preach'd at Charlestown, January 28, 1747, 8. 65077

Sermon, preached at Charlestown, June 19, 1796. 95175, note after 102616

Sermon, preached at Charlestown, November 29, 1798. 50949

Sermon preached at Charlestown, on a general thanksgiving. 65078

Sermon, preached at Charlestown, South-Carolina, after a most terrible fire. 83428

Sermon, preached at Charlestown, South-Carolina, in the year 1739. 83447

Sermon preached at Charlestown, South Carolina, March 27, 1763. 83463.

Sermon, preached at Charlotte Chapel, Pimlico. 61212

Sermon, preached at Chatham, at the request of St. John's Lodge. 92900

Sermon preached at . . . Cheltenham, Gloucestershire. 104613

Sermon preached at Cheshunt in Hertfordshire. 105494

Sermon preached at Chester, in Saybrook. 24273

Sermon preached at Christ-Church, Cambridge. 1855

Sermon, preached at Christ Church Chapel, Bridgwater. 91214

Sermon, preached at Christ Church, Philadelphia. (21054)

Sermon, preached at Christiana Bridge. 50153

Sermon preached at Cincinnati. 71559

Sermon preached at Cohansie, West-Jersey, 83794

Sermon, preached at Cohansy. 83795

Sermon preached at Colchester. 9107

Sermon, preached at Coldwater, Mich. 33210

Sermon preached at Columbia, Pa. 28850

Sermon preached at Commington, Mass. 28978

Sermon, preached at Concord, before His Excellency the Governor. 93954

Sermon, preached at Concord, before . . . the Governor. 4350

Sermon preached at Concord, before . . . the Legislature of . . . New-Hampshire. 7245

Sermon preached at Concord. [By Israel Loring.] 42088

Sermon, preached at Concord, June 3d, 1802. 105113

Sermon preached at Concord, Massachusetts, May 15, 1823. 13864

Sermon, preached at Concord . . . New-Hampshire. 17640

Sermon, preached at Concord, . . . New-Hampshire, June 3, 1813. 12989

Sermon, preached at Concord, on the day of the anniversary election. 97596

Sermon preached at Connecticut Farms in Elizabeth-Town. (20054)

Sermon preach'd at Coventry. 104370

Sermon preached at Crown-Point, at the close of the Campaign, 1762. 94524

Sermon preached at Cummington, October 5, 1819. 83541

Sermon preached at Danbury, September 19th, 1770. 18268

Sermon, preached at Dartmouth-Hall. 103203A

Sermon preached at Dedham, Second Church. 102749

Sermon preached at Deerfield, Novemb. 8. 1732. 104404

Sermon preach'd at Deerfield, Nov. 25, 1741. 2199

Sermon, preached at Dennis. 7942

Sermon preached at Dorchester, April 29th, 1774. 21242

Sermon . . . preached at Dorchester in New-England. (46729)

Sermon, preached at Dorchester, June 24, 1797. 95176

Sermon, preached at Dorchester, Third Parish. (71124)

Sermon preach'd at Douglass. 64313

Sermon, preached at Dunbarton, N. H. December 27, 1843. 7246

Sermon, preached at Dunbarton, N. H. May 17, 1835. 66824

Sermon, preached at Dunbarton, N. H., on the day of public thanksgiving. 66823

Sermon preached . . . at Dunstable . . . June 19. 103853

Sermon preached at Duxborough. 67774

Sermon preached at East Granville, Mass. 89774

Sermon preached at East Hartford, Dec. 23, 1801. (18419)

Sermon, preached at East-Hartford, March 6, 1760. 104215

Sermon, preached at East-Haven, April, 1777. 92777

Sermon, preached at East Windsor, at the national fast. 71849

Sermon, preached at East Windsor . . . November 21st, 1802. 66410

Sermon preached at Eastham, thanksgiving-day. (3880)

Sermon preached at Edgartown. 2869

Sermon preached at Enfield, at the interment. 71850

Sermon preached at Enfield, July 8, 1741. 21959

Sermon preached at Enfield, May 16, 1771. (8985)

Sermon, preached at Epping, in New-Hampshire. 90916

Sermon preached at Exeter. August the 27th, 1758. 96355

Sermon preached at Exeter on the 30th November, 1800. 19590

Sermon, preached at Fags Manor. 25267

Sermon preached at Fairfield, in New-Jersey. 4148

Sermon preached at Fairfield in New Jersey the 1st of December, 1756. 4147

Sermon preached at Farmington Aug. 28. 1726. 103746

Sermon, preached at Fitchburg. 77226

Sermon preached at Framingham. (21521)

Sermon preached at Fredericton. 71956

Sermon preached at Freehold in the Jersies. 50661

Sermon preached at Freehold, N. J. 16797

Sermon, preached at Friends' Meeting-House, Burlington. 104958

Sermon, preached at Glocester, N. E. 103402

Sermon preached at Gloucester, Nov. 29, 1759. (11871)

Sermon preached at Gorham. 51889

Sermon preached at Goshen. 4489

Sermon preach'd at Gosport. 24574

Sermon preached at Grace Street Church. 19886

Sermon, preached at Granville. 71836

Sermon preached at Greenfield, January 21, 1829. 89744

Sermon preach'd at Greenland. 43050

Sermon preached at Greenwich, Conn., 18th of Dec., 1777. 2479

Sermon preached at Greenwich, in Connecticut. 2480

Sermon preached at Greenwood, Indiana. 8551

Sermon preached at . . . Groton, Mass. 9104

Sermon preached at Guilford, December 15th, 1745. 73980

Sermon, preached at Hadley, on the 16th day of February, 1723. 12335

Sermon preached at Hadley upon a Lord's Day, 1731. 12335

Sermon preached at Halifax, July 3d, 1770. (78694)

Sermon preached at Hanover, New Hampshire. 64648

Sermon preached at Hanover, New-Hampshire, October 11, 1835. (105032)

Sermon, preached at Hartford, before the Board of Trustees. 92901

Sermon preached at Hartford before the Honorable General Assembly of the state of Connecticut. 8164

Sermon . . . preached at Hartford December 30th, 1739. 100927

Sermon preach'd at Hartford in His Majesty's colony of Connecticut. 91758

Sermon preached at Hartford, May 9, 1811. 91051

Sermon preached at Hartford on Conecticut [sic] in New-England. 100986

Sermon preached at Hartford on Connecticut in New-England, May 13th, 1686. 103699

Sermon preached . . . at Hartford on the anniversary election. 40810

Sermon . . . preach'd . . . at Hartford, on the day of election there. 21995

Sermon, preached . . . at Hartford, on the day of the anniversary election, March 14, 1795. 39696

Sermon, preached at Hartford, on the day of the anniversary election, May 9, 1799. 92895

Sermon preached . . . at Hartford, on the day of the anniversary election, May 9, 1793. 2623

Sermon, preached . . . at Hartford, on the day of the anniversary election, May 12th, 1796. 44744

Sermon, preached at Hartford, Vermont, May 24, 1812. 105160

Sermon preached at Hatfield, Sept. 2, 1741. 21967

Sermon, preached at Haverhill, Mass. 105141

Sermon preach'd at Hingham . . . May 10. 1738. 26785

Sermon preached at Hingham on a training day there. 26785

Sermon preached at his funeral by Dr. Holmes. 94367

Sermon, preached at Hollis, N. H. 68127

Sermon preach'd at Horsly-Down. 12335

Sermon preached at Indianapolis, Ind. (29839)

Sermon preached at Ipswich, November I. 1727. 103933

Sermon, preached . . . at Jamaica Plain. 103758

Sermon preached at King's Chapel, Boston. (25021)

Sermon preached at King's Chapel, Boston, September 9, 1813. 11206

Sermon preached at King's Town in Jamaica. (16752)

Sermon preached at Kingston in New-Hampshire. 78699

Sermon preached at Lancaster, before Captain Ross's Company. (10939)

Sermon, preached at Lee, Mass. 83738

Sermon, preached at Lexington, April 19, 1779. 105164

Sermon, preached at Lexington, April 19, 1777. 16350

Sermon, preached at Lexington, April 20th, 1778. 18104

Sermon preached at Lexington, on the nineteen-th of April, 1782. 59313

Sermon preach'd at Lexington, on the 13th of April, 1781. 17895

Sermon preach'd at Litchfield before the As-sociation of Litchfield County, June 8th, 1756. 4493

Sermon, preached at Litchfield, before the foreign Mission Society. 97598

Sermon preached at Litchfield, Conn., at the funeral of Colonel Benjamin Tallmadge. (31707)

Sermon preached at Litchfield in Connecticut. 1512

Sermon, preached at Littleton, Dec. 4, 1815. 25216

Sermon preached at Livepool, Nov. 19, 1782. 78322

Sermon, preached at Lynn, December 11, 1795. 95204

Sermon, preached at . . . Lynn, February 24, on the occasion. 42149

Sermon preach'd at Lynn, March 2. 1763. 72713

Sermon preached at Lynn . . . on the first day of December, 1803. 35872

Sermon preached at Machias. (24473)

Sermon preach'd at Malden. Decemb. 4th 1726. 22438

Sermon preached at Malden, June 24, 1705. 46318

Sermon preach'd at Malden, Setpember 28th. 1735. 22440

Sermon preach'd at Mansfield, Aug. 4. 1741. 104364

Sermon, preached at Mansfield, May 12, 1816. 81501

Sermon, preached at Mansfield, May 24, 1809. (71125)

Sermon preached at Marlborough. 65069

Sermon preached at Mattapoisett-Village. (71851)

Sermon preached at Medfield. 30892

Sermon, preach'd at Mendon Third Parish. 2870

Sermon preached at Middleboro', Mass. 3399

Sermon, preached at Middlebury, Vermont. 66227

Sermon preach'd at Millington. 23022

Sermon preached at Milton . . . and Dorchester. 30521

Sermon preach'd at Milton, Nov. 13. 1728. 25396

Sermon preached at Milton, Oct. 18, 1836. 14137

Sermon, preached at Montpelier. 101038

Sermon preached at Narragansett, March 15, 1741. 43664

Sermon preached at Narragansett, N. I. 1757. 97429

Sermon preach'd at Needham. 96386

Sermon preached at New Bedford. 30521

Sermon preach'd at New-Castle. 80793

Sermon preached at New-Court, Carey-Street. 104825

Sermon, preached at New Haven, Con. before the American Board of Commissioners for Foreign Missions, at their ninth annual meeting, Sept. 10, 1818. 89804

Sermon preached at New Haven, (Con.) before the American Board of Commissioners for Foreign Missions . . . Sept. 15, 1814. 70950

Sermon preached at New London, Dec. 20th, 1786. 11898

Sermon preach'd at New-London, Sunday, the 21st of February. 78554

Sermon preached at New London-derry. 9905

Sermon, preached at New-Preston. (82416)

Sermon, preached at New Town. 36859, 73408

Sermon preached at Newark, in New Jersey. (20062)

Sermon . . . preached at Newark, Jan. 19, 1742-3. (20062)

Sermon preached at Newark, N. J., May 8, 1751. 62793

Sermon preached at Newark, on the interment of the Rev. Edward D. Griffin. 89783

Sermon preached at Newbury, at the ordination. 43293

Sermon preached at Newbury, February 1st. 1772. 64801

Sermon preached at Newbury-Port, April 23, 1767. 97323

Sermon preached at Newbury-Port . . . February 15th, 1778. 37650

Sermon preached at Newbury-Port, June 25, 1767. (11858), (11861)-(11862), 97315

Sermon preached at Newport, March 27, 1715. 13202

Sermon, preached at Newport, on Rhode Island. 10073

Sermon preach'd at Newtown. 17095

Sermon preached at Norfolk. 101504

Sermon preach'd at North-Haven, December 25th 1760. 103213

Sermon preached at North Yarmouth. (11969)

Sermon, preached at Northampton, before the ecclesiatical convention. 104374

Sermon, preached at Northampton, before the Hampshire Missionary Society. 94206

Sermon, preached at Northampton, before the Hampshire Missionary Society; . . . August 25, 1808. 16366

Sermon preached at Northampton. . . . By Jonathan Edwards. 21936

Sermon preach'd at Northampton, Feb. 13. 1729. 104397

Sermon preached at Northampton . . . June 26, 1748. 21958

Sermon preached at Northampton, May 19th. 1723. 91943-91944.

Sermon, preached at Northampton, October 27, 1808. 104120

Sermon preached at Northampton, on the Lord's-Day, June 26. 1748. (21962)

Sermon preached at Northampton, on the twenty-eighth of November, 1781. 21556

Sermon preached at Northampton, the 17th. Decem. 1707. 91954

Sermon, preached at Northbridge, November 27, 1800. 17402

Sermon preach'd at Northfield, Jan 11, 1758. 2200

Sermon preach'd at Norton, January 3d, 1753. 47447

Sermon preached at Norwich . . . [by Joseph Morgan.] 50661

Sermon, preached at Norwich, on hearing of the death of General George Washington. 92936

Sermon preached at Norwich, on the continental thanksgiving. 97601

Sermon preached at Nottingham. 67117

Sermon preached at ordination of Rev. Joshua Young. 31218

Sermon, preached at Oswego, New York. 92243

Sermon preached at Ottumwa, Iowa. 75847

Sermon, preached at Oyster Ponds on Long Island. 65531

Sermon, preached at Pawlet. 28886

Sermon preached at Pennepeck in Pennsylvania. 36602

Sermon preached at Philadelphia April 15th 1744. 94699

Sermon, preached at . . . Philadelphia . . . April 23, 1865. 3864

Sermon preached at Philadelphia, December 7, 1865. 74740

Sermon, preached at Philadelphia, before the Reverend Synod of New York. (6789)

Sermon preach'd at Philadelphia December 24, 1747. 82872-82873, 94694

Sermon preached at Philadelphia, in the congregation of the Rev. Mr. Hemphill. 25527, 31295-31296

Sermon preach'd at Philadelphia, January 7. 1747-8. 94703

Sermon, preached at Philadelphia, Oct. 1, 1828. 70845

Sermon preach'd at Pinner's Hall, Jan. 4, 1735-36. 33871

Sermon preached at Plimmoth in New-England, December 9, 1621. (18132), 18135, 106053

Sermon preached at Plimmouth in New England in 1621. 18133

Sermon preached at Plymouth, December 22, 1793. (71761)

Sermon preached at Plymouth, Dec. 22, 1775. 2909

Sermon, preached at Plymouth, December 22d, 1773. 97474

Sermon preached at Plymouth, Dec. 23, 1776. 15090

Sermon preached at Plymouth, Feb. 22, 1789. (47818)

Sermon preached at Plymouth, in New-England, 1621. (18134)

Sermon preached at Plymouth, 1621. 19051

Sermon preached at . . . Portland . . . Jan. 30, 1853. 18182

Sermon, preached at Portsmouth, in New Hampshire. 8640

Sermon preached at Princeton, (Massachusetts,) April 8th, 1798. 74361

Sermon preached at Princeton on a general fast. 104931, 104934

Sermon preached at Princeton, on the 17th of May, 1776. 104931, 104934

Sermon preached at Princeton, September, 1775. 104933, 104947

Sermon preached . . . at Providence, . . . June 9, 1861. 9915

Sermon, preached at Providence, June 6, 1779. 73559

Sermon, preached at Provincetown, December 19, 1819. 92109

Sermon preached at Quebec, in 1854. 372

Sermon preached at Quebec on national schools. 43451

Sermon preach'd at Reading, April 30. 1758. 32315

Sermon, preached at Rehoboth (in the province of Massachusetts-Bay) May 14, 1766. 91735

Sermon preached at Rehoboth (. . . Massachusetts-Bay) May 14, 1766. 91734

Sermon preached at Richmond in Surry. 100977

Sermon preach'd at Road-Town. (67773)

Sermon, preached at Rochester, Oct. 15, 1769. 33211

Sermon preached at . . . Rochester, on the occasion of the funeral. 79921

Sermon preached at Roxbury, on a fast-day. 826

Sermon preached at Roxbury-Camp. 75928

Sermon preached at Rumney-Parish. 16640

Sermon preached at St. George's Church, Hanover Square. (74132)

Sermon preached at St. John's Church, Santa-Cruz. 30979

Sermon preached at St. Matthew's, Bethnal-Green. 102689

Sermon preached at St. Paul's Church, Richmond. 49313

Sermon preached at St. Pauls, Halifax. 71956

Sermon preached at St. Philip's Church. 26290

Sermon preached at St. Sepulchre's Church. 95421

Sermon preached at Saint Thomas' Church, Taunton. 85546

Sermon preached at Salem, February 14, 1827. 89744

Sermon preached at Salem, January 16, 1772. 20186

Sermon, preached at Salters-Hall, April 16th, 1783. 105502

Sermon, preached at Salters-Hall, April 12th, 1776. 91224

Sermon, preached at Salters-Hall, April 28th, 1784. 94435

Sermon preached at Savannah in Georgia. 103511

Sermon, preached at Scipio, N. Y., at the execution of John Delaware. 105117

Sermon, preached at Scipio, N. Y. Lord's Day. 105115

Sermon preached at Scituate on Lord's Day, May 29, 1838. 79393

Sermon, preached at Seekonk, Mass. 62742

Sermon preached at Shelburne. 88896

Sermon preach'd at Shrewsbury, North Precinct. 8938

Sermon, preached at Shrewsbury November 28, 1799. 93708

Sermon preached at . . . Shrewsbury . . . 7th of October, 1762. 25975

Sermon, preached at South Hadley, April 30, 1826. 89744

Sermon preach'd at Springfield, April 4, 1743. 79193

Sermon preach'd at Springfield, Dec. 13, 1770. 2905

Sermon preach'd at Springfield, January 26. 1736. 16640

Sermon preached at Springfield, March 26, 1724. 7755

Sermon, preached at Stafford. 102524

Sermon preached at Stamford, in Connecticut. 90122

Sermon preached at Stamford, Oct. 11, 1796. 40810

Sermon preached at Stanford by Mr. Noah Hobart. 103070

Sermon preached at Steuben. 4449

Sermon, preached at Stillwater. 90362

Sermon preached at Stockbridge. (72474)

Sermon preach'd at Stonington, Connecticut. 40772

Sermon preached at Stonington, June 14, 1733. 22005

Sermon, preached at Stoughton, May 22, 1808. (71126)

Sermon preached at Stourbridge and Cradley. 78278

Sermon, preached at Stow. 54957

Sermon preach'd at Stratford-le-Bow. (31807)

Sermon preach'd at Stratham. 43293

Sermon preached at Subdury, Mass. . . . November 21. (79949)

Sermon preached at Sudbury, Mass. . . . Nov. 24, 1864. (79946)

Sermon preached at Suffield, Conn. (18419)

Sermon preached at Suffield, the Sabbath after the news arrived. 32564

Sermon preach'd at Sunderland in the country of Hampshire. (67771)

Sermon preached at Sutton. 29750

Sermon preached at Swampfield. 91957

Sermon preached at Swanzey, N. H. (72453)

Sermon preached at Taunton, February the 18th and 25th, 1776. 96331

Sermon, preached at Tewksbury, February, 22, 1800. 9851

Sermon, preached at the anniversary election, Hartford, May 8, 1817. 43230

Sermon, preached at the anniversary election, Hartford, May 9, 1816. 24763

Sermon preached at the anniversary election, Hartford, May 12, 1814. 33949

Sermon preached at the anniversary election in Hartford, May 14, 1807. (3891)

Sermon, preached at the anniversary meeting of the Planter's Society. 79277

Sermon, preached at the anniversary of the Maine Missionary Society. 80179

Sermon, preached at the annual election, May 31, 1826. 19854

Sermon, preached at the annual election, May 25, 1831. 104953

Sermon, preached at the annual election, May 25, 1825. 89744

Sermon, preached at the annual election, May 26, 1830. 11919

Sermon preached at the annual fast, April 3, 1828. 16336-16337

Sermon [preached at the annual meeting of the Worcester Auxiliary Bible Society.] 105387

Sermon preached at the annual thanksgiving, December 7th, 1780. 92952

Sermon, preached at the annual thanksgiving, November 16th, 1797. 92968

Sermon preached at the audience of . . . Governor . . . Council, etc. 48007

Sermon preached at the Baptist Church in Charlestown. (26227)

Sermon preach'd at the Boston lecture, August 17. 1727. 79422

Sermon preach'd at the Boston Thursday-lecture. 12331

Sermon, preached at the Branch Church in Salem. 88891

Sermon preached at the burial of Thomas Powell. (8508)

Sermon preached at the celebration of the one hundred and fiftieth anniversary of the Society for the Propagation of the Gospel. 60977

Sermon preached at the centennial celebration of the opening of St. Peter's Church, Philadelphia. 19345

Sermon. Preach'd at the church of Petsworth. 33040

Sermon preached at the Church of the Advent. 88581

Sermon, preached at the Church of the Annunciation. 90831

Sermon preached at the Church of the Puritans. (12406)

Sermon preached at the Church of the Saviour. (23813)

Sermon preached at the city of New York. 44078

Sermon . . . preached at the consecrating of Trinity Church. (50329)

Sermon, preached at the consecration of Bishop Jarvis. 5883, 84692

Sermon preached at the consecration of Christ Church Cathedral. 88576

Sermon, preached at the consecration of Christ Church, Stratford. 1434, 1435A

Sermon preached at the consecration of Saint Alban's Church. (66876)

Sermon preached at the consecration of St. Peter's Church, Smyrna. 89021

Sermon, preached . . . at the consecration of the Parish Church, Leeds. 20391

Sermon preached at the consecration of the Polanen Chapel. (23813)

Sermon preached at the consecration of the Right Reverend Dr. Samuel Seabury. 81605-81606

Sermon preached at the consecration of the Rt. Rev. Samuel Seabury. 81607

Sermon preached at the consecration of Trinity Church, Chicago. (77574)

Sermon, preached at the consecration of Trinity Church, in . . . New-Haven. (32301)

Sermon preached at the Convention of the Protestant Episcopal Church. (21878)

Sermon preached at the coronation of King George III. 77122

Sermon, preached at the court of election, May, 24. 1682. 104073

Sermon preached at the dedication of a house for . . . worship. 17658

Sermon preached at the dedication of St. Paul's Church. 91659

Sermon preached at the dedication of the church in Hanover Street. 93213

Sermon; preached at the dedication of the Clinton Avenue Congregational Church. 38939

Sermon, preached at the dedication of the Congregational Church at the Upper Falls, Newton. 71580

Sermon, preached at the dedication of the Congregational Meeting-House, Claremont. 86675

Sermon, preached at the dedication of the Congregational Meeting-House in Franklin, Mass. 88676

Sermon preached at the dedication of the fifth house of worship of First Church. 22327

Sermon, preached at the dedication of the First Congregational Church in New-York. 23269

Sermon, preached at the dedication of the first Presbyterian Church, Benicia, California. 105090

Sermon, preached at the dedication of the Meeting-House, in the vicinity of Dartmouth College. 82879

Sermon preached at the dedication of the Meeting-House of the Evangelical Society in South Brookfield. 90287

Sermon preached at the dedication of the New Chapel. 85219

Sermon preached at the dedication of the New Church Temple. (3585)

Sermon, preached at the dedication of the New Congregational Church, in Andover. 89744

Sermon, preached at the dedication of the New Congregational Church in Barnstead, N. H. 13365

Sermon, preached at the dedication of the New Meeting-House, erected by the First Religious Society in North Danvers. (7370)

Sermon, preached at the dedication of the New Meeting House in the First Parish in Deerfield. 104121

Sermon, preached at the dedication of the New South Meeting House, in Salem. (32909)

Sermon preached at the dedication of the Presbyterian Church, at Little-Falls, Herkimer. 105117A

Sermon preached at the dedication of the Second Church, Boylston Street. 71793

Sermon, preached at the dedication of the Second Presbyterian Church, Charleston, S. C. 85300

Sermon preached at the dedication of the Third Reformed Protestant Dutch Church. 98997

Sermon preached at the dedication of the Union Meeting-House in Chester. 93546

Sermon preached at the dedication of the Unitarian Church in Athol, Mass. 13460

Sermon preach'd at the desire, and in the presence of the Ministers of the province of the Massachusetts-Bay. 96387

Sermon preached at the desire of the . . . Artillery-Company. 12312

Sermon, preached at the desire of the Committee, appointed for reparing of the Meeting-House. 25042

Sermon preach'd at the desire of the Honourable Artillery Company in Boston, June 6, 1737. 104408

Sermon preach'd at the desire of the Honourable Artillery-Company in Boston, June 3, 3, 1728. 26785

Sermon preached at the Dudleian lecture. 24553

Sermon preached at the East Precinct in Yarmouth. 103931

Sermon preached at the evening-lecture in the Old-Jewry. 9098

Sermon, preached at the execution of Moses Paul. 56635

Sermon preached at the farewell service. 31908

Sermon preached at the farewell service in Old Trinity Church. (77446)

Sermon preach'd at the Free-mens Meeting at New-Haven. 91757

Sermon preached at the French Meeting-House. 9907

Sermon preached at the French Meeting-House in Boston. 9906

Sermon preached at the funeral of Capt. Benjamin Sheppard. (32432)

Sermon, preached at the funeral of Deacon Asa Field. (69555)

Sermon preached at the funeral of Dea. Elijah Woodward. 9550

Sermon preached at the funeral of Eliakim Hall. 104314

Sermon, preached at the funeral of His Excellency William Eustis. 79799

Sermon preached at the funeral of Hon. William Jackson. 9551

Sermon, preached at the funeral of James William Blakey. 91155

Sermon preached at the funeral of John Belcher. 91223

Sermon preached at the funeral of Miss Mary Merchant. 91156

Sermon, preached at the funeral of Mr. Daniel Thurston. 22525

Sermon, preached at the funeral of Mr. Israel F. Morgan. 71593

Sermon preached at the funeral of Mr. William Huggeford. 99541

Sermon preached at the funeral of Mrs. Abby Woods. 93195

Sermon, preached at the funeral of Mrs. Freelove King. 95522

Sermon preached at the funeral of Mrs. Martha Horton. 64625

Sermon, preached at the funeral of Mrs. Susan Heard. (13397)

Sermon, preached at the funeral of Rev. David Ely. 102074

Sermon, preached at the funeral of Rev. Elisha Fiske. 92262

Sermon preached at the funeral of Rev. John E. Emerson. 90913

Sermon preached at the funeral of Rev. Matthias Bruen. 17270

Sermon preached at the funeral of . . . Reverend Mr. Samuel Cheever. 3471

Sermon, preached at the funeral of Rev. William Hart. 19830

Sermon preached at the funeral of the Honourable Col. John Pynchon. 91949

Sermon preached at the funeral of the Honourable, Wait Winthrop. 46355

Sermon, preached at the funeral of the Rev. David R. Downer. (73570)

Sermon preached at the funeral of the Rev. Eliphalet Porter. 66790

Sermon preached at the funeral of the Reverend John Davenport. 16345

Sermon: preached at the funeral of the Rev. John Elliott. (24569)

Sermon, preached at the funeral of the Rev. John Giles. 104352

Sermon preached at the funeral of the Rev. John Hunt. 32819

Sermon, preached at the funeral of the Rev. John Sabin. 72451

Sermon preach'd at the funeral of the Reverend Mr. John Hancock. 26785

Sermon, preached at the funeral of the Rev. Nathan Strong. 104312

Sermon, preached at the funeral of the Rev. Noah Wetmore. (77585)

Sermon preached at the funeral of the Rev. Stephen Williams. 7658

Sermon preached at the funeral of Woodbury Dommick. 20193

Sermon preached at the funeral solemnity of His Excellency Jonathan Trumbull. 22391

Sermon preach'd at the gathering of a church. 3476

Sermon, preached at the General Convention of Congregational Ministers in Boston, May 29, 1794. 71758

Sermon, preached at the general election at Hartford. 92937

Sermon, preached at the general election, May 10th, 1804. 22393

Sermon, preached at the general election, May 12th, 1791. 21563

Sermon preached at the high hills of Santee. (26227)

Sermon preached at the installation of Adams Ayer. 4575

Sermon preached at the installation of Rev. A. M. Bridge. 71794

Sermon, preached at the installation of Rev. Arthur Granger. 89680

Sermon preached at the installation of Rev. D. H. Barlow. (26240)

Sermon preached at the installation of Rev. George F. Simmons. 13418

Sermon preached at the installation of Rev. Grindall Reynolds. 71768

Sermon, preached at the installation of . . . Rev. James Flint. 14535

Sermon, preached at the installation of Rev. Jedediah Morse. 4441

Sermon preached at the installation of Rev. Rufus Ellis. 22309

Sermon preached at the installation of Rev. Samuel Osgood. 59362

Sermon, preached at the installation of Rev. William H. Gilbert. 70936

Sermon, preached at the installation of Rev. William Parsons Lunt. 26074

Sermon preached at the installation of the Rev. David Huntington. 92969

Sermon, preached at the installation, of the Rev. Elijah Gridley. 92889

Sermon preached at the installation of the Rev. George W. Bethune. 19877

Sermon, preached at the installation of the Rev. Holland Weeks. 22525

Sermon preached at the installation of the Rev. John M. C. Bartley. 18405

Sermon preached at the installation of the Rev. John Snelling Popkin. 62732

Sermon preached at the installment of the Reverend Mr. Ezra Carpenter. 26785

Sermon preached at the instalment of the Rev. Ethan Smith. 82740

Sermon preached at the instalment of the Rev. John Thompson. 14183

Sermon prached at the instalment of the Rev. Mr. James Wellman. (50913)

Sermon, preached at the institution of the Rev. Henry Whitlock. (37664)

Sermon preached at the interment of Rev. John Wilder. 42367

Sermon preached at the King's Chapel in Boston. 32783

Sermon preached at the King's-Chapel in Boston, N. E. 79278

Sermon preach'd at the King's Chapel in Boston, New England, March 23. 1737. 65463

Sermon preached at the last fast [Sept. 1, 1837.] 70210

Sermon preached at the last service in the Second Presbyterian Church. 83341

Sermon: preached at the Laurel Street Methodist Episcopal Church. 14043

Sermon preach'd at the lecture held in Boston. 101197

Sermon, preached at the lecture in Boston, after the funeral. 14504

Sermon preached at the lecture in Boston, April 1. 1731. 14486

Sermon preached at the lecture in Boston, April 29. 1742. (14525)

Sermon preach'd at the lecture in Boston, August 27. 1741. (14497)

Sermon preached at the lecture in Boston, Feb. 29. 1699. 104091-2 [sic] 1700

Sermon (preached at the lecture in Boston in New England the 18th day of the I moneth [sic] 1674.) 46736, 46758

Sermon (preached at the lecture in Boston in New-England the 18th of the I. moneth [sic] 1674.) 46736

Sermon preach'd . . . at the lecture in Boston, January 19. 1726,7. 16629

Sermon preach'd at the lecture in Boston. March 19, 1718-1719. 7119

Sermon preached at the lecture in Boston March 21. 1734. 14484

Sermon preached at the lecture in Boston, September 4. 1746. 14521

Sermon preached at the lecture in Boston the 5th. of July, 1705. 91942

Sermon preached at the lecture in Boston, two days after the death of the Reverend and Learned Cotton Mather. (14489), 46798

Sermon preached at the lecture in Boston; upon the death of the learned and venerable Solomon Stoddard. 14481

Sermon preached at the lecture in Dedham in Essex. 32837

Sermon preach'd at the lecture in Wenham. 12822

Sermon preach'd at the Ma'nor of Peace. 81636

Sermon preached at the Meeting-House near the Maze-Pond. 101123

Sermon preached at the Meeting-House of the people called Quakers. 77283

Sermon preach'd at the New-Building in Philadelphia. 103503

Sermon preached at the Old Church in Boston. 25395

Sermon, preached . . . at the Old-Church lecture, in Boston. 25408

Sermon preach'd at the opening an evening-lecture, in Brattle Street. 14519

Sermon, preached at the opening for public worship. 33222

Sermon preached at the opening of a Presbytery in Charlestown. 83442

Sermon preached at the opening of Christ's Church at Sorel. 20668

Sermon preached at the opening of St. Mark's Church, New York. 30493

Sermon preached at the opening of St. Paul's Chapel, in the city of New York. 2359

Sermon preached at the opening of the annual Convention of the Diocese of Pennsylvania, 1830. 19345

Sermon preached at the opening of the eighty-third annual Convention of the Diocese of New-Jersey. 83524

Sermon, preached at the opening of the Essex North Conference. 4296

Sermon preached at the opening of the General Convention, in Christ Church, Cincinnati. 82354

Sermon, preached at the opening of the New Scotch Church. 88953

Sermon, preached at the opening of the Reverend Presbytery of Salem. 103322

Sermon, preached at the opening of the said convention. 84582

Sermon preached at the opening of the Sixth General Council. 83520

Sermon preached at the opening of the Synod of Philadelphia. 20061A

Sermon preached at the opening of the Synod of the Presbyterian Church of the Lower Provinces. (37780)

Sermon preached at the opening of the Theological Institution in Andover. 21563

Sermon, preached at the ordination and installation of Rev. Richard H. Steele. 91128

Sermon preached at the ordination of a pastor, in the Church of the Baptists. 46241

Sermon preached at the ordination of Andrew Eliot. 22127

Sermon preach'd at the ordination of Edward Barnard. 3489

Sermon preached at the ordination of Frederick Frothingham. 90929

Sermon preached at the ordination of his son, Ammi Ruhamah Robbins. 71831

Sermon preached at the ordination of Jared M. Heard. 78369

Sermon: preached at the ordination of John Pierpont, Jr. 91372

Sermon preached at the ordination of John Pierpont, Jr., as pastor. 91374

Sermon preached at the ordination of . . . Joseph Howe. 18268

Sermon preached at the ordination of Mr. Frederick N. Knapp. 4575

Sermon preached at the ordination of Mr. Jabez Wight. 42013

Sermon preached at the ordination of Mr. James Francis Brown. 71770

Sermon, preached at the ordination of Mr. James H. Means. (5726)

Sermon preach'd at the ordination of Mr. Jeremiah Condy. (10077)

Sermon preached at the ordination of Mr. John E. Emerson. 13365

[Sermon preached at] the ordination of Mr. John Norton. 2199

Sermon preached at the ordination of Mr. John Sullivan Dwight. (71517)

Sermon preach'd at the ordination of Mr. Joshua Eaton. 29479

Sermon preach'd at the ordination of Mr. Nathaniel Gookin. 80795

Sermon, preached at the ordination of Mr.
Richard S. Storrs. 92257
Sermon preached at the ordination of Mr.
Samuel Barrett. note after 42429
Sermon preach'd at the ordination of Mr.
William Cooper. 14516, 16630
Sermon preach'd at the ordination of Mr.
William Rand. 12332
Sermon preached at the ordination of . . .
Penuel Bowen. 12331
Sermon preached at the ordination of Rev.
Calvin S. Locke. 90927
Sermon preached at the ordination of Rev.
Ebenezer Gancock. 30166
Sermon, preached at the ordination of Rev.
Eliphalet Gillett. 71760
Sermon preached at the ordination of Rev.
Enoch Pratt. 30521
Sermon preached at the ordination of Rev.
Frederick R. Newell. 91046
Sermon preached at the ordination of Rev.
Irem W. Smith. 82738
Sermon preached at the ordination of Rev. J.
Huntington. 42103
Sermon preached at the ordination of Rev.
John Pierce. 30521
Sermon preached at the ordination of Rev.
John R. Freeman. 70862
Sermon preached at the ordination of Rev.
Mr. Zedekiah Sarger. 8469
Sermon preached at the ordination of Rev.
William Richey. 21234
Sermon, preached at the ordination of the
Rev. Aaron Bancroft. 3492
Sermon preached at the ordination of the Rev.
Ashbald Green. 23327
Sermon, preached at the ordination of the
Rev. Azel Washburn. 89793
Sermon preached at the ordination of the Rev.
Caleb J. Tenney. (9490)
Sermon, preached at the ordination of the
Reverend Daniel Foster. 25231
Sermon, preached at the ordination of the
Rev. Daniel Merril. 89805
Sermon preached at the ordination of the Rev.
Edwards Whipple. 22525
Sermon, preached at the ordination of the
Reverend Eleazer Storrs. 75845
Sermon preached at the ordination of the
Rev. Ephraim Little. 13219
Sermon, preached at the ordination of the
Rev. George W. Briggs. (23813)
Sermon preached at the ordination of the
Rev. J. I. T. Coolidge. 82942
Sermon preached at the ordination of the
Reverend J. Rodgers. 24391
Sermon, preached at the ordination of the
Rev. James Milligan. 43569
Sermon preached at the ordination of the Rev.
James Otterson. 66230
Sermon preached at the ordination of the Rev.
John Cleaveland. 13595
Sermon preached at the ordination of the
Reverend John Eliot. 22128
Sermon, preached at the ordination of the Rev.
John Foster. 25234
Sermon preached at the ordination of the Rev.
Jonathan French. (25870)
Sermon preached at the ordination of the Rev'd
Jonathan Newell. 102751
Sermon, preached at the ordination of the Rev.
Jonathan Osgood. 25216
Sermon preached at the ordination of the Rev.
Joshua Crosby. 25206
Sermon preached at the ordination of the Rev.
Mather Byles. (9717)

Sermon, preached at the ordination of the
Rev. Miss Antoinette L. Brown. 39776
Sermon preached at the ordination of the Rev.
Mr. Abiel Leonard. 3511
Sermon preached at the ordination of the
Reverend Mr. Benjamin Wadsworth.
71828
Sermon preached at the ordination of the
Reverend Mr. Chandler Robbins. 71830
Sermon preached at the ordination of the Rev.
Mr. Daniel Thane. 2131
Sermon preach'd at the ordination of the
Reverend Mr. David Parsons. 67769
Sermon preach'd at the ordination of the Rev.
Mr. Ebenezer Gay. 26785
Sermon preach'd at the ordination of the
Reverend Mr. Edmund Noyes. 97313
Sermon preached at the ordination of the Rev.
Mr. Gyles Merrill. 3456
Sermon preached at the ordination of the
Reverend Mr. Jacob Biglow. 18106
Sermon preach'd at the ordination of the
Reverend Mr. James Diman. 32672
Sermon preach'd at the ordination of the Rev.
Mr. John Ballantine. 67772
Sermon preach'd at the ordination of the
Reverend Mr. John Brown. 17108
Sermon preached at the ordination of the Rev.
Mr. John Keep. 104376
Sermon preach'd at the ordination of the Rev.
Mr. John Lowell. 25398
Sermon preached at the ordination of the
Reverend Mr. Jonathan Judd. 21943
Sermon preach'd at the ordination of the
Reverend Mr. Jonathan Mayhew. 26780
Sermon preach'd at the ordination of the
Reverend Mr. Joseph Emerson. 22435
Sermon preached at the ordination of the
Reverend Mr. Joseph Roberts. 22129
Sermon preached at the ordination of the
Reverend Mr. Joseph Willard. 22126
Sermon preach'd at the ordination of the
Reverend Mr. Nathan Stone. 92093
Sermon, preached at the ordination of the
Reverend Nathan Strong. 92951
Sermon preached at the ordination of the
Reverend Mr. Nathanael Morril. 80796
Sermon preached at the ordination of the Rev.
Mr. Nicolas Dudley. 90917
Sermon preached at the ordination of the
Reverend Mr. Peter Thatcher. (71827)
Sermon preached at the ordination of the Rev.
Mr. Roger Newton. 27882
Sermon preached at the ordination of the
Reverend Mr. Samuel Cooper. (14503)
Sermon preached at the ordination of the Rev.
Mr. Samuel Payson. 59315
Sermon preach'd at the ordination of the
Reverend Mr. Solomon Lombard. 84351
Sermon preached at the ordination of the Rev.
Mr. Thomas Cary. 3456
Sermon preached at the ordination of the Rev-
erend Mr. William Symmes. (16346)
Sermon preached at the ordination of the Rev.
Munson C. Gaylord. 85394
Sermon, preached at the ordination of the Rev.
Nathan S. S. Beman. 4054
Sermon, preached at the ordination of the Rev.
Oliver Dodge. (25204)
Sermon preached at the ordination of the
Reverend Parson Thurston. 89806
Sermon, preached at the ordination of the Rev.
Rufus Anderson. (43391)
Sermon, preached at the ordination of the Rev.
Samuel Clark. 22465

Sermon preached at the ordination of the Rev. Samuel Presbury. 62772

Sermon preached at the ordination of the Reverend Samuel Shepard. 91807

Sermon preached at the ordination of the Rev. Timothy Clark. (9490)

Sermon preach'd at the ordination of the Rev. Ward Cotton. (17097)

Sermon, preached at the ordination of the Rev. Ward Cotton, to the pastoral care of the First Church. 71759

Sermon; preached at the ordination of the Rev. William C. Fowler. (24569)

Sermon, preached at the ordination of the Rev. William R. Chapman. 92245

Sermon preached at the ordination of the Rev. William Whitwell. 3488

Sermon preached at the Parish-Church of St. Mary. 103568

Sermon preached at the public lecture in Boston, . . . Jan. 29th 1756. 59604

Sermon preached at the public lecture in Boston, July 1st, 1725. (14525)

Sermon preach'd at the public lecture in Boston. On Thursday, Dec. 3, 1724. (47125)

Sermon preached at the publick lecture in Boston, February 1, 1739. (14525)

Sermon preach'd at the publick lecture in Boston July 18th. 1728. 79418

Sermon preached at the publick lecture, Tuesday, April 6. 1731. 103898

Sermon preached at the re-dedication of the Congregational Church in Union, Conn. 30092

Sermon, preached at the re-opening and dedication of the Church of the First Congregational Parish in Milton. 33983

Sermon preached at the re-opening of the Church of Augustus . . . Trappe. 51256

Sermon, preached at the request of the Ancient and Honourable Artillery Company, in Boston, June 3, 1799. 22465

Sermon, preached at the request of the Ancient and Honourable Artillery Company, June 4, 1792. (21792)

Sermon, preached at the request of the Ancient and Honorable Artillery Company, on the day of their election of officers, Boston. 97398

Sermon, preached at the Second Church in Boston, in November last. 71775, (71802)

Sermon preached at the Second Church in Boston, Sunday, April 17, 1864. 71786

Sermon preached at the Second Unitarian Church, Brooklyn. (23813)

Sermon preach'd at the South Church, in Boston, November 27th, 1746. 65595

Sermon preached at the South-Church in Boston: on the Lord's-Day after the death of the Honourable Josiah Willard. (79432)

Sermon preach'd at the South Church in Boston, on the Lord's Day after the funeral of the Reverend Mr. Alexander Cumming. 79409

Sermon preached at the South Church in Boston: on the Lord's-Day, after the funeral of the Reverend Mr. Thomas Prince. 79412

Sermon preach'd at the South Meeting House in Boston. 79413

Sermon, preached at the state fast, April 6th, 1798. 92973

Sermon, preached at the Stone Chapel in Boston. (4776)

Sermon preached at the Sunday Morning lecture in the Parish Church of St. Giles. 84347-84349

Sermon, preached at the Tabernacle, in Salem, December 29, A. D. 1799. 88894

Sermon, preached at the Tabernacle in Salem, July 23, 1812. 105301

Sermon preached at the Tabernacle, in Salem, (Mass.) 88887

Sermon preached at the Third Parish in Dedham. 95200

Sermon, preached at the Third Precinct in Brookfield. 101289

Sermon preach'd at the Thursday-lecture in Boston, August I. 1745. 101170

Sermon preached at the Thursday lecture in Boston 2, 1744. 22129

Sermon preached at the Thursday lecture in Boston, February 11th. 1730, 31. 102220

Sermon preached at the Thursday lecture, in Boston, January 1st, 1756. 65076

Sermon preached at the Thursday lecture in Boston, January 1st, 1740, 1. (79404)

Sermon preached at the Thursday lecture in Boston, Jan. 3, 1744-45. (1717)

Sermon preach'd at the Thursday-lecture in Boston January 28, 1741, 2. 79416

Sermon preach'd at the Thursday lecture in Boston, July 11. 1745. 79423

Sermon preach'd at the Thursday-lecture in Boston, June 19. 1729. 25390

Sermon preached at the Thursday lecture in Boston, May 6, 1742. 79429

Sermon, preached at the Thursday lecture in Boston, Novemb. 15. 1722. 102222

Sermon preached at the Thursday-lecture in Boston, September 16, 1762. (79430)

Sermon preached at the Thursday-lecture in Boston, September 3, 1778. (12309)

Sermon preached at the Thursday lecture, Nov. 24, 1859. 71776

Sermon preached at the Thursday lecture in Harvard College. 103899

Sermon preached at the union service. 83526

Sermon preached at the Unitarian Church in Jersey City. 26076

Sermon preached at the West-Church in Boston, July 27 A. M. 1766. 26781

Sermon . . . preached at the West Church in Boston, October 4th. 1741. 32880

Sermon preach'd at Thompson in Kellingley. 9803

Sermon preached at Topsfield, June 29, 1743. 13350

Sermon, preached at Trinity Church, April 6, 1810. 26624

Sermon preached at Trinity Church in New-York, before the administration of the Holy Sacrament. (37204)

Sermon preached at Trinity Church in New-York in America. 79839-79841

Sermon preach'd at Trinity-Church in New-York, the second Sunday after Trinity, 1728. 59640

Sermon preached at Trinity-Church, in New York, the 28th of November, 1703. 37197

Sermon preached at Utica, N. Y. Oct. 8, 1834. 89783

Sermon preached at Vergennes, state of Vermont. 76368

Sermon preached at Walthamstow. 67405

Sermon, preached at Warham, March 31st, [1793.] 8461

Sermon, preached at Warren, Connecticut. 94236A

Sermon preached . . . at Washington. 4575

Sermon preached at Weatherfield. (18419)

Sermon, preached at Weathersfield, No. 21. 1678. 73577

Sermon preached at Weaverham. 33931

Sermon, preached at Wellfleet. 103743

Sermon; preached at West Alexandria. 75795

Sermon, preached at West-Rutland. 94066

Sermon, preached at West Springfield. 89744

Sermon preached at Westerly. 24441

Sermon, preached at Westminister, (Mass.) 72452

Sermon preached at White-Chapel. 94125, 2d note after 99856

Sermon preached at Williamsburg. (28823)

Sermon preach'd at Wilmington. 50789

Sermon preached at Winchendon (Mass.) April 3, 1823. 13272

Sermon, preached at Winchendon, (Mass.) Oct. 18, 1820. 71844

Sermon, preached at Windham, A. D. 1721. 103707

Sermon preached at Windham, July 11th. 1721. 103707

Sermon, preached at Windham, November 29th, 1803. 102075

Sermon preached at Windsor, July 2, 1777. 34059, 99014

Sermon preached at Woodbury, Conn. 80365

Sermon, preached at York, Upper Canada. 92659

Sermon, preached at York Upper Canada, third of July, 1825. 92660

Sermon preached at York-Town. 3972

Sermon preached August 18, 1861. 7374

Sermon preached . . . August 1, 1830. 58325

Sermon, . . . preached August 9, 1832, being the fast day. 28686

Sermon, preached . . . August 9, 1832, the day appointed. 3622

Sermon preached . . . Aug. 7, 1842. note after 42429

Sermon preached August 6, 1863. (21443)

Sermon, preached August the 15th, 1798. 92276

Sermon, preached August the 19th, 1817. 66228

Sermon, preached August the 19th, 1817. 66228

Sermon, preached August 3, 1832. 89779

Sermon preach'd August 20th, 1727. (12368)

Sermon preached Aug. 24, 1862. (76474)

Sermon, preach'd . . . Aug. 23. 1730. (25399)

Sermon preached before a Convention of Ministers at Newington. (62819)

Sermon preached before a society of . . . free . . . masons. 57107

Sermon . . . preached . . . before a society of gentlemen. 99249

Sermon preached before . . . Francis Bernard, Esq; Governor . . . May 25th. 1763. 3489

Sermon preach'd before . . . Francis Bernard, Esq; Governor . . . of the province of the Massachusetts-Bay. 7805

Sermon preached before . . . Governour. (25976)

Sermon preach'd before His Excellency and General Assembly. 104259

Sermon, preached before His Excellency Caleb Strong. 3100

Sermon preached before His Excellency Francis Bernard, Esq; Governor and Commander in Chief. (3455)

Sermon preached before His Excellency Francis Bernard, Esq; Governor, His Honor Thomas Hutchinson, Esq; Lieutenant-Governor. 80802

Sermon preached before His Excellency Francis Bernard, Esq; Governor, the Honorable His Majesty's Council. (22124)

Sermon preached before His Excellency Isaac Tichenor, Esq. Governor. 76371

Sermon preached before His Excellency James Bowdoin, Governour. 102750

Sermon, preached before His Excellency John Brooks, Esq. 85405

Sermon preached before His Excellency John Davis, Governor. 100965

Sermon preached before His Excellency John Hancock, Esq. 94366

Sermon. Preached before His Excellency Jonh [sic] Hancock, Esq. Governour. 71757

Sermon, preached before His Excellency John Hancock, Esq. Governour: . . . of the Commonwealth of Massachusetts. 58878

Sermon preached before His Excellency John Hancock, Esq; Governour, . . . of the Commonwealth of Massachusetts, October 25, 1780. 16603

Sermon preached before His Excellency John T. Gilman. 105019

Sermon, preached before His Excellency Jonathan Trumbull. 60965

Sermon preach'd before His Excellency Jonathan Belcher. 104407

Sermon preach'd before His Excellency Jonathan Belcher, Esq; . . . May 29. 1734. 3471

Sermon, preached before His Excellency Jonathan Trumbull, Esq L. L. D. 9687, 91749

Sermon, preached before His Excellency Jonathan Trumbull, Esq. LL. D. Governour and Commander in Chief. 91750

Sermon preached before His Excellency Oliver Wolcott. 20746

Sermon preached before His Excellency Samuel Adams. (25868)

Sermon, preached before His Excellency Samuel Huntington, Esq. L. L. D. Governor, and the Honorable the General Assembly. 92129

Sermon, preached before His Excellency Samuel Huntington, Esq., LL. D., Governor, . . . of the state of Connecticut. 21970

Sermon preached before His Excellency Samuel Shute Esq. 92102

Sermon preached before His Excellency Sir Francis Bernard. (30885)

Sermon preached before His Excellency the Governour, and the Honourable Counsellors. 104071

Sermon preach'd before His Excellency the Governor, Council and Assembly of the Province of the Massachusetts-Bay. 104403

Sermon preached before His Excellency the Governor, etc. 29228

Sermon, preached before His Excellency the Governor . . . May 27, 1812. 25215

Sermon preached before His Excellency the Governor of Maryland. 91332

Sermon, preached before His Excellency the Governor, the Honorable Council and House of Representatives. 99021

Sermon preached before His Excellency the Governour, the Honourable Council, and Representatives of the province of

Massachusetts-Bay in New England: on
May 29, 1706. 72693

Sermon preached before His Excellency the
Governour the Honourable Council and
Representatives of the Province of the
Massachusetts-Bay. 79424

Sermon preached before His Excellency the
Governour, the Honourable Council and
Representatives of the Province of the
Massachusetts-Bay in New-England, on
May 30. 1711. 95161

Sermon preached before His Excellency the
Governor, the Honourable Council, and
the Representatives of the Province of
the Massachusetts-Bay in New-England.
On May 31. 1704. (74290)

Sermon, preached before His Excellency the
Governour, the Honourable Council, and
Representatives of the Province of the
Massachusetts-Bay in New-England: on
May. 25. 1709. (68105)

Sermonpreached before His Excellency, the
Governour, the Honoured Council and
Assembly of the Province of the Massa-
chusetts-Bay. 91968

Sermon, preached before His Excellency the
Goyenor [sic] of Maryland. 91331

Sermon preached before His Excellency
Thomas Hutchinson, Esq. 97475

Sermon preached before His Excellency
Thomas Pownall, Esq. (16601)

Sermon preached before His Excellency
William Burnet Esq. 104895

Sermon preached before His Excellency
William Shirley, Esq. 1836

Sermon, preach'd before His Excellency
William Shirley, Esq; May 29th, 1745.
26782

Sermon preached before His Excellency
William Shirley . . . May 31. 1749.
2873

Sermon preached before His Honor Thomas
Cushing, Esq; Lieutenant-Governor . . .
of Massachusetts. 17896

Sermon, preached before His Honor Thomas
Cushing, Esq; Lieutenant-Governor, the
Honorable the Council, and the two
branches of the General Court. 94123

Sermon preach'd before . . . His Majesty's
Council. (32671)

Sermon, preached before the American Society
for Meliorating the Condition of the
Jews. 89744

Sermon preached before the Ancient and Honorable Artillery Company, at the close
of the second century. (42147)

Sermon, preached before the Ancient and Honourable Artillery Company, in Boston,
June 5, 1809. 25238

Sermon preached before the Ancient and Honourable Artillery Company, in Boston,
June 2d, 1817. 76372

Sermon preached before the Ancient and Honourable Artillery Company, in Boston,
June 6, 1814. (11207)

Sermon, preached before the Ancient and Honourable Artillery Company, in Boston,
June 6, 1796. (4776)

Sermon preached before the Ancient and Honorable Artillery Company, June 7, 1830.
91375

Sermon, preached before the Ancient and Honorable Artillery Company, June 3, 1793.
95177

Sermon, preached before the Ancient and Honourable Artillery Company, on Monday,
June 2d, 1794. 102745

Sermon preach'd before the Ancient and Honourable Artillery-Company, on their
anniversary meeting for the election of
officers, June 6th 1748. (21246)

Sermon preached before the Ancient and Honourable Artillery Company, on their
anniversary meeting, June 2d. 1746.
101169

Sermon preached before the Ancient and Honorable Artillery Company, on their
CXCVIIth anniversary, June 6, 1836.
(71795)

Sermon, preached before the Antient and Honorable Artillery Company, on their 177th
anniversary. 19038

Sermon preached before the Ancient and Honourable Society of Free and Accepted
Masons, in Christ-Church, Boston. 8170

Sermon preached before the Ancient and Hon-
ourable Society of Free and Accepted
Masons, in the Parish Church of St.
Anne. 8185

Sermon preached before . . . the annual convention, in Boston. 12331

Sermon preached before the annual Convention
of Ministers in Boston. 2848

Sermon preached before the annual Convention
of the Congregational Ministers of Massachusetts, in Boston, May 29, 1830. 33794

Sermon preached before the annual Convention
of the Diocese of New-York. 82947

Sermon, preached before the Annual Convention
of the Protestant Episcopal Church.
40861

Sermon preached before the . . . Artillery
Company in Boston. 13347

Sermon preached before the . . . Assembly of
. . . Connecticut. 32308

Sermon, preached before the Associate Alumni
of the General Theological Seminary.
89342

Sermon, preached before the Associations for
Foreign Missions. 103380

Sermon preached before the Auxiliary Education
Society of Norfolk County, at their annual
meeting in Medway, June 11, 1823.
92265

Sermon, preached before the Auxiliary Education Society of Norfolk County, at their
annual meeting in Randolph, August 1,
1843. 88677

Sermon preached before the Auxiliary Education
Society of Norfolk County . . . in West
Roxbury, August 7, 1849. 71150

Sermon preached before the Auxiliary Education
Society of the Young Men of Boston.
35816

Sermon, preached before the Auxiliary Society
for the Reformation of Morals. 85406

Sermon preached before the Bladwin Place
Church. 21806

Sermon preached before the Bishop of Quebec.
102627

Sermon, preached before the Board of Directors
of the Domestic and Foreign Missionary
Society. 20391

Sermon, preached before the Buffalo Academy
of Music. 12527

Sermon, preached before the Charleston Union
Presbytery. 85288

Sermon preached before the Chitterden County
Consociation. 16210

Sermon preached before the churches of
Gloversville. (21335)

Sermon. Preached before the Commission
of the Synod. 59609

Sermon preached . . . before . . . the . . .
Concord Senate. 25875

Sermon, preached before the congregations
of Christ Church and St. Peter's. 16392

Sermon preached before the Connecticut
Society for the Promotion of Freedom.
21968

Sermon, preached . . . before the . . .
convention. (15815), 101999

Sermon, preached before the Convention of
Congregational Ministers in Boston,
May 31, 1804. 22525

Sermon, preached before the Convention of
the Clergy of Massachusetts. 42791

Sermon preached before the Convention of the
Clergy of the provinces of New-York
and New-Jersey. (77414)

Sermon, preached before the Convention of
the Congregational Ministers in Boston.
68556

Sermon, preached before the Convention of
the Protestant Episcopal Church, at New-
Brunswick. 73572

Sermon preached before the Convention of the
Protestant Episcopal Church in Pennsylvania, Philadelphia. 13385

Sermon preached before the Corporation for
the Relief of the Widows and Children
of Clergymen. 11880

Sermon preached before the Cortland County
Bible Society. 32448

Sermon preached before . . . the . . . Council
and . . . House of Representatives of
. . . New Hampshire. 8928

Sermon preached . . . before . . . the . . .
Council and . . . House of Representatives of . . . Vermont. 42781

Sermon preached before the Council and
Legislature of New Hampshire. 895

Sermon, preached before . . . the Council,
Senate, and House of Representatives,
of . . . Massachusetts, May 30, 1798.
22523

Sermon, preached before . . . the Council,
Senate, and House of Representatives
of . . . Massachusetts, May 29, 1799.
(14182)

Sermon preached before . . . the Council,
Senate and House of Representatives,
of . . . Massachusetts, May 27, 1789.
7808

Sermon preached before . . . the Council,
Senate, and House of Representatives,
of the commonwealth of Massachusetts,
25205

Sermon preached before the court of election
at Boston. 827

Sermon preached before the Eastern Convocation of Massachusetts. 82947

Sermon, preached before the Education Society
of the Young Men of Boston. 104356

Sermon preached before the election of
magistrates. 22793

Sermon preached before the Fatherless and
Widows' Society. 26536

Sermon preached before the First Congregational Church and Society. (69368)

Sermon, preached before the freemen of the
town of Middletown. (33958)

Sermon, preached before the General Assembly,
at Williamsburg. 91864

Sermon preach'd before the General Assembly
of . . . Connecticut at Hartford. (12338)

Sermon preached before the General Assembly
of . . . Connecticut, May 13th, 1756.
4259

Sermon preached before the General Assembly
of His Majesty's colony of Connecticut.
105091

Sermon preached before the General Assembly
of the colony of Connecticut, at Hartford
in New-England, May, 8th. 1712. 105161

Sermon preached before the General Assembly
of the colony of Connecticut, at Hartford
in New England, May 13. 1714. 103747

Sermon preached before the General Assembly
of the colony of Connecticut at Hartford
in New-England. May 13. 1697. 75853

Sermon preach'd before the General-Assembly
of the colony of Connecticut at Hartford,
May 14. 1713. (9106)

Sermon preached before the General Assembly
of the colony of Connecticut, at Hartford,
May the 11th, 1738. 22137

Sermon, preached before the General Assembly
of the colony of Connecticut, at Hartford
May 14, 1730. 74381

Sermon preach'd before the General Assembly
of the colony of Connecticut, at Hartford,
May 14. 1724. 105088

Sermon preach'd before the General Assembly
of the colony of Connecticut, at Hartford,
May 9th. 1734. 12336

Sermon preached before the General Assembly
of the colony of Connecticut, at Hartford,
May, 10, 1722. 9396

Sermon preach'd before the General Assembly
of the colony of Connecticut, at Hartford
May 13th. 1731. 103790

Sermon, preach'd before the General Assembly
of the colony of Connecticut, at Hartford,
on the day of election, May 11th, 1749.
96090

Sermon preach'd before the General Assembly
of the colony of Connecticut, at Hartford
on the day of election, May 14th, 1741.
104361

Sermon preached before the General Assembly
of the colony of Connecticut, at Hartford,
on the day of the anniversary election,
May 10th, 1753. 19829

Sermon, preached before the General Assembly
of the colony of Connecticut, at Hartford,
on the day of the anniversary election,
May 10th, 1764. 102572

Sermon, preached before the General Assembly
of the colony of Connecticut, at Hartford,
on the day of their anniversary election,
May 11, 1775. 61041

Sermon preach'd before the General Assembly
of the colony of Connecticut, at Hartford,
on the day of their anniversary election,
May 9th, 1745. 103733

Sermon, preached before the General Assembly
of the colony of Connecticut, at Hartford,
on the day of their anniversary election,
May 10th, 1770. 36322

Sermon preached before the General Assembly
of the colony of Connecticut, at Hartford,
on the day of their anniversary election,
May 12th, 1757. 68128

Sermon, preached before the General Assembly
of the colony of Connecticut, at Hartford,
on the day of their anniversary election.
May 12th, 1768. 75846

Sermon preached before the General Assembly
of the colony of Connecticut, at Hartford,

on the day of their anniversary election,
May the 12th, 1763. 103456
Sermon, preached before the General Assembly of the colony of Connecticut, at
Hartford, on . . . their anniversary
election, May 9th, 1771. 14216
Sermon preached before the General Assembly
of the colony of Connecticut, at Hartford,
on their anniversary election, May 10th,
1744. 105508
Sermon preached before the General Assembly
of the colony of Connecticut, in New-
England, at Hartford. 91930
Sermon, preached before the General Assembly
of the colony of Connecticut, on the day
of the anniversary election. 22004
Sermon, preached before the General Assembly
of the Presbyterian Church in the United
States, at their meeting at Washington
City, May, 1825. 9112
Sermon, preached before the General Assembly
of the Presbyterian Church in the United
States. . . . May 20, 1852. 3505
Sermon, preached before the General Assembly
of the state of Connecticut, at Hartford,
May 12th, 1785. 101028
Sermon, preached before the General Assembly
of the state of Connecticut, at Hartford,
on the day of the anniversary election,
May 8th, 1777. 19830
Sermon, preached before the General Assembly
of the state of Connecticut, at Hartford,
on the day of the anniversary election,
May 14th, 1778. 103788
Sermon preached before the General Assembly
of the state of Connecticut, on the day of
the anniversary election, May 13, 1779.
18417
Sermon preached before the General Assembly
of the state of Vermont, on the day of
their anniversary election, October 11,
1787. (64654)
Sermon preached before the General Assembly
of the state of Vermont, on the day of
their first election, March 12, 1778.
64802, note before 99021
Sermon preached before the General Assembly
of Virginia: at Williamsburg, March 1st
1752. 91865
Sermon preached before the General Assemely
[sic], of Virginia. 91863
Sermon preached before . . . the General
Convention of the Protestant Episcopal
Church. 43105
Serman [sic] preached before the General
Court of Election at Hartford. 104208
Sermon preached before the General Court,
on Friday, July the 4th, 1777. 28009
Sermon preached before the Generall Court
of the colony of New-Plimouth on the
first day of June 1669. 101120
Sermon preached before . . . the Governor,
. . . Council, and . . . Legislature of
. . . New Hampshire. 80792
Sermon preached . . . before . . . the
Governor, . . . Council, &c. of New
Hampshire. (49136)
Sermon preached before . . . the Governour
. . . May 28. 1707. 4404
Sermon preached before . . . the Governor
. . . of Connecticut. 22272
Sermon preached before . . . the Governor,
. . . of Massachusetts-Bay, . . . May
31, 1710. 59600
Sermon preached before the graduating class
in the University of Vermont. 59457

Sermon preached before the graduating class
of the Law School of Columbia College.
(64646)
Sermon, preached before the Grand Lodge, and
the other lodges of Ancient Freemasons,
of New York. (78578)
Sermon preached before the Grand Lodge, New
York. (34766)
Sermon preached before the Honorable Council,
and . . . Representatives of . . . Massachusetts-Bay, . . . at Boston, May 27,
1778. 59315
Sermon preached before the Honorable Council,
and the Honorable House of Representatives, of the colony of the Massachusetts-
Bay, in New-England. 102744
Sermon preached before the Honorable Council,
and the Honorable House of Representatives of the state of Massachusetts-Bay,
in New-England, at Boston, May 26, 1779.
91803
Sermon preached before the Honorable Council,
and the Honorable House of Representatives of the state of Massachusetts-Bay,
in New-England. At Boston, May 28,
1777. 102423
Sermon preached before the Honorable Council
. . . of the state of Massachusetts-Bay,
in New-England, May 31, 1780. 33279
Sermon, preached before the Honorable General
Assembly of the colony of Connectifut, at
Hartford. 103066
Sermon preached before the Honorable House
of Representatives, on the day intended
for the choice of Counsellors. 28010
Sermon preached before . . . the Hon. the
Council. 19059
Sermon preached before the Honorable Trustees
for Establishing the Colony of Georgia in
America. 4122
Sermon preached before the Honourable
Artillery-Company, in Boston, June 6th.
1720. 94106
Sermon preached before the Honourable General
Assembly of the state of Connecticut, at
the anniversary election, in the city of
Hartford, May 14, 1812. 102520
Sermon preached before the Honourable House
of Assembly in North Carolina. 83613
Sermon preached before the Honourable House
of Burgesses at Williamsburg. 31346
Sermon preached before the Honourable House
of Commons, at the Church of St.
Margaret's. 100860
Sermon preached before the Honorable Lieuten-
ant Governour, & Counsellors. 96302
Sermon preached before the Honourable the
Judges of the Superior Court. 92097
Sermon preach'd before the Honourable
Lieutenant Governour, Council & Repre-
sentatives of the province of the
Massachusetts-Bay in New-England,
May 26. 1725. 95228
Sermon preached before the Honourable the
Lieutenant Governor, the Council, and
Representatives of the province of the
Massachusetts-Bay, in New-England,
May 31. 1727. 4007
Sermon preached before the Honourable the
Lieutenant Governour, the Council &
Representatives of the Province of the
Massachusetts-Bay in New-England,
May 25, 1726. 96127
Sermon preached before the Honourable the
Lieut. Governour, the Council, and Repre-
sentatives of the Province of the

Massachusetts-Bay in New England, May
29th. 1728. 7657

Sermon preached before the Honourable, the
Lieutenant Governour, the Council & Representatives of the Province of the
Massachusetts Bay, in New-England, May
27, 1724. (79428)

Sermon preached before the Honourable
Trustees for Establishing the Colony of
Georgia in America, and the Associates
of the Late Rev. Dr. Bray; at their
anniversary meeting, March 15, 1743.
8725

Sermon preach'd before the Honourable
Trustees for Establishing the Colony of
Georgia in America, and the Associates
of the late Reverend Dr. Bray; at their
anniversary meeting, March 15, 1738-9.
(4986)

Sermon rpeached before the Honourable Trustees for Establishing the Colony of
Georgia, in America, and the Associates
of [the Late] Dr. Bray; at their anniversary meeting, March 19, 1740-1. 3918

Sermon preached before the Honourable Trustees for Establishing the Colony of
Georgia, in America, and the Associates
of the Late Rev. Dr. Bray; at their anniversary meeting, March 17, 1736-7.
101489

Sermon preached before the Honourable Trustees for Establishing the Colony of
Georgia in America, and the Associates
of the Late Rev. Dr. Bray, at their anniversary meeting, March 16, 1749-50.
25477

Sermon preached before the Honourable Trustees for Establishing the Colony of
Georgia, in America, and the Associates
of the Late Rev. Dr. Bray, at their
anniversary meeting, March 20, 1745-'6.
71296

Sermon preach'd before the Honourable Trustees for Establishing the Colony of
Georgia in America, and the Associates
of the Late Reverend Dr. Bray; at their
meeting, March 20, 1739-40. 17692

Sermon preached before the Honourable Trustees for Establishing the Colony of
Georgia in America, and the Associates
of the Late Reverend Dr. Bray, on their
anniversary meeting, March 17, 1747-8.
95612

Sermon preached before the Honourable Trustees for Establishing the Colony of
Georgia in America, . . . at their anniversary meeting, March 18. 1741-2.
(5054)

Sermon preached before the Honourable Trustees for Establishing the Colony of
Georgia, in America, . . . at their anniversary meeting, March 17, 1742/3.
37806

Sermon preached before the Honourable Trustees for Establishing the Colony of
Georgia in America, . . . at their anniversary meeting, March 16, 1748-9.
30767

Sermon preached before the . . . House of
Lords in the Abbey Church of Westminister, . . . Dec. 13, 1776. 40967

Sermon preached before the House of Lords,
in the Abbey Church of Westminister,
on Monday, January 30, 1769. 79279

Sermon preached before the Incorporated Society
for the Promotion [sic] of the Gospel in
Foreign Parts, 15th February, 1716.
31062

Sermon preached before the Incorporated Society
for the Propagation of the Gospel in
Foreign Parts, at the Parish Church of
St. Mary-le-Bow, on Friday, the 19th of
February, 1724 [i. e. 1725.] 105681

Sermon preached before the Incorporated Society
for the Propagation of the Gospel in
Foreign Parts; at the Parish-Church of
St. Mary-le-Vow, on Friday the 16th of
February, 1732. 82194

Sermon preached before the Incorporated Society
for the Propagation of the Gospel in
Foreign parts; at their anniversary meeting in the . . . [Parish] Church of St.
Mary-le-Bow, on . . . February 19, 1779.
106042

Sermon preached before the Incorporated Society
for the Propagation of the Gospel in
Foreign Parts; at their anniversary meeting in the Parish Church of St. Mary-le-
Bow, on February 19, 1773. (80505)

Sermon preached before the Incorporated Society
for the Propagation of the Gospel in
Foreign Parts; at their anniversary meeting in the Parish Church of St. Mary-le-
Bow, on February 20, 1767. 12318-12319,
23318-23319, 41642-(41644), 2d note after
99800

Sermon preached before the Incorporated Society
for the Propagation of the Gospel in
Foreign Parts; at their anniversary meeting in the Parish Church of St. Mary-le-
Bow, on Firday February 18, 1780. 95424

Sermon preached before the Incorporated Society
for the Propagation of the Gospel in
Foreign Parts; at their anniversary meeting in the Parish Church of St. Mary-le-
Bow, on Friday February 18, 1791. 82221

Sermon preached before the Incorporated Society
for the Propagation of the Gospel in
Foreign Parts; at their anniversary meeting in the Parish-Church of St. Mary-le-
Bow, on Friday, February 18, 1736. 13183

Sermon preached before the Incorporated Society
for the Propagation of the Gospel in
Foreign Parts; at their anniversary meeting in the Parish Church of St. Mary le
Bow, on Friday, February 15, 1822. 98521

Sermon preached before the Incorporated Society
for the Propagation of the Gospel in
Foreign Parts; at their anniversary meeting in the Parish Church of St. Mary-le-
Bow, on Friday February 15, 1750. 95423

Sermon preached before the Incorporated Society
for the Propagation of the Gospel in
Foreign Parts; at their anniversary meeting in the Parish Church of St. Mary-le-
Bow, on Friday February 15. 1744. 4123

Sermon preached before the Incorporated Society
for the Propagation of the Gospel in
Foreign Parts; at their anniversary meeting in the Parish Church of St. Mary-le-
Bow, on Friday February 15, 1765. 106017

Sermon preached before the Incorporated Society
for the Propagation of the Gospel in
Foreign Parts; at their anniversary meeting in the Parish-Church of St. Mary-le-
Bow, on Friday, February 19, 1741-2.
91002

Sermon preached before the Incorporated Society
for the Propagation of the Gospel in
Foreign Parts; at their anniversary

meeting in the Parish Church of St. Mary-le-Bow, on Friday, February 19, 1773. 80504, (80506)-80510

Sermon preached before the Incorporated Society for the Propagation of the Gospel in Foreign Parts; at their anniversary meeting in the Parish Church of St. Mary-le-Bow, on Friday February 17, 1786. 95767

Sermon preached before the Incorporated Society for the Propagation of the Gospel in Foreign Parts; at their anniversary meeting in the Parish Church of St. Mary-le-Bow, on Friday February 17, 1797. 93973

Sermon preached before the Incorporated Society for the Propagation of the Gospel in Foreign Parts; at their anniversary meeting in the Parish Church of St. Mary-le-Bow, on Friday February 17, 1792. 96143

Sermon preached before the Incorporated Society for the Propagation of the Gospel in Foreign Parts; at their anniversary meeting in the Parish Church of St. Mary-le-Bow, on Friday February 16, 1787. 101468

Sermon preached before the Incorporated Society for the Propagation of the Gospel in Foreign Parts; at their anniversary meeting in the Parish Church of St. Mary-le-Bow, on Friday February 16, 1749. 96797

Sermon preached before the Incorporated Society for the Propagation of the Gospel in Foreign Parts; at their anniversary meeting in the Parish Church of St. Mary-le-Bow, on Friday February 16, 1776. 94877

Sermon preached before the Incorporated Society for the Propagation of the Gospel in Foreign Parts; at their anniversary meeting in the Parish Church of St. Mary-le-Bow, on Friday, February 20, 1829. 93695

Sermon preached before the Incorporated Society for the Propagation of the Gospel in Foreign Parts; at their anniversary meeting in the Parish Church of St. Mary-le-Bow, on Friday, February 20. 1740-1. 78717

Sermon preached before the Incorporated Society for the Propagation of the Gospel in Foreign Parts; at their anniversary meeting in the Parish Church of St. Mary-le-Bow, on Friday February 20, 1746. 95420

Sermon preached before the Incorporated Society for the Propagation of the Gospel in Foreign Parts; at their anniversary meeting in the Parish Church of St. Mary-le-Bow, on Friday February 21. 1777. (44619)

Sermon preached before the Incorporated Society for the Propagation of the Gospel in Foreign Parts; at their anniversary meeting in the Parish Church of St. Mary-le-Bow, on Friday, February 21, 1766. 101276

Sermon preached before the Incorporated Society for the Propagation of the Gospel in Foreign Parts; at their anniversary meeting in the Parish-Church of St. Mary-le-Bow; on Friday the 18th of February, 1714. (2170)

Sermon preached before the Incorporated Society for the Propagation of the Gospel in Foreign Parts; at their anniversary meeting in the Parish-Church of St. Mary-le-Bow; on Friday the 18th of February, 1725. 103964

Sermon preached before the Incorporated Society for the Propagation of the Gospel in Foreign Parts; at their anniversary meeting in the Parish-Church of St. Mary-le-Bow; on Friday the 15th of February 1772 [i. e. 1723.] 102178

Sermon preached before the Incorporated Society for the Propagation of the Gospel in Foreign Parts; at their anniversary meeting in the Parish Church of St. Mary le Bow; on Friday, the 19th of February 1719. 7254

Sermon preached before the Incorporated Society for the Propagation of the Gospel in Foreign Parts; at their anniversary meeting in the Parish Church of St. Mary-le-Bow; on Friday the 19th of Feb. 1713. 90218-90218   14

Sermon preached before the Incorporated Society for the Propagation of the Gospel in Foreign Parts; at their anniversary meeting in the Parish-Church of St. Mary le Bow; on Friday the 17th of February, 1720. 100900

Sermon preached before the Incorporated Society for the Propagation of the Gospel in Foreign Parts . . . 18th of February, 1731. 4877, (4879)

Sermon preached before the Incorporated Society for the Propagation of the Gospel in Foreign Parts, . . . February 18th, 1785. 73369

Sermon preached before the Incorporated Society for the Propagation of the Gospel in Foreign Parts, . . . Feb. 15, 1782. 50407

Sermon preached before the Incorporated Society for the Propagation of the Gospel in Foreign Parts . . . February 15, 1739-40. 4751

Sermon preached before the Incorporated Society for the Propagation of the Gospel in Foreign Parts . . . on Friday February 16, 1798. 99250

Sermon preached before the Incorporated Society for the Propagation of the Gospel in Foreign Parts; . . . February 16, 1738-9. (6951)

Sermon preached before the Incorporated Society for the Propagation of the Gospel in Foreign Parts; . . . 16th of February, 1721. (6887)

Sermon preached before the Incorporated Society for the Propagation of the Gospel in Foreign Parts: . . . 20th of February, 1729. 1729. (59435)

Sermon, preached before the Kennebec-Baptist-Association. 91552

Sermon preached before the Legislature of His Majesty's Province of Nova-Scotia. 34765

Sermon preached before . . . the Legislature of Massachusetts. (5282)

Sermon, preached before the London Society for the Promotion of Christianity Amongst the Jews. 89744

Sermon preached before the Lords Spiritual and Temporal. 102146

Sermon, preached before the Massachusetts Missionary Society, at their annual meeting in Boston, May 24, 1808. 92929

Sermon preached before the Massachusetts Missionary Society, at their annual meeting, May 30, 1815. (76254)

Sermon, preached before the members of King Solomon's Lodge. 30521

Sermon preached before the members of the Church, in Chiechester. (40972)

Sermon preached before the Middlesex Lodge. 37281

Sermon, preached before the Military Company of Exempts. 58378

Sermon preach'd before the Ministers of the Province of Massachusetts-Bay. (1837)

Sermon preached before the Ministers of the Province of the Massachusetts-Bay . . . at their annual convention, in Boston; May 30. 1745. 13345

Sermon preached before the Ministers of the Province of the Massachusetts-Bay, . . . at their annual convention in Boston, May 28, 1772. 41734

Sermon preach'd before the Ministers of the Province of the Massachusetts-Bay in New-England, at their annual Convention in Boston; May 29. 1746. 26785

Sermon preached before the Ministers of the Province of the Massachusetts-Bay in New-England, at their annual convention in Boston, May 26, 1768. 97316

Sermon preached before the New-Hampshire Baptist State Convention. 17920

Sermon, preached before the New York Ministerium. 49017

Sermon preached . . . before the New-York Missionary Society. (43681)

Sermon, preached before the North Church and Society in Salem. 65562

Sermon preached before the Northern Missionary Society. 66228

Sermon preached before the Nova Scotia Philanthropic Society. (14225)

Sermon, preached before the Peace Society of Windham County. 37291

Sermon preached before the people commonly called Quakers. 77284

Sermon preached before the Plymouth Association of Ministers, . . . in Middleborough, Sept. 26, 1810. 68556

Sermon, preached before the Plymouth Association of Ministers; in the First Congregational Society in Plymouth. 71127

Sermon preached before the Presbyterian Churches of Cleveland. 5660

Sermon preached before the . . . Presbytery of West Lexington. 79746

Sermon preached before the Rensselaer County Bible Society. 91154

Sermon, preached before the Reverend Presbytery of New-Castle. 18764

Sermon, preached before the Rhode Island Baptist State Convention. 70976

Sermon preached before the Rhode Island Clerical Convention in Bristol. 13408

Sermon preached before the Right Honourable the Lord-Mayor. 96373

Sermon, preached before the Roxbury Charitable Society. (25239)

Sermon preached before the St. Andrew's Society of Montreal. 85470

Sermon preached before the St. George's Society of New York. 50690

Sermon preached before the Salem Female Charitable Society. 3493

Sermon preached before the Second Society in Lebanon. 103214

Sermon praeched . . . before . . . the Senate and House . . . New Hampshire. 20067

Sermon preached . . . before the Senate and House . . . of . . . New Hampshire. 9369

Sermon preached before the Society for Propagating Christian Knowledge . . . in . . . Edinburgh . . . January 1. 1750. 5743

Sermon preached before the Society for the Destitute Sick. 45463

Sermon preached before the Society for the Propagation of the Gospel in Foreign Parts. 90302

Sermon preached before the Society for the Propagation of the Gospel in Foreign Parts . . . at St. Mary le Bow, Feb. 18, 1708-9. 18925

Sermon preached before the Society for the Propagation of the Gospel in Foreign Parts. At the Parish-Church of St. Lawrence Jewry. 104258

Sermon preach'd before the Society for the Propagation of the Gospel in Foreign Parts, at the Parish Church of St. Mary le Bow, February 20th, 1707. 90318-90319 $\overline{8}$

Sermon preached before the Society for the Propagation of the Gospel in Foreign Parts, at the Parish-Church of St. Mary-le-Bow, on Friday the 17th of February, 1709. 96976 $\overline{10}$

Sermon preached before the Society for the Propagation of the Gospel in Foreign Parts, at the Parish-Church of St. Mary-le-Bow, on Friday the 16th of February 1710. 24690 $\overline{11}$

Sermon preached before the Society for the Propagation of the Gospel in Foreign Parts, at their anniversary meeting in the Parish of St. Mary-le-Bow, 21st February 1717. 5633

Sermon preach'd before the Society for the Propagation of the Gospel in Foreign Parts, at their anniversary meeting, . . . 20th of February, 1712. 50406 $\overline{13}$

Sermon preach'd before the Society for the PRopagation of the Gospel in Foreign Parts, at their first yearly meeting on Friday February the 20th. 1701. 104517 $\overline{2}$

Sermon preached before the . . . Society for the Propagation of the Gospel in Foreign Parts, . . . February 16, 1776. 31927

Sermon preached before the . . . Society for the Propagation of the Gospel in Foreign Parts, . . . February 21, 1783. 64328

Sermon preached before the Society for the Propagation of the Gospel in Foreign Parts . . . Feby 21, 1706-7. 5110

Sermon preached before the Society for the Propagation of the Gospel in Foreign Parts [on Matthew IV. 17.] 80353

Sermon preached before the Society for the Propagation of the Gospel in Foreign Parts, 1793. (20685)

Sermon preached before the . . . Society for the Propagation of the Gospel in Foreign Parts; . . . 17th of February, 1726. 40025

Sermon, preached before the Society in Scotland for Propagating Christian Knowledge, at their anniversary meeting. 91588

Sermon, preached before the Society in Scotland
for Propagating Christian Knowledge, at
their meeting on Tuesday, June 6. 1809.
102613

Sermon preached before the Society in Scotland
for Propagating Christian Knowledge,
. . . in the High Church of Edinburgh.
72005

Sermon, preached before the Society in Scotland
for Propagating Christian Knowledge, in
the King Church of Edunburgh. 104929

Sermon preached before the Society of Free
Masons. 88957

Sermon, preached before the Synod, at Glawya.
66228

Sermon preached before the Synod of New York.
9423

Sermon preached before the Taunton and
Raynham Volunteers. 5789

Sermon preach'd before the Trustees for
Establishing the Colony of Georgia, in
America. And before the Associates of
Dr. Bray. 9492

Sermon preached before the Trustees for
Establishing the Colony of Georgia in
America; and before the Associates of the
Late Dr. Thomas Bray. 29673

Sermon preach'd before the Trustees for
Establishing the Colony of Georgia in
America, and before the Associates of
the Late Rev. Dr. Thomas Bray. 38978

Sermon preached before the Trustees for
Establishing the Colony of Georgia in
America; at their anniversary meeting.
102173

Sermon: preached before the United Congregations of Wyoming, N. Y. 68022

Sermon preached before the University of
Cambridge, by P. Peckard. 59496

Sermon preached before the University of
Cambridge, on Friday, February 4th,
1780. 102147

Sermon preached before the University of
Cambridge, on Wednesday, May 29. 1776.
102145

Sermon preached before the University of
Dublin. (39975)

Sermon preached before the University of Oxford . . . December 13. 1776. 16589,
40514

Sermon preached before the University of
Oxford . . . February 21, 1781. 33019

Sermon preached before the Vermont Colonization Society at Montpelier, Oct. 20, 1830.
83756

Sermon, preached before the Vermont Colonization Society, at Montpelier, October 25,
1835. 103195

Sermon, preached before the Virginia troops
in New-Jersey. 34017

Sermon preached before the Wesleyan Conference in Toronto. (74585)

Sermon preached before the Wesleyan Methodist
Missionary Society. 102152

Sermon preached before the Young Men's
Christian Association of Columbia College.
70853

Sermon preached by A. B. Davidson. 100564

Sermon preached by a Swedish missionary.
89173-89175

Sermon preached by appointment before the
General Assembly. 89158

Sermon, preached by appointment before the
Northumberland Presbytery. 84851

Sermon preached by appointment, before the
Synod of New-York and New-Jersey.
83340

Sermon preached by appointment before the
Synod of New-York and New-Jersey, at
Newark, N. J. 89102

Sermon, preached by appointment of the Senior
Class. 44303

Sermon preached by . . . Archibishop Purcell.
66676

Sermon. Preached (by courtesy) in the German
Reformed Church. 92758

Sermon preached by G. K. 37213

Sermon, preached by him [i. e. John Williams],
upon his return. 104268-104270

Sermon preached by him [i. e. John Williams],
upon his return; at the lecture in Boston,
Decemb. 5. 1706. 104262

Sermon preached by him [i. e. John Williams],
upon his return, at the lecture in Boston,
December 5. 1706. 104264-104267

Sermon, preached by I. Mather. (46672)

Sermon preached by Isaac Stiles. 91759

Sermon preached by Jaazaniah Crosby. 17639

Sermon, preached by . . . John [Ewer], Lord
Bishop of Landaff. 12319, (34766)

Sermon preached by Mr. Edward Bulkley.
103200

Sermon preached by Nathaniel Whitaker. 103214

Sermon preached by order of the Honourable
Representatives. (80188)

Sermon preached by Peter Thacher. 95168

Sermon preached by request in St. Peter's
Church. 1674, 82732

Sermon, preached by request, in the Reformed
Presbyterian Church. 17438

Sermon preached by request of the Finance
Committee. 91570

Sermon preached by Rev. A. P. Putnam, at the
dedication. (66760)

Sermon preached by Rev. A. P. Putnam, in the
Church of the Savior. 66766

Sermon preached by Rev. B. Sadtler. 74829

Sermon preached by Rev. C. H. Spalding. 83495

Sermon preached . . . by Rev. Joel Hawes.
(65855)

Sermon preached by Rev. John C. Rankin.
67883

Sermon, preached by Rev. Josiah Spaulding.
88900

Sermon preached by Rev. Samuel T. Spear.
89084

Sermon preached by Rev. William P. Paine.
58256

Sermon preached by Rev'd William Shelton.
80156

Sermon preached by Rt. Rev. W. B. W. Howe.
87931

Sermon preached by the author to his own and
a neighbouring congregation. 24387,
95579

Sermon, preached by the Bishop of Gloucester.
(4670)

Sermon preached by the Most Reverend Dr.
Markham. 45418

Sermon preached by the Rev. Dr. Fuller. 26169

Sermon preached by the Rev. Dr. Fuller, on
Thursday, September 26, 1861. 26168

Sermon preach'd by the Rev. George Whitefield.
103530

Sermon preached by the Reverend Isaac Stiles.
91760

Sermon preached by the Reverend James Stone.
92064

Sermon preached by the Rev. John S. Ravenscroft. 67991

Sermon, preached by the Rev. John Wesley.
103508

Sermon preached . . . by the Rev. Joseph Fransioli. 25671

Sermon, preached by the Rev. Mr. Alexander Garden. 26594, 73406

Sermon preached by the Rev. Mr. Bradford of Rowley. 7240, 94361

Sermon preach'd by the Reverend Mr. George Whitefield, A. B. 103569

Sermon preached by the Rev. Mr. George Whitefield, on Kennington-Common. 103620

Sermon preached by the Reverend Mr. John Cotton. 17079

Sermon: preached by the Rev. P. D. Gurley. 29299

Sermon, preached by the Rev. Samuel T. Spear. 89097

Sermon, preached by the Rev. William R. De. Witt. 19879

Sermon preached by William Dewsbery. 84552

Sermon, preached Dec. 4, 1834. 91131

Sermon preached Dec. 17, 1865. 23239

Sermon preach'd . . . Decemb. 17. 1741. 12331

Sermon preached, December 16, 1825. 89744

Sermon preached Dec. 13, 1826. 22525

Sermon preached December 13th, 1776, being a day appointed for a public fast. 10760

Sermon preached December 13th, 1776, being the day appointed for a public fast. 1857

Sermon preached December 13, 1776. being the fast day on account of the troubles in America, at Beenham Berks. 91559

Sermon preached December 13, 1776, being the fast day on account of the troubles in America; at Hampstead. 33821

Sermon preached December 13, 1776, being the fast day, on account of the troubles in America, at Oxenden Chapel. (28304)

Sermon preached December 13, 1776, being the fast day on account of the troubles in America . . . . By C. de Coetlogon. (14155)

Sermon preached December 13, 1776, being the fast day on account of the troubles in America; . . . by G. Marriott. 44686

Sermon preached, December 13, 1776, being the fast day on account of the troubles in America. . . . By William Carpenter. 11007

Sermon preached December 13, 1776, being the fast day on account of the troubles in America, in a country church. 79280

Sermon preached December 13. 1776, being the fast day, on account of the troubles in America . . . . St. Michael, Cornhill, London. 24355

Sermon preached December 13, 1776, being the fast day on account of the troubles in America, to a congregation . . . at Bethnal-Green. 37276

Sermon preached December 13, 1776, being the fast day on account of the troubles in America. . . . To which is added a letter letter. 40793

Sermon preached Dec. 30. 1819, at the dedication of the House of Worship. 18404

Sermon preached December 30, 1819, at the . . . First Church in Dedham. 18405

Sermon preached December 12, 1787. 68555

Sermon, preached December 20, 1835. 38315

Sermon, preached, December 28th, 1825. (12182)

Sermon preached December 24, 1806. 82467

Sermon preached Dec. 29, 1861. 13849

Sermon preached December 29, 1799, in St. Peter's Church, Salem. (24480)

Sermon, preached December 29, 1799, in the North Meeting House, Salem. 3493

Sermon preached December 29, 1799, . . . the Lord's Day after the melancholy tidings. (32909)

Sermon preach'd December 27. 1739. 80794

Sermon preached December 23, 1767. 1567

Sermon preached . . . Eutaw. (42999)

Sermon preached . . . fast day, April 5th, 1855. 42149

Sermon preached February 18, 1767. 30892

Sermon preached . . . February 15th, 1835. 82732

Sermon preached February 15, 1802. Before the Honourable Senate and House of Representatives. 2921

Sermon preached Feb. 15, 1802, before the Senate and House of Representatives. 3101

Sermon, preached February 5th, 1800. 103767

Sermon, preached February 19, 1795. 92274

Sermon preached February 9, 1845. (16379)

Sermon preached February 2, 1845. 51614

Sermon, preached Feb. 28, 1798. 76517

Sernton preached Feb. 25, 1759. 43050

Sermon preached Feb. 25. 1761. 17906

Sermon preach'd February 27th. 1731, 2. 16640

Sermon preach'd February 26. 1741, 2. 79417

Sermon preached February 23, 1863. 20389

Sermon, preached 5th June, 1816. 92264

Sermon preached for the benefit of the poor. 71114

Sermon, preached for the benefit of the United Domestic Society. 70840

Sermon preached for the Board of Foreign Missions. 85270

Sermon preach'd for the reformation of manners. 31610

Sermon preached 14th March, 1815. 76373

Sermon preached . . . Hackensack, N. J. (19462)

Sermon preach'd in a new township. (16295)

Sermon preach'd in a time of great awakening. 102217

Sermon preached in . . . Albany, on . . . the twenty-third . . . July. (64646)

Sermon, preached in . . . Albany . . . MDCCXL. 37950

Sermon preached in All Soul's Church. 4575

Sermon preached in Armoy Hall, Oct. 9th, 1842. 13418

Sermon preached in Athens. 91579

Sermon preached in Augusta, Georgia. 87274

Sermon, preached in . . . Baltimore. (43338)

Sermon preached in Baltimore, November 28, 1861. 7456

Sermon preached in Baltimore, September 26, 1861. 26134

Sermon preached in Baltimore, thanksgiving day, August 6, 1863. 811

Sermon, preached in Barnstable, West Parish. (79923)

Sermon, preached in Berlin. note after 42429

Sermon preached in Beverly. (20758)

Sermon preached in Billerica, December 11, 1783. (17897)

Sermon preached in Billerica, Mass. 74374

Sermon, preached in Billerica, . . . 23d of November, 1775. 17894

Sermon preached . . . in Boston, and at Cambridge. 32588

Sermon preached in Boston, April 5, 1810. 11919

Sermon preached . . . in Boston, . . . April 16, 1837. 62772

Sermon preached in Boston, at the annual election, May 25, 1814. 1805

Sermon preached . . . in Boston, August 11. 1763. 10682

Sermon preached . . . in Boston, August 3d. 1773. 12331

Sermon preached . . . in Boston, before His Excellency Jonathan Belcher. (14487)

Sermon, preached in Boston, before the American Society for Educating Pious Youth. 12680

Sermon preach'd in Boston, before the Great and General Court or Assembly of the province of the Massachusetts-Bay in New-England. 104162

Sermon, preached in Boston before the Massachusetts Society for Promoting Christian Knowledge, May 28. 1817. 18405

Sermon, preached in Boston before the Massachusetts Society for Promoting Christian Knowledge, May 31, 1820. 90973

Sermon preached in Boston . . . before the Society for Encouraging Industry, and Employing the Poor. 16603

Sermon preached in Boston . . . before the Society for Encouraging Industry, and Employing the Poor, September 20, 1758. 3486

Sermon preached in Boston, before the Society for Encouraging Industry . . . Aug. 12. 1752. 12331

Sermon, preached in Boston, December 12, 1733. 79410

Sermon preach'd . . . in Boston, Feb. 8, 1728. (17094)

Sermon, preached in Boston, February 12, 1795. 93503, 95178

Sermon preached in Boston in New-England, April 29. 1668. 92351

Sermon, preached in . . . Boston, January 2, 1831. 42428

Sermon preached in Boston, July 2. 1719. 91955, 91966

Sermon preached in Boston, July 10th. 1726. 83448

Sermon preached in Boston, July 23, 1812. 11919

Sermon preached . . . in Boston, June 18, 1749. 7789

Sermon preached in . . . Boston, June 17, 1829. (51242)

Sermon preached . . . in Boston, March the 11th and 12th. 43293

Sermon preached in Boston, May 31. 1724. 46271

Sermon preached in Boston, May 29th, 1827. (64233)

Sermon, preached in Boston on the first anniversary of the American Society for Educating Pious Youth for the Gospel Ministry. 105315

Sermon preached in Boston, November 1, 1827. 64228

Sermon, preached in . . . Boston, on fast day, April 5, 1827. 62766

Sermon, preached in Boston, September 15. 1797. 91795

Sermon preach'd . . . in Boston, September 2d 1739. 12331

Sermon . . . . Preached . . . in Boston . . . September, 1742. 32880

Sermon preached . . . in . . . Boston, . . . September 27, 1798. 39187

Sermon preached in Boston, the 8th. of July, 1708. 91948

Sermon, preached in Braintree, before the Norfolk Auxiliary Society. 24519

Sermon preached in Braintree South-Parish. 79922

Sermon preached in Brighton. (25239)

Sermon preached in Brookfield, South Parish. 92090

Sermon preached in Brookfield, West Parish. 85395

Sermon preached in Brookline, Mass. (38779)

Sermon preached in Brooklyn, Connecticut. 104558

Sermon, preached in . . . Brooklyn, February 12, 1865. (72424)

Sermon preached in . . . Brooklyn, May 20th, 1866. (72425)

Sermon, preached in . . . Brooklyn, N. Y., February 2d, 1873. 66756

Sermon preached in Brooklyn, November 26, 1863. 10993

Sermon preached in Bulfinch St. Church. 760

Sermon preached in Calvary Church. 17277

Sermon, preached in Cambridge and Brighton. (25239)

Sermon preached in . . . Camden, N. J. 68591

Sermon preached in . . . Canandaigua, N. Y. 18269

Sermon preached in Chambersburg, November 28, 1861. 55163

Sermon preached in . . . Charlestown, . . . April 13, 1862. 26647

Sermon preach'd in Charlestown, South-Carolina. 83443

Sermon, preach'd in Charlestown, South Carolina, March 26th, Anno Domini 1740. 83430-83433, 103514, 103588, 103601

Sermon preached in Chicago, Aug. 3, 1862. 14417

Sermon preached in Chillicothe. 104682

Sermon preached in Christ Church and St. Peter's. 53

Sermon, preached in Christ-Church, Dover. (79281)

Sermon preached in Christ Church, Guysboro'. 80744

Sermon, preached in Christ-Church, in Newbern. 83612

Sermon, preached in Christ-Church, Philadelphia, at a general communication. 84584

Sermon, preached in Christ-Church, Philadelphia, before the Honourable Continental Congress. 21047

Sermon, preached in Christ-Church, Philadelphia; before the Provincial Grand Master. 84663-84664

Sermon preached in Christ-Church, Philadelphia, (for the benefit of the poor.) 84668

Sermon preached in Christ-Church, Philadelphia, (for the benefit of the poor) by appointment of the state of Pennsylvania. 84584

Sermon, preached in Christ-Church, Philadelphia, October 10, 1769. 84669-84670

Sermon preached in Christ-Church, Philadelphia, on Friday, October 7th, 1785. 84666

Sermon preached in Christ-Church, Philadelphia; on Sunday, January 10, 1762. 84626

Sermon preached in Christ Church, Quincy. 18162

Sermon preached in Christ Church, Savannah, on Friday, November 15th, 1861. 33235

Sermon preached in Christ Church, Savannah, on Thursday, September 18th, being the day set forth. 32279

Sermon preached in Christ M. E. Church, Pittsburgh. 85459

Sermon preached in Christ's Church, New York. 24334, 62859

Sermon preached in Christ's Church, New-York, on the fourth of July, 1794. 62859

Sermon, preached in Christ's-Church Philadelphia, before the Ancient and Honourable Fraternity of Free and Accepted Masons. 84667

Sermon preached in Christ's Church, Philadelphia, Friday, January 4, 1861. 20635

Sermon preached in Christ's Church, Savannah. 22277

Sermon preached in Chelmsford. 58118

Sermon preached in Cleveland, Nov. 28, 1861. 30933

Sermon preached in . . . Cleveland, Ohio. 5659

Sermon preached in Coeymans, New York. 39461

Sermon, preached in Cohasset. 92054

Sermon preached in Commemoration of the 220th anniversary. 8970

Sermon preached in Cross-Street Chapel, Manchester. 71733

Sermon preached in Cumberland-St. M. E. Church. 93629

Sermon, preached in . . . Dec. 30, 1860. (26098)

Sermon preached in Dedham and West Roxbury. (39263)

Sermon preached in Detroit, January 4, 1861. 43105

Sermon preached . . . in . . . Detroit, on thanksgiving day. 22100

Sermon, preached in . . . Detroit, September 26, 1861. 43104

Sermon preached in . . . Dighton. 18917

Sermon preached in . . . Dorchester, . . . Dec. 11, 1859. (29830)

Sermon preached in . . . Dorchester . . . January 1st, 1860. 62831

Sermon preached in . . . Dorchester, January 12, 1851. (29830)

Sermon preached in . . . Dover . . . December 27th, 1779. 43804

Sermon, preached in Dunstable, N. H. 90974

Sermon preached in Eastham, 24th February, 1730-31. (42038)

Sermon preached in Easton, Pennsylvania, November 28, 1861. 21839

Sermon preached in Easton, Pennsylvania, November 29, 1860. 21837

Sermon preached in 1852, on the occasion of the primary visitation. 5088

Sermon, preached in Enosburgh, Vermont. 84924

Sermon preached in Farmington, Connecticut. (64291)

Sermon preached in First Church. 22327

Sermon preached in . . . Foxborough, Mass. (20065)

Sermon, preached in Franklin, March 16, 1820. 24519

Sermon preached in Grace Church, Brooklyn Heights, N. Y. 32396

Sermon, preached in Grace Church, New-York. 100966

Sermon, preached in Grace Church, Orange, N. J. 9534

Sermon preached in Greenfield, Ohio. 17686

Sermon preached in Greenwich Church. 9361

Sermon preached in . . . Greenwich, New Jersey. 63424

Sermon preached in . . . Hackensack, N. J. 19461

Sermon, preached in Hadley, December 22, 1820. 105086

Sermon preached in Hamden, July 11th, 1792. (21975)

Sermon preached in Hanover County, Virginia. (18762)

Sermon preached in Hanover January 8, 1757. 18759

Sermon, preached in Harrisburg. 104622

Sermon, preached in . . . Hartford . . . 1843. 17277

Sermon, preached in Hartford, June 10th, 1797. 92970

Sermon preached in Hingham and Quincy. 14533

Sermon preached in Hingham, 17 December 1817. 14525

Sermon preached . . . in Holden, October 25th, 1863. 58256

Sermon preached in Hollis Street Church, . . . Dec. 8, 1844. 76988

Sermon preached in Hollis Street Church in Boston, . . . April 16th, 1837. 79282

Sermon preached in . . . Holmesburg, Pa. 30707

Sermon preached in Indiana-Place Chapel, Boston. 13418

Sermon preached . . . in Keene. 41558

Sermon preached in King's Chapel, August 6, 1843. 26074

Sermon preached in King's Chapel, Boston, December 7, 1856. 66791

Sermon, preached in Lebanon, at the funeral of Harry Bliss. 64647

Sermon; preached in Lenox. 102754

Sermon, preached in . . . Lexington . . . September 11, 1864. (41577)

Sermon preached in . . . Litchfield, Conn. 61060

Sermon, preached in Little Wild-Street. 91225

Sermon, preached in . . . Lockport. 17483

Sermon preached in London. 17425, note after 99858, note 2d after 100502

Sermon preached in Louisville, Kentucky. 31670

Sermon preached in Marblehead. 7310

Sermon preached in Marshfield First Parish. 79950

Sermon, preached . . . in May 27th, 1795. 24932

Sermon, preached in Medfield. 76374

Sermon, preached in Medway, December 14, 1817. 34172

Sermon preached in Medway Village. 76476

Sermon, preached in Middletown, Upper-Houses. 104305

Sermon, preached in Milton, November 1, 1797. 22169

Sermon preached in Milton, Pa. 104696

Sermon preached in . . . Montreal. (23810)

Sermon preached in New-Ark, June 12. 1744. 59608

Sermon, preached in . . . New Britain. 61010

Sermon preach'd in . . . New-Castle, . . . New-Hampshire. 60793

Sermon preached in . . . New Haven, August 8, 1810. 21563

Sermon, . . . preached in . . . New Haven, May 31, 1837. 2666

Sermon preached in . . . New London. 29866

Sermon preached in . . . New York, April 21, 1861. 4575

Sermon preached in . . . New York, April 23, 1865. 6393

Sermon, preached in . . . New York, at the opening of the General Synod of the Reformed Dutch Church. 73046

Sermon, preached in New-York, December 11th, 1783. 72473

Sermon preached in . . . New York . . . October 29th, 1865. 20349

Sermon, preached in . . . New-York, on thanksgiving-day. 13280

Sermon, preached in . . . New-York, on thanksgiving day, Nov. 27th, 1862. (13278)

Sermon, preached in . . . New York, on the day of national fasting. 43271

Sermon, preached in . . . New York, thanksgiving day, 1861. 20349

Sermon, preached in . . . New-York, . . . the 10th of December, 1835. 66878

Sermon preach'd in Newark, June 2, 1736. (20062)

Sermon preached in Newbury, June 10, 1804. 64138

Sermon preached in . . . Newburyport, . . . Dec. 25, 1837. (50978)

Sermon preached in . . . Newburyport, Oct. 4th, 1827. 66226

Sermon, preached in . . . Newton Lower Falls, Mass. 3991

Sermon preached in . . . Norfolk, Va., August 18, 1850. 35482

Sermon, preached in North Brookfield, August 20th, 1812. 85398

Sermon, preached in North Brookfield, July 23d, 1812. 85398

Sermon preached in Northampton, February 22, 1863. 33210

Sermon preached in Norton . . . 15th February, 1835. 5283

Sermon preached in . . . Norwich, Conn. 6279

Sermon, preached . . . in Norwich, December 13th, 1773. 42013

Sermon preached in . . . October, A. D. 1827. (32301)

Sermon preached in Old Lyme. 7338

Sermon preached in Old Saybrook, Conn. 42977

Sermon, preached in Orleans, at the ordination of the Rev. Daniel Johnson. 68556

Sermon preached in Oswego, New York. 29843

Sermon, preached in Park Street Church, Boston. 4339

Sermon preached in Park Street Church, on the Sunday succeeding the death of Daniel Webster. 92023

Sermon preached (in part) . . . July 24th 1729. 14472

Sermon, preached in Philadelphia, before the Provincial Grand Master. 84665

Sermon preached in . . . Philadelphia February 11, 1866. (3508)

Sermon preached in Philadelphia, Feb. 17, 1756. 94692

Sermon preached in Philadelphia, July the 15th, 1784. 90150

Sermon, preached in . . . Philadelphia, May 8th, 1822. 50148

Sermon preached in . . . Philadelphia . . . November 17. 1839. 4755

Sermon preached in . . . Philadelphia, on thanksgiving day. (6071)

Sermon, preached in . . . Philadelphia, on the 28th day of November, 1861. 6084

Sermon preached in . . . Philadelphia, . . . Sept. 7, 1862. 42344

Sermon preached in Philadelphia, 20th May, 1823. 17581

Sermon preached in . . . Pittsburg, Pa. (31854)

Sermon preached . . . in Plymouth (Massachusetts), June 8, 1794. 33213

Sermon preached . . . in . . . Plymouth, November 2. 1720. 40773

Sermon preached in Portsmouth; occasioned by the success in the late war. 30891

Sermon, preached in . . . Poughkeepsie, September 26th, 1830. (68558)

Sermon preached in private, May 6th, and afterwards in public. (12369)

Sermon preached in . . . Providence, on . . . April 19, 1865. 20984

Sermon preached in . . . Providence, R. I., May 12, 1861. 13222

Sermon, preached in Radnor Church, on Thursday. 65118, 79283

Sermon preached in Randolph, June 3, 1801. 82880

Sermon preached in Randolph, New York, Oct. 12, 1862. 17246

Sermon preached in Reading, North Parish. 5284

Sermon preached in Rochester, N. Y., Sept., 1843. 81643

Sermon preached in . . . Rochester . . . October 18, 1854. 21663

Sermon, preached in Roxbury, before Washington Lodge. 76375

Sermon preached in Rowley, West-Parish. 7367

Sermon, preached in St. Andrew's Church, Philadelphia. 91582

Sermon preached in St. Andrew's Church, Philadelphia, on Sunday, January 15, 1854. 91576

Sermon preached in St. Clement's Church, New York. (33493)

Sermon preached in St. George's Church, Montreal. 6287

Sermon preached in St. James' Church, Birmingham, Ct. 11780

Sermon, preached in St. James Church, by the Rev. J. H. Harris. 85853

Sermon, preached in St. James' Church, Greenfield. 93079

Sermon preached in St. James' Church, Hyde Park. 80450

Sermon preached in St. James' Church, Pointe a Cavagnol. 66865

Sermon preached in St. James' Church, New London. 78579

Sermon preached in St. John's Church, Bridgeport. 29866

Sermon, preached in St. John's Church, Clifton. 91709

Sermon preached in St. John's Church, Detroit. 2010

Sermon, preached in St. John's Church, Elizabeth-Town. (73883)

Sermon preached in St. John's Church, Providence. 20399

Sermon, preached in St. John's Parish, Passaic. 83523

Sermon preached in . . . St. Louis, Sept. 25, 1845. 64692

Sermon preached in . . . St. Louis, the Sabbath after the great fire. 64692

Sermon, preached in St. Luke's Church, New-York. 35311

Sermon preached in St. Mark's Church, Orange. 20391

Sermon preached in St. Mary's Church, Burlington. 20391

Sermon, preached in St. Mary's Church, Newton Lower Falls. (3990)

Sermon, preached in St. Michael's Church by the M. R. the Grand Chaplain. 87841

Sermon, preached in St. Michael's Church, Charleston, in behalf of the Protestant Episcopal Society. 89105

Sermon preached in St. Michael's Church, Charleston, S. C. 22267

Sermon preached in Saint Paul's Chapel, New York. 20347

Sermon, preached in St. Paul's Church, Albany, . . . January 13, 1861. 73886

Sermon preached in St. Paul's Church, Albany, on . . . December 1, 1861. (73887)

Sermon preached in St. Paul's Church, Alexandria. 67990

Sermon preached in St. Paul's Church, Boston. 93081

Sermon, preached in St. Paul's Church, Centreville. 90881

Sermon preached in St. Paul's Church, Montreal. 86471

Sermon preached in St. Paul's Church, Philadelphia. 62860

Sermon preached in St. Peter's Church, Albany. 13785

Sermon, preached in St. Peter's Church, Auburn. 73879

Sermon, preached in St. Peter's Church, Philadelphia. 84614

Sermon preached in St. Stephen's Church, New-York. 1675

Sermon preached in St. Thomas' Church, Bethel. (3356)

Sermon preached in Salem, April 13, 1865. 49119

Sermon, preached in Salem, before the Bible Society of Salem and its Vicinity. 100925

Sermon, preached in Salem, July 23, 1812. (22420)

Sermon, preached in Salem, on the anniversary thanksgiving. 82893

Sermon, preached in . . . Sandwich, Mass., September 15, 1856. 6409

Sermon preached in . . . Sandwich, November 21, 1861. 37755

Sermon preached in . . . Savannah . . . February 28th, 1862. 22281

Sermon, preached in . . . Savannah, . . . September 15, 1864. 22283

Sermon preached . . . in Seven Oaks, in Kent. (62788)

Sermon, preached in Sharon, Vermont. 21690

Sermon . . . preached in Somerville, Feb. 8, 1857. (64106)

Sermon preached in South Congregational Church, Boston. 29632

Sermon preached in South Dartmouth. 33270

Sermon preached in . . . South Parish, Andover. (64233)

Sermon preached in . . . Spencer, Mass. (17724)

Sermon, preached in Springfield, August 28, 1823. 89744

Sermon, preached in the audience of His Excellency Caleb Strong, Esq. Governor; His Honor, Edward H. Robbins, Esq. Lieutenant Governor. 80195

Sermon preached in the audience of His Excellency Caleb Strong, Esq. Governor . . . on the anniversary election. 937

Sermon, preached in the audience of His Excellency Samuel Huntington. 103760

Sermon preach'd in the audience of His Excellency William Shirley, Esq; Governour, . . . the Council, and the . . . Representatives. 47147

Sermon preached in the audience of His Excellency William Shirley, Esq. . . . on the day of election. 831

Sermon. Preached in the audience of His Honour Spencer Phips, Esq; Lieutenant Governour and Commander in Chief, the Honourable His Majesty's Council, and the Honourable House of Representatives. 102621

Sermon preach'd in the audience of His Honour Spencer Phips, Esq; Lieutenant Governour and Commander in Chief, the Honourable His Majesty's Council, and the House of Representatives. 17099

Sermon preached . . . in the audience of the Ancient and Honourable Artillery-Company in Boston. 62515

Sermon, preached in the audience of the General Assembly of the colony of Connecticut, at Hartford. 104217

Sermon preached in the audience of the General Assembly of the colony of Connecticut, on the day of their anniversary election in Hartford. (22007)

Sermon, preached in the audience of the General Assembly of the Massachusets [sic] colony, at Boston. 46645

Sermon preached in the audience of the General Assembly of the Massachusetts Colony, at Boston in New-England. 96301

Sermon, preached in the audience of the General Assembly of the province of the Massachusetts Bay in New-England. 46681

Sermon, preached in the audience of the General Assembly of the state of Connecticut. 104316

Sermon, preached in the audience of the Governour, Council, and Representatives. 46689

Sermon preached in the Baptist Church, Albany. 26195

Sermon preached in the Baptist Church, Shusham. (8488)

Sermon preached in the Baptist Meeting House in Providence. 47005

Sermon, preached in the camp at Roxbury. 44377

Sermon preached in the Central Presbyterian Church of Brooklyn. 72427

Sermon preached in the Central Reformed Protestant Dutch Church. 8173

Sermon preach'd in the Chapel of Harvard-College. 3470

Sermon preached in the Chapel of the Institute at Flushing, L. I. (51254)

Sermon preached in the Church at Falmouth. 14070

Sermon preached in the Church of Portsmouth. 8641

Sermon preached in the Church of St. Paul, Leavenworth. 22017

Sermon preached in the Church of the Advent, Boston. 21741

Sermon preached in the Church of the Advent, Boston . . . May 13, 1855. 88575

Sermon preached in the Church of the Advent, Boston, on the 9th of November, 1856. 88571

Sermon preached in the Church of the Advent, Boston, on the Sunday after the decease of its Rector. 93078

Sermon preached in the Church of the Advent, Boston: the fifth Sunday after Easter, May 13, 1855. 88575, 91719

Sermon preached in the Church of the Advent, Boston: the third Sunday after Trinity, June 20, A. D. 1858. 88577, 91720

Sermon preached in the Church of the First Parish, in Portland, Me. 91025

Sermon preached in the Church of the Holy Innocents, Albany. 68585

Sermon preached in the Church of the Messiah. 67782

Sermon, preached in the Church of the Pilgrims, Brooklyn, N. Y. 92272

Sermon preached in the Church of the Third Parish. 85603

Sermon, preached in the city of Boston. 33794

Sermon preached in the city of London. (82697)

Sermon preached in the city of New-Haven. (18419)

Sermon preached in the College at Cambridge, N. E. 72029

Sermon: preached in the College Church, Hampden Sidney [sic], Va. 18252

Sermon preached in the College of Philadelphia. 21983

Sermon, preached in the Congregational Church in Sharon. 72419

Sermon preached in the Congregational Meeting-House in St. Albans, Vt. 84926

Sermon, preached in the Court House, Auburn. 73884

Sermon preached in the Federal Street Meeting-House. (26530)

Sermon preached in the First Church, Dorchester. (29830)

Sermon preached in the First Church in Genoa. 84217

Sermon preached in the First Church, in Stonington, Conn. 79953

Sermon preached in the First Congregation at Chapel, Philadelphia. 26817

Sermon, preached in the First Congregational Church, Braintree. 92244

Sermon preached in the First Congregational Church, Litchfield, Conn. 70935

Sermon, preached in the First Parish Church, in Hingham, February 2, 1851. 71051

Sermon preach'd in the First Parish in Scituate. 21244

Sermon, preached in the First Presbyterian Church, Allegheny, Pa. 94065

Sermon preached in the First Presbyterian Church, April 19th, 1865. 89918

Sermon preached in the First Presbyterian Church, Brooklyn, N. Y. 72059

Sermon preached in the First Presbyterian Church, on the day of national humiliation. 28850

Sermon, preached in the First Presbyterian Church, South Bergen. 25858

Sermon preached in the First Reformed Church, New Brunswick, N. J. 91159

Sermon preached in the First Society in Dedham. 30886

Sermon preached in the Fourth Avenue Presbyterian Church. (17635)

Sermon preached in the Free Presbyterian Churches. 5433

Sermon, preached in the Hall of the House of Representatives. 89008

Sermon preached in the hearing, and at the request, of a man. 46572

Sermon, preached in the House of Prayer, Newark. 90882

Sermon preached in the Indiana Place Chapel. 13418

Sermon, preached in the Meeting at Savannah in Georgia. 106392-106393

Sermon, preached in the Meeting House of the Charles Street Baptist Society. 91873

Sermon, preached in the Meeting-House of the Harvard Church. 22309

Sermon, preached in the Mercer-Street Church. 65093

Sermon preached in the Methodist Church, Baton Rouge, La. 7363

Sermon, preached in the M. E. Church, Jamaica, L. I. 76437

Sermon, preached in the Middle Dutch Church, Nov. 17. 1822. 93067

Sermon preached in the New Presbyterian Church in Philadelphia. 24389

Sermon, preached in (the newly rebuilt) St. George's Church. 30645

Sermon, preached in the North Church in the city of Hartford. 89783

Sermon preached in the North Church, Portsmouth. 13365

Sermon, preached in the North Meeting-House in Salem. 88895

Sermon preached in the Old South Meeting-House in Boston. 14510

Sermon preach'd in the Parish-Church of Bexly in Kent. 103529

Sermon preach'd in the Parish-Church of Christ-Church, London. 85848, 95422

Sermon preached in the Parish-Church of Christ-Church, London, on Wednesday May the 7th, 1766. 97361

Sermon preached in the Parish-Church of Newbery, Berks. (60802)

Sermon preached in the Parish Church of Tottenham, Middlesex. 7290

Sermon preached in the Parish Church of West Bromwich. 96376

Sermon preached in the Pine Street Chapel. 2932

Sermon, preached in the Presbyterian Chapel at Quebec. 88958

Sermon preached in the Presbyterian Church at Caldwell. 89681

Sermon preached in the Presbyterian Church, Binghamton, April 16, 1865. 6064

Sermon preached in the Presbyterian Church, Binghamton, September 26, 1861. 6063

Sermon preached in the Presbyterian Church, Bound Brook, N. J. 72479

Sermon, preached in the Presbyterian Church, Charlottesville. 103485

Sermon preached in the Presbyterian Church, John's Island, S. C. 103379

Sermon preached in the Presbyterian Church, Mouth of Juniata, Penna. 17373

Sermon preached in the Presbyterian Church, New Bloomfield, Pa. 17371

Sermon preached in the Presbyterian Church, Norfolk, Va. 79326

Sermon preached in the Presbyterian Church, Vicksburg. 92740

Sermon preached in the Prison in Philadelphia. 21326

Sermon preached in . . . the province of the Massachusetts Bay in New-England. 13349

Sermon preached in the Reformed Dutch Church, at New Brunswick. 94442

Sermon, preached in the Reformed Dutch Shurch in Greenwich. 73534

Sermon preached in the Reformed Dutch Church, in Nassau-Street. 93620

Sermon preached in the Reformed Dutch Church of Kinderhook. 4991

Sermon, preached in the Rev. Doctor Stiles's Meeting. 96399

Sermon, preached in the School-House at the Goodrich Hollow. 101293

Sermon, preached in the Second Presbyterian Church in Brooklyn. 89327

Sermon, preached in the Second Society of Norwich. 92126

Sermon preached in the Second Society of Norwich, September 21st, 1777. 92125

Sermon, preached in the Scotch Church, in the city of Quebec. 88959

Sermon, preached in the Scotch Presbyterian Church at Quebec. 88960

Sermon, preached in the Second Church, Boston. (71796)

Sermon prached in the Second Presbyterian Church, Albany, April 27, 1856. 89744

Sermon preached in the Second Presbyterian Church, Albany, February 9, 1845. 89744

Sermon preached in the Second Presbyterian Church, Albany, July 13, 1856. 89744

Sermon preached in the Second Presbyterian Church, Albany, October 18, 1863. 89744

Sermon preached in the Second Presbyterian Church, Albany, Sabbath evening, May 11, 1834. 89744

Sermon preached in the Second Presbyterian Church, Albany, Sunday afternoon, September 21, 1857. 89744

Sermon, preached in the Second Presbyterian Church, Charleston. 2203

Sermon, preached in the Second Presbyterian Church, in Brooklyn, October 2, 1836. 89324

Sermon, preached in the Second Presbyterian Church in Brooklyn, on the day of the annual contribution for home missions. 89325

Sermon, preached in the Second Presbyterian Church, Lafayette, Indiana. 70825

Sermon preached in the Second Presbyterian Church, Lafayette, Indiana, December 11, 1859. 70824

Sermon preached in the Second Presbyterian Church, Newark, N. J. 83344

Sermon preached in the Second Presbyterian Church, Newark, N. J. Sunday, December 24th, 1871. 83346

Sermon preached in the Second Presbyterian Church, Newark, N. J., thanksgiving day, November 29, 1860. 83342

Sermon, preached in the Seventh Presbyterian Church, New-York. 84412

Sermon: preached in the Sixth Avenue Reformed Dutch Church. 83597

Sermon, preached in the South Congregational Church, Boston. 29629

Sermon, preached in the South Presbyterian Church, Brooklyn. 89092

Sermon preached in the South Presbyterian Church of Brooklyn, by the Pastor Rev. Samuel T. Spear, D. D., November 27th, 1862. 89095

Sermon preached in the South Presbyterian Church of Brooklyn, by the Pastor Rev. Samuel T. Spear, D. D. October 19th, 1862. 89100

Sermon preached in the South Presbyterian Church of Brooklyn, by the Pastor Rev.

Samuel T. Spear, D. D., October 7th, 1866. 89086

Sermon preached in the Tabernacle at Salem. 25038

Sermon preached in the Tenth Presbyterian Church, Philadelphia. 6078

Sermon preached in the Third Presbyterian Church in the city of Philadelphia. 21132

Sermon preached in the Third Presbyterian Church, Philadelphia, on the 30th of April, 1863. 7350

Sermon preached in the Thirteenth Street Presbyterian Church. 9203

Sermon preached in the time of the storm. 46485

Sermon preached in the Trinitarian Church, New Bedford. 17371

Sermon preached in the Unitarian Church at Waltham. 31864

Sermon: preached in the Unitarian Church, Vernon, N. Y. 22520

Sermon, preached in the United Presbyterian Church, Canonsburg, Pa. 2773

Sermon preached in the Village Church. 90990

Sermon, preached in Trinity Church, Cleveland. 90529

Sermon, preached in Trinity Church, Granville, N. Y. 89602

Sermon preached in Trinity-Church in New-York. 99325

Sermon preached in Trinity Church, New Haven. 30787

Sermon preached in Trinity Church, New York. 20638

Sermon preached in Trinity Church, New York, on Tuesday, May 7th, 1861. 78589

Sermon, preached in Trinity Church, Newark. 73882

Sermon preached in Trinity-Church, Newport, Rhode-Island. 5642

Sermon preached in Trinity Church, Newport, Rhode Island. 63882

Sermon preached in Trinity Church, Utica. 73880

Sermon preached in Troy, New York. (21443)

Sermon preached in Upper Canada. 92661

Sermon, preached in Watertown, December 14, 1787. 102085

Sermon, preached in Wendell, Dec. 22, 1820. 103920

Sermon, preached in West Springfield, March 30th, 1823. 89744

Sermon preached in West Springfield, on the resignation. 89744

Sermon preached in the Whitefield Church, Newburyport. 88923

Sermon preached in Windham, Newhampshire. 18163

Sermon preached in Windsor (Vt.), October 8th, A. L. 5811. (56356)

Sermon preached in the Winthrop Church, Charlestown. 67877

Sermon preached in Worcester, Aug. 17, 1862. (31806)

Sermon, preached in Worcester, Massachusetts, on the day of the national fast. 2422

Sermon preached in Worcester, Mass., on the occasion of the special fast. 2425

Sermon preached in Wrentham, January 1, 1701. 44335

Sermon preached in Wrentham, Mass., June 12, 1849. 24158

Sermon, preached in Zion Church, New-York. 88570

Sermon, preached in Zion Church, New York, the fifth Sunday after Easter. 88579

Sermon, preached January 18, 1809. 13852

Sermon, preached, January 11, 1804. 3941

Sermon preached January 14, 1829. 89744
Sermon preached January 4, 1861. (21334)
Sermon, preached . . . January 19, 1840.
  42148
Sermon preached January 4th. 1759. (72892)
Sermon preached . . . January 9th, 1853.
  42149
Sermon, preached January 9, 1805. 91804
Sermon preached, . . . Jan. 7, 1849. 26074
Sermon preached January 10th, 1810. 28818
Sermon, preached January 3d, 1804. 92971
Sermon, preached January 3, 1822. 89744
Sermon preached January 29th. 1772. (71763)
Sermon preached . . . Jan. 23, 1865. 22327
Sermon, preached July 5, 1829. 93090
Sermon preached July 4, 1764. 30888
Sermon preached . . . July 7th, 1775. 21051
Sermon preached July 7. 1728. 14474
Sermon preached July 19, 1863. 543
Sermon preached July 30, 1740. 11857
Sermon . . . preach'd July 30. 1740. 11894
Sermon, preached . . . July 4, 1854. 59354
Sermon preached . . . June 5th, 1847. 26065
Sermon, preached June 2, 1808. (71126)
Sermon preached . . . June 2d, 1803. (21710)
Sermon preached June 7th, 1835. 77007,
  89744
Sermon preached June 12, 1799. 95179
Sermon, preached . . . June 20, 1821. 35816
Sermon, preached, June 22, 1809. (25239)
Sermon preached Lord's-Day even, Feb. 1,
  1778. 23284
Sermon, preached March 18, 1778. 92972
Sermon, preached . . . March 4, 1838. 3621
Sermon preached March 4, 1736-37. (14525)
Sermon preach'd . . . March 4th. 1732-3.
  (12369)
Sermon preached March 4th to a prisoner.
  (12369)
Sermon preached March 9th, 1731, 2. 16633
Sermon preached March 7, 1855. 89744
Sermon preached . . . March 6, 1836. 66793
Sermon preached March 13th, 1808. (49064)
Sermon preached March 13, 1865. 20349
Sermon, preached March 31, 1828. 105087
Sermon, preached, March 12, 1795. 76516
Sermon preached March 28, 1867. (31806)
Sermon, preached, March 25th 1756. 102424
Sermon, preached, March 27, 1776. 91790
Sermon preach'd March 27. 1737. 1835,
  103899
Sermon preached March 23, A. D. 1828.
  92938
Sermon, preached May, 1847. 32627
Sermon preached May 11, 1808. (24795)
Sermon, preached May 4, 1806. 64136
Sermon preached May 14, 1841. (29753)
Sermon, preached May 14, 1841. 89328
Sermon preached May 14, 1795. (18419)
Sermon, preached May 14, 1732. 16640
Sermon preached May 15, 1821. 89744
Sermon, preached May 19, 1703. 46292
Sermon preached May 6, 1767. 12331
Sermon preached . . . May 30, 1855. 91709
Sermon preached . . . May 30, 1781. (13317)
Sermon preached, May 30th. 1770. 12330
Sermon, preached May 31, 1791. 91805
Sermon preached May 12, 1819. 70949
Sermon preached May 12, 1861. 58128
Sermon preach'd May 20th 1761. 7810
Sermon preached . . . May 28. 1718. 14512
Sermon preach'd . . . May 28. 1740. 16636
Sermon preach'd . . . May 28th. 1755. 12366
Sermon preached May 28. 1712. 12411
Sermon preached May 25. 1755. 91755
Sermon preached May 21, 1837. 47078

Sermon preached . . . May 29th. 1723. 14473
Sermon: preached . . . May 27, 1747. 12313
Sermon, preached . . . May 26, 1874. 31288
Sermon preached, May 23, 1856. 104824
Sermon, preached . . . New York, December
  14, 1843. 20069
Sermon preached . . . New York, May 12,
  1861. 6392
Sermon, preached 9th January, 1816. 76376
Sermon preached November 11, 1806. 90862
Sermon, preached November 15, 1786. 7809
Sermon, preached November 14, 1787. 79968
Sermon preached November 19, 1828. 66811
Sermon preached . . . November 19th. 1734.
  12331
Sermon, preached November 2, 1791. 44361
Sermon preached . . . Nov. 7, 1852. 76991
Sermon preached November 16, 1826. 98045
Sermon, preached November 10, 1836. 66824
Sermon, preached November 10. 1765. 12371
Sermon, preached November 28, 1861. 89780
Sermon preached . . . November 25, 1848.
  57741
Sermon preached November 21, 1792. 18102
Sermon, preached November 21, 1792. 76515
Sermon, preached November 29, 1821. 95523
Sermon preached November 27, 1862. 80083
Sermon preached November 26, 1843. 4575
Sermon preached November 23, 1826. (66810)
Sermon, preached October 8, 1811. 85417
Sermon, preached October 11th, 1797. (71128)
Sermon preached . . . October 15th, 1853.
  81401
Sermon, preached October 1, 1794. (18419)
Sermon, preached Oct. 4, 1840. 88672
Sermon preached October 14, 1772. 12389
Sermon preached, . . . October 19, 1862.
  21572
Sermon preached October 9. being a day of
  public thanksgiving, occasioned by the
  surrender of Montreal. (1839)
Sermon preached October 9, 1760. Being a
  day of publick thanksgiving. (25041)
Sermon preached October 9. 1760. Being a
  day of public thanksgiving on occasion of
  the reduction of Montreal. 105165
Sermon preached October 17, 1798. (18419)
Sermon preached October 7. 1683. 104086
Sermon, preached October 6, 1786. 103744
Sermon, preached October 10, 1792. 68556
Sermon, preached, October 3, 1792. 79969
Sermon, preached October 30, 1853. [By Henry
  W. Bellows.] 4575
Sermon, preached Oct. 30, 1853, on the occa-
  sion of the death. 62831
Sermon preached October 31, 1858. 38774
Sermon preach'd . . . October 31st. 1742.
  (14525)
Sermon preached October 25th. 1759. (22125)
Sermon, preached October 21st, 1801. 71129
Sermon, preached . . . October 22d, 1843.
  66875
Sermon, preached October 22, 1828. 71524
Sermon preach'd on a day of private fasting
  and prayer. (14514)
Sermon preached on a day when such a church
  was gathered. 46538, 2d note after
  94666
Sermon preached on a time of prayer. 46446
Sermon preached on All Saints' Day. 26074
Sermon, preached on board the Whitaker.
  103516, 103525
Sermon preached on December 13, 1776. 14321
Sermon, preached . . . on fast-day, April 8th,
  1841. 26074

Sermon preached on fast day, April 6, 1854.
90998

Sermon preached on fast day, 1854. 21978

Sermon preached on fast day, January 4, 1861.
28013

Sermon, preached on fast day, September 26,
1861. 20530

Sermon, preached on February 21st, 1777.
97572

Sermon preached on Friday, April 22, 1859.
(7957)

Sermon preached . . . on Friday, August 1st,
1834. 101369

Sermon preached on Friday, December 13,
1776. 1211, 79280

Sermon preached on Fryday [sic] forenoon.
103567

Sermon preached on . . . his death. (37232)

Sermon preached . . . on May 26. 1714.
18477

Sermon, preached on Monday, December 6,
1819. 104555

Sermon preeched on . . . New-Year's day.
4575

Sermon preached on occasion of leaving his
pastoral charge. 104623

Sermon, preached on occasion of the brief for
the American colleges. 102128

Sermon preached on occasion of the . . .
death of Mr. Timothy Metcalf. 19898

Sermon preached on occasion of the second
anniversary of the Holy Guild. 88578

Sermon preached on Sabbath afternoon, August
21, 1853. 89744

Sermon preached on Sabbath afternoon, January
25, 1857. 89744

Sermon, preached on Sabbath, April 30, 1865.
41219, 95516

Sermon, preached on Sabbath morning, April 1,
1855. 89744

Sermon, preached on Sabbath morning, April
16, 1865. 35227

Sermon, preached on Sunday, April 23, 1865.
9476

Sermon preached on Sunday morning, December
9, 1860. 89744

Sermon, preached on Sunday, October 20, 1850.
(14900)

Sermon, preach'd on Sunday Sept. 1, 1754.
84641

Sermon, preached on Sunday, September 27th,
1863. 83642

Sermon preached on thanksgiving day. (79284)

Sermon preached on thanksgiving day, December 7, 1865. 17924

Sermon, preached on thanksgiving day, December 12, 1850. 77588

Sermon preached on thanksgiving day, Nov.
19th, 1857. 82738

Sermon, preached on thanksgiving day, November 28, 1861. 75922

Sermon preached on thanksgiving day, November 28, 1867. 6080

Sermon preached . . . on thanksgiving day,
Nov. 25, 1852. 91153

Sermon preached on thanksgiving day, November 24, 1859. 4836

Sermon, preached on thanksgiving day, Nov. 29,
1860. 6085

Sermon preached on thanksgiving day, Nov. 22,
1855. 72639

Sermon, preached on thanksgiving day, November 27th, 1851. 90430A

Sermon preached on that occasion. [By
Cotton Mather.] 46577, 1st note after
99407

Sermon preached on that occasion by Right
Rev. Manton Eastburn. 21663

Sermon preached . . . on . . . the anniversary
election. 20063

Sermon preached on the anniversary of the
Boston Female Asylum. 100967

Sermon, preached on the annual thanksgiving
in Massachusetts, December 1, A. D.
1814. 95380

Sermon, preached on the annual thanksgiving
in Massachusetts, November 27, 1800.
22525

Sermon preached on the baptism of a grand-
child. 46560

Sermon preached on the completion of a general
repair. 71503

Sermon preached on the day for election of
officers. 100910

Sermon, preached on the day of annual thanksgiving. 100924

Sermon preached on the day of fasting and
prayer. 28014

Sermon, preached on the day of fasting, humiliation and prayer. 32381

Sermon, preached on the day of fasting, humiliation, and prayer, January 4, 1861. 66877

Sermon, preached on the day of general election,
at Montpelier. 105570

Sermon, preached on the day of general election,
at Montpelier, Oct. 10, 1816. 2425

Sermon preached on the day of general election
. . . before the . . . Legislature of
Vermont. 44728

Sermon preached on the day of national humiliation and prayer. 23876

Sermon preached on the day of national thanksgiving, November 24, 1864, at Easton,
Pennsylvania. 12839

Sermon preached on the day of national thanksgiving, November 24, 1864, in the Reformed Dutch Church, Easton, Pa. 21839

Sermon preached on the day of national thanksgiving, Thursday, November 24, 1864.
83519

Sermon preached on the day of thanksgiving,
November 28, 1861. 21839

Sermon, preached on the day of thanksgiving,
Nov. 28, 1833. 71897

Sermon, preached on the day of the annual
fast in Massachusetts, April 3, 1828.
(14221)

Sermon, preached on the day, of the annual
thanksgiving, November 26, 1829. 88592

Sermon, preach'd on the day of the continental
fast, at Tredyffryn. 36486

Sermon preached on the day of the funeral.
21965

Sermon preached on the day of the general
election, at Hartford, in the state of
Connecticut, May 5th, 1819. 22130

Sermon, preached on the day of the general
election, at Hartford, in the state of
Connecticut, May 9th, 1805. 32812

Sermon preached on the day of the general
election, at Hartford, in the state of
Connecticut, May 13th, 1813. 39720

Sermon, preached on the day of the national
fast. 32267

Sermon preached . . . on the . . . death of
Hon. Daniel Webster. 42141

Sermon preached . . . on the death of the Hon.
Harrison Gray Otis. 42149

Sermon preached on the death of the Honourable
Isaac E. Crary. 92914

Sermon preach'd, on the decease and at the
desire of Mrs. Katharine Mather.
(46578), 3d note after 99448

Sermon preached on the departure of . . . Mr. Thomas Bernard. 46573

Sermon preached on the eve of the battle of Brandywine. 97069

Sermon, preached on the 15th December, 1833. 104916

Sermon, preached on the fifth day of September, 1832. 28837

Sermon preached on the fiftieth anniversary of the organization. (42049)

Sermon. Preached on the first day of January, A. D. 1815. 91660

Sermon preached on the 1st March, 1857. 85474

Sermon preached on the first Sabbath in January, 1831. 104801

Sermon preach'd on the 4th. of January, 1729-30. 62812

Sermon, preached . . . on the fourth of July, 1791. (41342)

Sermon preached on the Friday evening-lecture. 79433

Sermon, preached on the general election at Hartford, in Connecticut, May 8, 1800. 82217

Sermon, preached on the general election at Hartford, in Connecticut, May 14, 1801. 97183

Sermon preached on the last day of the year, 1719. (46612)

Sermon preached on the last Sabbath of the year, 1794. (8444)

Sermon preached on the lecture at Boston, July 17. 1701. 104099

Sermon preached on the lecture in Boston; November 27th. 1692. 104103

Sermon preached on the Lord's-Day after the death. (26830)

Sermon preach'd on the Lord's-Day after the funeral of the Honourable John Appleton, Esq; 72692, 2d note after 97559

Sermon preach'd on the Lord's-Day after the funeral of William Harris Esq. (14492)

Sermon, preached on the melancholy occasion. (32139)

Sermon, preached on the morning of Easter Monday, April 16th, 1865. 20970

Sermon: preached on the national fast, August 3, 1849. 84544

Sermon, preached on the national fast day, at Church Green, Boston. 19860

Sermon preached on the national thanksgiving. 95524

Sermon preached . . . on the next Sabbath. 38468

Sermon preached on the ninth anniversary of the opening of the Church of the Holy Innocents. 68586

Sermon, preached on the 9th day of October, 1799. 17901

Sermon preached on the occasion of the death of Capt. Thomas Daniel. 50295

Sermon preached on the occasion of the death of Mrs. Sarah Milton Whipple. 70991

Sermon, preached on the occasion of the ordination of Geo. W. Lasher. 21721

Sermon preached on the opening of the Franklin College of Lancaster. 34048

Sermon preached on the opening of the Memorial Church. (77573)

Sermon preached on the public fast, April 19. 1753. 22122

Sermon preached on the publick lecture in Boston, July 8. 1731. 21944

Sermon, preached on the Sabbath after the death of General Wm. H. Harrison. 89329

Sermon, preached on the Sabbath following the burial. 88674

Sermon, preached on the Sabbath following the death. 88673

Sermon preached on the 7th d. of the 1st. m. 1686. 46244

Sermon, preached on the 7th Oct., 1862. 85472

Sermon, preached on the seventh of Jan. MDCCCI. 88886

Sermon preached on the sixtieth anniversary of the dedication. 90464

Sermon, preached on the state thanksgiving. 92959

Sermon, preached on the state thanksgiving, November 29, 1798. 92960

Sermon, preached . . . on the Sunday after the interment. 42149

Sermon . . . on the Sunday succeeding the death of Moses Grant. 42149

Sermon preached on the Sunday succeeding the death of the Hon. Daniel Webster. 50998

Sermon, preached on the Sunday succeeding the great fire. 101411

Sermon preached on the 13th of December, 1776. 27548

Sermon preached on the 30th of June, 1763. 103214

Sermon, preached on the twentieth anniversary of his ordination. 97399

Sermon preached on the twenty-fifth anniversary of his ordination. 71797

Sermon preached on the twenty fifth day of December, 1712. (46350)

Sermon preach'd on the 25th of December, being the nativity of Our Saviour. 78440

Sermon preached on the 24th . . . of June, 1789. 44680

Sermon preached on their occasion. [By Cotton Mather.] 46369

Sermon preached on third-day morning. 14413

Sermon: preached on Thursday, June 1, 1865. (29300)

Sermon preached on Wednesday evening, July 11, 1855. 89744

Sermon preach'd privately to a society of young men. 16640

Sermon preached privately, Sept. 27. 1706. 104089

Sermon preached September 18. 1741. (80798)

Sermon preached . . . September 11th, 1864. 36219

Sermon preached Sept. 5, 1855. (25185)

Sermon, preached, Sept. 1, 1811. 102579

Sermon preached Septem. 1. 1723. 14511

Sermon preached September 17. 1766. 22129

Sermon preached September 17th. 1727. 12367, 101016

Sermon, preached September 16, 1812. 76513

Sermon preached . . . September 12, 1830. 20391

Sermon, preached September 20th, 1793. 45461

Sermon preached September 25th, 1771. 33872

Sermon, preached September 29, 1771. 2656

Sermon, preached . . . September 26, 1830. 104038

Sermon preach'd . . . Sept. 23. 1733. 25397

Sermon preached 1707. (7358)

Sermon preached 16th November, 1748. (30165)

Sermon, preached 6 November 1817. (25239)

Sermon preached (summarily) at East-Hampton. 106212

Sermon preached Sunday, March 31, MDCCCXXXIII. 104968

Sermon preached the 18th of July, 1745. (12323)

Sermon preach'd the 5th of May. 7480

Sermon preach'd the 14th of June, 1749.
67770
Sermon preach'd . . . the Lord's Day after
. . . commencement. 12331
Sermon, preached the Lord's-Day after the
death of Mr. Edward Gray. 12331
Sermon preach'd the Lord's-Day after the
death of the Reverend Mr. Peter Thacher.
102224
Sermon preached the Lord's-Day after the
funeral of the late Reverend Mr. John
Webb. 22129
Sermon preached . . . the Lord's-Day after
the terrible earthquake. 12331
Sermon preached the Lord's-Day before the
execution of Levi Ames. 22121
Sermon, preached the second Lord's Day after
the death of his . . . wife. (9376)
Sermon, preached the 2d of October, 1757.
24388
Sermon preached the 7th of November. 12331
Sermon preach'd the 25th March, 1771. 22221
Sermon, preached there August 26, 1772.
360, 11967, 3d note after 96741
Sermon preached to a company of volunteers.
18760
Sermon, preached to a congregation of pro-
testant dissenters. 101045
Sermon preach'd to a numerous audience in
England. 103497
Sermon preach'd to a numerous gathering in
England. 103524
Sermon preached to a society of young men,
at Ipswich. 103932
Sermon . . . preached to a society of young
men, on a Lords-Day evening. 102223
Sermon preached to a very crowded audience.
14520
Sermon preached to an artillery-company at
Guilford. (73981)
Sermon preached to, and at the desire of, a
condemned prisoner. 12371
Sermon preached to, and at the request of the
Honourable Artillery Company of the
Massachusetts. 68014
Sermon preached to Captain Overton's Inde-
pendent Company of Volunteers. 18763
Sermon, preached to Essex Street Church and
Society. 74728
Sermon preached to God's Ancient Israel the
Jews. 16643
Sermon preached to his [i. e. William Ware's]
old flock. 4575
Sermon preached to Joshua Abbot. 47955
Sermon preached to Sir Thomas Warner.
23965
Sermon preached to some in New-England.
32810
Sermon preached to some miserable pirates.
14494
Sermon preach'd to the Ancient and Honourable
Artillery Company, in Boston, June 1st.
1752. 7806
Sermon, preached to the Ancient and Honour-
able Artillery Company in Boston, New-
England, June 1, 1772. (71826)
Sermon preached to the Ancient and Honourable
Artillery Company in Boston, New
England, June 1, 1767. 80801
Sermon preached to the Ancient and honourable
Artillery Company in Boston, New
England, June 4, 1770. 91806
Sermon preached to the Ancient and Honour-
able Artillery Company in Boston New
England, June 5, 1758. 3487

Sermon preached to the Ancient and Honourable
Artillery-Company, in Boston, New-
England, June 7th, 1773. 33278
Sermon preached to the Ancient and Honourable
Artillery-Company in Boston, New-
England, June 6th, 1774. 39186
Sermon preached to the Ancient and Honourable
Artillery Company, in Boston, New-
England, June 3d. 1771. (25039)
Sermon preached to the Ancient and Honourable
Artillery Company June 2. 1740. 9711
Sermon preached to the Ancient and Honourable
Artillery Company . . . June 6. 1768.
13430
Sermon preached to the Ancient and Honourable
Artillery Company . . . June 3. 1751.
(16597)
Sermon preached to the Ancient and Honourable
Artillery Company, on June 4. 1739.
46807
Sermon preached to the Artillery Company at
Boston, on June 5. 1699. 104093
Sermon, preached to the Artillery Company at
Boston, on their day of election of
officers. 95163
Sermon preached to the bereaved flock, March
4. 1739. 14482
Sermon preached to the Central Church and
Congregation. 94054
Sermon preached to the Church and Society
in Brattle-Street. 95180
Sermon preached to the Church in Brattle
Square. 58325
Sermon preached to the Coldwater Light Artil-
lery. 33209
Sermon preached to the congregation at the
Essex Street Church. 339
Sermon preach'd to the Convention of Ministers
of the Province of the Massachusetts-
Bay, N. E. 32667
Sermon, preached to the First Church, by its
minister, N. L. Frothingham. 26071
Sermon preached to the First Church, in re-
signing its pastoral charge. 26064
Sermon preached to the First Church, on the
close of the second century. 26073
Sermon preached to the First Congregational
Church in Brookline. 31218
Sermon preached to the First Congregational
Society in Leominster. 91048
Sermon preached to the First Evangelical
Congregational Church and Society. 90997
Sermon preached to the First Parish in Brain-
tree. 21243
Sermon preached to the First Society in
Lebanon. 104362
Sermon preached to the General Assembly of
the colony of the Massachusetts at Boston
in New-England. May 16. 1683. 96303
Sermon preached to the General Court of the
colony of New-Plimouth. 2079
Sermon preached, to the Great & General
Court of the province of the Massachusetts-
Bay, conven'd at Boston. 100914
Sermon preached to the Hampshire Missionary
Society. 39199
Sermon preached to the Honourable and Ancient
Artillery Company in Boston, June 5.
1738. (14471)
Sermon, preached to the Honourable Artillery
Company in Boston, on the day of their
election of officers. 7812
Sermon preached to the Honourable Convention
of the Governor, Council, and Repre-
sentatives. 46591

Sermon, preached to the Independent Congregational Society. 31217

Sermon preached to the ladies of the Cent Institution. 82530

Sermon preached to the members and families of the Nestorian Mission. 60963

Sermon preached to the militia of Hanover County. 18758

Sermon preached to the ministers of the Massachusetts-Bay. (67767)

Sermon preached to the . . . ministers of the province of the Massachusetts-Bay. (46800)

Sermon preached to the North and South Parishes in Portsmouth. 8930

Sermon preached to the Old Church in Boston. 25389

Sermon preach'd to the Old South Church. (16634)

Sermon, . . . preached to the orthodox people of Peterborough. 58687

Sermon preached to the provincials of the county of Suffolk. 65530

Sermon preached to the Pulaski Guards in Christ Church, Savannah. 22282

Sermon preached to the Second Church in Boston in New-England, March 17. 16<u>79</u> after that church had explicitly and <u>80</u> most solemnly renewed. 104079

Sermon preached to the Second Church in Boston in New-England, March 17. 16<u>79</u> when that church did solemnly and <u>80</u> explicitly renew. (46730)

Sermon preached to the Second Church . . . October 11, 1835. 71800

Sermon, preached to the Society in Brattle-Street. 95181

Sermon, preached to the Society in Brattle Street, Boston, November 14, 1790. 95182

Sermon, preached to the Society in Brattle Street, Boston, October 20, 1793. 95183

Sermon preached to the Society in Brattle Square. 58325

Sermon preached to the soldiers, Sept. 22, 1755. 22322, 36951

Sermon, preached to the South Church. (71784)

Sermon preached to the students of Bowdoin College. 85216

Sermon, preached to the students of the Wesleyan University. 32484

Sermon preached to the Third Congregational Society in Hingham. 90926

Sermon, preached to the Third Congregational Society in Hingham, on Sunday, March 2, 1851. 90925

Sermon, preached to the Third Congregational Society in Hingham; on Sunday, November 16, 1845. 90923

Sermon preached to the Third Gathered Church in Boston. 104076

Sermon preached to the United Congregations of Universalists. 21812

Sermon preached to the young men in the village church, Medway. 76477

Sermon preached to the young people at East Guilford. 96095

Sermon preached to Young people at the request of the deceased. 46518

Sermon, preached 20th November, 1816. 76377

Sermon preached 21st Feb., 1836. 26074

Sermon . . . preached 27 d. 3. m. 1715. 13204

Sermon preached unto some Godly young men. 95165

Sermon preached unto the Convention of the Massachusetts Colony in New-England. 45591, 46602

Sermon preached unto them on a special occasion. 46614

Sermon preached unto a day of generall humiliation. (32809)

Sermon preached upon Ezek. 22. 30, 31. 104104

Sermon preached upon the death, and at the desire of John Tappin. 100987

Sermon preach'd upon the death of the Honourable the truly virtuous Isaac Addington. 14488

Sermon, preached, with some special reference to the state of the public mind. (37232)

Sermon preacht [sic] on the weekly lecture in Boston. 50297

Sermon preche devant l'Universite de Cambridge 102144

Sermon predicado con termino de tres dais. 106319

Sermon predicado en el Castillo de San Felipe del Puerto de Callao. 47334

Sermon predicado el Domingo de Panes. 74855

Sermon predicado en la . . . ciudad de Cholula. 55348

Sermon predicado en la fiesta de la solemne colocacion de la Cruz. 6098, 6101

Sermon predicado en la Iglesia de San Juan de Dios de Zacatecas. 87245

Sermon predicado en la Iglesia del Convento Antiguo de Senoras Carmelitas Descalzas de Mexico. 76020

Sermon predicado en la Parroquia de Guanajuant 73037

Sermon predicado en la Santa Iglesia Metropolitana de Megico. (44939)

Sermon predicado en la solemne dedicacion del Nuevo Templo. 75993

Sermon predicado en las fiestas de la beatificacion. (79304)

Sermon predicado por el R. P. Fr. Mirano Cisneros. (13150)

Sermon . . . predico en las exequias del Illustrissimo Senor D. Pedro Nogales Davila. 55277

Sermon prepared for, and in part preached on September 18th. 1701. 104072

Sermon prepared for the ordination of Mr. Richard Pike. 59354

Sermon prepared for the Waco Baptist Association. 83863

Sermon . . . Presbyterian Church, Sag Harbor. 32994

Sermon, proceedings and addresses in commemo ration of the fiftieth anniversary of the settlement. 52315

Sermon, pronounce le 9 Octobre, 1834. 99283

Sermon pronunciado en la fiesta de la Sociedad "Maria." 71306

Sermon, . . . Providence, . . . October 14, A. D. 1798. 47005

Sermon, . . . Providence, R. I., . . . July 27, 1862. 19041

Sermon, public fast in New Hampshire. 13784

Sermon published for the service of others. 46351

Sermon que antes de descubrirse por su Muy Ilustre Ayuntamiento dijo. 57838

Sermon que el aniversario solemne de gracias. (19974)

Sermon que el dia 13 de Setiembre. 19976

Sermon que el R. P. F. Nicolas de Jesus Maria predico. 55246

Sermon, que en alabanza de S. Tomas de Aquino predico. 5024

Sermon que en complimiento del voto que hizo. 94872

Sermon, que en el dia de la Paraicion del Nra. Senora de Guadalupe. 60915

Sermon que en el tercer dia del solemne novenario. (47816)

Sermon que en la fiesta celebrata en accion de gracias. 77114

Sermon que en la reconquista de Guanaxuato. 7989

Sermon que en la solemne festividad del 20 Julio. 87247

Sermon que en la solemne funcion con que se dio principio. 74024

Sermon que en la solemne misa en accion de gracias. 94873

Sermon que en la toma de habito de Dona Mariana Samaniago y Canal. 49950

Sermon que en las solemnes honras celebradas en obsequio. 44440

Sermon que en los cultos. 62997

Sermon que predico . . . Eduardo Vazquez. 98712

Sermon que predico . . . el Doctor D. Francisco Pizarro de Orellana. 86546

Sermon que predico el Doctor Ysidro Sarinara. 48596

Sermon que predico el Doctor Ysidro Sarinana. Con licencia. 77050

Sermon que predico el Fr. Pedro Cortina. (52250)

Sermon, qve predico el M. R. P. M. Fr. Alonso de la Barrea. 98122

Sermon. Que . . . predico . . . el P. Fray Salvador y Valencia. 98347

Sermon, qve predico el P. Ivan de Robles. 72250

Sermon que se hizo en Mextitlan. 24134

Sermon que su primera fiesta, celebrada en el Convento Grande. (50627)

Sermon, read before the Suffolk South Association. 84294

Sermon realtive to Antichrist and the times. 68138

Sermon relating to the plantations. 27679

Sermon, . . . Roxbury Charitable Society. 22451

Sermon . . . Saint Andrew's Church, Montreal. 46853

Sermon. . . . St. Anne's Church, Lowell. (21878)

Sermon . . . St. Louis, Nov. 20, 1831. 64692

Sermon . . . Salem, December 15, 1814. 22421

Sermon . . . Salem, N. J., . . . April 23, 1841. 65244

Sermon . . . San Felipe de Jesus. 35335

Sermon, Santa Cruz, W. I. 30979

Sermon . . . Savannah, Dec. 21, 1845. 65381

Sermon, . . . Second Presbyterian Church. (28505)

Sermon . . . Sept. 14 and . . . September 28, 1862. 6082

Sermon . . . September 14, 1825. 28818

Sermon, . . . September 14, 1796. 47005

Sermon, September 19, 1852. 37848

Sermon . . . Sept. XIX. 58800

Sermon . . . September 2, 1828. 28818

Sermon . . . September 17, 1806. 64137

Sermon . . . Sept. 17, 1828. 4340

Sermon . . . September 7, 1777. (34760)

Sermon . . . September 16, 1804. 3272

Sermon . . . September 10th. 1741. 12331

Sermon, . . . September 3, 1788. (31895)

Sermon . . . September 12, 1860. 9243

Sermon . . . September 12, 1821. note after 42429

Sermon . . . Sept. 12, 1821, at the ordination of the Rev. George Fisher. 34175

Sermon . . . September 22nd, 1809. 26624

Sermon, . . . September 27, 1741. (28383)

Sermon . . . September 26, 1861. 43340

Sermon, September 24, 1823. 43790

Sermon . . . Sept. 29, 1819. (64233)

Sermon, . . . 7th of November, 1819. 49131

Sermon . . . 1715. (14525), (46522)

Sermon, . . . Sharon, June 11, 1828. (32235)

Sermon, shewing, that eternal hope is God's free gift. 4095

Sermon shewing that it is the interest of the people of God. 94116

Sermon shewing that the peace and quietness of a people. (23025)

Sermon shewing that the present dispensations of providence declare. 46737

Sermon shewing what is to be done in order. (46649)

Sermon, shewing what is wisdom for men. 100677

Sermon, . . . Shoreham. 50995

Sermon . . . Society for the Propagation of Christian Knowledge. 30362

Sermon, . . . Somerville, Dec. 28, 1862. (58103)

Sermon, South Church, Salem. 22421

Sermon, . . . Springfield, May 10, 1826. (23951)

Sermon . . . Stoughton . . . 18th of June, 1783. 30887

Sermon suggested by the death of President Lincoln. 75921

Sermon . . . Sunday . . . after the death of Bishop Doane. 56834

Sermon, . . . tenth of May, MDCCXC. 25042

Sermon . . . thanksgiving day. 45029

Sermon . . . thanksgiving day, December 8, 1842. 27634

Sermon, . . . thanksgiving day, November 27, 1862. 43340

Sermon . . . thanksgiving, December 11, 1783. 57778

Sermon . . . thanksgiving, December 7, 1865. (39694)

Sermon . . . thanksgiving for peace, May 5, 1763. 76348

Sermon, . . . thanksgiving, November 30, 1820. (59309)

Sermon, "the claims of seamen." 28818

Sermon . . . the Lord's Day after the funeral of the Reverend Mr. William Cooper. 14495

Sermon, the next after the death, of Zachary Taylor. 20391

Sermon, the next Lord's Day, by the Rev. Mr. Holmes. 39187, note after 102250, 104056

Sermon. The question of war with Great Britain examined. (18435), 43376, 79285

Sermon, the Sabbath preceding the ordination of S. C. Nartlett. 22377

Sermon. The story of David Rouge. 20028

Sermon, the substance of which was delivered at Hanover. 101511

Sermon, the substance of which was delivered at the evening-lecture. 59375

Sermon. The substance of which was delivered on the Lord's-Day April 11th 1725. (22439)

Sermon: the substance of which was preached at Strafford. 59605

Sermon, 3d April, 1811. (24759)

Sermon . . . 3d December, 1837. 62772

Sermon . . . third of April, 1825. 31415

[Sermon to a collection of young people.] 4397

Sermon to a military company, Upton. 24426
Sermon to a religious society of young men in Medford. 39187
Sermon, to a religious society of young people. 46264
Sermon to a society of young men, August 21. 1715. 16640
Sermon . . . to a society of young men, July 10. 1720. (14525)
Sermon to a society of young people in Sudbury. 16292
Sermon to aged people. 39199
Sermon to bring Lot's wife to remembrance. 26785
Sermon to Capt. Thomas Lawrence. 22445
Sermon to contrabands. (79286)
Sermon to . . . medical students. 51114
Sermon to officers and soldiers, Elizabeth-town. 37650
Sermon to swine. 79287
Sermon . . . to the Ancient and Honourable Artillery Company in Boston. (30884)
Sermon . . . to the Ancient and Honourable Artillery-Company, June 4. 1744. 58899
Sermon . . . to the Ancient and Honourable Artillery Company, . . . June 7, 1756. 59609
Sermon . . . to the Artillery Company in Boston. 59602
Sermon to the bucks and hinds of America. 79288
Sermon to the corporation of Freemen in Farmington. 30634
Sermon . . . to the females of the First Parish in Amherst. 13269
Sermon to the General Assembly of the Massachusetts-Province. (46545), note after 95317
Sermon to the General Assembly of the province of the Massachusetts-Bay. 46546
Sermon . . . to the . . . Honourable Artillery-Company, at Boston. 32317
Sermon to the New-England Forces on the expedition against Crown Point. 25940
Sermon to the North Church in Boston. (65591)
Sermon . . . to the scholars in the College Hall. (24927)
Sermon to the soldiers, Sept. 22, 1755. 36951
Sermon, to which is appended the family record. (44557)
Sermon . . . to youth. 24932
Sermon, . . . together with some occasional remarks. 106390
Sermon touching the application of religion to politics. 71014
Sermon . . . tirennial meeting of the General Convention of the Protestant Episcopal Church. 26138
Sermon . . . Troy, . . . May 19, 1861. 21442
Sermon, twenty-fifth anniversary of the author's ministry. 13589
Sermon, . . . 25 May, 1856. note after (58767)
Sermon, . . . 22nd November, 1840. 26074
Sermon, . . . 29th September, 1815. 58609
Sermon, two hundred and twenty-fifth anniversary of the First Church, 21978
Serm. II. On Tuesday, August 4, 1789. 84675-84675A
Sermon ueber Marcus am VI. v. 34. 94689
Sermon, . . . University of Virginia. 47242
Sermon, upon an artillery election. 71021-(71022)
Sermon upon intemperance. 104532
Sermon upon occasion of the death of our late soverign. 16602

Sermon upon . . . Rev. William B. O. Peabody. 33798, note after 89883
Sermon upon the assassination of President Lincoln. (26285)
Sermon . . . upon the death of a valuable relative. 46635
Sermon upon the death of Abraham Lincoln. 81700
Sermon upon the death of Mrs. Elizabeth Oliver. (65609)
Sermon . . . upon the death of Mrs. Mary Martyn. 24576
Sermon upon . . . the death of our late sovereign. 25394
Sermon upon the death of the Hon. Daniel Webster. 12890
Sermon upon the death of the Honourable Patrick Gordon. 17914
Sermon, upon the death of the Reverend Mr. Joseph Gerrish. 46283
Sermon upon the decease of the Rev. Dr. Samuel Johnson. 4095
Sermon, upon the development of the mystery. 96830
Sermon, upon the duties wherein. 46295
Sermon vpon the viii verse of the I. chapter of the Acts. (20601), 1st note after 99888
Sermon upon the purpose of God. 82492
Sermon upon the solemn fast ordered. 1513
Sermon upon the trial of the spirit, &c. 9905-9906
Sermon . . . Utica . . . Dec. 8, 1831. 20638
Sermon . . . Washington, November 18, 1860. 66877
Sermon when two Indians, Josias and Joseph were executed. 18479
Sermon wherein Godly parents are encouraged. 46721
Sermon wherein is declared that the blessed God is willing. 46716
Sermon wherein is shewed, I. That the ministers of the Gospel need. 46738
Sermon wherein is shewed, that fearful sights in heaven are the presages of great calamities. 46691, 46696
Sermon wherein is shewed that it is the duty and should be the care. 46772
Sermon wherein is shewed that the church of God is sometimes a subject. (46739)
Sermon wherein the great advantage of enjoying the oracles of God. 104066
Sermon which was preached to the Honoured Gentlemen of the Artillery Company. 104084
Sermon . . . with reference to the death of Prof. John Finley Smith. (44233)
Sermon . . . Worcester, June 10. 1747. 42995
Sremon . . . Yale College . . . fast day, April 6, 1860. 24465
Sermon, . . . Yale College, . . . fast day, January 4, 1861. 24465
Sermonario en lengua Mexicana, donde se contiene. 36798
Sermonario en lengua Mexicana. [Por Fr. J. de la Anunciacion.] 1726
Sermonario en lengua Mexicana. [Por Fray Juan Baptista.] 36133
Sermonario en lengua Nahuatl. 3999
Sermone Lation edidit. 77220
Sermones al milagroso aviso. 72552
Sermones de ramos y de pentecostes. 75612
Sermones de S. Elias, S. Jose, S. Miguel y otros. 76166
Sermones panegiricos y morales. 78925
Sermones. Para qve los cvras y otros ministros prediquen. 94838

Sermones. [Por Marcos de Saavedra.] 74650
Sermones. [Por Nicolas de Segura.] 78925
Sermones qvattuor. 47341
Sermones varios. [Por Nic. Gomez de
Cervantes.] 22762
Sermones varios. Por Pedro Quiros. (67352)
Sermones varios, predicados en la cuidad de
Lima. 526
Sermones y escritos sueltos. 51325
Sermons. 98181
Sermons addressed to the Baptist Church and
Society in Deerfield, Mass. 12393,
103736
Sermons, addresses & exhortations. (9201)
Sermons, addresses, and letters. (37232)
Sermons, addresses and statistics of the
Diocese of Montreal. 26139
Sermons and addresses. [By Beriah Green.]
28512
Sermons and addresses. [By Sewall S.
Cutting.] 18205
Sermons and charges. 25766
Sermons and discourses on several occasions.
59602
Sermons and essays by the Tennents and their
contemporaries. 83800
Sermons . . . and other writings. 33793
Sermons and sayings. 63917
Sermons and speeches of Gerrit Smith. 82656
Sermons and tracts. For the times. 77318
Sermons and tracts, separately published at
Boston, Philadelphia, &c. By Jonathan
Dickinson. (20062)
Sermons and tracts, separately published at
Boston. Philadelphia, etc. [By Samuel
Davies.] (18767)
Sermons, at the opening of a new Meeting-
House in Dennis. 92108, 97741
Sermons at the ordination of Charles Stearns.
366
Sermons at the ordination of William Gager.
200
Sermons by Albert William Duy. 21495
Sermons. By Alvan Lamson. 38775
Sermons [by Archbishop Secker.] 64328
Sermons [by Chauncey Lee.] 39720
Sermons [by Edward D. Griffin.] 89740
Sermons. [By Edward Payson.] (59309)
Sermons. [By J. P. Lesley.] 40185
Sermons, by James Muir. 51261
Sermons, by John Brazer. 7495
Sermons [by John Summerfield.] 93620
Sermons [by Jonathan Edwards.] 21948
Sermons. [By Jonathan Mayhew.] 47150
Sermon by Nahor Augustus Staples. 90473
Sermons by Nathan Parker. 58718, 101388
Sermons . . . [by P. P. Neely.] (52237)
Sermons. By Rev. C. W. Hodges. 32339
Sermons. By Rev. D. W. Clark. 13271
Sermons. By Rev. Daniel A. Clark. 13269
Sermons by . . . Rev. David Osgood. 57777
Sermons. By Rev. Ephraim Peabody. 59363
Sermons by Rev. Gregory T. Bedell. 4273
Sermons by Rev. J. B. Pitkin. 63040
Sermons . . . by Rev. John B. Romeyn. 73057
Sermons. [By Rev. John Braham.] 28226
Sermons, by Samuel Stanhope Smith. 84118
Sermons by the late David Barns. (3512)
Sermons . . . by the late Elijah Parish. 58609
Sermons by the late J. S. Buckminster. 8936
Sermons by the late Joseph Lathrop. 39200
Sermons by the late Rev. David Merrill.
47995
Sermons by the late Rev. George Shepard.
80180

Sermons by the late Rev. J. S. Buckminster.
8935
Sermons by the late Rev. James Richards.
70950
Sermons by the late Rev. Josiah D. Smith.
83456
Sermons by the late Rev. Samuel C. Thacher.
95190-95191
Sermons by the pastors of the First Church in
Dedham. 9241, 19212, 19898
Sermons by the Rev. James Spencer. 89333
Sermons by the Right Reverend Stephen Elliott.
22283
Sermons. [By Timothy Dwight.] 21566
Sermons by Thomas Wetherald, and Elias Hicks.
103059
Sermons. [By W. H. H. Murray.] 51549
Sermons . . . by William B. O. Peabody. 59384
Sermons: chiefly occasional. 42429
Sermons, chiefly of a practical nature. 25196
Sermons containing an illustration of the pro-
phecies. 82497
Sermons, delivered April the 6th, 1809. 89813
Sermons delivered by Elias Hicks & Edward
Hicks. 31715
Sermons delivered in Philadelphia, and Wilming-
ton. 103059
Sermons delivered on various occasions. By
Joseph Lathrop. 39197
Sermons delivered on various occasions. [By
Matthew Richey.] 71114
Sermons delivered on various occasions, with
addresses. 14135
Sermons delivered to the Baptist Church and
Society. 103736
Sermons . . . . Edited by Charles Lanman.
60930
Sermons, essays and strictures. 82373
Sermons, first published in the Providence
gazette. 79290
Sermons from the New-England fathers. 55889
Sermons from Universalist preachers. 84288
Sermons, historical and characteristical. 41348
Sermons in defence of the doctrine of universal
salvation. 81631
Sermons . . . in Memorial Church, Baltimore.
60930
Sermons . . . in Sandwich, Mass. (27938)
Sermons, journals, and letters [of George
Whitefield.] (69427)
Sermons, letters, and proceedings [of the
Colporteur Conventions.] (14757)
Sermons occasioned by the death of Mr. Breck.
94067
Sermons of Mr. Yorick. 91352, 91355
Sermons of Rev. Ichabod S. Spencer. 89330
Sermons of Rev. Joseph J. Foot. 25008
Sermons of Samuel Abbot Smith. 84012
Sermons of Samuel Stanhope Smith. 84120
Sermons of that memorable servant of Christ,
the Reverend, Mr. Joseph Stevens. 91548
Sermons of the late Nicholas Snethen. 85441,
85445
Sermons of the late Rev. Benjamin F. Stanton.
90386
Sermons of the Rev. Jacob Kirkpatrick. 38007
Sermons on a number of connected subjects.
82219
Sermons on church government. 36859
Sermons on different subjects. 37976
Sermons on important subjects. 91115, 91542
Sermons on important subjects; adapted to the
perilous state. 94704
Sermons on important subjects. By the late
Rev. David Tappan. 94367

Serrell & Co. firm see Stuart, Serrell & Co. firm
Serres, --------, Sieur. 79318
Serrill, Isaac. (30907)
Serrure, C. P. 30078
Serruto y Nava, Jose. (79319)-79320
Sertorius. pseud. Letter on the naval depot. (79321)
Serulan. pseud. Poems original. see Laurens, -------. supposed author
Servando, Jose de Mier y Guerra. see Mier y Guerra Servando, Jose de.
Servant Girl of 17 Years of Age. pseud. see Peters, Phillis (Wheatley) 1753?-1784.
Servant of Abraham. 46502
Servant of God concluding his labours. 90842
Servant of the Lord found ready. 46579, 1st note after 99604
Servant of the Lord not ashamed of his Lord. 46503
Servantes Carabajal, Juan Leonel de. defendant 86419
Servantes Casaus, Beatris Bernardina (de Andrada) de. plaintiff 86419
Servantes de Dieu en Canada. (10604), 19202
Servants of Christ, falsly called Ana-baptists. pseud. Preface. (72095)
Servants of the Lord Jesus Christ ought to be quickned. 104367
Servants on horse-back. 27713
Servastanoff, Pierre de. ed. 66508
Servertus, Mordecai. pseud. Mystic's plea. see Winchester, Elhanan.
Servetus, Michael, 1511-1553. (66483), 66485
Servetus, Michael, 1511-1553. supposed author (66481-(66483)
Service afloat. 79323
Service afloat and ashore. 27547, 52084
Service afloat and ashore during the Mexican war. 79075, 79083
Service among the Greeks. 9187
Service and its reward. 83302
Service of a glorious Christ. 46259
Service of God in the Gospel-ministry. 13350
Service of God recommended to the choice of young people. 16637
Service of the Lord must be chosen presently. 42088
"Service of the militia." 30386
Service, the end of living. 92024
Serviceable man. 46504
Services and addresses at the unveiling of the statue. 41231
Services. Arlington Street Church. 79324
Services at the centenary celebration. 10247
Services at the dedication of Green Mount Cemetery. 50219
Services at the dedication of the National Sailors' Home. (67297)
Services at the dedication of the School House. 55055B
Services at the designation of Mr. James Phillippo. 62469
Services at the Everett School, in Boston. (23276)
Services at the fortieth anniversary of the installation. 79802
Services at the funeral of Martha, wife of Hovey K. Clarke. 43494
Services at the funeral of the late Professor James J. Mapes. 4575
Services at the funeral of the Rev. Thomas Snell. 18098, 85409
Services at the induction of William E. Starr. 90565

Services at the installation of Rev. Daniel Temple Noyes. 70938
Services at the ordination of Mr. James de Normandie. 26536
Services at the public recognition of the Rev. Rufus Babcock. 52507
Services held by the Maryland Union Commission. 45250, 45359
Services in celebration of the fiftieth anniversary. 2340
Services in memory of Rev. Ezra Stiles Gannett. 26536
Services in memory of Rev. William E. Channing. 11926
Services of colored Americans, in the wars of 1776 and 1812. (52303)
Services of the Protestant Episcopal Church. 79325
Services on Bunker Hill. 9182
Services on the occasion of the ordination of Rev. F. P. Mullally. 85323
Seruicios que a Su Magestad ha hecho el Capitan Gaspar de Villagra. 99642
Seruicios que refiero a V. M. en el memorial. 68365
Serville, ------ Audient. see Audinet-Serville, ---------.
Servitude, and the duty of masters to their servants. 79326
Servius Sulpitius. pseud. Remarks on an address. see Fendall, Philip R. supposed author
Servor of the season. pseud. ed. and publisher 22144
Sese y Lacasta, Martin. 69327
Sesiones extraordinarias del Congreso Constituyente. (48656)
Sesma, Joaquin Ramirez y. see Ramirez y Sesma, Joaquin.
Sesqui-centennial gathering of the Clan Darlington. 18600
Sesse, Iosepe de. 79328
Session laws of the Legislative Council. 24880
Session laws of the Territory [of Minnesota.] 49307
Session of 1856. Report of Select Committee. 10019
Session of 1863. Pennsylvania Legislature. 60611
Session of the Teachers' Institute of the Third Assembly District. 50030
Sessional proceedings of the National Association for the Promotion of Civil Science. 51928
Sessions, Alexander J. 79329-79330
Sessions, John. 79331
Sesso e di Venafro, Ambrogio Spinola, Marchese del. 89456-89457
Set of anatomical tables. (82253)
Set of plans and forts in America. 79332
Set-off to Mr. Strong's off-set to Mr. Adams's letter!!! 92884
Seta tuomon tupa. 92523
Setabitani, Thomae. pseud. Thomae, Setabitani, Hispani malvendae de Antichristo. see Malvenda, T.
Sethonia, a tragedy. (79333)
Setier, L. P. tr. 79334, 91613-91614
Seton, Christopher. defendant at court martial 96932
Seton, Elizabeth Ann, Saint, 1774-1821. 79335-79336, 103358
Seton, R. ed. 79336
Seton, S. W. (79337)
Seton, William. 79338-79340
Settegart, H. 73282

Settentrione dell' Europa e dell' America. 18465
Settle, Dionyse. 25994-25996, 79341-79346
Settle, Elkanah. (79347)
Settled ministry. 42791
Settlement and early history Albany. 3528-3529
Settlement in the west. 57594
Settlement of Boston by the pilgrims. (6555)
Settlement of Boston by the puritan pilgrims. (79974), note after 97078
Settlement of emigrants from Ireland. 11796
Settlement of Germantown. 60746, 1st note after 97529
Settlement of Grants. Windham County. 99101
Settlement of Manamuskin. (14283)
Settlement of western country. 97028
Settler. pseud. Sketch of a plan. see Bannister, John W.
Settler at Stratford, Huron District, Canada West. pseud. Life of a backwoodsman. (41021)
Settler in Santo Domingo. pseud. In the tropics. 34420
Settler in Upper Canada. pseud. Six years in the bush. (10607), 2d note after 98090
Settler of Indiana. (36887)
Settler's guide. 24862
Settler's guide in the United States. 89292
Settlers' guide to Oregon and Washington Territory. 79348
Settlers in Canada. 44700
Settlers in the British colonies. pseud. Letters. 40593
Settlers in the Huron Tract, and others parts of Upper Canada. pseud. Letters and extracts of letters. 25769
Settlers in the woods. 26456
Settlers in Upper Canada. pseud. Copies and extracts from letters. 98071
Settlers in Upper Canada. pseud. Following are copies. 98078
Settlers in Upper Canada. pseud. Letters. 98082
Settlers in Upper Canada. pseud. Letters and extracts of letters. 98081
Settlers in Virginia. 12688, note after 100443
Settler's new home. 84224, 84226
Settlers new home or the emigrant's location. 84225
Settlers of Virginia, a national drama. 18155
Settlers on the Coast of Yucatan; and the Late Settlers on the Mosquito Shore. see British Honduras. Citizens.
Seu Ke-Yu. 79350
Seuda-defensa que el Senor Virgil hace. 26582
Seudo-liberales. 79349
Seul! 75542
Seve, Edouard. (79351)
Sevelinges, L. D. tr. 6819
Seven and a half years in the far west. 29728
Seven and nine years among the Camanches and Apaches. (79352)
Seven articles by Lord Denman. note after 92624
Seven articles from the Church of Leyden 1617. 79353
Seven brothers of Wyoming. 79354, 105692
Seven days; battles in front of Richmond. 79355
Seven day's contests. 42970
Seven discourses and three prayers. 25272

Seven discourses on miscellaneous subjects. 97399
Seven eventful years in Paraguay. (46189)
Seven features of Christianity. 92046
Seven hints for all who will take them. 62238, 79356
Seven letters. 10172, 21000
Seven letters from an emigrant. 101117
Seven letters on religious liberty. 25068
Seven letters to Amynton. 84844-84845
Seven letters to the Hon. Daniel Horsmanden. 57903
Seven letters to the Rev. George A. Calhoun. 2673
Seven Matroosen. 78896-78901 see also Seven Matroosen, op het Eyland Mauritius in Groenlandt. Seven Men on Greenland. Seven Sailors in Greenland.
Seven Matroosen, op het Eyland Mauritius in Groenlandt. 97528-97529 see also Seven Matroosen. Seven Men on Greenland. Seven Sailors in Greenland.
Seven Matrosen die op Spitsberghen. 97528-97529
Seven Men on Greenland. (28656), 92712 see also Seven Matroosen. Seven Matroosen, op het Eyland Mauritius in Groenlandt. Seven Sailors in Greenland.
Seven mile mirror to Canada. 60922
Seven months a prisoner. 79357
Seven months in prison. 74319
Seven per cent. gold bonds. 89898
Seven pointers of the new star. (47303)
Seven rational sermons. 79358
Seven Sailors in Greenland. 20518 see also Seven Matroosen. Seven Matroosen, op het Eyland Mauritius in Groenlandt. Seven Men on Greenland.
Seven select letters, of Mr. Cotton Mather. 46505
Seven sermons. 74292
Seven sermons . . . preached at a lecture. 47150
Seven sisters of sleep. (16325)
Seven stories, with basement and attic. 49680
Seven years' explorations in British America. 733
Seven years of a sailor's life. (13283)
Seven years of my life. (79359)
Seven years on the slave-coast of Africa. (9972)
Seven years' residence in the great deserts of North America. 20554
Seven years' resident in North America. pseud. Practical guide for emigrants. 64867
Seven years service on the slave coast of western Africa. 33981
Seven years' street preaching in San Francisco. 94548
Seven years' travel in Central America. 25992
Seventeen decisions of the Supreme Court of the United States. 79360
1788-1868. Memoir of Usher Parsons. 58877
1789 to 1889. Washington to Harrison. 84913
Seventeen hundred and seventy-six. (42134)
Seventeen hundred fifty-eight and eighteen hundred fifty-eight. 31218
Seventeen numbers. 24484
Seventeen proseltyes. 103293
MDCCXVII. An almanack. 72027
1775—Lexington—1875. 88689
1771. 1871. Addresses and proceedings. 74142
1776. Banner song. 1876. 84343
1776. 1876. 89488
1776. Independence, liberty, and glory! 96771

MDCCXVI. An almanack of the coelestial motions. 72027

1710. . . . An ephermeris of the coelestial motions. 72025

MDCCXXXVIII. The Rhode-Island almanack for the year, 1738. 90073

MDCCXXXV. The Rhode-Island almanack for the year, 1735. (70702)

MDCCXXXVII. The Rhode-Island almanack for the year, 1737. 90072

MDCCXII. An almanack of the coelestial motions. 62743

MDCCXX. An almanack . . . for the year . . . 1720. (24687)

MDCCXXVIII. The Rhode-Island almanac, for the year 1728. 70701

M DCC XXV. 52670

Seventeen years history. (43513)

Seventeen years travels of Peter de Cieza. (13056)

Seventeenth anniversary of the Corporate Society of California Pioneers. 9976

Seventeenth annual report . . . see Report . . .

Seventeenth jewel. 79361

Seventeenth jewel of the United States of America. (28021)

Seventh annual report . . . see Report . . .

Seventh biennial report . . . see Report . . .

Seventh census of the United States. 24492

Seventh census of the United States, 1850. 11669

Seventh census of the United States of America. 11671

Seventh census. Report of Jos. C. G. Kennedy. 11670, 34731

Seventh collection of papers. 9372, note after 14379, 81492, 86717

Seventh-Day Baptist anniversaries. 79373

Seventh-Day Baptist General Conference. New York. (79362)-79363

Seventh . . . debate, Oct. 6, 1864. 55840

Seventh essay on free trade and finance. 102409

Seventh fair of the St. Louis Agricultural and Mechanical Association. 75381

Seventh letter to the people of England. 80059

Seventh letter to the people of England upon political-writing. 80058

[Seventh letter to the Rev. Samuel Miller.] (49063)

Seventh National Congress, F. B. 24060

Seventh Presbyterian Church, New York. see New York (City) Seventh Presbyterian Church.

Seventh Regiment veterans. 79364

Seventh report . . . see Report . . .

Seventh seal opened. 79365

Seventh supplement [to the public laws of Rhode Island.] 70700

Seventh truth trumpet sounded. 79365

Seventy-eight persons. pseud. Counter testimonial. 37188

Seventy-fifth anniversary dinner of the Friendly Sons of St. Patrick. 86146

Seventy Quakers. see Friends, Society of. Philadelphia Yearly Meeting.

Seventy-six. pseud. To the people of Maryland. 97943

Seventy-six. [By John Neal.] 52157

Seventy-six; or the fall of the great republic. 79366

Seventy-Six Society, Philadelphia. publishers 2872, 19065, (26428), 45930, note after 79366

Sever, Nicholas. 79367

Sever & Francis. firm 11491

Several acts and law passed by the Great and General Court. 46120

Several acts of Assembly in relation to that canal. 69433, note after 93919

Several acts of Assembly providing for the education of children. 60612

Several acts respecting sales by the Surveyor General. 99110, 99113, 99119

Several Africans and Indians. pseud. Letters addressed to Dorothy Ripley. 71499

Several American authors. pseud. Tales of Gauber-Spa. see Bryant, William Cullen, 1794-1878. Leggett, William. Paulding, James Kirke, 1778-1860. Sands, Robert Charles, 1799-1832. Sedgwick, Catharine Maria, 1789-1867.

Several apologetical letters to a friend. (73968)

Several Assemblies of New Jersey, Pennsylvania, and Virginia, 79369

Several arguments proving, that inoculating the small pox is not contained in the law of physick. 46741, 104243

Several authentic and highly important letters from English emigrants. 13882, 14450

Several circular letters to the clergy of Maryland. 7482

Several conferences between some of the principal people. 59612

Several Cuban and Porto-Rican abolitionists. pseud. Abolition of slavery in Cuba and Porto Rico. 81723

Several curious letters which passed. 96932

Several declarations of the Company of Royal Adventures of England Trading into Africa. 79370

Several discourses on Acts XVI. 30. 3471

Several dissertations of Don Hippolito Ruiz. 38728

Several distinguished literary men. pseud. Views of New-York. 54712, note before 99588

Several divines. pseud. eds. Royal spiritual magazine. 73807

Several eminent divines of the congregational vvay. pseud. Judgment. see Mather, Increase, 1639-1723.

Several epistles given forth by two of the Lords faithful servants. 72199

Several essays. 13741

Several essays in political arithmetick. (61308)

Several extracts from a letter to his brother. 95252

Several extracts from a letter written to his brother. 95231-95233, 95235, 95247

Several eye-witnesses. pseud. Brief description. see Naish, William.

Several forms of prayer, for little children. 89811

Several Friends in Philadelphia. pseud. see Friends, Society of. Philadelphia Yearly Meeting.

Several gentlemen. pseud. comps. Geographical, historical, commercial, and agricultural view. 26974

Several gentlemen. pseud. Letters. 59066

Several gentlemen. pseud. Miscellany of knowledge. (49452)

Several gentlemen of eminence in Europe, and the continent of America. pseud. eds. 51507

Several gentlemen of this country. pseud. Virginia miscellany. 100560

Several gentlemen of unquestionable veracity. pseud. Letters. 7847, 27588

Several gentlemen who were of his council. pseud. Narrative of the proceedings. see Stoughton, William, 1632-1701.

Several hands. pseud. Collection of poems. (14381)

Several hands. pseud. Lives, English and forein [sic]. (41589)

Several hands. pseud. Papers concerning the boundary. 18936

Several hymns. 841

Several hymns out of the Old, and New, Testament. 3471

Several Incorporated Insurance Societies of the State of Pennsylvania. petitioners 60239

Several inhabitants there resident. pseud. Further account of New Jersey. see Hartshorne, Richard. Huckens, Ester. Pederick, Roger. S., Martha. Wade, Robert.

Several interesting public documents respecting the island of Trinidad. 103653

Several late acts of the legislature of the state of South-Carolina. 87711

Several laws and orders made at the General Courts. 47121

Several learned contemporaries. pseud. Appendix. 103663

Several letters . . . from A. A. Jones. 36447

Several letters from a gentleman of the medical faculty. 3106, 4th note after 93855

Several letters, from a rev. divine of the Church of England. 43662

Several letters from the President of the Council of New-Hampshire. 66514, 1st note after 99003

Several letters from the Secretaries of State. 32968, 1st note after 97146

Several letters to a member of Parliament. 2228, note after 105078, 105079

Several letters to the author, &c. 9926

Several letters to the Mayor and City Council of Washington. 79371, 88478

Several letters which passed to and from New York. 1456

Several literary gentlemen. pseud. eds. American magazine and repository of useful literature. 1134

Several medical gentlemen. pseud. Devotional somnium. 2846

Several members of New North Church, Boston. pseud. Vindication. see Lyman, Caleb. and Seares, Alexander.

Several members of that church. pseud. Vindication. see Lyman, caleb. and Seares, Alexander.

Several members of the court. pseud. Observations. 64131

Several messages which passed between His Honour the Lieutenant Governor and the two houses. 34084

Several methods by which meridional lines may be found. 22219

Several methods of making salt-petre. 79372-79374, note after 103712

Several ministers. pseud. Serious address. see Mather, Cotton, 1663-1728.

Several ministers. pseud. Testimony against evil customs. see Colman, Benjamin, 1673-1747. Mather, Cotton, 1663-1728. Wadsworth, Benjamin, 1669-1737.

Several ministers in and near Boston. pseud. Answer. see Allen, James, 1632-1710. Danforth, John, 1660-1730. Mather, Cotton, 1663-1728. Mather, Increase, 1639-1723. Morton, Charles, 1627-1698.

Sherman, James. Walter, Nehemiah. Willard, Samuel, 1640-1707.

Several ministers in New-York, &c. pseud. Introductory address. 104944

Several ministers of Boston. pseud. Attestation. see Colman, Benjamin, 1673-1747. Cooper, William, 1694-1743. Foxcroft, Thomas, 1697-1769. Gee, Joshua. Prince, Thomas, 1687-1758. Sewall, Joseph, 1688-1769. Webb, John.

Several ministers of Boston. pseud. Pastoral letter. see Mather, Cotton, 1663-1729.

Several ministers of the Gospel. pseud. Essay. see Danforth, John, 1660-1730. Danforth, Samuel, 1666-1727. Thacher, Peter, 1651-1727.

Several ministers of the Gospel. pseud. Testimony against evil customs. see Colman, Benjamin, 1673-1747. Mather, Cotton, 1663-1728. Wadsworth, Benjamin, 1669-1737.

Several ministers of the Gospel, in and near Boston. pseud. Warning. 46587, note after 101451

Several ministers of the Southern Presbytery. pseud. Statement of some recent transactions. 65227

Several miscellaneous pieces. 8559

Several new, pressing and weighty considerations. 47893

Several objections, made by the Agent on the part of New-York. (7884)

Several occasional papers. (35668), note after 99576, note after 105081

Several of the members of that church. pseud. Vindication. see Lyman, Caleb. and Seares, Alexander.

Several of the most ingenious pens of that island. pseud. Pattern for governors. 59127

Several of the sufferers. pseud. Writings. 5631

Several other pieces. 95255

Several other remarkable instances of persons. 105011-105012

Several other sermons occasionally preached. 105073

Several papers originally published in the New-York American. 8291, note after 101440

Several papers, written by several persons. 46295

Several pastors of adjacent churches, meeting in Cambridge, New-England. pseud. Thirty important cases, resolved. 46550, note after 95360

Several persons belonging to the flock of some of the injured pastors. pseud. Some few remarks. see Gill, Obadiah. Mather, Cotton, 1663-1728. Mather, Increase, 1639-1723.

Several persons who called themselves members of that Assembly. pseud. petitioners 35586

Several persons, who were dying in their youth. pseud. Extracts of some papers. 46295

Several petitions relative to the employment. (15793)

Several petitions which have been presented to the British House of Commons. 35640, 35666-35667, 2d note after 97478

Several planters and other inhabitants of the island of Barbadoes. petitioners see Barbadoes. Citizens. petitioners

Several planters, and others, inhabitants of Your Majesty's island of Barbadoes.

Sewall papers. (19639), note after 31743, (79447)

Sewanee review. 84837

Seward, Amos. 94271

Seward, Anna, 1747-1809. 51562, 79473-79489, 83421-83422

Seward, D. M. 79490

Seward, Edward S. 79491-79492

Seward, Frederick W. ed. (79507)

Seward, G. F. 79493 see also U. S. Legation. China.

Seward, James. (79494)

Seward, Olive Risley. ed. 79594

Seward, William. 79495, 103500

Seward, William, 1712-1782. 79496-79497

Seward, William Henry, 1801-1872. 316, 2823, 10169, 10190, 12480, 14984, (19659), 20031, (28415), 28493, 28835, 29864, 34725, 45451, 52200, 53633, 53687, (53783), (54729), (55610), (57591), 58467, 68604, 79498-79595, 79597-79598, 84463, 89208, 88295, 92395, 92452, 93510, 93644, 93663, 97124 see also New York (State) Governor, 1839-1843 (Seward) U. S. Department of State.

Seward Institute, Florida, N. Y. see S. S. Seward Institute, Florida, N. Y.

Seward memorial. (79599)

Sewel, Willem, 1653-1720. 13913, 18385, 20017, 21593, (66917), 79601-(79616), 100943, note after 103655

Sewell, Alfred L. 79617

Sewell, George. 67599, 79618-79619

Sewell, Jonathan, 1766-1839. 69403, 79620-79623, 93181

Sewell, Jonathan, 1766-1839. defendant at impeachment 42518, 96926-96927

Sewell, Joseph, 1688-1769. 24532, 79415

Sewell, Leonard. 82256-82257, 79624

Sewell, Mary. 79625

Sewell, Robert. 79626

Sewell, Samuel. 96820

Sewell, Stephen. ed. 42873

Sewell, Stephen. supposed author 98978

Sewell, William. 28078

Sewell, William Grant, 1829-1862. 79627

Sex predikninger. 4343

Sexagenary. 5985

Sexes mis-match'd. note after 88547

Sexta carta pastoral. 39284

Sexto informe annual. 66589

Sexto libro. 11385

Sexto puento de la relacion. 12799

Sexton, George. 79628

Sexton of the old school. pseud. Dealings with the dead. see Sargent, Lucius Manlius.

Sexton's monitor. 18696, 20627, 2d note after 79628

Seybert, Adam, 1773-1825. 79629-79632, 84305-84306, 105107

Seybt, Julius. 37000, 65295

Seyd, Ernest. 79633-79634

Seyfried, Johann Heinrich. 79635-79636

Seymour, Aaron C. ed. 27415

Seymour, Almira. 79637-(79638)

Seymour, Charles. 79639

Seymour, Charles C. B., 1829-1869. 79640

Seymour, David Lowrey, 1803-1867. 79641-79642

Seymour, E. Sandford. 79643-79644

Seymour, George F., 1829- 79645

Seymour, Horatio, 1810-1886. (8175), 16293, 30901, 37272, 42396, 51466, 53616, (68519), 79646-79660, 92850 see also New York (State) Governor, 1853-1855

(Seymour) New York (State) Governor, 1863-1865 (Seymour)

Seymour, J. engr. (82404), 97014

Seymour, John F. 53917, 69863, 79664-79665 see also New York (State) General Agent for the Relief of Sick, Wounded, Furloughed and Discharged Soldiers.

Seymour, Mary H. 79666

Seymour, Nelse. 79667

Seymour, Richard Arthur. 79668

Seymour, Samuel. engr. 85105

Seymour, Silas. 79669

Seymour, Thomas Hart, 1807-1868. 15843, 23271, (79670) see also Connecticut. Governor, 1850-1853 (Seymour)

Seymour, Truman, 1824- 79671-(79672)

Seymour, William N. 43741

Seymour and Blair. 17597

Seymour and Blair. Campaign edition. (79661)

Seymour and Blair Democratic platform of New Mexico. 53285

Seymour and vicinity: historical collections. 79855

Seymour campaign songster. (79662)

Seymour Democracy dissected. 20031

Seymour letter. 5821

Seymour, Vallandigham, and the riots of 1863. 79663

Seys, John. defendant 79673

Seywald, Blasius Vitalis. 38039, 79674-79675

Seyxas y Lovera, F. de. see Seixas y Lovera, F. de.

Sfera di Messer G. Sacrobosco. 32683

Sfera libri quattro in ottava rima. 90088

Sgaoyadih. pseud. tr. see Jemison, Jacob. tr.

Shackelford, B. 104884

Shackelford, J. O. 70037

Shackford, Charles C. (8636), 79676-79677

Shadd, Mary A. 79678

Shade, Maria. (58796)

Shade of "Alden." pseud. Notes on the seashore. see Homer, James Lloyd.

Shade of Plato. (32239)

Shades of the past. (26072)

Shadow, Ben. pseud. Echoes of a belle. (79680)

Shadow land. (82519)

Shadow of fate. 41040

Shadow of the rock. 79679

Shadows of the evergreen. 62925

Shadows of the metropolis. 39256

Shadows of the past. 87812

Shadowy land, and other poems. 33966 Shady side. 33462

Shadyside. 61375

Shaefer, Peter Wenrick, 1819- 80024-80027

Shaffer, David Henry. 13085

Shaffer, George W. ed. 51193

Shaffer, J. W. 79681

Shaffner, Taliaferro Preston, 1818-1881. 37526, 77499, 79682-79685

Shaffner's telegraph companion. 79683

Shafford, John Conrad. 79686

Shaftebury, Anthony Ashley Cooper, 1st Earl of, 1621-1683. (41726), 88005

Shaftesbury papers and other records. 88005

Shaftsbury Association. see Baptists. Vermont. Shaftsbury Association.

Shahcoolen. pseud. Letters. see Knapp, Samuel Lorenzo.

Shahgunahse ahnumeahwene muzzeneegun. 79688-79689

Shahmah in pursuit of freedom. 28594, 79691

Shailer, William H. 79692

Shaker Bible. 79723

Shaker lovers, and other tales. 95486

Shaker millennial praise. 79719, 97893, 4th
　　note after 102601
Shakerism detected. 82763, 82770B
"Shakerism detected, &c." examined & refuted.
　　82770B
Shakerism developed. 82768-82770A
Shakerism exposed; being an account. (21598)
Shakerism exposed. With the life of the
　　author. 28509
Shakerism unmasked; or, a narrative. 105124
Shakerism unmasked, or the history of the
　　Shakers. 30803
Shakers. 18508, (19181), 21309-21310, 21594,
　　(23152), 28513, 30803, 79694-79698,
　　79704, 79717, 79719, (79721)-79727,
　　92025, note before 93610, note after
　　94924, 97698, note after 97880, 97882,
　　97883-97884, 97886, 97888, 97893, 1st,
　　3d and 5th notes after 102601, 102602-
　　102603, note after 106196
Shakers. defendants 57844, note after 97893,
　　note after 105575
Shakers. petitioners 47632
Shakers. Canterbury and Enfield, N. H.
　　69858
Shakers. Canterbury and Enfield, N. H.
　　petitioners (52947), (79714), note after
　　97880, note after 103334
Shakers. Canterbury and Enfield, N. H.
　　Overseers. petitioners 21595-21596,
　　97894-97895, note after 104781 see also
　　Winkley, Francis. petitioner
Shakers. Canterbury and Enfield, N. H.
　　Trustees. 12595, 97895
Shakers. Enfield, N. H. see Shakers.
　　Canterbury and Enfield, N. H.
Shakers. New Lebanon, N. Y. 32664, 79706-
　　79708, note after 91701
Shakers. New Lebanon, N. Y. petitioners
　　97890-97891
Shakers. Pleasant Hill, Ky. 34961-34962,
　　79710-79711, note after 97880, 97896,
　　103874
Shakers. Pleasant Hill, Ky. petitioners
　　97892
Shakers. Union Village, Ohio. 97881
Shakers. Union Village, Ohio. defendants
　　57844, note after 97893, note after
　　105575
Shakers. Watervliet, N. Y. petitioners
　　97891, 97898
Shakers. Watervliet, Ohio. 97887
Shakers. Compendium of the origin, history,
　　principles, rules and regulations. (23152)
Shakers. Speech of Robert Wickliffe. 103870
Shakespear. pseud. Modern characters for
　　1778. 79728
Shakespeare, William, 1564-1616. 79729,
　　99866
Shakespeare Division no. 37, Sons of Temper-
　　ance. See Sons of Temperance of North
　　America. New York. Shakespeare
　　Division no. 37.
Shakespeare Division, no. 46, Sons of Temper-
　　ance. see Sons of Temperance of North
　　America. Massachusetts. Shakespeare
　　Division, no. 46, Boston.
Shakespeare in love. 83788
Shakespeare Society of Philadelphia. 62239
Shakespeare's works. 79729
Shaking dispensations. 46507
Shaking of the nations. 36219
Shakings. 4711
Shaler, Charles. 79730
Shaler, N. S. 85072

Shaler, William, 1778-1833. 49893-49894,
　　79731
Shales, W. 66686
Shall a great nation go abroad to pay its
　　interest? 79732
Shall America be rules by a monarch or by
　　the people? 44740
Shall criminals sit on the jury? (49198)
Shall England uphold the capture of private
　　property at sea? 44603
Shall I go to war with my American brethren?
　　22792-22793
Shall Indian affairs be placed under the control
　　of the military? 34648, note before
　　94525
Shall our government act? 79733
Shall our ocean mail service be performed
　　by foreign steamships? 79734
Shall slavery be extended? 74757
Shall slavery be permitted in Nebraska?
　　(52182)
Shall the church adopt the apostolic standard
　　of discipline? 17257
Shall the constitution and the union stand or
　　fall? 28450
Shall the constitution be repealed? (17271)
Shall the freedmen be admitted to the right of
　　suffrage. 79735
Shall the government surrender to the rebellion?
　　(5448)
Shall the new constitution be adopted? 49644
Shall the people or "the politicians," decide
　　the issue? (55107), 79736
Shall the President and Vice President of the
　　United States, be separately and directly
　　elected by the people? 73967
Shall the privilege of the writ of habeas corpus
　　ever be suspended in this state? 1683
Shall the republic be divided? 78161
Shall the republic stand on the foundation?
　　8669
Shall the society or the committee rule?
　　(47241), 93816
Shall the sword devour for ever. 105261
Shall the sword devour forever! 105265
Shall the territories be Africanized? 30386
Shall the war be for union and freedom, or
　　union and slaver? (16217)
Shall they be abolished or sustained? 49463
Shall we build? 82953
Shall we compromise? 63826
Shall we have a public library in Lexington?
　　40893
Shall we have an armistice? 79737
Shall we have liberty or slavery? 68661
Shall we have peace? 10842
Shall we keep the Canadas? (10605)
Shall we legislate? (3679)
Shall we licence or shall we suppress the
　　liquor shops? 63056
Shall we save our country. 21082
Shall we suffocate Ed. Green? (28520), (68530)
Shallus, Francis. 79738
Sham beggar. A farce. 79739
Sham-patriot unmasked; being an exposition of
　　the fatally successfully arts of dema-
　　gogues, to exalt themselves. 103846
Sham patriot unmasked. [By Harry Croswell.]
　　17677
Sham-patriot unmasked; or, an exposition of the
　　fatally successful arts of demagogues,
　　to exalt themselves. 32091, 75930, note
　　after 79739
Sham patriot unmasked: or an exposition of the
　　fatally successful arts of demagogues who

exalt themselves. 75929, note after
79739
Sham-robbery. (27930)
Shamokin, Pa. (79740)
Shamokin Valley and Oittsville Railroad
Company. Managers. 79742
Shamrock or Hibernian chronicle. 79743
Shamrock Society, New York. 47436
Shanafelt, J. R. (79744)
Shand, Peter J. 79745
Shane, J. D. 79746
Shangar, Marcus. 79747, 97319
Shank, David. (79748)
Shanklin, James M. 79749
Shanks, G. H. 79750
Shanks, John Peter Clever, 1826-1901. 79751-
79754
Shanks, William F. G., 1837- 79755
Shanly, Charles D., 1811-1875. 79756
Shanly, Walter, 1819- 57887, 79757-79758
Shannon, George. 19734, 79759, note after
95447
Shannon, Isaac N. 79760-79761
Shannon, James. 79762-79764
Shannon, Joseph. ed. 54369
Shannon, Mary Eulalie Fee. 79765
Shannon, Thomas Bowles, 1827-1879. (79766)
Shannon, William. 79767-(79768)
Shannon & Company. firm publishers see
Emmert, Shannon & Company. firm
publishers
Shannon and the Chesapeake. 79769
Shantz, J. Y. 79770
Shapahitamanash suyapu timtki. 88879
Shapard, E. R. ed. 88324
Shapley, E. Cooper. (79771)
Sharan, James. (79772)
Sharland, George. 79773
Sharon. 86564
Sharon Boarding School, Philadelphia. Female
Principal. 62240
Sharon Springs, N. Y. Teachers' Institute,
1861. see Schoharie County Teachers'
Institute, Sharon Springs, N. Y., 1861.
Sharp, -------. defendant (17400)
Sharp, -------. engr. (71242)
Sharp, -------, fl. 1830. 104196
Sharp, a country parson. pseud. Americans
roused. see Sewall, Jonathan, 1728-
1796.
Sharp, a country parson. pseud. Cure for
the spleen. see Sewall, Jonathan, 1728-
1796.
Sharp, Andre. 79774
Sharp, Anthony. pseud. Lancaster almanac.
see Rittenhouse, David.
Sharp, Bartholomew. 29473, 79781
Sharp, Daniel, 1783-1853. 79782-79806
Shart, Daniel, 1783-1853. defendant at court
martial 79807
Sharp, Granville, 1734-1813. 3689, 26898,
32288, 79808-79827, 79829-(79835),
93140, 93140, 95530
Sharp, Isaac. 83315
Sharp, Jacob, 1817-1888. petitioner 54135,
79836
Sharp, Jacob, 1817-1888. plaintiff (79837)
Sharp, James. 79838
Sharp, John. 79839-79841
Sharp, Joseph B. 79842
Sharp, Joshua. 3885A, 4718, (60298), 79843-
79845
Sharp, Leander J. 79846
Sharp, Pindar B. (79847)
Sharp, Rowland. defendant 6326, 1st note
after 97284

Sharp, Thomas. (79849)
Sharp, William S. 79850
Sharp-snout. 79851
Sharpe, Bartholomew, fl. 1678-1682. 29473
Sharpe, George. 104757
Sharpe, Horatio. 45094-45095, 45370 see also
Maryland (Colony) Governor, 1753-1769
(Sharpe)
Sharpe, Lynch Lawdon. 79852
Sharpe, R. Bowdler. 28401, 71032
Sharpe, W. C. 79854-79856
Sharpe, William. defendant 79853
Sharpe family. 78121
Sharpe genealogy and miscellany. 79856
Sharpey, Alexander. 66686
Sharpless, Joseph. 79857
Sharpless John Hebler, and others vs. the city
of Philadelphia. 58441
Sharpley, Sam. 79858
Sharpstein, John R. 79859
Sharron, J. supposed author 100878
Sharswood, George, 1810-1883. 15586, 79860-
79865, 92320
Sharswood, William, 1836- 79866-79868
Sharts, John. 79869
Shattock, Samuel. (73483)
Shattuck, Daniel. 103280
Shattuck, George C. 79872-79874
Shattuck, George Cheyne, 1783-1854. 79870-
79871
Shattuck, Jared. petitioner 79875
Shattuck, Lemuel, 1793-1859. 334, 6785, note
after 6785, 39399, 45986, 79876-79886
see also Massachusetts. Sanitary Com-
mission.
Shatzel, J. 79887
Shau-wau-nowe Kesauthwau. 79980
Shaveblock, Pasquin. pseud. Shaver's new
sermon. 79891-79892
Shaver. pseud. Priestcraft defended. see
Macgowan, John.
Shaver, Lewellyn A. (79889)
Shaver's new sermon for the fast day. 79891-
(79894)
Shaving mill. 42604
Shaw, -------, fl. 1850. 54651
Shaw, -------, fl. 1852. 79906
Shaw, -------, fl. 1855. 63660
Shaw, Benjamin. 79896
Shaw, Benjamin. defendant 79895
Shaw, Benjamin F. 79897
Shaw, Charles. 79899
Shaw, Charles, 1782-1828. 79898
Shaw, Charles B. 5894, 79900
Shaw, Charles P. (79901)
Shaw, Daniel. 53473, 54042, 79903, 83604
Shaw, Elijah. (79904)-79905
Shaw, Fred. 79907
Shaw, Gus. 79908
Shaw, Henry Wheeler, 1818-1885. 79909-79917
Shaw, J. 34253
Shaw, James, fl. 1867. (79918)
Shaw, James, fl. 1872. 79919
Shaw, James Boylan, 1808-1890. 79920-79921
Shaw, John, 1707?-1791. 79922-(79923)
Shaw, John, 1773-1823. defendant at court
martial 79925
Shaw, John, 1778-1809. 79924
Shaw, John, fl. 1856. 79926
Shaw, John A. (79927)-79930
Shaw, John C. 79931 see also Minnesota.
State Librarian.
Shaw, John Robert. 79932
Shaw, Joseph, 1778-1824. 79933-79934
Shaw, Joshua, b. 1776. illus. 79935-79937
Shaw, Joshua, fl. 1847. (79938)

Shelburne, William Petty Fitzmaurice, Earl of, 1737-1805. see Lansdowne, William Petty Fitzmaurice, 1st Marquis of, 1737-1805.

Shelburne, Mass. Congregational Church. 80114

Shelburne Falls, Mass. Academy. see Shelburne Falls Academy, Shelburne Falls, Mass.

Shelburne Falls Academy, Shelburne Falls, Mass. 80115

Shelby, Isaac, 1750-1826. 33150, 34461, 80116 see also Kentucky. Governor, 1812-1816 (Shelby)

Shelby and his men. 21925

Shelby College, Shelbyville, Ky. 80117

Shelbyville, Ky. Shelby College. see Shelby College, Shelbyville, Ky.

Sheldon, ---------, fl. 1779. 91933

Sheldon, Electra Maria. see Stewart, Electra Maria (Sheldon)

Sheldon, Elisha. defendant at court martial 80120

Sheldon, George. 80121, 104272, 104376

Sheldon, Henry Olcott. 80122-80123

Sheldon, Hezekiah Spencer. 80124

Sheldon, James. 80125-80127

Sheldon, James. reporter 95275-95276

Sheldon, James O. (80128)

Sheldon, L. H. 80130

Sheldon, Lionel Allen, 1828-1917. (80129)

Sheldon, M. L. petitioner 80131

Sheldon, W., of Norwich, Connecticut. (80132)

Sheldon, William, fl. 187-. 80134

Sheldon, William, d. 1871. 80133

Sheldon, Winthrop D. 80135

Sheldon magazine. 80123

Sheldonian prize essay. 42618

Sheldon's business . . . directory . . . of New York. (80136)

Shell and shell-guns. 18277

"Shell-fish" and their allies. 11000

Shellabarger, Samuel, 1817-1896. 80137-80146

Shellbarger and Cox contrasted. 34268

Shelley (M. M.) firm publishers (80147)

Shelley's petroleum, oil and railway guide. (80147)

Shells. 27419

Shelly, A. Fishe. pseud. Ostrea. see Gerard, James Watson.

Sheltering Arms, New York. Trustees. 80149

Shelton, Frederick William, 1814-1881. 80150-(80152), note after 97082

Shelton, Philo S. 80153-80154

Shelton, William, 1798-1883. (80155)-80156

Shelton. firm publishers 80157

Shelton's new almanac . . . 1815. 80157

Shelvocke, George. 31389, (54897), 80158-80160

Shemain, Theodorus van. pseud. Vision of hell. see Green, Jacob. supposed author

Shenandoah; or the last Confederate cruiser. (33842)

Sheston, Thomas S. (80161)

Shepard, A. K. 80162-80163

Shepard, Charles Upham, 1804-1886. 44416, 80164-(80171), 81038, 87534

Shepard, Mrs. D. E. G., 1820-1853. 80173

Shepard, Daniel. 80172

Shepard, E. Clarence. (80174)

Shepard, Elihu H. 80175-80176

Shepard, Enoch. 80177

Shepard, F. J. 85151

Shepard, G. 13269

Shepard, George. (65625), (80178)-80180

Shepard, Isaac F., 1816-1889. (80181)-80185

Shepard, J. H. 7836

Shepard, James. 80272

Shepard, James B. 80186

Shepard, Jeremiah, 1648-1720. 62743, 80187-80189

Shepard, L. H. 9334

Shepard, S. E. 80196

Shepard, Samuel, 1739-1815. (78487), 80190-80193

Shepard, Samuel, 1772-1846. 80194-80195

Shepard, Sylvanus. 80197

Shepard, Thomas, 1605-1649. (921), 18475, 18476, (21090), 22146-22147, 22165, 33698, 56382, 56385, 62483, 74696, 78431, 80198-80262, note before 92797, 101330, note after 104653, 104846, 106052

Shepard, Thomas, 1635-1677. 80212-(80213), 80258, 80263, 95195

Shepard, Thomas, fl. 1683. 89525-89530

Shepard, Thomas, 1792-1879. 80264-80268

Shepard, W. A. 44324, (80269)

Shepard, Charles. 80270-(80271)

Shepard, Isaac F. 39902

Shepard, Thomas, 1605-1649. see Shepard, Thomas, 1605-1649.

Shepheard, Thomas, 1605-1649. see Shepard, Thomas, 1605-1649.

Sheperd, Charles. (80273)

Shepherd, Daniel. 80274-80275

Shepherd, E. 80276

Shepherd, Forrest. (57371), 80169, (80277)-80279

Shepherd, J. W. reporter 80280

Shepherd, Jesse. see also Rochester, N. Y. City Attorney. (72346), 72353

Shepherd, Job. (64069)-64070, 80281-80282

Shepherd, Nathaniel. 2624

Shepherd, Richard Heren. (63569)

Shepherd, Samuel. 80283, 100406

Shepherd, Thomas James. 80284

Shepherd, William. 80285-80288

Shepherd boy of Minnesota. 39202

Shepherd of the sheep. 20391

Shepherd Smith, the Universalist. 84737

Shepherd's wanderings. 14426

Shepley, David. (55757), 59537, 80289

Shepley, Ether, 1789-1877. (80290)

Shepley, Samuel R. 62294

Sheppard, -------. 34576

Sheppard, F. H. 80291

Sheppard. Furman, 1823- 50152, 80292-80293 see also Philadelphia. Court of Chancery. Auditor.

Sheppard, George, 1820- 80294-80295

Sheppard, Mrs. J. C. 80296

Sheppard, J. H. (80297)

Sheppard, J. S. 34576, 80324

Sheppard, John Hannibal, 1789-1873. (80298)-80323

Sheppard, Moses, 1771-1857. 35563, (45211A), 80327

Sheppard, W. 80328

Sheppard, W. P. 80329

Sheppard, William. 14426

Sheppard (J. S.) & Co. firm publishers 34576, 80324-80326

Sheppard's Indiana state gazetteer and shipper's guide. 34576, 80324

Sheppard's Mississippi state gazetteer and shippers' guide. 80325

Sheppard's shippers' guide to the south and west. 80326

Sherbrooke, Sir John Coape. 12935
Sherburne, John Henry. 36554, 80335, 105047
Sherburne, Moses. 49299
Sherer, John. 80339
Sheridan, James B. reporter 31599, 60425
Sheridan, M. V. 84774
Sheridan, Philip. (70984)
Sheridan, Philip Henry. 31164
Sheridan, Richard Brinsley Butler, 1751-1816.
    8137, 38281-38282, 77817, 80340-(80344)
Sheridan, Thomas. 80345-(80348)
Sheridan and Kotzebue. 8137, 80342
Sheridan's play of Pizarro. 80341
Sheridan's ride. 68183-68184, (68986)
Sheridan's tragic play of Pizarro. 80342
Sheridan's troopers on the borders. 37172
Sherley, Sir Anthony. 66686, 80349
Sherley, Sir Robert. 66686, 80349
Sherley, Sir Thomas. 80349
Sherlock. pseud. Layman's apology. see
    Southwick, Solomon.
Sherlock. pseud. Letter extra. see South-
    wick, Solomon.
Sherlock. pseud. Letters. see Southwick,
    Solomon.
Sherlock, Thomas, successively Bishop of
    Salisbury, and London, 1678-1761. 5861,
    11878, 40537, 80350-80353, 1st note
    after 100484
Sehrlock, W. (80354)
Sherlock's letter extra. 88650
Sherlock's letters to Thomas Herttell. 88651
Sherman, David. 40318, 80355-(80356)
Serman, Eleazer. (80357)
Sherman, Eleazer. defendant before ecclesias-
    tical council 80358
Sherman, F. T. 86094
Sherman, Henry, 1808-1879. 80359-80363
Sherman, Henry Beers. 80364-80365
Sherman, J., fl. 1853. 92466, 92497
Sherman, James. (46631)
Sherman, John, 1613-1685. 18476, 46696,
    56382, 56384, 62743, 80261
Sherman, John, 1772-1828. 80366-80371,
    96777, note after 96778, 98479, note
    after 100602, 102522, note after 105520
Sherman, John, 1823-1900. 34923, (73953),
    80372-80389
Sherman, John H. 80390, 6th note after
    96930A
Sherman, Josiah. 40318, 80391-80393
Sherman, Richard C. 80394
Sherman, Richard C. supposed author 53602
Sherman, Roger, 1721-1793. 52971, 62743,
    69397, 80395-80405, 102402
Sherman, S. N. 80407
Sherman, S. S. 80408
Sherman, Sylvester G. 21129, (80409)-80410
Sherman, Watts. plaintiff 64285
Sherman, William Tecumseh, 1820-1891.
    15430, 19515, 31164, 40611, 69870,
    80411, 80413-(80418), 80420
Sherman & Co. firm see Duncan, Sherman
    & Co. firm
Sherman & Smith. firm cartographers/engrs.
    83930 see also Stiles, Sherman &
    Smith. firm cartographers/engrs.
Sherman and his campaigns. 7096
Sherman Institute for the Encouragement of
    Industry and Education, New York.
    80421-80422
Sherman Institute for the Encouragement of
    Industry and Education. Constitution,
    with explanatory remarks. 80422
Sherman-Johnston, light-draught monitors.
    69870

Sherman vs. Hood. 80419
Sherman's campaign through the Carolinas.
    39446
Sherman's march through the south. 16229
Sherman's marine insurance. (80361)
Shermer, -------. plaintiff 96925
Shermer, Henry B. 80423
Shereff, Emily. 80552-80553
Sherrard, Robert A. 59177, 80424
Sherrill, Hunting. (80425)-(80427)
Shervington, William. 83980
Sherwin, J. K. illus. 83421
Sherwin, W. T. (80428)
Sherwood, Abiel, 1791-1879. 80429-80433
Sherwood, George W. (80434)
Sherwood, H. H. 80439
Sherwood, Harold. 80435
Sherwood, Henry. 80436-80438
Sherwood, J. Ely. 80440-(80441)
Sherwood, James Manning, 1814-1890. (33170),
    (80442), (82704), 89330
Sherwood, John D., 1818- 17759, 80443
Sherwood, Lorenzo. 19511, 29996, 57592,
    80444-80449
Sherwood, Reuben, 1789-1856. 80450-80454,
    82920
Sherwood, S. R. 80457
Sherwood, Samuel. 80455-80456
Sherwood, Stephen. (80442)
Sherwood Forest. 86926
Sherzer, William Hittell. 85072
Shettles, E. L. 89305
Shewen, William, 1631?-1685. 80458-80460
Shewing . . . the sole right people have to call
    and dismiss their officers. 360, 6254,
    11968, 3d note after 96741
Sheys, James B. (69154), 80461, 83665
Shield, --------, fl. 1787. (64087), 86905
Shields, Benjamin Glover, 1808- (80462)
Shields, Charles Woodruff, 1825- 80463-80465
Shields, Ebenezer J., 1778-1846. (80466)-80467
Shields, James, 1810-1879. 18882, 80468-
    (80470), 91531
Shiells, William. pseud. Voyage round the
    world. see Defoe, Daniel, 1659?-1731.
Shiels, Andrew. 80471
Shier, J. 80472-80474
Shiffer, W. H. 601
Shifts and contrivances available in wild coun-
    tries. 26641
Shillaber, Benjamin Penhallow, 1814-1890.
    80475-80482
Shilling song book. (80486)
Shilling song book. No. 2. (80486)
Shilling song book. No. 3. (80486)
Shillinglaw, John J. 80488
Shilling's worth of good sense and a shilling's
    worth of common sense. 30611
Shilling's worth of the United States of America.
    80487
Shillitoe, Thomas, 1754?-1836. 80489-80490
Shimeall, Richard Cunningham, 1803-1874.
    80492-80495, note after 90579
Shinkin ap Shone, ap Griffith, ap Gearard, ap
    Shiles, ap Shoseph, ap Lewis, ap Laurence,
    ap Richard, ap Thomas, ap Sheffre, ap
    Sheames, ap Taffie, ap Harie, all Shentle-
    man in Wales. pseud. Honest Welch-
    cobler. 32778
Shinkwin, T. 8348
Shinn, Asa, 1781-1853. ed. 85443
Shinn, John L. 80497
Shinn, William M. 80498
Shinn, William Norton, 1782-1871. 64591
Ship Archer and the caulkers' strike. 80499
Ship canal. 18897

Ship canal around the falls of Niagara. 80500
Ship canal between the Atlantic and Pacific
　Oceans. 80501
Ship canal from the Mississippi to Lake
　Michigan. 2071
Ship canal to connect Mississippi River and
　Lake Michigan. (80502)
Ship canals. 78884
Ship Essex sails for California. 80456
Ship-fever, so called. (13297)
Ship Island canal. (73263)
Ship Lady Gage being arrived from London.
　95994
Ship-Owners' Association of the State of New
　York. 80531
Ship-Owners' Association of the State of New
　York, constitution and by-laws. 80531
Ship-wreck. 63582, 100804
Shipherd, Jacob R. 80503
Shipherd, Zebulon R. 101974
Shipherd (Jacob R.) & Co. firm bankers
　88211
Shipley, Jonathan, successively Bishop of
　Llandaff, and St. Asaph, 1714-1788.
　15150, 80504-80527, note after 89181,
　89183
Shipley, Jonathan, successively Bishop of
　Llandaff, and St. Asaph, 1714-1788.
　supposed author 89194
Shipley, Thomas. 95922
Shipman, George E. 55746
Shipman, S. V. 80528
Shipman, Thomas L. 80529-80530
Shipmates, avast! Here's a pretty kettle
　o'fish!! 98425
Shipp, Bernard, 1813- (80532)-80534, 98745
Shippen, Edward, fl. 1704. 66737
Shippen, Edward, 1726-1806. defendant at
　impeachment (30039), 1st note after
　96927
Shippen, John. supposed author 92342
　Shippen papers. 2871
Shipper's guide; containing a complete list.
　61380, (80535)
Shippers' guide to the south and west. 80326
Shippey, Josiah. (80536)
Shipping interest. 34030
Shipping list and town register from 1835.
　(52508)
Ships, colonies, and commerce. 59411
Shipwreck. A sentimental and descriptive
　poem. 99418
Shipwreck and adventures of Captain Nathaniel
　Uring. 102204
Shipwreck and adventures of Monsieur Pierre
　Viaud. 21020, 99415
Shipwreck and sufferings of Mrs. Maria
　Snethen. 85434
Shipwreck. [By William Falconer.] 92225
Shipwreck; or, the adventures of M. P. Viaud.
　99416
Shipwrecks, adventures at home and abroad.
　(76949)
Shipwrecks and disasters at sea; narratives
　of the most remarkable wrecks. 80538
Shipwrecks and disasters at sea; or historical
　narratives. 80537, 92355
Shipwrecks of December, 1839. 2502, 80539
Shiras, Alexander. 80540
Shiras, Charles P. 80541
Shiriff, Charles. see Shirreff, Charles.
Shirley, John, 1648-1679. supposed author
　(67567)-67569
Shirley, Walter. 80543, 86583
Shirley, William, 1694-1771. (774), (14497),
　15345, 16023, (47546)-(47548), note after

(47740), 47741, 47742, (56129), 62694,
　80545-80551, note after 96403 see also
　Great Britain. Commissioners on the
　Limits of St. Lucia and Nova Scotia.
　Massachusetts (Colony) Governor, 1741-
　1749 (Shirley) Massachusetts (Colony)
　Governor, 1753-1756 (Shirley)
Shirley, William, 1693-1771. supposed author
　80544, 91854
Shirreff, Charles. 80542, 95676
Shirreff, Patrick. 80554
Shirtleff, Roswell. see Shurtleff, Roswell.
Shively, J. M. 80555
Shoberl, Frederick. 47411, 80556
Shocco Springs, N. C. Public Meeting, 1824.
　Committee. 98414
Shock to Shakerism. 13263
Shocking calamity! 80557
Shocks from the battery. 63917
Shoe and canoe. 5360
Shoebinders of New York. 54829
Shoemaker, Abraham. 53165, (60298), 84948
Shoemaker, R. M. 80559
Shoepac recollections. 104128
Shoepac recollections: a way-side glimpse of
　American life. 104128
Shones and the bones. 80560
Shooting and fishing in the rivers, prairies,
　and backwoods. 70336
Shooting Niagara: and after? 10935
Shopkeepers of Philadelphia, and Places
　Adjacent. petitioners 102196
Shoppe, Sigismund van. see Schoppe, Sigis-
　mund van.
Shore, Edward. 51752
Shore and deep sea fisheries of Nova Scotia.
　(38129)
Shores, A. 95820
Shores of Vespucci. 97430
Short, Ben T. 92676
Short, Bob. pseud. Olio. see Gilley, William
　B.
Short, Bob. pseud. Patriotic effusions. see
　Gilley, William B.
Short, Beunaventura Arturo. defendant 103966
Short, Charles W. 80564
Short, Charles Wilkins, 1794-1863. 80562-
　(80563)
Short, John T. (80565)-(80567)
Short, Matthew, d. 1731. 80568
Short, Richard. illus. 80569-80570
Short, Thomas, 1690?-1772. (80571)-80575
Short, Thomas, fl. 1779. 80576
Short abstract. 98444
Short abstract of the history of New-York.
　50933
Short abstract of the statute and civil law.
　(36187), 36188, 36190
Short account from, and description of the
　isthmus of Darien. 78232
Short account of a late short administration.
　97117
Short account of a late short administration.
　[By Edmund Burke.] 9299, 80577
Short account of a long travel. 20757
Short account of a north west voyage. 36202
Short account of Algiers and its several wars,
　etc. 765, 80578-80579
Short account of Algiers, containing a descrip-
　tion. 765, 80578
Short account of Ann Rogers. 36233
Short account of five camp-meetings. 96318
Short account of George Fox. 25362
Short account of God's dealings with the
　Reverend Mr. George Whitefield. (36054),
　103591

Short account of the proceedings of the camp meeting. 89143

Short account of the proceedings of the Traveling Missionary Society. 85852

Short account of the procession of the brethren to and from church. 84584

Short account of the proposed South Shore Railroad. 88208

Short account of the province of New England. 80590

Short account of the publisher's difficulties. 8769

Short account of the . . . putrid bilious yellow fever. 32541

Short account of the religious exercise and experience of Betty. 104520

Short account of the religious Society of Friends. 4683

Short account of the revolutionary war. (13318)

Short account of the rise and progress of the African Methodist Episcopal Church in America. 74248

Short account of the rise and progress of the recent popular movements. 10606

Short account of the sickenss and death, of the Rev. Mr. John Wesley. 94540

Short account of the slave trade. 50864

Short account of the Society for the Conversion and Religious Instruction and Education of the Negroe Slaves in the British West India Islands. 85882, 2d note after 102867

Short account of the solar system. 9228

Short account of the state of Mendon Third Parish. 47821

Short account of the town of Milton. 46265

Short account of the yellow fever. 32645

Short account of the yellow fever in Philadelphia. 31268

Short account of this extraordinary writer. 103125

Short account . . . with quotations from the writings. (4687)

Short address, delivered before the sufferers by the late fire. 58118

Short address to his parishioners. 74483

Short address to military gentlemen. 72869

Short address to people who are scrupulous about bearing arms. 22386

Short address to persons of all denominations. 103592

Short address to the aged union citizens of Maryland. 45360

Short address to the disinterested and unprejudiced citizens. 80591

Short address to the English colonies in North-America. 9729

Short address to the free people of colour. 95386

Short address to the government. 2638, 80592

Short address to the people of Pennsylvania. 9836-9837, (68568)-(68569), 82725

Short address to the people of Scotland. (80593)

Short address to the public. (80348)

Short advice to the counties of New-York. 53957, 80594

Short American tramp in the fall of 1864. 80595

Short and brief account of the shipwreck of Capt. Joshua Winslow. 104806

Short and briefe narration of the two navigations. 11144

Short and candid enquiry into the proofs of Christ's divinity. 103097

Short and comprehensive history of the United States. 42872

Short and easy guide to arithmetick. 80596

"Short and easy method" with a late writer. (80597)

Short and easie method with the deists. 12365, 40191-40194, 80598, 101194

Short and faithful account of the conduct of Great Britain. 1023

Short and faithful narrative, of the late remarkable revival. 5759

Short-and-fat, Sampson. pseud. Daw's doings. see Kettell, Samuel.

Short and friendly caution to the good people of England. 80599

Short and hasty essay in favour of dancing and musick. 80600

Short and impartial view of the manner and occasion of the Scots colony's coming away from Darien. 9753, (78233)

Short and necessary observations in the settlement of the African trade. (80601)

Short and plain essay on, the withered hand revived & restored. 46473

Short and plain essay to answer [the] enquiry, what must I do to be saved? 46354

Short and plain introduction to astronomy and geography. 89057

Short and plain narrative of the late work of God's spirit. (13596)

Short and plain relation of some transactions. 21669

Short and sincere declaration. 80602

Short and true account of a young youth. 80603

Short and true account of the importance and necessity of settling the African trade. 80604

Short and trve description of the commodities and discommodities of that countrey. 31739, 31740, 106052

Short animadversion on the difference now set upon between gin and rum. 80605

Short answer to a late letter in the New-England courant. 104243

Short answer to A. S. 91382

Short answer to a subtle treatise. 70082

Short answer to "A true exposition of the doctrine." 103090, 103098

Short answer to an elaborate pamphlet, entitled, The importance of the sugar plantations, &c. 80606

Short answer to some criticisms, which were exhibited under the signature of Aristides. 84642

Short answer to some criticisms. Which were exhibited under the signature of Aristides: containing, a reasonable vindication. 2d note after 96428

Short answer to the appendix to the catholic question. 103090, 103098

Short answers to reckless fabrications. 8864

Short apology for infants. (68558)

Short appeal from the decrees of King Caucus. (80607)

Short appeal to the people of Great-Britain. 80608-80609

Short appendix, consisting of English publications. 90021

Short appendix of the statistics of Canada West. 20717

Short appendix to the remarks on the Lyme dispute. 101216

Short bibliographical memoir. 2181

Short biographical memoir. 93995-93996

Short biographical notice of the author. 79615

Short history of a long travel from Babylon to Bethel. 80627-(80630)

Short history of a long travel, from Babylon to Bethel, the house of God. (80631)

Short history of Algiers, with a concise view. 766, 80632

Short history of Algiers, with the origin of the rupture. 766, 80632

Short history of Barbados. 3281, 3288-3289

Short history of infant baptism. 82494

Short history of late administrations. 80633

Short history of late ecclesiastical oppressions in New-England and Vermont. 32178, 80634, 2d note after 99205

Short history of New England. (46509)

Short history of opposition. (56490)

Short history of paper-money and banking. 28074

Short history of T. E. Sickels' connection. 62242

Short history of the administration. 80635

Short history of the African Union Meeting and School-House. (66365), 80636

Short history of the agrostis cornucipiae. (25683)

Short history of the Bohemian-Moravian Protestant Church. (28190)

Short history of the case of Ives vs. Hazard. 35314

Short history of the conduct of the present ministry. 80637-(80638)

Short history of the discoveries and conquests of Spain. 8122

Short history of the extraordinary outpouring of the spirit of God. (52324)

Short history of the last session of Parliament. (80639)

Short history of the late extraordinary outpouring of the spirit of God. (43605), (52324), 89893

Short history of the life of Joshua Comstock. 15077

Short history of the life of William Vans. 98562

Short history of the Methodists in the United States of America. 39765

Short history of the nature and consequence of excise laws. 10071, (80640)

Short history of the opposition during the last session of Parliament. 27283, 43633, 68743, 80708, 104592

Short history of the persecution of Christians. 72052

Short history of the persecution of John Bamber. (80641)

Short history of the Peter Washingtonians. 30662, note after 101993

Short history of the poor black slaves who are employed in cultivating sugar. 51733

Short history of the public debt of Maryland. 45361

Short history of the rise, reign, and ruine of the familists. 103223

Short history of the treatment that Dr. Samuel Stearns hath met with. 90946, 90966

Short history of the war in America. 26443

Short history of the Westminister Forum. 103038

Short history of the yellow fever. 62241

Short hymns suited to the subjects. 79300

Short Indian catechism. (82267)

Short inquiry into its probable effects. 4988A

Short inquiry into the commercial policy of the United States. 32724, 34803, 80642

Short inquiry into the religious complaints of our American colonies. 36297

Short introduction to grammar. 80643-(80644)

Short introduction to Latin grammar. 80645-80651

Short introduction to Latin grammar, for the use of the University. 60758

Short introduction to the Latin tongue: for the use of the lower forms in the Latin schools. 12391, 68159, 80652-80662

Short introduction to the primitive faith. (80663)

Short introduction to the study of ethics. 13216

Short introduction to the study of the sciences. (36292)

Short journal of the labours and travels. 4451

Short journey in the West Indies. 80664, 1st note after 102866

Short letter to the Councils of Philadelphia. 5491

Short lives of the most interesting persons. 58957

Short meditations, fit for children. 101266

Short memoir. (35323)

Short memoir of Andrew Underhill. 97732

Short memoir of Courtland J. Fell. (71006)

Short memoir of her [i. e. Jane Bettle.] 5092

Short memoir of his [i. e. Jabez Kimball's] life. 64134

Short memoir of his [i. e. Samuel Emlin's] life. 22514

Short memoir of Lydia Ann Barclay. (32371)

Short memoir of Phebe Griffen. 28810

Short memoir of the author [i. e. John M. Mason.] 45463

Short memoir of the author [i. e. Thomas Romney Robinson.] 72197

Short memoirs of Thomas Coke. 93944

Short memorial of the life and death of a fellow labourer. 13025

Short method with the Unitarian nobility. 102082

Short missionary discourses. 63991

Short narrative and justification of the proceedings. 80665

Short narrative and military experience of Corp. G. A'Lord. 960

Short narrative of a late outrage committed. 46603-(46604)

Short narrative of Benjamin Crompton Chisley. 12844

Short narrative of several prodigies. 46602

Short narrative of the claim, title, and right. 864

Short narrative of the extraordinary work at Cambuslang. 80667

Short narrative of the extraordinary work at Cambuslang in Scotland. (80666)

Short narrative of the horrid massacre in Boston. 6739-6741, 80668-80673, 101479

Short narrative of the life and conversion of Rev. G. A. Lord. 42025

Short narrative of the life and sufferings of Matthew Bunn. (9185)

Short narrative of the life of Jack Saunders. 77183

Short narrative of the . . . life of Jacob Payne. 59281

Short narrative of the main passages of his earthly pilgrimage. 80993, note after 98499

Short narrative of the massacre in Boston. 80670

Short narrative of the mischief done by the French and Indian enemy. 20613

Short narrative of the second voyage of the Prince Albert. 37443

Short narrative of the state and progress of such errors. 101446

Short narrative of the sufferings, travel, present feelings and situation of M. Smith. 83624

Short notes on the Dred Scott case. 8244

Short notes on the winds of the Pacific. 73416

Short notice of Ariel. 80674

Short notices, by Professor Dickie. 34758

Short observations on slavery. 4688, 80675

Short patent sermons. 20760

Short, plain, comprehensive, practical Latin grammar. (73362)

Short—plain discourse. 82762

Short plan of Presbyterian church-government. 103322

Short poem. 91585

Short poem on the death of that great and good man. 103527

Short poem, on the death of the Rev'd. Mr. George Whitefield. 103650

Short poem spoken at the same time. (31889)

Short poem, with notes. 74747

Short poem, written by himself. 95489

Short postscript. (13597)

Short practical history of fragments collected. 31892

Short preface. 86045

Short reading lessons in the Ojibway language. 20679

Short reasons against the abolition of the slave trade. 80676

Short rejoinder. 67716

Short rejoinder to the Reverend Mr. Ramsay's reply. 96056

Short relation concerning a dream. 92710

Short relation, concerning a dream, which the author had on September 18, 1769. 80677

Short relation concerning the life and death of that man of God. 25171, 81375

Short relation of the papists late rebellion. 100546-100547

Short relation of the tryal, sentence, and execution, of William Leddra. 5629

Short remark on a letter. 86755

Short remarks relating to the African trade. 80678

Short remonstrance, in behalf of the public. 93880

Short reply to a pamphlet published at Philadelphia. 80679

Short reply to Mr. Stephen Hopkins's vindication. 32968, 1st note after 97146

Short reply to Mr. Whitefield's letter. 80680, 103560

Short reply to some of the layman's remarks. 47276, 97107

Short reply to the speech of Earl Aberdeen. 50859

Short representation of facts and circumstances. 80681-80682

Short representation of the calamitous state. (4670)

Short review of his former letters. 69501, 90377

Short review of leading and operating causes. 21640, 80683, 2d note after 102866

Short review of the British affairs. 80700, 101147, 101167

Short review of the history, government, constitution, fishery and agriculture of Newfoundland. 50859

Short review of the late proceedings at New-Orleans. 80684-80685

Short review of the political state of Great-Britain. 60819, 80686-80689

Short review of the reports of the African Institution. 46857, 95656

Short review of the slvae trade and slavery. 80690

Short scriptural catechism . . . by Cotton Mather. 46214

Short scripture catechism. 73806

Short sermon. 24700

Short sermon to the Calvinistic Baptists in Massachusetts. (82499)

Short sermons for idler readers. 19585

Short sermons to newsboys. 7158

Short sketch of a democratical form of government. 42945

Short sketch of families descended from the nobility or gentry of Europe. 83634

Short sketch of General Washington's life and character. 103903

Short sketch of his [i. e. William Clutter's] life. 96852

Short sketch of his [i. e. Effingham Warner's] life and character. 101434

Short sketch of his [i. e. Henri Gregoire's] writings, &c. 28724

Short sketch of the biography of General George Clinton. 430

Short sketch of the biography of Gen. George Clinton, and several essays. 13741

Short sketch of the evidence for the abolition of the slave trade. (17335), 80691-80692, 1st note after 102813

Short sketch of the history and conditions of Mexico. 69561, 71957

Short sketch of the history of Kingston. 20905

Short sketch of the life of Elijah Shaw. (79904)-79905

Short sketch of the life of Mr. Lent Munson. (28881)

Short sketch of the life of our dear friend, John Horn. 21872

Short sketch of the modern customs of mankind. 101371

Short sketch of the principal events of his [i. e. William Henry Harrison's] life. 92187

Short sketch of the province of Upper Canada. 6889

Short sketch on his [i. e. Albert Barnes'] character and last sickness. 8883

Short sketch on the government of God. 82776

Short sketches and family records of the early settlers of West Simsbury. 8433

Short specimen of the proceedings of the Baptist Church, and Council. 85542

Short state of the countries and trade of North America. 33552

Short state of the proceedings of the proprietors. (53236), (80693)

Short state of the progress of the French trade and navigation. 64568

Short statement of facts in reply to the attacks. 55294

Short statement of facts relating to the history. 67762

Short statement of the Earl of Stirling's case. 91841A

Short statement of the facts connected with the recent "breach." 20577

Short statement of the proceedings at Concord, N. H. (15145), 15156, (52825), note after (52943)

Short stories. 92428

Short stories and reminiscences of the last fifty years. 80694

Short stories for leisure moments. 86283

Short stories from the lives of remarkable women. 80695

Short story of the rise, reign, and ruin of the Antinomians. 104848

Short story of the rise, reign, and ruin of the Antinomians, Familists, and Libertines that infected the churches of New-England. 104849

Short summary and declaration of faith. 15157

Short summary and declaration of faith, of the First Baptist Church in Springfield. 89861

Short supply or amendment to the propositions. (39504)

Short system of book-keeping. 72087

Short testimony to the efficacy and sufficency of the teachings. 78294, (78296)

Short topographical description of His Majesty's province of Upper Canada. 85205

Short tract concerning the doctrine of "nullum tempus occurrit regi." 79832

Short tracts upon such subjects as appeared necessary. (5696)

Short treatise: containing observations. 106200

Short treatise, in favour of the Baptists. 104716

Short treatise of church discipline. 61497

Short treatise of magneticall bodies and motions. 71297

Short treatise, of the diseases most incident to seamen. 93166

Short treatise on a subject of greater importance to the people. 82955

Short treatise on dialling. 105574

Short treatise on gauging. 105474

Short treatise on military honors. 102230

Short treatise on the application of steam. 74127-74129

Short treatise on the causes and prevention of crime. 21238, 3d note after 95517

Short treatise on the deviation of the mariner's compass. 73375

Short treatise on the fulfillment of the prophecy. 91032

Short treatise on the milk-weed, or silk-weed. (38011)

Short treatise on the second appearing of Christ. (23152)

Short trip to America. 105969

Short trip to Rome. 103645

Short view. [By Daniel Perry.] 28884

Short view of New-Englands present government. 39640

Short view of our glorious Redeemer on His throne. 46510

Short view of our great Lord-Redeemer. 46336

Short view of Spanish America. 58180, 66627

Short view of the administrations in the government. 31310

Short view of the ancient and modern state of Great Britain. 8071

Short view of the dispute. 80696

Short view of the encorachments of France in America. 80697

Short view of the evidence, relative to that subject. 81811

Short view of the history of the colony. 46921

Short view of the history of the colony of Massachusetts' Bay, with respect to their original charter and constitution. (46920)

Short view of the history of the New England colonies. 46922

Short view of the life and character of Lieutenant-General Willets. 7014

Short view of the Lord High Admiral's jurisdiction. 80698

Short view of the political life and transaction of a late Right Honourable commoner. 80699

Short view of the present state of the eastern townships. 91661

Short view of the several nations of the world. 75823-75825

Short view of the state of affairs. (70269), 80700, 86751, 101147, 101167

Short vindication and explanation of part of a late mysterious printed sheet. 60693

Short vindication of Phil. Scot's defence of the Scots abdicating Darien. 18571, (32340), note after 72819, 78209-78210, 78211-78213, 78234

Short vindication of the conduct of the referees. 26630A

Short vindication of the French treaty. 80701, 99585

Short vindication of the religious society called Quakers. (80702)

Short vindication of the religious society of the people called Quakers. 80703

Short vocabulary in the language of the Seneca nation. 80704

Short way to know the world, being a new familiar method. (80705)

Short way to know the world; or, the rudiments of geography. (29404)

Short word of advice to all saints and sinners. 103965

Short word or two from Betty. 57344, 95797

"Short" yarn. (28574)

Shorte and briefe narration of the nauigation caused to be made. 11144, 80706

Shorte and briefe narration of the two nauigations. 11144, 80706

Shorter, Eli Sims, 1823-1879. 80707

Shorter answer to the short history of the opposition. 80708

Shorter catechism. 15445, (80719), 80722

Shorter catechism, agreed upon by the Assembly of Divines at Westminister. 80712, 80715, 80723

Shorter catechism, agreed upon by the Reverend Assembly of Divines at Westminister. 80718, (80721), 80725

Shorter catechism, and many things proper for children. note after 65546

Shorter catechism, by the Assembly of Divines. 95407

Shorter catechism composed by the Reverend Assembly of Divines. (80709), 80711, 80714

Shorter catechism composed by the Reverend Assembly of Divines at Westminister. 80710

Shorter catechism of the Assembly of Divines, with the proofs at large. (80713)

Shorter catechism of the Reverend Assembly of Divines. 80717

Shorter catechism of the Reverend Assembly of Divines at Westminister. 80720

Shorter catechism of the Westminister Assembly of Divines. 80728

Shorter catechism . . . with proofs. 80727

Shorter catechism . . . with scripture proofs. 80716, 80724, 80726

Shorter confession of faith, with scripture proofs. 99164

Shorter confession of faith, with scripture proofs, and a covenant. 99172

Shorter contributions to general geology. 83723

Shorter [preface] added by some of the ministers of Boston. 21939
Shortest and best route from Lake Ontario to the coal mines. 88318
Shortest route to California illustrated. 81358
Shortest route to California, via Vera Cruz and Acapulco. 48571
Shortfellow, Harry Wandsworth. pseud. Song of Drop O'Wather. see Clarke, Mary Cowden.
Shortfield, Luke. pseud. Life in the far west. see Jones, John Beauchamp, 1810-1877.
Shortfield, Luke. pseud. Western merchant. see Jones, John Beauchamp, 1810-1877.
Shortfield, Luke. pseud. Wild western scenes. see Jones, John Beauchamp, 1810-1877.
Shortness and afflictions of human life. 91125
Shortness and uncertainty of life. 104736
Shortness of time, a motive to moderation. 83450
Shortt, William Tayler Peter, b. 1801? 23964, 80733-80734
Shoshonee Valley; a romance. (24795), 80735
Shots from the monitor. 28762
Shotwell, Edmund. defendant 28120, 80736, 96938
Shotwell, Elizabeth. defendant (31332)
Shotwell, R. A. 54888
Shotwell, Thomas L. complainant (31332), 80737-80738, 105025-105026
Shotwell, Thomas L. defendant 19205, 23321, (31332), 88244
Should Republicans vote for James M. Ashley? 31811
Should the interest on the national debt be forced? 29929
Should the nullifiers succeed in their views of separation. 56315, 96073
Shoulder straps. 50630
Should straps for Negroes! (81727)
Shourds, Thomas. (80739)
Show your colors. Halt! 48973, 86297
Shower, John. 80740-80742
Shower, John. supposed author 86576
Showing the manner in which they do things. (40850)
Showman. 61264
Showman's rail-road guide. 80743
Shrady, George F. ed. 47323
Shrady, John. ed. 47324
Shreve, Charles J. 80744
Shreve, T. H. 102993
Shreveport, La. Centenary College of Louisiana. 11680, 42202
Shreveport, La. Charity Hospital. see Louisiana. Charity Hospital, Shreveport.
Shreveport & Southwestern Rail Road Company. see Southwestern and Rio Grande Railway Company.
Shrewsbury, Mass. Congregational Church. 80746
Shrewsbury, Mass. School Committee. 80746
Shrewsbury, N. J. Polytechnic Institute. see Polytechnic Institute, Shrewsbury, N. J.
Shrigley, Nathaniel. 80748
Shrimpton, Charles. 80749-80751
Shrines and sepulchres of the Old and New World. 43696
Shriver, James. 80753
Shuck, Oscar T. 80754-(80755)
Shuey, D. B. 80756
Shufeldt, George A. 80757
Shufeldt, Robert Wilson, 1822- 80758-80759
Shullsburg, Wisc. Primitive Methodist Western Annual Conference, 20th, 1864. see Primitive Methodist Church, Western

Annual Conference. 20th, Shullsburg, Wisc., 1864.
Shultz, Benjamin. 80760-80761
Shultz, Theodore, 1770-1850. 80762
Shulze, John Andrew, 1775-1852. (59996), note just before 60250, (60509) see also Pennsylvania. Governor, 1823-1829 (Shulze)
Shuman, B. 80763
Shumard, Benjamin Franklin. 80764-80765
Shumard, G. C. 68476
Shumway, D. B. ed. (59707), 102227
Shumway, Nehemiah. 80766
Shunammite. 80767
Shunk, Francis Rawn, 1788-1848. (59883), 60156, 60435, 80768 see also Pennsylvania. Governor, 1845-1848 (Shunk)
Shurtleff, J. B. 80770-80772
Shurtleff, James. 80769, 93363
Shurtleff, Nathaniel Brandstreet, 1810-1874. 34338, (45545), 45966, 53388, 63488, (66429), 80773-80779 see also Boston. Mayor, 1868-1870 (Shurtleff)
Shurtleff, Roswell. 80789-80792
Shurtleff, William, 1689-1747. 80793-(80798)
Shurtleff College, Alton, Ill. 80799
Shute, Daniel, 1722-1802. 26785, (80800)-80803
Shute, James M. 80804-80805
Shute, Samuel, 1653-1742. (15436), 34654, 80806, 80808 see also Massachusetts (Colony) Governor, 1716-1723 (Shute)
Shute, Samuel, 1653-1742. petitioner (80807) see also Massachusetts (Colony) Governor, 1716-1723 (Shute) petitioner
Shuttlesworth, Samuel. 80809
Shuttleworth, R. J. 80810
Shyrock, John. 101542
Si ecsiste el origen de la historia primitiva de Mexico en los monumentos egipcios. 48436
Si ecsiste el origen de la historia primitive de Mexico. 39078
Sia storia naturale. 27382
Sibbald, George. (80814)
Sibbard, Charles F. 80813
Sibbs, --------. supposed author 32847
Sibellius, C. (56742), (80815)
Siberie orientale et l'Amerique Russee. 74748
Sibiel, Alexander, 1709-1791. 80816-(80817)
Sibire, Antoine, b. 1757. 80818
Sibley, Henry Hastings, 1811-1891. 33150, 80919-80920, (80922), 80923 see also Minnesota. Governor, 1858-1860 (Sibley)
Sibley, Henry Hastings, 1811-1891. incorrectly supposed author 80821
Sibley, James. 80828
Sibley, John. 80824
Sibley, John Langdon, 1804-1885. 21247, 30730, 40824-40826, 78691, 80825-80828
Sibley, Solomon, 1769-1846. 80829
Sibleys, according to the records hunted up. 80828
Sibly, Job. reporter 77279-77280, 77283-77284, 77286-77287
Sibouette, ------ de. (47547)-(47548)
Sibs, Richard. 65369
Sibyllae Americanae Genethliacum Ludovico XVII. 80830
Sic in se sua per vestigia volvitur annua. Virg. 1678. 62743
Sicard, Felix. 80831
Sicardo, Jose. 80832-80833, 80835
Sicardo, Jose. petitioner 80834
Sicardo, Juan Bautista. 80836

Sicco, Seraphino. 20581
Sichem, ------ Van. see Van Sichem, ---------.
Sicilia, Mariano Jose. tr. (12261)
Sicilia y Montoya, Isidro. (29081), 80837-80838
Sicilius. pseud. Letters of Sicilius. 27067
Sicily. Sovereigns, etc., 1468-1516 (Fernando V) 39893 see also Fernando V, King of Spain, 1452-1516.
Sick woman. 31218
Sickels, T. E. 62242, 80839
Sickles, A. W. 80840
Sickles, Daniel Edgar, 1825-1914. 36136, 40611, 80841-80849, 87394 see also U. S. Army. Second Military District. Commander.
Sickles, Daniel Edgar, 1825-1914. defendant 80849
Sickness and mortality during the first year of the war. 80850
Sico de San Miguel, Phelipe, Bp. 59345 see also Segovia (Diocese) Bishop (Sico de San Miguel)
Siculus, Diodorus. pseud. see Diodorus Siculus. pseud.
Siddons, J. H. pseud. Union volunteer's hand-book. see Stocqueler, Joachim Haywood.
Siddons, Leonora. 80851
Side-glances at Harvard class-day. 20506
Side show of the southern side of the war. 5384, (82394)
Side splitting comic almanac. 93075
Siden, Thomas. pseud. History of the Sevarites. see Vairasse d'Allais, Denis.
Siderial messenger. (80852)
Sidi Hamet. 71397
Sidney. pseud. Appeal to Americans. see Webster, Noah, 1758-1843. supposed author
Sidney. pseud. Political papers. see Yates, Abraham, 1724-1796.
Sidney. pseud. Sidney's letters to William E. Channing. see Whitaker, Daniel Kimball.
Sidney, Algernon. pseud. Address to the people of New-England. see Granger, Gideon. and Leigh, Benjamin Watkins. incorrectly supposed author
Sidney, Algernon. pseud. Administration and the opposition. see Hale, Salma.
Sidney, Algernon. pseud. Principles and men. see Richmond, William E.
Sidney, Algernon. pseud. Vindication of the measures. see Granger, Gideon.
Sidney, Edward William. pseud. Partisan leader. see Tucker, Nathaniel Beverley.
Sidney, Henry. (80857)
Sidney, J. C. (80858)
Sidney, John. ed. (80862)
Sidney, Joseph. 80859
Sidney, Robert Y. 80860
Sidney, Samuel. 80861-(80862)
Sidney Daney, ------. 80863
Sidney & Adams. firm 61650
Sidney's emigrant's journal. (80862)
Sidney's letters to William E. Channing. 80853, 1st note after 95112, note after 103316
Sidons, C. pseud. Vereinigten Staten von Nordamerika. see Postl, Carl, 1793-1864.
Sidste Franklin-Expedition med "Fox." 61224
Sidste Mohicaner. 16458
Sieben Monate in den Rebellen-Staaten. 77535
VII. Theil America. (8784)

Siebende Schiffahrt in dans Goldreich Konigreich Guineam. 33661
Siebenjahriger Aufenthalt. 52062
Siebenzehende Schiffart. 33670, 89452
Siebert, John. 14894
Siebold, Philipp Franz von, 1796-1866. 47476, 49982, (58551), 80864
Shiebzehn grossen Zeichnungen in Steindruck. 71447
Siecle. 14935, 14938, 93411
Sieg, R. J. 80865
Siege and defence of Fort Stanwix. 54476
Siege de Quebec, en 1759. Copie d'apres un manuscrit. (80866)
Siege de Quebec en 1759 [par Jean Claude Panet.] 67024
Siege du Fort S. Philippe. 27650, (63966), 68421
Siege of Algiers. 83032
Siege of Babylon. 80867
Siege of Baltimore. 97705
Siege of Baltimore, and the battle of La Tranche. 97706
Siege of Belgrade. 92174D, 92177, 92177B
Siege of Charleston, by the British fleet and army. (12089), (33152)
Siege of Charleston; its history and progress. 48679
Siege of Chepacket. A poem. 12431, (80868)
Siege of Cuzco. 87203
Siege of Detroit. 43613
Siege of Mexico, a melo-drama. 80869
Siege of New Orleans. (13845)
Siege of Quebec. 80870
Siege of Quebec. An historical tragedy. 14109
Siege of Quebec, and conquest of Canada. (80871)
Siege of Quebec on 31st December, 1775. 80872
Siege of Richmond. 16279
Siege of Savannah, by the combined American and French forces. 33153, 80873
Siege of Savannah in December, 1864, and the Confederate operations in Georgia and South Carolina during Sherman's march. 36871, 80875
Siege of Savannah in December, 1864, and the Confederate operations in Georgia and the third military district of South Carolina. 36871, 80875
Siege of Savannah, in 1779. 36481, 80874
Siege of Spoleto. 42964
Siege of the Penobscot by the rebels. 9925
Siegel, A. L. 80876
Siegel, C. W. E. 80877
Sieges. (34773)
Siegvolck, Georg Paul. 80878-(80879), 104735
Siendo tan notorio. 98803
Sienitic granite, of Staten Island. 90791
Sierra, Jose de. 80880
Sierra, Justo. (80881)-80882, 80883-80884, 91301, 106281
Sierra Alta, Miguel de Salcedo y. see Salcedo y Sierra Alta, Miguel de.
Sierra, Justo. (80881)-80882, 80883-80884, 91301, 106281
Sierra y Rosso, Ignacio. 80889-80895
Sierra Leone, Bishop of. see Bowen, John Bishop of Sierra Leone, 1815-1859.
Sierra Leone. British Commissioner. see Great Britain. Consulate. Freetown, Sierra Leone.
Sierra Leone Company. 95656
Sierra Leone Company. petitioners 80887
Sierra Leone Company. Court of Directors. 80885-80886, 93372-93377
Sierra magazine. 80888

Sierragorda, ------, Conde de. 34185, (48815),
(76183) see also Michoacan
(Archdiocese) Comisionados para el
Funeral y Exequias del Antonio de San
Miguel Iglesias.
Siervos de Maria Santisima de los Dolores,
Mexico City. see Tercer Orden de los
Siervos de Maria Santisima de los
Dolores, Mexico (City)
Sierte angeles del apocalypsis en siete ser-
mones. 75621
Sieur de Beaulieu Hues o'Neil. pseud. tr.
see Baillet, Adrien, 1649-1706. tr.
Sieur Pontis's voyage to America. (17278)
Sieyes, Em. 101723 see also France.
Assemblee Nationale. Presidente.
Sifferath, N. L. 80896
Sigala, Geronimo Morales. 80897-80898
Sigaud, J.-F.-X. (80899)
Sigenische Katechismus. (80900)
Sigfrid, Isaac. 80901
Sighelmus, -------. 66686
Sights and notes. 80902
Sights and secrets of the national capital.
22320
Sights and sounds. 89424-89424A
Sights and wonders in New York. 80903
Sights in the gold region and scenes by the
way. 36329-36329
Sigismondo, Baron of Herberstein Neiperg &
Guttenhag. see Herberstein, Sigmund,
Freiherr von, 1486-1566.
Sigismund Ruestig, ou le naufrage du Pacifique.
44702
Siglio (Buenos Aires) 65549
Siglo (San Salvador) 80904
Siglo diez y nueve. (80905)
Siglo 18. 94352
Siglo XIX. 57719, 77138
Siglo 17. 94352
Siglo do oro y silvas de erple. 2863, 2d note
after 98300
Sigma. pseud. Ballad of the abolition blunder-
buss. see Sargent, Lucius Manlius.
Sigma Phi Fraternity. 80906
Sign-board. pseud. [Introduction.] 92282
Sign from heaven being a remarkable pheno-
menon. 101083
Signal and most gracious presence of God.
95165
Signal book for Boston harbor. 33500, 83020
Signal fires on the trail of the pathfinder.
80909
Signal, proposing a society. 105273
Signal work of the Holy Spirit in the United
States. 21663
Signatus. 46511
Signe el tejedor y so compadre. 94598
Signers of the Memorial to Congress, New
York, Feb. 11, 1834. Union Committee.
see Union Committee, New York, 1834.
Significance of the struggle between liberty and
slavery in America. 26060
Signs of apostacy lamented. 6792, 80910
Signs of our national atheism. 31262
Signs of the moral age. 57084
Signs of the times! A great debate! 85122,
85124
Signs of the times: a series of discourses.
18212
"Signs of the times." A sermon, before the
Foreign Missionary Society. (45438)
Signs of the times. A sermon, . . . before the
Society for Propagating the Gospel.
50951

Signs of the times. A sermon, delivered be-
fore the Pastoral Association. 14137
Signs of the times. A sermon delivered in
Brookfield. 85408
Signs of the times. A sermon . . . in Holles.
82468
Signs of the times; a sermon, . . . in Rochester.
58706
Signs of the times. A sermon, . . . in the
. . . Theological Seminary. (64233)
Signs of the times. A sermon . . . November
26, 1837. 42032
Signs of the times: a sermon occasioned by the
recent election. (75850)
Signs of the times. A sermon preached . . .
March 6, 1836. 66793
Signs of the times: a warning voice. 32749
Signs of the times. Addressed to the British
legislators. (71918)
Signs of the times. By G. Manignault. 44295
Signs of the times. [By Robert Possac Rogers.]
(72731)
Signs of the times, comprised in ten lectures.
2032
Signs of the times: comprising a history of the
spirit-rappers. (14203)
Signs of the times consider'd. 80911
Signs of the times favorable to peace. 44095
Signs of the times, illustrated and improved.
9098
Signs of the times, or a voice from Babylon.
13442
Signs of the times; or, reflections on nullifica-
tion. 87949
Signs of the times, or the moral meaning of
our present commercial difficulties. 4755
Signs of the times: . . . remarks . . . relative
to the remarkable phenomenon. 26754
"Signs of the times." Sermon for the General
Theological Seminary. 43679
Signs of the times. South Carolina toasts.
10889
ΦΙΛΟΜΑΘΗΣ. pseud. Letter to a cer-
tain gentleman, &c. see Robie, Thomas,
1689-1729.
Sigourney, A. M, 80918
Sigourney, Charles. 96034, 102001 see also
Trinity College, Hartford, Conn. Secre-
tary.
Sigourney, Henry H. W. 80912
Sigourney, Lydia (Huntley) 1791-1865. 13630,
44455, 69348, (69359), (69360), 3d note
after 69447, 79003, 80913-80967, 106207
Sigourney, Lydia (Huntley) 1791-1865.
supposed author 58021, note after (63501)
Sigsby, -------. 51474, 80968
Siguenza, ------- Gongora y. see Siguenza y
Gongora, Carlos de, 1645-1700.
Siguenza, Gabriel. 80969
Siguenza, Jose. (80970)
Siguenza y Gongora, Carlos de, 1645-1700.
27787, 80969, 80971-80987, 1st note after
106302
Sigur, -------, Conte di. 15017-15018, note
after 92196
Sijpesteyn, C. A. van. 80988-80992
Sikes, George. 80993, note after 98499
Sikes, William Wirt, 1836-1883. 80994-80995
S'il existe des sources de l'histoire primitive?
7440
Silabario de lengua Maya. 74519
Silas Mariner, the weaver of Raveloe. 40774,
51298
Silas Standfast. pseud. see Hillard, G.S.
Silas Wood's sketch of the town of Huntington,
L. I. 105071

SILBERMANN

Silbermann, J. T. 80996
Silent dead, or roll of honor. 37822, 80997
Silent influence of the Bible. 83345
Silentiarius. 46512
Silabario de la lengua Mexicana. 71622
Siles, Francisco, d. 1670. 80998-81000
Siles, Francisco de, fl. 1757. 72248
Silex. pseud. Letters on banks and banking. 81002
Silhouette, ------- de. (774), 16023, (47546)-(47547), note after (47740), 47741-47742, (56129), 69463, note after 96403 see also France. Commissaires sur les Limites de St. Lucie et de l'Acadie.
Silibario de idioma Mexicana. 26373
Silibario, del uso de etras y raiz de plabras. 74604
Siliceo, C. Manuel. (44966), 48543, 81005-81006, 81464-81465 see also Mexico. Secretaria de Fomento.
Siliceo, Ignacio Nunez. 81003
Siliceo, J. M. 81004
Siljestrom, O. A. (81007)
Silk culture in the United States. 81011
Silk culturist. (21542)
Silk culturist and farmer's manual. (81012)
Silk-grower and farmer's manual. 81013
Silk Growers and Silk Manufacturers National Convention, New York, 1843. see National Convention of Silk Growers and Silk Manufacturers, New York, 1843.
Silk manual. 24220
Silk question settled. 81014
Sill, E. N. 94271
Sill, Edward Rowland, 1841-1887. (81015)-(81017)
Sill, George S. 81018
Sill, Henry A. 81019
Sill, Thomas H. 81020
Sillem, ----------. defendant 34419
Sillery, Stephanie Felicite Brulart de, Comtesse de Genlis, 1746-1830. 26952, (81024)-81027
Sillibeer, J. 80483-80485
Silliman, Anna. 81028
Silliman, Augustus Ely, 1807-1884. 81029
Silliman, Benjamin, 1779-1864. 507-508, 1120, 14535, 18719, 24465, 35402, 44416, 62509, (69758), (71302), 81030-81048, 82810, 89199, 102319, 105796, 105800, 105836, 105842 see also Yale University. Inspector.
Silliman, Benjamin, 1816-1885. 1120, 1000, 12359, (14686), 70242, 81023-81034, (81049)-81066, 82998, 83003, 105792-105793
Silliman, Benjamin Douglas, 1805- 8291, 81067-81068
Silliman, Robert D. plaintiff 81069
Silloway, Thomas W. 81070
Siloam Lodge, no. 2, Boston. see Odd Fellows, Independent Order of. Massachusetts. Siloam Lodge, no. 2, Boston.
Silsbee, N. Jr. 81072 see also Salem, Mass. Mayor, 1850-1851 (Silsbee)
Silsbee, S. 81073-81074
Silurische Fauna des Westlichen Tennessee. 72592
Silva, -------- Vieira da. see Vieira da Silva, --------.
Silva, A. de Moraes da. see Moraes da Silva, A. de.
Silva, Antonio Carlos Ribeiro de Andrada Machado e. see Ribeiro de Andrada Machado e Silva, Antonio Carlos.
Silva, Antonio da. 81075-81076

Silva, Antonio Joaquim da. defendant 97697
Silva, Antonio Jose Caetano da. see Caetano da Silva, Antonio Jose, 1817-1865.
Silva, Antonio Luiz do Amaral e. see Amaral e Silva, Antonio Luiz do.
Silva, Antonio Telles da. 81078
Silva, Carlos Bento da, 1812- 81079
Silva, Domingos de Araujo e. see Araujo e Silva, Domingos de.
Silva, Felipe Narciso. 81080
Silva, Fernando de Alencastro Marona y. see Alencastro Marona y Silva, Fernando de, Marques de Valdafuentes.
Silva, Francisco Gomez da, 1791-1852. 81081
Silva, Galdino Augusto Nactividade e. see Nactividade e Silva, Galdino Augusto.
Silva, Galdino Augusto da Natividade. see Natividade Silva, Galdino Augusto de.
Silva, Henrique de Souza de Tavares da. see Souza de Tavares da Silva, Henrique de, Conde de Miranda.
Silva, I. F. da. see Silva, Innocencio Francisco da, 1810-
Silva, Ignacio Accioli de Cerquiera e. see Cerquiera e Silva, Ignacio Accioli de, 1808-1865.
Silva, Innocencio Francisco da, 1810- (81083), 98650
Silva, Joao Joaquim da. 81084
Silva, Joaquim Caetano da. (81085)-81086
Silva, Joaquim Norberto de Souza. see Souza Silva, Joaquim Norberto de, 1820-1891.
Silva, Joaquin Maria, d. 1807. 81087
Silva, Jose Antonio de Cerqueira e. see Cerqueira e Silva, Jose Antonio de.
Silva, Jose Bonifacio de Andrada e. see Andrada e Silva, Jose Bonifacio de.
Silva, Jose de Seabra da. 81088-81090
Silva, Jose Maria de Andrade e. see Andrade e Silva, Jose Maria de.
Silva, Jose Manuel Pereira da. see Pereira da Silva, Jose Manuel, 1819-1898.
Silva, Josino do Nascimento. 81091-81094
Silva, Juan de. 81095
Silva, Luis Ferreira de Araujo e. see Araujo e Silva, Luis Ferreira de.
Silva, Luiz Antonio Vieira da. 81096
Silva, Manoel de Nascimento Castro a. see Castro a Silva, Manoel de Nascimento.
Silva, Manuel Alves da, 1793- 81097
Silva, Miguel Antonio da. (81098)
Silva, Silvestre Ferreira da. see Ferreira da Silva, Silvestre.
Silva, Thomas Antonio dos Sanctos e. see Dos Sanctos e Silva, Thomas Antonio.
Silva, V. defendant 94225
Silva Araujo e Amazonas, Lourenco da. 81099-81100
Silva Berford, Sebastiao Gomes da. 81101
Silva Brandao, Luiz da. 81102 see also Rio de Janeiro (City) Santa Casa de Misericordia e Enfermarias Publicas. Hospital Geral. Gabinete Estadistico Medico-Cirurgico. Director.
Silva Caminha e Menezes, Antonio Telles da. see Telles da Silva Caminha e Menezes, Antonio, Marquez de Resende, 1790-1875.
Silva Castro, Francisco da. see Castro, Francisco da Silva.
Silva Costa, Jose da. ed. (70317)
Silva Coutinho, J. M. 81104
Silva e Sousa, Luis Antonio da. 81105
Silva Figueroa, Garcia. see Figueroa, Garcia Silva.
Silva Guimaraes, Aprigio Justiniano da. 19993, 24314, 81106-81107

Silva Guimaraes, Joao Joaquim da. 24314, 81108

Silva Leal, Antonio Carvalho. 85771

Silva Lisboa, Balthazar da. see Lisboa, Balthazar da Silva.

Silva Lisboa, Bento. 16153 see also Brazil. Ministerio das Relacoes Exteriores.

Silva Lisboa, Jose da. see Lisboa, Jose da Silva.

Silva Maia, Jose Antonio da. see Maia, Jose Antonio da Silva.

Silva Mello, Joaquim Guennes da. 81109

Silva Netto, A. de. 52356, 81110-81112

Silva Paranhos, -------- da. 58545, 81113

Silva Pontes, Rodrigo de Souza da. see Souza da Silva Pontes, Rodrigo de.

Silva Portilho, Joao Anastacio de Souza Pereira da. see Souza Pereira da Silva Portilho, Joao Anastacio de.

Silva Porto, Manuel Joaquim da. 81114

Silva Ramos, Joaquim Jose Pereira da. see Pereira da Silva Ramos, Joaquim Jose, b. 1818.

Silva Santisteban, Jose. see Santisteban, Jose Silva.

Silva Torres e Alvim, Francisco Cordeiro da. see Torres e Alvim, Francisco Cordeiro da Silva.

Silva Americana. 4561

Silva de sus frases i su declaracion. (29049)

Silva de varia leccion. (48242)

Silua d' varia lecio[n]. 48233

Silua de varia lecion. (48234), (48237), 48241

Silua varia lection. 48238

Silvanus Americanus. pseud. History of North America. see Nevill, Samuel.

Silveria, Joaquim Lobo da. 81116

Silveria, Manuel Joaquim da, Bp. 81117-81119 see also Maranhao (Diocese) Bishop (Silveira)

Silveira, Simao Estaco da. 81120

Silver, Abiel. 81121

Silver, Samuel. 81122

Silver and gold. 68067

Silver anniversary of the American Literary Union. 81123

Silver bugle. 67299

Silver Creek Copper and Lead Mining Company. 81124

Silver Jubilee of the Episcopate of the Most Rev. John Baptist Purcell, Cincinnati, 1858. see Cincinnati (Archdiocese) Silver Jubilee of the Episcopate of the Most Rev. John Baptist Purcell, 1858.

Silver jubilee of the University of Notre Dame. 42875

Silver knife. 72132

Silver Lake. 25778

Silver mines of Nevada. 81125

Silver mines of Virginia and Austin, Nevada. 81126

Silver question settled by enactment into law. 83886, 83891

Silver rifle. 29114

Silver trumpets of the sanctuary. 22282

Silver wedding memorial. 90976

Silversmith, Julius. 81127-81129

Silvester, David. (43923)

Silvester, Peter Henry, 1807-1882. 81130

Silvestris. pseud. Reflections. see Sylvestris. pseud.

Silvestro, P. F. tr. (67345)

Silvius, Aeneas. see Pius II, Pope, 1405-1464.

Sim, W. H. 81133

Sim. Cob. Junior. pseud. see Ward, Nathaniel.

Sima: romance historico do Alto-Amazonas. 81100

Simanes, Jose Javier de Tembra y. see Tembra y Simanes, Jose Xavier de.

Simao de Natua ou o Mercador de Feiras. (36942)

Simbolo de la serpiente. 89995

Simcock, John. 37178, 37205

Simcoe, John Graves, 1752-1806. 69508, 81134-note after 81138, 98064-98065E, 100896 see also Ontario. Lieutenant Governor, 1791-1796 (Simcoe)

Simcoe's military journal. 81135

Simeon, el Franco. (69220)

Simeon, Remi. 57232, 74951, 81139

Simeon Baxter. pseud. see Peters, Samuel. supposed author

Simeoni, --------, Cardinal. 84195

Simerwell, Robert. 81140-81141

Simes, Thomas. 81142, 84642

Simes (John W.) & Co. firm plaintiffs 43234

Similarity of Washington and Harrison. 84778

Simile of the apple tree. (81143)

Simitiere, Pierre Eugene du. 21446, 23112, 83761

Simlers, Johann Wilhelm. ed. 99534

Simmers, William. 81144

Simmonds, Peter Lund. 81145-81152, 85145

Simmonds, William. 82832, 92664

Simmonds' colonial magazine and foreign miscellany. 81150

Simmons, Mrs. --------. 81153

Simmons, -------, fl. 1839. 40240

Simmons, A. T. 81154

Simmons, Charles. (81155)

Simmons, Flora E. (81156)

Simmons, George Abel, 1791-1857. 81157-(81159)

Simmons, George Frederic, 1814-1855. 2415, (11920), 81160-(81163)

Simmons, Ichabod. 81164-81165

Simmons, J. L. A. (81172)

Simmons, James B. 81167

Simmons, James Fowler, 1795-1864. 81168-81171

Simmons, James Wright. (81173)-81177, 88390

Simmons, William. of Pennsylvania 81178

Simms, Jeptha Root, 1807-1883. 81179-81185

Simms, Thomas. (58740)

Simms, William Emmett, 1822-1898. 81186

Simms, William Gilmore, 1806-1870. 19836, 39260, 65736, 70907, 81187-81245, 81247-81250, 81251, (81253)-(81279), 82091, note after 88005, 7th note after 88114, note after 88297, 88390, 1st note after 106011

Simms, William Gilmore, 1806-1870. supposed author 73018, 81246, (81252)

Simm's poems. 81258

Simoes, Joaquim Isidoro. 85680

Simon. pseud. Dialogue between two gentle-men in New York. 19934

Simon. pseud. Dialogue shewing, what's there therein to be found. see Logan, James.

Simon. pseud. Reflections of a few friends of the country. 68690-68691

Simon, the tanner. pseud. Letter to the Reverend Andrew Croswell. 17670

Simon, Alexander. 81280

Simon, Mrs. Barbara Anne. 81281-81283

Simon, Jules. 15428

Simon, Menno. see Menno Simons.

Simon, Pedro Antonio, 1560?- 81285-81287

Simon, R. 4931-4934

Simon Ayanque. pseud. see Terralla y Landa, Esteban de.

Simon Hold-Fast. pseud. see Hold-Fast, Simon. pseud.
Simon in regimentals! 85454
Simon Question. pseud. see Norris, John.
Simon Search. pseud. see Search, Simon. pseud.
"Simon Snapping Turtle," Esq., the paradise of fools. 55392
Simon Snipe. pseud. see Snipe, Simon. pseud.
Simon Snodgrass. pseud. see Snodgrass, Simon. pseud.
Simond, Alfred, 1740-1801. 81288-81291
Simonde de Sismondi, Jean Charles Leonard. see Sismondi, Jean Charles Leonard Simonde de, 1773-1842.
Simonds, Artemas. 81292
Simonds, J. C. 81293-81294
Simonds, Thomas C. 81295- 95820
Simoni, Luis Vicente de, 1792- 81296-81303
Simonin, Amedee H. (81304)-81305
Simonin, Louis Laurent, 1830- 81306-81317
Simonis, Joh. Georgius. 100621
Simonis, Menno. see Menno Simons.
Simonis Maioli Astensis Episcopi Vultvrarien Dies canicvlares. 44056
Simonis Paulli, D. Medici Regij, ac Praelati Aarhasiensis Commentaris de abusu tabaci Americanorum Veteri. 59223
Simonot, -----. 81318
Simons, Benjamin B. 81319
Simons, Charles. illus. (35193)
Simons, G. J. 81320
Simons, James. 81321-81322
Simons, John Hume. 81323
Simons, John W. 45511, 81324
Simons, Leonard. defendant 81325
Simons, Menno. see Menno Simons.
Simons, N. W. ed. 36905
Simons, P. 81326
Simons, Thomas Young, 1828-1878. 81327-(81330)
Simons, William. see Symonds, William.
Simonton, A. G. (81331)
Simpathy with our suffering brethren, etc. 27292
Simpkins, John, 1768-1843. 81332-81333
Simpkinton, John Nassau. 81334
Simple, Sam. pseud. Autobiography. see Wilburn, George T. supposed author
Simple and easy plan to abolish slavery. 1425
Simple cobbler of Clerkenwell willing to help. 81335
Simple cobler of Aggawam in America. 7299, 19033, 32778, 101323-101329
Simple coblers boy. 101321
Simple exposition de la maniere dont se forment. 77362
Simple introduction to the common plants. (28370)
Simple notice sur le Rio de la Plata. 11400
Simple recit tire de l'histoire de l'eglise. (18223)
Simple settings, in verse. 81366
Simple sketches by Rev. John Todd. 96089
Simple story of a western home. 4327
Simple system of finance. 52010
Simple tales for my own children. 80955
Simple tradesman. pseud. Clear and certain truths. 13582
Simple truth. 95361
Simple truth vindicated. 81337
Simple notes sur l'Amerique Centrale. 80831
Simples observations d'un Mexicain. 74179
Simpleton, Jeremiah. pseud. Western emigration. see Trumbull, Henry.

Simplex. pseud. 95254
Simplex enumeratio distributa in singularum partium regiones. 52175
Simplicities defence against seven-headed policy. (28044)-28045, 104796
Simplicity of the Indians. (5339)
Simplicity that is in Christ. 64245
Simplicity's defence. (28046), 70719
Simplicivm medicamentorvm ex Novo Orbe. 49943
Simplicivm medicamentorvm ex Novo Orbe delatorvm, qvorvm in medicina vsvs est. 49942
Simplified anatomy. 89454
Simpson, -------, fl. 1782. 70138
Simpson, -------, fl. 1821. (69154), 83665
Simpson, -------, fl. 1865. 87803
Simpson, Alexander, 1811- 81338-81340
Simpson, Ann. defendant 81341
Simpson, Edward, 1824- 81342
Simpson, G. B. 81345
Simpson, Sir George, 1796-1860. 33595, (81343)-81344
Simpson, George P. petitioner 5620
Simpson, Henry, 1790-1868. 81346
Simpson, Henry I. 81347
Simpson, J. 81348
Simpson, J. B. 81349
Simpson, James. 87369 see also South Carolina (British Military Government) Intendant-General of Police.
Simpson, James, 1781-1853. 81350
Simpson, James Hervey, 1813-1883. 36377, 81351-81358, 84774
Simpson, John, fl. 1818. 10541, 98077
Simpson, John, 1812-1885. (81359)-81360
Simpson, John Hawkins. (81361)
Simpson, Joseph, fl. 1853. 81362
Simpson, Joseph, fl. 1865. 81363
Simpson, Joseph Cairn. 81364
Simpson, Matthew, Bp., 1811-1884. 41219, 81365-81367
Simpson, S. S. 81368-81369
Simpson, Sidrach, 1600?-1655, 21991, 27952-27954, 51773, 55888, (69679), 74624, 91383, 104343 see also Church of Scotland. General Assembly. Commission.
Simpson, Stephen, 1789-1854. 23759, 64329, 81370-81373
Simpson, Thomas, 1808-1840. 81374
Simpson, William, fl. 1671. 25171, 81375
Simpson, William, fl. 1761. 81376
Simpson, William, 1823-1899. (81377)
Simpson, William S. reporter 69815, 81378, note after 96856
Simpson. firm see Puttick and Simpson. firm
Simpson's retrospective review. 70138
Sims, Alexander Bromgoole, 1803-1848. 81379-81385
Sims, Clifford Stanley, 1839- 13127, 81386-81387
Sims, James. (81388)
Sims, Thomas. defendant 92068
Simsbury, Conn. Ecclesiastical Council, 1770. see Congregational Churches in Connecticut. Ecclesiastical Council, Simsbury, 1770.
Simsbury, Conn. First Church. 81389
Simsbury copper mine. 25430
Simson, John. plaintiff 81390
Simulacro y sitio de Atares. (42574)
Sin against God. 39776
Sin and danger of quenching the spirit. 16638

Sinner blinded to truth. 84123

Sinners in the hands of an angry God. 21959-21960

Sinners minded of a future judgment. 12371

Sinner's refusal to come unto Christ. 62517

Sinnett, Mrs. Percy. tr. 38219, 49915, 61338, 81432

Sinnonguiness Speaker. Indian Chief 628, 66062 see also Three Maquas Castles (Indians) Sachems.

Sinodo Diocesano celebrado por su Senoria Ilustrisima. 81433

Sins and dnagers of the times. 26297

Sins deadly wound. (17087)

Sins of a gainsaying and rebellious people. 73484

Sins of a nation. 82738

Sins of society. 47052

Sins of the government, sins of the nation. 81434

Sins of the land. 71559

Sins of youth, remembered with bitterness. 40773

Sinzendorf, Count Nicholas. see Zinzendorf, Nicolaus Ludwig, Graf von, 1700-1760.

Sion College, London. Library. 83977

Sion in distress. 71435

Siouan Indians. Treaties, etc. 96641

Sioune Indians. see Siouan Indians.

Sioux Indians. Treaties, etc. 96647, 96721 see also Michigan Indians. Treaties, etc.

Sioux Indians (Hunkpapas Band) see Hunkpapas Indians.

Sioux Indians (Medawah-Kanton Band) see Mdewakanton Indians.

Sioux Indians (Missouri Band) see Missouri Indians.

Sioux Indians (Omaha Band) see Omaha Indians.

Sioux Indians (Oto Band) see Oto Indians.

Sioux Indians (Santie Band) see Santee Indians.

Sioux Indians (Sissetong Band) see Sisseton Indians.

Sioux Indians (Susseton Band) see Sisseton Indians.

Sioux Indians (Upper Medawakanton Band) see Mdewakanton Indians.

Sioux Indians (Wa-ha-shaw Band) see Wahasha Indians.

Sioux Indians (Wahpaakootah Band) see Wahpekute Indians.

Sioux Indians (Wahpacoota Band) see Wahpekute Indians.

Sioux Indians (Wahpeton Band) see Wahpeton Indians.

Sioux Indians (Yancton Band) see Yankton Indians.

Sioux spelling book. 91536

Sipes, William B. 81436

Sipkins, Henry. 81437

Sipma, S. A. 81438-81439

Sir, ... 95898

Sir, a collection of books. 88964

Sir, a large number of respectable characters. 105398

Sir, a number of the citizens of this state. 87869

Sir, a stranger in your country. 94306

Sir: agreeably with your request. 89975

Sir and brother. I am directed by the Grand Lodge. 87846

Sir and brother, I have the honuor [sic] of enclosing you. 87846

Sir Anthonie Sherley's travels into Persia and Russia. 66686

Sir Anthony Avalanche. pseud. see Blauvelt, -------.

Sir, as the Committee of Safety is not sitting. 100003

Sir, as we have great reason to believe. 100035

Sir, as you have been pleased to address yourself. 95896

Sir, by the resolutions of Congress which accompany this. 100192

Sir Charles Henry Frankland, Baronet. 51887

Sir Charles Metcalfe defended. 74575

Sir Christopher Porcupine. pseud. see Porcupine, Sir Christopher. pseud.

Sir Copp. A poem for the times. 13464

Sir Edward Seaward. pseud. see Porter, William Ogilvie.

Sir Edward Seaward's narrative of his shipwreck. 64323

Sir F. B. Head. 31138

Sir F. B. Head and Mr. Bidwell. 5258

Sir F. Drake's and Sir J. Hawkins' farewell. 71896, 1st note after 97255

Sir Francis Alvarez's voyage unto the Court of Prete Janni. 66686

Sir Francis Bernard's answer. 4922, 4925

Sir Francis Drake his voyage, 1595. 47171

Sir Francis Drake, Knight, Generall of the Whole Fleete. (81440)

Sir Francis Drake revived. Being a full account of the dangerous voyages. 9500

Sir Francis Drake revived. Who is or may be a pattern. (18236), 20830, (20838)-20840, 20843, 20855-20856

Sir Fraunces Drakes and Sir John Hawkins farewell. 71895, 1st note after 97255

Sir George Calvert, created Baron of Baltimore. 52288

Sir George Jeoffrey Trustaff, Gent. pseud. see Trustaff, Sir George Jeoffrey. pseud.

Sir Guy Carleton. 50185, 82379

Sir, having been appointed. 86139

Sir, having received an application. 100209

Sir Henry Morgan. 50645

Sir Henry Morgan, the buccaneer. 33245

Sir Humphrey Mackworth's proposal. 43482

Sir, I enclose the copy of a letter. 101742, 101746

Sir, I enclose you . . . three acts of the last session. 100204

Sir: I have read your article in the city papers this morning. 90869

Sir, I have the pleasure of announcing to you. 94756

Sir, I have the pleasure of congratulating you upon the success. 101693

Sir, I understand several expressions have escaped you. 104027

Sir, in my former I frankly informed you. 95934

Sir, in the present state. 48895

Sir, in the settlement of the account of this commonwealth. 100218

Sir, it having been stated to me that a colouring. 97280

Sir John Franklin and the Arctic regions. 81145, 81151-81152, 85145

Sir John Franklin, die Unternehmungen fur seine Rettung. 7395

Sir John Narborough's voyage in the South-Sea. (72186)

Sir John Narborough's voyage to the South-Sea. 72187

Sir Morgan O'Doherty. pseud. see O'Doherty, Sir Morgan. pseud.

Sir, no doubt you have frequently heard the manner. 94757

Sir—on the 27th day of November, 1832. 105807

Sir, permit us to direct your attention to the subject. 89643

Sir, previous to my entering on a detail of what relates. 94023

Sir Richard Greenvil's engagement. 14414

Sir Richard Hawkins's voyage into the South Sea. 66686

Sir Robert Sherley's travels in Persia. 66686

Sir Roger de Coverley. pseud. see Sewall, Jonathan, 1728-1796.

Sir, so various and critical have been our American affairs. 94754

Sir, the act of October, 1780. 100208

Sir, the annexed resolution of the General Assembly is sent to you. 100224

Sir, the Commissioners for Surveying the Coast of North Carolina. 55696

Sir, the following act, etc. 100343

Sir, the freemen of the commonwealth. 100056

Sir, the General Court, in June last. 105367

Sir, the inclosed information being of the highest importance. 101690

Sir, the invasion of our country by the enemy. 100197

Sir, the late distress. 101132

Sir, the subscribers, a committee designated. 105406

Sir, the undersigned are appointed a committee. 105411

Sir, the undersigned having the honor to be constituted. 105412

Sir, there is due from [blank] to the President and Fellows. 105859

Sir: this association has been formed. 105429

Sir, this minute came to my hands. 95963

Sir, three months have elapsed. 85856

Sir Walter Ralegh's journal. 67555

Sir W. Ralegh's voyages of discovery to Guiana. 67560

Sir Walter Raleigh and his colony in America. 65646

Sir Walter Raleigh and his times. 37888

Sir Walter Raleigh sailing in the Low-lands. 67599

Sir Walter Raleigh's expedition to Guiana, &c., &c. 14414

Sir Walter Raleigh's instructions to his son. 67572

Sir Walter Raleigh's instructions to his sonne. 67578-(67579), 67599

Sir Walter Raleigh's observations on the British fishery. 67599

Sir Walter Raleigh's observations, touching trade and commerce with the Hollander. 67599

Sir Walter Raleigh's observations, touching trade and commerce with the Hollander, and other nations. 67578-67584, 67599

Sir Walter Raleigh's sceptick. 67573, 67588

Sir Walter Raleigh's sceptick, or specvlations. 67588

Sir Walter Rawleigh his apologie for his voyage to Guiana. 67561

Sir Walter Rawleigh his lamentation. 67599

Sir Walter Ravvleighs farewell to his lady. 67599

Sir Walter Rawleigh's ghost. (67586)

Sir Walter Ravvleighs ghost, or England fore-warner. (67586)

Sir Walter Rawleigh's ghost; or, his apparition. (67586)

Sir Walter Rawleigh's judicious and select essayes. 67587

Sir, when the treaty. 89652

Sir, whereas on the 10th day of March last. 98434

Sir; whereas on the 10th day of March last, immediately upon the death. 98436

Sir, while you were pleased. 95900

Sir William Alexander and American colonization. 65646, 81697, 91853

Sir William Alexander's Nova Scotia. 66686

Sir William Monson's naval tracts. 13015

Sir, you are desired to attend a special meeting. 81442

Sir, you are desired to attend a special meeting of the committee. 81441

Sir, you are returned one of the Overseers of the Poor. 81443

Sir, you desire my thoughts. 40289, (69691), 96960

Sire, Thomas Walpole & Consorts, contre Guillaume & Alexandre-Jean Alexander. 101149

Sirene de l'enfer. 70331

Siren's cruize. 102206

Siret, --------. 81444

Siri, Vittorio, 1608-1685. 81445-81448

Siria, Antonio, d. 1745. 81449

Siris. 65700

Sismondi, Jean Charles Leonard Simonde de, 1773-1842. (23230), (23234), 81450-81459, (82311)

Sisseton Indians. Treaties, etc. 81460, 96662, 96715

Sisseton and Whapeton treaty, of February, 1867. 81460

Sissetong Indians. see Sisseton Indians.

Sisson, George. 21622, 81461

Sisson, P. F. 21622, 81461

Sisson, Mrs. P. F. 81462

Siste Mohikanen. 16459

Sistema de Atole. 81463

Sistema Colombiano. (72272)

Sistema economico y rentistico de la Confederacion Argentina. 655

Sistema metrico-decima. 81464

Sistema metrico-decimal. Tablas que establecen la relacion. 81006, 81465

Sistema representativo y la cuestion del dia. 61162

Sistematice sistens animalia Groenlandiae Occidentalis. 23602

Sistens muscos hepaticos. (78103)

Sister. pseud. Memoir of Jonathan Leavitt. 39560

Sister of Charity. pseud. Escaped nun. 22822

Sister of one of the High Priests. pseud. Fifteen years' residence. see Smith, Mary Ettie V. (Coray) 1829-

Sister Rhody. pseud. Whatcheer. see Child, Anna P.

Sister Rhody's collection of historical facts. 12694

Sisters of Orleans. (81466)

Sisters of the Good Samaritan. 81467

Sisters of the Visitation, Georgetown, D. C. petitioners 27005

Sisti, Valerio Pucci. ed. 81468

Sisyphi opus. 101140

Sitgreaves, Charles, 1803-1878. 81469-81471

Sitgreaves, L. 35764, 81472-81473, 105714

Sitio de Puebla de Zaragoza. 81474

Sitio de Puebla, o apuntes para la historia de Mexico. (16767)

Sitio de S. Philipe de Portovelo. 40068

Six views of the most important towns.
101287
Six weeks in Fauquier. 81488, 2d note after
100605
Six weeks in South America. 90307
Six years in a Georgia prison. 58190
Six years in the bush. 10607, 2d note after
98090
Sixpenny volume library. 84181
Sixteen cases of Gen. Pincton's most horrid
cruelty. 62684
MDCLXXX. An almanack of coelestial motions.
62743
1680. Nisi Dominus frustra. 77593
MDCLXXXV. Cambridge ephemeris. 62743,
104394
1685. The Boston ephemeris. 46774, 62743
MDCLXXXIIII. Cambridge ephemeris. 62743
1684, the Boston ephemeris. 62743
MDCLXXXI. An almanack of coelestial
motions. 62743
MDCLXXXVII. Cambridge ephemeris. 62743,
104395
1686. The Boston Ephemeris. 62843
M.DC.LXXXIII. The Boston ephemeris. 46239
MDCL. An almanack for the year of Our
Lord 1650. 47210
MDCXLVI. An almanack for the year of Our
Lord 1646. 47209
Sixteen introductory lectures to courses of
lectures. note after 74241
Sixteen lectures. 24516
Sixteen letters, addressed to F. Childs and
J. H. Lawrence. 19001
Sixteen letters addressed to . . . Toler.
96122
Sixteen members of Assembly. pseud. Votes
and proceedings. 60045
Sixteen members of the Assembly of Pennsylvania. pseud. Address. 102415
Sixteen months at the gold diggins. 105123
1694. An almanack of the coelestiall motions.
62743
Sixteen plates, from the drawings of Isaac
Sprague. 56387, 57099
1670. An almanack of coelestiall motions.
62743
1678. An almanack of coelestial motions.
62743
1675. An almanack of coelestial motions.
62743
1674. An almanack. 62743
1679. An almanack of coelestial motions.
62743
1671. An almanack of coelestial motions.
62743
1677. An almanack of coelestial motions.
62743
1676. An almanack of coelestial motions.
62743
1673. an almanack of coelestial motions. 62743
M.DC.LXXIII. The Boston ephemeris. 46239
MDCLXVII An almanack of the coelestial
motions. 62743
1669. An almanack of coelestiall motions.
62743
1667. An almanack for the year of Our Lord
1667. 62743
1666. An almanack or astronomical calculations.
62743
Sixteen sermons preached on Christ's parable
of the fig-tree. 104065
Sixteen short sermons. 81489
1610. Dexter [genealogy.] 1857. 55017
1628-1658. Descendants of Jonathan Padelford.
55020

Sixteen years in Chile and Peru from 1822 to
1839. 93950
Sixteen years in Chili and Peru, from 1822 to
1839. 12805
Sixteen years in the West Indies. 10722
Sixteen years' preaching and procedure. 56049
Sixteene questions of seriovs and necessary
consequence. 81490
Sixteenth annual catalouge . . . see Catalogue
. . .
Sixteenth annual report . . . see Report . . .
Sixteenth report . . . see Report . . .
Sixteenth triennial festival [of the Massachusetts
Charitable Mechanic Association] . . .
Oct. 11, 1854. 45829
Sixth and seventh letters to the Rev. Samuel
Miller. 89009
Sixth annual advertisement of the . . . [New
England Female Medical] College. (52683)
Sixth annual address [before the Hartford
County Peace Society.] 103166
Sixth annual catalogue of the officers and stu-
dents of Bethel College. 5067
Sixth annual exhibition [of the Pennsylvania
Academy of the Fine Arts.] 60294
Sixth annual report . . . see Report . . .
Sixth annual session. First annual message of
Governor A. J. Faulk. 18297
Sixth book of records of the town of Southampton.
88230
Sixth census of the United States. 35806
Sixth census or enumeration of the inhabitants
of the United States. (81491)
Sixth collection of papers relating to the pre-
sent juncture of affairs in England.
9372, 81492
Sixth commandment friendly to virtue, honor
and politeness. 89807
Sixth . . . debate, Oct. 4, 1864. 55840
Sixth essay, comprising the substance of the
rejected essays. 65732, 103738
Sixth essay on free trade and finance. 102408
Sixth historical notice of the conquest of Tierra
Firme. 81285
Sixth lecture on colonial slavery. 95508
Sixth letter. (27898)
Sixth letter to the people of England. 80060
[Sixth letter to the Rev. Samuel Miller.]
(49063)
Sixth of August, or the Litchfield Festival.
41474, 81493
Sixth pastoral report of Trinity Church, Potts-
ville. 64695
Sixth reader. 73345
Sixth report . . . see Report . . .
Sixth semi-annual report . . . see Report
. . .
Sixth supplement [to the public laws of Rhode
Island.] 70700
Sixtieth anniversary sermon. 56043
Sixtum, Chr. tr. 73320
Sixtus V, Pope, 1521-1590. 42066, 48373-
(48374), 76223, 76332, note after 90828
see also Catholic Church. Pope, 1585-
1590 (Sixtus V)
Sixty-eight "home views." 32715
Sixty-eight testimonies. 59721-59722
Sixty-ninth anniversary address. 91615
Sixty sermons on various subjects. 58895
Sixty years in the north and twenty years in
the south. 7174
Sixty years of the life of Jeremy Levis. 57754,
81494
Sixty years since in America. 78784-78785
Sizer, Nelson. 8980, 81495-(81496)
Sizer, Thomas J. 81497

Sjoberattelse. 16501
Sjodahl, J. M. <u>tr</u>. 83229
Sjotrollet eller strovfvaren pa hafvet. 16538
Skandinaviens stjerne. 85513
Skaniadradigrono Indians. <u>see</u> Conoy Indians.
    <u>and</u> Nanticoke Indians.
Skating Club, New York. <u>see</u> New York
    Skating Club, New York.
Skeel, Theron. (81498)
Skeel, Thomas. (81499)
Skeleton exposed. 89294
Skeleton map to shew the probable line of rail-
    way communication. 85260
Skeleton of a proposal for a national bank.
    3184
Skeleton's cave. 94247
Skelton, -------. <u>engr</u>. 73385
Skelton, Charles, 1806-1879. 81500
Skelton, Thomas. 81501
Skeptic and other poems. (37736)
Sketch book. 84757-84757A
Sketch-book. 96334
Sketch-book of a German nobleman. 29004
Sketch-book of a manager of the . . . [Rosine]
    Association. 62198
Sketch book of Capt. G. F. Lyon. (42854)
Sketch-book of character. (81502)
Sketch book of distinguished authors. 81503
Sketch book of Geoffrey Crayon, Gent. 35197-
    35198
Sketch book of Geoffrey Crayon, Gent<u>n</u>. 35199
Sketch, by F. W. Chesson. 216, 27628
Sketch descriptive of the situation. (34260)
Sketch of a bill for a uniform militia. (18683)
Sketch of a comparison between the two great
    actions. 5791
Sketch of a discourse. 101884
Sketch of a journey through the western states
    of North America. 44375
Sketch of a journey through the western states
    of North America, from New Orleans.
    9139
Sketch of a journey to Jerusalem. 35267
Sketch of a plan for settling in Upper Canada.
    3214, note after 81503, 3d note after
    98090
Sketch of a railway judiciously constructed.
    81504
Sketch of a scheme for the maintenance and
    employment of the poor. 22973
Sketch of a South-Sea whaling voyage. 4108
Sketch of a voyage of discovery, undertaken
    by Mons. de la Perouse. (38967)
Sketch of Adjutant General Sumner's address.
    93719
Sketch of American literature. 79961
Sketch of an anniversary festival of the
    Mitchell family. 49736
Sketch of an argument. (42615)
Sketch of Arkensaw and Orleans Territory.
    (13299)
Sketch of Blockley Poor-House Hospital. 9840
Sketch of Brattleborough. 97621
Sketch of Bunker-Hill battle. 94059, 94060-
    94061
Sketch of Camden City, New Jersey. 81505
Sketch of Canadian history. 17591
Sketch of Chili. 33912, 1st note after 99449
Sketch of Colfax. 16702
Sketch of Connecticut forty years since.
    (80955)
Sketch of Dabney Carr Harnson. 32436
Sketch of Dacotah County, Minn. 49734
Sketch of debates in Congress on the subject.
    71575
Sketch of Detroit. (1142)

Sketch of Dr. Thomas Graeme. 84744
Sketch of Dover, N. H. 91556
Sketch of each town. 8058
Sketch of events in the life of George Law.
    39305
Sketch of Fairmount. 62245, (81506)
Sketch of grammar of the Chippeway language.
    93621
Sketch of Greenland and the Parry Isles.
    (44615)
Sketch of Henrew poetry. 42873, 79458
Sketch of . . . Henry Clay. (41503)
Sketch of Henry Hudson. 2184
Sketch of his [i. e. G. R. Clark's] campaign.
    (13287)
Sketch of his [i. e. Bela Jacobs'] character.
    35496
Sketch of his [i. e. Edward H. Edes'] life. 21831
Sketch of his [i. e. Isaac Child's] life. (12736)
Sketch of his [i. e. Jesse Appleton's] life.
    1802
Sketch of his [i. e. John Gardner Calkins
    Brainard's] life. 7332
Sketch of his [i. e. Stephen Burrough's] life.
    (9466)
Sketch of his [i. e. William G. Brownlow's]
    life. 8702
Sketch of his [i. e. William Lake's] life. 38655
Sketch of his [i. e. George Washington's] life,
    and an abstract of his last will. 101636
Sketch of his [i. e. Frederick Wing Cole's] life
    and character. 14286
Sketch of his [i. e. Lewis Wilber's] life and
    character, as originally given by him.
    103945
Sketch of his [i. e. Washington Irving's] life
    and writings. 35221
Sketch of his [i. e. Nahor Augustus Staples']
    life, by John W. Chadwick. 90473
Sketch of his [i. e. Francis L. Hawks'] life, by
    N. L. Richardson. 30972, 5th note after
    96966
Sketch of his [i. e. Ichabod S. Spencer's] life,
    by Rev. J. M. Sherwood. 89330
Sketch of his [i. e. James Richards'] life, by
    Samuel H. Gridley. (70947)
Sketch of his [i. e. Henry Winter Davis'] life,
    public services, and character. 18830
Sketch of His Majesty's province of Upper
    Canada. 6888
Sketch of his [i. e. William Reed Prince's]
    qualities as a preacher. (65625)
Sketch of Hon. James Hamilton. 84745
Sketch of Hon. Melville C. Smith. 83608
Sketch of Hon. Nathan Appleton. 80320
Sketch of Hon. Thomas Tolman. 80321
Sketch of Hull, Mass. (33649)
Sketch of incidents and adventures. (22373)
Sketch of idnustrial progress. (80567)
Sketch of its [i. e. Andover Theological
    Seminary's] rise and progress. 1437
Sketch of James Madison. 34734
Sketch of [John Quincy Adams.] (288)
Sketch of Joseph Ludwig. 42663
Sketch of Kenyon College. 55858
Sketch of Loudon Park Cemetery. 3084
Sketch of Miss Sophia Smith. 84961
Sketch of missionary proceedings at Cape
    Breton. (81507)
Sketch of missions. 104811
Sketch of Mr. Beecher and the lecture-room.
    4318, 50328
Sketch of Mr. Freeman's pastoral intercourse
    with Mr. Cotton. 91303
Sketch of Mr. Lincoln. 4319
Sketch of Mr. Randolph's first speech. 67832

Sketch of the late war. 95133, 6th note after 100603

Sketch of the laws relating to slavery. 93097-93098

Sketch of the life and a list of some of the works. 60937

Sketch of the life and character of Caleb Gannett. 26526

Sketch of the life and character of Charles Linsley. (61377)

Sketch of the life and character of Dr. Poedagogus. 81522, 103231

Sketch of the life and character of Ebenezer Lane. (55071)

Sketch of the life and character of . . . F. Ames. 20207, 52631

Sketch of the life and character of Gen. George Washington. 94893, note after 101884, 103093

Sketch of the life and character of his only child, Judge John Junius Burk. 10216

Sketch of the life and character of John D. Fisher. 11903

Sketch of the life and character of John Lacey. 18904

Sketch of the life and character of Mrs. A. E. Ranny. (67897)

Skecth of the life and character of Nathaniel Bowditch. 6995

Sketch of the life and character of President Dwight. 81044

Sketch of the life and character of Rev. Elias Cornelius. 21892

Sketch of the life and character of S. G. Morton. 28322

Sketch of the life and character of the author [i. e. John Blair Linn.] 41338

Sketch of the life and character of the late Dr. John D. Godman. 27665

Sketch of the life and character of the late Hon. Roger Minott Sherman. 80406

Sketch of the life and character of the late Joseph B. Skinner. 81647

Sketch of the life and character of the Rev. David Caldwell. 11169

Sketch of the life and character of William Penn. 59746

Sketch of the life and campaigns of General Whitelocke. 103671

Sketch of the life and death of Miss Hannah Dyckman. 25300

Sketch of the life and doctrine of the celebrated John Calvin. 74430

Sketch of the life and educational labors of Ebenezer Bailey. (2726)

Sketch of the life and labors of George Whitefield. 74595

Sketch of the life and labors of the Rev. Justin Edwards. 29910

Sketch of the life and millitary services of Gen. La Fayette. 38580

Sketch of the life and ministry of William T. Dwight. 85221

Sketch of the life and projects of John Law of Lauriston. 105051

Sketch of the life and public services of Amos Pilsbury. 62868

Sketch of the life and public services of Gen. Lewis Cass. 11358

Sketch of the life and public services of Gen. William Henry Harrison. 30596

Sketch of the life and public services of Theodore Frelinghuysen. (25831), (58651)

Sketch of the life and public services of William Henry Harrison. 30594, 81523

Sketch of the life and scientific work of Dr. John Lawrence Smith. 83003

Sketch of the life and services of Gen. Otho Holland Williams. (45211A)

Sketch of the life and services of Gen. W. O. Butler. (11353)

Sketch of the life and services of Isaac Craig. (17366)

Sketch of the life and services of William Henry Harrison. (81524)

Sketch of the life and times of Abraham Lincoln. (41232)

Sketch of the life and writings of the Rev. Micaiah Towgood. 44351

Sketch of the life, character, and public services of Joseph Ritner. 71584

Sketch of the life, character and writings of Rev. James Y. MacGinnis. 43276

Sketch of the life, character, and writings of the Rev. James Y. M'Ginnes. 33579

Sketch of the life, condemnation, and death of the three Thayers. 95263

Sketch of the life, last sickness and death of Annie R. Smith. 83749

Sketch of the life, last sickness and death, of Mrs. Mary Janes Grosvenor. 28953

Sketch of the life of Abraham Lincoln. 51238

Sketch of the life of Albert L. Starkweather. 90531

Sketch of the life of Alden March. 44482

Sketch of the life of Alexander Wilson. (57466)

Sketch of the . . . life of Alexander S. Byrne. 11076

Sketch of the life of an Indian hunter. 94680

Sketch of the life of Andrew Jackson Donelson. (24332)

Sketch of the life of Benjamin Banneker. (55505), note after 97651

Sketch of the life of Brig.-Gen. Francis Marion. 35723

Sketch of the life of Brissot. 8026

Sketch of the life of Clarence D. McKenzie. 5455

Sketch of the life of Com. Robert F. Stockton. 91904

Sketch of the life [of Edmund Burke.] 9304

Sketch of the life of Edward Everett. 4462

Sketch of the life of Elhanan Winchester. 99502

Sketch of the life of Elizabeth T. Stone. 92057

Sketch of the life of Francis William Greenwood. 28688

Sketch of the life of General Greene. 1187

Sketch of the life of Gen. Kilpatrick. 37744

Sketch of the life of General Lafayette. 38580

Sketch of the life of General Moreau. 93994

Sketch of the life of Gen. T. J. Chambers. 11805

Sketch of the life of Hannibal Hamlin. 3616

Sketch of the life of Hon. Wm. A. Graham. 78410

Sketch of the life of J. A. Lapham. 80408

Sketch of the life of Jacob Eshelman. 96889

Sketch of the life of James Benington. (4696)

Sketch of the life of James Wallack. 50785

Sketch of the life of John A. Andrew. 81525

Sketch of the life of John Bishop. 5610

Sketch of the life of John H. Sheppard. 80323

Sketch of the life of John Horne Tooke. 36912

Sketch of the life of John Howard Payne. 59288

Sketch of the life of John McLean, of Ohio. 43516

Sketch of the life of John Quincy Adams. 320-321

Sketch of the life of Lieut.-Gen. U. S. Grant. 16702

Sketch of the life of Lieut. Mathew Hughes. 33600

Sketch of the life of Lorenzo da Ponte. 64013

Sketch of the life of Louis Kossuth. 38269

Sketch of the life of Major General Daniel Denison. 81677

Sketch of the life of Major Gen. Henry Dearborn. 19072

Sketch of the life of Major General William Henry Harrison. (30595)

Sketch of the life . . . of Miss Anne Clay. (36471)

Sketch, of the life of Miss Ellen Jewett. 36111

Sketch of the life of Mrs. Eliza Garnaut. 62528

Sketch of the life of Mrs. Judith S. Grant. 21518

Sketch of the life of Okah Tubbee. 57096, 97294

Sketch of the life of Peter Starr. 94236A

Sketch of the life of President Brown. 105031

Sketch of the life of R. P. Robinson. 72167

Sketch of the life of Randolph Fairfax. 81709

Sketch of the life of Reuben E. Fenton. 24077

Sketch of the life of Rev. Michael Wigglesworth. 19034

Sketch of the life of Rev. N. A. Staples. 60465

Sketch of the life of Rev. Orin Fowler. 25315

Sketch of the life of Robert Raikes. 41702

Sketch of the life of said Wilson. 104606

Sketch of the life of Samuel Dexter. 92318

Sketch of the life of Samuel E. Godfrey. 96873

Sketch of the life of Samuel Neilson. 52298

Sketch of the life of Sir John Franklin. (36998)

Sketch of the life of the Apostle Eliot. 19077

Sketch of the life of the author [i. e. Abraham Van Dyck.] 98495

Sketch of the life of the author [i. e. John Stevens.] 91541

Sketch of the life of the author [i. e. Jonathan Dickinson.] (20062)

Sketch of the life of the Hon. George Mifflin Dallas. 31698, (63839)

Sketch of the life of the Hon. Isaac Fletcher. 68502

Sketch of the life of the illustrious Washington. (75207), 101885

Sketch of the life of the late Rev. David Merrill. 59452

Sketch of the life of the pirate Tardy. 11223

Sketch of the life of the Rev. H. D. Northrop. 91594

Sketch of the life of the Rev. Michael Eyster. (38860)

Sketch of the life of the Rev. Samuel Whiting. 103707

Sketch of the life of the Rev. William M. Jackson. (17931)

Sketch of the life . . . of the Right Rev. Alexander Viets Griswold. 39761

Sketch of the life of Timothy Claxton. 13530

Sketch of the life, personal appearance, character and manners of Charles S. Stratton. 92735

Sketch of the life, personal appearance, &c. of Chas. S. Stratton. 92734

Sketch of the life, public services and character of Henry Clay. 13555

Sketch of the life, public services, and character, of Major Thomas Stockton. 91912

Sketch of the life, travels, and sufferings of a reformed man. 81526

Sketch of the life, trial, and execution of Oliver Watkins. 102114

Sketch of the life, works and sufferings of a reformed man. 39667

Sketch of the Mendelssohn Quintette Club, of Boston. 81527

Sketch of the military bounty tract of Illinois. 94454

Sketch of the military system of France. 81528

Sketch of the mineralogy of Nova Scotia. (33218)

Sketch of the mining operations of that company. 9277

Sketch of the Montreal celebration of the Grand Trunk Railway. 93561

Sketch of the Mosquito Shore. 92722, 98925

Sketch of the official life of John A. Andrew. 8637

Sketch of the old Federal and Republican parties. 36630

Sketch of the olden time. 81529

Sketch of the 126th Regiment Pennsylvania Volunteers. (73539)

Sketch of the organization and powers of the Board. (54188)

Sketch of the organization, objects and membership of the Old Settlers Association of Minnesota. 49308

Sketch of the origin and history of the West Church. 44631

Sketch of the origin and progress of printing. 14200

Sketch of the origin and progress of the Adelphi School. 61446

Sketch of the origin and progress of the American Colonization Society. 82062

Sketch of the origin and progress of the causes. 81530

Sketch of the origin and progress of the . . . [Humane] Society [of New York.] 53696

Sketch of the origin and progress of the institutions. 60614

Sketch of the origin and progress of the Lyceum, by Jas. B. Congdon. 52474

Sketch of the origin, object and character of the Franklin Fund. 43008

Sketch of the origin, progress, and present condition of the system [of common schools in the state of New York.] 53645, 67801

Sketch of the overland route to British Columbia. 31938

Sketch of the Passaic Falls. 1903

Sketch of the personal character & qualities of General Zachary Taylor. 26370

Sketch of the physical description of the universe. (33727), 33729

Sketch of the pilgrims of Plymouth, etc. 81531

Sketch of the pilgrims who founded the church of Christ. (76482)

Sketch of the plans. 81532

Sketch of the policies. (81533)

Sketch of the political, social, and religious character. 77491

Sketch of the Presbyterian Tract and Sunday School Book Society. 65226

Sketch of the present state of Caracas. 79088

Sketch of the present state of our political relations. (23921)

Sketch of the present state of the Objebwa Nation. 16716

Sketch of the principal transactions. 58112, 62034

Sketch of the proceedings and trial of William Hardy, for murder. 5771

Sketch of the proceedings and trial of William Hardy, on an indictment. (30359)

Sketch of the progress of botany in western America. (80563)

Sketch of the progress of the malignant or epidemic cholera. 101460

Sketch of the public and private history of Major-General W. O. Butler. 11355

Sketch of the recent improvements at East-Boston. 6556

Sketch of the regiment. 12686

Sketch of the reign of George the Third. 27000-(27001), (81534)

Sketch of the remarks made by the President of the company. 54723

Sketch of the remarks of Mr. McLane. 43489

Sketch of the remarks of Mr. Stanly, on the bill. 90329A

Sketch of the remarks of Mr. Stanly, on the branch mint. 90330

Sketch of the remarks of Mr. Stilwell. 91820

Sketch of the remarks . . . upon the Nebraska resolutions. 66817

Sketch of the resources of the city of New York. 20340

Sketch of the revolution in chemistry. 84411

Sketch of the rise and progress of Grace Church, Providence. 21618

Sketch of the rise and progress of Methodism. 35465

Sketch of the rise and progress of the Church of England. 553

Sketch of the rise and progress of the First Baptist Church in New Haven. 53014

Sketch of the rise and progress of the yellow fever. 18002

Sketch of the rise of the Religious Society of Friends. 86066

Sketch of the rise of the state of Mississippi. 9655

Sketch of the rise, progress, and dispersion of the Mormons. 98494

Sketch of the route to California. 10042, 81535

Sketch of the Seminole war. (81536)

Sketch of the settlement and exploration of Lower California. 8662

Sketch of the slave trade. 24384

Sketch of the slave trade, a view of our national policy. 8490

Sketch of the state of affairs in Newfoundland. (81537)

Sketch of the temperance reform in America. 30605

Sketch of the times. 8815, 22409, 2d note after 106203

Sketch of the tour of General Lafayette. 25242

Sketch of the town of Bloomington. 81538

Sketch of the town of Huntington, L. I. 105071

Sketch of the trade of British America. 28122

Sketch of the travels and ministry of Elder Orson Hyde. (64970)

Sketch of the treatment of the insane. 13302

Sketch of the trial of George Coombs. 16395

Sketch of the trial of William Bevans. 5107

Sketch of the 29th Regiment of Connecticut Colored Troops. 31833

Sketch of the Union Library Company, Philadelphia. (50886)

Sketch of the U. S. Dry Docks at Philadelphia. 62244

Sketch of the United States of North America. 4173

Sketch of the various Indian tribes of Canada. (32347)

Sketch of the village in the last century. (39731)

Sketch of the voyages and discoveries of Columbus and Cortez. 8137

Sketch of the water works at Fairmount. 81539

Sketch of western Virginia. 81540, 3d note after 100521

Sketch of what remains to be ascertained by future navigators. 17312

Sketch of William Beardsley. 4136

Sketch of William Walcutt, the sculptor. 13678

Sketch on the life and doctrines of the celebrated John Calvin. 74430

Sketch prepared for the celebration of the opening. 50264

Sketch. With explanatory notes. 59109

"Sketchbook" of Washington Irving. 35187-35188

Sketcher's tour round the world. 22371

Sketches. 80957

Sketches accompanying the annual report of the Superintendent. 81541

Sketches and anecdotes of Americam Methodists. 81542

Sketches and anecdotes of many revolutionary patriots and heroes. 3200

Sketches and burlesques. (19665)

Sketches and business directory of Boston and its vicinity. 81543

Sketches and chronicles of the town of Litchfield. (37736)

Sketches and eccentricities of Col. David Crockett. 17573

Sketches and essays. (33412)

Sketches and illustrations of legal history and biography. 39329

Sketches and incidents. 81550

Sketches & incidents; or, a budget from the saddle-bags of a superannuated itinerant. 81544, 91480

Sketches and incidents of Rev. John Clark. 59482

Sketches and recollections of Lynchburg. 42821, (81545)

Sketches and recollections of the West Indies. (81546), 4th note after 102866

Sketches and statistics of Cincinnati in 1859. (13155)

Sketches and statistics of Cincinnati in 1851. 13154

Sketches and stories from life. 39738

Sketches, biographical and descriptive. 25305

Sketches, biographical and genealogical. 5701

Sketches by a sailor. (81547)

Sketches by a traveller. 81548, 3d note after 96481

Sketches: by N. P. Willis. 104515

Sketches by Rev. George Hale. 38007

Sketches by the way. 55118

Sketches connected with California history. 94438

Sketches describing his recollections of scenes. (4052)

Sketches during a campaign. (14231)

Sketches, essays, and translations. (27439)

Sketches for laying out Central Park. 4739

Sketches for the fireside. 81549

Sketches from a student's window. 27922

Sketches from history. 34146

Sketches from life. [By Seba Smith.] 84150, 84158

Sketches from life. [By W. F. Deacon.] 19010

Sketches from real life. (12727)

Sketches from the civil war in North America. (5709)

Sketches from the history of Pennsylvania. 51732, (60615)

Sketches from the history of yellow fever. 11016

Sketches from the life of the author. (57792)

Sketches from the study of a superannuated itinerant. 81550, note after 91480

Sketches, historical and bibliographical. 30893

Sketches, historical and descriptive. By Sidney D. Maxwell. 47054

Sketches, historical and descriptive, of Louisiana. 91928

Sketches, historical and topographical, of the Floridas. 25046

Sketches illustrative of the habits. 29788

Sketches in British North America. 21254

Sketches in Canada and rambles among the Red Men. (35728), (35731), 38914

Sketches in Mount Auburn Cemetery. 51152

Sketches in New Brunswick. 81551

Sketches in North America. 69006

Sketches in North America and the Oregon Territory. 101455

Sketches in prison camps. 56031

Sketches in prose and verse. By Mrs. E. W. F. Cheves. (12599)

Sketches in prose and verse, by Paulding, Halleck, Bryant, &c. 2298

Sketches in the Canadas. 85203

Sketches in verse. [By R. H. Rose.] 67377, 73248

Sketches in verse—namely, Dutch dignity, . . . death of La-Fayette, &c. (13435)

Sketches, miscellaneous, descriptive and statistical. (33006)

Sketches of a journey in Chili. 92669

Sketches of a plan for settling the vacant lands of Trinidada. 17530, 1st note after 91235, 2d note after 102829

Sketches of a New-England village. (39731)

Sketches of a running discourse. 2403

Sketches of a soldier's life. 67869

Sketches of a summer trip to New York and the Canadas. 104015

Sketches of a tour in the United States and Canada. 43355

Sketches of a tour to the lakes. 43407

Sketches of a tour to the western country. 17890

Sketches of adventures in California and Washoe. 8657

Sketches of Algiers, political, historical, and civil. 79731

Sketches of all the coloured churches in Philadelphia. 11558

Sketches of all distinguished women. 29670

Sketches of America. 23956

Sketches of America in 1854-55-56. 58260

Sketches of American character. 29668

Sketches of American life: a companion to "The Mayflower." 92449

Sketches of American life and manners. 63371

Sketches of American life. By C. F. Hoffman, Esq. 32387

Sketches of American missionaries. 12405

Sketches of American orators. 81552

Sketches of American policy. 102399

Sketches of American scenes and military adventure. 81029

Sketches of American society. By Seatsfield [pseud.] 41018, 64545

Sketches of American society from a residence of forty years. 34140

Sketches of an address delivered. (22345)

Sketches of Attleborough. 5930

Sketches of Bermuda. By Susette Harriet Lloyd. 41696

Sketches of Bermuda, or Somers' Islands. 17032

Sketches of border adventures. (33436)

Sketches of Boston. 32699, 1st note after 81552

Sketches of Brazil: including new views. 21271

Sketches of Buenos Ayres and Chile. 29536

Sketches of Buenos Ayres, Chile, and Peru. 29537

Sketches of Bunker Hill battle and monument with illustrative documents. By Charles P. Emmons. 22517

Sketches of Bunker Hill battle and monument: with illustrative documents. [By George E. Ellis.] 22309

Sketches of California. 9970, 26787

Skethhes of Canada and the United States. 43438

Sketches of Canadian life. 18591

Sketches of celebrated Canadians. (50648)

Sketches of . . . celebrated characters. 40017

Sketches of celebrated murders and pirates. 81553

Sketches of character. 81554

Sketches of character, chiefly in the "Old North State." 11167-11168

Sketches of character; moral and political condition of the republic. 48913, 95117, 1st note after 95515

Sketches of club-life, hunting, and sports. 81555

Sketches of contemporaneous history. 10889

Sketches of deceased laymen of the Methodist Episcopal Church. 84755

Sketches of Dingle Parish. 65119

Sketches of distinguished American authors. 81556

Sketches of domestic life. 81557

Sketches of East Tennessee life. 6180

Sketches of ecclesiastical history. 81558

Sketches of eminent freemasons. 50340-(50341)

Sketches of eminent Methodist ministers. 43047

Sketches of epidemic diseases in the state of Vermont. 26448

Sketches of Fairmount, Lemon Hill and the adjoining grounds. 62245, (81506)

Sketches of Farmington, Connecticut. (70957)

Sketches of French and English politicks in America. (81559)

Sketches of French society. 41846

Sketches of foreign travel and life at sea. 72420

Sketches of General Cass and Wm. O. Butler. 11359

Sketches of Georgia scenes. 12963

Sketches of Great Britain and Ireland. 91664

Sketches of Hayti. 30783

Sketches of his [i. e. Ezekiel Cheever Whitman's] life. 103737

Sketches of his [i. e. Job Swift's] life and character, and a sermon. 94066

Sketches of his [i. e. Robert Treat Paine's] life, character and writings. 58201

Sketches of his [i. e. Ebenezer Smith Thomas'] own life and times. 95387

Sketches of history, life and manners, in the farwest. 29792

Sketches of history, life and manners in the United States. 73822, (73824), 4th note after 96481

Sketches of history, life and manners, in the west. 29793-29794

Sketches of human manners. 100984

Sketches of Illinois. 34260, 34325

Sketches of imposture, deception, and credulity. (81560)

Sketches of incidents and adventures in the west. 81561

Sketches of Indian character and manners. (36355)

Sketches of Indian life and character. 85428, 3d note after 94249

Sketches of Iowa. 54998

Sketches of Iowa and Wisconsin. 63444

Sketches of Keokuk. 20810

Sketches of life and character in Louisiana. 42304

Sketches of life and landscape. 33413

Sketches of life in a South-American republic. 21699

Sketches of life in Newfoundland. 43116

Sketches of life in Texas. (64536)

Sketches of life in Virginia. 47483, (52419)

Sketches of life south of the Potomac. 14681

Sketches of living notables. (47791)

Sketches of Louisville and its environs. (43587)

Sketches of Lower Canada. 76706

Sketches of man "as he is." 42375

Sketches of Martha's Vineyard. (19809)

Sketches of men of mark. 81562

Sketches of men of progress. 58958

Sketches of military life. 68477

Sketches of Minnesota. 79644

Sketches of mission life. (81563)

Sketches of Mr. Mathews's celebrated trip to America. 46827

Sketches of Montreal, past and present. 76412

Sketches of Montana and Salt Lake. 6221

Sketches of Moravian missions. 97861

Sketches of my schoolmates. 28345

Sketches of naval life. 81564

Sketches of Nebraska. 7151

Sketches of New Brunswick. 30848

Sketches of New England character and manners. 78796

Sketches of New England divines. (80356)

Sketches of New England, or memories of the country. (20508)

Sketches of Newfoundland and Labrador. (26276)

Sketches of Newport and its vicinity. 9843

Sketches of Niagara Falls and River. 81565

Sketches of North America. 69004

Sketches of North Carolina, historical and biographical. 20528, 85333

Sketches of noted guerrillas and distinguished patriots. 7729

Sketches of Old Virginia family servants. 81566

Sketches of Paris. 76397, 76405

Sketches of past industrial exhibitions. 81567

Sketches of persons and scenes in America. 20346, 5th note after 96452

Sketches of persons, localities, and incidents of two centuries. 7774

Sketches of places and people abroad. 8586

Sketches of plans for settling in Upper Canada. 3214, note after 81567

Sketches of political frenzy. 63229

Sketches of Polynesia. 4726

Sketches of primitive races in the lands. 81432

Sketches of printers and printing in colonial New York. 85249

Sketches of Prominent female missionaries. 21808

Sketches of prominent places, persons and things. (8667)

Sketches of public characters. 38084

Sketches of public characters, discourses and essays. 8414

Sketches of remarkable characters. 21754

Sketches of remarkable conversions. 11123

Sketches of residence and travels in Brazil. 37708

Sketches of Rhode Island physicians. 58921

Sketches of Rio Janeiro. 14799

Sketches of Rochester. 57594

Sketches of St. Augustine. 79439

Sketches of scenery and manners in the United States. 21540

Sketches of scenery and notes of personal adventure. 43328

Sketches of scenes and characters among the descendants of the pilgrims. 92422, 92424

Sketches of several distinguished members of the Woodbee family. 81509, note after 105083

Sketches of slave life. 67853

Sketches of slavery in the United States. 41129

Sketches of society and manners in the West Indies. 44640

Sketches of society and travel. (81568)

Sketches of society in the United States. (66638)-66639

Sketches of soldiers in the war of rebellion. 17698

Sketches of some of his [i. e. George P. Barker's] most celebrated speeches. 8790

Sketches of some of the first settlers of Upper Georgia. (27440)

Sketches of some of the prominent public characters. 16074

Sketches of some of the speeches delivered in the House of Commons. 81569

Sketches of some of the western counties of New-York. 8558

Sketches of some Virginians. 40577, 88114

Sketches of south-western history. 81570

Sketches of southern and western life and adventure. 13848

Sketches of sport and natural history in the lower provinces. 30349

Sketches of Springfield, containing an account of the early settlements. 81571

Sketches of Springfield in 1856. 81572, note after 89893

Sketches of the acts and joint resolutions of the General Assembly of Virginia. (81573)

Sketches of the alumni of Dartmouth College. (11983)

Sketches of the ancient history of the Six Nations. 18142

Sketches of the Armies of the Potomac and the Shenandoah. 6292, 6861

Sketches of the author's [i. e. John Udell's] life. 97663

Sketches of the author's [i. e. Samuel Buell's] life. 8983

Sketches of the Baltimore pulpit. 85467

Sketches of the bench and bar. 24291

Sketches of the campaign in northern Mexico. 27330, 81574

Sketches of the campaigns of Generals Hull and Harrison. 8557

Sketches of the capital of Peru. 26118

Sketches of the character of the New-York press. (66884), 1st note after 105499

Sketches of the churches and pastors in Hampden County, Mass. 18814, 30130

Sketches of the city of Detroit. (19792)

Skinner, Orrin. 81619
Skinner, Otis Ainsworth, 1807-1861. 81620-
81631, 83585
Skinner, P. H. 81632
Skinner, R. C. 81633
Skinner, Roger Sherman. ed. 53799, 53836
Skinner, S. F. (9667), 81634
Skinner, St. John B. L. (81635)
Skinner, Thomas, 1710-1762. 81636-(81637)
Skinner, Thomas Harvey, 1791-1871. 81638-
(81648)
Skinner, Thomas Harvey, 1820-1892. 81649-
81650
Skinner, Warren. (81652)-81653
Skinners. firm publishers see Websters &
Skinners. firm publishers
Skipwith, Fulwar. 81654-81663, 102766 see
also West Florida. Governor, 1810
(Skipwith)
Skirmish drill for mounted troops. 15412,
81664
Skirmish made upon Quakerism. 59732
Skirmish of the West Indian heroes. (21101)
Skirmisher defeated and truth defended. 59732
Skirmishes and sketches. 20506
Skitt. pseud. Fisher's River. see
Taliaferro, H. E.
Skizze meiner Reise nach Brasilien. (26091)
Skizze von Brazilien. 81116
Skizzen Amerikanischen Lebens. 32388
Skizzen aus dem Amerkianischen Leben.
28808
Skizzen aus dem Leben des Kolumbus. 10301
Skizzen aus den Vereinigten Staaten von
Nordamerika. 38012
Skizzen aus der Amerikanischen Gesellschaft.
66640
Skizzen einer Reise durch Sud-America.
100686
Skizzen eines Deutschen Malers von Wilhelm
Heine. (31242)
Skizzen transatlantischen Lebens. 27194
Skizzen und Erinnerungen an die Reise nach
und in Amerika. 89440
Skizzen und Scenen von Charakteren unter den
Nachkommen der Pilger. 92435
Skizzen von Amerika entworfer auf einer Reise.
23957
Skizzen von Amerika. Zu einer Belehrenden
Unterhaltung fur gebildete Leser. 7455
Skizzen von Charakteren und Sitten in Neu-
England. 101086
Skizzen von Land und Leuten der Nord-
Amerikanischen Freistaaten. 28028
Skizzen zu meinem Tagebuch. 160
Skizzen zur Kenntniss seiner socialen und na-
turwissenschaftlichen Verhaltnisse. 37102
Skizzer af en tour til Vestindien. 65040
Skizzer af scener och karakterer ibland pil-
grimernas afkomlingar. 92439
Skizzer fra et kort besog par vore Vrstindiske
oer i sommeren 1841. 18274
Sklavengeschichte. 3702
Sklavenhandel. 7927
Sklavenleben in Amerika. 8520
Skalvenleben in den Freistaaten Amerikas.
92553
Sklavenleben in der Republik Amerika. 92550
Skalvenmacht. 23948
Sklaverei im Lander der Freiheit. 92564-92565
Sklaverei, Schutzzoll und Heimathsbill. 19798
Sklaverei, Seeherrschaft und die Preussische
Staatszeitung. 4842
Sklaverei und Emancipation der schwarzen
Rasse. 27681
Sklaverfrage in den Vereinigten Staaten. (37100)

Skoleundervusningen og den deraf fremgaaede
almindelige fulketplysning i Gronland.
35772
Skovdjaevelen. (5558)
Skowhegan, Me. Library Association. see
Skowhegan Library Association, Skowhegan,
Me.
Skowhegan Library Association, Skowhegan,
Me. 81666
Skowhegan Library Association, Skowhegan,
Me. Librarian. 81666
Skreen removed. 88168
Skrifwen och vtgifwen af thes Biskop, Doct.
Jesper Swedberg. 94034
Skrzynski, H. tr. 33726
Skully, William. 7512
Skunk Porcupine. pseud. see Porcupine,
Skunk. pseud.
Sky-lark. 81667
Sky-rocket. 81668
Slack, Charles W. (6765), 45859, note after
97006
Slack, David B. 81669-81670
Slack, Elijah, 1784-1866. 81671
Slack, James H., 1835-1874. 81672
Slack, Joshua P. 81673
Sladden, William. 81674-81675
Slade, Ann Maria. (64660)
Slade, Arthur. (81676)
Slade, Daniel D. 81677
Slade, William, 1786-1859. (6765), (61393)-
61394, 81678-81691, 95486, note after
97006, note after 99131, 99197 see also
Vermont. Secretary of State.
Slade's "laws" [of Vermont.] 95486
Slafter, Edmund Farwell, 1816-1906. 23122,
65646, 81692-81698, 91853
Slagle, J. F. 63116
Slamm, Levi D. defendant 35783
Slander refuted. (58152)
Slanders refuted. 59431
Slape, Albert H. 81699
Slappey. alias see William, George W.
defendant
Slashes at life with a free broad-axe. 36588
Slate, William, 1786-1859. 81691, 1st note
after 98997, 99024, 99049, note before
99075, 99077, 99079, 99081, 99085
Slater, Edward C. 81700
Slater, Lionel. 81701
Slaughter, Gabriel, 1767-1830. 37547 see
also Kentucky. Governor, 1816-1820
(Slaughter)
Slaughter, Linda Warfel. 81702
Slaughter, Philip. 81703-81710
Slaughter of the saints on Shoal Creek, Mo.
85505
Slauson, H. 81711
Slave. 2387, 92782
Slave; a musical drama. 51030
Slave. A poem. 11023
Slave among pirates. 51458, note after 92624
Slave & minstrel. 62826
Slave-auction. (38298)
Slave-catcher caught in the meshes of eternal
law. (67748)
Slave code of the District of Columbia. 82086
Slave colonies of Great Britain. 82063
Slave-dealer's daughter. 9091
Slave draver. pseud. How to abolish slavery
in America. 33233
Slave extention and protection. 13266
Slave girl. pseud. Deeper wrong. 19232
Slave girl. pseud. Incidents in the life of a
slave girl. see Brent, Lind.
Slave; his wrongs and their remedy. 82064

Slave-holder. pseud. Remarks upon slavery. see Gibbes, Morgan. supposed author
Slave: hunted, transported, and doomed to toil. 46186
Slave in Canada. 84422
Slave in the island of Cuba. pseud. Poems. 63605
Slave-labor system and free working-man's worst enemy. (55459)
Slave labor versus free labor sugar. 43600
Slave law. 42682
Slave law of Jamaica. 35629
Slave life in America. 92486
Slave life in Georgia. 27108
Slave life in Georgia; being a narrative. 8516
Slave-life in Missouri. 82012
Slave life in Virginia and Kentucky. 24002
Slave love in America. 81867
Slave mother. 75256
Slave oligarchy and its usurpations. Outrages in Kansas. 93674
Slave oligarchy and its usurpations. Speech of Hon. Charles Sumner. 93675
Slave: or, memoirs of Archy Moore. 31789-(31790), 82065
Slave power and its supporters. 19759
Slave power; its character, career, & probable designs: being an attempt to explain the real issues. 9856
Slave power; its character, career, and probable designs. [By John Stuart Mill.] 48987
Slave power: its heresies and injuries to the American people. 30022
Slave power of the Confederacy. 5187
Slave property in the Territories. 82066
Slave question. [By Henry C. Carey.] 10842
Slave question. Speech of Mr. William H. Bissell. 5637
Slave question. Speech . . . March 5, 1850. 9773
Slave question. Speech of Hon. J. Morton. (51005)
Slave representation. (6424)
Slave ships and slaving. 85380
Slave songs of the United States. 82067
Slave states of America. 8899
Slave taker, &c. 51733
Slave, the serf and the apprentice. 38668
Slave-trade: a full account of this species of commerce. 68106
Slave trade. A sermon by John Bidlake. 5252
Slave-trade, and its remedy. 93257
Slave trade at Rio Janeiro. (27978)
Slave trade. [By G. C. P. Knot.] (38139)
Slave trade. [By Henry, Lord Brougham.] 8419
Slave trade—Commerce. Report of Mr. Kennedy. 37404
Slave trade, domestic and foreign. 10840, 10842
Slave trade inconsistent with reason and religion. 7290
Slave-trade indespensable. 34789, 82068, 4th note after 102785
Slave trade, the African squadron, and Mr. Hutt's committee. 19578
Slave trade with Africa. 10947
Slave trader reformed. 7383
Slaveholder abroad, or Billy Buck's visit with his master to England. 36595, 82064, note after 90541, note after 95543, note after 95665
Slaveholder of West Virginia. pseud. Address to the people of West-Virginia. see Ruffner, Henry.

Slaveholders' conspiracy, an address by the Rev. William Henry Channing. 11931
Slaveholders' conspiracy, depicted by southern loyalists. 19505, 68242
Slaveholder's daughter. 57941
Slaveholders' rebellion. 63441
Slaveholders' rebellion and modern democracy. 60924
Slaveholders' rebellion; its internal causes. 73338
Slaveholder's war. A lecture. 36496
Slaveholder's war. An argument for the north and the Negro. 356
Slaveholding a malum in se. 97599
Slaveholding class dominant in the republic. 79556
Slaveholding examined in the light of the Holy Bible. 8009
Slaveholding not sinful. (33223)
Slaveholding piety illustrated. 82070
Slaveholding weighed in the ballance of truth. 24565
Slaven-emancipatie en slaven-arbeid in Suriname. 93864
Slaven en vrijen onder de Nederlandsche wet. 4585, 32380, 86209
Slaven-Geschiedenis. 92520
Slavenhouders en slavenvrienden. 93865
Slavernij. Vervolg en sleutel op de Negerhut. 92413
Slavery. 81952
Slavery a blessing. 18918
Slavery a curse and a sin. (42930)
Slavery, a divine trust. (58346)
Slavery a falling tower. (21691), 82072
Slavery: a lecture. (56412)
Slavery. [A poem.] 82071
Slavery. A poem. By Hannah More. 50538
Slavery, a public enemy, and ought therefore to be destroyed. 18190
Slavery, a sermon delivered in the First Congregational Church. 13229
Slavery a sin. (28800)
Slavery: a sin against God. 39776
Slavery a sin that concerns non-slaveholding states. 101307
Slavery: a treatise showing that slavery is neither a moral, political, nor social evil. 82073
Slavery abolished. Its relation to the government. 15621
Slavery among the ancient Hebrews. 48879
Slavery among the Puritans. 82074, 93197
Slavery: an essay in verse. (44610), 82075
Slavery an outlaw. 82649
Slavery and abolitionism, as viewed by a Georgia slave. 4989
Slavery and anti-slavery. 27849
Slavery and civil war. 3401
Slavery and civilization. 50955
Slavery and famine punishment for sedition. 21589
Slavery and freedom in the British West Indies. (9682)
Slavery and infidelity. [By Chalres D. Cleveland.] (82076)
Slavery and infidelity. Thompson. Barnes. Batton. 80281
Slavery and its contrasts. 55570, 74246
Slavery and its hero-victim. (29830)
Slavery and its prospects in the United States. 82077
Slavery, and its remedy. 43574
Slavery and secession. 2377
Slavery and secession in America. 22339
Slavery and serfdom considered. 82078

2675

Slavery and slaveholding in the United States.
1396
Slavery and southern Methodism. 9908
Slavery and the American Board of Commis-
sioners for Foreign Missions. 82079
Slavery and the American war. 49039
Slavery and the Bible. 82080
Slavery and the Bible. A tract for the times.
(77497)
Slavery and the Bible. By Rev. Enoch Pond.
63992
Slavery and the Bible. Slavery and the church.
80281
Slavery and the church. [By O. Scott.] 78345
Slavery and the church. By William Hosmer.
33114
Slavery and the church. Slavery and infidelity.
80281
Slavery and the church. Two letters addressed
to Rev. N. L. Rice. 82243
Slavery and the constitution, both sides of the
question. 7777
Slavery and the constitution. By William I.
Bowditch. 7010
Slavery and the domestic slave-trade in the
United States. 1497
Slavery and the episcopacy. 59472
Slavery and the internal slave trade in the
United States of North America. (82082)
Slavery and the north. 9324
Slavery, and the remedy. 56047-56048, 56050
Slavery & the slave trade. From Judge Story's
charge. 92319
Slavery and the slave trade: six articles.
19580, note after 92624
Slavery, and the slaveholder's religion. 8245
Slavery and the union. 82083
Slavery and the war. A historical essay.
18586
Slavery and the Wilmot proviso; with some
suggestions for a compromise. 10847
Slavery as it exists in the British West India
Islands. 102867
Slavery, as it relates to the Negro. 65491
Slavery, as recognized in the Mosaic civil law.
72184
Slavery at war with the moral sentiment of the
world. (78042)
Slavery, Biblical and American. 39544
Slavery. By a Marylander. 82085
Slavery. [By Francis Maseres.] 45417
Slavery: by J. L. Baker. 2832
Slavery. [By James Smith.] 82785
Slavery. [By William Ellery Channing.] 2414,
2415, (11920), 64948, 70190, 81162,
94057, 99583
Slavery. Con and pro. 82087
Slavery condemned by Christianity. 95560
Slavery considered with a view to its rightful
and effectual remedy. 103806
Slavery consistent with Christianity. 37603
Slavery defended from scripture. 42968
Slavery discussed in occasional essays. 2674
Slavery doomed. (21847)
Slavery examined by the light of nature. 3894
Slavery examined in the light of the Bible.
39776
Slavery gradually starved to death. 93468
Slavery illegal. 65683
Slavery illustrated in its effects upon woman
and domestic society. 82088
Slavery illustrated in the histories of Zangara
and Maquama. 82089
Slavery immoral. 30854
Slavery in a new light. 82090

Slavery in America. A history. By A. Rooker.
73089
Slavery in America. An essay for the times.
45480
Slavery in America; being a brief review of
Miss Martineau on that subject. 82091,
7th note after 88114
Slavery in America; or, an inquiry into the
character and tendency of the American
Colonization, and the American Anti-
slavery Societies. (35865)
Slavery in America shown to be peculiarly
abominable. 18994
Slavery in California and New Mexico. 25135
Slavery in Great Britain and the United States.
(82092)
Slavery in history. 29321
Slavery in its national aspects as related to
peace and war. 8453
Slavery, in its present aspects and relations.
90998
Slavery in its relation to God. 42030
Slavery in Maryland. An anti-slavery review.
45363
Slavery in Maryland briefly considered. 11201
Slavery in Maryland considered. (10848)
Slavery in Massachusetts. 50381
Slavery in New Jersey. (82093)
Slavery in rebellion. 82094
Slavery in South America. (5339)
Slavery in South Carolina. (25847)
Slavery in the Bible. 34880
Slavery in the capital of the republic. 72856
Slavery in the churches. 31377
Slavery in the District. (5774)
Slavery in the District of Columbia. (17694)
Slavery in the gentile churches. 82095
Slavery in the light of divine revelation. 92870
Slavery in the south: a review of Hammond's
and Fuller's letters. 30099, 82096
Slavery in the south. [By William Gilmore
Simms.] (81259)
Slavery in the south; or what is our present
duty to the slaves. (9744)
Slavery in the southern states. (65684)-65685,
note after 92624
Slavery in the territories. Speech . . . April
23, 1850. 59488
Slavery in the territories. Speech . . . in the
Senate of Michigan. 23691
Slavery in the territories. Speech of Caleb B.
Smith. 82366
Slavery in the territories. Speech of Hon. L.
B. Peck. 59488
Slavery in the territories. Speech of Hon.
Sidney Lawrence. 39370
Slavery in the territories. Speech of Hon.
T. H. Bayly. 4077
Slavery in the United States. A narrative of
the life and adventure of Charles Ball.
2934
Slavery in the United States. A sermon de-
livered in Amory Hall. 13418
Slavery in the United States. By J. K. Paulding.
59213
Slavery in the United States. . . . By M. B.
Sampson. 75946
Slavery in the United States; emancipation in
Missouri. 27611
Slavery in the United States: its evils, allevia-
tions, and remedies. 59364
Slavery in the United States of America.
(80361), 80363
Slavery in the West Indies. 82097
Slavery in the West Indies. [By James
Cropper.] 17621

Slavery in the West Indies. [By Thomas Perronet Thompson.] 95533
Slavery in the West Indies, with natural and physical history. 82098
Slavery in Trinidad. 82099
Slavery in Vermont. (82100), 3d note after 99205
Slavery inconsistent with justice and good policy. 5618, 70826-70827
Slavery inconsistent with the spirit of Christianity. 72172
Slavery indispensable to the civilization of Africa. 82101
Slavery inimical to the character of the great Father of all. 105610
Slavery irreconcilable with Christianity. (8493)
Slavery its nature, evils, and remedy. 50873
Slavery. Its origin, influence, and destiny. 58911
Slavery: its origin, nature and history. 92871
Slavery: its religious sanction. 32933
Slavery: its sin, moral effects, and certain death. 37144
Slavery justified; by a southerner. 82102
Slavery: letters and speeches, by Horace Mann. 44323
Slavery-limitation abandoned. 82103
Slavery no oppression. 82104
Slavery not a divine institution. (82105)
Slavery not forbidden by scripture. 55354, 74206-74207, (82106), note after 99798, 2d note after 102803
Slavery not sanctioned, but condemned by Christianity. 95560
Slavery not to be confined to the Negro race. 52587
Slavery of the British West India colonies delineated. (3352) 91238, 91243, 91248, 102798
Slavery of the United States. (81155)
Slavery or freedom . . . a discourse. 18202
Slavery or freedom: a strange matter, truely! (82107)
Slavery or freedom must die. 14901
Slavery: or, the times. 82108
Slavery ordained by God. 73356
Slavery past and present. note after 92624
Slavery plantations and the yeomanry. 40985
Slavery protected by the common law of the New World. (4705)
Slavery quarrel. 82109
Slavery question. Dred Scott decision. 82110
Slavery question settled. 37882
Slavery question. Speech . . . May 14, 1850. 36885
Slavery question. Speech of Hon. Amos P. Granger. (28280)
Slavery question. Speech of Hon. John Allison. 926
Slavery question. Speech of Hon. Samuel A. Bridges. 7826
Slavery question. Speech of Hon. William J. Alston. 967
Slavery. Rhymes addressed to the friends of liberty. 82111
Slavery sanctioned by the Bible. A tract for northern Christians. 82112
Slavery sanctioned by the Bible. The first part of a general treatiese. 36572
Slavery, secession and the constitution. 42016
Slavery sectional. 30109
Slavery, sovereignty, secession, and recogntiion considered. (23042)
Slavery—the Bible—infidelity. 59167
Slavery the cause of the war and all its evils. 2073

Slavery the crime and curse of America. 46186
Slavery; the evil—the remedy. 13536
Slavery the ground of southern secession. 1238
Slavery the mere pretext for the rebellion. 37420
Slavery: the nation's crime and danger. (20065)
Slavery unconstitutional. (28280)
Slavery viewed in the light of the golden rule. 90445
Slavery vindicated. 82113
Slavery's destruction, the union's safety. 20817
Slavery's last word. 21084
Slaves; a poem. 101060
Slaves and masters. 61229
Slaves and slavery. 80383
Slave's appeal. By E. Cady Stanton. 90405
Slave's appeal to Great Britain. 20716
Slave's friend. 82114
Slaves in Algiers. 73615
Slave's revenge. 93410
Slaves without masters. 24617
Sledgehammer, Aminadab. pseud. Farther defence. 23898
Sleep of twenty years. 71486
Sleeper, John Sherburne, 1794-1878. 73650, (73687), 73694, 73701, 82115-82123 see also Roxbury, Mass. Mayor, 1856-1858 (Sleeper)
Sleeper, John Sherburne, 1794-1878. defendant 85486
Sleeper, Samuel. 83410, 83411, 83413, 83419
Sleeper, Sarah. 83529
Sleeping sentinel. (35778)
Sleepy Hollow, N. Y. Reformed Dutch Church. 82124
Sleepy Hollow Cemetery, at Tarrytown. (82125)
Sleigh, Adderley W. 82126-82127
Sleigh, W. W. 82128-(82129)
Slemons, Thomas. 82131
Slender, Robert. pseud. Journey from Philadelphia to New York. see Freneau, Philip Morin, 1752-1832.
Slender, Robert. pseud. Letters on various interesting and important subjects. see Freneau, Philip Morin, 1752-1832.
Slicer, Henry, 1801-1874. 82132
Slichtenhorst, A. (82133)
Slick, Jonathan. pseud. High life in New York. see Stephens, Ann Sophia (Wintherbotham)
Slick, Samuel. pseud. Clock-maker. see Haliburton, Thomas Chandler.
Slick, Samuel. pseud. Letters of Sam Slick. see Haliburton, Thomas Chandler.
Slidell, Alexander. see Mackenzie, Alexander Slidell.
Slidell, John, 1793?-1871. 17811, (82136)-(82141)
Slidell, Thomas. 82142-82145, 93647
Slie, D. 22738, 82146
Slight, Benjamin. 82147
Slight slap at mobocratic snobbery. 95595
Slight touch of the serio-comic. 52969
Sligo, Howe Peter Browne, Marquis of. 9225, (82148), 93261
Slim Jim. 96582
Slingerland, John I., 1804-1861. 82149-82150
Sloan, E. L. 75842
Sloan, James, d. 1811. 82151-(82157), 89207
Sloan, James, fl. 1868. see Sloane, James.
Sloan, James A. (82159)
Sloan, Samuel, 1815-1884. (82160)-(82164)
Sloanaker, A. B. 82165
Sloane, Sir Hans, 1660-1753. 35585, (35636), 82166-82169, 98182

Sloane, James. 82158, 82170-82171
Sloane, James Renwick Wilson, 1833-1886. (82172)-82174
Sloane, Johann. 82168
Sloat, George B. plaintiff (82175)
Slocomb, William. 56962
Slocum, H. W. (82176), 90828
Slocum, J. J. supposed author (49992)-49993, (49996)-(49997), 84021, 92145
Slocum, John. 82177
Slocum, S. 82178
Slocum, William N. 82179
Sloetten, Cornelius van. pseud. Isle of Pines. see Neville, Henry.
Slonenbergh, Jasper van. pseud. Useful transactions. see King, William.
Sloo contract. Shall it be cancelled? (50980)
Sloot, F. W. van der. (82190)
Sloth contrasted with industry. 86825
Slothful servants neglecting their talents inexcusable. 30892
Slover, John. 38109, 38111, 48166
Slow and sure. (68570), 82191
Slow horses made fast and fast horses faster. 82192
Sluice club. 83974
Sluyter, Peter. 18503
Sly, Costard. pseud. Sayings and doings. 82193
Sly Sam, the Quaker spy. 36582
Slyck, ------ van. see Van Slyck, ---------.
Slygood, William. pseud. Universal kalendar. see Stearns, Samuel, 1747-1819.
Smacker, Isaac. (40970)
Smalbroke, Richard, successively Bishop of St. Davids, and Lichfield and Coventry, 1672-1749. 82194, 103596
Small, Elisha, d. 1842. 86804
Small, Henry Beaumont, 1831- 10628, 82195-82201
Small, Hugh. 82202
Small, John. 82204
Small, John. 98058A-98058B, 98059B-98059G, 98065E see also Ontario. Executive Council. Clerk.
Small, Jonathan. 82203
Small, Samuel. defendant (52925)
Small, William F. 29034, 82205
Small broom to sweep away the falshoods which Daniel Leeds has thrown into the way of Thomas Chalkley. 11753, (66742)
Small but earnest minority. see Congregational Churches in Massachusetts. Ecclesiastical Council, Danvers, 1852. Minority.
Small choice collection of precedents. 5643
Small fruit culturist. (26156)
Small man. pseud. Trip made by a small man. see Evans, Oliver.
Small offers towards the service of the tabernacle. 46486, 46513
Small pamphlet was published some little time since. 26630A, 95968
Small pox and the protective power of vaccination. 66366
Small singing book. 97421
Small singing book with 18 psalm tunes. 97421
Small singing book with 18 psalm tunes (both treble and bass) in the easy method of singing by letters. 97421
Small specimen of the genius of Canada West. 85240
Small success of the Gospel. 91588
Small tract, entitled, A candid exposition. 8773
Small treatise on the wilde and naked Indians. 963

Small voyages [of De Bry.] (8784)
Smallbroke, Richard. see Smalbroke, Richard, successively Bishop of St. Davids, and Lichfield and coventry, 1672-1749.
Smaller history of English and American literature. 79962
Smaller school history of the United States. 78255
Smaller standard speller. 76966
Smalley, David A., 1809- 82206
Smalley, Elam. (82207)-82211
Smalley, Eugene Virgil, 1841- 82212
Smalley, John, 1734-1820. (82213)-82220
Smallfield, A. G. 18722
Smallsense. pseud. see Parson All-sense, alias Smallsense, alis, Nonsense. pseud.
Smallwell, Edward, successively Bishop of St. Davids, and Oxford, d. 1799. 82221
Smallwood, Charles, 1812-1873. 82222
Smalridge, George, 1663-1719. 82223-(82225)
Smart, C. incorrectly supposed author 82226, 93133
Smart, Christopher, 1722-1771. 105486
Smart, Edwin. tr. 83138
Smart, Ephraim Knight, 1813-1872. 82227-82231
Smart, James H. 82232 see also Indiana. State Superintendent of Instruction.
Smart, James S. 82233-82235
Smart, John G. 90512
Smart, Stephen F. (82236)
Smart, T. B. (82238)
Smart, Theophilus. 82237
Smart, W. S. 82240
Smart, William. 82239
Smartest nation in all creation. 63371-63372
Smead, M. J. tr. 12240
Smead, Wesley, 1800-1871. 82241
Smead and Cowles. firm publishers 82242, note after 91325
Smead and Cowles' general business directory. 82242, note after 91325
Smectymnuus. pseud. Slavery and the church. see Waters, R. P. supposed author
Smedes, William C. 72047, 82244-82248
Smedt, Peter John de. see Smet, Peter John de, 1801-1872.
Smeducci, Girolamo Bartolomei gia. see Bartolomei, Girolamo.
Smeeks, H. 82249
Smeele, J. P. 66948, 82250
Smeeton's historical and biographical tracts. 17105
Smellie, T. 82251
Smellie, William, 1740-1795. 72254-72255
Smellie, William, d. 1763. 82252-(82253)
Smelt, Leonard. 79624, 82256-82259, 94134
Smet, Peter John de, 1801-1872. (34468), 82260-82277
Smethurst, Gamaliel. 82278
Smiles, Samuel. 82279-82281
Smiles and frowns for good and bad little children. 82282
Smiley, Thomas T. 82284-(82286)
Smilie, John, 1741-1812. 82287
Smillie, James. illus. 13606, 16778, (28695), 51149, (70963), 74169
Smirke, R. illus. 50143, 50145
Smissaert, W. J. E. 102933
Smissen, J. van der. 82288
Smith, -------, fl. 1742. Arctic explorer (19715)
Smith, -------, fl. 1742. of Philadelphia 82289
Smith, --------, fl. 1769. 90612
Smith, --------, fl. 1772. 71828
Smith, --------, fl. 1776. 35969

Smith, ---------, fl. 1816. 10210
Smith, --------, fl. 1837. 103969
Smith, --------, fl. 1845. 88294
Smith, --------, fl. 1848. 33500
Smith, --------, fl. 1853. engr. 92459,
   92485
Smith, --------, fl. 1860. (61367)
Smith, --------, fl. 1870. 28554, 83553
Smith, A. C. (82292)-82294
Smith, Mrs. A. C. see Smith, May Almeda
   Cary, 1859-
Smith, A. D. 58181
Smith, A. L. 83769
Smith, A. P. (82295)
Smith, A. W. 86094
Smith, Aaron, 1714?-1781. (82296)
Smith, Aaron, fl, 1823-1852. defendant 82297-
   82298
Smith, Abigail (Adams) 1765-1813. 168, 84905
Smith, Abijah. 82299
Smith, Abram D. 72300
Smith, Adam, 1723-1790. 22933, 64823, 81452,
   82301-82318, 93602
Smith, Albert, 1804-1863. 82319-82320
Smith, Albert, 1804-1862. reporter 95643
Smith, Albert, 1805-1870. 82321
Smith, Albert, fl. 1876. 82322
Smith, Alexander. pseud. Life of Alexander
   Smith. see Sargent, Charles L.
   supposed author
Smith, Alexander. see Smyth, Alexander.
Smith, Alexander H. 82325
Smith, Alfred Russell. 82326
Smith, Amasa. 82327-(82328)
Smith, Ann. alias see Carson, Ann.
   defendant
Smith, Annie R. 82329, 83749
Smith, Archibald, 1813-1872. 78172
Smith, Archibald, d. 1868. 82330
Smith, Asa. 83946, 83948-83950
Smith, Asa Dodge, 1804-1877. (82331)-82340
Smith, Ashbel, 1805-1886. (82341)-82347
Smith, Asher L. 82348
Smith, Augustus. 77765
Smith, B. H. 82349
Smith, Baker Peter. 82350
Smith, Ballard. 84479
Smith, Ballard, 1849- 84479
Smith, Barclay J. 84981
Smith, Baxter Perry. 82351
Smith, Ben. pseud. Motley book. see
   Mathews, Cornelius.
Smith, Benjamin. 82352
Smith, Benjamin Bosworth, Bp., 1794-1884.
   82353-82354
Smith, Benjamin F. 82355, 104222 see also
   Meeting of Working-Men and Other Per-
   sons Favorable to Political Principle,
   Albany, 1830. Chairman.
Smith, Benjamin G. see Smith Brothers &
   Co. firm
Smith, Benjamin J. 11770
Smith, Bernard. 82356
Smith, Bob. 82357
Smith, Buckingham. see Smith, Thomas
   Buckingham, 1810-1871.
Smith, C. B. M. (82358)
Smith, C. Billings. 82359-82360
Smith, C. H. 82361
Smith, Caleb, 1723-1762. 82362-82364
Smith, Caleb Blood, 1808-1864. 82365-82372
Smith, Calvin. 30796
Smith, Carey. 82373
Smith, Caroline Amelia. see De Windt,
   Caroline Amelia (Smith)
Smith, Charles, 1765-1836. 82374

Smith, Charles, 1768-1808. 50185, 82375-
   82379
Smith, Charles, fl. 1824. map seller 8215,
   82380-82381
Smith, Charles, fl. 1852. 82382
Smith, Charles, fl. 1865-1867. 82383-82384
Smith, Charles Adam, 1809-1879. 42735,
   82385-82389
Smith, Charles C. (71802)
Smith, Charles H. 82390
Smith, Charles H. J. (82391)
Smith, Charles Hamilton, 1790?- (82392)-
   82393
Smith, Charles Henry, 1826- 5384, (82394)-
   (82397)
Smith, Charles James. 82398
Smith, Charles Jeffrey, 1741?-1770. 82399
Smith, Charles James. 82400
Smith, Charles K. 82401
Smith, Charles Perrin, 1819-1883. 82402
Smith, Charles S. 84243
Smith, Charlotte, 1749-1806. 82403-(82404)
Smith, Chester W. 84132
Smith, Christen. tr. 20013
Smith, Clarence L. 84946-84947
Smith, Columbus. 82405-82415 see also
   Acting Gibbs Association of Vermont.
   Agent. Houghton Association. Agent to
   England.
Smith, Cotton Mather, 1731-1806. (82416)-
   82417
Smith, D. Junior 82418
Smith, D. Murray. 82419
Smith, Dabney Howard. 84322
Smith, Daniel, 1740?-1818. (82420)-82422, 2d-
   3d notes after 94805
Smith, Daniel, 1767-1846. (82423)
Smith, Daniel, 1789-1822. 49122
Smith, Daniel, 1806-1852. 82424-82428
Smith, Daniel D. 84948-84950
Smith, David. 82738
Smith, David H. 75544, 82429, 83300
Smith, David William. see Smyth, David
   William, 1764-1837.
Smith, Delavan. ed. 84789
Smith, Delazon, 1816-1860. 82430-82431
Smith, Denis E. 82432
Smith, Devereaux. 82433
Smith, Dexter. 82434
Smith, Don Carlos. 83496
Smith, E. (82436)
Smith, E. A. 82438
Smith, E. A. defendant at court martial 82437
Smith, E. C. 84342
Smith, E. Fitch. 82439-82440
Smith, E. G. ed. 47871
Smith, E. Perkins. ed. 53746
Smith, E. R. 15365
Smith, E. W. 102346
Smith, Ebenezer. 82441-82442
Smith, Edgar A. 28401, 71032
Smith, Edmund R. 82443
Smith, Edward, 1818?-1894. 82444
Smith, Edward, 1839-1919. 82445
Smith, Edward Darrell. (82446)
Smith, Edward Delafield, 1826-1878. 70131,
   82447-(82454), 83606 see also U. S.
   District Attorney (New York)
Smith, Edward Dunlap. 82455
Smith, Edward M. 82456
Smith, Edward Parmelee, 1827-1876. 82457
Smith, Edward Sutton. ed. 47329, 82811
Smith, Edward Worthington. 84925
Smith, Egbert T. 82458-82459
Smith, Elbert H. 1186, 47327, 82460-(82462)
Smith, Elbridge. (82463)-82465

Smith, Eleazer. 82466
Smith, Eli, 1759-1848. 82467-82468
Smith, Eli, 1787-1839. 82469
Smith, Eli, 1801-1857. 72067, 82470-82471
Smith, Elias. 82500
Smith, Elias. ed. 83500
Smith, Elias, 1769-1846. 31449, 80191, (82472)-(82499)
Smith, Elias, 1769-1846. supposed author 95300
Smith, Elias W. ed. 83276
Smith, Elihu Hubbard, 1771-1798. (82501)-(82504)
Smith, Eliza. supposed author 82435
Smith, Eliza Roxcy (Snow) see Young, Eliza Roxcy (Snow) Smith.
Smith, Elizabeth, 1776-1806. 82505
Smith, Elizabeth Lee (Allen) d. 1898. (82712)
Smith, Elizabeth (Oakes) 1806- 82506-82524, 84139-84141, 84151, 84862
Smith, Elizabeth P. 82986
Smith, Emeline (Sherman) 1823- (82525)-82526
Smith, Emily A. 83654
Smith, Emma. 82527
Smith, Englesfield. supposed author 104148
Smith, Erasmus Peshine, 1814-1882. (82528)-82529
Smith, Ethan, 1762-1849. 2722, 82530-(82540)
Smith, Eunice. (82541)-(82546), 86593, 86594-86602
Smith, Euphemia (Vale) 82547
Smith, Francis, fl. 1748-1749. 20808, 82549, 1st note after 94082
Smith, Francis, fl. 1784. 82550
Smith, Francis, 1812-1872. (82551)
Smith, Francis Gurney. ed. 20825, 84074
Smith, Francis H. 82552
Smith, Francis H. reporter 49244
Smith, Francis Henney, 1812-1890. (82553)-82558
Smith, Francis Louisa. 83504
Smith, Francis Osmond Jon, 1806-1876. 18906, (28603), 43958, 75835, 82559-(82570)
Smith, Francis Osmond Jon, 1806-1876. claimant 82559
Smith, Francis Osmond Jon, 1806-1876. defendant 82560
Smith, Francis Osmond Jon, 1806-1876. plaintiff 18028
Smith, Francis Osmond Jon, 1806-1876. reporter 44031
Smith, Franklin Webster. 55877, 82571, 82574, 84047, 84955-84956 see also Smith Brothers & Co. firm
Smith, Franklin Webster. defendant (82573), 82575-82576, 95377
Smith, Franklin Webster. defendant at court martial 82572, 82576
Smith, Frederic Cooke, d. 1839. see Smyth, Coke.
Smith, Frederick M. 83095
Smith, Gamaliel E. reporter 36735, 82577-82578, note after 96852
Smith, George. 83033-83034
Smith, George. defendant 102784 see also West India Dock Company, London. Treasurer. defendant
Smith, George. defendant at church trial 82580
Smith, George. plaintiff 82581
Smith, George, fl. 1777-1780. 62278 see also Philadelphia County, Pa. Sub-Lieutenant.
Smith, George, 1800-1868. 82582-82583
Smith, George, 1804-1882. (82584)
Smith, George, fl. 1808. 28755

Smith, George, fl. 1833. 82579
Smith, George Albert, 1817-1875. 64950, 70913, 82585, 83245, 83283, 83500, 85504, 85563
Smith, George B. 56759, 82586-(82588)
Smith, George F. 84954
Smith, George G. 82589
Smith, George Otis. 85010
Smith, George W. 82590
Smith, George Washington, 1800-1876. (23613), 82592-82593
Smith, George Washington, b. 1823. defendant 82591
Smith, George Williamson. (82594)
Smith, Gerrit, 1797-1874. 9794, 13536, 25641, 27850, 32532, 53491, 77725, (82595)-82673, 97549
Smith, Gideon B. ed. 36717, 81612, 82674
Smith, Gipsy. pseud. Forty years an evangelist. see Smith, Rodney, 1860-
Smith, Goldwin, 1823- 25147, 69464, 82675-82689
Smith, Gouverneur M. 82691
Smith, Grandma. pseud. Soldier's friend. see Smith, Susan E. (Drake?) 1817-
Smith, Green Clay, 1832-1895. (50082), (82692) see also Montana (Territory) Governor, 1866-1869 (Smith)
Smith, H. B. 82693
Smith, H. L. 52243
Smith, H. O. 82694
Smith, H. Perry. 82695
Smith, H. W. engr. 84352
Smith, Haddon. 83610
Smith, Hannah (Logan) 1720-1761. 41791, 82873
Smith, Hannah (Whitehall) 1832-1911. 82696
Smith, Harper A. 84981
Smith, Helen Grace. 84510
Smith, Heman C. 83246, 83256, 83292
Smith, Henry, 1550-1592? (82697)
Smith, Henry, 1805-1879. 82700-82701
Smith, Henry, b. 1815. 82698
Smith, Henry, 1784-1851. 94957 see also Texas (Provisional Government) Governor, 1835-1836 (Smith)
Smith, Henry, fl. 1858. 82699
Smith, Henry, fl. 1871. (82702)
Smith, Henry Barney. 82703
Smith, Henry Boynton, 1815-1876. 65654, (82704)-(82712)
Smith, Henry H. 82713
Smith, Henry Hollinsworth, 1815-1890. (82714)-82715
Smith, Henry Immanuel. see Schmidt, Henry Immanuel.
Smith, Henry M. 82717-82719
Smith, Henry More. 3947
Smith, Herbert H. 82720
Smith, Hervey. 82721
Smith, Hezekiah, 1737-1805. 82722-82723
Smith, Hezekiah Wright, 1828- illus. 30161
Smith, Horace Weymss, 1825-1891. 9836, 82696, 82724-82725, 82786, 84581, 84585, 84588, 84594-84595, 84604, 84609, 84610, 84614, 84616, 84622, 84628, 84648, 84662, 84674, 84678C, 84745
Smith, Horatio, 1779-1849. 82726
Smith, Hugh, 1736?-1789. 82727
Smith, Hugh, 1795-1849. 82728-82732, 97125
Smith, Hugh N. 82733
Smith, Humphrey, d. 1663. 82734-82735
Smith, Ira. 82736
Smith, Irem W. 82737-82738
Smith, Rev. Isaac. 82744
Smith, Isaac. of Indianapolis 82741

Smith, Isaac, 1744-1817. 82740
Smith, Isaac, 1749-1829. 82739 see also
 Harvard University. Librarian.
Smith, Isaac, 1817-1860. 82743
Smith, Isaac H. 82745
Smith, Isaac William, 1825- 82746-82748
 see also Manchester, N. H. Mayor,
 1869-1870 (Smith)
Smith, Ithamar. 82749
Smith, J. of Kingston, Canada. 82751
Smith, J. of Philadelphia 82750
Smith, J. Alden. 82752-82754 see also
 Colorado. State Geologist.
Smith, J. Augustine. 42764
Smith, J. C. 83926
Smith, J. F. tr. (32409)
Smith, J. Gray. 28398, 82755-82756
Smith, J. Henley. ed. 83509-83511
Smith, J. J. Pringle. 87931, 88005
Smith, J. M. defendant 64285
Smith, J. M. H. 82758
Smith, J. Massie. 82757
Smith, J. R. 82759
Smith, J. R. ed. 56189
Smith, Capt. J. S. 82760
Smith, J. V. reporter 57035
Smith, James. defendant at church trial
 82776
Smith, James. of Kingston, Jamaica 82761
Smith, James. of Sing Sing, N. Y. 82784
Smith, James. USA 82787
Smith, James. vicar of Lambourn 82762
Smith, James, 1737-1812. 48166, 82763-82771
Smith, James, 1771-1841. 70123, 82777-82778,
 82880 see also Maryland. State
 Vaccination Agent. U. S. Vaccine Agent.
Smith, James, 1771-1841. petitioner 82779
Smith, James, 1808-1868. 4710, 74983
Smith, James, d. 1812. 82772-82775
Smith, James, fl. 1832-1835. 82781-82783
Smith, James, fl. 1845. 82785
Smith, James, fl. 1856. 82786
Smith, Sir James Edward, 1759-1828. 25,
 (41354), 82788-(82789A)
Smith, James F. 12444, 82790
Smith, James H. 82791-82792
Smith, James McCune. 20714, 26677, 82793-
 82794
Smith, James Milton, 1823-1890. 82795 see
 also Georgia. Governor, 1872-1874
 (Smith)
Smith, James Stanley. see Strange, James
 Stanley-Smith, commonly styled Lord.
Smith, James Tinker, 1816-1854. 82796
Smith, James Wheaton, 1823-1900. 82797
Smith, James Youngs, 1809-1876. 66356, 70567,
 (70602), 70609, 82798-82799 see also
 Rhode Island. Governor, 1863-1866
 (Smith)
Smith, Jane. 82905
Smith, Jeremiah, 1759-1842. 78997, 82800-
 82801, 84704, 101803, 2d note after
 101883
Smith, Jeremiah, 1805-1874. 82802-82803
Smith, Jeremiah, 1837-1921. 85212
Smith, Jerome Van Crowninshield, 1800-1879.
 7042, (47319), 47329, 82804-82811, 97196
 see also Boston, Mayor, 1854 (Smith)
Smith, Jessie Willcox. illus. 83560
Smith, Johannes Erhard Valentin. see Valentin-
 Smith, Johannes Erhard.
Smith, John. pseud. "Honest John's" farmer's
 almanack. 82914
Smith, John. pseud. John Smith's letters.
 see Smith, Seba, 1792-1868.

Smith, John. pseud. Speech of John Smith.
 see Smith, Seba, 1792-1868
Smith, John, Jr. pseud. Romanism in Mexico.
 see Mayer, Brantz.
Smith, John, Jr., of Arkansas. pseud. Fete
 extraordinary. see Southworth, Sylvester S.
Smith, John. clockmaker. 82869-82870
Smith, John. geographer 82897
Smith, John. of New York 82911
Smith, John, of Quebec 67044, 82912
Smith, John. of Suffield 82878
Smith, John. Rector of St. Mary's, Colchester
 82868
Smith, John, 1580-1631. (8784), 13015, 19015,
 33667, 47885, 62957, 66686, 77538,
 78871, 82812-82857, 82859, 82863, note
 before 90030, 91853, 91860, note after
 92663, 92665, note after 99383C, 2d note
 after 100510, 3d note after 100533
Smith, John, 1580-1631. supposed author
 82862
Smith, John, fl. 1633-1673. 82864-82867
Smith, John, 1681-1766. 82871
Smith, John, 1722-1771. 41791, 82273,
 82873, 82982, 83984, 82972-92973, 94694-
 94695
Smith, John, 1735-1816. 82881-82882
Smith, John, 1735-1816. defendant 8434-(9435)
Smith, John, 1752-1809. 82879-82880
Smith, John, 1766-1831. 82885-82896
Smith, John, d. 1773. defendant 82874-82876
Smith, John, 1789-1858. 82913
Smith, John, 1790-1824. defendant 82898-
 82906, 82909-82910
Smith, John, fl. 1809. defendant 60470, 82884
 see also U. S. Marshall for the District
 of Pennsylvania. defendant
Smith, John, d. 1820. 82877
Smith, John, fl. 1821. defendant 102781
Smith, John Athelstane. see Carnota, John
 Athelstane Smith, Count of.
Smith, John Augustine, 1782-1865. 82918-82921
Smith, John Blair, 1756-1799. 82922-82923
Smith, John Broadfoot. 82924
Smith, John C., 1809-1883. 82925
Smith, John Calvin. 14797, 34335, 82926-
 82932, 103021
Smith, John Carpenter, 1816-1901. 82923-
 82935
Smith, John Cotton, 1765-1845. 33150, 82936-
 82939 see also Connecticut. Governor,
 1813-1818 (Smith)
Smith, John Cotton, 1826-1882. 64642, 82940-
 82947 see also New York (City) Church
 of the Ascension. Association. New York
 (City) Church of the Ascension. Rector.
Smith, John Cross, 1803-1878. 82948-82954
Smith, John F. 82955
Smith, John Fawcett. 82956
Smith, John Gregory, 1818-1891. 82957 see
 also Northern Pacific Railroad. Presi-
 dent.
Smith, John H. 34301, 82958-82968 see also
 Virginia. Commissioner of Revolutionary
 Claims.
Smith, John H. petitioner 82969-82971
Smith, John H., 1788- 82972
Smith, John Hyatt, 1824-1886. 82973
Smith, Mrs. John James. see Smith, Mrs.
 M. E.
Smith, John Jay, 1798-1881. 11649-11650,
 31858, (33066), 39255, 48984, (50852),
 61788, 82974-82987, 92135 see also
 Philadelphia. Library Company.

Librarian. Philadelphia. Library
Company. Loganian Library. Librar-
ian.
Smith, John Julius Pringle, d. 1894. 82988
Smith, John L. map publisher 82990
Smith, John L., d. 1898. 82989
Smith, John Lawrence, 1818-1883. 27419,
82991-83003 see also Interoceanic
Canal Convention, Paris, 1879. Repre-
sentative for San Francisco County and
City and Chamber of Commerce.
Smith, John Little, 1824-1890. 83004
Smith, John Mason. 83005
Smith, John Milton, 1823-1890. 82795 see
also Georgia. Governor, 1872-1876
(Smith)
Smith, John N. 83006
Smith, John Pye. 93199
Smith, John R. illus. 63894, 83007-83011
Smith, John Rubens, 1775?-1849. 83012
Smith, John Russell, 1810-1894. 83013-83017
Smith, John Spear, 1790-1866. (45211A),
83018
Smith, John Speed. (81524)
Smith, John Stafford. note before 90497
Smith, John T. 33500, 83020
Smith, John T. plaintiff 83019
Smith, John Thomas, 1766-1833. 83021
Smith, John W. 83022
Smith, John W., 1843- 83023
Smith, John Wheaton, 1835-1863. 83024
Smith, John William. defendant 6326, 1st
note after 96956, 1st note after 97284
Smith, John Yates, 1807-1874. 43740, 83025-
83029
Smith, Jonathan. defendant 25374
Smith, Jonathan B. 61493, 61734, 61794
Smith, Jonathan Bryan, d. 1872. 83030
Smith, Jonathan Kingsbury, 1797-1872. 83031
Smith, Jonathan S. 83032
Smith, Jorge. see Smith, George.
Smith, Joseph. of Grafton, Mass. 83306
Smith, Joseph. USN 84960 see also U. S.
Bureau of Yards and Docks.
Smith, Joseph, 1704-1781. see Smith, Josiah,
1704-1781.
Smith, Joseph, 1783-1881. 83316
Smith, Joseph, 1796-1868. 83304-83305
Smith, Joseph, fl. 1800. see Blyth, Joseph.
Smith, Joseph, 1805-1844. 50729, (50732),
58915, (59437), 83035-83037, 83241-
83280, 83282-83283, 83285-83289, 83293,
85168, 92675-92676, 92678-92680
Smith, Joseph, 1805-1844. defendant 50734,
83238-83240
Smith, Joseph, 1819-1896. 25362, 83307-83315
Smith, Joseph, 1832-1914. (50746), 69156,
75544, 83160, 83246, 83256, 83290-83302,
84431 see also Reorganized Church of
Jesus Christ of Latter Day Saints.
President.
Smith, Joseph, fl. 1853. 83529
Smith, Joseph A. 83318
Smith, Joseph Adams, 1837-1807. 83320
Smith, Joseph Adams, 1837-1907. defendant
at court of inquiry 83319
Smith, Joseph Aubin, 1832- 83317
Smith, Joseph Crouch, 1819-1857. 83321
Smith, Joseph Davis, 1828-1906. 83322
Smith, Joseph Edward Adams, 1822-1896.
28796, 83323-83336
Smith, Joseph Emerson, 1835-1881. 83337
Smith, Joseph Few, 1816-1888. 83338-83346
Smith, Joseph Fielding, 1838-1918. 83038,
83105, 83347
Smith, Joseph Fielding, 1876- 83348-83350

Smith, Joseph H. 83351
Smith, Joseph Jackson, 1817- 83352
Smith, Joseph Kencks. 83353-83355
Smith, Joseph Lee, 1776-1846. 83356
Smith, Joseph Mather, 1789-1866. 83357-
83363
Smith, Joseph Patterson, 1856-1898. 83365-
83366
Smith, Joseph Rowe, 1831-1911. 83367 see
also U. S. Army. Department of
Arizona. Medical Director. U. S. Army.
Department of Texas. Medical Director.
Smith, Joseph Russell, 1874- 83368-83384
Smith, Joseph Tate, 1818-1906. 83385-83391
Smith, Joseph Tate, 1850- 83392
Smith, Joseph Warren. 83396
Smith, Joseph Warren, 1831- 83393-83395
Smith, Joshua, d. 1731. 83397
Smith, Joshua, d. 1795. 83398-83419
Smith, Joshua, 1841- 83420
Smith, Joshua B. 84479
Smith, Joshua Hett, 1749-1818. 79487, 83421-
83422
Smith, Joshua Hett, 1749-1818. defendant
83423
Smith, Joshua Toulmin, 1816-1869. 83424-
83427
Smith, Josiah, 1704-1781. (24469)-24470,
83428-83454, 103514, 103588, 103601,
note after 103623
Smith, Josiah B. 83455
Smith, Josiah Dicket, 1815-1863. 83456
Smith, Josiah P. 83457
Smith, Judson. 83458
Smith, Julia (Crafts) 83459
Smith, Junius, 1780-1853. 83460-83462
Smith, Justin Almerin, 1819-1896. 83463-
83465
Smith, Justin Harvey, 1857- 83466-83472
Smith, L. incorrectly supposed author 83473,
83648
Smith, L. Bertrand, 1863- 83474
Smith, L. Eaton. 83475
Smith, L. M. 64405, 83476-83477, 84953
Smith, Laura Chase. 83479
Smith, Laura M. 83478
Smith, Lemuel. 83480
Smith, Leon Albert, 1863- 83481
Smith, Leonard Kingsley. 83482
Smith, Levi Ward, d. 1863. 83483
Smith, Lewis. 83484
Smith, Lewis Edwin, 1865- 83485
Smith, Lillian Clayton. 83486
Smith, Sir Lionel, Bart., 1778-1842. 83487
see also British Guiana. Governor (Smith)
Smith, Llewellyn Tarbox, 1845- 83488
Smith, Lloyd. 83489
Smith, Lloyd Pearsall, 1822-1886. 21321,
33202, 60360, 82987, 83490-83491, 84984
see also Philadelphia. Library Company.
Librarian.
Smith, Lloyd Waddell. 83492
Smith, Lorentz. appellant 83493
Smith, Lucius Edwin, 1822-1900. 83495
Smith, Mrs. Lucy, 1776-1855. 83496-83500
Smith, Mrs. Lydia Adeline, 1835- 83501
Smith, Lyndon Arnold, 1795-1865. 83502-83503
Smith, Mrs. Lyndon Arnold. see Smith,
Frances Louisa.
Smith, Mrs. M. A. 83505
Smith, Mrs. M. B. 83506
Smith, Mrs. M. E. 83507
Smith, Marcus A. 83508
Smith, Margaret (Bayard) 1778-1844. 83509-
83513, note after 84079, 2d note after
104829

Smith, Margaret Irvin, d. 1800. 82764
Smith, Margaret Mendenhall. 83514
Smith, Margaret Vowell. 83515-83516
Smith, Maria L. 38517
Smith, Marshall B., 1832-1882. 83518-83526
Smith, Martha, 1787-1841. 83527
Smith, Martha A. 83528
Smith, Martha (Hazeltine) 1809-1841. 83529
Smith, Martin F. 83530
Smith, Martin Leo. 83531-83532
Smith, Martin Luther, d. 1866. cartographer 83533-83534
Smith, Mary. 83535-83543
Smith, Mary Ann. 83545
Smith, Mary Constance. 83546-83547
Smith, Mary E. 83548
Smith, Mary Emily Estella. 83549
Smith, Mary Ettie V. (Coray) 1829- 28553-28554, 83550-83555
Smith, Mary Prudence (Wells) 1840- 83556-83560
Smith, Mary Rebecca Darby, 1814-1866. 83561-83565
Smith, Mary Roberts. 83556
Smith, Mary Stuart (Harrison) 1834- 83567
Smith, Mary Stuart (White) 1829- 83568, 83571
Smith, Matson Meier, 1826-1887. 83569-83570, 83571
Smith, Matthew. petitioner 19163, 19938, 60057, 64448 see also Pennsylvania (Colony) Citizens. petitioners
Smith, Matthew Hale, 1810-1879. 44324, 70570, 83572-83597
Smith, Maude Parsons (Canfield) 83599
Smith, May Almeda Cary, 1859- 83600
Smith, May Riley. 83601
Smith, Mayo Gerrish, d. 1901. 83602-83603
Smith, Melancthon, 1724-1798. 53473, 54042, 83604
Smith, Melancthon, 1810-1893. 83605
Smith, Melania (Boughton) 1789- 82449, 83606
Smith, Melville Clayton, 1833- 83607-83608
Smith, Meriwether, 1730-1790. 83609
Smith, Michael. missionary to South Carolina 83610-83614
Smith, Michael. Rector of Portland, Jamaica 83615
Smith, Michael. Minister of the Gospel 83616-83627
Smith, Miles Gilbert. 83628
Smith, Milton Hannibal, 1836-1921. 83629-83630 see also Louisville and Nashville Railroad Company. President.
Smith, Minna Carolina, 1860- 83631-83633
Smith, Montague. 83634
Smith, Moody B. 83635
Smith, Morgan L., 1801-1884. 83636
Smith, Mortimer J. defendant 83637-83638
Smith, Moses. of Huntington, N. Y. 83639-83640
Smith, Moses. USN 83641
Smith, Moses, 1830-1904. 83642-83646
Smith, Moses, fl. 1887. 83647
Smith, Mounson. 83473, 83648
Smith, Myrtle. 83649
Smith, N. 83650
Smith, N. E. 91531
Smith, Nancy W. Paine. 83652
Smith, Nathan. 83655, 101926 see also Association of Mechanics and Other Working Men, Washington, D. C. President.
Smith, Nathan. defendant 79945
Smith, Nathan, 1762-1829. 47328, 83653-83654, 83664
Smith, Nathan D. 83657, 85072

Smith, Nathan Ryno, 1797-1877. 47328, 83651, 83653-83654, 83658-83664
Smith, Nathan Ryno, 1797-1877. incorrectly supposed author 83664, note after 86785
Smith, Nathaniel. ed. and publisher (69154), 83665
Smith, Nathaniel, 1831-1877. 83666
Smith, Nathaniel R. 83667
Smith, Nathaniel Ruggles, 1784-1859. 83668
Smith, Neighbor. pseud. Cracked jug. see Williams, Moses.
Smith, Nelson Foot, 1813-1861. 83670
Smith, Nicholas, 1836-1911. 83671-83677 see also Republican Party. Wisconsin. State Central Committee. Press Secretary.
Smith, Nina L. 83678
Smith, Noah, 1755-1812. 83679
Smith, Noah E., 1808-1887. 83680
Smith, Nora Archibald. 83681-83682
Smith, Norman W. 75544, 83300
Smith, Nuima. 83683
Smith, O. W. ed. 83684
Smith, Oliver. 83685-83686
Smith, Oliver, 1766-1845. 7127, 83687
Smith, Oliver Hampton, 1794-1859. 83688-83695
Smith, Oreon (Mann) 83967
Smith, Oscar, 1887- 83697
Smith, Oscar L. 83698
Smith, Oskaloosa Minnewando, 1845-1910. 83699
Smith, Otis Alexander, 1862- 83700
Smith, P. M. 84342
Smith, Pascal B. (39340)
Smith, Percy Byshe. 83701
Smith, Percy Frazer, 1848- 83702-83703
Smith, Perry, 1783-1852. 83704-83705
Smith, Persifor Frazer, 1798-1858. 83706, 97562
Smith, Persifor Frazer, 1808-1882. 83707-83708 see also Pennsylvania. State Reporter.
Smith, Peter, 1753-1816. 83709-83710
Smith, Peter, 1802-1880. 83712
Smith, Peter, fl. 1856. 83711
Smith, Peter C. defendant 103189
Smith, Pewter. pseud. Mr. Printer, the following piece. 83713
Smith, Philip Anstie. 78964, 83714
Smith, Philip Henry, 1842- 83715-83719
Smith, Philip Sidney, 1877- 83720-83723
Smith, Platt. 83724-83725
Smith, Mrs. Pogson. see Smith, Sarah Pogson.
Smith, Preserved, 1759-1843. 83726-83728
Smith, Preserved, 1789-1881. 83729-83730
Smith, Prudence. 83731
Smith, Quintus Cincinnatus, 1842- 83732
Smith, R. A. 83733-83734
Smith, R. C., 1795-1832. 83735
Smith, R. F. 83736-83737
Smith, R. Inge. 83871
Smith, Ralph, 1810-1867. 83738
Smith, Ralph Clifton. 83739-83741
Smith, Ralph Dunning, 1804-1874. 83742-83743, 91200
Smith, Ralph J. 83744
Smith, Randolph Wellford. 83745-83747
Smith, Ray Burdick, 1867- 83738
Smith, Rebecca D. see Smith, Mary Rebecca Darby.
Smith, Rebekah Spalding. 83749
Smith, Reed, 1881- 83750-83751
Smith, Reeder. 83752-83754
Smith, Reeder. defendant at church conference 83755

Smith, Sarah. 84129-84130, 1st note after
95758
Smith, Sarah Eden. 84131
Smith, Sarah (Foote) 1829- 84132
Smith, Sarah Louisa (P   ), 1811-1832.
84135
Smith, Sarah (Pogson) 84136-84137
Smith, Sarah Saunders, 1843- 84138
Smith, Sarah Tappan. 32167
Smith, Seba, 1792-1868. 28463, 36147, 73524,
84139-84161, 84177-84187
Smith, Mrs. Seba. see Smith, Elizabeth
(Oakes) 1806-
Smith, Sebastian Bach, 1845-1895. 84188-
84216
Smith, Seth, 1785-1849. 84217
Smith, Seth, fl. 1826-1828. 84218-84219
Smith, Seymour R. 84220
Smith, Sheldon, 1788?-1835. 258, 84221-
84222
Smith, Sheldon, 1810- 84223
Smith, Sidney. 84224-84227
Smith, Sir Sidney, 1764-1840. see Smith,
Sir William Sidney, 1764-1840.
Smith, Sidney Irving, 1843-1926. 84228-84233
Smith, Simeon Conant. 84234
Smith, Snell. 84235
Smith, Sol. ed. 84241
Smith, Mrs. Sol. 84786
Smith, Solomon Franklin, 1801-1869. 84236-
84241
Smith, Sophia, 1796-1870. 84242
Smith, Sophia, 1847- 84243
Smith, Southwood. see Smith, Thomas South-
wood.
Smith, Spencer. 84244
Smith, Stephe R. 84245-84248
Smith, Stephen. defendant 84249
Smith, Stephen, 1739-1806. 84250
Smith, Stephen, 1823-1922. 1145, 54784,
84251-84277 see also New York (City)
Board of Health. New York (State)
Board of Social Welfare. Commissioners.
New York (State) Commissioner on
Lunacy. United States Sanitary Commis-
sion. Associate Medical Members.
Committee. Chairman.
Smith, Stephen C. 84278
Smith, Stephen Rensselaer, 1788-1850. 84279-
84292
Smith, Stephen Sanford, 1797- 84293-84294
Smith, Stevenson. 84295
Smith, Sumner S. 84296-84297 see also
U. S. Bureau of Mines.
Smith, Susan Augusta. 84298-84300
Smith, Susan E. (Drake?) 1817- 84301
Smith, Susan (Mason) 1765-1845. 82880, 84302
Smith, Susan Williamson. 84303
Smith, Sydney, 1771-1845. 84304-84321
Smith, Sydney K. 84322
Smith, Sylvanus, 1829-1917. 84323-84324
Smith, Sylvester, 1820-1911. 84325
Smith, T. of Edinburgh 84326
Smith, T. P. 84328
Smith, Mrs. T. P. ed. 41542
Smith, T. Rhys. 84329
Smith, Thaddeus. 84330
Smith, Theobald, 1859- 84331-84332
Smith, Theodate Louise. 84333
Smith, Theodore. 84334
Smith, Theodore Clarke, 1870- 84335-84342
Smith, Theodore Dehon. 84512
Smith, Theodore L. 84343-84344
Smith, Theophilus, 1800-1853. 84345
Smith, Theophilus Washington, 1784-1846.
84346, 103969

Smith, Thomas. Lecturer at St. Giles',
Cripplegate 84347-84349
Smith, Thomas. of Kentucky 84366
Smith, Thomas. of Liverpool 31982, 84355-
84356
Smith, Thomas. of St. Croix 84354
Smith, Thomas. painter 84372
Smith, Sir Thomas, 1558?-1625. 17425, 30120,
note after 99858, 99860, 99862, 99864,
99868, note after 99872
Smith, Thomas, 1702-1795. 84350-84353
Smith, Thomas, 1745-1809. defendant at
impeachment (30039), 1st note after 96927
Smith, Thomas, 1776-1844. 84368
Smith, Thomas, 1799-1876. 84369-84371
Smith, Thomas, 1808-1873. see Smyth,
Thomas, 1808-1873.
Smith, Thomas, d. 1830. 12891, 84357-84365
Smith, Thomas, fl. 1832. (22938), 84367
Smith, Thomas, d. 1868. 84373
Smith, Thomas Barlow. 84375-84378
Smith, Thomas Church Haskell, 1819-1897.
84385-84387
Smith, Thomas Edward Vermilye, 1857-1922.
84388-84390
Smith, Thomas Edwin. 84391-84392
Smith, Thomas F. 84393
Smith, Thomas Guilford, 1839-1912. 84394-
84395
Smith, Thomas Buckingham, 1810-1871. 2124,
9767, 9771, 21506, 28252, (73899),
84379-84384, 87205-87206
Smith, Thomas Kilby, 1820-1887. 84510, 84512
Smith, Thomas Kilby, 1871- 84397-84398
Smith, Thomas L. 84399
Smith, Thomas Lacey, 1805-1875. 12967,
84400-84403
Smith, Thomas Lacey, 1805-1873. supposed
author 12967, 61198, 84400
Smith, Thomas Laurens, 1797-1882. 84404-
84405
Smith, Thomas M. 92847
Smith, Thomas Marshall. 84406
Smith, Thomas Mather, 1797-1864. 84407
Smith, Thomas Mitchell. defendant 84409
Smith, Thomas P. 84410
Smith, Thomas Peters. 84411
Smith, Thomas Ralston, 1830-1903. 18959,
84412-84414
Smith, Thomas Rhett, 1768-1829. 84415
Smith, Thomas Southwood, 1788-1861. 84416-
84417
Smith, Thomas Timmis Vernon, 1824-1890.
84418-84419
Smith, Thomas W., fl. 1844. 84420
Smith, Thomas Washington. 84440
Smith, Thomas Watson. 84421-84422
Smith, Thomas West. 84423-84424
Smith, Thomas Wood, 1838-1894. 83293,
84425-84431
Smith, Timothy S. 84432-84433
Smith, Titus, 1768-1850. 84434-84435
Smith, Titus K. 84436-84439
Smith, Toulmin. see Smith, Joshua Toulmin,
1816-1869.
Smith, Truman, 1791-1884. 16008, 52200,
84441-84466, 93663
Smith, Tunstall. 84467-84468
Smith, Uriah, 1832-1903. 83749, 84469-84477
Smith, Valentin. 84478
Smith, Valentine, 1774-1869. 84479
Smith, Venture, 1729?-1805. 84480-84482
Smith, Victor, d. 1865. defendant 84483
Smith, Vivus Wood, 1804-1881. 84484 see
also New York (State) Superintendent of
Onondaga Salt Springs.

Smith, Volney Voltaire. 84485
Smith, W. A. 84486
Smith, W. G. 84487
Smith, W. H. N. 15402
Smith, W. J. ed. 95750
Smith, W. S. 86121
Smith, W. W. 84488
Smith, Walker C. 84489
Smith, Walter, 1836-1886. 84490-84499 see also Boston. Public Schools. Director of Drawing. Massachusetts. State Director of Art Education.
Smith, Walter A. 83071, 83289
Smith, Walter Allen, 1859-1882. 84505
Smith, Walter Brown, 1858- 84506
Smith, Walter Edward Clifton. 84507
Smith, Walter Gifford. 84517
Smith, Walter George, 1854-1925. 84397, 84508, 84516 see also American Bar Association. President. Commissioners of Uniform State Laws in National Conference. President. National Conference of Commissioners on Uniform State Laws.
Smith, Walter Ingelwood, 1862-1922. 84518-84520
Smith, Walter McCabe, 1886- 84521
Smith, Walter Robinson, 1875- 84522
Smith, Walter S., 1867- 84523-84524
Smith, Walter W. 83038, 83147, 83152
Smith, Warren. 84525-84526
Smith, Warren Du Pre, 1880- 84527-84533 see also Philippine Islands. Department of the Interior. Bureau of Science. Division of Geology and Mines. Chief.
Smith, Warren Slocum, 1891- 84534-84537
Smith, Wavell, d. 1756. 20721, 56481, 84539-84539, note after 97570
Smith, Wed. 47416
Smith, Wesley, 1815-1902. 84540-84541
Smith, Whitefoord, 1812-1893. 84542-84547
Smith, Wilder, 1835-1891. 84548
Smith, Willard J. 84549-84550
Smith, William. attorney at law see Smith, William Moore.
Smith, William. banker 84730
Smith, William. Chief Justice of Cape Breton 84697
Smith, William. Confederate seaman defendant 37272, 51456, 84728
Smith, William. defendant at impeachment 97092
Smith, William. F. S. A. S. 84731
Smith, William. of Glasgow 84713
Smith, William. of Hopewell, N. J. 84698
Smith, William. of Wisconsin 84729
Smith, William. schoolmaster in New York 84700
Smith, William. surveyor to the Royal African Company 65406, 84559-84562
Smith William, 1697-1769. 729, 731, 30380, (41650), 84554-84558, note after 91855, 98429
Smith, William, 1697-1769. supposed author 19341, 84557
Smith, William, d. 1673. 84551-84552
Smith, William, fl. 1716. 84553
Smith, William, 1727-1803. 96, (1133), 2464, 3849, 5883, 7876, 10666, 14395, 15526, 17463, (17766), 19370, 20040, (20046), 20049, 23179, 25279, 25577, (27219), 27658, 33694, 34476, 50865, 56629, 58214, 60451, 60742, 61642-61643, 62116, note after 63244, 72726-72727, 84577-84645, 84647-84678C, 84692, 84745, 85254, 94594, note after 97095, 2d-3d

notes after 97876, 1st note after 100814, note after 101995, 104455, note after 105999 see also Pennsylvania. University. Provost. Society of Noblemen and Gentlemen in London, for the Relief and Instruction of Poor Germans, and Their Descendants, Settled in Pennsylvania, and the Adjacent British Colonies in America. Trustees General. Secretary. United Illinois and Wabash Land Companies. Agent.
Smith, William, 1727-1803. defendant (32780)-32781, 69581
Smith, William, 1727-1803. petitioner 22337, 34294, 84577, 84628, 99771 see also Established or Parochial Schoolmasters in Scotland. Commissioner. petitioner United Illinois and Wabash Land Companies. Council. petitioners
Smith, William, 1727-1803. supposed author 10663, 10671, 15526, 20040, 23389, 23545, 40287, 40419, (41650), note after 63244, 66930, (74155), 84610, 84616-84619, 84627, 84642, 84676, 95730, 96804, 1st note after 101814
Smith, William, 1728-1793. 13171, 24958, (53066), 53730, 53732, 54472, 84558, 84564-84576, 90111
Smith, William, d. 1749? 84563
Smith, William, 1754?-1821. 51144, 56752, 66179, 84679-84696
Smith, William, 1756-1835. 84699
Smith, William, 1758-1812. see Smith, William Loughton, 1758-1812.
Smith, William, 1762-1840. 84705-84712
Smith, William, 1769-1847. 14566, 14701, 43858, 84570-84571, 84701, 99776
Smith, William, d. 1789. defendant 101087
Smith, William, 1797-1887. 84716-84724, 89208
Smith, William, 1799-1830. 84703-84704
Smith, William, 1812-1872. 13066, 84725-84727 see also Cincinnati. Chamber of Commerce and Merchant's Exchange. Superintendent.
Smith, Sir William, 1813-1893. ed. 79961-79962
Smith, William, fl. 1820. defendant at impeachment 84702
Smith, William, fl. 1824. defendant 103189
Smith, William, fl. 1832. 88083
Smith, William, fl. 1842. ed. 1630
Smith, William, fl. 1850. of New York 84714
Smith, William, fl. 1850. of Paris 84715
Smith, William A. 84732-84733
Smith, William Alexander, 1820-1911. 84735
Smith, William Alexander, 1843- 84734, 84910
Smith, William Anderson, 1842- 84736-84737
Smith, William Andrew, 1802-1870. (64773), 84739-84742
Smith, William Andrew, 1802-1870. complainant 84738, 84743
Smith, William Anthony, 1809-1887. 84744-84745
Smith, William Austin, 1872-1922. 84746
Smith, William B. comp. 84747
Smith, William B. defendant 84748 see also Philadelphia. Mayor, 1886 (Smith) defendant
Smith, William B. USA 84749
Smith, William Bartlett, 1806-1868. 43314, 84741, 84750
Smith, William Benjamin, 1850- 84751-84752
Smith, William C., 1809-1886. 84753
Smith, William Calvin, 1842-1921. 84754
Smith, William Chardo, 1818-1891. 84755-84757A

Smith, William Christopher, 1861- 84758-
84760
Smith, William D., d. 1848. 84761-84762
Smith, William Dexter. 84763
Smith, William E. 84764 see also Washing-
ton County, Oregon. Referee of Real
Estate.
Smith, William F., fl. 1852. 84766
Smith, William F., fl. 1864. 84767
Smith, William Farrar, 1824-1903. 36377,
69676, 84769-84774 see also Inter-
national Ocean Telegraph Company.
President. New York (City) Police
Commissioners. U. S. Agent on the
Improvement of Rivers and Harbors in
Delaware, in Maryland East of Chesa-
peake Bay, and of Inland Waterway from
Chincoteague Bay to Delaware Bay,
Virginia, Maryland, and Delaware.
Smith, William G. 84775
Smith, William George. 84776
Smith, William H. 84777
Smith, William Henry. of Canada 43858,
84779-84780
Smith, William Henry, 1788-1865. ed. and
tr. 4805, 85347
Smith, William Henry, 1806-1872. 84781-
84786
Smith, William Henry, 1833-1896. 75022,
84787-84791
Smith, William Henry, 1838- 84792
Smith, William Henry, 1839- 84793-84796
Smith, William Henry, 1846-1925. 84797-
84891
Smith, William Henry, d. 1860. 70537, 84778
see also Rhode Island. Secretary of
State.
Smith, William Henry Chatterton, d. 1893.
84802
Smith, William Hugh, 1826-1899. 84803-84809
see also Alabama. Governor, 1868-1870
(Smith)
Smith, William James. ed. 28776, 2d note
after 94663
Smith, William K. defendant 102578
Smith, William L. 84810
Smith, William L. G., 1814-1878. 84812-84813,
note after 92624
Smith, William Locke, 1844- 84814
Smith, William Loe, 1855- 84815
Smith, William Loughton, 1758-1812. 10983,
29948, (52392), (29973), 84816-84837,
87846, 2d note after 104983
Smith, William Loughton, 1758-1812. supposed
author 10663, 23545, 23994, (40365),
40434, 84819, 84829, 84331-84832, 87863,
2d note after 104983
Smith, William Moore, 1759-1821. 782, 17976,
34761, 84838-84842 see also Board of
Commissioners Under Article 6th of the
Treaty Between Great Britain and the
United States, London, Nov. 19, 1794.
Smith, William Pitt, 1760-1795. 84843-84845,
note after 94295
Smith, William Prescott, 1825?-1782. 84846-
84848 see also Baltimore and Ohio
Railroad Company. Assistant Master of
Transportation.
Smith, William Prescott, 1825?-1782. supposed
author 2992, 84847
Smith, William R. 84849
Smith, William Richmond, 1752-1820. 52562,
84850 see also Presbyterian Church in
the U. S. A. Presbytery of Newcastle.
Moderator.
Smith, William Richmond, 1849?- 84851

Smith, William Robert Lee, 1846- 84852-84853
Smith, William Robinson, 1813-1894. 84854
Smith, William Roy, 1876- 84855-84858
Smith, William Rudolph, 1787-1868. 84859-
84866 see also Wisconsin. State
Historian. U. S. Commissioner for
Treaty With the Chippewa Indians of the
Upper Mississippi
Smith, William Russell, 1815-1896. 2159,
18201, 30303, 73783, 84867-84895, 89208
Smith, William Russell, 1815-1896. supposed
author 38269, 84886
Smith, Sir William Sidney, 1764-1840. (1534),
(27337)
Smith, William Sooy, 1830-1916. 84897-84899
Smith, William Spooner, 1821-1916. 84990-
84902
Smith, William Stephens, 1755-1816. 10663,
16785, 84819, 84903
Smith, William Stephens, 1755-1816. defendant
84904
Smith, William Steuben, 1787-1850. 84906
Smith, William Thayer, 1839-1909. 84907-84908
Smith, William Thomas, 1844-1915. 84909
Smith, William Thomas, 1868- 84734, 84910
Smith, Mrs. William Walter. see Smith,
Maude Parsons (Canfield)
Smith, William White. (61541), 61969, 84911-
84913
Smith, William White. incorrectly supposed
author 63325, 85166
Smith, William Wragg, d. 1875. 84914-84915
Smith, William Wye, 1827-1917. 84916-84919
Smith, Wooster. 54915
Smith, Worthington, 1796-1856. 84920-84924,
84926-84930
Smith, Worthington Curtis, 1823-1894. 84931-
84933
Smith, Zachariah Frederick, 1827-1911. 84934-
84940
Smith, Zemro Augustus, 1837- 84941
Smith, Zoda G. 84942
Smith. firm publishers 84983
Smith. firm see Hall and Smith. firm
publishers Stiles, Sherman & Smith.
firm cartographers/engravers
Smith (Lloyd P.) firm publishers 84984
Smith (Pliny F.) firm publishers 84982
Smith (Sylvanus) & Co. firm 84324
Smith (T. J.) & Co. firm publishers see
Smith (Thomas J.) & Co. firm
publishers
Smith (Thomas H.) & Son. firm 84396
Smith (Thomas H.) & Son. firm debtors
84396
Smith (Thomas H.) & Son. firm Trustee.
84396
Smith (Thomas J.) & Co. firm publishers
84327
Smith (W. F.) & Co. firm see Smith
(William F.) & Co. firm publishers
Smith (William) & Co. firm 84583
Smith (William F.) & Co. firm publishers
84768
Smith (William L.) firm publishers 84810
Smith & Barrow. firm publishers 84943
Smith & Bartlett. firm 84944
Smith & Du Moulin. firm publishers 12641,
84945
Smith & Elliott. firm publishers 84946-84947
Smith & Forman. firm publishers 82291,
84948-84950
Smith & Swinney. firm 64405, 83477, 84953
Smith, Bleakley & Co. firm 84954
Smith Brothers & Co. firm 55877, 84955-
84960

Smith & Barrow's monthly magazine. 84843
Smith & Du Moulin's [directory] for the year ending May 1, 1860. 12641
Smith & Forman's New-York and New-Jersey almanac. 82291
Smith & Forman's New-York & New-Jersey almanac, for the year of Our Lord, 1808. 84948
Smith & Forman's New-York pocket almanac. 84949
Smith & Forman's New-York sheet almanac. 84950
Smith & Parmelee Gold Company. firm 84951-84952
Smith & Parmelee Gold Company. Capital, 125,000 shares $20 each. 84952
Smith & Parmelee Gold Company. President. George Warren Smith. 84951
Smith and Pocahontas. A poem. (44884)
Smith centennial memorial. 84223
Smith Centre, Kansas. Smith County Old Settlers Homecoming Association. see Smith County Old Settlers Homecoming Association, Smith Centre, Kansas.
Smith College, Northampton, Mass. 84961
Smith County Old Settlers Homecoming Association, Smith Centre, Kansas. 84962
Smith genealogy. 84390
Smith literary journal. 84090
Smithe, Sir Thomas. see Smith, Sir Thomas, 1558?-1625.
Smithee, James Newton, 1842-1905? 84962A see also Arkansas. Commissioner of State Lands.
Smither, Harriet. 84865, 84870
Smither, James. 84963-84964
Smithers, Nathaniel Barrett, 1818-1896. 84965-84968
Smithers, William Townsend, 1863- 84969
Smithey, Narvin, 1869- 84970
Smitherfield, R. I. 84972
Smithfield, R. I. Commissioners of the Town Asylum. see Smithfield, R. I. Town Asylum. Commissioners.
Smithfield, R. I. Committee of Investigation. 84974
Smithfield, R. I. Ordinances, etc. 84973
Smithfield, R. I. Overseer of the Poor. 84974
Smithfield, R. I. School Committee. 84971
Smithfield, R. I. Smithfield Seminary. see Smithfield Seminary, Smithfield, R. I.
Smithfield, R. I. Smithfield Union Institute. see Smithfield Union Institute, Smithfield, R. I.
Smithfield, R. I. Town Asylum. Commissioners. 84974
Smithfield, R. I. Town Asylum. Keeper. 84974
Smithfield, R. I. Town Clerk. 84976 see also Mann, Stafford.
Smithfield, R. I. Town Treasurer. 84976 see also Mann, Stafford.
Smithfield Academy, Union Village, R. I. see Smithfield Seminary, Smithfield, R. I.
Smithfield Seminary, Smithfield, R. I. 84977 see also Smithville Seminary, North Scituate, R. I.
Smithfield Union Institute, Smithfield, R. I. 84977 see also Smithfield Seminary, Smithfield, R. I.
Smithmeyer, John L., 1832-1908. 84978-84980
Smithmeyer and Pelz. firm 84980
Smithmeyer & Co. firm 84980
Smith's animadversions upon, and refutations of sundry gross errors. 82289

Smith's atlas. note before 83906, 83922, 83929, 83930-83935
Smith's atlas, for schools, academies, and families. note before 83906, 83928
Smith's atlas of modern and ancient geography. note before 83906, 83936
Smith's business chart. 83884, 83886
Smith's Canadian gazetteer. 84780
Smith's captivity with the Indians. 82766
Smith's Cash Store, San Francisco, Calif. firm 84981
Smith's comemrcial and travelling map of Canada West. 84780
Smith's continuation of the History of New-York. 84571
Smith's dollar magazine. 84982
Smith's English grammar, on the productive system. note before 83906, 83920
Smith's first book in arithmetic. 83910
Smith's first book in Geography. note before 83906, 83937-83945
Smith's first part. Intellectual and practical grammar. Part first. note before 83906, 83915-83916
Smith's geography for schools, academies, and families. 83936
Smith's geography. Geography on the productive system. note before 83906, 83922-83926
Smith's geography. Geography on the productive system for schools, academies, and families. 83927
Smith's guide to the southwest. 83737
Smith's hand-book and guide to Philadelphia. 84983
Smith's hand-book for travellers through the United States of America. 82930
Smith's homoeopathic directory of New York and vicinity. 82719
Smith's homoeopathic directory, of the United States. 82717
Smith's illustrated guide to and through Laurel Hill Cemetery. 83734
Smith's inductive arithmetic, and federal calculator. note before 83906, 83914
Smith's introductory arithmetic. The little federal calculator. note before 83906, 83910
Smith's modern and ancient geography. 83927
Smith's new arithmetic. Arithmetic on the productive system. note before 83906, 83911
Smith's new arithmetic or third book. 83911
Smith's new common school geography. 83775
Smith's new geography containing map questions. note before 83906, 83956
Smith's new grammar. 83918-83919
Smith's new grammar. English grammar on the productive system. note before 83906, 83918
Smith's New York and Brooklyn homoeopathic directory. 82718
Smith's oration. 84826
Smith's pocket commercial and travelling map of Canada West. 84780
Smith's primary arithmetic, and federal calculator. note before 83906, 83913
Smith's primitive psalmody. 84696
Smith's productive grammar. 83919
Smith's quarto, or second book in geography. 83951-83955
Smith's revised edition of the citizens' hand book and voter's manual. 84911
Smith's second book in arithmetic. 83908
Smith's street sweeping machine. 83845

Smith's universal guide, to the country along the line. 83737

Smith's weekly volume. 21321, 33202, 82987, 83491, 84984

Smithons, James. 84985, 85058

Smithson, Rumsey. 84991

Smithson, William T. 84992-84994

Smithsoni, Don Carlos. 84995-84996

Smithsonian bequest: an article from the Princeton review. 85068

Smithsonian bequest. Prof. Henry's exposition. 31403

Smithsonian bequest. (To accompany amendatory bill H. R. no. 1.) 85069

Smithsonian bequest. (To accompany H. R. no. 187.) 85070

Smithsonian catalogue system. 85071

Smithsonian collections. see Smithsonian miscellaneous collections.

Smithsonian contributions to knowledge. 232, 2739, 2740, (2588), (7760), 11480, 12008, 13612, 14174, 18806, 19648, 22204, 27419, 27280, 27484, 28097, 28373, 28374, 30782, 30893, 31021, (31800), 36577, 37003, 38976, 39664, 39903- 39904, (39906)-39908, 43042, 47101, 47171, (47371), 71333, (77905)-77912, 83657, note after 84996, 85007, 85010, 85072, 85088, 86970, 89950, 89954, 89955, 91824, 91921, 94010, 94011, 96295-96297, 97081, 101074-101075, 103821, 103824, 105674

Smithsonian Institution. 232, 2739-2740, (2588), 2804, 2805, 5499, 5502-(5503), (7760), 10905, 11480, 12008, 13612, 14174, 15899, 18806, 19648, (22053), 22204, 25992, 27280, 27301-(27302), 27419, 27484, 28097, 28373, 28374, 29510, 30782, 30893, 31021, (31800), 36108, 36577, 37003, 38976, 39664, 39903- 39904, (39906)-39908, 39662, 41775, 43042, 47101, 47171, (47371), 48986, 49668, 50664, 57823, 50842, 50845, 63754, 67966, 70122, 70476, 71333, 72586, 74014, 83657, 84985, 84987, 84988, 84990, note after 84996-84997, 84999, 85003, 85014, 85016-85017, 85019-85025, 85027-85039, 85040-85041, 85045-85047, 85049, 85051, 85063, 85065, 85067, 85069, 85072, 85075-85077, 85079-85080, 85085, 85087-85089, 85093, 86970, 89950, 89954, 89955, 90314, 91824, 91921, 92687, 94010-94011, 96295-96297, 97081, 100645, 101074, 101075, 103821-103824, 105674

Smithsonian Institution. Advisory Committee on the Langley Aerodynamical Labratory. 85027

Smithsonian Institution. Assistant Secretary. 85015, 85092, 85097 see also Abbot, C. G. Goode, George Brown.

Smithsonian Institution. Bache Scientific Trust. 85080

Smithsonian Institution. Board of Regents. 36107, note after 84996, 85024, 85026, 85030, 85032, 85042, 85043-85054, 85057-85059, 85060, 85066, 85080-85081 see also Choate, Rufus.

Smithsonian Institution. Board of Regents. Committees. 85080

Smithsonian Institution. Board of Regents. Minority. 85052

Smithsonian Institution. Board of Regents. Special Committee on the Communication of Prof. Henry. 85024

Smithsonian Institution. Board of Regents. Special Committee on the Distribution of the Income. 85059-85060

Smithsonian Institution. Board of Regents. Special Committee on the Distribution of the Smithsonian Fund. 85054

Smithsonian Institution. Board of Regents. Special Committee on the Distribution of the Smithsonian Fund. Majority. 85074

Smithsonian Institution. Board of Regents. Special Committee on the Distribution of the Smithsonian Fund. Minority. 85074

Smithsonian Institution. Board of Regents. Special Committee on the Proposal Submitted by the American Association of Agricultural Colleges and Experiment Stations. 85061

Smithsonian Institution. Chancellor. 85010, 85015 see also Taft, William Howard, Pres. U. S., 1857-1930.

Smithsonian Institution. Charter. 84998, 85018, 85045, 85058

Smithsonian Institution. Chief Clerk. 85007 see also Rhees, William Jones.

Smithsonian Institution. Committee on Cooperation. 85063

Smithsonian Institution. Committee to Consider What Will be the Best Use for the Large Room in the Second Story of the Main Building. 85056

Smithsonian Institution. Corcoran Gallery. 85080

Smithsonian Institution. Curator. 85065 see also Kidder, J. H.

Smithsonian Institution. Executive Committee. 85057

Smithsonian Institution. Executive Committee. Commission. 85071

Smithsonian Institution. Hamilton Bequest. 85080

Smithsonian Institution. Librarian. 85092 see also Adler, Cyrus. Jewett, Charles Coffin.

Smithsonian Institution. Memorial Meeting, 1906. 85067

Smithsonian Institution. Organization Committee. 85025, 85058

Smithsonian Institution. Reading-Room. 85011

Smithsonian Institution. Regents. see Smithsonian Institution. Board of Regents.

Smithsonian Institution. Secretary. 64753, 85000, 85002, 85005, 85014, 85024, 85026, 85043, 85048, 85052, 85062, 85084, 85086, 85090 see also Baird, Spencer Fullerton, 1823-1887. Henry, Joseph, 1797-1878. Walcott, Charles Doolittle.

Smithsonian Institution. Toner Lectures. 85080

Smithsonian Institution. Tyndall Trust. 85080

Smithsonian Institution. 85073

Smithsonian Institution. An article from the North American review. 85074

Smithsonian Institution annual reports. 85007, 85088

Smithsonian Institution, at Washington. 85075

Smithsonian Institution. [By Alonzo Gray.] 28365

Smithsonian Institution. By G. Brown Goode. 85091

Smithsonian Institution: documents, 1879. 85069

Smithsonian Institution: documents relating to its origin and history. Edited by William J. Rhees. 70476, 85076

Smithsonian Institution. Documents relative to its origin and history. 1835-1899. 85077

Smithsonian Institution, 1846-1896. The history of its first half century. 84986, 84988, 85097

Smithsonian Institution. Extracted from the American journal of science and arts. 85078

Smithsonian Institution. From the Smithsonian report for 1901. 85079

Smithsonian Institution. Its origin, growth, and activities. 85096

Smithsonian Institution: journals of the Board of Regents. 85080

Smithsonian Institution. March 3, 1855. 85081

Smithsonian Institution. Reports of explorations and surveys. 39666

Smithsonian Institution, Washington. 85082

Smithsonian library. 85083

Smithsonian meteorological observations. 85084

Smithsonian miscellaneous collections. 2739, 2804, 5499, 5502-(5503), 15899, (22053), 27301, (27302), 28374, 29510, 41775, 50664, 50842, 50845, 57823, 70476, 74014, (77216), (78525), (81352), 84985, 84987, 84990, note after 84996, 85004-85007, 85013, 85014, 85019, 85024, 85027, 85029, 85031, 85033, 85036-85037, 85039, 85046-85047, 85063, 85067, 85076, 85077, 85080, 85085, 85087-85088, 90314

Smithsonian miscellaneous publications. 85028, 85037, 85079, 85093

Smithsonian museum miscellanea. 85087

Smithsonian report for 1864. (4363)

Smithsonian report for 1869. (81352)

Smithsonian report for 1863. (4363)

Smithsonian report: on the construction of catalogues of libraries. 36108

Smithville Seminary, North Scituate, R. I. see Lapham Institute, North Scituate, R. I.

Smithwick, Nanna. see Donaldson, Nanna (Smithwick)

Smithwick, Noah, 1808-1899. 85099

Smitten household. 85100

Smoaking age. 94165

Smoaking flax, raised into a sacred flame. 46454

Smock, David, 1808?-1878. 85101

Smock, Finley M. 85101

Smoked glass. 54960

Smoker's and snuff-taker's companion. 47451

Smokers', chewer's, and snuff-taker's companion. 85102

Smoking and drinking. 58958

Smoking and smokers. 85103

Smollett, Tobias George, 1721-1771. 1601, 11228, 20518, 26815, 32163, 35753, 85104-85106

Smollett, Tobias George, 1721-1771. supposed author 102632

Smolnikar, Andreas Bernardus, b. 1795. 44088, 51096, 85107-85129, 3d note after 94085

Smolnikar, Andreas Bernardus, b. 1795. defendant 85129

Smoot, Joseph, d. 1857. petitioner 85130

Smoot, L. R. 85131 see also Virginia. Quartermaster General.

Smoot, Richmond Kelley, 1836-1905? 85132

Smooth preaching. 101059

Smothers, Samuel Henry. ed. 93249

Smucker, Isaac, 1807-1894. 13573, 85133-85144

Smucker, Israel, 1807-1894. 13573, (40970), 85133

Smucker, Samuel Mosheim. see Schmucker, Samuel Mosheim, 1823-1863.

Smucker, Samuel V. N. see Schmucker, Samuel Mosheim, 1823-1863.

Smuggler's son. 42903, 85171

Smuggler's son; and other tales and sketches. 42903, 85171

Smull, John Augustus, 1832-1879. 60233, 60595, 85172-85177 see also Pennsylvania. Legislature. House of Representatives. Resident Clerk.

Smull, William Pauli. 85177

Smull's legislative hand book, and manual. 85177

Smull's legislative hand book. Rules and decisions. 85177

Smylie, James, 1780?-1853. 85178-85180

Smyser, Daniel Martin. 85181-85182

Smyser, William Emery, 1866- 85182

Smyser Centennial Celebration. Committee. 85183

Smyth, Albert Henry, 1863-1907. 84586

Smyth, Alexander, 1765-1830. (68946), 82324, 85184-85200 see also U. S. Army. Inspector General.

Smyth, Alexander, 1765-1830. petitioner 85200

Smyth, Anson, d. 1886. 85101, 85202, 85348 see also Ohio. State Commissioner of Common Schools.

Smyth, Coke. 85203

Smyth, D. Clement, Bp. 72941 see also Dubuque (Diocese) Bishop (Smith)

Smyth, David William, 1764-1837. 85204-85205 see also Ontario. Surveyor General.

Smyth, Edward. 85206-85207

Smyth, Egbert Coffin, 1829-1904. 85208-85211, 85213-85224

Symth, Egbert Coffin, 1829-1904. defendant/appellant 85212

Smyth, Eliza Ann Carmichael. plaintiff 86225

Smyth, Emily (Lane) 85229

Smyth, Francis George. supposed author 85226

Smyth, Frederick, 1819-1899. 44211, (52938), 85227-85229 see also Manchester, N. H. Mayor, 1852-1854 (Smyth) Manchester, N. H. Mayor, 1864 (Smyth) New Hampshire. Governor, 1865-1867 (Smyth)

Smyth, George Washington, 1803-1866. 85230-85231

Smyth, J. F. D. 85616

Smyth, Sir James. 85234

Smyth, James Carmichael, 1741-1821. 85232-85233

Smyth, Sir James Carmichael, Bart., 1779-1838. 85234-85238

Smyth, Jane. 85240

Smyth, John. 85239-85240

Smyth, John F. 85241 see also New York (State) Insurance Department. Superintendent.

Smyth, John Ferdinand Dalziel, 1745-1814. 1367, 85243-85256

Smyth, Patrick, d. 1796. 85257

Smyth, Ralph D. see Smith, Ralph Dunning, 1804-1874.

Smyth, Robert Carmichael. see Carmichael Smyth, Robert Stewart, 1800?-1888.

Smyth, Robert Stewart Carmichael, 1800?-1888. see Carmichael Smyth, Robert Stewart, 1800?-1888.

Smyth, Thomas, 1808-1873. 85227, 85262-85341, 85344, 88045C

Smyth, W. S. ed. 85202

Smyth, Sir Warington Wilkinson, 1817-1890. 36879

Smyth, William, 1765-1849. 85343-85344

Smyth, William, 1797-1868. 85345
Smyth, William, 1800-1877. 85346
Smyth, William, fl. 1810. 85342
Smyth, William Henry, 1788-1865. 4805,
  85347
Smyth, William Henry Carmichael. defendant
  85225
Smyth, Winfield Scott, 1838-1908. ed 85202,
  85348
Smyth on presbytery and prelacy. 85314
Smythe, Charles R. 85349
Smythe, Charles Winslow, 1829-1865. 85350-
  85355
Smythe, Henry. 85356
Smythe, J. C. tr. 32992
Smythe, James M. 23089, (45041), 85357,
  88340
Smythe, Samuel. 85358
Smythe, Sir Thomas, 1558?-1625. see Smith,
  Sir Thomas, 1558?-1625.
Smythe, William Herbert. 85359-85360
Smythe's primary grammar. 85352
Smythe's school grammar. 85355
Smyth's lectures on the apostolical succession.
  85312
Snagg, Sir William, d. 1878. 85361-85362
Snake in the grass caught and crush't. 106107
Snake in the grass: or, satan transform'd into
  an angel of light. 40195-40197, 78185,
  85363-85365, 103655, 105650
Snapp, Henry, 1822-1895. 85366-86369
Snare broken. 47148
Snarest nulig t at ivaerksaette Negerslaveriets
  fuldkomme ophor paa de Dansk Vestin-
  diske oer. 18724
Snarly or Sharly. 85370
Snatch fleeting pleasures. 85371-85372
Snead, Claiborne, 1836-1909. 85373
Snead, Thomas Lowndes, 1828-1890. 85374
Sneak yclepid Copperhead. 85375
Sneath, Richard G. (76041) see also San
  Francisco. Chamber of Commerce.
  President.
Snedecor, Victoria Gayle, 1824-1888. 85375A
Sneed, Achilles. 85376
Sneed, John Louis Taylor, 1820-1901. 85377-
  85378 see also Tennessee. State
  Reporter.
Sneed, William C., d. 1862. 85379
Snelgrave, William. 85380-85382
Snell, Mrs. Charles. 85383
Snell, Daniel W. 85384-85385
Snell, Ebenezer Strong, 1801-1876. 85386
Snell, Thomas, 1774-1862. 65085, 85387-85409
Snelling, ----------, fl. 1851. 85410
Snelling, Anna L. (Putnam) 85411, 85415
Snelling, George Henry, 1801-1892. 85413
Snelling, George Henry, 1801-1892. petitioner
  85412
Snelling, Henry Hunt. 85411, 85414-85415
Snelling, Joseph. 85416
Snelling, Josiah, 1782-1828. 85417
Snelling, Richard, 1828?-1893. 85418, 85419-
  85420
Snelling, Richard, 1828?-1893. reporter 85421
Snelling, Richard E. 85422
Snelling, Thomas, 1712-1773. 85423
Snelling, William Joseph, 1804-1848. 43874,
  (59189), 85424-85426, 85428-85429,
  85431-85432, 3d note after 94249, 2d note
  after 97259
Snelling, William Joseph, 1804-1848. defendant
  85430
Snelling, William Joseph, 1804-1848. supposed
  author 1736, 67963, 85427, 85433
Snelson, J. B. ed. (75298)

Snethen, Maria. 85434
Snethen, Nicholas, 1769-1845. 85435-85443
Snethen, Reynold. 85444
Snethen, Worthington Garrettson. ed. 27318,
  85441, 85443, 85445-85447
Snethen on lay representation. 85442
Snider, Antonio. see Snider-Pellegrini,
  Antonio, 1802?-
Snider, Benjamin S., 1821- 85448
Snider, Benjamin S. 85449
Snider, Denton Jacques, 1841-1925. 85450-
  85451
Snider, Joseph. 85452
Snider-Pellegrin, Antonio, 1802?- 85453
Snip snags and snickerings of Simon Snodgrass.
  85468
Snipe, Simon. pseud. Sports of New York.
  85454
Snipe (Ship) in Admiralty 21993, 29308, 2d
  note after 92630
Sniter, James. defendant 96928
Snively, Jacob. 85455
Snively, Joseph, 1786-1872. 85456
Snively, William Andrew, 1833-1901. 63118,
  85457-85462
Snively, A. D. 1659-A. D. 1882. 85458
Snoblace ball. 85463
Snodgrass, Charles E. 85464
Snodgrass, John. 85465 see also Allegheny
  Portage Railroad. Superintendent of
  Motive Power.
Snodgrass, Joseph Evans, 1813-1880. 85466-
  85467
Snodgrass, Simon. pseud. Snip snaps and
  snickerings. 85468
Snodgrass, William, 1827-1906. 85469-85475
Snodgrass, William Davis, 1796-1886. 85476-
  85483
Snooks, Triptolemus. pseud. Cockney in
  America. 14112
Snorre Sturlusons andra band. 85484
Snorre Sturlusons Nordländske konunga sagor.
  85484
Snorri Sturluson, 1178-1241. 85484
Snow, Asa B., 1809?-1864. 85485
Snow, Azell. plaintiff 85486
Snow, Benjamin Poor, 1831-1907. 85487
Snow, Caleb Hopkins, 1796-1835. 85488-85489
Snow, Charles Andrew, 1829-1903. 85490
Snow, Charles Henry Boylston, 1822-1875.
  85481
Snow, Chauncey H., 1833?-1893. 85492 see
  also U. S. Government Director of the
  Union Pacific Railroad.
Snow, Edwin Miller, 1820-1888. (66238), 66245,
  66255, 66280, (66350)-(66352), 66356-
  66359, 66366, 66368, 66370, 70693,
  85493-85502 see also Providence, R. I.
  City Registrar. Providence, R. I. Super-
  intendent of Health. Rhode Island. Super-
  intendent of the Census.
Snow, Edwin Miller, 1820-1888. petitioner
  85498
Snow, Eliza Roxcy. see Young, Eliza Roxcy
  (Snow) Smith.
Snow, Erastus, 1818-1888. 83115, 83215,
  85508-85513
Snow, Francis Huntington, 1840-1908. 85514
Snow, George Knowles, 1826-1885. 85515
Snow, George Washington, 1809-1900. 85516
Snow, H. O. 85517
Snow, Henry, 1820-1880. 85518
Snow, Herman, 1812-1905. 85519-85520
Snow, James. respondent (70576)
Snow, Joseph Crocker, 1833-1901. 85521-85522
Snow, Josiah. 85523

Snow, Laura J. 85524
Snow, Lorenzo, 1814-1901. 83134, 83500, 85503-85504, 85525-85535
Snow, P. H. 85536
Snow, Samuel. 85537
Snow, Samuel Sheffield. 85538-85540
Snow, Samuel T., d. 1901. 85541
Snow, Samuel T., d. 1901. petitioner 47731, 85541 see also Revere Copper Company. Agent. petitioner
Snow, Simeon. 85542-85544
Snow, Theodore William, d. 1872. 85545-85546
Snow, Thomas. 97628
Snow, Thomas H. 85547
Snow, Thomas Hailes. 85548-85549
Snow, William. 85550
Snow, William Dunham, 1832-1910. (1992)
Snow, William Parker, 1817-1895. 85551-85560
Snow, William W., 1812-1886. 85561
Snow, Zerubbabel, 1809-1888. 70913, 85562-85563 see also Utah (Territory) Attorney General.
Snow. firm publishers see Noyes & Snow. firm publishers
Snow-drop: a gift for a friend. 85564
Snow drop; a juvenile magazine. 85565
Snow drop: by a lady. 85566
Snow flake: a Christmas, new year, and birthday gift. 85572
Snow flake: a Christmas, new-year, and birthday gift, for MDCCLIV. 85570
Snow flake: a Christmas, new-year, and birthday gift, for MDCCCLI. 85570
Snow flake: a Christmas, new-year, and birthday gift, for MDCCCLII. 85570
Snow-flake: a Christmas, new-year, and birthday present. 85571
Snow flake: a gift for innocence and beauty. 85568
Snow flake: a holiday gift, for MDCCCXLIX. 85569
Snow flake: a holiday gift, for MD CCL. 85569
Snow-flake: as exhibited. 85567
Snow flakes and sunbeams. 2952
Snow Fork Valley Railroad Company. 85573
Snow Fork Valley Railroad Company. Consulting Engineer. 85573
Snow Fork Valley Railroad Company. Directors. Committee. 85573
Snow-Hill messenger and Worcester County advertiser. 85574
Snow image, and other twice-told-tales. 30994
Snow ship. 75260
Snow storm, a ballad. 84156
Snow storm: an interesting tale for children. 85575
Snowden, Edgar. 85576
Snowden, Isaac Clarkson, 1791-1828. 85577
Snowden, James Ross, 1809-1878. 16807, 49330, 60144, 85578-85588 see also Pennsylvania. Historical Society. Building Committee. U. S. Bureau of the Mint. Director.
Snowden, Mrs. M. A. 86351
Snowden, Richard, d. 1825? 14856, 85589-85595
Snow's hand-book of northern pleasure travel. 85596
Snub, Citizen. pseud. Rub from Snub. see "Scotch Runaway." pseud. supposed author and Stanwick, John. supposed author
Sny Island levee bonds. 85598
Snyder, ------. illus. 63894
Snyder, Mr. ------, fl. 1852. 10009

Snyder, Adam Wilson, 1799-1842. 85599
Snyder, B. F. 85041
Snyder, F. A. 10021
Snyder, G. W. 85600
Snyder, George H. 60806, 85618 see also Snyder, Cook and Co. firm
Snyder, Henry. 85601
Snyder, John, 1793-1850. 85602
Snyder, John, 1842-1914. 85603
Snyder, Morgan, 1809-1883. 85604
Snyder, Oliver P., 1833-1882. 85605
Snyder, Peter. 85606-85607
Snyder, Philip. 85608-85609
Snyder, Philip F. 85610
Snyder, Silvenus. 85611
Snyder, Simon, 1749-1819. 33150, (43380), 57236, 60123, 60452, 60772 see also Pennsylvania. Governor, 1808-1817 (Snyder)
Snyder, Simon, fl. 1827-1828. 85612-85613
Snyder, Simon, fl. 1852-1853. 85614-85615
Snyder, William B. 85616
Snyder. land agents see Snyder and McFarlane. land agents
Snyder and McFarlane. land agents 32081, 85617
Snyder, Cook and Co. firm 60806, 85618 see also Cook, ------, fl. 1862. Higgins George. Snyder, George H.
So much of the King of England's proclamation of 1763 as relates. (37540)
So publicada todos los domingos. (16845)
Soane, George, 1790-1860. 85619
Soap-Boilers of Philadelphia. 62327, 70466
Soares, Gabriel. 88726
Soares, Joao Crispiniano. 85620-85621 see also San Paulo (Barzilian Province) Presidente (Soares)
Soares, Sebastiao Ferreira, 1820-1887. 24315, 85622-85634 see also Brazil. Thesouro Nacional. Chefe de Seccao.
Soares de Andrea, Francisco Jose de Souza. see Souza Soares de Andrea, Francisco Jose.
Soares de Souza, Gabriel. 85635
Soares de Souza, Paulino Jose, Visconde do Uruguay, 1807-1866. 85636-85648 see also Brazil. Ministerio das Relaçiones Exteriores. Brazil. Ministerio do Imperio. Rio de Janeiro (Province) Presidente, 1839-1840 (Soares de Souza)
Soares de Souza, Paulino Jose, 1834- 85649-85646 see also Brazil. Ministerio do Imperio.
Soares Ferreira Penna, Dominges. see Penna, Dominges Soares Ferreira.
Soares Franco, Francisco. (25483), 85657-85658
Soares Moreno, Martim, 1586?- 85659
Soares Vaz Preto, D. Marcos Pinto. see Preto, D. Marcos Pinto Soares Vaz.
Soaris, Gabriel. defendant 40988
Soave, Francesco. supposed author 11626, note after 98779
Sober address to all those who have any interest. 10887, 87818
Sober appeal to the Christian public. 85660
Sober attention to the scriptures of truth. 96398
Sober checks given to rash passions. 46338
Sober citizen. pseud. To the inhabitants of the city and county of New-York. 85661
Sober considerations, on a growing flood of iniquity. 46514, note after 85661
Sober dialogue between a country Friend, a London Friend, and one of G. K's. Friends 85662

Sober-mindedness explain'd. 79431

Sober remarks on a book lately re-printed at Boston, entituled, A modest proof. 12362, 12364, (25402), 25407, 99800, 101194, 103904

Sober remarks on the modest proof, &c. 12362

Sober reply to a mad answer. 17672, 85663

Sober reply to a serious enquiry. 106106

Sober sentiments. 46515

Sober thoughts on the state of the times. 101396

Sober view of the slavery question. 85664

Sober world. 83747

Soberania. 85665

Soberania temporal del Papa. 85666

Soberano estado de Oajaca al benemerito de la patria Vicente Guerrero. 29135

Sobersides, Solomon. pseud. Pretty new-year's gift. 65396, 85668

Sobolevskii, Sergiei Aleksandrovich, 1803-1870. (8784), 85669

Sobolewski, Serge. see Sobolevskii, Sergiei Aleksandrovich, 1803-1870.

Sobralia Elisabethae. note after 77796

Sobrarius, Ioannes. 85670

Sobre-carta al ciudadano Pacifico de San Francisco. 85676, note after 98910

Sobre el cultivo de la morera. 81009

Sobre el papel de Puebla el liberal. 85671

Sobre el sistema prohibitivo. 38825

Sobre eleccion de compromisarios. 85672

Sobre elecciones parroquiales. 62937

Sobre la convencion de 29 de Octubre de 1840. 98596

Sobre la execucion de los autos de conseho. 85673

Sobre la lengua de los Slavajes de la America. (49434)

Sobre las missiones llamadas de los Maynas. 72526

Sobre las turbaciones de Sur-America. 85674

Sobre leyes, jueces, y abogados. 98265

Sobre los derechos parroquiales de Indios. 71450

Sobre los inhustos, grandes, y excessivos arrauios. 76299

Sobre mitas de Potosi. 58411

Sobre obligar a los estranheros a pagar em-prestitos forzosos. 85675

Sobre qve no se cargven los Indios deste reyno. 98800

Sobre un escrito titulado Causa al D. D. J. C. Argomedo &c. 85677

Sobreira de Mello, Emilio Xavier, d. 1885. 85678-85680

Sobreviela, Manuel. (81617), 85681-85682, 97711

Sobrino, Rodrigo Alvarez de. see Alvarez de Sobrino, Rodrigo.

Sobron, Felix C. y. 85683

Sobry, A. tr. 35142

Soc Indians. see Sauk Indians.

Soccoro Rodriguez, Manuel del. see Rodriguez, Manuel del Soccoro.

Socher, Fr. Xav. ed. (52376), 91981

Sociable; or, one thousand and one home amuse-ments. 104233

Social and camp-meeting songs, for the pious. 85684

Social and domestic life. 22085

Social and domestic scenes and incidents in Barbadoes. 57504

Social and intellectual state of the colony. 1183

Social and political bearings of the American disruption. 32899

Social and sacred melodist. 79951

Social bliss carried out. 1604

Social bliss considered. 85685

Social Club, Worcester, Mass. 105371

Social compact exemplified. 302

Social companion, and songster's pocket book. 85686

Social condition of the southern states of America. 4020

Social Democratic Workingmen's Party of North America. 85687-85688

Social-Demokratischen Arbeiter-Partie von N. Amerika. see Social Democratic Work-ingmen's Party of North America.

Social destiny of man. 8004

Social development in Virginia. 86161

Social Division, no. 39, South Abington, Mass. see Sons of Temperance of North America. Massachusetts. Social Division, no. 93, South Abington.

Social duties. 57596

Social evenings. 39777

Social evils. 37823

Social Fraternity, New Hampton, N. H. see New Hampton, N. H. Academical and Theological Institution. Social Fraternity.

Social Fraternity, Williams College. see Williams College, Williamstown, Mass. Social Fraternity.

Social Friend's Library, Dartmouth College. see Dartmouth College. Social Friend's Library.

Social Gymnasium, Washington, D. C. see Washington Social Gymnasium, Washing-ton, D. C.

Social harmony. 4695

Social harmony; or, the cheerful songster's companion. 85691

Social history of Great Britain. 27867

Social independence of the American laborer. 84893

Social Law Library, Boston. see Boston. Social Law Library.

Social Library, Beverly, Mass. 85694

Social Library, New Haven, Conn. see New Haven Social Library, New Haven, Conn.

Social Library, Salem, Mass. Proprietors. 75745

Social Library, Stoneham, Mass. see Stone-ham, Mass. Social Library.

Social Library, Wareham, Mass. see Ware-ham Social Library, Wareham, Mass.

Social Library, Worcester, Mass. see Worcester Social Library, Worcester, Mass.

Social Library Company, New Haven, Conn. see New Haven Social Library Company, New Haven, Conn.

Social Library, No. 1, Boston. see Boston. Social Library, No. 1.

Social Library, No. I. Boston. Catalogue of books. 85695

Social life and national spirit of America. 40229

Social monitor. (32239)

Social Order of Temperance, Indianapolis. 85696

Social Party for the City of New York and Vicinity. 85697

Social pathology. 84068

Social pioneer, and herald of progress. 85698

Social principle. (81261)

Social psalmist. 84062, 92375

Social Reading Rooms, Stamford, Conn.
Library. 90123
Social record. 85699
Social reform. 8717
Social Reform Society of New York. 70528,
96395
Social relations in our southern states. 33831
Social relations of England and America.
85700
Social science and political economy. 85701
Social Science Association, Boston. see
Boston Social Science Association.
Social science review. see New York social
science review.
Social significance of our institutions. 35698
Social Society, Schenectady. 77601, 85703
Social spirit. 91785
Social standards. 84069
Social system. An address. 3454
Social thanksgiving a pleasant duty. 100924
Social Frage und ihre Losung. 85702
Sociale Fragen. 33472
Social Republik. 85704
Sociale Schriften. 11923
Sociale und politische Stellung. 77639
Socialism and the worker. 85705
Socialism of the Tribune examined. 28494
Socialiste. 85706
Socialistische Turner-Bund von Nord-Amerika.
see American Gymnastic Union.
Socialokonomie. (10838)
Sociedad (Medillon, Colombia) 85709
Sociedad (Mexico City) 47032, 71704
Sociedad Abolicionista Espanola, Madrid.
85710-85714
Sociedad Academica de Lima. see Sociedad
Academica de Amantes de Lima.
Sociedad Academica de Amantes de Lima.
(47935), 85681, 94564, 97711
Sociedad Academica de Amantes del Pais de
Lima. see Sociedad Academica de
Amantes de Lima.
Sociedad Agricola Mexicana. 84332
Sociedad Amigos del Pais, Panama. see
Sociedad de Amigos del Pais, Panama.
Sociedad Anonima del Ferro-Carril Cotoner,
Puerto Rico. 85715
Sociedad Anonima Denominada Banco Industrial,
Havana. 23038, 29431
Sociedad anomina "La Colonizadora," Havana.
85716
Sociedad Artistica, Mexico. 85717
Sociedad Benefica y Religiosa de los Espanoles
de Caracas. 85718
Sociedad Bienhechora, Puebla. 85719
Sociedad Bienhechora. Bases para su organiza-
cion. 85719
Sociedad de Agricultura, Valparaiso, Chile.
(12745)
Sociedad de Americanos. 5197
Sociedad de Amigos. pseud. eds. Registro
Yucateco. 68836
Sociedad de Amigos del Pais, Panama. 5228,
15000
Sociedad de Amigos del Pais, Panama.
Comision Revisora. 85720
Sociedad de Beneficencia, Buenos Aires. see
Sociedad de Beneficencia de la Capital,
Buenos Aires.
Sociedad de Beneficencia, Lima. see Sociedad
de Beneficencia de Lima.
Sociedad de Beneficencia.—Descripcion de la
funcion. 85721
Sociedad de Beneficencia de la Capital, Buenos
Aires. 58721
Sociedad de Beneficencia de Lima. 41125

Sociedad de Beneficencia Espanola, Mexico
City. 85723-85724
Sociedad de Beneficencia Espanola, Mexico
City. Junta Directiva. 85722
Sociedad de Beneficencia Publica, Lima. 85725
Sociedad de Beneficencia Publica, Lima. Direc-
tor. 85725 see also Carassa, Francisco.
Sociedad de Ciencias Fisicas y Naturales de
Caracas. 10773
Sociedad de Conocimientos Utiles. see Society
for the Diffusion of Useful Knowledge,
London.
Sociedad de Credito Industrial, Havana. 17781
Sociedad de Espanoles Regufiados en Inglaterra
y Francia. pseud. Emigrado observador.
56648
Sociedad de Geografia e Historia de Guatemala.
99643
Sociedad de Geografia y Estadistica de Mexico.
see Sociedad Mexicana de Geografia y
Estadistica.
Sociedad de la Union Americana de Cochabamba.
85726
Sociedad de la Union Americana de Santiago
de Chile. 85727
Sociedad de la Union Americana de Santiago
de Chile. Junta Directiva de la Union
Americana. 76857
Sociedad de Literados. pseud. Aventuras y
conquistas de Hernan Cortes en Mejico.
16945
Sociedad de Literatos. pseud. eds. Registro
trimestre. 68835
Sociedad de Literatos Distinguidos. pseud.
eds. Diccionario universal de historia
y de geografia. 579, 6834, 48429, 48599
Sociedad de los Fundadores de la Indepen-
dencia del Peru. 85728
Sociedad de Mejores Materiales y Morales de
Beneficencia y Socorros Mutuos, Texcoco,
Mexico. 68871, 85729-85730
Sociadad de Patriotas Granadinos. pseud. eds.
Semanario de la Neuva Granada. 9876,
79051
Sociedad de San Felipe de Jesus Para la
Propagacion de los Buenos Libros. 85731
Sociedad de Socorros Mutuos "Los Amigos del
Bien Publico," San Juan. 85732-85734
Sociedad de Subscritores del Teatro de la
Ciudad de Mexico. 48645, 85735
Sociedad del Canal de Maipo. 85736
Sociedad del Rio Bermejo. Comisionado.
34716, 85737
Sociedad Democratica de los Amigos de
America, New York. 16056, 84738-84739
Sociedad Democratica de los Amigos de
America, New York. Charter. 16056
Sociedad Economica de Amantes de Guatemala.
see Sociedad Economica de Amantes de
la Patria de Guatemala.
Sociedad Economica de Amantes de la Patria
de Guatemala. 29071, 85749-85750,
85752-85753
Sociedad Economica de Amantes de la Patria
de Guatemala. Comision. 85748
Sociedad Economica de Amantes de la Patria
de Guatemala. Secretario. 85751 see
also Milla, Jose.
Sociedad Economica de Amigos de Guatemala.
29088, 87213
Sociedad Economica de Amigos de Guatemala.
Junta Genera, 1864. 29088
Sociedad Economica de Amigos de Guatemala.
Secretario. 29088 see also Andreu,
Felipe.

Sociedad Economica de Amigos del Pais, Caracas. 85740-85741

Sociedad Economica de Amigos del Pais de la Havana. 1874, 11292, 17746, 17750, 27810, 29412, 29414, 29442-29443, 56746, 69227, 73006, 73008, 74915, 85742-85747, 98921 see also Comisiones Reunidas de la Real Sociedad Economica, Casa de Beneficencia y Demas Dependencias de Aquel Cuerpo, Havana.

Sociedad Economica de Amigos del Pais de la Havana. Comision Especial. eds. 17791, 85747

Sociedad Economica de Amigos del Pais de la Havana. Seccion de Historia. 85747

Sociedad Economica de Guatemala. 29085, 60933, 85753, 87214

Sociedad Economica de la Havana. see Sociedad Economica de Amigos del Pais de la Havana.

Sociedad Economica de Mexico. 48462

Sociedad Economica de Santiago de Cuba. 98165

Sociedad Economica Empleados de Aduana, Buenos Aires. 85754

Sociedad Filanthropica. pseud. Satelite del Peruano. 77135

Sociedad Filarmonica de Santa Cecilia, Havana. 85755

Sociedad Filitecnica, Bogota. 98611

Sociedad Itineraria del Norte, Cartago. Junta Directoria. 85756

Sociedad Latino-Americana Cientifico Literaria. 85757

Sociedad Literaria. pseud. trs. (39027)-39028, 73518

Sociedad Mexicana de Geografia y Estadistica. 29148, (48307), 48308, 48367, 48644, 62980, 59518, 73034, 73036, (74021), 85758-85759, 85762, 85764-85765, 94615

Sociedad Mexicana de Geografia y Estadistica. Charter. 48644, 85763

Sociedad Mexicana de Geografia y Estadistica. Comision Nombrada Para Escritar un Biografia de D. Jose M. Justo Gomez de la Cortina. 16975, 27760

Sociedad Mexicana de Geografia y Estadistica. Comision Nombrada Para Estudiar la Cuestion Relativa al Desague del Valle de Mexico. 85761

Sociedad Mexicana de Geografia y Estadistica. Comision Nombrada Para Examiner la Obra de D. Francisco Pimentel. 62878, 85760 see also Orozco y Berra, Manuel. Ramirez, Jose Fernando. Romero, Jose Guadalupe.

Sociedad Mexicana de Historia Natural. 52045

Sociedad Mexicana Promovedora de Mejores Materiales y Morales. 48644, 85766

Sociedad Patriotica de Carabobo. 68856

Sociedad Patriotica de Havana. see Sociedad Economica de Amigos del Pais de la Havana.

Sociedad Patriotica Promovedora de la Defensa Nacional, Mexico. 85767

Sociedad. Periodico politico y literario. 85708

Sociedad Sericiocola Americana, Santiago. 85768

Sociedad Sericocola America. Exposicion de los fines que se propone. 85768

Sociedad Auxiliadora da Industrial Nacional, Rio de Janeiro. 56370

Sociedade Commercio, Bahia. 85769

Sociedade da Bibliotheca Popular Itaborahyense, Rio de Janeiro. Directoria Respectiva. 85770

Sociedade de Beneficencia, Lima. see Sociedad de Beneficencia Publica de Lima.

Sociedade de Instruccao Elementar, Maranhao, Brazil. (36942)

Sociedade de Literatos. pseud. eds. Historia de Portugal. 32035

Sociedade de Vehiculos Economicos, Bahia. 85772

Sociedade de Vehiculos Economicos, Bahia. Comissao de Exame Contas. 85771

Sociedade Democratica Constitucional Limeirense. 85773

Sociedade em Commandita Transportes Urbanos na Bahia. 85774

Sociedade Estudiosa. pseud. eds. Revista universal Lisbonense. 70320

Sociedade Internacional de Immigracao, Rio de Janeiro. Director. 85775 see also Haupt, Herman. Tavares Bastos, Aureliano Candido, 1839-1875.

Sociedade Internacional de Immigracao, Rio de Janeiro. Directoria. 85775

Sociedade Portugueza de Beneficencia, Bahia. (69311)

Sociedades Americanas. 85776

Sociedades Americanas en 1828. 85776-85777

Societa di Filadelfia. see American Philosophical Society, Philadelphia.

Societa di Dotti e di Letterati. pseud. eds. 101352

Societa di Letterati. pseud. eds. Memorie istoriche. 47763

Societa di Mutuo Soccorso, St. Louis. 85778

Societa di Unione e Fratellanza Italiana, New York. 85779

R. Societa Geografia Italiana, Rome. 99281

Societa Italiana di Unione e Benevolenza in Nueva York. 85780

Societa Italiana in Nuova York. (16149)

Societas Jesu. see Jesuits.

Societas Jesu usque ad sanguinis et vitae profusionem militans. 94332

Societas Naturae Curiosorum, Leipzig. 78104

Societas Regia Antiqvariorum Septentrionalum. see K. Nordske Oldskrift-Selskab, Copenhagen.

Societat Zur Ausbreitung des Evangeliums Unter den Heiden. see Society of the United Brethren for Propagating the Gospel Among the Heathen.

Societatas Regia Antiqvariorum Septentrionalium. see K. Nordske Oldskrift-Selskab, Copenhagen.

Societe Americaine de France. 73305, 85781

Societe Amicale de Quebec. 85782

Societe Amicale de Quebec, fondee en Nov., 1810. 85782

Societe Bienveillante de Notre Dame de Bonsecours, Montreal. 85783

Societe Bienveillante de Quebec. 85784-85785

Societe Bienveillante des Ouvriers de Quebec. 85786

Societe Correspondante des Colons Francais, Paris. 85787-85789

Societe d'Agriculture, Lyon. 26013

Societe d'Agriculture, des Artes & du Commerce de Nantes. Commissaires. (40676)

Societe d'Agriculture du Bas-Canada. see Lower Canada Agricultural Society.

Societe d'Agriculture du Bas-Canada. Objet, statuts et reglements. 10347

Societe d'Agriculture du Comte de Beauharnois. 10347

Societe d'Agriculture du Departement de la Seine. 776, 47543, 48702

Societe d'Agriculture et d'Economie Politique
a la Martinique. 44971
Societe d'Anthropologie, Paris. 18332, 28058
Societe de Bienfaisance Franco-Canadienne de
Saint Paul. 85792
Societe Catholique de la Belgique. 51420
Societe de Cincinnatus. 44236
Societe de Colonisation Europeo-Americaine
au Texas, Brussels. 15026, 85793-85794
Societe de Construction de Quebec. 85795
Societe de Construction de Quebec, incorporee
par un acte de la Legislature Provinciale
en 1849. 85795
Societe de Construction du District de Montreal.
85796
Societe de Construction du Peuple, Quebec.
85797-85798
Societe de Construction du Peuple, incorporee
en 1849. 85798
Societe de Construction Metropolitaine,
Montreal. 85799
Societe de Construction Mutuelle, Quebec.
Directeurs. 85800
Societe de Construction Permanente de Levis,
Quebec. 85801
Societe de Construction Permanente de Levis,
fondee en 1869. 85801
Societe de Discussion de Quebec. 85802
Societe de Geographie, Geneva. 77203
Societe de Geographie, Paris. 1295, 2492,
2493A, 6893, 7420, 9128, 19741, 30599,
36431, 36433, 40764, 68443, 76841,
76845, 76848, 77204, 89982, 89990,
101361
Societe de Geographie, Paris. Commission
Speciale. 36434, 100990 see also
Jomard, Edme-Francois. Larenaudiere,
Philippe Francois de, 1787-1845. Walck-
enaer, Charles Athanase, Baron.
Societe de Geographie de France. 85803
Societe de Geographie et de Statistique de
Mexique. see Sociedad Mexicana de
Geografia y Estadistica.
Societe de la Morale Chretienne, Paris.
(81807)
Societe de l'Amerique Meridionale, Paris.
Ingenieur. 67921
Societe de l'Histoire du Protestantisme
Francaise, Paris. 9129, 69745
Societe de Nostre Dame de Montreal Pour la
Conuersion des Sauuages de la Nouuele
France. (50292), note after 98976
Societe de Savans. pseud. Geographie uni-
verselle. 47870
Societe de Savans. pseud. eds.
Revue des deux mondes. 70364
Societe de Savans et d'Hommes de Letters.
pseud. Bibliotheque Americaine. 5205
Societe d'Education du District de Quebec.
85790
Societe des Americainistes de Paris. 99362
Societe des Amis des Noirs, Paris. 8014,
13515, 20170, (78744), 81804-81805,
85804-85809
Societe des Amis des Noirs, Paris. petitioners
(68751)
Societe des Amis des Noirs, Paris. Secretaire.
85808 see also Brissot de Warville,
Jacques Pierre, 1754-1793.
Societe des Amis des Noirs a Arthur Dillon.
20170, 85807
Societe des Antiquaires de France. see
Societe Nationale des Antiquaires de
France.
Societe des Antiquaires de l'Amerique du Nord,
Copenhagen. see K. Nordske Oldskrift-
Selskab, Copenhagen.

Societe des Artes et des Sciences de Batavia.
see Bataviaasch Genootschap van Kuns-
ten en Wetenshcappen.
Societe des Chantiers et Ateliers de l'Ocean.
defendants 47527
Societe des Etangs Salins, St. Martin, Antilles.
61019
Societe des Etangs Salins, St. Martin, Antilles.
Charter. 61019
Societe des Ingenieurs Civils. 24638
Societe d'Ethnographie, Paris. 70371, 70373,
70376-73077, 73303, 73310, 85791
Societe d'Ethnographie Americaine et Orientale,
Paris. 1612, 70373-70374, 85791
Societe d'Etudes pour la Colonisation de la
Guyane. 29191, 39637, 94849
Societe d'Hommes de Couleur. pseud. eds.
70362
Societe du Departement de la Seine. 48698
Societe du Feu, Montreal. 85810
Societe du Feu, Montreal. Charter. 85811
Societe du Magnetisme de la Nouvelle-Orleans.
85812
Societe Ecclesiastique de St. Michel, Quebec.
85813
Societe Entomologique de France, Paris.
(6154)
Societe Etablie Pour la Propagation de l'Evan-
gelie Dans les Pays Etrangeres. see
Society for the Propagation of the Faith
in Foreign Parts, London.
Societe Ethnologique, Paris. 22076, 47544
Societe Francaise de Bienfaisance, New York.
85814-85815
Societe Francaise de Bienfaisance, Philadelphia.
62247-62248
Societe Francaise de Bienfaisance de Philadel-
phia. . . . Rapport. 62248
Societe Francaise Pour l'Abolition de l'Esclav-
age, Paris. 85816, 87133
Societe Geologique de France. 77205
Societe Historique de Montreal. 47549, 50255,
(50292), note after 98976, 99601
Societe Historique de Montreal. plaintiffs
5157
Societe Historique de Montreal vs. Maximilien
Bibaud. 5157
Societe Imp. de Lille. 12880
Societe Institutee en 1834 Pour l'Abolition de
l'Esclavage. see Societe Francaise
pour l'Abolition de l'Esclavage, Paris.
Societe Internationale des Etudes Pratiques
d'Economie Social. (57969)
Societe Linneenne de Paris. 2606, 24920
Societe Litteraire de Quebec. 85817
Societe Litteraire et Historique de Quebec.
see Literary and Historical Society of
Quebec.
Societe Litteraire et Historique de Quebec.
67019
Societe Montyon et Franklin, Paris. 85819
Societe Nationale des Antiquaires de France.
19648
Societe Orientale, Paris. 70359
Societe Permanente de Construction des
Artisans, Quebec. 85820
Societe Permanente de Construction Jacques
Cartier, Montreal. 85821
Societe Philanthropique d'Hayti. 85822
Societe Philologique, Paris. (72812), 85823
Societe Philomatique, Paris. 9127
Societe Pour la Conuersion des Sauuages de la
Nouuelle France, Montreal. see Societe
de Nostre Dame de Montreal Pour la
Conuersion des Sauuages de la Nouuelle
France.

Societe Pour la Propagation de l'Evangile. see
Society for the Propagation of the Faith.

Societe Pour la Propagation des Connaissances
Scientifiques et Industrielles, Paris.
19648

Societe Pour l'Abolition de l'Esclavage, Paris.
see Societe Francaise Pour l'Abolition
de l'Esclavage, Paris.

Societe Royale de Geographie, Paris. see
Societe de Geographie, Paris.

Societe Royal de Medecine, Paris. see
Academie de Medecine, Paris.

Societe Royale des Antiquaires du Nord, Copenhagen. see K. Nordske Oldskrift-
Selskab, Copenhagen.

Societe Royale des Antiquaires du Nord.
Seance annuelle du 14 Mai 1859. 85824

Societe Royale d'Agriculture de Lyon. see
Societe d'Agriculture, Lyon.

Societeit van Suriname. 46681, 56681, 68458,
93934, 93837-93838, note after 93841, 1st
note after 93862 see also Dutch Guiana.

Societeit van Suriname. plaintiffs 68458

Societeit van Suriname. Directeuren. (4868),
93835-93836, 93839-93841

Societes secretes, jugees par Washington.
85830

Societies for promoting manual labor in literary institutions. 85856

Society. pseud. Theophilanthropist. see
Fellows, John. ed.

Society, Edinburgh. (22979)

Society, Northampton, N. Y. see Northampton,
N. Y. Church.

Society for Abolishing Humbug. 5820

Society for Abolishing the Slave-Trade, Providence, R. I. 16078, (81943), 85831

Society for Abolishing the Slave-Trade, Providence, R. I. Charter. 85831

Society for Advancing the Christian Faith in
the British West India Islands, and Else-
where. see Society for the Conversion
and Religious Instruction and Education
of the Negro Slaves.

Society for Affording Relief to the Families of
Deceased Ministers, Hartford, Conn. 16127

Society for Alleviating the Miseries of Public
Prisons, Philadelphia. see Philadelphia
Society for the Alleviation of the Miseries
of Public Prisons.

Society for Bettering the Condition of the Poor,
Philadelphia. see Philadelphia Society
for Bettering the Condition of the Poor.

Society, for Charitable and Religious Purposes,
Richmond County, N. Y. see Richmond
County Society, for Charitable and
Religious Purposes.

Society for Colonizing the Free People of
Color. 14732

Society for Constitutional Information, London.
96175

Society for Converting and Civilizing the Indians
and Propagating the Gospel in Upper
Canada. 10466

Society for Detecting Horse-Thieves, and Re-
covering Stolen Horses, Wrentham,
Franklin, Medway, Medfield, Walpole,
Foxborough, Mansfield, and Attleborough,
Mass. 85833-85835, 105526

Society for Detecting Horse Thieves in the
Towns of Mendon, Bellingham and Milford,
Mass. 85836

Society for Educating Pious Young Men for the
Ministry of the Protestant-Episcopal
Church. 66209

Society for Educating the Poor of Newfoundland, London. 8950, 54987

Society for Educating the Poor of Newfoundland, London. Committee of Proceedings.
8950, 54987

Society for Employing the Female Poor, Boston.
(23420), 85837

Society for Employing the Female Poor, Boston.
Committee of Advice. 85838

Society for Employing the Female Poor, Boston.
Managers. 85837

Society for Employing the Female Poor, Boston.
School. (23420)

Society for Employing the Poor, Boston. see
Society for Employing the Female Poor,
Boston.

Society for Encouraging Industry and Employing
the Poor, Boston. 46122, 85839-85840

Society for Establishing Useful Manufactures,
in New Jersey. see Society for the
Establishment of Useful Manufactures in
New Jersey.

Society for Improvement in Practical Piety,
Boston. 85842

Society for Improving the Condition, and Elevating the Character of Industrious Females,
Philadelphia. 85843-85844

Society for Improving the Condition, and Elevating the Character of Industrious Females,
Philadelphia. Board of Managers. 85843,
85845

Society for Insuring of Houses, In and Near
Philadelphia. 61568

Society for Meliorating the Condition of the
Jews. see American Society for
Meliorating the Condition of the Jews.

Society for Mental and Moral Improvement,
New York. 85846

Society for Mental and Moral Improvement,
composed of members of Public School
no. 15. 85846

Society for Ministerial Relief, Boston. 85961

Society for Ministerial Relief, Boston. Committee of Investigation. Chairman. 3840,
85962 see also Brooks, Charles.

Society for Mitigating and Gradually Abolishing
the State of Slavery. see Society for
the Mitigation and Gradual Abolition of
Slavery Throughout the British Dominions.

Society for Political Enquiries, Philadelphia.
(62249)

Society for Printing, Publishing & Circulating
the Writings of the Honourable Emanuel
Swedenborg, Manchester. 85847

Society for Promoting Agriculture, Philadelphia.
see Philadelphia Society for Promoting
Agriculture.

Society for Promoting Agriculture in Massachusetts. see Massachusetts Society for
Promoting Agriculture.

Society for Promoting Agriculture in the Province of Nova-Scotia, Halifax. 29703,
29705, 2d note after 85847

Society for Promoting Agriculture in the State
of Connecticut. 15863

Society for Promoting Agriculture in Virginia.
see Society of Virginia for Promoting
Agriculture.

Society for Promoting and Improving Agriculture
and Other Rural Concerns, South Carolina.
see South-Carolina for Promoting and
Improving Agriculture and Other Rural
Concerns.

Society for Promoting Christian Knowledge,
London. 68369, 77358, 85848, note before
85932, 92211

Society for Promoting Christian Knowledge, London. Committee of General Literature and Education. 85851

Society for Promoting Christian Knowledge, London. Halifax Diocesan Committee. 85849

Society for Promoting Christian Knowledge, London. Newcastle District. Committee. 85852

Society for Promoting Christian Knowledge, London. Newcastle District. Traveling Missionary Society. 85852

Society for Promoting Christian Knowledge, London. Quebec Diocesan Committee. 85850

Society for Promoting Christian Knowledge, London. Toronto Committee. 85853

Society for Promoting Christian Knowledge and Piety, New York. see New York Society for Promoting Christian Knowledge and Piety.

Society for Promoting Christian Knowledge in Massachusetts. see Massachusetts Society for Promoting Christian Knowledge.

Society for Promoting Christian Knowledge, Piety and Charity, Boston. 85854

Society for Promoting Domestic Manufactures, Germantown, Pa. see Germantown Society for Promoting Domestic Manufactures.

Society for Promoting Education and Industry among the Indians and Destitute Settlers in Canada. see Central Auxiliary Society for Promoting Education and Industry Among the Indians and Destitute Settlers in Canada, Montreal.

Society for Promoting General Inoculation, at Stated Periods, and Preventing the Natural Small-Pox, Chester, England. 31031

Society for Promoting Manual Labor in Literary Institutions, New York. 85856, note after 102548

Society for Promoting Manual Labor in Literary Institutions, New York. General Agent. 85856, note after 102548 see also Weld, Theodore Dwight.

Society for Promoting Regular & Good Singing, Boston. 101197

Society for Promoting Religion and Learning in the State of New York. see Protestant Episcopal Society for Promoting Religion and Learning in the State of New York.

Society for Promoting Religious Instruction in the Isle of Shoals. 35259

Society for Promoting Religious Instruction in the Isle of Shoals. Directors. 85858

Society for Promoting the Abolition of Slavery, Liverpool. see Liverpool Society for Promoting the Abolition of Slavery.

Society for Promoting the Abolition of Slavery, and the Relief of Free Negroes, and Others, Unlawfully Held in Bondage, Maryland. see Maryland Society for Promoting the Abolition of Slavery.

Society for Promoting the Abolition of Slavery, and the Relief of Free Negroes Unlawfully Held in Bondage, Pennsylvania. see Pennsylvania Society for Promoting the Abolition of Slavery.

Society for Promoting the Abolition of Slavery in Maryland. see Maryland Society for Promoting the Abolition of Slavery.

Society for Promoting the Abolition of Slavery in Pennsylvania. see Pennsylvania Society for Promoting the Abolition of Slavery.

Society for Promoting the Abolition of Slavery in Virginia. see Virginia Society for Promoting the Abolition of Slavery.

Society for Promoting the Gospel Among Seamen in the Port of New York. 54668, 85859-85860

Society for Promoting the Gospel Among Seamen in the Port of New York. Charter. 85859

Society for Promoting the Manufacture of Sugar From the Sugar Maple-Tree, Philadelphia. 85861

Society for Promoting the Manumission of Slaves, New York. see New York Society for Promoting the Manumission of Slaves.

Society for Promoting the Mitigation and Ultimate Abolition of Negro Slavery, Edinburgh. 85862

Society for Promoting the United and Scriptural Education of the Poor of Ireland, Dublin. 96498

Society for Promoting Theological Education. see Society for the Promotion of Theological Education in Harvard University.

Society for Promoting Useful Knowledge, Philadelphia. 85863

Society for Propagating Christian Knowledge, Scotland. see Society in Scotland for Propagating Christian Knowledge.

Society for Propagating the Gospel Among the Destitute Settlers and Indians in Lower Canada. 10586

Society for Propagating the Gospel Among the Heathen. see Society of the United Brethren For Propagating the Gospel Among the Heathen.

Society for Propagating the Gospel Among the Indians and Others in North America. 12891, (34619), 84358-84362, 84365, 85864, note before 85932, 95170, 104013

Society for Propagating the Gospel Among the Indians and Others in North America. petitioners 85865

Society for Propagating the Gospel Among the Indians and Others in North America. Charter. 104913

Society for Propagating the Gospel Among the Indians and Others in North America. Secretary. 34619-34620, 35170, note after 95170 see also Thacher, Peter, 1752-1802.

Society for Propagating the Gospel Among the Indians and Others in North America. Select Committee. 30513, 34610, 85865-85866, 97386, 104913

Society for Propagating the Gospel Among the Indians and Others in North-America, . . . having requested and petitioned. 87865

Society for Propagation of the Gospel in New England. see Company for Propagation of the Gospel in New England and the Parts Adjacent in America, London.

Society for Protection of American Industry, Cleveland. 85868, 106060

Society for Protection of American Industry, Cleveland. Executive Committee. 85867

Society for Religious Inquiry, in the University of Vermont. see Vermont. University. Society for Religious Inquiry.

Society for Religious Liberty and Equality, Montreal. 85869

Society for Savings, Hartford, Conn. 85870

Society for Supplying the Poor with Soup, Philadelphia. 62250

Society for Suppressing of Intemperance in Massachusetts. see Massachusetts Temperance Society.

Society for Suppressing Vice and Immorality, Portland, Me. Committee. 64374

Society for the Abolition of Slavery, London. Committee. 82059

Society for the Abolition of Slavery in New Jersey. see New Jersey Society for the Abolition of Slavery.

Society for the Abolition of Slavery Throughout the British Dominions. (81747)

Society for the Abolition of the Slave Trade, London. see Society Instituted for the Purpose of Effecting the Abolition of the Slave Trade.

Society for the Advancement of Christianity. 60618, 60366

Society for the Advancement of Christianity. Trustees. 60618

Society for the Advancement of Female Education in Greece, Troy, N. Y. see Troy Society for the Advancement of Female Education in Greece, Troy, N. Y.

Society for the Advancement of General Education in the County of Bucks, Pa. 85871

Society for the Advancement of Learning in South Carolina. see South Carolina Society for the Advancement of Learning.

Society for the Advancement of Natural Sciences, Louisville. 85872

Society for the Advancement of Political and Social Science, New York. 58873

Society for the Advancement of Truth in Art. 53380

Society for the Alleviation of the Miseries of Public Prisons, Philadelphia. see Philadelphia Society for the Alleviation of the Miseries of Public Prisons.

Society for the Attainment of Useful Knowledge, Philadelphia. 62251

Society for the Benefit of Indians, Washington, D. D. 34597, (53400)

Society for the Care of Girls, Boston. see Boston Society for the Care of Girls.

Society for the Circulation of Dr. Channing's Works, Boston. 85874

Society for the Civilization and Improvement of the North American Indians Within the British Boundary, London. 66031

Society for the Colonization of Free Persons of Colour. 85875

Society for the Commemoration of the Landing of William Penn, Philadelphia. 85876

Society for the Commemoration of the Landing of William Penn, Philadelphia. Meeting, 1824. 85876

Society for the Conversion and Religious Instruction and Education of the Negro Slaves. 85878-85879, 85881-85883, 2d note after 102867

Society for the Conversion and Religious Instruction and Education of the Negro Slaves. Branch Associations of Antigua and St. Christopher. 85880

Society for the Conversion and Religious Instruction and Education of the Negro Slaves. Charter. 85883

Society for the Conversion and Religious Instruction and Education of Negro Slaves. St. Thomas in the East Branch Society, London. 75499

Society for the Defence of the Catholic Religion from Calumny and Abuse, Philadelphia. 62252, 85884

Society for the Development of the Mineral Resources of the United States. 12159

Society for the Diffusion of Christian Knowledge, New York. 85885

Society for the Diffusion of Christian Knowledge, New York. General Agent. 85885 see also Post, Israel.

Society for the Diffusion of Information on the Subject of Capital Punishments. 94515

Society for the Diffusion of Political Knowledge, New York. 12995, (17630), 33898, 47703, 58451, 69699, 85886-85888

Society for the Diffusion of Spiritual Knowledge, New York. 85889

Society for the Diffusion of Spiritual Knowledge, New York. Charter. 85889

Society for the Diffusion of Useful Knowledge, London. 8076, 8558, 26984, 41874, 80285-80288, 96441, 97307

Society for the Education and Advancement of Young Seamen, New York. 85890

Society for the Education and Maintenance of Young Deaf Mutes, New York. 85891

Society for the Education of Pious Young Men from the Ministry of the Protestant Episcopal Church. 85893

Society for the Elevation of Liberal Government, New York. 85894

Society for the Employment and Instruction of the Poor, Philadelphia. see Philadelphia Society for the Employment and Instruction of the Poor.

Society for the Employment and Relief of Poor Women, New York. 54669

Society for the Employment and Relief of the Poor, New York. see Society for the Employment and Relief of Poor Women, New York.

Society for the Encouragement of Agriculture, Arts, and Social Intercourse, Attleborough, Mass. 2331

Society for the Encouragement of American Industry. 85895-85897, 91009-91010

Society for the Encouragement of American Manufactures. 15649

Society for the Encouragement of Arts, London. see Royal Society of Arts, London.

Society for the Encouragement of Arts and Sciences in Canada. see Literary and Historical Society of Quebec.

Society for the Encouragement of Arts, Manufactures, and Commerce, Barbadoes. 34825, 3d note after 85897

Society for the Encouragement of Arts, Manufactures, and Commerce, London. see Royal Society of Arts, London.

Society for the Encouragement of Arts, Manufactures, and Commerce established in Barbadoes, 1781. 34725

Society for the Encouragement of Domestic Industry in Rhode Island. see Rhode Island Society for the Encouragement of Domestic Industry.

Society for the Encouragement of Faithful Domestic Servants, New York. see New York Society for the Encouragement of Faithful Domestic Servants.

Society for the Encouragement of Faithful Domestic Servants, Providence, R. I. see Providence Society for the Encouragement of Faithful Domestic Servants.

Society for the Encouragement of Faithful Domestics, Philadelphia. 62038, 85900

Society for the Encouragement of Faithful
Domestics, Philadelphia. Board of
Managers. 85899
Society for the Encouragement of Faithful
Domestics, Philadelphia. Committee.
62038
Society for the Encouragement of Manufac-
tures on Pennsylvania. see Pennsyl-
vania Society for the Encouragement
of Manufactures, Philadelphia.
Society for the Encouragement of the British
Troops, in German and North America.
100, 30276
Society for the Especial Study of Political
Economy, the Philosophy of History,
and the Science of Government. 25268
Society for the Establishment and Support of
Charity Schools, Philadelphia. (62039),
74199
Society for the Establishment and Support of
Charity Schools, Philadelphia. Board of
Managers. (63039), 62253
Society for the Establishment of Useful Manu-
factures in New Jersey. 85841
Society for the Establishment of Useful Manu-
factures in New-Jersey. Civil Engineer.
59061, 93535 see also Sullivan, John
Langdon.
Society for the Extinction of the Slave Trade,
and for the Civilization of Africa, London.
82040
Society for the Furtherance of the Gospel.
see Society of the United Brethren for
Propagating the Gospel Among the
Heathen.
Society for the Improvement of Domestic
Poultry in New-England. see New-
England Society for the Improvement of
Domestic Poultry.
Society for the Improvement of Philadelphia.
85901
Society for the Improvement of Schools, and
Diffusion of Useful Knowledge. 1130
Society for the Increase of the Ministry.
85902-85904
Society for the Increase of the Ministry.
Board of Directors. 85903
Society for the Increase of the Ministry.
Founded, 1857. 85904
Society for the Information and Assistance of
Persons Emigrating from Foreign Coun-
tries, New York. see New York Society
for the Information and Assistance of
Persons Emigrating from Foreign Coun-
tries.
Society for the Information and Assistance of
Persons Emigrating from Other Coun-
tries, South Carolina. see South-
Carolina Society, for the Information and
Assistance of Persons Emigrating from
Other Countries.
Society for the Institution and Support of First-
Day or Sunday Schools in . . . Philadel-
phia, and the Districts of Southwark and
the Northern Liberties. 62254
Society for the Instruction of the Deaf and
Dumb, and of the Blind, Toronto. 85905
Society for the Mitigation and Gradual Aboli-
tion of slavery Throughout the British
Dominions, London. 35639, 85906
Society for the Mitigation and Gradual Aboli-
tion of Slavery Throughout the British
Dominions, London. Committee. (81967),
85906
Society for the Moral and Religious Instruc-
tion of the Poor, Salem, Mass. see

Salem Society for the Moral and Religious
Instruction of the Poor.
Society for the Moral Improvement of Seamen,
New Bedford, Mass. see New Bedford
Port Society for the Moral Improvement
of Seamen.
Society for the Mutual Benefit of Female
Domestics and Their Employers, Boston.
85907
Society for the Permanent Support of Orphan
and Destitute Children, London. 85908
Society for the Permanent Support of Orphan
and Destitute Children, by means of
apprenticeship in the colonies. 85908
Society for the Prevention of Pauperism, Boston.
see Industrial Aid Society for the Pre-
vention of Pauperism.
Society for the Prevention of Pauperism in the
City of New York. 20480, (29552), 54670,
(63215), 85909
Society for the Prevention of Pauperism in the
City of New York. Committee on Erect-
ing a House of Refuge, for Vagrant and
Depraved Young People. 85957
Society for the Prevention of Pauperism in the
City of New York. Committee on Pauper-
ism. 54623, 85909
Society for the Promoting of Domestic Industry,
Philadelphia. see Philadelphia Society
for the Promotion of Domestic Industry.
Society for the Promotion of Agriculture,
Dutchess County, N. Y. see Society of
Dutchess County for the Promotion of
Agriculture, Poughkeepsie.
Society for the Promotion of Agriculture and
Domestic Manufactures in and for Cumber-
land. 85910
Society for the Promotion of Agriculture and
Domestic Manufactures in and for Cumber-
land. Charter. 85910
Society, for the Promotion of Agriculture and
Domestic Manufactures in Queens County,
N. Y. see Queen's County Society, for
the Promotion of Agriculture and Domes-
tic Manufactures.
Society for the Promotion of Agriculture and
Domestick Manufactures of the County
of Saratoga, N. Y. Executive Committee.
91099
Society for the Promotion of Agriculture, Arts
and Manufactures. see Society for the
Promotion of Useful Arts, New York.
Society for the Promotion of American Manu-
factures, Philadelphia. see Philadelphia
Society for the Promotion of American
Manufactures.
Society for the Promotion of Collegiate and
Theological Education at the West. 85911,
85913-85923 see also American College
and Education Society. Congregational
Education Society of Boston. Joint Com-
mittee from the American Education
Society, and the Society for the Promo-
tion of Collegiate and Theological Educa-
tion at the West.
Society for the Promotion of Collegiate and
Theological Education at the West.
Boston Consulting Committee. 85912
Society for the Promotion of Collegiate and
Theological Education at the West. Com-
mittee to Confer with the Trustees of
Western Reserve College. 85924
Society for the Promotion of Collegiate and
Theological Education at the West.
Quarter-Century Anniversary Meeting,
Marietta, Ohio. 1868. 85913, 85921

Society for the Promotion of Collegiate and
Theological Education at the West.
Select Committee [on the Proposed
Union With the American Education
Society.] 85920, 85923

Society for the Promotion of Domestic Indus-
try, Philadelphia. see Philadelphia
Society for the Promotion of Domestic
Industry.

Society for the Promotion of Freedom and the
Relief of Persons Unlawfully Holden in
Bondage in Connecticut. see Connecti-
cut Society for the Promotion of Free-
dom and the Relief of Persons Unlawfully
Holden in Bondage.

Society for the Promotion of Industry, New
York. 85925-85926

Society for the Promotion of Industry, New
York. Board of Managers. 85926

Society for the Promotion of Internal Improvement in Pennsylvania. see Pennsylvania Society for the Promotion of
Internal Improvement.

Society for the Promotion of Knowledge and
Industry, New York. see New York
Society for the Promotion of Knowledge
and Industry.

Society for the Promotion of National Industry,
Philadelphia. see Philadelphia Society
for the Promotion of National Industry.

Society for the Promotion of Permanent and
Universal Peace, London. 105298

Society for the Promotion of Public Economy,
Pennsylvania. see Pennsylvania Society
for the Promotion of Public Economy.

Society for the Promotion of Public Schools
in Pennsylvania. see Pennsylvania
Society for the Promotion of Public
Schools.

Society for the Promotion of Temperance in
Haverhill and Vicinity. Board of Council.
85927-85928

Society for the Promotion of Temperance in
New Hampshire. see New-Hampshire
Society for the Promotion of Temperance.

Society for the Promotion of Temperance in
New York. see New York State Temperance Society.

Society for the Promotion of Temperance in
South Carolina. see South Carolina
Society for the Promotion of Temperance.

Society for the Promotion of Temperance in
Virginia. see Virginia Society for the
Promotion of Temperance.

Society for the Promotion of the Rights and
Interests of Bona Fide Creditors, and
the Benefit and Relief of Honest Debtors,
Boston. 85929

Society for the Promotion of the Rights and
Interests of Bona Fide Creditors, and
the Benefit and Relief of Honest Debtors,
Boston. Committee. 85929

Society for the Promotion of Theological Educa-
tion, in Cambridge University. see
Society for the Promotion of Theological
Education in Harvard University.

Society for the Promotion of Theological Education in Harvard University. (22174),
(30723), 30740, 30765, 85930

Society for the Promotion of Theological Education in Harvard University. Committee.
85931

Society for the Promotion of Theological Education in Harvard University. Directors.
30765

Society for the Promotion of Useful Arts, New
York. 85998-86000 see also Albany
Institute.

Society for the Promotion of Useful Arts, New
York. Charter. 85998, 96743

Society for the Promotion of Useful Arts, New
York. Library. 85997

Society for the Propagation of the Faith. 1578-
1579A see also Catholic Church. Congregatio de Propaganda Fide.

Society for the Propagation of the Faith,
Louvain. (68446)

Society for the Propagation of the Faith,
Montreal. 50276

Society for the Propagation of the Gospel
Among the Indians. see Society for
Propagating the Gospel Among the Indians
and Others in North America.

Society for the Propagation of the Gospel in
Foreign Parts, London. 99, 101, 6325,
(13366), 14145, 30952, (33801), 37448,
(44619), 47140, 50192, 69247, (69273),
78713-78714, 78717, 82193, note before
85932, 85932-85933, 85934-85941, 85943-
85945, 85947-85950, 90108, 90218-90219,
91002, 91663, 93695, 93973, 94324, 95767,
96055, 96143, 96797, 98521, 99582,
100900, 101468, 102176, 102178, 103964,
105681, 106042

Society for the Propagation of the Gospel in
Foreign Parts, London. plaintiffs 31669

Society for the Propagation of the Gospel in
Foreign Parts, London. Charter. 84,
8641, 47140-47142, 47144-47145, 59035,
(69273), 5th note after 69412, 82194,
85933A-85934, 91002, 96143, 96797, note
after 99295, 101276, 101468, 103964

Society for the Propagation of the Gospel in
Foreign Parts, London. Codrington Trust.
Committee. 85942

Society for the Propagation of the Gospel in
Foreign Parts, London. Member. pseud.
see Chamberlayne, John. supposed
author

Society for the Propagation of the Gospel in
Foreign Parts, London. Missionaries to
the Mohawk Indians. trs. 57488-57489
see also Andrews, William. tr. Barclay,
Henry. tr. Ogilvie, John. tr.

Society for the Propagation of the Gospel in
Foreign Parts, London. Secretary. 38184,
85944, 95751 see also Burton, --------.

Society for the Propagation of the Gospel in
New England. see Company For Propagation of the Gospel in New England and
the Parts Adjacent in America, London.

Society for the Protection of American Industry.
see Society for Protection of American
Industry.

Society for the Purpose of Effecting the Abolition of the Slave Trade, London. 82011

Society for the Reformation of Juvenile Delinquents, New York. 54486, (54671), 85952

Society for the Reformation of Juvenile Delinquents, New York. petitioners 85956-
85957

Society for the Reformation of Juvenile Delinquents, New York. Board of Managers.
85891, 85958

Society for the Reformation of Juvenile Delinquents, New York. Board of Managers.
petitioners 85960

Society for the Reformation of Juvenile Delinquents, New York. Charter. 54486

Society for the Reformation of Juvenile Delinquents, New York. Committee for

Erecting an Institution for the House of Refuge. (54671), 85953

Society for the Reformation of Juvenile Delinquents, New York. House of Refuge. (54671), 85951, 85955, 85959

Society for the Reformation of Juvenile Delinquents, New York. House of Refuge. Managers. (54671), 85954

Society for the Reformation of Juvenile Delinquents, New York. House of Refuge. Managers. petitioners 85958

Society for the Reformation of Juvenile Delinquents, New York. House of Refuge. Managers. Special Committee. 85958

Society for the Reformation of Juvenile Delinquents, New York. House of Refuge. Superintendent. 30640 see also Hart, Nathaniel C.

Society for the Relief of Aged and Destitute Clergymen, Boston. see Society for Ministerial Relief, Boston.

Society for the Relief of Destitute Children of Seamen, New York. Board of Managers. 85963

Society for the Relief of Destitute Females and Their Helpless Children, New Orleans. 85964

Society for the Relief of Free Negroes, and Others, Unlawfully Held in Bondage, Philadelphia. 62255

Society for the Relief of Orphan and Destitute Children, Albany. 37976, 85967

Society for the Relief of Orphan and Destitute Children, Albany. Managers. 37976, 85967

Society for the Relief of Half-Orphan and Destitute Children, New York. 54672, 85965, 85966

Society for the Relief of Poor, Aged and Infirm Masters of Ships, Phialdelphia. 59782, 85968-85969

Society for the Relief of Poor, Aged and Infirm Masters of Ships, Philadelphia. Charter. 59782, 85968-85969

Society, for the Relief of Poor and Distressed Masters of Ships, Their Widows and Children, Philadelphia. see Society for the Relief of Poor, Aged and Infirm Masters of Ships, Philadelphia.

Society for the Relief of Poor Widows, New York. 54673

Society for the Relief of Poor Widows with Small Children, New York. see Ladies' Society for the Relief of Poor Widows with Small Children, New York.

Society for the Relief of Strangers in Distress, Toronto. 85976

Society for the Relief of the Destitute Blind of New York and Its Vicinity. 85977

Society for the Relief of the Destitute in the City of New York. 54674

Society for the Relief of the Insane, Hartford, Conn. 30674

Society for the Relief of the Ruptured and Crippled, New York. see New York Society for the Relief of the Ruptured and Crippled.

Society for the Relief of the Widows and Orphans of Deceased Clergymen in the Diocese of Virginia. 85978

Society for the Relief of the Widows Orphans of Medical Men, New York. see New-York Society for the Relief of the Widows and Orphans of Medical Men.

Society for the Relief of the Widows and Orphans of the Clergy of the Protestant Episcopal Church in South Carolina. 85979-85980

Society for the Relief of Worthy Aged and Indigent Colored Persons, New York. see New York (City) Lincoln's Hospital and Home.

Society for the Sale of Lands in America, London. 63284

Society for the Support of the Colored Home, New York. see New York (City) Lincoln's Hospital and Home.

Society for the Support of the Gospel Among the Poor in the City of New York. 54675, 85984

Society for the Suppression of Lotteries in Pennsylvania. see Pennsylvania Society for the Suppression of Lotteries.

Society for the Suppression of Vice, Bedford, N. Y. 85988

Society for the Suppression of Vice, Bedford, N. Y. Committee. 85987

Society for the Suppression of Vice, Portsmouth, N. H. see Portsmouth Society for the Suppression of Vice.

Society for the Suppression of Vice and Immorality. 85985-85986

Society for the Suppression of Vice and Immorality, New Jersey. see New Jersey Society for the Suppression of Vice and Immorality.

Society for the Suppression of Vice in the Town of Bedford, N. Y. Committee. 4280, 85987

Society for Theological Education. 85989

Society for Worcester County and Vicinity, Auxiliary to the Baptist Board of Foreign Missions for the United States. 105391-105392

Society in Aid of Social Improvements, Boston. 85990

Society in America. 44941, 44944, 103819, 103993

Society in New Jersey to Co-operate with the American Colonization Society. see New Jersey Colonization Society.

Society in Portland for Suppressing Vice and Immprality. see Society for Suppressing Vice and Immorality, Portland, Maine.

Society in Scotland for Propagating Christian Knowledge. (7340), note before 85932, 85992-85994, 102613, 104929

Society in Scotland for Propagating Christian Knowledge. Committee. 85991

Society in Scotland for Propagating Christian Knowledge. Correspondents. 34598

Society in Scotland for Propagating Christian Knowledge. Directors. 94428

Society in Scotland for Propagating Christian Knowledge. Secretary. 94427 see also Tawse, John.

Society Instituted at Halifax, for Promoting Agriculture in the Province of Nova Scotia. see Society for Promoting Agriculture in the Province of Nova Scotia, Halifax.

Society Instituted at London for the Encouragement of Arts, Manufactures and Commerce. see Society for the Encouragement of Arts, Manufactures and Commerce, London.

Society Instituted for the Purpose of Effecting the Abolition of the Slave Trade, London. Committee. 85995, 85996

Society Instituted in the State of New York for the Promotion of Agriculture, Arts and Manufactures. see Society for the Promotion of Useful Arts, New York.

Society Lately Established for the Suppression of Vice and Immorality. see Society for the Suppression of Vice and Immorality.

Society Library, New York. see New York Society Library.

Society Library, Rye, N. Y. 86001

Society Library, Salem, Mass. 75745

Society Library, Salem, Mass. Proprietors. 75745

Society, manners and politics in the United States. 12596

Society of Alumni of Hughes High School, Cincinnati. 86002

Society of American Republicans, Philadelphia. (62256)

Society of Ancient Masons, in Virginia. see Freemasons. Virginia.

Society of Antiquaries, Newcastle-Upon-Tyne. 86004

Society of Artists and Manufacturers of Philadelphia. 17296

Society of Artists of the United States. 62257, 86005-86006

Society of Artists of the United States. Annual Exhibition, 1st, 1811. 86006

Society of Artists of the United States. Annual Exhibition, 2d, 1812. 60616

Society of Artists of the United States. Annual Exhibition, 3d, 1813. 60616

Society of Artists of the United States. Committee to Examine Into the Rise, Progress, and Present State of the Society. 60616

Society of Arts and Manufactures of Philadelphia. petitioners 17296, (22964)

Society of Associates of the Cooper Union for the Advancement of Science and Art, New York. 86007

Society of Believers, Pleasant Hill, Ky. see Shakers. Pleasant Hill, Ky.

Society of California Pioneers, San Francisco. 9976, 86008-86014, 105053

Society of California Pioneers, San Francisco. Board of Directors. Committee. 86013

Society of California Pioneers, San Francisco. President. 86008 see also Cornwall, P. B.

Society of California Pioneers quarterly. 105053

Society of Christian Brethren, Harvard University. see Harvard University. Society of Christian Brethren.

Society of Christian Brethren in Harvard University, June, 1856. 30765

Society of Christian Independents, Gloucester, Mass. 1658, 27591-27592, 93506

Society of Christian Independents, Gloucester, Mass. plaintiffs 27591, 93506

Society of Cincinnati. see Society of the Cincinnati.

Society of Civil Engineers of Canada. see Canadian Society of Civil Engineers.

Society of Colonial Wars in the State of Rhode Island and Providence Plantations. 83760

Society of Commercial Travellers, New York. 86015

Society of Constitutional Republicans, Philadelphia. 62258

Society of Correspondence in New-York, With the Baptist Education Society in Philadelphia. 90209

Society of Dutchess County for the Promotion of Agriculture, Poughkeepsie. 21456, 86016

Society of Englishmen, and Sons of Englishmen, Established at Philadelphia, for the Advice and Assistance of Englishmen in Distress. see Society of the Sons of St. George, Philadelphia.

Society of First Steamship Pioneers, San Francisco. 86017

Society of First Steamship Pioneers, San Francisco. Committee. 86018-86019

Society of Friends. see Friends, Society of.

Society of Friends. A domestic narrative. 28915

Society of Friends as it was, and as it is. (33377)

Society of Friends in the United States: their views. 86067

Society of "Friends of the People," Philadelphia. 86072-86073

Society of Friends, Robert Barclay and Hai Ebn Yokdam. 83315

Society of Friends vindicated. 105026

Society of Gentlemen. pseud. eds. American magazine and monthly chronicle. (1133), 52440, 84585, 84678C

Society of Gentlemen. pseud. Halcyon luminary and theological repository. 29604

Society of Gentlemen. pseud. History of the British Empire. see Smollett, Tobias George, 1721-1771.

Society of Gentlemen in New-York. pseud. Universal receipt book. see Alsop, Richard. supposed author

Society of Gentlemen, in Philadelphia. pseud. eds. Remarks on the manufacturing of maple sugar. (69472)

Society of Husbandmen and Manufacturers of Middlesex, Mass. 48851

Society of Independent Democrats, Philadelphia. 39890, 98981 see also Democratic Party. Pennsylvania. Philadelphia.

Society of Inquiry, Marietta College. see Marietta College. Society of Inquiry.

Society of Inquiry Respecting Missions, Andover Theological Seminary. see Andover Theological Seminary. Society of Inquiry Respecting Missions.

Society of Inquiry Respecting Missions, Yale University. see Yale College Missionary Society.

Society of Inquiry Respecting the Advancement of Christianity. see New York (City) General Theological Seminary of the Protestant Episcopal Church in the U. S. Society of Inquiry Respecting the Advancement of Christianity.

Society of Jesus. see Jesuits.

Society of Literary & Scientific Chiffonniers. 103034

Society of Literati. pseud. eds. Level of Europe and North America. 22057

Society of Masons. see Freemasons.

Society of Mechanics and Tradesmen of the City of New York. see General Society of Mechanics and Tradesmen of the City of New York.

Society of Members of the New York Stock Exchange for Mutual Relief. 86076

Society of Moral Philanthropists, Providence, R. I. Celebration of the 97th Anniversary of the Birth Day of Thomas Paine, 1834. 70766

Society of Natural History, Boston. see Boston Society of Natural History.

Society of Natural History, Portland, Me. see Portland Society of Natural History, Portland, Me.

Society of Natural Sciences, Orleans County, N. Y. see Orleans County Society of Natural Sciences.

Society of Noblemen and Gentlemen in London, for the Relief and Instruction of Poor Germans, and Their Descendants, Settled in Pennsylvania, and the Adjacent British Colonies in America. Trustees General. 7876, 84588, 84625

Society of Noblemen and Gentlemen in London, for the Relief and Instruction of Poor Germans, and Their Descendants, Settled in Pennsylvania, and the Adjacent British Colonies in America. Trustees General. Secretary. 7876, 84588, 84625 see also Smith, William, 1727-1803.

Society of Paper Makers of Delaware. see Society of Paper Makers of Pennsylvania and Delaware.

Society of Paper Makers of Pennsylvania and Delaware. 60617

Society of Paper Makers of Pennsylvania and Delaware. petitioners (47713)

Society of Patriots. 86077

Society of People of Canterbury and Enfield commonly Called Shakers. see Shakers. Canterbury and Enfield, N. H.

Society of Perfectionists. see Oneida Community.

Society of Physicians. pseud. Vaccine enquirer. 98271

Society of Regulars, New York. 86078

Society of Regulars, New York. Delegation. 86079

Society of Regulars, New York. Special Committee. 86080

Society of St. George, Baltimore. 86081

Society of St. George, Baltimore. Committee. 86081

Society of St. George, New York. 86082-86083

Society of St. George, Philadelphia. see Society of the Sons of St. George, Philadelphia.

Society of St. Johnland, Smithtown, N. Y. Trustees. 86084

Society of St. Joseph, Philadelphia. 62197

Society of St. Tammany. see Tammany Society, New York.

Society of St. Vincent de Paul. New York. 86086

Society of St. Vincent de Paul. New York. Superior Council. President. 86085

Society of St. Vincent de Paul. St. Paul, Minn. 86087

Society of St. Vincent de Paul. U. S. 86086

Society of St. Vincent de Paul. U. S. Conferences. 86085

Society of St. Vincent de Paul. U. S. Councils. 86085

Society of St. Vincent de Paul. Explanatory notes upon the articles. 86086

Society of Separatists. U. S. see Separatists. U. S.

Society of Separatists of Zoar. 86088

Society of Shipowners of Great Britain. 2264, 69490

Society of Social Friends, Dartmouth College. see Dartmouth College. Society of Social Friends.

Society of Tammany. see Tammany Society, New York.

Society of Teachers, Baltimore. 86090

Society of Teachers in the city of Baltimore. 86090

Society of Teachers of the City and County of New York. (54678)

Society of Teachers of the City and County of New York. Charter. 54677

Society of the Alumni, Dartmouth College. see Dartmouth College. Society of the Alumni.

Society of the Alumni of the Hahnemann Medical College, Philadelphia. see Hahnemann Medical College, Philadelphia. Society of the Alumni.

Society of the Alumni of the Law Department of the University of Pennsylvania, Philadelphia. see Philadelphia. University. Law Department. Society of the Alumni.

Society of the Alumni of the University of Nashville. see Nashville, Tenn. University. Society of the Alumni.

Society of the Alumni of the University of Pennsylvania. see Pennsylvania. University. Society of the Alumni.

Society of the Army and Navy of the Gulf. 86093

Society of the Army of Georgia. 86094

Society of the Army of the Cumberland. 86094

Society of the Army of the James. 86095

Society of the Army of the Ohio. 86094

Society of the Army of the Potomac. 86096-86097

Society of the Army of the Tennessee. 86094, 86098

Society of the Burnside Expedition and of the Ninth Army Corps. 86099-86101

Society of the Church of the Puritans, New York. see New York (City) Church of the Puritans.

Society of the Cincinnati. 13117, 13125, 13131, 77035, 86102-86105, 86137

Society of the Cincinnati. General Meeting, Philadelphia, 1784. 13117, 86105

Society of the Cincinnati. Connecticut. 21561, 97126

Society of the Cincinnati. France. 27496

Society of the Cincinnati. Massachusetts. 13120-(13121), 13124, 13126, 86107-86112, 97403

Society of the Cincinnati. New Jersey. 13116, 13127, 86113, 86116

Society of the Cincinnati. New York. (13121), 13125, 86118-86122, 86124

Society of the Cincinnati. New York. Committee. 86124

Society of the Cincinnati. Pennsylvania. 13130-13131, 60382, (64310), 86125-86127

Society of the Cincinnati. Rhode Island. 13123, 86128

Society of the Cincinnati. South Carolina. 13129, 86136-86138, 86140-86141, 87950 see also Joint Committee of the South Carolina State Society of Cincinnati, and the American Revolution Society. petitioners

Society of the Constitutional Republicans. 401

Society of the Fifth Army Corps. petitioners 86142

Society of the Fifth Army Corps. 5th Army Corps memorial. 86142

Society of the Friendly Sons of St. Patrick, New York. 86143-86144, 86146

Society of the Friendly Sons of St. Patrick, New York. Charter. 86144

Society of the Friendly Sons of St. Patrick, New York State. 86145

Society of the Friendly Sons of St. Patrick, Philadelphia. 7852, (25951), 61720, 62259, 86147

Society of the Friendly Sons of St. Patrick, Philadelphia. Charter. 30135, 61720, 86147

Society of the Iron Man, New York. 86148

Society of the Lying-In Hospital, New York. (54508), 86149-86150

Society of the Lying-In Hospital, New York. Charter. (54508), 86149

Society of the New Jerusalem Church, Boston. see New Jerusalem Church. Boston Society.

Society of the New York Hospital, New York. (54480)-54481, 54484, 86151, 86154

Society of the New York Hospital, New York. petitioners 86155

Society of the New York Hospital, New York. Bloomingdale Asylum for the Insane. 54484, 86154, 86156

Society of the New York Hospital, New York. Charter. 54162, 54484, 86153-86154

Society of the New York Hospital, New York. Governors. (54480), 86156

Society of the New York Hospital, New York. Governors. Majority. 54484

Society of the New York Hospital, New York. Governors. Minority. 54484

Society of the New York Hospital, New York. Governors. Committee on a Village of Cottage Hospitals. 86158

Society of the New York Hospital, New York. Governors. Committee on the Occasional Prevalence of Erysipelas in That Hospital. 86157

Society of the New York Hospital, New York. Governors. Special Committee. 86159

Society of the New York Hospital, New York. Library. (54482), 86152, 86160

Society of the New York Hospital, New York. Pathological Cabinet. (54483)

Society of the Ninth Army Corps. see Society of the Burnside Expedition and of the Ninth Army Corps.

Society of the "Old Boys of Hampton Academy." 86161

Society of the Protestant Episcopal Church, for the Advancement of Christianity in Pennsylvania. see Society for the Advancement of Christianity.

Society of the Rosy Cross, United States and British North America. Department of General. 86162

Society of the Rosy Cross, United States and British North America. Supreme Council. 86162

Society of the Sixth Army Corps. 86163-86164

Society of the Sons of New England in Pennsylvania. see Sons of New England in Pennsylvania (1858-   )

Society of the Sons of New England of the City and County of Philadelphia. 86165

Society of the Sons of St. George, Philadelphia. 62260, (74070)-74071, 86166-86167

Society of the Sons of St. George, Philadelphia. Charter. 62260

Society of the United Brethren for Propagating the Gospel Among the Heathen. 387, (22872), note before 85932, 86171-86174, 93386, 97862, 1st note after 97862

Society of the United Brethren for Propagating the Gospel Among the Heathen. Charter. 86174, 97862

Society of the United Brethren for Propagating the Gospel Among the Heathen. Directors. 86168

Society of the War of 1812. Pennsylvania. 61959, 86175

Society of the War of 1812 in the Commonwealth of Pennsylvania. see Society of the War of 1812. Pennsylvania.

Society of Unitarian Christians at Philadelphia. see Unitarians. Philadelphia.

Society of United Christian Friends. see United Christian Friends, New York.

Society of United Fraternity, Dartmouth College. see Dartmouth College. United Fraternity.

Society of United Irishmen, Dublin. 86176

Society of Virginia for Promoting Agriculture. 86177, 1st note after 100527A, 100566

Society of Young Men, Hartford, Conn. 90152

Society of Young Men Belonging to Lynn. pseud. Review of Lynn. 42843, 70208

Society Quoit Club, Washington, D. C. see Washington Society Gymnasium, Washington, D. C.

Society to Establish Schools Among the Indians and the Settlers in Canada. 97586

Society without veil. 86178

Socini-Arian detected. 92025

Socinian. A narrative. 86179

Socio, Carlo Convivio, Junior. pseud. Post-chaise companion. 86180

Socio, Clio Convivius. pseud. Post-chaise companion. 86181

Socio de plebe pauperum. 86182

Sociology for the south. 24618

Sock Indians. see Sauk Indians.

Socke, David Ross. see Locke, David Ross.

Sockett, Grenville A. 63381

Sockett, Thomas, 1778?-1859. 22500, 40594, 86184-86187, note after 98068, note after 98069, 98070-98071, 1st-2d notes after 98076, 98078, 98081-98083

Soconusco (territorio de Centro-America,) ocupado militarmente. 86188

Socorro de Leon, Jose. see Leon, Jose Socorro de, 1831-1869.

Socorro (Colombian State) Gobernador, 1843 (Vega) 86189 see also Vega, . Francisco.

Socorro (Colombian State) Laws, statutes, etc. 86190

Socrates, Father of the House of Congress. pseud. Echo from the temple of wisdom. see Deane, Silas, 1737-1789. supposed author

Sodality Lyceum, St. Louis. 86194

Soden, Carl Theodor von. 86195

Soden, Friedrich Julius Heinrich, Graf von, 1754-1831. 27651, 86196-86197

Soder Compagniet. (68983), 91723-91724, 98188-98189, 98199, note after 98207, 98210

Sodet Compagniet. Charter. (68983), 98186, 98202-98205

Sodling, Carl Erik. 86198-86199

Sodor and Man, Bishop of. see Wilson, Thomas, Bishop of Sodar and man, 1663-1755.

Sodre, Francois de. 86198

Sodus, N. Y. Sodus Academy. see Sodus Academy, Sodus, N. Y.

Sodus Academy, Sodus, N. Y. 86201-86202

Sodus Bay Improvement Company. 86203

Sodus Canal Company. 86204-86206

Sodus Canal Company. Engineer. 86204

Sodus Canal Company. President. 86204-86205 see also Adams, William H. Greig, John.

Sodus Canal Company. Treasurer. 86205 see also Duncan, Alexander.

Sodus Canal Co. 86206

Sodus Canal. 1839. 86205
Sodus Point and Southern Rail Road Company of New York. 86207-86208
Sodus Point and Southern Rail Road Company of New York. Seven per cent. First mortgage convertible sinking fund bonds. 86207
Sodus Point and Southern Rail Road, of New York. Seven per cent. 86208
Soelen, Johan Gijsbert Verstolk de. see Verstolk de Soelen, Johan Gijsbert, d. 1845.
Soest, Gerardus Hubertus van. 86209
Soeurs jumelles. 79191
Sofficiente e vera descrittione de tutte la regioni al monarca di Moscouia soggette. 67738
Softly, brave yankees!!! 86210, 1st note after 102867
Softs the true Democracy of the state of New York. 86211
Sogro da rapasiada. 66902
Sohier, Elizabeth Putnam. supposed author 86212
Soho Company, incorporated the 27th November, 1801. 86213
Soi-disant bon Hollandois. pseud. Discours. (56478), 2d note after 93480
Soil-moisture one of its chief causes. 6992
Soil of the south. 86214
Soil, the seed, the sowers, the presidents and professors. 1316
Soiree in Honor of George Thompson, Esq., Paisley, Scotland, 1837. 95503
Soirees Bermudiennes. 11109
Soirees Canadiennes. 86215
Sojourn in the Old Dominion. (37421), (37423), 84812, note after 92624, 5th note after 93998
Sol (Mexico) 96216, 87167
Sol de Chile. 86217
Sol de Mayo. 46202
Sol del Nvevo Mvndo. 50071
Sol en el medio dia. 94862
Sol en el zodiaco. 96218-96219
Sol en Leon solmnes aplausos conque, el Rey N. S. D. Fernando IV. 24157, 44557B
Sol en su ocaso. 76168
Sol Smith Russell's character vocalist. 86220
Sol Smith Russell's "Jeremy Jollyboy" songster. 86221
Sol. Smith's theatrical apprenticeship. 84239
Sol y ano feliz del Peru. 29232
Sola, Magino. 88222-88223 see also Jesuits. Philippine Islands. Procurador General.
Sola y Fuente, Geronimo de. 56293, 86224
Solace for bereaved parents. 85325, 85331
Solana, Juan Blanco. see Blanca Solana, Juan.
Solana, Juan G. 86225
Solander, Daniel Charles, 1736-1782. (3201)-3203, 6864, 6867
Solano. pseud. Future of Vallejo. 86226
Solano, Fernando C. Moreno. 86227
Solano, Francisco Gallardo. illus. 86230
Solano, Joaquin. 98311
Solano, Jose. 86231
Solano, Jose Maria Diez de. see Diez de Solano, Jose Maria.
Solano, Matthew. 86232, 89686
Solano, Pedro Maria. 86233
Solano, Vicente, 1791 or 2-1865. 86234-86239
Solano, Zenon. 86240
Solano Astra-Buruaga, Francisco, 1817-1892. 86241-86246
Solano Constancio, Francisco. see Constancio, Francisco Solano.

Solano y Marcha, Jose Maria. 86249
Solano y Marcha, Jose Maria. petitioner 86247-86248
Solar, Fidelis Pastor del, 1836- 86250
Solar, Mercedes Marin del, 1804-1866. 86251-86252
Solar system displayed. 86253
Solchaga, Juan de. 86254
Solchaga, Miguel, d. 1718. 86255
Soldado. pseud. Debidas gracias al Zurriago. 86256
Soldado. pseud. Expedicion Goicuria. see Armas, Juan Ignacio de. supposed author
Soldado. pseud. Prision de un general Gachupin. 86258
Soldado. pseud. Situacion de la guerra de Cuba. see Estevan, Ricardo. supposed author
Soldado de la patria del Sabado 14 de Abril de 1827. 86260
Soldan, Felipe Paz. see Paz Soldan, Felipe.
Soldan, Jose Gregorio Paz. see Paz Soldan, Jose Gregorio.
Soldan, Manuel Rouard y Paz. see Rouard y Paz-Soldan, Manuel.
Soldan, Mariano Felipe Paz. see Paz Soldan, Mariano Felipe.
Soldan, Mateo Paz. see Paz Soldan, Mateo.
Soldaten Hand-Buch. 86261
Soldatenhandel Deutscher Fursten nach Amerika. 37101
Soldi, D. tr. 30862
Soldier. pseud. Lafitte; or, the Greek slave. see Rogers, J. W.
Soldier, b. 1743. pseud. Soldier's journal.
Soldier. pseud. Three voices. see Rosecrans, William Starke, 1819-1898.
Soldier. An affecting narrative of facts. 86262
Soldier and his lady. 86263
Soldier and sage. 86264
Soldier bird. 3615
Soldier boy and his father. 86265
Soldier boy and his father. A thrilling narrative. 88050
Soldier boy; or Tom Somers in the Army. 57216, 86266
Soldier caution'd and counsel'd. 32317
Soldier defended & directed. 59602
Soldier exhorted to courage. 50789
Soldier, God's minister. 26802
Soldier!—In Christ Jesus! 82954
Soldier in Company "H", 6th Regiment. pseud. Journal. see Daniels, Arthur M.
Soldier in the colored brigade. 86268
Soldier-life and every-day battles. 58973
Soldier of 1812. pseud. Appeal. see Abbott, Orrin. supposed author
Soldier of freedom. 44350
Soldier of Indiana in the war of the Union. 47992, 86270
Soldier of '77. pseud. Address to the freemen of Vermont. 99137
Soldier of the American revolution. pseud. Letter in answer to the speech. 86271
Soldier of the American revolution. pseud. Letter to John M. Mason. 45465
Soldier of the Cumberland. 32618
Soldier of the good cause. 55875
Soldier of the revolution of '76. 86272
Soldier, the battle, and the victory. 86273
Soldier, three years in the army of the Potomac. pseud. Views on the war. see H., W. J. pseud.
Soldier turned farmer. 86274
Soldiering in North Carolina. 38015

Soldiers must be paid. 29294

Soldiers National Cemetery Association. 27249

Soldiers National Cemetery Association.
Board of Commissioners. 27233-27235,
27242, 65830

Soldiers National Cemetery Association.
Board of Managers. see Soldiers
National Cemetery Association. Board
of Commissioners.

Soldiers National Cemetery Association.
Charter. 27235

Soldiers National Cemetery Association, Gettysburg, Pa. see Soldiers National
Cemetery Association.

Soldiers of the War of 1812. petitioners 86349

Soldiers of the War of 1812. Convention, Syracuse, 1854. see Convention of the Soldiers of the War of 1812, Syracuse, 1854.

Soldiers of Venezuela: a tale. 98883

Soldiers on their right to vote. 63762

Soldier's orphan. 86301

Soldiers' Orphans and Widows' Home, St.
Joseph, Missouri. 86350

Soldier's paper. 96302

Soldier's pocket-book. 86303

Soldier's pocket-companion. 86304

Soldier's prayer book. Arranged for the Book
of Common Prayer. 86305

Soldier's prayer book. [By Thomas Smyth.]
85309, 85326, 88045C

Soldiers read!! Citizens read!! 60619

Soldiers Reading Room, Philadelphia. 62262

Soldier's recollection of the West Indies and
America. 75025

Soldiers' record of Jericho, Vermont. 38852

Soldiers' register of Wayne County, Indiana.
64770

Soldiers' Relief Association, Columbia, S. C.
86351

Soldiers' Relief Association, New York. 86352

Soldiers' Relief Association of Maryland. see
Maryland Soldiers' Relief Association.

Soldiers Relief Fund Committee, San Francisco.
see United States Sanitary Commission.
Soldiers Relief Fund Committee, San
Francisco.

Soldiers' Relief Society, Charlestown, Mass.
86353

Soldiers' Relief Society. Originated April
nineteenth, 1861. 86353

Soldier's return. By F. R. Brunot, Esq. 8758

Soldier's return. By the author of Village
missionaries,'', &c. 86306

Soldier's right to vote. 11886

Soldier's sacrifice. 47223, 86307

Soldier's sacrifice. A poem for the times.
(29398)

Soldier's story of his captivity. 28057

Soldier's story of the war. 86308

Soldiers text book. 43200

Soldiers' Tract Association, Methodist Episcopal Church, South. 86294, 86302, 86318,
88402

Soldiers' Tract Society of the Virginia Conference, Methodist Episcopal Church, South.
see Methodist Episcopal Church, South.
Conferences. Virginia. Soldiers' Tract
Society.

Soldiers Valentine writer. 86354

Soldiers' visitor. 86309

Soldier's voting bill of the state of New York.
86310

Sole right people have to call and dismiss their
officers. 11968

Sole survivor. pseud. Voyage to South America. see Fracker, George.

Soleau, A. 29181, 86355, 1st note after 93861,
106315

Soledad Ortega de Arguello, Maria de la.
defendant 86356

Soledad Ortega de Arguello et al., Respondents.
86356

Soledade e Castro, Vicente da, Abp. 86357
see also Bahia (Archdiocese)
Archbishop (Soledade e Castro)

Solemn acknowledgment of publick sins. 80715,
86358

Solemn address, to Christians & patriots. 105513

Solemn address to distillers and venders of
ardent spirits. 102598

Solemn address to youth. 49105

Solemn admonitions unto all people. 46588

Solemn advice, . . . by the Council in Connecticut colony. 24577

Solemn advice of the Venerable Mr. Nathanael
Stone. 53311, 92107, 101174

Solemn advice to young men, not to walk in the
way of their hearts. 86359

Solemn advice of young men, not to walk in the
wayes of their heart. (46743)

Solemn and important reasons against becoming
an Universalist. 105036

Solemn and pathetic elegy. 95841

Solemn appeal to all persons at this tremendous
juncture. 94567

Solemn appeal to Christians of all denominations.
38528, 62433

Solemn appeal to the church. 32294, 36464

Solemn appeal to the good sense of the nation.
86360

Solemn appeal to the political wisdom of George
III. 40269

Solemn appeal to the President. 10862

Solemn call on Count Zinzendorf. 71406, 71408

Solemn call to the citizens of the United States.
86361-86362

Solemn charge given to ministers. 16349

Solemn convenanting with God. 8506

Solemn declaration of the late unfortunate
Jason Fairbanks. 23673

Solemn dirge. 70915

Solemn dirge [and] masonic hymn. 70929

Solemn discourse by a local preacher. 41189

Solemn elegy. 95841

Solemn farewell to Levi Ames. 86363

Solemn feasts solemn vows. 74728

Solemn league and covenant for reformation
and defence of religion. 80715, 86364

Solemn protest against the doctrine of universal
salvation. 92790

Solemn protest against the late declaration of
war. 57778

Solemn protest, directed to the Masonic brethren of Missouri. 50872

Solemn reasons. 93905

Solemn reasons for declining to adopt the
Baptist theory. 105274

Solemn review of the custom of war. 1st note
after 100993, 105253-105255, 105259-
105261, 105263, 105265, 105275-105295,
105298

Solemn truth. pseud. Abolition tract. No. 1.
81728

Solemn warning against free-masonry. 88652

Solemn warning against the dangerous doctrine.
10889, 96073

Solemn warning against the destructive doctrine
of a separation. 10889

Solemn warning by the Associated Presbytery.
(59899), 86365

Solemn warning on the banks of the Rubicon.
30053

Solemn warning on the banks of the Rubicon. No. 5. 10889
Solemn warning to all the dwellers upon earth. 33601
Solemn warning to the people of the United States. 86366
Solemn warning to the secure world. 94705-94706
Solemn week. 26074
Solemna proclamacion que 5 Oct. 1701 hizo. 41133
Solemne accion de gracias que tributaron al todopoderoso en la Metropolitana de Mexico. (48657)
Solemne acknowledgement of publick sins. 86358
Solemne aclamacion, y festivo movimiento. 67648
Solemne league and covenant. 80715
Solemnes accion de gracias que la Academia de Derecho Espanol. 48659
Solemnes aplausos conque, el Rey Nuestro Senor D. Fernando VI. 44557B
Solemnes exequias celebradas en la Iglesia del Tercer Orden de Nuestra Senora del Carmen de Mexico. 86367
Solemnes exequias de D. Matias de Galvez. 24152
Solemnes exequias de la Senora Dona Maria Josepha Aramburu de Itrubide. 35297
Solemnes exequias del D. Matias de Galvez Garcia. 26569
Solemnes exequias del Exmo. e Illmo. Senor D. Manuel Ignacio Gonzalez del Campillo. 47815, 86368, 98715
Solemnes exequias del Exmo. S. D. Juan Vicente Guemez Pacheco de Padilla Horcasitas, y Aguaya. 86369
Solemnes exequias del F. Antonio Bermond. 80880
Solemnes exequias del Illmo Senor Dr. Jose Gregorio Alonzo de Hortigosa. 44244
Solemnes exequias del S. D. J. Vicente Guemez. 29106
Solemnes exequias que celebro la Santa Yglesia Catedral de . . . Michoacan. 50698, 86370
Solemnes fiestas, que a la canonizacion del Mystico Doctor San Juan de la Cruz. 105731
Solemnes fiestas que a la canonizacion del Mystico Dr. S. Juan de la Cruz. 36800
Solemnes honras que a la buena memoria de los ciudadanos. 86371, 96275
Solemnidad fvnebre y exeqvias de la mverte del Catolico Avgvstissimo Rey. 86372
Solemnities at the Stone Chapel. 86373
Solemnization of the third centurial jubilee. 86374
Solensis, Aratus. see Aratus Solensis.
Soler, --------. 86375
Soler, Dionysio. defendant at court of inquiry 29458
Soler, Tomas Bertran. 86376
Soler Ruiz, Gaspar. 86377-86379
Soler y Gabarda, Geronimo. 86380-86381
Soles, Martin de. 9813, 98932 see also Mexico (City) Fiscal.
Soley, James Russell, 1850-1911. 86382
Solfeada y palo de ciego a todo autorcillo lego. 86383
Solger, Reinhold. 86384-86385
Solicitor of the Treasury and the Choctaw claims. 86386
Solicitous mother. pseud. Affectionate address. 40314

Solicitud de un ciudadano por la libertad de Davila. 86387
Solicitud de S. Ayuntamiento de Solima. 48814, (57235)
Solid and awakening discourse. 100986
Solid reasons for continuance of war. 74295
Solida narratio de moderno provinciae Virginiae statu. (8784), note before 90030, 92665
Solidi ac sphaerici corporis siue globi astronomici. (77799), 77808
Solidification of the coral reefs of Florida. 33052
Solier, Pedro Joseph Bermudez de la Torre y. see Torre y Solier, Pedro Joseph Bermudez de la.
Solignac, Armand de. 86388-86389
Soliloquies of "Brick" Pomeroy. 63933
Soliloquio entre el Dr. Pineres y Justo Festivo. 62937
Soliloquy. 94237
Soliloquy, by the Rev. William Smith. 84684-84685
Soliloquy. [By William Goddard.] (27643), 27645, 2d note after 97091
Soliloquy [of Lieut.-Governor Cadwallader Colden. By William Livingston.] (41651)
Soliloquy, upon his unfortunate situation. 83999
Soliloquy written in a country church-yard by Mr. Moore. 100663
Solima, Mexico. Ayuntamiento. 84414, (57235)
Solinus, C. Julius. (63921), 76838, 86390
Solinus Polyhistor, Julius. see Solinus, C. Julius.
Solis, Alonso Suarez de. see Suarez de Solis, Alonso.
Solis, Antonio de. see Solis y Ribadeneyra, Antonio de, 1610-1686.
Solis, Diego. 86395-86397
Solis, Francisco de, Bp. 34177, 47417, 86398 see also Aragon (Viceroyalty) Virrey (Solis) Cordova, Spain (Diocese) Bishop (Solis)
Solis, Francisco Lopez de, d. 1664. 86399-86422 see also Dominicans. Provincia de Santiago, Mexico. Abogado.
Solis, Gaspar Joseph de. see Solis, Gaspar Jose de.
Solis, Gaspar Jose de. 86423
Solis, Hernando de. 86424
Solis, Juan Alonso, d. 1641. 86425
Solis, Juan Bautista.⁻ 86426
Solis, Juan Diaz de. 86427-86428
Solis, Luis Gomez de. 86433-86435
Solis, Pedro. 86431
Solis, Aguirre, Ambrosio de. 86429-86431
Solis Calderon, Pedro de. 86432
Solis de Obando, Manuel A. 86436
Solis Holguin, Gonzalo de. 86437
Solis i Enriquez, Cristoval Alfonso de. petitioner (59589), 86394
Solis Osorio, Francisco de. 86438
Solis Valderabano i Bracamonte, Alonso. petitioner (59589), 86394
Solis Vango, Juan Prospero de. 86438
Solis y Alcazar, Francisco de. 86440
Solis y Barbosa, Antonio Sebastian de. 86441
Solis y Casanova, Francisco. 86442
Solis y Haro, Marcelino de. 86443-86444
Solis y Haro, Marcelino de. supposed author 58292, 86444
Solis y Quinones, Pedro de. 86445
Solis y Rabadeneyra, Antonio de, 1610-1686. 6124, 16944-16945, 16951-(16952), 16964, (27208), 32033, 56299, 75594-75595, 86391-86393, 86446-86493, 98758

Solis y Ribadeneyra, Antonio de, 1610-1686.
supposed author 16963, 48490, 65402
Solis y Rosales, Jose Vicente. 86494
Solis y Vlloa, Mathias de. petitioner 86495
Solis y Valenzuela, Bruno de. 86496-86498
Solis y Valenzuela, Pedro de. 86499-86501,
note after 98357
Solis y Zuniga, Jose. 86502
Solitaire. pseud. Streaks of squatter life.
see Robb, John S.
Solitaire. pseud. Swamp doctor's adventures
in the south-west. see Robb, John S.
Solitaire. pseud. Western scenes. see Robb,
John S.
Solitairo, A. C. Tavares Bastos do. see
Tavares Bastos, Aureliano Candido,
1839-1875.
Solitario de America. pseud. Argentiada.
see Tristani, Manuel Rogelio.
Solitary. 83788
Solitary of Juan Fernandez. 75543
Solitary rambles and adventures of a hunter
in the prairies. (58333)
Soll und Haben. 86385
Sollano, J. M. Diez de. see Diez de Solano,
Jose Maria, Bp., 1820-1881.
Sollers, Augustus Rhodes, 1814-1862. 86503
Sollicitudo omnium ecclesiarum. 73990
Solly, Samuel Edwin, 1845-1906. 86504
Solms-Braunfels, Carl, Prinz zu. see Carl,
Prinz zu Solms-Braunfels.
Solo en Durango. 86506
Sologuren, Jose. 86507
Sologuren, Juan de. 18508-86509
Solomon, Mr. -------. 86510
Solomon, Mrs. -------. 86510
Solomon, John. defendant 41268, note after
97069
Solomon Bell. pseud. see Snelling, William
Joseph, 1804-1848.
Solomon Irony. pseud. see Irony, Solomon.
pseud.
Solomon of the west. 86511
Solomon Secondsight. pseud. see McHenry,
James.
Solomon Secondthoughts. pseud. see Kennedy,
John Pendleton, 1795-1870.
Solomon Sobersides. pseud. see Sobersides,
Solomon.
Solomon's caution against the cup. 83450-
83451
Solomon's counsel to his son. 83453
Solon, or the rebellion of '61. (2818), 19455,
86512
Solorcano, Bernardino de. see Solorzano,
Bernardino de.
Solorcano, Justino de. see Solorzano, Justino
de.
Solorcano y Velasco, Alonso de. 86549
Solorzano, A. D. 86513
Solorzano, Bernardino de. petitioner 86514-
86515
Solorzano, Justino de. petitioner 86516
Solorzano Dieguez, Manuel. 86517-86519
Solorzano Paniagua i Trexo, Gabriel de. ed.
86532
Solorzano Pereira, Juan de, 1575-1655.
86520-86545 see also Spain. Consejo
de las Indias. Fiscal. plaintiff
Solorzano y Salcedo, Juan de. 86546
Solorzano y Velasco, Alonso de, d. 1680.
86547-86549
Solorzano's Politica Indiana. 86544
Solre, Prince Emmanuel de Croy-. see Croy,
Emmanuel, Duc de, 1718-1784.

Solucion de la Real, y Pontificia Vniuersidad
de Mexico. 86550
Solucion de los dificultades que embarazan la
pacification. (38992), 77063
Solucion del gran problema. 750
Solucion del problema en la cuestion capital de
la republica .Argentina. 86552
Soluciones posibles. 86553
Solvtae orationis fragmenta. 86555
Solvtae orationis fragmenta ad vsvs scholarvm
Latinitatis & rhetoricae. 86554
Solution de la question Mexicaine. (44116)
Solution des difficultes qui empechent la pacifi-
cation. 77065
Solution Mexicaine. 18370
Solution of our national difficulties. 86556
Solution of some of the mysteries. 86557
Solution of the labor problem. 84438
Solution of the scruples. (46516)
Solution of the silver question. 84439
Solution to the important question. 97346
Solvet, -------. 2815, 11484
Som free reflections upon occasion. 86646
Som njoe-singi vo da Evangelische Broeder-
Gemeente. 81419
Somano y Medinilla, -------. 65931
Sombra (Havana) 86559
Sombra (Mexico City) 86558
Sombra de Ayala. 86560
Sombra de Jarauta: periodico politico. 86561
Sombra de Hernan Cortes. 7074
Sombra de Moctheuzoma Xocoyotzin. 86562
Sombra de Zarogoza. 86563
Sombra funebre, oracion. 18505
Sombra imagen de la grandeza del D. Joseph
del Campillo y Cossio. 35286
Sombre, Samuel. pseud. Aquarelles. see
Gerard, James Watson.
Some account of a plant used in Lancaster
County. 3863
Some account of acts in relation to the construc-
tion. 633
Some account of Admiral Lord Graves. 86565
Some account of an entertainment. 43330
Some account of an existing correspondence.
86566
Some account of an existing correspondence
now carrying on between the inhabitants
of the moon, and the natives of this
country. 86566
Some account of Deacon John Butler. 9626
Some account of General Jackson. 21732
Some account of God's dealings with the Antioch
Baptist Church. 54087
Some account of Harvard Bible Class. 86567
Some account of his ancestors and relations.
103663
Some account of his [i. e. Benjamin Franklin's]
public life. 25573
Some account of Isaac Shoemaker. (80558)
Some account of Mr. Michael Diffendorffer.
94157
Some account of Mr. Shepard. 80210
Some account of J. S. (74619)
Some account of Maria Hughes. 86568
Some account of pestilence, famine, and in-
crease of crime. 25695, 65016
Some account of Portsmouth, N. H. 38871
Some account of some of the bloody deeds of
Gen. Jackson. 86569-86570
Some account of some of the deeds of General
Jackson. 35391
Some account of the author [i. e. Jonathan
Carver.] 11184, 3d note after 96502
Some account of the author, written by herself.
94202

Some account of the author's experience in the important business of religion. 33780

Some account of the . . . Azores. 100533

Some account of the baneful effects attending the use. 4678

Some account of the blessing which attends on a spirit. 4677

Some account of the British dominions. 20799

Some account of the case of Samuel Watson. 12000, 27969

Some account of the celebration of the fourth of July, 1857. 86571

Some account of the Charitable Corporation. 84669-84670

Some account of the Chicago Ministry-at-Large. 14466

Some account of the city of Philadelphia. (18750)

Some account of the commencement of St. John's College. 75289

Some account of the condition to which the protestant interest in the world is at this day reduced. 46535, 3d note after 93916

Some account of the conduct of the religious Society of Friends. 86572

Some account of the convincement, and religious progress of John Spalding. 88884

Some account of the design of the Trustees for Georgia. 27109

Some account of the designs both of the Trustees and Associates. 83978

Some account of the designs of the Trustees for Establishing the Colony of Georgia in America. 83978, 86573, 86574

Some account of the divine providence towards Benj. Church Esqr. 12996-12997

Some account of the dreadful havock made. (4674)

Some account of the early history and present state. 103759

Some account of the early poets and poetry of Pennsylvania. 84678C

Some account of the earthquake that shoot New-England. (46541), note after 94885

Some account of the Falkland Islands. (43461)

Some account of the Falkland Islands. To which is added a preliminary sketch. 86575

Some account of the formation of the Glasgow Ladies' Anti-slavery Association. 95505

Some account of the Gospel labours of Jonathan Burnyeat. (11744)

Some account of the grevious molestations. 46603

Some account of the holy life and death of Mr. Henry Gearing. 80742

Some account of the Hudson and Mohawk Railroad in 1831. 33508

Some account of the fever which existed in Boston. 26497

Some account of the holy life and death of Mr. Henry Gearing. 86576

Some account of the last sickness and death of . . . Wesley. 103662

Some account of the last yellow fever epidemic. (5737)

Some account of the late John Fothergill. 40724

Some account of the late work of God in North America. 102691

Some account of the life and death of Matthew Lee. 102692

Some account of the life and Gospel labours of William Reckitt. 68371

Some account of the life and religious exercises of Mary Neale. 52167

Some account of the life and religious labours of Samuel Neale. (52171)

Some account of the life and religious labours of Sara Grubb. 86577-86578

Some account of the life and writings by William Penn, Esq. 59715, note after 103670

Some account of the life, death and principles of Thomas Paine. 30372

Some account of the life of Spencer Houghton Cone. 15222

Some account of the life of the author. 91623

Some account of the life, sufferings, and death of Catharine Downing Williams. 78673

Some account of the life, writings, and speeches of William Pinkney. 103161

Some account of the lives and dying speeches of a considerable number. 47124

Some account of the lives and religious labours of Samuel Neale, and Mary Neale. 52172

Some account of the maranta, or Indian arrowroot. 74536

Some account of the medical school in Boston. 86579, 101476

Some account of the medicinal properties of the Hot Springs, Virginia. 86580

Some account of the mission of St. Margarets Bay, Nova Scotia. 90355

Some account of the missionary operations. 85950

Some account of the Mosquito Territory. 32363

Some account of the nature of the infection. (7141)

Some account of the North-American Indians. 84671

Some account of the origin and present condition of the Medical Institute of Louisville. 42330

Some account of the origin, objects and present state of the Pennsylvania Hospital. 60330, 86581

Some account of the Pennsylvania Hospital; from its first rise. 25588, 60329, 86582

Some account of the Pennsylvania Hospital, its origin, objects and present state. (44122)

Some account of the principles of the Moravians. 94707

Some account of the Prison at Philadelphia. 62263

Some account of the proceedings at the college of the Right Hon. the Countess of Huntingdon. 86583

Some account of the proceedings of the Legislature of New Hampshire. 79711

Some account of the proceedings on board ship Niagara of Boston. 33356

Some account of the province of Pennsylvania in America. 59710, (59719), 59733

Some account of the public life of the late Lieutenant-General Sir George Prevost, Bart. 65414

Some account of the religion, government, customs, and manners of the aborigines of North-America. (51798), 98626-98628, 2d note after 105691

Some account of the Rev. Mr. Piercy's farewell sermon. 96583

Some account of the rise and progress of the University of Maryland. 65659

Some account of the school for the liberal education of boys. 14218

Some account of the siren lacertina. 3824-3825

Some account of the small-pox. 86584

Some account of the so-called Church of the Latter-Day Saints. 86585

Some account of the Society for the Conversion and Religious Instruction and Education of the Negroe [sic] Slaves. 85882

Some account of the soil, climate, and vegetable productions. (33921)

Some account of the State Prison or Penitentiary House. 86586

Some account of the success of inoculation. 25589

Some account of the trade in slaves from Africa. (3147)

Some account of the trial of Samuel Goodere, Esq. 86587

Some account of the [White] Mountains of New Hampshire. 5301

Some account of the Woodward Institution. 105174

Some account of the work of God in North-America. 102693

Some account of their last hours. 90181

Some account of Thomas Dormer. 86587A

Some account of Thomas Paine, in his last sickness. 58252

Some account of those English ministers. 47124

Some account of two visits to the mountains. (68512)

Some account of what is said of inoculating or transplanting the small pox. 7143, 86588

Some additional considerations addressed unto the Worshipful Elisha Hutchinson, Esq. 52622, 86618

Some additional letters and documents. 7411

Some additional observations on the method of preserving seeds. 22319

Some additional remarks. 105296

Some additional remarks. By Juridicus. (17400)

Some additional remarks on the present state of Christianity in Pennsylvania. 102576

Some adventures of Captain Simon Suggs. 86589

Some advice for John Bull. 96396

Some advice to governesses and teachers. 86590-86591

Some aged non-conforming ministers. pseud. Letters. (40337)

Some allusion to the life and death of Andrew Jackson. 6078

Some ancient men which came out of Holland and Old England. pseud. Dialogues. 52630

Some anecdotes of the government of Jamaica. 33198-33199

Some animadversions and observations upon Sr Walter Raleigh's Historie of the world. (73325)

Some animadversions on a book, entitled Reliquiae Baxterianae. 4014

Some animadversions on a reply to a letter. 40289, (69681), 86592

Some animadversions on Mr. Adams's defence of the constitution and government. (41645), note after 91540

Some animadversions upon a tract by J. C. 11616

Some arguments against world-mindedness. 82545

Some arguments against worldly-mindedness. 86593-86602

Some authentic extracts. 16657

Some Baptist people, called Quakers, in New-London County. see Friends, Society of. New London Monthly Meeting.

Some benevolent gentlemen of the law. pseud. eds. 90521

Some brief account of those amazing things. 39443

Some brief hints of a religious scheme. (67956)

Some brief observations made on Daniel Leeds his book. 66743

Some brief observations upon George Keith's Earnest expostulation. 59657

Some brief observations, whether all the western lands, not actually purchased or conquered by the crown of Great-Britain. 69397, 80405, 102402

Some brief remarks on a book call'ed, though unjustly, An impartial account, &c. 9105, 103941

Some brief remarks on a piece published by John Cotton. 71762

Some brief remarks upon a late book entituled "George Keith once more brought to the test." 37216

Some brief remarks, upon a letter to a gentleman. 69700, 86603

Some brief remarks upon sundry important subjects. (28825)

Some brief remarks upon the result of a Council. 86604

Some brief sacramental meditations. 104106

Some brief sermon-notes on I. Cor. 10. 31. 2734

Some buds and blossoms of piety. 1721

Some by old words to fame have made pretence. 86605

Some calculations relating to the proposals made by the South-Sea Company. 86606

Some candid suggestions towards accomodation of differences with America. 86607

Some casual papers upon the "Alabama" and her commander. 56354, 86608

Some casual papers upon the American question. 86609

Some cautions to be used about swearing. 104080

Some chapters, of the Book of the Chronicles. 86610

Some church-members of the Presbyterian persuasion. pseud. Querists. see Evans, Thomas. supposed author

Some cogent arguments fetch'd from scripture. 105225-105227

Some collections for the information of those that are not acquainted with the principles and practices. 63335-63336

Some communications first published in the Brattleborough paper. 30798, 102608

Some communications of Christianity. 46224

Some comparison of the claims of Webster's . . . and Worcester's dictionaries. 47983

Some conjectures upon the great events. 46603

Some considerations against the setting up of a market in this town. 86611

Some considerations concerning the prejudice which the Scotch act establishing a company. 86612

Some considerations concerning the publick funds. (66641), 101148

Some considerations humbly offered on behalf of Jamaica. 86613

Some facts connected with the history of Professor Morse's picture. (51640)

Some facts respecting the measures taken by the members. 90778

Some facts respecting the treatment of slaves in the West Indies. 86642

Some facts stated, relative to the conduct of Walter Patterson. 59147

Some facts touching the Kohne legacy. (37613)

Some farraginous remarks. 86643

Some farther observations on the national debts. (66641), 101148

Some farther remarks on a late pamphlet. 1335A, (56514), 86644

Some farther remarks on naval affairs. 86645, 86748

Some few directions for ordering the voice. (66440)

Some few lines towards a description of the new heaven. 79443-79444, 91940, 104083

Some few remarks on the observations published in the Gazette. 56595

Some few remarks, upon a scandalous book. 27384, 46517

Some few verses, presented with an intention to soften the heart. 7919, note just before 53081

Some free men, states and presses. pseud. Anti-Texass [sic] Legion. 95069

Some free men, states and presses. pseud. Legion of liberty. 39868, 95097

Some fresh suggestions. 28821

Some friendly remarks on a sermon lately preach'd at Braintree. 7789

Some friendly remarks on said sermon. (64276)

Some friends to the truth of the Gospel. pseud. Remarks on several passages. (69427)

Some fruit of the spirit of love. 1721

Some fruits of solitude in reflections and maxims. 59699, (59734), 86647

Some fugitive thoughts on a letter signed Freeman. 86648

Some funeral verses occasioned by the death of the pious and much lamented, Mr. Jonathan French. 101217

Some further account from London. 46744

Some further considerations and proposals for the effectual and speedy carrying out of the Negro's Christianity. 27678, 3d note after 93806

Some general account of the New-England forces. (12320), (40382), 97569, 8th note after 100869, 7th note after 100870, note after 101077

Some general observations on American custom-house officers and courts of vice-admiralty. 23532, note after 96924

Some general observations on American customs-house officers, and courts of vice-admiralty. 39925-29926, 1st note after 87356, note after 87824

Some general observations on submissions and decrees-arbitral. 104492

Some general observations relative to the true principles. 94075, 102523

Some gentlemen of Pensilvania. pseud. Reflections on the printed case of William Penn. 68710

Some Gospel treasures. (23217)

Some helpes to stirre up to Christian duties. note after 103689

Some helps for the Indians. 22149, 59561

Some hints to people in power. 86649

Some hints to the delegates of the Rome Convention. (73952)

Some hints to the drummer and private soldier. 482, 28934

Some historical account of Guinea. 4689, 79818-79819

Some historical notices, connected with the origin of Geneva College. 86650

Some historical remarks, on the state of Boston. (46240)

Some honest opinions about autorial merits and demerits. (63522), 63570-63571

Some ideas and statements, the result of considerable reflection. 96363

Some important cases of consicence answered. 62834

Some important observations occasioned by, and adapted to the public fast, Dec. 18, 1765. 36323

Some important truths about conversion. 46745

Some incidents related by credible witnesses. 86651

Some information relative to the progress. 86652

Some information respecting America. 16611, 16615, (22509), 2d note after 59677

Some information respecting the use of Indian corn. 86653

Some inquiries with thoughts on religious subjects. 86654

Some instances of the oppression and male administration of Col. Parke. 58639

Some interesting letters written by Indians. 16794, 41538

Some interesting particulars of the life and untimely fate of Miss Harriot Wilson. 99425, 104621

Some judicious remarks and observations. 86655

Some leaves from the early history of Delaware & Maryland. 68195

Some lessons from his [i. e. Lincoln's] death. 9236

Some letters and an abstract of letters from Pennsylvania. 60621

Some letters, between him [i. e. Thomas Paine] and the late General Washington. 58231

Some letters occasioned by the proceedings of the Hopkinton Association. 23538

Some letters to a noble Lord. 99299

Some letters written by Mr. Robert Rich. 70896

Some lines in verse about Shakers. 79720

Some logical notions to initiate the Indians. 22163

Some material and very important remarks. 86656

Some materials to serve for a brief memoir of John Daly Burk. 10216

Some matters of fact relating to the present state of the African trade. 86656A

Some meditations (by way of essay) on the sense of that scripture. 50994

Some meditations concerning our honourable gentlemen. 104864

Some meditations in verse. 105231

Some melancholy heartfelt reflections. 102589

Some members of the Synod. pseud. Examination and refutation. see Presbyterian Church in the U. S. A. Synod of Philadelphia.

Some memoirs of his life, and of his departed children. 90185

Some memoirs of the first settlement of the island of Barbados. 3278, 3290

Some memoirs of the life and writings of the author. 52143

Some memoirs of the life and writings of the Rev. Thomas Prince. 20884

Some memoirs of the life, experience, and travels, of Elder Ephriam Stinchfield. 91835

Some memoirs of the life of Job. 6011

Some memoirs of the life of John Roberts. (71881)

Some memoirs of the religious life of William Penn. 59747

Some memorials of the Hon. John Richardson. 71035

Some miscellaneous remarks, and short arguments. 818, 98999

Some miscellaneous observations on our present debates. 21609, note after 104106

Some modern directions for the culture and manufacture of silk. 86658

Some modern observations upon Jamaica. 103104

Some modest and innocent touches on the letter from Zealand. (69679), 74624, 91382-91383

Some more friendly remarks on Mr. Porter and company. 7789

Some nameless Presbyterian ministers. pseud. Paper in manuscript. 86763-86764

Some necessary advertisements concerning the improvement. 10822

Some necessary and important considerations. 86659

Some necessary and important considerations, directed to all sorts of people; taken out of the writings of that late worthy and renowned Judge Sir Matthew Hale. 29642, 86660

Some necessary and important considerations, to be considered by all sorts of people. 86661

Some necessary precautions. 60622

Some necessary remarks on the education of the youth. 86662

Some new arguments and opinions against the idea of African liberty. 82104

Some new discoveries respecting the deates on the great calendar stone. 89996

Some new thoughts for the new year. 86663

Some news for Episcopalians. 86664

Some notes of a sermon taken in short hand. 7813

Some notes of Sr. Henry Vane's exhortation. 80993, note after 98499

Some notes on America to be written. 20005, 86665

Some notes, shewing the accomplishment of their prophecies. 5631

Some notes upon the discipline of their church. (62421), 1st note after 96924

Some notice of the remarks on S. Higginson. 31751

Some notive taken of his discourse. 103655

Some notices of his [i. e. Levi Frisbie's] life and character. (25978)

Some notices of Kentucky. 86666

Some notices of Samuel Gorton. 19051

Some notices of the character of Mrs. Sarah Parkman. 86667, note after 101396

Some objections against the treaty of Seville. 86668

Some objections to joint resolutions. 60623

Some objections to government demand notes. 86669

Some objections to Mr. Crawford as a candidate. 88115, 86670

Some observable & servicable passages in the life and death of Mr. Michael Wigglesworth. 46317

Some observations on divine providence. 84347-84349

Some observations and annotations upon the apologeticall narration. (27953), (69679), 74624, 91383

Some observations by N. H. Julius. 40985

Some observations concerning the increase of mankind. 25590

Some observations for the culture of madder. 86670A

Some observations in relation to the disputes. 43122, 2d note after 104889

Some observations in the weekly journal of June 8th. 1742. 9906

Some observations made in defence of the leag'd character. 69488, 86671

Some observations made upon the Angola seed. 86672

Some observations made upon the Barbado seeds. 86673

Some observations made upon the Bermudas berries. 86674

Some observations made upon the Brasillian root. 86675

Some observations made upon the herb cassiny. 86676

Some observations made upon the Mexico seeds. 86677

Some observations made upon the Virginian nutts. 56480, 86678

Some observations made upon the wood called lignum nephriticum. 86679

Some observations occasion'd by reading a speech. 20050

Some observations of consequence, in three parts. 86680

Some observations on a direct exportation of sugar. 2196

Some observations on a narrative by a citizen of New York. 105041

Some observations on a pamphlet, entitled, Taxation no tyranny. 2760, 36304, (80041)

Some observations on a pamphlet lately published entitled "The rights of Great Britain asserted" &c. 2761

Some observations on damages done by the Spaniards. 86681

Some observations on Dr. Huntington's letter, annexed to said sermon. 71889, 104315

Some observations on early currency of Maryland. (62491)

Some observations on extracts taken out of the report from the Lords-Commissioners for Trade and Plantations. 86682

Some observations on liberty: occasioned by a late tract. 102694

Some observations on Mr. Nevil's speech in the House of Assembly. 53067

Some observations . . . on public education based upon a report of the Superintendent of the Boston Schools. (6764)

Some observations on Richard Hakluyt and American discoveries. 29601

Some observations on the assiento trade. 1653, 19251, 86683

Some observations on the bill, intitled, "An act for granting to His Majesty an excise." 86684

Some observations on the charge. 19341, 84557

Some observations on the constitution for a federal government. 35441, 93506, 3d note after 95729

Some observations on the ethnography and archaeology of the American aborigines. (51024)

Some observations on the expediency of the petition of the Africans, living in Boston, &c. 1792, note after 45640, 81891

Some observations on the importance of the navigation-laws. 86685

Some observations on the . . . Indian natives. 89175

Some observations on the ministerial arguments, against putting the American prisoners on the same footing. 86686

Some observations on the new method of receiving the small-pox. 14502, 14518

Some observations on the occasional writer, numb. IV. 86687

Some observations on the proceedings against the Rev. Mr. Hemphill. 25591

Some observations on the proper management of new Negroes. 95446

Some observations on the Rev. Mr. Whitefield and his opposers. 86688-86689

Some observations on the Rev. Mr. Whitefield and his oppressers. 103506

Some observations on the Rev. Mr. Wesley's late reply. (23139)

Some observations on the scheme projected for emitting 60000£. in bills of a new tenour. 20725, 5th note after 98549

Some observations on the situation. 4691

Some observations on the state of the case of New-England. 15026

Some observations on the state of things prior to that catastrophe. 6739

Some observations on the two campaigns against the Cherokee Indians. 62558

Some observations on theatrical performances. 58933, 71187

Some observations on their peculiar fitness. 26964

Some observations published in part in the "Hartford courant." 86690

Some observations relating to the establishment of schools. 86692

Some observations relating to the establishment of schools, agreed to by the Committee. 86691

Some observations relating to the present circumstances of the province of the Massachusetts-Bay. 46124, 86693

Some observations, shewing the danger of losing the trade of the sugar colonies. 63322, 86694

Some observations, taken in part from an address. 102609

Some observations upon a late piece, entitled, "The detection detected." 26845

Some observations upon New-Englands government. 39641

Some observations upon the bill now depending in Parliament. 86695

Some observations upon the French tongue. 86696

Some observations; which may contribute to afford a just idea of the nature, importance, and settlement, of our new West-India islands. 106126

Some occasional observations. 49446

Some occasional thoughts on the influence of the spirit. 78700

Some of Bostons old planters and some other. pseud. Old mens tears. see Scottow, Joshua.

Some of Boston's old planters and some others. pseud. Old men's tears. see Scottow, Joshua.

Some of my brother trades-men in the city [of New York.] pseud. Letter. 103224

Some of his quondam dear friends, called, Quakers. pseud. Serious examination. see Whitehead, George.

Some of the acts of the Territory of Michigan. 48797

Some of the adventurers. pseud. Relation of the successful beginnings. (45316), 96291-96292, 103353

Some of the arguments that have been made. 86697

Some of the believers of the good tidings and joyful doctrine of Christ's dying for all men. pseud. Some short observations. 86763-86764

Some of the by-laws made by the Governor and Company of the city of London. 86698, 105694

Some of the causes of national anxiety. (81045)

Some of the descendants of William Holton. 86699

Some of the difficulties in the administration of a free government. 28617

Some of the dying speeches and declarations of John Battes. 86700

Some of the elders who were members of the Synod. pseud. Defence of the answer. see Mather, Richard.

Some of the exercises of a believing soul described. (82546)

Some of the first ministers of the Associate Church in America. see Associate Church in North America. Ministers.

Some of the fundamental truths of Christianity. 37205, 37217, 37219

Some of the gentlemen of the Council of New-York. see New York (Colony) Council.

Some of the glories of Our Lord. (14525)

Some of the honours that religion does unto the fruitful mothers in Israel. (14525)

Some of the last words of several dying persons. 13204

Some of the lessons of the tragedy at Harper's Ferry. 12396

Some of the letters which were writ to George Fox. 86701

Some of the many false, scandalous, blasphemous, & self-contradictory assertions of William Davis. 37218

Some of the members of the First Church in Newbury. see Newbury, Mass. First Church.

Some of the memorable events and occurences in the life of Samuel L. Mitchill of New York. From the year 1786 to 1823. 86702

Some of the memorable events and occurrences in the life of Samuel L. Mitchill of New York, from 1786 to 1821. 49749

Some of the ministers of Boston. pseud. Shorter [preface.] 21939

Some of the ministers in the country of Hampshire, Mass. see Congregational Churches in Massachusetts. Hampshire County Ministers.

Some of the ministers of Hampshire. see Congregational Churches in Massachusetts. Hampshire County Ministers.

Some of the most eminent evangelical ministers in the United States. pseud. Select discourses from the American preacher. 78983

Some of the objections against a division of the counties of Worcester and Middlesex. 86703

Some of the papers laid before the Governor. 86704

Some of the part-owners and proprietors of the patents of Minisink and Wawayanda. petitioners 47648

Some of the poetical fragments of a Washingtonian. 86705

Some of the providential lessons of 1861. 65093

Some of the Quakers contradictions. 86706

Some of the Quakers contradictory testimonies about oaths and swearing. 86707

Some of the Quakers principles and doctrines, laws & orders, &c. 86708

Some of the religious lessons which it teaches. 88570

Some of the representatives in the late General Assembly of the Colony of New York. see New York (Colony) General Assembly.

Some of the said people. pseud. Answer to part of a book. 66911

Some of the speeches delivered in the House of Commons. 81569

Some of the usages and abuses in the management of our manufacturing corporations. 2512

Some of the Vnivesitie of Oxford. see Oxford. University.

Some of the writings, and last sentences of Adolphus Dewey. 96360

Some of their evil conduct made manifest. 61368, 99240

Some of their people. pseud. Vindication of the ministers of Boston. 6565, 99812

Some original anecdotes of Mr. Burke. 9304

Some particular remarks on a letter. 25479

Some particulars of the Bishop's last illness. 100966

Some particulars of the commercial progress of the colonial dependencies. 18307

Some particulars of the last illness and death of Jane Wheeler. 103199

Some particulars of the late Boston Anti-slavery Bazaar. 86709

Some particulars relative to John Fisher and Lavina Fisher. 86710

Some particulars relative to the continuance of the endeavours. 86711

Some passages in the history of the First Church, Cambridge, Mass. 10125

Some passages in the life of Sir Frizzle Pumpkin. 86712

Some passages in the life of William Thom. (37423)

Some passages of divers letters from America. 41762, 63318

Some passages taken out of the history of Florence, &c. 78992

Some picture of the Pictes. (8784)

Some pieces in prose. 32786

Some poetical pieces by Mrs. Ann Beauchamp. 4159

Some poetical thoughts occasioned by the late public rejoicings. 86713

Some poetical thoughts on the difficulties. 86714

Some points relating to grain and other matters of interest. 88357

Some political remarks. 8769

Some practical observations on yellow fever. 86715

Some preliminary remarks and a sketch of Thomas Fysche Farmer. 21589

Some preliminary remarks. [By S. P. P. Fay.] 12097, 45038, 75208, 2d note after 98167-98158

Some proposals for a second settlement in the province of Pennsylvania. 59735

Some proposals for removing the principal disadvantages of Great Britain. 7867

Some proposals . . . for the . . . advancement of the British sugar colonies. 4732

Some proposals for the better securing of British trade. 19726

Some proposals to benefit the province. 86716

Some proposals towards promoting the propagation of the Gospel. 8190

Some queries concerning liberty of conscience. 9372, note after 14379, 81492, 86717

Some queries, concerning the operation of the Holy-Spirit. 86718

Some queries relating to the bill of engraftment. 86719

Some queries sent to the Rev. G. Whitefield. 18858

Some queries sent up to His Excellency the Earl of Bellomont. 86720

Some queries to the author of the Enquiry into the reasons. 86721

Some questions and answers, on the subject of the American Bible Society. 86722

Some questions proposed relative to the present disputes between Great Britain, and her American colonies. 16586

Some reasons for the immediate establishment of a national system. 8338

Some reasons agains the registry of slaves. 46857, 95656

Some reasons and arguments offered to the good people of Boston. 6732

Some reasons and causes of the late separation that hath come to pass. (23894), 37219

Some reasons for a farther encouragement for bringing naval stores from America. 86723

Some reasons for approving the Dean of Gloucester's plan. 86724, 97352

Some reasons for the question proposed. 86725

Some reasons given by the Western Association upon Merrimack River. 86726, 2d note after 103650

Some reasons offered by the late ministry in defence of their administration. 86727

Some reasons that influenced the Governor. 15855, 24589, 86728

Some reasons why I am opposed to the present war. 89786

Some reasons why the pending Cherokee treaty should be ratified. 20790

Some reasons why the votes of the state of New York ought to be given. 13566

Some recollections of our anti slavery conflict. 47078

Some recollections of the late Col. Hugh Maxwell. 47048

Some recollections of Washington's visit to Boston. 93720

Some reflections, occasioned by the death of the Rev. Habijah Weld. 95169

Some reflections on the disputes between New-York, New-Hampshire, and Col. John Henry Lydius of Albany. 42758, 106118

Some reflections on the law of bankruptcy. 51682

Some reflections on the proceedings of the church. 7095

Some reflections upon the invasion of the Spanish territory of West-Florida. 42450

Some reflexions on education. 84629

Some remarkable narratives of the success of the Gospel. 86729

Some remarkable passages relating to Archbishop Laud. (26315)

Some remarkable proceedings in the Assembly of Virginia anno 1718. 86730, 2d note after 99911

Some remarkable speeches in Parliament on the Spanish depredations. 32054

Some remarkables on the peaceful and joyful death of Mrs. Abiel Goodwin. 46372, 46518

Some . . . remarks and documents relating to the Massachusetts State Prison. 7247, note after 90640

Some remarks and explanatory observations on a petition to Parliament. 86731

Some remarks and extracts, in reply to Mr. Pickering's letter. 86732

Some remarks and observations by way of answer. 9331

Some remarks and observations respecting a certain species of population. 86733

Some remarks before the Joint Committee on Rivers and Canals. 15873

Some remarks by another hand. 71829

Some remarks, by Gen. Tallmadge, President. (31890)

Some remarks by Thomas Bulfinch. (81388)

Some remarks, &c. 52933

Some remarks, extracted from a letter. 103374

Some remarks, in prose and verse. (21065)

Some remarks in reference to recent proceedings. 86734

Some remarks in vindication of the constitution. 102417

Some remarks made before the Joint Committee of Rivers and Canals. 86734A

Some remarks of Ann Waring. 10142

Some remarks on a discourse deliver'd September 24th, 1763. (48178)

Some remarks on a late pamphlet, entitled, Observations on the conduct of Great Britain. 1335A, (56514), 86644

Some remarks on a late pamphlet, intitled, The state of religion in New England. 90595-90597, 103594

Some remarks on a late sermon, preached at Boston in New-England. (46746)

Some remarks on a pamphlet, call'd Reflections, on the constitution and management of the trade to Africa. 86735

Some remarks on a pamphlet, entitled "Don Quixote at College, & c." 11339

Some remarks on a pamphlet entitled, East and West India sugar. 86736

Some remarks on a pamphlet entitled, Rev. Mr. McIlvaine. 43324

Some remarks on a pamphlet, entituled, The enthusiasms of Methodists and Papists compar'd. 103595

Some remarks on a pamphlet, intitled, "Objections to the taxation of the American colonies, &c. considered." 6218

Some remarks on a pamphlet intitled Popular prejudices against the convention and treaty with Spain. 86737

Some remarks on a paper directed to all true patriots. (60625), note after 89175

Some remarks, on a pretended answer. 46639, 46747, 104255-104256

Some remarks on a speech said to have been delivered by Samuel Chew. 86738

Some remarks on Abel Morgan's answer to Samuel Finley. 86739

Some remarks on an account in the Boston evening-post. 360, 11967, 3d note after 96741

Some remarks on an article in the North American review. 55485

Some remarks on Canada and the United States. 56561

Some remarks on celibacy and nunneries. 70848

Some remarks on Dr. Trumbull's late appeal to the public. 66410, 97178

Some remarks on his second speech, and Mr. W——lk——r's. 88185

Some remarks on medicinal mineral waters. 84073

Some remarks on Mr. Adams's sermon, preached there August 26, 1772. 360, 11967, 3d note after 96741

Some remarks on Mr. Baring's pamphlet. 17184

Some remarks on Mr. Ebenezer Kinnersley's two letters. 86740

Some remarks on Mr. Goss's narrative. 360, 11968, 3d note after 96741

Some remarks on Mr. President Clap's history. 18587

Some remarks on Mr. Worth's appeal to the public, &c. 86741

Some remarks on religion. 34023

Some remarks on that reply. 82685

Some remarks on the Andover Institution. 65088, 96801

Some remarks on the assassination of Julius Caesar. 84703

Some remarks on the banking policy of Massachusetts. 15471

Some remarks on the barrier treaty. 86742, 94070

Some remarks on the character of the late Charles Chauncy. 6072

Some remarks on the city solicitor's opinions. 35406, 69886

Some remarks on the great and unusual darkness. 86743

Some remarks on the internal improvement system of the south. 96480

Some remarks on the late vigorous expedition against Canada. (62421), 1st note after 96964

Some remarks on the life and character of General David Cobb. 4068

Some remarks on the medical topography and diseases of this region. 8917

Some remarks on the memorial and remonstrance of the Corporation of Trinity Church. 86744

Some remarks on the most rational and effectual means that can be used in the present conjuncture. 952, 37244, 66015, 86745, 97575

Some remarks on the natural history of Beaver Islands. 92687

Some remarks on the pamphlet, entituled, "A compendious extract containing the chiefest articles of doctrine." 86746

Some remarks on the practice of taking down and publishing the testimonies of ministering Friends. 77285

Some remarks on the present high price of sugar. 8439

Some remarks on the proceedings of the late convention. 86747

Some remarks on the proposed changes in the constitution of the Protestant Episcopal Church in the United States. 18486

Some remarks on the public conduct of John C. Calhoun. 9955

Some remarks on the report of the Secretary of the Treasury. (26402)

Some remarks on the royal navy. 86645, 86748

Some remarks on the sentiments of the Rev. Messr. Hervey and Marshall. 4494

Some remarks on the settling of the island of Bermuda and Virginia. 49667

Some remarks on the slave trade, &c. 98662

Some remarks on the "toleration act" of 1819. 84704

Some remarks on the writings of a "Lover of Cudworth and truth." 86749

Some remarks relative to a standing army and a bill of rights. 44897

Some remarks shewing the advantages of the proposed railroad. 54839

Some remarks upon a late charge against enthusiasm. 103596

Some remarks upon a late pamphlet entitled, A letter from a minister of the Church of England. 86740

Some remarks upon a late pamphlet signed part by John Talbot. 66735, 66743

Some remarks upon a pamphlet, entitled, A Short view. 86751

Some remarks upon a second letter from the Church of England minister. 78732, 86752, 95355

Some remarks upon an oration delivered by Asa Child. 86753, note after 100786

Some remarks upon inland navigation. 5700, 105386

Some remarks upon Mr. Freeman's late performance, in Franklin's gazette. 60181, note after 97166

Some remarks upon said pamphlet, entituled, A discourse shewing, who is a true pastor of the church of Christ. 101194

Some remarks upon Sir Charles Bagot's Canadian government. 74576

Some remarks upon the bill for suspending the privilege of the writ of habeas corpus. 80684-80685

Some remarks upon the characters and genius of the Indians. 17463, 84673

Some remarks upon the conduct of the British ministry. 59332, 90292

Some remarks upon the consequences of the refusal. 38209

Some remarks upon the introduction of Africans into this state. 13309

Some remarks upon the progress of Canada. 11789

Some remarks upon the proposed election of February 22d. 86754

Some remarks upon the times. 86755

Some remarks upon two acts recently passed. 78840

Some remedies proposed. 67996

Some reminiscences of Lake Champlain. 789, 3525

Some reminiscences of the place. (11216)

Some rude & indigested thoughts. 86756

Some rules for preserving health by diet. 82870

Some rules of law, fit to be observed in purchasing land, &c. 42758, 106118

Some scruples propos'd in proper queries raised on each remark. 67116, 103664

Some seasonable advice from an honest sailor. 99248

Some seasonable advice to the poor. 46519

Some seasonable and modest thoughts partly occasioned by, and partly concerning the Scots East-India Company. 78235-78236

Some seasonable animadversions on exercises. 86757

Some seasonable considerations for the good people of Connecticut. 9095, 15856, (15860), 86758, note after 95296

Some seasonable considerations for those, who are desirous, by subscription, or purchase, to become proprietors of South-Sea Stock. 86759

Some seasonable enquiries offered. 46520

Some seasonable observations and remarks. 56463, 86760-86761

Some seasonable reflections upon the Quakers Solemn protestation. 37192

Some seasonable thoughts on evangelical preaching. 25405

Some select cases resolved. 80258

Some select portraitures and lives. 95341

Some sentiments on reviewers. 74598

Some serious and awful considerations. 86762

Some serious considerations on the present state of parties. 66940

Some serious remarks in reply to Rev. Mr. Jonathan Todd's Faithful narrative. 96092, 96094

Some serious remarks on that solemn and indispensable duty. 29747

Some serious thoughts on the design of erecting a college. (49754)

Some serious thoughts on the foundation, rise and growth of the settlements. 19899

Some short account of the experiences and dying testimony of Mr. Nathanael Shepherd. 2624

Some short account of the life and character of Rev. Joshua Eaton. 21733

Some short and easy rules, teaching the true pronunciation. 5762

Some short but interesting reflections on a future peace. 86645, 86748

Some short directions to the unexperienced in this method of practice. (7141)

Some short observations made on the Presbyterian doctrine. 86763-86764

Some short observations on our West India expedition. 9207

Some short observations upon H. M. his remarks. 103703

Some short remarks, on two pamphlets lately, printed. 86764A

Some stray recollections of the experience of the Albany Zouave Cadets. 86765

Some strictures of his [i. e. David Bostwick's] life and character. 6788

Some strictures on a pamphlet, intitled, "Objections to the taxation of the colonies." 68744

Some strictures on an act to provide a national currency. (24796)

Some strictures on certain scurrilous writers. 106040

Some strictures on church government. 86766

Some strictures on his [i. e. Abraham Bishop's] oration. 5591

Some strictures on the French proceedings in America. 8107

Some strictures on the "History of the United States of America." 84787

Some strictures on the late occurrences in North America. 86767

Some strictures on the plan of Mr. James Ramsey's steamboat. 17729

Some strictures on the preface to the Rev. Mr. Tennent's five sermons. 30173, 62419, 94687

Someruelos, Salvador Joseph de Muro y
Salzar, Marques de, 1754-1813.
86816-86819
Spmervill, M. 86820
Somerville, Alexander, 1811-1885. 86821-
86824
Somerville, Elizabeth. 86825
Somerville, Thomas, 1741-1830. 86826
Somerville, William Clarke, 1790-1826. 86827-
86828, note before 93468
Somerville, Mass. McLean Asylum for the
Insane. (43520)
Somerville, Arlington and Belmont directory.
86830
Somerville directory. 86829
Somerville Horse Railroad. 86831
Somerville Water Power Company. 86832
Somerville water power, at Somerville, N. J.
86832
Somes, Daniel Eton, 1815-1888. 86833-86835
Somes & Brown. firm 86835
Something. 52331, 86836
Something about Zack Chandler's campaign
lies. 86837
Something. Edited by Nemo Nobody, Esquire.
52331, 86836
Something for Douglas Democrats to remem-
ber. 80419
Something for everybody. 29730
Something in answer to a book printed in
1678. (70895)
Something in answer to a late performance.
60732, 2d note after 96752
Something in answer to a law. 25354
Something in answer to a law lately made at
the first sessions. 46123
Something in answer to a letter. (25355)
Something marvelous!! 86838
Something more about the whiskey tax. 95787
Something must be done. 89783
Something new. Being a picture of truth.
105182
Something new for the soldiers. 81121
Something new, or memoirs of that truely
eccentric character. (19908), 86840
Something to be known by all the churches.
46587, note after 101451
Something new. . . . To be published weekly,
by Michael H. Barton. 86839
Sometime. 83601
Somiology of North America. (67448)
Somis, ------. 86841
Somma, Agazio da. 86842
Sommaire de l'instance pendante au Conseil
Prieu du Roy. 86843
Sommaire des trios premieres parties de la
doctrine Chrestienne. (7742)
Sommaire d'observations sur les Etats-Unis
de l'Amerique. 94303
Sommaire, ou argument general du dernier des
manifestes. 93605
Sommaire recveil des raisons plvs importantes.
98208
Sommario della historia dell' Indie Occidentali.
67740
Sommario della natvrale et generale historia
dell' Indie Occidentali. 67740
Sommario delle Indie Orientali. 67730
Sommario di tvtti gli regni, citta, & popoli
orientali. 67730
Sommario istorico del Dottor Michele Zappvllo
Napolitano. 106256
Sommario scritto per Amerigo Vespvcci
Fiorentino di dve sve navigationi. 67730
Sommarsall, James. 86844

Sommary description. 86845
Sommation faite par le Marqvis de Spinola au
Gouuerneur de la ville de Breda. Auec
la responce dudit Gouuerneur a icelle
sommation. 89457
Sommation faite par le Marquis de Spinola au
Gouuerneur de la ville de Breda. En-
semble plusieurs particularitez. 89456
Sommelsdick, Francois van Aerssen, Heer van.
86846
Sommer, -----. 86857
Sommer, Johann Gottfired, d. 1848. 86849-
86850, 104704
Sommer, Karl von. 86847-86848
Sommer, Wilhelm, 1828-1906. 86851-86853
Sommer-Geiser, ------. 86854
Sommer Islands Company. see Bermuda Com-
pany.
Sommers, Charles George, 1793-1868. 86855-
86856, 93622
Sommers, John. see Somers, John Somers,
Baron, 1651-1716
Sommer's pocket director of Chicago. 86857
Sommersett, James. defendant 30374
Sommersett, James. plaintiff (15998), 23077,
1st note after 102801
Sommerville, J. 86858
Sommerville, William, 1832- 86859-86860
Sommervogel, Carlos, 1834-1902. 86861, 1st
note after 98488
Sommier verhael, vansekere Amerikaensche
voyagie. 27123, 27127-27128
Sommiere aenteyckeninge ende deductie inges-
telt. 20783
Somonte y Velasco, Jose Baltasar de. 86862
Somoza, Jeronimo Suarez de. pseud. Vida del
Venerable y Apostolico Padre Pedro
Claver. see Andrade, Alfonso de.
Son. pseud. Richmond alarm. A dialogue be-
tween father and son. 71195
Son, Francisco. alias see Santo, Francisco
dos. defendant
Son in the army. 86864
Son of a blacksmith. pseud. Catechism for
free workey men. (11498)
Son of a military officer. pseud. Four years'
residence in the West Indies. see
Bayley, W. F. N.
Son of candor. pseud. Principles of the late
changes impartially examined. see
Temple, Richard Temple Grenville-
Temple, Earl.
Son of freedom. pseud. following anonymous
letter. 86865
Son of Liberty. pseud. Address to a provincial
bashaw. see Church, Benjamin, 1734-
1776.
Son of liberty. pseud. Discourse delivered in
Providence. see Downer, Silas.
Son of liberty. pseud. New liberty song.
86866
Son of liberty. pseud. New song. 86867
Son of liberty. pseud. To the betrayed in-
habitants. see McDougall, Alexander.
Son of liberty. pseud. To the inhabitants.
95898
Son of liberty. pseud. Union, activity and
freedom. 86869
Son of Martin-Mar-Prelate. pseud. Essay upon
that paradox. see Walter, Thomas,
1696-1725.
Son of Mary Moore. pseud. Captives of Abb's
Valley. 10767
Son of Norfolk. pseud. State sovereignty re-
cord of Massachusetts. 90645

Son of temperance. pseud. ed. Fountain and the bottle. 25278

Son of the Church of England. pseud. Remarks on Dr. Mayhew's incidental reflections. see Browne, Arthur.

Son of the forest. A poem. 39448, 103694

Son of the forest. The experience of William Apes. (1733)

Son of the Huguenots. pseud. Crisis. 86870

Son of the mist. pseud. Letter to Robert Owen. 86871

Son of truth and decency. pseud. Vindication of the Bishop of Landaff's sermon. see Inglis, Charles, Bishop of Nova Scotia, 1734-1816.

Son preguntas, y respuestas, mas quien se queme, que sople. 98116

Sonambulo, pseud. Recompensa del merito. 86872

Sonambulo. pseud. Sistema de Atole. 81463

Sonata, sung by a number of young girls. 86873, 2d note after 101885

Sonderbare Entdeckung wieler sehr grossen Lander in Amerika. 31369

Sondermann, Johann Samuel. 86874

Sonet. 27351

Sonetos alusivos a la celestial imagen de Maria Santisima. 63305

Song. 37251, (73296), 86263, 101259, 103234

Song, adapted to the President's march. 32984

Song and chorus written for the national jubilee. 5434

Song, anticipating the arrival of General Washington. 101857

Song book. Containing a selection of upwards of two hundred of the most popular songs. 84178

Song book for the million. 86875

Song, composed by Mr. Story. 92315

Song composed by the British butchers. 86876, 86878

Song composed by the British butchers, after the fight at Bunker-Hill. 86877

Song, composed by the British soldiers. 86879

Song composed for the fraternity of Steben Lodge. 86880, 89434

Song composed in the year seventy five. 86881

Song, composed on the cause and progress, of the late American war. 86882

Song, composed on the evacuation of Boston. 86883, 3d note after 101885

Song, dedicated to the colored volunteer. 86884

Song for Sabbath-breakers. 105230

Song, for the anniversary of American independence, 1819. 86885

Song, for the first anniversary of the "Terrapin Aera." 86886

Song. For the Seventeenth anniversary of our national union. 86887

Song for the Sons of Liberty in New-York. 65527

Song made on the taking of General Burgoyne. 86888

Song made upon the election of new magistrates. 86889

Song made upon the foregoing occasion. 86889
Song of charity. 11978

Song of Deborah and Barak. 66431, (66433)-(66434), (66436), (66440)-(66441)

Song of deliverance for the lasting remembrance of God's wonderful works. 104655

Song of drop o'wather. 80729

Song of Floggawaya. 86890

Song of Hannah. 66431, (66433)-(66434), (66436), (66440)-(66441)

Song of Harmodius and Aristogeiton. (41324)

Song of Hiawatha. 41927, 86890

Song of iron and the song of slaves. 56727

Song of Jefferson and Liberty. 86891

Song of Milgenwater. (31325), note after 92903

Song of Milhanwatha. (31325), note after 92903

Song of Moses. 64431, (66433)-(66436), (66440)-(66441)

Song of praise and thanksgiveing [sic]. 90936

Song of praise and thanksgiving. 90935

Song of praise to God from United America. 94364

Song of Simeon. (66436), (66440)-(66441)

Song of Sion. 28344

Song of Songs which is Solomons. 66431, (66433)-(66436), (66440)-(66441), 89526-89527, 89529-89530

Song of the angels: from Luke, Chap. II. 93765

Song of the angels: from Luke, Chap. II: anthem. 86892

Song of the Blessed Virgin Mary. 66431, (66433)-(66434), (66436), (66440)-(66441)

Song of the old church at Williamstown. 8386

Song of the sexton. 639, 57138

Song of the Vermonters. note after 103816

Song of Washington. 86893

Song of Zacharias. 66431, (66433)-(66434), (66436), (66440)-(66441)

Song of Zion. 28978

Song on our country and her flag. 40985

Song on the arrival of General Washington. 101857

Song on the remarkable resurrection of above one hundred and fifty thousand pounds sterling. 86894

Song, on the surrender of General Burgoyne. 86895

Song on vacation. 95832

Song on Washington's birth day. 86896, 5th note after 101855

Song or, story, for the lasting remembrance. 104655

Song set for the day. 8447

Song that's-by-no-author. 95596

Song. The pilots whom Washington plac'd at the helm. 86897

Song, to the tune of Hearts of oak. 86898

Song, written on a Virginia cotton and tobacco merchant. 86899

Songe de Colomb. 11110

Songe: maide by yatte goode manne Schuyler ov Hobokuk. 105937

Songs and ballads: by George P. Morris. (50824)

Songs and ballads. [By Sydney Dyer.] 21601

Songs and ballads of freedom. 86900

Songs and ballads of the American revolution. 50369, 94431

Songs and ballads of the south. 81188

Songs and lullabies of the good old nurses. 86901

Songs and poems of the south. 47368

Songs and tales of American and patriotic subjects. (36483)

Songs by the way. (18603)

Songs, comic, satyrical, and sentimental. 91502-91503

Songs . . . composed in honour of the victories. (43813)

Songs duets & choruses. 86903

Songs, duets, &c. in the Fair American. 86904

Songs, duets, &c. in the Poor soldier. 86905

Songs, duets, trios, chorusses, &c. in the Cherokee. 86907

Songs, duetts, trios, &c. in the Two misers. 86906

Songs east and west. 83482

Songs, &c. in the Catawba travellers. 86902

Songs for emigrants. 86908

Songs for freemasons. 47466

Songs for gentlemen. Old and new. 86909

Songs for review day. 86910

Songs, for the amusement of children. 86911

Songs for the Boston Farm School. 86912

Songs for the cradle. 86917

Songs for the Dwight School. 86913

Songs for the grange. 86914

Songs for the great campaign of 1860; comprising a choice collection. 86915

Songs for the great campaign of 1860. Words and music. 13169

Songs for the million. 52512

Songs for the nursery, collected from the works. 86916

Songs for the nursery: or, Mother Goose's melodies. 86917

Songs for the people; comprising national, patriotic, and naval songs. 22417

Songs for the people, or Tippecanoe melodies. 86918

Songs for the politicians. 86919

Songs for the school room. 51888

Songs for the sons and daughters of temperance. 12971

Songs for the times. 86920

Songs for the union. 86921-86922

Songs for the union. A collection of patriotic, national, original, and selected songs. 86923

Songs for the Whig celebration, July 4, 1834. 6557, note after 103274

Songs for war time. 86924

Songs from Dixie's land. 8811

Songs from Revelation. 66431, (66433)-(66434), (66436), (66440)-(66441)

Songs from scripture. (81253)

Songs from the hearts of women. 83676

Songs, illustrating the enthusiastic feeling of the grateful. 30581

Songs in Henry Russell's vocal and pictorial entertainment. (74336)

Songs in many keys. 32621

Songs in the Castle of Andalusia. 86925

Songs in the comic opera of Robin Hood. 86925

Songs in the Deserter. 86927

Songs in the night, by a young woman under heavy afflictions. (30569)

Songs in the night. A thanksgiving sermon. 77575

Songs, in the Purse. 86928

Songs; national and moral. 2478

Songs. Naval and military. 86929

Songs, odes, and other poems. 42997

Songs of a wanderer. 74527

Songs of Alpha Delta Phi. Issued in the twenty-seventh year of the fraternity. 86930

Songs of Alpha Delta Phi. Published by the Union Chapter. 86931

Songs of Amherst. (1329)

Songs of Bowdoin. 86932

Songs of Columbia. 86933

Songs of creation, a poem. 50646

Songs of field and flood. 8342

Songs [of General Tom Thumb.] 92729, 92735

Songs of Judah, and other melodies. 94378

Songs of love and liberty. 37439

Songs of my summer nights. 12854

Songs of our land, and other poems. 31643, note after 91036

Songs of praise, with penitential cries to Almighty God. 89527, 89529-89530, 89536

Songs of praise with penitential cries to God. 89525

Songs of praise: with penitential cries upon several occasions. 89528

Songs of Robin Hood. 86934

Songs of Tammany. 30851

Songs of the College of the City of New York. 86935

Songs of the farmer. 86936

Songs of the free, and hymns of Christian freedom. 9751, 11996, note after 86936

Songs of the Mercury. 86937

Songs of the powow. 86938

Songs of the Prophet Isaiah. 66431, (66433)-(66436), (66440)-(66441)

Songs of the Psi Upsilon Fraternity. 86939

Songs of the redeemed. 46521

Songs of the redeemed, for the followers of the lamb. (82499)

Songs of the rivers. 4725

Songs of the sea. Consisting of a well-selected collection of naval songs. 74974

Songs of the sea, national, patriotic, satirical, and comic. 52086

Songs of the sea, with other poems. (76965)

Songs of the soldiers. (50370)

Songs of the south. 86940

Songs of the south. By W. Gilmore Simms. 81187

Songs of the war. 86941

Songs of the Washingtonians. 86942

Songs of the wilderness. 51187

Songs of Union [College.] 86943

Songs of victory. 173

Songs of Williams. 86944

Songs of Yale. 86945

Songs of Yale: a new collection. 22226

Songs of Zion: being a collection of hymns. 89839

Songs of Zion. By Ezekiel Cheever. 12393, 103736

Songs of Zion: for the use of the children. 84430

Songs of Zion; or, the Christian's new hymn book. 86946

Songs sung at the first commencement of Union College. 97786

Songs to the tune of "The tea tax." 86947

Songs we love to sing. 86948

Songs written for the dinner. (59370)

Songster. 97728

Songster, being a choice collection of new and popular patriotic, comic, sentimental, and descriptive songs. 86949

Songster's assistant. 94019

Songster's companion. 86950

Songster's magazine, containing a choice collection. 86952

Songster's magazine, a choice collection of the most approved patriotic, comic, sentimental, amatory and naval songs. 86953

Songster's magazine, a choice selection, 86951

Songster's miscellany. 86954

Songster's museum. A new and choice collection of popular songs. 86955

Songster's museum: a new selection of the most popular songs. 86956

Songster's museum: or, a trip to Elysium. 94020

Songsters of the grove. 86957

Songster's pocket book. 85686

Songster's pocket companion. 86958
Songsters repository; being a choice selection. 86959
Songster's repository; being a selection of the most approved sentimental, patriotic, and other songs. 14863
Sonmans, Peter. 86960
Sonmans, Peter. petitioner 57494, 99252
Sonneck, Oscar George Theodore. 84041, note before 90497, 105959, 105966
Sonnenstern, Maximilian von. 86961-86964
Sonneschmidt, Frederico Traugott, 1763-1824. 86965-86968
"Sonnet." 41356
Sonnet. For the fourteenth of October, 1793. 86969
Sonnets and other peoms. 26712
Sonnini de Manoncourt, Charles Nicolas Sigisbert, 1751-1812. 2541, 39687, (59572)
Sonntag, August. 85072, 86970-86971
Sonntags-Bibliothek. 6110
Sonntags-Schul-Verein der Deutschen Gemeiden, Allentown, Pa. 86972
Sonora, Jose de Galvez, Marques de. see Galvez, Jose de, Marques de Sonora.
Sonora (Diocese) Gobernador de la Mitra. 103966
Sonora (Mexican State) 86979
Sonora (Mexican State) Apoderado. 26519 see also Almada, Bartolome E.
Sonora. 21375
Sonora—and the value of its silver mines. 86974
Sonora et ses mines. 44173
Sonora, etendue, population, climat, produits du sol. 56358
Sonora Exploring and Mining Expedition. 96973-96974
Sonora Gold Mining Company, organized January 24th, 1852. 86975
Sonora Railway Company. 86976
Sonora Tunnel Company. 86977
Sonorense. pseud. Sonorense a sus conciudadanos. see Sinaloeno. pseud.
Sonorense (1840-1841) 86978
Sonorense a sus conciudadanos. 86980
Sonorense. Periodico oficial del gobierno del estado. 86979
Son's advice to his aged father. 67572-67573
Sons against fathers. 53408
Sons and Daughters of Connecticut. Festival, 1st, Galesburg, Ill., 1859. 86981
Sons and Daughters of Connecticut. Festival, 2d, Galesburg, Ill., 1860. 86981
Sons and Daughters of Delaware. 86982
Sons and Daughters of Temperance. (11210)
Sons of Africans. see Sons of the African Society.
Sons of Africa: an essay on freedom. 87108
Sons of Columbia, Boston. 101856
Sons of Liberty. see also United Sons of Liberty, New York.
Sons of Liberty. Boston. 86986
Sons of Liberty. New York. Committee. 69031, 86984-86985
Sons of liberty in New York. 18942
Sons of liberty in 1755 [sic]. 97203
"Sons of liberty," in 1776, and in 1856. 86987
Sons of Maine. 86988
Sons of Malta. see Independent Order of the Sons of Malta.
Sons of Malta exposed. An exposition of the ceremony. 86997
Sons of Malta exposed; being a complete expose. 86998

Sons of New England in Pennsylvania (1858-   ) 86999
Sons of New England in the City and County of Philadelphia. see Society of the Sons of New England of the City and County of Philadelphia.
Sons of New Hampshire. Festival, 1st, Boston, 1849. 52826, 92068
Sons of New Hampshire. Festival, 2d, Boston, 1853. 78731
Sons of Penn. Chicago. Annual Festival, 1st, 1850. (57586)
Sons of Revolutionary Sires, San Francisco. see Sons of the American Revolution. California Society.
Sons of Revolutionary Sires. Its origin, names of officers, constitution, by-laws, ... 87001
Sons of Revolutionary Sires. Organized in San Francisco. 87002
Sons of Rhode Island. 87003
Sons of St. Dominick. 75441, 87004
Sons of St. George. see Society of St. George, New York.
Sons of St. Patrick, Philadelphia. see Society of the Friendly Sons of St. Patrick, Philadelphia.
Sons of Temperance almanac. 87104
Sons of Temperance ministrel. 87018
Sons of Temperance of Canada East, instituted at Quebec. 87020
Sons of Temperance of North America. 87019, 87031, 92017
Sons of Temperance of North America. Grand Division. 87060, 87097
Sons of Temperance of North America. National Division. 51973, 87005-87009, 87011-87013, 87015-87017, 87031, 87060, 87093, 87097
Sons of Temperance of North America. National Division. Committee. 92017
Sons of Temperance of North America. Canada East. see Sons of Temperance of North America. Quebec.
Sons of Temperance of North America. Canada West. see Sons of Temperance of North America. Ontario.
Sons of Temperance of North America. Connecticut. Grand Division. 87022
Sons of Temperance of North America. Connecticut. Hancock Division, Centerville (Hamden) 87023
Sons of Temperance of North America. Connecticut. Harmony Division, no. 5, New Haven. 87024
Sons of Temperance of North America. Connecticut. Saltonstall Division, no. 37, East Haven. 87025
Sons of Temperance of North America. District of Columbia. Grand Division. 87026
Sons of Temperance of North America. East Tennessee. Grand Division. 87090
Sons of Temperance of North America. Eastern New York. Grand Division. 87016, 87060
Sons of Temperance of North America. Eastern New York. Grand Division. Session, 29th, New York, 1873. 87061
Sons of Temperance of North America. Eastern New York. Grand Division. Special Sessions, New York, 1851. 87062
Sons of Temperance of North America. Illinois. Grand Division. 87027
Sons of Temperance of North America. Illinois. Grand Division. Session, Pekin, 1863. 87027

Sons of Temperance of North America. Indiana. Grand Division. 34569

Sons of Temperance of North America. Maine. Grand Division. 87029

Sons of Temperance of North America. Maryland. Grand Division. 87030

Sons of Temperance of North America. Maryland. Grand Division. Quarterly Session, Reisterstown, 1864. 87030

Sons of Temperance of North America. Massachusetts. Grand Division. 45839, 87016, 87031-87033

Sons of Temperance of North America. Massachusetts. Grand Division. Committee of Publication. 87032

Sons of Temperance of North America. Massachusetts. Grand Division. Officers. 87034

Sons of Temperance of North America. Massachusetts. Calendonia Division, no. 90, Boston. 87035

Sons of Temperance of North America. Massachusetts. Corner Stone Division, no. 165, Hingham. 87036

Sons of Temperance of North America. Massachusetts. Excelsior Division, no. 16, Boston. 87037

Sons of Temperance of North America. Massachusetts. Gibson Division, no. 21, Dorchester. 87038

Sons of Temperance of North America. Massachusetts. Good Will Division, no. 17, New Bedford. 87039

Sons of Temperance of North America. Massachusetts. Henfield Division, no. 2, Salem. 87040-87041

Sons of Temperance of North America. Massachusetts. Independent Division, no. 111, West Amesbury. 87042

Sons of Temperance of North America. Massachusetts. Liberty Tree Division, no. 47, Boston. 87043

Sons of Temperance of North America. Massachusetts. Massachusetts Division, no. 71, 45839

Sons of Temperance of North America. Massachusetts. Merrimac Division, no. 138, West Newbury. 87044

Sons of Temperance of North America. Massachusetts. New Era Division, no. 175, Boston. 87045

Sons of Temperance of North America. Massachusetts. Old Cambridge Division, no. 26. 87046

Sons of Temperance of North America. Massachusetts. Pakachoag Division, no. 27, Worcester. 87047

Sons of Temperance of North America. Massachusetts. Roxbury Division, no. 78. 73730

Sons of Temperance of North America. Massachusetts. Salem Division, no. 61. 87048

Sons of Temperance of North America. Massachusetts. Shakespeare Division, no. 46, Boston. 87049

Sons of Temperance of North America. Massachusetts. Shawmut Division, no. 1, Boston. 87050

Sons of Temperance of North America. Massachusetts. Social Division, no. 93, South Abington. 87051

Sons of Temperance of North America. Massachusetts. Wingaesheek, Division, no. 183, Gloucester. 87052

Sons of Temperance of North America. Minnesota. Grand Division. 87053

Sons of Temperance of North America. New Jersey. 87054

Sons of Temperance of North America. New Jersey. Grand Division. 87055

Sons of Temperance of North America. New Jersey. Fidelity Division, no. 2, Trenton. Committee. 87056

Sons of Temperance of North America. New York. 53958

Sons of Temperance of North America. New York. Grand Division. 53958, 87057, 87062 see also Sons of Temperance of North America. Eastern New York. Grand Division. Sons of Temperance of North America. Western New York. Grand Division.

Sons of Temperance of North America. New York. Cayadutta Division, no. 504. 87064

Sons of Temperance of North America. New York. Coeymans Division, no. 185. 87065

Sons of Temperance of North America. New York. Grass River Division, no. 368. 87066

Sons of Temperance of North America. New York. Kinderhook Division, no. 164. 37775, 87067

Sons of Temperance of North America. New York. Mutual Alliance Division, no. 130. 87068

Sons of Temperance of North America. New-York. Shakespeare Division, no. 37. 87079

Sons of Temperance of North America. Nova Scotia. Howard Division, no. 26, Halifax. Worthy Patriarch. 50891, 87070 see also Morrison, E.

Sons of Temperance of North America. Ohio. Grand Division. Semi-annual Session, Marietta, 1851. 87071

Sons of Temperance of North America. Ontario. Grand Division. 87021

Sons of Temperance of North America. Pennsylvania. Grand Division. 87072, 87074, 87076-87077

Sons of Temperance of North America. Pennsylvania. Grand Division. Board of Discipline. 87073

Sons of Temperance of North America. Pennsylvania. Grand Division. Committee on Centennial Celebration, 1876. 87075

Sons of Temperance of North America. Pennsylvania. Bustleton Division, no. 173. 87078

Sons of Temperance of North America. Pennsylvania. Crystal Font Division, no. 20. 87079

Sons of Temperance of North America. Pennsylvania. Delaware Division, no. 22, New Hope. 87080

Sons of Temperance of North America. Pennsylvania. Fox Chase Division, no. 301. 87081

Sons of Temperance of North America. Pennsylvania. Friendship Division, no. 19, Philadelphia. 25th Anniversary Celebration, 1870. 87082

Sons of Temperance of North America. Pennsylvania. Hope Division, no. 3. 87083

Sons of Temperance of North America. Pennsylvania. Lancaster Temple of Honor, no. 48. 87084

Sons of Temperance of North America. Pennsylvania. Mercentile Division. no. 131. 87085

Sons of Temperance of North America. Pennsylvania. Neptune Division, no. 64. 87086

Sons of Temperance of North America. Pennsylvania. Niagara Division, bo. 14. 87087

Sons of Temperance of North America. Pennsylvania. Philadelphia Degree Temple of Honor, no. 1. 87088

Sons of Temperance of North America. Pennslyvania. Pleasant Grove Division, no. 386, Fulton Township. 87089

Sons of Temperance of North America. Quebec. Gough Division, no. 2, Quebec (City) 87020

Sons of Temperance of North America. Rhode Island. Channing Division, no. 5, Providence. 70568

Sons of Temperance of North America. Rhode Island. Olneyville Division, no. 10. 57252

Sons of Temperance of North America. Rhode Island. Providence Division, no. 2. (66367)

Sons of Temperance of North America. Rhode Island. William Penn Division, no. 8, Pawtucket. 59261

Sons of Temperance of North America. Tennessee. Knoxville Division, no. 3. 87091

Sons of Temperance of North America. Texas. La Grange Division, no. 48. 87092

Sons of Temperance of North America. Virginia. Grand Division. 87093

Sons of Temperance of North America. Virginia. Grand Division. Fifteenth Annual Session, Lynchburg, 1859. 87094

Sons of Temperance of North America. Virginia. Hutchinson Division, no. 63. 87095

Sons of Temperance of North America. Virginia. Wellsburg Division, no. 37. 87096

Sons of Temperance of North America. Western New York. Grand Division. 87063

Sons of Temperance of North America. Wisconsin. Grand Division. 87097-87099

Sons of Temperance of North America. Wisconsin. Geneva Lake Division, no. 26. 87100

Sons of Temperance of North America. Wisconsin. Green Bay Division, no. 2. 87101

Sons of Temperance of North America. Wisconsin. Magnolia Division, no. 93, Magnolia. 87102

Sons of Temperance of North America. Wisconsin. Racine Division, no. 4, Racine, 87103

Sons of Temperance of the United States. see Sons of Temperance of North America.

Sons of Temperance offering for all seasons. 87106

Sons of Temperance offering: for 1850. 87105

Sons of Temperance offering: for 1851. 87105

Sons of the African Society, Boston. 87107

Sons of the border. 91122

Sons of the Rechabites, Philadelphia. 87109

Sons of the sires. (32207), 87110

Sons of Vermont. Reunion, 1st, Worcester, Mass., 1874. 87111

Sontag, Anton. 87112

Sonthonax. pseud. Dialogue entre les deux egorgeurs de Saint-Domingue. see Theron, --------.

Sonthonax, Leger Felicte, 1763-1813. (42350), 62892, 75126, 75149, 87113-87126, 96343, note after 97172, 99242 see also France. Commission aux Isles Sous le Vent.

Sonthonax, Leger Felicite, 1763-1813. respondent 75163, 99242

Sonthonax, ci-devant Commissaire Civil. 87124

Sonthonax, Commissaire-Civil de la republique Francaise. 87125

Sonthonax, representant du peuple. 87126

Soon after the last European peace. 101150

Soon doth war that scourge of man exert its poignant rigours. 96002

Soper, Thomas N. 87128-87129

Soper (I. N.) and Company. firm 87127

Sophia. pseud. Whited sepulchure. see Olsen, Sophia B.

Sophia. 87131

Sophia Morton. (53426)

Sophie Sparkle. pseud. see Hicks, Jennie E. supposed author

Sophocles, Evangelinus Apostolides, 1807-1883. 105791

Sophomore. 87132

Sophronistes. 104218

ΣΟΦΙΑΣ, ΦΙΛΟΣ. pseud. Letter to a certain gentleman, &c. see Robie, Thomas, 1689-1729.

Soplamocos literario. 86238

Soplos en defensa de la pura concepcion de Nuestra Senora. 87133

Sopori Land and Mining Company. 87134

Sopori Land and Mining Company. Charter. 87134

Soran, Charles. 87135

Sorceress, or Salem delivered. (78326)

Sorces de l'histoire ante-Colombienne du Nouveau-Monde. (73309)

Sorciere des eaux. 16546

Sorehead war. 87136

Soren, John. plaintiff 87137-87138

Sorensen, Rasmus Moller. 87139-87142

Sorenson, Alfred. 87143

Sorenssen, Christian. tr. 49323

Soret, H. 87144

Sorg en raad, aang. de Evangelie-Prediking in Oost- en West-Indien. (32437)

Sorge, Rev. -------. 87145-87147

Sorge, F. A. 85705

Sorgel, Alwin H. 87148-87149

Sorgenti del Susquehanna ossia i coloni. 16505

Sorgo; or, the northern sugar plant. (31222)

Soria, Domingo de. 87150

Soria, Francisco de. 87151-87153

Soria, Francisco Joseph de. 87154-87155

Soria, Gabriel de. 87156-87157, 93575

Soria, Jose Soto y. see Soto Loria, Jose de.

Soria, Pablo. 85737

Soria Briviesca, Alvaro de. 87158

Soria Valesquez, Jeronimo de. 87159-87160

Soria y Mendoza, Manuel Ignacio de. 87161

Soriano, Juan Antonio. 87162

Soriano, Manuel S. 87163-87164

Sorlie, Sholto. 87165

Sorosis fourth anniversary at Delmonico's. 87166

Sorpresa del campo de Ahuatepec el ano de 1828. 87167

Sorrow of lent. 20389
Sorrow turned into joy. 96388
Sorrowful poem upon that desirable youth Isaac Stetson. 87168
Sorrowful specticle. (46522)
Sorrows and sympathetic attachments of Werter. 87169
Sorrows of slavery, a poem. 35740
Sorrows of Werter. A German story. 87170, 87172
Sorrows of Werter, an affecting story. 87171
Sorrows of Yamba: illustrating the cruelty of the slave-trade. 105945
Sorrows of Yamba; or the Negro woman's lamentation. 87173
Sort des Negres esclaves. 92527
Sort du commerce Francais. 19525
Sort of believers never saved. 80189
Sosa, Antonio de. 87174
Sosa, Diego de, 1696-1767. 87175 see also Augustinians. Provincia del Peru. Procurador y Difinidor General.
Sosa, Fernando de. 98726
Sosa, Francisco de. 87176-87177
Sosa, Francisco de Paula. 87178-87181
Sosa, J. A. Fernandez de Cordova y. see Souza, J. A. Fernandez de Cordova y.
Sosa, Jaime. see Sosa Escalada, Jaime, 1846?-1906.
Sosa, Jose Sandalio. 87182
Sosa, Jaun de. see Souza, Juan de.
Sosa, Miguel de. 87183
Sosa, Miguel Feijoo de. see Feyjoo de Sosa, Miguel, d. 1784.
Sosa, Pedro de, 1566- 87184-87188
Sosa Escalanda, Jaime, 1846?-1906. 87189
Sosa Troncoso, Antonio de. 87190
Sosa Victoria, Jose de. 87191-87192
Sosa Victoria, Nicolas de. 87193
Sosa y Lima, Jose. 87194
Sosa y Pena, Jose. 87195
Soscol Rancho. Register and Receiver. 87196
Sossa, Isidoro de Almedo y. see Olmedo y Sossa, Isidoro de.
Sossa, Pedro de. see Sosa, Pedro de, 1566-
Sostmanni, Johannis. 87198
Sot-weed factor. 16234, note after 80002
Sota, Juan Manuel de la. 39134, 44426, 87199-87200
Sota-cura. 87201
Sotelo, Luis. 87202
Sotheby, William. 87203
Sotheby, Wilkinson & Hodge. firm 90091
Sotillo, Antonio Jose. 98389
Soto, ------- de, fl. 1552. 11234, 39115
Soto, Basil Varen de. 44553
Soto, Bernardo de. defendant 27309, (51797), 69951, 93808, 96948
Soto, Francisco de. 87204
Soto, Hernando de, ca. 1500-1542. 7754, 20518, 25853, 66686, 84379, 87205-87206
Soto, Jos. M. Franco. see Rivas-Cacho, Jos. M. (Franco Soto) de.
Soto, Juan. 87207 see also Mexico. Ministerio de Guerra y Marina.
Soto, Juan de. 87208
Soto, Juan Estevan. 87209
Soto, Manuel Fernando. 56009, 87210-87212
Soto, Marco Aurelio. 87213-87214
Soto, Mariano. 87215-87223
Soto, Pedro de. petitioner 87224-87225 see also Dominicans. Provincia de San

Juan Buatista del Peru. Procurador General. petitioner
Soto Loria, Jose de. 87226-87229
Soto-Mayor, Juan de Villagutierre. see Villagutierre Soto-Mayor, Juan de, fl. 1701.
Soto y Marne, Francisco de. 87230-87235
Soto y Soria, Jose. see Soto Loria, Jose de.
Soto Zevallos Aranguren, Ignacio de. plaintiff 87236 see also Valladolid, Mexico. Iglesia. Canonigo Penitenciario. plaintiff
Sotomayor, Alonso de. petitioner 87237-87238
Sotomayor, Antonio Valladares de. see Valladares de Sotomayor, Antonio.
Sotomayor, Diego de Banos y. see Banos y Sotomayor, Diego de.
Sotomayor, Diego Sanchez de. 87239
Sotomayor, Fernando de. 87240
Sotomayor, Francisco Pimentel y. see Pimentel y Sotomayor, Francisco.
Sotomayor, Gabriel. 87241
Sotomayor, Gregorio Omana y. see Omana y Sotomayor, Gregorio.
Sotomayor, Jose Francisco. 87242-87245
Sotomayor, Juan de. 87246
Sotomayor, Juan de Villagutierre. see Villagutierre Soto-Mayor, Juan de, fl. 1701.
Sotomayor, Juan F. de. 87247
Sotomayor, Juan Gomez Tonel de. see Tonel de Sotomayor, Juan Gomez.
Sotomayor, Juliana (de Truxillo) Tonel de. see Tonel de Sotomayor, Juliana (de Truxillo)
Sotomayor, Urbano Feijoo de. 87248-87250
Sotomayor y Mendoza, Baltazar de Zuniga Guzman. see Zuniga Guzman Sotomayor y Mendoza, Baltazar de, Marques de Valero.
Sotomayor y Valdes, Ramon, 1830- 87251-87256
Sot's paradise. 101285
Sotweed redivivus. (16235)
Soublette, Carlos, Pres. Venezuela, 1790-1870. 14588, 87527-87529 see also Colombia. Secretaria de Marina. Venezuela. President, 1843-1845. (Soublette)
Souchu de Rennefort, Urbain. see Rennefort, Urbain Souchu de, ca. 1630-ca. 1689.
Souder, Casper, 1819-1868. 87260
Souder, Mrs. Edmund A. see Souder, Emily Bliss (Thacher)
Souder, Emily Bliss (Thacher) 87261-87262
Souillac, Jose Sourryere de. see Sourryere de Souillac, Jose, 1750-1820.
Sojourn in the Old Dominion. 5th note after 93998
Soul bound up in the bundle of life. 46325
Soul dejection. 103510
Soul of the soldiery. 87263
Soul prosperity. [By George Whitefield.] 103510
Soul prosperity. The prosperity of the soul proposed and promoted. 46570, note after 98363
Soul rising out of the vanity of time. (39324)
Soul-saving Gospel truths. 46748
Soul upon recollection. (46262)
Soul upon the wing. (46523)
Soul well-anchored. 46524
Soulastre, ------ Drovo-. see Drovo-Soulastre, ---------.
Souldier told what he should do. 46525
Souldiers counselled and comforted. 46526
Souldiery spiritualized. 50229
Soule, -------. 72412
Soule, Carolina Augusta (White) 1824-1904. 87264-87265

Soule, F. A. 87266-87267
Soule, Frank. 37662, 87268
Soule, Henry Birdsall. 87269
Soule, John Babson Lane. 22471, 87270
Soule, Joshua, 1781-1867. 87271-87274
Soule, Pierre, 1802-1870. 87275-87287
Soule, Pierre, 1802-1870. plaintiff 87280
Soule, Richard. 87288
Soule Female College, Nashville, Tenn. 87289
Soules, Francois, 1748-1809. 5911, 32545,
   (41296), 87290-87292
Soules benefit from vnion with Christ. 32850
Sovles effectvall calling to Christ. 32849,
   (32856), 32859
Sovles exaltation. 32850
Sovles hvmiliation. 32851-32853
Soules implantation. A treatise. (32854)
Soules implantation into the naturall olive.
   32855
Sovles ingrafting into Christ. (32854), (32856)
Soules justification. 32850
Soules possession of Christ. 87293
Sovles preparation for Christ. (32857)-32858
Soules vision with Christ. 32850
Sovles vocation or effectval calling to Christ.
   32859
Soulesbury Male College, Batesville, Ark.
   87294
Souleyet, L. F. A. 98298
Soulie, Emile. 87295
Soulie, Federico. 87296
Soulier, N. 87297
Souls flying to Jesus Christ pleasant and
   admirable to behold. 14519
Souls invitation unto Jesus Christ. 80226-
   80235, 80238
Souls of men do not dy. 87298
Soul's progress in the work of the new-birth.
   8192
Soult, Nicolas Jean de Dieu, Duc de Dalmatie.
   (38072)
Soulter, James T. plaintiff 87299-87301
Soumans, Peter. petitioner 53221
Sound beleever. 80200, 80239-(80243)
Sound believer. 80217, 80238, 80244-80251
Sound literature the safeguard of our national
   institutions. 21156
Sound repentance the right way to escape
   deserved ruine. 100986
Sound words, to be held fast, in faith and love.
   46527
Soundings from the Atlantic. 32621
Soundness of the policy of protecting domestic
   manufactures. 29984
Soup. pseud. Life and exploits of Gen. Scott.
   87302
Soupetard. pseud. Dish of frogs. 87303
Soupirs de l'Europe, &c. 21208
Source, Dominique Antoine Thaumur de la.
   see Thaumur de la Source, Dominique
   Antoine.
Source of discord, persecution and oppression
   demonstrated. 51310
Source of public prosperity. 35461
Sources du Rio de S. Francisco de Bresil.
   (75225)
Sources du Susquehanna. 16503
Sources for a history of the Mexican war.
   83471
Sources of a physician's power. 13365
Sources of American independence. 81261
Sources of cotton supply. 17125, 89973
Sources of military delusion. (31707)
Sources of national obligations. 52310
Sources of the Susquehanna. 16502

Sourel, A. illus. 505
Sourigny, --------. incorrectly supposed
   author 87304
Sourryere de Souillac, Jose, 1750-1820.
   87305-87306
Sourtauld, George. (17175), 87307
Sourville, ------ Generes. see Generes-
   Sourville, --------.
Sous les tropiques. 19917
Sousa, Jose Carlos Pinto de. see Pinto de
   Sousa, Jose Carlos.
Sousa, Jose Fernandez de Abascal y. see
   Abascal y Sousa, Jose Fernandez de.
Sousa, Luis Antonio da Silva e. see Silva e
   Sousa, Luis Antonio da.
Sousa, Manuel de Faria y. see Faria y
   Sousa, Manuel de.
Sousa, Pedro Lopes de. see Lopes de Sousa,
   Pedro.
Sousa, T. Faria y. see Faria y Sousa, T.
Sousa Azevedo Pizarro e Araujo, Jose de. see
   Azevedo Pizarro e Araujo, Jose de
   Sousa.
Sousa Brazil, Thomaz Pompeo de. see Souza
   Brazil, Thomaz Pompeo de, 1852-
Sousa Countinho, Francisco de, 1697?-1660.
   7543, 17197-17198, 88754-88757 see
   also Portugal. Legation. Netherlands.
Sousa Franco, Bernardo de. see Maldona-
   do, Theodoro de Sousa.
Sousa Maldonado, Theodoro de. see Maldona-
   do, Theodoro de Sousa.
Sousa Silva, Joaquim Norberto de. 56427
Souscription en faveur des affranchis des Etats-
   Unis d'Amerique. 87308
Souter, John. 87309
South; a letter from a friend in the north.
   14916
South Abington, Mass. Baptist Church. 85490
South Abington, Mass. Social Division, no. 93.
   see Sons of Temperance of North
   America. Massachusetts. Social Divi-
   sion, no. 93, South Abington.
South Adams, Mass. First Congregational
   Church. 87311
South after the war. (37380)
South alone, should govern the south. 96379,
   note after 97063
South America. A letter on the present state
   of that country. 7172, 87319
South America. A letter to J. Monroe. 7172,
   87319
South America and the Pacific. 77449
South-American. pseud. Outline of the revolu-
   tion in Spanish America. see Palacio
   Fajardo, Manuel.
South American, a metrical tale. 101062
South American and Colonial Gas Company.
   87320
South American emancipation. 1667
South American Gem Company. 87321
South American independence: or, the emanci-
   pation of Spanish America. (9314)-
   9315, 100594
South American independence. Speech of Simon
   Bolivar. 6189
South American journal. 87313
South American magazine. 87323
South American missionary magazine. 87322
South American Missionary Society. see
   Patagonian Missionary Society.
South American Navigation and Marine Railway
   Company. 87324
South American pilot. 87325
South American sketches of Sir W. Gore
   Ouseley. 29486

South Carolina (British Military Government) Intendant-General of Police. 87369 see also Simpson, James.

South Carolina. 87442, 87500, 87890, 96788 see also U.S. Army. Second Military District.

South Carolina. plaintiffs 83854, 97378

South Carolina. Acting Commissioner and Architect of the New State House. 87404

South Carolina. Adjutant and Inspector General. 87371-87372 see also Gist, States R.

South Carolina. Agent for Historical Records. 87547 see also Cruger, Henry N.

South Carolina. Agricultural Survey. 73919, 87374

South Carolina. Agricultural Surveyor. 73919, 87374 see also Ruffin, Edmund.

South Carolina. Appeals Court. 69454

South Carolina. Architect of the New State Capitol. see South Carolina. Acting Commissioner and Architect of the New State House. and South Carolina. Commissioner and Architect of the New State Capitol.

South Carolina. Attorney General. 87375-87382, 87469-87470, 92878 see also Chamberlain, Daniel Henry, 1835-1907. Hayne, Isaac William, 1809-1880. Hayne, Robert Young, 1791-1839.

South Carolina. Auditor. 87383-87385, 87681 see also Tupper, James.

South Carolina. Bank. see Bank of the State of South Carolina, Charleston.

South Carolina. Board of Public Works. 63308, 87388-87389

South Carolina. Board of Public Works. Member. pseud. see Member of the Board of Public Works, of the State of South Carolina. pseud.

South Carolina. Board of Visitors of the Military Academies. 87390

South Carolina. Bureau of Agricultural Statistics. 87391

South Carolina. Circuit Courts. Solicitors. 87392

South Carolina. Citizens. petitioners 87890

South Carolina. Civil and Military Engineer. 87393

South Carolina. College. see South Carolina. University.

South Carolina. Commissary-General. 87395

South Carolina. Commission on Charleston Harbor. (2588), 12081, 87297, 87396

South Carolina. Commission on Petigru's Code. see South Carolina. Commission on the Code.

South Carolina. Commission on the Code. 87398-87399, 87705 see also Petigru, James Louis.

South Carolina. Commission on the Revision and Consolidation of the Statute Laws of the State. 87400

South Carolina. Commission to Examine Into the Condition of the Assets of the State. 87401

South Carolina. Commission to Examine Into the Condition of the Catawba Indians. 87402

South Carolina. Commission to Examine the Militia System of the State. see South Carolina. Military Commission.

South Carolina. Commission to Negotiate With the Government of the United States,

1860-1861. (16860), note after 87402, 87436, 87438 see also Keitt, ----------. Miles, ---------.

South Carolina. Commissionar der Einwanderung. see South Carolina. Commissioner of Immigration.

South Carolina. Commissioner and Architect of the New State Capitol. 87403

South Carolina. Commissioner of Immigration. 87405-87406 see also Wagener, John A.

South Carolina. Commissioner of Public Works. see South Carolina. Superintendent of Public Works.

South Carolina. Commissioner of the Statutes. 87713

South Carolina. Commissioner to the Universal Exhibition at Paris, 1855. 87518 see also Elliott, William.

South Carolina. Commissioner to Virginia. 47489-47490 see also Memminger, C. G.

South Carolina. Commissioners for the Improvement of the Maffitt or Sullivan's Island Channel of the Harbor of Charleston. see South Carolina. Commission on Charleston Harbor.

South Carolina. Commissioners of the State of South Carolina, to the Government at Washington. see South Carolina. Commission to Negotiate With the Government of the United States, 1860-1861.

South Carolina. Commissioners on the Louisville, Cincinnati and Charleston Rail Road. see South Carolina. Commissioners on the Survey for a Railroad Between Charleston and Cincinnati.

South Carolina. Commissioners on the Survey for a Railroad Between Charleston and Cincinnati. 12080, 87407

South Carolina. Commissioners to Revise the Statutes, 1869. 87708

South Carolina. Commissioners to the Knoxville Convention. see South Carolina. Commissioners on the Survey for a Railroad Between Charleston and Cincinnati.

South Carolina. Comptroller General. 87409, 87411-87412 see also Harrison, Thomas.

South Carolina. Comptroller General. petitioner 87410

South Carolina. Constitution. 1269, 1271, 2071, 5316, 6360, 16086-16092, 16097, 16099-16103, 16107, 16113, 16118-16120, 16133, (19466), 25790, 33137, (47188), 59771, (66397), 87413-87418, 87436, 87440, 87445, 87477, 87525, 87666, 87668, 87675-87676, 87685, 87704, 87706, 87708, 87713, 87715, 100342, 104198

South Carolina. Constitutional Convention, Charleston, 1776-1776. 87413

South Carolina. Constitutional Convention. 1868. 87447, 87708

South Carolina. Constitutional Court. 87455, 87460-87462, 87464-87465, 87691

South Carolina. Convention, 1788. 22233, 87419, note after 106002

South Carolina. Convention, Columbia, 1832-1833. 46140, 48097, 69479, 87420-87426, 87428-87430, 87500, 87668, note after 90638

South Carolina. Convention, Columbia, 1832-
    1833. Committee of Twenty-One.
    46140, 48097, 87423, 87427-87428,
    note after 98638 see also Hayne,
    Robert Young, 1791-1839.
South Carolina. Convention, 1852. 87425,
    87431, 87500
South Carolina. Convention, Charleston, 1860-
    1862. (16860), 27102, 27093, note
    after 87402, 87432-87438, 87440,
    87443-87444
South Carolina. Convention, Charleston, 1860-
    1862. Committee on Relations with the
    Slaveholding States. 87441
South Carolina. Convention, Charleston, 1860-
    1862. Committee on the Address to
    the Southern States. Chairman. 27093,
    27102, 87436, 87443 see also De-
    Saussure, W. F.
South Carolina. Convention, Charleston, 1860-
    1862. Special Committee of Twenty-
    One. 87442
South Carolina. Convention, Charleston, 1865.
    87445-87446.
South Carolina. Convention, Charleston, 1865.
    Standing Committees. 87445
South Carolina. Convention, 1866. 87715
South Carolina. Council of Safety, 1775.
    88005
South Carolina. Council of Safety, 2d, 1776.
    88005
South Carolina. Court for the Correction of
    Errors. 87448
South Carolina. Court of Appeals. 28862,
    71403, 83854, 87449, 87454, 87461,
    87463, 87691, 89091
South Carolina. Court of Chancery. 87457
South Carolina. Court of Equity. 87464, 104663
South Carolina. Court of Errors. 87451
South Carolina. Courts. 87466, 87687, 87704,
    88013-88014
South Carolina. Department of Construction and
    Manufacture. Chief. 87471 see also
    Gist, W. H.
South Carolina. Department of Justice and
    Police. 87473
South Carolina. Department of Justice and
    Police. Chief. 87472-87473 see also
    Hayne, Isaac William, 1809-1880.
South Carolina. Department of the Military.
    Chief. 87474
South Carolina. Department of Treasury and
    Finance. Chief. 87475
South Carolina. Deputy Surveyor. 87687 see
    also Cooper, T. P.
South Carolina. District Court (C. S. A.) see
    Confederate States of America. District
    Court (South Carolina)
South Carolina. Executive Secretary. 87545
    see also Watts, Beaufort T.
South Carolina. General Assembly. 459, 933,
    9932, 9936, 9950, 16867, (22284),
    40343, 46058, 64808, 87411, 87417,
    87445, 87448, 87460, 87465, 87479,
    87480, 87481, 87483, 98499, 87500,
    87502-87506, 87508, 87514, note before
    87535, 87638-87639, 87644, 87648,
    87652-87664, 87666-87669, 87675-87676,
    87682, 87686, 87689, 87696, 87699-
    87700, 87702, 87708-87709, 87713-
    87714, 87727, 87862, 91428, 103875
South Carolina. General Assembly. petitioners
    64571, 87484-87485, 87509, 87905
South Carolina. General Assembly. Committee
    of Investigation of the Third Congres-
    sional District. 87492

South Carolina. General Assembly. Com-
    mittee of Ways and Means. 87497-
    87498
South Carolina. General Assembly. Com-
    mittee on Report that an Armed Force
    is Levying in this State. 87487
South Carolina. General Assembly. Com-
    mittee to Inquire How Much of the Leg-
    islation of Congress is Abrogated by the
    Secession of the State. 87486
South Carolina. General Assembly. Joint Com-
    mission on the Claims of the Legionaires
    of Luxembourg. 87489
South Carolina. General Assembly. Joint
    Committee on Federal Relations. 87478
South Carolina. General Assembly. Joint
    Committee to Inspect and Report upon
    the Affairs of the Bank of the State.
    87491
South Carolina. General Assembly. Joint
    Committee to Investigate the Affairs of
    the Charleston County Commissioners.
    87488
South Carolina. General Assembly. Joint
    Committee to Investigate the Bank of
    the State, at Charleston. 87490
South Carolina. General Assembly. Military
    Committee. 87372
South Carolina. General Assembly. Minority.
    87476
South Carolina. General Assembly. Special
    and Joint Committee to Inspect the Bank
    of the State of South Carolina at Charles-
    ton. 87492
South Carolina. General Assembly. Special
    Committee of Seven. Minority. 61297
South Carolina. General Assembly. Special
    Committee on the Communication of the
    British Consul. 87856
South Carolina. General Assembly. Special
    Committee on the Governor's Message,
    Transmitting Communications of the
    British Consul. 87501
South Carolina. General Assembly. Special
    Committee on the Message of Governor
    James H. Adams, Relating to Slavery
    and the Slave Trade. 87524
South Carolina. General Assembly. Special
    Committee on the Message of Governor
    James H. Adams, Relating to Slavery
    and the Slave Trade. Minority. 87524
South Carolina. General Assembly. Special
    Committee on the Subject of Encourag-
    ing European Immigration. 87493
South Carolina. General Assembly. Special
    Committee to Inquire Into the Liabilities
    and Assets of the Bank of the State.
    87494
South Carolina. General Assembly. Special
    Joint Committee Appointed to Investigate
    the Affairs of the Bank of the State.
    87495
South Carolina. General Assembly. Special
    Joint Committee in Regard to Certain
    Public Property on Hand at the Evacua-
    tion of Columbia, and the Surrender of
    Gen. Johnston's Army. 87496
South Carolina. General Assembly. House of
    Representatives. (22284) (23447),
    (71070), 87377, 87484, 87500, 87507,
    87511-87515, 87517, 87525, note before
    87535, 87843, 88100, 88333
South Carolina. General Assembly. House of
    Representatives. Speaker. 87522 see
    also Mackey, E. W. M.

South Carolina. Governor, 1856-1858 (Allston) 61297 see also Allston, Robert Francis Withers, 1806-1864.

South Carolina. Governor, 1858-1860 (Gist) 33150 see also Gist, William Henry, 1809-1874.

South Carolina. Governor, 1860-1862 (Pickens) 87371, 87442, 87550-87557 see also Pickens, Francis Wilkinson, 1805-1869.

South Carolina. Governor, 1862-1864. (Bonham) 87558 see also Bonham, Milledge Luke, 1813-1890.

South Carolina. Governor, 1865-1866 (Perry) 87445 see also Perry, Benjamin Franklin, 1805-1886,

South Carolina. Governor, 1866-1868 (Orr) 87559-87561 see also Orr, James Lawrence, 1822-1873.

South Carolina. Governor, 1868-1874 (Scott) (78353), 87562 see also Scott, Robert Kingston, 1826-1900.

South Carolina. Governor, 1874-1876 (Chamberlain) see also Chamberlain, Daniel Henry, 1835-1907.

South Carolina. Historical Commission. 87355, 87483

South Carolina. Hospital for the Insane. Physician. (37891), 87864

South Carolina. Inhabitants. petitioners see South Carolina. Citizens. petitioners

South Carolina. Laws, statutes, etc. 137, 12040, 12044, 12047, 12088, 16621, 16847, (18299), 23765, 33049, 39414, 46140, 48097, 52051, 57332, (57512), 69479, 70820-70821, 70864, (75307), 82438, 83854, 87371, 87377, 87398, 87413-87414, 87418, 87423, 87426-87429, 87431, 87433-87435, 87437-87440, 87444-87446, 87453, 87483, 87500, 87525, note before 87563, note before 87613, 87614-87635, 87636-87696, 87698-87705, 87706-87715, 87856,3d note after 87898, 87956-87957, 87980, 87983, 6th note after 88114, 88025, 88054, 89066, note after 90638, 91428, 97759, 104662

South Carolina. Lazaretto, Charleston. 87677

South Carolina. Legislative Library. see South Carolina. State Library, Columbia.

South Carolina. Medical College. see Charleston, S. C. Medical College of the State of South Carolina.

South Carolina. Military Academies. 87390

South Carolina. Military Commission. 87717-87718

South Carolina. Military Commission. Minority. (43114), 87716

South Carolina. Militia. 87627, 87630, 87676, 87691, 87696, 87698, 87704, 87713, 91428

South Carolina. Militia. Bratton's Brigade. 87803

South Carolina. Militia. Brooks Guards, Charleston. 8370

South Carolina. Militia. Cavalry. 87370

South Carolina. Militia. Phoenix Rifles, Charleston. 12047

SouthCarolina. Militia. South Carolina Rangers. see South Carolina Rangers.

South Carolina. Militia. Washington Light Infantry, Charleston. (12065), 88103, 88105, 88107-88109, 88111

South Carolina. Militia. Washington Light Infantry, Charleston. Charitable Association. see Washington Light Infantry Charitable Association.

South Carolina. Militia. Washington Light Infantry, Charleston. Easter Fair, 1875. 88104-88105, 88106, 88110

South Carolina. Militia. Washington Light Infantry, Charleston. Widow and Orphan Fund. 88105

South Carolina. Mineralogical, Geological, and Agricultural Survey. 87719-87722

South Carolina. Mineralogical, Geological and Agricultural Surveyor. 87719-97722 see also Lieber, Oscar Montgomery.

South Carolina. Nullification Convention, 1832. see South Carolina. Convention, Columbia, 1832-1833.

South Carolina. Registrar of Births, Marriages and Deaths. 87723

South Carolina. St. James Parish. see St. James Parish, South Carolina.

South Carolina. Secession Convention, 1860-1862. see South Carolina. Convention, 1860-1862

South Carolina. Second Council of Safety. see South Carolina. Council of Safety, 2d, 1775.

South Carolina. Secretary of State. 87507, 87724 see also Freneau, Peter. McGrath, A. G.

South Carolina. Special Envoy to Washington on Fort Sumter. 87552, 87555 see also Hayne, Isaac William, 1809-1880.

South Carolina. State Bank. see Bank of the State of South Carolina, Charleston.

South Carolina. State Geologist. 87534, 87722 see also Lieber, Oscar Montgomery. Tuomey, Michael.

South Carolina. State Library. 87725

South Carolina. State Reporter. see also Harper, William. M'Cord, David James.

South Carolina. Sundry Inhabitants of the Upper Counties. petitioners see Sundry Inhabitants of the Upper Counties of the State of South Carolina. petitioners

South Carolina. Superintendent of Public Works. 87726, 87729 see also Blanding, Abraham, 1776-1839.

South Carolina. Superior Courts. 87458, 87459

South Carolina. Supreme Court. 87414, 87452-87453

South Carolina. Supreme Court. Chief Justice. 20918 see also Drayton, William Henry, 1732-1779.

South Carolina. Survey. 87719-87722

South Carolina. Treasury. 87730

South Carolina. Union Bank. see Union Bank of South Carolina.

South Carolina. University. 83750-83751, 87969-87960, 87971, 87973-87975, 87980-87983, 88092-88099, 88102

South Carolina. University. Board of Trustees. 87971, 87980, 87983, 87991, 88091

South Carolina. University. Board of Trustees. Committee. 87970

South Carolina. University. Board of Trustees. Executive Committee. 88101

South Carolina. University. Charter. 87971, 87980, 87983

South Carolina. University. Clariosophic Society. 87995

South Carolina. University. Class of 1849. 87988

South Carolina. University. Class of 1858. Committee. 87989

South Carolina. University. Euphradian Society. 87996

South Carolina. University. Faculty. Chairman. 88100

South Carolina. University. Faculty. Committee. 87990

South Carolina. University. Library. 87997-88000

South Carolina. University. President. 87968, 87976, 87991 see also Cooper, Thomas, 1759-1839. Thornwell, James Henley.

South Carolina. University. Semi-Centennial Celebration, 1855. 87991

South Carolina. University. Southern Rights Association. 87967, 87986

South Carolina. University. Treasurer. 87992-87993

South Carolina. University. Trustees. see South Carolina. University. Board of Trustees.

South Carolina. Young Men's Missionary Society. see Young Men's Missionary Society of South Carolina.

"South-Carolina." 87732

South Carolina: a home for the industrious immigrant. Published by the Bureau of Agricultural Statistics. 87391

South Carolina:—a home for the industrious immigrant. Published by the Commissioner of Immigration. 87405

South-Carolina Academy of the Fine Arts. 87951

South Carolina Agricultural & Mechanical Society. see State Agricultural & Mechanical Society of South Carolina.

South Carolina Agricultural Convention. see State Agricultural Society of South Carolina (1839-1845)

South Carolina Agricultural Society. see State Agricultural & Mechanical Society of South Carolina. State Agricultural Society of South Carolina.

South Carolina agriculturalist—extra. 88060

South Carolina almanack. note after 96057

South-Carolina almanack and register for the year of Our Lord 1760. 87746

South-Carolina almanack and register, for the year of Our Lord, 1763. 87749

[South-Carolina] almanack and register, for the year of Our Lord, 1762. 87748

[South-Carolina almanack for 1765.] 87751

South Carolina and Georgia almanack and ephemeris for . . . 1787. 87763

South-Carolina and Georgia almanack, for . . . 1794. 101426

South-Carolina & Georgia almanac, for the year of Our Lord 1800. 87778

South-Carolina & Georgia almanac, for the year of Our Lord, 1789. 87767

South-Carolina and Georgia almanac, for the year of Our Lord, 1798. 87774

South Carolina and Georgia almanac for the year of Our Lord 1795. 87768

South-Carolina and Georgia almanac, for the year of Our Lord 1799. 87776

South-Carolina and Georgia almanac, for the year of Our Lord, 1797. 87772

South-Carolina and Georgia almanac, for the year of Our Lord, 1796. 87770

South-Carolina and Georgia almanac for the year of Our Lord 1793. 101426

South-Carolina and Massachusetts. 23169

South Carolina Anti-intemperance Society. 87952

South Carolina as a royal province, 1719-1776. 84858

South-Carolina Association, Charleston. 87366, 87953

South-Carolina. At a General Assembly begun and holden at Charles-Town. 87625A

South Carolian Bank. see Bank of the State of South Carolina, Charleston.

South-Carolina. By His Excellency James Glen. 87357

South-Carolina. By His Excellency the Right Honourable Lord Charles-Grenville Montagu. 87358

South Carolina. By Sir Henry Clinton. 87367

South Carolina Canal and Railroad Company. see South Carolina Railroad Company.

South Carolina Catholick Society. see Catholick Society of South Carolina.

South Carolina College. see South Carolina. University.

South Carolina Colportage Board. 88001

South Carolina Conference of the Methodist Episcopal Church. see Methodist Episcopal Church. Conferences. South Carolina.

South Carolina, disunion, and a Mississippi Valley Confederacy. 88002

South Carolina Domestic Missionary Society. 88003

South Carolina Domestic Missionary Society. Board of Managers. 88003

South Carolina Evangelical Knowledge Society. see Evangelical Knowledge Society in South Carolina.

South Carolina Female Collegiate Institute, Barhamville, S. C. 88004

South Carolina gazette. 86574, 87751, 87865, note after 96057, 103559, 103990

South Carolina historical and genealogical magazine. 84915

South Carolina Historical Commission, 1906-1909 publications. 87483

South Carolina Historical Society. 82988, 84915, note before 87456, 88005

South-Carolina. In a congress, begun and holden at Charles-Town. 87413

South-Carolina. In the Commons House of Assembly. 87354

South Carolina in the revolutionary war. 81262, note after 88005

South Carolina. In the Senate, December 21, 1793. 87507

South Carolina Indians. 33699

South Carolina Institute. 30101, 88006-88008

South Carolina Institute. Board of Directors. 88009

South Carolina Institute. Committee on Premiums. 30101, 88006

South Carolina Jockey Club. 88010-88012

South-Carolina justice of the peace. 88013-88014

South Carolina Land & Immigration Association. 88015

South Carolina legislative times. 87508

South Carolina Literary and Philosophical Society. see Literary and Philosophical Society of South Carolina.

South-Carolina Medical Association. 88016-88018, 88020

South-Carolina Medical Association. Board of Counsellors. 88017

South-Carolina Medical Association. Committee on the Medical Topography of South-Carolina. Chairman. 88019 see also Geddings, E.

South-Carolina Medical Society. see Medical Society of South Carolina.

South Carolina memorial upon the subject of duelling. 64571, 87905

South Carolina planter. pseud. Three letters. see Pinckney, Charles, 1757-1824.

South Carolina Planters' and Merchants' Bank. see Planters' and Merchants' Bank of South Carolina.

South-Carolina price-current. 88021

South Carolina protest against slavery. 39259

South-Carolina Protestant Episcopal Society for the Advancement of Christianity. see Protestant Episcopal Society for the Advancement of Christianity in South Carolina.

South Carolina Railroad Company. 87955-87959, 88024-88026, 88030

South Carolina Railroad Company. Charter. 87956-87957, 88025

South Carolina Railroad Company. Chief Engineer. 87962, 87965 see also Allen, Horatio.

South Carolina Railroad Company. Committee of Inspection. 88022, 88028

South Carolina Railroad Company. Committee on Cars. 87964

South Carolina Railroad Company. Directors. 87954

South Carolina Railroad Company. Directors and Stockholders. Committee. 87963

South Carolina Railroad Company. General Superintendent. 88023

South Carolina Railroad Company. President. 87966, 88022, 88029, see also Ravenel, J.

South Carolina Railroad Company. President and Directors. 88023

South Carolina Railroad Company. President and Directors. petitioners 87961

South Carolina Railroad Company. President and Directors. Committee of Inquiry. 87960

South Carolina Railroad Company. Stock-holders. 88022, 88027

South Carolina Railroad Company. Stock-holders. Committee of Seven. 88029

South Carolina Rangers. 88031

South Carolina Rangers' Charitable Association. 88032

South Carolina Republican Association. see Republican Party. South Carolina.

South Carolina St. David's Society. see St. David's Society of South Carolina.

South Carolina Salem Society. see Salem Society of South Carolina.

South-Carolina Society, Charleston. 12085, 88033, 88036-88038, note after 96180

South-Carolina Society, Charleston. Female Academy. 88034

South-Carolina Society, Charleston. First Centennial Celebration, 1837. 88036, note after 98180

South-Carolina Society, Charleston. Male Academy. 88035

South Carolina Society for Promoting and Improving Agriculture and Other Rural Concerns. 88039

South Carolina Society for the Advancement of Learning. 30446, 88041-88042

South Carolina Society for the Advancement of Learning. Publication no. 3. 88042

South-Carolina Society, for the Information and Assistance of Persons Emigrating from Other Countries. 87854

South-Carolina Society, for the Information and Assistance of Persons Emigrating from

Other Countries. Committee of Corres-pondence. 87854

South-Carolina Society for the Promotion of Temperance. 20093, note after 88042

South Carolina Society of the Cincinnati. see Society of the Cincinnati. South Carolina.

South Carolina State Agricultural Society. see State Agricultural Society of South Carolina.

South Carolina state gazette. 84836

South Carolina state gazetteer and business directory. 83905

South Carolina state gazetteer and business directory for 1880-'81. 83904

South Carolina State Press Association. 88043

South Carolina State Rights and Free Trade Association. see State Rights and Free Trade Association of South Carolina.

South Carolina State Temperance Convention, Charleston, 1844. 88073

South Carolina State Temperance Convention, Charleston, 1845. 88073

South Carolina State Temperance Society. Com-mittee. 88071

South Carolina Survivors' Association. see Survivors' Association of the State of South Carolina.

South Carolina Synod. see Presbyterian Church in the U.S.A. Synod of South Carolina. Presbyterian Church in the U.S.A. Synod of South Carolina and Georgia.

South Carolina Tax-Payers' Convention, Colum-bia, 1871. see Tax-Payers' Convention of South Carolina, Columbia, 1871.

South-Carolina. The actual commencement of hostilities. 87366

South Carolina. To the Honorable the President and other members of the Senate. 87531

South Carolina toasts. 10889

South Carolina Tract Society. 85326, 86265, 86291, 88043A-88051, note after 95649

South Carolina under Negro government. 62820

South Carolina Union and State Rights Party. see State Rights and Free Trade Party of Charleston, S.C.

South-Carolina weekly museum, and complete magazine of entertainment. 88052

South Carolina, with special reference to Aiken and vicinity. 88053

South Carolina Yazoo Company. 88054

South Carolina Yazoo Company. Certain Mem-bers. petitioners 88055

South Carolina Yazoo Company. Secretary. 88054

South-Carolinean [sic]. pseud. Some objec-tions. 86670, 88115

South Carolinian. pseud. American claim of rights. (1076)

South Carolinian. pseud. Appeal to the people. see Seabrook, Whitemarsh Benjamin, 1792-1855. supposed author

South Carolinian. pseud. Columbia's free-dom. 14888

South Carolinian. pseud. Confederate. see H. pseud.

South Carolinian. pseud. Economical causes of slavery. see Middleton, H.

South Carolinian. pseud. Emancipation. 22397

South Carolinian. pseud. Glimpses of New York City. see Bobo, William M.

South-Carolinian. pseud. Letter to the Rev. James C. Richmond. 40516, 88113

South-Carolinian. pseud. Letter to the Trus-tees of the South-Carolina College. 87985

South Carolinian. pseud. Letters by a South-Carolinian. 40577, 88114

South Carolinian. pseud. Life of Jefferson Davis. see Bacon, H. W. supposed author

South Carolinian. pseud. Observations to shew the propriety. see Pinckney, Charles, 1757-1824.

South Carolinian. pseud. Poems. see Hall, Samuel. supposed author and Hart, Samuel. supposed author

South-Carolinian. pseud. Practical considerations. see Dalcho, Frederick.

South-Carolinian. pseud. Refutation of the calumnies. see Holland, Edwin C.

South-Carolinian. pseud. Remarks on the decision. 69454

South-Carolinian. pseud. Remarks on the ordinance of nullification. 69479, 6th note after 88114

South Carolinian. pseud. Slavery in America. see Simms, William Gilmore, 1806-1870.

South Carolinian. pseud. Some objections to Mr. Crawford. 86670, 88115

South Carolinian. pseud. Three letters. see De Leon, Edwin.

South Carolinian. (30098)-30099

South Christian Church, New Bedford, Mass. see New Bedford, Mass. South Christian Church.

South Church, Andover, Mass. see Andover, Mass. South Church.

South Church, Boston. see Boston. South Church.

South Church, Dedham, Mass. see Dedham, Mass. South Church.

South Church, Eastham, Mass. see Eastham, Mass. South Church.

South Church, South Danvers, Mass. see South Danvers, Mass. South Church.

South Church, South Hadley, Mass. see South Hadley, Mass. South Church.

South Church, Springfield, Mass. see Springfield, Mass. South Church.

South Church: ecclesiastical councils viewed from celestial and satanic stand-points. 105621

South Company (Sweden) see Soder Compagniet.

South Congregational Church, Brooklyn. see Brooklyn. South Congregational Church.

South Congregational Church, Natick, Mass. see Natick, Mass. South Congregational Church.

South countryman. 88117

South Cove Corporation, Boston. Agent. 88118-88119 see also Jackson, Francis. Nichols, B. R.

South Cove Corporation, Boston. Board of Directors. 88118

South Cove Corporation, Boston. Charter. 88118

South Cove Corporation, Boston. Treasurer. 88118

South Danvers, Mass. see also Peabody, Mass.

South Danvers, Mass. Peabody Institute. see Peabody Institute, Danvers, Mass.

South Danvers, Mass. South Church. 88120

South defended. 47120

South devoted to the material interests of the southern states. 88121

South District Baptist Association. see Baptists. Illinois. South District Baptist Association.

South eastern . . . see Southeastern.

South End Provident Association, Boston. Public Meeting, 1851. 88123

South End Provident Association. A report presented and adopted. 88123

South Hadley Falls, Mass. Congregational Church. 88128

South Hadley Falls, Mass. Congregational Church. Pastor. 88127 see also Fisher, George E.

South Hadley Falls, Mass. Congregational Church. Semi-centennial Celebration, 1874. 88127

South Hadley, Mass. First Church. 88124

South Hadley, Mass. First Church. Standing Committee. 88124

South Hadley, Mass. Mount Holyoke Female Seminary. see Mount Holyoke Female Seminary, South Hadley, Mass.

South Hadley, Mass. South Church. 88125

South Hadley canal lottery. 88126

South Ham Gold and Copper Mining Company. 88130

South Hanover, Indiana. College. see Hanover College.

South Hanover, Indiana. Indiana Theological Seminary. see Hanover College.

South Hanover College. see Hanover College.

South Hanover College and Indiana Theological Seminary. Catalogue of the corporation, faculty, and students. 88138

South; her peril and her duty. (85346)

South in danger . . . . Address of the Democratic Association. 96362, 101069

South in danger; being a document. 96362, 101069

South in secession-time. 27448

South, in the union or out of it. 88139

South: its products, commerce, and resources. 36653

South—its resources and wants. 37272

South Jersey Cranberry Company. 88140

South Jersey Cranberry Company. Charter. 88140

South Jersey Institute, Bridgeton, N. J. 88141

South Kentucky District Association. see Baptists. Kentucky. South Kentucky District Association.

South Kingstown, R. I. First Baptist Church. 88143

South Limington Seminary. 88144

South Manchester, Conn. Manchester Library Association. see Manchester Library Association, South Manchester, Conn.

South Manchester and its silk manufactures. 88146

South Massachusetts Education Society. 88147

South Middlesex Conference of Churches. see Congregational Churches in Massachusetts. South Middlesex Conference of Churches.

South Middlesex peculiar. 88148

South Norwalk, Conn. Congregational Church. 88149

South now, heretofore and hereafter. 88150

South Pacific Railroad Company. petitioners 88153

South Pacific Railroad Company. plaintiffs 88152

South-Pacific Railroad Company. Land Department. 88151, 88154

South Parish, Ipswich, Mass. see Ipswich, Mass. South Parish.

South Parish, Portsmouth, N. H. see Portsmouth, N. H. South Parish.

South Parish, Weymouth, Mass. see Weymouth, Mass. South Parish.

South Parish Missionary Society, Lowell, Mass. see Lowell, Mass. South Parish Missionary Society.

South part of New-England, as it is planted this year, 1834. 105074

South Pennsylvania Railroad. 88155

South Pennsylvania Railroad. Charter. 88155

South Pewabic Copper Company. Directors. 88156

South Pewabic Copper Company. Mine. Superintendent. 88156 see also Frue, William B.

South Pewabic Copper Company. Treasurer. 88156

South Philadelphia Real Estate Association. 88157

South Reading, Mass. Baptist Church. 88159-88160

South Reading, Mass. Mechanic and Agricultural Institution. see South Reading Mechanic and Agricultural Institution.

South Reading Branch Railroad. 88161

South Reading Mechanic and Agricultural Institution. 88162

South Reading Mechanic and Agricultural Institution. Charter. 88162

South sacrificed. 33837

South Scituate, Mass. defendants 88163

South-sea ballad. 88164

South sea bubble. 88165

South Sea Company (Great Britain) 15028, (58935), 65865, 88167, 88177, 88189, 88192, 96767

South Sea Company (Great Britain) Agent in France. 88188

South Sea Company (Great Britain) Charter. 88166-88167, 88171-88173

South Sea Company (Great Britain) Directors. 65865, 88188-88189, 88191-88192

South Sea Company (Great Britain) General Court. 65865, 88192

South Sea Company (Great Britain) General Court. petitioners 75012

South Sea Company (Great Britain) Trustees. 88195-88196

South sea dream, a poem in Hudibrastic verse. 22318

South-sea herbal. 61288

South Sea islanders. 37148

South sea; or, the biters bit. 88199

South-sea scheme, as it now stands, considered. 88200

South sea scheme considered in a letter. 22931

South-sea scheme detected. 88201

South-sea scheme examin'd. 88201-88202

South Sea Surveying and Exploring Expedition. 70432

South seen with northern eyes. 2337

South Shore railroad. 88206

South Shore Railroad Company. 88206-88208

South Shore Railroad Company. Directors. 88207

South Shore Railroad Company. Stockholders' Committee. 88205

South Side Institute, Farmville, Va. see Longwood College, Farmville, Va.

South side of slavery. 92243

South Side Railroad Company, Long Island. 88210-88211

South Side Railroad Company, Virginia. Chief Engineer. 88213 see also Standford, C. O.

South Side Railroad Company, Virginia. President and Directors. 88212

South Side Railroad Company of Long Island. 88211

South side view of Cotton is king. 4476

South-side view of slavery. 340, 74741

South since the war. 1516

South. The political situation. 87310

South vindicated. [By James Williams.] (32924)

South vindicated from the treason and fanaticism of the northern abolitionists. 88214

South west. see Southwest.

South western. see Southwestern.

South Wharf Corporation, Boston. Charter. 88215

South Williamstown, Mass. Select Family School for Boys. see Select Family School for Boys, South Williamstown, Mass.

South Windsor, Conn. First Congregational Church. 88217

South Windsor, Conn. Second Congregational Church. 88218

South Woburn, Mass. Congregational Church. 88219

South Woodstock, Vt. Green Mountain Liberal Institute. see Green Mountain Liberal Institute, South Woodstock, Vt.

Southack, Cyprian. 88221

Southack, John. 88222

Southake, Cyprian. see Southack, Cyprian.

Southall, James Cocke. 88223-88225

Southall, Stephen O. 88226

Southampton, Mass. 88230

Southampton, Mass. Congregational Church. 88227-88228

Southampton, N. Y. 88229-88231

Southampton, N. Y. Committee. 88230

Southampton, N. Y. Town Clerk. 88230

Southampton, N. Y. Little South Division. 88232

Southampton, N. Y. Patent. 88230

Southampton, N. Y. Presbyterian Church. 88233

Southampton County, Va. Court. 97487

Southampton massacre. 35696

Southard, Milton Isaiah, 1836-1905. 88234-88236

Southard, Nathaniel. 48876, 81821, 88237-88239 see also Anti-slavery Cent-a-Week Society. General Agent.

Southard, Samuel Lewis, 1787-1842. 88240-88252

Southard, Samuel Lewis, 1819-1859. 19205, (20385), 88253-88254

Southborough, Mass. Protestant Episcopal Church. 88255

Southborough, Mass. Second Congregational Church. 88256

Southbridge, Mass. Congregational Church. 88260

Southbridge, Mass. Evangelical Free Church. 88261

Southbridge, Mass. First Baptist Church. 88262

Southbridge, Mass. Fourth of July Celebration, 1821. (5585)

Southbridge almanac, directory, and business advertiser. 88257

Southbridge business directory, for 1870. 88258

Southbridge directory for 1873. 88259

Southeastern Mining Company of Canada. Directors. 88263

Southeby, William. 88264-88266

Souther, John. 88267

Souther, Samuel. 26104, 88268-88269
Southerland, Thomas. defendant 42737, 88270
Southern, Henry. 69708
Southern, Sir Henry. 34437, 73210 see also Great Britain. Legation. Argentine Confederation.
Southern, Thomas. see Southerne, Thomas.
Southern Academy, Philadelphia. 88271
Southern adventures in time of war. (38177)
Southern agriculturist. 88272
Southern agriculturist, and register of rural affairs. 88273
Southern Aid Society, New York. 88275
Southern Aid Society, New York. Executive Committee. 88274
Southern Aid Society; its constitution. 88275
Southern almanac. 1852. 88276
Southern almanac, for . . . 1859. 88279
Southern almanac for 1875. 88287
Southern almanac for . . . 1860. 88280
Southern almanac for . . . 1868. 88285
Southern almanac for . . . 1865. 88283
Southern almanac for 1864. 70999
Southern almanac for . . . 1869. 88286
Southern almanac, for 1863. 88282
Southern almanac for the states of Georgia, Alabama, South Carolina, and Tennessee, for the year . . . 1862. 28806
Southern almanac for the states of Georgia, South Carolina, Alabama, Florida, Mississippi, Tennessee, and adjacent states. 88284
Southern almanac. With the courts of North and South Carolina, Georgia, Alabama, Tennessee & Florida. For . . . 1858. 88278
Southern almanac. With the courts of North and South Carolina, Georgia, Alabama, Tennessee & Florida. For . . . 1854. 88277
Southern almanac. With the courts of North and South Carolina, Georgia, Alabama, Tennessee and Florida. For . . . 1861. 88281
Southern amaranth. 88288
Southern and Atlantic Telegraph Company. defendants 88290
Southern and South-Western Presbyterian Convention, Cassville, Ga., 1840. 65182
Southern and south-western sketches. 88291
Southern and Western Commercial Convention, Baltimore, 1832. 3006
Southern and Western Commercial Convention, Memphis, 1853. 88292
Southern and western journal of progress. 88293
Southern and Western Liberty Convention, Cincinnati, 1845. (81765), 88294-88296
Southern and western literary messenger and review. see Southern literary messenger.
Southern and western masonic miscellany. 88297
Southern and western monthly magazine and review. (81263), 88393, note after 88297
Southern and Western Railroad Convention, New Orleans, 1851. 88298-88299
Southern and Western Railroad Convention, New Orleans, 1851. Committee. 88298
Southern and western songster: being a choice collection of the most fashionable songs. 28838, 88300

Southern and Western States Reform Medical Association. Georgia State Association. 88301
Southern apalachian. 88382
Southern Asylum Land Company. 88302
Southern Atlantic and California Railway. 88303
Southern Bank, New Orleans. Charter. 88304
Southern banner. 88305
Southern Baptist almanac and annual register. 88306
Southern Baptist, and general intelligencer. 88307
Southern Baptist Convention, Augusta, Ga., 1845. 3241, 88309
Southern Baptist Convention, Richmond, 1846. 88308
Southern Baptist Publication Society. 88310, 88486
Southern Baptist Publication Society. Meeting, Atlanta, 1853. 88310
Southern Baptist Theological Seminary, Greenville, S. C. 88311
Southern barrister. pseud. Recreations of a southern barrister. see Sands, Alexander Hamilton. supposed author
Southern Bible Society and Pilgrims' Depository. 88312
Southern Board of Foreign Missions. 85227, 88313
Southern book. (18896)
Southern boundary of Maryland. 45090
Southern boundary of Michigan. 88314
Southern boys and girls' monthly. 88315
Southern business directory and general commercial advertiser. 10258
Southern cabinet of agriculture. 88273
Southern cause and its prospects. 88316
Southern Central Agricultural Society. 88317
Southern Central Railroad. 88320
Southern Central Railroad. petitioners 88318
Southern Central Railroad. Chief Engineer. 88319
Southern Central Railroad. President. 88319
Southern central railroad. From Lake Ontario to Pennsylvania coal mines. 88320
Southern Central Medical Association of New York. see New York Southern Central Medical Association.
Southern Central New York Medical Association. see Medical Association of Southern Central New York.
Southern Cherokees. see Cherokee Nation (Southern)
Southern child's first book. 88321
Southern chivalry, and what the north ought to do with it. (67312)
Southern chivalry; the adventures of G. Whillikens. 88322
Southern Christian exemplified. 6133
Southern Christian Home Missionary Society, Philadelphia. 62265
Southern Christian Home Missionary Society, Philadelphia. Committee on the Organization and Conduct of a House of Industry. 62265
Southern citizen. pseud. Remarks on popular sovereignty. see Johnson, Reverdy, 1796-1876.
Southern clergyman. pseud. Defence of southern slavery. 81954
Southern college magazine. 88324
Southern Commercial Convention, New Orleans, 1855. 88327

Southern Commercial Convention, Richmond, 1856. 88328
Southern Commercial Convention, Savannah, 1856. 88328
Southern Commercial Convention, Knoxville, 1857. 56784, note after 88326
Southern Commercial Convention, Cincinnati, 1870. petitioners 88325
Southern Commercial Convention, Cincinnati, 1870. Committee of Arrangements. 88326
Southern Commercial Convention, Louisville, 1871. 88325
Southern confederacy. 10817, 64763
Southern confederacy and the African slave trade. 9857
Southern confederacy. Letters by James Robb. 71726-(71727)
Southern Convention, Nashville, 1850. 88329-88333
Southern Convention, Savannah, 1856. see Southern Commercial Convention, Savannah, 1856.
Southern cultivator. 88334
Southern delegate. pseud. Dialogue. 19933, 4th note after 98269
Southern Delegates in Congress, 1848-1849. 402, 88335
Southern Democracy! 88336
Southern dial, a monthly magazine. 88337
Southern dial and African monitor. 88338
Southern Directory and Publishing Company. firm 83903, 83905
Southern Dispensary for the Medical Relief of the Poor, Philadelphia. (62266)
Southern Dispensary for the Medical Relief of the Poor, Philadelphia. Charter. (62266)
Southern District Medical Society (Massachusetts) see Massachusetts Medical Society. Southern District Medical Society.
Southern eclectic and home gazette. 88340
Southern eclectic, composed chiefly of selections. 88341
Southern eclectic magazine. (71194)
Southern education for southern youth. 91771
Southern enterprize. 88342
Southern excitement, against the American system. 88343
Southern Express Company. 88344
Southern Famine Relief Commission. 88346-88347
Southern Famine Releif Commission. Executive Committee. 88345
Southern farm and fireside. 88348
Southern farm and home. 88348A
Southern farmer. pseud. Bondage, a moral institution. 6291, (24909)
Southern Female College, La Grange, Ga. see La Grange College, La Grange, Ga.
Southern Female Institute, Fredericksburg, Va. see Mary Washington College, Fredericksburg, Va.
Southern Female Institute, Richmond. 88351
Southern Fertilizing Company, Richmond. 88352-88358
Southern field and factory, 1873. 88359
Southern field and fireside. 88360
Southern field and fireside novellette, no. 2. 21852
Southern fifth reader: embracing copious and elegant extracts. 73345
Southern fifth reader. Prepared under the supervision of Prof. Geo. F. Holmes. 32601

Southern first reader. 32601
Southern first spelling book. 95448
Southern fourth reader. 32601
Southern friend. 88361
Southern generals, their lives and campaigns. 85554, 85557
Southern generals, who they are, and what they have done. 85558
Southern gentleman. 33244
Southern Gold Company. 88362
Southern hatred of the American government. 88363
Southern Historical Convention, Montgomery White Sulphur Springs, Va., 1873. 88369 see also Southern Historical Society.
Southern historical monthly. 88364
Southern Historical Society. 84724, 88366-88367, 88369-88371, 88395 see also
Southern Historical Convention, Montgomery White Sulphur Springs, Va., 1873.
Southern Historical Society. Executive Committee. 88365
Southern Historical Society. North Carolina Branch. 88368
Southern Historical Society papers. 84724, 88370
Southern history of the great civil war. (63849)
Southern history of the war. 63865, 63866
Southern history of the war. The last year of the war. 63864
Southern history of the war. The second year of the war. (63861)
Southern history of the war. The third year of the war. 63863
Southern history of the war in the United States. (63859)
Southern home. By a Virginian. 88372
Southern Home for Destitute Children, Philadelphia. 62354, note after 97815
Southern Home for Destitute Children, Philadelphia. Charter. 62354, note after 97815
Southern home journal devoted to choice literature. 88373
Southern Hotel Company. 88374
Southern Hotel Company. Charter. 88374
Southern husband outwitted by his union wife. 63253
Southern ichthyology. 32455
Southern illustrated news. 88375
Southern independence: an address. 89282
Southern Independence Association, London. 88374
Southern Independence Association, Manchester, Eng. 88377-88378
Southern Independence Association of London. 88376
Southern Independence Association, 26, Market Street, Manchester. 88378
Southern Insane Asylum. Report of Commissioners for 1869-70. 34258
Southern institutes. 77312
Southern insurrection: its elements and aspects. 97327
Southern intelligencer. 87867
Southern Jersey Indians. Treaties, etc. 53242
Southern journal of medicine and pharmacy. 83003
Southern Kansas immigrant. 88380
Southern Kansas Land Association. 88381
Southern ladies' book. 88382
Southern lady. pseud. Condition of the African race in the United States. 81935

Southern lady. pseud. Household of Bouverie. see Warfield, Catherine Ann Ware.

Southern lady. pseud. Letters on the condition of the African race. see Schoolcraft, Mary (Howard)

Southern lady. pseud. Plantation teacher. 88383

Southern lady. pseud. Southern child's first book. 88321

Southern lady. pseud. Southern scenes and scenery. 88486

Southern lady's companion, a monthly periodical. 88384

Southern lady's magazine. 88385

Southern Land, Emigration and Product Company. 88386

Southern Land, Emigration and Product Company, 71 Broadway. 88386

Southern land grants. Speech . . . February 4, 1868. 36885

Southern land grants. Speech . . . January 22 and 28, 1868. 36885

Southern library. 88387

Southern life as it is. 21683

Southern life as it was. 40036

Southern Life Insurance and Trust Company. Charter. 88388

Southern literary companion. 88389

Southern literary gazette (1828-1829) 88390

Southern literary gazette: an illustrated weekly journal. 88391

Southern literary journal. 103316

Southern literary journal and magazine of arts. 88392

Southern literary journal, and monthly magazine. 88392

Southern literary journal and monthly review. 103784

Southern literary messenger. 22975, (41520), 72064, 81263, 81908, 82091, 82848, 83513, 84162, 7th note after 88114, note after 88297, 88293, 92228, 92624, 95066, 4th note after 95515, 97299, 97608, 3d note after 100533, 100581

Southern Loyalists' Convention, Philadelphia, 1866. 69942, 88394

Southern Loyalists' Convention. Call for a convention. 88394

Southern magazine (1838?-   ) 84870

Southern magazine (1868-1875) 88371, 88395, 90799

Southern magazine and monthly review. 88396

Southern man. pseud. Slavery the mere pretext for the rebellion. see Kennedy, John Pendleton, 1795-1870.

Southern manufacturer. 90848

Southern martyrs: a poetical tale of Patagonia. 34044

Southern Maryland Railroad Company. 88397

Southern Maryland Railroad Company. Charter. 88397

Southern Maryland Railroad, from Washington City. 88397

Southern Masonic Female College, Covington, Ga. 88398

Southern Medical College, Savannah. 88399

Southern medical reports. (24068)

Southern Methodist almanac for . . . 1855. 88400

Southern Methodist almanac for . . . 1857. 88401

Southern Methodist almanac for . . . 1860. 88401

Southern Methodist almanac for . . . 1861. 88401

Southern Methodist primer. 88402

Southern Methodist Publishing House, 88401, 88403

Southern Methodist Publishing House. Agent. 88403-88404 see also Abbey, R.

Southern military manual. 88405

Southern minister, and his slave convert. (42656)

Southern Minnesota Land Grant Rail Road Company. see Southern Minnesota Railroad Company.

Southern Minnesota Railroad and its lands. 88415

Southern Minnesota Railroad Company. 88407-88412, 88416

Southern Minnesota Railroad Company. Charter. 88411

Southern Minnesota Railroad Company. Chief Engineer. 88413

Southern Minnesota Railroad Company. Receiver. 88414 see also McIlrath, Charles.

Southern Minnesota Railroad Company. Superintendent. 88414

Southern Minnesota Railroad Company. Trustee. 88406, 88410 see also Man, Albon P. Ruggles, Samuel B.

Southern Missouri, its resources. 39842

Southern monthly (1840-1843) see Magnolia; or southern monthly.

Southern monthly (1861-1862) 88417

Southern monthly collection of patriotic songs and heroic poems. 88418

Southern monthly magazine. 88419

Southern monthly magazine and review. 88420

Southern monthly novel library. 88417

Southern nabob. pseud. Slavery vindicated. 82113

Southern Normal University, Carbondale, Ill. see Illinois. Southern Normal University, Carbondale.

Southern notes for national circulation. 88421

Southern odes, by the outcast. 55843, note after 88421

Southern opinion's prize poems. 88422

Southern oppression. 88423

Southern orator, consisting of elements of elocution. 88424

Southern orator: being a collection of pieces in prose, poetry, and dialogue. (36849)

Southern outrages. 87310

Southern Pacific Railroad Company (California) petitioners 88427

Southern Pacific Railroad Company (California) Board of Directors. 88425

Southern Pacific Railroad Company (California) Land Agent. 88426 see also Madden, Jerome.

Southern Pacific Railroad Company (California) Secretary. 88427A see also Willcutt, J. L.

Southern Pacific Railroad Company (Texas) 88429, 88432, 88434, 88438 see also Texas and Pacific Railway Company.

Southern Pacific Railroad Company (Texas) Committee. 88437

Southern Pacific Railroad Company (Texas) Stockholders Convention, Memphis, 1858. 88433

Southern Pacific Railroad Company (Texas) Stockholders Meeting, Louisville, Ky., 1858. 88435-88436

Southern Pacific Railroad Company (Texas) Stockholders Meeting, New Orleans, 1858. 88436, 88438

Southouse, Edward. 88596

Southport, Wisc. Anti-secret Association. see Southport Anti-secret Association.

Southport Anti-secret Association. 88598

Southport Lodge, no. VII, Independent Order of Odd Fellows. see Odd Fellows, Independent Order of. Wisconsin. Southport Lodge, No. VII.

Southron. pseud. Prairiedom. see Page, Frederic Benjamin. supposed author

Southron. pseud. South-Carolina in the revolutionary war. see Simms, William Gilmore, 1806-1870.

Southron. pseud. To the people of South-Carolina. 88084

Southron. 88600

Southside consolidation act. 88601

Southside Sportsmen's Club of Long Island. 88602

Southville, Mass. Second Congregational Church. see Southborough, Mass. Second Congregational Church.

Southward ho! (81265), (81279)

Southward Railroad Company. petitioners 62267

Southwark, Pa. 62060

Southwark, Pa. Church of the Evangelists. see Southwark, Pa. Protestant Episcopal Church of the Evangelists.

Southwark, Pa. Citizens' Committee to Attend To and Alleviate the Sufferings of the Afflicted With the Malignant Fever, 1793. see Committee, Appointed on the 14th September, 1793, By the Citizens of Philadelphia, the Northern Liberties and the District of Southwark, to Attend to and Alleviate the Sufferings of the Afflicted With the Malignant Fever, Prevalent in the City and its Vicinity.

Southwark, Pa. First Presbyterian Church. 61666

Southwark, Pa. Library Company. see Southwark Library Company, Southwark, Pa.

Southwark, Pa. Ordinances, etc. 61899, 61905

Southwark, Pa. Protestant Episcopal Church of the Evangelists. 62103, 88603

Southwark, Pa. Protestant Episcopal Mission Church of the Evangelists. see Southwark, Pa. Protestant Episcopal Church of the Evangelists.

Southwark, Pa. Society for the Institution and Support of First-Day or Sunday Schools in . . . Philadelphia, and the Districts of Southwark and the Northern Liberties. see Society for the Institution and Support of First-Day or Sunday Schools in . . . Philadelphia, and the Districts of Southwark and the Northern Liberties.

Southwark, Pa. Temperance Beneficial Association. see Temperance Beneficial Association, Southwark, Pa.

Southwark, Pa. Theater. 88605

Southwark Library Company, Southwark, Pa. 88604

Southwark Library Company, Southwark, Pa. Directors. 88604

Southwell, Walter Sims. 88606

South-west. (34775), note after 105955

Southwest Pacific Railroad Company. Atlantic & Pacific Railroad Company, conveyances and documents. 88607

Southwest revisited. 88608

Southwest Virginia Agricultural Society. Annual Exhibition, 4th, Wytheville, 1872. 88609

Southwestern and Rio Grande Railway Company. 88610

Southwestern Bible Society of New-Orleans. (53376)

Southwestern Conference of Congregational Churches. see Congregational Churches in the United States. Southwestern Conference.

Southwestern Convention, Memphis, 1845. 88612

Southwestern Cooperative Association of the Order of Patrons of Husbandry. see Patrons of Husbandry. Southwestern Cooperative Association.

Southwestern Exposition Association of New Orleans. 88614

South-western farmer. 88615

South-western journal. 88616

South western literary journal and monthly review. 88617

Southwestern magazine, devoted to literature, art, and the prosperity of the country. 88618

South-western monthly. 88619

Southwestern Normal College, California, Pa. see Pennsylvania. State Normal School, California.

Southwestern Normal School and Business Institute, Lebanon, Ohio. see Lebanon University, Lebanon, Ohio.

Southwestern Normal School at Lebanon, Ohio. see Lebanon University, Lebanon, Ohio.

Southwestern Pacific Railroad. 88622

South-Western Railroad Bank, Louisville, Ky. 42324, 88023, 88027

Southwestern Railroad Company (Georgia) 88623-88624, 88626

Southwestern Railroad Company (Georgia) Chief Engineer. 88625

Southwestern Railroad Company (Georgia) President. 88625

Southwestern Railroad Company (Georgia) Superintendent 88625

Southwestern Railroad Company (Tennessee) 88627

Southwick, Edward W. 88628

Southwick, Francis M. 88629

Southwick, John B. 88630

Southwick, Josiah. (73483)

Southwick, Remington. 70706, 88631-88633

Southwick, Solomon. 14556, 35280, 63428, 78581, 88634-88657, note after 88657, 90594, 3d note after 99588

Southwick, Solomon. defendant 89295, 89298

Southwick. firm publishers see Barber & Southwick. firm publishers

Southwick, Mass. Baptist Church. 88658

Southwood, Marion. 88659, 95865, 95867

Southworth, Edward. 88660

Southworth, Emma Dorothy Eliza (Nevitte) 88661-88663

Southworth, George A. ed. 87444

Southworth, George Champlin Shepard. 88664

Southworth, John. 88665

Southworth, Mrs. S. A. 88666-88668

Southworth, Sylvester S. 88669-88670, 96905

Southworth, Sylvester S. supposed author 71857, 97198

Southworth, Tertius Dunning. 88671-88677

Southworth, William S. 88678 see also Lawrence Manufacturing Company. Agent.

Soutter, J. T. petitioner 88679

Souvenir: a monthly magazine. 88682

Souvenir. . . . A very few copies printed. 88680

Souvenir "America" testimonial to Rev. S. F.
Smith. 84062
Souvenir annual. 88683
Souvenir: by the Ladies' Literary Union,
Hillsdale College. 88684
Souvenir consacre a la memoire veneree de
M. L. J. Casault. 11296
Souvenir de Morristown. 88685
Souvenir de retraite. (35771)
Souvenir. Directions. Smith County Old
Settles Homecoming Association. 84962
Souvenir d'un sejour chez les planteurs du
sud. 39153
Souvenir d'une mission Indienne. 6295
Souvenir gallery. 88683, 88686
Souvenir of friendship, a Christmas and new-
year's present. 88687
Souvenir of friendship. Selections from
celebrated authors. 88688
Souvenir of overland travel. 30617
Souvenir of 1775. 88689
Souvenir of the Anchor Line Agents excursion.
88690
Souvenir of the Bal Costume. 85203
Souvenir of the lakes. 88691
Souvenir of the late polar search. (1924)
Souvenir of the Mississippi. 69062
Souvenir of the Trans-continental Excursion
of Railroad Agents, 1870. 88692
Souvenir. Our object use. 88681
Souvenir religieux d'un mission Indienne.
6296
Souvenir verse and story. 83334
Souvenirs Atlantiques. 59254
Souvenirs d'Amerique. [Par J. Dulien.]
12273
Souvenirs d'Amerique. Relations d'un voyage
au Texas et en Haiti. (44601)
Souvenirs de Guy-Joseph Bonnet. 6321
Souvenirs de la Guyane. 36941
Souvenirs de l'Amerique Centrale. 1997
Souvenirs de l'Amerique du Sud. 99741
Souvenirs de l'Amerique Espagnole. (67424)
Souvenirs de mes voyages aux Etats-Unis.
81313
Souvenirs de Mexique. 62706
Souvenirs de Rio de Janeiro. 71472
Souvenirs de Rio de Janeiro dessines d'apres
nature & publies par I. Steinmann.
88693, note before 91212
Souvenirs de trente annees de voyages. 39244
Souvenirs de voyage. [Par le Comte de la
Cornillere.] 38493
Souvenirs de voyage. [Par Paul Dhormoys.]
19917
Souvenirs de voyages. 93984
Souvenirs des Antilles. 50208
Souvenirs des Etats-Unis. (12300)
Souvenirs des Indes Occidentales. 44660
Souvenirs des invasions de 1814 et 1815.
93413
Souvenirs des voyages. 16802
Souvenirs, d'Italie, d'Angleterre et de
l'Amerique. 12269
Souvenirs du Mexique. 88694
Souvenirs du Rio de la Plata. 64702
Souvenirs d'un aveugle. 1866
Souvenirs d'un jeune voyageur. 88695
Souvenirs d'un medecin. 70330
Souvenirs d'un medicin Americain. 88696
Souvenirs d'un prisonnier d'etat Canadien en
1838. (64741)
Souvenirs d'un voyage dans l'Amerique
Centrale. 93416

Souvenirs d'un voyage dans l'ile d'Haiti. 19918
Souvenirs d'un voyage en Oregon et en
Californie. 73420
Souvenirs d'un voyageur. Par Isidore Lowen-
stern. 42506
Souvenirs d'un voyaguer. Par M. Isidore
Lowenstern. 42505
Souvenirs d'un voyageur. Par N. X. Marmier.
(44645)
Souvenirs et anecdotes. 78915
Souvenirs et reflexions d'un citoyen Americain.
39803
Souvenirs historiques de la guerre du Bresil en
1635. 19330, 38567
Souvenirs historiques du Canada. 67390
Souvenirs historiques sur la seigneurie de la
prairie. 99601
Souvenirs of a residence in Europe. (32705)
Souvenirs of a summer in Germany. 20091,
77466
Souvenirs of travel. 40750
Souvenirs ou recueil des ordres permanens.
88697
Souvenirs sur la vie privee du General La
Fayette. 13772
Souvenirs sur les commencements de l'Union
St. Joseph Montreal. (63420)
Souvestre, Emile. 88698
Souza, Aloysius de Vasconcellos &. see
Vasconcellos & Souza, Aloysius de.
Souza, Antonio Ennes de. 88699-88701
Souza, Antonio Jose de. 88702
Souza, Augusto Fausto de. 88703
Souza, Bernardo Avellino Ferreira e. see
Ferriera e Souza, Bernardo Avellino.
Souza, Bernardo Xavier Pinto de. 88704-88715
Souza, Domingo de. 88716
Souza, Feliciano Joaquim de. see Souza
Nunes, Feliciano Joaquim de.
Souza, Francisco Bernardino de. 88721-88722
Souza, Francisco de. 88718-88720
Souza, Gabriel Soares de. see Soares de
Souza, Gabriel.
Souza, J. A. Fernandez de Cordova y. 88723
Souza, Jose Carlos Pinto de. see Pinto de
Souza, Jose Carlos.
Souza, Jose Mariano Beristain de. see Beris-
tain de Souza, Jose Mariano, 1756-1817.
Souza, Juan de. 88725
Souza, Luis Antonio da Silva e. see Silva e
Souza, Luis Antonio de.
Souza, Manuel de Faria y. see Faria y Souza,
Manuel de.
Souza, Paulino Jose Soares de. see Soares de
Souza, Paulino Jose, Visconde do Uruguay,
1807-1866.
Souza, Paulino Jose Soares de. see Soares de
Souza, Paulino Jose, 1834-
Souza, Pedro Lopes de. 76833, 88726-88727
Souza, Rafael de. 88728-88729
Souza, I. Faria y. see Faria y Souza, T.
Souza Azevedo Pizarro y Araujo, Jose de.
see Azevedo Pizaxxo e Araujo, Jose de
Souza.
Souza Bandeira, Antonio Herculano de. 88730
Souza Bocayuva, Quintino de. 29123, 88731-
88738
Souza Brazil, Thomaz Pompeo de, 1852-
63950-63953, 88739-88747 see also
Ceara (Brazilian Province) Inspector
Geral da Instruccao Publica.
Souza Bueno, Maximiano de. 88748
Souza Coelho, Romualdo de, Bp. 88750-88753
see also Para, Brazil (Diocese) Bishop
(Souza Coelho) Para, Brazil (Diocese)
Delegado.

Spain. Casa de la Contratracion de las
Indias. 79140
Spain. Casa de la Contratacion de las Indias.
Tribunal. Presidente. 98594 see also
Varas y Valdes, Francisco.
Spain. Casa de Moneda de las Indias. 48615
Spain. Comendador de Ballesteros. 70095
see also Ayanz, Geronimo de.
Spain. Comision Nombrada Para Proponer
Medidas Conducentes al Bien y
Felicidad de Ambas Americas. 20107
Spain. Consejo de Castilla. (29358)
Spain. Consejo de las Indias. 15916-15917,
22550, 23516, 29029, 40050, note after
40960, (41092), 47616, 56265, 56282,
(57477), 57483, 58280, (58841), 70804,
(77142), 87176, 87224-87225, 99619
Spain. Consejo de las Indias. Fiscal. 36952,
70092, 86377
Spain. Consejo de las Indias. Fiscal.
defendant 16776, 39132, 93329, 93332,
99437, 99438
Spain. Consejo de las Indias. Fiscal.
plaintiff 86523-86524, 86541 see also
Solorzano Pereira, Juan de, 1575-1655.
plaintiff
Spain. Consejo de las Indias. Promotor
Fiscal de Cobrancas. defendant 16776,
39132
Spain. Consejo de las Indias. Sala de
Justicia. 25481
Spain. Consejo de Regencia. 87314
Spain. Consejo Real. (75562)
Spain. Consejo Real. plaintiffs 51041
Spain. Consejo Real. Fiscal. 51041 see
also Moscoso y Cordoua, Christoual de.
Spain. Constitution. 23587, (74905)
Spain. Contraduria General. 76306 see also
Sanchez Pereyra, Diego Joseph.
Spain. Correo General. 20447
Spain. Correo Maritimo. 98490
Spain. Cortes. 11099, 20252, 23587, 67141,
68428, 82430, 97044
Spain. Cortes. Congreso de los Diputados.
67141
Spain. Cortes. Diputados de America. (61092),
69971
Spain. Cortes. Diputados de Ultramar, 1821.
23436, 67655
Spain. Cortes. Senado. 67141
Spain. Direccion de Hidrografia. 1700-1701,
34828
Spain. Ejercito. 19949, (69238)
Spain. Fiscal. defendant 98315
Spain. Jueces Plenipotenciaros. 11698
Spain. Junta de Guerra de Indias. 57474
Spain. Junta Suprema de Gobierno, Seville.
68250, 97044, 99688
Spain. Laws, statutes, etc. (2229), 4419,
9044, (9891), 14126, 16058, 16668,
17747, 17749, 17774, 17799, 17800,
17801, 17808, 19208, 19422, 22452,
22550, 24159, 24892, (26482), 29028,
29359, 29360, 29422, 29425, 29447,
29450, (29879), 36899, 37756, (38993),
(39431), 40902-40905, 40959, note after
40960, (41092)-(41093), 41987, 42244,
44422, (47488), 48334, 48358, (48374),
48608, (48612), (48613), 48615, 48618,
48634, 48635, (48637), 56003, 56201,
56243, 56246-56247, 56254, 56259-56260,
56261, 56263-56264, 56288, (56292),
56300, 57516, 56747, 57472-57474,
57475, (57481)-57485, (57599), 58417,

58536, (58841), 59305, (60899), 61082,
(61088), (61114), 61135, 61251, 62441,
64914-(64915), 65039, 65048, 66408,
67108, 68222-68233, 68236, 68238,
(68245), 68247, 68249-68250, (68384),
68386-68388, 68389-68390, 68449, 68855,
68860, 68872-68873, (68890), 70462,
(70802), 72430, 72537, (72549), 73852,
75548-75552, 76293, 76306, 76312,
76861, (77142), (77671), 79140, 79823,
86398, 86411, 89647, 93303, 83586,
94352, 94628, 94947, note after 95563,
note after 96350, 96475, 97044, 98490,
99441, 99442, 99618, 103429, 103434,
105480, 105987A, 106408
Spain. Legacion. Great Britain. 23088,
(47531), 90292, 96526 see also Cardenas, Alonso de. Leyde, --------,
Marques de. Pozobueno, ----, Marques
de.
Spain. Legacion. Netherlands. 19125, 19154
Spain. Legacion. Netherlands. Secretary.
pseud. see Secretary to the Spanish
Embassy at the Hague. pseud.
Spain. Legacion. Portugal. 38998, 56001,
(74790) see also Chelemar, -------,
Prince de.
Spain. Legacion. United States. 25149,
57355-57356, 62655, 106214-106218 see
also Onis, Luis de, 1769-1830. Yrujo
y Tacon, Carlos Martineo de, Marques
de Casa Yrujo.
Spain. Ministerio de Estado. 34177, 38955,
47147, 86398, 90292 see also Mejorda,
-------, Marques de. Orendayn, Juan
Bautista, Marques de la Paz.
Spain. Ministerio de Hacienda. 17801
Spain. Ministerio de Marina. 34415, 74966,
98907-98908 see also Spain. Armada.
Spain. Ministerio de Ultramar. 47597
Spain. Regencia Provisional, 1840. 40905
Spain. Sovereigns, etc. 4419, 9044, 17812,
(26482), 29065, 38628, (44951), (48374),
51445, 56201, 56270, 58417, (58841),
(72549), 86411, 93586, 94352, 103429,
103434
Spain. Sovereigns, etc., 1479-1504 (Isabel I)
see Spain. Sovereigns, etc., 1479-1516
(Fernando V)
Spain. Sovereigns, etc., 1479-1516 (Fernando
V) 18792, 22550, note after 40960, 56338,
86398, 89647, 94352, see also Fernando
V, King of Spain, 1452-1516.
Spain. Sovereigns, etc., 1516-1556 (Carlos I)
(11229), 18782, 22550, 1st note after
39116, 40902-40904, note after 40960,
94352 see also Carlos I, King of Spain,
1550-1588.
Spain. Sovereigns, etc., 1556-1598 (Felipe II)
22550, 42066, 56201, 57483, 64171-
64172, 76223, 76332, note after 90828,
94352 see also Felipe II, King of Spain,
1527-1598.
Spain. Sovereigns, etc., 1598-1621 (Felipe III)
(48613), 56338, 70095, 98109 see also
Felipe III, King of Spain, 1578-1621.
Spain. Sovereigns, etc., 1621-1665 (Felipe IV)
10759, (41092), 44267, 45404, (48613),
51680, (57477), 57480, 59305, 61135,
64628, 65039, 65048, 65977, 96476,
98019, 98825, 99441-99442, 106408 see
also Felipe IV, King of Spain, 1605-1665.
Spain. Sovereigns, etc., 1665-1700 (Carlos II)
30155, (42067), 48608, 68231, 68386-
68390 see also Carlos II, King of Spain,
1661-1700.

Spain. Sovereigns, etc., 1700-1746 (Felipe V)
(9891), (16665), 16668, (16690), 17026,
19208-19209, 29422, 29359, (37863)-
37864, (48613), 48618, 56003, 56293,
(56589), 58536, 61094, 66408, 68231,
68238, 68249, (70381), 70382, 72044,
73852, (76658), 79140, 86398, 88181,
note after 93420, note after 96350, 96541,
98019, 99618 <u>see also</u> Felipe V, <u>King</u>
<u>of Spain</u>, 1683-1746.

Spain. Sovereigns, etc., 1700-1746 (Felipe V)
plaintiff 105732 <u>see also</u> Felipe V,
<u>King of Spain</u>, 1683-1746. <u>plaintiff</u>

Spain. Sovereigns, etc., 1724 (Luis I)
(48612) <u>see also</u> Luis I, <u>King of Spain</u>.

Spain. Sovereigns, etc., 1746-1759 (Fernando
VI) 96515, 96544, 96546 <u>see also</u>
Fernando VI, <u>King of Spain</u>, 1713-1759.

Spain. Sovereigns, etc., 1659-1877 (Carlos III)
16058, 17808, 19275, 26148, 26483,
29425, 29947, (29449), 32428, 32765,
36899, 48334, 48504, (48613), 48634-
48635, 56262, (61088), 68022, 68231-
68232, 68238, (68245), 68247, 68860,
68873, (68890), 76293, 76312, 88944,
93346, 93778, 96553, 98019, 98490 <u>see</u>
<u>also</u> Carlos III, <u>King of Spain</u>, 1716-
1788.

Spain. Sovereigns, etc., 1788-1808 (Carlos IV)
9031, 17800, 29028, 29094, 29450,
(56292), 56300, 56737, 66596, 67108,
68223, 68224, (68226), 68228-68229,
76861 <u>see also</u> Carlos IV, <u>King of</u>
<u>Spain</u>, 1748-1819.

Spain. Sovereigns, etc., 1808-1813 (Joseph
Bonaparte) 17747, 44422, (57599), 68225,
68229, (68243) <u>see also</u> Joseph Bonaparte, <u>King of Spain</u>, 1768-1844.

Spain. Sovereigns, etc., 1814-1833 (Fernando
VII) 17749, 17774, 17799, 17801,
24159, 29059, 48358, (48613), 66587,
68227, 68230, 68233, 68244, 68250,
(68384), (70383), 72430, 98650 <u>see also</u>
Fernando VII, <u>King of Spain</u>, 1784-1833.

Spain. Sovereigns, etc., 1833-1868 (Isabel II)
66593, (66597), 68855, 93303 <u>see also</u>
Isabel II, <u>Queen of Spain</u>, 1830-1904.

Spain. Treaties, etc. 416, (469), 1537, 2227,
2446-2447, 3557, 12689, 14300, 14371,
14399, 14566, 15930-15932, 16195,
(16197), (16202), 19274-19275, 24884,
24888, 26872-26873, 32773, (34358),
38998, 40047, 40319, 41849, 42054,
42889, 51083, 52223, 56001, (56519),
56582, 62457, 64837, 65044, 65046,
69589, 72044, (74790), 75240, 75534,
80700, 91092-91093, 94777, 95044,
95655, 95749, 96274, 96515, 96527-
96528,, 96541-96542, 96543-96545, 96547-
96548, 96551-96556, 96558, 96562,
96587-96589, 97298, 2d note after 97583,
note after 99260, 99314, 101144, 101147,
101167, 102888, 1st note after 102785

Spain. Universidad de Cargadores del Comercio. <u>see</u> Universidad de Cargadores del
Comercio de Espana.

Spain. Visitador General de Recidios. 19955
<u>see also</u> Rivera, Pedro de.

Spain. An account of the public festival.
88852

Spain and Cuba. 88853
Spain, Cuba and the United States. 88854
Spain yesterday and to-day. 87318
Spain yesterday and to-day. 1, 87318, 106195

Spalding, A. M. 88855
Spalding, Amos Fletcher. 88856-88859
Spalding, C. H. 83495, 88860
Spalding, Charles. 88861
Spalding, Charles C. 88862
Spalding, Edward H. 88863
Spalding, Erastus. 88864
Spalding, G. R. 88865
Spalding, George Burley. 88866-88872
Spalding, H. H. 58358
Spalding, Henry C. 88873
Spalding, Henry Harmon. (55110), 88873-
88880
Spalding, Henry W. 88881
Spalding, J. Willett, 1827- 88882
Spalding, James Reed, 1821-1872. 88883,
99213
Spalding, John. 88884
Spalding, John Lancaster, Bp., 1840-1916.
88885
Spalding, Joshua. Burden and heat of the day.
<u>see</u> Spalding, Josiah.
Spalding, Joshua, 1760-1825. 88886-88895,
101882 <u>see also</u> Salem, Mass. Taber-
nacle Church. Pastor.
Spalding, Josiah. 88896-88901
Spalding, Lyman. (64416), 88902-88907
Spalding, Martin John, Abp., 1810-1872. 72910,
82946, 72898-(72899), 88908-88912 <u>see</u>
<u>also</u> Baltimore (Archdiocese) Arch-
<u>bishop</u> (Spalding) Louisville (Diocese)
Bishop (Spalding)
Spalding, N. G. 88913
Spalding, R. C. <u>defendant at court martial</u>
88914
Spalding, Rufus Paine. 88915-88921
Spalding, Samuel Jones. 23002, note after
88921-88924
Spalding and Storrs. <u>firm</u> 83929
Spalding memorial. 88924
Spalding's monster North American circus.
88865
Spangenberg, August Gottlieb. (42110), 88925-
88934
Spangenberg, Eveque de l'Eglise des Freres.
71551
Spangler, Edward. <u>defendant</u> 41180-41182,
41235, 48935
Spanglers and tinglers; or the rival belles.
36537
Spaniard, a lover of his country. <u>pseud.</u>
South America. 88940
Spaniard in London. <u>pseud.</u> Letters. 40586
Spaniard, in Philadelphia. <u>pseud.</u> Observations
on the commerce of Spain. <u>see</u> Yrujo
y Tacon, Carlos Martinez de, <u>Marques</u>
de Casa Yrujo.
Spaniards cruelty and treachery to the English.
88936
Spaniards defeat. 99259
Spaniards in Peru. 80341-80342
Spaniards in Peru, or the death of Rolla.
38282, 97573
Spaniards perpetuall designes to an universal
monarchy. 78379
Spaniens och Portugalls Besittningar uti
America. 88937
Spanier in Mexiko. 88196
Spanier in Peru. 27651, 86196-86197
Spanier in Peru, oder Rolla's Tod. 97673
Spanier in Peru und Mexiko. 96196
Spanische Reich in Amerika. 10241, 88938
Spanischen Colonien. 12254
Spanischen Minister. <u>pseud.</u> Schreibens.
(58531)

Spanish account of Drake's attack on Puerto
Rico. 47171
Spanish America and the United States. 88941
Spanish America. Observations of an America.
64904, note after 88938
Spanish America. Observations on the in-
structions. 48580, 56524, 63694,
88939, 97925
Spanish America. Observations on the
present state of Spanish America. 88940
Spanish America; or a descriptive, historical,
and geographical account. 6333
Spanish American Bondholders Committee.
see Committee of Spanish American
Bondholders.
Spanish American Republics and the cause of
their failure. 89962
Spanish bibliography. 70887
Spanish books collected by the Reverend Dr.
Robertson. 96333
Spanish colonie. 11287, 1st note after 39118
Spanish colonies. 101226
Spanish conquest of America. (31278), 31280
Spanish cowardice expos'd. 22595, (35988)
Spanish cruelty and injustice. 96359
Spanish cruelty display'd. 30525, 57125
Spanish declaration relative to Falkland's
Island. 14371
Spanish domination. 26793
Spanish empire in America. 10240
Spanish exile, a play, etc. (70054)
Spanish gentleman in Philadelphia, this present
year, 1800. pseud. Communications
concerning the agriculture and commerce
of America. see Yrujo y Tacon, Carlos
Martinez de, Marques de Casa Yrujo.
supposed author
Spanish heroine. 88942
Spanish hireling. 9829-9830, 56845, 2d note
after 87848
Spanish hireling detected. 9829-9830, 56845,
2d note after 87848
Spanish inquisition under nine directors.
31687
Spanish insolence corrected by English gravery.
88943
Spanish insult repented. 100719
Spanish laws. 86544
Spanish manifesto. 88944
Spanish memorial of the 4th June considered.
18342
Spanish Merchants. petitioners see Portugal,
Italian, and Spanish Merchants, London.
petitioners
Spanish novel. 20585, 31381
Spanish outrages on the United States. 88945
Spanish papers and other miscellanies. 35202
Spanish Pilgrim. pseud. see Pilgrim
Spaniard. pseud.
Spanish pilgrime. 96752
Spanish Pirates. defendants 93808
Spanish practices. 78364, 78379
Spanish pretensions confuted. 8122
Spanish pretensions fairly discussed. 18343
Spanish regulations for the gradual enfranchise-
ment of slaves. 79823
Spanish revolution, and other poems. 8815
Spanish revolution in Cuba. 88946
Spanish rule of trade to the West-Indies.
98782
Spanish Town, Jamaica. Citizens. respondents
35603, 47918, note before 98976
Spanish West Indies. Cuba and Porto Rico.
39213, (57345), 88947
Spanish wife. A play, in five acts. 77714,
85169

Spann, J. R. 84743
Spare hours. 88948
Sparhawk, Ebenezer. 88949-88950
Sparhawk, Edward V. reporter 88951
Sparhawk, Thomas S. 88952
Sparke, Michael. 88961, 1st note after 100478
Sparkle, Sophie. pseud. Sparkles from
Saratoga. see Hicks, Jennie E.
supposed author
Sparkles from Saratoga. 88962
Spark, Alexander, d. 1819. 88953-88960
Sparks, Jared, 1789-1866. 1039, 7058, 9364,
11896, 12820, 16876, 23256, 25439,
25491, (25494), 25507, (25538), 25606,
26517, (28601), (30724), (30750), 36343,
(39692), 41591, 42143, 43424, (49054),
(49063), 55562, 64099, 65299, 68548,
68621, 74736, 78779, 85344, 88963-
89014, 89744, 90291, 1st note after
96495, 97106, 97833, 98041, 98046,
101411, 101686, 101710, 101747,
101765-101767, 102208, 102563, 103161,
103696, 105646 see also Harvard
University. President.
Sparks, Jared, 1789-1866. supposed author
29269
Sparks, William Henry. 89015
Sparks from a smith's forge. 82382
Sparks from the anvil. 9454
Sparrey, Francis. 66686
Sparrow, Patrick J. 89016-89017
Sparrow, William. (36157)-36158, 89018-89025
Sparrowgrass papers. 17325, 89026
Sparrow's ball. 89027
Sparry, C. ed. (52016), 55560
Spartanburg, S. C. Spartanburg Female Col-
lege. see Spartanburg Female College,
Spartanburg, S. C.
Spartanburg District, S. C. Citizens.
petitioners 89028
Spartanburg Female College, Spartanburg, S. C.
81266
Spartanburg Female College, Spartanburg, S. C.
Board of Trustees. President. 81266
see also Bobo, S.
Spartanburg Female College. Inauguration of
the Spartanburg Female College, on the
22d of August, 1855. 81266
Spatig, I. E. 84970
Spaulding, Anna Marie. 89029
Spaulding, Elbridge Gerry 89030-89043
Spaulding, Henry George. 89044-89046
Spaulding, James. defendant 7328
Spaulding, John H. 32077, 89047-89048
Spaulding, Justin. 89049
Spaulding, Mary. 89050-89051
Spaulding, Matilda (Davidson) 89052
Spaulding, Melville C. 89053-89054
Spaulding, Samuel S. 89055
Spaulding, Willard. 89056
Spaulding story. (58153)
Spaulding's history of Crown Point, N. Y.
89055
Spavens, William. 89057
Spawn of Ixion. 16362, 89058
Spayth, Henry G. 89059-89060
Spazier, ------. tr. 4189
Speaker Colfax and the Union League Com-
mittee. 89060
Speaker of the Children's Primary Association.
85507
Speakers of the House of Representatives.
84796
Speakership. (78468)
Speaking dead. 26177

Speakman, C. 89061
Speakman, Thomas Henry. 89062-89063
Spear, Antoinette A. plaintiff 89081
Spear, Charles. 65712, 89064, 89065-89072
Spear, David. 89074
Spear, James E. plaintiff 89081
Spear, John M. 51521
Spear, John Murray. 89071, 89075-89080
Spear, Laura A. W. plaintiff 89081
Spear, Samuel S. 89082
Spear, Samuel Thayer. 89083-89103
Spear, William S. defendant 89104
Spear, William W. 89105-89107
Spear, Denison & Co. firm publishers 89108
Spear, Denison, & Co's Cleveland city directory. 89108
Spec. pseud. Line etchings. see Keim, Beverley R. and Weston, William.
Special Commissioners to Investigate Indian Affairs in Canada. see Canada. Special Commissioners, Appointed on the 8th of September, 1856, to Investigate Indian Affairs in Canada.
Special Committee Appointed by the Friends of Judge Yates in the City of New York. 94676
Special Committee Concerning the City Bank of New Haven. see New Haven, Conn. Special Committee Concerning the City Bank of New Haven.
Special Committee of Nine on the Condition of Our Church as Affected by the Condition of Our Country. see Protestant Episcopal Church in the U. S. A. Special Committee of Nine on the Condition of Our Church as Affected by the Condition of Our Country.
Special Committee on Government Contracts—What it has done. 15630
Special Committee on Volunteering, New York County. see New York County, New York. Special Committee on Volunteering.
Special Committee to Make Suitable Arrangements for Bringing On From Mexico the Bodies of the Officers of the New York Regiment of Volunteers, New York. see New York (City) Special Committee to Make Suitable Arrangements for Bringing On From Mexico the Bodies of the Officers of the New York Regiment of Volunteers, and to Prepare and Present Medals to the New York Regiment of Volunteers.
Special directions to visiters. 85090
Special exemptions from Confederate state taxes, in kind. 15413
Special interview between the President of the United States and Omar. 105251, 105253, 105257, 105260, 105262-105263
Special-Karte der Bittleren Brittischen Colonien. 39937
Special laws of the state of Minnesota. 49309
Special meeting of the Proprietors of Hollis Street Meeting House. 62779
Special meeting of the stockholders . . . held at Wilmington, Delaware. 62051
Special message delivered to the House of Representatives of the state of Iowa. 35038
Special message of Governor A. G. Curtin. 18019
Special message of Gov. Andrew, Jan. 3, 1866. 46125
Special message of Governor Cannon, January 12, 1864. 19389

Special message of Governor Cannon, July 28, 1864. 19389
Special message of Governor Cannon, March 3, 1863. 19389
Special message of Gov. Joseph E. Brown. 27110
Special message of Governor Kirkwood, May 21, '61. 35024
Special message of Governor Lucas. 57051
Special message of Gov. Vance and accompanying documents. 55692
Special message of Gov. William H. Smith. 84809
Special message of His Excellency James Y. Smith. 70609
Special message of His Excellency Robert K. Scott. 87562
Special message of the Governor of Iowa. 35039
Special message of the Governor of Rhode Island. 70670
Special message [of the Governor of Rhode Island.] January 31, 1865. 70602
Special message of the ought-to-be Governor of Wisconsin. 89110
Special message (relating to war expenses.) 70602
Special notice. 87129
Special relief. 76663, 86316
Special Relief Committee, Philadelphia, 1865. see Philadelphia. Special Relief Committee, 1865.
Special report concerning the rebel hospitals in Richmond. 71178
Special report. Confederate States of America. Richmond, Va., July 31, 1861. 15414
Special report of a reconnoissance of the route. 71939
Special report of Directors . . . [of the North Missouri Rail Road Company] to the Governor and Legislature. 55723
Special report of Dr. E. Emmons. 51980
Special report of Mr. Dilke. 20156
Special report of Mr. George Wallis. (54494)
Special report of Mr. Joseph Whitworth. (54494)
Special report of Professor Wilson. (54494)
Special report of Sir Charles Lyell. (54494)
Special report of the African Institution. 7891, (81914)
Special report of the Auditor [of Ohio] containing abstracts. 56881
Special report of the Auditor [of Ohio] in reply to a resolution. 56881
Special report of the Auditor of State. 57026
Special report of the Board of Trustees of the Brookline Public Library. 8261
Special report of the [Bristol and Clifton Ladies' Anti-slavery] Society. 8062
Special report of the Commissioner of Education. 21885
Special report of the Commissioner of Public Schools. 70565
Special report of the Committee on City Property. 62237
Special report of the Committee on Legacies and Trusts. 62268
Special report of the Directors of the African Institution. 95560
Special report of the Directors of the African Institution . . . on the 12th of April, 1815. 95656
Special report of the Insurance Commissioner. 54323
Special report of the Librarian of Congress. 89556

SPECIAL

Special report of the measures which have
been adopted. 74577
Special report of the Secretary of the Treas-
ury. 95051
Special report of the Soldiers' Aid Society,
Bridgeport, Conn. 7819, 86311
Special report of the State Treasurer [of
Missouri]. (49646)
Special report of the Sup't of Public Schools.
76075
Special report on common school libraries.
67805
Special report on prisons and prison discipline.
46126, 76251
Special report on savings banks. 37681
Special report on separate school provisions.
(74578)
Special report on the present state of edu-
cation. 36167
Special report on the swamp lands belonging
to the Literary Board. 55618
Special report on the systems and state of
popular education. (74579)
Special reports, nos. 5 and 9 [of the United
States Revenue Commission.] 70175
Special returns received from every county.
13794
Special rules and regulations for the govern-
ment of the Salem Police. 75746
Special services at St. Philip's Church,
Charleston. 87931
Speciall [sic] treatise of that kind of nobility.
(48248)
Special verdict, in the chase of Lewis Le
Guen. 39877
Special view. 72643
Special vocation of the Protestant Episcopal
Church. 82354
Specie basis; how attainable. 89111
Specie basis: who are to be benefited? 89112
Specie better than small bills. 29850
Specie circular. 102301
Specie currency. pseud. Free banks. 89113
Specie currency. The true interests of the
people. 32877, note after 89113
Specie payments and no contraction. 89114
Specie payments and the Republican Party.
89115
Specie payments. Speech of Hon. Carl Schurz.
78025
Specie standard. 89116
Specific resolutions of the Board of Directors.
97759
Specification and description of the anthracite
coal furnace. 33521, 93530
Specification and description of the work and
materials. 54679
Specification of material and labor required.
75747
Specification of the various post offices. 64511
Specifications and contract, for the new public
buildings. (62269)
Specifications for a new High School House.
17919
Specifications . . . for a state arsenal. 57850
Specifications for . . . an engine house. 52493
Specifications for the rotunda and dome. 80528
Specifications, material and labor. 89117
Specifications of the work and materials neces-
sary. 37152
Specifications of two patents. 89118
Specifications of work and materials. 85959
Specifico antivernereo nouamente scoperto.
2981
Specimen florae Americanae Septentrionalis
cryptogamicae. (78103)

Specimen inaugurale de coloniis. 100769
Specimen juridicum inaugurale, de conditione
servorum. 58509, 98992
Specimen iuridicum inaugurale, de iure, et
officiis dominorum in servos. 103882
Specimen materiae medicae Brasiliensis.
44997
Specimen of a geographical view. 3826
Specimen of the surprizing performance.
89119
Specimen of a true dissenting catechism.
12365, 40192
Specimen of book and job cuts belonging to
Joel Munsell. 89120
Specimen of divine truths. A catechism. 8912
Specimen of divine truths, fitted for the use of
those. (31250)
Specimen of Isaiah Thomas's printing types.
95414
Specimen of modern and light face printing
types and ornaments. 103487
Specimen of modern and light face printing
types and ornaments, cast at the Thames-
Street Letter Foundry of E. White.
103371
Specimen of modern printing types. 103488
Specimen of naked truth. 99249
Specimen of printing type. (73068)
Specimen of printing types, from the foundry
of E. White. 103373
Specimen of printing types and oranments cast.
102612
Specimen of printing types, by R. Starr & Co.
90560
Specimen of printing types, from the foundry
of E. White. 103372
Specimen of printing types in the foundry of
Nathan Lyman. 89122
Specimen of republican institutions. 89123
Specimen of southern devotion. 89124
Specimen of the harmony of wisdom and felicity
78701, 89125
Specimen of the unrelenting cruelty of papists
in France. 89126
Specimen panopliae sacrae militantis ecclesiae.
67652
Specimen towards a new and compleat plan.
89127
Specimen quadraginta diversarum linguarum et
dialectorum. 47384
Specimen taken out of the new version of the
Psalms of David. (66440)-(66441)
Specimens of American eloquence. 89128
Specimens of American eloquence, consisting of
choice selections. 89129
Specimens of American poetry. 37655
Specimens of foreign standard literature. 71523
Specimens of metropolitan literature. (61971)
Specimens of newspaper literature. (8909)
Specimens of the American poets. 21659,
89130
Specimens of the garblings of letters. 28097
Specimans of the mosses collected in British
North America. 20975
Specimens of the northern register. 31075
Specimens of the stone, iron and wood bridges.
(21158)
Specimens of xylographic engraving. 89131
Specimens; or leisure hours poetically em-
ployed. (80536)
Speckman, Charles. 89132
Spectacle nouveau. 89134
Spectacle; par M. D'Aubigny. 101895
Spectacles, Timothy. pseud. Poetry on
different subjects. see Foster, William
C.

Spectacles. No. V. 89135
Spectateur American. 44238, 44240, note after 89135
Spectator. pseud. (60457)
Spectator. pseud. see Hall, Nathan H.
Spectator. pseud. Authentic account of the reduction of Louisbourg. 42174
Spectator. pseud. Bishop Onderdonck's trial. see Richmond, James C. supposed author
Spectator. pseud. Comments on the memorial from Williams College. 89138, 1st note after 104432
Spectator. pseud. Concise view of the late proceedings. see Woolny, William W. and Wolcott, Oliver. incorrectly supposed author
Spectator. pseud. Enquiry respecting the capture of Washington. see Armstrong, John, 1758-1843. supposed author and Winder, R. H. supposed author
Spectator. pseud. Faithful narrative of the transactions. 89140
Spectator. pseud. Good devised. 89141
Spectator. pseud. Influence of the Ministry at Large in the city of Boston. see Bartol, C. A.
Spectator. pseud. Our West Indian islands. 89142
Spectator. pseud. Short account of the proceedings of the camp meeting. 89143
Spectator. pseud. Snoblace ball. 85463
Spectator. pseud. Treatise on the proceedings of a camp meeting. 89144, 96751
Spectator. pseud. Union must be preserved! 97813
Spectator. pseud. Unparalleled law case. 71274
Spectator. pseud. Vore Vestindiske Øer. 89145
Spectator (London) 19994, (25283), 75945, 89136, 92340, note before 105976, 105983-105984
Spectator (Newport, Ala.) Carrier. 84896 see also Smith, William Russell.
Spectator Company, New York. firm publishers 89146
Spectator of the past. pseud. Book of nullification. see Memminger, C. G.
Spectator of the scenes. pseud. Past and present. see Carroll, J.
Specter & Ca. firm printers 89133
Spectral visitants. 89147
Spectre of the forest. 89148
Speculatien ende concepten. 89149
Speculatie op 't concept van reglement op Brasil. 7552, 7637-7637, note after 89149, note after 102886
Speculation: a poem. 27552
Speculation and the price of wheat. 83899
Speculation, or making haste to be rich. 89150
Specvlations. 67588
Speculations concerning the mineral wealth of California. 15074
Speculative ideas on the probable consequences of an invasion. 89151
Speculator. 105057-105058
Speculi orbis declaratio. 99327
Speculi orbis succintiss. sed neq₃ poenitenda neq₃ inelegens declaratio. 42638, note after 89151
Specvlvm astrologiae. note after 99383C

Specvlvm conivgiorvm. 29331, note before 89152, 98919
Speculum conjugiorum com Indicibus locuplentissimis et appendix. (29332), note before 89152
Speculum for looking into the pamphlet. 52270, 89152
Speculum orbis terrarum. 36826
Specvlum orientalis occidentalisqve Indiae navigationvm. 89450
Spedding, James, 1808-1881. ed. 67550, 89153
Spedon, Andrew Learmont. 89154-89157
Speece, Conrad. 89158-89168
Speece, Frederick C. (51619), 89169
Speech about colleges. 41315
Speech . . . advocating the great Pacific railroad. (43186)
Speech against a bridge, &c. 90671
Speech against abandoning or suspending the prosecution. 3454
Speech . . . against ceding seventy thousand square miles. 4787
Speech . . . against further delays in the trial. 9615
Speech . . . against receiving, referring, or reporting on abolition petitions. 8432
Speech . . . against the admission of Kansas. 20693
Speech . . . against the annexation of Texas. 13536
Speech . . . against the bill to incorporate the subscribers. 8862
Speech, against the bill to repeal the law. 103869
Speech . . . against the extension of slave territory. 20368
[Speech] against the force bill. 9936
Speech . . . against the proposed tariff. 34750
Speech . . . against the repeal of the metropolitan act. 56209
Speech . . . against the repeal of the Missouri compromise. 4727
Speech . . . against the repeal of the Missouri prohibition. 46882
Speech . . . against the revolutionary movement of the anti-slavery party. (13707)
Speech against the suspending and dispensing prerogative. 95750
Speech . . . against the tariff. 30016
Speech, . . . against the war and arming Negroes. (47067)
Speech and action. 72140
Speech . . . and comments on the national era. 29641
[Speech and motion in Parliament on the state of His Majesty's government.] 89171
Speech and motions made in the House of Commons. (30691)
Speech and motions, made in the House of Commons on Monday. 89172
Speech . . . and the debate on his amendment. 18830
Speech . . . April 11, 1864. 59646
Speech . . . April 11, 1862. 55361
Speech . . . April 15, 1869. 78046
Speech, April 15th, 1740. 10227
Speech . . . April 5th and 12th, 1871. 64024
Speech . . . April 5, 1842. 47332
Speech . . . April 5, 1860. 42367
Speech . . . April 5, 1869. [By Godlove S. Orth.] 57711
Speech . . . April 5, 1869. [By Thomas A. Jenckes.] 35982

Speech . . . at the Democratic . . . Convention in Salem. 42083

Speech . . . at the Democratic demonstration at Poughkeepsie, N. Y. (33929)

Speech . . . at the Democratic Meeting at the Capitol. 64285

Speech . . . at the dinner at Noble's Inn. 13550

Speech at the dinner given in honor of George Peabody, Esq. 23271

Speech at the first anniversary of the New England Anti-slavery Society. 12695

Speech at the International Commercial Convention at Detroit. (33315)

Speech at the Lexington Dinner. 35348

Speech at the Lexington Mass Meeting 13th November, 1847. 13550

Speech . . . at the mass meeting at Millstone, New Jersey. 25009

Speech . . . at the Mechanics' Collation . . . Cincinnati. 13550

Speech . . . at the meeting in favor of the re-annexation of Texas. 35336

Speech . . . at the meeting of the county of Montreal. 58489

Speech . . . at the Melodeon. 62528

Speech . . . at the New England Anti-slavery Convention. note after (58767)

Speech . . . at the N. Y. Academy of Music. 9615

Speech at the ninth anniversary of the American Colonization Society. (24620)

Speech, at the opening of the special session, October 27, 1813. 52896

Speech . . . at the Philadelphia Manufacturers' Dinner. 41427

Speech at the proroguing the Assembly. 35633

Speech, at the public banquet to the Chinese Embassy. (73973)

Speech . . . at the public dinner, at Fowler's Garden. 13550

Speech . . . at the public dinner given him by the citizens of New York. 9235

Speech . . . at the Republican Convention at Kingston Plains. 3772

Speech . . . at the Republican Ratification Meeting. 62785

Speech . . . at the Salisbury Beach Gathering. 62528

Speech, at the thirteenth anniversary meeting of the British and Foreign Bible Society. 45465

Speech . . . at the Tremont Temple. 13536

Speech at the Union League Reading Room. 16396

Speech . . . at the Union Mass Meeting, Marietta Ohio. 8402

Speech . . . at the Union Meeting at New Albany. 51020

Speech . . . at the Union Meeting in New York. 20031

Speech . . . at the war meeting at Faneuil Hall. 29996

Speech . . . at the Worcester Disunion Convention. 62528

Speech . . . at Toledo, May 30, 1851. 12200

Speech . . . at Vauxhall Garden, Nashville. 4461

Speech . . . at Warren, Ohio, July 31, 1872. 26664

Speech . . . at Warren, O., Sept. 1, 1866. 26664

Speech . . . at Washington, January 11, 1871. 71265

Speech . . . at Watertown, August 1, 1855. 42367

Speech . . . at Weymouth, Mass. (6977)

Speech . . . at Worcester . . . September 8th. 3206

Speech . . . Aug. 11, 1841. (41341)

Speech . . . August 15, 1866. (39376)

Speech . . . Aug. 1, 1854. 33195

Speech . . . August 2, 1852. 29383

Speech . . . August 2, 1861. 33337

Speech . . . August 17. (32398)

Speech . . . August 7, 1856. 61038

Speech . . . Aug. 7, 1848. 32596

Speech . . . August [16], 1842. 9936

Speech . . . Aug. 6, 1850. 21110

Speech, Aug. 27, 1862. 23271

Speech . . . before a committee of the Senate of the state of New York. 37646

Speech . . . before a convention of the people of Ontario County, N. Y. (28283)

Speech before a court of judicature in Connecticut. 1604

Speech . . . before . . . a legislative committee, Boston. 12860

Speech . . . before an auxiliary of the American Colonization Society. 36162

Speech . . . before the American Anti-slavery Society, in New York. 26079

Speech before the American Anti-slavery Society, . . . New York. 31755

Speech . . . before the American Colonization Society. 13550

Speech . . . before the Brooklyn McLellan Central Association. (36269)

Speech . . . before the Charleston State Rights and Free Trade Association. 30446

Speech . . . before the citizens of New Bedford. 68563

Speech . . . before the Constitutional Union Club of Boston. 55784

Speech before the Court of General Sessions. (28231)

Speech . . . before the Court of Sessions in New York. 8466

Speech . . . before the Democratic Union Association. (17271)

Speech . . . before the Democratic Union Association, Sept. 29th, 1862. 8384

Speech . . . before the electors of the fourth congressional district. 18830

Speech . . . before the Freedom Convention, in Louisville. 20817

Speech . . . before the General Conference of the Methodist Protestant Church. 42968

Speech . . . before the Joint Legislative Committee on Mercantile Affairs and Insurance. 67908

Speech . . . before the Joint Legislative Committee on Towns. 12860

Speech . . . before the Joint Legislative Rail Road Committee. 12860

Speech . . . before the Law Department of the University of Albany. 13550

Speech . . . before the Legislature—June session, 1816. 63450

Speech . . . before the Legislature of New Hampshire. 63450

Speech . . . before the Legislature of Pennsylvania. 9615

Speech . . . before the "Marion Grand Club." 24262

Speech . . . before the Mass Convention at Jefferson City. 20817

Speech . . . before the Massachusetts Constitutional Convention. 28909

Speech delivered at Turners-Hall. 106097A

Speech delivered at various political gatherings. 85608

Speech: delivered August 1st, 1857. 70828

Speech delivered before the Democratic Club of Lockport. 13281

Speech . . . delivered before the Democratic Union Association. (18048)

Speech delivered before the Municipal Court of the city of Boston. 21293

Speech . . . delivered before the National Union Association. 20817

Speech delivered by an Indian Chief, in America. 89175

Speech delivered by an Indian Chief in reply to a sermon. 89174

Speech delivered by Captain O'Halloran. 56855

Speech delivered by Daniel Webster. 102304

Speech delivered by Ed. Graham Hayward. (31093)

Speech delivered by H. M. Brackenridge. 7173

Speech delivered by him at the dinner. 8852

Speech delivered by him, at Washington. 41618

Speech delivered by him in Aug. '95. 95583

Speech delivered by Hon. J. M. Ashley. (2189)

Speech delivered by Hon. Josiah Quincy, Senior. 67242

Speech delivered by Horace Binney. (5495)

Speech delivered by James Wilson. 104631

Speech delivered by John Adams. 3431, 78743

Speech delivered by John S. Tyson. 97651

Speech delivered by Mr. John Randolph, in a committee. 67845

Speech delivered by Mr. John Randolph, March 5, 1806. (67843)

Speech delivered by Mr. Lewis Louaillier. 42158

Speech delivered by Senor Romero. (73030)

Speech delivered by Smith D. Atkins. (2277)

Speech delivered by the Honorable Joseph Howe. 33313

Speech delivered by William H. Seward, at Dubuque. 79534, 79592

Speech delivered by William H. Seward at St. Paul. 79514, 79534

Speech . . . delivered . . . February 10, 1860. 24200

Speech delivered from the bench in the Court of Common Pleas. (60625), note after 89175

Speech . . . delivered in a Union Meeting. 20817

Speech delivered in Congress, on the 15th April, 1806. 67243

Speech delivered in Essex County. 56837

Speech delivered in Faneuil Hall. 2415

Speech delivered in Glasgow. 20710

Speech delivered in . . . Indianapolis. 27989

Speech delivered in . . . Manchester. 95504

Speech delivered in Parliament by a person of honour. 89176

Speech delivered . . . in . . . St. Louis. 20817

Speech . . . delivered in . . . St. Louis, January 28, 1863. 20817

Speech delivered (in substance) at the dinner. 20093

Speech delivered in the city of Washington. 6005

Speech delivered in the Constitutional Convention of Illinois, 1862. 1683

Speech delivered in the Constitutional Convention of Illinois, February 12, 1862. 1682

Speech delivered in the Convention, held at Danville, Ky. 5618, 70826-70827

Speech . . . delivered in the Convention of the Protestant Episcopal Church of the Diocese of New York. 21107

Speech delivered in the Court House Square, at South Bend. 14344

Speech . . . delivered in the House . . . February 3, 1866. 11895

Speech . . . delivered in the House . . . February 27, '64. 5741

Speech . . . delivered in the House . . . July 14, 1868. 9615

Speech . . . delivered in the House . . . May 14, 1850. 8348

Speech, delivered in the House of Assembly. 20049-20050, 84678C

Speech delivered in the House of Delegates of Virginia. 94462

Speech delivered in the House of Lords. 36026

Speech . . . delivered in the House of Representatives, April 18, 1872. 76947

Speech . . . delivered in the House of Representatives, February 14, 1862. 43631

Speech . . . delivered in the House of Representatives, Feb. 6, 1862. 21994

[Speech] delivered in the House of Representatives, February 20, 1826. 1910

Speech . . . delivered in the House of Representatives, February 24, 1868. 9615

[Speech] delivered in the House of Representatives, in Committee of the Whole, Jan. 23, 1833. 1821

Speech . . . delivered in the House of Representatives, January 7, 1862. 20331

Speech . . . delivered in the House of Representatives, January 28, 1864. 22047

Speech . . . delivered in the House of Representatives, January 29, 1869. 30005

[Speech] delivered in the House of Representatives, January 29, 1834. 1911

Speech . . . delivered in the House of Representatives, Jan. 23, 1861. 23090

Speech . . . delivered in the House of Representatives, July 1, 1864. 39317

Speech . . . delivered in the House of Representatives, July 23, 1856. 18894

Speech . . . delivered in the House of Representatives, June 15, 1864. 22047

Speech delivered in the House of Representatives, March 30, 1812. 67847

Speech delivered . . . in the House of Representatives, March 18, 20, & 26, 1834. 9235

Speech . . . delivered in the House of Representatives, March 23, 1862. (47166)

[Speech] delivered in the House of Representatives, May 4, 1864. (6977)

Speech . . . delivered in the House of Representatives of Maine. 28084

Speech . . . delivered in the House of Representatives of Massachusetts. 11117

Speech, delivered in the House of Representatives, on the 6th January, 1812. 104189

[Speech] delivered in the House of Representatives U. S. on the 30th of May, 1832. 1820

Speech delivered in the Legislative Assembly. 21292

SPEECH

Speech . . . delivered in the Missouri State
    Convention. 20817
Speech . . . delivered in the . . . Senate,
    February 9, 1864. (20611)
[Speech] delivered in the Senate May 2, 1856.
    4707
Speech . . . delivered in the Senate . . . May
    16, 18, and 20. 4787
Speech . . . delivered in the Senate of
    Massachusetts. 9333
Speech delivered in the Senate of the state of
    New-York. 99268
Speech delivered in the Senate of the United
    States. 1411
Speech . . . delivered in the Senate of the
    United States, May 12-13, 1856. 11349
Speech, delivered in the Senate of the United
    States, on Monday, 28th November, 1808.
    83986
Speech, delivered in the Senate of the United
    States, on the mission to Panama.
    103391
Speech . . . delivered in the state capital.
    (24742)
Speech delivered in the Town Hall. 19483
Speech . . . delivered in the United States
    Senate, January 21st, 1858. (20611)
Speech . . . delivered in the United States
    Senate, January 24, 1860. (20611)
Speech . . . delivered . . . January 18 and 31.
    29641
Speech delivered . . . Jan. 25, 1866. 22101
Speech delivered on the 1st of Oct. 1830.
    7091
Speech delivered on the Peace Convention in
    Washington. 27892
Speech . . . delivered to the Legislature of
    the state of New York. 13724
Speech . . . Democratic meeting, . . . Phila-
    delphia. 24258
Speech . . . 1858. 30834
Speech . . . 1842. (47975)
Speech . . . establishing a deliberate design.
    13550
Speech, &c. 60006
Speech, . . . in favor of religious freedom.
    35819
Speech . . . [February 18, 1840.] 33428
Speech . . . Feb. 18, 1871. (37630)
Speech . . . February 8, 1866. (38854)
Speech . . . February 11, 1869. 50791
Speech, February 11th, 1780. 100754
Speech, . . . Feb. 15, 1854. 47214
Speech . . . February 15, 1853. 29640
Speech . . . February 15, 1848. (55256)
Speech . . . February 15, 1866. 54968
Speech . . . February 5, 1849. (33184)
Speech . . . February 5, 1869. 36885
Speech . . . February 5, 1867. 14344
Speech . . . February 1, 1861. (39163)
Speech . . . February 14, 1867. 18450
Speech . . . Feb. 14, 1839. 8862
Speech, . . . Feb. 14, 1826. 43205
Speech . . . February 4 and 5, 1868. 36838
Speech . . . February 4, 1868. 36885
Speech . . . February 4, 1862. 50791
[Speech] . . . February 19, 1864. 8384
Speech, Feb. 8, 1811. 22708
Speech . . . February 9, 1870. 51020
Speech . . . February 9, 1865. 36885
Speech . . . February 17, 1858. 42369
Speech . . . February 17, 1852. (33929)
Speech . . . February 17, 1864. (17271)
Speech . . . February 17, 1866. (39376)

Speech . . . February 7, 1865. 36885
Speech . . . February 7th, . . . [1867.]
    (28601)
Speech . . . Feb. 7, 1837. (41257)
Speech . . . February 7th, 1820. 43487
Speech . . . Feb, 7th, 8th, and 13th, 1855.
    8346
Speech . . . February 16, 1854. 2697
Speech . . . February 16, 1860. 24078
Speech . . . Feb. 6, 1855. 6G959
Speech . . . February 6, 1861. (47166)
Speech . . . February 6, 1827. 30016
Speech . . . February 10, 1849. (31890)
Speech . . . February 10, 1868. 30386
Speech . . . Feb. 10, 1864. 22175
Speech . . . February 3 and 4, 1852. 24006
Speech . . . February 3, 1854. 12200
Speech Feb. 13 and 14, 1866. 31319
Speech . . . Feb. 13, 1855. 39918
Speech . . . Feb. 12 and 19, 1852. 61382
Speech . . . Feb. 12, 1840. 32407
Speech . . . February 12, 1839. (35848)
Speech . . . February 20, 1872. 24590
Speech . . . February 20th, 1867. 31319
Speech . . . Feb. 28, 1851. 44324
Speech . . . February 28th, 1865. 51634
Speech . . . Feb. 28, 1863. 61046
Speech . . . February 25, 1868. (39376)
Speech . . . February 25, 1869. (32882)
Speech . . . February 21, 1854. 28997
Speech . . . February 21, 1866. 8886
Speech . . . February 24, 1858. 27942
Speech . . . Feb. 24, 1854. (33929)
Speech . . . February 24, 1859. (28280)
Speech . . . February 24, 1852. 57656
Speech . . . February 24, 1849. 11990
Speech . . . February 24, 1860. 43631
Speech . . . February 24, 1868. 42815
Speech . . . February 27, 1850. 43489
Speech . . . February 27, 1866. 31735
Speech . . . February 27, 1862. 30568
Speech . . . Feb. 26, 1857. (33929)
Speech . . . Feb. 23, 1849. 44324
Speech . . . February 23, 1861. 27828
Speech for a new trial. 18324
Speech for abolition of Negro apprenticeship.
    33365
Speech for Connecticut. 9547
Speech from America, on suppressing the
    rebels. 89177
Speech from His Excellency, William W.
    Ellsworth. 22347
Speech from the chancel. (35840)
Speech from the "North American." (29009)
Speech . . . General Assembly of the Presby-
    terian Church. 42987
Speech . . . House . . . Jan. 21, 1861. 16985
Speech . . . House . . . May 19, 1854. (19020)
Speech . . . House of Representatives, January
    14, 1861. (17271)
Speech . . . House of Representatives, January
    19, 1848. (29856)
Speech . . . House of R., March 4, 1852.
    7671
Speech . . . House of Representatives, on the
    neutrality laws. 80849
Speech . . . Jan. 25, 1847. 61049
Speech in answer to Mr. Calhoun. 102311
Speech . . . in behalf of the University of
    Albany. 37396
Speech in behalf of the University of Nashville.
    41315
Speech in case of Kneedler vs. Lane. 34727
Speech . . . in . . . . Chicago. (39041)

Speech . . . in the House of Commons on the
6th of March, 1828. 104595
Speech . . . in the House of Commons on the
state of the colonies. 49865
Speech . . . in the House of Commons, on the
13th of May, 1841. 33779
Speech in the House of Commons, previous to
the repeal of the Stamp Act. 52052
Speech in the House of Commons upon the
second reading. 44709
Speech in the House of Delegates of Virginia.
8527
Speech . . . in the House of Delegates of
Virginia on the policy. (23926)
Speech in the Ho-se of L——ds in Eng——d.
63065
Speech in the House of Lords, June 27, 1814.
105679
Speech . . . in the House of Representatives,
April 20, 1864. 8378
Speech . . . in the House of Representatives,
February 8, 1861. 11300
Speech . . . in the House of Representatives,
February 5, 1869. 32877
Speech . . . in the House of Representatives,
February 5th, 1861. (80845)
Speech . . . in the House of Representatives,
February 5, 1862. 62817
Speech . . . in the House of Representatives,
February 14 and 16, 1857. 33080
Speech . . . in the House of Representatives,
February 4, 1862. 15630
Speech . . . in the House of Representatives,
February 20, 1854. 23329
Speech . . . in the House of Representatives,
February 20, 1865. 22047
Speech . . . in the House of Representatives,
Feb. 21, 1837. 62904
Speech in the House of Representatives, Indian-
apolis, Ind. 36279, 36885
Speech in the House of Representatives, Jan-
uary 16, 1865. 36280
Speech, in the House of Representatives . . .
Jan. 6. (41562)
Speech . . . in the House of Representatives,
Jan. 13, 1854. 23329
Speech . . . in the House of Representatives,
January 12, 1860. 11120
Speech . . . in the House of Representatives,
January 28, 1861. 42369
Speech . . . in the House of Representatives,
January 29, 1862. 29296
Speech . . . in the House of Representatives,
June 2, 1862. (5231)
Speech . . . in the House of Representatives,
June 25, 1852. 27329
Speech, in the House of Representatives, March
11, 1850. 90434
Speech . . . in the House of Representatives,
March 25, 1858. 28997
Speech . . . in the House of Representatives,
May 8, 1854. 42847
Speech . . . in the House of Representatives,
May 17, 1854. 47214
Speech . . . in the House of Representatives,
May 27, 1852. 27892
Speech . . . in the House of Representatives,
. . . May 23, 1862. 36885
Speech . . . in the House of Representatives
of Kentucky. 47974
Speech . . . in the House of Representatives
of Kentucky, upon the bill. 13534
Speech . . . in the House of Representatives
of Massachusetts, March 19, 1836.
(28387)

Speech in the House of Representatives, of
the 3d and 11th of January, 1853.
90870
Speech in the House of Representatives of
the United States, January 19, 1809.
67225
Speech in the House of Representatives, of
the United States, on foreign relations.
26605
Speech, in the House of Representatives of
the United States. On the report of
the Committee of Foreign Relations.
67224
Speech in the House of Representatives, on
Mr. Gregg's bill. 67830
Speech . . . in the House of Representatives
on the bill. 18846
Speech in the House of Representatives on
the embargo. 26605
Speech . . . in the House of Representatives
. . . on the Indian annuity bill. (23282)
Speech . . . in the House of Representatives,
on the Mexican war. 14360
Speech . . . in the House of Representatives,
Thursday, December 12, 1861. (16217)
Speech . . . in the House . . . on the 8th day
of January, 1813. 13545
Speech . . . in the House . . . on the judiciary.
18496
Speech . . . in the Indiana Senate Chamber.
33586
Speech in the Legislative Assembly on the
financial condition of the province.
31932
Speech in the Legislative Council, 7 March,
1828. 74564
Speech in the Legislature of New-York. 105795
Speech in the Lower House by Sir E. Cicell
Colonell. 78379
Speech . . . in the Massachusetts House of
Representatives. 9133
Speech . . . in the Massachusetts Senate . . .
June 9th. 32474
Speech . . . in the Missouri House of Repre-
sentatives. 8453
Speech in the New York Diocesan Convention.
35837
Speech . . . in the Peace Conference at Wash-
ington. 20514
Speech in the Peace Convention, New York.
9437
Speech . . . in the Senate . . . April 8, 1850.
4787
Speech . . . in the Senate . . . April 15, 1870.
64024
Speech . . . in the . . . Senate, April 19, 1869.
11887
Speech . . . in the Senate . . . April 23, 1856.
33195
Speech . . . in the Senate . . . December 18,
19, 1851. 25020
Speech, in the Senate . . . December 1, 1808.
62659
Speech . . . in the Senate . . . December 10,
1867. 20817
Speech . . . in the Senate . . . December 12,
1859. 36170
Speech in the Senate, Dec 21 [1808.] 31884
Speech . . . in the Senate . . . Dec. 23, 1851.
33195
Speech . . . in the Senate . . . 8th of March,
1853. (13576)
Speech . . . in the Senate, . . . Feb. 8, 1854.
23271
Speech . . . in the Senate . . . February 11
and 20, 1868. 18818

SPEECH

Speech . . . in the Senate . . . February 14, 1860. 29641
Speech . . . in the Senate . . . February 7, 1849. 4787
Speech . . . in the Senate . . . February 16, 1848. 25020
Speech . . . in the Senate . . . February 10, 1847. 11349
Speech . . . in the Senate . . . February 20, 1860. 13266
Speech . . . in the Senate, Feb. 25, 1868. 59139
Speech . . . in the Senate . . . Feb. 25, 1833. 13550
Speech, in the Senate . . . February 21, 1809. 31884
Speech . . . in the Senate . . . February 23, 1859. 20693
Speech . . . in the Senate . . . January 9, 1860. 20368
Speech . . . in the Senate . . . January 6, 1829. 4787
Speech . . . in the Senate . . . January 10 and 11, 1860. 28533
Speech . . . in the Senate, January 10, 1861. 18837
Speech . . . in the Senate, January 3, 1861. 20693
Speech . . . in the Senate . . . January 31, 1868. 33337
Speech . . . in the Senate . . . January 12 and 16, 1854. (14 (13576)
Speech . . . in the Senate . . . January 29, 1868. 63940
Speech . . . in the Senate . . . January 24, 1870. 33335
Speech . . . in the Senate . . . January 22, 1869. (20611)
Speech . . . in the Senate . . . January 26, 1848. 20341
Speech . . . in the Senate . . . January 23, 1868. (20611)
Speech . . . in the Senate . . . July 15, 1854. 33195
Speech . . . in the Senate . . . July 10, 1848. (36269)
Speech . . . in the Senate . . . July 13, 1846. 40792
Speech . . . in the Senate, July 20th, 1861. (39163)
Speech . . . in the Senate . . . June 8, 1866. 31319
Speech . . . in the Senate . . . June 24, 1862. 20368
Speech . . . in the Senate . . . June 22 and 23, 1870. 33253
Speech . . . in the Senate . . . June 27, 1864, 17221
Speech . . . in the Senate . . . March 15, 1858. 13266
Speech . . . in the Senate, . . . March 5th, 1866. 63940
Speech . . . in the Senate, March 4, 1868. 31319
Speech . . . in the Senate . . . March 4, 1862. 17221
[Speech] . . . in the Senate, . . . March 6, 1840. 8862
Speech . . . in the Senate . . . March 3 and 4, 1852. 20493
Speech . . . in the Senate . . . March 31, 1871. 64024
Speech . . . in the Senate . . . March 12-13, 1856. 8437
Speech . . . in the Senate . . . March 29, 1848. 20341

Speech . . . in the . . . Senate, March 23 & 24, 1864. 33253
Speech in the Senate . . . of Hon. Thos. L. Clingman. (13707)
Speech . . . in the Senate of Maryland. 24398
Speech . . . in the Senate of Michigan. 23691
Speech . . . in the Senate of . . . New York, on repeal of laws. (14282)
Speech in the Senate of New-York, third and fourth of February, 1832. (47170)
Speech . . . in the Senate of the state of New York. 13724
Speech . . . in the Senate of the United States, April 30, 1834. 13550
Speech in the Senate of the United States, asking leave. 8397
Speech . . . in the Senate of the United States, February 23d, 1855. 27409
Speech in the Senate of the United States, Friday, December 2, 1803. 96420
Speech . . . in the Senate of the United States, Jan. 20, 1832. 4787
Speech . . . in the Senate of the United States, January 28, 1868. 25828
Speech . . . in the Senate of the United States . . . July 16, 1862. 11887
Speech . . . in the Senate of the United States, March 7, 1878. 76947
Speech . . . in the Senate of the United States, March 20, 21, and 22, 1861. 4030
Speech . . . in the Senate of the United States, March 26, 1850. 12200
Speech . . . in the Senate of the United States, May 2, 1876. 76947
Speech, in the Senate of the United States, on Mr. Hillhouse's resolution. 103450
Speech in the Senate of the United States, on the bill. 103449
Speech . . . in the Senate of the United States, . . . on the mission to Panama. 4787
Speech in the Senate of the United States, on the President's veto. 102279-102280
Speech . . . in the Senate of the United States, on the subject of the abolition petitions. 13550
Speech . . . in the Senate on establishing a government. 20031
Speech . . . in the Senate . . . on the bill for renewing the charter. 27376
Speech . . . in the Senate . . . on the mission to Panama, March, 1826. (32611)
Speech . . . in the Senate . . . on the mission to Panama, March 13, 1826. 20019
Speech . . . in the Senate . . . on the tariff of 1846. 18320
Speech. In the Senate, Wednesday, May 26th, 1852. 93676
Speech in the U. S. Senate, February 21, 1870. 64249
Speech . . . in the Virginia State Convention. 10923
Speech . . . in the Whig National Convention. 9373
Speech . . . in the Wisconsin Legislature. 82587
Speech . . . in vindication of Gen. McClellan. (17271)
Speech . . . in vindication of history and the constitution. 55858
Speech in vindication of Republican principles. 85609
Speech, . . . in which he gives a sketch of the political history. 18818
Speech, . . . independent treasury bill. (24915)
Speech . . . installing President Hall. 42959

Speech . . . June 3, 1862. [By William D. Kelley.] (37270)

Speech . . . June 3, 1862, on the bill. 22175

Speech . . . June 30, 1848. 44324

Speech . . . June 30, 1846. (36020)

Speech . . . June 30, 1862. (22378)

Speech . . . June 25, 1846. (33416)

Speech . . . June 25th, for a royal commission on the colonies. 49865

Speech . . . June 24, 1846. 30400

Speech . . . June 29, 1846. 37117

Speech . . . June 22d, 1859. 30386

Speech . . . June 22, 1842. 62621

Speech . . . June 23, 1862. 30568

Speech . . . Lansing, . . . January 25, 1864. 47053

Speech lately delivered to the Senate. (29314), 81981

Speech made by a black of Guardaloupe [sic]. 40304

Speech made by Gerrit Smith. 82670

Speech . . . made in the Senate. 14360

Speech made to Her Majesty. 89182

Speech made to the National Assembly of France. 44134

Speech made to the National Assembly, the 3d of November, 1791. 58932, note after 75175

Speech, made unto the inhabitants of Boston. (46541), note after 93885

Speech . . . March 18, 1840. 37818

Speech . . . March 18, 1842. (37389)

Speech . . . March 18, 1824. (37835)

Speech . . . March 11, 1852, . . . [by Edward Chauncey Marshall.] 44770

Speech . . . March 11, 1852, on the homestead bill. 44781

Speech . . . March 11, 1868. 22175

Speech . . . March 11, 1862. 31703

Speech . . . March 15, 1842. 49022

Speech . . . March 5, 1850. 9773

Speech . . . March 5, 1852. 10261

Speech . . . March 5, 1870. (39376)

Speech . . . March 5, 1863. (2723)

Speech . . . March 9, 1859. (32591)

Speech . . . March 9, 1842. 43656

Speech . . . March 9th, 1864. 43079

Speech . . . March 17, 1858. (17556)

Speech . . . March 7, 1860. 50463

Speech . . . March 7, 1868. 42815

Speech . . . March 7, 1866. 37272

Speech . . . March 7, 1836. 33428

Speech . . . March 16, 1854. 27329

Speech . . . March 16, 1866. 42815

Speech . . . March 6, 1868. 36885

Speech . . . March 10, 1870. [By Daniel J. Morrell.] 50780

Speech . . . March 10, 1870. [By John A. Logan.] 41801

Speech . . . March 10, 1866. [By Godlove S. Orth.] 57711

Speech . . . March 10, 1866. [By Sidney T. Holmes.] 32624

Speech . . . March 3, 1854. On the bill. 4461

Speech . . . March 3, 1854, on the Kansas and Nebraska Bill. 55506

Speech . . . March 3, 1871. 23873

Speech . . . March 3, 1868. 50791

Speech . . . March 3, 1869. 36615

Speech . . . March 3, 1863. 59646

Speech . . . March 13 and 14, 1856. 11349

Speech . . . March 13, 1856. (40238)

Speech . . . March 30, 1854. 42847

Speech . . . March 30, 1852. 28997

Speech . . . March 12, 1862. 50791

Speech . . . March 20, 1856. (35699)

Speech . . . Mar. 28, 1842. 68121

Speech . . . March 28, 1870. (17271)

Speech . . . March 28, 1868. 22101

Speech . . . March 25, 1850. (30527)

Speech . . . March 25, 1870. 37272

Speech . . . March 21, 1842. 33968

Speech . . . March 24, 1858. (28280)

Speech . . . March 24, 1866. 51634

Speech . . . March 29, 1869. 18818

Speech . . . March 22 and 23, 1871. 78314

Speech . . . March 22, 1858. 4030

Speech . . . March 27, 1868. (29841)

Speech . . . March 27, 1866. 58186

Speech . . . March 26, 1858. 50817

Speech . . . March 26, 1864. 50463

Speech . . . March 23, 1858. (33285)

Speech . . . March 23, 1854. (49124)

Speech . . . March 23, 1864. 43079

Speech . . . May, 1842. 29383

Speech . . . May 18, 1854. (40238)

Speech . . . May 18, 1860. 24078

Speech . . . May 1, 1860. 31703

Speech . . . May 14, 1850. 36885

Speech . . . May 14th, 1858. 44138

Speech . . . May 14, 1868. 35982

Speech . . . May 4, 1854. 42847

Speech . . . May 19th, 1862. (34047)

Speech . . . May 9 and 10, 1832. 4140

Speech . . . May 9, 1854. (39163)

Speech . . . May 9, 1870. 50791

Speech . . . May 16, 1838. 36573

Speech . . . May 10, 1854. [By Galusha A. Grow.] 28997

Speech . . . May 10, 1854. [By Thomas D. Eliot.] 22175

Speech . . . May 10, 1866. 4325

Speech . . . May 10, 1830. 9235

Speech . . . May 10, 1832. (31832)

Speech . . . May 3, 1852. (74285)

Speech . . . May 3, 1860. 27828

Speech . . . May 30 and 31, 1842. 43441

Speech . . . May 31, 1842. 33968

Speech . . . May 12, 1864. 36885

Speech . . . May 28, 1868. 43119

Speech . . . May 28, 1869. (28601)

Speech . . . May 21, 1850. 37791

Speech . . . May 24, 1860. 55361

Speech . . . May 29, 1867. 48987

Speech, May 27, 1840. 2268

Speech . . . May 26, 1846. (33184)

Speech . . . May 26, 1862. [By Alfred Ely.] (22378)

Speech . . . May 26, 1862. [By J. A. Gurley.] 29293

Speech . . . May 23, 1842. 29925

Speech . . . Monday, August 12, 1850. 11327

Speech . . . Nebraska and Kansas, April 4, 1854. (13707)

Speech . . . Nebraska and Kansas, March 23, 1864. 7671

Speech never intended to be spoken. 89183

Speech . . . New York City railroads. 39349

Speech . . . N. Y. Senate, June 2, 1853. 16362

Speech . . . New York Senate, on the bill to prevent illegal voting. 80849

Speech . . . 19th August, 1841. 13550

Speech . . . 19th May, 1826. (33076)

Speech . . . Norwich . . . 28th January, 1824. (29314)

Speech . . . November, 1864. 30022

Speech . . . Nov. 28, 1863. 31907

Speech . . . October 5, 1854. 44324

Speech . . . October 5th, 1860. 27286

Speech . . . October 4, 1864. 37271

Speech . . . October 17, 1856. 29890

Speech . . . October 3, 1864. 37271

Speech, October 12, 1859. 73977
Speech, Oct. 21, 1859. 73977
Speech . . . Oct. 21, 1853. 29890
Speech of a Creek-Indians, [sic] against the immoderate use of spirituous liquors. 17463, 84624, 84671, 84673
Speech of a General Officer in the House of Commons. 9254, 89184
Speech of A. Harding of Kentucky. 30329
Speech of a member of the General Assembly of New York. 8771
Speech of A. R. Sollers. 86503
Speech of a Right Honourable gentleman. 28767, (28772)
Speech of a Scots weaver. 89185
Speech of A. X. Parker. 58648
Speech of Aaron F. Perry. 61024
Speech of Abraham Lincoln. 41160
Speech of Abraham Van Vechten. 98581
Speech of Albert Gallatin, a representative. (26395)
Speech of Albert Gallatin, delivered in the House. 26396
Speech of Albert Smith. 82321
Speech of Alexander H. Stevens. 34484
Speech of Alex. Ramsey. 67724
Speech of Alexander Smyth, of Virginia. 85191
Speech of Alfred C. Hills. (31906)
Speech of Allen C. Spooner. 89600
Speech of Andrew Stewart. 91638
Speech of Anson Herrick. 31573
Speech of Appleton P. Clark. 13251
Speech of . . . April 19, 1864. 8348
Speech of Arnold Naudain. 52058
Speech of Aylett Buckner. 8940
Speech of B. H. Hill. 31808
Speech of Barkley Martin. (44856)
Speech of Benjamin Barstow. 3696
Speech of Benjamin G. Shields. (80462)
Speech of Benjamin H. Brewster. 7772
Speech of Benjamin Jones. 36458
Speech of Brig. Gen. Jas. S. Brisbin. 8011
Speech of C. Durkee. 21433
Speech of C. G. Baylor. 4072
Speech of C. H. Peaslee. 59470
Speech of C. Sitgreaves. 81471
Speech of Caleb B. Smith, of Indiana. 82366
Speech of Caleb B. Smith . . . on the veto power. 82365
Speech of Capt. R. F. Stockton, at the great Tyler Meeting. 91907
Speech of Capt. R. F. Stockton, delivered at the great Democratic Meeting. 91905
Speech of Capt. R. F. Stockton, in defence of the administration. 91906
Speech of Carl Schurz at Cooper Institute. (78044)
Speech of Carl Schurz, at the Milwaukee Ratification Meeting. 78038
Speech of Carl Schurz, delivered at Verandah Hall. 78043
Speech of Carl Schurz, delivered in Brooklyn. 78045
Speech of Carl Schurz, of Wisconsin, in Hampden Hall. 78027-78028
Speech of Carroll Spence. 89277
Speech of Caunonicus. 39187
Speech of Charles A. Sumner. 93690
Speech of Charles Ballance. (2949)
Speech of Charles C. Leigh. 39919
Speech of Charles Chauncey. 12302
Speech of Charles Durkee. 21433
Speech of Charles E. Clarke. 13398
Speech of Charles E. Haynes. 31048
Speech of Charles Francis Adams. 186
Speech of . . . Charles G. Ferris. 24187

Speech of Charles Hale. 29618
Speech of Charles Marsh. 44726
Speech of Charles Naylor. 52136
Speech of Charles O'Connor. 13291, 56660
Speech of Charles P. Johnson. 36200
Speech of Charles R. Buckalew. 8886
Speech of Chauncy F. Cleveland. 13653
Speech of Chesselden Ellis. 22294
Speech of Clement Dorsey. 20656
Speech of Col. A. O. Brewster. 7767
Speech of Col. Benj. Faneuil Hunt. 33839
Speech of Col. C. C. Crowe. 17690
Speech of Col. Curtis M. Jacobs. 35498
Speech of Colonel David Branson. (25261)
Speech of Col. James Page. 61883
Speech of Col. John C. Holland. 32508
Speech of Col. John H. Savage. 77241
Speech of Col. Joseph A. Nunez. 56318
Speech of Colonel T. C. H. Smith. 84387
Speech of Col. T. C. Macdowell. 43199
Speech of Col. W. R. Morrison. 50899
Speech of Colonel White. 103430
Speech of Com. Jesse Duncal Elliott. 22270
Speech of Commodore Robert F. Stockton. 91908
Speech of Commodore Stockton. 91909
Speech of . . . Cornelius Cole. 14284
Speech of Counsellor Sampson. (75956)
Speech of D. Reddington. (68487)
Speech of Daniel H. London. 41851
Speech of Daniel S. Dickinson. 54130
Speech of Daniel Webster, at the great mass meeting. 102315
Speech of Daniel Webster, in re[p]ly to Mr. Hayne. 102272
Speech of Daniel Webster, on the subject of the public lands. 102271
Speech of David Dudley Field. 24274
Speech of David S. Kaufman. 37117
Speech of death to Levi Ames. 89186
Speech of Dr. Alexander M. Ross. (73339)
Speech of Dr. Goodwin. (27935)
Speech of Dr. J. Augustine Smith. 82919
Speech of Dr. Lushington. (69713)
Speech of . . . E. C. Baker. 2819
Speech of E. S. Hamlin. 30074
Speech of Earl Aberdeen. 50859
Speech of Edmund Burke, Esq. At the Guildhall, in Bristol. 9298
Speech of Edmund Burke, Esq., on American taxation. 9295
Speech of Edmund Burke, Esq; on moving his resolutions. 9296
Speech of Edmund Burke, Esq.; spoken in the House of Commons. 80039
Speech of Edmund Burke . . . on presenting to the House of Commons. 9300
Speech of Edmund G. Ross. 73351
Speech of Edmund W. Hubard. (33416)
Speech of Edward L. Pierce. 62751
Speech of Edward Stanly, of North Carolina, defending the Whig Party. 90333
Speech of Edw. Stanly, of North Carolina, establishing proofs. 90331
Speech of Edward Stanly, of N. Carolina, exposing the causes. 90332
Speech of Edward Stanly, of North Carolina, in reply to Dr. Duncan. 90334
Speech of Eli K. Price, . . . in the Senate of Pennsylvania, April 6th and 7th, 1855. 65433
Speech of Eli K. Price, in the Senate of Pennsylvania, March 21, 1855. 65432
Speech of emancipation in colonies. 2205
Speech of Emerson Etheridge. 23090
Speech of Emory Washburn. 101519

Speech of Hon. E. M. Chamberlain. (11779)

Speech of Hon. E. S. Dargan. 18543

Speech of Hon. E. W. Chastain. 12223

Speech of Hon. Ebenezer Dumont. (21206)

Speech of Hon. Ebon C. Ingersoll. 34737

Speech of Hon. Edgar Cowan. 17221

Speech of Hon. Edmund G. Ross, of Kansas, in the Senate of the United States, May 5, 1870. 73350

Speech of Hon. Edmund G. Ross, of Kansas, in the United States Senate, December 20, 1866. 73349

Speech of Hon. Edmund G. Ross, of Kansas, in the United States Senate, March 24, 1869. 73352

Speech of Hon. Edson B. Olds. (57165)

Speech of Hon. Edward H. Rollins. 72853

Speech of Hon. Edward Joy Morris. 50817

Speech of Hon. Edward Stanly. 90335

Speech of Hon. Edwards Pierrepont. 62785

Speech of Hon. Eli S. Shorter. 80707

Speech of Hon. Eli Saulsbury. 77164

Speech of Hon. Elijah Babbitt, of Penn. 2569

Speech of Hon. Elijah Babbitt, of Pennsylvania. 2570

Speech of Hon. Elisha D. Standiford. 90163

Speech of Hon. Elisha R. Potter . . . March 14, 1863. (64637)

Speech of Hon. Elisha R. Potter, . . . upon the resolution. 64636

Speech of Hon. Ellis H. Roberts, of New York delivered in the House. 71886

Speech of Hon. Ellis H. Roberts, of New York, in the House. 71887

Speech of Hon. Emory B. Pottle. 64675

Speech of Hon. Ezra Cornell. 16796

Speech of Hon. F. A. Pike. 62817

Speech of Hon. F. C. Beaman. 4115

Speech of Hon. F. M. Kellogg. 37292

Speech of Hon. F. P. Blair, Jr., Jan 14, 1858. 79524

Speech of Hon. F. P. Blair, Jr. . . . on Fremont's defence. (5740)

Speech of Hon. F. P. Stanton, and letter of Governor Walker. 90411

Speech of Hon. F. P. Stanton, of Tennessee, delivered in the House. 90417

Speech of Hon. F. P. Stanton, of Tennessee, in the House of Representatives, February 13, 1850. 90408

Speech of Hon. F. P. Stanton, of Tennessee, in the House of Representatives, January 10, 1848. 90413

Speech of Hon. F. P. Stanton, of Tennessee, in the House of Representatives, March 14, 1848. 90427

Speech of Hon. F. P. Stanton, of Tennessee, in the House of Representatives, Thursday, July 2, 1848. 90419

Speech of Hon. F. P. Stanton, of Tennessee, in the House of Representatives, Tuesday, September 19, 1850. 90418

Speech of Hon. F. P. Stanton, of Tennessee, on improvements in the navy. 90420

Speech of Hon. Francis O. J. Smith, delivered at the New City Hall. 82567

Speech of Hon. Francis O. J. Smith, of Westbrook. 82568

Speech of Hon. Francis O. J. Smith to the Republican State Convention. (82570)

Speech of Hon. Frank C. Le Blond. 39598

Speech of Hon. Franklin Pierce. 62713

Speech of Hon. Frederick A. Sawyer, of South Carolina, delivered in the Senate. (77307)

Speech of Hon. Frederick A. Sawyer, of South Carolina, in the Senate. 77305

Speech of Hon. Frederick P. Stanton, late Acting Governor of Kansas. 90410

Speech of Hon. Frederick P. Stanton, of Tennessee. 90421

Speech of Hon. G. A. Grow, . . . February 29, 1860. (28994)

Speech of Hon. G. A. Grow, of Pennsylvania, in the House . . . June 30, 1856. 28993

Speech of Hon. G. A. Grow, of Pennsylvania, in the House of Representatives, February 29, 1860. 28995

Speech of Hon. G. A. Simmons, of New York, in the House of Representatives, July 11, 1856. 81157

Speech of Hon. G. A. Simmons, of New York, . . . in the House of Representatives, May 10, 1854. (81159)

Speech of Hon. G. A. Starkweather. 90533

Speech of Hon. G. Porter. 64250

Speech of Hon. G. R. Riddle. 71270

Speech of Hon. G. S. Houston. 33182

Speech of Hon. G. W. Dunlap. 21294

Speech of Hon. G. W. Jones. 36504

Speech of Hon. G. W. Scofield. 78160

Speech of Hon. George A. Brandreth. 7402

Speech of Hon. George E. Badger. 2697

Speech of Hon. George E. Spencer, of Alabama, delivered in the Senate of the United States, February 19, 1870. 89322

Speech of Hon. George E. Spencer, of Alabama, delivered in the Senate of the United States, March 17, 1870. 89317

Speech of Hon. George E. Spencer, of Alabama, in the Senate of the United States, June 28, 1870. 89321

Speech of Hon. George E. Spencer, of Alabama, in the Senate of the United States, May 20, 1870. 89319

Speech of Hon. George E. Spencer, of Alabama, in the Senate of the United States, May 20, 1872. 89320

Speech of Hon. George E. Spencer of Alabama, in the Senate of the United States, Tuesday, July 7, 1870. 89318

Speech of Hon. George F. Edmunds. 21871

Speech of Hon. George F. Miller. (49018)

Speech of Hon. George Fries. (25960)

Speech of Hon. George H. Pendleton. 59646

Speech of Hon. George I. Post. 64455

Speech of Hon. George P. Fisher. (24466)

Speech of Hon. George R. Davis. 18822

Speech of Hon. George R. Latham. 39159

Speech of Hon. George R. Robbins. 71817

Speech of Hon. George S. Boutwell. 9615

Speech of Hon. Geo. S. Fisher. 24467

Speech of Hon. George W. Julian . . . February 18th, 1863. 36885

Speech of Hon. George W. Julian . . . in the House of Representatives. 36884

Speech of Hon. Geo. W. Smyth. 85231

Speech of Hon. Gerrit Smith. (82595)

Speech of Hon. Glenni W. Scofield . . . in the House of Representatives, January 10, 1866. 78163

Speech of Hon. Glenni W. Scofield . . . in the House of Representatives, July 14, 1868. 78158

Speech of Hon. Glenni W. Scofield, of Pennsylvania. 78161

Speech of Hon. Glenni W. Scofield, of Pennsylvania, in the House of Representatives, April 28, 1866. 78159

Speech of Hon. John Sherman . . . on representation of southern states. 80388

Speech of Hon. John Sherman . . . on taxation of bank bills. 80385

Speech of Hon. John Sherman . . . on the general policy of the government. 80387

Speech of Hon. John Slidell, of Louisiana, delivered in the Senate of the United States, March 31, 1856. 82138

Speech of Hon. John Slidell, of Louisiana, in the Senate of the United States, May 1, 1854. (82141)

Speech of Hon. John Slidell, of Louisiana, on the neutrality laws. 82137

Speech of Hon. John V. L. Pruyn. (66414)

Speech of Hon. John W. Chandler. 11895

Speech of Hon. John W. Menzies. 47877

Speech of Hon. John W. Stebbins. 91027

Speech of Hon. John Wilkes. 105006

Speech of Hon. John Z. Goodrich. 27890

Speech of Hon. Jonas Martin. 44891

Speech of Hon. Joseph Bailey. 2742

Speech of Hon. Joseph Cable. (9797)

Speech of . . . Hon. Joseph J. McDowell. 43197

Speech of Hon. Joseph M. Blake. 5785

Speech of Hon. Joseph M. Root. 73133

Speech of Hon. Joseph P. Hoge. 32430

Speech of Hon. Joseph Segar, of . . . Virginia. 78894

Speech of Hon. Joseph Segar, on re-construction. (78890)

Speech of Hon. Joseph W. Jackson. 35444

Speech of Hon. Joseph W. McClurg. 43079

Speech of Hon. Justin S. Morrill, . . . April 23, 1860. 50791

Speech of Hon. Justin S. Morrill, . . . February 6, 1857. 50791

Speech of Hon. Justin S. Morill, January 25, 1865. 50790

Speech of Hon. Justin S. Morrill, . . . June 28, 1866. 50791

Speech of Hon. Kinsley S. Bingham. 5454

Speech of Hon. Kinsley S. Bingham, of Michigan. 5453

Speech of Hon. L. B. Peck. 59488

Speech of Hon. L. F. S. Foster. 25252

Speech of Hon. L. J. Gartrell. (26714)

Speech of Hon. L. M. Cox. 17263

Speech of Hon. L. M. Morrill. . . . On the confiscation of property. . . . March 5, 1862. 50792

Speech of Hon. L. M. Morrill. . . . On the confiscation of property. . . . May 1, 1862. 50792

Speech of Hon. L. Severance. (79381)

Speech of Hon. L. W. Powell, of Kentucky. 64756

Speech of Hon. L. W. Powell . . . on the bill. 64759

Speech of Hon. Lawrence M. Keitt. 37245

Speech of Hon. Lazarus W. Powell, . . . on executive usurpation. 64757

Speech of Hon. Lazarus W. Powell on the state of the union. 64758

Speech of Hon. Leonard Myers. 51634

Speech of Hon. Lewis B. Gunckell. 29279

Speech of Hon. Lewis Cass. 11349

Speech of Hon. Lewis D. Campbell. 10261

Speech of Hon. Lewis Selye. (79039)

Speech of Hon. Lewis Steenrod. 91173

Speech of Hon. Lewis W. Ross. 73395

Speech of Hon. Linus B. Comins, in defence of the financial institutions. (14951)

Speech of Hon. Linus B. Comins, of Massachusetts. (14950)

Speech of Hon. Lionel A. Sheldon. (80129)

Speech of Hon. Lucian Barbour. 3344

Speech of Hon. Luke P. Poland. 63728

Speech of Hon. M. A. Otero. 57841

Speech of Hon. M. F. Conway. (16217)

Speech of Hon. M. I. Southard. 88235

Speech of Hon. M. J. Crawford. 17442

Speech of Hon. M. Morris. 55506

Speech of Hon. M. Oliver. 57209

Speech of Hon. M. Schoonmaker of New York, on the disposition of the public lands. 77890

Speech of Hon. M. Schoonmaker of N. York, on the slave question. 77891

Speech of Hon. Marcus J. Parrott. 58851

Speech of Hon. Michael C. Kerr. (37630)

Speech of Hon. Milledge L. Bonham. 6301

Speech of Hon. Milton I. Southard, of Ohio, in the House of Representatives, January 7, 1874. 88234

Speech of Hon. Milton I. Southard, of Ohio, in the House of Representatives, May 19, 1874. 88235

Speech of Hon. Milton Sayler in the House. 77407

Speech of Hon. Milton Sayler in the Ohio Legislature. 77408

Speech of Hon. Mr. Bailey. (2723)

Speech of Hon. Mr. Prindle. 67679

Speech of Hon. Morris B. Corwin. 16984

Speech of Hon. Moses M. Strong. 92950

Speech of Hon. Moses Macdonald. 43166

Speech of Hon. Myron H. Clark. 13399

Speech of Hon. Myron Lawrence. 39365

Speech of Hon. N. B. Smithers, of Del., on the bill. 84965

Speech of Hon. N. B. Smithers, of Delaware, on the proposed amendment. 84966

Speech of Hon. N. Perry. 61045

Speech of Hon. Nathan F. Dixon. 20371

Speech of Hon. Nathaniel B. Smithers. 84967

Speech of Hon. Nehemiah Perry. 61046

Speech of Hon. Norman B. Judd. 36838

Speech of Hon. O. B. Flcklin. 24258

Speech of Hon. O. B. Matteson. 46882

Speech of Hon. O. H. Browning. 8695

Speech of Hon. O. R. Singleton. 81428

Speech of Hon. Oliver A. Morse. 50955

Speech of Hon. Oliver H. Smith. 83695

Speech of Hon. Oliver P. Snyder. 85605

Speech of Hon. Orange Ferris. 24194

Speech of Hon. Orlando Kellogg. (37298)

Speech of Hon. Owen Lovejoy. 79524

Speech of Hon. P. B. S. Pinchback. 62890

Speech of Hon. P. P. Barbour. 3345

Speech of Hon. P. Soule. 87281

Speech of Hon. Palmer E. Havens. (30902)

Speech of Hon. Paul Leidy. (39909)

Speech of Hon. Peleg Sprague. 89708

Speech of Hon. Peter Hitchcock. 32264

Speech of Hon. Peter M. Dox. 20795

Speech of Hon. Philemon Bliss. 5932

Speech of Hon. Philemon Bliss. (5931)

Speech of Honorable Preston S. Brooks. 8366

Speech of Hon. R. Barnwell Rhett, on the reference. 70482

Speech of Hon. R. Barnwell Rhett on the subject of taxation. 70483

Speech of Hon. R. Chapman. 11998

Speech of Hon. R. E. Fenton. 24078

Speech of Hon. R. F. Stockton. 91910

Speech of Hon. R. H. Duell. 21104

Speech of Hon. R. H. Stanton. 90435

Speech of Hon. R. McClelland. 43034

Speech of Hon. R. Milton Speer. 89250

Speech of Hon. R. R. Butler. 9659

Speech of Hon. R. Smith. 83840
Speech of Hon. Ralph Hill. 31855
Speech of Hon. Richard Brodhead. 8180
Speech of Hon. Richard I. Bowie. 7071
Speech of Hon. Robert B. Hall. (29841)
Speech of Hon. Robert B. Roosevelt, delivered
  at the Municipal Reform Meeting. 73114
Speech of Hon. Robert B. Roosevelt, of New
  York. (73110)
Speech of Hon. Robert B. Roosevelt, of New
  York, in the House of Representatives.
  73106
Speech of Hon. Robert C. Hutchings. (34036)
Speech of Hon. Robert C. Schenck, of Ohio,
  delivered in the House of Representa-
  tives, February 22, 1869. (77580)
Speech of Hon. Robert C. Schenck, of Ohio,
  delivered in the House of Representa-
  tives, March 31, 1870. 77584
Speech of Hon. Robert C. Schenck, of Ohio,
  in the House. 77578
Speech of Hon. Robt. McKnight. 43476
Speech of Hon. Robert Rantoul, Jr. (67902)
Speech of Hon. Robert Smith. 83836
Speech of Hon. Roger A. Pryor, of Virginia.
  66419
Speech of Hon. Roger A. Pryor on the prin-
  ciples. 66420
Speech of Hon. Roscoe Conkling. 15630
Speech of Hon. Rufus P. Spalding, of Ohio,
  delivered in the House of Representa-
  tives, January 24, 1864. 88915
Speech of Hon. Rufus P. Spalding, of Ohio,
  delivered in the House of Representa-
  tives, May 6, 1868. 88919
Speech of Hon. Rufus P. Spalding, of Ohio,
  in the House. 88920
Speech of Hon. Rufus P. Spalding, of Ohio,
  on the union. 88921
Speech of Hon. Russell Sage. 74895
Speech of Hon. S. A. Purviance. (66732)
Speech of Hon. S. A. Smith, of Tennessee, in
  defence. 84016
Speech of Hon. S. A. Smith, of Tennessee, on
  the admission of Kansas. 84019
Speech of Hon. S. A. Smith, of Tennessee, on
  the state of affairs. 84018
Speech of Hon. S. A. Smith, of Tenn., on the
  state of political parties. 84017
Speech of Hon. S. Breese. 7702
Speech of Hon. S. C. Pomeroy. 63937
Speech of Hon. S. F. Miller. (49069)
Speech of Hon. S. G. Andrews. 1515
Speech of Hon. S. Galloway. 26446
Speech of Hon. S. H. Rogers. 72734
Speech of Hon. S. L. Mayham. 47122
Speech of Hon. S. Mayall. 47087
Speech of Hon. S. O. Griswold. 29802
Speech of Hon. S. P. Brooks. 8367
Speech of Hon. S. R. Mallory. 44138
Speech of Hon. S. S. Prentiss. 65101
Speech of Hon. S. Shellabarger. 80140
Speech of Hon. S. Strong. 93070
Speech of Hon. S. W. Harris. 30503
Speech of Hon. S. W. Parker. 58736
Speech of Hon. Sam. Houston . . . exposing
  the malfeasance. 33194
Speech of Hon. Sam Houston of Texas. 33193
Speech of Hon. Sampson W. Harris. 30497
Speech of Hon. Samuel A. Bridges. 7826
Speech of Hon. Samuel A. Purviance. 66733
Speech of Hon. Samuel A. Smith, of Tennessee,
  delivered in the House of Representa-
  tives, April 5, 1854. 84014
Speech of Hon. Samuel A. Smith, of Tennes-
  see, delivered in the House of Repre-
  sentatives, December 9, 1856. 84015

Speech of Hon. Samuel A. Smith, of Tennes-
  see, on government expenditures. 84020
Speech of Hon. Samuel McKee. 43384
Speech of Hon. Samuel R. Curtis. (18064)
Speech of Hon. Samuel Shellabarger . . . at
  Springfield. (80144)
Speech of Hon. Samuel Shellabarger in reply
  to Messrs Vallandigham. 80146
Speech of Hon. Samuel Shellabarger . . . in
  the House of Representatives, January
  21, 1873. 80137
Speech of Hon. Samuel Shellabarger, of Ohio,
  delivered in the House of Representatives,
  February 24, 1862. 80141
Speech of Hon. Samuel Shellabarger, of Ohio
  . . . House of Representatives, July 25,
  1866. 80142
Speech of Hon. Samuel Shellabarger, of Ohio,
  in the House of Representatives, April
  6, 1871. (80138)
Speech of Hon. Samuel Shellabarger of Ohio
  . . . January 27, 1863. 80139
Speech of Hon. Samuel Shellabarger, of Ohio,
  on reconstruction. 80145
Speech of Hon. Samuel Shellabarger, of Ohio,
  on the habeas corpus. 80143
Speech of Hon. Samuel W. Smith. 84124
Speech of Hon. Shelby M. Cullom. (17864)
Speech of Hon. Sidney Clarke. 13463
Speech of Hon. Sidney Edgerton. 21850
Speech of Hon. Sidney Lawrence. 39370
Speech of Hon. Sidney Perham. 60924
Speech of Hon. Sidney T. Holmes. 32624
Speech of Hon. Simeon Corley. 16786
Speech of Hon. Solon Borland. (6429)
Speech of Hon. Stephen C. Foster. 25262
Speech of . . . Hon. Sydenham Moore. 50438
Speech of Hon. T. B. Robertson. (71972)
Speech of Hon. T. H. Bayly. 4077
Speech of Hon. T. J. D. Fuller. 26183
Speech of Hon. T. O. Howe. 33334
Speech of Hon. T. Smith. 84461
Speech of Hon. T. Stevens, of Pennsylvania.
  91561
Speech of Hon. T. Stevens . . . on the Presi-
  dent's message. 91562
Speech of Hon. T. T. Davis. 18892
Speech of Hon. T. W. Ligon. 41059
Speech of Hon. Thaddeus Stevens . . . in the
  U. S. House. 91563
Speech of Hon. Thaddeus Stevens . . . on the
  presidential question. 91564
Speech of Hon. Theodore G. Hunt. 33890
Speech of Hon. Theodore M. Pomeroy. 63943
Speech of Hon. Theophilus Callicot. 10079
Speech of Hon. Thomas A. R. Nelson. 52323
Speech of Hon. Thos. B. Florence. 24803
Speech of Hon. Thomas B. Shannon. (79766)
Speech of Hon. Thomas F. Foster. 25265
Speech of Hon. Thomas F. Smith. 84393
Speech of Hon. Thomas J. Speer. 89251
Speech of Hon. Thomas Fitch . . . in the
  House . . . April 1, 1869. 24590
Speech of Hon. Thomas Fitch . . . in the
  House . . . December 16, 1869. (24592)
Speech of Hon. Thomas G. Cary. 19662
Speech of Hon. Thomas J. Paterson. 59052
Speech of Hon. Thomas Laurens Jones. (36614)
Speech of Hon. Thomas Martin. 44921
Speech of Hon. Thos. Ross. 73409
Speech of Hon. Thomas Ruffin. 73921
Speech of Hon. Thomas S. Gholson. 27263
Speech of Hon. Thomas W. Ferry. 24200
Speech of Hon. Thompson Campbell. 10272
Speech of Hon. Timothy C. Day. (18992)
Speech of Hon. Truman Smith, of Conn., in
  support of the bill. 84462

SPEECH

SPEECH

SPEECH

Speech . . . on the annexation of Texas. [By William H. Haywood.] 31089

Speech . . . on the annexation of Texas; delivered in the House. 67951

Speech . . . on the annexation of Texas . . . in the House, . . . Jan. 6, 1845. 20693

Speech . . . on the annexation of Texas: . . . in the Senate. 20031

Speech . . . on the annexation of Texas. . . . January 11, 1845. (37423)

Speech . . . on the annexation of Texas. . . . Jan. 20, 1845. (33482)

Speech . . . on the annexation of Texas. January 24, 1845. 55506

Speech . . . on the annexation of Texas . . . Jan. 23, 1845. 24258

Speech on the anti-tariff resolutions. 9774

Speech . . . on the apportionment bill. 13691

[Speech on the] apportionment bill, May 3, 1842. 2268

Speech . . . on the . . . appropriation bill. (32611)

Speech . . . on the appropriation for Collins Ocean Steamers. (57165)

Speech . . . on the army appropriation bill. (40762)

Speech . . . on the army bills. 49040

Speech . . . on the arrest of Gen. Stone. (43186)

Speech . . . on the assault of Senator Sumner. (29841)

Speech, on the Assembly. 98581

Speech . . . on the bank bill, Jan. 22, 1811. 36278

Speech . . . on the bank bill, January 23, 1811. 55231

Speech . . . on the bankrupt bill. . . . August 11, 1841. 24222

[Speech] on the bankrupt bill. [By John C. Calhoun.] 9936

Speech . . . on the bankrupt bill. . . . May 25, 1840. 33428

Speech . . . on the bankrupt bill . . . June 23, 1840. 65101

Speech . . . on the bankrupt law. 27993

Speech on the basis question. [By J. Lyons.] 42874

Speech . . . on the basis question, delivered in the Virgina Reform Convention. (23926)

Speech . . . on the battle ground of Brandywine. 31703

Speech . . . on . . . the better organization of the treasury. 36504

Speech . . . on the "bill additional to the act." (37840)

Speech . . . on the bill . . . amendatory of the tariff law. 4078

Speech . . . on the bill authorizing the New York Protestant Episcopal School. 46765

Speech . . . on the bill commonly called the sub-treasury bill. 13550

Speech . . . on the bill "concerning the naval establishment." (41688)

Speech . . . on the bill creating a territorial government. 58325

Speech . . . on the bill designating and limiting the funds receivable for the revenues. 4787

Speech . . . on the bill "emancipating slaves of rebels." 39317

Speech . . . on the bill . . . entitled, "An act to repeal certain acts." 27376

Speech, on the bill for admitting the Territory of Orleans. (67227)

Speech . . . on the bill for arming the slaves. (33929)

Speech . . . on the . . . bill for enforcing the embargo. 51053

Speech . . . on the bill for establishing the Smithsonian Institution. 44737

Speech, on the bill for establishing the Western District Bank. 63356

Speech . . . on the bill for paying certain claims. 20341

Speech on the bill for raising a regiment of mounted riflemen. 10282

[Speech] on the bill for the admission of Michigan. 9936

Speech . . . on the bill for the apportionment of the representation. (13576)

Speech . . . on the bill for the more effectual collection. 18846

[Speech] on the bill for the occupation of the Oregon Territory. 9936

Speech . . . on the bill for the organization of the Smithsonian Institution. 58024

Speech on the bill for the protection of wool & woolen manufactures. 91635

Speech . . . on the bill for the release of certain persons. (34047)

Speech . . . on the bill for the relief of Yucatan. 33195

Speech . . . on the bill further to provide for the collection of duties. 63686

Speech . . . on the bill granting pensions to soldiers. 18007

Speech on the bill imposing additional duties as depositaries, in certain cases, on public officers, and for other purposes. 102310

Speech . . . on the bill imposing additional duties as depositaries, in certain cases, on public officials. 39855

Speech . . . on the bill imposing additional duties, as depositaries, in certain cases, on public officials. . . . In Senate . . . Sept. 25, 1837. 13550

Speech . . . on the bill imposing additional duties, as depositaries . . . on public officers; . . . September 23, 1837. 37818

Speech . . . on the bill imposing additional duties . . . February 13, 1838. 55322

Speech . . . on the bill imposing additional duties . . . on public officers. . . . September 29, 1837. 8862

Speech on the bill in relation to church tenures. 5624

Speech . . . on . . . the bill in relation to fugitive slaves. 2908

Speech . . . on the bill making appropriation of 10,000,000 dollars. 9936

Speech . . . on the bill making appropriations for certain rivers and harbors. 59293

Speech . . . on the bill making appropriations for the . . . Indian Department. 18095

Speech . . . on the bill making appropriations for the naval service. 23153

Speech . . . on the bill making appropriations for the suppression and prevention of Indian hostilities. 4461

Speech . . . on the bill organizing territorial governments. 27329

Speech . . . on the bill proposing a reduction of the duties on imports. 43205

Speech . . . on the bill providing for the prosecution of the war. 11349

Speech . . . on the bill to abolish the duty of alum salt. 4787

Speech on the bill to admit Kansas. 13531

Speech . . . on the bill to afford aid to the
Blue Ridge Rail Road. 47490

Speech . . . on the bill to amend the national
banking law. 32877

Speech . . . on the bill to appoint a Lieutenant
General. 20341

Speech . . . on the bill to appropriate ten
millions. 4787

Speech . . . on the bill to appropriate the
proceeds of the sales of the public lands,
. . . in the Senate. 23331

Speech . . . on the bill to appropriate the
proceeds of the sales of the public
lands. . . . July 6, 1841. 44781

Speech . . . on the bill to authorize an issue
of treasury notes. 23153

Speech . . . on the bill to authorize the issue
of treasury notes. 21250

Speech . . . on the bill to authorize the people
of the Territory of Kansas to form a
constitution. 8437

Speech . . . on the bill to confiscate the
property and free the slaves. 33337

Speech on the bill to construct a national road.
(31292)

Speech . . . on the bill . . . to distribute
annually among the several states. 68121

Speech on the bill to distribute the proceeds
of the public lands among the states . . .
July 2, 1841. 62621

Speech . . . on the bill to distribute the proceeds of the public lands among the states
. . . July 3, 1841. 43441

[Speech] on the bill to distribute the proceeds
of the public lands. [By John C. Calhoun.]
9936

Speech . . . on the bill to establish a railway
to the Pacific. 29383

Speech . . . on the bill to establish a territorial government in Oregon, Delivered
in the Senate . . . June 3, 1848. 20791

Speech . . . on the bill to establish a territorial government in Oregon. . . . in
the Senate . . . June 26, 1848. 20341

Speech . . . on the bill to establish a territorial government in Oregon: . . . March
30, 1848. (31890)

Speech . . . on the bill to establish a uniform
system of bankruptcy. (31042)

Speech . . . on the bill to establish governments in the territories. 20341

Speech on the bill to guarantee to certain
states, whose government is usurped or
overthrown. (17271)

Speech . . . [on] the bill "To guarantee to
certain states, whose governments have
been usurped or overthrown." 37272

Speech . . . on the bill to incorporate the
subscribers. 50581

Speech . . . on the bill to indemnify American
citizens. 20341

Speech . . . on the bill to indemnify General
Jackson. (41341)

Speech . . . on the bill to organize territorial
government in Nebraska. (11866)

Speech . . . on the bill to organize territorial
governments in Nebraska and Kansas.
(13576)

Speech . . . on the bill to organize the Territory of Arizuma [sic]. (20611)

Speech . . . on the bill to pay . . . for a slave
sent west. 27329

[Speech] on the bill to prevent the interference
of certain federal officers in elections.
9936

[Speech] on the bill to prohibit deputy post-
masters from receiving or transmitting
through the mails. 9936

Speech . . . on the bill to protect the rights
of American settlers in Oregon. 11349

Speech . . . on the bill to provide further
remedial justice. 12860

Speech . . . on the bill to provide further
remedial justice in the courts of the
United States. 8862

Speech . . . on the bill to provide homesteads.
36345

Speech . . . on the bill to provide increased
revenue from imports. 11556

Speech . . . on the bill to provide increased
revenue from imports; . . . in the Senate
. . . January 26, 1867. 31319

Speech . . . on the bill to raise a regiment of
mounted riflemen. 40756

Speech, on the bill to raise an additional military force. 90214

Speech . . . on the bill to reduce and graduate
the price of the public lands to actual
settlers. 7088

Speech . . . on the bill to reduce and otherwise
alter the duties on imports. 9235

Speech . . . on the bill to reduce the duties on
imports. 49079

Speech . . . on the bill to reduce the rates of
postage. 47989

Speech . . . on the bill . . . to reduce the
revenue. 16985

Speech . . . on the bill to refund the fine imposed on General Jackson. 20693

Speech . . . on the bill to regulate suffrage.
9380

Speech . . . on the bill to regulate the civil
service of the United States. 35982

Speech . . . on the bill to regulate the commercial intercourse between the United
States and the British colonies. 36380

[Speech] on the bill to repeal the force act.
9936

Speech . . . on the bill to repeal the fugitive
slave law. 25252

Speech . . . on the bill to secure the freedom
of elections. 4461

Speech . . . on the bill to separate the government from the banks. 4787

Speech . . . on the bill to strengthen the public
credit. 18818

Speech . . . on the boundary of Texas. (31890)

Speech . . . on the British colonial trade.
42466

Speech on the budger by the Honorable John
Rose. 63246

Speech . . . on the cabinet plan for a federal
exchequer. 4787

Speech . . . on the California claims. 4787

Speech . . . on the California question. 33317

Speech . . . on the canal bill. 32531

Speech . . . on the capitol bill. 14074

Speech . . . on the case of Alexander McLeod.
12860

[Speech] on the case of M'Leod. [By John C.
Calhoun.] 9936

Speech . . . on the case of McLeod. [By
Thomas Hart Benton.] 4787

Speech . . . on the causes of the rebellion.
5751

Speech . . . on the Central American treaty.
23271

Speech . . . on the change of the newspapers.
36211

Speech . . . on the motion of Mr. Benton. 11349

Speech . . . on the motion of Mr. C. T. Ingersoll. 27329

Speech . . . on the motion of Mr. Calhoun. (31832)

Speech . . . on the motion of Mr. Webster. 4787

Speech . . . on the Munroe [sic] doctrine. 20693

Speech . . . on the national currency. 31319

Speech . . . on the national finances. 20368

Speech . . . on the . . . naturalization laws and the origin of the Native American Party. 20368

Speech . . . on the naturalization laws. . . . In the House. 7088

Speech . . . on . . . the naval appropriation bill. 40756

Speech . . . on the naval appropriation bill; March . . . 1836. 4461

Speech . . . on the naval appropraitions for Pensacola. 103434

Speech . . . on the Naval Retiring Board. 4461

Speech . . . on the navigation laws of the United States. 37834

Speech . . . on the navy, Feb. 8, 1796. 30444

Speech on the navy: opposition to the motion of Mr. Gallatin. 30444

Speech . . . on the Nebraska and Kansas bill . . . House of Representatives. 13030

Speech . . . on the Nebraska and Kansas bill, . . . March 3, 1854. 33195

Speech . . . on the Nebraska and Kansas bill, May 24, 25, 1854. 4461

Speech . . . on the Nebraska Territory, January 30, 1854. 20693

Speech . . . on the necessity of regulating the currency. 32877

Speech . . . on the Negro enlistment bill. (47166)

Speech on the "Negro law." (13533)

Speech . . . on the New-Jersey contested election. 6832

Speech . . . on the nomination of J. J. Crittenden. (32611)

Speech . . . [on the ocean mail steamers appropriation bill.] (57165)

Speech . . . on the objections of the President. 6832

Speech on the occasion of Col. Lothrop's death. 79367

Speech . . . on the Oregon bill, delivered in the Senate. 18837

Speech . . . on the Oregon bill, . . . Jan. 29, 1845. 21250

Speech . . . on the Oregon bill. . . . June 27, 1848. 9936

Speech . . . on the Oregon question . . . April 16, 1846. (17556)

Speech . . . on the Oregon question . . . April 3, 1846. 2187

Speech . . . on the Oregon question; . . . April 13, 1845. 33968

Speech on the Oregon question. [By Archibald Yell.] 106008

Speech . . . on the Oregon question. [By John M. Niles.] 55322

Speech . . . on the Oregon question. Delivered in the House . . . February 7, 1846. 20493

Speech . . . on the Oregon question; delivered in the House of Representatives, Jan. 8, 1846. 13842

Speech . . . on the Oregon question. Delivered in the Senate . . . April 11, 1848. 4787

Speech . . . on the Oregon question. Delivered in the Senate of the U. S., on the 30th of March, 1846. 3652

Speech . . . on the Oregon question. Delivered . . . January 9, 1846. 27378

Speech . . . on the Oregon question. Delivered . . . March 4 & 5, 1846. 31089

Speech on the Oregon question . . . Feb. 5, 1846. 26956

Speech . . . on the Oregon question: . . . February 9, 1846. (37840)

Speech . . . on the Oregon question . . . Feb. 6, 1840. 25010

Speech . . . on the Oregon question . . . February 6, 1846. 33183

Speech . . . on the Oregon question. . . . in the House . . . February 5, 1846. (19352)

Speech . . . on the Oregon question. . . . in the House . . . February 6, 1846. 11517

Speech . . . on the Oregon question. . . . In the House . . . January 5, 1846. 7992

Speech . . . on the Oregon question, . . . in the House . . . January 6. 1846. 7088

Speech . . . on the Oregon question . . . in the House . . . January 27, 1846. 4078

Speech . . . on the Oregon question . . . in the Senate . . . February 18 & 19, 1846. 20341

Speech on the . . . Oregon question . . . in the Senate . . . March 9 and 10, 1846. 23153

Speech . . . on the Oregon question. . . . January 8, 1846. (43041)

Speech . . . on the Oregon question. . . . January 15, 1846. 36607

Speech . . . on the Oregon question. . . . January 9, 1846. 40756

Speech . . . on the Oregon question . . . Jan. 6, 1844. (31890)

Speech . . . on the Oregon question. . . . January 10, 1846. (37389)

Speech . . . on the Oregon question: . . . January 26, 1846. 59648

Speech . . . on the Oregon question . . . March 30, 1846. 11349

Speech . . . on the Oregon question. . . . March 12, 1844. 8862

Speech . . . on the Oregon question; . . . March 23, 1846. 49022

Speech . . . on the Oregon Territory bill. (33929)

Speech . . . on the . . . Oregon Territory; . . . in the House. 18095

Speech on the organization of the empire. (33315)

Speech . . . on the organization of the House. 43649

Speech . . . on the organization of the judiciary. 55231

Speech . . . on the origin of the war with Mexico. 21110

Speech . . . on the Pacific Railroad. . . . April 10, 1854. 29383

Speech . . . on the Pacific Railroad bill, April 17, 1858. 20693

Speech . . . on the passage of the bill. 13771

[Speech] on the passage of the tariff bill. 9936

Speech . . . on . . . the payment of revenue bonds. 63686

Speech . . . on the permanent prospective preemption bill. 33428

Speech . . . on the petition of the Troy and Greenfield Railroad. 61363

Speech . . . on the reduction of the army. 30444

Speech . . . on the reduction of the tariff. [By Ralph J. Ingersoll.] 34752

Speech . . . on the . . . reduction of the tariff. Delivered . . . June 27, 1846. 63886

Speech . . . on the reduction of the tariff, . . . January 23, 1832. 20019

Speech . . . on the reduction of the tariff, . . . July 1, 1846. 24258

Speech . . . on the reduction of the tariff of 1842. 10169

Speech . . . on the reference of the President's message. 20368

Speech . . . on the . . . rejection of petitions. (36347)

Speech . . . on the relation of the federal government to slavery. 27329

Speech on the 'remedial justice bill.' 3454

Speech on the removal of the deposites. (80290)

Speech . . . on the . . . removal of the deposites. December 19, 1833. 43205

Speech . . . on the removal of the deposites. Delivered in the House. 36498

Speech . . . on the removal of the deposites; delivered in the Senate. 23331

Speech on the removal of the deposites. March 27th, 1834. 22348

Speech . . . on the removal of the deposites; . . . Senate of the United States. (25831)

Speech . . . on the removal of the deposites . . . delivered in the Senate. (104020)

Speech . . . on the removal of the deposites . . . March 3 and 4, 1834. (31832)

Speech . . . on the removal of the public deposites. (29016)

Speech . . . on the removal of the Treasury Building. (41257)

Speech . . . on . . . the repeal of the liquor law. 42367

Speech . . . on the report and resolutions of the Committee on Elections. 3454

Speech on the report of Mr. Campbell. (67226)

Speech on the report of the Committee of Foreign Relations . . . December 16, 1811. 67833

Speech on the report of the Committee of Foreign Relations . . . December 10, 1811. 67832

Speech . . . on the report of the Committee of Thirteen. 13550

Speech . . . on the representation of the United States. 3206

Speech . . . on the resolution declaring Mr. Long, of Ohio, an unworthy member of the House. 14344

Speech . . . on the resolution of Mr. Ewing. 4787

[Speech on] the resolution of Mr. Foot, of Connecticut. (13575)

Speech . . . on the resolution of Mr. Mercer. (49726)

Speech . . . on the resolution of notice to Great Britain. (33929)

Speech . . . on the resolution of the twenty-eighth of March 1834. 8862

Speech . . . on the resolution offered by Mr. Hillhouse. 62659

Speech on the resolution proposed for his [i. e. Jesse D. Bright's] expulsion. 7964

Speech . . . on the resolution . . . proposing an inquiry. 43441

Speech . . . on the resolution proposing to examine. 4140

Speech . . . on the resolution proposing to retrocede the forts. (33929)

Speech . . . on the resolution submitted by Mr. Foote. 20791

Speech . . . on the resolution to expel Mr. Long. 57711

Speech . . . on the resolution to refer so much of the President's message. 27329

Speech on the resolution to repeal the embargo. 31882

Speech . . . on . . . the resolutions concerning Sabbath mails. (25831)

Speech . . . on the resolutions giving notice to Great Britain. 9936

Speech . . . on the resolutions of Kentucky and Massachusetts. 18095

Speech . . . on the resolutions of . . . Texas. (57155)

Speech . . . on the resolutions of the Hon. Edward Livingston. 44796

Speech . . . on the resolutions of the Legislature of New York. 27403

Speech . . . on the resolutions of the Massachusetts Legislature. (33929)

Speech . . . on the resolutions offered by Mr. Clay. 4787

Speech . . . on the resolutions relating to the Hon. John Quincy Adams. 62904

Speech . . . on the resolutions submitted by him, Dec. 23. 1828. 4787

Speech . . . on the restriction of slavery in Missouri. 47860

Speech . . . on the resumption of specie payments. 51020

Speech . . . on the revenue bill. 24333

Speech . . . on the revision of the tariff, and in defence of the protective policy. 50817

Speech . . . on the revision of the tariff, . . . February 10, 1859. 37173

Speech . . . on the revolutionary schemes of the ultra abolitionists. 5751

Speech . . . on the right of members elected by general ticket. 8432

Speech . . . on the right of members to their seats in the House of Representatives. Delivered . . . February 12, 1844. 67951

Speech on the right of members to their seats in the House of Representatives, . . . February 8, 1844. 4140

Speech . . . on the right of members to their seats in the House of Representatives: . . . February 10, 1844. 55506

Speech . . . on the right of petition. 18095

Speech . . . on the right to repeal bank charters. 34735

Speech . . . on the river and harbor appropriation bills. 11349

Speech . . . on the . . . river and harbor bill. 22175

Speech . . . on the . . . salary appropriated for the Minister to Russia. 9235

Speech . . . on . . . the sales of the public lands. (41341)

Speech on the same subject, by the Hon. Daniel Webster. 26390

Speech on the scafford. 67590, 67598

Speech on the second reading of his intestine estate bill. 72872

Speech . . . on the second reading of the Canada bill. 49865

Speech . . . on the sedition law. 57860

Speech . . . on the Seminole war. [By Charles Fenton Mercer.] (47902)

Speech . . . on the Seminole war. [By Henry Clay.] 13550

Speech . . . on the slavery question: . . . January 21, 1832. (43195)

Speech on the slave trade. 9850

Speech on the "slaveholder's rebellion." 82683

Speech . . . on the slavery question, delivered in the House. 36885

Speech . . . on the slavery question, . . . in the Senate. 8437

Speech on the slavery question, March 18 and 19, 1850. 2697

Speech . . . on the slavery question. . . . March 4, 1850. 9936

Speech on the slavery resolutions, 91765

Speech . . . on the Smithsonian Institution. 22608

Speech . . . on the specie circular. 13550

Speech on the state of the country. 36831

Speech . . . [on the state of the union] April 7, 1864. 41867

Speech . . . on the state of the union. [By William Brickly Stokes.] 92012

Speech . . . on the state of the union. Delivered in the House of Representatives . . . February 1, 1861. 29996

Speech . . . on the state of the union . . . in the House . . . February 24, 1864. 18946

Speech . . . on the state of the union. . . . In the Senate . . . January 28, 1861. 31291

Speech . . . on the state of the union; . . . In the Senate of the United States, February 5, and 6, 1861. 36170

Speech . . . on the state of the union. . . . January 18, 1861. 59646

Speech . . . on the state of the union, . . . January 16, 1861. 26681

Speech . . . on the state of the union, January 31, 1861. 29641

Speech . . . on the state of the union, March 29, 1828. 9235

Speech . . . on the status of the states. 50836

Speech . . . on the subject compromise. 33195

Speech . . . on the subject of a general system of internal improvements. 78885

Speech on the subject of an institution to be founded on the . . . Smithsonian legacy. (71743)

Speech . . . on the subject of congressional legislation. (13707)

Speech . . . on the subject of discriminating duties. (33482)

Speech . . . on the subject of fortifying Key West and Tortugas. 9773

Speech . . . on the subject of internal improvement. (32611)

Speech . . . on the subject of protecting American labor. 12860

Speech . . . on the subject of public lands. 63686

Speech . . . on the subject of retrenchment. 23271

Speech . . . on the subject of roads and canals. (31292)

Speech . . . on the subject of slavery, &c. 61394

Speech . . . on the subject of slavery in the territories. 44324

Speech on the subject of the admission of Kansas. 30834

Speech . . . on the subject of the Chesapeake and Ohio Canal. (47902)

Speech . . . on the subject of the finances. (57155)

Speech . . . on the subject of the New Jersey election. 21250

Speech . . . on the subject of the political parties. 9773

Speech . . . on the subject of the removal of the deposites, . . . in the Senate . . . December 26, 30, 1833. 13550

Speech . . . on the subject of the removal of the public deposites. 25150

Speech . . . on the subject of the retrocession of Alexandria to Virginia. (33929)

Speech . . . on the subject of the war with Mexico. (33482)

Speech . . . on the sub-treasury bill. 9936

Speech . . . on the sub-treasury bill, delivered June 27, 1840. (68563)

Speech on the sub-treasury bill. Delivered March 12, 1838. 102309

Speech . . . on the sub-treasury bill. . . . House . . . May 20 and 21, 1840. 18095

[Speech] on the sub-treasury bill, in reply to Mr. Webster. 9936

Speech . . . on the sub-treasury bill . . . in the House of Representatives, October 12, 1837. (36347)

Speech . . . on the sub-treasury bill . . . June 16 and 17, 1840. 4461

Speech . . . on the sub-treasury bill . . . June 12, 1840. 3454

Speech . . . on the sub-treasury bill . . . June 3, 1840. 33860

Speech on the sub-treasury scheme. 13550

Speech on the Sunday question. 9930

Speech on the tariff and revenue questions. 27892

Speech . . . on the tariff bill. . . . April 30, 1844. 44737

Speech . . . on the tariff bill, . . . April 24, 1820. (42531)

Speech . . . on the tariff bill, containing allusions. 8180

Speech . . . on the tariff bill, delivered in the House of Representatives. 63697

Speech . . . on the tariff bill . . . House of Representatives. 19077

Speech . . . on the tariff bill; . . . in the House. 9305

Speech . . . on the tariff bill. . . . June 9, 1842. 24333

Speech on the tariff bill . . . March 17, 1828. 3454

Speech . . . on the tariff bill, March 12, 1828. 18846

Speech . . . on the tariff bill . . . March 26, 1828. 3936

Speech . . . on the tariff bill . . . May 14, 1844. 3454

Speech . . . on the tariff bills. (33482)

Speech . . . on the tariff. [By John A. Dix.] 20341

[Speech] on the tariff, Dec. 23, 1841. 2268

Speech on the tariff, delivered in Broadhurst's Grove. 7173

Speech . . . on the tariff, delivered . . . July 2, 1846. 26956

Speech . . . on the tariff. Delivered in the Senate . . . July 25, 1846. (36269)

Speech . . . on the tariff. Delivered in the Senate of the United States, March 25, 1844. 4787

Speech . . . on the tariff. . . . February 15, 1832. (28916)

Speech . . . on the tariff in June 26, 1846. 14360

Speech . . . on the tariff, in reply to Messrs. Evans and Huntington. 43205

Speech . . . on the tariff. . . . in the House. 20368

Speech . . . on the tariff. [January 19, 1844.] 43205

Speech . . . on the tariff, . . . June 24, 1846. 33898

Speech . . . on the tariff . . . June 29, 1846. (33482)

Speech . . . on the tariff. . . . June 26, 1846. 12184

Speech . . . on the tariff; . . . May 1, 1844. (33416)

Speech . . . on the tariff. . . . May 3, 1844. 51466

Speech on the tariff, May 25, 1844. 2268

Speech . . . on the tariff question. . . . April 24th, 1860. 50817

Speech . . . on the tariff question. Delivered . . . July 1, 1846. 11069

Speech . . . on the tariff question, Jan. 20, 1859. 66733

Speech . . . on the tariff question, January 22, 1851. 30151

Speech . . . on the tariff question. . . . June 30th, 1846. 44737

Speech . . . on the ten regiment bill. Delivered in the Senate. (36269)

Speech . . . on the ten regiment bill, 1848. 9936

Speech. . . . On the ten regiment bill. . . . February 8, 1848. 49022

Speech . . . on the ten regiment bill . . . February 7, 1848. (33929)

Speech on the ten regiment bill . . . Jan. 18, 1848. 2697

Speech . . . on the ten regiment bill . . . United States Senate. 29641

Speech . . . on the territorial bill. 50919

Speech . . . on the territorial bills. 2908

Speech . . . on the territorial policy. 27942

Speech on the territorial question, August 2, 1850. 2697

Speech . . . on the territorial question. Delivered in Senate. 20693

Speech . . . on the territorial question, . . . in the Senate. 19003

Speech . . . on the territorial question; . . . March 19, 1850. 29641

Speech . . . on the territorial relations between the United States and Texas. 37117

Speech . . . on the Texas and New Mexico question. 23320

Speech . . . on the Texas and Oregon questions. 17871

Speech . . . on the third reading of the alien bill. (41617)

Speech, on the third reading, . . . of the bill for providing quarters. 63074

Speech . . . on the third reading of the tariff bill. 43205

Speech . . . on the thirty million bill. 20368

Speech . . . on the three million appropriation bill. (33482)

Speech . . . on the three million bill. Delivered in the Senate. 20341

Speech . . . on the three million bill. . . . In the House. (8154A)

Speech . . . on . . . the three million bill. . . . In the Senate. (36269)

[Speech] on the treasury note bill. [By John C. Calhoun.] 9936

Speech . . . on the treasury note bill. Delivered in the House. 68121

Speech . . . on the treasury note bill . . . February 6, 1862. 37302

Speech . . . on the treasury note bill; . . . February 3, 1862. 32877

Speech on the treasury note bill . . . in the House . . . Oct. 6, 1837. 18095

Speech . . . on the treasury note bill, in the Senate. 14360

Speech . . . on the treasury note bill . . . March 25, 1840. 3454

Speech . . . on the treasury order. 55322

Speech on the treatment of the Negro. 9615

Speech . . . on the treaty for the reannexation of Texas. 43205

Speech . . . on the trial of Preston S. Brooks. 27329

Speech . . . on the Troy and Greenfield Railroad bill. 42078

Speech . . . on the Turkish Mission. (41617)

Speech on the twelve million loan bill. 2268

Speech on the 20th of January, 1775. 63075

Speech on the union of the colonies. 43522

Speech . . . on the Vermont resolutions. 65099

Speech . . . on the veto message of the President. (13576)

SPeech . . . on the veto of the provisional tariff bill. 3454

Speech . . . on the veto of the revenue bill. 68121

Speech . . . on the veto power . . . April, 1842. 65387

Speech . . . on the Virginia and Tennesse Rail Road Belt. 78887

Speech . . . on the war and mail steamer bill. 49079

Speech . . . on the war and the public finances. 61394

Speech . . . on the war for the union. 36170

Speech . . . on the war with Great Britain. 30444

Speech . . . on the war with Mexico. Delivered in the Senate. 20791

Speech . . . on the war with Mexico. . . . January 19, 1848. 43489

Speech on the "water question." 89192

[Speech] on the West India emancipation. 20716

Speech . . . on the wheat trade of the country. (33482)

Speech . . . on the Wilmot proviso. [By George Rathbun.] 67951

Speech . . . on the Wilmot proviso . . . January 7, 1847. 28990

Speech . . . on the Wilmot proviso, . . . Senate, March 1, 1847. 11349

Speech . . . on the woollens' bill. 43205

Speech . . . on treason and its punishment. 57711

Speech on United States Bank. 36162

Speech . . . on unmanufactured cotton. 50792

Speech . . . on Walker's expedition to Nicaragua. 28918

Speech . . . on . . . war against Mexico. 11349

Speech . . . on wool and woolens. 14360

Speech or sermon made by way of a charge. 82289

Speech over his grave. 58891

Speech . . . peace and union; war and disunion. 43441

Speech . . . Philadelphia. 31703

Speech pronounced by William Kuhn. 38340

Speech, purporting to have been delivered [in] Senate. 60545

Speech recently delivered before the "Elders," in Utah. 28554, 83553

Speech relating to those letters. 34072

Speech . . . relative to the compromise measures. 49022

Speech, relative to the resignation of his pastoral charge. 45463

Speech . . . respecting the fortifications and defence of the country. 8862

Speech . . . respecting the powers of the Vice President. 36380

Speech reviewing the action of the Federal administration. 93662

Speech, said to be spoken at a General Court of the South-Sea Company. 8962, 1st note after 99795

Speech, said to have been delivered by him, [i. e. Mr. Levy, of Florida] at a meeting of Christians and Jews in London. 95762

Speech said to have been delivered by Samuel Chew. 86738

Speech said to have been delivered some time before the close of the last sessions. 89193

Speech . . . St. Louis . . . Oct. 21. 31319

Speech . . . Senate, 1848. 36221

Speech . . . Senate, Feb. 19, 1849. 18837

Speech, . . . Senate, Jan. 12, 1848. 20031

Speech . . . Senate, March 6, 1860. 51473

Speech . . . Senate, May 15 and 16, 1860. 20693

Speech . . . Senate . . . May 15, 1854. 11349

Speech . . . Senate . . . May 12-13, 1856. 11349

Speech . . . September 8th, 1868. 37272

Speech . . . September 16, 1856. 37272

Speech . . . September 28, 1864. 37271

Speech . . . September 26, 1864. 37271

Speech . . . September 23d, 1837. 37818

Speech . . . 7th of May, 1835. 31595

Speech . . . 16th of January, 1834. 4140

Speech . . . 6th and 7th January, 1829. 49201

Speech . . . sub-treasury scheme. (26670)

Speech that ought to have been on the bill. 89194

Speech . . . the constitutional validity of the act. 14360

Speech . . . the General Assembly at Cleveland. 28338

Speech . . . the resolution of Mr. Foot. 36380

Speech to a good number of people. 70906

Speech to Congress. 101578

Speech to Her Majesty on the 20th April. (25283)

Speech, to the Assembly held at Philadelphia, in Pensylvania [sic]. 60126

Speech . . . to the Assembly of the province of New Jersey. (50851)

Speech to the Assembly on his dissolving of them. 53108

Speech to the citizens of Baltimore. 30427

Speech to the citizens of Boston. 57860

Speech, to the Congress of the United States. 101678

Speech . . . to the convention of citizens of Onondaga County. 47078

Speech . . . to the Council and House of Representatives. 80808

Speech to the Governour. 35633

Speech to the Indians. 4035

Speech to the Legislature, 1840. 35629

Speech to the Legislature of Maine. 44043

Speech to the Legislature of Massachusetts. [By Christopher Gore.] 28017

Speech to the Legislature of Massachusetts, June 7, 1808. 93497

Speech to the Legislature of Massachusetts, . . . June 7, 1810. 46128

Speech . . . to the Legislature of the state of New York. 13724

Speech . . . to the Legislature of the state of New York, on the sixth day of January, 1819. 13724

Speech to the loyal refugees from Virginia. 28406

Speech . . . to the New Hampshire Legislature. 63450

Speech to the people of England. 89195

Speech to the Scots Lords and gentlemen. 104146

Speech to the Scots Lords and gentlemen met at St. James's. 9372, 81492

Speech, to the Senate and House of Representatives. 95008

Speech to the Senate of Carthage. 92802

Speech to the troops of Indiana. 32653

Speech . . . 12th April 1808. 31884

Speech . . . 12th January, 1813. (22541)

Speech . . . 28th July, 1869. 43447

Speech . . . 21st April, 1860. 29696

Speech . . . 29 May 1797. 30444

Speech . . . 21 February, 1859. 42367

Speech . . . 22d and 23d June, 1838. (37423)

Speech . . . 26th and . . . 28th of February, 1814. 62659

Speech under the gallows. 96905

Speech, U. S. House of Rep., on the tariff. 91647

Speech, United States Senate. 33195

Speech upon a motion, for the early consideration of measures, &c. 10693

Speech . . . upon a motion on 19th May, 1826. 22290

Speech . . . upon his [i. e. B. F. Butler's] bill to authorize the issue of a national currency. 9615

Speech, upon our relations with Great Britain. 4461

Speech upon proroguing the said session of the Legislature. 81138, 98064

Speech . . . upon . . . taxing bank stock. (32961)

Speech . . . upon the annexation of Texas. 27329

Speech upon the anti-rent question. (30474)

Speech . . . upon the army appropriation bill. 24222

Speech . . . upon the bill and resolutions relating to bank issues. 47490

Speech . . . upon the "bill to guarantee to certain states." (6977)

Speech . . . upon the bill "to reduce duties." 18846

Speech . . . upon the bill to supply the deficiency of appropriations, 27329

Speech upon the course to be pursued. (8154A)

Speech upon the executive patronage bill. 181, 102321, 103268

Speech upon the foreign slave trade. 89750

Speech upon the higher law. 8466

Speech . . . upon the improvement of the harbors on the lakes. 27329

Speech . . . upon the issues . . . before the American people. 27329

Speech . . . upon the issues . . . freedom and slavery. 27329

Speech, upon the loan bill. 101280

Speech upon the Mexican question in the Senate of Spain. (65521)

Speech . . . upon . . . the northeastern boundary. 23153

Speech . . . upon the proposition relative to a railroad. 47490

Speech . . . upon the resolution to correct abuses. 6289

Speeches of Hon. Joseph Lane. 91532
Speeches of Hon. Joseph Segar. 78891
Speeches of Hon. Joseph T. Buckingham. 8910, note after 89215
Speeches of Hon. Lewis Selye. (79040)
Speeches of Hon. Mr. Grundy. (29016)
Speeches of Hon. T. A. Plants. 63327
Speeches of Hon. T. Polk, of Missouri. 63847
Speeches of Hon. T. Polk, . . . on the admission of Kansas. 63847
Speeches of Hon. W. Dennison. 19593
Speeches of Hon. W. Y. Gholson. 27264
Speeches of Hon. William D. Kelly. 22713, note before 90885
Speeches of Hon. William E. Robinson. 72209
Speeches of Hon. William H. Koontz. 38236
Speeches of Hon. William I. Polk. 63850
Speeches of Hon. William M. Springer. 89840
Speeches of Hon. Z. Chandler. 11888
Speeches of Hons. John F. Driggs and Austin Blair. 20947
Speeches of Horace Greeley. 28492
Speeches of J. N. Wilder. 21100
Speeches of James T. Brady. 7313
Speeches of John A. Andrew. 1476
Speeches of John Bright. 7967
Speeches of John C. Calhoun and Daniel Webster. 9946, 102283
Speeches of John C. Calhoun. Delivered in the Congress. 9934
Speeches of Iohn Wilkes. 104008
Speeches of Joseph Hopkinson and Charles Chauncey. (32986)
Speeches of Judge Daly. 28452
Speeches of Judges Williams, Parsons, and Ellsworth. (30666)
Speeches of Maj. Hooker. 80417-(80418)
Speeches of Maj. Wm. A. Stokes. 92011
Speeches . . . of Messrs. Calhoun, Webster and Poindexter. 9947
Speeches of Messrs. Cameron and Seward. 10169
Speeches of Messrs. Collier, Haight, Matthews and Hulbert. (43001), 96901
Speeches of Messrs. Davis, Winthrop and others. 26126, 65915
Speeches of Messrs. Grundy, Wickliffe, and others. 89216, note after 102276
Speeches of Messrs. Hayne and Webster. (31043)
Speeches of Messrs. Webster, . . . and others. 52826, 92068
Speeches of Messrs. Webster, Frelinghuysen and others. 89216, note after 102276
Speeches of Messieurs Gardenieur & Tallmadge. 26606
Speeches of Mr. Bacon & Mr. Nicholson. 2658, note after 89216
Speeches of Mr. Boyd and John Randolph. 68198
Speeches of Mr. Cushing. 18095
Speeches of Mr. Giles and Mr. Bayard. 27377
Speeches of Mr. Jacob Barker and his counsel, on the trials for conspiracy. 89217
Speeches of Mr. Jacob Barker and his counsel, on the trials for conspiracy, &c. 3392
Speeches of Mr. Joseph Barker and his counsel, on the trials for conspiracy, with documents relating thereto. 89218-89219
Speeches of Mr. James Gowan and Mr. Haly. 2165
Speeches of Mr. King. 58482
Speeches of Mr. Leigh. (39916)
Speeches of Mr. Lloyd. (41688)
Speeches of Mr. Niles. 55322, 91637

Speeches of Mr. Randolph. (67843)
Speeches of Mr. Ross and Mr. Morris. 73360
Speeches of Mr. Smith, of South Carolina. 84816, 84823, 84835-84837
Speeches of Mr. Sprague. 89222, 89711
Speeches . . . of Mr. Van Ness. (29986)
Speeches of Mr. Wilberforce. 103959
Speeches of Mr. Wilde. 103975
Speeches of Mr. Wilkes in the House of Commons. 104010
Speeches of Mr. Wilkes in the House of Commons during the last session. 104009
Speeches [of Montgomery Balir.] 5751
Speeches of Ogden Hoffman. (72166)
Speeches of P. Henry. 89220
Speeches of R. A. Lockwood. 41752
Speeches of Richard Cobden. 14041
Speeches of Richard L. Sheil. 80105
Speeches of Sam Houston. 33195
Speeches of Senators Morton, . . . Stewart and Nye. 51020
Speeches of Senators . . . on the Pacific Rail Road question. (79093)
Speeches of Sir Samuel Romilly. (73063)
Speeches of Sir William Molesworth. 49865
Speeches of the Attorney General and Jared Ingersoll. 82884
Speeches of the Bishop of Huron. 38844
Speeches of the different Governors. 53960, 1st note after 89220
Speeches of the Duke of Richmond. (15052)
Speeches of the Governors of Massachusetts. (46131), 2d note after 89220
Speeches of the Hon. Colonel Burwell. 100896
Speeches of the Hon. David Wilmot. (31494)
Speeches of the Hon. DeWitt Clinton. 13723
Speeches of the Hon. Edgar Cowan. 17221
Speeches of the Hon. Gideon Haynes. 31051, 46130, 1st note after 89210
Speeches of the Hon. Henry Clay. 13543
Speeches of the Hon. Henry May. (47067)
Speeches of the Hon. Jefferson Davis. 18837
Speeches of the Hon. Matias Romero. 54594
Speeches of the Hon, Messrs. Grimes, Doolittle, and Nye. 52127
Speeches of the Hon. Messrs. Walsh and Cutting. 89221
Speeches of the Hon. Robert Y. Hayne. (31043), 102275
Speeches of the Hon. W. D. Kelley. 15909
Speeches of the late Right Honourable Sir Robert Peel. 59525
Speeches of the most celebrated American orators. 12209
Speeches of the Right Honourable the Earl of Chatham. 63078
Speeches of the Right Honourable . . . William Huskisson. 34028
Speeches of the Right Honourable William Pitt. 63099
Speeches of Thomas Corwin. 16985
Speeches of Thomas H. Russell. 74377
Speeches of W. Curtis Noyes. 28472, 56238
Speeches of William H. Seward, delivered at Albany and at Buffalo. 79583
Speeches of William H. Seward in Alaska. (79540)
Speeches of William H. Seward on the joint resolution. 79591
Speeches of William Sprague. 89724
Speeches . . . on alcohol and intemperance. 44812
Speeches, . . . on harbor and river bill. 51466
Speeches . . . on his [i. e. Henry Winter Davis'] bill. 18830

Spiegel der Spaense tyranny in West-Indien. 11266

Spiegel der Spaense tyrannye geschiet in West-Indien. 11254, 11262

Spiegel der Taufe, mit Geist. 89432

Spiegel der Tauffe mit Geist. 89431

Spiegel voor de Jeucht. 5100

Spieghel der Australische Navigatie. 14348, 14353, 44059, 77920

Spieghel der Spaenscher tirannije. (11249)-11251

Spieghel der Spaenscher tyrannye. 11251-11252

Spieghel der Spaenscher tyrannye in West-Indien. (11254), 11262

Spieghel der werelt. (31667)

Spieghel vande Spaensche tyrannie beeldelijcken af-gemaelt. 11253

Spier, Richard. petitioner 97891

Spierin, George Heartwell. 86880, 89433-89434

Spierin, George Heartwell, Jr. 89435

Spies, Johann Carolus. 89436-89437

Spies, William A. 89438

Spiess, Christian Heinrich. 89439

Spiess, Edmund. 89440

Spilberg, G. see Spilbergen, Joris van.

Spilbergen, Georgio von. see Spilbergen, Joris van.

Spilbergen, Joris van. (8784), 14349, 14957-14960, 30680, 33670, 66686, 68455, 74836, 77933, 89441-89452

Spilimberg, Fulquer. see Spirembergo, Placido.

Spillman, William. 89454

Spilman, Charles Harvey. 89453

Spilsbury, Johann. 13867

Spindler, Carl. ed. 91283

Spindler, Karl. ed. 92567

Spingler Institute, New York. 89455

Spinney, James W. 69858

Spinning wheel. 103135

Spinning-wheel of Tamworth. 84732

Spinola, Ambrogio. see Sesso e di Venafro, Ambrogio Spinola, Marchese del.

Spinola, Fabius Ambrosius. 89458-89460

Spinola, H. de. 89461

Spinosa, Rodrigo Saenz de Santayana y. see Saenz de Santayana y Spinosa, Rodrigo.

Spinoza, Francis. pseud. Strictures on a pamphlet. 89462

Spinoza. 71518

Spion. 16535

Spionen. 16537

Spiral Press. firm publishers 103923

Spirembergo, Placido. 89466

Spirit. An address delivered before the Philomathean Society. 89467

Spirit and duty of Christian citizenship. 31670

Spirit and philosophy of Uncle Tom's cabin. note after 92624

Spirit communication. 89468

Spirit congress. 89469

Spirit-intercourse. 85519-85520

Spirit messages from Franklin. 71149

Spirit of a discourse. (70928)

Spirit of adventure. (51491)

Spirit of an evening lecture. 70927

Spirit of contradiction. 89470

Spirit of despotism. 89471-89472

Spirit of discovery. 7086

Spirit of dissent. 89473

Spirit of 1862. 89474

Spirit of error. 62921

Spirit of evil and the spirit of good. 65495

Spirit of fanaticism. 89475

Spirit of Frazer, to General Burgoyne. 89476

Spirit of free-masonry. (55190)

Spirit of God a holy fire. 83448

Spirit of human liberty. 26323

Spirit of humanity, and essence of morality. 89477

Spirit of humanity, and the animal's friend. 89477

Spirit of humanity, extracted from the productions. 89478

Spirit of independence. 9235

Spirit of Jesus. (26240)

Spirit of John Jay. pseud. War with England. 101268

Spirit of laws. 96413

Spirit of liberty. An oration. (31890)

Spirit of liberty: or, Junius's loyal address. 36919

Spirit of life entering into the spiritually dead. 46529, 89479

Spirit of Madison. 89480

Spirit of man. 50994

Spirit of Methodism. 66541, 89481

Spirit of military institutions. 44651

Spirit of missions. 89482

Spirit of my sainted sire. 92177A

Spirit of our fathers, the nation's hope. 49036

Spirit of Paul the spirit of missions. 70950

Spirit of popery and the duty of protestants. 71115

Spirit of practical Godliness. 89483

Spirit of practical Godliness, and total abstience advocate. 89483

Spirit of prayer. (39324)

Spirit of railing Shimei. 37220, 66738

Spirit of Rhode Island history. 2084

Spirit of Roger Williams. 36254

Spirit of Seventy-Six. pseud. Candid examination. 64477

Spirit of '76. pseud. Spirit of '76, to the people of Kentucky. 89489

Spirit of '76 (Nashville) 89485

Spirit of '76: a weekly publication devoted to politics and local discussions. 32568, 89484

"Spirit of '76." First centennial report. 89486

Spirit of '76 in Rhode Island. 17235

Spirit of seventy-six; or, the coming woman. 18031, 89487

Spirit of 'seventy-six. 1776. 1876. 89488

Spirit of '76, to the people of Kentucky. 89489

Spirit of the age. 89936

"Spirit of the age." An address . . . before the two literary societies. 62904

Spirit of the age, and journal of humanity. 89491

Spirit of the age. Edited by Wm. H. Channing. 89490

Spirit of the annuals, for MDCCCXXX. 89492

Spirit of the annuals, for 1831. 89492

Spirit of the campaign. 89493

Spirit of the Chicago convention. 12662, 89494-89495

Spirit of the Christian ministry. 58800

Spirit of the conflict. 73487

Spirit of the Fair 1864. 89496

Spirit of the Fair for the Building Fund. 89497A

Spirit of the Fair. "None but the brave deserve the fair." 89497

Spirit of the Farmers' museum, and lay preacher's gazette. (19587), 89498

Spirit of the foreign magazines. 78991

Spirit of the foreign theological journals and reviews. 69354

Sprecher, Samuel P. 89754
Sprecher de Bernegy, J. A. 56240, note after 89754
Sprees and splashes. 50630
Sprengel, K. tr. (35457)
Sprengel, Matthias Christian, 1746-1803. 4964, 7544, 7929, 27381, 31186, 31207, 49480-49482, 51344, 67461, 89744, 89755-89765, 91079, 91304, 98444, 100690, note after 104633
Sprenger, Heinrich. 99383
Sprigg, Richard. 89764
Sprigg, Samuel. 45143 see also Maryland. Governor, 1819-1822 (Sprigg)
Sprightly widow. 49328
Spring, Arthur. defendant 89765-89766
Spring, Charles A. defendant (82175)
Spring, Gardiner. 17270, 30517, 32435, 49478, 2d note after 69442, (78821), 89767-89783, 104947
Spring, Lindley. 89784-89786
Spring, Samuel, 1746-1819. 44510, 62422, 89787-89813, 94368, 99826, 105136 see also Congregational Churches in Massachusetts. Ecclesiastical Council, Ipswich, 1805.
Spring, Samuel, 1792-1877. 89814-89815
Spring Arbor, Mich. Michigan Central College. see Hillsdale College, Hillsdale, Mich.
Spring blossoms, a daily paper. 89816
Spring Garden (District), Philadelphia. 61852
Spring Garden (District), Philadelphia. Charter. (59807), 60650
Spring Garden (District), Philadelphia. Commissioners. 62300
Spring Garden (District), Philadelphia. Free Reading Room. see Spring Garden Institute, Philadelphia.
Spring Garden (District), Philadelphia. Free Reading Room Association. see Spring Garden Institute, Philadelphia.
Spring Garden (District), Philadelphia. Ordinances, etc. (61589), 62300, 89817
Spring Garden (District), Philadelphia. Solicitor. 89817 see also Bethell, Robert.
Spring Garden (District), Philadelphia. Water Works. 62371 see also Joint Watering Committee of Northern Liberties and Spring Garden Water Works.
Spring Garden (District), Philadelphia. Watering Committee. 62371
Spring Garden Institute, Philadelphia. 62270, 89820
Spring Garden Institute, Philadelphia. Board of Managers. 62271, 89821
Spring Garden Institute, Philadelphia. Charter. 89821
Spring Garden Institute, Philadelphia. Library. 89818-89819
Spring Garden Institute, Philadelphia. Treasurer. 89821
Spring Grove Cemetery, Cincinnati. see Cincinnati. Spring Grove Cemetery.
Spring Grove Cemetery. Its history and improvements. 13114, note after 89825, note after 92746
Spring Hill Boarding School, Sandwich, Mass. 89826
Spring Hill College, Mobile, Ala. 89827
Spring Lane School, Boston. see Boston. Spring Lane School.
Spring notes. 89829
Spring of life. 101305
Spring Street Church, Newport, R. I. see Newport, R. I. Spring Street Church.

Spring Street Congregational Church, Milwaukee. see Milwaukee. Spring Street Congregational Church.
Spring Valley, N. J. Religious Society. Committee. 89839
Spring-Villa Seminary for Young Ladies, Bordentown, N. J. 89831
Spring water versus river water for supplying the city of New York. 29643, (54680)
Springbok (Barque) in Admiralty 58473-58474, note after 89831
Springer, Balthasar. 99363
Springer, Mrs. C. 85143
Springer, Cornelius. 89832
Springer, J. 89833-89834
Springer, J. J. 89835
Springer, Johann Christoph Eric. 89836
Springer, John S. 89837
Springer, Moses, Jr. 89838-89839
Springer, Rob. tr. 17936
Springer, William McKendree. 89840, 89842
Springer, William McKendree. defendant 89841
Springer. firm publishers 89843
Springer's Cleveland city guide. 89842
Springfield, Ill. Board of Trade. 64771, note after 89851
Springfield, Ill. Library Association. see Springfield Library Association, Springfield, Ill.
Springfield, Ill. National Lincoln Monument. 89850
Springfield, Ill. Old Settlers' Society. see Old Settlers' Society, Springfield, Ill.
Springfield, Ill. St. Paul's Church. 89851
Springfield, Ill. State Board of Equalization. see Illinois. State Board of Equalization.
Springfield, Ill. State Historical Library. see Illinois State Historical Library, Springfield, Ill.
Springfield, Ky. Presbytery. see Presbyterian Church in the U. S. A. Presbytery of Springfield.
Springfield, Mass. Cabot Institute. see Cabot Institute, Springfield, Mass.
Springfield, Mass. Chapin Family Meeting, 1862. see Meeting of the Chapin Family, Springfield, Mass., 1862.
Springfield, Mass. City Council. 89859
Springfield, Mass. City Hall. 89859
Springfield, Mass. City Library. 89884
Springfield, Mass. City Library Association. 89853
Springfield, Mass. City Library Association. Library. 89854
Springfield, Mass. Commemoration of the Birthday of Washington, 1862. 89872
Springfield, Mass. Debating Society. see Springfield Debating Society, Springfield, Mass.
Springfield, Mass. Firemen's Mutual Relief Association. see Firemen's Mutual Relief Association, Springfield, Mass.
Springfield, Mass. First Baptist Church. 89861
Springfield, Mass. First Church of Christ. 89862-89863
Springfield, Mass. First Congregational Church. 89864
Springfield, Mass. High School. Alumni Association. 89865
Springfield, Mass. Home for Friendless Women and Children. see Springfield Home for Friendless Women and Children, Springfield, Mass.
Springfield, Mass. Library Company. see Springfield Library Company, Springfield, Mass.

Springfield, Mass. Lincoln Funeral Day, 1865. 89868
Springfield, Mass. Mayor, 1872 (Spooner) 89623 see also Spooner, Samuel B.
Springfield, Mass. Mechanics' Mutual Benefit Association. see Mechanics' Mutual Benefit Association, Springfield, Mass.
Springfield, Mass. Meeting of the Chapin Family, 1862. see Meeting of the Chapin Family, Springfield, Mass., 1862.
Springfield, Mass. Memorial Church. 89867
Springfield, Mass. Monson Academy. see Monson Academy, Springfield, Mass.
Springfield, Mass. National Exhibition of Horses. see National Exhibition of Horses, Springfield, Mass.
Springfield, Mass. New England Agricultural Society Annual Exhibition, 1st, 1864. see New England Agricultural Society. Annual Exhibition, 1st, Springfield, Mass., 1864.
Springfield, Mass. North Congregational Church. 89869
Springfield, Mass. North Congregational Church. Pastor. 89870
Springfield, Mass. Olivet Congregational Church. 89871
Springfield, Mass. South Church. 89873-89876
Springfield, Mass. Third Congregational Church. Committee. 89883
Springfield, Mass. Washington Benevolent Society. see Washington Benevolent Society. Massachusetts. Springfield.
Springfield, Mass. Whig State Convention, 1851. see Whig Party. Massachusetts. Convention, Springfield, 1851.
Springfield, Mass. Young Men's Institute. Library. see Springfield, Mass. City Library.
Springfield, Mass. Young Men's Library Association. see Young Men's Library Association, Springfield, Mass.
Springfield, N. J. Centennial Celebration, July 4, 1876. 89888, note after 94615
Springfield, N. J. Centennial Celebration, July 4, 1876. Committee of Publication. 89888, note after 94615 see also Graves, Henry W. Lyon, Sylvanus.
Springfield, Ohio. Charter. 89889
Springfield, Ohio. Female College. see Springfield Female College, Springfield, Ohio.
Springfield, Ohio. Ordinances, etc. 89889
Springfield, Vt. Congregational Church. 89895
Springfield, Vt. Congregational Church. Pastor. 89897 see also Cobb, L. H.
Springfield almanac, directory, and business advertiser. 89855
Springfield and Illinois Southeastern Railway Company. 89898-89899
Springfield and Illinois Southeastern Railway Company. Financial Agents. 89899 see also Jones & Schuyler. firm
Springfield and Illinois Southeastern Railway Company. President. 89898 see also Ridgway, Thomas S.
Springfield and Illinois Southeastern Railway Company. First mortgage, sinking fund, gold bonds. 89899
Springfield and Mansfield Railroad Company. 89900
Springfield and Mansfield Railroad Company. Engineer. 89900
Springfield Aqueduct Company. petitioners 89877, 90684, 90873

Springfield Board of Trade. see Springfield, Ill. Board of Trade.
Springfield city directory and business advertiser. 89857
Springfield city directory and business mirror, for 1866. 89846
Springfield city directory and business mirror, for 1863. 89845
Springfield city directory, and Sagnamon County advertiser. 89844
Springfield city directory for 1873-74. 89887
Springfield city directory. For 1868-9. 89847
Springfield city directory, for 1869-70. 89848
Springfield City Library Association, Springfield, Mass. 89853
Springfield Debating Society, Springfield, Mass. 89878
Springfield directory, city guide and business mirror. 89890
Springfield directory, 1873-1874. 89891
Springfield directory [for 1858-59.] 89856
Springfield directory for 1851-1852. 89856
Springfield Female College, Springfield, Ohio. 89894
Springfield Home for Friendless Women and Children, Springfield, Mass. Managers. 89879
Springfield Horse Show. see National Exhibition of Horses, Springfield, Mass.
Springfield horse shows. 89880
Springfield Library Association, Springfield, Ill. 89852
Springfield Library Company, Springfield, Mass. 89881
Springfield, Mount Vernon & Pittsburg Railroad Company, 89901-89902
Springfield, Mount Vernon & Pittsburg Railroad Company. Engineer. 89901
Springfield musket. 89882
Springfield Presbytery. see Presbyterian Church in the U. S. A. Presbytery of Springfield.
Springfield republican. (69693), 89868
Springfield route. From New-York to Boston. 89903
Springfield, Union County, N. J. The history of its centennial fourth. 89888, note after 94615
Springfield, Urbana, Piqua, Sidney and Bellefontaine city directories. 89892
Springs. 89904
Springs, water-falls, sea-bathing resorts, and mountain scenery. 20322, 89905
Springwater, Dr., of North America. pseud. Cold-water-man. see Quaw, James E. supposed author
Sprint, John. supposed author 97128
Sprite. 89907
Sproat, Gilbert Malcolm. 89908-89910 see also British Columbia. Agent-General.
Sproat, Granville Temple. 89911
Sproat, James. 89912, 97570
Sproat, Nancy. 89913
Sproat, P. W. 89914-89916, note after 103973
Sprole, William Thomas. 89917-89918
Sprotto y Compania. firm see Schwartz, Sprotto y Compania. firm
Sproule, G. 3606
Sproule, Ziba. pseud. Brief epistle from Dr. Ziba Sproule. see Sargent, Lucius Manlius. supposed author and Trask, George. supposed author
Sproule, Ziba. pseud. Diary of the Rev. Solomon Spittle. see Sargent, Lucius Manlius. supposed author and Trask, George. supposed author

Stacy, George G.   43987
Stacy, George W., fl. 1844.   90031
Stacy, George W., fl. 1862.   90031A
Stacy, Nathaniel.   90032-90033
Stacy, William R.   87016
Stadacona Club, Quebec.   90034
Stadacona depicta.   90035
Stade, Hans.   see   Staden, Hans.
Staden, Hans.   (8784), 25472, 23999, 77677-
    77678, 90036-note after 90060, 105680
Staden, Johann.   see   Staden, Hans.
Stadnitski, Pieter.   90061
Stadnitski (Pieter) & Son.   firm   90061
Stadt New-York und Umgebung.   90062
Stadtbibliothek, Frankfurt a. M.   see   Frankfurt
    a. M.   Stadtbibliothek.
Staehlin von Storcksburg, Jacob.   90063-90064
Staempfli, Jakob.   see   Stampfli, Jakob.
Staff officer.   pseud.   Story of the march
    through Georgia.   80415
Staff officer.   pseud.   With General Sherman.
    see   Newhall, Frederic C.   supposed
    author
Staff officer serving in Virginia.   pseud.
    Mohun.   see   Cooke, John Esten, 1830-
    1886.
Staff surgeon.   pseud.   Trifles from my port-
    folio.   see   Henry, Walter.
Staff surgeon: or, life in England and Canada.
    90069, 1st note after 94147
Stafford, Cornelius William.   2998, (61605),
    1st-2d notes after 90069
Stafford, Edward.   90070
Stafford, Granville Leveson-Gower, 1st
    Marquis of, 1721-1803.   40467
Stafford, Hosea.   pseud.   see   Strong, Nehemiah.
Stafford, John.   engr.   82815
Stafford, John Nathan.   90071
Stafford, Joseph.   62743, 90072-90076
Stafford, Marshall P.   24525, 90077-90078
Stafford, Ward.   54274, 90079, 90083
Stafford & Ward.   firm   petitioners   90080
Stafford, Conn.   Ecclesiastical Councils, 1781.
    see   Congregational Churches in Con-
    necticut.   Ecclesiastical Councils, Staf-
    ford, 1781.
Stafford, Conn.   Inhabitant.   pseud.   see   In-
    habitant of Stafford.   pseud.
Stafford, Conn.   Second Church.   25232, 73562
Stafford-House address.   81840
Stafford Western Emigration Company.   90081
Stafford's almanack, for . . . 1780.   93031
Stafford's almanac, for . . . 1785.   93036
Stafford's almanack, for . . . 1784.   93035
Stafford's almanack, for . . . 1781.   93032
Stafford's almanack, for . . . 1787.   93038
Stafford's almanack, for . . . 1786.   93037
Stafford's almanack for . . . 1783.   93034
Stafford's almanac, for . . . 1782.   93033
Stafford's almanack, for . . . 1798.   93049
Stafford's almanack, for . . . 1791.   93042
Stafford's almanack, for . . . 1797.   93048
Stafford's almanack, for . . . 1792.   93043
Stafford's almanac, for . . . 1778.   93029
Stafford's Connecticut almanack, for . . . 1779.
    93030
Stage, canal, and steamboat register.   90082,
    1st note after 104412
Stage-coach.   90083
Stage register.   2707, 90084
Stage, steamboat and canal routes.   49721
Stage the high road to hell, &c.   1619
Stages and distances between Philadelphia and
    the falls of the Ohio.   24336, 24337
Stagg, Abraham.   90085-90086

Stagg, Edward.   90087
Stagio Dati, Leonardo di.   90088
"Stahl."   pseud.   New Orleans sketch book.   see
    Wharton, George M.
Stahle, William.   90089
Stahr, Adolf Wilhelm Theodor.   90090
Stainforth, Francis John.   90091
Stair, John Dalrymple, 5th Earl of, 1720-1789.
    16018, 18348, 81396, 90092-90102
Stair, John Dalrymple, 5th Earl of, 1720-1789.
    plaintiff   5378, (53066), 53082, 53098
    see also   Board of Proprietors of the
    Eastern Division of New Jersey.   plaintiffs
Stair, Nil.   90103
Stait, William A.   (61999)
Stake, Edward.   90104
Staley, Thomas Nettleship, Bishop of Honolulu,
    1823-1898.   90105-90108
Stalker, Eunice.   90109
Stallenge, William.   90110
Stallo, John Bernhard.   90111-90112
Stambaugh, Samuel C.   (12457), 12477, 90113-
    90115, 96664   see also   U. S. Commis-
    sioners to the Cherokee Indians.   U. S.
    Commissioners to the Menomonee Indians.
Stamer, William.   90116
Stamford, Conn.   Baptist Church.   90117
Stamford, Conn.   Baptist Church.   Sunday
    School.   90117
Stamford, Conn.   First Church.   see   Stamford,
    Conn.   First Congregational Church.
Stamford, Conn.   First Congregational Church.
    90118-90120
Stamford, Conn.   First Presbyterian Church.
    90121
Stamford, Conn.   Social Reading Rooms.   see
    Social Reading Rooms, Stamford, Conn.
Stamford Auxiliary Bible Society.   see Rutland
    and Stamford Auxiliary Bible Society.
Stamford registration of births, marriages
    and deaths.   90124
Stamford Seminary.   Judson Circulating Library.
    90125
Stamford soldiers' memorial.   (33956), 90126
Stamler, John.   90127-90128
Stamm, Anton.   90129
Stamm, August Theodor.   90130
Stamp act.   90134
Stamp Act Congress, New York, 1765.   (2444),
    15541, 17722, 53537, 65831
Stamp-act repealed.   106392-106393
Stamp collector's manual.   38052
Stamp duties.   90142
Stampfli, Jakob.   90065-90067
Stanard, Robert C.   90142A
Stanbery, Henry, 1803-1881.   90143-90146   see
    also   U. S. Department of Justice.
Stanbury, Arthur Joseph.   reporter   59476, 1st
    note after 90364
Stanbury, Henry.   see   Stanbery, Henry, 1803-
    1881.
Stanbury's expedition.   90370
Stanbury's report.   90370
Stancliff, John.   50399, 90147-90151
Stand.   90152
Stand by the flag!   90153
Stand by the government.   (82667)
Stand by the President!   1297
Stand by your colors.   26267
Stand from under.   71824
Stand und Ergebnisse der Europaischen und
    Amerikanischen Eisenbahnen.   4381
Stand up for Jesus!   91918
Standard (Chicago)   83465
Standard (London)   19580, note after 92624

Standard (Schenectady) see Schenectady and Saratoga standard.
Standard. A journal of reform and literature. 90154
Standard American authors. 88987
Standard bearer. Editor. 72491 see also Rodman, Washington.
Standard drama. 84784
Standard drama series. 85169
Standard fifth reader. 76966
Standard first reader, for beginners. 76966
Standard fifth reader, part two. 76966
Standard fourth reader. 76966
Standard fourth reader. Part two. 76966
Standard illustrated edition. 92487
Standard library. 84306
Standard library edition. American statesmen. 84335-84336
Standard library of popular modern literature. 97028
Standard novels. 92464
Standard of classification of American vessels. 54801
Standard of liberty; a poetical address. 73617
Standard of liberty, an occasional paper. 7192, note after 90154
Standard of the Lord lifted up in New-England. (55230)
Standard of trade in those parts of America. 20404
Standard second reader. 76966
Standard second reader. Part two. 76966
Standard school primer. 76966
Standard speaker. 76966
Standard speller. 76966
Standard third reader. 76966
Standard third reader, part two. 76966
Standard works of the Society for the Diffusion of Christian Knowledge. 85885
Standefer, James. 90155-90156
Stander by. pseud. Private thoughts on public affairs. (65727)
Standfast, Richard. 90157-90162
Standfast, Silas. pseud. Letters. see Hillard, G. S.
Standiford, Elisha David. 90163-90165
Standing Committee Appointed to Foreward the Application for a Rail-Road from this Place to the Hudson River, Opposite New-York, Paterson, N. J. see Paterson, N. J. Standing Committee Appointed to Foreward the Application for a Rail-Road from This Place to the Hudson River, Opposite New-York.
Standing Committee of the Diocese of Massachusetts, and the Free Church of St. Mary for Sailors. 67784
Standing Committee of the Diocese of New York. In the matter of Christ Church, New-Brighton. 52516
Standing Committee of the West India Planters and Merchants see West India Planters and Merchants. Standing Committee.
[Standing order of House relative to petitions claiming money.] 100085
Standing orders for the Garrison of Philadelphia. 62272
Standing orders of the Legislative Council. 56191
Standing rules and orders for conducting business. 16117
Standing rules and orders of the House of Representatives. 15595
Standing rules and orders of the Overseers of the college. 7019

Standing rules and regulations of the Legislative Assembly of Canada. 10502
Standing rules, confession of faith, convenant and catalogue of officers. 89876
Standing rules for conducting business in the House of Representatives. 94967
Standing rules for the government of the Convention of Texas. 94977, 94979
Standing rules for the government of the . . . ministers, elders, & deacons. 54616
Standish, George. 90166
Standish, Miles, Jr. pseud. Times: a poem. 48943, 90167, note after 95840
Standish: a story or our day. 90168
Standish memorial. 90170-90171
Standish Memorial Association. 90170-90172
Standish Memorial Association. Charter. 90173
Standish Memorial Association. Corresponding Secretary. 90169, 90173 see also Allen, Stephen M.
Standish Monument Association. see Standish Memorial Association.
Standish Monument Association. Honor to the first commissioned military officer. 90172
Standish monument. Exercises at the consecration. 90171
Standish monument on Captain's Hill, Duxbury. 90173
Standish, the puritan. (28423), note before 90174
Standley, Thomas. 97747
Standlichen Nachricht von der Beschaffenheit dieser beyden stadte. (74620)
Stanfield, James Field. 90174-90175
Stanford, Amasa Leland. see Stanford, Leland, 1824-1893.
Stanford, C. O. 88213 see also South Side Railroad Company, Virginia. Chief Engineer.
Stanford, John. 54183, 90176-90209 see also New York (City) Almshouse and Penitentiary, Bellevue. Chaplain.
Stanford, Leland, 1824-1893. 90210-90212 see also California. Governor, 1862-1864 (Stanford) Central Pacific Railroad Company. President.
Stanford, Richard. 90213-90214
Stanford, Thomas N. 54459, 90215-90216
Stanford (Edward) firm publishers 34111
Stanford and Swords. firm 90217
Stanford University publications. History and economics, Illl. 83566
Stanford's emigrant's guides. 34111
Stanford's postprandial New-Year's day soliloquy. 90212
Stanhope, Eugenia. 90223
Stanhope, George. 90218-90219
Stanhope, Sir John, fl. 1603. 67545
Stanhope, Sir John. see Stanhope of Harrington, John Stanhope, 1st Baron.
Stanhope, Leicester Fitzgerald Charles. see Harrington, Leicester Fitzgerald Charles Stanhope, 5th Earl of, 1784-1862.
Stanhope, Philip Dormer. see Chesterfield, Philip Dormer Stanhope, 4th Earl of, 1694-1773.
Stanhope, Philip Henry. see Stanhope, Philip Henry Stanhope, 5th Earl of, 1805-1875.
Stanhope, Philip Henry Stanhope, 5th Earl of, 1805-1875. (25054), 58325, 68621, 88978, 89000, 89003, 89004, 90287-90291
Stanhope, William. see Harrington, William Stanhope, 1st Earl of, d. 1756.

Stanhope of Harrington, John Stanhope, 1st Baron. 90220
Stanhope Burleigh. 90293
Staniford, Daniel. 90294-90295
Staniford's practical arithmetic. 90295
Stanislaus, Francis Alexander. see Wimpffen, Francis Alexander Stanislaus, Baron de.
Stanley, Charles. see Derby, Charles Stanley, 8th Earl of.
Stanley, Charles Henry. 90298
Stanley, Clinton W. 90299 see also Dartmouth College. Class of 1849. Permanent Secretary.
Stanley, E. G. 9398
Stanley, E. S. 90300-90301
Stanley, Edward, Bishop of Norwich, 1779-1849. 90302
Stanley, Edward George Geoffrey Smith. see Derby, Edward George Geoffrey Smith Stanley, 14th Earl of.
Stanley, Edward Henry. see Derby, Edward Henry Stanley, 15th Earl of.
Stanley, George Washington. 90308-90310
Stanley, Harvey. 90311
Stanley, Henry. ed. 21641, note after 90311
Stanley, Henry Edward John Stanley, 3d Baron, 1827-1903. 62806, note after 90319
Stanley, John. 90312
Stanley, John Mix. 69946, 85047, 90313-90314
Stanley, Mortimer D. defendant 90315
Stanley, Ruth. 90316
Stanley, S. supposed author (22963), note after 90316
Stanley, T. Lloyd. pseud. Outline of the future religion of the world. see Smith, Richard Morris, 1827-1896.
Stanley, Thomas. 90317
Stanley, W. 26314
Stanley, William. 90318-90319
Stanley-Brown, Joseph. ed. 84339
Stanley of Alderley, Henry Edward John Stanley, 2d Baron. see Stanley, Henry Edward John Stanley, 3d Baron, 1827-1903.
Stanley-Smith, James. see Strange, James Stanley-Smith, commonly styled Lord.
Stanley & Dickermann's North American Indian Portrait Gallery. 90313
Stanley-Pope discussion. 90304
Stanly, E. G. (10535)
Stanly, Edward, 1810-1872. 90320-90339 see also North Carolina. Military Governor, 1862-1863 (Stanly)
Stanly, John. 90340-90350
Stanly, John Wright. 90351
Stanly, William. 55078
Stanmore, Arthur Hamilton-Gordon, 1st Baron. 27968, note after 90353
Stannage, John. 90354-90355
Stansberry, ------. 90356
Stansbury, A. O. 90357
Stansbury, Arthur Joseph. 90358-90365
Stansbury, Arthur Joseph. reporter 59476, 96150, 96822, 96825
Stansbury, Charles Frederick. 90366-90368
Stansbury, Howard. 90370-90374
Stansbury, Joseph. 90375
Stansbury, Philip. 59510, 90376
Stanser, Robert. pseud. Examination of the Reverend Mr. Burke's letter. see Croke, Sir Alexander.
Stansfield, F. W. H. 90378
Stantibus &c. 96234
Stanton, Benjamin, 1809-1872. 23331, 89208, 90379-90384
Stanton, Benjamin Franklin. 90385-90386

Stanton, Daniel. 90387-90388, 97059
Stanton, Edwin L. 90389
Stanton, Edwin McMasters, 1814-1869. 15430, 80414, 90390-90394 see also U. S. War Department.
Stanton, Elizabeth Cady. 65869, (70344), 90395-90405
Stanton, Elizabeth Cady. petitioner 90404
Stanton, Frederick Perry, 1814-1894. 69887, 90406-90427 see also U. S. Congress. House. Committee on Naval Affairs. Chairman.
Stanton, Henry Brewster. 90428-90430
Stanton, J. M. 90430A
Stanton, John. 90431
Stanton, Lewis Elliott. 90432
Stanton, Phineas. 90433
Stanton, Phineas. defendant 90433
Stanton, Richard Henry, 1810-1891. 37539, 90434-90436
Stanton, Robert Livingston. 90437-90444
Stanton, Robert P. 90445
Stanton, Samuel. 90446
Stanton, Thomas. 22149, 59561 see also United Colonies of New England. Interpreter-General to the Indians.
Stanton, William. 90447
Stanton Copper Mining Company. 90448
Stanton Copper Mining Company. Charter. 90448
Stanton Street Baptist Church, New York. see New York (City) Stanton Street Baptist Church.
Stanwich, Conn. Congregational Church. 90450-90451
Stanwick, John. supposed author. 14032, 85597, 94025
Stanwix, John. 90452-90453
Stanwood, Arthur G. 90454
Stanwood, Avis A. (Burnham) 90455-90456
Stanwood, David. defendant at court martial 90457
Stanwood, Edward, 1841-1923. 90459-90460
Stanwood family. 90461
Stanzas to Queen Victoria. 9311, note after 90461
Stapfern, J. J. ed. 16958
Staple, W. C. 90462
Staple trade of Canada. 61032
Staples, ------. 97091
Staples, Carlton Albert. 47819, 90463-90465
Staples, Daniel. 90466
Staples, Franklin. 90467
Staples, Hamilton Barclay. 90468
Staples, John Bethune. 90469
Staples, John I. plaintiff 96865
Staples, M. W. 90470
Staples, Nahor Augustus. 90471-90473
Staples William Read. (28046), 65849, 70617, 90475-90478
Staples (Robert P.) and Co. firm 90474
Stapleton, Augustus Granville. 90479-90481
Stapp, Milton. 34525, 90482 see also Indiana. Fund Commissioner.
Stapp, William Preston. 90483
Star (Hartford, Conn.) 90484
Star (London) 91923, 99774
Star. A collection of songs. 90485
Star-banner song. 16297
Star Copper Company, Keweenaw Point, Mich. Directors. 90486
Star corps. (7279)
Star Fire Society, Newport, R. I. 90487
Star in the east, a tract for universal distribution. 90489

Star in the east. Edited by Elder G. J. Adams. 90488
Star in the west. 6856
Star of Columbia. 90490
Star of emancipation. 90491
Star of freedom. 90492
Star of freedom. A congressional & legislative journal. 90493
Star of freedom. Literary, political, & agricultural. 90493
Star of New York. 90494
Star of the south. (31081)
Star of the west (Steamship) in Admiralty 66109
Star of the west. 11065
Star of the west, of Kenyon College, in 1828. 12194
Star song book. 90495
Star songster. 90496
Star spangled banner. (37668), 83677, note before 90497, 90499, 90501, 90502, 105959, 105966
Star spangled banner: being a collection of the best naval, martial, patriotic songs, etc. 90503
Star spangled banner; being the latest and best selection ever offered to the public. 100655
Star-Spangled Banner Chapter, no. 96, Albany, N. Y. see Order of United Americans. Star-Spangled Banner Chapter, no. 96, Albany, N. Y.
Star spangled banner illustrated from drawings by F. O. Darley. 90500
Star spangled banner, sung by Messrs Darley & Nicholls. 90498
Starbird, Samuel Sylvester. 90504
Starbuck, Alexander. 90505
Starbuck, James F. 90506
Starbuck, Jethro. respondent 51752
Starbuck, Lucy Coffin. 90507
Starbock, Roger. 90508
Starbuck, Samuel. respondent 51752
Starbuck, Thomas. respondent 51752
Starbuck, Tristram. respondent 51752
Starck, Johann August. 90509
Starhemberg, Camillo Heinrich. 90510
Stark, Alexander W. 90511
Stark, Andrew. 30751, 56597, note before 90516
Stark, Andrew. defendant before Presbytery 90512, 90514
Stark, Andrew. reporter 90516, note after 96840, 1st note after 97091
Stark, Caleb. 72730, 90517-90518
Stark, James. 90519
Stark, John. 90518
Starke, James. 50269, note after 90523
Starke, Mariana. 90520
Starke, Mariana. supposed author 64088, note after 90519
Starke, Richard. 90521
Starke, Samuel. 90522
Starke, W. W. 90523
Starke. firm publishers see Mills & Starke. firm publishers
Starke's pocket almanack. 50269, note after 90523
Starkey, George R. 90524-90525
Starkey, James. supposed author 93472
Starkey, Thomas Alfred. 90526-90529
Starkey, N. Y. Starkey Seminary. see Starkey Seminary, Starkey, N. Y.
Starkey Seminary, Starkey, N. Y. 90530
Starksborough and Lincoln Anti-slavery Society. 81766, note after 90530

Starkweather, Albert L. defendant 90531
Starkweather, David Austin. 90532
Starkweather, George Anson. 90533-90534
Starkweather, Henry Howard. 90535
Starkweather, John. 90536
Starkweather, John Converse. 90537
Starkweather, Samuel. 90538
Starlight. 90539
Starling, Lyne. 90541
Starling, Samuel. 90540, 97265
Starling Medical College, Columbus, Ohio. 84070, 90541
Starnes, Ebenezer. 36595, 82069, note after 90541, note after 95543, note after 95665
Starnes, Henry. 90542
Starr, Ann Eliza. 90543
Starr, Chandler. 90544-90545
Starr, Eliza Allen, 1824-1901. 86272, 90547
Starr, F. Ratchford. 90548
Starr, Frederick. 40581, 90549-90551
Starr, George C. 90552
Starr, Gideon. 90553
Starr, J. Leander. 90554
Starr, J. W. 90555
Starr, Jeremiah. 90556
Starr, Leander. tr. 59582
Starr, M. B. 90557
Starr, Peter, 1744-1829. 90558
Starr, Peter, 1778-1860. 90559
Starr, Samuel. 90561-90562
Starr, Tarpley. 90564
Starr, W. H. ed. 23843, 69965
Starr, William E. 90676 see also Massachusetts. State Reform School, Westboro. Superintendent.
Starr, William G. 90566
Starr, William Henry. 90567
Starr, William Holt. 90568
Starr (R.) & Co. firm 90560
Starr (Samuel C.) firm publishers 90563
Starr Institute, Rhinebeck, N. Y. 90569
Starr Institute, Rhinebeck, N. Y. Circulating Department. 90569
Starr Institute, Rhinebeck, N. Y. Standard Library. 90569
Starring, Frederick Augustus. 90570
Starry calculator. 90571-90572
Starry flag. 57216
Stars and bars. 37327
"Stars and stripes." 68784
Stars and stripes. A poem pronounced before the Phi Beta Kappa Society. 31262
Stars and stripes in rebeldom. 3950, note after 90573
Stars and stripes; or, American impressions. (27723)
Stars and stripes songster. No. I. 90574
Stars and stripes songster. Original patriotic songs and marching choruses. 90574
Stars and stripes: the flag of the United States of America. 90573
Stars of Columbia. 90575
Startling and thrilling narrative. 90576
Startling confessions of Eleanor Burton. 90577
Starling confessions of the terrible deeds of Henry Madison. 90576
Startling developments of Crim. Con. 30355
Startling disclosure of the secret workings of the Jesuits. 90578
Startling disclosures concerning the death of John N. Maffit. 31680
Startling disclosures of Romanism. 64128
Startling disclosures of the great Mormon conspiracy. 98494
Startling disclosures of the wonderful ceremonies. 98494

Startling disclosures! The Bureau of Engraving and Printing and its head. 90579

Startling discoveries concerning the death of John Maffitt. 43790

Startling facts. A tract for the times (extra.) 80495, note after 90579

Startling facts for American protestants! 55878

Startling facts for native Americans called "Know-Nothings." (38146), 90580

Startling incidents and developments of Osowottomy Brown's insurrectionary and treasonable movements, &c. 8521, note after 90580

Startling revelations from the Department of South Carolina. 38176

Startling scenes and perilous adventures in the far west. 74890-74891

Startling truths concerning the management. 60278

Startling truths relating to the burning of New Jersey. 90581

State affairs. 90582

State Agricultural & Mechanical Society of South Carolina. 87692

State Agricultural & Mechanical Society of South Carolina. Annual Convention, Columbia, 1869. 88057

State Agricultural & Mechanical Society of South Carolina. Annual Fair, 1st, Columbia, 1856. 88060

State Agricultural & Mechanical Society of South Carolina. Annual Fair, 4th, Columbia, 1872. 88056

State Agricultural & Mechanical Society of South Carolina. Executive Committee. 88600

State Agricultural College, East Lansing, Mich. see Michigan. State University, East Lansing.

State Agricultural College, Michigan. 1866. Report of the President. (48716)

State Agricultural Convention, Albany, 1832. see New York State Agricultural Convention, Albany, 1832.

State Agricultural Society of California. see California State Agricultural Society.

State Agricultural Society of Illinois. see Illinois State Agricultural Society.

State Agricultural Society of Michigan. see Michigan State Agricultural Society.

State Agricultural Society of Minnesota. see Minnesota State Agricultural Society.

State Agricultural Society of New Jersey. see Agricultural Society of New Jersey.

State Agricultural Society of New York. see New York State Agricultural Society.

State Agricultural Society of North Carolina. Annual address. (13707)

State Agricultural Society of Oregon. 57571

State Agricultural Society of Pennsylvania. see Pennsylvania State Agricultural Society.

State Agricultural Society of South Carolina (1839-1845) 933, 78551, 87499, 87741, 88058-88059

State Agricultural Society of South Carolina (1839-1845) Committee on the Mill Constructed by Mr. John Ravenel. 67988, 87743

State Agricultural Society of South Carolina (1839-1845) Committee to Consider what Beneficial Effects Would Result to the Agricultural Interests of the State, by Importing Foreign Seeds. 87742

State Agricultural Society of South Carolina (1839-1845) Importing Committee. 87739

State Agricultural Society of South Carolina (1855-1861) see State Agricultural & Mechanical Society of South Carolina.

State Agricultural Society of South Carolina, Charleston. see State Agricultural Society of South Carolina (1839-1845)

State Agricultural Society of South Carolina, Columbia. Board of Curators. 87744

State Agricultural Society of Tennessee. see Tennessee State Agricultural Society.

State aid to railroads. 90583

State and case of the Quakers presented to all people. 44277

State and charity. 84068

State and national banks. 67147

State and national banks. The question of taxation, &c. (72141)

State and National Law School, Ballston Spa, N. Y. 2974, (53961)

State and prospects of Jamaica. 37795

State and prospects of religion in New York. (2796)

State and prospects of Utah. (64963)

State and the Baltimore & Ohio R. R. Co. 90584

State and the nation. 4575

State and the national governments. 33337

State and Union Law College, Ohio. see Ohio State and Union Law College.

State Archaeological and Historical Society of Ohio. see Ohio State Archaeological and Historical Society.

State armory & town hall. 45367

State Bank of Indiana. 34490

State Bank of Indiana. Bondholders. see Bondholders of the Indiana State Bank for 1844-1845. petitioners

State Bank of Indiana. Charter. 39435, 100879

State banks.—Taxation.—Legal tender notes. 89036

State Bible Society of Minnesota. see Minnesota State Bible Society.

State Board of Agriculture, and the management of the State Farm at Westborough. 24766

State Board of Health. A communication to a member of the Legislature. 84270

State book of Pennsylvania. 9470

State canals. 90585

State citizens, general citizens. (5931)

State Committee of Republicans, Appointed to Correspond With the Committees of the Several Counties of . . . Pennsylvania. see Democratic Party. Pennsylvania. State Committee.

State Convention for Rescuing the Canals from the Ruin With Which They are Threatened, Rochester, 1859. see New-York State Convention for Rescuing the Canals from the Ruin With Which They are Threatened, Rochester, 1859.

State Convention for Rescuing the Canals from the Ruin With Which They are Threatened, Utica, N. Y., 1859. see New-York State Convention for Rescuing the Canals from the Ruin With Which They are Threatened, Utica, 1859.

State Convention of Colored Citizens, Albany, N. Y., 1840. see New York State Convention of Colored Citizens, Albany, 1840.

State Convention of Coloured Citizens of Pennsylvania, Harrisburg, 1848. 60262

State Convention of Colored Men, Lexington, Ky., 1867. 37567

State Convention of Colored People, Albany, N. Y., 1851. see New York State Convention of Colored People, Albany, 1851.

State Convention of Delegates from the Several Counties of . . . New-York, Albany, 1828. see National Republican Party. New York. Convention, Albany, 1828.

State Convention of Mechanics, Utica, 1834. (65909)

State Convention of National Republican Young Men, Hartford, Conn., 1832. see Hartford, Conn. Natitional Convention of Republican Young Men, 1832.

State Convention of Sabbath School Teachers, 1st, Hartford, Conn., 1857. 15733

State Convention of Teachers and Friends of Education, Utica, N. Y., 1831. see New York State Convention of Teachers and Friends of Education, Utica, 1831.

State Convention of the Colored Citizens of Ohio, Columbus, 1849. 56961

State Convention of the Soldiers of the War of 1812, Syracuse, 1854. see Convention of the Soldiers of the War of 1812, Syracuse, 1854.

State Convention of the Southern Rights Party o of Kentucky, Frankfort, 1861. see Southern Rights Party of Kentucky. Convention, Frankfort, 1861.

State Convention of the Whig Young Men of Connecticut, Hartford, 1840. see Whig Party. Connecticut. State Convention of Whig Young Men, Hartford, 1840.

State Convention of the Young Men's Christian Association of New Hampshire. see Young Men's Christian Association of New Hampshire. State Convention.

State Convention of Whig Young Men, of Massachusetts, Worcester, 1839. see Whig Party. Massachusetts. Young Men's Convention, Worcester, 1839.

State Convention on Internal Improvements containing the resolutions, &c. 45368

State Convention to Consider Measures for Reforming the Management and Improving the Trade of the . . . Canals, Rochester, N. Y., 1870. (53869)

State Convention to Promote Common School Education, Harrisburg, Pa., 1850. see Pennsylvania State Convention to Promote Common School Education, Harrisburg, 1850.

State Convention to Select . . . Candidates for President and Vice-President of the United States of America, Albany, 1828. see National Republican Party. New York. Convention, Albany, 1828.

State, county and town tax. 74464

State creeds and their modern apostles. 90112

State debt. A plain statement of facts. 90586

State debt. An address. 83004

State debt of Tennessee. 92001

State Directors of the Delaware and Raritan Canal and Camden and Amboy Railroad Companies. see Joint Board of Directors of the Delaware and Raritan Canal, and Camden and Amboy Railroad Transportation Companies.

State Disunion Convention, Worcester, Mass., 1857. see Massachusetts State Disunion Convention, Worcester, 1857.

State documents relating to the conferences at Jalapa. 35540

State Education Convention, Columbus, 1837. see Ohio State Education Convention, Columbus, 1837.

State education not radically wrong. 45137

State ex rel. the Attorney-General vs. mandamus. 87469

State ex relatione the Attorney-General of South Carolina. 87470

State exaltation. 27505

State farce. 36936

State gazette and merchants and farmers' directory for Maryland. 90587

State gazette of North-Carolina. 99743

State gazetteer and business directory, for 1859 and 1860. (37514)

State geological survey of Iowa. (35001)

State Historical Society of Iowa. see Iowa State Historical Society.

State Historical Society of Kentucky. see Kentucky State Historical Society.

State Historical Society of Mississippi. see Mississippi Historical Society.

State Historical Society of Wisconsin. see Wisconsin. State Historical Society.

State Hospital, Fulton, Mo. see Missouri. State Hospital, Fulton.

State Hospital, St. Peter, Minn. see Minnesota. State Hospital, St. Peter.

State House, in Boston, Massachusetts. (66637)

State Independent Free Territory Convention of the People of Ohio, Cincinnati, 1848. 56873

State Industrial School for Girls, Lancaster, Mass. see Massachusetts. State Industrial School for Girls, Lancaster.

State Institution of Civil Engineers of New York. see New York State Institution of Civil Engineers.

State: its firms; political powers, centralization of the federal state. (72598)

State lecturer. pseud. Ritual and songs of the Cold Water Legions. 71599

State liabilities. 56881

State liberties. (33584)

State Lunatic Asylum, Fulton, Mo. see Missouri. State Hospital, Fulton.

State Medical Association of Kentucky. see Kentucky State Medical Society.

State Medical Convention, Lancaster, Pa., 1848. see Medical Society of Pennsylvania. Convention, Lancaster, 1848.

State Medical Society of Illinois. see Illinois State Medical Society.

State Medical Society of Indiana. see Indiana State Medical Society.

State Medical Society of Kentucky. see Kentucky Kentucky State Medical Society.

State Medical Society of Louisiana. see Louisiana State Medical Society.

State Medical Society of Minnesota. see Minnesota State Medical Society.

State Mechanics' Association of New York. see New York State Mechanics' Association.

State Military Convention, Syracuse, N. Y., 1853. 65911

State Military Convention, Worcester, Mass., 1835. see Military Convention, Worcester, Mass., 1835.

State military record. 53552

State Normal School. 53967

State Normal University, Normal, Ill. see Illinois. State Normal University, Normal.

State nullification discussed. 9948

State of additional propositions. 105707

State of Alabama. 29557

State of the account of John Forsyth. 106029

State of the account of John M'Clellan. 106032

State of the accounts and disputes. 90353

State of the accounts of Adam Hubley. (38801)

State of the accounts of Adam Orth. (38801)

State of the accounts of Andrew Boyd. 7102

State of the accounts of Andrew Kachline. 36970

State of the accounts of Archibald Thompson. 62277

State of the accounts of Benjamin Brannan. 7410

State of the accounts of Col. George Smith. 62278

State of the accounts of Col. Samuel Hunter. 55846

State of the accounts of Conrad Foos. (24998)

State of the accounts of Edward Batholomew. 3714-3716

State of the accounts of Edward Cook. 103040

State of the accounts of George Clingan. (13705)

State of the accounts of George Graff. 55774

State of the accounts of George Graff, Esq. Collector of Excise, Northampton County. . . . 1782 to . . . 1784. 55774

State of the accounts of George Graff, Esq. Collector of Excise, . . . to the 2d of August, 1784. 38802

State of the accounts of Gerardus Wyncoop, Esquire, Collector of Excise, Bucks County. 105677

State of the accounts of Gerardus Wyncoop, Esq. late Collector of Excise, Bucks County. 105678

State of the accounts of Gerardus Wyncoop, Esq. Collector of Excise for Bucks County. 105676

State of the accounts of Jacob Auld. 50164

State of the accounts of Jacob Barnitz Esquire, Collector of Excise, York County from November 20th 1782, to the 1st of May 1784. 3546, 106025

State of the accounts of Jacob Barnitz, Esq. Collector of Excise, York County, from the 1st of May, 1784, to 1st of May, 1785. 3547, 106026

State of the accounts of Jacob Barnitz, Esquire, late collector of Excise. 3548, 106027

State of the accounts of Jacob Engle. 62276

State of the accounts of Jacob Morgan. 50649

State of the accounts of James Ross. (38801)

State of the accounts of Jesse Jones. 55774

State of the accounts of John Buchanan. 8867

State of the accounts of John Christie. 12934

State of the accounts of John Gill. 27383

State of the accounts of John Hay. 106035

State of the accounts of John Lacy. (38456)

State of the accounts of John McLellan. 106031

State of the accounts of John Nixon. 60635

State of the accounts of Joseph Hart, Esq. 30629

State of the accounts of Joseph Hart, Esquire, Lieutenant of Bucks County. 30629

State of the accounts of Joseph Kirkbridge. (37979)

State of the accounts of Joshua Anderson. 8947

State of the accounts of Joshua Elder. (38801)

State of the accounts of Lewis Gronow. 28925

State of the accounts of Nicholas Brosius. 8383

State of the accounts of Peter Richards. 62275

State of the accounts of Robert Smith, Esquire. 83805

State of the accounts of Robert Smith, Esq. Lieutenant of Chester County. 83807

State of the accounts of Robert Wilson. 104678

State of the accounts of Samuel Adams. 23954

State of the accounts of Samuel Cunningham. 17970

State of the accounts of Samuel Dewees. 62274

State of the accounts of Samuel Turbett. 38802

State of the accounts of the Collectors of Excise for Bucks County. 8946

State of the accounts of the Collectors of Excise, for Lancaster County. 38802

State of the accounts of the Collectors of Excise for Northampton County. 55774

State of the accounts of the Collectors of Excise for York County. 106028

State of the accounts of the Collectors of Excise, of Berks County. 4890

State of the accounts of the Collectors of Excise of Cumberland County. 17889

State of the accounts of the Hon. George Wall. 101085

State of the accounts of the late Lieutenant and Sub-Lieutenants of Lancaster County. (38801)

State of the accounts of the late Lieutenant and Sub-Lieutenants of Northampton County. 55774

State of the accounts of the Lieutenant and Sub-Lieutenants of Chester County. 83806

State of the accounts of the Lieutenant and Sub-Lieutenants . . . 1780. (38801)

State of the accounts of the Lieutenant and Sub-Lieutenants . . . 1783. (38801)

State of the accounts of the Lieutenants & Sub Lieutenants of . . . Philadelphia, and Liberties. 62281

State of the accounts of the Lieutenants & Sub Lieutenants of Westmoreland County. 103040

State of the accounts of the Lieutenants & Sub Lieutenants of York County. 106036

State of the accounts of the Pennsylvania Hospital. 60330

State of the accounts of the Sub-Lieutenants of Washington County. 102012

State of the accounts of the taxes, of York County. 106038

State of the accounts of the Treasury of Pennsylvania. 60637

State of the accounts of Thomas Armor. 106024

State of the accounts of Thomas Cheney. 12546

State of the accounts of Thomas Levis. 40760

State of the accounts of Thomas Strawbridge. 92749

State of the accounts of Walter Clarke & William Murray. 55846

State of the accounts of Wm. Antes. (62279)

State of the accounts of William Coats. 13834

State of the accounts of William Crispin. 62273

State of the accounts of William Graham. 28238

State of the accounts of William Hay. 38802

State of the accounts of William Henry. (62280)

State of the accounts of William M'Henry. 43313

State of the accounts of William Scott. 106037

State of the accounts of William Webb. 60636

State of the accounts of William Wilson. 55846

State of the accounts . . . to the 20th of March 1780. (38801)

State of the action brought by William Fletcher. 24744, note before 90598, 2d note after 98664

State of the affairs of the La Crosse and Milwaukee Rail Road Company. 38508

State of the allegations and evidence produced. 90598

State of the application to Congress. 90599

State of the argument between Great Britain and her colonies. 90600

State of the asylum. 59900

State of the British and French colonies in North America. 90601

State of the British sugar-colony trade. 46183

State of the case and argument for the appellants. 30090, note after 90601

State of the case; and . . . Judge Reeves's opinion. 4731

State of the case between the South-Sea Company, and the proprietors. 88203, 90602

State of the case, briefly but impartially given. (36048), 37196

State of the case by which his candour to Mr. Edmund Jenings is manifested. 35985, 39258

State of the case in dispute between the Queen and the late Assembleis. 53974, note after 90602

State of the case now depending before the Court of Appeal. 81662

State of the case of the sugar plantations in America. 90603

State of the church. 90604

State of the claim of His Majesty's Bermuda subjects. 90605

State of the clergy, in Virginia, before the American revolution. 90606

State of the College in Rhode-Island. 90607

State of the colony and affaires in Virginia. 99873

State of the colony of Georgia. 27087

State of the commerce of Great Britain. 90608

State of the constitution of the colonies. 90609

State of the constitution of the colonies. [By Thomas Pownall.] 64833

State of the country. 7679

State of the country, a discourse, delivered in the First Presbyterian Church. 3507

State of the country: a discourse preached . . . in Boston. (26534)

State of the country. A sermon delivered in Grace Church, Providence. 13385

State of the country. Advanced sheets of the Princeton review. 28427, (32330), 90610

State of the country; an article published in the Boston recorder. 22381

"State of the country." An oration delivered at Buffalo. 13469

"State of the country," by the Rev. Robert Breckenridge. 7685

State of the country. Speech of Hon. A. G. Brown. 8437

State of the country. Speech of John A. Prall. 64924

State of the country. Speech of William H. Seward. 79584

State of the different fortifications. 85234

State of the Earl of Stirling's title. 90611, note after 91855

State of the embarrassments and difficulties. 90612

State of the English sugar with that of Portugal. 90603

State of the expedition from Canada. 9255-9256

State of the exports and imports of the British sugar colonies. 90613

State of the foreign slave trade. 104039

State of the great ship canal question. 90614

State of the importatations from Great Britain into the port of Boston, from January, 1769. 6558, 47406, note after 90614

State of the island of Jamaica. 35663, 90615

State of the land said to be once within the bounds. (15692), note after 90615

State of the licencees case. 4731

State of the nation, at the commencement of the year 1822. 90616

State of the nation consider'd, in a letter to a member of Parliament. 90617

State of the nation, considered in a sermon for thanksgiving day. note after (58767)

State of the nation for the year 1747. 90618-90619

State of the nation in respect to her commerce, debts, and money. 62454-62455

State of the nation, with a general balance of the publick accounts. 90620, note before 93779, note after 93808

State of the national debt. 18347, 27145, 65452, note after 71369

State of the national debt, the national income, and the national expenditure. 18348, 90100-90101

State of the navy consider'd. 90621

State of the New-York Hospital for the year 1803. 54484

State of the Newfoundland fishery. 14292

State of the present form of government of the province of Quebec. 56491

State of the present government of Trinidad. 90623

State of the proceedings in the House of Commons. 90624

State of the proceedings of the Corporation of the Governors of the Bounty of Queen Anne. 90625

State of the process, Peter Williamson against W. Fordyce. 104478

State of the province of Georgia. 27113, 91313, 91315-91316, 94215

State of the province of the Massachusetts-Bay considered. (49973)

State of the public debts. 18348, 90102

State of the public taxes, payable for the year 1786. 10415

State of the question, addressed to the petitions for the abolition. 90626

State of the question of jurisdiction and boundary. 90627

State of the question of Negro slavery. 90628

State of the representation of the people of England. 105707

State of the right of the colony of New-York. 792, 20987, 51825-51826, 90629, 4th-5th notes after 98997

State of the rights of the colony of New-York. 90629

State of the rise and progress of our disputes with Spain. 90630

State of the rise and progress of the disputes with Spain. 90631

State of the rules of the Brethren's Society for the Furtherance of the Gospel. 86174, 97862

State of the Society [in Scotland for Propagating Christian Knowledge.] 72005, note before 85932

State of the Society in Scotland, for Propagating Christian Knowledge; giving a brief account. 85994

State of the sugar-trade. 90632

State of the temperance reform. 77013, 91376

State of the trade and manufactory of iron in Great-Britain considered. 90633

State of the trade carried on with the French. 90634

State of the trade of Great Britain in its imports and exports. 103843

State of the trade of Great Britain with all parts of the world. 50562

State of the Treasury of Massachusetts. 46133

State of the union. A speech . . . delivered in the House. 23090

State of the union: being a complete documentary history. 90635

State of the union. Speech . . . House . . . Jan. 21, 1861. 16985

State of the union. Speech . . . in House of Representatives, February 27, 1861. 11120

State of the union. Speech . . . in the House of Representatives, February 8, 1861. 11300

State of the union. Speech . . . in the House of Representatives, January 28, 1861. 42369

State of the union. Speech . . . in the Senate, January 3, 1861. (20693A)

State of the union. Speech . . . January 11, 1861. 30386

State of the union. Speech . . . January 30, 1861. 33284

State of the union. Speech . . . January 31, 1861. 55133

State of the union. Speech . . . January 29, 1861. (30481)

State of the union. Speech of Hon. A. G. Porter. 64196

State of the union. Speech of Hon. James M. Quarles. 66946

State of the union: speech of Hon. Wm. Bigler. 5342

State of the union. Speech of J. M. Leach. 39509

State of the union. Speech of the Hon. Benjamin Stanton. 90383

State of the union. Speech of the Hon. Charles B. Sedgwick. 78813

State of things. A dramatic piece. 63819

State of things in North West Virginia. 95513

State of trade in the northern colonies considered. (41523), note before 90636

State of Vermont. An act regulating the choice of a Council of Censors. 99098

State of Vermont, Chittenden County, ss. Heman Allen against Usal Pierson. 96810

State of Vermont, in account current with the Hon. Samuel Mattocks. 99135

State of Vermont, in Council, Arlington, 10th Dec. 1779. 7286, 4th note after 99005

State of Vermont. In Council, Arlington, 23d of August, 1779. 803, 2d note after 99005

State of Vermont. In Council, Windsor, 7th June, 1779. 99074

State of Vermont. In General Assembly at Windsor, Oct. 9th, 1778. 99021

State of Vermont. In General Assembly, 10th October, 1795. 99045

State of Vermont. In General Assembly, Windsor, November 5th, 1799. 99048

State of Vermont. In General Convention, Windsor, 2d July, 1777. 99014

State of Vermont, Windsor, Feb. 12th, 1781. 99047

State of Wisconsin. Report of Caleb Corswell. 17676

State of Wisconsin–Supreme-Court. 10997

State on the present form of government. 90622

State or province? 62815

State ownership no remedy for existing evils. 89572

State Paper Office, London. see Great Britain. State Paper Office, London.

State papers and public documents of the United States from the accession of George Washington. 90637-90638

State papers and publick documents of the United States from the accession of Thomas Jefferson. 90637-90638

State papers and publick documents of the United States. Thomas B. Wait and Sons, propose to publish. 90636

State papers of New Hampshire. see Provincial and State Papers of New Hampshire.

State papers of Vermont. 81691, 1st note after 98997, note before 99008, 99024, 99049, 99077, 99079, 99081, 99085

State papers on nullification. 46140, 87423, note after 90638

State papers, on the negotiation and peace with America. 53975, 90639

State papers relating to the diplomatick transactions. 26822

State Poultry Society of Pennsylvania. 60638

State Press Association of South Carolina. see South Carolina State Press Association.

State printers. 99108

State prison life. 90640

State prison report. 70749

State prison reports. 70749

State prisons and the penitentiary system vindicated. 7247, note after 90640

State record for 1852. 45886

State record of North Carolina. note after 94720

State reference book. 43985

State Reform Farm, Lancaster, Ohio. see Ohio. Boys' Industrial School, Lancaster.

State Reform School. A discourse. 13384

State Reform School at Westborough. 46141

State reforms in Louisiana. 90641

State register and year book of facts. 10044-10045

State register; comprising an historical and statistical account. 4446

State register. No. 5. (15829)

State register, of civil, judicial, military, and other officers in Connecticut. 74340

State rights: a photograph from the ruins of ancient Greece. 40854

State rights and free trade almanac for the year of Our Lord 1833. 87784

State rights and free trade almanac for the year of Our Lord 1832. 90642

State Rights and Free Trade Association of South Carolina. 63815, 65912, 87784, 87827-87830, 88063-88064, 88067-88069, 90642, 94434, 2d note after 99578

State Rights & Free Trade Convention, Charleston, S. C., 1832. 65912, 88067

State rights and free trade evening post. 69479, 6th note after 88114

State Rights and Free Trade Party of Charleston, S. C. 39144, 88065, 88087-88089, 1st-2d notes after 97754, 101665

State Rights and Free Trade Party of Charleston, S. C. petitioners 88087

State Rights and Free Trade Party of Charleston, S. C. Celebration of the Fifty-Fifth Anniversary of American Independence, 1831. 20917, 97752, 97755 see also Charleston, S. C. Fourth of July Celebration, 1831.

State Rights and Free Trade Party of Charleston, S. C. Convention, Columbia, 1832. 56849, 97753

State Rights and Free Trade Party of Charleston, S. C. Convention, Columbia, 1832. Committee. 14852, 88087-88088, 1st-2d notes after 99754

State Rights and Free Trade Party of Charleston, S. C. Convention, Columbia, 1832. Committee. petitioners 14852, 88087-88088, 1st-2d notes after 99754

State Rights and Free Trade Party of Charleston, S. C. Meeting, Charleston, 1830. 88070

State Rights and Free Trade Party of Charleston, S. C. Meeting, Charleston, 1832. 20423, 56849

State Rights and Free Trade Party of Charleston, S. C. Public Meeting, Charleston, 1831. 88063

State rights and joint resolutions and report to the Ohio Legislature. 57054

State-rights and national union. 74414

State rights and state equality. 73921

State rights and the appellate jurisdiction of the Supreme Court. (9160), 2d note after 90642

State rights and the Supreme Court. (20611)

State rights. By Hon. T. Farrar. (23888)

State Rights Celebration, Charleston, S. C., 1830. see Charleston, S. C. State Rights Celebration, 1830.

State Rights' Convention, Jackson, Miss., 1834. Committee. 90643

State Rights Democratic Party. Pennsylvania. Convention, Harrisburg, 1859. 60429 see also Democratic Party. Pennsylvania.

"State rights man." pseud. Remarks on the devision. 69454

State Rights Meeting, Columbia, S. C., 1830. 65913, 88062

State Rights Party of South Carolina. see Union and State Rights Party (South Carolina)

State rights republican. pseud. Glance at state rights. 27531, note before 90644

State rights. Speech of Hon. Abram D. Smith. 82300

State Rights, Union and Jackson Party of Kershaw District, S. C. Committee. 90644

State Sabbath Convention, Harrisburg, Pa., 1844. 60431

State Sabbath Convention, Saratoga Springs, N. Y., 1844. see New York State Sabbath Convention, Saratoga Springs, 1844.

State Sabbath School Association of Minnesota. see Minnesota State Sabbath School Association.

State Sanitary Commission. Report on condition of troops. 34304

State School Convention of New York, 1831. see New York State School Convention, 1831.

State secrets for the people. (78429)

State securities. 99107

State Society of the Cincinnati of South Carolina. see Society of the Cincinnati. South Carolina.

State Soldiers' Depot, New York. see New York (State) Soldiers' Depot.

State sovereignty. A dialogue. 18944, note after 90644

State sovereignty, and a certain dissolution of the union. 72888

State sovereignty and the doctrine of coercion. 64321

State sovereignty and treason. 2897

State sovereignty. Rebellion against the United States. 30019

State sovereignty record of Massachusetts. 90645

State sovereignty . . . slavery. (28280)

State Sovereignty Society of Ohio. petitioners 90646

State specially the American state psychologically treated. 85450

State stocks and revenues. 90647

State street. A satire. 90648

State Street Church, Portland, Me. see Portland, Me. State Street Church.

State Street Presbyterian Church, Albany. see Albany. State Street Presbyterian Church

State substitute for a general bankrupt law. 90654

State Sunday School Convention, Delaware, Ohio, 1865. see Ohio State Sunday School Convention, Delaware, 1865.

State Sunday School Convention, St. Louis, 1866. see Missouri State Sunday School Convention, 1st, St. Louis, 1866.

State Sunday School Teachers' Association of New York. see New York State Sunday School Teachers' Association.

State system of education for New York. 68056

State Teachers' Institute of California. see California State Teachers' Institute.

State Temperance Alliance of Massachusetts. see Massachusetts State Temperance Alliance.

State Temperance Committee of Massachusetts. see Massachusetts State Temperance Committee.

State Temperance Committee, Augusta, Me., 1852. 44044

State Temperance Convention, Boston, 1840. see Massachusetts State Temperance Convention, Boston, 1840.

State Temperance Convention, Charleston, 1844. see South Carolina State Temperance Convention, Charleston, 1844.

State Temperance Convention, Charleston, 1845. see South Carolina State Temperance Convention, Charleston, 1845.

State Temperance Convention, Harrisburg, Pa., 1842. 60432

State Temperance Convention of New York, 1853. see New York State Temperance Convention, 1853.

State Temperance Society of Maryland. see Maryland State Temperance Society.

State Temperance Society of New York. see New York State Temperance Society.

State Temperance Society of Rhode Island. see Rhode Island State Temperance Society.

State Temperance Society of South Carolina. see South Carolina State Temperance Society.

State, territorial, and ocean guide book of the Pacific. 32486, 90655

State Texas Committee of Massachusetts. see Massachusetts State Texas Committee.

State thanksgiving during the rebellion. 89780

State Total Abstinence Society of Rhode Island. see Rhode Island State Total Abstinence Society.

State trial. 16608

State trials. 67590

State trials, court martial, 1838-9. 93241

State triumvirate, a political tale. (19995), 99276

State Union Convention of Ohio, 1862. see National Union Party. Ohio. Convention, 1862.

State University, East Lansing, Michigan. see Michigan. State University, East Lansing.

State University. . . . An address. 68147

State versus Ira Berry. 103041

State Woman's Rights Convention, Albany, 1854. see New York State Woman's Rights Convention, Albany, 1854.

Stated Preached to the Hospital and Almshouse in the City of New York. see New York (City) Hospital and Almshouse. Stated Preacher.

Stated rules of the Brethren's Society for the Furtherance of the Gospel. 97862

Stated rules of the Society of the United Brethren. 86174, 97862

Statement adopted by the Liverpool Antislavery Society. 5105

Statement addressed by the Association of the First Presbyterian Church. 62282

Statement addressed to the Episcopalians. (32230)

Statement affecting the proper disposition of the fund. 90659

Statement and appeal of the Bishop Seabury Mission. 90660

Statement and appeal of the Trustees of St. Thomas's Church. 8319, 75498

Statement and argument on their claims. 90115

Statement and arguments of Leland Stanford and D. C. McRuer. 90212

Statement and declaration of views. 7373, 90661

Statement and documents [relative to the controversy between Plymouth Church.] 90662

Statement and documents relative to the establishment of steam navigation. 90775, note after 103224

Statement and exposition of certain harmonies. 85072

Statement and exposition of the title of John Jacob Astor to the lands. 90663

Statement and memorial in relation to political affairs. 90664

Statement and plea of the New York City Council. 54438

Statement & review of the whole case of the Reverend Joy H. Fairchild. 23683

Statement and testimony. (61719)

Statement applicable to the case of the Olive Branch. 822

Statement . . . arguments . . . and opinion. (52437)

Statement as to the iron trade of Scotland. 90665

Statement . . . as to the labor and wants of the Commission. 4575

[Statement as to the labors and wants of the Commission.] 76579, 76647

Statement . . . before the Committee on Education and Labor. (33273)

Statement by A. B. Chambers. 11792, (75341)

Statement, by George Bradburn. 7201

Statement, by James C. Biddle and William M. Meredith. 5235

Statement, by James Schott, Jr. 77914

Statement [by Stanley Griswold.] 93066

Statement by the Association of the Western District of New Haven County. 90666

Statement by the First Baptist Church of Philadelphia. 90667

Statement by the President, Directors, and Company for Erecting a Permanent Bridge over the Ricer Schuylkill. 62231

Statement by the President of the Chester Valley Railroad Company. 59974

Statement by the Rev. Mr. How. (33225)

Statement . . . [by Theodore S. Fay.] (23949)

Statement concerning Abenaqui Springs. 51

Statement concerning the Army and Navy Calim Agent. 76681

Statement concerning the Colombian bonds. 14623

Statement concerning the Devon Mines of Lake Superior. 19825

Statement concerning the New-York and Erie Rail-Road Company. 90668

Statement concerning the property of the North American Petroleum Co. 55556

Statement concerning the recent assault upon the character. 32627

Statement, exhibiting the condition of institutions for savings. 70746

Statement, exhibiting the condition of the banks of Rhode Island. 70746

Statement, exhibiting the condition of the banks of Rhode Island, . . . the 25th day of November, 1863. (70545)

Statement, exhibiting the condition of the institutions for savings. (70545)

Statement, explanatory of the resignation of the officers. 90669

Statement for the consideration of workingmen. 25963

Statement for the Theological Seminary of the Protestant Episcopal Church. 90670

Statement from Dr. Bellows. 4575

Statement from the Bureau of Ordnance and Hydrography. 33468

Statement from the Executive Committee. 76682

Statement in behalf of Jubilee College, Ill. 36822, 1st note after 90670

Statement in behalf of the College of California. 37295, 2d note after 90670

Statement in behalf of the National Loan Fund Life Assurance Association. 90554

Statement in reference to the petition and memorial, &c. 1331

Statement in regard to bridging Lake Champlain. 90671

Statement in regard to the College of California. 104142

Statement in regard to the moral exposure and spiritual wants of Lowell. 42501

Statement in regard to the Soscol Ranch. 87197

Statement in relation to certain rights and privileges. 54723

Statement, in relation to . . . machine shops. 55827

Statement in relation to the case. 26630A

Statement in relation to the concerns. 90672

Statement in relation to the location. 55827

Statement in reply to the order of the House. 45098

Statement in reply to Mr. Stevenson's letter. 91604

Statement in reply to the calumnies of Lt. Gov. Jacob. (7678)

Statement indicating some of the advantages of the proposed city. 39113

Statement, July, 1860. 51996

Statement, letters, and documents. 26155

Statement . . . made before the Committee on Military Affairs. 26697

Statement made by a committee from the Vestry of St. George's Church. 75209

Statement made by a committee of the Vestry of "St. George's Church." 75213

Statement made by Dr. E. Pugh. 66610

Statement made by four physicians. 90673

Statement, made by Mr. Cambreleng. 10114

Statement made by the Association for the Exhibition of the Industry of All Nations. 2240, 90674

Statement made by the railroad companies. 90675

Statement made to the President of the United States. 90210

Statement of a case, Mess. Cabots, &c. versus the United States. 96930A

Statement of a majority of the corporation. 90676

Statement of accounts. (38807)

Statement of a committee . . . [of the Mass. Charitable Eye and Ear Infirmary.] 45827

Statement of A. E. Phillips. (62472)

Statement of Admiral David D. Porter. 64225

Statement of all the lands sold by the Comptroller. 53618

Statement of an argument on the memorials. 53979, note after 90676

Statement of appropriations heretofore made for the Cumberland Road. 17887

Statement of Benjamin H. Latrobe. 63126

Statement of Bishop Meade. 47239

Statement of case to . . . [Legislature] of Massachusetts. 30859

Statement of certain banks and savings institutions. 59905

Statement of certain banks. Read in the House. (59903)

Statement of Christian faith. 55099

Statement of circumstances attending the experiment. 90677

Statement of Col. H. K. Craig. 17359

Statement of Commander E. B. Boutwell. 6971

Statement of Comptroller Whittlesey. 89702, 89707

Statement of congressional documents, journals, registers and debates. 94670

Statement of D. B. Bouglass. 20708, 37590

Statement of David Leavitt. (39554)

Statement of deaths . . . in . . . Lowell. 42503

Statement of deaths, with the diseases and ages. 12090

Statement of devises, bequests, & grants to the Corporation. 62283

Statement of devises, . . . to the Corporation of . . . Philadelphia. 62284

Statement of Dr. Cheever's case. (12406)

Statement [of Dr. Jackson.] 38674

Statement of expenditure. 103265

Statement of Edward Mills. 49101

Statement of events previous and subsequent to the annual meeting. 11994

Statement of evidence before the Committee of the Legislature. 6785

"Statement of expences," etc. 2921

Statement of . . . expenses, from . . . 1852, to . . . 1853. 47302

Statement of Ex-Secretary Floyd. (24914)

Statement of F. A. Sawyer. 77308

Statement of facts. [ca. 1831.] 21820, 70221

Statement of facts. [ca. 1833.] 69683

Statement of facts, addressed to honest men of all parties. 15826, 15792, note just before 63828

Statement of facts addressed to the United-States Revenue Commission. 23944

Statement of facts, and a few suggestions. 90678

Statement of facts and circumstances connected with the recent trial of the Bishop of New-York. 57309, 71138

Statement of facts and circumstances connected with the removal of the author. (20707)

Statement of facts and circumstances of the trial of Dr. A. A. Muller. 51277

Statement of facts and figures relating to commerce with Brazil. 90679

Statement of facts and law relative to the persecution of the Rev. Clark Bentom. 4778, note after 90679

Statement of facts and reasons for its adoption. 88303

Statement of facts and remarks, in relation to the proceedings. 28677

Statement of facts, and the opinion of the court. 58611

Statement of facts, and the opinion of the Hon. Murray Hoffman. (66104)

Statement of facts and transactions of the Union Marine & Fire Insurance Company in Newburyport. 97810-97811

Statement of facts. By George McClellan. 43009

Statement of facts by S. E. Smith. 83971

Statement of facts by William Vans. 98563

Statement of facts. [By Zephaniah Moore.] 89128, 1st note after 104432

Statement of facts, concerning Joseph Ravara. 67979

Statement of facts, concerning the death of Samuel Lee. 4089

Statement of facts concerning the silver mines. 90680

Statement of facts, concerning the troubles in the Church. 88129

Statement of facts, confirmed by records of the Legislature. 98564

Statement of facts connected with his trial. 47239

Statement of facts connected with the Columbian loan. 14624

Statement of facts connected with the late reorganization. 60312-60313

Statement of facts, designed to correct some misrepresentations. 90681

Statement of facts exhibited at the Ecclesiastical Council. 105523

Statement of facts, exhibiting the causes that have led to the dissolution. 90682

Statement of facts from each religious denomination. 8340, 85962

Statement of facts, illustrating the administration. 90683

Statement of facts in a case between Ulysses Ward and Tucker & Thompson. 101343

Statement of facts, in a letter, to a member of of the Council. 8461, note just before 69458

Statement of facts, in answer to a bill book. 98565

Statement of facts, in connection with the petition of Charles Stearns. 90873

Statement of facts, in connection with the petition of the Springfield Aqueduct Company. 89877, 90684

Statement of facts in defence of the Congregational Church. 23751

Statement of facts in exposition of dangerous errors. 86870

Statement of facts in regard to the proposed division of the Diocese of Maryland. 58797, 1st note after 90684

Statement of facts in relation to the appointment of the Democratic delegation. 53980, 2d note after 90684

Statement of facts, in relation to the call and installation. 90685, 97370

Statement of facts in relation to the case of Rev. Jacob Knapp. 9200

Statement of facts in relation to the Charleston Union Presbytery. 87916

Statement of facts in relation to the claims of the inhabitants. 35279

Statement of facts in relation to the claims of the inhabitants of the county of Tompkins, for a bank in Ithaca. 5983

Statement of facts in relation to the delays. 78842

Statement of facts in relation to the dismissal of Mrs. Martha Bradstreet's suits. 7307, 90686

Statement of facts, in relation to the duty on foreign coal. 90687

Statement of facts in relation to the Howe Street Society. August 18, 1846. 70280, 90688

Statement of facts in relation to the Lancaster Mills. (5289)

Statement of facts in relation to the Norwich & Worcester Rail-Road Company. December, 1840. 55924, 105452

Statement of facts in relation to the Norwich & Worcester Rail-Road Company. June, 1841. 55924, 105452

Statement of facts in relation to the origin, progress, and prospects of the [New York & Harlem Rail Road] . . . Company. (54732)

Statement of facts in relation to the recent ordination. 82732

Statement of facts, . . . in relation to the steam boat ferries. 8291

Statement of facts in relation to wool and woolen goods. 90689

Statement of facts in reply to the allegations of certain Presbyters. 90690

Statement of facts in the matter betwixt Mr. Gowen and the Philadelphia Exchange Company. 28171

Statement of facts, in the nature of memoir. 9742

Statement of facts, in trial of Dea. Josiah Henshaw. 90691

Statement of facts on behalf of Daniel Parish. 58611

Statement of facts . . . on this . . . subject. 45245

Statement of facts pretaining to the case of Yale College. 105801-105804

Statement of facts, pertaining to the proclamation of martial law. 90740, 1st note after 101925

Statement of facts presented to an Ecclesiastical Council. 44203

Statement of facts regarding the admission of Colorado. 90692

Statement of facts. [Relating to] Richard W. Meade. 47236

Statement of facts relating to slavery. 45832

Statement of facts relating to the claim of J. W. Schaumburg. 77519-77520

Statement of facts, relating to the claim of Major Moses White. 103369

Statement of facts relating to the claim of O. De A. Santangelo. 76832

Statement of facts relating to the controversy. 90693

Statement of facts, relating to the demand of William Vans. 98566

Statement of facts, relating to the funds of Kingston Academy. 37914

Statement of facts relating to the late Democratic militia bill. 60640

Statement of facts, relating to the late ordination at Grace Church. 31429, note before 90694

Statement of facts relating to the negotiation of Cerro del Bote. 90694

Statement of facts relating to the ordination at Grace Church. 16312, 51262

Statement of facts, relating to the trespass on the printing press. 90695

Statement of facts, relative to an adjustment of a difficulty. 82745

Statement of facts relative to Canada wools and the manufactures of Worsted. 51935

Statement of facts relative to Canadian wools. 31026

Statement of facts relative to the Bergen Tunnel. 90696

Statement of facts relative to the circumstances by which he [i. e. Ephraim K. Avery] became involved in the prosecution. 2486

Statement of facts relative to the claims of Captain Wm. Tharp. 95214

Statement of facts relative to the claims of Capt. William Tharp and William Hobby. 95215

Statement of facts relative to the conduct of Henry Eckford. 55375

Statement of facts relative to the conduct of Mr. Benjamin Joy. 3598, (36777), 1st note after 90696

Statement of facts relative to the dismissal of James S. Howard. 33255, 2d note after 90696

Statement of facts relative to the establishment and progress. 33089

Statement of facts relative to the island of Jamaica. 90697

Statement of facts relative to the last will of the late Mrs. Badger. 2701, note after 90697

Statement of facts relative to the late fever. 90698

Statement of facts, relative to the late ordination at Grace Church. 31429

Statement of facts, relative to the late proceedings in Harvard College. 30762, 90699

Statement of facts, relative to the origin and causes of the present attempt to free the Schuylkill Permanent Bridge. 62231, note after 90699

STATEMENT

Statement of facts, relative to the petition and
    public hearing. 21674
Statement of facts, relative to the proceedings
    in Harvard College, Cambridge. 30762,
    90699, note after 103460
Statement of facts relative to the purchase of
    property. 90700
Statement of facts relative to the purchase of
    property from George W. Brown. (8482)
Statement of facts relative to the removal of
    six pupils. 90701
Statement of facts relative to the troubles in
    St. Paul's Church. 90702
Statement of facts respecting a contract.
    4208
Statement of facts respecting the American
    Colonization Society. 90703
Statement of facts respecting the Board of
    Missions of the Presbyterian Church.
    65143
Statement of facts respecting the condition &
    treatment of slaves. 31402
Statement of facts, respecting the dismission
    of the Rev. Mr. Andrews. 90704
Statement of facts, respecting the School for
    Colored Females. 90705, note before
    96855
Statement of facts respecting the Supreme
    Grand Council. 11299
Statement of facts set forth by the Wardens.
    90706
Statement of facts, showing the debt due to
    Vans. 98567
Statement of facts, submitted to the Right
    Hon. Lord Glenelg. 91339
Statement of facts, together with some obser-
    vations relating to the merits. 46886
Statement of facts, with accompanying docu-
    ments. 90707
Statement of facts, with remarks. 8291
Statement of Faculty to parents and guardians
    of students. (30752)
Statement of General Barton's lawsuit in
    Vermont. 51834
Statement of his own conduct and principles.
    38574
Statement of its separation. 8062
[Statement of its origin and objectives, Aug.
    13, 1861.] 76545, 76549, 76647
Statement of its purpose. 13092
Statement of its resources and merits, March,
    1868. 55821
Statement of James Ross Snowden. 85588
Statement of leading Republicans of Colorado.
    90708
Statement of Major-General Irwin McDowell.
    43193
Statement of measures contemplated. 8800,
    (60642)
Statement of Messrs. Miles and Keitt. (16860),
    note after 87402, 87436, 87438
Statement of military services of Brigadier
    General John C. Starkweather. 90537
Statement of Mr. David C. Claypoole. 101686
Statement of Mr. Madison's instructions.
    53975, 90639
Statement of Mr. Samuel A. Way's connection.
    102180
Statement of money placed to the credit of
    the special fund. 90709
Statement of objects and methods of the
    Sanitary Commission. (76595), 76647
Statement of premiums awarded by the Humane
    Society. 45765
Statement of premiums awarded by the Trustees.
    33681

Statement of President Quincy, June 4, 1834.
    (30752)
Statement of proceedings, against Mrs. Emily
    Richardson. 71003, note before 90710
Statement of proceedings in relation to the
    Mexican debt. 90710
Statement of proceedings in the First Society
    in Coventry, Conn. 17-18, 3d note after
    96123
Statement of proceedings on the part of the
    members of the Faculty. 90711
Statement of Prof. Henry. 85024
Statement of property belonging to the Corpo-
    ration. (62359)
Statement of property of the Chicago South
    Branch Dock Company. 12630
Statement of R. Morris Copeland. 16660
Statement of reasons against the assumption.
    (36921)
Statement of reasons against the confirmation.
    90712
Statement of reasons for not believing the
    doctrines of Trinitarians. 90713
Statement of reasons showing the illegality of
    that verdict. 90714
Statement of receipts and expenditures of the
    county of Middlesex. 48847
Statement of receipts, expenditrues, &c. 12096
Statement of relief on Unitarianism and spirit-
    ualism. 24095
Statement of St. Paul's School, Concord, N.H.
    75470
Statement of Senior Class. (30752)
Statement of some leading principles adopted
    by General Jackson. 9235
Statement of some leading principles and
    measures adopted by General Jackson.
    71751
Statement of some of the advantages attendant
    upon making St. John's. 75283
Statement of some of the advantages of the
    vicinity of Johnstown. 10115
Statement of some of the principal events.
    35291, (35296)
Statement of some of the principal facts.
    29857
Statement of some recent transactions in the
    Southern Reformed Presbytery. 65227
[Statement of supplies and aid furnished.]
    76690
Statement of the accounts of the Philadelphia
    Bank. 61961
Statement of the accounts of the United States.
    50867, note before 90715
Statement of the additional number of engineer
    officers. 85234
Statement of the adjustment of the insurance
    on the Pemberton Mill. 90715, note
    after 92226
Statement of the affairs of Amherst Institution.
    1330, 90716
Statement of the affairs of certain banks and
    savings institutions. 59905
Statement of the affairs of the Amherst Insti-
    tution. 1330, 90716
Statement of the affairs of the . . . [New
    Hampshire Missionary] Society. (52879)
Statement of the affairs of the Parish of Christ
    Church, Boston. (6639)
Statement of the amount of damages. 90717
Statement of the amount of internal duties.
    (60641)
Statement of the arts and manufactures of the
    United States of America. 17304
[Statement of the Auditor showing the balances
    due.] 100019

2820

Statement of the facts, pertaining to the proclamation of martial law. 90740

Statement of the Faculty in relation to trespasses by the students. 30765

Statement of the finances, with a plan of revenue and support. 638

Statement of the financial condition and history of the state of Alabama. 90741

Statement of the financial transactions of the banking firm of Truscott, Green & Co. 90742

Statement of the foreign debt. 43089

Statement of the frauds on the elective franchise. 27578

Statement of the funds of the corporation of the city. (54212)

Statement of the funds of the Missionary Society of Connecticut. 15633, 15812

Statement of the funds of the society, and a list of books. 15639

Statement of the funds of the state of New-York. 90743

Statement of the funds of the University . . . [of Pennsylvania.] 60758

Statement of the . . . Governors of the University of McGill College. 43273

Statement of the grievances, on account of which. 90744

Statement of the immediate government to the corporation. 30765

Statement of the income of Harvard College. 30765

Statement of the incumbrances at present on the property. (60341)

Statement of the Indian relations. 90745

Statement of the James River Company. (35727)

Statement of the judgments confessed by Evan Poultney. 45079

Statement of the Kennebeck claims. (37384), note before 90746

Statement of the Lake Contario and Hudson River Railroad. (38666)

Statement of the Lode Star Gold Mining Co. 41764

Statement of the measures adopted by the Trustees and Faculty. 8868

Statement of the measures contemplated against Samuel Bryan. (60642), 90746

Statement of the Memphis, Helena and St. Louis Levee Railroad. 47779

Statement of the merits that entitle them to preference. 84500

Statement of the method pursued by the Petworth Committee. 86186, 1st note after 98076

Statement of the . . . [Mutual Benefit Life Insurance] Co. 51607

Statement of the . . . National Bank of Commerce in New York. 54413

Statement of the national debt. 27145, 18347

Statement of the native and half-caste Indians. (33542)

Statement of the . . . Niagara Falls Hydraulic Company. 55124

Statement of the number of blind in Pennsylvania. 60339

Statement of the number of paupers and of the expenditures. (37483)

Statement of the objections of the Jamaica proprietors. 90747

Statement of the objections of the passage of th the bill. 105998

Statement of the objects and organization of the [American Geographical and Statistical Society.] 1091

Statement of the occurrences during a malignant yellow fever. (58982), 90748

Statement of the only practicable method by which the North Pole may be reached. 86971

Statement of the opinions given in the Board of Commissioners. 43158

Statement of the Oregon and Washington delegation. 90749

Statement of the origin, nature and operations of the Pennsylvania Domestic Missionary Society. 60317

Statement of the petitions in the case of the Walpole Company. 101150

Statement of the plan and objects of the Mariner's Church. 64380

Statement of the plan, objects, and effects of the Wesleyan missions. 90750

Statement of the plan of the St. Mary's Canal Mineral Land Company. 75423

Statement of the present depressed condition. 6576

Statement of the President and Directors, and of the Chief Engineer of said [St. Croix Railroad] Company. 75032

Statement of the President of the Board of Governors of the Alms House. 54073

Statement of the President on the affairs of the [Milwaukee and Beliot Rail Road] Company. (49165)

Statement of the principal facts in regard to the Stockbridge & Pittsfield Rail Road Company. 91874

Statement of the principle and practice of transacting marine insurance. 90751

Statement of the principles of the Christian Union. 90752

Statement of the proceedings in the First Church. 19221, 38776, note after 90752

Statement of the proceedings of citizens of Englewood. 90753

Statement of the proceedings of the Directors of the London Missionary Society. 82910

Statement of the proceedings of the justices of the Inferior Court. 103375

Statement of the proceedings of the . . . Presbyterian Church of Waterford, N. Y. 64760

Statement of the proceedings of the Yearly Meeting, held in London. 90754

Statement of the proceedings resulting in the purchase of the Newburyport Public Library Building. 54922

Statement of the proceedings that took place on the subject. 10884-10885

Statement of the professors in the Theological Department of Yale College. 105891

Statement of the public property belonging to the town. (75692)

Statement of the questions regarding the abolition of the slave trade. 90755

Statement of the reasons which induced the students of Lane Seminary, to dissolve their connection with that institution. 38861, note after 90755

Statement of the receipts and expenditures of the city of Chicago. (12651)

Statement of the receipts and expenditures of the town of Reading. (68211)

Statement of the receipts, expenditures, &c. of the city of Charlestown. 12124

Statement of the Rector, read by him. 69678

Statement of the . . . refusal to grant a patent. 50963

Statement of the relations of Rufus W. Griswold and Charlotte Myers. 28899

Statement of the relations of the Faculty of Medicine and Surgey. 90756

Statement of the resident members of the Board Board of Managers. (1235)

Statement of the rights and just reasons. 90757

Statement of the rights claimed by our colonists. 90758

Statement of the St. Paul & Chicago Railway Co. 75456

Statement of the satisfactory results which have attended emigration. 10609, note after 90758

Statement of the "Sayre-Ruppaner case." 90759

Statement of the Schenectady and Troy Railroad Company. 77604

Statement of the seizure of the British Schooner Lord Nelson. 90760

Statement of the Senior Class. 30765

Statement of the shareholders of the Bank of Commerce. 54109

Statement of the singular manner of proceedings of the Rev. Association. (28908), 90761

Statement of the situation, character and value of the lands. 90762

Statement of the South Carolina Railroad Company. 88024

Statement of the sugar crop made in Louisiana. 11850

Statement of the testimony taken at the trial of T. D. Huff. 97773

Statement of the theory of education. 90763

Statement of the title question. 52081

Statement of the town accounts. (75752)

Statement of the town . . . expenses. 47302

Statement of the trade and commerce of Buffalo, for 1853. 31323

Statement of the trade and commerce of Buffalo, for 1853. 31323

Statement of the trade and commerce of Buffalo, for the year 1851. 9048

Statement of the trade and commerce of Chicago. 12630

Statement of the trade and commerce of Cincinnati, for the commercial year. 84727

Statement of the trade and commerce of Cincinnati . . . for the year 1848. (13067)

Statement of the trade and commerce of Cincinnati; including a general view. 84726

Statement of the trade and commerce of Memphis. (47773)

Statement of the trade and commerce of Oswego. 57831

Statement of the trade and commerce of Saint Louis. 75334

Statement of the trade and commerce of Saint Louis, for the year 1865. 75335

[Statement of the trade and commerce of Saint Louis, for the years 1866-1872.] 75335

Statement of the trade and commerce, . . . with the general business, of . . . Milwaukee. (49150)

[Statement of the Treasurer.] 100416

Statement of the Treasurer of Harvard College. 30765

Statement of the Treasurer's account. 102014

Statement of the trial of Isaac B. Desha. 19734, note after 95447

Statement of the Trustees [of the Dudley Observatory.] 21096, (28096)

Statement of the Trustees of the Mount Auburn Cemetery. 51146

Statement of the Trustees relative to the reorganization of the Pittsburgh, Fort Wayne and Chicago Railway. 63129

Statement of the value of the property. 62288

Statement of the views and course of instruction. 105356

Statement of the works on the Sodus Canal. 86205

Statement of the yield [of the gold and silver fields of Oregon and Idaho.] 3558

Statement of Ury House School. 62362

Statement of various commercial transactions. 47109

Statement of votes in Congress. 78676, note after 90763

Statement on behalf of R. Shedden Patrick. 59076

Statement on the national debt. 18347, 27145, note after 71369

Statement on the part of the United States. 44046, note after 90764

Statement . . . on the present state of slavery. 27526

Statement on the present timber and deal trade. 90764

Statement . . . on the Troy and Greenfield Railroad. 30859

Statement . . . presented to the . . . House. 18095

Statement proving Millard Fillmore. 90765

Statemend read at the anniversary. 61805

Statemend read before the New England Historic Genealogical Society. 88387

Statement regarding certain charges. 17361

Statement regarding property, location, value, etc. 28970

Statement relating to southwest branch. (58090)

Statement relating to the double wharfage collected. 90766

Statement relating to the endowment of Washington University. (22178)

Statement relating to the Publication Fund. 60144

Statement relative to an intended theological seminary. 57056

Statement relative to Codrington College. 14145, 85947

Statement. [Relative to some business transactions.] 90656

Statement respecting St. Ann's Church for Deaf-Mutes. 74996, note after 90783

Statement respecting the Bible Society of the State of Rhode Island. 70750

Statement respecting the court martial. 8585

Statement respecting the Earl of Selkirk's settlement. (20699)-20700, 20703-20704, note before 90767

Statement respecting the necessity and advantages. 90767

Statement shewing that the University Lottery has not been exhausted. (45389)

Statement shewing the magnitude and progress of the work. (9174)

Statement shewing the reasons for the course pursued. 96141

Statement showing how the railroad companies have siezed. 90768

Statement, showing some of the evils and absurdities. 22620, 78819

Statement, showing the condition and prospects of the Paterson and Hudson River Railroad Co. 59062

Statement showing the effect that might be produced. 90769

Statement showing the funded debt. 15415

Statement, showing the . . . importance of the proposed railroad. 33538

Statement signed by the conservative members. 90739

Statement submitted by Lieutenant Colonel Desbarres. 19685

Statement. [Submitted by officers of the Navy.] 90657

Statement to its patrons and friends. (52683)

Statement to the congregation of the Church of the Epiphany. 61537, 97623

Statement . . . to the House of Representatives. 18095

Statement to the people of Connecticut. 90770

Statement to the public, by the Trustees of the College of California. 10001

Statement to the public in reference to the act of the Legislature. 90771

Statement to the public of . . . the work of the Children's Aid Society. 54177

Statement. [to the Senate of the United States.] 90658

Statement to the stockholders [of the Mill Creek Coal and Oil Company.] (48990)

Statement to the stockholders of the Norwich Mining Company. (55929)

Statement transmitted to the Legislature of New York. 84252

Statement; with notes and a supplement. 90772

Statement with reference to the Knights Baronets of Nova Scotia. 41739, 90773

Statements and arguments in behalf of the petitioners. 90774

Statements and documents in relation to imposing a sliding scale. (61169)

Statements and documents relative to the establishment of steam navigation. 90775

Statements and observations on the working of the laws. 90776

Statements and remarks addressed to Thomas Newton. 7951

Statements and remarks made before the Committee on Education. 90777

Statements by Colonel William H. Winder. 104748

Statements, calculations and hints relative to rail-roads. 72700

Statements concerning the Blodget Canal to Amoskeag Falls. 5960

Statements concerning the public printing. (71576)

Statements defining the powers and duties of the departments. 63821

Statements in relation to the proceedings of Friends in England. 90778

Statements in relation to the situation. 17444

Statements laid before the King of the Netherlands. 26393

Statements made by H. B. Skinner. 92056

Statements made in Congress. 29057

Statements made in the introduction. 87349

Statements of Cyrus H. McCormick. 84518

Statements of Dr. Lederer. 83287

Statements of fact, relative to the appointment. (57166)

Statements of facts in relation to the expulsion of James C. Cross. 17653, 90779

Statements of Henry Jones. 50218

Statements of John M. M'Calla. 32337

Statements of Joseph John Gurney. 9370

Statements of Lorenzo Sherwood, &c. 29996, 57592

Statements of Rev. A. Latham exposed. 90780

Statements of the coal and river trade. 90781

Statements of the Comptroller of Public Accounts. 55693

Statements of the receipts and disbursements. 14248

Statements of the receipts and expenditures of public monies. 50868

Statements of the Secretary of the New York Association for Colored Volunteers. 54427

Statements of the several banks in the commonwealth of Massachusetts. 45553

Statements on the part of Great Britain. 44046, note before 90764

Statements on the subject of British colonial slavery. 95504

Statements relating to a navy yard. 39519, note after 90781

Statements relating to the home and foreign trade. 59148

Statements relating to the pending application. 90782

Statements relating to trade, navigation, mining, etc. (50287)

Statements, reports, and accounts of the Grant Trunk Railway Company of Canada. (28269)

Statements respecting St. Ann's Church for Deaf-Mutes. 74996

Statements respecting the American abolitionists. 90783

Statements respecting the profits of mining in England. 94502

Statements showing the condition of certain banks in Maryland. 90785

Statements supported by evidence. 51032

Staten Generael der Vereenighde Nederlanden. 66513, (66523), 100936, 102907, 102909-102910

Staten Generael der Vereenighde Nederlanden: allen de genen die desen sullen sien ofte hooren lesen saluyt. 16664, 102889

Staten Island, N. Y. Executive Committee. 90785

Staten Island, N. Y. St. Andrew's Parish. Committee. 90786-90787

Staten Island Granite Company. 90791

Staten Island Hospital, New York. see New York (City) Staten Island Hospital.

Staten Island Improvement Association. 90788-90789

Staten Island Improvement Association. Committee on Transportation and Intercommunication. 90788-90789

Staten Island Railroad. 90792

Staten Island Railroad Company. Committee and Engineer. 90792

"States." pseud. Right to secede. 64321

States and territories of the great west. 24192

"States"-man. pseud. Letters to the London "Times." see Childe, Edward Vernon. and Lunt, George. incorrectly supposed author

States-man. pseud. To the people of the United States. see Leverson, Montague Richard.

States of central America. 89968, 89998

States of Mexico, their commerce, trade, &c. 43289

States of the River Plate. 39168

States Rights' Meeting, Columbia, S. C., 1830. 65913

States vs. territories. 90793

Statesman: a weekly journal of politics. 90797

Statesman and the man. 849

Statesman and the Senate. 20401

Statesman edition. Charles Sumner; his complete works. 93689

Statesman, or principles of legislation and law. (32611)

Statesman. Statistical almanac, and political manual for the state of New-Hampshire. 1865. 90796

Statesman. Statistical almanac, and political manual for the state of New-Hampshire. 1866. 36028

Statesman's manual. 90798

Statesman's manual brought down to President Taylor's inaugural address. 104205

Statesman's manual. [By Walker.] (24332)

Statesman's manual of the constitution of the United States. 90799

Statesman's manual. Presidents' messages. 104204

Statesman's manual. The address and messages of the Presidents. 104197, 104205

Statesman's year-book. 44875

Statesmanship, science, art, literature, and progress. 19495

Statesmen of America in 1846. (46977)

Statesmen of Podunk. 83719

Stati Uniti nel 1863. 5304

Statia (W. E.) firm publishers 90800-90802

Statias Hotel guide. 90800

Statia's hotel list guide. 90801

Statia's traveller's pocket companion. 90802

Station and duty of American teachers as citizens. 60947

Stationers' Hall almanack, for . . . 1835. 89587

Stationers' hand-book. 90803

Statistical account, 1815. note after 90803

Statistical account of several towns in the county of Litchfield. 50839, 2d note after 90803

Statistical account of the British empire. 43129

Statistical account of the British settlements in Australasia. 102636

Statistical account of the city of New Haven. 15858

Statistical account of the county of Middlesex. 24273, 2d note after 90803

Statistical account of the Schuylkill Permanent Bridge. 78065-(78066), 1st note after 90803

Statistical account of the Schuylkill Permanent Bridge, communicated to the Philadelphia Society of Agriculture. (61205)

Statistical account of the town of Middlebury. (29773)

Statistical account of the towns and parishes in the state of Connecticut. (15702), 15858, 21556, 21557, 24273, 50839, 2d note after 90803

Statistical account of the United States of America. (20599)

Statistical account of the valley, and adjacent country. (11986)

Statistical account of the West India islands. (24493)

Statistical account of Upper Canada. 28138, (28143)

Statistical address to the people of Austin and Washington Counties. 17436, note before 90804

Statistical almanac, and political manual for the state of New-Hampshire. 1865. 90796

Statistical almanac, and political manual for the state of New Hampshire. 1866. 36028

Statistical almanac 1846. 104206

Statistical & chronological view of the state of New-York. 90804

Statistical and chronological view of the United States of North America. 3774

Statistical and commercial history of the Kingdom of Guatemala. (36818)

Statistical and descriptive summary of the mines and minerals. 8662

Statistical and documentary evidence. 8897

Statistical and financial items. 48579

Statistical and historical account of the United States of America. 101363

Statistical and historical view of Fairmount Water Works. 90805

Statistical and historical view of the whole country. 81601

Statistical and practical observations, relative to the province of New-Brunswick. 102433

Statistical annals of the United States. 79631, 84305-84306

Statistical annual. 90806

Statistical chart of Newfoundland. 21275

Statistical classification of the occupations of the population. 22262

Statistical, commercial, and political description of Venezuela. 18674-18675

Statistical companion and pictorial almanac. 104206

Statistical companion for 1846. 104206

Statistical comparison, showing the progress. 55569

Statistical essay on New Spain. (33716)

Statistical facts in relation to the New-York and Albany Railroad. 90807

Statistical facts . . . showing the importance of the work. 54723

Statistical gazetteer of the states of Virginia and North Carolina. (21990)

Statistical gazetteer of the world. 82927

Statistical, geographical and other remarks. 11136, 69411

Statistical, historical, and political description of the colony. 102636

Statistical history of benevolent contributions in the past sixteen years. 90808

Statistical history of John Ridgway's vertical revolving battery. 90809

Statistical history of the first century of American methodism. (28054)

Statistical illustrations of the territorial extent and population. 44783

Statistical information relating to certain branches of industry. 46144

Statistical inquiry into the condition of the people of colour. 62289, note after 90809

Statistical list of the members and officers of the Assembly of . . . New-York. 53981

Statistical manual for the United States of America. 5956

Statistical memoranda of some of the affairs of the Committee of Police. (62290)

Statistical pocket manual. 90810

Statistical, political, and historical account of the United States. 35722, 101366

Statistical register. see Bankers' magazine and statistical register.

Statistical register and book of general reference. 48937

Statistical report . . . embracing a period of five years. 16381

STATISTICAL

Statistical report of the county of Albany for
the year 1820. 641, (65370), note after
90810
Statistical report of the Secretary of State.
57050
Statistical report [of the Secretary of State
of Ohio] for . . . 1869. 57049
Statistical report on the sickness and mortality
in the Army of the United States; compiled from the records of the Surgeon-
General's and Adjutant-General's Offices.
(39457)
Statistical report on the sickness and mortality
in the Army of the United States, compiled from the records of the Surgeon-
General's Office. 16380
[Statistical report on the sickness and mortality in the Army of the United States]
from January 1855, to January, 1860.
(39458)
[Statistical report on the sickness and mortality in the Army of the United States]
from January, 1839, to January, 1855.
(39458)
Statistical report on the sickness, mortality
& invaliding among the troops in the
West Indies. 97441
Statistical reports, Medical Department, U. S.
Army. 83367
Statistical sketch of Dr. Judson's missionary
life. 90811
Statistical sketch of its [i. e. Baltimore's]
institutions. 3026
Statistical sketch of the state of Michigan.
90812
Statistical sketches of Upper Canada. 10610,
21318, 90813
Statistical Society of Pennsylvania. 60643,
note after 90813
Statistical table, showing the influence of
intemperance on the churches. 3340
Statistical tables. 77544
Statistical tables and other important infor-
mation. 10609
Statistical tables and tables of distances, &c.
6848
Statistical tables: exhibiting the condition and
products of certain branches of industry.
5315
Statistical tables, exhibiting the return of votes
for electors. 63820, 104203
Statistical tables including the census of 1840.
32534, 53677
Statistical tables of population. 18636
Statistical tables of the state of New-York.
53982, note before 90814
Statistical tables relating to Massachusetts.
90814
Statistical view of American agriculture.
35849
Statistical view of the commerce of the United
States of America. 63046
Statistical view of the condition of the free
and slave states. 12179
Statistical view of the District of Maine.
(28665)
Statistical view of the executive and legis-
lative departments of the government of
Massachusetts. 45628, 64026-64027,
note after 90814
Statistical view of the number of sheep in the
several towns and counties. 4779
Statistical view of the operation of the penal
code of Pennsylvania. 60644, 90815

Statistical view of the population of Massa-
chusetts, from 1765, to 1840. (12675),
46145, note after 90815
Statistical view of the state of Illinois. 61324
Statistical view of the United States. 47435,
96484
Statistical view of the United States; containing
a geographical description. 47437
Statistical view of the United States, embracing
its territory. 19121
Statistiche Beschreibung der Besitzungen der
Hollander in Amerika. 42640
Statistiche und ethnographische Nachrichten.
(2711)
Statistics and causes of Asiatic cholera.
66368
Statistics by L. Chapin. 72342
Statistics connected with the Bear Valley coal
basin. 4121A
Statistics, etc. 31759
Statistics from the seventh annual report of
the Boston Board of Trade. 17115
Statistics in reference to the production of
silver. 42868
Statistics of American railroads. 37433
Statistics of British North America. 50008
Statistics of Cholera. 62291
Statistics of consumption in Roxbury. 17035
Statistics of Dane County, Wisconsin. 90816
Statistics of Dane County, Wisconsin: with a
sketch. 90817
Statistics of intemperance in Portsmouth.
90818
Statistics of Lowell manufactures. (42502)
Statistics of Madison and Dane County. 43749,
90817, note after 90818
Statistics of Mexico. 9666
Statistics of mines and mining. 68067
Statistics of Minnesota. 49310
Statistics of Niagara Falls, and vicinity. 36214
Statistics of Onondaga Salt Springs. 89390
Statistics of Philadelphia. 62292, note beofre
90819
Statistics of population of the city and county
of New York. 33154
Statistics of Saginaw Valley. 90819
Statistics of South Carolina. 49118
Statistics of the Boston Lying-In Hospital.
92191
Statistics of the British empire. 44784
Statistics of the class of 1859. (1442)
Statistics of the class of 1837. 105888
Statistics of the coal trade of the United States,
moved towards the seaboard, for 1867,
to which is added matter interesting to
coal operators. 90821
Statistics of the coal trade of the United States,
moved towards the seaboard, for 1867;
to which is added the prize essays.
90822
Statistics of the coal trade of the United States,
moved towards the seaboard, for 1866.
90820
Statistics of the colonies of the British empire
in the West Indies. 44911, (44917)
Statistics of the colored people of Philadelphia.
2639, 2682, 62293
Statistics of the common schools. 90823
Statistics of the condition and products of
certain branches of industry. 15857
Statistics of the condition and products of
certain branches of industry in Massachusetts. (46146)
Statistics of the Connecticut election sermons.
83743

Statistics of the cotton manufacture. 3911,
17115

Statistics of the cotton trade. (9356)

Statistics of the Lawrence Manufacturing
Company. (39390)

Statistics of the medical colleges of the
United States. 4238

Statistics of the meteorological observations
in the United States. 5950

Statistics of the New Jersey State Prison.
53196

Statistics of the operations of the Executive
Board of Friends' Association of
Philadelphia. 62294

Statistics of the present manufacturing centres.
5606

Statistics [of the proposed county of Erwin,
N. Y.] 22803, 90825

Statistics of the Senate and House of Representatives of Connecticut. 27956

Statistics of the state of Michigan. 48800

Statistics of the state of Oregon; containing
a description. 21151

Statistics of the state of Oregon. Published
by the State Agricultural Society. 57571

Statistics of the trade, industry, and resources
of Canada. 5927

Statistics of the United States, compiled under
the authority of the Secretary of the
Treasury. 19451

Statistics of the United States, (including
mortality, property, &c.) in 1860.
11676

Statistics of the United States of America,
for the use of emigrants and travellers.
96761

Statistics of the west. 29791, 29795

Statistics of the woollen manufactories in the
United States. 90824

Statistics of the world. 77543

Statistics of Trinity Church . . . Rochester.
72367

Statistics relating to elementary education.
10433

Statistics relating to the [proposed] county of
Erwin. 22803, 90825

Statistics relative to value of real estate.
90826

Statistics, showing the whole export of flour
and grain. 9054

Statisticus. pseud. Schedule of a revenue
tariff. 90827

Statisticus. (58508)

Statistik der Vereinigten Staaten von Nord-
Amerika. 8203

Statistik von Amerika. 41405

Statistique commerciale du Chili. 6451, note
after 89323

Statistique de la Martinique. (69623), 75537

Statistique de la population de la France et de
ses colonies. 6853

Statistique de l'Espagne. 50559

Statistique medicale de cet empire. (80899)

Statistisch-commerzielle Ergebnisse einer
Reise um die Erde. 77623

Statistische, politische und historische
Beschreibung. 101367

Statistische und ethnographische Nachrichten.
105519

Statistischen Gesellschaft zu New-York. 10842

Statistisches Hand- und Addressbuch der
Vereinigten Staaten von Nordamerika.
95835

Statistisk afhandling. 88937

Stato della religione cattolica in Terra-Nuova.
(24703)

Stato presente di terra ferma. 27382

Statte-Buch. 77201

Statu sarracenorum. 76838

Statue de l'Empereur Dom Pedro I. 59516

Statue of General Nathaniel Greene. 90828

Statue of Roger Williams. 89727

Statue of the Greek slave. 64796

Status of Georgia. 23893

Status of slavery. 40639, 43617, 56660

Status of the insurgent states. 9615

Statut du Parlement Provincial du Bas Canada.
85811

Statuta ab Illmo ac Rev.mo Dom. Richardo
Vinc. Whelan. 72974

Statuta dioecesana ab Illustrissimo et
Reverendissimo P. D. Joanne Baptista
Purcell. 72937

Statuta dioecesis Burlingtoniensis. 72936

Statuta dioecesis Clevelandensis. 72938

Statuta dioecesis Marianopolitanae in Michigan.
72972

Statuta dioecesis Novarcensis. 72954

Statuta dioecesis Pittsburgensis. 72964

Statuta dioecesis Pittsburgensis lata in Synodo
Dioecesana. 72963

Statuta dioecesis S. Ludovici. 72970

Statuta dioecesis Wayne Castrensis. 72942

Statuta lata et promulgata ab Illmo ac Revmo
D. Clementi Smyth. 72941

Statuta lata et promulgata ab Illmo. ac Revmo,
D. Petro Ricardo Kenrick. 72971

Statuta Novarcensis dioeceseos. 72952

Statuta ordinanta, a Sancto Concilio Provinciali
Mexicana Ill. 48373

Statvta ordinata, a Sancto Concilio Provinciali
Mexicano Ill. 42066, 76332, note after
90828

Statuta Synodi Mobiliensis. 72949

Statuta Synodi Richmondensis. 72965

Statute Law Book Company, Washington. firm
publishers 87666, note before 99075,
99076-99077, 99079-99080, 99083,
99090, 99094-99096, 99105, 99107-
99108

Statute law of Kentucky. (37540)

Statute laws of Connecticut. (15780)

Statute laws of the state of Tennessee. 31087

Statute laws of the territory. (35020)

Statute, passed at a meeting of the Board of
Trustees. 14844

Statute proposed by the Committee of the
Medical Faculty. 14843

Statuten der Europaisch-Amerikanischen
Colonisations-Gesellschaft in Texas.
85793

Statuten der West-Indische Mattschappij.
102931

Statuten des St. Petrus-Vereins in Albany.
75472

Statuten fur Deutsche Escompte (Discount)
Banken. 87112

Statuten van de Maatschappij van de
Protestantsche Surinaamsche Mettray op
Lustrijk. 93858

Statutes and laws of Harvard University.
(30749)

Statutes and laws of the University in Cambridge, Mass. (30749)

Statutes and regulations, institutes, laws, and
grand constitutions. 62815

Statutes at large and treatise of the United
States of America. 61208

Statutes at large; being a collection of all
the laws of Virginia. 31339, 2d note
after 99889, note before 99927, 100013,
100015, 100026, note after 100232,
100406, 100464

Statutes at large, of . . . Minnesota. (49311)

Statutes at large of . . . New York. 53983

Statutes at large of South Carolina. 87500, note before 87563, 87667, 87670, 87713-87714

Statutes at large of South Carolina; edited under the authority of the Legislature, by Thomas Cooper. 87713

Statutes at large of South Carolina: . . . 1682-1814. 16621

Statutes at large of the Confederate States of America. 15416

Statutes at large of the provisional government of the Confederate States of America. 15417

Statutes at large of Virginia, from October session, 1792. 80283

Statutes at large passed in the several General Assemblies. 56192

Statutes in relation to the public schools. 23707

Statutes of California, passed at the first session of the Legislature. 10029

Statutes of Columbia College and its associated schools. 14842

Statutes of Columbia College in New York. 14842

Statutes of Connecticut. 15781

Statutes of Dartmouth University relating to medical graduation. (18631)

Statutes of Dickinson College. 20084

Statutes of Dickinson College, including the course of study. 20085

Stautes of His Majesty's province of Upper-Canada. 98063

Statutes [of Illinois.] 34283

Statutes of Illinois . . . in force . . . 1857. 34290

Statutes of . . . Mississippi. 49548

Statutes of . . . Mississippi . . . with the constitutions. 33282

Statutes of . . . New Jersey. (53240)

Statutes of . . . New York. 53984

Statutes of New-York, in relation to highways. ·(53985)

Statutes of Nova Scotia passed in the first and second sessions of the General Assembly. (56193)

Statutes of Ohio, and of the Northwest Territory. (57030)

Statutes of Ohio, and of the Northwestern Territory. 12199

Statutes of . . . Ohio . . . in force at the present time. (57057)

Statutes of . . . Ohio . . . in force, August, 1854. (57057)

Statutes of . . . Ohio . . . in force, December 7, 1840. (57057)

Statutes of . . . Ohio . . . in force, January 1st, 1854. (57057)

Statutes of Ontario. 1867-68. 57365

Statutes of Rutgers College, in the city of New-Brunswick, N. J. (74441)

Statutes of the Albany Academy. ·589

Statutes of the British Parliament, in relation to the colonial trade. 90829

Statutes of the British Parliament relating to Canada. 10500

Statutes of the Centre College of Kentucky. 37507

Statutes of the Diocese of Louisiana and the Floridas. Issued by the Rt. Rev. Luis Ignatius Penalver y Cardenas, 1795. (80023)

Statutes of the Diocese of Louisiana and the Floridas, issued by the Rt. Rev. Luis Penalver y Cardenas, 1795. 72945

Statutes of the Mississippi Territory. (49547)

Statutes of the Naval Library and Institute. 12100

Statutes of the Province of Quebec passed in the . . . second session of the first Parliament. 67062

Statutes of the province of Upper Canada. 10499

Statutes of the state of Rhode Island. 66369

Statutes of the state of Vermont, passed by the Legislature. 99103

Statutes of the state of Vermont; revised and established by authority. 99110, 99113, 99119

Statutes of the state . . . relating to primary schools. 48801

Statutes of the territory of Kansas. (37065)

Statutes . . . of the territory of Oregon. 57572

Statutes of the territory of Washington. 101914

Statutes of the territory of Wisconsin. 104884

Statutes of the United States relating to revenue 31650

Statutes of the University of McGill College. 43273

Statutes of the University of William & Mary. 104155

Statutes of Upper Canada, passed in the 2d, 3d, and 4th sessions. 10499

Statutes of Upper Canada, to the time of the Union. 10499

Statutes [of Vermont.] note after 99131

Statutes regulating the practice of physic and surgery. (53987)

Statutes . . . relating to Common Schools. 53986

Statutes relating to elections other than for militia and town officers. 53988

Statutes relating to elementary education. 10433, (42517)

Statutes relating to Florida, in the Diocesan Synod. (80023), 90830

Statutes, rules, and ordinances. 43273

Statutes rules and ordinances of . . . King's College. 37873

Statuts de la Societe de Colonisation Europeo-Americaine au Texas. 85794

Statuts et autres documents. 61019

Staudenmayer, L. R. 90831

Staughton, James M. 90832-90833

Staughton, William. 90834-90842

Staughton, Sir George Leonard, Bart., 1737-1901. (59572), 90843

Staunton, Sir George T. ed. 27784

Staunton, Va. Albemarle Female Institute. see Albemarle Female Institute, Staunton, Va.

Staunton, Va. Meeting of Freeholders of Augusta County, Va., 1775. see Augusta County, Va. Meeting of Freeholders, Staunton, 1775.

Staunton, Va. Public Meeting, 1793. 90844

Staunton Baptist Female Institute. see Albemarle Female Institute, Staunton, Va.

Staunton embassy to the rump dynasty. (71959)

Staveley, E. 10627

Staveren, G. L. van Oosten van. see Oosten van Staveren, G. L. van.

Stay against straying. (2937)

Stay-law, and all the amendments. 87715

Stayner, Charles W. 90846

Steadfast, Jonathan. pseud. Address to the people of Connecticut. see Daggett, David. supposed author

Steadfast, Jonathan. pseud. Count the cost. see Daggett, David. supposed author

Steadfast people the pastor's joy and crown. 77576

Steadfastness and preparation in the day of adversity. 44487

Steadfastness in religion and loyalty recommended. 34765

Steadman, E. 90847-90848

Steadman, W. 21939

Steady habits vindicated. 15859, note after 90848

Steady progress of the Camden and Amboy Railroad Company. 90849

Steam Boiler Makers' and Iron Ship Builders' Benevolent & Protective Association, Boston. 90850

Steam communication between Boston and New Orleans. 6587, note after 90850

Steam doctor's defence. 95467

Steam engine, by J. C. Merriam. 22085

Steam engine. Hon. William H. Seward's argument. 79585

Steam engines. (68512)

Steam navigation between Boston and Europe. (31825)

Steam navy of the United States. 20018

Steam postal intercourse & traffic. 90851

Steam quack. 95568

Steam train boats for canal transportation. 90852

Steam trip to the tropics. 30932

Steam warfare in the Parana. 43463

Steamboat and railroad guide. 41701

Steamboat controversy. 27293

Steamboat directory, and disasters on the Western waters. 41691

Steamboat disasters and railroad accidents in the United States. (33386), 90853

Steamer Gray Jacket and cargo, Timothy Meaher, claimant, vs. the United States. 9615

Steamers between California China and Japan. 95464

Steamers to Ireland. 54731

Stearns, Asahel, 1774-1839. 45684, 45744, 98567

Stearns, Charles. abolitionist 22554, 90863-90866

Stearns, Charles, 1753-1826. 90854-90862

Stearns, Charles, 1788-1860. 17359, 51924, 66866, 90868-90871, 90874

Stearns, Charles, 1788-1860. petitioner 90873

Stearns, Charles, 1788-1860. plaintiff 90872

Stearns, Charles, fl. 1872. 90867

Stearns, Charles Woodward. 90875-90876

Stearns, Edward Josiah. 90877-90882

Stearns, Edwin. 14307, note after 90882

Stearns, Elisha. 90883

Stearns, Ezra Scollay. 90884

Stearns, F. P. note after 90885

Stearns, George B. defendant 104790

Stearns, George Luther, 1809-1867. 22713, note before 90885, 98005

Stearns, George Osborn. 36924, note before 90886

Stearns, Henry Putnam. 90886-90888

Stearns, Honestus. 90889

Stearns, Isaac. 90890-90891

Stearns, J. F. 83502

Stearns, J. M. ed. 23843

Stearns, J. N. 54489, 87061

Stearns, James S. 7336

Stearns, John, 1770-1848. 90892-90893, 105991

Stearns, John Glazier. 70157, 90894-90900

Stearns, John Milton. 90901-90902

Stearns, John Newton. 90903

Stearns, Jonathan French. (54912), 79451, 90904-90914

Stearns, Joseph Oliver. 90915

Stearns, Josiah. 90916-90919

Stearns, Norris. 90921

Stearns, O. S. 96966

Stearns, Oakman Sprague. 90922

Stearns, Oliver. 90923-90929

Stearns, Onslow, 1810-1878. 90930 see also New Hampshire. Governor, 1869-1871 (Stearns) Old Colony & Newport Railway Company. President.

Stearns, Robert Edwards Carter. 90931-90933

Stearns, Samuel, 1747-1819. 21833, 55530, 55536, 55539, 55567, 62743, 90934-90961, 90963-90966

Stearns, Samuel, 1747-1819. petitioner 90962

Stearns, Samuel, 1770-1834. 90967-90974

Stearns, Samuel Horatio. 90986-90988

Stearns, Silas. 90975

Stearns, Thomas C. 90976

Stearns, Timothy. 90977

Stearns, William. 90978

Stearns, William Augustus. 1323, 90979-90998, 93275

Stearns, William F. 90999-91000

Stearns, William G. 92312

Stearns, Zenus B. 91001

Stebbing, Henry, 1687-1763. 91002

Stebbing, Henry, 1716-1787. 91003

Stebbins, C. B. 91004

Stebbins, Daniel. 91005

Stebbins, G. R. 85895, 85897

Stebbins, George Stanford. 91006

Stebbins, Giles Badger. 85895, 85897, 91007-91015

Stebbins, Heman. plaintiff (8249), note after 91015

Stebbins, Henry A. 83234

Stebbins, Henry George, 1811-1881. 1774, 91016-91022

Stebbins, Horatio. 91023-91025

Stebbins, Jane E. 91026

Stebbins, John W. 91027

Stebbins, Jonathan. 91028

Stebbins, Josiah. 91029

Stebbins, Luke. 91030

Stebbins, Maria. 91031-91032

Stebbins, Mary Elizabeth (Moore) Hewitt. 26848, 31642-31643, 91033-91036, note after 91036

Stebbins, Rufus Phineas, 1810-1885. 31864, 47247, 84013, 91037-91049

Stebbins, Seymour L. 91050

Stebbins, Stephen Williams. 91051

Stebbins, Sumner. 91052-91054

Stedfastness in religion. 39198

Stedham, W. petitioner 44766

Stedman, A. J. 91055

Stedman, Charles. 13753, 91056-91057, 95606

Stedman, Charles J. 91058

Stedman, Edmund Clarence. 91060-91067

Stedman, James O. 91068-91069

Stedman, James S. 91070

Stedman, John Gabriel. 12723, 57458-57459, 91057, 91071-91084, 95606

Stedman, John W. 55925-55926, note after 91084-91085

Stelter, Robert U. ed. 83275
Stelzig, Ignaz Alfons. 91219
Stem uit Holland. 93865
Stem uit Pella, Iowa. 77773
Stem uit Suriname, beantwoord door een stem. 93865
Stem uit Suriname in het belag der negerslaven. 91220, note after 93865
Stemmata Rosellana. 91387
Stemme fra St. Croix. 9484
Stemmen uit Noord-Amerika. 8745
Stempelius, Gerardus Goudanus. 91221
Stenhouse, Fanny. 91222
Stenhouse, Thomas B. H. 91222
Stenio, Louis. tr. 69065
Stennett, Joseph. 91223
Stennett, Samuel. 91224-91225
Stenographer of the Atlas. pseud. reporter 96843
Stenographer of the House of Delegates. pseud. see Maryland. Legislature. House of Delegates. Stenographer. pseud.
Stenographer's minutes of the hearing. 84774
Stenographic report of the hearings. 85212
Stenographic reporter. 43531, 91226
Stenson, William. 91227
Stenstrom, Jaquinus. 91128
Stentorian eloquence and medical infallibility. 14111
Step-mother: a book founded on fact. 74247
Step-mother; a domestic tale from real life. 102592A-102593
Stephanini, J. 91229-91230
Stephanische Landverhuizing. 98775
Stephano, Hieronimo da Santo. see Santo Stephano, Hieronimo da.
Stephan'sche Auswanderung nach Amerika. 98774
Stephanus, Josephus Valentinus. 91231
Stephen. pseud. Night in Charleston. 91232
Stephen, Sir George. 19580, 91233-91234
Stephen, James, 1758-1832. (3352), 8514, 14726, 18487, 22590, (21855), 44704, 50827, (57413), 67839, (68265), 70254, 91235-91248, 95563, 101270, 102798
Stephen. James, 1758-1832. supposed author 17530, 42349, 42352, 91235-1st note after 91235, 2d note after 102829
Stephen, John. 75294
Stephen, Sir John. incorrectly supposed author 8514, 18487, 50827, 67839, note before 91236, 91240-91241, 91246-91247, 101270
Stephen, Leslie. 1st note after 91235, 2d note after 102829
Stephen A. Douglas on the cause and effect of the rebellion. 8802
Stephen Allen Benson, President of Liberia. (4752)
Stephen Bruton of Bristol, R. I. 84300
Stephen Girard. 85819
Stephen Girard's Heirs. plaintiffs see Heirs of Stephen Girard. plaintiffs
Stephen Grellet. 91249
Stephen, Prophet, Son of Douglas. pseud. see Prophet Stephen, Son of Douglas. pseud.
Stephen Smith, M. D., LL. D. 84277
Stephen Waring. 101425
Stephens, --------. illus. 16778, 91065
Stephens, Abednego. 91250
Stephens, Alexander Hamilton, 1812-1883. 10192, 13658, 27111, 39654, (48140), 51993, 65358, 91251-91279 see also Confederate States of America. Peace Commissioners to the Hampton Roads Conference.

Stephens, Ann Sophia (Winterbotham) 33620, 64364, 64368, 82134-(82135), 91280-note before 91289
Stephens, Edward. ed. note before 91289
Stephens, Ellen. 91289-91290
Stephens, George. ed. 71440
Stephens, Harriet Marion (Ward) 91291-91292
Stephens, Henry Louis. 91293-91294
Stephens, John. 91295
Stephens, John Lloyd. 7233, 11520, 69381, 91296-91301, 98812
Stephens, Joseph. 91302
Stephens, Lemuel. 91303
Stephens, M. D. supposed author 42349, 42352, 91235
Stephens, Philadelphie. 89763
Stephens, Philadelphie. supposed author 7929, 91304
Stephens, Stephen. 86053
Stephens, Thomas. 27055, (60861), 91305-91307 see also Georgia (Colony) Agent.
Stephens, Thomas, d. 1780? 71542, 91308-91309
Stephens, W. Hudson. ed. 95825
Stephens, William, 1671-1753. 27113, 91305, 91313-91316, 94215 see also Georgia (Colony) Secretary.
Stephens, William A. 91317
Stephens (Thomas) firm publishers 61604, 91310-91312
Stephens & Co. firm publishers 88389
Stephens' incidents of travel in Greece. 69381
Stephen's micellany. 91311
Stephenson, E. W. 75006
Stephenson, H. M. 88689
Stephenson, Marmaduke. 5629, 91318-91320
Stephenson, Oscar. 91321
Stephenson, Robert. 91322
Stephenson, Rowland Macdonald. 42982, 91323
Stephenson, Sarah. 91324
Stephenson, Thomas. 91325
Stephenson, William. 82242, note after 91325
Stephenson (I.) firm publishers 2d note after 100557, 104191
Stephens's Philadelphia directory, for 1796. 61604, 91312
Stephenstown, N. Y. Baptist Association. see Baptists. New York. Stephenstown Association.
Stephenstown Baptist Association. see Baptists. New York. Stephenstown Association.
Steps for organization and advice to managers. 88819
Steptoe, Eliza. 96121
Sterbende Monch in Peru. 100784
Sterett, Samuel. 91327
Sterfte der Slaven in Suriname. 38763
Sterility is laid. 71271
Sterling, Charles F. 91328-91329
Sterling, Edward. 99395
Sterling, James. 20405, 91330-91332
Sterling, John Canfield. 91334
Sterling, John Canfield. defendant before ecclesiastical court 91333
Sterling, William A. 91335
Sterling, Mass. Evangelical Church. 15454
Sterling, Mass. Washington Benevolent Society. see Washington Benevolent Society. Massachusetts. Sterling.
Stern, Samuel. 91336
Stern, Simon. ed. 54853
Sternberg, L. 91337
Sternberg, P. 91338

STERNE

Sterne, Henry. 91339
Sterne, Laurence. pseud. Koran. see
    Griffith, Richard.
Sterne, Laurence, 1713-1768. 91340-91341,
    91343-91356, 97293
Sterne's exposure of Jamaica justice. 91339
Sterne's letters to his friends. 91355
Sterns, Isaac. see Stearns, Isaac.
Sterns, Jonathan. 91357, note after 94546
Sterret, James. 91358-91359
Sterry, Abby H. 91360
Sterry, Consider. 91361-91363
Sterry, John. 91361-91362
Sterry, Louisa Ann. respondent 91365
Sterry, Peter. 91364
Sterry, Robert. respondent 91365
Stetson, Amasa. 91366-91369
Stetson, Caleb. 91370-91376
Stetson, Lemuel. 91377-91378
Stetson, Seth. 91379-91380
Steuart, Adam. (27953), 56461, (69679),
    74624, 91381-91384
Steuart, Andrew. 22785, 91385-91386
Steuart, Sir James, 1635-1715. 18570,
    78196, 2d note after 91386 see also
    Scotland. Lord Advocate.
Steuart, Sir James. see Denham, Sir James
    Steuart, 1712-1780.
Steuart, John. 91388-91389
Steuart, Richard Sprigg. 91390
Steuart, William. 91391
Steuart, Sir William Drummond, Bart. 91392
Steuban, Baron von. see Steuben, Friedrich
    Wilhelm August Heinrich Ferdinand,
    Freiherr von, 1730-1794.
Steuben, Friedrich Wilhelm August Heinrich
    Ferdinand, Freiherr von, 1730-1794.
    (44405), 48981, 50185, 68016, 74326,
    82379, 82979, 84906, 86300, 87696,
    91393-91465, 91428, 91459, 91464,
    94784, 94785, 104819
Steuben, N. Y. Teachers' Institute. see
    Steuben Teachers' Institute, Steuben,
    N. Y.
Steuben Teachers' Institute, Steuben, N. Y.
    91466
Steuben's manual exercise. 91432
Steuben's military discipline for the regulation
    of the troops of the United States.
    91441
Steuben's military discipline, for the regulation
    of the troops of the United States.
    Ornamented with cuts, &c. 91442
Steuben's military exercise for the government
    of the troops of the United States.
    91436
Steuben's regulations for the order and disci-
    pline of the troops of the United States.
    Illustrated by a frontispiece. 91456
Steuben's regulations for the order and disci-
    pline of the troops of the United States.
    To which is added, an act to regulate
    and discipline the militia. 91422
Steubenville, Ohio. Court. 28119, note after
    96937
Steubenville, Ohio. Presbyterian Church.
    91468
Steubenville, Ohio. Steubenville Female
    Seminary. see Steubenville Female
    Seminary, Steubenville, Ohio.
Steubenville, Ohio. Town Council. 91467
Steubenville, Ohio. Town Council. Committee
    on the Subject of a Western National
    Armory. 91467
Steubenville & Indiana Rail Road Company.
    Board of Directors. 91470

Steubenville and Indiana Railroad Company.
    91471
Steubenville Female Seminary, Steubenville,
    Ohio. 91469
Stevens, --------. 66686
Stevens, --------, fl. 1840. defendant 101436
Stevens, Abel. (52001), 81544, 81550, 91472-
    91480, 103172
Stevens, Alexander Hodgdon, 1789-1869, 34484,
    91481
Stevens, Augustus E. (64340) see also Port-
    land, Me. Mayor, 1866 (Stevens)
Stevens, B. F. 95301, 95958
Stevens, Benjamin. 91482-91485
Stevens, Beriah. 91486
Stevens, Byron. plaintiff (74472)
Stevens, Calvin F. (64499), 91487
Stevens, Charles. 91488-91489
Stevens, Charles Emery. 91490
Stevens, D. supposed tr. (74605)-74606, note
    after 91491, 2d note after 100518
Stevens, Daniel Waldo. 91492
Stevens, Ebenezer. 91725, 101814
Stevens, Edwin A. petitioner 91493
Stevens, Edwin J. 91494
Stevens, Ellen. defendant 90576
Stevens, Enos. 91495
Stevens, Ezra A. 91496
Stevens, Frank Everett. ed. 100978
Stevens, George. 91497
Stevens, George Alexander. 91498-91503
Stevens, George Alexander. supposed author
    25884
Stevens, George Lionel. 91504
Stevens, George W. 91505
Stevens, Henry, 1791-1867. 91506-91507
Stevens, Henry, 1819-1886. (5199), 25567,
    30599, 53058, 59367, 63857, 63960,
    69367, 70887, (73288), 77803, 77804,
    82823, 82850, 91508-91520
Stevens, Isaac Ingalls, 1818-1862. 19490,
    29890, 69900, 69946, 90740, 91521-
    91532, 101107, 101910-101911, 101918,
    2d note after 101924, 1st note after
    101925 see also Washington (Territory)
    Governor, 1853-1857 (Stevens)
Stevens, J. 91533
Stevens, James Wilson. 91534-91535
Stevens, Jedediah Dwight. 91536
Stevens, John, d. 1726. (1948), (13056),
    23802, 28002, 31557-31558, 39452,
    44553, (76429), 91537-91538, 98781-
    98782
Stevens, John, 1749-1838. (41645)-41646,
    61692, 91539-note after 91540
Stevens, John, fl. 1769. (7884), 95936
Stevens, John, 1750-1799. 91541-91542
Stevens, John, 1750-1799. supposed author
    (41645)-41646, note after 56495
Stevens, John, fl. 1851. claimant 54495
Stevens, John Austin. 2302, 53589, 86155
    see also Meeting to Further the Enter-
    prise of the Atlantic Telegraph, New
    York, 1863. Secretary.
Stevens, John Harrington. 91543
Stevens, John Hathaway. 91544-91547
Stevens, John Lloyd. see Stephens, John
    Lloyd.
Stevens, Joseph. 91548
Stevens, Judith. 91549-91550
Stevens, Levi Merriam. 10146, 30209, note
    after 91550
Stevens, Luther C. 91551-91552
Stevens, Philadelphia. see Stephens,
    Philadelphie.

2832

Stevens, Robert. petitioner 105694
Stevens, Robert. tr. 91553
Stevens, Samuel, 1778-1860. 45133, 45193,
45090, (45291) see also Maryland.
Governor, 1822-1826 (Stevens)
Stevens, Samuel C. 91554-91556
Stevens, Simon. 91557-91558
Stevens, T. 91559
Stevens, Thaddeus, 1792-1868. 91560-91567
Stevens, Thaddeus, 1792-1868. plaintiff
25807
Stevens, Thomas. see Stephens, Thomas, d.
1780?
Stevens, W. H. 93635
Stevens, William. 91568
Stevens, William, 1732-1806. 102145
Stevens, William Bacon, Bp., 1815-1887.
(36505), 83525, 84678C, 91569-91583
Stevens, William H. 60866, 90486
Stevens (Henry) Son and Stiles. firm publishers
93588, 94691
Stevens American nuggets. 91508
Stevens historical nuggets. 91508
Stevenson, -------. 60469 see also Penn-
sylvania. Legislature. Committee on
Domestic Manufactures. Chairman.
Stevenson, A. 54489, 87061
Stevenson, Alexander. 91585
Stevenson, Andrew. 91586-91587
Stevenson, Archibald. 91588
Stevenson, Carter Littlepage, 1817-1888.
15330, 15367
Stevenson, Charles L. 2891, note after 91588
Stevenson, David. 91589-91590
Stevenson, Edward, fl. 1836. 91592
Stevenson, Edward, fl. 1858. 91591
Stevenson, Edward O. 91593
Stevenson, George John. 91594
Stevenson, H. 91595
Stevenson, J. M. 91596
Stevenson, James S. 91597
Stevenson, John. 91598-91600
Stevenson, John Hall. see Hall-Stevenson,
John.
Stevenson, John White, 1812-1886. (37531),
91601 see also Kentucky. Commis-
sioners on the Code of Practice in Civil
and Criminal Cases.
Stevenson, Joshua Thomas. 91603-91605
Stevenson, Roger. 33403, 91607
Stevenson, V. K. 42822
Stevenson, William. complainant 91610
Stevenson, William, 1771-1829. (10237), 37631,
91609
Stevenson, William, fl. 1782. 91608
Stevenson, William Bennet. 79334, 91613-
91614
Stevenson, William J. 91615
Stevens's American bibliographer. 91520,
99362
Stevens's American nuggets. 91511
Steward, Austin. 91616 see also Wilberforce
Colony, London, Ontario. President.
Steward, Henry. 91617
Steward, James. 97192, 97196
Steward, Joseph. pseud. Poor Joseph. 62743,
64071, 91618
Steward, Joseph, 1752-1822. 91619, 92958
Steward, William. 91620-91621
Steward engages. 105831
Steward's healing art. 91621
Steward's thoughts upon Streeter's (isms.)
92790
Stewardship of wealth. 2956

Stewart, ---------, fl. 1805. defendant at
court martial (35978)
Stewart, ---------, fl. 1805. petitioner
(35978)
Stewart, ----------, fl. 1839. (45389)
Stewart, A. M. 91622
Stewart, Adam. 91623
Stewart, Alexander, d. 1771. 91624
Stewart, Alexander, 1794-1865. 91625
Stewart, Alvan. 91626-91632
Stewart, Arch. 91649
Stewart, Andrew. 22785, 55322, 91633-91648
Stewart, Catherine. 91650
Stewart, Charles, 1778-1869. 32655, 91651
Stewart, Charles, 1778-1869. petitioner
44138
Stewart, Charles James, Bishop of Quebec,
1775-1837. 91655-91663, 99582
Stewart, Charles Samuel. 52079, 91664-91672
Stewart, Charles William Vane. see London-
derry, Charles William Vane Stewart,
Marquis of Londonderry.
Stewart, Daniel. 85294
Stewart, David. 91673
Stewart, Dugald. 71988, 72007, 72011-(72012),
82304-(82305), 82314, 82318, 91674-
81676
Stewart, E. tr. 33556
Stewart, Electra Maria (Sheldon) 80119, note
after 91676
Stewart, Ellen (Brown) 91677
Stewart, F. H. 85589
Stewart, Fredinand Campbell. 91678
Stewart, George. 4355
Stewart, Isaac. 78263, note before 97104
Stewart, J. 91679
Stewart, J. B. 52136
Stewart, Jaime Z. tr. 83140-83141
Stewart, James. of Nova Scotia reporter
91682
Stewart, James, 1799-1864. supposed author
54277, note after 91682
Stewart, James, d. 1794. 91680-91681
Stewart, James Augustus. 91683-91687
Stewart, James W. 91688
Stewart, John. see Bute, John Stewart, 3d
Earl of, 1713-1792.
Stewart, John. of Jamaica 35557, 91691-
91692
Stewart, John, 1749-1822. (50495), 91693-
91695
Stewart, John, ca. 1758-1834. 91696
Stewart, John, ca. 1758-1834. petitioner
(61285), 65636, note after 93185
Stewart, John, d. 1797. defendant 91689-
91690
Stewart, John, d. 1823. 49704
Stewart, John G. (55830), 91697
Stewart, Kensey Johns. 91698
Stewart, L. L. 91699
Stewart, Maria W. (Miller) 91700
Stewart, Philemon. 32664, 79706-79708, note
after 91701
Stewart, Richard A. 91702
Stewart, Richard S. 11201
Stewart, Robert. A. M. 91704
Stewart, Robert, 1769-1822. see Londonderry,
Robert Stewart, 2d Marquis of, 1769-
1822.
Stewart, Robert, d. ca. 1844. 91703
Stewart, Robert Marcellus, 1815-1871. 33150
see also Missouri. Governor, 1857-
1861 (Stewart)
Stewart, Samuel. 91706

Stirling, William Alexander, calling himself 6th Earl of, 1726-1783. defendant 5279, 53074, 91855 see also Board of Proprietors of the Eastern Division of New Jersey. defendants

Stirling, William Alexander, calling himself 6th Earl of, 1726-1783. respondent 33874, 91855

Stirling peerage. 33828, 91841A, 91856

Stirling Peerage Committee. 93598

Stirling peerage. Trial of Alexander Humphrys or Alexander. 33828, 91841A, 91856, note after 97471

Stirpes Surinamenses selectae. 48907

Stirrat, David. 91857

Stirredge, Elizabeth. 91858

Stirring historical romance of the war. 70550

Stith, Ferdinand. ed. 76909

Stith, Mrs. Townshend. 91859

Stith, William. 76456, 91860-91865, 1st note after 99889

Stoa, -------- Quintianus. see Quintianus Stoa, ---------.

Stoaks, -------. (28474)

Stobnicza, John. see Stobniczy, Jan ze.

Stobniczy, Jan ze. 91866-91868

Stobo, Robert. 15205, 17365, (41650), (47511)-47512, 51661, 91869, 101710

Stock, John Edmonds. 91870

Stock, Joseph. 4882, 91871-91872

Stock and Exchange Board, New York. see New York (City) Stock Exchange.

Stock Exchange, New York. see New York (City) Stock Exchange.

Stock jobber turn'd gentleman. 23378

Stockbridge, C. petitioner (30658)

Stockbridge, John Calvin. 91873

Stockbridge, Mass. Centennial Commemoration of the Berkshire Association of Congregational Ministers, 1863. see Congregational Churches in Massachusetts. Berkshire Association. Centennial Commemoration, Stockbridge, Mass., 1863.

Stockbridge, Vt. Congregational Church. 91875

Stockbridge & Pittsfield Railroad Company. 91874

Stockbridge Indians. (15440), 86037

Stockbridge Indians. claimants 69881

Stockbridge Indians. Treaties, etc. 96736

Stockbridge, past and present. (36490)

Stockdale, John. tr. (38422)

Stockdale, Percival. 91876

Stockdale (John) firm publishers 102541

Stocker, John C. defendant 25374

Stockholder. pseud. Brief view of the important relations of the Morris Canal. 91878

Stockholder. pseud. Communication addressed to a committee. 68471

Stockholder. pseud. Considerations relating to the exclusive grant. 52566

Stockholder. pseud. Examination of some of the provisions of the act. 23352, 91879

Stockholder. pseud. Stockholder's views. 91882

Stockholder, pseud. Views of a stockholder. see Wurts, John.

Stockholder from the first. pseud. Reasons why the Directors. see Prescott, Luther. supposed author

Stockholder of the Morris Canal. pseud. Letter to John Wurtz [sic]. 91880-91881

Stockholder of the Morris Canal. pseud. Review. 91881, 105641

Stockholders of the Southern Pacific Railroad Company, met at Armory Hall. 88439

Stockholders of the Union Bank of Tennessee, Philadelphia. petitioners see Union Bank of Tennessee. Stockholders, Philadelphia. petitioners

Stockholder's view of the management. 91882

Stockholm. Svenska Vetenskapsakadamien. see Svenska Vetenskapsakademien, Stockholm.

Stockholm. K. Vetenskaps-Akademien. see Svenska Vetenskapsakademien, Stockholm.

Stocking, Abner. 91883

Stocking, Sabura S. 91884

Stocklein, Joseph, d. 1733. (52376), 91981-91982

Stocklein, P. 4043

Stockmar, Ernest Alfred Christian von. 91885

Stocks and stock-jobbing in Wall Street. 2039, note before 91886

Stockton, B. F. 10162

Stockton, Bayard. 91904

Stockton, Lucius Horatio. 32215, 91886-note after 91888

Stockton, R. F. 106236

Stockton, Mrs. Richard. 84107

Stockton, Richard, 1764-1828. 1795, note after 53697, note after 83791, 91889

Stockton, Robert Field, 1795-1866. (31177), 81832, 91890-91911

Stockton, Robert Field, 1795-1866. plaintiff (32969), 96929

Stockton, Thomas Hewings. 74634, 91913-91918

Stockton, Calif. Citizens. 37808, 97098

Stockton city directory. 91919

Stockton directory, and emigrant's guide to the southern mines. 91920

Stockton versus Hopkins. (32969)

Stockwell, John N. 85072, 91921

Stockwell, William. 91877

Stocqueler, Joachim Hayward. 91922-91923

Stoddard, Amos. 40628, 91924-91928

Stoddard, Anthony, d. 1687. 91929

Stoddard, Anthony, 1678-1760. 91930

Stoddard, Asa. 91931

Stoddard, Charles. 23315, 91932

Stoddard, Charles Warren. 9976

Stoddard, Darius. 91933

Stoddard, Elijah Woodward, 1799-1838. 91934

Stoddard, Elijah Woodward, 1820-1913. 23315, 91932

Stoddard, Enoch Vine. 84269

Stoddard, John S. 8328, note after 91935 see also Brooklyn. City Surveyor.

Stoddard, Mrs. M. 91936

Stoddard, Richard Henry. 28893, (63533), 84317, 91937-91938

Stoddard, Samuel. defendant 91939

Stoddard, Solomon. (46669), 79441, 79444, 91940-91968, 104083

Stoddard, Solomon. incorrectly supposed author 28052, 28506, 65689, 2d note after 74631, 79956-79957, 91945, 91953, note after 105090

Stoddard, William B. 91969

Stoddard, William Osborn. 71825, note after 91969, 2d note after 94296

Stoddard (Ashbel) firm publishers 91970-91979

Stoddard's diary. 91970-91979

Stoddart, John. 21873, 85217, note before 91980, 104689

Stony Brook Railroad. 92166
Stony Brook Railroad. Charter. 92166
Stony Brook Railroad. Directors. 92168
Stoopendall, ---------. illus. (26367)
Stop to the call of the unconverted. 97693
Storace, Stephen. 55370, 92169-92177C
Storchsburg, Jacob Staehlin von. see Staehlin
   von Storcksburg, Jacob.
Storer, Bellamy. 92178-92188
Storer, David Humphreys, 1804-1891. 23841,
   (46085), 59383, 82810, 92189-92191
   see also Massachusetts. Zoological
   and Botanical Survey.
Storer, Eliphalet G. 92192-92193
Storer, William, Jr. 92194
Storer, or the American syren. 92226
Stores of American life. 49753
Storey, Charles W. 46081
Storey, Isaac. see Story, Isaac, 1774-1803.
Storey, Thomas. see Story, Thomas.
Storia antica del Messico cavata da' migliori
   storici Spagnuoli. 13518
Storia de la vita, virtu, doni, e grazie della
   Venerabile Serva di Dio Suor Maria di
   Gesu. 92195
Storia degli stabilimenti Europei in America.
   9289, 92196
Storia degli Stati Uniti. 3126
Storia dei governo, della milizia, della
   religione. 24164
Storia del commercio e della navigazione.
   36657
Storia del regno di Ferdinando e Isabella.
   65288
Storia del regno di Filipo II. 65295
Storia del Signor di Cleveland figliuolo
   naturale di Cronvello. 65410
Storia dell' America, in continuazione del
   compendio della storia universelle del
   Sig. Conte di Sigur. 15017-15018, note
   after 92196
Storia dell' America Settentrionale. 68109
Storia dell' Indie Orientali. 43779
Storia dell' Isola di S. Domingo. 21899
Storia della California. 13524
Storia della Compagnia del' Opera Italiana.
   64009
Storia della conquista del Messico fatta da
   Cortez. 44442
Storia della guerra dell' independenza degli
   Stati Uniti. 6818, 86841
Storia della letteratura Italiana del Cav.
   Abate Girolamo Tiraboschi. 95861
Storia della lingua e letteratura Italiana in
   New-York. 64014
Storia della rivoluzione dell' America Inglese.
   92197, 94571
Storia della vita e dei viaggi di Cristoforo
   Colombo. 35178
Storia della vita e viaggi di Cristoforo
   Colombo. 35179
Storia della vita, virtu, doni, e grazie del
   Venerabile Servo di Dio P. F. Pietro
   di S. Giuseppe Betancur. 27517,
   92198
Storia della vita, virtu, donni, y grazzi del
   Pietro. 5062
Storia delle colonie Inglesi in America. 41865
Storia delle missioni apostoliche dello stato
   de Chile. (75805)
Storia delle religioni di tutti i regni del mondo.
   36771
Storia di America. (71997)
Storia di Cristoforo Colombo. 76522
Storia di Cristoforo Colombo compendiata.
   (73273)

Storia di Don Bernardino de Cardenas. 92199
Storia di Niccolo' I. Re del Paraguai. 92200
Storia di Niccolo' Rubiuni detto Niccolo'.
   92201
Storia, distinta, e curiosa del tabacco. 92202-
   92203
Storia galante. 100613
Storia generale de' viaggi. 92204
Storia incredibile ma vera. 94010
Storia letteraria della liguria. 4565
Storia universale. 10718
Storia universelle del Sig. Conte di Sigur.
   10517-10518, note after 92196
Stories about Arnold, Andre, and Champe.
   92335
Stories about Arnold, the traitor, Andre, the
   spy, and Champe, the patriot. 2063,
   note after 92204
Stories about Captain John Smith of Virginia.
   27920, note before 92205
Stories about Dr. Franklin. 92205
Stories about Gen. La Fayette. 92205A,
   92335
Stories about General Warren. 8546, note
   after 92205, 101478-101479
Stories about Indiana. 92206
Stories about the elephant. 97512
Stories about the whale. 92207
Stories about whale catching. 97512-97513
Stories about whales and the whale-fishery.
   92208
Stories, by Charles Nordhoff. 55460
Stories for children. 82521
Stories for good California children. 97724
Stories for the . . . family. 65374
Stories for young persons. (78802)-78803,
   note before 92209
Stories from American history. 92209
Stories from New England life. 74362
Stories from real life. 92210
Stories from the history of Mexico. 92211
Stories, not for good children, nor for bad
   children. 82508
Stories of early settlers in the wilderness.
   65492
Stories of frontier adventure. 14204
Stories of great men. 92212
Stories of great national songs. 83671-83672,
   83677
Stories of many lands. 13461
Stories of popular voyages and travels. 92213
Stories of success. 84057
Stories of the American revolution. 92214-
   92215
Stories of the discovery and conquest of
   America. 48899
Stories of the great prairies. 16539
Stories of the Hudson River counties. 75480
Stories of the Indians during the revolution.
   92216
Stories of the island world. 55463
Stories of the last battles of the American
   revolution. 92217
Stories of the Mississippi valley. 47378
Stories of the prairie, and other adventures.
   16539
Stories of the revolution. (65493)
Stories of the sea. 16540
Stories of the Spanish conquests in America.
   78817, note after 92217
Stories of the war of 1812. 92218
Stories of the woods. 16541
Stories of voyages. 92219
Stories of Washington and the American war.
   52036
Stories on the history of Connecticut. 27875

Stork, William. 24840, 92220-92223
Storm, Thomas. 12386
Storm. A novel. 92224
Storm, a poem. 92225
Storm, or the American syren. 92226
Storming of Quebec. A poem. By Alexander
    Coffin, Jr. 14159
Storming of Quebec, a poem, in three cantos.
    94535
Stormont, David Murray, Lord. see Mans-
    field, David Murray, 2d Earl of, 1727-
    1796.
Storrow, James Jackson. 90715, note after
    92226
Storrow, Samuel A. 92227
Storrow, Thomas W. 92228
Storrs, Charles Backus. 92229
Storrs, George. defendant 92230
Storrs, Henry Martyn. 92231-92232
Storrs, Henry Randolph, 1787-1837. 92233-
    92238
Storrs, John, 1735-1799. 92239
Storrs, John, 1801-1854. 92240
Storrs, Richard Salter, 1763-1819. 92241
Storrs, Richard Salter, 1787-1873. (66659)-
    66660, 92242-92265
Storrs, Richard Salter, 1821-1900. 41219,
    50041, 79299, 92266-92272
Storrs, William L. 15677
Storrs. firm see Spalding and Storrs. firm
Story, Augustus. 104884
Story, Enoch. 92273
Story, Isaac, 1749-1816. 92274-92276
Story, Isaac, 1774-1803. 92277-92282
Story, Isaac, 1774-1803. incorrectly supposed
    author (36061), 105979, 105983
Story, Joseph, 1779-1845. 1173, 7036, 7866,
    9559, 15586, 27488, 33154, 39355, 51133,
    75673, 89014, 92283-92320, 92331, 92333,
    93808, 95355, 96929, 97443-97444, note
    after 98101, 1st note after 100577
Story, Joseph, 1779-1845. supposed author
    (49444), note before 92310
Story, Joseph, 1779-1845. supposed author
    petitioner 47680, 1st note after 92309
Story, Sydney A., Jr. pseud. Caste. see
    Pike, Mary H.
Story, Thomas. 37367, 59726, 66737, 71080,
    92321, 92323-92330
Story, Thomas. supposed author 6108,
    92329
Story, William Wetmore. 92311, 92331-92332
Story, William Wetmore. reporter 92333
Story & Humphrey's Pennsylvania mercury.
    92273
Story. 39738, 94652
Story for boys. 64917
Story for boys, and a guide to persons visiting
    the city. 71212
Story for older boys and girls. (37359)
Story, for the lasting remembrance of diuers
    famous works. 104655
Story, founded in fact, of Leontine and Matilda.
    (25888), 1st note after 97876
Story, founded on facts. 104174
Story in verse. 57111
Story of a cavalry regiment. 84424
Story of a criminal. (81236)
Story of a famous book. 28557
Story of a great nation. (80021)
Story of a new parish in the west. 78057
Story of a penitent, Lola Montez. 50129
Story of a picture. 10989
Story of a regiment. 30233
Story of a revolutionary patriot. 92205A,
    92335

Story of a trooper. 202
Story of a very remarkable snake. 92336
Story of a working man's life. 45439
Story of adventure among the Black Hills.
    57294
Story of Aeneas and Dido burlesqued. 73932,
    92338, 2d note after 102599
Story of Aeneas and Dido burlesqued: from
    the fourth book of the Aeneid of Virgil.
    73932, 92337, 2d note after 102599
Story of American college life. 23657
Story of American life. 22185, 41040
Story of American western life. 84733
Story of candid-revised. 100729
Story of Canetucky. 37969
Story of Captain Sir F. L. McClintock's Arctic
    expedition. 9755
Story of civilization. 84524
Story of Columbus. 7259
Story of Conrad Mayer, the hunter. 65495
Story of David Rouge. 20028
Story of early colonial days. 84378
Story of eastern Oregon. 84746
Story of ever shifting scene on land and sea.
    84377
Story of 1861. 78704
Story of Fort Hill. 65558
Story of frontier life. 42962
Story of his own life. 31433
Story of Indian warfare. 48042
Story of Inkle and Yarrico. 92340
Story of Iris. 32621
Story of iron and steel. 83382
Story of Jack Halyard. 36539
Story of La Peyrouse. 38968
Story of land and ocean. (3118)
Story of life in a prairie home. 42825
Story of life in Mexico. 83682
Story of life . . . in the lumber region.
    (52154)
Story of life on the isthmus. 23590
Story of Meadville. 92341
Story of Mr. Anderson. 99138-99139
Story of my life. By a lady, who for fifty
    years belonged to the Society of Friends.
    66934, 70284
Story of my life. [By Rodney Smith.] 83893
Story of New England in war time. (31996)
Story of New York life. By C. Gayler.
    26799
Story of New York life. By Maria Maxwell.
    47052
Story of New York life, morals, and manners.
    (55215)
Story of northern New York in 1806. 77335
Story of northern Ohio. 71259
Story of old times. (57136)
Story of olden times. 12694
Story of one of Morgan's men. (17655)
Story of our civil war. (46846)
Story of our day. 90168
Story of Palemon and Eliza. 92342
Story of plebeians and patricians. (31890)
Story of ranch life in Wyoming. 83632
Story of Republican equality. 62828, note
    after 92320
Story of San Diego. 84517
Story of seashore life and manners. (78678)
Story of 1787. 80274
Story of Texas. 57139
Story of the age. 92478
Story of the Amazon. 42137
Story of the American navy. 80291
Story of the American revolution. A poem in
    three cantos. 55006

Story of the American revolution. By Mrs.
E. Oakes Smith. 82507
Story of the American revolution. Illustrated
by tales. 41075, 92343
Story of the American war. 90025
Story of the Atlantic and Pacific shores.
27946
Story of the battle of Ft. Ridgely, Minn.
83684
Story of the Black Hawk wars. 7061
Stork of the Book of Mormon. 83038
Story of the captivity and rescue from the
Indians of Luke Swetland. 94055
[Story of the civil war.] By E. Foxton.
58326
Story of the civil war. By George Ward
Nichols. (55198)
Story of the cruel giant Barbarico. 92344
Story of the early buccaneers. 51532
Story of the embarcation of Cromwell and
his friends. 17604, 19036
Story of the experiences and sufferings of the
unionists. 8702
Story of the Florida war. (26166)
Story of the fourth of July. 92334
Story of the Goth. 91245
Story of the great march. (55199)
Story of the great rebellion. By Mrs. Bella
Z. Spencer. 89303
Story of the great rebellion. By Oliver Optic.
57216, 86266
Story of the guard. 25834
Story of the last generation. 77460
Story of the life of Lafayette. 92339
Story of the lovely Miramichi Valley. 77254
Story of the march through Georgia. 80415
Story of the Mississippi. 24788
Story of the Mormons. 83038
Story of the New World. 59200
Story of the old Virginia frontier. 16323
Story of the pilgrim fathers. 104795
Story of the present day. 58024
Story of the present time. 39368
Story of the refugees. 61234
Story of the regiment. 41737
Story of the revolution. By Charles J.
Peterson. 61239
Story of the revolution. By the author of
"The scout." 81249
Story of the Santa Fe trail. 9553
Story of the Saranac Lakes. 29114
Story of the sea. 81189-81190
Story of the siege and fall of Fort Presq'Isle.
22297
Story of the south. 81269, 81277
Story of the stage. 84128
Story of the telegraph. 7940
Story of the Texan pampas. 9552
Story of the Thirty Eighth Regiment of Massa-
chusetts Volunteers. (64787)
Story of the Thirty-Third N. Y. S. Vols.
36832
Story of the upper Missouri. 3638
Story of the valley of Virginia. 16317,
(39543)
Story of the war in the Old Dominion. (57135)
Story of the war. In verse. By Cousin John.
(20972)
Story of the whaling grounds. 90508
Story of the white hills. 79666
Story of the world's struggles. 26191
Story of things actual and possible. 62829
Story of Thomas Ellwood. 58052
Story of thousands. 80995
Story of to-day. [By M. J. Savage.] (77244)

Story of to-day. . . . [By Mrs. Rebecca
Harding Davis.] 44531
Story of Tom Snell. 92345
Story of wild adventure in Mexico. 72130
Story of William Wilson, the whistling shoe-
maker. 89150
Story of Wyoming Valley. 84085, 84087-84088
Story teller. 92346
Story without a moral. (67188)
Story without fiction. (77613)
Stothard, -------. illus. 72733, 2d note after
100814
Stott, Elizabeth Phile. 92347
Stoughton, John. 92348
Stoughton, William, 1632-1701. 46731-46732,
49657-(49658), 65607, note after 70346,
92349-92351 see also Massachusetts
(Colony) Lieutenant Governor, 1692-1701
(Stoughton)
Stout, Benjamin. 51813, 92352-92355
Stout, Charles Bartolette. supposed author
90449, note after 92355
Stout, John W. 92356
Stout, Lansing. 92357
Stout, Marion Ira. 92358
Stout, Peter F. 92359
Stout, Susannah. 80603
Stout, William. see Stout, Benjamin.
Stout, Z. Barton. 92360
Stoutenburgh, Jacobus. 92361
Stover, Christian. respondent 92362
Stover, Johann Caspar. 91984
Stover, John. 34477
Stover, William Lilly. 92363
Stow, Alexander Wolcott. 92364
Stow, Baron. (14882), 84062, 92365-92375
Stow, Edward. 92376
Stow, Frederick H. 92377
Stow, Gardner. 92378
Stow, Horatio J. 92379
Stow, John, 1525?-1605. 82831
Stow, Joshua. respondent (16211), 92380
Stow, Silas. 92381-92383
Stow, Timothy. 92384-92385
Stow, Mass. Evangelical Church. 15454
Stoew, C. A. 92457, 92471
Stowe, Calvin Ellis, 1802-1886. 27415, 92386-
92394
Stowe, Harriet Elizabeth (Beecher) 1811-1896.
203, 13175, 13864, 17545, (17828), 19580,
(21176)-(21177), 21926, 28835, 30616,
31276, 31432-31433, 46842, 51458,
(52301), 58875, 59532, (65684)-65685,
69680, 79130-79131, (81837), 84812-
84813, 90880, 91234, 92395-note after
92624, 93648, 95491, 5th note after
95515, 95867
Stowe, William. 45808
Stowell, David. 92625-92626
Stowell, Francis. 92627
Stowell, Hugh. 92628
Stowell, Martin. 92629
Stowell, William Henry. 92630
Stowell, Sir William Scott, Baron, 1745-1836.
21993, 29308, 29517, 31125, 1st-2d
notes after 92630
Strabo. 67730, 106294, 106330-106331
Strachan, James. 92631
Strachan, John, Bishop of Toronto, 1778-1867.
13004, 14190, (30479), 43146, 50881,
69403, 74549, 79632, 92632, 92649-
92650, 92663, 93181
Strachey, William. 66686, 92664, 99866
Strachey, William. incorrectly supposed author
82832, note after 92664, 2d note after
100510

Stradanus, Joannes, 1523?-1605. 92665-
92667
Stradavits Reyse ter walvis-vangst. 74618
Strader, -------. plaintiff (5576)
Strader, P. W. defendant (77406)
Strader, Gorman, and Armstrong vs.
Christopher Graham. (5576)
Straet, Jan van der. see Stradanus, Joannes,
1523?-1605.
Strafford County, N. H. 92668
Strafford County, N. H. Court. (52925)
Strafford County, N. H. Supreme Court of
Judicature. 96867
Strafford Auxiliary Education Society. 92668
Strafford Bible Society. 92668
Strafford Conference of Churches. see
Congregational Churches in New
Hampshire. Strafford Conference of
Churches.
Strafford Home Missionary Society. 92668
Strafford Sacred Musical Society. 92668
Strafford Tract Society. 92668
Straight line railroad. 83696
Straight-Shanks, Hassan. pseud. see Hassan
Straight-Shanks. pseud.
Strain, I. C. see Strain, Isaac G.
Strain, Isaac G. 92669-92670
Strait gate and the narrow way. (26832),
92671
Strait-Creek Baptist Association. see
Baptists. Ohio. Strait-Creek Baptist
Association.
Straitsville Iron and Coal Mines, in Perry
County, Ohio. 92673
Straka, Cyril. ed. 99367, 99382
Stranding of the slave, "James Titus." 81991
Strane avventure avvenute in un viaggio
marittimo. 99417
Strang, Charles J. 92675, 92678, 92687
Strange, James Jesse. 48805, 83147, 92674-
92687
Strange, Jesse. defendant 92688-92693
Strang, Jesse James. see Strang, James
Jesse.
Strange, J. 103894
Strange, James Stanley-Smith, Lord. reporter
33548, 2d note after 92693
Strange, Sir John. 40451, 45099, 62542, 3d
note after 92693, 92694
Strange, Robert. 92695-92706
Strange account of the rising and breaking of
a great bubble. 92707
Strange actings of Sir John Heydon. 92708
Strange and dangerous voyage for the dis-
covery of a north-west passage. 13015,
35712
Strange and dangerovs voyage of Captaine
Thomas Iames. 35711, note after
92708
Strange and delectable history of the discouerie
and conquest of the prouinces of Peru.
106272
Strange and mysterious family of the cave of
Genreva. 5224
Strange and prodigious religious customs.
(18237)
Strange and remarkable Cape-Ann dream.
92709-92710
Strange and remarkable Swansey vision.
92709-92710
Strange and thrilling adventures of Miss
Madeline Moore. 50418
Strange and wonderful Indian dream. 66667,
92711
Strange and wonderfull news from Greenland.
(28656), 92712

Strange and wonderful predictions of Mr.
Christopher Love. 92713-92714
Strange and wonderful relation. 65952
Strange matter, truely! (82107)
Strange news from Virginia; being a full and
true account of the life and death of
Nathanael Bacon. (2679), 92716, 100488,
3d note after 100527A
Strange newes from Virginia, being a true
relation of a great tempest in Virginia.
92715, 4th note after 100527A
Strange phenomena of New England. (36506)
Strange relation of an old woman who was
drowned. 92717
Strange tale of Texas. 69049
Strange visitors. (33020)
Strangeness of God's ways. (21335)
Stranger. pseud. All the world's a stage.
see Story, Isaac, 1774-1803.
Stranger. pseud. Liberty, a poem. see
Story, Isaac, 1774-1803.
Stranger, a literary paper. 92718
Stranger at home. 39761
Stranger chieftan. 92127
Stranger in America. 84174
Stranger in America: containing observations.
35770
Stranger in America; or, letters to a gentleman
in Germany. 40984
Stranger in Charleston. (20756)
Stranger in Lowell. 103817
Stranger of the settlement. 7061
Stranger of the valley. 92719
Stranger, traveller, and merchant's guide
through the United States. 97931
Strangers and citizens guide to New York city.
54575
Stranger's apology for the general associations.
49984, note after 92719, 105297
Stranger's assistant and school-boy's instructor.
92720
Stranger's assistant, being a collection. 34878,
92721
Stranger's gift. 6176, note after 92721
Stranger's guide. An alphabetical list of all
the wards. (59263)
Stranger's guide and complete handbook to . . .
New York. (54681)
Stranger's guide and official directory for the
city of Richmond. 71210
Stranger's guide. By V. & C. 71171
Strangers' guide for 1839. (49780)
Stranger's guide in . . . Philadelphia. 61466
Stranger's guide in Philadelphia and its
environs. 62295
Strangers' guide in the city, for 1826. 67044,
82912
Stranger's guide in the city of Boston. 6561
Stranger's guide in the city of Boston. 1851.
1520
Stranger's guide in the city of Boston, no. 2.
1849. 6562
Stranger's guide; or, the daguerreotype of
Washington, D. C. 92783
Stranger's guide through . . . New York.
54682
Stranger's guide through the city of Montreal.
(50288)
Stranger's guide through the United States and
Canada. 97932
Stranger's guide to Baltimore. 3085
Stranger's guide to . . . New York. 54407
Stranger's guide to points of interest. 30202
Stranger's guide to the cities and principal
towns of Canada. (43366)

Stranger's guide to the city and adjoining districts. 61864, 94325

Strangers' guide to the city, for 1826. 82912

Strangers' guide to the city of Charleston. 12092

Stranger's guide to the city of New-York. 6033

Stranger's guide to the city of Washington. (50898)

Stranger's guide to the commercial metropolis. 54491, (54579)

Stranger's guide to the public buildings. 62061

Stranger's guide to the public buildings, places of amusement, streets, laines, alleys, roads, avenues . . . [of Philadelphia.] 62296, 94327

Stranger's hand-book. (54683)

Stranger's illustrated guide to . . . Montreal. (38888)

Strangeways, Thomas. 92722, 98925

Strasbourg (Diocese) Bishop [ca. 1834.] 92645

Strasburg Academy, Lancaster, Pa. 92723

Straten-Ponthoz, Gabriel Auguste van der. 92724-92727

Stratford, Conn. Congregational Church. 92728

Stratigraphy of the Skyomish Basin, Washington. 84534, 84537

Strattan, Oliver H. (42320)

Stratton, Charles Creighton, 1796-1859. 10739 see also New Jersey. Governor, 1844- 1848 (Stratton)

Stratton, Charles Sherwood. 92729, 92735

Stratton, Israel. petitioner 53226

Stratton, J. illus. 81134

Stratton, John. defendant 92736

Stratton, Joseph Buck. 92737-92740

Stratton, Ned. 92741

Stratton, Royal B. 92742-92743

Stratton, W. C. 9982

Straub, Christian M. 92744-92745

Straubenmuller, Johann. 92746

Strauch, Adolphus. 13114, note after 89825, note after 92746

Strauch, J. C. 92747

Strauss, F. 30000

Strawberry District, Va. Baptist Association. see Baptists. Virginia. Strawberry District Association.

Strawberry report. 13069

Strawbridge, Thomas. 92749 see also Chester County, Pa. Sub-Lieutenant.

"Straws." (19237)

Straws by Nemo. 52329, note after 92749

Stray leaves. By S. R. Chapin. 11959

Stray leaves from an Arctic journal. 57760

Stray leaves from students' port-folios. 92750

Stray subjects. 21432, 92751

Stray sunbeam. 92752

Stray sunbeams. 92753

Stray Yankee in Texas. 30083, 92754, 3d note after 95112

Straznicky, Edward Richard. 1091, note after 92754

Streaks of squatter life, and far-west scenes. 71729-71730, 94822

Stream of history. 30000

Streamlet. 92755-92756

Strebeck, George. 92757-92759, 93240

Strebeigh & Co. firm auctioneers see Leavitt, Strebeigh & Co. firm auctioneers

Streckfuss, G. F. 92760-92761

Streelende bespiegeling. 92762

Street, --------, fl. 1840. 83493

Street, Alfred Billings. 32707, 33391, 53972, 90428, 92763-92775, 92780

Street, Franklin. 92776

Street, Nicholas. 92777

Street, Owen. 50797, 92778-92780

Street, Robert. 92781

Street, Thomas George. supposed author 2387, 11023, 92782

Street life in Boston. 50646

Street Sweeping & Fertilizing Co. of Philadelphia. 62298

Street talk about an ordinance. 62297, note after 92782

Street tramways for London. 43358

Streeter, E. S. 92783

Streeter, Floyd Benjamin. ed. 83427

Streeter, Gilbert Lewis. 92784

Streeter, I. R. ed. 100558

Streeter, Milton W. defendant 95848

Streeter, Russell. 92785-92790, 92792

Streeter, Sebastian. 92790, 92791-92792, 98016

Streeter, Sebastian Ferris. (45211A), 92793

Streeter, Sereno Wright. 92794

Streeter, Squire. 92795

Streets of New-York. 89421

Streich, Leopold. 92578

Streif- und Jagdzuge durch die Vereiningten Staaten Nord-Amerikas. 27194

Streit, Philip B. 92796

Strejcek Tom. 92515

Strength and wisdom. 87841

Strength in weakness manifest in the life. 91858

Strength of the constitution. (18045)

Strength out of weakness. 3213, 74696, note before 92797, 92800-92801, 3d note after 103687, note after 103689

Strength out of weaknesse. note before 85867, note before 85932, 92797-92799, note after 103689

Strenuous motives for an immediate war with Spain. 5422, 92802

Strephon. pseud. Panegyrick. 92803

Stretch, L. M. 92804

Stribling, Benjamin F. W. 92805

Stric Tomaz. 92604

Stric Tomova koca. 92605

Stricker, W. ed. 92807

Stricker, Wilhelm Friedrich Karl. 92806-92808

Strickland, Agnes. ed. 92810

Strickland, Catherine Parr. see Traill, Catherine Parr (Strickland)

Strickland, Joe. pseud. Letter. see Arnold, George W. supposed author

Strickland, S. 101433A

Strickland, Samuel. 92810

Strickland, Susannah. see Moodie, Susannah (Strickland)

Strickland, William. of Yorkshire 92811, 94407

Strickland, William, 1787-1854. 62051, 92812, 92814-92817, 4th note after 101886

Strickland, William, 1787-1854. supposed author 60166, 92813

Strickland, William Peter, 1809-1884. 11160, 11162, 12952, (24378), 24382, 24732, 92818-92824, 94548

Strickney, John Charles. plaintiff 20630

Strict Congregational Churches. 92826

Strict Congregational Churches. Connecticut. 92825

Strict Congregational Churches. Long Island.
92826
Stricture on the "Elementa medicinae" of
Doctor Brown. 31223
Stricture on the judiciary of Massachusetts.
92827
Stricture on the letter of Chas. J. Ingersoll.
34735
Strictures addressed to James Madison. 16617,
17446, note after 92827
Strictures and familiar remarks. (80370),
102522
Strictures and observations upon the three
executive departments. 40101, 92828
Strictures and testimony on M. Thacher's
review. 63993
Strictures by Roderick M'Kenzie. 30226
Strictures of "Another who also knows" upon
the report. 12216
"Strictures" of Ebenezer Newcomb. 93080
Strictures of Gen. Duff Green. 28516, 1st-2d
notes after 101931, note after 101967
Strictures of Lord Mahon and others. 89003-
89004
Strictures [of Lord Sheffield.] 36646
Strictures on the sectarian character of the
common school journal. 83572
Strictures on a late publication, intitled,
"Considerations on the emancipation of
Negroes." (67717)
Strictures on a letter on the genius and
dispositions of the French government.
(30369), 1st note after 97909, 101165
Strictures on "A letter to the Hon. Henry
Clay." 92829, 4th note after 95112
Strictures on a Life of William Wilberforce.
13496
Strictures on a pamphlet, entitled a "Friendly
address to all reasonable Americans."
(3684), (11881), 16587-16588, 26867,
39714, 92830, 92850
Strictures on a pamphlet entitled a "Religious
tract." 92832
Strictures on a pamphlet, entitled, "An
examination of the President's reply to
the New-Haven remonstrance." 97440
Strictures on a pamphlet, entitled, Election
the foundation of obedience. 89462
Strictures on a pamphlet entitled Facts to
landholders. 96174, 100755
Strictures on a pamphlet entitled The case of
George McIntosh. 92833
Strictures on a pamphlet, intituled, "A friendly
address to all reasonable Americans."
(3684), (11881), 16587-16588, 26867,
92831
Strictures on a pamphlet purporting to be a
"Narrative of facts and circumstances."
51789, 2d note after 92833
Strictures on a pamphlet published by a minority
minority. 27320
Strictures on a pastoral letter. 32296
Strictures on a recent publication. 21820,
70221, 92834
Strictures on a sermon by Edward D. Griffin.
28818, 92835
Strictures on a sermon by Rev. H. J. Van
Dyke. 28013
Strictures on a sermon delivered by Mr.
Nathan Williams. 71889, 104315
Strictures on a sermon, entitled The principles
of the revolution vindicated. 102145
Strictures on a voyage to South America, &c.
7182, 35110, note after 92835

Strictures on an additional review of Mr.
Carey's letters. (2781)
Strictures on an address to the people of
Great Britain. 25378, 102868
Strictures on an article in the North American
review. 6533, 52586
Strictures on atonement. 92030
Strictures on Bishop Watson's "Apology for
the Bible." 92836
Strictures on Channing's letter on the annex-
ation of Texas. 11913
Strictures on Dr. Hodgkin's pamphlet on Negro
emancipation. 92837
Strictures on Dr. John M. Mason's plea.
92838
Strictures on Dr. Livingston's system of penal
laws. 40849
Strictures on female education. 92839
Strictures on Governor Morton's message.
31784
Strictures on Governor Seymour's veto of the
bill. 92840
Strictures on Harvard University. (37063),
note after 92840
Strictures on his essay concerning the
Perkiomen Zinc Mine. 105107
Strictures on J. Dickinson's defence of
Presbyterian ordination. 12362
Strictures on John Adams's defence of the
constitutions of government. (63799)
Strictures on Lt. Col. Tarleton's history.
43431, 94397
Strictures on Lord Kaims's discourse. 84103-
84106
Strictures on Lord Sheffield's pamphlet.
5458-(5459)
Strictures on Mercer's introductory discourse.
47904, 92841
Strictures on Mr. Burke's two letters. 92842
Strictures on Mr. Cambreleng's work. 10889,
1st note after 92842
Strictures on Mr. Galloway's private character.
26443
Strictures on Mr. Lacock's report. 38471,
note before 92843
Strictures on Mr. Lee's exposition of evidence.
10889, (39766), 92843
Strictures on Mr. Moore's reply. 11958
Strictures on Mr. Pattison's reply. 27323,
59151
Strictures on Mr. Thacher's pamphlet. 26184
Strictures on monopolies. 92844
Strictures on Montgomery on the cotton manu-
factures. 50150, note after 92844
Strictures on Nathan L. Rice's "Defence of
protestantism." 63438, (77444), 98169
Strictures on nullification. 23237, note before
92845
Strictures on Professor M'Vickar's pamphlet.
(43672), 92845
Strictures on Rev. Mr. Sullivan's last pamphlet.
72086
Strictures on Rev. Mr. Winslow's thanksgiving
sermon. 92846, 104805
Strictures on seceding masons. 92847
Strictures on select parts of Doctor Price's
"Additional observations." 20483
Strictures on that system. 8118
Strictures on the abolition of the slave trade.
92848
Strictures on the American state papers.
94261
Strictures on the attempt to establish con-
sociation. 3099

Strictures on the case of Ephraim K. Avery.
2485, note after 92848
Strictures on the conduct of John Adams.
9431, 12380, 2d note after 92859, 105044,
2d note after 106011
Strictures on the Court of Chancery. 30051
Strictures on the Edinburgh review. (3352)
Strictures on the establishment of colleges.
92849
Strictures on the friendly address examined.
(3684), (11881), 16587-16588, 26867,
39714, 92830-92831, 92850
Strictures on the graduates of the Military
Academy. 40484, 102946
Strictures [on the history of Oregon and
California.] (28630), (28632)
Strictures on the landed and commercial
interest. 62416
Strictures on the late message of the Presi-
dent. 66067, 88068
Strictures on the letter of Charles J. Ingersoll.
34735, 92851
Strictures on the lover of power in the prelacy.
66672
Strictures on the nature, necessity & practica-
bility of a system of national education.
(59533)
Strictures on the necessity of inviolably
maintaining the navigation and colonial
system of Great Britain. 32641
Strictures on the new political tenents of the
Right Hon. Edmund Burke. 62813
Strictures on the new school laws of Ohio
and Michigan. 39566
Strictures on the pamphlet of James Gallatin,
Esq. 9639
Strictures on the peace with America. 92852
Strictures on the Philadelphia mischianza.
92854
Strictures on the Philadelphia mischianza or
triumph upon leaving America uncon-
quered. (46925), 92853
Strictures on the proceedings of the General
Assembly. 92855
Strictures on the publication made in France.
44602
Strictures on the Queen Anne style of archi-
tecture. 84980
Strictures on the remarks of Dr. Samuel
Langdon. 7244
Strictures of the Rev. David Tappan's Letters
to Philalethes. 89794, 89797, 94368
Strictures on the Rev. Mr. Thacher's pamphlet.
93506, 95173
Strictures on the Rev. William Hague's Review
of Doctors Fuller and Wayland. 47943
Strictures on the said sermon [by William
Smith.] 5883
Strictures on the second part of the Age of
reason. 92856
Strictures on the slave trade. 92857
Strictures on the speech delivered by John
Adams. 3431, 78743
Strictures on the speech of John Adams.
3431, 78743
Strictures on the substance of a sermon.
14249, 102644
Strictures on two letters. 92026
Strictures passed by Mr. Robinson. (60572)
Strictures upon a "Review by members of
Essex South Conference." 75698-75699
Strictures upon Arator's attack. 60297
Strictures upon Bostwick. 13350
Strictures . . . upon certain parts of the
report. 22518

Strictures upon remarks on the emigration.
14000, note after 97538
Strictures upon the comments of Rev. Samuel
Willard. 42791, 104113, 104117
Strictures upon the conduct of the President
of the Long Island Rail-Road Company.
41899, note before 92858
Strictures, upon the constitutional powers of
the Congress. 92858
Strictures upon the declaration of the Congress
at Philadelphia. 34087, note after 92858
Strictures, upon the doctrine and discipline of
the Methodist Episcopal Church. 92859
Strictures upon the late correspondence between
Mr. Smith and Mr. Jackson. 42446
Strictures upon the letter imputed to Mr.
Jefferson. 35933, 1st note after 92859
Strictures upon the letter of General Joseph
Dickson. (32506)
Strictures upon the narrative of the suppression,
by Col. Burr. 9431, 12380, 2d note
after 92859, 2d note after 106011
Strictures upon the new doctrines. 97073
Strictures upon the observations of a 'Member
of Convention.' 52933
Strictures upon the second edition of a pamphlet.
92860
Strife for supremacy in the church. 33962
Strife of brothers. 92861
Strigliate del S. Rombusto Pogommega.
(51557)
Strike but hear! 92862
Strike but hear me. 52934
"Strike but hear me." An appeal to the
representatives. (22741), (22766),
92863
Strike for civil liberty. 92864
Striking scenes during a ministry of thirty-
five years. 59011
Striking similitude between the reign of terror.
322, note after 92864
Stringent license law the true policy. (13256)
Stringen usury laws the best defence against
hard times. 103304
Stringer, Samuel. 54002, 92865, note after
99543 see also Democratic Party.
New York. Albany. Corresponding
Committee. Chairman.
Stringfellow, Benjamin Franklin. 22263,
(27864), 92866-92867
Stringfellow, Thornton. 40799, 92868-92872
Stringfield, Thomas. 92873
Stringham, Joseph. 92874
Striped bass, trout, and black bass. (73115)
Striped pig. 92875
Stripes Surinamenses selectae. 49389
Stripling preacher. 11076
Strobel, B. B. 92876
Strobel, Martin. 87704, 92877-92878
Strock, Daniel. 92881
Stroeber, Ehrenf. 12251
Strohm, Isaac. ed. 16985
Stroke at the branch. 39971
Strokes and strictures. 85358
Stroller's pacquet open'd. note after 99547
Stromvaart op Amerika. 35769
Strong, Alexander. incorrectly supposed author
92882, 95532
Strong, Alexander Hanson. 92883
Strong, Caleb, 1745-1819. (23236), 33150,
42448, (45960), 46129, 92884-92886,
96874 see also Massachusetts.
Governor, 1800-1807 (Strong) Massa-
chusetts. Governor, 1812-1816 (Strong)
Strong, Cyprian. 92887-92901

Strong, Edward. 92902-92903
Strong, Ezra. (32197), 32182
Strong, George Augustus. (31325), note after 92903
Strong, George Crockett. 92904
Strong, George V. 92905
Strong, Harvey. 92906
Strong, Henry King, 1798-1860. 19848, 24270, (60152), 71931, 92907-92912 see also Swatara Mining Distrist Convention, Harrisburg, Pa., 1839. Committee. Chairman.
Strong, Henry N. 92913-92914
Strong, James, 1768-1839. 92915
Strong, James, 1783-1847. 92916-92920
Strong, James, 1822-1894. 92921-92922
Strong, Jonathan. 92923-92929
Strong, Joseph, 1728 or 9-1903. 92930-92934
Strong, Joseph, 1753-1834. 92935-92938
Strong, Joseph Dwight. 58088, 92939
Strong, Leonard. agent for the people of Providence, Md. 38886, 92940
Strong, Leonard, fl. 1838-1851. 28053, 92941-92944
Strong, Lewis. (8249), note after 91015
Strong, M. D. ed. 58088
Strong, M. M. 104884
Strong, Marshall M. 92945-92946
Strong, Moses McCure. 38508, 92947-92950
Strong, Nathan, 1717-1795. 92951
Strong, Nathan, 1748-1816. 92952-92975, 101824
Strong, Nathaniel. 92976-92977
Strong, Nathaniel T. 26253, 79105, 79110, 92978-92979
Strong, Nehemiah. (15661)-15662, 15669, (28908), 44258, 90761, note after 92979-93066, note after 105687
Strong, Pascal Neilson. 93067
Strong, Simeon. supposed author 58547, note after 93067
Strong, Solomon. 93068-93069
Strong, Stephen. 93070-93071
Strong, Theron Rudd. 93072
Strong, Thomas Morris. 93073-93074
Strong, Thomas W. 93075
Strong, Titus. 93076-93082, 104274
Strong, William. 93083-93085
Strong, William E. 86094
Strong, William Lightbourn. 93086-93090
Strong, William Lighthouse. see Strong, William Lightbourn.
Strong. firm publishers see Le Count & Strong. firm publishers
Strong consolation. (71798)
Strong fast. 93091
Strong rod broken and withered. (21962)
"Strong staff broken." A discourse in memory of Hon. Teunis Van Vechten. 72641
Strong staff broken. A discourse in memory of Kendall O. Peabody. 77253
Strong's almanac for . . . 1788. 93000
Strong's almanack, for . . . 1795. 93017
Strong's almanack, for . . . 1796. 93019
Strong's American almanac [for 1847.] 93075
Strong's astronomical diary, calender or, almanack, for . . . 1798. 93023
Strong's astronomical diary, calender, or, almanack, for . . . 1797. 93021
Strong's genuine almanack for the year of Our Lord, 1789. 92998
Strong's New York comic almanac. 93075

Strong's side splitting comic almanac. 1854. 93075
Strother, David Hunter. illus. 37405, (78409), note before 93092-93092, 1st note after 100557
Strother, J. R. 93093
Strother, John. 93094, 94806
Strother, John Hunt. 93095
Stroud, George McDowell. 93096-93099
Stroud, John H. 93100
Strozzi, Alberto. see Struzzi, Alberto.
Strubberg, Friedrich Armand. 93101-93108
Strubio, Jo. 9094
Struck oil. 83974
Strucker, W. ed. 92807-92808
Structure and distribution of the coral reefs. 18648
Structure of the nucleus. 85072
Structure of the visible heavens. 67447
Strudwick, Edmund. 93109
Struggle for freedom. 73615
Struggle for Kansas. (42656)
Struggle for liberty never in vain. (51518)
Struggle of the hour. 51540
Struggles of Capt. Thomas Keith, in America. 37237, 84129, note after 93109
Struggles through life. (30461)
Strunck, Amos K. 93110-93111
Strutt, John William. see Rayleigh, John William Strutt, Lord.
Struve, Burkhart Gotthelf. 93112
Struve, Gustav. 85704, 93113
Struzzi, Alberto. 93114
Stryc Tomas. 92516
Stryfe betwene the Spanyardes and Portugales. 1561
Stryker, James. 1197, 93115-93116
Stryker, Peter. 93117
Stryker, William S. 68571
Striker's American register and magazine. 93116
Stuart, -------. illus. 84677, 85105
Stuart, -------, fl. 1761. supposed author (40527)
Stuart, -------, fl. 1856. (12161), 14763, 30669, 65765
Stuart, Alexander Hugh Holmes. 93118-93125
Stuart, Alvan. see Steward, Alvan.
Stuart, Andrew, 1786-1840. 55976, 74939, 93126-93129
Stuart, Andrew, 1823-1872. 93130
Stuart, Archibald. 90844, 96015
Stuart, C. B. 55115
Stuart, Carlos D. 93131
Stuart, Charles, 1783?-1865. 8117, 82226, 93132-93144, 99799
Stuart, Charles A. 93185
Stuart, Charles Beebe. 28478, 41746, 55115, 72369, 93145-93151 see also Great Western Railroad Company, Canada. Chief Engineer. Lockport and Niagara Falls Railroad Company. Chief Engineer.
Stuart, Charles Edward. 93152-93158
Stuart, Charles Edward Louis Philip Casimir, 1720-1877. 68026
Stuart, D., fl. 1659. supposed author 32886
Stuart, D., fl. 1829. 74939
Stuart, David. 93159
Stuart, Ferdinand Smyth. see Smyth, John Ferdinand Dalziel, 1745-1814.
Stuart, George Okill. supposed author 47873, note before 93160
Stuart, Gilbert, 1755-1828. illus. 28897, 67695, 83842, 93160, 101686, 102484

Stuart, Henri L. 93161

Stuart, Isaac William. 30665, 93162-93164

Stuart, J. 93165

Stuart, James, M. D., of Philadelphia. 93166-93167

Stuart, James, fl. 1770. 3866, 95976

Stuart, James, 1775-1849. 93168-93170

Stuart, Sir James, Bart., 1780-1853. (10532), 27567, 79632, 93171-93181, 99597 see also Agent for Petitioners for Union of Upper and Lower Canada. Quebec (Province) Attorney General.

Stuart, Sir James, Bart., 1780-1853. petitioner 27567

Stuart, Sir James, Bart., 1780-1853. supposed author 69403, 93181

Stuart, James Ewell Brown, 1833-1864. 15364

Stuart, James F. 93182

Stuart, James P. 93183-93184

Stuart, John. R. N. M. C. 93186

Stuart, John, 1713-1792. see Bute, John Stuart, John, 3d Earl of, 1713-1792.

Stuart, John, 1749-1823. 93185

Stuart, John, fl. 1776. 87364

Stuart, John A. 93187

Stuart, John Ferdinand Dalziel Smyth. see Smyth, John Ferdinand Dalziel, 1745-1814.

Stuart, John Todd. 93188-93190

Stuart, Martinus Cohen. 93191-93193

Stuart, Moses, 1780-1852. 1240, 11919, 13362, 35863, 43980, 60952, 82074, 89744-note after 89744, 90713, 93184-93213, 101203, 101311

Stuart, Richardson. 3011, 93214 see also Baltimore County, Md. Court of Oyer and Terminer. Grand Jury. Foreman.

Stuart, T. C. 93215

Stuart, Thomas Middleton. 93216

Stuart, William, b. 1788? 93218

Stuart, William, fl. 1793. 93217

Stuart, William, fl. 1857. 93219

Stuart-Wortley, Emmeline Charlotte Elizabeth Manners. 93220-93221

Stuart. firm see Bankson & Stuart. firm

Stuart & Marsh. firm 72369

Stuart, Edwards & Brown. firm Lawyers 89841

Stuart, Serrell & Co. firm 72369, 93145

Stuart's three years in North America. 93169

Stubbe, Henry, 1606?-1678. 93222-93223

Stubbe, Henry, 1632-1676. 93224-93225

Stubbin, James. 93226

Stubbs, Alfred. 93227-93228

Stubbs, Robert. 13073, 56965, 93229-93231

Stubbs, Samuel. 10543, 93232

Stuber, -------. 102487

Stubs, John. 25363-(25364), 104337

Stubs, Philip. 99, 85932, 93233

Stuckder Warnungs-Predigt von Hn. Johann Tribecko. 2390, 32377, 98990

Stuck vande West-Indische Compagnie. 16732-(16734), 23344, 3d note after 102889A, 7th note after 102890

Stvcken gemencioneert in den bycorff die byde Edele Heeren Staten Generael. 98209

Stuckle, Henri. 93234

Stuckley, Lewis. see Stuckley, Sir Lewis.

Stucley, Sir Lewis. petitioner 67548, 67550, (67592)-(67593), 93235

Studdiford, Peter. 93236

Studdiford, Peter O. 93237

Student. pseud. Essayist. 93238

Student. pseud. Indian queen of Chenango. see Willoughby, Frederick Stanley Montgomery. supposed author

Student. pseud. Letter to Mr. Nicholas Chester. see Gunn, Alexander.

Student and preacher. 46400, 46532

Student at law. pseud. Digest of all the laws and ordinances. 54246

Student at law. pseud. Trial of Joseph N. Cardinal. 93241

Student at law. pseud. Twilight. see Knight, Frederick.

Student at Yale College. pseud. College almanack, 1761. see Huntington, Joseph. supposed author

Student-life. 57791

Student of Dickinson College. pseud. Story of Palemon and Eliza. see Shippen, John. supposed author

Student of Harvard University. pseud. Triumphs of superstition. see Harris, Thaddeus Mason.

Student of law. pseud. Fellow citizens. 93244

Student of Middle Temple. pseud. reporter Trial of Lieutenant General John Whitelocke. 103680

Student of the College of Philadelphia. pseud. Pennsylvania: a poem. 60292

Student of the Inner Temple. pseud. Political mirror. 63787

Student of the Inner Temple. pseud. reporter Trial at large of Thomas Paine. 96911

Student of the Temple. pseud. reporter Trial of Captain John Kimber. 96892

Student of Yale-College. pseud. College almanack. see Atwater, Noah. supposed author

Students' album. 97799

Students' cabinet library of useful tracts. 92297, 92303

Student's companion. 93246, note after 105852

Student's magazine. 93247

Students' miscellany. 93248

Students of Yale College. eds. see Yale University. Students. eds.

Students' repository. 93249

Studie. 31257

Studie illustrirt durch den Kampf um den Mississippi. 77536

Studie von Hermann A. Schumacher. 78017

Studien über die Nordamerikanische Verfassung. 12597

Studies and discipline of St. Paul's College. 75469

Studies and discipline of the Flushing Institute. 24922

Studies and discipline of the Institute at Flushing. 51256

Studies, discipline, etc., of St. James' Hall. 29515

Studies in Christian biography. 57791

Studies in language and literature. 2862, 1st note after 98300

Studies in southern history and politics. 84856

Studies in the field and forest. (24660)

Studies of nature. 75474

Studies of the town. 49674

Studies [of the University of Maine.] 84506

Studies on slavery. 24729

Studies sur l'economie politique. (81455)

Studio di dritto internazionale. 62705

Studios variados y cientificos. (72553)

Studley, Thomas. 82832, note after 92664, 2d note after 100510

Studley, William S. 93250

Study. 41165

Study for young men. (5498)

Study in Canadian immigration. 84776

Study of American nationality. 33844

Study of his life and writings. 63572

Study of natural history. 85182

Study of the classics on Christian principles. 78587

Study of the principles controlling the laws of exchange. 83890

Study of two hundred and twenty-eight women. 38566

Study on the Havana and Russian cigarette trade. 91001

Study, the only sure means of ultimate success. 91776

Stulpnagel, Fr. von. cartographer 4855

Stulta est clementia. 60645, 93252

Stultorum. A poem. 81699

Stumbling blocks. 20506

Stumbling stone. 14373

Stupor, Morpheus. pseud. Restivaliad. 93253

Sturbridge, Mass. Congregational Church. 93254

Sturbridge Association. see Baptists. Massachusetts. Sturbridge Baptist Association.

Sturbridge Baptist Association. see Baptists. Massachusetts. Sturbridge Baptist Association.

Sturge, John. 93257-93258

Sturge, Joseph. 93259-93264

Sturge and Harvey on the West Indies. 93264

Sturgeon, Robert. 93265

Sturges, Joseph. 93266

Sturgis, C. F. 43667, note before 93267

Sturgis, Russell. 53380

Sturgis, William. 17725, 93268-93270

Sturgis's Committee, 1852. 93269

Sturluson, Snorri. see Snorri Sturluson, 1178-1241.

Sturm, Daniel. 93271-93272

Sturm, Jacques. 93273

Strum von San Antonio. 93107

Sturtevant, Cornelius. ed. 93898

Sturtevant, Elisha. 94890

Sturtevant, Julian Monson. 93274-93281

Sturtevant, Peleg. 93282-93283

Sturtevant, Peleg. supposed author 57658, 103311

Sturz, Johann Jakob. 93284-93287

Stutson, Nelson. 93288

Stuttgart, Germany. Litterarischen Vereins. see Litterarischen Vereins, Stuttgart.

Stuven, -------- von. tr. 100721

Stuven, Johann Friedrich. 51478, 93251

Stuvenius. see Stuven, Johann Friedrich.

Stuyvesant, Peter G. plaintiff 90718

Stuyvesant Institute, New York. 54685, note after 93289

Stuyvesant Institute, New York. Charter. 54685, note after 93289

Stuyvesant Square Home Guard, New York. see New York (State) Militia. Stuyvesant Square Home Guard, New York.

Styles, Abel. see Stiles, Abel.

Styles, Ezra. see Stiles, Ezra, 1759-1784.

Styles, John. ed. 21928, 93291

Styles, Joseph C. defendant before Presbytery 65437

Stylus. 96382

Su assessor. pseud. Parecer. 22841

Su passion y muerte cantadas en octavas Castellanas. 10946

Svalander, Carl Edvard Otto. 93985-93986

Suanders, Charles. 75318

Suard, Jean Baptiste Antoine. 9734, 16249, 71991, 71994-71995, 72013, 93292

Suarez, Antonio. 93293-93294

Suarez, Buenaventura. 93295-93296

Suarez, Jose, fl. 1771. 93297

Suarez, Jose, fl. 1853. 93298

Suarez, Jose Bernardo. 93299

Suarez, Jose Ildefonso. 93300-93303, 94341

Suarez, Leonardo Santos. 93304

Suarez, Nicolas. 93305

Suarez, Pedro Suarez. 93306-93307

Suarez Argudin, Jose. 93308

Suarez de Arguello, Francisco. 93309

Suarez de Escobar, Pedro, Bp. 93310 see also Nueva Viscaya (Diocese) Bishop (Suarez de Escobar)

Suarez de Figueroa, Cristobal. (24317), 93311-93312

Suarez de Figueroa, Felix. 93313

Suarez de Figueroa, Jose. 93314-93318

Suarez de Figueroa, Miguel. 93319

Suarez de Gamoba, Juan. 93320-93321

Suarez de Giles, Tomas. 93322

Suarez de Melo, Matias. 93323

Suarez de Mendoza, Juan. 93324

Suarez de Peralta, Juan. 93325

Suarez de Peredo, Agustin. 93326 see also Mexico. Comisionado del Ramo de Coches de Providencia

Suarez de Peredo, Vicente del Nino Jesus. 93327-93328

Suarez de Solis, Alonso. 93329

Suarez de Somoza, Jeronimo. pseud. Vida de Venerable y Apostolico Padre Pedro Claver. see Andrade, Alfonso de.

Suarez de Zayas, Juan. 93331-93332

Suarez Iriarte, Francisco. defendant 35066, 93333 see also Mexico (Federal District) Asemblea Municipal. Presidente. defendant

Suarez Marrero, Diego. 93334

Suarez Navarro, Juan. see Suarez y Navarro, Juan.

Suarez Osorio de Cepeda, Juan. 93335

Suarez Pereda, Jose Rafael. 93336

Suarez Peredo, Francisco. 93337

Suarez Ponce de Leon, Nicolas. 93338

Suarez y Navarro, Juan. 52117, 60874, 76747, note after 93338-93344

Suarez y Romero, Anselmo. 93345

Suarez y Torquemada, Jose Francisco. 93346

Suarez Navarro, Juan. see Suarez y Navarro, Juan.

Sub-committee of the Celebration Committee. see Grand Trunk Railway. Celebration Committee. Sub-committee.

Subaltern. 27470, note after 93346

Subaltern in America. 27568, 27570, 27571, note after 93346

Subaltern's furlough. 14239

Subdivision du Bas-Canada. 10538, 10611

Subduing freedom in Kansas. 37092, 93347

Suberwick, -------- de. 93348

Subia, Juan de. 93349

Subida mas alta, la caida es muy lastimosa. 93350

Subject and spirit of the Christian minister. 1674, 92732

Subject and spirit of the ministry. (45438)

Subject discussed as a question of state policy and legislation. 41309

Subject-index of the General Library [of the New York State Library.] 53830

Subject of dispute, in the Tabernacle Church. 88890

Subject of study—acceptable delivery before large audiences. 105789

Subjection of kings and nations to Messiah. 104555

Subjection to Christ, in all his ordinances and appointments. 80252-80254

Subjection to civil rulers. 8349

Subjection to the powers that be. 88579

Subjects of baptism. 101216

Sublime and argumentative dissertation.
35900, 35936, 1st note after 99824

Sublime and beautiful of scripture. 93351

Sublime and ridiculous blended. 98493-98494

Submarine Armour Company. Charter. 93352

Submission of the rebels the sole condition
of peace. 82650

Submission to government. (64646)

Subordination to government the salvation of
our country. (19527)

Subordination to the civil authority the duty
of Christians. 17483

Subrecargue. pseud. Verite sur Haiti. see
Nonay, --------. supposed author

Subscriber. pseud. Brief appeal in behalf
of the Special Fund. 93354

Subscriber. pseud. petitioner To the President of the U. States. 104129

Subscriber. pseud. To the public. 103220

Subscriber has just taken notice of two publications of yesterday. 103220

Subscriber, having obtained patents of upwards
of 20,000 acres of land. 51175

Subscriber most respectfully solicits permission to submit. 104129

Subscriber would lease about 30,000 acres of
land. 101745

Subscribers. pseud. Legislature at their last
session. 104443

Subscribers agree to form themselves into a
society. 98006

Subscribers For Procuring a Survey of the
Western Rail-Road. Executive Committee.
103007 see also Western Railroad Corporation.

Subscribers have a merchant-mill on Redclay
Creek. 35317

Subscribers, Owners, and Insurers of the Ship
New Jersey, and Her Cargo. petitioners
53155

Subscribers, Proprietors of Lands in the State
of Pennsylvania. 93355

Subscribers, propretors of lands in the state
of Pennsylvania, finding it necessary to
protect their property. 93355

Subscribers, the Acting Committee of "The
Pennsylvania Society for the Promotion
of Internal Improvements in the Commonwealth," . . . submit the following essay.
10889

Subscribers to Malden-Bridge. (44100)

Subscribers to the Emmet Monument. 22516

Subscribers to the Funeral Fund of the Asso-
ciation of Mechanics and Manufacturers,
Providence, R. I. see Association of
Mechanics and Manufacturers, Providence,
R. I. Subscribers to the Funeral Fund.

Subscribers to the non-importation agreement
are desired to meet. 93356

Subscribers to the non-importation agreement,
are desired to meet at the Exchange.
93357

Subscribers to the Non-importation Agreement
in New York, 1770. see Non-importation
Association, New York, 1770.

Subscribers to the Non-importation Agreement
in Philadelphia, 1770. see Non-importation Association, Philadelphia, 1770.

Subscribers to the Petitions from the Province
of Quebec. see Quebec (Province)
petitioners

Subscribers to the Tontine Coffee-House, New
York. see New York (City) Tontine
Coffee House.

Subscribing inhabitants of the county of [blank]
respectfully represent. 100060

Subscripcion para imprimir una obra. 93358

Subscription assembly. 93359

Subscription Fund for the Benefit of Cambridge
Volunteers, Cambridge, Mass. Trustees.
10153, 69917

Subscription paper for the Deputy Commissary's
guide. 93360, 98392

Subsequent address to said Association. 90761

Subsequent letter on the failure of the late
effort. 30366

Subsequent observations, respecting the nature
of the principalities. 6219

Substance, of a Council held at Lancaster
August the 28th 1764. 60646, 93361

Substance of a course of lectures. 97308

Substance of a course of lectures on British
colonial slavery. 27671

Substance of a debate in the House of Commons. 93362

Substance of a debate on Christian baptism.
101063

Substance of a discourse, delivered at Haverhill. 93954

Substance of a discourse, delivered at the
Universal Meeting-House. 70916

Substance of a discourse, delivered at the
Universalist Meeting-House in Charlestown, Mass. April 13, 1815. 97478

Substance of a discourse, delivered at the
Universalists Meeting-House in Charlestown, Mass. September 14, 1815. 97479

Substance of a discourse, delivered at West-
ford. 89808

Substance of a discourse, delivered in . . .
Charleston, S. C. 22588

Substance of a discourse delivered in Danville,
Kentucky. 7681

Substance of a discourse, delivered in St.
Mark's Church. 102727

Substance of a discourse delivered in . . .
South Salem. 41311

Substance of a discourse delivered in Stokesley
Church, Cleveland, Yorkshire. 102728

Substance of a discourse delivered in the Adelaide Street Wesleyan-Methodist Church.
74547

Substance of a discourse delivered in the Council House, at Greenville. 70470

Substance of a discourse, delivered in the Methodist Protestant Church. 85443

Substance of a discourse, delivered in the New
Methodist Meeting House. 87273

Substance of a discourse delivered in the town
of Versailles. 94399

Substance of a discourse delivered in the
Wesleyan Chapel. 106096

Substance of a discourse, delivered Sabbath
day, August 9, 1812. 105303

Substance of a discourse, in two parts. 37752

Substance of a discourse; on divine providence.
104539

Substance of a discourse preached in the Hall
of the House of Representatives. 22588

Substance of a discourse, preached in the
Second Parish, Plymouth. 91379

Substance of a discourse preach'd lately in
the Royal Chappel [sic]. 30785

Substance of a discourse . . . September 12th,
1858. 42960

Substance of a discussion in the Senate. (1231),
note after 93362

Substance of a journal during a residence at
the Red River Colony. 102737-102738

Substance of remarks on episcopal resigna-
tions. 21043

Substance of sermons . . . given in his [i. e.
Samuel Davies'] own words. 18770

Substance, of several letters writ and sent.
97129

Substance of several sermons at Philadelphia.
24391

Substance of several sermons preach'd at
Cainhoy. 83438

Substance of several sermons preached at
York. (50312)

Substance of several sermons preached: by
Samuel Willard. 104098

Substance of several sermons preached on
that subject. 104074

Substance of sixteen sermons preached on
Christ's parable of the fig-tree. 104065

Substance of sixth lecture on colonial slavery.
35508

Substance of sundry sermons. By Joseph
Sewall. (79411)

Substnace of sundry sermons preached by Mr.
Cotton at Boston. (17072)

Substance of the argument was pleaded. 97177

Substance of the Bishop of Rochester's speech.
72333

Substance of the debate in the House of Commons. 93367

Substance of the debate in the House of Commons on Tuesday the 1st and on Friday
the 11th of June, 1824. 82906

Substance of the debate in the House of Commons respecting the trial and condemnation of the Rev. John Smith. 82906

Substance of the debates in the House of Commons. 93368

Substance of the debates on a resolution for
abolishing the slave trade. 93369

Substance of the debates on the bill for abolishing the slave trade, which was brought
into the House of Lords. 93370

Substance of the discourse . . . by Gerrit
Smith. (82669)

Substance of the evidence delivered to a Committee. 27609

Substance of the evidence of sundry persons
on the slave-trade. 13494, 1st note
after 93370

Substance of the evidence on the petition.
23302, (27606), (27610)

Substance of the following narrative was
taken. 98185

Substance of the Hon. John C. Spencer's remarks. 89359

Substance of the journal of Thomas Hulme.
84355

Substance of the memorial of the West India
Dock Company. 102782

Substance of the pleas made use of by two
parties. 51752

Substance of the proceedings in the House
of Commons. 93371

Substance of the remarks made before the
"American Association." 90001

Substance of the remarks made by John Minor
Botts. 6832

Substance of the remarks made by Mr. Joseph
Segar. 78892

Substance of the remarks of . . . at the Temperance Meeting. 23271

Substance of the remarks of Mr. Stuart of
Augusta. 93125

Substance of the report delivered by the Court
of Directors of the Sierra Leone Company . . . 1801. 93376

Substance of the report delivered by the Court
of Directors of the Sierra Leone Company, to the General Court of Proprietors,
on Thursday the 27th March, 1794.
80885, 93373-93374, 93377

Substance of the report of the Court of Directors of the Sierra Leone Company, delivered to the General Court of Proprietors.
80886, 93375, 93377

Substance of the report of the Court of Directors of the Sierra Leone Company to the
General Court held at London. 93372

Substance of the reports delivered by the
Court of Directors of the Sierra Leone
Company. 80885-80886, 93373, 93375,
93377

Substance of the speech delivered at the meeting of the Edinburgh Society for the
Abolition of Slavery. 95561

Substance of the speech delivered in the House
of Lords. 36026

Substance of the speech intended to be delivered from the t----e. 1685, note after
95790

Substance of the speech made by Gerrit Smith.
82670

Substance of the speech of Henry Beaufoy.
4167

Substance of the speech of John Cruger. 17721

Substance of the speech of John Quincy Adams.
310

Substance of the speech of the Duke of Clarence.
13236

Substance of the speech of the Rev. Mr. Walker.
101046

Substance of the speech of the Right Hon.
Frederick Robinson. 72072

Substance of the speech of the Right Hon. the
Earl of Westmoreland. 103039

Substance of the speech . . . on the . . .
tariff. 61394

Substance of the three reports. 21509, 102869

Substance of three lectures. 9436

Substance of three short sermons. 104209

Substance of three speeches in Parliament.
31682

Substance of XII. sermons. 91148

Substance of two discourses. By Samuel B.
Wylie. (24361), 105669

Substance of two discourses delivered in Park
Street Church. 8930

Substance of two discourses, delivered in . . .
Portsmouth. 8927

Substance of two discourses, occasioned by the
national breavement. 43222

Substance of two discourses on intemperance.
2705

Substance of two discourses, preached at
Haberdasher's-Hall. 27291

Substance of two discourses, preached to the
First Society in Lebanon. 104368

Substance of two lectures delivered at the
Town-Hall, Colchester. 11557

Substance of two lectures delivered in Halifax,
in November, 1849. 67761

Substance of two lectures on the history of
Mason. 31813

Substance of two letters concerning communion in the Lord's supper. 93378

Substance of two letters written to a friend.
92026

Substance of two reports of the Faculty of
Amherst College. 1332, note after 93378

Substance of two sermons, . . . at Bradford.
58900

Such an account of what the New-England governments have done. (12328), 97569

Such general laws of the state. 8297

Sucinta descripcion de las exequias que a Su Reina D.ª Maria Luisa de Borbon. 93393

Sucinta descripcion en verso. 93394

Sucinta esposicion documentada. 93395

Sucinta exposicion de los servicios prestados. 93396

Sucinta memoria sobre la segunda invasion de Buenos-Ayres. 93397

Sucinta noticia del ramo de la cera. 6241

Sucinta relacion del estado en que se hallaban las casa. 99305

Suckau, W. de. tr. 61340, 61343, (77657)

Suckling, George. 93398

Suckow, B. W. 43740, 83028

Sucre, ------, fl. 1864. (47807)

Sucre, Antonio Jose. 56450

Sucre, Antonio Jose de, Pres. Bolivia, 1795-1830. (6202), 93400 see also Bolivia. President, 1826-1828 (Sucre)

Sucre, Benigno Severo. 93401

Sucre, Jose Manuel. defendant 93402 see also Caracas. Administracion General de Tabaco. Administrador.

Sud. 93403

Sud America. 27186

Sud-America. Politica i comercio. 93404

Sud Americano. pseud. tr. 39523

Sud-Americano. pseud. Coleccion de los documentos. 14299

Sud-Carolina. 87406

Sudalegi udulvdiyu. 44088, 3d note after 94085

Sudamerika wie es War und wie es jetzt ist. 4245, second note before 93419

Sudamerikanische Tracten 1791. 99536

Sudamerikanischen Offizier. pseud. Freiheits-kampf im Spanischen Amerika. see Palacio Fajardo, Manuel.

Sudamerikanischer Roman. 5214

Sudbrasilien. Ein Handbuch. (33011)

Sudbrasilien in seinem Beziehungen. 6015

Sudbrasilien und seine Deutschen Kolonien. 92747

Sudbury, Mass. Evangelical Union Church. 93406

Sudbury, Mass. Wadsworth Monument. (6973), 93405

Suddards, William. 93407

Sudden and sharp doom. 34784

Sudden death made happy and easy. 46309

Suden bevorstehende Crisis. 27516

Suden und Norden. 64541, 64552

Suder Compagney im Konigreich Schweden. see Soder Compagniet.

Suder-Compagnie durch Schweden. see Soder Compagniet.

Sudlichen Provinzen. 9347

Sudlor, Elizabeth. petitioner 73625

Sudlor, Emory. petitioner 73625

Sudsee Inseln. 27186

Sue, Eugene. 93408-93418

Sue, Marie Joseph. see Sue, Eugene.

Sue Munday, the guerilla spy. 29482

Sueno alegorico. 86872

Sueno de un proscrito. 93419

Sueno de vna jouen oprimida de la guerra. 93420

Sueno infernal y extraordinario. 99697, 99718

Sueno intitulado Felipe el Grande en Jerusalen. 44104

Sueno segundo sin mentiras. 70314

Suenos y realidades. 28039

Sueur, ---- Le. see Le Sueur, -------.

Suez and Nicaragua Canal plans considered. (14287)

Sufferer. pseud. English cotejo. see Copi-thorne, R.

Sufferer in this titular conflict. pseud. Re-port, &c. &c. 94805

Sufferers mirrour. 44124

Sufferers of Wyoming, Pennsylvania, by Depre-dations Committed by the Indians in the Revolutionary War. petitioners see Wyoming, Pa. Citizens. petitioners

Suffering Greeks. 93421

Sufferings and escape of Capt. Chas. H. Brown. 93422

Sufferings of John Corbly's family. 44258, 105687-note after 105690

Sufferings of John Turner. 93423

Sufferings of Peter Williamson. 104489

Sufferings of the patriots. 7729

Sufferings of Union men. 8706

Sufferings of William Green. 28563

Sufficiency of one good sign. 91963

Sufficiency of the spirit's teaching. 93424

Sufficient answer to the late famous protest. 7918

Sufficit, Quantum. pseud. see Quantum Sufficit. pseud.

Suffield, Conn. First Congregational Church. 93425-93426

Suffisance de Maistre Colas Durand. 99725

Suffolk, Henry Howard, 12th Earl of, d. 1779. 93427

Suffolk, Thomas Howard, 1st Earl of, 1561-1626. 67545

Suffolk, Mass. Anti-slavery Committee. see Anti-masonic Party. Massachusetts. Suffolk County. Committee.

Suffolk, Mass. Bar. 21568

Suffolk, Mass. Lodge no. 8, Independent Order of Odd Fellows. see Odd Fellows, Independent Order of Massachusetts. Suffolk Lodge, no. 8.

Suffolk, Va. Democratic Party Convention, 1837. see Democratic Party. Virginia. Convention, Suffolk, 1837.

Suffolk County, Mass. petitioners 93434, 93438

Suffolk, County, Mass. Anti-masonic Commit-tee. see Anti-masonic Party. Massa-chusetts. Suffolk County. Committee.

Suffolk County, Mass. Bar. 83861, 93431-93432

Suffolk County, Mass. Convention, Dedham, 1774. 93430, 93439

Suffolk County, Mass. Grand Jury. 67236, 95187

Suffolk County, N. Y. petitioners 95462

Suffolk Bank in the City of New York. 93428

Suffolk Club, Boston. 93429

Suffolk County Bible Society. 93440

Suffolk County memorial. 93434

Suffolk County Temperance Society. 93435

Suffolk District Medical Society. see Massa-chusetts Medical Society. Suffolk Dis-trict Medical Society.

Suffolk Fire Society. 93436

Suffolk harmony. 5420

Suffolk Insurance Company. complainants 92312

Suffolk Lodge, no. 8, Independent Order of Odd Fellows. see Odd Fellows, Inde-pendent Order of. Massachusetts. Suffolk Lodge, no. 8.

Suffolk Railroad Company. Directors. 93443

Suffolk resolves. 93430, 93439
Suffolk surnames. 7002
Suffrage Association of Rhode Island. see
  Rhode Island Suffrage Association.
Suffrage confered by the fourteenth amend-
  ment. 89380
Suffrage constitutional amendment. 73351
Suffrage in the District of Columbia. Speech
  in the House. 36280
Suffrage in the District of Columbia. Speech
  . . . January 16, 1866. 36885
Suffrage in the District of Columbia. Speech
  . . . January 10, 1866. 37272
Suffrage in the District of Columbia. Speech
  of Hon. Glenni W. Scofield. 78163
Sufra. see Sufras de Santa Clara. Fray
Sufragante. Num. 1°. 93444
Sufras de Santa Clara. Fray 93445-93449
Sugada y Aquerrigui, Pedro. 93450
Sugar camp and other sketches. 38919
Sugar cane: a poem. (28249)
Sugar cane, and other poems. 28250
Sugar colonies. see British West Indies.
Sugar duties. An examination of the letter.
  26105
Sugar duties. By a West Indian. 93451
Sugar duties discussed. 52308
Sugar duties. Free and slave labour. 93452
Sugar planter's manual. 23195
Sugar plumb. 93453
Sugar question. 93454
Sugar question: being a digest of the evidence.
  93457
Sugar question. By an European and colonial
  sugar manufacturer. (40073), 57281,
  93456
Sugar question in relation to free trade and
  protection. 44918, note after 93457
Sugar question, West India question, Africa
  question. 93455
Sugar refiners. petitioners. 47649
Sugar Refiners of London. petitioners 4823,
  95700
Sugar River Valley Railroad Company. 93458
Sugar, slavery, and emancipation. 93459
Sugar taxes. 93460
Sugar trade and slave trade. 40022
Sugar trade, with the incumbrances thereon.
  2196, 1st note after 93460
Suggested outline of a plan for a University.
  8320, 2d note after 93460
Suggestion of a plan of uniting roads with rail-
  ways. 93528
Suggestion submitted to the British public.
  61183
Suggestions as to arming the state. 93461
Suggestions as to the spiritual philosophy of
  African slavery. 32469
Suggestions by a practical banker. 51968
Suggestions concerning a national bank. 93462
Suggestions concerning a national currency.
  (78265)
Suggestions for a domestic currency. 93463
Suggestions for a medal to record the dis-
  covery. 75541
Suggestions for an act to establish a uniform
  system of bankruptcy law. (35691)
Suggestions for certain improvements. 8467
Suggestions for making known the extent, value
  and importance. 93464
Suggestions for taxing tobacco. 26326
Suggestions for the consideration of the Legis-
  lature. 93465
Suggestions for the defence of Canada. 63370
Suggestions for the establishment of a poly-
  technic school. 93466

Suggestions for the establishment of an inter-
  national coinage. 22262
Suggestions for the immediate establishment of
  a direct communication. 93467
Suggestions for the improvement of the com-
  merce. 88074
Suggestions for the prevention . . . in the
  West Indies. (31327)
Suggestions for the speedy and secure convey-
  ance. 7081
Suggestions in reference to the metallic cur-
  rency. 79634
Suggestions of a plan of organizing a hospital
  system. 84271
Suggestions of amendments recommended.
  23380
Suggestions of amendments to the excise tax
  laws. 22425
Suggestions on education. (74391)
Suggestions on landscape gardening. 24953
Suggestions on library architecture. 84980
Suggestions on presidential elections. 86827,
  note before 93468
Suggestions on railroad communication. 61324
Suggestions on teachers' institutes. 74392
Suggestions on the abolition of slavery in the
  British colonies. 93468
Suggestions, . . . on the abolition of the slave
  trade. (23877)
Suggestions on the banks and currency of the
  several United States. 26397
Suggestions on the canal policy of Pennsylvania.
  93537
Suggestions on the defence of the Canadas.
  63370
Suggestions on the importance of the cultivation
  of cotton. 13827
Suggestions on the military resources of
  Canada. 72306, 93469
Suggestions on the organization of a system of
  common schools. 90823
Suggestions on the present crisis. 8046
Suggestions on the President's message. 93470
Suggestions on the propriety and practicability
  of securing colonization. 68155
Suggestions on the religious instruction of the
  Negroes. (36471)
Suggestions on the revision of the school law.
  34521
Suggestions on the slave trade. (24622)
Suggestions presented to the Judiciary Com-
  mittee. 3206, 42305
Suggestions relative to the improvement of the
  British West India colonies. 93471
Suggestions relative to the philosophy of geology
  81046
Suggestions relative to the sewerage and street
  grades in Saint Paul. 93472
Suggestions respecting improvements in educa-
  tion. 4292
Suggestions respecting sugar. 26263
Suggestions respecting the debt of the late
  republic of Texas. 94358
Suggestions respecting the formation of auxil-
  iaries. 93473
Suggestions respecting the reformation of the
  banking system. 30368
Suggestions respecting the revision of the con-
  stitution of New York. 24274
Suggestions respecting the Texian debt. 94358
Suggestions to accompany the communication.
  12477, 90115
Suggestions to Congress on the finances of the
  United States. 50707
Suggestions to emigrants. (34260), 34325
Suggestions to masters of ships. 93474

Suggestions to the class of sixty. 93475
Suggestions to the creditors of the United States. 30838
Suggestions to the people of the north. (68383)
Suggestions to young men engaged in mercantile business. (6083)
Suggestions touching the municipal government of New York. 93476
Suggestions towards a navy. (47066)
Suggestions towards . . . shortening the time of transit. 43259
Suggestions upon naval reform. 93477
Suggestions upon the bill introduced by Mr. Daws. (71079)
Suggestions urging the construction of a railroad. 19865
Sui generis. pseud. Pictures of a factory village. see Man, Thomas.
Suicide. 87172
Suicide. Dialogue exhibited on the stage. 93478, 105785B
Suire, Robert Mart le. see Le Suire, Robert Mart.
Suisse. pseud. Reve d'un Suisse. (36567)
Suisse. pseud. Reveries. 70186
Suisse. pseud. Voyage. see Girod-Chantrans, Justin.
Suit, Pleasant. 93479
Suite au memoire historique. 75161
Suite aux remarques de Mr. Demeunier. 19478
Suite de la correspondance de M. le General. 75088
Suite de la table generale. 70365
Suite de la vie du R. P. Pierre Joseph Marie Chaumonot. 12298, 2d note after 93480
Suite de l'article intitule Economie politique. 93480
Suite de l'enquete de M. Blondell. 5974, 17835
Suite de l'examen de la conduite de Sonthonax. 28286
Svite de l'histoire de la paix. (47931)
Suite de l'histoire generale des voyages. 65402
Suite des observations impartiales. (56478), 2d note after 93480
Suite des observations sur la geologie des Etats-Unis. 43555
Suite des observations sur Saint-Domingue. (67605)
Suite des voyages de Mr. le Baron de la Hontan. (38642)
Suite des voyages de Mr. le Baron de Lahontan. 38636
Suite du memoire de M. Loranger. (42005)
Suite du recueil des pieces concernant le bannissement. 63906
Suite du voyage de l'Amerique. 29142, (38643)
Svitte de l'histoire des choses plus memorables. 106227
Suitte des gverres civiles des Espagnols dans le Peru. 98750
Sukey. 101203
Sul y Amira, -------. 93481
Sull' arresto dei Commissari Americani. 19298
Sull' Italia. 64014
Sulla America Meridionale. 44399
Sulla guerra testi scoppiata fra gli Stati Uniti d'America. 47863
Sullivan, ------------, fl. 1855. defendant 64038-64039
Sullivan, Sir Edward Robert, Bart. 93482

Sullivan, George, 1771-1838. 393, 45698, note after 93482-93487, 102319 see also Massachusetts. Agent on the Claim Against the General Government.
Sullivan, George, 1783-1866. 93488-93490
Sullivan, J. H. 93491
Sullivan, James, 1744-1808. 1344, 20289, 27591, 22639, 30180, 32093, 45685, (48841), 62650, 62652, (79012), 84350, 2d note after 88111, 93492-93506, 94663, 95173 see also Massachusetts. Governor, 1807-1808 (Sullivan)
Sullivan, James, 1744-1808. complainant 94662-94663
Sullivan, James, 1744-1808. supposed author 93508, 95178, 101470
Sullivan, James, 1744-1808. incorrectly supposed author 35441, 93506, 3d note after 95720
Sullivan, James, 1813- 93507-93508
Sullivan, John. see Syllivan, Owen. alias defendant
Sullivan, John, 1740-1795. 52827, 84906, 93509-93510
Sullivan, John, d. 1784. defendant 1066, 3625, (31895), note before 93509, 103349A
Sullivan, John Langdon. (14282), 20225, 21002, 33521, 44101, (54070), 56521, 56061, 60467, 69726, 93511-93538, 105559 see also Society for the Establishment of Useful Manufactures in New Jersey. Chief Engineer. U. S. Board of Engineers for Internal Improvements.
Sullivan, John Langdon. appellant 93524
Sullivan, John T. 3189
Sullivan, John T. S. 93559
Sullivan, M. A. illus. 5384, (82394)
Sullivan, Richard. 93539-93541
Sullivan, Richard. supposed author (6603), (12116), 93541, 1st note after 101499
Sullivan, Robert Baldwin. 74561, 93542-93543
Sullivan, Thomas Russell. 40919, 72085-72086, 93544-93546
Sullivan, Thomas V. 93547
Sullivan, William. 92293, 93548-93560, note before 97919
Sullivan, William. supposed author (19522), (29661), 65082, note after 93549, 93554
Sullivan, William Baldwin. 93561
Sullivan County, N. H. Supreme Judicial Court. 18110
Sullivan County, N. H. Citizens. petitioners 47642
Sullivan County, N. Y. Monticello Academy. see Monticello Academy, Sullivan County, N. Y.
Sullivan Island; a satirical poem. 9480
Sullivan Railroad Company. 93562-93563
Sullivan Railroad Company. Charter. 93562
Sullivan Railroad Company. Directors. 93564
Sullivan Railroad Company. Treasurer. 93563-93564
Sullivan's Island, the raciad, and other poems. 17346, note after 93564
Sullivant, Joseph. 93565
Sullivant, W. S. 28366-28367, 69946
Sully. pseud. Remarks on the report. 93566
Sully, Charles. 93567
Sully, Thomas, 1783-1872. illus. 82857, 101660
Sully Brunet, E. 93568-93570
Sulpicius. pseud. Examination of the decision. 93571
Sulpicius. pseud. Letters. 93572

Sulpitius, Servius. pseud. Remarks on an address. see Fendall, Philip R. supposed author

Sum of a conference between some young men born in New England and sundry ancient men. 51017, 106053

Sum of Christian religion. 80258

Sum of Christian religion, in way of question and answer. 80199

Sum of saving knowledge. 80715, note after 93573

Sum of testimonies of truth. 93574

Sum of the Christian religion. 80201

Sum of the Christian religion: in way of question and answer. 80200

Sum of the matter. 46534

Suma de geographia que trata de todas las partidas. 22551-22553, note after 93574

Suma de las reglas, y constitvciones de la Congregacion de Nuestro Padre San Pedro. 87157, 93575

Svma de vna platica qve se predico a la Congregacion del Salvador. 93576

Sumarga, Juan. 93577

Sumaria averiguacion contra el General D. Vicente Guerrero. 29138

Sumaria mandada formar a pedimento del Sr. Coronel. 93578

Svmarias meditaciones. 93579

Svmario de algvnas indvlgencias. 33397

Sumario de la clarissima vida y heroicos hechos. 44587

Sumario de la residencia tomada a D. Fernando Cortes. 34154

Sumario de la residencia tomada a D. Fernando Cortes, Gobernador y Capitan General de la N. E. 48287, 93580

Sumario de las gracias, e indulgencias. 93581

Sumario de las indulgencias de Nuestra Senora del Carmen. 98724

Sumario de las indulgencias, gracias y privilegios autenticos. 29148

Sumario de lo sucedido en la Europa. 93582

Sumario de los instrvmentos qve ha remitido. 93584

Svmario del Concilio Provincial. 41088

Sumario del Concilio Prouincial, que se celebro en la Ciudad de los Reyes. 93584

Sumario del derecho popular. 93585

Svmario, y memorial aivstado de las probanzas. 99637

Svmarios de la recopilacion general de las leyes. 525

Svmarios de las sedvlas, ordenes, y provisiones reales. 93586

Sume. 93587

Sumien, Norbert. tr. 99383A-note after 99383C

Svmma de las reglas. 87157

Summa de los cinco sacramentos. 60913

Svmma tripartita scholasticae philosophiae. 57170

Summa triumphal. (43754)

Summa y recopilacion de cirugia. 41970

Summaria investigacion de el origen. 50111

Svmmarie and trve discovrse of Sir Francis Drakes VVest India voyage. 11505

Summarie and true discourse of Sir Francis Drakes West India voyage. 8500, 20840-20843, note after 93587-93588

Summaries and extracts from late European publications. 15637

Summario compendioso de las quentas de plata y ora. 36787

Summario de vida e morte da Ex.mo Senhora D. Leonor Josepha de Vilhena. 72301

Svmmario de la generale historia de l'Indie Occidentali. 1565, 45013, 1st-3d notes after 93588

Svmmario de la natvrale et general historia de l'Indie Occidentali. 1565, 1st-3d notes after 93588, 105724

Svmmario de las indvlgencias, concedidas por Nuestro Muy S. P. Papa Gregorio XIII. 93589

Svmmario de las indulgencias y perdones, co[n] cedias. 93590

Svmmario delle Indie Occidentali. 1565, (61097)

Svmmario di lettere del Capitano Francesco Vazquez di Coronado. 67740

[Svmmario. Por De Soto.] 11234-11235, 39115

Summarische Beschreibung der gantzen Welt. 38039, 79675

Summarische Nachricht von dem Bakkeljau-und Stockfischfang bei Terreneuf. 106373

Summarische Voorstellung aller Konigreiche. (55306)

Summarium additionale. 68434

Summary account of the first settlement of the country. 1592

Summary account of the late disgraceful fracas. (60642), 90746

Summary account of the late disgraceful fracus. 8800

Summary account of the life and death of Joseph Quasson. 50303

Summary account of the measures pursued. 93591

Summary account of the present flourishing state. (25309), 1st note after 93591, 1st note after 96048

Summary account of the Society. 85948

Summary account of the Society for the Propagation of the Gospel in Foreign Parts. 85949

Summary account of the Vice-Royalty of Buenos Ayres. 9041, note before 93590

Summary arguments in favor of episcopal church government. 93592

Summary case of the American loyalists. 93593, 3d note after 105598-9 [sic]

Summary declaration of the faith and practice of the Baptist Church in Boston. 93594

Summary declaration of the faith and practice of the Baptist Church of Christ in Salem. 75637, 93595

Summary declaration of the faith and practice of the First Baptist Church in Boston. 93596

Summary declaration of the faith and practice of the First Baptist Church in Charlestown. 12098

Summary declaration of the faith and practice of the Washington Street Baptist Church. 9063

Summary description, manifesting that greater profits are to bee done. 86845, 1st note after 93596

Summary description of the lead mines. 2419

Summary exposition of the case. 100949

Summary exposition of the social theory. (16356), 2d note after 93596

Summary geography of Alabama. 17926

Summary, historical and political. 20726-20728, 3d note after 93596

Summary historical, geographical, and statistical view of . . . New York. 54686, 4th note after 93596

Summary history of New England. 215

Summary imprisonment. 31234

Summary narrative of the exploratory expedition. (77862)-77863, 77878

Summary notes concerning John Sawin. (77293)

Summary observations and facts. 93597

Summary of agricultural statistics. 33154

Summary of all the early attempts to reach the Pacific. 4349

Summary of American & foreign literature. 6344

Summary of Archibald M'Lellan's trial. 81378

Summary of Canadian history. 7113

Summary of canons and resolutions. 32349

Summary of Christian doctrine and practice. 96511

Summary of Christian doctrines and duties. 95229

Summary of church-discipline. 87794

Summary of church-discipline. Shewing the qualifications and duties. 87796, 1st note after 93597

Summary of colonial law. 13260

Summary of colportage. (14767)

Summary of divinity. 15450

Summary of facts in relation to the late treaty. 79115

Summary of faith and rules of discipline. 41745

Summary of important arguments. 7873

Summary of meteorological observations. 61176

Summary of proceedings from the organization of the Medical and Chirurgical Faculty of Maryland. 45254

Summary of the art of war. 77504-77505

Summary of the case of Alexander, Earl of Stirling. 93598

Summary of the causes of the present most unnatural and indefensible of all rebellion's. 29391

Summary of the course of permanent fortification. 43863

Summary of the errors in the annual report. (72440)

Summary of the evidence produced before a Committee of the House of Commons. 93600

Summary of the evidence produced before the Committee of the Privy Council. 93599

Summary of the expeditions in search of Sir John Franklin. 8678

Summary of the facts and documents. 89567

Summary of the findings and conclusions of the Court of Inquiry. 83319

Summary of the history, doctrine, and discipline of Friends. 93601

Summary of the law of nations. 44848

Summary of the law of Pennsylvania. 8676

Summary of the law relative to . . . justice of the peace. 52581

Summary of the laws of commerce and navigation. 1646, 54991

Summary of the laws of Massachusetts. 39559

Summary of the laws of the several states. 94295

Summary of the practical principles of political economy. 93602

Summary of the principal events of the life. 101886

Summary of the proceedings of a convention of Republican delegates. 93603

Summary of the proceedings of the Grand Lodge of New Hampshire. 52835

Summary of the public exercises and honors at the interment. 93604

Summary of the salient features of the geology. 84533

Summary of the scientific, moral and religious progress. 2784

Summary of the statistical view of the Indian nations. 96499

Summary of the statistics of the meteorological observations. 5950

Summary of the trial of Robert M. Goodwin. 27951

Summary of the voyage. 28401, 71032

Summary of the voyages made by the Russians. 51285

Summary, or general argument of the last manifesto. 93605

Summary review of history, politics and literature. 1207, 3302, 101155

Summary review of the laws of the United States of North-America. 93606

Summary review of the present reign. (63789)

Summary statement of facts, or affirmation. 93607

Summary statement of the origin and present state. 32985

Summary statement of the origin, progress, and present state. 60778, 101992

Summary summing of the charges. 93608

"Summary view." (65447), 65457

Summary view of America. 10672, note after 93608

Summary view of Negro slavery. 93609

Summary view of the courses of crops. 6416, 45373, note after 93609

Summary view of the evidence before the House of Commons. (25380), 93600

Summary view of the Millennial Church. 28513, (79721)-79722, note before 93610, note after 97880, 5th note after 102601

Summary view of the progress of reform. 93610

Summary view of the rights of British America. (35918), note after 93610-93611

Summary view of the slave trade. 13495, note after 93611

Summary view of the statistics and existing commerce. 43479

Summary view of the U. S., geographical, historical, and statistical. 93612

Summe of certain sermons upon Genes: 15. 6. 46783

Summe of several sermons on Psal. 84. 10. 50298

Summer, A. G. 88060, 93613

Summer: a poem. 47212

Summer and fall campaign of the Army of the United States. 69088

Summer and winter in the country. 59639

Summer arrangements. 20323

Summer at Walnut Ridge. 29646

Summer book. 18051

Summer cruise on the coast of New England. 11122

Summer in the wilderness. (38916), 38925

Summer-Islands Company. see Bermuda Company.

Summer journey in the west. 91116

Summer-land. 93614

Summer month. 93615

Summer morning's converstaion. 12331, 13350, 102425

Summer of the pestilence. 2021

Summer on the borders of the Caribbean Sea. 30477

Summer on the lakes, in 1843. 57815

Summer rambles in the west. (22213)

Summer rest. 20506

Summer search for Sir John Franklin. 34758

Summer sketches. 86564

Summer stories of the south. 70968

Summer story, Sheridan's ride and other poems. 68183

Summer Street Christian Church, Boston. see Boston. Summer Street Christian Church.

Summer tour in Canada and the states. (43290)

Summer tour through Kansas. (47427)

Summer tourist's pocket guide to American watering places. 29762

Summer tours, or notes of a traveller. 21541, 95352

Summer voyage to Labrador and around Newfoundland. 55380

Summerbell, N. 93616

Summerfield, Charles. pseud. see Arrington, Alfred W. supposed author and Foster, Theodore. supposed author

Summerfield, John, 1798-1825. 93620

Summerfield, John, fl. 1834. 93621

Summerfield; or life on a farm. 39722

Summerings in the wilderness. 82695

Summers, Charles George. see Sommers, Charles George.

Summers, George William. 35738, 57125, 93623-93627

Summers, John. 3278, 3290

Summers, Thomas Osmond. 44537, 62718, 84742-84742A, 88401, 88402, 93628-93631

Summers, Thomas Osmond. supposed author 63631, 64473, 64921, 93631

Summer's jaunt across the water. 82987

Summer's journey to the Rocky Mountains. (7077)

Summerton, Winter. pseud. Will he find her? 93632

Summit Branch Rail Road Company. 93633-93634

Summit Branch Rail Road Company. Charter. 93633-93634

Summit Copper Mining Company. 93635

Summons, James B. 95778

Sumner, --------. reporter 4702

Sumner, Albert W. 93636

Sumner, Bradford. 92312, 93637-93638

Sumner, Charles, 1811-1874. 10190, 30732, 30609, 52200, 59002, 65336, (66786), 79130-79131, 80615, (81837), 85412, (82688), 84463, note after 92624, 93639-93689, 93721 see also Harvard University. Law Library. Librarian.

Sumner, Charles Allen. 93690

Sumner, Charles Pinckney. 93691-93694, 101803

Sumner, Charles Richard, successively Bishop of Llandaff and Winchester, 1790-1874. 93695

Sumner, Clement. 93696

Sumner, George, 1817-1863. (60384), 93697-93702

Sumner, Increase. 93703

Sumner, John Bird, Archbishop of Canterbury, 1780-1862. 70085, 85946, 93704

Sumner, Jospeh. 93705-93708

Sumner, Samuel. 93709

Sumner, William Hyslop. 26474, 45925, 48980, (56499), 39710-39720, 95086, 104842, 105111 see also Massachusetts. Adjutant General.

Sumner controversy. 93721

Sumner outrage. 93723

Sumner's letter on prison discipline. 93701

Sumpter, Arthur. 93724-93725

Sumter (Confederate Armed Raider) 79080

Sumter District, South Carolina. Anti-tariff Meeting, 1827. petitioners (47625)

Sumter anniversary, 1863. 42555, 57404, note after 93725

Sun (London) 17183, 32075

Sun (New York) see New York sun.

Sun Fire Society, Boston. 93728

Sun pictures of Rocky Mountain scenery. (31007)

Sunalei Akvlvgi Nu'gwisi Alikslvvsga Zvlvgi Gesvi. 104976

Sunbeam. 93729

Sunbeams through pagan clouds. 16297

Sunbury, Pa. Meeting on the Practicability and Utility of Immediately Constructing a Central Railway, from Pottsville to Sunbury and Danville, 1830. 60009, 64693

Sunbury, Pa. Susquehanna Railroad Convention, 1851. see Susquehanna Railroad Convention, Sunbury, Pa., 1851.

Sunbury & Erie Rail-Road Company. Board of Managers. 93730, 93733-93734

Sunbury & Erie Rail-Road Company. Charter. 93730

Sunbury & Erie Rail-Road Company. Chief Engineer. 93731, 93733 see also Miller, Edward.

Sunbury & Erie Rail-Road Company. Managers. see Sunbury & Erie Rail-Road Company. Board of Managers.

Sunbury & Erie Rail-Road Company. President. 93732, 93734 see also Fallon, Christopher.

Sunbury & Erie Rail-Road Company. Stockholders. 93733

Sunbury and Erie Railroad, and the state Legislature. 93735

Sunbury Baptist Association. see Baptists. Georgia. Sunbury Baptist Association.

Sunbury Canal and Water-Power Company, and the Sunbury Lumber and Car Manufacturing Company. 93738

Sunbury Water Power Canal. 93737

Sunbury Water Power Canal. Charter. 93737

Sunday and Adult School Union, Philadelphia. see Philadelphia Sunday and Adult School Union.

Sunday lager-beer trade. 93745

Sunday law unconstitutional and unscriptural. (51850)

Sunday legislation. 93739

Sunday liquor traffic. 93740

Sunday mails. Mr. Johnson's report on the transportation of the mail. 36278

Sunday mails; or, inquiries into the origin. 93741

Sunday of Constantine. 93742

Sunday question. Sabbath of the Jews. 93742

Sunday school. 99629

Sunday School Association, Norfolk County, Mass. see Norfolk County Sunday School Association.

Sunday School Association of Somerset County, N. J. 86810

Sunday School Convention, Delaware, Ohio, 1865. see Ohio State Sunday School Convention, Delaware, 1865.

Sunday-School Convention, St. Louis, 1866. see Missouri State Sunday School Convention, 1st, St. Louis, 1866.

Sunday school dial. 84919

Sunday-School Institute, New York. see New York Sunday-School Institute.

Sunday School picnic. First Congregational Society, New Bedford. 52509

Sunday School Society, Boston. see Unitarian Sunday School Society, Boston.

Sunday-School Society, North-Middlesex, Mass. see North-Middlesex Sunday-School Society.

Sunday School Society, Worcester, Mass. see Worcester Sunday School Society.

Sunday school teacher. pseud. Memoirs of David Brainerd. 7345

Sunday school teacher. pseud. St. Ann's Church. see Fish, T. G.

Sunday school teacher. see National Sunday school teacher.

Sunday School Teachers' Association of New York. see New York State Sunday School Teachers' Association.

Sunday-school teacher's reward. 28390, note after 93744

Sunday School Union, Chicago. see Chicago Sunday School Union.

Sunday School Union of Rhode-Island. see Rhode-Island Sunday School Union.

Sunday School Union of Southern New York. see New York Southern Sunday School Union.

Sunday-School Union of the Methodist Episcoapl Church. see Methodist Episcopal Church. Sunday-School Union.

Sunday School Union of the Protestant Episcopal Church. see General Protestant Episcopal Sunday School Union.

Sunday School Union Society, New York. see New York Sunday School Union Society.

Sunday service of the Methodists in His Majesty's dominions. 102695

Sunday service of the Methodists in North America. 102696

Sunday service of the Methodists in the United-States of America. 102697

Sunday service of the Methodists with other occasional services. 102695

Sunday services, "sacred concerts" and beer-gardens. 93745

Sunday travel. (26240)

Sunday vice and crime. 93745

Sunderland, Byron. 93747-93751

Sunderland, Charles Spencer, 3d Earl of, 1675-1722. 99390 see also Great Britain. Secretary of State for the Southern Department.

Sunderland, La Roy. 82203, 93752-93753

Sundius, Petrus. 93764

Sunrey errors, maxims, and corruptions. 23760

Sundry acts and laws . . . passed from June 17 to Nov. 10, 1785. 52935

Sundry American Citizens. Claimants 81514

Sundry anthems. 93765

Sundry articles. 78345

Sundry Banks of Philadelphia. petitioners see Philadelphia. Banks. petitioners

Sundry biographical sketches. 82534

Sundry British Merchants and Others, Subjects of His Britannic Majesty Within the United States. petitioners (69732)

Sundry choyce sermons. (17053)

Sundry Christian truths. 25563

Sundry Citizens of Alleghany County, Pa. petitioners see Alleghany County, Pa. Citizens. petitioners

Sundry Citizens of Colleton District, South Carolina. see Colleton District, South Carolina. Citizens.

Sundry Citizens of Massachusetts, Purchasers Under the Georgia Company. petitioners see Massachusetts. Citizens. petitioners

Sundry Citizens of Northumberland County, Pa. petitioners see Northumberland County, Pa. Citizens. petitioners

Sundry Citizens of Orangeburgh District, South Carolina. petitioners see Orangeburgh District, S. C. Citizens. petitioners

Sundry Citizens of Philadelphia. petitioners see Philadelphia. Citizens. petitioners

Sundry Citizens of Providence, R. I. petitioners see Providence, R. I. Citizens. petitioners

Sundry Citizens of Rhode Island. petitioners see Rhode Island. Citizens. petitioners

Sundry Citizens of the County of Washington, Pa. petitioners see Washington County, Pa. Citizens. petitioners

Sundry Citizens of the County of Wayne, in the Indiana Territory. petitioners see Wayne County, Indiana. French Citizens. petitioners.

Sundry Colored Citizens of Boston. petitioners see Boston. Colored Citizens. petitioners

Sundry discourses during the ravages of the French and Indians. 84599-84600

Sundry documents addressed to St. Mary's Congregation. (62214), note after 93765

Sundry documents, (copied from the original) relative to the claim of Gideon Olmsted. 57236, 93766

Sundry documents in relation to the extinguishment of the Indian title. 27073

Sundry documents in relation to the management of affairs on the Boston Station. 96807

Sundry documents referring to the Niagara and Detroit Rivers Railroad. 55121

Sundry documents relating to Asiatic cholera. 66356

Sundry documents submitted to the consideration of the pewholders of St. Mary's Church. 32425, (62214), note before 93767

Sundry facts and divers figures. 57929

Sundry false hopes of heaven. 62757

Sundry Farmers of Pennsylvania. petitioners see Pennsylvania. Sundry Farmers. petitioners

Sundry fugitive pieces. 42894

Sundry individuals. pseud. "Letter" addressed to the Church. 12403, 54184

Sundry Inhabitants of Louisiana. petitioners see Louisiana. Citizens. petitioners

Sundry Inhabitants of Pennsylvania. petitioners see Pennsylvania. Citizens. petitioners

Sundry Inhabitants of the Counties of Randolph and St. Clair, in the Indiana Territory. petitioners see St. Clair County, Indiana. Citizens. petitioners and Randolph County, Indiana. Citizens. petitioners

Sundry Inhabitants of the State of Massachusetts. petitioners see Massachusetts. Citizens. petitioners

Sundry Inhabitants of the State of Pennsylvania, Settled on the Lands Claimed under Grants from the State of Connecticut. petitioners see Pennsylvania. Citizens,

Settled on the Lands Claimed under Grants from the State of Connecticut.

Sundry Inhabitants of the Upper Counties of the State of South Carolina. petitioners 87891

Sundry laws of the commonwealth relating to town affairs. (6610)

Sundry letters and petitions. 93767

Sundry letters, directed to the public. (40939)

Sundry letters from divers ministers. 3213

Sundry Line Officers of the Navy. petitioners see U. S. Navy. Line Officers. petitioners

Sundry Manufacturers of Hats, in Philadelphia. petitioners see Manufacturers of Hats, Philadelphia. petitioners

Sundry Masters of Vessels Laying in the Port of Charleston, S. C. petitioners 12057

Sundry memorials against lighting the city with gas. 62150

Sundry memorials relating to the abolition of lotteries. 60503, 60508

Sundry Merchants. petitioners 47735

Sundry Merchants and Traders of Philadelphia. petitioners see Philadelphia. Merchants and Traders. petitioners

Sundry Merchants of Newburyport. 20249

Sundry Ministers. pseud. Preface. 104400

Sundry papers in the Lexington Church case. 81609

Sundry papers which have passed between the Lieut. Governor of Pennsylvania, and the Assembly there. 60025

Sundry passages taken out of Mr. Whitefield's printed sermons. 67116, 103644

Sundry persons. pseud. Substance of the evidence of sundry persons. 13494, 1st note after 93370

Sundry petitions, &c. from George A. Baker. 61563

Sundry petitions, &c. presented by Isaac Austin. 61563

Sundry petitions of the inhabitants of the city of New-York. 84556

Sundry petitions, praying that the Schuylkill Permanent Bridge should be made a free bridge. 62151

Sundry philosophical and other papers. 3855

Sundry Presbyters of the Protestant Episcopal Church. petitioners see Protestant Episcopal Church in the U. S. A. Sundry Presbyters. petitioners

Sundry Proprietors . . . of American Steam Vessels. petitioners (47652)

Sundry recommendations. 98010

Sundry resolutions and proceedings. 10663, 84842, 93768

Sundry resolutions of the state of Maine. 70614

Sundry sermons at Boston in New-England. 17074

Sundry sermons. By Joseph Sewall. (79411)

Sundry sermons, by Samuel Willard. 104094

Sundry sermons on . . . other subjects. (46671)

Sundry statements by the Secretary of the Treasury. 29985

Sundry Umbrella-Makers of Philadelphia. petitioners see Umbrella-Makers of Philadelphia. petitioners

Sundry votes passed by the Church of Christ in Dorchester. (20628), note after 93769

Sundstrom, Sveno. 93770

Sundzoll und die Vereinigten Staaten von Amerika. 93771

Sunlight and heartlight. 61398

Sunlight upon the landscape. 93772

Sunny side of life insurance. 83590

Sunny side; or, the country minister's wife. 61375, note after 93772

Sunny south. 34776, 93773

Sun's parallax deduced. 94678C

Sunshine and shadow in New York. 83582, 83587-83588, 83591-83592

Sunto delle navigazione e scoperte al Polo Australe. 67909

Sunto di alcune lezioni sulle antichita Americane. 5516

Sunzin de Herrera, Jose. 93774

Suo Georgio Reisch generosi Comitis de Zolrn. 69122, 69124

Suosa, Juan de Dios Fernandez de. see Fernandez de Suosa, Juan de Dios.

Super Cargo, vant Schip den Saeyervan Farnabock. pseud. Tijdinghe van Bresiel. 95816

Superannuate. (74538)

Superannuated. (80152)

Superannuated itinerant. pseud. Sketches & incidents. see Stevens, Abel. supposed author

Superannuated itinerant. pseud. Sketches from the study. see Stevens, Abel.

Superieur des Missions de la Mesme Compagnie. pseud. Relation de ce qvi s'est passe. see Le Mercier, Francois. and Ragueneau, Paul.

Superintendent. pseud. Cluster. see Page, Stephen Benson.

Superintendent's report for . . . 1853 [of the Philadelphia and Columbia Railroad.] (61945)

Superintendent's report [of the Alleghany Portage Railroad.] 778

Superintendent's report [of the Inebriates' Home for King's Count.] 37876

Superior Court: before His Honor Chief Justice Jones. 96842

Superior Court for the Counties of Plymouth, Barnstable, &c. 46875, 95436

Superior de las Missiones de los Maynas. pseud. Copia de dos cartas escritas. 16666, 47172

Superiour dignity of the office of the ministers. 67774

Superior fishing. (73115)

Superior Rail Road Company. see Milwaukee & Superior Rail Road Company.

Superior revocacion de las sentencias. 93775

Superiority of sanitary measures over quarantines. (13297)

Superlative love to Christ. (64275)

Supernumerary. pseud. Peep behind the curtain. see Ford, Thomas.

Supernumerary crisis. 93776-93777

Superstitions anciennes et modernes. 4931

Superstitions orientales. (4932)

Superunda, Joseph Antonio Manso de Velasco, Conde de. see Manso de Velasco, Joseph Antonio, Conde de Superunda.

Supervision of schools. 55839

Supervisors' book. (28055)

Suplement du voyage autour du monde. (18381)

Suplement ou description des cotes. 72757

Suplement to the state of the nation. 90620, note before 93779, note after 93808

Suplemento [a las constituciones de la Real y Pontificia Universidad de Mexico.] 48662

Suplemento a la exposicion breve y sencilla. 93779

Suplemento a la memoria del Sr. Iturbide.
99708
Suplemento a la memoria dirigida a la representacion del Peru. 71606
Suplemento a la miscelanea de comercio.
93780
Suplemento a la Quinologia. 74005
Suplemento a las cartas Americanas. 99498
Suplemento a las instrucciones para la eleccion de diputados. 93781
Suplemento a las semblanzas de los diputados a Cortes. 93782
Suplemento al Diario constitucional de 9 de Julio de 1820. 93783
Suplemento al Diario del gobierno constitucional de la Habana. 93784
Suplemento al Diario del gobierno de Megico, num. 1066. 19268, 93785
Suplemento al Espiritu publico, num. 23.
93787, 93796
Suplemento al mun. [sic] 73 del Diario oficial.
93788
Suplemento al n: 19 del Sabado 19 del corriente. 15082, 95074
Suplemento al num. 73 del Diario oficial del Jueves 12 de Octubre. 67910
Suplemento al papel titulado: La misma geringa con distinto palo. 93789
Suplemento al parte general sobre la campana de Puebla. 66571
Suplemento del cuadernito del tramite judicial.
96449
Suplemento del Diario de la Habana n°. 689.
1887
Suplemento del libro octavo del Codigo de la legislacion de Nicaragua. 72291
Suplemento interesante al numero 54 del Mexicano libre Potosinense. 93790
Suplemento, o ea tomo tercero-[tomo quarto] de los viages de Enrique Wanton. 79230, note after 99404, note after 101248
Suplicacion hecha a la Real Audiencia. 34721
Suplico de los Generales Bravo y Negrete.
93791
S'upl'im'int too thē hĭstĭre ōv Rōbinsĭn Kruzo.
(72223), note after 93791
Suplique des citoyens de couleur. 93792
Supper. 79254
Suppiger, Joseph. 75372, 93793
Supplement. 16019, 102826
"Supplement." (60625), note after 89175
Supplement a la denonciation de M. de la Luzerne. 42753, note after 93793
Supplement a la "Denonciation de M. de la Luzerne." 38698
Supplement a la monographie des Eumeniens.
77208
Supplement a la necrologie des hommes celebres. 99512
Svpplement a l'abrrege des annales ecclesiastiqves. 12294
Supplement a l'expose des eventualites.
93794, 95081
Supplement a l'histoire naturelle des oiseaux-mouches. 40215
Supplement a l'ouvrage de J. J. Ayme. 9369
Supplement and appendix to the arguments in behalf of the United States. 18095
Supplement au code [de la Martinique.]
61263
Supplement au journal historique du voyage.
38490
Supplement au Ministere de M. Pitt. (11826)
Supplement au Tableau chronologique des tremblements. (63666)

Supplement au voyage de M. de Bougainville.
(3202), 6867, 93292, note after 93794,
2d note after 100806
Supplement aux Affiches Americaines. (75044)
Supplement aux memoires concernant l'histoire des Chinois. 68352
Supplement aux nouvelles. 26810
Supplement aux travaux sur l'histoire du Canada. (5153)
Supplement aux voyages du Baron la Hontan.
38637
Supplement aux voyages du Capitaine Wood et de Fr. Martens. 4935-4936
Supplement, by George Whitehead. 105650
Supplement . . . by Henry Winthrop Sargent.
(20776)
Supplement. By J[oseph] W[yeth.] 22352,
105653
Supplement containing a brief account of the case. 30380, 84558
Supplement, containing a brief view of history.
67708
Supplement, containing an account of the turbulent and factious proceedings.
(13895), (14009), note after 101847
Supplement, containing official papers on the skirmishes at Lexington and Concord.
42860, note after 96144
Supplement, containing the five last protests.
65862, 88190
Supplement, containing the history of Peter Serrano. (35704), 79018
Supplement, containing the letters, and other authentic pieces. 38583, 98682
Supplement containing the receipts by Rev. H. W. Bellows. 76082, 76669
Supplement course of lectures. 105588,
105596
Supplement dated Feb. 1, 1863. 76585, 76647
Supplement de la methode pour etudier l'histoire. 40028
Supplement extraordinary to the independent journal. 93795
Supplement grammaticale. 80007
Supplement gratuit au n° 2970 du Monde illustre. 100745
Supplement independent patriot. 83302
Supplement instructions for the collectors of the war tax. 15418
Supplement January 1865. 18514, 59394
Supplement July 1857. 18514, 59394
Supplement, Lamoni gazette, April 1888.
83302
Supplement necessaire a l'adresse de la Societe des Amis des Noirs. 85808
Supplement no. 1. 87405
Supplement no. 3. [to the digest of the militia laws of Massachusetts.] 92039
Supplement no. 2. to the digest of the militia laws of Massachusetts. 92039
Supplement of additions during 1850 [to the Library of the St. Louis Mercantile Library Association.] 75358
Supplement of original papers and letters, relating to the Scots Company Trading to Africa and the Indies. 18574, 78238
Supplement [of the catalogue of books, belonging to the Library Company of Philadelphia.] 61785
Supplement on diseases of the external ear.
83664
Supplement on the present state of the slave trade. 104783
Supplement or continuation of the pioneer history. 97490

Supplement to the catalogue of the articles in the Museum. 75656

Supplement . . . [to the catalogue of the City School Library, Lowell, Mass.] 42475

Supplement [to the catalogue of the Free Public Library, New Bedford, Mass.] 52466

Supplement to the catalogue of the Library of Congress. 15566-(15567)

Supplement to the catalogue of the Library of Congress. December, 1840. 15573

Supplement to the catalogue [of the Library of Congress, December, 1831.] 15571

Supplement [to the catalogue of the Library of Harvard University.] 30729

Supplement to the catalogue of the library of Mr. T. W. Field. 74685

Supplement to the catalogue of the Library of the Athenaeum, in Salem. 75711

Supplement [to the catalogue of the Library of the Mercantile Library Association, New York.] 54391

Supplement [to the catalogue of the Library of the Peabody Institute.] 18514, 59394

Supplement [to the catalogue of the Library of the Young Men's Association of the City of Milwaukee.] 49182

Supplement [to the catalogue of the Lynn Free Public Library.] (42841)

Supplement [to the catalogue of the New York Society Library.] 54543

Supplement [to the catalogue of the New York State Library.] 53827

Supplement [to the catalogue of the Northampton Public Library.] 55763

Supplement [to the catalogue raisonee of the Medical Library of the Pennsylvania Hospital.] 60328

Supplement to the Chorister's companion. 36138, 93802

Supplement to the church manual. 88124

Supplement to the Columbian harmonist. 68145

Supplement to the Congressional globe. 36179

Supplement to the Conquest of Peru and Mexico. (67892), 2d note after 93802

Supplement to the Cyclopaedia of American literature. 21506

Supplement to the detection of the state and situation. 3291, note before 93803

Supplement to the digest of the acts of Assembly. 62300

Supplement to the digest of the laws, 1798. 70626

Supplement to the digest of the militia law of Massachusetts. 46148, 92038

Supplement to the educational directory. 102447

Supplement to the Emancipator. 93138

Supplement to the essay on monies. 93803

Supplement to the Farmers' register. (9721)

Supplement to the fourth part of Dr. Priestley's lectures on history. 93804, 105938

Supplement to the fourth report . . . [concerning aid and comfort given by the Sanitary Commission.] 38061

Supplement to the Gazette of the United States. 10889

Supplement to the general catalogue of the Library of the Linonian Society. 105906

Supplement to the history and genealogies of ancient Windsor, Conn. 71754

Supplement to the history of Robinson Crusoe. 72224, note before 93805

Supplement to the Independent journal, New-York. 93805

Supplement [to the index of the catalogue of books in the Upper Hall of the Boston Public Library.] 6759

Supplement to the Kentucky reporter. 93806

Supplement to the Kingston gazette. 98068

Supplement to the late analysis of the public correspondence. 42443, 42444, 1st note after 93806

Supplement to the Law reporter for January, 1859. 17552

Supplement to the laws of Rhode Island College. (8633), 2d note after 93806

Supplement to the laws of Tobago. 96045

Supplement to the letter of Americanus. 18239

Supplement to "the lost principle." 78307

Supplement [to the Maryland Code.] 45207

Supplement to the Mayor's report. 101427

Supplement to the Monthly literary journal. 98050

Supplement to the narrative. 96094

Supplement to the National observer. 88653

Supplement to the Negro's and Indian's advocate. 27678, 3d note after 93806

Supplement to the New York sun. 93727

Supplement to the ninth annual report of the Ohio Institution for the Education of the Blind. 11961

Supplement to the original papers and letters. 18574

Supplement to the original papers relating to the expedition to Carthagena. 40541, 99245

Supplement to the Pittsburgh gazette. (63148)

Supplement to the Political register, 1833, 102283

Supplement to the private correspondence between H. E. the Governor and Captain General of the Province of Buenos-Ayres. 9043, 93807

Supplement to the private correspondence between the Governor and Capt. General of Buenos Ayres. 9043, 93807

Supplement to the probability [of reaching the North Pole.] 3632

Supplement to the proceedings of the State Agricultural Society, of South Carolina. 88059

Supplement to the reasons for making void and annulling those fraudulent and usurious contracts. 86632

Supplement to the reply of His Majesty's subjects, the principal inhabitants. (32364)-32365, note after 96027-96028, note after 103448

Supplement to the report of the trial. 93808

Supplement to the reports of the Committee of Secrecy: containing I. A particular account. 88204

Supplement to the reports of the Committee of Secrecy; which compleats the abridgment. 88168

Supplement to the reports of the Committee of Secrecy. With the sums wherewith they are charged. 88187

Supplement to the representation of the case of Oliver Pollock. 105155

Supplement to the Republican. 75404

Supplement to the Saints' advocate. 83296

Supplement to the Saints' herald. 83160, 83284

Supplement to the Saints' herald, April 15, 1893. 83302

Supplement to the Saints' herald, August 23, 1916. 83202

Supplement to the Saints' herald, Lamoni, Decatur County, Iowa. 83202

Svpplice schiavo Indiano di Monsig. Reverendiss. D. Bartolomeo Dalle Case. 11230, 11247

Supplient humblement des habitants du pais de Canada. 39278

Supplies. 46396

Supplique et petition des citoyens de couleur. 93815

Svpply of the description of Monsier Pandorsvs Waldolynnatvs. 78189

Support in death. 90207

Support of slavery investigated. 17623

Support under trials. 104572

Supporter of Jackson, Van Buren, and Crawford. pseud. Mr. Van Buren and the war. 98425

Supporting ministers. 99105

Supports & comforts of the afflicted believer. 46432

Suppressed history of the adminisrtation of John Adams. 105047

Suppressed report in relation to difficulties. 4459

Suppressed tract! and the rejected tract! (47241), 93816

Suppression des barrieres entre la France et les colonies. 21059

Suppression of the liquor traffic. (38019)

Suppression of the rebellion. 30568

Supra-treasury bill. 93817

Supremacy of conscience. 78588

Supremacy of God over the nations. 89781

Supremacy of mind: a lecture. 24503

Supremacy of the British Legislature over the colonies. 93818

Supremacy of the constitution and laws. 10261

Supremacy of the seas. 14433, 93819

Supremacy of the written constitutional law. 19021

Supreme Court. E. Lockett versus the Merchants] Insurance Company. 82144

Supreme Court. In error. 3707

Supreme Court. Richard Wood and George S. Wood, against Daniel D. Comstock. 105055

Supreme Court. T. McCargo versus the Merchants' Insurance Company. (82143)

Supreme Court. T. McCargo versus the New Orleans Insurance Company. 82142

Supreme Court and Dred Scott. 27828

Supreme Court, City and County of New York, general term. 72589

Supreme Court of Illinois, January term, 1868. 89841

Supreme Court of New York. City and County of New York. 88290

Supreme Court of Pennsylvania, Eastern District. No. 246. 15097

Supreme Court of Pennsylvania . . . the Philadelphia and Erie Railroad Company and the Pennsylvania Railroad Co. 68169

Supreme Court of the State of Louisiana. Eastern District: New-Orleans. 96920

Supreme Court of the United States. Appeal from the Circuit Court. (26336)

Supreme Court of the United States, at its December term, at Washington. 46153

Supreme Court of the United States. December term, 1855. 70753

Supreme Court of the United States: December term, 1852. 46152, 70752

Supreme Court of the United States. February, 1863. (18446)

Supreme Court of the United States. Isaac Roach, Treasurer of the Mint. (7770)

Supreme Court of the United States: J. [i. e. S.] B. Stone, ads/ the United States of America. 93489

Supreme Court of the United States. January term, 1834. 103162

Supreme Court of the United States, no. 124. 42729

Supreme Court of the United States, No. 7. 5751

Supreme Court of the United States, No. 3. 46154

Supreme Court of the United States of America. James Carver, plaintiff in error, vs. James Jackson. 96888

Supreme Court of the United States. Rhode Island vs. Massachusetts. Papers put into the case by Massachusetts. 46154

Supreme Court of the United States. Rhode Island vs. Massachusetts. Papers put into the case of Rhode Island vs. Massachusetts. 70751

Supreme Court of the United States, September term, 1852. (46151)

Supreme Court of the United States. Speech. . . . Delivered . . . April 16, 1860. 15630

Supreme Court of the United States. The United States, appellants. 87287

Supreme Court of Vermont. General term, November, 1869. 91108

Supreme Court report no. 160. 2210

Supreme Court United States, December term, 1850. 87287

Supreme deity of Our Lord Jesus Christ. 9422, 93820

Supreme Governor of the Universe, having been pleased. 99056

Supreme Judicial Court. . . . John H. Clifford. 13689

Supremo Poder Executivo me ha dirigido el decreto siguiente. 106288

Supresion del trafico de esclavos Africanos. 74775

Sur-Americano. pseud. Coleccion de los documentos relativos a la navigacion fluviatil del Rio de la Plata. see Pereira Leal, F. J. supposed author

Sur Americano. pseud. Coleccion de varios documentos oficiales. see Pereira Leal, F. J.

Sur deux doubles arcs-en-ceil lunaires et colores observes a Cuba. 63667

Sur deux nouveaux types de nauges observes a la Havane. 63667

Sur la culture de tabac. 41711

Sur la detresse de colonies Francaises en general. 5026

Sur la methode d'observation adoptee. 63667

Sur la non-existence, sous le ceil du Mexique. 63667

Sur la publicacion des monuments de la geographie. 76840

Sur la remora & les halcyons. 12578, 40683

Sur la visite des vaisseaux neutres sous convoi. 77647

Sur l'admission des vaisseaux etrangers dans les colonies Francoises. 93821

Sur l'Amerique Meridionale. 1893

Sur le commerce et la navigation de la Grande-Bretagne. 26828

Sur le genre Houstonia. 67462

Sur le gisement de l'or en California. 44505

Sur le sort des astronomes. 27660, 38489

Sur le passage d'un quantite considerable de globules lumineaux. 63667

Sur l'education nationale dans les Etats-Unis d'Amerique. 21883, note after 93823
Sur l'emancipation de Saint-Domingue. 17193
Sur les colonies. 15 Octobre 1821. 93822
Sur les courans de l'ocean Atlantique. 1701, 73506
Sur les eclairs sans tonnerre observes a la Havane. 63667
Sur les finances, le commerce, la marine et les colonies. 48821, note after 93822
Sur les Incas et sur les langues Aymara-Quichua. 69655
Sur les maladies de St. Domingue. 12578, 40683
Sur les plantes de la meme isle. 12578, 40683
Sur les plantes usuelles de la Jamaique. 105627
Sur les prevenus d'emigration. 93823
Sur les races indigenes et sur l'archeologie du Mexique. 18332
Sur les tempetes electriques. 63667
Sur les troubles de Saint-Domingue. 48921
Sur l'etendue et les bornes des loix prohibitives du commerce etranger. 56473
Sur l'existence a la Havane des arcs surnumeraires. 63667
Sur l'idiome Libyen. 36435
Sur l'indemnite des anciens colons de Saint-Domingue. 93824
Sur l'independance de Saint-Domingue. 93825
Sur l'origine et l'epoque des monuments de l'Ohio. 12272
Sur Saint-Domingue. (19745,), note after 93825
Sur terre et sur mer. Excursions d'un naturaliste. 20960
Sur terre et sur mer, ou aventures de Miles Vallingford. 16410
Sur une gravure, Stances. Abraham Lincoln. (72971)
Sure advancement of Gospel truth. 88592
Sure and only foundation. 1491
Sure cure for the tetotal mania. 4286
Sure guide to gain both esteem and estate. 65310
Sure guide to hell. 93826-93827
Sure guide to hell, in seven sections. 93827
Sure road to competence in times of dearth. (25592), 6th note after 97146
Sure way to grow rich. 26654-26655, 93828
Surest way to the greatest honour. (46751)
Surette, Louis A. 93829
Surgeon. pseud. Examination of the legality of the general orders. see Ruschenberger, W. S. E.
Surgeon. pseud. Naval. see Ruschenberger, W. S. W.
Surgeon General's Office. Report on the extent and nature of the materials. 30116, 57853, 69954
Surgeon in the U. S. Navy. pseud. Principles of naval staff rank. see Clymer, George.
Surgeon of Norfolk, Virginia, pseud. Treatise on the gonorrhoea. 93830, note after 96747
Surgeon, U. S. Navy. pseud. Remraks on the condition of the Marine Hospital Fund of the United States. see Ruschenberger, W. S. W.
Surgery as a science and art. 84272
Surgical anatomy of the arteries. 83664
Surgical journal. 22431
Surgical memoirs of the war of the rebellion. 84276

Surgy, Jacques Philibert Rousselot de. see Rousselot de Surgy, Jacques Philibert.
Surigue, Sebastiao Fabregas. 93831-93833
Surinaamsche aangelegenheden. 93866
Surinaamsche adressen. 93867-93868
Surinaamsche almanak voor het jaar 1820. 93869
Surinaamsche artz. 100656
Surinaamsche hout bruikbaar en voordeeling bij den aanleg van spoorwegen. 80990
Surinaamsche Koloniale Bibliotheek. see Paramaribo, Dutch Guiana. Surinaamsche Koloniale Bibliotheek.
Surinaamsche leven. 93872
Surinaamsche Maatschappij van Weldadigheid. 93873
Surinaamsche mengelpoezy. 73101
Surinaamsche regerings-reglement van 1865. 68633
Surinaamsche staatkundige almanach voor den jaare 1793. 93870
Surinaamsche vlinders. (79169)
Surinam. 57765
Surinam justice. 76501
Surinam und seine Bewohner. 38207
Suriname (Dutch Colony) see Dutch Guiana.
Suriname. 93857
Suriname en de regering. 93874
Suriname, in deszelfs tegenwoordigen toestand. 93875
Suriname in losse tafereelen en schetsen. 51714, note after 93875
Suriname ontmaskerd of zaaklyke beschouwing. 44183
S[urinam]s Heer. pseud. Brief. 7913
Surius, Laurentius. 93881-93888
Surman, Robert. (58935)
Surnames. 20355, (20356)-20357
Surpreza de evora. 43301
Suprise de S^t. Eustache. 27650, (63966), 68421
Surprising account of the captivity and escape of Philip M'Donald & Alexander M'Lord of Virginia. (43167)
Surprising accounts of the revival of religion. 105173
Surprising adventures and sufferings of John Rhodes, a seman of Workington. 70763-70764, 71709, 93907-93908
Surprising adventures of John Roach, mariner, of Whitehaven. 70763-70764, 71709, 93907-93908
Surprising adventures of Bampfylde Moore Carew. 93889
Surprising adventures of four Russian sailors. 89544
Surprising adventures of Philip Quarll. 66951
Surprising adventures of Wild Tom. (36611)
Surprising and wonderful adventures of a voyage of discovery. (51308)
Surprising case of Rachel Baker. (44060)
Surprising history of Mr. Peter Williamson. 104490
Surprising life and death of Dr. John Faustus. 93890
Surprising life and sufferings of Peter Williamson. 104491
Surprising narrative of a young woman discovered in a cave. 93900
Surprising narrative of a young woman, discovered in a rocky cave. 59238, 93891
Surprising narrative of a yong woman who was discovered in a cave. 93895
Surprising, yet real and true voyages and adventures. 99419

Surprizing account of an old hermit. 93906
Surprizing adventures of John Roach, mariner. 70763-70764, 71709, 93907-93908
Surprizing appearance of a ghost. 93909
Surprizing relation, of a new burning-island. (46611), note after 105484
Surprizing variety of the acts of divine providence. 104368
Surprizing yet real and true voyages and adventures. 99418
Surra al Presidario Francisco Ivar el Falsario. 93910
Surratt, John H., b. 1844. defendant 62783
Surratt, Mary E., 1820-1865. defendant 41180-41182, 41235, 66001
Surrejoinder. 93880
Surrender of fugitive slaves. 9607
Surrender of Mason and Slidell. 20331
Surrender of seven eighth parts of Carolina. 10979, 93911
Surrender of slaves by the army. (28852)
Surrender of the British army. 97249
Surrender to the rebels advocated. 12662, 89494-89495
Surrey County, Jamaica. 70080
Surrey of Eagle's-Nest. 16320
Surrogate's Court. County of New York. 58611
Surrogate's Court, County of New York, in the matter of the last will. 12955
Surtees, Scott Frederick. 22488, note after 93911
Surtees, William Edward. 93912
Survey and report made for the Reading & Lehigh Rail Road. 68214
Survey [by Beale.] 43255
Survey for a proposed canal. 105562
Survey of a railroad. 3480
Survey of a route for the Southern Pacific R. R. 28375
Survey of Boston and its vicinity. 29672
Survey of church discipline. see Survey of the summe of church-discipline.
Survey of domestic and foreign politics. 63779
Survey of God's providence. 58800
Survey of Hudson River. 33525
Survey of Kennebec River. 37387
Survey of London. 82831
Survey of man. 93913
Survey of New Bedford harbor. 52488
Survey of Orange County. (19594)
Survey of the coal fields. 34529
Survey of the coast of the United States. 30819
Survey of the Colorado River of the West. 85086
Survey of the confession of fayth published in certayn conclusions. 72106
Survey of the fourth geological district [of New York.] 53793
Survey of the isthmus of Tehuantepec. 26549, note after 93913, 8th note after 94592
Survey of the knowledge and opinions. 6209
Survey of the line of operations of the U. S. Army. 56771, 83867
Survey of the Little Miami Rail Road. 49709
Survey of the modern state of American newspapers. 8110
Survey of the New Bedford harbor. 52488
Survey of the Ohio River. 71940
Survey of the roads of the United States. 14411
Survey of the second geological district [of New York.] 53791
Survey of the Spanish West Indies. 26302
Survey of the spiritvall Antichrist. 47759

Survey of the state of education. 93914
Survey of the state of Maine. 28666
Survey of the summe of church-discipline. 11615, 32860-32861, 33496, (74460), 92113
Survey of the survey of that summe of church-discipline. (74460)
Survey of the Theological Seminary, at Bangor, Me. 3160
Survey of the third geological district [of New York.] 53792
Survey of the trade of Great Britain and Ireland. (50807)
Survey of the West Indies. (26215)
Survey of the wonderful works of creation. 98017
Survey of trade. 105078
Surveyed route from Philadelphia to the New York state line. 60278
Surveyors. A tale of the Carolina settlements. 30044
Surveyor's pocket companion. 50321
Surveys in Arizona. (43102)
Surveys of the mainstream of history. 42619
Surville, J. F. de. 5912, (17716), 44594, 72371-(72372)
Survillier, Charlotte Julie (Bonaparte) Comtesse de. 93915
Surviving hunker. pseud. Epistolary lament. 22705
Surviving Officers of the Revolutionary Army. petitioners 47696
Surviving servants of God, carrying on the work. 95737, 100915
Survivor. pseud. Military memoirs of four brothers. (48968)
Survivors' Association of the State of South Carolina. 88075
Survivors inquiring after the God of their pious predecessors. (25406)
Sus hombres y sus actos en la rejeneracion Arjentina. 76128
Susanna Beckerin. 93916
Suspected daughter. 94160
Suspending power and the writ of habeas corpus. 36368, 2d note after 93916
Suspending power and writ of habeas corpus. 29465
Suspense and restoration of faith. 82947
Suspension of the habeas corpus! 48960
Suspension of the neutrality laws. (82141)
Suspension of the writ of habeas corpus. 91530, 101107, 101911, 1st note after 101924
Suspiria vinctorum. 46535, 3d note after 93916
Suspiros en la muerte del Virrey de Mexico. 76792
Suspiros espirituales. 93917
Suspiros magoados do Pastor Lidero. (22808)
Susquehanna County, Pa. Convention of Delegates, Tunkhannock, Pa., 1840. see Convention of Delegates from Luzerne, Susquehanna and Bradford Counties, Tunkhannock, Pa., 1840.
Susquehanna and Delaware Canal and Railroad Company. Charter. 93918
Susquehanna and Delaware Railroad. Charter. 93919
Susquehanna and Lehigh Canal Company. 69433, note after 93919
Susquehanna and Lehigh Canal Company. Charter. 69433, note after 93919
Susquehanna and Lehigh Canal Convention, Conyngham Town, Pa., 1832. see Nescopeck Canal Convention, Conyngham Town, Pa., 1832.

2865

Swamp dragons. 29482
Swamp lands of . . . North-Carolina. 55695,
2d note after 93999
Swamp robbers. 81268
Swampscott directory. 42837
Swan, Eliza. 94000
Swan, Godfried. defendant 94001
Swan, J. R. (57057)
Swan, James. 20294, 94002-94009
Swan, James Gilchrist. 85072-85073, 94010-
94011
Swan, Joseph. 94012
Swan, Joshua Augustus. 94013
Swan, R. 66686
Swan, Richard. 45370
Swan, Thomas. 94021
Swan, Timothy. 94014-94020
Swan, William Draper, 1809-1864. 93608
Swan Creek Band of Chippewa Indians. see
Chippewa Indians (Swan Creek Band)
Swan Point Cemetery, Providence, R. I. see
Providence, R. I. Swan Point Cemetery.
Swan Point Cemetery; its character, rules
and regulations. (66374), note after
94020
Swann, Thomas. 2992, 3037 see also Balti-
more and Ohio Railroad Company.
President.
Swanton, Hannah. 94022, 103387
Swanwick, John. supposed author 8110, 14031,
note after 94022, 94024-94025, note
after 100447, note after 102401
Swarton, Hannah. see Swanton, Hannah.
Swartwout, Samuel. 96771
Swartwout, Samuel. defendant 9426
Swartz. pseud. Sentiments veritables. see
Condorcet, Marie Jean Antoine Nicolas
Caritat, Marquis de.
Swartz & Tedrowe. firm publishers 89891
Swartz & Tedrowe's directory series. 89891
Swartzell, William. 94026
Swartzen. Model of an advertisement for a
Canadian furrier. 7121
Swatara and Good Spring Creek Rail Road
Company. Charter. 94027
Swatara Mining District Convention, Harris-
burg, Pa., 1839. Committee. 92910
Swatara Mining District Convention, Harris-
burg, Pa., 1839. Committee. Chairman.
92910 see also Strong, Henry King,
1798-1860.
Swaving, Justus Gerardus. 94028
Swaving's reizen en lotgevallen. 94028
Swayze, William. 94029
Swazey, Arthur. 8384
Swearing. 79254
Swearingen, George. defendant 94030-94032
Sweat, Moses. 94033
Swedberg, Jesper. 94034-94036
Swedberg, Johan Danielson. 94037
Sweden. 98194
Sweden. Academie Royale. (63350)
Sweden. Laws, statutes, etc. (68983), 75002,
98186, 98199, 98202-98205, note after
98207, 98210
Sweden. Sovereigns, etc., 1611-1632 (Gustaf II
Adolf) (68983), 98186, 98199, 98202-
98205, note after 98207, 98210 see also
Gustaf II Adolf, King of Sweden, 1594-
1632.
Sweden. Treaties, etc. 2149, (6361), 15493,
16119, 38259, 100931, 2d note after
102894
Swedenborg, Emanuel, 1688-1772. 55347,
93183
Swedenborgianism. 85517

Swedes in Pennsylvania. petitioners 60656,
94038
Swedes on the Delaware. 37716
Swedes petition to the House of Representatives.
60656, 94038
Swedish church in America. 70452
Swedish missionary. pseud. Sermon. see
Auren, Joen.
Swedish South Company. see Soder Compag-
niet.
Swedish West India Company. see Soder
Compagniet.
Sweedsche Robinson. 72237
Sweeney, Lawrence. 94039
Sweeny, Robert. 94040
Sweep, Terence. pseud. To the printur.
94041
Sweep of the lyre. (19522), note after 93549
Sweet, -------, fl. 1774. 95980
Sweet, C. A. engr. 82821
Sweet, Samuel Niles. 94042
Sweet, William Warren, 1881- 82776
Sweet-Scented, Thomas. pseud. Dialogue.
see Gooch, Sir William, Bart., 1681-
1751.
Sweet amidst the bitter. 34006
Sweet amusement for leisure hours. 93453
Sweet Auburn and Mount Auburn, with other
poems. 57635
Sweet Chalybeate Springs. 5143
Sweet home de la raison. 94385
Sweet psalmist of Israel. 101197
Sweeting, Whiting. defendant 94043-94053
Sweets of solitude! 104606
Sweetser, Seth. 94054
Swem, Earl Greg. ed. 97631, 100448-100449
Sweriges Rijkes General Handels Compagnies.
see Soder Compagniet.
Sweriges Rijkes General Handels Compagnies
contract, dirigerat til Asiam. 98210
Swetland, John. 94055
Swetland, Luke, 1729-1823. 94055
Swett, C. A. engr. 82816, 82819, 82823,
82834
Swett, John. 10001
Swett, Samuel, 1758-1820. 94056
Swett, Samuel, 1782-1866. (12696), 19075,
24022, 26080, 33805, 94058-94062
Swett, Samuel, 1782-1866. supposed author
(11920), 64948, 94057
Sweynheym, Conrad. cartographer 66470
Swick, Frank. 75297
Swieten, Gerard, Freiherr van. 94062
Swift, ----------. 5th note after 99205, 99236,
101230
Swift, Elisha Pope. 94064-94065
Swift, J. G. 8291
Swift, Job. 94066
Swift, John, 1679-1745. 94067-94068
Swift, Jonathan, 1667-1845. 482, 915, 15200,
28934, 68693, 86742, 94069-94070,
94240, 97363
Swift, Joseph Gardner, 1783-1865. 8291,
94071-94072 see also Baltimore and
Susquehanna Rail Road. Chief Engineer.
Swift, Samuel. (27857)
Swift, William Henry, 1800-1879. 29656, 94073
Swift, Zephaniah. 15558, (39424), 63946,
94074-94079, 102519, 102523
Swift (William, Jr.) firm publishers 72340
Swift & Chipman. firm publishers 5th note
after 99205, 99236, 101230
Swift & Chipman's Vermont register and alma-
nac. 5th note after 99205, 99236, 101230
Swift's digest of the laws of Connecticut.
15779

Swift's Vermont register and almanac. 5th note after 99205, 88236, 101230
Swigert, Jacob. 37534, 94080
Swildens, J. H. 94081-94082
Swinburne, John, 1820-1889. 31331, (39716)
Swindells, J. H. 105195
Swindler James Geo. Semple revived. 100863
Swindling by authority. 79982
Swindrage, Theodore. supposed author 20808, 28460, 82549, note after 94082
"Swingin round the cirkle." (41722), 2d note after 94082
Swinging round the circle. 41721, 86183, 2d note after 94082
Swinin, Paul. see Svin'in, Pavel Petrovich.
Swinney. firm see Smith & Swinney. firm
Swinson, William. 94083
Swinton, Alexander. reporter 33827
Swinton, Archibald. reporter 33827, 91841A, 94084
Swinton, William. 94085
Swiss. pseud. Great Britain's right to tax her colonies. see Zubly, Johann Joachim. supposed author
Swiss gentleman. pseud. Letter from South Carolina. see Nairn, Thomas. supposed author and Purry, Jean Pierre. supposed author
Swiss peasant. 44088, 3d note after 94085
Switch for the snake. 40197, 103655, 105650
Switser, woonachtig in German Town dat is Hoogduytse Stadt. pseud. Missive. see Wertmuller, Joris.
Sword and pike exercises for artillery. 94086
Sword and the distaff. 81269
Sword is now drawn, and God knows when it will be sheathed. 100012
Sword of General Richard Montgomery. A memoir. 40008
Sword of the Lord. A discourse delivered in St. Paul's Church, Troy. 14238
Sword of the Lord: a sermon, preached in the House of Prayer. 90882
Swords. firm see Stanford and Swords. firm
Swords of American independence; an oration. (81279)
Swormstedt, Leroy. defendant 84743
Sworn testimony of the witnesses examined. 61706
Svvymel-klacht des Spaenschen conincks Philippi Qvarti. 22075, note after 94086
Sybil the menomaniac. 103780
Sybrandt Westbrook eller Hollaenderens arne. 59187
Sydenham, Charles Edward Poulett Thomson, 1st Baron, 1799-1841. 42522, 72879 see also Canada. Governor General, 1839-1840 (Sydenham)
Sydenham, Edward. pseud. Man of two lives. see Boarden, James.
Sydney. pseud. Letters on the affairs of Spain. 94088
Sydney. pseud. Reply to the speech of Governor Cosby. see Sydney, John. pseud.
Sydney. pseud. Sydney, on retrocession. 94089
Sydney, Algernon. pseud. Address. see Leigh, Benjamin Watkins.
Sydney, Algernon. pseud. Administration and the opposition. see Adams, John Quincy, Pres. U. S., 1767-1848. and Hale, Salma.
Sydney, Algernon. pseud. Essays on the American system. 94090

Sydney, Algernon. pseud. Letters. see Leigh, Benjamin Watkins.
Sydney, Algernon. pseud. Principles and men. see Richmond, William E.
Sydney, John. pseud. According to my promise. 94092
Sydney, John. pseud. Men are subject to errors. 94093
Sydney, John. pseud. Reply to the speech of Governor Cosby. 94092
Sydney, Thomas Townshend, 1st Viscount, 1733-1800. 80040
Sydney A. Story, Jr. pseud. see Pike, Mary H.
Sydney Clifton; or, vicissitudes in both hemispheres. (23949), note before 94094
Sydney, on retrocession. 94089
Sydow, Ad. ed. 11923
Sykes, James N. 63162
Syllabus et formula juramenti pro ordinandis ad subdiaconatum. 72915
Syllabus of a course of lectures on botany. 33089
Syllabus of a course of lectures on chemistry. 74241
Syllabus of a course of lectures on natural experimental philosophy. 14411
Syllabus of a course of lectures on the institutes and practice of medicine. note after 74241
Syllabus of lectures on chemistry. (80171)
Syllabus of Mr. Webster's lectures. 102400
Syllabus of the lectures delivered to the senior students. 98221
Syllabus of the several courses of medical lectures. (54000)
Syllabus praelectionum de botanica pharmaceutico-medica. 44999
Syllacius, Nicolaus. see Scillacio, Niccolo.
Syllavan, Owen. alias defendant 94097-94098
Syllivan, Owen. alias see Syllavan, Owen. alias defendant
Sylph, and other poems. 95566
Sylphids' school, and other pieces of verse. 64994
Sylva, Jose de Seabra da. see Silva, Jose de Seabra da.
Sylva Americana. (8649)
Sylva Telluriana. 67464
Sylvan, enemy to human diseases. pseud. Formula of prescriptions. see Plinth, Octavius.
Sylvan, enemy to human diseases. pseud. Works of Sylvan. see Plinth, Octavius.
Sylvan Pen. pseud. see Pen, Sylvan. pseud.
Sylvanius, Lambertus. see Bos or Bosch, in Latin Sylvanius, Lambertus van den.
Sylvanus Americanus. pseud. History of North-America. see Nevill, Samuel.
Sylvanus Americanus. pseud. ed. New American magazine. see Nevill, Samuel. ed.
Sylvanus, Bernardus. pseud. [Dedication.] 66477
Sylvester, Joshua, 1563-1616. 96042, 97551
Sylvester, Matthew. 4013
Sylvester Daggerwood. pseud. see Pangloss, Peter. pseud.
Sylvestris. pseud. Reflections. 81132, 94100
Sylvia; or, the last shepherd. 68185
Sylvianus. pseud. [Pamphlet on the difficulties in the church.] see Duke, William. supposed author
Sylvie, Edouard. note after 94101
Sylvino et Anina. 1714
Sylvio, A. 58428
Sylvius. pseud. Letters. see Williamson, Hugh.

Sylvius, Aeneus. see Pius II, Pope, 1405-1464.
Sylvius, Lambertus. see Bos or Bosch, in
    Latin Sylvanius, Lambertus van den.
Symbol and word of encouragement. 91129
Symbola de la fe de S. Athanasio. (40080)
Symbolo Catholico Indiano. 57543
Symbols of the capital. 47181
Syme, David. defendant before Presbytery
    41652, 104681
Symes, Michael, 1753?-1809. (59572), 62957
Symmachia: or, a true-loves knot. 78370,
    78379
Symmachia or, the true-loves knot. 78378
Symmes, -------, fl. 1827. 70433
Symmes, John Cleves. (40339), 94102-94104
Symmes, Thomas. 8506, (37711), 94105-94118,
    97420
Symmes, William. 94119-94123
Symms, Thomas. see Symmes, Thomas.
Symonds, John. 94124
Symonds, William. 82832, note after 92664,
    94125, 2d note after 99856, 2d note after
    100510
Sympathes. pseud. Poetical essay. see
    Willard, Joseph. supposed author
Sympathizer. pseud. Prospectus of a new and
    highly interesting work. 20654
Sympathy. 79486
Sympathy in distress. 44618
Sympathy, its foundation and legitimate exer-
    cise considered. 37403
Sympson, Sidrach. see Simpson, Sidrach.
Symptoms of approaching evils. 104214
Symptson, Syd. 80205
Symzonia; a voyage of discovery. (78544)
Synagogue Beth Israel, Philadelphia. see
    Philadelphia. Synagogue Beth Israel.
Synagogue der Portugeesche Joodsche Ge-
    meente, Paramaribo. see Paramaribo,
    Dutch Guiana. Synagogue der Portu-
    geesche Joodsche Gemeente.
Synagogue Roudafe Sholum, Philadelphia. see
    Philadelphia. Synagogue Roudafe Sholum.
Synchronistical view of the events. (82707)
Syndic des Creanciers des Mr. Lioncey Freres.
    plaintiffs 63207, 94126
Syndic des Creanciers des Sieurs Lioncy
    Freres & Gouffre. 94126
Syndics de la Chambre de Commerce de Nor-
    mandie. see Normandie, France (Departe-
    ment) Chambre de Commerce. Syndics.
Synge, Millington Henry. 24181
Synod, Boston, 1716. see Congregational
    Churches in Massachusetts. Boston
    Synod, 1716.
Synod, Cambridge, Mass., 1641. see Congrega-
    tional Churches in Massachusetts. Cam-
    bridge Synod, 1641.
Synod, Cambridge, Mass., 1648. see Congrega-
    tional Churches in Massachusetts. Cam-
    bridge Synod, 1648.
Synod of Cumberland. see Cumberland Presby-
    terian Church in the United States.
Synod of Dort. see Dort (Synod)
Synod of Elders and Messengers of the
    Churches in Massachusetts-Colony in
    New England, Boston, 1662. see Congrega-
    tional Churches in Massachusetts. Boston
    Synod, 1662.
Synod of New York. see Presbyterian Church
    in the U. S. A. Synod of New York.
    Presbyterian Church in the U. S. A.
    Synod of New York and New Jersey.
    Presbyterian Church in the U. S. A.
    Synod of New York and Philadelphia.

Synod of New-York and Philadelphia vindicated.
    94127
Synod of Philadelphia. see Presbyterian
    Church in the U. S. A. Synod of New
    York and Philadelphia. Presbyterian
    Church in the U. S. A. Synod of Phila-
    delphia.
Synod of the Diocese of Toronto. see Toronto
    (Archdiocese) Synod.
Synod of the Evangelical Lutheran Ministerium
    of New York. see Evangelical Lutheran
    Synod of New York.
Synod van Zuyd-Holland. see Nederlandsche
    Hervormede Kerke. E. Christelyke Synod
    van Zuyd-Holland.
Synodens van Nederland. see Nederlandsche
    Hervormde Kerke. Synodens van Neder-
    land.
Synodical and dedicatory discourse. 20794
Synodical speech. 36933
Synodus diocesana Bostoniensis I. 72933
Synodo diocesana, con la carta pastoral. 11036
Synodo diocesana del Arzobispado de Santo
    Domingo. 52095
Synodus dioecesana Albanensis tertia. 72923
Synodus dioecesana Baltimorensis, mense Junio
    1853 habita. 72926
Synodus dioecesana Baltimorensis, mense Maii
    1863 habita. 72928
Synodus dioecesana Baltimorensis nona. 72932
Synodus dioecesana Baltimorensis octava.
    (72931)
Synodus dioecesana Baltimorensis I. 72924
Synodus dioecesana Baltimorensis II. 72925
Synodus dioecesana Baltimorensis septima.
    72930
Synodus dioecesana Buffalensis. 72932
Synodus dioecesana Detroitensis secunda.
    (72940)
Synodus Dioecesana Ludovicopolitana IV. (72948)
Synodus dioecesana Natchetensis mense Jan-
    uarii 1862. (72951)
Synodus dioecesana Natchetensis prima. 72950
Synodus dioecesana Natchetensis quarta.
    (72951)
Synodus dioecesana Neo-Eboracensis prima.
    72957
Synodus dioecesana Neo-Eboracensis quarta.
    72959
Synodus dioecesana Neo-Eboracensis tertia.
    72958
Synodus dioecesana Neu-Aurelianensis secunda.
    72956
Synodus dioecesana Novarcensis quinta. 72955
Synodus dioecesana Sancti Francisci. 72967
Synodus dioecesana Syracusana prima. 72973
Synodus tertia dioecesana Ludovicopolitana.
    72947
Synonyma geographica. 57692
Synonymia de diversos vegetaes. 75620
Synonymy of various conifers. 51487
Synopsis avium tanagrinum. 78145
Synopsis collectionis maximae conciliorum
    omnium Hispaniae. 531
Synopsis fungorum Carolinae. 78104
Synopsis in the form of a comprehensive index.
    81675
Synopsis of a plan for a national currency.
    note after 39323
Synopsis of a report made to the President
    and Directors. 9384
Synopsis of a report of the reconnaissance.
    69946
Synopsis of all the parts of learning. (80536)
Synopsis of American rails. (78146)
Synopsis of American wasps. (77216)

Syracuse, N. Y. Onondaga Whig Convention, 1834. see Whig Party. New York. Onondaga County. Convention, Syracuse, 1834.
Syracuse, N. Y. State Military Convention, 1853. see State Military Convention, Syracuse, N. Y., 1853.
Syracuse (Diocese) Bishop (Ludden) 72973 see also Ludden, Patritio A., Bp.
Syracuse (Diocese) Synod, 1887. 72973
Syracuse Convention; its spurious organization. 598
Syracuse daily standard. (12429)
Syren; a choice collection of sea, hunting, and other songs. 94130
Syren; or, musical bouquet. 94131
Syren, or vocal enchantress. 94132
Syria, Pedro de. 94133
Syria, ad Ptolomaici operis rationem. 66508, 106294, 106330
Syrobel, Philip A. 92879-92880
System; a tale of the West Indies. 96165
System; containing, the principles of the Christian religion. (73074)
System der Seehandlung und Politik Europa's. 2090
System for planting and managing a sugar estate. (73465)
System for the discipline of the artillery. 91568
System Francais. 12353
System maritime et politique des Europeens. 2089
System occasioned by the speech of Leonard Smelt. 82259, 94134
System of agricultural education. (6977)
System of American slavery "tested by scripture." 56344
System of arithmetic. note before 83906-83906
System of circulating medium. 93490
System of civil and criminal law. 20314
"System of colonial law." 79833
System of commercial travelling in Europe and the United States. 86015
System of credit foncier. 19114
System of credit for a republic. 91821
System of discipline and manoeuvres of infantry. (68946), 85187
System of doctrines. 7244
System of drill exercise. 104815
System of duties. (18016)
System of education for the Girard College for Orphans. 43068, 94135
System of education proposed for the improvement of common schools. 21708
System of education pursued at the free schools in Boston. 94136
System of education, the code of discipline, and professorships. 103026
System of exchange with almost all parts of the world. (35710), 94137
System of exercise and instruction of field-artillery. 104659
System of finance. 94138
System of free churches. 32397
System of general education. (70873)
System of general signals for night and day. 76948
System of geography. [By Joseph Randall.] 67792, 67794
System of geography, for . . . schools. 50971
System of geography: or, a new and accurate description. (49907)
System of geography, popular and scientific. 4453
System of infantry discipline. 20994, 2d note after 94138

System of instruction prepared by Prof. Walter Smith. 84502
System of laws of the state of Connecticut. 94078
System of liberal education. 84079
System of medical ethics. 53764, 3d note after 94138
System of mineralogy. 18424
System of modern geography. [By S. A. Mitchell.] 49722
System of modern geography, compiled from various sources. 70846
System of national finance. 12202
System of operating in railway stocks. 38884
System of operative surgery. 82715
System of organization, instruction, and manoeuvres. 96160
System of penal law for the United States of America. (41617)
System of penal laws . . . for . . . Louisiana. 40849
System of perfectible knowledge. 80465
System of public education adopted by the town of Boston. 21885
System of public education, adopted by the town of Boston. 94139
System of public instruction and primary school law of Michigan. 48802
System of public instruction in the state and city of New-York. 54688, 1st note after 94139
System of reformation recommended. 7781, 23464
System of rhetorick, in a method entirely new. 91848
System of speculative masonry. 45501, 96366
System of tactics. 87370
System of teaching geography. 52135
System of testaceous malacology. 63519
System of the laws etc. (4686)
System of truth pointed out. 94891
System of universal education. 77761
System of universal geography; comprising a physical, political, and statistical account of the world. 27922
System of universal geography, or a description of . . . the world. 44165
System of universal history, in perspective. 104049
System of universal science. 105156, 105157
System of writing the Seneca. (26277)
System unmasked, Greenbacks forever. 51938
System Africanvm. 104036
Systema de materia medica vegetal Brasileira. 57195
Systema financial do Brasil. 57193
Systema materiae medicae vegetabilis Brasiliensis. 44998
Systema metrico adoptado no imperio do Brasil. 67537
Systema theorico e practico para se organizer. 85633
Systema vegetabilium florae, Peruvianae et Chilensis. 74006
Systematic and analytical catalogue of the books. 75358
Systematic arrangement and description of all the plants hitherto discovered in the United States. 96294
Systematic arrangement and description of the plants of North America. 66728
Systematic arrangement of the list of foreign correspondents. 85032
Systematic arrangement of the species of the Genus Cusenta. 22580
Systematic beneficence. (39348)

T., W. pseud. Counterpoise. see Thornton, W. supposed author

T., W. pseud. Political economy. see Thornton, William, 1761-1828.

T., W. pseud. Three letters. see Tennent, William, 1705-1777.

T. C., M. G. pseud. Desengano de falsas imposturas. see Toral y Cabanas, Manuel German.

T. des P., M. O. pseud. see P., M. O. T. des. pseud.

T. I., J. pseud. Carta al Pensador Mejicano. 94161

T. P., J. G. pseud. Al que le venga. see Torres Palacios, Jose Gregorio de.

T. y C., M. pseud. Idea sucinta de las Cortes. 94162

T. A. pseud. see Abbay, Thomas.

T. Alston, Esq. (N. C.) who, from gambling, was shot by Capt. Johnson. 102473

T. A. Holland & Co.'s business directory of St. Louis. 75346

T. A. L. pseud. see Poyas, Elizabeth Anne.

T. B. pseud. see Brattle, Thomas.

T. C. pseud. see C., T. pseud.

T. C. pseud. see Carr, T.

T. C. pseud. see Chalkley, Thomas.

T. C. pseud. see Church, Thomas.

T. C. pseud. see Churchyard, Thomas.

T. C. pseud. see Crowley, Thomas.

T. C. M. pseud. see M., T. C. pseud.

T. C. P. pseud. see P., T. C. pseud.

T. C. R. pseud. see R., T. C. pseud.

T. D. pseud. see D., T. pseud.

T. D. pseud. see Dudley, Thomas.

T. D. H. pseud. see Hase, Theodore de. supposed author

T. D. L. pseud. see L., T. D. pseud.

T. F. pseud. see F., T. pseud.

T. F. pseud. see Foxcroft, Thomas.

T. G. pseud. see Gib, T.

T. Guilford Smith. 84395

T. H. pseud. see H., T. pseud.

T. H. pseud. see Hancock, Thomas.

T. H. pseud. see Hariot, Thomas.

T. H. pseud. see Hooker, Thomas.

T. H. pseud. see Johnson, Edward.

T. H. R. pseud. see Robinson, Thomas H.

T. H. S. pseud. see Stockton, Thomas Hewlings.

T. L. pseud. see Letchworth, Thomas.

T. L. C. W. pseud. see Chisholme, David.

T. Lloyd Stanley. pseud. see Smith, Richard Morris, 1827-1896.

T. M. pseud. see M., T. pseud.

T. M. pseud. see Blumeau, Jonathan.

T. M. pseud. see Maule, Thomas.

T. McCargo versus the Merchant's Insurance Company. 42985, (82143)

T. McCargo versus the New Orleans Insurance Company. 82142

T. N. pseud. tr. see Nicholas, Thomas. tr.

T. N. M. pseud. see M., T. N. pseud.

T. O***. pseud. see O***, T. pseud.

T. P. pseud. see P., T. pseud.

T. P. pseud. see Mather, Increase, 1639-1723.

T. Q. pseud. see Young, Samuel, fl. 1855.

T. R. pseud. see R., T. pseud.

T. R. pseud. see Rand, Thomas.

T. R. C. S. C. S. pseud. tr. see S., T. R. C. S. C. pseud. tr.

T. S. pseud. see S., T. pseud.

T. S. pseud. see Scott, Thomas, 1580?-1626.

T. S. pseud. see Sedgwick, Theodore, 1811-1859.

T. S. pseud. see Smith, Truman, 1791-1884.

T. S. pseud. see Sockett, Thomas, 1778?-1859.

T. S. pseud. see Stanley, Thomas.

T. S. of V. pseud. see Scott, Thomas, 1580?-1626.

T. T. pseud. see T., T. pseud.

T. T. pseud. see T., T., Junior. pseud.

T. T. pseud. see Thompson, Thomas, 1708?-1773. supposed author

T. T. B. D. pseud. see Thorowgood, Thomas.

T. True Briton. pseud. see Tod, Thomas.

T. T. M. T. pseud. see T., T. T. M. pseud.

T. W. pseud. see Chauncy, Charles, 1705-1787. and Walker, Timothy. supposed author

T. W. pseud. see Chuancy, Charles, 1705-1787.

T. W. pseud. see Wight, Thomas.

T. W., a Bostonian. pseud. see Chauncy, Charles, 1705-1787.

T. W. H. pseud. see Higginson, Thomas Wentworth.

Taaffe, Theobald. appellant (11193)

Taal- en Dichtlievende Genootschap, Leyden. 94163

Tabac. 94164

Tabacco. 91415

Tabacconists own book. 85102

Tabaci, seu nicotianae descriptio. (52173)

Tabaco Habano. 24179, 72554

Tabaco. The distinct and seuerall opinions. 94165

Tabacologia. (52173)

Tabacum poema libris duobus. 95622

Tabago: or, a geographical description. 94166

Tabares, Diego. 29424, note after 94166

Tabasca (Mexican State) Consulado. defendants 51043

Tabatinga am Amazonenstrome. 2474

Tabb, T. T. supposed author 94169, note after 100581

Tabellae geographicae. 77606

Tabelle der Arktischen Temperaturen. 7394

Tabelle uber die Aus- und Absonderungen des Korpers. 11773

Taber, Azur. 640, 73970, 73977

Taber, Joseph. 18893, 94170

Tabernacle Church, Salem, Mass. see Salem, Mass. Tabernacle Church.

Tabitha rediviva. 46536

Tabla de las materias mas fundamentales. 76154

Tabla de todas las religiosas. 94171

Tabla pacsual antigua anadida. 72463

Tabla synoptica de los tratados y convenciones. (73030)

Tabla y reglamento para las asistencias solemnes. 72814

Tablas acomodadas a la moneda de Indias. 50612

Tablas chronologicas. 13632

Tablas de Cassini y Halley. 8988

Tablas de latitudes y longitudes de los principales puntos. 44090

Tablas estadisticas del reyno de Espana. 33742

Tablas geografico-politicas del reyno de Nueva Espana. (33743)

Tablas mineralogicas dispuestas segun los discubrimientos. 37108

Tablas necrologicas del colera-morbis. 74936

Tablas que espresan la relacion entre los valores de las antiguas medidas Mexicanas y las del neuvo sistema legal. 71465

Tait, John. 63647, note after 94220
Tait, Jonathan. defendant 93450
Taiti. —Marquises. —Californie. 27477
Taix, Hieronimo. 94221
Take care!!! 94222
Take care! Major Sanderson. 48973, 86297
Take care of your health. 29863
Take care of your pockets. 64840
Take heed how ye hear. 26596
Taking of Naboth's vineyard. 12701
Taking of Teach, the pirate. 94554
Taking the census. 86589
Talamanca, Miguel de la Grua. see Grua
    Talamanca, Miguel de la, Marques de
    Branciforte.
Talancon y Salgado, J. Ramon. 94223
Talapusapaiain wanipt timas. 88880
Talavera, Lino. 94225
Talavera, Manuel Antonio. (42225A)
Talbot, Theodore, d. 1862. 97652
Talbot, ---------. USA 97652
Talbot, C. ed. 14869, note after 97998
Talbot, Charles C. 94226-94227
Talbot, Edward Allen. 94228-94231
Talbot, I. T. 52701
Talbot, John. 28453, 32146, 39817, 66735,
    66737, 66743, 94232
Talbot, Mary Anne. 94233
Talbot, Mary Elizabeth. 94234
Talbot, Silas. 94235-94236
Talbot, Silas. plaintiff 60180, 60582, 94236
Talbot, Theodore. 83706
Talbot, Theodore, d. 1862. 97652
Talbot, Sir William, Bart. tr. 39676
Talboys, D. A. ed. 31231-31232
Talboys, Thomas. 31995
Talcott, ---------, fl. 1854. 89199
Talcott, D. S. 80180
Talcott, George. defendant at court martial
    89356, note before 94236A, 1st note after
    96929
Talcott, Hart. 94236A
Tale. 9821, 16545, (16551), 29715, 33969,
    39722, 49421, 51216, 51730, (52149),
    52153, (52159), 59190, 59216, 71088,
    72189, 78800, 78806, 78846, 81206,
    83782, 89439, 2d note after 94271, 95481,
    98883, 101236, 101481, 102163, 1st note
    after 102052, note after 102637, note after
    103058, 103847
Tale and other poems. 34146
Tale by Byron Whippoorwill, Esq. 57658,
    103111
Tale, containing scenes from real life.
    96169
Tale. Designed for young people. 78806,
    96483
Tale designed for young persons. 78829,
    106134
Tale, edited by a New England minister.
    44526
Tale for the amusement and instruction of
    youth. 102376
Tale for the crisis. 4501, (36412)
Tale for the south and north. 29727
Tale for the times. By a lady of Virginia.
    74450
Tale for the times. By Dr. W. H. Brisbane.
    8006
Tale for young people. 32413
Tale, founded on fact. 72981
Tale, founded on fact. [By Laurence Stearne.]
    91354
Tale, founded on fact. [By Sarah Wentworth
    Apthorp Morton.] 51027, note after
    100593

Tale, founded on facts. 84237
Tale i skolehuset. 62595
Tale illustrative of Irish life. 74825
Tale illustrative of the early history of the
    Church of England. 90311
Tale, illustrative of the revolutionary history
    of Vermont. 95485
Tale, in two cantos. 81176
Tale, not stranger than true. 47981
Tale of a box. 94238
Tale of a country parish in the 17th century.
    81334
Tale of a New Yorker. 94239
Tale of a revolutionary soldier. 19127
Tale of a tub. 94240
Tale of a tub. Part second. 94240
Tale of Acadie. (41909)-41910
Tale of adventures in South America. 27922
Tale of Africa. 46186
Tale of Alabama. 70907, 81251
Tale of American life. 20655
Tale of an election. 84392
Tale of ancient Mexico. 75933
Tale of Arctic life. 21821
Tale of avarice and crime defeated. 95482
Tale of backwoods retribution. 69050
Tale of border life. 95477
Tale of Boston and our own times. 91829
Tale of California law. 10046, 37947, 3d note
    after 100684
Tale of Canada. 37907
Tale of Carolina. 73018, (81252)
Tale of Charlestown in 1834. 26057
Tale of Cherry Valley. 22297
Tale of colonial times. 33784
Tale of commercial life. 104135
Tale of country life. (49699)
Tale of Cuban patriotism. 88942
Tale of Detroit and Michillimackinac. 71041
Tale of disappointment and distress. 72053
Tale of disunion! and border war! (36534)
Tale of domestic life in Pennsylvania. 25158
Tale of Dutch Guiana. 57950
Tale of early times. 12718
Tale of 1838. 51637
Tale of 1824-1827. 82029
Tale of England, Ireland and America. 88606
Tale of Esquimaux land. 2952
Tale of Florida. 31466
Tale of frontier life and Indian character.
    48230, 72183
Tale of Georgia. 81216, (81218)
Tale of Harve de Grace. 59202
Tale of home trials. 21700
Tale of horror. 35509
Tale of hunters, Indians, and Banditti. 28848
Tale of Indian life among the Mohawks. 26545
Tale of Kentucky. By R. M. Bird. 5554
Tale of Kentucky. [By William Gilmore
    Simms.] (81200)
Tale of Lexington. 36829, 94241
Tale of life among the lowly. 92493, 92495
Tale of life in New York and Boston. 91825
Tale of life in the Old Dominion. 57191
Tale of Long Island Sound. 91329
Tale of Louisiana. By James S. Peacocke.
    59414
Tale of Louisiana. By Miss A. E. Dupey.
    21398
Tale of love and war. 29034, 82205
Tale of love and witchcraft. 75717
Tale of Lowell. 1971
Tale of Mexican treachery. 36516
Tale of Mexico. 21156
Tale of missionary life in the north-west.
    26165

Tale of Mississippi. 81194
Tale of Mormonism. 9985, (11475)
Tale of New-England. 104924
"Tale of New England." 92441
Tale of New England colonial life. (32509)
Tale of New Jersey. 17934
Tale of New Orleans life. 13237
Tale of New York, a poem. 2327
Tale of New York. By Harry Hazelton. 31120
Tale of New York. [By P. Hamilton Myers.] 51638
Tale of New York, founded on facts. 57134
Tale of Nova Scotia in three cantos. 80471
Tale of Ohio river life. 31324
Tale of olden times. (12425), 59527
Tale of our own times. By a lady. 23890
Tale of our own times. By the author of "Hope Leslie." 78769
Tale of Paraguay. 88567
Tale of past wars. 92698
Tale pf plantation life in South Carolina. 77883
Tale of planter life in the Old Dominion. 41065
Tale of race and social conflict. (81466)
Tale of real life. By Rev. John T. Roddan. 72465
Tale of real life. By the author of Way marks of a wanderer. 55570, 74246
Tale of Salt Lake City. 74982
Tale of 1782. 35089
Tale of 1773-75. (72176)
Tale of 1763. 59184
Tale of '76. 11600
Tale of Sherman's march. 59495
Tale of 1692. 75716
Tale of 1673. 51636, 59197
Tale of South Carolina. 72128
Tale of southern life. [By Caroline Lee Hentz.] 31436
Tale of southern life. By Logan. 41819, note before 95663
Tale of Tappan Zee. 32994
Tale of Texas. 81239
Tale of the Alamo. (34689)
Tale of the Alhambra. 103392
Tale of the American revolution. By Eldred Grayson. (28423), note before 90174
Tale of the American revolution. By Lawrence Labree. (38448)
Tale of the American revolution. By Mary S. B. Dana. 18437
Tale of the American revolution. By the author of "The bethroted [sic] of Wyoming.] 47950
Tale of the American revolution. By William Seton. 79339
Tale of the American woods. 33379
Tale of the Antarctic. 58356
Tale of the Antilles. 10787
Tale of the Arctic seas. (27416)
Tale of the Ashley River. 81197
Tale of the Brandywine. 68180
Tale of the bushwhackers in Missouri. 72129
Tale of the Canadas. 71041, 100881
Tale of the Canadian rebellion of 1837-8. (33869)
Tale of the Carolina settlements. 30044
Tale of the Creek war. (77836)
Tale of the crescent city. 81213, 81234
Tale of the cruises of the Sumter and Alabama. 59495
Tale of the crusades. 57658, 103311
Tale of the dark and bloody ground. (4724)

Tale of the dark days of Kentuck in the year 1861. 69552
Tale of the Dismal Swamp. 92409, note after 93950
Tale of the early days of the Texas republic. 69084
Tale of the early Kentucky settlements. 44802
Tale of the early toils. 57130
Tale of the east and the west. 22297
Tale of the far west; and other poems. 49702
Tale of the far west. By the author of "The silver bugle." 67299
Tale of the forest. 72046
Tale of the forked deer. 72133
Tale of the French and Indian wars. 25160
Tale of the frontier. A poem. 47862
Tale of the frontier. [By Emerson Bennett.] (4724)
Tale of the frontier. [By James S. French.] 25864
Tale of the future. 97374
Tale of the good woman. 59214
Tale of the great American war. 24304, (31081)
Tale of the Great Dismal Swamp. 92396-92397, 92408
Tale of the Great Kanawha. 53020
Tale of the great rebellion. By Hon. Jere. Clemens. 13620
Tale of the great rebellion. [By Jane Hay Fuller.] (26166)
Tale of the great transition. (76959)
Tale of the hospital. 103446
Tale of the Hudson. 13760, note after 101036
Tale of the Huguenots. 24986
Tale of the Indian country. 35115
Tale of the last war. 95411
Tale of the late American war. 71036, 71039
Tale of the late war. (45040)
Tale of the liberating expedition of 1851. (30325)
Tale of the massacre of 1778. 22297
Tale of the Mexican war. (18061)
Tale of the Minnesota massacre. 22297
Tale of the Mississippi. 81195
Tale of the Mohawk Valley in revolutionary times. 36582
Tale of the neutral ground. (3559)-3562, 16533, 89934
Tale of the New World. 33969
Tale of the Niagara fountier. 67075
Tale of the nineteenth century. (23949), note before 94094
Tale of the north and south. 91291
Tale of the northwest. By Kah-ge-ga-gah-bowk. (16718)
Tale of the northwest in 1862. 22297
Tale of the ocean. 39833
Tale of the Old Dominion; by a Virginian. 94169, note after 100581
Tale of the Old Dominion. By one of her daughters. 13693
Tale of the olden time. 50487
Tale of the outbreak of 1837. (43466)
Tale of the Pacific. 16426, 16474
Tale of the pilgrimage of the Moravian Indians. 50525
Tale of the polar seas. 75248
Tale of the primitive Moravians. 50983
Tale of the puritans. 57185
Tale of the Quaker City during the revolution. 27159
Tale of the Ramapo in 1779. 35317
Tale of the real and ideal. 36840

Tale of the rebellion. By Wesley Bradshaw. 7291

Tale of the rebellion. Facts and figures. 59652, 1st note after 94241

Tale of the republic of Texas. 2108A, note after 93619

Tale of the revolution. 31475

Tale of the revolution, and other sketches. 27922

Tale of the revolution. By Charles F. Sterling. 91329

Tale of the revolution. [By David Murdoch.] 51435

Tale of the revolution. By Sylvanus Cobb, Jr. (13858)

Tale of the revolution. By the author of "The Yemassee." 81243

Tale of the revolution. By W. Gilmore Simms, Esq. 81209

Tale of the revolution. For children. 103263

Tale of the revolution founded on fact. 90522

Tale of the revolution, founded upon fact. 81179-81181

Tale of the revolution. In two volumes. 76931

Tale of the revolution of Paraguay, from authentic sources. (80174)

Tale of the revolutionary era. 83567

Tale of the Rocky Mountains. By R. M. Ballantyne. 2952

Tale of the Rocky Mountains. With the Rose of Wisconsin. 75261

Tale of the Schoharie Valley. 85611

Tale of the sea. By Hawser Martingale. 82119

Tale of the sea. [By James Fenimore Cooper.] 16595

Tale of the Seminole war. (81242)

Tale of the seventeenth century. [By W. H. C. Hosmer.] (33116)

Tale of the seventeenth century. In two volumes. 80067

Tale of the south. [By Caroline Lee Hentz.] 31436

Tale of the south. [By Mary A. Denison.] (19574)

Tale of the south. [By Theresa J. Freeman.] 25778

Tale of the southern seas. 27666

Tale of the southern states. [By William Wells Brown.] 8590

Tale of the southern states. With other poems. 27118

Tale of the southwest. 72127

Tale of the ten-mile trace. 72133

Tale of the Tennessee mountains. (36220)

Tale of the tents. 31324

Tale of the thousand islands. 75257

Tale of the times. By Allen Hampden. 30123

Tale of the times. [By Thomas L. Nichols.] (55215)

Tale of the times of Aaron Burr. 13620

Tale of the times of the iron hoof. 41526

Tale of the times. Serio-comical. 19816

Tale of the tory ascendency. 37413, (37423)

Tale of the two worlds. 69033

Tale of the Ursuline Convent. 12962

Tale of the voyage of Hendrick Hudson. 104514

Tale [of the war.] 32617

Tale of the war of independence. 31719

Tale of the wars of King Philip. 21659, 89130

Tale of the Washington Soldiers' and Sailors' Orphans' Fair. 19837

Tale of the west. 104176

Tale of the west. . . . In two volumes. 43311, 1st note after 101905, 103986

Tale of the West Indies. 96165

Tale of the witches. 92147

Tale of thirty years ago. (64195)

Tale of times not long ago. 35697

Tale of treason. (7653)

Tale of Troy. 59526

Tale of truth. [By Jane Ermina Locke.] 41725

Tale of truth. By Mrs. Rowson. 73604, 73606

Tale of Tucuman. 36927, 2d note after 94241

Tale of two cities. 84144

Tale of Upper Canada. (37692)

Tale of Venezuela. (21638)

Tale of Virginia. 31720

Tale of West India piracy. 34784

Tale of West Tennessee. 88417

Tale of woe. 103438

Tale of Wyoming: a poem. 26011, 1st note after 105691

Tale of Wyoming, a poem, in five cantos. 25673

Tale relative to the slave trade. 50805

Tale unveiling some of the mysteries. 36537

Talekesuhsutaduks? How are you to be saved? 67765, 3d note after 94241

Tales. 63571

Tales about Canada. 27924, 94242

Tales about Europe, Asia, Africa, and America. 94243

Tales about the United States of America. 94243

Tales about the world. 27923

Tales and ballads. 27431

Tales and essays for children. 80958

Tales and jests of Mr. Hugh Peters. 61196, 106018

Tales and miscellanies now first collected. 35730

Tales and pencilings. 92427

Tales and sketches, by a cosmopolite. 94244

Tales and sketches. By a country school master. 39866, 1st note after 94244

Tales and sketches. By the author of "Hope Leslie." 78804, 2d note after 94244

Tales and sketches collected during a trip to the Pictures Rocks of Lake Superior. 38923, 57814, note after 95662

Tales and sketches from the Queen City. 20812

Tales and sketches of New England life. 92451, 92455

Tales and sketches. Second series. (78805), 2d note after 94244

Tales and sketches,—such as they are. 92147, 92152, 92154

Tales and sketches: to which is added the Raven. 63554

Tales and souvenirs of a residence in Europe. 71683, 3d note after 94244

Tales and traditions of the Eskimo. 71439

Tales. By Edgar A. Poe. 63553

Tales by the the author of "Three experiments of living." 39738, 4th note after 94244

Tales from American history. 71807, 71809, 5th note after 94244

Tales from American history. [Second series.] 71808-71809, 5th note after 94244

Tales from American history. Third series. 71809, 5th note after 94244

Tales from Blackwood. 64533

Tales. Lives of Franklin & Washington. 101848

TALES

Tales, national and revolutionary. 104172, 104175-104176
Tales, national, revolutionary. 104172
Tales of a traveller. 35203-(35204), note before 94245
Tales of a wayside inn. 41930
Tales of an American landlord. 94245
Tales of an Indian camp. 36521, 94246
Tales of Barbados. 19773
Tales of five lands. 104514
Tales of Glauber-Spa. 94247
Tales of mystery and imagination. 63555
Tales of mystery, imagination, and humor. 63556
Tales of old travel. Re-narrated. 37890
Tales of other days. 35135, (35148)
Tales of Passaic. 94658
Tales of passed times by Mother Goose. 86917
Tales of Peter Parley, about America. 27911, 94248
Tales of St. Augustine. 83678
Tales of Somerville. 99630
Tales of the border. (29796)
Tales of the Canadian forest. 89156-89157
Tales of the colonies. By John Howison. 33367
Tales of the colonies; or the adventures of an emigrant. 73538
Tales of the Emerald Isle. 103049
Tales of the fireside. 94249, 103049
Tales of the garden of Kosciusko. 38084
Tales of the good woman. 59214, 1st note after 94249
Tales of the grotesque and arabesque. 63557
Tales of the Indians. 95220
Tales of the night. 105060
Tales of the North American Indians. 30916
Tales of the northwest. 85426, 85428, 3d note after 94249
Tales of the ocean, and essays for the forecastle. 82122
Tales of the olden times. 73613
Tales of the prison. 33237
Tales of the puritans. 94250
Tales of the revolution, and thrilling stories. 94252
Tales of the revolution; being rare and remarkable passages. 94253, note after 95220
Tales of the revolution. By a young gentleman of Nashville. 94251
Tales of the revolution. By John H. Mancur. 44228
Tales of the sea. (55298)
Tales of the tripod. 102121
Tales of the war. 1140
Tales of travel in Central America. 85429
Tales of travels in the north of Europe. 95429
Tales of travels west of the Mississippi. 85429
Tales of Venezuela. 10193, note before 94254, note after 98870
Tales, sketches, and lyrics. (43265)
Tales, sketches, &c. 102535
Taletell, George. pseud. Recreations of George Taletell. see Holmes, Isaac Edward. supposed author
Talgarth, Wales. Trevecca College. see Trevecca College, Talgarth, Wales.
Taliaferro, H. E. 94255
Taliaferro, John. 94256-94257
Taliaferro, Lawrence. 96715 see also U. S. Commissioner to the Wahpaakootah, Susseton, and Upper Medawakanton Tribes of Sioux Indians.

Talisman. see Cabinet & talisman. Worcester talisman.
Talisman for MDCCCXXX. 94258, note after 99271, note after 99276
Talisman for MDCCCXXVIII. 94258, note after 99271, note after 99276
Talisman for MDCCCXXIX. 94258, note after 99271, note after 99276
Talk on southern affairs. 16203
Talk with my pupils. 78808
Talk with the camp. 19862
Talks with slaves in the southern states. 68529
Talks with the people of New York. 17394
Tall- en Dichtlievende Genootschap, Leyden. 94163, note after 101819, 3d note after 101888
Tallahassee, Fla. Constitutional Convnetion, 1861. see Florida. Constitutional Convention, Tallahassee, 1861.
Tallahassee, Fla. Constitutional Convention, 1868. see Florida. Constitutional Convention, Tallahassee, 1868.
Tallcot, Joseph. 90778
Taller de coheteria. 18784
Talleyrand-Perigord, Charles Maurice de, Prince de Benevent, 1754-1838. 16863, 47492, 59593, 62702, 76325, 99303, 94259-94261, 903848 see also France. Ministere des Affaires Etrangeres.
Talleyrand's defence. 94261
Tallis, A. illus. 54691
Tallis' New York street views. 54691
Tallmadge, Benjamin, 1754-1835. 26606
Tallmadge, Daniel Bryant, 1793-1847. 94262-94263
Tallmadge, James, 1778-1853. (31890), 58482, 94264-94267
Tallmadge, Nathaniel Pitcher, 1795-1864. 94268-94270
Tallmadge, S. W. 69636
Tallmadge, Ohio. Fiftieth Anniversary Commemoration, 1857. 94271
Tallow Chandlers, Baltimore. see Baltimore. Tallow Chandlers.
Tallulah and Jocassee. (70969)
Tally Rhand. pseud. see Rhand, Tally. pseud.
Talmage, James Edward, 1862- 83263-83270, 83272, 73273, 83275
Talmanaco, Mexico. Franciscan Convent. 40960, note after 47585, note after 47850
Talon, Jean Baptiste. supposed author 67020, 1st note after 94271
Talvera, Gabriel de. 94224
Talvi. pseud. History of the colonization of America. see Robinson, Therese Albertine Louise (Von Jakob) 1797-1869.
Talvi's history of the colonization of America. 72191, 2d note after 94271
Talvj. pseud. History of the colonization of America. see Robinson, Therese Albertine Louise (Von Jakob) 1797-1869.
Tamaio de Vargas, Thomas. see Tamayo de Vargas, Tomas.
Tamajuncosa, Antonio. 94272
Tamakoce. Dakota Indian sobriquet see Riggs, Stephen R.
Tamakoce kaga. 18293, (71344)
Tamakoce okaga. 18291, 71336
Tamara, Francisco. 6119, 94273
Tamariz, A. defendant (70796)
Tamariz, Antonio de Haro y. see Haro y Tamariz, Antonio de.
Tamariz, Jose Nicholas de Escalona y. see Escalona y Tamariz, Jose Nicolas de.

2880

Tamariz, Josef Tobar y. see Tobar y Tama-
riz, Josef.
Tamariz, Mariano. 94274
Tamariz de Carmona, Antonio. 94275
Tamaron, Pedro. 94276
Tamás bátya. 92584-92585
Tamás bátya kunyhója. 92583
Tamás bátya kunykójához. 92417
Tamaulipas (Mexican State) Cuarto Congreso
Constitucional, 1831. 94277-94278
Tamaulipas (Mexican State) Laws, statutes,
etc. 13810, 39405, 94948
Tamayo, Antonio. 94279
Tamayo de Vargas, Tomas. 94280
Tamayo y Mendoza, Garcia de. 94281-94284
Tamayo y Negron, Francisco. 94285
Tambien al berdugo Azotan. 94286
Tamburini, Giacomo. 94287-94288
Tamerlane, and minor poems. (63518)
Tamerlane and other poems. (63569), note
after 94288
Tammanial Tontine Association, New York.
see New York Tammanial Tontine
Association.
Tammany, Father. pseud. Father Tammany's
almanac. 23911
Tammany Hall, and other miscellaneous poems.
19537
Tammany, Philadelphia and Illinois letters.
39655
Tammany Society, Alexandria, Va. 747
Tammany Society, New York. 32052, (54024),
84843, 94289, 94291-note after 94295,
104984
Tammany Society, New York. Committee of
Amusement. 84843, note after 94295
Tammany Society, New York. Committee
to Revise and Amend the Constitution.
94291
Tammany Society, New York. Fourth of July
Celebration, 1863. 50629
Tammany Society, New York. Wallabout Com-
mittee. 54021, (54024), 94289, 94298,
note after 101092
Tammany Society—Committee of Amusement.
On the discussion of the following ques-
tion. 84843, note after 94295
Tammany Society.—In Committee of amuse-
ment. On the discussion of the following
question. 84843
Tammany Society, no. 1, twenty fourth anni-
versary address. 72889
Tamoc Caspipina. pseud. see Duche, Jacob.
Tampico. Cantada heroico. 94300
Tam's fortnight ramble. 43400
Tamworth tune. 94335
Tan Teladakadidjik Apostalewidjik. (67763),
note after 94300
Tana, ------. (67737)-67739
Tanagrarum catalogus specificus. 78148
Tanc, Xavier. 94301
Tanco, Diego Martin. ed. 79054
Tanco, Luis Becerra. see Becerra Tanco,
Luis.
Tandel, Emile. tr. 25993
Taney, Roger Brooke, 1777-1864. (29463),
37667, 48029, 58696, 78257-78259, note
after 94301-94302 see also U. S.
Supreme Court. Chief Justice.
Tangencies of circles and of spheres. 85072
Tangui, ------. 22057, 40744
Tanguy de la Boissiere, C. C. 94303-94308
Tank, Otto. 57322
Tanker ofver Daniel och Uppenbarslen. 84475
Tannatt (A. G.) & Co. firm publishers 94719
Tannehill, Wilkins. 40575, 94309, 94799

Tanner, A. H. 90828
Tanner, B. engr. 8215, 50185, 82375-82379,
102484, 104597-104598
Tanner, Henry Schenck. 2594, 61863-61864,
62296, 94310-94327, note after 94327,
99586
Tanner, John. 12833, 26773, 35684-(35686),
94328-94330
Tanner, Mathias. 94331-94332
Tanner, Halpin & Co. firm 75346
Tanner-boy, and how he became Lieutenant-
General. 59762, note after 94332
Tans'ur, William. 91716, 94333-94339, 101196
Tanto le pican al buey hasta que embiste.
94340
Taopi. 31964
Tap of the drum. 63816, 63777
Tapaboca; o sea contestacion. 94341
Tapaboca al libelista autor del anonimo pub-
licado. (70091)
Tapado. pseud. A los semi-eruditos. 94342
Tapatio, el Pensador. pseud. Pensador Tapa-
tio a sus censores. 94343
Tapatio, el Pensador. pseud. Todos pensamos.
94344-94345, note after 96100
Tapfere Spanier wahrend des Feldzuges in
Florida. 98761
Tapia, Andreas de. 34153
Tapia, Diego de. 94346
Tapia, Francisco de. 94347
Tapia, Francisco Pichardo y. see Pichardo
y Tapia, Francisco.
Tapia, Juan Antonio de. 94348
Tapia, Mathias de. 94349-94350
Tapia Centeno, Carlos de. see Tapia Zen-
teno, Carlos de.
Tapia de Vargas, Juan. 94351
Tapia y Rivera, Alejandro. 94352
Tapia Zenteno, Carlos de. 94353-94355
Tapp, John. 16968
Tappan, Benjamin, 1773-1857. 92884-94356-
94358
Tappan, Benjamin, 1788-1863. 92884, 94356-
Tappan, David, 1752-1803. 7241, 62535, 89794,
89797, 94361-94368, 101751, 104054
Tappan, Henry Philip. (34343), 48804, 54706,
1st note after 94368
Tappan, Lewis, 1788-1873. 21232, 40642,
67184, (70193), 81791, note after 90732,
2d-3d notes after 94368, 94369-note after
94370 see also American and Foreign
Anti-slavery Society. Secretary.
Tappan, Lewis, 1788-1873. defendant before
church session (54136), 94370
Tappan, Lewis, 1788-1873. supposed author
69423, note after 94370
Tappan, William Bingham. 94371-94378, note
after 104633
Tappan and Dennet. firm publishers defend-
ants 93585
Taracena, Manuel. 94379
Tarado, Jos. Atan. Diaz y. see Diaz y Tarado,
Jos. Atan.
Tarafa, Franciscus. see Tarrafa, Francis-
cus.
Tarahumarisches Woterbuch. 91187
Taraia, --------. supposed author 41117
Taralla, -------. supposed author see
Taraia, -------. supposed author
Taramete, Hemi E. tr. 83277
Taranaltos, F. de. 16929
Taraphus, Franciscus. see Tarrafa, Francis-
cus.
Tarasca de los ladrones y prison de medio
rey. 94380
Tarascon, Louis Anastasius. (61433), 94381-
94385

Tasman, Abel Janszoon, 1603-1659. 4937A, 16782, 21211-21215, (72185)-72197

Tassel, Isaac van. see Van Tassel, Isaac.

Tassel, Truman van. see Van Tassel, Truman.

Tassoni, Alessandro. 94402

Tassy, ------- Garcin de. see Garcin de Tassy, ---------.

Taste, Timothy. pseud. Freaks of Columbia. 20314, 94403

Tatam, William. 92811

Tatar, Peter. tr. 92585

Tate, Nahum, 1652-1715. 3471, 7315, 64998-(64999), (66440)-(66441), 66448-66449

Tate, Robert. 94404

Tatem, H. (25794), 89359, 101509

Tatem, William. complainant 94405

Tates, Edward. supposed author 40550, note 94405

Tatham, William. 15004, 92811, 94406-94415, note after 106213

Tatham, William. reporter 36994, 94411, note after 95882, 3d note after 96891

Tatton, John. 66686

Taunay, Felix Emile. tr. 94418

Taunay, Hippolyte. 94416-94417

Taunay, Theodore Maria. 94418

Taunton, Mass. Bristol Academy. see Bristol Academy, Taunton, Mass.

Taunton, Mass. Bristol County Whig Convention, 1837. see Whig Party. Massachusetts. Bristol County. Convention, Taunton, 1837.

Taunton, Mass. Convention of Ministers, 1745. see Number of Ministers Conven'd at Taunton, Mass., 1745.

Taunton, Mass. County Convention of Delegates of All the Towns in Bristol County, 1837. see Whig Party. Massachusetts. Bristol County. Convention, Taunton, 1837.

Taunton, Mass. Lunatic Hospital. see Massachusetts. State Hospital, Taunton.

Taunton, Mass. Number of Ministers. see Number of Ministers Conven'd at Taunton, Mass., 1745.

Taunton, Mass. West Congregational Church. 94421A

Taunton Baptist Association. see Baptists. Massachusetts. Taunton Baptist Association.

Taunton Union, for the Relief and Improvement of the Colored Race. 94421

Taunton Union, for the Relief and Improvement of the Colored Race. Board of Managers. 94421

Taunton whig. 90891

Tausia-Bournos, -----. 94422-94423

Tauste, Francisco de. 94424

Tavares, -------Villela. see Villela Tavares, ---------.

Tavares, Jeronymo Villa de Castro. see Castro Tavares, Jeronymo Villa de.

Tavares, Joas Fernandes. 7513, 94425-94426

Tavares Bastos, Aureliano Candido, 1839-1875. (3901), 85775 see also Sociedade Internacional de Immigracao, Rio de Janeiro. Director.

Tavares Bastos, Jose. see Bastos, Jose Tavares.

Tavares Bastos do Solitario, Aureliano Candido. see Tavares Bastos, Aureliano Candido, 1839-1875.

Tavares da Silva, Henrique de Souza de. see Souza de Tavares da Silva, Henrique de, Conde de Miranda.

Tavares de Brito, Francisco. see Brito, Francisco Tavares de.

Tavares de Sequeira e Sa, Manoel. see Sequeira e Sa, Manoel Tavares de.

Taver, Joseph. 94170

Tavola di bronzo. 89647

Tavola di bronzo, il pallio di seta ed il codice. 3093

Tavole moderne di geografia de la maggior parte del mondo. 5000

Ta-wa karo Indians. Treaties, etc. 96719

Tawse, John. 94427-94428 see also Society in Scotland for Propagating Christian Knowledge. Secretary.

Tax-act and estimate, passed the 22d day of July, 1766. 87604

Tax-act and estimate, passed the 23d day of August, 1769. 87609

Tax act of 1866. 87715

Tax act. Passed in January, 1777. 87625

Tax-act, passed the first day of June, 1749. 87577

Tax-act, passed the 31st day of July, 1760. 87595

Tax-act, passed the 29th day of May, 1761. 87598

Tax bill. Speech . . . April 19, 1864. 50791

Tax bill. Speech of William Sprague. 89724, 89728

Tax bill, with all the amendments. (43876)

Tax-exemption no excuse for spoliation. 67274

Tax for . . . 1821. (44047)

Tax law of Ohio. (57060)

Tax on cotton. 17229

Tax or no tax. March 17, 1836. 94138

Tax payer. pseud. City finances. 94429

Tax payer. pseud. Comparison of the taxes. 54207, note after 94429

Tax payer. pseud. New-York and Erie Rail Road. 94430

Tax payer. pseud. Remarks. (69391)

Tax payer. pseud. Tax payer's reply. 8327

Tax-Payers' Convention of South Carolina, Columbia, 1871. 88077, 1st note after 94434

Tax-Payers' Convention of South Carolina, Columbia, 1871. petitioners 87942, 88078, 1st note after 94434

Tax-payer's guide. 71570

Tax-payer's manual. (6977)

Tax payer's reply to "An advocate for water." 8327

Tax reform in South Carolina. 83751

Taxable resources of the United States. 91022

Taxable valuation of the polls and estates. 10715

Taxable valuation of the polls and estates of the town of Dorchester. (20628)

Taxation. 106079

Taxation in the United States. (31029)

Taxation.—Legal tender notes. 89036

Taxation no tyranny. 106-107, 1657, 2760, 15523, (19253), 36302-36303, 36306-36307, 36309, 50452, 56060, 58399, 63216, 63771, 78302, (80441), 90317, note before 94431, note before 94434, 96184, 97635, 102647

Taxation of America. 94431

Taxation of intangible property in Ohio. 83965

Taxation of learning, charity, and religion. 62119, 65434

Taxation of North America. 94432

Taxation of the British empire. 44918

Taxation royal tyranny. 94433

Taxation, tyranny. 36308, note before 94434

Taxes. 99099

TAXES

Taxes assessed and received in the several
  counties. 60762
Taxes! Taxes! Taxes! 94434
Taylder, T. W. P. 64949
Tayler, Arthur. 54306, note before 94435
Tayler, Asher. see Tayler, Arthur.
Tayler, John. defendant (35991), 98547
Tayler, Thomas. 94435
Taylor, ---------, fl. 1795. 102346
Taylor, --------, fl. 1801. 30150
Taylor, ---------, fl. 1816. 635, 13786
Taylor, ---------, fl. 1819. 94267
Taylor, ----------, fl. 1830-1854. 89199,
  97594, 104917
Taylor, ---------, fl. 1860. defendant 6021
Taylor, ---------, fl. 1869. defendant 31669
Taylor, A. D. 94436
Taylor, A. E. (21904)
Taylor, Alexander Smith. 8662, 94437-94438
Taylor, Alma I. tr. 83135
Taylor, Amos. 94439, 94448-94450
Taylor, Bayard, 1825-1878. 32707, 51019,
  58958, 71017, 80419, 91937, 94440-
  94441
Taylor, Benjamin Cook. 94442
Taylor, C. 94443
Taylor, C. B. 9444-94446
Taylor, C. W. 92513
Taylor, C. W. L. 90555
Taylor, Caleb Jarvis. 94447
Taylor, Creed. 16686
Taylor, Dolly. see Taylor, Dorothy.
Taylor, Dorothy. 94448-94450
Taylor, E. G. ed. 93744
Taylor, Emily. 94451-94452
Taylor, F., fl. 1839. 94454
Taylor, F., fl. 1841. 94453
Taylor, Fennings. (56025)
Taylor, Fitch Waterman. 94455-94456
Taylor, Frances. (26877), 59703, (66925)
Taylor, G. 94457
Taylor, G. C. 55956
Taylor, George. 82979
Taylor, George, fl. 1763. 94458
Taylor, George, 1820-1894. 94461
Taylor, George, fl. 1833-1834. 94459-94460
Taylor, George Braxton. 94473
Taylor, George Keith. 94462
Taylor, George Watson. see Watson-Taylor,
  George.
Taylor, Gustavus N. supposed author (70978),
  note before 94463
Taylor, H. R. reporter 101907
Taylor, Hannis. 102402
Taylor, Henry. 94463-94465
Taylor, Hezekiah. 94466
Taylor, Isaac. of Pennsylvania 59957, note
  after 94466
Taylor, Isaac, 1759-1829. 94467-94469
Taylor, J., fl. 1649. (74457)
Taylor, J., fl. 1866. ed. 10628, (82198)
Taylor, J. L. 55641
Taylor, J. W. 76930
Taylor, Jacob. 94470
Taylor, James. 94498
Taylor, James. of Crowle, England. 94471
Taylor, James B. of Missouri 51809, note
  before 94472
Taylor, James Barnett. 94472-94474
Taylor, James Bayard. see Taylor, Bayard,
  1825-1878.
Taylor, James D. 94476
Taylor, James W. 8663-8664 see also U. S.
  Special Commissioners on the Mineral
  Resources of the United States.
Taylor, Janette. ed. (36551), note after 94476

Taylor, John. alias see Talbot, Mary Anne.
Taylor, John. of Bristol, England. 94480
Taylor, John. Rector of Trinity Church, Pitts-
  burgh 94504
Taylor, John, 1580-1653. supposed author
  54972, note after 94477
Taylor, John, 1638?-1708. 94478-94479
Taylor, John, 1750-1824. supposed author
  11587, 105034
Taylor, John, 1752-1833. 94481-94482
Taylor, John, 1753?-1824. 18070, (19272),
  22647, 29952, 94483-94495
Taylor, John, 1762-1840. 94496-94499,
  104268-104271
Taylor, John, 1779-1857. 94500-94501
Taylor, John, 1779-1863. ed. (33750), note
  after 94501-94502
Taylor, John, 1781-1864. 49965, 94503
Taylor, John, 1790-1863. plaintiff 19369,
  note after 94503
Taylor, John, fl. 1808. defendant (35991)
Taylor, John, 1808-1887. 28554, 50749, 64962,
  83122-83123, 83124-83128, 83169, 83252,
  83264, 83283, 83553, 94505-94506A
Taylor, John B. 94507
Taylor, John E. tr. 162
Taylor, John Lord. ed. 1440, note after
  94507
Taylor, John Louis, 1769-1829. (55687),
  94508-94509
Taylor, John Orville, 1807-1890. 14996, 94510,
  94514
Taylor, John Sydney. 94515
Taylor, John W., 1784-1854. 58482, 65760,
  76930, 94516
Taylor, Jonathan. 69746
Taylor, Joseph. defendant 94518-94521
Taylor, Joseph, d. 1816. 1829, 94517, 104056
Taylor, Joshua. 4497, 94522-94523, 101314
Taylor, Miles, 1805-1873. (19491), 42213,
  85081
Taylor, N. W. 105842
Taylor, Nathaniel. supposed author 4497,
  94524
Taylor, Nathaniel Green, 1819-1887. 1253,
  19593, 34648, note before 94525
Taylor, Oliver Alden. 1433, note after 94525
Taylor, R., fl. 1823. 52269, 94526
Taylor, R., fl. 1864. 3143
Taylor, Richard Cowling. 60569, 94527-94530,
  97803
Taylor, Robert Barraud. 94531-94533
Taylor, Robert Barry. 94534
Taylor, Samuel. Junior 38868, 3d note after
  94534
Taylor, Samuel D. supposed author 41787,
  4th note after 94534
Taylor, Samuel H. 58663
Taylor, Samuel Leiper. 60140, 5th note after
  94534 see also Pennsylvania. Histori-
  cal Society. Librarian.
Taylor, Samuel Priestly, 1779-1874. 84680
Taylor, Samuel W. 94535
Taylor, Simon. 94536
Taylor, Stephen. 94537-94538
Taylor, Thomas. of South Carolina 88087
Taylor, Thomas, 1738-1816. 94539-94540
Taylor, Thomas, fl. 1833. 94541
Taylor, Thomas, fl. 1848. 9860
Taylor, Thomas House. supposed author
  51786, note after 89350, 1st note after
  94541
Taylor, Timothy. 29402, 103659
Taylor, Tom. 41167, note before 94542
Taylor, Vermilye. 94542-94543, note before
  95353

2884

Taylor, W. B. S. tr. 96070
Taylor, W. H. S. (15392)
Taylor, Willett. 94544
Taylor, William. defendant 95557
Taylor, William. of Maine (3438), 94545
Taylor, William. of Nova Scotia 91357,
    note after 94536
Taylor, William, fl. 1660. 80212
Taylor, William, 1821-1902. 94547-94548
Taylor, William J. R. 74435
Taylor, William Stanhope. ed. 63067
Taylor, Zachary, Pres. U. S., 1784-1850.
    9923, 26099, 48117, 58025, 59488,
    74757, 78765, 90434, 91562-91563,
    91565, note after 95665, 96707, 104205
    see also U. S. Commissioner to the
    Sioux of Wa-ha-shaw's Tribe of Indians.
    U. S. President, 1849-1850 (Taylor)
Taylor, Cass and Van Buren compared.
    90866
Taylor anecdote book. 58025, note after
    95665
Taylorism examined. 95205
Taylour, Joseph. 54976, 94549
Tayse, D. Jacobszoon. 94550
Tazewell, Henry, 1753-1799. 96572
Tazewell, Littleton Waller, 1744-1860.
    (45087), 94551, 95419, 98425 see also
    Virginia. Governor, 1834-1836 (Tazewell)
Tchipayatek-o-mikan. Kanachtageng. 70905,
    1st note after 94551
Te Deum laudamus. 30879
Te leeuwarden. 5046
Te parau i papaihia e te rima o Mormona.
    83144
Te perdiste America. 99719
Tea-ship being arrived, every inhabitant.
    94552
Tea-ship having arrived, every inhabitant.
    (49957)
"Tea tax." 86947
Tea tax, and humble wish. 94553
Teachem, Mrs. pseud. Governess. 94556
Teacher. pseud. Address. 94557
Teacher. pseud. Scholar's manual. 77766
Teacher. 92040
Teacher and the parent. 66783
Teacher of common sense. 94558
Teachers and educators. 3465
Teachers' Association, Milwaukee. see Mil-
    waukee Teachers' Association.
Teachers' Association of Massachusetts. see
    Massachusetts Teachers' Association.
Teachers' Association of Michigan. see
    Michigan Teachers' Association.
Teachers' Association of New York State. see
    New-York State Teachers' Association.
Teachers' Association of Ohio. see Ohio
    Teachers' Association.
Teachers' Association of Ontario. 57366
Teachers' Association of the Pilgrim Sunday
    School, San Francisco. see San Fran-
    cisco. Pilgrim Sunday School. Teachers'
    Association.
Teachers at Port Royal and its Vicinity.
    pseud. Extracts of letters. 23529
Teacher's guide, and parent's assistant.
    94559
Teachers' Institute, Cheshire County, N. H.
    see Cheshire County Teachers' Institute.
Teachers' Institute, Cobleskill, N. Y. see
    Schoharie County Teachers' Institute
    (Second District) Cobleskill, N. Y., 1862.
Teacher's Institute, Kennebec County, Me. see
    Kennebec County, Me. Teachers' Insti-
    tute.

Teachers' Institute, Philadelphia. 62302
Teachers' Institute, Rockingham County, N. H.
    see Rockingham County, N. H. Teachers'
    Institute, Exeter.
Teachers' Institute, Schoharie County, N. Y.
    see Schoharie County Teachers' Insti-
    tute.
Teachers' Institute of the Third Assembly
    District of Monroe County, N. Y. 50030
Teachers' Institute, Second District, Schoharie
    County, N. Y. see Schoharie County
    Teachers' Institute (Second District)
    Cobleskill, N. Y., 1862.
Teachers' magazine. 48766
Teacher's manual. 58380
Teacher's reunion. Hawthorne Street, Feb-
    ruary 4th, 1861. 15471
Teachers' Society of Georgia. 94561
Teachers' Society of Georgia. Committee.
    94560
Teachers' Society of the State of Georgia.
    see Teachers' Society of Georgia.
Teaching elders. pseud. Several qvestions of
    serious and necessary consequences.
    17080
Teaching of the holy Catholic Church. 84216
Teachings of Christ. 84289
Teachings of patriots and statesmen. 12174
Teachings of the crisis. 26702
Teachings of the dead. 85329
Teachings of the past. 50975
Teackle, Littleton Dennis. note after 45370,
    94563
Teagnes. pseud. Examen historico-critico.
    94564
Teale, Isaac. 94565
Teall, Benjamin. 94566
Tear drop. 77008
Teardrop. 77009
Tears drop'd on dust and ashes. 46608, note
    after 105465
Tears of Britannia. 94567
Tears of Columbia. 93082
Tears of contrition. 43789
Tears of ministry. (9793)
Tears of repentence. 22166
Tears of sympathy. 94568
Tears of the Foot Guards. 1664A, 94569
Tears of the Indians. (11286), note before
    94570
Teasdale, Thomas C. 94570
Teatro critico Americano. 71445-71446
Teatro de la legislacion Columbiana. 11429
Teatro de la legislacion universal de Espana
    e Indias. (60899)
Teatro de la Santa Iglesia Metropolitano de
    Mexico. 80987
Teatro de todo el mundo. 35774
Teatro del cielo, e della terra. 73198
Teatro del mondo de Abrahamo Ortelio. 57703
Teatro del mondo . . . nel qvale distintamente
    si dimostrano. 57702
Teatro della guerra marittima e terrestre fra
    la Gran Bretagna. 94571
Teatro eclesiastico de la primitiva iglesia de
    las Indias. 18777
Teatro gerarquico de la luz. 6100
Teatro historico, juridico, y politico-militar.
    50216, 98165
Teatro historico juridico y politico militar de
    la misma isla. 98164
Teatro Mexicano descripcion breve de los
    svcessos exemplares. 99386, 99388
Teatro moderno applaudito. 100725
Tebar, Pedro de. 81286
Tebbs, William P. 94572

TECHNICAL

Technical appreciation of the first American
   printers. 106398
Technical instruction. 21885
Techo, Nicolas del, Originally Du Toict, 1611-
   1685. 4644, 5101, 13015, (69246),
   94573-94576
Techo's history of the provinces of Paraguay.
   13015, 94575
Tecla, Dona. pseud. Algo de masones. 94577
Tecumseh; a novel. 71046
Tecumseh and the prophet of the west. 36503
Tecumseh. By a young American. 3970
Tecumseh, or the battle of the Thames.
   22530
Tecumseh; or the death of the Shawnee chief.
   2
Tecumseh; or the warrior of the west. 94578
Tecumseh; or, the west thirty years since.
   14786
Tedrowe. firm publishers see Swartz &
   Tedrowe. firm publishers
Teele, Albert Kendall, 1823-1901. 50893,
   93430
Teelinck, Ewout. 94579
Teellinck, Willem. 94580
Teenstra, Marten Douwes. 94581-94588
Tee-totalism unmaksed! 58774
Tefft, Benjamin Franklin. 24381, 39073,
   92819, 94589-94590
Tega, R. de la. (30295)
Tegen-advys, op de presentatie van Portugal.
   94591
Tegen-vertooch op seecker discours. 19671,
   4th note after 102890
Tegenwoordige staat der Vereenigde Staaten
   van Amerika. 50925
Tegenwoordige staat van alle volkeren. 32096
Tegenwoordige staat van Amerika. 32096
Tegenwoordige-verschillen de volkplantingen
   in Amerika. 106, 102647
Tegg, Thomas. ed. 44592, 93423
Tegg's mariner's marvellous magazine.
   44592, 93423
Tehuantepec Railroad Company. 3480
Tehuantepec Transit Company. 18094
Teixeira, -------. 91538
Teixeira, Domingos. 94593-94594
Teixeira, Jose. supposed author 96752
Texieira de Freitas, Augusto. 68335
Teixeira de Macedo, Joaquim. see Macedo,
   Joaquim Teixeira de.
Teixeira Pinto, Bento. see Pinto, Bento
   Teixeira.
Tejada, Antonio del Monte. see Delmonte y
   Tejada, Antonio, 1783-1861.
Tejada, Antonio Delmonte y. see Delmonte
   y Tejada, Antonio, 1783-1861.
Tejada, Bernardo de. 94596
Tejada, M. M. Lerdo de. see Lerdo de
   Tejada, M. M.
Tejada, Miguel Lerdo de. see Lerdo de
   Tejada, Miguel.
Tejada, Sebastian Lerdo de. see Lerdo de
   Tejada, Sebastian, Pres. Mexico.
   1824-1889.
Tejado, Fran Lerdo de. see Lerdo de
   Tejado, Fran.
Tejas y los Estados-Unidos de America.
   36659, 96208
Tejeda, ------, fl. 1859. 58566
Tejedor. pseud. Para estos lances sirve la
   imprenta; dialogo. 94597
Tejedor. pseud. Signe el tejedor y su com-
   padre. 94598
Tejocote. pseud. Libertad de imprenta.
   99706

Tekel ofte vveech-schale vande groote monarch
   van Spaignien. 31663, 94599
Tela praevisa. 46537
Telaya y Santiso, Luis. 94600
Telegrafo. 48638, 68834
Telegrafo de Guadalajara. 94602
Telegrafo extraordinario. 94603
Telegrafo Habanero y "El liberal." 94604
Telegrafo Megicano. 94605
Telegrafo mercantil. 94606
Telegrafo Mexicano. 94607
Telegrafo. Santiago Viernes 7 de Mayo de
   1819. 94601
Telegraph companion. 79683
Telegraph dictionary, and seamen's signal
   book. 72676
Telegraph manual. (79685)
Telegraph or star-banner song. 16297
Telegraph papers. 89531, 94608
Telegraphic epic for the times. (70973)
Telegraphic union of the old and new worlds.
   65483
Telegrapho Americano. 94609
Telemachus. pseud. Dialogue. 19934, note
   after 94609
Telemachus. pseud. Wonderful narrative.
   94610
Telescope, Timothy. pseud. Philadelphia
   newest almanack for 1776. 62021, note
   after 94610
Telescope (Leominster) 93900
Telescope (New York) 94611
Telescopio Brasiliense nos acores. 94612
Telesforo de Trueba y Cosio, Joaquin. see
   Trueba y Cosio, Joaquin Telesforo de.
Telford, Thomas. 94613
Tell, William. spirit author 1081A, 101770
Tell tale. 61376
Tell Truth, John. pseud. Patriote Anglois.
   see Le Blanc, Jean Bernard. supposed
   author
Tell truth and shame the devil. 94614
Tellechea, Miguel. 94615
Teller, H. W. 89888, note after 94615
Teller, Romanus. 94616
Teller, Thomas. ed. 91537
Teller, William. defendant 94617
Telleria, Manuel. 94618 see also Peru.
   Congreso. Senado. Presidente.
Teller's amusing instructive and entertaining
   tales. 97513
Telles, Baltazar. 36944, 68430
Telles da Silva, Antonio. see Silva, Antonio
   Telles da.
Telles da Silva Caminha e Menezes, Antonio,
   Marquez de Resende, 1790-1875. 81103-
   94619-94620
Telles de Faro, Fernando. 17452, 68494,
   94621-94622 see also Portugal. Lega-
   tion. Netherlands.
Tellez, Fernando. 94623
Tellez, Gabriel, 1571-1648. (49898)
Tellez Calderon, Bernardo. 94624
Tellez Calderon, Jose. 94625
Tellez Carvajal, Pedro. 94626
Telliamed; or, the world explain'd. 43892,
   note after 94626
Telliamed ou entretiens d'un philosophie Indien.
   43891
Tellier, Michel le. see Le Tellier, Michel,
   1643-1719.
Tellier de Courtanvaux, F. C. le. see Le
   Tellier de Courtanvaux, F. C.
Tello, Josef Espinosa y. see Espinosa y
   Tello, Josef.
Tello, Pedro. 94627

Tello de Guzman, Maria. see Guzman, Maria Tello de.
Tello de Guzman y Medina, Juan. 94628
Tello de Mayorga, Francisco Javier. 94630
Tello de Meneses, Francisco. 94631
Telltruth, Timothy. pseud. Collected wisdom. 94632
Telltruth, Timothy. pseud. To Morris Morris. 60671, 94633
Temblores en San Salvador. 76205
Temblores sentido en Guatemala. 41668
Tembra y Simanes, Jose Javier de. 94635-94636
Temixtitla, Mexico. (48387), 98919
Temixtitla, Mexico (Diocese) (48387), 98919
Temoin actif dans ce grand drame de feu. pseud. see Fortunio, Temoin actif dans ce grand drame de feu. pseud.
Temoin oculaire. pseud. Journal historique. see Desevres, F. X. supposed author and Paquin, Jacques. supposed author
Temoin oculaire. pseud. Origine et progres de la mission de Kentucky. see Badin, S. T.
Temoin oculaire. pseud. Rapport. see Junes, John.
Temoinage donne devant un Comite de la Chambre des Communes. 13488
Temoinages du Comite Sepcial de la Cahmbre d'Assemblee du Bas-Canada. 10568
Tempe Argentino. 77130
Tempe Arjentino. 77131
Templehof, Georg Friedrich von, 1737-1807. 41301
Temper, C. G. ed. 94639
Temperance. pseud. Hints to the honest tax payers of Boston. note after 6785, 94640
Temperance address . . . at Runsom, N. J. (58827)
Temperance address, . . . in West Chester, Conn. (50637)
Temperance advocate. 46314
Temperance Alliance, New York. see New York Temperance Alliance.
Temperance Alliance of Massachusetts. see Massachusetts State Temperance Alliance.
Temperance and popery. 9114
Temperance and revivals. 52354
Temperance anecdotes, and interesting facts. 94641
Temperance battle not man's but God's. (44749)
Temperance Beneficial Association, New York. 94642
Temperance Beneficial Association, Southwark, Pa. Female Branch, No. I. 94643
Temperance bill. 91027
Temperance bulletin. 94644
Temperance cause. 26536
Temperance Committee, Boston. 89627
Temperance Committee of Massachusetts. see Massachusetts State Temperance Committee.
Temperance Convention, Augusta, Me., 1852. see State Temperance Convention, Augusta, Me., 1852.
Temperance Convention, Boston, 1835. 6547
Temperance Convention, Boston, 1840. see Massachusetts State Temperance Convention, Boston, 1840.
Temperance Convention, Charleston, 1844. see South Carolina State Temperance Convention, Charleston, 1844.
Temperance Convention, Charleston, 1845. see South Carolina State Temperance Convention, Charleston, 1845.

Temperance Convention, Greenville Court House, S. C., 1842. 88072
Temperance Convention, Harrisburg, Pa., 1842. see State Temperance Convention, Harrisburg, Pa., 1842.
Temperance Convention, Pittsburgh, 1839. 94646
Temperance Convention, Worcester, Mass., 1833. see Massachusetts Temperance Convention, Worcester, 1833.
Temperance Convention, Worcester, Mass., 1852. see Massachusetts Temperance Convention, Worcester, 1852.
Temperance Convention of New York, 1853. see New York State Temperance Convention, 1853.
Temperance. Extracts from an address delivered before . . . the inhabitants of the town of Caroline, N. Y. 89234
Temperance. Gerrit Smith to John Stuart Mill. (82671)
Temperance herald. 94646
Temperance. In which was the convention right? 74611
Temperance journal. 84648
Temperance lecturer; being facts gathered from a personal examination. 12829
Temperance ledger. 94649
Temperance magazine. 87006
Temperance manual. [By Justin Edwards.] 21979
Temperance manual, comprising the constitution of the Westchester County Temperance Society. 102956
Temperance Meeting, Boston, 1867. see Boston. Great Temperance Meeting, Tremont Temple, 1867.
Temperance odes. 98576
Temperance oration. 82973
Temperance organization . . . in Massachusetts. (43977)
Temperance poem. [By McDonald Clarke.] (13435)
Temperance poem; delivered at the anuual meeting. 101372
Temperance prize essays. 94650
Temperance recollections. (44749)
Temperance recorder. 94651
Temperance reform. 94652
Temperance reformation, its history. 2034
Temperance reformation of this XIX century. 2033
Temperance reformation the cause of Christian morals. 28862
Temperance report. 1838. 104767
Temperance sermon . . . December 12, 1847. (43359)
Temperance Society, Albany, N. Y. see Albany City Temperance Society.
Temperance Society, Baltimore. see Baltimore Temperance Society.
Temperance Society, Columbia, S. C. see Columbia Temperance Society, Columbia, S. C.
Temperance Society, Dorchester, Mass. see Dorchester Temperance Society.
Temperance Society, New York. see New York City Temperance Society.
Temperance Society, South Berwick, Me. see South Berwick Temperance Society.
Temperance Society, Worcester, Mass. see Worcester Temperance Society.
Temperance Society, a national institution. 105995
Temperance Society of Columbia, S. C. see Columbia Temperance Society, Columbia, S. C.

Tempore, Disciplus de, Junior. pseud.
 Irenicvm. 35063
Temps. . . . Journal bi-hebdomadaire.
 94672
Temptations of city life. 18139
Temptations of the times. 71523
Tempted Christian triumphing over his
 temptations. 46353
Temps nunc. pseud. Address. 94673
Ten acres enough. 50815, note after 94673
Ten Brink, Barend. see Brink, Barend ten.
Ten Broeck, Abraham. see Broeck, Abraham
 ten.
Ten Broek, Joachim George le Sage. see
 Broek, Joachim George le Sage ten,
 1775-1847.
Ten Eick, Coanrod. 94677
Ten Entel, W. see Entel, W. ten.
Ten Have, J. L. see Have, J. L. ten.
Ten Hoorn, Jan. see Hoorn, Jan ten.
Ten Hove, Michiel. 69587, 5th note after
 102911, 102913
Ten cent novels. 95611
Ten chapters from the story of a life. 89406
Ten chapters in the life of John Hancock.
 31748-(31749), note after 94676, 1st
 note after 105630
Ten colored views taken during the Arctic
 expedition of Sir James C. Ross. 8678
Ten colored views taken during the Arctic
 expedition of the Enterprise. 73366
Ten commandments, the Lord's prayer.
 44123
Ten commandments, the Lord's prayer, etc.
 67764
Ten days in the Tombs. 43275
Ten fac-simile reproductions relating to New
 England. 94172, 96153-96154, 104653
Ten facsimile reproductions relating to old
 Boston. 95192, 104110
Ten hints addressed to wise men. (31970),
 42449, 94678, 4th note after 98684
Ten hours in New York! 68489
Ten letters, addressed to the taxpayers of
 England. 13882
Ten letters on the church and church estab-
 lishments. 96371
Ten letters on the subject of slavery. 70857
Ten letters to a niece. 92370
Ten minutes before three. 101092
Ten months among the tents of the Tuski.
 (32883)
Ten months at the south. 83506
Ten months in Brazil. Notes on the Para-
 guayan War. 14141
Ten months in Brazil: with incidents of voy-
 ages and travels. (14140)
Ten months in Libby Prison. 11717
Ten months residence in the United States.
 19228
Ten months with the 153d Penn'a Volunteers.
 81144
Ten particvlar rules to be practice. 32834-
 32835
Ten precepts to his second son, Robert Cecil.
 90233, 90236-90237, 90246
Ten sermons composed by himself. 31243
Ten sermons preached on various important
 subjects. 103597
Ten thousand American citizens robbed.
 (64967)
Ten thousand Christians invited to protest.
 24610
Ten tribes of Israel historically identified.
 81283
Ten years a Methodist preacher. 8393, 45422

Ten years among the mail bags. 32447
Ten years in Oregon. By D. Lee and J. H.
 Frost. (39724)
Ten years in Oregon. Travels and adventures
 of Doctor E. White and lady. 781,
 103377
Ten years in the United States. 49671
Ten years in Wall Street. (25332)
Ten years' ministry. 64670
Ten years of colportage in America. 1249
Ten years of experience. (6704), 81912
Ten years of my life. 75811
Ten years of preacher life. 48919
Ten years of the world's progress. 66801
Ten years' parochial work in the tropics.
 30979
Ten years' progress. 62304
Ten years' record of the "Republican" Party.
 26712, 81716-81717
Ten-year's resident. pseud. Emigrant's guide.
 98075
Ten years' services in the navy of the United
 States. 9187
Ten years' work among the Tsimshean Indians.
 21264, 47174
Tenant houses. 21156
Tenant of the spring. 103491
Tence, Ulysse. ed. 40234
Tendencies of the age to peace. 906
Tendencies of the principles . . . and system.
 51157
Tendency of evil speaking against rulers.
 79803
Tendency of infidelity and Christianity con-
 trasted. (24711)
Tendency of religious obedience to promote
 national prosperity. 17640
Tendency of the Christian religion to promote
 genuine liberty. 31859
Tender heart pleasing to God. (79432)
Tender husband. 88605
Tendilla, Antonio de Mendoza, Conde de. see
 Mendoza, Antonio de, Conde de Tendilla.
Tenderness to mothers. 86825
¿Tenemos constitucion? 94679
Teneriffe. 39300
Tenesles, Nicola. 94680-94682
Tenison, Thomas, Archbishop of Canterbury,
 1636-1715. 28230
Tennant, Charles. 79132, 94683-94684
Tennant, John. see Tennent, John, fl. ca.
 1700-ca. 1760.
Tennent, Charles. 40455, 47276, 65149,
 (78736), 97107, 103622 see also Eighteen
 Presbyterian Ministers, in America.
Tennent, Gilbert, 1703-1764. 21664, 30172,
 40455, 47276, 62419, 65149, 67117,
 69400, (78736), 79292, 82872-82873,
 83794-83795, 83800, 90595-95096, 84685-
 84709, 94719, 95744, 97107, 103515,
 103593-103594, 103597, 3d note after
 103650 see also Eighteeen Presbyterian
 Ministers, in America.
Tennent, John, fl. ca. 1700-ca. 1760. 23299,
 24459, 94710-94717
Tennent, John, 1706-1732. 83800, 97405-97406
Tennent, William, 1740-1777. 40455, 47276,
 65149, (78736), 79292, 83800, 94709,
 94718-94719, 95744, 97107 see also
 Eighteen Presbyterian Ministers, in
 America.
Tennessean. pseud. Plan for abolishing the
 American Anti-slavery Society. 81729
Tennessean. 73825
Tennessean abroad. 26775, 43257
Tennessee (Franklin Governmental District)
 Constitution. 94720

TENNESSEE

Tennessee (Franklin Governmental District)
    Constitutional Convention, Greeneville,
    1785. 94720
Tennessee (Franklin Governmental District)
    Declaration of Rights. 94720
Tennessee (Territory) petitioners note after
    94720
Tennessee (Territory) Charter. note after
    94720
Tennessee (Territory) General Assembly.
    94777
Tennessee (Territory) General Assembly.
    House of Representatives. 94721-94722
Tennessee (Territory) General Assembly.
    Legislative Council. 94723-94724,
    94777
Tennessee (Territory) Governor. 94777
Tennessee (Territory) Governor, 1790-1796
    (Blount) 69834, note after 94720, 94725
    see also Blount, William, 1749-1800.
Tennessee (Territory) Judges. 94777
Tennessee (Territory) Laws, statutes, etc.
    94764, 94765, 94777
Tennessee. (19178), 37577, (47286), 69859
Tennessee. plaintiffs 25694
Tennessee. Assistant Inspector General.
    94761 see also Hays, Robert.
Tennessee. Commissioner of Immigration.
    6177 see also Bokum, Hermann.
Tennessee. Commissioners on the Boundary
    Line with Kentucky. 37547
Tennessee. Constitution. 1269, 1271, 2071,
    5316, 6360, 16097, 16099-16103, 16107,
    16113, 16133, 25790, 33137, (34358),
    (47188), 59771, (66397), 82422, 94726-
    94730, 94731, 94777, 104198
Tennessee. Constitutional Convention, Knoxville,
    1796. 94728, 94731
Tennessee. Court of Errors and Appeals.
    94737
Tennessee. Department of Education. Division
    of Library and Archives. 94750
Tennessee. East Tennessee College. see
    Tennessee. University.
Tennessee. East Tennessee University. see
    Tennessee. University.
Tennessee. Evangelical Lutheran Synod. see
    Evangelical Luthern Tennessee Synod.
Tennessee. General Assembly. 23382, 37577,
    69859, 94722-94724, 94745, 94785,
    94803
Tennessee. General Assembly. petitioners
    94744-94745
Tennessee. General Assembly. House of
    Representatives. 94746-94748, 94750
Tennessee. General Assembly. Senate.
    94749-94751
Tennessee. Governor, 1796-1801 (Sevier)
    94745, 94752-94756 see also Sevier,
    John, 1745-1815.
Tennessee. Governor, 1803-1809 (Sevier)
    94757 see also Sevier, John, 1745-
    1815.
Tennessee. Governor, 1809-1815 (Blount)
    33150, 94758-94761 see also Blount,
    Willie, 1768-1835.
Tennessee. Governor, 1845-1847 (Brown)
    see also Brown, Aaron Venable, 1795-
    1859.
Tennessee. Governor, 1857-1862 (Harris)
    23372, 33150, 37577, 69859 see also
    Harris, Isham Green, 1818-1897.
Tennessee. Governor, 1865-1869. (Brownlow)
    (8707) see also Brownlow, William
    Gannaway, 1805-1877.

Tennessee. High Court of Impeachment.
    25694
Tennessee. Laws, statutes, etc. 11171, 23765,
    31087, 39414, (34358), (47778), 51870,
    52051, 70820-70821, 82438, 89066, 94762-
    94763, 94766-94772, 94773-94782, 94784,
    94785-94786, 94812, note after 97760
Tennessee. Legislature. see Tennessee.
    General Assembly.
Tennessee. Militia. 94783, 94784-94786
Tennessee. State Library. 94750
Tennessee. State Reporter. see also Sneed,
    John Louis Taylor, 1820-1901.
Tennessee. Superior Courts of Law & Equity.
    94734-94735
Tennessee. Supreme Court of Errors and
    Appeals. 94732-74933, 94735-94736,
    94738-94739
Tennessee. Union Bank. see Union Bank of
    Tennessee. and Union Bank of the State
    of Tennessee.
Tennessee. University. 94740
Tennessee. University. Board. 94742
Tennessee. University. President and Trus-
    tees. petitioners 94743
Tennessee and her bondage. 85378
Tennessee Association of Baptists. see
    Baptists. Tennessee. Tennessee Associ-
    ation.
Tennessee Company. 94806-94807
Tennessee Company to Messrs. Strawbridge
    Jackson and Dexter. 94807
Tennessee farmer. 94808
Tennessee farmer: or, farmer Jackson in New-
    York. 35391, 94809
Tennessee gazette. 94770
Tennessee gazette. see Democratic clarion
    and Tennessee gazette.
Tennessee gazetteer, or topographical diction-
    ary. 50811
Tennessee handbook and immigrant's guide.
    6177
Tennessee historical magazine. 94785
Tennessee Historical Society. 94750
Tennessee history for boys and girls. (58986)
Tennessee letters. 94810
Tennessee Manumission Society. see Manu-
    mission Society of Tennessee.
Tennessee Medical Society. see Medical
    Society of the State of Tennessee.
Tennessee (North-America) gefundenen Fossilen
    knochen des Megalonyx Lagueatus.
    30389
Tennessee quarterly. 94720
Tennessee reports. 95378, 94734-94735
Tennessee state gazette. see Clarion and
    Tennessee state gazette.
Tennesseean. pseud. Abolitionism exposed,
    corrected. 91729
Tennesseean. pseud. Christian advocate. see
    Haywood, John. supposed author
Tenney, Caleb Jewett, 1870-1847. 94815
Tenney, Francis V. 44203
Tenney, Samuel. 94815
Tenney, Tabitha Gilman. 94816
Tenney, William J. ed. 49223
Tenney. firm publishers see Carpenter &
    Tenney. firm publishers
Tenny, Joseph. 61064, 94817
Tennyson, Alfred Tennyson, 1st Baron, 1809-
    1892. 83876
Tenorio, Danres Arias. 86408
Tenorio, Francisco Joseph Caldas y. see
    Caldas y Tenorio, Francisco Joseph.
Tenorio, Gonzalo. 94818-94819

Tenorio Carvajal, Tomas. 94820
Tensas, Madison. pseud. Old leaves. see Lewis, Henry Clay.
Tensas, Madison. pseud. Swamp Doctor's adventures. see Lewis, Henry Clay.
Tent pitch'd. 104504, 104509
Tentamen florae Brasiliensis. 29512
Tentamen medicum inaugurale. 92006
Tentativa del Pensador en favor del Canonigo San-Martin. 94823
Tentivas para la pacificacion de la republica Oriental del Uruguay. 38719
Tenth and eleventh annual discourses after the half-century. 42007
Tenth anniversary of the North Reformed Dutch Church. 54884
Tenth annual address to the Convention of the Protestant Episcopal Church in Pennsylvania. 64617
Tenth annual meeting . . . Paris, Ill., May 8th and 9th, 1860. 34265
Tenth annual report . . . see Report . . .
Tenth baccalaureate . . . [in Miami University.] (36934)
[Tenth letter to the Rev. Samuel Miller.] (49063)
Tenth muse lately sprung up in America. 7296, note after 94832
Tenth Presbyterian Church, Philadelphia. see Philadelphia. Tenth Presbyterian Church.
Tenting on the old camp ground. 83677
Tenure of office. . . . Government House, Halifax, N. S. 56195
Tenure-of-office law. Speech . . . March 29, 1869. 18818
Tenure-of-office law. Speech of Hon. Edmund G. Ross. 73352
Teodoro Parker ossia Cristianesimo e patriottismo estratto dalla riforma del secolo XIX. 58762
Teologal discurso y reflexion piadosa. (73044)
Teologo imparcial. pseud. Respuesta. see San Bartolome, Jose de.
Teomoxtli o libro que contiene todo lo interesante. 9570
Teone: or the magic maid. 83545
Teoria de un sistema administrativo y economica por la republica de Chile. 12807
Teoria de un sistema administrativo y economico para la republica de Chile. 94825
Teotamachilizti inyiuliliz auh iny miquiliz tu Temaquizticatzim Iesu Christo. 94826
Tepeyac, Juan Diego del. 94827
Tepic, Mexico. Ayuntamiento. 94828
Tepiton teotlatolli. 20421
Tepotzotlan, Mexico. Real Colegio Seminario. 30411
Tequenos encausados ante S. E. la Corte Superior y al publico. 94829
Teques, Venezuela. see Los Teques, Venezuela.
Ter Beck, J. see Beck, J. ter.
Ter gelegenheid van het beloofd en gewijgerd convo convoy naar de West-Indien. 94830
Ter ordonnantie van de Hove. 93847
Teran, Jose Maria. 44540, 94831
Teran, Juan Francisco. 94832
Teran, Manuel de Mier y. see Mier y Teran, Manuel de.
Teran de Gonzalez, Antonio. supposed author 68789, 94833
Teran de la Torre, Antonio. 94834
Teran Rubin, Pedro de. 94835
Tercentenary Celebration of the Birth of Shakespeare, Boston, 1864. see

New-England Historic-Genealogical Society, Boston. Tercentenary Celebration of the Birth of Shakespeare, 1864.
Tercentenary celebration of the birth of Shakespeare. 80322
Ter-centenary celebration of the Birth of William Shakespeare, Lowell, Mass., 1864. 42493
Tercer amonestacion al Muy Reverendo Padre Fray "Americano." 94836
Tercer manifiesto de D. Gabriel Claudio Sequeira. 1885
Tercer Orden de los Siervos de Maria Santisima de los Dolores, Mexico (City) (68897), note after 94835
Tercer sermon de un padre santo. 93448
Tercera Brigada del Ejercito Mexicano. 67865
Tercera carta del Venrable Siervo de Dios Don Juan de Palafox y Mendoza. 58307
Tercera carta pastoral del Illmo. Sr. Arzobispo de Mexico. 26719
Tercera guia judicial. 48906
Tercera Inglesia de terceros dominicos. 99729
Tercera Junta Publica de la Real Sociedad Economica de Guatemala. 29085
Tercera noticia de la segunda parte. 81286
Tercera parte de "Clamor de la justicia." 98959
Tercera parte de la Pajarotada. 94837
Tercera parte de los veinte i vn libros rituales i monarchia Indiana. 96212
Terceras observaciones. 48264
Tercero cathecismo y exposicion de la doctrina Christiana. 94838
Tercero por antonomisia o rey tres veces coronado. 93346
Tercerta Junta Publica de la Real Sociedad Economica de Amantes de la Patria de Guatemala. 85749
Terence Sweep. pseud. see Sweep, Terence. pseud.
Terencio, -----. 94839
Terentius Phlogobombos. pseud. see Judah, Samuel B. H.
Teresa de Chantal. Sister 56853
Teresa, Gio. Giuseppe de S. see Santa Teresa, Giovanni Gioseppe di.
Teresa, Giovanni Gioseppe di Santa. see Santa Teresa, Giovanni Gioseppe di.
Teresa, Luis de Santa. see Santa Teresa, Luis de.
Teresa. Novel original. 99692
Terhune, Mary Virginia Hawes. 94840
Terminacao da soie lade e do seguro de loterias. 88715
Termination of the Pennsylvania Rail Way. 60358
Termino de la cuestion. 11408
Termometro de la opinion. 97375
Terms, condition, and circumstances. 97933
Terms of admission, course of studies, expenses, &c. 102002
Terms of contract between the state of Nicaragua, and the Atlantic & Pacific Ship Canal Company. (55162)
Terms of enlistment of the officers and seamen. 94841
Terms of peace. A sermon at the dedication of the Church. (14532), 14535
Terms of peace. Remarks of Hon. Wm. H. Seward. 79530
Terms of peace. Speech of William H. Seward. 79529, (79531)

Terms of treaties hereafter to be made with certain tribes of Indians. 57656

Ternaux, Guillaume Louis. 94842

Ternaux, L.-G. see Ternaux, Guillaume Louis.

Ternaux-Compans, Henri. 994, 2860, (7559), 9574, 9767, 9770, 11140, 11379, 20888, 23997-(23998), 24854, 24894, 29182, 35319-35320, 43794-(43795), 50126, 2d note after 51715, (57186), 57996, 77686, 91287, 86231, 87205-87206, 90059, 94843-94856, 95146, 98647, 98793, note after 99605, 99728, 105725, 106401, 106405

Teron y Prieto, Jose de. 94857

Terquem, P. A. 46970

Terra Rossa, Vitale. 94858

Terra Australis cognita. (8388), 10053, 89452, 1st note after 94857, note after 99383C

Terra Australis incognita. 67357-(67358)

Terra beata. (46539), 2d note after 94857

Terra Mariae. 52288

Terracina, Miguel. tr. 65407

Terrada, Carlos. 94859

Terrae Sanctae, qvam Palaestinum nominant. 106331

Terrain carbonifere dans l'Amerique du Nord. 44504

Terralla y Landa, Esteban de. 2503-2504, 41117, 94860-94863

Terranoua, Estefana Cortes, Duquesa de. see Cortes, Estefana, Duquesa de Terranoua.

Terrasa y Rejon, Dionisio. 94864

Tarraube, Louis Antoine Marie Victor de, Marquis Galard de. see Galard de Terraube, Louis Antoine Marie Victor de, Marquis, 1765-1840.

Terrazas, Matias. 94867, 94868-94873

Terre Australe connue. 74819

Terre chaude, scenes de moeurs Mexicaines. 5141

Terre et l'homme ou apercu historique de geologie. (46975)

Terre promise. 39580

Terre temperee, scenes, de la vie Mexicaine. 5142

Terrell, W. H. H. 34526, (34557), 34563 see also Indiana. Adjutant General. Indiana. Financial Secretary.

Terremoto de Cuba. 93394

Terremotos. (56731)

Terrentius, Joannes. (31515)-31516

Terrero, Leopoldo. 89285

Terreros Ochoa, Antonio. 94874

Terreros Ochoa, Antonio. plaintiff 94874

Terreros y Trebuesto, Maria Michaela Romero de, Marquesa de San Francisco. defendant. 76223

Terres dans l'Amerique Septentrionale. 96173

Terres d'or. 4903F

Terres situees dans les Comtes de Jefferson et de Lewis. 55985

Terrestrial air-breathing mollusks of the United States. 5467

Terrestrial air-breathing mollusks of the United States, and the adjacent territories of North America. 5505

Terrett, --------. plaintiff 31669

Terri, D. J. 58566

Terri, D. J. M. 58566

Terribilia Dei. 46540

Terrible calamities that are occasioned by war. 94347-84349

Terrible mysteries of the Ku-Klux-Klan. 20360

Terrible tractoration!! 24213, 24218-24219, note after 94875

Terrible tragedy at Washington 41233

Terrible transactions at the seat of the muses. 30755, 59539

Terribles cargos contra el Ministro Poinsett. 94876

Terrick, John, successively Bishop of Peterborough, and London, 1710-1777. 94877

Terrien, --------. 56471

Terriere, Pierre de Salles la. see La Terriere, Pierre de Salles.

Terriere, Peter de Sales la. see Sales la Terriere, Peter de.

Terrific register. 94878

Territorial abstractions ignored. 29605

Territorial company, Philadelphia. (63287), 94879

Territorial government in Oregon. (29856)

Territorial governments. 5454

Territorial legislation in Wisconsin. 92950

Territorial limits of the Iroquois. 54476

Territorial obstructions ingnored as now immaterial. (81814)

Territorial policy. Speech. 28553

Territorial question . . . in the Senate. 19003

Territorial question. Speech . . . in the House. 21110

Territorial rights of New York. 1st note after 98997

Territorial slave policy. 22175

Territorial slave question. (81907)

Territories of Kansas and Nebraska. (49834)

Territories. Speech . . . delivered in the Senate. 11349

Territory of Florida. 104284

Territory of New Mexico and its resources. 43886

Territory of the United States, North-West of the River Ohio. see Northwest Territory, U. S.

Territory of the United States, South of the River Ohio. see Tennessee (Territory)

Territory of Wyoming. 9327

Terrones, Lorenzo de. petitioner 94885

Terror of the Lord. (46541), note after 94885

Terror of the west. 66942

Terroristes de S. Domingue denounces. 94886

Terrors of the pestilence. 92272

Terrors of the storm at Barbadoes. (42634)

Terrors of war, and the consequence thereof. 94887

Terrours of hell demonstrated. 46572

Terry, Adrian Russell. 94888

Terry, Alfred. 105883

Terry, David Smith. defendant 94889

Terry, Edward. 66686

Terry, Ellen F. 76663, 86316

Terry, Ellwood. 16922

Terry, Ezekiel. 94890-94893, note after 101884, 103093

Terry, John Orville. 94894

Terry, Money. pseud. New Bedford money matters. see Congdon, James B.

Tersteegen, Gerhard, 1797-1769. 72590

Tertia Ferdinandi Cortesii Sac. Caesar. et Cath. Maiesta. 16948

Tertiary formation of Alabama. (39486)

Tertiary invertebrate fossils. 10008

Tertre, Jean Baptiste du. see Du Tertre, Jean Baptiste.

Tertulia de Don Sirindico. 97041

Tertulia de la aldea. 94895

Tertulia de la Havana. 98147

Tertullian. 94093

Teruel, Juan Diego. 94896
Terwecoren, Edouard. 82260, 92263, 92271
Terza parte delle historie dell' Indie. 13052
Terza relatione di Fernando Cortese. 67740
Terzo volvme delle navigationi et viaggi.
  16951
Terzo volvme delle navigationi et viaggi nel
  qvale si contengono la nauigationi al
  Mondo Nuouo. 67740
Terzo volvme delle navigationi et viaggi rac-
  colto gia da M. Gio. Gattista Ramvsio.
  67741
Teschemacher, J. E. 45862
Tesillo, Santiago de. 94897-94899
Tesis sobre la libre navegacion de los rios.
  11029
Tesora de medicina y de las plantas de la
  Nueva Espana. 41980
Tesorero actual de la benditas animas. 98948
Tesorero de esta case de moneda. 98344
Tesoro. 74039
Tesoro catequistico Indiano. 24321
Tesoro de comerciantes. 9044
Tesoro de la Iglesia Catolica. 86393
Tesoro de la lengua Castellana o Espanola.
  57647
Tesoro de la lengva Gvarani. 74027, 74037
Tesoro de la lengva Gvarani, segvnda parte.
  74027
Tesoro de la virtud. 9815
Tesoro de medecina. 42578, 75605
Tesoro escondido en el campo fertil. 73182
Tesoro Guarani-Espanol. 74039
Tesoro Guarani (o Tupi)-Espanol. (74041)
Tesoro Peruano. 94900
Tesoros verdaderos de la Unidas en la
  historia. 47423
Tessan, U. de. 21354
Test of experience. 31968
Test of friendship. (68538)
Test of the religious principles of Thomas
  Jefferson. 35934
Testacea novissima insulae Cubanae et Ameri-
  cae Centralis. 50594
Testament de mort d'oge. 94901
Testament nutak. 22873
Testament politique de l'Angleterre. 94902
Testamentaria de D. M. Ajuria. plaintiff
  (67640), 67643
Testamentaria de la Sra. Dona Maria Teresa
  Castaneda de Basoco. 98823
Testamentaria de la Senora Dona Teresa
  Castanza de Bascoso. 99687
Testamentaria del Presbytero D. Sib. Lecaros.
  plaintiff 26208
Testamente nutak. 22041
Testamente nutak kaladlin okauzennut nukter-
  simarsok. (22874)
Testamentetak tamedsa nalegapta piulijipta.
  22875
Testamentitokab. Makpersegejsa illanoet
  Mosesim. 28657
Testamentitokab. Profetib mingnerit Danieliblo
  agleit. (28658)
Testamentitokamit. 22868
Testamentitokamit Mosesim aglegij siurdleet.
  22852
Testamentitokamet profetib Esaisim aglegij
  okauzeenut N. G. W. 22870
Testamentitokamet Salomonis ajokaersutej
  erkairseksaet okauzeenut. 22869
Testamento codicilo. 94903
Testamento de D. Francisco de la Parra.
  (58837)
Testamento de la Federacion Mexicana.
  48661

Testamento del ano de 1839. 94904
Testamento del difunto. 94905
Testamento del difunto del ano de 1840.
  94906
Testamento del gallo. 94907
Testamento del gato. 94908
Testamento del General D. Juan Fernandez de
  la Fuente. 74858
Testamento del Jeneral Francisco Morazan.
  50527
Testamento del Pare Arenas y nueva noticia de
  los conspiradores. 99721
Testamento del Padre Arenas, y verdadera
  noticia. 99720
Testamento enforma. (40080)
Testamento hecho por un pobre que se canso
  de serlo. 94910-94911
Testamento, y benedicion, que dexo a sus
  hijas. 11461
Testamento y codicilo de Cristo Ntro. Sr.
  (75564)
Testigo ocular. pseud. Terremoto de Cuba.
  see Alvarez, M.
Testigos oculares. pseud. Noticias sobre los
  sitios. 56016
Testimonial Dinner to Henry C. Carey, Phila-
  delphia, 1859. 10841, note after 94911
Testimonial dinner to Joseph Green Cogswell.
  14218
Testimonial of members of the medical pro-
  fession. 51032
Testimonial of mercantile and manufacturing
  houses. 82575
Testimonial of merchants and manufacturers.
  (82573)
Testimonial of respect of the bar of Chicago.
  44261
Testimonial of respect of the bar of New York.
  (20032)
Testimonial of respect to the memory of
  Abbott Lawrence. 73977
Testimonial of respect to the memory of
  General Washington. 86126
Testimonial to Col. Rush C. Hawkins. (30959)
Testimonial to the editor of the Knickerbocker
  magazine. 38098
Testimonial to the memory of General Wash-
  ington. 13131
Testimonials presented by Alfred Stille. 91783
Testimonials, submitted to the consideration
  of the Trustees [of the University of
  Pennsylvania.] 60758
Testimonials . . . submitted to the Trustees
  of the University of Pennsylvania.
  (30369)
Testimonials in favor of the plan of Horace H.
  Day. 18968
Testimonials of respect ot the memory of
  John Quincy Adams. 323
Testimonials to Henry C. Carey. 10841, note
  after 94911
Testimonials to the life and character of the
  late Francis Jackson. 35409
Testimonials to the merits of Thomas Paine.
  50567
Testimonies and cases by eminent physicians
  and surgeons. 94912
Testimonies and depositions of His Majesty's
  Officers. 2451
Testimonies. . . . By William Penn. 59722
Testimonies concerning slavery. 16222
Testimonies concerning the character and
  ministry of Mother Ann Lee. 102603
Testimonies in favor of the Amherstburg
  Missionary Society. 1335
Testimonies of Capt. John Brown. 8522

TESTIMONIES

Testimonies of his [i. e. Anthony J. Bleecker's] devotions. (5898)

Testimonies of many persons in Bolton. 360, 6254, 11968, 3d note after 96741

Testimonies of the life, character, revelations and doctrines of our ever blessed mother Ann Lee. 102602

Testimonio autorizado. 94913

Testimonio avtentico. 98766

Testimonio de la sentencia que dio. 98154

Testimonio de P.-Fr.-Bernardino Sahagun. 9567

Testimonio del sumario instruido en Cocha-bamba. 94914

Testimonios de los titulos antiguos de Costa-Rica. (49880)

Testimonios relativos de legitimadad. 94915

Testimony. . . . A sermon preached at the re-opening of the church of Augustus. 51256

Testimony against Elias Hicks. 40802, 53779

Testimony against evil customs. 46542, 94916

Testimony against John Fenwick. 24082

Testimony against prophaneness in Philadelphia. 88266

Testimony against several prophane and superstitious customs. 46752

Testimony against that false and absurd opinion. 37186, (37221), (37225)

Testimony against the antichristian practice. 14305

Testimony against the corruptions of the market-place. (46545), note after 95317

Testimony against the fashionable vice of swearing. 1845

Testimony against the prophaneness of some of the public disputes. 17675

Testimony against the publications of Marcus. 105142

Testimony and advice of a number of laymen. 94917

Testimony and advice of an Assembly of Pastors of Churches in New-England. 16199, 94918, 4th note after 103650

Testimony and brief of facts, etc. (33466)

Testimony and caution to such as do make a profession of faith. 86068, note after 94918

Testimony, and epistle of advice. 34498, 70194

Testimony and exhibits. 58611

Testimony and practice of the Presbyterian Church. 72118

Testimony and warning given forth in the love of truth. 24012

Testimony before Coroner's Jury. 57253

Testimony before the Harper's Ferry Committee. 1476

Testimony before the Select Committee to Inquire Into the Alleged Frauds in Army Contracts. (60663)

Testimony concerning our dear and wellbeloved friend. (13817)

Testimony concerning the life, death, trials, travels, and labours of Edward Burroughs. 33364

Testimony deliver'd to the people in Philadelphia Market. 102576

Testimony finished by Dr. Increase Mather. (49658)

Testimony for prosecution and defence in the case of Edward Spangler. 88935

Testimony from the Monthly Meeting of Friends of Jericho. 31718, note before 94920

Testimony from the scripture against idolatry & superstition. 46787

Testimony given forth from our Monthly-Meeting, held at Philadelphia. 94920

Testimony in favour of Judson. 56050

Testimony in reference to charges of corruption. 63126

Testimony in the case of the Rev. Mr. Jones. (36465)

Testimony in the Forrest divorce case. 25112

Testimony in the Forrest divorce case. Verbatim report. 25113

Testimony of a club convened at Boston. 6563, 94924

Testimony of a number of ministers conven'd at Taunton, in the county of Bristol, March 5. 1744, 5. (22007), 94921, note after 103533, 5th note after 103650

Testimony of a number of ministers in the county of Bristol. 94923

Testimony of a number of New England ministers. 94922, note after 103402

Testimony of a refugee from East Tennessee. 6178

Testimony of a thousand witnesses. 102547

Testimony of Alexander H. Stephens. 51993

Testimony of an association of ministers convened at Marlborough. 94923

Testimony of an association or club of laymen. 9563, 94924

Testimony of an escaped novice. 9183

Testimony of atheists. 74377

Testimony of Burlington Monthly Meeting. 91249

Testimony of Captain Charles H. Davis. 18807

Testimony of Charles H. Dalton. 83856

Testimony of Christ's second appearing. 18608, 79723-79727, note after 94924, note after 97880, note after 106196

Testimony of Clear Lake Monthly Meeting. 57745

Testimony of conscience a most solid foundation for rejoicing. 18268

Testimony of Drs. Salisbury and Swinburne. (39716)

Testimony of Francis M. Fowler and Evan Poultney. 45079

Testimony of Gen. Hancock. 36781

Testimony of God against slavery: a collection of passages from the Bible. 93762

Testimony of God against slavery, or a collection of passages from the Bible. 82203, 93761

Testimony of God against slavery: with notes. 93763

Testimony of his call to that service. 72199

Testimony of Nine-Partners Monthly Meeting of Friends. 95625

Testimony of Purchase Monthly Meeting. 28815

Testimony of southern witnesses. 50314-50315

Testimony of the civilized nations against slavery. 93762

Testimony of the Father's love unto all that desire after Him. 13815

Testimony of the gentleman at College. 99827

Testimony of the Monthly Meeting of Friends, at Prymont. 59615, 94925

Testimony of the Monthly Meeting of Friends in Philadelphia. 97059

Testimony of the New York Association of Friends. 32996, 44685

Testimony of the North Association in the country of Hartford. 94926, 6th note after 103650

Testimony of the pastors of the churches in the province of the Massachusetts-Bay in New England. 26831, 46160, 94927

Testimony of the people called Quakers, given forth by a meeting of the representatives of the said people in Pennsylvania. 21632

Testimony of the people called Quakers, given forth by a meeting of the representatives of the said people, in Pennsylvania and New-Jersey. 94928

Testimony of the President, Professors, Tutors, and Hebrew Instructor of Harvard College. (30764), 1st note after 94928, 103566

Testimony of the religious society of Friends, against slavery. 86069, 2d note after 94928

Testimony of the Rev. J. Thorpe. 95654

Testimony of the Society of Friends, on the continent of America. 86070, 3d note after 94928

Testimony of the two witnesses. 2632

Testimony of the truth. (60663)

Testimony of Washington, and of the Congress of 1776. 94929, 2d note after 101745

Testimony of William G. Read. 45079

Testimony . . . on the causes of the decadents of American tonnage. (47352)

Testimony on the wrongs of the Negro in Jamaica. 41298

Testimony relating to the great election frauds of 1838. 94930

Testimony taken before a Committee of the House of Delegates. 45375

Testimony taken before a Special Committee of the House of Delegates. 45376

Testimony taken before the Committee of Grievances and Courts of Justice. 94931

Testimony taken before the Committee of Privileges and Elections. 42397

Testimony taken before the Joint Committee of the Legislature. 45233

Testimony taken by the Joint Select Committee. 78314

Testimony taken before the Select Committee. 60665

Testimony taken before the Senate Committee in the matte of bridging the Hudson at Albany. 33528

Testimony taken before the Senate, on charges against John F. Smyth. 85242

Testimony taken before the Special Committee of the House of Delegates. 2992

Testimony taken before the United States Revenue Commission. 17132

Testimony taken by the Committee appointed by the House. 60666

Testimony taken by the Committee of the House of Delegates. 45084

Testimony taken . . . in the investigation of charges. 36180

Testimony to the cause of God. 31743

Testimony to the 4[th.] paper presented. 104336

Testimony to the order of the Gospel. 31746, (46789), 94932, 104900

Testimony to the people called Quakers. 104547

Testimony to the said fourth paper. 104336

Testimony to the truth as it is in Jesus. 70896

Testimony to the truth of God. 59737

Testis. pseud. Expose and review of the vindication. 94933

Testman, Peter. 94934

Testory, -------. 78908

Tests of divine inspiration. (23152)

Tete-plate. 12570

Tetherington, ---------. supposed author 90589

Tetlow, Richard John. 94935

Teton Indians. Treaties, etc. 96640

Teucro duce nil desperandum. 60662

Teutsche Pilgrim. 60667

Teutschen Geringen Handwercks Mann. pseud. Klare und gewisse Wahrheit. (38036)

Teutschen Gesellschaft in Philadelphia. see Deutsche Gesellschaft von Pennsylvanien, Philadelphia.

Teutshcen und die Amerikaner. (31246)

Tevebaugh, -------. petitioner 75019

Tevet, Andrea. see Thevet, Andre.

Tevius, Jacobius. 27691, 51646

Tew, --------. defendant 32182, (32197)

Tewksbury, Mass. State Alms House. see Massachusetts. State Alms House, Tewksbury.

Texada, J. Lerdo de. see Lerdo de Texada, J.

Texada, J. Prudencio Moreno de. see Moreno de Texada, J. Prudencio.

Tedaxa, Manuel Saenz de. see Saenz de Texada, Manuel.

Texada y Guzman, Juan de. 94936

Texan. pseud. Brief remarks on Dr. Channing's letter to Henry Clay. 11913

Texan. pseud. Life of Monroe Edwards. (21980)

Texan emigrant. 91726-91727, note after 95104

Texan Emigration and Land Company. 94937

Texan revolution. 12702, note after 94937, note just before 95113

Texas (Mexican State) see Coahuila and Texas (Mexican State)

Texas (Provisional Government) Army. 94541

Texas (Provisional Government) Constitution. 30694, note after 94951

Texas (Provisional Government) Consultation, Austin, 1835. 94952-94953

Texas (Provisional Government) Declaration of Independence. 94954-94955, 94974, 94976, 94994, 95114

Texas (Provisional Government) General Council. 94957-94959

Texas (Provisional Government) Governor, 1835-1836 (Smith) 94957 see also Smith Henry, 1784-1851.

Texas (Provisional Government) Laws, statutes, etc. 2427, note before 94938, note after 94951, 94957, 94959, 94994

Texas (Provisional Government) Secretary of State. 94959

Texas (Republic) 15082, 26885, 85455, 94965, 95074, 103113

Texas (Republic) Adjutant General. 94960

Texas (Republic) Army. 94961, 95017, 95057-95059

Texas (Republic) Army. Commander in Chief. 33189, 94961 see also Houston, Samuel, 1793-1863.

Texas (Republic) Attorney General. 95009 see also Birdsall, John.

Texas (Republic) Board of Travelling Commissioners. see Texas (Republic) Travelling Commissioners for Detection of Fraudulent Land Certificates.

Texas (Republic) Commissioner of the General Land Office. see Texas (Republic) General Land Office. Commissioner.

Texas (Republic) Congress. 50350, 94960, 94962, 94965, 94970, 94982, 94988, 95004, 95010-95011, 95015, 95018-95019,

Texas et sa revolution. 39652
Texas. Extract of a letter from a western citizen. 95116
Texas; extracts from the address of John Quincy Adams. 311
Texas gazette. 94944
Texas. Geschildert in Beziehung auf seine geographischen, socialen und urbrigen Verhaltnisse. 10898
Texas heroes. 37627
Texas Historical Association. see Texas State Historical Association.
Texas im Jahre 1848. 7161
Texas in 1850. 67885
Texas in 1840. 95091, 95122
Texas in 1824. 95122
Texas in sein wahres Licht gestellt. 101208
Texas: its claims to be recognized as an independent power. 78154
Texas: its geography, natural history, and topography. 37441
Texas Land Company. see Galveston Bay & Texas Land Company.
Texas. Mit besonderer Rucksicht. 72593
Texas. Observations, historical, geographical and descriptive. (32528)
Texas, or an answer to the objections. 95123 '
Texas, ou notice historique sur le Champ d' Asile. 30706
Texas Pacific Railroad. Speech of Hon. E. D. Standiford. 90165
Texas pan-handle. 24665
Texas. [Par H. Castro.] 11453
Texas; par Theodore Barbey. 3336
Texas question discussed by prominent individuals. 95124
Texas question, reviewed by an adopted American citizen. 95125
Texas Railroad, Navigation and Banking Company. Charter. 94991
Texas ranger. 24640
Texas revolution. 12702
Texas rifle hunter. 24641
Texas San Saba Company. 95216
Texas secessionists, versus, Lorenzo Sherwood in 1856. 80445
Texas sentinel. 94965
Texas: sketches of character. 48913, 95117, 1st note after 95515
Texas State Historical Association. 84858
Texas: the rise, progress, and prospects of the republic. 37440
Texas treason. 89687
Texas and Seine Revolution. 22072
Texas Western Railroad Company. see Southern Pacific Railroad Company (Texas)
Texcoco, Mexico. Sociedad de Mejores Materiales y Morales de Beneficencia y Socorros Mutuos. see Sociedad de Mejores Materiales y Morales de Beneficencia y Socorros Mutuos, Texcoco, Mexico.
Texcoco en los ultimos tiempos. 6835
Texeda, Antonio de. 95136
Texeda, Pedro Alexandro de. 95138-95140
Texian. pseud. Brief remarks on Dr. Channing's letter. see Hammekin, George L. supposed author
Texian. pseud. Life of the celebrated Munroe Edwards. 95142
Texian. pseud. Mexico versus Texas. see Ganihl, Anthony.
Texian Loan Contractors. petitioners 95102 see also Gray, William F. petitioner Triplett, Robert. petitioner

Texier, Edmond. 92536, 92546
Text. 14775, note after 95143
Text-book. 21708
Text-book of conchology. 63519
Text book of modern universalism in America. 30843
Text book of the origin and history, &c. &c. of the colored people. 59765
Text-book of the Washington Benevolent Society. 63786, 5th note after 101872, 101982
Text-book of Universalism. 83593
Texte, documents, et commentaires de la legislation des brevets d'invention. 3588
Texte & documents. 64703
Texte Quichua. 57224
Textvs de sphaera Ioannis de Sacrobosco. 74801
Texugo, F. T. see Torres Texugo, F.
Texugo, F. Torres. see Torres Texugo, F.
Teyoninhokarawen. Indian name see Norton, John, fl. 1805.
Tezozomoc, Fernando Alvarado. 95146
'Tgeestelyck roer van't coopmans schip. 97664
Th. Dufruit. pseud. see Cabet, Etienne.
Thaboriano. pseud. Examen comparativo. 23339
Thacher, Anthony. 106052
Thacher, John Boyd, 1847-1909. 94095, note after 99383C
Thacher, James. 95147-95153
Thacher, Moses, 1795-1878. 52749, 63993, 95154-95156, 105523
Thacher, Moses, 1795-1878. petitioner (69256), 105524 see also North Wrentham, Mass. Church. petitioners
Thacher, Moses, 1795-1878. plaintiff 95157-95158
Thacher, Oxenbridge, 1720-1765. 95160
Thacher, Oxenbridge, 1720-1765. supposed author (15954), 95159
Thacher, Peter, 1651-1727. 18469, 22472, 22929, (81422), 95161-96165
Thacher, Peter, 1677-1737. 95166-95167
Thacher, Peter, 1688-1744. 95168
Thacher, Peter, 1715-1785. 26184, 95169
Thacher, Peter, 1752-1802. (6737), (34619), 34620, 93503, 93506, 95170-95183, note after 102616 see also Society for Propagating the Gospel Among the Indians and Others in North America. Secretary.
Thacher, Peter, 1776-1843. see Thacher, Peter Oxenbridge, 1776-1843.
Thacher, Peter Oxenbridge, 1776-1843. 2599, 19583, (69415), 95184-95187, 96850, 4th note after 103741
Thacher, Samuel. 95188
Thacher, Samuel Cooper. 11924, 70224, 95189, 105305
Thacher, Samuel Cooper. supposed author 1441, 70224, 95190-95191, note after 97996
Thacher, T. A. 89199
Thacher, Thomas, 1620-1678. 51012, 80263, 95192-95195, 104654
Thacher, Thomas, 1756-1812. 95196-95202
Thacher, Thomas Cushing. 95230-95204
Thacher, Tyler. 95205
Thacher, William. 95206-95207
Thaddaus Kosciuszko. (23730)
Thaddeus Hyatt's contributions. (12406)
Thadee Kosciusko. 23731
Thal, Andreas. 95208
Thalberg, Friedrich. tr. 21376
Thalhimer, B. 95209
Thamara, Francisco. see Tamara, Francisco.

Thanksgiving sermon at Hatfield. 42791

Thanksgiving sermon . . . at King's Chapel. 34742

Thanksgiving sermon at Lee. 34117

Thanksgiving sermon at Littleton. 25216

Thanksgiving sermon at Middlebury. 45483

Thanksgiving sermon, . . . at Nottingham-West. 47994

Thanksgiving sermon, at Pepperrell. (22447)

Thanksgiving sermon at Pittsfield. 2751

Thanksgiving sermon at Portland. 37288

Thanksgiving sermon . . . at Staten Island. 36484

Thanksgiving sermon, at Three Rivers, Michigan. 67894

Thanksgiving sermon at Upton. 24428

Thanksgiving sermon at Wilton, N. H. (24539)

Thanksgiving sermon at Woodstock. 40092

Thanksgiving sermon, Bloomingdale. 35816

Thanksgiving sermon [by Ebenezer Bradford.] 7241

Thanksgiving sermon [by Jonathan Mayhew.] 13593

Thanksgiving sermon. By Rev. David Inglis. 34767

Thanksgiving sermon. By Rev. I. N. Hays. 31060

Thanksgiving sermon. By Rev. Joseph Kimball. 37763

Thanksgiving sermon by Rev. Richard H. Steele. 91159

Thanksgiving sermon. [By Samuel Stillman.] 91808

Thanksgiving sermon, . . . by the Rev. S. Morais. (50490)

Thanksgiving sermon. [By William Andrew Snively.] 85461

Thanksgiving sermon, December XV. MDCCLXXIV. 92275

Thanksgiving sermon: December 7th, 1865. (21139)

Thanksgiving sermon delivered at Boston December 11, 1783. 104056

Thanksgiving sermon, delivered at Logansport, Ind. 64464

Thanksgiving sermon, delivered at South Reading. 5915

Thanksgiving-sermon, deliver'd at the lecture in Boston. (65600)

Thanksgiving sermon, delivered before the Second Society in Plymouth. 91480

Thanksgiving sermon, delivered by Rev. Everard Kempshall. 37344

Thanksgiving sermon, delivered in . . . Brooklyn. 62738

Thanksgiving sermon, delivered in Calais, Maine. 88868

Thanksgiving sermon, delivered in . . . Harrisburg, Pa. 35440

Thanksgiving sermon, delivered in Meadville, Penn. (70436)

Thanksgiving sermon. Delivered in . . . Philadelphia. 7415

Thanksgiving sermon, delivered in the Evangelical Lutheran Church. (23162)

Thanksgiving sermon: delivered in the First Unitarian Church. 18183

Thanksgiving sermon, delivered in the Third Street Presbyterian Church. 89265

Thanksgiving sermon delivered in Winchester, Va. 7106

Thanksgiving sermon delivered November 28, 1861. 49036

Thanksgiving sermon, delivered November 28, 1862. 43237

Thanksgiving sermon, delivered November 30th, 1843. 13270

Thanksgiving sermon, delivered November 27th, 1800. 92975

Thanksgiving sermon delivered November 27, 1862. 33405

Thanksgiving sermon. Delivered November 26, 1835. 73121

Thanksgiving sermon . . . Farmington, 1822. (64297)

Thanksgiving sermon . . . Fisherville, N. H. 27446

Thanksgiving sermon for the entire reduction of Canada. 29748

Thanksgiving sermon, . . . in Boston, February 19, 1795. 51522

Thanksgiving sermon . . . in Catskill, on the fifth of December, 1822. (64216)

Thanksgiving sermon: . . . in . . . Chicago. (38019)

Thanksgiving sermon . . . in . . . Elizabeth-town. 51536

Thanksgiving sermon, . . . in . . . Harrisburg. (50373)

Thanksgiving sermon . . . in Milford, N. H. (50391)

Thanksgiving sermon, . . . in . . . New Haven. 42650

Thanksgiving sermon, . . . in New-York. 43473

Thanksgiving sermon . . . in . . . Newark, N. J. 52418

Thanksgiving sermon . . . in Providence, November 26th, 1846. 28284

Thanksgiving sermon . . . in Say-brook. 33126

Thanksgiving sermon . . . in Shelburne. (58122)

Thanksgiving sermon, July 25, 1745. 22138

Thanksgiving sermon . . . New York, July 31. 59609

Thanksgiving sermon . . . November 11, 1860. 30879

Thanksgiving sermon, Nov. 5th, 1656. 91364

Thanksgiving sermon, November 28, 1861. 71272

Thanksgiving sermon, . . . November 28, 1839. 52315

Thanksgiving sermon . . . November 24, 1864. 36218

Thanksgiving sermon . . . Nov. 29, 1804. 42791

Thanksgiving sermon, Nov. 26, 1858. 21722

Thanksgiving sermon, November. 26, 1812. 18405

Thanksgiving sermon, occasion'd by the glorious news. 96513

Thanksgiving sermon, on occasion of the smiles of heaven. 104365

Thanksgiving sermon on the total repeal of the stamp-act. 1840

Thanksgiving sermon [on the victory over the French in Canada.] (62788)

Thanksgiving sermon, . . . Portsmouth, N. H. 38874

Thanksgiving sermon preached at Brillerica. 17901

Thanksgiving sermon preach'd at Boston. 104108

Thanksgiving sermon preached at Harlem. 27404

Thanksgiving-sermon preach'd at Pepperrell. (22446)

Thanksgiving sermon, preached at . . . Philadelphia. 8365

Thanksgiving sermon preached at Staten Island. 36484

Thanksgiving sermon preached at the First Baptist Church. (33417)

Thanksgiving sermon, preached at the Second Church in Boston. 71799, (71902)

Thanksgiving sermon preached at Vergennes, Vt. 88870

Thanksgiving sermon, preached before the Thirty-Ninth O. V. 12686

Thanksgiving sermon, preached by Rev. Noah Hunt Schenk. (77568)

Thanksgiving sermon, preached in Baltimore. (33885)

Thanksgiving sermon, preached in Baltimore November 24, 1864. 77569

Thanksgiving sermon, preached in . . . Brooklyn. 4324

Thanksgiving sermon preached in Buffalo. 50343

Thanksgiving sermon preached in Christ M. E. Church. 85457

Thanksgiving sermon preached in Christ M. E. Church, Pittsburgh. 85462

Thanksgiving sermon, preached in Easton, Penn. 34006

Thanksgiving sermon, preached in Emmanuel Church, Baltimore. 77575

Thanksgiving sermon, preached in Grace Church, Jamaica, L. I. (82594)

Thanksgiving sermon, preached in Lebanon. 8168

Thanksgiving sermon: preached in Newburyport. 31755

Thanksgiving sermon preached in Pittsburgh. 22009

Thanksgiving sermon: preached in . . . Scranton, Pa. (31708)

Thanksgiving sermon, preached in the National Palace. 83867

Thanksgiving sermon preached in the Presbyterian Church. (17372)

Thanksgiving sermon, preached in the Third Presbyterian Church. 36219

Thanksgiving sermon preached in Washington, August 6, 1863. 66877

Thanksgiving sermon, preached November 30, 1854. 38780

Thanksgiving sermon, preached Nov. 24, 1853. 52310

Thanksgiving sermon, preached November 29, 1798. 89809

Thanksgiving sermon, preached . . . the 24th of November, 1803. 36151

Thanksgiving sermon, . . . San Francisco, California. (23810)

Thanksgiving sermon. The religious character of a people. (21137)

Thanksgiving sermon. The virtues and public services of William Penn. (3508)

Thanksgiving sermon, to the Chapel Society. 17474

Thanksgiving sermon, 25 November 1847. 4322

Thanksgiving sermon, upon the occasion. 95761

Thanksgiving sermon . . . West-Springfield, February 19, 1795. 39199

Thanksgiving story of the Peabody family. 11935, 46830-46831

Tharp, Peter. 95212-95213

Tharp, William. claimant 95214-95215

The Great Britain will one day fall. 95972

That old serpent, the devil, and satan. 90030

That Presbyterian ministers may justly challenge. 92934

That servant so imperious in his masters absence revived. (28044)

That the impartial world may be acquainted with the proceedings. 99006

That there is but one covenant. 4497

That this meeting do unanimously nominate Daniel Webster. 103275

That we may have peace we must now make war. 20098

That which is morally wrong. 82132

Thatcher, Anthony. see Thacher, Anthony.

Thatcher, Benjamin Bussey. 6488, 95216-95221

Thatcher, Benjamin Bussey. supposed author 94253, note after 95220

Thatcher, George. 96820

Thatcher, Moises. tr. 83140-83141

Thatcher, Moses. see Thacher, Moses, 1795-1878.

Thatcher, Peter. see Thacher, Peter, 1752-1802.

Thaumatographia Christiana. 46544

Thaumur de la Source, Dominique Antoine. 9079, note before 95222

Thavenet, --------. 95222

Thaxter, Thomas. 95223

Thayendanegea. see Brandt, Joseph, 1742-1807.

Thayer, Abijah W. 96224

Thayer, Caroline Matilda (Warren) 51616, 95225-95226, 101457-101458

Thayer, Christopher Toppan. 95227

Thayer, Ebenezer. 95228

Thayer, Elihu. 95229

Thayer, Elisha. 95230

Thayer, Isaac. defendant 95263-95277

Thayer, Israel, Jr. defendant 95263-95277

Thayer, John. note before 95231-95256

Thayer, Nathaniel. 62051, 95257-95262

Thayer, Nelson. defendant 95263-95277

Thayer, Thomas B. 63162

Thayer, William A. (26277), 95278, 105546

Thayer, William M. ed. 31170

Thayer. firm see Martin & Thayer. firm

Thayer & Eldridge. firm publishers 88421

Thayer & Eldridge's national library. 88421

Thayer expedition. 30714

Theater: a discourse. 16222

Theater; a discourse . . . at the Bromfield Street M. E. Church. 54993

Theater defended. 85330

Theater-repertoire, part 26. 92574

Theatre, New York. see New York (City) Theatre.

Theatre, Philadelphia. see Philadelphia. Theatre.

Theatre. 62306-62307

Theatre, a school of religion, manners and morals! 85330

Theatre Anglais. 17876

Theatre. Argument. The town being collected in Faneuil-Hall. 95280

Theatre. By Mr. J. H. Waddell. 100892

Theatre contemporian illustre. 92539, 92546

Theatre de l'univers. 57691, 57695

Theatre d'education. 81025

Theatre dv monde d'Abraham Ortelivs. (57688)

Theatre du monde. [Par M. Richer.] 71108

Theatre naval hydrographique. 78963

Theatre of education. 95281

Theatre of politically flying-insects. 66688

Theatre of the empire of Great Britain. 89228

Theatre of the present war in North America. 106064-106065

Theatre of the whole world. 57708

Theatre on fire. Awful calamity! 95282

Theatre-Royal, Covent-Garden, London. see
London. Theatre-Royal, Covent-Garden.
Theatre-Royal, Drury-Lane, London. see
London. Theatre-Royal, Drury-Lane.
Theatri geographiae veteris tomus prior.
66497
Theatri orbis terrarum enchiridion. 23935
Theatri orbis terrarvm parergon. 66494,
66497
Theatri Orteliani. 57689
Theatri Orteliani praecipuatum orbis regionum
delineationes. (57690)
Theatrical apprenticeship. 84239-84240
Theatrical apprenticeship and anedoctical
recollections. 84236-84238
Theatrical budget. Being an excellent col-
lection of recitations. 95284
Theatrical budget; or actor's regalio. 95283
Theatrical censor. 95285
Theatrical censor and critical miscellany.
95285-95286
Theatrical censor and musical review. 95287
Theatrical censor for the ensuing winter.
95286
Theatrical comicalities. 95288
Theatrical contributions of "Jacques" to the
U. S. Gazette. 35518, 95289
Theatrical journey-book and anecdotical re-
collections. 84240
Theatrical management in the west and south
for thirty years. 84241
Theatrical news. 89635
Theatrical register. 95290
Theatrical songster. 95291
Theatrical songster, and musical companion.
95292
Theatrical songster, or amusing companion.
94293
Theatricus. 10872
Theatro Americano. 99686
Theatro Americano descripcion general. 1716
Theatro Belgico, o vero ritratti historici.
40248
Theatro de virtudes poleticas. 80985
Theatro del mondo. Nel quale si da notitia
distinta. 57704
Theatro del mondo . . . ridotto in forma
piccola. 57701
Theatro geographico-historico de Ingelsia de
Espana. 24834
Theatro herioco. 60856
Theatro historico. 43300
Theatro naval hidrographico. (78962)
Theatro naval hydrographico, de los flvxos.
78961
Theatrical trip for a wager! 70773
Theatrum Apollineum. 76302
Theatrvm geographiae veteris. 66497
Theatrum oder Schawbuch des Erdtkreys.
57707
Theatrum oder Schawplatz des Erdbodems.
57706
Theatrum orbus terrarum. 35773, (57693)-
(57694), 57696-57700, 57705-57706,
57708
Theatrum orbis terrarum, sive atlas novis.
5720
Theatrum urbum praecipuarum mundi. (7449)
Theatrum victoriae. (31477), note before
95294
Thebiade en Amerique. 73478
Theban club. 95294
Thebaudieres, ------. 95295
Theca, Marcos de. petitioner 100623
Theft and murder! 95296

Their chaplain. pseud. Discourse delivered.
see Eliot, William Greenleaf.
Their humble servant, the Shaver. pseud. see
Shaver. pseud.
Their idealism; what and whence is it? 5932
Their Majesties colony of Connecticut in New-
England vindicated. 15856, (15860),
86758, note after 95296
Their nephew. pseud. Life of Vice-Admiral
Sir Charles Vinicombe Penrose. see
Penrose, John.
Their old friend. pseud. One more letter.
57326
Their position defined, in the summer of 1844.
91627
Their tutor. pseud. Supplement to the fourth
part. see Marsh, Ebenezer Grant.
Their voyage to New Jersey. (66937)
Theller, Edward Alexander. 95297
Thellez Calderon, Bernardo. see Tellez
Calderon, Bernardo.
Thello y Batbero, Antonio Domingo. 95298
Thellusson, George Woodford. 95299, 102861
see also Martinique. Principal Inhabi-
tants and Proprietors. Agents. peti-
tioners
Them in the time of their imprisonment,
pseud. Certain writings. 5629
Them that would be counted Quakers and are
not. 9064
Theme presentee et soutenue a la Faculte de
Medecine de Paris. 94426
Themenide et Paleno. 97025
Themistocles. pseud. Letters. see Welles-
ley, Richard Colley Wellesley, Marquis,
1769-1842.
Themistocles. pseud. Reply to Sir Henry
Clinton's narrative. 16814, note before
95301
Themistius. pseud. Madison and religion.
see Smith, Elias. supposed author
Thenessa, Francisco. 95302
Theo. S. Fay, to C. C. Jewett, Esq. 90656
Theobald, Lewis. 67599, 95303
Theocratic watchman. 60920
Theodat, Gabriel Sagard. see Sagard Theo-
dat, Gabriel.
Theodor Jan Kiewitch de Miriewo, Sravnitel
niy Slovar. (37727)
Theodor Parker. Sein Leben und Wirken.
70291
Theodor Parker's Sammtlicke Werke. 58766
Theodora. A dramatic sketch, in two acts.
95304
Theodore, Adolfo. 95305-95309
Theodore, or the Peruvians. 39626
Theodore Parker: a sermon. 26079
Theodore Parker and liberal Christianity.
64307
Theodore Parker. [By A. D. Mayo.] 47181
Theodore Parker. Sa vie et ses oeuvres.
58763, 70290
Theodore Parker's experience as a minister.
58764
Theodore Parker's lesson for the day. 6505,
9404
Theodore Parker's review of Webster. 58765
Theodore Parker, the reform pulpit, and the
influences that oppose it. 76991
Theodorus, Lodewijk, Grave van Nassau la
Leck. 51890, 95310
Theogonie Newtonienne. 39999
Theologian. 68677
Theological and miscellaneous works. 74490
Theological and Religious Library Association
of Cincinnati. 10392

Theological and Religious Library Association of Cincinnati. Board of Directors. 13092

Theological and western eclogue. 27355

Theological discussion held in Americus, Ga. 80104

Theological education. 58625

Theological Education Society of the State of New York. see Protestant Episcopal Theological Education Society in the State of New York.

Theological Institute of Connecticut, East Windsor, Conn. see Hartford Theological Seminary.

Theological Institution, Bangor, Me. 3157, 3158, 3168

Theological Institution in Andover, Mass. see Andover Theological Seminary.

Theological Institution in Phillips Academy, Andover, Mass. see Andover Theological Seminary.

Theological Library, Boston. see Boston. First Church (Unitarian) Theological Library.

Theological magazine see New York theological magazine.

Theological perceptor. 56824

Theological pretenders. 43790, note after 95312

Theological review. 5201, 12909-12910, 12921, 65654, 72361 see also American Presbyterian and theological review.

Theological School at Cambridge, Mass. see Harvard University. Divinity School.

Theological School at New Hampton, N. H. see Academical and Theological Institution, New-Hampton, N. H.

Theological School of the Diocese of Virginia. see Alexandria, Va. Protestant Episcopal Seminary in Virginia.

Theological seminaries in the west. 7695

Theological Seminary, Andover, Mass. see Andover Theological Seminary.

Theological Seminary, Bangor, Me. see Theological Institution, Bangor, Me.

Theological Seminary, Chicago. see Chicago Theological Seminary.

Theological Seminary, Columbia, S. C.

Theological Seminary, Galena, Ill. see Galena Theological Seminary.

Theological Seminary, Hartford, Conn. see Hartford Theological Seminary.

Theological Seminary, N. Y. see New York (City) General Theological Seminary of the Protestant Episcopal Church in the U. S. New York (City) Union Theological Seminary.

Theological Seminary, Salem, N. Y. see Washington Academy, Salem, N. Y. Theological Seminary.

Theological Seminary of Ohio. see Kenyon College, Gambier, Ohio. Theological Seminary.

Theological Seminary of St. Charles Borromeo, Philadelphia. 62308

Theological Seminary of the Associate Synod of New York, Newburgh, N. Y. see Associate Reformed Presbyterian Church. Theological Seminary, Newburgh, N. Y.

Theological Seminary of the General Synod of the Evangelical Lutheran Church in the U. S., Gettysburg, Pa. see Gettysburg, Pa. Theological Seminary of the Evangelical Lutheran Church in the U. S.

Theological Seminary of the Presbyterian Church at Danville, Ky., 1865. 18521

Theological Seminary of the Presbyterian Church in the U. S. A., Danville, Ky. see Danville, Ky. Theological Seminary of the Presbyterian Church in the U. S. A.

Theological Seminary of the Presbyterian Church, Princeton, N. J. see Princeton Theological Seminary, Princeton, N. J.

Theological Seminary of the Protestant Episcopal Church in Kentucky, Lexington. (37568), 2d note after 95313

Theological Seminary of the Protestant-Episcopal Church in Kentucky, Lexington. Charter. (37568), 2d note after 95313

Theological Seminary of the Protestant-Episcopal Church in Kentucky. Charter, regulations, and course of study. (37568), 2d note after 95313

Theological Seminary of the Protestant Episcopal Church in the United States, Hartford, Conn. 63297

Theological Seminary of the Reformed Dutch Church, New Brunswick, N. J. see Reformed Church in America. Theological Seminary, New Brunswick, N. J.

Theological system of government. 95314

Theological theses. 80901

Theological works [of Charles Leslie.] 85364

Theological works of Richard Sprigg. 89764

Theologicarum de Indis quaestionum. 106406

Theologies. 82673

Theol. Jahresbericht. 5421

Theology, explained and defended. (21558)

Theology in America. 47181

Theology of Edwards. 85222

Theology of New England. 42045

Theophilanthropist. 95315

Theophili Spitzelii Elevatio relationis Montezinianae. 89546

Theophilus. pseud. Defence of the dialogue. see Dickinson, Jonathan, 1688-1747.

Theophilus. pseud. Friendly dialogue. see Towers, John.

Theophilus. pseud. Letters between Theophilus and Eugenio. 25528, note after 95316

Theophilus, John. 95317

Theophilus, William. 37707

Theophilus Philadelphus. pseud. Sequel to Common sense. 79187

Theophilus Americana. (46545), note after 95317

Theoretical and practical grammar of the Otchipwe language. 3248

Theoric and practic principles of the art of navigation. 75852

Theorica y practica de comercio, y marina. 97690, 98249-98250

Theoricae novae planetarvm. 66670

Theorie des sentiments moraux. 82315-82317

Theorie et pratique du commerce et de la marine. 98251

Theories of currency. 42024

Theory according to art. 95603

Theory and practice of commerce and maritime affairs. 98252

Theory and practice of gunnery. 30275

Theory and practice of heavy artillery. 91568

Theory and practice of life assurance. 80295

Theory and practice of the international trade. (3688)

Theory and principles of civil liberty and government. 27926

Theory and regulation of public sentiment. 82731

Theory and treatment of fevers. 76909

Theory and history of earthquakes. 95318

Theory of agency. 60958, note after 95318, 8th note after 102552

Theory of centripetal storms. (68512)

Theory of good light. 62336

Theory of government. 102399

Theory of investment and speculation. 83900

Theory of money and banks investigated. 97304

Theory of moral sentiments. 22933, 82314

Theory of politics. (31785)

Theory of the blending of the races. 49433

Theory of the north-west passage to India. 94443

Theory of William Miller. 81629

Theosophischer Entwurf. 72590

Theosoro de virtudes. 16949

Theran de los Rios, Thomas. defendant 98154

Therapeutic Institute of Philadelphia. (62309)

There is a snake in the grass!!! 95319

There is no reason to be ashamed of the Gospel. (18419)

There is nothing true but heaven! 77169

Theremin, Charles. 95320

Theresa. pseud. Breechiad. 95321

Theresia, Baronesse van ***. see Hoog, Theresia, Baroness van.

Theriaca Andromachi. 30785

Theriault, Cesaree. see Berube, Cesaree (Theriault)

Thermomtrical navigation. 104300

Thermopilae. pseud. [Dedication.] 89185

Theroff, E. J. 95324

Theron. pseud. Letters and dialogues. see Bellamy, Joseph.

Theron and Aspasio. 76339

Theron, Paulinus and Aspasio. 17834

Therou, ----------. 87116, 95325-95327

Thesaur. Antiq. VII. 60934

Thesaurus expticorum. 30279

Thesavrvs geographicvs. (57709)

Thesaurus juris Romani. 86521

Thesaurus of American, English, Irish and Scotch law books. 45032

Thesaurus poetarum. (75554)

Thesaurus rerum Indicarum. 35791

These. 98512

These apresentada a Faculdade de Medicina do Rio de Janeiro. (47852)

These are some things in the house. 57878

These are to give notice, that it is proposed. (66038)

These bad times the product of bad morals. 47078

These people. pseud. Answer to a scandalous paper. 66910

These presents witness, that we the subscribers. 97871

These presents witness: that we who have hereunto subscribed. 95328

These, proposed for explanation. 103360

These three. 80365

[Theses and catalogue of the Collegiate School of Connecticut.] 105855

Theses hasce, huvenes in artibus initiati. 96467

Theses hasce . . . quas, . . . pro viribus defendere. 105856A

Theses . . . quas sub . . . Reverendi D. Crescentii Matheri. 30765

Theses sabbaticae. 80255-(80257)

Thesis; presented to the faculty of Michigan University. 84798

Thesoro de virtudes vtil & copioso. note after 27585, 40960, note after 47850

Thesoro spiritual de pobres. 27360, 47342, note just before (71416)

Thesoro spiritual de pobres en lengua de Michuaca. 27360

Thespian mirror. 59288, 95329

Thespian monitor, and dramatick miscellany. 95330

Thespian oracle. 95331

Thespis. pseud. Review of the Rev. Thomas Smyth's two sermons. note after 85330

Thevenot, Melchisedec. 88, 152, 10328, 26298-26316, 30482-30483, 31370-31372, 41659, 42918, 44666, 95332-95334

Thevet, Andre. 95335-95341

They steer to liberty's shores. 95342

Thibaud, ------- Larchevesque. see Larchevesque-Thibaud, -------.

Thibault de Chanvalon, Jean Baptiste. see Chanvalon, Jean Baptiste Thibault de.

Thiboust, B. engr. 98370

Thickens, J. (49154)

Thicknesse, Philip. 95343

Thiere und Pflanzen des tropischen America. 44999

Thiergeschichte der Nordlichen Polarlander. 59760

Thierry, J. B. S. 21383, 41611, 95344-95347

Thierry, J. B. S. defendant 56303

Thierry, Warin. 7787

Thiers, ------. 4484

Thiery de Menonville, Nicolas Joseph. 62957, 95348-95349

Thimble's wife. 95880

Thing, Samuel. 95350

Things and thoughts in America and Europe. 57813

Things as they are. 95351

Things as they are in America. 11807

Things as they are, or federalism turned inside out! (55313), note after 95351

Things as they are, or notes of a traveller. 55955, 95352 1st note after 96481

Things as they have been! 94542

Things as they have been, are and ought to be. 60668

Things as they will be, &c. 94542

Things as they will be; or, all barkers are not biters. 94543, note before 95353

Things for a distress'd people to think upon. 46546

Things for northern men to do. 28512

Things lovely and of good report. 43804

Things necessary to be settled in the province of Quebec. 95353

Things new and old. 31755

Things of earth and things of heaven. (81547)

Things relating to moral behavior. 36291

Things relating to the mind or understanding. 36291

"Things that make for peace." 62772

Things that young people should think upon. (46547), 46615

Things to be look'd for. 46548

Things to be more thought upon. 46549

Things to be seen by the sea at Nahant. 51725

Think and act. 60794

Think twice ere you speak once. 60030

Thinking bayonet. 33106

Third address of the Rev. Robert Heys. 94506A

Third address [to the people of Maryland.] 14455

Third relation. (1618)
Third report . . . see Report . . .
Third semi-annual report . . . see Report
. . .
Third . . . series of bibliographical col-
lections and notes. 97139
Third series of historical documents. 67023
Third series of lectures. 26796
Third series of the Breitmann ballads.
(39963)
Third Social Library, Boston. see Boston.
Third Social Library.
Third Social Library of Boston. By-laws
[and catalogue.] 95359
Third supplement [to the public laws of Rhode
Island.] 70700
Third trial of Jacob Barker. 3392
Third triennial catalogue of the officers and
graduates [of Miami University.] 48682
Third triennial charge to the clergy of the
Diocese of Rhode Island. 13385
Third year of the war. 63862-63863
Thirsty invited to come. 79433
Thirteen essays on the policy of manufactur-
ing. 10889, 22989, 66530, 95360
Thirteen historical discourses. 2675
Thirteen hymns, suited to the present times.
104733
Thirteen letters from a gentleman to his
friend. 35585, (35636), 82167
Thirteen letters to a friend. (24363), 70265
Thirteen portraits of American legislators.
21446
13 witnesses. pseud. Description of the
province of New Albion. 63310
Thirteen years' experience in the itinerancy.
44388
Thirteen years in the south. (63321)
Thirteenth annual catalogue of Monticello Female
Seminary. (50204)
Thirteenth annual report . . . see Report . . .
Thirteenth article of the bar rules. 105393
Thirteenth report . . . see Report . . .
Thirten [sic] lecturs. (70874)
Thirtieth anniversary discourse. 24606
Thirtieth annual report . . . see Report
. . .
Thirty days in New Jersey ninety years ago.
30874
Thirty different draughts of Guinea. 65406,
84559-84560, 84562
Thirty-first annual report . . . see Report
. . .
Thirty-first report . . . see Report . . .
Thirty-five anti-Federal objections refuted.
619, 35929
Thirty-fourth catalogue of Oneida Conference
Seminary. (57340)
Thirty important cases, resolved. 46550,
note after 95360
Thirty miles around New York by railroad.
54693
Thirty million bill. 79586
Thirty-nine men for one woman. (12572)
Thirty-ninth annual meeting, held at Hamilton,
Madison Co., N. Y. 53540
Thirty-ninth annual register of the Rensselaer
Polytechnic Institute. 69641
Thirty-ninth annual report . . . see Report
. . .
Thirty-ninth circular of Castleton Medical
College. 11440
Thirty-one. pseud. Penitential tears. see
Withington, Leonard.
Thirty-One Boston Schoolmasters. see Asso-
ciation of Boston School Masters.

Thirty poems [of] William Cullen Bryant.
(8824)
Thirty practical essays, founded on common
sense. 102351
Thirty-second annual report . . . see Report
. . .
Thirty-seventh annual report . . . see Report
. . .
Thirty-seventh report . . . see Report . . .
Thirty-Six American Citizens Confined at
Carthagena. petitioners 69841
Thirty-six days in the woods. 79357
Thirty-six voyages to various parts of the
world. 14195
Thirty-six years of a seafaring life. 95361
Thirty-sixth annual report . . . see Report
. . .
Thirty-third annual report . . . see Report
. . .
30,000 Disfranchised Citizens of Philadelphia.
petitioners see Philadelphia. Citizens.
petitioners
£30,000 for the cow-pox!!! 85250
Thirty-three articles extracted from, and con-
tracting of, the Platform of church-
discipline. 46439
32 questions. 23094, note after 106353
Thirty-two years of the life of an adventurer.
20858
Thirty years ago. (21308), 95362
Thirty years' facts against one reviewer's
opinion. 10889
Thirty years from home. 39812
Thirty years in the Arctic regions. 25632
Thirty years' ministry. 76510
Thirty years of army life on the border.
44516
Thirty years of Boston. 29632
Thirty years of foreign policy. (43477)
Thirty years passed among the players in
England and America. 17236
Thirty years reformer. pseud. Star of the
east. 90489
Thirty years' resident. pseud. Jamaica;
who is to blame? 35606
Thirty years' view. 4783, 4785, 4787, 84151,
note after 95362
This chart shows the undevemoped resources
of & general condition of the state of
Arkansas. 1996
This declaration of trust, made at Boston.
88255
This great and good man died at his seat in
the state of Virginia. 101817
This highly important report. 103010
This House being deeply impressed. 99926
This indented bill of ten shillings. 77246
This indenture made the seventeenth day of
September. 10979, 93911
This indenture, made this twenty-second day
of May. 96986
This indenture witnesseth. 34440
This is a white workingman's government.
18895
This is the house that Jonathan built. 95363
This is to notify the citizens. 103251
This morning Congress received the following
letter. 101693
This morning the Committee of Correspondence
met. 100012
This pamphlet is humbly dedicated. 1384
This paper will be devoted exclusively to the
presidential election. 97990
This night will be performed at the steps.
95364

Thomas' Buffalo city directory for 1865.
9056, (55873), note after 95451
Thomas' Buffalo city directory for 1864.
9056, note after 95451
Thomas' Buffalo city directory for 1867.
9056, 91134, note after 95451
Thomas' Buffalo city directory for 1863.
9056, note after 95451
Thomas Campanella. 10199
Thomas Casuisticus. pseud. see A., E.
H. M. pseud.
Thomas Clarkson; a monograph. 22358
Thomas Clarkson, his life and labours.
13499
Thomas Coryate's travels. 66686
Thomas Crane Public Library, Quincy, Mass.
255, (67288), 67293
Thomas Crawford; his career, character,
and works. 31721
Thomas Doyle. pseud. see More, John J.
Thomas Gage's proclamation versified.
97240
Thomas H. Smith and Son. Letter from the
Secretary of the Treasury, in relation
to a compromise. 84396
Thomas H. Smith & Son. Letter from the
Secretary of the Treasury, showing the
terms of a compromise of the claim.
84396
Thomas H. Smith & Son. Letter from the
Secretary of the Treasury, transmitting
the information required by a resolution.
84396
Thomas H. Smith and Son. May 26, 1832.
84396
Thomas H. Wentworth, of Oswego, New-York.
102633
Thomas Jackson. 41065
Thomas Jefferson writings. 85376
Thomas Judd and his descendants. 36844
Thomas Lee, Esq. 99989
Thomas' New England almanac, 1772. 45826
Thomas Paine: a celebration. 16222
Thomas Paine. An address delivered before
the Goethean and Diagnothian Societies
of Franklin and Marshall College. 92011
Thomas Paine the author of the letters of
Junius. 36914
Thomas Paine to the citizens of Pennsylvania.
58240
Thomas Paine's letter. 58225
Thomas Paine's letter to the late General
George Washington. 58227
Thomas Ritchie's letter. 71577
Thomas Shepard's memoir of his own life.
106052
Thomas Singularity. pseud. see Hopkins,
Jeremiah.
Thomas Singularity, Journeyman printer.
pseud. see Nott, Henry Junius.
Thomas Smith. 84374
Thomas Starr King. 47181
Thomas Starr King. For the benefit of the
Sanitary Commission. (37849)
Thomas Sweet-Scented. pseud. see Gooch,
Sir William, Bart., 1681-1751.
Thomas the Rhymer. pseud. XLV. chapter
of the prophecies. see Arnot, Hugh.
supposed author
Thomas the Seer. pseud. American's dream.
1268, 2d note after 95453
Thomas Thompson. pseud. see Hedworth, H.
supposed author
Thomas Thumb. pseud. see Brandon, Ben-
jamin. supposed author Church, Ben-
jamin, 1734-1776. supposed author

Mayhew, Jonathan, 1720-1766. supposed
author Waterhouse, Samuel. supposed
author
Thomas Thumb, Esq; Surveyor of the Customs.
pseud. see Waterhouse, Samuel.
Thomas von Westen und Hans Egede. (7445)
Thomas Williams's centurial sermon. 104389
Thomas Zealot. pseud. see Zealot, Thomas.
pseud.
Thomason, A. pseud. Men and things in
America. see Bell, Andrew.
Thomason, John. 61187
Thomason's men, etc. 4447
Thomas's much approved almanack. 90958
Thomas's New-England almanack. 2d note
after 95414
Thomassen a Thuessink, Evart Jan. 95455
Thomasson, William Poindexter, 1797-1882.
83833
Thomaston election. 1832. 95456
Thomaz de Negreiros, Antonio. 52251, 95457
Thome, Anastasia. 95458
Thome, James A. (19087), 38861, 95459-
95460
Thome de Gamond, Aime de, 1807-1875.
2768, 26518, note after 95460
Thompkins, Ray. defendant 1680
Thompson, --------. defendant 101343
Thompson, --------, fl. 1794. 53019
Thompson, -------, fl. 1827. 88951
Thompson, -------, fl. 1856. 45874, note
after 89212
Thompson, Abraham. 95461
Thompson, Abraham G. petitioner 95462
Thompson, Ambrose W. 95463-95464
Thompson, Amira (Carpenter) 95465
Thompson, Ann. appellant (11193)
Thompson, Archibald. 62277 see also Phila-
delphia County, Pa. Sub-Lieutenant.
Thompson, Augustus Charles. 73641, note after
95465
Thompson, Benjamin, Count Rumford. see
Rumford, Sir Benjamin Thompson, Count,
1753-1814.
Thompson, Benjamin, fl. 1833. 95467
Thompson, Benjamin, fl. 1848. 37683
Thompson, Benjamin Franklin. 54476, 95468-
95472
Thompson, Mrs. C. M. petitioner 53978
Thompson, Charles. 87364
Thompson, Charles. tr. 57516
Thompson, Daniel Pierce. 95473-95486, note
after 99131, note before 99222
Thompson, David. 95487
Thompson, David Decamp, 1852-1908. 84064
Thompson, Denman. 91288
Thompson, Edward. 95488
Thompson, Francis. appellant (11193)
Thompson, G., fl. 1794. 21589
Thompson, G. Burton. 95489
Thompson, George, 1804-1878. 28277, 28853,
52273, 81854, 89204, note after 92624,
95490-95509
Thompson, George, 1804-1878. supposed
author (81854), note after 95491
Thompson, George Alexander. 683, 95510-
95512
Thompson, George Western. 7116, note after
95512-95513
Thompson, Gilbert. 95514
Thompson, Henry. supposed author 48913,
95117, 1st note after 95515
Thompson, J. Edgar. 88441
Thompson, J. R. ed. 88393
Thompson, J. S. ed. 84281
Thompson, J. S. T. ed. 43634

Thorne, Jaime. defendant 99484
Thorne, Master R. 29592, 66686
Thorne, William. 95626
Thorne's address, to Dr. Ley. 29592
Thornhill, Henry. 95627
Thornton, Abel. 95628
Thornton, De Mouncie. 95629
Thornton, Elisha. 70704-70705
Thornton, Jessy Quinn. 95630
Thornton, John. 95631
Thornton, John Wingate, 1818-1878. 12315,
    16292, 28005, 33278, 38872, 47131,
    91749, 91853, 39499, 95632-95642,
    102744
Thornton, Robert John. 85246
Thornton, Samuel Yardley. defendant 95643
Thornton, Thomas. 97086, 101841, 2d note after
    101887
Thornton, W. supposed author 17147, 2d note
    after 95643
Thornton, William, 1761-1828. 57959, 95645-
    95648
Thornton, William, fl. 1806. 95644
Thorntown Party of Miami Indians. see Eel
    River Indians.
Thornwell, James Henley. 396, 65130, 87991,
    88049, 95649-note after 95649 see also
    South Carolina. University. President.
Thoron, Enrique. Vicomte Onffroy de. see
    Onffroy de Thoron, Enrique, Vicomte.
Thorowgood, Thomas. 95650-95653
Thorp, George B. 96876
Thorpe, Francis Newton, 1857-1926. note
    after 94720, note after 94725
Thorpe, George B. 2879, 72619, 101441
Thorpe, John. 95654
Thorpe, Robert. 42954, 46857, 95655-95661
Thorpe, Thomas Bangs. 58025, 95662-note
    after 95665
Thorpe, Thomas Bangs. incorrectly supposed
    author 36595, 38923, 38959, 57814,
    82069, note after 90541, note after 95543,
    1st note after 95662, note after 95665, 2d
    note after 102991
Thorpe, Thomas Bangs. supposed author
    41819, note before 95663
Those Freemen, of the City of Philadelphia,
    Who are Now Confined in the Mason's
    Lodge, by Virtue of a General Warrant.
    59610
Those parts of the custom of the Viscounty
    and Provostship of Paris. (66985)
Those taught by God the Father, to know God
    the Son; are blessed. 91964
Those Who Deliver the Pennsylvania Ledger
    to the Subscribers. see Pennsylvania
    Ledger. Delivery Boys.
Those who knew. pseud. Olden time in New-
    York. see De Forest, T. R.
Those who know. pseud. Collins steamers.
    14433
Those who lived them. pseud. Memorials
    written on several occasions. 47747
Tho'ts of impediments to reformation. 42037,
    92099
Thou shalt love thy neighbour as thyself.
    79429
Thou shalt do no murder. 95666
Thou shalt not seethe a kid in his mother's
    milk. 17833, 44577
Thouars, Abel Aubert du Petit. see Dupetit-
    Thouars, Abel Aubert, 1793-1864.
Thouars, Aristide Aubert Dupetit. see
    Dupetit-Thouars, Aristide Aubert.
Though, in a legal sense, I might stand ex-
    cused. 94458

Thought for the crisis. (57641)
Thoughts about the city of St. Louis. 32420,
    1st note after 95666
Thoughts about water. 6785, 2d note after
    95666
Thoughts and reflections on the present posi-
    tion of Europe. (29009)
Thoughts and sentiments on the evil of slavery.
    17856
Thoughts and sentiments on the evil and wicked
    traffic of the slavery. 17857
Thoughts and things, at home and abroad.
    9452
Thoughts and ways of God. 77420
Thoughts concerning the bank of North America.
    17305, 60391, 63266, 95667
Thoughts concerning the bank, with some facts.
    95668
Thoughts concerning the present revival of
    religion in New-England. 21963, note
    after 102697
Thoughts during the Easter recess of Parlia-
    ment. 81668
Thoughts, &c. 44705
Thoughts for a birth-day. 46333
Thoughts for a Lord's-Day morning. 97576
Thoughts for Christians. 59167
Thoughts for the afflicted. 85100
Thoughts for the age. 18791
Thoughts for the crisis. 35998
Thoughts for the day of rain. 46496, 46551
Thoughts for the new-year. (77421)
Thoughts for the people. 82672
Thoughts for the times: addressed to the con-
    siderate people of the northern states.
    1278, note before 95669
Thoughts for the times. By Joel Prentiss
    Bishop. (5609)
Thoughts for the young men of America.
    (68313)
Thoughts for the young women of America.
    (68314)
Thoughts from nature. 21593
Thoughts in a series of letters. 54669
Thoughts in favor of the abolition of the slave
    trade. 92058
Thoughts in rhyme. (58827)
Thoughts of a dying man. 46552, note after
    95669
Thoughts of a traveller upon our American
    disputes. 20904, note before 95670, 5th
    note after 96481, note after 99409
Thoughts of an American in the wilderness.
    (47303)
Thoughts of leisure hours. 81462
"Thoughts of peace and not of affliction."
    1535B
Thoughts of the elective franchise. 39887
Thoughts on a militia and standing army.
    17147, 2d note after 95643
Thoughts on a new order of missionaries.
    82548
Thoughts on a plan of economy. 5957
Thoughts on a question of importance pro-
    posed to the public. 95670
Thoughts on African colonization. (26708)
Thoughts on agency; wherein the article of
    motive (as necessitating human action)
    is particularly examined. 60958, note
    after 95670
Thoughts on American slavery. 95671
Thoughts on "annexation." 51187
Thoughts on attending the funeral. 99300
Thoughts on banking and the currency. 95672
Thoughts on British colonial slavery. 104614

Thoughts on British Guiana. 29197, note after 95672

Thoughts on civilization. 95673

Thoughts on colonial representation. 95674

Thoughts on colonization. 6889

Thoughts on currency and finance. 31096

Thoughts on Daniel and the Revelation. 84472-84473

Thoughts on education. 94025

Thoughts on education: a poem. 8788

Thoughts on educational topics and institutions. (6977)

Thoughts on emigration. 95675

Thoughts on emigration and on the Canadas. 80542, 95676

Thoughts on emigration as a means of surmounting our present difficulties. 95677

Thoughts on emigration, education, &c. 22508

Thoughts on emigration in a letter from a Gentleman in Philadelphia to his friend in England. 16611, 16615, (22509), 2d note after 95677

Thoughts on emigration. To which are added, miscellaneous observations. (19708), 96327-96328

Thoughts on evangelizing the world. (81648)

Thoughts on executive justice. 56487, 73061

Thoughts on experimental religion. 91541-91542

Thoughts on female education: by Benjamin Rush, M. D. 90240

Thoughts on female education. By Mrs. Townshend Smith. 91859

Thoughts on finance and colonies. 66538, 4th note after 95677

Thoughts on government: applicable to the present state of the American colonies. 251, 5th note after 95677

Thoughts on government, with a short view of the comparative political freedom. 102155

Thoughts on his letters to Mr. Hervey. 76339

Thoughts on inland navigation, &c. 95678

Thoughts on labor, capital, currency, &c. 44298, note after 95678

Thoughts on labor in the south. 43107

Thoughts on liberty and the rights of Englishmen. 95679

Thoughts on modern politics. 95680

Thoughts on Negro slavery. 95681, 104025

Thoughts on our affairs with England. 12383

Thoughts on peace and war. An address. (11905)

Thoughts on peace and war; the result of twenty odd years reflection. 39069

Thoughts on peace in the present situation of the country. 95682

Thoughts on penitentiaries and prison discipline. 10889

Thoughts on political economy. 68042

Thoughts on popular and liberal education. 9899

Thoughts on prison discipline. 35683, note after 102092

Thoughts on quarantine and other sanitary systems. 9899

Thoughts on religion, &c. 69346

Thoughts on religious education and early piety. 63454

Thoughts on shaving. 95684

Thoughts on slavery. 95685

Thoughts on slavery. By John Wesley. 102699

Thoughts on slavery occasioned by the Missouri Question. 17537, (31888), 81944

Thoughts on slavery. With a useful extract from the Massachusetts spy. 1792, note after 45640, 81891

Thoughts on speculative free-masonry. 11853

Thoughts on taxation, in a letter to a friend. 95686

Thoughts on the abolition of slavery. 95687

Thoughts on the abolition of the slave trade, and civilization of Africa. 44709, 95689

Thoughts on the abolition of the slave trade. By an inhabitant of Lynn. 95688

Thoughts on the abolition of the slave trade, &c. 102148

Thoughts on the act for making more effectual provision. 95690

Thoughts on the affair between the Leopard and the Chesapeake. (12491), 1st note after 100681

Thoughts on the Anglican and Anglo-American churches. 8052

Thoughts on . . . the approaching state convention. 36162

Thoughts on the banking system of Upper Canada. 98091

Thoughts on the Baptist controversy. 95691

Thoughts on the Canada bill. (10614), note after 95691

Thoughts on the career of life. 70408

Thoughts on the cause of the present discontents. 9303, 42946, 95692

Thoughts on the causes of the present distresses. 95693

Thoughts on the causes of the present failures. 95694

Thoughts on the certainty and near approach of death. 91541

Thoughts on the colonization of the free blacks. 95695

Thoughts on the condition and prospects of popular education in the United States. 95113, 95696

Thoughts on the conduct of the late minority. 97531

Thoughts on the constitution. 30051

Thoughts on the constitution of the state of South-Carolina. 88079

Thoughts on the crisis. 95697

Thoughts on the currency. (52340), note after 95697

Thoughts on the death penalty. 9324

Thoughts on the destiny of man. 95698

Thoughts on the destructive influence of quackery. 95699

Thoughts on the difficulties and distresses in which the peace of 1783. 37812

Thoughts on the discontents of the people last year. 4823, 95700

Thoughts on the division of dioceses. 95701, 103820

Thoughts on the duty of the Episcopal Church. (35848)

Thoughts on the education of girls. 42421

Thoughts on the education of youth. 14107

Thoughts on the ensuing election. 95702

Thoughts on the entertainments of the stage. 95703

Thoughts on the erection of the theatre in 1793. 95704

Thoughts on the examination and trials of candidates for the sacred ministry. 929, 5746

Thoughts on "the excitement" in reply to a letter. 815, 95705

Thoughts on the five per cent. 95706

Thoughts on the French revolution. 91808

Thoughts upon the fatal consequences of losing the present opportunity. 92802

Thoughts upon the mode of education, proper in a republic. 60393

Thoughts upon the political situation of the United States. 35441, 93506, 3d note after 95729

Thoughts upon the present contest. 95730

Thoughts upon the proper means and measures. 23895, (26248)

Thounens, J. B. 95731-95733

Thouret, Michel Augustin, 1749-1810. 25579, 92135

Thousand chances to make money. (25733)

Thousand miles' walk across the Pampas. 5614

Thousand years of prosperity promised to the Church of God. 4497

Thousands. pseud. Address of Thousands to the people of the United States. 62652, note before 93501

Thousands. pseud. Essays. see Snethen, Nicholas, 1769-1845.

Thouvenel, Edouard Antoine, 1818-1866. 45451 see also France. Ministere des Affaires Etrangeres.

Thrasher, J. S. (5059), 33721

Threads of Maryland colonial history. 52288

Threatening ruin. (78944)

Three addresses delivered to the prisoners in Toronto Gaol. 37896

Three addresses, on various public occasions. 105588

Three apprentices. A tale of life in New York and Boston. 91825

Three apprentices. By A. L. Stimson. 91828

Three articles on the suffrage question. 35993

Three articles sett downe by the Councell of Virginia. 99863

Three beauties. 67042

Three brief discourses. 46501

Three brief essays to sum up the whole Christian religion. 46422

Three brothers. 80349

Three chief safeguards of society. note after (58767)

Three choice and profitable sermons upon severall texts of scripture. 55889

Three communications. 95155

Three conservative replies. 20255

Three considerations proposed to Mr. William Pen. 9372, note after 14379, 81492

Three cruel mothers. 104971

Three curious pieces. 95734

Three dangers of the republic. 58701

Three daring trappers. 10906

Three days at Nauvoo. 11476

Three days' battle of Chattanooga. 47393

Three days of blood in Paris. (81279)

Three days on the White Mountains. 2933

Three days reign of terror. 54695, note after 95734

Three degrees of banking. 95735

III. Demerara. Further reports. 82904

Three dialogues, adapted to the meanest capacities. 103069

Three dialogues. [By Thomas Doolittle.] 20614

Three discourses at the Salem Street Church. 71077

Three discourses. [By Mason Locke Weems.] 102467, 102470, 102477

Three discourses. [By Samuel Stanhope Smith.] 84096, 84097, 84117, 84121-84123

Three discourses . . . by the Hon. Harnes Frisbie. 25977

Three discourses concerning the reality and extremity. 16639

Three discourses delivered before the Mercantile Library Association. (78400)

Three discourses, delivered January 24, 1841. (25314)

Three discourses, . . . delivered . . . November 18, 1838. 38773

Three discourses from Ezekiel VII. 12. 104615

Three discourses . . . May 28th, June 4th and June 11th, 1854. (26240)

Three discourses of S^r. Walter Ralegh. 67589

Three discourses, on national subjects. 50800

Three discourses on several subjects. 42088

Three discourses, preached at Watertown, N. Y. 70409

Three discourses preached before the Congregational Society in Watertown. 25440

Three discourses, preached in the South Evangelical Church. 39264

Three discourses. . . . To which may be added, a short scriptural catechism. 46214

Three discourses upon the religious history of Bowdoin College. 85223

Three discourses written by Mr. Monis himself. 14477

Three dissertations on Boylston prize questions. 79871

Three duetts, for two performers. 84334

Three English statesmen. 82689

Three eras of New England. 42707

Three essays. 46608, note after 105465

Three excellent new songs. 95736

Three experiments of living. 39738, 4th note after 94244

Three financial problems and their attempted solution. (57930)

Three fingered Jack. 86903

Three first letters to the Rev. Mr. Whitefield. (17668), note after 103614

Three former sermons. 55889

Three French Prisoners Taken by the Maquase. 66062

Three friends of Indiana. pseud. Letter 26164

Three funeral sermons preach'd at Cambridge. (1834), 14499, 95737, 100915

Three great battles. 39226, 1st note after 95737

Three great points of practical Christianity. 46501

Three historic flags and three September victories. 65013

Three hundred and twenty-eight laymen. pseud. Communication. 57309

Three hundred millions of dollars. 15928

Three Indians, Who Were Educated at Dartmouth College. pseud. When shall we th[ree meet again.] 103235

Three interesting tracts. 104005

Three judgments given forth by a party of men. 8956, (37333), 47171, 97113

Three lectures. . . . By John D. Ogilby. 56836

Three lectures, by the Rev. Francis L. Hawks. 16352, (30969)

Three lectures delivered at Southold, L. I. 27721

Three lectures delivered before the American Institute of Instruction. (55765)

Three lectures, delivered by request. 32895

Three lectures delivered in . . . Cincinnati. 47178

Tillforlitliga underrattelser on Nord-Amerikas forenta stater. 93986

Tillier, Rodolphe. 12220, 19728, 33140-33141, 95824-95825

Tillinghast, Allen. defendant at court martial 62977, 96942

Tillinghast, George. 95826

Tillinghast, Joseph Leonard. 95827-95830

Tillinghast, Pardon. 37212, 95831

Tillman, Ben. 85000

Tillotson, D. ed. 14876, 1st note after 101785

Tillotson, Daniel. 95832

Tillotson, Romants. (23455), (30625)

Tillotson, Thomas. (53678, see also New York (State) Secretary of State.

Tilly, Alexandre-Francois-Auguste, Comte de Grasse. see Grasse-Tilly, Alexandre-Francois-August, Comte de.

Tilly, Francois Joseph Paul, Marquis de Grasse. see Grasse-Tilly, Francois, Joseph Paul, Marquis de, 1722-1788.

Tilt at our best society. 55977

Tilton, James. 95833-95834

Tilton, John E. ed. 54915

Tilton, N. H. Tilton Seminary. see Tilton Seminary, Tilton, N. H.

Tilton Seminary, Tilton, N. H. V. A. S. Association. (52868)

Tim Trimmer. pseud. see Trimmer, Tim. pseud.

Timaeus, Johann Jacob Carl. 95835

Timandro. pseud. Coloquio de Aristo y de Timandro. 14734

Timber rail-ways-economical plan. 95746

Timberlake, Henry. 95836-95837

Timberly, Hendrick. 66686, 78871

Time and change. 85507

Time and the end of time. 25370

Time-piece. (49449)

Time piece. 67607

Time spend as it should be. 46361

Time when the first Sabbath was ordained. (66872)

Timely articles on slavery. 32954

Timely remembrancer. 95838

Timely warning against surfeiting and drunkenness. 36859

Timely warning to the people of England. 95839

Times, London. 8092, 8420, (12729), 21107, 27527, 30299, 30301, (31209), (31378), (37800), 40650, 41212, 43444, 51103, 69420, 72912, 74179-(74180), 86792, 90794, note after 92624, 95659, 3d note after 95742, note after 98924, 99278, 99821

Times. A discourse delivered in . . . Boston. 14535

Times: a poem. By an American. 12985, 2d note after 95839

Times; a poem. By Peter Markoe. 44623, 95840

Times; a poem, addressed to the inhabitants of New-England. 48943, 90167, note after 95840

Times, a satirical poem. 56713

Times, a solemn and pathetic elegy. 95841

Times, a solemn elegy. 95841

Times and gazette. 87976

Times and seasons. 83035, 83037-83038, 83147, 83153, 83236, 83240-83243, 83245-83246, 83252, 83254, 83259, 83288, 83289

Times, and signs of the times. 78321

Times. By a young Bostonian. 89928, 1st note after 95839

Times. By the author of Monmouth. 82108

Times, mankind is highly concerned to support that. 95842

Times, morally considered. 26291

Times of birth and death. 24778

Times of India. 84005

Times of men. 46753, 46758

Times of men are in the hand of God. 46753

Times of Tecumseh. 82523

Times of the "bloody Brandt." 51435

Times of the first settlers. 12915

Times of the rebellion in the west. 33303

Times: or, the pressure and its causes examined. 95843

Times store-hovse. (48248)

Timo. Titterwell, Esq. see Kettell, Samuel. supposed author

Timoleon. pseud. Biographical history of Dionysius. see Tilton, James.

Timoleon. pseud. Epistle from Timoleon. see Bollan, William.

Timoleon. pseud. Free thoughts on the American contest. see Anderson, James.

Timoleon. pseud. Solemn address. see Worman, Tunis.

Timon. pseud. Indios bravos. 57735

Timoniclus. pseud. Enquiry into the Caledonian project. see Harris, Walter. supposed author

Timonius, Emmanuel. 7143, 86588

Timorous revilers slighted. 95527

Timorous soul's guide. (65514)

Timosthenes. 76838

Timothy. pseud. Dialogue shewing, what's therein to be found. see Logan, James.

Timothy. pseud. Letter to the Moderator of the New Hampshire Association. see Worcester, Thomas.

Timothy, Lewis, d. 1738. 87865

Timothy, Peter. 87413, 87439

Timothy Spectacles. pseud. see Foster, William C.

Timothy Taste. pseud. see Taste, Timothy. pseud.

Timothy Telescope. pseud. see Telescope, Timothy. pseud.

Timothy Telltruth. pseud. see Telltruth, Timothy. pseud.

Timothy Tickle, Esq. pseud. see Kendall, B. F.

Timothy Tickler. pseud. see Tickler, Timothy. pseud.

Timothy Tickletoby. pseud. see Bradford, Samuel F.

Timothy Titcomb. pseud. see Holland, Josiah Gilbert.

Timothy Titcomb's letters to young people. 32512

Timothy Wheelwright. pseud. see Wheelwright, Timothy. pseud.

Timpson, Thomas. 95844

Tin-Plate, Copper, and Sheet-Iron Workers' Association of Massachusetts. see Massachusetts Tin-Plate, Copper, and Sheet-Iron Workers' Association, Boston.

Tincker. pseud. To the free and respectable mechanicks. 95845

Tinelli, Luigi. 95846-95847

Tingley, H. F. 95848

Tinker, Edward. defendant 95849

Tinker spy. 68643

Tinne, A. 95850

Tinne, A. supposed author 106045

Tintin. pseud. Tintin Veracruzano. 95851

Tintin Veracruzano. 95851

Tintinnabulum. pseud. Sporting intelligencer. 89632

Tioga County, N. Y. Court of Common Pleas. 95852

Tiphys Aegyptus. pseud. Navy's friend. (52129)

Tippecanoe: a legend of the border. 97171

Tippecanoe almanac. 50142

Tippecanoe almanac, for the year 1841. 95853

Tippecanoe and log cabin almanac. 95853

Tippecanoe Club songster. 95854

Tippecanoe melodies. 86918

Tippecanoe song book. 95855

Tippecanoe text-book. (55338), note after 95855

Tipper (Samuel) firm publishers 70380, 103679

Tipper's edition of General Whitelocke's trial. 103679

Tipper's edition of General Whitelocke's trial at large. 103680

Tippett, Edward D. 95856-95858

Tipton, John, 1786-1839. 95859, 96655 see also U. S. Commissioner to the Eel River or Thorntown Party of Miami Indians.

Tipton, William. 95860

Tipvs orbis vniversalis ivxta Ptolomei cosmographie traditionem. 86390

Tiraboschi, Girolamo. 95861

Tiradores en Mexico. 69073

Tirailleurs au Mexique. 69074-69076

Tirana Americana que conmovio a toda la tierra dentro. 95862

Tired soldier. 95863

Tirel, ------ Darinel de. see Darinel de Tirel, --------.

Tirpenne, ------. illus. 73935, 48916

"'Tis eighty years since." (35322), 55111

'Tis fifty years since. 11902

Tisdale, E. engr. 50185, 82379, 92375, 97220, 97223

Tisdale, Joseph. 95864

Tisdale, W. S. 8347, 38140

Tit for tat. A novel. 95865

Tit for tat, a sea kick, for a land cuff. 95866

Tit for tat, in your own way. 78475, 104455

Tit for tat; or, a purge for a pill. 14018, note after 95866

Tit for tat; or, American fixings of English humanity. 95867

Tit for tat, or the score wip'd off. 78452, note after 95867

Tit for tat; t'other side; or, bounce-about. 95868

Tit-bit for Billy Pitt, &c. &c. (65019)

Titania's banquet, a mask. (73989), 2d note after 100820

Titcomb, Jonathan. 95869

Titcomb, Timothy. pseud. Gold foil. see Holland, Josiah Gilbert.

Titcomb, Timothy. pseud. Letters to the Joneses. see Holland, Josiah Gilbert.

Titcomb, Timothy. pseud. Timothy Titcomb's letters. see Holland, Josiah Gilbert.

Titian, 1477-1576. illus. 98732

Title of John Stevens. 54495

Title papers of the Clamorgan grant. 95870, 102303

Titles and documents relating to the seigniorial tenure. 10601

Titles, and legal opinions thereon, of lands in East Florida. 24900, (29478)

Titles, extracts, and characters of old books in English literature. 8829, 25999, 79342

Titles of acts and resolutions. (60669)

Titles of Jesus. 89066

Titles of private acts. 87697, 1st note after 97056

[Titles of the bills for the members of the General Assembly.] 100054

Titles of the perpetual acts, 1692-1734. 87697, 1st note after 97056

Titles to land in the city of San Francisco. 76101

Titles to land in the city of San Francisco. Supreme Court of California, December, 1859. 67822

Titres des anciennes concessions de terre. 100763

Titterwell, Timo., Esq. pseud. Yankee notions. see Kettell, Samuel. supposed author

Tittle, Walter. illus. 84054

Titus, ----------. 72134

Titus Antigallicus. pseud. Ode, for the thanksgiving day. 56700

Titus Ironicus. pseud. 95979

Tivoli, J. de. (19981)

Tizenkét eredeti rajzok után keszut kö- és egynehány fametszettel. 35273, 105715

Tiziano Vecelli, 1477-1576. see Titian, 1477-1576.

Tjassens, Johan. 95872

Tlalpam, Mexico. Ayuntamiento. 68862, note after 95874

Tlalpam, Mexico. Ordinances, etc. 68862, note after 95874

Tlalpam, Mexico (State) Consejo. 68862, note after 95872

Tlascala, Mexico. Ayuntamiento. petitioners 95878

Tlascala, Mexico. Diputacion. 95877

Tlaxcala (Diocese) 34836

To a friend in London. 103599

To a gentleman in Barbadoes. 97289

To a planter, about the manufactury of cotton. 97289

To a planter of sugar. 97289

To a republican, with Mr. Paine's Rights of man. 95879

To A. S. 74624

To ——— a stockholder in the Bank of the U. S. 94021

To ——— a stockholder in the Bank of the United States. 83765, 102505

To a woodman's hut. 95880

To Aaron Clark. 95881

To Abraham Lincoln. 30820

To Abraham Lincoln. . . . To whom it may concern. 84763

To all and singular to whom these presents come, greeting: Treaty between the United States of America, and the Mingoes. 96663

To all and singular to whom these presents come, Greeting: whereas a treaty between the United States of America, and the Sioux and the Chippewa. 96647

To all and singular to whom these presents come, greeting: whereas articles of agreement between the United States of America and the band of Delaware Indians, upon the Sandusky River. 96660

To all and singular to whom these presents shall come, greeting. Articles of agreement and convention between the United States of America, and the Seneca Tribe of Indians. 96665

To all and singular to whom these presents shall come, greeting. Treaty between the United States of America and the Cherokee Nation of Indians, West of the Mississippi. 96656

To all and singular to whom these presents shall come, greeting: whereas a supplementary article to the treaty. 96661

To all and singular to whom these presents shall come, greeting: whereas a treaty between the United States of America and the Belantse-etoa or Minnetaree Tribe of Indians. 96644

To all and singular to whom these presents shall come, greeting: whereas, a treaty between the United States of America and the Chippeway, Menomonie and Winnebago Tribes of Indians. 96652

To all and singular to whom these presents shall come, greeting: whereas a treaty between the United States of America and the Choctaw Nation of Indians. 96635

To all and singular to whom these present[s] shall come, greeting: whereas a treaty between the United States of America and the Confederated Tribes of Sacs and Foxes. 96662

To all and singular to whom these presents shall come, greeting: whereas a treaty between the United States of America and the Creek Nation of Indians. 96636

To all and singular to whom these presents shall come, greeting: whereas a treaty between the United States of America and the Crow Tribe of Indians. 96646

To all and singular, to whom these presents shall come, greeting: whereas, a treaty between the United States of America, and the Eel River or Thorntown Party of Miami Indians. 96655

To all and singular to whom these presents shall come, greeting: whereas a treaty between the United States of America and the Great and Little Osage Tribes of Indians. 96637

To all and singular to whom these presents shall come, greeting: whereas a treaty betwen the United States of America and the Hunkpapas Band of the Sioux Tribe of Indians. 96642

To all and singular to whom these presents shall come, greeting: whereas a treaty between the United States of America and the Ioway Tribe of Indians. 96632

To all and singular to whom these presents shall come, greeting: whereas a treaty between the United States of America and the Kanzas Nation of Indians was made and concluded. 96638

To all and singular to whom these presents shall come, greeting: whereas a treaty between the United States of America and the Maha Tribe of Indians. 96650

To all and singular to whom these presents shall come, greeting: whereas a treaty between the United States of America and the Mandan Tribe of Indians. 96645

To all and singular to whom these presents shall come, greeting: whereas a treaty, between the United States of America and the nation of Winnebago Indians. 96659

To all and singular to whom these presents shall come, greeting: whereas a treaty between the United States of America and the Ottoe and Missouri Tribe of Indians. 96648

To all and singular to whom these presents shall come, greeting: whereas a treaty between the United States of America and the Pawnee Tribe of Indians. 96649

To all and singular to whom these presents shall come, greeting: whereas a treaty between the United States of America and the Poncar Tribe of Indians. 96639

To all and singular to whom these presents shall come, greeting: whereas, a treaty between the United States of America and the Potawatamie Tribe of Indians. 96653

To all and singular to whom these presents shall come, greeting: whereas a treaty between the United States of America and the Quapaw Nation of Indians. 96634

To all and singular to whom these presents shall come, greeting: whereas a treaty between the United States of America and the Ricara Tribe of Indians. 96643

To all and singular to whom these presents shall come, greeting: whereas a treaty between the United States of America and the Shawonee Nation of Indians. 96651

To all and singular to whom these presents shall come, greeting: whereas a treaty between the United States of America and the Sioune and Ogallala Tribes of Indians. 96641

To all and singular to whom these presents shall come, greeting: whereas a treaty between the United States of America and the Sock and Fox Tribes of Indians. 96633

To all and singular to whom these presents shall come, greeting: whereas a treaty between the United States of America and the Teton, Yancton, and Yanctonies Bands of the Sioux Indians. 96640

To all and singular to whom these presents shall come, greeting: whereas, a treaty was made and concluded at the Forks of the Wabash. 96737

To all and singular to whom these presents shall come, greeting: whereas, a treaty was made at Stockbridge, in the Territory of Wisconsin. 96736

To all brave, healthy able bodied, and well disposed young men. 95882

To all charitable persons, and patrons. 84622

To all charitable persons, patrons of literature. 84622

To all Christian people. 95883

To all evangelical Christians. (47241), 93816

To all farmers and tradesmen. 95884

To all friends of American liberty. 102195

To all friends of religion and patrons of useful knowledge. 84623

To all gentlemen, merchants, and pilots. 11144, 80706

To all my beloved brethren in Christ, greeting. 72686

To all officers and ministers ecclesiastical and civil. 53671

To all people in Jamaica. 13816

To all people to whom these presents shall come. 95885

To all people whom these may concern. 95886

To all patriots and real lovers of liberty. 95887

To all that are faithful in Christ Jesus. 63332

To all good people of Virginia. 99907
To all the worthy and reverend, the clergy
  and ministers of the Gospel. 84674
To all those citizens of Cambridge who deal
  in intoxicating liquors. 10153
To all to whom these presents shall come—
  greeting: whereas a treaty of peace
  and friendship between the United States
  of America and the Tribes of Indians.
  96605
To all to whom these presents shall come.
  Greeting. Whereas Low Jackson.
  99989
To all to whom these presents shall come
  or may any way concern. 98433
To all true patriots and real lovers of
  liberty. 60670
To all who are advertised by G. Keith.
  105653
To all, who are desirous of the spread of
  the Gospel. 95888
To all who desire to worship God in the
  spirit. 78442
To all who may have seen and heard the
  dying groans. 95127
To all whom these presents may concern.
  95889
To American youth. 94641
To Anacreon in heaven. 90497
To any member of Congress. 95890-95891
To any of the flock of Christ that may be
  scattered. 72685-72686
To be performed at the Brattle-Street Church.
  95892
To be performed at the Old-Church, on
  Saturday. 95893
(To be published in numbers.) No. I. 96947,
  4th note after 98168
To be sold, a tract of land of one hundred
  thousand acres. 90611
To be sold, by public venue. 55978
To be sold by the subscriber. 91190
To be sold, one of the best stands for busi-
  ness. 105369
To be sold, one of the most fertile and well
  cultivated estates. 96178
To be sold, or lett from eight hundred to
  four thousand acres. 24365, note after
  98632
To be sold or rented, Marlbro' Iron-works.
  106250
To be sosd [sic], by William Prince. (65619)
To beso til Sydamerikas fastland med briggen
  St. Croix in 1826. 18274
To [blank] By virtue of His Majesty's royal
  commission. 99990
To C. C. Jewett, Esq. 90656
To capitalists and citizens of Baltimore.
  3086
To capitalists, relative to Milwaukee city
  loan. 49180
To Captain Alexander Patterson. 82550
To citizens of the United States, and particu-
  larly to those not born therein.
  22108
To . . . Congress. 5811, (35448)
To . . . Congress . . . : the memorial and
  petition of John Barney. 3539
To . . . Congress . . . : Memorial of . . .
  [the Chesapeake and Ohio Canal Com-
  pany.] 12502
To C. P. Kirkland. 82517
To Cuba and back. 18447
"To cut the Gordian knot." 69824, 100796
To Daniel O'Connell, the great agitator.
  (56653)

To day a man, to morrow none. 67599
To-day. A romance. 37767
To Doctor Cheever. 82618
To Dr. Coke, Mr. Asbury, and our brethren
  in North-America. 102700
To Doctor Johnson from his very humble
  servant the author. 84693
To Dr. Levi Ives. 103489
[To each Inspector of the Sanitary Commision.]
  sion.] 76642
To Edwin Croswell. 82619
To emigrants; John Almy, State Agent, 1845.
  48803
To emigrants to the gold region. 71919
To enable the freemen of this colony to form
  a true judgment of the proposals.
  101333
To every courteous reader. 104331
To F——— H——— Esq. 95894
To farmers, mechanics, and others in the
  northwest. 91008
To Federalists, attached to Republican gov-
  ernment. 13747
To Friends in Barbadoes, Virginia, and New-
  England. 9462
To Friends in Barbadoes, Virginia, Maryland,
  New-England, and elswhere [sic]. 25356
To Friends in England. 59661
To Friends of Ireland, and else-where. 98098
To Friends of the Island of Tortola. 25273
To General Andrew Jackson. 93797
To General Conway. 59410
To General Lafayette. 38583
To General Lee. 82620
To General U. S. Grant. 13651
To [blank] Gentlemen, you are hereby appointed
  Commissioners. 100193
To George Bancroft. 55760
To George M'Duffie. 103818
To George Thompson. 82621
To Governor Seymour. 82622
To his beloved friends the inhabitants of
  Groton. 104110
To His Catholic Majesty, Ferdinand the
  Seventh. 95895
To his constituents. 82623
To his countrymen. 61696
To His Excellency Abraham Lincoln. 73972
To His Excellency Andrew Johnson. (35248)
To His Excellency Edward Viscount Corn-
  bury. (37179), 104070
To His Excellency George Washington. 50652
To His Excellency Governor Belcher. 9716
To His Excellency Henry J. Gardner. 30247
To His Excellency Henry Laurens. 93814
To His Excellency John Wentworth. 103217
To His Excellency, Sir Henry Clinton. 79477
To His Excellency the Governor . . . of Mas-
  sachusetts. 17609
To His Excellency the Governor of the pro-
  vince of the Massachusetts-Bay. 1037,
  81585
To His Excellency the Governor of the state
  of Massachusetts. 98562
To His Excellency the Governor, the Honorable
  Council, and House of Representatives,
  of the state of Vermont. 99134
To His Excellency William Shirley. 100928
To His Excellency William Tyron. 95896
To His fellow citizens of the United States of
  America. 94384
To his friends. 37297
To his friends, &c. &c. &c. 94383
To His Grace, Her Majesty's High Commis-
  sioner. (78239)
To His Grace the Duke of Portland. 95299

To His Most Excellent Majestje [sic], Charles. 66682
To Hon. E. M. Stanton. 41967
To Horace Greeley. 82624
To J. Collins. 54976, 94549
To James Earl of Perth. 78186
To John A. Gurley. 82625
To John Cruger. 95897
To John Ellis. 72992
To John M. S————, Esq. 95898
To John Stuart Mill. (82671)
To Lord North. 51899
To loyal Democrats! (42546)
To Luther Martin. 95899
To Maj. Gen. Fitz John Porter. 64249
To marry a wife's sister, no inconsistent with the divine law. 66410, 97178
To members of the General Court. 48009
To merchants, underwriters, and others interested. 25050
To Messieurs Edward Payne & Henderson Inches. 26630A, 1st note after 95889
To Messrs. N. Goddard. 10889
To Miss Seward. 79478
To Mr. A. C. 95900
To Mr. Garrison. 82626
To Mr. Isaac Low. 98982
To Montgomery Blair. 82627
To Morris Morris. 60671, 94633
To mothers in the free states. 24955
To Mrs. Leonard, on the death of her husband. 103140
To Mrs. Moore. (76683)
To my constituents of the counties of Clarke, Fayette, Woodford, and Franklin. 30927
To my constituents of the fourth congressional district. 84888
To my fellow citizens. (68186)
To my fellow-citizens, friends to liberty. 45021
To my fellow-countrymen of Powhatan. 16340
To my friends in Pensilvania [sic]. 98986
To my honest capitaine, the author. 82819
To my loving and dearly beloved Christian friends. 2734
To my respected friend I. N. 60672, note after 95900
To my reverend dear brother, N. Samuel Stone. 92113
To New-England's pretended Christians. 82735
To old Republicans. 95901
To our beloved brethren and neighbours. (53384)
To our friends and brethren. 62312, note after 95901
To our friends and brethren of the several meetings. 95902
To our . . . legislative councillors. 98065B
To Owen Lovejoy. 82628
To P. V. B. Livingston. 105223
To Pacificus in reply to his essay. 62564
To perpetuate the memory of peace. 95903, 2d note after 97010
To persons, incluned to emigrate to America. 95904
To Philip S. Physick, M. D. 95905
To please Christ, the great business of a Gospel minister. (71763)
To President Buchanan. 76386
To President Grant. 82629
To prevent, as much as possible, the evil consequences. 15146, 98439
To prevent impositions. 100037
To R. G. Payne. 33823
To Republicans. 3570

To Robert Jordan. 60673, 1st note after 95905
To S. C. Phillips. 96509
To Samuel Allison. 100973
To Senator Sumner. 82630
To sing of mercy and judgment recommended and exemplified. 26777
To Sir Guy Carleton. 93776
To Sir Iohn Norris and Sir Frauncis Drake. 59526
To Sir Thomas Robinson, Bart. 102451
To southern states citizens in Europe. 88469
To such as are d[e]sirious of settling on the lands of the crown. 98065E
To such of his deluded subjects. 87367
To Thaddeus Stevens. 82631
To Thad. Stevens & Co., greeting. 89480
To the advocates of ministerial oppression. 60674, 3d note after 95905
To the Agents of Their High Mightinesses the Dutch East-India Company. 95906
To the alumni of Yale College. 105920
To the American public. 19841
To the Associate Congregation of Cambridge. 90512
To the Associate Congregation of Grand-Street, New-York. 90515
To the author of a letter to Doctor Mather. 95907
To the author of the book. 97296
To the author of those intelligencers. 95908
To the banks of . . . New York. 54696
To the betrayed inhabitants of the city and colony of New-York. 86868
To the Board of Education of the Pennsylvania Society for Promoting the Abolition of Slavery. 59989
To the Board of National Popular Education. 4293
To the bondholders of the Central and Western Pacific Railroad Companies. 24523
To the British nation is presented by Colonel Venault de Charmilly. 98839
To the Building Committee . . . of the . . . [American] Academy [of Music.] 61458
To the candid reader. 28506, 28052, 65689
To the candid public. 91747
To the Catholic voters of the city of Baltimore. 104445
To the Chancellor of the state of New-York. 104500
To the children of light. 95909
To the Christian reader. (46670), 46783, 72687, 72691, 79341, 80199, 80200, 80209, note after 92797, 104093
To the church and inhabitants of Northampton. (46626)
To the Church of Christ at Wester. 72682
To the churches and congregations of Vermont. 99234
To the churches in New-England. 9462
To the citizens and legislators of the United States. 97934
To the citizens of America. 95910
To the citizens of Baltimore. (3087)
To the citizens of Baltimore and others interested. 45205
To the citizens of Boston. March, 1846. 58912
To the citizens of Boston [on the new plan of public schools.] (58630)
To the citizens of Connecticut. 79255
To the citizens of Greenville District. 28676
To the citizens of Jefferson, Oldham, Nelson & Bullitt Counties. 103860-103861
To the citizens of . . . Louisiana. (42307)
To the citizens of Massachusetts. 94207

To the citizens of Missouri. (49648)

To the citizens of New Haven. 105805

To the citizens . . . of Pennsylvania. [ca. 1825] 60677

To the citizens . . . of Pennsylvania. [ca. 1832] 60678

To the citizens of Pennsylvania. [By George Grey, Speaker, for a majority of the Assembly.] 60675

To the citizens of Pennsylvania. [By the Constitutional Society, Philadelphia.] 60398

To the citizens of Pennsylvania. [By the Federal Party of Pennsylvania.] (60676)

To the citizens of Pennsylvania, on the proposal for calling a convention. 58240

To the citizens of Pennsylvania. Pennsylvania Academy of the Fine Arts. 60294

To the citizens of Pennsylvania; read for yourselves. 100680

To the citizens of Philadelphia. [ca. 1771.] (62314)

To the citizens of Philadelphia. [ca. 1826.] (62313)

To the citizens of Philadelphia. Pennsylvania Academy of the Fine Arts. 60294

To the citizens of Philadelphia, relative to John Hendree. 98099

To the citizens of Philadelphia . . . Robert Morris. 50869

To the citizens of South Carolina. [ca. 1823.] 71117

To the citizens of South-Carolina. [By Appius.] 87733

To the citizens of South Carolina. [By Matthew Carey.] 10889

To the citizens of the ninth congressional district. 103862

To the citizens of the tenth congressional district of Kentucky. 105946

To the citizens of the twenty-first ward. 54697

To the citizens of the United States, and particularly to the citizens of New-York. 97937

To the citizens of the United States. [By A native of Maryland.] 97935

To the citizens of the United States. [By Hamilton, i. e. Mathew Carey.] 10889

To the citizens of the United States. [By the Soldier's Home, Philadelphia.] 86336

To the citizens of the United States of America. 97938

To the citizens of the United States. Review of the address of the Free Trade Convention. 10889

To the citizens of the United States. Robert Fulton. 97936

To the citizens of the village of Utica. 98225

To the citizens of Walnut Ward. [By the American Party of Pennsylvania.] (62315)

To the citizens of Walnut Ward. [By the Whig Party of Pennsylvania. (62316)

To the citizens of Washington County. Fellow-citizens. 102013

To the citizens of York. 95911

To the claimants under the sixth article of the treaty. 84842

To the clergie of the foure great parties. 104333

To the clerical and lay members. 45310

To the clergy and congregations of the Diocese of Pennsylvania. 60679

To the clergy and laity of Long Island. 41901

To the clergymen and other well informed gentlemen. 102343

To the close of the peninsula campaign of 1862. 29113

To the colored citizens of the American republic. 36276

To the Commissioners Appointed by the East-India Company. 95912

To the Committee for the Construction of a Ship Canal. 95913

To the Committee of the Washington Monument Association. 25692

To the Committee on Corporations of the Senate. 103437

To the Committee on Plans for the Philadelphia Academy of Music. 61937

To the Committee on Post-Offices and Post-Roads. 56238

To the Committee who fitted out William Kittletas. 95914

To the . . . Committees of both . . . Houses of Parliament. 101508

To the Committee of the Senate & House of Representatives, on the Illinois and Wabash memorial. 34294, 84577-84578, 2d-3d notes after 97876

To the congregation of the first Presbyterian Church. 43595

To the Congress of the Confederate States. 15421

To the Congress of the United States. [ca. 1854] 70597

To the Congress of the United States: [asking that a special act be passed.] 78882

To the Congress of the United States. Bridging the Ohio & Mississippi Rivers. 13071

To the Congress of the United States. [By Hamilton.] (70349)

To the Congress of the United States. [By Sydney.] 94089

To the Congress. The remonstrance of the subscribers. 62317

To the conservative people of Virginia. (23926)

To the constituents of the 37th Congress. (28570)

To the contributors. 60330

To the courteous reader. 77289, 73577, 82844

To the creditors of the Bank of Maryland. 45079

To the daughters of Washington! 51177

To the Delaware pilots. 19402-19403

To the delegates of the Democratic National Convention. 60680

To the delegates to the Convention of the Democratic Party. 60681

To the Democracy of Indiana. 73254

To the Democracy of the border states. 19490

To the Democracy of the fifth congressional district of South Carolina. 88080

To the Democracy of the United States. (19491)

To the Democratic and conservative voters of the state. 34578

To the Democratic citizens of Pennsylvania. 60682

To the Democratic delegates of Pennsylvania. 60683

To the Democratic Party of Rhode Island. 70754

To the Democratic Party of the U. S. 91653

To the Democratic Republican electors. 2589

To the Democrats of Pennsylvania. (60684)

To the dissenting electors. 95915

To the dis-united inhabitants. 95916
To the doctors. 39820, 1st note after 94666
To the editor of the Advertiser. 19200
To the editor of the United States Gazette. 101742, 101746
To the editors of . . . religious periodicals. (29837)
To the editors of the Albany register. (39070)
To the editors of the first American edition. 99822
To the editors of the National intelligencer. [By E. G. Squier.] 89967
To the editors of the National intelligencer. [By Hamilton.] 30056
To the editors of the National intelligencer. [By Henry Clay.] 96362
To the electors at the ensuing election. 95917
To the electors of Chenango County, N. Y. 13303
To the electors of Great-Britain. 95918
To the electors of Massachusetts. 46162, note after 103275, 1st note after 104862
To the electors of Middlesex District. 101346
To the electors of . . . Pennsylvania. [By the Democratic Party of Pennsylvania.] 60687
To the electors of Pennsylvania. [By the Federal Party of Pennsylvania.] (60685)
To the electors of the Borough and County of Lancaster. (38798), note after 92058
To the electors of the city of New-York. 54698
To the electors of the counties of Johnston, Wayne, Greene, Lenoir, Jones, Craven and Carteret. 90347
To the electors of the counties of Johnston, Wayne, Greene, Lenoir, Jones, Craven, and Carteret——Gentlemen. 90346
To the electors of the county of Madison. (43728)
To the electors of the county of Middlesex. 48852, 103279
To the electors of the county of Norfolk. (55475)
To the electors of the county of Plymouth. 95432
To the electors of the Eastern District. 95919
To the electors of the First Western District. 78830
To the electors of the fourth congressional district. 48852, 103279
To the electors of the ninth congressional district. 72863
To the electors of the second congressional district. 60686
To the electors of the sixteenth congressional district. 92238
To the electors of the Southern District. 95920
To the electors of the state of New-York. 94676
To the electors of Worcester County. 105413
To the farmers, manufacturers and mechanics of Rensselaer County. 69640
To the farmers, mechanics, laborers, and all voters of the western & north-western states. 85895, 91009
To the farmers of Rhode Island! 70755
To the Federalists of the United States. (30057)
To the flock of God father'd out of the world. 13816

To the free Africans and other free people of color. 95921
To the free and independent electors, of the state of New-York. 26908, 100693
To the free and respectable mechanicks, and other inhabitants. 95845
To the free electors of the state. 54699
To the free-holders and freemen of the city. 97165
To the free-holders of the province of Pennsylvania. 60692
To the free inhabitants of West-Chester County. 102953
To the free people of colour in the United States. 95922
To the free voters of Ohio. 82110
To the freeholders and electors of the city and county of Philadelphia. 62318
To the freeholders and electors, of the province of Pennsylvania. 60688
To the freeholders and freemen a further information. 60689, note after 95922
To the freeholders and freemen, in Pennsylvania. 60690
To the freeholders, and freemen, of the north-ward. 100894A
To the freeholders and other electors for the city and county of Philadelphia. 62319
To the freeholders and other electors of Assembly-men. 60691
To the freeholders, etc., of Philadelphia. 61676
To the freeholders, merchants, tradesmen and farmers. 62320, 62337
To the freeholders of Charlotte, Buckingham, Prince-Edward, and Cumberland. 67847
To the freeholders . . . of . . . Pennsylvania. 5233
To the freeholders of the counties of Campbell, Pittsylvania and Halifax. 97305
To the freeholders of the county of Providence. 94458
To the freeholders of the District of Fairfax. 95923
To the freeholders of Washington, Wythe, Grayson, Russell, Tazewell, Lee, and Scott. 85198
To the freeholders, to prevent mistakes. 60693
To the freemen and freeholders of the city and county of New-York. 95768
To the freemen and freeholders of the colony aforesaid. 101252
To the freemen, citizens of Philadelphia. [By a Philadelphian, June 16, 1773.] 62322
To the freemen, citizens of Philadelphia. [By a Philadelphian, May 29, 1773.] 61807, 62321
To the freemen of America. 51227, 95924
To the freemen of Arkansas. 106008
To the freemen of Columbia. 95880
To the freemen of Connecticut. 96423
To the freemen of Kentucky. 103948
To the freemen of New-England. (30196), 74359, 103849
To the freemen of North Carolina. 55588
To the freemen of Pennsylvania. [ca. 1784.] 60698
To the freemen of Pennsylvania. [ca. 1764.] (60694)
To the freemen of Pennsylvania. [By A. P.] (60696)
To the freemen of Pennsylvania. [By Civis.] (60695)
To the freemen of Pennsylvania. [By Regulus.] (60697)

To the Honorable Robert Dinwiddie, Esq; His Majesty's Lieutenant-Governor, and Commander in Chief of the Colony and Dominion of Virginia; the humble address of the Council. [ca. 1757] 99905

To the Honourable Robert Dinwiddie, Esq; His Majesty's Lieutenant-Governor, and Commander in Chief, of the Colony and Dominion of Virginia, the humble address of the House of Burgesses. [ca. 1753] 99922

To the Honorable Robert Dinwiddie, Esq; His Majesty's Lieutenant-Governor and Commander in Chief, of the Colony and Dominion of Virginia' the humble address of the House of Burgesses. [ca. 1756] 99904

To the Honorable Robert Dinwiddie, Esq; His Majesty's Lieutenant-Governor, and Commander in Chief of the Colony and Dominion of Virginia; the humble address of the House of Burgesses. [ca. 1757] 99923

To the Hon. Secretary of the United States Treasury. 91001

To the Honorable Senate and House of Representatives. 86324

To the Honorable Senate and House of Representatives, in General Court assembled. 98569

To the Honorable Senate and House of Representatives in General Court assembled. Gentlemen representatives of the people 98570

To the Honorable Senate and House of Representatives of the state of South Carolina. 87401

To the Honorable Senate and House of Representatives of the United States, in Congress assembled. 99207

To the Hon. Senate and House of Representatives of the United States. Memorial of the Philadelphia Society for the Promotion of American Manufactures. 62324

To the Honourable Senate, and the House of Representatives of the commonwealth of Massachusetts. 8707

To the Honourable Simon Broadstreet. 78434

To the Honourable, Sir William Ashvrst Knight. 79443

To the Honble. Sir William Gooch, Bart. His Majesty's Lieutenant-Governor, and Commander in Chief, of the Colony and Dominion of Virginia. 99901

To the Honourable Sir William Gooch, Bart. . . . The humble address of the Council. 99900

To the Honourable Sir William Gooch, Bart. . . . The humble address of the House of Burgesses. [ca. 1747] 99920

To the Honble Sir William Gooch, Bart. . . . The humble address of the House of Burgesses. [ca. 1748] 99921

To the Honourable, the Commissioners "Appointed by His Most Gracious Majesty, for Ascertaining, Settling, Adjusting, and Determining, the Boundary." 95936

To the Honourable the Committee appointed to receive claims of such as have right and property in the Narraganset Country. 95937

To the Honorable, the Committee of the House of Representatives. 1254

To the Honourable the Commons of Great Britain, in Parliament assembled. The humble petition of the merchants. 95938-95939

To the Honourable the Commons of Great Britain, in Parliament assembled: the petition of the merchants. 95940

To the Honorable the Congress of the United States of America. 97921

To the Hon. the Corporation of New-York. 98482

To the Hon. the Corporation of the city of New-York. 95801

To the Honorable the General Assembly of Maryland. 12206

To the Honorable the General Assembly of the commonwealth of Virginia. 100528

To the Honorable the General Assembly of the state of Connecticut. 105797-105798

To the Honourable the Governor and Council. 100527

To the Honorable the Governor Charles S. Whitman. 83848

To the Hon. the House of Representatives. (26907)

To the Honourable the House of Representatives of the commonwealth of Massachusetts. 88994

To the Honourable the House of Representatives of the United States. The memorial of the subscribers, citizens of ——— in Massachusetts. 97939

To the Honourable the House of Representatives of the United States. The Memorial of the subscribers, merchants and traders of ———. 97940

To the Honourable the Knights, Citizens, and Burgesses in Parliament assembled. 33697, 52428

To the Honourable the Legislature of . . . Pennsylvania. (60702)

To the Honorable the Legislature of the state of New-York. (54000)

To the Honorable the Legislature of the state of New York: . . . [By Tax or no tax.] 94138

To the Honorable the Legislature of the state of New York. [By the Managers of the Society for the Reformation of Juvenile Delinquents.] 85960

To the Honorable the Legislature of the state of New-York. [By the Trustees of Union College.] 97787

To the Honourable the Legislature of the state of New-York, in Senate and Assembly convened. The directors of the Western and Northern Inland Lock Navigation Companies, respectfully report. 69857, 102964

To the Honorable the Legislature of the state of New York, in Senate and Assembly convened——the remonstrance of the subscribers. 102952

To the Honourable, the members of both Houses of Congress. 101108

To the Honourable the People's Council and House of Representatives. 1037, 81585

To the Honorable, the President and Members of the Council. 94957

To the Honourable the Preisdent and members of the Senate, and the Honourable the Speaker. 86141

To the Honourable, the President and members of the Senate of South Carolina. 87387

To the Honorable the President and other
members of the Senate of the said state
[of South Carolina.] 87531

To the Honorable the President, and other
members of the Senate of the said state
[of the South Carolina]: the Committee
appointed 20th December last. 87528

To the Honourable the Senate and House of
Representatives . . . in Congress
assembled. (47621), 60704

To the Honourable, the Senate and House of
Representatives, in Congress assembled:
we the undersigned petitioners. 86349

To the Honorable the Senate, and House of
Representatives of Massachusetts. 93434,
93438

To the Honourable the Senate and House of
Representatives . . . of Pennsylvania.
(60703)

To the Honourable the Senate, and House of
Representatives, of the commonwealth of
Massachusetts, in General Court, as-
sembled. 103404

To the Honorable the Senate and House of
Representatives of the state of New-
Hampshire. 95535

To the Honorable the Senate and House of
Representatives of the United States.
[By Henry P. Scholte.] 77775

To the Honourable the Senate and House of
Representatives of the United States, in
Congress assembled——the memorial
of the subscribers. 97942

To the Honorable the Senate and House of
Representatives of the United States, in
Congress assembled. The memorial
of the undersigned. 101953

To the Honorable the Senate and House of
Representatives of the United States of
America. 103163

To the Honourable the Senate and House of
Representatives of the United States of
America, in Congress assembled. 97941

To the Honorable the Senate and House of
Representatives of the United States of
America, in Congress assembled: . . .
[By W. J. Poorman.] 86325

To the Honourable the Senate and House of
Representatives of the United States of
America, in Congress assembled——the
memorial of Augustus V. Van Horne.
98516

To the Honble. the Senate and House of
Representatives of the United States, the
memorial of James Smith. 82779

To the Hon. the Senate and House of Representatives of the United States. The
petition of Daniel Renner and Nathaniel
H. Heath. 69618

To the Honourable the Senate and House of
Representatives of the United States:
the petition of Samuel Ward. 101336

To the Hon. the Senate and . . . Representatives . . . in Congress assembled.
46165

To the Hon. the Senate . . . of . . . Massachusetts. 46164

To the Honorable the Senate of the United
States. 95538

To the Honourable the Senate of the United
States. Memorial of First Lieutenant
James W. Schaumburg. 77521

To the Hon. the Senators of the first senate
district. 95462

To the Hon. the Speaker and House of
Delegates of Virginia. 100060

To the Honorable the Speaker, and the other
members of the House of Representatives
of the state of South-Carolina. 86140

To the Hon. Timothy Pickering. 95933

To the Hon'ble Thomas Hubbard. 103141

To the Trustees of the Colony
of Georgia. 104690

To the Hon. W. J. Grayson. 88081

To the Honourable W. Pitt. 56704

To the Honourable William Gooch, Esq; His
Majesty's Lieutenant-Governor, and
Commander in Chief, of the Colony and
Dominion, of Virginia. The humble addres
of the Council. 99893

To the Honourable William Gooch, Esw; His
Majesty's Lieutenant-Governor, and
Commander in Chief, of the Colony of
Virginia. 99899

To the Honourable William Gooch, Esq; . . .
the humble address of the House of
Burgesses. [February 1745-46.] 99919

To the Honourable William Gooch, Esq; . . .
The humble address of the House of
Burgesses. Presented, on Monday, the
6th day of November, 1738. 99914

To the Hon. William Lawrence. 88404

To the Honorary Council of the Citizens'
Association of New York. (54188)

To the . . . House of Representatives of . . .
Massachusetts. 45918

To the impartial publick. 96442

To the independent electors of Pennsylvania.
60705

To the independent freeholders and freemen.
95941

To the indepen[de]nt voters of Middlesex
County. 103280

To the independent voters of . . . Philadelphia.
61911

To the independent yeomanry of the Jackson
Party. 95942

To the individual members of the General
Assembly. 55697

To the ingeneous and candid. (50333), 101849

To the inhabitants of America. 2059

To the inhabitants of Canada. 101689

To the inhabitants of Great Britain. 15596,
30179, 97533

To the inhabitants of New-York. 86124

To the inhabitants of Pennsylvania. 60706

To the inhabitants of Philadelphia. (62326)

To the inhabitants of Thames-Street. 71721

To the inhabitants of the city and county of
New-York. [By a sober citizen.] 85661

To the inhabitants of the city and county of
New-York. [By a son of liberty.] 95898

To the inhabitants of the city and county of
New-York. [By the watchman.] 102044

To the inhabitants of the city and county of
New-York. Friends and fellow citizens.
95769

To the inhabitants of the city and county of
Philadelphia. 62325

To the inhabitants of the city and liberties of
Philadelphia. 62328

To the inhabitants of the city, county and
province of New-York. 103261

To the inhabitants of the city of Philadelphia,
and parts adjacent. 62327, 70466

To the inhabitants of the colony of New York.
15583, 98439

To the inhabitants of the county of Essex.
93421

To the inhabitants of the province of Pennsylvania. 60707

To the inhabitants of the Province of Quebec. 15526, (15528), note after 63244, 84642

To the inhabitants of the state of Vermont. Friends and fellow citizens. 99005

To the inhabitants of the state of Vermont. Friends and fellow-countrymen. 99004

To the inhabitants of the state of Vermont. Gentlemen. 99002

To the inhabitants of the states of Pennsylvania, New-Jersey and Delaware. 101704

To the inhabitants of the towns bordering upon and near to the River Merrimack. 95943

To the inhabitants of the township of ———. 95944

To the inhabitants of Vermont. 106119

To the judicious reader. (66867)

To the King of Greate Britaine. 86845, 1st note after 93596

To the Kings Most Excellent Maiestie. 67550, 93235

To the King's Most Excellent Majesty. [By John Allen.] 1037, 81585

To the King's Most Excellent Majesty. [By Philo Caledon.] 78211

To the King's Most Excellent Majesty in Council, the humble petition and memorial. 35587, 35664

To the King's Most Excellent Majesty in Council. The memorial of the Honourable Thomas Walpole. 101150

To the King's Most Excellent Majesty; the humble address and petition of the merchants, traders, and others. 95945

To the King's Most Excellent Majesty. The humble address of divers of the gentry, merchants and others. 6474, 95946

To the King's Most Excellent Majesty. The humble petition of Roger Williams. 104344

To the Kings Most Excellent Majesty, the humble remonstrance of John Blande. 100529

To the ladies of Massachusetts. 19663

To the landholders of the state of Maryland. (45378)

To the legatees of Gen. Washington. 101764

To the legal voters of the Church of the Epiphany. 61537

To the Legislature 60758

To the Legislature of Maine. 89703

To the Legislature of . . . New York. 43441

To the Legislature of South Carolina. 88082

To the Legislature of the state of New-York. 97898

To the Legislature of Virginia, on the subject of militia fines. 100525

To the Legislature of Virginia. The memorial and petition of the religious society of Friends. 100527A

To the Liberty Party in Ohio. 93565

To the . . . Lord President, and Counsell of State. note after 100560, 104190

To the . . . Lords of the Councell of Virginea. 99866

To the loyal women of America. 76684

To the Managers of the . . . Society. 62349

To the manufacturers and mechanics of Philadelphia. 62329

To the Mayor and City Council of Baltimore. 93938

To the mechanics, manufactures, [sic] and working men. 37422

To the mechanics of New-York. 93538

To the members of both houses of the Legislature of Virginia. 100530

To the members of St. Mary's Congregation. (62214)

To the members of the American Institute. 95948

To the members of the American Peace Society. 5830

To the members of the Baltimore Bar. 104318

To the members of the Carmine Street Church. 95947

To the members of the Congregation of St. Peter's Church. (13787)

To the members of the Convention for Amending the Constitution of Massachusetts. (5827)

To the members of the First Presbyterian Church, Albany. 616

To the members of the Free and Easy Club. 95949

To the members of the General Assembly of Rhode Island. 63054

To the members of the General Court of Massachusetts: being a counter remonstrance. (52687)

To the members of the . . . General Court of . . . Massachusetts. [By Josiah Little.] (41521)

To the members of the General Court of Massachusetts, friendly to temperance. 46166

To the members of the House of Representatives of the United States. 95648

To the members of the Louisville Commercial Convention. 85447

To the members of the Magdalen Society. (61801)

To the members of the Moral Reform Society of Salem. 10588

To the members of the Mount-Pleasant Church. 92028

To the members of the Parish of Grace Church. 100968

To the members of the . . . [Pennsylvania State Agricultural] Society. 60376

To the members of the Protestant Episcopal Church in . . . St. James's. 67992

To the members of the Protestant Episcopal Church in the United States of America. 103474

To the members of the religious society of Friends. 93262

To the members of the Roman Catholic Church. 104446

To the members of the Society for Propagating the Gospel Among the Indians, and Others, in North-America. 11203, (34627), 95950

To the . . . members of the U. S. Senate from La. 3392

To the memory of Daniel Webster. 103819

To the memory of John Woolman. 47080

To the memory of Mary Callahan. 88575

To the memory of Mrs. Betsey Porter. 64263

To the memory of the departed. 86667, note after 101396

To the memory of the martyrs. 54700

To the memory of William Foster Otis. 91720

To the men of New-York. 85199

To the men of Rhode Island. 71148

To the merchants and manufacturers of Great Britain. 95951

To the merchants and other inhabitants of Pennsylvania. 60708

To the merchants, and traders, of the city of Philadelphia. 62330

To the Merchants Committee, the dry goods merchants, &c. 62331

To the merchants of Chicago. 12668

To the military officers, select-men, and committee of correspondence. 95952

To the militia of Pennsylvania. (60709)

To the millers. 95317

To the ministers and elders of the Presbyterian Church. 5579

To the minority, lay and clerical, in the Anglican Synod of Toronto. 89632

To the Most High and Excellent Prince Charles. 82835

to the Most High and Excellent Prince, Charles, Prince of Wales. 66683

To the Most Illustrious and Hopefull Prince Charles. 67591

To the Most Noble Prince Henry Duke of Beaufort. 44822

To the Most Reverend Father in God, George. 66682

To the Most Reverend Father in God, George, Lord Archb. of Canterburie. 66686

To the New Capitol Commissioners. 64203

To the New England professors. (25346)

To the nobility, gentry, and commvnaltie of England. 78369

To the nobility, gentry, and communalty of England. 78369

To the non-commissioned officers and privates. 62332

To the officers & members of the Centennial Legion. 84343

To the officers of the Army. 102216

To the officers of the late war, the following proceedings had in reference. 95953

To the officers of the late war, the second of independence. (38814), 95954

To the officers of the Navy and Marine Corps. 95955, 96014

To the ouer-wise, ouer-wilfull, ouer-curious, or ouer-captious reader. 78189

To the parents and guardians of the children of Public School no. I. 35673

To the parishioners. 643

[To the parishioners.] 28186

To the parishioners of Trinity Church. 79020

To the patriotic citizens of Pompton Plains. (19527)

To the patrons and friends of the American Tract Society. (14757)

To the people. An address in five numbers. 71069

To the people and the Honorable the Legislature of the state of New York. 42024

To the people. No. 3. 95956

To the people of America. [By a British officer.] 95958

To the people of America. Common sense. 93777

To the people of Canada. 73340

To the people of Clarke County. 100495

To the people of Colorado. 12855

To the people of Connecticut. 17539

To the people of Connecticut. "The extention of slavery." 15862

To the people of Daviess County. 96993

To the people of England and America. 17514

To the people of Florida. 103432-103433

To the people of Georgia. [By A. H. Stephens.] 91279

To the people of Georgia. [By Wm. H. Stiles.] 91777

To the people of Great Britain and Ireland. 95959

To the people of Great Britain, from the delegates appointed by the several English colonies. 40509, 95960

To the people of Ireland. 47380

To the people of Kentucky. [By Achilles Sneed.] 85376

To the people of Kentucky. [By Cassius M. Clay.] 13535

To the people of Maine. 44045

To the people of Maryland and of the United States of America. 97943

To the people of Massachusetts, and to the friends of rail-roads. 19305

To the people of Massachusetts. [By Robert C. Winthrop.] 103276, 2d note after 104862

To the people of Mississippi. 28351

To the people of New-York . . . . [By a citizen.] 95987

To the people of New-York. [By Jesse Buel.] 101159

To the people of North-America. 102870

To the people of North-Carolina. 55698

To the people of Pennsylvania. (60710)

To the people of Pennsylvania, and to the Legislature now in session. 60711

To the people of Pennsylvania. [By Devereaux Smith.] 82433

To the people of Pennsylvania. [By Jacob Dewees.] 19841

To the people of Rhode Island. 30194

To the people of South-Carolina. An address on the subject of the approaching Presidential election. 88084

To the people of South Carolina. [By William Smith.] 88083

To the people of Suffolk. 35535, note after 93439

To the people of Suffolk County. 35535

To the people of Suffolk, of all parties. 35535

To the people of the congressional district. 13550

To the people of the county of Oneida. 27704

To the people of the first congressional district Ky. 96974

To the people of the south. Senator Hammond and the Tribune. 30101, note after 97063

To the people of the southern states. (39520)

To the people of the state of Missouri. 61303

To the people of the state of New York. 54468

To the people of the state of New-York. [By Cato.] 11547, 95781

To the people of the state of New-York. [By the Committee appointed at Mrs. Vandewater's.] 53473, 54042, 83604

To the people of the state of New-York. [By the Virginia Anti-Jackson Convention, 1827.] 100497

To the people of the state of North Carolina. 90338

To the people of the state of South-Carolina. 88085

To the people of the United States. [ca. 1807] 25881

To the people of the United States. [ca. 1828] 97945

To the people of the United States. [ca. 1844] 66066

To the people of the United States. [ca. 1864] (23149)

To the people of the United States. Andrew County, Missouri. 58400

To the people of the United States, announcing his intention of retiring from public life. 101599

To the people of the United-States. British pretentions and American rights. 97947

To the people of the United States. [By a U.S. Senator.] 97946

To the people of the United States. [By George Washington]. note before 101548, 101572, 101584

To the people of the United States. [By Nehemiah R. Knight.] (38121)

To the people of the United States. [By the U. S. Anti-masonic Convention, 1830.] 32529, 97957

To the people of the United States. [By William Maclure.] (43556), 97944

To the people of the United States. (From the American citizen.) 97948

To the people of the United States. (From the Pennsylvania inquirer.) 97949

To the people of the United States [of America: an address from A. V. Brown and others.] 8431

To the people of the United States of America this engraved copy of Washington's farewell address. 101660

To the people of the United States, on the choice of a president. [By Touchstone.] 96326

To the people of the United States on the choice of a president. [By Washington.] 101526

To the people of the United States . . . . [On the reorganization of the south.] 23777

To the people of the United States, or, to such Americans, as value their rights. 14400

To the people of the United States. What says the law? 90795

To the people of Tyrrell, Washington, Hyde, Pitt, Beaufort and Edgecombe Counties, North Carolina. 90339

To the people of Vermont. [By William Slade.] 81690

To the people of Vermont. Mr. Phelps's rejoinder to Mr. Slade's "Reply." 61394

To the people of Virginia. [By F. H. Pierpoint.] 62756

To the people of Virginia. [By Franklin.] 99807, note after 100544

To the people of Virginia. [By P. Williams.] 100531, note after 104322

To the people of Virginia . . . . [By the Virginia Anti-Jackson Convention, 1827.] 100497

To the people of Virginia! John Letcher and his antecedents. (40237)

To the people. The bargain proved by the testimony of Mr. Clay's friend's. 13567

To the people. The officers of the Grand Division of the Sons of Temperance. 87034

To the people. The real state of the case. 95957

To the persons belonging to the Protestant Episcopal Church. 95961

To the pewholders and other contributors of St. Paul's Church. 3088

To the philharmonical merchants, and others. 61920

To the planters of South-Carolina. (56466), 87904

To the poor, trapan'd, simple deluded people in Pennsylvania. 97693

To the President and Council of Pennsylvania. (59611), 61671

To the President, . . . and Directors, of the Massachusetts Hospital Life Insurance Company. 42432

To the President and Directors of the New Jersey Zinc Company. (53197)

To the President and Directors of the South Side Rail Road Company. 88213

To the President and Directors of the Williams' Valley Railroad and Mining Company. 104434

To the President and Executive Council. 60712

To the President and Managers of the Union Canal Company. 60750

To the President and Officers of the various life insurance companies. 76527, 76549, 76647

To the President of the U. States, and the Honourable the members of both houses of Congress. The subscriber. 104129

To the President of the United States, and the members of both houses of Congress, on the subject of the tariff. 104129A

To the President of the United States, and the members of both houses of Congress, The subscriber most respectfully solicits. 104129

To the President of the United States. The address of the [people] of South-Carolina. 87509

To the presidents and officers of the various life insurance companies of the United States. 76527, 76549, 76647

To the principal landholders of England. 95962

To the printer. 103253

To the printer of the Pennsylvania packet. 93439

To the printer. Sir, this minute came to my hands the post-script to the Boston gazette. 95963

To the printer. The rise of goods at vendue. 95964

To the printers of the Pennsylvania gazette. 51164, (61916)

To the printur of the Penselvaney kronical mr Godard. 94041

To the privates of the several battalions of military associators. (60713)

To the proprietors of a tract of land. 95965

To the Proprietors of Mount Auburn Cemetery. 44331

To the Proprietors . . . of Trinity Church, Boston. 39762

To the provisional committee. 84496

To the public. 6838, 10889, 15583, 23891, 24581, 24582, 26630A, 27642, 29325, 32147, 35226, 37918, (41995), (43409), 60714-60720, 62333, 64363, 74126, 80116, 83754, 83929, 84281, 84452, 84466, 84681, 86747, 88851, 90350, 90871, 91748, 92877, 94776-94777, 94974, 95329, note after 95866, 95966-95962, 95984-95990, 95993-96000, 96002-96009, 96011-96015, 97060, 97740, 97999, 98439, 984534, 98583, 100787, 101295, 101335, 101610, 101852, 103386, 103944, 103973, 105032, 105672, 106120

To the public. A few plain facts for gas consumers! 62336

To the Reverend Mr. William Hubbard. (33445)-33446, 106052

To the Right Honourable, Algernon, Lord Percy. 82814

To the Right Honorable and Most Generous Lords of England. 82812, 82839

To the Right Honourable and my singular good Lord, George Earle of Cumberland. 79341

To the Right Honourable, and Right Reverend Father in God: Iohn, Lord Bishop of Lincolne. 66685

To the Right Honorable and Right Worthy Adventurers. 82835

To the Right Honorable and Worthy Aduenters to all discoueries and plantations. 82833

To the Right Honourable and Worthy Lords, Knights, & Gentlemen. 82819

To the Right Honorable, both houses of the High Court of Parliament. 104331

To the Right Honourable Charles Baron Glenelg. 96026

To the Right Honourable George, Earl of Halifax. 84566

To the Right Honovrable Henry Lo: Cary. 80620

To the Right Honourable, My Very Good Lady, the Lady Bridget Countess of Lincoln. (21090), 33698, 78431, 104846

To the Right Honorable Sir Edward Coke. 82833

To the Right Honourable Sr. Edward Semer Knight. 82832, note after 92664, 2d note after 100510

To the Right Honourable Sir Henrie Sidney, Knight. 95338

To the Right Honourable, Sir Iohn Egerton. 82833

To the Right Honourable the Lords & Commons assembled in High Court of Parliament. 80205

To the Right Honovrable, the Lords and others of His Majesties Most Honourable Priuie Councell. 96027

To the Right Honourable the Lords of His Majesty's Most Honourable Privy Council. 72848

To the Right Honourable the Lords of Trade and Plantations. Supplement to the reply. (32364), 32365, note after 96027-96028, note after 103448

To the Right Honourable the Lords of Trade and Plantations. The reply of H. M.'s subjects. (32364)-32365, note after 96027-96028, note after 103448

To the Right Honourable the Lords Spiritual & Temporal in Parliament assembled. 95940

To the Right Honourable the Secretary at War. 85243

To the Right Reverend, and Reverend the Bishops. 96029

To the Right Rev. William Bacon Stevens. 83525

To the Right Worshipfull Aduenturers for the countrey of New England. 82819

To the Right VVorshipful Edmund Bray, Esquire. 11144, 80706

To the Right VVorshipfull Sir Robert Heath, Knight. 82812

To the Right Worshipfvl the Maister, the Wardens, and the Comapnie of the Fish-Mongers. 82833

To the Right Worshipful, the Mayor, Aldermen and Commonalty of the city of New-York. 30379-30380

To the Right Worshipfvll Thomas Watson, and Iohn Bingley, Esqvires. 82832, note after 92664, 2d note after 100510

To the Right Worthy . . . Sir William Wade Knight, &c. 99866

To the Roman Catholics of the state of Maryland. 103099

To the rulers of New Haven town. 86714

To the Second-Day's Morning Meeting. 76415

To the Secretary of the Treasury of the United States. 94487

To the Select Council. (62188)

To the Senate and House of Representatives, a respectful memorial. 95928

To the Senate and House of Representatives. [By George Wilkes.] 104000

To the . . . Senate and House of Representatives. [By Moyers & Dedrick.] 51222

To . . . the Senate and House of Representatives in Congress assembled. 30248

To the Senate and House of Representatives of Pennsylvania. 60726

To the Senate and House of Representatives of . . . Pennslyvania [in favor of consolidation.] 61834

To the . . . Senate and House of Representatives . . . of Pennsylvania: the memorial of . . . members. (62214)

To the Senate and House of Representatives of . . . Pennsylvania. The memorial of the . . . Schuylkill and Shsquehanna Navigation. 60725, 78072

To the Senate and House of Representatives of the Commonwealth of Pennsylvania. [By Edwin A. Stevens.] 91493

To the Senate and House of Representatives of the Commonwealth of Pennsylvania. The address and petition of the people called Quakers. 61936

To the Senate and House of Representatives of the United States. [By citizens of Albemarle County, Virginia.] 100532

To the . . . Senate and House of Representatives, of the United States. [By Harriet G. Peale, and others.] 59421

To the Senate and House of Representatives of the United States of America in Congress assembled. [By Joseph Scattergood.] 77451

To the Senate and House of Representatives of the United States of America in Congress assembled. The memorial of Joseph Smoot. 85130

To the Senate and House of Representatives of the United States. The undersigned, citizens of the town of Providence. 97951

To the . . . Senate . . . of Massachusetts in behalf of the Corporation . . . of [Harvard University.] 38005

To the . . . Senate of . . . New York. 54158

To the Senate of the United States. 95513

To the . . . Senators and Representatives of . . . Massachusetts. 1477

To the Senators and Representatives of the United States. 90885

To the Seneca Nation. 47332, 79107

To the Seneca Nation of Indians, residing at Cattaraugus and Alleghany. 79116

To the serious reader. 33442

To the settlers in Austins settlement. 94938

To the settlers in what is called 'Austin's colony,' in Texas. 94945

To the Seventy-Day Baptists. 72682
To the several battalions of the Military
  Associators. (60727)
To the several persons claiming under the
  Indian purchases. 56801
To the shareholders of the New-York Society
  Library. (43580)
To the Society for Promoting the Abolition of
  Slavery. 96030
To the Society of United Brethren for
  Propagating the Gospel Among the
  Heathen. 106297
To the soldiers of the Army of the Centre.
  85184
To the Sons of Liberty in this city. 96031
To the Sons of Liberty in this city. Gentle-
  men, it's well known. 86985
To the south. 96032
To the Speaker and members of the House
  of Representatives. 97952
To the stock-holders of the Bank of North
  America. 59907
To the stock-holders of the Bank of North
  America, on the subject of the old and
  new banks. 102416
To the stockholders in the Northern and West-
  ern Inland-Lock-Navigation Companies.
  102985
To the stockholders of Phoenix Bank. 96033
To the stockholders of the Bank of the United
  States. [By Richard Smith.] 83765,
  102505
To the stockholders of the Bank of the United
  States. [By Thomas Swann.] 94021
To the stockholders of the Morris Canal and
  Banking Company. 50890
To the stockholders of the Phoenix Bank.
  96034
To the subscribers of the Rotunda. 98483
To the stockholders of the Schuylkill Perma-
  nent Bridge Company. 78067
To the stockholders of the South-Carolina C.
  & R. R. Company. 87966
To the stockholders of the Spot Pond Aqueduct
  Company. 89645
To the stockholders of the Washington,
  Alexandria and Geo'town Steam Packet
  Company. 101975
To the stockholders of the West Philadelphia
  Passenger Railway Company. 62383
To the stockholders, or charter members,
  and patrons. 83012
To the students of Yale-College. 13215,
  105894-105895
To the subscribers for Rivington's New-York
  gazetteer. 71692
To the supervisors of [blank] in the county of
  [blank]. 96035
To the Supreame Authoritie of the nation.
  note before 92797
To the Supreme Authority, the Parliament of
  the commonwealth of England: a serious
  charge and accusation. 7487
To the Supreme Authority the Parliament of
  the commonwealth of England; the humble
  petition. 101443
To the Supreme Court of the United States.
  27048
To the Tabernacle Congregation. 87147
To the teachers of Toryism. 96036
To the thinking and reflecting supporters of
  Gen. Andrew Jackson. 65349
To the three generals. 96037
To the tobacco planters of the United States.
  96038, 2d note after 96993
To the Tories. 96039

To the town of Boston in New-England. 78753
To the tradesmen, farmers, and other
  ants of . . . Philadelphia. 62320, 62337
To the tradesmen, mechanics, &c., of the
  province of Pennsylvania. 60728
To the tribunal of the American people. 64223
To the true-hearted British readers. 73878
To the truely Honourable, & Venerable, . . .
  Rector. 46554
To the truly Christian reader. 104336
To the Union Party of South Carolina. 33886
To the U. S. San. Com. 86312
To the University of Oxford. 84646
To the unprejudiced reader. 6531, note after
  103702
To the upright in heart. 61021
To the Ursa Major. 101397
To the very learned, loqaucious, rhetorical,
  oratorical, disputative, flexible, incom-
  prehensible, impenetrable, pathetic and
  irresistably eloquent chairman. 96313
To the virtueous and patriotic citizens of
  New-York. 89189
To the voters of Maryland. (45379)
To the voters of Richmond County. 37818
To the voters of the county of Middlesex.
  92356
To the voters of the electorial district.
  103286
To the voters of the fifth congressional district
  [of Virginia.] 71656
To the voters of the fifth district. (68200)
To the voters of the first congressional district
  of Virginia. 78893
To the voters of the second congressional dis-
  trict of Tennessee. (39499)
To the voters of the second electorial district
  of the state of Missouri. 5623
To the voters of Worcester, Somerset, &
  Dorchester. 94563
To the voting citizens of the United States.
  51927
To the Wednesday Evening Club. 91603
To the Whig Party of Virginia. 59648, 1st
  note after 100532
To the Whig voters of . . . Philadelphia.
  (62388)
To the Whig voters of the fourth congressional
  district. 46167
To the Whigs and conservatives of the United
  States. 103266
To the Whigs of Maryland. 64980
To the Whigs of Virginia. 6832, 2d note after
  100532
To the whole Whig Party of the United States.
  6832, 2d note after 100532
To the Worshipfvll Sir Thomas Smith Knight.
  77962
To the Worshipfull the Master Wardens &
  Societe of the Cordwayners. 82824
To the . . . worthie friends. 99866
To the worthy Am*r*c*ns. 94558
To the worthy and generous friends of religion
  and learning. 94708
To the worthy freeholders and freemen.
  96040
To the worthy gentlemen, adventurers and
  planters in Virginia. 100450, note after
  100560, 104190
To the worthy inhabitants of the city of New-
  York. 93244
To the young men . . . of the American union.
  26334
To their brother reformers in Upper Canada.
  98087

To Their Excellencies Richard Viscount Howe, Admiral; and William Howe, Esq. 20920

To this awful wreck, let there be a remedy. 104064

To Thomas Scott and John Alexander, Esquires. 101096

To Thomas Scott, Esq. of Chillicothe. 101097

To those born on the soil. 38144, note before 96041

To those who have sworn to support the constitution. 82775

To Walter Tolley. 96041

To William Denny. 60729

"To whom it may concern." "A big thing." 89230

To whom it may concern. Written by W. Dexter Smith. 84763

To William Lloyd Garrison. 82633

To worship God in spirit, & in truth. 6225

To you is committed the safety of your country. 100680

To young men. (70939)

Tobacco: a poem in two books. 95622

Tobacco and internal revenue. 62745

Tobacco and its adulterations. 64248

Tobacco battered. 96042

Tobacco Convention, Washington, D. C., 1840. 96038, 2d note after 96993

Tobacco Convention, Washington, D. C., 1840. Committee to Prepare the Address. 96038, 2d note after 96993 see also Triplett, Robert

Tobacco Convention, which met in the city of Washington. 96038

Tobacco Cutter's Association of Michigan. petitioners 47728

Tobacco: its history and associations. 23708

Tobacco: its history, cultivation, manufacture, and adulterations. 91212

Tobacco manufacture in the United States. 9306

Tobacco Manufacturers of Cincinnati, Ohio. 13102

Tobacco Planters in His Majesty's Colony of Virginia. petitioners 100442

Tobacco: the outlook in America for 1875. 88358

Tobacco; what it is, and what it does. (37790)

Tobago (British Colony) Assembly. Committee on the Increase of Population. 96043

Tobago (British Colony) Commissioners for the Sale of Lands. see Great Britain. Commissioners for the Sale of Lands in the Island of Tobago.

Tobago (British Colony) Laws, statutes, etc. 96044-96045

Tobago (French Colony) Commissaire et Ordonnateur. 2931, 73468-73470 see also Roume, Philippe Rose.

Tobago (French Colony) Creanciers Anglais. see Creanciers Anglais des Colons de Tobago.

Tobago insulae Caraibicae in America sitae fatum. (58059), 64912, 96049

Tobar, Mateo de. 96050-96051

Tobar, Pedro de. plaintiff 96052 see also Dominicans. Province of San Antonio de la Nuevo Reyno de Granada. Procurador General. plaintiff

Tobar y Buendia, Pedro de. 96052-96053

Tobar y Tamariz, Josef. 38381, 56007, (75765) see also Spain. Armada. Primer Piloto.

Tobiae Wagneri D. Cancellarii Tubingens. 100955

Tobin, James. 67716, 96054-96056

Tobin, John. 96057

Tobias Wilson, a tale of the great rebellion. 13620

Tobler, John. note after 96057

Tobocoh. Choctaw Indian Chief 96601

Toca Velasco, Jose Ignacio de. 96058

Tocantins e o Anapu. 58503

Tochman, G. (36269)

Tocornal, Joaquin. 96059 see also Chile. Ministerio del Interior y Relaciones Exteriores.

Tocornal, M. A. 39151, 70301

Tocqueville, Alexis Charles Henri Maurice Clerel de, 1805-1859. 4189-4192, 9574, 18724, 19371, 21074, 33618, 92278-92280, 96060-note after 96072

Tocsin: a solemn warning against the dangerous doctrine of nullification. 10889, 96073

Tocsin: or, the call to arms! 96074

Tocsin the third. (71918)

Tod, Nicolas. pseud. Good humor. see Manwaring, Mr. -------. supposed author

Tod, Thomas. 2559, 56492, 96048, 96076-96080

Tod, William. petitioner 73468-73469, 96047-96048, 96078-96080 see also Creanciers Anglois des Colons de Tobago. petitioners

Todas las costas meredionales. 100767

Todavia arrastramos las cadenas del despotismo. 96081

Todd, Alfred. 10487

Todd, Charles R. (81524)

Todd, Charles Stewart. 96082

Todd, Charles W. 96083, note after 105147

Todd, David. defendant at impeachment 96084

Todd, Francis. plaintiff 26705

Todd, Henry Cook. 96085-96086

Todd, Henry Cook. supposed author (35275), note after 96084

Todd, Henry J. ed. 83976-83977

Todd, James. plaintiff 65221

Todd, John, 1800-1873. 12733, 52321, 96088-96089

Todd, John, d. 1812. 96087

Todd, Jonathan. (30647), 96090-96095

Todd, Lewis C. 96096

Todd, Thomas. 72464

Todd, Timothy. 96097

Todd genealogy. (28609)

Toddy-mill. 96098

Toderighrono Indians. Treaties, etc. 36337

Toderini, Giambattista. 96099

Todeskampfe des Sclaventhums. 5889

Todkill, Anas. 82832, note after 92664, 2d note after 100510

Todo de los medicos. 73079

Todo tiene remedio siendo el aviso oportuno. 96100

Todos pensamos. 94344-94345, note after 96100

Toebast, Ignatius. 96101, note after 104997

Toekomstige betrekkingen der beschaafde wereld. (77691)

Toelichting van eenige punten. 67413

Toespraak van de schrijfter aan de jeugd. 92522

Toestand der zamenleven in den Vereen. Staten v. N. A. 96102

Toestant der swevende verschillen tusschen de Oost- ende West-Indische Compagnien van Engeland. 20781

Toestant der swevende verschillen, tusschen de Oost, ende West-Indische Compagnien, van Engelant, ende van de Vereenighde Nederlanden. 96103, 3d note after 102913

Toets-steen, toets-sende waar het by toekomst men hun Hoog Mogende. 96104

Tofino de San Miguel, Vincente. 98306

Togkunkash, tummethamunate matchesecongana-nemehtug. 39409, 96105

Togno, Joseph. 96106

Togt van het Engelsche schip Pagoda. 8775

Togte naar Para in Suriname. 24936

Toict, Nicolas du. see Techo, Nicolas del, originally Du Toict, 1611-1685.

Toil and the toilers, etc. 31197

Toilers of the sea. 89622

Toilet and ladies' cabinet of literature. 85523

Tokeah; or, the white rose. (64554)-64555, 2d note after 96106

Token. 3d note after 96106

Token; a Christmas and new year's present. 104516

Token for children. 35754, 46555, 4th note after 96106, 1st note after 96107

Token for mariners. 35755, 96107

Token for mourners. 24682

Token for the children of New England. 35754, 46555, 4th note after 96106, 1st note after 96107

Token for the children of New-England, or some examples of children. 35754, 46555, 4th note after 96106, 1st note after 96107

Token for youth. (68488), 2d note after 96107

Token of a nation's sorrow. 324, 3d note after 96107

Token of God's protection. 8729

Token of remembrance for 1848. 84143, 84146

Token of respect to the New England mothers. 71782

Tokens. 27960, 30153, note after 95748

Tokens at the tomb. 44252

Tokens of the divine displeasures. 104556

Tokens of wrath from the Lord unto a sinful people. 104615

Tolar, William J. defendant before military commission (31083)

Tolck, Joseph Joosten. see Joosten, Jacob, fl. 1649.

Toledo, Domingo Albarez de. see Albarez de Toledo, Domingo.

Toledo, F. Alvarez de. see Alvarez de Toledo, F.

Toledo, Fadrique de. see Toledo Osorio y Mendoza, Fadrique de.

Toledo, Francisco de, 1532-1596. 96108

Toledo, Francisco de, d. 1584. (41092), 69239, 98800 see also Peru (Viceroy-alty) Virrey, 1569-1581 (Toledo)

Toledo, Joaquim Floriano de. 85621

Toledo, Jose Alvarez de. see Toledo y Dubois, Jose Alvarez de.

Toledo, Juan Baptista Alvarez de. see Alvarez de Toledo, Juan Baptista, Bp.

Toledo, Luys Tribaldos de. see Tribaldos de Toledo, Luys.

Toledo Osorio y Mendoza, Fadreque de. 69217, 96109-96116

Toledo y Dubois, Jose Alvarez de. 977-978, 16159, 96117-96118

Toledo y Dubois, Jose Alvarez de. supposed author 48270, 96118

Toledo y Leiva, Pedro de, Marques de Mancera, 1585-1654. 2245, (35238), 96119-96120 see also Peru (Viceroyalty) Virrey, 1639-1647 (Toledo y Leiva)

Toledo al Indio patriote. 96117

Toledo blade. 85202

Tolendal, T. G. Lally. see Lally-Tolendal, T. G. 38694

Toler, Henry. 96121-96122

Tolerancia, opusculo politico. (46203)

Tolerancia politica. 16990

Toleration. pseud. Bishop's bonus. 96123, 1st note after 105926

Toleration: a discourse . . . in Brooklyn. 36208

Toletus. pseud. Friendly dialogue between Philalethes and Toletus. see Spring, Samuel, 1746-1819.

Toletus. pseud. Two friendly letters. see Tappan, David.

Toletus, Franciscus. see Toledo, Francisco de, 1532-1596.

Tolhausen. firm publishers see Gardissal & Tolhausen. firm publishers

Toll, Daniel. supposed author 69421, 2d note after 96123

Toll toll the knell. 92177C

Tolland County Association of Ministers. see Congregational Churches in Connecticut. Tolland County Association of Ministers.

Tollius, H. 100768

Tollo, Luis B. de. 96124

Tolman, Thomas. (12851), 96125, 99073, note after 99131, 99134 see also Vermont. Militia. Paymaster.

Tolon, Miguel T. 5061

Tolosan, J. de. supposed author 96126

Tolosani, Gio. M. 90088

Toluca, Mexico. Exposicion de Objetos Naturales e Industriales, 2a., 1851. see Exposicion de Objetos Naturales e Industriales, 2d, Toluca, Mexico, 1851.

Toluca, Mexico. Instituto Literario. see Instituto Literario, Toluca, Mexico.

Toluqueno. pseud. Elecciones de Toluca. 96127

Tom and Kate. A song. 86263

Tom bell. 83974

Tom Brown. pseud. Trip to Jamaica. see Ward, Edward, 1667-1731.

Tom-Cod catcher. 96140

Tom Cringle's log. 78339, 96128

Tom Gage's proclamation versified. 96129

Tom Paine's jests. (58242), 96130

Tom Russell's far west songster. 74378

Tom Somers in the army. 57216, 86266

Tom Thumb. sobriquet see Stratton, Charles Sherwood, 1838-1883.

Tom Thumb. 12982

Tom Thumb's folio, for little giants. 96133

Tom Thumb's folio, or a new play-thing. 96134

Tom Thumb's folio: or, a new threepenny play thing. 96135

Tom Thumb's little book. 96136

Tom Thumb's play book. 96137

Tom Tickle, Esq. pseud. see Tickle, Tom, Esq. pseud.

Tom Trueblue. pseud. see Trueblue, Tom. pseud.

Tom Wiley, the scout to the northwest. 55208

Tomajuncosa, Antonio. see Tamajuncosa, Antonio.

Tomas, Domingo de Santo. see Domingo de Santo Tomas.

Toplady, Augustus Montague. 77231, 96184
Topliff, Nathaniel. 96185
Topografia medica de la isla de Cuba. 62981
Topographia medica portus Novi-Archangel-
scensis. 5874
Tpopgraphical analysis, of the commonwealth
of Virginia: compiled for 1790-1. 94413-
94414
Topographical analysis of Virginia for 1790.
35908
Topographical and historical description of
Boston. By Nathaniel B. Shurtleff.
80788
Topographical and historical description of
Boston. [By Thomas Pendleton.] 59619
Topographical and historical description of
Boston, from the first settlement.
79898
Topographical and historical notices of the
town. 3939
Topographical and historical sketch of Epsom.
18055
Topographical and historical sketch of the
town of Andover. 50397
Topographical and historical sketches of the
town of Lancaster. 104061
Topographical and historical sketches of the
town of Leicester. 101520
Topographical and pictorial guide. 55132, 4th
note after 97444
Topographical and political description of the
Spanish part of Saint-Domingo. 50572
Topographical and statistical account of the
province of Louisiana. 42308, 2d note
after 96185
Topographical and statistical description of
the provinces of Lower and Upper
Canada. 6848
Topographical description and historical sketch
of Plainfield. 64264
Topographical description of Georgetown in the
county of Lincoln. 93506
Topographical description of such parts of
North America as are contained. (64835)
Topographical description of Texas. 6317
Topographical description of the counties of
Frederick, Berkeley & Jefferson. 98630
Topographical description of the island of
Grenada. 59051
Topographical description of the province of
Lower Canada. 6849
Topographical description of the state of Ohio,
Indiana Territory, and Louisiana.
18170, 3d note after 96185
Topographical description of the western
territory of North America. 24337,
34053-34056, (34358), 82422
Topographical description of Thomaston.
93506
Topographical description of Virginia, Pennsyl-
vania, Maryland, and North Carolina.
(34053)-34054
Topographical description of Virginia, Pennsylvania, Maryland, and North-Carolina, by
Mr. Tho. Hutchins. (34358)
Topographical description of Wisconsin.
(39192)
Topographical dictionary; containing a description of the several counties. 50811
Topographical dictionary, containing a description of the several counties, towns,
villages, settlements, . . . in the state
of Ohio. 37730
Topographical dictionary; containing a description of the several counties, towns,
villages, settlements, roads, lakes,

rivers, creeks, and springs, in the state
of Indiana. 34532, 78305
Topographical dictionary, containing a descrip-
tion of the several counties, towns,
villages, settlements, roads, lakes, rivers,
creeks, springs, &c., in the state of
Indiana. 78304
Topographical dictionary of the province of
Lower Canada. 6851
Topographical dictionary of the state of Indiana.
34533
Topographical geology. 45751
Topographical, historical and other sketches
of the city of Charleston. (80068)
Topographical, historical, and political view
of Texas. 17566, 83778
Topographical map of the island of Barbados.
77785
Topographical sketch of Nahant. (11905)
Topographical sketch, with remarks on the
diseases of West Tennessee. 102117
Topographical sketches of parts of the states.
96186
Topographical war map of the United States.
61015
Topographical work, by Joseph Lesley. 34529
Topographie, ou description succincte. 25292
Topographie medicale de San-Domingue.
73513
Topographie-moeurs-histoire-documents
diplomatiques et politiques. 18495
Topography of the state of Mississippi.
100778
Toppan, Charles, illus. 101660
Toppan prize essay of 1896. 84338
Toppans of Toppan's Lane. 14179
Toprell, Edward. tr. 27288
Topsfield, Mass. Meeting of Delegates from
the Several Towns of Essex County,
1808. see Essex County, Mass. Meeting
of Delegates from the Several Towns,
Topsfield, 1808.
Toral y Cabanas, Manuel German. 96188-
96189
Torally, Carlos Augusto. see Torralli,
Carlos Augusto.
Torch light. 96190
Torchet de Bois-Mesle, Jean-Baptiste. see
Bois-Mesle, Jean-Baptiste Torchet de.
Tordesillas, Antonio de Herrera y. see
Herrera y Tordesillas, Antonio de,
1559-1625.
Toree, Olof. see Toren, Olaf.
Toren, Olaf. 5691, 65025, 96091
Toreen, -----. see Toren, Olaf.
Torfaeus, Thormodus. 96192-96193
Toriano, --------, fl. 1785. 2195, 56484
Toribio, --------. 29430, 96194
Toribio Polo, Jose. see Polo, Jose Toribio.
Toribio Alfonso Mogrovesio il Santo Arci-
vescovo di Lima. 98360
Toribio Alfonso Mogrovesio Santo Arcivescovo
di Lima. 49836
Toribius. Saint see Mogroveius, Toribius
Alphonsius, Saint, Abp. of Lima.
Torija, Antonio Torres. see Torres Torija,
Antonio.
Torija Ortuno, Francisco de. plaintiff 87193
Torino, Italy. Academia Imperiale della
Scienze. 10705, 14654, 51758-51760,
51762
Torino, Italy. Academia Reale della Scienze.
see Torino, Italy. Academia Imperiale
della Scienze.
Tormentos executados por el Senor Coronel
Don Manuel de la Concha. 96195

Tornado Committee, Medford, Mass., 1851. see Medford, Mass. Tornado Committee, 1851.

Tornado Committee, Waltham, Mass., 1851. see Waltham, Mass. Tornado Committee, 1851.

Tornado Committee, West Cambridge, Mass., 1851. see West Cambridge, Mass. Tornado Committee, 1851.

Tornado dos vassalas de Coroa do Portugal. 29126

Tornado of 1851. 8339

Torne, Pierre Anastase. 96196

Tornel, Jose Maria. see Tornel y Mendivil, Jose Maria.

Tornel y Mendivil, Jose Maria. 36659, 36761, 93786-93787, 96197-96208

Tornos, Alberto de. tr. (66886)

Toro, Agustine de la Rosa. see La Rosa Toro, Agustin de.

Toro, Anjel Mariano. plaintiff 96209

Toro, ------- Coucha i. see Coucha i Toro, --------.

Toro, Francisco de Paulo. see Paulo Toro, Francisco de.

Toro, Francisco Rodriguez de. 96210

Toro, J. Rodriguez del. see Rodriguez del Toro, J.

Toro Zambrano y Ureta, Mateo de. 96211

Toro dialogos critico-jocoserios. 18785

Toronto, Bishop of. see Strachan, John, Bishop of Toronto.

Toronto. Annual Session of the Grand Division of the Sons of Temperance of Ontario, 1855. see Sons of Temperance of North America. Ontario. Grand Division. Annual Session, Toronto, 1855.

Toronto. Athenaeum. President. (77432) see also Scadding, Henry.

Toronto. Common Council. 33779

Toronto. Grand Jury, March 8th, 1838. 72120

Toronto. International Geological Congress, 12th, 1913. see International Geological Congress. 12th, Toronto, 1913.

Toronto. Library of Parliament. see Canada. Parliament. Library.

Toronto. Magnetical Observatory. (37898)

Toronto. Meeting on the Clergy Reserved Lands and the King's College, 1830. petitioners 98072, 98092

Toronto. Public Meeting, 1830. petitioners 98072, 98092

Toronto. Reform Convention, 1859. see Reform Convention, Toronto, 1859.

Toronto. Royal Canadian Yacht Club. see Royal Canadian Yacht Club, Toronto.

Toronto. Society for the Instruction of the Deaf and Dumb, and of the Blind. see Society for the Instruction of the Deaf and Dumb, and of the Blind, Toronto.

Toronto. Society for the Relief of Strangers in Distress. see Society for the Relief of Strangers in Distress, Toronto.

Toronto (Archdiocese) 32349

Toronto (Archdiocese) Bishop [ca. 1840] 100896

Toronto (Archdiocese) Bishop (Charbonnel) 10420, 74553, 74555 see also Charbonnel, Armand Francois Marie de, 1802-1891.

Toronto (Archdiocese) Synod. 32349

Toronto & Georgian Bay Ship Canal. 8385

Toronto Colonist. 10571

Toronto Committee of the SPCK. see Society for Promoting Christian Knowledge, London. Toronto Committee.

Toronto of old. 77433

Toronto to Quebec. 52322

Torpedo-boat policy. 83960

Torpedo war, and submarine explosions. 26199

Torquemada, Jose Francisco Suarez y. see Suarez y Torquemada, Jose Francisco.

Torquemada, Juan de. 96212-96214

Torquenada, Juan de, fl. 1600. 47812

Torralli, Carlos Augusto. 96215-96216

Torrano, Gines Rocamora y. see Rocamora y Torrano, Gines.

Torrboll, Christian Friis. 73441-73442

Torre, ------- de la, fl. 1825. 48336, 76116

Torre, Aloisius de la. see Torre, Luis de la.

Torre, Antonio de Olmedo y. see Olmedo y Torre, Antonio de.

TorreAntonio Teran de la. see Teran de la Torre, Antonio.

Torre, Geronimo Alonso de la. plaintiff 98600

Torre, Giovanni Battista. 14645

Torre, Gonzalo Cayetano de la. 96217

Torre, J. M. de la. see Torre, Jose Maria de la.

Torre, Jose Isidro Inana y. see Inana y Torre, Jose Isidro.

Torre, Jose Maria de la. 39212-39213, (57345), 88947, 1st note after 96217

Torre, Juan del Corral Calvo de la. see Corral Calvo de la Torre, Juan del, 1666-1737.

Torre, Luis de la. 96218

Torre, Manuel de la. 96219

Torre, Manuel Ortiz de la. see Ortiz de la Torre, Manuel.

Torre, Martin de la. see De la Torre, Martin.

Torre, Matias Rubin de la. see Rubin de la Torre, Matias.

Torre, Miguel de la. (19966), 50703, 96220-96222

Torre, Pedro Bermudes de la. see Bermudez de la Torre y Solier, Pedro Joseph.

Torre, Pedro de la. 96223 see also Peru. Ministerio de Relaciones Esteriores.

Torre, Pedro Jose Bermudez de la. see Bermudez de la Torre, Pedro Jose.

Torre, Rafael Martinez de la. see Martinez de la Torre, Rafael.

Torre, Ramond de la. (14362)

Torre Barrio y Lima, Lorenzo Phelipe. 96225-96226

Torre, Lloreda, Manuel de la. 96227-96228

Torre Miranda, Antonio de la. 96229

Torre Rezzonico, Carlo de la. see Clement XIII, Pope, 1693-1769.

Torre-Tagle, Jose Bernardo de Tagle y Portocarrero, Marques de. see Tagle y Portocarrero, Jose Bernardo de, Marques de Torre-Tagle.

Torre y Solier, Pedro Joseph Bermudez de la. see Bermudez de la Torre y Solier, Pedro Joseph.

Torrejon, Miguel de Valdivieso y. see Valdivieso y Torrejon, Miguel de.

Torrens, Jose Anastasio. 96232

Torrens, Robert. 96233

Torrensus, Iacobus. see Torres Bollo, Diego de.

Torrent, Bernardino. 96234

Torrente, Mariano. 96235-96237
Torres, --------, Marquesa de las. plaintiff
    98967
Torres, Agustin Salazar y. see Salazar y
    Torres, Agustin.
Torres, Andres. 96238-96239, 99790
Torres, Andres, supposed author 10711,
    note after 96237
Torres, Antonio de. 96240
Torres, Bernardo de. 96241
Torres, Cristobal de. 96242
Torres, Diego de. see Torres Bollo, Diego
    de.
Torres, Francisco Caro de. see Caro de
    Torres, Francisco.
Torres, Francisco de. plaintiff 96243
Torres, Gaspar de Guzman, Duque de Medina
    de la. see Olivares, Gaspar de Guz-
    man, Conde Duque de, 1587-1645.
Torres, Geronimo. 96244
Torres, Ignacio de. 96245-96246
Torres, Jakuba. see Torres Bollo, Diego
    de.
Torres, Jose de. 86494
Torres, Joseph de. see Torres y Vergara,
    Jose de.
Torres, Joseph Julio Garcia de. see Garcia
    de Torres, Joseph Julio.
Torres, Juan de. 76007
Torres, Julian del Molino. 96247
Torres, Ludovico Antonio de. see Torres
    Tunon, Luis Antonio.
Torres, Luis de. see Torres Tunon, Luis
    Antonio.
Torres, Manuel. 96248
Torres, Manuel Gaytan de. see Gayton de
    Torres, Manuel.
Torres, Miguel de. 96249-96250
Torres, Nicolas de. 99400
Torres, Nicolas de. M. D. 96251
Torres, Pedro Antonio de. 96252
Torres, Sebastian Santander y. see Santander
    y Torres, Sebastian.
Torres, V. G. 74969
Torres, Vidente Garcia. see Garcia Torres,
    Vicente.
Torres Bollo, Diego de. 96253-96259
Torres Caicedo, Jose Maria. 96260
Torres Castillo, Juan de. 11424, 50109,
    note after 96260
Torres de Mendoza, Luis. ed. 58072,
    106405
Torres e Alvim, Francisco Cordeiro da Silva.
    96261-96264
Torres Escribiala, N. J. 24156
Torres Palacios, Jose Gregorio de. 96265-
    96266
Torres Rubio, Diego de. 96267-96271
Torres Rubio, Diego de. supposed author
    5020, 20565, 32492, 100643
Torres Rubio, P. ed. 67161
Torres Texugo, F. 95144, note before 96272
Torres Torija, Antonio. 96272
Torres Tunon, Cayetano Antonio, 1719-1787.
    4216, 9814
Torres Tunon, Luis Antonio. 9814, 38624,
    96273-96274
Torres Vargas, Diego de. 94352
Torres y Guzman, Jose Maria. 86371, 96275
Torres y las Plazas, Ramon Casaus. see
    Casaus Torres y Las Plazas, Ramon.
Torres y Morales, Rodrigo de. 96276
Torres y Vergara, Jose de. 96277-96278,
    97707
Torrescano, Geronimo. 96279

Torrescauo, Geronimo. see Torrescano,
    Geronimo.
Torrey, --------, fl. 1739. defendant (65578)
Torrey, Almira. 96280
Torrey, Charles Turner. (28349), 96281
Torrey, Jason. 96282
Torrey, Jsees. 96283-96290
Torrey, John, fl. 1795. 96291
Torrey, John, 1796-1873. 22538, 35308,
    44739, 53788, 54705, 67461, 68476,
    69946, 81472-81473, 85072, 96292-96297
Torrey, Joseph. 84929
Torrey, Joseph. defendant 43663, 96298
Torrey, Mary C. 96299
Torrey, Mrs. Erasmus. see Torrey, Susanna
    (Eastman)
Torrey, Paul. supposed author 103085
Torrey, Rufus Campbell. 96300
Torrey, Samuel. 96301-96303
Torrey, Susanna (Eastman) plaintiff 96304
Torrey, Thomas. plaintiff 25124, 96305
Torrey, William. 95947
Torrey, William Turner. 96306
Torrey. firm see Fleming & Torrey. firm
Torrez, Simon Perez de. see Perez de
    Torrez, Simon.
Torribo, D. (14367)
Torrijos, ------. tr. 49029
Torrontegui, Joseph Manuel de. 96307
Torrubia, Giuseppe. see Torrubia, Jose.
Torrubia, Jose. 23338, 96308-96311
Torrubiano Ripoli, Jaime. see Ripoli, Jaime
    Torrubiano.
Torry, Susanna. see Torrey, Susanna
    (Eastman)
Tort, --------. Sieur. 29240
Történeti konyvtár. 89010
Torti, Joao. 81299
Tortillera. pseud. Desengano a los Indios.
    see V., A., el Mexicano. pseud.
Torts apparens ou la famille Ameriquaine.
    96312
Tory. pseud. To the very learned. 96313
Tory. pseud. True Whig displayed. 97161
Tory, Jack. pseud. Choice dialogue. see
    Walter, Thomas, 1696-1725.
Tory and his league. (13858)
Tory guardian. 90522
Tory medley. 96314
Tory medley written in the year 1780. 96314
Tory outwitted. 27268
Tory squib. 90356
Tory's daughter. 95485
Toscanneli, Paolo. 40224
Toscano. pseud. Observazioni. 14661
Tosier, John. 96315
Tosinus, E. 66475-(66476)
Tosoquatho. Indian Chief 628, 66062 see
    also Three Maquas Castles (Indians)
    Sachems.
Tossiat Ferrer, Manuel. 96316
Tot den Leser. 77930-77932, 77939
Total abstinence advocate. 89483
Total eclipse of liberty. 12982, 25296
Total loss of the American ship Hercules.
    92355
Total refutation and political overthrow of
    Doctor Price. 91681
T'other congress convened. 97010
"'Tother side of Ohio." 57154, 96317
T'other side; or, bounce-about. 95868
Totivs orbis situ. 20210
Totten, Joseph. 96021, 96318
Totten, Joseph Gilbert, 1788-1864. 6723,
    60203, 96319

Tottenham Court Chapel, London. see
London. Tottenham Court Chapel.

Totton, J. A. 105886

Totyerenhton kahyatonhsera ne royatadogenhti
Paul shagohyatonni ne Corinthians.
49851

Toucey, Isaac, 1796-1869. 54725, 89926 see
also Connecticut. Governor, 1846-1847
(Toucey)

Touch at the times. A dialogue. 19421,
104590

Touch at the times. A poem. 105618

Touch at the times. A satire. 101140

Touch at the times, a satirical poem. (74426)

Touch at the times. [By Daniel Clement
Colesworthy.] 96320

Touch of the times. 37176, 96321

Touch on the times. 96322

Touch stone for the clergy. 96323

Touche, Louis Charles Le Vassor de la. see
Le Vassor de la Touche, Louis Charles.

Touching a marriage between Prince Henry
of England. 67599

Touchstone. pseud. Touchstone to the people
of the United States. see Herring,
Elbert. supposed author

Touchstone, Geoffry. pseud. He wou'd be a
poet. see Carey, James. supposed
author

Touchstone, Geoffry. pseud. House of
wisdom in a bustle. see Carey, James.
supposed author

Touchstone for the leading partymen in the
United States. 101525

Touchstone for Tryon. (55611)

Touchstone of sincerity. 24682

Touchstone to the people of the United States.
96326

Toug, Claude. 3308

Toulette, E. L. J. see Toulotte, E. L. J.

Toulmin, Harry. (19708), (37533), 49499,
96327-96328

Toulmin, J. R. 96329

Toulmin, Joshua. 52143-52145, 96330-96331

Toulotte, E. L. J. incorrectly supposed author
96332

Toulza, Philippe de. ed. and tr. 86485

Toup, Jonathan. 96333

Tour, ------- Leschenault de la. see
Leschenault de la Tour, --------.

Tour, Bertrand de la. see La Tour, Bertrand
de.

Tour, Charles de Saint Estienne, Seigneur
de la. see Saint Estienne, Charles
de, Seigneur de la Tour.

Tour, Louis Brion de la. see Brion de la
Tour, Louis.

Tour, Serres de la. 17165

Tour across the Pampas to Buenos Ayres.
6299

Tour among the planters. 58875

Tour around Hawaii. (76380)

Tour beyond the mountains. (23790), 24651

Tour dans les prairies a l'ouest des Etats-
Unis. 35143

Tour du monde. 29109

Tour en Sicile. 16928

Tour from London to Paris. 90963, 90965

Tour from the city of New-York to Detroit.
18533

Tour in America. 58786

Tour in Holland, in MDCCLXXXIV. 102136

Tour in the prairies. 35141

Tour in the southern states of America.
39353

Tour in the United States; with two lectures on
emigration. (65059)

Tour in the United States of America. 84616,
85246, 85251, 85254-85255

Tour in the west. 2958, 81520

Tour in Virginia, Tennessee, etc. 16795,
62509, 76707

Tour of almost fourteen months. 19129, note
before 98445, 98445, 98447, 98451-
98453, 98455-98456, 98461, 98463,
98465

Tour of Cowneck and North Hempstead. 96335

Tour of duty in California. 70182

Tour of exploration in the south. (73750)

Tour of four great rivers. 83761

Tour of General La Fayette from the United
States. 33856

Tour of H. R. H., Albert Edward. 657

Tour of James Monroe. 101011

Tour of James Monroe, President of the United
States. 101012

Tour of the American lakes. 14783

Tour of Virginia, Tennessee, etc. 19795,
62509, 76707

Tour on the prairies. 35139, note before
96334

Tour round the world. Being a short but
comprehensive description. (26983)

Tour round the world. [By Robert Davidson.]
18737

Tour through Arizona and Nevada. (8656)

Tour through North America. 80554

Tour through part of the Atlantic. 91161

Tour through part of the north provinces of
America. 43655

Tour through part of Virginia, in the summer
of 1808. Also, some account of the
. . . Azores. 100533

Tour through part of Virginia, in the summer
of 1808. In a series of letters. 9917,
1st note after 96334, 4th note after
100532

Tour through parts of the United States and
Canada. 4168, 2d note after 96334

Tour through the British colonies. 92512

Tour through the British West Indies. 43456

Tour through the island of Jamaica. 104182

Tour through the land of the west. 83650

Tour through the several islands of Barbadoes,
St. Vincent, Antigua, Tobago, and Grenada.
(21895)

Tour through the several islands of Barbadoes,
St. Vincent, Antigua, Tobago, and Grenada,
in the years 1791, and 1792. 21901,
106128

Tour through the southern and western territories. 64109

Tour through the western country. 30331

Tour through universalism, unitarianism and
skepticism. 83582

Tour through Upper and Lower Canada. 10615,
(56818)-(56819), note after 98091, 3d
note after 96334

Tour through Virginia, Tennessee, &c. 67617

Tour to Quebec, in the autumn of 1819.
62509, (71302), 81047

Tour to the River Saguenay. 38926

Tour to the springs. 20325, note after 55831

Tour to the White Hills. 88628

Tour to Virginia. 76707

Tourbe ardante. 72764

Tourette, James la. see La Tourette, James.

Tourist. pseud. Guide for emigrants to
Minnesota. (49250)

Tourist, or pocket manual for travellers on
the Hudson River. 98487

Tourist; or, pocket manual for travellers on the Hudson River, the Western Canal, and stage road. 98484

Tourist, or pocket manual for travellers on the Hudson River, the Western Canal, and stage road, to Niagara Falls. 98485

Tourist, or pocket manual for travellers on the Hudson River, the Western Canal and stage road to Niagara Falls, down Lake Ontario and the St. Lawrence to Montreal and Quebec. 98486

Touriste. pseud. Excursion d'un touriste. see Roy, J. J. E.

Tourist's companion to Niagara Falls, Saratoga Springs, the lakes, Canada, etc. 55128

Tourists' guide-book through the United States. (14793)

Tourist's guide . . . . Edited and published by Mrs. S. S. Colt. 53820

Tourists' guide; giving a description of Canadian lake and river scenery. (82198)

Tourist's guide . . . including notices of the whirlpool. 19804

Tourist's guide, or pencillings in England and on the continent. 80337

Tourist's guide through Canada and the United States. 12841

Tourist's guide to Quebec. 56431

Tourist's guide to the city of Montreal. 38887

Tourist's guide to the Upper Mississippi River. 20325

Tourist's guide to the Yo-Semite Valley. 10041, 34045

Tourneaux, L. E. le. see Le Tourneaux, L. E.

Tournee a la monde dans les Etats-Unis. (23903), 69336, 96487

Tournefort. 3603

Touron, Antoine. 96337

Tours through England. 106063

Tourte-Cherbuliez, ---------. tr. 41931

Tous, --------, Marques de, fl. 1823. 96338

Tousard, Anne Louis de. 96339-96341

Tousard, Lieutenant-Colonel du Regiment du Cap. 96341

Tousey, W. G. reporter 89627

Toussaint de la Rue, Amelie Eugenie (Caron de Beaumarchais) petitioner 4176-4176, (4179)-4180, 96342

Toussaint-Louverture, Francois Dominique, 1743-1803. 3885, (42350), 43255-(43256), (75482), 96343, 96345-96349 see also Haiti. Armee. General en Chef.

Toussaint l'Ouverture: a biography. (42356)

Toussaint l'Ouverture, de bevrijder des Negers op Haity. 4126

Toussaint Louverture, General en Chef de l'Armee de Saint-Domingue. 96346

Toussaint Louverture, General en Chef de l'Armee de Saint-Domingue, a tous les bons Francais. 96349

Toussaint Louverture; poeme dramatique. 38710

Tovar, Balthasar de. (9891), note after 96350

Tovar, Joseph Pellicer de Ossav y. see Pellicer de Ossav y Tovar, Joseph.

Tovar, Martin. 96351

Tower, Reuben. 96352

Tower of Babel. 36525

Towers, John. 96353

Towers, Joseph. 96354

Towers, Joseph. supposed author 36305, 95353

Towgood, Micaiah. 96355-96358, 96359, 99418, 103403

Towle, Nancy. 96360-96361

Towles, James. 95128, 96362, 101069 see also Whig Party. Massachusetts. State Central Committee. Chairman.

Town, -------. Grammatician 102370

Town, Ithiel. 19775, 96363-96364

Town, Robert. 74459

Town, Salem. 45501, 96365-96366

Town, Thomas. 96367

Town accounts [of Brunswick, Me.] 8767

Town and country almanack, (formerly published by Mr. Zachariah Poulson.) for . . . 1808. 5520

Town and country almanac, for . . . 1789. 64721

Town and country almanac for 1798. 95921

Town and country almanac, for . . . 1797. 44258, note after 105687

Town and country almanac for 1774. 47256

Town and country. By the author of "Allen Prescott." 78828

Town and country; or, life at home and abroad. 326

Town and country song book. 96368

Town being collected in Faneuil-Hall. 95280

Town in its truest glory. (46556), note after 96368

Town meeting. 30667, 62338

Town-meeting; a Tory squib. 90356

Town-meeting. [By John Trumbull.] 97210-97211

Town Meeting of Citizens, Without Distinction of Party, to Hear the Report of Their Delegates to the National Convention of Business Men, Philadelphia. 1837. see Philadelphia. Town Meeting of the Citizens, Without Distinction of Party, to Hear the Report of Their Delegates to the National Convention of Business Men, 1837.

Town-meeting.----treaty. Citizens! 96369

Town of North Hempstead vs. town of Hempstead. 55717

Town of Boston in New England. 88221

Town of Huron at the foot of Lake Huron. 34008

Town of New-Bedford in account with the Overseers of the Poor. (52510)

Town of Saco. Annual reports of the several departments. (47482)

Town of Smithfield year book. 84972, 84976

Town of Southold, Long Island. 50331

Town of Southold: personal indexes prior to 1698 and index of 1698. 88595

Town officer. 27945, 95377

Town records of Salem. 75757

Town Temperance Committee, New Bedford, Mass. 52505

Town topics of Boston in 1682. 52641, note after 100866

Towndrow, Thomas. 54693, 96882

Towne, Benjamin. pseud. Defence of Messrs. Galloway and Wharton. 3d note after 96369

Towne, Benjamin. pseud. Humble Confession. see Witherspoon, John.

Towne, Benjamin. 27642, 60721

Towne, Richard. 96370, 2d note after 96741

Townley, Adam. 96371

Townley, Charles. 64962

Townley, Daniel O'Connell. 54071, 96372

Townley, James. 96373
Towns and cities. 77919
Townsend, Alexander. 96374-96375
Townsend, C. C. ed. 1588
Townsend, Charles, 1725-1767. see Townshend, Charles, 1725-1767.
Townsend, Charles, fl. 1828. 96376
Townsend, David. 96377
Townsend, G. H. (47791)
Townsend, Isaiah. ed 13773, (24993), note after 96377, note after 101800
Townsend, James. tr. 40160
Townsend, John. of South Carolina 20615, 87530, 96378-96379, 96380, note after 97063
Townsend, John, 1783-1854. note after 89744
Townsend, John Kirk. 96381-96383
Townsend, Jonathan, 1697-1762. 96384-96387
Townsend, Jonathan, 1721-1776. 96388
Townsend, Joseph. 96389
Townsend, Micah. 99020, 99098, 99104 see also Vermont. Secretary.
Townsend, Peter S. 96390-96392
Townsend, Peter S. supposed author 54376, note after 96392
Townsend, Richard H. 57616, 96393-96394
Townsend, Robert. 96395
Townsend, Samuel P. 96396
Townsend, Shippie. 78500, 96397-97398, 98012
Townsend, Solomon. 96399
Townsend, Theyer Lawrence. 96400
Townsend, Thomas, 18th cent. tr. 86487-86491
Townsend, Thomas, 1733-1800. see Sydney, Thomas Townshend, 1st Viscount, 1733-1800.
Townsend, Walter. 96401-96402
Townshend, Charles, 1725-1767. (774), 12482, 13645, 41678, note after (47740), 47742, note after 96403
Townshend, Charles, 1725-1767. supposed author 20684, 40263, 40293, 40862, 47546-47547, 47741-47742, 69470
Townshend, Charles, 1725-1767. incorrectly supposed author 69671, 96403
Townshend, Charles, 1725-1767. mediumistic author 19947, note after 96403
Townshend, George, 1715-1769. 96404
Townshend, George, 1724-1807. see Townshend, George Townshend, 1st Marquis, 1724-1807.
Townshend, George Townshend, 1st Marquis, 1724-1807. (15052), 45934, 45547, 69535, 104749-104755
Townshend, J. K. see Townsend, John Kirk.
Townshend, Lord James. 104651
Townshend, Thomas, 1733-1800. see Sydney, Thomas Townshend, 1st Viscount, 1733-1800.
Townshend, Vt. Leland Seminary. see Leland Seminary, Townshend, Vt.
Towson, Nathan. 16875, 22270, 96405
Toxus. Indian Chief 4391, 15429
Toze, Eobald. 96406
Tozen, --------. 51478
Tr—n, William. pseud. Speech. 89190
Traanen van een gryzen Hollander. 96407
Trabajos coronados. 76791
Traccia del Licenziato Luis de Neve y Molina. 52412
Tracditionary history of a norrow and providential escape. 34480
Tracey, Daniel. plaintiff 96930

Trachsler, Heinrich. 96408
Traconis, Juan Bautista. 20442 see also Puerto Rico. Gobernador (Traconis)
Trackt [sic] for the soldiers. 77128
Tract Association of Dublin Friends. see Dublin Friends Tract Association.
Tract Association of Friends, Dublin. see Dublin Friends' Tract Association.
Tract Association of Friends, New York. 1045, 86029
Tract Association of Friends, New York. Committee of Management. 96410
Tract Association of Friends, Philadelphia. 86063, 86409, 97731, 105196
Tract Association of the Society of Friends, London. 27665, 33264, 105204, 105206 see also Friends, Society of. London Yearly Meeting.
Tract. [By Sumner Stebbins.] 91054
Tract. By which is vindicated the obvious practicability. 42414
Tract V. 97358
Tract for churchmen. 28158
Tract, for missionary distribution. 105333
Tract for northern Christians. 82112
Tract for the day. 29626, note after 95129, 2d note after 96410
Tract for the times. 30286
Tract for the times [against Southard.] 54140
Tract for the times. [By Caleb Sprague Henry.] (31388)
Tract for the times. By Jubal Hodges. 32343
Tract for the times, by Rev. Philip Schaff. (77497)
Tract for the times. [By T. G. Clark.] (13379)
Tract for the times (extra.) 80495, note after 90579
Tract for the times. No. I. 13557
Tract for the times, on the question. 12410
Tract for the times. Prepared by order of Willis Green. 93380
Tract for the tropics. 30979
Tract for universal distribution. 90489
Tract, in simple style, founded on science and scripture. 106067
Tract in verse by R. Rich. 70891
Tract, no. 2. New York, June 26th, 1860. (41203)
Tract of the times for every man who can read. 21467
Tract, on man's primitive rectitude. 104211
Tract on missions. 76382
Tract on religious experience. 3622
Tract on the alteration of the tariff. 10868
Tract on the "close communion" of the Baptist. 82973
Tract on the proposed alteration of the tariff. 16618
Tract VI. An epostulatory letter. 97358
Tract Society, Hartford, Conn. see Hartford Tract Society.
Tract Society, Philadelphia. see Philadelphia City Tract Society.
Tract Society of Friends, New York. see Tract Association of Friends, New York.
Tract Society of Friends, Philadelphia. see Tract Association of Friends, Philadelphia.
Tract Society of New England. see New England Tract Society.
Tract Society of South Carolina. see South Carolina Tract Society.
Tract Society of Strafford County, N. H. see Strafford Tract Society.
Tract Society of the Methodist Episcopal Church. see Methodist Tract Society.

Tracts on the Unitarian controversy. 4596, 96412

Tracts published by the Tract Association of Friends in New York. 96410

Tracts relating to the aborigines. 391, 34705

Tracts relating to the attempts to convert to Christianity the Indians of New England. 22146-22147, 80207-80208, 101330, note after 104653

Tracts relating to the corn trade and corn laws. 35492

Tracts relating to the currency of the Massachusetts Bay. 6711, 9449, 14536, 14538, 21088, (40332), 42824, 52622, 79377, 86618, 86630, 86716, 1st note after 99800, 103900, note after 103907, 105085

Tracts relative to the aborigines. (23623A), 26254-26255, 34651-34652, 34667, 34674, 69883, 103180

Tracts: the Molucco nutts, serpent stones, Barbados seeds, Mexican seeds. 44639

Tracy, -------, fl. 1840. 98425

Tracy, Alexandre de Prouville, Marquis de. see Prouville, Alexandre de, Marquis de Tracy.

Tracy, Antoine Louis Claude Destutt de, Comte. 96071, 96413-96415

Tracy, F. P. 96416

Tracy, John. 96417

Tracy, Joseph. (19992), 32124, 76454, 96418-96419

Tracy, Uriah. 29982-29983, 96420-96423

Tracy, W. S. 96424

Tracy, William, 1805-1881. (53951), 96425

Trade and commerce inculcated. 96426

Trade and fishing of Great Britain displayed. 82864, 82866

Trade & fishing of Great-Britain displayed. 82867

Trade and letters. (78400)

Trade and navigation of Great-Britain considered. 26827, note after 96426

Trade Convention, Baltimore, 1835. Committee of International Improvement. 3067

Trade granted to the South-Sea Company. 19251, (58160), 96427

Trade language of Oregon. 27301

Trade preferred before religion. 27679

Trade relations of British North America. 50282

Trade review. 30769

Trade to the East Indies. 17504

Trade-winds explained. 55068

Trade with British America. Speech . . . March 7, 1866. 37272

Trade with England and her colonies. 8348

Trade with the West Indies, Brasil, etc. 50282

Trader's best companion. 11970

Trader's useful assistant. 68217

Trader's useful assistant, in buying and selling all sorts of commodities. 23977, 68217

Traders useful guide in navigating the Monongahela. 17384-17385

Trades increase. 30394, 71899

Trades-Men in the City of New York. 103224

Trade's release. 96428

Tradescant, John, d. 1637? 29941

Tradescant der Aeltere, 1618, in Russland. 29940

Tradesman. pseud. Letter from a tradesman. 40315

Tradesman. pseud. To the tradesmen, farmers, and other inhabitants, 62320 62337

Tradesman. pseud. Tradesman's address to his countrymen. 60730, 62341, note after 96429

Tradesman of Germantown. pseud. Sundry Christian truths. 25563

Tradesman in Lancaster. pseud. Letter. 38209

Tradesman of Philadelphia. pseud. Observations on the late popular measures. see Drinker, John.

Tradesman of Philadelphia. pseud. Plain truth. see Franklin, Benjamin, 1706-1790.

Tradesman of Philadelphia. pseud. Short answer to some criticisms. 2d note after 96428

Tradesman of San Francisco. pseud. Conversation. (16204)

Tradesman of the city. pseud. Nature of contracts consider'd. 96429

Tradesman's address to his countrymen. 60730, 62341, note after 96429

Tradesman's calling. 91149

Tradesmen, artificers. 61921

Tradesmen, artificers and other inhabitants. 96430

Tradesmen's protest against the proceedings of the merchants. 96432

Tradicion historica del Christo de la Piedad. 22921

Tradicion historical original. 24153

Tradition of Hawaii. 35799

Tradition of Hi-a-wat-ha. (13330), 57605

Tradition of Pennsylvania. 5551

Tradition of the Old Cheraw. 87798

Tradition. Pamphlet. 85332

Traditional account of the life of Tammany. 44517-44518

Traditional ballad and its South Carolina survivals. 83751

Traditional history and characteristic sketches of the Ojibway Nation. (16722)

Traditionary tale of the cocked hat gentry. 11173 , 100482

Traditions Americaines. (29103)

Traditions and reminiscences chieflt of the American revolution in the south. (36245)

Traditions of De-coo-dah. 62698

Traditions of the North American Indians. 36521, 94246

Traditions of Venture. 84482

Traduccao de hum artigo inserido no periodico de Philadelphia. 96433

Traduccion de el Cathecismo Castellano del G. de Ripalda. 27794, (71491)

Tradvccion de la dedicatoria real. 86532

Traduccion de una noticia biografia. 69628

Traducteur, Monsieur. pseud. tr. see Clopper, Jonas.

Traduction de diverses notes sur cette colonie. 42895, 101246

Traduction de la demonstration de la Compagnie des Indes Occidentales. 47825

Traduction de la procuration de Jean Alexander. 101149

Traduction du catechisme et de cantiques dans la langue des Sauteux. 4408

Traduction et preface d'A. de Montluc. 74762

Traductor. pseud. [Poemas.] 81299

Traductor Mexicano. 48582, 96434

Tragedia del Voltaire. 100724

Tragedia di Voltaire. 100725

Tragedia en cinco actos, con la segunda parte. 63031

Tragedia en cinco actos. Por el Capitan Graduado D. Jose de Urcullu. 98119

Tragedia famosa intitulada La ridiculez andado. 96435

Tragedia Francesa. 10095, 100726

Tragedia por D. J. G. de Magalhaes. 43792

Tragedie. (39841)

Tragedie de M. de Voltaire. 100696-100708

Tragedie en cinq actes. 77221

Tragedie en 5 actes. 23859, 73846

Tragedie en quatre actes. 77222

Tragedie-lyrique en cinq actes. 63175

Tragedie Mexicaine. 4588

Tragedie. [Par De Sourigny.] 87304

Tragedie . . . par M. Le Blanc. 39595

Tragedie. Representee . . . Janvier 1744. 63021

Tragedie tiree des amours de Pistion & de Fortunie. 29938

Tragedie, tiree des amous de Pistion et Fortunie. 29939

Tragedies. [By Laughton Osborn.] 57755

Tragedies of the wilderness. 20883, 30266

Tragedies of unbelief. 2267

Tragedy. 7185, 33287, 33965-33966, 34733, 34735, 39447, 39449, (39960), 44622, 51055, 50440, 55914, (56702), 71087, 73603, (72729), (79333), 80337, 82517, 87203, 87802, 88519-88524, 88526-88527, 88531-88539, 88542, 88545, 88547, 90520, 100710-100719, 101480, note after 101861, 103483, 105586

Tragedy and other plays. 88525

Tragedy as lately acted near Saratoga. 51508

Tragedy, as lately performed. 102474

Tragedy by J. Hawkesworth. 88528

Tragedy, by Thomas Southern. 88537

Tragedy, in five acts. As performed at the Charleston Theatre . . . by John B. White. 103413

Tragedy in five acts. As performed at the Charleston Theatre, South Carolina. 103414

Tragedy in five acts as performed at the Theatre Royal in Drury-Lane. 4792, 38281, 80340

Tragedy in five acts. [By Cornelius Mathews.] 46840

Tragedy in five acts. By Epes Sargent. 76961, 76966

Tragedy, in five acts. By Horace Twiss. 97543

Tragedy, in five acts. By Mrs. E. Oakes Smith. 82514

Tragedy, in five acts. By Henry K. Strong. 92907

Tragedy, in five acts. By Horatio Hubbell. 33458

Tragedy, in five acts; by Thomas Southern. 88544, 88546

Tragedy, in five acts; by William Charles White. 103478

Tragedy, in five acts; translated from the German . . . . By James Lawrence. 38282

Tragedy, in four acts. 106395

Tragedy of Amboyna. 1002

Tragedy of errors. 66835, note after 96435

Tragedy of Louis Capet. 96436

Tragedy of Oroonoko. 88543

Tragedy of Sir Walter Raleigh. 67599, 79618-79619

Tragedy of success. 66836, note after 96436

Tragedy, of three acts. 105986

Tragedy; with other miscellaneous poems. (58115)

Tragic drama. (52668), 103731

Tragic drama in three acts. (52668), 103731

Tragic plan. In five acts. 83006

Tragic farce. In one act. 31130, 63891, 93647

Tragic play of Pizarro. 80342

Tragic scenes in the history of Maryland. 3233

Tragica descripcion que bosquexa la momentanea l amentable desolacion. 79314

Tragical account of the defeat of Gen. St. Clair. 96437

Tragical death of Miss Jane M'Crea. 63622

Tragical poem on the oppression of the human species. 7375

Tragico comico: or, melo-dramatico burlesco. (37861)

Tragi-comedy of five acts. 39512

Tragi-comedy, or rather a comico-tragedy. 83457

Tragi-comic memoirs. 96438

Tragi-comi-pastoral farce. 88199

Trago discretio aplicado con sosiego. 96439

Traicion y muerte en Guilapa. 93449

Traicte de la navigation et des voyages de descouverte et conquestes modernes. 4850, 5073, note before 96440

Traicte de la navigation et des voyages de descouuerte & conqueste modernes. 32016

Traicte entre le Roy Louis XIII. 96516

Traicte politique touchant les ambassades. 26342

Trail of blood: a tale of New York. 31120

Trail of history. 48017

Traill, Catherine Parr (Strickland) 1802-1899. 1622, 96440-96441

Traill, Robert. 96442

Traill, Thomas Stewart, 1781-1862. 51501

Training for citizenship. 83396

Training School for Idiotic and Feeble-Minded Children, Elwyn, Pa. see Pennsylvania Training School for Feeble-Minded Children, Elwyn.

Training School for Primary Teachers, Oswego N. Y. see New York (State) State Normal School, Oswego.

Traite abrege des anciens loix. 17853

Traite d'agriculture adapte au climat de Bas-Canada. 61005

Traite d'Amerique, droits et reclamations de Francais. 96443

Traite d'amitie et de commerce, conclu entre le Roi. 96565

Traite d'amitie et de commerce entre S. M. Britannique. 28292

Traite d'amitie et de commerce entre Sa Majeste le Roi de Prusse. 96570, 96590

Traite d'amitie et de commerce entre Sa Majeste le Roi de Suede. 100931

Traite dans le quel le Chretien peut apprendre a vaincre. 96790

Traite de la couleur de la Peau humaine en general. (39627)

Traite de la culture du Nopal. 95348-95349

Traite de la defence et de la conservation des colonies. 21190

Traite de la fievre [sic] jaunte d'Amerique. 98354

Traite de la loi des fiefs. 17854

Traite [de la nature et qualite de chocolate.] 14544

Traite de la police. 17855

Traite de la procedure criminelle en Angleterre. 49764

Traite de la sphere de Leonardo Dati de Florence. 76838

Traite de la sphere, &c. 15019

Traite de le predour et les interets de la France. (5813)

Traite de l'arte metallique. 3255

Traite de navigation. 62805

Traite de neutralite. 96530

Traite de neutralite conclu a Londres le siezieme Novembre 1686. 96531

Traite de paix conclu a Paris le 10 fevrier 1763. 56582

Traite de paix entre la France et a'Angleterre conclu a Ryswick. 96534

Traite de paix entre la France et l'Angleterre fait a Westminster. 96521

Traite de paix entre le Roi et le Roi de la Grande-Bretagne. 96557

Traite de paix entre le Roi, le Roi d'Espagne et le Roi de la Grande-Bretagne. 96551

Traite de paix entre le Roy, le Roy de la Grande Bretagne, et les Etats Generaux des Provinces-Unies de Pays-Bas. 96543

Traite de paix entre le Royaume de France et la Republique d'Angleterre. 96521

Traite de paix, entre les citoyens blancs & les citoyens de couleur. 75083, 96738

Traite de paix entre les covronnes de France et d'Angleterre. 96526

Traite de paix et amitie, entre la Serenissime & Tres-Puissante Princesse Anne. 96538

Traite de Pierre d'Ailly. 76838

Traite d'economic politique et de commerce des colonies. 58158

Traite d'economie politique. 77362

Traite des banques et de la circulation. 67507

Traite des fievres de l'isle de St.-Domingue. 19754, (63713)

Traite des fougeres de l'Amerique. 63458

Traite des maladies de plus frequentes. (24121)

Traite des maladies des regions intertropicales. 75505

Traite des Negres. 96444

Traite des Noirs, drame en cinq actes. 19750

Traite des pelleteries, le Labrador. (12573)

Traite des plantes usuelles des colonies Francaises. 19693

Traite des vents alisez de regles. 18384

Traite du Castor. 44580

Traite du 4 Juillet 1831. 27274, 96445

Traite du mais. 6262

Traite elementaire d'agriculture a l'usage des habitants Franco-Canadiens. 57810

Traite elementaire de botanique a l'usage des ecoles. 66235

Traite en conventions pour les malades. 96548

Traite et convention pour les malades. 96549

Traite et description des animavx, arbres & fruicts des Indes Orientales. 66879, (66881)

Traite et l'esclavage des noirs. 77150

Traite general du commerce de l'Amerique. 11814, 1st note after 96445

Traite historique sur les Amazones. 61258

Traite nouv. et curieux du cafe. 21146

Traite ou abrege des plantes usuelles de Saint Domingue. 64730

Traite sur la politique coloniale du Bas-Canada. 49959, 2d note after 96445

Traite sur le commerce des grains du royaume & de l'etranger. 11814, 1st note after 96445

Traite sur le gouvernement des esclaves. (61253)

Traite sur le venin de la vipere. 24988

Traite sur les lois civiles du Bas-Canada. 19761

Traite sur les terres noyees de la Guiane. 29256, (44145)

Traite sur son histoire naturelle. 77269

Traite theorique et pratique de droit publique et administratif. 3903A

Traites le predour doivent etre ratifies. 6905

Traites le predour. Noticie au point de vue du droit international. 6904

Traitez de paix conclus entre S. M. le Roy de France et les Indiens du Canada. 96559

Traitez de paix entre la France, l'Angleterre, la Savoye et la Hollande. 96540

Traitez de paix et de commerce, navigation et marine. 96539

Traitor detected. 96446

Traitorous advertisements of the bankrupts of Virginia. 14008

Traits de patriotisme de Polverel et de Sonthonax. 96447

Traits of American humour. 29696

Traits of American life. (29669)

Traits of character. 105528

Traits of colonial jurisprudence. 35111

Traits of Indian character. 97483

Traits of Mexican tradition. 65485

Traits of the aborigines of America. 80959, 3d note after 96447

Traits of the tea party. 95221

Traits requisite in the character of modern reformers. 20531

Traitte provisional sur le nouvel incident. (74790)

Traktaat van vrede, geslooten op het Hof tot Ryswyk. 96535

Traktat o zemi svate. 99367

Tram road a vapordo Paraguassi na provincia de Bahia. 50656

Tramarria, Mariano. 96448

Tramezzino, Michele. 56340

Tramites de los jusgados inferiores. 96449

Tramp in the Chateaugay woods. 30107

Tramp in the Chateaugay woods, over the hills. 30108

Trampler, Johann Christoph. 96450

Tramping tragedian. 84246

Tramps in New York. 68315

Tranan, over den doodt van den Grooten Admirael van Hollandt. 89746

Tranquillisador dos povos ou tranquillisantes reflexoens. 96451

Tranquillisantes reflexoens. 96451

Transaction of the Novodamus of Nova Scotia. 741, 11684, 91853

Transactions of a convention of delegates. 96452

Transactions of the Aborigines' Protection Society. (14687)

Transactions of the Academy of Science of St. Louis. 75326-(75327)

Transactions of the Agricultural and Horticultural Society of Hingham, Mass.
31956

Transactions of the agricultural societies.
43908

Transactions of the Agricultural Society and
Institute of Newcastle County, Delaware.
54930

Transactions of the Alabama Historical
Society. 569

Transactions of the Albany Institute. 32733,
33145

Transactions of the American Antiquarian
Society. 1049, 26399 31374, 65936,
89542, 95406, 99841-99853

Transactions of the American Art-Union.
(1055)

Transactions of the American Association of
Social Sciences. (36714)

Transactions of the American Ethnological
Society. 1084, 4608, 29636, 89983

Transactions of the American Historical
Society. 51810, 86574, 91316, 2d note
after 100494

Transactions of the American Institute. 1106

Transactions of the American Medical
Association. 83363, 83503, 90467,
93978-93980

Transactions of the American Medical Society.
89946

Transactions of the American Philosophical
Society, Philadelphia. 1136, 1181-1182,
3816, (3821), 10915, 13179, 13821,
30818, 31206, 39489, 39666, (40206),
51022, 52130, 52131, 62622, (68512),
74201, 77039, 77376, 77381, (77387),
79731, 84411, 84678C, note before
91856, 95646, 104297, 104300, 106301

Transactions of the Apollo Association. 1760

Transactions of the Art Union of Philadelphia.
61480

Transactions of the Barnstable County Agricultural Society. 3556

Transactions of the Belmont Medical Society.
4584

Transactions of the Berkshire County Agricultural Society. 4898

Transactions of the Board of Agriculture of
Ontario. (10343)

Transactions of the California State Agricultural Society. 9993

Transactions of the Canadian Society of Civil
Engineers. 84419

Transactions of the Chicago Academy of
Sciences. 12618

Transactions of the Cincinnati Horticultural
Society. 13069

Transactions of the College of Physicians of
Philadelphia. 61548

Transactions of the Connecticut Academy of
Arts and Sciences. 15704

Transactions of the Connecticut State Agricultural Society for the year 1854.
15658

Transactions of the Convention of the Ohio
Wool Growers' Association. 67790

Transactions of the Council called for the
ordination of the Rev. Mr. Hubbard.
33432

Transactions of the Eclectic Medical Society.
(53655)

Transactions of the eighth family reunion.
67896

Transactions of the Essex Agricultural Society.
23005, 97257-97258

Transactions of the fifth annual meeting of the
Kansas Academy of Science. 85514

Transactions of the first annual meeting of
the, Kentucky State Medical Society.
37525

Transactions of the fourth annual meeting of
the Western Literary Institute. 102990

Transactions of the Franklin County Agricultural Society. 25662

Transactions of the Geological Society, London.
(5258), 91210

Transactions of the Geological Society of
Pennsylvania. 26987, (60117)

Transactions of the Grand Chapter of the State
of Iowa. 35022

Transactions of the Grand Council of Royal
and Select Masters. 87833

Transactions of the Grand Lodge . . . of Free
. . . Masons of . . . New-York. (53692)

Transactions of the Grand Lodge of Free . . .
Masons of the state of New York.
(53692)

Transactions [of the Grand Lodge of Texas.]
95085

Transactions of the Hampden County Agricultural
Society. 30131

Transactions of the Hampshire Agricultural
Society. 30138

Transactions of the Hampshire, Franklin and
Hampden Agricultural Society. 30146

Transactions of the Hartford County Agricultural
Society. (30679)

Transactions of the Hingham Agricultural and
Horticultural Society. 21588

Transactions of the Historical and Literary
Committee of the American Philosophical
Society. 1183, 7668

Transactions of the Historical and Philosophical
Society of Ohio. (56932), 101080

Transactions of the Historical Society of
Cincinnati. 31799

Transactions of the Historical Society of Ohio.
30571

Transactions of the Homoeopathic Medical
Society. (53695)

Transactions of the Housatonic Agricultural
Society. (33171)

Transactions of the Illinois Natural History
Society. (34262)

Transactions of the Illinois State Agricultural
Society. 34198

Transactions of the Illinois State Medical
Society. 34265

Transactions of the Jefferson County Agricultural Society. (35945)

Transactions of the Journal of medicine.
(80563)

Transactions of the Kansas Academy of Science.
85514

Transactions of the Kansas State Board of
Agriculture. (37017), 85514

Transactions of the Kansas State Historical
Society. (68629)

Transactions of the Literary and Historical
Society of Quebec. 11141, 11143,
38901, 67018, 72307, 93129, 104014

Transactions of the Literary and Philosophical
Society of New York. 54362, (74699)

Transactions of the Lower Canada Board of
Agriculture. (10342)

Transactions of the Maine Medical Association.
43982

Transactions of the Marshfield Agricultural
and Horticultural Society. (44818)

Transactions of the Martha's Vineyard Agricultural Society. 44852

Transactions of the Maryland Academy of Science and Literature. 45198

Transactions of the Massachusetts Baptist Charitable Society. 45821

Transactions of the Massachusetts Horticultural Society. 45862

Transactions of the Massachusetts Society for Promoting Agriculture. (45896)

Transactions of the Massachusetts Teachers' Association. 45907

Transactions of the Medical and Chirurgical Faculty of Maryland. 45254, 83664

Transactions of the Medical and Surgical Society of the University of the State of New York. (54000)

Transactions of the Medical Association of Southern Central New York. (47312)

Transactions of the Medical Society of New Jersey. 53152

Transactions of the Medical Society of Pennsylvania. 60235

Transactions of the Medical Society of the State of New York. 4225, 53765, 72477, 75604, 90893, 103419

Transactions of the Medical Society of the State of Tennessee. 94802

Transactions of the Michigan State Agricultural Society. 48717

Transactions of the Middlesex Agricultural Society. (48840)

Transactions of the Minnesota State Medical Society. (49289)

Transactions of the Moravian Historical Society. 50526, 68988, 68993

Transactions of the Nantucket Agricultural Society. 51755

Transactions of the National Association of Wool Manufacturers. 51935

Transactions of the Natural History Society of Hartford. 30675

Transactions of the New England Agricultural Society. 52645

Transactions of the New England Methodist Historical Society. 14198

Transactions of the New Hampshire Agricultural Society. (52888)

Transactions of the New-Hampshire Medical Society. 52878, 84907

Transactions of the New-Haven County Horticultural Society. 52990

Transactions of the New Haven Horticultural and New Haven County Agricultural Societies. 52994

Transactions of the New York Academy of Medicine. 54423

Transactions of the New York Ecclesiological Society. 54769

Transactions of the New York Historical Society. 26399

Transactions of the New York Life-Saving Benevolent Association. 54506

Transactions of the New York Southern Central Medical Association. 54855

Transactions of the New York State Agricultural Society. (19594), 53811, 75792-75793

Transactions of the New-York State Institution of Civil Engineers. 53823

Transactions of the Ninth International Medical Congress. 83367

Transactions of the Norfolk Agricultural Society. (55467)

Transactions of the North-Western Fruit Growers Association. 55744

Transactions of the Northern Illinois Horticultural Society. (55799)

Transactions of the Nova-Scotia Literary and Scientific Society. 56157

Transactions of the Ohio mob. 106197

Transactions of the Ohio State Medical Society. 57008

Transactions of the Old Settlers' Association, of Sauk County, Wisconsin. 77159

Transactions of the Onondaga County Agricultural Society. 57360

Transactions of the Pennsylvania Horticultural Society. 60326

Transactions of the Pennsylvania Momological Society. 60352

Transactions of the Philological Society. (62550)

Transactions of the Physico-Medical Society of New-York. 54577

Transactions of the Plymouth County Agricultural Society. 63493

Transactions of the Queen's County Agricultural Society. 67068

Transactions of the Queens County Agricultural Society. 67068

Transactions of the Rensselaer County Agricultural Society. 69638

Transactions of the Rhode-Island Medical Society. 70727, 85502

Transactions of the Rhode Island Society for the Encouragement of Domestic Industry. (70736), 85493

Transactions of the Rock County Agricultural Society and Mechanics' Institute. 29117

Transactions of the Rockingham Fair. 72392

Transactions [of the Royal Irish Academy.] 21322

Transactions of the Royal Society, London. 74704

Transactions of the Royal Society of Northern Antiquarians. 23717

Transactions of the St. Louis Academy of Sciences. 84244

Transactions of the Society for Promoting Agriculture in the State of Connecticut. 15657, 15863

Transactions of the Society, for the Promotion of Agriculture, Arts and Manufactures, Institute in the State of New-York. 86000

Transactions of the Society, Instituted in the State of New York, for the Promotion of Agriculture, Arts, and Manufactures. 85999

Transactions of the Society of California Pioneers. 86014

Transactions of the Society of Dutchess County for the Promotion of Agriculture. 21456, 86016

Transactions of the Society of Husbandmen and Manufacturers, Middlesex, Mass. 48851

Transactions of the Society of Literary & Scientific Chiffonniers. 103034

Transactions of the South-Carolina Medical Association. 88016-88017

Transactions of the South-Carolina Medical Association, at the extra meeting in Greenwood. 88020

Transactions of the Southern Central Agricultural Society. 88317

Transactions of the Southern Historical Society. 88371

Transactions of the State Board of Agriculture. 34489

Transactions of the State Board of Agriculture, 1861. 34198

Translyvania journal of medicine, extra.
96470-96471
Transylvania Presbytery. see Presbyterian
Church in the U. S. A. Presbytery of
Transylvania.
Transylvania Seminary. see Transylvania
University, Lexington, Ky.
Transylvania University, Lexington, Ky.
96461-96464, 96467
Transylvania University, Lexington, Ky.
Botanic Garden. 67450, 96468
Transylvania University, Lexington, Ky.
Exercises on the Arrival of General
Lafayette, 1825. 38583, 96464
Transylvania University, Lexington, Ky.
Faculty and Board of Trustees. 96465
Transylvania University, Lexington, Ky.
Library. 96469
Transylvania University, Lexington, Ky.
Medical Department. 96470-96471
Translyvanian trilogy. 96328
Trap'em, Tristram. pseud. Boston assem-
blage. 6486, 96472
Trap for a scold. 100502
Trapham, Thomas. 96473
Trapham, Thomas. supposed author 86674
Trappan'd maiden. 96474
Trapper's bride. 75253, 75261
Trapper's bride and White stone canoe, &c.
&c. 75262
Trapper's bridge; or spirit of adventure.
(51491)
Trapper's guide. 55000
Trappers of Arkansas. 543
Trappers of New York. 81185
Trappers of Umbagog. 95477
Trapper's retreat. 14171
Trappeurs de la Baie d'Hudson. (12573)
Trappeurs de l'Arkansas. 543
Trappeurs du Kansas. 56738
Trarado y parcero sobre el servicio personal.
513
Trarahumarisches Worterbuch. 91187
Trasitvs ad occasum. 33490, 67355
Trask, George. supposed author 77003,
(77005), 77993, 88919, 89539, note
before 96474, note before 96475
Trask, J. B. 10006
Trask, W. L. 47771
Trask, William B. (20619), 46784, 93714
Trask, William Blake. 93772
Traslado bien y fielmente sacado de una
Cedula. 96475
Traslado de una carta. 7640, note after
96475
Traslado del despacho del servicio personal
de los Indios. 96476
Trasvina, Antonio. 96477
Tratado a cerca del mineral de Pasco.
96796
Tratado a lo vltimo de la doctrina Christiana.
94424
Tratado breve de la antigvedad de linaie de
vera. 66580
Tratado breve de medicina y de todas las
enfermedades. (23797)
Tratado breve del dvlcissimo nombre de
Maria. 24320
Tratado comprobatorio. 11237, 11239
Tratado co[m]probatorio del imperio soberano
y principado uniuersal. 11231, 11235,
note after 39114
Tratado consolatorio a la Princesa de
Portugal. 57714
Tratado contra la carta del Prothonotario de
Lucena. 57714

Tratado contra las bubas, sive Fruto de Todos
Santos. 35250, note after. 74024
Tratado da sphera com a theorica do sol e
da lua. 56320
Tratado, das batalhas. 23207
Tratado de la esfera, en 200 fojas. 80987
Tratado de amistad, limites y navegacion.
96587
Tratado de avisos, y puntos importantes.
99693
Tratado de confirmaciones reales de encomi-
endas. 40057
Tratado de economica politica. 77364
Tratado de ensayos, tanto por al via seca
como por la via humeda. (20561)
Tratado de escripturacao mercantil. 85634
Tratado de la amalgamacion de Mexico.
86967
Tratado de la amalgamacion de Nueva Espana.
86968
Tratado de la ciudad de Mexico. 99389
Tratado de la ciudad de Puebla de los Angeles.
99389
Tratado de la fiebre epidemica. (72566)
Tratado de la geografia politica. 96478
Tratado de la humilidad y obediencia. 78921
Tratado, de la importa[n]cia del medio.
98331
Tratado de la paz del alma en Megicano.
(70807)
Tratado de la propiedad. 59304
Tratado de las antiguas minas de Espana.
(3253)
Tratado de las presas maritimas. 50106
Tratado de las relaciones verdaderas de los
reynos de China. 57523
Tratado de limites de conquistas entre . . .
D. Joao V. Rey de Portugal. 96546
Tratados de limites das conquistas entre os
Muito Altos, e Poderosos Senhores.
96515
Tratados de los comentarios, dificvltades, y
discvrsos literales y misticos sobre los
euangelios de la Qvaresma. 99674-
99675
Tratado de los funerales y de las sepulturas.
2545
Tratado de los usos y abusos del propriedades
y virtudes del tobacco. 39290
Tratado de operacoes de banco. 95457
Tratado de paz, ajustado entre las coronas
de Espana, y de Inglaterra. 96542
Tratado de paz, concluido en veinte de
Setiembre de 1697. 96536
Tratado de paz entre el Director Provisorio
de la Confederacion Argentina. 58062
Tratado de que se deben administrar los
Sacramentos a los Indios. 59517
Tratado de violencias judiciales y enormidad
de ministros. 36128
Tratado definitivo de paz concluido entre el
Rey Nuestro Senor. 96558
Tratado definitivo de paz concluido entreel
Rey Nvestro Senor y S. M. Christianisima
96552
Tratado definitivo de paz concluido entre os
Muitos Altos, e Muito Poderosos Sen-
hores. 96544
Tratado definitivo de paz concluido entre SS.
MM. Christianissima, y Britanica.
96545
Tratado definitivo de paz e uniao entre . . .
Joseph I. 19275, 96553
Tratado del agua mineral caliente de San
Bartholome. 42066

Tratado del arbol de la quina o cascarilla. 74003

Tratado del real derecho de las midias-anatas seculares. 70462

Tratado del sistema de marcacion. 47834

Tratado del ziquilite y anil de Guatemala. 51224

Tratado dela herida del rey. 57714

Tratado descriptivo do Brazil em 1587. 85635

Tratado domestico de algunas enfermedades bastante comunes en esta capital. (10650)

Tratados dos descobrimientos antigos. (26468)

Tratado firmado en Madrid. 96547

Tratado general sobre las aguas que fertilizan los valles de Lima. (38824)

Tratado historico, politico, y legal de la comercio. 29360, 73852

Tratados historicos, politicos, ethicos, y religiosos. 52095

Tratado juridico das pessoas honradas. 85647

Tratado para componer las controversias. 96527

Tratado prelimina sobre los limites de los paises pretenecientes en America Meridional. 96555

Tratado prelimina de paz, e de limites na America Meridional. 96554

Tratado prelimina sobre los limites de los estados. 96556

Tratado que compos o nombre e notauel capitao Antonio Galuao. 26467

Tratado sobre el ganado lanar de Espana. 39152

Tratado sobre el oficio de Protector General de los Indios. 74660

Tratado sobre las aguas de los valles de Lima. 47937

Tratado sobre los eclipses del sul. 80987

Tratado vnico, y singvlar del origen de los Indios Occidentales. (72290)

Tratado verdadero del viage y navegacion deste ano de seiscientos y veinte y dos. 98726

Tratados del Doctor Alonso Ortis. 57714

Tratados que la republica de Colombia ha celebrado. 14625

Tratando del remedio que puede tener la inundacio de Mexico. 96479

Tratantes en el Ramo de Pulques. petitioners 69969

Tratatto naturale, medico, morale, e curioso. 91215

Trate de mesures. 59172

Trattado das tregoas. 96519

Trattado . . . della historia. 114

Trattado del veleno della vipera de' veleni Americani. (24990)

Trattato della sfera. 32678, 74810

Trattato della neue & del beuer fresco. 57670

Trattato della sphera, nel quale si dimostrano. 32678, 74810

Trattato di navigazione. (62804)

Trauerrede, auf die ersten Helden und Opfer des Vaterlandes. 1945

Trauer-Rede gehalten am 19ten April, 1865. (22089)

Trauerspiel. 100720

Trauerspiel in einer Handlung. 105986

Trauerspiel in funf Aufzugen. 100722

Trauerspiel in Mexiko. 77614

Traunholds des Jungeren Begebenheiten, Reisen (72225)

Trautwine, John Cresson. (38466), 60187, note after 96479-96480

Travail general sur la famille des Graminees par C. S. Kunth. 33766

Travail, liberte, propriete pour tous. 50695

Travaux d'ameliorations interieures. 64732, (64740)

Travaux publics de l'Amerique du Nord. 91590

Travaux sur la meteorologie. 63667

Travel and description series. 94934

Travel letters. 83489

Travel, life, and adventures, in the British North American provinces. 82126

Travel notes of an octogenarian. 84901-84902

Travel through the two Louisianas. 62506

Traveller and tourist's route-book through the United States. 24487

Traveler's directory for Illinois. 59486

Traveler's observations on cotton and slavery. 57240

Traveler's own book. 30617

Traveler's sketch. 62342

Traveling Missionary Society of the Newcastle District. see Society for Promoting Christian Knowledge, London. Newcastle District. Traveling Missionary Society.

Traveller. pseud. Account of Abimelech Coody. see Clinton, De Witt, 1769-1828.

Traveller. pseud. California, from its discovery. see Kells, Charles E. supposed author

Traveller. pseud. Description of the Great Western Canal. 19721

Traveller. pseud. Geographical sketch of St. Domingo. see Clark, Benjamin C.

Traveller. pseud. Gleanings in America. (27561)

Traveller. pseud. Letter to the Hon. Daniel Webster. see Cleveland, Henry R.

Traveller, pseud. Letters to the Hon. Daniel Webster. 40645

Traveller. pseud. Life and manners in the United States. 41008

Traveller. pseud. Notes of a traveller. 55955, 95352, 1st note after 96481

Traveller. pseud. Notes upon Canada and the United States. see Todd, Henry Cook.

Traveller. pseud. Notes upon Canada and the United States of America. see Todd, Henry Cook.

Traveller. pseud. Sketches by a traveller. 81548, 3d note after 96481

Traveller. pseud. Sketches of history. see Royall, Anne.

Traveller. pseud. Summer tours. see Dwight, Theodore, 1796-1866.

Traveller. pseud. Things as they are. 55955, 95352, 1st note after 96481

Traveller. pseud. Thoughts of a traveller. see Draper, Sir William.

Traveller. pseud. Visit to Texas. 95133, 6th note after 100603

Traveller, Jack. pseud. Letters from a gentleman in Transilvania. see Hunt, Isaac.

Traveller (Boston) 66789

Traveller. 26316

Traveller and emigrant's hand-book to Canada. 29757

Traveller and monthly gazetteer. 96481A

Traveller and tourist's guide-book through the western states. 14796

Traveller in Basaruah. pseud. History of the kingdom of Basaruah. 96482

Traveller in the province. pseud. Notices of East Florida. (24889)

Traveller in the Caribbees. pseud. Letter. 3291, note before 93803

Traveller in the United States. pseud. Ritual and illustrations of Freemasonry. 71598

Traveller; or, meditations on various subjects. 47402

Traveller recently returned from California. pseud. Emigrant's guide to California. 10002

Traveller, some years resident in that and the other American states. pseud. Notes and reflections on Mexico. 96481

Traveller: spirit of the times and life in New-York. 89508

Traveller through some of the middle and nothern states. pseud. Things as they are. see Dwight, Theodore, 1796-1866.

Traveller through those parts. pseud. Visit to Texas. 95133

Traveller to Florida. pseud. Journal of a traveller to Florida. 24869

Travellers. A tale. Designed for young people. 78806, 96483

Traveller's and emigrant's guide to Wisconsin and Iowa. 49

Travellers' and tourists' guide-book through the United States. (14793)

Travellers benighted. 91998

Traveller's breviat. 36287, 1st note after 96483

Traveller's companion: being a complete guide. 35714

Traveller's companion. Containing each day's observations. 64036

Traveller's companion through the great interior. 91127

Traveller's directory, and emigrant's guide. 91144, 2d note after 96483

Traveller's directory, and statistical view of the United States. 96484

Traveller's directory: exhibiting the distances on the principal land and water thorough-fares. 96485

Traveller's directory; or, a pocket companion. 50436

Traveller's directory through the United States. 47435

Traveller's dream and other poems. 31119

Travellers' guide and descriptive journal. (26095)

Travellers guide and statistical view of the United States. 102324

Traveller's guide for Montreal and Quebec. 50290, note after 96485

Traveller's guide from New York to Phila-delphia. 46899

Traveller's guide in New England. 96486

Traveller's guide; or, pocket gazetteer of the United States. (50953)

Traveller's guide, or table of distances on the principal rail road, canal and stage routes in the state. 96763

Traveller's guide through North America. 18695

Traveller's guide through the commercial metropolis of the United States. 49746

Travellers' guide through the middle and northern states and . . . Canada. 18910, 96487

Traveller's guide: through the middle and northern states, and the provinces of Canada. 6899, 18728, 18910, (73502), 96487, 3d note after 100806

Traveller's guide through the state of New-York, Canada, &c. 96488

Traveller's guide through the United States. [By H. Phelps.] (61379)

Traveller's guide through the United States. [By S. A. Mitchell.] 49717

Traveller's guide to America. 96489

Traveller's guide to Madeira and the West Indies. 96490, 1st note after 102871, note after 106194

Traveller's guide to Montreal and its vicinity. (52091), note after 96490

Traveller's guide to the Hudson River. 20325

Traveller's guide to the west. 104013

Traveller's hand-book of . . . Quebec and its environs. 57347

Travellers hand-book of the city of Quebec and its environs. 67063

Traveller's illustrated pocket guide. 31929

Travellers in America. 84304-84305

Travellers in America. A farce. 21309

Travellers' legal guide and directory. 18796

Traveller's library. (35728), 38914, 84315

Traveller's manual. 96491

Traveller's memorandum. 70960

Travellers', miners', and emigrants' guide and hand-book. (29758)

Traveller's observations on cotton and slavery. 57240

Travellers' own book, to Saratoga Springs. 19805

Traveller's pocket companion and advice to the travelling public. 90802

Traveller's pocket dictionary and stranger's guide. 96492

Traveller's pocket directory and stranger's guide. 96493

Traveller's pocket directory and stranger's guide: exhibiting distances. 96493

Traveller's pocket medical guide. 96494

Traveller's report; or, abroad and at home. 3794

Traveller's rest. 4847

Traveller's steamboat and railroad guide to the Hudson River. [By H. Phelps.] (61379)

Traveller's steamboat and railroad guide to the Hudson River, describing the cities, towns, and places of interest along the route. (33526), 1st note after 96494

Travelling bachelor. pseud. Notions of the Americans. see Cooper, James Feni-more, 1789-1851.

Travelling book-agent's guide and instructor. 30649

Travelling gentleman in America: a satire. 80151, note after 97028, 2d note after 97036

Travelling to and in Upper Canada. 96495

Travels across the Isthmus of Darien. 100942

Travels and adventures in Canada and the Indian territories. 31383

Travels and adventures in Mexico. (11017)

Travels and adventures in South and Central America. 58140

Travels and adventures of Capt. John Smith. 66686

Travels and adventures of celebrated travelers. 33304

Travels and adventures of David C. Bunnell.
9187
Travels and adventures of Doctor E. White
and lady. 781, 103377
Travels and adventures of John Ledyard.
(39692), 1st note after 96495
Travels and adventures of Sir Anthony, Sir
Robert, & Sir Thomas Sherley. 80349
Travels and extraordinary adventures of
Henry Sidney in Brazil. (80857)
Travels and labors in Europe and America.
20755
Travels and labors of Lorenzo Dow in Europe
and America. 20757
Travels and providential experience of Lorenzo
Dow. 20757
Travels and relations of Friar William de
Rubriquis. 66686
Travels and researches of Alexander von
Humboldt. 33744
Travels and residence in the free states of
America. 91706
Travels and sketches in North and South
America. 27880
Travels and voyages in Europe, Asia, Africa,
and America. 52454
Travels and voyages in the north by Giles
Fletcher. 66686
Travels and voyages into Africa, Asia, and
America. 49794
Travels and works of Captain John Smith.
82857
Travels around the world. 79594
Travels [by Carver.] 40827
Travels. By Kinahan Cornwallis. 16820
Travels: comprising a journey from England
to Ohio. 23566
Travels continued in the United States.
73821
Travels from Buenos Ayres, by Potosi, to
Lima. 31265, 62506
Travels from New York to Detroit. 74122
Travels from Vienna to Brazil. 61337
Travels in America and Italy. 12276
Travels in America. [By Frances Milton
Trollope.] 97028
Travels in America. By George Fibbleton.
28585, 2d note after 96495
Travels in America. [By George William
Frederick Howard, Earl of Carlisle.]
33248-33249
Travels in America. By John Eyre. 23563,
23566
Travels in America. By Theodore Dwight.
(21542), 96352
Travels in America, performed in 1806.
2180, 62506-62507, 96495
Travels in Bolivia and across the pampas.
19111
Travels in Bolivia; with a tour across the
pampas. 6299
Travels in Brazil. By Henry Koster. 38272
Travels in Brazil, Cape Colony, and part of
Caffreland. 32567
Travels in Brazil, in 1815, 1816, and 1817.
47022, 62509
Travels in Brazil, in the years 1815, 1816,
1817. (47021)
Travels in Brazil, in the years 1817-1820.
89551
Travels in British Columbia. 40030
Travels in Buenos Ayres. 4194
Travels in California. 104616
Travels in Canada and the United States in
1816 and 1817. (29769), 84304-84306,
84320-84321

Travels in Canada, and through the states of
New York and Pennsylvania. 38219
Travels in Central America; being a journal
of nearly three years' residence.
(21317)
Travels in Central America including accounts
of some regions unexplored. 50592
Travels in Central America, particularly in
Nicaragua. 89999
Travels in Chile and La Plata. 48889
Travels in Denmark, Norway, and Sweden.
(59572)
Travels in India. (59572)
Travels in Kamtschatka, during the years
1787 and 1788. 40209, (59572)
Travels in Louisiana and the Floridas.
4965, note after 96496
Travels in Louisiana, &c. [By Claude C.
Robin.] 72041
Travels in Lower Canada. 10616, 62509,
76707
Travels in Mexico and California. 13393
Travels in Mexico, South America, etc. etc.
99606
Travels in New England and New York. 21559
Travels in North America, by Emanuel Crespel.
(17479)
Travels in North America. [By George
Philips.] 62456, 96497
Travels in North America, by Mr. Isaac
Weld. 46984, 102540
Travels in North America. By Whitman Mead.
(47229)
Travels in North America. [By William
Mavor.] 46984, 102540
Travels in North America during the years
1834, 1835, & 1836. 51490-(51491)
Travels in North America, from modern
writers. 5463
Travels in North America in 1840-42.
(42761)
Travels in North America, in the years 1827
and 1828. 5247, 29725
Travels in North America, in the years 1780,
1781, and 1782. 12229-12230, 12233,
69508, 81137
Travels in Oregon. (23868)-23869
Travels in parts of South America. 19644.
62506-62507
Travels in Peru and India. 44616
Travels in Peru and Mexico. 31862
Travels in Poland. (59572)
Travels in Portugal. (59572)
Travels in Prince Edward Island. 36401
Travels in Siberia. 22771
Travels in some parts of North America.
93943
Travels in South America. 96498
Travels in South America, during the years
1801, 1802, 1803, and 1804. 19643
Travels in South America, during the years
1819-20-21. 9877
Travels in South America. From modern
writers. 5464
Travels in South America from the Pacific
Ocean to the Atlantic Ocean. 44508,
1st note after 96498
Travels in South and North America. 44609
Travels in southern California. 105714
Travels in the Californias. 23867, 23871
Travels in the central portions of the Missis-
sippi Valley. 77880
Travels in the east by W. Biddulph. 66686
Travels in the eastern and western world.
8893

Travels through the United States and Canada. (5872), 96503

Travels through the United States of America. (81136)

Travels through the United States of North America. 102542

Travels through the United States, the country of the Iroquois, and Upper Canada. 39057, 46984, 102540

Travels through the western country in the summer of 1816. 95384

Travels through the western interior of the United States. 37599

Travels through Upper and Lower Canada. (10617)

Travels to the frozen ocean. 43808

Travels to the source of the Missouri River. 40829-(40831)

Travels to the west of the Alleghany Mountains, in the states of Ohio, Kentucky, and Tennessea [sic]. (48705)

Travels to the westward of the Allegany Mountains, in the states of Ohio, Kentucky, and Tennessee. (48704)

Travels to the westward of the Allegany Mountains, in the states of Ohio, Kentucky, and Tennessee, in the year 1802. 48706, 62506

Travels to the westward, or the unknown parts of America. 98446, 98449, 98454, 98457-98460

Travels to the westward or the unknown parts of America: in the years 1786 & 1787. 98448

Travels, trial and conviction of the Mormon apostle, Lorenzo Snow. 85535

Travers, De Val. supposed author 93597

Travers, George. defendant 96504

Travers, John. 86809, 96505

Traves de la razon. 96506

Travestie in one act. 95594A

Travis, Daniel. 62743

Travis, Daniel Charles. defendant before Military Commission 9381

Travis, M. Charles E. 26688

Travis, Robert. 96507

Traycion que dos sargentos avian maqvinado hacer en Badajos. 96508

Tre bref. 93985

Tre delarne. (77966)

Tre drammi. 64014

Tre navigationi fatte da gli Olandesi. 67742

Treacherous dealer slighted. 103702

Treacherous husband caught in his own trap. (37720)

Treachery and tyranny of administration. (39703)

Treachery in Texas. 89688

Treacle fetch'd out of a viper. (46557), note after 96508

Treadway, James. ed. 100595, 2d note after 105939

Treadway, W. R. H. reporter 87455

Treadwell, Daniel. 6493, 96509

Treadwell, Francis C. (20647), note after 96509-96510

Treadwell, John. 96511

Treadwell, John G. (56691)

Treadwell, Seymour Boughton. 96512

Treadwell, Thomas. comp. 22988, 1st note after 96762

Treason and its treatment. 32653

Treason and law. 30287

Treason and the fate of traitors. 26647

Treason defined. 96510

Treason detected. 23020, (31399)

Treason discovered but not punished. 97206

Treason in Congress. 26664

Treason of Charles Lee. 50380

Treason of the Romish bishops in America. 4303

Treason of West Point. 33458

Treason should not be dignified by concessions from patriots. 86833

Treason should not be dignified by concessions to traitors. 86834

Treason triumphant. 30022

Treason unmasked. An exposition of the origin, objects and principles of the Knights of the Golden Circle. 76471

Treason unmasked. By a Virginian. 43148, 2d note after 100582

Treasure of the fathers, inheritable by their posterity. 95165

Treasure of the Inca. (32409)

Treasure of traffike. (71910)

Treasured moments. 77296

Treasurer and Company of Adventurers and Planters of the City of London. see Virginia Company of London.

Treasurer of a corporation. pseud. Profits on manufactures at Lowell. see Cary, Thomas Graves.

Treasurer of Trinity Church, Boston. see Boston. Trinity Church. Treasurer.

Treasurer takes this method to inform the public. 99134

Treasurer's account current. 89821

[Treasurer's account, with the report of the Committee thereon.] 100417

Treasurer's address to the Legislature in June last. 99133

Treasurer's annual report [i. e. at Newburyport, Mass.] 54913

Treasurer's report, a list of members, etc. [of the Norfolk Auxiliary Education Society.] 2744

Treasurer's report [i. e. of North Carolina.] 55699

Treasurer's report of the receipts and expenditures of the town of Brighton. 7976

Treasurer's report of the receipts and expenditures of the town of Brookline. 8262

Treasurer's report [of the Vermont Antislavery Society.] 99220

Treasurer's report, showing the receipts and payments, 1839-40. 62343

Treasurer's report to the Honorable Board of Trustees of South Carolina College. 87992

Treasurer's report to the Honorable the Board of Trustees of the South Carolina College. 87993

Treasurer's report to the Legislature of New Jersey. (53241)

Treasurer's statement . . . for 1859 [of the Arch Street Presbyterian Church, Philadelphia.] 61477

Treasurer's statement, Jan. 1, 1825. 46169

Treasurer's statement of the annual expense of printing. 46169

Treasurer's statement [of the Maine Missionary Society.] (5978)

Treasvrie of avncient and moderne times. 58247

Treasury and the taxes. 71887

Treasury Department and its various fiscal bureaus. 47192

Treasury Department, Register's Office, 1st June, 1833. 101546-101546A

Treasury note bill. Speech . . . delivered in the House of Representatives, February 6, 1862. 21994

Treasury note bill. Speech of Hon. Jno. A. Bingham. 5446

Treasury notes a legal tender. 64285

Treasury of divine and useful knowledge. 13028

Treasury of geography. 46942

Treasury of history. 46940

Treasury of knowledge. 38069

Treasury of politics and literature. 69963

Treasury; or, impartial compendium. 69963

Treasury report. Report of the Special Commissioner and Auditor of State. 57062

Treat, Joseph, 1734-1797. 96513

Treat, Joseph, 1775-1853. 96514

Treat, Joseph, 1775-1853. defendant at court martial 96514

Treat, Robert, 1622-1710. 15860, note after 95296 see also Connecticut (Colony) Governor, 1689-1698 (Treat)

Treat, Robert, 1695-1770. 62743

Treat, S. B. 71343

Treat, Salmon. 91944

Treat, Samuel H. 34290

Treaties. 61208

[Treaties between two or more European states.] 26601, 27262, 30866, 38201, (38742), 40234, 43889, 44839-44949, 66396, 68429, (69476), 73495

Treaties between the United States and Great Britain, and the United States and France. 96560

Treaties between the United States and Great-Britain: viz. the definitive treaty, signed at Paris, 1783. 96563

Treaties between the United States of America, and the Chiefs, Headmen, and Warriors, of the Potawattamie Indians. 96595

Treaties between the United States of America and the several Indian tribes, from 1778 to 1837. 96597

Treaties lately made between the United States and sundry tribes of Indians. 96592

Treaties made between Great Britain and the United States, from the year 1783 to 1814. 96564

Treaties of alliance, amity & commerce, between the United States of America, and the French government. 96568

Treaties of amity and commerce, and of alliance eventual and defensive, between His Most Christian Majesty and the Thirteen United States of America. 96556

Treaties of amity and commerce, and of alliance eventual and defensive, between His Most Christian Majesty and the Thirteen United States of America; the difinitive treaty between Great Britain and the Thirteen United States of America. 96562

Treaties of amity and commerce, and of alliance, with France. 96565-96568

Treaties [of 1778] between His Most Christian Majesty and the Thirteen United States of America. 96567

Treaties of the United States, with the Choctaw and Chickasaw Indians. 96596

Treaties, which have lately been entered into. 96591

Treaties with certain Indian tribes. 96593

Treaties with France, Great Britain, and the United States. 96561

Treaties with the Indians in the state of New York. 54781

Treaties with various Indian tribes and nations. 15493

Treatise against detraction. (39990)

Treatise annexed, written by that learned mathematician Mr. Henry Briggs. 99885

Treatise. By John De Witt. 78992

Treatise by William Law, M. A. (39324)

Treatise by William Law, M. A. . . . with some thoughts on the nature of war. 93925

Treatise, concerning Christ the foundation. 83541

Treatise concerning civil government. 97358, 97364

Treatise concerning conversion. 91966

Treatise concerning marriage. 84552

Treatise, concerning political enquiry. 105514

Treatise concerning religious affections. 21967

Treatise concerning the ancient orders and manner of worship. 66869

Treatise concerning the Lord's Supper. 20614

Treatise concerning the malignant fever in Barbados. 101466

Treatise concerning the properties and effects of coffee. (51048)

Treatise concerning thoughts and imaginations. 80459

Treatise containing a plan for the internal organization and government. (3862)

Treatise containing, the broken heart. (32854)

Treatise containing the soules vision with Christ. 32850

Treatise declaring from the word of truth the terms on which we stand. 49657-(49658), 65607, 92351

Treatise designed to promote peace and harmony. 65340, note before 95775

Treatise, detecting first, the plots of the devil. 46225

Treatise, discovering the intrigues and arbitrary proceedings. 104036

Treatise, etc., 1748. 25563

Treatise explanatory of the various figures. 96490, 1st note after 102871, note after 106194

Treatise, for justices of the peace. 29555

Treatise of affaires maritime, and of commerce. 49924

Treatise of bloud. 97551

Treatise of church discipline. 36602

Treatise of commerce. 103192-103193

Treatise of contrition. (32857), 32858

Treatise of effectual calling. 24400

Treatise of evangelical conversion. 80244-80246, (80249)-80251

Treatise of evangelicall conversion. 80239-(80243), 80247-80248

Treatise of extraordinary divine dispensations. 8192

Treatise of gardening. 96739

Treatise of hem-husbandry. 67182

Treatise of holy time. (66872)

Treatise of ineffectual hearing the word. 80252-80254

Treatise of liturgies. 80259

Treatise, of M. Edward Hayes. (7730)

Treatise of military exercise. 96740

Treatise of Mr. Cotton's. 17088, note after 97545

Treatise of New England. 96741

Treatise of oaths, &c. 66926

Treatise of practical information for farmers. 72180

Treatise on the deluge, containing remarks on the Lord Bishop of Clogher's account of that event. 11496

Treatise on the "democratic principle." 82001

Treatise on the discipline of the cavalry. 96747

Treatise on the diseases of Negroes. 95575

Treatise on the diseases of Virginia and the neighbouring colonies. 94716

Treatise on the distillation of ardent spirits. 93094

Treatise on the effects of musketry and artillery. 88405

Treatise on the elements of written language. 95646

Treatise on the fevers of Jamaica. 35456

Treatise on the fullness of the everlasting Gospel. 44905

Treatise on the glandular disease of Barbadoes. 31334-(31335)

Treatise on the gonorrhoea. 93830, note after 96747

Treatise on the great rebellion of 1861. 19465

Treatise on the human teeth. 81633

Treatise on the importance of extending the British fisheries. 61392

Treatise on the improvement and emancipation of slaves. 13499

Treatise on the improvement of canal navigation. 26201

Treatise on the inalienable rights of women. 77401

Treatise on the inhalation of ether for the prevention of pain. 83602-83603

Treatise on the inherent rights and obligations of man. 74534

Treatise on the intellectual character and civil and political condition of the colored people of the United States. (21692), 21723

Treatise on the jurisdiction and proceedings of justices of the peace. 28832

Treatise on the justice, policy, and utility of establishing an effectual system for promoting the progress of useful arts. (2522)

Treatise on the law and practice of ejectment. 95421

Treatise on the law and the Gospel. 96748

Treatise on the law of copyright in books. 18046

Treatise on the law of descents. 68666

Treatise on the law of libel and the liberty of the press. 16619

Treatise on the law of the American rebellion. 26641

Treatise on the law of the Protestant Episcopal Church. 32404

Treatise on the law relating to banks and banking. 50954

Treatise on the law relating to the powers and duties of justices of the peace. 94012

Treatise on the lawfulness of defensive war. 10944, 17999A

Treatise on the lawfvlnes of hearing of the ministers in the Church of England. 72109

Treatise on the laws of patents for useful inventions. 18047

Treatise on the lien of mechanics and material men. 79192

Treatise on the martial power of the President. 26641

Treatise on the military art. 33403

Treatise on the millenium, shewing its near approximation. 96749

Treatise on the millennium. [By Samuel Hopkins.] 32955

Treatise on the millennium, or latter-day glory of the church. 64666

Treatise, on the mode and manner of Indian war. 82771

Treatise on the mulberry tree and silk worm. 13425

Treatise on the nature and cultivation of coffee. 39127

Treatise on the nature and cure of the yaws. (52325)

Treatise on the nature, source, and probability of a permanent supply. 52276

Treatise on the necessity of holding fast the truth. 94697, 94707

Treatise on the new sword exercise, for cavalry. 87165

Treatise on the office and duty of a justice of the peace. 23326

Treatise on the organization and jurisdiction of the courts. (28025)

Treatise on the organization, jurisdiction and practice of the courts. 15618

Treatise on the organization, properties, and uses of hair and wool. 8676

Treatise on the origin and principles of courts martial. 91568

Treatise on the patriarchal, or co-operative system of society. 96750

Treatise on the patriarchal system of society. 37895

Treatise on the plague and yellow fever. 97656

Treatise on the practice of the Supreme Court of Judicature. 105647

Treatise on the principal diseases of the interior valley. 20825, 84074

Treatise on the principal trades and manufactures of the United States. (25730), (25733)

Treatise on the principles of currency and banking. (67505)

Treatise on the principles, practice, & history of commerce. 43130

Treatise on the proceedings of a camp-meeting. 89144, 96751

Treatise, on the raising and culture of Wheat. 91338

Treatise on the regeneration and eternal duration of matter. 64969

Treatise on the relation of the church, Rome and dissent. 85360

Treatise on the right of personal liberty. 33992

Treatise on the right of suffrage. 36604

Treatise on the scarlatina anginosa. 13372

Treatise on the seven apocalyptic vials. (82531)

Treatise on the slave trade. 90446

Treatise on the steam engine. 69654

Treatise on the subject of prayer. (4673)

Treatise on the symbolism and mythology of the red race in America. 7998

Treatise on the Synochus Icteroides. 18003

Treatise on the theory and practice of landscape gardening. (20776)

Treatise on the trade of Great Britain to America. 10242

Treatise on the typhus fever. 8845

Treatise on the venom of the viper. 24989

Treatise on the vine. 65623

Treatise on the West Indian encumbered estates act. 18149

Treatise on the work which has now appeared in the German language. 85129

Treatise on the writ of habeas corpus. 5485

Treatise on the . . . yellow fever. 31877

Treatise on the yellow fever, as it appeared in the island of Dominica. 13301

Treatise on tobacco, tea, coffee, and chocolate. 59225

Treatise on tropical diseases. 51050

Treatise on turning tables. 26734

Treatise on turpentine farming. (61033)

Treatise on usury, addressed to men of sense. 96411

Treatise on . . . yellow fever. 8553

Treatise opening the true nature of faith. 39796

Treatise paraenetical. 96752

Treatise relating to the origin, history, and present position. 8332

Treatise, shewing the intimate connection. 14071

Treatise shewing the need we have to rely upon God. 60732, 2d note after 96752

Treatise showing that slavery is neither a moral, political nor social evil. 82073

Treatise showing the best way to California. 71919

Treatise tending to prove human learning to be of no help. 93424

Treatise theologicall, morall, and historicall. (72111)

Treatise upon common-school education. 55783

Treatise upon husbandry or planting. 4423

Treatise upon the estate and rights of the corporation. 32405

Treatise upon the law of Pennsylvania relative to the proceedings. 79215

Treatise upon the laws of extradition. 13400

Treatise upon the navigation of St. Domingo. (66858)

Treatise upon the powers and duties of justices of the peace. 18854

Treatise upon the trade from Great-Britain to Africa. 96753

Treatise wherein are contained several particular subjects. 66754

Treatise wherein many great evangelical truths. 55887

Treatise wherein there is a clear discovery. 101120

Treatises of the Abbe Boissier de Sauvages and Pullien. 6163

Treatises on astronomy and geography. 97654

Treatises, wherein is demonstrated. 14241

Treatment of crime. 84068

Treatment of fractures of the lower extremity. 83664

Treatment of gunshot wounds. 84273

Treatment of liquor dealers. 74541

Treats of life. 37767

Treaty. 96754

Treaty and convention, for the sick, wounded, and prisoners of war. 96549-96550

Treaty and conventions entered into and ratified by the United States of America and the French republic. 42309

Treaty at Washington. Speech . . . in the Senate. (13576)

Treaty between France and Great Britain. 2144, 96526

Treaty between France and the United States of America. 14378

Treaty between . . . George Clinton . . . Governor of the province of New-York . . . and the Six United Indian Nations. 13740

Treaty between Governor Peregrine Thomas Hopson, and the Mickmack Indians. 33004

Treaty between Great Britain and France in relation to the wounded, prisoners of war, etc., 1759. 96548-96550

Treat between Great Britain and France, 1783. 96557

Treaty between Great Britain and Spain, concluded at Madrid, 1770. 96527-96528

Treaty between Great Britain and Spain, 1783. 96558

Treaty between Great Britain and the Netherlands. 2147, 2158, 96524-96525

Treaty between Great Britain and the United States, signed at Paris, Sept. 3, 1783. 19273, note before 96570

Treaty between Portugal and Spain, 1750. 1537, 96546-96547

Treaty between Portugal and the Netherlands, 1661. 2157, 96522-96523, 98987

Treaty between Spain and Portugal, 1777. 1537, 96554-96556

Treaty between the government of New Jersey, and the Indians. 53242

Treaty between the President and Council of the province of Pennsylvania, and the Indians of Ohio. (60738)

Treaty between the Seneca Nation of Indians and Oliver Phelps. 96610

Treaty between the States General of the United Netherlands and the United States of America. 14378

Treaty between the United States and His Catholic Majesty. 96588

Treaty between the United States and the Chickasaw Nation of Indians. 96629

Treaty between the United States and the Otoes 96714

Treaty between the United States and the Potawattamie Tribe of Indians. 96709

Treaty between the United States and the Pottawatomie Indians. 64607

Treaty between the United States of America and Mes-quaw-buck. 96699

Treaty between the United States of America and Miami Tribe of Indians. 96731

Treaty between the United States of America and the Appalachicola Band of Indians. 96690

Treaty between the United States of America and the Appalachicola Tribe of Indians. 96669

Treaty between the United States of America and the Caddo Nation of Indians. 96696

Treaty between the United States of America and the Cherokee Nation of Indians, west of the Mississippi. Concluded February 14, 1833. 96685

Treaty between the United States of America and the Cherokee Nation of Indians, west of the Mississippi . . . made and concluded at the city of Washington. 96656

Treaty between the United States of America and the Chickasaw Indians. Concluded May 24, 1834. 96694

Treaty between the United States of America and the Chickasaw Indians. Concluded October 20, 1832. 96677

Treaty between the United States of America and the Chief and Headmen of Aub-ba-nauba's Band of the Pottawatamie Indians. 96701

Trelles y Govin, Carlos Manuel, 1866-
    978, note after 96117, 98165
Tremaine, Lyman. 28472, 56238
Tremais, Querdisien. supposed author
    67020
Tremarec, Y. J. de Kerguelen. see
    Kerguelen-Tremarec, Y. J. de.
Tremayne, Edward. ed. 54823
Tremblement de terre de la Guadeloupe.
    38460
Tremblement de terre de la Martinique.
    (38607)
Tremblor de Lima del ano 1599. 57303
Tremblo de tierra de Lima. 58304
Tremebundo. pseud. Revolucion de Santa-
    Anna. 96765
Tremeda. The dreadful sound with which the
    wicked are to be tunderstruck. 46559,
    96766
Tremont Temple, Boston. see Boston.
    Tremont Temple.
Tremont Temple enterprise. 36985
Trench, T. B. tr. 24106
Trenchard, J. illus./engr. 14869, 50865,
    84620, note after 97998
Trenchard, John, 1662-1723. 15028, 34453,
    69523, 86631, 96767-note after 96768
Trenchard, John, 1662-1723. supposed author
    15028, 96767
Trent, W. H. 93507
Trent, William. petitioner 25595, 34579-
    34580, 82979, 96769, 99584, note just
    before 103108
Trent and San Jacinto. 13261
Trent case, and the means of averting foreign
    war. 37272
Trent, Council of, 1545-1563. 42066, 57101,
    63165, 68461, 75884, 76223, note after
    90828, 94221, 98773, 99441
Trent-Gall. 44662
Trente annees dans les deserts de l'Amerique
    du Nord. (35686), 94329
Trente mois de ma vie. 20736
Trent-neuf hommes pour une femme. (12571)
Trente-quatre etoiles de l'Union Americaine.
    23557
Trenton, N. J. Adams Convention, 1824. see
    Democratic Party. New Jersey. Con-
    vention, Trenton, 1824.
Trenton, N. J. Anti-monopoly State Conven-
    tion, 1868. see Anti-monopoly State
    Convention, Trenton, N. J., 1868.
Trenton, N. J. Committee . . . of the Friends
    of Education. see Committee . . . of
    the Friends of Education, Trenton, N. J.
Trenton, N. J. Convention, 1776. see New
    Jersey. Convention, Trenton, 1776.
Trenton, N. J. Convention, 1787. see New
    Jersey. Convention, Trenton, 1787.
Trenton, N. J. Convention, 1812. see New
    Jersey. Convention, Trenton, 1812.
Trenton, N. J. Convention of the Friends of
    John Quincy Adams, 1824. see Demo-
    cratic Party. New Jersey. Convention,
    Trenton, 1824.
Trenton, N. J. Democratic State Convnetion,
    1824. see Democratic Party. New
    Jersey. Convention, Trenton, 1824.
Trenton, N. J. Fidelity Division, No. 2. see
    Sons of Temperance of North America.
    New Jersey. Fidelity Division, No. 2,
    Trenton.
Trenton, N. J. Jackson Convention, 1828.
    see Democratic Party. New Jersey.
    Convention, Trenton, 1828.

Trenton, N. J. Meeting of the New Jersey
    Prison Reform Association, 1850. see
    New Jersey Prison Reform Association.
    Annual Meeting, 1st, Trenton, 1850.
Trenton, N. J. Provincial Congress, 1775.
    see New Jersey (Colony) Provincial
    Congress, Trenton, 1775.
Trenton, N. J. Rutgers Scientific School. see
    Rutgers Scientific School, Trenton, N. J.
Trenton, N. J. St. Michael's Church. Wardens
    and Vestrymen. 90562
Trenton, N. J. State Hospital. see New
    Jersey. State Hospital, Trenton.
Trenton, N. J. State Lunatic Asylum. see
    New Jersey. State Hospital, Trenton.
Trenton, N. J. State Teachers College and
    Normal School. see New Jersey. State
    Teachers College and Normal School,
    Trenton.
Trenton, N. J. Trenton Library Company.
    see Trenton Library Company, Trenton,
    N. J.
Trenton, N. J. Washington Benevolent Society.
    see Washington Benevolent Society. New
    Jersey. Trenton.
Trenton Delaware Falls Company. 96774
Trenton Delaware Falls Company. Board of
    Managers. 96776
Trenton Delaware Falls Company. President
    and Managers. 96775
Trenton Falls. [By John Sherman.] 96777
Trenton Falls, picturesque and descriptive.
    80369, note after 96778
Trenton Falls. With a brief description of the
    scenery. 96778, 101233
Trenton federal post. 87419
Trenton, June 5. 87419
Trenton Library Company, Trenton, N. J.
    96772-96773
Treny, ------. 96779
Trepidantium Malleus. pseud. Trepidentium
    Malleus intrepidanter Malleatus. see
    Young, Samuel, fl. 1690-1700.
Tres-Palacios y Verdeja, Felipe Jose de, Bp.
    96781 see also Havana (Diocese) Bishoc
    (Tres-Palacios y Verdeja)
Tres cartas de un Sacerdote Religioso.
    (75765)
Tres cartas, qve el Capitan Garcia de Tamayo
    y Mendoza. 94282-94284
Tres clerigos herederos. 98868
Tres cosas son las que obligan a credito.
    93321
Tres dialogos Latinos que Francisco Cervantes
    Salazar escribio. 75566
Tres discursos do Illmo. e Exmo. Sr. Paulino
    Jose Soares de Sousa. 85648
3 epocas de Peru. 16780
Tres gemidos del aguila Mexicana. 35283
Tres-Illvstre, Genereux & Puissant Prince,
    Henry de Lorraine. 74883
Tres merveilleuses victoires des femmes de
    Nouveau Monde. 64526-64529
Tres Mexicanos honrados. pseud. Opusculo
    de la verdad y de la razon. 96780
Tres primeros historiadores de . . . Cuba.
    98165
Tres primeros historiadores de la isla de
    Cuba. 98307
Tres siglos de la dominacion Espanola en
    Yucatan. 14211, 14973
Tres siglos de la dominnion Espanola en
    Yucatan. 14211, 41973
Tres siglos de Mexico durante el gobierno
    Espanol. 11613
Treschow, Johannes. 96782

Tribunal de Protomedicato, Mexico. see Mexico (Viceroyalty) Tribunal de Protomedicato.
Tribunal de Consulado, Havana. see Havana. Tribunal del Consulado.
Tribunal del Consulado, Lima. see Lima. Tribunal del Consulado.
Tribunal de Protomedicato, Havana. see Havana. Tribunal del Protomedicato.
Tribunal historico. 80987
Tribunal of Arbitration under the Treaty of Washington. see Geneva Arbitration Tribunal, 1871-1872.
Tribunal y Real Audiencia de Cunetas, Havana. see Havana. Real Audiencia de Cuentas.
Tribunales de Commercio y la constitucion. 38834
Tribune (Minneapolis) 49233
Tribune (New York) see New York tribune.
Tribune almanac. 63823, 103264
Tribune essays. (15463)
Tribune lecture series, vol. I. 81050
Tribune tracts. 28995, 78033, (79500), 88394
Tribune war tracts, no. 1. 15212, 69849
Tribune's annual exhibit of the manufacturing and commercial industry. 49233, note before 96959
Tribuno de la plebe. 96959
Tribunus. pseud. Preface. see Lee, Arthur.
Tribunus populi. pseud. Reply to a letter. 40289, (69681), 86592, 96960, note after 96961
Tribut de reconnaissance. 96962
Tribute book. (27887), 1st note after 96962
Tribute for the Negro. 2007
Tribute of a mourning husband. 89744
Tribute of affection to John Roulstone. 10743, 2d note after 96962
Tribute of affection to the memory of Professor Irah Chase. (12182), 3d note after 96962
Tribute of affection to the memory of Rev. Samuel B. Swaim. 90922
Tribute of Boston merchants to the memory of Joshua Bates. 3944, 5th note after 96962
Tribute of filial respect to the memory of his mother. 30521
Tribute of gratitude and respect for the services and memory of General Washington. 86124
Tribute of gratitude to the Hon. M. B. Lowry. 42540, 7th note after 96962
Tribute of gratitude to the memory of that celebrated navigator. 16252, (69383)
Tribute of respect and friendship to the memory of the Rev. Samuel Cary. 11208, 14535, 8th note after 96962
Tribute of respect by the citizens of Troy. 29736, 9th note after 96962, note after 97070
Tribute of respect offered by the citizens of Louisville. 39792
Tribute of respect, paid to his memory. 101595
Tribute of respect to departed friends. 5619
Tribute of respect to the character and memory of Mr. Ensign Lincoln. (79804)
Tribute of respect to the memory of a good man. 46853
Tribute of respect to the memory of Benjamin West. 96963
Tribute of respect to the memory of her fallen heroes. 2381

Tribute of respect to the memory of Mrs. Eliza Crocker. 103785
Tribute of respect to the memory of Mrs. Sarah Bowdoin Dearborn. 30521
Tribute of respect, to the memory of Samuel Adams. 95201
Tribute of respect, to the memory of the Hon. James Dowdoin. 30519
Tribute of respect to the memory of the Rev. Daniel Sharp. 92374
Tribute of respect to the memory of the Rev. George Whitefield. 98889
Tribute of the affection to John Roulstone. 10743, 2d note after 96962
Tribute of the Chamber of Commerce. 52595, 2d note after 96963
Tribute of the Massachusetts Historical Society to the memory of Edmund Quincy and John Lothrop Motley. 67189
Tribute of the Massachusetts Historical Society to the memory of Edward Everett. 23277, 3d note after 96963
Tribute of the Massachusetts Historical Society to the memory of George Livermore. 41570, 4th note after 96963
Tribute of the Massachusetts Historical Society to the memory of Josiah Quincy. 45859, 5th note after 96963
Tribute of the muses through the carriers of the Columbian centinel. 96964
Tribute of William Ellery Channing. 11924
Tribute to a beloved son and brother. 83502
Tribute to Abraham Lincoln. 31003
Tribute . . . to . . . Alvan Lamson. 2725
Tribute to Brig.-Gen. Charles Russell Lowell. 3794
Tribute to Caesar. (62421), 1st note after 96964
Tribute to Edward Everett. 13689
Tribute to Florence Nightingale. 55300
Tribute to Gallaudet. 3469
Tribute to Judge Sprague. 18450, 89718
Tribute to Kane. 11984
Tribute to Major Sidney Willard. 3794
Tribute to New-England. 30517, 2d note after 69442, (78821), 89782
Tribute to our soldiers and the sword. 3794
Tribute to the Anti-slavery cause. 97400
Tribute to the character and position of Washington. 87128
Tribute to the fair. 44561, 3d note after 96964
Tribute to the life and character of Jonas Chickering. 58728, 4th note after 96964
Tribute to the memory, character and position of Washington. 87129
Tribute to the memory of a faithful public servant. (64646)
Tribute to the memory of Abraham Lincoln. 41236, 6th note after 96964
Tribute to the memory of Alden March. 44482, 7th note after 96964
Tribute to the memory of Alexander McLeod. 73537
Tribute to the memory of Alexander von Humboldt. 33746
Tribute to the memory of Azariah E. Stimson. 89744, note after 91829
Tribute to the memory of Benjamin Bussey. 28412
Tribute to the memory of Charles F. Hovey. 33204, 62528, 10th note after 96964
Tribute to the memory of De Witt Clinton. 13737, 90019
Tribute to the memory of departed infants. 71800

Tried and true. 89303
Tried stability of our government. 29843
Triennial and annual catalogues, course of
    study, &c. [of Hanover College.] 30241
Triennial Baptist register. 97961
Triennial catalogue . . . see Catalogue . . .
Triennial charge to the clergy of the Diocese
    of Rhode Island. 13385
Triennial Convention of Ministers and Dele-
    gates of the Congregational Churches in
    the North West. see Congregational
    Churches in the Northwest. Triennial
    Convention of Ministers and Delegates,
    Chicago, 1858.
Triennial register of the . . . State Normal
    School [of New Jersey.] 53195
Triennial report . . . see Report . . .
Triennial sermon, before the . . . Board of
    Missions. 57842
Triennial visitation and proceedings of the
    Church Synod of the Diocese of Toronto.
    92663
Trifles from my portfolio. 31416, note after
    96968
Trifles, in verse. 13156
Trigault, E. 24319
Trigavlt, Nicolas. 32027
Trigault, Nicolas. incorrectly supposed author
    67498, 96969
Trigautius, Nic. 66686, 67498
Trigo de Loureiro, Lorenco. see Loureiro,
    Trigo de.
Trigonometrical survey for the new map of
    Maryland. (45156)
Trigoso de Aragao Morato, Francisco Manuel.
    see Morato, Francisco Manuel Trigoso
    de Aragao.
Trigueros, Ignacio. (23061) see also Mexico
    (Federal District) Gobernador
    (Trigueros)
Trim, a barber. pseud. Americans roused.
    see Sewall, Jonathan, 1728-1796.
Trim, a barber. pseud. Cure for the spleen.
    see Sewall, Jonathan, 1728-1796.
Trimble, David. 96970-96974
Trimble, I. (3074), 45098 see also Balti-
    more. Engineer.
Trimmer, Tim. pseud. Now in the press.
    96975
Trimnell, Charles, successively Bishop of
    Norwich and Winchester, 1663-1723.
    96976
Tri-Mountain. (79974), note after 97078
Tri-mountain; or, the early history of Boston.
    6564, 97079
Trinidad, Bernardo de la. see Bernardo de
    la Trinidad.
Trinidad, Juan de la. 96977-96978
Trinidad. 103653
Trinidad. Governor (Hinslop) 31995 see also
    Hinslop, -------.
Trinidad. Laws, statutes, etc. 46855
Trinidad almanac and pocket register for
    . . . 1840. 96979
Trinidad; its geography, resources, administra-
    tion, present condition, and prospects.
    19813
Trinitarian Church, Concord, Mass. see
    Concord, Mass. Trinitarian Church.
Trinitarian Church, Fitchburg, Mass. see
    Fitchburg, Mass. Trinitarian Church.
Trinitarian Congregational Church, Waltham,
    Mass. see Waltham, Mass. Trinitarian
    Congregational Church.
Trinitarian review. 105247
Trinitarian Society. Committee. 16861

Trinite. 101350
Trinity Church, Albany. see Albany. Trinity
    Church.
Trinity Church, Boston. see Boston. Trinity
    Church.
Trinity Church, Bridgewater, Mass. see
    Bridgewater, Mass. Trinity Church.
Trinity Church, New York. see New York
    (City) Trinity Church.
Trinity Church, Newport, R. I. see Newport,
    R. I. Trinity Church.
Trinity Church, Pottsville, Pa. see Pottsville,
    Pa. Trinity Church.
Trinity Church, Rochester, N. Y. see
    Rochester, N. Y. Trinity Church.
Trinity Church, Washington, D. C. see
    Washington, D. C. Trinity Church.
Trinity Church. (6378)
Trinity Church case. 50655, 1st note after
    96986
Trinity Church title. 30381, 2d note after
    96986
Trinity College, Hartford, Conn. (15815),
    65961, 101997-102003
Trinity College, Hartford, Conn. Athenaeum
    Society. 102004
Trinity College, Hartford, Conn. Athenaeum
    Society. Library. 102004
Trinity College, Hartford, Conn. Charter.
    101998
Trinity College, Hartford, Conn. Library.
    102005
Trinity College, Hartford, Conn. Secretary.
    102001 see also Sigourney, Charles.
Trinity College, Hartford, Conn. Washington
    College Association. 102006
Trinity College Historical Society. 104450
Trinity Hall School, Boston. see Boston.
    Trinity Hall School.
Trinity House, Montreal. see Montreal.
    Trinity House.
Trinity House, Quebec. see Quebec (City)
    Trinity House.
Trinity School, New York. see New York
    (City) Trinity School.
Trino Usauna. pseud. see Usauna, Trino.
    pseud.
Trio. pseud. 43204, 51919
Trio, V. N. D. et S. S. S. pseud. Squint at
    a "co-presbyter." see Cox, Samuel H.
    supposed author
Triolus. pseud. Boarding school. A poem.
    96989
Triomphe du beau sexe. 96990
Triomphe du nouveau monde. 8747, 1st note
    after 96990
Trionfo della S. Chiesa su la rovina della
    monarchia. 36883
Trip across the plains. 37250
Trip from Boston to Littleton. 106231
Trip from Boston to New Hampshire. 38376
Trip from the Missouri River to the Rocky
    Mountains. 89109
Trip made by a small man. 96991
Trip of the Oceanus to Fort Sumter and
    Charleston, S. C. 25863
Trip of the steamer Oceanus to Fort Sumter
    and Charleston, S. C. 25863, 1st note
    after 96991
Trip through the lakes of North America.
    29324, 2d note after 96991
Trip through the Mississippi Territory. 17890
Trip to America. A farce in two acts. 98180
Trip to America, etc., etc., etc. 22615
Trip to America, in a dialogue. 67997
Trip to Boston. 104774

Trip to Canada. 38850
Trip to Cuba. (33319)
Trip to Elysium. 94020
Trip to Holy-Head. 96992
Trip to Jamaica. 101285
Trip to Jamaica, with a true character of the people and island. (8571)
Trip to Mexico. 25047, 2d note after 96992
Trip to New-England. 101286
Trip to Newfoundland. 51273
Trip to Niagara. 21309
Trip to Rome. 84731
Trip to Saratoga. 50338
Trip to the far west. 82350
Trip to the springs, Niagara, Quebeck, and Boston. 76915, 96487
Trip to the tropics and home through America. 10251
Trip to the United States and Cuba. 4210
Trip to the west and Texas. 58643
Tripartito del Christianissimo y consolatorio Doctor Iuan Gerson de doctrina Christiana. 27168
Tri-party war of 1861 and 1862. 17600
Triplet, Robert. see Triplett, Robert.
Triplett, Philip. 96038, 96993
Triplett, Robert. 6260, 96038, 2d note after 96993 see also Tobacco Convention, Washington, D. C., 1840. Committee to Prepare the Address.
Triplett, Robert. petitioner 95102
Triplex, Brothers. pseud. see Brothers Triplex. pseud.
Tripoli, Guillaume de. 76838
Tripoli. Treaties, etc. 96562
Trippett, John. 96994
Tripple-plea. 96995
Trist, Nicholas Philip. 96996-97002, 4th note after 102623 see also U. S. Consulate. Havanna.
Trist, Nicholas Philip. supposed author 40555, 43695, note after 96999
Tristan, Flor. see Tristan y Moscozo, Flore Celestine Therese Henriette.
Tristan y Moscozo, Flore Celestine Therese Henriette. 97003
Tristani, Manuel Rogelio. 97004
Tristes ayes dela aguila Mexicana. 72540, 1st note after 96790
Tristia. 57983
Tristitiae ecclesiarum. 55332
Tristram Shandy. 97293
Tristram Trap 'Em, Esq. pseud. see Trap 'Em, Tristram. pseud.
Tritemius, Joannis. see Trithemius, Joannes.
Trithemius, Joannes. 97005-97006
Triumph and unity of truth. 72112
Triumph at Pittsburgh. 83788
Triumph of divine mercy. 102701
Triumph of equal school rights in Boston. (6765), note after 97006
Triumph of faith. 97007
Triumph of infidelity; a poem. 21560, note after 97007
Triumph of liberty and peace with America. 97008
Triumph of liberty, or Louisiana preserved a national drama. 103417
Triumph of liberty in the chariot of praise. (39794)
Triumph of nature; a comic opera. 44623
Triumph of nature. Founded on truth. 64784
Triumph of philanthropy. 97009
Triumph of religion over infidelity. 82894
Triumph of suffering. 89783
Triumph of the Whigs. 97010

Triumph of truth, a poem. 8785
Triumph of truth. History and vision of Clio. 44890, 1st note after 97010
Triumph of truth over popery. 84022, 84034
Triumph upon leaving American unconquered. (46925), 92853-92854
Triumphal arch, and looking glass. 95903, 2d note after 97010
Triumphal pompa. 97011
Triumphale. 97012
Triumphales latices mediciae. 76302
Triumphant deaths of pious children. 12878, 105540
Triumphant deaths; or brief notices of the happy deaths. 97013
Triumphant defence of slavery! 7982, note after 92624
Trivmphe van vveghen de gheluckighe ende voer-rijcke victorie. 89747
Trivmpho de San Elias. 76291, 97024
Trivmpho parthenico. 80986
Triumphos de la fe. 74025
Triumphs of faith. 59543
Triumphs of genius, a poem. (40886)
Triumphs of liberty. 2727
Triumphs of love. 97014
Triumphs of redemption. 85483
Triumphs of science, a poem. 101110
Triumphs of science, and other poems. 101109
Triumphs of superstition: an elegy. 30520, 93243, 1st note after 97014
Triumphs of temper; a poem. 31035
Triumphs of temperance. (44749)
Triumphs of the reformed religion, in America. (46561)
Triumphs of war. 59354
Triumphs of ways and means. 64520
Triumphs over troubles. 46562
Triumphus super capta Olind . 3407
Triumvirat. 86476-86478, 86480
Triumvirate of Pennsylvania. 60741, 2d note after 97014
Triumvirato espiritual, e historico. 76785
Trivnfal aclamacion. 97015
Triunfo. 97824
Triunfo de Fernando VII. 97016
Triunfo de la constitucion. 97017
Triunfo de la constitucion celebrado en Caracas 97018
Triunfo de la iglesia. 50606
Triunfo de la justicia. (67109)
Triunfo de la justicia en los viles insurgentes. 74607, 97019
Triunfo de la libertad sobre el despotismo. (73223)-73224, note after 97019
Triunfo de la moral Christiana. 10095, 100726
Triunfo de la religion. 97020
Triunfo de la religion y muerte de la demogogi 93481
Triunfo de la virtud y del patriotismo. 97021
Triunfo de los escritores por la libertad de imprenta. 97023
Triunfo de S. Elias. 76291, 97024
Triunfo del amante de la constitucion. 97022
Triunfo del silencio. 11462
Triunfo mas glorioso de la religion. 105738
Triunfo sosaya. 36784
Trivnfos del Santo Oficio Peruano. 96224
Trivigiano, Angelo. tr. 1547, 40995
Trivnio de la lyra. Poema. 106324
Trobe, Benjamin la. see La Trobe, Benjamin.
Trobe, Christian Ignatius la. see La Trobe, Christian Ignatius.
Trobe, P. la. see La Trobe, P.

Trobriand, Philippe Regis Denis de Keredern, Comte de, 1816-1897. 68813-(68814), 70368
Trobriand, Regis de. see Trobriand, Philippe Regis Denis de Keredern, Comte de, 1816-1897.
Trodden dovvn strength. 20864
Trofeo de la justicia Espanola. 80987
Trognon, A. pseud. Campagne de l'Armee du Potomac. see Joinville, Francois Ferdinand Philippe Louis Marie d'Orleans, Prince de.
Trois ages des colonies. 64907
Trois ans aux Etats-Unis. 14939
Trois ans chez les Oricaras. 23922
Trois ans d'esclavage chez les Patagons. (29241)
Trois Babylones. (12574)
Trois derniers mois de l'Amerique Meridionale. 23915, 64908
Trois dialogues. 48244
Trois etrangers. pseud. Offrandes a Bonaparte. see Walsh, Robert, 1784-1859.
Trois etudes critiques. 75538
Trois fils du Capitaine Amerique du Sud Antilles. 29109
Trois hommes de couleur de la Martinique. petitioners (47421)
Trois lettres addressee par un Mexicain. 28032
Trois lettres de Lafayette. 8040
Trois lettres escrittes en annees 1625. et 1626. (38679)
Trois lettres interessantes sur le meme dispute. 11701, 32012
Trois liures de l'histoire des Indes. 43229
Trois memoires interessans. 12017
Trois Merlettes. 100745
Trois mois de la Louisiane. (39619)
Trois mondes. 39008
Trois nations, contes nationaux. 97025
Trois navigations de Martin Frobisher. 4936, 68414
Trois navigations dont la premiere est de Cuba. 23542
Trois navigations pour chercher un passage a la Chine. 25999
Trois Pasteurs Presbyteriens des Etats-Unis. pseud. Memoires et journaux. 7803
Trois Rivieres, Quebec. Court. 96845
Troisieme lettre [a M. le Duc de Broglie.] 61262
Troisieme lettre d'un colon de St. Domingue. 97026
Troisieme notice sur les progres des sciences physiques et naturelles. 98352
Troisieme voyage de Cook, ou journal d'un expedition. 16260
Troisieme voyage de Cook, ou voyage a l'Ocean Pacifique. 16261
Trojanski, -------. tr. (67481)
Trollipania. 36358
Trollope, Frances (Milton) 1780-1863. 14766, 16930, 50115, 80151, 97027-97035, 97914
Trollope, Nicodemus. 97036
Trollope, Mrs. T. A. see Trollope, Frances (Milton) 1780-1863.
Trollopiad. 80151, note after 97028, 2d note after 97036
Tromp, ----- van. pseud. New milk cheese. see Sargent, Lucius Manlius.
Trompeta de verdades del bayamo numero I. 97037

Tronchoy, ------ Gautier du. see Gautier du Tronchoy, -------.
Troncon du Coudray, ------. (1534), (27337)
Troncoso, Antonio de Sosa. see Sosa Troncoso, Antonio de.
Troncoso, Francisco Javier. 39215
Troncoso, Juan Antonio Segura. see Segura Troncoso, Juan Antonio.
Troncoso, Juan Nepomuceno. 23607, 52334, 97038-97049
Troncoso, M. de la Barrera y. see La Barrera y Troncoso, M. de.
Trono de Mexico. 57685
Trono Mexicano. 59627
Trooper. pseud. Leaves from a trooper's diary. (39551)
Trooper's manual. 18857
Troost, G. tr. 100852
Troost, Gerard. 97050-97051
Troost, P. 97052
Tropas acuarteladas pidan se cumpla la ley. 97053
Tropheo de la victoria mas celebre. 48267
Tropical agriculturist. (64253)
Tropical fibres. 90000
Tropical free labour. 97054
Tropical Free Labour Company, London. 97054
Tropical hygiene. 36224
Tropical world. 30720
Troschel, Franz Hermann, 1810-1882. 77780
Trosne, G.-F. le. see Le Trosne, G.-F.
Tross, Edwin. ed. 40172, 40174, 74886
Trott, John. 97055
Trott, Nicholas. note before 87563, 87697, 97056-97097
Trott, Nicholas. defendant 2d note after 97056
Trott, Perient. 97057, 97142
Trott, Perient. petitioner 105694
Trotter, Alexander. 97058
Trotter, George, Sr. 97060
Trotter, George, Jr. 97060
Trotter, Isabella Strange. 24407, note after 97060
Trotter, J. Pope. 97061
Trotter, Choker & Company exhibited. 97062
Trotting record for 1869. 25454, 29674, 29930
Troubadour and other poems. 42975
Troubadours at home. 83468
Trouble from the north, exemplified in the south. 20757
Troubles . . . had with the Indian savages. 46693
Troubles in the north, exemplifying in the south. (17742), 20757
Troublesome trio. 10166, 1st note after 97062
Trou-hertighe onderrichtinge. 9757, 2d note after 97062
Trouin, ------ du Guay-. see Guay-Trouin, ------ du.
Trouloosheyt Englesche. 97063
Troup. pseud. To the people of the south. 30101, note after 97063
Troup, George Michael, 1780-1856. 27074, 27076, 27080 see also Georgia. Governor, 1823-1827 (Troup)
Troup, Robert. (22680), 29542, 30566, (34385), (34385), note after 53697, 54581, (68287), note after 93791, 96982, 97064-97067 see also New York (City) Common Council. Committee on Fuel. Chairman.
Trout, Joab. 97068-97069
Trouw bericht. 97664

Trovas Mexicanas. 77058
Trow, John Fowler. 41268, 54459, 84074,
note after 97069
Trowbridge, Edmund. 32362, 37712, 96946,
96951, 2d-3d notes after 102623
Trowbridge, J. M. 90788
Trowbridge, John Townsend. 97070
Trowbridge, T. J. ed. 52305, 57942, 76692
Trow's . . . directory. 54459
Trow's . . . directory, 1855-6. 54459
Trow's . . . directory . . . 1859-60. 54459
Trow's . . . directory, for 1853-4. 54459
Trow's New York city directory, for 1852-3.
54459
Trow's New York . . . directory. 54459
Troy, N. Y. Citizens. 29736, 9th note after
96962, note after 97070
Troy, N. Y. Commercial Bank. see Com-
mercial Bank of Troy, Troy, N. Y.
Troy, N. Y. Common Council. 22763, note
after 97071
Troy, N. Y. Common Council. Committee.
22763, note after 97071
Troy, N. Y. Emma Willard School. see
Emma Willard School, Troy, N. Y.
Troy, N. Y. Female Seminary. see Emma
Willard School, Troy, N. Y.
Troy, N. Y. First Presbyterian Church.
97073
Troy, N. Y. Library. see Troy Library,
Troy, N. Y.
Troy, N. Y. Mortuary Record. 7997
Troy, N. Y. Rensselaer Polytechnic Institute.
see Rensselaer Polytechnic Institute,
Troy, N. Y.
Troy, N. Y. Society for the Advancement of
Female Education in Greece. see Troy
Society for the Advancement of Female
Education in Greece, Troy, N. Y.
Troy, N. Y. Troy Academy. see Rensselaer
Polytechnic Institute, Troy, N. Y. Troy
Academy.
Troy, N. Y. Troy University. see Troy
University, Troy, N. Y.
Troy, N. Y. Union Village Academy. see
Union Village Academy, Troy, N. Y.
Troy, N. Y. Walnut Grove School. 101141
Troy, N. Y. Washington Benevolent Society.
see Washington Benevolent Society.
New York. Troy.
Troy Academy, Troy, N. Y. see Rensselaer
Polytechnic Institute, Troy, N. Y. Troy
Academy.
Troy and Greenfield Railroad. petitioners
32889, 61363, 103002
Troy and Greenfield Railroad. Commissioners.
Chairman. 8358
Troy and Greenfield Railroad. Argument.
19662
Troy Bridge case. 614
Troy city directory. 97072
Troy Commercial Bank. see Commercial
Bank of Troy, Troy, N. Y.
Troy Conference miscellany. 58809, note
after 97074
Troy directory, for the year 1829. 97072
Troy Female Seminary, Troy, N. Y. see
Emma Willard School, Troy, N. Y.
Troy for fifty years. 8975
Troy Library, Troy, N. Y. 97074
Troy Presbytery. see Presbyterian Church
in the U. S. A. Presbytery of Troy.
Troy Society for the Advancement of Female
Education in Greece, Troy, N. Y.
104043, 104049

Troy University, Troy, N. Y. Trustees.
73088
Trozos selectos del libro de Mormon. 83139
Truair, John. 97075-97078
Truant chicken. 79756
Trubenhach, Kurt. ed. 99378
Trvbino, Fernando. 100637
Trubner, Charles. 44896
Trubner, Nicholas. 607, 1537, 42643, (54365)
Trubsalen. 20016
Trudaine de la Sabliere, ------. see
Sabliere, Trudaine de la.
True, Charles Kittredge. (6555), (79974), note
after 97078-97079
True, Eliza S. 97080
True, Frederick William, 1858-1914. 85072,
97081
True, H. 2604, 99795
True, firm publishers see Dunham and True.
firm publishers
True . . . . A discourse 16222
True account. 88046
True account of all the Presbyterian and
Congregational ministers. 36621
True account of an American revival. (5573)
True . . . account of Andrew Frey. 71406
True account of Captain Kidd. 89557
True account of eight years' exports. 73778
True account of the Aloe Americana, or
African. 17238, 2d note after 97081
True account of the barbarous, inhuman and
cruel treatment of Isaac H. Hunt. 33867,
92057
True account of the colonies of Nova-Scotia,
and Georgia. 97082
True account of the country. 8952-8953
True account of the defalcation of the Hills-
borough Bank. (31914)
True account of the design. 19736, 97083
True account of the dying words of Ockanickon.
8952, 17510, 56650
True account of the forts and castles. 73779
True account of the government and people.
2346
True account of the Jews. 95653
True account of the late pyracies of Jamaica.
note before 97084, 100958
True account of the loss of the ship Columbia.
97084
True account of the most considerable occur-
rences. 20878-20879, 97085
True account of the most remarkable assaults.
(23479), 23481
True account of the murder of Abraham
Suydam. 72164, 1st note after 97085
True account of the Netherlanders insupportable
insolencies. 13514
True account of the proceedings, sense and
advice of the people called Quakers.
30235
True account of the province of Cuzco. 105720
True account of the singular sufferings of
John Fillmore. 24330
True account of the tryals, examinations,
confessions, condemnations, and execu-
tions of divers witches, at Salem.
46563, 2d note after 97085
True account of the voyage of the Nottingham-
Galley of London. 19029, 3d note after
97085
True account of their grievous and extreme
sufferings. 3271, 20242, note after
28914
True agreement between Jehovah's being a
wall of fire. 24579
True aim of life. 21721

True aims of American ambition. 15898

True American (Philadelphia) 101797

True American citizen. 20335

True American; containing the inaugural addresses. (14151)

True American system of finance. 10207

True American's manual for 1856. 38140

True and affecting history of Henrietta De Bellgraves. 19109

True and authentic account of Andrew Frey. (71410)

True and authentic account of the Indian war in Florida. 24901, (79063)-79064, 4th note after 97085

True and authentic history of His Excellency George Washington. 97086, 101841, 2d note after 101887

True and authentic narratives of captives. 20883

True and candid statement of facts. 23642, note after 97086

True and complete history of the lives. 103349A

True and complete narrative of all the proceedings. 97087

True and concise narrative of the origin and progress. 18632, 1st note after 97087, 2d note after 103214

True and concise narrative of the voyage and sufferings of James Washburn. 101522

True and doleful ditty. 5584

True & exact history of the island of Barbados. 41057-41058, note before 105976

True and exact history of the Jesuit refugees. 97088

True and exact history of the Jesuits. 64576

True and exact relation of the late prodigious earthquake. 104744

True and faithful account of an intire [sic] and absolute victory. 97089

True and faithful account of the four chiefest plantations of the English. 13444, 13448, 13450

True and faithful account of the great conspiracy. 3270

True and faithful account of the island of Veritas. 97090

True and faithful account of the loss of the Brigantine Tyrrell. 37135

True and faithful account of the most material circumstances attending the mysterious disappearance of Samuel Field. 97091

True and faithful history of the trial of the Rev. Alexander Bullions. 90516, note after 96840, 1st note after 97091

True and faithful narrative of a most remarkable phaenomenon. 12982, 25296, 86684, 3d note after 95765, 2d note after 102065

True and faithful narrative of the modes and measures pursued at the anniversary election. 55104, 2d note after 97091

True and faithful narrative of the proceedings of the House of Burgesses of North-Carolina. 97092

True and faithful narrative of the surprising captivity and remarkable deliverance of Captain Isaac Stewart. 78263, note before 97104

True and faithful narrative of what passed at a conference. 34329

True and faithful relation of the proceedings. 89383

True and false democracy. 48988

True and false faith distinguished. 20059

True and false philanthropist. 3400

True and genuine account of the life and doctrine. 103651

True and genuine account of the result of the Council of Fourteen Churches. 97093

True and genuine account of the whole transaction. 97094

True and genuine copy of the trial of Sir Chaloner Ogle. 56842

True and genuine discovery of animal electricity. 90965

True and graphic accounts of the many perils and privations. 70448

True and historical narrative of the colony of Georgia in America. 94215-94218

True and historical narrative of the said colony [of Georgia.] (5054)

True and impartial account of the rise and progress of the South Sea Company. 97095

True and impartial journal of a voyage to the South-Seas. 95437

True and impartial state of the province of Pennsylvania. 60742, 84589, 84594, note after 97095

True and infernal friendship. 97096

True and interesting travels of W. Lee. 39805

True and just view of Trinity Church. 4972

True and just vindication of Mr. Alexander Campbell. 93809, 97097

True and last relation of the dreadful accident which happened at Witticombe. 54942, 65017

True and living God. 89369

True and minute history of the assassination of James King. 37808, 97098

True and particular account contained in the lives. 97099

True and particular account of the horrid, cruel and barbarous murder. 97100

True and particular history of earthquakes. 42592

True and particular narrative by way of vindication. 74871

True and particular narrative of the late tremendous tornado. 97101

True and particular relation of the dreadful earthquake, which happen'd at Lima. (42593)-42594, 97102

True and particular relation of the dreadful earthquake which happened at Lima. (42595), 97102

True and particular relation of the dreadful ruin in which Lima . . . was involved. (42593), 97102

True and perfect account brought by Caleb More. (50536), 101454

True and perfect account brought in by Caleb More. (50536), 101454

True and perfect account of the disposal of the one hundred shares. 8955

True and perfect description, of the last voyage or nauigation. (39635), 1st note after 97102

True and perfect description of three voyages. 98738

True and perfect narrative of the late dreadful fire. 9535

True and perfect relation of that most sad and terrible earthquake. 64185

True and perfecte newes of the woorthy and valiaunt exploytes. 28701, 97103

Trve and sincere declaration of the purpose and ends of the plantation begun in Virginia. 99859

True and single [i. e. simple] account of the conduct. 98366

True and surprising adventures. 99420

True and tragicall discourse. (55183)

True and wonderful narrative of the surprising captivity and remarkable deliverance of Mrs. Frances Scott. 78263, note before 97104

True and wonderful relation of the appearance of three angels. 97104

True Baptist. pseud. Age of inquiry. 510

True basis and ends of civil government. 51439

True basis for an union among the people of God. 46241

True basis of the restored representation. 47927

True basis of American independence. 79587

True basis of civil government set forth and ascertained. 97364

True basis of reconstruction. 57711

True believers, hated by the world. 84290

True believer's testimony of the work of true faith. 72602

True believer's vade-mecum. 28509

True-born Englishman's unmasked battery. 97166

True born Pennsylvania. pseud. Quakers assisting. (66936), 1st note after 97104

True Briton. pseud. Consolatory thoughts. see Tod, Thomas.

True Briton. pseud. Observations on American independency. see Tod, Thomas.

True Briton of the nineteenth century. 97105

True catholic. 85120

True cause of all contention. (32910)

True character of fate and destiny. 12609

True character of the people and island. (8571)

True child. 82522

True Christian both in life and death. 46334

True Christian patriot. (12406)

True Christianity explained. 42013

True Christian's support under affliction. 39531

True churchman. 47242

True commercial and revenue policy of Pennsylvania. (43059)

True complaint of a peaceable people. 28045

True condition of American loyalty. (18048)

True condition of the south. 20795

True constitvtion of a particular visible church. 17089

True constitutional means for putting an end to the disputes. 97106

True copies of I. The agreement between Lord Baltimore and Messers Penn. (45073), 60743, note after 97106

True copy of a genuine letter. 47276, (78736), 97107

True copy of a letter as it came to our hands. 91318

True copy of a letter, from a member of St. P[au]l's. 97108

True copy of a letter from that clergyman to his friend. 12358, 40302, 59267, 62218

True copy of a letter which was sent from one who was a magistrate in New-England. (74383)

True copy of a letter written by Mr. Thomas Parker. 58770

True copy of a letter wrote by Mr. Vale. 98339

True copy of a manuscript found hanging on a post at Gorham Corner 1819. 91779, 97109

True copy of a paper given in to the Yearly Meeting. 37222

True copy of an inimitable and incomprehensible doggrel poel. 97110

True copy of eight pages. 97111

(True copy) of Judge Symme's pamphlet. 94104

True copy of Queen Elizabeth's heroic speech. 68259

True copy of the address of the members of the Assembly. 68710

True copy of the grant of King Charles the First. 98637

True copy of the last will and testament of the late Rev. George Whitefield. 103600

True copy of the minutes. 99047

True copy of the oaths that are appointed by act of Parliament. 97112

True copy of the paper left behind him. 98339

True copy of the proceedings of John A. Graham. 28230, 1st note after 99204

True copy of three judgments given forth. 8956, (37333), 47181, 97113

True copy of two letters. 91318

True countryman. pseud. Historical account, of the late disturbance. 32053, 60137-(60138), 60145, 97114, 2d note after 102552

True crisis of the colonies. 22400

True date of the English discovery. (44071)

Trve declaration of the estate of the colonie in Virginia. 99860

True declaration of the troublesome voyage. 30954

True democracy. A speech . . . at East Cambridge. 42367

True democracy contrasted with false democracy 104593

True Democrat. pseud. To the public. see Stearns, Isaac.

True Democrat. 7201

True description of a number of tyrannical pedagogues. 13633, 2d note after 97114

True description of Carolina. 97115

True description of Gviana. 67574

True description of Jamaica. 97116

True description of the Lake Superior country. 75246

True designs of the Chicago Convention. (12663)

True dignity of politics. 36842

Trve discovrse historicall of the svcceeding Governovrs. 13033

True discourse of the late voyages of discouerie. (5051), 25994, 79345, 2d note after 97116

Trve discovrse of the present estate of Virginia. (30120)-30121, note after 99872

True discovery of certain strange and inhumane proceedings. 38886, 92940

True divinity of Jesus Christ. 3471

True economy of human life. 90279

True English interest. (70402)

True Englishman. pseud. War as it is. 101260

True excellency of a minister of the Gospel. 21967

True exposition of the doctrine of the Catholic Church. 103090, 103098

True exposition of the transactions which led to the failure of the late Franklin Bank. 9503

True faith makes the best soldiers. (21246)

True faith will produce good works. 2632

True fast: a fast-day sermon. 11964

True fortitude delineated. 25267

True friend of his country. pseud. Address to the people of America. 424

True friend of liberty. pseud. Good of the community impartially considered. see Rusticus. pseud.

True friend of liberty. pseud. Letter to a merchant in Boston. see Rusticus. pseud.

True friendship: a discourse. 29530

True friendship distinguished from that which is false. 77183

True genealogy of the Dunnel and Dwinnel family of New England. 21330

True glory of a nation. 91583

True God but one person. 105334

True grace distinguished from the experience of devils. 21967

True grandeur of nations. 93652, 93683

True greatness: a discourse on . . . Rev. Wilbur Fisk. 32484

True greatness, a sermon on the death of Gen. George Washington. (43097)

True greatness, as illustrated by the character of Wesley. 94590

True greatness of our country. 79588

True ground of estime for the ministry. 85482

True grounds of Christian unity. (66794)

True guide to Prince Edward Island. 65643

True history. By the author of "Peep of day." 88297

True history, found amongst the papers of Father Quesnel. 100748

True history of a late short administration. 97117

True history of a late short administration. [By Charles Lloyd.] 41681, 4th note after 97116

True history of Catherine Kendall. 89375

True history of Deacon Giles' distillery. 12397

True history of Deacon Giles's distillery. 12397, 2d note after 97117

True history of men's hearts and habits. 21156

True history of the captivity & restoration of Mrs. Mary Rowlandson. 73579

True history of the conquest of America. 19985

True history of the conquest of Mexico. (19984)

True history of the Kansas wars. (48003)

True history of the late division in the anti-slavery societies. 45810

True history of the originall undertakings of the advancement of plantations. 28020

True history of the Spaniards proceedings. 28020

True history of the wild Methodist. 97118, 97273

True history. Translated from the French of M. de Voltaire. 100747, 100749

True history. Translated from the French of Voltaire. 100750

True honor of nauigation and nauigators. 105040A

True idea of female education. 88883

True idea of the university. (31388)

True interest of America impartially stated. 97119

True interest of Great-Britain, in regard to the trade and government. 97120

True interest of Great Britain, Ireland and our plantations. (51483)

True interest of Great Britain set forth in regard to the colonies. 2d note after 96428, 97121, 97346, 97365

True interest of Great Britain, with respect to her American colonies. 97121

True interest of the United States, and particularly of Pennsylvania. 97122

True interest of the United States, and particularly of Pennsylvania, considered, &c. (60744)

True interests of the European powers and the Emperor of Brazil. 101227

True interests of the people. 32877, note after 89113

True interpretation of the American civil war. 57351

True Irishman. pseud. Address to the Irish inhabitants. 97123

True issue, and the duty of the Whigs. 58702

True issue. [By a Kentuckian.] 64782

True issue. [By a meeting of the citizens of Auburn, N. Y.] 97124

True issue for the true churchman. 82732

True issue of the American civil war. 18225

True issue of the convent question. 18044

True issue sustained. 97125

True issues of the presidential campaign. 28492

True issues now involved. 8669

True journey from Newcastle to London. 96502

True Latter Day Saints' herald. 83037, 83048, 84431

True liberality. 105315

True liberty, as exhibited in the life, precepts, and early disciples of the Great Redeemer. 43840

True light of the political system of Amsterdam. 22011

True life of the nation: an address. 43567

True life of William Poole. 64039

True limits of the Lords Day. (66872)

True, lively, and experimentall description of that part of America, commonly called Nevv England. 105074-105076

True lover of his country. pseud. True state of the present difference. 97157

True lover of his country, and an hearty promoter of trade at home and commerce abroad. pseud. South-Sea scheme. 88200

True lover of His Majesty and native country. pseud. Englands interest asserted. see Carter, William.

True lover of the people. pseud. Letter to a member of Parliament. 40399

True-loves knot. 78370, 78378-78379

True loyalty in a citizen is fidelity to his state. 8496

True means of establishing public happiness. 21561, 97126

True means to avert national judgments. 1513

True merits of a late treatise. 97127

True method of studying and teaching history. 19017

True mode of reconstruction. (49018)

True, modest, and just defence of the petition for reformation. 97128

True motives exposed for the attacks upon the South Carolina College. 87994

True narrative. [By John Morrison Duncan.] (74653)

True narrative of an unhappy contention in the church at Ashford. 3889, 55332

True narrative of the capture of David Ogden. 65494

True narrative of the capture of the Rev. O. M. Spencer. 89367

True narrative of the dispute between the governors and assemblies. 60742, note after 97095

True narrative of the late svccess which it hath pleased God to give. 97129

True narrative of the late successe which it hath pleased God to give. (6361)

True narrative of the life. 97130

True narrative of the Lords providences. 25007, 103200

True narrative of the origin and progress of the difference. 103661, 103665

True narrative of the sufferings of Mary Kinnan. 97131

True national greatness. 23691

True nature and cause of the tails of comets. 60957, 97132

True nature and method of Christian preaching. 10684

True nature of the beautiful. 80082

True office of civil government. 82673

True origin and source of the Mecklenburg and national declaration of independence. 85313, 85333

True patriot. pseud. Letters. see Warren, Joseph, 1741-1775.

True patriot. 97996

True patriot: on an oration. 102494

True patriotism. A discourse delivered on fast day. 11947

True piety, a source of individual happiness. 82239

True piety the best policy for times of war. 100916

True physician. 67335

True picture of abolition. 42045

True picture of America. 86210

True picture of emigration. 97133

True picture of the American church and clergy. 25263

True picture of the King of England. 64163

True picture of the United States of America. 97134-97135

Trve pictvres and fashions of the people. (8784), 30377, 103395

True pleasure, chearfulness, and happiness. 97136

True policy in Canada. (8853)

True policy of the south. 10842

True policy of the state of Pennsylvania. 60745

True policy of the United States. 97137

True policy. Speech . . . January 21, 1870. 22092

True position, interests, and policy of the south. 25826

True position of Rev. Theodore Parker. 76992, note after 97137

True position of the controversy regarding Mr. Gough's dead letter. 28082

True position of the medical profession. 84256

True Presbyterian layman. pseud. see Old covenanting, and true Presbyterian layman. pseud.

True principles of American greatness. 102729

True principles of political economy. 91857

True principles of the Christian & protestant religion defended. 37209

True prophecies or prognostications of Mich. de Nostradamus. 55936

True protestant. pseud. Plain reasons. 63227

True protestant: a dissertation. 78595, (78596)

True protestant. A tale for the times. 74450

True Quaker reproving the false one. 9064

True question of the day. 72643

True reasons for Mr. Daniel White and Mr. Thomas Byles disposing. 103361

True reasons on which the election of the Hollis Professor. 50952

True Reformed Dutch Church in the United States of America. 8189, 97138

True relation of a bloody battle fought between George and Lewis. 37121, 78535

Trve relation of a late very famous sea-fight. 97139

True relation of a most bloody, treacherous and cruel design of the Dutch. 1002

True relation of all that hath passed and beene done. 102498

Trve relation of of [sic] a wonderfvll sea fight. 97140

True relation of Sir Henry Morgan his expedition. 79781

Trve relation of such occurrences and accidents of noate as hath hapned in Virginia. 19051, 82823, 82844-82847, 82855, 3d note after 100533

Trve relation of that vvich lately hapned. 97141

True relation of the barbarous cruelty. 74814

True relation of the flette which went vnder the Admirall Jaquis Le Hermite. 31510, 1st note after 97141

True relation of the illegal proceedings. 97057

True relation of the just and unjust proceedings. 92708, 97142

True relation of the late action between the French and Dutch. 97143

True relation of the late battell fought in New England. 99763-99766

True relation of the late battell fought in New England, between the English, and the salvages: vvith the present state of things there. 99760-99762

Trve relation of the most prosperous voyage made this present yeere 1605. (73288)

True relation of the murder committed by David Wallis. 46493

True relation of the proceedings against the Quakers, &c. 22359, 59659

Trve relation of the travailes. (18774)

Trve relation of the vnivst, crvell, and barbarovs proceedings. 1001

True relation of the vanquishing of the towne Olinda. 97144

True relation of the voyage undertaken by Sir Anthony Sherley. 80349

True relation of things very remarkable at the plantation of Plimoth in Nevv-England. 104795, 106053

True relation of Virginia. 82849-82850, 3d note after 100533

True relation of Virginia and Maryland. 80748

True religion delineated. 4497

True religion: extracted from Job Scott's journal. 78294, (78296)

True remedy for the wrongs of woman. 4294

True remedy. Speech of Hon. Charles Sumner. 93647

True report of Martin Frobisher's his last and third voyage. 22330

True report of the laste voyage into the west and northwest regions. 8829, 79341

Trueba y Cosio, Joaquin Telesforo de.
16045, 97162-97164
Trueba y Cosio's life of Cortez. 16045
Trueblue, Tom. pseud. To the free-holders.
97165
Trueman, Mr. pseud. Mr. Trueman's ob-
servations. 60181, 97167
Trueman, Andrew. pseud. Dialogue. 19926,
79242, 97168
Trueman, Timothy. 53165
Trueno de la libertad en Mexico. 97169
Trueno de los gachupines en Mejico. 97170
Truesdell, Mary Van Hogel. 97171
Truest and largest account of the late earth-
quake. (35559), 35665, 97172
Truguet, Laurent Jean Francois, comte.
87118, note after 97172
Trujillo, Jose Sanchez. see Sanchez Trujillo,
Jose.
Trulle, Rafael. 97173 see also Guatemala.
Real Consulado. Tesorero.
Truly blessed man. 104109
Truman, ———. 7313
Truman, Andrew. pseud. see Trueman,
Andrew. pseud.
Truman, B. F. 89214
Truman, G. 50430
Truman, Thomas. 97174
Trumbull. pseud. Mischiefs of legislative
caucuses. 97175
Trumbull, ------, fl. 1826. 105712
Trumbull, Benjamin, 1735-1820. 33431,
52984, 66410, 97176-97190 see also
Congregational Churches in Connecticut.
New Haven County Association. Scribe.
Trumbull, Benjamin, 1735-1820. supposed
author 97176, 105925, 105935
Trumbull, David. 97191
Trumbull, Henry. 82808, 84616, 97192-97201,
note after 100770
Trumbull, Henry. supposed author (6370),
40997, 71857, 97198
Trumbull, Henry Clay, 1830-1903. 52025
Trumbull, James. pseud. Life of George
Washington. 97202, 101779, note after
101843, 101851
Trumbull, James Hammond, 1821-1897. 15797,
39642, 51773, 59561, 66519, 85254,
96618, 97203, 97210, 97232, 104340
Trumbull, John, 1750-1831. 1795, 1365,
21778, 22112, 22392, 22971, (28481),
note after 53697, 71321, (82501), 82978,
note after 83791, 94663, 97204-97240,
2d note after 105927, 2d note after
105937
Trumbull, John, 1756-1843. 168, 28897,
50959, (65028), 75022, 84791, 84824,
84905, 97241-97249, 101818, 105921-
105921A see also American Academy
of the Fine Arts. President.
Trumbull, John M. defendant 97250
Trumbull, John M. plaintiff 97250
Trumbull, Jonathan, 1710-1785. 36925,
93936, 97252-97254, 97290 see also
Connecticut (Colony) Governor, 1769-1873
(Trumbull)
Trumbull, Lyman, 1813-1896. 17221
Trumbull, Mary. petitioner note before
91856
Trump kards. 79916
Trumpet air. 78217
Trumpet and Universalist magazine. Editor.
103802 see also Whittemore, Thomas.
Trumpet of fame. 71895-71896
Trumpet of the Lord sounding there. (55230)

Trumpet sounded out of the wilderness of
America. 39821
Trunbull, Robert James, 1775-1833. 8776,
17534
Truscott, Green & Co. firm 90742
Trusdell, William. plaintiff 731, 30380,
84558
Trusler, John. ed. 90225, 90231-90232,
90234, 90239-90245, 90248-90249
Trust, Joseph William. reporter 58783, 2d
note after 97255
Trust deed, from Eliphalet Nott and wife.
56036
Trust deed [of the Galveston Bay and Texas
Land Company.] 93710, 95086, 105111
Trust deed of the Southern Minnesota Railroad
Company. 88416
Trust in God. 12330
Trust in God in public commotions. 105032
Trust in God, the strength of a nation. 43105
Trust on which the Sanitary Commission holds
its funds. 21544, 76611
Trust, power and duty of the Grand Juries of
England. 86800
Trusta, H. pseud. Last leaf from Sunny Side.
see Phelps, Elizabeth (Stuart)
Trustaff, Sir George Jeoffrey. pseud.
Foreigner's scribble for amusement.
97256
Trustee. speud. Objections to re-organization.
60758
Trustees' account of the Agricultural Ex-
hibition. 97257
Trustees' account of the Cattle Show. 97258
Trustees for Establishing the Colony of Georgia
in America. see Georgia (Colony)
Trustees for Establishing the Colony of
Georgia in America.
Trustees for Georgia, and the places of their
abode. 23335
Trustees for Raising Money on the Estates of
the Late South Sea Directors and Others.
see South Sea Company. Trustees.
Trustees of Obadiah Brown's Benevolent Fund,
Providence, R. I. 52637
Trustees of Andrew Grant, of Grenada.
plaintiffs 28294
Trustees of Donations for Education in Liberia.
40923
Trustees of Phillips Academy, a corporation.
85212
Trustees of Phillips Academy vs. the Attorney-
General et al. 85212
Trustees of Phillips Academy, v. the Attorney
General, the Visitors of the Theological
Institution in Phillisp Academy in Andover
et al. 85212
Trustees of St Mary's Church, Philadelphia.
see Philadelphia. St. Mary's Church.
Trustees.
Trustees of the Leake and Watts Orphan House
v. Lawrence et al. 54701
Trustees of the McDonogh Estate. see
McDonogh Educational Fund and Institute,
Baltimore. Trustees.
Trustees of the . . . [Massachusetts General]
Hospital, to the public. 45846
Trustees of the Missionary Fund, Roxbury,
Mass. see Ministry at Large, Roxbury,
Mass. Trustees of the Missionary Fund.
Trustees of the Subscription Fund for the
Benefit of the Cambridge Volunteers,
Cambridge, Mass. see Subscription
Fund for the Benefit of the Cambridge
Volunteers, Cambridge, Mass. Trustees.
Trustees to Receive Contributions for the
Ransom of the Captives Taken by the

Indians, Hatfield, Mass. see Hatfield,
Mass. Trustees to Receive Contributions
for the Ransom of the Captives Taken
by the Indians.
Trusty. pseud. Dialouge between Freeman
and Trusty. 60056
Trusty and well-beloved, wee greet you well.
104147
Trvth. pseud. Bloudy tenent. see Williams,
Roger, 1604?-1683.
Truth. pseud. Letters of James Stephen.
see Stephen, James.
Truth. pseud. Reply to the attacks in the
Boston morning post. (69701), 1st note
after 97258
Truth. pseud. Very new pamphlet indeed!
(57146), 99320, note after 99776
Truth, John Tell. pseud. Patriote Anglois.
see LeBlanc, Jean Bernard.
Truth a general enemy. 95734
Truth, a gift for scribblers. 85433
Truth, a gift for scribblers; with additions
and emendments. 85432
Truth; a new year's gift for scribblers.
(59189), 85431, 2d note after 97259
Truth about Centralia. 84489
Truth about Cuba. 81154
Truth: addressed to the people at large.
(57146), 99320, note after 99776
Truth advanced in the correction of many
gross and hurtful errors. 37224
Truth advocated. 99781
Truth against error. (28349)
Truth and character vindicated. 1492, 60842
Truth and error contrasted. 81281
Truth and falsehood. 97260
Truth and innocency. (37221), (37225)
Truth and innocency defended. 5631, note
after 103702
Truth and justice. 56655
Truth and our times. 17277
Truth and reason, versus calumny and folly.
9002, 103675
Truth and righteousness triumphant. 30977
Truth as it is. 97261
Truth at home. 104611
Truth, being a discourse which the author
delivered at his baptism. 49979
Truth brought to light. Being a discovery of
some facts. 15205, (41650), (47511)-
47512, 51661
Truth brough to light; or, murder will out.
97262
Truth. [By Judah Monis.] 14477
Truth by majority. (81015)
Truth defended and Methodism weighed in the
balance. 94506A
Truth discriminated from error. 89812
Truth disentangled from error and delusion.
(43002)
Truth displayed, in a letter addressed to
young persons. 89513
Truth displayed; in a series of elementary
principles. (57744)
Truth espoused, relative to the difficulties.
58916
Truth exalted in the writings of that eminent
and faithful servant of Christ John
Burnyeat. 9417
Truth exploded. 97263
Truth from an honest man. 41159
Truth further defended. 103939
Trvth gloriously appearing. 103441
Truth held forth and maintained according to
the testimony of the Holy Prophets.
46934, (46935)

Truth in its nudity. 44186
Truth in love. 83456
Truth, in plain English. 98979
Truth is great, and will prevail. 2632, note
after 97263
Truth is mighty and will prevail. 90868,
90874
Truth is no slander. 97264
Truth made known. 104771
Truth not to be overthrown. (29830)
Truth. No. I. 35100, 1st note after 97259
Truth of Christ Jesus with the professors
thereof. (21671)
Truth of history vindicated. 36885
Truth of the Christian religion, demonstrated.
46477
Truth owned and the lying tongue rebuked.
78185
Truth plainly spoken. 27286
Truth prevailing and detecting error. 22353
Truth rescued from imposture. 90540, 96265
Truth revealed. 23683
Truth stated and illustrated. 97266
Truth stifled and appeal to the genius of the
ancient Romans. 94717
Truth stranger than fiction. 4295
"Truth the foundation of genuine liberty."
43582
Truth the strongest of all. 103703
Truth, the whole truth, and nothing but the
truth. 97267
Truth triumphant through the spiritual warfare.
3367
Trith, truth, truth. 97268
Truth unveiled. 62346, note after 97268
Truth versus fiction. 93946
Truth vindicated. [By Joseph C. Dean.] 105465
Truth vindicated; or, a spiritual essay. 97269
Truth vindicated. Senator Price and the Ex-
ecutive Committee. 65434
Truth will out! 20994, 97270
Truth without controversy. 83759
Truth without guile &c. 97271
Truthful elucidation of the attractions of the
country. 73108
Truthful epic. 103938
Truthful minister. 35998
Truth's advocate and monthly anti-Jackson
expositor. 97272, 99545
Truths come out at last. 97118, 97273
Truths for voters. 3454
Truths from the West Indies. 32366
Truths in a true light. 44082
Truths in rhyme. 93999
Truth's proofs that masonic oaths do not
impose any obligations. 97274
Truth's resurrection. 77434
Truxillo, Ildefonso. 97276
Truxillo, Juan Ignacio de. 97277
Truxillo, Juliana de. see Tonel de Sotomayor,
Juliana (de Truxillo)
Truxillo, Manuel Maria. 97278 see also
Franciscans. Comisario General de
Indias.
Truxillo y Guerro, Felipe Ignacio de, Bp.
97279 see also Michoacan (Diocese)
Bishop (Truxillo y Guerro)
Truxton, Thomas. 97280-97282
Truxton's victory. 97283
Truxton's victory. A naval patriotic song.
97284
Truxton's victory: or brave yankee boys.
97283
Truxton's victory—together with the Beggar
girl. 97284
Tryal of assurance. 91967

Tufts College, Medford, Mass. petitioners
45990
Tufts Library, Medford, Mass. see Medford,
Mass. Tufts Library.
Tugnot de Lanoye, Ferdinand, 1810-1870.
11542, 31601, 38931
Tuhi, John. defendant 97432
Tuke, Henry. 21591, 97433
Tuke, Samuel. 12913, (25353), (66917),
97434, note after 103655-103656
Tuksiantit attuagaesit illageennut innuit
nunaennetunnut. 22857
Tuksiautillo illaejartortut. 95618
Tuksiautit attuagaekset illageennut innuit
nunaennetunnut. 97435
Tuksiutit sabbatit ulloinnut napertorsaket.
95618
Tulane University of Louisiana. 42225,
42310
Tulane University of Louisiana. Adminis-
trators. 42310
Tulane University of Louisiana. Medical
Department 42310
Tulasne, ------. 75224
Tullar, Martin. 97436
Tulley, David. 97437
Tulley, John. 62743, 97438
Tulley, Samuel. see Tully, Samuel.
Tulley 1687. An almanack. 62743, 97438
Tulley's farewel 1702. 62743
Tullidge, Edward W. 83302
Tullius. pseud. Three letters. 97439
Tullius Americus. pseud. Strictures on a
pamphlet. see Bishop, Abraham.
supposed author
Tulloch, Alexander Murray. 97441
Tullulah, and other poems. (35419)
Tully, Kivas. 45475
Tully, Samuel. defendant 97442-97444
Tully, William. (2883), 49203-49204, 1st-2d
notes after 97444
Tumulo imperial. 75569
Tvmvlo imperial dela gran ciudad de Mexico.
75569
Tumultos y rebeliones acaecidos en Mexico.
11424, 50109, note after 96260
Tune book. 85507
Tune is, Let us to Virginny go. 100502
Tunes of the Pslams. (66440)-(66441)
Tunis, ------. 55132, 4th note after 97444
Tunis's topographical and pictorial guide.
55132, 4th note after 97444
Tunkhannock, Pa. Convention of Delegates
from Luzerne, Susquehanna and Bradford
Counties, 1840. see Convention of
Delegates from Luzerne, Susquehanna
and Bradford Counties, Tunkhannock,
Pa., 1840.
Tunkhannock, Pa. North Branch Canal Con-
vention, 1840. see North Branch Canal
Convention, Tunkhannock, Pa., 1840.
Tunnel loan bill. 30859
Tunnel pump and measure guard. (70768)
Tunon, Cayetano Antonio Torres. see Torres
Tunon, Cayetano Antonio, 1719-1787.
Tunon, Cayetano Torres. ed. 55262
Tunon, Luis Antonio Torres. see Torres
Tunon, Luis Antonio.
Tuomey, Michael. 87532-87534 see also
South Carolina. Geological Surveyor.
South Carolina. State Geologist.
Tupac-Amaru, Jose Gabriel de. 97447
Tupac-Amaru, Juan. 97446
Tupinambas, chronique Bresilienne. 6842,
(26774)
Tupper, ------. 97448

Tupper, E. W. (8152)
Tupper, Ferdinand Brock. (8152), 97449
Tupper, James. 87681 see also South
Carolina. Auditor.
Tupper, W. de Vic. (8152)
Turbett, Samuel. 38802 see also Lancaster
County, Pa. Collector of Excise.
Turbill, Hannah. appellant (11193)
Turc a 81 queues. pseud. Poesie et la
philosophie. see Zannovich, Stiepan,
1751-1786.
Turcarum liturgia. 60934
Tvrcici imperii descriptio. 98222
Turckey, ------. 4858A
Turckse grammatica. (36639)
Turcotte, J. E. 34041, 69661
Turell, Ebenezer. (14513), 17672, (28200),
69400, 90595-90596, 97450-97455, 103594,
3d note after 103650, 103935 see also
Congregational Churches in Massachusetts.
Ecclesiatical Council, Grafton, 1744.
Scribe.
Turell, Jane (Colman) d. 1735. (14513), 97451
Turf and the trotting horse of America.
(22099)
Turgot, Anne Robbert Jacques, Baron de
l'Aulne, 1727-1781. 234-236, 49393-
49394, 65450, 97456-97457
Turkey. 44605
Turkish fast. 97458
Turkish lady. 95736
Turks are all confounded. 96428
Turmeau de la Morandiere, ------. 97459
Turn-pike system. 87729
Turn-Spit, Moses. pseud. Modern eloquence.
97499
Turn-Zeitung. 85707
Turbull, --------. cartographer 56771,
83867
Turnbull, David. 62506, 97460
Turnbull, Gordon. 97461-97464, note after
102819
Turnbull, John D. 97465-97466
Turnbull, Robert James, 1775-1833. 46140,
48097, 87420, 87423, 87426, 87428, note
after 90638, 97467-97471
Turnbull, Robert James, 1775-1833. supposed
author 8776, 17534, note after 97466
Turnbull, William. 33828, note after 97471-
97472
Turnbull, William. reporter 33828, 91841A
Turnbull and Marsenie hand-bills. 97472
Turncoat, Robert Rusty. pseud. Wasp. see
Croswell, Harry.
Turned from the door. 50630
Turner, ------, fl. 1652. 104336
Turner, ------, fl. 1849. defendant 82581
Turner, A. A. illus. (41053)
Turner, Benjamin. illus. 36666
Turner, Charles. 97473-97475
Turner, Daniel. 103038 see also Westminster
Forum. President.
Turner, Edward. 97476-97479
Turner, Edward. ed. (49547)
Turner, Francis, successively Bishop of
Rochester, and Ely, 1638?-1700. 43178
Turner, Francis, fl. 1833. 97480
Turner, George. 17641 see also Rhode
Island. Committee on the Registered
State Debt.
Turner, George. Judge of the Northwest
Territory 97481-97484, note after 98679
Turner, George. of Newport, R. I. 20646,
20649, 87920, 1st-2d notes after 97484
Turner, George. reporter 20649, 29888,
45506

Tweede bericht ofte relaas van William Penn.
59701, 59738

Tweede boeck enz. 35775

Tweede brief van den nu geweezen Zee-
Officier. 100642

Tweede catalogus. 51282

Tweede deel van William Dampiers reystogt
rondom de werreld. 18385

Tweede deel vande waeractige verclaringe
nopende de goude en silvere mihne.
17129, 17131

Tweede journael, of dagh-register. 78899

Tvveede nootwendiger discovrs ofte vertoogh
aan alle landtlievende. 39241, 97530

Tweede stem uit Pella, Iowa. 77774

Tweede vervolg der bijlagen behoorende tot
zijne memorie. 67412

Tweede voyagie van Iacob van Neck. 55440,
2d note after 105014

Tweede wachter. 94579

Tweedie, A. 97531

Tweejaarige reyze rondom de wereelde. 72770

Tween sententien. 16681, 24085

Twelfth anniversary address before the Mount
Holyoke Female Seminary. 32250

Twelfth annual report . . . see Report . . .

Twelfth annual review of the trade and commerce. 12629

12th April 1786. note after 94720

Twelfth-Night at the Century Club. 99278

Twelfth-Night at the Century Club, January 6,
1858. (54160)

Twelfth Regiment R. I. Volunteers. 51618

Twelfth report . . . see Report . . .

Twelfth triennial and thirty-sixth annual
catalogue of the officers and students
of Centre College. 11688

Twelve acts of outlawry. 98998

Twelve anniversary sermons preached before
the Society for the Propagation of the
Gospel in Foreign Parts. 101276,
104258, 104517

Twelve articles exhibited by several of its
separating members. 104756

Twelve cents worth of wit. 97532

Twelve chapters on the struggles of the age.
70139

Twelve days' campaign. 20954

Twelve days in the tombs. 28535

Twelve discourses on government. 89079

Twelve lectures on primitive civilizations.
(43860)

Twelve lectures on the natural history of man.
37924

Twelve letters. Addressed to the Levant
Company. 23407, 96745

Twelve letters to young men. 105747

Twelve messages from the spirit John Quincy
Adams. 91766

Twelve months' history of the United States.
9471

Twelve months residence in the West Indies.
(43697)

Twelve-month's tour of observations through
America. (49452), 98634

Twelve month's tour thro' America. 98632

Twelve month's volunteer. (26217)

Twelve nights in the hunter's camp. 34653

Twelve plates, drawn from nature by G. W.
Fasel. 54153

Twelve practical and occasional discourses.
83610

Twelve propositions [of William Wilberforce.]
103959

Twelve resolutions of Mr. Joseph Hume.
58159

Twelve seasons at the "States." 83317

Twelve sermons. [By Michael Smith.] 83615

Twelve sermons: delivered at Antioch College.
44324

Twelve sermons on the following seasonable
and important subjects. 12331

Twelve sermons, on the most interesting subjects. 83610

Twelve sermons on various important subjects.
83433, 103601

XII. Sermons. Preached to a country coungre-
gation. 91148

Twelve sermons, preached upon several
occasions. 83614

Twelve sketches illsutrative of Sir Walter
Scott's demonology and witchcraft. 78382

Twelve Spanish Pirates. defendants see
Spanish Pirates. defendants

Twelve United Colonies, by their delegates in
Congress. 15596, 30179, 97533

Twelve views in the interior of Guiana. 4770,
77796

Twelve views of churches. 60747

Twelve views of Quebec, in 1759. 80570

Twelve years a Roman Catholic priest. 47116

Twelve years a slave. 55847

Twelve years in America. (79918)

Twelve years in the mines of California.
59140

Twentieth anniversary. A commemorative
discourse. 9548

Twentieth annual catalogue of Springfield
Female College. 89894

Twentieth annual circular of Hanover College.
30241

Twentieth annual report . . . see Report . . .

Twentieth report . . . see Report . . .

Twenty articles of charge against Rev. Samuel
Bacheller. 2603

XX articles of charge against the Rev^d Mr.
Bacheller. 31052

Twenty-eight judges. pseud. Appeal from the
twenty eight judges. see Keith, George.

Twenty-eight Quakers. see Friends, Society
of. Philadelphia Monthly Meeting.

Twenty-eighth annual report . . . see
Report . . .

Twenty Eighth Congregational Society, Boston.
see Boston. Twenty Eighth Congregational Society.

Twenty-fifth anniversary discourse. 14949

Twenty-fifth anniversary of Friendship Division,
No. 19. 87082

Twenty-fifth anniversary of the installation of
George W. Blagden. 5724

Twenty-fifth anniversary of the Mt. Holyoke
Female Seminary. 51159

Twenty-fifth anniversary sermon preached
. . . in Uxbridge. 13454

Twenty-fifth annual report . . . see Report
. . .

Twenty-first annual report . . . see Report
. . .

Twenty-first annual catalouge of . . . Kings-
ville Academy. 37919

Twenty-five years in the west. (44246)

Twenty-five years of a congregation. 57791

Twenty-four discourses. 60968

Twenty-four Journeymen Tailors, Philadelphia.
defendants 28121, note after 96948

Twenty-four letters from labourers in America.
97536

Twenty-four views of the vegetation of the
coasts. 38025

Two discourses delivered in Harvard Church. 22309

Two discourses delivered in Park Street Church, Boston. 8930

Two discourses delivered in . . . Portsmouth. 8927

Two discourses, delivered in the College Chapel, at Hanover. 101512

Two discourses, delivered in the First Baptist Meeting House. 102185

Two discourses delivered in the First Congregational Meeting-House in Canton. (72731)

Two discourses delivered in the Prison of Philadelphia. (78660), 2d note after 97555

Two discourses, delivered in the public assemblies. 92328

Two discourses delivered in the said church. 11989

Two discourses, delivered July 14, 1774. 103770

Two discourses, delivered July 4, 1830. 30516

Two discourses, delivered July 23, 1812. 101073

Two discourses delivered November 23d. 1758. 47138

Two discourses delivered Oct. 1st, 1780. (18419)

Two discourses delivered October 25th, 1759. (47149)

Two discourses delivered October 25th, 1759. 46804

Two discourses delivered on taking leave of the Old Church. 24779

Two discourses delivered on the anniversary of the author's ordination. 90911

Two discourses; delivered on the Lord's Day preceding a removal. 64138

Two discourses, delivered . . . on the occasion. 85300

Two discourses, delivered on the opening of the new theatre in Charleston. 85330

Two discourses, delivered on the public fast in Massachusetts. 1417

Two discourses, delivered to the Second Presbyterian Society in Newburyport. 27371

Two discourses, exhibiting an historical sketch of the First Baptist Chruch in Boston. 104718

Two discourses for the times. 10846

Two discourses, from I. Cor. iii. 6. 1841

Two discourses from Isaiah vii. on January 28th. 1747, 8. 1842

Two discourses. God in the ptestilence. 22788

Two discourses . . . Hartford, March 5, 1848. 30925

Two discourses from Lev. 26. 3, 4. (82296)

Two discourses in commemoration of the founding of the First Presbyterian Church in Northern Liberties. 80284

Two discourses in consequence of the war. 4054

Two discourses . . . in Ipswich, April 4, 1799. (25981)

Two discourses . . . in . . . New-York, February, 1805. (49064)

Two discourses . . . in Taunton . . . April 7, 1840. (5280)

Two discourses, . . . January 26 and February 2, 1845. (26240)

Two discourses, occasioned by a sentence of death. 46588

Two discourses, occasioned by the approaching anniversary of the declaration of independence. (26240)

Two discourses occasioned by the cruel oppression of the Protestants in France. 27292

Two discourses, occasioned by the death of General George Washington. 56825

Two discourses, occasioned by the death of Jared Sparks. 54967

Two discourses occasioned by the death of the Rev. Mr. John Lowell. 97317

Two discourses, occasioned by the severe droughts in sundry parts of the country. 18770

Two discourses, October 19, 1851. 47943

Two discourses of the author [i. e. Thomas Bromley] never before printed. 8192

Two discourses on a new system of society; as delivered in . . . Washington. 58016

Two discourses . . . on a publick fast. 39199

Two discourses on April 5, 1770. 1845

Two discourses on intemperance. 2705

Two discourses, . . . on January 1, 1832. 76479

Two discourses, on John vith, 44th. (82213), 82215

Two discourses, on June 11. 1769. 1844

Two discourses on liberty. 55326

Two discourses on man's inability to comply with the Gospel. 82220

Two discourses on our own religious affairs. (58372)

Two discourses on providence. 832

Two discourses on slavery. (20529)

Two discourses on the character of Rev. Thomas Chalmers. 79805

Two discourses on . . . the close of a century. (50978)

Two discourses, on the completion of the second century from the landing. 32587

Two discourses on the death of Rev. Nathaniel Taylor. (28908)

Two discourses on . . . the death of William Henry Harrison. 61034

Two discourses on the divine faithfulness. (66812)

Two discourses on the divinity of Christ. 80180

Two discourses on the fiftieth anniversary of the author's ordination. 66809

Two discourses on the most improtant duties of townsmen. (31767)

Two discourses on the occasion of the great fire in Charleston. 85334

Two . . . discourses on the prudent apprehensions of death. 46279

Two discourses on the same subject by the Rev. Mr. Witter. 2623

Two discourses on the state of the country. 82947

Two discourses, on the sudden deaths. (62699)

Two discourses on . . . the war between the U. States and Mexico. 29612

Two discourses: I. On the commencement of the new year. 18418

Two discourses, preached at Haberdasher's-Hall. 27291

Two discourses preached at Lexington. 1843

Two discourses preached at Rindge. (59317)

Two discourses preached before the First Congregational Society in Medford. 91376

Two discourses, preached December 29, 1861. 65093

Two discourses, preached . . . February 10, 1850. 3622

Two discourses, preached . . . in Boston. 43374

Two discourses preached in St. Andrew's Church, Philadelphia. 91578

Two discourses preached in the Presbyterian Church, Natchez. 92737

Two discourses preached in Tremont Temple. 36985

Two discourses preached . . . July 12 and July 19, 1863. 26536

Two discourses, preached to the First Society in Lebanon. 104368

Two discourses, Sept. 12, 19, 1858. 91578

Two discourses . . . Sept. 21, 1851. 37847

Two discourses . . . September 29, 1839. 42714

Two discourses shewing, I. That the Lord's ears are open. (46754)

Two discourses; the first about redemption of time. 25370

Two discourses; the first, delivered on taking leave of the Old Meeting-House. 95202

Two discourses; the first delivered on the 25th of May, 1856. 89767, 89775

Two discourses: the first occasioned by the death of General Washington. (64216)

Two discourses, the first on the day of fasting and prayer. 103929

Two discourses. The whole adapted to the weakest capacities. 4497

Two discourses to the Second Church and Society in Berwick. (31893)

Two discourses which were delivered in the Chapel of the University. 82921

Two dissertations. First. The nature and constitution of the law. 76473

Two dissertations: I. Concerning the end for which God created the world. 21967

Two distinguished members of the Philadelphia Bar. pseud. Eulogies. 27712, 95821-95822

Two donkeys. 20642

Two Dutch Men. pseud. Account of the present state and strength of Canada. 4035

Two-edged sword; being an impartial address. 19827, 27619

Two edged sword. Extraordinary disclosure of arbitrary power. 95858

Two editorials from the Boston courier. 82083

Two elders. pseud. Epistle. 43595

Two elegiac poems. 90446

Two elegies, on the death of Mr. Lunsford. 96121

Two eminent authors. pseud. Voice from the tombs. 100663

Two eminent merchants at Port-Royal in Jamaica. pseud. reporters (37982)-37983, note after 99766, note after 100901

Two Englishmen. pseud. Reminiscences of America in 1869. 69562

Two episcopal charges by Rt. Rev. John Henry Hobart. (32305)

Two epistles of free stricture. 102335

Two epistles of that excellently wittie Doctor, Francis Rablais. 31037

Two epistles. The angels' address, or the glorious message. 35706

Two epistles to my cousin Tom, in New York. 56311

Two epistles to Presbyterians. 5618

Two essays: I. on the foundation of civil government. 16620

Two essays sent in a letter from Oxford. 58061, 3d note after 97555

Two exact lists. 99249

Two excellent court ballads dedicated to the Right Honourable Sir Robert Walpole. 99249

Two excellent hymns. 84553

Two experienced reporters. pseud. reporters 102290

Tvvo famovs sea-fights. 97556

Two farewell sermons, by the late Reverend Mr. Geo. Whitefield. 103580, 103602

Two favorite new songs at the American camp. 97557

Two favorite songs, made on the evacuation of the town of Boston. 97558, 97574

Two favorite songs made on the evaculation of the town of Boston by the Britons. 97559

Two first parts of his life, with his journals, revised. 103550, 103603

Two-fold slavery of the United States. 29825

Two following depositions were laid before the House. (60748)

Two for one. 30611

Two friendly letters from Toletus to Philalethes. 89794, 89797, 94368

Two Friends (Ship) in Admiralty 59584, 93383, 96934

Two fruitful sisters Virginia, and Mary-land. 30102, 82976

Two funeral discourses. 84599-84600

Two funeral hymns. 103604

Two funeral sermons. . . . In Otis, at the interment. 49110

Two funeral sermons on the death of the Honourable John Appleton. 72692, 2d note after 97559

Two funeral sermons: the first, occasioned by the death of the Right Honourable Katherine, Countess of Effingham. 101490

Two General Assemblies ought not to be united. 92862

Two gentlemen in New York. pseud. Dialogue. 19935

Two gentlemen of law-knowledge. pseud. reporters Trial of Charles Vattier. see Turner, George.

Two geological reports. 44503

Two great breavements commemorated. 18469

Two great ladies. pseud. Dialogue. 19936

Two great questions consider'd. 69516, 97560

Two great questions further considered. 97560

Two great wars in America. 35702

Two hemispheres. 38722

Two hemispheres; a romance. 74166

Two historical discourses occasioned by the close of the first ten years' ministry. 104141

Two hundred and thirty-seventh annual record of the Ancient and Honorable Artillery Company of Massachusetts. (77244)

Two hundred dollars reward. 105372

Two hundred temperance anecdotes. (44749)

Two hundred years ago. A sermon preached to the First Church. 26073

Two hundred years ago. By the author of "The Green-Mountain boys." 95476

Two hundred years ago; or, a brief history of Cambridgeport. 81369

Two Hundredth Anniversary Celebrations of the Incorporation of the Town of Dartmouth, New Bedford, Mass., 1864. see

Dartmouth, Mass. Two Hundredth Anniversary Celebration, New Bedford, Mass., 1864.

Two hundredth anniversary of the First Protestant . . . Dutch Church. 77593

Two hundredth anniversary of the formation of the First Congregational Church in Dover, N. H. 73119

Two hundredth anniversary of the incorporation of the town of Chatham. 84760

Two imaginary letters. 51255, 75280

Two Indian treaties the one held at Conestogoe in May 1728. 97561

Two interesting letters. 95241

Two interests reconciled. 34882-34884, 97562

Two Jonathans agreeing to settle the slave question. 58091

Two journals. 13015

Two journeys of the present Emperour of China. (24865)

Two kingdoms. 64795

Two last sermons preached at Christ's-Church in Philadelphia. 61202

Two lectures [by Charles Brooks.] 8340

Two lectures. [By Charles Gayarre.] 26797

Two lectures. [By Edward Palmer.] (58350)

Two lectures. [By Horace Mann.] 44324

Two lectures. . . . By Rev. G. G. Lawrence. 39352

Two lectures. By the Rev. Adam Lillie. (41070)

Two lectures . . . by the Rev. Louis Heylen. 31651

Two lectures. [By Thomas Coltrin Keefer.] 37146

Two lectures, delivered at Berlin. 77491

Two lectures delivered at the Town-Hall, Colchester. 11557

Two lectures delivered at Torquay. 78183

Two lectures . . . delivered before the Lowell Institute. 22300

Two lectures delivered before the Young Men's Association of the City of Utica. 96425

Two lectures delivered in Halifax, in November, 1849. 67761

Two lectures delivered to the Leeds Mechanics' Institution and Literary Society. 33248-33249

Two lectures, delivered to the students of the Columbian College. 79468

Two lectures . . . 11th and 25th January, 1853. 33818

Two lectures, . . . in . . . New-York and . . . in Brooklyn. (51253)

Two lectures . . . in the Law School of Harvard College. 58699

Two lectures . . . January 29th and February 26th, 1858. 35309

Two lectures on Canada. 10266

Two lectures on comets, by Professor Winthrop. 57199, 104858

Two lectures on comets, read in the Chapel of Harvard-College. 104857

Two lectures on intemperance. 44324

Two lectures on Newfoundland. 51299

Two lectures on political economy. 39383

Two lectures on the advantages of a republican condition of Society. 103348

Two lectures on the connection between the Biblical and physical history of man. 56040

Two lectures on the constitution of the United States. 40985

Two lectures on the history of Mason. 93813

Two lectures on the history of the American union. 68548

Two lectures on the natural history of the Caucasian and Negro races. 56040

Two lectures on the parallax and distance of the sun. 104859

Two lectures, on the poetry of Pope, and on his own travels in America. 33248

Two lectures on the present American war. 4945

Two lectures on the present crisis. 30833

Two lectures upon the pleasures of the senses. note after 74241

Two lesser poems. 96329

Two lessons from the future. 51641

Two letter [sic] written by G. Fox to Coll. Lewis Morris. 39817

Two letters. A circular letter. 97562

Two letters, adapted to the present critical juncture. 105503

Two letters, addressed to a member of the present Parliament. 92842

Two letters addressed to General William Hull. 101078

Two letters addressed to Rev. N. L. Rice. 82243

Two letters addressed to Sir Thomas Charles Bunbury. 97564

Two letters addressed to the Bishop of the Diocese. 51262

Two letters addressed to the editor of the "Church." 71114

Two letters addressed to the Right Honourable Thomas Lord Denman. 33825, 91841A

Two letters, addressed to the Right Rev. Prelates. 97565

Two letters and several calculations on the sugar colonies and trade. 4732

Two letters by Bollan. 6220

Two letters: by Solomon Southwick. 88655

Two letters cited by the Rev. Mr. Clap. 21932

Two letters concerning Archbishop Tillotson. 26596

Two letters concerning communion in the Lord's Supper. 93378

Two letters concerning some farther advantages and improvements. 10733, 97566

Two letters. . . embracing a history of the re-charter. 5243

Two letters, extracted from the life of Benedict Joseph Labre. 95232

Two letters from a dismissed usher. 68596

Two letters from a gentleman to his friend. 26144

Two letters from a merchant retired from business. 25883, note after 59281

Two letters from Agricola to Sir William Howe. 33344

Two letters from an English gentleman in China. 90279

Two letters from D. Hartley Esq. 30693

Two letters from Dr. Franklin. 97567

Two letters from himself [i. e. John Avery.] 2487

Two letters from his wife. 92714

Two letters from . . . John Jay. (70071)

Two letters from Mr. John Bushel. 9535

Two letters from Nathaniel Lovetruth. 103560

Two letters from Robert G. Harper. 20439

Two letters from Robert G. Harper, Esq., Member of Congress. (20438)

Two letters from Robert G. Harper, Esq. of South Carolina. 20437

Two letters from Tallahassee. 20924

Two letters from the author of Siris. 65700

Two letters from the Reverend Mr. Williams
& Wheelock. 104369

Two letters from W. Graves. 28354

Two letters in defence of the present. 26434

Two letters in reply to certain publications.
102564

Two letters, lately written from Boston to
London. 103100

Two letters from Col. Orne and Gen. Duff
Green. 14898

Two letters of Gen. H. M. Naglee about Gen.
McClellan. 51720

Two letters of Helvetius on the merits of the
same book. 96413

Two letters of May 19, 1727. 10894, 27312-
(27313), 71968

Two letters of the Hon. Michael Hoffman.
(5302), (37656)

Two letters of the Late Right Honorable
Edmund Burke. 105483

Two letters of the Lord Bishop of London.
10894, 27312-(27313), 71968

Two letters of William Roscoe. 98707

Two letters on cases of cure. 92872

Two letters of Christian fellowship. 72110

Two letters on free masonry. 74276

Two letters on political subjects and one
describing a bisit. 3540

Two letters on public subjects. (74277)

Two letters on slavery in the United States.
30099

Two letters on the slave trade. 96956

Two letters on the subject of slavery. 97568

Two letters. One addressed to the academical
faculty. 96465

Two letters one from an American gentleman
to the author. 42945

Two letters published by the Rev. Mr. John
Tucker. (11861)

Two letters published in the Hamilton gazette.
9354

Two letters relating to the subject. 93591

Two letters . . . relative to the slave-cultured
estates. 71390

Two letters relative to the vaccine institution.
82780

Two letters respecting the conduct of Rear-
Admiral Graves. (28355)

Two letters, supposed to be written some
years hence. 75279

Two letters, the first written by a gentleman
at New-York. 16729

Two letters to a clergyman. 95572

Two letters to a friend. 57500, 90601

Two letters to a friend. [By Moses Brown.]
22115, (78492)-78493

Two letters to a friend. [By Titus Strong.]
93076

Two letters to a friend, on the present critical
conjuncture of affairs in North America.
(12320), (12328), (40382), 97569, 7th
note after 100870

Two letters to a friend on the present critical
conjuncture of affairs. 16603

Two letters to a friend, on the removal of
the Rev. Mr. J[ame]s S[proa]t. 97570

Two letters to a friend. Wherein a practical
plan is laid down. 56104

Two letters to a merchant in London. 4920

Two letters to a noble lord. [By Charles
Lee.] 38707

Two letters to a noble lord: one from a
gentleman in the navy. 56104

Two letters to Dr. Joseph Priestley. 102401

Two letters to Dr. Priestley. 77231

Two letters to Gen. Grant. (37290)

Two letters to his friend in the country. 86740

Two letters to John Armstrong. 81663

Two letters to Lord Onslow. 58243

Two letters to Mr. Wood. 84539, note after
97570

Two letters to Rev. Edward W. Hale. 1478

Two letters . . . to the Board of Managers
and Executive Committee of the Episcopal
Sunday School Union. 47242

Two letters to the citizens of the United States.
3433

Two letters to the Colonial Secretary. 49686

Two letters to the editor of the New Bedford
mercury. (18048)

Two letters to the Hon. S. P. Chase. 26403

Two letters to the Marquis of Londonderry.
97471

Two letters to the preachers in Boston. 37207-
37208

Two letters to the printer. 80684-80685

Two letters to the Rev. Horatio Bardwell.
17628

Two letters to the Reverend Moses Stuart.
63990, 93902, 103728, 103730

Two letters to the Right Honourable the Earl
of B———. 63091

Two letters to the Right Reverend the Bishop
of London. 103498

Two letters upon this subject. 103067

Two letters: viz. I. A letter to the Earl of
Abingdon. 97572

Two letters, which they writ to the Lords
people. 91318

Two letters. Written by a person of quality.
37703

Two letters written by G. Fox to Coll. Lewis
Morris. 28453, 39817, 66735, 66743

Two letters written by George Fox to Coll.
Lewis Morris, deceased. 28453

Two letters, written by himself [i. e. John
Smith.] 82874-82876

Two letters written by Queene Mary from
Heauen. 78374-78375, 100799

Two letters written to a friend. 92026

Two letters wrote originally in German.
87145

Two letters wrote originally in German, from
the Reverend Mr. Sorg. 87147

Two letters, write originally in German, from
the Reverend Mr. Sorge. 87146

Two maidens. 34776

Two masonic addresses. 90900

Two Meetings, Held in Boston, on the 7th &
14th July [1852], to Protest Against the
Nomination of Gen. Scott, for the Presidency, and to Recommend Hon. Daniel
Webster for that Office. see Whig
Party. Massachusetts. Suffolk County.
and Boston. Webster Meetings, July,
1852.

Two Meetings of Citizens Respecting Col.
Clark's Plan for Ascending Rapids in
Rivers, Philadelphia, 1824. see Phila-
delphia. Two Meetings of Citizens
Respecting Col. Clark's Plan for As-
cending Rapids in Rivers, and Thereby
Improving the Navigation of the River
Delaware, Beyond Trenton, 1824.

Two Meetings, on the 7th & 14th July, 1852,
to Protest Against the Nomination of
Gen. Scott. see Whig Party. Massachusetts. Suffolk County. and Boston.
Webster Meetings, July, 1852.

Two memorable relations. 102498

Two memoranda on the objects and construction of the American ephemeris. 18807

Two memorial discourses. (27943)

Two memorials. 64835-64836

Two men of Padua. pseud. eds. Portico. see Simpson, Stephen. and Watkins, Tobias.

Two metrical romances. 97573

Two millions. (9663A)

Two misers. A comic opera. 86906

Two Missouri historians. 85374

Two mites on some of the most important and much disputed points. 78322

Two modes of spending it. 34442

Two months among "the bankers." (78687)

Two months in Fort Lafayette. (65709)

Two Mormon apostles exposed . . . in Boston. 30355

Two most aged ministers of the Gospel, yet surviving in the countrey. pseud. Testimony, to the order of the Gospel. see Higginson, John. and Hubbard, William.

Two most masterly letters of Junius. (36398)

Two narratives, by men that were wounded. 18602

Two narratives of maritime discovery. 49935

Two nations. 63878

Two New England gentlemen. petitioners 9372

Two new songs. 97558, 97574

Two notices of Mr. Upham his reply. 46623, 64043, 98039

Two Neighbouring Associations of Ministers in the Country. pseud. Letter. 103631

Two objects to be gained at once. 104503

Two occasional sermons, delivered at North-Haven. 103786

Two odes and an acrostic. 96139

Two of Bp. Gibson's letters on that subject. 33800

Two of his friends. pseud. Brief sketch of the life of the deceased. 102458

Two of the brethren. pseud. Reply. see Goodwin, John. supposed author

Two olive-trees. 42791

Two orations. 30178, 101477

Two ordination sermons. 47354

Two other discourses. (24539)

Two pagents. 38310

Two papers, on the subject of taxing the British colonies in America. 952, 37244, 66015, 86745, 97575

Two pastoral letters addressed to the congregation of St. Paul's Church. 37950

Two persons under a window. pseud. Conversation. 97621

Two petitions to Congress. (13299)

Two pictures in one. 92452

Two pieces descriptive of Cuban slavery. 63605

Two pieces of the intended jubilee. 17224

Two plain and practical discourses concerning I. Hardness of heart. 46755

Two plans for forming the town of Boston. 6714, note after 97575

Two poems against tobacco and coffee. 97551

Two poems. By Arthur Slade. (81676)

Two poems. By Benjamin Whitman Jr. Esq. 103721

Two poems. First. On a soul pleading with God. 97576

Two poems, founded on texts of scripture. 97577

Two poems, one delivered in 1811. (27436)

Two points of the West Indian question considered. 97578

Two political odes. (65036)

Two prefaces by the editor [i. e. Mathew Carey.] 29979

Two Presidents secretly assassinated by poison. (21579)

Two princes. 94555

Two principal arguments of William Wirt. 104883

Two proclamations. 8348

Two proposals becoming England at this juncture to undertake. 40877, 1st note after 97578

Two protestant sisterhoods. 51256

Two protests against the bill to repeal the American stamp act. 16839

Two public lectures in the Hall of Harvard-College. 103903

Two questions. 80260

Two rare tracts printed in 1649-'50. 20596, note after 98474, note after 99310

Two rebellions. A few words to His Excellency the Hon. C. F. Adams, &c. 12993

Two rebellions: Benjamin and American slave-holders. 91112

Two rebellions; or, treason unmasked. 43148, 2d note after 100582

Two records Nephite Jewish. 83251

Two rejoinders, on slave holding. 20255

Two relations not vnfit for these times. 97556

Two relations, one of the northeasterne parts. 66682

Two reports, and appeal to the people of New-York. (32516), 84221

Two reports concerning the aid and comfort given by the Sanitary Commission. 76559, 76647

Two reports . . . from the Committee of the Honourable House of Assembly. 35640, 35666-35667, 2d note after 96578

Two reports, made by Committees appointed by the Directors of the Association for Improving the Navigation of Connecticut River above Hartford, etc. (15874), 3d note after 97578

Two reports of a Committee of His Majesty's Council. 97479

Two reports of the Faculty of Amherst College. 1332, note after 93378

Two reports: on the coal lands. 94530

Two reports on the condition of military hospitals. 76565, 76647

Two reports on the matter of complaint of Mr. Livius against Governor Wentworth. (41657), 1st note after 97579, note after 102630

Two reports (one presented the 16th of October, the other on the 12th of November, 1788.) 35640, 35666-35667, 2d note after 97578

Two reports . . . September 23, 1861. 38061

Two respectable writers. pseud. Treaty of commerce and navigation. 96582

Two series of essays, originally published in the "Columbian centinel." 99823

Two sermons addressed to the Second Congregational Society. 89813

Two sermons, addressed to the Second Presbyterian Congregation. 89744

Two sermons . . . [after] the interment of John W. Foster. 59354

Two sermons . . . April 25, 1799. 18405

Two sermons . . . at a particular fast. 58204

Two sermons at Ashburnham, Mass. 18112

Two sermons . . . at Berlin. 66604

Two sermons, at Boston-lecture in the month of July 1697. 46540

Two sermons, . . . at Bradford, March 11th and 25th, 1743,4. 58900

Two sermons on the nature of regeneration opened. 94706

Two sermons, on the party spirit and divided state of the country. 104965

Two sermons on the Presbyterian Church, Madison, Wis. (28569)

Two sermons, on the promotion of Christianity amongst the Jews. 89744

Two sermons, . . . on the second centennial anniversary of the organization of the First Church. 44363

Two sermons on the signs of the times. (58346)

Two sermons; one delivered in . . . Cincinnati. 31671

Two sermons; one in proof of the Christian religion. 34063

Two sermons, one on a fast day. 4397

Two sermons—one on beneficence. 30239

Two sermons, one on leaving the old, and the other on entering the new house of worship. 22464

Two sermons: I. On leaving the old chapel. II. On entering the new. (64308)

Two sermons. One on leaving the old, the other on entering the new, Meeting House, in Stoughton. (71126)

Two sermons. I. Signs of our national atheism. 31262

Two sermons; part of the opening and applying the parable. 80189

Two sermons preached. 46559, 96766

Two sermons preached . . . after her funeral. (14513), 97451

Two sermons, preached after the conclusion of the treaty of peace. (24711)

Two sermons preached . . . April 23, 1865. (31445)

Two sermons preached at a few small churches only. 78385

Two sermons, preached at and after the ordination of the Revd. Mr. Charles-Jeffry Smith. 103214

Two sermons preach'd at Burlington. 94709

Two sermons preached at Cambridge. 32588

Two sermons, preached at Dominica. 61188

Two sermons preach'd at Dorchester. 17098

Two sermons, preached at Epping. 90919

Two sermons, preached at Haverhill. 82722

Two sermons, preached at King's Chapel, Boston. (11209), 2d note after 97579

Two sermons preached at Maldon. 12414

Two sermons preach'd at Needham. 96384

Two sermons preached at New-Brunswick. 94697

Two sermons. Preached at Pequea. 83797-83798

Two sermons preach'd at Philadelphia. 94696

Two sermons preached at Plymouth. 17102

Two sermons preach'd at Portsmouth. 16638

Two sermons preached at Ragged Island and Boston. 44676

Two sermons, preach'd at Rowley. 11860

Two sermons preach'd at Salem-Village. 13346

Two sermons, preached at Sandwich. 13854

Two sermons, preached at Stephey. 92887

Two sermons preached at the lecture in Boston, 1699. 104102

Two sermons, preached at the opening of the Baptist Meeting-House. 90837

Two sermons, preached at the Second Church in Boston. 71775, 71799, (71802)

Two sermons preached at Thetford in Norfolke, Anno 1620. (78365)

Two sermons preached at Watertown. 22170

Two sermons, preached before the First Congregational Church and Society. 84293

Two sermons preached before the First Congregational Church and Society in Leominster. 91049

Two sermons preached before the Synods of New York and Philadelphia. 771

Two sermons preached by him [i. e. Frederick T. Gray.] 28390, 51592, 54993

Two sermons: preached by Robert Smith. 83799

Two sermons, preached by the Rev. C. G. Finney. 24393

Two sermons preached by the Rev. Gregory T. Bedell. 4271

Two sermons preached by Thomas Shepard. 80226-80228, 80233, 80235

Two sermons preached December 13. 1776. 19203

Two sermons preached Feb. 26. 1740, 1. 59312

Two sermons, preached in a congregation of Black slaves. 2685, 2687, 3d note after 97579

Two sermons preached in a few small churches only. 78384

Two sermons preached in Boston. 16641

Two sermons preached in Boston, N. E. (47136)

Two sermons, preached in Boylston. (76502)

Two sermons, preached in Dover, Massachusetts. 76510

Two sermons preached in . . . Eckley. 74363

Two sermons, preached in Newbury. 104949

Two sermons preached in . . . Providence. 57791

Two sermons preached in . . . Rensselaerville. 26173

Two sermons preached in said [Christ] Church. 20638

Two sermons, preached in St. Armand. 91662

Two sermons preached in . . . Savannah. 22283

Two sermons, preach'd in the First Church of Christ in Braintree. 30175

Two sermons preached in the First Church in Plymouth, Mass. 7948

Two sermons, preached in the First Presbyterian Church, Yonkers, N. Y. 84414

Two sermons, preached in the Tabernacle Church, in Salem. 103317

Two sermons, preached . . . Oct. 24, 1841. 58885

Two sermons preach'd on March 21st. 1727, 8. 96385

Two sermons, preached on the lecture in Boston. 104074

Two sermons, preached on the lecture, in the year, 1700. 104111

Two sermons, preached, the first on the evening of June 30. 13853

Two sermons, preached to a new assembly of Christians. 37234

Two sermons, preached 21st November, 1830. 6969

Two sermons shewing how to begin. (25387)

Two sermons, shewing, that sin is the greatest evil. (46653)

Two sermons testifying against the sin of drunkenness. 46759

Two sermons. The almost Christian. 103497, 103530, 103605

Two sermons: the Christian's behaviour under severe and repeated bereavements. 3471

Two sermons; the first addressed to seamen. 97580

Tyler, John, Pres. U. S., 1790-1862. 448,
    18005, 24888, 30779, (48107)-48111,
    62465, 63811, 70577, 70725, 78647,
    79115, 86503, 93121, 96737, 97605-
    97613, 102287, 104204-104205 see also
    U. S. President, 1841-1845 (Tyler)
Tyler, John, 1819-1896. 97614
Tyler, Lyon Gardiner, 1853-1935. ed. 82832,
    82950
Tyler, R. ed. (52353)
Tyler, Royal, 1757-1826. 97615-97621, 3d
    note after 105973
Tyler, Samuel. 45312
Tyler, W. S. 84961
Tyler, Texas. Camp Ford (Confederate
    Military Prison) Union Prisoners.
    eds. (57129)
Tyler Davidson Fountain, given by Mr. Henry
    Probasco. (64048)-64049
Tymbiras. Poema Americano. 19963
Tyndall, John, 1820-1893. 76966
Tyng, Dudley Atkins, 1760-1829. 97622
Tyng, Dudley Atkins, 1825-1858. 61537,
    91918, 92078, 97623
Tyng, Stephen Higginson, 1800-1885. 4273,
    49131, 64642, 92082, 97624-97629
Tyng, Stephen Higginson, 1839-1898. defendant
    at church trial 97630
Tyng, Stephen Higginson, 1839-1898. plaintiff
    50655, 1st note after 96986
Types of border life in the western states.
    43087
Types of mankind. 56040
Types of womanly attributes of all lands and
    ages. 13436
Typhus d'Amerique. 70463
Typhus syncopalis. 49202
Typis orbis terrarvm. 98222
Typography. 97631
Typographical Association of New-York. 97632
Typographical gazetteer. 17041
Typographical miscellany. (51375)
Typographical Society, New York. see New
    York Typographical Society.
Typographical Society, Philadelphia. see
    Philadelphia Typographical Society.
Typvs cosmographicvs vniversalis. 34100,
    (34104)
Tyrannic administration of St. Francisco.
    12978
Tyrannical libertymen. 97633
Tyrannical nature of the government and dis-
    cipline. 51576
Tyrannicide proved lawful. 4015, note after
    97633
Tyrannies et crvavtez des Espagnols. 11271
Tyrannies et crvavtez des Espangols, perpe-
    trees es Indes Occidentales. 11227-
    11228, 11230, 11233-11234, 11267-11268
"Tyranny anatomized" in four letters. 43275
Tyranny and injustice of sumptuary law.
    24308
Tyranny exposed. 49427, 82020
Tyranny exposed, true liberty discovered.
    47907
Tyranny in disguise. 49815
Tyranny stripped of the garb of patriotism.
    (24212)
Tyranny the worst taxation. 73804, 97634
Tyranny unmasked. An answer to a late
    pamphlet. 36309, 97635
Tyranny unmasked. By John Taylor, of
    Virginia. 94495
Tyrant caught in his own toils. 97636
Tyro. pseud. Banker. see Taylor, Vermilye.
Tyron, George W. 1111, (67449)

Tyron, Thomas. 25947, note after 97286
Tyso, Jonathan. 28926
Tysoe, John. (23054)
Tyson, Edward. 97637
Tyson, Elisha. 97638
Tyson, J. Washington. 97639
Tyson, James Lawrence. 97640
Tyson, Job Roberts. 1183, 7908, (27492),
    42151, 97641-97649
Tyson, John Shoemaker, 1797-1864. 7183,
    97650-97651, note after 105507
Tyson, Martha (Ellicott) 1795-1873. 32917,
    (45211A), (55505), note after 97651
Tyson, Philip Thomas, 1799-1877. 45158,
    83706, 97652
Tyssod de Patot, Simon, b. 1655. 97653
Tythe no Gospel maintenance, for Gospel
    ministers. 41763
Tythingman. pseud. Remarks on the ob-
    servation of the Lord's Day. see Wyman
    Rufus. supposed author
Tytler, James, 1747-1805. 97654-97656
Tytler, Patrick Fraser, 1791-1848. 67599,
    67657-67659
Tytler's poem. 97655

U

U., A. G. pseud. tr. 9604, 27215, note after
    97659
U., E. P. pseud. Some casual papers. see
    Nye, G.
U., Y. A. pseud. Carta de un sacerdote.
U. A. O. D. see United Ancient Order of
    Druids.
U. L. A. see United League of America.
U. S. A tale of Upper Canada. (37962)
Ubanumpa isht vtta vhicha hvt Westminsta.
    80728
Ubelin, Georgius. ed. (66478), (66480)
Uber Auswanderungen. 2438
Uber Brasilien. 7533
Uber Chile. 5217
Uber das Klima der Argentinischen Republik.
    9350
Ueber das Klima von Buenos Aires. 9351
Ueber den Aufstand der Englischen Colonien in
    Amerika. 97665
Ueber den Cortex Adstringens Brasil. 47982
Ueber den Einfluss des Separatismus. (77151)
Uber den gegenwatigen Zustand der Geographie
    von Sud-Amerika. 4000
Uber den gegenwartigen Zustand der Hudsonsbay
    97703
Ueber den geselzichen Zustand der Negersklaven
    in Westindien. 68977
Ueber den jetzigen Nordamericanischen Krieg.
    89761
Ueber d. Negersklaverei in d. Vereinigten
    Staaten. 97666
Uber Deutsche Colonisation in Mexico. 6138
Ueber die alt-Amerikanischen Denkmaler.
    7457
Ueber die altesten Karten des neuen Continents.
    (27261)
Ueber die altesten Volkerstamme. 48686
Ueber die Amerikanische Pflanzen Agave und
    Begonia. 2982
Uber die Anlegung. 5521
Ueber die Auswanderungen nach Amerika.
    29518
Uber die Aztekischen Ortsnamen. 9531
Ueber die Bedeutung der ersten Kampfes.
    28180

Unanue, Jose Hipolito. 61130, 85681, 97711-
    97721 see also Peru. Ministerio de
    Hacienda Publica.
Unanue, Jose Hipolito. supposed author
    60804, note after 97719
Unavailing cry. 13246
Unavoidable ignorance preferable to corrupt
    Christianity. 83610
Unbegreifliche Ereignisse und geheimniszvolle
    Thaten. 63576
Unbekante Neue Welt. 50087, 1st note after
    97721
Uvbeleevers preparing for Christ. 32862
Unbelief detected and condemned. 95165
Unbeliever. pseud. Practical language inter-
    preted. see Smith, Eunice.
Unbiased Irishman. pseud. Orangeism exposed.
    97722
Unbiased view of the American crisis. 32925
Unbridled tongue. 12331
Unca Eliza Winkfield. pseud. see Winkfield,
    Mrs. Unca Eliza. pseud.
Uncas, Old John. Mohegan Indian Chief
    appellant 15749-15750
Uncas, Young John. Mohegan Indian Chief
    appellant 15750
Uncas and Miantonomoh. 92153
Uncertain doom of kingdoms. 18757
Uncertainty of a death-bed repentance. 14373
Uncle. pseud. Dialogue between an uncle and
    his kinsman. 97723
Uncle, T. 85247
Uncle Ben. pseud. Brief sketch of the life
    of Charles Baron Metcalfe. see
    Crofton, Walter Cavendish.
Uncle Daniel. pseud. Traits of character.
    see Wrifford, Alison or Anson.
Uncle John. pseud. Uncle John's stories.
    97724
Uncle John's stories for good California
    children. 97724
Uncle Juvinell. pseud. Farmer boy. see
    Heady, Morrison.
Uncle Ned. pseud. Stories of the fourth of
    July. 92334
Uncle Philip. pseud. Adventures of Daniel
    Boone. see Hawks, Francis Lister,
    1798-1866. supposed author
Uncle Philip. pseud. American forest. see
    Hawks, Francis Lister, 1798-1866.
Uncle Philip. pseud. Conversations with the
    children about the whale fisher and
    Polar Seas. see Hawks, Francis List,
    1798-1866.
Uncle Philip. pseud. Conversations with the
    children about Virginia. see Hawks,
    Francis Lister, 1798-1866.
Uncle Philip. pseud. History of the United
    States, no. 2. see Hawks, Francis
    Lister, 1798-1866.
Uncle Philip. pseud. History of the United
    States: N°. III. see Hawks, Francis
    Lister, 1798-1866.
Uncle Philip. pseud. Lost Greenland.
    (28652)
Uncle Philip. pseud. Uncle Philip's conversa-
    tions with young persons. see Hawks,
    Francis Lister, 1798-1866.
Uncle Philip. pseud. Uncle Philip's conversa-
    tions with young persons. History of
    Virginia. see Hawks, Francis Lister,
    1798-1866.
Uncle Philip's conversations. (6371), 82858
Uncle Philip's conversations about the lost
    colonies of Greenland. (28652)

Uncle Philip's conversations . . . about the
    trees of America. 30962, 1st note after
    97724
Uncle Philip's conversations with the children
    about Massachusetts. 97725
Uncle Philip's conversations with the children
    about New York. (30966), 3d note after
    97724
Uncle Philip's conversations with the children
    about the whale fishery and Polar Seas.
    30971, 2d note after 97725
Uncle Philip's conversations with the children
    about Virginia. 30970, 2d note after
    97726, 2d note after 100480
Uncle Philip's conversations with the young
    people about the whale fisher and polar
    regions. 97726
Uncle Philip's conversations with young persons.
    97725
Uncle Richard. pseud. Northern regions.
    55829, 3d note after 97726
Uncle Richard's relation of Captain Parry's
    voyages. 55829, 3d note after 97726
Uncle Robin, in his cabin in Virginia. 58154
Uncle Sam and his country. 58260
Uncle Sam series for American children.
    91067
Uncle Sam's debts. 57122
Uncle Sam's emancipation. 92453-92454
Uncle Sam's farm fence. 49126
Uncle Sam's pecularities. 4776
Uncle Solomon and the Homan family. 97727
Uncle Solon's almanac. 88276
Uncle Tim. 92448
Uncle Tim, and other tales. 92455
Uncle Tim and Uncle Jaw. 92456
Uncle Tom at home. 203, 92624
Uncle Tom in England. note after 92624
Uncle Tom in Paris. 30616, note after 92624
Uncle Timitudes. 92586
Uncle Tom's cabin. 203, 17545, 18590, 21926,
    30616, 31276, 31432-31433, 51428,
    59532, (65684)-65685, 69680, 79130-
    79131, (81837), 84812-84813, 90880,
    92396, 92411-92412, 92521, 92522, 92424-
    92425, 92430, 92452, 92458-92501, 92502-
    92513, 92616, 92624-note after 92624,
    95491, 4th note after 95514
Uncle Tom's Cabin and Relief Society, Amher-
    stsburgh, Ontario. 70835
"Uncle Tom's cabin" as it is. 84812, note
    after 92624
Uncle Tom's cabin as it is, or, life at the
    south. 84813, note after 92624
Uncle Tom's cabin, Bleak house, slavery and
    the slave trade. 19580, 91234, note
    after 92624
"Uncle Tom's cabin" contrasted with Buckingham
    Hall. 17545, note after 92624
[Uncle Tom's cabin, in Armenian.] 92514
[Uncle Tom's cabin in German.] 92566
Uncle Tom's cabin in ruins. 7982, note after
    92624
[Uncle Tom's cabin translated into Greek.]
    92581
[Uncle Tom's cabin translated into Hindustani.]
    92582
[Uncle Tom's cabin translated into Roumanian.]
    92600
[Uncle Tom's cabin translated into Roumanian
    from the French of L. Pilatte.] 92599
[Uncle Tom's cabin translated into Russian.]
    92601-92602
[Uncle Tom's cabin translated into Serbian.]
    92603

Uncle Tom's companions. 21926, 92479, note after 92624

"Uncle Tom's" many editors. 51458, note after 92624

Uncle true, songster. 97728

Unconditional loyalty. 4574

Unconditional Union Central Committee, New York. 54040

Unconditional Union Party. Maryland. 43784, (44366), 45197

Unconditional Union Party. Maryland. State Central Committee, Baltimore. 43785, 45197

Unconditional Union State Central Committee, Baltimore. see Unconditional Union Party. Maryland. State Central Committee, Baltimore.

Unconnected Whig. pseud. Unconnected Whig's address to the public. 97729

Unconnected Whig's address to the public. 97729

Unconquerable, all conquering, & more than conquering souldier. 56385

Unconstitutionality of Congressional action. 25963

Unconstitutionality of slavery. 89617

Unconstitutionality of slavery, including parts first and second. 89618

Unconstitutionality of the fugitive act. 58181

Unconstitutionality of the fugitive slave act. 26130

Unconstitutionality of the laws of Congress. 89619

Unconstitutionality of the nine million debt bill. 59273

Uncrowned nation. 9103

Uncultivated heritage. 2400

Unda, Pablo Victor. 87167, 97730

Undeceived Englishman. 23756

Undelivered speech on executive arrests. 34727

Under canvas. (64024)

Under-currents of Wall-Street. 37767

Under his banner. 58683

Under-ground railroad. 48735

Under the cactus flag. 83682

Under the stars. 30190

Under the sun. 75547

Under the willows and other poems. 42438

Under-world of the great city. 22223

Undercliff. 104514

Undergraduate of Jesus College, Oxford. pseud. Io triumphe! 34967, 63595, 99249

Undergraduate of Jesus College, Oxford. pseud. Poem upon Admiral Vernon. 34967, 63595, 99249

Undergraduates of Bowdoin College. see Bowdoin College, Brunswick, Me. Undergraduates.

Underhil, E. B. ed. 104332

Underhill, --------, fl. 1866. 41298

Underhill, Abraham I. respondent 98438

Underhill, Andrew. 97731-97732

Underhill, David Harris. 97733

Underhill, Edward Fitch, 1830-1898. 95594

Underhill, Edward Fitch, 1830-1898. reporter 53863

Underhill, John. 97733

Underhill, Joshua. respondent 98438

Underhill, Joshua S. complainant 104500 see also Friends, Society of. New York Monthly Meeting. Property Committee. complainants

Underhill, Samuel. 97734

Underhill, Solomon. 97735

Underhill, Thomas. 97736

Underhill, Updike. 97615

Underhill Society of America. 97733

Underrattelse om den Fordna Svenska Kolonien i Norra Amerika. 94855

Undersigned, a Committee of the Board of Managers of the Washington National Monument Society, respectfully address you. 102033

Undersigned Citizens of the State of Vermont. petitioners see Vermont. Citizens. petitioners

Undersigned citizens of the state of Vermont . . . not to express at least, a distrust in the restrictive measures. 99207

Undersigned, citizens of the town of Providence, respectfully shew. 97951

Undersigned have entered into an association. 88015

Undersigned, Plenipotentiaries from the republic of Texas to the United States of America, respectfully present. 94974

Undersogelse om Amerikas opdagelse har mereskadet end gavnet het menneskelige kion? 13512

Undersogelese-reise til Ostkysten af Gronland. (28178)

Undersogelsereize til Ostkysten af Gronland i aarene 1828-31. 62945

Understanding of church music. 91815

Underwood, A. B. 37717

Underwood, Alvan. 97737

Underwood, James. 97738

Underwood, Joseph Rogers. 97739-97740

Underwood, Nathan. 92108, 97741

Underwriter. pseud. Opinion of the Supreme Judicial Court of Massachusetts. see Wells, Samuel Adams.

Underwriters and Merchants of the City of Baltimore. petitioners see Baltimore. Underwriters and Merchants. petitioners

Undeveloped northern portion of the American continent. 78485

Undiano y Gastelu, Sebastian. 97742

Undoubted art of thriving. 20589

Undoubted certainties. (46567)

Une annee de sejour a Londres. 23923, 73377

Unentbehrliche Buch fur die Duetschen Buerger in Nord America. 97743

Unentbehrlicher Rathgeber fur Stadt und land. 68349

Unequal conflict. 97744

Unexpected hostile attack. 1941

Unexpected observations on the writings of our present scribblers. 67166

Unfaithful hearers detected & warned. 101174

Unfeigned and hearty lover of England. pseud. Some seasonable and modest thoughts. see K., C. pseud.

Unfeigned friend. pseud. Some meditations. see Winthrop, Wait Still.

Unfortunate Englishman, or, a faithful narrative. 14096, 14098, note after 97744

Unfortunate Englishman; or a narrative. 32703

Unfortunate hero; a Pindaric ode. 65528, 97745

Unfortunate prisoner. pseud. Journal. see Egerton, Charles Calvert.

Unfortunate shipwright. 3403

Ung-eish-neut Teu-au-geh neh-huh yoh-weh-neut-dah Eng-lish. 80704

Ungar, Robert d'. see D'Ungar, Robert.

Ungava. 2952

Ungedruckten Handschrift der Verfassers. 104708

Ungeheuchelte theologische Unterredung. 97746

Ungewitter, F. H. <u>tr</u>. 21187, 35180, 92560, 92568

Ungodly nations doomed. 90443

Unhang der Spanischen Monarchi Camoanellae. 10201

Unhappiness of England as to its trade by sea and land. (64644)

Unhappy beggar. 27615, 65465

Unhappy life of Stephen Frothingham. 90902

Uniacke, Crofton. 97747

Uniacke, R. J. <u>ed</u>. 56192

Unico asilo de las republicas Hispano Ameri-canas. 97748

Uniform and dress of the army of the Con-federate States. 15424

Uniform and dress of the navy of the Con-federate States. 15425

Uniform and dress of the officers of the volunteer forces. 87371

Uniform dress for the students of Yale College. 105840

Uniform divorce laws. 84516

Uniform national currency. By a western banker. 97749

Uniform national currency. Speech of Hon. John Sherman. 80389

Uniform of the army of the republic of Texas. 95057-95058

Uniform of the militia of South Carolina. 87372

Uniform record of all political parties in Maine. (82570)

Uniform social laws, a lecture. 84516

Uniform system of public instruction. 45137

Uniform trade list circular. 11755

Uniform trade list directory. 11755

Uniformity of gold coinage. (73973)

Uniformity of legislation. 84516

Unio reformantium sive examen Hoornbecki. 5111

Union de Cuba, Miguel Tacon y Rosique, Marques de la. <u>see</u> Tacon y Rosique, Miguel, Marques de la Union de Cuba, 1777-1854.

Union (Paris) 12347

Union a blessing. 49036

Union. A poem. 42708

Union a revocable compact. 71376

Union. A sermon . . . in . . . Savannah. (13285)

Union Academy, Philadelphia. Trustees. 62347

Union Academy, Plainfield, N. H. Charter. 97750

Union, activity and freedom. 86869

Union Ameircaine. 89283

Union Americaine apres la guerre. 63742

Union Americaine et l'Europe. 69624

Union Americana. 85726

Union among the friends of religious order. 92264

Union: an address by the Hon. Daniel S. Dickinson. 20031

Union and American. 8432

Union and anti-slavery speeches. 20816

Union and emancipation. 3405

Union and freedom: a drama, in three acts. 91504

Union and freedom without compromise. 12200

Union and liberty. An ode. 97755

Union and liberty. Power of Congress in relation to the slaves. (40254)

Union and protection tracts. 97751

Union and secession. 10272

Union and State Rights Meeting, Berkley, S. C., 1831. 97754

Union and State-Rights Parties of Georgia. 35444

Union and State Rights Party of South Carolina. <u>see</u> State Rights and Free Trade Party of Charleston, S. C.

Union and the human race. 42714

Union and the war. 80083

Union and the state-rights parties. 12223

Union annual. 1837. 97756

Union Anti-Lecompton Mass Meeting of the Citizens of Erie County, Buffalo, N. Y., 1858. <u>see</u> Erie County, N. Y. Union Anti-Lecompton Mass Meeting, Buffalo, 1858.

Union as our fathers designed it. 64763

Union Bank of Florida. Board of Directors. 97757

Union Bank of Louisiana. 97758

Union Bank of Louisiana. Charter. 97758

Union Bank of Louisiana. Directors. 97758

Union Bank of Maryland. 97760

Union Bank of Maryland. Charter. 45081, 97760

Union Bank of Maryland. Stockholders. 45081

Union Bank of South-Carolina. 97759

Union Bank of South-Carolina. Board of Directors. 97759

Union Bank of South-Carolina. Charter. 97759

Union Bank of Tennessee. Stockholders, Philadelphia. <u>petitioners</u> 94811

Union Bank of the State of Tennessee. 94811

Union Bank of the State of Tennessee. Board of Directors. 94812, note after 97760

Union Bank of the State of Tennessee. Charter. 94812, note after 97760

Union banner. 97761

Union Baptist Association. <u>see</u> Baptists. Connecticut. Union Baptist Association.

Union Benevolent and Trade Society, New Brunswick, N. J. 97764

Union Benevolent Association, Philadelphia. 62184, 62348-62349, note after 97764-97765

Union Benevolent Association, Philadelphia. Executive Board. 62349

Union Benevolent Association, Philadelphia. Ladies' Branch. 92349, note after 97794

Union: being a condemnation of Mr. Helper's scheme, 97763

Union Brigade of New Jersey. <u>see</u> New Jersey. Militia. Union Brigade.

Union campaign documents. 79530, 89495

Union canal. 95381

Union Canal Company of Pennsylvania. (60749)-60750, 96749-96750, note after 97766-97767 <u>see also</u> Delaware and Schuylkill Canal Navigation. Schuylkill and Sus-quehanna Navigation Company.

Union Canal Company of Pennsylvania. <u>petitioners</u> 58312, 60750, note after 97766

Union Canal Company of Pennsylvania. <u>plaintiffs</u> 97771

Union Canal Company of Pennsylvania. Charter. 58312, (60749), note after 97766

Union Canal Company of Pennsylvania. Com-mittee of Bondholders. 60750

Union Canal Company of Pennsylvania. Engineer. 60750

Union Canal Company of Pennsylvania. Engineers. 60750

Union Canal Company of Pennsylvania. President. 60750, note after 97766-97767 see also Watson, Joseph, fl. 1819.

Union Canal Company of Pennsylvania. President and Managers. 60750, note after 97766

Union Canal Company of Pennsylvania vs. William W. Young and James McAllister, Jr., Joseph Fox and Philip M. Price. 97771

Union Canal Convention, Harrisburg, Pa., 1838. 60750, note after 97766

Union Canal Convention, Harrisburg, Pa., 1838. petitioners 97770

Union Church, Boston. see Boston. Union Church.

Union Church, Groton, Mass. see Groton, Mass. Union Church.

Union Church, Worcester, Mass. see Worcester, Mass. Union Church.

Union Club of Philadelphia. 62350

Union College, Schenectady, N. Y. 24838, 25927, (59006), 97774-97775, 97782-97783, 97786, 97788, 97799

Union College, Schenectady, N. Y. Adelphic Society. 97790

Union College, Schenectady, N. Y. Adelphic Society. Library. 97789

Union College, Schenectady, N. Y. Anti-slavery Society. 97799

Union College, Schenectady, N. Y. Association of Graduates. see Union College, Schenectady, N. Y. Graduates Association.

Union College, Schenectady, N. Y. Bible Society. 97791

Union College, Schenectady, N. Y. Charter. 97776

Union College, Schenectady, N. Y. Class of 1827. 97774

Union College, Schenectady, N. Y. Class of 1828. 97774

Union College, Schenectady, N. Y. Class of 1830. 97774

Union College, Schenectady, N. Y. Class of 1831. 97774

Union College, Schenectady, N. Y. Class of 1833. 97774

Union College, Schenectady, N. Y. Class of 1840. Senate. 97792

Union College, Schenectady, N. Y. Equitable Union. 97793

Union College, Schenectady, N. Y. Graduates Association. 97784

Union College, Schenectady, N. Y. Library. 97794

Union College, Schenectady, N. Y. One of the Graduates, 1806. pseud. see Van Vechten, Teunis A. supposed author

Union College, Schenectady, N. Y. Phi Beta Kappa Society. see Phi Beta Kappa. New York Alpha, Union College.

Union College, Schenectady, N. Y. Philomathean Society. 97798

Union College, Schenectady, N. Y. Philomathean Society. Library. 97797

Union College, Schenectady, N. Y. Students. 97778

Union College, Schenectady, N. Y. Students. defendants. 97773

Union College, Schenectady, N. Y. Trustees. 89345, 97777, 97783, 97787

Union College, Schenectady, N. Y. Trustees. defendants 97779-97781

Union College, Schenectady, N. Y. Trustees. Committee on Finance. 97785

Union College, Schenectady, N. Y. Trustees. Select Committee. 97785

Union College, Schenectady, N. Y. Undergraduates. 58927, 97799

Union College, a fragment, poem. 97788

Union Colonization Society, Wilmington, Del. see Wilmington Union Colonization Society, Wilmington, Del.

Union Commission of Maryland. see Maryland Union Commission.

Union Committee, New York, 1834. 26399, 51938, 54653, 69918, note after 97799 see also Meeting of the signers of the Memorial to Congress, New York, 1834.

Union Committee of the Sunday Schools of the Three Baptist Societies in Boston. see Baptists. Boston. Union Committee of the Sunday Schools of the Three Baptist Societies.

Union Company. Charter. 97814

Union Congregational Anti-slavery Society, Providence, R. I. 97800

Union Congregational Church, Portland, Me. see Portland, Me. Union Congregational Church.

Union Congregational Church, Providence, R. I. see Providence, R. I. Union Congregational Church.

Union Congressional Committee, 1875. see Republican Congressional Committee, 1875.

Union Congressional Executive Committee, 1875. see Republican Congressional Committee, 1875.

Union Considered as the only safety of the United States. 102209

Union Convention, Worcester, Mass., 1860. see Union Party. Massachusetts. Convention, Worcester, 1860.

Union Convention, of Ohio, 1862. see National Union Party. Ohio. Convention, 1862.

Union de l'eglise et de l'etat dans la Nouvelle Angleterre. 97802

Union Defence Committee of the Citizens of New York. see New York (City) Union Defence Committee.

Union des provinces de l'Amerique Britannique du Nord. 11560

Union District, South Carolina. Citizens. petitioners 47667

Union, disunion, and reunion. 57826

Union Female Missionary Society, Philadelphia. Managers. 97801

Union Ferry Company of Brooklyn. Proceedings and testimony. 8291

Union Fire Company, Washington, D. C. 101955

Union for Christian Work, Providence, R. I. (66376)

Union, for the Relief and Improvement of the Colored Race, Taunton, Mass. see Taunton Union, for the Relief and Improvement of the Colored Race.

Union for the sake of the union. 36831

Union forever. 32653

Union foundations: a study of American nationality as a fact of science. 33844

Union Gold-Mining Company. 97803

Union Gold-Mining Company. Directors. 97803

Union harmony. 32475

Union in Christ. 85340

Union in the church and the nation. 73969, 73974

Union Philosophical Society, Dickinson College.
see Dickinson College, Carlisle, Pa.
Union Philosophical Society.

Union policy contrasted with that of the
President. (80144)

Union Potomac Company. Charter. 97814

Union prayer meeting, held by the Christian
Commission. 45383

Union preserved. 43467

Union Press. firm publishers 105576

Union principle through un-denominational not
anti-denominational. 6076

Union Prioners at Camp Ford, Tyler, Texas.
see Tyler, Texas. Camp Ford (Confederate Military Prison) Union Prisoners.

Union question. 68057

Union Railway Company vs. God's law. 10154

Union rangers. 72131

Union Ratification Meeting, San Francisco,
1867. see San Francisco. Union
Ratification Meeting, 1867.

Union record. (31847)

Union Reform Party of South Carolina.
88090

Union Reform Party of South Carolina.
Executive Committee. 88090

Union Relief Association, Baltimore. 3017

Union Relief Association, Baltimore. Executive Committee. 3017

Union Republican Congressional Committee,
1868. see Republican Congressional
Committee, 1868.

Union Republican Party of Connecticut. see
Democratic Party. Connecticut.

Union Republican Party of South Carolina.
see Republican Party. South Carolina.

Union Republican State Convention, Williamsport, Pa., 1867. see Republican Party.
Pennsylvania. Convention, Williamsport,
1867.

Union Republican ticket for 1820. 97815

Union restored by legal authority. (33876)

Union Safety Committee. 79007

Union School and Children's Home, Moyamensing, Pa. see Moyamensing Union
School, and Children's Home, Moyamensing, Pa.

Union School and Children's Home, Philadelphia. see Southern Home for Destitute Children, Philadelphia.

Union School, Lockport, N. Y. see Lockport Union School, Lockport, N. Y.

Union School, Salem, Ohio. see Salem Union
School, Salem, Ohio.

Union.—Secession. 22390

Union Seminary, Richmond, Va. see Richmond, Va. Union Theological Seminary.

Union Seminary, Richmondville, N. Y. see
Richmondville Union Seminary, Richmondville, N. Y.

Union Seminary bulletin. 97820

Union sketch-book. 27623

Union.-Slavery.-Secession. 10049

Union Society, Boston. 97816

Union Society, Hamilton College. see Hamilton
College, Clinton, N. Y. Union Society.

Union Society, Newburyport, Mass. 97817

Union Society, Savannah. 65381

Union song book. 97818

Union: speech of William H. Seward in the
Senate. (79589)

Union Square and the Sanitary Commission.
73975

Union State Central Committee. Maryland.
see Republican Party. Maryland.
State Central Committee.

Union State Central Committee. Pennsylvania.
see Republican Party. Pennsylvania.
State Central Committee.

Union State Central Committee. Proceedings
Dec. 16, 1863. 45382

Union State Executive Committee. Maryland.
see Union Party. Maryland. State
Executive Committee.

Union State Executive Committee versus the
Union City Convention. 45382

Union Tabernacle or movable tent-church.
41873

Union Temporary Home for Children, Philadelphia. 62356

"Union, the constitution, and the laws."
Message of Governor Seymour. 79660

Union, the constitution and the laws. Secession, a national crime and curse. 21808

Union—and constitution—peace. A thanksgiving
sermon. 35440

Union the paramount good. (32478)

Union, the true source of disunion. 85324

Union Theological Seminary, New York. see
New York (City) Union Theological
Seminary.

Union Theological Seminary, Prince Edward
County, Va. see Richmond, Va. Union
Theological Seminary.

Union Theological Seminary, Richmond, Va.
see Richmond, Va. Union Theological
Seminary.

Union Theological Seminary of the Presbyterian
Church, Prince Edward County, Va. see
Richmond, Va. Union Theological
Seminary.

Union to be restored. 19819, 21430

Union to Christ, and to His church. 85335

Union Turnpike Road. President, Directors,
and Company. plaintiff 97890, 97822

Union University, Schenectady, N. Y. see
Union College, Schenectady, N. Y.

Union, victory and freedom. 47063

Union Village, Ohio. 97882

Union Village, Ohio. United Society. see
Shakers. Union Village, Ohio.

Union Village, R. I. Smithfield Academy. see
Smithfield Academy, Union Village, R. I.

Union Village Academy, Troy, N. Y. 97823

Union volunteer's hand-book. 91922

Union vor dem Richterstuhle des gesunden
Menschenverstandes. 93113

Union wie sein soll. 51294

Union with France a greater evil than union
with Britain. 7367

Union with the Son of God by faith. 46235

Unionist. pseud. Abolition and secession.
81714-81715

Unionist—extra, Charleston, Dec. 22, 1832.
88087-88088, 1st-2d notes after 97754

Unionists versus traitors. 10249

Unipersonal con intermedios de music. 97824

Unipersonal del General Don Antonio Lopez
de Santa-Anna. 97825

Unipersonal que represento D. Antonio Rosal.
97826

Unipkautsit. 3703

Unique: a series of portraits of eminent
persons. 101816

Unis labor multorum laborem allevat. 62743

Unitarian. pseud. Charge of ignorance and
misrepresentation proved against "A
lover of Cudworth and Truth." see
Upham, Charles Wentworth.

Unitarian. pseud. Charge of ignorance and
misrepresentation proved against Rev.

George B. Cheever. see Upham, Charles Wentworth.

Unitarian. pseud. Letter to the editor of the Charleston observer. see Upham, Charles Wentworth.

Unitarian. pseud. Salem controversy. see Upham, Charles Wentworth.

Unitarian. 97827

Unitarian advocate. 97828

Unitarian advocate, and religious miscellany. 97829

Unitarian Association, Boston. see Unitarian Churches. Massachusetts. Boston Association.

Unitarian Association in the County of Worcester, Mass. see Unitarian Churches. Massachusetts. Worcester Association.

Unitarian Association of Maine. see Unitarian Churches. Maine. Church Association.

Unitarian Association of New-Hampshire. see Unitarian Churches. New Hampshire. Association.

Unitarian autumnal convention, a sermon. 31755

Unitarian Body, London. (81841), 82050

Unitarian Book and Pamphlet Society. 97830

Unitarian Book and Tract Society, Charleston. 12092

Unitarian Book Society, Baltimore. see Baltimore Unitarian Book Society.

Unitarian Book Society, New York. see New York Unitarian Book Society.

Unitarian Christianity. 13460

Unitarian Church Association of Maine. see Unitarian Churches. Maine. Church Association.

Unitarian Church of Charleston, S. C. see Charleston, S. C. Unitarian Church.

Unitarian Churches. U. S. 89002 see also National Conference of Unitarian and Other Christian Churches.

Unitarian Churches. U. S. National Convention, 1865. see National Unitarian Convention, New York, 1865.

Unitarian Churches. U. S. Western Association. 102993

Unitarian Churches. Maine. Church Association. Annual Meeting, 1st., Bangor, 1853. 43914

Unitarian Churches. Maine. Church Association. Convention, Portland, 1852. 43914

Unitarian Churches. Massachusetts. Boston Association. 97835

Unitarian Churches. Massachusetts. Worcester Association. 105389, 105415

Unitarian Churches. New Hampshire. Association. 52890

Unitarian Churches. One Hundred and Seventy-Three Unitarian Ministers. petitioners see Disciples of Christ. Rhode Island and Massachusetts Conferences.

Unitarian denomination—past and present. 66765

Unitarian: devoted to the statement, explanation, and defence of the principles. 97831

Unitarian essayist. 97832

Unitarian Home Mission, New Orleans. 53319

Unitarian miscellany and Christian monitor. (49063), 88970, 88972, 88975, 89002, 89006, 89009, 89014, 97833

Unitarian monitor. 97834

Unitarian of Baltimore. pseud. Eighth and ninth letters. see Sparks, Jared, 1789-1866.

Unitarian of Baltimore, pseud. Fourth and fifth letters. see Sparks, Jared, 1789-1866.

Unitarian of Baltimore. pseud. Second and third letters. see Sparks, Jared, 1789-1866.

Unitarian of Baltimore. pseud. Sixth and seventh letters. see Sparks, Jared, 1789-1866.

Unitarian of New York. pseud. Appeal from the denunciation. 45465

Unitarian register and universalist leader. 93729, 93827, 101391, 105441

Unitarian review and religious magazine. (70413)

Unitarian Society, Philadelphia. see Philadelphia. First Unitarian Society.

Unitarian Society, Washington, D. C. see Washington, D. C. Unitarian Society.

Unitarian Sunday School Society, Boston. 93743

Unitarianism an exclusive system. 16336-16337

Unitarianism delineated. (12406)

Unitarianism in America. 97835

Unitarianism in Brooklyn. 66766

Unitarianism not a negative system. 26536

Unitarianism; or the doctrine of the Trinity confuted by scripture. 97836

Unitarianism unmasked. 92029

Unitary Building Association, Philadelphia. see Philadelphia Unitary Building Association.

Unitas. pseud. Friendly letter to a member of the Episcopal Church in Maryland. 97837

Unitas Fratrum. see United Brethren.

Unite or fall. 97838

United Agricultural Societies of Virginia. petitioners 102201

United Agricultural Societies of Virginia. Delegation. 94492

United Ancient Order of Druids. Pennsylvania. Grand Board, Philadelphia. 60127

United Ancient Order of Druids. Pennsylvania. Covenant Lodge. 60752

United Ancient Order of Druits. Pennsylvania. Pride of Oak Lodge. 60752

United Associate Synod of Scotland. 98181

United Bands of Oto and Missouri Indians. see Missouri Indians. and Oto Indians.

United Baptist Association. see Baptists. North Carolina. United Baptist Association.

United Baptist Churches of Christ in Virginia. see Baptists. Virginia. Baptist General Committee.

United Brethren. 2462, 2463, 7846, (7935), 12477, 12891, 17418, 29010, 39979, 50522, 50523-50524, 51292-51293, 51692, 59984, 60753, 60766, 60786, 60932, 65035, 66467, (75836), 75905, 84358-84362, 84365, 86171, 86746, 88928, 93385-93386, 4th-6th notes after 97845, 97846, 97848, 97849, 97851-97852, 97855-97857, 97858, note after 97858, 97860, 1st note after 97862, 97863, 4th note after 97895, 100687, 106360, note after 106412 see also Bohemian Brethren. Congregation of God in the Spirit. Moravians.

United Brethren. Directors of the Missionary Concerns. petitioners 17977, 86170 see also Cunow, John G. petitioner

United Brethren. Missionaries. trs. 55362 see also Austen, C. A. tr. Latrobe, C. J. tr.

United Brethren. Society for Propagating the Gospel Among the Heathen. see Society of the United Brethren, for Propagating the Gospel Among the Heathen.

United Brethren. Antigua. Missionary Meeting, St. John's, 1840. 97848

United Brethren. England. Secretary. 97849 see also Latrobe, Christian Ignatius. United Brethren. Great Britain.

United Brethren. Great Britain. Deputies. 69853

United Brethren Great Britain. Deputies. petitioners 69731, 1st note after 97845, 97847

United Brethren. Pennsylvania. 2462-2463, 59958, 60766, 60786, 4th note after 97845

United Brethren. Pennsylvania. Dritten Confernz, 174½. 4th note after 97845

United Brethren. Pennsylvania. Vierte General-Versammlung, Germantown, 174½. 4th note after 97845

United Brethren. West Indies. 58940, 97850, 97858

United Brethren in Christ. 97864-97866

United Brethren Missionary Meeting, St. John's, Antigua, 1840. see United Brethren. Antigua. Missionary Meeting, St. John's, 1840.

United Brethren's Historical Society. see Moravian Historical Society.

United Brethren's Missionary intelligencer, and religious miscellany. 60753, 97863

United Brethren's Missionary Society. 97859

United Brothers' Society, Brown University. see Brown University. United Brothers' Society.

United Christian Friends, New York. 97868

United Church of England and Ireland in Canada. see Church of England in Canada.

United Colonies of New England. (7962) see also New Haven (Colony)

United Colonies of New England. Commissioners. 22149, 45706, 51774, 53388, 59561, 63488, 83790, 104844

United Colonies of New England. Commissioners. President. 45706, 51774, 104844 see also Winthrop, Jonathan, 1588-1649.

United Colonies of New England. Interpreter-General to the Indians. 22149, 59561 see also Stanton, Thomas.

United Colonies of New England. Laws, statutes, etc. 63488, 90609

United Colony of Demerara & Essequibo. see Demerara.

United Companies Under the Name of the Philadelphia, Wilmington and Baltimore Rail Road Company. see Philadelphia, Wilmington and Baltimore Rail Road Company.

United Congregational Church, Newport, R. I. see Newport, R. I. United Congregational Church.

United Congregational Society, New Haven, Conn. see New Haven, Conn. United Congregational Society.

United Democracy for regular nominations. 611

United Domestic Missionary Society, New York. 54078, 97870 see also Convention of Delegates for the Formation of a Domestic Missionary Society, New York, 1822.

United Domestic Missionary Society, New York. Executive Committee. 54078, 97869

United Empire loyalist. pseud. Sir F. B. Head and Mr. Bidwell. 5258

United Empire minstrel. (79768)

United Evangelical Lutheran Synod, Philadelphia, 1785. see Evangelical Lutheran Ministerium of Pennsylvania and Adjoining States.

United Fire Club, Newport, R. I. 97871

United Fire Society, Boston (1773-1816) see Franklin United Fire Society, Boston.

United Fire Society, Boston (1789-   ) 97873

United Foreign Missionary Society (1817-1825) 97874 see also American Board of Commissioners for Foreign Missions.

United Foreign Missionary Society. Domestic Secretary. pseud. Letter to a member of Congress. 40394

United Fraternity, Dartmouth College. see Dartmouth College. United Fraternity.

United Fraternity's Library, Dartmouth College. see Dartmouth College. United Fraternity. Library.

United German Lutheran Churches in New York. see Vereinigte Deutsche Gesellschaften der Stadt New York.

United Illinois and Wabash Land Companies. 96, 34295-34296, 34314, 84577-84578

United Illinois and Wabash Land Companies. petitioners 34294-34296, 84577-84578, 2d-5th notes after 97876-97877

United Illinois and Wabash Land Companies. Agents. 84577-84578, 2d-3d notes after 97876 see also Morris, Robert, 1734-1806. Nicholson, John. Smith, William, 1727-1803. Steinmetz, John. Wilson, James, 1742-1798.

United Illinois and Wabash Land Companies. Council. petitioners 34294, 84577 see also Morris, Robert, 1734-1806. Nicholson, John. Smith, William, 1727-1803. Steinmetz, John.

United Illinois and Wabash Land Companies. President. 84577-84578, 2d-3d notes after 97876 see also Wilson, James, 1742-1798.

United Illinois and Wabash Land Companies. President. petitioner 34294, 84577 see also Wilson, James, 1742-1798. petitioner

United Illinois and Wabash Land Companies. Secretary. 34295, 4th note after 97876

United Insurance Company, in the City of New York. appellant 96896, 97879

United Insurance Company, in the City of New York. defendant 37475, 96813

United Insurance Company, in the City of New York. plaintiff 100777

United Insurance Company of New York. Charter. 97878

United Kingdom. 17818, note after 95370

United Mexican Mining Association. Court of Directors. 97880

United Mexican Mining Association. 97880

United Moravian Churches. Deputies. see United Brethren. Great Britain. Deputies.

United Nation of Chippewa, Ottawa, and Potawatomi Indians. see Chippewa Indians. Ottawa Indians. Potawatomi Indians.

United North and South Columbia. see Colombia.

United Order of Independent Odd Ladies. Samaritan Institute, No. 1, Boston. 75898

U. S.

U. S. Army. Courts Martial (Arbuthnot)'
1893-1895, 48077, 51782, 56758
U. S. Army. Courts Martial (Arnold) 2060-
2061
U. S. Army. Courts Martial (Bache) (2591)
U. S. Army. Courts Martial (C. Burbank)
(9196)
U. S. Army. Courts Martial (G. Burbank)
9197
U. S. Army. Courts Martial (B. M. Burne)
9726
U. S. Army. Courts Martial (P. Burne)
(9727)
U. S. Army. Courts Martial (Chambers)
(11802)
U. S. Army. Courts Martial (Cranston)
17409
U. S. Army. Courts Martial (Cushing)
18123
U. S. Army. Courts Martial (Drane) 20886
U. S. Army. Courts Martial (Eastman)
21689
U. S. Army. Courts Martial (Edmands)
21861
U. S. Army. Courts Martial (Fremont)
25840
U. S. Army. Courts Martial (Gardner)
26639
U. S. Army. Courts Martial (Gates) 26759
U. S. Army. Courts Martial (C. W. Hall)
29742
U. S. Army. Courts Martial (J. C. Hall)
(65814)
U. S. Army. Courts Martial (Hammond)
(30112), 30115, 30116, 2d note after
90723
U. S. Army. Courts Martial (Hastings)
30821
U. S. Army. Courts Martial (Henley)
(31343)-31344
U. S. Army. Courts Martial (Henshaw)
31426
U. S. Army. Courts Martial (Howe) 33328
U. S. Army. Courts Martial (Hull) 25045,
(33642), 33644-33646
U. S. Army. Courts Martial (King) 37854
U. S. Army. Courts Martial (Learned)
39537
U. S. Army. Courts Martial (Lee) 39711-
39713
U. S. Army. Courts Martial (Loring) 42094,
(42096)
U. S. Army. Courts Martial (Marston)
44824
U. S. Army. Courts Martial (Norwood)
(65814)
U. S. Army. Courts Martial (Osbon) 6230
U. S. Army. Courts Martial (Paulding)
(12825), 59185
U. S. Army. Courts Martial (Porter) 32653,
(36267), 64247
U. S. Army. Courts Martial (Ragland)
67490
U. S. Army. Courts Martial (Revere) 43179,
70180-70181
U. S. Army. Courts Martial (Runkle)
(74135)-74137
U. S. Army. Courts Martial (St. Clair)
(75021)
U. S. Army. Courts Martial (Sanderson)
76395
U. S. Army. Courts Martial (Schuyler)
78059
U. S. Army. Courts Martial (Sheldon)
80120

U. S. Army. Courts Martial (Six Militiamen)
56778
U. S. Army. Courts Martial (Smith) 82437
U. S. Army. Courts Martial (Stanwood)
90457
U. S. Army. Courts Martial (Talcott) 89356,
note before 94236A, 1st note after 96929
U. S. Army. Courts Martial (Treat) 96514
U. S. Army. Courts of Inquiry (Andre)
1453-(1458), 21296-21297, 83423, 96812
U. S. Army. Courts of Inquiry (Dyer) 21581
U. S. Army. Courts of Inquiry (Felt) 24207
U. S. Army. Courts of Inquiry (Ferris)
24188
U. S. Army. Courts of Inquiry (Gaines)
78420
U. S. Army. Courts of Inquiry (Harmar)
30401
U. S. Army. Courts of Inquiry (Latimer)
(36269)
U. S. Army. Courts of Inquiry (McDowell)
43193
U. S. Army. Courts of Inquiry (D. H. Miles)
48922
U. S. Army. Courts of Inquiry (S. D. Miles)
(36270)
U. S. Army. Courts of Inquiry (Pillow)
(52854), 62853-(62854)
U. S. Army. Courts of Inquiry (Ripley)
71527
U. S. Army. Courts of Inquiry (Scott)
78420-78421
U. S. Army. Courts of Inquiry (Voorkers)
100771
U. S. Army. Crockett's Regiment. 34301,
82960
U. S. Army. Department of Arizona. Medical
Director. 83367 see also Smith,
Joseph Rowe, 1831-1911.
U. S. Army. Department of Texas. Medical
Director. 83367 see also Smith,
Joseph Rowe, 1831-1911.
U. S. Army. Department of the Cumberland.
Headquarters. (73255)
U. S. Army. Department of the Cumberland.
Indiana Soldiers. see Indiana Soldiers
in the "Department of the Cumberland."
U. S. Army. Department of the Cumberland.
Quartermaster. 20588
U. S. Army. Department of the East.
26893
U. S. Army. Department of the Gulf. 9613,
53320
U. S. Army. Department of the Gulf. Bureau
of Free Labor. 16233
U. S. Army. Department of the Gulf.
Financial Commission of New Orleans,
1864. Majority. 53372
U. S. Army. Department of the Gulf.
Financial Commission of New Orleans,
1864. Minority. 53372
U. S. Army. Engineer Department. see
U. S. Army. Corps of Engineers.
U. S. Army. Engineers. see U. S. Army.
Corps of Engineers.
U. S. Army. General Headquarters. 74091
U. S. Army. General in Chief. 29883-
29884 see also Halleck, Henry Wager,
1815-1870.
U. S. Army. General of the Army. 53362
see also Grant, Ulysses Simpson,
Pres. U. S., 1822-1885.
U. S. Army. Hospital, York, Pa. (11147)
U. S. Army. Illinois Regiment. 32301,
82960

U. S. Army. Inspector General. 85188
see also Smyth, Alexander, 1765-1830.
U. S. Army. Judge Advocate General. see
U. S. Judge Advocate General's Office
(Army)
U. S. Army. Medical Department 2051,
25121, 39456-(39457), 83367
U. S. Army, Military Commission. Ander-
son. 1865. 3981
U. S. Army. Military Commission. Beall.
1865. 4109
U. S. Army. Military Commission. Bell.
1862. 8979
U. S. Army. Military Commission. Bowles.
1865. 96953
U. S. Army. Military Commission. Cantril.
1865. 9381
U. S. Army. Military Commission. Dexter.
1866. 9622
U. S. Army, Military Commission. Dodd.
1865. 96953
U. S. Army. Military Commission. Grenfell.
1865. 9381
U. S. Army. Military Commission. Lincoln's
Assassinators. 1865. 41180-41182,
41235, 66001, 88935
U. S. Army. Military Commission. McRae.
1867. 43648
U. S. Army. Military Commission. Marmaduke. 1865. 9381
U. S. Army. Military Commission. Morris.
1865. 9381
U. S. Army. Military Commission. Powers.
1867. (31083)
U. S. Army. Military Commission. Sander-
son. 1865. 76395
U. S. Army. Military Commission. Semmes.
1865. 9381
U. S. Army. Military Commission. Tolar.
1867. (31083)
U. S. Army. Military Commission. Travis.
1865. 9381
U. S. Army. Military Commission. Walsh.
1865. 9381
U. S. Army. Military Commission. Watkins.
1867. (31083)
U. S. Army. Military Railroads. Director
and General Managers. 42980 see also
McCallum, D. C.
U. S. Army. New Jersey Volunteers. 53209
U. S. Army. Officers. petitioners 389,
47646
U. S. Army. Officers and Soldiers. 87485
U. S. Army. Ordnance Board. 50531
U. S. Army. Ordnance Department. 49633,
68948, 71528-71529, (72488) see also
Ripley, James Wolfe.
U. S. Army. Pay Department. 68951
U. S. Army. Provost Martial (1st Congres-
sional District, New York) 67070
U. S. Army. Quartermaster's Department.
see U. S. Quartermaster's Depart-
ment.
U. S. Army. Recruiting Service. 68954
U. S. Army. Second Military District. see
also South Carolina.
U. S. Army. Second Military District.
Commander. 87394 see also Sickles,
Daniel Edgar, 1825-1914.
U. S. Army. Signal Corps. 51626
U. S. Army. Subsistence Department. see
U. S. Subsistence Department.
U. S. Army. Surgeon General. see U. S.
Surgeon General's Office.
U. S. Army. Twenty Sixth Michigan Infantry.
(57910)

U. S. Army. Western Army. 34301, 82960
U. S. Articles of Confederation. 1074, 1241,
1270-1271, 2142, 4023, 11701, 15770,
16086, 16100, 16113, 16119, 16133,
(23985), 23987, 23990, 28421, 32012,
34739, 42215, (45189), 51471, (52845),
56507, 59107, (59821), 60014, 68448,
70628, 70626, 70627, 94777, 99578,
100039
U. S. Articles of War. 2143, 20308, 26903,
31621, 45925, 74054-74066, 74069,
74080, 87704, 91428, 91431, 91437,
91442, 91454, 91458
U. S. Assistant Agent for the Reception of
Recaptured Negroes on the Western
Coast of Africa. 2641, 81740-81742
see also Bacon, E.
U. S. Attorney General. see U. S. Department of Justice.
U. S. Bank. see Bank of the United States.
U. S. Bill of Rights. see U. S. Constitution.
1st-10th Amendments.
U. S. Board of Commissioners, Appointed
Under the Eleventh Article of the Treaty
of Amity, Settlement, and Limits, Between
the United States and His Catholic Majesty,
Concluded at Washington, on the 22d of
February, 1819. see Board of Commis-
sioners, Under the Eleventh Article of
the Treaty of Amity, Settlement, and
Limits, Between the United States and
His Catholic Majesty, Concluded at
Washington, on the 22d of February, 1819.
U. S. Board of Commissioners, for the Ad-
justment of French Spoliation Claims.
37006
U. S. Board of Commissioners of Sinking
Fund. 69765, 96783-96784, 96817
U. S. Board of Commissioners on the Claims
Against Mexico. 69904
U. S. Board of Commissioners Under Article
Sixth of the Treaty Between Great
Britain and the United States, London,
Nov. 19, 1794. see Board of Commis-
sioners Under Article Sixth of the Treaty
Between Great Britain and the United
States, London, November 19, 1794.
U. S. Board of Commissioners Under the
Cherokee Treaty, 1835-1836. 90113
U. S. Board of Commissioners Under the
Convention With France, of the 4th of
July, 1831. see U. S. Board of Com-
missioners, for the Adjustment of French
Spoliation Claims.
U. S. Board of Commissioners Under the
Eleventh Article of the Treaty of Amity,
Settlement, and Limits, Between the
United States and His Catholic Majesty,
Concluded at Washington, on the 22d of
February, 1819. see Board of Commis-
sioners Under the Eleventh Article of
the Treaty of Amity, Settlement, and
Limits, Between the United States and
His Catholic Majesty, Concluded at
Washington, on the 22d of February,
1819.
U. S. Board of Engineers on Internal Improve-
ments. see U. S. Board of Internal
Improvement.
U. S. Board of Indian Commissioners.
(34609), 34680, 69763 see also U. S.
Office of Indian Affairs.
U. S. Board of Internal Improvement. 4946,
48087, 93538
U. S. Board of Land Commissioners. 76046
see also U. S. General Land Office.

U. S.   Board of Naval Examiners.   90809
U. S.   Board of Navy Commissioners.   74115
see also U. S. Navy Department.
U. S.   Board of Treasury.   (18173), 69948,
70072 see also U. S. Treasury
Department.
U. S.   Board of Trustees of the Sinking Fund.
see U. S. Board of Commissioners of
Sinking Fund.
U. S.   Board of War.   see U. S. War
Department.
U. S.   Board to Determine on a Standard of
Construction of the Pacific Railroad,
1866.   (69748)
U. S.   British and American Joint Commission
for the Final Settlement of the Claims
of the Hudson's Bay and Puget's Sound
Agricultural Companies.   see British
and American Joint Commission for the
Final Settlement of the Claims of the
Hudson's Bay and Puget's Sound Agri-
cultural Companies.
U. S.   Bureau of American Ethnology.   85007
U. S.   Bureau of Animal Industry.   84331-
84332
U. S.   Bureau of Construction.   84957 see
also Lenthall, John.
U. S.   Bureau of Education.   see U. S.
Office of Education.
U. S.   Bureau of Fisheries.   84223, 84228-
84232, 94125 see also Baird, Spencer
Fullerton, 1823-1887.
U. S.   Bureau of Indian Affairs.   see U. S.
Office of Indian Affairs.
U. S.   Bureau of Mines.   1067, (22054),
84296-84297 see also Raymond,
Rossiter W. Smith, Sumner S.
U. S.   Bureau of Naval Personnel.   41459
U. S.   Bureau of Navigation.   see U. S.
Bureau of Naval Personnel.
U. S.   Bureau of Ordnance.   18277, 69771,
84958 see also Wise, Henry Augustus,
1819-1869.
U. S.   Bureau of Ordnance and Hydrography.
33465, 33468
U. S.   Bureau of Refugees. Freedmen, and
Abandoned Lands.   (9127)
U. S.   Bureau of Refugees, Freedmen, and
Abandoned Lands. Board of Education
for Freedmen. Department of the Gulf.
(6053), 69762
U. S.   Bureau of Refugees, Freedmen, and
Abandoned Lands. Commissioner.
(33273)-(33274) see also Howard,
Oliver Otis, 1830-1909.
U. S.   Bureau of Refugees, Freedmen, and
Abandoned Lands. Department of
Kentucky. Chief Superintendent.   (74134)
see also Runkle, Benjamin O.
U. S.   Bureau of Refugees, Freedmen, and
Abandoned Lands. Department of
Tennessee and Arkansas.   14751, 21728-
21729
U. S.   Bureau of Refugees, Freedmen, and
Abandoned Lands. Department of
Tennessee and Arkansas. General
Superintendent.   21728-21729, 25746
see also Eaton, John.
U. S.   Bureau of Refugees, Freedmen, and
Abandoned Lands. Department of the
Gulf.   (6053) 69762
U. S.   Bureau of Refugees, Freedmen, and
Abandoned Lands. General Superintendent
of Negro Affairs.   37938 see also
Kinsman, J. Burnham.

U. S.   Bureau of Refugees, Freedmen, and
Abandoned Lands. General Superintendent
of Schools for Freedmen.   (9217), 25743
see also Alvord, John Watson, 1807-
1880.
U. S.   Bureau of Statistics.   see U. S. Navy
Department. Bureau of Statistics.
U. S.   Bureau of Steam Engineering.   (35249),
84959 see also Isherwood, Benjamin
Franklin, 1822-1915.
U. S.   Bureau of the Mint.   (7770)
U. S.   Bureau of the Mint. Director.   (43135),
(43137), 48055, 49329-49331, (69835),
85579 see also Snowden, James Ross,
1809-1878.
U. S.   Bureau of Topographical Engineers.
see U. S. Army. Corps of Topographical
Engineers. U. S. Engineer Department.
U. S.   Bureau of Yards and Docks.   84960
see also Smith, Joseph. USN
U. S.   Census.   5606
U. S.   Census, 1st, 1790.   11662, 19121,
70144-(70145)
U. S.   Census. 2d, 1800.   1074, 19121,
20994, (53576), (70145)-(70147), 102347
U. S.   Census. 3d, 1810.   (11663), 19121,
(20141), 44429, 79226, note just before
94178, 103306-103307
U. S.   Census. 4th, 1820.   512, 11664,
19121, (20141)
U. S.   Census. 5th, 1830.   11665-11666,
19121, (45273), (59966)
U. S.   Census. 6th, 1840.   8246, 11667-
11668, 19121, 17728, 20325, 30796,
31074, 32534, 36021, 49722, 53677,
74161, 74301, (81491)
U. S.   Census. 7th, 1850.   2923, 2925,
11669-11670, 11671-11676, 16115, 19119,
19121, (19171), 20150, (23786), 24485,
24488, 24490, 24492, (37426), 37430-
37433, (53030), (70447), 83935
U. S.   Census. 8th, 1860.   11673-11676,
20325, 37425, 37427-37428, 44428,
61804, 90810
U. S.   Census Office.   11670, 34731
U. S.   Census Office. Superintendent.   11670,
11672-11674, 19119, 37425, 37428,
37431 see also De Bow, James
Dunwoody Brownson, 1820-1867.   Kennedy,
Joseph Camp Griffith, 1813-1867.
U. S.   Centennial Exposition, Philadelphia,
1876.   see Philadelphia. Centennial
Exposition, 1876.
U. S.   Circuit Court (1st Circuit)   1480,
(12856), 24736, 27309, 28621, 36663,
39377, (41584), 42729, 44630, 45488,
46110, (51797), (58767), 69915, 74097,
90872, 92294, 92312, 92313, 92314,
92333, 93230, 93808, 96504, 96943-
96944, 96948-96949, 1st note after
96930A, 1st note after 96936, 103418,
104281, note after 104281, 105383
U. S.   Circuit Court (1st Circuit) Grand Jury.
92285, 92286, 92287, 92318-92319
U. S.   Circuit Court (2d Circuit)   1337, 2189,
2896, 5879, 24274, 28097, 31850, 53098,
53520, 74084, 79505, 79546, 79585,
81069, 81809, 82206, 84738, 84904,
88951, 93524, 96837, 96888, 101243
U. S.   Circuit Court (3d Circuit)   2210, 7970,
(11324), 12928, (25961), 27488, 51456,
(59056), 60597, (74111), 84728, 96866,
note after 101528, 103111, 103162,
103227

U. S. Circuit Court (4th Circuit) 9426, 9429, 9433-9435, 32341, 33371, 44873, 101907, 101975, 103854

U. S. Circuit Court (4th Circuit) Grand Jury. 104626

U. S. Circuit Court (5th Circuit) 7328, 12956, (26336), 83971, 84809

U. S. Circuit Court (6th Circuit) (16986), (61025), 84743, 93736, 94735, 105043

U. S. Circuit Court (7th Circuit) 87299-87301

U. S. Circuit Courts. 7904, (14989), 20148, 71828, 80359, (80361), 84842

U. S. Citizens. petitioners see U. S. petitioners

U. S. Citizens in Paris. Meeting, 1843. see Meeting of the Citizens of the United States in Paris, at the Athenee Royale, 1843.

U. S. Coast and Geodetic Survey. 2739, 13821, 18804, 28097, 30816, 30819, 49687, 52488, 57612, 65661, 85072

U. S. Coast and Geodetic Survey. Committee of Twenty. see American Association for the Advancement of Science. Committee of Twenty.

U. S. Coast and Geodetic Survey. Superintendent. 13821, 40338, 81541, 87396 see also Bache, Alexander Dallas, 1806-1867.

U. S. Coast Survey. see U. S. Coast and Geodetic Survey.

U. S. Collector of Customs, Charleston, S. C. see U. S. Customs House, Charleston. Collector.

U. S. Commissary General of Subsistence. see U. S. Subsistence Department.

U. S. Commission for the Revision of the Revenue System. see U. S. Revenue Commission, 1865-1866.

U. S. Commission for Investigations to Test the Practicability of Cultivating and Preparing Flax or Hemp as a Substitute for Cotton, 1863. 40356

U. S. Commission of Claims Against Mexico. 48369

U. S. Commission of Claims Under the Convention of February 8, 1853, Between the United States and Great Britain. see Commission of Claims Under the Convention of February 8, 1853, Between the United States and Great Britain.

U. S. Commission of Inquiry and Advice In Respect of the Sanitary Interests of the United States Forces. see United States Sanitary Commission.

U. S. Commission of Inquiry to Santo Domingo, 1871. 75191

U. S. Commission on Ordnance and Ordnance Stores. see U. S. War Department. Commission on Ordnance and Ordnance Stores.

U. S. Commission on the Keiler Vouchers, St. Louis. 37167

U. S. Commission to Examine the Causes of the Explosion of the Parrott Cannon During the First Attack on Fort Fisher. 19802

U. S. Commission to Negotiate with the Crow Indians in Montana Territory. 69773

U. S. Commission to Negotiate with the Ute Indians in Colorado Territory. 69774

U. S. Commission to Negotiate with the Shoshone Indians in Wyoming Territory. 69772

U. S. Commission to Run and Mark the Boundary Between the United States and Mexico, 1850-1851. 3745

U. S. Commission to the Paris Exposition, 1867. 23523, 40200, (42161), (51235)-51236, 55872, 56763, (58595), 73959, 83003 see also Hayes, John L. Hazard, George S. Hewitt, Abram S. Mudge, E. R. Norton, Charles Benjamin, 1825-1891. Nourse, B. F. Ruggles, Samuel B. Valentine, W. J.

U. S. Commissioner for Determining the Boundary Between the United States and the Possessions of His Catholic Majesty in America, 1796-1800. (22216)-22217 see also Ellicott, Andrew.

U. S. Commissioner for Treaty with the Chippewa Indians of the Upper Mississippi. 84862 see also Smith, William Rudolph, 1787-1868.

U. S. Commissioner of Agriculture. see U. S. Department of Agriculture.

U. S. Commissioner of Education. see U. S. Office of Education.

U. S. Commissioner of Fisheries. see U. S. Bureau of Fisheries.

U. S. Commissioner of Indian Affairs. see U. S. Office of Indian Affairs.

U. S. Commissioner of Internal Revenue. see U. S. Office of Internal Revenue.

U. S. Commissioner of Mining Statistics. see U. S. Bureau of Mines.

U. S. Commissioner of Patents. see U. S. Patent Office.

U. S. Commissioner of Pensions. see U. S. Pension Bureau.

U. S. Commissioner of Public Lands. see U. S. General Land Office. Commissioner.

U. S. Commissioner of the Revenue. see U. S. Special Commissioner of the Revenue, 1866-1870.

U. S. Commissioner on the Claims of Creditors of the Potawatomi Indians of the Wabash. 21868 see also Edmonds, John Worth.

U. S. Commissioner to New Orleans. 36268 see also Johnson, Reverdy, 1796-1876.

U. S. Commissioner to the Apalachicola Indians. 96669, 96690 see also Gadsden, James.

U. S. Commissioner to the Band of Delaware Indians, Upon the Sandusky River, in the State of Ohio. 96660 see also M'Elvain, John.

U. S. Commissioner to the Caddo Indians. 96696 see also Brooks, Jehiel.

U. S. Commissioner to the Chickasaw Indians. 96694 see also Eaton, John H.

U. S. Commissioner to the Cherokee Nation of Indians, West of the Mississippi. 96656 see also Barbour, James, 1775-1842.

U. S. Commissioner to the Chippewa Indians. 96716, 96720, 96728 see also Dodge, Henry, 1782-1867. Schoolcraft, Henry Rowe, 1793-1864.

U. S. Commissioner to the Swan Creek and Black River Bands of the Chippewa Nation.

U. S. Commissioner to the Chippewa Indians (Saganaw Tribe) see U. S. Commissioner to the Saganaw Tribe of Chippewas.

U. S. Commissioner to the Choctaw Indians. 96635 see also Calhoun, John Caldwell, 1782-1850.

U. S.

U. S. Commissioner to the Confederate
Tribes of Sauk & Fox Indians. 96713
see also Dodge, Henry, 1782-1867.

U. S. Commissioner to the Creek Indians.
96671 see also Cass, Lewis, 1782-
1866.

U. S. Commissioner to the Eel River or
Thorntown Party of Maimi Indians.
96655 see also Tipton, John.

U. S. Commissioner to the First Christian
and Orchard Parties of the Oneida
Indians. 96729 see also Harris,
Carey A.

U. S. Commissioner to the Four Confederated
Bands of Pawnees. 96693 see also
Ellsworth, Henry Leavitt, 1791-1858.

U. S. Commissioner to the Fox Indians.
see U. S. Commissioner to the Confederate Tribes of Sauk & Fox Indians.
U. S. Commissioner to the Iowa Tribe
of Indians and the Band of Sauk and
Foxes of the Missouri. U. S. Commissioner to the Sauk and Fox Tribe of
Indians.

U. S. Commissioner to the Foxes of Missouri.
see U. S. Commissioner to the Sauk
and Foxes of Missouri.

U. S. Commissioner to the Great and Little
Osage Indians. 96637, 96733 see also
Arbuckle, M Clark, William, 1770-1838.

U. S. Commissioner to the Iowa Indians.
96725, 96730 see also Dougherty,
John. Pilcher, Joshua.

U. S. Commissioner to the Iowa Tribe of
Indians and the Band of Sauk and Foxes
of the Missouri. 96708 see also
Clark, William, 1770-1838.

U. S. Commissioner to the Kansas Indians.
96638 see also Clark, William, 1770-
1838.

U. S. Commissioner to the Little Osage
Indians. see U. S. Commissioner to
the Great and Little Osage Indians.

U. S. Commissioner to the Mdewakanton
Indians. see U. S. Commissioner to
the Wahpaakootah, Susseton, and Upper
Medawakanton Tribes of Sioux Indians.

U. S. Commissioner to the Menomonie Indians.
96706 see also Dodge, Henry, 1782-
1867.

U. S. Commissioner to the Miami Indians.
96695, 96731 see also Marshall,
William. Pepper, Abel C.

U. S. Commissioner to the New York Indians.
96726 see also Gillet, Ransom H.

U. S. Commissioner to the Oneida Indians.
see U. S. Commissioner to the First
Christian and Orchard Parties of the
Oneida Indians.

U. S. Commissioner to the Orchard Party
of the Oneida Indians. see U. S. Commissioner to the First Christian and
Orchard Parties of the Oneida Indians.

U. S. Commissioner to the Ottawa Indians.
96668, 96687 see also Gardiner,
James B. Porter, George B.

U. S. Commissioner to the Potawatomi
Indians. 96595, 96653, 96699-96702,
96705, 96709, 96711, 96718 see also
Cass, Lewis, 1782-1866. Douglass, John
T. Pepper, Abel C. Marshall, William.

U. S. Commissioner to the Quapaw Indians.
96634, 96689 see also Crittenden,
Robert. Schermerhorn, John F.

U. S. Commissioner to the Saganaw Tribe of
Chippewas. 96734-96735 see also
Hulbert, John.

U. S. Commissioner to the Sauk and Fox
Tribe of Indians. 96712 see also Dodge
Henry, 1782-1867.

U. S. Commissioner to the Sauk and Foxes
of Missouri. 96722 see also Harris,
Carey A.

U. S. Commissioner to the Sauk Indians. see
U. S. Commissioner to the Confederate
Tribes of Sauk & Fox Indians. U. S.
Commissioner to the Iowa Tribe of
Indians and the Band of Sauk and Foxes
of the Missouri, U. S. Commissioner
to the Sauk and Fox Tribe of Indians.

U. S. Commissioner to the Seneca Indians.
96665 see also Gardiner, James B.

U. S. Commissioner to the Shawonee Indians.
96651 see also Clark, William, 1770-
1838.

U. S. Commissioner to the Sioux Indians.
96721 see also Poinsett, Joel Roberts,
1779-1851. U. S. Commissioner to the
Wahpaakootah, Susseton, and Upper
Medawakanton Tribes of Sioux Indians.

U. S. Commissioner to the Sioux of Wah-ha-
Sahw's Tribe of Indians. 96707 see also
Taylor, Zachary, Pres. U. S., 1784-
1850.

U. S. Commissioner to the Sioux Indians
(Yankton Tribe) see U. S. Commis-
sioner to the Yankton Tribe of Sioux
Indians.

U. S. Commissioner to the Sisseton Indians.
see U. S. Commissioner to the Wahpaakootah, Susseton, and Upper Medawakanton Tribes of Sioux Indians.

U. S. Commissioner to the Stockbridge and
Munsee Indians. 96736 see also
Gallup, Albert.

U. S. Commissioner to the Swan Creek and
Black River Bands of the Chippewa
Nation. 96704 see also Schoolcraft,
Henry Rowe, 1793-1846.

U. S. Commissioner to the United Bands of
the Otos and Missouris. 96691 see
also Ellsworth, Henry Leavitt, 1791-
1858.

U. S. Commissioner to the Universal Exposition, Paris, 1867. see U. S. Commission to the Paris Exposition, 1867.

U. S. Commissioner to the Wahpaakootah,
Susseton, and Upper Medawakanton
Tribe of Sioux Indians. 96715 see also
Taliaferro, Lawrence.

U. S. Commissioner to the Wahpekute Indians.
see U. S. Commissioner to the Wahpaakootah, Susseton, and Upper Medawakantor
Tribes of Sioux Indians.

U. S. Commissioner to the Winnebago Indians.
96724 see also Harris, Carey A.

U. S. Commissioner to the Wyandot Indians.
96703 see also Bryan, John A.

U. S. Commissioner to the Yankton Tribe of
Sioux Indians. 96723 see also Harris,
Carey A.

U. S. Commissioner Appointed to Lay Out a
Road From Cumberland, Md. to the State
of Ohio. 17887

U. S. Commissioners Appointed to Negotiate
With the Cherokee Indians, for a Certain
Portion of Their Country, 1828. 52249,
69778

U. S. Commissioners Appointed to Survey
the River Potomac. see Commissioners

of Maryland and Virginia Appointed to Survey the Potomac River.

U. S. Commissioners for Purchasing the Public Debts. 69781

U. S. Commissioners for Settlement of Limits of Georgia. 27042, 27072, 27097, 95390

U. S. Commissioners for Settling a Cartel for the Exchange of Prisoners with Great Britain, 1779. 15323, 18775, 69750 see also Davies, William. Harrison, R. H.

U. S. Commissioners for Surveying the Coast of North Carolina. 55696

U. S. Commissioners of Sinking Fund. see U. S. Board of Commissioners of Sinking Fund.

U. S. Commissioners on French Spoliation Claims, 1807, (1077), 25881

U. S. Commissioners on the Georgia-Mississippi Territory. 27043

U. S. Commissioners on the Northeastern Boundary. (55710)-(55711)

U. S. Commissioners to Buenos Aires. see U. S. Legation. Buenos Aires.

U. S. Commissioners to Confer With the Insurgents in the Western Counties of Pennsylvania. 60475

U. S. Commissioners to Survey the Potomac River. see Commissioners of Maryland and Virginia Appointed to Survey the Potomac River.

U. S. Commissioners to the Belantse-etoa or Minnetaree Indians. 96644 see also Atkinson, Henry. O'Fallon, Benjamin.

U. S. Commissioners to the Cherokee Indians. (12457), 69778, 90114, 94745, 96600 see also Clarke, M. St. Clair. Hawkins, Benjamin. Kendall, Amos. M'Intosh, Lacklan. Martin, Joseph, 1740-1808. Paschal, George W. Pickens, Andrew. Stambaugh, Samuel C.

U. S. Commissioners to the Cherokee Indians, West of the Mississippi. 96685 see also Ellsworth, Henry Leavitt, 1791-1858. Schermerhorn, John F. Stokes, Montfort.

U. S. Commissioners to the Chickasaw Indians. 96601, 96607 see also Hawkins, Benjamin. Martin, Joseph, 1740-1808. Pickens, Andrew. Wilkinson, James, 1757-1825.

U. S. Commissioners to the Chippewa Indians. see U. S. Commissioners to the United Nation of Chippewa, Ottawa, and Potawatomi Indians.

U. S. Commissioners to the Chippewa, Menominee and Winnebago Indians. 96652 see also Cass, Lewis, 1782-1866. M'Kenney, Thomas L.

U. S. Commissioners to the Choctaw Indians. 96601, 96663 see also Coffee, John. Eaton, John H. Hawkins, Benjamin. Martin, Joseph, 1740-1808. Pickens, Andrew.

U. S. Commissioners to the Comanche and Wichita Indians. 96697 see also Armbuckle, M. Armstrong, J. W. Stokes, Montfort.

U. S. Commissioners to the Confederate Tribes of Sauk and Fox Indians. 96674 see also Reynolds, John, 1788-1865. Scott, Winfield, 1786-1866.

U. S. Commissioners to the Confederated Tribes of Sauk and Foxes; the Mdewwakanton, Wahpekute, Wahpeton and Sisseton Bands or Tribes of Sioux; the Omahas, Iowas, Ottos, and Missouri Indians. 96662 see also Clark, William, 1770-1838. Morgan, Willoughby.

U. S. Commissioners to the Creek Indians. 96636, 96654, 96732 see also Armbuckle, M. Armstrong, William. Campbell, Duncan G. Crowell, John. McKenney, Thomas L. Meriwether, James. U. S. Commissioners to the Muskogee or Creek Indians.

U. S. Commissioners to the Crow Indians. 96646 see also Atkinson, Henry. O'Fallon, Benjamin.

U. S. Commissioners to the Delaware Indians. see U. S. Commissioners to the Shawnee and Delaware Indians.

U. S. Commissioners to the Fox Indians. see U. S. Commissioners to the Confederate Tribes of Sauk and Foxes.

U. S. Commissioners to the Hunkapa Indians. 96642 see also Atkinson, Henry. O'Fallon, Benjamin.

U. S. Commissioners to the Kaskaskia and Peoria Indians. 96676 see also Allen, Frank J. Clark, William, 1770-1838. Kouns, Nathan.

U. S. Commissioners to the Ka-ta-ka Indians. see U. S. Commissioners to the Kioway, Ka-ta-ka, and Ta-wa-karo Indians.

U. S. Commissioners to the Kickapoo Indians. 96679 see also Allen, Frank J. Clark, William, 1770-1838. Kouns, Nathan.

U. S. Commissioners to the Kioway, Ka-ta-ka, and Ta-wa-karo Indians. 96719 see also Chouteau, A. P. Stokes, Montfort.

U. S. Commissioners to the Maha Indians. 96650 see also Atkinson, Henry. O'Fallon, Benjamin.

U. S. Commissioners to the Mandan Indians. 96645 see also Atkinson, Henry. O'Fallon, Benjamin.

U. S. Commissioners to the Menominee Indians. 96664, 96681 see also Eaton, John Henry, 1790-1856. Porter, George B. Stambaugh, Samuel C.

U. S. Commissioners to the Miami Indians. 96737 see also Hamilton, Allen. Milroy, Samuel.

U. S. Commissioners to the Michigan Indians. 96647 see also Cass, Lewis, 1782-1866. Clark, William, 1770-1838.

U. S. Commissioners to the Missouri Indians. see U. S. Commissioners to the Otos, Missouri, Omaha, and Yankton and Santee Bands of Sioux.

U. S. Commissioners to the Mixed Bands of the Seneca and Shawnee Indians. 96666 see also Gardiner, James B. McElvain, John.

U. S. Commissioners to the Muskogee or Creek Indians. 96686 see also Ellsworth, Henry Leavitt, 1791-1858. Schermerhorn, John F. Stokes, Montfort. U. S. Commissioners to the Creek Indians.

U. S. Commissioners to the Omaha Indians. see U. S. Commissioners to the Otos, Missouri, Omaha, and Yankton and Santee Bands of Sioux.

U. S. Commissioners to the Oto Indians. see U. S. Commissioners to the Oto and Missouri Indians. and U. S. Commissioners to the Oto, Missouri, Omaha, and Yankton and Santee Bands of Sioux.

U. S.

U. S. Commissioners to the Oto and Missouri Indians. 96648 see also Atkinson, Henry. O'Fallon, Benjamin.

U. S. Commissioners to the Oto, Missouri, Omaha, and Yankton and Santee Bands of Sioux. 96714 see also Dougherty, John. Pilcher, Joshua.

U. S. Commissioners to the Ottawa Indians. see U. S. Commissioners to the United Nation of Chippewa, Ottawa, and Otawatomi Indians.

U. S. Commissioners to the Paris Exposition, 1867. see U. S. Commission to the Paris Exposition, 1867.

U. S. Commissioners to the Pawnee Indians. 96649 see also Atkinson, Henry. O'Fallon, Benjamin.

U. S. Commissioners to the Peoria Indians. see U. S. Commissioners to the Kaskaskia and Peoria Indians.

U. S. Commissioners to the Piankeshaw and Wea Indians. 96683 see also Allen, Frank J. Clark, William, 1770-1838. Kouns, Nathan.

U. S. Commissioners to the Ponca Indians. 96639 see also Atkinson, Henry. O'Fallon, Benjamin.

U. S. Commissioners to the Potawatomi Indians. 96658 see also Cass, Lewis, 1782-1866. Menard, Pierre. U. S. Commissioners to the United Nation of Chippewa, Ottawa, and Potawatomi Indians.

U. S. Commissioners to the Potawatomi Indians of the Prairie. 96678 see also Crume, Marks. Davis, John W. Jennings, Jonathan.

U. S. Commissioners to the Ricara Indians. 96643 see also Atkinson, Henry. O'Fallon, Benjamin.

U. S. Commissioners to the Santee Indians/ see U. S. Commissioners to the Oto, Missouri, Omaha, and Yankton and Santee Bands of Sioux.

U. S. Commissioners to the Sauk Indians. see U. S. Commissioners to the Confederated Tribes of Sauk and Fox Indians.

U. S. Commissioners to the Seminole Indians. 96688 see also Ellsworth, Henry Leavitt, 1791-1858. Schermerhorn, John F. Stokes, Montfort.

U. S. Commissioners to the Seneca and Shawnee Indians. 96684 see also Ellsworth, Henry Leavitt, 1791-1858. Schermerhorn, John F.

U. S. Commissioners to the Seneca Indians. see U. S. Commissioners to the Mixed Bands of Seneca and Shawnee Indians.

U. S. Commissioners to the Shawnee and Delaware Indians. 96675 see also Allen, Frank J. Clark, William, 1770-1838. Kouns, Nathan.

U. S. Commissioners to the Shawnee Indians. 96602, 96667 see also Gardiner, James B. McElvain, John. U. S. Commissioners to the Mixed Bands of the Seneca and Shawnee Indians. U. S. Commissioners to the Seneca and Shawnee Indians.

U. S. Commissioners to the Sioune and Oglala Indians. 96641 see also Atkinson, Henry. O'Fallan, Benjamin.

U. S. Commissioners to the Six Nations of Indians. 96598 see also Butler,

Richard. Lee, Arthur, 1740-1792. Wolcott, Oliver.

U. S. Commissioners to the Ta-wa-karo Indians. see U. S. Commissioners to the Kioway, Ka-ta-ka, and Ta-wa-karo Indians.

U. S. Commissioners to the Teton, Yancton, and Yanctonies Sioux Indians. 96640 see also Atkinson, Henry. O'Fallon, Benjamin.

U. S. Commissioners to the United Nation of Chippewa, Ottawa, and Potawatomi Indians. 96692 see also Owen, Thomas J. V. Porter, George B. Weatherford, William.

U. S. Commissioners to the Wea Indians . see U. S. Commissioners to the Piankeshaw and Wea Indians.

U. S. Commissioners to the Wiandot, Delaware, Chippewa and Ottawa Indians. 96599

U. S. Commissioners to the Winnebago Indians. 96659, 96673 see also Atwater, Caleb. M!Neil, John. Menard, Pierre. Reynolds, John, 1788-1865. Scott, Winfield, 1786-1866.

U. S. Commissioners to the Winnebago Tribe, and the United Tribes of Potawatomie, Chippewa, and Ottawa Indians. 96657 see also Cass, Lewis, 1782-1866. Menard, Pierre.

U. S. Commissioners to the Wichita Indians. see U. S. Commissioners to the Comanche and Wichita Indians.

U. S. Commissioners to the Yankton Indians. see U. S. Commissioners to the Oto, Missouri, Omaha, and Tankton and Santee Bands of Sioux.

U. S. Commissioners Under the Convention of April 1803 With France, Paris. (20534)

U. S. Commissioners Under the Fourth Article of the Treaty of Ghent, Dec. 24, 1814. see Commissioners Under the Fourth Article of the Treaty of Ghent, Dec. 24, 1814.

U. S. Commissioners Under the Treaty of Ghent. see Commissioners Under the Fourth Article of the Treaty of Ghent, Dec. 24, 1814.

U. S. Committee Appointed by the Postmaster General, to Examine and Revise the Postal Code. see U. S. Post Office Department. Committee Appointed by the Postmaster General, to Examine and Revise the Postal Code.

U. S. Committee to Investigate the Capacities and Advantages of the New McCarty Gun. (9227) see also Burger, Louis.

U. S. Comptroller of the Currency. 17994, 44632, 69847, 89702, 89707 see also Whittlesey, Elisha.

U. S. Congress. 324, 762, 764, 1128-1129, 1162, 1338, 3046, 3299, 4783, 4787, 7161, 8348, (8325), 10067, 13562, 13577, (13897), 15006, 15062, 15119, 15508, 15515, 15519, 15527, (15532)-(15534), 15587, (15588), 15591, 15592, (15594), 15601, 15606, (15607)-15610, 16092, 16117, (16864), (18789), 20151-(20152), (20299), 20314, 20428, 20477, (20696), 23106, 23510, (23526), 24223, 26916, 27015, 28488, 28517, (28601), 29057, 29952, 30443, 30597, 30819, 31723, (33581), (34203), 34481, 35834, 35887-35888, 36179, 36324, 37693, (37858), (40339), (42178), 43710, 43716,

U. S.

U. S. Congress. Committee to Whom Was Referred So Much of the President's Speech as Relates to the Naval Establishment. 69837

U. S. Congress. Committee to Whom Was Referred the Correspondence Between Mr. Monroe and Mr. Channing. 12489

U. S. Congress. Committee to Whom Was Referred the Memorial and Remonstrance of the Legislature of the State of Georgia. 69839

U. S. Congress. Committee to Whom Was Referred the Memorial of the Legislative Council and House of Representatives of the Mississippi Territory. 69735

U. S. Congress. Committee to Whom Was Referred the Memorial of the Representatives of the People South of the Ohio. note after 94720

U. S. Congress. Committee to Whom Was Referred the Message from the President Accompanying the Copy of a Letter from the Governor of the Territory South of the River Ohio. 69834

U. S. Congress. Committee to Whom Was Referred the Motion of the 17th of January Last, Respecting the Territory of the United States Southward and Westward of the State of Georgia. 69836

U. S. Congress. Committee to Whom Was Referred the Petition of Thirty-Six American Citizens Confined at Carthagena. 69841

U. S. Congress. Committee to Whom Was Referred the Report of a Select Committee Appointed to Prepare and Report Articles of Impeachment Against Samuel Chase. (69840)

U. S. Congress. Committee to Whom Was Referred the Several Petitions on the Subject of Mails on the Sabbath. 36278

U. S. Congress. Committee to Whom Was Referred Certain Memorials and Petitions Complaining of an Act, Intitled "An Act Concerning Aliens." (69843)

U. S. Congress. Committee to Whom Were Referred the Memorial of Return Jonathan Meigs, Junior. 47399

U. S. Congress. Committee to Whom Were Referred the Memorials and Petitions of the Board of Trustees of Jefferson College in the Mississippi Territory, and of W. Dunbar. 69844

U. S. Congress. Committee Upon the Survey of the Coast. 30817

U. S. Congress. Conference Committee of the Kansas Question, 1858. 44781

U. S. Congress. Democratic Delegation. see Democratic Party.

U. S. Congress. Democratic Delegation from New York. see Democratic Party. New York.

U. S. Congress. Democratic Republican Members. see Democratic Party.

U. S. Congress. Independent Democratic Delegation. see Free Soil Party.

U. S. Congress. Joint Committee on Foreign Affairs. 34404

U. S. Congress. Joint Committee on the Library. 29987, (35919), 84835

U. S. Congress. Joint Committee on Reconstruction. 15593, 24222

U. S. Congress. Joint Committee on the Conduct of the War. 748, 2052, 15212, (23154), 25164, 25639, 37646, 69825, (69826), 69848-69849, 69867-69870

U. S. Congress. Joint Committee to Consider What Further Measures Ought to be Taken for the Accomodation of the President of the United States; and to Whom Was Referred the Message From the President 69866

U. S. Congress. Joint Select Committee to Inquire Into the Condition of Affairs in the Late Insurrectionary States. 78314

U. S. Congress. Joint Special Committee, Appointed Under Joint Resolution, March 3, 1865. 15189, 20610

U. S. Congress. Joint Special Committee on the Condition of the Indian Tribes. 15188, 20610

U. S. Congress. Massachusetts Members. 45959

U. S. Congress. Massachusetts Members. petitioners (82573), 82575

U. S. Congress. Oregon and Washington Members. 90749

U. S. Congress. Select Committee of Thirty-Three on the Disturbed Condition of the Country. 69952

U. S. Congress. Select Committee on a Resolution Relating to the Claim of Massachusetts, for Expenditures of Their Militia. 45469

U. S. Congress. Select Committee on Alleged Corrupt Combination of Members of Congress, 1857. 15514

U. S. Congress. Select Committee on Emancipation and Colonization. 22403

U. S. Congress. Select Committee on New York Election Frauds. (39375)

U. S. Congress. Select Committee on the Claims of Col. James Monroe. 98363

U. S. Congress. Select Committee on the New Orleans Riots. 53368

U. S. Congress. Select Committee on the New Orleans Riots. Minority. 53368

U. S. Congress. Select Committee on the Pacific Railroad. Majority. 69950

U. S. Congress. Select Committee on the Pacific Railroad. Minority. 69950

U. S. Congress. Select Committee on the Rhode Island Controversy. (43041)

U. S. Congress. Select Committee on the Sale of Fort Snelling. Minority. (23926)

U. S. Congress. Select Committee to Answer the Speech of the President, 1797. 250

U. S. Congress. Select Committee to Investigate Matters Connected With the New Orleans Massacre of July 30, 1866. 53367

U. S. Congress. Select Committee to Whom Were Referred the Resolutions of the Legislature of Maine. 43922

U. S. Congress. South Carolina Members. 39144, 88065

U. S. Congress. Southern Delegates, 1848. 402, 33930, 88335

U. S. Congress. Treasury Investigating Committee. Minority. 2840, 29386

U. S. Congress. Washington Members. see U. S. Congress. Oregon and Washington Members.

U. S. Congress. Whig Members. see Whig Party. Congressional Executive Committee. and Whig Congressional Committee, 1844.

U. S. 1st Congress, 1789-1791. 15554, 83991

U. S. 1st Congress, 1789-1791. House. 15554, 20463, note after 36724

U. S. 1st Congress, 1st session, 1789-1790.
House. 15554-15555, 36725
U. S. 1st Congress, 1st session, 1789-1790.
Senate. 15551
U. S. 1st Congress, 2d session, 1790. Senate.
15551
U. S. 1st Congress, 3d session, 1790-1791.
Senate. 15551
U. S. 2d Congress, 1791-1793. 15554, 83991
U. S. 2d Congress, 1791-1793. House. 15554,
20463, note after 36724
U. S. 2d Congress, 1791-1793. Senate.
15551
U. S. 2d Congress, 2d session, 1792-1793.
Senate. 80759
U. S. 3d Congress, 1793-1795. 15521, 15551,
15554, 83991
U. S. 3d Congress, 1793-1795. House. 20463
U. S. 3d Congress, 1st session, 1793-1794.
House. 15554, note after 36724, 85230
U. S. 4th Congress, 1795-1797. 15554, 83991
U. S. 4th Congress, 1st session, 1795-1796.
House. 8128, 15520
U. S. 4th Congress, 1st session, 1795-1796.
Senate. 15552
U. S. 4th Congress, 2d session, 1796-1797.
11006
U. S. 4th Congress, 2d session, 1796-1797.
House. 84577
U. S. 5th Congress, 1797-1799. 15554, 83991
U. S. 5th Congress, 1st session, 1797-1798.
15549
U. S. 5th Congress, 3d session, 1798. 15548,
15556, 15585
U. S. 6th Congress, 1799-1801. 15554, 83991
U. S. 6th Congress, 2d session, 1800-1801.
82939
U. S. 7th Congress, 1801-1803. 15554, 83991
U. S. 7th Congress, 1st session, 1801-1802.
19101, 19105, 82939
U. S. 8th Congress, 1803-1805. 15554, 83991
U. S. 9th Congress, 1805-1807. 15554, 83991
U. S. 10th Congress, 1807-1809. 15554,
83991
U. S. 10th Congress, 1st session, 1807-1808.
(4181), 17887, 20465
U. S. 10th Congress, 1st session, 1807-1808.
Senate. 82881, 82883
U. S. 10th Congress, 2d session, 1808-1809.
17887
U. S. 11th Congress, 1809-1811. 15554, 83991
U. S. 12th Congress, 1811-1813. 15554,
(31832), 83991
U. S. 13th Congress, 1813-1815. 15554,
83991
U. S. 13th Congress, 2d session, 1814-1815.
House. 15535
U. S. 13th Congress, 3d session, 1815. House.
10219, (15563)
U. S. 14th Congress, 1815-1817. 83991
U. S. 14th Congress, 1st session, 1815-1816.
10219
U. S. 15th Congress, 1st session, 1817-1818.
Senate. 13821
U. S. 15th Congress, 2d session, 1818-1819.
House. 1894-1895
U. S. 16th Congress, 2d session, 1820-1821.
House. 87891
U. S. 17th Congress, 1st session, 1821-1822.
15525
U. S. 17th Congress, 1st session, 1821-1822.
House. (12059), 82780
U. S. 17th Congress, 2d session, 1822-1823.
85189
U. S. 17th Congress, 2d session, 1822-1823.
House. 12057

U. S. 17th Congress, 2d session, 1822-1823.
Senate. 14965
U. S. 18th Congress, 1st session, 1823-1824.
20147
U. S. 18th Congress, 1st session, 1823-1824.
House. 82780
U. S. 19th Congress, 1st session, 1825-1826.
4067
U. S. 19th Congress, 1st session, 1825-1826.
House. 15489
U. S. 19th Congress, 2d session, 1825-1826.
House. 23268, 37387, 82780
U. S. 20th Congress, 1827-1829. House.
2992
U. S. 20th Congress, 1st session, 1827-1828.
3552, 36996, 37639, (49354)
U. S. 20th Congress, 1st session, 1827-1828.
House. 1596, 4165A, 10114, 17337,
37484, 70887, 87410, 87484
U. S. 20th Congress, 1st session, 1827-1828.
Senate. 87529
U. S. 20th Congress, 2d session, 1828-1829.
87961
U. S. 20th Congress, 2d session, 1828-1829.
Senate. 36277
U. S. 21st Congress, 1st session, 1829-1830.
34663
U. S. 22d Congress, 1st session, 1831-1832.
312, 3189, 70599
U. S. 22d Congress, 1st session, 1831-1832.
House. 12502, 84396, 87890
U. S. 22d Congress, 2d session, 1832-1833.
15610
U. S. 22d Congress, 2d session, 1832-1833.
House. 3189, 48097, 86545, 87423
U. S. 22d Congress, 2d session, 1832-1833.
Senate. 48097, 87423
U. S. 23d Congress, 1st session, 1833-1834.
34671
U. S. 23d Congress, 1st session, 1833-1834.
House. 5492, 14236
U. S. 23d Congress, 1st session, 1833-1834.
Senate. 34637, 102287
U. S. 23d Congress, 2d session, 1834-1835.
2189, 88135
U. S. 23d Congress, 2d session, 1834-1835.
House. 23961, 84396
U. S. 24th Congress, 1st session, 1835-1836.
9936
U. S. 24th Congress, 1st session, 1835-1836.
House. 84314, 85070, 88314, 103385,
105102
U. S. 24th Congress, 1st session, 1835-1836.
Senate. (23963), 84396
U. S. 24th Congress, 2d session, 1836-1837.
House. 3299
U. S. 25th Congress, special session, 1837.
23168
U. S. 25th Congress, 2d session, 1837-1838.
House. 3299, 39853, 80500
U. S. 25th Congress, 2d session, 1837-1838.
Senate. 88136
U. S. 26th Congress, 1st session, 1839-1840.
House. 3299, 82968, 85069
U. S. 26th Congress, 1st session, 1839-1840.
Senate. 28633, 91822, 95370
U. S. 26th Congress, 2d session, 1840-1841.
Senate 83239
U. S. 27th Congress, 2d session, 1841-1842.
House. 25174, (80502), 82969-82970
U. S. 27th Congress, 2d session, 1841-1842.
Senate. 87504-87505
U. S. 27th Congress, 3d session, 1842-1843.
House. 37404
U. S. 27th Congress, 3d session, 1842-1843.
Senate. 85161

U. S.

U. S. 28th Congress, 1st session, 1843-1844.
22235
U. S. 28th Congress, 1st session, 1843-1844.
House. 70725, 70728, 51462
U. S. 28th Congress, 2d session, 1844-1845.
12673, 12834
U. S. 28th Congress, 2d session, 1844-1845.
House. 51465
U. S. 29th Congress, 1st session, 1845-1846.
12878
U. S. 29th Congress, 1st session, 1845-1846.
(10747), 83832
U. S. 29th Congress, 2d session, 1846-1847.
Senate. 85052
U. S. 30th Congress, 1st session, 1847-1848.
Senate. 15584, 31186, 84384
U. S. 30th Congress, 2d session, 1848-1849.
Senate. 83533
U. S. 31st Congress, 1st session, 1849-1850.
9063
U. S. 31st Congress, 1st session, 1849-1850.
House. 25249, 69887, 72135, 90427,
98220
U. S. 31st Congress, 1st session, 1849-1850.
Senate. 83534, 83706, 84774, 97652
U. S. 31st Congress, 2d session, 1850-1851.
36613
U. S. 32d Congress, special session, 1851.
25249
U. S. 32d Congress, special session, 1851.
Senate. 90372
U. S. 32d Congress, 1st session, 1851-1852.
(28215)
U. S. 32d Congress, 1st session, 1851-1852.
Senate. 1498, 3745
U. S. 32d Congress, 2d session, 1852-1853.
31524
U. S. 32d Congress, 2d session, 1852-1853.
Senate. 3750, 31524, 81472, 81541
U. S. 33d Congress, special session, 1853.
Senate. 3742
U. S. 33d Congress, 1st session, 1853-1854.
House. 4258, 5802, 5809, 11314, 69900
U. S. 33d Congress, 1st session, 1853-1854.
Senate. (76485), 81473
U. S. 33d Congress, 2d session, 1854-1855.
4258
U. S. 33d Congress, 2d session, 1854-1855.
House. 11672, 19119, 69946, 85055,
85081
U. S. 33d Congress, 2d session, 1854-1855.
Senate. 5809, 20456, (30968), 69946
U. S. 34th Congress, 1st session, 1855-1856.
House. (37053), 37087
U. S. 34th Congress, 1st session, 1855-1856.
Senate. 14982, 16380, 37040
U. S. 34th Congress, 3d session, 1856-1857.
Senate. (28216)
U. S. 35th Congress, 1st session, 1857-1858.
House. 37041
U. S. 35th Congress, 1st session, 1857-1858.
Senate. 14983, 28219, 37081
U. S. 35th Congress, 2d session, 1858-1859.
12813
U. S. 35th Congress, 2d session, 1858-1859.
Senate. 18807, 69946, 81354
U. S. 36th Congress, special session, 1859.
Senate. 64337
U. S. 36th Congress, 1st session, 1859-1860.
House. 69946
U. S. 36th Congress, 1st session, 1859-1860.
Senate. 12813
U. S. 36th Congress, 2d session, 1860-1861.
House. 42913
U. S. 36th Congress, 2d session, 1860-1861.
Senate. 69946

U. S. 37th Congress, 1861-1863. 47393
U. S. 37th Congress, 1861-1863. Senate.
29882
U. S. 37th Congress, 2d session, 1861-1862.
16903, 25159, 28191
U. S. 37th Congress, 2d session, 1861-1862.
House. (20809), 28157, 35092, 38665,
69907
U. S. 37th Congress, 3d session, 1862-1863.
(16869), 16882, 19003, 36268
U. S. 37th Congress, 3d session, 1862-1863.
House. 84956
U. S. 38th Congress, 1863-1865. 3206, 42305
U. S. 38th Congress, 1863-1865. House.
646, 10039
U. S. 38th Congress, 1863-1865. Senate.
748, 42305
U. S. 38th Congress, 1st session, 1863-1864.
30313
U. S. 38th Congress, 1st session, 1863-1864.
House. 1415, 5741-5742, 17219, 19014,
(26689), 43054
U. S. 38th Congress, 1st session, 1863-1864.
Senate. 9406, 24450, 24526, 35504,
41439, 44072, 82056
U. S. 38th Congress, 2d session, 1864-1865.
House. 1994, 30821, 37275
U. S. 38th Congress, 2d session, 1864-1865.
Senate. 42247, 44073, 69870, 85064
U. S. 39th Congress, 1865-1867. House. 23901
U. S. 39th Congress, 1st session, 1865-1866.
15583, 78035
U. S. 39th Congress, 1st session, 1865-1866.
House. 33130, 41175, 86334
U. S. 39th Congress, 1st session, 1865-1866.
Senate. 34941, 85498
U. S. 39th Congress, 2d session, 1866-1867.
36180
U. S. 40th Congress, 1st session, 1867. 36180
U. S. 40th Congress, 2d session, 1867-1868.
7705, 41707
U. S. 40th Congress, 2d session, 1867-1868.
House. 9615
U. S. 41st Congress, 1st session, 1869. Senate.
82957
U. S. 41st Congress, 2d session, 1869-1870.
34677
U. S. 41st Congress, 2d session, 1869-1870.
Senate. 88505
U. S. 41st Congress, 3d session, 1870-1871.
House. 71940
U. S. 41st Congress, 3d session, 1870-1871.
Senate. 20398
U. S. 42d Congress, 1st session, 1871. House.
(27705)
U. S. 42d Congress, 3d session, 1872-1873.
House. 85062, 85492
U. S. 43 Congress, 1st session, 1873. House.
64753, note after 85023, 85048, 85086
U. S. 44th Congress, 1st session, 1875-1876.
88428
U. S. 45th Congress, 2d session, 1877-1878.
House. 82757
U. S. 49th Congress, 1st session, 1885-11886.
Senate. 85492
U. S. 60th Congress, 1st session, 1807-1908.
Senate. 102402
U. S. 61st Congress, 1st session, 1909. House.
85043
U. S. 63d Congress, 3d session, 1914-1915.
House. 85042
U. S. 63d Congress, 3d session, 1914-1915.
Senate. 85000
U. S. Congress. House. 299-300, 393, 3189,
4071, 6002, 8978, (9325), 11684, 12203-
12204, 12207, 13437, (13897), 14008,

14010, 14990, 15456, 15489, 15509,
15514, 15531, 15535, 15539, 15540,
15554-15555, 15595, 16104-(16106),
16117, (16126), 17121, 17457, 18830,
19092, 19097, 19104, 19618, (20152),
20253, 20463, 20478, 24223, 24383,
24513, 25011, 26399, 27085, 27256,
28890, (29980), 31723, 34294, 34455,
34482, 35391, 35887, 36172, 36178-
-36179, 36181, note after 36724-36725,
37038, 37070, (37858), (38264), 38739,
41443, 42216, 42370, 43627, 44413,
44416, 49576, 52032, 53362, 59476,
63145, 64606, (65305), 65775-65776,
65863, 67197, (67700), 67796, 69765,
(69769), 69783, 69800, 69808, 69936,
70144, 70146, 70887, 71366, 74073,
(75020), 77036, 77041, 77417-77418,
79067, 79399, (79402), 81010, 81038,
82757, 83987, 84396, 84577, 84825,
85017, 85032, 85052, 85054, 85059,
85064, 85076, 1st note after 90364,
90535, 91903, note after 93482, note
after 94720, 94744-94745, 96996-96998,
96999, 97001-97002, 99292,
101545, 101772, note after 101860,
4th note after 102623, 102717, 103865
U. S. Congress. House. Clerk. 39425
U. S. Congress. House. Speaker. 101093
U. S. Congress. House. Bank Committee.
see U. S. Congress. House. Committee on Banking and Currency.
U. S. Congress. House. Committee. (18453)
U. S. Congress. House. Committee Appointed
Under the Resolutions Offered by the
Hon. John Covode, March 6, 1860.
17219
U. S. Congress. House. Committee of
Investigation on the Capture of Washington
by the British, on the 24th August, 1814.
see U. S. Congress. House. Com-
mittee on the Invasion of Washington,
1814.
U. S. Congress. House. Committee of
Investigation Into the Accounts of William
Cullom, late Clerk. (47190)
U. S. Congress. House. Committee of
Privileges. see U. S. Congress.
House. Committee on Elections.
U. S. Congress. House. Committee on
Banking and Currency. 3189, 102120
U. S. Congress. House. Committee on
Banking and Currency. Minority. 3189,
103778
U. S. Congress. House. Committee on
Claims. (77416)-77418, 82939, 91366
U. S. Congress. House. Committee on
Commerce. 37404, 37418, 47878
U. S. Congress. House. Committee on
Commerce and Navigation. 10110-
(10111)
U. S. Congress. House. Committee on
Elections. 1994, 3454, 8431, 28890,
(36246), (37053), 42862, 60091, (66732),
69806, 69808, 91259
U. S. Congress. House. Committee on
Elections. Minority. 53049
U. S. Congress. House. Committee on
Foreign Affairs. 57711, (67223)-67224,
(67226), 67832-67833, 84454, 89595
U. S. Congress. House. Committee on
Foreign Affairs. Majority. 23271,
(44075)
U. S. Congress. House. Committee on
Foreign Affairs. Minority. 23271

U. S. Congress. House. Committee on
Kansas. 37083, 37092, 93347
U. S. Congress. House. Committee on
Manufactures. (75861)
U. S. Congress. House. Committee on
Manufactures. Minority. 325
U. S. Congress. House. Committee on
Military Affairs. 19014, 25174, 51465
U. S. Congress. House. Committee on Naval
Affairs. 572, 27256, 37274, 69887,
70816, 90427
U. S. Congress. House. Committee on Naval
Affairs. Majority. 44073
U. S. Congress. House. Committee on Naval
Affairs. Minority. 44073
U. S. Congress. House. Committee on Naval
Affairs. Chairman. 69887, 84956,
90427 see also Sedgwick, Charles B.
Stanton, Frederick Perry.
U. S. Congress. House. Committee on Post
Offices and Post Roads. 64509
U. S. Congress. House. Committee on Public
Buildings and Grounds. 101200
U. S. Congress. House. Committee on Public
Expenditures. 69822
U. S. Congress. House. Committee on Public
Lands. (15688), 71375, 101093
U. S. Congress. House. Committee on Public
Printing. Minority. 37830
U. S. Congress. House. Committee on
Revolutionary Claims. 82968, 82970-
82971, 103369, 103439
U. S. Congress. House. Committee on Roads
and Canals. 28290, 80500, 83832
U. S. Congress. House. Committee on
Territories. 42291, 48780, 69831,
85230
U. S. Congress. House. Committee on the
Assassination of Lincoln. see U. S.
Congress. House. Committee on the
Judiciary.
U. S. Congress. House. Committee on the
Expediency of Opening a Road from
Vincennes, in the Indiana Territory, to-
wards Dayton, in the State of Ohio.
69795
U. S. Congress. House. Committee on the
Invasion of Washington, 1814. 10219,
(22650), 69795, 89138, note after 101937,
104746
U. S. Congress. House. Committee on the
Judiciary. 37056, 41175, (59430),
64622, 69828, 70261, 84396, 89702,
89707, 91268
U. S. Congress. House. Committee on the
Judiciary. Majority. (41210)
U. S. Congress. House. Committee on the
Judiciary. Minority. (41210)
U. S. Congress. House. Committee on the
Library. (15563), 70887
U. S. Congress. House. Committee on the
Memorial of the American Colonization
Society. 14732
U. S. Congress. House. Committee on the
Memorial of the American Philosophical
Society. 47653
U. S. Congress. House. Committee on the
Memorials of the United Illinois and
Ouabache Land Companies. 34294,
84577-84578, 2d-3d notes after 97876
U. S. Congress. House. Committee on the
Petition of Oliver Evans. (23182)
U. S. Congress. House. Committee on the
Resolutions of the State of Georgia.
17458

U. S. Congress. House. Committee on the Suppression of the Slave Trade. (82047)

U. S. Congress. House. Committee on Ways and Means. 3138, 3189, (31424), 34916, 56559, (69730), (69814)-69817

U. S. Congress. House. Committee on Ways and Means. Minority. 5492

U. S. Congress. House. Committee on Ways and Means. Chairman. 16859, 40340

U. S. Congress. House. Committee to Enquire Into the Causes of the Failure of the Late Expedition Under Major General St. Clair. 75018

U. S. Congress. House. Committee to Enquire Into the Official Conduct of Winthrop Sargent, Governor of the Mississippi Territory. 77036, 77041

U. S. Congress. House. Committee to Enquire Into the Spirit and Manner in Which the War Has Been Waged by the Enemy. 3296

U. S. Congress. House. Committee to Examine and Report, Whether Monies Drawn from the Treasury, Have Been Faithfully Applied to the Objects For Which They Were Appropriated, and Whether the Same Have Been Regularly Accounted For. 104982

U. S. Congress. House. Committee to Examine Into the State of the Treasury Department. 69800

U. S. Congress. House. Committee to Examine Into the State of the Treasury Department. Minority. 2840

U. S. Congress. House. Committee to Examine the Books and Proceedings of the Bank of the United States. see U. S. Congress. House. Committee on Banking and Currency.

U. S. Congress. House. Committee to Inquire Into the Causes and Particulars of the Invasion of the City of Washington, By the British Forces in the Month of August, 1814. see U. S. Congress. House. Committee on the Invasion of Washington, 1814.

U. S. Congress. House. Committee to Investigate the Bank of the United States. see U. S. Congress. House. Committee on Banking and Currency.

U. S. Congress. House. Committee to Investigate the Causes of the Late Duel, 1838. 90326

U. S. Congress. House. Committee to Prepare and Report Articles of Impeachment Against William Blount. 6000-6001, (6003)

U. S. Congress. House. Committee to Which Was Referred the Letter of the Hon. Choate. 85055

U. S. Congress. Committee to Whom Was Referred the Communication of Patrick Magruder. see U. S. Congress. House. Committee on the Library.

U. S. Congress. House. Committee to Whom Was Referred the Message From the President of the United States, of the Second Ultimo, Accompanying the Copy of a Letter from the Governor of the Territory South of the River Ohio. note after 94720

U. S. Congress. House. Committee to Whom Was Referred the Remonstrance and Petition of the Legislature of the State of Tennessee. 94745

U. S. Congress. House. Committee to Whom Were Referred the Message From the President of the United States, on the 8th Instant. note after 94720

U. S. Congress. House. Committee Upon So Much of the President's Message As Relates to Louisiana. 42291

U. S. Congress. House. Massachusetts Representatives, 1808. 69677, 98641

U. S. Congress. House. Select Committee Charged With the Memorial of Dr. James Smith, and His Letter of December 19, 1825. 82780

U. S. Congress. House. Select Committee of Fifteen on the Lecompton Constitution. 91261

U. S. Congress. House. Select Committee on Abstracted Indian Trust Funds. 24913

U. S. Congress. House. Select Committee on Deposite Banks. 103779

U. S. Congress. House. Select Committee on Foreign Paupers and Naturalization Laws. 74321

U. S. Congress. House. Select Committee on Gold and Silver Coins. 14236

U. S. Congress. House. Select Committee on Harbor Defences of the Great Lakes and Rivers. 30292

U. S. Congress. House. Select Committee on Internal Revenue Frauds. (34917)

U. S. Congress. House. Select Committee on Postal Telegraph. (64519)

U. S. Congress. House. Select Committee on the Ether Discovery. Minority. 90329

U. S. Congress. House. Select Committee on the Memorial of the Democratic Members of the Legislature of Rhode Island. 70725

U. S. Congress. House. Select Committee on the Memorial of the Democratic Members of the Legislature of Rhode Island. Minority. 70728

U. S. Congress. House. Select Committee on the Memorial of William T. G. Morton. 51032

U. S. Congress. House. Select Committee on the Memorial of William T. G. Morton. Minority. 51032

U. S. Congress. House. Select Committee on the Memphis Riots. 47782

U. S. Congress. House. Select Committee on the Smithsonian Bequest. 85070

U. S. Congress. House. Select Committee to Investigate the Affairs of the Post Office Department. 3693

U. S. Congress. House. Select Committee to Investigate the Assault Upon the Hon. W. D. Kelley. 37275

U. S. Congress. House. Select Committee to Prepare and Report Articles of Impeachment Against Samuel Chase. (69840)

U. S. Congress. House. Select Committee to Which Was Referred the Memorial of Dr. James Smith. 82780

U. S. Congress. House. Select Committee to Which Was Referred the Memorial of the Officers and Soldiers of the Rhode Island Brigade. 9235

U. S. Congress. House. Select Committee to Which Was Referred the Messages of the President of the 5th and 8th February, and 2d March, 1827. 69903

(44820), 46031, 46095-46096, 46098,
47187, 47193, 48065, 48369, (48747),
48966-48967, 48978-48980, 49244, 49318,
49492, 49499, (49547), 49764, (50099)-
50100, (50398), 50814, 50954, 51058,
51311, 51340, 51936-(51937), (51963)-
51966, 52027, 52028, 52051, 52072,
52122, 52180, 52200, 52810, (53024),
53295, (53306), (53409), 55632, 55821,
55951, 56537, 56913, 57409, (57507)-
57509, 57567, 57583, 56898, 56913,
58149, 58358, (59003), (59039), 59040-
(59042), 60198, 60293, 60806-60811,
61206, 61208, 61604, (63726), (64481),
(64483)-64485, (64499)-64504, 65566,
65725, 66517, 67434, 67435, 67610,
68448, 68497, 68943, 69099, 69473,
(69606), 69760, (69926), 70076, (70084),
70241, 70820, 70821, (70885)-70886,
70913, 71092, 71570, (71820), 72589,
73153, 73253, 74103, 75032, 75840,
77749, 78124, 78269, 78996, 79104,
79189, 79626, 80865, 81129, 81984,
82008, 82438, 82779, 83886, 83968,
84401-84402, 84463, 84478, 84998,
85018, 85045, 85058, 85197, 85563,
85618, 86169, 87467, 87685, 87691,
87698, 87704, 88505, 88607, 89033,
note after 89216, 89607, 90829, 90864,
91001, 91089, 91312, 91423, 91425-
91427, 91428-91431, 91437, 91450,
91452, 91454, 91456, 92320, 92720,
93096-93098, 93606, 93663, 94078,
94392, 94394, 94394A, 94395, note after
94720, note after 94725, 94777, 94784-
94785, 95464, 96073, 96092, 96328,
note after 96593-96594, 97381, 98391,
99587, 100075, 100375, 100398, 100401,
101914, 101942, 101955, 102016, 102594,
103155, 103160, 103434, 104201-104202,
104207, 104688

U. S. Legation. Buenos Aires (Province)
9021, 72494 see also Bland, Theodric.
Graham, John, 1774-1820. Rodney,
Caesar Augustus, 1772-1824.

U. S. Legation. Central American Confederation. (48119) see also Squier,
Ephraim George, 1821-1888.

U. S. Legation. China. 12813, 34866, 48134,
79493 see also McLane, Robert
Milligan, 1815-1898. Parker, -------.
Seward, G. F.

U. S. Legation. Chile. 5865 see also
Bland, Theodric.

U. S. Legation. France. 16863, 25497,
25605-25606, (42161), 48054, (48088),
56775, (58595), 59593, 62702, 69499,
94261, 99303, 103949 see also Franklin,
Benjamin, 1706-1790. Gerry, Elbridge,
1744-1814.

U. S. Legation. Great Britain. 1010, 4549,
16887, (40345), 43707, 45451, (55531),
(58464), 62908, 74264-74266, 74272-
74274, 87138, 101270 see also Adams,
Charles Francis, 1807-1886. Madison,
James, Pres. U. S., 1751-1836. Pinckney,
Thomas, 1750-1828. Pinkney, William,
1764-1822. Rush, Richard, 1780-1859.

U. S. Legation. Japan. 68945 see also
De Long, C. E.

U. S. Legation. Mexico. (20115), 23433,
48397, 58076, 63687

U. S. Legation. Netherlands. 230, 247-248,
(15934), (39804), 47760, 92762, 98504,
104130 see also Adams, John, Pres.

U. S., 1735-1826. Lee, William, 1739-
1795.

U. S. Legation. Panama. (16986), 58408
see also Corwine, Amos B.

U. S. Legation. Paraguay. (58515) see also
Washburn, Charles A.

U. S. Legation. Spain. 25149 see also
Forsyth, John, 1780-1841.

U. S. Library of Congress. 10053, 15560-
(15562), (15563)-15579, 84041, 1st note
after 98997, 4th note after 99888

U. S. Library of Congress. Law Department.
47364

U. S. Library of Congress. Librarian.
89556 see also Spofford, Ainsworth
Rand, 1825-1908.

U. S. Light House Board. see U. S.
Treasury Department. Light House
Board.

U. S. Marine Corps. 26904, 29943, 68958,
68960

U. S. Marine Corps. Courts Martial (Devlin)
19822, 70424

U. S. Marine Corps. Courts Martial (Heath)
61047

U. S. Marine Corps. Courts Martial
(Reynolds) 70425-70426

U. S. Marine Corps. Quartermaster's Department. 68958

U. S. Marine Hospital Fund. (70294)

U. S. Marshall for the District of Pennsylvania.
defendant 60470, 82884 see also Smith,
John. defendant

U. S. Military Academy, West Point, N. Y.
48975

U. S. Military Academy, West Point, N. Y.
Board of Visitors. 12216, 95806

U. S. Military Academy, West Point, N. Y.
Corps of Cadets. First Class, 1848.
(82343)

U. S. Mine Inspector for Alaska. see U. S.
Bureau of Mines.

U. S. Mixed Commission on British and·
American Claims. see Mixed Commis-
sion on British and American Claims
Under Article XII of the Treaty of
Washington, 1871.

U. S. Mixed Commission on Private Claims
Established Under the Convention Between
Great Britain and the United States, 1853.
see Mixed Commission on Private
Claims Established Under the Convention
Between Great Britain And the United
States, 1853.

U. S. National Cemetery, Antietam, Md. see
U. S. Antietam National Cemetery.

U. S. National Cemetery, Gettysburg, Pa.
see U. S. Gettysburg National Cemetery.

U. S. National Currency Bureau. First
Division. Chief. 69940 see also
Clark, S. M.

U. S. National Department of Education. see
U. S. Office of Education.

U. S. National Museum, Washington, D. C.
83739, 84230, 85007, 80521-80522,
80552

U. S. National Museum, Washington, D. C.
Traveling Exhibit of Graphic Arts.
83739

U. S. National Observatory, Washington, D. C.
see U. S. Naval Observatory, Washington, D. C.

U. S. National Zoological Park, Washington,
D. C. see Washington, D. C. National
Zoological Park.

U. S.

U. S. Naval Academy, Annapolis. 1594-
1594B, 56781, 68947, 68966
U. S. Naval Academy, Annapolis. Board of
Officers. 68947
U. S. Naval Astronomical Expedition, 1845-
1852. see United States Naval Astro-
nomical Expedition, 1849-1852.
U. S. Naval Commission to Examine League
Island. see U. S. Navy Department.
Board of Officers to Decide Between
League Island and New London for a
Naval Station.
U. S. Naval Observatory, Washington, D. C.
2258-2259, 18803
U. S. Naval Retiring Board. 64322
U. S. Naval Ranks Board. (69888)
U. S. Navy. 7045, 7411, 18277, 19133,
22940, 23510, (23526), 25058, 25060,
25722, 26904, 29943, 39356, 40765,
41446, 51641, 51743, 52083, 56779,
56787, 57503, 62408, 68949, 68960-
(68962), 70541, 70611, 77540, 82958,
92320, 95355, 1st note after 99448
U. S. Navy. Courts Martial (Abbot) 24,
96807, 1st note after 101000
U. S. Navy. Courts Martial (Babbit) 2568
U. S. Navy. Courts Martial (Barron) 3644
U. S. Navy. Courts Martial (Binney) 5465,
48976, 8th note after 96930A
U. S. Navy. Courts Martial (Bolton) 6251
U. S. Navy. Courts Martial (Coxe) 17286
U. S. Navy. Courts Martial (Craven) 17430
U. S. Navy. Courts Martial (Cromwell)
86804
U. S. Navy. Courts Martial (Follansbee)
24952
U. S. Navy. Courts Martial (Glynn) 96872
U. S. Navy. Courts Martial (Gordon) 3644
U. S. Navy. Courts Martial (Grayson)
28422
U. S. Navy. Courts Martial (Hall) 3644
U. S. Navy. Courts Martial (Hook) 3644
U. S. Navy. Courts Martial (Kennon) 37456
U. S. Navy. Courts Martial (Kenny) (37458)
U. S. Navy. Courts Martial (McBlair)
(42957)
U. S. Navy. Courts Martial (Mackenzie)
16515, 43421, 43426
U. S. Navy. Courts Martial (May) 47084
U. S. Navy. Courts Martial (Meade) 47236
U. S. Navy. Courts Martial (Newell) 54963
U. S. Navy. Courts Martial (Perry) 61047
U. S. Navy. Courts Martial (Porter) 64221-
64222
U. S. Navy. Courts Martial (Rhind) (70488)
U. S. Navy. Courts Martial (Shaw) 79925
U. S. Navy. Courts Martial (Sheburne)
80338
U. S. Navy. Courts Martial (Small) 86804
U. S. Navy. Courts Martial (Smith) 82572,
82576
U. S. Navy. Courts Martial (Spalding) 88914
U. S. Navy. Courts Martial (Spencer) 86804
U. S. Navy. Courts of Inquiry (Baldwin)
(72747)
U. S. Navy. Courts of Inquiry (Barron)
3643
U. S. Navy. Courts of Inquiry (Bartlett)
3780
U. S. Navy. Courts of Inquiry (Hull)
(33636)
U. S. Navy. Courts of Inquiry (Latimer)
(39027)
U. S. Navy. Courts of Inquiry (Renshaw)
75957, note after 96922

U. S. Navy. Courts of Inquiry (Lockwood)
(41754)
U. S. Navy. Courts of Inquiry (Long) 41868
U. S. Navy. Courts of Inquiry (Meade)
47236
U. S. Navy. Courts of Inquiry (Morris)
50862
U. S. Navy. Courts of Inquiry (Porter)
64217, 64221
U. S. Navy. Courts of Inquiry (Riell) 78352
U. S. Navy. Courts of Inquiry (Ringgold)
(71426)
U. S. Navy. Courts of Inquiry (Rodgers)
72475
U. S. Navy. Courts of Inquiry (Shaw) 79963
U. S. Navy. Courts of Inquiry (Smith) 83319
U. S. Navy. Courts of Inquiry (Somers
Mutiny) 86804
U. S. Navy. Officers. petitioners 47647,
(53592), 71589, 75342, 90657
U. S. Navy. Sundry Line Officers. petitioners
see U. S. Navy. Officers. petitioners
U. S. Navy Board, Philadelphia. Paymaster.
60636 see also Webb, William.
U. S. Navy Department. 24, 646, 3644,
3828, 5465, 14978, 15119, 18805, 18807,
20449, 20451, 25722, 26648, 34415,
35092, (35249), 39519, 36613, 39519,
43180, 47285, 51743, 53252, 53373,
56762, 56787, 61047, (62493), 65733,
68960, (69688), (69923), 72024, 74109,
74966, 75957, 82574, 84956, note after
90781, 91900, 93951, 96807, note after
96922, 97280, 97282, 1st note after
101000, 101913 see also Robeson,
George Maxwell, 1829-1897. U. S.
Board of Navy Commissioners.
U. S. Navy Department. Agents. 48059,
55877, 84955 see also Norton, Eugene
L.
U. S. Navy Department. Board of Naval
Officers Upon a Trial of an Amoskeag
Steam Fire Engine, 1866. 69749
U. S. Navy Department. Board of Officers
to Decide Between League Island and
New London for a Naval Station. 39518-
31519, 69764, 90707 see also Com-
mittee Appointed by the Secretary of the
Navy and the Legislature of Connecticut,
on the Navy Yard at New London.
U. S. Navy Department. Board of Officers
to Decide Between League Island and
New London for a Naval Station.
Majority. 44073
U. S. Navy Department. Board of Officers
to Decide Between League Island and
New London for a Naval Station.
Minority. 39519, 44073, 70242
U. S. Navy Department. Board of Naval
Examiners. see U. S. Board of Naval
Examiners.
U. S. Navy Department. Bureau of Construc-
tion, see U. S. Bureau of Construction.
U. S. Navy Department. Bureau of Navigation.
see U. S. Bureau of Naval Personnel.
U. S. Navy Department. Bureau of Naval
Personnel. see U. S. Bureau of Naval
Personnel.
U. S. Navy Department. Bureau of Ordnance.
see U. S. Bureau of Ordnance.
U. S. Navy Department. Bureau of Ordnance
and Hydrography. see U. S. Bureau
of Ordnance and Hydrography.
U. S. Navy Department. Bureau of Statistics.
Chief. (41436)

U. S. Navy Department. Bureau of Steam Engineering. see U. S. Bureau of Steam Engineering.

U. S. Navy Department. Bureau of Yards and Docks. see U. S. Bureau of Yards and Docks.

U. S. Navy Department. Judge Advocate. see U. S. Judge Advocate General's Office (Navy)

U. S. Navy Department. Permanent Commission. 90809

U. S. North Pacific Exploration Expedition, 1853-1856. see North Pacific Exploring Expedition, 1853-1856.

U. S. Northwest Territory. see Northwest Territory, U. S.

U. S. Office of Education. 21884-21885, 33408, 70977, 84499, 90763 see also Hoyt, John W. Richards, Zalmon, 1811-1899.

U. S. Office of Indian Affairs. 9658, 12443, (12457), 12471-(12472), (32746), 34607, 34630, 34648, 34668, 40341, 40346, (44438)-(44439), (48718), 77838, 77849, 77855, (79113), 96597, 96632-96633, 96661, 96689, 96708, 96712-96714, (96754), 96732 see also Armstrong, William. Clark, William, 1770-1838. Dodge, Henry, 1782-1867. Dougherty, John. Hulbert, John. Long, Stephen H. Manypenny, George W. Schermerhorn, John F. Schoolcraft, Henry Rowe, 1793-1864. U. S. Board of Indian Commissioners.

U. S. Office of Internal Revenue. 6975, 6977, 34913-34914, 68497

U. S. Patent Office. 8495, 22247, (22345), 59037-59040, 59043, 59047-59048, 70122

U. S. Patent Office. Commissioner. 20144, (22344), (22345), 59037-(59038), 59040-59041, 59043, (69775) see also Burke, Edmund, 1809-1882. Ellsworth, Henry Leavitt, 1791-1858.

U. S. Patent Office. Library. 59036

U. S. Peace Commissioners, Paris, 1782. 66394 see also Franklin, Benjamin, 1706-1790. Laurens, Henry, 1724-1792.

U. S. Peace Commissioners, Ghent, 1814. 53975, 90639

U. S. Peace Commissioners to the Hampton Roads Conference, 1864. (48140)

U. S. Pension Bureau. 25037, 73253

U. S. Pension Office. see U. S. Pension Bureau.

U. S. Post Office Department. 7055, 8215, 10250, 20325, 25169, 30070, 40883, 41690, 47397, 52431, 53389, (57020), (64475)-64476, 64482, 64484, (64486)-64491, 64492-64498, (64499), (64501), 64502, 64505, 64511-64513, 64984, 69674, 69889, 72466, 91487, 94173, 94507, 102347 see also Barry, William Taylor, 1785-1835. Granger, Gideon, 1767-1822. Holt, Joseph, 1807-1894. Meigs, Return Jonathan, 1764-1824.

U. S. Post Office Department. Auditor. (28233)

U. S. Post Office Department. Committee Appointed By the Postmaster General, to Examine and Revise the Postal Code. 64508

U. S. Postmaster General. see U. S. Post Office Department.

U. S. Presidnet. 15539-15540, 57406, 61208, 82976

U. S. President, 1789-1797 (Washington) (445)-449, 6001, 14010, (14151), 15176-15178, 15517, 16180, 18005, 24886, 25876, 25980, (29967)-29968, 33150, 34900, 36361, 40343, 48045-48050, 48141, 59593, 60418, 63811, 65343-65344, 65359, 69834, 78647, 87862, 89198, note after 94720, 96583-96584, 96586, 96589, 96603-96605, 96754, 100222, 101529, 101545, 2d note after 101545, 101708-101709, 2d note after 101709, 101734, 101747, 101748, 101765-101767, 101837, 101873, note after 101900, 104204-104205, 104459 see also Washington, George, Pres. U. S., 1732-1799.

U. S. President, 1797-1801 (Adams) 227, (238), 250, 259, (445)-449, 1016, (1230), 2446, 3431, 14008, (14151), 14990, 15456, 18005, 24886, 25876, 25886, 34865, (48051)-48056, 48141, 48148, 59593, 62656, 62702, 63811, 65359, 69837-69838, 69866, 78647, 78743, 79399, (79402), note after 97538, 89198, 94261, 96590, note after 99292, 101712-101716, 103848, 104204-104205 see also Adams, John, Pres. U. S., 1732-1826.

U. S. President, 1801-1809 (Jefferson) (445)-449, 1226, 2025, 9428-9429, 11027, 12877, 12488, (14151), 14312, 18005, 20449, 22291, (23365), 25876, 26259, 27072, 29953, 34544, 35885-(35886), 35893, 35916-35917, (35919), (35925), 40696, 40824-40827, 40832-40833, 41610, 42177-42179, 42192, 42264, 42266, 42291, (48057)-48065, 48148, (48755), (49519), 50013, 52083, 56434, 58478, 63811, 65004, 65359, 69789, 78647, 83811, 89198, 95390, 2d note after 96498, 96499, 96591-96592, 96613, 96625, 96627, 96631, 97440, note after 101839, 103334, 104204-104205, 104647, 105157 see also Jefferson, Thomas, Pres. U. S., 1743-1826.

U. S. President, 1809-1817 (Madison) (445)-448, 3299, (14151), 15945, 17448, (17885), 18005, 20450, 21533, 22412, 23502, 25876, 26399, (31832), 34398, 34400, (35886), 42265, 42267, 42456, 46031, 48065-(48074), 48148, 53975, 57627, (56498), 56959, 63811, 65359, 69737, 69816, 70237, 72475, 72847, 74353, 78647, 83809-83810, 83812-83817, 89198, 90639, 93470, 97901, 99315, note after 102768, 104204-104205 see also Madison, James, Pres. U. S., 1751-1836.

U. S. President, 1817-1825 (Monroe) (445)-448, (14151), 14849, 14981, (15594), 18005, 24859, 24887, 25876, 27073, 35345, (35378), 37456, 38739, 46068, 48075-48086, 48148, 63811, 65359, 78647, (79068)-79069, 89198, 93270, 96593, 96632-96635, 101011, 104204-104205 see also Monroe, James, Pres. U. S., 1758-1831.

U. S. President, 1825-1829 (J. Q. Adams) (445)-448, (14151), 15489, 18005, 24892, 25876, 48087-48095, 48148, 48580, 56524, 58405, 63694-63695, 63697, 63611, 69903, 71712, 78403, 78647, 88939, 89595, 96636-96657, 97913, 97925, 103434, 104204-104205 see also Adams, John Quincy, Pres. U. S., 1767-1848.

U. S. President, 1829-1837 (Jackson) (445)-448, 3138, (14151), 18005, 20314, 21445,

U. S.

25429, 25876, 29932, 31769, 33120, 34607, 34641, 35342, 35347, 35350-35359, 35391, 40370, 47200, 48096-48104, 48148, 63811, 64585, 65933, 66067, 69479, (77238), 78647, (79065), 85070, 87423, 88068, 6th note after 88114, 96559, 96659-96662, 96665, 98411, 98425, 102279-102281, 102291, 104204-104205 <u>see also</u> Jackson, Andrew, <u>Pres</u>. <u>U</u>. <u>S</u>., 1767-1845.
U. S.　President, 1837-1841 (Van Buren) (445)-448, (14151), 18005, 25876, 43927, 48105-48106, 48148, 54781, 55709-(55711), 59043, 63811, 78647, 96736, 98411, 98416, 102318-102319, 104240-104205 <u>see also</u> Van Buren, Martin, <u>Pres</u>. <u>U</u>. <u>S</u>., 1782-1862.
U. S.　President, 1841 (William Henry Harrison) 447-448, 18005, 25876, 63811, 78647, 104240-104205 <u>see also</u> Harrison, William Henry, <u>Pres</u>. <u>U</u>. <u>S</u>., 1773-1841.
U. S.　President, 1841-1845 (Tyler) 448, 18005, 24888, (48107)-48111, 62465, 63811, 70577, 70725, 78647, 79115, 86503, 93121, 96737, 104204-104205 <u>see also</u> Tyler, John, <u>Pres</u>. <u>U</u>. <u>S</u>., 1790-1862.
U. S.　President, 1845-1849 (Polk) 25840, 41162, 43091, 48112-48116, 48493, 48574, 49207, (52854), 55712, 70482, 72439, 73134, 73135, 80440, 90413, 90417, 90419, 91648, 104204-104205 <u>see also</u> Polk, James Knox, <u>Pres</u>. <u>U</u>. <u>S</u>., 1795-1849.
U. S.　President, 1849-1850 (Taylor) 9963, 48117, 59488, 74757, 78765, 90434, 91562-91563, 91565, 104205 <u>see also</u> Taylor, Zachary, <u>Pres</u>. U. S., 1784-1850.
U. S.　President, 1850-1853 (Fillmore) (17792), (24332)-24333, 36885, 48118-48122, 91278 <u>see also</u> Fillmore, Millard, <u>Pres</u>. <u>U</u>. <u>S</u>., 1800-1874.
U. S.　President, 1853-1857 (Pierce) 4785, 11585, (17762), 48122-48129, 49332, (68967) 70277, (82658), 84015 <u>see also</u> Pierce, Franklin, <u>Pres</u>. <u>U</u>. <u>S</u>., 1804-1869.
U. S.　President, 1857-1861 (Buchanan) 6130, 12813, (16860), 22917, 33077, 37023, 37071, 40330, 40663, 48130-48135, 50955, 52997, (65356), 70749, note after 87402, 87436, 87438, 86788, 101913 <u>see also</u> Buchanan, James, <u>Pres</u>. <u>U</u>. <u>S</u>., 1791-1868.
U. S.　President, 1861-1865 (Lincoln) (2650), 3616-(3617), 5641, 8158, 14978, (16860), 16882, 17632, 20214, 28191, 29628, 35504, 36268, (37994), 37996, (39163), 40347, 40981, 41150-41159, 41162, 45353, 48136-(48141), 48922, 53946, (55179), 58467, (65305), 65932, 68047, 68049, 76524, 76549, 76647, 76684, 78035, 84483, 86277, 87552, 87555, 89850 <u>see also</u> Lincoln, Abraham, <u>Pres</u>. <u>U</u>. <u>S</u>., 1809-1865.
U. S.　President, 1865-1869 (Johnson) 2652, 25253, 36168, 36170, 36174, (48142)-48145, 51085, (58468-(58469), (69754), 71366, 87445 <u>see also</u> Johnson, Andrew, <u>Pres</u>. <u>U</u>. <u>S</u>., 1818-1875.
U. S.　President, 1869-1877 (Grant) (37076), (68475), 75191 <u>see also</u> Grant, Ulysses Simpson, <u>Pres</u>. <u>U</u>. <u>S</u>., 1822-1885.

U. S.　President, 1881 (Garfield) <u>see also</u> Garfield, James Abram, <u>Pres</u>. <u>U</u>. <u>S</u>., 1831-1881.
U. S.　President, 1897-1901 (McKinley) 83366 <u>see also</u> McKinley, William, <u>Pres</u>. <u>U</u>. <u>S</u>., 1843-1901.
U. S.　President, 1909-1913 (Taft) <u>see also</u> Taft, William Howard, <u>Pres</u>. <u>U</u>. <u>S</u>., 1857-1930.
U. S.　Provost Marshall of Rhode Island. 70682 <u>see also</u> Hamlin, William E.
U. S.　Quartermaster's Department. 1430, 20449, (45016), 47393, 48059, 51875, 63263, 66974, 68962, 72819-(72836), (72838)-(72845) <u>see also</u> Meigs, M. C.
U. S.　Receiver of the Land Office, Fort Wayne, Ind. <u>see</u> U. S. General Land Office. Receiver, Fort Wayne, Ind.
U. S.　Register of the Treasury. 50868
U. S.　Revenue Commission, 1865-1866. 16703, 17132, (20295), 70170, 70173-70175 <u>see also</u> Colwell, Stephen. Hayes, Samuel Snowden, 1820?-1880. U. S. Special Commissioner of the Revenue, 1866-1870. Wells, David Aimes, 1828-1898.
U. S.　Sanitary Commission. <u>see</u> United States Sanitary Commission.
U. S.　Second Auditor of the Treasury. <u>see</u> U. S. Treasury Department. Second Auditor.
U. S.　Secretary of Agriculture. <u>see</u> U. S. Department of Agriculture.
U. S.　Secretary of State. <u>see</u> U. S. Department of State.
U. S.　Secretary of the Interior. <u>see</u> U. S. Department of the Interior.
U. S.　Secretary of the Navy. <u>see</u> U. S. Navy Department.
U. S.　Secretary of the Treasury. <u>see</u> U. S. Treasury Department.
U. S.　Secretary of War. <u>see</u> U. S. War Department.
U. S.　Smithsonian Institution. <u>see</u> Smithsonian Institution.
U. S.　Solicitor General. <u>see</u> U. S. Department of Justice.
U. S.　Solicitor of the Treasury. 57402
U. S.　Special Agent to Georgia. 27080
U. S.　Special Commissioner of the Revenue, 1866-1870. 10842, 37272, 70171-70172, 71803 <u>see also</u> U. S. Revenue Commission, 1865-1866. Wells, David Ames, 1828-1898.
U. S.　Special Commissioners on the Mineral Resources of the United States. 8664 <u>see also</u> Browne, John Ross, 1817-1875. Taylor, James W.
U. S.　Special Counsel on the Suit of Richmond Banks Claiming Coin, 1866. 89232
U. S.　State Department. <u>see</u> U. S. Department of State.
U. S.　Subsistence Department. 34637-(34638), (68954)
U. S.　Superintendent of Finance. 50866-50868, 70072, note before 90715 <u>see also</u> Morris, Robert, 1734-1806.
U. S.　Superintendent of Indian Affairs. <u>see</u> U. S. Office of Indian Affairs.
U. S.　Superintendent of Public Schools. <u>see</u> U. S. Office of Education.
U. S.　Superintendent of the Census. <u>see</u> U. S. Census Office. Superintendent.
U. S.　Superintendent of the Coast Survey. <u>see</u> U. S. Coast and Geodetic Survey. Superintendent.

U. S. Supreme Court. 274, 2210, 2895, 3924, 5472, (5576), 5751, 6602, (7770), 7904, (8482), 9426, 9612, 9615, 10927, 10995, 11308, 12031, 12045, 12197, (14989), 16134, (17390), (18036), (18446), (19399), 20148, (20647), 21621, 23453, 23887, 25009, (26336), 26640, 26916, 27082, 27293, 27488, (29463), 29534, 29889, (30089), 30090, (31093), 31317, 31669, (31825), 33240-(33241), 34738, 42206, 42729, 43255, 44794-44795, 45686, 46149, (46151)-46154, 48029, 49087, 49669, (52437), 56050, 58473-58474, 58696, (59653), 60817, 61206, 64251, 65520, 69402, (69606), 70249, 70497, 70546, 70732, 70751-70753, 70820, 71728, (74111)-74112, 74316, 78256-(78262), (79360), 80359, (80361), 82581, 83725, 84842, 85190, 87287, 88152, 88584, 89224, note after 89831, 90390, 90394, note after 90601, 90759, 93489, 93524, note after 96509, note after 96853, 2d note after 96883, 96888, 2d note after 100462, 101425, 2d note 101499, 101975, 102261, 103153-103154, 103160, 103162, 103424A, 103431, 104413, 105215, 105321, 105476, 105479

U. S. Supreme Court. Chief Justice. 35832, 48029, 82655, note after 94301 see also Chase, Salmon Portland, 1808-1873. Jay, John, 1745-1829. Taney, Roger Brooke, 1777-1864.

U. S. Surgeon General's Office. 2049, 2523, 3523, 16380, 18032, 22683-22684, 30116, 39456-(39458), 42382, 47307, 50347, 57853, 69757, 69911, 69920, 69954, 76524, 76549, 76565, 76647, 84268, 105991 see also Barnes, Joseph K. Hammond, William Alexander, 1828-1900. Lawson, Thomas. Lovell, Joseph. Mann, James, 1759-1832.

U. S. Surveyor General. 86169 see also Putnam, Rufus, 1738-1824.

U. S. Survey General of Kansas and Nebraska. 37022

U. S. Tax Commissioner. 71570

U. S. Territory South of the River Ohio. see Tennessee (Territory)

U. S. Thirty-Six American Citizens, Confined at Carthagena. petitioners see Thirty-Six American Citizens Confined at Carthagena. petitioners

U. S. Treasurer of the Mint. see U. S. Bureau of the Mint.

U. S. Treasury Department. 1823, (3179), (3187), 3189, 3191, 7258, 8659, 8723, 12200, 14965, 14978, 16703, 16859, 17126, 17132, 17444, (17760), 19305, 19451, (20295), (20472), 26399, (26402), (26931), 29975, 29976-(29981), 29985, 29987, 29988, 30819, 35441, 36485, 26968, (37841), (38264), 40338, 40340, 42177, 42192, 44416, 45121, (47191)-47192, 62167, 66067, (69498), 69784, 70171, 70173, 70175, 70240, 70262, 72434, (72438), (72440), 72675, 74077, 74736, 76045, (80166), 81010, 81038, 84396, 85076, 86169, 88068, 89042, 91639, 91648, 94395, 96396, 97751, 103265, 103385, 105102, 106114 see also Chase, Salmon Portland, 1808-1873. Corwin, Thomas, 1794-1865. Gallatin, Albert, 1761-1849. Hamilton, Alexander, 1755-1804. Meredith, William Morris, 1799-1873. Rush, Richard, 1780-1859. U. S. Board of Treasury. Walker,

Robert John, 1801-1869. Woodbury, Levi, 1789-1851.

U. S. Treasury Department. Bureau of Statistics. 50197

U. S. Treasury Department. Light House Board. 41044-41046, (41048)

U. S. Treasury Department. Register's Office. 101546-101546A

U. S. Treasury Department. Second Auditor. 34642-(34643)

U. S. Treasury Department. First Comptroller. 40763 see also Whittlesey, Elisha.

U. S. Treaties, etc. 276-277, 775, 1059, 1074, 1228, 2461, 2447-2449, (6582), (7164), (7904), 8126-8127, 9021, 9080, 9199, 10663, 10883, 10889, 11006, 11825, 12477, (12830), 12877, 13578, (13895), 14008-(14009), 14378, 14389, 15493, 15531, (15559), 15770, 16086-16090, 16119, 16196, (11759), 17184, (17531), 18875, 19273, (20464), (22015), 22231, 22234, 23422, 23962, 23966, 24884, 24888, 25640, (26388), 27095, 27274, 27995, 28069, 28421, (30030), 30335, 30825, (32223), 33854, (34358), 34481, 35779, 35849, 37723, 38815, 38820, 39383, 39423, 39430, 39431-39432, 42211, 42227, 42308-42309-42309, 42895, 44046, 47770, (48060), (48062), 48065, 48073, 48086, 48107, 48115, 48145, 48369, 48398, 50016, 50018, 51311, 52776, 52843, 53913, 54781, 56163, (56519), 56569, 56898, 57656, 57738, 58340, 61206, 61208, 63286, (64480), 64516-64517, 64605, 64607, 65446, 65110, (65757), 65935, 66394, (69090), 69440, 69443, note after 69528, 69760, 69884, 74337, 76747, 77548, 79115, 81460, 82008, 83609, 84448, 84842, 89975, 89991, 90115, 91092-91093, 92762, 93129, 94777, 2d note after 96185, 96445, 96560-96578, 96580-96590, 96591-96737, 96754, 97298, 97545, 99303, 99307, 99314, 2d note after 99216, 100039, 100931, 101246, note after 101847, 102401, 2d note after 102806

U. S. United States and Mexican Boundary Survey. 22538

U. S. Vaccine Agent. 82780 see also Smith, James, 1771-1841.

U. S. War Department. 57-58, 2045, 2804, 2992, 3926, 5809, 9063, 12474, 14978, 15002, 15430, 15456, 15832, 16868, 17459, 17865, 17866, 20449, (20809), (24103), 24913-(24914), (26689), (26892), 26894, 27065, 27080, 29523, 29883, (30030), 30409, 30574, 33525, 34481-34482, 34628, note after 34645, 34664-(34666), 34703, 34867, (35321), (35734), 36377, 37387-37388, 37854, (43014), (43017), 43022, 48961, 51739, 56435, 55127, 56778, 56787, 58456, note just before 60250, (60810), 63150, 63691, 63696, 64116-(64117), 64247, 65338, 66689, (68129), (68946), 68957, 69900, (69923), 69946, 69697, 70293, 70592, 70731, 71713, 71715, 71940, (72488), (73259), 73393, 74079-74080, 74091, 74212, (75020), (76081), (77847), 78405, 78407, 79112, 80414, 83533, 83534, 83706, 83724, 84774, 85187-85188, 86232, 86282, 86289, 88413, 89686, 90537, 94745, note after 96593, 96656, 96664, 101911, 101913, note after 104493 see also Barbour, James, 1775-1842. Cameron, Simon, 1799-1889. Davis, Jefferson, Pres.

Confederate States, 1808-1889. Eaton, John Henry, 1790-1856. Eustis, William, 1753-1825. Floyd, John Buchanan, 1807-1863. Marcy, William Learned, 1786-1857. Poinsett, Joel Roberts, 1779-1851. Porter, Peter Buell, 1773-1844. Stanton, Edwin McMasters, 1814-1869. Wilkins, William, 1779-1865.

U. S. War Department. Bureau of Military Justice. 20142

U. S. War Department. Bureau of Topographical Engineers. see U. S. Army. Corps of Topographical Engineers. and U. S. Engineer Department.

U. S. War Department. Clerk. 19618

U. S. War Department. Commission on Ordnance and Ordnance Stores. 70260

United States. 83370

United States acts, 1st session, 4th Congress. 85197

United States advertising circular. 61606

United States against Franklin W. Smith. 82572

United States against Franklin W. Smith. A review of the argument. 82576

United States against Henry Hertz. 52394

United States Agricultural Academy. 85446

United States Agricultural Society. 36747, 66960

United States album. 25623

United States almanac. 84218

United States almanac and national register for the year 1850. 20325

United States' almanac. Comprising ca[l]culations for the latitudes and meridians. 84218

United States almanac. . . . For . . . 1820. (51849)

United States almanack, or complete ephemeris for 1843. 20769

United States almanac. . . . With a variety of public information. (19739)

United States and British provinces contrasted. 31853

United States and Canada. (1943)

United States and Cuba. 62470

United States and England: being a reply to the criticism of Inchiquin's letters. 59215

United States and England. By an America. (28518)

United States and foreign postage directory. 10250

United States and France. 38444

United States and Mexican Boundary Survey. see U. S. United States and Mexican Boundary Survey.

United States and Mexican Claims Commission, 1869-1876. 48342, (58272), (72513)

United States and New-Hampshire register, for the year 1797. 97953

United States and Mexican Mail Steamship Lines. 9666

United States and New York Foreign and Domestic Exchange Company. 97954

United States and other divisions of the American continent. 24789

United States Anti-masonic Convention, Philadelphia, 1830. 32529, 45492, 97955-97959

United States Anti-masonic Convention, Philadelphia, 1830. Committee. Chairman. 32529, 97957 see also Halley, Myron.

United States Anti-masonic Convention, Philadelphia, 1830. Committee to Report a

Succinct and Lucid Account of the Abduction and Murder of William Morgan. 97955, note after 103826

United States Anti-masonic Convention, Philadelphia, 1830. Committee to Report a Succinct and Lucid Account of the Abduction and Murder of William Morgan. Chairman. 97955, note after 103826 see also Whittlesey, Frederic.

United States Anti-masonic Convention, Baltimore, 1831. 97960

United States Anti-masonic Convention, 1833. 50682, 97958

United States Assessors. Convention, Cleveland. see Convention of United States Assessors, Cleveland, 1863.

United States autography. (69100)

United States Bank. see Bank of the United States.

United States bankrupt law. 70821

United States Baptist annual register and almanac. 97961

United States Baptist annual register, for 1832. 97961

United States Beneficial Society of Philadelphia. 97962

United States bonds and securities. (4417)

United States bonds, the various issues. (24350)

United States business directory for 1867. 47879

United States calendar. (15829), 52884

United States calendar; for 1801. (24688), 45887

United States' calendar, for . . . 1822. 43985

United States calendar, for the year 1820. 70733

United-States calendar, for the year 1823. 15660

United States calendar, for . . . 1822. 52885

United States catholic almanac. 11521

United States catholic almanac; or, laity's directory. 48217, 97963

United States catholic historical magazine. 72918, 72945, 79993, 80004, 80014, 80018, (80023), 96193

United States Catholic Historical Society. 99357, 99362, note after 99383C. 101017, 106398

United States catholic magazine. (37410)-37411, 47103, (69337), 80001

United States Christian Commission. 12905, 68401, 86276, 86292

United States Christian Commission. Army Committee, Pittsburgh. 63144

United States Christian commission. Baltimore. see Baltimore Christian Commission.

United States Christian Commission. Maryland. 45383-45385 see also Maryland State Fair, for the Christian and Sanitary Commissions, Baltimore, 1864.

United States Christian Commission. New York Branch. 54385

United States Christian Commission. Philadelphia. (61525)

United States Christian Commission. Union Prayer Meeting, Baltimore, 1863. 45383

United States Christian Commission. Second report of the Committee of Maryland. 45385

United States chronicle. 103175

U. S. Circuit Court, Vermont, 1861. In the matter ex parte, Anson Field. 82206

U. S. Circuit Court. Myra C. Gains vs. City of New Orleans. (21256)

United States Coast Survey. 18807

"United States Coast Survey." 86964

United States Coast Survey. [By Albert Gallatin.] 26398

U. S. Coast Survey report for 1855. 5810

United States commercial and statistical register. 31107

United States commercial register. 65693

United States complete bankrupt's gazette. 45823

United States constitution, a pro-slavery instrument. 7011

United States constitutional manual. 43459

United States consulates in China. 79493

United States criminal calendar. 29935, 75023, 2d note after 97963

United States criminal history. 29935, 75023, 2d note after 97963

United States customs guide. 1525

United States debt. 51317

United States Democratic review. 97973

U. S. Department of the Interior. Report of the Board of Indian Commissioners. 34680

United States deposites. 97964

United States diary. 62505

United States digest; being a digest of decisions. 66825, 66827, 76506

U. S. Digest of common law and admiralty reports. 66826

United States directory. 79937

United States during the war. 39240

United States elevated to glory and honor. 6987, 91749

United States elevated to glory and honour. 91750

United States' equity digest. 66826

United States, et al., libellants and captors, vs. the steamship Peterhoff. 80449

United States, ex. rel. John H. Wheeler vs. Passmore Williamson. 10696

United States Exploring Expedition, 1838-1842. 7193, (7692), 7845, 11370, 14850, 18422-(18423), 18425-18427, 23780, 25836, 25837, (25841), 25843, (25845), 27484, 28089, 28368, 29635, 36014, 62622-(62623), 103994

United States Exploring Expedition . . . ethnography and philology. 29635

United States Exploring Expedition . . . herpetology. 27484

United States express guide and shipping directory. 30918

United States farmer's almanac, for . . . 1845. 89591

United States farmers' almanac, for . . . 1846. 89580, 89591

United States farmers' almanac, for . . . 1843. 89578, 89590

United States, 15th January, 1794. 87862

United States Fire Company, Philadelphia. 62357, 97965

United States Fire Company, Philadelphia. Charter. 62357, 97965

United States gazette. 8227, 26008, 35518, 70238, 85612, 85613, 95289, 2d note after 102863

United States gazetteer. 78331

United States' general directory. 97931

United States Geological Exploration of the fortieth parallel. 29523

United States George Washington Bicentennial Commission. 33005, 101545, 101696, 101700, 101702, 101767

U. S. Grand Jury as a political engine. (53420)

U. S. Grinnell Expedition in search of Sir John Franklin. (36998)

United States Guano Company. 29046

United States herald. 94784

United States historical and statistical index. 29491

United States historical magazine. (80006)

United States illustrated. 18396

United States in 1861. 26730

United States in prophecy. 83481

United States in the light of prophecy. 84469-84471

United States Insurance Company. see Washington Association and United States Insurance Company. 101977

United States internal revenue and tariff law. 20925

United States Insurance Company of Baltimore. 97966

United States Insurance Company of Philadelphia. Charter. 97967

United States; its power and progress. 64736

United States journal. 84162

United States kalendar and army and navy register. 97968

United StatesLand Company. 97969

United States law register and official directory for 1860. 41629

United States lawyer's directory and official bulletin. 41629

United States literary gazette. 49445, 93602, note after 97969

United States Lloyd's register of American and foreign shipping. 30711

United States lottery. 97971

United States lottery; 1776. 97970

United States magazine and Democratic review. 5302, 6503, 7671, 23232, (41993), 53080, (69707), 76952, (78742), 84151, 84162, 89595, 95110, 97550, 97972-97973, 100582, 102328

United States magazine, or, general repository of useful instruction and rational amusement. 97974

United States manual of biography and history. 44786

United States, Massachusetts District: SS. Special District Court. 96929

United States mercantile guide. (25730), (25733)

United States mercantile register. 37301

United States, Mexico, Japan. 84489

United States Military Academy, at West Point. 44387

United States Military Philosophical Society. 97975

United States military railroads. Report of Bvt. Brig.-Gen. D. C. McCallum. 42980

United States militia act. 91423, 91425-91427, 91429-91430, 91450

United States militia acts. 91456

United States' Mining Company. Board of Directors. 97976

United States mint. 74133

United States national almanac. 43070

United States national register and calendar for 1851-1852. 20325

United States nautical magazine. (50189)

United States Naval and Military Academy. Candidates book of information. 83697

United States' naval and miscellaneous almanac. 97977

United States Naval Astronomical Expedition, 1849-1852. 83001

U. S. Naval Astronomical expedition to the southern hemisphere. 27419

United States Naval Benevolent Association. 97978

United States naval chronicle. (27715)

United States Naval Engineers. petitioners (47692)

United States Naval Fraternal Association. 97979

United States Naval Institute, Annapolis. 83828, 83960

United States Naval Lyceum, Brooklyn. 97980

United States Naval Lyceum, Brooklyn. Administration Committee. 97981

United States Naval Lyceum, Brooklyn. Special Committee. 52079, 97982

U. S. naval magazine. (68512)

United States Navy. What is its use? (17138)

United States of America. (18536)

United States of America; a history. 43433

United States of America. Circuit Court of the United States, for the Northern District of Illinois. James F. Soulter et al. vs. the Peoria & Oquawka Railroad Company et al. In chancery. Foreclosure of second mortgage. Argument of counsel. 87300

United States of America. Circuit Court of the United States, for the Northern District of Illinois. James F. Soulter et al. vs. the Peoria & Oquawka Railroad Company et al. In chancery. Forclosure of second mortgage. In the matter of the title to 119 bonds. 87301

United States of America compared with some European counties. (32301)

U. S. A. "Going home to vote." 12200

United States of America. In the Supreme Court of the United States. Stephen Waring, a citizen of the state of Connecticut. 101425

United States of America. Joint Memorial and resolutions of the Nevada Legislature. 52410

United States of America. Northern Pacific Railroad Company, charter, organization, and proceedings. 55821

United States of America: their climate, soil, productions, population, manufactures, religion, arts, government, &c. &c. 91704

United States of America; their history from the earliest period. 51503

United States of America vs. International Harvister Company et al. 84518

United States of America, vs. the President, Directors, and Company of the Bank of the United States. 82145

United States of North America. 51417

United States of North America as they are. 1265

United States of North America as they are in their political, religious, and social relations. 64559, note after 97982

United States of North America as they are; not as they are generally discribed. 8398

United States of the world. 63631

United States passport and Russia. 83966

United States patent law. 51340

United States' political looking-glass. 97983

United States Post Office directory. 64984

United States Post Office directory and postal guide. 72466

United States Post Office directory [for Columbus, O.] 14894

United States Post Office Director [for Lexington, Ky.] 40883

United States Post Office directory [for New Albany, Ind.] 52431

United States Post Office guide. 7055

United States postal guide, and official advertiser. 64514

United States practical navigator. 72312

United States primer, containing, besides other useful and instructive matter. 97984

United States primer, improved. 97983A

United States railroad and ocean steam navigation guide. 54459

United States railroad & ocean steam navigation guide, illustrated with a map of the United States. 20528

United States railroad directory. 32690

United States record, for . . . 1827, 28, 29. 15666, 68816

United States record for the year 1829. 74340

United-States record from 1785 to 1857 inclusive. 15665

United States register. 1122, (5261), 22238, 63823, (66942), 95835, 97905, 97986-97985, 103264

United States register, and New York pocket almanac for 1805. 26331, 49221, 50441

United States register, geographical, historical and statistical. 97987

United States register of the officers of the Army. 32689

United States register, or, blue book for 1866. 20325

United States repository, and New-Hampshire register. 97988

United States review. 11117, 97973

United States Sanitary Commission. 4575, 5995, (12061), 13112, 13681, 20718, 21544, 22262, 25696, 27245, 30113, 32427, (33118), 34822, 34868, 38061, 40454, 40512, 52305, 54892-54893, 54896, 57539, (57918), 57942, 61910, 68940, 68965, 76523-76660, 76664-76679, 76681-76686, 76688-76689, 76692, 76695-(76696), 84268, 84276, 86287 see also Northwestern Sanitary Commission.

United States Sanitary Commission. Army and Navy Claim Agency. 76681

United States Sanitary Commission. Army Relief Bazaar, Albany, 1864. see Army Relief Bazaar, Albany, N. Y., 1864.

United States Sanitary Commission. Associate Medical Members. Committee. 84268

United States Sanitary Commission. Associate Medical Members. Committee. Chairman. 84268 see also Smith, Stephen, 1823-1922.

United States Sanitary Commission. Auxiliary Finance Committee. (76618), 76647

United States Sanitary Commission. Baltimore. see also Maryland State Fair, for the Christian and Sanitary Commissions, Baltimore, 1864.

United States Sanitary Commission. Boston Branch. Executive Committee. 76690

United States Sanitary Commission. Bureau of Information and Employment. 76617, 76647

United States Sanitary Commission. California Branch. 2698, 7906, 76636, 76687

United States Sanitary Commission. Central Finance Committee. 76535, 76647

United States Sanitary Commission. Central Office. 76578, 76647

United States Sanitary Commission. Central Treasury. 76686

United States Sanitary Commission. Chicago Branch. 12657

United States Sanitary Commission. Cincinnati Branch. 13097, 13112, 33438, 76568, 76647, 76660

United States Sanitary Commission. Commission of Inquiry On the Treatment of Prisoners of War. 34341, 76651

United States Sanitary Commission. Committee of Inquiry. 51791

United States Sanitary Commission. Committee to Visit the Military General Hospitals, In and Around Washington. 76540, 76546, 76647 see also Agnew, C. R. Van Buren, William Holme, 1819-1883.

United States Sanitary Commission. Department of Special Inspection of the General Hospitals of the Army. 76581, 76591, 76605, 76647

United States Sanitary Commission. English Branch. Agent. (76648) see also Fisher, Edmund Crisp.

United States Sanitary Commission. European Branch. (7076), (76649)

United States Sanitary Commission. Executive Committee. 76682

United States Sanitary Commission. Executive Finance Committee on the State of New York. (76538)

United States Sanitary Commission. Executive Service. 76608, 76612, 76647

United States Sanitary Commission. Field Relief Agency. see United States Sanitary Commission. Field Relief Corps.

United States Sanitary Commission. Field Relief Corps. 68940, (76598), (76607), 76647

United States Sanitary Commission. Field Relief Corps. Chief Inspector. (76598), 76647 see also Steiner, Lewis H.

United States Sanitary Commission. Field Relief Service, 76618, 76647

United States Sanitary Commission. General Aid Society for the Army, Buffalo. 9057, 76629

United States Sanitary Commission. General Aid Society for the Army, Buffalo. Delegates. (33100)

United States Sanitary Commission. General Secretary. see United States Sanitary Commission. Secretary.

United States Sanitary Commission. Great Central Fair, Philadelphia, 1864. see Philadelphia. Great Central Fair, 1864.

United States Sanitary Commission. Kentucky Branch. (76654)

United States Sanitary Commission. New-England Women's Auxiliary Association, Boston. Supply Department. 76661

United States Sanitary Commission. New York Agency. 76570, 76647

United States Sanitary Commission. New York City Branch. 76581, 76668 see also New York (City) Committee Who Presented the Report on Ambulance and Camp-Hospital Corps to the Authorites in Washington, 1862.

United States Sanitary Commission. New York City Branch. Executive Finance Committee. (76538), 76549, 76647

United States Sanitary Commission. Northwestern Sanitary Commission. see Northwestern Sanitary Commission.

United States Sanitary Commission. Philadelphia Associates. see United States Sanitary Commission. Philadelphia Branch.

United States Sanitary Commission. Philadelphia Branch. 61577, 62358, (76637), 76693-(76694)

United States Sanitary Commission. Philadelphia Branch. General Superintendent. 61971

United States Sanitary Commission. President. 67537, 76082, 76549-76550, 76574, 76579, (76589), 76622, 76647, 76669, 76672, (76675), 76687 see also Bellows, Henry Whitney, 1814-1882.

United States Sanitary Commission. Protective War Claim and Pension Agency, Philadelphia. Solicitor. 62168, 66097, 76652

United States Sanitary Commission. Secretary. 76655, (76674)

United States Sanitary Commission. Soldiers' Aid Society of Northern Ohio, Cleveland. 13681, 76561, 76647, 86312, 86316-86317

United States Sanitary Commission. Soldiers Relief Fund Committee, San Francisco. Secretary. 76082, 76669

United States Sanitary Commission. Soldiers Relief Fund Committee, San Francisco. Treasurer. 76082, 76669

United States Sanitary Commission. Statistical Bureau. (76696)

United States Sanitary Commission. Supply Department. 68965, 76588, 76592, 76647

United States Sanitary Commission. Western Department. 76580, 76610, 76647, 76680

United States Sanitary Commission. Western Department. Secretary. (76590), 76601, 76610, 76623 see also Newberry, James Strong, 1822-1892.

United States Sanitary Commission. Women's Central Association of Relief, New York. (54620), (76556), 76630-76634, 76647, 76697

United States Sanitary Commission. Women's Maryland Branch. 45397

United States Sanitary Commission. Women's Pennsylvania Branch. 62358, 76698

United States Sanitary Commission. Women's Relief Association of Brooklyn. 76679

United States Sanitary Commission. California Branch. Document no. 2. How and where the money goes. 76687

U. S. Sanitary Commission. [Circular calling attention to the "Army and Navy Claim Agency."] (76688)

United States Sanitary Commission. Classified statement of the expenditures and receipts of the Central Treasury. 76686

U. S. Sanitary Commission. Classification of the financial report. 76689

U. S. Sanitary Commission. Document no. 1. New series. 76624

United States Sanitary Commission. (Executive Committee of Boston Associates.) No. 1. 76690

United States Sanitary Commission. (Executive Committee of Boston Associates.) II. 76690

U. S. Sanitary Commission. First annual report of the Soldiers' Aid Society, of Northern Ohio. 76691

United States Sanitary Commission in the valley of the Mississippi. 54896, 76623

U. S. Sanitary Commission. Nelly's hospital. 52305, 57942, 76692

United States Sanitary Commission. Philadelphia associates. An appeal to the people of Pennsylvania. 62358, 76693

U. S. Sanitary Commission. Preamble and resolutions. (76694)

Universal calendar, and the North American almanack, for the year of the creation, according to Sacred Writ, 5750. 90949

Universal calendar, and the North American almanack, for the year of the creation, according to Sacred Writ, 5751. 90951

Universal calendar, and the North-American almanack, for the year of the creation, according to Sacred Writ, 5749. 90948

Universal calendar, and the North-American almanack, for the year of the creation according to the scriptures 5751. 90952

Universal calendar, and the North-American's almanack, for the year of the creation, according to Sacred Writ, 5750. 90950

Universal cambrist and commercial instructor. 37316

Universal chronicle. 73791

Universal chronologist, and historical register. 75419

Universal church gazetteer. 25382

Universal dictionary of arts, sciences and literature. (68634)

Universal dictionary of knowledge. 102370

Universal dictionary of trade and commerce. 77276-77278

Universal emancipation. 10889, 97999

Universal empire of love. A poem. 55363

Universal evening post. 10732

Universal exposition, Paris, 1867. see Paris. Exposition Universelle, 1867.

Universal extension of Messiah's kingdom. 66228

Universal friend. 92790

Universal friend to all mankind. pseud. Some considerations. see Wilkinson, Jemima.

Universal friend's advice, to those of the same religious society. 104031-104032

Universal gazette. 84079

Universal gazetteer; a dictionary, geographical, statistical, and historical. 43130

Universal gazetteer; ancient and modern. 105237-105238

Universal gazetteer of ancient and modern geography. (78598)

Universal gazetteer of the eastern and western continents. (50953)

Universal gazetteer; or, a new geographical dictionary. (18534)

Universal gazetteer, remodelled and brought down to the present time. 8246

Universal geographical dictionary. 7791

Universal geography. [by T. Milner.] 49127

Universal geography, or a description of all the parts of the world. 44166

Universal geography, together with sketches of history. (73602)

Universal grace. 68122

Universal guide. 83737

Universal harmony. 4050

Universal history Americanized. 67708

Universal history, ancient and modern. (46985)

Universal history: arranged to illustrate Benn's charts of chronology. 59358

Universal history. [By Comte Louis Philippe de Segur.] 15017, note after 92196

Universal history. [By Samuel Goodrich.] 27915

Universal history: in which the history of every nation. 27900

Universal history of the U. S. of America. 94445

Universal history of the United States of Ame America. 94446

Universal history on the basis of geography. 27922

Universal instructor in all arts and sciences. 37176, 60754, 98000

Universal jest book. 98001

Universal kalender. 90946

Universal kalendar, comprehending the landman's and seaman's almanac. 90946

Universal kalendar, and the North-American's almanack. 90947

Universal library. 92481

Universal love. 63883

Universal Lyceum, Philadelphia. 98002

Universal magazine. 1162

Universal masonic record. 34137

Universal medicine. 23216

Universal pathfinder. 57247

Universal peace-maker. (52429)

Universal Peace Society, with the basis of co-operation. 4263

Universal picturesque album. 57923

Universal pocket almanack, 1756. 64083

Universal popular statistics. 17728

Universal pronouncing gazetteer. 2925

Universal psalmodist. 94335-94339

Universal receipt book. 98003

Universal register of the Baptist denomination. 2223, 100434

Universal repository of instruction and amusement. 34077, 73781-73782

Universal repository of knowledge and entertainment. 62019

Universal republic of truth and righteousness. 85129

Universal restitution, a scriptural doctrine. 92162

Universal restoration. 104734-104735

Universal review of literature, domestic and foreign. 41488

Universal right of sufferage [sic] is in danger. 98004

Universal salvation. (31056)

Universal signal book. 90013

Universal spread of the Gospel. 16366

Universal statistical table. 77544

Universal suffrage, an address. 8453

Universal suffrage: an argument. 4323

Universal suffrage, and complete equality of citizenship. 98005

Universal tablet of memory. 30317

Universal tontine. 98006

Universal traveller and commercial and manufacturing directory. 31634

Universal traveller and monthly gazetteer. 96481A

Universal traveller: or, a compleat description of the several nations of the world. 75829

Universal traveller; or, a complete account of the most remarkable voyages and travels. 3362

Universal traveller . . . with woodcuts. 27875

Universale descrittione di tutto di mondo. 73194

Universale fabrica del mondo overo cosmografia. 1364

Universali historia. 6118, 6120, 94273

Universalior [sic] cogniti orbis tabula ex recentibus confecta. 76838

Universalis astrolabii facilis depingendi modus. 91221

Vniversalis tabvla ivxta Ptolemeum. 66490-66491, 66494, 66497-66498

Universalism: a modern invention. 73834

Universalism against suicide. 103792

Universalism as it is. 30843

Universalism confounds and destroys itself. 88901

"University project." Report of Special Committee. (13088)
University quarterly. 8624
University record. 60761
University settlement. 84067
Universum, or views of the remarkable places and objects. 8204, 48674
Universums Neue Welt. 8204
Universus terrarum orbis scriptorum calamo delineatus. 39133, 2d note after 98594
Unjust reproaches. 17277
Unknown. pseud. Slave among pirates. see Murphy, George Mollett.
Unknown author, of Virginia. pseud. Treatise on slavery. 96744
Unknown foreigner. pseud. Inchiquin, the Jesuit's letters. see Ingersoll, Charles Jared.
'Unknown' library. 84128
Unknown or lays of the forest. 30987
Unknown parts of America. 19129, note before 98445-98449, 98451-98461, 98463, 98465
Unletter'd laick. pseud. Layman's answer to Dr. Trapp. 39472
Unmasked nabob of Hancock County. 98021
Unmasking of a politick atheist. 106018
Unnersoutiksak ernisuksiortunnut kaladlit nunaen netunnut. 40133
Uno de los Ministros de la Corte Suprema de Justicia. see Mexico. Corte Suprema de Justicia.
Uno de sus amigos. pseud. Defensa de D. Ildefonso Villamel. see Roel, Juan.
Uno de sus colaboradores. pseud. tr. 59573
Unofficial. Contrast of expenses of the government. 103265
Unofficial letter from General Harrison. 30572
Unos amigos de la disciplina eclesiastica. pseud. Juicio imparcial. see Solano, Vicente, 1791 or 2-1865.
Unos catolicos. pseud. Capilla protestante en Valparaiso. see Solano Astra-Buruaga, Francisco, 1817-1892.
Unos Centro Americanos. pseud. Soconusco (territorio de Centro-America.) 86188
Unos conciudadanos. pseud. Reflexiones sobre la urgencia. (68737), 5th note after 98882
Unos cuenteros. pseud. Va de cuento. 98270
Unos eclesiasticos. pseud. Verdadera idea del poder. 98939
Unos emigrados de la villa de Chilapa. pseud. Representacion calumniosa. 48527
Unos Michoacanos. pseud. see Michoacanos. pseud.
Unos Nicaraguenses. pseud. publishers 89961
Unos Peruanos. pseud. Articulo sobre la republica de Chile. 16157
Unos republicanos. pseud. Ojeada al Congreso de 1830. 98882
Unos Salvadorenos. pseud. publishers 89961
Unos Valenciano. pseud. A nuestros compatriotas. 98022
Unos Venezolanos. pseud. Principales acontacimientos de Puerto Cabello. 65662
Unparalleled exhibition. 11535
Unparalleled law case. 71274
Unparallel'd sufferings and surprising adventures of Philip Quarll. 66952
Unparalleled sufferings and surprising adventures of Philip Quarll. (66950)
Unparalleled sufferings and surprising adventures of Philip Quarll, an Englishman. 66949
Unpartheyische gedancken in reimen. 98032
Unprejudiced observer. pseud. Letter to a great M-------r. 40391, note after 98023

Unprejudiced refutation of Hogan's farewell address. 32426
Unpublished journal of Job Scott. 78285
Unpublished letters of Mrs. Isabella Graham. 28212
Unpublished manuscript on Shaker history. 23501, 79705
Unpublished parody of Voltaire's Alzire. 100728
Unpublished records of the craft. 33576
Unreasonable pleas made by some against their duty to their ministers. 1703, (37480), note after 97417
Vnreasonablenesse of the separation. 72103
Unseen glory of the children of God, asserted. 104073
Unseen hand. 31324
Unselfish patriotism. 2010
Unsere grossen Feldherren. 85148
Unsere Lehre uberhaupt und dieses Schriftgen. 42642, note after 106351, 106359
Unseres Landes wohlstand einer Probe Gottlicher Huld. (82190)
Unspeakeable gift of God. (14525)
Unspotted life. 3794
Untaught bard. 98024
Unter den Penchuenden. 27194
Unterhaltende Belehrungen. 5099
Unterhaltende Darstellung der Entdeckungen. 106341
Unternehmung jenseits der Felsengebirges. 35132
Unternehmungen fur seine Rettung. 7384
Unterrichtendes Handbuch fur Alle. (57820)
Unterschiedliche Gotterdienste in der gantzen Welt. 73321
Untersuchungen uber Amerika's Bevolkerung. 33748, 98679
Untersuchung uber das gelbe Fieber. 46883
Untersuchungen uber die Geographie America's. (57257)
Untersuchungen uber die Geographie des Neuen Continents. 33747
Untersuchungen und Aufschlusse uber die Entdeckung von Amerika. 98025
Vnterhanige Supplication. (8784)
Untimely death of a man of God lamented. 26785
Unum, E. Pluribus. pseud. Broadside for the times. 8142
Unum necessarium. 46568
Unvorgreiffliches Bedencken. 98357
Unveiling of divine justice. (72196)
Uvzueta, Gabriel Bocangel y. see Bocangel y Vnzueta, Gabriel.
Unzueta, Juan Antonio de. 98026-98028 see also Mexico. Contrador Jeneral de las Rentas Nacionales de Tabaco y Polvora. Mexico. Oficia de Rezagos. Gefe.
Up country letters. 44384
Up the river. (80152)
Up to the light. 84134
Upcott, William. ed. 23208
Updike, Wilkins. 43662, 71144, 98029-98030
Updike, Wilkins. supposed author 70538, note after 98028
Upfold, George. 90182
Upham, Charles Wentworth. (288), 9927, (12406), 25838, 46623, 60643, 62642, 64042-64043, 75653, 85081, 98031-98046, 3d note after 101723
Upham, D. A. J. 49011
Upham, Ebenezer P. defendant 103686
Upham, Nathaniel Gookin. 98047
Upham, Phineas. 105365
Upham, Thomas Cogswell. 1216, (32709), 46475, 94112, 98048-98051

Upham, Timothy. plaintiff 98052-98053
Upholsterer. pseud. Upholsterer's letter.
98054
Upholsterer's letter. 98054
Upland, Pa. Court. 68399
Upon American slavery. 56652
Upon Mr. Samuel Willard, his frist coming
into the Assembly. (79448), note after
98054, 104082
Upon the death of that aged, pious, sincere-
hearted Christian, John Alden. 98055
Upon the death of that reverend and aged man
of God, Mr. Samuel Arnold. 98056
Upon the death of that virtuous and religious
Mrs. Lydia Minot. 98057
Upon the drying up of that ancient river, the
River Merrymak. 98058
Upon the elaborate survey. (33445), 106052
Vpon the elaborate survey, etc. 33446
Upon the first invention of shipping. 67561
Upon the history, condition and prospects of
the University [of Miami, Ohio.] 1385
Upon the history, principles, and prospects of
the Bank of British North Ameirca.
106075
Upon the joyfull and vvelcome return of His
Sacred Majestie. (47153)
Upon the peace. A sermon. 33040
Upon the present state of commerce and manu-
factures. 8417
Upon the tariff; April, 1824. 102265
Upon the visitation of neutral vessels under
convoy. 77648
"Upon the whole, I will beg leve to tell the
House" what is realy my opinion. 63761
Upon whom rests the guilt of the war? 38445
Upper Alton, Ill. Anti-slavery Convention,
1837. see Illinois Anti-slavery Conven-
tion, Upper Alton, 1837.
Upper Canada Baptist Association. see Bap-
tists. Ontario. Baptist Association.
Upper Canada. By His Excellency John G.
Simcoe. 98065C
Upper Canada Celtic Society. 52296 .
Upper Canada Celtic Society prize essay.
55296
Upper Canada Clergy Society. 98093
Upper Canada. Copy of a petition to the Im-
perial Parliament. 98072, 98092
Upper Canada. Council-Chamber, Navy Hall,
February 2, 1793. 98059A
Upper-Canada. Council-Office, Sept. 24, '99.
98059F
Upper Canada gazette. 98061
Upper Canada herald. 74564
Upper Canada law list or directory. 73152
Upper Canada Law Society. see Law Society
of Upper Canada.
Upper Canada Loyal and Patriotic Society. see
Loyal and Patriotic Society of Upper
Canada.
Upper Canada Reform Alliance Society. see
Reform Alliance Society of Upper Canada.
Upper Canada Religious Tract and Book Society.
98094-98095
Upper Canada Religious Tract and Book Society.
Committee. 98094
Upper Canadian. pseud. Military defences of
Canada. 48957
Upper Canadian Convention of Friends to En-
quiry. 98096
Upper Canadian Travelling Mission Fund.
91679
Upper Granville Baptist Association. see
Baptists. Nova Scotia. Baptist Associa-
tion in Upper Granville.

Upper Medawakanton Indians. see Medwakanton
Indians.
Upper Merion, Pa. Christ Church. (62359)
see also Corporation of the United Swedish
(Lutheran) Churches of Wiccacoe, Kinguss-
ing, and Upper Merion, Pa.
Upper Mississippi. 26357
Upper Mississippi Company. petitioners 98097
Upper Peru. 61082
Upper Sandusky, Ohio. Wyandotte Mission.
see Methodist Episcopal Church. Con-
ferences. Ohio Annual Conference. Wyan-
dotte Mission, Upper Sandusky.
Upper ten thousand. 8047
Uppingham tune. 94335
Upright happy in death. 102085
Upright lives of the heathen briefly noted.
105218
Upright man. 91492
Uprising of a great people. 26731-26732
Ups and downs in America. 55005
Ups and downs in the life of a distressed gentle-
man. 92154
Ups and downs of Lot Wyman. 84162
Upsala. University. Library. Palmskold
Collection. 1941
Upsher, Thomas. 98098
Upshur, Abel Parker, 1791-1844. 7866, 92291,
98099-98102, 1st note after 100577
Upshur, Abel Parker, 1791-1844. supposed
author 100463
Upson, A. J. 22520
Upton, F. S. supposed author 90714
Upton, F. V. supposed author 90714
Upton, Francis Henry. supposed author 90714
Upton, George P. (80028), (80031)
Upton, Samuel. 98103
Upton, Sarah M. 95624
Upton, Wheelock Samuel. 42205, 42209, 98104
Uraga, Jose Lopez. see Lopez Uraga, Jose.
Uranga, Jose Maria Orruno Irasusta y. see
Irasusta y Uranga, Jose Maria Orruno.
Uraguay: poema. 26487
Urania: a rhymed lesson. 32621
Urania; or, a choice collection of psalm-tunes.
42856
Uranian Society for Promoting the Knowledge
of Vocal Music, Philadelphia. 62361
Urano, C. M. tr. 6464
Urbain, Frere. see Gaillet, Urbain.
Urbain, Ismayl. 98106
Urbair, B. von Wullerstorf-. see Wullerstorf-
Urbair, B. von.
Urban VIII, Pope, 1568-1644. (68844), 68844,
76885, 98108-98109 see also Catholic
Church. Pope, 1623-1644 (Urban III)
Urban, Fortia d'. see D'Urban, Fortia.
Urban, Silvanus. ed. (26954)
Urbana, Ohio. Oak Dale Cemetery. Trustees.
56377
Urbaneja, Diego Bautista. tr. (43761), 77739
Urbaneja, Manuel M. 3251
Urbano de Mata, Nicolas. 98107
Urbanus Catholicus. pseud. Waare oosprong.
98110
Urbanus Filter. pseud. New England magazine.
see Mecom, Benjamin, b. 1732.
Urbina, Thelesforo Jose de. 98111-98116
Urbium praecipuarum totius orbis brevis et
methodica descriptio. 73000
Vrbivm rervmqve Hispanicarvm, academiarvm,
bibliothecarvm, clarorvm deniqve in omni
disciplinarvm genere scriptorum auctores.
77904
Urcullu, Jose de. 98117-98119
Urdaneta, Amenodoro. 98120

Urdinola, Francisco de. 98121
Ureta, Mateo de Toro Zambrano y. see
  Toro Zambrano y Ureta, Mateo de.
Uribe, Francisco de. 98122
Uribe, J. P. de Fernandez de. see Fernandez
  de Uribe, J. P. de.
Uriburu, Beeche y Compania. Sindicos del
  Concurso. see Sindicos del Concurso
  de Uriburu, Beeche y Compania.
Urim and Thummim. 90208
Urim, or halcyon cabala. 98123, 100670
Uring, Nathaniel. 98124-98127, 102204
Urizar y Bernal, Antonio Joaquin de. petitioner
  98128-98129
Urizar y Estrada, Juan de. 98130
Urlsperger, Johann August. 27084, 31209,
  98131
Urlsperger, Johann August. respondent 31209,
  note after 98130
Urlsperger, Samuel. 98131-98139
Vrlspergervs, Ioannes Avgvstvs. see Urls-
  perger, Johann August.
Urmston, Nathaniel M. 98140
Urquhart, David. 93647, 98141-98143
Urquhart, Thomas. 98144-98146
Urquinaona, Jose Maria. 98147
Urquinaona y Pardo, Pedro de. (69223), 98148-
  98149
Urquiza, Justo Jose de. 9021, 16166
Urquizu Ibanez, Gaspar. 98150
Urrabieta, Mariano. 12165, note after 99383C
Urraca, Maria. 98151
Urrea, Jose. 98152-98153
Urruha Montayo, Ignacio Joseph de. see
  Urrutia y Montoya, Ignacio Jose de.
Urrutia, ------- Cordova y. see Cordova
  y Urrutia, -------.
Urrutia, Carlos de. (24978)
Urrutia, Fernando de. 98154
Urrutia, Francisco Xavier Maria de. petitioner
  98155
Urrutia, Juan Antonio de. defendant 98156
Urrutia, Manuel Jose de. 98157
Urrutia de Vergara, Antonio. petitioner
  98159-98161
Urrutia de Vergara y Estrada, Manuel. 98162-
  98163
Urrutia y Arana, Juan Antonio Guerrero y
  Davila. see Guerrero y Davila Urrutia
  y Arana, Juan Antonio.
Urrutia y Montoya, Ignacio Jose de. 50216,
  98164-98165
Urrutigoyti, Miguel Antonio Francisco de.
  98166
Ursino, Alex. 66686
Ursprung, Lehre, Constitution und Zucht-
  Ordung [der Vereinigten Bruder in
  Christo.] 97866
Ursprung und Fortgang der Revolution daselbst
  bis 1819. 4245, second note before 93419
Urstandliche und Erfahrungs-Volle hohe Zeug-
  nusse. 106363
Ursua, Antonio Maria Bucareli y. see
  Bucareli y Ursua, Antonio Maria.
Ursua, Juan Ignacio Castorena y. see
  Castorena y Ursua, Juan Ignacio.
Ursuline Convent, Charlestown, Mass. see
  Charlestown, Mass. Ursuline Convent.
Ursuline Convent, Quebec (City) see Quebec
  (City) Ursuline Convent.
Ursuline Convent. A poem. 62438, (77444),
  98169
Ursulines de Quebec. 98171
Ursus griseus. 9127
Urtassum, Juan de. 98172
Urteaga, H. H. 99633, 105724

Urtiaga, Pedro de la Concepcion. 98173
Uruena, Atanasio Jose de. 98174
Uruguay, Paulino Jose Soares de Souza, Ves-
  conde de. see Soares de Souza, Paulino
  Jose, Vesconde do Uruguay, 1807-1866.
Uruguay. (20435), (20441), 38719, 98175
Uruguay. Director del Estado, 1818. defendant
  99459 see also Pueyrredon, Juan
  Martin. defendant
Uruguay. Ministerio de Relaciones Exteriores.
  8996, 38988
Uruguay. Secretario del Gobierno. 99459
  see also Tagle, Gregorio.
Uruguay. Treaties, etc. 38719
Urville, Jules Sebastien Cesar Dumont d'. see
  Dumont d'Urville, Jules Sebastian Cesar.
Ury House School, Philadelphia. see Phila-
  delphia. Ury House School.
Us. pseud. Appendix to a late essay. 1793,
  2d note after 98175
Usage du compas et proprotion. 33563
Usauna, Trino. pseud. Algo sobre cierto
  discurso. 98176
Use and excellency of vocal music. (13317)
Use of Christianity . . . a sermon. (65513)
Use of Christianity, especially in difficult times.
  (65513)
Use of the round-leaf-cornel. (72125)
Useful and amusing book to every traveller.
  81535
Useful discovery in a letter. 98177
Useful essays, and instructive stories. 98178
Useful extract from the Massachusetts spy.
  1792
Useful family guide. 104250, 104252, 104254
Useful family herb bill. 104249, 104251
Useful family herbal. 104253
Useful hints in every daily life. 30210
Useful hints to travellers. 98178
Useful instruction and rational amusement.
  97974
Useful instructions for a professing people.
  104110
Useful life and peaceful death. 43841
Useful man. A sermon delivered at the funeral
  of Hon. Charles Paine. 26536
Useful man; or a trip to America. 98180
Useful selections from ecclesiastical records
  and printed sermons. 98181
Useful transactions for the months. 98182
Useful transactions in philosophy. 98182
Usefulness and expedience of souliers as dis-
  covered. (73981)
Uses and values of Congress, Empire and
  Columbian Waters. 76925
Uses of music. 55513
Uses of solitude. 84895
Uses of the dead to the living. 84417
Usher, Ellis Baker, 1852- 91117
Usher, Freeman L. pseud. Signal. see
  Worcester, Noah, 1758-1837.
Usher, James, Archbishop. see Ussher, James,
  Archbishop of Armagh, 1581-1656.
Uslar, Justus Ludwig von. 98183 see also
  Mexican Company of Mines. Chief Direc-
  tor.
Uslegung der Mercarthen oder Cartha marina.
  98184
Uso de la lengua vulgar. 24010
Uso manual de los llamados indigenas de
  Tlaxcala. 74604
Uso y eficacia de las aguas de los manatiales
  de Saratoga. 76926
Usos y costumbres de los Indios Pampas.
  3295
Uss, Francis. defendant 98185

Usselinx, Willem. 38260, 44661, 63830, (68646), (68983), note before 98186-98216, note after 101026, 3d note after 102894

Usselinx, Willem. supposed author 55449, (57379), 99316, 100773, 102879, 102893

Ussher, James, Archbishop of Armagh, 1581-1656. 7996, 16037, 101877

Ussieux, Louis d'. 21447, 98217

Ustariz, Geronymo de. see Uztariz, Geronymo de.

Ustariz, Mariano Eduardo de Rivero y. see Rivero y Ustariz, Mariano Eduardo de.

V. Sᵃ reserua de tributo, mitas, y seruicios personales. 98801

Usteri, Martin. 85371-85372

Usual manner of the procession of proclaiming the declaration of war against Spain. 98218

Usurpation of the Senate. 93685

Usurpation of the war powers. 78048

Usurpations of slavery. (79590)

Usurpations of the federal government. 30900

Usurpations of the federal government. The dangers of centralization. (34036)

Usurpations of the Senate in the origination of appropriation bills. 93684

Usurpations of vice through popular negligence. 105565-105566

Usury, funds, and banks. 56616

Usury laws. 18450

Usury, or interest proved to be repugnant to the divine and ecclesiastical laws. 56616

Vsvs annuli astronomici Gemma Frisio mathematico authore. (26856)

Vt fluctus fluctum. (55010), 62743

Ut vocatur volgo comptus ecclesiasticus. 23681

Utah (Territory) (28464), 75840

Utah (Territory) Attorney General. 85562 see also Snow, Zerubbabel, 1809-1888.

Utah (Territory) Constitution. 19731, 98220

Utah (Territory) Governor, 1874 (Vaughan) 85562 see also Vaughan, Vernon H.

Utah (Territory) Laws, statutes, etc. (28464), 75840

Utah (Territory) Supreme Court. 85563

Utah and the Mormons. Speech of Hon. John Cradlebaugh. 17331

Utah and the Mormons——The history, government, doctrines, customs, and prospects of the Latter-Day Saints. 24184

Utah bill. A plea for religious liberty. (32882)

Utah expedition. 16214

Utah journal. 83296, 83298

Utah problem. 24590

Utazás Kalifornia déli részeiben. 35764, 105714

Utenhovius, Carolus. (6799), 98222

Vthforligh forklaring ofwer Handels Contractet. 98211

Utica, N. Y. 98224

Utica, N. Y. petitioners 98227

Utica, N. Y. Anti-Masonic Convention, 1830. see Anti-masonic Convention, Utica, N. Y., 1830.

Utica, N. Y. Anti-masonic Republican State Convention, 1832. see Anti-masonic Republican State Convention, Utica, N. Y., 1832.

Utica, N. Y. Bank. see Bank of Utica.

Utica, N. Y. Census, 1816. 98232

Utica, N. Y. Charter. 98225

Utica, N. Y. Committee to Revise the Village Charter. 98225

Utica, N. Y. Constitutional Convention, 1837. see New York (State) Constitutional Convention, Utica, 1837.

Utica, N. Y. Convention of Loayl Leagues, 1863. see Loyal National League of the State of New York.

Utica, N. Y. Convention of the Young Men of the State of New York, 1828. see Convention of Young Men of the State of New York, Utica, 1828.

Utica, N. Y. Cornell University. see Cornell University, Utica, N. Y.

Utica, N. Y. Democratic State Convention, 1848. see Democratic Party. New York Convention, Utica, 1848.

Utica, N. Y. Fair of the Oneida County Agricultural Society, 1853. see Oneida County Agricultural Society. Annual Fair, Utica, 1853.

Utica, N. Y. Female Academy. see Utica Female Academy.

Utica, N. Y. First Presbyterian Church. 98226

Utica, N. Y. Hamilton Female Seminary. see Hamilton Female Utica, N. Y.

Utica, N. Y. Library. see Utica, N. Y. School District Library.

Utica, N. Y. Loyal Leagues. see Loyal National League of the State of New York.

Utica, N. Y. Lunatic Asylum. see New York (State) State Hospital, Utica.

Utica, N. Y. Merrill & Hastings Circulating Library. see Merrill & Hastings Circulating Library, Utica, N. Y.

Utica, N. Y. Neptune Fire Engine Company, No. 5. see Neptune Fire Engine Company, No. 5, Utica, N. Y.

Utica, N. Y. New York State Convention of Teachers and Friends of Education, 1831. see New York State Convention of Teachers and Friends of Education, Utica, 1831.

Utica, N. Y. New-York State Lyceum Annual Meeting, 1st, 1831. see New York State Lyceum. Annual Meeting, 1st, Utica, 1831.

Utica, N. Y. Oneida Bible Society. see Oneida Bible Society, Utica, N. Y.

Utica, N. Y. School District Library. 98231

Utica, N. Y. School District Library. Charter. 98231

Utica, N. Y. State Convention For Rescuing the Canals From the Ruin With Which They Are Threatened, 1859. see New York State Convention For Rescuing the Canals From the Ruin With Which They Are Threatened, Utica, 1859.

Utica, N. Y. State Convention of Mechanics, 1834. see State Convention of Mechanics, Utica, 1834.

Utica, N. Y. State Hospital. see New York (State) Hospital, Utica.

Utica, N. Y. Whig Party Convention, 1840. see Whig Party. New York. Convention, Utica, 1840.

Utica, N. Y. Young Men's Anti-masonic State Convention, 1830. see Young Men's Anti-masonic State Convention, Utica, N. Y., 1830.

Utica, N. Y. Young Men's Association. see Young Men's Association, Utica, N. Y.

Utica, N. Y. Young Men's State Convention, 1838. see New York Young Men's State Convention, Utica, 1838.

Utica Academy. 98235

V.

V., P. pseud. Defensa del Pensador Mexicano.
see Villavicencio, Pablo de.
V., P. pseud. Grandes bailes. see Villavi-
cencio, Pablo de.
V., S. de. pseud. tr. see Vries, Simon de.
V., S. von. pseud. tr. see Vries, Simon de.
V. C., J. M. pseud. see Villasenor Cervantes,
Jose Maria.
V. G., N. pseud. see Geelkercken, Nic. van.
V: S., P: P: see S., P: P: v:
V. W., G. S. pseud. see W., G. S. van.
pseud. tr.
V. y M., J. B. de. pseud. tr. 33720
V. A. S. Association of the New Hampshire
Conference Seminary, Northfield, N. Y.
see Tilton Seminary, Tilton, N. H. V.
A. S. Association.
V. & C. pseud. City intelligencer. 71171
V. Blanda. pseud. see Volck, Adalbert John,
1828-
V. C. pseud. see C., V. pseud.
V. D. B. pseud. see Bos or Bosch, in Latin,
Sylvanius, Lambertus van der.
V. D. C. pseud. see Cullion, F. Val de.
V. N. D. et S. S. S. pseud. see Cox, Samuel
H. supposed author
V. P. pseud. see P., V. pseud.
V. R. A. pseud. see A., V. R. pseud.
V. V. Smith, Lieutenant Governor of Arkansas,
vs. A. H. Garfield. 84485
V. W. C. pseud. see C., V. W. pseud.
Va de cuento. 98270
Vaamonde, Simon. 89285
Vaca, Alvar Nunez Cabeza de. see Cabeza de
Vaca, Alvar Nunez, 1490?-1557.
Vaca de Guzman, Jose Maria. see Vaca de
Guzman y Manrique, Jose Maria.
Vaca de Guzman y Manrique, Jose Maria.
29375, note after 98270
Vacancies in offices. 99108
Vacation voyage. 18447
Vacaville, Calif. Pacific Methodist College.
see Pacific Methodist College, Vacaville,
Calif.
Vacca, Alvaro Nunez Capo di. see Cabeza
de Vaca, Alvar Nunez, 1490?-1557.
"Vaccination." 85246
Vaccination. March 1, 1827. 82780
Vaccine enquirer. 82780, 98271
Vaccine Society, Philadelphia. 98272
Vaccinae vindicia. 85246
Vade, Jean Joseph. 98273
Vade mecum for America. 98274
Vade mecum: or, the dealers pocket com-
panion. 98275
Vaderlandsche afgezant naar Noord-Amerika.
98277
Vaderlandsche Dichter. 98276
Vaderlandsche Historie. 100950
Vaderlandsche merkwaerdigheden in het merk-
waerdig jaar 1782. 98277
Vaderlandsche merkwaerdigheden in het wonder-
jaar 1783. 98277
Vadiano, Iochimo. see Vadianus, i. e. Joachim
von Watt, 1484-1551.
Vadianus, i. e. Joachim von Watt, 1484-1551.
63956-63960, 76838, 98278-98283, note
after 102155
Vadianus, Joachimus. see Vadianus, i.e.
Joachim von Watt, 1484-1551.
Vadillo, Jose Manuel de. 1859, 98284
Vadius, Angelus. ed. 66469
Vae ri 9utubal 8habal. 98285
Vaez, Francesco. 96253
Vagabond. 101048
Vagabond. A novel. 101049
Vagabond adventures. 37149

Vagabond life in Mexico. 4534
Vagabond, or new looking-glass. 62914
Vagad, Gaubert Fabricius de. 98286
Vagaries of Vandyke Brown. 7412
Vagliente, Piero. 99353, 99374, 99379, 99393,
99383C
Vahl, Martin Hendriksen, 1749-1804. 67461,
98287-98288
Vaigem de Cayaba ao Rio de Janeiro. 4201
Viaggio fatto da gli Spagnivola a torno a'l
mondo. 47042
Viaje a los Estados-Unidos del Norte de
America. 106281
Vail, Aaron. 98289
Vail, Alfred. 98290-98292
Vail, Alfred. petitioner 50963
Vail, Eugene A. 98293-98294
Vail, Joseph. see Vaill, Joseph, 1751-1838.
Vail, Thomas H. 59258
Vail (Aaron) & Co. firm 98289
Vaill, Joseph, 1751-1838. 98295
Vaill, Joseph, 1790-1869. 98296-98297
Vaillant, Auguste Nicolas. 39111, 98298
Vaillant, Francois le. see Le Vaillant,
Francois.
Vain prodigal life. 31252, 2d note after 98298
Vain youth summoned to appear at Christ's bar.
50303
Vairasse d'Allais, Denis. 74822, 98299
Vaisseaux pris sur les Anglois. 94179
Val, ----- du. see Du Val, -------.
Val, Marcus du. see Du Val, Marcus.
Val, P. du. see Du Val, P.
Val, S. du. see Du Val, S.
Valades, Diego, fl. 1580. (24934), 98300
Valadesius, Didacus. see Valades, Diego, fl.
1580.
Valance, Henry L. 50681
Valasco, Luis de. 24894
Valasquez, Pedro. supposed author 91301
Valazquez, Jose. defendant 93808, 96948
Valbuena, Bernardo de. 2862-(2864), 1st-2d
notes after 98300
Valbuena, Pedro. defendant 48476
Valcarce, Joseph Bruno Magdalena Santin y.
see Magdalena Santin y Valcarce, Joseph
Bruno.
Valcarce Velasco, Manuel Antonio. 98301
Valcarcel, -------. (64436)
Valcarcel, Francisco de. 16825, note after
98301, note after 98720
Valckenaer, J. 100768
Valckenburgh, Johan. 98302
Valckenier, F. 49565
Valckenier, Frederiko. 98303
Valdafuentes, Fernando de Alencastro Marona
y Silva, Marques de. see Alencastro
Marona y Silva, Fernando de, Marques de
Valdafuentes.
Valdenebro, J. de. 19260
Valdeosera, Miguel Gonzales de. see Gonzales
de Valdeosera, Miguel.
Valderabano i Bracamonte, Alonso de Solis.
see Solis Valderabano i Bracamonte,
Alonso de.
Valderrama, Manuel. 98304
Valdes, -------, fl. 1683. 48608
Valdes, Alejandro. 98305
Valdes, Antonio. 98306
Valdes, Antonio Jose. 71309, 98307
Valdes, Cayetano. ed. 681, 69221
Valdes, Clemente. (48613), 98019 see also
Universidad de Mercaderes de Mexico.
Prior.
Valdes, Didaco. 98300
Valdes, Didacus. 25934

Valdes, Diego de Hevia y. see Hevia y Valdes,
Diego de, Bp.
Valdes, F. de Llano y. see Llano y Valdes,
F. de.
Valdes, Francisco Varas y. see Varas y
Valdes, Francisco.
Valdes, Gabriel de la Concepcion. 98308
Valdes, Garcia Ossorio de. plaintiff 86420
Valdes, Gonzalo Fernandez de Oviedo y. see
Oviedo y Valdes, Gonzalo Fernandez de,
1478-1557.
Valdes, Gonzalo Hernandez de Oviedo y. see
Oviedo y Valdes, Gonzalo Fernandez de,
1478-1557.
Valdes, Jose Eugenio. 98310
Valdes, Jose Manuel. 98311-98313
Valdes, Juan de. 98314-98315
Valdes, Juan de Salas y. see Salas y Valdes,
Juan de.
Valdes, Juana de. defendant 86422
Valdes, Leonor Ribera. see Ribera Valdes,
Leonor.
Valdes, Manuel. 98316
Valdes, Manuel Antonio, 48484, 75607, 98307,
98309, 98317-98320
Valdes, Miguel Anselmo Alvarez de Abreu y.
see Abreuy y Valdes, Miguel Anselmo
Alvarez de, Bp.
Valdes, Rafael. 98321
Valdes, Ramon Francisco. 73012
Valdes, Ramon Sotomayor y. see Sotomayor
y Valdes, Ramon, 1830-
Valdes, Rodrigo de. 98322
Valdes, Rodrigo Garcia Flores de. see
Flores de Valdes, Rodrigo Garcia.
Valdespino, Juan de. defendant 86417 see
also Dominicans. Vicario General.
defendant
Valdez, -------. 57224
Valdez, Gonzalo Hernandez de Oviedo y. see
Oviedo y Valdes, Gonzalo Fernandez de,
1478-1557.
Valdivia, Juan Antonio. 98323
Valdivia, Luis de, 1562-1642. 41085, 42669-
42671, 98324-98330, 98334
Valdivia, Luis de, 1562-1642. petitioner
98331-98333
Valdivia, Pedro de. 12754
Valdivia und Chiloe fur Deutsche Auswanderer.
(11363)
Valdivieso y Torrejon, Miguel de. 98335
Vale, Gilbert. 98336-98338
Vale, Mauritius. defendant 98339
Vale of Guasco. 98340
Vale of Louisiana. 98341
Vale of Norma. 77857
Vale of Tallulah. (69545)
Vale of Yumuri. 106372
Valedicion, for New Year's Day. 98342
Valedictions of the class then first graduated.
5468
Valedictory address, ... Amherst College.
33794
Valedictory address before the First Church
and Congregation in Saybrook. 33129
Valedictory address, . . . before the Social
Fraturnity [sic]. 41571
Valedictory address by Newton Edwards.
64278
Valedictory address, delivered at the anniver-
sary of the Oneida Institute. 28512
Valedictory address delivered at the third
annual commencement. 91207
Valedictory address, delivered before the
Athenaeum of Toronto. (77432)

Valedictory address delivered before the Homoeopathic Medical College of Pennsylvania.
90525
Valedictory address, delivered December 6,
1837. 105121
Valedictory address, delivered September 13,
1837. 28512
Valedictory address. . . designed to be delivered
at the gallows. 96873
Valedictory address, . . . July 26, 1810. 82713
Valedictory address . . . March 11, 1846.
(58191)
Valedictory address of Erastus Fairbanks.
23667
Valedictory address of General George Washing-
ton. 101606
Valedictory address of George Washington.
101686
Valedictory address of His Excellency, Frederick
Smyth. 52938, 85228
Valedictory address of His Excellency John A.
Andrew. 1479
Valedictory address of His Honor John S. Sleeper.
82123
Valedictory address of Mayor Weston. 44222
Valedictory address of the class. 87872
Valedictory address of the deceased. (50942)
Valedictory address of the late illustrious
George Washington. 101618, 101632-
101642
Valedictory address of the late President.
(38001)
Valeidctory address of the late Rev. John
Stevens. 91541-91542
Valedictory address of Washington to the people
of the United States. 101609-101610,
101615-101616
Valedictory address on reconstruction. 81525
Valedictory address, on relinquishing the charge
of Gorham Academy. 51889
Valedictory address on retiring from the Office
of President. 40866
Valedictory address on some of the duties and
qualifications of a physician. 9899
Valedictory address on the subject of recon-
struction. 8637
Valedictory address to his congregation.
91541
Valedictory address to the Adelphic Union
Society. 92883
Valedictory address to the class of medical
graduates. 82715
Valedictory address . . . to the graduates of
the Jefferson Medical College. 43009
Valedictory address to the graduates of the
Medical Department of Pennsylvania
College. 91784
Valedictory address to the graduates of the
Medical Department of Pennsylvania
College . . . March 2, 1861. 67749
Valedictory address to the graduating class
. . . March 16, 1864. 65365
Valedictory address to the graduating class
. . . March 12th, 1870. 65365
Valedictory address to the graduating class
of the Female Medical College of
Pennsylvania. 65365
Valedictory address to the graduating class of
the Female Medical College of Pennsyl-
vania. 79002
Valedictory address to the graduating medical
class of Harvard University. 6989
Valedictory address to the people of the United
States. 10666, 10671, 10674-10675,
10678-10680, 10683-10684

Valedictory address to the people of the United
States, published in September, A. D.
1796. 101669
Valedictory address to the Senior Class of
Oneida Institute. 28512
Valedictory address to the young gentlemen.
21562, note after 98342, 105785C
Valedictory address, upon resigning the
Mastery. 103074
Valedictory address . . . Women's Medical
College. (13655)
Valedictory addresses. 9235
Valedictory admonitions. 12944
Valedictory and inaugural addresses of the
Mayor. 49181
Valedictory and mintory writing. 27859
Valedictory charge to the graduates. 65944
Valedictory delivered at the forum. 75936
Valedictory delivered before the Mercantile
Library Association. 2824
Valedictory discourse: . . . Baltimore,
October 3, 1842. (36157)
Valedictory discourse . . . before the Second
Universalist Congregation. 65565
Valedictory discourse delivered at Durham.
14147
Valedictory discourse, delivered at the South
Church. 709
Valedictory discourse, delivered before the
Cincinnati of Connecticut. (33815)
Valedictory discourse, delivered before the
Society of United Christian Friends.
33476
Valedictory discourse, delivered by the Rev.
Arthur J. Stansbury. 90365
Valedictory discourse, delivered in the Ancient
Church. 92791
Valedictory discourse delivered in the First
Church. 95227
Valedictory discourse, . . . [in] Weymouth.
55879
Valedictory discourse, preached to the First
Church and Society. 104122
Valedictory discourse, preached to the First
Church and Society in Dorchester. 30521
Valedictory discourse preached to the South
Church and Parish. 14224
Valedictory discourse . . . 30th of October,
1836. 39201
Valedictory in the Senate. 13540
Valedictory lecture before the Philosophical
Society of Delaware. 98686
Valedictory lecture, delivered by Professor
Draper. 20899
Valedictory letter to the Trustees of Dart-
mouth College. 29615
Valedictory: . . . March 2, 1867. 60147
Valedictory message of Hon. Isaac W. Smith.
82748
Valedictory of Paul to the Corinthians. (76492)
Valedictory oration, at Yale College. 18183
Valedictory oration . . . before the Senior
Class of Yale College. (81017)
Valedictory oration, by Alexander Johnston.
72142
Valedictory oration by C. F. Burnam. 32553
Valedictory oration by Charles Andrew Johnson.
2690
Valedictory oration, by Donald G. Mitchell.
77913
Valedictory oration, by Henry C. Deming.
78460
Valedictory oration, by Homer B. Sprague.
89672
Valedictory oration by Joseph Fenton. (36362)
Valedictory oration, by Rufus Putnam Cutler.
83483

Valedictory oration [on American civilization.]
(7782)
Valedictory oration, pronounced at the com-
mencement. 98343
Valedictory oration, pronounced at the departure
of the Senior Class. 91785
Valedictory oration, pronounced . . . [before
the] Brothers in Unity. (72208)
Valedictory oration, Senior Class, Philadelphia
Academy. 50840
Valedictory oration, which closed the public
performances. 91029
Valedictory poem and oration. 32649
Valedictory peom before the class of 1830.
101465
Valedictory remarks of Henry O'Reilly. 72355
Valedictory sermon . . . April 4, 1858. 26323
Valedictory sermon, Apr. 19, 1840. 104822
Valedictory sermon, delivered on . . . resign-
ing his pastoral charge. 72450
Valedictory sermon, . . . in . . . Albany.
37976
Valedictory sermon . . . in Dorchester, 1st
December 1816. 30521
Valedictory sermon . . . on fifteenth Sunday
after Trinity. 77626
Valedictory sermon, on leaving the Old Meeting
House. 62733
Valedictory sermon, preached at Milton.
43379, 2d note after 98343
Valedictory sermon, preached . . . at the
Patapaco Female Institute. 58797
Valedictory sermon, preached in Trinity Church,
Chicago. 77576
Valedictory sermon, to the First Baptist Church
and Congregation. 104319
Valedictory to the graduating class. 84766
Valedictory, to the people of the United States.
101615
Valencia, Antonio. 98344
Valencia, Jose de. 47606
Valencia, Martin de. see Martin de Valencia.
Valencia, P. F. 98345
Valencia, Pedro de, Bp. 16066, 98346 see
also La Paz (Diocese) Bishop (Valencia)
Valencia, Slavador de. 98347
Valenciana, Mexico. 98348
Valenciennes, Achille, 1794-1865. 21354,
78689
Valencuela Monge Cartuxo, Bruno de. see
Valenzuela, Bruno de.
Valens. pseud. Letters. see Burke, Edmund.
Burke, Richard. Burke, William.
Valente, Christovao. 19556, 73458
Valentin, Louis, 1758-1829. 98350-98352
Valentin, Louis Francois Marie. 98353-98354
Valentin Romero, Jose. see Romero, Jose
Valentin.
Valentine, Abraham M. defendant 48019
Valentine, D. P. (54569)
Valentine, David Thomas, 1801-1869. 18941,
54208-(54209), 54369, 65439, (69567)
see also New York (City) Common
Council. Clerk.
Valentine, David Thomas, 1801-1869. supposed
author 59219
Valentine, John. 46875, 95436, 98355
Valentine, W. J. 55872 see also U. S.
Commission to the Paris Exposition,
1867.
Valentine, ou la nina Canadienne. 44499
Valentine's gift. 98356
Valentine's manuals of the Common Council.
(69567)
Valentini, Michael Bernhard. 98357
Valenzuela, Bruno de. 86499, note after 98357

Van Buren, John, 1810-1866. 611, 25111,
(31494), 65645, 79659, 89205, 98412
Van Buren, Martin, Pres. U. S., 1782-1862.
(445)-448, 13653, (14151), 18005, 25876,
43976, 43976, 44324, 46091, 48105-48106,
48148, 53484, 54781, 55709-(55711),
59043, 63811, 78647, 88669, 95067,
96736, 98409-98425, 102318-102319,
104204-1 04205 see also U. S. President, 1837-1841 (Van Buren)
Van Buren, William Holme, 1819-1883. 30113,
76540, 76546, 76647, 76657, 76695 see
also United States Sanitary Commission.
Committee to Visit the Military General
Hospitals, In and Around Washington.
Van Buren and Harrison contrasted. 98425
Van Caerden, P. see Caerden, P. van.
Van Campen, Moses. (51798), 98626-98628,
2d note after 105691
Van Carnbee, Pieter, Baron Melvill. see
Melvill van Carnbee, Pieter, Baron,
1816-1856.
Vance, Clarence H. ed. 2d note after 99553
Vance, Hugh. see Vans, Hugh.
Vance, Joseph, 1786-1852. 57044 see also
Ohio. Governor, 1836-1838 (Vance)
Vance, R. H. 98437
Vance, Zebulon Baird, 1830-1894. 55692
see also North Carolina. Governor,
1862-1865 (Vance)
Van Cortland, Jacobus. see Cortland, Jacobus
van.
Van Cortlandt, Philip. appellant 98438
Van Cortlandt, Pierre. 15583, 98439 see
also New York (Colony) Committee of
Safety. Chairman.
Van Cortlandt, Pierre. appellant 98438
Van Cott, J. M. 98440
Vancouver, George, 1758-1798. 21211-21215,
38966, (59572), 98441-98444
Vancouver, John. ed. 98443
Vancouver Island and British Columbia. Their
history, resources, and prospects. 43253
Vancouver Island and British Columbia, where
they are. 67964
Vancouver Island; its resources and capabili-
ties as a colony. 25036
Vancouver's Island sailing directions. 70955
Vancouver's Island, the Hudson's Bay Company
and the government. 24609
Van Craesbeecke, Paulus. see Craesbeecke,
Paulus van.
Van Cuelebroek, Edouard Blondel. see
Blondel van Cuelebrouk, Edouard.
Van Cumberland, Georg, Graaf. see
Cumberland, George de Clifford, 3d
Earl of, 1558-1605.
Van D., W. pseud. tr. see D., W. van.
pseud. tr.
Van Dalen, Corn. illus. 67591, 71906
Van Dam, Rip. 98433-98434, 98436
Van Dam, Rip. complainant (53693)
Van Dam, Rip. defendant 84557, 98429
Van Dam, Rip. plaintiff 50849, (53693),
84557, 98430-98432, 98435-98436
Van Dam, W. van Irhoven. see Irhoven van
Dam, W. van.
Van Dam van Isselt, E. W. see Isselt, E. W.
van Dam van.
Van Deinse, And. see Deinse, And. van.
Vandeleur, John. pseud. see Decalves,
Amonso. pseud.
Vandeluer, John. pseud. see Decalves,
Alonso. pseud.
Van Delure, John. pseud. see Decalves,
Alonso. pseud.

Van den Bergh, L. Ph. C. see Bergh, L.
Ph. C. van den.
Van den Bergh, S. J. see Bergh, S. J. van
den.
Van den Biesen, J. J. see Biesen, J. J. van
den.
Van den Bos, Lambertus. see Bos or Bosch,
in Latin Sylvanius, Lambertus van den.
Van den Bosch, J. see Bosch, J. van den.
Van den Bosch, Lambertus. see Bos or Bosch,
in Latin Sylvanius, Lambertus van den.
Van den Brandhof Ez, A. see Brandhof Ez,
A. van den.
Vanden Broeck, Matheus. see Broeck,
Matheus vanden.
Van den Broeck, Pieter. see Broeck, Peiter
van den.
Van den Broek, Reinier. 98471
Van den Broek, Wilhelm. see Broek, Wilhelm
van den.
Van den Heuvell, H. H. see Heuvell, H. H.
van den.
Vanden Heuval, Jacob Adrien. see Van Heuvel,
Jacob Adrien.
Van den Vondel, Joost. see Vondel, Joost
van den.
Van de Perre, J. see Perre, J. van de.
Van der Aa, Peter. see Aa, Pieter van der,
1659-1733.
Vanderauwera, ------. ed. 57458
Vanderbilt, John. 98473-98474
Van der Broeck, P. see Broeck, P. van der.
Van der Brugge, Jacob Segersz. see Segersz
van der Brugge, Jacob.
Van der Capellan, Alexander. see Capellan,
Alexander van der.
Van der Capellen, Johan Berk, Baron. see
Capellen, Johan Berk, Baron van der.
Van der Capellan, Robert Jasper. see Capel-
lan, Robert Jasper van der.
Van der Donck, Adriaen. see Donck, Adriaen
van der, d. 1655.
Van der Gon Netscher, A. D. see Netscher,
A. D. van der Gon.
Van der Groben, J. see Groben, J. van der.
Van der Hagen, ------. see Hagen, ------
van der.
Van der Hagen, Et. see Hagen, Et. van der.
Van der Hagen, Steven. see Hagen, Steven
van der.
Vander Hammen y Leon, Lorenzo. see Ham-
men y Leon, Lorenzo vander.
Vanderheyden, Levinus. 89345
Van Derhoven, Orrin. defendant 79985
Van der Keere, Pieter. see Keere, Pieter
van der.
Van der Kemp, Francis Adrian, 1752-1829.
36925, 37335, 79664, 97252, 98475-98479,
note after 105520
Van der Kemp, Francis Adrian, 1752-1829.
supposed author 52219
Van der Kemp, Francis Adrian, 1752-1829.
supposed tr. 17498, 98479
Vanderlandsch magazijn. 84110
Vanderlandsche droon. 31622
Van der Linden, Johannes. see Linden,
Johannes van der, 1756?-1835.
Vanderlyn, John. 98482-98483
Van der Maelen, Ph. see Maelen, Ph. van
der.
Vander Mander Schilder, Karel. see Schilder,
Karel Vander Mander.
Van der Meulen, M. E. see Meulen, M. E.
van der.
Van der Myle, Arnold. see Mylius, Arnold,
1540-1604.

Van der Mylius, Arnold. see Mylius, Arnold, 1540-1604.
Vander Neck, ------. pseud. Account of the first settlement. see Burgh, James.
Van der Platts, -------. see Platts, ------ van der.
Vanderpoel, -------, fl. 1831. 102448
Van der Schley, J. see Schley, J. van der.
Van der Sloot, F. W. see Sloot, F. W. van der.
Van der Smissen, J. see Smissen, J. van der.
Van der Steere, Dionysius. see Steere, Dionysius van der.
Vander Stell, Adrien. see Steel, Adrien vander.
Van der Straet, Jan. see Stradanus, Johannes.
Van der Straten-Ponthoz, Gabriel Auguste. see Straten-Ponthoz, Gabriel Auguste van der.
Van der Veer, C. 67130
Van der Vegt, A. Helmig. see Helmig van der Vegt, A.
Van der Velde, Karl Franz. see Velde, Karl Franz van der.
Van der Vlag, M. M. pseud. see Vlag, M. M. van der. pseud.
Vander Water, Guillelmus. see Water, Guillelmus van der.
Van der Worm, A. W. see Worm, A. W. van der.
Van de Sande, J. see Sande, J. van de.
Vandewater, Robert J. 98484-98487
Vandiera, Domenico. of Siena supposed author 12835, 24135-24138, 1st note after 98488
Vandike, John. pseud. Narrative. 98488
Van Dissel, S. see Dissel, S. van.
Vando sobre limpieza de las calles de Mexico. 17592, (48663)
Van Doren, Isaac. 98489
Van Doren's Collegiate Institute, for Young Ladies. see Brooklyn Collegiate Institute for Young Ladies.
Van Dorn, Earl. (15326)
Vandos publicados a consequencia de reales ordenes. 98490
Van Driessen, Petrus. 98491-98492
Van Dulmanhorst, Salomon Davidssoon. see Dulmanhorst, Salomon Davidssoon van.
Van Dusen, Increase McGee. 98493-98494
Van Dusen, Maria. 98493-98494
Van Dussen Muilkerk, W. E. J. Berg. see Berg van Dussen Muilkerk, E. W. J.
Van Dyck, Abraham. 98495
Van Dyck, Henry. respondent 64285 see also New York (State) Banking Department. Superintendent. respondent
Van Dyck, Leonard B. 69416, 98495
Van Dyke, Henry J. 515, 2669, 6369, 28013, 82173
Vandyke, Jonathan P. 85179-85180
Vandyke, Kensey J. 98497
Vane, Charles. 104336
Vane, Charles William. see Londonderry, Charles William Stewart Vane, 3d Marquis of, 1778-1854.
Vane, Sir Henry, d. 1662. 80993, 98498-note after 98499
Vane, Sir Henry, d. 1662. defendant 98500
Vaneechout, E. tr. 46964
Van Effen, J. see Effen, J. van.
Vanegas, Francisco. 86523-86524
Vanegas de Busto, Alejo. 98501-98502
Van Engelen, Jacobus Voegen. see Voegen van Engelen, Jacobus.

Van Enghuysen, Jan Outghersz. see Enghuysen, Jan Outghersz van.
Van Evrie, J. H. 78259
Van Eyndhoven, Jan. see Eyndhoven, Jan van.
Van Fhelgum, ----- Murk. see Murk van Fhelgum, -------.
Van G., N. pseud. see Geelkercken, Nic. van.
Van Garretson, Hans. see Garretson, Hans van.
Van Geelkercken, Nic. see Geelkercken, Nic. van.
Van Geuns, Jan. see Geuns, Jan van.
Vango, Juan Prospero de Solis. see Solis Vango, Juan Prospero de.
Van Geons, Rijklof Michael. 230, (15934), 27638, 98503-98510
Van Gogh, M. 98511 see also Netherlands. Legatie. Great Britain.
Vangrifter, Zachary Philemon. pseud. ed. 82193
Van H., J. pseud. see H., J. van, Patriot van't vaderlandt. pseud.
Van Hagen, Peter Albrecht, d. 1800? 84845
Van Hall, H. C. see Hall, H. C. van.
Van Hann, Nancy. see Van Haun, Nancy.
Van Haun, Nancy. plaintiff 9478, 96842
Vanheddeghem, Alexandre. 98512
Van Heeckeren, -------, Baron. see Heeckeren, -------, Baron van.
Van Heede, Michiel Joostens. see Heede, Michiel Joostens van.
Van Heemskerck, Cornelis. see Heemskerck, Cornelis van.
Van Heemskerck, Jacob. see Heemskerck, Jacob van.
Van Heenrick, Gustav. (39192) see also New York (State) Commissioners of Emmigration.
Van Heuvel, Jacob Adrien. 98513-98514
Van Heuvel, Jacob Adrien. petitioner 98472
Van Hextor, J. see Hextor, J. van.
Van Hilten, Jansz, Jan. see Hilten, Janszoon Jan van.
Van Hoek, S. see Hoek, S. van.
Van Hoesen, J. A. 49498
Van Hoevell, W. R. see Hoevell, W. R. van.
Van Hogel, Mary. see Hruesdell, Mary (Van Hogel)
Van Hogendorp, D. J. see Hogendorp, D. J. van.
Van Hogendorp, Gijsbert Karel. see Hogendorp, Gijsbert Karel, Graaf van, 1762-1834.
Vanhollen, George Speth. defendant 98515
Van Holly, D. Muys. see Muys van Holly, Nicolaes.
Van Holly, Nicolaes Muys. see Muys van Holly, Nicolaes.
Van Hoog, Theresia, Baroness. see Hoog, Theresia, Baroness van.
Van Hoogstraten, F. see Hoogstraten, F. van.
Van Horn, -------. 79781
Van Horn, W. O. pseud. Lebensgang Georg Washingtons. see Oertel, Phillip Friedrich.
Van Horne, Augustus V. petitioner 98516
Van Horne, David. 98517-98518
Van Horne, John. ed. 2862, 1st note after 98300
Van Horn's Lessee. plaintiffs (59056)
Van Hove, -----. illus. 67589
Vaniere, Jacques. 75949, 2d note after 96930A, 98519-98520

Van Ingen, James. 54002, 92865, note after 99543 see also Democratic Party. New York. Albany. Corresponding Committee. Secretary.

Van Ingen, James. defendant 14637-14638

Van Irhoven van Dam, W. see Irhoven van Dam, W. van.

Vanishing things. 46573

Van Isselt, E. W. van Dam. see Isselt, E. W. Van Dam van.

Vanity and impiety of judicial astrology. 17687

Vanity and unsatisfactory nature of earthly possessions. 24779

Vanity fair. 91065

Vanity of every man at his best estate. (9717)

Vanity of human institutions in the worship of God. (20062)

Vanity of man as mortal. 14521

Vanity of man considered in a sermon delivered February 22d, 1800. 55335

Vanity of the Quakers' pretence of their being the one only catholic church of Christ. 9072

Vanity of trusting to an army of flesh. 63622

Vanity of vanities, &c. 103921

Vanity of zeal for fasts. 65077

Van Kampen, N. G. see Kampen, N. G. van.

Van Kannenburch, Hendrick. see Kannenburch, Hendrick van.

Van Keulen, Gerard. see Keulen, Gerard van.

Van Keulen, J. see Keulen, J. van.

Van L., B. pseud. see L., B. van. pseud.

Van Laer, Arnold Johan Ferdinand, 1869- ed. 84558

Van Lansberge, Henrique. see Lansberge, Henrique van.

Vanleason, James. pseud.?? see Vandeleur, John. pseud.??

Van Lede, Ch. see Lede, Ch. van.

Van Lennep, J. H. see Lennep, J. H. van.

Van Lennep, Jacob. see Lennep, Jacob van.

Van Lennep Coster, G. see Lennep Coster, G. van.

Van Leson, James. pseud. see Declaves, Alonso. pseud.

Van Liebergen, Arnout. see Liebergen, Arnout van.

Van Lil, Herman. see Lil, Herman van.

Van Linschoten, Jan Huygen. see Linschoten, Jan Huygen van, 1563-1611.

Van Loon, Geraard. see Loon, Geraard van.

Van Loon, J. see Loon, J. van.

Van Loven, Hermes. see Loven, Hermes van.

Van Mander, -----. see Mander, ----- van.

Van Marle, Egb. see Marle, Egb. van.

Van Meteren, Emanuel. see Meteren, Emanuel van.

Van Meteron, ------. see Meteron, ----- van.

Van Middelburch, Andries Jasszoon. see Middelburch, Andries Jasszoon van.

Van Middelgeest, Simon. see Middelgeest, Simon van.

Van Mildert, William, successively Bishop of Llandaff, and Durham, 1765-1836. 98521

Van Montlong, Wilhelm. see Montlong, Wilhelm van.

Van Muyden, G. see Muyden, G. van.

Van Nassau la Leck, Lodewijk Theodorus, Grave. see Theodorus, Lodewijk, Grave van Nassau la Leck.

Van Neck, Jacob Corneliszoon. see Neck, Jacob Corneliszoon van, 1564-1638

Van Neck, Jacques Corneliszoon. see Neck, Jacob Corneliszoon van, 1564-1638.

Van Ness, Cornelius Peter. 98523-98526

Van Ness, John Peter. 98527-98528, 101942A

Van Ness, P. see Van Ness, William Peter.

Van Ness, William Peter. 17677, 18863, 18866, (29986), 35362, 35921, 53744, 98529-note after 98533, 102037

Van Ness, William Peter. supposed author 1977, 2d note after 98528, 102364, 104541

Van Ness, William Peter. incorrectly supposed author 23995, 29960, 102361

Van Ness, William W. (43001), 96901, 98534

Van Nispen, A. see Nispen, A. van.

Van Noort, Olivier. see Noort, Olivier van, 1568-1611.

Van Nyenborgh, Johan. see Nyenborgh, Johan van.

Van Oelen, A. Jsz. see Oelen, A. Jsz. van.

Van Oosten van Staveren, G. L. see Oosten van Staveren, G. L. van.

Van Opdam, ------ van Wassenaer, Baron. see Wassenaer, ----- van, Baron van Opdam.

Van Os, P. see Os, P. van.

Van Otterloo, A. see Otterloo, A. van.

Van Paddenburg, G. G. see Paddenburg, G. G. van.

Van Patten, John F. defendant 98535

Van Pelt, Peter I. 71216, 98536-98537

Van Pradelles, -----. 98538

Van Pumpkin, Isaac. pseud. To the agents. 95906

Van Quelen, Augustus. see Guelen, Auguste de.

Van Raalte, A. C. 8746

Van Raders, J. E. W. F. see Raders, J. E. W. F. van.

Van Raders, R. F. see Raders, R. F. van.

Van Raders, S. F. see Raders, S. F. van.

Van Draders, W. see Raders, W. van.

Van Raemdonck, J. see Raemdonck, J. van.

Van Ranst, C. W. 98539

Van Rechteren, ------. see Rechteren, ----- van.

Van Rees, O. see Rees, O. van.

Van Renselaar, A. see Renselaar, A. van.

Van Rensselaer, Anne. appellant 98438

Van Rensselaer, Cortlandt, 1808-1860. 10162, 20255, (31177), 32714, 65199, note after 91895, 98540

Van Rensselaer, James. 101698

Van Rensselaer, Jeremiah. 98541-98542

Van Rensselaer, John S. 98543

Van Rensselaer, Kiliaen. see Rensselaer, Kiliaen van.

Van Rensselaer, Maunsell, 1819-1900. 54476

Van Rensselaer, Philip S. appellant 98438

Van Rensselaer, Solomon, 1744-1852. 98548

Van Rensselaer, Solomon, 1774-1852. defendant (35991), 98547

Van Rensselaer, Solomon, 1774-1852. plaintiff (35991), 98547

Van Rensselaer, Stephen, 1765-1839. 1795, 4039, 21701-21703, 22755, 31792, 33523, 53566, (53688), note after 53697, note after 83791, 98549-3d note after 98549, 3d note after 103741 see also New York (State) Commissioners on Internal Navigation.

Vanresviqui, Nicolas. plaintiff 98315

Van Ripperda, Joan Willem. see Ripperda, Joan Willem van, Duque, d. 1737.

Van Roosbroeck, Gustave L. 100728

Van Rosenthal, J. Th. H. Nedermeyer. see Nedermeyer van Rosenthal, J. Th. H.

Vans, Miss ------. supposed author 52329, note after 92749

Vans, Hugh. 20725, 34810, 4th-5th notes after 98549

Van Zandt, Tobias. 98591
Vappaus, J. E. (77074)
Vapulacion mas cruel a escritores miserables. 98592
Vara, Francisco Antonio Velasco de la. see Velasco de la Vara, Francisco Antonio.
Varahinca, Domingo de. (48613), 98019 see also Universidad de Mercaderes de Mexico. Consules.
Varaigne, ------. ed. and tr. 56332
Varanda, Diego Porres. see Porres Varanda, Diego.
Varaorna, Sancho de. 98593
Varas, A. ed. 70301
Varas y Valdes, Francisco. 98594 see also Spain. Casa de Contratacion de las Indias. Tribunal. Presidente.
Varas extrangeras, reducidas a Catellanas. 47848
Varca, Miguel Calderon de la. see Calderon de la Varca, Miguel.
Vardill, John. supposed author 101737-101743
Varea, Alhponso Lasor a. see Lasor a Varea, Alphonso.
Varela, F. ed. 63330
Varela, Felix. see Varela y Morales, Felix, 1788-1853.
Varela de Montes, Jose. 98597
Varela y Ulloa, Pedro. tr. (56309)
Varela y Morales, Felix, 1788-1853. 48162
Varen, Bernhard, 1622-1650. (2308)
Varen de Soto, Basil. see Soto, Basil Varen de.
Varenne, Jacques Nicolas Billaud. see Billaud-Varennes, Jacques Nicolas.
Varennes, Jacques Nicolas Billaud. see Billaud-Varennes, Jacques Nicolas.
Varga, ------ Ramirez de. see Ramirez de Varga, -------.
Varga y Ponce, Jose de. 1729, 16771-16772, 98612-98614,4th note after 100814
Varga y Ponce, Jose de. supposed author 16765, note after 98613
Vargara, Augustin de. 71623
Vargas, -------, fl. 1831. 34413, 98624-98625, 106224
Vargas, Agustin Francisco Esquibel y. see Esquibel y Vargas, Agustin Francisco.
Vargas, Alonso Ramirez de. see Ramirez de Vargas, Alonso.
Vargas, Diego de Torres. see Torres Vargas, Diego de.
Vargas, Ignacio. 98698
Vargas, Ildefonso de Esquivel y. see Esquivel y Vargas, Ildefonso de.
Vargas, Jose Mariano de. 98599
Vargas, Juan de. 36794
Vargas, Juan Pison y. see Pison y Vargas, Juan.
Vargas, Juan Tapia de. see Tapia de Vargas, Juan.
Vargas, Luis de. 98600
Vargas, M. M. 98601
Vargas, Manuel Antonio de. 98602
Vargas, Melchior de. 98603
Vargas, Tomas Tamayo de. see Tamayo de Vargas, Tomas.
Vargas Machuca, Bernardo de. 98604
Vargas Machuca, Francisco de. 98608
Vargas Machuca, Juan de. 87224-87225, 98605-98607
Vargas Machuca, Pedro de. 98609-98610
Varhaftige Beschreibung eyner Landschafft der Wilden nacketen. 25472, 77677-77678, 90039

Varia historia de la Nueva Espana y Florida. 18781
Variaciones interesantes. 98615
Varian, Isaac L. (54205) see also New York (City) Mayor, 1839-1841 (Varian)
Varian, Isaac L. defendant 98616
Varias cartas dirigidas al Soberano. 94352
Varias cartas, escritas al Rey Nuestro Senor. 97671
Varias cartas sobre diversas materias. 26721
Varias cartas y representaciones. 98805
Varias cedulas y cartas del Rey. 94352
Varias litteras missas a Religiosis Societatis Iesu. 106367
Varias notas para mayor inteligencia de la historia. 39294, (44427), note after 98763
Varias observaciones contra un opusculo titulado: Apuntamientos sobre derecco publico ecclesiastico. (48664)
Varias Personas de Mexico. petitioners see Mexico. Varias Personas. petitioners
Varias poezias do Fr. Ag. da Cruz. (4949)
Varias reales cedulas de 1538 a 1561. 94352
Varias reflecsiones sobre el estado de la republica. 99440
Variation charts of the whole terraqueous globe. 13026
Variation of sun and clock. 93040
Variation of the compass, &c. &c. &c. 97281
Variations of the magnetic needle. 6026
Varick, Richard. 53735, 79372-79373 see also U. S. Continental Congress, 1775. Secretary.
Variedad del gobierno de los Romanos. 58048
Variedades. 98617
Variedades litterarias. (60886)
Varieties and oppositions of criticisms on the play of Pizarro. 8137, 80342
Varieties in human life. (67304)
Varieties of human greatness. 106055, 106057
Varieties of literature. 98618
Variety of anecdotes and remarks. 8110
Variety of favorite hymn tunes and anthems. 94335-94339
Variety of human life. 104370
Variety of interesting particulars. (10064)
Variety of original and select poems. 5528
Variety of original designs for rural buildings. (82160)
Variety of original poetical pieces. 99838
Varillas, Antoine. 98619-98620
Varin, Charles. 23093, note after 98620
Variorum in Europa itinerum deliciae. 13037
Varios autores. pseud. Mexicanos pintados por si mismos. 48577
Varios ciudadanos. petitioners see Mexico. Varios Ciudadanos. petitioners
Varios Ciudadanos de los Estados-Unidos de America. petitioners 95103
Varios Comerciantes. petitioners 101294
Varios cosecheros. pseud. Breves reflecsiones. 98621
Varios documentos del siglo XVI. (34156)
Varios Dominicanos Amandes de su Pais. pseud. Vida politica de Pedro Santana. (76807)
Varios electores. pseud. Documentos importantes. 20437
Varios Estudiantes de Buen Humor. pseud. eds. 71385
Varios extractos de huma carta escripta a seu Irmao. 95252
Varios Gefes Mexicanos. pseud. Vindicacion del General Bravo. 99788
Varios Gualtemaltecos. pseud. Noticia biographia. 39095

Vassor de la Touche, Louis Charles Le. see
   Le Vassor de la Touche, Louis Charles.
Vast importance of the herring fishery. 41741
Vastey, Pompee Valentine, Baron de. 14553,
   52245, 98666-98678, note after 100785
Vater, Abraham. tr. 79074
Vater, Johann Severin, 1771-1826. 453, 5269,
   11042, 31066, 33748, 42643, 98679
Vater-Unser in Mehr als 200 Sprachen und
   Mundarten. 2373
Vater-Unser in Mehr als Sechshundert Sprachen
   und Mundarten. 2373
Vater Unsrer Republik in ihrem Leben und
   Wirken. (25617), 38318
Vaticinio. 9221
Vaticinio feliz. 98347
Vattemare, Alexander. 34931, 65799, 80996
Vattemare, Hippolyte. tr. (24257), (47902)
Vattier, Charles. defendant 97484, note after
   98679
Vaublanc, Vincent Marie Vienot, Comte de.
   38583, 39289, 96348, 98679A-98682, note
   after 99533
Vauchelles, F. de Lowencourt, Sieur de. see
   Lowencourt, F. de, Sieur de Vauchelles.
Vaudevil, sung by the characters at the con-
   clusion of a new farce. 98683
Vaudicault, A. (19781)
Vaudreuil, --------, Comte de. 47519 see
   also Santo Domingo (French Colony)
   Commissaires.
Vaudreuil de Cavagnal, Pierre Francois de Ri-
   gaud, Marquis de, 1698-1765. 42283, 98684
   see also Louisiana (Province) Governeur,
   1743-1752 (Vaudreuil de Cavagnal)
Vaudreuil de Cavagnal, Pierre Francois de
   Rigaud, Marquis de, 1698-1765. defendant
   98684
Vaughan, --------. of New York supposed
   author 49811, 1st note after 98684
Vaughan, Benjamin. 25599, 2d note after 98684
Vaughan, Benjamin. supposed author (31970),
   42449, 69412, (74176), 94678, 3d-4th
   notes after 98684
Vaughan, H. S. ed. 101044
Vaughan, John, 1775-1807. 98685-98686
Vaughan, John, fl. 1833. 98687
Vaughan, John C. 7201, 43864, 98688
Vaughan, Mary C. 8162
Vaughan, Robert. illus./cartographer 5967,
   6812, note after 41144, 56761, 67572-
   67573, 67577-67584, 67587, 71906, 82823
Vaughan, Samuel. (51453), 98689-98690
Vaughan, Vernon H. 85562 see also Utah
   (Territory) Governor, 1874 (Vaughan)
Vaughan, William. 31037, 98691-98694
Vaughan, John M. (42320)
Vaugondy, Didier Robert de. see Robert
   de Vaugondy, Didier, 1723-1786.
Vaugondy, Gilles Robert de. see Robert
   de Vaugondy, Gilles, 1688-1766.
Vaugues, Lauriston Joseph. 98695
Vaul, Jacques de. 76838
Vaux, Charles Grant, Vicomte de. see Grant,
   Charles, Vicomte de Vaux.
Vaux, G. 98696
Vaux, Henry Brougham, Baron Brougham and.
   see Brougham and Vaux, Henry
   Brougham, Baron.
Vaux, James. 98697
Vaux, Roberts. 4694, 41617, 60373, 79203,
   98698-98707
Vaux, W. S. W. 20856
Vaux & Company. firm see Olmsted, Vaux
   & Company. firm
Vauxcelles, Simon-Jerome Bourlet de. ed.
   93292

Vaya un pliego de papel conque se obsequia a
   Tornel. 96208
Vayer, ------- de la Mothe le. pseud. see
   La Peyrere, Isaac de.
Vaz, -------. 26875
Vaz, Antonio Jose. 98708-98710
Vaz, Lopez. 66686
Vaz Coutinho, Goncalo. 17201, 98711
Vaz Preto, D. Marcos Pinto Soares. see
   Preto, D. Marcos Pinto Soares Vaz.
Vazquez, Eduardo. 98712
Vazquez, F. P. tr. 13521
Vazquez, Francisco, 1647-ca. 1714. 98713
Vazquez, Francisco Pablo, Bp., 1769-1847.
   10313, 47815, (49770)-49772, 86368,
   98714-98716 see also Puebla, Mexico
   (Diocese) Bishop (Vazquez)
Vazquez, Francisco Xavier. 98717-98718
Vazquez, J. M. 98719
Vazquez, Jesus Maria. 47036, 58273
Vazquez, P. see Vazquez, Francisco Pablo,
   Bp., 1769-1847.
Vazquez Coronado, Carlos. plaintiff 16825,
   note after 98301, note after 98720
Vazquez de Cisneros, Alonso. 98721-98722
Vazquez de Coronado, Carlos. see Vazquez
   Coronado, Carlos.
Vazquez de Coronado, Francisco, 1510-1549.
   16951, 66686, 67740, 84379, 98723
Vazquez de Espinosa, Antonio. (22889), 98724-
   98726
Vazquez de Figueroa, Jose. 24322, 98727-
   98729 see also California (Alte
   California) Comandante General y Gefe
   Politico.
Vazquez de Medina, Ivan. 98730
Vazquez de Medina, Juan. plaintiff 98730
Vazquez di Coronado, Francesco. see Vazquez
   de Coronado, Francisco, 1510-1549.
Vazquez Gaztelu, Antonio. 24312, 26746-(26751),
   1st-2d notes after 98659-98660
Vazquez Salgado, Antonio. see Salgado,
   Antonio Vazquez.
Veatch, John A. 98731
Veaux, S. de. see De Veaux, S.
Veazey, Thomas Ward, 1774-1848. 45068 see
   also Maryland. Governor, 1835-1838
   (Veazey)
Veazey, W. G. 27249
Vec, Joseph de Vega y. see Vega y Vec,
   Joseph de.
Vecellio, Cesare. 98732
Vechten, Abraham van. see Van Vechten,
   Abraham.
Vechten, Philip van. see Van Vechten, Philip.
Vechten, Teunis A. van. see Van Vechten,
   Teunis A.
Vecina de ella. pseud. Tertulia de la aldea.
   94895
Vecindario de Morelia. see Morelia, Mexico.
Vecino de esa ciudad. pseud. Cosas del Plata
   explicadas. (16988)
Vecino de esta ciudad. pseud. Obsequio.
   (56440)
Vedia, Agustin de. ed. 35073
Vedia, Enrique de. 16942, 32043
Veech, James. 98733-98736
Veedor, Jose. 98737
Veen, Corneille de. 68455
Veer, C. van der. see Van der Veer, C.
Veer, Gerart de. see Veer, Gerrit de.
Veer, Gerrit de. 14957-14960, (32028), 33655,
   (40035), 41366, 66686, 98738-98740
Vega, Alfonso Carillo Laso de la. see Carillo
   Laso de la Vega, Alfonso.
Vega, Alonso Carrillo Laso de la. see
   Carrillo Laso la Vega, Alfonso.

Vega, Antonio de Cordova Laso de la. see Laso de la Vega, Antonio de Cordova.

Vega, Bernardo de la. see La Veta, Bernardo de.

Vega, Dionisio Martinez de la. see Martinez de la Vega, Dionisio.

Vega, Feliciano de la. 98741-98742 see also La Paz (Diocese) Bishop (Vega) Mexico (Archdiocese) Archbishop (Vega)

Vega, Francisco. 86189 see also Socorro (Colombian State) Gobernardo (Vega)

Vega, Francisco Nunez de la. see Nunez de la Vega, Francisco.

Vega, Gabriel Lasso de la. see Lasso de la Vega, Gabriel.

Vega, Carcilaso de la. see Garcilaso de la Vega, called El Inca, 1539-1616.

Vega, Gonzales de la. see La Vega, Gonzales de.

Vega, Ildefonso. ed. 87245

Vega, Jos. Antonio Garcia de la. see Garcia de la Vega, Jos. Antonio.

Vega, Jose Maria Gonzalez de la. see Gonzalez de la Vega, Jose Maria.

Vega, Joseph de la. 98762

Vega, Juan de. 98763

Vega, Luis Lasso de la. see Lasso de la Vega, Luis.

Vega, Manuel de la. 39294, (44427), note after 98763

Vega, Matheo de la. plaintiff 61136

Vega, Nicolas del Valle y de la. see Valle y de la Vega, Nicolas del.

Vega, Pedro de la, fl. 1626. 98764

Vega, Pedro de la, fl. 1752. 98765

Vega, Pedro Saenz. see Saenz Vega, Pedro.

Vega, R. de la. see La Vega, R. de.

Vega, Silvestre Diaz de la. supposed author 48645, 85735

Vega, Ventura de la. 11654

Vega Bazan, Estanislao de. 98766

Vega Carpio, Lopez Felix de, 1562-1635. 98767-98772

Vega y Vec, Joseph de. 98773

Vegetable materia medica of the United States. 3863

Vegetation a remedy for the summer heat of cities. 84275

Vegetation sauvage. 74902

Vegt, A. Helmig van der. see Helmig van der Vegt, A.

Vehse, Karl Eduard. 98774-98775

Veiga, Evaristo Ferreira da. see Ferreira da Veiga, Evaristo.

Veiga, Manuel Luis da. 98776

Veigal, Franz Xavier. (51480), (51482), 98777

Veil lifted. 73284

Veil removed; or, reflections on David Humphreys' essay. 24022, 94058

Veil removed, or W. W. Seligh unmasked. 82130. note after 98777

Veil removed. Peace-reconciliation-reconfederation. 44339

Veil withdrawn. 98778

Veillard, ------ le. see Le Veillard, --------.

Veillees Americaines. 98779

Veillees de Cayenne. 11626, note after 98779

Veillees du tropique. 63708

Veilles de Chasse. 69077

Veilles des Antilles. 19681

Veilles Canadiennes. 57810

Veir, G. de. 14349

Veitia, Mariano Jose Fernandez de Echeverria y. see Veytia, Mariano, 1718-1779.

Veitia Linage, Jose de. see Veitia Linaje, Jose de, 162-?-1688.

Veitia Linaje, Jose de, 162-?-1688. 98780-98782

Veitia Linaje, Jose de, fl. 1690. 98783

Veiviser for Norske emigranter. (69098)

Vijamen hecho a la Universidad. 72564

Vel, O. Saint. see Saint-Vel, O.

Velarde, Diego Calderon. 98784

Velarde, Pedro Murillo. see Murillo Velarde, Pedro.

Valarde y Cienfuegos, Juan Antonio. petitioner 98785

Velasco, Alonso Alberto de. 98786-98788

Velasco, Alonso de Solorcano y. see Solorcano y Velasco, Alonso de.

Velasco, Alonso de Solorzano y. see Solorzano y Velasco, Alonso de, d. 1680.

Velasco, Antonio Perez. see Perez Velasco, Antonio.

Velasco, Baltasar de Zurita de. see Zurita de Velasco, Baltasar de.

Velasco, Diego de. 98789-98790

Velasco, Diego de. petitioner 98789

Velasco, Francisco. 98852

Velasco, Francisco Antonio. see Velasco de la Vara, Francisco Antonio.

Velasco, Francisco de Paula Rodriguez. see Rodriguez Velasco, Francisco de Paula.

Velasco, Gaspar de Borja y. see Borja y Velasco, Gaspar de, Abp.

Velasco, Ignacio Alonso de. 98791-98792

Velasco, J. Banos de. (34196)

Velasco, Jo. Fernandez de. 91231

Velasco, Joaquin de la Pezula y Sanchez Munoz de. see Pezula y Sanchez Munoz de Velasco, Joaquin de la, l. Marques de Viluma, 1761-1830.

Velasco, Jose Baltasar de Somonte y. see Somont y Velasco, Jose Baltasar de.

Velasco, Joseph Antonio Manso. see Manso de Velasco, Joseph Antonio, Conde de Superunda.

Velasco, Juan de. 98793

Velasco, Lvdovico de. 96218

Velasco, Luis de, Marques de Salinas, 1534-1617. 24894, note after 94854, 94856, 98794-98801 see also Mexico (Viceroyalty) Virrey, 1590-1595 (Velasco) Peru (Viceroyalty) Virrey, 1596-1604 (Velasco)

Velasco, Manuel Antonio Valcarce. see Valcarce Velasco, Manuel Antonio.

Velasco, Pedro de. petitioner 98804-98805 see also Jesuits. Mexico. Provincial. petitioner

Velasco, Pedro Regil. see Regil Velasco, Pedro.

Velasco de la Vara, Francisco Antonio. 98806

Velasco y Arellano, Jose Luis. 98807

Velasco: a tragedy in five acts. 76966

Velasques de Leon, Joaquin. 76824

Velasquez, Alonso. defendant 98600

Velasquez, Alvaro. petitioner 98816

Velasquez, Andres. 98808

Velasquez, Jeronimo de Soria. see Soria Velasquez, Jeronimo de.

Velasquez, Juan. 98809-98811

Velasquez, Juan Antonio. 58290

Velasquez, Pedro. 98812

Velasquez Cardenas Leon, Carlos Celedonio. see Velasquez de Cardenas y Leon, Carlos Celedonio.

Velasquez de Cardenas y Leon, Carlos Celen Celedonio. 10809, 98813

Velasquez de Leon, Joaquin. 34348, 40076-40078, 42724, note after 98813-98814

Velasquez de Leon, Joaquin. petitioner 39135, note after 98814-98815

Velasquez Minaya, Francisco. 49191, note after 98817

Valazquez, Jose. defendant 27309, (51797), 69915, 93808, 96948

Velazquez, Juan. see Velasquez, Juan.

Valazquez de Leon, Joaquim. see Velasquez de Leon, Joaquin.

Velazquez de Salazar, Juan. petitioner 98817

Velazquez Minaya, Francisco. see Velasquez Minaya, Francisco.

Velde, Karl Franz van der. 98818-98821

Veldwijk, E. G. 93849, 98822

Veledictory [sic] address. 101874

Velez, Pedro. (48665), 98823, 1st note after 99783

Velez, Santos. 98824

Velez de Escalante, Silvestre. (80023)

Velez de Guevara, Luis. (4587)

Velez de Guevara y Salamance, Juan. 98825

Velez de Ulibarri y Olasso, Jose Manuel. 98826

Velez de Ulivarri y Olasasso, J. M. (44542)

Velez Herrera, Ramon. 31571, note after 98827

Velez Sarsfield, Dalmacio. see Sarsfield, Dalmacio Velez.

Velho, Alvaro. supposed author 98649

Vellerino de Villalobos, Balthasar de. see Villalobos, Balthasar.

Vellini, Giovanni Ricuzzi. see Camers, Joannes, i. e. Giovanni Ricuzzi Vellini, 1448-1546.

Vello de Bustamante, Fernando. see Bustamente, Fernando Vello de.

Velloso, Jose Mariano. see Velloso Xavier, Jose Mariano da Conceicao.

Velloso de Oliveira, Antonio Rodrigues. 98828-98829

Velloso Pederneiras, I. see Pederneiras, I. Velloso.

Velloso Xavier, Jose Mariano de Conceicao. 19993, 75615, 98830-98834

Vellozo de Miranda, J. incorrectly supposed author 98828-98829

Veloren arbeyt ofte klaar en kortbondigh vertoogh. 27120

Velos antiguos i modernos. 62934

Velse, H. tr. (32437)

Velserus, Marcus. 66497

Veluti in speculum; or, a scene in the High Court of Admiralty. 8514

Veluti in speculum. The devil and his subjects in Hartford. 98835

Velvet cushion. 105490

Venable, Abraham B. 28890, 69808

Venables, G. H. tr. (37609)

Venables, Thomas. pseud. Reviewer (in the Christian observer) reviewed. see Hibbert, George.

Venafro, Ambrogio Spinola, Marchese del Sesso e di. see Sesso e di Venafro, Ambrogio Spinola, Marchese del.

Venancio, ------. 29430, 96194

Venancio Malo, Felix. see Malo, Felix Venancio.

Venant, Barre Saint. see Barre Saint-Venant, Jean.

Venant, Jean Barre Saint. see Barre Saint-Venant, Jean.

Venault de Charmilly, -----. 98837-98839

Ven den Bergh, S. J. tr. 7712

Vendel Chaudron, Adelaide de. see Chaudron, Adeliade de Vendel.

Vendryes, B. 98840

Venegas, Alexio. see Vanegas de Busto, Alexio.

Venegas, Francisco Xavier. see Venegas de Saavedra, Francisco Xavier.

Venegas, Juan Manuel. 98841

Venegas, Miguel. 98842-98849

Venegas de Saavedra, Francisco Javier. 98850-98857, 98859-98861 see also Mexico (Viceroyalty) Virrey, 1810-1816 (Venegas de Saavedra)

Venema, Pieter. 98862

Venerabilibus Fratribus Antistibus Brasiliae. 63904

Venerable Senor Don Juan de Palafox y Mendoza, . . . justificado. 58301

Venerando in Christo, F. Augustino Lustiniano. (66468)

Venero, Alonso. 98863-98865

Venetian exile. 103413

Venezolano. pseud. Apuntes historicos con algunas observaciones. 98866

Venezolano. pseud. Manual politico del Venezolano. 98867

Venezolanos. "Diez y siete anos de desgracias." 96222

Venezuela (Spanish Colony) Gobernador, 1624-1630 (Meneses y Padilla) defendant 51043 see also Meneses y Padilla, Juan de, Marques de Marianela. defendant

Venezuela (Spanish Colony) Real Audiencia, Caracas. see Caracas, Venezuela. Real Audiencia.

Venezuela (Colombian Department) petitioners 101790

Venezuela. (40899), 47803, 2d note after 98873, 98878

Venezuela. Act of Independence. 10775, (34898), note after 98877

Venezuela. Colegio de Ingenieros de la Republica. see Colegio de Ingenieros de Venezuela, Caracas.

Venezuela. Comision Encargada de Proponer Arbitrios Para el Ejercito. 53258

Venezuela. Congreso Constituyente. 98872

Venezuela. Congreso Nacional. 23438

Venezuela. Congreso Nacional, 2d. 6189

Venezuela. Constitution. 10775, (34898), note after 98877

Venezuela. Corte Superior. 94829

Venezuela. Declaration of Independence. see Venezuela. Act of Independence.

Venezuela. Ejercito. Hospitales Militares. 74887

Venezuela. Ejercito. Medico Cirujano Mayor e Inspector de los Hospitales. 68875 see also Arvelo, Carlos.

Venezuela. Ejercito. Servicio Sanitario. 68875

Venezuela. Fiscal Agent. 29371 see also Guzman, Antonio Leoncadio.

Venezuela. Laws, statutes, etc. (34898), (40899), 56450, 65982, (68737), 68787, 68882, 73887, 76232, 98871, 98872, 1st and 5th notes after 98882, 101294

Venezuela. Ministerio de Credito Publico. 47602

Venezuela. Ministerio de Geurra y Marina. 23445

Venezuela. Ministerio de Hacienda. (23437), 47602, 101294

Venezuela. Ministerio de Interior. 47605

Venezuela. Ministerio de Interior, Justicia, y Relaciones Exteriores. 29370 see also Guzman, Antonio Leoncadio.

Venezuela. Ministerio de Interior y Justicia. 23440

Vermont. Governor, 1790-1797 (Chittenden) 99063-99069 see also Chittenden, Thomas, 1730-1797.

Vermont. Governor, 1797-1809 (Tichenor) 99070-99072, 99199 see also Tichenor, Isaac, 1754-1838.

Vermont. Governor, 1809-1813 (Galusha) 99199 see also Galusha, Jonas, 1753-1834.

Vermont. Governor, 1813-1815 (Chittenden) 55323 see also Chittenden, Martin, 1769-1840.

Vermont. Governor, 1815-1820 (Galusha) 33150 see also Galusha, Jonas, 1753-1834.

Vermont. Governor, 1858-1860 (Hall) 33150 see also Hall, Hiland, 1795-1885.

Vermont. Governor, 1860-1861 (Fairbanks) 23666-23667 see also Fairbanks, Erastus, 1792-1864.

Vermont. Governor and Council. see Vermont. Supreme Executive Council.

Vermont. Laws, statutes, etc. 18117, 22765, 25880, 28722, 37938, 39414, 50238, 52051, 55930, 65098, 70820-70821, 74465-74466, (74472), 81691, 82438, 89066, 91421, 95486, 99002, note before 99008, 99018-99020, 99022, 99051, note before 99075-99091, 99092-99110, 99111-99132, 105048

Vermont. Militia. 99060, 99104, 99114, 99122

Vermont. Militia. Pay-master. 99134 see also Tolman, Thomas.

Vermont. School Commissioners. 83908

Vermont. Secretary. 803, 7286, 2d and 4th notes after 99005, 99020, 99008, 99104, 99125 see also Fay, Joseph. Hopkins, Roswell. Townsend, Micah.

Vermont. Secretary of State. 81691, 99089 see also Slade, William, 1786-1859.

Vermont. State Library. 61280, 2d note after 98997

Vermont. State Prison. 74289

Vermont. Superior Court, Westminster. 99074

Vermont. Supreme Court. 6379-6380, (12821), 19019, 91108, 96839-96841, 99132

Vermont. Supreme Executive Council. 801, 803, 806, 7286, 52791, 56564, 66514, 1st note after 98997, 98998, note after 98998, 98999, 2d note after 99000, 99001-99002, 1st note after 99003, 99005, 2d-3d, and 6th notes after 99005, note before 99008-99008, 99009, 99018-99019, 99053-99059, 99068, 99073, 99090, 101077 see also Vermont. Council.

Vermont. Supreme Executive Council. Secretary. 7286, 4th note after 99005 see also Fay, Joseph.

Vermont. Treasurer. 99000-1st note after 99000, 4th note after 99005, 99045-99046, 99133-99135 see also Allen, Ira. Mattocks, Samuel.

Vermont. Undersigned Citizens. petitioners see Vermont. petitioners

Vermont. University. 99208-99209, 99212-99213

Vermont. University. College of Natural History. 99214

Vermont. University. Faculty. 99210-99211

Vermont. University. Library. 99215

Vermont. University. Semi-centennial Anniversary Celebration, 1854. 99213

Vermont. University. Society for Religious Inquiry. 99216

Vermont Academy of Medicine, Castleton. see Castleton Medical College, Castleton, Vt.

Vermont agriculturalist. 77820

Vermont almanac and register, for . . . 1795. 99141

Vermont almanac and register, for . . . 1797. 99142

Vermont almanac and register, for . . . 1796. 99142

Vermont almanac for 1784. note after 99139

Vermont American. 81681, 99197

Vermont and Maine elections. 96032

Vermont and the New York land jobbers. 83717, 83719

Vermont anti-masonic almanac, for the year of Our Lord 1831. 99143

Vermont Anti-masonic State Convention, Montpelier, 1829. see Anti-masonic State Convention, Montpelier, Vt., 1829.

Vermont Anti-masonic State Convention, Montpelier, 1830. see Anti-masonic State Convention, Montpelier, Vt., 1830.

Vermont Anti-masonic State Convention, Montpelier, 1831. see Anti-masonic State Convention, Montpelier, Vt., 1831.

Vermont Anti-masonic State Convention, Montpelier, 1833. see Anti-masonic State Convention, Montpelier, Vt., 1833.

Vermont Anti-slavery Society. 99220

Vermont Anti-slavery Society. Treasurer. 99220

Vermont Association. see Baptists. Vermont. Vermont Association.

Vermont autograph and remarker. 99221

Vermont Baptist Sunday School Union 99121

Vermont Bible Society. 89744, 99222

Vermont Branch of the Northern Baptist Education Society. see Northern Baptist Education Society. Vermont Branch.

Vermont Central Railroad. Directors. 67264

Vermont Colonization Society. 99223

Vermont Delegation to the National Republican Party Convention, Baltimore, 1831. see National Republican Party. Vermont.

Vermont Domestic Missionary Society. 99224, 99226-99227, 99234

Vermont Domestic Missionary Society. Directors. 99224

Vermont Domestic Missionary Society. Treasurer. 99224

Vermont gazette. 91413, 99058, 99206

Vermont Gibson Association. see Gibson Association of Vermont.

Vermont harmony. 99225

Vermont historical gazetteer. 31284

Vermont Historical Society. 801, 29781, 34059, 61280, 83679, 1st-2d notes after 98997, 98990-99000, 6th note after 99005, 99014

Vermont journal. 93896, 99056, 99059, 99159

Vermont Juvenile Missionary Society. see Vermont Domestic Missionary Society.

Vermont Literary and Scientific Institution. 99228

Vermont magazine. 50188, 1st note after 99197

Vermont Medical College, Woodstock, Vt. 99229-99230, 102104

Vermont Medical Society. 99232

Vermont Medical Society. Charter. 99232

Vermont miniature register, and gentleman's pocket almanac. 99160

Vermont miniature register, for . . . 1833. 99233

Vermont Missionary Society. see Vermont Domestic Missionary Society.

Vermont Mutual Fire Insurance Company. 99235

Vermont quarterly gazetteer, 31284

Vermont register. 95555

Vermont register and almanac. 5th note after
99205, 99236, 101230
Vermont register and almanac, for . . . 1803.
5th note after 99205, 99236, 101230
Vermont register and almanac, for . . . 1810.
99027
Vermont Religious Society. 99138
Vermont Religious Tract Society. 99138
Vermont repository. see Rural magazine;
or, Vermont repository.
Vermont Republican Convention Friendly to the
Election of Andrew Jackson to the Next
Presidency of the United States, Mont-
pelier, 1828. see Democratic Party.
Vermont. Convention, Montpelier, 1828.
Vermont resolutions on the admission of Texas.
65099
Vermont Sabbath-School Union. 99238
Vermont State Agricultural Society. Fair,
Brattleborough, Vt., 1866. see Fair of
the New England and Vermont State
Agricultural Societies, Brattleborough,
Vt., 1866.
Vermont state papers. 81691
Vermont townsman. 37938
Vermont Washington Benevolent Society. see
Washington Benevolent Society. Vermont.
Vermont year-book. 101230
Vermonter. pseud. Review of a "Letter from
the Right Rev. John H. Hopkins."
(32928)
Vermonters unmasked. 61368, 99240
Vermont's appeal to the candid and impartial
world. 7286, 4th note after 99005
Vernal de Salvatierra, Andres. see
Salvatierra, Andres Vernal de.
Vernero, Ioanne. see Werner, Joannes.
Verneuil, -------. 96447, 99241-99242
Verneuil, -------. petitioner (2765), 75163,
99242
Verneuil, Enrique Leopoldo de. tr. 89337,
89338
Verneuil, F. T. A. Chalumeau de. see
Chalumeau de Verneuil, F. T. A.
Vernieuden Nederlandschen waersegger. 78474
Vernon, Edward, 1684-1757. 2455, 11131-
11132, 11134, 11518, 11794, 40540-
40541, 56843, 99243, 99245-1st note
after 99245, 99249
Vernon, Edward, 1757-1847. see Harcourt,
Edward, Archbishop of York, 1757-1847.
Vernon, Francis V. 99251
Vernon, James. 99252
Vernon, Roland. 72053
Vernon, William Henry. 99253-99254
Vernon-Harcourt, William George Granville.
see Harcourt, William George Granville
Vernon.
Vernon, Conn. First Congregational Church.
99255
Vernon, N. Y. School. (55911)
Vernon H. Quincey. pseud. see Sewall,
Jonathan Mitchell, 1748-1808. supposed
author
Vernon-iad. 99257
Vernon's glory. Containing fourteen new songs.
99258
Vernon's glory; or, the Spaniards defeat.
99259
Vero ritratti historici. 40248
Veron de Forbonnais, Francois de. 99260
Veron de Forbonnais, Francois Louis.
supposed tr. 97691
Verordnung Wegen des West-Indischen und
Guineischen Handels. 102941
Verot, Augustine, Bp., 1804-1876. 47103

Verovering van Mexico. 98821
Veroveringh van de Stadt Olinda. 41849, note
after 99260
Verplanck, Gulian Crommelin, 1786-1870.
1358, (19995), 21107, 84258-note after
94258, 99261-99276, 99278, 99821
Verplanck, Gulian Crommelin, 1786-1870.
defendant 99277
Verplanck, Isaac. 99279
Verplanck, Johnston. 98534
Verplanck, Philip. 91365
Verrazzano, Giovanni da. 67740-67742, 99281
Verrazzano, Giovanni da. supposed author
29592
Verre, Pierre Alexandre Jacques de. 99282
Verren, Antoine. 3707, 99283
Verrichtung der Special-Conferenz der Evang.
Luth. Prediger und Abgeordneten. 100485
Verrichtung der Special-Conferenz . . . gehalten
. . . den 4ten und 5ten October, 1807.
100485
Verrichtungen der Evangelisch-Lutherischen
Synode fur Nord-Carolina und angranzende
Staaten. 55702
Verrichtungen der Special-Conferenz . . .
gehalten den ersten und zweyten October,
1809. 100485
Verrier Prestre, Jean de. see Prestre, Jean
de Verrier.
Verrill, Addison Emery, 1839-1926. 84233
Verritt, Paul. see Verity, Paul.
Versailles, France. Concours General des
Lycees et Collages de Paris et de
Versailles, 1854. see Concours General
des Lycees et Colleges de Paris et de
Versailles, 1854.
Versailles, Ky. Convention of the Synod of
Kentucky, 1840. see Presbyterian Church
in the U. S. Synod of Kentucky. Conven-
tion, Versailles, Ky., 1840.
Versalg geschreven door de hand van Mormon.
83120-83121
Versameling van stukken tot de dertien
Vereenigde Staaten. 97252
Versammlung Deutscher Philologen Orientalisten
und Schulmanner, Halle. (64601)
Versammlungen Deutscher Naturforscher und
Aerzte. see Gesellschaft Deutscher
Naturforscher und Aerzte.
Versassung der Vereinigten Staaten. 9672
Verscheide zee en land-togten gedaan in de
West-Indien. 31551
Verscheyde brieven en schriften. 7577
Verscheyde journalen. (74845), 98740
Verscheyde memorien van den Heer Resident
Charisius. 69585
Verscheyde noornaame reysen. 17874
Verscheyde Oost-Indische voyagien. (74830),
102500
Verscheyde scheeps-tegten na Florida. 24902,
39236, note before 99284
Verscheyden lessen, waarin beschreven worden.
48152
Verscheyden notabele consideratien. (57376),
2d note after 102903
Verschiedene alte und neuere geschichten.
99284
Verschiedene Christliche wahrheiten. 88824
Verschiedene Deutsche Volker. pseud.
Nachrichten und erinnerungen. 51693
Verschiedenen Gesichtern solcher die auch
jeto Noch am Leben sind. 99284
Verschuldigd dank-adres aan de Staaten van
Holland. 60764
Verse. By H. W. P. 58677
Verse memorials. 38704

Vert, Octavia Walton le. <u>see</u> Le Vert, Octavia Walton.
Vertebrals, including fossil mammals. 71033
Vertellende zyne vreemde vonderlijke avontueren. 11605
Vertelling voor de jeugd. 38241
Verteuil, Louis Antoine Amie Gaston de. <u>see</u> De Verteuil, Louis Antoine Aime Gaston, b. 1807.
Vertheidigung der Franzosischen Regierung. 99303
Vertheidigung der Freyen Kirche von Nord-Amerika. 27625
Vertholen, Andries Cornelissen. 47766, 3d note after 102895
Verthooninge, ghedaen aen die van de Vereenichde Nederlanden. 99304
Vertidas en las exequias del Senor D. Fernando de Borbon. 38624
Vertiz, Joaquin Maria Oteiza y. <u>see</u> Oteiza y Vertiz, Joaquin Maria de.
Vertiz, Pedro de. 99305
Vertoman, Lewis. <u>see</u> Barthema, Lewis.
Vertooch aen de Ed. Ho. Mo. Heeren Staten Generael. 99306
Vertooch aan de Hooch-Mogende Heeren Staten Generael. 55449, (57379), 99316
Vertooch aen de Hoogh en Mogende Heeren Staten Generael. 7595, 7643, note after 99306
Vertoog over het aanbelang van een tractaat van commercie. 99307
Vertoog van alle de religionen en ketteryen in Asia. 73319
Vertoog van de redenen die den Capitein Thomas Danielsz. 18500
Vertoogh. 98201
Vertoogh aan alle landtlievende. 39241, 97530
Vertoogh aende Hog: Mog: Heeren Staten Generael. (63197), 102908
Vertoogh by een lief-hebber des vaderlandts vertoont. 7575-7576, 99308
Vertoogh, door de Generaale West-Indische Compagnie deezer landen. 47824, 102441, 102889A
Vertoogh, hoe nootwendich, nut ende profijtelick het sy voor de Vereenighde Nederlanden. 98212-98213
Vertoogh, over den toestant der West-Indische Compagnie. 99309, note after 102917
Vertoogh teghen het ongefonderde ende schadelijck sluyten der cryen handel in Brazil. 7575-7576, 99308
Vertoogh van de considerabele colonie. 99310
Vertoogh van Nieu Neder-Landt, weghens de gheleghentheydt. 5045, 20595, note after 98474, note before 100436
Vertoogh van Nieu Nederland. 20596, note after 98474, note after 99310
Vertoonen met behoorlyk respect Bewinthebberen. 102889A
Vertrag brieff der Australischen oder Suder Compagney im Konigreich Schweden. 98199-98189
Vertrauliche briefe, aus Kanada und Neu England. 99311
Vertue, ------. <u>illus</u>. 67560
Vertus. <u>pseud</u>. Letters. <u>see</u> Sterling, Edward.
Vertus et bienfaits des missionnaires. 6903
Verum, Dic. <u>pseud</u>. <u>see</u> Your Wellwisher, Dic Verum. <u>pseud</u>.
Verungluckte reise von Hamburg. 99312
Verus. <u>pseud</u>. Calumnies of Verus. <u>see</u> Verax. <u>pseud</u>.

Verus. <u>pseud</u>. Letters lately published in the Diary. <u>see</u> Burges, J. Bland. <u>supposed author</u>
Verus. <u>pseud</u>. Letters of Verus. <u>see</u> Armstrong, John. <u>supposed author</u> and Fatio, Philip. <u>supposed author</u> and Yrujo y Tacon, Carlos Martinez de, Marques de Casa Yrujo. <u>supposed author</u>
Verus. <u>pseud</u>. Observations on the conduct of our executive towards Spain. <u>see</u> Onis, Luis de.
Verus. <u>pseud</u>. Observations on the existing differences. <u>see</u> Onis, Luis de.
Verus. <u>pseud</u>. Passage of the President's message. <u>see</u> Onis, Luis de.
Vervaerilijcken Oost-Indischen eclipsis. 55449, (57379), 99316
Vervaetende een duydelycke beschryvingh. 6442
Vervesserte A-B-C- oder Namenbucher. 98927
Vervolg der bijlagen. 67412
Vervolg en sleutel op de Negerhut. 92413
Vervolg op het Engelsche en Amerikaansche kaart-spel. 77516
Vervolg van de zeeven dorpen en Brandt. 98510
Vervolg van den Surinaamschen landman. 5964
Vervolgh op de t'samen-sprack tusschen teeuwes ende keesje maet. 99317
Verwandtschafts-verhaltnisse der Athapaskischen Sprachen dargestellt. 9529
Very, Nathaniel. 99318-99319
"Very age." A comedy in five acts. 28102
Very brief account of the wretched state of man by the fall. 92106
Very brief and plain essay on those acts of complaince. 46298
Very brief and very comprehensive life of Ben. Franklin. (80481)
Very brief essay, in the methods of piety. 46600
Very brief essay, on fidelity in keeping of promises and engagements. 46397
Very brief essay, on the enjoyment of God. (46284)
Very brief essay, on the union between the Redeemer and the beleever. [sic] 46402
Very brief essay, on tokens for good. 46411
Very brief essay, to detect and prevent hyporcrisy. 46566, 4th note after 97284
Very brief essay to offer some instructions of piety. 46464
Very brief essay, to show the light. (46374)
Very brief essay upon divine desertions. 46351
Very brief essay upon the caution to be used. 46312
Very brief essay upon the methods of piety. 46448
Very brief notice of the ecclesiastical and moral condition of North-Carolina. 11169
Very curious and modest address. 103238
Very extensive, important and valuable medical and surgical library. 84093
Very extraordinary narrative of Whiting Sweeting. 94048
Very hopeful young scholar. <u>pseud</u>. Ingenious poem. <u>see</u> Byles, Mathew.
Very important debate of the House of Commons. 53287
Very interesting and remarkable trial of Matthias. 46896
Very interesting letter from a minister in London. 7847, 27588
Very necessarie and profitable booke concerning nauigation. 94220
Very needful cuation. 46576, note after 99319
Very new pamphlet indeed! (57146), 99320, note after 99776

Viaggio nell' interno del Brasile. 46994
Viaggio per il Napo al Para. (57768)
Viaggio pittoresco intorno al modo ossia riassunto
generale de viaggi e scoperte. (21213)
Viaggio scritto per vn Comito Venitiano. 67730
Viaggio verso la India Orientale descritto da
Plinio. 67730
Viagio ed paese de lisola de loro. (36789)
Viaje a la Habana por la Condesa de Merlin.
(47979)
Viaje a la Luna. 63564
Viaje a Loja. 86239
Viaje a los Estados-Unidos del Norte de
America. 106280
Viaje a Rio de Janeiro. (48710)
Viaje al rededor del mundo. 16266
Viaje de D. Desiderio del Final Experto
Caballero. 99407
Viaje de Emperador Maximiliano y de la
Emperadriz Carlota. 47036
Viaje de Lionel Wafer al istmo del Darien.
100947
Viaje del Atlantico a Bogota. (26575)
Viaje e las cataratas de Niagara. 98364
Viaje pintoresco al rededor del mundo. 21212
Viaje pintoresco de las dos Americas, Asia
y Africa. 57459
Viaje pintoresco y arqueolojico sobre la parte
mas interesante. 52178
Viajero. pseud. Indios del Andaqui. see
Albis, --------.
Viajero. pseud. Juicio critico de los minis-
terios de la Inquisicion. 93348
Viajeros modernos. 12165, note after 99383C
Viajes a las cinco partes del mundo. 10204
Viajes cientificos a los Andes Ecuatoriales.
6941
Viajes de Amerigo Vespucio. note before
99327, 99380
Viajes de orden suprema. 65517
Viajes de un Colombiano en Europa. (75919)
Viajes en Europa, Africa, y America. 77085
Viajes menores. 99380
Viajes por al America del Sud. (2543)
Viajes y descubrimientos de los companeros
de Colon. 35211
Viaji practicado desde el calles. 11472
Vial poured out upon the sea. 46577, 1st note
after 99407
Viana, Miguel Pereira. note before 99408
Viana Zavala Saenz de Villaverda, Francisco
Leandro de. 48644, 99408
Vianen, J. van. cartographer 31359
Vianna, Antonio de Rocha. see Rocha
Vianna, Antonio da.
Vianna, B. L. tr. (12268)
Viator. pseud. Baltimore and Ohio Rail Road
Company. 2992, 99409
Viator. pseud. Thoughts of a traveller. see
Draper, Sir William.
Viator, John. pseud. Answer to Dr. Inglis's
defence. see Peters, Samuel. supposed
author
"Viator," on the Baltimore & Ohio Rail Road
Co. 2992
Viator; or, a peep into my note book. 32395
Viaud, Pierre. pseud. see Dubois-Fontanelle,
Jean Gaspard.
Vicar of Bray. 80812
Vicar of Wrexhill. 97028
Vicars, John. 31037
Vice Grand Commander of the Grand Council.
pseud. Sons of Malta exposed. 86997
Vice in its proper shape. 99421
Vicente, Francisco Antonio Garcia. ed. 87230

Vicente, Juan Manuel de San. see San Vicente,
Juan Manuel de.
Vicente, Nicolas Garcia de San. see Garcia
de San Vicente, Nicolas.
Vicenzo Piccolomini, Enea Silbo. see Piccolo-
mini, Enea Silbo Vicenzo, Conte.
Vicepresidente de Colombia da cuenta a la
republica. (25459), 76809
Vicepresidente de la republica a los Venezolanos.
87259
Viceroy's dream. 79852
Vicery, Eliza. 99422
Vicissitudes illustrated. 96361
Vicissitudes in both hemispheres. (23949),
note before 94094
Vicissitudes in the wilderness. 20759
Vicissitudes of human life. 99423
Vicissitudes of life. (20752)
Vicissitudes, or the journey of life. 20757
Vickers, Thomas. (47182), 66675
Vickers and Purcell controversy. 66676
Vicksburg, Miss. Citizens. 33250, note before
91708
Vicksburg, Miss. State Colored Convention,
1865. see Mississippi State Colored
Convention, Vicksburg, 1865.
Vicksburg, Miss. Southern Railroad Company
Committee. see Southern Railroad Com-
pany. Committee, Vicksburg, Miss.
Vicksburg and El Paso Railroad Company. see
Southern Pacific Railroad Company (Texas)
Vicomte de Chateaubrun. 4540
Victim. pseud. Astounding disclosures! see
Hunt, Isaac H.
Victim of revenge. 103415
Victim of seduction. An affecting narrative.
99424
Victim of seduction!—some interesting particu-
lars. 99425, 104621
Victima real legal. 76
Victimas-algozes quadros da escravidao. 43214
Victimas del Japon. 99426
Victims of fate. 91162
Victims of gaming. 99427
Victims of the rebellion. 80005
Victoire du Nord aux Etats-Unis. (50066)
Victor. pseud. Nouveaux voyages en diverses
parties de l'Amerique. 99428
Victor, Benjamin. supposed author 12553-
12557, 55285, 1st note after 99428-99431,
note after 100822
Victor, Jacques Maximilien Benjamin Bins de
Saint. see Saint Victor, Jacques Maxi-
milien Benjamin Bins de.
Victor, Metta Victoria (Fuller) 59373, 99432
Victor, Orville James. 39874-39875, 47792,
99433-99434
Victor Unda, Pablo. see Unda, Pablo Victor.
Victor Hugo's letter on John Brown. 33620,
note before 91289
Victor y festivo parabien y aplavso gratvlatorio.
86498
Victoria, Queen of Great Britain, 1819-1901.
85203 see also Great Britain.
Sovereigns, etc., 1837-1901 (Victoria)
Victoria, Francisco. 99435
Victoria, Francisco de, fl. 1633. 99436-99438
Victoria, Franciscus de. see Francisco de
Vitoria, 1486?-1546.
Victoria, Guad. ed. 19679
Victoria, Jeronimo. plaintiff 86402
Victoria, Jose de Sosa. see Sosa Victoria,
Jose de.
Victoria, Manuel Felix Fernandez Guadalupe,
Pres. Mexico, 1789-1843. 19679, 48565,
(64442), 99439-99440, 100849 see also
Mexico. President, 1824-1829 (Victoria)

Vida del D.ͬ Benjamin Franklin. 99454

Vida del esclarecido P. Juan Gumersvac. 2985

Vida del Il^{mo} i Exmo Senor D. Juan de Pala-fox i Mendoza. 73280

Vida del Ilvstr. i Revend. Don Toribio Alfonso Mogrovejo Arzobispo de Lima. (40058)

Vida del Ilvstrissimo i Reverendissimo D. Toribio Alfonso Mosgrovejo. (40058)

Vida del Inclyto Mexicano San Felipe de Jesus. (76029)

Vida del joven Rene. 12267

Vida del Padre Antonio Ruiz de Montoya. 74042

Vida del P. Fr. Diego Romero. 41411

Vida del Padre Francisco Maria Galluzzi. 47488

Vida del P. Francisco Xavier Lazcano. (39480)

Vida del P. Gaspar de Carvajal de la Comp. de Jesus. 9880

Vida del P. Ignacio de Loyola. 70781

Vida del P. Jose Campoi. 11446

Vida del Padre Joseph de Ancheta de la Compania de Jesvs. 4828

Vida del Padre Joseph de Anchieta de la Compania de Jesus. (1373)

Vida del Rmo. P. Fr. Rodrigo de la Cruz. 26571

Vida del Siervo de Dios Gregorio Lopez. 42578

Vida del Ven. Arzobispo de Mexico, D. Alonzo de Guevas Davalos. 80987

Vida del Ven. Hermitano Juan Bautista. 75777

Vida del V. P. Alonso Messia. 75581

Vida del Ven. Padre Antonio Baldinucci. 26447

Vida del Venerable Padre Bartholome Castano. 22817

Vida del Venerable Padre Don Pedro de Arellano y Sossa. 22066

Vida del Ven. P. Fr. Antonio Margil. 81087

Vida del Ven. P. Francisco Maria Picoli. 2986

Vida del Ven. P. Mtro. Fr. Diego Basalenque. 75778

Vida del Ven. P. Miguel Wadingo. 75817

Vida del Ven. Padre, y exemplarissimo varon, el Mtro. Fr. Diego Basalenque. 75779

Vida del V. Siervo de Dios Antonio de los Angeles, Bustamente. (22895)

Vida del Venerable y apostolico Padre Pedro Claver de la Compania de Iesvs. 93330

Vida del Vice Almirante Lord Vizconde de Nelson. 99455

Vida di Sebastiano Giuseppe di Carvalho e Melo. 63912

Vida do Apostolico Padre Antonio Vieyra. 3645

Vida do P. Joao de Almeida. 98656

Vida de proto martyr do Peru o Padre Frey Diego Ortis. 76785

Vida do Veneravel Padre Belchior de Pontes. (24981)

Vida do Venerauel Padre Ioseph de Anchieta. 98644

Vida dos pretos na America. 92598

Vida, e peregrinacoens de irmdo Bartholomeu Lourenco. 76785

Vida exemplar, heoricas virtudes, y apostolicos ministerios de el V. P. Antonio Nunes de Mirande. 58002

Vida exemplar, mverte santa, y regicijada de el angelical Hermano Migvel de Omana. 99463

Vida exemplar y admirable del Venerable siervo de Dios, y Padre de San Joseph Betancvr. 26571

Vida exemplar, y mverte dichosa de el Padre Juan Carnero. 99648

Vida exemplar y muerte dichosa del Ven. P. Bartolome Castano. 11394

Vida exemplar, y muerte preciosa de la Madre Barbara Josepha de San Francisco. 96250

Vida exemplar, y virtudes heroicas del Venerable Padre Juan Antonio de Oviedo. (39480)

Vida exemplares, y venerables memorias de algunos claros varones de la Compania de Iesvs. 55272

Vida interio o confesiones. 58304

Vida interior [de Juan de Palafox y Mendoza.] (36797), 99456

Vida interior del Excel. Senor Don Juan de Palafox y Mendoza. 58303

Vida interior del Excelentissimo Senor Don Jvan de Palafox y Mendoza. 99456

Vida interior del Ilvstrissimo, Excelentissimo, y Venerable Senor D. Juan de Palafox y Mendoza. 99456

Vida la patria. 100630

Vida, martyrio, y beatificacion del invicto proto-martyr de el Japon. 47337

Vida militar y politica del General Don Juan Lavalle. (38452)

Vida, muerte y funeral del Iltmo. Sr. D. Feliciano de la Vega. 86431

Vida politica de Pedro Santana. (76807)

Vida portentosa del Americano Septentrional apostol el V. P. Fr. Antonio Margil de Jesus. 31498, 99614

Vida prodigiosa del Venerable siervo de Dios, Fray Sebastian de Aparicio. (72520)

Vida prodigiosa, en lo vario de los svcesos. 105717

Vida qve el Siervo de Dios Gregorio Lopez hizo. 42576-42577

Vida que hizo el servo de Dios Gregorio Lopez. 42579

Vida que hizo el siervo de Dios Gregorio Lopez. 42575

Vida, virtudes, y milagros de la Venerable sierva de Dios, Mariana de Jesus. 27514

Vida, virtudes, trabajos . . . de la Ven. M. Sor Maria de Jesus. 40020, 74863

Vida, virtudes y dones sobrenaturales de la Ven. sierva de Dios Sor Maria de Jesus. 36090

Vida, virtudes y milagros del nvevo apostol del Pirv el Venerable P. F. Francisco Solano. 86228

Vida y virtudes de la Ven. Isabel de la Encarnacion. 75816

Vida, y virtudes de la Ven. Madre Sor Maria Ynes de los Dolores. 50479

Vida y virtudes del P. Juan de Ledesma. (39679)

Vida y escritos de D. Bernardo Monteagudo. (51348)

Vida y escritos de . . . Las Casas. 98604

Vida y escritos de Las-Casas, noticia importante. (49434)

Vida, y escritos del Venerable varon Gregorio Lopez. 1944, 28739

Vida y hechos del Almirante D. Christoval Colon. (14674)

Vida y martirio del glorioso Padre Fray Diego Ruiz Ortiz. 93305

Vida y martyr de Cristoval. 99457

Vida y martyrio de el Ven. Padre Diego Lvis de Sanvitores. 26565

Vida y memorias del Dr. Don Mariano Moreno. 50614

Vida y muerte del P. Antonio Tempis. 38234

Vida, y milagros del glorioso S. Antonio de
Padua. 48160

Vida y milagros del glorioso S. Nicolas To-
lentino. (47339)

(*) Vida (*) y milagros del Sancto Confessor
de Christo, F. Sebastian de Aparicio.
96214

Vida y muerte de el P. Pablo de Salceda.
56645

Vida y muerte del siervo de Dios S. Francisco
de Cordova y Bocanegra. 16773

Vida y prodigiosas virtudes del P. Francisco
German Glandorf. 7447

Vida y viajes de Cristobal Colon. 35177

Vida y virtudes de el siervo de Dios el Ven.
Padre D. Domingo Perez de Barcia.
18779

Vida, y virtudes de el Venerable, y Apostolico
Padre Juan de Ugarte. 99694

Vida y virtudes de la Venerable Madre
Francisca Maria de el Nino Jesvs.
99655

Vida y virtudes de los PP. Keler y Provincial
Mateo Ansaldo. 37246

Vida y virtudes de majestad. 58302

Vida y virtudes del Exmo i Illmo Senor D.
Juan de Palafox y Mendoza. 73279

Vida, y virtudes del V. P. Juan Buatista
Zappa. 98849

Vida y virtudes heroycas de el exemplar y
fervoroso Hermano Juan Nicolas. 50480

Vidas de Espanoles celebres. 67324-67325

Vidas de los Venerables Padres del Convento
de S. Agustin de Salamanca. 80835

Vidas y virtudes de algvnos varones. 26571

Vidal, -------. plaintiff 5472, 27488

Vidal, --------. 27499, 29178, 99458

Vidal, Benito. 99459

Vidal, E. E. 99460

Vidal de Figueroa, Jose. 99461-99463

Vidal de Figueroa, Lorenzo. plaintiff 99464

Vidal de Negreiros, Andrea. 85659

Vidal y Mico, Francisco. 99465

Vidal vs. the city of Philadelphia. 5472

Vidalin, Argrimur Jonsson, 1568-1648. 2058,
(28646), 36637, 66686, 74880

Vidalin, Lavmand Povel. 99466

Vidaure, ------, Abbe. see Vidaurre, Felipe
Gomez de. incorrectly supposed author

Vidaure, Felipe Gomez de. see Vidaurre,
Felipe Gomez de.

Vidaurrazaga, Aparicio de. 99467-99468

Vidaurre, Felipe Gomez de. incorrectly supposed author 12756, 38366, note after
99468-99469

Vidaurre, M. L. see Vidaurre y Encalada,
Manuel Lorenzo del.

Vidaurre y Encalada, Manuel Lorenzo de.
(14600)-14601, 44285, (61137), 93812,
99470-99500 see also Peru. Ministerio
de Relaciones Esteriores.

Vidaurre contra Vidaurre. 99499

Vide de Bolivar. 14578

Vide de el Capuchino Espanol, Francisco de
Pamplona. 1574

Videa, Francisco de Ugarte. see Ugarte-
Videa, Francisco de.

Videla, Zenon. defendant 73214

Videns, Fabricus. pseud. ed. Spy-glass.
89937

Videto, Stephen. defendant 99501

Vidette; a tale of the Mexican war. (18061)

Vidler, William, 1758-1816. 99502, 104734

Vidono, -------, Cardinal. (64173), 99503

Vidua, Carlo, Conte. 99504

Vie a New-York. (12573)

Vie chez les Indiens. 11542

Vie correspondance et ecrits de Washington.
89011, 101747

Vie d'Abraham Lincoln. 47292

Vie d'Adele Coulombe. 17141

Vie d'Anna Jane Linnard. 2799

Vie d'Anne Gertrude. 4424

Vie dans la Nouveau-Monde. 23558

Vie de Benjamin Franklin. 25543

Vie de Buxton. 9694

Vie de Christophe Colomb par l'Abbe Eug.
Cadoret. (9831)

Vie de Christophe Colombe, par M. le Baron
de Bonnefoux. 6313

Vie de Corneille Tromp. (71104)

Vie de Cristophe Colomb. 14677

Vie de famille dans le Nouveau Monde. 7714

Vie de Franklin. 25585, 78116

Vie de Franklin. [Par Jared Sparks.] 88997

Vie de Franklin. . . . Par M. Mignet. 48903

Vie de Frederick Douglass. 20712

Vie de George Fox. 97433

Vie de George Washington. 27502, (44793),
1st note after 99504, 101888

Vie de Georges Washington General en Chef.
(67696)

Vie de Gregoire Lopez. 42583

Vie de Gregoire Lopez dans la Novvelle-
Espagne. 42580-42581

Vie de Guillaume Penn. (44820)

Vie de J. J. Dessalines. 21029

Vie de J. Tuckerman. 11915

Vie de la B. Soevr Rose de Sainte Marie.
24227, 73176

Vie de la Bienhevrevse epovse de Jesus-Christ
Soevr Rose de Sainte Marie. 27793

Vie de la Mere Catherine de Saint Avgvstin.
(67499)

Vie de la Mere Marie de l'Incarnation. 12141,
3d note after 99504

Vie de la Soeur Bourgeoys. (47529)

Vie de la Soeur Bourgeoys et l'histoire de la
Congregation de Villemarie. 47551

Vie de la Soeur Bourgeoys, fondatrice de la
Congregation de Notre-Dame de Villemarie. 23655, 4th note after 99504

Vie de la Soeur Marguerite Bourgeois. 67898,
4th note after 99504

Vie de la Venerable Mere Marie de l'Incarnation. 44861, 5th note after 99504

Vie de la Venerable Soeur Marguerite Bourgeois
(67899), 4th note after 99504

Vie de la Venerable Soeur Marguerite Bourgeoys
50131, 4th note after 99504

Vie de Lafayette. 99505

Vie de l'auteur, par Philemon Louis Savary.
(77270)

Vie de l'illustre serviteur de Dieu, Noel Bru-
let de Sillery. 81023

Vie de M. Olier. 23652

Vie de Madame d'Youville. (47529)

Vie de Mme d'Youville, fondatrice de Soeurs
de la Charite de Villemarie. 23653

Vie de Madame Mance. (47529)

Vie de Mlle. Le Ber. 23650, 39588

Vie de Mlle Mance et histoire de l'Hotel-Dieu
de Villemarie. 23654

Vie de Michel de Ruiter. 7406

Vie de Phil. Emm. de Lorraine. 50220

Vie de Rene du Guay-Trouin. 71107

Vie de Ruiter. 71108

Vie de S. Torribio de Lima. 30415

Vie de Sainte Rose de Ste. Marie. (73189)

Vie de Toussaint l'Ouverture, chef des noirs
insurges. 21030

Vie de Toussaint-L'Ouverture par Saint-Remy.
75484

Vie de Washington. 88997, 89011-89012
Vie des femmes chez les Mormons. 70332,
   note after 101315
Vie des Negres dans les etats a esclaves
   d'Amerique. 92535
Vie des Negres en Amerique. 92530-92532
Vie dv bienhevrevx Gregoire Lopez. 42582
Vie du bien-heureux Pere Francois Solano.
   17187
Vie du Capitaine Cook. 37955
Vie du Cardinal de Cheverus. 33555
Vie du General J. M. Borgella. 1928
Vie du P. Marcel Francois Mastrilli. 15098
Vie du Pere Pierre Claver. 99506
Vie du R. P. Joseph Varin. 29216
Vie du R. P. Pierre Joseph Marie Chaumonot.
   (12297)-12298, 2d note after 93480
Vie du Venerable Dom Jean de Palafox. 20101,
   99507, 100609
Vie du Venerable Pere Pierre Claver. 24745
Vie et aventures de Martin Chizzlewit. 20007
Vie et les actions memorables de Michel de
   Ruyter. 74514
Vie et les aventures de Ferdinand Vertamont.
   99508
Vie et les aventures de Robinson Crusoe.
   99510
Vie et les aventures de Robinson Crusoe,
   contenant sa naisance. 99509
Vie et les aventures surprenantes de Robinson
   Crusoe. 77218, 99509
Vie et voyages de Christophe Colomb, d'apres
   des documents authentiques. (73271)
Vie et voyages de Christophe Colomb; traduit
   de l'Anglois par G. Renson. 35175
Vie et voyages de William Dampier. 38240
Vie, les avantures, & le voyage de Groenland
   du Reverend Pere Cordelier Pierre de
   Mesange. 97653
Vie, lettres, voyages, memoires et opuscules
   d'Aristide-Aubert du Petit-Thouars.
   61260
Vie militaire du General Grondel. 3980
Vie miraculeuse du P. Joseph Anchieta. 4829
Vie politique de Marie—Paul—Jean—Roch—
   Yvres—Gilbert Motier, Marquis de Lafay-
   ette. 99511
Vie privee, impartiale, politique, militaire et
   domestique, du Marquis de la Fayette.
   99512
Vie privee, politique et litteraire de Beau-
   marchais. 99513
Vie privee politique et militaire de Toussaint-
   Louverture. 96350
Vie publique et privee de M. le Marquis de
   Lafayette. 99514
Vie souterraine ou les mines et les mineurs.
   81317
Viedma, Antonio de. 99515
Viedma, Francisco de. 99516-99517
Viefville des Essars, -------- de. 99518
Viega Cabral, P. G. T. da. note after 99518
Vieillard. pseud. Reflexions. see Dubucq,
   --------.
Vieillard du pays de Medoc. pseud. Reflex-
   ions. see Lemesle, Charles.
Vieira, Antonio. 34186, note before 99519-
   99530
Vieira, Joao Fernandes. ed. 36088-36089
Vieira Cansancao, Joao Lins. see Sinimbu,
   Joao Lins Vieira Cansancao, Visconde
   de, 1810-1906.
Vieira Couto, J. see Couto, J. Vieira.
Vieira da Silva, -------. 99531
Vieira da Silva, Luis Antonio. see Silva,
   Luis Antonio Vieira da.

Viejra, Antonio. see Vieira, Antonio.
Viel-Castel, Henri. 99532
Viele, Egbert Ludovickus, 1825-1902. 54158,
   54655 see also New York (City) Board
   of Commissioners of the Central Park.
   Engineer-in-Chief.
Viele, John Jay. 99533
Vielen Original-Correspondenzen und historisc-
   hen Aktenstucken. (22002)
Vienna. Akademie der Wissenschaften. see
   K. Akademie der Wissenschaften, Vienna.
Vienna. K. K. Brasilianer-Museum. 63677
Vienna. Burgtheater. 100721
Vienna. Congress, 1814-1815. 38201, 52387
Vienna. K. K. Nationaltheater. 2581, 104839
Vienne Jourdan, ------ de la Haute. see
   Jourdan, ------ de la Haute-Vienne.
Vienot, Vincent Marie. see Vaublanc, Vincent
   Marie Vienot, Comte de.
Vienot-Vaublanc, Vincent Marie. see Vaublanc,
   Vincent Marie Vienot, Comte de.
Vier Jahre in Cayenne. 2329
Vier loblicher Staat. 89554A, 99534
Vier maanden onder de goudzoekers in Opper-
   Californie. 8351, 1st note after 99534,
   1st note after 100641
Vier Monate unter den Goldsuchern im Sacra-
   mento-Thale in Obercalifornien. 8352,
   1st note after 100641
Vier Monate unter Goldfindern in Ober Kali-
   fornien. 8353, 2d note after 99534, 1st
   note after 100641
Vier Schweizern. pseud. Kurze Nachricht.
   87855
Vier vnd zwantzigste Schiffahrt. 33677, 67981
Viera, Juan de. 99535
Vierdte Buch von der Neuwen Welt. (8784)
Vierdte Schiffart. 77682
Vierge du Canada. 23102
Vierge Iroquoise. (18223)
Viernes sagrado en culto y obsequio del Cora-
   zon. 76282
Viero, Theodore. 99536
Vierte General Versammlung der Kirche Gottes
   aus allen Evangelischen Religionen in
   Pennsylvania. 60766, 4th note after 97845
Vierte Schiffart. 33656, (67562), 77680-77681
Viertzehende Schiffart. 33667, 82819
Vierzehender Theil Americanischen Historien.
   (8784)
Vierzehn jahrige Ost-Indische Kreig-und Ober-
   Kaufmanns-Dienste. 105639
14 Taf. von J. H. von Minutoli. 71445
Vies de Jean d'Estrees. 71106
Vies de Sainte Rose de Lima. (39608)
Vies des plus celebres marins. (71104)-71108
Vies du Capitaine Cassard, et du Capitaine
   Paulin. 71105
Vies et aventures remarquables des plus cele-
   bres voyageurs modernes. 11933
Vietor, Johann Daniel. 99537-99538
Viets, Roger. 99539-99541
Vieux commandeur. pseud. Bambois. see
   Bourdillon, --------.
Vieux philanthrope. pseud. Quelques considera-
   tions sur l'Amerique. see Carlet,
   Joseph Antoine. supposed author
Vieux planteur. pseud. De l'exploitation des
   sucreries. see Poyen Sainte-Marie,
   --------.
Vievigne, ------ Petit de. see Petit de
   Veivigne, -------.
View and defence of the Christian religion.
   95383
View and description of the Eastern Penitentiary.
   60080, note after 99542

View and opinions of William Wheeler Hubbell.
33467

View and survey of such ships as were in the
River Thames. 67574

View, by A. Vaudincault. (19781)

View of a Christian church, and church government. 99543

View of all religions. 71852

View of all religions in the world. 73313-
73317

View of America. (8016), 8030

View of America. To which is prefixed, a
narrative. 41305

View of American unitarian missions. 59129

View of an American steamer. 92216

View of astronomy. 59284

View of Carney Mission. 84433

View of certain proceedings in the Legislature.
54002, 92865, note after 99543

View of certain proceedings in the two houses
of the Legislature. 54002, 92865, note
after 99543

View of congregationalism. 66658-(66659)

View of congregationalism, its principles and
doctrines. 66660

View of ecclesiastical proceedings in the county
of Windham, Connecticut. (80370)-80371,
note after 100602, 102522

View of exertions lately made for the purpose
of colonizing the free people of colour.
99544

View of General Jackson's domestic relations.
99545

View of Governor Jay's administration. 16363

View of Holliston in its first century. 24565

View of home life during the American revolution. 43538

View of Major Anderson's garrison family.
25168

View of Niagara. 102633

View of North America. 99546

View of our national policy and that of Great
Britain. 8490

View of politics. 105566, 105567

View of Quebec. 50185, 82379

View of religions. 209-210

View of river rights. 34735

View of Russian America. 72307

View of science and quackery. 95588

View of slavery in connection of With Christianity. 106096

View of slavery in the United States. 67189

View of slavery, moral and politica. 81385

View of slavery outside the cabin. 30616

View of some of the first operations of the
war. (63785)

View of some of the more prominent features
of that state of society. 52269, 94526

View of South-America and Mexico. 99547

View of South Carolina. (20915)

View of spiritual, or anti-typical Babylon.
28040

View of the absurd practice, in the yellow, or
bilious fever. 62364

View of the action of the federal government.
35866

View of the administration of the federal government. 99548

View of the advantages of . . . Texas. 22475

View of the agricultural, commercial, manufacturing, financial, political, literary,
moral and religious capacity and character.
8050

View of the alien question unmasked. 14436

View of the American Indians. 105493

View of the American slavery question. 3675

View of the application for an amendment of
the charter. 99549

View of the Archiepiscopal Palace at Scrooby.
33926

View of the arguments . . . in the case of the
United States vs. Brigantine William.
(5766)

View of the British possessions in North-
America. 83617, 83626

View of the calumnies lately spread in some
scurrilous prints. 60767, 60771, 99550

View of the Calvinistic clubs in the United
States. 99551

View of the campaigns of the North-Western
Army, &c. 8557

View of the cause and consequences of the
American revolution. 6839

View of the causes of the superiority of the
men. 19333

View of the causes of the suspension of cash
payments at the banks. 10889, 23366

View of the character, manners, and customs
of the North-Americans. 99551A

View of the city of New-Orange. (51132)

View of the city of Quebec. 67001

View of the claims of American citizens.
81514, 99552

View of the climate and soil of the United
States. 100693

View of the coasts, countries and islands.
99553

View of the coins struck by the East India
Company. 85423

View of the commerce between the United
States and Rio de Janeiro. 2836

View of the commerce of the United States
and the Mediterranean sea-ports. 2837

View of the commerce of the United States as
it stands at present. 10883, 23966,
96561

View of the comparative claims of W. H.
Harrison and M. Van Buren. 55810

View of the condition of the Negroes in Jamaica
in 1824. 63326

View of the conduct of the executive, in the
foreign affairs of the United States.
29982-29983, 50020, 96421-96422

View of the conduct of the executive of Virginia.
100544

View of the constitution of the British colonies.
91992, 91994

View of the constitution of the United States of
America. 68003

View of the controversy between Great-Britain
and her colonies. 29955-29956, 78579-
78581, 2d note after 99553, 4th note after
100862

View of the controversy subsisting between
Great-Britain and the American colonies.
90978

View of the course of crops in England and
Maryland. 6416, 45373, note after 93609

View of the cultivation of fruit trees. (17313)

View of the debts and expenses of the commonwealth of Pennsylvania. 60768

View of the Democratick Republican Celebration,
at Westmoreland, N. H. 99554

View of the depredations and ravages committed
by the Spaniards. 99555

View of the diseases most prevalent. 18003

View of the diseases of the army in Great
Britain, America, and West Indies. 69097

View of the doctrine of Smith. 82304

View of the doctrines held by Judge Cooper in
1813. 10889

View of the doctrines of Smith. 82304

View of the Dutch trade in all the states. 33568

View of the economy of Methodism. 99556

Vievv of the English acquisitions in Guinea. 99557

View of the evidence relative to the conduct of the American war. 19774, 99558

View of the exertions lately made for the purpose of colonizing the free people of colour. 14732, 99544

View of the expected Christian millenium. 65496

View of the finances of the state of Maryland. 45390

View of the government of the United States. 43459

View of the Grand Canal. 99559

View of the Greenland trade and whale-fishery. 22196, 28659, note after 99559-99560

View of the Hebrews; exhibiting the destruction of Jerusalem. 82538

View of the Hebrews; or the tribes of Israel in America. (82539)-(82540)

View of the history of Great-Britain. (31901), 31903, 55515, 99561

View of the history, politics, and literature of the year. 1614

View of the history—religion—manners and customs of the Hindoos. 71841

View of the impending political crisis. 71549

View of the importance of the British American colonies. 1391

View of the interior of the Park Theatre. (69154), 83665

View of the internal policy of Great Britain. 101106

View of the island of St. Helena. 99557

View of the jurisdiction and proceedings of the Court of Probate. 103370

View of the lake coast from Sandusky to Detroit. 8557

View of the land laws of Pennsylvania. 79216

View of the law and practice in the Spanish colonies. 99562

View of the lead mines of Missouri. 77858, 77877, 77881

View of the Livingston County High-School. 41655, 99563

View of the management of the Schuylkill Navigation Company. 91882

View of the missions, funds, expenditures and prospects. 99564

View of the missions of the American Board of Commissioners for Foreign Missions. 99566

View of the missions of the American of the American Board of Commissioners of Foreign Missions. 99565

View of the missions under the direction of the American Board of Commissioners fore Foreign Missions. 99567

View of the moral and political epidemic. 99568

View of the moral state of Newfoundland. (74729)

View of the moral world. 66071

View of the New-England illuminati. 99569

View of the New-York State Prison in the city of New-York. 54711, 99570

View of the Ohio State Fair Grounds, 1854. 57064

View of the opinions . . . May 16, 1816. 103054A

View of the ordination of the author of these books. 78322

View of the origin, powerful influence and pernicious effects of intemperance. 88656

View of the past and present state of the island of Jamaica. 91692

View of the Patowmac River. 102541

View of the policy of permitting slaves in the states. (39538)

View of the political and civil situation of Louisiana. 99571

View of the political conduct of Aaron Burr, Esq. 12387, 1st note after 99571, note after 105047

View of the political situation of the province of Upper Canada. 35438, 2d note after 99571

View of the political transactions of Great-Britain. 99572

View of the practicability and means of supplying the city of Philadelphia with wholesome water. 39219, 60451, 62116, 84648

View of the present condition of the slave population. 24801

View of the present increase of the slave trade. 95661

View of the present seat of war at and near New York. 42402

View of the present situation of the United States of America. (50924)

View of the present state of the western parts of the state of New-York. 51355, 99573, note after 104444

View of the present state of all the empires, kingdoms, states, and republics in the known world. 50926

View of the present state of the African slave trade. 60769, 99574

View of the present state of the currency. 5243

View of the present state of the Penitentiary and Prison in the city of Philadelphia. 60644, 90815

View of the present state of the political and religious world. 43474

View of the present state of the slave trade. 60769, 99574

View of the present state of the world. 50970

View of the President's conduct, concerning the conspiracy of 1806. (18684)

View of the principal causes that have produced the present extraordinary advance of the stock of the U. S. Bank. 3189, note after 99574

View of the principles, operation and probable effects of the funding system of Pennsylvania. 60770, 99575

View of the principles upon which the Independent Society for Public Worship, under the ministry of the Rev. Mr. Frey, is established. 99576

View of the proceedings of the Assemblies of Jamaica, for some years past. (35668), note after 99576, note after 105081

View of the proceedings of the Convention of 1776. 60435, 80768

View of the proceedings of the House of Representatives. 4071

View of the proceedings of the last session of Congress. 99577

View of the progress of society in Europe. 72003

View of the progressive improvement of England. 5647

View of the proposed constitution of the United States. 99578

View of the proposed Grand Junction Canal. 94415

View of the province of Upper Canada. 35438
View of the quarterly diminution of the present 6 per cent. stock. 73891
View of the relative situation of Great Britain and the United States of North America. (5542), 1st note after 99578
View of the remedies proposed for existing evils. 88069, 2d note after 99578
View of the rights and wrongs, power and policy, of the United States of America. 34735
View of the rise and progress of French influence. 11004
View of the ruinous consequences of a dependence on foreign markets. 10889
View of the Russian empire. (59572)
View of the scandals lately spread. 60767, 60771, 99579
View of the several schemes with respect to America. 41781, 99580
View of the social condition of the white, coloured, and Negro population of the West Indies. 10938
View of the soil and climate of the United States of America. 100694
View of the state of parties in America. 15032, 99581
View of the state of the Church in the Canadas. 91663, 99582
View of the state of the colonies of Great Britain. 8842
View of the subject of slavery contained in the Biblical repertory for April, 1836. 70193, 99583
View of the Texas revolution. 24283
View of the theory and practice of the . . . governments. 44372
View of the title to Indiana, a tract of country on the River Ohio. 25595, 34579-34580, 96769, 99584, note just before 103108
View of the trade of South-Carolina. 106016
View of the treaty of commerce with France. 80701, 99585
View of the Trinity. (82540)
View of the United States. By John Hayward. 31078
View of the United States; for the use of schools and families. (31763), 31768
View of the United States, historical, geographical, and statistical. 18535
View of the United States of America, in a series of papers. 17307
View of the universe. 91537
View of the valley of the Mississippi. 2594, note after 94327, 99586
View of the wants and prospects of our country. 32708
View of the West India question. (25622)
View of the whole ground. A brief history of the proposed impeachment of the Governor. (43380), 60772, note after 99586
View of the whole ground: being the whole correspondence. 42992
View of the whole ground: comprising the constitution. 99587
View of universal history. 226
View of Upper Canada & British possessions. 83624
View of West Florida. 104285
View on the Hudson River. 102541
View on the Patowmac River from Mount Vernon. 102541
View to preserve from contamination and crime destitue and neglected female children. 8856
Views a-foot. 94440

Views and assumptions of the radicals. 5750
Views and map, illustrative of the scenery and geology. 52834
Views and opinions of American statesmen. (76406)
Views and plans of the Smithsonian Institution. 58020
Views and reviews in American literature. 81272
Views around Ithaca. 13401
Views for freedom. 49709
Views from drawings by W. G. Wall. 33529, note after 101087
Views from Plymouth Rock. 51239
Views in Mexico. 22044
Views in . . . New York. 54129
Views in New-York, and its environs. 54712, note before 99588
Views in New York city. (9120)
Views in Philadelphia and its environs. (12731) 99588
Views in Philadelphia, and its vicinity. (12731), 99588
Views in South America. 57947
Views in the island of Dominica. 64193
Views in the vicinity of the city of Kingston Jamaica. 103829
Views of a stockholder, in relation to the Delaware and Hudson Canal. 91881, 105641
Views of American constitutional law. 27850
Views of American slavery, taken a century ago 4693, 102699
Views of ancient monvments in Central America 11520, 91301
Views of Canada and the colonists: embracing the experience of a residence. 10618
Views of Canada and the colonists, embracing the experience of an eight years; residence 8501
Views of colonization. 56057
Views of duty adopted to the times. 59354
Views of Elmira. 88657
Views of General Grant, Sherman, Dix, Wood Butler, Edward Everett, J. A. Griswold, etc. 19515
Views of Ithaca and its environs. 35280, note after 88657, 3d note after 99588
Views of J. W. Schuckers. 77998
Views of Jalapa, Guadalazara, Tlalpuxahua, and other parts of Mexico. 101288
Views of Judge Woodward and Bishop Hopkins. 37330
Views of life. 50454
Views of life and death. 90466
Views of Louisiana. (7168), 7176-7177
Views of nature: or contemplations on the sublime phenomena of creation. (33708)
Views of New-Haven and its vicinity. (3329), note after 99587
Views of Philadelphia. 103971
Views of Philadelphia, and its vicinity. 62366
Views of Philadelphia, consisting of 20 small and 4 large panorama plates on India paper. 62365
Views of religion. 99589
Views of Saratoga. 76927
Views of slavery and emancipation. 44944, 103819
Views of society and manners in America. 18640-18641, note after 99589-99590, 105597
Views of the actual commerce of the United States with the Spanish colonies. 88941
Views of the juvenile, youthful, and adult population. 105097

Views of the minority of the Committee
. . . . January 12, 1819. 1895
Views of the minority of the Committee on
Manufactures, presented by Mr. Cleveland.
13664
Views of the origin and migrations of the
Polynesian nations. (38867)
Views of the powers and policy of the govern-
ment of the United States. 83243-83245,
83242, 83286-83288
Views of the present state, progress, and pros-
pects of the colony. 8501
Views of the profile mountain and profile rock.
89679
Views of the public debts. 26399
Views of the remarkable places and objects of
all countries. 8204, 48674
Views of the Society of Friends in relation to
civil government. 99591
Views of Wilberforce, Clarkson, and others.
91011
Views on Philadelphia and its vicinity. (12731)
Views on political economy, from the descrip-
tion of the United States. 47437
Views on the Chinese question. 37272
Views on the formation of a British & Ameri-
can Land and Emigration Company.
(32394)
Views on the government and policy of the
United States. 83257
Views on the Hudson. 33527, 52322
Views on the liberal and restrictive systems.
10889
Views on the location of the port of entry.
14288
Views on the powers and policy of the govern-
ment of the United States. 83279
Views on the St. Lawrence. 52322
Views on the subject of internal improvements.
99592
Views on the subject of systematic British
pauper immigration to Canada. 17449
Views on the war. 99593
Views relative to the construction of a rail-
way from Halifax to Quebec. 14215
Views respecting the Chesapeak and Delaware
Canal. 99594
Views, sustained by facts and authorities.
68169
Views taken during the Arctic Expedition.
8579
Views, with ground plans, of the Highland
cottages at Roxbury. 99595
Vieyra, Antonio. see Vieira, Antonio.
Vieyra, E. R. del Rio Laubyan y. see
Laubyan y Vieyra, E. R. del Rio.
Vieyra, Luis Gonzaga. 99595
Viger, Denis Benjamin, 1774-1861. 10350,
(57399), 73520, (80866), 93177, note
after 99595-99598 see also Quebec
(Province) Legislature. Legislative
Assembly. Agent.
Viger, Denis Benjamin, 1774-1861. appellant
99598
Viger, Denis Benjamin, 1774-1861. supposed
author 1764, 16024, note after 99596
Viger, Jacques. 23609, 34041, 44867, 69661,
99599-99601 see also Montreal.
Surveyor of Roads and Bridges.
Viger, Marie Amable (Foretier) appellant
99598
Vigier, George. note after 99601
Vigil of faith, and other poems. 32390
Vigilance Committee, San Francisco. see
San Francisco. Vigilance Committee.

Vigilance Committee of San Francisco. . . .
Speeches of R. A. Lockwood. 41752
Vigilant Fire Company, Philadelphia. 99602
Vigilante (Ship) (81922), 99603-99604
Vigilantius. Or, a servant of the Lord found
ready for the coming of the Lord. 46579,
46613, 1st note after 99604
Vigilius. Or, the awakener. 46580, 2d note
after 99604
Vignal, -------. 99605
Vignaud, Henry, 1830-1922. 99383A-99383C
Vignaud, Jean Henry. see Vignaud, Henry,
1830-1922.
Vigne, Charles de la. supposed author 24854,
note after 99605
Vigne, Godfrey Thomas, 1801-1863. 99606
Vigne, Magdeleine (Buree) de la. plaintiff
67035
Vigne en Amerique. 21221
Vignes de Cap-Breton. 6166
Vignettes. 12248, (12261)
Vignettes of American history. 33375
Vignoles, Charles Blacker. 99607-99608
Vigo Roussillon, F.-P. 99609
Vigor. A novel. (78466)
Vigornius. pseud. Essays on slavery. see
Palmer, ------. supposed author and
Worcester, Samuel Melanchthon. supposed
author
Vigors, N. A. 71031
Vijf verscheyde jorunalen van Pieter van den
Broeck. 74837
Vijil, Juan Antonio. 99611
Vilalliave Circus. 105344-105345
Vilaplana, Hermenegildo de. 31498, 99612-
99615
Vilbort, Joseph. 50763
Vile prophanations of prosperity by the degene-
rate among the people of God. 18470,
(19157), 104088
Vilela, Francisco de Auendano y. see Auendano
y Vilela, Francisco de.
Vilette, Dapres de Manne. see Manne-Vilette,
Dapres de.
Villa, Jose. 14576-14577, 16905, note after
99615-99616 see also Peru. Legacion.
Colombia. Peru. Ministerio de Guerra
y Marina.
Villa. Juan de. see Villa Sanchez, Juan de.
Villa Franca y Cardenas, Jose Ruiz de. see
Ruiz Villafranca y Cardenas, Joseph.
Villa Real, Christoval de. 99618-99619
Villa Sanchez, Juan de. 99620-99622
Villa Senor y Sanchez, Joseph de. 23606
Villa Rica de Oropeza de Guancanelica. see
Oropeza, Bolivia.
Villa Rica; poema. 44356
Villabrille, F. F. tr. 10300
Villada, Vicente Jose. 99623
Villadarias, Manoel Duarte Caldeiras Centenera
da. note after 99623
Villademoros, Domingo Rico. 99624
Villaflor, Luis Henriquez de Guzman, Conde de
Alva de Aliste y de. see Henriquez de
Guzman, Luis, Conde de Alva de Aliste
y de Villaflor.
Villafranca y Cardenas, Jose Ruiz de. see
Ruiz Villafranca y Cardenas, Joseph.
Villagagnon, Nicolas Durand de. see Villegag-
non, Nicolas Durand de.
Villagagnon, Nicolaus. see Villegagnon,
Nicolas Durand de.
Villagagnonis in America gesta. 32041, 40153-
(40154)
Villagarcia, Feliz Anotnio de. 99626

Village; a poem. With an appendix. (41247), note after 99626
Village Americain. 41931
Village green. 99627
Village harmony. 1st note after 99627
Village in the mountains. 103984-103985
Village life in New England. An original dramatic comedy of American life. 18354
Village life in New England. By Henry Ward Beecher. 4317, 18354
Village life in the west. 58024
Village maid, a drama. 77171
Village merchant: a poem. To which is added the Country printer. 25902, 2d note after 99627
Village missionaries. 86306
Village of Hermonia. 101372
Village pastor. pseud. Records of a village 68403
Village pastor. 99628
Village poems. 89913
Village poet or dreams of the pound master. 104715
Village reformed or the Sunday school. 99629
Village register, prepared to accompany the Worcester talisman. 105374, 105542
Village sketches. 99630
Village tales. 64685, 99631
Villager's daughter. 99632
Villagomez, Pedro de, Abp. 99633-99637 see also Lima (Archdiocese) Archbishop (Villagomez)
Villagra, Gaspar de. (80006)
Villagra, Gaspar Perez de. 99638-99642
Villagutierre Soto-Mayor, Juan de, fl. 1701. 50592, 99643
Villahermosa de Alfaro, -------, Marques de. defendant 68333
Villahumbrosa, -------, Duque de. 94275
Villalobos, Arias de. 99644-99646
Villalobos, Baltasar de. 99647
Villalobos, Joachin Antonio de. 99648-99649
Villalobos, Juan de. 99650
Villalobos, Juan Julian de. 34710, 1st note after 99650
Villalon, Juan San Diego y. see San Diego y Villalon, Juan.
Villalon, Pedro de Rivera. see Rivera Villalon, Pedro de.
Villalpando, C. defendant 11295
Villalpando, Luis de. 2d note after 99650
Villalta, Jose Garcia de. tr. 35176
Villalta, Manuel. 99651
Villalva, Estevan. 99652
Villalva, Jose Arcadio de. 99653
Villamil, Ildefonso. 72587, 99654
Villamor, Pedro Pablo de. 99655
Villanovanus, Michael. see Servetus, Michael.
Villaneuva, Joaquin Lorenzo. 99656
Villany unmasked. 96880
Villapando Abarca de Bolea, Ambrosio Funes. see Abarca de Bolea, Ambrosio Funes Villapando, Conde de Ricla.
Villar, Blas de la Pena y. see Pena y Villar, Blas de la.
Villar, Francisco de Paula de. 99657
Villar, Pedro de. 99658
Villar de Francos, Juan Isidro Pardinas. see Pardinas Villar de Francos, Juan Isidro.
Villar de Fuente, ------. 26112, 44291, 76158
Villaran, Manuel. 41103, 99659
Villaran, Manuel Vicente. 38702

Villareal, Christoval de. see Villa Real, Christoval de.
Villares, Vicente. 99660
Villaret-Joyeuse, Louis Thomas. 99661-99663
Villarguide, Juan. 99664
Villarino, Basilio. 99665-99666
Villaroel, Gaspar de. 99668-99675
Villarreal, Juan Joseph de. 99667
Villarroel, Hipolito. supposed author 9582, 2d note after 98255, note after 99675
Villars, Charles Hautin de. see Hautin de Villars, Charles.
Villars, -------Miette de. see Miette de Villars, -------.
Villasenor, Jose Maria. see Villasenor Cervantes, Jose Maria.
Villasenor Cervantes, Jose Maria. 63634, 99676-99684
Villasenor Cervantes, Jose Maria. supposed author 95874
Villasenor y Sanchez, Jose Antonio de. 99685-99686
Villaurrutia, Jacobo de. 99687-99688
Villaurrutia y Puente, Wenceslao de. 99690
Villauscencio, Nunez de. defendant 44289, 74862
Villaverde, Cirilo Simon de la Paz. 99691-99692
Villaverde, Francisco Leandro de Viana Zavala Saenz de. see Viana Zavala Saenz de Villaverde, Francisco Leandro de.
Villavicencio, Diego Jaymes Ricardo. 99693
Villavicencio, Joannes a Malo de. 32719
Villavicencio, Juan Joseph de. 99694
Villavicencio, Pablo de. 34149, 93910, 99695-99702, 99704-99823
Villavicencio, Pablo de. defendant 99703
Villavicencio Nunez, Jos. Philippus de. see Nunez, Jos Philippus de Villavicencio.
Villavicencio y Horozco, Nuno Nunez de. defendant 87161
Villavicensio, Damian de. plaintiff (34719)
Villavicencio, J. J. L. Xaso Gamboa y. see Gamboa y Villavicenzio, J. J. L. Xaso.
Ville, Jean Ignace de la. see De la Ville, Jean Ignace.
Ville et la Vallee de Mexico. 64727
Ville-Marie. 76412
Villebrune, Jean Baptiste Lefebvre. 10912
Villebrune, Le Febvre de. see Le Febvre de Villebrune, -------.
Villefranche, Carlos P. note after 99723
Villegagnon, Nicolas Durand de, 1510-1571? 32041, 40148, 40153-(40154), 79443, 99724-99728
Villegaignon: founder and destroyer of the first Huguenot settlement. 84390
Villegas, Alonso de. tr. 5022, note after 99728
Villegas, Antonio Claudio de. 99729
Villegas, Manuel Jose de. 99730
Villegas, Simon Bergano y. see Bergano y Villegas, Simon.
Villegas de Echeverria, Jose. 99731-99732
Villela Barbosa, Francisco. 99733-99735
Villela Tavares, ------. 78957
Villemain, E. 99736
Villeneuve, ------. illus. 48916, 73935
Villeneuve, ------ Belin de. see Belin de Villeneuve, ------.
Villeneuve, A. Champion de. 29569, 75078, note after 98577
Villeneuve, Gabrielle Suzanne Barbot Gallon de. 99738
Villeneuve, Jerome Petin de. see Petin de Villeneuve, Jerome.

Villeneuve, L. P. Couret de. see Couret de
  Villeneuve, L. P.
Villeon, --------. 99739
Villeon, Contre-Amiral, a la Convention Na-
  tionale. 99739
Villerias, Mateo de. 99740
Villers, Charles de. supposed author 38959,
  note after 99840
Villetard, --------. tr. 35147
Villette, John. 99742
Villeveque, ------. 29099
Villeveque, ------- Laisne de. see Laisne de
  Villeveque, -------.
Villiagomez, Petrus de. see Villagomez,
  Pedro de.
Villiers, ------ de, fl. 1757. 15205, 17365,
  (41650), (47511)-47519, 51661, 101710
Villiers, George, 1628-1687. see Buckingham,
  George Villiers, 2d Duke of, 1628-1687.
Villiers, George William Frederick. see
  Clarendon, George William Frederick
  Villiers, 4th Earl of, 1800-1870.
Villiers, Jean Pierre. note before 99743
Villiers, Sir John Abraham Jacobs de. see
  De Villiers, Sir John Abraham Jacobs,
  1863-1931.
Villiers, Marius. 99741
Villiers, R. 99743
Villifranchi, Giovanni. 99744
Villot, ------. 67626
Vilton, ------. 6978
Viluma, Joaquin de la Pezula y Sanchez Munoz
  de Velasco, 1. Marques de. see Pezula
  y Sanchez Munoz de Velasco, Joaquin de
  la, 1. Marques de Viluma, 1761-1830.
Vimeur, Donatien Marie Joseph de, Vicomte
  de Rochambeau. see Rochambeau,
  Donatien Marie Joseph de Vimeur,
  Vicomte de.
Vimeur, Jean Baptiste Donatien de, comte de
  Rochambeau. see Rochambeau, Jean
  Baptiste Donatien de Vimeur, Comte de.
Vimont, Barthelemy. ed. 99748-99753
Vinadio, Cesare Balbo, Conte di. see Balbo,
  Cesare, Conte di Vinadio, 1789-1853.
Vinal, William. 99754
Vincard, Pierre. 23096
Vincent, ------ de, General du Genie. 99755-
  99756
Vincent, Benjamin. ed. 31014-31015
Vincent, J. 99757
Vincent, J. H. ed. 93744
Vincent, Jean Baptiste Georges Bory de Saint.
  see Bory de Saint Vincent, Jean Baptiste
  Georges, 1778?-1846.
Vincent, M. see Vincent, N.
Vincent, N. 1288A, note before 99759-99759
Vincent, Philip. 99760-99766
Vincent, Samuel. defendant at court martial
  (37982)-37983, note after 99766, note
  after 100901
Vincent, Thomas. 41854, 99767-99769
Vincent, de Paul, Marie Joseph. 99770
Vincent Centinel. pseud. see Centinel.
  Vincent. pseud.
Vincentius Beluacensis. 66686
Vincentius, P. see Vincent, Philip.
Vinculos de Ollanta y Cusi-Kcuyllor. 55398
Vindel, Francisco. 93319, 93325
Vindel, Pedro, Madrid. ed. 105717
Vinder. pseud. Clerge Canadien venge par
  ses ennemis. see Maguire, Thomas.
Vindex. pseud. Candid animadversions. see
  Allison, Patrick.
Vindex. pseud. Clerge Canadien vengee par
  ses ennemis. see Maguire, Thomas.

Vindex. pseud. Conduct of the British govern-
  ment. 99773
Vindex. pseud. Considerations submitted in
  defence of the orders in Council. 99774
Vindex. pseud. Defence. (62666)
Vindex. pseud. Honest politician. (32777),
  note after 99774
Vindex. pseud. Letter. 20657
Vindex. pseud. Letters on the West India
  question. 99775
Vindex. pseud. Observations d'un catholique.
  see Maguire, Thomas.
Vindex. pseud. Old truths and established
  facts. see Paine, Thomas, 1737-1809.
  supposed author
Vindex. pseud. On the maritime rights of
  Great Britain. see Eden, Sir Frederick
  Morton.
Vindex. pseud. Prelatical usurpation exposed.
  see Ireland, John. supposed author
Vindex. pseud. Review and refutation. 70189,
  99779
Vindex. pseud. To the public friends and
  fellow citizens. 99780
Vindex. pseud. Truth advocated. 99781
Vindex on the liability of the abolitionists.
  99782
Vindex: or the doctrines of the strictures
  vindicated. 92030
Vindicacion al R. P. Gutierrez. 99783
Vindicacion ante el Supremo Consejo de
  Regencia. 86819
Vindicacion coleccion de los ultimos articulos.
  72797
Vindicacion de D. Francisco Carabajal. 10797
Vindicacion de D. Francisco J. Moreiras.
  96239
Vindicacion de D. Gerano Montoto. 50215
Vindicacion . . . de Jose Manuel Selva. 79037
Vindicacion de la Primera Sala de la Suprema
  Corte de Justicia. (48665), 1st note after
  99783, 98823
Vindicacion de los agravios infundados. 98858
Vindicacion de los crimenes que gratiutamente
  se le imputan. 76747, 99784
Vindicacion de los ex-consejales presos.
  76000
Vindicacion de seis maracayberos calumniados
  atrozmente en Caracas. 67653
Vindicacion del cuidadano Coronel de Ingenieros
  Jose Antonio Rincon. (71415)
Vindicacion del ciudadano Francisco Sains de
  la Pena. 99785
Vindicacion del ciudadano Manuel R. Veramendi.
  98920
Vindicacion del ciudadano Miguel Guzman.
  99786
Vindicacion del clero catolico. 47425
Vindicacion del clero Mexicano vulnerado en
  los anotaciones. 26577
Vindicacion del difunto Senor Coronel D. Juan
  de Noriega. 99787
Vindicacion del General Bravo. 99788
Vindicacion del General Manuel Rincon. 71419
Vindicacion del General Presidente. 99789
Vindicacion del Intendente del Provincia de
  Colchagua. 96238-96239, 99790
Vindication del Juez de Circuito de Sinora,
  Sinaloa y Baja California. 29333
Vindicacion del Ldo. D. Gaspar Acosta. 21003
Vindicacion del Lic. D. Jose Antonio Lopez
  Salazar. 75571
Vindicacion del papel continuacion al numero
  4 del "Censor." 99791
Vindicacion del Provincial de Carmelitas.
  (62930)

Vindication of the American, French, and Irish characters. 14029

Vindication of the appendix to the Sober remarks. 12362, 12364, (25402), 25407, 99800, 103904

Vindication of the author from several injurious aspersions. 71756

Vindication of the author from the infamous charges. 33591

Vindication of the authority of Parliament. (36947)

Vindication of the Bank of Credit projected in Boston. 6711, 9449, 21088, 42824, 1st note after 99800

Vindication of the Bishop of Landaff's sermon. 12318-12319, 23319, (34766), 41642-(41644), 2d note after 99800

Vindication of the Brethren who were unjustly and illegally cast out. 5760

Vindication of the British colonies. 40281, 57868, 3d note after 99800

Vindication of the calling of the Special Superior Court. 94079

Vindication of the capacity of the Negro race for self-government. 32565

Vindication of the captors of Major Andre. 4746-4748, 4th note after 99800

Vindication of the character and condition of the females. 3730

Vindication of the character of Alford Richardson. 70988

Vindication of the character . . . of Andrew Jackson. 39752

Vindication of the character of Geo. Fox. 99801

Vindication of the character of Mrs. Elizabeth Dana. 18410

Vindication of the character of Nathaniel G. M. Senter. 79150

Vindication of the character of the late Col. Solomon P. Sharp. 79846

Vindication of the character of the pilgrim fathers. 81618

Vindication of the charitable plea for the speechless. 24391

Vindication of the Cherokee claims. 12476, (30369), note after 99801

Vindication of the civil establishment of religion. 11870

Vindication of the claim of Alexander M. W. Ball. 50955

Vindication of the claim of Elkanah Watson. 97067

Vindication of the claim of the late General Schuyler. 97067

Vindication of the claims of Sir Fernando Gorges. 64060

Vindication of the conduct and character of Henry D. Sedgwick. 78822

Vindication of the conduct and character of John Adams, Esq. 261, 29961, 99802

Vindication of the conduct of the Agency of Texas. 95127, 95132

Vinduction of the conduct of the General Assembly of the state of Vermont. 825, 1st note after 99005

Vindication of the conduct of the House of Representatives. 57869

Vindication of the conduct of the late great c------r. 99803

Vindication of the conduct of the present war. 99804

Vindication of the constitutional power. 3189

Vindication of the currency of the state of New York. 66528, 2d note after 99804

Vindication of the disciplinary proceedings. 70198

Vindication of the dissenters. (59550)

Vindication of the district. 61314

Vindication of the divine authority of ruling elders. 103400

Vindication of the divine authority of ruling elders in the churches of Christ. 99805, 103400

Vindication of the doctrine advocated by John Randolph. 105157

Vindication of the doctrine of the final perseverance of the saints. 64666

Vindication of the Dutch Westindia trade. 99806

Vindication of the Earl of Shelburne. 80112

Vindication of the essence and unity. 33496-33497

Vindication of the exclusive right of jurisdiction. 65042, 99778

Vindication of the four laymen. 20397

Vindication of the General Assembly of the Presbyterian Church (O. S.) 90444

Vindication of the general ticket law. 99807, note after 100544

Vindication of the government, doctrine, and worship. 43700, 52147

Vindication of the government of New-England churches. (63341), 103400, 104900-104901

Vindication of the Governour and government of His Majesty's colony of Rhode-Island, &c. 99808

Vindication of the great ordinance of God. 14427

Vindication of the honour and justice of Parliament. 80329, 88168

Vindication of the hospital report of 1848. 6998

Vindication of the keyes of the kingdome of heaven. 11616, 17091

Vindication of the Land Agent. 32779, 43947-(43948)

Vindication of the late Governor and Council of Jamaica. 35669, 1st note after 99808

Vindication of the late New Jersey Assembly. 53243

Vindication of the late pastoral letter of the Synod of Philadelphia. (62367), 2d note after 99808

Vindication of the laws, limiting the rate of interest on loans. 99809

Vindication of the legislative power. 37241, (41792)

Vindication of the legislative powers, submitted to the representatives. 60773, note after 99809

Vindication of the measures of government, with respect to America. 1789

Vindication of the measures of the present administration. (28283), 80856, 99810

Vindication of the measures of the President and his commanding generals. (57981), 99811

Vindication of the military character and services of General Franklin Pierce. 91531

Vindication of the ministers of Boston. 6565, 99812

Vindication of the minority in opposition. 33028

Vindication of the minority of the Congregational Church in the South Parish, Augusta. 103042

Vindication of the negociators of the treaty of 1783. 30045

Vindication of the New-England churches. 26753, 103320

Vindication of their [i. e. Wetmore and Caner's] cause and characters. 4091

Vindication of Thomas Jefferson. 13724, note after 99831

Vindication of those ministers and churches. 7661

Vindication of volume first of the Collections of the Vermont Historical Society. 29781

Vindication of West Point and the regular army. (79672)

Vindication of William Penn. 25067

Vindication: to the congregation of the First Presbyterian Church. 43595

Vindicator. pseud. Reviewer of Mrs. E. Willard reviewed. 104049

Vindicatory address and appeal of Lieutenant Weaver. 76498, 95779

Vindicatory address and appeal, to the public. 102207

Vindiciae Americanae. 99832

Vindiciae anti-Baxterianae. 4014

Vindiciae clavium. 11616, 17091, note after 99832

Vindiciae Judaecoram. 95653

Vindiciae Lusitanae. 41329

Vindiciae Lusitaniae. 34780

Vindiciae ministerii evangelici. 14427

Vindiciae vindiciarum. 11615

Vinditiae clavium. 32861

Vine, Peter. defendant 101449

Vine: its culture in the United States. (61385)

Vineto, Elia. 32680-32681, 74804-(74807)

Vining, John. 99833

Vinne, Daniel de. see De Vinne, Daniel.

Vinous, vivacious monthly. 17325

Vins, ------- de, Marques de Peysac. 99834

Vinton, ---------. 6978, 17481

Vinton, David. 99835

Vinton, John Adams. 44315

Vinton, Samuel Finley. 99836

Vio esta capital el dia 30 de Junio. 99837

Viola, Miguel Navarro. 9021, 64440

Viola oder Abenteuer im fernen Sudwesten. (4724)

Viola or the heiress of St. Valverde. 99838

Violations of the contract exposed. 37353

Violations of the federal constitution. 2966

Violence of party spirit. 63780, (77040)

Violencia de dos terremotos. 98380

Violent destroyed. 16350

Violet, Alphonse. tr. see Viollet, Alhponse.

Violet, Edmund. 99839

Violet. 99840

Violett, Alhponse. tr. 21067, 92430, 92433, 92541, 98870

Viollet le Duc, Eugene Emmanuel, 1814-1879. 12153

Vireau, Jean. tr. 32007

Vireinato del Rio de la Plata 1776-1810. (67127)

Virey a los habitantes de esta capital. 98859

Virey de Nueva Espana a todos sus habitantes. 98861

Virey und die Aristokraten; oder, Mexiko im Jahre 1812. 64541, 64560-64561, 1st note after 99840

Virgen Mexicana. 74023

Virgidemiae. (29819)

Virgil. see Vergilius Naso, Publius.

Virgilius Christianus. 39625

Virgin, Henry. defendant 6326, 1st note after 96956, 1st note after 97284

Virgin of the sun. 8137, 80342

Virgin of the sun, a play, in five acts. 38283

Virginalia; or songs of my summer nights. 12854

Virginia. pseud. Two rebellions. see Mac-donald, Angus W.

Virginia (Colony) 14008, 32968, 2d note before 99889, 99976, 100464

Virginia (Colony) Charter. 12162-12163, (37540) 66686, 91860-91862, 99889, 1st note after 99889

Virginia (Colony) Clergy. see Clergy of Virginia. pseud.

Virginia (Colony) Commissioners to the Catawba and Cherokee Indians. 100006 see also Byrd, William, 1728-1777. Randolph, Peter.

Virginia (Colony) Commissioners to Treat With the Six Nations of Indians, 1744. 60736-60737, 1st-2d notes after 100005

Virginia (Colony) Committee of Correspondence, 1775. 100012

Virginia (Colony) Convention, Williamsburg, 1774. 2d note after 99925, 100008

Virginia (Colony) Convention, Williamsburg, 1774. Moderator. 100008 see also Randolph, Peyton, 1721?-1775.

Virginia (Colony) Convention, Richmond, 1775. 100009-100011, 100024

Virginia (Colony) Council. 99890-99893, 99895-99908, 100904

Virginia (Colony) Council. defendants 99894

Virginia (Colony) Council. Clerk. 99907-99908 see also Blair, John. Scott, U.

Virginia (Colony) Council. President. 99909-99911

Virginia (Colony) Court. 99908-note after 99908, 99975

Virginia (Colony) General Assembly. 16688, 79369, 2d note after 99889, 100002

Virginia (Colony) General Assembly. House of Burgesses. 86730, 99890, 99891, 99893, 99897-99899, 99901-99904, 99908, 2d note after 99911, 99912-99974, 99991, 99999, 100002, 100006, 100381, 100389 see also Non-importation Association of Virginia, 1774.

Virginia (Colony) General Assembly. House of Burgesses. Clerk. 100380 see also Randolph, Henry.

Virginia (Colony) General Assembly. House of Burgesses. Speaker. 99909-99911, 99913 see also Randolph, Sir John, 1793-1737.

Virginia (Colony) General Court. see Virginia (Colony) Court.

Virginia (Colony) Governor and Council. defendants see Virginia (Colony) Council. defendants Virginia (Colony) Governor, 1727-1749 (Gooch) defendant

Virginia (Colony) Governor, 1610-1618 (De la Warr) 102756 see also De la Warr, Thomas West, 3d Lord, 1577-1618.

Virginia (Colony) Governor, 1645-1652 (Berkeley) 99976 see also Berkeley, Sir William, 1606-1677.

Virginia (Colony) Governor, 1661-1662 (Moryson) 100380 see also Moryson, Francis.

Virginia (Colony) Governor, 1662-1676 (Berkeley) 4889A, 41460, 99976 see also Berkeley, Sir William, 1606-1677.

Virginia (Colony) Governor, 1710-1722 (Spots-wood) 86730, 2d note after 99911 see also Spotswood, Alexander, 1676-1740

Virginia (Colony) Governor, 1727-1749 (Gooch) 99975, 99977-99988 see also Gooch, Sir William Bart., 1681-1751.

Virginia (Colony) Governor, 1727-1749 (Gooch) defendant 99894 see also Gooch, Sir William, Bart., 1681-1751. defendant

100084, 100206, 100208, note before
100232, 100281-100316, 100319-100379,
100392-100406, 100410-100411, 100427,
100429-100430, note after 100447, 100462,
100464, 2d-3d notes after 100486, 100492-
100493, 100519, 100528, 100544-note
after 100544, 100548, note after 102401,
104743
Virginia. Lieutenant Governor, 1790 (Wood)
100407 see also Wood, James, 1747-
1813.
Virginia. Marine Corps. 82961
Virginia. Militia. (59274), 82959, 82962,
82964-82965, 100350, 100365, 100372,
100375, 100379, 100401, 100410-100412
Virginia. Militia. Board of War and Ordnance.
100408
Virginia. Militia. Continental Line. see
Virginia. Militia.
Virginia. Militia. Courts Martial (Yancey)
105947
Virginia. Militia. War Office. 100409
Virginia. Navy. 82959, 82961, 82964
Virginia. Privy Council. see Virginia. Coun-
cil of State.
Virginia. Quartermaster General. 85131 see
also Smoot, L. R.
Virginia. Second Centennial Anniversary Jubilee,
Jubilee, Jamestown, 1807. 35739
Virginia. Second Centennial Anniversary
Jubilee, Jamestown, 1807. Select Com-
mittee. 35739
Virginia. State Library, Richmond. 91860,
99908, 99927, 100037, 100118, 100192,
100209-100210, 100212
Virginia. State Line. see Virginia. Militia.
Virginia. Superior Court of Chancery. 93479
Virginia. Supervisor's Office. 100413
Virginia. Supreme Court, Richmond. 33371
Virginia. Treasurer. 100414-100417 see also
Ambler, Jaquelin.
Virginia. Treasury Office. 100414-100418
Virginia. 250th Anniversary Celebration, James-
town, 1857. 35737
Virginia. United Agricultural Societies. see
United Agricultural Societies of Virginia.
Virginia. University. 100535-100536, 100540,
100543
Virginia. University. Commissioners. 100539,
100542
Virginia. University. Commissioners Appointed
to Fix the Site of the University. see
Virginia. Commissioners Appointed to
Fix the Scite [sic] for the University.
Virginia. University. Faculty. 100538
Virginia. University. Library. 100534
Virginia. University. Rector. 100540 see
also Jefferson, Thomas, Pres. U. S.,
1743-1826.
Virginia. University. Rector and Visitors.
100537
Virginia. University. Students. 35947
Virginia. University. Visitors. 100539
Virginia (Anti-secession Government) Governor,
1861-1865 (Pierpont) (62753), 62756 see
also Pierpont, Francis Harrison, 1814-
1899.
Virginia (Schooner) in Admiralty 100576
Virginia. 104190
Virginia. A copy of the record. 99975
Virginia: a pastoral drama. 33005, 100545
Virginia, a pastoral poem. 33005, 100545
Virginia. A sermon preached at White-Chappel.
94125, 2d note after 99856
Virginia address. A Convention of Delegates,
appointed by public meetings. 100499

Virginia. Address before the Washington and
Jefferson Societies. 65372
Virginia addresses. 100545A
Virginia almanac, for the year of Our Lord
1800. 102495
Virginia and Kentucky resolutions of 1798 and
1799. (22237), note after 100545A
Virginia and Maryland campaign. (43594)
Virginia and Maryland. Or, the Lord Balta-
more's [sic] case, uncased and answered.
100546
Virginia and Maryland. Or, the Lord Balta-
more's [sic] printed case. 100547
Virginia and New England Mining Company.
100548
Virginia and New England Mining Company.
Charter. 100548
Virginia & North Carolina almanac. 102496
Virginia and North Carolina almanac for . . .
1865. 71000
Virginia and North Carolina almanac, for 1864.
70998
Virginia & North Carolina almanac, for the
year . . . 1865. (71001)
Virginia & North Carolina almanac, for the
year of Our Lord 1800. 102496
Virginia and North Carolina Presbyterian
preacher. 100549
Virginia and Tennessee Railroad. see Lynch-
burg and Tennessee Railroad.
Virginia Anti-Jackson Convention. see National
Republican Party. Virginia.
Virginia Anti-Jackson Convention. Saturday,
Dec. 12, 1827. 100497
Virginia argus. (44479), 58933, 71187, 83826,
100480, 104875
Virginia argus. Correspondent. pseud.
Observations on the letters. (56531),
100506
Virginia Assembly. Report of the Select Com-
mittee on Revolutionary Claims. 82967
Virginia Baptis. 95383
Virginia Baptist Educational Society. 100550,
100552
Virginia Baptist ministers. 94473
Virginia Baptist Seminary, Richmond. see
University of Richmond. Richmond
College.
Virginia Bible Society. Managers. 100436
Virginia campaign of 1865. 69350
Virginia chronicle. 100553
Virginia chronicle . . . dated Orange County,
Virginia. 39971
Virginia Collegiate Institute, Salem, Va. see
Roanoke College, Salem, Va.
Virginia colonial decisions. 99975
Virginia Colonization Society. 100445-100446
Virginia Colonization Society. Board of Man-
agers. 100445-100446
Virginia comedians. 16321
Virginia Company of London. 16691, 17425,
20601, (24896), (30120), 13998, 35676,
(36286), 52285, 52288, 53249, 55946-
55947, 57488, (57499), 70889-70891,
99854-note after 99858, 99859-99883, 2d
note after 99883, 99885-4th note after
99888, 100450, 2d note after 100502,
102756, 104974, 1st note after 105510
Virginia Company of London. Charter. 66686
Virginia Company of London. Clerk. 99854
see also Atkinson, Richarde.
Virginia Company of London. Council. 103313
Virginia Company of London. Wardens. 99860,
99862
Virginia Company of London. Extracts from
their manuscript transactions. 52288

Virginia confederate. pseud. In vinculis.
see Keiley, A. M.
Virginia Conference sentinel. 84743
Virginia convention question in 1827. 100554
Virginia Convention of 1829-30. 28843
Virginia Convention of 1776. (28844)
Virginia Democrat. pseud. Lecompton question. 39655
Virginia doctrine considered. 100581
Virginia doctrines, not nullification. 100555
Virginia edition, of the various charges exhibited. 98530
Virginia, ein Landschafft Americae. (69296)
Virginia, especially Richmond, in by-gone days.
50534
Virginia evangelical and literary magazine.
note after 100555
Virginia Foundry Company. firm 96760
Virginia 1492-1892. 83516
Virginia gazette (Richmond) 10072, 44478,
80405
Virginia gazette (Williamsburg: Dixon and
Hunter) 100501
Virginia gazette (Williamsburg: Parks) 103529,
103569
Virginia gazette (Williamsburg: Purdie)
100022
Virginia gazette (Williamsburg: Purdie and
Dixon) 100464
Virginia gazette (Williamsburg: Rind) 23500,
90521, 99967, 100465
Virginia gazette & Petersburg intelligencer.
83826, 101576
Virginia gazette and weekly advertiser. 100093
Virginia georgics. (39717)
Virginia Graham, the spy of the grand army.
(36581)
Virginia Historical and Philosophical Society.
72062, 93185, 100556 see also Virginia
Historical Society.
Virginia Historical and Philosophical Society.
Standing Committee. 100556
Virginia historical register. 55993, 85254,
2d note before 99889
Virginia Historical Society. 44081, 4th note
after 99888, 2d note after 99889, 99908,
99976, 99994, 100006, 100381, 2d note
after 100507, 100545A, note after 100556,
3d note after 102552 see also Virginia
Historical and Philosophical Society.
Virginia house-wife. 100557
Virginia illustrated. 93092, 1st note after
100557
Virginia impartially examined. (9145)
Virginia in America, richly valued. 2d note
after 100557, 104191
Virginia: in the High Court of Chancery, March
16, 1798. 100231
Virginia, in the High Court of Chancery, March
the 19th, 1800. 100231
Virginia. In the House of Delegates. January
13, 1786. 100088
Virginia. In the House of Delegates, Thursday,
28th November, 1793. 100098
Virginia. In the House of Delegates, Tuesday,
December the 13th, 1796. 100103
Virginia independent chronicle. (50137), (55169),
100213, 100415, 100451
Virginia justice. 90521
Virginia literary museum and journal of belles
lettres. 100543
Virginia lyceum. 100558
Virginia magazine of history and biography.
44081, 2d note after 99889, 99908, 99976,
100006, 100381, 2d note after 100507,
100545A, 3d note after 102552

Virginia, Maryland, Pennsylvania, & New Jersey
weekly advertiser. 60343
Virginia Military Institute, Lexington. 100559
Virginia mineral springs. 9319
Virginia miscellaneous records, 1606-1692.
100464
Virginia miscellany. 100560
Virginia: more especially the south part thereof, richly and truly valued. 82976,
100450, note after 100560, 3d note after
100571, 104190, 104192
Virginia navy commutation claims. 90142A
Virginia nightingale. 100561
Virginia Non-importation Association, 1769.
see Non-importation Association of
Virginia, 1769.
Virginia non-importation Association, 1774.
see Non-importation Association of
Virginia, 1774.
Virginia, North and South Carolina, and Georgia.
30964, 2d note after 100461
Virginia, North Carolina, Maryland and District
of Columbia almanac for 1850. 70997
Virginia; or, the fatal patent. 100562
Virginia orator. 5528
Virginia palladium. 40577, 88114
Virginia patriot. 65086
Virginia religious magazine. 100563
Virginia Religious Tract Society. 100564
Virginia resolutions of '98 and '99. (23627)
Virginia resolutions of 1798. see Kentucky
and Virginia Resolutions of 1798.
Virginia richly and truly valued. 104193
Virginia richly valued, by the description of
the maine land of Florida, her next
neighbour. (24864), (24896), 29600, 87206,
3d note after 99856, 1st note after 105510
Virginia, SS. By the Hon. Robert Dinwiddie.
99992
Virginia SS. Pleas at the capitol in Williamsburg. 99975
Virginia scrivener. 100565
Virginia series no. I. 82849, 3d note after
100533
Virginia Society for Promoting Agriculture.
see Society of Virginia for Promoting
Agriculture.
Virginia Society for Promoting the Abolition
of Slavery. 100567
Virginia Society for Promoting the Abolition
of Slavery. petitioners 47745
Virginia Society for the Promotion of Temperance. 100568
Virginia springs, and springs of the south and
west. 50470
Virginia springs, with their analysis. 50469
Virginia Students at the University of Pennsylvania, 1812. see Pennsylvania. University. Virginia Students, 1812.
Virginia Synod. see Presbyterian Church in
the U. S. Synod of Virgina. Presbyterian
Church in the U. S. A. Synod of Virginia.
Virginia text-book. 20740
Virginia. The Right Honourable Thomas Lord
Fairfax, Petitioner. 99894
Virginia, to wit: General Assembly begun and
held at the capitol. 100351
Virginia, to wit: in General Assembly, Friday,
the 20th November, 1788. 100025
Virginia, to wit: in General Assembly, Friday,
the 20th November, 1788. Sir, the freemen of the commonwealth in convention
assembled. 100056
Virginia, to wit. In the House of Delegates.
100105

Virginia, to wit. Thomas Lee, Esq; President of His Majesty's Council. 99989

Virginia Tobacco Palnters. petitioners 99909-99911

Virginia tourist. 63879

Virginia Tract Society. 100569

Virginia trade stated. 100570

Virginia tragedies. 57755

Virginia United Agricultural Societies. see United Agricultural Societies of Virginia.

Virginia vs. Peter N. Garner and others. 99836

Virginia White Sulphur Springs, with the analysis of its waters, etc. 50470

Virginia wreath. 103102

Virginia Yazoo Company. petitioners 100571, 2d note after 106003

Virginia Yazoo Company. Agent. 69389, 1st note after 100571

Virginia Yazoo Company. Agent. petitioner 100571, 2d note after 106003 see also Cowan, William. petitioner

Virginian. pseud. tr. 1st note after 100572, 100837

Virginian. pseud. American wanderer. see Lee, Arthur. supposed author

Virginian. pseud. Baltimore and Ohio Rail Road Company. see Viator. pseud.

Virginian. pseud. Biographical sketch of Hon. Linn Boyd. see Thompson, George Western.

Virginian. pseud. Bride of Ossano. 100577

Virginian. pseud. Brief enquiry into the true nature. see Upshur, Abel Parker, 1791-1844.

Virginian. pseud. Defence of the character of Thomas Jefferson. see Tucker, George.

Virginian. pseud. Don Paez, and other poems. see Price, James C. and Price, James H. supposed author

Virginian. pseud. Edge Hill. see Heath, James Ewell.

Virginian. pseud. Kentuckian in New York. see Caruthers, William Alexander ca. 1800-1848.

Virginian. pseud. Land of Powhatan. see Carter, St. Leger L.

Virginian. pseud. Letter from a Virginian. see Boucher, Jonathan, 1738-1804. supposed author

Virginian. pseud. Letters on the Richmond Party. 40631, 100578

Virginian. pseud. Life and death of Sam. see Gardner, -----. supposed author and Wise, Henry A. supposed author

Virginian. pseud. Life of Stonewall Jackson. see Cooke, John Esten, 1830-1886. and Daniel, John M. incorrectly supposed author

Virginian. pseud. Odes and other poems. see Davies, ---------.

Virginian. pseud. Reflections excited by the present state of banking operations. 3183

Virginian. pseud. Remarks on the bill of rights. 100519

Virginian. pseud. Review of the slave question. see Harrison, Jesse Burton.

Virginian. pseud. Right of instruction. see Roane, -------.

Virginian. pseud. Rose-Hill. see Tabb, T. T.

Virginian. pseud. Second war of the revolution. see Garland, Hugh A.

Virginian. pseud. Slavery in Maryland. 45363

Virginian. pseud. Southern home. 88372

Virginian. pseud. Southern politics! see Gilmer, John H.

Virginian. pseud. Two rebellions. see Macdonald, Angus W. supposed author and McDonald, William Naylor. supposed author

Virginian born and bred. pseud. Remarks on the bill of rights. 100519

Virginian boy's progress to renouwn. (57135)

Virginian confederate. pseud. In vinculis. see Keiley, A. M.

Virginian girl. pseud. Virginian girl's address to her Maryland lover. 88492

Virginian girl's address to her Maryland lover. 88492

Virginian history of African colonization. 81710

Virginia's cure. 26274, 2d note after 100571

Virginia's danger and remedy. 18770

Virginia's discovery of silk-vvormes, with their benefit. note after 100560, 3d note after 100571, 104190, 104192

Virginia's God be thanked. 16691, 2d note after 99888

Virginias verger. 66686

Virginie. 101350

Virginiensis. pseud. Defence of the alien and sedition laws. see Lee, Charles. supposed author

Virginiensis. pseud. [Poems.] see Wharton, John.

Virginius. pseud. Lines on a serenade. see Somerville, William Clarke, 1790-1826.

Virginius. pseud. Political truth. 1st note after 100510, 100564

Virgo triumphans. 104192-104193

Virrey de N. E. a los habitantes de los pueblos del sur. 98860

Virrey que fue de Nueva Espana vindicado. 35299

Virtual representation. 100585

Virtud juiziosa. 47843

Virtudes de las aguas del Penol. 96251

Virtudes del Indio. 58294, (58299), 58307, 2d note after 100585

Virtue and innocence. 100586

Virtue and vice. 100587-100591

Virtue given up. 66232

Virtue in it's verdure. 46581, note after 100591

Virtue triumphant, or, Elizabeth Canning in America. 100592

Virtue triumphant; or, the victory of the planters in Parliament. 100593

Virtue vs. defeat. 16222

Virtues and public services of William Penn. (3508)

Virtues of a prudent wife. 97436

Virtues of nature. 2654, 51026

Virtues of society. A tale, founded on fact. 51027, note after 100593

Virtuous rulers a national blessing. 21563

Virtuous woman found. (46308)

Virtutis, Amator. pseud. Youth's companion. see Witherspoon, John.

Virtutum comes inviada. 78369

Viscardo y Guzman, Juan Pablo. 9315, 100594

Vischer, M. tr. 10957, note after (28941), 38647, 39453, 57158, 72220

Vischer, N. J. cartographer 20594, note after 98474, note after 99310

Vischer, Nic. cartographer (71907)

Visible church, in covenant with God. 4495, 46769

Visible church, in covenant with God; further illustrated. 4486, 46770

Visible display of divine providence. 28746

Visite a la Prison de Philadelphie. 97471
Visite chez Soulouque. 19918
Visite du Dairo a l'Empereur du Japon. 68455
Visite du General de la Fayette a la Louisiane. 38582, 1st note after 100605
Visiter. pseud. Essay on the Red Sulphur Springs, of Virginia. see S., J. H. pseud.
Visiter. pseud. Six weeks in Fauquier. 81488, 2d note after 100605
Visiting Committees of the Directors of Public Schools. (62368)
Visitor. pseud. Guide to rambles from the Gatskill Mountain House. 11552
Visitor. pseud. Peculiarites of the Shakers. 59506, 79716, note after 97880, 3d note after 100605
Visitor. pseud. Pencillings about Ephrata. 22681
Visitor. pseud. Rambles in the Mammouth Cave. see Croghan, John.
Visitor. pseud. Trotter, Choker & Company exhibited. 97062
Visitor; a Christmas and New Year's token. 100606
Visitor's companion to Niagara Falls. 9281
Visitors' guide, and a catalogue of the Eighth Industrial Exhibition. 76054
Visitors' guide to Passaic Falls. 58998
Visitor's guide to Richmond and vicinity. (71211)
Visitor's guide to the city of New York. 54713
Visitor's guide to the Smithsonian Institution. 85089
Visitor's hand-book to the city. 54490, 77178
Visitor's manual [of the Association for Improving the Condition of the Poor, New York.] 54099
Visitor's manual, of the Roxbury Charitable Society. (73726)
Visitors of the . . . [Union Benevolent] Association. 62349
Visits and sketches at home and abroad. (35729)
Visits and sketches at home and abroad. With tales and miscellanies. 35730
Visits of mercy. 22384
Visits to Brunswick, Georgia, and travels south. 83394
Visits to Massasoit. 51017
Visits to Presbyterian schools for foreign population. 89261
Viso, Julian. 56450
Visorrei, ------. 84379
Visscher, Nikolass. cartographer note after 100606
Vissier, Paul. 100607
Vista, Barao da Boa. see Boa Vista, Barao da.
Vista del Fiscal de la Ilustrisma Corte de Apelaciones. 100608
Vistas en la provincia de Tarapaca. 83034
Vita B. Augusti Hermanni Franckii. 46805
Vita Beatae Rosae Lovanij. 30250
Vita Beati Patris Ignatii Loyolae. (70783)
Vita Beati Turribii Archiepiscopi Limani in Indiis. 98370
Vita brevis. 46583
Vita candidissima S. Philippi Nerri. 67647
Vita candissima S. Philippi Nerii. 59523
Vita Caroli Magni. 41067
Vita condatta dal servo di Dio Gregorio Lopez. 42587
Vita dei Negri in America. 92588
Vita del B. Martino de Porres. 49799, 64175
Vita del Beato Giovanni Massias. 46179

Vita del Beato Giovanni Massias, (O. S. B.) 13138
Vita del Catolico Re Filippo II. 40249
Vita . . . del . . . Fr. Giuseppe da Carabantes. (67345)
Vita del P. C. Spinola. 89458
Vita del P. Carlo Spinola. 89459
Vita del P. Gioseppo Anchietto. 4830
Vita del P. Guiseppe Anchieta. 1374, 56697, 100610
Vita del Padre F. Diego Ortiz. (57715)
Vita del Padre Gioseffo Anchieta. (4831)-(4832)
Vita del servo di Dio D. Torivio Alfonso Mogrovejo. 38981
Vita del Vener. Mons. G. di Palafox. 20201, 99507, 100609
Vita del Venerabil servo di Dio P. Giuseppe Anchieta. 100610
Vita del Venerable P. Fr. Francesco Camacho. 100611
Vita del Venerabile servo di Dio Monsignor D. Giovanni di Palafox. (58305)
Vita del Venr. Mons. G. di Palafox. 100609
Vita della Beata Rosa di Santa Maria. (44495), 73190
Vita della gloriosa Santa Rosa. 100612
Vita della Madre Suor Madre dell' Incarnazione. 12142
Vita della Madre Suor Maria Catterina di S. Agostino. 67500
Vita dell' Invitissimo Imperator Carlo Quinto. 97679-97680
Vita dell' Invittissimo, e Sacratissimo Imperator Carlo V. 97681-97682
Vita di Christoforo Colombo. (6463)
Vita di Cristoforo Colombo per Professore Angelo Sanguineti. 76522
Vita di S. Rosa de Lima Domenicana. 27475
Vita di S. Toribio Alfonso Mogrovesio. (55263)
Vita di Santa Rosa di Lima. 73191
Vita e la avventure di Robinson Crusoe. 100613
Vita e lettere di Amerigo Vespvcci. 3149, 99383A, note after 99383C
Vita e martirio del Venerabil P. Ignazio de Azevedo. (34193)
Vita e miracoli del Fr. Sebastiano d'Apparisio. 24394
Vita e viaggi di Cristoforo Colombo. 10649
Vita ed avventure di Robinson Crusoe. 100614
Vita et historia S. Rosae A. S. Maria. (73192)
Vita et historia S. Rosae A. S. Maria quae nata Limae. 98379A
Vita, et mors eorum qui ex Societe Jesu in causa fidei. 94332
Vita et obitus Ven. P. Henrici Wenceslai Richter. 7128
Vita Franckii. 25474
Vita Gregorii. (43784)
Vita historia India. (43784)
Vita Ignatii Loiolae. (70782)
Vita Ignatii Loyolae. 43770, 43776
Vita interiore. (58306)
Vita interiore del Venerabile . . . G. di Palafox e Mendoza. 100615
Vita interiore del V. servo di Dio Monsig. D. Giovanni di Palafox e Mendoza. 100616
Vita Josephi Juliani Parreni. 11614
Vita mirabilis et mors pretiosa B. Rosae de S. Maria Limensis. 30250
Vita mirabilis et mors pretiosa Venerabilis Sororis Rosae de S. Maria. (30249)
Vita mirabilis mors pretiosa sanctitas thaumaturgae inclytae virginis sponsae

Christi B. Rosae a S. Maria Peruanae. 30251
Vita partis Johannis de Almeida. 43207
Vita P. Caroli Spinolae. 89460
Vita P. Ignatii Loiolae. 70784
Vita Petri Mali. 44243
Vita R. P. Iosephi Anchietae. (4827)
Vita Sancti Thomae Aquinatis. 74772
Vita Venerabilis Alfonsi Torrebio Mongrovegii. (43208)
Vita Venerabilis Patris Emmanuelis Correae. (16831), 1st note after 100616
Vitae Sixti IV. (43766)
Vitae viorum illustrum Americae. 8362
Vital Christianity. (46584), 78441-78443, 2d note after 100616
Vital statistics of Boston. 79886
Vital statistics of New Orleans. 90519
Vitalis, Louis. petitioner (81718), 100617
Vite parallele di Mirabeau e Washington. 10718
Vitellio, R. tr. 67355
Vitman, -------. 67461
Vitoria, Francisco de. see Francisco de Vitoria, 1486?-1546.
Vitoria, Paulo de. see Victoria, Paulo de.
Vitoria, Pedro Gobeo de. see Victoria, Pedro Gobeo de.
Victoria Barahona, Francisco. petitioner 100623-100625
Vitringa, Lambertus Julius. 100626
Vitruve, -----. 76838
Vittnesbord af de lefvande och de dode. 85511
Viuda e Hijos de D. Jose Foribino Larrain. defendants (12764)
Viva copia del M. Sagrado Machabeo Joan Hyrcano. 9818
Viva el Ejercito Imperial Mexicano de las tres garantias. 100627
Viva la federacion. Rasgos de la vida publica. 73221
Viva la federacion y que muera el centralizmo! 100628
Viva la patria. 100629
Viva Nuestro Rey. 98260
Vivanco, Diego de. 100631
Vivar, Andres de. 100632
Vivar, Rodrigo Diaz de. see Infantado, Rodrigo Diaz de Vivar, 6. Duque del.
Viverius, Jacobus. ed. 38881, note after 100632
Vives, Francisco Dionisio. 17783, 100633-100635 see also Cuba. Gobernador, 1823-1832 (Vives)
Vives, Ludovico. (75565), 75567-75568
Vives, Luys. see Vives, Ludovico.
Vivid representation of the dangers to American liberty. (38146), 90580
Vivien de Saint-Martin, Louis. note after 100635
Vivier-Bourgogne, Charlotte de Cossas du. see Argoult, Charlotte de Cossas (du Vivier-Bourgogne) d'.
Vivier-Bourgogne, Marie-Anne (Godefroy) du. see Bourgogne, Marie-Anne (Godefroy) du Vivier-.
Viviparous quadrupeds of North America. 2367
Vizarron y Eguiarreta, Juan Antonio de, Abp. 100637-100639 see also Mexico (Archdiocese) Archbishop (Vizarron y Eguirreta) Mexico (Viceroyalty) Virrey, 1734-1740 (Vizarron y Eguiarreta)
Vizcainas, Colegio de las. 66053
Vizcayno, Antonio. 100640
Vizetelly, Henry. (8350)-8353, 8804, 100641

Vlackenburgh, Johan van. 102912-102912A see also Nederlandsche West-Indische Compagnie. Directeur-Generael.
Vlag, M. M. van der. pseud. Tweede brief. 100642
Vlas-Bloem, Lvdovicvs. 77959-77961
Vleck, Abraham H. van. see Van Vleck, Abraham H.
Vleck, William van. see Van Vleck, William.
Vleet, Abraham van. see Van Vleet, Abraham.
Vleet, Abram van. see Van Vleet, Abram.
Vlierden, Petrus van. see Van Vlierden, Petrus.
Vliet, Jeremie van. tr. 31473
Vloten, J. van. ed. and tr. 70324
Vlugtige beschouwing. 94588
Vlugtige blik. 48223
Vocabulaer, of tale van eenige eylanden. 77941
Vocabvlaer: ofte tale van de eylanden. 77930
Vacabulaire de la langue des Miamis. 100692
Vocabulaire et un abrege de la grammaire. 35514
Vocabulaire Francais et Galibi de noms. 66412, 1st note after 100802
Vocabulaire Francais-Galibi. 44474
Vocabulaire Oceanien-Francais et Francaise-Oceanien. 51037
Vocabulaires de plusieurs contress de l'Afrique. 68443
Vocabularies of the languages of several Indian nations. 20404
Vocabulario Brazileiro. 73855
Vocabvlario breve en la lengva Qvichva. 96269, 100643
Vocabulario da lingua indigena geral. (78951)
Vocabulario das Arvores Brasileiras. 50588
Vocabulario de la lengua Abigira. 93307
Vocabvlario de la lengva de Chile. 42669, 98324
Vocabulario de la lengua de los naturales de la Mision de San Antonio. 81475
Vocabulario de la lengua general de Perv. 20565
Vocabulario de la lengua general de todo el Peru Llamada Quichua. 32492, 100643
Vocabulario de la lengva Gvarani. 74032
Vocabulario de la lengua Mejicana. (73309)
Vocabulario de la lengua Otomi. (70807)
Vocabulario de la lengua Teguima y platicas doctrinales en ella. (41842)
Vocabulario de la lengua Zapoteca. 24105
Vocabulario del idioma Misteco. (971)
Vocabulario dela lengva general de todo el Perv. (33495)
Vocabvlario desta lengva ZaElohpaEap. 70459
Vocabulario en la lengua Aymara. 5023
Vocabulario en la lengua Castellana y Mexicana. (49866), 49867
Vocabvlario en la lengva general del Perv llamada Quichua y en la lengua Espanola. [Par D. G. Holguin.] 23492, (67160), 100643
Vocabulario en la lengua general del Peru, llamada Quichua y en la lengua Espanola. [Par Juan Martinez.] (44955)
Vocabulario en lengua Castellana, y Cora. 57683
Vocabulario en lengua de Mechuacan. 27361
Vocabvlario en lengva Mexicana y Castellana. 49867
Vocabulario en lengua Misteca. 49652
Vocabulario en lengua Nevome. 2124, 84380
Vocabulario Espanol-Guarani. 74039, (74041)
Vocabulario (Kechua-Spanish) 32492, 100643
Vocabulario manual de las dos lenguas Castellana y Mexicano. 1934

Vocabulario manual de las lenguas Castellana
y Mexicana. 1935-1937
Vocabulario y tesoro de la lengua Guarani.
(74041)
Vocabularium Catharinaeum. (37727)
Vocabularium linguae Brasilicae. 69242
Vocabularium Pocomamum. 16828
Vocabulary and rudiments of grammar of the
Tsoneca language. 77663
Vocabulary by Buckingham Smith. 28252
Vocabulary of Indian languages. 77390
Vocabulary of the Algic, or Chippeway language.
43407
Vocabulary of the Algonquin language. 31489
Vocabulary of the Cataba language. 40987
Vocabulary of the Catawba language, by Oscar
M. Lieber. 88005
Vocabulary of the Chinook jargon. 100644
Vocabulary of the Chippeway language. 41878
Vocabulary of the Cochinchinese language.
1183
Vocabulary of the jargon or trade language of
Oregon. 49668, 100645
Vocabulary of the language of the San Antonio
Mission. 81475
Vocabulary of the Massachusetts (or Natick)
Indian language. 17104
Vocabulary of the Sioux language. 2335
Vocabulary of words in the Hawaiian language.
100646
Vocabulary: or, collection of words and
phrases. 102363
Vocabulary, or collection of words and phrases
which have been supposed to be peculiar
to the United States. 62637-62638
Vocabulary or phrase book of the Mutsun
language. 2118
Vocabulary and instrumental musical miscellany.
106078
Vocal cabinet. 100647
Vocal charmer. 100648
Vocal companion, and masonic register.
100650
Vocal companion. Being a choice collection.
100649
Vocal enchantress. 94132
Vocal lyre. 100651
Vocal medley. 100652
Vocal muse. 100653
Vocal remembrancer. 100654
Vocal standard. 100655
Vocation. 79191
Vocation de la colonie de Montreal. 73520
Voces a la alma. 20567
Voces de Triton Sonoro. (22837)
Voces del postor en el retrio. 75981
Voces el silencio. 48881
Voe, Thomas Farrington de. see De Voe,
Thomas Farrington, 1811-1892.
Voe, W. M. de. see De Voe, W. M.
Voegen van Engelen, Jacobus. 100656
Voeu de toutes les nations. 4178, 100657
Voeu patriotique d'un Americain. 100658
Voeux des colons de Saint-Domingue. 4966
Voeux des Hurons et des Abnaquis. 20673
Vogages [sic] autour du monde et anufrages
celebres. 38606
Vogdes, --------. 60774, 62173
Vogel, Charles. 77607
Vogel aus Asien. (29532)
Voiage au Japon. 68455
Voiage de C. Matelief. 68455
Voiage de Corneille de Veen aux Indes Orien-
tales. 68455
Voiage de G. Spilberg aux isles Moluques.
68455

Voiage de Guillaume Isbrantsz Bontekou.
68455
Voiage de l'Amiral Verhoeven aux Indes Orien-
tales. 68455
Voiage de ll vaisseaux Hollandois. 68455
Voiage de P. van Caerden. 68455
Voiage de P. van der Broeck. 68455
Voiage de Wolphart Harmansen. 68455
Voiage d'Olivier de Noort. 68455
Voiages du R. P. E. Emmanuel Cressel dans
le Canada. (17476)
Voice and influence of the pious dead. (69368)
Voice for South America. 87322
Voice from a friend. (11351)
Voice from America. [By J. Caughey.] 11562
Voice from America to England by an Ameri-
can gentleman. 14784, 100659
Voice from Babylon. 13442
Voice from bleeding Africa. 6047
Voice from Connecticut. 35815
Voice from Greece. 100660
Voice from Harper's Ferry. 1414
Voice from Heaven. (71269)
Voice from Jamaica. (7823)
Voice from Jerusalem. (64970)
Voice from Kentucky. pseud. Appeal to the
people of the North. see Coleman,
William, fl. 1861.
Voice from Kentucky. April, 1864. 42567
Voice from Leverett Street Prison. (17599),
note after 100660
Voice from Nazareth. 7960
Voice from North Carolina. pseud. Seces-
sionists. 78711
Voice from old Tammany! 94297
Voice from Pennsylvania. 100661
Voice from prison. 70418
Voice from Richmond. . . . By the late Rev.
Robert May. 47074
Voice from Richmond. The southern history
of the war. (63859)
Voice from Sing Sing. (9442)
Voice from South America. 26612
Voice from the "Aged guard of '62" in the
city of Baltimore. 3089
Voice from the East. A reply from the west.
(17742), 20757
Voice from the east. . . . A sermon. (66665)
Voice from the forge. 9454
Voice from the Green Mountains. 22243
Voice from the interior. 100662
Voice from the main deck. 39812
Voice from the mother land. 13175
Voice from the mountains and from the crowd.
43358
Voice from the newsboys. 50901
Voice from the past. (79680)
Voice from the prison. 72484
Voice from the sanctuary concerning the civil
war. 22354
Voice from the south. 42942
Voice from the steerage. 84714
Voice from the tombs. 100663
Voice from the Washingtonian home. 30605
Voice from the west. 35497
Voice from the West Indies. (33053)
Voice from the wilderness. 3955, note after
104356
Voice from twenty graves. 51737
Voice from Virginia! 100500
Voice in Ramah. 91213
Voice in the great conflict. 83646
Voice of Christ in the story. (28279)
Voice of days. 69010
Voice of duty. 2967
Voice of Elias. 85540

Voice of episcopacy in the wilderness. 39277
Voice of glad tidings to Jews and gentiles.
  13442
Voice of God. Being serious thoughts on the
  present alarming crisis. 100664
Voice of God in a tempest. 46585
Voice of God in calamity. 85338
Voice of God, in stormy winds. 46757
Voice of God: or, an account of the inparalel-
  led fires. 25695, 65016
Voice of God to the American congregational
  churches. 58370
Voice of God to the young people in the late
  terrible judgment. 96095
Voice of God upon the waters. 90831
Voice of gratitude: a discourse delivered on
  22d November, 1804. 6126
Voice of gratitude. An anniversary sermon.
  104821
Voice of Joseph. 85534-85535
[Voice of Joseph. In French.] 85533
[Voice of Joseph. In Italian.] 85532
Voice of jubilee. 13312
Voice of Lancaster County. 38803, 100665
Voice of loyal Democrats in the army. 9073
Voice of New York. pseud. Ohio canal. see
  Clinton, De Witt, 1769-1828. supposed
  author
Voice of one crying in the wilderness. 79956-
  79958
Voice of peace. 100667
Voice of pity for South America. 87322
Voice of the Church and the times. 100668
Voice of the dead. 71733
Voice of the departed. 20391
Voice of the Empire State in condemnation of
  freemasonry. 100669
Voice of the glorious God in the thunder.
  46243
Voice of the hour. (26240)
Voice of the Lord, from the deep places of the
  earth. 25408
Voice of the midnight cry. 100670
Voice of the ministry. 100671
Voice of the minority. 100671
Voice of the people. 100672
Voice of the people: a collection of addresses
  to His Majesty. 100674
Voice of the people, a poem. 100675
Voice of the people, and the facts. 100676
Voice of the people! General Republican ad-
  dress. 26908, 100673
Voice of the prophets considered in a discourse
  or sermon. 100677
Voice of the rod: a sermon, delivered at
  Albany. 89744
Voice of the rod. A sermon: preached on
  Thursday, June 1, 1865. (29300)
Voice of the times. 9364
Voice of the turtle. 100678
Voice of the West Indies. 100679
Voice of the yeomanry! 106023
Voice of truth, containing General Joseph Smith's
  correspondence. 83254, 83288
Voice of truth: or, an examination of the pro-
  ceedings, 100681
Voice of truth; or, thoughts on the affair between
  the Leopard and the Chesapeake. (12491),
  1st note after 100681
Voice of truth. To the citizens of Pennsylvania.
  100680
Voice of truth, uttered forth against the un-
  reasonableness. (13373)
Voice of twenty years. 3794
Voice of warning and instruction to all people.
  64971-64972

Voice of warning, to Christians. 45463, 2d
  note after 100681
Voice of warning to religious republicans.
  35932, 79263
Voice of wisdom. 102338
Voice to the United States of America. 100682
Voices from America. 11564
Voices from prison. 89071-89072
Voices from the army. (80418)
Voices from the pulpit of New York and
  Brooklyn. 41219
Voices from the street. A series of poems.
  29678
Voices in American history. 66757
Voices of flowers. 80961
Voices of history. 64471
Voices of home. By Mrs. L. H. Sigourney.
  80962
Voices of home, on the sea. 80967
Voices of life. 40182
Voices of nature, and thoughts in rhyme.
  21602
Voices of nature. By William Cullen Bryant.
  8826
Voices of the border. 59117
Voices of the night; and other poems. 65948
Voices of the night. [By Henry Wadsworth
  Longfellow.] (41932)
Voices of the past. 78644
Voices of the spirit. 47056
Voices of the wind and other poems. 68574
Voices of thought and counsel. (81208)
Voici, of pourtrait en byzonderheeden aangaande
  den politiek-vertoog-schryver. (40761)
Voies de communication aux Etats-Unis. 93234
Voila donc connu de secret plein d'horreur.
  98678
Voisin, Charles Antoine. 1st note after 100682
Voisin, Pierre Joseph. 2d note after 100682
Voisin de la Popelliniere, Lancelot. see La
  Popelliniere, Lancelot Voisin de.
Voiture, Nicolas Auguste. 3d note after
  100682
Vojagie naar Groenland of Spitsbergen. 44836
Vokins, Joan. 100683
Vol maeckte lauwer-crans. 100684
Volafan, Genero H. de. pseud. ed. see
  Varnhagen, Francisco Adolfo de, Conde
  de Porto Seguro, 1816-1878.
Volante de Ocariz, Jose. 55274, 57103, 1st
  note after 100684
Volaterranus, Raffaello. see Maffei, Raffaello.
Volcanic diggings. 10046, 37947, 3d note
  after 100684
Volcano diggings. 10046, 37947, 3d note after
  100684
Volcano Quartz Mining Company, located at
  Colvanoville. 100684
Volcanos. 78509
Volcanos of Central America. 90001
Volcans des Cordilleres de Quito et du
  Mexique. 33749
Volck, Adalbert John, 1828- (5709)
Volckart, Adrian Gottlieb. 100685A
Volgens den Parysschen Druk in 't Nederduitsch
  vertaald. 6467
Volght de beschryvinge der Neuwe Werelt.
  77776
Volker, John W. F. tr. 83120-83121
Volker der fremden Welttheile. (19649)
Volker des Erdballs nach ihrer Abstammung
  und Verwandtschaft. 4857A
Volker ehtnalten. 6468
Volker und Sprachen des Britischen Ostlandes.
  (9527)
Volker und Sprachen Neu-Mexiko's und der
  Westseite. 9530

Volunteer Zouave. pseud. Baltimore, A. D. 1862. 2988
Volunteer Zouave in Baltimore. 2989
Volunteers; a farce. 73619
Volunteers' camp and field book. 18008
Volunteer's hand book. 39766
Volunteers' manual. 71095
Volunteer's manual; or, ten months with the 153d Penn'a Volunteers. 81144
Volunteer's role of honor. 7293
Volunteer's text book. 86289
Voluntier's march [sic]. 100759
Volzius, Paulus. 69122
Vom Elend und Eriosung der Menschen. 106384
Vom Kriege. 22087, 38322
Vom Ursprung des Negerhandels. 89763
Vom Rumford, Benjamin Thompson, Count. see Thompson, Benjamin, Count vom Rumford, 1753-1814.
Von America dem vierdten Theyl der Welt. 12957, 1st note after 91211
Von America ein teyl dauonhie Beschriben. 25965, 1st note after 98183
Von dem auch new erfundenen Lande Virginia. 20926
Von dem Ligno Gvayaco. 104966
Von dem new erfundnem vierten Theil der Welt. 67354
Von dem Rechtszustande unter den Ureinwohnern Brasiliens. 44999
Von dem Unterschiede der Feinde und Freunde des Kreuzes Jesu. 94616
Von den Hessen in Amerka. 31617
Von den nawen Insulen vnnd Landen so itzt kurtzliche[n] den sint durch den Konigk von Portugal. note before 99327, 99346
Von den newen Insulen vnd Landen so yetz kurtzlichen erfundenn. note before 99327, 99349
Von den new[n] Insule[n] vnd La[n]den so yetz kurtzliche[n] erfunde[n] synt durch den Kunig von Portugall. note before 99327, 99345
Von den newen Insulen vnd Landen so yttz kurtzlichen erfunden seynd durch den Kunigk von Portigal. note before 99327, 99348
Von den nuwen Insule[n] vnd Landen so yetz kurtzlichen erfunden synt durch den Kunig von Portugall. note before 99327, 99347
Von den Quakern. 54944
Von der Arbeit der Evangelischen Bruder unter den Heiden. 88934
Von der Beschreibung der Newen Welt. 67978
Von der Bezaubernden Kraft. (3818)
Von der Holzaxt zum Prasidentenstuhl. 41238
Von der Krankheiten. 82168
Von der nawen Werlt. 99346
Von der neu gefunden Region die wol ein Welt genent mag Werden. note before 99327, 99343
Von der neu gefunden Region so wol ein Welt genempt mag Werden. note before 99327, 99340
Von der neuw gefunden Region die wol ain Welt genent mag Werden. note before 99327, 99341
Von der neuwen gefunde[n] Region, die wol ein wellt genennt mag Werden. note before 99327, 99342
Von der new gefunnde[n] Region die wol ein Welt genennt mag Werden. note before 99327, 99344
Von der newen Welt. 99345

[Von der nuwen Insulen und Landen so yetz kurtzlichen erfunden synt durch den Kunig von Portugall.] note before 99327, 99351
Von der nuwen Welt. 99347
Von Georg Weitfields Predigten, der dritte Theil. 103607
Von Georg Weitfields Predigten, der erste Theil. 103607
Von Georg Weitfields Predigten, der zweyte Theil. 103607
Von Gottes gnaden Wir Wilhelm, Landgraf und Erbprinz zu Hessen. 103991
Von Ocean zu Ocean. 7078
Von Sant Brandon ein hubsch lieblichen Lesen. 100760
Von Albensleben, Ludwig. see Albensleben, Ludwig von.
Von Ambach, Ed. see Ambach, Ed. von.
Von Angliara, Joan. see Anghiera, Pietro Martire d'.
Von Antersen, Johann Peter. see Antersen, Johann Peter von.
Von Archenholtz, Johann Wilhelm. see Archenholtz, Johann Wilhelm von.
Von B. . . ., Constantia. pseud. see B. . . ., Constantia von. pseud.
Von Baer, Karl Er. see Baer, Karl Er. von.
Von Behr, Ottomar. see Behr, Ottomar von.
Von Berger, Frederick Ludwig. see Berger, Frederick Ludwig von.
Von Berkel, Adriaan. see Berkel, Adriaan von.
Von Bibra, Ernst. see Bibra, Ernst, Freiherr von.
Von Blumencron, Leopold R. see Blumencron, Leopold R. von.
Von Boguslawski, B. see Boguslawski, B. von.
Von Borcke, Heros. see Borcke, Heros von.
Von Bourignon, Haubold Xaverius, Graf. see Bourignon, Haubold Xaverius, Graf von.
Von Braunschweig, Johann Daniel. see Braunschweig, Johann Daniel von.
Von Breitenbauch, Georg August. see Breitenbauch, Georg August von.
Von Brentano, Carl August. see Brentano, Carl August von.
Von Buch, Christoph Leopold. see Buch, Christian Leopold von, Baron, 1744-1853.
Von Buckholtz, L. see Buckholtz, L. von.
Von Bulich, J. D. see Bulich, J. D. von.
Von Bulow, Adam Heinrich Dietrich. see Bulow, Dietrich, i. e. Adam Heinrich Dietrich, Freiherr von, 1757-1807.
Von Bulow, Dietrich. see Bulow, Dietrich, i. e. Adam Heinrich Dietrich, Freiherr von, 1757-1807.
Von Bunsen, Christian Karl Josias, Freiherr. see Bunsen, Christian Karl Josias, Freiherr von, 1791-1860.
Von Buss, Franz Joseph, Ritter. see Buss, Franz Joseph, Ritter von, 1803-1878.
Von Carlscroon, Jean Dumont, Baron. see Dumont, Jean, Baron de Carlscroon, d. 1725.
Von Caspar, F. X. see Caspar, F. X. von.
Von Chamisso, Adelbert. see Chamisso, Adelbert von, 1781-1838.
Von Chamisso, Louis Charles Adelbert. see Chamisso, Adelbert von, 1781-1838.
Von Coelln, Johann. see Coelln, Johann von.
Von Cordoua, Didacum. see Cordova, Diego de.
Von Czarnowsky, Otto. see Czarnowsky, Otto von.
Vondel, Joost van den. 100761-100762
Vondenvelden, William. 100763

Von der Gabelentz, H. C. see Gabelentz, H. C. von der.
Von Dille, Goszwin Theodor. see Dille, Goszwin Theodor von.
Von Duben, C. see Duben, C. von.
Von Dunderhead. pseud. Budget. 100764
Von Dusch und Eiselein, Al. see Dusch und Eiselein, Al. von.
Von Eelking, Max. see Eelking, Max von.
Von Egloffstein, F. W. see Egloffstein, F. W. von.
Von Epplen Hartenstein, Clara. see Gerstner, Clara (von Epplen Hartenstein) von.
Von Eschwege, L. W. see Eschwege, L. W. von.
Von Eschwege, W. C. see Eschwege, W. C. von.
Von Eschwege, W. L. see Eschwege, W. L. von.
Von Esenbeck, C. G. Nees. see Nees von Esenbeck, C. G.
Von Esslingen, ------- Mayor. see Mayer von Esslingen, --------.
Von Etzel, Anton. see Etzel, Anton von.
Von Feldner, W. Chr. G. see Feldner, W. Chr. G. von.
Von Fenneherg, F. F. see Fenneherg, F. F. von.
Von Firsch, Valentin Marquard. see Firsch, Valentin Marquard von.
Von Floos, Ph. von Roesgen. see Roesgen von Floss, Ph. von.
Von Franckenberg, Hans. see Franckenberg, Hans von.
Von Frantzius, A. see Frantzius, A. von.
Von Furstenwarther, Moritz, Freiherr. see Furstenwarther, Moritz, Freiherr von.
Von Gagern, Hans Christoph Ernst, Freiherr. see Gagern, Hans Christoph Ernst, Freiherr von, 1766-1852.
Von Gallenberg, Wenzel Robert, Graf. see Gallenberg, Wenzel Robert, Graf von, 1783-1839.
Von Gentz, F. see Gentz, F. von.
Von Gernsbach, Weil. see Gernsbach, Weil von.
Von Gerstner, Clara (von Epplen Hartenstein) see Gerstner, Clara (von Epplen Hertenstein) von.
Von Gerstner, Franz Anton, Ritter. see Gerstner, Franz Anton, Ritter von.
Von Goellm, Johannes. see Goellm, Johannes von.
Von Goethe, Johann Wolfgang. see Goethe, Johann Wolfgang von, 1749-1832.
Von Gortz, C. G. see Gortz, C. G. von.
Von Graffenried, Friedrich. see Graffenried, Friedrich von.
Von Griepel, E. W. see Greipel, E. W. von.
Von Grone, A. C. E. see Grone, A. C. E. von.
Von Guion, Ludwig Heinrich, Graf. see Guion, Ludwig Heinrich, Graf von.
Von Hagen, P. A. 101811
Von Hagen (P. A.) & Company. firm publishers 101811
Von Halfern, Albert. see Halfern, Albert von.
Von Haller, Albrecht. see Haller, Albrecht von, 1708-1777.
Von Haller, Victor Albrecht. see Haller, Albrecht von, 1708-1777.
Von Harten, Gerard. defendant 100765
Von Hefner, Jos. see Heffner, Jos. von.
Von Hellwald, Friedrich. see Hellwald, Friedrich von.

Von Herberstein, Sigmund, Freiherr. see Herberstein, Sigmund, Freiherr von, 1486-1566.
Von Hock, Carl, Freiherr. see Hock, Carl, Freiherr von.
Von Horn, W. O. pseud. Benjamin Franklin. see Oertel, Philipp Friedrich.
Von Horn, W. O. pseud. Lebensgang Georg Washingtons. see Oertel, Philipp Friedrich.
Von Humboldt, Alexander, Freiherr. see Humboldt, Alexander, Freiherr von, 1769-1859.
Von Humboldt, Friedrich Heinrich Alexander, Freiherr see Humboldt, Alexander, Freiherr von, 1769-1859.
Von Hutten, Ulric. pseud. see Hutten, Ulric von. pseud.
Von Karwinsky, Wilhelm Friedrich, Freyherr. see Karwinsky, Wilhelm Friedrich, Freiherr von.
Von Kittlitz, Friedrich Heinrich, Freiherr. see Kittlitz, Friedrich Heinrich, Freiherr von, 1799-1874.
Von Kloden, G. A. see Kloden, G. A. von.
Von Kobbe, Peter Ludwig Christian. see Kobbe, Peter Ludwig Christian von.
Von Konige, A. see Konige, A. von.
Von Konigshofen, Nicolaus Honiger. see Konigshofen, Nicolaus Honiger von.
Von Kotzebue, August Friedrich Ferdinand. see Kotzebue, August Friedrich Ferdinand von, 1761-1819.
Von Kotzebue, Otto. see Kotzebue, Otto von, 1787-1846.
Von Kronfels, L. see Kronfels, L. von.
Von Krusenstern, Adam Johann. see Kursenstern, Adam Johann von.
Von la Roche, Sophie. see La Roche, Sophie von.
Von Langsdorff, Georg Heinrich. see Langsdorff, Georg Heinrich von.
Von Lengerke, H. see Lengerke, H. von.
Von Lery, Johann. see Lery, Jean de.
Von Leubelfing, J. see Leubelfing, J. von.
Von Lienau, J. F. see Lienau, J. F. von.
Von Lindenau, Karl Friedrich. see Lindenau, Karl Friedrich von, 1742-1817.
Von Linne, Carl. see Linne, Carl von, 1707-1778.
Von Loebell, Heinrich. see Loebell, Heinrich von, 1816-1901.
Von M***. pseud. see M***, von. pseud.
Von Martels, Heinrich. see Martels, Heinrich von.
Von Martens, Georg Friedrich. see Martens, George Friedrich von, 1756-1821.
Von Martius, Karl Friedrich Philipp. see Martius, Karl Friedrich Philipp von, 1794-1868.
Von Massow, F. see Massow, F. von.
Von Megerle, Therese. see Megerle, Therese von.
Von Mendieta, Alhponsum. see Mendieta, Alphonsum von.
Von Meyer, Ph. A. G. see Meyer, Ph. A. G. von.
Von Millern, Alexander. see Millern, Alexander von.
Von Minutoli, J. H. see Minutoli, J. H. von.
Von Mohl, Robert. see Mohl, Robert von.
Von Moosthal, Erwin. see Moosthal, Erwin von.
Von Mueller, Ferdinand, Freiherr. see Mueller, Ferdinand, Freiherr von, 1825-1896.

Von Murr, Christoph Gottlieb. see Murr, Christoph Gottlieb von.

Von N., S. pseud. see N., S. von. pseud.

Von Noort, Olivier. see Noort, Olivier von, 1558-1628.

Von Pelzeln, August. see Pelzeln, August von.

Von Petersen, B. see Petersen, B. von.

Von Pufendorf, Samuel, Freiherr. see Pufendorf, Samuel, Freiherr von, 1632-1694.

Von Rango, F. L. see Rango, F. L. von.

Von Rarop, Symon Gilde. see Rarop, Symon Gilde von.

Von Raumer, Friedrich Ludwig Georg. see Raumer, Friedrich Ludwig Georg von, 1781-1873.

Von Raumer, Karl Georg. see Raumer, Karl Georg von, 1783-1865.

Von Rechberg und Rothelowen, Bernhard, Graf. see Rechberg und Rothelowen, Bernhard, Graf von, 1806-1899.

Von Reck, P. G. F. see Reck, P. G. F. von.

Von Reden, Friedrich Wilhelm. see Reden, Friedrich Wilhelm von.

Von Rehfues, Ph. J. see Rehfues, Ph. J. von.

Von Reiswitz, G. L. see Reiswitz, G. L. von.

Von Rhein, Franco. see Rhein, Franco von.

Von Richtofen, Emil Heinrich, Freiherr. see Richtofen, Emil Karl Heinrich, Freiherr von.

Von Riedesel, Frederica Charlotte Louise (von Massow Baroness see Riedesel, Frederica Charlotte Louise (von Massow) Baronness von.

Von Riedesel, Friedrich Adolph, Freiherr. see Riedesel, Friedrich Adolph, Freiherr von.

Von Roesgen von Floss, Ph. see Roesgen von Floss, Ph. von.

Von Ronne, ------. see Ronne, ------- von.

Von Rosen, W. see Rosen, W. von.

Von Ross, G. M. see Ross, G. M. von.

Von Rotteck, Karl. see Rotteck, Karl von.

Von Sack, Albert. see Sack, Albert, Baron von.

Von Scelter, Helter. pseud. Schemer. see Ridley, J.

Von Schaeffer, -------, Ritter. see Schaeffer, ------, Ritter von.

Von Scheliha, ------. see Scheliha, ----- von.

Von Schirach, G. B. see Schirach, G. B. von.

Von Schlagintweit, Robert. see Schlagintweit, Robert von.

Von Schlechtendal, Diedrich Franz Leonhard. see Schlechtendal, Diedrich Franz Leonhard von, 1794-1866.

Von Schlieben Wilhelm Ernst August. see Schlieben, Wilhelm Ernst August von.

Von Schmettow, W. F. see Schmettow, W. F. von.

Von Schmidt-Phiseldek, Conrad Friedrich. see Schmidt-Phiseldek, Conrad Friedrich von.

Von Schriebers, Carl Franz Anton. see Schriebers, Carl Franz Anton von, 1775-1852.

Von Schriebers, Karl. see Schriebers, Carl Franz Anton von, 1775-1852.

Von Schweinitz, Lewis David. see Schweinitz, Lewis David von, 1780-1834.

Von Siebold, Philipp Franz. see Siebold, Philipp Franz von, 1796-1866.

Von Sivers, Jegor. see Sivers, Jegor von.

Von Soden, Carl Theodor. see Soden, Carl Theodor von.

Von Soden, Friedrich Julius Heinrich. see Soden, Friedrich Julius Heinrich,

Von Soden, Friedrich Julius Heinrich. see Soden, Friedrich Julius Heinrich, Graf von, 1754-1831.

Von Someren, A. see Someran, A. von.

Von Sommer, Karl. see Sommer, Karl von.

Von Sonnenstern, Maximilian. see Sonnenstern, Maximilian von.

Von Spilbergen, Georgio. see Spilbergen, Joris van.

Von Spix, Johann Baptist. see Spix, Johann Baptist von.

Von Spruner, Karl. see Spruner, Karl von.

Von Sprunger, Karl. see Sprunger, Karl von.

Von Spuyten, Henry. pseud. Few thoughts. see Brewer, William A.

Von Steuben, Friedrich Wilhelm August Heinrich Ferdinand, Baron. see Steuben, Friedrich Wilhelm August Heinrich Ferdinand, Baron von.

Von Stiernman, Anders Anton. see Stiernman, Anders Anton von, 1695-1765.

Von Stockmar, Ernest Alfred Christian. see Stockmar, Ernest Alfred Christian von.

Von Storcksburg, Jacob Staehlin. see Staehlin von Storcksburg, Jacob.

Von Stulpnagel, Fr. see Stulpnagel, Fr. von.

Von Stuven, -----. see Stuven, ----- von.

Von Tempelhof, Georg Friedrich. see Tempelhof, Georg Friedrich von, 1737-1807.

Von Thurstein, Herr. pseud. see Zinzendorff, Nicolaus Ludwig, Graf von, 1700-1760.

Von Treskow, A. see Treskow, A. von.

Von Tschudi, Johann Jakob. see Tschudi, Johann Jakob von.

Von Tschudi, John James. see Tschudi, Johann Jakob von.

Von Uchteritz, Heinrich. see Uchteritz, Heinrich von.

Von Uslar, Justus Ludwig. see Uslar, Justus Ludwig von.

Von V., S. pseud. see Vries, Simon de.

Von Voss, Julius. see Voss, Julius von.

Von Vries, Simon. see Vries, Simon de.

Von Wallwille, Maria (Owliam) Grafin. see Wallwille, Maria (Owlaim) Grafin von.

Von Wangenheim, Friedrich Adam Julius. see Wangenheim, Friedrich Adam Julius von.

Von Watt, Joachim. see Vadianus, i. e. Joachim von Watt, 1484-1551.

Von Wedell, L. M. see Wedell, L. M. von.

Von Weech, J. Friedrich. see Weech, J. Friedrich von.

Von Werndel, Johann Georg. see Werndle, Johann Georg von.

Von Wiesner, F. R. see Wiesner, F. R. von.

Von Wiesner, Franz, Ritter. see Wiesner, Franz, Ritter von, 1748-1823.

Von Wrangel, Ferdinand Petrovich, Baron. see Wrangel, Ferdinand Petrovich, Baron von.

Von Wullerstorf-Urbair, B. see Wullerstorf-Urbair, B. von.

Von Wurtemberg, Paul Wilhelm Friedrich, Herzog. see Wurtemberg, Paul Wilhelm Friedrich, Herzog von.

Von Zach, Franz Xavier, Freiherr. see Zach, Franz Xavier, Freiherr von, 1754-1832.

Von Zimmermann, C. A. W. see Zimmermann, C. A. W. von.

Von Zimmermann, Eberhard August Wilhelm. see Zimmermann, Eberhard August Wilhelm von.

Von Zinzendorff, Nicolaus Ludwig, Graf. see Zinzendorff, Nicolaus Ludwig, Graf von, 1700-1760.

Vostey, Gabriel Henry. note after 100785

Votaries of twilight. (55220)

Vote of censure on Jacob Kerr. 37628

Vote of the members of the Pennsylvania Convention. 25371

Voted and resolved, that Jonathan Freeman, Esq; and Capt. David Woodward, be desired to wait upon the Reverend Eden Burroughs. 99021

Voted, that the class meet five years from the present time. 105883

Voter. pseud. Fellow citizens and fellow voters. 100786

Voter. pseud. Some remarks upon an oration. 86753, note after 100786

Voter. pseud. To the public. 100787

Voter. pseud. To the Republican electors of . . . New Hampshire. 52937

Voters' guide. 5272

Voter's new catechism. 100788

Voter's text book; comprising a collection of the most important documents. 31675

Voter's text-book; or, the Maryland citizen's companion to the pools. (5866), 1st note after 100788, 2d note after 104412

Votes and proceedings of the American Continental Congress. (15528), note after 23535

Votes and proceedings of the Assembly of the state of New-York; at the first meeting of the fourth session. 54010

Votes and proceedings of the Assembly of the state of New-York, at their first session, begun and holden . . . at Kingston. 54009

Votes and proceedings of the freeholders and other inhabitants of the town of Boston. 6567-6569

Votes and proceedings of the General Assembly of the colony of New York. [From July 29, 1746, to December 6, 1746.] 54005

Votes and proceedings of the General Assembly of the colony of New York. [From June 27, 1749, to Aug. 4, 1749.] 54007

Votes and proceedings of the General Assembly of the colony of New York. [From June 3, 1746, to July 15, 1746.] 54004

Votes and proceedings of the General Assembly of the colony of New York. [From September 29, 1747, to Nov. 25, 1747.] 54006

Votes and proceedings of the General Assembly of the colony of New York, Feb. 15-17, 1757. 54008

Votes and proceedings of the General Assembly of the province of New-Jersey. At a sitting at Burlington. 53244

Votes and proceedings of the House of Assembly of Bahama Islands. 2721

Votes and proceedings of the House of Assembly of the Delaware state. 19404

Votes and proceedings of the House of Representatives of the province of Pennsylvania. 60775-60777

Votes and proceedings of the House of Representatives: recommended to the consideration of all the free men of the province. 60045

Votes and proceedings of the Lower House of Assembly of the province of Maryland. 45391

Votes and proceedings of the Senate of the state of Maryland. 45392

Votes and proceedings of the Senate of the state of New-York. 54011

Votes and proceedings of the town of Boston. 6570

Votes and proceedings of the twenty-sixth General Assembly of . . . New Jersey. 53245

Votes and resolves of the Lower House of Assembly of the province of Maryland. 45393

Votes and speeches of Martin Van Buren. 98425

[Votes of Assembly of Vermont.] 99049

Votes of delegates in the Whig National Convention. 93724

Votes of the General Assembly of New-Jersey. (53246)

Votes of the General Assembly of the colony of New York. 54003

Votes of the Honourable Assembly of the island of Jamaica. 35671

Votes of the Honorable House of Assembly of Jamaica. 35672

Votes of the Honorable House of Representatives of the province of the Massachusetts Bay, 1721-1722. 46171

Votes of the House of Assembly of the province of Nova Scotia. (56128)

Votes of the House of Assembly, of the province of Pennsylvania. 60096

Votes of the Overseers and Corporation of Harvard University. 30765

Votes passed by the School Committee [of Roxbury, Mass.] 73738

Voting for propositions to become law. 23211

Votivae Angliae. 78372-(78373), 78379, 2d note after 100788

Votive pillar. 4274

Voto a favor de los primeros caudillos de la libertad Americana. 29337

Voto consultivo que ofrece al Exc. Senor Don Jose. Ant. Manso de Velasco. 7463

Voto consultivo que ofrece al Excelentissimo Senor D. Joseph Antonio Manso de Velasco. 38630

Voto de America. 100789, 105745

Voto be Venezuela. 100790

Voto del Marques de Tous, Diputado de Sevilla. 96338

Voto del Senador que suscribe sobre la renuncia. 96244

Voto fundado de uno de los Ministros de la Corte Suprema de Justicia. 100791

Voto general de la nacion contrario al particular. 98658

Voto nacional. 100792

Voto particular al proyecto de reformas de las leyes constitucionales. (67651)

Voto particular del Sr. Senador Lic. D. Manuel Larrainzar. (39080)

Voto particular que sobre el punto de patronato presento. (67651)

Voto qui di en la Junta Jeneral tenida en Mejico. 99688

Voto que ofference Domingos Alves Branco Moniz Barreto. 100793

Votos de la razon por el actual estado de la independencia. 100794

Votos de los Americanos a la naciona Espanola. 99500

Vouchers. 10514

Vought, John G. 100795-100796

Vought, John G. defendant 96824, 100796

Vous etes prie de la parte du Ministre Plenipotentaire de France. 100797

Vous trouverez sous ce pli nos adresses a l'Assemblee Nationale. 75070

Vouves, P.-L.-C.-F. Rezard de. see Rezard de Vouves, P.-L.-C.-F.

Voux, Roberts. 4694, 98704

Vowell, Ebenezer. 100798

Vowell, Richard Longeville. supposed author 10193, (21638), note before 94254, 98870, note after 98870

Vox coeli. 78374-78375, 78379, 100799

Vox Dei. 78378-78379

Vox populi. pseud. Taxation royal tyranny. 94433

Vox populi. Liberty, property, and no stamps. 100800

Vox popvli. Or nevves from Spayne, translated according to the Spanish coppie. 78362, 78366, (78376)-78379, 100801

Vox populi; vox Dei; being true maxims of government. (19280), 86795

Vox regis. 78378-78379

Vox vera. 78187

Vox veritatis. 100802

Voyage a Berlin, en 1784. 44236

Voyage a Buenos-Ayres et a Porto-Alegre. (35239)

Voyage a Cayenne. 63057-63059

Voyage a Guazaca. 95348-95349

Voyage a la Baye de Hudson. (22313)

Voyage a la Cochinchine. 3658

Voyage a la Guiane et a Cayenne. 66412, 1st note after 100802

Voyage a la Guyane et a Catenne. 44474, 2d note after 100802

Voyage a la Havana. (73274)

Voyage a la Louisiane et sur le continent de l'Amerique, fait dans les annees 1794 a 1798. 21487

Voyage a la Louisiane, et sur le continent de l'Amerique Septentrionale. 3979, 2d note after 100802

Voyage a la Martinique, contenant diverses observations. 11936, 5th note after 100802

Voyage a la Martinique. Vues et observations politiques. 72987, 4th note after 100802

Voyage a la mer du Sud, completant la relation du Voyage d'Anson. 9735

Voyage a la mer du Sud, entripris pour intro- duir aux Indes Occidentales. 5911

Voyage a la mer du Sud, fait par quelques officiers. 1639, 100803

Voyage a la nouvelles galles du Sud. 103406

Voyage a la partie orientale de la Terre-Ferme. 19641

Voyage a l'isle de Terre Neuve. 2606

Voyage a l'Ocean Pacifique. 16261

Voyage a l'ouest de Monts Alleghanys. 48703

Voyage, a poem in seven parts. 63582, 100804

Voyage; a poem written at sea. 57798

Voyage a Rio-Grande do Sul (Bresil) 75235

Voyage a Saint-Domingue. 104711

Voyage a Surinam. Description des possessions Neerlandaises. 4737

Voyage a Surinam et dans l'interieur de la Guiane. 91082-91084

Voyage a Surinam, par M. Leschenauld de la Tour. 40180

Voyage a Terre-Neuve. (11020)

Voyage a travers l'Amerique du Sud. (44507)

Voyage along the eastern coast of Africa. 62509, 65696

Voyage among the treetops. 69018

Voyage and discovery of the West Indies. 40914

Voyage and historie of AEthiopia Orientalis. 66686

Voyage and shipwreck of Richard Castelman. 99429, note after 100822

Voyage anecdotique de Marcel Bonneau. 14936

Voyage au Bresil, dans les annees 1815, 1816, et 1817. (47023)-47024

Voyage au Bresil. Par Francois Biard. 5135

Voyage au Bresil; . . . traduit de l'Anglais par Francois Soules. (41296)

Voyage au Canada, par Edward Allen Talbot. 94231

Voyage au Canada, pendant les annees 1795, 1796 et 1797. 102544

Voyage au centre de la terre. 100805-100806

Voyage au Chili, au Perou, et au Mexique. 29719

Voyage au Golfe de Californie. (14925)

Voyage au Guazacoalcos. 8040

Voyage au Kentoukey. 42898, 1st note after 100806

Voyage au Lac Superieur. 71695

Voyage au Mexique. 77217

Voyage au Minnesota. 20556

Voyage au Nouveau-Mexique. (62838)

Voyage au Nouveau-Monde. 17477

Voyage au pays des Mormons. (69595)

Voyage au pays des Osages. 16928

Voyage au Pol Sud. 21216

Voyage au Pole Boreal. 62574

Voyage au relions equinoxiales du Nouveau Continent. 33768

Voyage au Spitzberg et a la Nouvelle-Zemble. 89545

Voyage autour de monde, commence en 1708 & fini en 1711. Par le Capitaine. Woodes Rogers. 72757, note after 93778

Voyage autour du monde, commence en 1708 et fini en 1711. Traduit de l'Anglais. (72758)

Voyage autour du monde, contenant la descrip- tion geographique et pittoresque. 11821

Voyage autour du monde de Cook. 3575

Voyage autour du monde de M. Le Grand. 81414

Voyage autour du monde . . . en 1766-69. 6866

Voyage autour du monde, entrepris en 1803, 1804, 1805 et 1806. 38327

Voyage autour du monde entrepris par ordre de Sa Majeste Britannique. 30941

Voyage autour du monde entrepris par ordre du gouvernement. 40214

Voyage autour du monde, entrepris par ordre du Roi. 25916

Voyage autour du monde, et principalement a la cote nord-ouest de l'Amerique. 20366, 64391

Voyage autour du monde, execute par ordre de Sa Majeste l'Empereur Nicolas Ier. (42739)

Voyage autour du monde, execute par ordre du Roi, sur le corvette de Sa Majeste, la Coquille. 21353

Voyage autour du monde pendant les annees 1836 et 1837. 98298

Voyage autour du monde, fait dans les annees 1803, 1804, 1805 et 1806. 38332

Voyage autour du monde, fait dans les annees 1740, 41, 42, 43 and [sic] 44. 1637, 101186-2d note after 101186, 1st note after 101187

Voyage autour du monde fait dans les annees 1740, 41, 42, 43, et 44. 1638, 101186, 3d-4th notes after 101186

Voyage autour du monde, fait dans les annees MDCCXL, I, II, III, IV. 1637, 101186-2d note after 101186, 1st note after 101187

Voyage autour du monde, fait en 1764 et 1765. 9734

Voyage autour du monde, par la fregate du Roi le Boudeuse. 6864-6866, 6868, 2d note after 100806

Voyage de Francis Drach a l'entour du monde. 20844-20845

Voyage de Francois Pyrard, de Laval. (66881)-66882

Voyage de Francois Pyrard de Laual contenant sa nauigation. 66880

Voyage de Georges Anson. 100803

Voyage de Guillaume Dampier. (18381)-18383, 100944

Voyage de Hafenaar aux Indes Orientales. 68455

Voyage de Jacqves Cartier av Canada en 1534. 11141

Voyage de Jean Huyghen de Linschoten. 4935-4936

Voyage de la Corvette l'Astrolabe. (6153), 21210

Voyage de la Flote de Nassau. 68455

Voyage de la France Eqvinoxiale en l'isle de Cayenne. 5269

Voyage de la Louisiane. 39276, 98393

Voyage de la Mer Atlantique a l'Ocean Pacifique. 44111

Voyage de La Perouse autour du monde, publie conformement au decret du 22 Avril 1791. 38961

Voyage de La Perouse autour du monde, publie conformement au decret du 22 Avril 1791, et redige par M. L. A. Milet-Mureau. (38960)

Voyage de La Perouse, pendant les annees 1785, 1786, 1787, et 1788. 38959

Voyage de La Perouse, redige d'apres ses manuscrits originaux. 38965

Voyage de la Riviere des Amazones. 38491, 62957

Voyage de l'Ambassade de la Compagnie des Indes Hollandais. (33133)

Voyage de l'Amerique, contenant ce qui s'est passe. 2692, 100808

Voyage de l'Amerique, ou dialogues de Monsieur le Baron de Lahontan. 29142, (38643)

Voyage de l'Atlantique au Pacifique. 49144

Voyage de l'Empereur de la Chine. 4935-4936

Voyage de l'Entrecasteaux. (22671)

Voyage de "l'Erbe" et de la "Terreur." 38931

Voyage de l'Illvstre Seignevr et Cheualier Francois Drach. 20844-20846

Voyage de Lionel Wafer. (18381)-18383, 100944

Voyage de Madame *** aux Etats-Unis et au Mexique. (23581), 31532, note before 95090

Voyage de Marseille la Lima. 21437, note after 100808, 3d note after 102871

Voyage de M. de Bougainville. 6867, 93292

Voyage de M. de Surville. (17716), 72371

Voyage de M. J. M. Duncan. 84231, 94228

Voyage de Mr. le Chevalier de Chastellux en Amerique. 12226

Voyage de Mr. Wafer. 100946

Voyage de Moscou a la Chine. 4936

Voyage de Narborough a la Mer du Sud. 16781

Voyage de Newport a Philade[l]phie. 12225, 12227, 100809

Voyage de quinze vaisseaux Hollandois. 68455

Voyage de Rechteren aux Indes Orientales. 68455

Voyage de Samvel Champlain. (11834)

Voyage des isles Camercanes. 46987

Voyage des pais septentrionavx. 38711

Voyage des pays septentrionavx. 38711

Voyage d'exploration et de decouvertes. 2493

Voyage d'Iberville. 67023

Voyage down the Ohio and Mississippi Rivers. 17890

Voyage du Chevalier des Marchais en Guinee. (38414)

Voyage du Fort du Prince de Galles. 31183

Voyage du General Lafayette aux Etats-Unis. 38583, 100811

Voyage du poete, poeme. 75507

Voyage d'un Allemand au Lac Oneida. 10309, note after 100811

Voyage d'un Ambassadevr qve le Tartar de Moscovie envoya par terre. 95332

Voyage d'un Americain a Londres. 25212

Voyage d'un Francois. 1st note after 100572, 100837

Voyage d'un jeune Marin a travers les tenebres. 69042

Voyage d'un Suisse dans differentes colonies d'Amerique. 27510, 100812

Voyage d'une femme autour du monde. 61340

Voyage en Africque et en Amerique. 33355

Voyage en Amerique, en Italie, en Sicile et en Egypte. (50229)

Voyage en Amerique. [Par F. A. de Chateaubriand.] (12228), 12248, 12255, (12261), 12273

Voyage en Amerique. Par Marie Mallet. 44133

Voyage en Amerique, notes envoyees a G. le Vavasseur. 64927

Voyage en Araucanie. 79334, 91613-91614

Voyage en Californie. Description de son sol. 8805

Voyage en Californie 1850-1851. 74988, note after 100812

Voyage en Californie par Edouard Auger. 2376

Voyage en Californie. Par H. de Chavennes de la Giraudiere. 12350

Voyage en Californie pour l'observation du passage de Venus. 12003

Voyage en Chine. 39300

Voyage en Guinee, isles Voisines, et a Cayenne. (19459)

Voyage en Gujane. 152, 52380

Voyage en Icarie. 9787

Voyage en Islande et au Groenland. 26330

Voyage en 1815 et 1816. 50208

Voyage en un pays plus grand que l'Europe. 4936

Voyage et aventures au Mexique. (4535)

Voyage et aventures de Lord Villiam Carisdall. 100813

Voyage et decouverte de quelques pays et nations. 44666

Voyage et decouverte de quelques pays et nations . . . pat le P. Marquette et Sr. Joliet. 95332

Voyage et nauigation faict par les Espaignolz. 62803

Voyage fait autour du monde, par le Capitaine Woodes Rogers. (72759), note after 93778

Voyage fait autour du monde, traduit de l'Anglois. 72760

Voyage fait aux terres Australes par M. de Loziers Bouvet. 18336

Voyage fait dans les annees 1816 et 1817, de New-Yorck a la Nouvelle-Orleans. 50209-50210, note after 100813

Voyage fait par ordre de l'Emperatrice de Russie. 77153

Voyage fait par ordre du Roi en 1771 et 1772. 98960

Voyage fait par ordre du Roi en 1768 et 1769. 24760

Voyage fait par ordre du Roi, en 1768, pour eprouver les montres marines. (11372)

Voyage fait par ordre du Roi en 1750 et 1751. (11723)

Voyage pittoresque et historique au Bresil. 19122

Voyage pittoresque et industriel dans le Paraguay-roux et la Palingenesie Australe. 19453

Voyage qui contient une relation exacte. 31352-31353, 31355

Voyage round the globe. 29473

Voyage round the world. 55448

Voyage round the world. Being an account of a remarkable enterprize. 5057

Voyage round the world, between the years 1816-1819. 62509, 73150

Voyage round the world; but more particularly to the north-west coast of America. (20364), 64389-64390

Voyage round the world by a course never sailed before. 19290

Voyage round the world. [By G. F. Gemelli-Careri.] 13015

Voyage round the world. [By Turnbull.] 62506

Voyage round the world, by the way of the great South Sea: performed in a private expedition during the war. 80159

Voyage round the world by the way of the great South Sea, perform'd in the years 1719, 20, 21, and 22. 80158

Voyage round the world. Compiled from his [i. e. George Anson's] papers, & c. 1630, 2d note after 101180, 1st-3d notes after 101185

Voyage round the world. Containing an account of Captain Dampier's expedition. 18373, 18378, (26213)

Voyage round the world during the years 1785, 1786, 1787, and 1788. (59572)

Voyage round the world, from 1806 to 1812. 10210

Voyage round the world, in His Britannic Majesty's Ship Resolution. 25130, 101031

Voyage round the world, in His Majesty's Frigate Pandora. 30011

Voyage round the world, in His Majesty's Ship the Dolphin. 9732, 97668

Voyage round the world in the Gorgon man of war. 58715, 3d note after 100816

Voyage round the world in the United States Frigate Columbia. 94456

Voyage round the world, in the years 1803, 1804, 1805, & 1806. (38331)

Voyage round the world, in the years 1803, 4, 5, & 6. 41416

Voyage round the world, in the years 1785, 1786, 1787, and 1788. By J. F. G. de La Perouse. 38963

Voyage round the world, in the years 1785, 1786, 1787, and 1788. Performed in the King George. 100817

Voyage round the world, in the years 1740, 1, 2, 3, 4. 101192

Voyage round the world, in the years M DCCXL, I, II, III, IV. 1625-1629, 101175-101185

Voyage round the world; including an embassy to Muscat and Siam. 74197

Voyage round the world, including travels in Africa. 32566

Voyage round the world. Performed by order of His Most Christian Majesty, in the years 1766, 1767, 1768, and 1769. (6869)

Voyage round the world, performed during the years 1790, 1791, and 1792. 24752

Voyage round the world, performed in 1785, 1786, 1787, and 1788. 20365

Voyage round the world, performed in the years 1785, 1786, 1787, and 1788. 38962

Voyage round the world, performed in the years 1785, 1786, 1787, 1788, by M. de La Perouse. 38966, (59572), 98444

Voyage round the world: with a history of the Oregon Mission. (31952)

Voyage, shipwreck and miraculous preservation of R. Castelman. 99430, note after 100822

Voyage, shipwreck, and miraculous preservation of Richard Castleman, gent. 12553, 2d note after 99428

Voyage sur le Rio Parahybe. 3382A

Voyage sur l'isthme de Tehuantepec. 7441

Voyage the first. 30630

Voyage through the islands of the Pacific Ocean. 100818

Voyage thro' the streights of Magellan. 29473

Voyage to Boston; a poem. 6571, 25903, 26319, 96502, 1st note after 100818

Voyage to Buenos Aires. 62509

Voyage to Buenos Ayres, performed in the years 1817 and 1818. 7180

Voyage to Cadiz. 66686

Voyage to California, to observe the transit. 12004

Voyage to California, via Panama. 94440

Voyage to Cathay. 16477

Voyage to Cochin China. 103411

Voyage to Cochinchina, in the years 1792 and 1793. 3657

Voyage to Congo. 67565

Voyage to Georgia. 50352

Voyage to Guiana. 67599

Voyage to Guinea, Brasil, and the West-Indies. 2274-2275

Voyage to Hudson's Bay. 62509

Voyage to Hudson's Bay, by the Dobbs Galley and California. 22312

Voyage to Hudson's Bay, during the summer of 1812. 43396

Voyage to London, and an acrostic. 17261

Voyage to Madagascar by the Sieur Cauche. 91538

Voyage to Madagasgar and the East Indies. (59572), 62957

Voyage to Maryland. A satyr. 16234, note after 80002

Voyage to Mexico and Havana. 3383

Voyage to Mountseradoe in Africa. 13015

Voyage to New Holland, &c. 18373, 18376, 100940

Voyage to Newfoundland and Sallee. 12004

Voyage to North America. 62509

Voyage to North America, and the West Indies. 50230

Voyage to North America, perform'd by G. Taylor. 94457

Voyage to North-America: undertaken by command of the present King of France. 12143

Voyage to Peru. 3605, 6876, 62957, 69148

Voyage to Peru; performed by the Conde de St. Malo. 17177, 2d note after 100818

Voyage to Quebec in an Irish emigrant vessel. 56638

Voyage to Quebec, in two cantos. 8696

Voyage to Saint Domingo. 104712

Voyage to South America and the Cape of Good Hope. 37230, 62506

Voyage to South America: describing at large the Spanish cities. 36813, 6th note after 97689

Voyage to South America, performed by order of the American government. 7179, 7182, 35110, note after 93835

Voyage to South America, with an account of a shipwreck in the River La Plata. 25412, 3d note after 100818

Voyage to Spitzbergen and Greenland. 72187

Voyage to Surat. 5691

Voyage to Terra Australis. (24758)

Voyage to the coast of Africa, in 1758. 41304

Voyage to the Demerary. 6182, 62506-62507

Voyage to the East Indies by Francois Pyrard de Laval. 66686

Voyage to the East Indies; giving an account of the isle of Madagascar. (19447)

Voyage to the eastern part of Terra Firma. 19642

Voyage to the Greenland whale fishery. 3659

Voyage to the internal world. (78544)

Voyage to the island of philosophers. (105117B)

Voyage to the islands Madera, Barbadoes . . . and Jamaica. 82169, 98182

Voyage to the islands Madera, Barbados, Nieves, St. Christophers and Jamaica. 82169, 98182

Voyage to the Massachusetts, and their entertainment there. (51198), note after 104797

Voyage to the moon. 97307

Voyage to the new island Fonseca. 24983, 4th note after 100818

Voyage to the north Pacific. 19883

Voyage to the North Pole, by Benjamin Bragg. 7322, 5th note after 100818

Voyage to the North Pole. By Commodore Phipps. (30938)

Voyage to the North Pole, in the frigate the Syrene. 43396

Voyage to the Pacific . . . . Being a copious, comprehensive, and satisfactory abridgment. 16251

Voyage to the Pacific Ocean, for making discoveries in the northern hemisphere. (59572), 100819

Voyage to the Pacific Ocean; undertaken by the command of His Majesty, for making discoveries in the northern hemisphere, performed under the directions of Captains Cook, Clerke, and Gore. (16259)

Voyage to the Pacific Ocean, undertaken, by the command of His Majesty, for making discoveries in the northern hemisphere. To determine the position and extent. 16250

Voyage to the River Sierra-Leone. 46888

Voyage to the slave coast of Africa. (31852)

Voyage to the South Atlantic and round Cape Horn. 14546

Voyage to the South Sea, and along the coasts of Chili and Peru. (25926)

Voyage to the South Sea, and round the world. 16303

Voyage to the South-Sea. [By Sir John Narborough.] 72187

Voyage to the South Sea, undertaken by command of His Majesty. 5910

Voyage to the South Seas and round the world. 72756

Voyage to the South Seas and to other parts of the world. (1632)

Voyage to the South-Seas, by His Majesty's Ship Wager. 100820

Voyage to the South Seas, in the years 1812, 1813, and 1814. 64220

Voyage to the South-Seas, in the years 1740-1. 9108-9109

Voyage to the West Indies by David Middleton in 1601. 66686

Voyage to Virginia, made in 1609. 13015, 55933

Voyage to Virginia: or, the valliant souldier's farwel. 100572

Voyage towards the North Pole. 62509

Voyage towards the North Pole undertaken by His Majesty's command 1773. 62572

Voyage towards the South Pole, and round the world. (16245)

Voyage towards the South Pole, performed in the years 1822-24. 102431

Voyage up the Mississippi, etc. 37949

Voyage up the River Amazon. 21999

Voyage up the River of Plata. 152

Voyage up the Thames. 105986

Voyage vers le Pole Arctique dans la Baie de Baffin. 23923, 73377

Voyager. pseud. Ruins of Athens. see Hill, George.

Voyager's companion. 44591

Voyages, adventures, and discoveries of the following circum-navigators. 100821

Voyages, adventures & situation of the French emigrants. 100822

Voyages and adventures of Capt. Barth. Sharp and others. 79781

Voyages and adventures of Captain Robert Boyle. 99430-99431, note after 100822

Voyages and adventures of Capt. Robert Boyle, in several parts of the world, &c. 12553, 2d note after 99428

Voyages and adventures of Capt. Robert Boyle, who was taken into slavery. 99429

Voyages and adventures of Capt. William Dampier. 18379

Voyages and adventures of Edward Teach. 104034

Voyages and adventures of Edward Teach, commonly called Black Beard, the notorious pirate. To which is added, The two princes. 94555

Voyages and adventures of Jack Halliard. 35337, 100823

Voyages and adventures of John Willock, mariner. 104534

Voyages and adventures of Miles Philips. 62460

Voyages and adventures of Sir Amyas Leigh, Knight. 37889

Voyages and adventures of Sir Francis Drake. 100824

Voyages and adventures of Sir Walter Raleigh. 67594

Voyages and adventures of the Chevalier Dupont. 21386

Voyages and adventures of Thomas Randall, of Cork, pilot. 23723, 100846

Voyages and cruizes of Commodore Walker. 101044

Voyages and descriptions. 18375

Voyages and discoveries in South-America. 152, 1st note after 100824

Voyages and discoveries in the Arctic regions. 47173

Voyages and discoveries of Capt. William Dampier. 18380

Voyages and discoveries of Christopher Columbus. (14672)

Voyages and discoveries of Henrie Hudson. 66686

Voyages and discoveries of the companions of Christopher Columbus. (35007), 35182

Voyages and discoveries of the companions of Columbus. 35205

Voyages and discoveries of the companions of Columbus. Mit Noten zur Erklarung des Textes. 35208

Voyages and travels, containing all the circum-navigators. 10243

Voyages and travels in various parts of the world. (38896)

Voyages and travels of a sea officer. 99251

Voyages and travels of an Indian interpreter and trader. 41878

Voyages and travels of Captain Uring. 98126

Voyages and travels of Captains Parry, Frank-lin, Ross, and Mr. Belzoni. 19582, 100825

Voyages and travels of Fletcher Christian, and a narrative of the mutiny. 12896, 100846

Voyages and travels of Marco Paul. 34

Voyages & travels of that renowned captain, Sir Francis Drake. 20850, 100827

Voyages and travels of that renowned Captain Sir Francis Drake into the West Indies and round the world. 20851

Voyages and travels in the Holy Land and the east by John Newberie. 66686

Voyages au Grand-Desert, en 1851. 82271

Voyages au Perou. (81617)

Voyages autour du monde et dans les contrees les plus curieuses du globe. 84715

Voyages autour du monde et vers les deux poles. 58169

Voyages aux Antilles Francaises. 28287

Voyages aux cotes de Guinee et en Amerique. 51677, note after 100827

Voyages aux iles du Grand Ocean. 49829

Voyages aux Montagnes Rocheuses chez les tribus Indiennes du vaste territoire de l'Oregon. 82273-82274

Voyages aux Montagnes Rocheuses et sejour chez les tribus Indiennes de l'Oregon. (82275)

Voyages aux Montagnes Rocheuses, et une annee de sejour chez les tribus Indiennes. 82270, 82272

Voyages aux terres Magellaniques. 79774

Voyages, aventures, etc., d'une famille Alle-mande. 39287

Voyages avantvrevx dv Capitaine Iean Alphonse Saintongeois. 100828-100834

Voyages chez differentes nations sauvages. 41879

Voyages chez les peuples sauvages. 2580, 70904

Voyages curieux et nouveaux des Messieurs Hennepin & De la Borde. 31354

Voyages, dangerous adventures and imminent escapes of Captain Richard Falconer. 23723, 100846

Voyages dans la mer du Sud. 18344

Voyages dans la partie septentrionale du Bresil. 38273

Voyages dans l'Amerique. 6873

Voyages dans l'Amerique Meridionale. 2541

Voyages dans l'Amerique Septentrionale. Oregon par le R. Pere P. J. de Smet. 82276

Voyages dans les Ameriques, mers du Sud. 38606

Voyages dans les cinq parties du monde. 52092, note after 100836

Voyages dans les colonies du melieu de l'Amerique-Septentrionale. 4254

Voyages dans les colonies du milieu de l'Ameri-que Septentrionale. 9360

Voyages dans les countrees desertes de l'Ameri-que du Nord. 35131

Voyages dans les deux oceans. 19429

Voyages dans les glaces du pole Arctique. 31601

Voyages dans les mers du Sud et dans l'Oceanie. 19534

Voyages dans les parties interieures de l'Ameri-que. 1368, 100835

Voyages dans les regions Arctiques. (2614)

Voyages dnas les solitudes Americaines. 20556

Voyages dans l'interieur de la Louisiane. 72031, (72039)

Voyages dans l'interieur de l'Aemrique Septen-trionale. 43416

Voyages . . . dans l'Ocean Pacifique. 55134

Voyages de Americ Vespuce. 2493A

Voyages de Coreal. 4937A

Voyages de decouverte au Canada. 10620, 67020

Voyages de decouverte en Canada entre les annees 1534 et 1542. 11143

Voyages de Francois Coreal. 16781, 67554

Voyages de la Chine a la Cote du nord-ouest d'Amerique. 47262

Voyages de la Novvelle France Occidentale. 7652, 11839-11840

Voyages de La Perouse autour du monde. 5838

Voyages de l'empereur de la Chine. 98928

Voyages de Lionnel Waffer. 100944

Voyages de Magellan. 5839

Voyages de Marco Polo. 68334

Voyages de M. le Marquis de Chastellux. 8019, 12225, 12227, 100809

Voyages de Sieur de Champlain. 11841

Voyages des Capitaines Lewis et Clarke. 26742

Voyages des flottes de Salomon et d'Hiram en Amerique. (57353)

Voyages des premiers navigateurs au Nouveau-Monde. 10296

Voyages des premiers navigateurs dans le Nouveau Monde. (10287)

Voyages, distresses, and wonderful adventures of Captain Winterfield. Containing a genuine succinct account. 104836

Voyages, distresses, and adventures of Capt. Winterfield. Written by himself. 104837

Voyages du Baron la Hontan. 38637

Voyages du Barron de la Hontan dans l'Ameri-que Septentrionale. 38641

Voyages du Capitaine Cook dans la Mer du Sud. 100836

Voyages du Capitaine Robert Lade. (38530), 65412

Voyages du Lieutenant Henri Timberlake. 95837

Voyages du Sr de Champlain Capitaine Ordin-aire. 11838

Voyages dv Sievr de Champlain Xaintongeois. (11835)

Voyages d'un etudiant dans les cinq parties du monde. 52092, note after 100836

Voyages d'un naturaliste. (19695)

Voyages d'un philosophe. (63716)-63719, note after 100837

Voyages en Afrique, Asie, Indes Orientales et Occidentales. 49790

"Voyages en Amerique." 42989

Voyages en Amerique, en France, et en Italie. 12272

Voyages en Amerique et en Italie. 12262

Voyages en Amerique; par Christophe Colomb. 50115

Voyages en Amerique . . . . Par M. de Chateau-briand. 12273

Voyages en Asie, en Afrique, & en Amerique. 73492, 100838

Vue de la Riviere de Patowmac. 102544
Vue des Cordilleres. (33751)
Vue pittoresque de la Jamaique. 4249
Vuelos de la Paloma. 72522
Vuenherus, Adam. 69122, 69124
Vues de la colonie Espagnole du Mississippi.
  4963
Vues des Cordilleres et les monumens des
  peuples indigenes de l'Amerique. (33752)
Vues des Cordilleres, et monumens des peuples
  indigenes de l'Amerique. 33750, (33754)
Vues des terres. 104505
Vues et paysages des regions equinoxiales.
  12885
Vues et observations politiques. 72987, 4th note
  after 100802
Vues et scenes. 11411
Vues et souvenirs de l'Amerique du Nord.
  11412
Vues generales sur les moyens de concilier
  l'interet. 95295
Vues historiques. 98838
Vues pittoresques de l'Amerique. 93915
Vues politiques. 68741
Vueyer, Hieronymus. 71582
Vulcan's peak. 16426
Vulgar error. 102394
Vulgarity of treason. 22113
Vulkane der Republik Mexiko. 62798
Vy fluctus fluctum. 62743
Vyage abowte the worlde. 1561
Vyerighe Colom. 14548
Vyner, -------. 9257
Vyse, William. 100860

W

W. pseud. Battle of Lepanto. 100861
W. pseud. Consise statement of the awful
  conflagration. 100862
W. pseud. National finances. see Walley,
  Samuel Hurd.
W. pseud. Notice sur la province de Texas.
  see Warden, David Baillie, 1778-1845.
W. pseud. Owl Creek letters. see Prime,
  W. C.
W***. pseud. Selections from Les recherches
  philosophiques. see Webb, Daniel, 1719-
  1798.
W —lk—r, --------. pseud. [Speech.] 88185
W. pseud. Tribute of respect to the memory
  of Mrs. Eliza Crocker. see Whitridge,
  Joshua Barker.
W——, A——. pseud. reporter 104518
W*****, A***. pseud. reporter 104519
W., A. pseud. [Letters to Hamilton.] see
  Wilkins, Isaac.
W., A., Farmer. pseud. Congress canvassed.
  see Seabury, Samuel, Bp., 1729-1796.
  and Wilkins, Isaac.
W., A., Farmer. pseud. Free thoughts. see
  Seabury, Samuel, 1729-1796. and Wilkins,
  Isaac.
W., A., Farmer. pseud. View of the controversy.
  see Seabury, Samuel, 1729-1796. and
  Wilkins, Isaac. and Cooper, Myles.
  incorrectly supposed author Chandler,
  Thomas Bradbury. incorrectly supposed
  author Inglis, Charles, Bishop of Nova
  Scotia, 1734-1816. incorrectly supposed
  author
W., A. J. pseud. tr. 94576
W., B. pseud. To the courteous reader.
  73577

W., C. pseud. Two years journal in New-York.
  see Wooley, Charles.
W., C. H. pseud. Elegy. see Wharton,
  Charles Henry.
W., C. K. pseud. American Tract Society,
  Boston. see Whipple, Charles King.
W., C. L. pseud. tr. 74166
W., D. pseud. Poetical nosegay. 100863
W., E. pseud. Certain errors in navigation.
  see Wright, Edward.
W., E. pseud. Good newes from New England.
  see Winslow, Edward.
W., E. pseud. Interesting detail. see Eaton,
  William.
W., E. pseud. Little selection. see MacNe-
  mar, Richard.
W., E. pseud. New-England's present suffer-
  ings. see Wharton, Edward.
W., E. pseud. Series of lectures. see Mac-
  Nemar, Richard.
W., E., Gent. pseud. Virginia. see Williams,
  Edward, fl. 1650.
W., E. A. pseud. Our first year of army life.
  see Walker, Edward Ashley.
W., E. B. V. pseud. ed. 86943
W., E. T. pseud. Biography of Mr. Edwin
  Forrest. (25106)
W., Ernest. pseud. tr. 35143
W., F. H. pseud. Envoy. see McDougall,
  Frances Harriet (Whipple) Greene.
W., G. pseud. tr. 12254
W., G. pseud. Antidote against the venome.
  see Whitehead, George. 1636?-1723.
W., G. pseud. Cvres of the diseased. see
  Wateson, George. supposed author and
  Whetstone, George. supposed author
W., G. pseud. To the Tabernacle congregation.
  see Whitefield, George, 1714-1770.
W., G. C. pseud. Geneenzaame leerwyze.
  see Weygandt, G. C.
W., G. S. von. tr. (67932)
W., H. pseud. Elegiac ode. see Wheaton,
  Hannah.
W., H. pseud. Poem, descriptive of the
  terrible fire. 100864
W., H. pseud. Proposals for traffick and
  commerce. 66039
W., H. pseud. Retrospect. see Whiting,
  Henry.
W., I. H. pseud. Dartmoor massacre. see
  Waddell, John Hunter.
W., I. L. pseud. Hispanicae dominationis
  Arcana. see Weidner, Johann Leonhard.
W., I. P. pseud. Sketch of the life and pro-
  jects of John Law. see Wood, John
  Philip.
W., J. pseud. Address to the freeholders of
  New Jersey. 53055
W*******, J***. pseud. Baseness and perni-
  ciousness. see Winthrop, John, 1714-
  1779. supposed author
W., J. pseud. Catalogue of Friends books.
  see Whiting, John, 1656-1722.
W., J. pseud. Churches quarrel espoused.
  see Wise, John.
W., J. pseud. Copy of a letter. see Wads-
  worth, James.
W., J. pseud. Farewell to Pittsburgh and the
  mountains. 100865
W., J. pseud. Judicious observation. see
  Wiswall, Ichabod.
W., J. pseud. Letter from a gentleman in
  Nova-Scotia. 100866
W., J. pseud. Letter from New England.
  see Ward, Edward, 1667-1731.

W******

W*****, J****. pseud. Meditations on the incomprehensibility of God. see Wolcott, Josiah. supposed author

W., J. pseud. Mode of elections considered. 100867

W*********, J***. pseud. Narrative. see Williamson, John, d. 1840.

W., J. pseud. On the memory of Mr. Robert Rich. 70893

W., J. pseud. Supplement. see Wyeth, Joseph.

W., J. A. pseud. Hessische Officier in Amerika. 100879

W., J. G. pseud. ed. Letters from John Quincy Adams. see Whittier, John Greenleaf, 1807-1892.

W., J. H. pseud. Dartmoor massacre. see Waddell, John Hunter.

W., J. H. pseud. Preface. see H., W. J. pseud.

W., J. O. pseud. comp. Catalogue of Mr. J. H. V. Arnold's library. 50876

W., J. R. pseud. Interesting sketch. see Willson, James Renwrick, 1780-1853.

W., M. pseud. Our navy. see Woodhull, Maxwell.

W., N. pseud. Almanach. see Whittemore, N.

W., N. G. pseud. tr. see Wolf, N. G. tr.

W., R. pseud. Answer to a letter sent from Mr. Coddington. see Williams, Roger, 1604?-1683.

W., R. pseud. Fourth paper. see Williams Roger, 1604?-1683.

W., R. pseud. George Fox digg'd out of his burrovves. see Williams, Roger, 1604?-1683.

W., R. pseud. Manvdiction for Mr. Robinson. see Ames, William.

W., R. pseud. Names of some. see Whitbourne, Sir Richard.

W., R. H. pseud. see Wilde, R. H.

W., S. pseud. Sketch of the life of Lorenzo da Ponte. 64013

W., S. pseud. Some particulars. see Wheeler, Sarah.

W., S. pseud. Wonderful appearance of an angel, devil & ghost. 105002

W., T. pseud. Letter to a friend. see Chauncy, Charles, 1705-1787. and Walker, Timothy. supposed author

W., T. pseud. Salvation for all men. see Chauncy, Charles, 1705-1787.

W., T. pseud. Second letter to a friend. see Chauncy, Charles, 1705-1787. and Walker, Timothy. supposed author

W., T. pseud. Truth further defended. 103939

W., T. pseud. Two letters to a friend. see Chauncy, Charles, 1705-1787. and Walker, Timothy. supposed author

W., T. J. pseud. Drama. 100871

W., T. L. C. pseud. Lower-Canada watchman. see Chisholme, David.

W., W. Gent. pseud. tr. see Wright, William, fl. 1619. tr.

W., W. pseud. Aduise concerning the philosophy of these late discoueryes. see Watts, William.

W., W. pseud. Prophetic controversy. see Watson, Wingfield.

W., W. pseud. Some meditations. see Winthrop, Wait Still.

W., W. A. pseud. Poems by a priest. 63603

W., W. H. pseud. Genealogy of the Norton family. see Whitmore, William Henry.

W., W. J. D. pseud. Report of the late Bishop of Qeubec's Upper Canadian Mission Fund. see Waddilove, William James Darley.

W., Z. pseud. Melancholy case of Mrs. Ackerman. 100873

W., A., a minister in Virginia. pseud. see A., W., a minister in Virginia. pseud.

W. A. W. pseud. see W., W. A. pseud.

W. B. pseud. see B., W. pseud.

W. B. pseud. see Bingham, William.

W. B. Pseud. see Bradford, William.

W. B. pseud. see Broedleth, Wilhelm.

W. B. pseud. see Burroughs, W.

W. B. B. pseud. see Buchanan, W. B.

W. B. C. pseud. see Crafton, William Bell.

W. C. pseud. see C., W. pseud.

W. C. pseud. see Castell, William. supposed author

W. C. pseud. see Courten, Sir William. supposed author

W. C. pseud. see Crane, William.

W. D. pseud. see D., W. pseud.

W. D. pseud. see Douglass, William, d. 1752.

W. D. pseud. see Duane, William.

W. D. pseud. see Williamson, Hugh.

W. D. B. pseud. see Bickham, William D.

W. D. G. pseud. see Gallagher, William D.

W. D. H. pseud. see H., W. D. pseud.

W. E. pseud. see Wharton, Edward.

W. E. Forster's speech on the "slaveholder's rebellion." 82683

W. F. F. pseud. see F., W. F. pseud.

W. G. pseud. see G., W. pseud.

W. G. pseud. see Gauntley, William.

W. H. pseud. see Hodgson, William.

W. H. pseud. see Hornsnell, William.

W. H. M. B. pseud. tr. see B., W. H. M. pseud. tr.

W. H. S. pseud. see Smith, William Henry, d. 1860.

W. H. W. pseud. see Whitmore, William Henry.

W. J. pseud. see J., W. pseud.

W. H. pseud. see Jordan, W.

W. J. against J. W. 35331

W. J. D. W. pseud. see Waddilove, William James Darley.

W. J. H. pseud. see H., W. J. pseud.

W. K. pseud. see Kingsford, William.

W. L. pseud. see Loddington, William.

W. L. I. Easter Fair, 1875. 88105-88106, 88110

W. M. pseud. see M., W. pseud.

W. M. pseud. see Masters, William.

W. M. a witness for the truth. pseud. see Mather, W.

W. N. pseud. see N., W., of the Middle-Temple. pseud.

W. P. pseud. see P., W. pseud.

W. P. pseud. see Penn, William, 1644-1718.

W. P. pseud. tr. see Phillip, William. tr.

W. P. psued. see Pitkin, William. supposed author

W. P. a protestant. pseud. see Penn, William, 1644-1718.

W. R. pseud. see R., W. pseud.

W. R. pseud. see Rathband, William.

W. R. pseud. see Richmond, William.

W. R. pseud. see Robinson, William.

W. R. pseud. see Roscoe, William.

W. R. his testimony to his call to that service 72199

W. S. pseud. see S., W. pseud.

Waikna. 90002
Wailes, L. C. 49540
Wailly, Leon de. tr. (31792), 92536, 92546
Wain, Nicholas. 66737
Wainwright, Jonathan Mayhew, Bp., 1792-
1854. 39199, 64678, 99815, 100964-
100968
Wainwright, Jonathan Mayhew, Bp., 1792-1854.
supposed author (15980), note after
100964
Wait, Mrs. B. 100969
Wait, Benjamin. 100969
Wait, T. G. 601, 41956
Wait (Thomas B.) and Sons. firm publishers
90636-90638
Waite, Eliza. 100970
Waite, John. 100971
Waite, Josiah K. 100972
Waiting on God. 174
Wakantanka ti ki canku. 67994
Wake, Baldwin. 100973
Wake, Sir William. (15052)
Wake Forest College, Wake Forest, N. C.
100974-100975
Wake Forest College, Wake Forest, N. C.
Charter. 100974
Wake Forest Institute. see Wake Forest
College, Wake Forest, N. C.
Wakefield, Edward Gibbon. 82304
Wakefield, Edward Gibbon. supposed author
14036, 100976
Wakefield, Gilbert. 34108, 100977
Wakefield, Horace P. petitioner (32988)
Wakefield, John Allan. 100978
Wakefield, Priscella (Bell) 100979-100984
Wakefield, Ala. Meeting of the Inhabitants of
Washington County. see Washington
County, Ala. Citizens.
Wakefield, Mass. 58710
Wakefield's history of the Black Hawk war.
100978
Wakeley, Joseph B. (6115)
Wakely, Charles. defendant 100985
Wakeman, George. 49433
Wakeman, Samuel. 100986-100987
Wakeman, Thaddeus B. 100988
Waking dreams of a foreigner during the five
years of his probation. 9491
Wakondah; the master of life. 46840
Walaeus, Ant. 72110
Walch, Johann Georg. 100989
Walchersche Robinson. 72238
Walckenaer, Charles Athanase, Baron. 2541-
(2544), 36434, 52105, 76838, 84560, 100990,
106394 see also Societe de Geographie,
Paris. Commission Speciale.
Walcot, James. 100991-100992
Walcott, Charles Doolittle. 84997 see also
Smithsonian Institution. Secretary.
Walcott, Eliza. incorrectly supposed author
100993, 104981
Walcott, R. F. see Wallcut, Robert Folger.
Walcott, Samuel Baker. 46054, 46150
Walcott, Sarah G. incorrectly supposed author
100993, 104981
Walcott, William. 28337, 86895
Walcutt, Robert Folger. 88363, 89507, 1st note
after 100993
Walde-Warren. (4724)
Waldeck, Frederico. see Waldeck, Jean Fred-
eric Maximilien, Comte de.
Waldeck, Jean Frederic Maximilien, Comte de.
7434-7435, 15196, (34151), 71446, 85781,
100994
Walden, Isaac. 100995

Walden, Jacob T. defendant 100996
Walden, Jacob T. respondent 100997
Walden, P. E. 15248
Walden, Thomas. defendant 100996
Walden, Thomas. respondent 100997
Walden, Thomas Howard, 1st Baron Howard
de. see Suffolk, Thomas Howard, 1st
Earl of, 1561-1626.
Walden. 11929
Walden spring. 11929
Walderande, J. B. de. tr. 98208, note after
101026
Waldesbraut. (4724)
Waldganger. 4536
Waldie (Adam) firm publishers (29722),
40821, (44696), 48984, 61788, 71041,
73381, 77097, 82983, 82987, 96381,
97401, 99419, 100998
Waldie's Circulating library. see Waldie's
Select circulating library.
Waldie's library. 48984
Waldie's port folio and companion to the Select
circulating library. 61788, 82983
Waldie's Select circulating library. (29722),
40821, (44696), 71041, 73381, 77097,
82987, 96381, 97401, 99419, 100998
Waldimar, a tragedy. (2736)
Waldlaufer. 4539
Waldleben in Amerika. 5203
Waldo, Alibgence. 100999, 103763
Waldo, Daniel. 100000, 105401, 105406
Waldo, David. 105406
Waldo, Francis W. reporter 24, 44902-44903,
96807, 1st-2d notes after 101000
Waldo, Loren Pinckney, 1802-1881. 15763,
15778
Waldo, S. supposed author (40748)
Waldo, Samuel, 1696-1759 101001, 101003-
101005
Waldo, Samuel, 1696-1759. appellant 101002
Waldo, Samuel, 1696-1759. supposed author
(40748)
Waldo, Samuel Putnam, 1780-1826. 31054,
74171, 96830, 101006-101012
Waldo County, Maine. Bar. 101013
Waldron, Henry. 101015
Waldseemuller, Martin, 1470-1521? 910,
1740-(1741), 1743, 1746, (66478), 66481,
69126, 77803, 77804, 91866, 99354-99356,
99358, 99368-99369, 99379-99380, note
after 99383C, 101017-101026
Waldspinne. 74167
Waldteufel. 5555
Wales, Ebenezer. 101027
Wales, Samuel. 101028
Wales, T. E. (9338)
Wales, William. 25128, 101029-101031
Wales, Mass. 26610
Walford, Edward. (47791)
Walk from sea to sea by the southern route.
64804
Walk of the upright, with its comfort. (46806)
Walk through Fifth Avenue. 40115
Walk with God characterized. (46340)
Walkenaer, Charles Athanaes, Baron. see
Walckenaer, Charles Athanase, Baron.
Walker, -------, fl. 1779. 87696, note before
91395, 91428
Walker, -------. illus. (19919)
Walker, Adam. 101032
Walker, Alexander. 101033-101034
Walker, Amasa. 101035-101036
Walker, Ambrose. supposed author 31760,
note after 101036
Walker, B. ed. (36557)
Walker, C. engr. 85346

Walton, Augustus Q. 51552, note after 91708, 101209
Walton, Daniel. 101210
Walton, George. alias see Allen, James. defendant
Walton, George. of Ontario, Canada 101212-101213
Walton, George, 1740-1804. 101211
Walton, Isaac. 71906
Walton, John, 1694-1764. 13350, 101215-101218
Walton, Joseph S. ed. 95396
Walton, William, 1740-1824. 27348, 42165, note before 101219-101219
Walton, William, 1784-1857. 1446, 1473, 7646, 101220-101228
Walton, William, 1784-1857. supposed author 9024, note after 101223
Walton, William Claiborne. 101229
Walton (E. P. & G. S.) firm publishers 95555, 101230
Walton (G. S.) firm publishers see Walton (E. P. & G. S.) firm publishers
Walton's register. 101230
Walton's Vermont register. 95555
Walton's Vermont register and almanac. 101230
Waltzemuller, Martin. see Waldseemuller, Martin, 1470-1521 ?
Walum-olum. 89965
Walvischvangst, met veele byzonderheden daartoe betrekkelyk. 101231
Walvischvangt. 55284
Walwille, Frau von. see Wallwille, Maria (Owliam) Grafin von. pseud.
Walworth, Reuben H. 95273-95276
Wame ketoohomae uketoohomaaongash David. 22157
Wame ketoohamae uketoohomaongash David. (22165), note before 101232
Wan teladeget? 76675
Wanderbilder aus Central-Amerika. (31242)
Wanderbuch eines Ingenieurs. 23569
Wanderbuchlein nach Nordamerika. 6461
Wanderer. pseud. At home in the wilderness. see Lord, John Keast.
Wanderer. pseud. Journal of a wanderer. (36698)
Wanderer. pseud. Narraganset chief. see Peirce, I.
Wanderer (Schooner) 1480
Wanderer. 101232
Wanderer: a poem. 33156
Wanderer, a rambling poem. 68635, 68644, 101234
Wanderer in America. 104611
Wanderer in Jamaica. A poem. 102169
Wanderer in Washington. 102170
Wanderer, or Horatio and Laetitia: a poem. 101235
Wanderer. Trenton Falls. 96778, 101233
Wanderers. 93220
Wandering guerilla. (13858)
Wandering Jew. pseud. Thoughts on shaving. 95684
Wahdering Jew's advice to Bank Directors. 95684
Wandering philanthropist. 25304, 1st note after 101235
Wandering recollections of a somewhat busy life. 52160
Wandering sketches of people and things in South America. 105083
Wandering sybil. 101318
Wandering Will's adventures in South America. 42136
Wanderings and death of Father Rawle. 37949

Wanderings and fortunes of some German emigrants. 27176
Wanderings in Europe, and in the orient. (17271)
Wanderings in Peru, Chili, and Polynesia. 104892-104893
Wanderings in some of the western republics of America. 9699
Wanderings in South America. 84305-84306, 84309, 84313, 84316-84317
Wanderings in South America, the north-west of the United States. 102094
Wanderings north and south. 6180
Wanderings of a travelling merchant. 72133
Wanderings of an artist. 37007
Wanderings of William. 101236
Wanderings round Lake Superior. 38215
Wanderung in den Prairien. 35144
Wanderungen durch Chile und Peru. 9701
Wanderungen durch die mittel-Amerikanischen Freistaaten. 77624
Wanderungen durch die Prairien und Westen des westlichen Nordamerika. 49916
Wanderungen durch Portugal, Spanien und Nord-Amerika. (42157), note after 101236
Wanderungen durch Prairien und das Nordliche Mexico. 28716
Wanderungen durch Sudamerikanische Republiken. 9700
Wanderungen durch Texas. 57245
Wanderungen eines Heimathlosen in Nord Amerika. 100954
Wanderungen eines Jungen Norddeutschen durch Portugal. 42157
Wanderungen in Peru, Chili und Polynesien. 104891
Wanderungen . . . unter den Indianern Nord-amerika's. 37008
Wanderungen zwischer Hudson und Mississippi. 9520
Wandesforde, J. B. illus. 85162
Wandlende Seel. 77470
Wangenheim, Friedrich Adam Julius von. 101237-101238
Wanhoopige Britten. 101239
Wanley Penson; or, the melancholy man. 92345
Wanmdiduta kaga. 63996
Wanneer zullen onze West Indische slaven vrij worden? 20520
Wanostrocht, N. ed. (44652)
Wansey, Henry. 43808, 1 01240-101242
Wanskaps och handels tractat. 100931
Wansley, Thomas J. defendent 101243
Want of patronage the principle cause of the slow progress. 35816
Want of universality no just objection to the truth. 19581
Wante, Charles Etienne Pierre. 101244-101245
Wante, Charles Etienne Pierre. supposed author 42895, 101246
Wanted, a male cook. 90153
Wanted, a number of hands to cut wood. 101247
Wanted by the barrack-master, a number of wood-cutters. 101248
Wanton, Enrico. pseud. Viages. see Seriman, Zaccaria.
Wanton, Enrico. pseud. Viaggi. see Seri-man, Zaccaria.
Wanton, John. 30081
Wanton, Joseph. 95980, 1 01252-101253
Wanton, William. 101254
Wanton wife. 101255
Waping Indians. Treaties, etc. 60255
Wapinger Indians. see Wappinger Indians.

Wappaus, J. E. ed. 19436, 91197
Wappinger Indians. 49348
Wappinger Indians. defendants 26969, 101256
War a necessary evil. 18164
War, a poem, in three parts. 102253
War a revolutionary agent. (16217)
War a school of surgery. 84276
War against the Gospel by its friends. 5529
War against the New England Female Medical
    College. 28745
War: an heroic poem. 14110-14111, 101257
War an occasion for thanksgiving. 10846
War and Christianity; an address before the
    American Peace Society. (17138)
War and Christianity irreconcilable. 25250
War and emancipation. 4324
War, and how to end it. 82179
War, and its cause. (79949)
War and its close. 20526
War and its lessons. (33845)
War, and its moral: a Canadian chronicle.
    14190, 92649
War and its remedies. 4262
War and peace. 34929
War and peace: the evils of the first, and a
    plan for preserving the last. 35867
War and peace with America. 3659
War and slavery; and their relations to each
    other. 3680
War and the Christian Commission. 17651
War: and the duty of a loyal people. 19041
War and the workers. 84489
War and Washington. A song. 101259
War as it is, and the war as it should be.
    101260
War-atlas. 10858
War begun. 31262
War. Being a faithful record of the transactions
    of the war. 101258
War between Spain and England. 66686
War between the United States and Mexico
    illustrated. 37362
War-chess, or the game of battle. (70989)
War claimant's guide. 67435
War commenced by the rebels. 19296
War contrary to the Gospel. 37291
War declared against Great Britain. 101261
War expenses. [By Albert Gallatin.] 26399
War expenses of Washington and Oregon Terri-
    tories. 91532
War for the union; a lecture by Wendell Phillips.
    62528
War for the union. By William Swinton. 94085
War for the union, or the rights of the republic.
    (26540)
War for the unity, and life of the American
    nation. 15893
War Hawk (Ship) in Admiralty 101262
War hoop. 101263
War in America. A sermon. By Rev. H. R.
    Bromwell. 8223
War in America. A sermon preached August
    18, 1861. 7374
War in America: being an historical and political
    account of the southern and northern states.
    77499, 79685
War in America. 1863-64. 63880
War in Arkansas. 19465
War in disguise. 8514, 1 8487, 50827, 67839,
    note before 91236, 91240-91241, 91246-
    91247, 101270
War in Florida. 64673, 2d note after 101263
War in Heaven. 31679
War in Kansas. 77 65
War in New-England, visibly ended. (40436),
    101454

War in Texas. 95134
War in the light of divine providence. 51703
War in the River Plate in 1865. 39004
War in the United States. 39661
War in the west. 21925
War inconsistent with the doctrine and example
    of Jesus Christ. (78297)
War inconsistent with the religion of Jesus
    Christ. 20495, 101264
War is lawful, and arms are to be proved.
    46807
War: its cause and cure. (18898)
War, its causes and consequences. 23881
War, its causes and the remedy. 43658
War, its evils and their compensations. 11082
War; its necessity. 26323
War: its origin. (56388)
War-lyrics and other poems. 8688
War lyrics. By W. A. Devon. 19826
War meeting. (2941)
War must be prosecuted with more vigot.
    29296
War necessary, just and beneficial. 9235
War not for emancipation or confiscation.
    18818
War of 1861. (26021)
War of 1812. First series. 71045
War of independence. (42134)
War of Ormuzd and Ahriman in the nineteenth
    century. 18829, 18833
War of posts. 104302
War of races. 27444
War of secession. 5831
War of slavery upon the constitution. 20817
War of the gauges. 22738, 82146
War of the giants. 101265
War of the gulls. 33647, 101507
War of the rebellion. 25020
War of the South vindicated. 85339
War Office, Williamsburg, November 11,
    1779. 100409
War on Texas by Henry Clay and by Mexico.
    95128
War on the Bank of the United States. 28003,
    1st note after 101265
War, or no war? 42755, 2d note after 101265
War path. 36533, (36535)
War pictures. Experiences and observations
    of a chaplain. 72702
War pictures from the south. 23075
War poems. (18168)
War poetry of the south. 81274
War power of the President. 31234
War power outside the constitution. (10998)
War powers of Congress, and of the President.
    (58703)
War powers of the general government. 11065
War Premium Claimants. petitioners 89570-
    89571
War record of the State of Illinois. 34306
War sermon preached by him [i. e. H. D.
    Walker] in September, 1864. 7960
War-songs and ballads from the Old Testment.
    63453
War. Speech of Hon. E. C. Benedict. (4656)
War. Speech of Hon. William Sawyer, of Ohio.
    (77327)
War spirit of the present day is Antichrist.
    19141
War system of the commonwealth of nations.
    93687
War, temporal and spiritual, considered.
    101266
War the duty and destiny of the nation. 32458
War; the great crime of our civilization.
    36670

War the only means of preserving our nationality. (3698)

War, the work of the Lord, and the coward cursed. 104674-104675

War to end only when the rebellion ceases. 4575

War trail; or, the hunt of the wild horse. 69079

War! United States, Mexico, Japan. 84489

War unreasonable and unscriptural. 105752

War with Algiers, and the treaty of peace. 18875

War with Amalek! (22089)

War with America. (17529), 101267

War with England. 101268

War with Mexico. A sermon preached in the North Church, Portsmouth, N. H. 13365

War with Mexico. By Justin H. Smith. 83472

War with Mexico. By R. S. Ripley. 71530

War with Mexico reviewed. 41558

War with Mexico. Speech . . . in the House . . . February 2, 1848. 13843

War with Mexico. Speech . . . in the Senate . . . January 26, 1848. 20341

War with Mexico. Speech of Hon. F. P. Stanton. 90427

War with Mexico. Speech of Hon. Isaac E. Morse. 50919

War with Mexico. Speech . . . Senate, 1848. 36221

War with the devil. (37125), note after 101268

War with the Indians—address to the reader. 52445

War with the monopoly. 53096

War without disguise; or, brief considerations on the political and commercial relations. 101269

War without disguise; or, the frauds of neutral commerce. 101270

War without hope. 42455, note after 105966

Warachtich cort bericht vanden handel ende zeden der Tuppin Imbas. 90040

Warachtige historie ende beschrivinge eens lants in America ghelegen. 90040

Warachtighe ende grondige beschryvinghe van het groot en gout-rijck coningrijck van Guiana. 37690, 97597

Warachtighe ende grondighe beschryvinghe van het groot en gout-rijck coningrijck van Guiana. 37689, 67596

Warachtighe ende seer verschrickelijcke geschiendenisse. 101271

Warachtighe historie ende beschriivinghe eens lants in America gelegen. 90041

Warberten, Sir Peter. see Warburton, Sir Peter, 1540?-1621.

Warbler. 101272

Warburg, Daniel. 101273

Warburton, A. F. reporter 82452, 97630

Warburton, Bartholomew Elliott George. ed. 101275

Warburton, George Brought, 1816-1857. 84779, 101274-101275

Warburton, Sir Peter, 1540?-1621. 67545

Warburton, William, Bishop of Gloucester, 1698-1779. (4670), (17674), 101276, 101287, 103574

Ward, --------. plaintiff (31825)

Ward, Andrew. supposed author 97570

Ward, Andrew Henshaw. 101277-101278

Ward, Artemas. 101279-101280

Ward, Artemus. pseud. Artemus Ward among the Mormons. see Browne, Charles Farrar, 1834-1867.

Ward, Artemus. pseud. Artemus Ward; his book. see Browne, Charles Farrar, 1834-1867.

Ward, Artemus. pseud. Artemus Ward; his travels. see Browne, Charles Farrar, 1834-1867.

Ward, Artemus. pseud. Artemus Ward (his travels) among the mormons. see Browne, Charles Farrar, 1834-1867.

Ward, Berkeley. 101281

Ward, Bernardo. 101282

Ward, D. S. 101283

Ward, Dana. ed. (45495)

Ward, E. C. 101286

Ward, Edward, 1667-1731. (8571), 52641, note after 100866, 101285-101286

Ward, Emily Elizabeth Swinburne, Lady. illus. 101287-101288

Ward, Ephraim. 101289-101290

Ward, Ferdinand De Wilton. 101291

Ward, Francis. 101292-101293

Ward, G. 101294

Ward, Gamaliel H. defendant 101295

Ward, George Atkinson. 18075-18077, 101296

Ward, Mrs. H. 101293

Ward, H. D. supposed author 63602

Ward, Mrs. H. G. see Ward, Emily Elizabeth Swinburne, Lady.

Ward, Henry. 101297

Ward, Henry Dana, 1797-1884. 45495, 45501, 101298-101299

Ward, Henry George. 73892, 101300-101304

Ward, J. G. 101305

Ward, James. 101306

Ward, James Warner. 101307

Ward, James Warner. supposed author 101308, note after 106019-20 [sic]

Ward, Jasper. (53929)

Ward, John William. see Dudley, John William Ward, 1st Earl of, 1781-1833.

Ward, Jonathan, 1769-1860. 94522-94523, 101309-101314

Ward, Malthus Augustus. 101315

Ward, Marcus Lawrence, 1812-1884. 53130 see also New Jersey. Governor, 1866-1869 (Ward)

Ward, Maria. supposed author 24185, 70332, note after 101315

Ward, Matthew F. defendant (70981)

Ward, Milton. 101316

Ward, Minus. 101317

Ward, Molly. 101318

Ward, Nahum, 1785-1860. (18173), 18175, 47394, 101319-101320

Ward, Nathaniel, 1578?-1652. 7299, 19033, 22146-22147, 32778, 45652, 70082, 80207-80208, 101321-101330, note after 104653

Ward, R. 99808 see also Rhode Island (Colony) Secretary.

Ward, Samuel. 44124

Ward, Samuel, 1725-1776. 101332-101335 see also Rhode Island (Colony) Governor, 1765-1757 (Ward)

Ward, Samuel 1756-1832. 101336-101337

Ward, Samuel, 1786-1839. 101338

Ward, Samuel Dexter. 66784, 101331, 101339

Ward, Seth, Bishop of Salisbury, 1617-1689. 97551

Ward, Thomas. 70516 see also Rhode Island (Colony) Secretary.

Ward, Thomas, 1788- 101340

Ward, Thomas, 1807-1873. 50165, 101341-101342

Ward, Thomas, fl. 1845. 83155

Ward, Thomas W. 99814, note after 101342, 105364, 105439 see also Worcester County, Mass. Sheriff.
Ward, Ulysses. defendant 101343
Ward, Ulysses. plaintiff 101343
Ward, Valentine. 101344
Ward, William, Jr. 101346
Ward, William, 1769-1823. 71841, 101345
Ward. firm petitioners see Stafford & Ward. firm petitioners
Ward (Samuel) & Brothers. firm 101336-101337
Ward, Locke and Company. firm publishers 79913, 84183, 84307
Ward family. 101278
Warden, David Baillie, 1778-1845. 23795, 25173, (28728), 31623, 35379, 35722, 40010, 40038, 68443, 71995, 101347-101367
Warden, David Baillie, 1778-1845. incorrectly supposed author 5248
Warden. firm publishers (36227), (75954), note after 96890
Warden refuted. 35722, 101366
Wardenburg, Dieterich. see Waerdenburgh, Dirk van.
Warden's estimate of the affairs to the State Prison. 52939
Warden's report of the trial of James Johnson. (36227), (75954), note after 96890
Warder, W. S. 101368
Wardlaw, J. C. G. 87803
Wardlaw, Ralph. 101369, 102189
Ward's magnet. 80323
Ward's Mexico. 101302
Wards of Mount Vernon. 83567
Wardsborough, Vt. Washington Benevolent Society. see Washington Benevolent Society. Vermont. Wardsborough.
Wardwell, Joseph. 101370-101371
Wardwell, Stephen S. 101372
Ware, Arthur. 101373-101374
Ware, Asher. see Ware, Arthur.
Ware, Camilla. supposed author (82100), 3d note after 99205
Ware, Charles E. ed. (52738)
Ware, Charles Pickard. 82067
Ware, Henry, 1764-1845. 101375-101385, 105132, 105135-105136
Ware, Henry, 1794-1843. 12909, (26418), 58718, 86667, 88979, 90713, 92305, 101386-101400, 102563, 105646
Ware, John, 1795-1864. 6493, 82255, 101401-101403
Ware, Jonathan. 101404
Ware, Joseph A. (64501)
Ware, Joseph E. 101405
Ware, Nathaniel A. 55963, note after 88444A
Ware, Samuel. 101406
Ware, Thomas. 101407-101408
Ware, William, 1797-1852. 63729, 97831, 101409-101411
Ware, Mass. East Evangelical Church. 101412
Ware gedagt'nis, gelovige navolging. 73076
Ware Manufacturing Company. 101413
Ware Manufacturing Company. Charter. 101413
Ware oorsprong . . . der Jesuites. 101414
Ware Robinson. 19557
Wareham, Mass. Ex-parte Council, 1845. see Congregational Churches in Massachusetts. Ex-parte Council, Wareham, 1845.
Wareham, Mass. Social Library. see Wareham Social Library, Wareham, Mass.
Wareham Social Library, Wareham, Mass. 101415

Warehouse manual and general custom house guide. 8723
Warehousing Company of Philadelphia. 62374
Warehousing Company of Philadelphia. Charter. 62374
Wareing, Elijah. 101416
Warfield, Catherina Ann Ware. 101417
Warfield, Charles. 37866, note after 101417
Warfield, Perry S. 101418
Warfield, Susanna. 101419
Warford, A. B. 60211
Warhafft, umbstand und grundlicher Bericht. 7649, note after 101419
Warhaffte Beschreibung der wunderbarlichen Rayse vnd Schiffart. 77955
Warhaffte Beschreibung, welcher gestalt Don Antonii Armada. (76756)
Warhaffte Nachricht von einer Hochteutschen Evangelischen Colonie zu Germantown. 27160, 101420
Warfaffter Bricht. 101421
Warhafftig Historia vnnd Beschreibung. 90037
Warhafftige Beschreibung aller furnemen und gedenckwurdigen Historien. (69296)
Warhafftige Beschreibung der Newen Insl Pines genannt. 82186
Warhafftige . . . Beschreibung der vierdent Schiffahrt. (8784)
Warhafftige Beschreibung dess Niederlandischen Krieges. 48177
Warhafftige Beschreibung desz Newen Engellands. (8784), note after 99383C
Warhafftige Beschreibung aller chronick-wirdiger namhaff iger Historien und Geschichten. 36776
Warhafftige Beschreibung aller schonen Historien. 77678, 90039
Warhafftige Beschreibunge aller vnd mancherley sorgfeltigen Schiffarten. 25472, 77677, 90039
Warhafftige Contrafacturen. (8784)
Warhafftige Contrafrey einer wilden Frawen. 101422
Warhafftige Historia vnnd Beschrebung einer Landtschaft der Wilden. 90039
Warhafftige Historia von Erfindung Calecut. 11390
Warhafftige Historien einer wunderbaren Schiffart. 33656, (67562), 77680-77682
Warhafftige Relation. 33655
Warhafftige und eygentliche Beschreibung der Langwierigen. (8784)
Warhafftige vnd grundtliche Historia desz Zugs, 101423
Warhafftige vnd liebliche Beschreibung. (8784), 25472, 77677-77678, 90039
Warhafftiger Bericht. (18220)
Warhafftiger vnd grundtlicher Bericht. 11278
Warhafftiger vnd Zuvor nie erhorter Bericht. 33668
Warhaftig Historia vnd Beschreibung. 90036, 105680
Warhaftige Beschreibung aller und mancherley sorgfeltigen Schiffarten. 25472, 77677
Warhaftige vn grundliche Beschreibung. 76764
Warhaftige Vorweisung desz Lebens. 72603
Warin, Jean Regnault. see Regnault-Warin, Jean.
Waring, Ann (Cromwell) 101424
Waring, E. supposed author 59713
Waring, Horatio S. 87889
Waring, James J. 77263, 101427
Waring, Noell E. 106370
Waring, Stephen. plaintiff 101425
Waring, William. 53165, 101426
Waring, William R. 101427

WARLAND

Warland, J. H. (70831)
Warland, William. 101428
Warley, Felix B. 101429
Warm as yourselves in the glorious cause of liberty. 102870
Warm hearts in cold regions. 21821
Warne, Jonathan. 101430-101431
Warner, -------. plaintiff 36136
Warner, Aaron. 101432
Warner, Anna Bartlett. 101433
Warner, Ashton. 101433A
Warner, Daniel B., Pres. Liberia. (40928) see also Liberia. President, 1864-1868 (Warner)
Warner, Edmund. defendant 24083, note after 97149
Warner, Edward. 57977
Warner, Effingham. 101434
Warner, Effingham H. plaintiff 101435-101436
Warner, Fannie. ed. 57933
Warner, G. J. engr. 50185, 82376, 82379
Warner, George James. 101437
Warner, George Washington. 101438
Warner, Harriot W. 9893
Warner, Henry Whiting. 2879, 8291, 22642, 101439-101441
Warner, J. J. 30282 see also California. Board of State Viticulture Commissioners.
Warner, M. F. ed. 96739
Warner, Oliver. 45554, (45638), 45963, 46144 see also Massachusetts. Secretary of the Commonwealth.
Warner, Orson C. 101442
Warner, Richard. petitioner 101443
Warner, Samuel. 101444
Warner, Thomas. 101445
Warner, W. S. 83706
Warner, Walter. ed. 30376
Warnes, Jose Maria Quintana. see Quintana Warnes, Jose Maria.
Warnicke, J. G. engr. 104597-104598
Warning against Hopkinsian, and other allied errors. 101446
Warning for the crisis. 3895
Warning for tobacconists. 105468
Warning from the death. 103197
Warning, in the bonds of love. 86627, note after 104031
Warning of an old Kentuckian. 40959
Warning of God unto young people. (14525)
Warning of the Presbytery of New-Castle. 101447
Warning of the trumpet vnto ludgement [sic]. 44820
Warning of war. 15464
Warning piece. A poetical thought. 101448
Warning piece to all clergymen. 101449
Warning-piece to England. 67599
Warning to all people. 92687
Warning to the Canadian Land Company. 101450
Warning to the Democracy. 101451
Warning to the flocks against wolves in sheeps-cloathing. 46587, note after 101451
Warning to the inhabitants of Barbadoes, entitled, the voice of truth. (13373)
Warning to the inhabitants of Barbadoes, who live in pride. 73485
Warning to the inhabitants of the said province. 70292
Warning to the north. 77631
Warning to the people of the United States of America. 95300
Warning to the rulers and magistrates of Boston. 8654

Warning to them from one among them. 103197
Warning to young & old. 101452
Warning voice from a watery grave! 101453
Warning voice; or, clerical and political corruption exposed. 32749
Warning voice: or what is the object of this war? 66903
Warning voice to the cotton and tobacco planters. 10889, note after 101453
Warning words to young men. (50450)
Warnings from the dead. 46588
Warnings to the people of the United States. 50963
Warnings to the unclean. 104275
Warningen und Rathschlage der Deutschen Gesellschaft in New-York. (9676)
Warr, Thomas West, 3d Lord de la. see De la Warr, Thomas West, 3d Lord, 1577-1618.
Warr in New-England visibly ended. (50536), 101454
Warrdenau, D. de. see De Warrdenau, D.
Warre, Sir Henry James. 101455
Warre was a blessing. (78359)-78360
Warren. pseud. Antidote to John Wood's poison. see Cheetham, James.
Warren. pseud. Rights of the judiciary in a series of letters. 101456
Warren, A. C. engr. 84154
Warren, Caroline Matilda. see Thayer, Caroline Matilda (Warren)
Warren, Charles. 101459
Warren, Edward. 101460, note after 101476
Warren, George, fl. 1667. 57765, 101461-101463
Warren, George, d. 1856. 101464
Warren, George Washington. 68376, 101465
Warren, Gouveneur Kemble, 1830-1882. (47371), 69900, 69946, 85072
Warren, Henry, fl. 1739. 101466
Warren, Henry, fl. 1821. 101467
Warren, Ira. supposed author 38651, note before 96806
Warren, J. 62743
Warren, John, successively Bishop of St. Davids, and Bangor, 1730-1800. 101468
Warren, John, 1753-1815. 25798, 30507, (45498), note after 45694, 101469-101471 see also Freemasons. Massachusetts. Grand Lodge. Chairman.
Warren, John B. 101472
Warren, John Borlase, 1753-1822. 101473
Warren, John Collins. 86579, 101460, 101474-101476
Warren, Joseph, 1741-1775. 833, (7637)-6739, 6741, 8546, 30178, 32551, 45924, 80668-80673, 82976, 93430, 7th note after 97146-97147, 101477-101479 see also Boston. Committee to Prepare "A Short Narrative of the Horrid Massacre in Boston," 1770.
Warren, Joseph, 1829-1876. 17150
Warren, Leron. 3950, note after 90573
Warren, Mary. see Warren, Mercy (Otis) 1728-1814.
Warren, Mercy (Otis) 1728-1814. 2160, 5220, 56539, 101480-101487
Warren, Mercy (Otis) 1728-1814. supposed author 5945, 51110, (76703), 101481, 101485, 101487
Warren, Owen Grenliff. 74795, 101488
Warren, Robert. 83978, 101489
Warren, Thomas. 101490
Warren, William. defendant 32362, 96946, 96951, 2d-3d notes after 102623

Warren. firm publishers see Canfield and
Warren. firm publishers
Warren & Co. firm publishers 9968
Warren, Ohio. Convention, 1833. see Warren
Convention, 1833.
Warren, Ohio. see Convention on Connecting
the Pennsylvania and Ohio Canals, 1833.
see Convention on Connecting the Penn-
sylvania and Ohio Canals, Warren, Ohio,
1833.
Warren, Ohio. Convention on Connecting the
Pennsylvania and Ohio Canals, 1833.
Philadelphia Board of Trade Delegation.
see Philadelphia. Board of Trade.
Delegates to the Warren Convention,
Warren, Ohio, 1833.
Warren, R. I. Baptist Church. 101492
Warren, R. I. Committee on the Providence
and Bristol Railroad. see Committee
Appointed by the Citizens of Providence,
Warren and Bristol, R. I., on the Provi-
dence and Bristol Railroad.
Warren, R. I. First Baptist Church. Centennial
Celebration, 1864. 88856
Warren, R. I. Library Society. see Warren
Library Society, Warren, R. I.
Warren, R. I. Washington Lodge, No. 3. see
Freemasons. Rhode Island. Washington
Lodge, No. 3, Warren.
Warren County, N. Y. Citizens. see Meeting
of the Inhabitants of Saratoga and Warren
Counties, Cornish, N. Y., 1846.
Warren County, Ohio. 101500
Warren Anatomical Museum, Harvard University.
see Harvard University. Warren An-
atomical Museum.
Warren Association. see Baptists. Rhode
Island. Warren Association.
Warran Baptist Association. see Baptists.
Rhode Island. Warren Association.
Warren Bridge Company, Boston. see Proprie-
tors of Warren Bridge.
Warren Bridge Proprietors. see Proprietors
of Warren Bridge.
Warren Convention, 1833. 60299, 101491
Warren Convention, 1833. Philadelphia Dele-
gation. 61970
Warren County administration meeting. 101500
Warren County Railroad. Commissioners.
101501
Warren Gamaliel Harding. 82744
Warren Insurance Company. Charter. 101494
Warren Library Society, Warren, R. I. 101495
Warren Street Chapel, Boston. see Boston.
Warren Street Chapel.
Warreniana; with notes, critical and explanatory.
19011, 101502
Warrhaftiger und grundlicher Bericht. (11280)
Warriner, Francis. 101503
"Warrington." sobriquet see Robinson,
William S.
Warrington, Thomas. 101504
Warrington, Thomas. defendant 96949
"Warrington" pen-portraits. (72216)
Warrington's manual. 72217
Warrior of the west. 94578
Warriors gazetteer of places remarkable for
sieges or battles. 81142
Warriors of the Genesee. (33116)
Warriors of the west. 85411
Warrock. firm publishers 71000
Warrock's Virginia and North Carolina almanac.
71000
Warrs with forraign princes dangerous to our
common-wealth. 67599

Warry, Augustine. 101505
Wars and rumers of wars. A sermon preached
at . . . Groton, Mass. 9104
Wars, and rumors of wars, heaven's decree
over the world. 25940
Wars between England and America. 84341-
84342
Wars of America. 101506
Wars of New-England. (46641)
Wars of the gulls. 33647, 101507
Wars of the western border. 7765
Wartenberg, Dirk van. see Waerdenbergh,
Dirk van.
Warville, Anacharsis Brissot de. see
Brissot de Warville, Anacharsis.
Warville, Jean Pierre Brissot de. see
Brissot de Warville, Jean Pierre, 1754-
1793.
Warwick, Robert Dudley, Earl of. see
Dudley, Sir Robert, styled Duke of
Northumberland and Earl of Warwick,
1574-1649.
Warwick, Robert Rich, 2d Earl of. 101508
Warwick, R. I. First General Baptist Church.
101509
Warwick and Coventry Baptist Church, Cromp-
ton, R. I. see Crompton, R. I. War-
wick and Coventry Baptist Church.
Warwick Baptist Association. see Baptists.
New York. Warwick Baptist Association.
Warwijck, Wybrand van. 14957-14960, (52214)-
52215, 3d note after 100931
Was die Militair-Journale uber die Expedition
nach Mexico erzahlen. 41770
Was gestalt der schone Portus und Hafe Todos
los Sanctos. 7567, (7585), 33674
Was hat die Katholische Kirche seit der Ent-
deckung Amerikas? 44530
Was is dem Christen die Trubsal dieser Zeit?
91989
Was ist Calvinismus? 84762
Was it a pistol? A nut for lawyers. 84896
Was it an original tenet of the Church of
Jesus Christ of Latter Day Saints?
82325
Was it murder? The truth about Centralia.
84489
Was Joseph Smith a divinely inspired prophet?
80134
Was Joseph Smith sent by God? 64942
Was Man von die Erde Weiss. 4857A
Was secession a constitutional right previous
to the war of 1816? 5893
Was the formation of the San Francisco
Vigilance Committee justifiable? 103177
Wasa, Gustav. see Equiano, Olaudah.
Waschington's Abschieds Addresse an das
Volk der Vereinigten Staaten. 101672-
101673, 101676, 101682
Washchington's Abschieds Addresse an das
Volk der Vereinigten Staaten, bekannt
gemacht im September, A. D. 1796.
101670
Washashe wageressa pahugreh tse. 57737,
note after 101510
Washburn, ------. plaintiff 92333
Washburn, Andrew. (71209), 86344 see also
Soldiers' Memorial Society, Boston.
Free White Schools, Richmond. Super-
intendent.
Washburn, Azel. 101511-101512
Washburn, Charles A. (58515), 58528 see
also U. S. Legation. Paraguay.
Washburn, D. 64695
Washburn, E. H. 86010

Washburn, Emory, 1800-1877. 7827, 101513-
101520 see also Massachusetts.
Governor, 1854-1855 (Washburn)
Washburn, Ichabod. 101514
Washburn, Israel, 1813-1883. 43943 see also
Maine. Governor, 1861-1863 (Washburn)
Washburn, James. plaintiff 101521-101522
Washburn, John. defendant 101523
Washburn, P. T. (5763)
Washing and Bathing Association, New York.
see New York Washing and Bathing
Association.
Washington. pseud. Constitution of the United
States defended. 101524
Washington. pseud. Touchstone for the leading
partymen in the United States. 101525
Washington. pseud. Washington to the people
of the United States. 101526
Washington, -----, fl. 1704. ed. 81, note after
100381
Washington, Bailey. 101528
Washington, Bushrod, 1762-1829. 14732, (25961),
36543, 44788, 44791-44792, 96866, 99544,
100038, 100066, note after 101528, 101764,
101843 see also Virginia. General
Assembly. Committee to Superintend an
Edition of all Legislative Acts Concerning Lands.
Washington, George, Pres. U. S., 1732-1799.
12, (445)-449, 854, 1093, 1123, 1189,
1241, 3137, 4746-4748, 5325, 5361, 5477,
6001, note after 7269, 7754, 9257, 9672,
9837, 10663, 11071, (11731), 12114,
12230, (13318), (13744), (13897), 14010,
(14151), 14378, 14379, 15176-15178,
15205, 15517, 15601, 16060, (16121),
16126, (16141), 16180, 16814, 17365,
18005, 19066, 19175, 20623, (20989),
23989, 24886, 25040, 25173, 25876,
25980, (26320), 27140, 27496, (29967)-
(29968), 32784-32785, 33150, 33473,
34900, 36361, (38001), (39521), 39614,
39711-39712, 40343, 41601, (41650),
(43681), 45394, (47511)-(47512), 48045-
48050, 48148, 49393, 49398, (50137),
(50333), (50942), 51175, 51338, 51661,
52038, 52346, 53515, 54069, 54900,
(55169), (56044), 58231, 58234, 59107-
59108, 59593, 60418, 60778, 61204,
(61900), 63586, 63587-63588, 63786,
63795, 63811, 65343-65344, 65359, 68621,
69834, (70117), 70350, 70626-70628,
(71282), 71301, (74021), (74155), 74870,
77766, 77983-(77984), 78059, 78647,
(78703), 78997, (79403), (80023), 81394,
81857, 82974-82976, 82979, 84579, 84819,
84904, 84906, 85595, 86004, 86264,
87862, 88089, 88963, 88977-88978, 88986,
88989, 88998, 89000, 89003-89004, 89011,
89013-89014, 89198, 89200, 90291, 91396,
note after 91855, 92817, 94163, 94663,
note after 94720, 94929, 95301-note after
95301, 96583-96584, 96587, 96589, 96603-
96605, 96754, note after 96799-96800,
97202, 98041, note after 99300, 4th note
after 99800, 100007-100008, 100022,
100451, 101418, 101529-101736, 101742-
101743, 101745-101767, 101777, 101779,
101786, 101807, note after 101819, note
before 101837, 101837, 101841, note after
101843, 101846A, 101849, 101851, 101854,
note after 101860, 1st, 3d and 5th notes
after 101872, 101873, 101874, 101882,
2d note after 101883, 6th note after
101885, 4th note after 101886, 3d note

after 101888, 101899-note after 101900,
101981-101984A, 101986-101990, 101992,
101994, 1st note after 102036A, note
after 102121, 102492, 102746, 103696,
104204-104205, 104459 see also U. S.
Constitutional Convention, 1787. President. U. S. President, 1789-1797
(Washington)
Washington, George, Pres. U. S., 1732-1799.
supposed author 25293
Washington, George, Pres. U. S., 1732-1799.
mediumistic author 1081A, 38845,
101770
Washington, George, Pres. U. S., 1732-1799.
spurious author 89518, 101726, 101737-
101744, 101746
Washington, George Corbin, 1789-1854. 64591
Washington, H. A. ed. (35919)
Washington, Irwin. see Irving, Washington,
1783-1859.
Washington, John. 101906
Washington, L. reporter 101907
Washington, Martha (Dandridge) Custis, 1732-
1802. 82979
Washington, Thomas. 101908
Washington (Territory) Citizens. petitioners
91523, 2d note after 101924
Washington (Territory) Court (Third Judicial
District) 84483, 101909
Washington (Territory) Court (Third Judicial
Circuit) Bar. 101925
Washington (Territory) Court Martial. 90740,
1st note after 101925
Washington (Territory) Governor, 1853-1857
(Stevens) 69946, 90740, 91530, 101107,
101910-101911, 101918, 1st note after
101925 see also Stevens, Isaac Ingalls,
1818-1862.
Washington (Territory) Governor, 1857-1861
(McMullen) 91523, 101912-101913, 2d
note after 101924 see also McMullen,
Fayette, 1805-1880.
Washington (Territory) Indian Council, Walla
Walla, 1855. 37945
Washington (Territory) Laws, statutes, etc.
101914-101915
Washington (Territory) Legislative Assembly.
101916-101917, 101920, 101922
Washington (Territory) Legislative Assembly.
Council. 101917-101919
Washington (Territory) Militia. 101911
Washington (Territory) Secretary and Acting
Governor. 101922-101923 see also
Mason, C. H.
Washington (Territory) Secretary of State.
101915 see also Mason, C. H.
Washington (Territory) Surveyor General's
Office. 101924
Washington (Territory) University. see
Washington (State) University.
Washington (State) University. 84295
Washington, D. C. 74256-74257, (74270)-74271,
99301, 90301, 2d note after 101951
Washington, D. C. African Education Society.
see African Education Society, see
Washington, D. C.
Washington, D. C. Andrew Jackson Statue.
(35369)
Washington, D. C. Aqueduct. Engineer in
Charge. (75907) see also Samo,
Theodore B.
Washington, D. C. Association of Mechanics
and Other Working Men. see Association
of Mechanics and Other Working Men,
Washington, D. C.

Washington, D. C. Asylum. Guardians.
101963

Washington, D. C. Bank. see Bank of
Washington, D. C.

Washington, D. C. Bible Society. see
Washington Bible Society, Washington,
D. C.

Washington, D. C. Burns Club. see Burns
Club, Washington, D. C.

Washington, D. C. Capitol. 65758, 101947-
101948

Washington, D. C. Central Executive Committee
of Irish Citizens. see Central Executive
Committee of Irish Citizens, Washington,
D. C.

Washington, D. C. Citizens. 101943

Washington, D. C. Citizens. petitioners
101953

Washington, D. C. City Hall. 101928

Washington, D. C. Clerks in the Executive
Departments. petitioners see Clerks
in the Executive Departments, at Washington City. petitioners

Washington, D. C. Clerks of the Executive
Departments. petitioners see Clerks
of the Executive Departments at Washington. petitioners

Washington, D. C. Colored People's Education
Monument Association in Memory of
Abraham Lincoln. see Colored People's
Educational Monument Association in
Memory of Abraham Lincoln, Washington,
D. C.

Washington, D. C. Congressional Total Abstinence Society. see Congressional Total
Abstinence Society, Washington, D. C.

Washington, D. C. Columbia Typographical
Society. see Columbia Typograhical
Society, Washington, D. C.

Washington, D. C. Columbian College. see
George Washington University, Washington,
D. C.

Washington, D. C. Columbian Horticultural
Society. see Columbian Horticultural
Society, Washington, D. C.

Washington, D. C. Columbian Institute for the
Promotion of Arts and Sciences. see
Columbian Institute for the Promotion of
Arts and Sciences, Washington, D. C.

Washington, D. C. Common Council. Select
Committee on Colored Suffrage. 61314

Washington, D. C. Conference Convention, 1861.
see Washington, D. C. Peace Convention,
1861.

Washington, D. C. Conference on the Future of
the Smithsonian Institution, 1927. see
Conference on the Future of the Smithsonian Institution, Washington, D. C., 1927.

Washington, D. C. Congressional Temperance
Society. see Congressional Temperance
Society, Washington, D. C.

Washington, D. C. Connecticut Soldiers' Relief
Association. see Connecticut Soldiers'
Relief Association, Washington, D. C.

Washington, D. C. Criminal Court. 27003,
28227

Washington, D. C. Democratic Association.
see Democratic Association, Washington,
D. C.

Washington, D. C. Dinner for Louis Kossuth,
1852. see Dinner for Louis Kossuth,
Washington, D. C., 1852.

Washington, D. C. Dinner in Honor of the
Centennial Anniversary of Washington,
1832. see Public Dinner in Honor of
the Centennial Anniversary of Washington,
Washington, D. C., 1832.

Washington, D. C. Educational Monument
Association, to the Memory of Abraham
Lincoln. see Colored People's Educational Monument Association, in Memory
of Abraham Lincoln, Washington, D. C.

Washington, D. C. Federal Lodge, No. 15.
see Freemasons. Washington, D. C.
Federal Lodge, No. 15.

Washington, D. C. Fourth Presbyterian Church.
Sabbath School Library. 101941

Washington, D. C. Franklin Fire Company.
see Franklin Fire Company, Washington,
D. C.

Washington, D. C. Friends of African Colonization Convention, 1842. see Friends
of African Colonization. Convention,
Washington, D. C., 1842.

Washington, D. C. Gonzaga Fair, 1865. see
Gonzaga Fair, Washington, D. C., 1865.

Washington, D. C. Grand Convocation and
Supreme Grand Council of the Independent
Order of the Sons of Malta, 1860. see
Independent Order of the Sons of Malta.
U. S. Grand Convocation and Supreme
Grand Council, Washington, D. C., 1860.

Washington, D. C. Granite State Lincoln Club.
see Granite State Lincoln Club, Washington, D. C.

Washington, D. C. Howard University. see
Howard University, Washington, D. C.

Washington, D. C. Institut Francais. see
Institut Francais de Washington.

Washington, D. C. International Medical Congress, 9th, 1887. see International
Medical Congress, 9th, Washington, D. C.
1887.

Washington, D. C. Jackson Democratic Association. see Jackson Democratic
Association, Washington, D. C.

Washington, D. C. Jockey Club. see Washington Jockey Club, Washington, D. C.

Washington, D. C. Library Company. see
Washington Library Company, Washington,
D. C.

Washington, D. C. Literary, Scientific, &
Military Gymnasium. see Washington
Literary, Scientific, & Military Gymnasium,
Washington, D. C.

Washington, D. C. Loyal Pennsylvanians, 1864.
see Loyal Pennsylvanians at Washington,
1864.

Washington, D. C. Lyceum. 101960

Washington, D. C. Mayor, 1856. 20306

Washington, D. C. Meeting, 1833. 101942A

Washington, D. C. Meeting for the Promotion
of the Cause of Temperance, in the
United States, 1833. see Meeting for
the Promotion of the Cause of Temperance
in the United States, Washington, D. C.
1833.

Washington, D. C. Meeting for the Promotion
of Temperance in the United States, 1832.
see Meeting for the Promotion of Temperance in the United States, Washington,
D. C., 1832.

Washington, D. C. Meeting of Ministers of
All Religious Denominations in the
District of Columbia, 1865. see Meet-
ing of Ministers of All Religious De-
nominations in the District of Columbia,
Washington, D. C. 1865.

Washington, D. C. Tobacco Convention, 1840. see Tobacco Convention, Washington, D. C., 1840.

Washington, D. C. Trinity Church. 101954

Washington, D. C. Union Congressional Committee, 1875. see Republican Congressional Committee, 1875.

Washington, D. C. Union Fire Company. see Union Fire Company, Washington, D. C.

Washington, D. C. Unitarian Society. 101955A

Washington, D. C. White House. 41230

Washington, D. C. Young Men's Temperance Society. see Young Men's Temperance Society, Washington, D. C.

Washington, Ga. Washington Female Seminary. see Washington Female Seminary, Washington, Ga.

Washington, Miss. Jefferson College. see Jefferson College, Washington, Miss.

Washington, Miss. Lyceum. publishers 88616

Washington, N. C. Meeting of Delegates from Newburn, Washington, . . . , 1827. 101972

Washington, Pa. Meeting of Friends of the Administration, 1827. see National Republican Party. Pennsylvania. Washington, Pa.

Washington, Pa. Washington College. see Washington College, Washington, Pa.

Washington, Texas. Convention, 1836. see Texas (Republic) Convention, Washington, 1836.

Washington, Texas. General Convention, 1836. see Texas (Republic) Convention, Washington, 1836.

Washington County, Ala. Citizens. 102008

Washington County, Me. Supreme Judicial Court. 96895

Washington County, Md. College of St. James. see Saint James College, Washington County, Md.

Washington County, N. Y. Convention of Young Men, Hartford, 1830. see Antimasonic Convention of Young Men of the County of Washington, Hartford, N. Y., 1830.

Washington County, N. Y. Convention of Young Men Opposed to the Masonic Institution, 1830. see Antimasonic Convention of Young Men of the County of Washington, Hartford, N. Y., 1830.

Washington County, N. Y. Meeting of Committees from the Different Towns, 1808. 102009

Washington County, N. Y. Washington Agricultural Society. see Washington Agricultural Society, Washington County, N. Y.

Washington County, N. Y. Washington Benevolent Society. see Washington Benevolent Society. New York. Washington County.

Washington County, Oregon. Referee of Real Estate. 84764 see also Smith, William E.

Washington County, Pa. Citizens. petitioners 60499

Washington County, Pa. Collector of Excise. 28238 see also Graham, William.

Washington County, Pa. Democratic Meeting, 1808. see Democratic Party. Pennsylvania. Washington County.

Washington County, Pa. Lieutenant. 102012

Washington County, Pa. Sub Lieutenants. 102012

Washington County, Pa. Sundry Citizens. see Washington County, Pa. Citizens. petitioners

Washington County, Texas. Committee on Railroads. see Committee on Railroads in Austin and Washington Counties, Texas.

Washington County, Vt. Bar. 59488

Washington (Brig) 101527

Washington. [c. 1789] 94163, note after 101819, 3d note after 101888

Washington. [c. 179-?] 101768

Washington. [c. 1834?] 101889

Washington. [A poem.] 5361, 101777

Washington: a biography. 28901

Washington a free mason. 20706

Washington, a national poem. 9168

Washington Academy, Salem, N. Y. 63296, 101973

Washington Academy, Salem, N. Y. Theological Seminary. 63296, 101973

Washington Agricultural Society, Washington County, N. Y. 101974

Washington, Alexandria, And Georgetown Steam Packet Company. 101975

Washington, Alexandria, and Georgetown Steam Packet Company. defendants 101975

Washington, Alfred and William Tell. 1081A, 101770

Washington almanac. 84219

Washington almanack, for the year of Our Lord 1845. 84219

Washington als Prasident I. 69109

Washington and Alexandria Steamboat Company. defendants 20018

Washington and his army. 30873

Washington and his generals. By J. T. Headley. 31161

Washington and his generals; or legends of the revolution. (41399)

Washington and his masonic compeers. 31011

Washington and independence. 101890

Washington and Jacksonian class book, for Schools. 101891

Washington and Lee University, Lexington, Va. 102006A

Washington and Napoleon. 40985

Washington and other poems. 9134

Washington and our own times. 42708

Washington and the generals of the American revolution. 28900

Washington and the union. 58373

Washington Artillery, Boston. see Massachusetts. Militia. Washington Artillery, Boston.

Washington Artillery Battalion, New Orleans. see Louisiana. Militia. Washington Artillery Battalion, New Orleans.

Washington as a freemason. 43447

Washington Association and United States Insurance Company. 101977

Washington Association, Chester County, Pa. 102036A

Washington Association of Philadelphia. 101978

Washington Bank in the City of New-York. 101980

Washington Benevolent Society. 63786, 101646, 101648, 101649, 101658, 5th note after 101872, 101981-101982

Washington Benevolent Society. Connecticut. Glastonbury. 101649

Washington Benevolent Society. Connecticut. Hartford. 101649

Washington Benevolent Society. Connecticut. Hebron. 101649

Washington Benevolent Society. Connecticut. Oxford. 101648

Washington Benevolent Society. Connecticut.
Weathersfield. 101656

Washington Benevolent Society. Massachusetts.
101625, 101991

Washington Benevolent Society. Massachusetts.
Berkshire County. 101629

Washington Benevolent Society. Massachusetts.
Brimfield. 101626, 101769

Washington Benevolent Society. Massachusetts.
Brookfield. 101626

Washington Benevolent Society. Massachusetts.
Cambridge. 101985

Washington Benevolent Society. Massachusetts.
Fitchburg. 101655

Washington Benevolent Society. Massachusetts.
Franklin County. 101628

Washington Benevolent Society. Massachusetts.
Hampden County. 101638, 101654 see
also Washington Benevolent Society.
Massachusetts. Springfield.

Washington Benevolent Society. Massachusetts.
Hampshire County. 101624, 101635

Washington Benevolent Society. Massachusetts.
Lancaster. 101655

Washington Benevolent Society. Massachusetts.
Leominster. 101655

Washington Benevolent Society. Massachusetts.
Newburyport. 54928

Washington Benevolent Society. Massachusetts.
Pittsfield. 101629

Washington Benevolent Society. Massachusetts.
Southern Part of Worcester County. see
Washington Benevolent Society. Massa-
chusetts. Worcester County.

Washington Benevolent Society. Massachusetts.
Springfield. 101654 see also Washington
Benevolent Society. Massachusetts.
Hampden County.

Washington Benevolent Society. Massachusetts.
Sterling. 101655

Washington Benevolent Society. Massachusetts.
Worcester. 101624 see also Washington
Benevolent Society. Massachusetts. Wor-
cester County.

Washington Benevolent Society. Massachusetts.
Worcester County. 101655 see also
Washington Benevolent Society. Massa-
chusetts. Worcester.

Washington Benevolent Society. Massachusetts.
Worcester County. Committee. 105416

Washington Benevolent Society. New Hampshire.
Concord. 63786, 101981-101982

Washington Benevolent Society. New Hampshire.
Marlborough. 101630

Washington Benevolent Society. New Jersey.
101619, 101651

Washington Benevolent Society. New Jersey.
Cranberry. 101634

Washington Benevolent Society. New Jersey.
Gloucester County. 101639, 101657

Washington Benevolent Society. New Jersey.
Mount Holly. 101651

Washington Benevolent Society. New Jersey.
Princeton. 101634

Washington Benevolent Society. New Jersey.
Sussex County. 101634

Washington Benevolent Society. New Jersey.
Trenton. 101639

Washington Benevolent Society. New York.
Albany. 101607, 101622-101623, 101645

Washington Benevolent Society. New York.
Augusta. 101983 see also Washington
Benevolent Society. New York. Oneida
County.

Washington Benevolent Society. New York.
Berkshire County. 101617

Washington Benevolent Society. New York.
Berlin. 101984 see also Washington
Benevolent Society. New York. Rens-
selaer County.

Washington Benevolent Society. New York.
Brookfield. 101984A

Washington Benevolent Society. New York.
Cayuga County. 101986

Washington Benevolent Society. New York.
Charlton. 101987

Washington Benevolent Society. New York.
Chittenden County. 101621

Washington Benevolent Society. New York.
Columbia County. 101605, 101617

Washington Benevolent Society. New York.
Florida. 101607, 101988 see also
Washington Benevolent Society. New
York. Montgomery County.

Washington Benevolent Society. New York.
Galway. 101989 see also Washington
Benevolent Society. New York. Saratoga
County.

Washington Benevolent Society. New York.
Greene County. 101617

Washington Benevolent Society. New York.
Herkimer County. 101990

Washington Benevolent Society. New York.
Hudson. 101650

Washington Benevolent Society. New York.
Montgomery County. 101607, 101988
see also Washington Benevolent Society.
New York. Florida.

Washington Benevolent Society. New York.
New York City. 101605, 101630,
101643

Washington Benevolent Society. New York.
Oneida County. 101983 see also Washingt
Benevolent Society. New York. Augusta.

Washington Benevolent Society. New York.
Onondaga County. 101614

Washington Benevolent Society. New York.
Rensselaer County. 101612 see also
Washington Benevolent Society. New
York. Berlin.

Washington Benevolent Society. New York.
Saratoga County. 101621, 101640
see also Washington Benevolent Society.
New York. Galway.

Washington Benevolent Society. New York.
Troy. 101641

Washington Benevolent Society. New York.
Washington County. 101620, 101637

Washington Benevolent Society. Pennsylvania.
60778, 101992

Washington Benevolent Society. Vermont.
101618, 101632

Washington Benevolent Society. Vermont.
Cornish. 101644

Washington Benevolent Society. Vermont.
Jefferson County. 101618

Washington Benevolent Society. Vermont.
Jerico. 101631

Washington Benevolent Society. Vermont.
Randolph. 101643

Washington Benevolent Society. Vermont.
Wardsborough. 101643

Washington Benevolent Society. Vermont.
Windsor. 101642-101644

"Washington Benevolents." 25295, 30662,
101993

Washington Bible Society, Washington, D. C.
101958-101959

Washington Bible Society, Washington, D. C.
Board of Managers. 101959

Washington Birthday Celebration, Paris, 1866. see Paris, France. Washington Birthday Celebration, 1866.

Washington Blues, Philadelphia. see Pennsylvania. Militia. Washington Blues, Philadelphia.

Washington Bridge Company. Board of Directors. Committee. 101956

Washington Building Company. 101957

Washington. By Monsieur Guizot. 29269

Washington Centennial Celebration, New York, 1832. see New York (City) Washington Centennial Celebration, 1832.

Washington chronicle. 14738

Washington Circulating Library, New York. 101995

Washington circulating library. Catalogue of books, at the Washington Circulating Library. 101995

Washington City Bible Society. see Washington Bible Society, Washington, D. C.

Washington City, February 1, 1806. 102143

Washington city gazette. 103867

Washington city general advertiser. 22321

Washington City Lyceum. see Washington, D. C. Lyceum.

Washington City Orphan Asylum. Board of Managers. 101962

Washington College, Chestertown, Md. Charter. 101996

Washington College, Chestertown, Md. Visitors and Governors. 84579, note after 101995

Washington College, Hartford, Conn. see Trinity College, Hartford, Conn.

Washington College, Lexington, Va. see Washington and Lee University, Lexington, Va.

Washington College, Washington, Pa. Board. 105664

Washington College, Washington, Pa. Board. Committee on the Union With Jefferson College. 102007, 105664

Washington College, Washington, Pa. Trustees. 102007, 105664

Washington College. 102001

Washington College Association. see Trinity College, Hartford, Conn. Washington College Association.

Washington College, Hartford, Conn. 1829. 102003

Washington College, Hartford, Connecticut. Terms of admission. 102002

Washington, Commandant-general des Etats-Unis. 101892

Washington County Grammar School, Montpelier, Vt. 102015

Washington County Bible Society. 102014

Washington County Bible Society. Directors. 102014

Washington County Bible Society. Treasurer. 102014

Washington County post. 88643, 88651

Washington County post extra. 88651

Washington, December, 14th, 1807. 104027

Washington described. (62565)

Washington directory and government register. 69120

Washington directory, showing the name, occupation, and residence. 101936-101937

Washington, D. C.——January 19, 1864. 90885

Washington. Drama historique. 40183

Washington. Eine Vorlesung gehalten in Jena. 91885

Washington en Necker. Lierzang. 101893

Washington et Bonaparte. 12264

Washington evening star. 84807

Washington expositor. 102016

Washington family relics. 36615

Washington, February 27th. 1823. 96971

Washington Federalist. pseud. Look before you leap. 41944

Washington Federalist. pseud. Proposed treaty with Texas. 102017

Washington federalist. 93900

Washington Female Seminary, Washington, Ga. 102018

Washington Fire Club, Salem, Mass. 75758

Washington Fire-Engine Company, Louisville, Ky. 42343

Washington; foundation de la republique. 89011-89012

Washington Funeral Celebration, Newburyport, Mass., 1800. see Newburyport, Mass. Washington Funeral Celebration, 1800.

Washington garland. 101894

Washington globe. 81794, 94780

Washington Grays, Philadelphia. see Pennsylvania. Militia. Light Artillery Corps Philadelphia.

Washington guide. [By Peter Force.] 25061

Washington guide: containing an account of the District of Columbia. 22248-22249, 101965-101966, 102166

Washington, Hamilton, and Fisher Ames. 1081A, 101770

Washington historical quarterly. 103997

Washington. Historisch-epische Dichting in vier Gesangen. 35759

Washington Hotel Lottery, Boston. 41449, 102019-102020

Washington in arms. 89924

Washington in domestic life. 74269, 74278

Washington Insurance Company in Providence, R. I. Charter. 102022

Washington Insurance Company of Philadelphia. Charter. 102021

Washington Irving. 35221

Washington Irving and his literary friends. 81503, 81556

Washington Irving. Ein Lebens- und Charakterbild. 38930

Washington Jockey Club, Washington, D. C. 101968

Washington letters. 86004

Washington letters to the Vermont journal. (15221)

Washington Library Company, Washington, D. C. 101969

Washington Light Infantry, Charleston. see South Carolina. Militia. Washington Light Infantry, Charleston.

Washington Light Infantry Charitable Association. 88111 see also South Carolina. Militia. Washington Light Infantry, Charleston.

Washington, Lincoln, and the fathers of the revolution. 44387

Washington Literary, Scientific, & Military Gymnasium, Washington, D. C. 101970

Washington Lodge, No. 3, Warren, R. I. see Freemasons. Rhode Island. Washington Lodge No. 3, Warren.

Washington Lyceum, Washington, Miss. see Washington, Miss. Lyceum.

Washington Medical College of Baltimore. see Washington University, Baltimore. Medical Department.

Washington military directory for . . . 1863. 64096

Washington Military Society, New York. see New York Washington Military Society.

Washington Military Union of the American Army, Quincy, Ill. (67282)

Washington miracle refuted. 46848, (64900), 102024

Washington Monument Association, Boston. 65821, 102026

Washington Monument Association, Boston. President. 65821, 102026 see also Brooks, John.

Washington Monument Association, Boston. Secretary. 65821, 102026 see also Russell, Benjamin.

Washington Monument Association, Boston. Trustees. 102025

Washington Monument Association, Philadelphia. 62376

Washington Monument Association of the First School District of Pennsylvania. see Washington Monument Association, Philadelphia.

Washington monument. Shall it be buit? [sic] (42855)

Washington Mutual Assurance Company, New York. see New York Washington Mutual Assurance Company.

Washington Mutual Assurance Company of the City of New York. see New York Washington Mutual Assurance Company.

Washington National Monument Society. 102031-102033

Washington National Monument Society. Board of Managers. 102029-102030

Washington National Monument Society. Board of Managers. Committee. 102033

Washington National Monument Society. Treasurer. 102033

Washington, November 13, 1839. 102033

Washington, or a vision of liberty. 2706

Washington, or liberty restored. 55838

Washington, or l'Orpheline de la Pensylvanie. 3978, 101895

Washington Orphan Asylum Society. 101964

Washington, ou la liberte du Nouveau-Monde. 5389, 77222

Washington, ou les represailles. 98956

Washington, ou l'orpheline de la Pensylvanie. 3978, 101895

Washington, our example. 78627

Washington. Par M. Guizot. 29268

Washington pillory. 72706

Washington pocket almanac. 22238

Washington, Por M. Guizot. 29270

Washington reporter. pseud. Remarkable trial of Richard Lawrance. 39366

Washington republican. 40631, 100578

Washington Section No. 2, Cadets of Temperance, Providence, R. I. see Cadets of Temperance. Rhode Island. Washington Section No. 2, Providence.

Washington Social Gymnasium, Washington, D. C. '101971

Washington Social Quoit Club. see Washington Social Gymnasium, Washington, D. C.

Washington Society, Boston. 32089, 102034

Washington Society, Charleston, S. C. 102035-102036

Washington Society of Maryland. 45394, 101608, 101615-101616, 1st note after 102036A

Washington spy. 101562

Washington Street Baptist Church, Buffalo. see Buffalo, N. Y. Washington Street Baptist Church.

Washington Street Church, Brooklyn, N. Y. see Brooklyn, N. Y. Washington Street Church.

Washington St. Wharf Company, San Francisco. (76102)

Washington Temperance Society, New Haven, Conn. see Martha Washington Temperance Society, New Haven, Conn.

Washington Territory. The great north-west. 47899

Washington Territory west of the Cascade Mountains. 47373

Washington, the one in prophecy like the Son of Man. 89670

Washington to Harrison. 84913

Washington to the people of the United States. 101526

Washington Total Abstinence Society, New Bedford, Mass. Auditor. 52487

Washington Total Abstinence Society of Massachusetts. see Massachusetts Washington Total Abstinence Society.

Washington Total Abstience Society of Providence, R. I. see Providence Washington Total Abstinence Society, Providence, R. I.

Washington und die Amerikanische Revolution. 101896

Washington und die Befreiung der Nordamerikanischen Freistaaten. 101897

Washington und die Franzosische Revolution. 101898

Washington und die Nordamerikanische Revolution. 28048, 42171, note after 101898

Washington under der Franzosische Staat. 42170

Washington union. 9305

Washington University, Baltimore. Medical Department. 102023

Washington University, Baltimore. President and Board of Visitors. 102023

Washington University, St. Louis. Mary Hemenway Foundation Lectures. 82522

Washington Universtiy, St. Louis. School of Law. 75369

Washington vision. 7294

Washingtonian. pseud. Some of the poetical fragments. 86705

Washingtonian. pseud. Washington's birth day see Lovett, John.

Washingtonian Mass Convention, Boston, 1845. (65754)

Washingtonian reform. (2833)

Washingtonian songster. 62761

Washingtoniana: a collection of papers. 101899

Washingtoniana: containing a biographical sketch. 101900

Washingtoniana; containing a sketch of the life and death of the late Gen. George Washington. 36361, 84115, note after 101900

Washingtoniana: or, memorials of the death of George Washington. 33154, 92304

Washingtonisch-Wohltatigen Gesellschaft Pennsylvaniens. see Washington Benevolent Society. Pennsylvania.

Washingtons. 81334

Washington's Abschiedsadresse. 9672

Washington's accounts, from June, 1775, to June, 1783. 101546-101546A

Washington advertiser. see National intelligencer and Washington advertiser. 84079

Washington's agricultural correspondence. 101722

Washingtons Ankunft in Elisium. 101901
Washington's birth-day. Admit🖙Dinner on
table at half past 2 o'clock. 101902
Washington's birth day: an historical poem.
101903
Washington's Birth Day Celebration, Hoosick
Falls, N. Y., 1862. see Hoosick Falls,
N. Y. Washington's Birth Day Celebration,
1862.
Washington's Birth-day. Patriotism. (22178)
Washington's birthday. Centennial celebration.
62375
Washington's Birthday Centennial, Philadelphia,
1832. see Philadelphia. Centennial
Celebration of Washington's Birthday,
1832.
Washington's diary. note after 7269
Washington's elete. 89010
Washington's farewell address. 45394, 60778,
101611, 101653, 101846A, 101998, 101992,
1st note after 102036A
Washington's farewell address, and the constitution of the United States. 101631, 101648
Washington's farewell address in facsimile.
note after 101547
Washington's farewell address; the constitution
of the United States. 101662
Washington's farewell address, to his fellow-
citizens on his retiring from the Presidency of the United States. 101598,
101603
Washington's farewell address to the people of
the United States. 101605, 101607-
101608, 101612, 101614, 101617, 101619-
101626, 101628-101629, 101634-101635,
101637-101641, 101643, 101645-101646,
101649-101652, 101654, 101657-101659,
101667, 101677, 101725
Washington's farewell address to the people of
the United States. Also, the constitution
of the United States. 101644
Washington's farewell address to the people of
the United States of America. 101686
Washington's farewell address to the people of
the United States, September 19, 1796.
101681
Washington's farewell address to the people of
the United States. September 1796.
101661
Washington's farewell address, to the people of
the United States, September, 1796. 101668
Washington's farewell address to the people of
the United States. September 17, 1796.
101663
Washington's farewell address to the people of
the United States, 1776. [sic] 19175
Washington's farewell address, to the people
of the United States. To which is added
the constitution of the United States.
101650, 101656
Washington's farewell address to the people of
the United States. Together with the
constitution. 101655
Washington's farewell address to the people of
the United States. With an abstract of
his last will and testament. 101636
Washington's farewell . . . [portrait] . . .
address to the people. 101660
Washington's first campaign. 17367
Washingtons hinterlassene Schriften. 89014
Washingtons Junglingsjahre. 103989
Washington's Leben. 101904
Washington's legacy. 101595, 101651
Washington's legacy & the constitution. 101650

Washington's legacy, published for the Union
and State Rights Party. 88089, 101665
Washington's legacy, with a sketch of his life.
101636
Washington's letter, declaring his acceptance
of the command. 101717
Washington's letter to the President of Congress.
101725
Washington's masonic character and standing.
25850
Washington's monuments of patriotism. 35473,
101748-101749
Washingtons overgang ter onsterfelijkheid.
3301
Washington's papers. 89013
Washington's political legacies. 94369,
101750-101751, 101841
Washington's prophecy; or facts concerning
the rebellion. 44740
Washington's valedictory address to the people
of the United States. 101666, 101669,
101671, 101674-101675, 101678-101680,
101683-101684
Washington's valedictory, to the people of the
United States. 101615
Washington's valuable advice to his fellow
citizens. 101578
Washington's veledictory [sic] address.
101874
Washinton [sic], o los prisoneros Ingleses.
101905
Washoe Mines. A directory of all mines.
42104
Wasp. By Robert Rusty-Turncoat. 17677,
note after 98533, 102037
Wasp stinging frolick. 102038
Wasselinx, Wilhelm. see Usselinx Willem.
Wassell, W. H. 83699
Wassenaer, ----- van, Baron van Opdam.
98972
Wassenaer, Nicolaes van, d. 1631? 77957,
102039, 102920
Wassenaer, Wilhelmus Fredericus Henricus
van. 100769
Wassenbergh, Eberhard, b. 1610. 95777
Wassernixe. 16547
Waste book. No. I. 102040
Watch, an ode, humbly inscribed to the Rt.
Hon. the Earl of M—F——D. 101041
Watch, an ode, suggested to the author.
102042
Watch for a wise man's observation. 102043
Watch: the prophecy of the scripture and
truth. 77223
Watch-tower. (30352), (41640), (41651), 44080
Watch-word from our Lord Iesus Christ unto
his churches. 80263, 95195
Watchfulness, essential to wisdom. 70929
Watchman. pseud. Cochranism delineated.
see Stinchfield, Ephraim.
Watchman. pseud. To the inhabitants of the
city and county of New-York. 102044
Watchman. pseud. Watchman's alarm to
Lord N---h. see British Bostonian.
pseud.
Watchman. pesud. Whoever has candidly
traced. 102045, 1st note after 103846
Watchman. 84059, 84585
Watchman and Jamaica free press. 102867
Watchman, No. V. 102050
Watchman, No. IV. 102049
Watchman. No. I. 102046
Watchman, No. III. 102048
Watchman. No. II. 102047
Watchman's alarm to Lord N---h. 102051-
102052

Watchman's answer to the question, What of the night? &c. 9423

Watchman's warning to the house of Israel. (25221)

Watchword of New Orleans. 88659

Water, Guillelmus van der. 66498

Water-baptism plainly proved by scripture. 95831

Water birds. 56350

Water boundary. 14077

Water Committee, Brooklyn. see Brooklyn, N. Y. Common Council. Water Committee.

Water-drops. 80963

Water from Brooklyn and Williamsburgh. 8334

Water from the White Sulphur Springs. 50470

Water power of Maine. By Walter Wells. 44053

Water-power of Maine. Reports of the Commissioners and Secretary of the Hydrographic Survey of 1867. (44052)

Water question. 8333

Water supply. Address to the citizens of South Bend. 87334

Water-weereld, waer in vertoont werden alle de zee-kusten. 27962, 106290

Water witch. [By Richard Penn Smith.] 83788

Water-witch; or, the skimmer of the seas. 16545, 1st note after 102052

Water-works for the metropolitan city of Washington. 49118

Water-works of the United States. 93151

Water works. The misconduct of the present City Councils. 62369, 2d note after 102052

Water-world. 78539

Waterbury, Jared Bell, 1799-1876. 85100, 102053

Waterbury, Vt. Baptist Anti-slavery Convention, 1841. see Baptist Anti-slavery Convention, Waterbury, Vt., 1841.

Watered stock. 89842

Waterford, N. Y. Citizens. petitioners 102054

Waterford, N. Y. Presbyterian Church. 64760

Waterhouse, Benjamin, 1754-1846. 31031, 102055-102065, 105649

Waterhouse, Edward, 1619-1670. 99885

Waterhouse, George R. 18649

Waterhouse, Samuel. 102066-102067

Waterhouse, Samuel. supposed author 12982, 25296, 86684, 3d note after 95765, 2d note after 102065

Waterland, -------. 5745, (20062)

Waterloo, N. Y. Friends of Human Progress. see Friends of Human Progress, Waterloo, N. Y.

Waterman, A. G. 62164

Waterman, Andrew J. defendant 85212 see also Massachusetts. Attorney General. defendant

Waterman, Catherine Harbeson. 102069

Waterman, Elijah. 102070-102075

Waterman, Henry. 102076

Waterman, J. W. 90702

Waterman, Jotham. 102077-102082

Waterman, Julius A. 102083

Waterman, Nehemiah. 102084

Waterman, Rhoda Elizabeth. see White, Rhoda Elizabeth (Waterman)

Waterman, Simon. 102085

Waterman, Thomas. 102086

Waterman, Thomas T. 70662

Waterman Street Baptist Church, Providence, R. I. see Providence, R. I. Waterman Street Baptist Church.

Waterous, Timothy, Sr. 102087-102088

Waterous, Timothy, Jr. 102087-102088

Waterous, Zachariah. 102087-102088

Waters, R. P. supposed author 82243

Waters, Samuel. 102089-102090

Waters, Thomas Franklin. 101326

Waters of Marah sweetened. 46299

Waterspook. 16548

Waterston, Robert Cassie. 76992, note after 97137, 102091-102092

Waterston, Robert Cassie. supposed author 95683, note after 102092

Waterton, Charles. 84305-84306, 84309, 84313, 84316-84317, 102093-102094

Watertown, Mass. Council of Fourteen Churches, 1722. see Congregational Churches in Massachusetts. Ecclesiastical Council, Watertown, 1722.

Watertown, Mass. Ecclesiastical Council, 1722. see Congregational Churches in Massachusetts. Ecclesiastical Council, Watertown, 1722.

Watertown, Mass. Provincial Congress, 1775. see Massachusetts. Provincial Congress, Watertown, 1775.

Watertown, N. Y. Black River Literary and Religious Institute. see Jefferson County Institute, Watertown, N. Y.

Watertown, N. Y. Jefferson County Institute. see Jefferson County Institute, Watertown, N. Y.

Watertown, Wisc. Northwestern University. 55754

Watertown directory, for 1840. 102096

Watertown in '75. 74874

Watertown, (Massachusetts-Bay) April 19. 102195

Waterville, Me. Colby College. see Colby College, Waterville, Me.

Waterville, Me. College. see Colby College, Waterville, Me.

Waterville, Me. Eastern mail. see Eastern mail, Waterville, Me.

Waterville, Me. First Baptist Church. 10209

Waterville, Me. Maine Literary and Theological Institution. see Colby College, Waterville, Me.

Waterville, Me. Sabbath School. Superintendent. 102097 see also Page, Stephen Benson.

Waterville, Me. Waterville College. see Colby College, Waterville, Me.

Waterville, N. Y. Sangerfield Meeting, 1830. see Sangerfield Meeting, Waterville, N. Y., 1830.

Waterville College Clinical School of Medicine, Woodstock, Vt. see Vermont Medical College, Woodstock, Vt.

Waterville College. Origin, progress, and present state. 102102

Waterville College, Waterville, Me. see Colby College, Waterville, Me.

Watervliet Turnpike. 102108

Watervliet Turnpike Company. Charter. 102109

Waterwereld beschouwd. (8948)

Waterwereld, waer in vertoont werden alle de zee-kusten van het bekende des aerdbodems. 27962

Watery war. 4664, note after 102109

Wateson, George. supposed author 103258

Watkins, David. defendant (31083)

Watkins, George. petitioner 102110

Watkins, John W. 102111

Watkins, Joseph S. 102112

Watkins, Miles Selden. 84705

Watkins, N. 102113
Watkins, Oliver. defendant 102114-102115
Watkins, Miss R. 102113
Watkins, Robert. 102116
Watkins, Thomas. defendant before military
  commission (31083)
Watkins, Thomas G. 102117
Watkins, Tobias, 1780-1855. 854, 40351,
  57356, 96329, 102118-note after 102121
Watkins, Tobias, 1780-1855. defendant 101907
Watkins, W. J. 20717
Watkins, William Henry. 102122-102123
Watkins, William W. plaintiff 101343
Watmough, Edward Coxe. 8583, 102124
Watmough, John Goddard. 102125-102127
Watson, -------, fl. 1775. 62743
Watson, Daniel. 102128
Watson, David. (15142), 104878
Watson, Ebenezer. ed. 87322
Watson, Elkanah. 27961, 32120, 50837, 102128-
  102136
Watson, George. see Watson-Taylor, George.
Watson, Henry C. (51502), (54134)
Watson, John, d. 1826. 102137-102139
Watson, John Fanning. 82974-82978, 102140-
  102143
Watson, Joseph, fl. 1819. 97767 see also
  Union Canal Company of Pennsylvania.
  President.
Watson, Joseph, fl. 1826. (38814), 95954
  see also New York (City) Committee of
  Officers of the War of 1812. Agent.
Watson, Juan. 97672
Watson, Paul Barron, 1861- 93251
Watson, Richard, Bishop of Llandaff, 1737-
  1816. 92836, 102144-102147
Watson, Richard, 1781-1833. 102148-102152
Watson, Samuel. defendant at court martial
  96952, 102153
Watson, Thomas. supposed author 82844-82845
Watson, William. 102154
Watson, Willam R. 70526, 70680, 70746
  see also Rhode Island. Auditor. Rhode
  Island. State Insurance Commissioner.
Watson, William R. supposed author 30058
Watson, Wingfield. 84549, 92674-92675, 92685,
  92687
Watson, Winslow C. 27417, 102133
Watson-Taylor, George. 102155
Watson (Ebenezer) firm publishers 15669,
  92981
Watson-Blair debate. 84549
Watson's Connecticut almanac, for . . . 1777.
  92982
Watson's register, and Connecticut almanack.
  92980
Watson's register and Connecticut almanac, for
  . . . 1776. 15669, 92981
Watt, Frederick. 88441 see also Southern
  Pennsylvania Iron and Railroad Company.
  Trustees.
Watt, G. D. reporter 64962
Watt, J. 16816, (61931)
Watt, Joachim von. see Vadianus, i. e.
  Joachim von Watt, 1484-1551.
Watters, William. 102156
Watterston, George. 101965, 102157-102170
Watterton, -------. 50115
Watts, Beaufort T. 87545 see also South
  Carolina. Executive Secretary.
Watts, Charles. 96929, 102171
Watts, Ephraim. 102172
Watts, George, d. 1736. 83978, 102173
Watts, H. M. 102174

Watts, Isaac, 1674-1748. 12878, 21939, 46624,
  69649, 71539, 73540, 77366, 79196,
  80716, 82979, 83419, 84553, 91150, 96036,
  101812, 103604, 105534
Watts, J. ed. 51574
Watts, John. appellant 102175
Watts, Joseph. 67599
Watts, Robert. 37447, 102176
Watts, Samuel. (34857), 36736, 62579, 5th
  note after 102623 see also Massa-
  chusetts (Colony) Commissioners to Treat
  With the Eastern Indians.
Watts, Stephen. 25279, 84611-84612
Watts, Thomas Hill, 1819-1892. 15244
  see also Confederate States of America.
  Attorney General.
Watts, Thomas. 92620
Watts, Washington. 102177
Watts, William. 35711, note after 92708
Wau-bun, the "early day" in the north-west.
  12660, (37941)
Waugh, -------, fl. 1853. 5341
Waugh, B. 33398
Waugh, John. 102178
Waugh (B.) firm publishers 102681
Waukesha and Mississippi Rail Road Company.
  see Milwaukee, Waukesha, and Mississip-
  pi Rail Road Company.
Wawawanda. A legend of old Orange. 55013
Wawasi lagidamwoganek mdala chowagidam-
  woganal tabtagil. 105710
Waw-ke-wa. Potawatomi Indian Chief 96700
Waw-ke-wa Band of Potawatomi Indians. see
  Potawatomi Indians (Waw-ke-wa Band)
Wawrzin tzy petrowi de Medicis pozdrawenije.
  99367
Way, J. 102179
Way, Samuel A. 102180
Way Americans are treated for aiding the
  cause of liberty at home. 20911
'Way down east; or, portraitures of yankee
  life. 84150, 84158-84159, 84161
Way for a people to live long in the land.
  91968
Way marks of a wanderer. 74246
Way of churches walking in brotherly equalitie,
  or coordination. 11616, (17090)-17091,
  note after 99832
Way of directing souls that are under the
  work of conversion. 91950-91953
Way of fortune. 22521
Way of God in the story. 20349
Way of God vindicated. 32729
Way of God with his people in these nations.
  91364
Way of Israels welfare. 103699
Way of life. By T. W. Smith 84425
Way of life or, Gods vvay and course.
  (17087)
Way of peace. 88051
Way of the churches of Christ in New England.
  11616, (17090)-17091, note after 99832
Way of the congregational churches cleared.
  17091
Way of the cross. 70905
Way of the world. 101371
Way of truth laid out. A catechism. 46589
Way of truth, laid out, with a threefold cate-
  chism. 46396
Way-side glimpse of American life. 104128
Way to a blessed estate in this life. 102181
Way to abolish slavery. 90866
Way to avoid the centre of our violent gales.
  6034
Way to be happy here, and for ever. 104109

Way to bless and save our country. 33794

Way to excel. 46590

Way to grow rich. 26655, 93828

Way to health, long life, and happiness. 97285, 97289

Way to heaven made plain. 74292

Way to know hypocrisy cleared up. 91955

Way to know sincerity and hypocrisy cleared up. 91966

Way to outdo England without fighting her. 10842

Way to peace. 51660

Way to prosperity. 46591

Way to . . . rest. 30696

Way to secure peace and establish unity as one nation. 33468

Way to the Sabbath of rest. 8192

Way to trauell. 27842

Way to wealth, as clearly shewn in the preface. 102182

Way to wealth as clearly shown. 25597

Way to wealth, honour and distinction. 90221

Way to wealth, or Poor Richard improved. 25596

Way to wealth; or, the admonition of Poor Richard. 25567, (25598), 78109, 102351

Way to wealth, to which is added the prompter. (25598)

Way, truth, and life. 90473

Way with the colonies. 96075

Wayawa tokaheya. 71340

Wayes and joyes of early piety. 46592

Wayland, Francis, 1796-1865. (26170), 28944, 29526, 47943, (70542), 70662, 82785, 89736, 94538, 102183-102190

Wayland, John. (79795)

Waymouth, George. (74131)

Wayne, Anthony, 1745-1796. 99605

Wayne, Isaac. (50388)

Wayne, James Moore. 102191

Wayne County, Indiana. French Citizens. petitioners 47641, 102192

Wayne County, Indiana. Sundry Citizens. petitioners see Wayne County, Indiana. French Citizens. petitioners

Wayne County, Michigan. Court. 41064

Ways and means for the inhabitants of Delaware to become rich. 60058, 67997, note after 102192

Ways and means of payment. 14917

Ways and means of make the South-Sea stock more intrinsically worth. 102193

Ways of God vindicated. 71764

Ways of living on small means. 102194

Ways of pleasure and the paths of peace. 78702, note after 102194

Ways of providence. 72189, 2d note after 94271

Ways of the hour. (16549)

Ways to attain and secure peace. 37272

Ways to attain glory by inheritance. 92107

Wayside flowers. 42162

Wayside glimpses, north and south. 25253

Wayside songs. (27937)

Wa-zah-wah-wa-doong. sobriquet see Pitezel, John H.

We are coming, Father Abraham. 83677

We are favoured with the general orders. 101701

We conceive the sense of our fellow citizens. 96022

We four villagers. 25158

We have had frequent intimations from England. 95993

We have just received the following important intelligence. 102195

We have presumed to address you on the subject. 105414

We have this day entered into a copartnership. 98289

We His Majesty's faithful subjects, the Council of this colony. 99907

We ordaine and requre, that . . . the foure ancient burroughs. 99876

We rejoice with trembling. 39187

We still live as a nation. 43237

We thanked God and took courage. 83570

We the Commissioners for Managing & Causing to be Levied His Majestys Customs & Other Duties in America do hereby depute and impower. 95885

We the committee, who were appointed. 95999

We, the delegates of the people of the state of South Carolina. 87415

We, the shopkeepers of Philadelphia, and places adjacent. 102196

We the subscribers do voluntarily contribute the sums. 86124

We the subscribers having been appointed as a committee. 95990

We the subscribers . . . having taken into . . . consideration. 100528

We the subscribers, inhabitants of the town of [blank] having taken into our serious consideration. 101479

We the subscribers proprietors and claimants in and of sundry townships. 61280, 2d note after 98997

We the subscribers severally agree. 105366

We the undersigned petitioners. 86349

We, the underwritten having associated. 100573

We think it incumbet on us. 96041

We whose names are hereunto subscribed. 100532

Wea Indians. Treaties, etc. 96683

Wea mission. 102197

Wea primer. 102198

Weak oppressed believer victorious. 83795

Weakley, R. 40575, 94790, 94799

Weakness and inefficiency of the government. 47901

Weakness of American exposed. 15993, note after 103935

Weaknesses of Brutus exposed. 102417

Wealth and beauty. (34004)

Wealth and biography of the wealthy citizens of Philadelphia. 62377

Wealth and resources of the state of Oregon. 57574

Wealth discovered. (17332)

Wealth, industry, and resources of Portsmouth. 59354

Wealth of Great Britain in the Ocean. 102199-102200

Wealth of nations. 64823, 82301, 93602

Wealth of society. 102201

Wealth, resources, and power of the people. 22097

Wealthy men and women of Brooklyn and Williamsburgh. 41833

Weaned Christian. 46593

Weare, M. 52897

Weariness in well-doing. 92265

Wearing of the gray. (16322)

Weas Indians. Treaties, etc. 96620

Weas Kickapoo Indians. see Kickapoo Indians.

Weather book for . . . 1857. 54720

Weather diary. 82979

Weatherford, William. 96692 see also U. S. Commissioners to the United Nation of Chippewa, Ottawa, and Potawatomi Indians.

Weathford times. 85356
Weatherhead, W. Davidson. 102202
Weathermore, J. 15664
Weathersfield, Conn. 14122
Weathersfield, Conn. Joseph Emerson's
    Female Seminary. see Joseph Emerson's
    Female Seminary, Weathersfield, Conn.
Weathersfield, Conn. Washington Benevolent
    Society. see Washington Benevolent
    Society. Connecticut. Weathersfield.
Weatherwise, Abraham. pseud. Father
    Abraham's almanack. 23909
Weatherwise, Abraham. pseud. New England
    town and county almanac, 1769. 52752,
    62743
Weatherwise, Abraham. pseud. New-Hampshire
    calendar. 52864
Weaver. pseud. Letter. 40318, 80391
Weaver, Isaac. supposed author 20986, 3d
    note after 102203
Weaver, John. 98124, 102204
Weaver, William Augustus. 102205-102208
Weaver, William Augustus. plaintiff 76498,
    95779, 102207
Weaver of Raveloe. 40774, 51298
Weaver's wife cunningly catch'd in a trap.
    100575
Web of many textures as woven by Ruth her-
    self. (80478)
Web of many textures, wrought by Ruth Parting-
    ton. 80475
Webb, Conrad. 102209
Webb, Daniel. English Woolen Manufacturer
    102210
Webb, Daniel, 1719?-1798. 59250-29252, 3d
    note after 100862, 1st-3d notes after
    102210
Webb, Elizabeth. 1 02211-102212
Webb, George, 1708?- 102213
Webb, George, d. 1758. 102214
Webb, George James. 38583, 102215
Webb, James Watson. 91392, 102216
Webb, John. 17675, 20057, (20271), 21946,
    46274, 95166, 101016, 102217-102224
    see also Eight Ministers Who Carry On
    the Thursday Lecture in Boston.
Webb, Mary, d. 1861. supposed author 89073,
    102224
Webb, Mary E. 92504
Webb, R. 102225
Webb, Robert. 59707, 102226-102227
Webb, Samuel. 102228-102229, 103804
Webb, Thomas. 102230
Webb, Thomas Hopkins. (67486), (70634),
    102231
Webb, Thomas Smith. (25810), 102232-102244
Webb, William. 60636 see also U. S. Navy
    Board, Philadelphia. Paymaster.
Webb, William, d. 1754. defendant 102245
Webbe, John. supposed author 102246
Webber, Charles Wilkins. 102247-102249
Webber, George. 102250
Webber, Horace H. 6242
Webber, Mabel L. 87751
Webber, Samuel, 1759-1810. 39187, 50926, note
    after 102250-102251, 104056
Webber, Samuel, 1797-1880. 1 02252-102253
Webster, --------. 25591
Webster, C. ed. 69356
Webster, Chauncy. 102253A
Webster, Clement L. 85041
Webster, Daniel, 1782-1852. 181, 4785, (6527),
    7127, 8397, 9170, 9175-9176, 9945-9947,
    (13173), 13362, 14535, 15983, (16141),

(16573), 17471, 19655, 20253, 26390,
28386, (29016), note after 30759, (31043)-
31044, (33650), 35856, 35863, 36741,
(36917), 37050, 38066, 38269, (39344),
(42795), 45686, 52200, (52746), 52801,
52826, (53746), 60952-60953, 62525,
63449, 65098, 68636, (69758), 70732,
(70978), 71585, 72390, 76244, 77712,
82074, 84463, 85154, 85164-85165, 88496,
88910, 89211, 89213, 89216, 92068,
92331, 93197, 93208, 93487, 93663, note
before 94463, 95806, 95870, 96013,
96893, 98425, 102254-102321, 103268,
103427, 103490A see also Boston.
Citizens. Committee to Prepare the
Memorial. Chairman. Boston. Committee of Merchants and Others, 1820.
Bunker Hill Monument Association.
Directors. Bunker Hill Monument As-
sociation. President. U. S. Department
of State.
Webster, Daniel, 1782-1852. plaintiff (42801),
    102321, 1st note after 103741
Webster, Daniel, 1782-1852. mediumistic
    author 71149
Webster, David. ed. (60342)
Webster, Ezekiel. 102322-102323
Webster, J. W. (52746)
Webster, Jacob. 102325
Webster, James. 22668, 102324
Webster, James. Merchant's Clerk 102327
Webster, James. of New York 53080, 102328
Webster, James, 1803-1854. 102326
Webster, John White, 1793-1850. 6493
Webster, John White, 1793-1850. defendant
    4627, 81553, 90714, 102329
Webster, Josiah. 102330
Webster, M. M. see Mosby, M. M. (Webster)
Webster, M. P. 93430
Webster, Matthew Henry. 102331
Webster, Noah, 1758-1843. 1135, 1314, 2914,
    5598, 14007, 15645, 15672, 17549, 18071,
    (20541), (25598), 37892, (44480), 47983,
    (56489), 62637-62638, 70345, 78614,
    76952, 78614, 96561, 96580, 102332-
    102401, 102998, 104945, 104847, 105266
Webster, Noah, 1758-1843. supposed author
    1977, 5591, 12279, (15640), 15644, 15875,
    23995, 29960, 95742, 102333-note after
    102333, 102361, 102364, 105939
Webster, Pelatiah, 1726-1795. (20303), (22937),
    69397, 80405, 102402-102417
Webster, Pelatiah, 1726-1795. supposed author
    60442, 94024, note after 100447, note
    after 102401, 102414
Webster, Pelatiah, 1726-1795. incorrectly
    supposed author 22994, 56536, note after
    102409, note before 102412, 104937
Webster, Redford. 102418-102419
Webster, Redford. supposed author 6529,
    79004, 102419, note after 102419
Webster, Samuel, 1719-1796. 13350, 102420-
    102426
Webster, Samuel, 1743-1777. 5977, 102427
Webster, Santiago. see Webster, James.
    Merchants' Clerk
Webster, Sarah E. plaintiff 89380
Webster, Sidney. 21414
Webster, Stephen P. 102428
Webster, William Henry Bayley. 102429
Webster (J. L.) firm publishers 102324
Webster Meetings, Boston, 1852. see Boston.
    Webster Meetings, 1852.
Webster on the currency. 102316

Websterian orthography. 64049
Websters & Skinners. firm publishers (51376), 81598
Webster's Bunker Hill speech. 88910
Webster's calendar. 81598
Webster's calendar or the Albany almanac. (51376)
Webster's grammar. 102337
Webster's traveller's guide. 102324
Weddell, ------. supposed author 105986
Weddell, James. 102430-102431
Wedderburn, ------. tr. 14526, note after 105986
Wedderburn, -------. incorrectly supposed author 14526, note after 105986
Wedderburn, A. Alias see Colville, A.
Wedderburn, Alexander. of St. John, New Brunswick 102432-102433
Wedderburn, Alexander, 1733-1805. see Rosslyn, Alexander Wedderburn, 1st Earl of, 1733-1805.
Wedderburn, J. W. 36544
Wedderburn, John. defendant 102434-102437
Wedderburn, Robert. 102438
Wedderburne, Alexander. see Rosslyn, Alexander Wedderburn, 1st Earl of, 1733-1805.
Wedding: an epic poem. 102439
Wedding days of former times. 33895
Wedding ring, fit for the finger. 78720
Wedell, L. M. von. tr. 103989
Wederleggende aanteeekeningen van een Hollandsch rechtgeleerden. 100768
Wederlegging eener memorie. 102440
Wederlegging van de argumenten. 102441, 102889A
Wederlegginge van de argumenten opgestelt van wegen de Heeren Bewinthebberen. 40712, 102442
Wedgwood, William B. ed. 33061
Wednesday, January 1. 1701. 79444-79445, 79449, note after 102442
Wednesday, July 14, 1779. 104435
Wee Davie. 43544
Weeas Kickapoo Indians. see Kickapoo Indians.
Weech, J. Friedrich von. 102443-102444
Weeckwercken der ghedenckwaerdighe historien. 56360
Weed, Enos. 102445-102447
Weed, Thurlow, 1797-1882. 23658, (62905), 3d note after 97148
Weed, Thurlow, 1797-1882. defendant (57388), 57390, 102448
Weed, Parsons & Co. firm publishers 34052
Weeden, Job. 102449
Weeden, John. defendant 98638
Weeds of Maine. (78479)
Week among autographs. 27429, (27436)
Week at Newport. 9842, 4th note after 100603
Week at Port Royal. (31857)
weekes, George. 102450
Weekes, Nathaniel. 102451
Weekes, Refine. 102452-102455
Weekly advertiser. see Pennsylvania gazette and weekly advertiser. Pennsylvania journal and weekly advertiser. Virginia gazette and weekly advertiser.
Weekly advertiser, or Pennsylvania journal. 60779
Weekly essays on sundry important subjects. 34452, (41651), 84576, 90011
Weekly family journal. 88340
Weekly for boys and girls. (9313)
Weekly gazette. 88391
Weekly industrial worker. 84489

Weekly inspector. 24220
Weekly journal. 9906, 30174, 104272
Weekly journal (Milton, Mass.) 46265
Weekly journal, designed to improve the soil and the mind. 88615
Weekly journal, devoted to literature and the fine arts. 54818
Weekly journal;—devoted to literature, arts and sciences. 88389
Weekly journal devoted to politics, literature, science and art. 51909
Weekly journal . . . devoted to the exposition of the mutual interests. 34454
Weekly journal devoted to the science, history, philosophy, and teachings of spiritualism. 89524
Weekly journal of politics, literature, science and art. 90797
Weekly Lecture, Boston. 50297
Weekly literary, entertaining, and scientific journal. 49215
Weekly magazine. see North American miscellany: a weekly magazine.
Weekly magazine of ministerial and anti-ministerial essays. 63759
Weekly magazine of tales, poetry, and engravings. 84154
Weekly mercury. see New-York gazette: and the weekly mercury. Ruddiman's weekly mercury.
Weekly miscellany. see Companion and weekly miscellany. Yankee. A weekly miscellany.
Weekly miscellany devoted to public amusements. 65992
Weekly miscellany of theatricals. 65993
Weekly news-letter (Boston) (12323), 12325, 104272
Weekly paper, devoted chiefly to the cause of Christianity and education. 13009
Weekly paper, devoted to agriculture, horticulture, and rural economy. 26922
Weekly periodical. see Review. A weekly periodical.
Weekly periodical of literature, science, and art. 87323
Weekly political journal devoted to the discussion and development of the principles of social democracy. 93729
Weekly political register. 14017
Weekly post boy. see New York gazette and weekly post boy. New-York gazette revived in the weekly post boy.
Weekly publication, containing documents. 26951
Weekly publication devoted to politics and local discussions. 32568, 89484
Weekly record of the notable, the useful and the tasteful. 73473
Weekly register (New York) see New York journal, and weekly register.
Weekly register (Norristown, Pa.) 89472
Weekly register (Norwich, Vt.) 83402
Weekly register (Philadelphia) see Philadelphia repository and weekly register.
Weekly register. see Niles' weekly register.
Weekly register: containing political, historical, geographical, scientifical, astronomical, statistical, and biographical documents. 55314
Weekly register. Jan. 15, 1808. 14906
Weekly register of science and the arts. 41489
Weekly republication of standard literature. 70006

Welcome to Albert, Prince of Wales. 80435
Welcome to Charles Dickens. 20005
Welcome to Charles Dickens. The Boz Ball.
　　To be given under the direction.
　　54715
Welcome to George Peabody, Esq. (59370)
Welcome to Goldwin Smith. (82690)
Welcome to Kossuth. 79591
Welcome to Louis Kossuth, Governor of Hun-
　　gary. 81632
Welcome to the ransomed. 59280
Weld, Angelina Grimke. 102550
Weld, Charles Richard. (38912)
Weld, Edmund. 102528-102531
Weld, Mrs. Edmund. 102529-102530
Weld, Ezra. 102532-102534
Weld, Horatio Hastings. 25493, 102535
Weld, Isaac. 46984, (71330), 102536-102544
Weld, Lewis. 1 02545
Weld, Ludovicus. 102546
Weld, Theodore Dwight. 11575, (20309), 85856,
　　102547-102550 see also Society for
　　Promoting Manual Labor in Literary
　　Institutions, New York. General Agent.
Weld, Thomas. see Welde, Thomas.
Welde, Thomas. (52617)-52618, (66428)-66430,
　　(67947), 102551-102552, 1st note after
　　102552, 2d note after 103846, 104848
Welde, Thomas. supposed author 104843
Welderen, -------, Graaf van. 93427
　　see also Netherlands. Legatie.
　　Great Britain.
Weldon, Sir Anthony. pseud.??? 31654
　　Aulicus coquinariae.
Weldon, Joseph. 731, 30380, 84558
Weleerwaarde Classis van Amsterdam. see
　　Nederlandsche Hervormde Kerk. Classis
　　van Amsterdam.
Welford. firm see Barrett and Welford.
　　firm
Well-accomplish'd soldiers, a glory to their
　　king. 26785
Well-bred scholar or practical essays. 14868
Well in the valley. 85335, 85340
Well-known Democrat. pseud. To the conser-
　　vative people of Virginia. (23926)
Well received and candid examination. 23545,
　　84819
Well tempered self-love a rule of conduct.
　　34059, 99015
Well-willer to England and Holland. pseud.
　　Second part of Vox populi. see Scott,
　　Thomas, 1580?-1626.
Well-willer, who wisheth, that the poore of
　　England might be prouided for, as none
　　should neede to go a begging within this
　　realme. pseud. Greevovs grones. see
　　Sparke, Michael.
Well-wisher. pseud. pseud. Historical account,
　　of the late disturbance. see True
　　Countryman. pseud.
Well-wisher of the commonwealth. pseud.
　　True relation. 31510
Well-wisher of the West-Indians. pseud.
　　Some remarks. 86736
Well-wisher to all men. pseud. tr. 80619
Well-wisher to both governments. pseud.
　　Pleain and friendly perswasive. see
　　Makemie, Francis.
Well-wisher to Brazilian independence. pseud.
　　Brazilian improvements. 7542
Well wisher to his countrey. pseud. New
　　Englands crisis. see Thompson, Ben-
　　jamin.

Well-wisher to his country. pseud. True state
　　of the case. 97153
Well-wisher to his king and country. pseud.
　　Principles of trade. see Whately,
　　George.
Well wisher to his king and country. pseud.
　　Short but serious address. 80610
Well-wisher to mankind. pseud. Teacher of
　　common sense. see Murray, James.
Well-wisher to mankind. pseud. Theory of
　　agency. see Perkins, John.
Well-wisher to the common-wealth. pseud.
　　True relation of the fleete. 31510, 1st
　　note after 97141
Well-wisher to the labouring classes and the
　　collony at large. pseud. Dialogue or
　　conversation. 8105, 19945
Well wisher to the prosperity both of Great-
　　Britain and North America. pseud.
　　Proposed appendix. see Carlisle,
　　Frederick Howard, 5th Earl of, 1748-
　　1825.
Well-wisher to the Royal Navy of England.
　　pseud. Observations on a pamphlet.
　　90621
Well-wisher to the trade and navigation of
　　Graet-Britain. pseud. Miserable case
　　of the British sugar planters. 49455
Well-wisher to truth. pseud. Brief essay on
　　the number seven. 7868
Well-wishing souldier. pseud. Experimental
　　discoverie of Spanish practises. see
　　Scott, Thomas, 1580?-1626.
Welladay. 67599
Welland Canal Company. Board of Directors.
　　102554, 102557, 102559
Welland Canal Company. President and Direc-
　　tors. 102558
Welland Canal Company, incorporated by acts
　　of the Provincial Parliament, of Upper
　　Canada. 102559
Wellendarfer, Virgilius, Bp. 102560
Weller, Catharine. 102561
Weller, George. 102562-102564
Weller, John B., 1812-1875. 33150 see also
　　California. Governor, 1858-1860 (Weller)
Weller, Samuel. 102565
Weller, William H. 102566
Welles, Arnold. 102567
Welles, Elijah G. 102568
Welles, Noah. 4093, 4094, (25392), 30530-
　　30531, 78494, 102569-102574, 103067
Wellesley, Richard Colley Wellesley, 1st
　　Marquis, 1760-1842. 1010-1012, 50766,
　　note after 102574 see also Great
　　Britain. Foreign Office.
Wellfare, Michael. 102575-102576
Wellfleet, Mass. First Congregational Church.
　　102577
Wellford, Beverley Randolph. 57439, 3d note
　　after 95515, 102578
Wellington, Charles. 102579
Wellington, E. 102580
Wellington, James. alias see Monroe,
　　Michael. defendant
Wellington, Jeduthan. petitioner (10144)
Wellman, Arthur H. 85212
Wellman, Joshua W. complainant 85212
Wellman, Mary W. 102581
Wellmore, E. engr. 75022, 84791
Wellons, W. B. 90566
Wells, -------, fl. 1769. 90612
Wells, -------, fl. 1803. defendant 55182
Wells, -------, fl. 1835. defendant 69454
Wells, Amos. 102582

Wentworth, Sir John, 1737-1820. defendant 41656-(41657), 1st note after 97579, note after 102630 see also New Hampshire (Colony) Governor, 1767-1775 (J. Wentworth) defendant Nova Scotia. Lieutenant Governor, 1792-1808 (Wentworth) defendant

Wentworth, John, 1768-1816. 102631

Wentworth, John, 1815-1888. 83236

Wentworth, P. H. 73719

Wentworth, Paul. petitioner 93593, 3d note after 105598-9 [sic]

Wentworth, Thomas. supposed author 102632

Wentworth, Thomas H. 102633

Wentworth, Trelawney. 102634-102635

Wentworth, William Charles. 102636

Wentworth Fitzwilliam, William. see Milton, William Fitzwilliam, Viscount, 1839-1877.

Wentz, Samuel. defendant before Presbytery 102637

Wenzel, G. T. tr. 25581, (54080)

Wept of Wept-ton-Wish. 16416

Wept of Wish-ton-Wish. 16441

Wept of Wish-ton-Wish: a tale. 16416, (16551), note after 102637

Wer kaan das heil erlangen? 83302

Wer soll und darf auswandern, wer nicht? 8206

Werden, Peter. 78281, 102638

Werdenbvrch, Dirk van. see Waerdenburgh, Dirk van.

We're all teetotalers here. 90153

Were slave holders members of the apostolic church? 17257

Werelt-spiegel, beschryvinge des gehelen aertbodems. 25473

Wereltboeck, spieghel ende beletenisse der gheheelen aertbodems. (25470)

Werfel, J. 102639

Werke [von Adelbert von Chasisso.] 11817

Werke [von J. F. Cooper.] 16562

Werke [von William Ellery Channing.] 11923

Werken uitgegeven door de Linschoten Vereeniging. 98738, 100852

Werkhoven, M. van. tr. 55077

Werndle, Johann Georg von. tr. 86229

Werneck, Luiz Peixoto de Lacerda. see Lacerda Werneck, Luiz Peixoto de.

Werner, A. G. 71443

Werner, Charles J. 95469-95470

Werner, Johannes. see Vernero, Ioanne.

Werninck, I. tr. 44792

Wert, Sebald de. see Weert, Sebald de.

Werter and Charlotte. 87172

Werter to Charlotte. 87172

Werth, John J. 102640

Werth der gangbarsten gold- und Silber-Munzen. 2093

Wertheste Landes-Leute. 77199

Wertmuller, Adolphus Ulrich. 102641

Wertmuller, Joris. 60746, 1st note after 97529, note after 102641

Wesche, W. L. tr. 4519, 4536

Wescott, Isaac. ed. 88682

Wescott, James D. 86232

Wescott, Thompson. 77510

Wesentlicker Berucksichtigung der biblischen Urgeschichten. 8478

Wesley, Charles, 1707-1788. 83419, 102642-102643, 102685, 103519-103520, 103526-103528, 103604, 103663

Wesley, Charles, 1707-1788. supposed author 102644

Wesley, John, 1703-1791. 106-107, 4671, (4674), 4678, 4693, 9080-9081, 11599, 20757, (21935), 21955-(21956), 21963, 23138, (23139), (23141), 23499, (24726), 26420, 26429, (27219), (30147), 32106, 33327, 34135, (35331), (35744), 41780, (41882), 50452, 51504, (52054), (57218), 60919, 63764, 63771, 70066, 73140, 78346, 80543, 84662, 85207, 90317, 93800, 96184, 96354, 96354, 97367, 100776, 102643, note before 102645-102702, 103508, 103556, 103617, 103663, 105746

Wesley, John, 1703-1791. supposed author (68714), note after 102685

Wesley, Samuel. 27047, note after 102702

Wesley and his coadjutors. 39072

Wesley and his times. [By George Smith.] 82582

Wesley and his times. By Rev. D. Holmes. 32593

Wesley his own historian. (35744)

Wesley offering. 32593

Wesley on slavery. 78346

Wesleyan Academy, Wilbraham, Mass. 102703

Wesleyan Academy, Wilbraham, Mass. petitioners 45990

Wesleyan anti-slavery review. 78345

Wesleyan Anti-slavery Society, New York. Publishing Committee. 102699

Wesleyan College, Macon, Ga. 27024

Wesleyan Conference memorial on the question of liberal education. 74584

Wesleyan Juvenile Benevolent Society, Boston. 102704

Wesleyan Juvenile Benevolent Society, in Boston. 102704

Wesleyan manual. 39776

Wesleyan Methodism in Upper Canada. (74585)

Wesleyan Methodist. pseud. Methodist error. 102705

Wesleyan Methodist Church. Canadian Conference. 69673, 74580-(74581), 74584, 74587, 102706

Wesleyan Methodist Church. Canadian Conference. petitioners 74584

Wesleyan Methodist Church. English Conference. 69673

Wesleyan Methodist Church. Jamaican Conference. Missionaries. 106096

Wesleyan Methodist Missionary Society. Committee. 90750

Wesleyan-Methodist missions in Jamaica and Honduras delineated. 75966

Wesleyan Methodist Relief Society, New York. see New-York Wesleyan Methodist Relief Society.

Wesleyan Missionary Society, London. 14248, 102707

Wesleyan repository. 85422-85443

Wesleyan Seminary and Female College, Kent's Hill, Me. see Maine Wesleyan Seminary and Female College, Kent's Hill.

Wesleyan Seminary Hallowell, Me. see Maine Wesleyan Seminary, Hallowell, Me.

Wesleyan student. 32484

Wesleyan University, Florence, Ala. see Florence Wesleyan University, Florence, Ala.

Wesleyan University, Iowa. see Wesleyan University.

Wesleyan University, Middletown, Conn. (36839), 88628, 102708-102709

Wesleyan University, Middletown, Conn. Library. 102710

Wesleyan University, Middletown, Conn.
Peithologian Society. 102711
Wesleyan University, Middletown, Conn.
Peithologian Society. Library. 102711
Wesleyan University, Middletown, Conn.
Philorhetorian Society. 102712-102713
Wesleyan University, Middletown, Conn. Philo-
rhetorian Society. Library. 102712
Wesleyan University, Middletown, Conn. Alumni
records, 1833 to 1869. (36839)
Wesley's thoughts on slavery, etc. 4671, (4674),
4678, 102699
Wesley's visit to America. 35465
Wesselhoeft, Robert. (7443)
West, -------, fl. 1748. 19238
West, -------, fl. 1787-1990. (45307)
West, Benjamin. Ex-Shaker 102714
West, Benjamin, 1730-1813. 52200, 52648,
(52650), 55541, 55543, 62743, (70707),
74327, 93891, 102715, 105008
West, Benjamin, 1730-1813. supposed author
39053
West, Benjamin, 1738-1820. 21050, 26457-
(26458), 72116, 82978, 84617, 84647,
96963, 102713
West, Cato. petitioner 102717
West, David. 102718
West, Elizabeth H. 95117
West, Francis Athon. 102719
West, George Montgomery. 89348, 102720-
102729 see also Protestant Episcopal
Church in the U. S. A. Ohio (Diocese)
Agent.
West, H. Byrd. 20865
West, Hans. 102730-102732
West, James. 102733
West, John, 1780?-1845. 102737-102738
West, John, 1794-1870. note after 102738,
106019-20 [sic]
West, John, fl. 1796-1820. note after 6696,
102734-102736
West, Lucy (Brewer) 2839, 7758, 89409,
102739-102742
West, Moses. 84552
West, Preston C. F. lithographer 84774
West, Robert. (53078), (59679) see also
Board of Proprietors of the Eastern
Division of New Jersey.
West, Samuel, 1731-1807. 95642, 102743-
102744
West, Samuel, 1738-1808. 102745-102751
West, Stephen. (32953), 36039, 102752-102755
West, Thomas. see De La Warr, Thomas
West, 3d Lord, 1577-1618.
West (David) bookseller, Boston 102718
West (John) & Company. firm 102736
West & Blake. firm booksellers 102757
West African stories. 85380
West almanac. 103176
West-Amerikanische Geschichte. 103989
West Amesbury, Mass. Independent Division,
No. 111. see Sons of Temperance of
North America. Massachusetts. Indepen-
dent Division, No. 111, West Amesbury.
West and north to be victims. 91007
West Boston Bridge Company. see Proprietors
of the West Boston Bridge.
West Boylston, Mass. Congregational Church.
24604
West Boylston, Mass. First Congregational
Church. Maternal Association. 102759
West Boylston, Mass. Sabbath School Teachers
Convention. see Baptists. Massachusetts.
Worcester Baptist Association. Sabbath

School Teachers Convention, West
Boylston, Mass.
West Brookfield, Mass. Church. 90691
West Brookfield, Mass. Church. Pastor.
90691
West Brookfield, Mass. Ecclesiastical Council,
1843. see Congregational Churches in
Massachusetts. Ecclesiastical Council,
West Brookfield, 1843.
West Cambridge, Mass. Tornado Committee,
1851. 8339
West Cambridge on the nineteenth of April,
1775. 84013
West Chester, Pa. Chester County Cabinet
of Natural History. see Chester County
Cabinet of Natural History, West Chester,
Pa.
West Chester County, N. Y. see Westchester
County, N. Y.
West-Chester Copper Mine Company. 102951
West Chester Extended Rail Road Company.
defendants 102761
West Chester Rail Road Company. plaintiffs
102761
West Chester Rail Road Company. Charter.
102760
West Chester Rail Road Company. Directors.
102762
West Church, Boston. see Boston. West Church.
West Church and its ministers. 3794
West coast signal. 105053
West Congregational Church, Taunton, Mass.
see Taunton, Mass. West Congregational
Church.
West End Association, New York. Committee.
83849
West Feliciana Railroad Company. 102763
West Feliciana Railroad Company. Charter.
102763
West Florida (Spanish Territory) Gobernador,
1796-1812 (Folch y Juan) 102764 see
also Folch y Juan, Vicente.
West Florida. 99315, note after 102768
West Florida. petitioners 24847, 102767,
102768
West Florida. Convention, 1810. 24903,
102765
West Florida. Governor, 1810 (Skipwith) 1 02766
see also Skipwith, Fulwar.
West Florida. Laws, statutes, etc. 24903,
102765
West Florida. Ordinances adopted by the
convention. 24903, 102765
West for the union, now and forever. 29296
West illustrated. 12625
West India agricultural distress. 10277 0
West-India almanack for the year 1819. 5 8669
West-India atlas. (35970)
West-India Body, London. 93459, 102792
West India claims on the mother country.
102771
West India colonies. (43643)
West-India common-place book. 106128
West India Company (Danish) see West-
Indiske og Guineiske Compagnie.
West India Company (Dutch) see Neder-
landsche West-Indische Compagnie.
West India Company (French) see Compagnie
des Indes Occidentales.
West India Company (Great Britain) see
West India Company, London.
West India Company, London. 102775
West India Company. 102775
West India customs and manners. 50620
West India directory. (55488), 102776

West India Dock Company, London. 31684-31685, 102782

West India Dock Company, London. petitioners 102782

West India Dock Company, London. plaintiffs 102781

West India Dock Company, London. Charter. 44707, 102780

West India Dock Company, London. Directors. Committee. 102777

West India Dock Company, London. General Court. 102777

West India Dock Company, London. Treasurer. defendant 102784 see also Smith, George. defendant

West India Dock Company. 102783

West India Dock Company. The important trial. 102784

West India emancipation. 26712

West India interest considered. 34346

West India interests, African emigration, and slave trade. 19578

West-India islands. 35971

West-India legislatures vindicated. 43172

West-India merchant. pseud. Brief account of the present declining state. 102785

West-India merchant. pseud. Letter from a West-India merchant. 40319

West India merchant. pseud. Letter to the members of Parliament. see Innes, William.

West India merchant. pseud. Permanent and effectual remedy suggested. see Robley, John. supposed author

West-India merchant. pseud. Slave trade indispensable. see Innes, William.

West India merchant. pseud. West India merchant. Being a series of papers. 102786

West India merchant. 102786

West-India merchant, factor and supercargoes daily assistant. 105607

West India Merchants, London. see West India Planters and Merchants, London.

West India Mission. 102787

West India, or Jamaica almanack 1674. 102788

West-India pilot. 89247-89249

West India plantation journal. 91238

West India planter. pseud. Considerations on the emancipation of Negroes. 15982, (67717), 1st note after 102788

West India planter. pseud. Considerations on the state of the sugar islands. 16012, 2d note after 102788

West India planter. pseud. Letter to the Most Honorable the Marquis of Chandos. 40501, 3d note after 102788, 1st note after 102846

West-India planter. pseud. Remarks on the evidence. see Glover, Richard.

West India Planters and Merchants, London. 1779, 23302, 57601, 69744, 91599, 5th note after 102788, 102790, 102793-102794 see also Macarty, --------. Meeting of the West India Planters and Merchants, London.

West India Planters and Merchants, London. petitioners 23302, (27606)-27607, (27610), 40546, 56506, 69690, 4th note after 102788, 3d note after 102846, note after 102851

West India Planters and Merchants, London. Committee on a Bill Depending in Parliament for Forming Wet Docks, &c. 69744, 102793

West India Planters and Merchants, London. Standing Committee. Sub-committee. 97492

West India Planters . . . in Scotland. petitioners 61270

West-India planters vindicated from the charge of inhumanity. 97461, note after 102819

West India proprietor. pseud. Brief observations on the West India question. 102795

West India proprietor. pseud. Refutation of various calumnies. 102796

West India Proprietors. petitioners see West India Planters and Merchants, London. petitioners

West India question considered. 40022

West India question. Immediate emancipation would be safe for the masters. 93144

West India question plainly stated. 21510

West India question practically considered. 22590, 40358, 46855, 91237, 102797, 102845

West India question. The outline of a plan. 62503

West India savage. pseud. New system of fortification. 53404

West India sketch book. 102634-102635

West India slavery. 102798

West India sugar. 102799

West-India trade and islands. 14980, 102800

West Indian. pseud. Comparison between distressed English labourers and the coloured people and slaves of the West Indies. 102801

West Indian. pseud. Considerations on the Negro cause. see Estwick, Samuel.

West Indian. pseud. Epitome of the West India question. 81964, 4th note after 102832

West Indian. pseud. Hints on the propriety of establishing by law the civil rights. 102835A

West Indian. pseud. Jamaica under the new form of government. 35605

West Indian. pseud. Letter . . . on the claims of the West India proprietors. see Hurd, S. P.

West-Indian. pseud. Letter to the Lord Chancellor. 40495, 1st note after 102802

West-Indian. pseud. Maniacs. see Estwick, Samuel. supposed author

West Indian. pseud. No colonies no funds. 55365, 3d note after 102802

West Indian. pseud. Notes in defence of the colonies. 102803

West-Indian. pseud. Rev. Mr. Cooper and his calumnies against Jamaica. (16626), 1st note after 102803

West Indian. pseud. Slavery not forbidden by scripture. see Nisbet, Richard. supposed author

West Indian. pseud. Some considerations. see Clarke, Sir Simon Houghton. supposed author

West Indian. pseud. Sugar duties. 93451

West Indian: a comedy. 17876, 4th note after 102803

West Indian. A novel. 102592

West Indian adventurer. 50161

West Indian converted and slave grateful. 102804

West-Indian eclogues. 102805

West Indian humanity. 102806

West Indian magazine. 10625

West Indian marine shells, with some remarks. 38313

West Indian, mit Anmerkingen. 17878

West Indian; or, memoirs of Frederic Charlton. 102807

West Indian: or, the happy effects of diligence and self-control. 102808

West-Indian pretensions refuted. 91248

West Indian proprietor. pseud. Some considerations on the present state of our West India colonies. 86623, note after 102808

West-Indian sketches. 38243

West-Indian sketches. Drawn from authentic sources. 81852, 102809

West Indian slavery traced to its actual source. 102810

West India story. 37767

West Indian tale. 91074

West Indianische Compagnia. 102923

West-Indianische Reisze und Beschreibung. 710

West-Indianisk reese-beskriffning. 31290

West-Indians. pseud. Maniacs. see Estwick, Samuel.

West Indians defended. 102811

West-Indie. 106334

West-Indie. Bijdragen tot de bevordering von de kenniss de Nederlandsch West Indische kolonien. (24937), 2d note after 93879

West Indies (British Colonies) see British West Indies.

West Indies. 102872

West Indies. A novel. 102592

West Indies, and other poems. 50146

West Indies and other poems, on the abolition of the slave trade. 50147

West Indies as they are. 5218

West Indies, before and since slave emancipation. 18915

West Indies: being a description of the islands. (65571)

West Indies in 1837. 93261, 93264

West Indies, Mauritius, and Ceylon. 58820

West Indies rendered independent of America. 86210, 1st note after 102867

West Indies: the natural and physical history of the Windward and Leeward colonies. 29899

West Indies: . . . with the history of the past and present state of British Guiana. 29900

West-Indisch discours. 102873

West-Indische Compagnie. De ghemeene Directeurs. 27260, 102925

West Indische Compagnie. Reglement by de West-Indische Compagnie. 102928

West-Indische Compagnie. Reglement by de West-Indische Compagnie. 102927

West-Indische Compagnie. Reglement byde West-Indische Compagnie. 68899, note after 102936

West-Indische Compagnie waerschouwinge. 102929

West-Indische klapper. 102930

West-Indische Maatschappij, Amsterdam. 102931-102933

West-Indische Maatschappij, Amsterdam. Charter. 102931

West-Indische Maatschappij, behandeld in een gesprek. 102932

West-Indische Maatschappij, gevestigd te Amsterdam. 102933

West-Indische spieghel. 34722, note after 102933

West-Indische trivmph-basvyne. 1350

West-Indiske og Guineiske Compagnie. 102935, 102938-102941

West-Indiske og Guineiske Compagnie. Charter. 102934, 102936-102937

West-Injes-huys spreekt. 100761

West: its commerce and navigation. 29797

West: its culture and its collages. 43844

West: its destiny and its duty. 97534, 97592

West: its soil, surface, and productions. 29798

West Lexington Presbytery. see Presbyterian Church in the U. S. A. Presbytery of West Lexington.

West Market Street Meeting. Termination of the Pennsylvania Rail Way. 60358

West Medford, Mass. Mystic-Hall Seminary. see Mystic-Hall Seminary, West Medford, Mass.

West Newbury, Mass. Merrimac Division, No. 183. see Sons of Temperance of North America. Massachusetts. Merrimac Division, No. 138, West Newbury.

West-Newton, Mass. Normal School. see Massachusetts. State Normal School, West-Newton.

West-Newton, Mass. State Normal School. see Massachusetts. State Normal School, West-Newton.

West on the resurrection. 19238

West Parrish Association, Boston. 102943

West Parish Association, Boston. Committee on the Library. 102943

West Parish Association, Boston. Committee on the State of Religion. 102944

West Parish Association, Boston. Committee on the Sunday Schools. 102943

West Philadelphia. 62379

West Philadelphia. Committee to Consider Plans for Erecting Water Works. 62379

West Philadelphia. Council. 62379

West Philadelphia. Ordinances, etc. 61565, 62379

West Philadelphia (District), Philadelphia. see West Philadelphia.

West Philadelphia Canal Company. petitioners 62231

West Philadelphia Children's Home. 62380

West Philadelphia Homestead Association. (62381)

West Philadelphia Institute. Managers. 62382

West Philadelphia Institute. Treasurer. 62382

West Philadelphia Passenger Railway Company. 62383

West Philadelphia Passenger Railway Company. Charter. 62383

West Philadelphia Railroad Company. 62384, 102945

West Philadelphia Railroad Company. Charter. 62384, note after 102944

West Philadelphia Railroad Company. Chief Engineer. 102945

West Philadelphia Railroad Company. President. note just before 60250

West Point, N. Y. Military Academy. see U. S. Military Academy, West Point, N. Y.

West Point cadet. 64100

West Point; or a tale of treason. (7653)

West Point oration. 43020-(43021)

West proposed line of steam communication. 85240

West Roxbury, Mass. note before 102947

West Roxbury, Mass. Brook Farm Association. see Brook Farm Association for Industry and Education, West Roxbury, Mass.

West Roxbury, Mass. Mount Hope Cemetery. see Dorchester, Mass. Mount Hope Cemetery.

West Roxbury directory. 8251

West Side Association, New York. 54716

West Side Association, relating to New York city improvements. 54716

West Side Improvement and its relation to all the commerce. 83850

West Springfield, Mass. Celebration of the One Hundredth Anniversary of the Ordination of the Rev. Joseph Lathrop, D. D., 1856. 89729

West Stafford, Conn. Ecclesiastical Councils, 1781. see Congregational Churches in Connecticut. Ecclesiastical Councils, West Stafford, 1781.

West Stafford, Conn. Second Church. 25232, 73562, 102947

West Stafford, Conn. Second Church. Committee. 25232, 73562, 102947 see also Blodget, Silas. Davis, Samuel. Johnson, Nathan.

West Stafford, Conn. Second Church. Pastor. 25232, 73562, 102947 see also Foster, Isaac.

West Stafford Association. see Congregational Churches in Connecticut. West Stafford Association.

West thirty years since. A poem. 14786

West-vnnd Ost Indische Lustgart. (22657), 1st note after 102874, note after 102948

West-vnnd Ost Indischer Lustgart. (22657), 42742

West Virginia. Constitution. 1269, 16113, 33137, (66397)

West Virginia. Laws, statutes, etc. 82438, 70820-70821

West Virginia. Office of the Commissioner of Immigration. 19085

West Virginia Iron Mining and Manufacturing Company. 102948

West Virginia; its farms and forests, mines and oil fields. 20500

West Vriesland (Province) see Holland (Province)

West Washington market case. 6021

Westborough, Mass. Reform School. see Massachusetts. Reform School, Westborough.

Westbrook, G. W. 50755

Westbrook, Me. First Congregational Church. 102949

Westbrook; or, the outlaw. 71046

Westbusch, Passchier van. 4804

Westchester County, N. Y. Auxiliary Bible Society. see Westchester County Auxiliary Bible Society.

Westchester County, N. Y. Citizens. petitioners 84556, 102957

Westchester County, N. Y. Court. 46896

Westchester County, N. Y. Owners of Real Estate. petitioners see Owners of Real Estate in the County of Westchester. petitioners

Westchester County, N. Y. Rip Van Winkle Club. see Rip Van Winkle Club of Westchestre County, N. Y.

Westchester Agriculgural Society. 102950

Westchester American republican. see American republican.

Westchester Associated Presbytery. see Presbyterian Church in the U. S. A. Associate Presbytery of Westchester.

Westchester County Auxiliary Bible Society. 102954

Westchester County Bank. Charter. 102955

Westchester County directory. (27954)

Westchester County Historical Society. 2d note after 99553

Westchester County Temperance Society. 102956

Westchester farmer. pseud. Congress canvassed. see Seabury, Samuel, Bp., 1729-1796. and Wilkins, Isaac.

Westchester farmer. pseud. Free thoughts. see Seabury, Samuel, Bp., 1729-1796. and Wilkins, Isaac.

Westchester farmer. pseud. Remarks on a petition. 102957

Westchester farmer. pseud. View of the controversy. see Seabury, Samuel, Bp., 1729-1796. and Wilkins, Isaac. and Cooper, Myles. incorrectly supposed author and Chandler, Thomas Bradbury. incorrectly supposed author and Inglis, Charles, Bishop of Nova Scotia, 1734-1816. incorrectly supposed author

Westchester gazette. 18936

Westcott, James D. 57440, 102958

Westcott, James Diament, 1802-1880. 102959

Westcott, Thompson, 1820-1888. (51742), 75510, 83793, 84589

Westerlo, E. tr. 65677

Westerly, R. I. Pawcatuck Library Association. Library. see Pawcatuck Library Association, Westerly, R. I. Library.

Westerman, Hans. note after 102959

Western, Henry M. 3707, 102961

Western academician and journal of education and science. 102961

Western Academy of Natural Sciences of Cincinnati. (56889)

Western address directory. (42767)

Western Agency of the Presbyterian Education Society. see Presbyterian Education Society. Western Agency.

Western agriculturist, and practical farmer's guide. see Farmer's guide, and western agriculturalist.

Western almanac for 1816. 62569

Western almanac for . . . 1824. 9050

Western America, including California and Oregon. 103995

Western and Atlantic Railroad. 102963

Western and Northern Inland Lock Navigation Companies. Directors. 69857, 102964, 102984

Western antiquary. (67547)

Western Association of Ladies for the Relief and Employment of the Poor, Philadelphia. 62385

Western Association of New-Haven County, Conn. see Congregational Churches in Connecticut. New Haven County Western Association.

Western Association of Universalists, New York. see Universalist Church in the U. S. New York. Western Association.

Western Association upon Merrimack River. see Congregational Churches in Massachusetts. Western Association Upon Merrimack River.

Western banker. pseud. Uniform national currency. see R., J. J. pseud.

Western Baptist Association of Nova Scotia. see Baptists. Nova Scotia. Western Baptist Association.

Western Baptist Educational Association. Executive Committee. 102970

Western Baptist Theological Institute, Covington, Ky. 17216

Western Baptist Theological Institute, Covington, Ky. Board of Trustees. 69694

Western Board of Agency of the American Sunday School Union. see Western Sunday School Board of Agency.

Western border life. 33916, 23787

Western calendar, or the Cincinnati almanac. 43243, 93229

Western campaign of the Agents of the "American Free Trade League." 91014

Western Canal Convention, Rochester, N. Y., 1839. 22752, 102972

Western Canal Convention, Rochester, N. Y., 1839. Executive Committee. 22752, 102972

Western captive, or the times of Tecumseh. 82523

Western Central Railroad Company of Pennsylvania. 59964

Western Central Railroad Company of Pennsylvania. defendants 68169

Western characters or types of border life in the western states. 43087

Western Cherokees. Statement and argument on their claims. 12477, 90115

Western Cherokees, their claims under treaties of 1835-36. 12477, 90115

Western Christian advocate. 89367

Western Christian monitor. 102973

Western citizen. pseud. Examination of the opinion. 23362, note after 102973

Western citizen. pseud. Texas. 95116

Western clearings. (37993)

Western Clinical Infirmary, Philadelphia. 62386

Western Clinical Infirmary, Philadelphia. Charter. 62386

Western College Society. see Society for the Promotion of Collegiate and Theological Education at the West.

Western Consocia tion in Fairfield County, Conn. see Congregational Churches in Connecticut. Fairfield County Western Consociation.

Western conspiracy against the railroad interests of Maryland. (29382)

Western conspiracy in aid of the southern rebellion. 32652, 69874

Western continent. 4618

Western Department, etc. 69869

Western Department of the United States Sanitary Commission. see United States Sanitary Commission. Western Department.

Western District Agricultural and Horticultural Society. Directing President. 102974

Western Domestic Missionary Society of the State of New York. 102974A

Western ecclesiastical court. 83755

Western Education Society Cincinnati. Directors. 102975

Western Education Society of the State of New York. Directors. 102976

Western emigration. Journal of Doctor Jeremiah Smipleton's [sic] tour to Ohio. 97201

Western emigration. Narrative of a tour. 104013

Western emigrants' magazine. 102977

Western ephemens. 63123

Western examiner. 102978

Western farmer and gardener. 102979

Western farmer, devoted to agriculture, horticulture, and rural economy. 102979

Western farmer's almanac. 93230

Western farms & factories. 91015

Western Foreign Missionary Society. 12891, 49466, 84358-84362, 84365

Western Foreign Missionary Society. Board of Directors. (65229), note after 102979

Western fruit-book. A compendiouⁿ collection of facts. 32870

Western fruit book; or, American fruit-grower's guide. (22266)

Western gazetteer. [By Edward H. Hall.] 29762

Western gazetteer; or emigrant's directory. 8558

Western general advertiser. 13153

Western grape grower. pseud. My vineyard at Lakeview. 51624

Western guide book, and emigrant's directory, containing different routes. 91141-91143

Western guide book, and emigrant's directory; containing general descriptions of different routes. 91145, 102980

Western home, and other poems. 80965

Western House of Refuge for Juvenile Delinquents, Rochester, N. Y. see New York (State) State Industrial School, Rochester.

Western Inland Lock Navigation Company. 102986

Western Inland Lock Navigation Company. Charter. 102981

Western Inland Lock Navigation Company. Directors. 69857, 102964, 102982, 102984, 102986

Western journal of medicine and surgery. 93810, 102992

Western journal of the medical and physical sciences. 102992

Western Kansas Immigration Society. (37074)

Western Ladies of Philadelphia for the Relief . . . of the Poor. Board. see Board of Western Ladies of Philadelphia for the Relief . . . of the Poor.

Western Land Agency and Commission Office, St. Louis, Mo. 4224

Western Land Company. 102987

Western lands and western waters. 27189

Western layman. pseud. Serpent uncoiled 79305

Western Library Association of Philadelphia. 62387

Western Literary and Scientifick Academy, Buffalo. 102988

Western Literary Institute, and College of Professional Teachers, Cincinnati. 102961, 102989-102990

Western literary journal, and monthly review. 88617, 102991

Western lyre. 85616

Western man. pseud. Essay, on hemp and flax in the west. see Bragdon, C. D.

Western man. pseud. Legends of a log-cabin. see Gilman, Chandler R. and Thorpe, Thomas Bangs. incorrectly supposed author

Western Maryland Rail Road. 3086

Western Maryland Rail Road. plaintiffs 45396

Western Maryland Rail Road. Attorney. 45396 see also Fisher, William A.

Western Maryland Rail Road. President and Directors. 45396

Western Maryland Rail Road, its agricultural and mineral resources. (45395)

Western Maryland Railroad and His Honor the Mayor of Baltimore. 45396

Western medical and physical journal, original
and eclectic. 1 02992
Western memorabilia. pseud. see Gowan
(William) publisher
Western merchant, a narrative. 80731
Western messenger. 11918
Western messenger: devoted to religion and
literature. 102993
Western Methodist Historical Society of the
Mississippi Valley. Board of Managers.
102994
Western metropolis. 81590
Western Military Institute, Nashville, Tenn.
Collegiate Department. 51880
Western miscellany. 91838
Western Missionary Society of Pennsylvania.
60780, 102995
Western Missionary Society of Pennsylvania.
Trustees. 60780, 102995
Western missions and missionaries. 82277
Western monitor. 25172, 33905, 96466
Western monthly magazine. see Hesperian:
or, western monthly magazine.
Western monthly magazine, a continuation of
the Illinois monthly magazine. see
Western monthly magazine, and literary
journal.
Western monthly magazine, and literary journal.
13074, (34261), 85144, 92448, 101080,
102996, 104448
Western monthly review. 102997
Western navigator: containing charts of the Ohio
River. 17902
Western navigator: containing directions for
the navigation. 17903
Western neptune, or pilot for America. 35965
Western New York Sabbath school advocate.
106205
Western Pennsylvania Hospital, Dixmont, Pa.
see Dixmont, Pa. Western Pennsylvania
Hospital.
Western Pennsylvania Hospital, Harrisburg, Pa.
see Dixmont, Pa. Western Pennsylvania
Hospital.
Western pilot. (17904)
Western portraiture, and emigrant's guide.
18069
Western prairie life; an autobiography. (29388)
Western primer, or introduction to Webster's
spelling book. 102998
Western rail-way. 103011
Western Railroad Company. petitioners 90774
Western Railroad Corporation. 102999-103000,
103004, 103008, 103010-103011 see also
Committee of the Boston and Worcester
and Western Railroad Corporations on
Uniting the Two Railroads. Subscribers
for Procuring a Survey of the Western
Rail-Road. Executive Committee.
Western Railroad Corporation. petitioners
32889, 103002
Western Railroad Corporation. Charter.
103001
Western Railroad Corporation. Delegation to
Albany, 1840. 103006
Western Railroad Corporation. Directors.
103001
Western Railroad Corporation. Directors.
petitioners 101519
Western Railroad Corporation. Engineers.
103009
Western Railroad Corporation. Transportation
Department. 103005
Western reader. 103012

Western Reserve almanac for 1818. 71917
Western Reserve Branch of the American
Education Society. see Western Re-
serve Education Society.
Western Reserve chronicle. 58092
Western Reserve College, Hudson, Ohio. see
Western Reserve University, Cleveland,
Ohio.
Western Reserve College catalogue. 33506
Western Reserve Education Society. Directors.
103015
Western Reserve Foreign Missionary Society.
Directors. 103016
Western Reserve Historical Society, Cleveland,
Ohio. 21092
Western Reserve Historical Society, Cleveland,
O., August, 1870. 21092
Western Reserve University, Cleveland, Ohio.
33506, 103014
Western review. see Evangelical record and
western review.
Western review (1819-   ) 67453
Western review (1851-   ) see Ohio
teacher.
Western review. [By Richard McNemar.]
105575
Western Sanitary Commission, St. Louis, Mo.
(22178), note after 103016
Western Sanitary Commission; a sketch of its
origin. 25097, note after 103016
Western scenes and reminiscences. 77837,
77867, (77882)
Western scenes; or, life on the prairie. 71730
Western Shore Association. see Baptists.
Maryland. Western Shore Association.
Western Shore treasury. 45080
Western sketch-book. 26380
Western Society of Engineers. 84898
Western South American and its relation to
American trade. 83383
Western souvenir, a Christmas and New Year's
gift for 1829. 29799, 103018
Western spy and literary cadet. (59554),
(62740)
Western star (Lebanon, Ohio) 82770B, 92768
Western star (Stockbridge, Mass.) 93937
Western State Normal School, Farmington, Me.
see Maine. State Normal and Training
School, Farmington.
Western states: their pursuits and policy.
22097
Western Sunday School Board of Agency.
103019
Western Teachers' Institute, Marietta, O.
see Marietta College, Marietta, Ohio.
Western Theological Seminary of the Pres-
byterian Church, Alleghany City, Pa.
65230
Western tour. 103020
Western tourist. pseud. Ma-Ka-Tai-Me-She-
Kia-Kiak. see Smith, Elbert H.
Western tourist and emigrant's guide. 82931
Western tourist or emigrant's guide. 14797,
82931-82932, 103021
Western tourist or pocket manual. 103022
Western trader. pseud. Letters on the
necessity of cheapening transport. 40625
Western traveler's pocket directory and
stranger's guide. 103023
Western traveller, and northern tour. (55833)
Western traveller, embracing the canal and
railroad routes. 20325
Western traveller's pocket directory and
stranger's guide. 103024
Western Union Telegraph Company. 83961

Western Unitarian Association. see Unitarian Churches. U. S. Western Association.

Western University of Pennsylvania. see Pittsburgh. University.

Western wanderings; or, a pleasure tour in the Canadas. 37907

Western watchman. 89372

Western wilds of America. 68799

Western windows, and other poems. 62598

Western woodpecker. 41799

Western woods and waters. 72

Western world. 105043

Western world; or, travels in the United States in 1846-47. 43351

Western world revisited. 11479

Westervelt, Jacob A. 54158 see also New York (City) Mayor, 1853-1854 (Westervelt)

Westerwyk, Gerard. tr. 38648

Westfield, Mass. Congregational Church. 103027

Westfield, Mass. Normal School. see Massachusetts. State Normal School, Westfield.

Westfield, Mass. State Normal School. see Massachusetts. State Normal School, Westfield.

Westfield, Mass. Westfield Academy. see Westfield. Academy, Westfield, Mass.

Westfield, a view of home life. 43538

Westfield Academy, Westfield, Mass. 103028

Westfield Baptist Association. see Baptists. Massachusetts. Westfield Baptist Association.

Westhuysen, Abrahamus A. 103031

Westindian. pseud. Charleston, South Carolina. 12042

Westindian. 17877

Westindianischen Kleinen Albertus. 102874

Westindien. 106345

Westindien und der Kontinent von Sudamerika. 42169

Westindien und die Sudpolar-Lander. 91197, 91436

Westindische Compagnie. Notificatie. 56018, 102926

Westland. 103032

Westliche Welt. Reise durch die Vereinsstaaten van Amerika. 37122, 43352

Westliche Welt. Reisen in den Vereinigten Staaten. 43553

Westman, Georg A. 103033

Westman, Habakkuk O. pseud. Spoon. see Ewbank, Thomas. supposed author

Westminster, England. Court of King's Bench. see Great Britain. Court of King's Bench.

Westminster, England. Genera Meeting of the Electors, 1782. 25337

Westminster, Mass. 100 Anniversary Celebration, 1859. 103035

Westminster, Vt. Congregational Church. 103036

Westminster, Vt. Superior Court. see Vermont. Superior Court, Westminster.

Westminster and foreign quarterly review. (44754), 79542

Westminster Assembly of Divines. 1649, 15445, 20223, 24678, 27952-27954, 39031-39032, 46534, 49859, 51586, (52713)-52716, 52726, 52730, note after 65546, (80709)-80728, 84713, 85297, 86358, 86364, note after 93573, 95407, 97984, 103037, 104075

Westminster Assembly's catechism. note after 65546

Westminster catechism. 20223, (80709)-80728

Westminster Church, Buffalo, N. Y. see Buffalo, N. Y. Westminster Church.

Westminster Church of Christ, Providence, R. I. see Providence, R. I. Westminster Church of Christ.

Westminster Congregational Society, Providence, R. I. see Providence, R. I. Westminster Church of Christ.

Westminster Forum. 103038

Westminster Forum. President. 103038 see also Turner, Daniel.

Westminster Glaubens-Bekenntniss in Uebereinstimmung. 84762

Westminster review. 8119, 10645, (44262), 75940, 84417, 92882, 95532-95533

Westmoreland, John Fane, 10th Earl of, 1759-1841. 102039

Westmoreland County, Pa. Collector of Excise. 28238 see also Graham, William.

Westmoreland County, Pa. Friends of the General Administration Meeting, Greensburgh, 1827. see National Republican Party. Pennsylvania. Westmoreland County.

Westmoreland County, Pa. Lieutenant. 103040 see also Cook, Edward.

Westmoreland County, Pa. Sub-Lieutenant. 103040

Westmoreland: or, secession ferocity. 19607

Weston, ------. 44222 see also Manchester, N. H. Mayor, 1869 (Weston)

Weston, --------. engr. 86169

Weston, Cyrus. plaintiff 103041

Weston, Daniel Cony. 103042

Weston, Edward. supposed author 96358, note after 103042, note after 103067

Weston, Edward Payson. ed. 7039, 103043

Weston, Ezra. 103044

Weston, Gershom B. 21492, 103045

Weston, Isaac. 103046

Weston, John E. 103047

Weston, Jonathan Delesdernier. 103048

Weston, Miss M. A. supposed author 94249, 103049

Weston, Nathan. 103050

Weston, Nathan. incorrectly supposed author 103042

Weston, Plowden Charles Jennett. ed 103051

Weston, Richard. 103052

Weston, Silas. 103053-103054

Weston, Stephen. 103054A

Weston, Theodore. 8331

Weston, William. engineer 54645, 69857, 102964, 102984, 103057

Weston, William. Merchant 103055-103056

Weston, William, fl. 1875. 89109

Weston. firm see Paris and Weston. firm

Weston, Mass. Reunion of the Sons of Weston, 1853. (82331)

Weston & Atchison Rail Road Company. President. 49607

Westover manuscripts. (9721)

Westtown Boarding School. 103058

Westtown Boarding School. Committee. 103058

Westward by rail. 67430

Westward empire. 43841

Westward ho! A tale. 59190, 59216, note after 103058

Westward ho! or, the voyages and adventures of Sir Amyas Leigh. 37889

Westward hoe for Avalon. 103332

Wet days at Edgewood. 49680

Wetenhall, Edward, successively Bishop of Cork, and Kilmore and Ardagh, 1636-1713. 59691, 73398-73400, (73402), 91385

What I saw in the army. 3536
What I saw on the west coast of South and North America. 4002
What is a ghost? 7718
What is a monopoly? 78845, 3d note after 103115
What is a revenue standard? 1823
What is Calvinism? 84762
What is Christ to me, if He is not mine? 17675
What is contraband of war and what is not. 51054
What is done for the poor. 24634, 54419
What is education? 29615
What is fair and equal reciprocity? 43092
What is gentility? 83511
What is it? 55106
What is monopoly? 78845, 3d note after 103115
What is needed. 51968
What is our constitution, league, pact, or government? 40985
What is our present duty to the slaves. (9744)
What is our situation? and what our prospects? 32985, 6th note after 103115-103116
What is Presbyterianism? (32330)
What is resistance? 35418
What is sauce for a goose is also sauce for a gander. 78475, 104455
What is slavery? 17257
What is slavery? By Jehu Geeup, of Jackass Alley. 82025
"What is that hath been? the same thing shall be." 1535A
What is the character of the late tariff law? 96380
What is the matter? 105598-9 [sic]
What is the object of this war. 66903
What is the result of the election? fully answered. 103117
What is the true policy of the state of New York? 8359
What is treason? 89718
What is true civilization 78875
What is truth? 66676
What is unconditional unionism? 29533
What it was, is, and ought to be. 56753
What "Jeems Pipes of Pipesville" saw—and—did. 46175
What Jeff Davis said. (27453), 68322
What makes slavery a question of national concern? 188
What may be accomplished in a lifetime. 78100
What may be done by the public in anticipation of the cholera. 61504
What may or may not be done. 93560
What measures the English ought to take. 69516, 97560
What miscegenation is! 78613
What New York might be with a good government. (54188)
What ought the Diocese to do? (47245)
What ought to be done with the freedmen and the rebels? 19896
What our generals say. 8285
What our soldiers say about the Copperheads. 21781
What President Lincoln did for his country. (67312)
What religion may do for a man. note after (58767)
What Santa Anna's professions of republicanism are worth. 76747
What says the law? 90795
What shall be done? 57931

What shall be done with the confiscated Negroes? 44253
What shall be done with the people of color? 90551
What shall be done with the practice of the courts? 24274
What shall we do? (29839)
What shall we do with Canada? (10621), 103118
What shall we do with the Hudson's Bay Territory? 68008
What shall we do with the insane of the western country? 35805
What she is, what she lacks, and what her position is. 66189
What should be done: or, remarks on the political state of things. 103119
What should be most of all tho't upon. 46594, 1st note after 103119
What some did then, others are seeking to do now. 49972
What sort of armistice the rebels will accept. 8285
What the French king will do with respect to the Spanish monarchy. 69516, 97560
What the North has to do with slavery. 22175
What the people of the Pacific coast think of the Coolie invasion. 90557
What the people ought to know about the national banks. 16313
What the pious parent wishes for. 46595
What the President proclaims!! (68246)
What the rebels say. (42546)
What the Republican Party have accomplished. 90641
What the soldiers think of northern traitors. 9073
What the Supreme Court decided in the prize (18444)
What the U. S. Sanitary Commission is doing in the Valley of the Mississippi. 54896, (76590), 76647
What they have to do who stay at home. 76575, 76647
What they suffered and what they sought. 48681
What think ye of Christ? 103583, 103610
What think ye of Congress now? A plan of a proposed union. 11882, 16590-16591, 2d note after 103119
What think ye of the Congress now? Or, an enquiry. 11882, 16590-16591, 2d note after 103119
What to see, and how to see it. (54683)
What to see and how to see it. . . . Gude to New York City. (61379)
What traitors say. (55793)
What was said at giving the right hand of fellowship. (65613)
What we are and what we will be. 27443
What we are coming to! 44339
What we are to expect now that Mr. Lincoln is re-elected. 78613
What we did at Gettysburg. 27249
What we have secured by the war. 82384
What will be the place assigned by history to Abraham Lincoln? 41239
What will Congress do? 103120
What you please. 5347
Whatcheer, a story of olden times. 12694
Whatcheer! or Roger Williams in banishment. (21426)
Whatcoat, Richard, Bp. 62582, note after 103120
Whately, George. supposed author 38180, 65678, 103121

3143

Whately, R. 32048
Whately, Thomas. (5859), 10243, 28770-28771, 103122-103123
Whately, Thomas. supposed author (1969), (3111), 28768-28769, 38180, 54979, 56562, 1st-2d notes after 103122
Whately, W. (23712)
Whatever is, is right. 12693
Whatly, George. see Whately, George. supposed author
Wheat, J. Thomas. 102124
Wheat, Josiah. see Wheet, Josiah.
Wheat and silk. 14535
Wheat fields and amrkets of the world. 83901
Wheat plant: its origin, culture, growth, development. (38054)
Wheatley, John. 103136
Wheatley, Phillis. see Peters, Phillis (Wheatley) 1753?-1784.
Wheaton, Eber. defendant 81325
Wheaton, Hannah. 103143-103150
Wheaton, Henry, 1785-1848. 39377, (74252), 103151-103159, 103161
Wheaton, Henry, 1785-1848. plaintiff 103160, 103162
Wheaton, Henry, 1785-1848. reporter 27293, (33241), 103153
Wheaton, Joseph. petitioner 103163
Wheaton, Josephus. 103164
Wheaton, Levi. 103165
Wheaton, Nathaniel Sheldon. (69512), 1st note after 101998, 103166-103169
Wheaton, Nathaniel Sheldon. incorrectly supposed author 15720-15721, 36334, 2d note after 101998, 103169
Wheaton College, Norton, Mass. 103170
Wheaton Female Seminary, Norton, Mass. see Wheaton College, Norton, Mass.
Wheaton on captures. (74252), 103155
Whedon, Daniel Denison. 103171-103173
Wheel in the middle of a wheel. 83803
Wheeler, A, J. ed. (45513)
Wheeler, Alfred. 103174
Wheeler, Bennett. 103175-103176
Wheeler, C. B. 103177
Wheeler, C. Gilbert. tr. (5952)
Wheeler, Charles. 103178
Wheeler, Charles Stearns. 103179
Wheeler, Daniel, Jr. ed. 103182
Wheeler, Daniel, 1771-1840. 103180-103182
Wheeler, Ephraim. defendant 103183
Wheeler, George. auctioneer 103184
Wheeler, George B. 9857
Wheeler, Ira B. 103190
Wheeler, Jacob D. 96943, 103185-103189
Wheeler, James. 103191
Wheeler, John, 1553?-1610? 103192-103193
Wheeler, John, 1798-1862. 99213, 103194-103195
Wheeler, John H. plaintiff 10696
Wheeler, John Hill. 103196
Wheeler, Jonathan. 48852, 103279 see also Whig Party. Massachusetts. Middlesex County. Convention, Concord, 1838. Committee.
Wheeler, Mercy. 103197
Wheeler, O. G. 99213
Wheeler, Peter. 103198
Wheeler, Sarah. 103199
Wheeler, Sophia W. 101453
Wheeler, T. cartographer 3606
Wheeler, Thomas, 1620?-1686. 25007, 52872, 103200
Wheeler, W. A. 86917
Wheeler's Manchester chronicle. 16612
Wheeler's North American calendar. 55543
Wheeling, W. Va. 2992

Wheeling, W. Va. City Engineer. 2992
Wheeling, W. Va. People's League of the Old and New World. see People's League of the Old and New World, Wheeling, W. Va.
Wheeling (Diocese) Bishop (Whelan) 72974 see also Whelan, Richard Vinc., Bp.
Wheeling (Diocese) Synod, 1873. 72974
Wheeling and Belmont Bridge Company. defendants 30333, 74316, 90390, 90394
Wheeling Bridge. 22209
Wheeling directory and advertiser. 103201
Wheelock, ------- Capt. 48099
Wheelock, Eleazar, 1711-1779. 19372, (43066), 103202-1st note after 103214, 104369
Wheelock, Eleazar, 1711-1779. supposed author 103217
Wheelock, James. 18632, 1st note after 97087, 2d note after 103214 see also Hanover, N. H. Congregational Church. Committee.
Wheelock, James R. defendant before presbytery 103215
Wheelock, James Ripley. 103216
Wheelock, John. 18630, 18633, (21281), (25775), 58598, note after 99814, 103217-103220
Wheelock, Matthew. 103221
Wheels of the world govern'd by a wise providence. 919
Wheelwright, I. W. 103222
Wheelwright, John. of New York 43188, note after 103223 see also New York Female Benevolent Society. Auditing Committee. Chairman.
Wheelwright, John, 1592-1679. 19051, 103223
Wheelwright, Lot. 6604
Wheelwright, Timothy. pseud. 103224 Mr. Zenger. 103224
Wheelwright, William, 1798-1873. 43150, 90775, note after 103224, 104607
Wheems, M. L. see Weems, Mason Locke, 1759-1825.
Wheet, Josiah. 103225
Wheildon, William Willder. 103226
Whelan, Richard Vinc., Bp. 72974 see also Wheeling (Diocese) Bishop (Whelan)
Wheland, William. 103227
Whelp, Treumund. tr. 17936
Whelpley, Ann. 103232
Whelpley, Philip Melancthon. 103228
Whelpley, Samuel. 81522, 103229-103232
Whelpley, Samuel W. 103233
When America first at heaven's command. 103234
When I was young and in my prime. 105489
When shall we th[ree meet again.] 103235
When the chimneys of the barracks of the different regiments want sweeping. 60168, 103236
When the conduct of individuals in a community is such as to attract public attention. 103237
When the Godly cease and faithful fail. (79434), 103899
When the people, and the rulers among them, willingly offer themselves. 65078
When was the drama introduced in America? 18358
When will the day come? (45898)
Whence came the oil? (50883)
Where are the remains of Columbus? 80022
Where are the spoils of the slave? 28442
Where are ye all now? 103238
Where do the gold and silver go? 82806
Where Governor Seymour got his "lessons." 80419

Where there is prefixed unto a late pamphlet. 65689

Where to emigrant, and why. (27633)

Where to go, and who should go. 34015

Where to settle in the River Plate states. 36216

Where will it end? 67189

Where would be the harm of a speedy peace? 103239

Whereas a certain congregation in Boston. 103240

Whereas a great handle is made against Messrs. De Lancey and Walton. 103241, 103250

Whereas a great number of people have express'd a desire. 103242

Whereas a great number of people have exprest a desire. 103243

Whereas a publick library, whould be very useful. 103244

Whereas a supplementary article to the treaty between the United States and the Delaware Indians. 96661

Whereas a treaty between the United States of America and the Belantse-etoa or Minnetaree Tribe of Indians. 96644

Whereas, a treaty between the United States of America and the Chippeway, Menomonie and Winnebago Tribes of Indians. 96652

Whereas a treaty between the United States of America and the Choctaw Nation of Indians. 96635

Whereas a treaty between the United States of America and the Confederated Tribes of the Sacs and Foxes. 96662

Whereas a treaty between the United States of America and the Creek Nation of Indians was made and concluded. 96654

Whereas a treaty between the United States of America and the Creek Nation of Indians, was made and concluded on the twelfth day of February. 96636

Whereas a treaty between the United States of America and the Crow Tribe of Indians. 96646

Whereas, a treaty between the United States of America; and the Eel River or Throntown Party of Miami Indians. 96655

Whereas a treaty between the United States of America and the Great and Little Osage Tribes of Indians. 96637

Whereas a treaty between the United States of America and the Hunkpapas Band of the Sioux Tribe of Indians. 96642

Whereas a treaty between the United States of America and the Ioway Tribe of Indians. 96632

Whereas a treaty between the United States of America and the Kanzas Nation of Indians was made and concluded. 96638

Whereas a treaty between the United States of America and the Maha Tribe of Indians. 96650

Whereas a treaty between the United States of America and the Mandan Tribe of Indians. 96645

Whereas a treaty, between the United States of America and the Nation of Winnebago Indians. 96659

Whereas a treaty between the United States of America and the Ottoe and Missouri Tribe of Indians. 96648

Whereas a treaty between the United States of America and the Pawnee Tribe of Indians was made and concluded. 96649

Whereas a treaty between the United States of America and the Poncar Tribe of Indians was made and concluded. 96639

Whereas, a treaty between the United States of America, and the Potawatamie Tribe of Indians, was entered into. 96653

Whereas a treaty between the United States of America and the Quapaw Nation of Indians. 96634

Whereas a treaty between the United States of America and the Ricara Tribe of Indians was made and concluded. 96643

Whereas a treaty between the United States of America and the Shawonee Nation of Indians was made and concluded. 96651

Whereas a treaty between the United States of America and the Sioune and Ogallala Tribes of Indians. 96641

Whereas a treaty between the United States of America, and the Sioux and Chippewa. 96647

Whereas a treaty between the United States of America and the Sock and Fox Tribes of Indians. 96633

Whereas a treaty between the United States of America and the Teton, Yancton, and Yanctonies Bands of the Sioux Indians. 96640

Whereas a treaty of commerce and navigation. 65935

Whereas a treaty of peace and friendship. 99605

Whereas, a treaty was made and concluded at the Forks of the Wabash. 96737

Whereas, a treaty was made at Stockbridge. 96736

Whereas an advertisement was yesterday dispers'd about this town. 98696

Whereas an association has lately been entered into. 103245

Whereas an uncommon and rittous disturbance prevails. 103246

Whereas an unhappy dispute has subsisted between some of the citizens. 99007

Whereas articles of agreement between the United States of America and the Band of Delaware Indians. 96660

Whereas articles of agreement between the United States of America, and the Winnenbago Tribe. 96657

Whereas by letters received from His Grace the Duke of Portland. 98058B

Whereas Colonel Sheldon, has by insinuations base and dishonorable. 91933

Whereas during the incursions which have been made. 100198

Whereas . . . for the better setling of the colony and plantation in Virginia, etc. 99856

Whereas great quantities of English copper half-pence have been lately imported into this province. 103247

Whereas [blank] hath paid in readie money to Sir Thomas Smith Knight. 99854

Whereas His Britannic Majesty. 106119

Whereas His Most Excellenty Majesty having received advice. 78201

Whereas His Most Excellent Majesty having received advice, that several ships of force fitted out in Scotland. 78202

Whereas it appears by letters lately received. 98058A

Whereas it appears by the minutes of the Council. 98065C

Whereas it has been expedient. 103249

Whereas it has been reported that a permit will be given. 103248

Whereas, it is declared in the preamble of the constitution. 99205

Whereas it is industriously reported. 100104

Whereas it is pretended by an advertisement. 103241, 103250

Whereas it is reported, that an effigy or effigies will be exhibited. 103251

Whereas it is represented to me. 100219

Whereas it is the prevailing rage of the present time. 103252

Whereas Lord Dunmore, not contented. 103253

Whereas Low Jackson. 99989

Whereas many persons have settled upon lands. 98059E

Whereas on the death of the late Governour Montgomerie. 98433

Whereas on the late examination before the Honourable House of Assembly. 103254

Whereas [blank] paid in ready money to Sir Thomas Smythe Knight. 99862

Whereas Rip Van Dam, Esq; 98436

Whereas, several persons, inhabitants of the United States of America. 101696

Whereas since my return from St. George's River. 101005

Whereas sundrie the aduenturers to Virginia. 99870

Whereas sundry persons, inhabitants of this state. 99053

Whereas the enemy have invaded this state. 87535

Whereas the . . . exertions of the good people of this state. 99051

Whereas the existing state of the province renders the continuation. 98059B

Whereas the General Assembly of this state did appoint me. 99002

Whereas the General Court of the commonwealth of Massachusetts. 99058

Whereas the good shippe, called the Hercules. 99857

Whereas the Governor and Company of the English colony of Rhode-Island. 103255

Whereas the ladies of Charlestown. 86353

Whereas the Legislature of this state, at their session in June last. 99054

Whereas the ministerial army have abandoned the town of Boston. 101691

Whereas the number of poor in and around the city. 103256

Whereas the rapid and alarming depreciation of the currency. 103257

Whereas the . . . situation of the United States. 100087

Whereas the statute laws are now completed and promulgated. 99059

Whereas there is prefixed unto a late pamphlet. 28052, 28506, 65589, 88506, 91945

Whereas Thomas Charles Williams. 95992

Whereas vpon the return of Sir Thomas Dale Knight. 99874

Whereas we are credibly informed that in many of our plantations. 85933A

"Wherefore change?" (50550), 105470

Wherein you have the narration of the two late dreadful judgements. 99768-99769

Whereupon an act passed in the ninth year of Her Majesty's reign. (24957)

Wheten, George. 62743

Whether an account of the work of grace? 80260

Whether the Turkey was known before the discovery of America. 2628

Whether the whole church is to be the judge thereof? 80260

Whether to go, and whither? 84226-84227

Whetstone, George. supposed author 103258

Whewell, William. 103259

Which do you like best, the peer or the farmer? 34970, note after 96638

Which? Fillmore or Buchanan? 11065

Which first—the loyal Negro or the white rebel? 20817

Which is the traitor. 105195

Which is the true Democracy? 54780

Which society shall you join, liberal or orthodox? 103260

Which will you have as President, Jackson or the Bank? 103261

Whidden, Joseph. 56161, (56168)

Whig. pseud. 78581

Whig. pseud. To the inhabitants of the city, county and province of New-York. 103262

Whig (Baltimore) 30254

Whig against tory. 103263

Whig almanac, and politician's register. 63823, 103264

Whig almanac and United States register. 63823, 103264

Whig and Democratic platforms. 16179

Whig and the Jimmy. 18713, 64454

Whig and tory. 28812

Whig anti-subscription council ticket. (62388)

Whig Celebration, Boston, July 4, 1834. see Whig Party. Massachusetts. Boston.

Whig Central Committee of Vigilance of Fuaquier County, Virginia. see Whig party. Virginia. Fauquier County. Central Committee.

Whig Club, New York. see New York Whig Club, New York.

Whig Committee address to the people of Arkansas. 103269

Whig Congressional Committee, 1839-1841. 103265

Whig Congressional Committee, 1844. 93380, 96362, 101069

Whig Congressional Committee, 1844. Chairman. 93380, 96362, 101069 see also Green, Willis.

Whig Congention, Concord, Mass., 1838. see Whig Party. Massachusetts. Middlesex County. Convention, Concord, 1838.

Whig extra. 94760

Whig Investigating Committee on the Irregular Proceedings of the Selectmen on the Portsmouth Check List, Portsmouth, N. H. see Whig Party. New Hampshire. Portsmouth. Investigating Committee.

Whig journal of politics, literature, science, and arts. 1212

Whig Members of the Massachusetts Legislature. see Whig Party. Massachusetts.

Whig mirror. 103267

Whig nominations. 48852, 103279

Whig of Ohio. pseud. Pacificus. 58092

Whig of '76. pseud. Reply to the resolutions and address. see Macomb, Robert.

Whig of the free states. pseud. Northern no! 55816

Whig of the old school. pseud. Appeal from the new to the old whigs. see Adams, Charles Francis.

Whig Party. 9170, (14786), 16179, 20429, 28493, note after 102315

Whig Party. Congressional Executive Committee. Chairman. 93380 see also Green, Willis.

Whipper, William. 103297
Whipple, --------, fl. 1848. 70732
Whipple, Amiel Weeks, 1818-1863. 69900,
　69946, 88607
Whipple, Augustus Oliver. 103298
Whipple, Charles King. (47241), 81973, 93816,
　103299-103300
Whipple, Charles King. supposed author
　23309, 103300
Whipple, Elise D. defendant 103301
Whipple, Frances Harriet. see McDougall,
　Frances Harriet (Whipple) Greene.
Whipple, Henry Benjamin, Bp., 1822-1901.
　31964, 49474
Whipple, John. (57858), 103304-103305
Whipple, Mrs. John. defendant 92691
Whipple, John M. 52901, 52950 see also
　New Hampshire. Commissioners to Make
　Examination of the Public Lands.
Whipple, Joseph. 103306-103307, 103631
Whipple, Levi. 103308
Whipple, Oliver. 103309
Whipple, Thomas J. 103310
Whippo, Charles T. (59996), 103310A
Whippoorwill, Byron, Esq. pseud. Orondalee.
　see Sturtevant, Peleg. supposed author
Whippoorwill, Byran, Esq. pseud. Orondalie.
　see Sturtevant, Peleg. supposed author
Whirlwind storms. (68512)
Whirlwinds excited by fire. (68512)
Whiskey and tobacco. 23206
Whiskey rebellion. (24360)
Whiskey war in Adrian. 82235
Whisper to a bride. 80966
Whistelo, Alexander. defendant 103312
Whistle, a true story. 102394
Whiston, -------, fl. 1729-1730. 62812
Whiston, William. 46438
Whitaker, Alexander, 1585-1617? 66686, 103313
Whitaker, Benjamin. 87356 see also South
　Carolina (Colony) Court of General Sessions
　of the Peace, Oyer and Terminer, Assize
　and General Gaol Delivery. Chief Justice.
Whitaker, Daniel Kimball. 11913, 88392, 88452,
　103314-note after 103316
Whitaker, Daniel Kimball. supposed author
　80853, 1st note after 95112, note after
　103316
Whitaker, Henry C. 32997
Whitaker, Jeremy. 80205
Whitaker, Nathaniel. 13594, 26753, 30646,
　103202-103203, 103214, 103317-103327
Whitaker, Nathaniel H. auctioneer 103328
Whitall, J. 83769
Whitbey, John. 103329
Whitbourne, Sir Richard. (8784), (33673),
　66686, 103330-103333, 104786
Whitbourne's New-found-land. 66686
Whitbridge, Joshua Barker. 103784-103785
Whitburn, T. ed. 103332
Whitby, Henry. defendant 96803, 103334
Whitcher, John. supposed petitioner (52947),
　(79714), note after 97880, note after
　103334
Whitchurch, Samuel. 103335
Whitcomb, Chapman. 69341, 93900, 103336-
　103344, 105690
Whitcomb, Elihu. 103345
Whitcomb, James. 103346
Whitcomb, Samuel. 103347-103348
White, -------. Captain 103349
White, ---------. defendant 32182, (32197)
White, ---------. explorer 4935-4936
White, -------. Keeper of the Goal at Win-
　chester 31839

White, ---------, fl. 1764. defendant before
　Ecclesiastical Council 23697, 99820
White, --------, fl. 1798. 104735
White, --------, fl. 1857. 63467
White, A. D. 75191
White, Adam. 14374, 28400-28401, 71032
White, Agnes. defendant 18178
White, Alexander, d. 1784. defendant 1066,
　3625, (31895), note before 93509,
　103349A, 103350
White, Andrew. 103351-103353
White, Andrew. supposed author (45316),
　69291-69292, note after 80002, 103353
White, Andrew Dickson, 1832-1918. 85067
White, Anthony Walton. 103353
White, B. 80790
White, Carleton. 51814, 103355
White, Carleton. defendant 51814
White, Charles. defendant 86587
White, Charles, 1728-1813. 84106, 103356
White, Charles Abiathar, 1826-1910. (35001)-
　35003
White, Charles Ignatius. 103357-103358
White, Charles Washington. 103359-103360
White, Daniel. 103361
White, Daniel Appleton. 103361-103370
White, Diaz de Leon y. see Leon y White,
　Daiz de.
White, Ebenezer. defendant before Church
　Consociation 103374
White, Edward. defendant 103375
White, Edward. supposed author 102811
White, Edward D. 1529
White, Elihu. 103371-103373
White, Elijah. 781, 103376-103378
White, Elipha. 103379-103380
White, Elizabeth. 103381
White, Ezra. plaintiff 103382-103383
White, Francis. 61600, note after 103383
White, G. S. 89517
White, George. an African 103384
White, George, fl. 1711. 19029, 3d note after
　97085
White, George F. 36259
White, George S. defendant 96921
White, George Savage, 1784-1850. 103385
White, Henry, fl. 1775. 103386
White, Henry, 1790-1858. 94022, 103387
White, Henry, 1800-1850. 103388
White, Henry, fl. 1831. 105883
White, Hugh. 103389
White, Hugh. defendant 32362, 96946, 96951,
　2d note after 102623, 3d note after 102623
White, Hugh Lawson, 1773-1840. 54781, 78343,
　103390-103391
White, J. J. 103392
White, Mrs. J. W. see White, Rhoda
　Elizabeth (Waterman)
White, James. supposed author 31971, 1st
　note after 102835
White, Jesse. defendant 92736
White, John, 1575-1648? 17075, 68261, (75668),
　96357, 99805, 103396-103397 103397,
　103400, 104901, 106052
White, John, 1575-1648? supposed author
　(21090), 33698, 78431, 104846
White, John, fl. 1585-1593. illus. (8784),
　30377, 103394-103395
White, John, 1677-1760. 27584, 94922, 99805,
　103398-note after 103402 see also
　Gloucester, Mass. First Church. Pastor.
White, John, 1685-1755. 96356-96357, 103403
White, John, d. 1760. incorrectly supposed
　author 103403
White, John, fl. 177-? petitioner 103404

White, John, 1787-1852. 103408-103410
White, John, fl. 1790. 103405-103406
White, John, fl. 1806. 103407
White, John, fl. 1825. 103412
White, John, d. 1840. 103411
White, John Blake. 103413-103417
White, John Duncan. defendant 103418
White, Joseph, 1755?-1836. 103420
White, Joseph, 1763-1832. 103419
White, Joseph Blanco, 1775-1841. 11094,
22884, 78907, 103421
White, Joseph M., 1781-1838. 24892, 49669,
86544, 103422-103434
White, Joseph M., 1781-1839. supposed author
35384, (65342), note after 103429
White, Josiah. of Northampton, Mass. 103435
White, Josiah, 1781-1850. 103436-103437
White, K. 103438
White, M. E. ed. 30332
White, Moses. claimant 103369, 103439
White, Nathaniel. 103440-103441
White, Nathaniel, d. 1819. defendant 96944,
note after 104181
White, Noah. 103442
White, Philip S., d. 1868. 103443
White, R. G. 6362, 70160, 103445
White, R. L. C. 94750
White, Rhoda Elizabeth (Waterman) 103444
White, Richard Grant. 6359, 103445-103446
White, Richard Grant. supposed author 6937,
58028, 68317
White, Richard W. plaintiff 27020 see also
Chatham County, Georgia. Superior Court.
Clerk. plaintiff
White, Richmond W. plaintiff 18815
White, Robert. 32365, 51077, note after 96027-
96028, note after 103446-note after 103448
White, Robert. petitioner (11313), 103447-103448,
1st-2d notes after 106221 see
also British Honduras. Agent. petitioner
White, S. Frances. ed. 92752
White, Samuel. of Adams County, Pa. 32157,
103452
White, Samuel, fl. 1800. 2403, 97766, note
after 101874
White, Samuel, 1770-1809. 89207, 103449-
103451
White, Seneca. 103453-103454
White, Steele. 103455
White, Stephen. 103456-103457
White, T. W. 39912, 88393, 94091
White, Thomas. 103458-103459
White, Thomas. petitioner 94813
White, Timothy. 103460
White, Vincent. see Le Blanc, Vincent.
White, W. M. 15787
White, William. defendant 46271
White, William. petitioner 105694
White, William. Jr. 71583, 103476A
White, William. of Watertown supposed author
30762, 90699, note after 103460
White, William, Bp., 1748-1836. 6350, 60778,
62102, 66171, 82976, 82979, 84678C,
101992, 103461-103474
White, William, Bp., 1748-1836. supposed
author 59013, note after 103465
White, William, 1783-1831. 103475-103476
White, William, fl. 1808. 96318
White, William, fl. 1844. 93267
White, William Charles. 45687, 103477-103484
White, William H. 85055
White, William Spotswood. 103485
White. firm publishers see Mitchell, Ames
and White. firm publishers
White (James) bookseller 103393

White and Gillingham. firm 62371
White, Hager & Co. firm 103487-103488
White acre vs. black acre. 26269
White chief: a legand of northern Mexico.
69080
White-faced pacer. 52161
White Haven, Conn. Meeting House. Commit-
tee. 103489
White Hills; their legends, landscape, and
poetry. 37848
White-jacket. 47482
White Mountain girl. 50387
White Mountain guide book. 21687
White Mountain history. 89047
White Mountain notch. 31865
White Mountain pilgrim. pseud. Brief
illustration. see Rollins, Edward B.
White oak. pseud. Riddle. 60593, 71257,
103490
White Oak Farm. A tale of life in the Old
Dominion. 57191
White Plains, N. Y. Bloomingdale Asylum.
see Bloomingdale Asylum, White Plains,
N. Y.
White preacher and the black slave lecturer.
89925
White, red, black. (66638)-66639
White republican. pseud. Flag of truce.
24644
White republican. pseud. North and south.
see Fuller, Hiram.
White rose. (64554), 2d note after 96106
White rose. An Indian tale. 64555, 2d note
after 96106
White rose in Acadia. 36037
White rover. 72133
White slave, by R. Hildreth. 92476, 92494,
92528
White slave; or memoirs, of a fugitive.
(31786)
White slave; or, memoirs of a fugitive, a new
picture of American slave life. (31787)
White slave; or Negro life in the slave states.
31788
White slavery: a new emancipation cause.
(9508), note after 103490
White slavery in the barbary states. 93688,
93689
White slavery!! or selling white men for debt!
103490A
White spirit of the wilderness. 36536
White squaw. 69081
White squaw, and the yellow chief. 69082
White stone canoe. 72563, 75262
White Sulphur papers. 59638, note after
103490A
White swan. (38371)
White tiger of the woods and prairies. 28912
White widows and orphans compelled to wait!
34459
White wing; or, the pirate and the rigolets.
34776
White wolf. 9553
Whited sepulchre. 87130
Whitefield, E. engr. 84779
Whitefield, George, 1714-1770. (3218), 15027,
26596, 27270-27271, 27415, 28794, 30399,
32670, (36054), (36750), 38813, (47545),
(59659), 67116, 69400, (69427), 71860,
80680, 82974, 82976, 83433, 87145,
87147, 90595-90596, 95527, 101314,
102565, 102701, 103202-103203, 103492-
103518, 103521-103525, 103529-103603,
103605-103613, note after 103616, 103622,
103644, 103645, 103647, 3d note after
103650, note after 103656, 103901, 105926

Whitefield, George, 1714-1770. supposed author (48178)
Whitefield, George, 1714-1770. incorrectly supposed author 103519-103520, 103526-103528, 103604, 103643
Whitefield, Henry. note before 92797, 103688, 103698
Whitefield, and Tennent, their conduct and preaching vindicated. 94709, 103652
Whitefield, Derguson. (103541)
Whitehall, J. 103653
Whitehall evening-post. 3285, 88178
Whitehall treaty of neutrality, 1686. 96529-96532
Whitehead, Charles. 67599
Whitehead, David. 103654
Whitehead, George, 1636?-1723. 12913, 37198, 377222, 53083, 59663, (59689), (66917), 66926, 78661, 95527, 103655-103660, 105450
Whitehead, John, 1740?-1804. 37198, 37222, 59663, 94539, 103661-103665
Whitehead, William, 1715-1785. 101866
Whitehead, William Adee, 1810-1884. 50850, 53058, 78186, 83982, note before 91508
Whitehead's funeral sermon. 6915
Whitehook. pseud. Remarks upon usury and its effects. see Kellogg, Edward.
Whitehouse, Henry John. 103666
Whitehouse, W. F. 103667
Whitelocke, Sir Bulstrode, 1605-1675. 59715, note after 103670
Whitelocke, John. 103676
Whitelocke, John. defendant at court martial 103671, 103674-103675, 103677-103681
Whitelocke, John. supposed author 2453, 9000, 103782
Whitelow; or, Nattie of the Lake Shore. 72133
Whitely, Edward. 61606
Whitely, George M. 78142
Whitely, Henry. 103668-103670
Whitely's directory for 1820. 61606
Whiteoak anthem. 103682
White's brief relation. 106052
White's new recopilacion of the laws of Spain and the Indies. 103429
White's new recopilacion of the laws of Spain and the Indies, and of colonial charters, commissions, &c. 103434
Whitesboro, N. Y. Academy. see Whitesboro Academy, Whitesboro, N. Y.
Whitesboro, N. Y. Congregational Church. 103683
Whitesboro, N. Y. Oneida Baptist Association. see Baptists. New York. Oneida Baptist Association.
Whitesboro, N. Y. Oneida Institute. see Oneida Institute, Whitesboro, N. Y.
Whitesboro, N. Y. Presbyterian Church. 103684
Whitesboro Academy, Whitesboro, N. Y. 103685
Whiteside, Robertson. plaintiff 103686
Whitestown and Oneida Institute Anti-slavery Societies. Executive Committee. 103687
Whitfield, George. see Whitefield, George, 1714-1770.
Whitfield, Henry, 1597-1660? supposed author 3213, 74696, 82978, note before 85867, note before 85932, note before 92797-92801, 3d note after 103687-note after 103689
Whitfield, J. M. 20717
Whitfield, James, Apb., 1770-1834. (51839), 59019, 72925 see also Baltimore (Archdiocese) Archbishop (Whitfield)
Whitfield, James M. 36210

Whitfield, John. 91268
Whitford, Helena (Wells) 102592-102593
Whithead, George. (40196)
Whithington, Nicholas. see Withington, Nicholas.
Whiting, Daniel W. 105885
Whiting, H. 103690
Whiting, H. C. 36377, 84774
Whiting, Henry. 32062, 39448, 77876, 103691-103696
Whiting, J. R. 3707, 103383
Whiting, John. see Whiting, Jonathan.
Whiting, John. USA 104696
Whiting, John, 1635?-1689. 24579, 103699
Whiting, John, 1652-1722. 5631, (28341), 103700-103703
Whiting, Jonathan. 13220, 105826-105827 see also Yale University. Tutors.
Whiting, Lyman. 18098, 85409
Whiting, Nathan. defendant at court martial 62977, 96942
Whiting, Samuel. of Connecticut 103710-103711
Whiting, Samuel, 1597-1679. 31743, 41005, 55885, 103704-103706
Whiting, Samuel, 1670-1725. supposed author 103707
Whiting, Samuel, 1744-1819. 103709
Whiting, Samuel, 1750-1819. 103708
Whiting, Thurston. 103712
Whiting, William. Banker 103713
Whiting, William. M. D. 79373, note after 103712
Whiting (Isaac N.) firm booksellers 103697-103698
Whiting (Samuel) firm publishers (32358)
Whitington, G. T. 103714
Whitley, Hiram C. defendant 71265
Whitlock, Henry. 103715
Whitlock, Samuel. 103716
Whitlock, William. 33939, 78737, 103717
Whitlocke, Sir Bulstrode. see Whitelock, Sir Bulstrode, 1605-1675.
Whiteman, Benjamin, 1768-1840. 45772, 103718-103720
Whitman, Benjamin, 1797-1840. 103721
Whitman, Bernard. 63990, 93202, 97827, 103722-103730
Whitman, E. B. 47183
Whitman, Elnathan. 103732-103733
Whitman, Ezekiel. 43906, 103734
Whitman, Ezekiel Cheever. see Cheever, Ezekiel.
Whitman, George G. 65732, 103738
Whitman, George H. 65732, 103738
Whitman, Jason, 1799-1848. 10165, 103739-103741
Whitman, John Winslow. reporter 2599, (12703), 16608, (42801), 102321, 1st-2d, 4th notes after 103741
Whitman, Kilborn. 103742
Whitman, Levi. 103743-103744
Whitman, Nathaniel. 103745
Whitman, R. W. Z. G. see Whitman, Zachariah Gardner.
Whitman, Samuel, 1676-1751. 103746-103747
Whitman, Samuel, 1751-1826. 83541, 103748
Whitman, Sarah Helen. 66292
Whitman, Zachariah Gardner. 103749-103751
Whitmarsh, Joseph A. defendant 103752
Whitmarsh, Samuel. 103753
Whitmer, John. 83147
Whitmerism unmasked. 84550
Whitmore, W. G. ed. 21343

Whitmore, William Henry. 9708, 21343, 46244, (46637), 46642, 46689, 46709, 46712, 46723-46725, 46731-46732, (46749), 46756, 52598, 52611, (65323), 1st note after 65324, 65582, 65646, note after 80346, 80621, 92350, 101755, 103754-103755, 104068
Whitmore, Matthew. see Aylmer, Matthew Whitmore, 5th Baron, 1775-1850.
Whitney, -------. defendant 76498, 95779, 102207
Whitney, Anne. 83859
Whitney, C. L. ed. 48773
Whitney, Charles. defendant 67796
Whitney, D. R. 83857
Whitney, Eli. 103756, 105796
Whitney, George. 103757-103759
Whitney, J. D. 10001, 10007, 10009, 15248-25249, 34253, (35000), 48738, 69571, 81055
Whitney, John. ed. 71239
Whitney, Josiah. 103760-103764
Whitney, Milton. 24447
Whitney, Moses. 103296
Whitney, N. K. 83154
Whitney, Parkhurst. defendant 103765
Whitney, Peter, 1744-1816. 58686, 103766-103771, 105017
Whitney, Peter, 1770-1843. 103772-103776
Whitney, Phineas. 103777
Whitney, Reuben M. petitioner 103778-103779
Whitney, Reuben M. supposed author 56603, note after 103779
Whitney, Richard. 99048 see also Vermont. Council. Secretary.
Whitney, Sybil. 103780
Whitney, Thomas R. ed. 37814, 70004
Whitney & Bliss. firm publishers 601
Whitney family of Connecticut. (62584)
Whitney's railroad to the Pacific. 72135
Whiton, E. V. 104884
Whiton, John Milton. 103781-103782
Whiton, Joseph. 45599, 67205, 103783 see also Boston. Meeting of Citizens From Every Part of the State, 1815. President.
Whitsitt, William H. 84852
Whittaker, Alexander. 52287
Whittaker, James. 97884'
Whittelsey, Chauncey, 1717-1787. 13220, 103786-103789, 105825-105826, 105927 see also Yale University. Tutors.
Whittelsey, Samuel, 1686-1725. (52975), 91756, 103618, 103790-103791
Whittemore, B. F. 90828
Whittemore, Benjamin. 103792
Whittemore, G. H. 84041
Whittemore, Joseph. 103793-103796
Whittemore, N. 62743
Whittemore, Samuel. (2927), note after 103796
Whittemore, Thomas. (18515), 51524, 103797-103803
Whittemore, William Henry. see Whitmore, William Henry.
Whitten, Wilfred. ed. 83021
Whittenhall, Edward, Bp. see Wetenhall, Edward, successively Bishop of Cork, and Kilmore and Ardagh, 1636-1713.
Whittier, John Greenleaf, 1807-1892. 285, 7332, 9751, 11996, 12213, 37655, 44455, 49422, 49900, 55730, (63623), 65062, 70902, 79003, 84139-84141, 84143, 84146, 85431, note after 86936, 2d note after 97725, 103804-103819, 106207
Whittingham, William Rollinson, Bp. 66152, (71134), 95701, 103820

Whittlesey, Charles. 85072, 103821-103824
Whittlesey, Elisha. 40763, 89702, 89707, 103826 see also U. S. Comptroller of the Currency.
Whittlesey, F. 95961
Whittlesey, Frederic. 97955, note after 103826 see also United States Anti-masonic Convention, Philadelphia, 1830. Committee to Report a Succinct and Lucid Account of the Abduction and Murder of William Morgan. Chairman.
Whittlesey, Joseph. 103827
Whittlestick. pseud. California characters. (9966)
Whitty, Mrs. E. 103828
Whitty, I. S. illus. 103829
Whitwell, Benjamin. 103830-103834
Whitwell, Richard. 103835
Whitwell, Samuel. 103836
Whitwell, William. 103837-103838
Whitwell & Bond. firm auctioneers 22169, 103839-103840
Whitwell & Seaver. firm auctioneers 103841
Whitwell, Bond & Co. firm auctioneers 103841
Whitworth, Sir Charles. 12708, 18687, 103842-103843
Whitworth, Joseph. (54494)
Who and what is John Tyler. 63816
Who are the agitators? 9392
Who are the agressors? 27922
Who are the authors of the rebellion? 80146
Who are the canters? 9857
Who are the schismatics? 81882, 103844
Who are the sympathizers with the rebellion? (42546)
Who are their friends? 36885
Who are to be benefited by an immediate return to a specie basis? 89112
Who burnt Columbia? 80420
Who caused the crisis? (65435)
Who caused the reduction of postage in 1845? 89620
Who caused the reduction of postage?· ought he to be paid? 89619, 89621
Who commenced and who can end it? 81816
Who d'ye think? pseud. Things as they will be. see Taylor, Vermilye.
Who ever saw the like! 83457
"Who framed and ratified the constitution of the United States." 6643
Who goes there? 6129
Who goeth a warfare at his own charges? 62772
Who has a right to vote? 30186
Who has hindered reconstruction? December, 1867. 36171
Who have violated compromises. 31703
Who he is and what he has done. 103998
Who is entitled to the credit of it. 84441, 84446
Who is entitled to the credit of making great discovery? 84442
Who is first? A poem. 13388, 90648
Who is John Bell? (4463)
Who is my neighbor? 26195
"Who is on the Lord's side?" 59464
Who is responsible? A story of American western life. 84733
Who is responsible for public calamities? 42977
Who is right? Rev. Dr. Dewey, or Dr. James M'Cure Smith? 19862
Who is to blame? 67765
Who is to blame? or a cursory review. 28246

Who ought we to send to Congress, John Geddes, or, J. R. Poinsett? 103845

Who shall administer? 84426-84427

Who shall be governor, Strong or Sullivan? 103846

Who shall be governor? The contrast. 46172, note after 103845

Who shall be our next sheriff? 62389

Who shall be President? 100662

Who shall be the Republican nominee for President? 78546

Who shall count the electoral votes and declare the result. 73130

Who should and who should not emigrate. 22485

Who then can be saved? 83301

Who they are, and what they were. 54095

Who troubles Israel. 17629

Who was the first Governor of Massachusetts? 24037

Who were the early settlers of Maryland? 812, (45211A)

Who withholds co-operation? 21100

Whoever has candidly traced the rapid growth. 102045, 1st note after 103846

Whoever seriously considers the improverished state of this city. 95973

Whole and true discouerye of Terra Florida. 70792

Whole book of psalms, in metre, with hymns. 6350

Whole booke of psalmes faithfully translated into English metre. (66428), 1st note after 102552, 2d note after 103846

Whole book of psalmes, faithfully transled into English metre. 66430

Whole course of catechetical instruction. 7483

Whole duty of man. 26596, 103506, 103557-103557A

Whole duty of sheriffs. 13162

Whole duty of woman. 103847

Whole history of navigation. 13017

Whole method of bleaching or whitening linen-cloth. 78985

Whole of Mr. Erskine's admirable speech. 96916

Whole of the celebrated speech of the Rev. Dr. Jonathan Shipley. (80526)

Whole of the documentary evidence. 97787

Whole of the proceedings in the case of Olmstead and others. 57236

Whole of the proceedings of the trial of James Hill. 31841

Whole of the public and secret correspondence. 16814, note before 95301

Whole official correspondence between the envoys of the American states, and Mons. Talleyrand. 59593, 62702, 103848

Whole proceedings of the American Continental Congress. 15598

Whole proceeddings of the Court Martial, held on General Whitelock. 103681

Whole proceedings on the trail of an information. 96918

Whole prophecie of Daniel explained. 33630

Whole service as performed in the congregation. 97496

Whole story of the sorrows of Maria, of Monlines. 91353

Whole story of the sorrows of Maria, of Moulines. 91354

Whole truth. Address to the freemen of New England, Nov. I, 1808. (30196), 74359, 103849

Whole truth. An address to the freemen of New-England. 103850

Whole truth, being a discourse. 14477, 49979

Whole truth of the question of "the fire fiend." 26607

Whole truth: or, the Essex Junto exposed. 103852

Whole truth relative to the controversy. (32464)

Whole truth. The Essex Junto exposed. (30196), 103851

Whole truth. To the freemen of New-England. (30196), 74359, 103849

Whole world governed by a Jew. (82499)

Wholesale business directory. 61606

Wholesale business intelligencer and southern and western merchants' pocket directory. 61606

Wholesome severity reconciled with Christian liberty. note before 17046, 17046, 2d note after 103852

Wholesome words. 46596, 1st note after 103852

Whom do the English tories wish elected to the Presidency? (21847)

Whore of Babylon unmasked. 105575

Who's the croaker? 25485

Why a national literature cannot flourish. (72285)

Why and how. 16225

Why are we still at war? 15110, 3d note after 103852

Why are you a federalist? 67206, 92886

Why do I live? 85341

Why do we mourn departing friends? 103604

Why does the history of the world oscillate? 49934

Why I am a whig. 28492

Why I have not gone to the south. 72261

Why is allegiance due? and where is it due? 1499

Why is Canada not a part of the United States? (80023)

Why is this country periodically in such deep distress? 91626

Why M'Clellan was removed. 15212, 69849

Why men hate the ministers of Christ. 83597

Why not paid. 29294

Why Pennsylvania should become one of the Confederate States. 43308

Why shall you vote for Gov. Strong? 67206, 92886

Why the Chinese emigrate. 16225

Why the early inhabitants of Vermont disclaimed the jurisdiction. 29781

Why the north cannot accept the separation. 38446

Why the south can't stand. 58967

Why was the continet of America not discovered till so late a period? 43141

Why was their introduction permitted? 81908

Why we should recognize the confederates. 69005

Why will ye die? (40843), 106353

Why work for the slave? 88238-88239, 4th note after 103852

Whyley, G. E. 103853

Wiandot Indians. Treaties, etc. 96599

Wiccacoe, Pa. Gloria Dei Church. (62359) see also Corporation of the United Swedish (Lutheran) Churches of Wiccacoe, Kingussing, and Upper Merion, Pa.

Wichita Indians. Treaties, etc. 96697

Wichtige Aufschlusse. 85120

Wichtige Beytrage zur Geschichte des menchlichen Geschlechts. 59248

Wichtigkeit und Vortheil des Kap-Breton. 6217, 2d note after 103853

Wijnandts, Willem. see Wynandts, Willem.
Wikoff, Isaac. 56205, (61430), 7th note after 103943, 103944
Wilber, C. D. (34262)
Wilber, Lewis. defendant 103945-103947
Wilberforce. pseud. To the freemen of Kentucky. 103948
Wilberforce, Robert Isaac. 103949-103950, 103952
Wilberforce, Samuel, successively Bishop of Oxford and Winchester, 1805-1873. 4992, 13496, 103949-103950, 103952
Wilberforce, William, 1759-1833. 13496, 14021, (22402), 22630, 34789, 44880, 81932, (81976), 82068, 91011, 93371, 95661, 102770, 4th note after 102785, 103951-103959
Wilberforce, William, 103949-103950, 103952
Wilbour, Charles E. reporter 95877
Wilbour, Nathaniel. pseud. Prayer. 99554
Wilbraham, Mass. Wesleyan Academy. see Wesleyan Academy, Wilbraham, Mass.
Wilbur, Anne T. tr. 75543
Wilbur, Hervey, 1787-1852. ed. 49985, 103960
Wilbur, Horace. pseud. Biglow papers. see Lowell, James Russell, 1819-1891.
Wilbur, James Benjamin, 1856-1929. 97617, 99000, 99024, 99049, note before 99075
Wilbur, John. 10082, 94129
Wilbur, Marguerite E. tr. 98842
Wilbur, Thomas. 70522
Wilburn, George T. supposed author 103961
Wilckens, O. ed. 84531
Wilcocke, Samuel Hull. 103962-103963
Wilcocks, Joseph, successively Bishop of Gloucester and Rochester, 1673-1756. 103964
Wilcocks, Thomas. 103965
Wilcoks, Santiago Smith. 103966
Wilcox, Carlos. 103967-103968
Wilcox, De Lafayette. defendant 84346, 103969
Wilcox, G. B. 53255
Wilcox, Julius. (54721), 54831
Wilcox, Leonard. 103970
Wilcox, Orlando Bolivar. see Willcox, Orlando Bolivar.
Wilcox, Richard. see Willcox, Richard.
Wilcox, Thomas. see Wilcocks, Thomas.
Wilcox, Adams & Co. firm publishers 68240
Wilcoxson, David B. 95832
Wild, -------. tr. 9360
Wild, J. C. illus. 61913, 62365-62366, 103971-103972
Wild, James. ed. 88534
Wild achievements, and romantic adventures. 103973
Wild American. pseud. Savage beauty. see Sproat, P. W.
Wild Bill, the Indian-slayer. 65376
Wild brier; or, lays by an untaught minstrel. (41738)
Wild fire. 69008
Wild flower. 68171
Wild flowers of Nova Scotia. By M. Morris. 84435
Wild flowers of Nova Scotia. By Mrs. Maria Miller. 49038
Wild flowers, sacred poetry. 73479
Wild goose. 69009
Wild hunter of the Rocky Mountains. (57149)
Wild huntress. (69083)
Wild life in the interior of Central America. 9702
Wild life; or, adventures on the frontier. 69084

Wild man of the west. 2952
Wild Methodist. pseud. Truths come out at last. see Abrams, Isaac.
Wild Nell, the White Mountain girl. 50387
Wild northern scenes. 30109
Wild oats sowings. 18121
Wild scenes in Kansas and Nebraska. 74894
Wild scenes in South America. 58140
Wild scenes in the forest. 32386
Wild scenes in the forest and prairie. 32387
Wild scenes of a hunter's life. (26054)
Wild scenes on the frontiers. (4724)
Wild shrubs of Alabama. 30598
Wild southern scenes. A tale of disunion! (36534)
Wild sports in the far west. 27191
Wild western scenes. 36533, (36535), (80732), note after 89943
Wild western scenes; or, the white spirit of the wilderness. 36536
Wilde, Richard Henry. 103431, 103974-103976
Wilde, Samuel Summer. 103977-103978
Wilde Europaerin. 101130
Wilde life among the backwoods. 64919
Wilde notes from the back woods. (58179)
Wilde Scenen in Wald und Prairie. 32388
Wilde van Aveyron en de Robinsons. 19557
Wilder, Alexander. 1113
Wilder, J. N. 21100
Wilder, James H. 103979
Wilder, John, 1759?-1836. 76515, 103980-103982
Wilder, Joshua. 103983
Wilder, Lewis. 6674, 103983
Wilder, O. 103983A
Wilder, Sampson Vryling Stoddard. 103984-103985
Wilder, Solomon Van S. see Wilder, Sampson Vryling Stoddard.
Wilder. firm publishers see Adams and Walder. firm publishers
Wilder (F. J.) firm publishers 94815
Wilder, Pickard & Co. firm publishers 85515
Wilder Holbrook vs. the President, Directors and Company of the Worcester Bank. 105383
Wilderness. 89148
Wilderness and the war-path. 29800
Wilderness journeys in New Brunswick. 27968, note after 90353
Wilderness; or Braddock's times. 43311, 1st note after 101905, 103986
Wilderness; or the youthful days of Washington. 103987
Wilderness shall bloom as the rose. 103217
Wilderness; together with the union of the states. 103988
Wilder's genealogical reprints, 1919, series M, no. 3. 94815
Wildes Leben im Innern von Central-America. 9703
Wildfire, Walter. pseud. Comet. 14933
Wildniss oder Washingtons Junglingsjahre. 103989
Wile, Benjamin F. 103896
Wileman, H. 84558
Wiles of Popery. 103990
Wiley, Albert. plaintiff 37593
Wiley, Calvin H. 55586
Wiley, John. 53473, 54042, 83604
Wiley, Thomas. 82803
Wilford, Major -------. supposed author 69403, 93181
Wilford, John. see Wilsford, John.
Wilful and malicious loss. 29861

Wilhelm, Landgraf und Erbprinz zu Hesse. see Wilhelm IX, Landgraf von Hessen-Kassel.

Wilhelm IX, Landgraf Von Hessen-Kassel. 103991

Wilhelm Penn's Kurze Nachricht von dem Ursprunge. 59739

Wilhelm Penn's Kurze Nachricht von der Netziehung. 59740

Wilh. Thomas Raynals Philosophische und politische Geschichte. 68115

Wilhelmina; a legendary, dramatic tale. 103992

Wilkes, -------. supposed author 103993

Wilkes, Charles, 1798-1877. 36014, 47084, 103994-103995 see also United States Exploring Expedition, 1838-1842.

Wilkes, Fabian Sebastian. ed. 100774

Wilkes, George. 74081, 89508, 103996-note after 104000

Wilkes, George. petitioner 83832

Wilkes, Henry. 67872

Wilkes, J. C. ed. 63759

Wilkes, John, 1727-1797. 1660, 1662, 26150, 36910, 58483, 95918, 104002-104010

Wilkes, John, 1727-1797. supposed author 5270, 27282, note after 104001

Wilkes, John A. ed. 49837, 49841-49844, 49848

Wilkes-Barre, Pa. Meeting of a Number of Sufferers at Wyoming During the Revolutionary War, Their Descendants and Others, 1837. 105693A see also Wyoming, Pa. Citizens.

Wilkes Barre, Pa. Wyoming Historical and Genealogical Society. see Wyoming Historical and Genealogical Society, Wilkes Barre, Pa.

Wilkes' spirit of the times. 74081, 89508, note after 104000

Wilkeson, Samuel. 104011-104012

Wilkey, Major Walter. pseud. Western emigration. see Deming, Ebenezer.

Wilkie, Daniel. 104014

Wilkie, David. 104015

Wilkie, John. tr. 67018

Wilkin, Simon. ed. 8677

Wilkins, -------, fl. 1845. 6785

Wilkins, David. ed. (78975)

Wilkins, Gouverneur Morris. 78581

Wilkins, Gouverneur Morris. supposed author 104016

Wilkins, Isaac. 11882, 29955, 29956, 53957, 78559, (78562)-78565, 78574-78575, 78580-78581, 80594, 2d note after 99553, 4th note after 100862, 1st-6th notes after 104016

Wilkins, Isaac. incorrectly supposed author 2d note after 99553

Wilkins, J. ed. 56189

Wilkins, Jacob. 66686

Wilkins, James. 96607 see also U. S. Commissioners to the Chickasaw Indians.

Wilkins, John. 104017

Wilkins, Peter. Cornishman 58394, 74631, note after 104017

Wilkins, Peter. of Massachusetts 104018

Wilkins, William, 1779-1865. 398, (53675), 73393, 102287, 104019-104020 see also U. S. War Department

Wilkins Wylder; or, the successful man. 49073

Wilkinson, -------, fl. 1840. 83493

Wilkinson, Abraham. defendant 92314

Wilkinson, Benjamin R. defendant 104022

Wilkinson, David. 104021

Wilkinson, Eliab. (52663)

Wilkinson, Eliza (Yonge) 104023

Wilkinson, J. B. 104024

Wilkinson, J. W. 95682, 104025

Wilkinson, James, 1757-1825. 14162-14163, (45589), (71362), (71402), 96607, 104026-104029 see also U. S. Commissioners to the Chickasaw Indians.

Wilkinson, James. 1757-1825. defendant 105478

Wilkinson, James, 1757-1825. defendant at court martial 104030

Wilkinson, Jemima. 86627, 104031-104032

Wilkinson, John. 94773

Wilkinson, M. S. (49305), 66943

Wilkinson, Madge W. 84295

Wilkinson, S. 94555, 104034

Wilkinson, Thomas. 104035

Wilkinson, William. Commander of the ship "Henry and William" 104036

Wilkinson, William, fl. 1683. (23054)

Wilkinson, William, 1760-1852. 104037

Wilkinson & Hodge. firm see Sotheby, Wilkinson & Hodge. firm

Wilks, Henry. 104001

Wilks, Samuel Charles. 104038-104039

Will the rover. pseud. Rambles in Chili. 12800

Will, J. G. F. tr. 65479

Will, John Still. pseud. see Still-Will, John. pseud.

Will. Adams. pseud. see Neal, John.

Will and codicil of William Price. 65469

Will and schedule of his property. 101900

Will and the affections. 59354

Will laboring men vote for Seymour? 15910

Will of a father submitted to. 46598

Will of Charles McMicken. 43575

Will of General G. Washington. 101756

Will of Gen. George Washington. 101763

Will of General George Washington. To which is annexed, a schedule of his property, directed to be sold. 101752, 101759, 101761

Will of General George Washington: to which is annexed a schedule of his property, directed to be sold; also, an interesting correspondence. 101755

Will of General George Washington. To which is annexed, a schedule of his property directed to be sold; also, the oration, delivered by Major-General Lee. 101758

Will of General George Washington. To which is annexed a schedule of his property directed to be sold. Printed from the record of the County Court of Fairfax. 101753

Will of General Washington. 101757

Will of George Cheyne Shattuck. 79870

Will [of George Fox.] 28794

Will [of George Washington.] 101636, 101722, 101751

Will of God performed on earth. 89783

Will of James R. Wilson. 104643

Will of Mr. Girard. 1940, (27494)

Will of Mrs. Elizabeth Stott. 92347

Will of Rev. Richard Mather. 46784

Will of Samuel Appleton. 1847

Will of Stephen Girard. 27488, 81371

Will of the late Mrs. Badger, of Natick. 2276, 56235

Will of the late Stephen Girard, Esq. 27486

Will of the majority against the rule of a minority. 31703

Will of the people. 62352

Will of Thomas Boylston. 7140

Will of Thomas Dows. 20792

William Hate-Smoke. pseud. Smoking and 85103
William Henry Harrison versus Martin Van Buren. 16181, 31772, 98425
William Jackson, an importer. 86986
William Jackson Davis. In memoriam. 18943
William Judd's address to the people of . . . Connecticut. 36846
William King's Lessee. defendant 85190
William Knibb: missionary in Jamaica. 83507
William McC. pseud. see McC., Wm. pseud.
Wm. Machie et als., vs. Dan Lord et als. 96900
William Morgan abducted and murdered by masons. 2035
Wm. N. Seymour's Madison director. 43741
William Madir. pseud. see Douglass, William, 1691?-1752.
William Oronoco. pseud. see Gooch, Sir William, Bart., 1681-1751.
William Palmer, empoisonneur et faussaure. (34129)
William Parks. 99977
Williams Park Club, Richmond, Va. 96739
William Pen, secundus. pseud. tr. see Deken, Agatha. supposed author and Wolff, Elizabeth Bekker. supposed author
William Penn. An historical biography, founded on family and state papers. (20377)
William Penn: an historical biography, from new sources. 20376
William Penn and the Quakers either impostors, or apostates. 106108-106108A
William Penn and Thomas B. Macaulay. 25146
William Penn Beneficial Institution of Pennsylvania. 104158
William Penn. [By Richard Penn Smith.] 83788
William Penn Division, No. 8, Pawtucket. see Sons of Temperance of North America. Rhode Island. William Penn Division, No. 8, Pawtucket.
William Penn his own interpreter. 71005
William Penn oder die zustande Englands. 59748
Wulliam Penn Parlor in the Great Central Fair, Philadelphia, 1864. see Philadelphia. Great Central Fair, 1864. William Penn Parlor.
William Penn, Proprietary of Pennsylvania, his ancestry and descendants. 59749
William Penn, the founder of Pennsylvania. 92348
William Peters of Boston, in N. E., 1634. 61211
William Pitt. pseud. see Wickliffe, Robert, 1815?-1850.
William Pitt Fessenden. 65015
William R. Trusty and Well-Beloved, Wee greet you well. 104147
William Slygood. pseud. see Stearns, Samuel, 1747-1819.
William Spotswood's Book-Store, Philadelphia. see Spotswood, William.
William Spotswood's catalogue of books, &c. 89651
William Stenson, at his grocery-store. 91227
Wm. T. Coleman & Co.'s circular and market review. 14316
Wm. T. G. Morton and his designs on the U. S. Treasury. 84442
William Tell (Ship) in Admiralty 104160
William Thompson, a native and freeholder of this town. 95540
William Tyndale at home and abroad. 45006

William Weston. 104161
William Wilberforce. 14758
William Wood; appellant. David Philhill, Esq.; and others. 105082
William Wood's description of Massachusetts. 106052
William Young, Jr. (of Philadelphia) 106129
William Young's catalogue for 1787. Books. 106123
Williams, ---------. Chief Justice of Vermont 96823
Williams, --------. defendant 5161
Williams, ---------, fl. 1823. defendant 68042
Williams, Aaron. 91715, 94333-94339
Williams, Abraham. 104162
Williams, Albert. 104163
Williams, Amos A. 104164
Williams, Avery. 104165-104166
Williams, Benjamin. 104167
Williams, Benjamin P. 104168
Williams, Brooke. 20312
Williams, C. S. 14894, 19005, 104169
Williams, Catherine R. (Arnold) 104170-104176
Williams, Catherine R. (Arnold) supposed author 48898
Williams, Charles, 1796-1866. 104177-104179
Williams, Charles Kilborn. 104562
Williams, Charles Richard. 84789
Williams, Charles Wye. 104181
Williams, Cynric R. 104182
Williams, Daniel. 12333-12334, 104183-104184
Williams, David, 1738-1816. 104185-104187
Williams, David, fl. 1826. 104188
Williams, David Rogerson, 1776-1830. 33150, 104189 see also South Carolina. Governor, 1814-1816 (Williams)
Williams, Edward. defendant 54320
Williams, Edward. English Slave in Turkey 104194
Williams, Edward, fl. 1650. 82976, 100450, 2d note after 100557, note after 100560, 3d note after 100571, 104190-104193
Williams, Edward, 1746-1826. 104195
Williams, Edward, fl. 1830. defendant 104196
Williams, Edwin. 6360, 53799, 54459, 63820, 104197-104207
Williams, Eleazar, 1688-1742. 104208-104209
Williams, Eleazer, 1787-1858. 6353, 49838, 104210-104213
Williams, Eliphalet. 104214-104218
Williams, Elisha. 22990, 104219-104221
Williams, Emma. plaintiff 83637-83638
Williams, Ennion. 73596
Williams, F. G. 83147
Williams, Frederick. plaintiff 104223
Williams, Frederick G. 83152
Williams, G. W. reporter 19734, note after 95447
Williams, George C. 52901, 52950 see also New Hampshire. Commissioners to Make Examination of the Public Lands.
Williams, George W. defendant 104224
Williams, Gilbert Tennent. 104225
Williams, Griffith. 104226
Williams, H. W. 45874, note after 89212
Williams, Helen Maria. (33751), 33770, 104227-104230
Williams, Henry. of Boston 3184, (11905), 104231
Williams, Henry F. 104232
Williams, Henry Llewellyn. 104233
Williams, Hercules. 104234
Williams, Hugh. 92621, 92623

Williams, William R. 45439, 79801, 86855, 93622

Williams. firm publishers 52431 see also James & Williams. firm publishers

Williams (C. S.) firm publishers 13085, 57010

Williams (J. D. & M.) firm 102180

Williams & Company. firm publishers 14894, (17215), 23197, 25169, 30070, 57004, 89890

Williams Alumni Association of New York. see Williams College, Williamstown, Mass. Alumni Association, New York.

Williams and Pen. pseud. Voter's text-book. see Bland, Theodric.

Williams biographical annals. (21423)

Williams' calendar. (23847)

Williams' Cincinnati directory. 13085

Williams College, Williamstown, Mass. 104415-104417, 104418-104423

Williams College, Williamstown, Mass. petitioners 23271, 30765, 89138, 1st note after 104432

Williams College, Williamstown, Mass. Adelphic-Union. Library. 104428-104430

Williams College, Williamstown, Mass. Alumni Association, New York. 104421

Williams College, Williamstown, Mass. Botanical Class. 21706-21708, 44408

Williams College, Williamstown, Mass. Library. 104426-104431

Williams College, Williamstown, Mass. Social Fraternity. 104432

Williams College, Williamstown, Mass. Trustees. 104414

Williams College, Williamstown, Mass. Trustees. petitioners 104424-104425

Williams College. At a meeting of a large number of gentlemen. 69401, 104433

Williams College necrological annals. (21423)

Williams' Columbus directory for 1867-8. 14894

Williams' Columbus directory for 1866-7. 14814

Williams' Covington and Newport directory. (17215)

Williams' Evansville directory for 1866. 23197

Williams' Fort Wayne directory for 1866-67. 25169

Williams Lake and Cariboo. 58355

Williams' map of New York. 90082, 1st note after 104412

Williams' New Albany directory. 52431

Williams' Ohio state directory and shippers' guide. 57004

Williams' Ohio state register and business mirror. 57010

Williams' Springfield directory. 89890

Williamsburg, Va. Committee of Correspondence. 100012

Williamsburg, Va. Convention, 1774. see Virginia (Colony) Convention, Williamsburg, 1774.

Williamsburg, Va. Convention, 1776. see Virginia. Convention, Williamsburg, 1776.

Williamsburg, Va. William and Mary College. see William and Mary College, Williamsburg, Va.

Williamsburg, August 6, 1778. 100192

Williamsburg, August 20, 1776. 100035

Williamsburg, May 31, 1774. 100008

Williamsburg, Saturday, April 29, 1775. 100012

Williamsburg to wit. 104435

Williamsburg, Wednesday the 17th of May, 1769. 100504

Williamsburgh, N. Y. Bank. see Williamsburgh Bank, Williamsburgh, N. Y.

Williamsburgh, N. Y. Charter. (70442), 104436

Williamsburgh Bank, Williamsburgh, N. Y. 104438

Williamsburgh directory and yearly advertiser, for 1847-8. 104437

Williamsburgh Fire Insurance Company. 104439

Williamsburgh Fire Insurance Company. Charter. 104439

Williamson, --------. plaintiff 33257

Williamson, Mrs. -------, fl. 1796. 89593

Williamson, A. J. 104440

Williamson, Sir Adam, 1736-1798. 98837 see also Jamaica. Lieutenant Governor, 1790-1794 (Williamson)

Williamson, Charles. 59284, 104441-104444

Williamson, Charles. supposed author 50009, 51355, 53643, 99573, 104441, note after 104444

Williamson, D. 104445-104446

Wiliamson, George T. 13074, 104448

Williamson, Hugh. 14452-14453, 54362, 59853, 78475, 104449-104455, 1st note after 106233

Williamson, Hugh. supposed author 2330, 13731, 63401-63402, note after 104453, note after 104454

Williamson, Hugh. incorrectly supposed author (63213), 104444, 104453, 1st note after 106233

Williamson, Isaac Dowd. 104456

Williamson, Isaac Halsted, 1767-1844. 13747, 53156, 104457-104458, 105025-105026 see also New Jersey. Governor, 1817-1928 (Williamson)

Williamson, John. 104460

Williamson, John. Officer in the Revolution supposed author 16180, 2d note after 101545, 104459

Williamson, John, d. 1840. 104461

Williamson, John Brown. 104462

Williamson, John P. 57380, 71328

Williamson, Passmore. defendant 10696

Williamson, Passmore. plaintiff 31770

Williamson, Peter. 36555, 104463-104475, 104476-104484, 104486, 104488-104492

Williamson, Peter. plaintiff 104475, 104478, 104485, 104487

Williamson, Robert Stockton, 1824-1882. 69900, 69946, 83706, 97652

Williamson, Thomas S. 18288, 18289, 69646-69649

Williamson, William Durkee. 93499, 104493

Williamson. firm publishers 42326

Williamson et al vs. Coulter's Ex'rs. et al. 33257

Williamsport, Pa. Convention, 1850. 59924

Williamsport, Pa. Court of Oyer and Terminer. see Lycoming County, Pa. Court of Oyer and Terminer, Williamsport.

Williamsport, Pa. Dickinson Seminary. see Dickinson Seminary, Williamsport, Pa.

Williamsport, Pa. Internal Improvement Convention, 1836. see Internal Improvement Convention, Williamsport, Pa., 1836.

Williamsport, Pa. Republican Party Convention, 1867. see Republican Party. Pennsylvania. Convention, Williamsport, 1867.

Williamsport, Pa. Union Republican State Convention, 1867. see Republican Party. Pennsylvania. Convention, Williamsport, 1867.

Williamsport and Philadelphia Lumber Company.
104494
Williamsport and Philadelphia Lumber Company.
Committee. 104494
Williamsport Convention, 1850. see Williams-
port, Pa. Convention, 1850.
Williams's Hamilton directory. 30070
Williams's statistical companion and pictorial
almanac. 104206
Williamstown, Mass. Church of Christ. 104495
Williamstown, Mass. Williams College. see
Williams College, Williamstown, Mass.
Williard, S. see Willard, Samuel,
1640-1707.
Willimantic, Conn. Congregational Church.
104496
Willinck, G. 104497
Willinck, J. P. M. 104497
Willing captive. 31324
Willington, Conn. Baptist Church of Christ.
104498
Willis, -------, fl. 1730. 86743
Willis, J. H. 104499
Willis, John R. complainant (16787), 104500
see also Friends, Society of. New York
Monthly Meeting. Trustees. complainants
Willis, Lydia. 104501-104502
Willis, Nathaniel. ed. 104503, 106204
Willis, Nathaniel Parker, 1806-1867. 1157,
3784, 3786-3787, 16923, 32707, 50825,
(53288), 62965, 63534, 63570-63571,
(69590), (70978), 79003, 80369, 85431,
note before 94463, note after 96778, 2d
note after 97259, 104502-104516, 106207
Willis, Richard. 104517
Willis, Sarah. defendant 96847
Willis, Thomas, fl. 1812-1831. 31710, 104521-
104523
Willis, Thomas, fl. 1820-1830. 78347, 104518-
104520
Willis, William. of New Bedford 104524
Willis, William, 1794-1870. 43971, 84352,
104525
Willis, William, fl. 1825. 101707
Willis genealogy. 50911
Willison, John, fl. 1742. 21934, 101877
Williston, Ebenezer Bancroft. 72468, 84837,
92297, 96420, 101477, 101478, 102269,
104526
Williston, Payson. (28126), 55388, 104527-
104528
Williston, Seth. 104529-104533
Williston, Vt. (9201)
Willman, Lewis. defendant 51591, note after
104533
Willmore, -------. engr. 3784, 3787, 8899,
note after 104504-104505
Willock, John. 104534-104535
Willoughby, Frederick Stanley Montgomery.
supposed author 93239
Willoughby, Sir Hugh, d. 1554. 29941, 66686
Willoughby, Ohio. Willoughby University of Lake
Erie. see Willoughby University of Lake
Erie, Willoughby, Ohio.
Willoughby Association. 82414
Willoughby University of Lake Erie, Willoughby,
Ohio. 104536
Willow, George. petitioner 9372, 81492
Willow. Composed by Storace. 92174B
Willow Grove Turnpike Company. Charter.
104537
Willox, -------. 104538 see also Great
Britain. Guernsey Commissioners.
Wills, Archibald. 63585, 104539
Wills, Elizabeth. 7879

Wills, Guillermo. 104540
Wills, Thomas. 104542
Wills, Thomas. supposed author 2d note
after 98528, 104541
Wills, William. defendant 104543
Wills Hospital, Philadelphia. see Philadelphia.
Wills Hospital.
Wills of William Bordman Senior. 39374
Willsford, John. 104544-104545
Willson, David. 104546-104547
Willson, Estevan Julian. 104548
Willson, James M. ed. 17212
Willson, James Renwick, 1770-1853. 55373,
104549-104556, 104644-104645
Willson, John. 104557
Willson, Luther. 104558-104559
Willson, Marcius. 104560
Willson, R. W. 92133
Willson, Shipley W. 104561
Willson, W. P. 104562
Willyams, Cooper. 104563
Wilmer, -------. 25615, 1st note after
104563
Wilmer, James I. see Wilmer, James Jones.
Wilmer, James Jones. 1166, 101778, 104564-
104572
Wilmer, John. 104573-104574
Wilmer, Simon. 20391, 20396, note after
104574-104576
Wilmer, William H. 104577-104578
Wilmere, Alice. 11842
Wilmington, Del. Census, 1859. 19380
Wilmington, Del. Library Company. see
Library Company of Wilmington.
Wilmington, Del. Meeting of Merchants and
Other Inhabitants, 17th June, 1801.
Committee. 104579
Wilmington, Del. Meeting of Merchants and
Other Inhabitants, 20th July, 1801.
104579
Wilmington, Del. Meeting of the Stockholders
of the Philadelphia, Wilmington and
Baltimore Rail Road Company, 1855.
see Philadelphia, Wilmington and Balti-
more Rail Road Company. Stockholders.
Meeting, Wilmington, Del., 1855
Wilmington, Del. Military College. see
Military College, Wilmington, Del.
Wilmington, Del. Newcastle County Agricultural
Society and Institute. see Newcastle
County Agricultural Society and Institute,
Wilmington, Del.
Wilmington, Del. Wilmington Academy. see
Wilmington Academy, Willmington, Del.
Wilmington, Del. Wilmington Union Coloni-
zation Society. see Wilmington Union
Colonization Society, Wilmington, Del.
Wilmington Academy, Wilmington, Del. Trustee
104583
Wilmington almanac or ephemeris. 25375
Wilmington & Raleigh Railroad Company.
Stockholders. 104585
Wilmington and Susquehanna Rail Road Com-
pany. 104587
Wilmington and Susquehanna Rail Road Com-
pany. Charter. 104586
Wilmington Company. see Compagnie de
Wilmington, dan la Caroline du Nord,
Sur la Riviere de Cape-Fear, aux Etats-
Unis de l'Amerique.
Wilmington Union Colonization Society, Wilming-
ton, Del. 104599, 104589
Wilmingtoniad: being a touch at the times.
19421, 104590
Wilmore, John. see Wilmer, John.

Wilmot, Montague, d. 1766. 84583 see also Nova Scotia. Governor, 1764-1766 (Wilmot)
Wilmot, David. (31494)
Wilmot, John Eardley. 104591-104592
Wilmot, Robert. 104593
Wilmot-Horton, Sir Robert John, Bart., 1784-1841. 33073-(33076), 82902-82904, 93371, 104594-note after 104595
Wilmot-Horton, Sir Robert John, Bart., 1784-1841. 22590, 40358, 46855, 91237, 102797, 102845
Wilmot proviso. 37830
Wilmot proviso—Martin Van Buren. 5561
Wilmot proviso. Speech of Hon. Jacob Brinkerhoff. 7993
Wilmsen, Friedrich Philipp. 104596
Willsford, John. see Willsford, John.
Wilson, --------, Commissary of General Amherst's Army, 1759. 1311
Wilson, ---------, fl. 1836. 95079, 95093
Wilson, ---------, fl. 1854. (54494) see also Great Britain. Commissioners to the New York Industrial Exhibition, 1854
Wilson, ---------, fl. 1861. (74581), 74583
Wilson, Alexander, 1766-1813. 6264, 6266, 16045, (57467), 104597-104604
Wilson, Amos. 104605-104606
Wilson, B. C. 12359
Wilson, Belford Hinton. 43150, 104607
Wilson, Bird. 84678C, 104608, 104632
Wilson, Charles Henry. of Northallerton 104611
Wilson, Charles Henry, d. 1808. 104609-104610
Wilson, Daniel, d. 1774. defendant 104612
Wilson, Daniel, Bishop of Calcutta, 1778-1858. 104613-104614
Wilson, Sir Daniel, 1816-1892. 10630, 92630
Wilson, David. 104615
Wilson, E. (8636)
Wilson, E. L. ed. 62025
Wilson, Edward. 104616
Wilson, Edward C. ed. 39498
Wilson, Elizabeth. defendant 104617
Wilson, Estevan Julian. see Willson, Estevan Julian.
Wilson, George. defendant 47464
Wilson, H. N. 104620
Wilson, Harriot. defendant 99425, 104621
Wilson, Henry. 54459, (54905)
Wilson, Henry, 1812-1875. 10190, 89627, 93644
Wilson, Henry R. 104622
Wilson, J. D. see Wilson, Joshua Lacy.
Wilson, J. H. 18397
Wilson, J. Q. (25793)
Wilson, James. attorney 104625
Wilson, James. defendant 6326, 1st note after 96956, 1st note after 97284
Wilson, James, M. D. of London ed. 101175
Wilson, James. Presbyterian preacher 104623-104624
Wilson, James, 1742-1798. 11005, 16144, 15967, 23356, 34294, 60040, (61411), 69398, 84577-84578, 2d-3d notes after 97876, 98626, note after 99172, 104626-104632 see also United Illinois and Wabash Land Companies. President.
Wilson, James, 1742-1798. petitioner 84677-84678, 2d-3d notes after 97876 see also United Illinois and Wabash Land Companies. President. petitioner
Wilson, James, 1759?-1814. 28820, (49480)-49482, (59572), note after 104633
Wilson, James, 1760-1839. 104634-104639

Wilson, James, 1777-1851. 51501, 97657, 104640
Wilson, James, 1799-1827. 104641
Wilson, James Grant. 29876
Wilson, James J. 104642
Wilson, James R., d. 1819. 104643
Wilson, James Renwick, 1780-1853. see Wilson, James Renwick, 1780-1853.
Wilson, Jasper. pseud. Letter. see Currie, James, 1756-1805.
Wilson, Jasper, Jr. pseud. Lie direct!! 104647
Wilson, Jeremiah Morrow, 1828-1901. 85492
Wilson, Job. 104648
Wilson, John. explorer 66686
Wilson, John, 1588-1677. 3213, 31743, 46783, 58769, 80202, note before 92797, note after 92800, 3d note after 103687, 104653-104655
Wilson, John, 1588-1677. supposed author 22146-22147, 74696, 80207-80208, 101330, note after 104653
Wilson, John. 1750. 104649
Wilson, John, fl. 1751. 104650
Wilson, John, 1788-1870. 104656
Wilson, John, 1804-1875. (22167), 104657
Wilson, John, d. 1807. defendant at Court Martial 104651-104652
Wilson, John, fl. 1830. 82355, 104222 see also Meeting of Working-Men and Other Persons Favorable to Political Principles, Albany, N. Y., 1830. Secretary.
Wilson, John Fanning. ed. 82974-82978
Wilson, John Grover. 104657A-104658
Wilson, John Lyde, 1784-1849. 87984, 104659-104663 see also South Carolina. Governor, 1822-1824 (Wilson)
Wilson, Joseph. printer 104665-104666
Wilson, Joseph. temperance writer 104664
Wilson, Joseph G. 104667
Wilson, Joshua Lacy. 61186, 96825, 104668-104676
Wilson, Montgomery. supposed author 16705
Wilson, N. (35584)
Wilson, Peter. 53048, 54476
Wilson, Rachel. 104677
Wilson, Ralph. 66686
Wilson, Richard. 100952
Wilson, Robert, 1747- 104680
Wilson, Robert, fl. 1770. 3866, 95976
Wilson, Robert, fl. 1779. 104678 see also Chester County, Pa. Sub-Lieutenant.
Wilson, Robert, fl. 1806. 21211-21215, 104679
Wilson, Robert, fl. 1837. 104681
Wilson, Robert G. 57015, 104682 see also Ohio. University, Athens. President.
Wilson, S. ed. 601
Wilson, Samuel. of Kentucky 104683
Wilson, Samuel. of South Carolina 104684
Wilson, Samuel, fl. 1678-1682. 10963, 104685
Wilson, Samuel, 1703-1750. 104686
Wilson, Samuel Farmer. 104687
Wilson, T. pseud. ed. see Clark, Samuel.
Wilson, T. ed. 27923
Wilson, T. S. 83725
Wilson, Thomas. of Manchester 104688
Wilson, Thomas. USA 90457
Wilson, Sir Thomas, 1560?-1629. 66686
Wilson, Thomas, 1655?-1725. 20033, 104689
Wilson, Thomas, Bishop of Sodor and Man, 1663-1755. 104690-104692
Wilson, Thomas, 1768-1828? 47269, 61606, 104693-104694

Wilson, Thomas L. V. supposed author
6479
Wilson, William. illus. (49480)-49482,
(59572), note after 104633
Wilson, William, fl. 1783. 55846 see also
Northumberland County, Pa. Collector
of Excise.
Wilson, William, fl. 1796-1798. (59572)
Wilson, William, fl. 1825. 104695
Wilson, William, fl. 1831. 105696
Wilson, William Dexter. 104697
Wilson, William Hasell, 1811-1902. 60567
Wilson Philip, A. P. see Philip, A. P. Wilson.
Wilson. firm publishers see Heckendorf &
Wilson. firm publishers MacArthur &
Wilson. firm publishers Prescott &
Wilson. firm publishers
Wilson (George M.) firm. 104619
Wilson (James) and Co. firm appellants 69087
Wilson (James) and Sons. firm appellants
69087
Wilson Association. 82694
Wilson the ornithologist. 59071
Wilson's business directory. 54459
Wilson's business directory . . . 1867-8.
54459
Wilson's . . . copartnership directory, for
1856-57. 54459
Wilson's . . . co-partnership directory . . .
for 1869-70. 54459
Wilson's . . . copartnership directory, for 1860-
61. 54459
Wilson's illustrated guide to the Hudson River.
33530
Wilson's Newburgh directory for 1856-'57.
(54905)
Wilson's plea in the cause of Lyman Beecher.
104676
Wiltbank, John. 60311
Wiltberger, C. 104698
Wilton, William. 104699
Wilton, N. H. Academy (Proposed) 104701
Wilton, N. H. Church of Christ. 104700
Wilton, N. H. Selectmen. 104701
Wilupupki 1842, lapwai hipaina takta hwait
tamalwiawat kimakespkinih. 103378
Wimmer, Gottlieb August. 33738, 104702-
104704
Wimon, Sally. 104705
Wimpey, Joseph. 104706
Wimpffen, Francois Alexandre Stanislaus,
Baron de. 104707-104712
Win and wear. (51620)
Winch, Silas. 104713
Winchell, A. 47635, 52243
Winchell, Horace. 104714
Winchell, J. F. 104715
Winchell, Jacob. 104716
Winchell, James Manning. 104717-104718
Winchell, N. H. 49247 see also Minnesota.
State Geologist.
Winchester, B. ed. 50739
Winchester, Benjamin. 85508, 104719
Winchester, Elhanan. 99502, 104720-104736
Winchester, Elhanan. supposed author 69519,
note after 104732
Winchester, George. 104737
Winchester, James. 32047, 104738
Winchester, Samuel G. 104741
Winchester, Samuel Gover. 104739-104741
Winchester, Bishop of. see Sumner, Charles
Richard, successively Bishop of Llandaff,
and Winchester, 1790-1874. Thomas,
John, successively Bishop of Peterborough,
Salisbury, and Winchester, 1696-1781.

Tomline, Sir George Pretyman, Bart.,
successively Bishop of Lincoln, and
Winchester, 1750-1827. Trimnell,
Charles, successively Bishop of Norwich,
and Winchester, 1663-1723. Wilberforce,
Samuel, successively Bishop of Oxford,
and Winchester, 1805-1873.
Winchester, England. Court of King's Bench.
see Great Britain. Court of King's
Bench.
Winchester, Mass. Industrial School for Girls.
see Massachusetts. Industrial School
for Girls, Winchester.
Winchester, Va. Meeting of the Friends of the
Present Administration, 1828. see
National Republican Party. Virginia.
Winchester.
Winchester, Va. Western Shore Association
Meeting, 1792. see Baptists. Mary-
land. Western Shore Association.
Winchester and Potomac Rail Road Company.
104742-104743
Winchester Potomac Railroad Company.
Charter. 104743
Winchester and Potomac Railroad Company.
Committee of Finance. 104743
Winchester and Potomac Railroad Company.
President and Directors. 104742-104743
Winchilsea, Heneage Finch, 2d Earl of.
104744
Winckelmann, Johann Justus. see Wynkelmann,
Johann Just.
Wind, S. de. ed. 72767
Wind and current charts. (46965)
Wind Mill Island cash lottery. (62392)
Wind Mill Island cash lottery, &c. . . . June
27, 1774. 104745
Winder, C. M. 47285
Winder, R. H. supposed author (22650),
89139, note after 101937, 104746
Winder, William H. 93938 see also
Maryland. Susquehannah Commissioners.
Winder, William H. of Philadelphia 104747
Winder, William Henry, 1775-1824. 104748
Windham, William, 1717-1761. 45934, 45547,
104747-104755
Windham, William, 1750-1810. 101166
Windham, Conn. Ecclesiastical Council, 1813.
see Congregational Churches in Con-
necticut. Ecclesiastical Council, Windham,
1813.
Windham, Conn. First Church. 90704
Windham, Conn. Third Church. Pastor and
Brethren. 104756
Windham, Conn. Third Church. Separating
Members. 104756
Windham, N. H. Old Nutfield Celebration,
1869. see Celebration of the One
Hundred and Fiftieth Anniversary of the
Settled Part of Old Nutfield, N. H., 1869.
Windham County, Conn. Association of Con-
gregational Ministers. see Congregational
in Connecticut. Windham County As-
sociation.
Windham County, Conn. Convention of Churches,
1800. see Congregational Churches in
Connecticut. Windham County Consocia-
tion.
Windham County, Conn. Eastern Association.
see Congregational Churches in Connecticut. Windham County Eastern Association.
Windham County, Conn. Peace Society. see
Windham County Peace Society.
Windham County, Conn. Superior Court.
96921

Windham County Agricultural Society. 104758
Windham County Associated Ministers. see
  Congregational Churches in Massachusetts.
  Windham County Association.
Windham County Association. see Congrega-
  tional Churches in Connecticut. Windham
  County Association. and Congregational
  Churches in Vermont. Windham County
  Association.
Windham County Charitable Society. Directing
  Committee. 104764
Windham County Consocation. see Congrega-
  tional Churches in Connecticut. Windham
  County Consocation.
Windham County Eastern Association. see
  Congregational Churches in Connecticut.
  Windham County Eastern Association.
Windham County Peace Society. 59407, 104765-
  104766
Windham County Temperance Society. 104767
Windham herald. 63946, 94075, 102523
Winds of the globe. 85072
Winds of the northern hemisphere. 14174,
  85072
Windsor, Conn. 14122
Windsor, Nova Scotia. King's College. see
  King's College, Windsor, Nova Scotia.
Windsor, Vt. Connecticut-Passumpsic Rivers
  Railroad Convention, 1836. see Conven-
  tion for Taking Preliminary Measures for
  a Railroad Through the Valleys of the
  Connecticut and Passumpsic Rivers to
  the St. Lawrence, Windosr, Vt., 1836
Windsor, Vt. Constitutional Convention, 1777.
  see Vermont. Constitutional Convention,
  Windsor, 1777.
Windsor, Vt. Constitutional Convention, 1793.
  see Vermont. Constitutional Convention,
  Windsor, 1793.
Windsor, Vt. Convention, 1825. see Convention,
  Windsor, Vt., 1825.
Windsor, Vt. Convention for Taking Into
  Consideration Subjects Connected With
  the Improvement of the Navigation of
  Connecticut River, 1830. see Convention
  for Taking Into Consideration Subjects
  Connected With the Improvement of the
  Navigation of Connecticut River, Windsor,
  Vt., 1830.
Windsor, Vt. Convention for Taking Preliminary
  Measures for a Railroad Thought the
  Valleys of the Connecticut and Passumpsic
  Rivers to the St. Lawrence, 1836. see
  Convention for Taking Preliminary Measures
  for a Railroad Through the Valleys of
  the Connecticut and Passumpsic Rivers to
  the St. Lawrence, Windsor, Vt., 1836.
Windsor, Vt. Convention for Taking Preliminary
  Measures to Effect an Imporved Navigation
  on Connecticut River, 1825. see Conven-
  tion for Taking Preliminary Measures to
  Effect an Improved Navigation on Con-
  necticut River, Windsor, Vt., 1825.
Windsor, Vt. Convention for the Purpose of
  Taking Preliminary Measures for a Rail
  Road, 1836. see Convention for the
  Purpose of Taking Preliminary Measures
  for a Rail Road, Windsor, Vt., 1836.
Windsor, Vt. Washington Benevolent Society.
  see Washington Benevolent Society.
  Vermont. Windsor.
Windsor County, Vt. Meeting, Woodstock, 1833.
  petitioners 104769
Windsor Association. see Congregational
  Churches in New Hampshire. Windsor
  Association.

Windsor Forest. 21547
Windt, Caroline Amelia (Smith) de. see
  De Windt, Caroline Amelia (Smith)
Wine for Gospel wantons. 80261
Winebrenner, John. 104770-104771
Wines, Enoch Cobb. 21324, 50177, 104772-
  104776
Winfield Scott, Franklin Pierce, their qualifi-
  cations and fitness. 65341
Winfield Scott und Seine Verlaumder. 78430
Winfield, the lawyer's son, and how he became
  Major-General. 19562, 59762
Wing, Austin E. 104777
Wing, C. P. 104778
Wingaersheek Division, No. 183, Gloucester,
  Mass. see Sons of Temperance of
  North America. Massachusetts. Wingaer-
  sheek Division, No. 183, Gloucester.
Wingate, Edmund, 1596-1646. 81, note after
  100381
Wingate, James. 45238
Wingate, Joseph F. supposed author (20226),
  (37853), 37856, 104779
Wingfield, Edward Maria. 19051, 66686
Wingfield, Rowland. 104780
Wingfield's Portugall voyage. 66686
Winke fur Auswanderer. 29409
Winkelmann, Hans Just. see Wynkelmann,
  Johann Just.
Winkelmann, J. C. A. 9297
Winkfield, Mrs. Unca Eliza. pseud. Female
  American. 104781
Winkle, C. S. Van. see Van Winkle, C. S.
Winkle, S. W. van. see Van Winkle, S. W.
Winkler, E. T. 88111
Winkler, E. W. ed. 94970
Winkles; or, the merry monomaniacs. 36537
Winkley, Francis. petitioner 21595, 97895,
  note after 104781 see also Shakers.
  Canterbury and Enfield, N. H. Overseers.
  petitioners
Winn, T. S. 104782-104784
Winne, Edward. 103330-103333, 104786
Winnebago Indians. Treaties, etc. 96647,
  96652, 96657, 96673, 96724 see also
  Michigan Indians. Treaties, etc.
Winnebago renegade. 7061
Winning his way. 14170
Winnipiseogee Canal Corporation. Charter.
  104787
Winnipiseogee Canal Corporation. Directors.
  52913, 104787
Winnipiseogee Canal Corporation. Directors.
  Committee to Prepare a Statement.
  52913, 104787
Winnipiseogee Canal Corporation. Directors.
  Committee to Procure a Survey. 104788
Winnisimmet Company. Directors. 104789
Winnowings in American history. 80594
Winsamius, Pieruis, 1586-1644. ed. 29937
Winship, G. P. 52641, note before 85867, note
  before 92797, note after 100866, 100940,
  101286, 104846
Winship, O. F. USA 91531
Winslett, David. 17461, (51587), 51589, 72017-
  72020
Winslow, Benjamin. defendant 104790
Winslow, Benjamin Davis. 104791
Winslow, Charles Frederick 104792
Winslow, Edward, 1595-1655. 7263, (12705)-
  12706, (22152), 45664, 51017, (51198)-
  51201, 63332, 66686, note before 92797,
  1st note after 98664, 104794-note after
  104797, 106053
Winslow, Edward Lee. 29697

Wisconsin. Commissioners of Public Lands. 88415 see also Conant, M.

Wisconsin. Commissioners to Ascertain and Settle the Liabilities of the State . . . to the . . . Milwaukee and Rock River Canal Company. (49169)

Wisconsin. Committee on Improvement of the Rock River. 62415

Wisconsin. Consitution. 1269, 5316, 9672, 16113, 29731, 33137, (66397), 71572

Wisconsin. Constitutional Convention, 84861

Wisconsin. Court of Chancery. 96860

Wisconsin. Geological Survey. 18498

Wisconsin. Governor, 1854-1856 (Barstow) 84866 see also Barstow, William Augustus, 1813-1865.

Wisconsin. Governor, 1858-1862 (Randall) 33150 see also Randall, Alexander Williams, 1819-1872.

Wisconsin, Governor, 1862-1864 (Salmon) defendant 10997 see also Salmon, Edward, 1830- defendant

Wisconsin. Land Commissioners. see Wisconsin. Commissioners of Public Lands.

Wisconsin. Laws, statutes, etc. 23765, 29555, 29731, 37460, 38508, 43734, 43736-(43737), 43744, 49151, 49153, (49165)-49166, (49169), 49171-49173, 49177, 49208, (49210), 52051, (52300), 70820-70821, 75032, 80064, 82438, note after 92947

Wisconsin. Legislature. 17676, 84861

Wisconsin. Legislature. Committee to Investigate into the Alleged Frauds . . . in the Disposition of the Land Grant By . . . the Legislature of 1856. 43748

Wisconsin. Legislature. Select Committee to Investigate the Milwaukee and Superior Railway Company. 49171

Wisconsin. Legislature. Assembly. 74529

Wisconsin. Legislature. Senate. 33461, 37728

Wisconsin. Legislature. Senate. Court of Impeachment. 74529

Wisconsin. State Historian. 84861, 84866 see also Smith, William Rudolph, 1787-1868.

Wisconsin. State Historical Society. 20901, 84132, 84337, 83026, 83029, 85428, 85433, 92227, 3d note after 94249

Wisconsin. State Teachers College, Plattesville. 63361

Wisconsin. Superintendent of Public Instruction. 20901 see also Draper, Lyman Copeland, 1815-1891.

Wisconsin. Supreme Court. 3699, 3883, 10997, 26130, 80096

Wisconsin. (39192)

Wisconsin almanac and annual register, 1856. 33878

Wisconsin and her resources. 73364

Wisconsin and its resources. 71572

Wisconsin Canal Conventions. petitioners 47715

Wisconsin enquirer. (20667), 1st note after 104889

Wisconsin gazetteer. 33879

Wisconsin Historical Society. see Wisconsin. State Historical Society.

Wisconsin in the war of the rebellion. 42364

Wisconsin Mining Company. 104889

Wisconsin railroad grant. (40238)

Wisconsin reports. 80096

Wisconsin State Historical Society. see Wisconsin. State Historical Society.

Wisconsin state journal. 73365

Wisconsin territory. (20667), 1st note after 104889

Wisconsin. Zwei Abetheilungen. 29410

Wisdom, an essential requisite. 62517

Wisdom and duty of magistrates. 22393

Wisdom and goodness of God. 79806

Wisdom and knowledge, the main pillars of a republican government. 101406

Wisdom and knowledge the nation's stability. 92394

Wisdom and policy of the French in the construction of their great offices. 43122, 2d note after 104889

Wisdom is justified of all her children. 22442

Wisdom justified in her children. 58895

Wisdom, knowledge, and the fear of God recommended. 17099

Wisdom of Eve. 97096

Wisdom of fleeing from persecution. 15027, note after 103616

Wisdom of God crying and calling to the sons and daughters of men. 102576

Wisdom of God in the permission of sin, vindicated. 4497

Wisdom of God in the redemption of man. 1845

Wisdom of observing the footsteps of providence. (18419)

Wisdom taught by man's mortality. 104736

Wisdome, the cae of the spiritual souldier. 104084

Wisdom's favorite. 95880

Wise, Henry Alexander, 1806-1876. 305, (12727), (32207), (33150), 38148, 39655, 69350, 87100, 104890 see also Virginia. Governor, 1856-1860 (Wise)

Wise, Henry Alexander, 1806-1876. supposed author 41004, 1st note after 100578

Wise, Henry Augustus, 1819-1869. 69771, 84958, 104891-104893 see also U. S. Bureau of Ordnance.

Wise, Jeremiah. 104894-104895

Wies, John, 1652-1725. 15449, 25948, (63341), 103320, 103400, 104896-104902, note after 105459

Wise, R. 104903

Wise, Thomas Turner. 104904

Wise and faithful steward. 1675

Wise and foolish virgins. 103516, 103582

Wise & good civil rulers. 95167

Wise builder, a sermon. 13269

Wise devision. 83526

Wise expectation of, and preparation for, troublesom changes. 46537

Wise man is strong. 9630

Wise mans counsel to the young man. 80187

Wise men of the east confounded! 30662, note after 101993

Wise saws. 29696

Wise sayings of the Honorable Isaac Hill. (31832)

Wishart, William. (51141)

Wislizenus, Frederick Adolphus. 104905

Wisner, Benjamin Blydenburg. 104906-104915

Wisner, William. 104916-104918

Wissenschaftliche Wurdigung der Reiseberichte Springers. 99363

Wissenschaftlichen Erlauterungen von Alexander von Humboldt. 33702-33703

Wisshart, William. 78448

Wistar, Caspar. 104919-104920

Wister, Johannes. 104921

Wister, Sally. 82979

Wiswall, Ichadod. 98056, 104922
Wiswell, Ichabod. see Wiswall, Ichabod.
Wit, Frederick de. cartographer 78539
Wit and honest of James Hoskins. 6108,
    92329
Wit and humor. 79917
Wit and humor in paragraphs. 65064-65065
Wit and wisdom of the Rev. Sydney Smith.
    84317-84319
Wit by folly vanquished. 71135
Witch hill. 51240
Witch of Blagge's Cove. 105195
Witch of New England. 19457
Witch of New England, a romance. 104923
Witch of the Wescot. 80471
Witchcraft. 46840
Witchcraft delusion in New England. 9927,
    20884
Witchcraft delusion of 1692. (34088)
Witchcraft: or the art of fortune-telling unveiled.
    62891
Witches: a tale of New-England. 104924
Witches of New York. 95597
Witchetaw Indians. see Wicheta Indians.
With, Jan. (8784)
With, Witte Cornelisszoon de, 1599-1658.
    100772, 104925
With, Witte de. see With, Witte Corneliss-
    zoon de, 1599-1658.
With astonishment I read a late publication.
    96008
With General Sheridan in Lee's last campaign.
    90068
With the French in Mexico. 22367
With the Winnebagoes. 83485
Withall, Benjamin. petitioner 104926
Wither, George, 1588-1667. 31037, 39820,
    1st note after 94666
Wither'd hand stretched forth at the command
    of Christ. (14522)
Witherell, George. 104927
Withers, Alexander Scott. 65720, 104928
Withers, Robert. 66686
Witherspoon, John, 1723-1794. 22944, (32117),
    51511, 60346, 65156-65157, 99005, note
    after 102409, 104929-104947 see also
    Presbyterian Church in the U. S. A.
    Committee to Draught a Plan of Govern-
    ment and Discipline. Chairman.
Witherspoon, John, 1723-1794. supposed author
    104629
Within Fort Sumter. 25168
Within the meshes. 91162
Withington, George M. petitioner (45948)
Withington, George R. M. petitioner 11117,
    (45948)
Withington, Leonard. 104355, 104948-104953
Withington, Nicholas. 14095, 14097, 66686
Withington, O. W. 101395
Withington, William. 104954-104956
Withy, George. 104957-104958
Witlbank, --------. 4107
Witness for the truth. pseud. Brief character.
    see Mather, W.
Witness of the spirit. A sermon preached at
    Newark. (20062)
Witness of the spirit in the hearts of believers.
    13350
Witness to truth, and lover of religion and
    learning. pseud. Letter to a member
    of the House of Representatives. see
    Graham, John.
Witness unto the truth. 78589
Witnesses' address. 92031

Witnesses to several captures and outrages.
    pseud. Depositions. 48052, note after
    87538
Witsius, Hermann. 104959
Witt, Benjamin de. see De Witt, Benjamin,
    1774-1819.
Witt, Cornelis de. tr. 47083
Witt, Francis de. see De Witt, Francis.
Witt, Johan de. 78761
Witt, John de. see De Witt, John.
Witt, Simeon de. see De Witt, Siemon,
    1745-1834.
Witt, Thomas de. see De Witt, Thomas,
    1791-1874.
Witt, W. G. 86815
Witt, W. R. de. see De Witt, W. R.
Witt, Wallace de. see De Witt, Wallace.
Witt, William R. de see De Witt, William R.
Witte, August. 104960
Witte, Henning. 104961
Witte, J. 86814
Witte, William H. 85081
Wittenberg, A. tr. 2091, 31902, (37956)
Witter, Ezra, 1768?-1833. 2623, 104962-
    104965
Witterungs-Beobachtungen. (2711)
Wittich, Johann. 104966
Witticisms of the late President Lincoln.
    6346
Wix, Edward. 104967-104969
Wizard. 97788
Wizard of Conlin. 84392
Wizard of the wave. (72071)
Wjffin, Richard. see Wiefin, Richard.
Wlkr potrwatome msina'kin; kewrnpinukatr.
    81141
Wo and a warning. 104971
Wo occasioned to the inhabitants of the earth.
    19818
Wo to drunkards. 46759
Wo to sleepy sinners. (46210)
Wobanaki kimzowi awighigan. 57817, 105711
Woburn, Mass. Church. 82483
Woburn, Mass. Council of Six Churches, 1746.
    see Congregational Churches in Massa-
    chusetts. Ecclesiastcail Council, Woburn,
    1746.
Woburn, Mass. Ecclesiastical Council, 1746.
    see Congregational Churches in Massa-
    chusetts. Ecclesiastical Council, Wo-
    burn, 1746.
Woburn, Mass. First Church. 35407, 104972
Woburn, Mass. First Church. Pastor. 35407,
    104972 see also Jackson, Edward.
Woburn Agricultural and Manufacturing Com-
    pany. Directors. 104973
Wochentliche Philadelphische Staatsbote. 62393
Wodenoth, Arthur. 100450, 2d note after
    100521, 104974
Wodurch unterscheiden sie sich von einander
    und was sind sonach der Deutsche Bund.
    90017
Woe to the city. 16170
Woensel, P. van. ed. 68097
Woerl, J. E. mapmaker 8221
Woerner, J. G. 75345
Woes of youth. 104975
Wofford, J. D. 104976
Woful effects of drunkenness. 18479
Wohin soll der Deutsche Auswandern? 38323
Wohl-eingerichtetes Veih-Arznen-Buch.
    104977
Wohl-gemeindter und Ernstlicher Rath. 102508
Wohlfahrt, J. J. 93847
Wohlfahrt, Joanna Susan. 97091
Wohlfahrt, Johan Fransocis. [sic] 97091

Wohlfahrt, Michael. 100775
Wohlfeile Hand-Bibliothek fur Auswanderer.
8200, 8205, 8207-8208, 8222
Wohlversuchte Sud-lander. 4378
Wo[h]richende Narde. 106363
Wokumayaan. 67765
Wolcott, ---------, fl. 1866. (39672)
Wolcott, Alexander. 104978-104980
Wolcott, Alexander. supposed author 15847,
104980
Wolcott, Eliza. 100993, 104981
Wolcott, Josiah. supposed author 100869
Wolcott, Oliver, 1760-1833. 10889, 22987,
69815, 96598, 104982-104984, 105844
see also Connecticut. Governor, 1818-
1827 (Wolcott) U. S. Commissioners to
the Six Nations of Indians.
Wolcott, Oliver, 1760-1833. supposed author
23994, 84829, 84831, 84832, 2d note
after 104983
Wolcott, Oliver, 1760-1833. incorrectly sup-
posed author 15121, note before 89139,
1st note after 104983, 105212
Wolcott, Roger. 104985-104986
Wolcott, Samuel. 82057
Wolcott, Sarah G. 100993, 104981
Wolcott, William. 28337, 2d note after 104986
Wole booke of psalmes. (66428)
Wolf, Adolf. Tr. 35536
Wolf, Ferdinand. 35536
Wolf, George, 1777-1840. 60503, 60508, 60513
see also Pennsylvania. Governor, 1829-
1835 (Wolf)
Wolf, Henry. illus. 83740
Wolf, John d'. see D'Wolf, John.
Wolf, L. E. de. see De Wolf, L. E.
Wolf, Miels. tr. 22868
Wil¹ . G. tr. 22869, 22870, (28637)
Wo; Thaddeus K. de. see De Wolf, Thaddeus
K. de.
W)lᶠ in sheep's clothing. 9110
Wolfe, J. M. (21040), 38507, 57261
Wolfe, James, 1726-1759. 26630, 104987-
104989
Wolfe, James, 1726-1759. mediumistic author
19937, 19947, 67002, note after 96403
Wolfe, Nathaniel. (70981)
Wolfe of the Knoll. 44723
Wolfeborough, N. H. Convention of New-
Hampshire Publishers, Editors, and
Printers, 1868. see Convention of New-
Hampshire Publishers, Editors, and
Printers, Wolfeborough, 1868.
Wolfert's Roost and other papers. 4777, (35213)
Wolff, E. Th. tr. 42762
Wilff, Elizabeth Bekker. 104990
Wolff, Elizabeth Bekker. supposed author
18260, 59622, 104991
Wolford, George. 53952
Wolfson, D. L. 67409
Wolgemuth, Michael. engr. 77523
Woll, Adrian. 20548, 104992-104993
Wolley, Charles. 104994
Wolves in sheep-skins detected. (42163)
Woman. pseud. England, the civilizer. 22592
Woman; a poem. (7120)
Woman adventurers. 94233
Woman and her era. 23862
Woman and her needs. 82524
Woman and her wishes. 31755
Woman and the higher education. 104042
Woman and the way. 5562
Woman, her education and influence. 69013
Woman, in all ages and nations. (55215)

Woman in America; being an examination.
28346
Woman in America: her character and position.
(22450)
Woman in America. Her work and her re-
ward. 43336
Woman in prison. 105122
Woman in the nineteenth century. 58716
Woman of the town. 104995
Woman outwitted. 100575
Woman that lives without eating. 49126
Woman who dared. 76966
Woman's Alliance of the First Church of Port-
land, Me. see Portland, Me. First
Church. Woman's Alliance.
Woman's Central Association of Relief, March
23, 1863. 33228
Woman's defence. 24182
Woman's destiny. 29670
Woman's duty to vote. 4325
Woman's endurance. 80749, 80751
Woman's example. 55300
Woman's hospital of the State of New York.
see New York (State) Woman's Hospital
of the State of New York.
Woman's influence in politics. 4325
Woman's journal round the world. 61339
Woman's reason why women should not vote.
13629
Woman's record. 29670
Woman's relation to education. 18304
Woman's relation to it. 52330
"Woman's right to labor." 18305
Woman's right to the ballot. 23679
Woman's rights. An essay. 33216
Woman's Rights Committee of New York State.
see New York State Woman's Rights
Committee.
Woman's Rights Convention, Rochester, N. Y.,
90397
Woman's Rights Convention, Seneca Falls,
N. Y., 1848. 90397
Woman's Rights Convention, Albany, 1854.
see New York State Woman's Rights
Convention, Albany, 1854.
Woman's rights tracts, no. 10. 90403
Woman's rights under the law. 18306
Woman's suffrage in the Supreme Court of
the District of Columbia. 89380
Woman's temperance movement. 91100
Woman's thoughts about women. 85202
Women's trial, a play, in five acts. 83779
Woman's Union Missionary Society of America.
49471
Woman's wanderings in the western world.
8199
Woman's work in the civil war. 8162
Woman's wrongs: a counter-irritant. 20506
Women artists in all ages and countries.
22214
Women have a work to do. (61018)
Women invited to war. 104996
Women ministering to Christ. 85409
Women of beauty and heroism. (27887)
Women of England. pseud. Address. 13864,
43335
Women of Methodism. note after 91480
Women of New York; or, the under-world of
a great city. 22223
Women of New York. Written and illustrated.
By Marie L. Hankins. 30228
Women of the American revolution. 22214
Women of the revolution. 83567
Women of the south distinguished in literature.
25114

Women of the war. 50371
Women vs. ballot. 26195
Women's Branch of the Centennial Association of Connecticut. see Centennial Association of Connecticut. Women's Branch.
Women's Central Association of Relief, New York. see United States Sanitary Commission. Women's Central Association of Relief, New York.
Women's Christian Association, Providence, R. I. (66382)
Womens complaint against tobacco. 104997
Women's Maryland Branch of the U. S. Sanitary Commission. see United States Sanitary Commission. Women's Maryland Branch.
Women's Pennsylvania Branch of the United States Sanitary Commission. see United States Sanitary Commission. Women's Pennsylvania Branch.
Women's Reform and Relief Association, New Bedford, Mass. see New Bedford Women's Reform and Relief Association.
Women's Relief Association of Brooklyn. see United States Sanitary Commission. Women's Relief Association of Brooklyn.
Women's rights. 77401
Women's Rights Convention, Akron, Ohio, 1851. see Ohio Women's Rights Convention, Akron, 1851.
Women's Rights Convention, Cleveland, 1853. see National Women's Rights Convention, Cleveland, 1853.
Women's suffrage. 9549
Wonder leven, van de H. Rosa de S. Maria. 105516
Wonder of the age. 37837
Wonder of the Lorde most admirable. 57926, 71894
Wonder of wonders! Or, the wonderful appearance. 105002
Wonder upon wonder. A tale. 89439
Wonder-working providence. 28020, (36203), 36205
Wonderbaere reyze na d'uytterste paelen van America. 96101, note after 104997
Wonderbaerlijcken strydt tusschen de kickvorschen ende de muysen. 104998
Wonderbare reyzen van Whil. Retchir. (72235)
Wondere beschryvinge ende vindinge van het landt Canada. 104999, 105014A
Wonderful account of the death and burial of the old hermit. 105000
Wonderful advantages of adventuring in the lottery!!! 105001
Wonderful adventurer. 90456
Wonderful adventures of A. Gordon Pym. 63527
Wonderful adventures of a lady of French nobility. 84034
Wonderful adventures of Beelzebub Bubble. 55392
Wonderful adventures of Captain Priest. 30084
Wonderful and eccentric museum. 37961
Wonderful and horrible thing is committed in the land. 19608, 31915
Wonderful and melancholy transformation of several naught masters and misses. 99241
Wonderful and scientific museum. 94233
Wonderful appearance of an angel, devil & ghost. 105002
Wonderful curiosity. 36628
Wonderful deliverance of the Rev. J. Rodgers. 105178
Wonderful disclosure! 42101
Wonderful discovery! Being an account of a recent exploration. 40240

Wonderful discovery of a hermit. 105005-105007
Wonderful discovery of a hermit being a most remarkable narrative. 105003
Wonderful discovery of an old hermit. 105004, 105008
Wonderful dream. 104033
Wonderful escapes! Containing the interesting narrative of the shipwreck. 92355, 105009
Wonderful facts from the gold regions. 101210
Wonderful instance of the goodness of God. 19817
Wonderful lamp. 82973
Wonderful life and adventures of Three-Fingered Jack. 105010
Wonderful life and terrible death of Morgan. 50692
Wonderful magazine and extraordinary museum. 42166
Wonderful monitor. 94518, 94521
Wonderful narrative of an Indian. 2478
Wonderful narrative of two families. 94610
Wonderful narrative: or, a faithful account of the French prophets. 105011, 105012
Wonderful phenomenon explained. 28548
Wonderful prodigies of judgment and mercy. 9502
Wonderful prophecies concerning popery. 59230
Wonderful providence, in many incidents at sea. (32460)
Wonderful providence of God. 101124
Wonderful quiz. pseud. Fable for critics. see Lowell, James Russell, 1819-1892.
Wonderful revelation of the present rebellion. 89509
Wonderful signs of wonderful times. 52342
Wonderful sleeper. 91067
Wonderful, startling and thrilling narrative. 50418
Wonderful, surprising, and uncommon voyages and adventures of Captain Jones. (41685)
Wonderful trial of Caroline Lohman. 41829
Wonderful vision of Nicodemus Haven's. 105013
Wonderful vision of . . . the city of New York. 30899
Wonderful works of God. A narrative. (8639)
Wonderful works of God commemorated. 46591, 46602
Wonderfull history of the Morristown ghost. 72722, 106070
Wonderlicke avontuer, van twee Goelieven. 105014
Wonderlijcke ende warachtighe historie. 106274
Wonderlijcke ende warachtighe historie vant coninckrijck van Peru. 106257-106258, 106273
Wonderlijcke historie van de noordersche landen. 57106
Wonderlijcke histoire van de Noordersche Landen beschreuen door Heere Olaus de Grote. 43835
Wonderlijcke voyagie, by de Hollanders gedaen. 55440, 2d note after 105014
Wonderlijcke voyagie, by de Hollanders ghedaen. 55441, 55443, (55445)
Wonderlijcke voyagie . . . ghedaen . . . des aerdtbodems om. 55442
Wonderlyk leven van Gust. Landkroon. 72237
Wonderlyke reyze, by de Hollanders gedaan. 55448
Wonders of American patience. 8110, note after 94022
Wonders of Christianity. 46544

Wonders of creation. 65366
Wonders of geology. 27913
Wonders of nature and art. 84363, 84865
Wonders of nature and providence, displayed.
  65496, note after 105014A
Wonders of the gold diggins of British Columbia.
  8094
Wonders of the hatred of liberty. (65019)
Wonders of the invisible world. 4009, 5196,
  9926-9927, (19046), 20884, 27384, 46603-
  46607, (46648), 75736, 82976, 89927,
  97495
Wonders of the ocean. 44592, 93423
Wonders of the west Indies. 42811
Wonders of the world. 105015
Wonders of the world. And the answer.
  105016
Wonders of the world, in nature, art, and mind.
  (78656)
Wonders of the Yellowstone. 71017
Wonders of the Yellowstone region in the Rocky
  Mountains. (71018)
Wonders of trauell. 27842
Wonders. The birth of Washington. And the
  tars of Columbia. 105016
Wont we be a happy people, when this war is
  over. (41607)
Wood, -------. 42527
Wood, -------. D. D. 93205
Wood, -------, fl. 1857. 66107
Wood, A. E. 105074
Wood, Abraham. 92083, 103771, 105017-
  105018
Wood, Amos. 105019
Wood, Anthony a, 1632-1695. 27351, 67599
Wood, Barnabas. 1134
Wood, Benjamin. explorer 66686
Wood, Benjamin. Pastor of the Church at Upton
  105020-105023
Wood, E. F. (49781)
Wood, Elder. 48777
Wood, Fernando. (33273)
Wood, G. 104500
Wood, George, 1789-1860. 105025-105026
Wood, George, 1799-1870. 605
Wood, George Bacon, 1797-1879. 60330, 60332,
  105027-105030
Wood, George S. plaintiff 105055
Wood, H. C. 85072
Wood, Henry. Yorkshire Journalist supposed
  author 20004, note after 105032
Wood, Henry, fl. 1834-1835. 105031-105032
Wood, Hewing. petitioner 33440
Wood, Horatio C. 85072
Wood, Isaiah. 105033-105033A
Wood, Jacob. 105035-105037
Wood, James. of Ipswich 105038
Wood, James. supposed author 11587, 105034
Wood, James, 1747-1813. 100226-100227,
  100407 see also Virginia. Governor,
  1796-1799 (Wood) Virginia. Lieutenant
  Governor, 1790 (Wood)
Wood, James, 1799-1867. 105039
Wood, James, fl. 1902. 84762
Wood, Jean. 4935-4936
Wood, Jesse. defendant 105040
Wood, John. complainant 104500 see also
  Friends, Society of. New York Monthly
  Meeting. Property Committee. com-
  plainants
Wood, John. explorer (72185)-72187
Wood, John. of Woburn 105049
Wood, John, fl. 1618. 105040A
Wood, John, fl. 1670. 29473

Wood, John, 1775?-1822. 9431, 12380, 2d note
  after 92859, 105041-105047, 2d note after
  106011
Wood, John, 1775?-1822. incorrectly supposed
  author 12387, 1st note after 99571, note
  after 105047
Wood, John, fl. 1798. 105048
Wood, John Philip. 39307-39315, 105050-
  105051
Wood, John S. 1134
Wood, Joseph. (31800), 77911, 85072, 105052
Wood, L. 100415 see also Virginia. Junior
  Solicitor.
Wood, Lewis K. 105053
Wood, Nathaniel. petitioner 45470
Wood, Nicholas. 105054
Wood, Nicholas. defendant 31940
Wood, Nicholas L. defendant 45313
Wood, Richard. plaintiff 105055
Wood;, S. S. 28799
Wood, Sally Sayward Barrell Keating. 105056-
  105062
Wood, Samuel. New York bookseller 105063
Wood, Samuel. Unitarian minister 105064
Wood, Samuel, 1752-1836. 105061-105062
Wood, Samuel R. 95808, 105064
Wood, Samuel Simpson. 105066
Wood, Silas. 89598, 105067-105072
Wood, Susan. defendant 89081
Wood, T. 69522
Wood, Thomas. supposed author 78364
Wood, Thomas, d. 1778. 105073
Wood, Thomas John, 1823-1906. 19515, 40611
Wood, W. 65646
Wood, W. B. 69155
Wood, William. appellant 11194
Wood, William. of Jamaica 2228, 35660,
  (35668), 1st note after 97148, note after
  99576, note after 105078-105080, 105081-
  note after 105081
Wood, William. of Jamaica appellant 105082
Wood, William, 1580-1639. 65646, 82823,
  82974, 82976, 105074-105077, 106052
Wood, William, 1679-1765. 78984, 105078
Wood, William, fl. 1818. defendant 30365
Wood, William, fl. 1855. defendant (21627)
Wood, William Maxwell. 105083
Wood County, West Virginia. Circuit Court.
  89363
Wood daemon. 97466
Wood daemon, or, the clock has struck!
  97466
Wood demon. 65068
Wood engraved work of Timothy Cole. 83741
Wood-yard mystery. 31324
Woodbridge, Miss A. D. 89744
Woodbridge, Ashbel. 105084
Woodbridge, Benjamin. 58769
Woodbridge, John, 1613-1696. 79377, 105085
Woodbridge, John, 1784-1869. 105086-105087
Woodbridge, Samuel. 105088
Woodbridge, Sylvester, fl. 1840. 105089
Woodbridge, Sylvester, fl. 1851. 105090
Woodbridge, Timothy. supposed author 28052,
  28506, 65689, 91945, note after 105090
Woodbridge, William, 1755-1836. 105092-
  105093
Woodbridge, William, 1780-1861. 105094-
  105095
Woodbridge, William Channing. 104045,
  105096-105097
Woodward, William Elliot. ed. and publisher
  20867, 20884, 33453, 62489, (68405)
Woodbury, Augustus. 3694, 8524, 55721, 66292,
  note after 89213

Woodbury, Fanny, <u>d</u>. 1814. 105098
Woodbury, I. B. <u>ed</u>. (54824)
Woodbury, Levi, 1789-1851. 103385,
  105099-105102 <u>see also</u> U. S. Treasury
  Department.
Woodbury, Levi, 1789-1851. <u>supposed author</u>
  269, (50398), note after 99796, note after
  105101
Woodbury, Peter P. (4279)
Woodbury Library Company, Philadelphia.
  105103
Woodbury's tables and notes on the cultivation,
  manufacture, and foreign trade of cotton.
  105102
Woodcock, A. H. 77031
Woodcock, Henry Iles. 105104
Woodcock, T. S. <u>engr</u>. 12891, 84358-84362,
  84365
Woodcraft; or hawks about the dovecote. 81277,
  (81279)
Woode, Abraham. 52518-52519, note after
  100495, 104191
Wooden booksellers and miseries of authorship.
  24219
Wooden-legged soldier. <u>pseud</u>. Answer to a
  colonel's letter. 1654
"Wooden nutmegs" at Bull Run. 26096
Wooden walls well manned. 18850, 64472
Woodfall, --------. <u>defendant</u> 40490
Woodfall, --------. <u>printer</u> 97362
Woodhill; or, the ways of providence. 72189,
  2d note after 94271
Woodhouse, James. 105105-105108
Woodhouse, S. W. 81472-81473
Woodhull, Alfred Alexander. 53088
Woodhull, John. 105109
Woodhull, Maxwell. 105110
Woodland adventures in the middle states.
  (31462)
Woodland lays, legends, and charades. 29621
Woodland warbler. 89157
Woodlands Cemetery, Philadelphia. <u>see</u>
  Philadelphia. Woodlands Cemetery.
Woodlawn Cemetery, Charlestown, Mass. <u>see</u>
  Charlestown, Mass. Woodlawn Cemetery.
Woodlawn Cemetery in North Chelsea and
  Malden. 26161
Woodman, --------, <u>fl</u>. 1793. (78487), 80190
Woodman, Cyrus. <u>ed</u>. 14183
Woodman, David. 26474, 83710, 95086, 105111
Woodman, H. <u>reporter</u> 95187
Woodman, Jonathan. 105112
Woodman, Joseph. 105113
Woodman, Woodville. 64962
Woodman. 11929
Woodman, and other poems. 11929
Woodnoth, Arthur. <u>see</u> Wodenoth, Arthur.
Woodrangers. 4537
Woodreve Manor. 20655
Woodruff, Ephraim Treadwell. 105114
Woodruff, Hezekiah North. 105115-105117A
Woodruff, J. <u>reporter</u> 87447
Woodruff, J. H. 13085
Woodruff, Sylvester. <u>supposed author</u> (105117B)
Woodruff, Wilford. 83193, 83207-83208, 83220,
  83245, 83283 <u>see also</u> Church of Jesus
  Christ of Latter Day Saints. President.
Woods, --------, <u>fl</u>. 1808. 105118
Woods, Alva. 105119-105121
Woods, Caroline H. 105122
Woods, Daniel Bates. 105123
Woods, James W. 42828
Woods, John, <u>fl</u>. 1695. 66741
Woods, John, 1780- 105124
Woods, John, <u>d</u>. 1829. 105125

Woods, Joseph. 81895, 105126
Woods, Leonard, 1774-1854. 41954, 54955-
  54956, 54962, 89736-89737, 93205, 101375,
  101379-101380, 105127-105142
Woods, Leonard, 1774-1854. <u>supposed author</u>
  25535, 41024, 1st note after 105132
Woods, Leonard, 1807-1878. <u>ed</u>. 41479
Woods and by-laws of New England. 24662
Woods and waters. 92775
Wood's New-England's prospect. 65646
Woodside, -------. <u>illus</u>. 25722, 1st note
  after 99448
Woodstock, Conn. Anti-masonic Convention,
  1829. <u>see</u> Anti-masonic Convention,
  Woodstock, Conn., 1829.
Woodstock, Conn. Second Church of Christ.
  105146
Woodstock, Pa. Charter. 105147
Woodstock, Vt. 92787
Woodstock, Vt. Clinical School of Medicine.
  <u>see</u> Vermont Medical College, Wood-
  stock, Vt.
Woodstock, Vt. Court. 96304
Woodstock, Vt. Medical College. <u>see</u> Vermont
  Medical College, Woodstock, Vt.
Woodstock, Vt. Meeting of the Citizens of
  Windsor County, 1833. <u>see</u> Windsor
  County, Vt. Meeting, Woodstock, 1833.
Woodstock, Vt. School of Medicine. <u>see</u>
  Vermont Medical College, Woodstock, Vt.
Woodstock, Vt. Vermont Medical College.
  <u>see</u> Vermont Medical College, Wood-
  stock, Vt.
Woodstock Association. <u>see</u> Baptists. Vermont.
  Woodstock Baptist Association.
Woodstock circular. 105144
Woodville, N. Y. Mechanics' and Gardeners'
  Mutual Education, and Manual Labour
  Association. <u>see</u> Mechanics' and
  Gardeners' Mutual Education, and Manual
  Labour Association, at Woodville, Long
  Island.
Woodville; or, the anchoret reclaimed. 96083,
  note after 105147
Woodward, --------. <u>defendant</u> 31669
Woodward, Augustus Brevoort. 105148-105157
Woodward, B. B. 3788
Woodward, Beza. 66514, 1st note after 99003,
  99021 <u>see also</u> Vermont. Committee
  to Draw Up a Public Defence of the
  Right of the New-Hampshire Grants.
  Vermont. General Assembly. Clerk.
Woodward, E. 105158
Woodward, George A. 60619
Woodward, George Washington, 1799-1875.
  4107, 16298, 37330, 60619, 60755
Woodward, Israel Beard. 105159
Woodward, James W. 105160
Woodward, John. <u>of New York</u> 105162
Woodward, John, 1671-1746. 105161
Woodward, John, <u>fl</u>. 1837. 105163
Woodward, Joseph J. 30116, 57853, 69954
Woodward, S. B. 32944
Woodward, Samuel. 105164-105165
Woodward, Samuel Bayard. 45910, 105166
Woodward, Thomas. 105167
Woodward, William Elliot, <u>d</u>. 1892. 20867,
  20884, 33453, 48819, 62489, (68405)
  <u>see also</u> Woodward (William Elliot)
  <u>firm publishers</u>
Woodward, William H. <u>defendant</u> 23887
Woodward, William Henry. (57444), 105168-
  105169
Woodward, William R. 30732 <u>see also</u>
  Harvard University. Law Library.
  Librarian.

Woodward, William W. 34434, 44483, 105169A-
105173
Woodward, William W. defendant 18613,
18623, 18625, 102261
Woodward (Charles L.) firm publishers
101507
Woodward (William Elliot) firm publishers
20867, 20884 see also Woodward,
William Elliot, d. 1892.
Woodward & Rowland. firm publishers 63128
Woodward & Rowland's Pittsburgh directory for
1852. 63128
Woodward College, Cincinnati, Ohio. 105174
Woodward College, Cincinnati, Ohio. President.
105174
Woodward High School, Cincinnati, Ohio. see
Cincinnati. Woodward High School.
Woodworth, --------. defendant 12045
Woodworth, --------. ed. 105193
Woodworth, James. tr. 14545
Woodworth, John, 1768-1858. 53744, 63362,
105175-105176
Woodworth, John, 1768-1858. supposed author
89923, note after 105176
Woodworth, Joseph. (105176A)
Woodworth, Samuel, 1784-1842. 38536, 38538,
(54092), 54819, 58929, (69154), (70978),
82726, 83665, note before 94463, 100636,
101258, 105177-105195
Woodworth, Samuel, 1784-1842. supposed author
31528, note after 105184
Woodworth, William W. plaintiff (82175)
Wooing and warring in the wilderness. 37969
Wool, John Ellis, 1784-1869. 34037, 101911
Wool-gathering. 20506
Wool Growers and Manufacturers Convention,
New York, 1831. (65779)
Wool Growers and Manufacturers of Berkshire
County, Mass. petitioners 47694
Wool Growers' Association of Ohio. see Ohio
Wool Growers' Association.
Woolaston, --------. illus. 28897
Wooleagunoodumakun tan tula saneku. 67765
Wooley, Benjamin, 58938, note after 105195
Woolley, --------. ed. 85527
Woolley, E. M. 84285
Woolman, John. 33264, 40618, 82978, 105196-
105211
Woolny, William W. 15121, note before 89139,
1st note after 104983, 105212
Woolsey, Jane Stuart. 105213
Woolsey, Melancton L. 105214
Woolsey, Theodore Dwight. 40974, 69402,
105215
Woolverton, Charles. 69333, 105216-105218
Woolworth, Aaron. 105219
Woolworth, James M. 105220
Woolworth, Ainsworth & Co. firm publishers
84500-84501, 84503
Woonspe itakihna. (69644)
Woord des oogenbilks. 93193
Woord voor den konink. 105221
Woorden ter aanprijzing van den mais-bouw in
de kolonie Surineam. 67410, 1st note
after 93855
Woordenboek van Americanismen. 3739
Wooster, Charles Whitney. 105222
Wooster, David. 105223
Wooster, Hezekiah Calvin. (57747)
Wooster, Ohio. Bank of Wooster. see Bank of
Wooster, Ohio.
Wootanin waxte Luka qu Jan. 18292
Worcester, Francis. 105225-105231
Worcester, Isaac Redington. 105232
Worcester, Jesse. 105233-105235

Worcester, Joseph Emerson. 1039, 17520,
47983, (69695), 93608, 105236-105238
Worcester, Leonard. 3105, 97296, 105239-
105245
Worcester, Noah. 2914, 12908, (23519), 25944,
(82540), 93905, 1st note after 100993,
102253, 105246-105299, 105455
Worcester, Noah. supposed author 49984,
note after 92719, 105297
Worcester, Samuel. of Boston 105316
Worcester, Samuel, 1770-1821. 11924, 24593-
24594, 24600, 96412, 101400, 105137,
105300-105315
Worcester, Samuel Austin. 12442, 12460-12461,
105317-105321
Worcester, Samuel Austin. plaintiff 27081,
44794-44795, 105321
Worcester, Samuel Melanchthon. 75655, 85651,
2d note after 94170, 105315, 105322-
105324 see also Salem, Mass. Tabernacle Church. Pastor.
Worcester, Samuel Melanchthon. supposed
author 99610, note after 105324
Worcester, Thomas. (52836), 52946, 68540,
8th note after 95843, 105299, 105325-
105334, 105455
Worcester, Bishop of. see Hough, John,
successively Bishop of Oxford, Lichfield
and Coventry, and Worcester, 1651-1743.
Hurd, Richard, successively Bishop of
Lichfield and Coventry, and Worcester,
1720-1808. Johnson, James, successively
Bishop of Gloucester, and Worcester,
1705-1774. Maddox, Isaac, successively
Bishop of St. Asaph, and Worcester,
1697-1759.
Worcester, Mass. 105366
Worcester, Mass. Academy. see Worcester
Academy, Worcester, Mass.
Worcester, Mass. Agricultural Society. see
Worcester Agricultural Society.
Worcester, Mass. Associate Library Company.
see Worcester Associate Library Com-
pany, Worcester, Mass.
Worcester, Mass. Baptist Convention, 1825.
see Baptists. Massachusetts. Massa-
chusetts Baptist Convention, Worcester,
1825.
Worcester, Mass. Baptist Sabbath School
Library. 105338
Worcester, Mass. Calvinist Church. 105340
Worcester, Mass. Center School District.
see Worcester Center School District,
Mass.
Worcester, Mass. Central Church. Pastor.
94054 see also Sweetser, Seth.
Worcester, Mass. Clarendon Harris's Circu-
lating Library. see Clarendon Harris's
Circulating Library, Worcester, Mass.
Worcester, Mass. College of the Holy Cross.
see College of the Holy Cross, Wor-
cester, Mass.
Worcester, Mass. Committee of Correspondence.
105346-105347
Worcester, Mass. Committee of Correspondence.
Chairman. 105346-105347 see also
Baldwin, Nathan. Young, William.
Worcester, Mass. Committee on the Black-
stone Canal. see Worcester County,
Mass. Committee on the Blackstone
Canal.
Worcester, Mass. Convention of the Church
Anti-slavery Society, 1859. see Church
Anti-slavery Society.

Worcester, Mass. Convention of the Ministers of Worcester County, 1837-1838. see Convention of the Ministers of Worcester County, Worcester, Mass., 1837-1838.

Worcester, Mass. Convention of the Young Men of Massachusetts, Friendly to the Cause of Temperance, 1836. see Convention of the Young Men of Massachusetts, Friendly to the Cause of Temperance, Worcester, 1836.

Worcester, mass. Convention of Whig Young Men, 1839. see Whig Party Massachusetts. Convention of Young Men, Worcester, 1839.

Worcester, Mass. Convention of Worcester County, 1779. see Worcester County, Mass. Convention, 1779.

Worcester, Mass. Convention of Worcester County, 1782. see Worcester County, Mass. Convention, 1782.

Worcester, Mass. Ecclesiastical Council, 1820. see Congregational Churches in Massachusetts. Ecclesiastical Council, Worcester, 1820.

Worcester, Mass. Female Classical Seminary. see Female Classical Seminary, Worcester, Mass.

Worcester, Mass. Fire Society. see Worcester Fire Society, Worcester, Mass.

Worcester, Mass. First Church. 57602, 69468, 105357-2d note after 105357, 105358

Worcester, Mass. Herbert Hall. see Herbert Hall, Worcester, Mass.

Worcester, Mass. Houghton Association Meeting, 1847. see Houghton Association. Meeting, Worcester, 1847.

Worcester, Mass. Lunatic Hospital. see Massachusetts. Lunatic Hospital, Worcester.

Worcester, Mass. Lyceum. see Worcester Lyceum, Worcester, Mass.

Worcester, Mass. Meeting of the National Republican Young Men, 1812. see Democratic Party. Massachusetts. Worcester.

Worcester, Mass. Military Convention, 1835. see Military Convention, Worcester, Mass., 1835.

Worcester, Mass. Mutual Fire Society. see Mutual Fire Society, Worcester, Mass.

Worcester, Mass. National Republican Party Convention, 1832. see National Republican Party. Massachusetts. Convention, Worcester, 1832.

Worcester, Mass. National Republican Young Men's Meeting, 1832. see National Republican Party. Massachusetts. Worcester. Young Men's Meeting, 1832.

Worcester, Mass. New England Manufacturers' Convention, 1868. see New England Manufacturers' Convention, Worcester, Mass., 1868.

Worcester, Mass. Old Church. see Worcester, Mass. First Church.

Worcester, Mass. Old South Church. see Worcester, Mass. First Church.

Worcester, Mass. Pakachoag Division, No. 27. see Sons of Temperance of North America. Massachusetts. Pakachoag Division, No. 27, Worcester.

Worcester, Mass. Republican Party Convention of Worcester County, 1812. see Democratic Party. Massachusetts. Worcester County. Convention, Worcester, 1812.

Worcester, Mass. Salisbury Mansion School. see Salisbury Mansion School, Worcester, Mass.

Worcester, Mass. Second Congregational Society. (31806)

Worcester, Mass. Second Parish. Library. 105370

Worcester, Mass. Social Club. see Social Club, Worcester, Mass.

Worcester, Mass. Social Library. see Worcester Social Library, Worcester, Mass.

Worcester, Mass. Sons of Vermont Reunion, 1874. see Sons of Vermont. Reunion, 1st, Worcester, Mass., 1874.

Worcester, Mass. State Convention of Whig Young Men, 1839. see Whig Party. Massachusetts. Young Men's Convention, Worcester, 1839.

Worcester, Mass. State Disunion Convention, 1857. see Massachusetts State Disunion Convention, Worcester, 1857.

Worcester, Mass. State Lunatic Hospital. see Massachusetts. Luntaic Hospital, Worcester.

Worcester, Mass. Sunday School Society. see Worcester Sunday School Society.

Worcester, Mass. Temperance Convention, 1833. see Massachusetts Temperance Convention, Worcester, 1833.

Worcester, Mass. Temperance Convention, 1852. see Massachusetts Temperance Convention, Worcester, 1852.

Worcester, Mass. Temperance Society. see Worcester Temperance Society, Worcester, Mass.

Worcester, Mass. Union Church. 105373

Worcester, Mass. Union Convention, 1860. see Union Party. Massachusetts. Convention, Worcester, 1860.

Worcester, Mass. Wachusett Club. (41788) see also Wachusett Club, Worcester, Mass.

Worcester, Mass. Washington Benevolent Society. see Washington Benevolent Society. Massachusetts. Worcester.

Worcester, Mass. Whig State Convention, 1837. see Whig Party. Massachusetts. Convention, Worcester, 1837.

Worcester, Mass. Whig State Convention, 1848. see Whig Party. Massachusetts. Convention, Worcester, 1848.

Worcester, Mass. Whig State Convention, 1849. see Whig Party. Massachusetts. Convention, Worcester, 1849.

Worcester, Mass. Whig State Convention, 1855. see Whig Party. Massachusetts, Convention, Worcester, 1855.

Worcester, Mass. Whig Young Men's Convention, 1839. see Whig Party. Massachusetts. Young Men's Convention, Worcester, 1839.

Worcester, Mass. Worcester Bank. see Worcester Bank, Worcester, Mass.

Worcester, Mass. Worcester County Institute for Savings. see Worcester County Institute for Savings, Worcester, Mass.

Worcester, Mass. Worcester County Institution for Savings. see Worcester County Institution for Savings, Worcester, Mass.

Worcester, Mass. Young Men's Temperance Convention, 1835. see Young Men's Temperance Convention, Worcester, Mass., 1835.

Worcester, Mass. Young Men's Temperance Convention, 1834. see Young Men's Temperance Convention, Worcester, Mass., 1834.

Worcester County, Mass. 86703

Worcester County, Mass. Auxiliary Bible Society. see Worcester County Auxiliary Bible Society.

Worcester County, Mass. Auxiliary Unitarian Association. see Unitarian Churches. Massachusetts. Worcester Association.

Worcester County, Mass. Bar. 105393-105394

Worcester County, Mass. Blackstone Canal Committee. see Worcester County, Mass. Committee on the Blackstone Canal.

Worcester County, Mass. Committee of Correspondence. 105395-105396

Worcester County, Mass. Committee on the Blackstone Canal. 5700, 105386

Worcester County, Mass. Committee on the Blackstone Canal. Engineer. 5700, 105386

Worcester County, Mass. Convention of Committees for the County, 1775. see Non-Importation Association, Worcester County, Mass., 1775.

Worcester County, Mass. Convention, 1779. 105365

Worcester County, Mass. Convention, 1782. 105419

Worcester County, Mass. Court. 96936

Worcester County, Mass. Court of Common Pleas. 93068, 96937

Worcester County, Mass. Court of General Sessions. 105397

Worcester County, Mass. Federal Party Convention, 1812. see Federal Party. Massachusetts. Worcester County. Convention, 1812.

Worcester County, Mass. Friends of the American Colonization Society. see Worcester County Auxiliary Colonization Society.

Worcester County, Mass. Grand Jury. 93068

Worcester County, Mass. Ministers' Convention, 1837-1838. see Convention of the Ministers of Worcester County, Worcester, Mass., 1837-1838.

Worcester County, Mass. Non-importation Association, 1775. see Non-importation Association, Worcester County, Mass., 1775.

Worcester County, Mass. Religious Charitable Society. see Religious Charitable Society of Worcester County, Mass.

Worcester County, Mass. Sheriff. 105364, 105372 see also Greenleaf, William. Ward, Thomas W.

Worcester County, Mass. Unitarian Association. see Unitarian Churches. Massachusetts. Worcester Association.

Worcester County, Mass. Washington Benevolent Society. see Washington Benevolent Society. Massachusetts. Worcester County.

Worcester County, Mass. Washington Benevolent Society of the Southern Part of the County of Worcester. see Washington Benevolent Society. Massachusetts. Worcester County.

Worcester Academy, Worcester, Mass. 105375-105376

Worcester Agricultural Society. 7963, 105377

Worcester Agricultural Society. Anniversary Cattle Show and Exhibition of Manufactures, 1820. 5319

Worcester almanac, directory, and business advertiser, for 1844. 105444

Worcester and Hartford Railroad Company. Charter. 105446

Worcester and Middlesex counties, made . . . April 23d, 1856. (6977)

Worcester and Middlesex North Sabbath School Union. 105378

Worcester and Norwich Rail Road Company. 105447-105448 see also Norwich and Worcester Rail Road Company.

Worcester & Norwich Rail-Road Company, 1835. 105448

Worcester as it is. 33382

Worcester Associate Library Company, Worcester, Mass. 105379

Worcester Association of Mutual Aid in Detecting Thieves. 105380-105381

Worcester Auxiliary Bible Society. see Worcester County Auxiliary Bible Society.

Worcester Bank, Worcester, Mass. see Worcester County National Bank.

Worcester Bank and Trust Company. see Worcester County National Bank.

Worcester Baptist Association. see Baptists. Massachusetts. Worcester Baptist Association.

Worcester Book Store, Worcester, Mass. 105386

Worcester business directory and advertiser. 105444

Worcester Central School District, Mass. Charter. 105342

Worcester Central School District, Mass. Committee. 105341

Worcester Central School District. Incorporation. By an act of the Legislature. 105342

Worcester Central Association Auxiliary Foriegn Mission Society. see Congregational Churches in Massachusetts. Worcester Central Association. Auxiliary Foreign Mission Society.

Worcester collection of sacred harmony. 2d note after 95414

Worcester county advertiser. 85574

Worcester County Auxiliary Bible Society. 105387-105388

Worcester County Auxiliary Colonization Society. 105418

Worcester County Auxiliary Colonization Society. Committee. 105418

Worcester County Auxiliary Unitarian Association. see Unitarian Churches. Massachusetts. Worcester Association.

Worcester County Cattle Show and Exhibition of Manufactures. 105377

Worcester County convention. 105419

Worcester County Horticultural Society. 35781

Worcester County Institute for Savings, Worcester, Mass. 105420, 105423

Worcester County Institution for Savings, Worcester, Mass. 105421-105424

Worcester County Institution for Savings, Worcester, Mass. Charter. 105420

Worcester County Institution for Savings, Worcester, Mass. Treasurer. 105423

Worcester County Institution for Savings. At the annual meeting. 105423

Worcester County Institution for Savings, in the town of Worcester. 105424

Worcester County Manual Labor High School. see Worcester Academy, Worcester, Mass.

Worcester County National Bank. 105382

WORCESTER

Worcester County National Bank. defendants 105383

Worcester County Religious Charitable Society. see Religious Charitable Society, Worcester County, Mass.

Worcester County Republican convention. 105425

Worcester County Society Auxiliary to the Baptist Board of Foreign Missions for the United States. see Society for Worcester County and Vicinity, Auxiliary to the Baptist Board of Foreign Missions for the United States.

Worcester County Unitarian Association. see Unitarian Churches. Massachusetts. Worcester Association.

Worcester daily spy. 92867

Worcester District Medical Society. see Massachusetts Medical Society. Worcester District Medical Society.

Worcester, February 21st, 1838. 105439

Worcester Female Samaritan Society. 105327

Worcester Fire Society, Worcester, Mass. 105428

Worcester Historical Society. 105429

Worcester Historical Society (1831). 105429

Worcester Historical Society. Sir: this association has been formed. 105429

Worcester, January 4th, 1793. 105367

Worcester, January 3d, 1793. 105366

Worcester, June 13th. 1774. 105346

Worcester, June 20, 1808. 105411

Worcester Lyceum, Worcester, Mass. 105431

Worcester Lyceum, Worcester, Mass. Library. 105430

Worcester magazine and historical journal. 15411, 17628, 32583, 95409, 2d note after 95414, 101277, 101520, 104061, 105432, 105433

Worcester, March 1, 1819. 105406

Worcester, March 13, 1815. 105403

Worcester, March 23, 1813. 105402

Worcester, Massachusetts, Feb. 1, 1790. 95412

Worcester Mutual Fire Insurance Company. 105434

Worcester news-paper. 95413

Worcester North Auxiliary Education Society. 105435

Worcester North District Medical Association. see Massachusetts Medical Society. Worcester North District Medical Association.

Worcester North Vicinity Auxiliary Foreign Mission Society. see Congregational Churches in Massachusetts. Worcester North Association. Auxiliary Foreign Mission Society.

Worcester, [Oct. 15th, 1808.] 105412

Worcester, October 23, 1812. 105401

Worcester pulpit. 82211

Worcester Social Library, Worcester, Mass. 105437

Worcester Society of Mutual Aid in Detecting Thieves. see Worcester Association of Mutual Aid in Detecting Thieves.

Worcester South Auxiliary Education Society. 105438

Worcester South Division Anti-slavery Society. 105439

Worcester South-West United Architectural Society. 105440

Worcester speculator. 24549

Worcester Sunday School Society. 105441

Worcester Sunday School Society. President. 105441

Worcester Sunday School Society. Secretary-Treasurer. 105441 see also Hill, Alonzo, 1800-1871.

Worcester talisman. 105374, 105442, 105445

Worcester Temperance Society, Worcester, Mass. 76996, 105443

Worcester traveller. 93678

Worcester village directory. 105444

Worcester village register. 105374, 105442, 105445

Word about slavery. 39973

Word about slavery and the colored race. 35235

Word and will of the Lord. 83163

Word at parting to the Earl of Shelburne. 80113, 105453

Word for old Roxbury. (73739)

Word for peace. (26240)

Word for soldiers. 31307

Word for the African. 30047

Word for the armie. 101130, note after 105462

Word for the armie, and two words to the kingdome. 61196

Word for the church. (32305)

Word for the merchant. 79633

Word for Trinity Church. 33483, 3d note after 96986

Word from the author.. 99283

Word in behalf of the Lord. 106221

Word in season. Fellow citizens, ... 105454

Word in season, in behalf of the Holy Scriptures. 34035, (67748)

Word in season; or review of the political life. 105456

Word in season. Or, the duty of the people. 62517

Word in season. The writings of Noah and Thomas Worcester. 105299, 105455

Word in season to all true lovers of their liberty. 25770, note after 105456

Word in season, to the church and the country. (77564)

Word in season, touching the present misunderstanding. 35124, 105457-8 [sic]

Word of advice to all who adhere to those doctrines. 64973, 72688

Word of advice to straight-haired folks. 2161

Word of advice, to such as are settling new plantations. 105459

Word of comfort to a melancholy country. 25948, 104899, 104902

Word of comfort to a melancholy country. Or the bank of cerdit erected. 104902, note after 105459

Word of comfort to Mrs. S. Rowson. 14032, 85597

Word of consolation for the kindred. (26240)

Word of encouragement to their sons. 5619

Word of friendly counsel to young men. 6086

Word of God a volume for the world. 100925

Word of God and its means. 88581

Word of God is not bound. 59354

Word of God our supreme rule in religion. 78626

Word of God preached. 104371

Word of instruction. 17050

Word of peace on the American Question. (26733)

Word of peace on the difference between England and the United States. 26730

Word of remembrance and caution to the rich. 105208, 105210

Word of self-defence. 90562
Word of understanding. 46608, note after 105465
Word on behalf of the slave. (81904)
Word on the laws against popery in Great Britain. 36297
Word or two about the war. 4096
Word or two to Melchizedech. 101127
Word paintings of the beautiful. 9507
Word to a right honourable commoner. 105460
Word to all true Americans. 105461
Word to commanders. (58808)
Word to Federalists. 105461-105462
Word to his defenders. 97055
Word to Mr. Peters. 101130, note after 105462
Word to the friends of temperance. (44749)
Word to the north and to the south. 80363
Word to the present and succeeding generations. 46760
Word to the public in regard to the difficulties. 90787
Word to the well-inclin'd of all perswasions. 92330
Word to the well-wishers of the good work of God. 24682
Word to the Whigs of Pennsylvania. 60784
Word to the wise, for setling the government. 9372, 91492
Word to the wise in heart. 8372
Word to the wise is sufficient. 106119
Word to the wise; or, an appeal to the honour and good sense. 105463
Word to the wise; or, the Bishop of Cloyne's exhortation. 4880
Word to the world in general. 44347
Word to those that are afflicted very much. 22443
Word to those whom it concerns. 105464
Word to women. 20092
Word upon our example as a nation. 14913
Word with Bishop Hopkins. 43498
Worden, Peter. 105465
Words about the war; or, plain facts for plain people. 33846
Words at the burial of Mrs. Bradford. 23091
Words for the hour. (33319)
Words for the people. 57596
Words of a grand selection of sacred music. (62395)
Words of consolation to Mrs. Robert Stetson. 87168
Words of counsel to men of business. 19509
Words of Daniel O'Connell. 28747
Words of patriotism and wisdom for the consideration of freemen. 15864
Words of patriotism and wisdom now presented. 41
Words of understanding. 46608
Words, phrases, and short dialogues. 1183
Words spoken in . . . Albany. 7833
Words to young gentlemen and young ladies. 84292
Wordsworth, Christopher, 1774-1846. 59497
Wordsworth, William, 1770-1850. 105466
Worfield, Beulah. 105467
Worinnen auch der Ost- und West-Indien b. cersch. heidn. Lander. 7408
Work and the workmen. (21571)
Work and wages. (25266)
Work done, . . . by the Society for the Advancement of Christianity in Pennsylvania. 50801
Work for chimney-sweeps. 105468
Work in the colonies. 85950
Work of a Christian. 17645

Work of a cooper. 105684
Work of a Gospel minister opened and applied. 66753
Work of faith. (17863)
Work of God in Philadelphia. 60812
Work of ministers and the duty of hearers. 104404
Work of ministers represented. 16640
Work of preaching Christ. 43324
Work of the Army Committee of the New York Young Men's Christian Association. 7335
Work of the Bishop Seabury Mission. 78591
Work of the church in America. (1519)
Work of the Lord in the earthquake. 24576
Work of the ministry. A sermon . . . before the . . . Meadville Theological School. 59354
Work of the ministry, described. 46718
Work of the Sanitary Commission. 4575
Work of the two great captains. 72148
Work-people's companion. (50654)
Work under the ark. 46609
Work within doors. 46610, note after 105468
Workers in Iron of Philadelphia. petitioners 47695 see also Iron Workers of Philadelphia. petitioners
Workes [of Thomas Scott.] 100799
Working classes of the United States. 51223
Working-man. 67171
Working man defended. 105469
Working man's advocate. 67418 see also Radical reformer and working man's advocate.
Working man's destiny. 84526
Working man's manual. 81373
Working man's miscellany. 89974
Working man's political economy. 62638
Working man's views. 72643
Working men of Boston. 6572
Working Men of Pittsburgh. 63105 ·
Working-Men's Convention, Boston, 1833. 65916, 105471
Working of British free trade. 10842
Working woman of Boston. pseud. Aristocrat and trade union advocate. 105473
Working women's advocate. 54822
Workingman. pseud. More than one hundred reasons. (50550), 105470
Workingman. pseud. "Wherefore Change?" (50550), 105470
Workingman's advocate-extra. 98413
Workingman's reasons for the re-election of Abraham Lincoln. 41240
Workingmen of Charlestown, Mass. Grand Rally, 3d, 1840. see Grand Rally of the Workingmen of Charlestown, Mass. 3d, 1840.
Workingmen's Democratic Republican Association. 21475, 28451, (35097)
Workingmen's library. 67900
Workingmen's State Convention, Salina, N. Y., 1830. 105472
Workman, Benjamin. 105474
Workman, Giles. 105475
Workman, James. 105476, 105478-105483
Workman, James. defendant 105477, 106484
Workman, James supposed author 53325, 104030, note after 105480
Workmen, and their work. 80454
Works by Rev. William Cook. 16297
Works connected with American history. 59667
Works, in verse and prose, of the late Robert Treat Paine. 58201

Works issued by the Hakluyt Society. 29593, 89452, 90060, 92664, 98738, 98757, 99363, 99375, 99376, 100940, 105720
Works of Adam Smith. 82318
Works of Alexander Hamilton; comprising his correspondence. 29988, 84835
Works of Alexander Hamilton, comprising his most important official reports. 29987
Works of Ann Bradstreet. 7299, note after 94823
Works of Barton Warren Stone. 92031
Works of Benjamin Franklin. 25606, 88984, 97106, 103121
Works [of C. C. Heyne.] 26762
Works [of Captain John Smith.] 82812, 82815, 82819, 82823-82824, 82830-82834, 82837, 82850-82852, 82855-82856
Works of Catharine M. Sedgwick. 78807
Works [of Charles Kingsley.] 67599
Works [of Charles Summer.] 93689
Works of Dr. Benjamin Franklin. 25514, 25516, 25604
Works of Dr. Benjamin Franklin, consisting of essays. 25599
Works of Dr. Benjamin Franklin, in philosophy, politics, and morals. 25513, 25605
Works of Edgar Allen Poe. Edited by John H. Ingram. 63573
Works of Edgar Allen Poe, including political and prose works. 63574
Works of Edgar Allen Poe. Including the choicest of his critical essays. 63572
Works of Elihu Burritt. 9454
Works of Fisher Ames. Compiled by a number of his friends. 273, 1303, 43375, 42459
Works of Fisher Ames. With a selection from his speeches. 1304
Works of Flavius Josephus. 36666
Works [of Francis Blackburne.] 5689
Works of George Berkeley. 4881, 91873
Works [of George Colman.] 14526, note after 105986
Works of George Fox. 25347, 25358
Works of George Lord Lyttleton. (42890)
Works of George Washington. 89013
Works of God in relation to the church in general. 39199
Works of Henry Clay. 13551
Works [of Henry Ware, Jr.] 101400
Works [of Horace Walpole.] 101143
Works [of Humphrey Smith.] 82735
Works of Isaac Penington. 58658, 59662
Works, of J. P. Kennedy. (37423)
Works of . . . J. S. Ravenscroft. 67992
Works [of J. Wise.] 15449
Works of James Fenimore Cooper. 16559
Works of James Houstoun. 33199, 97095
Works [of Jeremy Bentham.] 4765
Works of Jeremy Peeters. 12967, 61198, 84400
Works of Jesse Appleton. 1808
Works of John Adams. 253, 80405, 90629, 2d note after 95677
Works of John C. Calhoun. 9932, 9936
Works of John Cleveland. 13662
Works [of John Dryden.] 20979
Works [of John Fletcher.] 24726
Works of John Fothergill. 25271
Works of John Robinson. 72110
Works [of John Wesley.] 85207, note after 102680-102681
Works of John Woolman. 105201, 105211
Works of Jonathan Edwards. 21974
Works of Jonathan Edwards the younger. (21975)

Works [of Jonathan Swift.] 94069-94070
Works of Joseph Bellamy. 4497
Works [of Joseph Stevens Buckminster.] 8936
Works of Laurence Stearne. 91352, 91355
Works of Lord Bolingbroke. 75240
Works of Lyman Beecher. 4344
Works of Nathaniel Emmons. 22526
Works of Orville Dewey. 19862
Works [of Palafox y Mendoza.] 73280
Works [of Peele.] 78597
Works of Philip late Duke of Wharton. 103104
Works of Philip Lindsley. 41316
Works of President Edwards. 21967
Works of Rev. Leonidas L. Hamline. 30077
Works of Rufus Choate. 12860
Works of Samuel Dexter Bradford. 7257
Works of Samuel Hopkins. 32955
Works of Sir Thomas Brown[e]. 8677
Works of Sir Walter Ralegh, Kt. Now first published. 67599
Works of Sir Walter Ralegh, Kt. political, commercial, and philosophical. 67498, 67554
Works [of Soame Jenyns.] 36053
Works of Stephen Olin. 57174
Works of Sylvan. 63423
Works of that eminent minister of the Gospel, Job Scott. 78298
Works of the devil destroyed. 88677
Works of the English poets. 42894
Works of the Hakluyt Society. (74131)
Works of the Honourable James Wilson. 104608, 104628, 104629, 104632
Works of the late Dr. Benjamin Franklin: consisting of memoirs of his early life. 25603
Works of the late Doctor Franklin: consisting of his life. (25600)-25602, 102487
Works of the late Edgar Allan Poe. (63522), 63570-63571
Works of the most famous and reverend Divine Mr. Thomas Scot. 78379
Works of the Reverend George Whitefield. 103579, 103611
Works of the Rev. John Wesley. 102702
Works of the Rev. John Witherspoon. 104940, 104946
Works of the Rev. Samuel Blair. 5761
Works of the Rev. Sydney Smith. 84313-84314, 84320
Works of the Rev. Sydney Smith. Essays. 84321
Works of the Right Honorable Edmund Burke. 9304
Works of the Right Rev. John England. 22588
Works of the Right Reverend Jonathan Shipley. 80527
Works of Thomas Paine. 58244
Works of Thomas Paine, Secretary of Foreign Affairs. 58245
Works of Thomas Paine. With an account of his life. 58246
Works of Thomas Secker. 78719
Works of Thomas Shepard. 80262
Works of Washington Irving. 35215-35218
Works of Washington Irving. With a memoir of the author. (35214)
Works of Will. Adams. 52153
Works [of William Cobbett.] 94025
Works of William E. Channing. 11921-(11922)
Works of William H. Seward. 79547, 79595
Works [of William Miller.] 49076
Works [of William Penn.] 59706, (64411)
Works of William Robertson. 72006-(72012)

Worthington, -------. illus. 72008
Worthington, Erastus. 22957, 45723, 2d note after 105499-105501
Worthington, Hugh. 105502-105503
Worthington, Thomas, 1769-1827. 33150, 105504-105505 see also Ohio. Governor, 1814-1819 (Worthington)
Worthington, V. G. D. 7183, 105506-note after 105507
Worthington, William. 105508
Worthington, Ohio. Annual Communication of the Grand Royal Arch Chapter of Ohio, 5829. see Freemasons. Ohio. Grand Royal Arch Chapter. Annual Communication, Worthington, 1829.
Worthington Manufacturing Company. 105509
[Wo]rthy example of a married daughter. 105510
Worthy oration appropriated. 78364
Worthy student of Harvard College. 58325
Worthye and famovs history of the travailes. 24897, 3d note after 99856
Wortley, Emmeline Charlotte Elizabeth Manners Stuart. see Stuart-Wortley, Emmeline Charlotte Elizabeth Manners.
Wortman, Tunis. 105511-105514
Wotanin waxte Markus owa kin Dee. 69648
Wotherspoon, George. 22225
Wotton, Sir Henry, 1568-1639. 67545, 67599, 105515
Woudlooper. 4540
Would immediate abolition be a blessing? 25705
Wounded soldier. pseud. Series of intercepted letters. see Smith, Robert Hall.
Wouters, Johan Bautista. see Wouters, Joannes Baptista.
Wouters, Joannes Baptista. (4367), 105516
Wowapi inonpa. 63996
Wowapi mitawa. 18293, (71344)
Wowapi nitawa. 71345
Wowapi wakan etanhan taku wanjikji oyakapi kin he dee. 63996
Wrack and weeds. 83851
Wragg, William. (25788), (87588), 87858, 87865
Wrangel, Carl Magnus. 105517
Wrangel, Ferdinand Petrovich, Baron von. (2711), 26376, 105518, 105519
Wrath of Herr Vonstoppelnoze. 77338
Wrath to come. 92759
Wraxal, ------, fl. 1752. 84673
Wraxall, Lascelles. tr. 27178
Wraxall, Sir Nathaniel William. supposed author 60819, 80686-80689
Wreath for St. Crispin. 65564
Wreath for the Rev. Daniel Dow. 98479, note after 105520
Wreath of gems. (60863)
Wreath of love. 74139
Wreath of wild flowers from New England. 47781
Wreath; or verses on various subjects. 105520
Wreck-elections of a busy life. 7072
Wreck of the Arctic regions. (34021)
Wreckmaster. 38095
Wren, Roger. pseud. Sentiments. 105521
Wren and eagle in contest. 102082
Wrentham, Mass. petitioners 16140
Wrentham, Mass. First Church. 102533, 105523
Wrentham, Mass. Ecclesiastical Council, 1830. see Congregational Churches in Massachusetts. Ecclesiastical Council, Wrentham, 1830.
Wrentham, Mass. North Parish. 105523-105524
Wrentham, Mass. North Parish. Committee. 105523

Wrentham, Mass. Original Congregational Church of Christ. 105525
Wrentham, Mass. St. Alban's Lodge. see Freemasons. Massachusetts. St. Albany's Lodge, Wrentham.
Wrentham, Mass. Society for Detecting Horse-Thieves, and Recovering Stolen Horses. see Society for Detecting Horse-Thieves, and Recovering Stolen Horses, Wrentham, Franklin, Medway, Medfield, Walpole, Foxborough, Mansfield, and Attleborough, Mass.
Wrentham jubilee. 24518
Wretched slave sung in the new opera. 105527
Wrifford, Alison or Anson. 105528
Wright, ------. 60468 see also Pennsylvania. Commissioners to Investigate the Affairs of the Bank of Susquehanna County.
Wright, -------. cartographer 38880, 95757, note after 100632
Wright, -------. illus. (70963)
Wright, -------, fl. 1862. 85618
Wright, A. E. 105529
Wright, Alfred. 12864-12865, 12868, 12872, 12874, 12876, 12878, note after 12878, 89272-89273, 105530-105541
Wright, Andrew. 105542
Wright, Andrew. defendant 105543
Wright, Asher. 20330, (26277), (28168), 47868, 105544-105557
Wright, Benjamin. (54729), 60467, 72157, note after 93534, 94430, 98088, 105558-105562
Wright, Benjamin Hall. 66589, 105563
Wright, Charles. 105564-105567
Wright, Charles Cushing. 89131
Wright, Chester. 105568-105570
Wright, Crafts J. 15433
Wright, David. 105571
Wright, Edward, 1558?-1615. 27356, 105572-105574, 106246
Wright, Eleazar. pseud. Little selection of choice poetry. see MacNemar, Richard.
Wright, Eleazar. pseud. Other side of the question. see MacNemar, Richard.
Wright, Eleazar. pseud. Review of the most important events. see MacNemar, Richard.
Wright, Eleazar. pseud. Series of lectures. see MacNemar, Richard.
Wright, Eliphalet. 105578
Wright, Elizur. 22713, 45888, 66954, note before 90885, 105579-105580
Wright, Ephraim. (46158)
Wright, Frances. see D'Arusmont, Frances (Wright)
Wright, George B. 56893 see also Ohio. Commissioner of Railroads and Telegraphs.
Wright, Guy W. ed. 102992
Wright, J. ed. (11601)-11602, 2d note after 105598-9 [sic]
Wright, J. tr. 104712
Wright, J. le. see Le Wright, J.
Wright, James. petitioner 93593, 3d note after 105598-9 [sic]
Wright, Sir James, Bart., 1714-1785. (27056), 36718 see also Georgia (Colony) Governor, 1761-1776 (Wright)
Wright, Joel. 105600
Wright, John. accountant 105606-105607
Wright, John. M. D. 21709, 105611
Wright, John. of Lancaster County, Pa. 105608
Wright, John. Presbyterian minister 105601

Wunder-wurdige Juden- und Heiden-Tempel.
73324
Wunderbare Geschichte von Ambrose Gwinnett.
105634
Wunderbare jedoch grundlich- und warhaffte
Geschichte und Reise. 49793
Wunderbare Lebennchicksale. 8520
Wunderbare Lebensbeschreibung. 105635
Wunderbare Prophezeihungen uber das Pabstthum.
59229
Wunderbare Reisen und Abentheuer zu Wasser
und zu Lande. 2616
Wunderbare Rettung aus grosser Gefahr.
105636
Wunderbare Welte in einer kurtzen Cosmographia
furgestellet. 30278
Wunderbaren Schiffart und Reise Beschreibung.
105680
Wunderbaren Schiffart, welche Vlrich Schmidel
von Straubing. 77681-77682
Wunderbarliche, doch warhafftige Erklarung.
(8784)
Wunderbarliche Leben. 30252, (73193)
Wunderbarliche vnd seltsame Raiss. 99446
Wunderthaetige Kraft der Kleider. 105637
Wunderwurdige Juden- und Heiden-Tempel.
73323
Wunnamptamoe Sampooaonk wussampoowontamun
nashpe moeuwehkomunganash ut New-
England. 89013
Wunnissoo, or the vale of Hoosatunnok. 900
Wurdiman, F. supposed author 76993, 105638
Wurffbain, Johann Sigmund. 105639
Wurffbain, L. 105640
Wurtemberg, Paul Wilhelm Friedrich, Herzog
von. see Paul Wilhelm Friedrich,
Herzog von Wurtemberg.
Wurtemberger. pseud. Nord-Amerika. (55456)
Wurts, John. 91881, 105641
Wurtz, Georg Christian. 105642-105643
Wurzburger, J. W. tr. 30158
Wusku wuttestamentum nul-lordum Jesus Christ
nuppoquohwssuaenenmum. 22155
Wvskv wuttestamentamentum nul-lordumum
Jesus Christ nuppoquohwussuaeneumunx.
22157
Wuskus wuttestamentum nul-lordum Jesus
Christ nuppoquohwussuaeneumum. note
after 22155
Wwaerachtighe ende grondighe beschryvinge van
het groot ende goudt-rijck coninckrijck
van Guiana. 67595
Wy Mr Joan Jacob Mauricius. 93844
Wy Mr. Wolpert Jacob Beeldsnyder Matroos.
93845
Wyandot chief. 54933
Wyandot Indians. Treaties, etc. 96618, 96630-
96631, 96670, 96703, 99605
Wyandotte Mission, Upper Sandusky, Ohio. see
Methodist Episcopal Church. Conferences.
Ohio Annual Conference. Wyandotte
Mission, Upper Sandusky.
Wyandotte; or, the hutted knoll. 16570
Wyandotte. Traduit . . . par A. J. B. De-
fauconpret. 16571
Wyatt, Henry H. plaintiff (20933)
Wyatt, James, 1707- 105645
Wyatt, William Edward. 88979, 102563, 105646
Wyche, George. ed. 47314
Wyche, William. 105647
Wyck, Catharine van. see Van Wyck, Catharine.
Wyckof, Simon. 25755, 25974, 98572
Wycliffe, Thomas. 105648
Wyeth, John B. 105649
Wyeth, Joseph. 22352, (40196)-40197, 103655,
105650-105653

Wyeth, Nathaniel J. 90790
Wygentliche Erzehlung. 42742
Wyland, J. P. 105654
Wyld, James. 10004, 21846, 27709, 85259-
85260, 105655-105657
Wylie, Andrew. 102007, 105658-105667
see also Jefferson College, Canonsburg,
Pa. President.
Wylie, Samuel Brown. (24361)-(24362), 105668-
105669
Wylie, Robert Crichton. 105670-105671
Wylly, William. 105672-105673
Wylly, William. supposed author 80583,
105673
Wyman, Jacob. defendant 17642
Wyman, Jeffries, 1814-1874. 27419, 77249,
85072, 105674
Wyman, Mary Alice. 84142, 84145, 84157,
84162
Wyman, Oliver C. 193296
Wyman, R. H. tr. (37621)
Wyman, Rufus. supposed author 69477, 1st
note after 97653, note after 105674
Wyman, W. ed. 84665
Wyman, William. 105675
Wymberly-Jones, George. see De Renne,
George Wymberley Jones, 1827-1880.
Wynandts, Williem. 41714, 41779, 5th-6th
notes after 103943, 1st-2d notes after
105675
Wyncoop, Gerardus. 105676-105678 see also
Bucks County, Pa. Collector of Excise.
Wyndham, Henry Penruddocke. ed. 20516
Wyndham, William. see Grenville, William
Wyndham, Baron.
Wynkeep, Gerardus. see Wyncoop, Gerardus.
Wynkelmann, H. J. 90039
Wynkelmann, Johann Just. 105680
Wynne, Charles H. 86294
Wynne, Edward. see Winne, Edward.
Wynne, James, 1814-1871. 9495, (45211A)
Wynne, John, successively Bishop of St. Asaph,
and Bath and Wells, 1667-1743. 105681
Wynne, John Huddlestone. 105682-105682B
Wynne, Thomas. 105683-105684
Wynne, Thomas H. (9722), 23778-23779,
40785, 2d note before 99889
Wynne, W. 64746
Wynne, William. ed. 40914
Wynne. firm publishers (71001)
Wynne's edition. Richardson's Virginia &
North Carolina almanac. (71001)
Wyoming. pseud. Letters. 105685
Wyoming, Pa. Citizens. (59830), 105686A,
105693A see also Allen, Ethan, of
Pennsylvania, fl. 1786. Franklin, John,
fl. 1786. Jenkins, John, fl. 1786.
Wilkes-Barre, Pa. Meeting of a Number
of Sufferers at Wyoming During the
Revolutionary War, Their Descendants,
and Others, 1837.
Wyoming, Pa. Citizens. petitioners (70351)
Wyoming County, N. Y. Perry Academy. see
Perry Academy, Wyoming County, N. Y.
Wyoming, and its history. 92150
Wyoming and Lehigh Rail Road Company.
Charter. 105686
Wyoming chief and woodman's boy. 105693
Wyoming claim. 105693A
Wyoming Historical and Genealogical Society,
Wilkes Barre, Pa. 93937
Wyoming; its history, stirring incidents, and
romantic adventures. 59472
Wyoming magazine. 84090
Wyoming magazine annex. 84090
Wyoming sufferers. (70351)

Wyoming valley in 1892. 84087, 84089-84090
Wyoming valley in the nineteenth century.
    84087, 84090
Wyoming valley in the 19th century. 84088
Wyse, John. petitioner 105694
Wyse, Sir Thomas, 1791-1862. (25200)
Wysgeerige bespiegelingen over Amerika.
    59249, 105695
Wysgeerige en staatkundige geschiedenis.
    68116
Wytfliet, Cornelius. 105696-105701
Wyth, John. see White, John, fl. 1585-1593.
Wythe, pseud. Power of Congress over the
    District of Columbia. see Weld, Theodore
    Dwight.
Wythe, George, 1726-1806. 100040, 100066,
    100230, 105702-105703 see also Virginia.
    General Assembly. Committee to Super-
    intend an Edition of All the Legislative
    Acts Concerning Lands.
Wytheville, Va. Fourth Annual Exhibition of
    the Southwest Virginia Agricultural
    Society, 1872. see Southwest Virginia
    Agricultural Society. Annual Exhibition,
    4th, Wytheville, 1872.
Wyttenbach, Daniel. 80901
Wyvill, Christopher. 105704-105707
Wyze and dwaaze maagden. 103609
Wzokhilain, Peter Paul. 57827, 105708-105711

X

X. pseud. Defence of the Lehigh Coal and
    Navigation Company. note after 39878
X. pseud. Don Augustin Arambul. see Soler
    y Gabarda, Geronimo.
X. pseud. Jugglery. see Smith, Gerrit, 1797-
    1874.
X. pseud. Reply to Trumbull on the improve-
    ment of the Connecticut River. 105712
X, author of nothing. pseud. Experiment.
    see Ranken, ---------.
X., P. D. R. pseud. Elogios. 105713
X.-B. Saintine. pseud. see Boniface, Joseph
    Xavier.
X. Y. pseud. see Y., X. pseud.
X. Y. Z. pseud. see Z., X. Y. pseud.
X. Y. Z., Gentleman. pseud. see Z., X. Y.,
    Gentleman. pseud.
X. Z. pseud. see Watts, William.
Xaintoigne, Jean Alfonse de, i. e. Jean
    Fonteneau, known as. 11143, 100828-
    100834
Xalo, Joachin Casses de. see Casses de Xalo,
    Joachin.
Xanctoigne, Jean Alfonse de. see Xaintoigne,
    Jean Alfonce de, i. e. Jean Fonteneau,
    known as.
Xantus, Janos. 35273, 35764, 105714-105715
Xantus Janos levelei Ejszakamerikábol. 35273,
    105715
Xara & Zegio, Pietro di Osma & di. see Osma
    & di Xara & Zegio, Pietro di.
Xarque, Francisco. 105716-105718
Xaso Gamboa y Villavicenzio, J. J. L. see
    Gamboa y Villavicenzio, J. J. L. Xaso.
Xaveiro de Meunrios, Francisco. pseud.
    Description historique. see Louis
    XVIII, King of France, 1775-1824.
Xavier, -------, Conde de San. see San
    Xavier, ------, Conde de.
Xavier, Boniface. see Boniface, Joseph Xavier.
Xavier, Francisco. 2375, (11100), note after
    105718

Xavier, Jose Marianno da Conceicao Velloso.
    see Velloso Xavier, Jose Marianno da
    Conceicao.
Xavier de la Fita y Carrion, Francisco. see
    Fita y Carrion, Francisco Xavier de la.
Xavier de Sancta Rita Bastos, Francisco. see
    Sancta Rita Bastos, Francisco Xavier de.
Xavier Fluvia, Francisco. see Gluvia,
    Francisco Xavier.
Xavier Pinto de Souza, Bernardo. see Souza,
    Bernardo Xavier Pinto de.
Xavier Sarria, Francisco. see Sarria,
    Francisco Xavier.
Xaviero de Meunrios, Francisco. pseud.
    Description historique. see Louis
    XVIII, King of France, 1775-1824.
Xavierr, Marco de Guadalajara y. see
    Guadalajara y Xavierr, Marco de.
Xenia Springs Joint Stock Association, Grene
    County, Ohio. 81074
Xenophon. pseud. Fragment. see Brizard,
    Gabriel.
Xeres, Francisco de. see Xerez, Francisco
    de, b. 1500.
Xerez, Francisco de, b. 1500. 3350, 57989,
    66686, 67740-67742, 105720-105725
Xerxes the great. 105726
Ximena. 94441
Ximenez de Bonilla, Joaquim Ignacio. 105731
Ximenez, Francisco. tr. 32045, (77618),
    105727
Ximenez, Gonzalo. 94853
Ximenez, Juan. tr. 93885-83886
Ximenez, Mateo. 105727A-105728
Ximenez, Miguel Maria. 105729
Ximenez de Bonilla, Joaquin Ignacio. 78910,
    105731
Ximenez de Mondragon, Carlos. 87236
Ximenez de Quesada, Conzalo. see Quesada,
    Conzalo Ximenez de.
Ximenez Pantoja, Thomas. 105732
Ximenez Panton, Bartolome. 105734
Ximenez Samaniego, Jose. 105733
Ximenez y Frias, Jose Antonio. 27470,
    105730
Ximeno, Fabian Perez. 86429
Ximeno, Jose. of Valencia 105736-105739
Ximeno, Jose, 1697-1765. 105735
Ximeno, Rafael. 105740
Xiu, Gaspar Antonio, also called Chi or
    Herrera. note after 105740
Xivrey, J. B. de. 105741
Xochitl o la ruina de Tula. 71703
Xufre del Aguila, Melchor. 105742

Y

Y****. pseud. To the Ursa Major. see
    Ware, Henry, 1794-1843.
Y****, A. pseud. Theatre of the present war
    in North America. see Young, Arthur.
Y., A., Esq; author of the Theatre of the
    present war in North America. pseud.
    Reflections. see Young, Arthur.
Y., D. T. V. pseud. Estats, empires et
    principalvtez dv monde. see Davity,
    Pierre.
Y., J. pseud. Adonde las dan las toman.
    105743
Y., J. M. Y. pseud. ed. 48283
Y., J. R. pseud. Defensa del voto. see
    Indarte, Jose Rivera.
Y., J. R. pseud. Defensa del voto de America.
    see Indarte, Jose Rivera.

Yale University. Lycurgan Association. 105907
Yale University. Medical Institution. see Yale University. School of Medicine.
Yale University. Missionary Society. see Yale College Missionary Society.
Yale University. Moral Society. Library. 105864-105865, 105901-105902
Yale University. Phenix Society. Library. 105907A
Yale University. Phi Beta Kappa Society. see Phi Beta Kappa. Connecticut Alpha, Yale University.
Yale University. President. 13215, 13220, 105786, 105787, 105805, 105806, 105826-105827, 105895 see also Clap, Thomas, 1703-1767. Day, Jeremiah, 1773-1867. Dwight, Timothy, 1752-1817.
Yale University. President and Fellows. petitioners 105797-105798 see also Day, Jeremiah, 1773-1867. petitioner
Yale University. Rector. see Yale University. President.
Yale University. Rector and Tutors. 13220, 105826-105827
Yale University. School of Medicine. 105786, 105909-105918
Yale University. School of Medicine. Temperance Society. 105919
Yale University. Sheffield Scientific School. Visitors. (80103)
Yale University. Society of the Alumni. 105920
Yale University. South Dining Hall. 105830 see also Yale University. Dining Hall.
Yale University. Steward. 105859 see also Beers, Nathan.
Yale University. Student Body, 1828. 105941
Yale University. Students. eds. 105853
Yale University. Theological Department. see Yale University. Divinity School.
Yale University. Treasurer. 105857-105859
Yale University. Trumbull Gallery. 97244, 105921-105921A
Yale University. Tutors. 13220, 105826-105827 see also Darling, Thomas. Whiting, John. Whittelsey, Chauncey, 1717-1787.
Yale University scheme. 18427
Yamba. 87173, 105946
Yamoyden, a tale of the wars of King Philip. 21659, 89130
Yan' Dargent, -----. illus. 44250
Yancey, Bartlett, 1785-1828. (29016), 55641
Yancey, Joel. 105946
Yancey, Robert. defendant at Court Martial 105947
Yancton Indians. see Yankton Indians.
Yancton Indians (Sioux) see Yankton Indians.
Yanctonies Sioux Indians. see Yankton Sioux Indians.
Yandell, Lunsford Pitts. 105948-105950
Yandiola, Juan Jos. 57421
Yanes, Francisco Javier. 14679, note after 98871, 105951
Yanez, Jose Isidro. 105952
Yanez, Juan. defendant 105953
Yanez, Remigio. 105953A
Yanguas, Diego de Nagera. see Nagera Yanguas, Diego de.
Yangues, Manuel de. 74017, 105954
Yankee. pseud. Glance at the times. 27533
Yankee. pseud. Humbug. 105955
Yankee. pseud. South-west. see Ingraham, Joseph H.
Yankee. see Yankee and Boston literary gazette.

Yankee. A weekly miscellany. 52161
Yankee among the nullifiers. 28586, note after 105956
Yankee and Boston literary gazette. 105956
Yankee and the nigger at the exhibition. 81925
Yankee arguments. 90575
Yankee blade. 92751
Yankee champion. (13858)
Yankee chronology. 21309, 105957
Yankee conscript. ·24461
Yankee Doodle. 83677, 105958-105966
Yankee Doodle court. 69103
Yankee Doodle, illustrated. 18583
Yankee Doodle's defeat. (64855)
Yankee drolleries. 84181-84182, 84185-84187
Yankee farmer. pseud. Peace without dishonor. see Lowell, John.
Yankee frolics, brought down to April 27th, 1813. 105967
Yankee fun and frolic books. 84180
Yankee idyll. 42435
Yankee in England. 105968
Yankee in London. pseud. Guesses. see Stevens, Henry, 1819-1886.
Yankee in London. 105969
Yankee Jack. 36517
Yankee land. A comedy. 41789
Yankee land the the Yankee. 44487
Yankee management. 105970, 106050
Yankee middy. 359
"Yankee Ned", of Lynn, Massachusetts. Seven years of a sailor's life. see Clark, George Edward.
Yankee notes for English circulation. 91844
Yankee notions. 95871, note after 104970
Yankee officer among the rebels. (23206)
Yankee prisoner loose in Dixie. 26835
Yankee privateering. 105971
Yankee scout. 7061
Yankee slave driver. 63325, 85166, 85170
Yankee song. 105958, 105963
Yankee songster's pocket companion. 105972
Yankee spy. 55350, 105973
Yankee stories and yankee letters. 29696
Yankee tar. 33394
Yankee traveller: or the adventures of Hector Wigler. 103943, 1st note after 105973
Yankee travels through the island of Cuba. 17816, 62423
Yankee. Whole no. 12. 89578
Yankeeland in her trouble. 91923
Yankees fondateurs de l'esclavage aux Etats-Unis. 19425
Yankees made southerners. 31907
Yankee's return from camp. 105964-105965
Yankey in London. 97621, 3d note after 105973
Yankey's return from camp. 105960
Yankey's return from camp. Together with the favorite song of the Black bird. 105966
Yankies war-hoop. 105974
Yankton Indians. Treaties, etc. 96640, 96662, 96714, 96723
Yankton Indians (Sioux) see Yankton Indians.
Yanktonies Sioux Indians. Treaties, etc. 96640
Yannez, Christopher Garcia. see Garcia Yannez, Christopher.
Yapuguay, Nicolas. 74033
Yaradee; a plea for Africa. 25757
Yard, Joseph. supposed author 95807, 105975
Yarico to Inkle. note after 92282
Yarico to Inkle, a poem. 105980

Yarico to Inkle. An epistle. (36061), 105976, 105979, 105981-105982, 105985
Yariko. Ein Trauerspiel in einer Handlung. 105986
Yariza. an Indian Maid 17463, 34476, 84624, 84671, 86473
Yariza, an Indian Maid's letter. 34476
Yarleme, I. D. Dralymont, Lord of. see Dralymont, I. D., Lord of Yarleme.
Yarnall, Ellis. defendant 23168, 32936, 69768, 2d note after 105986
Yarns of the sea. 82117
Yarrico. 92340, 105977
Yarrow, Thomas. 105987
Yarrow revisited & other poems. 105466
Yarza, Joseph Antonio de. 105987A
Yarza, Remigio de. 105987B
Yates, Abraham, 1724-1796. 63791, 70072, 105988
Yates, Andrew. 105989
Yates, Andrew J. 105900
Yates, Christopher Columbus. 105991-105993
Yates, Edmund. ed. 46824
Yates, Henry. complainant 97779-97781, 97785
Yates, J. B. 98088
Yates, John. (72107)-(72108)
Yates, John Ashton. 105996
Yates, John Austin. 105994-105995
Yates, John B. 105997-105998
Yates, John B. complainant 97779-97781, 97785
Yates, John Van Ness. 51330, 84569, 105999-note after 105999
Yates, John Van Ness. defendant (78979)
Yates, Joseph Christopher, 1768-1837. 54960, 1st note after 89220 see also New York (State) Governor, 1822-1824 (Yates)
Yates, Peter W. 106000-106001
Yates, Richard, 1818-1873. 34298, 34270, 34306 see also Illinois. Governor, 1861-1865 (Yates)
Yates, Robert. 22233, (26931), 40471, 57362, 78749, 106002-note after 106002 see also New York (State) Commissioners for Settling the Titles to Land in the County of Onondaga.
Yates, Sarah. plaintiff 105702
Yates, William. 106003
Yates, William. plaintiff 105702
Yazoo County, Miss. Southern Rights Association. see Southern Rights Association, Yazoo County, Miss.
Yazoo Company of South Carolina. see South Carolina Yazzo Company.
Ybanes, Diego. plaintiff 106003A see also Dominicans. Mexico. Provincia de Gvaxaca. Jues Conservador. plaintiff
Yeadon, Richard. 106004
Year: a poem, in three cantoes. (59556), 62747
Year and a life well concluded. (46612)
Year, and other poems. 43524, 106005
Year-book and almanac of British North America. 10622
Year book of facts. 10044-10045
Year book of general information. see Massachusetts state record and year book of general information.
Year-book of general information, for 1830. 8076
Year-book of missions for 1847. 32868
Year-book of the nations. (8453)
Year in Canada; and other poems. (24699), 38101

Year in Spain. 78542
Year of Jubilee. (65534)
Year reviewed in New-Brunswick's oldest church. 91157
Year, with other poems. 43524, 106005
Yearly annals of the Protestant Episcopal Church of the Evangelists. 62103
Yearly astronomical magazine. 97997
Yearly Meeting epistle of London. 4676
Yearly meeting, Philadelphia, 4 mo. 1801. 86071
Yearly record. 54720
Yearly verses of the printer's lad, who carrieth about the Pennsylvania gazette. 106006
Year's life. 42438
Years of many generations considered. (76502)
Year's remembrances. 54967
Year's residence, in the United States of America. 14021
Year's wanderings over untrodden ground. (51600)
Yearsley, Ann. 106007
Yearwood, Randolph. 46735
Yeates, Jasper. (52568)
Yeates, Jasper. defendant at impeachment (30039), 1st note after 96927
Yeates, Sir Joseph. supposed author 40793
Yeghelick segget den anderen voort. 27260, 102925
Yell, Archibald. 106008
Yellott, Coleman. 55571
Yellow, and remitting, and intermitting fevers. 67169, 1st note after 102848
Yellow beard. sobriquet see Pitezel, John H.
Yellow bird. pseud. Life and adventures of Joaquin Murieta. see Ridge, John R.
Yellow book. 49686
Yellow Creek, Carrollton and Zoar Rail-Road. 106009
Yellow Creek, Carrollton and Zoar Rail-Road. Charter. 106009
Yellow fever. 62396, 106010
Yellow fever, considered in its historical, pathological, etiological, and therapeutical relations. 39048
Yellow or malignant bilious fever. 36104
Yellow Springs, Ohio. Antioch College. see Antioch College, Yellow Springs, Ohio.
Yellowplush correspondence. 106011
Yemassee. 81190, 81196-81197, 81199, 81205, (81232), 81237, 81243, 81245, 81264, 81272, 81275, 81278-(81279), 1st note after 106011
Yeoman. pseud. Strictures upon the narrative. 9431, 12380, 2d note after 92859, 2d note after 106011
Yeoman Association, Roxbury, Mass. see Roxbury Yeoman Association, Roxbury, Mass.
Yoemans, John William. 106012
Yepes, Joaquin Lopez. 60903, 106013
Yerba Buena island. 76947
Yerrington, J. M. W. reporter 6500, (19090), 34924, (45950), 70995
Yesterday with authors. 24301
Yet one warning more, to thee o England. 2817
Ying hwan che leo. 79350
Ylarregui, Jose Salazar. see Salazar Ylarregui, Jose.
Ymago mundi incipit. 66508
Ymant Adams. pseud. see Middelgeest, Simon van. supposed author
Ymparciales. pseud. Examen del merito. 105492, 106013A

Yndemnisacion plean de Don Isidoro Palacio.
106013B
Ynderweisung vnd vszlegung der Cartha Marina.
25965, 1st note after 98183
Ynka Garcilasso de la Vega. see Garcilaso
de la Vega, called el Inca.
Ynstruccion del modo de substanciar. 98157
Yo Fray Francisco de S. Antonio. 61165,
(75986)
Yockahoopoie. Choctaw Indian Chief 96601
Yockanahoma. Choctaw Indian Chief 96601
Yohn, Albert B. ed. 90803
Yoncker. pseud. Green hand's first cruise.
28575
Yong, -------. Botaniste de Pensylvanie see
Young, William, Jr., fl. 1753-1771.
Yonge, Francis. 11067, 106014-106016
Yonge, Philip, successively Bishop of Bristol
and Norwich, d. 1783. 106017
Yonge, William, fl. 1663. 106018
Yonge, Sir William, fl. 1751. 66643
Yonge-Street. Notice is hereby given. 98059C
Yonkers, N. Y. Rising-Star Lodge, No. 393.
see Freemasons. New York. Rising-
Star Lodge, No. 393, Yonkers.
Yonley, T. D. W. 84485
Yonnondio, or warriors of the Genesee. (33116)
Yorick. pseud. Letters. see Sterne,
Laurence, 1713-1768.
Yorick. pseud. Sentimental journey. see
Sterne, Laurence, 1713-1768.
Yorick. pseud. Sermons. see Sterne,
Laurence, 1713-1768.
Yorick, and other poems. 101308, note after
106019-20 [sic]
Yorick's sentimental journey continued. 91351
Yorick's sentimental journey through France
and Italy. 91356
York, James A. alias see Allen, James.
defendant
York, Joseph. 26908, 100693 see also
Democratic Party. New York. Albany.
Corresponding Committee. Secretary.
York, Manassah M. 33566
York, Archbishop of. see Dawes, Sir William,
Bart., Archbishop of York, 1671-1724.
Drummond, Robert Hay, Archbishop of
York, 1711-1776. Gilbert, John, Arch-
bishop of York, 1693-1761. Harcourt,
Edward, Archbishop of York, 1757-1847.
Harsnet, Samuel, Archbishop of York,
1561-1631. Herring, Thomas, Arch-
bishop of Canterbury, 1693-1757. Hutton,
Matthew, Archbishop of Canterbury, 1693-
1758. Markham, William, Archbishop of
York, 1719-1807. Monteigne, George,
Archbishop of York, d. 1628.
York, Canada. see Toronto.
York, England. 89180, note after 101126-101127
York, England. International Congress, 1864.
see International Congress, York, England,
1864.
York, England. Meeting, 1779. 82259, 84134
York County, England. petitioners 82258
York County, Maine. Congregational Churches
Semi-centennial, 1872. see Congregational
Churches in Maine. York County Conference.
Semi-centennial, 1872.
York County, Maine. Convention, Alfred. 1812.
106023
York County, Maine. Convention, Portland, 1795.
see Maine (District) Convention, Portland,
1795.
York County, Ontario. Assizes. (20701), 79016,
note after 96860, 2d note after 106023

York County, Pa. 106038
York County, Pa. Anti-masonic Committee.
see Anti-masonic Party. Pennsylvania.
York County. Committee.
York County, Pa. Collector of Excise. 3546-
3548, 106024-106033 see also Armor,
Thomas. Barnitz, Jacob. Forsyth, John.
Hahn, Michael. McClellan, John. Miller,
Henry.
York County, Pa. Committee, 1779. 106034
York County, Pa. Inhabitants' Committee,
1779. see York County, Pa. Committee,
1779.
York County, Pa. Lieutenant. 106036-106037
see also Scott, William.
York County, Pa. Sub Lieutenant. 106035-
106036 see also Hay, John.
York Academy. 106041
York and Cumberland Rail-Road Company.
Directors. 82569
York Baptist Association. see Baptists.
Maine. York Baptist Association.
York commercial directory. 101213
York, Council-Office, July 8, 1799. 98059E
York, Council-Office, July 3d, 1799. 98059D
York, Cumberland, and Lincoln Counties Con-
vention, Portland, Me., 1795. see
Maine (District) Convention, Portland,
1795.
York County Conference of Churches. see
Congregational Churches in Maine. York
County Conference.
Cork Count Conference Semi-Centennial, 1872.
see Congregational Churches in Maine.
York County Conference. Semi-centennial,
1872.
York museum. 106040
Yorke, Chevalier. see Dover, Joseph Yorke,
Baron.
Yorke, Henry Readhead. (10237), 28724
Yorke, James, successively Bishop of Gloucester
and Ely, d. 1808. 106042
Yorke, Joseph. see Dover, Joseph Yorke,
Baron.
Yorke, Philip. see Hardwicke, Philip Yorke,
Earl of, 1692-1764.
Yorke, Zaida. 41735
Yorkshire farmer. 98634
Yorkshireman's trip to the United States and
Canada. 84731
Yorktown, N. Y. Congregational Church.
106047
Yorktown: an historical romance. 106048
Yorkville, S. C. King's Mountain Celebration,
1855. 11652
Yosemite: its wonders and its beauties. 32274
You are earnestly requested to meet a number
of the freeholders of this city. 61926,
106049
You are once more summoned of Faneuil-Hall.
87339
You have agreed to support this man at the
election. 95929
You have heard of them. 73277
You have no doubt been informed. 101764
You Parliament of England. 105970, 106050
You-Sing: the Chinaman in California. 33108
Youmans, E. L. ed. 64144
Young, -------, fl. 1721. 65865, 88192
Young, Alexander, fl. 1800. plaintiff 106058,
106131
Young, Alexander, 1800-1854. 13208, 18135,
31739, (33445), 467777, (51198), 80198,
82837, 103397, 104795-104796, note after
104797, 105074, 106051-106057

Young, Andrew White. 106059-106060
Young, Arthur. 62954, 63775, (74176), 3d
   note after 98684, 106061-106065
Young, Arthur. incorrectly supposed author
   106125
Young, Bennett H. defendant 4710, 74983
Young, Brigham, 1801-1877. 83163, 83237,
   83245, 83283, 83284, 83496, 93500
   see also Church of Jesus Christ of Latter
   Day Saints. President.
Young, C. P. reporter 43648
Young, Charles. 106066
Young, David. 48189, (54719), 54739, 54774,
   64076, 72720-72722, 80439, 106067-
   106070
Young, Edward, 1683-1765. 79459
Young, Edward J. 84012
Young, Edward R. 106071
Young, Eliza Roxcy (Snow) Smith. 83496,
   85503-85507
Young, George. ed. 99374
Young, George Renny. (29707), 106072-106075
Young, Gilbert Ainslie. 106076
Young, J. tr. 79118
Young, J. H. cartographer 84865
Young, James. of Edinburgh 101970
Young, James, d. 1789. 7937, 75199, 106077
Young, Jo. 23113
Young, John, D. D., Minister of Hawick,
   Scotland 106079
Young, John. of Halifax 40607, 106083
Young, John. of New Hampshire 106081-
   106082
Young, John. Philadelphia musician 106078
Young, John, d. 1797. defendant 106080
Young, John Clarke, 1803-1857. (47241), 93816,
   106084-106087
Young, Peter. 106088-106089
Young, Robert, 1750-1779. defendant 106090-
   106093
Young, Robert, fl. 1787. 30954, (64400),
   106094
Young, Robert, of Jamaica, 1796-1865. 106095-
   106098
Young, Robert Alexander. 106097
Young, Robert Anderson. 74626
Young, Samuel. of Baltimore ed. 3053
Young, Samuel, fl. 1690-1700. 106097A-
   106108A
Young, Samuel, 1789-1850. 53566, (70188),
   106109-106114
Young, Samuel, fl. 1855. 106115
Young, Samuel B. 106116
Young, Capt. Thomas. 103051
Young, Thomas, 1731-1777. 42758, 99008,
   104989, 106117-106119
Young, W. supposed author 105747
Young, W. A. 26216, 32147, 106120-106121
Young, William. Philadelphia bookseller
   106122-106123
Young, Sir William, Bart., 1725?-1799.
   106124-106126
Young, Sir William, Bart., 1749-1815. (21895),
   21901, 89293, 106127-106128
Young, Sir William, Bart., 1749-1815. in-
   correctly supposed author 106125
Young, William, Jr., fl. 1753-1771. 106129
Young, William, fl. 1774. 105346 see also
   Worcester, Mass. Committee of Corre-
   spondence. Chairman.
Young, Sir William, 1799-1887. 56161, (56188)
Young, William, 1809-1888. (41053)
Young, William P. 106130
Young, William W. defendant 97771
Young Abel dead, yet speaketh. 65597, 65617

Young abolitionists. 36538
Young against Chipman. 106058
"Young America." A play in five acts. 89422
Young America. A poem. (29877)
Young America afloat. 57216
Young American. pseud. Battle of the Thames.
   3970
Young American, detained in that country.
   pseud. Journal of a residence in Chili.
   see Coffin, J. F.
Young American ephemeris for the year 1715.
   62743
Young American; his dangers, his duties, and
   his destinies. 20390
Young American lady. pseud. see Young
   lady, native of America. pseud.
Young American: or book of government and
   law. 27922
Young American's first book of rights and
   duties. 61381
Young American's library. 59750
Young American's magazine of self-improvement.
   (41038)
Young and old puritans of Hatfield. 83560
Young artillerist's pocket companion. 91568
Young Baltimorean. pseud. Rhymes. see
   Townsend, Richard H.
Young Benjamin Franklin. 47127
Young Bostonian. pseud. Times. see Spurr,
   Josiah. supposed author
Young captain of the Ucayga Steamer. 57216
Young captain: a memorial of Captain Richard
   C. Derby. 30162
Young Carolinian of 1776. 8003
Young Catholics Friend Society, Boston.
   106132
Young cautioned against vice. 98295
Young chemist's pocket companion. 105108
Young Christian soldier: his life and death.
   5456
Young Christians' Missionary Association,
   Philadelphia. 62397
Young citizen's catechism. 33291
Young citizen's manual. (15620)
Young clergyman. 106133
Young clerk's magazine. 89384
Young disciple. 13313
Young emigrant. 10899
Young emigrants. A tale designed for young
   persons. 78829, 106134
Young Englishman of rank. pseud. British
   spy. see Wirt, William, 1772-1834.
Young female slave. pseud. Beautiful poem
   on providence. see Peters, Phillis
   (Wheatley) 1753?-1784.
Young fisherman of Cape Ann. 57216
Young folks' library for school and home.
   83633
Young folks' series. 84057
Young follower of a great saviour. 46579,
   46613
Young freemason's guide. (25258)
Young fur traders. 2952
Young gent. pseud. Squints through an opera
   glass. 90010
Young gentleman. pseud. Choice. see Church,
   Benjamin.
Young gentleman. pseud. Law given at Sinai.
   see Dawes, Thomas.
Young gentleman. pseud. New voyage to
   Georgia. 27079, 3d note after 106134
Young gentleman and lady's monitor. 90270
Young gentleman in the 23d year of his age.
   pseud. Confession of faith, or a summary
   of divinity. 15450

Young gentleman lately deceased. pseud.
Pious remains. 63003
Young gentleman of Nashville. pseud. Tales
of the revolution. 94251
Young gentleman of New-York. pseud. Mis-
cellaneous works. see Linn, J. B.
Young gentleman of Philadelphia. pseud.
Hamiltoniad. 30072
Young gentleman of Philadelphia. pseud.
Victors. 99449
Young gentleman of rank. pseud. British spy.
see Wirt, William, 1772-1834.
Young gentleman of this city. pseud. Alfred
the great. 106135
Young gentleman of Trinity College, Dublin.
pseud. Yarico to Inkle, a poem. see
Anketell, John.
Young gentleman who went to reside there.
pseud. Vicissitudes of human life.
99423
Young gentleman's and lady's assistant. 25678
Young gold-digger. 27194
Young heroes of Shiloh. 88001
Young invincibles. 59100
Young John Uncas. see Uncas, Young John.
Mohegan Indian Chief
Young knighthood. 58326
Young Ladies Academy, Philadelphia. see
Philadelphia. Young Ladies Academy.
Young Ladies' Association for the Promotion
of Literature and Missions in the Colle-
giate Institution of Young Ladies, Phil-
adelphia. see Collegiate Institution for
Young Ladies, Philadelphia. Young Ladies'
Association for the Promotion of Literature
and Missions.
Young Ladies Association of the New-Hampton
Female Seminary, for the Promotion of
Literature and Missions. see New
Hampton Female Seminary, New Hampton,
N. H. Young Ladies Association for the
Promotion of Literature and Missions.
Young Ladies' High School, Providence, R. I.
see Providence, R. I. Young Ladies'
High School.
Young Ladies' Institute, New Haven, Conn.
see New Haven Young Ladies' Institute,
New Haven, Conn.
Young Ladies' Institute, Philadelphia. 106138
Young Ladies' Institute, Pittsfield, Mass.
(63157)
Young ladies library vol. 3. 106143
Young Ladies of the Albany Female Academy.
pseud. eds. Stray sunbeams [sic].
92753
Young ladies' selection of elegant extracts.
note just before 71069
Young lady. pseud. Appeal to young soldiers.
88043B
Young lady. pseud. Epistle from a young lady.
(22690)
Young lady. pseud. Humble intercession.
86866, 106139
Young lady. pseud. Letter. see Pitt, Miss
------.
Young lady. pseud. Poem, spoken extempore.
63594, note after 106139
Young lady lately received by him into the
church. pseud. Letter. see Pitt,
Miss --------.
Young lady, native of America. pseud. Effusions
of female fancy. 106140
Young lady of Boston. pseud. George Allen,
the only son. 106141
Young lady of Charleston. pseud. Poems.
63607

Young lady of seventeen. pseud. Caroline
Westerley. 10982
Young lady of the state of New-York. pseud.
Fortunate discovery. 106142
Young lady of Worcester county. pseud.
Emily Hamilton. see Vicery, Eliza.
Young lady received by him into the church.
pseud. Letter. see Pitt, Miss -------.
Young lady, who was lately a resident of that
unhappy town. pseud. Humble inter-
cession. 106139
Young lady's book. 106145
Young lady's book of elegant poetry. 106143
Young lady's book of elegant prose. 106144
Young lady's equestrian manual. 106145
Young lady's friend. 106147
Young lady's gift, a common-place book.
106146
Young lady's library, vol. 4. 106144
Young lady's perceptor. 103711
Young lieutenant. 57216
Young lion of the woods. 84378
Young man. pseud. Conversion of Juvenis.
see Stanford, John.
Young man, a Quaker in Pennsylvania. pseud.
Copy of a letter. see Bringhurst,
Joseph.
Young man, in a declining state of health.
pseud. Address to youth. see Wood-
worth, John.
Young man spoken to. 46614
Young man warn'd. 83453
Young man who embraced the same principles.
pseud. Dying expressions. 86655
Young man who was prisoner nearly six
months in the island of Barbadoes.
pseud. Concise narrative. see Cole-
man, Simeon.
Young man who went from Glasgow about four
years ago. pseud. Three letters. see
D., W. pseud.
Young mans claim unto the sacrament of the
Lords-Supper. 67164-67165, 91945
Young man's companion. 78754-(78760),
106148
Young man's conflict with the powers of dark-
ness. (37125), note after 101268
Young-mans duty. 102223
Young man's guide. 102194
Young Man's Institute, Philadelphia. 62399
Young Mans' Institute, Philadelphia. Trustees.
62399
Young man's legacy to the rising generation.
100987
Young man's magazine, containing the substance
of moral philsophy. 106149
Young man's monitor. 106150
Young man's monitor. [By Cotton Mather.]
(46547), 46615
Young man's own book. 106143
Young marooners on the Florida coast. 28130
Young mason's monitor. Containing some
necessary hints. 89428, 103176
Young mason's monitor, and vocal companion.
91712
Young mason's monitor. To which is annexed
a collection of masonic songs, odes, etc.
91713
Young men, born in New England. pseud.
Dialogues. 52630
Young men of America. 3912
Young Men of New York Convention, Utica,
1828. see Convention of the Young Men
of New York, Utica, 1828.
Young Men of Philadelphia. see Philadelphia.
Young Men.

Young Men's Anti-masonic Association for the Diffusion of Truth, Boston. 50682, 97958, 106152

Young Men's Anti-masonic State Convention, Utica, N. Y., 1830. 106153

Young Men's Anti-slavery Society, New York. see New York Young Men's Anti-slavery Society.

Young Men's Association, Buffalo, N. Y. see Buffalo Library, Buffalo, N. Y.

Young Men's Association, Rochester, N. Y. (72354), 106159 see also Rochester, N. Y. Athenaeum—Young Men's Association.

Young Men's Association, Schenectady. see Young Men's Association for Mutual Improvement in the City of Schenectada. [sic]

Young Men's Association, Utica, N. Y. 98234

Young Men's Association, Utica, N. Y. Charter. 98234

Young Men's Association, Utica, N. Y. Library. 98234

Young Men's Association for Mutual Improvement, Saratoga Springs, N. Y. 76192, 1st note after 106156

Young Men's Association for Mutual Improvement, Saratoga Springs, N. Y. Charter. 76192, 1st note after 106156

Young Men's Association for Mutual Improvement, Saratoga Springs, N. Y. Executive Committee. 76192, 1st note after 106156

Young Men's Association for Mutual Improvement, Saratoga Springs, N. Y. Treasurer. 76192, 1st note after 106156

Young Men's Association for Mutual Improvement in the City of Schenectada. 77602

Young Men's Association for Mutual Improvement in the City of Schenectada. Library. 106156A

Young Men's Association for Mutual Improvement in the City of Schenectada. President. 77602, 2d note after 106156 see also Clute, John B.

Young Men's Association for Mutual Improvement in the Village of Saratoga Springs, N. Y. see Young Men's Association for Mutual Improvement, Saratoga Springs, N. Y.

Young Men's Association for Mutual Improvement, of the City of Albany. Charter. 106156

Young Men's Association for Mutual Improvement, of the City of Albany. Library. 106155

Young Men's Association for Mutual Improvement, of the City of Albany. President. 106154

Young Men's Association for the Suppression of Intemperance, Philadelphia. Executive Committee. 106157

Young Men's Association of the City of Albany. 640, 73970, 73977

Young Men's Association of the City of Albany. Committee. 640, 73970

Young Men's Association of the City of Buffalo. see Buffalo Library, Buffalo, N. Y.

Young Men's Association of the City of Chicago. Executive Committee. 12672

Young Men's Association of the City of Chicago. Library. 12672

Young Men's Association of the City of Chicago. President. 12672

Young Men's Association of the City of Milwaukee. 49183

Young Men's Association of the City of Milwaukee. Library. 49182-48183

Young Men's Association of the Madison-Square Presbyterian Church, New York, see New York (City) Madison-Square Presbyterian Church. Young Men's Association.

Young Men's Auxiliary Education Society of the City of New-York. Directors. 106160

Young Men's Benevolent Society, Boston. 106161

Young Men's best companion. 24459

Young Men's Bible Society of Baltimore. 106162

Young Men's Bible Society, of Brooklyn. 106163

Young Men's Bible Society of Cincinnati. 106164

Young Men's Bible Society of Frederick County, Maryland. 106165

Young Men's Bible Society of New York. see New York Bible Society.

Young Men's Bible Society of Philadelphia. see Philadelphia Young Men's Bible Society.

Young Men's Bible Society of Providence, R. I. see Providence Young Men's Bible Society.

Young Men's Central Home Mission, Philadelphia. 62400

Young Men's Charitable Association, Charlestown, Mass. 106166

Young Men's Christian Association. 66963-(66965)

Young Men's Christian Association, Baltimore. (3030)

Young Men's Christian Association, Boston. 86292, 86339

Young Men's Christian Association, Boston. Army Committee. 5456, 6787

Young Men's Christian Association, Boston. Fair For the Building Fund, 1858. 89497A

Young Men's Christian Association, Bristol. 8054

Young Men's Christian Association, Brooklyn. 8268

Young Men's Christian Association, Brooklyn. Army and Navy Committee. 86290

Young Men's Christian Association, Germantown, Pa. 62401

Young Men's Christian Association, Nashua, N. Y. (51862)

Young Men's Christian Association, Natick, Mass. (51907)

Young Men's Christian Association, New Bedford, Mass. (52494)

Young Men's Christian Association, New Hampshire. State Convention, 2d, Nashua, 1869. 52940

Young Men's Christian Association, New York. 54561, 86290

Young Men's Christian Association, New York. West Side Branch. Educational Department. 83381

Young Men's Christian Association, Newton, Mass. 55097

Young Men's Christian Association, Newton, Mass. Directors. 55097

Young Men's Christian Association, Philadelphia. 60812, 62401

Young Men's Christian Association, Philadelphia. Army Committee. 86295

Young Men's Christian Association, Philadelphia. Charter. 62401

Young Men's Christian Association, Providence, R. I. 66340

Young Men's Christian Association, Richmond, Va. 71213

Young Men's Christian Association, Rochester, N. Y. 72364

Young Men's Christian Association, Roxbury, Mass. 73735

Young Men's Christian Association, St. John, N. B. 75277

Young Men's Christian Association, St. Louis. 75402-(75403)

Young Men's Christian Association, St. Paul, Minn. 89257

Young Men's Christian Association, San Francisco. 76103-76104

Young Men's Christian Associations in North America. see Young Men's Christian Association.

Young Men's Christian Associations of the United States and British Provinces. see Young Men's Christian Association.

Young Men's Christian Union, Buffalo, N. Y. 9063

Young Men's Christian Union, Providence, R. I. see Providence Young Men's Christian Union.

Young Men's City Bible Society, of New-York. Board of Managers. 106167

Young Men's Colonization Society, Baltimore. 81769

Young Men's Colonization Society, New York. 106168

Young Men's Colonization Society of Pennsylvania. Board of Managers. 60785, 106169-106171

Young Men's Colonization Society of Pennsylvania. At a meeting of the Board of Managers, held on Friday evening. 60785, 106171

Young Men's Convention, Worcester, Mass., 1839. see Whig Party. Masscahusetts. Young Men's Convention, Worcester, 1839.

Young Men's Democratic Republican Club of the City and County of San Francisco. 93690 see also Republican Party. California. San Francisco.

Young Men's Education Society of New-York City. 106172

Young Men's Education Society of the Cities of New York and Brooklyn. 106173

Young Men's Evangelical Union, Charlestown, Mass. (12107)

Young Men's Home, Philadelphia. see Philadelphia. Young Men's Home.

Young Men's Institute, Hartford, Conn. Charter. 30677

Young Men's Institute, Hartford, Conn. Executive Committee. 30677

Young Men's Institute, Hartford, Conn. Library and Reading Room. 30678

Young Men's Institute, Hartford. First annual report of the Executive Committee. 30677

Young Men's Institute, New Bedford, Mass. 106174

Young Men's Institute, New Haven, Conn. see New Haven Young Men's Institute, New Haven, Conn.

Young Men's Institute, Northampton, Mass. Library. 55763

Young Men's Institute, Springfield, Mass. Library. see Springfield, Mass. City Library.

Young Men's Library Association, Springfield, Mass. 89885

Young Men's Mercantile Library, Pittsburgh. see Pittsburgh Library Association.

Young Men's Mercantile Library Association and Mechanics' Institute, Pittsburgh. see Pittsburgh Library Association.

Young Men's Mercantile Library Association of Cincinnati. see Cincinnati. Young Men's Mercantile Library Association.

Young Men's Missionary Society of New-York. 106176-106177

Young Men's Missionary Society of St. Andrew's Church, Philadelphia. see Philadelphia. St. Andrew's Church. Young Men's Missionary Society.

Young Men's Missionary Society of South-Carolina. 106178

Young Men's Missionary Society of the Reformed Dutch Church. 106179

Young Men's Moral Reform Society, New York. see New York City Young Men's Moral Reform Society.

Young Men's New-York Bible Society, Auxiliary to the American Bible Society. see New York Bible Society.

Young Men's Republican Union, New York. 41194 see also Republican Party. New York. New York City.

Young Men's Sodality, St. Louis. see Sodality Lyceum, St. Louis.

Young Men's Society, Baltimore, see Baltimore Young Men's Society.

Young Men's Society, Detroit. see Detroit Young Men's Society.

Young Men's Society, New York. see New York Young Men's Society.

Young Men's Society, Philadelphia. 62053

Young Men's Society, Philadelphia. Second Division. (62403)

Young Men's Society for the Promotion of Temperance, New York. 53514, 106182-106183

Young Men's State Convention, Utica, N. Y., 1838. see New York Young Men's State Convention, Utica, 1838.

Young Men's State Temperance Convention, Ann Arbor, Mich., 1836. 106184

Young Men's State Temperance Convention, Michigan. 106184

Young Men's Temperance Association in Salisbury and Amesbury, Mass. 106185

Young Men's Temperance Convention, Worcester, Mass., 1834. 105417, (106185A)

Young Men's Temperance Convention, Worcester, Mass., 1835. Committee. 105417

Young Men's Temperance Society, Albany. 106186

Young Men's Temperance Society, Boston. 106187

Young Men's Temperance Society, New Bedford, Mass. 52478, 106188

Young Men's Temperance Society, New Haven, Conn. 92072, 106189

Young Men's Temperance Society, Philadelphia. 106190

Young Men's Temperance Society, Providence, R. I. see Providence Young Men's Temperance Society.

Young Men's Temperance Society, Washington, D. C. 106191-106192

Young Men's Temperance Society, of the City of Albany. see Young Men's Temperance Society, Albany.

Young Men's Union, Salem, Mass. see Salem Young Men's Union, Salem, Mass.

Young Men's Unitarian Book and Pamphlet Society. 106193

Young Mexican. 12810

Young mill-wright & miller's guide. (23182)

Young millionaire. 51638

Young minister; or, memoirs and remains of Stephen Beekman Bangs. 43852

Young Narragansett. pseud. Address to the people of Rhode Island. 70539, 106194

Young Negro. pseud. Negro Servant. 52266

Young nobleman. pseud. Poems. see Lyttleton, Thomas Lyttleton, 2d Baron, 1744-1799.

Young of the crayfishes Astacus and Cambarus. 85072

Young pastor's wife. 51127

Young patriot; a memorial of James Hall. 29809

Young patriot. A tale of the American revolution. 18437

Young patriot, and other poems. 9510

Young patroon; or, Christmas in 1690. 51638

Young people called upon to consider. 91811-91812

Young people solemnly warn'd both against enticing, and consenting whem enticed to sin. 62517

Young people warned. 96095

Young people's magazine. 84162

Young People's Society of the State Street Presbyterian Church. 90653

Young pilot of Lake Champlain. 57216

Young pilot of the Belle Creole. 31436

Young pioneers of the north-west. 59440

Young poetess. (52237)

Young prince of Annamaboe. pseud. Memoirs. 47577

Young puritans in captivity. 83560

Young puritans in King Philip's war. 83560

Young puritans of Old Hadley. 83560

Young puritans series. 83560

Young quartermaster. (4357)

Young sailor's assistant, etc. 7316

"Young Sam" or native American's own book! (34062)

Young speaker. (42381)

Young stripling. pseud. Choice dialogue. see Walter, Thomas, 1696-1725.

Young student. pseud. On the death of the Reverend Benjamin Colman. see Seccombe, Joseph, 1706-1760.

Young student. (36232)

Young Tennessean, . . . an Indian tale. 44537, 93630

Young traveller. pseud. Traveller's guide to Madeira and the West Indies. see Miller, George. supposed author

Young traveller from Ohio. 10982

Young traveller in South America. 1, 87318, 106195

Young travellers in South America. 1, 87318, 106195

Young 'un. pseud. Stray subjects. see Burnham, George P.

Young voyager to the South Seas. 106196

Young voyageurs; or, adventures in the fur cuntries. 69085

Young voyageurs; or, the boy hunters in the north. 69086

Young woman, d. 1693. defendant 46588

Young woman, who dyed on June 8. 1693. defendant see Young woman, d. 1693. defendant

Young woman's gift, of literature, science and morality. 62902

Young women in convents. 17651

Young wrecker of the Florida reef. 2595

Youngs, Benjamin Seth. 18608, 79723-79727, note after 94924, note after 97880, note after 106196-106197

Youngs, Daniel K. 67068

Youngs, Isaac Newton. 79712, 106198-106200

Youngs, James. 106201

Young's vocal and instrumental musical miscellany. 106078

Your attendance at the court house 106202

Your attendance at the court-house tomorrow evening. 61917

Your committee have obtained for you a copy. 106119

Your faithful adherents, and most obedient admirers. pseud. Useful discovery. 98177

Your humble servant. pseud. Observations on the case. 100505

Your humble wagoner. pseud. Beginning and the end. 4364

Your Majesty's loyal subjects not for fear only, but for conscience' sake, unjustly called Ana-Baptists. petitioners 104331

Your own book. 71345

Your wellwisher, Dic Verum. pseud. Observations upon remarks on Mr. Whitefield. 103638

Youth. pseud. Poems. 106203

Youth. pseud. Some thoughts on religion. 86772

Youth a flower. 100926

Youth in its brightest glory. 46616

Youth: its weapons; its armor. 80908

Youth of eighteen. pseud. see One of the Bachelors; a youth of eighteen. pseud.

Youth of his [i. e. Rev. Joshua Belding's] parish. pseud. Elegy, on the death of Mrs. Anne Belding. (4413)

Youth of Jefferson. 16323

Youth of the Old Dominion. 32958

Youth of thirteen. pseud. Embargo. see Bryant, William Cullen, 1794-1878.

Youth, or scenes from the past. 63453

Youth persuaded to obedience. 11753

Youthful days of Washington. 103987

Youthful pleasure. 14784

Youthful pleasures must be accounted for. 30878

Youth's companion. 106204

Youth's companion and western New York Sabbath school advocate. 106205

Youth's companion; or a safe guide to eminence. 104932-104933, 104947

Youth's companion, or an historical dictionary. 75931

Youth's essay. 92742

Youth's gazette. 88483

Youth's history of California. 55495

Youth's history of Kentucky from the earliest discoveries and settlements. 84940

Youth's history of the great civil war in the United States. 33078

Youth's history of the United States. 50105

Youth's instructor. note after 65546

Youth's keep-sake; a new-year, Christmas, and birth-day present. 106206

Youth's keepsake; a Christmas and new year's gift. 106207

Youth's manual of the constitution of the United States. 106208

Youth's Missionary Society, Philadelphia. 62404, 106209

Youth's Missionary Society of Philadelphia. see Youth's Missionary Society, Philadelphia.

Youth's religious instructor. see Guardian;
  or youth's religious instructor.
Youth's religious instructor. Containing a
  summary of the principles. 56824
Youth's sketch book. 106210
Youth's sketch book for 1836. 106210
Youths' Tract Society, Philadelphia. 62405,
  106211
Youths' Tract Society of Philadelphia. see
  Youths' Tract Society, Philadelphia.
Youth's triumph. 106212
Yr esgusodion drosto, a'r feddyginiaeth.
  93682
Yramategui, Juan de. respondent 19912
Yriarte, Bernardo. 70079, 72232, 77094
Yrolo Calar, Nicolas de. 86414, 106213
Yrujo, Carlos Martinez de Yrujo y Tacon,
  Marques de Casa. see Casa Yrujo,
  Carlos Martinez de Yrujo y Tacon,
  Marques de, 1763-1824.
Yrujo y Tacon, Carlos Martinez de. see
  Casa Yrujo, Carlos Martinez de Yrujo y
  Tacon, Marques de, 1763-1824.
Ysartius, Antonius. cartographer 2987, 47336
Ysla, Ruy Diaz de. 106219
Yta y Parra, Bartolome Felipe de. 35283-35284,
  106220
Yturbide, Augustin de. see Iturbide, Augustin
  de, Emperor of Mexico, 1783-1824.
Yturgoyen, Pedro Phelipe de Azua e. see
  Azua e Yturgoyen, Pedro Phelipe de.
Yturgoyen, Phelipe de Azura e. see Azura e
  Yturgoyen, Phelipe de, Abp.
Yturrigaray, Joseph de. see Iturrigary, Jose
  de, Abp.
Yturrizara, Miguel de. 106221
Yuba County, Calif. Citizens. petitioners
  97497
Yucatan (Diocese) 34836
Yucatan (Diocese) Bishop (Guerra) see also
  Guerra, Jose Maria, Bp.
Yucatan (State) Laws, statutes, etc. 98622
Yucatan (State) Legitimo Congreso Constitucional.
  98622
Yucatan (State) Presidio de San Felipe de
  Bacalar. see Mexico (Viceroyalty)
  Ejercito. Presidio de San Felipe de
  Bacalar, Yucatan.
Yucatan (State) Special Commissioner. 95040
  see also Peraza, --------.
Yucatano. pseud. Observaciones. 86453
Yucatecan grammar. 74526
Yucateco. pseud. A hildago. 106222
Yucateco. pseud. Observaciones que en 19
  del ultimo Octubre. 34413, 98624
Yucateco. pseud. Observaciones sobre las
  inciativas. 56453, 106223
Yucatecos imparciales. pseud. Impugnacion a
  las observaciones. 34413, 98624, 106224
Yuh-po, Lew. see Lew Yuh-po.
Yule, Patrick. 106225
Yulee, David Levy, 1811-1886. (49762), 95762
Yulenbroek, Pieter Johannes. 98245, note after
  101848
Yunibarbia, Bernardo de. 106226
Yuririapundaro, Mexico. Convent (Augustinian)
  plaintiffs 69973
Yuste de Quintero, Mariana. see Quintero,
  Mariana Yuste de.
Yves de Saint-Prest, Jean. see Saint-Prest,
  Jean Yves de.
Yves d'Eveux. Pere 106227
Yvonnet, Francis V. 106228
Yzaguerri, Francisco de. 106228A

Z

Z. pseud. Remarks on slavery in the United
  States. see Sewall, Samuel E.
Z., A.——. pseud. see A.——Z. pseud.
Z., A. pseud. Animadversions. see Welles,
  Noah.
Z——h, A——r. pseud. Considerations on
  the dispute. 15979, 2d note after 106233
Z., A. pseud. Debate between the Rev'd
  Mr. Byles. see Gale, Benjamin.
  supposed author
Z., A. pseud. Esposicion sobre las analogias
  i diferencias. 106230
Z., A. pseud. Present state of the colony of
  Connecticut. see Gale, Benjamin.
Z., A. pseud. Reply to a pamphlet. see
  Gale, Benjamin.
Z., B. K. pseud. Trip from Boston to Little-
  ton. see Hall, Frederick.
Z., C. A. pseud. Estado presente. 106232
Z., F. A. V. pseud. Introducion. 98957
Z., G. pseud. Amerique en 1826. see
  Zenouwitz, G.
Z., R. G. pseud. Observaciones. 106233
Z., T. Q. pseud. tr. (3204)
Z., X. pseud. Aduise concerning the philosophy.
  see Watts, William.
Z., X. Y. pseud. Expositor of certain news-
  paper publications. 8622
Z., X, Y. Gentleman. pseud. Plain dealer:
  number II. (63213), 104453, 1st note
  after 106233
Z. Cano, Gabriel de Cardenas. anagram
  see Barcia, Andres Gonzalez.
Z. O. A. pseud. see Villela Barbosa,
  Francisco.
Z. P. pseud. see Mansfield, L. W.
Z. P. pseud. see Panneah, Zaphnath.
Z Prachu Knihoven. 99367, 99382
Z. W. pseud. see W., Z. pseud.
Z, W, X, Y, pseud. Advertisement. 91499
Zaak der Negerslaaven. 26014
Zaaklyke inhoud van de missive en memorie.
  196234
Zaamenspraak tusschen een Hollander en Zeeuw.
  106235
Zabala, Antonio. 44557A
Zabriskie, James C. 106236
Zacatecanos resuscitados. 14060
Zacatecas, Mexico (City) (34445)
Zacatecas, Mexico (City) Real Colegio de San
  Luis Gonzaga de Nuestra Senora. see
  Real Colegio de San Luis Gonzaga de
  Nuestra Senora de los Zacatecas.
Zacatecas, Mexico (State) 15041, 49444
Zacatecas, Mexico (State) Congreso. (29023),
  34412, 68680, 68684
Zacatecas, Mexico (State) Law, statutes, etc.
  86225
Zach, Franz Xavier, Freiherr von, 1754-
  1832. 4565
Zacharia, Friedrich Wilhelm. 106241
Zachariae Lilii Vicentini canonici regvlaris
  Orbis breviarvm. 41066
Zachary Philemon Vangrifter. pseud. see
  Vangrifter, Zachary Philemon. pseud.
Zadkiel. pseud. Prophecy on the great
  rebellion. 78872
Zadkiel's prophecy. 78872
Zafrilla, Marcos Moriana y. see Moriana y
  Zafrilla, Marcos, Bp.
Zahlreichen Holzschnitten und 3 Stahlstichen.
  8732

ZWOTE